The Good Pub Guide 2014

Edited by Alisdair Aird and Fiona Stapley

Associate Editor: Patrick Stapley

Editorial Research: Fiona Wright
Contributing Editor: Tim Locke
Office Manager: Sarah White
Administrative Assistant: Jan Jones

EBURY PRESS
LONDON

Please send reports on pubs to:

The Good Pub Guide
FREEPOST TN1569, Wadhurst, East Sussex, TN5 7BR

or **feedback@goodguides.com**

or visit our website: **www.thegoodpubguide.co.uk**

If you would like to advertise in the next edition of *The Good Pub Guide*,
please email **goodpubguide@tbs-ltd.co.uk**

10 9 8 7 6 5 4 3 2 1

Published in 2013 by Ebury Press, an imprint of Ebury Publishing

A Random House Group Company

Text © Random House Group Ltd 2013
Maps © PerroGraphics 2013

The Random House Group Limited Reg. No. 954009

Addresses for companies within the Random House Group can be found at
www.randomhouse.co.uk

A CIP catalogue record for this book is available from the British Library

The Random House Group Limited supports The Forest
Stewardship Council (FSC®), the leading international forest
certification organisation. Our books carrying the FSC label are
printed on FSC® certified paper. FSC is the only forest certification
scheme endorsed by the leading environmental organisations,
including Greenpeace. Our paper procurement policy can be found
at www.randomhouse.co.uk/environment

To buy books by your favourite authors and register for offers,
visit www.randomhouse.co.uk

Typeset from authors' files by Jerry Goldie Graphic Design
Project manager and copy editor Cath Phillips
Proofreader Tamsin Shelton

Printed and bound by CPI Group (UK) Ltd, Croydon, CR0 4YY

ISBN 9780091951818

Cover design by Two Associates
Cover photographs reproduced by kind permission of the pubs:
Front: The Acorn Inn, Evershot, Dorset
Spine: The Walnut Tree Inn, Blisworth, Northamptonshire
Back top left: The Rose & Crown, Snettisham, Norfolk
Back top right: The Potting Shed Pub, Malmesbury, Wiltshire
Back bottom left: The White Horse Inn, Compton Bassett, Wiltshire
Back bottom right: The Red Lion Inn, Babcary, Somerset

Contents

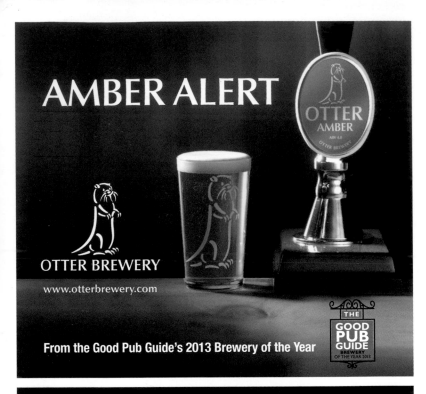

We brew Pale Ale, others brew pale imitations.

Marston's Pedigree is still brewed the best way known to Master Brewers; using Burton well water and the Union system, maintained by our own cooper, Mark, with a passion for the result. Whilst other breweries 'Burtonise' their water, we use water from the source.
Marston's - Proud of our Pedigree.

It's all about **Pedigree**

Introduction & The Good Pub Guide Awards 2014

In the next 12 months, between 2,500 and 4,000 pubs will go out of business. This sounds dire, and of course it's bad news for their staff and regular customers. But these are the pubs at the bottom of the pecking order, the Bad Pubs, which still behave as if we were stuck in the 1980s, happy with indifferent food, drink, service and surroundings. It's high time they closed their doors. As one eminently successful landlord told us: 'There are probably still far too many pubs in the wrong place and often chasing the wrong market. The bad pubs are still being culled, just like lions pick off the slowest of the herd. It makes the pub industry more robust and far better placed for the future. I do not know of a single good pub that has got into trouble in recent years, despite our harsh economy, unsupportive banks and horrible weather.'

In this same coming year, we expect well over 1,000 new pubs to open – often by visionary and energetic new licensees bringing fresh life to former pubs that were shuttered for months or years. Many of these will join the Good Pubs: the 4,800 or so excellent places that fuel *The Good Pub Guide* with its raw material.

Between these two extremes are the remaining 40,000 or so Average Pubs. These range from straightforward locals to the big chains of standard-pattern eateries and drinkeries with their reliably consistent offerings: you always get what you expect, no less – but no more.

This year we carried out an interview survey of a small sample of top publicans, to find out how they lift their pubs so far above the average. The most interesting finding was that they were unanimous in being extremely positive about the future of British Pubs. These clear-sighted landlords see a trend away from large generally brewery-owned chains and instead favour much more diversity, with great scope for real professionalism in pub management. We'd agree with that: as one of them told us, the legal, fiscal and operational demands of running a pub are now so great that really there's no room for the enthusiastic amateur.

Based on our top landlords' frank answers, here is *The Good Pub Guide*'s recipe for success:

- Realise that today's pub-goers know more and expect more – so guarantee consistently high standards
- Don't just run the pub to your own satisfaction – take time to identify your market, then match its needs relentlessly
- Don't be distracted – you can't be everything to everyone, and if you try to be, you'll fail
- Always be ready to adapt to changing pressures – there's no point trying to compete with cheap supermarket deals or the lure of home cinema, so tempt customers in with something quite distinct
- Good food is virtually essential and at least brings a chance of success; mediocre food means no chance
- Don't be greedy with your pricing, as too-high prices lead to a vicious spiral of falling trade
- The key word is hospitality, which demands real warmth and service quality – 'Anyone can do food and drink, but it's what comes with that, that makes the difference'
- Getting the right staff is paramount – even though 'You have to kiss a lot of frogs before you find a prince'

This last point is crucial. This year, as so often before, we have found that poor service is the Number One reason for writing off a pub. The UK pub industry (including bars and nightclubs) employs about 330,000 people, the great majority of them under 30 years old, and typically in their late teens or early twenties.

Landlords and landladies who motivate and inspire these young people are the driving force behind improving pub service standards. And they're bringing a search for real professionalism into the industry, with an increase in vocational training and qualifications, and recently launched schemes for work placements and apprenticeships.

The biggest problem is that the UK is almost alone in undervaluing its chefs, and waiting and bar staff. In other countries, these are valued jobs, held with professional pride. Here, there's an absurd status gap between the growing horde of TV superstar chefs and pub chefs, who typically earn £15,000 to £20,000 a year (in the hope of one day landing a head chef job, paying £20,000 to £45,000), but who often cook every bit as well.

Many pubs now name-check their chefs, on menus and websites. This is a good practice, which we'd like to see happen everywhere – with photos and potted biographies.

Drinks: the search for fair prices and top quality

On price, the basic rule is: steer clear of the South-east. Our national survey of drinks prices shows a staggering 65p-a-pint difference in the price of beer between Staffordshire, the cheapest area, and London, the most expensive. How does your area rank? Here are the details, in average price order:

Bargain beer
Staffordshire, Derbyshire, Herefordshire, Worcestershire, Cornwall, Nottinghamshire, Shropshire, Northumbria

Fair-priced beer
Yorkshire, Lincolnshire, Cumbria, Lancashire, Northamptonshire, Somerset, Wales

Average-priced beer
Cheshire, Cambridgeshire, Gloucestershire, Devon, Dorset,

Suffolk, Norfolk, Essex, Leicestershire, Warwickshire, West Midlands, Hampshire, Bedfordshire, Wiltshire, Oxfordshire

Expensive beer
Scotland, Kent, Isle of Wight, Buckinghamshire, Hertfordshire, Berkshire, Sussex

Rip-off beer
Surrey, London

When *The Good Pub Guide* launched in 1983, the pub scene was dominated by a handful of national beer brands, with little variation in taste. Good publicans even then were trying to search out interesting, lesser-known beers for their customers, and we've always highlighted their efforts. Over these three decades, just as everyone's expectations of pub food quality and variety have risen, so has our interest in what we drink.

The range of beers on offer, to match this interest, has grown dramatically. Now, you can find more than 7,000 different beers, produced by many hundreds of craft brewers. These are not always long-lived ventures – of all the breweries that have set up since 1970, around 650 have disappeared. But some make it big. Sharps Doom Bar, which we remember starting off in a very small way in Cornwall 20 years ago, has become a part of one of the world's biggest breweries and is now Britain's top-selling real ale.

Among the most interesting beers are those brewed by pubs themselves, on the premises. These have the big plus of lower prices. Our national price survey this year shows that own-brew beers typically cost 40p a pint less than the local average.

Our Top Ten Own-Brew Pubs are The Driftwood Spars at Trevaunance Cove (Cornwall), Drunken Duck near Hawkshead, Beer Hall at Hawkshead Brewery in Staveley and Watermill at Ings (Cumbria), Church Mill at Uppermill (Lancashire), Grainstore in Oakham (Leicestershire and Rutland), Dipton Mill at Diptonmill and Ship at Newton-by-the-Sea (Northumbria), Weighbridge Brewhouse in Swindon (Wiltshire) and Fox & Hounds in Houston (Scotland).

For the superb quality and value of the ten different beers it brews, the Grainstore in Oakham is **Own-Brew Pub of the Year 2014**.

In this edition we pick out over 300 pubs as outstanding for the quality, and often the range, of beers they sell – each gets a Beer Award ◖. This year's Top Ten Beer Pubs are the

Bhurtpore at Aston and Mill in Chester (Cheshire), Watermill at Ings (Cumbria), Tom Cobley at Spreyton (Devon), Old Spot at Dursley (Gloucestershire), Fat Cat in Norwich (Norfolk), Malt Shovel in Northampton (Northamptonshire), Fat Cat in Ipswich (Suffolk), Nags Head in Malvern (Worcestershire) and Kelham Island Tavern in Sheffield (Yorkshire). All have not just a great changing choice of interesting beers kept in fine condition, but knowledgeable landlords, plenty of character and a cheerful lively atmosphere. The Tom Cobley, tucked away in the little village of Spreyton and unusual for a beer specialist in having a thriving restaurant too, is our **Beer Pub of the Year 2014**.

As we've already said, there are now not just dozens but hundreds of breweries producing good beers. One of the longest-running is Fullers, going strong since 1829 – and beers were being produced at their London brewery site for over 150 years before that. They're still very much a family-run company, and have combined traditional virtues (they have a very good tenanted pub estate) with a go-ahead attitude to modern conditions. Their beers are top notch. One in 12 Good Pubs now stocks at least one Fullers beer (and many also stock good farm cider from Cornish Orchards, recently bought by

Fullers – who have also always deserved the good reputation their wines have). Fullers are **Brewery of the Year 2014**.

Well over one-third of all Good Pubs now take such care over their wines that they qualify for our Wine Award ♀. Many have an outstanding offering, with a devoted following for their tutored tastings, bin-end specials and sometimes their own wine shops – all on top of an interesting range by the glass. This year's Top Ten Wine Pubs are the Old Bridge in Huntingdon (Cambridgeshire), Harris Arms at Portgate and Nobody Inn at Doddiscombsleigh (Devon), Yew Tree at Clifford's Mesne (Gloucestershire), Inn at Whitewell (Lancashire), Olive Branch at Clipsham (Leicestershire and Rutland), Woods at Dulverton (Somerset), Crown at Stoke-by-Nayland (Suffolk), Inn at West End (Surrey) and Vine Tree at Norton (Wiltshire). Not for the first time, Woods at Dulverton gains the title of **Wine Pub of the Year 2014**. Here, Patrick Groves is really rewarding to talk to about wine, and will open any of his 400 listed bottles for just a glass – he may even tempt you to one of his unlisted collection of 500 well aged New World wines.

Whisky now accounts for 80% of Scotland's food and drink export earnings – and a quarter of the UK's. The choice is almost endless, with nearly 100 single malt distilleries producing endless variants. To taste at home even a small fraction of what's available, the number of bottles you'd have to buy would cost a fortune. Luckily, quite a few pubs stock such a fine choice that you can start an odyssey through the world of whisky at much more modest cost. Our Top Ten Whisky Pubs, all with a choice of over 100 malts, are the Bhurtpore at Aston and Old Harkers Arms in Chester (Cheshire), Nobody Inn at Doddiscombsleigh (Devon), Britons Protection in Manchester (Lancashire), Orchard in West London, Pack Horse at Widdop (Yorkshire), and Bow Bar in Edinburgh, Bon Accord in Glasgow, Sligachan Hotel and Stein Inn, both on Skye (Scotland). The Bon Accord in Glasgow, with its fantastic range of 380 whiskies, is **Whisky Pub of the Year 2014**.

Pub food: the great quest for value and flavour

Value isn't just about cost, it's about getting a really worthwhile deal, whether it's for a simple but hearty lunchtime bowl of soup, or for a celebration birthday treat.

This year, faced with rising food costs, pubs have found it hard to keep their prices down. But their efforts to source food economically (which usually means locally), and real ingenuity in menu planning, have brought great results. Our national survey of food prices in Good Pubs shows that this year a typical two-course pub meal costs 9% less than it did last year, with a quarter of pubs cutting the price of their most popular dish. Our Value Award £ picks out those pubs – one in six or seven of all Good Pubs – that have had outstanding success in giving a good choice at rewarding prices. Our Top Ten Value Pubs are the Three Tuns at Fen Drayton (Cambridgeshire), Drake Manor at Buckland Monachorum (Devon), Anchor at Oldbury-on-Severn (Gloucestershire), Yew Tree at Lower Wield (Hampshire), Red Lion at Preston (Hertfordshire), Sun at Cottesmore (Leicestershire and Rutland), Lord Nelson in Southwold (Suffolk), Six Bells at Chiddingly (Sussex), Lamb in Marlborough (Wiltshire) and Crown & Trumpet at Broadway (Worcestershire). With its interesting choice from hearty pub staples to imaginative vegetarian, fish and game dishes, the Red Lion at Preston – the very first of the UK's growing number of community-owned pubs – is **Value Pub of the Year 2014**.

More than a third of Good Pubs now qualify for our Food Award ⑪, showing outstanding quality. This reflects real dedication in the kitchen, with chefs often building networks of local farmers, growers, gamekeepers and other suppliers to ensure top-quality seasonal produce, and more and more establishments growing their own fruit and veg or keeping chickens and even livestock. This year's Top Ten Dining Pubs, all exceptional places for a special meal out, are the Royal Oak at Bovingdon Green (Buckinghamshire), Yew Tree at Spurstow (Cheshire), Treby Arms at Sparkwell (Devon), Purefoy Arms at Preston Candover (Hampshire), Stagg at Titley (Herefordshire), Olive Branch at Clipsham (Leicestershire and Rutland), County at Aycliffe (Northumbria), Lord Poulett Arms at Hinton St George (Somerset), Bell & Cross at Holy Cross (Worcestershire) and Pipe & Glass at South Dalton (Yorkshire). A particular favourite, for its informal atmosphere, thoughtful and unusual drinks choice and hospitable little bar, as well as its amazing food, the Stagg at Titley is **Dining Pub of the Year 2014**.

The country's top pubs

It's hard enough to run just one good pub. To run several successfully demands extraordinary skill and brilliant organisation. So it's a tremendous achievement that the last decade or so has seen the emergence of several small groups of good pubs. An outstanding example is Becky Salisbury's Salisbury Pubs, with four in and around the Chilterns, all quite special: each has a Food and Wine Award, and two are County Dining Pubs (for Buckinghamshire and Hertfordshire). Salisbury Pubs is **Pub Group of the Year 2014**.

With food the driving force in so many pubs, it's heartening that so many genuinely unchanging and unpretentious places still thrive on pure character, without depending on meals as their mainstay.

Our Top Ten Unspoilt Pubs are the Barley Mow at Kirk Ireton (Derbyshire), Rugglestone near Widecombe (Devon), Digby Tap in Sherborne and Square & Compass at Worth Matravers (Dorset), Viper at Mill Green (Essex), White Horse near Petersfield and Harrow at Steep (Hampshire), Victoria in Durham (Northumbria), and Crown at Churchill and Halfway House at Pitney (Somerset). The time-warp White Horse near Petersfield – long known as The Pub With No Name, thanks to its empty inn-sign gantry by the lonely road over the downs – is **Unspoilt Pub of the Year 2014**.

In towns and cities, pubs generally fall into two groups. On the one hand, there are all the local pubs, which can rely on their regulars being within walking distance and piling in at

Welcome to The

EARL SPENCER

Located in pretty Southfields the gateway to Wimbledon Park & The All England Lawn Tennis & Croquet Club.

This grand Edwardian drinking palace hums with activity from the open kitchen specialising in freshly prepared and cooked food, to the regulars enjoying the traditional pub atmosphere.

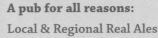

A pub for all reasons:

Local & Regional Real Ales

Single Malt & World Whiskies

Fine Cuban Cigar Selection

Open Log Fires or Terrace Garden in season

Winner *Evening Standard* Pub of the Year

Southfields Tube, situated at 260-262 Merton Road, Southfields, London, SW18 5JL.

BOOKINGS NOT ESSENTIAL   020 8870 9244
CHECK OUT OUR DAILY CHANGING MENU ONLINE
www.theearlspencer.com

lunchtime and the early evening. At the other end of the scale are the pubs that have set their sights much higher, aiming to give something special and attracting a much wider range of customers at all times of day – shoppers for a relaxing coffee, ladies who lunch, crossword puzzlers warming in front of the fire with a pint, people having a confidential meeting away from the office. Our Top Ten Town Pubs are all ideal for this, and are worth seeking out by connoisseurs of interesting and individual pubs of character: the Park in Bedford (Bedfordshire), Punter in Cambridge (Cambridgeshire), Eight Bells in Chipping Campden (Gloucestershire), Wykeham Arms in Winchester (Hampshire), Britons Protection in Manchester (Lancashire), Olde Mitre in Central London, Kings Head in Woodstock (Oxfordshire), Old Green Tree in Bath (Somerset), Crown in Southwold (Suffolk) and Old Joint Stock in Birmingham (Warwickshire and West Midlands). The Park in Bedford, an eye-opening new entry, is **Town Pub of the Year 2014**.

The ideal country pub has a good warm fire in winter and a pretty garden in summer, surroundings that provide tempting opportunities for walkers (and their dogs), honest-to-goodness food and drink, a relaxing atmosphere and easy-going comfort – and the really genuine welcoming feel given by cheerful landlords, landladies and locals. Our Top Ten Country Pubs are the Crown & Garter at Inkpen (Berkshire), White Horse at Hedgerley (Buckinghamshire), Pheasant at Burwardsley (Cheshire), Duke of York at Iddesleigh (Devon), Brace of Pheasants at Plush (Dorset), Royal Oak at Fritham (Hampshire), Butchers Arms at Sheepscombe (Gloucestershire), Hatchet at Lower Chute and Malet Arms at Newton Tony (Wiltshire) and Harp at Old Radnor (Wales). In the lovely streamside village of Newton Tony, and run so enthusiastically by its countryman landlord, the Malet Arms is **Country Pub of the Year 2014**.

This year, we have added 163 new main entries to *The Good Pub Guide* – about one in five. They cover a great range from simple taverns to grand inns, but all share the stamp of real quality. From the new finds that have given us particular personal pleasure, our Top Ten New Pubs are the Park in Bedford (Bedfordshire), White Oak at Cookham and Fox at Peasemore (Berkshire), Tickell Arms at Whittlesford (Cambridgeshire), Three Greyhounds at Allostock and Bulls Head at Mottram St Andrew (Cheshire), Compasses at Littley Green (Essex), Slaughters at Lower Slaughter (Gloucestershire), Woodbridge at Coalport (Shropshire) and Talbot at Mells (Somerset). With their latest Cheshire pub, the Brunning & Price group have surpassed themselves; this lovely pub, the Bulls Head in Mottram St Andrew, is **New Pub of the Year 2014**.

Good Pubs have really cottoned on to their potential for overnight, weekend or longer breaks. Every year, more and more open bedrooms, either upstairs or in well converted outbuildings – almost half of our Main Entries now offer bedrooms, and most of these are really nice places to stay in. Our Top Ten Inns, all in lovely parts of the country, are the New Inn at Cerne Abbas (Dorset), New Inn at Coleford (Devon), Kings Head at Bledington (Gloucestershire), Inn at Whitewell (Lancashire), Olive Branch at Clipsham (Leicestershire and Rutland), Talbot at Mells (Somerset), Cat at West Hoathly (Sussex), King John at Tollard Royal (Wiltshire), Blue Lion at East Witton and Horseshoe at Levisham (Yorkshire). Run by Paul and Helen Klein for more than 20 years, the charming Blue Lion at East Witton is **Inn of the Year 2014**.

Running a pub has always been really hard work involving very long hours, complex admin and staffing, and an ability to stay charming and cheerful when lesser mortals would be tearing their hair out. Recent years have added heavy extra burdens, with additional health & safety and employment rules and paperwork, financial complications – even the rotten weather. So our Top Ten Licensees – who don't just run their pubs well but really *are* their pubs – are exceptional people: Philip and Lauren Davison of the Fox at Peasemore (Berkshire), Mike Norris of the Red Lion at Chenies (Buckinghamshire), Julie and Justin Satur of the Church Inn at Chelmorton (Derbyshire), Peter and Angela Gatling of the Merry Harriers at Clayhidon (Devon), Simon and Sally Jackson of the Horse & Groom at Upper Oddington (Gloucestershire), Tim Gray of the Yew Tree at Lower Wield and Kerry Dutton of the Rock & Thistle at Rockbourne (Hampshire), Glenn Williams of the Bell at Tillington (Herefordshire), Martin Coldicott of the Rose & Crown at Shilton (Oxfordshire) and Peter and Veryan Graham of the George at Croscombe (Somerset). Tim Gray at his Yew Tree in Lower Wield, so hard-working, so ever-present and so consistently cheerful, is **Landlord of the Year 2014**.

Each year, a number of pubs stand out as being absolutely at the top of their game – they crop up again and again in readers' reports as giving really special enjoyment. This year's Top Ten Pubs, between them notching up over 4,000 votes on our website, www.thegoodpubguide.co.uk, are

* * * * *

TOP TEN PUBS 2014
(in county order)

Cock Hemingford Grey (Cambridgeshire)

Horse & Groom Upper Oddington
(Gloucestershire)

Olive Branch Clipsham (Leicestershire
and Rutland)

Rose & Crown Snettisham (Norfolk)

Olde Ship Seahouses (Northumbria)

Kings Arms Woodstock (Oxfordshire)

Crown Southwold (Suffolk)

Horse Guards Tillington (Sussex)

Woods Dulverton (Somerset)

Crown Roecliffe (Yorkshire)

* * * * *

the Cock at Hemingford Grey (Cambridgeshire), Horse
& Groom at Upper Oddington (Gloucestershire), Olive
Branch at Clipsham (Leicestershire and Rutland), Rose &
Crown at Snettisham (Norfolk), Olde Ship at Seahouses
(Northumbria), Kings Arms in Woodstock (Oxfordshire),
Crown in Southwold (Suffolk), Horse Guards at Tillington
(Sussex), Woods at Dulverton (Somerset) and Crown at
Roecliffe (Yorkshire). The civilised Olive Branch prompts
readers to superlatives: 'service as good as it gets', 'sublime
food', 'one of our favourites', 'how have they managed to
maintain such consistently high standards?', 'the ultimate
pub experience', 'fabulous place', 'wonderful pub'. The Olive
Branch at Clipsham is **Pub of the Year 2014**.

YOU'LL JUST LOVE AN INDIVIDUAL INN

What is a good pub?

The Main Entries in this *Guide* have been through a two-stage sifting process. First of all, some 2,000 regular correspondents keep in touch with us about the pubs they visit, while double that number report occasionally. We also get a flow of reports sent to us at feedback@goodguides.com or via our website, www.thegoodpubguide.co.uk. This keeps us up to date about pubs included in previous editions: it's their alarm signals that warn us when a pub's standards have dropped (after a change of management, say) and it's their continuing approval that reassures us about keeping a pub as a full entry for another year.

New Entries

Particularly important are the reports we receive on pubs we don't know at all. It's from these new discoveries that we create a shortlist, to be considered for possible inclusion as new Main Entries. The more people that report favourably on a new pub, the more likely it is to win a place on this shortlist – especially if some of the reporters belong to our hardcore of trusted correspondents whose judgement we have learned to rely on. These are people who have each given us detailed comments on dozens of pubs, and shown that (when we ourselves know some of those pubs too) their judgement is closely in line with our own.

This brings us to the acid test. As well as inspection, the editors have to find some special quality that would make strangers enjoy visiting it. What often marks out the pub for special attention is good value food (and that might mean anything from a well made sandwich, with good fresh ingredients at a low price, to imaginative cooking outclassing most restaurants in the area). The drinks may be out of the ordinary – maybe several hundred whiskies, remarkable wine lists, interesting ciders, a wide range of well kept real ales (perhaps even brewed by the pub itself) or bottled beers from all over the world. Perhaps there's a special appeal about it as a place to stay, with good bedrooms and obliging service. Maybe it's the building itself (from centuries-old parts of monasteries to extravagant Victorian gin-palaces), or its surroundings (lovely countryside, attractive waterside, extensive well kept garden), or what's inside it (charming furnishings, extraordinary collections of bric-a-brac).

Above all, though, what makes the good pub is its atmosphere. You should be able to feel at home there, and feel not just that you're glad you've come but that they're glad you've come. A good landlord or landlady makes a huge difference here – they can make or break a pub.

It follows from this that a great many ordinary local pubs, perfectly good in their own right, don't earn a place in the *Guide*. What makes them attractive to their regular customers (an almost clubby chumminess) may even make strangers feel rather out of place.

Another important point is that there's not necessarily any link between charm and luxury. A basic unspoilt village tavern, with hard seats and a flagstone floor, may be worth travelling miles to find, while a deluxe pub-restaurant may not be worth crossing the street for.

Those pubs featured with Main Entries do pay a fee, which helps to cover the *Guide's* research and production costs. But no pub can gain an entry simply by paying a fee. Only pubs that have been inspected anonymously, and approved as meeting our very high standards, are invited to join.

The Cock Inn

Family-run pub ◆ Food served 7 days a week:
lunchtimes and evenings, and all day on Sundays ◆ Large garden and sun terrace
◆ Cask Marque accredited real ales ◆ Roasts served all day on Sundays ◆ Open all day
on Bank Holidays ◆ Vegetarian menu always available (five choices)
◆ Home-cooked food – something for every taste, diet and budget!

Old Uckfield Road (A26), Near Ringmer, East Sussex BN8 5RX
Tel 01273 812040 • **www.cockpub.co.uk**

Using the *Guide*

The Counties

England has been split alphabetically into counties. Each chapter starts by picking out the pubs that are currently doing best in the area, or are specially attractive for one reason or another.

The county boundaries we use are those for the administrative counties (not the old traditional counties, which were changed back in 1976). We have left the new unitary authorities within the counties that they formed part of until their creation in the most recent local government reorganisation. Metropolitan areas have been included in the counties around them – for example, Merseyside in Lancashire. And occasionally we have grouped counties together – for example, Rutland with Leicestershire, and Durham with Northumberland to make Northumbria. If in doubt, check the Contents pages.

Scotland, Wales and London have each been covered in single chapters. Pubs are listed alphabetically (except in London, which is split into Central, East, North, South and West), under the name of the town or village where they are. If the village is so small that you might not find it on a road map, we've listed it under the name of the nearest sizeable village or town. The maps use the same town and village names, and additionally include a few big cities that don't have any listed pubs – for orientation.

We list pubs in their true county, not their postal county. Just once or twice, when the village itself is in one county but the pub is just over the border in the next-door county, we have used the village county, not the pub one.

Stars ★

Really outstanding pubs are awarded a star, and in one case two: these are the aristocrats among pubs. The stars do NOT signify extra luxury or specially good food – in fact, some of the pubs that appeal most distinctively and strongly are decidedly basic in terms of food and surroundings. The detailed description of each pub shows what its particular appeal is, and this is what the stars refer to.

Food Award ⑪

Pubs where food is quite outstanding.

Stay Award 🛏

Pubs that are good as places to stay at (obviously, you can't expect the same level of luxury at £60 a head as you'd get for £100 a head). Pubs with bedrooms are marked on the maps as a square.

Wine Award ♀

Pubs with particularly enjoyable wines by the glass – often a good range.

Beer Award ◖

Pubs where the quality of the beer is quite exceptional, or pubs that keep a particularly interesting range of beers in good condition.

Value Award £

This distinguishes pubs that offer really good value food. In all the award-winning pubs, you will find an interesting choice at under £10.

Recommenders

At the end of each Main Entry we include the names of readers who have recently recommended that pub (unless they've asked us not to use their names).

Important note: the description of the pub and the comments on it are our own and not the recommenders'.

Also Worth a Visit

The Also Worth a Visit section at the end of each county chapter includes brief descriptions of pubs that have been recommended by readers in the year before the *Guide* goes to print and that we feel are worthy of inclusion – many of them, indeed, as good in their way as the featured pubs (these are picked out by a star). We have inspected and approved nearly half of these ourselves. All the others are recommended by our reader-reporters. The descriptions of

The HOOP

The Hoop is a freehouse which dates back 450 years. It is famous for its extensive range of guest beers which change daily and range from light summer ales through to dark winter stouts.

The Hoop holds an annual beer festival during the late May Bank Holiday with over 150 real ales, 50 ciders, a hog roast and BBQ.

You can also enjoy traditional fresh food in our AA Rosette awarded Oak Room Restaurant open Tues-Fri and Sunday lunch times for a set 3 course menu, Tues-Sat for full a la carte dining experience.

WEDDINGS AND SPECIAL OCCASSIONS CATERED FOR
BYO WINE NIGHTS, CURRY NIGHTS & QUIZ NIGHTS

The Hoop, High Street, Stock, Essex, CM4 9BD. Tel: 01277 841137
Email: thehoopstock@yahoo.co.uk Website: www.thehoop.co.uk

these other pubs, written by us, usually reflect the experience of several different people.

The pubs in Also Worth a Visit may become featured entries in future editions. So do please help us know which are hot prospects for our inspection programme (and which are not!), by reporting on them. There are report forms at the back of the *Guide*, or you can email us at feedback@goodguides.com, or write to us at The Good Pub Guide, FREEPOST TN1569, Wadhurst, East Sussex TN5 7BR.

Locating Pubs

To help readers who use digital mapping systems we include a postcode for every pub. Pubs outside London are given a British Grid four-figure map reference. Where a pub is exceptionally difficult to find, we include a six-figure reference in the directions. The Map number (Main Entries only) refers to the maps at the back of the *Guide*.

Motorway Pubs

If a pub is within four or five miles of a motorway junction we give special directions for finding it from the motorway. The

Special Interest Lists at the end of the book include a list of these pubs, motorway by motorway.

Prices and Other Factual Details
The *Guide* went to press during the summer of 2013, after each pub was sent a checking sheet to get up-to-date food, drink and bedroom prices and other factual information. By the summer of 2014 prices are bound to have increased, but if you find a significantly different price please let us know.

Breweries or independent chains to which pubs are 'tied' are named at the beginning of the italic-print rubric after each Main Entry. That generally means the pub has to get most if not all its drinks from that brewery or chain. If the brewery is not an independent one but just part of a combine, we name the combine in brackets. When the pub is tied, we have spelled out whether the landlord is a tenant, has the pub on a lease, or is a manager. Tenants and leaseholders of breweries generally have considerably greater freedom to do things their own way, and in particular are allowed to buy drinks including a beer from sources other than their tied brewery.

The Orange Tree
Thornham

Norfolk's
Best
Just
Keeps
Getting
Better

01485 512213 www.theorangetreethornham.co.uk

Free houses are pubs not tied to a brewery. In theory they can shop around, but in practice many free houses have loans from the big brewers, on terms that bind them to sell those breweries' beers. So don't be too surprised to find that so-called free houses may be stocking a range of beers restricted to those from a single brewery.

Real ale is used by us to mean beer that has been maturing naturally in its cask. We do not count as real ale beer that has been pasteurised or filtered to remove its natural yeasts.

Other drinks. We've also looked out particularly for pubs doing enterprising non-alcoholic drinks (including good tea or coffee), interesting spirits (especially malt whiskies), country wines, freshly squeezed juices and good farm ciders.

Bar food usually refers to what is sold in the bar, we do not describe menus that are restricted to a separate restaurant. If we know that a pub serves sandwiches, we say so – if you don't see them mentioned, assume you can't get them. Food listed is an example of the sort of thing you'd find served in the bar on a normal day.

Children. If we don't mention children at all, assume that they are not welcome. All but one or two pubs allow children in their garden if they have one. 'Children welcome' means the pub has told us that it lets them in with no special restrictions. In other cases, we report exactly what arrangements pubs say they make for children. However, we have to note that in readers' experience some pubs make restrictions that they haven't told us about (children only if eating, for example). If you come across this, please let us know, so that we can clarify with the pub concerned for the next edition. The absence of any reference to children in an Also Worth a Visit entry means we don't know either way. Children's Certificates exist, but in practice children are allowed into some part of most pubs in this *Guide* (there is no legal restriction on the movement of children over 14 in any pub). Children under 16 cannot have alcoholic drinks. Children aged 16 and 17 can drink beer, wine or cider with a meal if it is bought by an adult and they are accompanied by an adult.

Dogs. If Main Entry licensees have told us they allow dogs in their pub or bedrooms, we say so; absence of reference to dogs means dogs are not welcome. If you take a dog into a pub you should have it on a lead. We also mention in the text any pub dogs or cats (or indeed other animals) that we've come across ourselves, or heard about from readers.

Parking. If we know there is a problem with parking, we say so, otherwise assume there is a car park.

Credit cards. We say if a pub does not accept them; some that do may put a surcharge on credit card bills, to cover charges made by the card company. We also say if we know that a pub tries to retain customers' credit cards while they are eating. This is a reprehensible practice, and if a pub tries it on you, please tell them that all banks and card companies frown on it – and please let us know the pub's name, so that we can warn readers in future editions.

Telephone numbers are given for all pubs that are not ex-directory.

Opening hours are for summer; we say if we know of differences in winter, or on particular days of the week. In the country, many pubs may open rather later and close earlier than their details show (if you come across this, please let us know – with details). Pubs are allowed to stay open all day if licensed to do so. However, outside cities many pubs in England and Wales close during the afternoon. We'd be grateful to hear of any differences from the hours we quote.

Bedroom prices normally include full english breakfasts (if available), VAT and any automatic service charge. If we give just one price, it is the total price for two people sharing a double or twin-bedded room for one night. Prices before the / are for single occupancy, prices after it for double.

Meal times. Bar food is commonly served from 12-2 and 7-9, at least from Monday to Saturday. We spell out the times if they are significantly different. To be sure of a table it's best to book before you go. Sunday hours vary considerably from pub to pub, so it's advisable to check before you leave.

Disabled access. Deliberately, we do not ask pubs about this, as their answers would not give a reliable picture of how easy access is. Instead, we depend on readers' direct experience. If you are able to give us help about this, we would be particularly grateful for your reports.

Electronic Route Planning

Microsoft® AutoRoute™, a route-finding software package, shows the location of pubs in *The Good Pub Guide* on detailed maps and includes our text entries for those pubs on screen.

Our website (www.thegoodpubguide.co.uk) includes every pub in the *Guide*.

iPhone and iPad

You can search and read *The Good Pub Guide* both on our website (www.thegoodpubguide.co.uk) and as a download on your smartphone or iPad. They contain all the pubs in this *Guide*. You can also write reviews and let us know about undiscovered gems.

There are apps available for iPhone and iPad – and the *Guide* can be downloaded as an eBook to your reader.

Changes during the year – please tell us

Changes are inevitable during the course of the year. Landlords change, and so do their policies. We hope that you will find everything just as we say, but if not please let us know. You can find out how by referring to the Report Forms section at the end of the *Guide*.

Editors' acknowledgements

We could not produce the Guide without the huge help we have from the many thousands of readers who report to us on the pubs they visit, often in great detail. Particular thanks to these greatly valued correspondents: N R White, Paul Humphreys, George Atkinson, Michael and Jenny Back, John Wooll, Tony and Wendy Hobden, Susan and John Douglas, Chris and Angela Buckell, Phil and Jane Hodson, Phil Bryant, Clive and Fran Dutson, Mike and Wena Stevenson, Simon and Mandy King, David Jackman, Roger and Donna Huggins, Brian and Anna Marsden, Sara Fulton, Roger Baker, Gordon and Margaret Ormondroyd, Ann and Colin Hunt, Michael Doswell, Ian Herdman, Comus and Sarah Elliott, Gerry and Rosemary Dobson, Pat and Tony Martin, Guy Vowles, Peter Meister, Richard Tilbrook, Dr Kevan Tucker, Taff Thomas, Derek and Sylvia Stephenson, Richard and Penny Gibbs, Brian Glozier, Ian Phillips, Val and Alan Green, Dennis Jones, Martin and Pauline Jennings, Steve Whalley, Dave Braisted, Paul Rampton, Julie Harding, Tony and Jill Radnor, Martin and Karen Wake, John Beeken, Michael Butler, John Saville, Ross Balaam, R K Phillips, Tracey and Stephen Groves, Conor McGaughey, John Evans, Brian and Janet Ainscough, Mr and Mrs P R Thomas, Giles and Annie Francis, John and Sylvia Harrop, Mrs Margo Finlay, Jörg Kasprowski, Stanley and Annie Matthews, Mike and Mary Carter, GSB, Pauline Fellows and Simon Robbins, Pete Walker, Di and Mike Gillam, M G Hart, R L Borthwick, Torrens Lyster, Simon Collett-Jones, J F M and M West, Lucien Perring, Reg Fowle, Helen Rickwood, Tina and David Woods-Taylor, John and Eleanor Holdsworth, R T and J C Moggridge, Ryta Lyndley, Neil and Anita Christopher, R C Vincent, Edward Mirzoeff, B and M Kendall, Mark Barker and Tony Shepherd, Gerry Price, Susan Loppert, Jane Caplan, Peter F Marshall, David M Smith, Roger Fox, Christian Mole, Ron and Sheila Corbett, Howard and Margaret Buchanan, Andy and Jill Kassube, Sheila Topham, Dr and Mrs A K Clarke, Pat and Stewart Gordon, Conrad Freezer, Dr A J and Mrs B A Tompsett, Eddie Edwards, Les and Sandra Brown, Jeremy Whitehorn, Mike and Jayne Bastin, Roy Hoing, Dr D J and Mrs S C Walker, Tom McLean, Henry Fryer, Tim Maddison, Neil and Angela Huxter, Stephen Funnell, David and Stella Martin, David Heath, David Lamb, Ian and Rose Lock, Jenny and Brian Seller, C and R Bromage, Barry Collett, Michael Tack, Patrick and Daphne Darley, D and M T Ayres-Regan, Michael Mellers, Dave Webster, Sue Holland, S G N Bennett, David and Sally Frost, Richard Cox, Nigel and Sue Foster, KC, Adrian Finn, David and Sue Atkinson, Colin McKerrow, G Jennings, Bill Adie, David Howe, Robert Wivell, Dennis and Doreen Haward, David and Ruth Hollands, Leslie and Barbara Owen, Lynda and Trevor Smith, Steve and Liz Tilley, John Branston, Alex Rorke, J A Snell, Ron Clementson, David and Judy Robison, P and D Carpenter, Paul and Marion Watts, Adrian Johnson, Barbara and Peter Kelly, Roger and Anne Newbury, Phil and Sally Gorton, Tom Evans, David Handforth, Chris and Val Ramstedt, Robert W Buckle, P and J Shapley, Peter and Avril Hanson, David and Julie Glover, Ted George, John and Nan Hurst, Penny and Peter Keevil, John Coatsworth, Mike and Eleanor Anderson, Mrs P Sumner, David McCullagh, Jane Hoskisson, Philip and Susan Philcox, James Stretton.

Thanks, too, to the ladies at The Book Service for their cheerful dedication: Maria Tegerdine, Michele Csaforda, Kerry Rusch and Carol Bryant. And particularly to John Holliday of Trade Wind Technology, who built and looks after our all-important database.

Alisdair Aird and Fiona Stapley

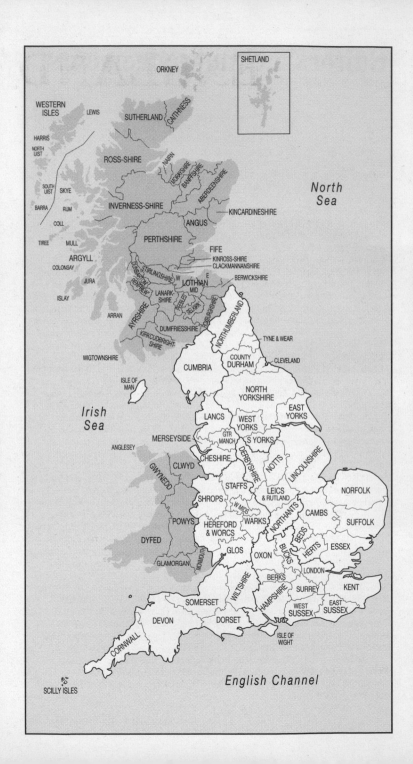

ENGLAND

Bedfordshire

New pubs this year are the Park in Bedford (a civilised and individual town oasis with imaginative cooking), Flying Horse at Clophill (much extended but with plenty of character and serving good modern food) and Fox & Hounds in Riseley (attractively refurbished by its new owners and offering super steaks). Other places doing well are the Black Horse in Ireland (attractive, character rooms and imaginative food), Hare & Hounds at Old Warden (lovely gardens and thoughtfully presented dishes), Horse & Jockey at Ravensden (carefully run, with highly thought-of food and drink), Bedford Arms in Souldrop (an honest local with a lively landlord and landlady), French Horn at Steppingley (comfortable pub with modern touches, elegant dining room and tempting food) and Birch in Woburn (family-run dining pub with impressive modern food). Our Bedfordshire Dining Pub 2014 is the Black Horse in Ireland.

AMPTHILL   TL0338 Map 5
Prince of Wales
Bedford Street (B540 N from central crossroads); MK45 2NB

Civilised with contemporary décor and up-to-date food; bedrooms

From the outside, this red-brick town house looks typically traditional; inside, it's anything but. Stylish, comfortable and on two levels, it's more of an open-plan bar-brasserie with good lighting and modern prints on the mainly cream walls (dark green and maroon accents at either end). The slightly sunken flagstoned area with a log fire in an exposed brick fireplace leads to a partly ply-panelled dining room with dark leather dining chairs set around a mixed batch of sturdy tables, and there are plenty of church candles and big leather deco-style armchairs and sofas at low tables on wood-strip flooring; background music. Wells & Youngs Bombardier and Eagle on handpump, plenty of wines by the glass and good coffee. There are picnic-sets out on a nicely planted two-level lawn, and a terrace by the car park.

As well as lunchtime sandwiches, tortilla wraps and baguettes, the wide choice of popular, interesting food might include sharing platters, chicken liver and pistachio terrine with home-made piccalilli, bubble and squeak with poached duck egg, bacon and home-made ketchup, sausages of the week with mash and red onion gravy, steak burger with bacon, stilton, coleslaw and fries, baked portobello mushroom with stilton and leek rarebit with pepper and roasted vegetable couscous, bass fillets on wilted spinach with tiger prawns, dill, spring onion and avocado oil, and prosciutto-wrapped chicken breast filled with leek and herb ricotta and chablis crème fraîche, and puddings; Thursday is steak night. *Benchmark main dish: coke and Jack Daniels-marinated rack of ribs £12.95. Two-course evening meal £17.50.*

Wells & Youngs ~ Lease Richard and Neia Heathorn ~ Real ale ~ (01525) 840504 ~ Open 12-3, 6-11(12-midnight Fri, Sat); 12-5 Sun; closed Sun evening ~ Bar food 12-2.30 (3 Sun), 6.30-9.30 ~ Restaurant ~ Children welcome ~ Dogs allowed in bar and bedrooms ~ Bedrooms: £55/£70 ~ www.princeofwales-ampthill.com *Recommended by Ruth May*

BEDFORD
Park ♀

TL0550   Map 5

Corner of Kimbolton Road (B660) and Park Avenue, out past Bedford Hospital; MK40 2PA

Civilised and individual oasis – a great asset for the city

This is a relaxing refuge throughout the day, suiting all sorts of people from young mums with toddlers, through business colleagues sorting out deals, to couples and groups simply enjoying themselves. You can choose your mood, from the more or less conventional bar with its heavy beams, panelled dado and leaded lights in big windows, the light and airy conservatory sitting room with easy chairs on carpet, or the extensive series of softly lit rambling dining areas, carpeted or flagstoned. The appealing décor has all sorts of thoughtful touches without being too obtrusive. Neat efficient staff serve Wells & Youngs Eagle, Bombardier and Bitter with a guest such as Holts Two Hoots from handpump, inventive bar nibbles and an excellent choice of wines by the glass (even half a dozen sparklers); well reproduced background music. The sheltered brick-paved terrace has good timber furniture, some under dark red canopies, and attractive shrub plantings.

They make their own bread, pasta, pickles, chutneys and ice-cream and grow their own herbs for the imaginative food: sandwiches (until 6pm), rabbit and chicken terrine with apricot and ginger chutney, white and black pudding with crispy bacon, stilton glaze and parsnip crisps, sharing platters, a risotto, pasta and fish dish of the day, steak, mushroom and oxtail pudding, corn-fed chicken breast wrapped in speck on gnocchi with taleggio and tarragon, slow-roast pork with prune stuffing, osso bucco, saffron risotto and greens, and puddings such as espresso panna cotta with bourbon biscuit and Amaretto ice-cream or dark chocolate brownie with white chocolate ice-cream. *Benchmark main dish: steak and coriander burger with swiss cheese, bacon, tomato chutney and chips £11.50. Two-course evening meal £19.00.*

Wells & Youngs ~ Lease Steve Wilkins ~ Real ale ~ (01234) 273929 ~ Open 11.30-11(11.30 Fri, Sat); 12-10.30 Sun ~ Bar food 12-3, 6-10; 12-8 Sun ~ Restaurant ~ Children welcome ~ Dogs allowed in bar ~ www.theparkbedford.co.uk
Recommended by Emma Scofield

CLOPHILL
Flying Horse

TL0837   Map 5

Corner A6 and the High Street; MK45 4AD

Interestingly refurbished dining pub with much character, bar with snug corners, two-level dining room, friendly staff and interesting modern food

Completely refurbished, this is a much extended and well run dining pub with a great deal of character. The split-level beamed bar has standing timbers and a log fire in the fine old brick fireplace, comfortable armchairs, tub chairs and cushioned stools around small copper-topped tables on the stripped bare floorboards, a rustic sideboard set with church candles, and contemporary wood-block bird paintings on the brown-painted or white-planked walls. This leads to the beamed and timbered open-plan dining area with its central raised log fire and huge conical hood, white-painted dining chairs and very long upholstered wall banquette, pale wooden tables on more floorboards and large farmyard-style paintings; there's also a lower dining area through open-timbered walls. Purity Pure Ubu and Sharps Doom Bar on handpump and several wines by the glass, served by bright young staff. There are plenty of seats outside under parasols on a side terrace and in front of the pub.

As well as inventive sharing platters, the wide choice of tempting food includes lunchtime sandwiches, pancetta hash (savoy cabbage, pancetta lardons and potato with béchamel sauce, topped with free-range egg and crispy pancetta), crispy risotto balls filled with mozzarella and roasted sweet peppers served with green chilli mayonnaise, good pizzas, tiger prawn, crab and chorizo linguine with tomato and chilli, crispy duck tossed with mooli, sesame seeds, carrot and cucumber in plum and hoisin sauce, spit-roasted gammon with free-range egg and smoked salt-seasoned frites, burger with onion, gherkin, mustard mayonnaise, cheese and relish, chicken, leek and cheese pie with lemon thyme mash, and puddings such as white chocolate brûlée and apple and blackcurrant brûlée with vanilla custard. *Benchmark main dish: rump steak £14.95. Two-course evening meal £20.00.*

Mitchells & Butlers ~ Manager David Brown ~ Real ale ~ (01525) 860293 ~ Open 11-11 ~ Bar food 12-10 ~ Restaurant ~ Children welcome ~ Dogs allowed in bar ~ www.theflyinghorse.co.uk *Recommended by Ruth May, Toby Jones*

FLITTON
White Hart ♀

TL0535   Map 5

Village signed off A507; MK45 5EJ

Simply furnished and friendly village pub with bar and dining area, real ales, interesting food, and seats in the garden

At the centre of this quiet village with a 13th-c church on one side and Flitton Moor on the other, this friendly pub is popular for its often enterprising food. The minimally decorated front bar has dark leather tub chairs around low tables, contemporary leather and chrome seats at pedestal tables, and Farrow & Ball painted walls. B&T Dragon Slayer and a guest such as Buntingford Twitchell on handpump and 20 wines – as well as champagne and prosecco – by the glass; TV. Steps lead down to a good-sized, simply furnished back dining area with red plush seats and banquettes on dark wood floorboards. The nice garden has neat shrub borders, and teak seats and tables on a terrace shaded by cedars and weeping willows.

As well as their famous steaks, the highly thought-of food includes open sandwiches, crayfish, prawn and apple cocktail, chicken liver pâté, chicken with creamed leeks, bacon and brie, duck breast with apple and red onion tarte tatin and truffle oil, chargrilled whole bass, slow-roasted pork belly with bubble and squeak, cider gravy and crackling, and puddings like white chocolate, raspberry and lavender bread and butter pudding and rum and raisin crème brûlée; they also offer a midweek two- or three-course set menu. *Benchmark main dish: fresh fish £13.25. Two-course evening meal £22.00.*

Free house ~ Licensees Phil and Clare Hale ~ Real ale ~ (01525) 862022 ~ Open
12-2.30, 6-midnight; 12-3, 6-1am Sat; 12-5 Sun; closed Sun evening, Mon ~ Bar food
12-2(2.30 Sun), 6.30-9(9.30 Fri, Sat) ~ Restaurant ~ Children welcome ~ Dogs allowed
in bar ~ www.whitehartflitton.co.uk *Recommended by Richard and Penny Gibbs*

IRELAND   TL1341   Map 5

Black Horse 🍴 🍷

Off A600 Shefford–Bedford; SG17 5QL

Bedfordshire Dining Pub of the Year

Contemporary décor in old building, imaginative food, good wine list
and lovely garden with attractive terraces; bedrooms

Our readers really enjoy their visits to this well run cottage – and you
can be sure of a friendly welcome from the attentive staff. The bars
have beams and timbering, fresh flowers and house plants, comfortable
banquettes and red leather armchairs on wood-strip and stone flooring,
Adnams Bitter, Sharps Doom Bar and St Austell Tribute on handpump, 15
wines by the glass, a dozen malt whiskies, and good coffee from the long
green slate bar counter. The rambling, two-level dining room has a mix
of elegant high-backed chairs around wooden tables on polished boards,
more wall banquettes, artwork on the walls, and a woodburning stove.
French windows open on to various terraces with individual furnishings
and mature topiary, giving a pleasant, almost garden-room feel – one
terrace is prettily surrounded by white wicket fencing and gives on to
a neatly kept garden with a play area. The bedrooms are across the
courtyard in a separate building. The Birch at Woburn is under the same
ownership.

Imaginative food includes lunchtime ciabattas, as well as crab cake with
pickled thai vegetable salad and lemongrass aioli, rope-grown mussels in
garlic, shallot and cider broth, ham roasted in orange, stout and honey with free-
range eggs, home-made vegetable haggis with crushed swede, red peppercorns and
vegetarian gravy, pie of the day, fillet of plaice filled with white crab meat in lobster
sauce on sweet potato mash with roast leeks and celery drizzled with watercress oil,
venison loin with peeled prawns on cauliflower purée, sherry-pickled prunes and
parisienne potatoes, and pudding such as blackberry soufflé with roasted pear and
apple and ginger purée and chocolate and banana brownie with candied walnuts
and clotted cream. *Benchmark main dish: pork shoulder £14.95. Two-course
evening meal £21.00.*

Free house ~ Licensee Darren Campbell ~ Real ale ~ (01462) 811398 ~ Open 11-3,
6-11; 12-5 Sun; closed Sun evening ~ Bar food 12-2.30, 6.30-10; 12-5 Sun ~ Restaurant ~
Children welcome ~ Bedrooms: /£55 ~ www.blackhorseireland.com
*Recommended by Phillip Jackson, Marianne and Peter Stevens, John and Alison Hamilton,
Peter Wiser, Andy Lickfold, Edward Heaney*

OAKLEY   TL0053   Map 5

Bedford Arms

High Street; MK43 7RH

Updated 16th-c village inn with several individual rooms, real ales and
wines by the glass, fish and other popular food in two dining rooms
and seats in an attractive garden

The four cosy, individually decorated rooms leading off the main bar
are the nicest places for a drink and chat in this updated 16th-c village

inn. One has a large circular pine table (just right for a private party), the second has farmhouse chairs and a cushioned pew beside a small fireplace, another has ladder-back chairs and shiny tables on ancient floor tiles and the last is Victorian in style. The pubbiest part, with a baby grand piano, has straightforward wooden furniture on bare boards, flower prints on the walls, daily papers, a decorative woodburning stove with a flat-screen TV above it, and Courage Directors and Wells & Youngs Eagle IPA and Special on handpump; darts. The stone-floored dining rooms have tartan-covered seating or wicker chairs and the light, airy conservatory overlooks the pretty garden, where there are seats for warm-weather meals.

As well as daily fish choices and lunchtime sandwiches, the good food includes stuffed fig with camembert, honey and walnuts, scallops with black pudding and parma ham, home-cooked ham and eggs, lemon linguine with pine nuts, sunblush tomatoes and parmesan, home-made beef burger with cheese, bacon and chips, steak, kidney and smoked oyster pudding, duck with pak choi, spring onions, cucumber and seaweed, seafood pie, and puddings like lemon and lime meringue and bread and butter pudding. *Benchmark main dish: fresh fish £14.00. Two-course evening meal £21.00.*

Wells & Youngs ~ Tenants Tim and Yvonne Walker ~ Real ale ~ (01234) 822280 ~ Open 12-11(10.30 Sun) ~ Bar food 12-2.30, 6-9.30; 12-5 Sun ~ Restaurant ~ Children welcome ~ Dogs allowed in bar ~ www.bedfordarmsoakley.co.uk
Recommended by Richard and Karen Clark

RAVENSDEN   TL0754 Map 5

Horse & Jockey 🍴 ⚲

Village signed off B660 N of Bedford; pub at Church End, off village road; MK44 2RR

Contemporary comfort, with enjoyable food and good range of drinks

Thoughtfully run and offering a genuinely friendly welcome, this enjoyable pub is popular with both drinkers and diners. The refurbished interior is pleasantly modern with a quiet colour scheme of olive greys and dark red, careful lighting, modern leather easy chairs in the bar, a meticulously designed wall of old local photographs, a rack of recent *Country Life* issues and daily papers; background music and board games. Service is charming, and there are 30 wines by the glass and four guest ales from brewers such as Adnams, Cottage, Fullers and St Austell on handpump. The bright dining room has nice chunky tables and high-backed seats, well lit prints and a contemporary etched glass screen, and overlooks a sheltered terrace with smart modern tables and chairs under cocktail parasols, a few picnic-sets on the grass beside; further off is a handsome medieval church with churchyard.

Good, carefully cooked food includes open sandwiches with chips, chicken and duck liver pâté with fruit chutney, seared scallops with pea purée and pork belly, chicken caesar salad, home-made beef burger, aubergine parmigiana with bean and olive salad, seafood linguine, slow-cooked lamb shoulder with cider red cabbage and celeriac and potato gratin, smoked haddock florentine with poached egg and citrus salad, and puddings like sticky toffee fig sponge pudding with crème anglaise and toffee sauce and chocolate mousse with vanilla ice-cream. *Benchmark main dish: braised shoulder of lamb £17.00. Two-course evening meal £22.50.*

Free house ~ Licensees Darron and Sarah Smith ~ Real ale ~ (01234) 772319 ~ Open 12-3, 6-11; 12-midnight Sat; 12-10 Sun ~ Bar food 12-2, 6-9; 12-8 Sun ~ Restaurant ~

Children welcome ~ Dogs allowed in bar ~ www.horseandjockey.info
Recommended by Michael Sargent, Jack and Sandra Clarfelt

RISELEY
Fox & Hounds
TL0462   Map 5

Off A6 from Sharnbrook/Bletsoe roundabout; High Street, just E of Gold Street; MK44 1DT

Cut-to-order steaks in attractively reworked country pub

Lots of low dark beams, stripped boards and an imposing stone fireplace with a warm winter blaze provide a sturdy skeleton, fleshed out comfortably with a mix of sofas, armchairs and housekeeper's chairs, plenty of tables, and dark green or ochre paintwork with tasteful grey floral wallpaper. Young staff are friendly and considerate, and they have Wells & Youngs Eagle and Bombardier on handpump. The separate dining room on the left is cosy yet roomy, with more low beams, soft seats and a thick carpet. This overlooks a back terrace with teak tables and verandah, and picnic-table sets on the grass beyond. There are more picnic-table sets – circular with cocktail parasols – out in front.

 Their famous steaks are hand-cut to the weight you want at the butcher's counter next to the bar, then sizzled and flamed on a monster griddle in the dining room; they come with a choice of five sauces. Other good food includes sandwiches, black pudding, chorizo and poached egg, mushroom pepper pot with stilton, fish and chips with tartare sauce, all sorts of home-made burgers with coleslaw, chilli con carne, broccoli bake, gammon and eggs, chicken dijonnaise, daily specials, and puddings such as apple crumble and jam roly-poly with custard. *Benchmark main dish: 8oz rump steak £15.65. Two-course evening meal £22.00.*

Wells & Youngs ~ Lease Antony and Diane Goodman ~ Real ale ~ (01234) 709714 ~ Open 11.30-11(11.30 Fri, Sat); 12-10.30 Sun ~ Bar food 12-2.30, 6.30-9.30(10 Sat); 12-8 Sun ~ Restaurant ~ Children welcome ~ Dogs allowed in bar ~ www.foxandhoundsriseley.co.uk *Recommended by Michael Sargent*

SOULDROP
Bedford Arms ✦ £
SP9861   Map 4

Village signposted off A6 Rushden–Bedford; High Street; MK44 1EY

Proper country tavern with good value homely food in cottagey dining area

This is a true pub – the games room is a former brew house – with chatty regulars at the bar, lively, welcoming licensees, traditional décor and an easy-going atmosphere. As well as bar chairs by the counter, there are a few more seats in the small low-beamed room, including a table in a low-ceilinged alcove. Black Sheep, Copper Kettle Cornucopia (brewed just a mile away), Greene King IPA, Hopping Mad Brainstorm and Phipps Red Star on handpump, several wines by the glass and local farm cider from Evershed's. The cottagey dining area has more low beams (one way through is potentially a real head-cracker) and a central fireplace – and, like the rest of the pub, broad floorboards, shelves of china, and original artwork (for sale). Come evenings and weekends, the spacious, mansard-ceilinged public area comes to life, with hood skittles, darts, games machine, shove-ha'penny, board games and TV; it has a big inglenook fireplace and opens on to a neat garden containing a new pétanque court.

Honest food includes sandwiches, baguettes, garlic mushrooms, home-made pâté, sausage and mash, honey-roast ham and egg, beef stew with dumplings, vegetable lasagne, various curries, and puddings such as apple crumble and sticky toffee pudding. *Benchmark main dish: steak in ale pie £9.95. Two-course evening meal £14.50.*

Free house ~ Licensees Sally Rushworth and Fred and Caroline Rich ~ Real ale ~ (01234) 781384 ~ Open 12-3, 6-11; 12-midnight Fri, Sat; 12-10 Sun; closed Mon except bank holidays ~ Bar food 12-2, 6.30-9; 12-4 Sun ~ Restaurant ~ Children welcome ~ Dogs allowed in bar *Recommended by Edward Heaney*

STEPPINGLEY TL0135 Map 5
French Horn ♀
Off A507 just N of Flitwick; Church End; MK45 5AU

Comfortable pub serving thoughtfully prepared food with modern touches

There's plenty of real character in the interconnected rooms in this attractive old pub. An eclectic mix of chesterfield sofas, leather armchairs, cushioned antique dining chairs and other furniture old and new works well with the stippled beams, standing posts and wall timbers – there are even two armchairs tucked into an old brick inglenook (another houses a woodburning stove). Some appealing pews, lamps, cushions, paintings on the wonky walls and rugs on flagstones or floorboards keep it homely and welcoming. Greene King IPA and St Edmunds on handpump, a farm cider, ten wines by the glass from a very good list and an interesting selection of malt whiskies; background music and TV. The dining room is softly lit and elegantly furnished.

 Tempting food includes lunchtime sandwiches, scotch egg with spicy mayonnaise, devilled kidneys on fried bread, roasted butternut squash risotto with blue cheese dumpling, ham and egg, chilli cheeseburger with harissa mayonnaise and triple-cooked chips, fish crumble with parsley and cheddar crust, chicken breast with sautéed potatoes, baby carrots and red wine jus, and puddings such as sticky toffee pudding with caramel sauce and clotted cream ice-cream and rice pudding with roasted plum and dark rum compote. *Benchmark main dish: beef and mushroom pie £9.95. Two-course evening meal £20.00.*

Greene King ~ Lease Richard Hargroves ~ Real ale ~ (01525) 720122 ~ Open 12-1am; 12-10.30 Sun ~ Bar food 12-3, 6-10; 12-10 Sat; 12-9 Sun ~ Restaurant ~ Children welcome ~ Dogs allowed in bar ~ www.frenchhornpub.co.uk *Recommended by Caroline Prescott*

WOBURN SP9433 Map 4
Birch ♀
3.5 miles from M1 junction 13; follow Woburn signs via A507 and A4012, right in village then A5130 (Newport Road); MK17 9HX

Well run dining establishment with focus on imaginative food, good wines and attentive service

This family-run, edge-of-town inn has several individually and elegantly furnished linked rooms with contemporary décor and paintwork. The upper and lower dining areas contain high-backed leather or wooden dining chairs around a mix of tables on polished floorboards, comfortable leather sofas, plenty of fresh flowers, house plants and candles, and modern prints on deep red or cream walls with splashes of bright blue dotted about. The bustling bar is similarly furnished, with a few high bar chairs next to the sleek, smart counter where they serve Adnams Bitter and Sharps Doom Bar on handpump, 15 good wines by the glass, a dozen malt whiskies and several teas and coffees. The airy back conservatory has a continental feel thanks to its ceramic tile floor, light-coloured furnishings and glazed pitched roof; unobtrusive background music and daily papers. There are tables out on a sheltered deck and in summer the front of the pub has masses of lovely pink hanging baskets and tubs. The Black Horse at Ireland is under the same ownership.

🍴 Choose your size of beef or venison steaks, bass fillets, swordfish and crevettes, cooked to order on a griddle; other good food includes lunchtime ciabattas, stuffed roast pear with blue cheese and red wine spiced syrup, home-made fishcake topped with poached egg and meunière sauce, beef burger with smoked bacon, melted cheese and battered onion rings, a pie and pasta dish of the day, corn-fed chicken breast with bacon, pearl onions and roasted hazelnuts in cream sauce, gressingham duck breast with honey and thyme glaze, red cabbage and raisins, and puddings such as crumble of the day and calvados apple brûlée. *Benchmark main dish: cider-cooked ham hock with roasted apple and mustard sauce £14.50. Two-course evening meal £22.50.*

Free house ~ Licensee Mark Campbell ~ Real ale ~ (01525) 290295 ~ Open 11-3, 6-11; 12-5 Sun; closed Sun evening ~ Bar food 12-2.30, 6.30-10; 12-5 Sun ~ Restaurant ~ Children welcome ~ www.birchwoburn.com *Recommended by Michael Sargent, John Saville, David and Ruth Shillitoe, Gerry and Rosemary Dobson, Roy Hoing*

Also Worth a Visit in Bedfordshire

Besides the fully inspected pubs, you might like to try these pubs that have been recommended to us and described by readers. Do tell us what you think of them: feedback@goodguides.com

AMPTHILL TL0337
Albion (01525) 634857
Dunstable Street; MK45 2JT Drinkers' pub with up to 12 well kept real ales including local B&T and Everards, three ciders and a perry, friendly knowledgeable staff, no food apart from lunchtime rolls; dogs welcome, beer garden, open all day. *(G Holmes)*

BEDFORD TL0549
Embankment (01234) 261332
The Embankment; MK40 3PD Airy L-shaped bar in refurbished mock-Tudor hotel adjacent to the river, mix of modern furniture on wood floor, Wells & Youngs ales, several wines by the glass, good choice of food all day including deli boards and daily roast, nice coffee, cheerful helpful service, back restaurant; background music; seats out at front, 20 bedrooms (best ones with river views), good breakfast. *(Harvey Brown)*

BIDDENHAM TL0249
Three Tuns (01234) 354847
Off A428; MK40 4BD Refurbished part-thatched village dining pub, food (not Sun evening, Mon) from traditional favourites to more ambitious modern cooking (evening set menu Tues-Thurs), extensive wine list, well kept Greene King ales, swift friendly service; spacious garden with picnic-sets, more contemporary furniture on terrace and decked area, open all day. *(Michael Sargent, Peter Wiser)*

BLETSOE TL0157
⋆**Falcon** (01234) 781222
Rushden Road (A6 N of Bedford); MK44 1QN Refurbished 17th-c building with comfortable opened-up bar, low beams and joists, seating from cushioned wall/window seats to high-backed settles, woodburner in double-sided fireplace, snug with sofas and old pews, panelled dining room, fairly traditional food plus some interesting specials, Wells & Youngs and a guest ale, decent choice of wines by the glass, good coffee, daily papers; unobtrusive background music; decked and paved terrace in lovely big garden down to the Ouse, open all day. *(Edward Heaney)*

BOLNHURST TL0858
⋆**Plough** (01234) 376274
Kimbolton Road; MK44 2EX Stylish conversion of ancient building with a thriving atmosphere, charming staff and top notch food, real ales such as Adnams and Hopping Mad, good carefully annotated wine list

(including organic vintages) with over a dozen by the glass, home-made summer lemonade and tomato juice, airy dining extension; children welcome, dogs in bar, attractive tree-shaded garden with decking overlooking pond, remains of old moat, closed Sun evening, Mon and for 2 weeks after Christmas. *(Ryta Lyndley, Michael Sargent, Sarah Flynn, Robert Wivell and others)*

BROMHAM   TL0050
Swan (01234) 823284
Bridge End; near A428, 2 miles W of Bedford; MK43 8LS Refurbished beamed pub in quiet village, wide food choice including deals, good separate restaurant menu, quick friendly service, well kept Greene King ales and a guest, good choice of wines by the glass, log fire, lots of pictures, locals' bar, quiz nights; children welcome, disabled access, picnic-sets out by car park. *(Peter Wiser, Michael Tack)*

BROOM   TL1742
White Horse (01767) 313425
Southill Road; SG18 9NN Comfortable country pub with rooms off small front bar, Greene King ales, enjoyable reasonably priced straightforward food from sandwiches up, friendly staff; picnic-sets in big back garden, campsite. *(Edward Heaney)*

CARDINGTON   TL0847
∗Kings Arms (01234) 838533
The Green; off A603 E of Bedford; MK44 3SP Much extended Mitchells & Butlers village dining pub with interestingly furnished linked rooms; easy-going bar with cushioned wall seats, tub chairs around trestle-style or copper-topped tables, driftwood mirrors, Adnams, Everards and Purity from rustic counter, dining room with church chairs and white-painted tables on coir, sepia photographs of airships, enjoyable food from light lunches up, good tea and coffee, more formal room with Victorian furniture, portraits and unusual log-end wallpaper, comfortable end room with leather banquettes and big log fire; background music, small TV; well behaved children and dogs welcome, disabled facilities, modern seats on terrace, picnic-sets under willows to one side. *(Peter Wiser)*

CHALTON   TL0326
Star (01525) 872248
Luton Road (B579 3 miles from M1 junction 12, via Toddington); LU4 9UJ Big comfortable Chef & Brewer pub with decent range of real ales and wines, their usual well priced food all day, friendly efficient service, main dining area separate from bar, beams and open fires; big garden,

good for families. *(Andrew Jeeves, Carole Smart, Ross Balaam)*

CLOPHILL   TL0838
Stone Jug (01525) 860526
N on A6 from A507 roundabout, after 200 metres, second turn on right into backstreet; MK45 4BY Secluded old stone-built local, cosy and welcoming, with enjoyable pubby lunchtime food at bargain prices from sandwiches up, efficient service, good choice of well kept ales, pleasantly unpretentious comfortable bar with family area and darts in small games extension; background music; roadside picnic-sets and pretty little back terrace. *(N R White)*

GREAT BARFORD   TL1351
Anchor (01234) 870364
High Street; off A421; MK44 3LF Recently refurbished open-plan Wells & Youngs pub by medieval bridge and church, their ales and guests kept well, good food (all day Sat, Sun) from snacks up, back restaurant (children welcome here); background music; picnic-sets overlooking River Ouse, three bedrooms, open all day weekends. *(Vanessa Treacle)*

HARLINGTON   TL0330
Old Sun (01525) 877330
Sundon Road, by Methodist church; LU5 6LS Recently redecorated 18th-c village pub, friendly and welcoming, with good value home-made food and decent range of well kept beers; dogs welcome, open all day. *(Lesley McKenzie)*

HENLOW   TL1738
Crown (01462) 812433
High Street; SG16 6BS Small inviting beamed pub being refurbished as we went to press; good choice of popular food all day including children's, several wines by the glass, well kept Caledonian Flying Scotsman, Courage Directors and a guest, daily newspapers, woodburner; background music; terrace and small garden, open all day. *(Harvey Brown)*

HENLOW   TL1738
∗Engineers Arms (01462) 812284
A6001 S of Biggleswade; High Street; SG16 6AA Traditional spic-and-span village pub, up to a dozen changing ales plus good choice of ciders/perries, bottled belgian beers and wines by the glass, helpful knowledgeable staff, limited range of good value snacks, comfortable carpeted front room with old local photographs on fleur-de-lys wallpaper, bric-a-brac collections and good log fire, smaller tiled inner area and another comfortable carpeted one,

occasional live music, beer/cider/country wine festivals; sports TVs, juke box, silenced fruit machine, board games; dogs allowed in bar, picnic-sets out in front and on heated back terrace, open all day. *(Anon)*

HOUGHTON CONQUEST   TL0441
Knife & Cleaver (01234) 930789
Between B530 (old A418) and A6, S of Bedford; MK45 3LA Refurbished and recently extended 17th-c dining pub, food all day from 7am, Courage, Wells & Youngs and a guest; garden with terrace, nine bedrooms. *(D C Poulton)*

KEYSOE   TL0763
⋆Chequers (01234) 708678
Pertenhall Road, Brook End (B660); MK44 2HR Good value tasty home-made food from sandwiches to blackboard specials in peaceful down-to-earth village local, friendly long-serving licensees, two homely, comfortably worn-in beamed rooms divided by stone-pillared fireplace, beers such as Bass, Boddingtons and McEwans, Weston's cider, reasonably priced wines; background music/radio, no credit cards; children welcome, wheelchair access through side door, seats on front lawn and terrace behind, play area, closed Mon evening, Tues. *(Michael and Jenny Back and others)*

MAULDEN   TL0538
⋆Dog & Badger (01525) 860237
Clophill Road E of village, towards A6/A507 junction; MK45 2AD Attractive neatly kept bow-windowed cottage, family run, with good generous well priced bar food including set weekday lunches (booking advised weekends), Wells & Youngs and guests served by friendly staff, beams and exposed brickwork, high stools on bare boards by carved wooden counter, mix of dining chairs including high-backed leather ones around wooden tables, two-way fireplace, steps down to two carpeted areas and restaurant; background music; children welcome, tables and smokers' shelter in front, back garden with sturdy play area, open all day Fri-Sun. *(Peter Wiser)*

MAULDEN   TL0537
White Hart (01525) 406118
Ampthill Road; MK45 2DH Immaculate 17th-c thatched and beamed pub, enjoyable nicely presented food from pubby choices up including good value weekday set lunch, friendly helpful service, Greene King IPA and Timothy Taylors Landlord, good choice of wines by the glass, large well divided dining area; background music; children welcome, plenty of tables in sizeable gardens with pleasant back decking, play area, open all day. *(George Atkinson)*

NORTHILL   TL1446
⋆Crown (01767) 627337
Ickwell Road; off B658 W of Biggleswade; SG18 9AA Prettily situated refurbished village pub; cosy bar with copper-topped counter, heavy low beams and bay window seats, big open fire, modern tables and chairs on wood floor in dining room, good brasserie-style food (not Sun evening), friendly helpful service, Greene King ales and a guest; background music; children welcome, no dogs inside, tables out at front and on sheltered side terrace, more in big back garden with good play area, open all day. *(M and GR, Keith MacBrayne)*

ODELL   SP9657
Bell (01234) 720254
Off A6 S of Rushden, via Sharnbrook; High Street; MK43 7AS Popular thatched village pub with several low-beamed rooms around central servery, mix of old settles and neat modern furniture, log or coal fires, good service under friendly licensees, well kept Greene King ales, good choice of generous usual food (not Sun evening) from sandwiches and baked potatoes up; background music; children welcome away from counter, delightful big garden backing on to River Ouse, handy for Harrold-Odell country park. *(Brian Brooks, Philip Sewell)*

OLD WARDEN   TL1343
⋆Hare & Hounds (01767) 627225
Village signposted off A600 S of Bedford and B658 W of Biggleswade; SG18 9HQ Contemporary styling blending cleverly with attractive old features; four cosy beamed rooms with dark standing timbers, décor in reds and creams, tweed upholstered armchairs and sofas on stripped flooring, all manner of dining chairs around light wood tables on tiling, woodburner, prints and photographs of aircraft in the Shuttleworth Collection (just up the road), Courage Directors and Wells & Youngs Eagle, several wines by the glass, attractively presented food (not Sun evening); background music; children welcome, dogs in bar, glorious garden stretching up to pine woods behind, nice thatched village and local walks, closed Mon. *(Michael Sargent, Derek Thomas, Dr Matt Burleigh)*

SOUTHILL   TL1441
White Horse (01462) 813364
Off B658 SW of Biggleswade; SG18 9LD Comfortable well run country pub with extensive eating area, enjoyable generous pubby food from baguettes up, friendly staff, good choice of changing ales and decent wines; background music; children welcome, lots of tables in big neatly kept garden with play area. *(Lois Dyer, D C Poulton)*

STAGSDEN   SP9848
Royal George (01234) 823299
High Street; MK43 8SG Cleanly refurbished modern interior, enjoyable food including signature pizzas from open kitchen, beers such as Greene King Abbot and Sharps

Doom Bar, pleasant attentive staff; children welcome, small lawn at the back and terrace. *(S Holder)*

STUDHAM TL0215
Red Lion (01582) 872530
Church Road; LU6 2QA Character community pub with hands-on landlord, and public bar and eating areas filled with all manner of bric-a-brac collected over many years, house plants, wood flooring, carpeting and old red and black tiles, homely pubby furnishings, open fire, Adnams Southwold, Fullers London Pride, Greene King IPA on handpump, themed food nights; green picnic-sets in front under pretty window boxes, more on side grass. *(Anon)*

THURLEIGH TL0558
Jackal (01234) 771293
High Street; MK44 2DB Friendly part-thatched village pub with easy chairs and fire in tiled-floor bar (where dogs allowed), another fire in comfortable carpeted dining lounge, good home-made food and service, well kept Wells & Youngs ales; background music; seats and pretty hanging baskets/tubs out by road, nice rambling garden behind, closed Mon. *(D C Poulton)*

TOTTERNHOE SP9721
⋆**Cross Keys** (01525) 220434
Off A505 W of A5; Castle Hill Road; LU6 2DA Well restored thatched and timbered two-bar pub below remains of a motte and bailey fort, low beams and cosy furnishings, good straightforward food, several real ales including well kept Adnams Broadside, friendly service, dining room; big-screen TV; good views from big attractive garden. *(Ross Balaam)*

TURVEY SP9352
Three Fyshes (01234) 881463
A428 NW of Bedford; Bridge Street, W end of village; MK43 8ER Refurbished early 17th-c beamed pub, big inglenook with woodburner, mix of easy and upright chairs around tables on tiles or ancient flagstones, enjoyable interesting home-made food (all day weekends), good friendly service, ales such as Banks's, Greene King and Marstons, decent choice of wines, daily papers, extended side restaurant; background music; dogs welcome, children in eating areas, decking and canopy in charming garden

overlooking bridge and mill on the Great Ouse, open all day. *(George Atkinson)*

UPPER DEAN TL0467
Three Compasses (01234) 708346
On road to Melchbourne, W of village; PE28 0NE 17th-c beamed and thatched pub with carpeted L-shaped bar and separate dining room, good value traditional food cooked by landlady, well kept Courage Directors, Wells & Youngs Eagle and a guest, table skittles and cribbage; garden picnic-sets, closed Mon lunchtime. *(D C Poulton)*

WILDEN TL0955
Victoria Arms (01234) 772437
Off B660 NE of Bedford; MK44 2PB Village pub under newish management in attractive spot by green next to church, Greene King IPA, Abbot and guests, standard food; open all day Fri-Sun. *(D C Poulton)*

WOBURN SP9433
Bell (01525) 290280
Bedford Street; MK17 9QJ Small beamed bar area, longer bare-boards dining lounge up steps, pleasant décor and furnishings, decent good value food all day (including OAP deals), friendly helpful service, Greene King ales, good choice of wines by the glass, nice coffee; background music, games; children welcome at lunchtime, back terrace, hotel part across busy road, handy for Woburn Park. *(John Wooll)*

WOOTTON TL0046
Legstraps (01234) 854112
Keeley Lane; MK43 9HR Extensively refurbished dining pub (was the Rose & Crown), food from sandwiches to pricey restaurant-style dishes, Adnams, Brains and Timothy Taylors ales, lots of wines by the glass including champagne. *(D C Poulton)*

WRESTLINGWORTH TL2547
Chequers (01767) 631841
High Street; SG19 2EP Smallish convivial 17th-c pub with generally well liked food including OAP lunch Weds, changing ales from central servery, open fire and woodburner, side dining area, pool; children welcome, garden with summer barbecues and bouncy castle, open all day Thurs-Sun, closed Mon lunchtime. *(Claire and Aruna Karunathilake)*

Post Office address codings confusingly give the impression that some pubs are in Bedfordshire, when they're really in Buckinghamshire or Cambridgeshire (which is where we list them).

Berkshire

Strong new entries are the White Oak at Cookham and Greene Oak in Oakley Green (carefully designed dining pubs under the same ownership with good, interesting food), Dundas Arms in Kintbury (canalside pub with a new landlord offering enjoyable food and thoughtful drinks), Fox at Peasemore (newly opened by the expert licensees formerly at the Sun in the Wood at Ashmore Green) and Pheasant at Shefford Woodlands (smartly refurbished by new, keen race-going owners). Other pubs doing notably well are the Hinds Head in Bray (owned by Heston Blumenthal and with exceptional food), Queens Arms at East Garston (smart, chatty dining pub with impressive cooking), Pot Kiln in Frilsham (very well run and popular with both drinkers and diners), Horse & Groom at Hare Hatch (thriving Brunning & Price pub with fantastic range of drinks and bistro-style food), Plume of Feathers in Hungerford (consistently reliable and deservedly busy town-centre pub), Swan in Inkpen (run by organic farmers, with a farm shop next door), Ale House in Reading (cheerful, no-frills tavern with smashing beers), Bull in Sonning (fine old place near the Thames), George & Dragon in Swallowfield (run by genuinely friendly, long-serving licensees), Beehive at White Waltham (popular food and drink in carefully run, busy pub), Winterbourne Arms in Winterbourne (bustling village pub with attractively presented meals) and Royal Oak in Yattendon (civilised but informal, serving ales brewed in the village and delicious food). The Royal Oak in Yattendon is our Berkshire Dining Pub 2014.

BRAY   SU9079   Map 2

Crown 🍴 �

1.75 miles from M4 junction 9; A308 towards Windsor, then left at Bray signpost on to B3028; High Street; SL6 2AH

Ancient low-beamed pub with knocked-through rooms, imaginative pubby food (the owner is Heston Blumenthal), real ales and plenty of outside seating

Though emphasis in this 16th-c pub is on the interesting food, you would not feel out of place just dropping in for a pint and a chat as the atmosphere is friendly and informal. The partly panelled main bar has heavy old beams – some so low you may have to mind your head – plenty of timbers handily left at elbow height where walls have been knocked through, two log fires in winter and neatly upholstered dining chairs and cushioned settles. Courage Best and Directors and a couple of changing guest beers on handpump and around 17 wines by the glass. There are modern slatted chairs and tables in the heated covered courtyard, and plenty of picnic-sets in the large, enclosed back garden.

Enjoyable food with imaginative touches includes lunchtime sandwiches, chicken liver parfait with sweet and sour onions, whitebait with lemon and horseradish mayonnaise, broccoli and blue cheese linguine, cornish mussels with cider and granny smith apple, chicken, ham and mushroom pie, fillet of hake with charred leeks, celeriac purée and cep sauce, rare-breed burger with cheese and fries, and puddings such as earl grey panna cotta with lemon crumble and banana bread with vanilla custard; also, takeaway fish and chips (Monday-Thursday) and a hamper menu for four people. *Benchmark main dish: rare-breed burger £13.00. Two-course evening meal £21.50.*

Scottish Courage ~ Lease Nick Galer ~ Real ale ~ (01628) 621936 ~ Open 11.30-11; 12-10.30 Sun ~ Bar food 12-2.30(3 Sat), 6-9.30(10 Fri, Sat); 12-8 Sun ~ Restaurant ~ Children welcome ~ Dogs allowed in bar ~ www.thecrownatbray.co.uk
Recommended by Simon Collett-Jones, Ruth May

BRAY   SU9079   Map 2

Hinds Head ❍ ♀

High Street; car park opposite (exit rather tricky); SL6 2AB

First class food in top gastropub, traditional surroundings, local ales, fine wines by the glass and quite a choice of other drinks

They're keen to keep the atmosphere in this handsome 15th-c pub informal and welcoming and it's just the place for a pint of local ale and a snack (though, of course, most customers are here to sample the inventive main courses). The thoroughly traditional L-shaped bar has dark beams and panelling, polished oak parquet, blazing log fires, red-cushioned built-in wall seats and studded leather carving chairs around small round tables, and latticed windows. They keep a couple of beers from local breweries such as Rebellion and Windsor & Eton on handpump, 14 wines by the glass from an extensive list, several malt whiskies and a dozen specialist gins with interesting ways of serving them. It's owned by Heston Blumenthal, as are the nearby Crown and renowned Fat Duck restaurant.

Beautifully presented, if not cheap, food includes nibbles like devils on horseback and scotch eggs, hash of snails, brûlée of chicken liver parfait, oxtail and kidney pudding, free-range chicken thighs with bacon, mushrooms, baby onions and red wine sauce, wild mushroom macaroni with slow-cooked egg, fillet of lemon sole with samphire, pickled cucumber and horseradish cream sauce, free-range pork belly with pearl barley and wheat beer, and puddings such as treacle tart with milk ice-cream and rhubarb trifle. *Benchmark main dish: veal chop, cabbage with onion and sauce 'reform' £29.95. Two-course evening meal £28.50.*

Free house ~ Licensee Kevin Love ~ Real ale ~ (01628) 626151 ~ Open 11-11; 12-7 Sun ~ Bar food 12-2.30, 6.30-9.30; 12-4 Sun ~ Restaurant ~ Children welcome ~ Dogs allowed in bar ~ www.hindsheadbray.com *Recommended by Ruth May*

COOKHAM

SU8885   Map 2

White Oak 🍴 ♟

The Pound (B4447); SL6 9QE

Convivial well run dining pub with good interesting food and wines

The focus here – our current favourite in the local trio of 'Oak' pubs – is the main back dining area, on the left. Three rows of round or square light-wood tables, in varying sizes, are matched by comfortably cushioned or upholstered dining chairs on polished floorboards, with brown leather wall banquettes on either side. A big skylight, white-framed mirrors on soft grey walls, and floral blinds for the french windows at the end keep things light and airy. The convivial atmosphere comes from a great mix of people really enjoying their meals, and the smiling considerate service. The linked front bar has wing armchairs, other seats on a slightly raised platform facing small high tables and high stools, big prints on the walls, and cosier areas at each side that can be closed off for private parties. There's Greene King Abbot on handpump, and an interesting choice of wines. Sturdy wooden tables and chairs on the sheltered back terrace have large canvas parasols, and steps lead up to white wirework tables on the grass.

🍴 Cooked by the chef/patron using the best local, seasonal produce, the inventive food might include oak-smoked pollack, crab mayonnaise and pickled cucumber, chorizo, goose rillette, comte cheese and capers, fresh pasta with basil, mushrooms, pine nuts, artichoke and parmesan, short rib chilli with creamed corn, lettuce and sour cream, skate wing with spinach, caper butter and chips, confit duck leg with delmonico potatoes, cress salad and celeriac remoulade, daily specials, and puddings like hot brioche doughnuts with raspberry purée and vanilla sauce and crème brûlée; they also offer a two- and three-course set menu (not Sunday lunch). *Benchmark main dish: shoulder of lamb, shepherd's pie, breast of lamb and crispy sweetbreads £16.00. Two-course evening meal £23.50.*

Greene King ~ Lease Henry and Katherine Cripps ~ Real ale ~ (01628) 523043 ~ Open 12-11.30; 12-10.30 Sun ~ Bar food 12-2.30, 6-9.30; 12-3, 5.30-8.30 Sun ~ Restaurant ~ Children welcome ~ www.thewhiteoak.co.uk *Recommended by P Waterman*

COOKHAM DEAN

SU8785   Map 2

Chequers 🍴 ♟

Dean Lane; follow signpost Cookham Dean, Marlow; SL6 9BQ

Friendly, civilised dining pub with neat, comfortable bar and restaurant, airy conservatory, first rate food and three real ales

In fine weather, there are plenty of picnic-sets under smart green parasols on the grass in front of this neatly kept, civilised brick dining pub. Inside is a busy little bar where helpful, professional staff provide a warm welcome, whether it's just a pint and a chat that you want rather than a full meal – though most customers are here to sample the imaginative food. There are comfortable old sofas on flagstones, Rebellion IPA and Smuggler on handpump, good wines by the glass, and fresh flowers and crisp white linen on the assorted dining tables on either side of the bar; a relaxed atmosphere and maybe background music. The area on the left, with an open stove in a big brick fireplace, leads back to a conservatory that overlooks the neat sloping lawn.

🍴 They offer a very good value two- and three-course set lunch menu plus other interesting choices such as roast marrow bone with parsley, garlic and croutons, tempura king prawns with sweet chilli sauce, ham hock and pistachio with pickled beetroot and spiced pear chutney, sweet potato, red pepper and chickpea risotto, pork platter (belly, tenderloin and black pudding) with herb stuffing, apple purée and crackling, bass fillet with balsamic-glazed red onion, lyonnaise potato and basil and cucumber sauce, and puddings such as blood orange, apple and blackberry crumble with custard and chocolate and hazelnut cake with tonka bean ice-cream. *Benchmark main dish: calves liver with smoked bacon and buttery mash £14.95. Two-course evening meal £22.00.*

Free house ~ Licensee Peter Roehrig ~ Real ale ~ (01628) 481232 ~ Open 11-3, 5.30-11; 12-11 Sat; 11-6 Sun; closed Sun evening ~ Bar food 12-2.30, 6.30-9.30; 12-5 Sun ~ Children welcome ~ www.chequersbrasserie.co.uk *Recommended by Harvey Brown*

 EAST GARSTON   SU3676   Map 2

Queens Arms ♀ 🛏

3.5 miles from M4 junction 14; A338 and village signposted Gt Shefford; RG17 7ET

Smart but chatty dining pub with good food and friendly country bar

This is an enjoyable place to stay in – the spacious bedrooms are attractively decorated and spotlessly clean, and the breakfasts are very good indeed. Run by helpful, friendly people, it attracts a wide mix of customers, though much of the local chat is about horse racing as the pub is at the heart of racehorse-training country. The roomy opened-up bar has plenty of antique prints (many featuring jockeys), daily papers on a corner table (the most prominent being *Racing Post*), wheelbacks and other dining chairs around well spaced tables on the wooden floor, Wadworths IPA and guest beers like Loddon Hullabaloo and West Berkshire Good Old Boy on handpump, several wines by the glass and a fair choice of whiskies. Background music and live horse racing on TV. To the right is a lighter dining area with bigger horse and country prints and a pleasing array of furniture. There are seats on a sheltered terrace. They can arrange fly fishing and shooting, and there are numerous downland walks nearby.

Using the best local, seasonal produce the enticing food includes lunchtime sandwiches, pork and sage pâté with chutney, roast pigeon with bacon, black pudding, lentils and pan juices, stuffed and roasted pork shoulder with pease pudding, apple sauce and crackling, bass fillet with sautéed potatoes, creamed cabbage and caper jus vinaigrette, partridge with game chips and bread sauce, and puddings like jam roly-poly and custard and dark chocolate brownie with chocolate sauce and vanilla ice-cream. *Benchmark main dish: fish and chips £14.50. Two-course evening meal £19.50.*

Free house ~ Licensee Adam Liddiard ~ Real ale ~ (01488) 648757 ~ Open 11-11(10.30 Sun) ~ Bar food 12-2.30, 6.30-9.30 ~ Restaurant ~ Children welcome ~ Dogs allowed in bar and bedrooms ~ Bedrooms: /£90 ~ www.queensarmshotel.co.uk
Recommended by Richard Tilbrook, Ian Herdman, Simon Lewis

 HARE HATCH   SU8077   Map 2

Horse & Groom ♀ 🍺

A4 Bath Road W of Maidenhead; RG10 9SB

Spreading pub with attractively refurbished, timbered rooms, friendly staff, enjoyable food, a fine range of drinks and seats outside

A former coaching inn on what was the great road to Bath, this place has been offering sustenance to customers for 300 years. Visitors still get a warm welcome, and plenty of space in several interlinked areas: beams and timbering, a pleasing variety of well spread individual tables and chairs on mahogany-stained floorboards, oriental rugs and some carpet to soften the acoustics, open fires in attractive tiled fireplaces, house plants and a profusion of mainly old or antique prints. The long bar counter has a splendid choice of drinks, including a good changing range of 20 wines by the glass, Brakspears Bitter and Oxford Gold and rotating guests like Brakspears Special and Wychwood Hobgoblin on handpump, two Weston's farm ciders, plenty of spirits including malts of the week, and several coffees; also several different daily papers. Busy well trained staff are kind and friendly. A sheltered back terrace has teak tables under square canvas parasols.

Good, interesting food cooked by the landlord includes sandwiches, ham hock and chicken terrine with piccalilli, king scallops with cauliflower purée, crisp smoky pancetta and peach dressing, moules marinière with white wine and shallot cream, honey and mustard ham with free-range eggs, pork and leek sausages with red wine and onion gravy, calves liver on spring onion and cabbage mash with crispy bacon and sherry jus, smoked salmon and haddock fishcakes with tomato salad, butternut squash and butter bean goulash with wild mushroom pilaff and sour cream, and puddings like belgian waffle with butterscotch sauce and vanilla ice-cream and chocolate marquise with pistachio mascarpone and black cherries. *Benchmark main dish: braised lamb shoulder with red wine and rosemary gravy £17.95. Two-course evening meal £20.00.*

Brunning & Price ~ Manager Mark Hider ~ Real ale ~ (0118) 940 3136 ~ Open 11.30-11(10.30 Sun) ~ Bar food 12-10(9.30 Sun) ~ Children welcome ~ Dogs allowed in bar ~ www.horseandgroom-harehatch.co.uk *Recommended by Paul Humphreys, Simon Collett-Jones, DHV*

HUNGERFORD SU3368 Map 2

Plume of Feathers

High Street; street parking opposite; RG17 0NB

At the heart of a bustling little town with well liked bar food and a relaxed family atmosphere

This welcoming and very well run town pub is the sort of place our readers return to again and again. It's unspoilt, friendly and full of the sound of happy chatter and the fairly priced food is very good indeed. The open-plan rooms stretch from the smallish bow-windowed façade around the island bar to an open fire in the stripped-wood fireplace at the back. There are armchairs and a black leather sofa next to low tables under lowish beams on the left at the front, and elsewhere a mix of tables with padded chairs or cushioned small pews on floorboards. There's a decent choice of wines by the glass, alongside a beer named for the pub from Greene King, Ruddles Best and a changing guest on handpump and good coffee, and the scottish landlord and his staff are unfailingly helpful. The sheltered back courtyard isn't large, but is well worth knowing about on a warm day; prettily planted, it has a swing seat as well as green-painted metal tables and chairs.

The good quality, consistently reliable food includes lunchtime sandwiches, smoked salmon terrine with horseradish cream and pickled cucumber, seared scallops with pea purée and crispy bacon, spicy three-bean tortilla wrap with cheese, sour cream and salad, roast corn-fed chicken with wild mushroom risotto and crisp pancetta, local venison sausages with beetroot mash, red onion marmalade and gravy, seared swordfish with couscous and cherry tomato salsa, and puddings such as chocolate brownie with vanilla ice-cream and passion-fruit panna cotta with tropical fruit salad. *Benchmark main dish: home-made lamb and oregano burger with feta and tzatziki £9.95. Two-course evening meal £17.50.*

Greene King ~ Lease Haley and James Weir ~ Real ale ~ (01488) 682154 ~ Open 11-3, 5.30(6 Sat)-11; 12-4 Sun; closed Sun evening ~ Bar food 12-2.30, 7-9 ~ Children welcome ~ Dogs allowed in bar *Recommended by Richard Tilbrook, Stuart Paulley, Mike and Mary Carter, Mr and Mrs P R Thomas, Pat and Graham Williamson, Martin and Sue Day, Susan and Nigel Brookes*

INKPEN SU3764 Map 2
Crown & Garter

Inkpen Common: Inkpen signposted with Kintbury off A4; in Kintbury turn left into Inkpen Road, then keep on to Inkpen Common; RG17 9QR

Remote-feeling pub with appealing layout, character bars, good food and beer and particularly friendly landlady; lovely garden and nearby walks

Run by a long-serving, friendly landlady, this is a neatly kept pub tucked away down a country lane. The low-ceilinged and relaxed panelled bar has West Berkshire Good Old Boy and a beer brewed just for the pub from the nearby Two Cocks Brewery called Gibbet Ale (it's worth asking about the name) on handpump, decent wines by the glass and several malt whiskies; a cosy small sitting area just off here has armchairs and a leather sofa in front of the woodburning stove, and shelves of books. Three original areas radiate from the bar; our pick is the parquet-floored section by the raised woodburning stove, with a couple of substantial old tables and a huge old-fashioned slightly curved settle. Other parts are slate and wood with a good mix of well spaced tables and chairs, and original black and white or sepia photographs of local scenes on the walls. The half-panelled restaurant has comfortable, padded dark sea-green leather dining chairs around a mix of freshly scrubbed wooden tables on slate flooring. There's a front terrace for outside eating, a lovely long side garden with picnic-sets, and plenty of good downland walks nearby. The bedrooms are in a separate single-storey building that forms an L around a pretty garden. King James II is reputed to have used the pub on his way to visit his mistress who lived locally.

Good, popular food includes sandwiches, deep-fried camembert with rhubarb chutney, chicken liver parfait with cranberry sauce, grazing boards, spinach and cheese tortelloni, line-caught cod fillet and chips with mushy peas, fresh crab lasagne, chargrilled chicken breast with chasseur sauce and sautéed potatoes, guinea fowl breast with wild mushroom sauce, and puddings like raspberry and almond tart with vanilla ice-cream and dark and white chocolate pots with orange sherbert. *Benchmark main dish: steak and kidney pudding £12.95. Two-course evening meal £20.00.*

Free house ~ Licensee Gill Hern ~ Real ale ~ (01488) 668325 ~ Open 12-3, 5.30-11; 12-5, 7-10.30 Sun; closed Mon and Tues lunchtimes ~ Bar food 12-2(2.30 Sun), 6.30(7 Sun)-9.30(9 Sun) ~ Restaurant ~ Children allowed in bar, but over-7s only in evening and in bedrooms ~ Bedrooms: £85/£99 ~ www.crownandgarter.co.uk
Recommended by John and Gloria Isaacs, N R White, Mrs P Sumner, Mrs J A Taylar

Post Office address codings confusingly give the impression that some pubs are in Berkshire, when they're really in Buckinghamshire, Oxfordshire or Hampshire (which is where we list them).

INKPEN
Swan

SU3564 Map 2

Lower Inkpen; coming from A338 in Hungerford, take Park Street (first left after railway bridge); RG17 9DX

Extended country pub with rambling rooms, traditional décor, friendly staff, real ales and plenty of seats outside; comfortable bedrooms

This much-extended country pub, surrounded by walks in the North Wessex Downs, has picnic-sets outside on tiered front terraces overlooking a footpath. The rambling beamed rooms have cosy corners, traditional pubby furniture, eclectic bric-a-brac and three log fires, and there's a flagstoned games area and a cosy restaurant too. Friendly helpful staff serve Butts Jester and Traditional and a changing guest on handpump and several wines by the glass; darts and board games. The bedrooms are quiet and comfortable. The interesting farm shop next door sells the owners' own organic beef and ready-made meals and groceries.

 Using beef and other produce from their organic farm and making some of their own bread and pasta, the food (with italian influences from the chef) includes mussels with onions, white wine and cream, beef ravioli with basil and tomato sauce, home-made sausages with mash and gravy, burger with cheese and chips, vegetable lasagne, beer-battered cod with tartare sauce, spaghetti napoletana, steak and kidney pudding, swordfish in spicy tomato sauce with capers, peppers, olives and pine nuts, and puddings such as blackberry and apple pie and warm chocolate fudge cake. *Benchmark main dish: home-cured bresaola with olive oil, salad, olives and balsamic dressing £14.95. Two-course evening meal £20.00.*

Free house ~ Licensees Mary and Bernard Harris ~ Real ale ~ (01488) 668326 ~ Open 12-3, 6-11; 12-11 Sat; 12-10.30 Sun; closed two weeks Christmas ~ Bar food 12-2(4 Sun), 7-9; not Sun evening or winter Mon ~ Restaurant ~ Children must be well behaved ~ Bedrooms: £70/£90 ~ www.theswaninn-organics.co.uk
Recommended by Alec and Susan Hamilton, Mr and Mrs P R Thomas, Terry Mercy

KINTBURY
Dundas Arms 🍷 🛏

SU3866 Map 2

Village signposted off A4 Newbury–Hungerford about a mile W of Halfway; Station Road – pub just over humpback canal bridge, at start of village itself; RG17 9UT

Handsomely updated inn with relaxed informal bar, good two-level restaurant, comfortable bedrooms and lovely waterside garden

In summer the large pretty garden is one of the nicest spots for miles around; the inn is on what amounts to an island in the Kennet & Avon Canal, with water each side of the garden, which has plenty of well spaced tables on the grass among shrubs and trees. This is overlooked by the big windows of the smart two-level restaurant. At the other end, the smallish bar has a relaxed informal mood thanks to the cheerful helpful staff. There are sporting prints above the high oak dado, neat little cushioned arts-and-crafts chairs around a few stripped or polished tables on the broad floorboards, and high chairs by the counter, which serves Tutts Clump farm cider from handpump as well as Arkells Wiltshire Golden, Two Cocks Cavalier and West Berkshire Good Old Boy. Outside are a few picnic-table sets on canalside decking. Between the bar and restaurant, a cosy tartan-carpeted sitting room has wing armchairs and a splendid leather and mahogany sofa, daily papers, a good winter log fire flanked by glass-fronted bookcases, and big silhouette portraits on topiary-print wallpaper. There are pleasant walks nearby.

{fork/knife icon} The thoughtful, seasonally changing menu uses local produce and includes sandwiches, eggs benedict, duck and foie gras pâté with pickles, beer-battered daily fish with crushed peas and tartare sauce, risotto with wild mushrooms, fresh herbs, parmesan wafer and truffle oil, prime rib burger with beer-battered onion rings, rabbit, pheasant and venison pie with spicy red cabbage, whole baked line-caught bass wrapped in greaseproof paper with marjoram, olives, piquillo peppers and garlic, slow-roast belly of middle white pork with mash and grain mustard, and puddings such as home-made lemon curd meringue pie with lemon crisp and sticky toffee, date and banana pudding with hot toffee sauce and clotted cream. *Benchmark main dish: slow-roast pork belly £14.50. Two-course evening meal £21.50.*

Free house ~ Licensee Tom Moran ~ (01488) 658263 ~ Open 12-11(10.30 Sun) ~ Bar food 12-2.30, 6-10; 12-9 Sun ~ Restaurant ~ Children welcome ~ Dogs allowed in bar and bedrooms ~ Bedrooms: £90/£120 ~ www.dundasarms.co.uk
Recommended by Alex Macdonald, Mrs P Sumner, Stella and Geoffrey Harrison

{logo: THE GOOD PUB GUIDE} OAKLEY GREEN SU9276 Map 2

Greene Oak {fork/knife icon} {wine glass icon}

Off A308 Windsor–Maidenhead at Twyford (B3024) signpost; Dedworth Road; SL4 5UW

Spacious well organised dining pub, good food choice with something interesting for everyone

The prototype for what is now a group of three deservedly popular places owned by Henry and Katherine Cripps (daughter of Sir Terry Wogan), it established their pattern of turning typical straightforward roadside pubs into carefully designed dining pubs, each with a good chef-patron masterminding the food side (always their focus). This one, far from its former days as a Hungry Horse chain eatery, has several eating areas rambling together, with a variety of dining chairs and wall banquettes around unusual green-painted kitchen-style tables with polished tops, on dark boards or flagstones. It's well organised for coping with large groups. Like its two offshoots, it has some country-landscape wallpaper, prints of cutlery and oak trees, and floral blinds. Those wanting just a drink will find a few chairs near the inner back bar counter, which has Greene King IPA and Abbot on handpump. There are tables and picnic-table sets out on a sizeable paved and gravelled terrace behind, and a heated shelter for smokers.

{fork/knife icon} Inventive food might include loin of rabbit stuffed with pork and truffle with pea purée and fennel salad, gratinated scallops with chorizo and herb crust, herb gnocchi with mushrooms, roast vine tomato sauce and pecorino, slow-cooked pork belly with caramelised onion and sage mash and honey-roast parsnips, cod fillet with cornish crab and salsify risotto, boned and rolled corn-fed chicken, ballontine of plaice, watercress and radish salad and pea purée, and puddings such as hot chocolate fondant with honeycomb ice-cream and steamed ginger pudding with clotted cream. *Benchmark main dish: dry-aged steak £18.55. Two-course evening meal £23.00.*

Greene King ~ Lease Henry and Katherine Cripps ~ Real ale ~ (01753) 864294 ~ Open 12-11(9.30 Sun) ~ Bar food 12-2.15, 4.30-9.15; 12-3, 5.30-8 Sun ~ Children welcome ~ www.thegreeneoak.co.uk *Recommended by Gerald Lee*

PEASEMORE
Fox

4 miles from M4 junction 13, via Chieveley: keep on through Chieveley to Peasemore, turning left into Hillgreen Lane at small sign to Fox Inn; village also signposted from B4494 Newbury–Wantage; RG20 7JN

Friendly downland pub on top form under its expert new licensees

Philip and Lauren Davison made many friends among *Guide* readers at their last pub (the Sun in the Wood at Ashmore Green), and when we visited in the spring shortly after they'd opened here, they'd already fired up that trademark buoyant atmosphere that always made the Sun such a pleasure. They've opened the place up very appealingly, breaking up the long bare-boards bar with strategically placed high-backed settles made comfortable with plenty of colourful cushions, and a woodburning stove in the stripped-brick chimneybreast; for real sybarites, there are two luxuriously carpeted end areas, one with velour tub armchairs. Friendly and efficient black-clad staff serve West Berkshire Good Old Boy and Berkshire Beauty from handpump and 15 wines by the glass; faint nostalgic pop music. This is downland horse-training country, and at the front a couple of picnic-table sets look out to rolling fields beyond the quiet country lane – on a clear day as far as the Hampshire border hills some 20 miles south; there are more tables on a smallish sheltered back terrace.

Quite a choice of enjoyable food includes pork and liver pâté with port jelly and toasted brioche, warm pigeon breast salad with black pudding, roasted shallots and raspberry jus, steak and mushroom pie, burger topped with caramelised red onions, cheddar and beer-battered onion rings, nut roast and wild mushroom strudel with sweet pepper and roasted tomato sauce, bass fillet on braised fennel with olive and basil tapendade, peppered venison steak with roasted root vegetables and game chips, and puddings such as sticky toffee and date pudding with treacle sauce and toffee ice-cream, and iced nougatine with minted raspberry coulis and tuile biscuit. *Benchmark main dish: fillet of beef wellington with stilton and port sauce £16.95. Two-course evening meal £20.45.*

Free house ~ Licensees Philip and Lauren Davison ~ Real ale ~ (01635) 248480 ~ Open 12-2.30, 6-11; 12-midnight Sat; 12-10.30 Sun; closed Mon ~ Bar food 12-2, 6-9; 12-9 Sat; 12-5 Sun ~ Restaurant ~ Children welcome ~ Dogs allowed in bar
Recommended by Ruth May, Ian Herdman

READING
Ale House

Broad Street; RG1 2BH

No-frills pub with small panelled rooms, cheerful atmosphere, and eight quickly changing ales

The lively bar in this cheerful basic pub – our readers love the place – is for those in search of interesting, quickly changing ales. Mobile phones, children and dogs are banned here, but allowed in the rest of the pub. The eight beers on handpump might include Binghams Vanilla IPA, Bristol Beer Factory Milk Stout, Burscough Mere Blonde, Stonehenge Sign of Spring, Sunny Republic Dorset Cross, West Berkshire Auntie Ruths Kitchen Porter and Brick Kiln Bitter, and Wild Weather Stormbringer. Pump clips cover practically every inch of the walls and ceiling of the simple bare-boards bar – a testament to the enormous number of brews that have passed through the pumps over the years (now over 6,650). They also have lots of different bottled beers, czech lager on tap and farm ciders and perry. Up a step is a small seating area, but the best places to sit are the three or four tiny panelled rooms reached by a narrow corridor leading from the bar; cosy and intimate, each has barely enough space for one table and a few chairs or wall seats, but they're very appealing if you're able to bag one; the biggest also manages to squeeze in a fireplace; background music and TV.

Community Taverns ~ Manager Katrina Fletcher ~ Real ale ~ No credit cards ~ (0118) 950 8119 ~ Open 11-11(midnight Fri); 12-10.30 Sun ~ Children allowed away from main bar ~ www.hobgoblinpubreading.co.uk *Recommended by Andrea Rampley*

RUSCOMBE
Royal Oak 🍴 ◀

SU7976   Map 2

Ruscombe Lane (B3024 just E of Twyford); RG10 9JN

Wide choice of popular food at welcoming pub with interesting furnishings and paintings, local beer and wine, and adjoining antiques and collectables shop

Before a visit to this notably well run pub, do pop into the landlady's antiques and collectables shop, which is open during pub hours. The open-plan carpeted bars are cleverly laid out so that each area is fairly snug, but still manages to keep the overall feel of a lot of people enjoying themselves. A good variety of furniture runs from dark oak tables to big chunky pine ones with mixed seating to match – the two sofas facing one another are popular. Contrasting with the old exposed ceiling joists, modern paintings and prints, mostly unframed, decorate the walls, which are mainly dark terracotta over a panelled dado. Binghams (the brewery is just across the road) Brickworks and Twyford Tipple and Fullers London Pride on handpump, champagne and a dozen wines by the glass (they stock wines from the Stanlake Park Vineyard in the village), several malt whiskies and attentive service. Picnic-sets are ranged around a venerable central hawthorn in the garden behind (where there are ducks and chickens); summer barbecues. The pub (known locally as Buratta's, so don't drive past) is on the Henley Arts Trail.

🍴 Using local produce and their own eggs, the highly thought-of food might include deep-fried salt and pepper squid with chilli dressing, field mushrooms stuffed with stilton mousse, various platters, marinated artichoke risotto with tomato sauce topped with parmesan, fillet of chicken with wild mushrooms, pak choi and red wine sauce, duck breast with black cherry sauce and dauphinoise potatoes, braised lamb shoulder with champ, and puddings. *Benchmark main dish: fillet of cod with creamed leeks and crushed peppered potatoes £13.00. Two-course evening meal £21.00.*

Enterprise ~ Lease Jenny and Stefano Buratta ~ Real ale ~ (0118) 934 5190 ~ Open 12-3, 6-11; 12-3 Sun; closed Sun and Mon evenings ~ Bar food 12-2.30, 6-9.30; 12-3 Sun ~ Restaurant ~ Children welcome ~ Dogs allowed in bar ~ www.burattas.co.uk *Recommended by Martin and Karen Wake, Paul Humphreys, Michael Rugman*

SHEFFORD WOODLANDS
Pheasant

SU3673   Map 2

Under 0.5 miles from M4 junction 4 – A338 towards Wantage, first left on B4000; RG17 7AA

Recently refurbished inn under new owners with bustling bars, separate dining room, enjoyable food and beer and seats outside; bedrooms

Reopened after a refurbishment just as we went to press and with a new landlord at the helm, this friendly, bustling inn now provides even more of an excuse to leave the nearby M4. The various interconnecting bar rooms have plenty of horse-related prints, photos and paintings (including a huge mural) on the walls – the owners are keen racegoers – a warm fire in a little brick fireplace, a mix of elegant wooden dining chairs and settles around all sorts of tables, and big mirrors here and there; one snug little room, with log-end wallpaper, has armchairs, a cushioned chesterfield and a flat-screen TV. There's also a separate dining room. Butts Jester, Ramsbury Gold and Upham Punter on handpump and quite a few good wines by the glass. There are seats in the garden and attractive views. The comfortable modern bedrooms are in a separate extension; the continental breakfasts (cooked is also available) are good.

Using seasonal, local produce, the food includes sandwiches, chicken liver pâté with relish, crispy salt and pepper squid with garlic mayonnaise, sharing boards, creamy wild mushroom and truffle linguine, burger with smoked cheddar, bacon and fries, beer-battered cod with samphire, chips and tartare sauce, steak and Guinness pie, risotto with lobster, rocket and parmesan crisp, and puddings such as apple and mixed berry crumble and chocolate brownie pudding with salted caramel ice-cream; on Sunday evening they offer pizzas from their stone-bake oven. *Benchmark main dish: pork belly with crackling and apple sauce £13.95. Two-course evening meal £20.00.*

Free house ~ Licensee Rupert Fowler ~ Real ale ~ (01488) 648284 ~ Open 11-11; 12-10.30 Sun ~ Bar food 12-2.30, 6.30-9.30(6-8.30 Sun) ~ Children welcome ~ Dogs welcome ~ Bedrooms: /£85 ~ www.thepheasant-inn.co.uk *Recommended by Tess White*

SONNING
Bull 🍺

SU7575   Map 2

Off B478, by church; village signed off A4 E of Reading; RG4 6UP

Pretty timbered inn in attractive spot near Thames, plenty of character in old-fashioned bars, Fullers beers, friendly staff and good food; bedrooms

Always bustling and friendly and with a wide mix of chatty customers, this fine old black and white timbered inn is picture-postcard pretty when the wisteria is flowering and the courtyard is full of tubs of bright flowers. The two old-fashioned bar rooms have low ceilings and heavy beams, cosy alcoves, leather armchairs and sofas, cushioned antique settles and low wooden chairs on bare boards, and open fireplaces. Fullers Chiswick, Discovery, HSB, London Pride and a couple of guests on handpump served by helpful staff, and good wines by the glass. The dining room has a mix of wooden chairs and tables, rugs on parquet flooring and shelves of books. If you bear left through the ivy-clad churchyard opposite, then turn left along the bank of the River Thames, you come to a very pretty lock. The Thames Valley Park is close by. The bedrooms are well equipped and comfortable.

Enjoyable food includes baguettes, a good brunch, eggs florentine with bacon, chicken liver parfait with ginger and apricot chutney and toasted brioche, fig and blue cheese tart with a fig and honey glaze, pork and ale sausages with onion gravy and crispy leeks, jerk-spiced ham with soft poached duck egg, dauphinoise potatoes and fresh grilled pineapple, chicken and leek pie with goosefat roast potatoes, trout with bean, pea and pancetta fricassée, caper butter and minted new potatoes, slow-roast gressingham duck leg with sweet tamarind sauce, and puddings such as sticky toffee pudding with salted caramel ice-cream and the italian chef's special, tiramisu. *Benchmark main dish: home-made pies £15.00. Two-course evening meal £22.50.*

Fullers ~ Manager Dennis Mason ~ Real ale ~ (0118) 969 3901 ~ Open 11-11(11.30 Sat); 12-11 Sun ~ Bar food 10-9.30 ~ Restaurant ~ Children welcome ~ Dogs allowed in bar ~ Bedrooms: /£99 ~ www.fullershotels.com
Recommended by John Saville, Sam and Christine Kilburn, Jack and Sandra Clarfelt, Susan and John Douglas, John Ecklin, Paul Humphreys

STANFORD DINGLEY   SU5771   Map 2
Old Boot
Off A340 via Bradfield, coming from A4 just W of M4 junction 12; RG7 6LT

Country furnishings and open fires in welcoming beamed bars, a choice of bar food, real ales, and rural views from seats in the garden

The beamed bar in this stylish 18th-c pub is just the place for a cosy winter drink with its two open fires (one in an inglenook), and they keep West Berkshire Good Old Boy and a guest such as Fullers London Pride on handpump and several wines by the glass, served by the warmly welcoming landlord and his staff. There are also fine old pews, settles, country chairs and polished tables, as well as some striking pictures and hunting prints, boot ornaments and fresh flowers. There's a conservatory-style restaurant too. From picnic-sets on the terrace and in the large, quiet garden, there are pleasant rural views; a swing and a slide for children. More picnic-sets at the front are dotted between flowering tubs.

 As well as sandwiches and pizzas (takeaway pizzas too), the well liked food includes smoked salmon with home-cured gravadlax and dill dressing, baked goats cheese salad with roasted beetroot, sausages of the day with onion gravy, linguine with roasted cherry tomatoes, spinach and pesto, battered fish and chips with home-made tartare sauce, pie of the week, chicken curry, duck breast with apple and cider sauce and dauphinoise potatoes, daily specials, and puddings like treacle tart with vanilla ice-cream and sticky toffee pudding. *Benchmark main dish: calves liver and bacon £10.50. Two-course evening meal £20.50.*

Free house ~ Licensee John Haley ~ Real ale ~ (0118) 974 4292 ~ Open 11-3, 6-11; 11-11 Sat, Sun ~ Bar food 12-2, 7-9 ~ Restaurant ~ Children welcome ~ Dogs allowed in bar ~ www.oldbootinn.co.uk *Recommended by Julie Preddy*

SWALLOWFIELD   SU7364   Map 2
George & Dragon ♀
Church Road, towards Farley Hill; RG7 1TJ

Busy country pub with good nearby walks, enjoyable bar food, real ales, friendly service, and seats outside

Both the long-serving licensees and their staff are sure to make you feel genuinely welcome, and there's always a good, bustling atmosphere. It's a well run comfortable pub and the various interconnected rooms have plenty of character – as well as beams (some quite low) and standing timbers, a happy mix of nice old dining chairs and settles around individual wooden tables, rugs on flagstones, lit candles, a big log fire and country prints on red or bare-brick walls; background music. Fullers London Pride, Ringwood Best and Sharps Doom Bar on handpump, quite a few wines by the glass and several gins and whiskies. In the garden there are picnic-sets on gravel or paving.

The pub website gives details of a four-mile walk that starts and ends at the pub.

🍴 Interesting and very good, the food might include sandwiches, barbecue-marinated sticky ribs with dipping sauce, beetroot and gin-cured gravlax with herb and mustard crust on pickled vegetables with lemon dressing, stuffed aubergine with pine nuts, mozzarella and basil on wilted spinach with tomato fondue, burger with bacon, cheese and guacamole served with chips and paprika mayonnaise, bacon-wrapped rabbit loin on confit pork belly with caponata and red wine jus, yellowfin tuna steak with stir-fried chinese greens and soy, and puddings like fresh fruit and marshmallows with chocolate and Amaretto dipping sauce and orange and Grand Marnier pancakes with vanilla ice-cream. *Benchmark main dish: slow-cooked lamb shoulder with rosemary jus £14.95. Two-course evening meal £19.00.*

Free house ~ Licensee Paul Dailey ~ Real ale ~ (0118) 988 4432 ~ Open 12-11(10 Sun) ~ Bar food 12-2.30(3 Sun), 7-9.30(9 Sun) ~ Restaurant ~ Children welcome ~ Dogs allowed in bar ~ www.georgeanddragonswallowfield.co.uk
Recommended by Simon Collett-Jones, DHV, Ian Herdman, Mrs P Sumner

UPPER BASILDON   SU5976   Map 2
Red Lion ♀ 🍴

Off A329 NW of Pangbourne; Aldworth Road; RG8 8NG

Laid-back country pub with friendly family atmosphere, popular food, and a good choice of drinks

After a walk along the Ridgeway, this friendly country pub is just the place to end up – and dogs are welcome in the bar too. There's a relaxed atmosphere, chapel chairs, a few pews and miscellaneous stripped tables on bare floorboards, a green leather chesterfield and armchair, and pale blue-grey paintwork throughout – even on the beams, ceiling and some of the top-stripped tables. Beyond a double-sided woodburning stove, a pitched-ceiling area has much the same furniture on cord carpet, but a big cut-glass chandelier and large mirror give it a slightly more formal dining feel. Brakspears Bitter, Otter Bitter, West Berkshire Good Old Boy and a weekly changing guest such as White Horse Brewery Bitter on handpump and an extensive wine list; the *Independent* and *Racing Post*, occasional background music and regular (usually jazz-related) live music. There are sturdy picnic-sets in the sizeable enclosed garden, where they have summer barbecues and hog roasts.

🍴 As well as lunchtime sandwiches and baguettes, the interesting food includes a coarse terrine with tomato chutney, smoked duck breast with beetroot and watercress salad and orange dressing, wild mushroom risotto, minty lamb burger with tzatziki, feta and red onion salad, home-cooked ham and eggs, calves liver with smoked bacon, roasted button onions and red wine gravy, pork and leek sausages with onion gravy, home-made chicken kiev, and puddings such as treacle tart with clotted cream and dark chocolate mousse with kirsch cherries, whipped cream and toasted almonds. *Benchmark main dish: cornish seafood spaghetti (prawns, clams, mussels, calamari) with garlic and chilli £14.50. Two-course evening meal £21.00.*

Enterprise ~ Lease Alison Green ~ Real ale ~ (01491) 671234 ~ Open 11-3, 5-11; all day weekends ~ Bar food 12-2.30, 6-9.30; 12-3.30, 6-9 Sun ~ Restaurant ~ Children welcome ~ Dogs allowed in bar ~ www.theredlionupperbasildon.co.uk *Recommended by Paul Humphreys, William Davies, Jeremy Hebblethwaite, Alan and Audrey Moulds*

WHITE WALTHAM

SU8477 Map 2

Beehive

Waltham Road (B3024 W of Maidenhead); SL6 3SH

Enjoyable bar food and welcoming staff at a traditional village pub

'This seems to personify rural England,' says one of our reporters, who was watching a game of cricket on the village field opposite, in sunshine, with a pint in his hand. It's a popular, well run pub with a bustling atmosphere and efficient, courteous staff who serve Brakspears Bitter, Fullers London Pride, Greene King Abbot and a changing guest from Loddon on handpump, ten wines by the glass and a good choice of soft drinks. To the right, several comfortably spacious areas have leather chairs around sturdy tables; to the left is a neat bar brightened up by cheerful scatter cushions on comfortable built-in wall seats and captain's chairs. A brick-built room has glass doors opening on to the front terrace (where teak seats and picnic-sets take in the pub's rather fine topiary). Background music, board games and a quiz evening on the last Thursday of the month. A good-sized sheltered back lawn has seats and tables. Disabled access and facilities.

As well as sandwiches (the hot ones come with fries), the well prepared food includes chicken liver pâté, seared scallops with bacon, home-baked ham with eggs, home-made burgers with cheese and onion rings, pie of the day, calves liver and bacon with champ and red wine jus, thai-style salmon fishcakes with sweet chilli sauce, jambalaya with chicken, chorizo, shrimps and prawns, and puddings such as banana bakewell tart and white chocolate and raspberry cheesecake. *Benchmark main dish: smoked haddock on spinach with poached egg £13.95. Two-course evening meal £21.00.*

Enterprise ~ Lease Guy Martin ~ Real ale ~ (01628) 822877 ~ Open 11-3, 5-11; 11-11 Sat; 12-10.30 Sun ~ Bar food 12-2.30, 5.30-9.30; 12-9.30 Sat; 12-8.30 Sat ~ Restaurant ~ Children welcome ~ Dogs allowed in bar ~ www.thebeehivewhitewaltham.co.uk
Recommended by Paul Humphreys, Susan and John Douglas

WINTERBOURNE

SU4572 Map 2

Winterbourne Arms ♀

3.7 miles from M4 junction 13; at A34 turn into Chieveley Services and follow Donnington signs to Arlington Lane, then follow Winterbourne signs; RG20 8BB

Bustling village pub with quite a choice of bar food, real ales, lots of wines by the glass, and a large landscaped garden

Our readers enjoy this warmly friendly old inn, and the pretty village is surrounded by lovely countryside and walks; it's handy for the M4 too. The traditionally furnished bars have early prints and old photographs of the village on pale washed or exposed stone walls, stools along the counter, a mix of pine dining chairs and tables, and a collection of old irons around the big fireplace; background music. Big windows take in peaceful views over rolling fields. Ramsbury Gold and Winterbourne Whistle Wetter (a guest beer brewed for the pub by West Berkshire) on handpump and a dozen wines by the glass including sparkling and sweet wines. There are seats outside in the large landscaped side garden and pretty flowering tubs and hanging baskets.

As well as freshly baked baguettes, the good, well presented food includes smoked duck breast with apple and red onion chutney, deep-fried butterfly prawns with lemon and sweet chilli dipping sauce, burger with cheese and bacon and straw fries, pie of the week, organic pork sausages on mash with onion gravy, beer-battered haddock with mushy peas and tartare sauce, boned chicken leg stuffed with mozzarella and bacon on ham and pea risotto with fennel seed gremolata, daily specials, and puddings such as chocolate brownie with popcorn ice-cream and apple and rhubarb crumble with custard. *Benchmark main dish: aged sirloin steak with flat cap mushrooms and skinny chips £18.95. Two-course evening meal £22.00.*

Free house ~ Licensee Frank Adams ~ Real ale ~ (01635) 248200 ~ Open 12-3, 6-11; 12-10.30 Sun ~ Bar food 12-2.30(3 Sun), 6-9.30(9 Sun) ~ Children welcome ~ Dogs allowed in bar ~ www.winterbournearms.com *Recommended by Martin and Sue Day, Jack and Sandra Clarfelt, Andrea Rampley, Michael Butler, David Fowler, Alistair Forsyth, R K Phillips*

WOOLHAMPTON
Rowbarge ♀ ◀
Station Road; RG7 5SH

SU5766 Map 2

Carefully refurbished canalside Brunning & Price pub with lots of outside seating, rambling rooms with open fires, antiques and hundreds of prints and photographs, six real ales and good, bistro-style food

In fine weather, the wooden chairs and tables on a decked terrace and the picnic-sets among trees by the edge of the Kennet & Avon Canal are quickly snapped up – it's best to arrive promptly. The six rambling rooms are connected by open doorways and knocked-through walls: beams and timbering, plenty of nooks and crannies, open fires, and décor that's gently themed to represent the nearby canal. There are oars on walls and hundreds of prints and photographs (some of rowing and boats), old glass and stone bottles, fresh flowers, big house plants and evening candles; the many large mirrors create an impression of even more space. Throughout, there are antique dining chairs around assorted nice old tables, settles, built-in cushioned wall seats, armchairs, a group of high stools around a huge wooden barrel table, and rugs on polished boards, stone tiles or carpeting. Friendly, helpful staff serve Brunning & Price Bitter (named for them by Phoenix) on handpump plus guests such as Andwell Ruddy Darter, Ramsbury Grand Slam, Stonehenge Spire and Three Castles Tiddly Dyke, 18 wines by the glass and over 50 malt whiskies; background music and board games.

Interesting modern dishes might include sandwiches, potted salmon, smoked mackerel and trout with piccalilli, pigeon breast with cauliflower purée, pancetta crisp and red wine jus, mushroom rösti with soft poached egg and blue cheese and leek sauce, crispy beef salad with cashew nuts and sweet chilli dressing, steak burger topped with grilled bacon and cheddar with coleslaw and chips, calves liver and bacon with onion and red wine gravy, braised pork belly with carrot purée, roasted shallots and star anise jus, and puddings like crème brûlée and white chocolate parfait with honeycomb and raspberry coulis. *Benchmark main dish: fish pie (salmon, smoked haddock, cod, prawns and boiled egg) with french-style peas £12.95. Two-course evening meal £19.50.*

Brunning & Price ~ Manager Stephen Butt ~ Real ale ~ (0118) 971 2213 ~ Open 11.30-11; 12-10.30 Sun ~ Bar food 12-10(9.30 Sun) ~ Restaurant ~ Children welcome ~ Dogs allowed in bar ~ www.rowbarge.hcpr.co.uk *Recommended by Belynda Mitchell, Debbie Cleminson*

We checked prices with the pubs as we went to press in summer 2013. They should hold until around spring 2014.

YATTENDON   SU5574   Map 2

Royal Oak 🍴 🍷 ⇦

The Square; B4009 NE from Newbury; right at Hampstead Norreys,
village signed on left; RG18 0UG

Berkshire Dining Pub of the Year

**Handsome old inn with beamed and panelled rooms, lovely flowers,
local beers, imaginative modern bar food, friendly service and seats in
pretty garden; comfortable bedrooms**

By the square in a pretty village, this is an elegantly handsome brick-
built inn with a lot of civilised character. The charming rooms have
plenty of space for an imaginative meal or a quiet drink; with the West
Berkshire brewery actually in the village, the four real ales on handpump
are on tip-top form, and the wines by the glass are well chosen. There
are beams and panelling, an appealing choice of wooden dining chairs
around interesting tables, some half-panelled wall seating, rugs on quarry
tiles or wooden floorboards, plenty of prints on brick, cream or red
walls, lovely flower arrangements and four log fires. Under the trellising
in the walled back garden are wicker armchairs and tables, and there
are picnic-sets beneath parasols at the front. The light and attractive
bedrooms overlook the village square or garden. The pub is only ten
minutes from Newbury Racecourse and gets pretty busy on race days.

Using beef and game from the Yattendon Estate and other carefully chosen
local produce, the excellent, beautifully presented food includes sandwiches,
grilled crevettes and chorizo with harissa mayonnaise, devilled ox kidneys on toast,
leek and gruyère tart with pomegranate and mustard leaf salad, wild boar and
apple sausages with sage and apple mash and stout gravy, crab linguine with tomato
concasse, chilli, chervil and garlic butter, roast breast and leg of guinea fowl with
fennel purée, crisp black pudding and balsamic lentils, and puddings such as apple,
cinnamon and pecan crumble with vanilla custard and white and dark chocolate
pavé with chocolate sauce; they also offer a two- and three-course weekday set
lunch. *Benchmark main dish: rabbit and mustard pie with celeriac mash and
parsnip crisps £14.00. Two-course evening meal £21.00.*

Free house ~ Licensee Rob McGill ~ Real ale ~ (01635) 201325 ~ Open 11-11; 12-10.30
Sun ~ Bar food 12-2.30(3 Fri-Sun), 6.30-9.30(10 Fri, Sat, 9 Sun) ~ Restaurant ~
Children welcome ~ Dogs welcome ~ Bedrooms: /£100 ~ www.royaloakyattendon.co.uk
Recommended by Richard Endacott, Lisa-Marie Heenan

Also Worth a Visit in Berkshire

Besides the fully inspected pubs, you might like to try these pubs that
have been recommended to us and described by readers. Do tell us what
you think of them: feedback@goodguides.com

ALDWORTH   SU5579
⋆**Bell** (01635) 578272
*A329 Reading–Wallingford; left on to
B4009 at Streatley; RG8 9SE* Unspoilt
and unchanging (in same family for over 250
years), simply furnished panelled rooms,
beams in ochre ceiling, ancient one-handed
clock, woodburner, glass-panelled hatch
serving Arkells, West Berkshire and a
monthly guest, Upton cider, nice house wines,

maybe winter mulled wine, good value rolls,
ploughman's and winter soup, traditional pub
games, no mobile phones or credit cards; can
get busy weekends; well behaved children
and dogs welcome, seats in quiet, cottagey
garden by village cricket ground, animals
in paddock behind pub, maybe Christmas
mummers and summer morris, closed Mon
(open lunchtime bank holidays). *(Richard
Endacott, Ray Carter, Franklyn Roberts, Andrea
Rampley)*

pizzas up, real ales and several wines by the glass, friendly attentive service; open all day. *(Anon)*

ALDWORTH   SU5579
✴ Four Points (01635) 578367
B4009 towards Hampstead Norreys; RG8 9RL Attractive 17th-c thatched pub with low beams, standing timbers and panelling, nice fire in bar with more formal seating area to the left and restaurant at back, good value home-made food from baguettes up, local Two Cocks and Wadworths 6X, friendly helpful young staff; children welcome, garden over road with play area. *(Paul Humphreys)*

ARBORFIELD CROSS   SU7667
Bull (01189) 762244
On roundabout; RG2 9QD Light open-plan dining pub with good popular food including some french dishes, best to book at busy times, well priced house wines, good service; children welcome, closed Mon, otherwise open all day. *(Paul Humphreys)*

ASHMORE GREEN   SU4969
Sun in the Wood (01635) 42377
B4009 (Shaw Road) off A339, right to Kiln Road, left to Stoney Lane; RG18 9HF The long-serving licensees who built an excellent reputation here for food have left – reports on new regime please; high-beamed bare-boarded front bar with nice mix of light wood cushioned dining chairs around stripped tables, Wadworths ales, more beams in big back dining area with dark wooden tables and chairs on carpet, conservatory; decked terrace with seats under parasols, old-fashioned street lights, lots of picnic-sets in big woodside garden, nine-hole woodland crazy golf. *(Anon)*

ASTON   SU7884
✴ Flower Pot (01491) 574721
Off A4130 Henley–Maidenhead at top of Remenham Hill; RG9 3DG Roomy popular country pub with nice local feel, roaring log fire, array of stuffed fish and fishing prints in airy country dining area, enjoyable food from baguettes to fish and game, well kept ales including Brakspears, quick friendly service, snug traditional bar with more fishing memorabilia; very busy with walkers and families at weekends; lots of picnic-sets giving quiet country views from big dog-friendly orchard garden, side field with poultry, Thames nearby, bedrooms. *(Alan and Liz Haffenden, D J and P M Taylor, Susan and John Douglas, DHV, Roy Hoing and others)*

BEEDON   SU4976
Coach (01635) 247271
3 miles N of M4 junction 13, via A34; RG20 8SD Modernised pub/restaurant with good food from pub staples and stone-baked

BURCHETTS GREEN   SU8381
Crown (01628) 826184
Side road from A4 after Knowl Green on left, linking to A404; SL6 6QZ Popular village dining pub with sensibly short choice of good food cooked to order, own-baked bread, well chosen wines (many from small producers), compact log-fire bar for drinkers (and dogs) with well kept Morland and Aspall's cider, good service, other areas set for eating, stripped-pine tables on wood floors, motor racing pictures (swiss landlady used to race BMWs); children welcome, picnic-sets out at front, garden with vegetable patch, some classic car meetings, open all day Sun till 9pm (no evening food then), closed Mon lunchtime. *(Paul Humphreys, Susan and John Douglas)*

CHEAPSIDE   SU9469
✴ Thatched Tavern (01344) 620874
Off A332/A329, then off B383 at Village Hall sign; SL5 7QG Civilised dining pub with a good deal of character and plenty of room if you just want a drink; interesting up-to-date food, competent friendly staff, good choice of wines by the glass, Fullers London Pride, a beer brewed for the pub and a guest ale, Weston's cider, big inglenook log fire, low beams and polished flagstones in cottagey core, three smart dining rooms off; children welcome, dogs in bar, tables on terrace and attractive sheltered back lawn, handy for Virginia Water, open all day weekends. *(John and Annabel Hampshire, Susan and John Douglas)*

CHIEVELEY   SU4773
✴ Olde Red Lion (01635) 248379
Handy for M4 junction 13 via A34 N-bound; Green Lane; RG20 8XB Attractive red-brick village pub with friendly landlord and helpful staff, three well kept Arkells beers, nice varied choice of generously served food from good sandwiches and baguettes up, reasonable prices, low-beamed carpeted L-shaped bar with panelling and hunting prints, log fire, extended back restaurant; background music, games machine, TV; wheelchair accessible throughout, small garden, bedrooms in separate old building, open all day weekends. *(Phil and Jane Hodson)*

COOKHAM   SU8985
✴ Bel & the Dragon (01628) 521263
High Street (B4447); SL6 9SQ Smartly refurbished 15th-c inn with panelling and heavy Tudor beams, log fires, bare boards and

---

Virtually all pubs in this book sell wine by the glass. We mention wines if they are a cut above the average.

simple country furnishings in two-room front bar and dining area, hand-painted cartoons on pastel walls, more formal back restaurant, helpful friendly staff, interesting well presented food (at prices you might expect for the area), Rebellion IPA and a local guest, good choice of wines; children welcome, dogs in bar, well kept garden with terrace tables, five new bedrooms, Stanley Spencer Gallery almost opposite, open all day. *(Brian Glozier)*

COOKHAM
SU8985

Ferry (01628) 525123

Sutton Road; SL6 9SN Splendidly placed riverside pub/restaurant with relaxing contemporary décor, wide choice of food all day including sharing plates and fixed-price menu (Mon-Fri 12-7pm), good service, Rebellion IPA and Timothy Taylors Landlord, some interesting lagers, comprehensive wine list, light and airy Thames-view dining areas upstairs and down, sofas and coffee tables by fireplace, small servery in beamed core; background music; children welcome, extensive terrace overlooking river. *(Martin and Karen Wake, Geoffrey John, Alistair Forsyth)*

COOKHAM DEAN
SU8785

★ Jolly Farmer (01628) 482905

Church Road, off Hills Lane; SL6 9PD Traditional pub owned by village consortium; old-fashioned unspoilt bars with open fires, five well kept ales including Brakspears, farm cider and decent wines, sensibly priced popular food from baguettes up, pleasant attentive staff, good-sized more modern eating area and small dining room, old and new local photographs, pub games; well behaved children and dogs welcome (friendly resident black lab called Czar), tables out in front and on side terrace, nice garden with play area, open all day. *(Susan and John Douglas)*

COOKHAM DEAN
SU8785

Uncle Toms Cabin (01628) 483339

Off A308 Maidenhead–Marlow; Hills Lane, towards Cookham Rise and Cookham; SL6 9NT Welcoming small-roomed local, good food from sandwiches and traditional choices up including popular Sun lunch, low beams, wood floors and half-panelling, open fire; children in eating areas, sheltered sloping back garden. *(Paul Humphreys and others)*

CRAZIES HILL
SU7980

Horns (0118) 940 6222

Warren Row Road off A4 towards Cockpole Green, then follow Crazies Hill signs; RG10 8LY Comfortable and individual old beamed pub refurbished under newish licensees, enjoyable interesting food (not Sun evening) from good lunchtime sandwiches up, friendly helpful service, Brakspears and a guest, good choice of wines by the glass, stripped furniture and open fires, raftered barn dining room with

woodburner; background music; well behaved children welcome in eating areas, dogs in bar, big garden, open all day weekends. *(Paul Humphreys and others)*

EAST ILSLEY
SU4981

★ Crown & Horns (01635) 281545

Just off A34, about 5 miles N of M4 junction 13; Compton Road; RG20 7LH Refurbished Georgian pub in horse-training country, rambling beamed rooms, log fires, reasonably priced home-made food from sandwiches, baked potatoes and pizzas up, five real ales, friendly efficient staff; background music; children, dogs and muddy boots welcome, tables in pretty courtyard, modern bedroom extension, open all day from 10am. *(Ann and Colin Hunt, Roger and Donna Huggins)*

FINCHAMPSTEAD
SU7963

Queens Oak (0118) 973 4855

Church Lane, off B3016; RG40 4LS Friendly country local named for the oak planted by Queen Victoria on green opposite; largely open-plan with mix of simple seats and tables, some in airy parquet-floored area on right, well kept Brakspears ales, enjoyable good value food (all day Sat, not Sun evening) including Mon meal deal, Thurs quiz, some live music; children, dogs and walkers welcome, picnic-sets in good-sized garden with play area, summer barbecues, open all day. *(Janice Lord)*

FRILSHAM
SU5573

★ Pot Kiln (01635) 201366

From Yattendon take turning S, opposite church, follow first Frilsham signpost, but just after crossing motorway go straight on towards Bucklebury ignoring Frilsham signposted right; pub on right after about half a mile; RG18 0XX Bustling country inn with good mix of locals and visitors, pubby feel despite emphasis on interesting food; little bar has West Berkshire ales, several wines by the glass and maybe a couple of ciders, efficient service; main bar area with dark wooden furniture on bare boards and a winter log fire, extended lounge at back leading to large dining room with nice jumble of furniture and old-looking stone fireplace; darts and board games; children and dogs welcome, idyllic spot with wide views from big suntrap garden, woodland walks nearby, open all day weekends, closed Tues. *(Paul and Penny Dawson, Rob Winstanley, Simon Rodway, Pat and Tony Martin, Robert Watt)*

GREAT SHEFFORD
SU3875

Swan (01488) 648271

2 miles from M4 junction 14, A338 towards Wantage (Newbury Road); RG17 7DS Low-ceilinged, bow-windowed pub doing well under present management, nice food from interesting sandwiches and sharing plates up, well kept ales such as

Butts, Sharps Doom Bar and Timothy Taylors Landlord, friendly efficient young staff, sofas in bar area, nice river-view dining room; children welcome, tables on attractive waterside lawn and terrace. *(Mark and Ruth Brock, Charlotte Drake, Lizie Flower, Val and Alan Green)*

HAMSTEAD MARSHALL   SU4165
White Hart   (01488) 657545
Off A4 W of Newbury; RG20 0HW
Comfortably refurbished beamed dining pub with good fresh food from sandwiches, deli boards and pub standards up, friendly prompt service, Greene King ales and a local guest like West Berkshire, plenty of wines by the glass, L-shaped bar with flagstones, half-panelling and central log fire, more contemporary dining room with woodburner and open-view kitchen; children and dogs welcome, disabled facilities, pretty tree-sheltered garden, eight bedrooms in two converted barns, open all day. *(Lisa Sumner)*

HENLEY   SU7682
⋆Little Angel   (01491) 411008
Remenham Lane (A4130, just over bridge E of Henley); RG9 2LS Civilised dining pub, more or less open-plan but with distinct seating areas, bare boards throughout, little bar with leather cube stools, tub and farmhouse chairs, woodburner, other parts with mix of dining tables and chairs, artwork on Farrow & Ball paintwork, contemporary food (all day weekends), Brakspears ales and several wines by the glass, pleasant attentive service, airy conservatory; soft background music; well behaved children allowed, dogs in bar, tables on sheltered floodlit back terrace looking over to cricket pitch, open all day. *(Simon Rodway, Tom and Ruth Rees, Susan and John Douglas, Ian Phillips, Simon Collett-Jones, DHV and others)*

HOLYPORT   SU8977
George   (01628) 628317
1.5 miles from M4 junction 8/9, via A308(M)/A330; The Green; SL6 2JL
Attractive old pub with colourful history, open-plan low-beamed interior, cosy and dimly lit, with nice fireplace, good choice of enjoyable food from baguettes up, Adnams, Courage Best and Fullers London Pride, several wines by the glass, ebullient landlord and friendly helpful service; picnic-sets on appealing terrace, lovely village green.
(Paul Humphreys, Alistair Forsyth)

HURLEY   SU8281
Dew Drop   (01628) 824327
Small yellow sign to pub off A4130 just W; SL6 6RB Old flint and brick pub tucked way in nice rustic setting, well liked traditional food from generously filled sandwiches up, Brakspears and a guest ale, friendly staff, Tues quiz; children and dogs welcome, french windows to terrace,

pleasant views from landscaped back garden, good local walks, open all day (till 6pm Sun). *(Simon Collett-Jones, Paul Humphreys, Ross Balaam)*

HURLEY   SU8382
Red Lyon   (01628) 823558
A4130 SE, just off A404; SL6 5LH Large pub with several linked low-beamed areas, stone floors and panelling, log fires, enjoyable food from sandwiches and deli boards up using local produce (some home-grown), ales such as Rebellion and White Horse; children welcome, picnic-sets in good-sized pretty garden (summer hampers and rugs available). *(Paul Humphreys)*

HURST   SU7973
Castle   (0118) 934 0034
Church Hill; RG10 0SJ Popular old dining pub still owned by the church opposite; good fairly priced food (not Sun evening, Mon) including meal deals, well kept Binghams and Rebellion, good selection of wines by the glass, well trained helpful staff, bar and two restaurant areas, beams, wood floors and old brick walls, some visible wattle and daub; children welcome, garden picnic-sets.
(Paul Humphreys, DHV)

HURST   SU8074
Green Man   (0118) 934 2599
Off A321 just outside village; RG10 0BP Partly 17th-c pub with enjoyable fairly standard food from sharing plates to steaks, weekday set menu choices too, Brakspears and a guest ale, pleasant uniformed staff, old-fashioned bar with dark beams and standing timbers, cosy alcoves, cushioned wall seats and built-in settles, hot little fire in one fireplace, old iron stove in another, dining area with modern sturdy wooden tables and high-backed chairs on solid oak floor; children welcome, sheltered terrace, picnic-sets under big oak trees in large garden with play area, open all day weekends (food all day then too). *(David and Sue Smith, Paul Humphreys)*

HURST   SU7972
Jolly Farmer   (01189) 341881
Davis Street; RG10 0TH Smartly revamped under welcoming new licensees, good value food from traditional choices to chinese and thai dishes, Greene King ales, restaurant at back; sports TVs, Weds quiz; children welcome, big enclosed garden, open all day. *(Paul Humphreys)*

KNOWL HILL   SU8178
⋆Bird in Hand   (01628) 826622
A4, handy for M4 junction 8/9; RG10 9UP Relaxed, civilised and roomy, with cosy alcoves, heavy beams, panelling and splendid log fire in tartan-carpeted main area, wide choice of popular home-made food all day (special diets catered for), well kept Brakspears and local guests, good choice

of other drinks, much older side bar, smart restaurant; soft background and occasional live music; tables on front terrace and in neat garden, Sun summer barbecues, 20 bedrooms (some in separate block). *(Susan and John Douglas, DHV, Simon Collett-Jones)*

LAMBOURN SU3180
Malt Shovel (01488) 73777
Upper Lambourn; RG17 8QN Décor and customers reflecting race-stables surroundings, traditional locals' bar, enjoyable home-made food in smart modern dining extension including good Sun carvery, nice choice of wines by the glass, well kept ales, friendly helpful staff; racing TV. *(Michael Sargent)*

LITTLEWICK GREEN SU8379
Cricketers (01628) 822888
Not far from M4 junction 9; A404(M) then left on to A4 – village signed on left; Coronation Road; SL6 3RA Welcoming refurbished country pub, Badger ales and good choice of wines by the glass, enjoyable traditional food from lunchtime sandwiches and baguettes to blackboard specials, huge clock above brick fireplace, Tues quiz; background music, can get crowded; children and dogs welcome, charming spot opposite cricket green, open all day, closed Mon in winter. *(Paul Humphreys, DHV and others)*

MARSH BENHAM SU4267
Red House (01635) 582017
Off A4 W of Newbury; RG20 8LY Attractive thatched dining pub with good fairly traditional food with a twist from french chef/owner including set menu choices (Mon-Sat till 6.30pm), West Berkshire and a guest ale, lots of wines by the glass, afternoon tea, roomy flagstoned/ wood floor bar with woodburner, refurbished restaurant; background music; children and dogs welcome, terrace and long lawns sloping to water meadows and the River Kennet, open all day. *(Dr and Mrs R E S Tanner)*

MIDGHAM SU5566
Coach & Horses (0118) 971 3384
Bath Road (N side); RG7 5UX Comfortable main-road pub with wide choice of food including good value lunchtime specials, cheerful helpful service, Fullers London Pride and Ringwood Best, flagstoned bar with sofa by brick fireplace, steps up to small half-panelled carpeted dining area, also a second dining room; children welcome, garden behind, closed Sun evening, Mon. *(Roger and Donna Huggins)*

PALEY STREET SU8675
Bridge House (01628) 623288
B3024; SL6 3JS Extended low-beamed cottage with comfortably refurbished traditional log-fire bar, friendly helpful landlady, well kept Rebellion and Fullers London Pride, decent reasonably priced pubby food (all day weekends) from shortish menu, pleasant back dining room; soft background music, TV, Weds quiz; children welcome, gardens front and back, two smokers' shelters, open all day. *(Dave Braisted)*

PALEY STREET SU8676
✳ Royal Oak (01628) 620541
B3024 W; SL6 3JN Attractively modernised and stylish 17th-c restauranty pub owned by Sir Michael Parkinson and son Nick; good british cooking (not cheap) and helpful service, Fullers London Pride, wide choice of wines by the glass including champagne, smallish informal beamed bar with open fire, leather sofas and cricketing prints, dining room split by brick pillars and timbering with mix of well spaced wooden tables and leather dining chairs on bare boards or flagstones; piped jazz; children welcome (but no pushchairs in restaurant), closed Sun evening. *(Julia and Richard Tredgett, Christopher Smith)*

READING SU7174
Griffin (0118) 947 5018
Church Road, Caversham; RG4 7AD Popular roomy Chef & Brewer in beautiful Thames-side spot overlooking swan sanctuary, separate areas with log fires, five well kept ales including Wells & Youngs, good value generously served food all day, cafetière coffee, friendly efficient young staff; soft background music and some live jazz; children welcome, tables in attractive heated courtyard. *(Dave Braisted)*

READING SU7272
Jolly Anglers (0118) 376 7823
Kennetside; RG1 3EA Simple two-room pub on River Kennet towpath originally built for workers at the former Huntley & Palmers biscuit factory; four or more well kept changing ales and up to ten ciders/perries, good value home-made food including vegetarian/vegan choices, piano, original fireplaces, darts and other pub games, open mike night Mon, quiz Thurs; resident black lab called Stella, back roof terrace, open all day. *(Susan and John Douglas)*

READING SU7174
Moderation (0118) 375 0767
Caversham Road; RG1 8BB Modernised airy Victorian pub with some eastern influences, enjoyable reasonably priced food including thai/indonesian choices, pleasant prompt service, Greene King IPA and three other well kept ales; enclosed garden behind. *(C and R Bromage)*

READING SU7073
Nags Head 07765 880137
Russell Street; RG1 7XD Friendly local with good mix of customers, a dozen well kept changing ales and 13 real ciders, baguettes and pies, open fire, darts and

cribbage; background and occasional live music, TV for major sporting events; beer garden, open all day. *(Anon)*

READING   SU7173
⁕ **Sweeney & Todd** (0118) 958 6466
Castle Street; RG1 7RD Pie shop with popular pub/restaurant behind, warren of private little period-feel alcoves and other areas on various levels, good home-made food all day including own range of pies such as venison and wild boar, cheery service, small bar with four well kept ales including Wadworths 6X, Weston's cider, nice wines; children welcome in restaurant area, open all day (closed Sun evening and bank holidays). *(Susan and John Douglas)*

SHINFIELD   SU7367
⁕ **Magpie & Parrot** (0118) 988 4130
2.6 miles from M4 junction 11, via B3270; A327 just SE of Shinfield on Arborfield Road; RG2 9EA Unusual homely little roadside cottage with warm fire, lots of bric-a-brac (miniature and historic bottles, stuffed birds, dozens of model cars, veteran AA badges and automotive instruments) in two cosy spic-and-span bars, Fullers London Pride and local guests from small corner counter, weekday lunchtime snacks and evening fish and chips (Thurs, Fri), hospitable landlady; no credit cards or mobile phones; pub dog (others welcome), seats on back terrace and marquee on immaculate lawn, open 12-7.30, closed Sun evening. *(Greg Powell, Susan and John Douglas)*

SHURLOCK ROW   SU8374
⁕ **Shurlock Inn** (0118) 934 9094
Just off B3018 SE of Twyford; The Street; RG10 0PS Village-owned pub with new landlady and some recent refurbishment; a few beams, new oak flooring, panelling and light grey walls, log fire in double-sided fireplace dividing bar and larger dining room, four local ales including West Berkshire Mr Chubb, enjoyable food (all day Sun) from pubby choices up; background music; children welcome, dogs in bar, black metal furniture on side and back terraces, garden with picnic-sets under parasols and fenced play area, open all day Fri-Sat, till 9pm Sun. *(Paul Humphreys, Simon Collett-Jones and others)*

STOCKCROSS   SU4368
Lord Lyon (01488) 608366
Off A34; RG20 8LL Welcoming 19th-c roadside pub, enjoyable home-made food using local produce including own vegetables and eggs, well kept Arkels ales; small garden, five bedrooms, open all day Sun. *(Anon)*

SUNNINGHILL   SU9367
Carpenters Arms (01344) 622763
Upper Village Road; SL5 7AQ Village pub and restaurant run by french team, good authentic french country cooking including well priced set lunch (Mon-Sat), nice wines; terrace tables, open all day.
(Hunter and Christine Wright)

SUNNINGHILL   SU9367
Dog & Partridge (01344) 623204
Upper Village Road; SL5 7AQ Modern feel with emphasis on good reasonably priced home-made food, friendly helpful staff, Fullers London Pride and Sharps Doom Bar, good range of wines; background music; children and dogs welcome, disabled facilities, sunny courtyard garden with fountain, play area, open all day weekends, closed Mon. *(Anon)*

THEALE   SU6471
Fox & Hounds (0118) 930 2295
2 miles from M4 junction 12; best to bypass restricted-access town centre – take first left at town-edge roundabout, then at railway turn right into Brunel Road, then left past station on Station Road; keep on over narrow canal bridge to Sheffield Bottom S of town; RG7 4BE Large neatly kept dining pub, friendly and relaxed, with well priced food (all day Fri-Sat, not Sun evening) from baguettes up, several Wadworths ales, Weston's cider, decent wines and coffee, L-shaped bar with dividers, traditional mix of furniture on carpet or bare boards including area with modern sofas and low tables, two open fires, daily papers, pool and darts, Sun quiz; children and dogs welcome, outside seating at front and sides, lakeside bird reserve opposite, open all day Fri-Sun. *(Anon)*

TIDMARSH   SU6374
Greyhound (0118) 984 3557
A340 S of Pangbourne; RG8 8ER Prettily restored old thatched pub, warm and friendly, with good choice of enjoyable food including early-evening discount (Mon-Thurs), pleasant service, Fullers ales, two carpeted bars, woodburner, back dining extension; good walks nearby, open all day (till 9pm Sun). *(Paul Humphreys)*

WALTHAM ST LAWRENCE   SU8376
⁕ **Bell** (0118) 934 1788
B3024 E of Twyford; The Street; RG10 0JJ Heavy-beamed and timbered 15th-c village local with cheerful landlord and chatty regulars, good home-made food (not Sun evening) from bar snacks to local

---

'Children welcome' means the pub says it lets children inside without any special restriction; some may impose an evening time limit earlier than 9pm – please tell us if you find this.

game, efficient service (may ask to keep your credit card while you eat), five very well kept changing local ales (summer beer festival), real cider, plenty of malt whiskies and nice wines, good log fires, compact panelled lounge, daily papers; children and dogs welcome, tables in back garden with extended terrace, open all day weekends. *(Paul Humphreys and others)*

WEST ILSLEY SU4782
Harrow (01635) 281260
Signed off A34 at E Ilsley slip road; RG20 7AR Appealing country pub in peaceful spot overlooking cricket pitch and pond, Victorian prints in deep-coloured knocked-through bar, some antique furnishings, log fire, good choice of enjoyable sensibly priced food (not Sun or Mon evenings), well kept Greene King ales and nice selection of wines by the glass; children in eating areas, dogs allowed in bar, big garden with picnic-sets, more seats on pleasant terrace, handy for Ridgeway walkers, may close early Sun evening if quiet. *(Helen and Brian Edgeley)*

WICKHAM SU3971
Five Bells (01488) 657300
3 miles from M4 junction 14, via A338, B4000; Baydon Road; RG20 8HH Refurbished 17th-c thatched village pub in racehorse-training country, nine changing real ales and three ciders, good choice of bottled belgian beers, popular fairly traditional home-cooked food including wood-fired pizzas, friendly staff, open-plan (but snug) beamed interior with wood floor; children welcome, garden and heated terrace, bedrooms, interesting church nearby with overhead elephants, open all day weekends. *(Paul Humphreys)*

WINDSOR SU9676
⋆ **Carpenters Arms** (01753) 863739
Market Street; SL4 1PB Nicholsons pub rambling around central servery with good choice of well kept ales and several wines by the glass, reasonably priced pubby food all day from sandwiches up including range of pies, friendly helpful service, sturdy pub furnishings and Victorian-style décor with two pretty fireplaces, family areas up a few steps, also downstairs beside former tunnel entrance with suits of armour; background music, no nearby parking, no dogs; tables out on cobbled pedestrian alley opposite the castle, handy for Legoland bus stop. *(D J and P M Taylor, Ian Herdman, George Atkinson)*

WINDSOR SU9676
Duchess of Cambridge
(01753) 864405 *Thames Street; SL4 1PL* Refurbished McMullens pub opposite the castle, their ales along with a good selection of wines and cocktails, food from lunchtime sandwiches to grills, friendly helpful staff; open all day from 9.30am. *(Alistair Forsyth)*

WINDSOR SU9676
Two Brewers (01753) 855426
Park Street; SL4 1LB In the shadow of the castle with three compact unchanging bare-board rooms, well kept Fullers London Pride with guests such as Sharps Doom Bar, good choice of wines by the glass, enjoyable food (not Fri-Sun evenings) from shortish menu, friendly efficient service, thriving old-fashioned pub atmosphere, open fire, daily papers; background music, no children inside; dogs welcome, tables out by pretty Georgian street next to Windsor Park's Long Walk, open all day. *(Ian Herdman)*

WINDSOR SU9576
Vansittart Arms (01753) 865988
Vansittart Road; SL4 5DD Friendly three-room Victorian pub, interesting local prints, some old furniture and cosy corners, open fires, well kept Fullers ales and enjoyable home-made food (not Sun evening); background and some live music, sports TV, pool; children welcome, garden with heated smokers' area, open all day. *(David M Smith)*

WOODSIDE SU9270
Rose & Crown (01344) 882051
Woodside Road, Winkfield, off A332 Ascot–Windsor; SL4 2DP Welcoming pub with low-beamed bar and neat extended dining area, good choice of enjoyable food with some spanish influences, good Sun roasts (meat from Royal Farms Windsor), attentive courteous service, Greene King ales; background music – live Sat; children welcome, tables out in front and in side garden backed by woodland, open all day. *(Martin Page)*

Buckinghamshire

A fine clutch of new entries include the Kings Head in Aylesbury (a beautiful and interesting place – part pub, part coffee shop and with an arts and crafts shop and tourist information centre), Three Oaks in Gerrards Cross (well run dining pub with comfortable and relaxed bar too), Hand & Flowers in Marlow (exceptional food in very busy inn, four real ales and character bedrooms), Swan in Milton Keynes (town-edge place given an attractive, contemporary makeover), Chandos Arms in Oakley (cheerful village pub with enthusiastic owners and tasty pubby food), Red Lion in Penn (proper character village-green pub with plenty to look at) and Jolly Cricketers at Seer Green (civilised and easy-going with enjoyable food and drink). Look out too for the Royal Oak in Bovingdon Green (pubby bar but with fine food as well), Red Lion in Chenies (smashing village pub with cheerful, long-serving landlord), Royal Standard of England at Forty Green (own brews plus guest beers, all-day food and lots of character and history), Black Horse at Fulmer (carefully run and liked by both drinkers and diners), White Horse in Hedgerley (a country gem with eight beers and an informal atmosphere), Queens Head in Little Marlow (readers return here regularly), Crown at Little Missenden (long-serving licensees, honest food and five ales), Old Queens Head at Penn (extremely helpful service plus good wines and food), Polecat at Prestwood (rather smart with thoughtful drinks and well presented food) and Chequers in Wooburn Common (a lively bar in a busy hotel). Many of these pubs serve really special food, but to become a Dining Pub award winner, it is vital to also have a thriving bar – somewhere drinkers and diners feel at ease and mix happily together. For this reason, and because its imaginative food gets better every year, the Royal Oak in Bovingdon Green is our Buckinghamshire Dining Pub 2014.

ADSTOCK   SP7330   Map 4

Old Thatched Inn

Main Street, off A413; MK18 2JN

Pretty thatched dining pub with keen landlord, friendly staff, real ales and enjoyable food

The emphasis at this pretty thatched dining pub is on the good, attractively presented food, but they do also have a front bar area with low beams, flagstones, high bar chairs and an open fire, and they do keep Fullers London Pride, Hook Norton Hooky Bitter and Sharps Doom Bar on handpump, several wines by the glass and a dozen malt whiskies; service is friendly. A dining area has more beams and a mix of pale wooden dining chairs around miscellaneous tables on stripped wooden flooring. There's also a modern conservatory restaurant at the back, with well spaced tables on bare boards. The sheltered terrace has tables and chairs under a gazebo. This is an attractive village.

 Using local, often organic, produce the popular food might include devilled kidneys with caramelised onions on toast, smoked mackerel rillette with cucumber and dill salad and granary crostini, cumberland sausages with bubble and squeak and onion gravy, lamb neck fillet with roasted root vegetables and minted red wine gravy, guinea fowl with dauphinoise potatoes and creamy mushroom sauce, bass fillet on olive oil-crushed potatoes with tomato and chorizo provencale, and puddings like raspberry cheesecake with pink champagne jelly and belgian dark chocolate parfait with honeycomb; they also offer a two- and three-course set weekday lunch and on Fridays have fish specials. *Benchmark main dish: roast aylesbury duck breast, confit leg and braised savoy cabbage £15.50. Two-course evening meal £21.00.*

Free house ~ Licensee Andrew Judge ~ Real ale ~ (01296) 712584 ~ Open 12-midnight ~ Bar food 12-2.30, 6-9.30; 12-8 Sun ~ Restaurant ~ Children welcome ~ Dogs allowed in bar ~ www.theoldthatchedinn.co.uk *Recommended by Harvey Brown*

AYLESBURY   SP8113   Map 4

Kings Head ◖

Kings Head Passage (off Bourbon Street), also entrance off Temple Street; no nearby parking except for disabled; HP20 2RW

Handsome town-centre pub with civilised atmosphere, good local ales (used in the food too) and friendly service

Our readers really enjoy this interesting place. Owned by the National Trust, it's a rather special 15th-c building, with the pub being just one part – the others are a coffee shop, arts and crafts shop, Tourist Information Office and conference rooms. It's such a surprise, tucked away as it is in a modern town centre, with particularly beautiful early Tudor windows and stunning 15th-c stained glass in the former Great Hall showing the royal arms of Henry VI and Margaret of Anjou. Three truly timeless rooms have been restored with careful and unpretentious simplicity: stripped boards, cream walls with minimal decoration, gentle lighting, a variety of seating including upholstered sofas and armchairs, cushioned high-backed settles and some simple modern pale dining tables and chairs dotted around. Most of the bar tables have circular glass tops supported on low casks. It's all nicely low-key – not smart, but thoroughly civilised. The neat corner bar has Chiltern Ale, Beechwood Bitter and a couple of guests on handpump (they are the brewery tap for Chiltern) and some interesting bottled beers. Service is friendly and there's no background music or machines; disabled access and facilities. The atmospheric medieval cobbled courtyard has teak seats and tables, some beneath a pillared roof, and a second-hand bookshop.

🍴 Good, tasty food includes sandwiches made with beer bread (the brunch muffin is popular), ham with free-range eggs, a trio of fishcakes with citrus mayonnaise, roasted vegetable parcel in creamy garlic sauce, a changing pie, beef cobbler topped with scones, and puddings such as porter cake with chocolate sauce or sticky toffee pudding. *Benchmark main dish: beer-battered fish and chips with home-made mushy peas and tartare sauce £10.95.*

Chiltern ~ Manager George Jenkinson ~ Real ale ~ (01296) 718812 ~ Open 11-11; 12-10.30 Sun ~ Bar food 12-2(3 Sat); not evenings ~ Children welcome ~ Occasional live entertainment ~ www.farmersbar.co.uk *Recommended by Tim and Ann Newell, Doug Kennedy*

BOVINGDON GREEN

Royal Oak 🍴 ♟

SU8386 Map 2

0.75 miles N of Marlow, on back road to Frieth signposted off West Street (A4155) in centre; SL7 2JF

Buckinghamshire Dining Pub of the Year

Civilised dining pub with nice little bar, a fine choice of wines by the glass, real ales, good service and excellent food

Of course, the imaginative british cooking is always going to draw customers into this friendly little whitewashed pub, but this is a proper pub and locals tend to head for the low-beamed cosy snug, closest to the car park: three small tables, a woodburning stove in an exposed brick fireplace (with a big pile of logs beside it), Rebellion IPA and Smuggler on handpump, 22 wines by the glass (all from Europe), nine pudding wines, a good choice of gins and farm cider. Several attractively decorated areas open off the central bar with the half-panelled walls painted in pale blue, green or cream (the dining room ones are red). Throughout, there's a mix of church chairs, stripped wooden tables and chunky wall seats, with rugs on the part-wood, part-flagstone floors, co-ordinated cushions and curtains, and a very bright, airy feel. Thoughtful extra touches enhance the tone: a bowl of olives on the bar, carefully laid-out newspapers and fresh flowers or candles on the tables. Board games and background music. A sunny terrace with good solid tables leads to an appealing garden; there's also a smaller side garden, a kitchen herb garden and a pétanque court. Red kites regularly fly over.

🍴 Enticing and beautifully presented, the food might include steamed mussels with bombay-spiced coconut curry cream, home tea-smoked salmon with fennel, sesame seeds and blood orange dressing, feta goats cheese with sweet potato gnocchi with spinach and toasted hazelnut pesto, local pork sausage and black pudding cassoulet with spring onion mash, chargrilled free-range chicken breast with wild mushroom and leek lasagne and truffled porcini cream, specials such as venison carpaccio with beetroot remoulade and chocolate wine syrup, and crispy bass fillet with stir-fried vegetables, pak choi, noodles and hot and sour caramel, and puddings such as baked dark chocolate soup with salted peanut ice-cream and warm prune and almond bakewell tart with maple syrup ice-cream. *Benchmark main dish: beef shin and confit onion wellington £15.25. Two-course evening meal £21.00.*

Salisbury Pubs ~ Lease Philip Daley ~ Real ale ~ (01628) 488611 ~ Open 11-11; 12-10.30 Sun ~ Bar food 12-2.30(3 Sat, 4 Sun), 6.30-9.30(10 Fri, Sat) ~ Restaurant ~ Children welcome ~ Dogs allowed in bar ~ www.royaloakmarlow.co.uk *Recommended by Simon Collett-Jones, Ellie Weld, David London, John Watson, Martin and Karen Wake, Di and Mike Gillam*

CHENIES
Red Lion ★ 🍺

TQ0298   Map 3

2 miles from M25 junction 18; A404 towards Amersham, then village signposted on right; Chesham Road; WD3 6ED

Delightful pub with long-serving licensees, a bustling atmosphere, real ales and good food

' A thoroughly good, proper village pub,' is how a couple of readers describe this white-painted brick house. The cheerful Mr Norris has been here for 27 years and the place has a loyal local following – but there's always a warm welcome for visitors too. The L-shaped bar is very traditional and unpretentious (no games machines or background music) and has comfortable built-in wall benches by the front windows, other straightforward seats and tables, and original photographs of the village and of traction engines. There's also a small back snug and a neat dining extension with more modern décor. Well kept Lion Pride is named for the pub by Rebellion and served on handpump alongside Vale Best Bitter and a couple of changing guests such as Thwaites Best Bitter and Wadworths 6X, and they have up to ten wines by the glass and some nice malt whiskies. The hanging baskets and window boxes are pretty in summer, there are picnic-sets on a small side terrace, and local walks. They now call themselves an autarkic free house. No children.

 Enjoyable food includes sandwiches, filled baked potatoes, crisp fishcake with home-made tartare sauce, lambs kidneys in creamy mustard and cayenne sauce, spinach and oyster mushoom-filled crêpes with cream and gruyère, a proper curry, smoked haddock with welsh rarebit topping, toulouse sausages with white bean and tomato cassoulet, coq au vin, flat fish of the day with parsley butter, pork belly with crackling and cider and apple sauce, daily specials and home-made puddings; the takeaway service is popular. *Benchmark main dish: lamb pie £12.50. Two-course evening meal £18.00.*

Free house ~ Licensee Mike Norris ~ Real ale ~ (01923) 282722 ~ Open 11-2.30, 5.30-11; 11-11 Sat; 12-10.30 Sun ~ Bar food 12-2, 7-10; 12-10 weekends ~ Restaurant ~ Dogs allowed in bar ~ www.theredlionchenies.co.uk *Recommended by Barry and Anne, M G Hart, Roy Hoing, Nick Gill, John Branston*

COLESHILL
Harte & Magpies

SU9594   Map 4

E of village on A355 Amersham–Beaconsfield, by junction with Magpie Lane; HP7 0LU

Friendly and busy roadside dining pub with enjoyable all-day food, well kept local ales, and seats in big garden

T his enthusiastically run pub certainly attracts a wide mix of customers – dogs (who get their own jar of treats) and owners with wellingtons are welcome, as are families (there's a children's play area) and those keen to hear live music and attend various events. Although it's a large, open-plan place, the rambling collection of miscellaneous pews, high-backed booths and some distinctive tables and chairs, plus cosy boltholes to the right, give it a pleasantly snug feel. There's a profusion of vigorously patriotic antique prints, candles in bottles, and Scrumpy Jack the self-possessed young labrador. Chiltern Ale, Rebellion

Smuggler and a changing guest beer on handpump and a good choice of other drinks too; service is friendly. Outside, a terrace has picnic-sets by a tree picturesquely draped with wisteria and the big sloping informal garden has more trees, and more tables on wood chippings. With plenty of nearby walks, it's really useful that this bustling pub serves food all day – starting at 10am with breakfast. It shares owners with the Royal Standard of England at Forty Green.

From a long menu, the popular food includes all-day breakfast, lunchtime baguettes, moroccan-spiced lamb koftas with tzatziki, garlic prawns, spaghetti carbonara, various pizzas, ham and eggs, burger with caramelised onions and chips, lambs liver and bacon, fish pie, chicken, leek and mushroom pie, daily specials (game in winter), and puddings such as hot chocolate fondant with ice-cream and treacle tart. *Benchmark main dish: fish and chips with mushy peas £12.00. Two-course evening meal £16.00.*

Free house ~ Licensee Stephen Lever ~ Real ale ~ (01494) 726754 ~ Open 10am-11pm; 11-10 Sun ~ Bar food 10-9.45; 12-8 Sun ~ Children welcome ~ Dogs welcome ~ Live music Sat evening ~ www.magpiespub.com *Recommended by Brian Glozier*

DENHAM
Swan ⑪ ⏺
Village signed from M25 junction 16; UB9 5BH

TQ0487 Map 3

Double-fronted dining pub in quiet village with interesting furnishings in several bars, open fires, good food and a fine choice of drinks

In May, when the wisteria is flowering, this civilised pub and the other old tiled village buildings are a very pretty sight. The bar rooms are stylishly furnished with a nice mix of antique and old-fashioned chairs and solid tables, individually chosen pictures on cream and warm green walls, rich heavily draped curtains, inviting open fires, newspapers and fresh flowers. Caledonian Flying Scotsman, Rebellion IPA and a summer guest beer on handpump, 22 european wines by the glass, plus nine pudding wines and a good choice of vodkas and liqueurs; background music. The extensive garden (floodlit at night) leads from a sheltered terrace with tables to a more spacious lawn. It can get busy at weekends, when parking may be tricky.

Using local, seasonal produce, the inventive food might include sandwiches, juniper-spiced fillet of beef carpaccio with waldorf salad, potted crab and crayfish with caper crème fraîche, borlotti bean, chestnut mushroom and root vegetable stew with parsley dumplings and beetroot crisps, braised pig cheeks with black and white pudding, pea mash and grain mustard gravy, beer-battered whiting fillet with tartare sauce and pea purée, specials such as whitebait with lemon mayonnaise and pork, sage and black pepper sausages with onion rings and red wine gravy, and puddings like lemon curd and treacle tart with salted caramel ice-cream and custard panna cotta with poached rhubarb and ginger snap. *Benchmark main dish: free-range coq au vin £14.75. Two-course evening meal £21.00.*

Salisbury Pubs ~ Lease Mark Littlewood ~ Real ale ~ (01895) 832085 ~ Open 11-11; 12-10.30 Sun ~ Bar food 12-2.30(3 Sat, 4 Sun), 6.30-9.30(10 Fri, Sat) ~ Restaurant ~ Children welcome ~ Dogs allowed in bar ~ www.swaninndenham.co.uk
Recommended by Kevin Thomas, Nina Randall

The knife-and-fork award ⑪ distinguishes pubs
where the food is of exceptional quality.

FINGEST SU7791 Map 2

Chequers

Off B482 Marlow–Stokenchurch; RG9 6QD

Friendly, spotlessly kept old pub with big garden, real ales and interesting food

Dating from the 15th c, this white-shuttered brick and flint pub is charmingly placed and surrounded by good walks. There's an unaffected public bar with real country charm, plus other neatly kept old-fashioned rooms that are warm and cosy, with large open fires, horsebrasses, pewter tankards, and pub team photographs on the walls. Brakspears Bitter and Special and a guest such as Banks's Sunbeam on handpump alongside quite a few wines by the glass and several malt whiskies; board games and a house cat and dog. French doors from the smart back dining extension open on to a terrace (plenty of picnic-sets), which leads to the big, beautifully tended garden with fine views over the Hambleden valley. Over the road is a unique Norman twin-roofed church tower – probably the nave of the original church.

 As well as top-selling steaks (which come from a farm just three miles away), other tempting dishes include lunchtime sandwiches, king prawns with waldorf salad and garlic mayonnaise, welsh rarebit, tagliatelle with rocket pesto and parmesan, sausage and mash with deep-fried onions, beer-battered line-caught cornish haddock with home-made tartare sauce, ballontine of chicken with lemon and thyme stuffing and creamed cabbage with pancetta, lemon sole meunière, and puddings such as treacle tart and vanilla crème brûlée with home-made shortbread. *Benchmark main dish: local steak £15.95. Two-course evening meal £20.00.*

Brakspears ~ Tenants Jaxon and Emma Keedwell ~ Real ale ~ (01491) 638335 ~ Open 12-3, 5.30-11; 12-11 Sat; 12-10.30 Sun ~ Bar food 12-2(3 Sat, 4 Sun), 7-9(9.30 Fri, Sat) ~ Restaurant ~ Children welcome ~ Dogs allowed in bar ~ www.chequersfingest.com
Recommended by Susan Loppert, Jane Caplan, John Wooll, Roy Hoing, Tracey and Stephen Groves

FORD SP7709 Map 4

Dinton Hermit 🛏

SW of Aylesbury; HP17 8XH

Carefully furnished dining pub with well liked food, big inglenook in the bar, cosy restaurant and seats in pretty garden; bedrooms in main building and converted barn

This carefully extended 16th-c stone inn is tucked away and surrounded by lots of country walks. The little bar has timbered walls, quite a choice of chairs and wooden tables on the nice old black and red tiled floor, white-painted plaster on thick uneven stone walls, an old print of John Bigg (the supposed executioner of King Charles I and the man later known as the Dinton Hermit) and a huge inglenook fireplace. The back dining area has similar furniture on quarry tiles, and church candles. Adnams Bitter and a guest from Vale on handpump and several wines by the glass. In summer, the window boxes and flower-filled wooden tubs are pretty, and there are picnic-sets under parasols in the quiet back garden. The contemporary bedrooms are comfortable, with some in the converted barn.

 Good food includes lunchtime baguettes, crispy goats cheese with red pepper essence, moules frites, steak burger topped with cheddar, assorted warm salads, pork and leek sausages with mash and apple gravy, deep-fried haddock with chips and mushy peas, a daily special, and puddings such as sticky toffee pudding and fruit with vanilla syrup and clotted cream. *Benchmark main dish: peppered rump steak £16.95. Two-course evening meal £22.00.*

Free house ~ Licensee David White ~ Real ale ~ (01296) 747473 ~ Open 11am-midnight; 11-10.30(8.30 winter) Sun ~ Bar food 12-2(3 Sun), 7-9(6.30-8.30 Sun) ~ Restaurant ~ Children welcome ~ Dogs allowed in bar ~ Bedrooms: /£110 ~ www.dintonhermit.co.uk
Recommended by Richard and Penny Gibbs, Mel Smith

FORTY GREEN
Royal Standard of England

SU9291   Map 2

3.5 miles from M40 junction 2, via A40 to Beaconsfield, then follow sign to Forty Green, off B474 0.75 miles N of New Beaconsfield; keep going through village; HP9 1XT

Full of history and character, with fascinating antiques in rambling rooms, and good choice of drinks and food

Our readers thoroughly enjoy this ancient place – one has been coming here for 50 years and says it still looks the same inside. It's been trading for nearly 900 years (the leaflet documenting the pub's history is really interesting) and there are some fine old features to look out for. The rambling rooms have huge black ship's timbers, lovely worn floors, carved old oak panelling, roaring winter fires with handsomely decorated iron firebacks and cluttered mantelpieces, and there's a massive settle apparently built to fit the curved transom of an Elizabethan ship. Nooks and crannies are filled with a collection of antiques, including rifles, powder-flasks and bugles, pewter and pottery tankards, lots of tarnished brass and copper, needlework samplers and richly coloured stained glass. As well as brewing their own Britannia Pale and Gold, they keep six changing guests from other breweries such as Brakspears, Chiltern, Elgoods, Rebellion and Windsor & Eton; there's also a carefully annotated list of bottled beers and malt whiskies, farm ciders, perry, somerset brandy and around a dozen wines by the glass. You can sit outside in a neatly hedged front rose garden or under the shade of a tree; look out for the red gargoyle on the wall facing the car park. The inn is used regularly for filming TV programmes such as *Midsomer Murders*. They also own the Harte & Magpies in Coleshill and Red Lion at Penn.

Some kind of food from the popular, wide-ranging menu, is served all day: sandwiches (until 5pm), home-made pâté, moules marinière, home-made sausages and mash with onion gravy, ham and eggs, seasonal vegetarian risotto, steak and kidney pudding, lambs liver and bacon, pork belly with bubble and squeak and apple sauce, duck breast with dauphinoise potatoes and orange sauce, and puddings such as sticky toffee pudding and pear and almond frangipane with ice-cream. *Benchmark main dish: fish and chips £12.50. Two-course evening meal £18.50.*

Own brew ~ Licensee Matthew O'Keeffe ~ Real ale ~ (01494) 673382 ~ Open 11-11; 12-10.30 Sun ~ Bar food 12-9 ~ Children welcome ~ Dogs allowed in bar ~ www.rsoe.co.uk
Recommended by N R White, Iain Clark, Paul Humphreys, Roy Hoing, Dave Braisted, Susan and John Douglas, Simon Collett-Jones, Tracey and Stephen Groves

---

The letters and figures after the name of each town are its Ordnance Survey map reference. 'Using the Guide' at the beginning of the book explains how it helps you find a pub, in road atlases or large-scale maps as well as in our own maps.

FULMER   SU9985 Map 2

Black Horse 🍴 ♟

Village signposted off A40 in Gerrards Cross, W of junction with A413;
Windmill Road; SL3 6HD

Appealingly reworked dining pub, friendly and relaxed, with
enjoyable up-to-date food, exemplary service and pleasant garden

If you can't find this 17th-c place – once craftmen's cottages – just head
for the church. It's been gradually extended over the years to form
a charming and thoughtfully run country pub with bags of character
and a welcome for both drinkers and diners. There's a proper bar in
the middle and two cosy areas to the left with low black beams, rugs
on bare boards, settles and other solid pub furniture and several open
log fires. Greene King IPA, H&H Olde Trip and a changing guest beer on
handpump and most of the wines on the list are available by the glass.
Service is friendly and efficient; background music. The main area on the
right is set for dining and leads to the good-sized suntrap back terrace.
As we went to press, they were just about to open two bedrooms. This is
a charming conservation village.

🍴 Using the best, carefully chosen local produce, the interesting food includes
sharing boards, chicken liver parfait with fig chutney, crab and avocado with
gazpacho dressing, thai vegetable curry with sticky rice, home-made beef burger
with mature cheddar, skinny chips, gherkins and coleslaw, beer-battered fish with
mushy peas and tartare sauce, chicken kiev with garlic and tomato potatoes, duck
breast with fondant potatoes and roast figs, and puddings like syrup sponge with
custard and chocolate tart with chantilly cream; between 3-6pm they also offer
light dishes such as croque monsieur, caesar salad, ham with eggs and triple-
cooked chips. *Benchmark main dish: sticky pork ribs £14.00. Two-course evening
meal £20.00.*

Greene King ~ Lease Richard Coletta ~ Real ale ~ (01753) 663183 ~ Open 8.30am-11pm;
12-10.30 Sun ~ Bar food 12-3, 6-9.30(10 Fri, Sat); 12-7 Sun ~ Restaurant ~ Children
welcome ~ Dogs allowed in bar ~ www.theblackhorsefulmer.co.uk
Recommended by Richard and Penny Gibbs, David Jackman, Dave Braisted, M G Hart, Susan and
John Douglas, R K Phillips

GERRARDS CROSS   TQ0089 Map 2

Three Oaks

Austenwood Lane, just NW of junction with Kingsway (B416); SL9 8NL

Well run dining pub with comfortable and relaxed bar too

Facing the scrub woodland of Austenwood Common, this former
roadhouse is the latest in the trio of 'Oak' pubs started in Berkshire
by Henry and Katherine Cripps (she's Sir Terry Wogan's daughter). It
struck us as the most 'pubby' of the three, with fireside bookshelves
in the more prominent two-room front bar, tartan wing armchairs and
pouffes, scatter cushions on a couple of sturdy wall settles, comfortable
banquettes and a rather broader beer choice – Fullers London Pride
and Marlow Rebellion IPA and Infiltrator on handpump. The good-sized
dining area has tartan-backed leather-seat banquettes and padded dining
chairs in three linked rooms, and a flagstoned side terrace has sturdy
wooden tables. Service is by well trained, neatly dressed young staff.

🍴 As well as a two- and three-course set menu, the impressive food includes ham
hock terrine with mustard and piccalilli, cured salmon with beetroot dressing,

grapefruit and coriander, butternut squash with sage gnocchi and mediterranean vegetable pastilla, steak and Guinness pie, megrim with pine nut and caper butter and wild garlic, chargrilled lemon and thyme chicken with salt-baked celeriac and turnip, truffle mayonnaise and frites, and puddings such as ginger loaf with pineapple and lime and chocolate brownie with blackcurrant sorbet and almond crumble. *Benchmark main dish: pork belly with roast apple, parsnip crush and chorizo and apple jam £16.90. Two-course evening meal £23.00.*

Free house ~ Licensees Henry and Katherine Cripps ~ Real ale ~ (01753) 899016 ~ Open 12-11; 12-10 Sun ~ Bar food 12-2.30, 6.30-9.30; 12-3, 5.30-8.30 Sun ~ Restaurant ~ Children welcome ~ www.thethreeoaksgx.co.uk *Recommended by Caroline Prescott, Harvey Brown*

GREAT MISSENDEN
SP9000 Map 4

Nags Head 🍴 🛏
Old London Road, E – beyond abbey; HP16 0DG

Well run and pretty inn with beamed bars, an open fire, a fine range of drinks and good modern cooking; comfortable bedrooms

The beamed bedrooms in this pretty brick and flint inn, built in the late 15th c, are well equipped and comfortable, and the breakfasts are very good. It's a quietly civilised and neatly kept place with a low beamed area on the left, a loftier part on the right, a mix of small pews, dining chairs and tables on carpet, Quentin Blake prints on cream walls and a log fire in a handsome fireplace. Fullers London Pride, Sharps Doom Bar and a changing guest from Tring, Rebellion or Vale on handpump from the unusual bar counter (the windows behind face the road) and over a dozen wines by the glass from an extensive list. There's an outside dining area beneath a pergola and seats on the extensive back lawn. This was Roald Dahl's local, and the Roald Dahl Museum & Story Centre is just a stroll away.

🍴 Imaginative meals using the freshest organic produce, local game and meat and home-smoked fish, meat and vegetables might include crab with home-smoked salmon, blinis and chive cream, shredded ham hock with scotch egg and spiced balsamic jus, beef burger with black bean and barbecue mayonnaise and fries, sausages of the day with red wine gravy, steak and kidney in ale pie, slow-cooked lamb shank in local ale, a daily vegetarian and fresh fish of the day, and puddings like chocolate and honey fondant with maple and walnut ice-cream and apple and red fruit crumble; there's also a two- and three-course weekday set menu (not Friday evening). *Benchmark main dish: beer-battered haddock and chips with mushy peas £14.95. Two-course evening meal £21.50.*

Free house ~ Licensee Adam Michaels ~ Real ale ~ (01494) 862200 ~ Open 12-11 ~ Bar food 12-2.30(3.30 Sun), 6.30-9.30(8.30 Sun) ~ Restaurant ~ Children welcome ~ Dogs allowed in bar ~ Bedrooms: /£95 ~ www.nagsheadbucks.com *Recommended by John Wooll, Ruth May*

HEDGERLEY
SU9687 Map 2

White Horse ★ 🍺 £
2.4 miles from M40 junction 2; at exit roundabout take Slough turn-off following alongside M40; after 1.5 miles turn right at T junction into Village Lane; SL2 3UY

Old-fashioned drinkers' pub with lots of beers tapped straight from the cask, regular beer festivals, home-made lunchtime food and a cheery mix of customers

Thankfully, little changes at this country gem – you can still be sure of a warm friendly welcome and a fine choice of up to eight real ales. As well as Rebellion IPA, they keep up to seven daily changing guests, sourced from all over the country and tapped straight from casks in a room behind the tiny hatch counter. Their Easter, May, Spring and August Bank Holiday beer festivals (they can get through about 130 beers during the May event) are a highlight on the local calendar. This marvellous range of drinks extends to three farm ciders, still apple juice, a perry, belgian beers, 11 wines by the glass, 11 malt whiskies and winter mulled wine. The cottagey main bar has plenty of unspoilt character, with lots of beams, brasses and exposed brickwork, low wooden tables, standing timbers, jugs, ballcocks and other bric-a-brac, a log fire, and several leaflets and notices about village events. A little flagstoned public bar on the left has darts and board games. A canopied extension leads out to the garden where there are tables and occasional barbecues, and there are numerous hanging baskets and a couple more tables in front of the building overlooking the quiet road. Good walks nearby, and the pub is handy for the Church Wood RSPB reserve and popular with walkers and cyclists; it can get crowded at weekends.

🍴 Lunchtime bar food includes good sandwiches, a salad bar with home-cooked quiches and cold meats, and a changing menu of hot dishes such as soup, sausages, lamb casserole, and proper puddings like plum sponge and bread and butter pudding. *Benchmark main dish: steak and mushroom pie £7.45.*

Free house ~ Licensees Doris Hobbs and Kevin Brooker ~ Real ale ~ (01753) 643225 ~ Open 11-2.30, 5-11; 11-11 Sat; 12-10.30 Sun ~ Bar food 12-2(2.30 weekends); not evenings ~ Children welcome in canopied extension area ~ Dogs allowed in bar
Recommended by Brian Glozier, Roy Hoing, N R White, Susan and John Douglas, Tracey and Stephen Groves

LEY HILL   SP9901   Map 4

Swan 🍺

Village signposted off A416 in Chesham; HP5 1UT

Charming, old-fashioned pub with friendly licensees, chatty customers, four real ales, and quite a choice of popular food

This lovely old country pub has a chatty and relaxed atmosphere and is kept spic and span – not easy given the antiquity of the interior – by the hands-on, friendly licensees. The main bar is cosily old-fashioned with black beams (mind your head) and standing timbers, an old range, a log fire, an appealing mix of old furniture and a collection of old local photographs. St Austell Tribute, Timothy Taylors Landlord, Tring Side Pocket for a Toad and a guest such as Sharps Doom Bar on handpump and several wines by the glass. The light and airy dining area has a raftered ceiling, cream walls and curtains and all sorts of old tables and chairs on timber floors. It's worth wandering over the common (where there's a cricket pitch and nine-hole golf course), which is opposite this little timbered 16th-c pub, to turn back and admire the very pretty picture it makes, with picnic-sets among tubs of flowers and hanging baskets (there are more in the large back garden).

🍴 Enjoyable bar food includes sandwiches, lambs kidneys with mushrooms and herbs on toasted brioche, tiger prawns in garlic, chilli and ginger butter, vegetarian tagliatelle, home-made burger with cheddar, mustard mayonnaise and chips, smoked haddock with free-range poached egg and wholegrain mustard sauce, calves liver and bacon with onion gravy, pork belly with crackling, fondant potato, apple purée and red wine jus, and puddings such as raspberry and white chocolate cheesecake and apple and rhubarb crumble with ice-cream. *Benchmark main dish: beer-battered haddock and chips with mushy peas and tartare sauce £11.95. Two-course evening meal £20.50.*

Free house ~ Licensee Nigel Byatt ~ Real ale ~ (01494) 783075 ~ Open 12-3, 5.30-11; 12-4 Sun; closed Sun evening, Mon ~ Bar food 12-2.30(3 Sun), 6.30-9 ~ Restaurant ~ Children welcome until 9pm ~ www.swanleyhill.com
Recommended by John Taylor, R E Munn, Ross Balaam

LITTLE MARLOW
SU8787 Map 2

Queens Head 🍴

Village signposted off A4155 E of Marlow near Kings Head; bear right into Pound Lane cul-de-sac; SL7 3SR

Charmingly tucked away country pub, with good food and beers, friendly staff and seats in an appealing garden

Our readers return again and again to this unpretentious, easy-going and friendly country pub – as one says, 'they just get everything right'. The main bar, with a table of magazines by the door, has simple but comfortable furniture on polished boards, and leads back to a sizeable squarish carpeted dining extension with good solid tables. Throughout are old local photographs on cream or maroon walls, panelled dados painted brown or sage, and lit candles. On the right is a small, separate, low-ceilinged public bar with Rebellion IPA and Zebedee and Sharps Doom Bar on handpump, several wines by the glass, quite a range of whiskies and good coffee; neatly dressed efficient staff and unobtrusive background music. On a summer's day, the garden in front of this pretty tiled cottage is a decided plus, though not large: sheltered and neatly planted, it has teak tables and quite close-set picnic-sets, and white-painted metal furniture in a little wickerwork bower.

As well as lunchtime sandwiches and ciabattas, the extremely popular food includes duck liver parfait with apricot and date chutney and toasted brioche, cornish scallops on black pudding with balsamic glaze, smoked salmon and scrambled eggs, pumpkin and butternut squash tartlet with chestnut purée and thyme and maple syrup shallots, pork tenderloin wrapped in parma ham with dauphinoise potatoes and red onion and beetroot jam, beer-battered fish and chips with home-made pea purée and tartare sauce, and puddings such as bakewell tart with vanilla ice-cream and pear and blackberry crumble with custard. *Benchmark main dish: steak and kidney pudding £14.95. Two-course evening meal £20.00.*

Punch ~ Lease Daniel O'Sullivan and Chris Rising ~ Real ale ~ (01628) 482927 ~ Open 12-11(10 Sun) ~ Bar food 12-2.30(4 Sat, Sun), 6.30-9.30 ~ Restaurant ~ Children welcome ~ www.marlowslittlesecret.co.uk *Recommended by Simon and Mandy King, Paul Humphreys, Ian Wilson, Jamie and Sue May, Martin and Karen Wake, Roy Hoing, D and M T Ayres-Regan*

LITTLE MISSENDEN
SU9298 Map 4

Crown £

Crown Lane, SE end of village, which is signposted off A413 W of Amersham; HP7 0RD

Long-serving licensees and pubby feel in little brick cottage, with several real ales and traditional food; attractive garden

A good mix of customers, including a loyal bunch of regulars, adds to the cheerfully chatty atmosphere in this traditional brick-built local. It's been run by the same family for more than 90 years, and the friendly landlord continues to keep it spotless. There are old red floor tiles to the left, oak parquet to the right, built-in wall seats, studded red leatherette chairs, a few small tables and a winter fire. Adnams Bitter, Exmoor Ale, St Austell Tribute and a guest or two such as Rebellion Roasted Nuts and Woodfordes Wherry on handpump or tapped from the cask, farm cider, summer Pimms and several malt whiskies; darts, bar billiards and board games. The large attractive sheltered garden behind has picnic-sets and other tables, and there are also seats out in front. The interesting church in the pretty village is well worth a visit. Bedrooms are in a converted barn (continental breakfasts in your room only).

 Honest lunchtime food includes sandwiches, soup, their famous buck's bite, home-made pies, lasagne and salads. *Benchmark main dish: buck's bite £6.75.*

Free house ~ Licensees Trevor and Carolyn How ~ Real ale ~ (01494) 862571 ~ Open 11-2.30, 6-11; 12-3, 7-11 Sun ~ Bar food 12-2; not evenings or Sun ~ Bedrooms: £65/£75 ~ www.the-crown-little-missenden.co.uk *Recommended by Roy Hoing*

MARLOW   SU8486 Map 2

Hand & Flowers
West Street (A4155); SL7 2BP

Busy little inn with sophisticated food in beamed dining rooms, four real ales in more informal extension and friendly, courteous and professional service; bedrooms

This is an exceptional place for a meal – but Tom and Beth Kerridge's busy little inn is to get an extension, which will create an area for drinkers too. Details were not finalised as we went to press, but plans were for high stools at the bar, for those popping in for a pint (or to eat at the counter) and for several tables and chairs to be available on a first come, first served basis; the bar counter in the main building will be removed to free up more dining space. The three interconnected beamed restaurant rooms are cosy and surprisingly informal, with high-backed, leather-seated chairs and brown suede wall seats around an attractive mix of chunky tables on bare floorboards or flagstones, plus pretty posies of fresh flowers, and candles in brass candlesticks or hurricane jars. They keep Greene King Abbot and IPA, Rebellion IPA and a beer named for the pub on handpump, lots of good wines by the glass from a fine list and specialist gins; service is impeccable. The character bedrooms are comfortable and well equipped – one even has its own jacuzzi terrace – with a cooked breakfast available downstairs or a continental picnic basket or bacon sandwiches in your room. Thames walks are close by.

 As well as an incredibly good value two- and three-course set lunch, the accomplished and highly enjoyable food includes parfait of duck and foie gras with orange chutney and toasted brioche, scallops with warm roast chicken bouillon, morels, nasturtium leaves and apple, red mullet with beef dripping, oxtail and bay leaf dressing, pork tenderloin with pickled mustard leaf, loin of venison with hispi cabbage, swiss chard farci and rye bread sauce, and puddings such as tonka bean panna cotta with poached rhubarb, ginger wine jelly and rhubarb sorbet and warm pistachio sponge cake with melon sorbet and marzipan. *Benchmark main dish: slow-cooked duck with fat chips £27.00. Two-course evening meal £36.00.*

Greene King ~ Lease Tom Kerridge ~ Real ale ~ (01628) 482277 ~ Open 12-5.30, 6.30-midnight; 12-6 Sun; closed Sun evening ~ Bar food 12-2.45, 6-9.45; 12-3.15 Sun ~ Restaurant ~ Children welcome ~ Dogs allowed in bedrooms ~ Bedrooms: /£140 ~ www.thehandandflowers.co.uk *Recommended by Tess White, Ruth May*

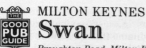

MILTON KEYNES
Swan

SP8939 Map 4

Broughton Road, Milton Keynes village; MK10 9AH

Close to the original village with plenty of space in well throught-out rooms, contemporary furnishings, open fires and woodburners, enjoyable food and drink and seats outside

With its smart new thatch and fresh white paintwork, this is an attractive pub with plenty of space both inside and out. The interconnecting rooms have been thoughtfully refurbished recently and the atmosphere throughout is easy-going and friendly – helped along by courteous service. The beamed main bar area has an open fire in an inglenook fireplace with logs piled neatly on each side and two striped plush armchairs in front, several high tables and chairs dotted about, a cushioned wall banquette with scatter cushions, wooden dining chairs and chunky tables on flagstones; Everards Yakima and Wells & Youngs Bombardier on handpump, several wines by the glass, good coffees and large glass jars of nuts. Off to the left is a cosy room with a woodburning stove, more cushioned banquettes and similar tables and chairs on parquet flooring, bookcase-effect wallpaper, some photos of the pub and a TV. The spreading, partly beamed restaurant with open kitchen views has all manner of wooden and pretty fabric-covered dining chairs, cushioned settles and wall seats and a few curved banquettes (creating snug, private areas) on floorboards, and another woodburning stove; steps lead up to an airy room overlooking the garden, which has seats and picnic-sets on grass.

 Using their own herbs, vegetables from regulars' allotments and carefully sourced local produce, the tempting food might include fennel and lemon-stuffed baby squid with chilli oil, chicken liver parfait with red onion marmalade, home-made pasta dish of the day, butternut squash, chickpea and spinach parcel with spicy tomato sauce, sausages with mash and onion gravy, pie of the day, roasted gressingham duck breast with black pudding, dauphinoise potatoes and griottines cherries, grilled fillet of bass with sautéed samphire and braised shallots, and puddings such as orange crème brûlée with chocolate-coated almonds and banana and coconut pie with rum and raisin ice-cream. *Benchmark main dish: slow-roast pork belly with creamed cabbage and bacon £14.50. Two-course evening meal £19.50.*

Front Line Inns ~ Manager Tyrone Bentham ~ Real ale ~ (01908) 665240 ~ Open 11-11(midnight Fri, Sat); 12-10.30 Sun ~ Bar food 12-3, 6-9.30; 12-10 Fri, Sat; 12-8 Sun ~ Restaurant ~ Children welcome ~ Dogs allowed in bar ~ www.theswan-mkvillage.co.uk
Recommended by Isobel Mackinlay

PENN
Old Queens Head ⑪ ♀

SU9093 Map 4

Hammersley Lane/Church Road, off B474 between Penn and Tylers Green; HP10 8EY

Stylishly updated pub with interesting food, a good choice of drinks, and woodland walks nearby

There are plenty of different areas to sit in this extended dining pub, all with different aspects, and the open-plan rooms are decorated in a stylish mix of contemporary and chintz. The various linked areas have well spaced tables, comfortably varied seating, a modicum of old prints, and floors of flagstones or broad dark boards. Stairs lead up to

an attractive (and popular) two-level dining room, part carpeted, with
stripped rafters. The active bar side has Greene King IPA and Ruddles
County on handpump, 22 wines by the glass, nine pudding wines and
several liqueurs; the turntable-top bar stools let you swivel to face
the log fire in the big fireplace. There are lots of daily papers and well
reproduced background music. The sunny terrace overlooks the church
of St Margaret's and there are picnic-sets on the sheltered L-shaped lawn.
You can walk through the nearby ancient beechwoods of Common or
Penn Woods.

🍴 Good, imaginative food might include lunchtime sandwiches (not weekends),
confit duck leg hash with puy lentils and poached local duck egg yolk, potted
home-smoked mackerel with beetroot and horseradish relish, salsify and swede
risotto with wild mushrooms, tempura oyster mushrooms and parmesan crisps,
roast sea bream fillet with confit tomato, lemon butter sauce, saffron oil and
dauphinoise potatoes, pheasant, leek and mushroom pie, specials such as free-
range pork and herb scotch egg with piccalilli or barbary duck breast with celeriac
dauphinoise, broccoli purée and pan juices, and puddings like white chocolate tart
with pineapple carpaccio and coconut ice-cream and poached saffron pears with
vanilla ice-cream and meringue. *Benchmark main dish: slow-cooked local pork
belly £14.75. Two-course evening meal £21.00.*

Salisbury Pubs ~ Lease Tina Brown ~ Real ale ~ (01494) 813371 ~ Open 11-11; 12-10.30
Sun ~ Bar food 12-2.30, 6.30-9.30(10 Fri); 9.30-3, 6.30-10 Sat; 12-9 Sun ~ Restaurant ~
Children welcome ~ Dogs allowed in bar ~ www.oldqueensheadpenn.co.uk
Recommended by Richard and Penny Gibbs, I D Barnett, Edward Mirzoeff

PENN
Red Lion 🍺
Elm Road, B474; HP10 8LF

SU9093   Map 4

**Bustling village pub with lots to look at in character rooms, a good
mix of customers, well kept ales and tasty, pubby food; seats outside**

Opposite the green and duck pond – and there's a cheery sign by
the door welcoming both dogs and ducks inside – this is a proper
village pub with a lot of character. There are original 17th-c features
here and there and some fine old pieces of furniture, and throughout
the various bar rooms you'll find rugs on ancient parquet flooring, old
quarry tiles, a happy mix of rustic tables each set with a candle in a
nice old brass candlestick, chairs ranging from cushioned mates' ones
to leather and brass-studded dining chairs, all sorts and sizes of settles
(the curved one beside the woodburner in the main bar is noteworthy)
and various homely sofas and armchairs. The walls are covered with a
fantastic collection of British Empire prints and paintings, the beams are
draped with hops and the window sills and mantelpieces are crammed
with Staffordshire china dogs and plates and stone and glass bottles.
It's all very friendly and relaxed – helped by the good mixed crowd of
customers. Efficient staff serve Britannia Pale (brewed by their sister
pub), as well as ales from Chiltern and Elgoods on handpump, farm cider
and wines by the glass. There are wood and metal seats and tables on
the front terrace, and settles lined along the walls facing the pond. This
shares ownership with the Royal Standard of England at Forty Green.

🍴 Carefully chosen produce is used in their good, honest food, which might
include sandwiches, chicken liver parfait with chutney, a charcuterie plate,
quiche lorraine, vegetarian cassoulet, sausages and mash with onion gravy,
beef burger with bacon and cheese, steak pie with mash or chips, coq au vin,

daily specials and puddings like chocolate and dark rum tart and ginger crème brûlée. *Benchmark main dish: fish and chips with tartare sauce £11.00. Two-course evening meal £16.00.*

Free house ~ Licensee Matthew O'Keeffe ~ Real ale ~ (01494) 813107 ~ Open 11-11; 12-10.30 Sun ~ Bar food 12-9 ~ Children welcome ~ Dogs allowed in bar ~ www.redlionpenn.co.uk *Recommended by Harvey Brown*

PRESTWOOD

SP8799 Map 4

Polecat

170 Wycombe Road (A4128 N of High Wycombe); HP16 0HJ

Enjoyable food, real ales and a chatty atmosphere in several smallish civilised rooms; attractive sizeable garden

The garden around this rather smart country pub is most attractive with lots of spring bulbs, colourful summer hanging baskets and tubs and plenty of herbaceous plants; there are quite a few picnic-sets under parasols on neat grass in front beneath a big fairy-lit pear tree, and more on a large well kept back lawn. Inside, it's civilised and well run with a quietly chatty atmosphere and helpful, friendly staff. Several smallish rooms, opening off the low-ceilinged bar, have slightly chintzy décor: an assortment of tables and chairs, various stuffed birds, stuffed white polecats in one big cabinet, small country pictures, rugs on bare boards or red tiles, and a couple of antique housekeeper's chairs by a good open fire. Brakspears Bitter, Greene King Old Speckled Hen, Marstons Pedigree and Ringwood Best on handpump, 16 wines by the glass, 20 malt whiskies and home-made summer elderflower pressé. They don't take bookings at lunchtime (except for groups of six or more), so do arrive promptly at weekends to be sure of a table.

Well presented and reasonably priced, the very popular food includes lunchtime sandwiches, chicken liver and pistachio pâté with apricot chutney, twice-baked stilton soufflé with red onion marmalade, smoked haddock and spinach fishcakes, cumberland sausage with onion gravy and cheddar bubble and squeak, roast parsnip bake with puy lentils, leeks, cream and white wine, chicken curry with poppadums, specials such as rabbit casserole with grain mustard mash or daube of beef with parsnip gnocchi and blue cheese glaze, and puddings such as sherry trifle and blackcurrant syllabub with shortbread biscuit. *Benchmark main dish: steak and mushroom in ale pie £11.30. Two-course evening meal £17.50.*

Free house ~ Licensee John Gamble ~ Real ale ~ (01494) 862253 ~ Open 11.30-2.30, 6-11; 12-3 Sun; closed Sun evening ~ Bar food 12-2, 6.30-9 ~ Children allowed in gallery or drovers' bar only ~ Dogs allowed in bar
Recommended by Peter and Jan Humphreys, Roy Hoing, Mel Smith

SEER GREEN

SU9691 Map 2

Jolly Cricketers

Chalfont Road, opposite the church; HP9 2YG

Bustling and friendly village pub with cricketing paraphernalia, a thoughtful choice of drinks, enjoyable food and seats on a back terrace

Opposite the flint church, this 19th-c red-brick dining pub has a chatty and gently civilised atmosphere. The parquet-floored bar is divided by a big chimney into two rooms, with a woodburning stove in each room (one had a bowl of chestnuts for roasting beside it), nice cushioned seats in bow windows, a mix of pale farmhouse and antique dining chairs around wooden and painted tables set with candles in glass jars and fresh flowers, and plenty of old cricketing photos, prints and bats on the walls. The bar stools are well used by locals, and friendly, helpful staff serve Fullers London Pride, Rebellion Smuggler, Sharps Doom Bar and Vale VPA on handpump – they hold regular beer festivals – and good wines by the glass; big glass jars of nuts and dried fruit behind the bar, board games, daily papers and background music. The separate restaurant is similarly furnished and has a tiny little cushioned settle, teddies in cricket gear and a basket of cricket bats, and a chandelier over the table by the window. There's a handsome wisteria at the front and picnic-sets on a back terrace; occasional live music.

🍴 Enticing food with imaginative touches might include nibbles like home-made scotch egg or sausage rolls, pressed ox tongue with pickled shallots and mustard, soft boiled quails eggs with caviar and anchovy mayonnaise, steak burger with mature cheddar, aioli and chips, gorgonzola, parmesan and spinach risotto with garlic and herb butter, ale-braised ham with colcannon and parsley sauce, beer-battered fish and chips, braised chicken and rabbit with pea purée, potato galette and walnut jus, and puddings such as bread and butter pudding with vanilla custard and Valrhona chocolate brownie with cherries and pistachio ice-cream. *Benchmark main dish: beer-battered fish and chips £14.50. Two-course evening meal £21.00.*

Free house ~ Licensees Amanda and Chris Lillitou ~ Real ale ~ (01494) 676308 ~ Open 12-11.30(midnight Fri, Sat); 12-10.30 Sun ~ Bar food 12-2.30(3 Sat, 3.30 Sun), 6.30-9; not Sun evening ~ Restaurant ~ Children welcome ~ Dogs welcome ~ www.thejollycricketers.co.uk *Recommended by Kevin Thomas, Nina Randall, Tracey and Stephen Groves*

WOOBURN COMMON
SU9187 Map 2
Chequers ♀ 🛏

From A4094 N of Maidenhead at junction with A4155 Marlow road, keep on A4094 for another 0.75 miles, then at roundabout turn right towards Wooburn Common and into Kiln Lane; if you find yourself in Honey Hill, Hedsor, turn left into Kiln Lane at the top of the hill; OS Sheet 175 map reference 910870; HP10 0JQ

Busy and friendly hotel with a bustling bar, four real ales, good food in both bar and smart restaurant; comfortable bedrooms

The friendly bar at the heart of this busy hotel and restaurant continues to thrive as a welcoming local. It feels nicely pubby, with low beams, standing timbers and alcoves, characterful rickety furniture and comfortably lived-in sofas on bare boards, a bright log-effect gas fire, pictures, plates, a two-man saw and tankards. In contrast, the bar to the left, with dark brown leather sofas at low tables on wooden floors, feels plain and modern; the smart restaurant has high-backed black leather dining chairs around white-clothed tables. Greene King Old Speckled Hen, Rebellion Smuggler, XT4 from the new XT Brewing Company and a changing guest on handpump, a good sizeable wine list (with a dozen by the glass) and a fair range of malt whiskies and brandies; background music. The spacious garden, set away from the road, has seats around cast-iron tables and summer barbecues.

🍴 As well as afternoon tea and a two- and three-course set menu, the good, inventive food includes sandwiches, potted ham hock with pea custard and toasted raisin brioche, beetroot salmon gravadlax with watercress coulis, lemon jam, watermelon and pickled onions, chicken caesar salad with anchovies, cumberland sausage with onion gravy, thai-style fishcakes, calves liver and bacon with red onion gravy, loin of cod with black pudding and sweet potato purée, roast lamb rump with rosemary jus, and puddings like bitter chocolate and toffee tart with rosemary ice-cream and strawberry and rhubarb compote tortellini. *Benchmark main dish: home-made burger with bacon, cheese, chips and coleslaw £9.95. Two-course evening meal £23.50.*

Free house ~ Licensee Peter Roehrig ~ Real ale ~ (01628) 529575 ~ Open 10am-midnight ~ Bar food 12-2.30, 6-9.30; all day weekends; also light snacks all day ~ Restaurant ~ Children welcome ~ Dogs allowed in bar ~ Bedrooms: £99.50/£107.50 ~ www.chequers-inn.com *Recommended by Roy Hoing, R K Phillips*

Also Worth a Visit in Buckinghamshire

Besides the fully inspected pubs, you might like to try these pubs that have been recommended to us and described by readers. Do tell us what you think of them: feedback@goodguides.com

ASKETT   SP8105
⋆ **Three Crowns** (01844) 347166
*W off A4010 into Letter Box Lane;
HP27 9LT* Handsome, well run pub in small hamlet among the Chiltern Hills; main emphasis on the particularly good interesting food, but also real ales such as Vale from herringbone brick counter, good wine list, two contemporary-styled beamed dining rooms with mix of high-backed pale wood or black leather chairs around dark wood tables, light flooring, minimal décor; some picnic-sets outside under parasols, pretty front flower beds and baskets. *(Peter and Jan Humphreys, David and Katharine Cooke, Mel Smith)*

ASTON CLINTON   SP8811
Bell (01296) 632777
London Road; HP22 5HP Refurbished old Mitchells & Butlers village pub/restaurant (former Duck Inn back to its original name); ales such as Adnams, Greene King and Wells & Youngs, plenty of wines by the glass including champagne, good choice of food all day (weekend breakfast from 9am); tables under trees in garden, 11 Innkeepers Lodge bedrooms. *(Toby Jones)*

AYLESBURY   SP7510
Bottle & Glass (01296) 748444
A418 just over a mile towards Thame, beyond Stone; HP17 8TY Rambling thatched dining pub with nice modern layout and décor, enjoyable food (all day weekends) from sandwiches and sharing boards up, well kept beer and plenty of wines by the glass, friendly efficient staff; children welcome, disabled facilities, terrace tables, open all day. *(Mel Smith)*

BENNETT END   SU7897
Three Horseshoes (01494) 483273
Horseshoe Road; from Radnage on unclassified road towards Princes Risborough, left into Bennett End Road, then right into Horseshoe Road; HP14 4EB Country pub in lovely quiet spot – seemingly off the beaten track but close to M40; well kept Rebellion IPA and a guest, several wines by the glass, good choice of food including some traditional options (not cheap and service charge added), flagstoned softly lit snug bar with log fire in raised fireplace, original brickwork and bread oven, two further sitting areas, one with long winged settle, the other enclosed by standing timbers, stone-floor dining room with big windows overlooking garden, red telephone box half submerged in duck pond, unspoilt valley beyond; children welcome till 9pm, dogs in bar, six bedrooms, closed Sun evening, Mon lunchtime. *(Roy Hoing)*

BOURNE END   SU8987
Bounty (01628) 520056
Cock Marsh, actually across the river along the Cookham towpath, but shortest walk – still about 0.25 miles – is from Bourne End, over the railway bridge; SL8 5RG Welcoming take-us-as-you-find-us pub tucked away in outstanding setting on bank of the Thames accessible only by foot or boat; bar counter made from a boat, collection of flags, well kept Rebellion ales, basic standard food including children's meals, back dining area, bar billiards; background music inside and out; dogs and muddy walkers welcome, picnic-sets with parasols on front terrace, play area to right, open all day in summer (may be boat trips), closed winter weekdays. *(N R White)*

BRADENHAM   SU8297
Red Lion (01494) 562212
A4010, by Walters Ash turn-off; HP14 4HF Charming NT-owned pub under friendly new licensees, three or four Rebellion ales, enjoyable home-made food from good baguettes up, small simple bar, good-sized smarter low-beamed dining room;

well behaved children welcome, dogs in bar, picnic-sets on terrace and lawn, pretty village green nearby, closed Sun and Mon evenings. *(Bob Dizon)*

BRILL SP6514
⋆ **Pheasant** (01844) 239370
Windmill Street; off B4011 Bicester–Long Crendon; HP18 9TG More or less open-plan with some beams, chatty bar with smart chairs by counter, leather tub chairs in front of woodburner, well kept Vale Best and a guest, enjoyable food, friendly helpful service, dining areas with high-backed leather or dark wooden chairs, attractively framed prints, books on shelves; background music; children welcome, dogs allowed in bar, seats on decked area and in garden, fine views over post windmill (one of the oldest in working order), comfortable bedrooms, good breakfast, open all day. *(Bruce and Sharon Eden, Paul Bates, John Evans, Neil and Angela Huxter)*

BUCKINGHAM SP6933
Villiers (01280) 822444
Castle Street; MK18 1BS Pub part of this large comfortable hotel with own courtyard entrance, big inglenook log fire, panelling and stripped masonry in flagstoned bar, beers from Hook Norton and Black Sheep, reliably good food from shortish menu (also set choices Mon-Fri), competent friendly staff, sofas and armchairs in more formal front lounges, restaurant with two large tropical fish tanks; no dogs; children welcome till 9pm, terrace, tables, open all day. *(George Atkinson)*

BUTLERS CROSS SP8407
Russell Arms (01296) 624411
Off A4010 S of Aylesbury, at Nash Lee roundabout; or off A413 in Wendover, passing station; Chalkshire Road; HP17 0TS Refurbished beamed pub, a former 18th-c coaching inn and servants' quarters for nearby Chequers, now owned by the village and under new management; bar with woodburner, separate light and roomy dining room, real ales such as Aylesbury, Chiltern, Rebellion and Vale, good wine choice, food from bar snacks up including children's menu, afternoon teas, village shop; background music; small sheltered garden, well placed for Chilterns walks, closed Sun evening, Mon. *(Anon)*

CADSDEN SP8204
Plough (01844) 343302
Cadsden Road; HP27 0NB Extended former coaching inn with airy open-plan bar/dining area, well spaced tables on flagstones, exposed brick and some faux beams, very popular with families and Chilterns ramblers, good choice of real ales and hearty home-made food (not Sun evening), cherry pie festival (first Sun in Aug), efficient service; lots of tables in delightful quiet front and

back garden, pretty spot on Ridgeway path, bedrooms, open all day weekends. *(Roy Hoing, Mel Smith, N R White)*

CHALFONT ST GILES SU9895
⋆ **Ivy House** (01494) 872184
A413 S; HP8 4RS Old brick and flint beamed coaching inn tied to Fullers, their ales, good food including some interesting choices, decent wines by the glass, espresso coffee, friendly young staff, comfortable fireside armchairs in carefully lit and elegantly cosy L-shaped tiled bar, lighter flagstoned dining extension; dogs allowed in bar, pleasant terrace and sloping garden (some traffic noise), five bedrooms. *(Bratzz, Mrs S Watkins, Roy Hoing)*

CHALFONT ST GILES SU9893
Milton's Head (01494) 872961
Deanway; HP8 4JL Pub/restaurant with good mainly italian food cooked by sardinian landlord, also pizzas and traditional Sun roasts, reasonable prices, nice italian wines and coffee, no real ales but Peroni on draught; children and dogs welcome, small side terrace, handy for John Milton's Cottage, closed Sun evening, Mon. *(Dr Paul Glover)*

CHEARSLEY SP7110
Bell (01844) 208077
The Green; HP18 0DJ Cosy traditional thatched and beamed pub on attractive village green, Fullers beers and good wines by the glass, decent choice of bar food from sandwiches up, friendly service, enormous fireplace; quiz and bingo nights; children in eating area, dogs welcome, plenty of tables in spacious back garden with heated terrace and play area, open all day summer weekends. *(David Lamb)*

CHESHAM SP9604
Black Horse (01494) 784656
Vale Road, N off A416 in Chesham; HP5 3NS Neatly extended popular black-beamed country pub, good choice of enjoyable food including meal deal Weds and Thurs, well kept ales such as Fullers and Tring, decent wines, good service, inglenook log fire; fortnightly quiz Mon; dogs welcome, picnic-sets out in front and on back grass, closed Sun evening. *(D and M T Ayres-Regan)*

CHESHAM SP9501
Queens Head (01494) 778690
Church Street; HP5 1JD Popular, well run Fullers corner pub, two traditional beamed bars with scrubbed tables and log fires, their ales and a guest such as Brakspears kept well, enjoyable thai food along with modest range of pub staples, restaurant, friendly staff and chatty locals; sports TV; children welcome, tables in small courtyard used by smokers, next to little River Chess, open all day. *(Paul A Moore)*

COLESHILL SU9495
Red Lion (01494) 727020
Village Road; HP7 0LH Small popular local with welcoming long-serving landlord, generous good value pubby food (not Sun evening) from sandwiches up, ales such as Eton & Windsor, Sharps and Vale, log fire, thriving darts and dominoes teams; sports TV; children and dogs welcome, front and back gardens, good walks, open all day Sat. *(Mrs S Watkins, Roy Hoing, David Lamb, N R White)*

COLNBROOK TQ0277
Ostrich (01753) 682628
1.25 miles from M4 junction 5 via A4/ B3378, then 'village only' road; High Street; SL3 0JZ Spectacular timbered Elizabethan building (with even longer gruesome history) given contemporary makeover, comfortable sofas on stripped wood and a startling red plastic and stainless steel bar counter, well kept changing ales, good choice of wines by the glass including champagne, some emphasis on the enjoyable food from sandwiches and pub favourites up, efficient friendly service, attractive restaurant with open fire; soft background music, comedy and live music nights upstairs; children welcome, open all day Sun. *(Hunter and Christine Wright, Susan and John Douglas)*

CUBLINGTON SP8322
Unicorn (01296) 681261
High Street; LU7 0LQ Extended low-beamed 17th-c village pub, supposedly haunted, with popular sensibly priced food from interesting menu, Sharps, Shepherd Neame, XT and guests (May, Aug beer festivals), handsome fireplace at one end, Mon quiz and some live music; big enclosed garden behind, open all day. *(Mel Smith)*

CUDDINGTON SP7311
✶ Crown (01844) 292222
Spurt Street; off A418 Thame–Aylesbury; HP18 0BB Convivial refurbished thatched cottage with nice chatty mix of customers, comfortable pubby furnishings including cushioned settles in two low-beamed linked rooms, big inglenook log fire, well kept Fullers and guests, around 20 wines by the glass, good home-cooked food (not Sun evening), competent friendly service, carpeted two-room back dining area with country kitchen chairs around nice mix of tables; children welcome; neat side terrace with modern garden furniture and planters, picnic-sets in front. *(Jim Lyon, Doug Kennedy, Mrs S Watkins, Roy Hoing, Mel Smith, Dave Braisted and others)*

DINTON SP7610
Seven Stars (01296) 749000
Signed off A418 Aylesbury–Thame, near Gibraltar turn-off; Stars Lane; HP17 8UL Pretty 17th-c community-owned pub with newish french landlady, inglenook

bar, beamed lounge and refurbished dining room, well kept ales such as Black Sheep, Fullers and Timothy Taylors, plenty of wines by the glass, enjoyable home-made food from pub staples up, friendly service; tables in sheltered garden with terrace, pleasant village, open all day weekends. *(Doug Kennedy, Dick O'Driscoll, Mel Smith, David Lamb)*

DORNEY SU9279
Palmer Arms (01628) 666612
2.7 miles from M4 junction 7, via B3026; Village Road; SL4 6QW Modernised and extended dining pub in attractive conservation village, good popular all-day food from snacks and pub favourites to more restaurant dishes, friendly competent service, Greene King ales and lots of wines by the glass, nice coffee too, daily newspapers, civilised front bar, back dining room, open fires; background music; children welcome, dogs in certain areas, disabled facilities, terrace overlooking mediterranean-feel garden, enclosed play area, good riverside walks nearby, open all day. *(C and R Bromage, Cliff Sparkes, I D Barnett, Alistair Forsyth)*

DORNEY SU9279
Pineapple (01628) 662353
Lake End Road: 2.4 miles from M4 junction 7; left on A4 then left on B3026; SL4 6QS Nicely old-fashioned pub, shiny low Anaglypta ceilings, black-panelled dados, leather chairs around sturdy country tables (one very long, another in big bow window), woodburner and pretty little fireplace, china pineapples and other decorations on shelves in one of three cottagey carpeted linked rooms on left, well kept Fullers London Pride, Sharps Doom Bar and Windsor & Eton Guardsman, up to 1,000 varieties of sandwiches in five different fresh breads; background music, games machine; children and dogs welcome, rustic seats on roadside verandah, round picnic-sets in garden, fairy-lit decking under oak tree, some motorway noise, open all day. *(R T and J C Moggridge)*

EASINGTON SP6810
✶ Mole & Chicken (01844) 208387
From B4011 in Long Crendon follow Chearsley, Waddesdon signpost into Carters Lane opposite indian restaurant, then turn left into Chilton Road; HP18 9EY Calls itself a restaurant-with-rooms; opened-up beamed interior, cream-cushioned chairs and high-backed leather dining chairs at oak and pine tables, flagstones or tiles, dark leather sofas, fabric swatches hung as wall decorations, winter log fires, modern food including set menu choices, also some traditional favourites, real ales such as Hook Norton and Vale; background music; children welcome, no dogs inside, attractive raised terrace with country views, five comfortable bedrooms, open all day. *(JJW, CMW, Karen Eliot, Dennis and Doreen Haward)*

FRIETH   SU7990
Prince Albert (01494) 881683
Off B482 SW of High Wycombe; RG9 6PY
Friendly cottagey Chilterns local with low
black beams and joists, high-backed settles,
big black stove in inglenook and log fire
in larger area on right, decent lunchtime
food from sandwiches up (also Fri and Sat
evenings), well kept Brakspears and guests,
quiz and folk nights; children and dogs
welcome, nicely planted informal side garden
with views of woods and fields, good walks,
open all day. *(Anon)*

GAWCOTT   SP6831
Crown (01280) 822322
Hillesden Road; MK18 4JF Well run,
traditional beamed village pub, popular very
good value food using local meat including
carvery (Weds and Sun), well kept ales such
as Sharps Doom Bar from herringbone brick
counter, restaurant area, pool; background
music, Sky TV; children welcome, long back
garden with swings, open all day. *(Michael
Tack)*

GREAT HAMPDEN   SP8401
⋆ Hampden Arms (01494) 488255
*W of Great Missenden, off A4128;
HP16 9RQ* Friendly village pub opposite
cricket pitch, good mix of locals and visitors,
comfortably furnished front and back rooms
(back one more rustic with big woodburner),
Adnams, Hook Norton and a guest from
Vale, several wines by the glass and maybe
Addlestone's cider from small corner bar,
good choice of reasonably priced pubby food,
cheerful efficient service; children and dogs
welcome, seats in tree-sheltered garden,
good Hampden Common walks.
(Brian Patterson, N R White, David Lamb)

GREAT KINGSHILL   SU8798
⋆ Red Lion (01494) 711262
A4128 N of High Wycombe; HP15 6EB
Carefully refurbished pub with contemporary
décor, interesting, popular brasserie-style
food, local beers, good wine list, plenty of
space in 'lobby' plus cosy little flagstoned
bar with brown leather sofas and tub
armchairs, log fire, spacious candlelit
dining room on left, relaxed atmosphere;
well behaved children welcome, closed Sun
evening. *(Anon)*

GREAT LINFORD   SP8542
Nags Head (01908) 607449
High Street; MK14 5AX Thatched 15th-c
pub with big inglenook in low-beamed
lounge, several real ales including Fullers
London Pride and Timothy Taylors Landlord,
straightforward inexpensive food, friendly
staff coping well when busy, darts in public
bar, some live music; children welcome,
picnic-sets outside, pleasant walks (next to
park and canal), open all day. *(Paul Rampton,
Julie Harding, Peter Martin)*

GREAT MISSENDEN   SP8901
⋆ Cross Keys (01494) 865373
High Street; HP16 0AU Relaxed and
friendly village pub, unspoilt beamed bar
divided by standing timbers, traditional
furnishings including high-backed settle,
log-effect gas fire in huge fireplace, well
kept Fullers ales and often an unusual guest,
decent food from sandwiches to Sun roasts,
cheerful helpful staff, spacious beamed
restaurant; children and dogs welcome, back
terrace with picnic-sets, open all day. *(Anon)*

GROVE   SP9122
⋆ Grove Lock (01525) 380940
*Pub signed off B488, on left just S
of A505 roundabout (S of Leighton
Buzzard); LU7 0QU* Overlooking Grand
Union Canal and usefully open all day;
open-plan with lofty high-raftered pitched
roof in bar, squashy brown leather sofas on
oak boards, eclectic mix of tables and chairs
including butcher's block tables by bar, big
open-standing winter log fire, steps down to
original lock-keeper's cottage (now a three-
room restaurant area), more winter log fires,
Fullers ales and lots of wines by the glass;
background music; children welcome, seats
on canopied deck and waterside lawn by
Lock 28. *(John Branston, Mel Smith,
Taff Thomas)*

HADDENHAM   SP7408
Green Dragon (01844) 291403
*Village signposted off A418 and A4129,
E/NE of Thame; then follow Church End
signs into Churchway; HP17 8AA* 18th-c
village pub with shuttered cottagey front and
neat window boxes, contrasting open-plan
modernised interior with mix of old tables
and chairs and leather sofas, two log fires,
well kept ales such as Holts and Vale, several
wines by the glass, traditional local food all
day, friendly landlord and staff; background
music; children and dogs welcome, big
sheltered gravel terrace, picnic-sets in
appealing garden. *(Tony and Wendy Hobden)*

HAMBLEDEN   SU7886
⋆ Stag & Huntsman (01491) 571227
Off A4155 Henley–Marlow; RG9 6RP
Major refurbishment at this handsome brick
and flint pub; enjoyable generously served
food from sandwiches up, Loddon Hoppit,
Rebellion IPA and Sharps Doom Bar, good
wines by the glass, efficient service; they may
ask for a credit card if you run a tab; children
and dogs (not in dining room) welcome, nice
garden, pretty Chilterns village popular with
walkers, new bedrooms, open all day. *(Paul
Humphreys, Susan and John Douglas)*

HAWRIDGE   SP9505
⋆ Rose & Crown (01494) 758386
*Signed from A416 N of Chesham;
The Vale; HP5 2UG* Roomy open-plan pub
dating from the 18th-c; welcoming licensees,

good traditional home-made food (not Sun evening, Mon) from snacks up, well kept local beers, proper cider and perry, big log fire, peaceful country views from upper restaurant area; children and dogs welcome, pretty hanging baskets, broad terrace with lawn dropping down beyond, play area, open all day Thurs-Sun, closed Mon lunchtime. *(Mrs P Sumner)*

HAWRIDGE COMMON   SP9406
★**Full Moon** (01494) 758959
Hawridge Common; left fork off A416 N of Chesham, follow for 3.5 miles towards Cholesbury; HP5 2UH 18th-c pub with low-beamed little bar, ancient flagstones and chequered floor tiles, built-in floor-to-ceiling oak settles, hunting prints and inglenook fireplace, Adnams, Bass, Fullers London Pride, Timothy Taylors Landlord and a guest, several wines by the glass, popular bar food from sandwiches up; background music; seats in pleasant garden or on heated covered terrace with views over fields and windmill beyond, paddock for hitching horses, walks on common. *(John Branston, N R White, Roy Hoing, Mel Smith)*

HUGHENDEN VALLEY   SU8697
★**Harrow** (01494) 564105
Warrendene Road, off A4128 N of High Wycombe; HP14 4LX Small cheerful brick and flint roadside cottage surrounded by Chilterns walks; traditionally furnished with tiled-floor bar on left, black beams and joists, woodburner in big fireplace, pewter mugs, country pictures and wall seats, similar but bigger right-hand bar with sizeable dining tables on brick floor, carpeted back dining room, decent pubby food (not Sun evening) from sandwiches up including meal deal Mon-Thurs, Courage Best, Fullers London Pride and Shepherd Neame Spitfire, friendly staff; Tues quiz; children and dogs welcome, disabled access, plenty of picnic-sets in front with more on back lawn, play area, open all day. *(Richard and Penny Gibbs, David Lamb)*

HYDE HEATH   SU9300
Plough (01494) 783163
Off B485 Great Missenden–Chesham; HP6 5RW Prettily placed pub overlooking village green, traditional bare-boards bar and carpeted dining extension, good value food including some thai dishes, Fullers London Pride and St Austell Tribute, real fires; background music, TV; open all day Fri-Sun. *(Roy Hoing)*

ICKFORD   SP6407
Rising Sun (01844) 339238
E of Thame; Worminghall Road; HP18 9JD Pretty thatched local with cosy low-beamed bar, friendly staff and regulars, four real ales including Adnams Broadside and Black Sheep, simple reasonably priced home-made food; pleasant garden. *(David Lamb)*

IVINGHOE ASTON   SP9518
Village Swan (01525) 220544
Aston; signed from B489 NE of Ivinghoe; LU7 9DP Friendly village-owned pub, enjoyable home-made pubby food including Sun carvery, good choice of real ales; handy for Ivinghoe Beacon and Icknield Way. *(Alan Weedon)*

LACEY GREEN   SP8200
Black Horse (01844) 345195
Main Road; HP27 0QU Friendly mix of customers in this two-bar beamed country local, popular good value home-made food (not Sun evening, Mon) from baguettes up, breakfast from 9am Tues-Sat, four real ales including Brakspears, nice choice of wines by the glass, quotations written on walls, inglenook woodburner, darts; sports TV; children welcome, picnic-sets in garden with play area and aunt sally, closed Mon lunchtime, open all day Thurs-Sun. *(Mel Smith, Paul Humphreys)*

LACEY GREEN   SP8100
Whip (01844) 344060
Pink Road; HP27 0PG Cheery and attractive hilltop local welcoming walkers, mix of simple traditional furnishings in smallish front bar and larger downstairs dining area, popular good value food from sandwiches up (booking advised weekends), six interesting well kept/priced ales, Oct beer festival with jazz, friendly helpful service and good landlord; TV, fruit machine; tables in mature sheltered garden looking up to windmill, open all day. *(N R White, Mel Smith, Tracey and Stephen Groves)*

LANE END   SU8091
Grouse & Ale (01494) 882299
High Street; HP14 3JG Welcoming beamed pub with good food from pub standards up, helpful friendly staff, great range of wines by the glass including champagne, well kept changing ales, comfortable bar and smartly laid out restaurant with flowers on tables, newspapers and books, log fires; soft background music; children welcome (toys provided), seats outside. *(Martin and Karen Wake, D and M T Ayres-Regan)*

LITTLE KINGSHILL   SU8999
Full Moon (01494) 862397
Hare Lane; HP16 0EE Picturesque brick and flint village pub with good choice of popular well presented food, well kept Adnams, Fullers London Pride, Wells & Youngs and a guest, nice wines, friendly helpful service from busy staff, traditional beamed and quarry-tiled bar with open fire, bigger dining room, live music first and third Mon of month; children and dogs welcome, round picnic-sets out at front, lawned garden with swings, good walks. *(LM)*

LITTLE MARLOW   SU8788

⋆**Kings Head** (01628) 484407

*Church Road; A4155 about 2 miles E of
Marlow; SL7 3RZ* Long, flower-covered
local with open-plan bar, low beams,
captain's chairs and other traditional seating
around dark wooden tables, cricketing
memorabilia (pitch opposite), log fire, half
a dozen well kept ales such as Adnams
Broadside and Wychwood Hobgoblin, popular
pubby blackboard food from sandwiches up
(booking advised weekends), OAP specials
Mon, free bar nibbles Sun, helpful friendly
service, gingham-clothed tables in attractive
dining room; big walled garden with modern
terrace furniture, open all day. *(Ross
Balaam, D and M T Ayres-Regan, Roy Hoing, Paul
Humphreys and others)*

LITTLE MISSENDEN   SU9298

⋆**Red Lion** (01494) 862876

*Off A413 Amersham–Great Missenden;
HP7 0QZ* Unchanging pretty 15th-c cottage
with long-serving landlord; small black-
beamed bar, plain seats around elm pub
tables, piano squashed into big inglenook
beside black kitchen range packed with
copper pots, kettles and rack of old guns,
little country dining room with pheasant
décor, well kept Greene King IPA, Marstons
Pedigree and Wadworths 6X, fair-priced
wines, good coffee, enjoyable inexpensive
pubby food and good friendly service, live
music Tues and Sat; children welcome, dogs
in bar (there's a friendly pub dog), picnic-
sets out in front and on grass behind wall,
back garden with little bridge over River
Misbourne, some fancy waterfowl, stables
farm shop, open all day Fri, Sat. *(John Taylor,
Mrs Margo Finlay, Jörg Kasprowski, Susan and
John Douglas, Roy Hoing, N R White)*

LITTLE TINGEWICK   SP6432

Red Lion (01280) 848285

*Off A421SW of Buckingham; pub
towards Finmere, over the Oxon border;
MK18 4AG* 16th-c stone and thatch country
dining pub, food from sandwiches and pub
favourites to more restauranty choices,
Fullers ales and a guest, decent wines by the
glass, helpful service, inglenook log fire, low
beams, mixed simple new furniture on wood
floor; background music; tables out in front
and in small garden behind with aunt sally,
open all day weekends. *(David Lamb)*

LITTLEWORTH COMMON   SP9386

Blackwood Arms (01753) 645672

*3 miles S of M40 junction 2; Common
Lane, OS Sheet 165 map ref 937864;
SL1 8PP* Small brick pub in lovely spot on
edge of beechwoods with good walks, sturdy
mix of furniture on bare boards, roaring log
fire, enjoyable home-made food (not Sun
evening), well kept Brakspears and guests,
friendly staff; children, dogs and muddy
boots welcome, good garden with paved area,

closed Mon, otherwise open all day (Sun till
9.30). *(Eva Drewett, Cliff Sparkes)*

LONG CRENDON   SP6908

⋆**Eight Bells** (01844) 208244

*High Street, off B4011 N of Thame; car
park entrance off Chearsley Road, not
'Village roads only'; HP18 9AL* Character
17th-c beamed pub, unassuming and
unchanging, with good cheerful staff; little
bare-boards bar on left serving a house
beer (Hel's Bells – named for landlady),
Wadworths IPA and three changing guests
from the cask, Thatcher's cider and decent
choice of wines; bigger low-ceilinged room on
right with log fire and a pleasantly haphazard
mix of tables and simple seats on ancient red
and black tiles, good modestly priced food
(not Sun evening, Mon), daily papers and
darts, also a snug hidey-hole with just three
tables devoted to the local morris men –
frequent visitors; children and dogs welcome,
well spaced picnic-sets in colourful little
back garden, aunt sally, interesting village
featured in TV's *Midsomer Murders*, open all
day weekends, closed Mon lunchtime; goes
up for sale in 2014. *(David Lamb, Mel Smith,
John Branston, David Jackman)*

LUDGERSHALL   SP6617

⋆**Bull & Butcher** (01844) 238094

*Off A41 Aylesbury–Bicester; bear left
to The Green; HP18 9NZ* Nicely old-
fashioned country pub facing village green,
bar with low beams in ochre ceiling, wall
bench and simple pub furniture on dark tiles
or flagstones, inglenook log fire, back dining
room, decent bar food, a couple of changing
ales, aunt sally and dominoes teams, quiz
(second Sun of month); children welcome,
picnic-sets on pleasant front terrace, play
area on green, open all day weekends, closed
Mon. *(David Lamb)*

MAIDS MORETON   SP7035

Wheatsheaf (01280) 815433

*Main Street, just off A413 Towcester–
Buckingham; MK18 1QR* Attractive
17th-c thatched and low-beamed local under
cheerful chatty landlord, quickly served
pubby food including bargain over-50s
lunch (Tues), Tring Side Pocket and a
couple of local guests, old settles, pictures
and bric-a-brac, two working inglenooks,
conservatory restaurant with woodburner;
children welcome, no dogs inside, seats on
front terrace, hatch service for pleasant quiet
enclosed garden behind, open all day Sat,
closed Sun evening, Mon. *(George Atkinson)*

MARLOW   SU8587

Britannia (01628) 485066

Little Marlow Road; SL7 1HL Fully
refurbished McMullens pub, three of their
ales in good condition, decent choice of
wines, all-day food from extensive reasonably
priced menu, well trained staff.
(D and M T Ayres-Regan)

MARLOW SU8586
⋆ **Two Brewers** (01628) 484140
St Peter Street, first right off Station Road from double roundabout; SL7 1NQ
Interesting layout with low beams, shiny black woodwork and nice mix of furniture on bare boards, nautical pictures and brassware, well kept Brakspears, Fullers London Pride and Rebellion, several wines by glass, well liked food (all day Sat, not Sun evening), friendly service, River View room and Cellar both set for dining; children welcome, dogs in bar, cheerfully painted picnic-sets out at front with glimpse of the Thames, more seats in sheltered back courtyard, limited parking, open all day. *(David Fowler)*

MARLOW BOTTOM SU8588
Three Horseshoes (01628) 483109
Signed from Handy Cross roundabout, off M40 junction 4; SL7 3RA Welcoming much-extended former coaching inn tied to nearby Rebellion, their full range kept well, brewery photographs, knowledgeable helpful uniformed staff, extensive choice of reasonably priced generous blackboard food (not Sun evening), good value wines, comfortable traditional furnishings on different levels, beams and log fires; children and dogs welcome, big back garden, good walks nearby, open all day Fri-Sat. *(David Lamb, Tony and Wendy Hobden, Alicia Garrett, Andy and Jill Kassube)*

MARSWORTH SP9114
Red Lion (01296) 668366
Vicarage Road; off B489 Dunstable–Aylesbury; HP23 4LU Partly thatched 18th-c pub close to impressive flight of locks on Grand Union Canal; plain public bar on right with quarry tiles, straightforward furniture and small coal fire, Fullers London Pride, Nethergate Growler and Skinners Cornish Knocker, traditional food at low prices, friendly service, raised ceiling area with red leather stools and sofas, multi-level lounge to left with comfortable black sofas in one part and various knick-knacks, two-roomed games area with bar billiards, darts and juke box; children and dogs welcome, picnic-sets out in front, back terrace with heated smokers' gazebo, steps up to sizeable garden, more seats on village green opposite with old stocks. *(Susan and John Douglas, John Wooll, Alan Weedon and others)*

MEDMENHAM SU8084
Dog & Badger (01491) 571362
Bockmer (A4155); SL7 2HE Spacious low-beamed pub under welcoming newish landlord, nice décor with good mix of old furniture on polished boards, open fire, enjoyable food in bar and restaurant, well kept local ales; children welcome, terrace tables. *(R C Tiptaft)*

MOULSOE SP9141
Carrington Arms (01908) 218050
1.25 miles from M1 junction 14: A509 N, first right signed Moulsoe; Cranfield Road; MK16 0HB Wide food choice including chargrilled meats and fish sold by weight from refrigerated display, up to three changing real ales, friendly helpful staff, open-plan layout with comfortable mix of wooden chairs and cushioned banquettes; children allowed, long pretty garden behind, 16 bedrooms in two adjacent blocks, open all day. *(John Saville)*

NEWPORT PAGNELL SP8743
Cannon (01908) 211495
High Street; MK16 8AQ Friendly bay-windowed drinkers' pub with military theme, four real ales including Banks's and Marstons, darts, regular live music in room behind; small back terrace, smokers' shelters, open all day. *(David John)*

NEWTON LONGVILLE SP8431
⋆ **Crooked Billet** (01908) 373936
Off A421 S of Milton Keynes; Westbrook End; MK17 0DF Thatched pub with good enterprising restauranty food plus some cheaper pub favourites including sandwiches, set menu choices too (Tues-Sat lunch, Tues-Thurs dinner), Greene King ales, extensive choice of wines by the glass, modernised extended pubby bar, log-fire dining area; background and monthly live music, no dogs; children welcome away from bar, tables out on lawn, closed Mon. *(Toby Jones)*

OAKLEY SP6312
Chandos Arms (01844) 238296
The Turnpike; brown sign to pub off B4011 Thame–Bicester; HP18 9QB 16th-c part-thatched village pub under temporary management; two smallish rooms, one for locals and one for diners, low black beams, some stripped stone, padded country kitchen chairs on patterned carpet, inglenook housing big basket of books, Courage Best, Greene King IPA and Sharps Doom Bar, sensibly priced pubby food (not Mon, Tues lunchtime), darts, Tues quiz; games machine, maybe quiet radio, TV; picnic-sets on terrace and aunt sally, open all day. *(David Lamb)*

OLNEY SP8851
Bull (01234) 711470
Market Place/High Street; MK46 4EA 18th-c former coaching inn with sofas and other seats in three smallish front rooms, big

airy eating area on right, popular food (not Sun evening) from bar snacks up including mussels done in six ways, set menu choices lunchtime/early evening, pleasant efficient service, well kept Wells & Youngs and guests (Aug Bank Holiday festival), good coffee, open and log-effect gas fires; children and dogs welcome, seats in courtyard and big back garden with climbing frame, start of the famous Shrove Tuesday pancake race, open all day from 10am. *(D P and M A Miles)*

PENN STREET SU9295

✶ **Hit or Miss** (01494) 713109

Off A404 SW of Amersham, keep on towards Winchmore Hill; HP7 0PX Traditional pub with friendly licensees, heavily-beamed main bar with leather sofas and armchairs on parquet flooring, horsebrasses, open fire, two carpeted rooms with interesting cricket and chair-making memorabilia, more sofas, wheelback and other dining chairs around pine tables, Badger ales (summer beer festivals), interesting if not cheap food; background music; children welcome, dogs in bar, picnic-sets on terrace overlooking pub's cricket pitch, open all day. *(Roy Hoing)*

PENN STREET SU9295

Squirrel (01494) 711291

Off A404 SW of Amersham, opposite the Common; HP7 0PX Friendly sister pub to nearby Hit or Miss, open-plan bar with flagstones, log fire, comfortable sofas as well as tables and chairs, good value home-made traditional food from baguettes up (not Sun evening), good children's meals, well kept Black Sheep, Brains and two guests, free coffee refills, bric-a-brac and cricketing memorabilia, darts; big garden with good play area and village cricket view, lovely walks, open all day weekends (till 8pm Sun), closed Mon lunchtime. *(Susan and John Douglas)*

POUNDON SP6425

Sow & Pigs (01869) 277728

Main Street; OX27 9BA Small beamed village local with L-shaped bar, Brakspears ales and maybe a Marstons-related guest, good value straightforward food from short menu; Sky TV; children and dogs welcome, tables in good-sized back garden, open from 4pm weekdays, all day Sat, till 6pm Sun. *(David Lamb)*

SKIRMETT SU7790

✶ **Frog** (01491) 638996

From A4155 NE of Henley take Hambleden turn and keep on; or from B482 Stokenchurch–Marlow take Turville turn and keep on; RG9 6TG Pretty pub

in Chilterns countryside; nice public bar with log fire, prints on walls, cushioned sofa and leather-seated stools on wood floor, high chairs by counter serving Rebellion IPA, Gales Seafarer and a changing guest, a dozen wines by the glass including champagne and 24 malt whiskies, two different styled dining rooms, one light and airy with country kitchen tables and chairs, the other more formal with dark red walls, smarter furniture and candlelight, good, interesting food served by friendly helpful staff; background music; children welcome, dogs in bar (they have a black lab), side gate to lovely garden with unusual five-sided tables, attractive valley views, nearby hikes, comfortable bedrooms, closed Sun evening Oct-May. *(Susan Loppert, Jane Caplan, Maureen and Keith Gimson, D J and P M Taylor, Paul Humphreys, Ian Herdman and others)*

ST LEONARDS SP9107

White Lion (01494) 758387

Jenkins Lane, by Buckland Common; off A4011 Wendover–Tring; HP23 6NW New management for this unspoilt little open-plan pub, highest in the Chilterns, with old black beams and inglenook, ales such as Greene King IPA, Sharps Doom Bar and Tring, good value pub food (not Sun evening); children and dogs welcome, sheltered garden, good walks, open all day. *(David Lamb)*

STOKE GOLDINGTON SP8348

✶ **Lamb** (01908) 551233

High Street (B526 Newport Pagnell–Northampton); MK16 8NR Chatty village pub with friendly helpful licensees, up to four interesting changing ales, Weston's farm cider, good range of wines and soft drinks, good generous home-made food (all day Sat, not Sun evening) from baguettes to bargain Sun roasts, lounge with log fire and sheep decorations, two small pleasant dining rooms, table skittles in public bar; may be soft background music, TV; children and dogs welcome, terrace and sheltered garden behind with play equipment. *(JJW, CMW)*

STOKE MANDEVILLE SP8310

✶ **Woolpack** (01296) 615970

Risborough Road (A4010 S of Aylesbury); HP22 5UP Boldly decorated thatched pub with contemporary and stylish bar rooms, high-backed black or beige leather dining chairs on rugs or stone flooring, cushioned wall seats, open fire, Brakspears, Purity UBU and Sharps Doom Bar, several wines by the glass, cocktails, nice choice of food including fixed price weekday menu (till 7pm) and good Sun roasts,

---

efficient service; well behaved children allowed, seats in back garden and on the heated front terrace, open all day. *(Paul Hiskens, Mel Smith, Tracey and Stephen Groves)*

STONE   SP7912
Bugle Horn (01296) 747594
Oxford Road, Hartwell (A418 SW of Aylesbury); HP17 8QP Long 17th-c stone-built Vintage Inn (former farmhouse), comfortable linked rooms with mix of furniture, usual choice of reasonably priced food all day including set menu till 5pm, three real ales and lots of wines by the glass, log fires, conservatory; children welcome, attractive terrace, lovely trees in big garden with pastures beyond. *(Tony Halford, Mel Smith)*

STONY STRATFORD   SP7840
Old George (01908) 562181
High Street; MK11 1AA Attractive beamed and timbered inn dating to the 16th c, enjoyable good value food from sandwiches and wraps up, quick friendly staff, real ales such as Marstons, Ringwood and Wychwood, back dining room; background and some live music; upstairs lavatories; tables in courtyard behind, 11 bedrooms, parking nearby can be tricky. *(George Atkinson)*

SWANBOURNE   SP8027
Betsy Wynne (01296) 720825
Mursley Road; MK17 0SH Popular new pub (part of the Swanbourne Estate) built in traditional timbered style, emphasis on landlord/chef's enjoyable food using Estate and other local produce, good choice of real ales, welcoming efficient staff, spacious layout with plenty of exposed oak beams including raftered dining room, wood or terracotta-tiled floors, woodburner in central brick fireplace; children and dogs welcome, tables on terrace and lawn, play house and old tractor, open all day.
(Brian Glozier, Dennis and Doreen Haward)

THE LEE   SP8904
★ **Cock & Rabbit** (01494) 837540
Back roads 2.5 miles N of Great Missenden, E of A413; HP16 9LZ Stylish place run for over 25 years by same friendly italian family, although much emphasis on the good italian cooking they do keep Flowers and a guest ale and are happy to provide lunchtime baps, carefully decorated plush-seated lounge, cosy dining room and larger restaurant; seats outside on verandah, terraces and lawn, good walks. *(Paul Humphreys, Roy Hoing)*

THE LEE   SP8904
★ **Old Swan** (01494) 837239
Swan Bottom, back road 0.75 miles N of The Lee; HP16 9NU Welcoming tucked-away 16th-c dining pub, three attractively furnished linked rooms, low beams and flagstones, cooking-range log fire

in inglenook, enjoyable sensibly priced food, well kept Chiltern, Sharps Doom Bar and an occasional guest, attentive service; children welcome, big back garden with play area, good walks, open all day weekends (till 7pm Sun), closed Mon lunchtime. *(Toby Boyle)*

TURVILLE   SU7691
★ **Bull & Butcher** (01491) 638283
Valley road off A4155 Henley–Marlow at Mill End, past Hambleden and Skirmett; RG9 6QU Black and white pub in pretty village (famous as film and TV setting), two traditional low-beamed rooms with inglenooks, wall settles in tiled-floor bar, deep well incorporated into glass-topped table, Brakspears ales in good condition and decent wines by the glass, traditional food including lunchtime sandwiches, friendly staff; background and some live music; children and dogs welcome, seats by fruit trees in attractive garden, good walks, closed Sun evening in winter otherwise open all day. *(John Saville, John Wooll, Jim and Frances Gowers, Brian Glozier)*

WADDESDON   SP7316
Long Dog (01296) 651320
High Street; HP18 0JF Well renovated village pub (formerly the Bell), enjoyable food from varied menu including good burgers, bar area with open fire, friendly accommodating service, well kept ales and nice choice of wines by the glass; background music; children and dogs welcome (resident dachshund), tables out front and back, very handy for Waddesdon Manor.
(Colin McKerrow)

WEEDON   SP8118
Five Elms (01296) 641439
Stockaway; HP22 4NL Cottagey two-bar thatched pub, low beams and log fires, good traditional food cooked by landlord (best to book), Tring Side Pocket for a Toad or Skinners Betty Stogs kept well, good reasonably priced wines, old photographs and prints, separate dining room, games such as shove-ha'penny; a few picnic-sets out in front, pretty village, closed Sun evening. *(Martin Warne, Chris Birks, Taff Thomas)*

WENDOVER   SP8609
Village Gate (01296) 623884
Aylesbury Road (B4009); HP22 6BA Usefully open and serving good popular food all day (reduced afternoon menu); carefully updated décor in interconnected rooms with contemporary paintwork and furnishings, bar with woodburner in brick fireplace, chunky leather stools and assortment of dining chairs, animal prints on walls, Fullers London Pride and guests from unusual modern counter, other rooms laid out for eating with high-backed dining chairs around mix of tables on bare boards, carpet and stone tiles, occasional live bands; children and dogs (in bar) welcome, lots of outside

seating on decked and gravel areas, long-reaching country views. *(Tracey and Stephen Groves, Ruth May, Taff Thomas)*

WEST WYCOMBE   SU8394
George & Dragon (01494) 535340
High Street; A40 W of High Wycombe; HP14 3AB Popular rambling hotel bar in preserved NT Tudor village, massive beams and sloping walls, dim lighting, big log fire, four ales including Rebellion, fairly priced food from sandwiches and baguettes up, good friendly staff, small family dining room; dogs welcome, grassed area with picnic-sets and fenced play area, character bedrooms (magnificent oak staircase), handy for West Wycombe Park and the Hell Fire Caves, open all day. *(Dr A Y Drummond, C and R Bromage, Paul Humphreys)*

WESTON UNDERWOOD   SP8650
Cowpers Oak (01234) 711382
Signed off A509 in Olney; High Street; MK46 5JS Wisteria-clad beamed pub brightened up under present owners, enjoyable country cooking (all day weekends), Hopping Mad, Sharps Doom Bar, Wychwood Hobgoblin and Woodfordes Wherry, friendly helpful staff, nice mix of old-fashioned furnishings including pews, painted panelling and some stripped stone, two open fires, back restaurant; background

music; children and dogs welcome, small suntrap front terrace, more tables on back decking and in big orchard garden, fenced play area, pretty thatched village, open all day weekends. *(George Atkinson)*

WINCHMORE HILL   SU9394
Plough (01494) 259757
The Hill; HP7 0PA Refurbished village pub/restaurant with italian-influenced food including pizzas (landlord is from Campania), flagstones, low beams and open fires, linked dining area with polished wood floor, real ales and imported lagers, good coffee, little shop selling italian wines and other produce; children welcome, tables on terrace and lawn, pleasant walks nearby, open all day from 9.30am for breakfast. *(C and R Bromage)*

WING   SP8822
Queens Head (01296) 688268
High Street; LU7 0NS Welcoming refurbished 16th-c pub, enjoyable freshly cooked food (not Sun evening) in bar, restaurant or snug, well kept Courage Directors, Wells & Youngs and a guest, decent wines, afternoon tea with home-made scones, log fires; children welcome, disabled facilities, sunny terrace and garden with marquee, open all day; for sale as we went to press so things may change. *(John Wooll)*

Post Office address codings confusingly give the impression that some pubs are in Buckinghamshire, when they're really in Bedfordshire or Berkshire (which is where we list them).

Cambridgeshire

G ood new entries, or pubs that are back in these pages after a break, include the Eltisley in Eltisley (interestingly laid-out rooms and enjoyable food in village-green inn), Brewery Tap in Peterborough (fantastic own-brewed Oakham beers, knowledgeable staff and good and cheap thai food) and Tickell Arms in Whittlesford (a light and airy dining pub with enterprising food). This county is full of particularly well run pubs such as the Black Bull in Balsham (a smashing all-rounder), Willow Tree in Bourn (smart dining pub with impressive modern cooking), Free Press in Cambridge (consistently reliable local with six ales and fairly priced meals), John Barleycorn in Duxford (charming country pub with a helpful landlord and good choice of ales and food), Crown in Elton (enterprising food cooked by the landlord and comfortable bedrooms too), Carpenters Arms at Great Wilbraham (our readers love the place for its food, drinks choice and welcome), Cock at Hemingford Grey (a first class pub with a fine choice of ales and exceptional food), Old Bridge in Huntingdon (a proper pubby bar in an exceptional inn – super drinks and food choice and exemplary staff), Pheasant in Keyston (delicious modern cooking and fine wines in pretty thatched dining pub), New Sun in Kimbolton (spotlessly kept, deservedly busy and much enjoyed) and Bell in Stilton (the perfect break from the A1). Our Cambridgeshire Dining Pub 2014 is the Pheasant in Keyston.

 BALSHAM   TL5850   Map 5
Black Bull
Village signposted off A11 SW of Newmarket, and off A1307 in Linton;
High Street; CB21 4DJ

Pretty thatched pub with bedroom extension and enjoyable food too – a good all-rounder

R un with care and thought for both the pub and their customers, this black and white timbered inn is much enjoyed by our readers. The beamed bar spreads around a central servery where they keep Adnams Bitter, Greene King IPA, Woodfordes Wherry and a guest beer on handpump and 12 wines by the glass from a good list. Dividers and standing timbers break up the space, which has an open fire (and leather sofas in front of it), floorboards, low black beams in the front part, and furniture that includes dining chairs with leatherette seats. A restaurant extension has a high-raftered oak-panelled roof and a network of standing posts and steel ties. The front terrace offers teak tables and chairs by a long, pleasantly old-fashioned verandah and there are more seats in a small sheltered back garden. Smart, comfortable bedrooms are in a neat single-storey extension. The pub is under the same good ownership as the Red Lion at Hinxton.

As well as four smashing home-made pies daily, the imaginative food includes sandwiches and filled baguettes, potted rabbit with chargrilled baby carrots, coriander purée, pickled onions and vegetable crisps, truffled dressed crab tian with apple, avocado and red pepper jelly with mustard endive and blue cheese dressing, home-made burger with smoked cheese and tomato sauce, grilled smoked haddock with poached egg and wholegrain mustard sauce, artichoke risotto with mushroom, asparagus, pine nuts, olive, rocket, truffle and balsamic vinegar, and puddings such as chilled chocolate fondant with minted panna cotta, strawberry soup and honeycomb ice-cream, and lemon posset – lemon sponge, candied orange and lemon with raspberry sorbet. *Benchmark main dish: pie of the day £13.00. Two-course evening meal £20.00.*

Free house ~ Licensee Alex Clarke ~ Real ale ~ (01223) 893844 ~ Open 11-3, 5.30-11; 11-11 Sat; 12-10.30 Sun ~ Bar food 12-2 (2.30 Fri-Sun), 6.30 (7 Sun)-9 (9.30 Fri, Sat) ~ Restaurant ~ Well behaved children welcome ~ Dogs allowed in bar ~ Jazz singer regular Sats ~ Bedrooms: £79/£99 ~ www.blackbull-balsham.co.uk
Recommended by Mrs Margo Finlay, Jörg Kasprowski, M and GR, Simon Watkins

BOURN
Willow Tree 🍴 ♟

TL3256   Map 5

High Street, just off B1046 W of Cambridge; CB23 2SQ

Light and airy dining pub with versatile choice of good up-to-date food and stylish garden

Now a free house and run by friendly, considerate staff, this is a relaxed and informal place – even if your first impression feels a bit misleading given the cut-glass chandeliers, sprinkling of Louis XVI chairs and sofas in velvet and gilt, and profusion of silver-plate candlesticks. In fact, there's a great variety of seating and of tables – many with stripped tops and painted lower parts. The uncluttered décor is mostly fresh cream, with one area papered to resemble shelves of books. They have a good range of wines by the glass, some inventive cocktails and Milton Pegasus and Tiki and Woodfordes Wherry on handpump. A back deck has smart chairs and tables beneath an extendable canopy, and beyond the car park a huge weeping willow serves as the 'pole' for a circular purple tent, with teak tables and chairs, and matching purple deckchairs on the grass by fruit trees.

Using the best local seasonal produce, the tempting food includes tapas, lunchtime sandwiches, sharing platters, rabbit, venison and bacon terrine with apple compote, scotch duck egg wrapped in pork, herb and black pudding with parsnip dipping crisps, several good pizzas, burger with cheese, onions, bacon and gherkins, braised oxtail stew, corn-fed chicken breast with carrot and puy lentil stew, chard, ricotta and root vegetable roulade with pickled beetroot salad, lamb rump with creamed, bacony savoy cabbage, parmentier potatoes and rosemary hollandaise, and puddings like caramelised banana crêpes with cinnamon ice-cream and chocolate delice with salted caramel, milk ice-cream and cherries; they also hold monthly supper clubs. *Benchmark main dish: beer-battered fish and chips £11.00. Two-course evening meal £20.50.*

Free house ~ Licensee Shaina Galvin-Scott ~ Real ale ~ (01954) 719775 ~ Open 11am-midnight; 12-11 Sun ~ Bar food 12-3, 5.30-9.30; 12-8 Sun ~ Children welcome ~ www.thewillowtreebourn.com *Recommended by John Saville, Mike and Mary Carter*

CAMBRIDGE
TL4558   Map 5

Free Press  £

Prospect Row; CB1 1DU

Quiet and unspoilt with interesting local décor, up to six real ales, and good value food

With well kept, changing real ales and reasonably priced, good food, this charming little backstreet pub remains as popular as ever – and there are no mobile phones, background music or games machines to disturb the peace. In a nod to the building's history as the home of a local newspaper, the characterful bare-boarded rooms are hung with historic newspaper pages and printing memorabilia, as well as old printing trays that local customers are encouraged to top up with little items; there's also a log fire. Greene King IPA, Abbot and Mild and regularly changing guests such as Milestone St Georges Legend, Thwaites Wainwright, Timothy Taylors Golden Best and Wadworths St George & the Dragon on handpump, 25 malt whiskies, a dozen wines by the glass, and plenty of rums, gins and vodkas; assorted board games. There are seats in the sheltered and paved suntrap garden, and sometimes morris men in summer. Wheelchair access.

The enjoyable, fairly priced food includes sandwiches, an antipasti plate, chunky chilli beef, whiting fillet with parsley sauce, red lentil and mixed nut roast with sweet tomato sauce, ham hock and black pudding hash with fried egg, leg of lamb with sweet potato mash, purée of peas, bacon, mint and garlic and redcurrant sauce, and puddings such as sticky toffee pudding with custard and lemon sponge with raspberry coulis. *Benchmark main dish: pork schnitzel with braised red cabbage and sautéed potatoes £8.50. Two-course evening meal £13.00.*

Greene King ~ Lease Craig Bickley ~ Real ale ~ (01223) 368337 ~ Open 12-2.30, 6-11; 12-11 Fri, Sat; 12-3, 7-10.30 Sun ~ Bar food 12-2 (2.30 Sat, Sun), 6 (7 Sun)-9 ~ Children welcome ~ Dogs allowed in bar ~ www.freepresspub.com *Recommended by Chris and Angela Buckell, Clive and Fran Dutson, David and Gill Carrington, John Honnor, John Wooll, Roger Fox*

CAMBRIDGE
TL4459   Map 5

Punter

Pound Hill, on corner of A1303 ring road; CB3 0AE

Good enterprising food in relaxed and interestingly furnished surroundings

The rambling and informal linked rooms with their old dark floorboards have quite a bit of character, and are filled with paintings, antique prints and a pleasing choice of seating – pews, elderly dining chairs, Lloyd Loom easy chairs. One prized corner is down a few steps, behind a wooden railing. The scrubbed tables have candles in bottles or a variety of candlesticks, and the staff are quick and friendly. They have Adnams Ghost Ship and a Nethergate ale named for the pub on handpump, and decent wines by the glass; board games and maybe unobtrusive piped music. The flagstoned and mainly covered former coachyard has tables and picnic-sets; beyond is a raftered barn bar, similar in style, with more pictures on papered walls, a large rug on dark flagstones, and a big-screen TV. This is sister pub to the Punter in Oxford.

As well as the bargain £5 lunch, the interesting food might include potted shrimps on toast, venison and pork terrine with pickles, chilli con carne with crème fraîche, leek risotto with chive mascarpone and truffle oil, venison sausages with mash and caramelised onions, confit duck leg with puy lentils, red cabbage and crispy bacon, beef shin with roast carrots and turnips and half a roast guinea fowl with truffled potatoes, spinach and pickled mushrooms. *Benchmark main dish: burger with cheese and chips £12.50. Two-course evening meal £20.00.*

Punch ~ Lease Paul Fox ~ Real ale ~ (01223) 363322 ~ Open 12-11 ~ Bar food 12-3, 6-10 (6-9 Sun) ~ Restaurant ~ Children welcome ~ Dogs welcome ~ Occasional acoustic guitar Sun evenings ~ www.thepuntercambridge.com
Recommended by Clive and Fran Dutson

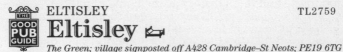

ELTISLEY   TL2759   Map 5

Eltisley 🛏

The Green; village signposted off A428 Cambridge–St Neots; PE19 6TG

Village-green inn with interestingly laid out dining bar and more formal restaurant area

The interestingly shaped bar twists so much it could do with 'S-bend' warning signs – and that's not even counting the cosy, very low-beamed library room tucked down steps, past the serving counter with its line of five hurricane lamps. Pale flagstones here, dark boards there, leatherette wall seats, curved high-backed fabric-covered settles and all sorts of chairs, a similar mix of tables including some with zinc tops – all unified by grey paintwork throughout, even on the heavy-beamed ceiling. A classic deco three-piece leather suite sits by the cast-iron stove in the massive central chimneypiece. There's Wells & Youngs Eagle on handpump, decent wines in three glass sizes; piped pop music. The separate dining room with pitched rafters suits more formal occasions. Canopied decking in a sheltered area behind has wicker-style seating, with a small group of silver birches on the side grass. We have not yet heard from readers staying in the bedroom block beyond.

From a good varied menu, the enjoyable food includes sandwiches, chicken and ham hock terrine with apricot chutney, fried pigeon breast with honey-roasted figs and pea-shoot salad, a trio of local sausages with baby onions, bacon and grain mustard mash, chicken burger with basil pesto, mozzarella and chips, wild mushroom and tarragon pappardelle with white wine cream sauce, roast fish of the day with ratatouille and fondant potato, roast lamb rump with coriander crust, potato and celeriac gratin and red cabbage, pork chop with sautéed potatoes, chorizo and roasted roots, and puddings such as chocolate and griottine cherry brownie and bitter chocolate sauce, and sticky toffee and banana pudding with toffee and rum sauce; 6-7pm Tues-Fri they do a few takeaway dishes. *Benchmark main dish: burger with bacon, cheese, mayonnaise and chips £11.95. Two-course evening meal £21.00.*

Free house ~ Licensee John Steans ~ Real ale ~ (01480) 880308 ~ Open 12-3, 6-11; 12-11 Sat; 12-3.30 Sun; closed Mon (except bank holidays), Sun evening ~ Bar food 12-2,

6-9; 12-9 Sat; 12-3 Sun ~ Children and dogs welcome ~ Bedrooms: £40/£65 ~
www.theeltisley.co.uk *Recommended by Michael Sargent, Dave Braisted, Simon Watkins, Lucien Perring*

ELTON
Crown ⊕ ♀ ⇔

TL0894   Map 5

Off B671 S of Wansford (A1/A47), and village signposted off A605 Peterborough–Oundle; Duck Street; PE8 6RQ

Lovely thatched inn in charming village, interesting food, several real ales, well chosen wines and a friendly atmosphere; stylish bedrooms

The bedrooms in this lovely thatched stone inn are smart, comfortable and well equipped and the breakfasts are notably good. The very attractive layout includes a softly lit beamed bar with an open fire in the stone fireplace, good pictures and pubby ornaments on pastel walls, and leather and antique dining chairs around an attractive mix of chunky tables on bare boards. The beamed main dining area has candles, fresh flowers and similar furniture on stripped wood floors; a more formal, circular, conservatory-style restaurant is open at weekends. High bar chairs against the counter are popular with locals, and they keep Golden Crown (brewed for them by Tydd Steam), Greene King IPA and a guest or two such as Burton Bridge Sovereign Gold and Slaters Top Totty on handpump, well chosen wines by the glass and farm cider. There are tables outside on the front terrace. Elton Mill and Lock are a short walk away.

 Impressive food, cooked by the landlord, includes lunchtime sandwiches, mussels with white wine, garlic, bacon and cream, home-smoked duck breast with toasted pine nuts, blood orange and chargrilled fennel, omelettes, beef and mushroom in ale pie, beef burger with cheese, bacon or free-range egg, millefeuille of wild mushrooms and celeriac with poached duck egg, baby spinach and truffle oil, corn-fed chicken breast and crsipy wings with herb dumplings and baby vegetable stew, lamb rump with leek and potato dauphinoise, beetroot fondant and baby onion and rosemary jus, and puddings such as rhubarb and plum crumble and citrus sponge with Baileys clotted cream. *Benchmark main dish: home-made cider and apple sausages with colcannon, crispy bacon and onion gravy £13.95. Two-course evening meal £21.00.*

Free house ~ Licensee Marcus Lamb ~ Real ale ~ (01832) 280232 ~ Open 12-11 ~ Bar food 12-2 (3 Sun), 6.30-9; not Sun evening ~ Restaurant ~ Children welcome ~ Dogs allowed in bar ~ Bedrooms: £73/£120 ~ www.thecrowninn.org *Recommended by Ian and Helen Stafford, Michael Doswell, Howard and Margaret Buchanan, R L Borthwick, Lesley Dick*

FEN DRAYTON
Three Tuns £

TL3468   Map 5

Off A14 NW of Cambridge at Fenstanton; High Street; CB24 5SJ

Charming old pub, traditional furnishings in bar and dining room, real ales, tasty food and seats in garden

The friendly licensees have struck just the right balance between drinkers and diners in this ancient thatched pub, and the open fires in each room help create a warm, relaxed atmosphere. The three rooms are more or less open-plan with a mix of burgundy cushioned stools, attractive old dining chairs and settles in the friendly bar, and wooden dining chairs and tables on the red-patterned carpet in the dining room, along with framed prints of the pub. Greene King IPA and Old Speckled

Hen, a beer named for the pub and a guest such as St Austell Trelawny on handpump and 16 wines by the glass; friendly service. A well tended back lawn has seats and tables, a covered dining area and a children's play area.

🍴 Reasonably priced food, using local produce and free-range eggs, includes lunchtime sandwiches (the jumbo hot dog with home-made chilli is popular, as are the sizzling fajitas), chicken liver terrine with own-made red onion marmalade, crispy breaded mushrooms with garlic mayonnaise, french onion tart, home-baked honey-roast ham with egg or grilled pineapple, shredded duck salad, lasagne, chicken jalfrezi and bass fillets with herb and lemon butter; they also offer a two-course set lunch for OAPs during the week. *Benchmark main dish: home-made pies £8.95. Two-course evening meal £14.50.*

Greene King ~ Tenant Sam Fuller ~ Real ale ~ (01954) 230242 ~ Open 12-2 (3 Sat), 6-11; 12-3 Sun; closed Sun evening ~ Bar food 12-2, 6-9 (9.30 Fri, Sat) ~ Restaurant ~ Children welcome ~ Dogs allowed in bar ~ www.the3tuns.co.uk *Recommended by Barry and Anne, Dave Braisted, Simon Watkins, Jeremy King, R L Borthwick*

GREAT WILBRAHAM   TL5558   Map 5

Carpenters Arms 🍴 ♍ ◧ £

Off A14 or A11 SW of Newmarket, following The Wilbrahams signposts; High Street; CB21 5JD

Inviting village pub with traditional bar, good food in both bar and back restaurant; pleasant garden

' A delightful place all round,' says one of our readers – and many agree. It's even more likeable now they've opened their own microbrewery to offer Craft Beers Carpenters Cask and Sauvignon Blonde on handpump, alongside their bottled ale Sixteen Strides, plus a guest like Greene King IPA. The properly pubby, low-ceilinged village bar on the right has a carefully chosen wine list (strong on the Roussillon region), bar billiards, a sturdy settle by the big inglenook with its woodburning stove, copper pots and iron tools, and cushioned pews and simple seats around the solid pub tables on floor tiles; background music. Service is spot on: thoughtful, helpful and cheerful. On the left, a small, cosy, carpeted dining area has another large stone fireplace and overflowing bookshelves; this leads through to a sitting area with comfortable sofas and plenty of magazines. The light and airy extended main dining room has country kitchen chairs around chunky tables. A huge honeysuckle swathes the tree in the pretty back courtyard, and further on, an attractive homely garden, with fruit and vegetables, has round picnic-sets shaded by tall trees.

🍴 Excellent food using some own-grown produce and their own sauces and chutneys includes sandwiches, toasties and filled baguettes, grilled scallops with toasted hazelnut and coriander butter, mushroom, thyme and goats cheese tartlet, pork and black pudding sausages with onion gravy, mushroom-stuffed chicken breast with brandy and mushroom cream sauce, slow-roast pork belly with sage and onion mash and apple sauce, vegetable strudel, and puddings such as catalan crème brûlée and triple chocolate delight. *Benchmark main dish: beef in ale pie £9.95. Two-course evening meal £15.00.*

Free house ~ Licensees Rick and Heather Hurley ~ Real ale ~ (01223) 882093 ~ Open 11.30-3, 6.30-11; 11.30-3 Sun; closed Sun evening, Tues ~ Bar food 12-2.30 (3 Sun), 7-9 ~ Restaurant ~ Children welcome ~ www.carpentersarmsgastropub.co.uk
Recommended by M and GR, Edward Mirzoeff, R P Knight, Paul and Corinna Goldman

HEMINGFORD ABBOTS

Axe & Compass £

TL2870   Map 5

High Street; village signposted off A14 W of Cambridge; PE28 9AH

Thriving proper village community pub, popular too for good value food

Dating back to the 15th c, this bustling pretty thatched pub is in a lovely village and always has a happy mix of customers. Various linked rooms have mainly traditional pub furnishings on tiled floors, with cheery pictures and an inglenook fireplace in one red-walled room, heavy black Tudor beams and local photographs in another, and a well lit pool table and TV on the left. At the back are an old leather sofa and comfortable library chairs by shelves of books, and a dresser with their own chutneys and jams for sale. The central island servery has Greene King IPA and Old Speckled Hen and Sharps Doom Bar on handpump, and around a dozen wines by the glass; darts, pool, TV and board games. Leading off is a long dining room decorated with prints, and the garden, next to the tall-spired church, has swings and a play area for children and a chicken run. Good disabled facilities.

As well as a very good value two- and three-course set menu (weekday lunchtimes only), the honest, home-made and reasonably priced food includes sandwiches (the soup and sandwich deal is popular), whitebait with lemon mayonnaise, macaroni cheese and garlic bread, sausages and mash with onion gravy, cheese burger with onions, mushrooms or bacon, home-cooked ham and eggs, chilli beef, and various puddings. *Benchmark main dish: pie of the day £9.50. Two-course evening meal £17.00.*

Enterprise ~ Lease Nigel Colverson ~ Real ale ~ (01480) 463605 ~ Open 12 (10 Sat, Sun)-11 (10 Sun) ~ Bar food 12-2.30 (3 Sat, Sun), 6-9; not Sun evening ~ Restaurant ~ Children in bar until 5pm, in dining area after 5pm ~ Dogs allowed in bar ~ Bedrooms: £70 ~ www.axeandcompass.co.uk *Recommended by Mrs Margo Finlay, Jörg Kasprowski, Simon Watkins*

HEMINGFORD GREY

Cock 🍴 ♀ 🍺

TL2970   Map 5

Village signposted off A14 eastbound and (via A1096 St Ives road) westbound; High Street; PE28 9BJ

Imaginative food in pretty pub, extensive wine list, four interesting beers, a bustling atmosphere and smart restaurant

As well run and as popular as ever, this is a favourite with many – as one reader says, 'it never disappoints'. The bar rooms have dark or white-painted beams, lots of contemporary pale yellow and cream paintwork, assorted artworks, fresh flowers and church candles, and throughout a really attractive mix of old wooden dining chairs, settles and tables. They've sensibly kept the traditional public bar on the left for drinkers only: an open woodburning stove on the raised hearth, bar stools, wall seats and a carver, steps that lead down to more seating, Brewsters Hophead, Great Oakley Wots Occurring, Nethergate IPA and Oldershaw Newtons Drop on handpump, 18 wines by the glass mainly from the Languedoc-Roussillon region and local farm cider; they hold a beer festival every August Bank Holiday weekend. In marked contrast, the stylishly simple, spotless restaurant on the right – you must book to be sure of a table – has flowers on each table, pale floorboards and another woodburning stove. The neat garden has seats and tables among stone troughs and flowers, and lovely hanging baskets.

🍴 Using the best local, seasonal produce, the enticing food might include lunchtime sandwiches, ham hock, leek and mustard terrine with blood orange jelly, smoked chicken breast with grapes, crispy shallots and juniper dressing, home-made sausages such as pork, five spice and hoisin, or pork with green peppercorns and stilton with a choice of four sauces and four kinds of mash, pearl barley and braised leek risotto, pork tenderloin with roasted celeriac and beetroot, sage and garlic mash and red wine sauce, daily fresh fish dishes such as clam and mussel chowder with brioche croutons and coriander oil or cod steak with walnut crust, bacon rösti, wilted spinach and apple purée, and puddings such as dark chocolate and Cointreau terrine with chantilly cream and orange shortbread, and pistachio and sea-salt cake with lemon granita; the two- and three-course set lunch (weekdays only) is extremely good. *Benchmark main dish: venison haunch steak with roasted shallot, spinach, cherries and red wine sauce £18.50. Two-course evening meal £20.50.*

Free house ~ Licensees Oliver Thain and Richard Bradley ~ Real ale ~ (01480) 463609 ~ Open 11.30-3, 6-11; 11.30-11 summer Sat; 12-10.30 Sun; 12-4, 6.30-10.30 winter Sun ~ Bar food 12-2.30, 6.30 (6 Fri, Sat)-9 (8.30 Sun) ~ Restaurant ~ Children allowed in bar lunchtime only; in restaurant must be over-5 in evening ~ Dogs allowed in bar ~ www.thecockhemingford.co.uk *Recommended by Michael Sargent, Pat and Stewart Gordon, Barry and Anne, Howard and Margaret Buchanan, M Mossman, Gordon and Margaret Ormondroyd, Derek and Sylvia Stephenson, John Saville, S Holder*

HINXTON
Red Lion 🍴 ⏛ 🛏

TL4945   Map 5

2 miles off M11 junction 9 northbound; take first exit off A11, A1301 N, then left turn into village – High Street; a little further from junction 10, via A505 E and A1301 S; CB10 1QY

16th-c pub with friendly staff, interesting bar food, real ales and a big landscaped garden; comfortable bedrooms

Handy for the Imperial War Museum at Duxford and at the heart of a pretty conservation village, this pink-washed inn is run by a cheerful, attentive licensee. The low-beamed bar has oak chairs and tables on wooden floorboards, two leather chesterfield sofas, an open fire in the dark green fireplace, an old wall clock and a relaxed, friendly atmosphere. Adnams Bitter, Greene King IPA, Woodfordes Wherry and a guest such as Brandon Rusty Bucket on handpump, 12 wines by the glass (they have regular wine tastings), a dozen malt whiskies and first class service. An informal dining area has high-backed settles, and the smart restaurant with its oak rafters made with traditional dry-peg construction is decorated with assorted pictures and clocks. The large, neatly kept garden has a pleasant terrace with teak tables and chairs, picnic-sets on the grass, a dovecote and views of the village church; another terrace outside the porch door has a huge parasol for sunny days. The bedrooms are in a separate flint and brick building. They also own the Black Bull in Balsham just up the road.

🍴 As well as noteworthy sandwiches, the sophisticated food includes pigeon breast with beetroot purée, waldorf salad, beetroot crisps and honey and mustard dressing, scallops on potato rösti with salmon mousse and celeriac nut butter, home-made burger with smoked cheese and tomato chutney, beer-battered fish and chips with home-made tartare sauce, cauliflower risotto with truffle foam, parsley oil, nut butter and chocolate, lamb cutlet, saddle and braised breast with fondant potato, pea purée and fried sweetbread jus, bream fillet with chargrilled artichokes, thai aspargus, tarragon-crushed new potatoes and garlic butter, and puddings such as vanilla panna cotta with raspberry coulis and lemon sorbet and chocolate tart with crème fraîche ice-cream, coffee anglaise, chocolate tuile and pistachio praline. *Benchmark main dish: steak in ale pie £12.00. Two-course evening meal £21.00.*

Free house ~ Licensee Alex Clarke ~ Real ale ~ (01799) 530601 ~ Open 11-11; 12-4, 7-10.30 Sun ~ Bar food 12-2 (2.30 Fri-Sun), 6.30-9 (7-9 Sun) ~ Restaurant ~ Well behaved children welcome ~ Dogs allowed in bar ~ Bedrooms: £90/£135 ~ www.redlionhinxton.co.uk *Recommended by KC, Charles Gysin*

HUNTINGDON

Old Bridge Hotel 🍽 ♟ 🛏

TL2471 Map 5

1 High Street; ring road just off B1044 entering from easternmost A14 slip road; PE29 3TQ

Georgian hotel with smart pubby bar, splendid range of drinks, first class service and excellent food; fine bedrooms

This really is an excellent all-rounder – extremely civilised, warmly welcoming and with sparkling service and top class food and drinks. And while the hotel side clearly dominates, there's a wide mix of customers who very much enjoy the traditional pubby bar. This has a log fire, comfortable sofas and low wooden tables on polished floorboards, and Adnams Bitter and City of Cambridge Hobsons Choice on handpump; service is first rate. There's also an exceptional wine list (up to 30 by the glass in the bar) and a wine shop where you can taste a selection of the wines before you buy. You can dine in the big airy 'Terrace' (an indoor room, but with beautifully painted verdant murals suggesting the open air) or in the slightly more formal panelled restaurant. There are seats and tables on the terrace by the Great Ouse, and they have their own landing stage. This is a lovely place to stay and some bedrooms overlook the river.

Delicious food includes nibbles such as home-made crisps and salt-cod croquettes, terrine of confit chicken, foie gras, shiitake mushrooms and tarragon, wrapped in prosciutto, with toasted brioche and truffle mayonnaise, smoked mackerel salad with celery, fennel and crème fraîche with lemon and horseradish dressing, fish and chips with mushy peas and tartare sauce, pork and leek sausages with white onion and mustard sauce, poached and grilled saddle of rabbit with borlotti beans, violetta artichokes and tarragon sauce, slow-braised sticky rib of beef with spicy noodles and asian salad of red cabbage, pink grapefruit and mint and candied pecans, and puddings such as panna cotta with champagne rhubarb and sticky toffee pudding with toffee sauce and jersey cream; they also offer a two- and three-course set menu Monday-Saturday lunchtimes and 6.30-7.30 evenings (not Saturday or Sunday). *Benchmark main dish: crab linguine with chilli, lemon and parsley £12.95. Two-course evening meal £21.50.*

Huntsbridge ~ Licensee John Hoskins ~ Real ale ~ (01480) 424300 ~ Open 11-11 ~ Bar food 12-2, 6.30-10 ~ Restaurant ~ Children welcome ~ Dogs welcome ~ Bedrooms: £89/£160 ~ www.huntsbridge.com *Recommended by Michael Sargent, Kay and Alistair Butler, Martin and Pauline Jennings*

The details at the end of each featured entry start by saying whether the pub is a free house, or if it belongs to a brewery or pub group (which we name).

KEYSTON

TL0475   Map 5

Pheasant 🍴 ♔

Just off A14 SE of Thrapston; brown sign to pub down village loop road, off B663; PE28 0RE

Cambridgeshire Dining Pub of the Year

Good civilised country dining pub with appealing décor and attractive garden

This neatly kept and thatched white building has come a long way since it was the village smithy. It's now a civilised dining pub offering several real ales and excellent food cooked by the landlord. The main bar has pitched rafters high above with lower dark beams in side areas, and the central serving area has dark flagstones, with hop bines above the handpumps for Adnams Southwold and Broadside and Nene Valley NVB, a tempting array of 17 wines by the glass, and padded stools along the leather-quilted counter. Nearby are armchairs, a chesterfield, quite a throne of a seat carved in 17th-c style, other comfortable seats around low tables, and a log fire in a lofty fireplace. The rest of the pub is mostly red-carpeted with dining chairs around polished tables, and large sporting prints – even hunting-scene wallpaper in one part. Lighted candles and tea-lights throughout, and neat friendly attentive staff add to the feeling of well-being. The attractively planted and well kept garden behind has tables on lawn and terrace; from the picnic-sets in front of the pretty thatched building you may see the neighbours' hens pottering about by the very quiet village lane.

As well as tasty nibbles such as pork crackling with apple sauce, thai green cashews and home-made bread, the exceptional food might include tempura tiger prawns with pickled pink ginger, mizuna, coriander and asian dipping sauce, gnocchi with cime di rapa, duck sauce and parmesan, local mussels with white wine, garlic, parsley cream and chips, burger with caramelised onions and blue cheese, calves liver with grilled polenta, roast beetroot, pancetta, rhubarb and red wine sauce, corn-fed chicken with sprouting broccoli, pancetta, baby onions and mushrooms duxelle, saddle of rabbit with purple potatoes, cauliflower purée, braised baby gem and thyme and red wine sauce, and puddings such as lemongrass and lime leaf crème brûlée and treacle tart with cinnamon ice-cream; they also offer a two- and three-course set lunch (not Sunday) and early supper (not Saturday). *Benchmark main dish: chargrilled cushion of lamb with borlotti beans, shallot purée and salsa verde £16.95. Two-course evening meal £21.00.*

Free house ~ Licensee Simon Cadge ~ Real ale ~ (01832) 710241 ~ Open 12-3, 6-11; 12-11 Fri, Sat; 12-5 Sun; closed Sun evening, Mon ~ Bar food 12-2, 6.30-9.30; 12-3.30 Sun ~ Restaurant ~ Children welcome ~ Dogs allowed in bar ~ www.thepheasant-keyston.co.uk
Recommended by Michael and Jenny Back, Michael Sargent, Ryta Lyndley, J F M and M West

KIMBOLTON

TL0967   Map 5

New Sun 🍴 ♔

High Street; PE28 0HA

Interesting bars and rooms, tapas menu plus other good food, and a pleasant back garden

On a lovely high street, this interesting and consistently well run pub is somewhere you can drop into for a morning coffee, a chatty pint or an enjoyable meal – the friendly, efficient staff make everyone welcome. The cosiest room is perhaps the low-beamed front lounge with standing timbers, exposed brickwork, shelves of books, and a couple of comfortable armchairs and a sofa beside a log fire. This leads into a narrower locals' bar with Wells & Youngs Bombardier and Eagle and a weekly changing guest on handpump, and 15 wines by the glass (including champagne and pudding wines); background music, board games, piano and quiz machine. The traditionally furnished dining room opens off here. The airy conservatory with high-backed leather dining chairs leads to the terrace, where there are smart seats and tables under giant umbrellas. Note that some of the nearby parking spaces have a 30-minute limit.

As well as popular tapas such as spicy chorizo sausages, fried squid with aioli and belly pork nuggets with quince paste, the reliably good, tasty food includes lunchtime sandwiches, filled baked potatoes, home-cooked ham with free-range eggs, wild mushroom and truffle oil risotto, beef stroganoff, duck breast with confit leg, spinach and port jus, slow-cooked shoulder of lamb, and puddings such as Malteser cheesecake; they also hold regular themed food evenings. *Benchmark main dish: steak and kidney pudding £10.75. Two-course evening meal £18.00.*

Wells & Youngs ~ Lease Stephen and Elaine Rogers ~ Real ale ~ (01480) 860052 ~ Open 11.30-11; 12-10.30 Sun; 11.30-2.30, 5-11 winter Mon-Thurs ~ Bar food 12-2.15 (2.30 Sun), 7-9.30; not Mon or Sun evenings ~ Restaurant ~ Children welcome ~ Dogs allowed in bar ~ www.newsuninn.co.uk *Recommended by Simon Watkins, Ryta Lyndley, Alan Sutton*

PETERBOROUGH   TL1899   Map 5

Brewery Tap 🍺 £

Opposite Queensgate car park; PE1 2AA

Fantastic range of real ales including their own brews, and popular thai food in huge conversion of old labour exchange

It may be an unusual combination, but the popular thai food and notably good own-brewed real ales in this striking modern conversion of an old labour exchange consistently draw in many happy customers. There's an easy-going feel to the contemporary open-plan interior, with an expanse of light wood and stone floors and blue-painted iron pillars holding up a steel-corded mezzanine level. Stylish lighting includes a giant suspended steel ring with bulbs running around the rim and steel-meshed wall lights. A band of chequered floor tiles traces the path of the long sculpted pale wood bar counter, which is backed by an impressive display of bottles in a ceiling-high wall of wooden cubes. There's also a comfortable downstairs area, a big-screen TV for sporting events, background music and regular live bands and comedy nights. A two-storey glass wall divides the bar from the brewery, giving fascinating views of the newly installed 10-hectolitre microbrewing plant. They produce their own Oakham beers (Bishops Farewell, Citra, Inferno, JHB, Scarlet Macaw and seasonal ales) and also keep up to eight guests; quite a few whiskies and several wines by the glass. The place gets very busy in the evening.

The thai food remains incredibly popular. As well as set menus and specials, you might find tom yum soup, chicken, beef, pork, prawn, duck and vegetable curries, stir-fried crispy chilli beef, talay pad cha (prawns, squid and mussels with crushed garlic, chilli and ginger), various noodle dishes, assorted salads and stir-fries and five kinds of rice. *Benchmark main dish: chicken pad thai £7.25. Two-course evening meal £13.00.*

Own brew ~ Licensee Jessica Loock ~ Real ale ~ (01733) 358500 ~ Open 12-11 (10.30 Sun) ~ Bar food 12-2.30, 5.30-10.30; 12-10.30 Fri, Sat ~ Restaurant ~ Children welcome during food service times only ~ Dogs allowed in bar ~ Live bands and comedy Sat evenings ~ www.oakham-ales.co.uk *Recommended by Ian and Helen Stafford*

STILTON

TL1689 Map 5

Bell ♀ ⇐

High Street; village signposted from A1 S of Peterborough; PE7 3RA

**Fine coaching inn with several civilised rooms including a residents'
bar, bar food using the famous cheese, and seats in the very pretty
courtyard; bedrooms**

Our readers really enjoy this lovely example of a 17th-c coaching
inn, and it's a perfect break from the busy A1. The left-hand side is
a civilised hotel, but the two neatly kept right-hand bars (which have
the most character) are where many customers head for. There are
bow windows, sturdy upright wooden seats on flagstone floors, plush
button-back built-in banquettes and a large log fire in a handsome stone
fireplace; one bar contains a large cheese press. The partly stripped
walls have big prints of sailing and coaching scenes and a giant pair
of blacksmith's bellows hangs in the middle of the front bar. Digfield
Fools Nook, Greene King IPA and Old Speckled Hen, Oakham Bishops
Farewell and a guest beer on handpump, quite a few malt whiskies and
around nine wines by the glass; service is helpful and welcoming. Other
rooms include a residents' bar, a bistro and a restaurant. Through the
handsome coach arch is a very pretty sheltered courtyard with tables and
a well that dates from Roman times.

 Using the famous cheese in many dishes, the good, popular food includes
stilton pâté with pineapple, passion-fruit jam and toast, slow-cooked pigs
cheek with rhubarb salad and mustard glaze, basil linguine with ratatouille and
focaccia croutons, coq au vin, home-made burger with barbecue sauce topped
with stilton, fresh beer-battered haddock, assiette of duck (breast, leg, wrap, liver
stuffing) with apricot chutney and sage fondant, cannon of lamb with rosemary
potatoes and cooking liquor, and puddings like hot chocolate fondue with toasted
marshmallows and caramel rice pudding with roast pears and salted caramel; you
can try a stilton cheese sampler too. *Benchmark main dish: sausage and mash
with onion rings and gravy £10.95. Two-course evening meal £20.00.*

Free house ~ Licensee Liam McGivern ~ Real ale ~ (01733) 241066 ~
Open 12-2.30 (3 Sat), 6-11 (midnight Sat); 12-10.30 Sun ~ Bar food 12-2.15 (2.30 Sat),
6-9.30; 12-3, 6-9 Sun ~ Restaurant ~ Children allowed in bistro ~ Bedrooms: £73.50/£105
~ www.thebellstilton.co.uk *Recommended by Barry and Anne, Mike and Mary Carter, J F M
and M West, Aimee, B and M Kendall, Lee and Liz Potter*

SUTTON GAULT

TL4279 Map 5

Anchor ⑪ ♀ ⇐

Bury Lane off High Street (B1381); CB6 2BD

**Tucked-away inn with charming candlelit rooms, inventive food,
real ales and thoughtful wine list; bedrooms**

The food here is so impressive under the new licensee that you'll need
to book well ahead to reserve a table at the weekend. But this isn't
just a restaurant – although space for drinkers can be tight on Friday
and Saturday evenings and Sunday lunchtime, at other times you can
pop in for a pint of Nethergate Growler tapped from the cask or one
of the dozen wines by the glass. The four heavily timbered rooms are
stylishly simple with two log fires, antique settles and wooden dining
chairs around well spaced scrubbed pine tables with candles on gently
undulating old floors, and attractive lithographs and big prints on the
walls. Service is helpful and friendly. Bedrooms are comfortable, well

equipped and overlook the river. There are seats outside and you can walk along the high embankment; the bird-watching is said to be good.

 Using the best local produce, the modern british food might include grilled dates wrapped in bacon with mild mustard cream, pigeon breast on black onion seed pasta with pickled red cabbage and port syrup, beer-battered haddock fillet with pea purée and tartare sauce, goats cheese with curried cauliflower and cashew nut millefeuille with butternut squash purée, chilli jam and cucumber salad, ballotine of chicken stuffed with pheasant breast, wrapped in bacon with champ mash, chantenay carrots and madeira jus, fillet of bass with citrus crème fraîche, pak choi and sauce vierge, and puddings such as chocolate fondant with beetroot sorbet and marshmallow sauce and sticky toffee pudding with butterscotch sauce and double cream ice-cream; they also offer a two- and three-course set lunch on weekdays. *Benchmark main dish: venison steak with chestnut purée, braised red cabbage, potato rösti and port jus £17.95. Two-course evening meal £23.00.*

Free house ~ Licensee Jeanene Flack ~ Real ale ~ (01353) 778537 ~ Open 12-2, 7-9 (6-9.30 Sat); 12-2.30, 6.30-9 Sun ~ Bar food 12-2, 7-9 (6-9.30 Sat) ~ Restaurant ~ Children welcome ~ Bedrooms: £89.50/£115 ~ www.anchor-inn-restaurant.co.uk
Recommended by M and GR, Mr and Mrs P R Thomas, Andrew Conway, Mrs Margo Finlay, Jörg Kasprowski, Sally Anne and Peter Goodale, R and M Tait, Ryta Lyndley, George Atkinson

WHITTLESFORD
Tickell Arms ⑪ ♐
TL4648   Map 5

2.4 miles from M11 junction 10: A505 towards Newmarket, then 2nd turn left signposted Whittlesford; keep on into North Road; CB22 4NZ

Light and refreshing dining pub with good enterprising food and pretty garden

The main emphasis is on the dining area on the right, through an ornate glazed partition, but there's also a proper L-shaped bar with tiled floor, on the left, containing some mementoes of the legendarily autocratic regime of Wagner-loving former owner Kim Tickell, such as his prohibition of 'long-haired lefties'. The three porcelain handpumps of his era are now orphaned, decorating a high counter that's suspended between a pair of ornate cast-iron pillars and lined with bentwood bar stools. The beer itself is still available: well kept Milton Pegasus and Nethergate IPA and Old Growler. On the right are tables varying from sturdy to massive, with leather-cushioned bentwood and other dining chairs and a single dark pew, and fresh minimalist décor in palest buff. This opens into an even lighter limestone-floored conservatory area, partly divided by a very high-backed ribbed leather banquette. There's a friendly buzz of relaxed conversation, confident and neatly informal staff, and a good range of fairly priced wines by the glass including champagne and other sparklers. The side terrace has comfortable tables, while the secluded garden beyond has pergolas and a pond.

Interesting food using the best seasonal produce might include tempura squid with chilli, lime and black onion seeds, warm potato and black pudding terrine with sweet chilli sauce, home-cured corned beef hash rösti with smoked cherry-tomato sauce and poached egg, swede and gorgonzola gratin with beetroot purée, parsnip crisps and salsa verde, thyme-roasted chicken with wild mushroom and spinach gnocchi, crispy pancetta and truffle oil, steak and kidney suet pudding, sea bream with ratatouille, black olive caramel and sautéed potatoes, and puddings such as dark chocolate marquise, kirsch cherries and chocolate sauce, and bramley apple, prune and armagnac parfait with brandy snaps and caramel sauce; the two-

and three-course weekday set menu is particularly good value. *Benchmark main dish: star anise and liquorice braised beef cheek with oyster dumpling and roast celeriac £18.00. Two-course evening meal £23.00.*

Free house ~ Licensees Oliver Thain, Richard Bradley, Max Freeman ~ Real ale ~ (01223) 833025 ~ Open 12-2.30 (3 Sat, Sun), 6-11 (9.30 Sun) ~ Bar food 12-2.30 (3 Sat), 6.30 (6 Sat)-9; 12-8 Sun ~ Restaurant ~ Children welcome, over-10s only in pub, over-5s only in restaurant in evening ~ Dogs allowed in bar ~ www.cambscuisine.com/the-tickell-whittlesford *Recommended by Giles and Annie Francis*

Also Worth a Visit in Cambridgeshire

Besides the fully inspected pubs, you might like to try these pubs that have been recommended to us and described by readers. Do tell us what you think of them: feedback@goodguides.com

ABINGTON PIGOTTS   TL3044
Pig & Abbot (01763) 853515
High Street; SG8 0SD Spotless Queen Anne local with two small traditional bars and restaurant, good choice of enjoyable reasonably priced food, friendly efficient staff, well kept Adnams, Fullers London Pride and guests, log fires, quiz night second Weds of month; back terrace, pretty village with good walks, open all day weekends – very busy then. *(Lucien Perring)*

ARRINGTON   TL3250
☀ **Hardwicke Arms** (01223) 208802
Ermine Way (A1198); SG8 0AH Handsome 18th-c coaching inn with 13th-c origins and 1792 work by Sir John Soane; enjoyable food from sandwiches and pub favourites up including good value Sun roasts, Greene King IPA and two or three interesting guests, good friendly service, dark-panelled dining room, huge central fireplace, daily papers; background music; 12 bedrooms, handy for Wimpole Hall, open all day. *(Simon Watkins)*

BARRINGTON   TL3849
Royal Oak (01223) 870791
Turn off A10 about 3.7 miles SW of M11 junction 11, in Foxton; West Green; CB22 7RZ Rambling thatched Tudor pub with tables out overlooking classic village green, heavy low beams and timbers, mixed furnishings, beers from Adnams, Potton and Wells & Youngs, Aspall's cider, enjoyable food from pub favourites up, good friendly service, airy dining conservatory; background music; children welcome. *(Rghmsmith, Mr and Mrs M Walker)*

BOXWORTH   TL3464
Golden Ball (01954) 267397
High Street; CB23 8LY Attractive partly thatched building with comfortably contemporary open-plan bar, three-part restaurant in original core, friendly helpful staff, popular food from baguettes through suet puddings and pies to grills, well kept Courage and Wells & Youngs ales, good whisky choice; children welcome, nice garden and heated terrace, pastures behind, 11 quiet bedrooms in adjacent block, open all day. *(Jeremy King)*

BRAMPTON   TL2170
Black Bull (01480) 457201
Church Road; PE28 4PF 16th c and later with updated low-ceilinged interior, stripped-wood floor and inglenook woodburner in split-level main bar, restaurant area with light wood furniture on tiles, enjoyable well priced food (not Sun evening) including own sausages and pies, four real ales, friendly staff; children welcome and dogs (home-made treats for them), garden play area, open all day. *(John and Elspeth Howell)*

BRANDON CREEK   TL6091
☀ **Ship** (01353) 676228
A10 Ely–Downham Market; PE38 0PP Lovely spot on Norfolk border at confluence of Great and Little Ouse, plenty of tables out by the moorings; welcoming helpful staff, good choice of enjoyable pub food including specials, Adnams and up to four guests, spacious tastefully modernised bar with massive stone masonry in sunken former forge area, big log fire one end, woodburner the other, interesting old photographs and prints, restaurant; children and dogs welcome, open all day weekends, closed Mon in winter. *(Anon)*

BROUGHTON   TL2877
☀ **Crown** (01487) 824428
Off A141 opposite RAF Wyton; Bridge Road; PE28 3AY Attractively tucked away opposite church, fresh and airy décor, sturdy furnishings including nicely set dining end, good well presented enterprising food, friendly service, real ales such as Church End and Nethergate; disabled access and facilities, tables out on big stretch of grass behind, open all day Sun till 8pm. *(David, Roy Shutz)*

BUCKDEN   TL1967
★ **George** (01480) 812300

High Street; PE19 5XA Handsome and
stylish Georgian-faced hotel with bustling
informal bar, fine fan beamwork, leather
and chrome chairs, log fire, Adnams Best
and a changing guest from chrome-topped
counter, lots of wines including champagne
by the glass, nice choice of teas and coffees,
friendly well trained staff, good modern
food in popular brasserie with smart cream
dining chairs around carefully polished
tables; background music; children and dogs
welcome, tables under large parasols on
pretty sheltered terrace with box hedging,
charming bedrooms, open all day. *(Michael
Sargent, George Atkinson, David and Ruth
Hollands, J F M and M West)*

BUCKDEN   TL1967
★ **Lion** (01480) 810313

High Street; PE19 5XA Partly 15th-c
coaching inn, black beams and big inglenook
log fire in airy and civilised bow-windowed
entrance bar with plush bucket seats,
wing armchairs and sofas, good food from
lunchtime sandwiches up, fine choice of
wines, Adnams Bitter and a guest, prompt
friendly staff, panelled back restaurant
beyond latticed window partition; children
welcome, back courtyard, 14 bedrooms, open
all day. *(Anon)*

CAMBRIDGE   TL4658
★ **Cambridge Blue** (01223) 471680

85 Gwydir Street; CB1 2LG Smashing
little backstreet local, knowledgeable
landlord and a dozen interesting ales (some
tapped from the cask – Feb/June festivals),
bottled beers, traditional bar food, small,
attractive conservatory and two simply
decorated peaceful rooms with lots of
breweriana, bare-boards-style furnishings,
board games; can get busy weekends;
children and dogs welcome, seats in
surprisingly rural-feeling back garden,
open all day. *(Tony Hobden)*

CAMBRIDGE   TL4459
Castle (01223) 353194

Castle Street; CB3 0AJ Full Adnams beer
range and several interesting guests in big
airy bare-boards bar, several pleasantly
simple rooms, wide range of good value quick
pubby food from sandwiches up, friendly
staff, peaceful upstairs (downstairs can be
louder, with background music); picnic-sets
in good walled back courtyard, open all day
Fri-Sat. *(Roger Fox)*

CAMBRIDGE   TL4657
Devonshire Arms (01223) 316610

Devonshire Road; CB1 2BH Popular, light
and airy Milton-tied pub with two linked
bars, their ales plus guests, Crone's cider,
great choice of bottled beers, well chosen
wines and a dozen malts, decent low-priced

food from sandwiches and snacks to steaks,
cheerful chatty staff and locals, creaky
wood floors, mix of furniture including long
narrow refectory tables, architectural prints
and steam engine pictures, woodburner in
back bar; disabled access, handy for the
station. *(Chris and Angela Buckell, Mr and
Mrs M Walker)*

CAMBRIDGE   TL4458
★ **Eagle** (01223) 505020

Bene't Street; CB2 3QN Original
architectural features (once the city's most
important coaching inn); rambling rooms
with two medieval mullioned windows
and the remains of possibly medieval wall
paintings, two fireplaces dating to around
1600, lovely worn wooden floors and plenty
of pine panelling, dark red ceiling left
unpainted since World War II to preserve
signatures of British and American airmen
made with Zippo lighters, candle smoke and
lipstick, Greene King ales including Eagle
DNA (Crick and Watson announced the
discovery of DNA's structure here in 1953)
and two guests, enjoyable efficiently served
food despite the crowds; children welcome,
disabled facilities, heavy wooden seats in
attractive cobbled and galleried courtyard,
open all day. *(Chris and Angela Buckell, Michael
Sargent, John Wooll, Barry Collett, Susan and
Nigel Brookes, Giles and Annie Francis and others)*

CAMBRIDGE   TL4558
Elm Tree (01223) 363005

Orchard Street; CB1 1JT Traditional
one-bar backstreet drinkers' pub, ten well
kept ales including Wells & Youngs, good
range of continental bottled beers, local
ciders/perries usually poured from the barrel,
friendly knowledgeable staff, nice unspoilt
interior with breweriana, basic lunchtime
snacks; some outside tables at side. *(Chris
and Angela Buckell, David and Gill Carrington,
Rob Jones)*

CAMBRIDGE   TL4559
Fort St George (01223) 354327

Midsummer Common; CB4 1HA
Picturesque old pub (reached by foot only)
in charming waterside position overlooking
ducks, swans, punts and boathouses;
extended around old-fashioned Tudor core,
good value bar food including traditional Sun
lunch, well kept Greene King ales, decent
wines, cheery helpful young staff, oars on
beams, historic boating photographs, stuffed
fish and bric-a-brac; children welcome,
wheelchair access via side door, lots of tables
outside. *(Chris and Angela Buckell, John Wooll)*

CAMBRIDGE   TL4657
★ **Kingston Arms** (01223) 319414

Kingston Street; CB1 2NU Victorian
pub with well kept interesting ales from 11
handpumps, over 50 bottled beers and good
choice of wines by the glass, enjoyable freshly
prepared food including some bargains,

discounts for students, companionably big plain tables and basic seating, thriving chatty atmosphere, friendly staff; children and dogs welcome, back beer garden – torch-lit, heated and partly covered, open all day Fri-Sun. *(Tony Hobden)*

CAMBRIDGE TL4557
Live & Let Live (01223) 460261

Mawson Road; CB1 2EA Popular backstreet alehouse, friendly and relaxed, with well kept Nethergate Umbel Magna and seven changing guests, lots of bottled belgians, local cider and over 120 rums, good value bar food, heavily timbered brickwork rooms with sturdy varnished pine tables on bare boards, country bric-a-brac and some steam railway and brewery memorabilia, gas lighting (not always lit), cribbage and dominoes; children and dogs welcome, disabled access awkward but possible. *(Chris and Angela Buckell)*

CAMBRIDGE TL4458
Mill (01223) 311829

Mill Lane; CB2 1RX Pleasant, recently reopened pub in picturesque spot overlooking mill pond where punts can be hired; eight local real ales, reasonably priced pubby food (all day weekends) including children's choices, Mon quiz. *(Richard Tilbrook, John Wooll)*

CAMBRIDGE TL4458
Mitre (01223) 358403

Bridge Street, opposite St Johns College; CB2 1UF Welcoming Nicholsons pub close to the river, rambling bar on several levels, their usual good value food cooked well and served all day including set price menu (from 5pm), good friendly service, eight well kept mainly mainstream ales, farm cider, well priced wines by the glass; background music; children welcome, disabled access. *(Paul Spring, John Saville, Gerry and Rosemary Dobson)*

CAMBRIDGE TL4559
☆ Old Spring (01223) 357228

Ferry Path; car park on Chesterton Road; CB4 1HB Extended Victorian pub, roomy and airy, with smartly old-fashioned scrubbed-wood décor, bare boards, lots of old pictures, enjoyable well priced home-made food including enterprising dishes and Sun roasts, efficient welcoming service, well kept Greene King IPA, Abbot and three guests, good coffee and choice of wines by the glass, two log fires, long back conservatory; background music, no under-21s in the evening, dogs outside only; disabled facilities, large heated well planted terrace, open all day. *(Chris and Angela Buckell, P and D Carpenter)*

CASTLE CAMPS TL6343
Cock (01799) 584207

High Street; CB21 4SN Small village pub run by friendly enthusiastic couple, beers such as Cottage, Fullers and Greene King, nice selection of wines, enjoyable good value food cooked by landlord (not Mon); dogs welcome. *(Adele Summers, Alan Black)*

CASTOR TL1298
☆ Prince of Wales Feathers

(01733) 380222 *Off A47; PE5 7AL* Friendly stone-built local with well kept local Castor, Woodfordes and interesting guests, farm cider and perry, landlady does good value food (not weekend evenings) including Sun roasts, side dining area; Sky TV, games machines, pool (free Thurs), Sat live music, Sun quiz; children and dogs welcome (they have a friendly setter), attractive front terrace, back one with shelters, open all day, till late weekends. *(Ian and Helen Stafford, David Moody)*

COTON TL4158
Plough (01954) 210489

Just off M11 junction 13; High Street; CB23 7PL Emphasis on food from tapas to full meals, prompt helpful service, three ales such as Adnams, Greene King and Woodfordes, good choice of wines by the glass, airy clean-cut contemporary décor with pale wood, pastel colours, sofas and big log fire; no dogs inside; children welcome, sizeable garden with play area, open all day (food all day Sun). *(John Saville)*

DUXFORD TL4746
☆ John Barleycorn (01223) 832699

Handy for M11 junction 10; right at first roundabout, then left at main village junction; CB22 4PP Pretty 17th-c thatched pub with shuttered windows; bars with standing timbers and brick pillars creating alcoves, hops on heavy beams, log fires and nice old floor tiles, eclectic mix of seating including some rather fine antique farmhouse chairs, lots to look at on blue or yellow walls, Greene King and guests, comprehensive wine list, good food served by friendly helpful staff; background music; children and dogs welcome, hanging baskets and blue-painted picnic-sets on front terrace, more tables in back garden, comfortable bedrooms, Air Museum nearby, open all day. *(Rghmsmith, Dave Braisted, Mrs Margo Finlay, Jörg Kasprowski, Mr and Mrs M Walker)*

ELSWORTH TL3163
☆ George & Dragon (01954) 267236

Off A14 NW of Cambridge, via Boxworth, or off A428; CB23 8JQ Neatly

---

kept popular dining pub with courteous staff and easy-going atmosphere; pleasant panelled main bar decorated with a fishy theme opening on the left to a slightly elevated dining area, woodburner, garden room overlooking attractive terraces, more formal restaurant on the right, wide choice of enjoyable food from baguettes to good steaks and grills, Thurs fish night, Greene King ales and a guest, decent wines; steps down to lavatories; children welcome, dogs in bar, open all day Sun. *(Michael and Jenny Back and others)*

ELY   TL5479

✳ **Cutter**   (01353) 662713

Annesdale, off Station Road (or walk S along Riverside Walk from Maltings); CB7 4BN Beautifully placed contemporary riverside pub with carpeted dining bar and smart restaurant, enjoyable promptly served food from sandwiches up including good value Sun roasts, well kept Sharps Doom Bar and Woodfordes Wherry from boat-shaped bar, nice wines by the glass, decent coffee, good views from window seats and front terrace. *(John Saville, Ryta Lyndley, Val and Alan Green)*

ELY   TL5480

High Flyer (01353) 771110

Newnham Street; CB7 4PQ Refurbished Youngs pub with enjoyable good value food including daily carvery, friendly service; children welcome, five comfortable bedrooms. *(Anon)*

ELY   TL5480

Lamb (01353) 663574

Brook Street (Lynn Road); CB7 4EJ Good choice of food in popular hotel's panelled lounge bar or restaurant, friendly welcoming staff, Greene King ales and plenty of wines by the glass, decent coffee; children welcome, close to cathedral, 31 clean comfortable bedrooms, good breakfast. *(Sue and Mike Todd)*

ETTON   TF1406

Golden Pheasant (01733) 252387

Just off B1443 N of Peterborough, signed from near N end of A15 bypass; PE6 7DA Yellow brick Georgian pub with friendly chatty landlady, restaurant next to comfortable bar with open fire, very well kept Adnams Lighthouse, Oakham JHB and guests, decent choice of wines and spirits, enjoyable food including good value bar menu, some live music; children welcome, big tree-sheltered garden with play area, vintage car meetings, on Green Wheel cycle route, open all day Fri-Sat. *(Howard and Margaret Buchanan)*

FEN DITTON   TL4860

Plough (01223) 293264

Green End; CB5 8SX Big Mitchells & Butlers dining pub with wide choice of tasty food all day, pleasant service, well kept Adnams and guests such as Sharps and Wells & Youngs, extensive choice of wines (many by the glass), rowing décor, dining area down steps; background music; children welcome, tables on decking and riverside lawns, nice walk from town. *(John Marsh, Jeremy King)*

GRANTCHESTER   TL4355

✳ **Blue Ball** (01223) 840679

Broadway; CB3 9NQ Particularly well kept Adnams and a guest ale in character bare-boards village local, said to have the area's oldest, proper hands-on landlord (there's a list of previous publicans back to 1767), good log fire, cards and traditional games including shut the box and ring the bull, lots of books; no food; dogs welcome, tables on small terrace with lovely views to Grantchester Meadows, good heated smokers' shelter, nice village, open from 2pm (midday weekends), till 7pm Sun. *(Anon)*

GRANTCHESTER   TL4355

Green Man (01223) 844669

High Street; CB3 9NF Friendly pub with heavy beams, mix of old tables and chairs on bare boards, leather sofa and armchairs, log fire, well cooked/presented food (all day weekends) from traditional to more sophisticated dishes – popular so best to book, good range of changing local ales tapped from the cask, decent wine list, separate dining room with linen napkins, Sun night jazz; children and dogs welcome, disabled facilities, tables in big back garden with own bar, Grantchester Meadows views, open all day. *(Simon Watkins, Eddie Edwards, P and D Carpenter, S J and C C Davidson)*

GRANTCHESTER   TL4355

Red Lion (01223) 840121

High Street; CB3 9NF Comfortable and spacious thatched pub, wide choice of enjoyable food including plenty of fish dishes and bargain weekday specials, children's menu, good friendly service, well kept Greene King ales, four modernised open areas with beams, timbers and panelling; background music; sheltered terrace and good-sized lawn, play area, easy walk to river, open all day. *(John Saville)*

GREAT CHISHILL   TL4239

✳ **Pheasant** (01763) 838535

Follow Heydon signpost from B1039 in village; SG8 8SR Popular split-level flagstoned pub with beams, timbering, open fires and some elaborately carved (though modern) seats and settles, good freshly made food (not Sun evening) using local produce, welcoming friendly staff, two or three ales including one for the pub from Nethergate, good choice of wines by the glass, small dining room (best to book), darts, cribbage, dominoes; no under-14s inside; dogs allowed, charming secluded back garden with small play area, open all day weekends. *(Mrs Margo Finlay, Jörg Kasprowski)*

GREAT SHELFORD   TL4652
Square & Compasses
(01766) 810250 *High Street; CB22 5EH* Small well kept village local with friendly welcoming staff, popular sensibly priced food, Greene King ales. *(Phil and Jane Hodson, Eddie Edwards)*

HARDWICK   TL3758
Blue Lion (01954) 210328
Signed off A428 (was A45) W of Cambridge; Main Street; CB23 7QU Attractive old dining pub, beams and timbers, leather armchairs by copper-canopied inglenook, good food from landlord/chef in bar and extended dining area with conservatory, friendly young uniformed staff, Greene King IPA and guest ales; children welcome, pretty roadside front garden, more seats on decking and lawn with play area, handy for Wimpole Way walkers, open all day. *(Simon Humphrey, John Saville, M and GR)*

HELPSTON   TF1205
✴ Blue Bell (01733) 252394
Woodgate; off B1443; PE6 7ED The charming, professional, hands-on landlord at this homely pub has retired; refurbishment under way as we went to press with restaurant, mediterranean-style menu and bedrooms planned – news please. *(Anon)*

HEYDON   TL4339
✴ King William IV (01763) 838773
Off A505 W of M11 junction 10; SG8 8PW Rambling dimly lit rooms with fascinating rustic jumble (ploughshares, yokes, iron tools, cowbells) along with copperware and china in nooks and crannies, log fire, Fullers, Greene King and Timothy Taylors Landlord, good varied choice of well presented food including proper home-made pies, helpful staff; background music; children welcome, dogs in bar area, teak furniture on heated terrace and in pretty garden, open all day weekends. *(John Wooll, Howard and Margaret Buchanan)*

HISTON   TL4363
✴ Red Lion (01223) 564437
High Street, off Station Road: 3.7 miles from M11 junction 1; signposted off A14 E via B1049; CB24 9JD A shrine to real ale; ceiling joists in L-shaped main bar packed with hundreds of beer mats and pump clips among hop bines and whisky-water jugs, fine collection of old brewery advertisements and rack of real ale campaign literature, impressive choice of draught and bottled beers along with a farm cider and perry, spring and early autumn festivals, limited lunchtime food (nothing on Sun), cheerful efficient service, comfortable brocaded wall seats, matching mate's chairs and pubby

tables, log fires, nice antique one-arm bandit, bar on left with darts, TV and huge collection of beer bottles; no credit cards; well behaved children allowed in one part only, picnic-sets in neat garden, play area, limited parking, open all day. *(Anon)*

HORSEHEATH   TL6147
Old Red Lion (01223) 892909
Linton Road; CB21 4QF Neatly kept Greene King pub, good value food, efficient staff; 12 cabin bedrooms. *(Simon Watkins)*

HOUGHTON   TL2772
Three Jolly Butchers
(01480) 463228 *A1123, Wyton; PE28 2AD* Popular 17th-c beamed pub with wide choice of enjoyable home-made food from baguettes and baked potatoes up (not Sun evening), cheerful attentive service, four well kept ales including Greene King Old Speckled Hen, inglenook woodburner; background music; children and dogs allowed in one area, covered back terrace, huge garden with play area, own moorings on River Ouse, pretty village, open all day. *(John and Nan Hurst)*

LITTLE WILBRAHAM   TL5458
✴ Hole in the Wall (01223) 812282
High Street; A1303 Newmarket Road to Stow cum Quy off A14, then left at The Wilbrahams signpost, then right at Little Wilbrahams signpost; CB1 5JY Tucked-away pub/restaurant with cosy carpeted ochre-walled bar on right, log fire in big brick fireplace, 16th-c beams and timbers, snug little window seats and other mixed seating around scrubbed kitchen tables, similar middle room with fire in open range, rather plusher main dining room with another fire, really good inventive cooking, Fellowes ales with guests like Brandon, Potton and Woodfordes, ten wines by the glass and some unusual soft drinks, helpful service; well behaved children allowed, dogs in bar, neat side garden with good teak furniture and small verandah, interesting walk to nearby unspoilt Little Wilbraham Fen, closed Sun evening, all day Mon and for two weeks in Jan. *(J F M and M West, Mrs D Crew, Mr and Mrs T R Leighton)*

MADINGLEY   TL3960
✴ Three Horseshoes (01954) 210221
High Street; off A1303 W of Cambridge; CB23 8AB Civilised thatched restauranty pub – most customers come here for the inventive if not cheap italian-influenced food; there is also a small pleasantly relaxed bar, with simple wooden furniture on bare boards and open fire (can be a bit of a crush at peak times), Adnams and Jennings Cumberland, outstanding wine list with 23 by the glass, friendly service, pretty dining conservatory; children welcome, picnic-sets under parasols in sunny garden. *(Tom and Ruth Rees)*

NEEDINGWORTH   TL3571
⋆ **Pike & Eel** (01480) 463336
*Pub signed from A1123; Overcote Road;
PE27 4TW* Peacefully placed old riverside
hotel with spacious lawns and small marina;
plush bar opening into room with easy chairs,
sofas and big open fire, civilised eating area
(also separate smart restaurant) in light and
airy glass-walled block overlooking water,
boats and swans, good food and service,
Adnams, Black Sheep and Greene King IPA,
good coffee and wines; background music;
children welcome, 12 clean simple bedrooms,
good breakfast. *(Simon Watkins)*

NEWTON   TL4349
⋆ **Queens Head** (01223) 870436
*2.5 miles from M11 junction 11; A10
towards Royston, then left on to B1368;
CB22 7PG* Lovely traditional unchanging
pub run by same welcoming family for many
years, lots of loyal customers, peaceful bow-
windowed main bar with crooked beams in
low ceiling, bare wooden benches and seats
built into cream walls, curved high-backed
settle, paintings, big log fire, Adnams ales
tapped from the cask, farm cider, hearty
simple food, small carpeted saloon, pubby
games including table skittles, shove-ha'
penny and nine men's morris; no credit
cards; children on best behaviour allowed in
games room only, dogs welcome, seats out in
front by vine trellis. *(Sarah Flynn)*

OFFORD D'ARCY   TL2166
Horseshoe (01480) 810293
High Street; PE19 5RH Extended former
17th-c farmhouse, emphasis on good food
including popular Sun carvery, friendly
service, five changing ales, well chosen
wines, two bars and restaurant, beams and
log fires; children welcome, garden with
play area, open all day Fri-Sun.
(P and D Carpenter)

PAMPISFORD   TL4948
⋆ **Chequers** (01223) 833220
*2.6 miles from M11 junction 10: A505
E, then village and pub signed off; Town
Lane; CB22 4ER* Traditional neatly kept
old pub with friendly licensees, low beams
and comfortable old-fashioned furnishings,
booth seating on pale ceramic tiles in cream-
walled main area, low step down to bare-
boards part with dark pink walls, Greene
King IPA, Woodfordes Wherry and two guests,
enjoyable fairly priced food including good
Sun carvery; TV; children and dogs welcome
(their collie is called Snoopy), picnic-sets in
prettily planted simple garden lit by black
streetlamps, parking may be tricky, open all

day (till 4pm Sun). *(D and M T Ayres-Regan,
David and Gill Carrington, Evelyn and Derek
Walter, Roy Hoing, David Jackman and others)*

PETERBOROUGH   TL1998
⋆ **Charters** (01733) 315700
Town Bridge, S side; PE1 1FP
Remarkable conversion of dutch grain barge
moored on River Nene; a dozen real ales
including Oakham, good value pan-asian
food, sizeable timbered bar on lower deck,
restaurant above, lots of wooden tables and
pews, regular beer festivals, live bands (Fri
and Sat after 10.30pm, Sun from 3.30pm);
background music, games machines; children
welcome till 9pm, dogs in bar, huge riverside
garden (gets packed in fine weather), open
all day. *(Anon)*

PETERBOROUGH   TL1898
Drapers Arms (01733) 847570
Cowgate; PE1 1LZ Roomy open-plan
Wetherspoons in sympathetically converted
draper's, fine ale range, food all day; can
get very busy Fri and Sat evenings; children
welcome, open from 9am. *(Roger Fox)*

REACH   TL5666
Dyke's End (01638) 743816
*From B1102 follow signpost to
Swaffham Prior and Upware; village
signposted; CB25 0JD* Newish owners
for this 17th-c farmhouse; simply decorated
bar with kitchen chairs and heavy pine
tables on dark boards, panelled section on
left and step down to carpeted part with
servery, own-brewed Devils Dyke beers plus
guests, enjoyable food (not Sun evening,
Mon) from pub favourites up; children and
dogs welcome, picnic-sets on front grass,
attractive spot next to church and village
green, open all day weekends, closed Mon
lunchtime. *(Bruce M Drew, M and GR,
Simon Watkins)*

SPALDWICK   TL1372
George (01480) 890293
*Just off A14 W of Huntingdon;
PE28 0TD* Friendly well run 16th-c pub,
stylish décor, sofas in bar, larger bistro
area, nice food from good value bar snacks
up, local real ales; children welcome.
(Roy Shutz)

ST NEOTS   TL1761
Eaton Oak (01480) 219555
*Just off A1, Great North Road/Crosshall
Road; PE19 7DB* Under same ownership as
the George & Dragon at Elsworth and Rose
at Stapleford; wide choice of popular food
including grills, fresh fish and good value
lunchtime set menus (Tues-Fri), Wells &

Post Office address codings confusingly give the impression that some pubs are
in Cambridgeshire, when they're really in Bedfordshire, Lincolnshire, Norfolk or
Northamptonshire (which is where we list them).

Youngs ales and an occasional guest, efficient friendly service, spacious dining area, conservatory; children and dogs (in bar) welcome, disabled access throughout, tables outside under parasols, nine bedrooms, open all day (breakfast for non-residents). *(Michael and Jenny Back and others)*

STAPLEFORD   TL4651
✳ **Rose** (01223) 843349
London Road; M11 junction 11; CB22 5DG Comfortable sister pub to George & Dragon at Elsworth and Eaton Oak at St Neots, emphasis on dining and can get very busy, wide choice of well cooked reasonably priced food, pleasant uniformed staff, well kept Wells & Youngs ales, small low-ceilinged lounge with inglenook woodburner, roomy split-level dining area, some refurbishment after recent flooding; faint background music; picnic-sets on back grass. *(Michael and Jenny Back)*

STIBBINGTON   TL0898
Sibson Inn (01780) 782227
Off A1 northbound; PE8 6ND Former 17th-c farmhouse – a handy stop if travelling north on A1; decent food all day from 7am (8am weekends); 19 bedrooms. *(John Coatsworth)*

STOW CUM QUY   TL5260
White Swan (01223) 811821
Off A14 E of Cambridge, via B1102; CB25 9AB Cosy 17th-c beamed village pub/restaurant under newish licensees, five well kept ales, Weston's cider and several wines by the glass, enjoyable home-made food from bar snacks and pubby choices to more ambitious restaurant dishes, big fireplace, friendly atmosphere; children and dogs welcome, terrace picnic-sets, handy for Anglesey Abbey (NT), open all day. *(Phil and Jane Hodson, M and GR, Mrs M Baxter, Hazel Miller)*

THORNEY   TL2799
Dog in a Doublet (01733) 202256
B1040 towards Thorney; PE6 0RW Friendly riverside pub with good food and well kept ales, open fire; handy for Hereward Way walks. *(Middlemass Ryan)*

THRIPLOW   TL4346
Green Man (01763) 208855
3 miles from M11 junction 10; A505 towards Royston, then first right; Lower

Street; SG8 7RJ This simply furnished unpretentious place has been bought by the village and new licensees installed (same people who run the Hole in the Wall at Little Wilbraham); it's unclear as we go to press what changes will be made – so news please; has closed Sun evening, Mon. *(Andy Lickfold, Phil and Jane Hodson, P and D Carpenter, Roger and Lesley Everett)*

TILBROOK   TL0769
White Horse (01480) 860764
High Street (B645); PE28 0JP Welcoming and relaxed two-room country pub, enjoyable reasonably priced food (not Sun evening, Mon), cosy bar with traditional games such as table skittles, Wells & Youngs ales, nice range of coffees, some low beams, conservatory; big garden with play equipment, goats, chickens and ducks, closed Mon lunchtime, otherwise open all day. *(John Allman, George Atkinson, Ryta Lyndley)*

UFFORD   TF0904
✳ **White Hart** (01780) 740250
Main Street; S on to Ufford Road off B1443 at Bainton, then right; PE9 3BH Friendly village pub dating from the 17th c, informal, chatty bar with wood floor and exposed stone walls, railway memorabilia, farm tools and chamber pots, high-backed settles and leather sofa by woodburner, well kept Adnams Bitter, Black Sheep, Grainstore Ten Fifty and Oakham JHB, several wines by the glass, good food including some imaginative choices, beamed restaurant and small orangery; children and dogs welcome, three acres of gardens, comfortable bedrooms, good breakfast, open all day (till 9pm Sun). *(Phil and Jane Hodson, F and M Pryor, Michael Doswell, Gordon and Margaret Ormondroyd)*

WANSFORD   TL0799
Paper Mills (01780) 782328
London Road; PE8 6JB Attractively refurbished old stone pub with friendly buzzy atmosphere, Fullers London Pride and a couple of guests, good wine selection, enjoyable popular food from changing menu, good sandwiches too, friendly well trained young staff, beamed and flagstoned bar with fireplaces either side, conservatory; children and dogs welcome, tables in nicely tended terrace garden, open all day. *(Phil and Jane Hodson, Sam and Christine Kilburn, G Jennings, Lois Dyer)*

A very few pubs try to make you leave a credit card at the bar, as a sort of deposit if you order food. They are not entitled to do this. The credit card firms and banks that issue them warn you not to let cards out of your sight. If someone behind the counter used your card fraudulently, the card company or bank could in theory hold you liable, because of your negligence in letting a stranger hang on to your card. Suggest instead that if they feel the need for security, they 'swipe' your card and give it back to you. And do name and shame the pub to us.

WARESLEY TL2454
Duncombe Arms (01767) 650265
*Eltisley Road (B1040, 5 miles S of
A428); SG19 3BS* Comfortable welcoming
old pub, long main bar with fire at one end,
enjoyable traditional food and well kept
Greene King ales, friendly service, back room
and restaurant; occasional live music; picnic-
sets in small shrub-sheltered garden.
(Simon Watkins, Roger Fox)

WHITTLESFORD TL4648
Bees in the Wall (01223) 834289
*North Road; handy for M11 junction
10; CB22 4NZ* Comfortably worn-in,
split-level timbered lounge with flowers on
polished tables and country prints, small
tiled public bar with old wall settles, darts,
decent good value food (not Tues and Sun
evenings) from sandwiches up, well kept
Timothy Taylors Landlord and guests, open
fires; may be classical background music,
games machine, no dogs; picnic-sets in big
paddock-style garden with terrace, bees'
nest visible in wall, handy for Imperial War
Museum Duxford, closed Mon. *(Anon)*

WHITTLESFORD TL4748
Red Lion (01223) 832047
Station Road; CB22 4NL Modernised
old coaching inn handy for the Imperial
War Museum Duxford; beamed bar with an
array of well kept Adnams beers, enjoyable

reasonably priced home-made food, friendly
helpful staff, warm fires; tables out on lawn
(overlooked by A505), 18 bedrooms, adjacent
to station and Duxford Chapel (EH).
(P and D Carpenter)

WICKEN TL5670
Maids Head (01353) 720727
High Street; CB7 5XR Old thatched
dining pub under newish ownership; good
choice of enjoyable home-made food all
day, Greene King IPA and three guests,
fairly priced house wines, unpretentious
bar with pool and darts, restaurant
(children welcome here), two open fires,
occasional quiz nights; dogs allowed in
bar, tables out at front and side, village-
green setting, handy for Wicken Fen
nature reserve (NT), open all day (till 1am
Fri, Sat). *(David Brown, Jamie and Sue May)*

WOODDITTON TL6558
Three Blackbirds (01638) 731100
Signed off B1063 at Cheveley; CB8 9SQ
Sympathetically restored two-bar thatched
pub, low 17th-c beams, mix of old country
furniture on bare boards, pictures and
knick-knacks, open fires, some enterprising
food together with pub favourites and
lunchtime sandwiches, Adnams, Timothy
Taylors and changing local guests,
restaurant; children welcome, garden,
closed Sun evening and Mon (except bank
holidays). *(Simon Watkins)*

Cheshire

New places here are the Three Greyhounds Inn at Allostock (carefully renovated and with plenty of original features and thoughtful food), Architect in Chester (interestingly refurbished pub by the racecourse with super food and drinks), Fishpool at Delamere (stylish changes for former country inn), Bells of Peover at Lower Peover (peacefully located dining pub with enterprising food) and Bulls Head in Mottram St Andrew (a newly opened Brunning & Price pub). Other good pubs include the Grosvenor Arms at Aldford (the Brunning & Price flagship), Egerton Arms in Astbury (charming, long-serving licensees and good pubby food), Dysart Arms in Bunbury (a smashing all-rounder), Pheasant at Burwardsley (usefully serving good food all day), Albion in Chester (very long-serving licensees and interesting World War I décor), Sutton Hall at Macclesfield (a wonderful building and a buzzing pub too), Davenport Arms at Marton (thoroughly traditional and welcoming), Bulls Head at Mobberley (everything is special here), Old Hall at Sandbach (a stunning building and our readers love it), Swettenham Arms at Swettenham (ancient country pub with nicely traditional rooms) and Dusty Miller at Wrenbury (right beside the canal). For a fine choice of real ales, head for the Bhurtpore in Aston, and the Mill and Old Harkers Arms, both in Chester – they all source their interesting beers from across the country. Many pubs here are fantastic for food, but our Cheshire Dining Pub 2014 is the Yew Tree in Spurstow.

 ALDFORD SJ4259 Map 7

Grosvenor Arms ★ (🍴 ♟ 🍺)

B5130 Chester–Wrexham; CH3 6HJ

Spacious place with buoyantly chatty atmosphere, impressive range of drinks, wide-ranging imaginative menu, good service; lovely big terrace and gardens

In a pretty village, this sizeable Victorian brick and half-timbered pub is the Brunning & Price flagship. Staff are genuinely friendly and attentive and the various rooms have plenty of interest and individuality.

Spacious cream-painted areas are sectioned by big knocked-through arches with a variety of wood, quarry tile, flagstone and black and white tiled floor finishes – some richly coloured turkish rugs look well against these natural materials. Good solid pieces of traditional furniture, plenty of interesting pictures and attractive lighting keep it all intimate. A handsomely boarded panelled room has tall bookshelves lining one wall; good selection of board games. Half a dozen real ales including Phoenix Brunning & Price Original and Weetwood Eastgate, with guests like Titanic Lifeboat and Weetwood Cheshire Cat, are served from a fine-looking bar counter; they also offer 20 wines by the glass, more than 80 whiskies and distinctive soft drinks such as peach and elderflower cordial and Willington Fruit Farm pressed apple juice. Lovely on summer evenings, the airy terracotta-floored conservatory has lots of gigantic low-hanging flowering baskets and chunky pale wood garden furniture. It opens out to a large elegant suntrap terrace, and a neat lawn with picnic-sets, young trees and an old tractor.

From a wide choice of thoughtful dishes, the good food might include sandwiches, pork and chorizo meatballs in tomato sauce, salmon, watercress and fennel salad with lemon, herb and crème fraîche dressing, malaysian vegetable, cashew nut and coconut curry, venison cottage pie with sweet braised red cabbage, ham with free-range eggs, sausages and mash with gravy, beer-battered haddock with mushy peas and tartare sauce, grilled tandoori chicken with mango, toasted almonds and yoghurt dressing, braised shoulder of lamb with garlic mash and red wine and thyme gravy, and puddings such as crème brûlée and bread and butter pudding with apricot sauce and clotted cream. *Benchmark main dish: steak burger topped with bacon and cheddar with coleslaw and chips £11.95. Two-course evening meal £20.00.*

Brunning & Price ~ Manager Tracey Owen ~ Real ale ~ (01244) 620228 ~ Open 11.30-11; 12-10.30 Sun ~ Bar food 12-9.30(10 Fri, Sat, 9 Sun) ~ Children welcome ~ Dogs allowed in bar ~ www.grosvenorarms-aldford.co.uk *Recommended by John Andrew, W K Wood, Claes Maurvy, Clive Watkin, Mike and Wena Stevenson*

ALLOSTOCK
SJ7271 Map 7

Three Greyhounds Inn ♀

4.7 miles from M6 junction 18: A54 E then fork left on B5803 into Holmes Chapel, left at roundabout on to A50 for 2 miles, then left on to B5082 towards Northwich; Holmes Chapel Road

Relaxing, civilised and welcoming, with enjoyable food all day

In winter the prime spot is by the cheerful fire on the left, with its leather wing armchairs – but any time of year this prominent grey-painted crossroads pub is equally welcoming, thanks to the friendly young staff. Soft lighting (candles even in daytime) and an abundance of luxurious deep purple scatter cushions are guaranteed to soothe even the most unquiet spirit; the décor generally, with dark grey walls nicely pointing up the crisp modern black-on-white prints, and thick rugs, is very restful, with unobtrusive background music. A good choice of drinks majors on interesting wines by the glass, with three house ales – Almighty Allostock Ale (from Mobberley), Biley Bomber (from Caledonian) and Three Greyhounds Bitter (from Weetwood) – plus guests such as Merlins Gold and Tatton Best on handpump. The big side lawn has picnic-table sets under cocktail parasols, with more tables on the decking of a Perspex-roofed side verandah. Just across the road is Shakerley Mere, with a nature reserve walk. This belongs to the small Cheshire Cat Pubs & Bars group.

As well as lunchtime sandwiches and thoughtful nibbles, the enjoyable food includes various platters of meats, cheeses and fish, potted beef with stout piccalilli, wild mushrooms in white wine and cream on granary toast, steak burger with bacon, cheese, coleslaw and chips, salmon and smoked haddock fishcake in light mustard sauce with lemony green beans, root vegetable cobbler with cheddar scone, ale-braised sausage and red onion casserole, chicken, smoked ham, leek and tarragon pie, slow-cooked pork belly in cider with creamy smoked bacon mash, and puddings like apple and calvados crumble with custard and warm chocolate tart with raspberry compote. *Benchmark main dish: chicken, leek and tarragon pie £11.95. Two-course evening meal £18.50.*

Free house ~ Licensee James Griffiths ~ Real ale ~ (01565) 723455 ~ Open 12-11 (11.30 Sat, 10.30 Sun) ~ Bar food 12-9.15(9.45 Fri, Sat, 8.45 Sun) ~ Children welcome ~ Dogs allowed in bar ~ www.thethreegreyhoundsinn.co.uk *Recommended by Ruth May*

ASTBURY SJ8461 Map 7

Egerton Arms £ 🛏

Village signposted off A34 S of Congleton; CW12 4RQ

Friendly and cheery village pub with popular bar food, four real ales and large garden; nice bedrooms

Dating in part from the 16th c, this is a smashing pub with a warm welcome for all from the charming licensees and their long-serving staff. The pubby cream-painted rooms are decorated with newspaper cuttings relating to 'Grace' (the landlady's name), the odd piece of armour, shelves of books and quite a few mementoes of the Sandow Brothers (one of whom was the landlady's father) who performed as 'the World's Strongest Youths'. In summer, dried flowers replace the fire in the big fireplace; background music and TV. Robinsons Dizzy Blonde, Double Hop, Frederics and Unicorn on handpump, 11 wines by the glass, 16 malt whiskies, and alcoholic winter warmers. Well placed tables outside enjoy pleasant views of the church, and a play area has a wooden fort; handy for Little Moreton Hall (National Trust).

 Enjoyable, fair-priced food might include sandwiches (the fish finger version is popular) and hot baguettes, sharing boards, potted stilton and walnut pâté, black pudding and bacon salad, mushroom and goats cheese risotto, spicy chilli con carne, super steak and kidney pudding, chicken curry, a huge cod fillet (battered or grilled), a choice of roasts, lambs liver and bacon in rich gravy, and puddings like apricot and lavender tart and lemon cheesecake. *Benchmark main dish: salmon with honey and walnuts £10.50. Two-course evening meal £15.50.*

Robinsons ~ Tenants Allen and Grace Smith ~ Real ale ~ (01260) 273946 ~ Open 11.30-11(10.30 Sun) ~ Bar food 11.30-2, 6-9; 12-8 Sun ~ Restaurant ~ Children welcome until 8.30 ~ Bedrooms: £50/£80 ~ www.egertonarms.co.uk *Recommended by Dave Webster, Sue Holland, Paul Humphreys, Dr D J and Mrs S C Walker, Mike and Wena Stevenson*

ASTON SJ6146 Map 7

Bhurtpore ★ ♀ 🍴 £

Off A530 SW of Nantwich; in village follow Wrenbury signpost; CW5 8DQ

Fantastic range of drinks (especially real ales) in warm-hearted pub with some unusual artefacts; big garden

Beer lovers flock here, which isn't surprising given that they get through more than 1,000 different ales a year, sourced from all over the country. They usually keep 11 on at any one time, with fantastic names like Acorn Amber, Beowulf English Horseman, Copper Dragon Golden Pippin, Heavy Industry Collaborator and Electric Mountain, Lancaster Java, Oakham Citra, Purple Moose Snowdonia Ale, Salopian Automaton and Requiem, and Spitting Feathers Empire IPA. They also stock dozens of unusual bottled beers and fruit beers, a great many bottled ciders and perries, over 100 different whiskies, carefully selected soft drinks and wines from a good list; summer beer festival. The pub's name commemorates the siege of Bhurtpore (a town in India) during which local landowner Sir Stapleton Cotton (later Viscount Combermere) was commander in chief. The connection with India also explains some of the quirky artefacts in the carpeted lounge bar – look out for the sunglass-wearing turbaned figure behind the counter; also good local period photographs and some attractive furniture in the comfortable public bar; board games, pool, TV and games machine. Weekends tend to be pretty busy.

From a varied menu, the food includes sandwiches, toasties and baguettes, spicy lamb samosas with yoghurt and mint dip, curries such as vegetarian or kashmiri chicken, beer-battered haddock with mushy peas and chips, gammon with egg or pineapple, steak and kidney in ale pie, chicken in stilton and smoked bacon sauce, and puddings such as sticky toffee pudding and warm chocolate fudge cake. *Benchmark main dish: game pie £11.95. Two-course evening meal £15.00.*

Free house ~ Licensee Simon George ~ Real ale ~ (01270) 780917 ~ Open 12-2.30, 6.30-11.30; 12-midnight Fri, Sat; 12-11 Sun ~ Bar food 12-2, 6.30-9.30; 12-9.30 Sat (9 Sun) ~ Restaurant ~ Children welcome till 8.30 ~ Dogs allowed in bar ~ www.bhurtpore.co.uk
Recommended by Dave Webster, Sue Holland

BICKLEY MOSS
Cholmondeley Arms ♀

SJ5550 Map 7

Cholmondeley; A49 5.5 miles N of Whitchurch; the owners would like us to list them under Cholmondeley village, but as this is rarely marked on maps we have mentioned the nearest village which appears more often; SY14 8HN

Imaginatively converted high-ceilinged schoolhouse with decent range of real ales and wines, well presented food and a sizeable garden

This former schoolhouse with its lofty ceilings and high gothic windows has been refurbished with a great deal of individuality – the huge old radiators and historic school paraphernalia (hockey sticks, tennis rackets, trunks and so forth) are all testament to its former identity. Also, armchairs by the fire with a massive stag's head above it, big mirrors, all sorts of dining chairs and tables, warmly coloured rugs on bare boards, fresh flowers and church candles; background music. Cholmondeley Best and Teachers Tipple (both Weetwood beers) and three guests from brewers such as Coach House, Dunham Massey and Salopian on handpump, and an impressive range of 87 gins, all served by friendly, professional staff. There's plenty of seating outside on the sizeable lawn, which drifts off into open countryside, and more in front overlooking the quiet road. The pub is handily placed for Cholmondeley Castle Gardens. This belongs to the small Cheshire Cat Pubs & Bars group; others include the Three Greyhounds in Allostock and Bulls Head in Mobberley (both in this chapter) and the Red Lion in Weymouth (Dorset).

Good food includes nibbles like potted shrimps and home-made black pudding 'scotch egg', chicken liver pâté with rhubarb chutney, mini yorkshire puddings filled with pork, crackling and brandy apple sauce, crispy duck and watercress salad with spiced plums and honey dressing, burger with bacon, melted cheese, fennel coleslaw and chips, chicken wrapped in bacon with pistachio and lemon stuffing, bubble and squeak and coq au vin sauce, cod loin with brown shrimps and lemon butter and spicy sausage and butternut squash hash cake, slow-roasted pork belly with salt-and-pepper spare rib with smoked mash and red cabbage, and puddings such as sticky hot chocolate pudding with toasted marshmallows and iced Grand Marnier soufflé. *Benchmark main dish: steak and kidney pie £12.95. Two-course evening meal £19.00.*

Free house ~ Licensee Steven Davies ~ Real ale ~ (01829) 720300 ~ Open 12-11 (11.30 Sat, 10.30 Sun) ~ Bar food 12-9.30(9.45 Sat, 8.45 Sun) ~ Children under 10 till 8pm in pub, 9pm in garden ~ Dogs welcome ~ quiz monthly ~ Bedrooms: £80/£110 ~ www.cholmondeleyarms.co.uk *Recommended by Peter Harrison, Mike Proctor, David and Lin Short, Claes Mauroy, Steve Whalley, Dave Webster, Sue Holland, R T and J C Moggridge*

BUNBURY SJ5658 Map 7

Dysart Arms

Bowes Gate Road; village signposted off A51 NW of Nantwich; and from A49 S of Tarporley – coming in this way on northernmost village access road, bear left in village centre; CW6 9PH

Civilised chatty dining pub attractively filled with good furniture in thoughtfully laid-out rooms, enjoyable food and a lovely garden with pretty views

Our readers love this particularly well run village pub with its easy-going atmosphere, enjoyable food and drink and warmly friendly staff. And although opened up, the neatly kept rooms still retain a cottagey feel as they ramble around the pleasantly lit central bar. Cream walls keep it light, clean and airy, with deep venetian red ceilings adding cosiness, and each room (some with good winter fires) is nicely furnished with an appealing variety of well spaced sturdy wooden tables and chairs, a couple of tall cases of books and just the right amount of carefully chosen bric-a-brac, properly lit pictures and plants. Flooring ranges from red and black tiles to stripped boards and some carpet. Phoenix Brunning & Price Original, Timothy Taylors Landlord and three guests such as Adnams, Caledonian Deuchars IPA and Fullers London Pride on handpump, alongside a good selection of 17 wines by the glass from a list of about 70 bottles, and just over 20 malts. Sturdy wooden tables on the terrace and picnic-sets on the lawn in the well cared for, slightly elevated garden are lovely in summer, with views of the splendid church at the end of this pretty village and the distant Peckforton Hills beyond.

Attractively presented and very good, the enterprising food includes thai-style crab bonbons with sweet chilli jam, pickled ginger and candied lime, juniper-cured pigeon breast with roasted mushroom and chestnut salad, parsnip crisps and cranberry relish, honey-roast ham with free-range eggs, king prawn linguine with chorizo, oven-dried tomatoes, capers and rocket, puy lentil and aubergine moussaka with greek salad, confit pork belly, braised pigs cheek and black pudding croquette with spinach, red cabbage and crackling, fried cod supreme with ratatouille, crispy polenta parmentier and pesto dressing, and puddings like hot waffle with butterscotch sauce and honeycomb ice-cream and apple and rhubarb crumble with custard. *Benchmark main dish: braised lamb shoulder £16.75. Two-course evening meal £22.00.*

Brunning & Price ~ Manager Chris Ridsdale ~ Real ale ~ (01829) 260183 ~ Open 11.30-11; 12-10.30 Sun ~ Bar food 12-9.30(9 Sun) ~ Restaurant ~ Children welcome ~ Dogs allowed in bar ~ www.dysartarms-bunbury.co.uk *Recommended by Mark Delap, David Jackman, Mrs P Abell, Claes Mauroy, Mike and Wena Stevenson, Dave Webster, Sue Holland*

BURLEYDAM
SJ6042 Map 7

Combermere Arms ⊕ ◀

A525 Whitchurch–Audlem; SY13 4AT

Roomy and attractive beamed pub successfully mixing a good drinking side with imaginative all-day food

An extended pub with a 16th-c heart, this has an attractive but understated interior in many rambling yet intimate-seeming rooms. The various nooks and crannies have a happy mix of furnishings and décor that take in antique cushioned dining chairs around dark wood tables, rugs on wood (some old and some new oak) and stone floors, prints hung frame to frame on cream walls, deep red ceilings, panelling and open fires. Friendly staff provide an equally pleasant welcome to drinkers and diners, with both aspects of the business seeming to do well. Phoenix Brunning & Price Original, Joules Pale Ale, Montys Mojo, Weetwood Cheshire Cat and Wincle Sir Philip on handpump, around 70 whiskies, 14 wines by the glass from an extensive list and three farm ciders; board games. Outside are good solid wood tables in a pretty, well tended garden and a restored tractor for children to play on.

🍴 Enjoyable and attractively presented, the food includes sandwiches, duck liver and port pâté with red onion marmalade, garlic wild mushrooms on toasted brioche, warm harissa chicken with pomegranate and pearl barley salad, steak and kidney pudding, cheshire cheese, potato and leek pie with wholegrain mustard cream sauce, beer-battered haddock with mushy peas and tartare sauce, braised lamb shoulder with dauphinoise potatoes and redcurrant gravy, and puddings such as chocolate and chilli tart with orange and mint salad and rhubarb crumble with cinnamon ice-cream. *Benchmark main dish: steak burger with bacon and cheese, coleslaw and chips £11.95. Two-course evening meal £19.00.*

Brunning & Price ~ Manager Lisa Hares ~ Real ale ~ (01948) 871223 ~ Open 11.30-11(10.30 Sun) ~ Bar food 12-9.30(10 Thurs-Sat, 9 Sun) ~ Restaurant ~ Children welcome ~ Dogs allowed in bar ~ www.combermerearms-burleydam.co.uk
Recommended by Mike and Shirley Stratton, Paul and Gail Betteley, Roger Fox

BURWARDSLEY
SJ5256 Map 7

Pheasant ★ ⌇ ⇤

Higher Burwardsley; signposted from Tattenhall (which is signposted off A41 S of Chester) and from Harthill (reached by turning off A534 Nantwich–Holt at the Copper Mine); follow pub's signpost up hill from Post Office; OS Sheet 117 map reference 523566; CH3 9PF

Fantastic views and enjoyable food at this fresh conversion of an old heavily beamed inn; open all day

The views right across the Cheshire plains from seats on the terrace of this 17th-c half-timbered and sandstone pub are glorious, and on a clear day the telescope sees as far as the pier head and cathedrals in Liverpool. The attractive low-beamed interior is quite airy and modern-feeling in parts and the various separate areas have comfy leather armchairs and nice old chairs spread spaciously on wooden floors, and a log fire in a huge see-through fireplace. Local Weetwood Best and Eastgate on handpump, a local farm cider and apple juice served by friendly, helpful staff; quiet background music, daily newspapers and large-screen TV for sporting events. A big side lawn has picnic-sets. This is a great stop if you're walking the scenic Sandstone Trail along the

Peckforton Hills, and a nice play to stay. Sister pub is the Bears Paw at Warmingham (also in this chapter).

🍴 As well as interesting sandwiches (until 6pm), the thoughtful choice of good food includes potted shrimps, sticky ginger chicken with spring onion and sesame salad, deli boards (charcuterie, fish and cheese), chilli and crab linguine with coriander and lime, beef, mushroom and ale pie, steak burger with cheese, bacon and chips, half a pot-roast corn-fed chicken with sage and chicken juices, confit shoulder of lamb with rissole potatoes and toasted almond dressing, whole roasted plaice with nut butter, and puddings. *Benchmark main dish: steak and mushroom in ale pie £11.95. Two-course evening meal £21.00.*

Free house ~ Licensee Andrew Nelson ~ Real ale ~ (01829) 770434 ~ Open 11-11 (10.30 Sun) ~ Bar food 12-9.30(10 Fri, Sat, 9 Sun) ~ Restaurant ~ Children welcome ~ Dogs allowed in bar and bedrooms ~ Bedrooms: £75/£85 ~ www.thepheasantinn.co.uk
Recommended by Dr Kevan Tucker, Mrs P Abell, David and Lin Short, Claes Mauroy, Dave Webster, Sue Holland, S Holder

CHESTER
Albion ★ ◖ £
SJ4066 Map 7

Albion Street; CH1 1RQ

Strongly traditional pub with comfortable Edwardian décor and captivating World War I memorabilia; pubby food and good drinks

After a walk along the city wall, this genuinely friendly and old-fashioned pub is just the place to head for; dogs might be offered a sausage and a bowl of water. The charming licensees have been here for more than 40 years and have collected an absorbing collection of World War I memorabilia; this is actually an officially listed site of four war memorials to soldiers from the Cheshire Regiment. The peaceful rooms are filled with big engravings of men leaving for war and similarly moving prints of wounded veterans – as well as flags, advertisements and so on. There are leatherette and hoop-backed chairs around cast-iron-framed tables, lamps, an open fire in the Edwardian fireplace and dark floral William Morris wallpaper (designed on the first day of World War I). You might even be lucky enough to hear the vintage 1928 Steck pianola being played; there's an attractive side dining room too. Adnams and a couple of guests from brewers such as Hook Norton and Titanic on handpump, new world wines, fresh orange juice, organic bottled cider and fruit juice, over 25 malt whiskies and a good selection of rums and gins. Small but comfortable bedrooms are furnished in keeping with the pub's style (free parking for residents and a bottle of house wine if dining).

🍴 Even the trench rations (helpings are so generous they don't offer starters) are in period: lunchtime sandwiches, corned beef hash with pickled red cabbage, lambs liver, bacon and onions in rich cider gravy, cumberland sausage with mash and apple sauce, haggis with tatties and specials such as chilli con carne and local sausage casserole. *Benchmark main dish: gammon pease pudding £10.50.*

Punch ~ Lease Michael Edward Mercer ~ Real ale ~ No credit cards ~ (01244) 340345 ~ Open 12-3, 5(6 Sat)-11; 12-2.30 Sun; closed Sun evening ~ Bar food 12-2.30, 5-8 (8.30 Sat) ~ Restaurant ~ Dogs allowed in bar ~ Bedrooms: £75/£85 ~ www.albioninnchester.co.uk *Recommended by Trevor Graveson, D H Bennett, Simon J Barber, Dave Webster, Sue Holland*

> If we don't specify bar meal times for a featured entry, these are normally 12-2 and 7-9; we do show times if they are markedly different.

Architect 🍺

Nicholas Street (A5268); CH1 2NX

Bustling, newly refurbished Brunning & Price pub by the racecourse; lots of interesting furnishings and décor, attentive staff, a good choice of drinks and super food

Overlooking the racecourse at Roodee, this newly refurbished Georgian pub has hit the ground running – our readers love it. It consists of two almost separate places connected by a glass passage, with the original building to the right and the new open-plan garden room to the left. Throughout there are hundreds of interesting paintings and prints on green, cream or yellow walls, house plants and flowers on window sills and mantelpieces, elegant antique dining chairs around a mix of nice old tables on rugs or bare floorboards, and lots of bookcases. Also, open fires, armchairs in front of a woodburning stove or tucked into cosy nooks, candelabra and big mirrors, and a friendly, easy-going atmosphere. The garden room is the pubbiest part with more of a bustling feel, where they serve Phoenix Brunning & Price Original, Acorn Saphir IPA, Barngates Cracker, Hawkshead Stout, Hobsons Mild, Tatton Blonde and Weetwood Eastgate on handpump, 17 wines by the glass, 74 whiskies and farm cider. Big windows and french doors overlook the terrace, where there are plenty of good quality wooden seats and tables under parasols.

 Tempting food includes sandwiches, red pepper panna cotta with sweet pickled peppers and artichokes, seared pigeon breast with wild mushroom sausage and beetroot fondant, meat or vegetarian platters, king prawn and chorizo linguine, pork sausages with mash and onion gravy, chicken and ham suet pudding, smoked haddock and salmon fishcakes with tomato and spring onion salad, roast duck breast with cabbage, bacon and a juniper and port sauce, and puddings such as warm treacle tart with citrus syrup and crème fraîche and bread and butter pudding with apricot sauce. *Benchmark main dish: braised lamb shoulder with red wine and rosemary gravy £16.95. Two-course evening meal £19.50.*

Brunning & Price ~ Manager Jon Astle-Rowe ~ Real ale ~ (01244) 353070 ~ Open 10.30am-11pm(11.30 Fri, Sat, 10.30 Sun) ~ Bar food 12-10(9.30 Sun) ~ Restaurant ~ Children welcome ~ Dogs allowed in bar ~ www.brunningandprice.co.uk/architect
Recommended by Isobel Mackinlay

Mill 🍺 £

Milton Street; CH1 3NF

Big hotel with huge range of real ales, good value food and cheery service in sizeable bar

It's quite a surprise to find a smart modern hotel with such a fantastic range of real ales. They always have at least ten (and up to 16) beers on handpump and get through over 2,000 guests a year. Weetwood Best and Mill Premium (brewed for them by Coach House) are always available, with other regulars coming from Abbeydale, Caledonian, Dark Star, Ossett, Phoenix and Titanic; also a dozen wines by the glass, two farm ciders and 25 malt whiskies. You'll find a real mix of customers in the neatly kept bar, which has some exposed brickwork and supporting pillars, local photographs on cream-papered walls, contemporary seats around marble-topped tables on light wood floors, and helpful, friendly staff. One comfortable area is reminiscent of a bar on a cruise liner; quiet background music and unobtrusively placed big-screen sports TV. Converted from an old mill, the hotel straddles the Shropshire Union Canal, with a glassed-in bridge connecting the two halves. Bedrooms are comfortable and rather smart.

There's a wide choice of food and several menus: sandwiches, pizzas, lambs kidneys with red wine sauce, breaded tiger prawns with chilli jam, stuffed red peppers on couscous, burger with chips, cheese and bacon, corn-fed chicken with spring onion mash and port sauce, pork fillet wrapped in bacon with apricot stuffing and red wine and rosemary sauce, venison with mediterranean pepper and shallot sauce, and puddings like sherry trifle and raspberry crème brûlée. *Benchmark main dish: a changing curry £12.50. Two-course evening meal £22.00.*

Free house ~ Licensees Gary and Gordon Vickers ~ Real ale ~ (01244) 350035 ~ Open 9-midnight ~ Bar food 11.30-11; 12-10 Sun ~ Restaurant ~ Children welcome ~ Bedrooms: £73/£140 ~ www.millhotel.com *Recommended by Ian Malone, Dave Webster, Sue Holland*

CHESTER
SJ4166   Map 7
Old Harkers Arms ♀ ◖
Russell Street, down steps off City Road where it crosses canal; CH3 5AL

Well run spacious canalside building with a lively atmosphere, a great range of drinks (including lots of changing real ales) and tasty food

Beside the Shropshire Union Canal – you can watch the boats from the tall windows that run the length of the main bar – this is a clever conversion of an early Victorian warehouse. The striking high-ceilinged industrial interior is divided into user-friendly spaces by brick pillars. Walls are covered with old prints hung frame to frame, there's a wall of bookshelves above a leather banquette at one end, the mixed dark wood furniture is set out in intimate groups on stripped-wood floors, and attractive lamps lend some cosiness; board games. Cheerful staff add to the lively bustle. There's around nine real ales on handpump, including Phoenix Brunning & Price Original and Weetwood Cheshire Cat, and half a dozen regularly changing guests from brewers such as Bradfield, Lancaster, Salopian and Titanic; also, more than 100 malt whiskies, lots of wines from a well described list and farm cider.

Interesting food includes sandwiches, king prawns in hot garlic and chilli oil, smoked trout rillettes with rhubarb chutney, honey-glazed ham with free-range eggs, steak burger topped with grilled bacon and cheddar with coleslaw and chips, fennel and red onion tarte tatin with roast celeriac, spinach and blue cheese salad, chicken breast wrapped in parma ham with white wine cream sauce and parmentier potatoes, seared five-spice breast and spring roll of gressingham duck with squash fondant, pak choi and plum sauce, and puddings such as hot waffle with butterscotch sauce and honeycomb ice-cream and crème brûlée. *Benchmark main dish: lamb shoulder with dauphinoise potatoes and redcurrant gravy £16.95. Two-course evening meal £19.50.*

Brunning & Price ~ Manager Paul Jeffery ~ Real ale ~ (01244) 344525 ~ Open 10.30am-11pm; 12-10.30 Sun ~ Bar food 12-9.30 ~ Children welcome but no babies, toddlers or pushchairs ~ Dogs allowed in bar ~ www.harkersarms-chester.co.uk
Recommended by Trevor Graveson, Andy and Jill Kassube, D H Bennett, Simon J Barber, Dr Kevan Tucker, Dave Webster, Sue Holland

Pubs close to motorway junctions are listed at the back of the book.

COTEBROOK
SJ5765   Map 7

Fox & Barrel

A49 NE of Tarporley; CW6 9DZ

Attractive building with stylishly airy décor, an enterprising menu and good wines

---

Although many customers are here for the excellent food, this is no straightforward dining pub – drinkers feel at home perched on the high chairs next to the counter enjoying a chat and a pint of Caledonian Deuchars IPA, Weetwood Eastgate and a couple of guests from brewers such as Merlin and Lancaster on handpump. They also have a good array of wines with about 20 by the glass. Subtle refurbishments have made the most of the building's nice character. A big log fire dominates the bar, while a larger uncluttered beamed dining area has attractive rugs and an eclectic mix of period tables on polished oak floorboards, with extensive wall panelling hung with framed old prints. The terrace has plenty of smart tables and chairs and there are picnic-sets on grass, old fruit trees and a tractor.

Imaginative dishes from a wide menu include sandwiches, quail and pistachio terrine with golden raisin chutney, pea and mint risotto with poached egg and air-dried ham, spicy vegetable tagine with quinoa and pomegranate salsa, honey-glazed gammon with pineapple, fried egg and chips, salmon and smoked haddock fishcakes with dill mayonnaise, calves liver with garlic mash, pancetta and balsamic onion sauce, venison and rabbit suet pudding with truffle mash, and puddings such as rhubarb and custard panna cotta and dark chocolate and blood orange cheesecake. *Benchmark main dish: beer-battered haddock £12.75.*

Free house ~ Licensee Gary Kidd ~ Real ale ~ (01829) 760529 ~ Open 12-11(10.30 Sun) ~ Bar food 12-9.30(9 Sun) ~ Restaurant ~ Children welcome but no pushchairs ~ Dogs allowed in bar ~ www.foxandbarrel.co.uk *Recommended by Dennis Jones*

DELAMERE
SJ5667   Map 7

Fishpool

Junction A54/B5152 Chester Road/Fishpool Road, a mile W of A49

Something for everyone in extensive and interestingly laid out pub, good range of food all day

---

The clever layout here combines an open main area that's large, bright and happy, with plenty of other intimate smaller places. Throughout, furnishings are carefully chosen and rather unusual, with lots of variety – everything's been done with great style and wit. The lofty central part, partly skylit and full of contented diners, has a row of booths facing the long bar counter, plenty of other tables with banquettes or overstuffed small armchairs on pale floorboards with rugs, then a conservatory overlooking picnic-table sets on a flagstone terrace, and a lawn beyond. Off on two sides are many rooms with much lower ceilings, some with heavy dark beams, some with bright polychrome tile or intricate parquet flooring, William Morris wallpaper here, dusky paintwork or neat bookshelves there, sofas, armchairs, a twinkling fire in an old-fashioned open range, lots of old prints and some intriguing objects such as carved or painted animal skulls. The efficient staff in neatly informal 'uniforms' make a point of greeting everyone warmly. They have a good choice of wines by the glass and a fine range of local and other real ales, such as Beartown Bearly Literate, Caledonian Deuchars IPA, Keswick Thirst Quencher, Ministry of Beer False Economy and Weetwood Best,

Cheshire Cat and Eastgate on handpump; unobtrusive piped music; upstairs lavatories.

 As well as sandwiches (until 6pm), the very popular food includes tiger prawns in garlic and chilli, sticky barbecue pork ribs, chicken caesar salad, steak burger with bacon, cheese, red onion jam, pickles and chips, roasted vegetable lasagne, good proper pies, pizzas from a wood-fired oven, grills from a special charcoal oven, roast lamb rump with redcurrant and mint jus, roast duck with stir-fried vegetables and plum sauce, and puddings such as sticky toffee pudding with toffee sauce and ice-cream and glazed lemon and lime tart with raspberry compote and raspberry tuile. *Benchmark main dish: beer-battered fish and chips with mushy peas and tartare sauce £11.50. Two-course evening meal £20.00.*

Free house ~ Licensee Andrew Nelson ~ Real ale ~ (01606) 883277 ~ Open 11-11 ~ Bar food 12-9.30(10 Fri, Sat, 9 Sun) ~ Restaurant ~ Children welcome ~ Dogs allowed in bar ~ www.thefishpoolinn.co.uk *Recommended by Harvey Brown*

 EATON   SJ8765   Map 7

Plough 🛏

A536 Congleton–Macclesfield; CW12 2NH

Neat and cosy village pub with up to four interesting beers, bar food and views from big attractive garden; good bedrooms

With a fairly traditional feel, the carefully converted bar at this tidy red-brick 17th-c pub has plenty of beams and exposed brickwork, a couple of snug little alcoves, comfortable armchairs and cushioned wooden wall seats on red patterned carpets, long red curtains, leaded windows and a big stone fireplace. Service is friendly and attentive, and they keep Storm Desert Storm and PGA plus a couple of guests from brewers such as Cottage and Hydes on handpump, and around ten wines by the glass from a decent list; background music and occasional TV. Moved here piece by piece from its original home in Wales, the heavily raftered barn at the back makes a striking restaurant. You get good views of the fringes of the Peak District from the big tree-filled garden, which has picnic-sets on the lawn and a covered decked terrace with heaters. The appealingly designed bedrooms are in a converted stable block. Dogs are only allowed in the pub outside food service times.

 Well liked food includes sandwiches, chicken liver parfait, garlic mushrooms topped with brie, mediterranean vegetable linguine with tomato sauce topped with goats cheese, thai green chicken curry, lamb henry (in mint and honey), duck breast on stir-fried vegetables with sesame noodles and oriental cherry sauce, tuna with prawns and capers in garlic butter, and puddings such as bakewell tart with custard and a cheesecake of the day. *Benchmark main dish: beer-battered haddock and chips £9.95. Two-course evening meal £18.00*

Free house ~ Licensee Mujdat Karatas ~ Real ale ~ (01260) 280207 ~ Open 12-11 (12 Sat, 10.30 Sun) ~ Bar food 12-2.30, 6-9.30; 12-9.30 Fri, Sat; 12-7.30 Sun ~ Restaurant ~ Children welcome ~ Dogs allowed in bedrooms ~ Bedrooms: £60/£75 ~ www.theploughinnateaton.co.uk *Recommended by Richard and Penny Gibbs*

 KETTLESHULME   SJ9879   Map 7

Swan 🍺

B5470 Macclesfield–Chapel-en-le-Frith, a mile W of Whaley Bridge; SK23 7QU

Charming 16th-c cottagey-pub with enjoyable food (especially fish), good beer and an attractive garden

Just in the Peak District National Park, this pretty wisteria-clad white cottage is close to plenty of good walks. The front terrace has teak tables, another two-level terrace has more tables and steamer benches under parasols, and there's also a sizeable streamside garden. The interior, beneath the heavy stone roof, is snug and cosy, with latticed windows, very low dark beams hung with big copper jugs and kettles, timbered walls, antique coaching and other prints and maps, ancient oak settles on turkish carpet, and log fires. Marstons on handpump with a couple of guest beers such as Marble Lagonda IPA and Storm Windgather; service is polite and efficient.

They specialise in fresh fish dishes such as a hearty bouillabaise, smoked haddock and goose egg omelette, thai monkfish and tiger prawns in light coconut curry sauce, and cod fillet with herb crust and anchovy and caper tapenade; also, sandwiches, wild mushrooms on toast in cream sauce topped with prosciutto, lambs kidneys in green peppercorn and brandy cream, steak pie with home-made chips, warm duck rillette with orange and cranberry sauce, guinea fowl roulade with curried parsnip and apple purée and lentils in red wine sauce, and puddings like queen of puddings and warm chocolate brownie with chocolate sauce. *Benchmark main dish: beer-battered fish and chips £12.00. Two-course evening meal £17.00.*

Free house ~ Licensee Robert Cloughley ~ Real ale ~ (01663) 732943 ~ Open 12-11; closed Mon lunchtime ~ Bar food 12-8.30(7 Thurs, Fri, 9 Sat, 4 Sun) ~ Children welcome ~ Dogs allowed in bar ~ www.verynicepubs.co.uk/swankettleshulme
Recommended by Richard and Penny Gibbs, David Cotterill

LANGLEY SJ9569 Map 7
Hanging Gate ♀

Meg Lane, Higher Sutton; follow Langley signpost from A54 beside Fourways Motel, and that road passes the pub; from Macclesfield, heading S from centre on A523 turn left into Byrons Lane at Langley, Wincle signpost; in Sutton (0.5 miles after going under canal bridge, ie before Langley) fork right at Church House Inn, following Wildboarclough signpost, then 2 miles later turn sharp right at steep hairpin bend; OS Sheet 118 map reference 952696; SK11 0NG

Remote old place with fires in traditional cosy rooms, tasty food and fantastic views from the airy extension and terrace

After a windswept walk on the nearby moors, the log fire in this old drovers' pub is just the ticket. It's a tucked away place on the side of a hill high up in the Peak District with stunning panoramic views – on a clear day you can see Liverpool's Anglican cathedral and Snowdonia. Still in their original layout, the three cosy little low-beamed rooms are simply furnished. The tiny snug bar, at its pubbiest at lunchtime, has a welcoming log fire in a big brick fireplace, just one table, plain chairs and cushioned wall seats and a few old pub pictures and seasonal photographs on its creamy walls. The second room has just a section of bar counter in the corner and five tables; the third is an appealing little oak-beamed blue room. Hydes Original and a Hydes seasonal beer with a couple of guests such as Charles Wells Bombardier on handpump, quite a few malt whiskies and ten wines by the glass; background music, board games, dominoes, books. It can get busy, so it's best to book a table in advance at weekends. You can camp here for free if you eat at the pub. It's claimed that the last hanging from the gallows outside (hence the pub's name) took place in 1940.

🍴 Sandwiches are made with their own home-made bread, and other good food dishes might include chicken liver and gloucester old spot pork pâté with red onion chutney, local wild duck breast with blood orange and smoked bacon with potato croutons, mussels in white wine with cream, a trio of home-made sausages with mash and gravy, rabbit, leek and ham hock pie, beer-battered fish with mushy peas and chips, wild mushroom and herb risotto, slow-braised lamb shank with rosemary and garlic, honey-glazed gressingham duck breast glazed with apple and clementine tart and red wine reduction, and puddings. *Benchmark main dish: pork belly with black pudding and mash £12.95. Two-course evening meal £19.00.*

Hydes ~ Tenants Ian and Luda Rottenbury ~ Real ale ~ (01260) 252238 ~ Open 12-3, 6-11; 10-11 Sat, Sun ~ Bar food 12-2(3.30 Sat), 6-9; 12-8 Sun ~ Restaurant ~ Children in blue room only ~ Dogs allowed in bar ~ www.thehanginggate.co.uk
Recommended by Rob and Catherine Dunster, Stuart Paulley, David Crook

LOWER PEOVER
SJ7474   Map 7

Bells of Peover

Just off B5081; The Cobbles; WA16 9PZ

Wisteria-covered pub in pretty setting with real ales and interesting food; lots of seating areas in garden

Off the beaten track in a peaceful hamlet, this is a well run dining pub with plenty of space outside for fine weather. Seats on the front terrace overlook the black and white 14th-c church, while at the side a spacious lawn beyond the old coachyard spreads down through trees and under rose pergolas to a little stream. Inside, the various rooms have beams and panelling, open fires and antiques, comfortable seating ranging from brown leather cushioned wall seats to high-backed upholstered or leather dining chairs around an assortment of tables on bare boards, and various prints, paintings and mirrors on the walls. Robinsons Dizzy Blonde, Hartleys XB and Unicorn on handpump and several wines by the glass served by friendly staff; background music.

🍴 A wide choice of interesting food includes lunchtime sandwiches, potted salmon with watercress mousse, hand-dived scallops with cauliflower, pomegranate and capers, butternut squash risotto with pumpkin seeds and popcorn, steak burger with mayonnaise and fries, home-made sausages with a changing mash and duck fat chips, slow-cooked casserole of duck, sausage, pork belly and white haricot beans, moroccan-style lamb with aubergine caviar and couscous, sea bream fillet with brown shrimps and pink fir apple potatoes, and puddings such as apple tatin with spiced caramel sauce and vanilla ice-cream and chocolate pave with salted caramel and kirsch; they also offer a two- and three-course set menu. *Benchmark main dish: pie of the day £12.95. Two-course evening meal £19.50.*

Robinsons ~ Manager Andre Sievers ~ Real ale ~ (01565) 722269 ~ Open 11-11; 12-10.30 Sun; closed Mon ~ Bar food 12-2.30, 6-9.30; 12-9.30 Sat; 12-8 Sun ~ Restaurant ~ Children welcome ~ www.thebellsofpeover.com *Recommended by Trevor Swindells, Hugh Roberts*

MACCLESFIELD
SJ9271   Map 7

Sutton Hall 🍴 🍺

Leaving Macclesfield southwards on A523, turn left into Byrons Lane signposted Langley, Wincle, then just before canal viaduct fork right into Bullocks Lane; OS Sheet 118 map reference 925715; SK11 0HE

Historic building set in attractive grounds, with a fine range of drinks and impressive food

Our readers return to this rather splendid 16th-c manor house on a regular basis – it's particularly well run and the food and drink are extremely good. The original hall that forms the heart of the building is highly impressive, particularly in its entrance space. A charming series of bar and dining areas, some divided by tall oak timbers, are warm and cosy with plenty of character, antique oak panelling, warmly coloured rugs on wide flagstones, bare boards and tiles, lots of frame-to-frame pictures and a raised open fire – all very Brunning & Price. The atmosphere has just enough formality, with cheerful staff and an enjoyable mix of customers, to keep it nicely relaxed. A good range of drinks includes Phoenix Brunning & Price Original, Flowers Original, Wincle Lord Lucan and a couple of guests from brewers such as Titanic and Weetwood on handpump, and well over a dozen wines by the glass from an extensive list. The gardens are lovely, with spaciously laid out tables (some on their own little terraces), sloping lawns and fine mature trees.

🍴 Highly thought-of food includes sandwiches, thai potted fish with mango and lime salsa, brie, crisp parma ham and caramelised red onion salad with sweet grape dressing, crab and asparagus risotto with samphire and crispy poached egg, portobello mushroom, spinach and gruyère cheese wellington with roasted beetroot and madeira wine sauce, chicken, ham and leek pudding with mash and gravy, braised lamb shoulder with redcurrant jelly, slow-roast pork belly with black pudding fritter and watercress mash, and puddings such as banoffee panna cotta with caramelised bananas and peach and prosecco jelly with strawberry and mint salad. *Benchmark main dish: beer-battered fish and chips £12.25. Two-course evening meal £19.00.*

Brunning & Price ~ Manager Syd Foster ~ Real ale ~ (01260) 253211 ~ Open 11.30-11; 12-10.30 Sun ~ Bar food 12-10(9.30 Sun) ~ Children welcome ~ Dogs allowed in bar ~ www.suttonhall.co.uk *Recommended by Dennis Jones, Hugo Buckley, Rob and Catherine Dunster, Pat and Tony Martin, Brian and Anna Marsden, Claes Mauroy, Michael Butler*

MARTON
Davenport Arms 🍺 £
SJ8568 Map 7

A34 N of Congleton; SK11 9HF

Handsome pub with welcoming bar, comfortable restaurant, good food and drink, and good-sized sheltered garden

Welcoming and most enjoyable, the two linked front bar rooms here have a good traditional feel. There's a woodburning stove, ticking clock, comfortably cushioned wall settles, wing armchairs and other hand-picked furnishings on patterned carpet, old prints on the cream walls, and colourful jugs hanging from sturdy beams. You can eat (or just have a drink or coffee) in any of these rooms and there's also a pleasantly light and airy more formal dining area behind; background music. Courage Directors, Theakstons Black Bull and a couple of guests from brewers such as Merlin and Slaters on handpump, and staff are friendly and helpful. Outside is a terrace with metal garden furniture, a fairy-lit arbour, and a timber shelter, well spaced picnic-sets and a set of swings in the garden beyond, and a substantial separate play area. The 14th-c timbered church opposite is well worth a look. They do take caravans but you must book.

🍴 Popular food includes baguettes and wraps, a pâté of the day with home-made chutney, black pudding stack with creamed leeks and bacon, home-made fishcakes with citrus mayonnaise and sweet chilli dip, burger with blue cheese, bacon, red onion marmalade and home-made chips, a lunchtime curry of the day, beer-battered fresh haddock with mushy peas and tartare sauce, cajun chicken with mango salad, lambs liver with onion gravy and mash, a pie of the day and puddings; Tuesday is curry night. *Benchmark main dish: rack of pork ribs with garlic mayonnaise and chips £12.50. Two-course evening meal £18.50.*

Free house ~ Licensees Ron Dalton and Sara Griffith ~ Real ale ~ (01260) 224269 ~ Open 12-2.30, 6-11; 12-11 Sat; 12-10.30 Sun; closed Mon lunchtime ~ Bar food 12-2.30, 6-9; 12-9 Sat; 12-8 Sun ~ Restaurant ~ Children welcome ~ www.thedavenportarms.co.uk
Recommended by David Heath, Mike and Wena Stevenson

MOBBERLEY
Bulls Head 🍴

SJ7879   Map 7

Mill Lane; WA16 7HX

Terrific all-rounder just over six miles from the M6 and with interesting food

'This has got everything right,' says one of our enthusiastic readers about this well run village pub – and many agree. It's been kept nice and pubby with just a touch of modernity, and there's plenty of room round the counter where they serve three Weetwood beers and three guests from local brewers Merlin and Mobberley on handpump (useful tasting notes too); dogs are made equally welcome, with the friendly staff dispensing doggie biscuits from a huge jar. Several rooms are furnished quite traditionally, with an unpretentious mix of wooden tables, cushioned wall seats and chairs on fine old quarry tiles, black and pale grey walls contrasting well with warming red lampshades, pink stripped-brick walls and pale stripped-timber detailing, and there are lots of mirrors, hops, candles and open fires. This pub is part of the small Cheshire Cat Pubs & Bars group, which also include the Cholmondeley Arms at Bickley Moss and Three Greyhounds at Allostock (both Cheshire) and the Red Lion in Weymouth (Dorset).

As well as their 'nibble and natter' dishes such as pork pie with real ale chutney and crispy salt and pepper whitebait with tartare sauce, the wide choice of enjoyable food includes lunchtime sandwiches, sharing plates, fried duck livers with warm chicory and fig salad on toasted home-made beer bread, butternut squash hash with spiced carrot chutney and beetroot leaf and sorrel salad, organic pork sausages with mash and shallot gravy, cheese-crumbed chicken with wild mushroom sauce, smoked fish pie in creamy white wine sauce with carrot and celeriac mash, and puddings like whiskey sticky toffee pudding with vanilla ice-cream and chocolate brownie with warm chocolate sauce. *Benchmark main dish: steak in ale pie £12.95. Two-course evening meal £19.00.*

Free house ~ Licensee Ben Redwood ~ Real ale ~ (01565) 873395 ~ Open 12-11 (11.30 Sat); 12-10.30 Sun ~ Bar food 12-9.15(9.45 Sat, 8.45 Sun) ~ Children over 10 till 7pm in pub ~ Dogs allowed in bar ~ quiz monthly, jazz alternate Sun ~ www.thebullsheadpub.co.uk *Recommended by Gavin McLaughlin, Paul Allott, Jane Taylor and David Dutton, Michael and Angela Prior, Mike and Wena Stevenson, Dave Webster, Sue Holland*

MOBBERLEY
Plough & Flail 🍷

SJ8179   Map 7

Off B5085 Knutsford–Alderley Edge; at E end of village turn into Moss Lane, then left into Paddock Hill Lane (look out for small green signs to pub); WA16 7DB

Extensive family dining pub, comfortable and well run, with enjoyable food and plenty of outside tables

Really well worth tracking down, tucked away as it is down narrow lanes, this spacious place has an easy-going atmosphere and cheerful, attentive staff. It's well laid out and feels gently up-to-date; the softly lit main area around the bar has plain cream walls and bare panelled dado, chunky cushioned dining chairs around sturdy stripped tables, low rustic beams and flagstones. Near the entrance, a handsomely floored side area has low sofas with scatter cushions, and sports TV. At the far end is a smaller, comfortable, light and airy dining room, and a further conservatory dining room. Joules Bitter and Lees Best and Governor on handpump and a good choice of wines by the glass; well reproduced nostalgic background music. There are lots of teak tables on heated flagstoned terraces and picnic-sets on neat lawns around the car park; robust play area.

As well as a two- and three-course set menu (12-7 Monday-Thursday), the good food includes sandwiches (until 5pm), ham hock terrine with plum and apple chutney, crab in lime and tarragon dressing, sharing platters, burger with cheese, bacon, tomato relish and triple-cooked chips, turkey, ham and leek pie with mash and gravy, wild mushroom stroganoff, shin of beef with horseradish mash and red wine jus, grilled red mullet with spiced potatoes and salsa verde, and puddings like chocolate fudge brownie with chocolate ganache and mixed fruit crumble with custard. *Benchmark main dish: steak pie £12.50. Two-course evening meal £19.00.*

Lees ~ Manager Jose Lourenco ~ Real ale ~ (01565) 873537 ~ Open 12-11; 12-10.30 Sun ~ Bar food 12-9(10 Fri, Sat, 8 Sun) ~ Restaurant ~ Children welcome
Recommended by Michael Butler, Dr and Mrs A K Clarke, W K Wood

MOTTRAM ST ANDREW
Bulls Head ♥ ◀

SJ8878   Map 7

A538 Prestbury–Wilmslow; Wilmslow Road/Priest Lane; E side of village

Superb new country dining pub, an excellent retreat at any time of day

The star feature here is the dining zone at the far end. Four levels stack up alongside or above each other, each with a distinctive décor and style, from the informality of a sunken area with rugs on a tiled floor, through a comfortable library/dining room, to one with an upstairs conservatory feel and another, higher-windowed, with more of a special-occasion atmosphere. The rest of the pub has the usual appealing Brunning & Price mix of abundant old prints and pictures and a great variety of comfortable seating, with a coal fire in one room, a blazing woodburning stove in a two-way fireplace dividing two other rooms, and an antique black kitchen range in yet another. In addition to a lengthy changing range of real ales such as Phoenix Brunning & Price Original, Bollington Dinner Ale, Hawkshead Lakeland Gold, Pennine Amber Necker, Tatton Blonde and Wincle Sir Philip, lots of wines by the glass and a fine range of spirits, they have an attractive separate tea and coffee station with pretty blue and white china cups, teapots and jugs all hung ready for action; lots of daily papers, a shelf of board games. Staff clearly enjoy their work and each other's company – always a good sign. There are picnic-table sets under cocktail parasols out on the lawn.

The good interesting food includes sandwiches, pressed terrine of goats cheese with basil and roasted red pepper and black olive tapenade, lime-cured sea trout with wasabi crème fraîche and sesame shrimp toast, crab, dill and asparagus quiche, steak burger topped with bacon and cheddar with coleslaw and chips, steak and kidney pudding, tandoor roasted cod with spiced crab samosa, fennel and cucumber salad and almond pilaf rice, braised lamb shoulder with red wine and rosemary gravy and carrot purée, and puddings such as peach, apricot and pistachio bakewell tart with raspberry ripple ice-cream and dark chocolate ganache with Cointreau mascarpone. *Benchmark main dish: beer-battered haddock and chips with minted mushy peas £12.15. Two-course evening meal £19.00.*

Brunning & Price ~ Manager Andrew Coverley ~ Real ale ~ (01625) 828111 ~ Open 10.30am-11pm ~ Bar food 12-10(9.30 Sun) ~ Children welcome ~ Dogs allowed in bar ~ www.brunningandprice.co.uk/bullshead *Recommended by Brian and Anna Marsden*

NETHER ALDERLEY
SJ8576   Map 7
Wizard 🍴

B5087 Macclesfield Road, opposite Artists Lane; SK10 4UB

Bustling dining pub on National Trust land with interesting food, real ales, a friendly welcome and relaxed atmosphere

Most customers come to this well run dining pub to enjoy the highly rated food, but they do keep Thwaites Wainwright and a guest from Storm on handpump, ten wines by the glass and several malt whiskies, all served by friendly, helpful staff. The various rooms are connected by open doorways and are cleverly done up in a mix of modern rustic and traditional styles: beams and open fires, a happy assortment of antique dining chairs (some prettily cushioned) and settles around all sorts of tables, rugs on pale wooden floorboards, prints and paintings on contemporary paintwork and decorative items ranging from a grandfather clock to staffordshire dogs and modern lampshades; lovely fresh flowers and plants dotted about. The pub is just a few minutes from lovely walks along Alderley Edge (a dramatic red sandstone escarpment with fine views), and there are seats and tables in the sizeable back garden that are just right for a relaxing lunch afterwards. The pub is part of the Ainscough group.

Particularly good food might include lunchtime sandwiches, various platters, tomato, pesto and mozzarella tart, venison scotch egg with cumberland dressing and pickled cabbage, king prawn caesar salad with bacon, anchovies and parmesan, burger with cheese, bacon and triple-cooked chips, trio of bangers with parsley mash and braised shallot jus, home-made chicken kiev, slow-braised ox cheek with bacon lardons, baby onions and button mushrooms, and puddings like jam roly-poly with custard and chocolate cappuccino mousse with marshmallows. *Benchmark main dish: steak in ale suet pudding £12.95. Two-course evening meal £18.50.*

Free house ~ Licensee Dominic Gottelier ~ Real ale ~ (01625) 584000 ~ Open 12-3, 5.30-11; 12-11 Sat; 12-10 Sun ~ Bar food 12-2, 6.30-9.30; 12-9.30 Sat; 12-8 Sun ~ Children welcome ~ Dogs allowed in bar ~ www.ainscoughs.co.uk
Recommended by Richard and Penny Gibbs, Brian and Anna Marsden, David Cotterill

PEOVER HEATH
SJ7973   Map 7
Dog 🍺

Off A50 N of Holmes Chapel at the Whipping Stocks, keep on past Parkgate into Wellbank Lane; OS Sheet 118 map reference 794735; note that this village is called Peover Heath on the OS map and shown under that name on many road maps, but the pub is often listed under Over Peover instead; WA16 8UP

Homely pub with interesting range of beers and generously served food; bedrooms

Our readers feel genuinely welcomed by the friendly, efficient staff in this cottagey place. The neatly kept bar is gently old fashioned with tied-back floral curtains at little windows, a curved cushioned banquette built into a bay window and mostly traditional dark wheelbacks arranged on a patterned carpet. A coal fire, copper pieces and pot plants add to the homely feel. A genuine local atmosphere is maintained by areas that are set aside for drinkers. Dunham Massey Big Tree Bitter, Hydes (very good value), Mobberley Barn Buster and Weetwood Best, Cheshire Cat and Old Dog on handpump, a good range of malt whiskies and several wines by the glass; games room with darts, dominoes, board games and TV (for sport). There are picnic-sets beneath colourful hanging baskets on the peaceful lane, and more in the pretty back garden. It's a pleasant walk from here to the Jodrell Bank Centre and Arboretum.

A wide choice of interesting food includes sandwiches, giant scotch egg with brown sauce, duck liver and thyme pâté with quince jelly, sunblush tomato and roasted baby artichoke risotto, sausages with onion gravy, shin of beef pie in ale with rib gravy and mash, curried soft-shell crab fritters with avocado and tomato salad, poached rabbit ragout on tagliatelle, salt and pepper pork belly with mustard greens and pan gravy, and puddings such as bitter chocolate and Cointreau mousse and apricot bread and butter pudding. *Benchmark main dish: fish and chips with mushy peas £11.95. Two-course evening meal £19.00.*

Free house ~ Licensee Edward Barlow ~ Real ale ~ (01625) 861421 ~ Open 11.30-11; 12-10.30 Sun ~ Bar food 12-2.30, 6-9; 12-9 Sat; 12-8.30 Sun ~ Restaurant ~ Children welcome ~ Dogs allowed in bar ~ Bedrooms: £65/£85 ~ www.thedogpeover.co.uk
Recommended by Brian and Anna Marsden, Mike and Wena Stevenson

SANDBACH
SJ7560   Map 7

Old Hall 🍴 ♀ ◀

1.2 miles from M6 junction 17: A534 into town, then right into High Street; CW11 1AL

Stunning mid-17th-c hall-house with impressive original features, plenty of drinking and dining space, six real ales and imaginative food

As one of the very few Grade I listed pubs in Britain, this glorious 17th-c manor house is a masterpiece of timbering and fine carved gable-ends. There are many lovely original architectural features, particularly in the room to the left of the entrance hall, which is much as it has been for centuries, with a Jacobean fireplace, oak panelling and priest's hole. This leads into the Oak Room divided by standing timbers into two dining rooms, with heavy beams, oak flooring and reclaimed panelling. Other rooms in the original building have more hefty beams and oak boards, three open fires and a woodburning stove; the cosy snugs are carpeted. The Garden Room is big and bright, with reclaimed quarry tiling and exposed A-frame oak timbering, and opens on to a suntrap back terrace with teak tables and chairs among flowering tubs. Throughout, the walls are covered with numerous interesting prints, there's an appealing collection of antique dining chairs and tables of all sizes, and plenty of rugs, bookcases and plants. From the handsome bar counter, efficient and friendly staff serve Phoenix Brunning & Price Original, Redwillow Feckless, Three Tuns XXX and three guests such as Derby Double Mash, Thornbridge Jaipur and Wincle Life of Riley on handpump, 15 good wines by the glass and 40 malt whiskies; board games. There are picnic-sets in front by rose bushes and clipped box hedging.

🍴 Tempting food includes sandwiches, fried mackerel and soused vegetables with saffron and orange dressing, potted pork belly with spiced caramelised apple, crackling and toffee apple sauce, crab linguine with ginger, chilli and coriander, gloucester old spot sausages with onion gravy and mash, crispy beef salad with satay sauce and toasted peanuts, chicken and ham hock pie, potato, thyme and parmesan gnocchi with mint crème fraîche, aubergines, courgettes and fennel, gilt-head bream with garlic and chive mash, fricassée of mussels, broad beans, spinach and roasted cherry tomatoes, and puddings such as walnut and cranberry tart and chocolate brownie with chocolate sauce and vanilla ice-cream. *Benchmark main dish: braised shoulder of lamb with dauphinoise potatoes and rosemary gravy £16.95. Two-course evening meal £19.50.*

Brunning & Price ~ Manager Chris Button ~ Real ale ~ (01270) 758170 ~ Open 11.30-11; 12-10.30 Sun ~ Bar food 12-10(9.30 Sun) ~ Restaurant ~ Children welcome ~ Dogs allowed in bar ~ www.oldhall-sandbach.co.uk *Recommended by Richard and Penny Gibbs, Sandra McGechan, Brenda Keogh, Susan and Nigel Brookes, Dave Webster, Sue Holland, Brian and Anna Marsden, Dr and Mrs A K Clarke, Mike and Wena Stevenson, R Anderson*

SPURSTOW
Yew Tree ★ 🍴 ♍ 🍺 SJ5657   Map 7

Off A49 S of Tarporley; follow Bunbury 1, Haughton 2 signpost into Long Lane; CW6 9RD

Cheshire Dining Pub of the Year

Plenty of individuality, smashing food and drinks and a bouncy atmosphere

A thoroughly top notch all-rounder, this thriving place is genuinely individual and entertaining. An elegant mix of nice old tables and chairs mixes with Timorous Beasties' giant bees papered on to the bar ceiling and a stag's head that looms proudly out of the wall above a log fire. Nicely simple pale grey, off-white and cream surfaces explode into striking bold wallpaper; there's a magnified hunting print and surprisingly angled bright tartans. And the doors to the loos are quite a puzzle – which of the many knobs and handles actually work?! The island bar has half a dozen sensibly priced ales such as Acorn Barnsley Gold, Merlins Gold, Redwillow Wreckless, Stonehouse Station, Weetwood Eastgate and Woods Shropshire Lass on handpump, a beer of the month, a local cider, over two dozen malts and a good range of wines by the glass from an interesting bin-ends list of about 50. The informal service is quick even when they are busy. A more dining-oriented area shares the same feeling of relaxed bonhomie – a favourite table is snugged into a stripped wood alcove resembling a stable stall. A terrace outside has teak tables, with more on the grass.

🍴 Impressive food includes sandwiches, goats cheese bonbons with chicory and red pepper marmalade, salt beef hash cake with horseradish and thyme rösti and poached egg, butternut squash and chickpea tagine with apricot and coriander couscous, maple- and mustard-glazed ham with eggs, braised beef brisket chilli with paprika rice and sour cream, a home-made pie of the day, ballontine of chicken stuffed with tarragon mousse wrapped in parma ham with onion and thyme purée and coq au vin sauce, slow-cooked crispy pork belly with black pudding mash, apple fritter and sage jus, and puddings such as toffee popcorn cheesecake and pear and ginger pudding with cinnamon ice-cream. *Benchmark main dish: home-made fish pie topped with cheshire cheese mash £11.00. Two-course evening meal £19.50.*

Free house ~ Licensees Jon and Lindsay Cox ~ Real ale ~ (01829) 260274 ~ Open 12-11; 11-10.30 Sun ~ Bar food 12-2.30, 6-9.30(10 Fri); 12-10 Sat; 11-8 Sun ~ Children welcome

~ Dogs welcome ~ Live acoustic music last Fri of month ~ www.theyewtreebunbury.com
Recommended by Edward Leetham, R T and J C Moggridge, Jane Taylor and David Dutton, Dave Webster, Sue Holland

 SWETTENHAM   SJ7967   Map 7

Swettenham Arms

Off A54 Congleton–Holmes Chapel or A535 Chelford–Holmes Chapel; CW12 2LF

Big old country pub in a fine setting with shining brasses, five real ales and tempting food

At the start of walks in the lovely surrounding countryside, this spacious country pub is also handy for Quinta Arboretum. Said to be as old as the interesting village church (which dates in part from the 13th c), this former nunnery has three interlinked areas that are still nicely traditional, with dark heavy beams, individual furnishings, a polished copper bar, three welcoming open fires, plenty of shiny brasses, a sweep of fitted turkey carpet and a variety of old prints – military, hunting, old ships, reproduction Old Masters and so forth. Friendly efficient staff serve Beartown Kodiak Gold, Brains Hancocks HB, Hydes Bitter, Moorhouses Pride of Pendle and a changing guest on handpump, Weston's cider and over 50 malt whiskies; background music. Behind are tables on a lawn that merges into a lovely sunflower and lavender meadow.

 Using produce from their own garden, bees and hens, the creative food might include sandwiches, a meat or fish platter, hot home-smoked duck breast with rhubarb and soft herb salad and thyme dressing, black pudding fondant with hot mustard mayonnaise, watercress velouté and poached egg, spiced fish bubble and squeak with raita and apricot chutney, pork wiener schnitzel with onions and parma ham, sautéed potatoes and lemon hollandaise, seared sea bream fillet with leeks, chorizo and white wine sauce, and puddings such as rhubarb steamed sponge with tonka bean crème anglaise and caramelised pears with macadamia praline parfait and earl grey and prune jelly. *Benchmark main dish: steak in ale pie £12.75. Two-course evening meal £21.00.*

Free house ~ Licensees Jim and Frances Cunningham ~ Real ale ~ No credit cards ~ (01477) 571284 ~ Open 11.30-11(midnight Sat); 12-10.30 Sun ~ Bar food 12-2.30, 5-9.30; 12-9.30 Sat; 12-8.30 Sun ~ Restaurant ~ Children welcome ~ Dogs allowed in bar ~ www.swettenhamarms.co.uk *Recommended by Mike and Wena Stevenson*

TARPORLEY   SJ5562   Map 7

Rising Sun £

High Street; village signposted off A51 Nantwich–Chester; CW6 0DX

Friendly, bustling and quaint, with pubby food

There's a happy mix of regulars and visitors in this charmingly friendly and down-to-earth old pub – it's been in the same family for over 25 years. The low-ceilinged interior has plenty of character and is prettily furnished with eye-catching old seats and tables, including creaky 19th-c mahogany and oak settles. An attractively blacked iron kitchen range nestles next to gleaming old cupboard doors, and sporting and other old-fashioned prints decorate the cream walls. Accommodating staff serve Robinsons Dizzy Blonde and Unicorn and a seasonal ale from handpumps. There are a couple of seats and a TV for sporting events in a tiny side bar; background music.

🍽 Popular, fair value food includes sandwiches and baked potatoes, asparagus and cheese pancake, braised ox liver with bacon and onion gravy, cod mornay, veal in white wine and mushroom sauce, home-made pies, chicken kiev, cantonese-style prawns, and puddings like profiteroles with hot chocolate sauce and strawberry cheesecake. *Benchmark main dish: battered cod, chips and mushy peas £8.65. Two-course evening meal £13.50.*

Robinsons ~ Tenant Alec Robertson ~ Real ale ~ No credit cards ~ (01829) 732423 ~ Open 11.30-3.30, 5-11; 11.30-11 Sat; 12-11 Sun ~ Bar food 11.30-2, 5-9.30; 12-9 Sat, Sun ~ Restaurant evening ~ Children welcome ~ www.therisingsuntarporley.co.uk
Recommended by Mike Proctor

THELWALL
SJ6587   Map 7

Little Manor ♀ ◀

Bell Lane; WA4 2SX

Restored manor house with lots to look at, plenty of room, well kept ales and interesting bistro-style food; seats outside

The six beamed rooms in this handsome 17th-c house are all linked by open doorways and standing timbers, and the carefully preserved nooks and crannies have plenty of character. There are leather armchairs (the carved wooden one is lovely) by open fires, all manner of antique dining chairs around assorted tables (small, large, circular, square), flooring that ranges from rugs on bare boards through carpeting to some fine old black and white tiles, and lighting from wall lamps, standard lamps and metal chandeliers. As well as fresh flowers and house plants, the décor includes hundreds of interesting prints and photographs, books on shelves and lots of old glass and stone bottles on window sills and mantelpieces. They keep Coach House Cromwell, Phoenix Brunning & Price Original, Wincle Sir Philip and three guests from brewers such as Moorhouses, Tatton and Weetwood on handpump, about 15 wines by the glass and around 60 whiskies; the young staff are consistently helpful. In fine weather you can sit at the chunky teak chairs and tables on the terrace; some are under a heated shelter.

🍽 Good bistro-style food includes sandwiches, teriyaki bream with pak choi and sesame seed salad, pineapple crisp and wasabi hollandaise, seared scallops with smoked haddock and fennel brandade and crispy chorizo, crispy beef salad with sweet chilli and cashew nuts, beetroot and red wine risotto with crème fraîche, pumpkin seeds and parmesan, steak burger topped with grilled bacon and cheddar with coleslaw and chips, braised shoulder of dauphinoise potatoes with rosemary gravy, duck breast with parsnip fondant, vanilla bean celeriac purée and Drambuie syrup, and puddings like warm treacle, apple, sultana and whisky tart and bread and butter pudding with apricot sauce. *Benchmark main dish: sausages and mash with onion gravy £10.95. Two-course evening meal £19.00.*

Brunning & Price ~ Manager Andrew Cloverly ~ Real ale ~ (01925) 261703 ~ Open 12-11(10.30 Sun) ~ Bar food 12-10(9.30 Sun) ~ Children welcome ~ Dogs allowed in bar ~ www.littlemanor-thelwall.co.uk *Recommended by Richard and Penny Gibbs, Dr and Mrs A K Clarke*

Real ale to us means beer that has matured naturally in its cask – not pressurised or filtered. We name all real ales stocked. We usually name ales preserved under a light blanket of carbon dioxide too, though purists – pointing out that this stops the natural yeasts developing – would disagree (most people, including us, can't tell the difference!).

WARMINGHAM   SJ7161 Map 7

Bears Paw 🍺

School Lane; CW11 3QN

Nicely maintained place with enjoyable food, half a dozen real ales and well equipped bedrooms

A maze of rooms work their way into one another in this extensive Victorian inn – each with plenty of individual character. You'll find several cosy places to sit; we particularly like the two little sitting rooms with their panelling, fashionable wallpaper, bookshelves and slouchy leather furniture with plumped-up cushions comfortably arranged by magnificent fireplaces with woodburners; stripped wood flooring and dado keep it all informal. There's an eclectic mix of old wooden tables, with some nice old carved chairs, well spaced throughout the dining areas, with lofty windows providing a light and airy feel and big pot plants adding freshness. There are stools at the long bar counter where cheerful and efficient staff serve half a dozen real ales on handpump from Beartown, Weetwood and a guest brewer such as Moorhouses, and a dozen wines by the glass. There are tables in a small front garden by the car park. This is sister pub to the Pheasant in Burwardsley (also in this chapter).

🍴 The interesting food includes lunchtime sandwiches and wraps, various deli boards, beetroot with goats cheese and candied walnuts, roast pigeon breast with pickled wild mushrooms, pancetta and onion purée, smoked salmon, pea and mint risotto with white truffle oil, steak burger with bacon, melted cheese and crispy onion rings, roasted sweet potato, chickpea and lentil dhal, roast lamb rump with boulangère potatoes, creamed cabbage and pancetta with dijonnaise sauce, and puddings such as white chocolate cheesecake with poached rhubarb and bread and butter pudding with apricot compote. *Benchmark main dish: steak and mushroom in ale pie £12.95. Two-course evening meal £20.50.*

Free house ~ Licensee Andrew Nelson ~ Real ale ~ (01270) 526317 ~ Open 11-11(midnight Fri, Sat); 11-10.30 Sun ~ Bar food 12-9.30 Mon-Thurs; 12-10 Fri, Sat; 12-9 Sun ~ Restaurant ~ Children welcome ~ Dogs allowed in bar and bedrooms ~ Bedrooms: £75/£85 ~ www.thebearspaw.co.uk *Recommended by Richard and Penny Gibbs, Dave Webster, Sue Holland*

Also Worth a Visit in Cheshire

Besides the fully inspected pubs, you might like to try these pubs that have been recommended to us and described by readers. Do tell us what you think of them: feedback@goodguides.com

ALPRAHAM   SJ5759
Travellers Rest (01829) 260523
A51 Nantwich–Chester; CW6 9JA
Unspoilt four-room country local in same friendly family for three generations, well kept Tetleys and Weetwood, no food, leatherette, wicker and Formica, some flock wallpaper, fine old brewery mirrors, darts and dominoes; may be nesting swallows in the outside gents', dogs welcome, back bowling green, 'Hat Day' last Sun before Christmas with locals sporting some unusual headgear, closed weekday lunchtimes. *(Claes Mauroy)*

ALVANLEY   SJ4973
White Lion (01928) 722949
Manley Road; handy for M56 junction 14; WA6 9DD Refurbished 16th-c village pub with low beams, cosy corners and open fire, wide choice of enjoyable well priced food all day from sandwiches and sharing plates up, Robinsons ales and plenty of wines by the glass, friendly service; Tues quiz; children welcome, teak furniture in landscaped garden. *(John Szostek)*

AUDLEM   SJ6543
Shroppie Fly (01270) 811772
Shropshire Street; CW3 0DX Popular
three-room former warehouse by Locks
12/13 of Shropshire Union Canal, friendly
helpful staff, good range of real ales and
plenty of wines by the glass, well liked food
from sandwiches and wraps up, bar made
from original barge, canal memorabilia,
mainly modern furnishings, central fire,
pool in public bar; background music – live
Sat; children and dogs welcome, waterside
terrace, open all day. *(Mike and Wena
Stevenson, Claes Mauroy)*

BARBRIDGE   SJ6156
Barbridge Inn (01270) 528327
Just off A51 N of Nantwich; CW5 6AY
Open-plan family dining pub by lively
marina at junction of Shropshire Union and
Middlewich canals, enjoyable well cooked
food served by friendly staff, local Woodlands
beers, conservatory; no dogs inside; play
area in riverside garden, open all day.
(Dave Webster, Sue Holland)

BARTHOMLEY   SJ7752
★ White Lion (01270) 882242
*M6 junction 16, B5078 N towards
Alsager, then Barthomley signed on left;
CW2 5PG* Charming, unspoilt 17th-c
thatched tavern with wide mix of customers,
good value straightforward tasty food
(lunchtime only), five well kept ales, friendly
timeless main bar with latticed windows,
heavy low beams, moulded black panelling,
prints on walls and blazing open fire, steps
up to room with another fire, more panelling
and a high-backed winged settle; children
allowed away from bar, dogs welcome, seats
out on cobbles overlooking attractive village
and early 15th-c red sandstone church, open
all day. *(David Jackman, Mike Horgan, Di
Wright, Mike Proctor, Dr D J and Mrs S C Walker,
Dave Webster, Sue Holland, Stuart Doughty
and others)*

BARTON   SJ4454
★ Cock o' Barton (01829) 782277
*Barton Road (A534 E of Farndon);
SY14 7HU* Stylish and witty contemporary
décor and furnishings in spreading bright
and open skylit bar, good enterprising
up-to-date food, plenty of wines by the glass,
Moorhouses Pride of Pendle and Stonehouse
Station, neat courteous staff; unobtrusive
background music; children welcome,
tables in sunken heated inner courtyard
with canopies and modern water feature,
picnic-sets on back lawn, open all day, closed
Mon. *(Bradley Beazley)*

BELL O' TH' HILL   SJ5245
Blue Bell (01948) 662172
Just off A41 N of Whitchurch; SY13 4QS
Heavily beamed partly 14th-c country pub
with friendly licensees and chatty locals,
three or four well kept ales, traditional food
from sandwiches up, two cosy attractive
rooms, folk night first Tues of month, Weds
quiz; children and dogs welcome, pleasant
garden, small caravan site in paddock, closed
Mon. *(MLR, Claes Mauroy)*

BOLLINGTON   SJ9377
Church House (01625) 574014
Church Street; SK10 5PY Welcoming
village pub with good value home-made
food including OAP menu, efficient friendly
service, well kept frequently changing ales,
roaring fire, separate dining room; good place
to start or end a walk, bedrooms.
(Dr D J and Mrs S C Walker)

BOLLINGTON   SJ9377
Holly Bush (01625) 573073
Palmerston Street; SK10 5PW
Three-room pub with panelling and
traditional décor, good food from spanish
chef including tapas, well kept Robinsons
ales, friendly service. *(Anne and Steve
Thompson)*

BOLLINGTON   SJ9477
Poachers (01625) 572086
Mill Lane; SK10 5BU Stone-built village
local prettily set in good walking area,
comfortable and welcoming, with five well
kept ales including Storm and Weetwood,
good pubby food including bargain lunches,
daily newspapers; sunny back garden, open
all day Sun, closed Mon lunchtime.
(Brian and Anna Marsden)

BOLLINGTON   SJ9377
Vale (01625) 575147
Adlington Road; SK10 5JT Friendly tap
for Bollington Brewery in three converted
19th-c cottages, their full range and a couple
of local guests (tasters offered), good range
of freshly made food, efficient knowledgeable
young staff, interesting photos, newspapers
and books, roaring fire; picnic-sets out
behind overlooking cricket pitch, near
Middlewood Way and Macclesfield Canal,
open all day Fri-Sun. *(Mike and
Wena Stevenson)*

BRERETON GREEN   SJ7764
Bears Head (01477) 544732
*Handy for M6 junction 17; set back off
A50 S of Holmes Chapel; CW11 1RS*
Beautiful 17th-c black and white timbered

Most pubs with any outside space now have some kind of smokers' shelter. There
are regulations about these – for instance, they have to be substantially open to the
outside air. The best have heating and lighting and are really quite comfortable.

Vintage Inn, welcoming and civilised linked rooms with low beams, old-fashioned furniture, flagstones, bare boards and log fires, enjoyable well prepared food, ales such as Thwaites and Timothy Taylors; 25 bedrooms in modern Innkeepers Lodge block, open all day. *(Dr D J and Mrs S C Walker)*

BURTONWOOD   SJ5692
Fiddle i'th' Bag (01925) 225442
3 miles from M62 junction 9, signposted from A49 towards Newton-le-Willows; WA5 4BT Eccentric place (not to everyone's taste) crammed with bric-a-brac and memorabilia, three changing ales, enjoyable home-made food, friendly staff; may be nostalgic background music; open all day weekends. *(Stuart Travis)*

CHELFORD   SJ8175
⋆ Egerton Arms (01625) 861366
A537 Macclesfield–Knutsford; SK11 9BB Cheerful rambling old place usefully serving food all day; various separate areas with beams and nice mix of furniture including carved settles, wooden porter's chair by grandfather clock, Copper Dragon Golden Pippin, Wells & Youngs Bombardier and five guests, steps down to little raftered games area with squishy sofas and antique farm-animal prints on stripped-brick walls, pool and darts; background music, sports TV and games machines; dogs welcome in bar, deck with canopied picnic-sets, more on grass and toddlers' play area. *(John Taylor, David Cotterill, Dr D J and Mrs S C Walker)*

CHESTER   SJ4065
⋆ Bear & Billet (01244) 351002
Lower Bridge Street; CH1 1RU Handsome 17th-c timbered Okells pub with four changing guest ales, belgian and american imports and nice range of wines by the glass, reasonably priced home-made pubby food, interesting features and some attractive furnishings in friendly and comfortable open-plan bar with fire, sitting and dining rooms upstairs; sports TVs; pleasant courtyard, open all day. *(Dave Webster, Sue Holland)*

CHESTER   SJ4065
Brewery Tap (01244) 340999
Lower Bridge Street; CH1 1RU Tap for Spitting Feathers Brewery in interesting Jacobean building with 18th-c façade, steps up to lofty bar (former great hall) serving their well kept ales plus mainly local guests, real cider, hearty home-made food all day using local suppliers including some unusual choices like devilled kidneys and home-cured veal; open all day. *(D H Bennett, Simon J Barber, Dave Webster, Sue Holland, Allan and Joan Spencer)*

CHESTER   SJ4066
Coach House (01244) 351900
Northgate Street; CH1 2HQ Refurbished 19th-c coaching inn by town hall and cathedral, comfortable lounge with central bar, Bass, Thwaites and guests, decent choice of locally sourced food from semi-open kitchen, afternoon tea with home-made scones, prompt friendly service; children and dogs welcome, tables out in front, eight bedrooms, open all day from 9am for breakfast. *(D H Bennett)*

CHESTER   SJ4066
Olde Boot (01244) 314540
Eastgate Row N; CH1 1LQ Good value in lovely 17th-c Rows building, heavy beams, dark woodwork, oak flooring, flagstones, some exposed Tudor wattle and daub, old kitchen range in lounge beyond, old-fashioned settles and oak panelling in upper area popular with families, standard food, bargain Sam Smiths OBB kept well, good cheerful service, bustling atmosphere; background music. *(D H Bennett)*

CHESTER   SJ4066
Pied Bull (01244) 325829
Upper Northgate Street; CH1 2HQ Old beamed and panelled coaching inn with roomy open-plan carpeted bar, own-brewed Bull Hit ale along with Adnams Broadside and four guests, enjoyable reasonably priced food all day from sandwiches and baked potatoes up, friendly staff and locals, imposing stone fireplace with tapestry above, divided inner dining area; background music, games machines; children welcome, handsome Jacobean stairs to 13 bedrooms, open all day. *(Trevor Graveson, Derek Wason, Dave Webster, Sue Holland)*

CHESTER   SJ4066
Red Lion (01244) 321750
Northgate Street; CH1 2HQ Pleasant old Nicholsons pub with traditional décor, good choice of ales and their usual fairly priced food from sandwiches and sharing plates up; open all day. *(Dave Braisted)*

CHESTER   SJ4066
Telfords Warehouse (01244) 390090
Tower Wharf, behind Northgate Street near railway; CH1 4EZ Well kept interesting ales in large converted canal building, generous fresh up-to-date food including good sandwich menu, efficient staff, bare brick and boards, high pitched ceiling, big wall of windows overlooking water, massive iron winding gear in bar, some old enamel signs, steps up to heavy-beamed area with sofas, artwork and restaurant; late-night live music, bouncers on door; tables out by water, open all day (till late Weds-Sun). *(Anon)*

CHRISTLETON   SJ4465
Cheshire Cat (01244) 332200
Whitchurch Road; CH3 6AE Large canalside Vintage Inn in restored early 19th-c building, popular good value food all day including set menu till 5pm (not Sun),

well kept ales and attentive cheerful service, open fires; garden, 14 bedrooms. *(Steven Hunter)*

CHRISTLETON SJ4565
Plough (01244) 336096
Plough Lane; CH3 7PT Popular 18th-c country local with three linked areas, ales such as Caledonian and Theakstons, good home-made local food (not Sun), friendly helpful staff; garden with play area, good setting. *(Ann and Tony Bennett-Hughes)*

CHURCH MINSHULL SJ6660
Badger (01270) 522607
B5074 Winsford–Nantwich; handy for Shropshire Union Canal, Middlewich branch; CW5 6DY Refurbished 18th-c coaching inn in pretty village next to church, good imaginative food all day from sharing boards up (pub favourites too), Black Sheep, M&B Mild and Timothy Taylors Landlord, interesting range of wines and several malt whiskies, friendly helpful staff, bar and spacious lounge leading to new back conservatory; children till 6pm, five bedrooms, good breakfast. *(Edward Leetham, John and Hazel Sarkanen, Bob Scott)*

COMBERBACH SJ6477
⋆ Spinner & Bergamot
(01606) 891307 *Warrington Road; CW9 6AY* Comfortable 18th-c beamed village pub (named after two racehorses) with two-room carpeted lounge, good home-made bar and restaurant food (12-7.30pm Sun) including fresh fish, service pleasant but can be slow at busy times, well kept Robinsons ales, good wines, log fires, hunting prints, toby jugs and brasses, some Manchester United memorabilia, daily papers, pitched-ceiling timber dining extension, simple tiled-floor public bar; unobtrusive background music; dogs welcome, picnic-sets on sloping lawn, flowers, small verandah, bowling green, open all day. *(Mike and Wena Stevenson, Simon J Barber)*

CONGLETON SJ8659
Horseshoe (01260) 272205
Fence Lane, Newbold Astbury, between A34 and A527 S; CW12 3NL Former 18th-c coaching inn set in peaceful countryside; three small carpeted rooms with decorative plates, copper and brass and other knick-knacks (some on delft shelves), mix of seating including plush banquettes and iron-base tables, log fire, well kept predominantly Robinsons ales, popular good value hearty food, friendly staff and locals; no dogs; children welcome, rustic garden furniture, adventure play area with tractor, good walks. *(Dr D J and Mrs S C Walker)*

CREWE SJ7055
Borough Arms (01270) 748189
Earle Street; CW1 2BG Own microbrewery and lots of changing guest ales, good choice

of continental beers too, friendly staff and regulars, two small rooms off central bar and downstairs lounge; occasional sports TV; picnic-sets on back terrace and lawn, open all day Fri-Sun, closed lunchtime other days. *(Steven Edgar, Dave Webster, Sue Holland)*

DUNHAM MASSEY SJ7288
Rope & Anchor (0161) 927 7901
Paddock Lane; WA14 5RP Minimalist feel with neutral colours throughout and lots of varnished wood and chrome, swish brasswork around the bar, light wooden floors with inset slate tiling, limed tables and bench seating, mix of armchairs, large log-effect gas fire behind glass, Lees beers and good range of wines by the glass, nice food from sandwiches and pub staples to more upscale dishes like scallops with pork belly, efficient friendly staff, additional upstairs dining area; background music turned down on request; children welcome, lots of outside seating with heaters and umbrellas, luxurious smokers' shelter, open all day. *(Mike and Wena Stevenson)*

FADDILEY SJ5852
⋆ Thatch (01270) 524223
A534 Wrexham–Nantwich; CW5 8JE Attractive, thatched, low-beamed and timbered dining pub carefully extended from medieval core, open fires, raised room to right of bar, back barn-style dining room (children allowed here), well kept ales such as Salopian and Weetwood, good choice of enjoyable popular food (booking advised weekends), friendly helpful service, relaxing atmosphere; soft background music; charming country garden with play area, open all day weekends, closed Mon and Tues lunchtimes. *(M J Winterton)*

FIVECROSSES SJ5276
Travellers Rest (01928) 735125
B5152 Frodsham–Kingsley; WA6 6SL Comfortably refurbished dining pub with really nice food (booking advised), well kept beers, efficient pleasant service; superb views across Weaver Valley. *(Glenwys and Alan Lawrence)*

FRODSHAM SJ5278
Bears Paw (01928) 731404
Main Street (A56), near M56 junction 12; WA6 7AF 16th-c stone-built pub (Original Pub Co) with long bar split into four areas, open fire one end, woodburner the other, well kept Black Sheep, Timothy Taylors and Wells & Youngs, good value fairly traditional food all day (till 6pm Fri-Sun); children welcome, back parking fee refunded at bar. *(Dennis Jones)*

FULLERS MOOR SJ4954
Sandstone (01829) 782333
A534; CH3 9JH Light and airy dining pub with wide choice of good sensibly priced fresh food from sandwiches and snacks up,

well kept local ales such as Beartown, Coach House, Stonehouse and Weetwood, friendly staff, modern décor, woodburner, dining conservatory, Tues quiz, may be wine tasting; children and dogs welcome, spacious garden with lovely views, handy for Sandstone Trail, open all day weekends (food all day then too). *(Frank Smits, Tom Barton, Lucy Charles)*

GAWSWORTH
SJ8869

⋆**Harrington Arms** (01260) 223325

Church Lane; SK11 9RJ Rustic 17th-c farm pub with four unchanging rooms, friendly landlord and locals, Robinsons Hatters Mild, Unicorn and two guests from fine carved oak counter, traditional food plus a few specials, good service; children and dogs welcome, sunny benches out on small front cobbled area, more seats in garden overlooking fields, events such as morris dancing and Sept giant onion competition. *(Claes Mauroy, Mike and Wena Stevenson, Dr D J and Mrs S C Walker)*

GOOSTREY
SJ7770

Crown (01477) 532128

Off A50 and A535; CW4 8PE Extended and recently refurbished 18th-c village pub, beams and open fires, good choice of enjoyable food with many main courses available in smaller sizes, friendly service, well kept local beers including Weetwood; close to Jodrell Bank, open all day. *(Anon)*

GRAPPENHALL
SJ6386

⋆**Parr Arms** (01925) 212120

Near M6 junction 20 – A50 towards Warrington, left after 1.5 miles; Church Lane; WA4 3EP Charming, solidly traditional black-beamed pub in picture-postcard setting with picnic-sets out on cobbles by church, more tables on canopied back deck, well kept Robinsons ales, friendly personal service, decent reasonably priced food from sandwiches up, central bar serving lounge and smaller public bar (both comfortable), open fire, Weds quiz; open all day Fri-Sun. *(Anon)*

GREAT BUDWORTH
SJ6677

⋆**George & Dragon** (01606) 892650

Signed off A559 NE of Northwich; High Street opposite church; CW9 6HF Smartly refurbished building owned by Lees and dating in parts to the 1720s; their beers kept well and plenty of wines by the glass, welcoming friendly young staff, good choice of enjoyable reasonably priced food from lunchtime sandwiches and baguettes to specials, dark panelled bar with grandfather clock and leather button-back banquettes, back area more restauranty with tables

around central woodburner; children welcome, delightful village, open all day Fri-Sun. *(Mike and Wena Stevenson, Simon J Barber)*

LANGLEY
SJ9471

⋆**Leather's Smithy** (01260) 252313

Off A523 S of Macclesfield, OS Sheet 118 map reference 952715; SK11 0NE Isolated stone-built pub in fine walking country next to reservoir, well kept Theakstons and two or three guests, lots of whiskies, good food from sandwiches to interesting blackboard specials such as local boar, good welcoming service, beams and log fire, flagstoned bar, carpeted dining areas, interesting local prints and photographs; unobtrusive background music; children welcome, no dogs but muddy boots allowed in bar, picnic-sets in garden behind and on grass opposite, lovely views, open all day weekends. *(Brian and Anna Marsden, Dr D J and Mrs S C Walker, David Cotterill, John Wooll)*

LITTLE BOLLINGTON
SJ7387

Swan With Two Nicks

(0161) 9282914 *2 miles from M56 junction 7 – A56 towards Lymm, then first right at Stamford Arms into Park Lane; use A556 to get back on to M56 westbound; WA14 4TJ* Extended village pub full of beams, brass, copper and bric-a-brac, some antique settles, log fire, welcoming helpful service, good choice of enjoyable food from filling baguettes up, including popular Sun lunch (best to book), several good local ales, decent wines and coffee; children and dogs welcome, tables outside, attractive hamlet by Dunham Massey (NT) deer park, walks by Bridgewater Canal, open all day. *(Don Bryan, Mike and Wena Stevenson)*

LITTLE BUDWORTH
SJ5966

Shrewsbury Arms (01829) 760240

Chester Road (A54); CW6 9EY Comfortable little Robinsons country pub, friendly and welcoming, with good well priced traditional food (smaller helpings available on some main courses); children welcome, garden overlooking farmland, open all day weekends. *(Anon)*

LITTLE LEIGH
SJ6076

Holly Bush (01606) 853196

A49 just S of A533; CW8 4QY Ancient timbered and thatched pub, spotlessly clean, with enjoyable good value food including several vegetarian options, helpful friendly staff, Tetleys and a couple of mainstream guests, restaurant; children welcome, no dogs inside, courtyard tables and garden with play

We mention bottled beers and spirits only if there is something unusual about them – imported belgian real ales, say, or dozens of malt whiskies; so do please let us know about them in your reports.

area, 14 bedrooms in converted back barn, open all day weekends. *(Christopher Mobbs, Mike and Wena Stevenson)*

LITTLE LEIGH   SJ6076
Leigh Arms (01606) 853327
A49 by swing bridge; CW8 4QT
Welcoming straightforward beamed pub next to Acton swing bridge, flagstone, tile or wood floors, interesting pictures, leather chesterfields and armchairs, country kitchen tables and chairs, good choice of well priced pub food, Robinsons and guest ales, music night Thurs; riverside garden with play area. *(Paul Humphreys)*

LOWER WHITLEY   SJ6178
Chetwode Arms (01925) 730203
Just off A49, handy for M56 junction 10; Street Lane; WA4 4EN Rambling low-beamed dining pub dating from the 17th c, good food with some south african and austrian influences including early-bird deal (before 7pm), also steaks cooked on a hot stone, welcoming efficient service, solid furnishings all clean and polished, small front bar with warm open fire, Adnams and a local guest, good wines by the glass; well behaved children allowed – but best to ask first, limited wheelchair access, bowling green, closed lunchtimes apart from Sun (may open by prearrangement).
(Roger and Gillian Holmes)

LYMM   SJ7087
Barn Owl (01925) 752020
Agden Wharf, Warrington Lane (just off B5159 E); WA13 0SW Comfortably extended popular pub in nice setting by Bridgewater Canal, Marstons and four guest ales, decent wines by the glass, reasonable choice of good value all-day pub food including OAP deals, efficient service even when busy, friendly atmosphere; children welcome, disabled facilities, may be canal trips, moorings (space for one narrow boat). *(Ben Williams, Mike and Wena Stevenson)*

MACCLESFIELD   SJ9173
Treacle Tap (01625) 615938
Sunderland Street; SK11 6JL Small one-room pub with simply furnished bare-boards interior, three interesting changing ales and good selection of bottled beers (particularly belgian and german), other drinks too, tasty locally made pies, regular events such as a book club, french, spanish, german conversation evenings, a stitch'n'bitch night and Sun quiz; children welcome till 8pm, open all day.
(John Wooll)

MACCLESFIELD   SJ9173
Waters Green Tavern
(01625) 422653 *Waters Green, opposite station; SK11 6LH* Seven quickly changing and interesting largely northern ales in roomy L-shaped open-plan local,

good value home-made lunchtime food (not Sun), friendly staff and regulars, back pool room. *(Anon)*

MOBBERLEY   SJ7879
Frozen Mop (01565) 873234
Faulkners Lane; WA16 7AL Comfortably modernised Vintage Inn, with their usual fairly priced food including set menu, real ales and plenty of wines by the glass, armchairs in lounge by bar, airy dining area with light wood furniture; children welcome, tables outside, open all day. *(Michael and Angela Prior)*

MOBBERLEY   SJ7879
Roebuck (01565) 873322
Mill Lane; down hill from sharp bend on B5085 at E edge of 30mph limit; WA16 7HX Reopened after refurbishment – reports please. *(Hilary Forrest)*

MOULDSWORTH   SJ5170
Goshawk (01928) 740900
Station Road (B5393); CH3 8AJ Comfortable family dining pub (former station hotel); mix of furniture in extensive series of rooms including small 'library' area, masses of pictures, double-sided log fire, good popular food from sandwiches to restauranty dishes, attentive cheerful uniformed staff, some enterprising wines by the glass, well kept ales such as Theakstons and Weetwood; background music, no dogs; disabled facilities, good spot near Delamere Forest with big outdoor space including play area and bowling green, open all day. *(Simon J Barber)*

NANTWICH   SJ6452
⋆Black Lion (01270) 628711
Welsh Row; CW5 5ED Old black and white building smartened up but keeping beams, timbered brickwork and open fire, good food from short interesting menu, three well kept Weetwood ales and three regularly changing guests, good service, upstairs rooms with old wooden tables and sumptuous leather sofas on undulating floors; open all day.
(Dave Webster, Sue Holland)

NANTWICH   SJ6551
Globe (01270) 623374
Audlem Road; CW5 7EA Full range of well kept Woodlands ales and a guest, ten wines by the glass, good regularly changing food all day using local produce, lunchtime deals, friendly helpful staff, comfortable open-plan layout keeping distinct areas, local artwork, newspapers and magazines, occasional live music; garden tables. *(Dave Webster, Sue Holland)*

NANTWICH   SJ6552
Leopard (01270) 480454
London Road; CW5 6LJ Victorian hunting lodge-style pub recently fully restored as Joules brewery tap, stained-glass windows,

panelling and oak floors, their ales in top condition, decent range of competitively priced pub food; terrace picnic-sets, open all day. *(Edward Leetham)*

NANTWICH   SJ6552
Vine (01270) 624172
Hospital Street; CW5 5RP Dates from 17th c, sympathetically modernised and stretching far back with old prints, books and dimly lit quiet corners, well kept Hydes Original and four guests, friendly staff and locals, lunchtime sandwiches, wraps, baked potatoes and simple hot dishes, raised seating areas; unobtrusive background music and TV; children welcome, small outside area behind, open all day. *(Steven Edgar, Clive and Fran Dutson)*

NESTON   SJ2976
Harp (0151) 336 6980
Quayside, SW of Little Neston; keep on along track at end of Marshlands Road; CH64 0TB Tucked-away two-room country local with well kept Holts and up to five interesting guests, some good malt whiskies, no food, woodburner in pretty fireplace, pale quarry tiles and simple furnishings, interesting old photographs, hatch servery in one room; children (in lounge) and dogs welcome, garden behind, picnic-sets up on front grassy bank facing Dee marshes and Wales, glorious sunsets with wild calls of wading birds, open all day. *(MLR)*

PARKGATE   SJ2778
Boathouse (0151) 336 4187
Village signed off A540; CH64 6RN Popular black and white timbered pub with attractively refurbished linked rooms, wide choice of good food from snacks up including fresh fish, cheerful attentive staff, well kept changing ales such as local Brimstage, several wines by the glass and nice coffee, big conservatory with great views to Wales over silted Dee estuary (RSPB reserve), may be egrets and kestrels. *(John and Verna Aspinall, Mike and Wena Stevenson)*

PARKGATE   SJ2778
Ship (0151) 336 3931
The Parade; CH64 6SA Bow-window estuary views from hotel's refurbished bar, well kept Marstons Pedigree with guests like Brimstage, Spitting Feathers and Woodlands, several wines by the glass and over 50 whiskies, good home-cooked food including daily specials and popular Sun roasts, afternoon tea, pleasant service, log fire, Weds quiz night; children welcome, no dogs inside,

a few tables out at front and to the side, 25 bedrooms, open all day. *(Justin Lang, Paul Whitehead, Gillian Turner, Geoff Jones)*

PLUMLEY   SJ7275
Golden Pheasant (01565) 722125
Plumley Moor Lane (off A556 by The Smoker); WA16 9RX Civilised well extended pub with good locally sourced food including Sun carvery, friendly efficient service, Lees ales, comfortable lounge areas, roomy restaurant and conservatory; children welcome, spacious gardens with play area, bowling green, six bedrooms, open all day. *(Leo and Barbara Lionet)*

PLUMLEY   SJ7075
✶ Smoker (01565) 722338
2.5 miles from M6 junction 19: A556 towards Northwich and Chester; WA16 0TY Neatly kept 400-year-old thatched coaching inn, three spotless lounges with dark panelling, deep sofas and other comfortable seats, open fires in impressive period fireplaces, generous reasonably priced bar food (all day Sun) including weekday deals, five Robinsons beers and a good choice of wines and whiskies, slick service; background music may be intrusive; children welcome away from bar, sizeable garden with roses and play area, open all day weekends. *(Lesley and Peter Barrett, Andy Dolan, Paul Humphreys, Dennis Jones, Adrian Johnson)*

RAVENSMOOR   SJ6250
Farmers Arms (01270) 623522
Barracks Lane; CW5 8PN Popular and welcoming with wide range of good fairly priced food in big dining lounge, ales such as Joules, Salopian and Woodlands, separate bar, pool room; garden with terrace and play area. *(Edward Leetham)*

SALE   SJ7890
Belmore (0161) 973 2538
Brooklands Road; M33 3QN Part of hotel but nice local feel, enjoyable food and well kept Lees ales, good friendly service; sunny garden. *(Anon)*

STOAK   SJ4273
Bunbury Arms (01244) 301665
Little Stanney Lane; a mile from M53 junction 10, A5117 W then first left; CH2 4HW Big but cosy beamed lounge with antique furniture, pictures and books, small snug, wide choice of enjoyable food (all day Sun) from sandwiches to interesting specials including fresh fish, good changing

---

'Children welcome' means the pub says it lets children inside without any special restriction. If it allows them in, but to restricted areas such as an eating area or family room, we specify this. Places with separate restaurants often let children use them, and hotels usually let children into public areas such as lounges. Some pubs impose an evening time limit — let us know if you find one earlier than 9pm.

ales, extensive wine list, open fires, board games and Mon quiz; can get busy; garden tables (some motorway noise), short walk for Shropshire Canal users from Bridge 136 or 138, handy for Cheshire Oaks shopping outlet, open all day. *(Anon)*

WHITEGATE SJ6268
Plough (01606) 889455

Foxwist Green, OS Sheet 118 map ref 624684; off A556 just W of Northwich, or A54 W of Winsford; CW8 2BP Bar/taproom and extended dining area, wide choice of good home-made food all day, cheerful efficient service, four well kept Robinsons ales and plenty of wines by the glass; background music, no under-14s or dogs inside; disabled access, a few picnic-sets out in front, more in back garden, popular walks nearby. *(James Morrell)*

WHITELEY GREEN SJ9278
Windmill (01625) 574222

Off A523 NW of Bollington; Hole House Lane; SK10 5SJ Modernised and extended open-plan pub with heavy-beamed core, good well presented food (all day weekends) from new landlord/chef, efficient friendly staff, Marstons EPA and local Storm, lots of wines by the glass, light wood furniture along with leather sofas and armchairs on stone or wood-strip floors, daily newspapers; children welcome, plenty of tables in attractive big garden, close to Middlewood Way and Macclesfield Canal (Bridge 24), open all day Fri-Sun. *(Dr Kevan Tucker)*

WILLINGTON SJ5367
⋆ **Boot** (01829) 751375

Boothsdale, off A54 at Kelsall; CW6 0NH Attractive hillside dining pub in row of converted cottages, views over Cheshire plain to Wales, popular food from pub staples to daily specials (they may ask to keep a credit card while you run a tab), Greene King and local Weetwood ales, decent wines and 30 malt whiskies, friendly staff, small opened-up unpretentiously furnished rooms, lots of original features, woodburner, extension with french windows overlooking garden, pub cats, dog and donkey; well behaved children welcome (no pushchairs), picnic-sets in front on raised suntrap terrace, open all day. *(Anon)*

WINCLE SJ9665
⋆ **Ship** (01260) 227217

Village signposted off A54 Congleton–Buxton; SK11 0QE 16th-c stone-built country pub under new management, bare-boards bar leading to carpeted dining room, old stables area with flagstones, beams, woodburner and open fire, good food from varied menu, three Lees ales and a dozen wines by the glass, quick attentive service; children and dogs welcome, tables in small side garden, good Dane Valley walks, open all day weekends, closed Mon. *(David Cotterill)*

WRENBURY SJ5947
⋆ **Dusty Miller** (01270) 780537

Cholmondeley Road; village signed from A530 Nantwich–Whitchurch; CW5 8HG Well converted 19th-c corn mill with fine canal views from gravel terrace and series of tall glazed arches in bar, spacious modern feel, comfortably furnished with tapestried banquettes, oak settles and wheelback chairs around rustic tables, quarry-tiled area by bar with oak settle and refectory table, old lift hoist up under the rafters, four Robinsons beers, farm cider, enjoyable generously served food (all day weekends), friendly staff; background music; children and dogs welcome, closed Mon, otherwise open all day. *(Rebecca Patel, Mike and Wena Stevenson, Dave Webster, Sue Holland)*

Post Office address codings give the impression that some pubs are in Cheshire, when they're really in Derbyshire (and therefore included under that chapter) or in Greater Manchester (see the Lancashire chapter).

Cornwall

Many of the pubs here are close to stunning walks or the sea and can get pretty crowded at peak holiday times – it's always best to arrive early to be sure of a seat. Places our readers have enjoyed particularly this year are the Blisland Inn at Blisland (lots to look at and honest food and drink), Trengilly Wartha at Constantine (thoughtfully run and enjoyable inn with quite a mix of customers), Old Quay in Devoran (good food and drink in light and airy pub near the quay), Gurnards Head Hotel at Gurnards Head (civilised but informal with contemporary food and comfortable bedrooms), Globe in Lostwithiel (our readers return constantly for the super food, beer and welcome), Old Coastguard in Mousehole (brasserie-style cooking, sea-view bedrooms and idyllic garden), Pandora at Mylor Bridge (lovely character pub in a stunning creekside position), Turks Head in Penzance (lively and well run town pub), Victoria at Perranuthnoe (imaginative food, a warm welcome and airy bedrooms), Blue Peter in Polperro (long-serving licensees in charming little harbour place) and Driftwood Spars at Trevaunance Cove (hands-on landlady, own-brewed beers and a cheerful mix of customers). Just three pubs here have Food Awards: the Gurnards Head Hotel, Old Coastguard and Victoria; the Victoria is also Cornwall Dining Pub 2014.

BLISLAND   SX1073   Map 1
Blisland Inn 🍺 £

Village signposted off A30 and B3266 NE of Bodmin; PL30 4JF

Village local by the green with fine choice of real ales, beer-related memorabilia, pubby food and seats outside

Our readers very much enjoy this old-fashioned, traditional pub, where the friendly licensees offer a warm welcome to both locals and visitors. Every inch of the beams and ceiling is covered with beer badges (or their particularly wide-ranging collection of mugs), and the walls are similarly filled with beer-related posters and the like. Tapped from the cask or on handpump, the ales include two brewed for the pub by Sharps – Blisland Special and Bulldog – as well as five or six quickly changing guests; also, farm cider, fruit wines and real apple juice; good service. The carpeted lounge has several barometers on the walls, toby jugs on the beams and a few standing timbers, while the family room has pool, table skittles, euchre, cribbage and dominoes; background music. Plenty of picnic-sets outside. The popular Camel Trail cycle path is close by – though the hill up to Blisland is pretty steep. As with many pubs in the area, the approach involves negotiating several single-track roads.

 Honest, home-cooked food includes lunchtime baps, whitebait, butterfly prawns with sweet and sour dip, popular sausage and mash, and ham and eggs, leek and mushroom bake, rabbit or steak in ale pies, and puddings like sticky toffee pudding and coconut treacle tart. *Benchmark main dish: home-made pies £9.95. Two-course evening meal £15.00.*

Free house ~ Licensees Gary and Margaret Marshall ~ Real ale ~ (01208) 850739 ~ Open 11.30-11.30(midnight Sat); 12-10.30 Sun ~ Bar food 12-2, 6.30-9 ~ Children in family room only ~ Dogs welcome *Recommended by John and Bernadette Elliott, P and J Shapley, Fiona Loram, B J Thompson, Paul and Karen Cornock*

BOSCASTLE
SX0991   Map 1
Cobweb
B3263, just E of harbour; PL35 0HE

Heavy beams, flagstones, lots of old jugs and bottles, a cheerful atmosphere, several real ales, straightforward food and friendly staff

This tall stone pub, very near the tiny steeply cut harbour and the pretty village, has two interesting bars. Both have heavy beams hung with hundreds of bottles and jugs, lots of pictures of bygone years, quite a mix of seats (from settles and carved chairs to more pubby furniture) and cosy log fires. They keep four real ales such as St Austell Tribute, Sharps Doom Bar, Tintagel Cornwalls Pride and a guest on handpump and a local cider, and there's a cheerful, bustling atmosphere, especially at peak times; games machine, darts, juke box and pool. The restaurant is upstairs. There are picnic-sets and benches outside, some under cover. A self-catering apartment is for rent.

 Traditional bar food includes sandwiches, chicken liver pâté with a changing compote, baked potatoes, pasties, ham or sausages with egg, lamb curry, beef stew, beer-battered fish and chips with home-made tartare sauce, mixed grill, specials such as fried chicken and tiger prawns in creamy garlic sauce, and puddings like cheesecake and crumble. *Benchmark main dish: steak in ale pie £9.80. Two-course evening meal £14.50.*

Free house ~ Licensees Ivor and Adrian Bright ~ Real ale ~ (01840) 250278 ~ Open 10.30am(12.30 Sat)-11.30pm ~ Bar food 11.30-2.30, 6-9.30 ~ Restaurant ~ Children welcome ~ Dogs allowed in bar ~ Live music Sat evening, some Sun afternoons ~ www.cobwebinn.co.uk *Recommended by John and Sharon Hancock, Lee and Liz Potter, George Atkinson*

CADGWITH
SW7214   Map 1
Cadgwith Cove Inn
Down very narrow lane off A3083 S of Helston; no nearby parking; TR12 7JX

Bustling inn at the bottom of a fishing cove with traditionally furnished bars, real ales and quite a choice of all-day food; fine coastal walks; bedrooms

Under new ownership since our last edition, this bustling place now serves food all day, takeaway meals and drinks, and offers picnic lunches to residents. The two front rooms have pubby seats and tables on parquet flooring, a log fire, lots of local photographs and memorabilia such as naval hat ribands, fancy knot-work and compass binnacles; some of the dark beams have blue spliced rope hand-holds. Otter Bitter, Sharps Doom Bar and Skinners Betty Stogs on handpump. A back bar has a huge and colourful fish mural. Seats on the good-sized front terrace look down to the fish sheds by the bay, and the comfortable bedrooms overlook the sea. The coastal walks in either direction are fantastic. It's best to park at the top of the village and meander down through the thatched cottages, but it's quite a steep hike back up again.

As well as serving breakfasts to non-residents (8.30-9.30am) and cream teas with home-made cakes, the wide-ranging menu includes sandwiches, pasties, crab tian with beetroot gazpacho, moules marinière, ham and eggs, burger with cheddar and chips, pie of the day, fish and chips with home-made tartare sauce, goats cheese tart with salad, lobster salad, mixed grill, and puddings like lemon panna cotta with strawberry compote and chocolate mousse. *Benchmark main dish: seafood medley £11.70. Two-course evening meal £18.50.*

Punch ~ Lease Garry and Helen Holmes ~ Real ale ~ (01326) 290513 ~ Open 11-midnight ~ Bar food 12-9; 12-3, 6-9 in winter ~ Children welcome ~ Dogs welcome ~ Folk night Tues, local singers Fri ~ Bedrooms: £73.70/£82.70 ~ www.cadgwithcoveinn.com *Recommended by Dr A McCormick, David and Sue Atkinson*

CONSTANTINE
Trengilly Wartha ♀ 🛏
SW7328 Map 1

Nancenoy; A3083 S of Helston, signposted Gweek near RNAS Culdrose, then fork right after Gweek; OS Sheet 204 map reference 731282; TR11 5RP

Well run inn surrounded by big gardens with a friendly welcome for all, popular food and drink and an easy-going atmosphere; bedrooms

There's always a cheerful mix of customers in this thoughtfully run, tucked away inn, and a genuine welcome from the courteous licensees and their helpful staff. The long low-beamed main bar has a sociable feel (especially in the evening when the locals drop in), all sorts of tables and chairs, a woodburning stove, cricket team photos on the walls, two ales from Dartmoor Legend, Otter Amber, Potton No Ale and Skinners Betty Stogs on handpump, up to 20 wines by the glass and 60 malt whiskies. Leading off the bar is a conservatory family room and there's also a cosy bistro. The six acres of gardens are well worth a wander and offer plenty of seats and picnic-sets under large parasols; lots of surrounding walks too. The cottagey bedrooms are comfortable and the breakfasts are very good.

Enjoyable food using local produce includes sandwiches, hot crab pot, pigeon breast with wild mushrooms on home-made granary toast, local mussels in white wine and garlic, stir-fried vegetables in filo parcel with rich tomato sauce, whole lemon sole with herb butter, duck breast with red onion and plum marmalade, and puddings such as sticky toffee pudding and a trio of brûlées. *Benchmark main dish: chicken satay £13.50. Two-course evening meal £20.00.*

Free house ~ Licensees Will and Lisa Lea ~ Real ale ~ (01326) 340332 ~ Open 11-3.15, 6-midnight ~ Bar food 12-2.15, 6-9.30 ~ Restaurant ~ Children welcome away from bar area ~ Dogs allowed in bar and bedrooms ~ Live music Weds evening ~ Bedrooms: £60/£84 ~ www.trengilly.co.uk *Recommended by J R Simmons, Guy Vowles, Chris and Angela Buckell, David and Sharon Collison, Ron and Sheila Corbett, John and Bryony Coles, Tony and Rachel Schendel*

CRAFTHOLE
Finnygook ♀
SX3654   Map 1

B3247, off A374 Torpoint road; PL11 3BQ

Carefully renovated former coaching inn with interesting furniture and décor, enjoyable food and real ales; bedrooms

There are stunning views across the Lynher and Tamar rivers through the hop-hung windows of this 15th-c former coaching inn, and good surrounding walks as the South West Coast Path is nearby. It's a civilised place and the bar has beams and joists, long, attractively cushioned wall pews and carved cushioned dining chairs around various wooden tables on stripped floorboards, and a central log fire that warms both sides of the room. There are also a couple of high wooden tables and chairs near the bar counter, black and white local photographs, big warship and other prints on the walls and, in one large window, an old compass. Cottage Duchess, St Austell Tribute and Skinners Cornish Trawler on handpump, a decent choice of wines by the glass, 15 malt whiskies and ciders. The carefully lit dining room on the other side of the building has all manner of dining chairs and tables, rugs on floorboards, an unusual log-effect gas fire in a big glass cabinet, church candles and plants, and walls hung with more black and white photographs (this time of local people, houses and beaches) and some vinyl records; there's a library at one end.

As well as a two- and three-course set lunch, there's quite a choice of good food such as baguettes, duck liver pâté with date chutney, local sardines with roasted vine tomatoes, burger with bacon, cheddar, gherkins, pickled chilli and fries, curry of the day, rabbit and mushroom ragout on tagliatelle, baked aubergine moussaka, beer-battered haddock and chips with mushy peas, crab linguine, daily specials and puddings; Wednesday is curry night. *Benchmark main dish: shellfish bowl with king prawns, mussels, clams, scallops and crab claws in ginger broth £14.00. Two-course evening meal £19.00.*

Free house ~ Licensee Max Earle ~ Real ale ~ (01503) 230338 ~ Open 12-11.30 (11 Sun); closed Mon Oct-Apr ~ Bar food 12-2.30, 6-9; all day weekends in summer ~ Restaurant ~ Children welcome ~ Dogs allowed in bar and bedrooms ~ Live music every second Fri ~ Bedrooms: £55/£75 ~ www.finnygook.co.uk *Recommended by R T and J C Moggridge, M G Hart, John and Sharon Hancock*

DEVORAN
Old Quay
SW7938   Map 1

Devoran from new Carnon Cross roundabout A39 Truro–Falmouth, left on old road, right at mini-roundabout; TR3 6NE

Light and airy bar rooms in friendly pub with four real ales, good wines by the glass, imaginative food, helpful staff and an informal atmosphere; seats on pretty back terraces; bedrooms

At the head of Restronguet Creek and next to the coast-to-coast Portreath to Devoran Mineral Tramway path, this is a welcoming place at the end of a residential terrace. The spacious bar has an interesting 'woodburner' set halfway up one wall, a cushioned window seat, wall settles and a few bar stools around just three tables on stripped boards, and bar chairs by the counter (much favoured by the friendly and chatty locals), where Bass, Otter Bitter, Sharps Doom Bar and Skinners Betty Stogs on handpump and good wines by the glass are served by cheerful, helpful staff; you can buy their own jams and chutneys. Off to the left is an airy room with black and white yacht photographs on white walls, and built-in cushioned wall seating, plush stools and a couple of big tables on the dark slate floor. On the other side of the bar is another light room with additional settles and farmhouse chairs, attractive blue and white striped cushions dotted about and more sailing photographs; darts and board games. As well as benches at the front, from where you can look down through the trees to the water, there's a series of snug little back terraces with picnic-sets and chairs and tables. Nearby parking is limited, unless you arrive early. There is wheelchair access through a side door.

As well as moreish nibbles such as home-made pork scratchings with apple sauce and home-made scotch egg, the particularly enjoyable food includes sandwiches, chicken and chorizo terrine with own-made piccalilli, mackerel fillet topped with garlic langoustine and herb oil, creamy pea and mint risotto, burgers (meat, fish, vegetarian) with cheese, bacon, onion rings and chips, seafood pasta (local crab, mussels and king prawns with chilli, ginger and coriander in thai-style coconut sauce), and puddings like lemon syllabub and bread and butter pudding with chocolate sauce. *Benchmark main dish: home-made pies (steak and kidney, chicken and ham, salmon and spinach, three cheese and red onion) £10.50. Two-course evening meal £18.00.*

Punch ~ Tenants John and Hannah Calland ~ Real ale ~ (01872) 863142 ~ Open 11-11 ~ Bar food 12-3, 6-9; all day July, Aug ~ Restaurant ~ Children welcome ~ Dogs allowed in bar ~ Bedrooms: £45/£75 ~ www.theoldquayinn.co.uk *Recommended by H Jones, Chris and Angela Buckell, Dan Thompson, Linda Pelham*

GURNARDS HEAD
SW4337 Map 1
Gurnards Head Hotel 🍴 ♀ 🛏
B3306 Zennor–St Just; TR26 3DE

Interesting, well run inn close to the sea, with real ales, lots of wines by the glass and very good inventive food; fine surrounding walks and comfortable bedrooms

'An oasis in the middle of old engine houses and ruins,' as one reader put it, is really rather apt. This civilised but informal inn just 500 metres from the Atlantic has glorious walks all around in the outstanding bleak National Trust scenery. Inside, the bar rooms are painted in bold, strong colours, there are paintings by local artists, open fires and a happy mix of wooden dining chairs and tables on stripped boards. Skinners Betty Stogs and guests like Harbour IPA, Rebel Penryn Pale Ale and a beer named for the pub from Cornish Crown on handpump, ten wines by the glass and a couple of ciders; background music, darts and board games. There are seats in the large back garden, and the comfortable bedrooms have views of the rugged moors or the sea. This is under the same ownership as the civilised Griffin at Felinfach (see Wales) and Old Coastguard in Mousehole, also in Cornwall.

Using local, seasonal produce, the impressive food includes carpaccio of local beef, white crab salad with pear and avocado, beetroot risotto with walnuts and blue cheese, line-caught cod with leek, apricot, cashew, lime and coriander curry, pork with creamy mash, faggot and onion, lamb rump with parsley risotto, confit garlic and oyster mushrooms, ray wing with spinach, cockles and vermouth cream, and puddings such as vanilla rice pudding with rhubarb and honeycomb and passion-fruit crème brûlée with orange shortbread; they also offer a two- and three-course set lunch. *Benchmark main dish: fresh fish of the day £16.00. Two-course evening meal £22.50.*

Free house ~ Licensees Charles and Edmund Inkin ~ Real ale ~ (01736) 796928 ~ Open
11-11 ~ Bar food 12-2.30, 6(6.30 in winter)-9.30 ~ Restaurant ~ Children welcome ~
Dogs allowed in bar and bedrooms ~ local singers Mon evening ~ Bedrooms: £85/£100 ~
www.gurnardshead.co.uk *Recommended by Stephen Shepherd, Robert Wivell, Bruce and Sharon
Eden, Paul Holmes, M A Borthwick, Di and Mike Gillam, Richard Tilbrook, Andrea Rampley, David
and Katharine Cooke, Clifford Blakemore*

HELSTON   SW6522   Map 1
Halzephron ♀ 🛏
*Gunwalloe, village about 4 miles S but not marked on many road maps; look
for brown sign on A3083 alongside perimeter fence of RNAS Culdrose; TR12 7QB*

**Bustling pub in lovely spot with tasty bar food, local beers; bedrooms;
good nearby walks**

Friendly new licensees have taken over this bustling inn – which,
usefully, is now open all day. The neatly kept bar and dining areas
have an informal, friendly atmosphere, comfortable seating, a warm
winter fire in the woodburning stove and St Austell Proper Job, Sharps
Doom Bar and Skinners Betty Stogs on handpump, ten wines by the
glass and quite a few malt whiskies. The dining gallery seats up to 30
people; darts and board games. Picnic-sets outside look across National
Trust fields and countryside, and there are lovely coastal walks in both
directions. Gunwalloe fishing cove is just 300 metres away and Church
Cove with its sandy beach is nearby – as is the church of St Winwaloe
(built into the dunes on the seashore).

Well thought of food includes sandwiches, seafood chowder, roast brie with
garlic and red onion marmalade, wild boar sausages with red wine gravy,
butternut squash and leek crumble, chicken stuffed with crab, sea bream with garlic
butter, bass with mediterranean vegetables and sautéed potatoes, and puddings such
as bread and butter pudding and raspberry vacherin. *Benchmark main dish: crab
cakes with sweet chilli dip £14.50. Two-course evening meal £20.00.*

Free house ~ Licensee Claire Murray ~ Real ale ~ (01326) 240406 ~ Open 10.30am-
11pm; 12-10.30 Sun ~ Bar food 12-2(3 Sun), 6-9 ~ Restaurant ~ Children welcome ~
Dogs allowed in bar ~ Bedrooms: £55/£94 ~ www.halzephron-inn.co.uk
*Recommended by Bryan and Helen Lee, David and Sue Smith, Stephen and Jean Curtis,
P J Checksfield, Paul Rampton, Julie Harding, Nigel Morton, Dave Webster, Sue Holland*

LOSTWITHIEL   SX1059   Map 1
Globe ♀ 🍺
North Street (close to medieval bridge); PL22 0EG

**Unassuming bar in traditional local, interesting food and drinks and
friendly staff; suntrap back courtyard with outside heaters**

This particularly well run town pub is the sort of place customers
return to again and again. The food and ales are consistently good,
there's a cheerful, bustling atmosphere and genuinely friendly staff.
The unassuming bar is long and somewhat narrow, with a mix of pubby
tables and seats, photographs of locals on pale green plank panelling at
one end, nice largely local prints (for sale) on canary yellow walls above
a coal-effect stove at the snug inner end, and a small red-walled front
alcove. The ornately carved bar counter, with comfortable chrome and
leatherette stools, dispenses Sharps Doom Bar, Skinners Betty Stogs
and a changing guest on handpump, plus 11 reasonably priced wines
by the glass, 20 malt whiskies and two local ciders; background music,

darts, board games and TV. The sheltered back courtyard is not large, but has some attractive and unusual plants and is a real suntrap (with an extendable overhead awning and outside heaters). You can park in nearby streets or the (free) town car park. The 13th-c church is worth a look and the ancient river bridge, a few metres away, is lovely.

Reliably good, extremely popular food includes moules marinière, mushrooms topped with stilton and baked in port sauce, home-made pie of the day, pork and leek sausages with mash and onion gravy, much loved posh home-made 'fish fingers' with mushy peas and tartare sauce, chilli con carne, specials such as vegetarian roast, a smashing fish pie or honey-roast duck breast with port and redcurrant sauce and sautéed potatoes, and puddings like ginger and black treacle sponge with custard and banoffi pie. *Benchmark main dish: bass stuffed with pesto and wrapped in prosciutto with mediterranean vegetables £14.95. Two-course evening meal £20.00.*

Free house ~ Licensee William Erwin ~ Real ale ~ (01208) 872501 ~ Open 12-2.30, 6(5 Fri)-11(midnight Fri, Sat) ~ Bar food 12-2, 6.30-9 ~ Restaurant ~ Children welcome but no pushchairs in restaurant ~ Dogs allowed in bar ~ Live music Fri evening ~ Bedrooms: /£70 ~ www.globeinn.com *Recommended by R K Phillips, R T and J C Moggridge, B and M Kendall, Peter Salmon, Mr and Mrs Richard Osborne, Dr and Mrs S G Barber*

MOUSEHOLE   SW4726   Map 1

Old Coastguard ⑪ ♀ 🛏
The Parade (edge of village, Newlyn coast road); TR19 6PR

Lovely position for carefully refurbished inn, with a civilised, friendly atmosphere, character furnishings, a good choice of wines and first rate food; bedrooms with sea views

In warm weather, the garden behind this well run place is delightful – seats on the terrace overlook Mount's Bay and St Clement's Island, tropical palms and dracaenas, and a path leads down to rock pools. The bar rooms have boldly coloured walls hung with paintings of local scenes and sailing boats, stripped floorboards and an atmosphere of informal but civilised comfort. The Upper Deck houses the bar and the restaurant, with a nice mix of antique dining chairs around oak and distressed pine tables, lamps on big barrel tables and chairs to either side of the log fire, topped by a vast bressumer beam. There's St Austell and Skinners beers on handpump and a good choice of wine in bottle, carafe and two glass sizes. The Lower Deck has glass windows running the length of the building, several deep sofas and armchairs, and shelves of books and games. Most of the comfortable bedrooms overlook the water. This is sister pub to the Gurnards Head (also Cornwall) and the Griffin at Felinfach (Wales).

Interesting, brasserie-style food includes scallops with curry and herb butter, chicken and leek terrine with creamy walnut vinaigrette, caramelised onion, potato and blue cheese tart, roast chicken with braised leeks, wild mushrooms and roasting juices, beef skirt with vegetable and herb broth and horseradish, duck confit with puy lentils and herb dressing, plaice with spinach and a mussel and parsley ragout, and puddings like brown sugar cheesecake with figs and madeira and hot chocolate pudding with marmalade ice-cream and pistachios; they also offer a two- and three-course set lunch (not Sunday). *Benchmark main dish: fresh fish dishes £16.00. Two-course evening meal £19.00.*

Free house ~ Licensees Charles and Edmund Inkin ~ Real ale ~ (01736) 731222 ~ Open 11-11 ~ Bar food 12-2.30, 6-9.30(9 in winter) ~ Children welcome ~ Dogs welcome ~ Light jazz monthly Sun afternoon ~ Bedrooms: £70/£110 ~ www.oldcoastguardhotel.co.uk *Recommended by Richard and Penny Gibbs*

MOUSEHOLE
Ship 🛏

SW4626 Map 1

Harbourside; TR19 6QX

Bustling harbourside local in pretty village

Just across the road from the harbour in a lovely village, this is a
bustling local with a welcoming, pubby atmosphere. The opened-up
main bar, where fishermen and other regulars enjoy the St Austell HSD,
Trelawny and Tribute on handpump, has black beams and panelling, and
built-in wooden wall benches and stools around low tables; also, sailors'
fancy ropework, granite flagstones and a cosy open fire. Several wines
by the glass and maybe background music. Six of the comfortable, airy
bedrooms overlook the sea. It's best to park at the top of the village and
walk down (traffic can be a bit of a nightmare in summer). The elaborate
harbour lights at Christmas are worth seeing.

Well liked bar food includes sandwiches and baked potatoes, moules
marinière, citrus tiger prawns with sweet chilli, honey-roast ham and
egg, burger topped with cheddar and onion rings, fresh fishcakes with shellfish
mayonnaise, lamb stew in rich tomato and cider gravy, fresh local seasonal crab
salad and puddings. *Benchmark main dish: beer-battered fresh fish £10.50.
Two-course evening meal £17.00.*

St Austell ~ Manager Melanie Matthews ~ Real ale ~ (01736) 731234 ~ Open
11am-11.30pm; 11-10.30 Sun ~ Bar food 12-2.30, 6-8.30; 12-3, 6-9 in summer ~ Restaurant
~ Children welcome ~ Dogs allowed in bar and bedrooms ~ Bedrooms: £90/£105 ~
www.shipinnmousehole.co.uk *Recommended by Isobel Mackinlay*

MYLOR BRIDGE
Pandora ♀

SW8137 Map 1

*Restronguet Passage: from A39 in Penryn, take turning signposted Mylor
Church, Mylor Bridge, Flushing and go straight through Mylor Bridge following
Restronguet Passage signs; or from A39 further N, at or near Perranarworthal, take
turning signposted Mylor, Restronguet, then follow Restronguet Weir signs, but turn
left downhill at Restronguet Passage sign; TR11 5ST*

**Beautifully placed waterside inn with seats on long floating pontoon,
lots of atmosphere in beamed and flagstoned rooms, and some sort of
food all day**

As ever, this lovely medieval thatched pub gets full marks from our
readers. Its sheltered waterside position is hard to beat on a warm
day, so you must arrive early to bag one of the picnic-sets on the long
floating jetty or just beside the front door; many customers arrive by
boat at high tide. Inside, several rambling, interconnecting rooms have
low wooden ceilings (mind your head on some of the beams), beautifully
polished big flagstones, cosy alcoves with leatherette benches built into
the walls, old racing posters, model boats in glass cabinets, and three
large log fires in high hearths (to protect against tidal floods). St Austell
HSD, Proper Job, Trelawny and Tribute on handpump and a dozen wines
by the glass. The upstairs dining room has exposed oak vaults and dark
tables and chairs on pale oak flooring. Because of the pub's popularity,
parking is extremely difficult at peak times; wheelchair access.

Some sort of food is served all day, including afternoon cream teas, with
produce from cornish fishermen and farmers: sandwiches, wild mushroom
and chicken liver terrine with citrus and herb butter, seared scallops and smoked
salmon with tarragon aioli dressing, chargrilled chicken caesar salad, vegetable and

chickpea curry, burger with bacon, wholegrain mustard coleslaw and chips, beer-battered fish of the day with mushy peas and home-made tartare sauce, peppered pork chop with honey and sweet potato mash, toasted pistachios and madeira sauce, and puddings such as chocolate and crème fraîche marquise and baked vanilla egg custard tart with blackcurrant liquorice poached pear and blackcurrant sorbet. *Benchmark main dish: steamed mussels in white wine, garlic and cream £14.00. Two-course evening meal £20.00.*

St Austell ~ Tenant John Milan ~ Real ale ~ (01326) 372678 ~ Open 10.30am-11pm ~ Bar food 12-9.30 ~ Restaurant ~ Children welcome away from bar area ~ Dogs allowed in bar ~ www.pandorainn.com *Recommended by David Crook, Andrea Rampley, John Marsh, Chris and Angela Buckell, Pat and Tony Martin, R Elliott*

 PENZANCE   SW4730   Map 1

Turks Head

At top of main street, by big domed building (Lloyds TSB), turn left down Chapel Street; TR18 4AF

Cheerfully run pub with a good, bustling atmosphere and popular food and beer

For both us at the *Guide* and our readers, this bustling town pub has always been a favourite. It's just the place to drop into on a wet and windy day – there's always a lively mix of locals and visitors, and the landlord and his staff offer a friendly welcome to all. The bar has old flat-irons, jugs and so forth hanging from beams, pottery above the wood-effect panelling, wall seats and tables and a couple of elbow-rests around central pillars; background music. Sharps Doom Bar, Skinners Betty Stogs and a changing guest beer on handpump and several wines by the glass. The suntrap back garden has big urns of flowers. There's been a Turks Head here for over 700 years, though most of the original building was destroyed by a Spanish raiding party in the 16th c.

Well liked bar food includes lunchtime sandwiches, ham hock terrine with chutney, tiger prawns in sweet chilli sauce, burger with creamy coleslaw, salad and chips, pork and leek sausages with caramelised red onion gravy, lasagne, moules marinière, beer-battered fish and chips, specials like sunblush tomatoes, pepper and spinach tagliatelle in creamy pesto sauce or lamb shank in redcurrant and mint jus with roasted root vegetables, and puddings. *Benchmark main dish: sizzling tandoori monkfish £11.95. Two-course evening meal £18.00.*

Punch ~ Lease Jonathan and Helen Gibbard ~ Real ale ~ (01736) 363093 ~ Open 11.30-midnight; 12-midnight Sun ~ Bar food 12-2, 7-9 ~ Restaurant ~ Children welcome ~ Dogs welcome ~ www.turksheadpenzance.co.uk *Recommended by Trevor Graveson, David Crook, Robert Wivell, Alan Johnson*

 PERRANUTHNOE   SW5329   Map 1

Victoria ♙

Signed off A394 Penzance–Helston; TR20 9NP

Cornwall Dining Pub of the Year

Carefully furnished inn close to Mount's Bay beaches, friendly welcome, local beers, interesting fresh food and seats in pretty garden; bedrooms

With particularly good food and a warm welcome, this well run place gets consistently enthusiastic reports from our readers. The L-shaped bar has a bustling atmosphere, a cheerful mix of customers, an attractive array of dining chairs around wooden tables on oak flooring, various cosy corners, exposed joists and a woodburning stove; also, china plates, all sorts of artwork on the walls and fresh flowers. The restaurant is separate. Sharps Doom Bar and Skinners Betty Stogs on handpump and several wines by the glass; background music, and Bailey the pub labrador. The pretty tiered garden has white metal furniture under green parasols, and the beaches of Mount's Bay are a short stroll away. There are light and airy bedrooms, plus a cottage to rent in nearby St Hilary.

Imaginative and very good, the food might include tempura of local ling and tiger prawns with spicy vegetable salsa, duck liver and port pâté with spiced pear, apple and raisin chutney, local mussel risotto with parsley and parmesan, ham with free-range eggs and home-made tomato ketchup, roast sirloin of beef with bubble and squeak potato cake, poached free-range egg and horseradish cream, cod with herbs, savoy cabbage and bacon, and puddings like sticky ginger pudding with apple compote, toffee sauce and calvados ice-cream and rhubarb, apple and almond crumble with Amaretto ice-cream. *Benchmark main dish: slow-cooked local pork with black pudding, dauphinoise potatoes and apple sauce £14.95. Two-course evening meal £21.00.*

Pubfolio ~ Lease Anna and Stewart Eddy ~ Real ale ~ (01736) 710309 ~ Open 12-2.30, 5.30-midnight; 12-2.30 Sun; closed Sun evening and winter Mon ~ Bar food 12-2, 6-9; 12-3 Sun ~ Restaurant ~ Children welcome ~ Dogs allowed in bar ~ Bedrooms: $50/$75 ~ www.victoriainn-penzance.co.uk *Recommended by S Chaudhuri, Robert Wivell, Paul and Claudia Dickinson, Bruce and Sharon Eden, Paul Holmes, Evelyn and Derek Walter, R and S Bentley*

PERRANWELL
SW7739 Map 1

Royal Oak ♀

Village signposted off A393 Redruth–Falmouth and A39 Falmouth–Truro; TR3 7PX

Welcoming and relaxed, with well liked food and real ales

This is a fine little pub surrounded by plenty of walks and cycle tracks. The roomy, carpeted bar has a relaxed atmosphere, horsebrasses and pewter and china mugs on black beams and joists, plates and country pictures on cream-painted stone walls, and cosy wall and other seats around candlelit tables. It rambles around beyond a big stone fireplace (with a winter log fire) into a snug little nook of a room, with just a couple more tables. Sharps Doom Bar and IPA and Skinners Betty Stogs on handpump, as well as good wines by the glass and farm cider.

Under the new licensees, the popular food (listed on oak tree-shaped boards) includes lunchtime sandwiches, terrine of the day with chutney, scallops with sherry, cream and chorizo, a tapas plate, beer-battered cod with chips, seafood pie, pork tenderloin with thyme, cream and capers, hake fillet with herb butter, chicken stew with chorizo, confit duck, and puddings such as caramel apple pie and hot chocolate brownie with ice-cream. *Benchmark main dish: crab bake topped with breadcrumbs and cheese £12.25. Two-course evening meal £20.00.*

Free house ~ Licensees Tim Cairns and Lizzie Archer ~ Real ale ~ (01872) 863175 ~ Open 11-3, 6-11; 12-4, 6-11 Sun ~ Bar food 12-2.30, 6.30-9.30 ~ Restaurant ~ Children welcome ~ Dogs allowed in bar *Recommended by Stephen Shepherd, Jim Banwell, Chris and Angela Buckell, John Marsh, Gene and Tony Freemantles*

We say if we know a pub allows dogs.

POLKERRIS

SX0952 Map 1

Rashleigh

Signposted off A3082 Fowey–St Austell; PL24 2TL

Lovely beachside spot, with heaters on sizeable sun terrace, five real ales and quite a choice of food

The position of this friendly pub is really splendid. There's a front terrace with seats under a big awning, heaters and marvellous views across St Austell and Mevagissey bays; a fine beach with restored jetty is just a few steps away. Inside is a cosy bar with comfortably cushioned chairs around dark wooden tables at the front, and similar furnishings, local photographs on the walls and a winter log fire at the back. Otter Bitter, Skinners Betty Stogs, Timothy Taylors Landlord, Wells & Youngs Special and Wooden Hand Pirates Gold on handpump, several wines by the glass, two farm ciders and organic soft drinks. All the tables in the restaurant have a sea view. There's plenty of parking either in the pub's own car park or the large village one. The local section of the Cornish Coastal Path is renowned for its striking scenery.

Popular food includes ciabatta sandwiches (the open crab one is lovely), chicken liver pâté with spiced pear chutney, thai-style crab cakes with sweet chilli mayonnaise, butternut squash, beetroot and crème fraîche tart, steak in ale pie, trio of local sausages with creamy mash and caramelised onion gravy, grilled chicken breast topped with bacon, barbecue sauce and cheddar with home-made coleslaw, and puddings. *Benchmark main dish: beer-battered cod with chips and home-made tartare sauce £9.95. Two-course evening meal £17.00.*

Free house ~ Licensees Jon and Samantha Spode ~ Real ale ~ (01726) 813991 ~ Open 11-11 ~ Bar food 12-3, 6-9; afternoon cream teas and snacks ~ Restaurant ~ Children welcome ~ Dogs allowed in bar ~ www.therashleighinnpolkerris.co.uk
Recommended by David and Sue Atkinson, Paul Rampton, Julie Harding, Paul and Karen Cornock, Dave Webster, Sue Holland, Di and Mike Gillam, Ian Herdman

POLPERRO

SX2050 Map 1

Blue Peter £

Quay Road; PL13 2QZ

Friendly pub overlooking pretty harbour, with fishing paraphernalia, paintings by local artists and carefully prepared food

Overlooking the small working harbour, this bustling little pub is just the place to shelter in inclement weather. The charming licensees and their staff welcome all customers and there's always a happy mix of locals and visitors. The cosy low-beamed bar with its solid wood bar counter has a chatty, relaxed atmosphere, St Austell Tribute, Sharps Special and guests like Bays Gold, Cornish Crown St Michaels Bitter and O'Hanlons Port Stout on handpump, and traditional furnishings that include a small winged settle and a polished pew on the wooden floor, photographs and pictures by local artists, fishing regalia and lots of candles. A window seat has views of the harbour, another looks out past rocks to the sea. Families must use the upstairs room; background music. There are a few seats outside on the terrace and more upstairs in an amphitheatre-style area. It gets crowded at peak times. They have a cash machine (there's no bank in the village).

Deserving a Bargain Award for offering several dishes under £10 (mainly for lunch), the popular food here includes lunchtime sandwiches, wraps and baguettes, fish and shellfish soup, chicken liver pâté with red onion chutney, local crab linguine with garlic and chilli, moroccan mushrooms with chickpeas, tomatoes and onions, chicken fajitas, goan curry, gammon with egg and pineapple, and puddings. *Benchmark main dish: beer-battered fish and chips £9.95. Two-course evening meal £16.00.*

Free house ~ Licensees Steve and Caroline Steadman ~ Real ale ~ (01503) 272743 ~ Open 11-11; 12-10.30 Sun ~ Bar food 12-2.30, 6.30-8.30; food all day from 9am peak season ~ Children in upstairs family room only ~ Dogs allowed in bar ~ Live music weekends ~ www.thebluepeter.co.uk *Recommended by Richard Tilbrook, Ruth Mann, Adrian Johnson, Peter Thornton*

 PORT ISAAC   SX0080   Map 1

Port Gaverne Inn 🛏

Port Gaverne signposted from Port Isaac and from B3314 E of Pendoggett; PL29 3SQ

Busy small hotel near the sea and fine cliff walks, with a lively bar, plenty of locals and well liked food and drink; bedrooms

Although the hotel side of this 17th-c inn is very popular, what our readers enjoy is the bustling bar, which is always full of lively locals. The bar has a relaxed atmosphere, low beams, flagstones and carpeting, some exposed stone and a big log fire; the lounge has interesting old local photographs. You can eat in the bar or the 'Captain's Cabin'– a little room where everything is shrunk to scale (old oak chest, model sailing ship, even the prints on the white stone walls). St Austell Tribute, Sharps Doom Bar, Cornish Coaster and maybe a guest beer such as Fullers London Pride on handpump, a decent choice of wines and several whiskies; cribbage and dominoes. There are seats in the terraced garden and splendid clifftop walks all around.

🍴 Bar food includes sandwiches, calamari with lemon and garlic mayonnaise, smoked mackerel pâté with salad, ham and eggs, wild mushroom and garlic tagliatelle in cream sauce, pie of the week, local crab salad, pork escalopes with prosciutto, sage, white wine and madeira, baked guinea fowl with port jus, whole grilled dover sole with herb butter, and puddings. *Benchmark main dish: beer-battered haddock with chips £10.50. Two-course evening meal £18.00.*

Free house ~ Licensee Graham Sylvester ~ Real ale ~ (01208) 880244 ~ Open 11-11; 12-10.30 Sun ~ Bar food 12.30-2(2.30 in holiday season), 6.30-9 ~ Restaurant ~ Children welcome ~ Dogs welcome ~ Bedrooms: £75/£120 ~ www.port-gaverne-hotel.co.uk *Recommended by Mike and Shirley Stratton, John and Bernadette Elliott, R T and J C Moggridge, Clifford Blakemore, Barry and Anne*

 PORTHTOWAN   SW6948   Map 1

Blue

Beach Road, East Cliff; car park (fee in season) advised; TR4 8AW

Informal, busy bar right by wonderful beach with modern food and drinks; lively staff and customers

This bustling bar – certainly not a traditional pub – is right beside a fantastic beach, and attracts a wide mix of cheerful customers from serious surfers to dog walkers to families. The atmosphere is easy and informal, and big picture windows look across the terrace to the huge expanse of sand and sea. The front bay windows have built-in pine seats, while the rest of the large room has chrome and wicker chairs around plain wooden tables on a stripped-wood floor, several bar stools and plenty of standing space around the counter; powder blue-painted walls, ceiling fans, some big ferny plants; fairly quiet background music, pool table. St Austell Tribute and Skinners Betty Stogs on handpump, several wines by the glass, cocktails and shots, and all kinds of coffees, hot chocolates and teas served by perky, helpful young staff.

🍴 Starting with brunch at 10am, they serve food all day: starters to share include various nachos and chips with dips like chilli jam, aioli, hummus, and sour cream with chives, four stone-baked pizzas with lots of extra toppings, meat and vegetarian burgers, fajitas, beer-battered fish with minted pea purée and tasty daily specials. *Benchmark main dish: burger with mushroom and blue cheese sauce and chips £10.00. Two-course evening meal £16.50.*

Free house ~ Licensees Tara Roberts and Luke Morris ~ Real ale ~ (01209) 890329 ~ Open 10am-11pm(10pm Sun) ~ Bar food 10-9 ~ Children welcome ~ Dogs allowed in bar ~ Acoustic music Sat evening ~ www.blue-bar.co.uk *Recommended by David Crook, David and Sue Smith, John Marsh*

ST MERRYN
Cornish Arms
SW8874   Map 1

Churchtown (B3276 towards Padstow); PL28 8ND

Busy roadside pub, liked by locals and holidaymakers, with bar and dining rooms, real ales, pubby food, friendly service and seats outside

Once the summer crowds have gone, this bustling roadside pub returns to being a local again with plenty of regulars and euchre teams. The main door leads into a sizeable, informal area with a pool table, plenty of cushioned wall seating and a shelf of paperbacks; to the left is a light, airy dining room overlooking the terrace. There's an unusual upright modern woodburner with tightly packed logs on each side, photographs of the sea and former games teams, and pale wooden dining chairs around tables on quarry tiles. You can walk from here to two more linked rooms with ceiling joists; the first has pubby furniture on huge flagstones, an open fire in a stone fireplace and black and white photographs, while the end room has more cushioned wall seating, contemporary seats and tables and parquet flooring. St Austell Proper Job, Trelawny and Tribute on handpump, friendly service, background music and TV. In summer, the window boxes are pretty and there are picnic-sets on a side terrace and more on grass.

🍴 Popular food might include sandwiches, pork and herb terrine with beetroot chutney, piri-piri prawns, ham and egg, lamb curry, pork sausages with mash and onion gravy, grilled cod with mushy peas and tartare sauce, burger with cheese and chipotle relish, and puddings such as apple pie and treacle tart; Saturday is steak night. *Benchmark main dish: mussels and chips £12.50. Two-course evening meal £18.00.*

St Austell ~ Tenant Luke Taylor ~ Real ale ~ (01841) 532700 ~ Open 11.30-11 ~ Bar food 12-2, 6-9 ~ Restaurant ~ Children welcome ~ Dogs welcome ~ www.rickstein.com/the-cornish-arms.html *Recommended by Robert Watt, Chris and Val Ramstedt*

'Children welcome' means the pub says it lets children inside without any special restriction. If it allows them in, but to restricted areas such as an eating area or family room, we specify this. Some pubs may impose an evening time limit. We do not mention limits after 9pm as we assume children are home by then.

TREVAUNANCE COVE   SW7251 Map 1
Driftwood Spars
Off B3285 in St Agnes; Quay Road; TR5 0RT

Friendly old inn, with plenty of history, own-brew beers and wide range of other drinks, popular food and beach nearby; attractive bedrooms

Originally a marine warehouse and fish cellar, this deservedly busy pub is run by a hands-on, hardworking landlady. Just up the lane from a dramatic cove and beach, it always has a wide mix of customers including families, walkers with their dogs and surfers. The bustling bars are timbered with massive spars (the masts of great sailing ships, many of which were wrecked along this coast), and there are dark wooden farmhouse and tub chairs and settles around a mix of tables, padded bar stools by the counter, old ship prints, lots of nautical and wreck memorabilia and woodburning stoves. It's said that an old smugglers' tunnel leads from behind the bar up through the cliff. Seven real ales on handpump might include their own Driftwood Bolsters Blood, Bawden Rocks and Montol, Otter Bright, Rebel Henri and Sharps Doom Bar; they hold two beer festivals a year. Also, 30 malt whiskies, ten rums, seven gins and several wines by the glass; table football and pool. The modern dining room overlooks the cove; service is friendly and helpful. There are pretty summer hanging baskets, seats in the garden and many of the attractive bedrooms overlook the coast.

Using local, seasonal produce, the highly rated food includes sandwiches, several platters, chicken liver terrine with ale chutney, moules marinière, burger topped with emmenthal and shallot chutney with chips, honey-roasted ham and free-range eggs, crab linguine with lemon, chilli and artichokes, sausages with onion gravy and creamy mash, roasted vegetable lasagne, fish pie, and puddings like crème brûlée with home-made shortbread biscuit and chocolate and Grand Marnier. *Benchmark main dish: beer-battered fish and chips £9.95. Two-course evening meal £16.00.*

Own brew ~ Licensee Louise Treseder ~ Real ale ~ (01872) 552428 ~ Open 11-11 (1am Sat); 11-10.30 Sun ~ Bar food 12-2.30, 6.30-9 ~ Restaurant ~ Children welcome away from bar ~ Dogs welcome ~ Live music Sat evening ~ Bedrooms: £50/£86 ~ www.driftwoodspars.com *Recommended by Michael and Maggie Betton, David and Sharon Collison, John Marsh*

WAINHOUSE CORNER   SX1895 Map 1
Old Wainhouse
A39; EX23 0BA

Usefully open and serving food all day, this cheerful pub has friendly staff, a good mix of customers, plenty of seating, real ales and good food

As this cream-painted and black-shuttered place is close to the South West Coast Path, it's handy for walkers that food is available all day. The main bar has an easy-going, cheerful atmosphere, an attractive built-in settle, stripped rustic farmhouse chairs and dining chairs around a mix of tables on enormous old flagstones, a large woodburner with stone bottles on the mantelpiece above it, and beams hung with scythes, saws, a horse collar and other tack, spiles, copper pans and brass plates; do note the lovely photograph of a man driving a pig across a bridge. Off from here is a simpler room with similar furniture, pool table, flat-screen

TV and background music. The dining room to left of the main door has elegant high-backed dining chairs around pale wooden tables, another woodburner and more horse tack. Sharps Cornish and Doom Bar on handpump and friendly service. Outside, there's a grass area to one side with picnic-sets. Bedrooms are clean and comfortable.

Being a local farming family, the licensees are keen to use only produce from the area: chicken liver parfait with onion jam, thai scallop salad, beer-battered pollock with home-made tartare sauce, red wine and blue cheese risotto with spiced walnuts, tarragon-stuffed chicken breast wrapped in parma ham with jerusalem artichoke purée and red wine sauce, and puddings such as apple and cherry crumble and crème brûlée. *Benchmark main dish: chargrilled rump steak with home-made fries £12.50. Two-course evening meal £18.50.*

Enterprise ~ Lease Peter Owen ~ Real ale ~ (01840) 230711 ~ Open 10-midnight ~ Bar food 10-9 ~ Restaurant ~ Children welcome ~ Dogs welcome ~ Bedrooms: £50/£80 ~ www.oldwainhouseinn.co.uk *Recommended by Reg Fowle, Helen Rickwood*

Also Worth a Visit in Cornwall

Besides the fully inspected pubs, you might like to try these pubs that have been recommended to us and described by readers. Do tell us what you think of them: feedback@goodguides.com

ALTARNUN SX2280
Kings Head (01566) 86241
Five Lanes; PL15 7RX Old stone-built beamed roadside pub, Greene King Abbot, Skinners Betty Stogs and a couple of guests, real ciders, reasonably priced pubby food from sandwiches and baguettes up including good Sun carvery, carpeted lounge with big log fire, slate-floored restaurant and public bar with another fire; darts, pool and TV; children and dogs welcome, picnic-sets on front terrace and in garden behind, four bedrooms, open all day. *(John Marsh)*

ALTARNUN SX2083
⋆**Rising Sun** (01566) 86636
NW; village signed off A39 just W of A395 junction; PL15 7SN Tucked-away 16th-c pub with traditionally furnished L-shaped main bar, low beams, slate flagstones, coal fires, good choice of food including excellent local seafood and generous Sun roasts, Penpont and Skinners ales, farm cider, good friendly service; background music; dogs and well behaved children allowed in bar but not restaurant, seats on suntrap terrace and in garden, pétanque, camping field, beautiful church in nice village, open all day weekends. *(John and Bernadette Elliott, David Crook)*

BODINNICK SX1352
Old Ferry (01726) 870237
Across the water from Fowey; coming by road, to avoid the ferry queue, turn left as you go downhill – car park on left before pub; PL23 1LX Old inn (new management) just up from the river with lovely views from terrace, dining room and

some of the 12 bedrooms; traditional bar with nautical memorabilia, old photographs and woodburner, back room hewn into the rock, well kept Sharps, enjoyable food from lunchtime sandwiches up including children's menu; good circular walks, lane by pub in front of ferry slipway is extremely steep and parking limited, open all day. *(B and M Kendall, Dave Webster, Sue Holland, Peter J and Avril Hanson, Di and Mike Gillam)*

BOSCASTLE SX0990
⋆**Napoleon** (01840) 250204
High Street, top of village; PL35 0BD Welcoming 16th-c thick-walled white cottage at top of steep quaint village (fine views halfway up); slate floors and cosy rooms on different levels including small evening bistro, oak beams and log fires, interesting Napoleon prints and lots of knick-knacks, good food from daily changing menu, well kept St Austell tapped from casks, decent wines and coffee, traditional games; background music – live Fri, sing-along Tues; children and dogs welcome, small covered terrace and large sheltered garden, open all day. *(Clifford Blakemore, Wilburoo, David Crook, Stanley and Annie Matthews)*

BOTALLACK SW3632
⋆**Queens Arms** (01736) 788318
B3306; TR19 7QG Friendly old pub with good home-made food including local seafood, meat sourced within 3 miles, well kept Sharps and Skinners, good service, log fires (one in unusual granite inglenook), dark wood furniture, tin mining and other old local photographs on stripped-stone walls, family extension; dogs welcome, tables out in front and pleasant back garden, wonderful cliff-top

walks nearby, lodge accommodation, open all day. *(J D O Carter, David and Sue Smith, Richard Tilbrook)*

BREAGE   SW6128
⋆ **Queens Arms** (01326) 573485
3 miles W of Helston just off A394; TR13 9PD Friendly chatty pub with L-shaped bar and smallish restaurant, seven well kept ales including Cornish Chough, Sharps and Skinners, farm cider, decent wines by the glass, good well priced food from baguettes with cornish brie and cranberry to seafood and steaks, good helpful service, warming coal fires, plush banquettes, brass-topped tables, daily papers, games area with pool; background music; children and dogs welcome, some picnic-sets outside, covered smokers' area, two bedrooms, medieval wall paintings in church opposite, open all day Sun. *(Dennis Jenkin, Pat and Tony Martin)*

BUDE   SS2006
Brendon Arms (01288) 354542
Falcon Terrace; EX23 8SD Popular pub (particularly in summer) near canal, two big friendly pubby bars and back family room, well kept ales such as St Austell and Sharps, decent wines by the glass, enjoyable food from doorstep sandwiches up, bargain OAP lunch Tues, nice coffee and maybe hot spicy apple juice, good cheery service; juke box, sports TV, pool and darts; dogs allowed in public bar, disabled access, picnic-sets on front grass, heated smokers' shelter, bedrooms and holiday apartments, good walks nearby. *(Dennis Jenkin, John Marsh, Mike and Wena Stevenson)*

BUDE   SS2006
Falcon (01288) 352005
Breakwater Road; EX23 8SD Popular 19th-c hotel overlooking canal, enjoyable good value food in carpeted bar with lots of plush banquettes and fire, good friendly service, well kept St Austell ales, restaurant; attractive well maintained gardens, comfortable bedrooms, good breakfast. *(Ryta Lyndley)*

CALLINGTON   SX3569
Bulls Head (01579) 383387
Fore Street; PL17 7AQ Ancient unspoilt local under new management since death of veteran landlady; relaxed friendly atmosphere, handsome black timbering and stonework, well kept cornish ales, some live acoustic music; good pasties from shop next door; open all day. *(Giles and Annie Francis)*

CALSTOCK   SX4368
⋆ **Tamar** (01822) 832487
The Quay; PL18 9QA Cheerful relaxed local dating from the 17th c, just opposite the Tamar with its imposing viaduct, dark stripped stone, flagstones, tiles and bare boards, pool room with woodburner, more

modern fairy-lit back dining room, good generous straightforward food, summer cream teas, well kept Sharps Doom Bar and other cornish ales, good service and reasonable prices, darts, some live music; children away from bar and well behaved dogs welcome, nicely furnished terrace, heated smokers' shelter, hilly walk or ferry to Cotehele (NT). *(Giles and Annie Francis)*

CAWSAND   SX4350
⋆ **Cross Keys** (01752) 822706
The Square; PL10 1PF Slate-floored traditional local with lots of matchboxes, banknotes and postcards, some cask tables, steps up to carpeted dining room with nautical décor, enjoyable generous food especially seafood (book in season), reasonable prices, changing ales, flexible helpful service; may be background music, pool; children and dogs welcome, seats outside, pleasant bedrooms but no parking nearby. *(Simon J Barber)*

CHAPEL AMBLE   SW9975
Maltsters Arms (01208) 812473
Off A39 NE of Wadebridge; PL27 6EU More busy country restaurant than pub and they like you to book, good food and thriving atmosphere, drinkers confined to bar counter or modern back extension (if not used by diners); St Austell Tribute and Sharps Doom Bar; contemporary styling with splendid fire, beams, painted half-panelling, stripped stone and partly carpeted flagstones, light wood furniture; picnic-sets in sheltered sunny corner. *(Anon)*

CHARLESTOWN   SX0351
Rashleigh Arms (01726) 73635
Quay Road; PL25 3NX Modernised early 19th-c pub with nautical touches, public bar, lounge and dining area, well kept St Austell ales and two guests, good wine choice and coffee, enjoyable competitively priced food all day including popular Sun carvery, friendly obliging service; background music (live Fri), free wi-fi; children welcome, dogs in bar, disabled facilities, front terrace and garden with picnic-sets, eight bedrooms (some with sea views). *(Robert Watt)*

COVERACK   SW7818
Paris (01326) 280258
The Cove; TR12 6SX Comfortable Edwardian seaside inn above harbour in beautiful fishing village, carpeted L-shaped bar with well kept St Austell ales, large relaxed dining room with white tablecloths and spectacular bay views, nice food including good fresh fish, Sun lunchtime carvery, helpful friendly service, large model of namesake ship (wrecked nearby in 1899); children welcome, more sea views from garden, four comfortable bedrooms. *(John and Sharon Hancock, Stanley and Annie Matthews)*

CRACKINGTON HAVEN   SX1496
✶ Coombe Barton   (01840) 230345
Off A39 Bude–Camelford; EX23 0JG
Much-extended old inn in beautiful setting
overlooking splendid sandy bay, modernised
pubby bar with plenty of room for summer
crowds, neat welcoming young staff, wide
range of simple bar food including local
fish, popular carvery Sun lunch, Sharps and
St Austell, good wine choice, lots of local
pictures, surfboard hanging from plank
ceiling, big plain family room, restaurant;
darts, pool, fruit machines, background
music, TV; dogs allowed in bar, side terrace
with plenty of tables, fine cliff walks, roomy
bedrooms, good breakfast, open all day in
season. *(Dr A McCormick, Mick and Moira
Brummell)*

CREMYLL   SX4553
✶ Edgcumbe Arms   (01752) 822294
End of B3247; PL10 1HX Splendid setting
by Plymouth foot-ferry with great Tamar
views and picnic-sets beside the water;
attractive layout and décor, slate floors,
big settles and comfortably old-fashioned
furnishings including fireside sofas, old
pictures and china, well kept St Austell ales,
cheerful staff, reasonably priced food from
doorstep sandwiches up, lunchtime carvery
(plus evenings Fri-Sun), good family room/
games area; pay car park some way off;
children in eating area, dogs allowed in one
bar (where most tables too low to eat at),
four bedrooms, open all day. *(David Crook,
Simon J Barber)*

CROWS NEST   SX2669
Crows Nest   (01579) 345930
*Signed off B3264 N of Liskeard; OS Sheet
201 map reference 263692; PL14 5JQ*
Old-fashioned 17th-c pub under newish
management, enjoyable traditional food
and well kept St Austell ales, attractive
furnishings under bowed beams, big log fire,
chatty locals; children and dogs welcome,
picnic-sets on terrace by quiet lane, handy
for Bodmin Moor walks. *(John and Bernadette
Elliott)*

CUBERT   SW7857
✶ Smugglers Den   (01637) 830209
Off A3075 S of Newquay; TR8 5PY
Big open-plan 16th-c thatched pub, good
locally sourced food and four well kept beers
(May pie and ale festival), plenty of wines by
the glass, efficient friendly young staff, neat
ranks of tables, dim lighting, stripped stone
and heavy beam and plank ceilings, west
country pictures and seafaring memorabilia,
steps down to area with huge inglenook,
another step to big side dining room, also
a little snug with woodburner and leather
armchairs; background music; children and
dogs welcome, small front courtyard, terrace
with nice country views, sloping lawn with
play area, camping opposite, open all day

summer, closed Mon-Weds lunchtime in
winter. *(P and J Shapley)*

EDMONTON   SW9672
✶ Quarryman   (01208) 816444
*Off A39 just W of Wadebridge bypass;
PL27 7JA* Welcoming busy family-run pub,
part of a small holiday courtyard complex;
three-room beamed bar with interesting
decorations including old sporting
memorabilia, generous pubby lunchtime
food plus good individual dishes (signature
sizzling steaks), quick friendly service, four
changing ales and seven wines by the glass,
no mobile phones or background music;
well behaved dogs and children welcome,
disabled access (but upstairs lavatories),
picnic-sets in front and courtyard behind,
open all day. *(Anon)*

FALMOUTH   SW8132
✶ Chain Locker   (01326) 311085
Custom House Quay; TR11 3HH
Busy place in fine spot by inner harbour
with window tables and lots of seats outside,
well kept Sharps and Skinners ales, good
value generous food from sandwiches and
baguettes to fresh local fish and interesting
vegetarian choices (smaller appetites also
catered for), cheery young staff, bare boards
and masses of nautical bric-a-brac, darts
alley; games machine, background music;
well behaved children and dogs welcome,
self-catering accommodation, open all
day. *(David and Sue Smith, Simon J Barber)*

FALMOUTH
Front   (01326) 212168
Custom House Quay; TR11 3JT
Bare-boards drinkers' pub with good
changing selection of ales, some tapped from
the cask, foreign beers and ciders/perries,
friendly knowledgeable staff, no food but
can bring your own (good fish and chip shop
above), mix of customers from students to
beards; seats outside, open all day. *(Thomas
Readings, Mike and Eleanor Anderson)*

FALMOUTH   SW8032
Seven Stars   (01326) 312111
The Moor (centre); TR11 3QA Quirky
17th-c local, unchanging and unsmart (not
to everyone's taste), friendly atmosphere and
chatty regulars, no gimmicks, machines or
mobile phones, half a dozen well kept ales
tapped from the cask, home-made rolls, big
keyring collection, quiet back snug; corridor
hatch serving roadside courtyard. *(Ted
George)*

FLUSHING   SW8033
Seven Stars   (01326) 374373
Trefusis Road; TR11 5TY Old-style waterside pub with welcoming local atmosphere,
well kept ales and pubby food, coal fire,
separate dining room, darts; pavement picnic-
sets, great views of Falmouth with foot-ferry
across, open all day. *(Mike and Eleanor Anderson)*

FOWEY   SX1251
Galleon (01726) 833014
*Fore Street; from centre follow car ferry
signs; PL23 1AQ* Superb spot by harbour
and estuary, good ale range including local
microbrews, good generous straightforward
food, reasonable prices, nice choice of wines,
fast friendly service, fresh modern nautical
décor, lots of solid pine, dining areas off, jazz
Sun lunchtime; pool, big-screen TV, evenings
can get loud with young people; children
welcome, disabled facilities, attractive
extended waterside terrace and sheltered
courtyard with covered heated area, estuary-
view bedrooms. *(Mick and Moira Brummell,
Dave Webster, Sue Holland)*

FOWEY   SX1251
✳ King of Prussia (01726) 832450
Town Quay; PL23 1AT Handsome
quayside building with spacious, neatly
kept upstairs bar, bay windows looking over
harbour to Polruan, good welcoming service,
enjoyable pubby food including nice crab
sandwiches and carve-your-own Sun roasts,
well kept St Austell ales and sensibly priced
wines, family restaurant; background music,
pool; seats outside, six pleasant bedrooms,
open all day in summer. *(Nick Lawless, Alan
Johnson, John Edwell, Ian Herdman, Mr and
Mrs A H Young)*

FOWEY   SX1251
Lugger (01726) 833435
Fore Street; PL23 1AH Centrally placed
St Austell pub with unpretentious bar and
small back dining area, good mix of locals
and visitors (can get busy), enjoyable food
including local fish; children welcome,
pavement tables, open all day in summer.
(Nick Lawless, Dave Webster, Sue Holland)

FOWEY   SX1251
Safe Harbour (01726) 833379
Lostwithiel Street; PL23 1BP
Redecorated 19th-c former coaching inn set
away from main tourist area, with lounge/
dining area and regulars' bar, good value
locally sourced home-made food, well kept
St Austell ales, welcoming landlord, old local
prints, upstairs overflow dining room; pool,
darts, games machine; heated side terrace,
seven bedrooms and self-catering apartment,
open all day till midnight. *(Nick Lawless, Dave
Webster, Sue Holland)*

FOWEY   SX1251
✳ Ship (01726) 832230
Trafalgar Square; PL23 1AZ
Bustling local with friendly staff, good
choice of well priced generous food from
sandwiches up including fine local seafood,
well kept St Austell ales, coal fire and
banquettes in tidy bar with lots of yachting
prints and nauticalia, newspapers, steps up
to family dining room with big stained-
glass window, pool/darts room; background

music, small sports TV; dogs allowed,
comfortably old-fashioned bedrooms, some
oak-panelled. *(Nick Lawless, Ted George, Ian
Herdman, Mr and Mrs A H Young)*

GERRANS   SW8735
Royal Standard (01872) 580271
The Square; TR2 5EB Friendly little local
– now a free house, and quieter alternative to
the nearby Plume of Feathers in Portscatho;
narrow doorways linking carpeted rooms, up
to three well kept local ales, Sharps cider and
Skinners lager, short choice of well chosen
wines, enjoyable pub food from sandwiches to
local fish, old photographs on white plaster
or black-boarded walls, brass shell cases
and kitchen utensils, woodburner, lakeland
terrier called Millie; children welcome away
from bar, disabled access, sunny beer garden,
interesting church opposite (15th-c, rebuilt
in 19th c after fire). *(Chris and Angela Buckell)*

GOLANT   SX1254
✳ Fishermans Arms (01726) 832453
Fore Street (B3269); PL23 1LN
Bustling partly flagstoned small waterside
local with lovely views across River Fowey
from front bar and terrace, good value
generous home-made food including nice
crab sandwiches and seafood, efficient
friendly service, up to five well kept cornish
ales, good wines by the glass, log fire,
interesting pictures; dogs welcome, pleasant
garden, open all day summer, all day Fri-Sun
winter. *(Stuart Paulley)*

GORRAN CHURCHTOWN   SW9942
Barley Sheaf (01726) 843330
*Follow Gorran Haven signs from
Mevagissey; PL26 6HN* Old village pub
extensively refurbished by present owner,
good reasonably priced home-made food,
well kept Sharps Doom Bar and guests,
friendly staff, some live music; dogs welcome,
garden. *(Bill Shelton, Jeremy Whitehorn, Stephen
and Judy Parish)*

GRAMPOUND   SW9348
Dolphin (01726) 882435
A390 Street Austell–Truro; TR2 4RR
Friendly St Austell pub under newish local
management, their ales and decent wines,
pub food done well, two-level bar with
black beams and panelling, polished wood
or carpeted floors, pubby furniture with
a few high-backed settles, pictures of old
Grampound, log fire, quiz nights; children
welcome, dogs in bar, wheelchair access from
car park, beer garden, smokery opposite,
handy for Trewithen Gardens. *(Chris and
Angela Buckell)*

GULVAL   SW4831
Coldstreamer (01736) 362072
*Centre of village by drinking fountain;
TR18 3BB* Welcoming place with good food
and several well kept local ales, traditional
bar with woodburner, old photographs

and traditional games, updated restaurant has modern pine furniture on wood floor; children welcome, quiet pleasant village very handy for Trengwainton Garden (NT) and Isles of Scilly heliport, comfortable bedrooms, open all day. *(John and Jackie Chalcraft)*

GUNNISLAKE SX4371
Rising Sun (01822) 832201
Calstock Road, just S of village; PL18 9BX Attractive 17th-c two-room village pub, beams, stripped stone, panelling and flagstones, lovely fireplaces, cheerful service, six real ales, enjoyable food (not Mon) including early-bird menu, may be weekend live music; pleasant valley views from terraced garden, open all day. *(Paul, Peter Thornton)*

HARROWBARROW SX4069
Cross House (01579) 350482
Off A390 E of Callington; School Road – towards Metherell; PL17 8BQ Substantial stone building (former farmhouse) with spreading carpeted bar, booth seating, cushioned wall seats and stools around pub tables, enjoyable reasonably priced home-made food, well kept St Austell ales and nice wines by the glass, friendly smiling service, open fire and woodburner, darts, restaurant; children and dogs (in bar) welcome, disabled facilities, plenty of picnic-sets on good-sized lawn, play area, handy for Cotehele (NT), open all day. *(Dennis Jenkin, John and Nan Hurst)*

HELFORD SW7526
Shipwrights Arms (01326) 231235
Off B3293 SE of Helston, via Mawgan; TR12 6JX Thatched 18th-c pub by beautiful wooded creek, at its best at high tide, terraces make the most of the view, plenty of surrounding walks and summer foot-ferry from Helford Passage; now run by local consortium and refurbished in simple contemporary style, woodburner, Sharps Doom Bar and a couple of cornish guest ales, good locally sourced food (booking advised) including fresh fish from daily changing menu, nice crab sandwiches using landlady's organic bread, friendly helpful young staff, occasional live music; children, dogs and muddy boots welcome, small car park (parking nearby may be tricky), pontoon mooring, open all day. *(Andrea Rampley, Ian and Carol King, Henry Fryer)*

HELSTON SW6527
⋆ Blue Anchor (01326) 562821
Coinagehall Street; TR13 8EL Many (not all) love this no-nonsense, highly individual, thatched 15th-c local; quaint rooms off corridor, flagstones, stripped stone, low beams and well worn furniture, family room, traditional games and skittle alley, limited bargain food at lunchtime (perhaps best time to visit), ancient back brewhouse still

producing distinctive and very strong Spingo IPA, Middle and seasonals like Bragget with honey and herbs; seats out behind, four bedrooms, open all day. *(Anon)*

HESSENFORD SX3057
Copley Arms (01503) 240209
A387 Looe–Torpoint; PL11 3HJ 17th-c village pub with slightly old-fashioned feel, popular with families and passing tourists, enjoyable reasonably priced food from sandwiches to grills in linked carpeted areas, friendly service, well kept St Austell ales and nice choice of wines, teas and coffees, log fires, tables in cosy booths, one part with sofas and easy chairs, big family room; background and some live music, Thurs quiz; dogs allowed in one area, a few roadside picnic-sets by small River Seaton, fenced play area, five bedrooms. *(Adrian Johnson)*

KINGSAND SX4350
Devonport (01752) 822869
The Cleave; PL10 1NF Character pub with lovely bay views from front bar, three changing local ales and enjoyable well priced bar food, friendly service, scrubbed floorboards and Victorian décor, lots of ship photographs and bric-a-brac, mix of cast-iron-framed pub furniture with window seats and pine settles, log fire, back snug; dogs welcome, tables out by sea wall, good value bedrooms. *(Suzy Miller)*

LANLIVERY SX0759
Crown (01208) 872707
Signposted off A390 Lostwithiel–St Austell (tricky to find from other directions); PL30 5BT A new landlord for this ancient place, just ten minutes from the Eden Project; main bar with log fire in huge fireplace, traditional settles on big flagstones, some cushioned farmhouse chairs, Penpont, Sharps, Skinners and a changing guest, several wines by the glass, malt whiskies and summer farm cider, food has been popular, a couple of other similarly furnished rooms, also a dining conservatory and huge glass-topped well by the porch; children welcome away from servery, dogs allowed in bar, plenty of picnic-sets in quiet garden, bedrooms. *(Dennis Jenkin, Steven Green, Michelle, Richard and Marilyn Bradford, Robert Parker)*

LELANT SW5436
Old Quay House (01736) 753445
Griggs Quay, Lelant Saltings; A3047/ B3301 S of village; TR27 6JG Large pub in great spot by bird sanctuary estuary; newish management and some redecoration, enjoyable home-made pub food, Sharps and Skinners ales, dining area off well divided open-plan bar, upstairs restaurant; children and dogs (in bar) welcome, garden and small roof terrace with views over saltings, play area, nine motel-type bedrooms, open all day. *(Anon)*

LELANT   SW5436
Watermill (01736) 757912
Lelant Downs; A3074 S; TR27 6LQ Mill-conversion family dining pub; working waterwheel behind with gearing in dark-beamed central bar opening into brighter airy front extension, upstairs evening restaurant, Sharps Doom Bar, Skinners Betty Stogs and a guest, enjoyable food served by friendly staff; dogs welcome, good-sized pretty streamside garden, open all day. *(Anon)*

LERRYN   SX1356
★Ship (01208) 872374
Signed off A390 in Lostwithiel; Fore Street; PL22 0PT Lovely spot especially when tide is in, well kept local ales, farm cider, good wines (including country ones) and whiskies, sensibly priced food both imaginative and traditional, cheerful service, huge woodburner, adults-only attractive dining conservatory, (booking advisable evenings and weekends), games room with pool; children welcome, dogs on leads (friendly resident black lab), picnic-sets and pretty play area outside, near famous stepping-stones and three signposted waterside walks, decent bedrooms in adjoining building and self-catering cottages, open all day weekends. *(Nick Lawless, B and M Kendall, Evelyn and Derek Walter)*

LIZARD   SW7012
Top House (01326) 290974
A3083; TR12 7NQ Neat clean pub doing well under friendly landlord, good local food from sandwiches and snacks up including fresh fish, children's meals and cream teas, well kept ales such as St Austell Tribute and Skinners Betty Stogs, lots of good local sea pictures, fine shipwreck relics and serpentine craftwork (note the handpumps), warm welcoming log fire; sheltered terrace, interesting nearby serpentine shop, eight bedrooms in adjoining building (three with sea views), open all day summer, all day weekends winter. *(M P Mackenzie, Dave Webster, Sue Holland, Clifford Blakemore)*

LIZARD   SW7012
Witchball (01362) 290662
Lighthouse Road; TR12 7NJ Small pub with good food including fresh local fish and seafood (booking advised), ales such as Chough, St Austell and Skinners, cornish cider, helpful friendly staff; children and dogs welcome, terrace tables, open all day. *(Clifford Blakemore, Dave Webster, Sue Holland)*

LOOE   SX2553
Olde Salutation (01503) 262784
Fore Street, East Looe; PL13 1AE Good welcoming bustle in big squareish, slightly sloping, beamed and tiled bar, reasonably priced food from notable crab sandwiches to

wholesome specials and Sun roasts, friendly service, well kept Sharps Doom Bar, red leatherette seats and neat tables, blazing fire in nice old-fashioned fireplace, lots of local fishing photographs, side snug with olde-worlde harbour mural, step down to simple family room; may be background music, forget about parking; lots of hanging baskets, handy for coast path, open all day. *(George Atkinson)*

LUDGVAN   SW5033
★White Hart (01736) 740574
Off A30 Penzance–Hayle at Crowlas; TR20 8EY Appealing old village pub, friendly and welcoming, with well kept Atlantic and Sharps tapped from the cask, own summer cider and premium range of spirits, enjoyable blackboard food from pub standards up including good value Sun lunch, small unspoilt beamed rooms with wood and stone floors, nooks and crannies, woodburners, quiz first Weds of month; dogs welcome, beer garden and little decked area at back, interesting church next door, two refurbished bedrooms, open all day in summer. *(Mick and Moira Brummell, Bruce and Sharon Eden, John and Jackie Chalcraft, R and S Bentley)*

MARAZION   SW5130
Godolphin Arms (01736) 710202
West End; TR17 0EN Former coaching inn with great views across beach and Mount's Bay towards St Michael's Mount, traditional food including good crab sandwiches and popular Sun carvery, St Austell and Sharps ales, helpful friendly staff, upper lounge bar and dining area, informal lower bar with pool table, sports TV and live music (Fri); children and dogs welcome, decked beachside terrace, ten bedrooms (most with sea view, some with balconies), good breakfast, open all day. *(John and Sharon Hancock)*

MARAZION   SW5130
Kings Arms (01736) 710291
The Square; TR17 0AP Old one-bar pub in small square, comfortable and welcoming with warm woodburner, good well presented food including local fish from regularly changing menu, St Austell ales; children and dogs welcome, picnic-sets out front, open all day. *(Mr and Mrs P R Thomas, Alan Johnson)*

MAWNAN SMITH   SW7728
★Red Lion (01326) 250026
W of Falmouth, off former B3291 Penryn–Gweek; The Square; TR11 5EP Old thatched and beamed pub, popular and chatty, with cosy series of dimly lit lived-in rooms including the raftered bar, open kitchen doing good food from interesting menu especially seafood (book summer evenings), quick friendly service, lots of wines by the glass, well kept real ales such as Sharps Doom Bar, good coffee, daily papers, fresh flowers, woodburner in huge

stone fireplace, dark woodwork, country and marine pictures, plates and bric-a-brac; background music, TV; children (away from bar) and dogs welcome; disabled access, picnic-sets outside, handy for Glendurgan (NT) and Trebah Gardens, open all day. *(Chris and Angela Buckell, Richard and Liz Thorne, R Elliott)*

MEVAGISSEY   SX0144
⋆**Fountain**   (01726) 842320
Cliff Street, down alley by Post Office; PL26 6QH Popular low-beamed fishermen's pub, slate floor, some stripped stone and a welcoming coal fire, old local pictures, piano, well kept St Austell ales, good food at reasonable prices including local fish/seafood, friendly staff, back bar with glass-topped pit, small upstairs evening restaurant; children and dogs welcome, pretty frontage with picnic-sets, bedrooms, open all day in summer. *(Trevor Graveson, Ian Phillips, Henry Fryer, Martin Lewis, Di and Mike Gillam, Stephen and Judy Parish)*

MEVAGISSEY   SX0144
Ship   (01726) 843324
Fore Street, near harbour; PL26 6UQ 16th-c pub with interesting alcove areas in big open-plan bar, low beams and flagstones, nautical décor, woodburner, cheery uniformed staff, fairly priced pubby food including good fresh fish, small helpings available, St Austell ales kept well, back pool table; games machines, background and some live music; dogs allowed, children welcome in two front rooms, five bedrooms, open all day in summer. *(Anon)*

MINIONS   SX2671
Cheesewring   (01579) 362321
Overlooking the Hurlers; PL14 5LE Popular well run village pub useful for Bodmin Moor walks, well kept ales including Sharps, good choice of reasonably priced home-made food, lots of brass and ornaments, chatty locals; children and dogs welcome, bedrooms, open all day. *(M A Borthwick)*

MITCHELL   SW8554
⋆**Plume of Feathers**
(01872) 510387/511125   *Off A30 Bodmin–Redruth, by A3076 junction; take southwards road then first right; TR8 5AX* Well run 16th-c coaching inn with several linked bar and dining rooms, appealing contemporary décor, paintings by local artists on pastel walls, old stripped beams and standing timbers, painted wooden dados, farmhouse dining chairs and table and two open fires, good interesting food, Sharps Doom Bar, Skinners Betty Stogs and St Austell Tribute, several wines by the glass, impressive conservatory; background music; children (away from bar) and dogs welcome, picnic-sets under parasols in well planted garden areas, comfortable stable-conversion

bedrooms, open all day from 8am. *(R J Hord, Bernard Stradling, Katherine Bright, Ron and Sheila Corbett, David Elfman)*

MITHIAN   SW7450
⋆**Miners Arms**   (01872) 552375
Off B3285 E of Street Agnes; TR5 0QF Cosy stone-built pub with traditional small rooms and passages, pubby furnishings, fine old wall painting of Elizabeth I in squint-walled, irregular beam and plank-ceilinged back bar, open fires, popular good value food, Sharps and Skinners ales kept well, friendly helpful staff, board games; background music; children welcome, dogs in some rooms, seats on back terrace, in garden and on sheltered front cobbled forecourt, open all day. *(David and Sharon Collison, Dennis Jenkin, John Marsh)*

MORWENSTOW   SS2015
⋆**Bush**   (01288) 331242
Signed off A39 N of Kilkhampton; Crosstown; EX23 9SR New licensees expected to take over this well liked 13th-c beamed pub in autumn 2013 – news please; character bar with flagstones, woodburner in big stone fireplace, horse tack and copper knick-knacks, several rooms set for dining; picnic-sets on grass plus a couple of heated dining huts overlooking the sea; children and dogs have been welcome, bedrooms and self-catering, fantastic walks all around, has been open all day from 9am. *(Anon)*

MULLION   SW6719
Old Inn   (01326) 240240
In small one-way street opposite church – not down in the cove; TR12 7HN Thatched and beamed 16th-c pub with enjoyable home-made food, well kept St Austell ales and a guest, decent wines, narrowish bar with linked eating areas, lots of brasses, plates, clocks, nautical items and old wreck pictures, big inglenook; TV; children and dogs welcome, picnic-sets on terrace and in garden, five bedrooms, open all day. *(David and Sue Smith, Paul Rampton, Julie Harding)*

MULLION COVE   SW6618
Mullion Cove Hotel   (01326) 240328
End of road of Cove Road; TR12 7EP Imposing Victorian cliff-top hotel overlooking sea and harbour, friendly and hospitable, with good food in bistro bar, ales such as Sharps Doom Bar, more formal and expensive sea-view restaurant; children welcome, 30 bedrooms, useful coast path stop. *(Anon)*

MYLOR BRIDGE   SW8036
Lemon Arms   (01326) 373666
Lemon Hill; TR11 5NA Popular and friendly traditional village pub, opened-up bar area with stripped-stone walls and panelling, well kept St Austell ales, enjoyable sensibly priced food (no credit cards); children and dogs welcome, wheelchair

access with help, back terrace, good coastal walks. *(Jim Banwell, John Marsh)*

NEWLYN   SW4629
Tolcarne (01736) 363074
Tolcarne Place; TR18 5PR Traditional 17th-c quayside pub redecorated under new landlord/chef – reports please; daily changing menu with much emphasis on local fish/ seafood, no meals Sun evening or Mon, St Austell, Skinners and maybe a guest, live jazz Sun; children and dogs welcome, terrace (but harbour wall cuts off view), good parking. *(Anon)*

NEWLYN EAST   SW8256
Pheasant (01872) 510237
Churchtown; TR8 5LJ Friendly traditional village pub in quiet backstreet, enjoyable reasonably priced food including popular Sun carvery, Dartmoor and Sharps beers, good service; not far from Trerice (NT). *(Stanley and Annie Matthews)*

NEWQUAY   SW8061
Fort (01637) 875700
Fore Street; TR7 1HA Massive recently built pub in magnificent setting high above surfing beach and small harbour, decent food all day from sandwiches, hot baguettes and baked potatoes up, open-plan areas well divided by balustrades and surviving fragments of former harbourmaster's house, good solid furnishings from country kitchen to button-back settees, soft lighting, friendly staff coping well at busy times, St Austell ales, games section with two pool tables, excellent indoor children's play area; great views from long glass-walled side section and sizeable garden with terrace and further play areas, bedrooms, open all day. *(Alan Johnson)*

NEWQUAY   SW8061
Lewinnick Lodge (01637) 878117
Pentire headland, off Pentire Road; TR7 1NX Modern flint-walled bar-restaurant built into the bluff above the sea, big picture windows with terrific views, light and airy bar with wicker seating, spreading dining areas with contemporary furnishings on light oak flooring, bistro-style food from shortish menu, three or four well kept ales, several wines by the glass, good service and pleasant relaxed atmosphere even when busy; children welcome, modern seats and tables on terraces making the most of stunning Atlantic views, ten new bedrooms; under same management as the Plume of Feathers, Mitchell. *(Peter Humble)*

PADSTOW   SW9175
☆ Golden Lion (01841) 532797
Lanadwell Street; PL28 8AN Old inn dating from the 14th c, cheerful black-beamed locals' bar, high-raftered back lounge with plush banquettes, three well kept ales such as Sharps Doom Bar, reasonably priced simple bar lunches including good crab sandwiches, evening steaks and fresh fish, friendly staff, coal fire and woodburner; pool in family area, background music, sports TV; dogs welcome, colourful floral displays at front, terrace tables, three bedrooms, open all day. *(Anon)*

PADSTOW   SW9175
Harbour Inn (01841) 533148
Strand Street; PL28 8BU Attractive pub set just back from the harbour and a quieter alternative; long room with nautical bric-a-brac, front area with comfy sofas, woodburner, well kept St Austell ales, enjoyable home-made food, good coffee, friendly staff; children and dogs welcome, open all day. *(Anon)*

PADSTOW   SW9275
Old Custom House (01841) 532359
South Quay; PL28 8BL Large, bright, airy open-plan seaside bar, comfortable and well divided, with rustic décor and cosy corners, beams, exposed brickwork and bare boards, raised section, big family area and conservatory, good food choice from baguettes up, four local ales including St Austell, efficient friendly service, adjoining fish restaurant; background and live music, TV, machines, pool; good spot by harbour, attractive sea-view bedrooms, open all day and can get very busy. *(Ted George)*

PELYNT   SX2054
☆ Jubilee (01503) 220312
B3359 NW of Looe; PL13 2JZ Popular early 17th-c beamed inn with wide range of locally sourced home-made food (best to book in season) from good sandwiches up including Sun roasts, well kept St Austell ales, good wines by the glass, friendly helpful young staff, spotless interior with interesting Queen Victoria mementoes (pub renamed in 1897 to celebrate her diamond jubilee), some handsome antique furnishings, log fire in big stone fireplace, separate bar with darts, pool and games machine; children and dogs welcome, disabled facilities, large terrace, 11 comfortable bedrooms, open all day weekends. *(Dennis Jenkin, Peter Thornton, Stanley and Annie Matthews)*

PENDOGGETT   SX0279
Cornish Arms (01208) 880263
B3314; PL30 3HH Picturesque old coaching inn with traditional oak settles on front bar's polished slate floor, fine prints, above-average food from good sandwiches up, also good authentic thai food (not Sun, Mon), Sharps Doom Bar and a couple of guests, decent wines by the glass, friendly helpful staff, comfortably spaced tables in small dining room, proper back locals' bar with woodburner and games; provision for children, dogs welcome in bars, disabled access, terrace with distant sea view, bedrooms, open all day. *(Chris Macey, Dennis Jenkin)*

PENELEWEY
SW8140
Punch Bowl & Ladle
(01872) 862237 *B3289; TR3 6QY*
Thatched dining pub with several room
areas, generous sensibly priced home-made
food from good sandwiches to local steaks,
children's menu, OAP lunch on Mon, efficient
helpful service, St Austell ales and good
wine choice, big sofas and rustic bric-a-brac;
background music; dogs welcome, small side
terrace, handy for Trelissick Garden (NT),
open all day. *(R K Phillips, Paul Rampton,
Julie Harding)*

PENTEWAN
SX0147
Ship
(01726) 842855
*Just off B3273 Street Austell–
Mevagissey; West End; PL26 6BX*
Big 17th-c beamed pub opposite tiny village's
harbour, comfortable and clean with bar,
snug and lounge/dining area, lots of dark
tables, open fire, up to four well kept St
Austell ales, maybe draught perry, enjoyable
reasonably priced pub food including good
fish and chips, friendly service; background
and some live music; children and dogs
welcome, views from tables outside, near
good sandy beach and big caravan park,
open all day summer, all day weekends
winter. *(Colin Woodward, Stephen Funnell)*

PENZANCE
SW4730
Admiral Benbow
(01736) 363448
Chapel Street; TR18 4AF Well run
rambling pub, full of life and atmosphere
and packed with interesting nautical gear,
friendly staff, good value above-average food
including local fish, real ales such as Sharps,
Skinners and St Austell, cosy corners, fire,
downstairs restaurant in captain's cabin
style, upper floor with pool, pleasant view
from back room; children and dogs welcome,
open all day in summer. *(John and Gloria
Isaacs, David Crook, Robert Wivell)*

PENZANCE
SW4730
Crown
(01736) 351070
Victoria Square, Bread Street; TR18 2EP
Small, friendly backstreet local with neat bar
and snug dining room, own-brewed Cornish
Crown beers plus Otter, several wines by the
glass, enjoyable good value home-made food
(not Sun evening, Mon or Tues), Tues quiz,
board games (beat the landlady at Snatch
for a free pint); children and dogs welcome,
seats outside, open all day. *(Anon)*

PENZANCE
SW4729
⋆ Dolphin
(01736) 364106
*Quay Street, opposite harbour after
swing-bridge TR18 4BD* Part old-
fashioned pub and part bistro, good value
food especially fresh fish (landlady's
husband is a fisherman), St Austell ales,
good wines by the glass, friendly helpful
service, roomy bar, great fireplace, dining
area a few steps down, cosy family room;

big pool room with juke box etc, no obvious
nearby parking; pavement picnic-sets, open
all day. *(Mr and Mrs C F Turner)*

PERRANARWORTHAL
SW7738
⋆ Norway
(01872) 864241
A39 Truro–Penryn; TR3 7NU Large
beamed pub with half a dozen linked areas,
helpful friendly service, good choice of
generous well presented food using local
produce including vegetarian options,
OAP lunch Tues, all-day Sun carvery, good
selection of St Austell ales and several wines
by the glass, open fires, old-style wooden
seating and big tables on slate flagstones,
restaurant, Mon quiz; children welcome,
tables outside, four bedrooms, open all
day. *(Mick and Moira Brummell)*

PHILLEIGH
SW8739
Roseland
(01872) 580254
*Between A3078 and B3289, NE of St
Mawes just E of King Harry Ferry;
TR2 5NB* In a small hamlet and handy for
the King Harry ferry and Trelissick Garden
(NT), but a bit rundown at the moment;
two bar rooms, one with flagstones, the
other carpeted, wheelbacks and built-in red
cushioned seats, open fires, old photographs
and some giant beetles and butterflies in
glass cases, tiny lower area for locals, back
restaurant too, Skinners Betty Stogs and
Sharps Doom Bar (the pub no longer brews
its own beer); children and dogs welcome,
seats on paved front courtyard, open all day
school summer holidays. *(R K Phillips, Peter
Thornton, Dennis Jenkin, Mr and Mrs Richard
Osborne, R and S Bentley, Chris and Angela
Buckell and others)*

PILLATON
SX3664
⋆ Weary Friar
(01579) 350238
*Off Callington–Landrake back road;
PL12 6QS* Tucked-away welcoming 12th-c
inn, good generously served food from
wide-ranging menu in bar and restaurant
(best to book), friendly helpful staff, well
kept St Austell and Sharps beers, farm
cider, knocked-together carpeted rooms,
dark beams, copper and brass, log fires in
stone fireplaces; no dogs inside; children
welcome, tables out in front and behind,
church next door (Tues evening bellringing),
14 comfortable bedrooms. *(Ted George, Jackie
Cranmer, Drs J and J Parker)*

POLGOOTH
SW9950
Polgooth Inn
(01726) 74089
*Well signed off A390 W of St Austell;
Ricketts Lane; PL26 7DA* Big welcoming
country pub, separate servery for good
generous food from doorstep sandwiches
up (only roasts on Sun), children's helpings
and reasonable prices, well kept St Austell
ales, good wine choice, eating area around
sizeable bar with woodburner, good big
family room; fills quickly in summer (handy
for nearby caravan parks); dogs welcome,

steps up to play area, tables on grass, pretty countryside. *(P and J Shapley, Stephen Funnell)*

POLMEAR   SX0853
Ship (01726) 812540
A3082 Par–Fowey; PL24 2AR Flower-decked 18th-c pub with chatty locals and welcoming staff, enjoyable straightforward food including evening carvery, well kept Fullers London Pride, Sharps Doom Bar and a guest from rowing-boat counter, roomy bar with lots of hanging whisky-water jugs and big stove; background and live music, TV, cash machine; children and dogs welcome, two garden areas (one with summer bandstand), camping and self-catering cabin, open all day. *(Liz and Brian Barnard)*

POLPERRO   SX2051
Crumplehorn Mill (01503) 272348
Top of village near main car park; PL13 2RJ Converted mill and farmhouse with original beams, flagstones and some stripped stone, snug lower beamed bar leading to long main room with cosy eating area at end, well kept cornish ales, wide choice of reasonably priced food from snacks to blackboard specials (booking advised), friendly speedy service, log fire; children welcome, outside seating and working mill wheel, refurbished bedrooms, self catering, open all day. *(Neil and Brenda Skidmore)*

POLPERRO   SX2050
Three Pilchards (01503) 272233
Quay Road; PL13 2QZ Small low-beamed local behind fish quay, good choice of reasonably priced food all day from baguettes to fresh fish and thai specials, Otter, Sharps and Timothy Taylors ales, efficient obliging service even when busy, lots of black woodwork, dim lighting, simple furnishings, open fire in big stone fireplace; children and dogs welcome, picnic-sets on upper terrace up steep steps. *(Neil and Brenda Skidmore)*

POLRUAN   SX1250
Lugger (01726) 870007
The Quay; back roads off A390 in Lostwithiel, or passenger/bicycle ferry from Fowey; PL23 1PA Steps up to beamed and carpeted waterside local, high-backed wall settles, ship pictures, model boats etc, good food from bar snacks up, Sun carvery, well kept St Austell ales, restaurant on upper level; children and dogs welcome, good walks, limited parking, open all day. *(Dave Braisted)*

PORT ISAAC   SW9980
⋆ Golden Lion (01208) 880336
Fore Street; PL29 3RB Friendly local atmosphere in simply furnished old rooms, open fire in back one, window seats and three balcony tables looking down on rocky harbour and lifeboat slip far below, straightforward food including good local fish, St Austell ales, darts, dominoes, cribbage; background music, games machine;

dogs welcome, children in eating areas, dramatic cliff walks, open all day. *(Anon)*

PORTHALLOW   SW7923
Five Pilchards (01326) 280256
SE of Helston; B3293 to Street Keverne, then village signed; TR12 6PP Sturdy old-fashioned stone-built local in secluded cove right by shingle beach, lots of salvaged nautical gear, interesting shipwreck memorabilia and model boats, woodburner, cornish ales and enjoyable, reasonably priced, straightforward food including local fish, conservatory; children and dogs welcome, seats in sheltered yard, refurbished bedrooms, in winter closed Sun evening, Mon lunchtime and Tues. *(Henry Fryer)*

PORTHLEVEN   SW6325
Atlantic (01326) 562439
Peverell Terrace; TR13 9DZ Friendly buzzy pub in great setting up above harbour, good value tasty food, real ales including Skinners and St Austell, big open-plan lounge with well spaced seating and cosier alcoves, good log fire in granite fireplace, dining room with amazing trompe l'oeil murals; lovely bay views from front terrace, open all day. *(Simon Lindsey, Rose Rogers)*

PORTHLEVEN   SW6225
Harbour Inn (01326) 573876
Commercial Road; TR13 9JB Large neatly kept pub-hotel in outstanding harbourside setting, well organised friendly service, expansive lounge and bar with impressive dining area off, big public bar with panelling, well kept St Austell ales, good range of pubby food including catch of the day, lunchtime carvery Weds (OAP deal) and Sun; quiet background music (live Sat), Thurs quiz; children welcome, picnic-sets on big quayside terrace, 15 well equipped bedrooms, some with harbour view, good breakfast, open all day. *(John and Gloria Isaacs, David Crook, John and Sharon Hancock, Pat and Tony Martin)*

PORTHLEVEN   SW6225
⋆ Ship (01326) 564204
Mount Pleasant Road (harbour) off B3304; TR13 9JS
Friendly fishermen's pub built into cliffs, fine harbour views (interestingly floodlit at night) from seats on terrace and in knocked-through bar, well kept Courage Best and Sharps Doom Bar, honest bar food like good crab sandwiches and home-made pies (may ask to hold a credit card if you eat outside), good service, log fires in big stone fireplaces, some genuine individuality, family room (converted from old smithy) with huge fire, candlelit dining room also looking over sea; background music, games machine; dogs welcome in bar, open all day; for sale as we went to press. *(John and Gloria Isaacs, Stephen Shepherd, Clifford Blakemore, David and Sue Smith, Alan Johnson)*

PORTLOE SW9339
✳ Ship (01872) 501356
At top of village; TR2 5RA Bright unspoilt
L-shaped local; popular generous food
including good fresh fish (excellent if pricey
crab sandwiches), well kept St Austell ales,
Healey's cider/perry and good choice of
wines, friendly welcoming staff, interesting
nautical and local memorabilia, amazing beer
bottle collection; background music; children
and dogs welcome, disabled access to main
bar (but road very steep), smokers' gazebo,
sheltered and attractive streamside garden
over road, pretty fishing village with lovely
cove and coast path above, bedrooms, open
all day Fri-Sun in summer. *(Dr A McCormick,
Chris and Angela Buckell, Henry Fryer, Barry
Collett, John and Sharon Hancock and others)*

PORTREATH SW6545
Portreath Arms (01209) 842259
*By B3300/B3301 N of Redruth;
TR16 4LA* Victorian hotel's lounge bar
with steps down to dining room, slightly
old-fashioned lived-in feel, but good choice
of enjoyable food from sandwiches to steaks
and fresh fish, reasonable prices, friendly
attentive waitresses, Greene King Abbot
and Skinners Betty Stogs, Sharp's Orchard
cider, separate public bar; children welcome,
seven bedrooms, well placed for coastal
walks. *(Stanley and Annie Matthews)*

PORTSCATHO SW8735
Plume of Feathers (01872) 580321
The Square; TR2 5HW Cheerful largely
stripped-stone pub in pretty fishing village,
well kept St Austell and other ales, Healey's
cider, pubby food from sandwiches and
huge ploughman's up, bargain fish night
Fri, sea-related bric-a-brac in comfortable
linked room areas, small side locals' bar
(can be lively in the evening), restaurant;
very popular with summer visitors, warm
local atmosphere out of season; background
music; children, dogs and muddy boots
welcome, disabled access, lovely coast walks,
open all day in summer (and other times
if busy). *(Chris and Angela Buckell, Clifford
Blakemore, Robert Watt)*

PRAZE AN BEEBLE SW6335
St Aubyn Arms (01209) 831425
The Square; TR14 0JR Welcoming
refurbished pub with two bars and a
contemporary restaurant, well kept Otter,
St Austell and Skinners, enjoyable food with
emphasis on local steaks, attentive friendly
service, Tues quiz; background music;
children and dogs welcome, picnic-sets in
large attractive garden. *(David and Sue Smith)*

ROSUDGEON SW5529
Falmouth Packet (01736) 762240
A394; TR20 9QE Nice place with quite a
history, stone walls and open fires, enjoyable
good value food using organic local produce,

well kept Bays and Penzance, friendly
landlord and good service, conservatory;
garden, self-catering cottage. *(John and
Jackie Chalcraft)*

RUAN LANIHORNE SW8942
✳ Kings Head (01872) 501263
*Village signed off A3078 St Mawes Road;
TR2 5NX* Country pub in quiet hamlet,
relaxed small bar with log fire, Skinners and
a guest, maybe farm cider, well liked food
especially local fish, friendly helpful service,
two dining areas, lots of china cups hanging
from ceiling, plenty of copper and brass,
hunting prints, cabinet filled with old bottles,
separate restaurant; background music; well
behaved children allowed in dining areas
only, dogs in bar, terrace across road and nice
lower beer garden, interesting church nearby
and walks along Fal estuary, closed in winter
Sun evening and Mon. *(M J Winterton, Bob and
Margaret Holder, Nick Lawless, Penny Simpson,
Peter Thornton, M and A H and others)*

ST DOMINICK SX4067
✳ Who'd Have Thought It
(01579) 350214 *Off A388 S of
Callington; PL12 6TG* Large, comfortable
and welcoming country pub under mother
and (chef) daughter management,
wide choice of good food from generous
sandwiches to blackboard specials, well kept
St Austell ales, decent wines, superb Tamar
views especially from conservatory, cosily
plush lounge areas with open fires; dogs
allowed in public bar, garden tables, handy
for Cotehele (NT). *(Ted George, Peter Thornton,
John Evans)*

ST GERMANS SX3557
Eliot Arms (01503) 232733
Fore Street; PL12 5NR Welcoming stone-
built slate-roofed pub with two bars and a
restaurant, reasonably priced home-made
food (not Sun evening), St Austell ales; pool,
darts and sports TV; picnic-sets in walled
area at front with flowers and hanging
baskets, four bedrooms. *(Anon)*

ST IVES SW5140
Lifeboat (01736) 794123
Wharf Road; TR26 1LF Thriving family-
friendly beamed quayside pub, wide choice of
good value food all day, well kept St Austell
ales, spacious interior with harbour-view
tables and cosier corners, nautical theme
including lifeboat pictures, friendly helpful
staff, Sept music festival; sports TV, fruit
machine, no dogs; disabled access and
facilities. *(Christopher Vallely)*

ST IVES SW5441
Pedn Olva (01736) 796222
The Warren; TR26 2EA Hotel not pub,
but has well kept reasonably priced St
Austell ales in roomy bar, panoramic views
of sea and Porthminster beach, especially
from tables on rooftop terrace, all-day bar

food and separate restaurant, good service; comfortable bedrooms. *(Alan Johnson)*

ST IVES   SW5441
Queens (01736) 796468
High Street; TR26 1RR Georgian inn with friendly relaxed atmosphere, bare-boards bar with open fire, scrubbed pine tables, tartan banquettes and comfy leather armchairs, wall of barometers, good sensibly priced food, St Austell ales; children welcome, eight bedrooms. *(David White, Zoe Freeman)*

ST IVES   SW5140
★Sloop (01736) 796584
The Wharf; TR26 1LP Busy low-beamed, panelled and flagstoned harbourside pub with bright St Ives School pictures and attractive portrait drawings in front bar, booth seating in back bar, good value food from sandwiches and interesting baguettes to lots of fresh local fish, quick friendly service even when busy, ales including Greene King Old Speckled Hen and Sharps Doom Bar, good coffee; background music, TV; children in eating area, a few beach-view seats out on cobbles, open all day (breakfast from 9am), cosy bedrooms, handy for Tate gallery. *(Bruce and Sharon Eden, Roger and Donna Huggins, Andrew Goddard, Alan Johnson, Stanley and Annie Matthews, Clifford Blakemore and others)*

ST IVES   SW5140
Union (01736) 796486
Fore Street; TR26 1AB Popular and friendly low-beamed local, roomy but cosy, with good value food from sandwiches to local fish, well kept Sharps Doom Bar and Weston's Old Rosie cider, decent wines and coffee, small hot fire, leather sofas on carpet, dark woodwork and masses of ship photographs; background music; dogs welcome. *(Alan Johnson)*

ST JUST IN PENWITH   SW3731
Kings Arms (01736) 788545
Market Square; TR19 7HF Three separate carpeted areas, granite walls, beamed and boarded ceilings, open fire and woodburner, well kept St Austell ales, shortish menu of enjoyable home-made food (not Sun evening), good helpful service; background music (live Sun), TV, Weds quiz; children and dogs welcome, tables out in front. *(Neil Alford, Alan Johnson)*

ST JUST IN PENWITH   SW3731
★Star (01736) 788767
Fore Street; TR19 7LL Relaxed and informal low-beamed two-room local, friendly landlord, five well kept St Austell ales, no food (at lunch bring your own sandwiches or

pasties), dimly lit main bar with dark walls covered in flags and photographs, coal fire, sleepy pub cat, darts and euchre, nostalgic juke box, live celtic music Mon, open mike Thurs; tables in attractive backyard with smokers' shelter, open all day. *(Alan Johnson)*

ST KEW   SX0276
★St Kew Inn (01208) 841259
Village signposted from A39 NE of Wadebridge; PL30 3HB Grand-looking 15th-c pub with neat beamed bar, stone walls, winged high-backed settles and more traditional furniture on tartan carpeting, assorted jugs dotted about, log fire in stone fireplace, three dining areas, St Austell beers from cask and handpump, good choice of enjoyable well presented food (not Sun evening in winter), friendly attentive service, live music every other Fri; children (away from bar) and dogs welcome, pretty flowering tubs and baskets outside, picnic-sets in garden over the road, open all day in summer. *(Paul and Penny Dawson, Barry and Anne, Andrea Rampley, John Marsh, Chris and Val Ramstedt)*

ST MAWES   SW8433
Rising Sun (01326) 270233
The Square; TR2 5DJ Light and airy pub across road from harbour wall; relaxed bar on right with end woodburner, sea-view bow window opposite, rugs on stripped wood, a few dining tables, sizeable carpeted left-hand bar with dark wood furniture, well prepared tasty food served by friendly young staff, well kept St Austell ales and nice wines by the glass, wood-floored conservatory; background music; awkward wheelchair access, picnic-sets on sunny front terrace, bedrooms. *(Phil and Jane Villiers, Stanley and Annie Matthews, John and Sharon Hancock)*

ST MAWES   SW8433
Victory (01326) 270324
Victory Hill; TR2 5DQ Tucked up from the harbour and still for sale; carpeted locals' bar on left, dining area to the right, more formal upstairs restaurant with balcony, well kept Otter, Sharps and Skinners ales, good food including local fish, log fires, friendly staff; background music, no wheelchair access; children welcome, one or two picnic-sets outside, two good value bedrooms, open all day. *(M J Winterton, Henry Fryer, Barry Collett)*

ST MAWGAN   SW8765
★Falcon (01637) 860225
NE of Newquay, off B3276 or A3059; TR8 4EP Attractive wisteria-clad old stone inn, log-fire bar with antique coaching prints and falcon pictures, St Austell ales kept well,

---

Cribbage is a card game using a block of wood with holes for matchsticks or special pins to score with; regulars in cribbage pubs are usually happy to teach strangers how to play.

pubby food, good friendly service, compact stone-floored dining room, darts; children welcome, front cobbled courtyard and peaceful back garden with wishing well (they ask to keep a credit card if you eat outside), pretty village, two bedrooms, open all day in summer. *(Anon)*

ST TUDY   SX0676
Tudy Inn (01208) 850656

Off A391 near Wadebridge; PL30 3NN Nicely refurbished 16th-c village pub under newish welcoming landlord, good freshly cooked food at reasonable prices, well kept cornish beers from small breweries, helpful service, some interesting photographs taken by landlord, warm log fire in raised hearth, closed Sun evening, Mon. *(Dr and Mrs M P Bracy, Jason Caulkin, Mrs Jill Silversides, Barry Brown)*

STITHIANS   SW7640
Cornish Arms (01872) 863445

Frogpool – not shown on many road maps but is NE of A393, ie opposite side to Stithians itself; TR4 8RP Unspoilt 18th-c village pub under brother and sister team (he cooks), long beamed bar with fires either end, cosy snug, low priced wholesome food (not Mon) from sandwiches and four types of ploughman's up, local ales and ciders; pool, euchre, piped radio; well behaved children and dogs welcome, closed Mon lunchtime. *(John Marsh)*

TIDEFORD   SX3459
Rod & Line (01752) 851323

Church Road; PL12 5HW Small old-fashioned local set back from road up steps, friendly lively atmosphere, Greene King Abbot and St Austell Tribute kept well, lots of fish from local market including good crab, angling theme with rods etc, low-bowed ceiling, settles, good log fire; children and dogs welcome, tables outside. *(Julian Distin, Ian Phillips, Andrea Rampley)*

TINTAGEL   SX0588
Olde Malthouse (01840) 770461

Fore Street; PL34 0DA Well looked after beamed pub with inglenook bar and restaurant, good value food from lunchtime sandwiches to good local fish, ales such as Skinners Betty Stogs and Heligan Honey; children and dogs welcome, tables on roadside terrace, seven bedrooms. *(George Atkinson)*

TOWAN CROSS
Victory (01209) 890359

Off B3277; TR4 8BN Comfortable roadside local with above average good value food, four ales including Skinners, helpful staff; pool, euchre and Tues quiz; children and dogs welcome, beer garden, camping, handy for good uncrowded beaches, open all day. *(Richard Fulbrook, John Marsh)*

TREBURLEY   SX3477
Springer Spaniel (01579) 370424

A388 Callington–Launceston; PL15 9NS Relaxed country pub popular with locals, clean décor with high-backed settle by woodburner, farmhouse chairs and other seats, further cosy room with big solid teak tables, attractive restaurant up some steps, good locally sourced food (some from own organic farm), well kept Sharps and Skinners, good wine choice; dogs welcome in bar, children in eating areas, covered terrace. *(Stanley and Annie Matthews)*

TREEN   SW3923
★ Logan Rock (01736) 810495

Just off B3315 Penzance–Land's End; TR19 6LG Low-beamed traditional bar with well kept St Austell ales, generous tasty food from sandwiches and home-made pasties up, good vegetarian options too, inglenook fire, small back snug with excellent cricket memorabilia (welcoming landlady eminent in county cricket association), family room (no under-14s in bar); dogs welcome on leads (resident cat), pretty split-level garden behind covered area, good coast walks including to Logan Rock itself, handy for Minack Theatre, open all day in season and can get very busy. *(Dennis Jenkin, David Crook, Di and Mike Gillam, Robert Wivell, Jennifer Banks)*

TREGADILLETT   SX2983
★ Eliot Arms (01566) 772051

Village signposted off A30 at junction with A395, W end of Launceston bypass; PL15 7EU Creeper-covered with series of small rooms, interesting collections including 72 antique clocks, 400 snuffs, hundreds of horsebrasses, barometers, old prints and shelves of books/china, fine mix of furniture on Delabole slate from high-backed settles and chaises longues to more modern seats, open fires, well kept St Austell Tribute, Theakstons XB and a guest, decent good value food, friendly service; background music, games machine and darts; children and dogs welcome, seats out front and back, lovely hanging baskets and tubs, two bedrooms, open all day. *(John and Bernadette Elliott)*

TREGONY   SW9244
Kings Arms (01872) 530202

Fore Street (B3287); TR2 5RW Light and airy 16th-c coaching inn, long traditional main bar and two beamed and panelled front dining areas, St Austell ales, Healey's cider/perry, nice wines, good quality reasonably priced pub food using local produce, tea and coffee, welcoming prompt service and chatty landlord, two fireplaces, one with huge cornish range, pubby furniture on carpet or flagstones, old team photographs, back games room; well behaved children welcome, disabled access, tables in pleasant suntrap garden, charming village. *(Chris and Angela Buckell)*

TRELEIGH   SW7043
Treleigh Arms (01209) 315095
Near Redruth, A3047; TR16 4AY
Hospitable place, clean and tidy, with good
food (special diets catered for), well kept
beers such as Bass, Sharps and Skinners,
real cider, efficient staff coping well at
busy times, Tues quiz; children and dogs
welcome, garden with boules, open all day
Fri-Sun. *(Mick and Moira Brummell, John and
Jackie Chalcraft)*

TRURO   SW8244
Old Ale House (01872) 271122
Quay Street; TR1 2HD Town-centre tap
for Skinners brewery, five of their ales plus
guests, some from casks behind bar, several
wines by the glass including country ones,
tasty bargain food such as 'sizzling skillets'
from open kitchen, cheerful service, dimly lit
beamed bar with engaging mix of furnishings,
sawdust on floor, free monkey nuts, some
interesting 1920s bric-a-brac, life-size cut-out
of Betty Stogs, beer mats on walls and
ceiling, daily newspapers, upstairs room with
table football; juke box; children (away from
bar) and dogs welcome, open all day. *(David
Crook, B and M Kendall, Alan Johnson)*

TRURO   SW8244
White Hart (01872) 277294
*New Bridge Street (aka Crab & Ale
House); TR1 2AA* Compact old city-centre
pub with nautical theme, friendly landlord
and locals, three or four well kept ales
including St Austell Tribute and Sharps Doom
Bar, good helpings of enjoyable reasonably
priced pub food. *(John and Sarah Perry,
Stanley and Annie Matthews)*

TYWARDREATH   SX0854
New Inn (01726) 813901
Off A3082; Fore Street; PL24 2QP
Timeless 18th-c local, friendly and relaxed,
with Bass tapped from the cask and St
Austell ales on handpump, caring friendly
landlord, back games/children's room with
juke box, open fires; large secluded garden
behind, nice village setting, bedrooms, open
all day. *(Anon)*

VERYAN   SW9139
New Inn (01872) 501362
Village signed off A3078; TR2 5QA
Comfortable and homely one-bar beamed
local continuing well under present landlord;
straightforward good value food from
sandwiches up (can get busy in evening, so
worth booking), St Austell ales, Healey's
cider, good wines, friendly attentive service,
inglenook woodburner, polished brass and old
pictures; background music, nearby parking
difficult in summer; dogs and well behaved
children welcome, wheelchair access
with help, secluded beer garden behind,

bedrooms, interesting partly thatched village
not far from nice beach. *(R K Phillips, Chris
and Angela Buckell, M Mossman)*

WATERGATE BAY   SW8464
Beach Hut (01637) 860877
*B3276 coast road N of Newquay;
TR8 4AA* Great views from bustling modern
beach bar with customers of all ages, surfing
photographs on planked walls, cushioned
wicker and cane armchairs around green
and orange tables, weathered stripped-wood
floor, unusual sloping bleached-board ceiling,
big windows and doors opening to glass-
fronted deck looking across sand to the sea,
simpler end room, three real ales including
Skinners, decent wines by the glass and
lots of coffees and teas, good modern food
served by friendly young staff; background
music; dogs welcome in bar, easy wheelchair
access, open summer 8.30am-11pm, winter
10am-5pm (9am-9pm weekends). *(Chris and
Val Ramstedt, Jason Caulkin)*

WATERGATE BAY   SW8464
Phoenix (01637) 860353
Trevarrian Hill; TR8 4AB Popular
surfers' haunt with great coast and sunset
views from open balcony, bar-restaurant
upstairs with enjoyable food including
interesting fish dishes, downstairs bistro
bar, good friendly service, well kept St
Austell Tribute, Sharps Doom Bar and
Skinners Betty Stogs, decent wines, sensible
prices; live music, TV and pool; well behaved
children and dogs welcome, disabled
facilities, plenty of outside seating, open all
day weekends. *(Anon)*

WENDRON   SW6731
New Inn (01326) 572683
B3297; TR13 0EA Friendly little 18th-c
granite-built village pub, three well kept
changing ales, enjoyable good value food
from landlady including popular Sun lunch;
children and dogs welcome, open all day in
summer. *(Ken and Tammy Lewis)*

ZELAH   SW8151
Hawkins Arms (01872) 540339
A30; TR4 9HU Homely 18th-c stone-built
beamed local, well kept Bays and guests such
as Skinners, decent good value food including
blackboard specials, nice coffee, friendly
landlord and staff, copper and brass in bar
and dining room, woodburner; children and
dogs welcome, back and side terraces, four
bedrooms. *(Stanley and Annie Matthews)*

ZENNOR   SW4538
☀ Tinners Arms (01736) 796927
B3306 W of St Ives; TR26 3BY Friendly
welcome and good food from ploughman's
with three cornish cheeses up, long unspoilt
bar with flagstones, granite, stripped pine
and real fires each end, back dining room,
well kept St Austell and Sharps ales, farm
cider, sensibly priced wines and decent

coffee, quick service even when busy, friendly mix of locals and visitors, Thurs folk night; children, dogs and muddy boots welcome, tables in small suntrap courtyard, lovely peaceful windswept setting near coast path and by church with 15th-c carved mermaid bench, bedrooms in building next door, open all day. *(Rod and Chris Pring, Robert Wivell, Paul and Claudia Dickinson, Roger and Donna Huggins, John and Jackie Chalcraft, Di and Mike Gillam and others)*

ISLES OF SCILLY

ST AGNES SV8808
★**Turks Head** (01720) 422434
The Quay; TR22 0PL One of the UK's most beautifully placed pubs, idyllic sea and island views from garden terrace, can get very busy on fine days, good food from pasties to popular fresh seafood (best to get there early), well kept ales and cider, friendly licensees and good cheerful service; children and dogs welcome, closed in winter, otherwise open all day. *(Bob and Margaret Holder, Michael Sargent, David and Katharine Cooke)*

ST MARY'S SV9010
★**Atlantic Inn** (01720) 422323
The Strand; next to but independent from Atlantic Hotel; TR21 0HY Spreading and hospitable dark bar with well kept St Austell ales, good range of food including daily specials, sea-view restaurant, low beams, hanging boat and other nauticalia, mix of locals and tourists – busy evenings, quieter on sunny lunchtimes; darts, pool,

games machines, piped and live music; nice raised verandah with wide views over harbour, good bedrooms in adjacent hotel. *(Bob and Margaret Holder)*

ST MARY'S SV9110
Old Town Inn (01720) 422301
Old Town; TR21 0NN Nice local feel in welcoming light bar and big back dining area, wood floors and panelling, enjoyable food (not Mon-Weds in winter) cooked by landlady including good pizzas, well kept Ales of Scilly, Sharps Doom Bar and guests, monthly folk club; pool and darts; children and dogs welcome, tables in tidy garden behind, three courtyard bedrooms, handy for airport, open all day in summer (from 5pm weekdays, all day weekends in winter). *(Jacky Chadwick)*

TRESCO SV8815
★**New Inn** (01720) 423006
New Grimsby; TR24 0QG Handy for ferries and close to the famous gardens; main bar with comfortable old sofas, banquettes, planked partition seating and farmhouse tables and chairs, a few standing timbers, boat pictures, collection of old telescopes and large model yacht, pavilion extension has cheerful yellow walls and plenty of seats on blue-painted floors, Ales of Scilly and Skinners, a dozen good wines by the glass, quite a choice of spirits and several coffees, enjoyable food including daily specials; background music, board games, darts and pool; children and dogs (in bar) welcome, seats on flower-filled sea-view terrace, bedrooms, open all day in summer. *(R J Herd, Bernard Stradling, Michael Sargent, David and Katharine Cooke and others)*

Cumbria

As many of the pubs here are in stunning scenery with wonderful hikes all around, it makes sense to provide hearty, good value lunchtime food at honest prices – which a large number of places do. Pubs our readers have particularly enjoyed this year while out walking include the Wateredge Inn in Ambleside (stunning lakeside position, good food all day and stylish bedrooms), Pheasant at Bassenthwaite Lake (head for the pubby little bar), Hare & Hounds near Bowland Bridge (local beers and interesting food in attractive bars), Blacksmiths Arms at Broughton Mills (log fires, cosy bars, reliable food and a friendly atmosphere), Masons Arms in Cartmel Fell (fantastic choice of drinks and food and amazing views), Sun in Coniston (eight real ales, tasty food and a dramatic setting), Britannia near Elterwater (fine choice of beers and food, lots of cheerful customers and popular bedrooms), Drunken Duck near Hawkshead (informal lunchtime bar in civilised inn, own-brewed beers and exceptional evening restaurant), Watermill at Ings (eight own-brewed beers, popular food and a lovely landlord), Kirkstile Inn at Loweswater (deservedly busy little place with own brews and well liked meals), Black Swan in Ravenstonedale (thriving bar in family-run hotel, nice food and good drinks choice) and Langstrath in Stonethwaite (some sort of enjoyable food served all day by friendly staff). For a really special meal and pubs with exceptional chefs, we recommend the Masons Arms at Cartmel Fell (you could stay in their self-catering apartments too), George & Dragon at Clifton (impressive food using Estate produce), Punch Bowl at Crosthwaite (an absolutely first class all-rounder), Plough at Lupton (some sort of impressive food all day in civilised inn, and lovely bedrooms), Queens Head at Troutbeck (character bars, imaginative cooking, popular bedrooms), Derby Arms in Witherslack (a fine range of drinks, enticing meals and elegant furnishings) and the Gate Inn at Yanwath (exceptional food served by courteous, helpful staff). Our Cumbria Dining Pub 2014 award goes to the Plough at Lupton.

AMBLESIDE

NY3704 Map 9

Golden Rule

Smithy Brow; follow Kirkstone Pass signpost from A591 on N side of town;
LA22 9AS

Simple town local with a cosy, relaxed atmosphere and real ales

This is an honest Lakeland local where nothing changes at all – which is just the way the regulars and walkers with their dogs like it. The bar area has built-in wall seats around cast-iron-framed tables (one with a local map set into its top), horsebrasses on the black beams, assorted pictures on the walls, a welcoming winter fire and a relaxed atmosphere. Robinsons Cumbria Way, Hatters Dark Mild, Dizzy Blonde, Double Hop, Enigma and Hartleys XB on handpump and Weston's cider. A brass measuring rule hangs above the bar (hence the pub's name). There's also a back room with TV (not much used), a room on the left with darts and a games machine, and another room, down a couple of steps on the right, with lots of seating. The backyard has benches and a covered heated area, and the window boxes are especially colourful. There's no car park.

There might be scotch eggs and pies but they tend to run out fast, so don't assume you'll be able to get something to eat.

Robinsons ~ Tenant John Lockley ~ Real ale ~ No credit cards ~ (015394) 32257 ~ Open 11-midnight ~ Children welcome away from bar and must leave by 9pm ~ Dogs welcome ~ www.goldenrule-ambleside.co.uk *Recommended by G Jennings*

AMBLESIDE

NY3703 Map 9

Wateredge Inn ♀ ⇔

Borrans Road, off A591; LA22 0EP

Family-run inn in beautiful spot by Lake Windermere, plenty of room both inside and out, up to six ales on handpump and enjoyable all-day food; comfortable bedrooms.

There's always a really easy-going, bustling atmosphere here, with a wide mix of customers keen to make the most of the lovely setting at the tip of Lake Windermere. The modernised bar – originally two 17th-c cottages – has splendid views through big windows looking over the sizeable garden that runs down to the water. There are leather tub chairs around wooden tables on flagstones, and several different areas leading off with similar furniture, walls with exposed stonework here and there hung with interesting old photographs and paintings (some wood panelling too) and a much-favoured cosy beamed room with timbers, sofas, armchairs and an open fire. The six real ales on handpump served by friendly, cheerful staff come from breweries like Barngates, Cumberland, Jennings, Theakstons and Tirril and there are lots of wines by the glass; quite a choice of coffees too. Background music and TV. There are plenty of seats outside and they even have their own moorings. The bedrooms are stylish and comfortable, many with water views.

Some sort of food is available all day and might include sandwiches, baby rack of pork ribs in sweet chilli glaze, a charcuterie plate, corned beef hash with poached hen or duck egg, tempura fresh haddock with mushy peas and triple-cooked chips, spicy five-bean chilli with coriander couscous, corn crisps and sour cream, a pie of the day, free-range chicken breast stuffed with haggis in creamy whisky sauce, sweet-cured bacon chop with caramelised pineapple and dripping chips, and puddings like knickerbocker glory and sticky toffee pudding with butterscotch sauce. *Benchmark main dish: beer-battered fish and chips £11.95. Two-course evening meal £18.00.*

Free house ~ Licensee Derek Cowap ~ Real ale ~ (015394) 32332 ~ Open 10am-11pm ~ Bar food 12-4, 5-9; light snacks 4-5 ~ Children allowed in eating area of bar ~ Dogs allowed in bar and bedrooms ~ Live music Fri evening ~ Bedrooms: £52/£99 ~ www.wateredgehotel.co.uk *Recommended by Ruth May, Caroline Prescott*

BASSENTHWAITE LAKE NY1930 Map 9
Pheasant ★

Follow Pheasant Inn sign at N end of dual carriageway stretch of A66 by Bassenthwaite Lake; CA13 9YE

Charming, old-fashioned bar in smart hotel with enjoyable bar food, and a fine range of drinks; comfortable bedrooms

At the heart of this rather smart and civilised hotel is a surprising little bar of proper character. It's nicely old-fashioned – and much used by chatty locals – with mellow polished walls, cushioned oak settles, rush-seat chairs and library seats, and hunting prints and photographs. Coniston Bluebird, Cumberland Corby Ale and Eden Dark Knight on handpump, a dozen good wines by the glass, over 50 malt whiskies and several gins and vodkas all served by friendly, knowledgeable staff. There's a front bistro, a formal back restaurant overlooking the garden, and several comfortable lounges with log fires, beautiful flower arrangements, fine parquet flooring, antiques and plants. The garden has seats and tables and is surrounded by attractive woodland; plenty of walks in all directions.

You can eat in the bar, bistro or lounges at lunchtime and only in the bistro and restaurant in the evening. As well as sandwiches, the well liked food might include twice-baked goats cheese soufflé with spinach, beetroot and walnut salad, potted shrimps with lemon and toast, cumberland sausage with braised red cabbage and onion gravy, smoked ham with egg and triple-cooked chips, braised pork belly with smoked bacon, savoy cabbage and creamed potatoes, calves liver with bacon, red onion marmalade and sherry vinegar jus, thai green chicken curry, and puddings such as orange crème caramel with orange and basil salad and rum and raisin cheesecake with sour cherry ice-cream. *Benchmark main dish: beer-battered haddock £13.95. Two-course evening meal £19.00.*

Free house ~ Licensee Matthew Wylie ~ Real ale ~ (017687) 76234 ~ Open 11.30-2.30, 5.30-11; 12-2.30, 6-10.30 Sun ~ Bar food 12-2, 7-9 ~ Restaurant ~ Children over 8 only ~ Dogs allowed in bar and bedrooms ~ Bedrooms: £95/£170 ~ www.the-pheasant.co.uk *Recommended by Jeremy and Ruth Preston-Hoar, Martin and Sue Day, Pat and Stewart Gordon, Colin McLachlan, Hugh Roberts*

BOWLAND BRIDGE SD4189 Map 9
Hare & Hounds

Signed from A5074; LA11 6NN

17th-c inn in quiet spot with a friendly, cheerful landlady, real ales, popular food and fine views; comfortable bedrooms

Comfortable bedrooms and especially good breakfasts make this attractive 17th-c former coaching inn a good base for the area – Lake Windermere is just three miles away. There's a little bar with a log fire, daily papers, and high chairs by the wooden counter where they serve Hare of the Dog (named for the pub by Tirril) and guests from Keswick and Tirril on handpump, a farm cider from half a mile away and ten wines by the glass. Leading off here, other rooms are appealingly furnished with a pleasing mix of interesting dining chairs around all sorts of tables on black slate or old pine-boarded floors, numerous hunting prints on painted or bare-stone walls, a candlelit moroccan-style lantern in a fireplace with neatly stacked logs to one side, and a relaxed atmosphere; background music and board games. The collie is called Murphy. There are teak tables and chairs under parasols on the front terrace, with more seats in the spacious side garden and fine valley views.

As well as a two-course weekday light lunch menu, the good, enjoyable food includes hot and cold sandwiches, local game terrine with sweet berry chutney, smoked trout, smoked salmon and crayfish platter with pickled cucumber and dill mascarpone, cajun hot chicken and bacon salad with lemon mayonnaise, sweet potato gateau with herb crumb and basil and garlic pesto sauce, lamb hotpot topped with dauphinoise potatoes, specials like aubergine layer with spicy tomato sauce and creamy goats cheese or pork, mango and stilton sausage with caramelised gravy on spring onion mash, and puddings such as chocolate terrine with raspberry coulis and sticky ginger pudding. *Benchmark main dish: beef in ale pie £11.50. Two-course evening meal £18.00.*

Free house ~ Licensee Kerry Parsons ~ Real ale ~ (015395) 68333 ~ Open 12-11(10.30 Sun) ~ Bar food 12-2, 6-9; all day weekends ~ Children welcome ~ Dogs welcome ~ Bedrooms: /£85 ~ www.hareandhoundsbowlandbridge.co.uk *Recommended by Martin Hickes, Mr and Mrs P R Thomas, Patricia White, Steve Pye, R J Herd, David Heath, Michael Doswell*

BOWNESS-ON-WINDERMERE
Hole in t' Wall

SD4096 Map 9

Fallbarrow Road, off St Martins Parade; LA23 3DH

Lively and unchanging town local with popular ales and friendly staff

This is an interesting tavern that happily never changes – it's the town's oldest pub. There's always a good crowd of customers in the split-level rooms, which have beams, stripped stone and flagstone floors, lots of country knick-knacks and old pictures, and a splendid log fire beneath a vast slate mantelpiece; the upper room has some noteworthy plasterwork. Robinsons Double Hop, Dizzy Blonde, Hartleys XB and Unicorn on handpump. Friendly staff and a juke box in the bottom bar. The small flagstoned front courtyard has sheltered picnic-sets and outdoor heaters.

Bar food includes pâté, salt and pepper squid, a prawn platter, beer-battered cod goujons, a curry of the day, and puddings like jam sponge with custard and sticky toffee pudding. *Benchmark main dish: chicken and mushroom pie £11.25. Two-course evening meal £20.00.*

Robinsons ~ Tenant Susan Burnet ~ Real ale ~ (015394) 43488 ~ Open 11-11(11.30 Fri, Sat); 12-11 Sun ~ Bar food 12-2.30, 6-8.30; 12-8 Fri-Sun ~ Children welcome ~ Live music Fri and alternate Sun *Recommended by David Bedford*

'Children welcome' means the pub says it lets children inside without any special restriction. If it allows them in, but to restricted areas such as an eating area or family room, we specify this. Places with separate restaurants often let children use them, and hotels usually let children into public areas such as lounges. Some pubs impose an evening time limit – let us know if you find one earlier than 9pm.

BROUGHTON MILLS   SD2190 Map 9

Blacksmiths Arms ⑪

Off A593 N of Broughton-in-Furness; LA20 6AX

Friendly little pub with imaginative food, local beers and open fires; fine surrounding walks

Maintaining high standards year after year, this amiable small pub remains popular with our readers. It's surrounded by quiet countryside and the four little bars have log fires, a relaxed, friendly atmosphere and are simply and attractively decorated with straightforward chairs and tables on ancient slate floors. There's Barngates Cracker Ale, Cumberland Corby Blonde and Tirril Nameless Ale on handpump, nine wines by the glass and summer farm cider; darts, board games and dominoes. The hanging baskets and tubs of flowers in front of the building are very pretty in summer, and there are seats and tables under parasols on the back terrace.

 Reliably good food includes sandwiches, warm confit shredded duck leg with hoisin sauce, goats cheese with rocket, red onion, walnut and sun-dried tomato salad, honey-roast ham with poached egg, rhubarb chutney and home-made chips, chargrilled cajun-spiced chicken with sour cream dressing, cumberland sausage with spring onion mash, black pudding and red onion and balsamic gravy, pork tenderloin wrapped in pancetta with chorizo and chickpea casserole and duck fat roasted potatoes, and puddings like lime and ginger crème brûlée and dark chocolate brownie with warm chocolate sauce; they also offer a two-course set lunch. *Benchmark main dish: slow-braised shoulder of minted lamb £13.95. Two-course evening meal £19.50.*

Free house ~ Licensees Mike and Sophie Lane ~ Real ale ~ (01229) 716824 ~ Open 12-11(5-11 Mon); 12-10.30 Sun; 12-2.30, 5-11 Tues-Fri in winter; closed Mon lunchtime ~ Bar food 12-2, 6-9; not Mon ~ Restaurant ~ Children welcome ~ Dogs welcome ~ www.theblacksmithsarms.co.uk *Recommended by Miss J F Reay, Tina and David Woods-Taylor*

CARLETON   NY5329 Map 9

Cross Keys ◀

A686, off A66 roundabout at Penrith; CA11 8TP

Friendly refurbished pub with several connected seating areas, real ales and popular food

As this well run pub is always deservedly busy, you should book in advance to be sure of a table. There's a good mix of customers, a friendly, bustling atmosphere and the beamed main bar has pubby tables and chairs on light wooden floorboards, modern metal wall lights and pictures on the bare stone walls, and Tirril 1823 and a changing guest on handpump. Steps lead down to a small area with high bar stools around a high drinking table, and then upstairs to the restaurant: a light, airy room with big windows, large wrought-iron candelabras hanging from the vaulted ceiling, pale solid wooden tables and chairs, and doors to a verandah. At the far end of the main bar is yet another couple of small connected bar rooms with darts, games machine, pool, juke box and dominoes; TV and background music. There are fell views from the garden. This is under the same ownership as the Highland Drove in Great Salkeld.

Enjoyable food includes chicken liver pâté with onion and apricot chutney, warm salad of slow-roasted pork belly with black pudding and caramelised apple, roast vegetable and feta tart with tomato and aubergine stack, beer-battered haddock with mushy peas and tartare sauce, cumberland lamb hotpot, a fish dish of the day, chargrilled piri-piri chicken with tomato and onion salsa and sour cream, flat-iron steak with mushrooms, tomatoes and chips, and puddings such as passion-fruit crème brûlée and chocolate brownie with chocolate sauce and vanilla ice-cream. *Benchmark main dish: steak in ale pie £10.95. Two-course evening meal £16.00.*

Free house ~ Licensee Paul Newton ~ Real ale ~ (01768) 865588 ~ Open 12-3, 5-midnight; 12-1am Sat; 12-midnight Sun ~ Bar food 12-2.30, 6(5.30 Fri, Sat)-9(8.30 Sun) ~ Restaurant ~ Children welcome ~ Dogs allowed in bar ~ www.kyloes.co.uk
Recommended by Richard J Holloway, Gregg Davies, Comus and Sarah Elliott

CARTMEL   SD3778   Map 7

Kings Arms

The Square; LA11 6QB

Bustling village pub with five real ales and well liked food

This 18th-c former coaching inn has seats and picnic-sets out in front facing the lovely square. Inside, the cosy bars have beams, open log fires, flagstones and wooden floorboards and an attractive range of seats, from nice old wooden or leather and brass-studded dining chairs around a mix of wooden tables, to comfortable leather armchairs. Bass and Hawkshead Bitter, Brodies Prime, Lakeland Gold and Windermere Pale on handpump, served by friendly staff. The village has a notable priory church and is surrounded by good walks.

Popular bar food includes sandwiches, various platters, tiger prawns with sweet chilli dip, duck and orange pâté, confit chicken breast, steak in ale pie, roasted chicken breast and confit leg with wild mushrooms and pancetta jus, beer-battered fish and chips, lamb shoulder hotpot, venison steak with red wine jus and celeriac purée, and puddings like whiskey rice pudding and lemon tart. *Benchmark main dish: steak in ale pie £11.95. Two-course evening meal £15.50.*

Enterprise ~ Lease Richard Grimmer ~ Real ale ~ (015395) 33246 ~ Open 10-midnight(1am Fri, Sat) ~ Bar food 12-9 ~ Restaurant ~ Children welcome ~ Dogs welcome ~ www.thekingsarmscartmel.com *Recommended by Pauline Fellows and Simon Robbins*

CARTMEL FELL   SD4189   Map 9

Masons Arms ⏺ ♀ ⏺

Strawberry Bank, a few miles S of Windermere between A592 and A5074; perhaps the simplest way to find the pub is to go uphill W from Bowland Bridge (signposted off A5074) towards Newby Bridge and keep right then left at the staggered crossroads – it's then on your right, below Gummer's How; OS Sheet 97 map reference 413895; LA11 6NW

Stunning views, beamed bar with plenty of character, interesting food and real ales plus many foreign bottled beers; self-catering cottages and apartments

'If this place was nearby, we'd go every week,' enthuses one of our more discerning readers; many others agree. The main bar has plenty of character, with low black beams in the bowed ceiling and country chairs and plain wooden tables on polished flagstones. A small lounge has oak tables and settles to match its fine Jacobean panelling, there's also a plain little room beyond the serving counter with pictures and a fire in an open range, a family room with the atmosphere of an old parlour and an upstairs dining room; background music and board games. Cumbrian Legendary Loweswater Gold, Hawkshead Bitter, Thwaites Wainwright and a guest beer on handpump, several foreign bottled beers, 12 wines by the glass and ten malt whiskies; service is friendly and helpful. Rustic benches and tables on the heated terrace take in the stunning views down over the Winster Valley to the woods below Whitbarrow Scar. The stylish and comfortable self-catering cottages and apartments also have fine views.

Enticing and extremely good, the food includes lunchtime sandwiches, sticky ribs, devilled crab cakes with chilli jam and chive sour cream, cumberland sausages with black pudding mash and onion gravy, creamy butternut squash risotto with toasted pine nuts, parmesan and truffle oil, excellent steak pudding, lambs liver and bacon with roasted onions, creamy mash and gravy, fillet of smoked haddock with spring onion mash, soft poached egg and cheese and chive sauce, and puddings such as baked new york-style cheesecake with berry compote and sticky toffee pudding. *Benchmark main dish: lamb shank with roasted root vegetables, dauphinoise potatoes and rich gravy £17.95. Two-course evening meal £18.50.*

Individual Inns ~ Managers John and Diane Taylor ~ Real ale ~ (015395) 68486 ~ Open 11.30-11; 12-10.30 Sun ~ Bar food 12-2.30, 6-9; all day weekends ~ Restaurant ~ Children welcome ~ Dogs allowed in bar and bedrooms ~ www.strawberrybank.com
Recommended by Karen Eliot, Christian Mole, Mr and Mrs P R Thomas, Peter Armstrong, Tina and David Woods-Taylor, Pauline Fellows and Simon Robbins, Roger Fox

CLIFTON   NY5326   Map 9

George & Dragon 🍴 🍷 🛏

A6; near M6 junction 40; CA10 2ER

18th-c former coaching inn with attractive bars and sizeable restaurant, local ales, well chosen wines, imaginative food and seats outside; smart bedrooms

With excellent food, stylish bedrooms and very helpful, friendly staff, this carefully restored former coaching inn is on top form. There's a relaxed reception room with leather chairs around a low table in front of an open fire, bright rugs on flagstones, a table in a private nook to one side of the reception desk (just right for a group of six) and a comfortable bed for Porter, the patterdale terrier. Through some wrought-iron gates is the main bar area with additional cheerful rugs on flagstones, assorted wooden farmhouse chairs and tables, grey panelling topped with yellow-painted walls, photographs of the Lowther Estate and of the family with hunting dogs, various sheep and fell pictures and some high bar stools by the panelled bar counter. Cumberland Corby Blonde, Hawkshead Bitter and Hesket Newmarket High Pike on handpump, a dozen wines by the glass from a well chosen list and home-made soft drinks. A further room with another open fire is similarly furnished. The sizeable restaurant to the left of the entrance is made up of four open-plan rooms: plenty of old pews and church chairs around tables set for dining, a woodburning stove and a contemporary open kitchen. Outside, there are tables on the decoratively paved front area and in a high-walled enclosed courtyard, and a herb garden.

Using produce from the Estate of which this inn is part, the impressive food might include sandwiches, wild mushroom and black pudding fricassée, eggs benedict, omelette of the day, butter bean and tomato ragout with chilli and sour cream, burger (using Estate beef) with chips and salad, chicken schnitzel with lemon butter, baked salmon fillet, curried leeks and prawns, roast duck served two ways with pak choi and honey and clove sauce, and puddings like a crumble of the day and chocolate pot with home-made biscotti; there's also a two- and three-course set menu (not Saturday evening or Sunday lunchtime). *Benchmark main dish: venison burger with hand-cut chips £12.50. Two-course evening meal £21.00.*

Free house ~ Licensee Charles Lowther ~ Real ale ~ (01768) 865381 ~ Open 12-midnight ~ Bar food 12-2, 6-9 ~ Restaurant ~ Children welcome ~ Dogs allowed in bar and bedrooms ~ Bedrooms: £79/£95 ~ www.georgeanddragonclifton.co.uk
Recommended by Richard J Holloway, Malcolm and Jo Hart, Richard Chinn, Chris Pease, David Heath, Chris Hoyer Millar, Pat and Stewart Gordon, Steve Whalley, David and Katharine Cooke

CONISTON
SD3098 Map 9
Sun
Signed left off A593 at the bridge; LA21 8HQ

Lovely position for extended old pub with a lively bar, plenty of dining space, real ales, well liked food and seats outside; comfortable bedrooms

The choice of drinks in this stunningly placed 16th-c pub is worthy of high praise: eight real ales from breweries such as Barngates, Bluebird, Copper Dragon, Hawkshead, Keswick and Loweswater on handpump, eight wines by the glass, two farm ciders and 20 malt whiskies. The heart of the inn is the cheerful bar, which has a good mix of customers (and their dogs), exposed stone walls, beams and timbers, flagstones and a Victorian-style range. Also, cask seats, old settles and cast-iron-framed tables and quite a few Donald Campbell photographs (this was his HQ during his final attempt on the world water-speed record). Above the bar is another room, open to the ceiling, with extra seating for families and larger groups, and there's also a sizeable side lounge that leads into the dining conservatory; pool, darts and TV. The seats and tables on the terrace and in the big tree-sheltered garden make the most of the dramatic fell views. The quiet and comfortable bedrooms have pretty special views too.

Tasty food includes sandwiches, soup, various pizzas, honey- and mustard-glazed ham and egg, beer-battered fish or burger with chips, tagliatelle with mushroom, wine and tarragon sauce, lasagne, steaks, and puddings such as egg custard tart and brown sugar meringue with berries. *Benchmark main dish: cumberland sausage and mash £10.50. Two-course evening meal £15.00.*

Free house ~ Licensee Alan Piper ~ Real ale ~ (015394) 41248 ~ Open 11am-midnight ~ Bar food 12-2.30, 5.30-8.30 ~ Restaurant ~ Children welcome ~ Dogs allowed in bar and bedrooms ~ Bedrooms: £50/£100 ~ www.thesunconiston.com *Recommended by Kim Skuse, Dr Kevan Tucker, Ben Dobson, Roger Fox*

CROSTHWAITE
SD4491 Map 9
Punch Bowl
Village signed off A5074 SE of Windermere; LA8 8HR

Smart dining pub with a proper bar and several other elegant rooms, real ales, a fine wine list, impressive food and friendly staff; seats on terrace overlooking the valley; lovely bedrooms

A first class all-rounder, this civilised inn has outstanding food and service – but also a proper bar. This public bar has rafters, a couple of eye-catching rugs on flagstones, bar stools by the slate-topped counter, Barngates Tag Lag and Westmorland Gold, and Winter Valley Old School on handpump, 22 wines by the glass and around a dozen malt whiskies. To the right are two linked carpeted and beamed rooms with well spaced country pine furniture of varying sizes, including a big refectory table, and walls painted in neutral tones with an attractive assortment of prints; winter log fire, woodburning stove, lots of fresh flowers and daily papers. On the left, the wooden-floored restaurant area (also light, airy and attractive) has comfortable high-backed leather dining chairs. Throughout, the pub feels relaxing and nicely uncluttered. There are some tables on a terrace stepped into the hillside overlooking the lovely Lyth Valley, and the stylish and comfortable bedrooms make this a fine place to stay. This is sister pub to the Plough at Lupton (also in this chapter).

Using the best local, seasonal produce, the accomplished food might include black pudding with bubble and squeak, crispy egg and caramelised onions, baked scallops with leeks, pancetta and gruyère, loin of rabbit with crayfish mousse, lemongrass, apricot and fondant potato, spinach risotto with poached duck egg and chargrilled artichokes, brisket of beef with roast garlic mash, dates and chard, fried bass with fennel, blackberries and red wine jus, and puddings such as baked lemon tart with basil, iced tea and black pepper meringue and raspberry soufflé with white chocolate and tarragon ice-cream. *Benchmark main dish: breast of guinea fowl with truffle gnocchi £16.95. Two-course evening meal £22.00.*

Free house ~ Licensees Richard Rose and Abi Lloyd ~ Real ale ~ (015395) 68237 ~ Open 11-11 ~ Bar food 12-9; light snacks 4-5.30 ~ Restaurant ~ Children welcome ~ Dogs allowed in bar ~ Bedrooms: £95/£130 ~ www.the-punchbowl.co.uk
Recommended by Michael Doswell, Steve Pye, Joss Mitchell

ELTERWATER   NY3204   Map 9
Britannia
Off B5343; LA22 9HP

Much loved inn surrounded by wonderful walks and scenery; up to six real ales and well liked food; bedrooms

With a stunning position, half a dozen well kept real ales and good food, it's not surprising that this friendly place is always so busy; there are walks of every gradient right from the front door. The atmosphere is old-fashioned and the little front bar has beams and a couple of window seats that look through the trees across to Elterwater. The small back bar is traditionally furnished: thick slate walls, winter coal fires, oak benches, settles, windsor chairs and a big old rocking chair. Coniston Bluebird, Hawkshead Red, Hesket Newmarket Catbells, Jennings Bitter, Thwaites Wainwright and a guest from Coniston named for the pub on handpump, and 15 malt whiskies. The lounge is comfortable and there's a hall and dining room. Plenty of seats outside, and summer morris and step and garland dancers.

Generously served and popular (book in advance to avoid disappointment), the food might include lunchtime sandwiches, cumberland pâté with port sauce, grilled haggis with plum jam, puff pastry tartlet with mediterranean vegetables in tomato and basil sauce topped with goats cheese, beer-battered fresh haddock with home-made tartare sauce, burger with home-made red onion marmalade, vine tomatoes and chips, grilled bass fillet with basil and parmesan crust and lemon and chive butter, specials like slow-braised lamb shoulder in mint and honey and venison haunch steak with candied red cabbage, crisp pancetta and port and redcurrant jus, and puddings such as profiteroles with warm dark chocolate sauce and a brûlée of the day. *Benchmark main dish: steak and mushroom in ale pie £13.95. Two-course evening meal £18.50.*

Free house ~ Licensee Andrew Parker ~ Real ale ~ (015394) 37210 ~ Open 10.30am–
11pm ~ Bar food 12-2, 6-9; afternoon snacks 2-5 ~ Restaurant ~ Children welcome ~
Dogs allowed in bar and bedrooms ~ Bedrooms: £85/£95 ~ www.britinn.co.uk
Recommended by Dr Kevan Tucker, Christian Mole, G Jennings, Tina and David Woods-Taylor

GREAT SALKELD   NY5536   Map 10
Highland Drove 🍴
B6412, off A686 NE of Penrith; CA11 9NA

**Bustling place with a cheerful mix of customers, good food in several
dining areas, fair choice of drinks, and fine views from the upstairs
verandah; bedrooms**

This old place has been welcoming customers for hundreds of years
– the earliest were scottish drovers walking their cattle from the
Highlands to markets in northern England. Today, the hard-working,
hands-on landlord is always there to offer a warm welcome, and
everything is kept spotlessly clean. The chatty main bar has sandstone
flooring, stone walls, cushioned wheelback chairs around a mix of
tables and an open fire in a raised stone fireplace. The downstairs eating
area has more cushioned dining chairs around wooden tables on pale
boards, stone walls and ceiling joists and a two-way fire in a raised
stone fireplace that separates this room from the coffee lounge with its
comfortable leather chairs and sofas. There's also an upstairs restaurant
– best book to be sure of a table. Theakstons Black Bull, John Smiths
and a guest beer on handpump, several wines by the glass and 30 malt
whiskies; background music, juke box, darts, pool and dominoes. The
lovely views over the Eden Valley and the Pennines are best enjoyed
from seats on the upstairs verandah. There are additional seats on the
back terrace. Same ownership as the Cross Keys in Carleton.

🍴 Highly enjoyable food includes lunchtime ciabattas, potato and pea samosas
with garlic and mushroom spring roll, leek, celery and ginger wontons and
sweet chilli dipping sauce, lamb kofta on mini naan bread with baba ganoush, a
charcuterie or fish platter, aubergine stuffed with cream cheese, sultanas and
pine nuts on tagliatelle, beer-battered haddock with mushy peas, a trio of lamb
(cutlet, mini shepherd's pie and braised shoulder) with onion sauce, and puddings
like creamy vanilla rice pudding with honey-roast fruit and sticky toffee pudding.
Benchmark main dish: steak in ale pie £10.95. Two-course evening meal £15.00.

Free house ~ Licensees Donald and Paul Newton ~ Real ale ~ (01768) 898349 ~ Open
12-3, 6-11; 12-midnight Sat; 12-3, 6-11 Sun; closed Mon lunchtime ~ Bar food 12-2, 6-9 ~
Restaurant ~ Children welcome ~ Dogs allowed in bar ~ Bedrooms: £42.50/£75 ~
www.kyloes.co.uk *Recommended by Richard J Holloway*

HAWKSHEAD   NY3501   Map 9
Drunken Duck 🍴 🍷 🍽 🛏
*Barngates; the hamlet is signposted from B5286 Hawkshead–Ambleside,
opposite the Outgate Inn; or it may be quicker to take the first right from B5286, after
the wooded caravan site; OS Sheet 90 map reference 350013; LA22 0NG*

**Stylish little bar, several restaurant areas, own-brewed beers and
bar meals as well as innovative restaurant choices; lovely bedrooms,
stunning views**

At lunchtime, the small, smart bar in this civilised inn is an extremely
popular place for a drink or a meal. In warm weather, sit at the
wooden tables and benches on grass opposite the building, where

there are spectacular views across the fells; the thousands of spring and summer bulbs are lovely. With an informal, pubby feel, the bar has leather bar stools by the slate-topped counter, leather club chairs, beams and oak floorboards, photographs, coaching prints and hunting pictures on the walls, and horsebrasses and some kentish hop bines as decoration. From their Barngates brewery, there might be Brathay Gold, Cat Nap, Cracker, Red Bull Terrier and Tag Lag on handpump, as well as 17 wines by the glass from a fine list, quite a few malt whiskies and belgian and german draught beers. The three restaurant areas are elegant, and the beautifully furnished bedrooms get booked up months in advance; some have their own balcony and overlook the garden and tarn.

🍴 The lunchtime bar menu runs until 4pm and might include sandwiches, omelette arnold bennett, barnsley chop with champ mash and mint jelly, roasted hake with romesco sauce, grilled leeks and almonds, and puddings such as dark chocolate pot with poppy seed and orange tuile and bread and butter pudding with custard. In the evening the delicious and enticing dishes include scallops with cauliflower purée, cockles and chive and cauliflower dressing, spelt risotto with sheeps cheese and roasted tomatoes, roast cod with white bean purée and smoked ham, and roasted rump and braised breast of lamb with wild garlic and baby turnips. *Benchmark main dish: fillet steak and onion sandwich with thick-cut chips and wholegrain mayonnaise £10.95. Two-course evening meal £22.00.*

Own brew ~ Licensee Steph Barton ~ Real ale ~ (015394) 36347 ~ Open 11.30-11; 12-10.30 Sun ~ Bar food 12-4, 6.30-9 ~ Restaurant ~ Children welcome ~ Dogs allowed in bar ~ Bedrooms: £78.75/£105 ~ www.drunkenduckinn.co.uk *Recommended by Angela Horsley, Christian Mole, Colin McLachlan, John Evans, Dave Webster, Sue Holland*

INGS
Watermill 🍺 🛏

SD4498 Map 9

Just off A591 E of Windermere; LA8 9PY

Busy, cleverly converted pub with fantastic range of real ales including own brews, and well liked food; bedrooms

At peak times, there may be up to 16 real ales on handpump here including their own brews: Watermill A Bit'er Ruff, Blackbeard, Collie Wobbles, Dogth Vader, Isle of Dogs, Windermere Blonde and Wruff Night – plus guests such as Coniston Bluebird, Cumbrian Legendary Grasmoor Dark Ale, Hop Back Summer Lightning, Keswick Thirst Ascent, Kirkby Lonsdale Tiffin Gold, Theakstons Old Peculier and Ulverston Another Fine Mess. Also, scrumpy cider, a huge choice of foreign bottled beers and 40 malt whiskies. It's a particularly well run place with a friendly, hard-working, hands-on landlord who genuinely loves his pub and his customers – and it shows. The building, cleverly converted from a wood mill and joiner's shop, has plenty of character and the bars have a lively atmosphere, a happy mix of chairs, padded benches and solid oak tables, bar counters made from old church wood, open fires, and interesting photographs and amusing cartoons by a local artist. The spacious lounge bar, in much the same traditional style as the other rooms, has rocking chairs and a big open fire. There's also darts, board games, seats in the gardens and lots to do nearby. Dogs may get free biscuits and water. And it's a smashing place to stay.

🍴 As well as sandwiches (served until 5pm), the popular food includes pork, chicken liver and brandy pâté with home-made cumberland sauce, creamy garlic mushrooms, cumberland sausage on wholegrain mustard mash with beer and onion gravy, fish pie topped with parmesan mash, gammon with free-range egg and pineapple, vegetarian pot, chilli and coriander burger with tomato chutney and home-made chips, and puddings such as eton mess and hot chocolate fudge cake. *Benchmark main dish: beef in ale pie £10.25. Two-course evening meal £16.00.*

Own brew ~ Licensee Brian Coulthwaite ~ Real ale ~ (01539) 821309 ~ Open 11.15-11(10.30 Sun) ~ Bar food 12-9 ~ Children welcome ~ Dogs allowed in bar and bedrooms ~ Bedrooms: £43/£79 ~ www.lakelandpub.co.uk *Recommended by the Didler, Lee and Liz Potter, Dennis Jones, Karen Eliot, Mike Proctor, David Bedford, Paul Goldman, Ian and Jane Irving, Tina and David Woods-Taylor, Dave Webster, Sue Holland*

LANGDALE

NY2806 Map 9

Old Dungeon Ghyll 🍺 £

B5343; LA22 9JY

Straightforward place in lovely position with real ales, traditional food and fine walks; bedrooms

This is a good place to stay, with warm bedrooms and highly thought-of breakfasts. A traditional pub, full of character and atmosphere, it's a real fell-walkers' and climbers' haven as it's right at the heart of the Great Langdale Valley. As the whole feel is basic but cosy there's no need to remove boots or muddy trousers – you can sit on seats in old cattle stalls by the big warming fire and enjoy the fine choice of six real ales on handpump: Dent Bitter, Jennings Cumberland, Theakston Old Peculier, Thwaites Lancaster Bomber and Yates Best Bitter; also, around 20 malt whiskies. It may get lively on a Saturday night (there's a popular National Trust campsite opposite).

Decent helpings of honest food includes their own bread and cakes, lunchtime sandwiches, a changing pâté, cumberland sausages with onion gravy, a pie of the day, beer-battered fish with mushy peas and various curries. *Benchmark main dish: home-made pies £9.50. Two-course evening meal £15.00.*

Free house ~ Licensee Neil Walmsley ~ Real ale ~ (015394) 37272 ~ Open 11-11 (10.30 Sun) ~ Bar food 12-2, 6-9 ~ Restaurant ~ Children welcome ~ Dogs allowed in bar and bedrooms ~ Live music Weds evening ~ Bedrooms: £58/£116 ~ www.odg.co.uk *Recommended by the Didler, David Bedford, Dave Braisted*

LEVENS

SD4987 Map 9

Strickland Arms 🍷 🍺

4 miles from M6 junction 36, via A590; just off A590, by Sizergh Castle gates; LA8 8DZ

Friendly, open-plan pub with popular food, local ales and a fine setting; seats outside

Handy for the M6, this civilised inn gets pretty busy at peak times, when it would be best to book a table. Largely open-plan and with a light and airy feel, the bar on the right has oriental rugs on flagstones, a log fire, Loweswater Gold, Thwaites Wainwright and a couple of local guest beers on handpump, several malt whiskies and nine wines by the glass. On the left are polished boards and another log fire, and throughout there's a nice mix of sturdy country furniture, plus candles on tables, hunting scenes and other old prints on the walls, heavy fabric for the curtains and some staffordshire china ornaments. Two of the dining rooms are upstairs; background music and board games. The flagstoned front terrace has plenty of seats; disabled access and facilities. The castle, a lovely part-medieval house with beautiful gardens, is open in the afternoon (not Friday or Saturday) from April to October. This is part of the Ainscough group.

🍴 Enjoyable food includes sandwiches, potted shrimps in lemon butter, black pudding fritters with garlic mayonnaise, chicken caesar salad, mushroom pasta, organic burger (from their own herd) with sweet chilli sauce and chips, their own sausages with mash and onion gravy, pork loin with free-range egg and griddled pineapple, seafood platter, lamb hotpot, beer-battered fish with mushy peas and tartare sauce, and puddings. *Benchmark main dish: steak and mushroom in red wine pie £11.95. Two-course evening meal £18.00.*

Free house ~ Licensee Martin Ainscough ~ Real ale ~ (015395) 61010 ~ Open 12-11 (10.30 Sun); 12-3, 5.30-11 in winter ~ Bar food 12-2(2.30 Sat), 6-9; 12-8.30 Sun ~ Children welcome ~ Dogs welcome ~ www.thestricklandarms.com
Recommended by Ray and Winifred Halliday, Mr and Mrs P R Thomas, John and Sylvia Harrop

LITTLE LANGDALE   NY3103   Map 9
Three Shires 🍺 🛏

From A593 3 miles W of Ambleside take small road signposted The Langdales, Wrynose Pass; then bear left at first fork; LA22 9NZ

Fine valley views from seats on the terrace, local ales, quite a choice of food and comfortable bedrooms

Our readers enjoy their visits to this reliably well run inn, where there's always a good mix of chatty customers from walkers with their dogs to families. The comfortably extended back bar has green Lakeland stone and homely red patterned wallpaper (which works rather well), stripped timbers and a beam-and-joist stripped ceiling, antique oak carved settles, country kitchen chairs and stools on big dark slate flagstones, and Lakeland photographs. Coniston Old Man, Cumbria Legendary Esthwaite, Hawkshead Red and Jennings Cumberland on handpump, over 50 malt whiskies and a decent wine list; service is helpful and friendly. The front restaurant has chunky leather dining chairs around solid tables on wood flooring, fresh flowers, and wine bottle prints on the dark red walls; a snug leads off here; darts, TV and board games. This is a lovely spot with views across the valley from seats on the terrace to the partly wooded hills below; there are more seats on a neat lawn behind the car park, backed by a small oak wood, and award-winning summer hanging baskets. The three shires are the historical counties of Cumberland, Westmorland and Lancashire, which meet at the top of the nearby Wrynose Pass.

🍴 Very good and popular, the food includes sandwiches (the soup and sandwich deal is well liked), smoked salmon with beetroot and vodka crème fraîche, scallops with toasted hazelnut butter, pea and gorgonzola risotto, steak burger with blue cheese, caramelised onions and chips, daube of beef in pancetta and red wine with herby mash, pheasant breast with leg meat burger with celeriac and potato purée and port and red wine sauce, bass on steamed coconut and herb rice with thai mussel broth, and puddings such as maple crème brûlée with pecan brittle and lemon posset with home-made shortbread. *Benchmark main dish: chicken and leek pie £12.95. Two-course evening meal £21.50.*

Free house ~ Licensee Ian Stephenson ~ Real ale ~ (015394) 37215 ~ Open 11-10.30 (11 Sat); 12-10.30 Sun; 11-3, 8-10.30 in winter; closed 3 weeks Jan ~ Bar food 12-2, 6-8.45; no evening food midweek Dec, Jan ~ Restaurant ~ Children welcome ~ Dogs allowed in bar ~ Bedrooms: /£114 ~ www.threeshiresinn.co.uk *Recommended by Ann Balmforth, Hugh Roberts, Christian Mole, Tina and David Woods-Taylor, G Jennings, Barry Collett, J R Wildon*

LOWESWATER
NY1421　Map 9

Kirkstile Inn 🍺 🛏

From B5289 follow signs to Loweswater Lake; OS Sheet 89 map reference 140210; CA13 0RU

Well run, popular inn in lovely spot with busy bar, own-brewed beers, good food and friendly welcome; bedrooms

Even though this friendly little country pub is off the beaten track, it's always deservedly busy and full of walkers; there are marvellous surrounding hikes of all levels. The bustling main bar has low beams, carpets, comfortably cushioned small settles and pews, partly stripped stone walls, a roaring log fire and a friendly atmosphere; board games and a slate shove-ha'penny board. As well as their own-brewed Cumbrian Legendary Esthwaite, Langdale and Loweswater Gold, they keep a guest such as Watermill Collie Wobbles on handpump; nine wines by the glass and ten malt whiskies. The stunning views of the surrounding peaks can be enjoyed from picnic-sets on the lawn, from the very attractive covered verandah in front of the building or from the bow windows in one of the rooms off the bar; if you're lucky, you might spot a red squirrel. Dogs are allowed in the bar lunchtime only.

🍴 Offering some kind of food all day, there might be lunchtime sandwiches and baguettes, chicken and duck terrine with date and damson chutney, haggis and black pudding croquettes with red onion marmalade, omelettes, goats cheese, spinach and roasted vegetable lasagne, mixed game pudding, pork tenderloin wrapped in air-dried ham with bubble and squeak and mustard and brandy cream, lamb stew with black pudding, beetroot and horseradish chutney, specials like sea bream fillet in lemon, honey and marjoram dressing with sautéed potatoes, and puddings such as crumble of the day and fudge and chocolate brownie with vanilla ice-cream. *Benchmark main dish: steak in ale pie £9.95. Two-course evening meal £18.00.*

Own brew ~ Licensee Roger Humphreys ~ Real ale ~ (01900) 85219 ~ Open 11-11; 12-11 Sun ~ Bar food 12-2, 6-9; sandwiches and soup 2-4.30 ~ Restaurant ~ Children welcome ~ Dogs allowed in bar and bedrooms ~ Bedrooms: £63.50/£99 ~ www.kirkstile.com
Recommended by the Didler, Margaret Dickinson, John and Sylvia Harrop, Tim Maddison, Pat and Stewart Gordon, Simon Collett-Jones, Martin and Sue Day

LUPTON
SO5581　Map 7

Plough 🍴 ♀ 🛏

A65, near M6 junction 36; LA6 1PJ

Cumbria Dining Pub of the Year

Stylish inn with sofas and antique furniture, woodburning stoves, daily papers, real ales and top class food; well equipped bedrooms

The bedrooms in this carefully refurbished 18th-c inn are attractive, warm and comfortable and the breakfasts are extremely good. There are spreading open-plan bar rooms with beams, hunting prints and Punch cartoons on the contemporary grey paintwork, rugs on wooden floors, a nice mix of antique dining chairs and tables, comfortable leather sofas and armchairs in front of a large woodburning stove with impressive log piles to each side, and fresh flowers and daily papers; background music. High bar stools sit beside the granite-topped bar counter, from where neatly dressed, friendly staff serve Coniston Bluebird, Hawkshead Bitter, Jennings Cumberland and Kirkby Lonsdale Monumental on handpump.

There are rustic wooden tables and chairs under parasols behind a white picket fence, with more in the back garden; plenty of fine surrounding walks. This is sister pub to the Punch Bowl at Crosthwaite.

🍴 As well as sandwiches and afternoon tea, the impressive food might include tasters such as courgettes in tempura batter with cheese and honey or crispy fried whitebait, plus chicken liver parfait with fig chutney, salt and pepper tempura squid with soy and sesame dipping sauce, several boards (ploughman's, fisherman's, gardener's), free-range pork sausages with mash and onion gravy, aberdeen angus burger with tomato salsa and french fries, roasted cod with horseradish mash and baby beetroots, rösti potato-topped chicken and mushroom bake, asparagus and ricotta tortellini with truffle and lemon butter and parmesan salad, and puddings such as bread and butter pudding with vanilla poached apricots and bramley apple crumble and custard. *Benchmark main dish: sirloin steak with confit field mushroom, crispy onion rings, slow-roasted tomato and chips £19.95. Two-course evening meal £21.00.*

Free house ~ Licensees Richard Rose and co-owner ~ Real ale ~ (015395) 67700 ~ Open 11-11 ~ Bar food 12-9 ~ Restaurant ~ Children welcome ~ Dogs allowed in bar and bedrooms ~ Bedrooms: £95/£115 ~ www.theploughatlupton.co.uk
Recommended by Karen Eliot, W K Wood, Michael Doswell, David Heath

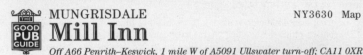

MUNGRISDALE
NY3630   Map 10
Mill Inn
Off A66 Penrith–Keswick, 1 mile W of A5091 Ullswater turn-off; CA11 0XR

Bustling pub in fine setting with marvellous surrounding walks, real ales, home-cooked bar food and seats in garden; bedrooms

With good nearby walks and some strenuous hillwalking further on, this friendly 17th-c Lakeland pub – in a striking spot below the fells – is just the place for a break; there are seats in the garden by the river. Inside, the open log fire in the stone fireplace is just right for colder weather, and the neatly kept bar has a wooden counter with an old millstone built into it, traditional dark wooden furnishings, hunting pictures on the walls, and Robinsons Cumbria Way, Dizzy Blonde, Hartleys XB and a guest beer on handpump; there's also a separate dining room. Darts, winter pool and dominoes.

🍴 Using meat from local farms, free-range eggs and other local produce, the tasty food includes sandwiches (until 6pm), crispy-coated salt and pepper calamari with aioli, fresh crabcakes on fennel slaw with seafood sauce, cumberland sausage and mash with onion gravy, a curry and pie of the day, venison burger with crumbled stilton and onion marmalade, duck lasagne, fell-bred lamb shoulder in port and redcurrant with rosemary and mint jus, vegetarian filo pastry roll with dauphinoise potatoes and honey and mustard dressing, specials such as slow-cooked pork belly with apple cider reduction and fondant potatoes, and puddings. *Benchmark main dish: steak in ale pie £10.90. Two-course evening meal £17.00.*

Robinsons ~ Tenant Andrew Teasdale ~ Real ale ~ (017687) 79632 ~ Open 11-11; 12-11 Sun ~ Bar food 12-9 ~ Restaurant ~ Children welcome ~ Dogs welcome ~ Bedrooms: £47.50/£75 ~ www.the-millinn.co.uk   *Recommended by Isobel Mackinlay*

If a service charge is mentioned prominently on a menu or accommodation terms, you must pay it if service was satisfactory. If service is really bad, you are legally entitled to refuse to pay some or all of the service charge as compensation for not getting the service you might reasonably have expected.

 NEAR SAWREY SD3795 Map 9

Tower Bank Arms

B5285 towards the Windermere ferry; LA22 0LF

Backing on to Beatrix Potter's farm, with well kept real ales, tasty bar food and a friendly welcome; nice bedrooms

Many illustrations in the Beatrix Potter books can be traced back to their origins in this village, including the pub, which features in *The Tale of Jemima Puddle-Duck*. It does get packed at weekends during the school holidays, when it's best to book a table in advance. But no matter how busy it is, you can be sure of a genuinely friendly welcome from the landlord and his welcoming staff – this extends to dogs too. The low-beamed main bar has plenty of rustic charm, with seats on the rough slate floor, game and fowl pictures, a grandfather clock, a log fire and fresh flowers; there's also a separate restaurant. Barngates Cracker Ale and Pride of Westmorland, Cumbrian Legendary Loweswater Gold and Hawkshead Bitter and Brodies Prime on handpump, several wines by the glass, ten malt whiskies and Weston's organic perry; board games. There are pleasant views of the wooded Claife Heights from seats in the extended garden. This is an enjoyable place to stay and the breakfasts are particularly good.

 Generous helpings of pubby food include lunchtime sandwiches, local brie wrapped in air-dried ham, chicken liver pâté with cumberland sauce, baked smoked haddock with cheese topping, cumberland sausage with mustard mash and onion gravy, roasted red peppers stuffed with goats cheese, pine nuts and caramelised mango, braised shoulder of lamb, and puddings such as chocolate brownie with vanilla ice-cream and banana and gingerbread sundae. *Benchmark main dish: beef in ale stew £11.95. Two-course evening meal £19.00.*

Free house ~ Licensee Anthony Hutton ~ Real ale ~ (015394) 36334 ~ Open 11.30-11; 12-10.30 Sun; 11.30-2.30, 5.30-10.30 in winter; closed 1 week mid Jan ~ Bar food 12-2, 6-9(8 Sun, winter Mon-Thurs and bank holidays) ~ Restaurant ~ Children welcome ~ Dogs allowed in bar and bedrooms ~ Bedrooms: /£95 ~ www.towerbankarms.com
Recommended by Margaret Dickinson, Christian Mole, G Jennings, Ian and Rose Lock, Roger Fox

RAVENSTONEDALE NY7203 Map 10

Black Swan

Just off A685 SW of Kirkby Stephen; CA17 4NG

Bustling hotel with thriving bar, several real ales, enjoyable food and good surrounding walks; comfortable bedrooms

Run with enthusiasm, this is a neatly kept and smart Victorian hotel with a bustling bar and plenty of customers. The U-shaped bar has quite a few original period features, stripped-stone walls, plush stools by the counter, a comfortable green button-back banquette, various dining chairs and little stools around a mix of tables, and fresh flowers. Black Sheep Ale and Bitter, John Smiths and a couple of changing guests such as Cumberland Corby Ale and Thwaites Nutty Black on handpump, eight wines by the glass, more than 20 malt whiskies and a good choice of fruit juices and pressés; background music, TV, darts, board games,newspapers and magazines. Service is genuinely friendly and helpful. There are picnic-sets in the tree-sheltered streamside garden across the road, and lots of good walks from the door (they have leaflets describing the routes). This is an enjoyable place to stay, with individually decorated bedrooms and big breakfasts; this year they've added three new rooms that have disabled access and are dog friendly. They also run the village store with outside café seating.

Using local, seasonal produce, the interesting food might include smoky barbecue chicken with herb and tomato couscous, seared scallops with lime and coriander soy reduction, root vegetable and beef cottage pie with thyme gravy, roasted rosemary and rock salt butternut squash filled with mushrooms and spinach with port syrup, teriyaki beef with noodle and vegetable stir-fry, lime marmalade-glazed chicken with onion and mushroom stuffing and lime crème fraîche, specials like cumbrian salami and lamb cutlets with carrot purée and red wine sauce, and puddings. *Benchmark main dish: beer-battered haddock with home-made tartare sauce £10.95. Two-course evening meal £19.50.*

Free house ~ Licensees Louise and Alan Dinnes ~ Real ale ~ (015396) 23204 ~ Open 11am-midnight(1am Fri, Sat) ~ Bar food all day ~ Restaurant ~ Children welcome ~ Dogs allowed in bar and bedrooms ~ Bedrooms: £55/£75 ~ www.blackswanhotel.com
Recommended by Mr and Mrs M Wall, David Hunt, Michael Doswell, Claes Mauroy, J R Wildon

STAVELEY   SD4798 Map 10

Beer Hall at Hawkshead Brewery

Staveley Mill Yard, Back Lane; LA8 9LR

Hawkshead Brewery showcase plus a huge choice of bottled beers, knowledgeable staff, brewery memorabilia and interesting food

The full range of ales from the Hawkshead Brewery are showcased in this spacious, modern glass-fronted building, and they hold regular beer festivals too. From the 14 handpumps there might be Bitter, Brodies Prime, Cumbrian Five Hop, Dry Stone Stout, Lakeland Gold and Lager, Red, Windermere Pale and seasonal beers. They also keep an extensive choice of bottled beers and whiskies with an emphasis on independent producers – all served by friendly, interested staff. The main bar is on two levels with the lower level dominated by the stainless-steel fermenting vessels. There are high-backed chairs around light wooden tables, benches beside long tables, nice dark leather sofas around low tables (all on oak floorboards), and a couple of walls are almost entirely covered with artistic photos of barley and hops and the brewing process; darts. You can buy T-shirts, branded glasses, mini casks and polypins and there are brewery tours. Parking can be tricky at peak times.

As well as constantly changing tapas to complement your beer, there might be cumberland sausage and mash, fish and chips with minted mushy peas and tartare sauce, venison and damson casserole with dumplings, confit duck leg and toulouse sausage casserole, and puddings like fruit crumble and a trio of puddings (sticky toffee with caramel sauce, cherry bakewell with cherry brandy sauce, vanilla ice-cream). *Benchmark main dish: brewers lunch (platter of sausages, ham, black pudding, BBQ ribs, pork pie and pickles) £11.00.*

Own brew ~ Licensee Alex Brodie ~ Real ale ~ (01539) 825260 ~ Open 12-5(6 Tues-Thurs); 12-11 Fri, Sat; 12-8 Sun ~ Bar food 12-3; 12-7 Fri, Sat; 12-6 Sun ~ Children welcome away from bar until 8pm ~ Dogs allowed in bar ~ www.hawksheadbrewery.co.uk
Recommended by Michael Doswell, Caroline Prescott

Real ale may be served from handpumps, electric pumps (not just the on-off switches used for keg beer) or – common in Scotland – tall taps called founts (pronounced 'fonts') where a separate pump pushes the beer up under air pressure.

STAVELEY SD4797 Map 9

Eagle & Child  £

Kendal Road; just off A591 Windermere–Kendal; LA8 9LP

Welcoming inn with warming log fires, a good range of local beers and enjoyable food; bedrooms

At lunchtimes, this friendly, well run place is always deservedly full with walkers from the Dales Way. There's a bustling atmosphere, a log fire under an impressive mantel beam, a roughly L-shaped flagstoned main area with plenty of separate sections furnished with pews, banquettes, bow window seats and high-backed dining chairs around polished dark tables. Also, police truncheons and walking sticks, some nice photographs and interesting prints, a few farm tools, a delft shelf of bric-a-brac and another log fire. The five real ales on handpump come from breweries such as Barngates, Cumbrian Legendary, Hawkshead, Jennings and Loweswater, and they keep several wines by the glass, 30 malt whiskies and farm cider; background music, darts and board games. An upstairs barn-themed dining room (with its own bar for functions) doubles as a breakfast room. There are picnic-sets under cocktail parasols in a sheltered garden by the River Kent, with more on a good-sized back terrace and a second garden behind. This is a lovely spot and makes a perfect base for exploring the area; the bedrooms are comfortable and the breakfasts very generous.

 As well as their bargain Lunch for a Fiver deal, the popular, generously served food includes sandwiches, chicken liver and port pâté with chutney, thai-style salmon fishcakes with chilli and basil dip, cheddar, leek and potato pie, cumberland sausage with mash and red wine and caramelised onion gravy, lasagne, beer-battered haddock with mushy peas and tartare sauce, chicken breast wrapped in smoked bacon and barbecue sauce with melted cheese, and puddings like hot chocolate fudge cake and apple crumble. *Benchmark main dish: steak in ale pie £9.95. Two-course evening meal £14.00.*

Free house ~ Licensees Richard and Denise Coleman ~ Real ale ~ (01539) 821320 ~ Open 11-11 ~ Bar food 12-2.30, 6-9; 12-9 Sun ~ Restaurant ~ Children welcome ~ Dogs allowed in bar ~ Bedrooms: £50/£75 ~ www.eaglechildinn.co.uk
Recommended by the Didler, Margaret Dickinson, David and Katharine Cooke, David Bedford, John and Sylvia Harrop, G Jennings, Tina and David Woods-Taylor

STONETHWAITE NY2513 Map 9

Langstrath

Off B5289 S of Derwentwater; CA12 5XG

Civilised little place in lovely spot, traditional food with a modern twist, four real ales, good wines and malt whiskies, and seats outside; bedrooms

In a quiet village beautifully surrounded by the steep fells above Borrowdale, this is a small and civilised inn with friendly licensees. The neat and simple bar (at its pubbiest at lunchtime) has a welcoming log fire in a big stone fireplace, new rustic tables, plain chairs and cushioned wall seats, and walking cartoons and attractive Lakeland mountain photographs on textured white walls. Four real ales on handpump from breweries like Black Sheep, Hawkshead, Keswick and Jennings and 25 malt whiskies; background music and board games. The small room on the left (actually the original cottage built around 1590) is a residents' lounge; the restaurant has fine views. Outside, a big sycamore shelters several picnic-sets with views up to Eagle Crag. There are fine surrounding walks and both the Cumbrian Way and the Coast to Coast Walk are not far away.

Enjoyable and usefully served all day, the food includes hand-potted local brown shrimps, black pudding and chorizo salad, cumberland sausage on wholegrain mustard mash with nettle jelly and onion gravy, roasted squash and mixed nut bake with red wine and shallot sauce, beer-battered fresh haddock with mushy peas and chips, free-range corn-fed chicken on bubble and squeak with crispy pancetta and wild mushroom and creamy white wine sauce, a suet pudding of the day, and puddings. *Benchmark main dish: slow-roasted lamb with red wine gravy £16.95. Two-course evening meal £19.00.*

Free house ~ Licensees Guy and Jacqui Frazer-Hollins ~ Real ale ~ (017687) 77239 ~ Open 12-10.30; closed Mon, closed Jan, Dec ~ Bar food 12-4, 6-9 ~ Restaurant ~ Children over 10 in restaurant before 7.30pm only ~ Dogs allowed in bar ~ Bedrooms: /£110 ~ www.thelangstrath.com *Recommended by Mike Proctor, Martin and Sue Day, Graham and Jane Bellfield, Stephen Funnell, Tina and David Woods-Taylor*

TALKIN   NY5457   Map 10

Blacksmiths Arms ♀ ⇔

Village signposted from B6413 S of Brampton; CA8 1LE

Neatly kept and welcoming with tasty bar food, several real ales and good surrounding walks; bedrooms

There are several neatly kept, traditionally furnished bars to choose from in this friendly 18th-c former blacksmiths. The cosy lounge on the right has a log fire, upholstered banquettes and wheelback chairs around dark wooden tables on patterned red carpeting, and country prints and other pictures on the walls. The restaurant is to the left, and there's a long lounge opposite the bar, with another room up a couple of steps at the back. Black Sheep Bitter, Geltsdale Brampton Bitter and Cold Fell, and Yates Bitter on handpump, 20 wines by the glass and 35 malt whiskies; background music, darts and board games. There are a couple of picnic-sets outside the front door with more in the back garden. This is a quiet and comfortable place to stay (two rooms have been completely refurbished this year, the rest have been redecorated), with numerous walks in the vicinity.

Reliably good food includes sandwiches, chicken liver pâté with cumberland sauce, smoked haddock and spring onion fishcakes with tartare sauce, vegetable curry, steak and kidney pie, sweet and sour chicken, cumberland sausage with fried egg, beef stroganoff, specials such as haggis and black pudding, fish medley with sweet chilli dip, duck breast in port and plum sauce, and puddings. *Benchmark main dish: beer-battered haddock £8.95. Two-course evening meal £16.00.*

Free house ~ Licensees Donald and Anne Jackson ~ Real ale ~ (016977) 3452 ~ Open 12-midnight ~ Bar food 12-2, 6-9 ~ Restaurant ~ Children welcome ~ Bedrooms: £50/£70 ~ www.blacksmithstalkin.co.uk *Recommended by Ruth May*

TIRRIL   NY5026   Map 10

Queens Head

B5320, not far from M6 junction 40; CA10 2JF

18th-c Lakeland pub with two bars, real ales and speciality pies, and seats outside; bedrooms

As well as running this busy inn, the hard-working licensees also run the Pie Mill (you can eat their pies here) and the village shop. The building dates from 1719 and the oldest parts of the main bar have low beams, black panelling and original flagstones and floorboards, with nice little tables and chairs on either side of the inglenook fireplace (always lit in winter). Another bar to the right of the entrance has pews and chairs around sizeable tables on a wooden floor and candles in the fireplace, while the back locals' bar has heavy beams and a pool table; there are three dining rooms as well. Robinsons Cumbria Way, Dizzy Blonde and Unicorn and a guest beer on handpump and several wines by the glass. At the front of the building are some picnic-sets, with modern chairs and tables under cover on the back terrace. The pub is very close to a number of interesting places, including Dalemain at Dacre, and Ullswater is nearby.

As well as lunchtime sandwiches and popular pies, bar food might include salmon and smoked haddock fishcake with caper mayonnaise, deep-fried camembert with red onion marmalade, mediterranean vegetable lasagne, venison sausage on black pudding mash with red wine gravy, a curry of the day, gammon with eggs or pineapple, bass topped with brown shrimps with parsley mash, and puddings. *Benchmark main dish: steak in ale pie £10.00. Two-course evening meal £18.00.*

Robinsons ~ Tenants Margaret and Jim Hodge ~ (01768) 863219 ~ Open 11-11(midnight Sat); 12-10.30 Sun ~ Bar food 12-2.30, 5.30-8.30 ~ Restaurant ~ Children welcome ~ Dogs allowed in bar and bedrooms ~ Bedrooms: £50/£75 ~ www.queensheadinn.co.uk
Recommended by Richard and Penny Gibbs

TROUTBECK NY4103 Map 9

Queens Head ⑪ ♀ 🍺 🛏
A592 N of Windermere; LA23 1PW

Civilised inn with several rambling rooms, interesting food, quite a few real ales and friendly staff; comfortable bedrooms

There's still a great deal of character and atmosphere in this rather smart 17th-c coaching inn as the extensions over the years have been very carefully done. The big rambling, original U-shaped bar has beams, flagstones, an attractive mix of cushioned settles and mate's chairs around sizeable tables, and a log fire in the raised stone fireplace flanked by horse harnesses and so forth; there's also a coal fire, country pictures, stuffed pheasants in a big glass case and a stag's head. A massive Elizabethan four-poster bed is the basis of the finely carved counter, from where they serve Robinsons Cumbrian Way, Dizzy Blonde, Hartleys XB, Old Tom and Unicorn on handpump and eight wines by the glass; background music. Other dining rooms are decorated similarly to the main bar, with oak beams and stone walls, settles along big tables, trumpets, cornets and saxophones on the walls, and lots of scatter cushions. Seats outside have a fine view over the Troutbeck Valley to Applethwaite Moors. The highly thought-of bedrooms are in the inn itself or in the carefully transformed barn opposite.

Quite a choice of imaginative food includes nibbles, sandwiches and baguettes (until 6pm), corned ham hock and black pudding with an egg and home-made brown sauce, foie gras terrine with poached cherries, sour cherry gel and warm orange brioche, honey-roasted goats cheese salad with peanut and herb crumb and a trio of beetroot, sausage whirl of the day with smoked cheese mash, crispy onion rings and onion gravy, a choice of mussels done three ways with chips, free-range duck breast with honey-roasted cashew nuts and watermelon salad with soy and honey dressing, and puddings like passion-fruit soufflé with dark chocolate sorbet and hot white chocolate fondue and crème brûlée with rhubarb gel and ginger eggy-bread soldiers. *Benchmark main dish: fish pie £14.95. Two-course evening meal £21.50.*

Robinsons ~ Lease Ian and Annette Dutton ~ Real ale ~ (015394) 32174 ~ Open 8am-midnight ~ Bar food 12-9 ~ Restaurant ~ Children welcome ~ Dogs allowed in bar and bedrooms ~ Bedrooms: £75/£120 ~ www.queensheadtroutbeck.co.uk
Recommended by Lesley and Peter Barrett, Christian Mole, Ian and Rose Lock, Clifford Blakemore

 ULVERSTON   SD3177 Map 7

Bay Horse ♀ 🛏

Canal Foot signposted off A590, then wend your way past the huge Glaxo factory; LA12 9EL

Civilised waterside hotel with lunchtime bar food, three real ales and a fine choice of wines; smart bedrooms

Six of the bedrooms in this civilised and friendly hotel have french windows that open out on to a terrace giving a panoramic view over the Leven Estuary; the bird life is wonderful, the breakfasts are excellent and our readers enjoy staying here very much. At its most informal at lunchtime, the bar has a relaxed atmosphere despite smart furnishings: attractive wooden armchairs, some pale green plush built-in wall banquettes, glossy hardwood traditional tables, a huge stone horse's head, black beams and props, and lots of horsebrasses. Magazines are dotted about, there's an open fire in the handsomely marbled grey slate fireplace and decently reproduced background music; board games. Jennings Cocker Hoop and Cumberland and a guest beer on handpump, 16 wines by the glass (including champagne and prosecco) from a carefully chosen and interesting wine list and several malt whiskies. The conservatory restaurant has lovely views over Morecambe Bay and there are some seats out on the terrace.

With their own bread and delicious shortbread, the consistently good food includes lunchtime dishes such as interesting hot and cold sandwiches, button mushrooms in creamy tomato and brandy sauce on peanut butter crouton, chicken liver pâté with cranberry and ginger purée, fresh crab and salmon fishcakes with white wine and fresh herb cream sauce, grilled lambs liver with black and white puddings on rich madeira sauce, aberdeen angus minced beef with kidney beans, ginger and chilli pepper and white pudding mash; you can only eat in the bar in the evening if the restaurant is full. *Benchmark main dish: braised lamb shank £14.75. Two-course evening meal £25.25.*

Free house ~ Licensee Robert Lyons ~ Real ale ~ (01229) 583972 ~ Open 11-11(10.30 Sun) ~ Bar food 12-2(3 Tues-Fri, 4 weekends), 7-9 ~ Restaurant ~ Children welcome but over-9s only in evening or in bedrooms ~ Dogs allowed in bar and bedrooms ~ Bedrooms: £80/£100 ~ www.thebayhorsehotel.co.uk *Recommended by John and Sylvia Harrop, W K Wood*

 WITHERSLACK   SD4482 Map 10

Derby Arms 🍽 🍺 🛏

Just off A590; LA11 6RH

Bustling country inn with half a dozen ales, good wines, particularly good food and a friendly welcome; reasonably priced bedrooms

They keep a fine choice of drinks in this enjoyable pub, including up to six real ales on handpump, such as Cumbrian Legendary Loweswater

Gold and a beer named for the pub from them, Hardknott Cool Fusion, Hawkshead Bitter and Windermere Pale Ale and Thwaites Wainwright; also, 11 wines by the glass and 22 malt whiskies. Service is friendly and courteous. The main bar has an easy-going atmosphere, lots of sporting prints on pale grey walls, elegant old dining chairs and tables on large rugs over floorboards, some hops above the bar counter and an open fire. A larger room to the right is similarly furnished (with the addition of cushioned pews) and has lots of political cartoons and local castle prints, a cumbrian scene above another open fire, and alcoves in the back wall full of nice bristol blue glass, ornate plates and staffordshire dogs and figurines; large windows lighten up the rooms, helped at night by candles in brass candlesticks. There are two further rooms – one with dark red walls, a red velvet sofa, more sporting prints and a handsome mirror above the fireplace. The bedrooms are comfortable. The inn is handy for Levens Hall with its topiary garden and for Sizergh Castle. This is part of the Ainscough group.

From a sensibly short menu, the impressive food might include lunchtime baguettes, fresh haddock, smoked salmon and chive fishcakes with home-made tartare sauce, chicken liver and brandy pâté with spiced fruit chutney, burger with chorizo, cheese, onion rings and chips, cumberland sausage with rich onion gravy on cheesy champ mash, pasta in creamy mushroom and rosemary sauce topped with gruyère, lamb hotpot with pickled red cabbage, and puddings like apple crumble with vanilla custard and strawberry and black pepper crème brûlée with lemon shortbread. *Benchmark main dish: beer-battered fish and chips £10.50. Two-course evening meal £18.00.*

Free house ~ Licensee Jessica Brown ~ Real ale ~ (015395) 52207 ~ Open 11.30-11; 12-10.30 Sun ~ Bar food 12-2, 6-9; all day weekends ~ Restaurant ~ Children welcome ~ Dogs allowed in bedrooms ~ Bedrooms: £55/£65 ~ www.thederbyarms.co.uk
Recommended by David Heath, Michael Doswell, Hugh Roberts

YANWATH   NY5128   Map 9

Gate Inn 🍴 ♟

2.25 miles from M6 junction 40; A66 towards Brough, then right on A6, right on B5320, then follow village signpost; CA10 2LF

Emphasis on imaginative food but also local beers and thoughtful wines, a pubby atmosphere and a warm welcome from helpful staff

'A real joy to revisit' and 'wonderful food' are just two comments from readers on this civilised, friendly and immaculately kept 17th-c dining pub. Despite the emphasis on the impressive cooking, locals do still drop in for a chat and ales from breweries such as Barngates, Tirril and Yates are on handpump – as well as around a dozen good wines by the glass, 12 malt whiskies and Weston's Old Rosie cider. There's a cosy bar of charming antiquity with country pine and dark wood furniture, lots of brasses on the beams, church candles on all the tables and a good log fire in the attractive stone inglenook; staff are courteous and helpful. Two restaurant areas have oak floors, panelled oak walls and heavy beams; background music. There are seats on the terrace and in the garden. They have a self-catering cottage to let, and the pub is handy for Ullswater and the M6.

Carefully prepared and exceptionally good food might include interesting tapas like teriyaki-marinated beef strips, red snapper and tiger prawn ceviche and courgette fritters with sweet chilli dipping sauce, plus steamed mussels with white wine, garlic, cream and chives, pheasant and smoked pancetta terrine with apricot chutney, cumberland sausage and black pudding with mash and cumberland gravy, burger in home-baked bun with cheese and chips, sunblush tomato, basil and globe artichoke risotto with ricotta, venison liver with pancetta and sautéed potatoes, roasted goose breast with ginger and honey jus and bubble and squeak, and puddings like white chocolate brûlée and sour cranberry compote and orange panna cotta with pickled lemons. *Benchmark main dish: loin of mutton with black pudding, rosemary and smoked garlic jus £21.95. Two-course evening meal £25.00.*

Free house ~ Licensee Matt Edwards ~ Real ale ~ (01768) 862386 ~ Open 12-11 ~ Bar food 12-2.30, 6-9 ~ Restaurant ~ Children welcome ~ Dogs allowed in bar ~ www.yanwathgate.com *Recommended by Richard J Holloway, Graham and Elizabeth Hargreaves, Pat and Stewart Gordon, Michael and Maggie Betton, Ray and Winifred Halliday, Catherine Pritchard, Stephen Sumner, David and Katharine Cooke, Tina and David Woods-Taylor, Walter and Susan Rinaldi-Butcher, Dr and Mrs A K Clarke, Michael Doswell*

Also Worth a Visit in Cumbria

Besides the fully inspected pubs, you might like to try these pubs that have been recommended to us and described by readers. Do tell us what you think of them: feedback@goodguides.com

AMBLESIDE   NY4008
★ **Kirkstone Pass Inn** (01539) 433624
A592 N of Troutbeck; LA22 9LQ
Lakeland's highest pub, in grand scenery, hiker-friendly décor of flagstones, stripped stone and dark beams, lots of old photographs and bric-a-brac, open fires, good value food all day from 9.30am (they may try to keep your credit card while you eat), changing ales such as Hesket Newmarket Kirkstone Pass and Tirril Old Faithful, hot drinks, daily papers, games and books; soft background music; well behaved children and dogs welcome, tables outside with incredible views to Windermere, camping field next door, three bedrooms, open all day. *(Simon J Barber)*

APPLEBY   NY6819
★ **Royal Oak** (01768) 351463
B6542/Bongate; CA16 6UN Attractive old beamed and timbered coaching inn on edge of town, popular generously served bar food including early-bird and OAP deals, up to five well kept local ales, friendly efficient young staff, log fire in panelled bar, armchair lounge with carved settle, traditional snug, restaurant; background music, TV; children and dogs welcome, terrace tables, 11 bedrooms and self-catering cottage, good breakfast, open all day. *(Jane Bailey, Comus and Sarah Elliott, Richard and Penny Gibbs)*

ARMATHWAITE   NY5045
★ **Fox & Pheasant** (01697) 472400
E of village, over bridge; CA4 9PY Well run friendly old coaching inn with lovely River Eden views, well kept Robinsons ales and decent wines by the glass, sensibly short choice of good fresh food, log fire in main beamed and flagstoned bar, dining bar in converted stables with exposed stone walls and woodburner, also, small more formal Victorian dining room; picnic-sets outside, comfortable bedrooms. *(Jean and Douglas Troup, Lucien Perring)*

ASKHAM   NY5123
Punch Bowl (01931) 712443
4.5 miles from M6 junction 40; CA10 2PF Attractive 18th-c village pub under new management; spacious beamed main bar, locals' bar, snug lounge and dining room, open fires, ales such as Cumberland, Eden and Thwaites; picnic-sets in front, on edge of green opposite Askham Hall. *(Anon)*

ASKHAM   NY5123
Queens Head (01931) 712225
Lower Green; off A6 or B5320 S of Penrith; CA10 2PF Traditional 17th-c beamed pub with enjoyable good value food all day including gluten-free choices, well kept beers such as Black Sheep, friendly landlady, red upholstered seating including banquettes, dark wood tables, brasses and old photographs, open fires, games room, yorkshire terrier called Oscar; background music; tables out at front and in pleasant garden, four bedrooms. *(David and Katharine Cooke)*

BAMPTON GRANGE   NY5218
Crown & Mitre (01931) 713225
Opposite church; CA10 2QR Old inn in attractive country hamlet (*Withnail and I* was filmed around here); opened-up interior with comfortable modern décor, leather sofas by log fire, four beers such as Black Sheep and Hesket Newmarket, good food from pub favourites up, nice coffee, efficient friendly

young staff; children and dogs welcome, walks from the door, eight bedrooms and self-catering apartment, open all day summer, from 5pm (12pm weekends) winter. *(Stephen Funnell)*

BASSENTHWAITE   NY2332
✳ **Sun** (017687) 76439
Off A591 N of Keswick; CA12 4QP
White-rendered slate house in charming village; rambling bar with low 17th-c black beams, big winter log fires in two good stone fireplaces, built-in wall seats and plush stools around heavy wooden tables, Jennings ales and a guest, well liked food served by friendly staff, cosy dining room; children (till 9pm if eating) and dogs welcome, seats under parasols on terrace with fine views of the fells and Skiddaw, handy for osprey viewing at Dodd Wood, open all day weekends, closed weekday lunchtimes. *(Christian Mole, Mr N and Mr G Webb)*

BEETHAM   SD4979
✳ **Wheatsheaf** (015395) 62123
Village (and inn) signed off A6 S of Milnthorpe; LA7 7AL Striking old building with fine black and white timbered cornerpiece, handily positioned on the old road to the Lake District; traditionally furnished rooms, opened-up lounge with exposed beams and joists, main bar (behind on the right) with open fire, two upstairs dining rooms, residents' lounge, Cross Bay Nightfall, Tirril Queen Jean and a guest beer, several wines by the glass and quite a few malt whiskies, wide choice of food including deals; children welcome, dogs in bar, plenty of surrounding walks, pretty 14th-c church opposite, bedrooms, open all day. *(Ray and Winifred Halliday, David and Katharine Cooke)*

BOOT   NY1701
Boot Inn (01946) 723711
Aka Burnmoor; signed just off the Wrynose/Hardknott Pass road; CA19 1TG Recently refurbished beamed pub with three or more real ales, decent wines and enjoyable locally sourced home-made food, log-fire bar, conservatory; children and dogs welcome, garden with play area, lovely surroundings and walks, nine bedrooms, open all day. *(Anon)*

BOOT   NY1701
✳ **Brook House** (01946) 723288
From Ambleside, W of Hardknott Pass; CA19 1TG Good views and walks, friendly service and wide choice of good sensibly priced country cooking including interesting dishes and unusual sandwiches, great whisky selection (over 160) and up to seven well kept ales such as Barngates, Cumbrian Hawkshead and Yates, Weston's farm cider or perry, decent wines, relaxed and comfortable raftered bar with woodburner and stuffed animals, smaller plush snug, peaceful separate restaurant; children and dogs

welcome, tables on flagstoned terrace, eight reasonably priced bedrooms, good breakfast (for nearby campers too), mountain weather reports, excellent drying room, handy for Eskdale railway terminus, open all day. *(the Didler, David Uren, David Bedford, Kay and Alistair Butler)*

BOOT   NY1901
Woolpack (019467) 23230
Bleabeck, midway between Boot and Hardknott Pass; CA19 1TH Last pub before the notorious Hardknott Pass; refurbished and welcoming with main walkers' bar and more contemporary café bar, also an evening restaurant (Fri, Sat), enjoyable home-made food all day including wood-fired pizzas, up to eight well kept ales, real cider and over 50 vodkas, June beer festival, pool room, some live music; children and dogs welcome, mountain-view garden with play area, eight bedrooms. *(Anon)*

BOUTH   SD3285
✳ **White Hart** (01229) 861229
Village signed off A590 near Haverthwaite; LA12 8JB Cheerful bustling old inn with Lakeland feel, six changing ales and 25 malt whiskies, popular generously served food (all day Sun), good friendly service, sloping ceilings and floors, old local photographs, farm tools and stuffed animals, collection of long-stemmed clay pipes, two woodburners; background music; children welcome, no dogs at mealtimes, seats outside, fine surrounding walks, five comfortable bedrooms, open all day. *(Anon)*

BOWNESS-ON-WINDERMERE   SD4096
Royal Oak (015394) 43970
Brantfell Road; LA23 3EG Handy for steamer pier, interconnecting bar, dining room and big games room, lots of bric-a-brac, open fire, well kept ales such as Coniston, Everards, Greene King and Jennings, generous reasonably priced pub food from baguettes to specials, friendly efficient service; pool, darts and juke box; children welcome, tables out in front, bedrooms. *(Dennis Jones)*

BRAITHWAITE   NY2323
Royal Oak (017687) 78533
B5292 at top of village; CA12 5SY Bustling local atmosphere, four well kept Jennings ales and reasonable choice of food including children's helpings, prompt helpful service, well worn-in flagstoned bar; background music, Sky TV; dogs welcome except mealtimes, open all day. *(Anon)*

BRIGSTEER   SD4889
Wheatsheaf (01539) 568254
Off Brigsteer Brow; LA8 8AN This attractive dining pub should have reopened under new owners by the time you read this – reports please.

BROUGHTON-IN-FURNESS SD2187
Manor Arms (01229) 716286
The Square; LA20 6HY Fine choice of
interesting well priced changing ales in this
end-of-terrace drinkers' pub on quiet sloping
square, flagstones and nice bow-window seat
in front bar, coal fire in big stone fireplace,
chiming clocks, old photographs, limited
food (rolls and soup), pool; stairs down to
lavatories; children allowed, bedrooms, open
all day. *(Dr Peter Crawshaw)*

BUTTERMERE NY1716
Fish (017687) 70253
B5289 SE of Buttermere; CA13 9XA
Spacious, light and airy former coaching
inn on NT property between Buttermere
and Crummock Water, fine views, well kept
Jennings and Keswick ales, wide range
of good value food, friendly helpful staff;
suntrap terrace attracting greedy sparrows
and finches, popular with walkers and
anglers, bedrooms. *(Simon Collett-Jones,
M S and M Imhoff)*

CARLISLE NY4056
Kings Head (01228) 533797
Fisher Street (pedestrianised); CA3 8RF
Heavy beams, lots of old local prints,
drawings and black and white photographs,
friendly bustling atmosphere, generous
bargain pub lunches, Yates and two or three
guests, raised dining area; background
and live music, TV, silent fruit machine,
no children or dogs; interesting historical
plaque outside, partly covered courtyard,
open all day. *(the Didler, Jeremy King, Eric
Larkham)*

CARLISLE NY4055
Woodrow Wilson (01228) 819942
Botchergate; CA1 1QS Large busy
Wetherspoons with up to a dozen real ales,
their usual bargain food, pleasant raised side
area with booths; back terrace, open all day
from 7am. *(Dave Braisted)*

CARTMEL SD3778
Cavendish Arms (01539) 536240
*Cavendish Street, off the Square;
LA11 6QA* Former coaching inn with simply
furnished open-plan beamed bar, roaring
log fire (even on cooler summer evenings),
three or four ales including a house beer
from Cumberland, several wines by the
glass, friendly attentive staff, good range of
popular local food (all day) from lunchtime
sandwiches up, ample helpings and fair
prices, restaurant; children welcome, dogs in
bar, tables out in front and behind by stream,
nice village with notable priory church,
good walks, ten bedrooms (and three more
above their shop in the square). *(Mrs F H
Banaclough, Pat and Stewart Gordon, Steve and
Claire Harvey, Dennis Jones)*

CARTMEL SD3778
Royal Oak (015395) 36259
The Square; LA11 6QB Low-beamed
flagstoned local now under same
management as the Kings Arms next door
(see Main Entries); cosy nooks and big log
fire, good value food including traditional
choices, home-made pizzas and pasta, early-
bird deals, Thwaites and two changing local
guests, welcoming helpful staff; background
and weekend live music, two sports TVs;
children and dogs welcome, nice big riverside
garden with new heated terrace, four
refurbished bedrooms, open all day (till 1am
Fri, Sat). *(Anon)*

CASTERTON SD6379
★ Pheasant (015242) 71230
A683; LA6 2RX Traditional 18th-c inn with
neat beamed rooms, good home-made food
including some interesting choices, changing
local ales and several malt whiskies,
restaurant; background music; children and
dogs welcome, a few roadside seats, more
in pleasant garden, near church with pre-
Raphaelite stained glass and paintings, ten
bedrooms. *(Anon)*

CASTLE CARROCK NY5455
Duke of Cumberland
(01228) 670341 *Geltsdale Road;
CA8 9LU* Popular cleanly refurbished
village-green pub with friendly family owners,
upholstered wall benches and mix of pubby
furniture on slate floor, coal fire, dining area
with old farmhouse tables and chairs, well
kept Geltsdale and a guest, enjoyable good
value pub food; children welcome, no dogs
inside, open all day. *(Dr Kevan Tucker, David
and Katharine Cooke)*

CHAPEL STILE NY3205
Wainwrights (015394) 38088
B5343; LA22 9JH White-rendered former
farmhouse, half a dozen real ales including
Banks's and Jennings, plenty of wines by the
glass, enjoyable quickly served pubby food
from good sandwiches up, friendly service,
spacious new-feeling bar welcoming walkers
and dogs, slate floor and log fire, other
spreading carpeted areas with beams, some
half-panelling, cushioned settles and mix
of dining chairs around wooden tables, old
kitchen range; background music, TV and
games machines; children welcome, terrace
picnic-sets, fine views, open all day. *(Dr
Kevan Tucker, Jane and Alan Bush, G Jennings)*

COCKERMOUTH NY1230
★ Bitter End (01900) 828993
Kirkgate, by cinema; CA13 9PJ
Welcoming pub with three cosy bars, well
kept local ales including their own (no longer
brewed on site), lots of bottled beers, good
choice of enjoyable traditional food, unusual
pictures of old Cockermouth, also framed
beer mats, various bottles and jugs, coal

stove and woodburner; background music; no dogs; children welcome, public car park at the back, open all day weekends, from 4pm weekdays. *(J Chilver, the Didler)*

COCKERMOUTH   NY1231
Trout (01900) 823591
Crown Street; CA13 0EJ Busy extensively refurbished hotel, welcoming helpful staff, good imaginative food, well kept local ales including Jennings, nice wines by the glass; gardens down to river, 49 bedrooms. *(Dr and Mrs Leach, Pat and Stewart Gordon)*

CONISTON   SD3097
Black Bull (01539) 441335/41668
Yewdale Road (A593); LA21 8DU Own-brewed Coniston beers remain a draw to this bustling old inn; back area (liked by walkers and their dogs) has slate flagstones, more comfortable carpeted front part has open fire and Donald Campbell memorabilia, bar food served all day, residents' lounge with 'big toe' of Old Man of Coniston (large piece of stone in the wall), restaurant; they ask to keep a credit card if you run a tab; children welcome, plenty of seats in former coachyard, bedrooms, open all day from 8am (parking not easy at peak times). *(Dr Kevan Tucker, Mike Lee, David Bedford, Robin Constable)*

CROOK   SD4695
⋆ Sun (01539) 821351
B5284 Kendal–Bowness; LA8 8LA Comfortable welcoming atmosphere in low-beamed bar with two dining areas off, good generously served traditional food, reasonable prices, prompt cheerful service, well kept ales such as Coniston and Hawkshead, good value wines, roaring log fire; children and dogs (in bar) welcome, open (and food) all day weekends. *(Hugh Roberts)*

DENT   SD7086
George & Dragon (01539) 625256
Main Street; LA10 5QL Two-bar corner pub in cobbled street, the Dent Brewery tap, with their full range kept well plus real cider and perry, old panelling, partitioned tables and open fire, enjoyable food from snacks up, prompt friendly service, steps down to restaurant, games room with pool and juke box; sports TV; children, walkers and dogs welcome, ten bedrooms, lovely village, open all day. *(David Heath, Claes Mauroy, Comus and Sarah Elliott)*

ENNERDALE BRIDGE   NY0716
Fox & Hounds (01946) 861373
High Street; CA23 3AR Popular community-owned pub, smart and clean with flowers on tables, five well kept ales including local Ennerdale and Jennings, tasty reasonably priced home-made food; picnic-sets in streamside garden, three bedrooms, open all day. *(Mr and Mrs C R Little, Stephen Funnell)*

ENNERDALE BRIDGE   NY0615
Shepherds Arms (01946) 861249
Off A5086 E of Egremont; CA23 3AR New management for this well placed walkers' inn by car-free dale, bar with log fire and woodburner, up to five local beers, good choice of home-made food, can provide packed lunches, panelled dining room and conservatory; children welcome, seats outside by beck, eight bedrooms. *(Anon)*

ESKDALE GREEN   NY1200
⋆ Bower House (01946) 723244
0.5 miles W of Eskdale Green; CA19 1TD Civilised old-fashioned stone-built inn extended around beamed and alcoved core, good fires, well kept local ales such as Jennings Cocker Hoop, decent freshly made food in bar and biggish restaurant, friendly relaxed atmosphere; nicely tended sheltered garden by cricket field, charming spot with great walks, bedrooms, open all day. *(Paul J Robinshaw, Tina and David Woods-Taylor, Martin and Sue Day)*

ESKDALE GREEN   NY1400
King George IV (01946) 723470
E of village; CA19 1TS Cheerful beamed and flagstoned bar with log fire, good range of well kept ales and malt whiskies, sensibly priced plentiful food from sandwiches to grills, friendly staff, restaurant; children and dogs welcome, fine views from garden tables (road nearby), lots of good walks, self-catering accommodation. *(Margaret and Jeff Graham)*

FAUGH   NY5054
String of Horses (01228) 670297
S of village, on left as you go downhill; CA8 9EG Welcoming 17th-c coaching inn with cosy communicating beamed rooms, log fires, panelling and some interesting carved furniture, tasty traditional food alongside some central american/mexican dishes, two Geltsdale beers, restaurant; children welcome, no dogs at mealtimes, tables out in front, 11 comfortable bedrooms, good breakfast, closed lunchtimes, all day Mon. *(Anon)*

FOXFIELD   SD2085
⋆ Prince of Wales (01229) 716238
Opposite station; LA20 6BX Cheery bare-boards pub with half a dozen good changing ales including bargain beers brewed here and at their associated Tigertops Brewery, bottled imports, farm cider, huge helpings of enjoyable home-made food including lots of unusual pasties, good service and character landlord, hot coal fire, bar billiards and other pub games, daily papers and beer-related reading matter; children very welcome (games for them), four reasonably priced bedrooms, open all day Fri-Sun, from mid-afternoon Wed, Thurs, closed Mon, Tues. *(Pauline Fellows and Simon Robbins)*

GOSFORTH   NY0703
Gosforth Hall (019467) 25322
*Off A595 and unclassified road to
Wasdale; CA20 1AZ* Friendly well run
Jacobean inn with interesting history,
beamed carpeted bar (popular with locals)
with fine plaster coat-of-arms above
woodburner, lounge/reception area with huge
fireplace, ales such as Hawkshead, Keswick
and Yates, enjoyable home-made food
including good range of pies, restaurant; TV;
nice big side garden, 22 bedrooms (some in
new extension), open all day, food from 5pm
(not Sun). *(David and Katharine Cooke)*

GREAT URSWICK   SD2674
General Burgoyne (01229) 586394
Church Road; LA12 0SZ Flagstoned early
17th-c village pub overlooking small tarn,
four cosy rambling rooms with beams and
log fires (look for the skull in a cupboard),
three Robinsons ales, some creative cooking
from landlord/chef along with pub favourites,
dining conservatory; children and dogs
welcome, picnic-sets out at front, closed Mon
and Tues lunchtimes, otherwise open all
day. *(Genevieve Horsted)*

GREYSTOKE   NY4430
Boot & Shoe (01768) 483343
By village green, off B5288; CA11 0TP
Cosy two-bar pub by green in pretty 'Tarzan'
village; low ceilings, exposed brickwork and
dark wood, good generous reasonably priced
food including popular theme nights, well
kept Black Sheep and local microbrews,
bustling friendly atmosphere; sports TV; on
national cycle route, bedrooms. *(Anon)*

HARTSOP   NY4013
Brotherswater Inn (01768) 482239
A592; CA11 0NZ Walkers' and campers'
pub in magnificent setting at the bottom
of Kirkstone Pass, Jennings ales and good
choice of malt whiskies, decent reasonably
priced pubby food served by friendly staff;
beautiful fells views from picture windows
and terrace tables, six bedrooms, bunkhouse
and campsite, open all day (from 8am for
breakfast). *(Tina and David Woods-Taylor)*

HAVERTHWAITE   SD3284
Anglers Arms (01539) 531216
Just off A590; LA12 8AJ Popular split-
level pub with good generous fresh food at
fair prices, friendly helpful staff, Thwaites
and a guest ale, separate upstairs dining
room; handy for steam railway. *(Dennis Jones)*

HAWKSHEAD   SD3598
Queens Head (015394) 36271
Main Street; LA22 0NS Timbered pub
in charming village, low-ceilinged bar with
heavy bowed black beams, red plush wall
seats and stools around hefty traditional
tables, decorative plates on panelled walls,
open fire, snug little room off, several eating

areas, well kept Robinsons ales and a guest,
good wine and whisky choice, enjoyable bar
food and more elaborate evening meals,
friendly staff; background music, TV, darts;
children welcome, seats outside and pretty
window boxes, 13 bedrooms, open all
day. *(Lesley and Peter Barrett, Dave Webster, Sue
Holland)*

HESKET NEWMARKET   NY3438
★ Old Crown (016974) 78288
*Village signed off B5299 in Caldbeck;
CA7 8JG* Straightforward cooperative-
owned local in attractive village, own good
Hesket Newmarket beers (can book brewery
tours); small friendly bar with bric-a-brac,
mountaineering kit and pictures, log fire,
dining room and garden room, well presented
good value pub food, folk night first Sun
of month; juke box, pool and board games;
children and dogs welcome, closed Mon-
Thurs lunchtimes (open Weds and Thurs
lunchtimes in school holidays). *(Dr Kevan
Tucker)*

HIGH NEWTON   SD4082
Crown (015395) 30613
*Just off A590 Lindale–Newby Bridge,
towards Cartmel Fell; LA11 6JH*
Refurbished 17th-c coaching inn with
beamed and flagstoned bar, log fire in stone
fireplace, local ales such as Hawkshead
and decent wines by the glass, enjoyable
home-made food (all day weekends), sizeable
restaurant; children and dogs welcome, beer
garden, good local walks and fishing, seven
bedrooms. *(Walter and Susan Rinaldi-Butcher)*

KENDAL   SD5192
Riflemans Arms (01539) 723224
Greenside; LA9 4LD Village-green setting
on edge of town, friendly locals and staff,
well kept Tetleys and three guests, no food,
Thurs folk night; children and dogs welcome,
closed weekday lunchtimes, open all day
weekends. *(Hugh Roberts)*

KESWICK   NY2623
★ Dog & Gun (01768) 773463
*Lake Road; off top end of Market Square;
CA12 5BT* Unpretentious town pub liked
by locals and their dogs (menu for them),
friendly bustling bar with low beams and
timbers, part slate, part wood, part carpeted
flooring, fine collection of striking mountain
photographs, brass and brewery artefacts,
half a dozen well kept ales, reasonably priced
hearty food all day including signature
goulash in two sizes, log fires; children
welcome before 9pm if eating, can get very
busy in season. *(Dr Kevan Tucker, Mike Proctor,
S Chaudhuri, John and Gloria Isaacs, Eddie
Edwards, Adrian Johnson and others)*

KESWICK   NY2623
George (017687) 72076
St Johns Street; CA12 5AZ Handsome
17th-c coaching inn with open-plan main

bar and attractive traditional dark-panelled side room, old-fashioned settles and modern banquettes under black beams, log fires, daily papers, four Jennings ales and a couple of guests kept well, plenty of wines by the glass, generous home-made food including signature cow pie, prompt friendly service, restaurant; background music, quiz night; children welcome in eating areas, dogs in bar, 13 bedrooms, open all day. *(Eddie Edwards)*

KESWICK
NY2624
Pheasant (017687) 72219
Crosthwaite Road (A66, a mile out); CA12 5PP Small friendly beamed local with enjoyable straightforward home-made food, well kept Jennings and guests, good service, log fire, dining room; children welcome if eating, bedrooms, near ancient church of St Kentigern. *(Martin and Sue Day)*

KIRKBY LONSDALE
SD6178
Orange Tree (01524) 271716
Fairbank; LA6 2BD Family-run inn acting as tap for Kirkby Lonsdale brewery, well kept guest beers too and good choice of wines, beams, sporting pictures, old range, enjoyable food in back dining room; pool, darts, background music; children and dogs welcome, comfortable bedrooms (some next door), open all day. *(Anon)*

KIRKBY LONSDALE
SD6178
★**Sun** (015242) 71965
Market Street (B6254); LA6 2AU Cheerful busy 17th-c inn striking good balance between pub and restaurant; unusual-looking building with upper floors supported by three sturdy pillars above pavement, attractive rambling beamed bar with flagstones and stripped-oak boards, pews, armchairs and cosy window seats, big landscapes and country pictures on cream walls, two log fires, comfortable back lounge and modern dining room, good contemporary food (booking advised), well kept Hawkshead, Kirkby Lonsdale and Thwaites, good service; background music; children and dogs welcome, nice bedrooms, no car park, open all day from 9am, closed Mon till 3pm. *(Karen Eliot, Mrs Debbie Tether, D W Stokes, Malcolm and Pauline Pellatt, John and Dinah Waters)*

KIRKOSWALD
NY5641
Fetherston Arms (01768) 898284
The Square; CA10 1DQ Busy old stone inn with enjoyable food at reasonable prices including steak and pie nights, interesting changing beers, friendly helpful service; bedrooms. *(David and Katharine Cooke)*

LANGDALE
NY2906
Sticklebarn (015394) 37356
By car park for Stickle Ghyll; LA22 9JU Lovely views from this roomy walkers' and climbers' bar now owned and run by the NT; five changing ales and a real cider, home-

made locally sourced food (meat from next-door farm), mountaineering photographs, two woodburners, upstairs bar with pool; background music (live Sat); children, dogs and boots welcome, big terrace with inner verandah, outside pizza oven, open all day. *(Jane and Alan Bush, Dr and Mrs Leach)*

LORTON
NY1526
★**Wheatsheaf** (01900) 85199
B5289 Buttermere–Cockermouth; CA13 9UW Friendly local atmosphere in neatly furnished bar with two log fires and vibrant purple walls, affable hard-working landlord, Jennings and regular changing guests, several good value wines, popular home-made food (all day Sun) from sandwiches up, curry night Weds, fresh fish Thurs and Fri evenings, smallish restaurant (best to book), good friendly service, live music Sat; children and dogs welcome, tables out behind and campsite, open all day weekends, closed Mon lunchtime (Mon-Fri lunchtimes in winter). *(Chris and Anne Thompson, Mr and Mrs M Wall, Pat and Stewart Gordon, Simon Collett-Jones)*

MARYPORT
Captain Nelsons Tavern (01900) 816697 *South Quay; CA15 8AB* Small refurbished single-storey pub under friendly family ownership, enjoyable generously served home-made food, good local beers. *(Sue Brandon)*

MELMERBY
NY6137
Shepherds (01768) 881741
A686 Penrith–Alston; CA10 1HF Friendly family-run split-level country pub, comfortable heavy-beamed dining room off flagstoned bar, spacious end room with sofa and leather chairs by woodburner, good choice of popular tasty food including bargain lunchtime/early evening two-course menu, well kept changing ales, seven wines by the glass, darts; children and dogs welcome, terrace tables, open all day in summer. *(Marcus Byron, M A Borthwick)*

NETHER WASDALE
NY1204
★**Strands** (01946) 726237
SW of Wast Water; CA20 1ET Lovely spot below the remote high fells around Wast Water, brews its own Strands ales (lots of varieties), popular good value food, well cared for high-beamed main bar with woodburner and relaxed friendly atmosphere, smaller public bar with pool, separate dining room, pleasant staff; background music; children and dogs welcome, neat garden with terrace and belvedere, 14 bedrooms, open all day. *(Anon)*

NEWBY BRIDGE
SD3686
Swan (015395) 31681
Just off A590; LA12 8NB Substantial refurbished 17th-c hotel in fine setting below fells and next to river; extensive bar serving

locally sourced food and ales, good coffee, helpful friendly staff, restaurant; background music; children welcome in eating areas, waterside picnic-sets by old stone bridge, comfortable bedrooms, swimming pool and spa, open all day. *(Margaret and Jeff Graham)*

PENRUDDOCK   NY4227
✶ Herdwick (01768) 483007
Off A66 Penrith–Keswick; CA11 0QU
Attractively cottagey and sympathetically renovated 18th-c inn, warm welcoming atmosphere, well kept Jennings and summer guests from unusual curved bar, decent wines, enjoyable sensibly priced pubby food, Sun carvery, friendly efficient staff, good open fire, stripped stone and white paintwork, nice dining room with upper gallery, games room with pool and darts; children in eating areas, five good value bedrooms, open all day weekends. *(Anon)*

RAVENSTONEDALE   NY7401
Fat Lamb (01539) 623242
Crossbank; A683 Sedbergh–Kirkby Stephen; CA17 4LL Isolated inn surrounded by great scenery (good walks), pews in comfortable beamed bar with fire in traditional black inglenook range, good local photographs and bird plates, propeller from 1930s biplane over servery, friendly helpful staff, wide choice of good proper food from filled baguettes to enjoyable restaurant meals, well kept Black Sheep, decent wines and around 60 malts; children and dogs welcome, disabled facilities, tables out by nature-reserve pastures, 12 refurbished bedrooms, open all day. *(Comus and Sarah Elliott)*

RAVENSTONEDALE   NY7204
Kings Head (015396) 23284
Pub visible from A685 W of Kirkby Stephen; CA17 4NH Spacious country inn with nicely opened-up interior, central woodburner and another log fire, well kept ales such as Jennings, Tirril and Kirkby Lonsdale (tasting trays available), good wines by the glass, enjoyable freshly made traditional food from sensibly short menu, attentive welcoming staff, restaurant, games room with pool and shove-ha'penny; seats out in front, stream across lane, six well equipped comfortable bedrooms, open all day in summer, all day weekends winter. *(J R and P D Holt, Gary Topham)*

ROSTHWAITE   NY2514
Scafell (017687) 77208
B5289 S of Keswick; CA12 5XB Hotel's big slate-floored back bar useful for walkers,

weather forecast board, six well kept ales, blazing log fire, enjoyable reasonably priced food from sandwiches up, afternoon teas, also appealing cocktail bar/sun lounge and dining room, friendly helpful staff; background music, pool; children and dogs welcome, tables out overlooking beck, 23 bedrooms, open all day. *(Dr Kevan Tucker, Mike Proctor)*

RYDAL   NY3606
Glen Rothay Hotel (015394) 34500
A591 Ambleside–Grasmere; LA22 9LR Attractive small 17th-c hotel with up to five well kept changing local ales in back bar, banquettes and stools, some badger pictures, good choice of enjoyable locally sourced food from sandwiches up, beamed and panelled dining lounge with open fire, restaurant, helpful friendly staff, acoustic music first Weds of month; walkers and dogs welcome, tables in pretty garden, eight comfortable bedrooms, open all day. *(Anon)*

SANDFORD   NY7316
✶ Sandford Arms (01768) 351121
Village and pub signposted just off A66 W of Brough; CA16 6NR Neat former 18th-c farmhouse in peaceful village, enjoyable food (all day weekends Apr–Oct) from chef/landlord, L-shaped carpeted main bar with stripped beams and stonework, Black Sheep, Lancaster and a house beer from Tirril, comfortable raised and balustraded eating area, more formal dining room and second flagstoned bar, woodburner; background music; children and dogs welcome, seats in front garden and covered courtyard, three bedrooms and self-catering cottage, closed Tues and lunchtime Weds. *(Anon)*

SANTON BRIDGE   NY1101
Bridge Inn (01946) 726221
Off A595 at Holmrook or Gosforth; CA19 1UX Old inn under newish management; charming riverside spot with fell views, beamed and timbered bar bustling with locals, log fire, some booths around stripped-pine tables, Jennings and guest ales, traditional food including Sun carvery, family dining room, friendly helpful staff, small reception hall with log fire and daily papers; background music; dogs welcome in bar, seats outside by quiet road, plenty of walks, 16 bedrooms, open all day. *(Anon)*

SATTERTHWAITE   SD3392
✶ Eagles Head (01229) 860237
S edge of village; LA12 8LN Pretty and prettily placed on the edge of beautiful Grizedale Forest (visitor centre nearby); low

---

Stars before the name of a pub show exceptional character and appeal. They don't mean extra comfort. And they are nothing to do with food quality, for which there's a separate knife-and-fork symbol. Even quite a basic pub can win stars, if it's individual enough.

black beams and big log fire, comfortable traditional furnishings, lots of local photographs and maps, welcoming and obliging landlord, good fairly priced generous pubby food, wider evening choice, well kept local ales including Barngates and two named for the pub, pool room, occasional live music; children and dogs welcome, picnic-sets in attractive tree-shaded courtyard garden with pergola, closed Mon (and Tues in winter). *(Anon)*

SEATHWAITE　　　　　　　SD2295
⋆ **Newfield Inn**　(01229) 716208
Duddon Valley, near Ulpha (not Seathwaite in Borrowdale); LA20 6ED
Friendly 16th-c cottage with good local atmosphere in slate-floored bar, wooden tables and chairs, interesting pictures, woodburner, three changing local beers and good straightforward food, comfortable side room, games room; children and dogs welcome, tables in nice garden with hill views, play area, good walks, two self-catering flats, open all day. *(Anon)*

SHAP　　　　　　　　　　NY5614
⋆ **Greyhound**　(01931) 716474
A6, S end, handy for M6 junction 39; CA10 3PW This honest pub, popular with locals, walkers and families, was closed as we went to press – news please.

ST BEES　　　　　　　　　NX9711
Queens　(01946) 822287
Main Street; CA27 0DE Friendly 17th-c two-bar pub with well kept Jennings and good reasonably priced home-made food, dining area and conservatory, log fires, Thurs quiz and monthly live music; two-tier garden behind, coast walks, 14 bedrooms, good breakfast. *(Stephen Funnell)*

STAINTON WITH
ADGARLEY　　　　　　　　SD2472
Stagger Inn　(01229) 462504
Long Lane; LA13 0NN Big helpings of straightforward tasty food, prompt attentive service, good local beers, roaring log fire. *(Alec and Susan Hamilton)*

THRELKELD　　　　　　　NY3225
⋆ **Horse & Farrier**　(017687) 79688
A66 Penrith–Keswick; CA12 4SQ
New people have taken over this 17th-c inn; linked mainly carpeted rooms (some flagstones) with mix of furniture from comfortably padded seats to pubby chairs and wall settles, some beams and open fires, Jennings Bitter, Cumberland, Mild and Sneck Lifter, quite a choice of food, partly stripped-stone restaurant; children welcome, dogs allowed in bar, disabled facilities, a few picnic-sets outside and fine views towards Helvellyn range, walks from the back door, bedrooms, open all day. *(Anon)*

TORVER　　　　　　　　　SD2894
⋆ **Church House**　(015394) 41282
A593/A5084 S of Coniston; LA21 8AZ
Rambling 14th-c coach house with welcoming licensees; pubby bar with heavy beams, straightforward tables and chairs on slate flooring, Lakeland bric-a-brac and big log fire in sizeable stone fireplace, generous helpings of good home-made food, Barngates, Coniston, Copper Dragon, Cumbrian and Hawkshead ales, several wines by the glass and quite a few malt whiskies, comfortable lounge, separate yellow-walled dining room; children welcome, dogs allowed in bar and bedrooms (they have a jack russell called Molly), standing for six caravans, good nearby walks to Coniston Lake, open all day. *(Chris and Anne Thompson, Tina and David Woods-Taylor, Dennis Jones, Dr Peter Crawshaw, Martin Lewis)*

TORVER　　　　　　　　　SD2894
Wilson Arms　(01539) 441237
A593; LA21 8BB Old family-run roadside inn, beams, nice log fire and some modern touches, well kept Coniston and other local ales, good locally sourced food cooked to order (more evening choice) in bar or dining room; children and dogs welcome, hill views (including Old Man of Coniston) from tables outside, nine refurbished bedrooms and two holiday cottages, open all day. *(Jane Walker)*

TROUTBECK　　　　　　　NY4103
Mortal Man　(015394) 33193
A592 N of Windermere; Upper Road; LA23 1PL Beamed and partly panelled bar with cosy room off, log fires, well kept local ales including a house beer from Hawkshead, several wines by the glass, well liked food in bar and picture-window restaurant, but some reader concerns over service, quiz Weds, folk night Sun; children and dogs welcome, great views from sunny garden, lovely village, bedrooms, open all day. *(David and Katharine Cooke, Ian and Rose Lock)*

ULVERSTON　　　　　　　SD2878
⋆ **Farmers Arms**　(01229) 584469
Market Place; LA12 7BA Convivial attractively modernised town pub, front bar with comfortable sofas, contemporary wicker chairs and original fireplace, daily newspapers, quickly changing real ales and a dozen wines by the glass, interesting fairly priced food, second bar leading to big raftered dining area (children here only); unobtrusive background music, Thurs quiz; seats on attractive heated front terrace, lots of colourful tubs and hanging baskets, Thurs market day (pub busy then), three cottages to rent, open all day from 9am. *(Anon)*

ULVERSTON　　　　　　　SD2978
Stan Laurel　(01229) 582814
The Ellers; LA12 0AB Beamed pub with good choice of enjoyable food (not Mon)

including deals Tues-Thurs, efficient friendly service, six mainly local ales, woodburner, pool room; children and dogs (in bar) welcome, bedrooms, open all day Sun, closed Mon lunchtime. *(R M Webberley)*

WASDALE HEAD NY1807

Wasdale Head Inn (019467) 26229

NE of Wast Water; CA20 1EX Mountain hotel worth knowing for its stunning fellside setting; roomy walkers' bar with nice fire, enjoyable home-made food, several local ales and good choice of wines; residents' bar, lounge and panelled restaurant; children welcome, dogs in bar, nine bedrooms, also nine apartments (six self-catering) in converted barn, camping, open all day. *(the Didler, Margaret and Jeff Graham, Martin and Sue Day)*

WINDERMERE SD3801

Langdale Chase (015394) 32201

A591, N of Ecclerigg; LA23 1LW Imposing Victorian country-house hotel, good bar food including hot or cold sandwiches in conservatory with stunning Windermere views, nice coffee, more formal restaurant, efficient pleasant staff; children welcome, extensive lakeside grounds, 29 bedrooms (some in separate building, one above boathouse), open all day. *(Margaret and Jeff Graham)*

WINSTER SD4193

✳**Brown Horse** (015394) 43443

A5074 S of Windermere; LA23 3NR Refurbished 19th-c coaching inn, welcoming bustling bar with beams, pubby furniture on flagstones, some half-panelling and woodburner, own-brew Winster Valley ales plus local guests, several wines by the glass, ten malt whiskies, good food using own estate-reared produce, smart but relaxed restaurant with candles and flowers, pleasant prompt service; darts and board games; children welcome, dogs in bar, sturdy furniture on front terrace and in side garden with Winster Valley views, nine bedrooms, open all day. *(Walter and Susan Rinaldi-Butcher, Mr and Mrs M Wall, Martin Hickes, Steve Pye, Tina and David Woods-Taylor, Dennis Jones and others)*

Please keep sending us reports. We rely on readers for news of new discoveries, and particularly for news of changes – however slight – at the fully described pubs: feedback@goodguides.com, or (no stamp needed) The Good Pub Guide, FREEPOST TN1569, Wadhurst, E Sussex TN5 7BR.

Derbyshire

With so much wonderful countryside to walk in, it's worth making a weekend of it and staying overnight at one of the pubs here. Places with Stay Awards are the Old Poets Corner at Ashover (ten real ales and warmly welcoming), Devonshire Arms in Beeley (a clever mix of contemporary furnishings and original features), Church Inn at Chelmorton (charming landlord and an easy-going atmosphere), Plough at Hathersage (good food and fine riverside grounds), Cheshire Cheese in Hope (friendly and traditional), John Thompson in Ingleby (unchanging pub with own brews), Barley Mow at Kirk Ireton (lots of character and lovely landlady) and Devonshire Arms in Pilsley (civilised place with four real ales and popular food); breakfasts are usually very good and generous. New this year are the Old Hall in Chinley (charming, small Peak District inn), Chequers at Froggatt Edge (smart dining pub with interesting food and spotless bedrooms), Scotsmans Pack in Hathersage (warm welcome for all, popular food and ales and lots of knick-knacks), Royal in Hayfield (handsome former coaching inn with thoughtful food and drink), Royal Oak at Hurdlow (carefully renovated with much enjoyed all-day food), Yorkshire Bridge near Ladybower Reservoir (fine views and handy for walks) and Red Lion at Litton (cosy and unspoilt near good walking country). Other pubs enjoyed by our readers are the Bear at Alderwasley (beamed cottage rooms and good ales), Olde Gate in Brassington (lots of character and some unspoilt features), Lathkil at Over Haddon (popular buffet-style lunches), Flying Childers at Stanton in Peak (charming, with delightful licensees) and White Horse in Woolley Moor (neatly kept and in lovely countryside). In general, food is fairly priced and honest, but for a special meal try our Derbyshire Dining Pub 2014: the Devonshire Arms at Beeley.

ALDERWASLEY

SK3153 Map 7

Bear ★ ♀ ◀

Left off A6 at Ambergate on to Holly Lane (turns into Jackass Lane),
then right at end (staggered crossroads); DE56 2RD

Unspoilt country inn with beamed cottagey rooms, good range of
real ales, tasty food and a peaceful garden; bedrooms

With welcoming log fires and high standards of food and drink
continuing under the new landlord, this characterful tavern remains
extremely popular. The lovely dark low-beamed rooms have a cheerful
miscellany of antique furniture including high-backed settles and locally
made antique oak chairs with derbyshire motifs. One little room is filled
right to the built-in wall seats by a single vast table. Other décor includes
staffordshire china ornaments, old paintings and engravings. There's no
obvious front door – just a plain back entrance by the car park – and
it can get busy, so you may need to book. A beer named for the pub
(from Derby), Bass, Thornbridge Jaipur and Timothy Taylors Landlord
on handpump, several wines by the glass from a decent list, as well as
malt whiskies; service is very good. Well spaced picnic-sets in the lovely
garden have wonderful country views.

Well thought-of food in generous helpings includes sandwiches, chicken
liver pâté with home-made chutney, beer-battered mushrooms stuffed with
stilton and garlic with tomato sauce, lasagne, brie and caramelised red onion
tartlet, ham with free-range eggs, black pudding and wild mushroom sausages
with mash and onion gravy, chicken breast with creamy wild mushroom and
tomato sauce, lamb shank with mint gravy, salmon fillet with champagne sauce,
and puddings. *Benchmark main dish: steak and potato pie with chips £10.95.*
Two-course evening meal £19.00.

Free house ~ Licensee Keith Marshall-Clarke ~ Real ale ~ (01629) 822585 ~ Open 11-11
~ Bar food 12-3, 6-9; 12-9 Fri-Sun ~ Restaurant ~ Children welcome ~ Dogs allowed
in bar ~ Bedrooms: /£65 ~ www.bear-hotel.com *Recommended by Lindsay White, Stephen*
Shepherd, David Heath, Brian and Jacky Wilson, David and Sue Atkinson, R and S Bentley, Richard
Cole, Peter F Marshall

ASHOVER

SK3462 Map 7

Old Poets Corner ◀ £ ⇌

Butts Road (B6036, off A632 Matlock–Chesterfield); S45 0EW

A fine range of interesting real ales (some own brew) and ciders in
characterful village pub with enthusiastic owners; hearty, reasonably
priced food

'If only it was my local,' says one reader wistfully. This is a smashing
all-rounder – even on a bitter winter's day there are usually plenty
of customers enjoying the warm welcome, roaring open fires and
candlelight. The informal bar with its mix of chairs and pews has an
easy-going atmosphere. There's a fine range of ten or so real ales on
handpump, four of which come from their own microbrewery (Ashover
Light Rale, Coffin Lane Stout, Hydro and Poets Tipple – you can do a
brewery tour), plus guests like Abbeydale Deception, Batemans XXXB,
Blue Monkey Infinity, Raw Grey Ghost and Slaters Top Totty; also, a
terrific choice of eight farm ciders, a dozen fruit wines, 20 malt whiskies
and belgian beers. They also hold regular beer festivals. A small room
opening off the bar has a stack of newspapers and vintage comics,
and french doors leading to a tiny balcony with a couple of tables;

background music. The music-loving landlord runs acoustic, folk and blues sessions, and posters advertise forthcoming events, such as quiz nights, poetry evenings and morris dancers. The bedrooms are attractive, and there's a holiday cottage sleeping eight.

 As well as baguettes and baked potatoes, the very reasonably priced food includes battered king prawns with chilli dip, creamy garlic mushrooms on toasted sourdough, five-bean chilli with rice and yoghurt, nine types of sausages, braised liver and onions with mash and gravy, rustic beef stew, beer-battered haddock fillet with mushy peas and chips, bacon-wrapped chicken breast with barbecue sauce, and puddings; Sunday evening is curry night. *Benchmark main dish: meat and potato pie with mushy peas and chips £8.25. Two-course evening meal £15.50.*

Own brew ~ Licensees Kim and Jackie Beresford ~ Real ale ~ (01246) 590888 ~ Open 12-11.30 ~ Bar food 12-2(3 Sat), 6.30-9(6-9.30 Fri, Sat); 12-4, 7-9 Sun ~ Restaurant ~ Children welcome away from bar until 9pm ~ Dogs allowed in bar and bedrooms ~ Open mike Tues, quiz Weds, live bands some Fri, 50s/60s singalong Sun ~ Bedrooms: £55/£80 ~ www.oldpoets.co.uk *Recommended by David Heath, George Atkinson, Steve Short, Ken and Lynda Taylor, Laurence Sillars, Peter F Marshall, Derek and Sylvia Stephenson*

BEELEY
Devonshire Arms 🍴 ♈ 🍺 🛏
SK2667 Map 7

B6012, off A6 Matlock–Bakewell; DE4 2NR

Derbyshire Dining Pub of the Year

Contemporary twist to lovely old interior; local beers, good wine list, interesting carefully sourced food; attractive comfortable bedrooms

An unusual feature here is the game rotisserie in a raised area of the bar – in season they have grouse, partridge, pigeon, pheasant, rabbit and venison (out of season, other meats are used). We feel Charles Dickens, a frequent visitor, would have approved. It's a handsome 18th-c building in an attractive Peak District village on the fringes of the Chatsworth Estate, and within walking distance of Chatsworth House. It's at its most pubby at lunchtime (when table bookings aren't taken) and they keep up to six changing real ales, such as Abbeydale Daily Bread, Peak Ales Chatsworth Gold, Sharps Doom Bar, Theakstons Old Peculier, Thornbridge Jaipur and Whim Hartington, several wines by the glass from a well chosen list, a good range of malt whiskies and local mineral water. Contemporary colours contrast with the attractive traditional interior: amid black beams, flagstones, stripped stone, traditional settles and cheerful log fires, you'll find bright candy-coloured modern furnishings, prints and floral arrangements. Although dogs are permitted in the stylishly comfortable bedrooms, they are not allowed in the bar.

 Sourcing ingredients from the Chatsworth Estate, the imaginative food includes sandwiches (served all afternoon), smoked fish with red and yellow chicory, caramelised marmalade and thyme croutons, potted duck with plum sauce, caesar salad, sausages with red wine and onion gravy, spaghetti with roasted tomatoes, rocket, basil and parmesan, honey-roast ham and eggs with skinny chips, crispy belly pork with white and black pudding, haricot beans and parmentier potatoes, venison with smoked aubergine, piquillo pepper, churros and chilli chocolate sauce, and puddings such as lemon tart with chantilly cream and sticky toffee pudding with toffee sauce and vanilla ice-cream. *Benchmark main dish: honey and herb-glazed poussin £13.95. Two-course evening meal £21.00.*

Free house ~ Licensee Alan Hill ~ Real ale ~ (01629) 733259 ~ Open 12-11(10.30 Sun)
~ Bar food 12-3, 6-9.30; sandwiches 3-6 ~ Restaurant ~ Children welcome ~
Dogs allowed in bedrooms ~ Bedrooms: £79/£139 ~ www.devonshirebeeley.co.uk
Recommended by David Heath, Mr and Mrs D Hammond, Derek and Sylvia Stephenson,
R and S Bentley, Di and Mike Gillam, Tracey and Stephen Groves

BRASSINGTON
SK2354   Map 7

Olde Gate ★ £

Village signed off B5056 and B5035 NE of Ashbourne; DE4 4HJ

**Lovely old interior, candlelit at night, with tasty, fair-priced food,
real ales and country garden**

Just a few minutes' drive from Carsington Water, this unspoilt old place
with mullioned windows has a very inviting garden with tables looking
out to idyllic silvery-walled pastures; there are also benches in the small
front yard. The interior is full of fine furnishings, including an ancient
wall clock, rush-seated old chairs and antique settles, among them a
lovely example in black solid oak. Log fires blaze, gleaming copper pots
sit on a 17th-c kitchen range, pewter mugs hang from a beam, and a side
shelf boasts a collection of embossed Doulton stoneware flagons; there's
also a Georgian panelled room. To the left of a small lobby (served from
a hatch), a cosy beamed room has stripped panelled settles, scrubbed-
top tables and a blazing fire under a huge mantelbeam. Brakspears
Oxford Gold, Jenning Cumberland and Marstons Pedigree on handpump,
and a good choice of malt whiskies; cribbage, dominoes, cards and
maybe Sunday evening boules in summer.

Fair-priced, popular food includes sandwiches and baguettes, chicken liver
pâté, creamy garlic mushrooms, trio of sausages with mash and onion gravy,
gammon, egg and chips, curry of the day, beer-battered cod with mushy peas,
chicken breast in tarragon sauce, rack of lamb with redcurrant and rosemary jus,
duck with orange and cointreau sauce, and puddings. The Bargain Award is for the
lunchtime dishes. *Benchmark main dish: steak in Guinness pie £9.95. Two-course
evening meal £15.50.*

Marstons ~ Lease Peter Scragg ~ Real ale ~ (01629) 540448 ~ Open 12-2.15, 6-11; 12-3,
6-10 Sun; closed Mon except bank holiday lunchtimes, Tues lunchtime, Sun evening in
winter ~ Bar food 12-2(2.30 Sun), 6.30-8.45 ~ Restaurant ~ Children welcome ~ Dogs
welcome ~ www.oldgateinnbrassington.co.uk *Recommended by Peter F Marshall, George
Atkinson, JJW, CMW, Ann and Colin Hunt*

BRETTON
SK2078   Map 7

Barrel

*Signposted from Foolow (which is signposted from A623 just E of junction
with B6465 to Bakewell); can also be reached from the B6049 at Great Hucklow, or the
B6001 via Abney, from Leadmill just S of Hathersage; S32 5QD*

**Remote dining pub with traditional décor, popular food and
friendly staff**

Magnificently situated on the edge of an isolated ridge in excellent
walking country, this former turnpike inn enjoys unparalleled views
– when the weather is right, you can see five counties. Inside, everything
is kept spic and span, and the friendly staff are smartly dressed. Stubs of
massive knocked-through stone walls divide the place into several areas.
The cosy dark oak-beamed bar is charmingly traditional, with gleaming
copper and brass, warming fire, patterned carpet, low doorways and

stools lined up at the counter: Marstons Pedigree and EPA and Wychwood Hobgoblin on handpump, and tankards hanging above; background radio. Seats on the front terrace by the road and in a courtyard garden are nicely sheltered from the inevitable breeze at this height.

🍴 Enjoyable food includes sandwiches, stilton mushrooms, devilled whitebait, beer-battered fish and chips with mushy peas and tartare sauce, lamb chops, finnan haddock with chive and cream sauce, roast venison, and puddings like fruit crumble and profiteroles with warm chocolate sauce. *Benchmark main dish: steak in ale pie £11.95. Two-course evening meal £18.00.*

Free house ~ Licensee Philip Cone ~ Real ale ~ (01433) 630856 ~ Open 11-3, 6-11; may open all day in high summer; 11-11 Sat, Sun ~ Bar food 12-2, 6-9; 12-9 Sun ~ Well behaved children welcome ~ Dogs allowed in bar ~ Bedrooms: /$85 ~ www.thebarrelinn.co.uk *Recommended by Ann and Colin Hunt, David Heath, Peter F Marshall, Hilary Forrest*

CHELMORTON
Church Inn 🍷 £ 🛏

SK1170   Map 7

Village signposted off A5270, between A6 and A515 SE of Buxton; keep on up through village towards church; SK17 9SL

Cosy, convivial traditional inn beautifully set in High Peak walking country – good value food

Our readers enjoy staying here very much – and the breakfasts are good too. It's a welcoming place where the hospitable landlord and his friendly staff get customers, locals or visitors, talking to each other. The chatty, low-ceilinged bar has a warming fire and is traditionally furnished with built-in cushioned benches and simple chairs around polished cast-iron-framed tables (a couple still with their squeaky sewing treadles). Shelves of books, Tiffany-style lamps and house plants in the curtained windows, atmospheric Dales photographs and prints, and a coal-effect stove in the stripped-stone end wall all add a cosy feel. Adnams, Marstons Bitter and Pedigree and a couple of guests such as Thornbridge Kipling and Wincle Life of Riley on handpump; darts in a tiled-floor games area on the left; TV, background music and board games. The inn is opposite a largely 18th-c church and is prettily tucked into woodland; there are fine views over the village and hills beyond from good teak tables on the two-level terrace.

🍴 Sensibly priced food includes hot and cold baps, cheesy melts, black pudding fritters with spiced chutney, chicken goujons with garlic mayonnaise, lasagne, chickpea tagine, gammon with egg and pineapple, daily specials like lamb shank in red wine and rosemary sauce, fresh battered haddock with chips and peas or bacon-wrapped chicken with creamy mushroom sauce, and puddings. *Benchmark main dish: rabbit pie £12.00. Two-course evening meal £15.00.*

Free house ~ Licensees Julie and Justin Satur ~ Real ale ~ (01298) 85319 ~ Open 12-3, 6-11; 12-11 Sat, Sun ~ Bar food 12-2.30, 6-8.30; 12-8.30 weekends ~ Children welcome ~ Dogs allowed in bar ~ Bedrooms: £50/£75 ~ www.thechurchinn.co.uk
Recommended by J and E Dakin, David and Sue Atkinson, R and S Bentley, Ann and Colin Hunt, Mike and Margaret Banks, Peter F Marshall

---

Please tell us if the décor, atmosphere, food or drink at a pub is different from our description. We rely on readers' reports to keep us up to date: feedback@goodguides.com, or (no stamp needed) The Good Pub Guide, FREEPOST TN1569, Wadhurst, E Sussex TN5 7BR.

CHINLEY
Old Hall ★ 🛏 🍺

SK0382   Map 7

Village signposted off A6 (very sharp turn) E of New Mills; also off A624 N of Chapel-en-le-Frith; Whitehough Head Lane, off B6062

Charming small Peak District inn, great range of beers and ciders, good country food, striking ancient dining hall, comfortable bedrooms

This 16th-c stone-built inn nestles prettily in a steep hamlet huddled below the moors. The warm bar is basically four small friendly rooms opened into a single area tucked behind the inn's massive central chimney – open fires, some broad flagstones, some patterned red carpet, sturdy country tables, a couple of long pews and various other seats including a leather chesterfield and wing armchair. Their beers are exceptional, a great, mainly local, changing range from half a dozen or more handpumps – on our visit, they had examples from Buxton, Marble, Marstons, Phoenix and Tatton, as well as Thatcher's farm cider, some interesting lagers on tap and a rare range of bottled ciders and (mainly belgian) beers. They also run beer festivals, with music, in late February and September. The list of wines by the glass is also unusual, mainly new world. Service is friendly and helpful. Even if you're here just for a drink or bar meal, do poke your nose into the dining room – a surprisingly grand space with a great stone chimney soaring into high eaves, splendid refectory tables on a parquet floor, lovely old mullioned windows and a splendid minstrel's gallery. The pretty walled garden has picnic-sets under sycamore trees.

 Quite a choice of popular food includes lunchtime sandwiches, chicken liver, bacon and port pâté with onion marmalade, corned beef hash with fried egg, cumberland pork sausages on creamy mash with onion gravy, sunblush tomato, red onion, fine bean and ricotta tagliatelle, fresh tuna niçoise, chicken burger with coleslaw, tarragon mayonnaise and chips, curried monkfish with thai sweet potato and coconut sauce, gammon with egg and pineapple, and puddings such as lemon meringue cheesecake and toffee and apple tart with local ice-cream; they have a good cheeseboard and an early-bird menu (lunchtimes, not weekends). *Benchmark main dish: steak and kidney pudding £12.00. Two-course evening meal £15.50.*

Free house ~ Licensee Daniel Capper ~ Real ale ~ (01663) 750529 ~ Open 12-12 ~ Bar food 12-2, 5-9(9.30 Fri, Sat); 12-7.30 Sun ~ Restaurant ~ Children welcome ~ Dogs allowed in bar ~ Bedrooms: £75/£89 ~ www.old-hall-inn.co.uk
Recommended by Annette and John Derbyshire, Malcolm and Pauline Pellatt, Frank Blanchard

FENNY BENTLEY
Coach & Horses £

SK1750   Map 7

A515 N of Ashbourne; DE6 1LB

Cosy former coaching inn with pretty country furnishings, roaring open fires and food all day

In winter, the two log fires in this comfortable 17th-c coaching inn are very welcoming. The traditional interior has all the trappings you'd expect of a country pub, from exposed brick hearths and flagstones to

---

The letters and figures after the name of each town are its Ordnance Survey map reference. Using the Guide at the beginning of the book explains how it helps you find a pub, in road atlases or large-scale maps as well as in our own maps.

black beams hung with horsebrasses, wagon wheels and pewter mugs, and hand-made pine furniture that includes wall settles with floral-print cushions. There's also a conservatory dining room. Marstons Pedigree and a guest such as Abbeydale Moonshine on handpump, and the landlord is knowledgeable about malt whiskies – he stocks just under two dozen; quiet background music. There are views across fields from tables in the side garden by an elder tree, and modern tables and chairs under cocktail parasols on the front roadside terrace. The pub is a few minutes' walk from the popular Tissington Trail (which follows a former railway line) – it's best to join the trail at the nearby picture-book village of Tissington.

Hot and cold sandwiches are served until 5pm, and other fairly priced dishes include brandied chicken liver and tarragon pâté with apple chutney, goats cheese and red onion marmalade wrapped in filo pastry, griddled vegetables on ratatouille, venison and rosemary sausages on horseradish mash with cranberry gravy, chorizo-stuffed chicken breast with leek and wholegrain mustard sauce, duck breast with fig and cointreau sauce, and puddings. *Benchmark main dish: gammon steak with egg or melted cheese and pineapple £11.50. Two-course evening meal £17.00.*

Free house ~ Licensees John and Matthew Dawson ~ Real ale ~ (01335) 350246 ~ Open 11-11; 12-10.30 Sun ~ Bar food 12-9 ~ Restaurant ~ Children welcome
Recommended by Tony W Dickinson, Mrs P M Chapman, J and E Dakin, Ann and Colin Hunt, Dave Webster, Sue Holland, Tracey and Stephen Groves

FROGGATT EDGE   SK2476   Map 7
Chequers 🛏
A625, off A623 N of Bakewell; S32 3ZJ

Bustling dining pub in Peak District country, several real ales, quite a choice of interesting food and seats in quiet garden; bedrooms

Just below Froggatt Edge, this smart, well run dining pub is particularly popular with walkers and cyclists at weekends – when it sensibly serves food all day. The opened-up bar and dining rooms are cosily attractive, with solid country furnishings like farmhouse and captain's chairs and cushioned settles around all manner of tables on bare floorboards or carpeting, plus a woodburning stove, longcase clock and antique prints. Bradfield Farmers Blonde, Peak Ales Bakewell Best Bitter and Wells & Youngs Bombardier on handpump and eight wines by the glass; background music. There are seats in the peaceful back garden. Bedrooms are clean and comfortable and the breakfasts very good.

Impressive food includes sandwiches, game terrine with pear jelly, crispy pheasant leg with bacon, cabbage and quince purée, home-cooked ham with duck egg, fat chips and tomato chutney, burger with smoked cheddar, bacon and home-made coleslaw and relish, spinach and goats cheese tagliatelle, seafood pancakes with fresh haddock, smoked haddock, salmon and prawns, braised pork belly with chorizo, sage and a red onion sauce, fillet of brill with mussel linguine and chilli lemon squid, and puddings such as bakewell pudding with custard and rich chocolate torte with orange syrup and choc-chip ice-cream. Their preserves, chutneys and marmalade are for sale. *Benchmark main dish: moroccan lamb £17.00. Two-course evening meal £20.50.*

Pubmaster ~ Lease Jonathan and Joanne Tindall ~ Real ale ~ (01433) 630231 ~ Open 12-11(10.30 Sun) ~ Bar food 12-2.30, 6-9.30; 12-9.30 Sat; 12-9 Sun ~ Children welcome ~ Bedrooms: /£85 ~ www.chequers-froggatt.com *Recommended by Emma Scofield, Caroline Prescott*

GREAT LONGSTONE   SK1971 Map 7

Crispin

Main Street; village signed from A6020, N of Ashford in the Water; DE45 1TZ

Spotless traditional pub with emphasis on good, fairly priced pubby food; good drinks choice too

In excellent walking country at the heart of the Peak District, this well established, family-run pub offers a warm welcome to all. Décor throughout is thoroughly traditional, running from brass or copper implements, decorative plates, horsebrasses on the beams in the red ceiling, and a collage of regulars' snapshots to built-in cushioned wall benches, upholstered chairs and stools around polished tables on red carpet, and a fire. A corner area is snugly partitioned off, and on the right is a separate, more formal dining room; darts, board games and maybe faint background music. Cheerful staff serve a good choice of wines and whiskies, as well as Robinsons Dizzy Blonde, Double Hop, Frederics, Hoptimus and Unicorn on handpump and Weston's Old Rosie cider. There are picnic-sets out front (one under a heated canopy), set well back above the quiet lane, and more in the garden.

The well liked food includes sandwiches, oatcakes with goats cheese, spinach and walnuts, omelettes, lasagne, burger topped with cheddar, bacon and portobello mushroom, fish pie, chilli con carne, rainbow trout with parma ham, garlic and lemon butter, slow-braised lamb shank, ham hock with cider and apples, and puddings. *Benchmark main dish: steak and kidney in ale pie £12.95. Two-course evening meal £19.00.*

Robinsons ~ Tenant Paul Rowlinson ~ Real ale ~ (01629) 640237 ~ Open 12-3, 6-11; 12-11 Sat, Sun ~ Bar food 12-2.30, 6-9 ~ Restaurant ~ Children welcome ~ Dogs welcome ~ www.thecrispin.co.uk *Recommended by Brian and Jacky Wilson, David Eberlin*

HASSOP   SK2272 Map 7

Eyre Arms

B6001 N of Bakewell; DE45 1NS

Comfortable, neatly kept comfortable pub with decent food and beer, and pretty views from the garden

At any time of year, this 17th-c former coaching inn is a fine sight – the hanging baskets make a lovely display in summer and the creeper bursts into spectacular colour in autumn. Inside, it's snug and cosy with cheery log fires warming the low-ceilinged oak-beamed rooms. Traditional furnishings include cushioned oak settles, comfortable plush chairs, a longcase clock, old pictures and lots of brass and copper. The small public bar has an unusual collection of teapots, as well as Black Sheep, Peak Ales Swift Nick and a guest from Bradfield on handpump, nine wines by the glass and 25 malt whiskies; classical background music. The dining room is dominated by a painting of the Eyre coat of arms above a stone fireplace. The delightful garden, with its gurgling fountain, looks straight out into fine Peak District countryside.

Using some home-grown produce, the choice of food includes sandwiches, whitebait with salad, deep-fried garlic mushrooms with a dip, mushroom stroganoff, venison pie, salmon fillet with orange and basil sauce, lamb cooked in indian spices and coconut with naan bread and mango chutney, specials such as baked camembert with garlic bread or rabbit pie with cider and bacon, and puddings. *Benchmark main dish: chicken stuffed with leeks and stilton in creamy sauce £13.40. Two-course evening meal £19.00.*

Free house ~ Licensees Nick and Lynne Smith ~ Real ale ~ (01629) 640390 ~ Open 11-3, 6-11; 12-3, 6-10.30 Sun; closed Mon evening Nov-Easter ~ Bar food 12-2, 7-9 ~ Children welcome ~ Dogs allowed in bar ~ www.eyrearms.com *Recommended by J and E Dakin*

HATHERSAGE

Plough

SK2380 Map 7

Leadmill; B6001 towards Bakewell; S32 1BA

Comfortable dining pub usefully placed for exploring the Peak District, with good food, beer and wine, and seats in the waterside garden; comfortable bedrooms

This is an enjoyable place to stay – especially in the well equipped beamed bedrooms in the converted barn across the cobbled courtyard. An immaculately kept 16th-c inn in the Peak District National Park, it has cosy and traditionally furnished rooms. There are rows of dark wooden chairs and tables (with cruets showing the emphasis on dining) and a long banquette running almost the length of one wall, on bright tartan and oriental patterned carpets. Also, a big log fire and a woodburning stove, decorative plates on terracotta walls and pewter tankards hanging from a dark beam; the neat dining room is slightly more formal. There's a good wine list (with nearly two dozen by the glass), 25 malt whiskies and Adnams, Black Sheep and Timothy Taylors on handpump; quiet background music. The nine-acre grounds are on the banks of the River Derwent – the pretty garden slopes right down to the water – and a new terrace offers wonderful valley views.

A thoughtful choice of good food includes sandwiches, tea-smoked trout fillet with home-made crumpet, poached egg and sweet mustard, platter of mixed hors d'oeuvres, corn-fed chicken with stilton, leeks and port jus, red pepper couscous, vegetable tagine and grilled halloumi, lambs liver and bacon with champ and onion jus, beer-battered cod with mushy peas and fries, lamb shank with vegetable risotto, sea bream with sweet potato, marinated cherry tomatoes and salsa verde, and puddings such as bakewell pudding with dried fruit compote and custard and fromage frais with berry compote and their own-recipe granola. *Benchmark main dish: steak and kidney pudding £14.00. Two-course evening meal £25.00.*

Free house ~ Licensees Bob, Cynthia and Elliott Emery ~ Real ale ~ (01433) 650319 ~ Open 11-11; 12-10.30 Sun ~ Bar food 11.30-9.30; 12-8.30 Sun ~ Restaurant ~ Occasional live jazz ~ Dogs welcome ~ Bedrooms: £95/£130 ~ www.theploughinn-hathersage.co.uk *Recommended by Richard Cole, Mike and Mary Carter*

HATHERSAGE

Scotsmans Pack

SK2381 Map 7

School Lane, off A6187; S32 1BZ

Well run inn with five real ales, plenty to look at and popular food; bedrooms

With a warm welcome for both drinkers and diners, this is a relaxed and well run inn that takes its name from the scottish packmen who used to sell their tweeds to local farmers. The various dark panelled rooms are full of interesting knick-knacks (plates on delft shelving, brass and copper items and old photographs on the walls, hanging tankards), and there are upholstered gingham stools and dining chairs, cushioned wall seats, captain's and other solid dining chairs around an assortment of wooden tables, and a woodburning stove. Black Sheep,

Jennings Cumberland, Marstons Pedigree and a couple of guest beers on handpump; TV, darts and background music. There are picnic-sets on a pleasant terrace by a trout stream, and the inn is well placed for walks.

 Tasty bar food includes sandwiches, game terrine, smoked salmon and crayfish salad, chicken wrapped in bacon with white wine and leek sauce, lambs liver and bacon with onion gravy, braised lamb shanks with mint gravy, mixed grill, and puddings. *Benchmark main dish: steak pie £10.25. Two-course evening meal £18.00.*

Marstons ~ Lease Nick Beagrie, Steve Bramley and Susan Concannon ~ Real ale ~ (01433) 650253 ~ Open 11-midnight; 12-midnight Sun; 11-3, 5.30-midnight Mon-Thurs in winter ~ Bar food all day in summer, Fri-Sun in winter; 12-2, 6-9.30 Mon-Thurs in winter ~ Restaurant ~ Children welcome ~ Live music last Fri of month ~ Bedrooms: £45/£75 ~ www.scotsmanspack.com *Recommended by Alan Bowker, Peter F Marshall, Malcolm and Pauline Pellatt*

HAYFIELD SK0388 Map 7
Lantern Pike £
Glossop Road (A624 N) at Little Hayfield, just N of Hayfield; SK22 2NG

Friendly retreat from the surrounding moors of Kinder Scout, with reasonably priced food; bedrooms

This homely place is handy if you're in the area and need a break from the windswept moors. It's in the Peak District National Park, and tables on a stone-walled terrace look over a big-windowed weaver's house towards Lantern Pike. The traditional red plush bar proudly displays photos of the original *Coronation Street* cast, many of whom were regulars here, along with Tony Warren, one of its earlier script writers, and Arthur Lowe of *Dad's Army* fame. It's quite possible that the interior hasn't changed much since those days. You'll find a warm fire, brass platters in numbers, china and toby jugs, fresh flowers on the tables and a counter lined with red plush stools. Castle Rock Harvest Pale and Timothy Taylors Landlord on handpump; TV and background music. Dogs may be allowed in at the licensees' discretion, and if clean.

 Chalked up on blackboards, the menu includes chicken pâté with toast, haddock fishcake with sweet chilli dip, vegetable bake, a special prawn curry, pork in stilton sauce, liver and bacon with onion gravy, slow-braised lamb shank in rosemary and red wine sauce, and puddings like lemon cheesecake and crème brûlée. *Benchmark main dish: daily fresh fish dishes £11.00. Two-course evening meal £15.50.*

Enterprise ~ Lease Stella and Tom Cuncliffe ~ Real ale ~ (01663) 747590 ~ Open 12-3, 5-11; 12-11 Sat; closed Mon lunchtime ~ Bar food 12-2.30, 5-8.30; all day weekends ~ Restaurant ~ Children welcome ~ Dogs allowed in bar ~ Bedrooms: £52/£64 ~ www.lanternpikeinn.co.uk *Recommended by Dennis Jones, David and Sue Atkinson*

HAYFIELD SK0387 Map 7
Royal
Market Street; SK22 2EP

Big, bustling inn with fine panelled rooms, friendly service and thoughtful choice of drinks and food; bedrooms

A handsome 18th-c stone-built former coaching inn at the heart of an attractive village by the River Sett. The oak-panelled bar and lounge areas have a good mix of locals and visitors, open fires, a fine collection of seats, from long settles with pretty scatter cushions through elegant upholstered dining chairs to tub chairs and chesterfields, around an assortment of solid tables on rugs and flagstones; house plants, daily papers. There's Thwaites Original and guests such as Dunham Massey Stamford Bitter, Happy Valley Sworn Secret, Thwaites Wainwright and Titanic Anchor Bitter on handpump (they hold a beer festival every October), and 11 wines by the glass. There are seats on the sunny front terrace. The bedrooms are spotlessly clean and comfortable and the breakfasts are good.

Using produce from local farmers and suppliers, the food includes sandwiches, chicken liver and brandy pâté with red onion marmalade, prawn cocktail, all-day breakfast, macaroni cheese, trio of sausages with wholegrain mustard mash and onion gravy, cajun chicken with chips, gammon steak with egg and pineapple, beef and horseradish or lamb and mint burgers with bacon and fries, steak in ale pie, and puddings like cheesecake of the day and apple pie with custard. *Benchmark main dish: beer-battered fish and chips £9.50. Two-course evening meal £15.50.*

Free house ~ Licensees Mark Miller and Lisa Davis ~ Real ale ~ (01663) 742721 ~ Open 10am-11.30pm; 12-10.30 Sun ~ Bar food 10-9(8 Sat) ~ Restaurant ~ Children welcome ~ Dogs allowed in bar and bedrooms ~ Bedrooms: £50/£70 ~ www.theroyalathayfield.com
Recommended by Ruth May

HURDLOW
Royal Oak

SK1265 Map 7

Monyash–Longnor Road, just off A515 S of Buxton; SK17 9QJ

Bustling, carefully renovated pub in rural spot with beamed rooms, friendly staff and tasty, all-day food

This carefully renovated pub is on the Tissington Trail, so it's popular with walkers, cyclists and horse riders (they offer overnight stabling) and, usefully, a wide choice of nicely presented food is available all day. The beamed two-room bar has an open fire in a stone fireplace, lots of copper kettles, bed-warming pans, horsebrasses and country pictures, cushioned wheelback chairs and wall settles around dark tables, and stools against the bar counter, where friendly, helpful staff serve Sharps Doom Bar, Whim Hartington IPA and Wincle Life of Riley on handpump, eight wines by the glass and several malt whiskies; background music and board games. The attractive dining room has bare floorboards with country dining chairs, more wheelbacks and a cushioned pine settle in one corner, pretty curtains and another open fire. For large groups, there's also a downstairs flagstoned cellar room with benches flanking long tables. The terraced garden has plenty of seats, with picnic-sets on the grass. A self-catering barn has bunk bedrooms and there's a campsite too.

Popular, honest, all-day food includes sandwiches, soup, antipasti plate, spicy chicken wings, gammon and eggs, burger with smoked bacon, stilton and coleslaw, cranberry barbecue ribs, butternut squash, spinach and walnut lasagne, chilli con carne, thai green chicken curry, slow-cooked lamb shank with spring onion mash, jumbo beer-battered haddock with home-made chips and mushy peas, pork fillet in Grand Marnier cream sauce and black pudding mash, and puddings such as white chocolate cheesecake and apple and mixed berry crumble; they also offer a hearty breakfast menu (10-11.30 weekdays, 8.30-11.30 weekends). *Benchmark main dish: beef and stilton pie £11.95. Two-course evening meal £18.00.*

Free house~ Licensee Justin Heslop ~ Real ale ~ (01298) 83288 ~ Open 10am-11pm (midnight Sat) ~ Bar food 10-9 ~ Children welcome ~ Dogs welcome ~ www.peakpub.co.uk
Recommended by Brian and Jacky Wilson, Graham Parker

INGLEBY
SK3427 Map 7
John Thompson 🍺 £ 🛏

NW of Melbourne; turn off A514 at Swarkestone Bridge or in Stanton by Bridge; can also be reached from Ticknall (or from Repton on B5008); DE73 7HW

Own-brew pub that strikes the right balance between attentive service, roomy comfort and good value lunchtime food

Unchanging and friendly, this own-brew pub has been in every edition of this *Guide* since it started 31 years ago – it's also the longest established microbrewery in the county. It takes its name from the licensee's father. The simple but comfortable and immaculately kept modernised lounge has ceiling joists, old oak settles, button-back leather seats, sturdy oak tables, antique prints and paintings and a log-effect gas fire; background music. A couple of smaller, cosier rooms open off from here; piano, games machine, board games, darts, TV, and pool in the conservatory. Friendly staff serve a couple of their own brews such as JTS XXX, Gold, St Nicks and Rich Porter alongside a guest such as Timothy Taylors Landlord. There are lots of tables by flower beds on the neat lawns, or you can sit on the partly covered terrace, surrounded by pretty countryside and near the River Trent. If you stay in one of the self-catering detached chalet lodges, breakfast is delivered to your fridge.

🍴 The short lunchtime menu includes sandwiches, baked potatoes, three-cheese and broccoli pasta bake, salads, and puddings such as fruit crumble and Mrs Thompson's famous bread and butter pudding – a speciality of the pub for the past 40 years. *Benchmark main dish: roast beef £8.95.*

Own brew ~ Licensee Nick Thompson ~ Real ale ~ (01332) 862469 ~ Open 11-2.30, 6-11; 11-11 Sat; 12-10.30 Sun; closed Mon lunchtime except bank holidays ~ Bar food 12-2 ~ Restaurant ~ Children welcome in main bar till 6pm, in conservatory till 9pm ~ Dogs allowed in bar ~ www.johnthompsoninn.com *Recommended by Andy Dolan, David Eberlin, Ian and Jane Irving, Tracey and Stephen Groves*

KIRK IRETON
SK2650 Map 7
Barley Mow 🍺 🛏

Village signed off B5023 S of Wirksworth; DE6 3JP

Welcoming old inn that focuses on real ale and conversation; bedrooms

Much enjoyed by both regulars and visitors, this is a special place with a kindly landlady who's been here for well over 30 years. An inn since around 1800, it shows how some grander rural pubs might have looked a century or so ago. The small main bar has a relaxed very pubby feel, with antique settles on the tiled floor or built into the panelling, a roaring coal fire, four slate-topped tables and shuttered mullioned windows. Another room has cushioned built-in pews on oak parquet and a small woodburning stove; a third has more pews, a tiled floor, low beams and big landscape prints. In casks behind a modest wooden counter are five well kept, often local, changing real ales mostly from smaller brewers such as Blue Monkey, Northumberland, Peak Ales, Storm and Whim; french wines and farm cider too. There's a good-sized garden, a couple of benches out in front and a shop in what used to be the stable. This very pretty hilltop village is within walking distance of Carsington Water. Bedrooms are comfortable, and readers enjoy the good breakfasts served in the stone-flagged kitchen.

Very inexpensive lunchtime rolls are the only food; the decent evening meals (no choice) are reserved for those staying here.

Free house ~ Licensee Mary Short ~ Real ale ~ No credit cards ~ (01335) 370306 ~ Open 12-2, 7-11(10.30 Sun) ~ Bar food lunchtime sandwiches only ~ Children welcome ~ Dogs allowed in bar and bedrooms ~ Bedrooms: £45/£65 *Recommended by Tich Critchlow, Josh Greaves*

 LADYBOWER RESERVOIR SK1986 Map 7

Ladybower Inn

A57 Sheffield–Glossop, just E of junction with A6013; S33 0AX

All-day food in comfortable proper pub nestling above reservoir in good walking country; good value bedrooms

Taking its name from the huge reservoir nearby, this well run and friendly inn is extremely popular at weekends and during the holidays. The various carpeted areas are homely with traditional furnishings that take in peach cottagey wallpaper and curtains, little pictures, cast-iron fireplaces, wall banquettes, captain's and country kitchen chairs and the like; the most relaxing place to eat is at the end on the right, with leather-padded traditional dining chairs around heavier tables, lancaster bomber pictures recalling the Dambusters' practice runs on the reservoir, and a coal-effect fire; unobtrusive background music and darts. Cheerful, helpful staff serve Acorn Barnsley, Bradfield Farmers Blonde, Greene King Ruddles County and a couple of guests such as Black Sheep and Sharps Doom Bar on handpump, and decent wines by the glass. If you stay in the annexe bedrooms, you won't be disturbed by traffic noise – but the road is busy, so crossing from the car park opposite needs care; picnic-sets out in front.

Using pheasants from the landlord's farm and other local produce, the generous home cooking includes hot and cold sandwiches, hot smoked salmon and smoked salmon salad, warm partridge salad with pears, bacon and honey dressing, chicken, ham and mushroom pie, pork medallions on butter beans and leeks, aubergine, pumpkin and chilli salad with crumbled cheese, venison haunch steak with apple and blue cheese tart, and puddings such as warm chocolate brownie with beer ice-cream and vanilla and green tea panna cotta with rhubarb compote. *Benchmark main dish: steak in ale pie £10.50. Two-course evening meal £20.00.*

Free house ~ Licensee Deborah Wilde ~ Real ale ~ (01433) 651241 ~ Open 10am-11pm ~ Bar food 12-9 ~ Restaurant ~ Children welcome ~ Dogs allowed in bedrooms ~ Bedrooms: £45/£80 ~ www.ladybower-inn.co.uk *Recommended by Mike Proctor, Richard and Andrea Bion*

LADYBOWER RESERVOIR SK2084 Map 7

Yorkshire Bridge

A6013 N of Bamford; S33 0AZ

Popular inn handy for the reservoir with several real ales, friendly staff, tasty food and fine views; bedrooms

This pleasantly genteel inn sits in dramatic country beneath the forested and moorland slopes just south of the Ladybower Reservoir dam. The cosy bar has countless tankards hanging from beams, lots of china plates, photographs and paintings on red walls, horsebrasses and copper items, red plush dining chairs around a mix of tables on a red patterned carpet, and a woodburning stove. There's lots more space in several other rooms – including a light and airy garden room with fine valley views – with an assortment of seating ranging from wicker and metal through bentwood-style chairs around quite a choice of wooden tables, on more carpeting or flagstones, plus many more decorative plates and photographs. Friendly staff serve Abbeydale Moonshine, Bradfield Farmers Blonde, Buxton Moor Top and Peak Ales Bakewell Best on handpump and nine wines by the glass. Dogs are allowed in some bedrooms, but not in the bar at mealtimes.

🍴 Tasty bar food includes sandwiches, crab fishcakes with sweet chilli dip, giant yorkshire pudding filled with onion gravy, italian-style pork steaks with basil and tomato sauce, trout with lemon and caper butter, lasagne, beer-battered fish of the day with mushy peas and chips, mediterranean vegetable moussaka, slow-roasted pork belly with cider and honey sauce, and puddings such as bakewell pudding and a sponge of the day. *Benchmark main dish: steak and kidney pie £10.75. Two-course evening meal £15.00.*

Free house ~ Licensees Trevelyan and John Illingworth ~ Real ale ~ (01433) 651361 ~ Open 11-11(10.30 Sun) ~ Bar food 12-2.30, 6-9(9.30 Fri, Sat); 12-8.30 Sun ~ Children welcome ~ Dogs allowed in bedrooms ~ Bedrooms: £65/£96 ~ www.yorkshire-bridge.co.uk *Recommended by Simon Pyle, Barry Collett*

LITTON
SK1675   Map 7
Red Lion
Village signposted off A623, between B6465 and B6049 junctions; also signposted off B6049; SK17 8QU

Unspoilt charm in friendly village pub, cosy bars, real ales and well liked food

Converted from three farm cottages, this friendly village pub – under a new landlady as we went to press – is popular with walkers as there are lots of hikes in the nearby Dales. The two linked front rooms are homely, with low beams and panelling, cushioned settles and wall seats around pubby tables, paintings, horsebrasses, open fires and Abbeydale Absolution and Moonshine and Barnsley Oakwell on handpump, decent wines and several malt whiskies. There's also a bigger stripped-stone back room; darts and evening TV. You'll find seats and tables out in front and on the village green.

🍴 As well as daily specials, the tasty food might include sandwiches, chicken liver pâté, deep-fried brie with cranberry sauce, home-made fishcakes with tomato chutney, burger with fries, goats cheese, roasted courgettes and red pepper with pasta, steak and kidney pie, beer-battered fish and chips, and puddings like cheesecake of the day and chocolate brownie. *Benchmark main dish: steak and kidney pie £10.95. Two-course evening meal £17.50.*

Enterprise ~ Lease Louise Parker ~ Real ale ~ (01298) 871458 ~ Open 12-11(midnight Fri, Sat); 12-10.30 Sun ~ Bar food 12-9(8 Sun) ~ Children over 6 welcome ~ Dogs allowed in bar ~ www.theredlionlitton.co.uk *Recommended by Robin Constable, Mr and Mrs D J Nash, Brian and Anna Marsden, Greta and Guy Pratt, Steve and Sue Griffiths, David Hunt, David and Jenny Billington, Mike and Wena Stevenson, Barry Collett*

'Children welcome' means the pub says it lets children inside without any special restriction. If it allows them in, but to restricted areas such as an eating area or family room, we specify this. Places with separate restaurants often let children use them, and hotels usually let children into public areas such as lounges. Some pubs impose an evening time limit – let us know if you find one earlier than 9pm.

OVER HADDON
SK2066 Map 7
Lathkil 🍺
Village and inn signposted from B5055 just SW of Bakewell; DE45 1JE

Traditional pub well placed for Lathkill Dale with super views, good range of beers and well liked food

The views from this unpretentious hotel are spectacular, and can be enjoyed from seats in the walled garden – and from windows in the bar. It's extremely popular with walkers (muddy boots must be left in the lobby), and dogs are welcome in the bar. The airy room on the right has a nice fire in an attractively carved fireplace, old-fashioned settles with upholstered cushions and chairs, black beams, a delft shelf of blue and white plates, and original prints and photographs. On the left, the sunny spacious dining area doubles as an evening restaurant. Everards Tiger, Peak Ales Swift Nick and Whim Hartington IPA with guests from brewers such as Abbeydale and Blue Monkey on handpump, a reasonable range of wines (including mulled wine) and a decent selection of malt whiskies; background music, darts, TV and board games.

 Lunch (served buffet-style) includes rolls, pork pâté, quiche of the day, steak and kidney pie, beef in Guinness casserole with dumplings and butternut squash lasagne, with evening choices like crayfish tails with lemon mayonnaise, gammon and eggs, roasted mediterranean vegetable risotto, bass fillets with tomato and caper sauce, loin of lamb with parma ham and herb stuffing and plum and port sauce, and puddings such as Mars bar banoffi pie and Baileys cheesecake. *Benchmark main dish: venison and blackberry casserole £10.95. Two-course evening meal £16.75.*

Free house ~ Licensee Alice Grigor-Taylor ~ Real ale ~ (01629) 812501 ~ Open 11-11; 12-10.30 Sun ~ Bar food 12-2(2.30 weekends), 6-8(7-8.30 Fri, Sat) ~ Restaurant ~ Children welcome ~ Dogs allowed in bar and bedrooms ~ Bedrooms: £60/£75 ~ www.lathkil.co.uk *Recommended by Mrs P Bishop, Dennis Jones*

PILSLEY
SK2371 Map 7
Devonshire Arms 🍷 🍺 🛏
Village signposted off A619 W of Baslow, and pub just below B6048; High Street; DE45 1UL

Simple yet stylish country inn, good all round; nice place to stay

On the Chatsworth Estate and handy if visiting Chatsworth House and Gardens, this is a civilised little country inn given a gentle contemporary slant. The flagstoned bar has four ales from local brewers such as Bakewell, Peak, Thornbridge and Whim on handpump, and a good choice of wines by the glass. Several fairly compact, mainly carpeted areas open off from the bar, each with a distinct character: stripped stone here, soft grey paintwork there, rather sumptuous crimson and gold wallpaper in one part, soft heather curtains and big modern paintings, log fires in stone fireplaces, comfortable seating in leather or fabric, and thick wooden table tops on either sturdy modern metal columns or old cast-iron bases – at least one still has its old sewing-machine treadle. Service is polite and efficient. There are some tables outside. The renowned Chatsworth Estate farm shop is at the top of the lane.

 Using Estate produce, the well liked food includes open sandwiches with salad and crisps, crispy bacon, black pudding and brie salad with walnut and honey dressing, cheddar cheese omelette, home-made corned beef hash with fried egg, creamy mushrooms, leek, spinach and stilton topped with pastry, chargrilled tuna with niçoise salad and cajun potato wedges, mixed grill, and puddings such as tiramisu and iced chocolate parfait. *Benchmark main dish: steak and kidney pudding £12.85. Two-course evening meal £19.00.*

Free house ~ Licensee Alan Hill ~ Real ale ~ (01246) 583258 ~ Open 11-11(10.30 Sun) ~ Bar food 12-2.30, 5-9; 12-8 Sun ~ Children welcome ~ Bedrooms: /£99 ~ www.devonshirepilsley.co.uk *Recommended by R and S Bentley*

 STANTON IN PEAK   SK2364 Map 7
Flying Childers  £
Village signposted from B6056 S of Bakewell; Main Road; DE4 2LW

Top notch beer and inexpensive simple bar lunches in warm-hearted, unspoilt pub – a delight

Named after an unbeatable racehorse of the early 18th c, this homely village pub is very popular with our readers. The friendly landlord keeps his regular Wells & Youngs Bombardier and a couple of guests such as Abbeydale Deception and Black Sheep on handpump, and wines by the glass. The best room in which to enjoy them is the snug little right-hand bar, virtually built for chat, with its dark beam-and-plank ceiling, dark wall settles, single pew, plain tables, coal and log fire, a few team photographs, dominoes and cribbage; background music. There's a bigger, equally unpretentious bar on the right. The well tended back garden has picnic-sets, and there's a couple more out in front; this beautiful steep stone village overlooks a rich green valley; good walks lead off in most directions.

Prepared by the landlady – as friendly as her husband – lunchtime bar food includes soup, filled cobs, toasties and casseroles. They sell home-made produce in the little porch shop and sometimes use vegetables from their allotment.

Free house ~ Licensees Stuart and Mandy Redfern ~ Real ale ~ No credit cards ~ (01629) 636333 ~ Open 12-2(3 weekends), 7-11; closed Mon and Tues lunchtimes ~ Bar food 12-2 ~ Children in lounge bar only ~ Dogs allowed in bar ~ Live acoustic music first Thurs evening of month ~ www.flyingchilders.com *Recommended by Brian and Anna Marsden, Ann and Colin Hunt*

 WOOLLEY MOOR   SK3661 Map 7
White Horse ♀
Badger Lane, off B6014 Matlock–Clay Cross; DE55 6FG

Attractive old dining pub with good food, pretty countryside

In lovely rolling countryside, this attractive old pub was built on the original packhorse route from the toll-bar cottage at Stretton to Woolley Moor toll-bar. A neat and uncluttered place, it has tidily arranged rows of furniture (including a leather sofa) on stone floors or wooden boards, boldy patterned curtains and blinds, little to distract on the cream walls and uniform lamps on window sills. The buoyantly chatty tap room has Peak Ales Bakewell Best and Chatsworth Gold and a guest on handpump, and a dozen wines by the glass from the brick counter; background music. There's also a conservatory. In the sloping garden you'll find a boules pitch, picnic-sets and a children's play area with a wooden train, boat, climbing frame and swings. Ogston Reservoir is just a couple of minutes' drive away.

🍴 Well thought-of food includes ciabattas, trout and lemon pâté, home-made crab croquettes with dill crème fraîche, brie and beetroot tart, steak and stilton slice with gravy and chips, sausages with mash and red wine sauce, roast chicken with stuffing and yorkshire pudding, battered cod loin and crushed peas, thick gammon with eggs and chunky chips, lambs liver and black pudding with onion gravy, and puddings such as apple and banana crumble and strawberry panna cotta; they also offer a two- and three-course set menu (all day Tues-Thurs, lunchtimes Fri, Sat). *Benchmark main dish: pork belly with smoked bacon sauce £13.95. Two-course evening meal £18.00.*

Free house ~ Licensees David and Melanie Boulby ~ Real ale ~ (01246) 590319 ~ Open 12-3, 5.30-11; 12-5 Sun; closed Sun evening, Mon except bank holidays ~ Bar food 12-1.45, 6-8.45; 12-4 Sun ~ Restaurant ~ Children welcome ~ www.thewhitehorsewoolleymoor.co.uk *Recommended by Ian Phillips, Peter Robson, R and S Bentley, Derek and Sylvia Stephenson*

Also Worth a Visit in Derbyshire

Besides the fully inspected pubs, you might like to try these pubs that have been recommended to us and described by readers. Do tell us what you think of them: feedback@goodguides.com

ASHBOURNE SK1846
Horns (01335) 347387
Victoria Square; DE6 1GG
Attractive 18th-c pub with bay window overlooking steep cobbled street, enjoyable home-made food, well kept Marstons Pedigree and a couple of guests, friendly staff, rooms on different levels, open fire; seats outside. *(David and Sue Atkinson)*

ASHBOURNE SK1846
Olde Vaults (01335) 346127
Market Place; DE6 1EU Attractive old building overlooking market square, cheerful staff, generous bargain food (not winter evenings), well kept Bass and Marstons Pedigree, good local atmosphere in simple open-plan bar (busy on Thurs and Sat market days); seats out in front, four bedrooms, open all day. *(Aidan Long)*

ASHFORD IN THE WATER SK1969
⋆ **Bulls Head** (01629) 812931
Off A6 NW of Bakewell; Church Street (B6465, off A6020); DE45 1QB
Traditional 17th-c village inn run by same welcoming family for 60 years, cosy two-room beamed and carpeted bar with fires, one or two character gothic seats, spindleback and wheelback chairs around cast-iron-framed tables, local photographs and country prints on cream walls, daily papers, Robinsons ales and gently imaginative food (not Thurs evening in winter), friendly efficient service; background jazz; children welcome in some areas, dogs in bar, overshoes for walkers, hardwood tables and benches in front and in good-sized garden behind with boules and Jenga. *(Derek and Sylvia Stephenson)*

ASTON-UPON-TRENT SK4129
Malt Shovel (01332) 792256
Off A6 SE of Derby; The Green (one-way street); DE72 2AA Comfortably revamped village pub with enjoyable food and several well kept ales, friendly atmosphere; children and dogs welcome, back terrace. *(Anon)*

BAKEWELL SK2168
Castle Inn (01629) 812103
Bridge Street; DE45 1DU Bay-windowed, Georgian-fronted pub dating from the 17th c, well kept Greene King ales and a guest such as Abbeydale Moonshine, good competitively priced straightforward food, three candlelit rooms with two open fires, flagstones, stripped stone and lots of pictures, good friendly service; background music and fruit machine; dogs welcome, level inside for wheelchairs but steps at front, tables out by road, gets busy Mon market day, four bedrooms. *(David and Jenny Billington, Derek and Sylvia Stephenson, Paul Goldman)*

BASLOW SK2772
Robin Hood (01246) 583186
A619/B6050; DE45 1PQ Fairly modern comfortable pub with good sensibly priced food (not Sun or Mon evenings) from sandwiches up, three well kept Marstons-related ales, friendly staff, back room overlooking golf course, open fires; walkers, climbers and dogs welcome, good walking country near Baslow Edge, can get very busy, open all day weekends. *(Brian and Anna Marsden)*

BELPER
Black Bulls Head (01773) 882654
Openwoodgate, Kilburn Lane; DE56 0SF
Edwardian pub refurbished by current

licensees; two rooms with open fires, Oakham and several guests such as Blue Monkey, Castle Rock and Whim, real ciders and perry; open all day. *(Yvonne and Rob Warhurst)*

BIRCHOVER
SK2362

Druid (01629) 650302

Off B5056; Main Street; DE4 2BL
Updated 17th-c pub with stone-floor bar area, dining room either side and upstairs restaurant with grand piano, good varied food including some unusual choices, friendly willing service, a couple of own-badged beers brewed by Titanic plus guests; children welcome, dogs in bar, tables out in front on two levels, good area for walks, Nine Ladies stone circle nearby, open all day in summer. *(Brian and Anna Marsden, Nick Simms)*

BIRCHOVER
SK2362

Red Lion (01629) 650363

Main Street; DE4 2BN Friendly early 18th-c stone-built pub with popular good value italian-influenced food (landlord is from Sardinia), also make their own cheese and have a deli next door, well kept ales (up to five in summer), four ciders, microbrewery planned, glass-covered well inside, woodburners; children and dogs welcome, nice rural views from outside seats, popular with walkers, open all day weekends, closed Mon in winter. *(Nick Simms)*

BOLSOVER
SK4770

Blue Bell (01246) 823508

High Street, off A632; S44 6HF Former 18th-c coaching inn, pleasant and friendly, with several well kept ales including Marstons and Wychwood, good value pub meals (not Sun evening, Mon or Tues evening), two rooms, beams and log fire, conservatory; children welcome, garden with pizza oven and wide views. *(Anon)*

BONSALL
SK2758

☆ Barley Mow (01629) 825685

Off A5012 W of Cromford; The Dale; DE4 2AY Basic one-room stone-built local with friendly colourful atmosphere, beams, character furnishings and coal fire, pictures and bric-a-brac, well kept local ales and real ciders, microbrewery planned, hearty generously served food (be prepared to share a table), live music Fri and Sat; short walk out to lavatories; children and dogs welcome, nice little front terrace, events such as hen racing and world-record-breaking day, popular with UFO enthusiasts, walks organised from the pub, camping, open all day weekends, closed Mon and lunchtimes Tues-Fri. *(Anon)*

BRACKENFIELD
SK3658

Plough (01629) 534437

A615 Matlock–Alfreton, about a mile NW of Wessington; DE55 6DD Much modernised, oak-beamed, stone-built 16th-c

former farmhouse in lovely setting, tidy and welcoming three-level bar, cheerful log-effect gas fire, well kept ales including interesting local brews, plenty of wines by the glass, good value enjoyable fresh food (not Sun evening), lunchtime set deal (Mon-Sat), appealing lower-level restaurant extension; large neatly kept gardens with terrace, open all day. *(Ian Phillips)*

BUXTON
SK1266

☆ Bull i' th' Thorn (01298) 83348

Ashbourne Road (A515), 6 miles S of Buxton, near Flagg and Hurdlow; SK17 9QQ Fascinating medieval hall doubling as straightforward roadside dining pub, handsome panelling, old flagstones and big log fire, armour, longcase clocks and all sorts of antique features, decent choice of generous good value food including vegetarian options, well kept Robinsons ales, friendly smartly dressed landlord, plain games room and family room; dogs welcome, terrace, big lawn and play area, rare-breeds farm behind, good walks, three bedrooms and big breakfast, camping too, open all day in summer, all day weekends in winter (closed Mon lunchtime then). *(Ann and Colin Hunt)*

BUXTON
SK0573

☆ Old Sun (01298) 23452

High Street; SK17 6HA Charming old building with several cosy and interesting traditional linked areas, well kept Marstons-related ales and good choice of wines by the glass, simple bargain home-made food from good sandwiches up, low beams, bare boards or tiles, soft lighting, old local photographs, open fire; background music and some live acoustic evenings, Sun quiz, no dogs; children till 7pm, roadside garden, open all day. *(Ann and Colin Hunt, Barry Collett)*

BUXWORTH
SK0282

Navigation (01663) 732072

S of village towards Silkhill, off B6062; SK23 7NE Friendly inn by restored canal basin, five well kept ales including Robinsons Unicorn and Timothy Taylors Landlord, good value pubby food from sandwiches up, cheery welcoming staff, linked low-ceilinged rooms, canalia, brassware and old photographs, open fires, games room with pool and darts, Thurs quiz; background music; children allowed away from main bar, dogs in some areas, disabled access, tables on sunken flagstoned terrace, play area, four bedrooms, breakfast 8-11am (non-residents welcome), open all day. *(Brian and Anna Marsden)*

CALVER
SK2374

Derwentwater Arms (01433) 639211

In centre, bear left from Main Street into Folds Head; Low Side; S32 3XQ Largely bright and modern inside (some recent redecoration), big windows looking down from village-centre knoll to cricket pitch, good fairly priced food from varied menu, ales such as Adnams and Peak; children and dogs welcome, terraces on slopes below (disabled access), boules, open all day weekends. *(Bruce and Sharon Eden)*

CASTLETON SK1582
Bulls Head (01433) 620256
Cross Street (A6187); S33 8WH Imposing building spreading through several attractive linked areas, handsome panelling and pictures, appealing mix of comfortable seating including sofas and easy chairs, heavy drapes and coal fires, well kept Robinsons ales, food from sandwiches and hot ciabattas to pub standards and specials, helpful friendly service; background music; some roadside picnic-sets, five bedrooms. *(David Heath)*

CASTLETON SK1482
✶Castle Hotel (01433) 620578
High Street/Castle Street; S33 8WG Roomy and welcoming Vintage Inn with usual good choice of well priced food all day from sandwiches up, ales such as Bass, Mansfield and Marstons, plenty of wines by the glass, decent coffee, friendly efficient staff even at busy times, log fires, stripped-stone walls, beams and some ancient flagstones; background music; children welcome, seats out in front and on heated terrace, 15 comfortable bedrooms, good breakfast, open all day. *(David Heath)*

CASTLETON SK1482
✶George (01433) 620238
Castle Street; S33 8WG Busy but relaxed old pub with flagstoned bar and restaurant, well kept ales such as Courage and Wells & Youngs, good choice of malts, enjoyable home-made food at reasonable prices, decent coffee, friendly staff, ancient beams and stripped stone, copper and brass, log fires; children and dogs welcome, tables out at front and back, castle views, good walks, bedrooms, open all day Fri-Sun. *(Ann and Colin Hunt, David Heath)*

CASTLETON SK1583
Olde Cheshire Cheese
(01433) 620330 *How Lane; S33 8WJ* Family-run 17th-c inn with two linked beamed and carpeted areas, cosy and spotless, with six well kept ales such as Acorn, Bradfield and Peak, good range of reasonably priced wholesome food all day, nice house wine, quick friendly service, two gas woodburners, lots of photographs, toby jugs and brassware, back dining room; background music; children welcome in restaurant, dogs in bar, ten bedrooms, parking across road. *(David Heath, David M Smith, Eddie Edwards, David and Jenny Billington)*

CASTLETON SK1582
✶Olde Nags Head (01433) 620248
Cross Street (A6187); S33 8WH Small solidly built refurbished hotel dating from the 17th c, interesting antique oak furniture and coal fire in civilised beamed and flagstoned bar with nice pictures, well kept Black Sheep, Sharps Doom Bar and guests, nice coffee, helpful staff, good locally sourced food in bars and bistro; attractive village, comfortable bedrooms, good breakfast choice, open all day. *(Ann and Colin Hunt, David Heath)*

CHESTERFIELD SK3871
Chesterfield Arms (01246) 236634
Newbold Road (B6051); S41 7PH Restored 19th-c pub with up to 16 ales including Everards, Fullers London Pride and three house beers from Leatherbritches, six ciders and good choice of wines and whiskies, basic snacks along with Mon pie night and Thurs curry, open fire, oak panelling and stripped wood/flagstoned floors, new conservatory linking weekend barn room, beer festivals, some live music and Wed quiz; outside tables on decking, open all day. *(Christian Yapp, Andrew Bosi)*

CHESTERFIELD SK3670
Rose & Crown (01246) 563750
Old Road (A619); S40 2QT Owned by Brampton Brewery with their full range plus Everards and two changing guests, Weston's cider, enjoyable home-made food, spacious traditional refurbishment with leather banquettes, panelling, carpet or wood floors, brewery memorabilia and cast-iron Victorian fireplace, cosy snug area, Tues quiz; tables outside; open all day. *(Anon)*

CLIFTON SK1645
Cock (01335) 342654
Cross Side, opposite church; DE6 2GJ Unpretentious two-bar beamed village local, comfortable and friendly, with jovial landlord, reasonably priced home-made pub food from baguettes up, well kept Marstons Pedigree, Timothy Taylors Landlord and a couple of guests, ten wines by the glass, darts, quiz last Tues of month; children really welcome, revamped garden with play equipment. *(Simon Cattley)*

COMBS SK0378
Beehive (01298) 812758
Village signposted off B5470 W of Chapel-en-le-Frith; SK23 9UT Roomy, neat and comfortable, with emphasis on good freshly made food (all day Sun) from baguettes to steaks and interesting specials, also very good value weekday set menu,

Marstons Pedigree and a house beer from Wychwood, good choice of wines by the glass, log fire, heavy beams and copperware; background music, TV, Tues quiz; plenty of tables out in front, by lovely valley tucked away from main road, good walks, one-bed holiday cottage next door, open all day. *(Anon)*

CROWDECOTE   SK1065
Packhorse   (01298) 83618

B5055 W of Bakewell; SK17 0DB Small three-room 16th-c pub in lovely setting, welcoming landlord and staff, good reasonably priced food from weekday light bites and sandwiches up, four changing well kept ales, split-level interior with brick or carpeted floors, stripped-stone walls, open fire and two woodburners, pool room; tables out behind, beautiful views, popular walking route, closed Mon and Tues. *(Dennis Jones, Brian and Jacky Wilson, Graham Parker)*

DERBY   SK3538
Abbey Inn   (01332) 558297

Darley Street; DE22 1DX Former abbey gatehouse opposite Derwent-side park (pleasant riverside walk from centre), massive 15th-c or older stonework remnants, brick floor, studded oak doors, coal fire in big stone inglenook, stone spiral staircase to upper bar with oak rafters and tapestries, bargain Sam Smiths and reasonably priced bar food; the lavatories with their beams, stonework and tiles are worth a look too; children and dogs welcome, open all day. *(Anon)*

DERBY   SK3635
Alexandra   (01332) 293993

Siddals Road; DE1 2QE Imposing Victorian pub, popular locally; two simple rooms with traditional furnishings on bare boards or carpet, railway prints/memorabilia, well kept Castle Rock ales and quickly changing microbrewery guests, lots of continental bottled beers with more on tap, snack food such as pork pies and cobs; background music; children and dogs welcome, nicely planted backyard, four bedrooms, open all day. *(Anon)*

DERBY   SK3535
Babington Arms   (01332) 383647

Babington Lane; DE1 1TA Large well run open-plan Wetherspoons with up to 18 real ales and four proper ciders, good welcoming service, usual well priced food, comfortable seating with steps up to relaxed back area; attractive verandah, open all day from 8am for breakfast. *(Anon)*

DERBY   SK3635
⋆ Brunswick   (01332) 290677

Railway Terrace; close to Derby Midland Station; DE1 2RU One of Britain's oldest railwaymen's pubs with fantastic range of ales tapped from casks or on handpump

(seven from own microbrewery), cheap traditional lunchtime food (not Sun), welcoming high-ceilinged panelled bar with whisky-water jugs, another room with little old-fashioned prints and high-backed wall settle by coal fire, chatty family parlour, wall displays showing history and restoration of building, interesting old train photographs, darts, jazz upstairs on Thurs evening; TV, games machines, no credit cards; dogs welcome, two outdoor seating areas, open all day; landlord is retiring, so things may change. *(Ian and Helen Stafford, John Honnor, Pat and Tony Martin)*

DERBY   SK3534
Falstaff   (01332) 342902

Silver Hill Road, off Normanton Road; DE23 6UJ Basic unsmart local, aka the Folly, brewing its own good value ales, guest beers too, left-hand bar with games, coal fire in quieter lounge, some brewery memorabilia; open all day. *(Anon)*

DERBY   SK3436
Mr Grundys Tavern   (01332) 349959

Georgian House; Ashbourne Road; DE22 3AD Hotel bar serving own Mr Grundys ales (brewed here) and plenty of guests, two inviting dimly lit rooms, coal fires, panelling, old bench seating, superb collection of hats, a wall of classic film-star pictures, lots of breweriana and an old red telephone box, decent food (not Sun evening); garden picnic-sets, 18 bedrooms, open all day. *(Anon)*

DERBY   SK3536
Old Silk Mill   (01332) 369748

Full Street; DE1 3AF Refurbished keeping traditional feel, cosy inside with two open fires, nine changing ales from main bar including a house beer from Blue Monkey, second hop-adorned bar (open Thurs and Fri evenings, all day Sat, Sun lunchtime) with usually four cask-tapped beers, friendly service, regular live music; open all day. *(Anon)*

DERBY   SK3536
Olde Dolphin   (01332) 267711

Queen Street; DE1 3DL Quaint 16th-c timber-framed pub just below cathedral, four small dark unpretentious rooms including appealing snug, big bowed black beams, shiny panelling, opaque leaded windows, lantern lights and coal fires, half a dozen predominantly mainstream ales (good July beer festival), cheap simple food all day, upstairs steak bar (not always open); no under-14s inside; sizeable outside area for drinkers/smokers, open all day. *(Anon)*

DERBY   SK3335
Rowditch   (01332) 343123

Uttoxeter New Road (A516); DE22 3LL Popular character local with own microbrewery, well kept Marstons Pedigree and guests too, country wines, friendly landlord, attractive small snug on right, coal fire, pianist every other Sat; no children or dogs; pleasant back garden, closed weekday lunchtimes. *(Anon)*

DERBY   SK3536
Smithfield   (01332) 370429
Meadow Road; DE1 2BH   Unusual bow-fronted pub recently reopened after refurbishment, good choice of well kept ales, friendly service; riverside terrace. *(Anon)*

DERBY   SK3436
☆**Standing Order**   (01332) 207591
Irongate; DE1 3GL   Cavernous Wetherspoons in grand and lofty-domed former bank, main part with large island bar, booths down each side, handsome plasterwork, pseudo-classical torsos, high portraits of mainly local notables; good range of ales including some unusual ones, standard popular food all day, reasonable prices, daily papers; good disabled facilities. *(Anon)*

DRONFIELD   SK3479
Coach & Horses   (01246) 413269
Sheffield Road (B6057); S18 2GD   Well managed comfortable pub next to Sheffield FC ground, up to five Thornbridge ales, home-made food, some live music; open all day, closed Mon lunchtime. *(Anon)*

EARL STERNDALE   SK0966
☆**Quiet Woman**   (01298) 83211
Village signed off B5053 S of Buxton; SK17 0BU   Old-fashioned unchanging country local in lovely Peak District countryside, simple beamed interior with plain furniture on quarry tiles, china ornaments and coal fire, character landlord serving well kept Marstons Pedigree and guests, own-label bottled beers (available in gift packs), good pork pies, family room with pool, skittles and darts; picnic-sets out in front along with budgies, hens, turkeys, ducks and donkeys, you can buy free-range eggs, local poetry books and even hay, good hikes across nearby Dove Valley towards Longnor and Hollinsclough, small campsite next-door, caravan for hire. *(Dennis Jones, Ann and Colin Hunt, Barry Collett)*

EDALE   SK1285
Old Nags Head   (01433) 670291
Off A625 E of Chapel-en-le-Frith; Grindsbrook Booth; S33 7ZD   Relaxed well used traditional pub at start of Pennine Way, good friendly staff coping well, generous pubby food, good local ales, log fire, flagstoned area for booted walkers, airy back family room with board games; TV, can get very busy weekends; front terrace and garden, open all day, closed Mon and Tues lunchtimes out of season. *(Anon)*

ELMTON   SK5073
Elm Tree   (01909) 721261
Off B6417 S of Clowne; S80 4LS   Softly lit and popular country pub with good food all day including set menu, up to seven well kept ales such as Black Sheep, wide choice of wines, quick friendly service, stripped stone and panelling, back barn restaurant (mainly for functions); children welcome, garden tables, play area, closed Tues. *(Derek and Sylvia Stephenson, Rob and Catherine Dunster)*

ELTON   SK2260
☆**Duke of York**   (01629) 650367
Village signed off B5056 W of Matlock; Main Street; DE4 2BW   Unspoilt local kept spotless by very long-serving amiable landlady, bargain Marstons Burton Bitter, lovely little quarry-tiled back tap room with coal fire in massive fireplace, glazed bar and hatch to flagstoned corridor, nice prints and more fires in the two front rooms – one like a private parlour with piano and big table, the other with pool, darts, dominoes, friendly chatty locals; outside lavatories; in charming village, open 8.45pm-11pm and Sun lunchtime, no food. *(Anon)*

FOOLOW   SK1976
☆**Bulls Head**   (01433) 630873
Village signposted off A623 Baslow–Tideswell; S32 5QR   Friendly pub by green in pretty upland village; simply furnished flagstoned bar with interesting collection of photographs including some risqué Edwardian ones, Adnams, Black Sheep, Peak and a guest, over two dozen malts, good food (all day Sun) with more elaborate evening choices, step down to former stables with high ceiling joists, stripped stone and woodburner, sedate partly panelled dining room with plates on delft shelves; background music (live Fri evening), quiz Thurs; children welcome and dogs (resident westies Holly and Jack), side picnic-sets with nice views, paths from here out over rolling pasture enclosed by dry-stone walls, three bedrooms, closed Mon. *(Michael Butler, Ann and Colin Hunt, Roger and Diana Morgan, Barry Collett)*

FROGGATT EDGE   SK2577
Grouse   (01433) 630423
Longshaw, off B6054 NE of Froggatt; S11 7TZ   Nicely old-fashioned with proper landlady, plush front bar, log fire and wooden benches in back bar, big dining room, enjoyable honest home-made food from nice sandwiches to blackboard specials, well kept Banks's, Caledonian Deuchars IPA, Greene King Abbot and Marstons Pedigree, friendly prompt service, handsome views; dogs welcome, verandah and terrace, good moorland walking country, open all day. *(Anon)*

GLOSSOP
SK0394
Star (01457) 853072
Howard Street; SK13 7DD Unpretentious alehouse opposite station with Black Sheep and six well priced changing ales, real cider, friendly helpful staff, no food (you can bring your own), interesting layout including flagstoned tap room with hatch service, old local photographs; background music; bedrooms, open all day from 2pm (4pm Mon, Tues, 12pm Sat, Sun). *(Anon)*

HARDWICK HALL
SK4663
Hardwick Inn (01246) 850245
Quite handy for M1 junction 29; S44 5QJ Golden stone building dating from the 15th c at the south gate of Hardwick Park; several busy linked rooms including proper bar, open fires, fine range of some 220 malt whiskies and plenty of wines by the glass, well kept Black Sheep, Theakstons, Wells & Youngs and an ale brewed for the pub by Brampton, popular well priced bar food served all day, carvery restaurant, long-serving landlord and efficient friendly staff; unobtrusive background music; children allowed, pleasant back garden, more tables out in front, open all day. *(Derek and Sylvia Stephenson, Andy Dolan)*

HARTINGTON
SK1260
Charles Cotton (01298) 84229
Market Place; SK17 0AL Popular four-square stone-built hotel in attractive village centre; large comfortable bar/bistro with open fire, good food from lunchtime sandwiches and snacks up (more restaurant evening choice), up to five ales including local Whim, bottled beers and real cider, nice wines and italian coffee, friendly helpful service, restaurant and summer tearoom; background and some live music; children welcome, dogs in bar, seats out at front and in small back garden, 17 bedrooms, open all day. *(Dennis Jones, J and E Dakin, Ann and Colin Hunt)*

HARTINGTON
SK1260
Devonshire Arms (01298) 84232
Market Place; SK17 0AL Traditional unpretentious two-bar pub in attractive village, welcoming landlord, ales including Marstons Pedigree, generous home-made food, log fires; may be background music; children and dogs welcome, tables out in front facing duck pond, more in small garden, good walks, open (and food) all day weekends. *(Dennis Jones, Alan Johnson)*

HEAGE
SK3750
Black Boy (01773) 856799
Old Road (B6013); DE56 2BN Smart village pub/restaurant with welcoming licensees, popular food in bar and upstairs dining area including fish specials, a house beer brewed by Marstons and well kept regularly changing guests, open fire; TV

for major sports events, no dogs; children welcome, small outside seating area, open all day. *(Michael Mellers)*

HEANOR
SK4445
Marlpool Ale House (01773) 711285
Breach Road; DE75 7NJ Tiny old-fashioned alehouse in former butcher's shop, own good Marlpool beers and a couple of guests served from pulpit counter, cheery atmosphere and some impromptu acoustic music; dogs welcome, open 3-9pm Fri, 12-9pm Sat, Sun. *(Yvonne and Rob Warhurst, Frank Hazeldine)*

HEANOR
SK4445
Queens Head (01773) 768015
Breach Road, Marlpool; DE75 7NJ Five-room Victorian alehouse with traditional clean interior, tiled floors, cast-iron tables, padded stools around old barrel tables, two open fires and woodburner, up to 20 well kept beers including Castle Rock, Oakham and Thornbridge (many served from cellar where customers welcome), 28 ciders, half a dozen perries, good range of wines and spirits too, some snacky food (can bring your own), daily papers; children and dogs welcome, back terrace with open-fronted log-fire room, beer garden, open all day. *(Anon)*

HEATH
SK4467
Elm Tree (01246) 850490
Just off M1 junction 29; A6175 towards Clay Cross, then first right; S44 5SE Popular roadside pub with half-panelled lounge/dining areas, good well priced blackboard food (all day weekends) including generous Sun carvery, well kept Jennings ales and a guest, wide choice of wines, good helpful service, mix of traditional wooden furniture and leather armchairs on wood and stone floors, woodburner in stone fireplace, darts in smallish bar; soft background music; children and dogs welcome, some picnic-sets out at front, attractive garden with play area and lovely views to Bolsover and beyond (but traffic noise). *(C A Hall)*

HOGNASTON
SK2350
⋆ Red Lion (01335) 370396
Off B5035 Ashbourne–Wirksworth; DE6 1PR Traditional 17th-c inn with open-plan beamed bar, three fires, attractive mix of old tables, curved settles and other seats on ancient flagstones, friendly licensees, good well presented home-made food from shortish menu in bar and conservatory restaurant, nice wines by the glass, Marstons Pedigree and guests; background music; picnic-sets in field behind, boules, handy for Carsington Water, three good bedrooms, big breakfast. *(Anon)*

HOLBROOK
SK3645
⋆ Dead Poets (01332) 780301
Chapel Street; village signed off A6 S of Belper; DE56 0TQ Reassuringly pubby and

unchanging drinkers' local with nine real ales (some served from jugs), farm cider, country wines, filled cobs and good value weekday bar food, simple cottagey décor with beams, stripped-stone walls and broad flagstones, high-backed settles forming booths, big log fire, plenty of tucked-away corners, woodburner in snug, children allowed in back conservatory till 8pm; quiet background music, no credit cards; dogs welcome, seats in heated verandah room, more in yard, open all day Fri-Sun. *(Anon)*

HOLYMOORSIDE SK3369
Lamb (01246) 566167
Loads Road, just off Holymoor Road; S42 7EU Small spotless village pub with half a dozen particularly well kept ales such as Black Sheep, Daleside Blonde, Fullers London Pride, Timothy Taylors Landlord and Theakstons, charming comfortable lounge, coal fire in cosy bar, friendly locals, pub games; tables outside, leafy spot, closed weekday lunchtimes. *(Anon)*

HOPE SK1783
⁎ Cheshire Cheese (01433) 620381
Off A6187, towards Edale; S33 6ZF Bustling 16th-c traditional inn, snug oak-beamed rooms on different levels, open fires, red carpets or stone floors, straightforward furnishings and gleaming brasses, friendly staff serving ales such as Bradfield, Greene King, Peak and Whim, a dozen malts, pubby food including sandwiches, folk night first Thurs of month; children welcome, dogs allowed in bar, good local walks in the summits of Lose Hill and Win Hill or the cave district around Castleton, four bedrooms, limited parking, open all day weekends in summer, closed Mon. *(Peter F Marshall, Malcolm and Pauline Pellatt, R and S Bentley, Brian and Anna Marsden)*

HORSLEY WOODHOUSE SK3944
Old Oak (01332) 881299
Main Street (A609 Belper–Ilkeston); DE7 6AW Busy roadside local linked to nearby Bottle Brook and Leadmill microbreweries, their ales and weekend back bar with another half-dozen well priced guests tapped from the cask, farm ciders, good basic snacks, beamed rooms with blazing coal fires, chatty friendly atmosphere, occasional live music; children and dogs welcome, hatch to covered courtyard tables, nice views, closed weekday lunchtimes, open all day weekends. *(Anon)*

ILKESTON SK4742
Dewdrop (0115) 932 9684
Station Street, Ilkeston junction, off A6096; DE7 5TE Large Victorian corner

local in old industrial area, not strong on bar comfort but popular for its well kept beers (up to eight) including Blue Monkey, Castle Rock and Oakham, simple bar snacks, back lounge with fire and piano, connecting lobby to front public bar with pool, darts and TV, some Barnes Wallis memorabilia; sheltered outside seating at back, walks by former Nottingham Canal, open all day weekends, closed weekday lunchtimes. *(Anon)*

ILKESTON SK4641
Spanish Bar (0115) 930 8666
South Street; DE7 5QJ Busy bar with well kept and well priced changing ales, bottled belgians, friendly efficient staff, evening overspill room, Tues quiz; small back garden and skittle alley, open all day. *(Anon)*

KELSTEDGE SK3463
Kelstedge Inn (01246) 590448
Matlock Road (A632); S45 0DX Popular and friendly with good choice of enjoyable well priced food (not Sun evening), ales such as Black Sheep, Bradfield and Buxton, decent wines by the glass, beams and open fires; open all day. *(Peter F Marshall)*

LITTLE LONGSTONE SK1971
Packhorse (01629) 640471
Off A6 NW of Bakewell via Monsal Dale; DE45 1NN Three comfortable linked beamed rooms, pine tables on flagstones, well kept Thornbridge and usually Theakstons Bitter, good choice of wines by the glass, popular good value food (Sat breakfast from 8.30am), coal fires; hikers welcome (on Monsal Trail), terrace in steep little back garden. *(Peter Waller, J and E Dakin)*

LULLINGTON SK2513
Colvile Arms (01827) 373212
Off A444 S of Burton; Main Street; DE12 8EG Popular 18th-c village pub with high-backed settles in simple panelled bar, cosy comfortable beamed lounge, pleasant atmosphere and friendly staff, four well kept ales including Bass, Marstons Pedigree and a guest, enjoyable good value food; may be background music; picnic-sets on small sheltered back lawn, closed weekday lunchtimes. *(Anon)*

MAKENEY SK3544
⁎ Holly Bush (01332) 841729
From A6 heading N after Duffield, take first right after crossing River Derwent, then first left; DE56 0RX Down-to-earth two-bar village pub (former farmhouse) with three blazing coal fires (one in old-fashioned range by snug's curved high-backed settle), flagstones, beams, black panelling and tiled floors, lots of brewing advertisements, half

---

Virtually all pubs in this book sell wine by the glass. We mention wines if they are a cut above the average.

a dozen or so well kept changing ales (some brought from cellar in jugs), real cider, cheap food including rolls and pork pies, may be local cheeses for sale, games lobby with hatch service (children allowed here), regular beer festivals; picnic-sets outside, dogs welcome, open all day. *(Anon)*

MATLOCK
SK2960
Thorn Tree (01629) 580295
Jackson Road, Matlock Bank; DE4 3JQ
Superb valley views to Riber Castle from this homely 19th-c stone-built local, Bass, Greene King, Timothy Taylors Landlord and four guests, simple well cooked food including their locally renowned pies, friendly staff and regulars; closed Mon lunchtime, open all day weekends. *(Ian and Helen Stafford)*

MILFORD
SK3545
King William IV (01332) 840842
Milford Bridge; DE56 0RR Friendly and relaxing stone-built riverside pub, long room with low beams, bare boards, quarry tiles, old settles and a coal fire, well kept Marstons Pedigree, Timothy Taylors Landlord and guests, simple food; three bedrooms, closed weekday lunchtimes, open all day weekends. *(Anon)*

MILLERS DALE
SK1473
Anglers Rest (01298) 871323
Just down Litton Lane; pub is PH on OS Sheet 119 map reference 142734; SK17 8SN Ivy-clad pub in lovely quiet riverside setting on Monsal Trail, two bars and dining room, log fires, well kept Adnams, Storm and two usually local guests, enjoyable simple home-made food, cheery helpful service, reasonable prices, darts, pool, muddy walkers and dogs in public bar (they have their own dogs); children welcome, wonderful gorge views and river walks, self-catering apartment, open all day weekends. *(John Griffiths)*

MONSAL HEAD
SK1871
★**Monsal Head Hotel** (01629) 640250
B6465; DE45 1NL Popular inn in outstanding hilltop location, cosy stables bar with stripped timber horse-stalls, harness and brassware, cushioned oak pews on flagstones, big open fire, ales such as Bradfield, Buxton, Oakwell and Wincle, german bottled beers, several wines by the glass, locally sourced food from lunchtime sandwiches up (they may ask to keep your credit card while you eat); children (over 3), well behaved dogs and muddy walkers welcome, big garden, stunning views of Monsal Dale with its huge viaduct, seven bedrooms, open all day till midnight.
(Mr and Mrs D J Nash, Dennis Jones)

MONYASH
SK1566
★**Bulls Head** (01629) 812372
B5055 W of Bakewell; DE45 1JH Rambling stone pub with high-ceilinged rooms, straightforward traditional furnishings including plush stools lined along bar, horse pictures and a shelf of china, log fire, Black Sheep and a couple of guests, restaurant more cottagey with high-backed dining chairs on heated stone floor, generous fairly traditional food (all day weekends), small back room with darts, board games and pool; background music; children and dogs welcome, plenty of picnic-sets under parasols in big garden, gate leading to well equipped public play area, good surrounding walks, open all day Fri-Sun. *(Mr and Mrs D J Nash, Mrs P Bishop)*

NEW MILLS
SJ9886
Fox (0161) 427 1634
Brook Bottom Road; SK22 3AY Tucked-away unmodernised country local at end of single-track road, a nice summer family outing; long-serving landlord serving Robinsons ales and good value basic food (not Tues evening) including sandwiches, log fire, darts and pool; no credit cards; lots of tables outside, good walking area, open all day Fri-Sun. *(Brian and Anna Marsden)*

NEWTON SOLNEY
SK2825
Brickmakers Arms (01283) 703170
Main Street (B5008 NE of Burton); DE15 0SJ 19th-c beamed village pub now owned by Burton Bridge Brewery; their ales kept well and occasional guests, no food; two rooms off bar, one with original panelling and a delft shelf displaying jugs and plates, pubby furniture, built-in wall seats and open fires, area with piano and books; tables on terrace and a little shop, closed Mon-Thurs lunchtimes, open all day Sat. *(Casper Leaver)*

OCKBROOK
SK4236
Royal Oak (01332) 662378
Off B6096 just outside Spondon; Green Lane; DE72 3SE Quiet 18th-c village local run by same friendly family since 1953, bargain honest food (not Sat or Sun evenings) from good lunchtime cobs to steaks, Sun lunch and OAP meals, well kept Bass and interesting guest beers, good soft drinks' choice, tile-floored tap room, carpeted snug, inner bar with Victorian prints, larger and lighter side room, nice old settle in entrance corridor, open fires, darts and dominoes; children welcome, sheltered cottage garden and cobbled front courtyard, separate play area. *(MP)*

Anyone claiming to arrange, or prevent, inclusion of a pub in the *Guide* is a fraud. Pubs are included only if recommended by genuine readers and if our own anonymous inspection confirms that they are suitable.

OSMASTON   SK1943
Shoulder of Mutton (01335) 342371
Off A52 SE of Ashbourne; DE6 1LW
Down-to-earth red-brick pub with enjoyable
generous home-made food, quick friendly
service, three well kept ales including
Marstons Pedigree; attractive garden,
farmland views, peaceful pretty village with
thatched cottages, duck pond and good
walks. *(MP)*

PARWICH   SK1854
✶**Sycamore** (01335) 390212
By church; DE6 1QL Chatty old country
pub well run by cheerful welcoming landlady,
generous wholesome food lunchtimes and
most Weds-Sat evenings, Robinsons ales,
good log fire in neat traditional back bar,
pool in small front hatch-served games room,
another room serving as proper village shop;
children welcome, tables in front courtyard,
picnic-sets on neat side grass, good walks.
(Ann and Colin Hunt)

PENTRICH   SK3852
✶**Dog** (01773) 513360
*Main Road (B6016 N of Ripley);
DE5 3RE* Extended pub popular for its
enjoyable all-day food, three well kept ales
from carved church-look counter, nice
wines by the glass, woodburner, pubby
bar furniture, smarter modern dining
area beyond part with leather sofas etc;
background music; well behaved children
(over 8) allowed if eating, extensive garden
behind, nice views, good walks. *(Anon)*

REPTON   SK3026
Bulls Head (01283) 704422
High Street; DE65 6GF Well reworked
beamed pub with interesting mix of old and
new furniture on bare boards or flagstones,
woodburners, good food including popular
wood-fired pizzas, four well kept usually local
ales, good choice of wines and decent coffee,
upstairs restaurant; children welcome till
9pm, dogs away from dining areas, garden
with sizeable terrace, attractive village, open
all day. *(Stephen Shepherd)*

RIPLEY   SK3950
Talbot Taphouse (01773) 742626
Butterley Hill; DE5 3LT Full range of local
Amber ales and changing guests kept well by
knowledgeable landlord, farm ciders, draught
belgians and bottled beers too, long narrow
panelled room with new bar counter, comfy
chairs, brick fireplace; friendly staff; open all
day weekends, from 5pm other days. *(Anon)*

ROWARTH   SK0189
Little Mill (01663) 743178
*Signed well locally; off A626 in Marple
Bridge at Mellor sign, sharp left at
Rowarth sign; SK22 1EB* Beautifully
tucked-away 18th-c pub with welcoming
landlord, well kept Banks's, Marstons and

guests, good value generous food all day (till
7pm Sun) including weekend carvery, roomy
open-plan bar and recently refurbished
upstairs restaurant, big log fire, unusual
features like working waterwheel and vintage
Pullman-carriage bedrooms; background
music (live Fri evenings); children and dogs
welcome, disabled access, verandah with
terrace below, pretty garden dell across
stream, good play area, open all day. *(Anon)*

ROWSLEY   SK2565
Grouse & Claret (01629) 733233
A6 Bakewell–Matlock; DE4 2EB
Attractive family dining pub in old stone
building, spacious, clean and comfortable,
with welcoming licensees and friendly staff,
enjoyable low-priced food (all day weekends)
from sandwiches up, well kept Jennings
Cumberland and Marstons Pedigree, decent
wines, open fires, tap room popular with
walkers; tables outside, play area, good value
bedrooms, campsite, open all day. *(Ann and
Colin Hunt, Mr and Mrs D Hammond)*

ROWSLEY   SK2565
✶**Peacock** (01629) 733518
Bakewell Road; DE4 2EB Civilised small
17th-c country hotel with comfortable chairs
and sofas and a few antiques in spacious
uncluttered lounge, interesting stone-floored
inner bar, restful colours, enjoyable if not
cheap food from lunchtime sandwiches to
restaurant meals, Peak ales, good wines
and beautifully served coffee; attractive
riverside gardens, trout fishing, good
bedrooms. *(George Atkinson)*

SAWLEY   SK4931
Trent Lock (0115) 972 5159
Lock Lane; NG10 2FY Refurbished
Vintage Inn placed between the River Trent
and Erewash Canal; three real ales and their
usual food including good value set menu
till 5pm (not Sun), friendly efficient service;
children welcome, tables outside, open all
day. *(MP)*

SHARDLOW   SK4430
Malt Shovel (01332) 792066
*3.5 miles from M1 junction 24, via A6
towards Derby; The Wharf; DE72 2HG*
Canalside pub in 18th-c former maltings,
interesting odd-angled layout with cosy
corners, Marstons-related ales, good value
tasty home-made food from lunchtime
sandwiches and baked potatoes up (evening
food only Thurs, Fri), quick friendly service,
beams, panelling and central open fire, live
music from 5pm Sun; lots of terrace tables
by Trent & Mersey Canal, pretty hanging
baskets, open all day. *(Alistair Forsyth)*

SHARDLOW   SK4429
Old Crown (01332) 792392
*Off A50 just W of M1 junction 24;
Cavendish Bridge, E of village;
DE72 2HL* Good value pub with great range

of Marstons-related ales and guests all kept well, nice choice of malt whiskies, pubby food (not Fri or Sun evenings) from sandwiches and baguettes up, beams with masses of jugs and mugs, walls covered with other bric-a-brac and breweriana, big inglenook; children and dogs welcome, garden with play area, open all day. *(Anon)*

SHELDON   SK1768
★ **Cock & Pullet** (01629) 814292
Village signed off A6 just W of Ashford; DE45 1QS Charming no-frills village pub with friendly courteous licensees and plenty of locals; low beams, exposed stonework, flagstones and open fire, cheerful mismatch of furnishings, large collection of clocks and various representations of poultry (some stuffed), well kept Hartington, Timothy Taylors and a guest, good simple food from shortish menu, reasonable prices, pool and TV in plainer public bar; quiet background music, no credit cards; children and dogs welcome, seats and water feature on pleasant back terrace, pretty village just off Limestone Way and popular all year with walkers, clean bedrooms, open all day. *(Sara Fulton, Roger Baker, J and E Dakin, Mrs P Bishop and others)*

SHIRLEY   SK2141
Saracens Head (01335) 360330
Church Lane; DE6 3AS Nicely modernised late 18th-c dining pub in attractive village; good range of interesting well presented food from pubby to more expensive restaurant dishes, four Greene King ales, speciality coffees, simple country-style dining furniture, two pretty little working art nouveau fireplaces; background music; children welcome, dogs in bar area, picnic-sets under parasols on front and back terraces, self-catering cottage, open all day Sun. *(Anon)*

SMISBY   SK3419
Smisby Arms (01530) 412677
Nelsons Square; LE65 2UA Ancient low-beamed village local with popular range of good reasonably priced food, friendly efficient service, well kept Marstons Pedigree and a changing guest, decent coffee, bright little dining extension down steps; no dogs; children welcome, a few tables out in front. *(Brian and Jacky Wilson)*

SPONDON   SK3935
★ **Malt Shovel** (01332) 674203
Off A6096 on edge of Derby, via Church Hill into Potter Street; DE21 7LH Homely traditional pub with several well kept mainly Marstons-related ales (some tapped from the cask) in tiny bar or from hatch in tiled corridor, various other little rooms, old-fashioned décor and a huge inglenook, generous inexpensive home-cooked food, friendly helpful staff, steps down to big games bar with darts and pool; lots of picnic-sets, some under cover, in large back

garden with good play area, open all day Fri-Sun. *(Anon)*

STRETTON EN LE FIELD   SK2913
Cricketts (01283) 760359
Burton Road; DE12 8AP Stylishly modernised 19th-c pub with enjoyable good value food including some interesting specials, Sun carvery, Marstons Pedigree, good friendly service; children welcome, garden with play area, open all day. *(Howard Bradley)*

SUTTON CUM
DUCKMANTON   SK4371
Arkwright Arms (01246) 232053
A632 Bolsover–Chesterfield; S44 5JG Friendly mock-Tudor pub with bar, pool room (dogs allowed here) and dining room, all with real fires, good choice of well priced food all day (not Sun evening), up to 16 changing ales including local Raw, ten real ciders and four perries (beer/cider festivals Easter/ Aug bank holidays); TV, games machine; children welcome, seats out at front and on side terrace, attractive hanging baskets, play equipment. *(JJW, CMW)*

TICKNALL   SK3523
★ **Wheel** (01332) 864488
Main Street (A514); DE73 7JZ Stylish contemporary décor in bar and restaurant, enjoyable interesting home-made food (all day weekends), friendly staff, well kept Marstons Pedigree and a guest; children welcome, nice outside area with café tables on raised deck, near entrance to Calke Abbey. *(Anon)*

TIDESWELL   SK1575
Horse & Jockey (0845) 498 9009
Queen Street; SK17 8JZ Family-run pub reworked in old-fashioned style, with beams, flagstones, cushioned wall benches and coal fire in small public bar's traditional open range, bare boards, button-back banquettes and woodburner in lounge, ales such as Bradfield, Sharps, Tetleys and Thornbridge, modestly priced enjoyable food, stripped stone and flagstones in sparely decorated dining room; children and dogs welcome, five bedrooms, good walks, open all day. *(David Hunt)*

WARDLOW   SK1875
★ **Three Stags Heads** (01298) 872268
Wardlow Mires; A623/B6465; SK17 8RW Basic unchanging pub (17th-c longhouse) of great individuality, flagstoned floors, old country furniture, heating from cast-iron kitchen ranges, old photographs, long-serving plain-talking landlord, locals in favourite corners, well kept Abbeydale ales including Black Lurcher (brewed for the pub at a hefty 8% ABV), lots of bottled beers, hearty seasonal food on home-made plates (licensees are potters and have a small gallery), may be free roast chestnuts or cheese on the bar, folk music Sun afternoon;

no credit cards; well behaved children and dogs welcome, hill views from front terrace, good walking country, open only Fri evening and all day weekends. *(Dennis Jones)*

WHITTINGTON MOOR SK3873

☀ Derby Tup (01246) 454316

Sheffield Road; B6057 just S of A61 roundabout; S41 8LS Spotless no-frills Castle Rock local with up to a dozen well kept interesting ales from long line of gleaming handpumps, farm cider and irish whiskeys too, friendly service, simple furniture, coal fire and lots of standing room as well as two small side rooms, daily papers, no food (sandwiches from nearby deli); can get very busy weekend evenings and on match days, no children; dogs welcome, closed Weds lunchtime, open all day Fri-Sun. *(Peter F Marshall)*

WINDLEY SK3244

Puss in Boots (01773) 550316

S on B5023; DE56 4AQ Former mill nicely situated above the Ecclesbourne in wooded countryside; two character rooms with open fires, low beams and oak panelling, lots of plates and brass, well kept Bass and Marstons Pedigree, enjoyable home-made lunchtime food from good sandwiches, well run popular place with friendly regulars; pleasant garden, good walks. *(David Heath)*

WINSTER SK2460

☀ Bowling Green (01629) 650219

East Bank, by NT Market House; DE4 2DS Traditional old stone pub with good chatty atmosphere, character landlord and welcoming staff, enjoyable reasonably priced food, at least three well kept changing local ales, good selection of whiskies, end log fire, dining area and family conservatory; nice village, good walks, closed Mon, Tues and lunchtimes, open all day Sun. *(Anon)*

WINSTER SK2360

Miners Standard (01629) 650279

Bank Top (B5056 above village); DE4 2DR Simply furnished 17th-c stone local, relaxed at lunchtime, livelier in the evening, well kept Brampton, Marstons

Pedigree and guests, good value generous pubby food including huge pies, big woodburner, lead-mining photographs and minerals, lots of brass, backwards clock, ancient well, snug and restaurant; background music; children allowed away from bar, attractive view from garden, campsite next door, interesting stone-built village below, open all day weekends. *(David Heath, Dennis Jones)*

WIRKSWORTH SK2854

Royal Oak (01629) 823000

North End; DE4 4FG Small, chatty old-fashioned terraced local, five well kept ales including Bass, Timothy Taylors Landlord and Whim Hartington, dominoes, may be good filled cobs, old copper kettles, key fobs and other bric-a-brac, interesting old photographs; opens at 8pm, closed lunchtimes except Sun. *(Cliff Sparkes)*

YEAVELEY SK1840

Yeaveley Arms (01335) 330771

On by-road S of Ashbourne; DE6 2DT Comfortable modern open-plan interior with bar, lounge and big airy restaurant, enjoyable food from pub favourites up, friendly efficient service, Marstons Pedigree and three guests; no dogs inside; children welcome, seats out at front and on back terrace with smokers' shelter, closed Sun evenings, Mon and Tues; sister pub to the Saracens Head at Shirley. *(Peter Watts)*

YOULGREAVE SK2164

George (01629) 636292

Alport Lane/Church Street; DE45 1WN Handsome 17th-c stone-built inn opposite Norman church, comfortably worn inside, with banquettes running around three sides of main bar, flagstoned tap room (walkers and dogs welcome) and games room, generous helpings of reasonably priced home-made food (all day) from extensive menu including children's choices, John Smiths, Theakstons Mild and a local guest, friendly service; roadside tables, attractive village handy for Lathkill Dale and Haddon Hall, simple bedrooms. *(Ann and Colin Hunt, Dennis Jones)*

Post Office address codings confusingly give the impression that a few pubs are in Derbyshire, when they're really in Cheshire (which is where we list them).

Devon

We are pleased with this year's new entries to the *Guide's* largest county: the Rockford Inn at Brendon (small, friendly inn surrounded by wild countryside), Bickley Mill in Kingskerswell (spotlessly kept, comfortable bedrooms and sub-tropical hillside garden), Dartmoor Inn at Lydford (stylish and civilised with imaginative food, carefully chosen drinks and spacious bedrooms), Horse in Moretonhampstead (rustic bars, mediterranean-influenced food and continental-style courtyard), Millbrook at South Pool (creekside local with french-influenced country cooking), Oxenham Arms in South Zeal (full of history and character, with four-posters and antiques in bedrooms) and Treby Arms in Sparkwell (delicious food and carefully chosen drinks). Other places our readers have enjoyed include the Watermans Arms at Ashprington (friendly streamside inn and a nice place to stay), Turtley Corn Mill at Avonwick (very popular converted watermill), Fountain Head in Branscombe (unchanging tavern with own-brew beers), Drake Manor in Buckland Monachorum (welcoming long-serving landlady and charming bars), Merry Harriers in Clayhidon (incredibly popular, and genuinely welcoming licensees), New Inn at Coleford (our readers love staying here), Turf at Exminster (seasonal openings, in a lovely remote waterside spot), Rock at Haytor Vale (at its most informal at lunchtime, super food and smart bedrooms), Grove in King's Nympton (an enjoyable all-rounder), Cleave in Lustleigh (hands-on landlord, interesting all-day food and local ales), Church House in Marldon (neatly kept with enticing food), Church House at Rattery (ancient inn with original features and very good landlord), Sea Trout in Staverton (well equipped bedrooms and enterprising food), Old Church House in Torbryan (super place tucked away down small lanes), Rugglestone near Widecombe (charmingly unspoilt, with honest food and drink) and Diggers Rest in Woodbury Salterton (well run village pub, interesting beers and food). Many places hold a Food Award, meaning the food is pretty special – but our Devon Dining Pub 2014 is the Treby Arms in Sparkwell.

ASHPRINGTON
Watermans Arms 🛏

SX8056 Map 1

Bow Bridge, on Tuckenhay Road; TQ9 7EG

Bustling pub with plenty of riverside seats, several rambling rooms, lots to look at, friendly staff, real ales, cider, several wines by the glass and enjoyable food; bedrooms

If staying overnight in this bustling old pub (as many of our readers do), you can choose from a bedroom in the 17th-c inn itself or (a more spacious) one in a purpose-built annexe; the generous breakfasts include eggs from their own free-range chickens and home-made marmalade. This is a fine spot, with lots of picnic-sets across the lane beside the little Harbourne River, where you might see swans and kingfishers; the garden has more seats and a small play area. Inside, the quarry-tiled main bar has heavy beams and standing pillars creating a stable-like effect, built-in green-painted and cushioned wall seats and wheelback chairs around stripped wooden tables, a woodburning stove and stone bottles and copper implements – including a large alembic. A dining room has fishing rods on beams, stuffed fish and lanterns; from here, steps lead down to a comfortable area with leather chesterfields and tub chairs. There's also a front bar with a log fire, oars on beams and old sailing blocks. Sizeable mirrors here and there give the feeling of even more space. Palmers Best, Copper and Dorset Gold on handpump, a farm cider and several wines by the glass, served by the charming landlord and his friendly staff; darts, board games, TV and maybe Radio 2.

The wide choice of good, popular food includes open sandwiches, baguettes, omelettes, a cheese slate with home-made red onion marmalade, chilli king prawns, chicken liver pâté with cumberland sauce, organic vegetarian bean burgers with relish, pizzas with lots of toppings, steak in ale pie, sausage and mash with gravy, slow-cooked beef with red cabbage, pork curry, whole grilled lemon sole with lemon and herb butter, and puddings such as treacle sponge with custard and home-grown apple or pear crumble with crunch topping. *Benchmark main dish: burger (local beef) with cheese, relish, coleslaw and chips £10.00. Two-course evening meal £18.00.*

Jersey ~ Tenants Rob and Jane Crawford ~ Real ale ~ (01803) 732214 ~ Open 10am-11pm; closed Jan ~ Bar food 12-2.30, 6-9 ~ Restaurant ~ Children welcome ~ Dogs welcome ~ Bedrooms: /£70 ~ www.thewatermansarms.net
Recommended by Rob Oliver, Dave Moorleigh, Richard Marks, David Jackman

AVONWICK
Turtley Corn Mill ♀ 🛏

SX6958 Map 1

0.5 miles off A38 roundabout at SW end of South Brent bypass; TQ10 9ES

Clever conversion of tall mill house with interestingly furnished areas, local beers, modern bar food and huge garden; bedrooms

This carefully converted watermill is so popular that it's sensible to book a table in advance. It's a pretty setting and the extensive garden has plenty of well spaced picnic-sets, a giant chess set and a small lake with unusual ducks; dogs are welcome but must be kept on a lead. Inside, the spreading linked areas are decorated with some individuality. There are bookcases, fat church candles and oriental rugs in one area, dark flagstones by the bar, a strategically placed woodburning stove dividing off one part, and a side enclave with a modern pew built in around a really big table. Lighting is good, with plenty of big windows overlooking the grounds, and there's a pleasant array of prints, a history of the mill and framed 78rpm discs on pastel-painted walls, elderly wireless sets, house plants and a mix of comfortable dining chairs around heavy baluster-leg tables. Dartmoor Legend, St Austell Tribute, Sharps Doom Bar and Summerskills Tamar on handpump, nine wines by the glass and around 30 malt whiskies. The bedrooms are comfortable and the breakfasts good.

❙❙❙ Starting with breakfast (available to non-residents too), they serve some kind of enjoyable food all day: sandwiches, shredded duck salad with hoisin sauce, potted salmon, smoked mackerel and trout with pickled vegetables, teriyaki chicken with sesame noodles and stir-fried vegetables, red pepper, spinach and blue cheese lasagne, beef in Guinness pie, cumberland sausages with creamy mash, black pudding and gravy, chilli-braised pork belly with coleslaw and skinny fries, seafood risotto, and puddings like baked raspberry cheesecake and chocolate brownie with chocolate sauce; they also offer a two- and three-course set lunch menu. *Benchmark main dish: beer-battered local haddock with mushy peas and frites £13.50. Two-course evening meal £18.50.*

Free house ~ Licensees Lesley and Bruce Brunning ~ Real ale ~ (01364) 646100 ~ Open 11-11; 12-10.30 Sun ~ Bar food 8.30am-9pm(9.30 Fri, Sat) ~ Children welcome ~ Dogs allowed in bar ~ Bedrooms: £80/£99 ~ www.turtleycornmill.com *Recommended by Helen and Brian Edgeley, Lynda and Trevor Smith, Colin and Angela Boocock, Christian Mole, Nicki Spicer, M G Hart, Roger and Donna Huggins, N R White*

AXMOUTH   SY2591   Map 1

Harbour Inn

B3172 Seaton–Axminster; EX12 4AF

Family-run thatched pub by the Axe estuary with heavily beamed bars, plenty of boating memorabilia, real ales and well liked food

Many customers here are walkers and bird-watchers – the Axe estuary is just a stone's throw away. A striking entrance hall with seats on huge flagstones leads into two heavily beamed connected bar rooms with plenty of character: brass-bound cask seats, a high-backed oak settle and one or two smaller ones, leather-topped bar stools and all manner of tables on bare floorboards, pots hanging from pot-irons in a huge inglenook fireplace, glass balls in nets, a large turtle shell and lots of model boats and accounts of shipwrecks. There are also two dining rooms with more heavy beams, a little snug alcove leading off, built-in blue cushioned wall, window and other seats, and more model yachts, ships in bottles, pulleys and blocks; they hope to install a large-scale model of HMS *Victory* in a cabinet. Badger Best, First Gold, Pickled Partridge and Tanglefoot on handpump and several wines by the glass; pool, skittle alley. There are contemporary-style seats and tables on the front terrace and plenty of picnic-sets on grass. The handsome church opposite has some fine stone gargoyles. Sister pub is the Wheelwright in Colyford.

❙❙❙ As well as breakfasts from 9am, the popular food includes sandwiches, crispy whitebait with tartare sauce, deep-fried brie with redcurrant jelly, honey-roast ham and eggs with triple-cooked chips, burger with red onion marmalade, melted cheese, gherkins and fries, lasagne, pie of the day, lambs liver and bacon with caramelised onion gravy, chicken breast wrapped in parma ham, stuffed with leeks, bacon, cheese and pine nuts on mint and pea risotto, specials like moules marinière or lamb tagine, and puddings such as apple and rhubarb crumble with custard and sticky toffee pudding with toffee sauce. *Benchmark main dish: trio of beef patties with red onion marinade, cheese and skinny fries £9.00. Two-course evening meal £15.00.*

Badger ~ Lease Gary and Toni Valentine ~ Real ale ~ (01297) 20371 ~ Open 9am-11.30pm(midnight Sat); 9am-11pm Sun ~ Bar food 9am-9.30pm ~ Restaurant ~ Children welcome ~ Dogs allowed in bar ~ www.theharbour-inn.co.uk
Recommended by Jonathan Alexander

BEESANDS
Cricket 🍴 🛏

SX8140 Map 1

About 3 miles S of A379, from Chillington; in village turn right along foreshore road; TQ7 2EN

Welcoming pub with enjoyable food (especially fish) and real ales; clean, airy bedrooms

The crab, lobster, scallops and much of the fish on the menu come straight out of the sea in front of this well run pub. It gets pretty busy at peak times, so book a table in advance. It's popular locally, but the cheerful licensees are warmly welcoming to all and the atmosphere is relaxed and chatty. The light, airy décor is new england in style, with dark wood or leather chairs around big, solid light wood tables on stripped-wood flooring by the bar and light brown patterned carpet in the restaurant. Big TV screens at either end roll through old local photographs, sport or the news. Otter Ale and Bitter and St Austell Tribute on handpump, several wines by the glass and local cider; background music. The cheerful black labrador is called Brewster. There are picnic-sets beside the sea wall (a little bleak but essential protection) with pebbly Start Bay beach just over the other side. The South West Coast Path runs through the village.

As well as fish dishes, such as crab soup, grilled sardines with herb and spring onion couscous and chilli and peanut crust, white beer-battered cod with mushy peas, mackerel fillets with chorizo and leeks with crispy shallot rings, scallops with celeriac purée, chicken and curried lentils, and king prawn linguine, the very good food might include sandwiches, chicken liver and madeira parfait, chicken and ham pie, vegetarian dish of the day, home-smoked duck leg with carrot and cumin purée, pak choi and honey jus, and puddings. *Benchmark main dish: seafood pancake £12.50. Two-course evening meal £19.00.*

Heavitree ~ Tenant Nigel Heath ~ Real ale ~ (01548) 580215 ~ Open 11(12 Sun)-11; 12-3, 6-10 in winter ~ Bar food 12-8.30; 12-2.30, 6-8.30 in winter ~ Restaurant ~ Children welcome ~ Dogs allowed in bar ~ Bedrooms: £80/£100 ~ www.thecricketinn.com
Recommended by DHV, Jane and Rowena Leverington, Ian Roe, R L Borthwick, Roy Hoing, S Holder

BRAMPFORD SPEKE
Lazy Toad 🍴

SX9298 Map 1

Off A377 N of Exeter; EX5 5DP

Well run dining pub in pretty village, delicious food, real ales, friendly service and pretty garden; bedrooms

By the time this *Guide* is published, there will be two new bedrooms in an annexe attached to this friendly 18th-c inn, and a new residents' garden. The pretty village with its thatched cottages is well worth a wander, and there are fine walks beside the River Exe and on the Exe Valley Way and Devonshire Heartland Way. The interconnected bar rooms have beams, standing timbers and slate floors, a comfortable sofa and rocking chair (much prized in winter) by the open log fire, and cushioned wall settles and high-backed wooden dining chairs around a mix of tables; the cream-painted brick walls are hung with lots of pictures and there's a rather fine grandfather clock. Dartmoor Jail Ale, Otter Bitter and St Austell Tribute on handpump and 14 nice wines by the glass are served by attentive staff; the resident cocker spaniel is called Sam. There are green-painted picnic-sets in the courtyard (once used by the local farrier and wheelwright) and in the walled garden.

🍴 They bake their own sourdough daily, smoke their own meat and fish, cure bacon and hams and use local, seasonal ingredients for their enticing food: sandwiches, tian of cornish crab with guacamole salad and crab foam, confit of duck salad with linguine and coriander, sausages with mash and onion gravy, steak and kidney pie with duck fat roast potatoes, red onion and goats cheese tart with polenta chips and beetroot crisps, smoked haddock and thyme risotto with free-range egg, chicken with cauliflower and truffle purée and pommes anna potatoes, fried pigs cheek, crispy ears, sage soubise and rosemary potatoes, and puddings like pear and walnut frangipane tart with vanilla pod custard and pecan nut sauce and stem gingerbread pudding with butterscotch sauce. *Benchmark main dish: oxtail stew with braised short ribs, ravioli, celeriac and horseradish foam £18.00. Two-course evening meal £19.50.*

Free house ~ Licensees Clive and Mo Walker ~ Real ale ~ (01392) 841591 ~ Open 11.30-2.30, 6-11; 11.30-11 Sat; 12-3 Sun; 11.30-2.30, 6-11 Sat in winter; closed Sun evening, Mon ~ Bar food 12-2(2.30 Sun), 6.30-9 ~ Children welcome but over-12s only in bedrooms ~ Dogs allowed in bar and bedrooms ~ Bedrooms: £68/£90 ~ www.thelazytoadinn.co.uk
Recommended by R F Sawbridge, Mary Graham, Jan and Alan Summers

BRANSCOMBE
SY1888   Map 1

Fountain Head 🍺 £

Upper village, above the robust old church; village signposted off A3052 Sidmouth–Seaton, then from Branscombe Square follow road uphill towards Sidmouth, and after about a mile turn left after the church; OS Sheet 192 map reference SY188889; EX12 3BG

Old-fashioned and friendly stone pub with own-brewed beers and reasonably priced, well liked food

Thankfully unchanging over the years, this warmly welcoming 14th-c pub remains as popular as ever with locals and visitors. There's a nicely old-fashioned atmosphere and no background music, TV or games machines. The room on the left (formerly a smithy) has forge tools and horseshoes on high oak beams, cushioned pews and mate's chairs and a log fire in the original raised firebed with its tall central chimney. They brew their own Branscombe Vale Branoc, Summa That and a changing guest beer, which they keep on handpump, and hold a beer festival in June; several wines by the glass and local cider. On the right, an irregularly shaped, more orthodox snug room has another log fire, a white-painted plank ceiling with an unusual carved ceiling-rose, brown-varnished panelled walls and rugs on a flagstone and lime ash floor. Local artists' paintings and greeting cards are for sale; darts and board games. You can sit outside on the front loggia and terrace listening to the stream gurgling under the flagstoned path, and the surrounding walks are very pleasant.

🍴 Reasonably priced and well liked, the bar food includes sandwiches, local mussels in creamy white wine and garlic sauce, confit duck leg with spicy red onion marmalade, honey-roast ham and eggs, local crab and pawpaw salad with lime and chilli dressed salad, lambs liver and crispy bacon with champ potato and onion gravy, moroccan-style vegetable stew with couscous and mint yoghurt, chicken supreme filled with smoked cheese and bacon with white wine sauce, and puddings. *Benchmark main dish: beer-battered cod and chips £10.50. Two-course evening meal £16.00.*

Free house ~ Licensees Jon Woodley and Teresa Hoare ~ Real ale ~ (01297) 680359 ~ Open 11-3, 6-11; 12-10.30 Sun ~ Bar food 12-2, 6.30-9 ~ Restaurant ~ Children welcome away from main bar area ~ Dogs allowed in bar ~ www.fountainheadinn.com
Recommended by Peter Thornton, C and R Bromage, Chris Johnson, Christine and Neil Townend, N R White, R K Phillips, George Atkinson, Kerry Law, Patrick and Daphne Darley

 BRANSCOMBE   SY2088 Map 1

Masons Arms

Main Street; signed off A3052 Sidmouth–Seaton, then bear left into village; EX12 3DJ

Rambling low-beamed rooms, woodburning stoves, a fair choice of real ales, popular food and seats in quiet terrace and garden; cottagey bedrooms

This picturesque 14th-c longhouse is in an especially pretty village and just a stroll from the sea, so it gets busy at peak times – best to arrive early if you want a parking space. The rambling main bar is the heart of the place; with a good mix of locals and visitors, you can be sure of a cheerful, bustling atmosphere and a warm welcome from the licensees. There are comfortable seats and chairs on slate floors, ancient ships' beams, a log fire in a massive hearth and St Austell Proper Job and Tribute and two guest beers on handpump. A second bar also has a slate floor, a fireplace with a two-sided woodburning stove and stripped pine; there are also two dining rooms. A quiet flower-filled front terrace, with thatched-roof tables, extends into a side garden. This is a nice place to stay, with bedrooms in converted cottages.

Usefully serving food all day, such as sandwiches, steamed mussels in white wine, garlic and cream, pâté with ale chutney, pie of the day, sausage and mash with caramelised onions and red wine sauce, mushroom, chive and tomato pancake with wine and wholegrain mustard cream, chargrilled burger with bacon, gruyère, chips and tomato and basil chutney, slow-roast pork belly with mustard mash, cider sauce and braised red cabbage, beer-battered local fish, and puddings. *Benchmark main dish: crab ploughman's £12.00. Two-course evening meal £19.00.*

St Austell ~ Managers Simon and Alison Ede ~ Real ale ~ (01297) 680300 ~ Open 11-11; 12-10.30 Sun ~ Bar food 12-9 ~ Restaurant ~ Children welcome ~ Dogs allowed in bar and bedrooms ~ Bedrooms: /£80 ~ www.masonsarms.co.uk *Recommended by Noel Thomas, Chris Johnson, Mr and Mrs M Wall, George Atkinson*

BRENDON   SS7547 Map 1

Rockford Inn

Rockford; Lynton–Simonsbath Road, off B3223; EX35 6PT

Homely and cosy small inn surrounded by fine walks and scenery, open fires, real ales, a friendly welcome and honest food; bedrooms

In the remote Brendon Valley surrounded by Exmoor National Park, this is a friendly and traditional 17th-c inn by the East Lyn River; seats overlook the water and they have fishing permits. The small spotless linked rooms have open fires, cushioned settles, wall seats and wheelback chairs around sturdy tables on carpet, a shelf of books (several about fishing), lots of country prints on the walls and horse tack.

Stools line the bar, where they keep Clearwater Real Smiler, Cotleigh
Harrier and Exmoor Gold tapped from the cask, farm cider and wines by
the glass, and behind the counter there are lots of pump clips and toby
jugs; board games and background music. The refurbished bedrooms are
comfortable and cottagey, and the breakfasts are good. Splendid walks
all around.

There are home-made pizzas plus pâté of the day, crispy fried brie with
walnut and cranberry salad, bean and vegetable chilli, steak in ale or game
pies, chicken in mushroom and garlic sauce, beer-battered cod and chips, lamb
shank, beef madras and puddings such as banoffi pie and apple and blackberry
crumble. *Benchmark main dish: braised beef £11.95. Two-course evening
meal £17.00.*

Free house ~ Licensees Kathryn and Sarah Ward ~ Real ale ~ (01598) 741214 ~ Open
12-11; 12-2.30, 6-10.30 Sun ~ Bar food 12-2.30, 6-8.30; 12-2, 6-8 Sun ~ Children welcome
~ Dogs allowed in bar ~ Bedrooms: £40/£80 ~ www.therockfordinn.co.uk
Recommended by Sheila Topham

BUCKLAND BREWER   SS4220   Map 1
Coach & Horses

*Village signposted off A388 S of Monkleigh; OS Sheet 190 map reference
423206; EX39 5LU*

**Friendly old village pub with a mix of customers, open fires and
real ales; good nearby walks**

In fine weather you can sit outside this old pub at picnic-sets on the
front terrace and in the side garden, while in winter there are warm
fires in cosy rooms. It's been run by the same friendly family for over
25 years, and the heavily beamed bar (mind your head on some of
the beams) has comfortable seats, a handsome antique settle and a
woodburning stove in an inglenook; there's also a good log fire in the
big stone inglenook in the small lounge. A little back room has darts
and pool; the three-legged cat is called Marmite. Forge Litehouse, Otter
Ale and Sharps Doom Bar on handpump, Winkleigh cider and several
wines by the glass; skittle alley (which doubles as a function room),
background music, games machine and occasional TV for sports. The
RHS garden Rosemoor is about five miles away. They have a holiday
cottage next to the pub.

Bar food includes sandwiches and paninis, chicken liver pâté, mushrooms
baked with stilton, ham and egg, steak in ale pie, burger with bacon and
cheese, crispy chicken goujons in parmesan and thyme crumb with garlic
mayonnaise, home-made curries, baked salmon steak with sweet chilli glaze and
lime crème fraîche, duck with smoked bacon and chestnut stuffing and port and
onion sauce, and puddings like fruit crumble and chocolate brownie with hot
chocolate fudge sauce. *Benchmark main dish: steak and Guinness pie £9.50.
Two-course evening meal £20.00.*

Free house ~ Licensees Oliver and Nicola Wolfe ~ Real ale ~ (01237) 451395 ~ Open
12-3, 5.30(6 Sun)-midnight ~ Bar food 12-2, 6.30-9.30 ~ Restaurant ~ Children welcome
~ Dogs allowed in bar ~ www.coachandhorsesbucklandbrewer.co.uk
*Recommended by Pat and Tony Martin, Christopher Turner, M and GR, Mark Flynn, John Marsh,
Bob and Margaret Holder, Ryta Lyndley*

The ◖ symbol shows pubs which keep their beer unusually well,
have a particularly good range or brew their own.

BUCKLAND MONACHORUM

Drake Manor 🍺 £ 🛏

SX4968 Map 1

Off A386 via Crapstone, just S of Yelverton roundabout; PL20 7NA

Nice little village pub with snug rooms, popular food, quite a choice of drinks and pretty back garden; bedrooms

Built to house masons constructing the nearby church in the 12th c, this popular old place has a good local atmosphere and a welcoming landlady who's been here for 23 years. The heavily beamed public bar on the left has brocade-cushioned wall seats, prints of the village from 1905 onwards, horse tack and a few ship badges, and a woodburning stove in a really big stone fireplace; a small door leads to a low-beamed cubbyhole. The snug Drakes Bar has beams hung with tiny cups and big brass keys, a woodburning stove in another stone fireplace, horsebrasses and stirrups and a mix of seats and tables (note the fine stripped-pine high-backed settle with hood). On the right is a small, beamed dining room with settles and tables on flagstones. Shove-ha'penny, darts, euchre and board games. Dartmoor Jail Ale, Otter Bitter and Sharps Doom Bar on handpump, ten wines by the glass and 20 malt whiskies. There are picnic-sets in the prettily planted and sheltered back garden and the front floral displays are much admired; morris men perform regularly in summer. Bedrooms are comfortable and there's also an attractive self-catering apartment.

Using their own home-reared and other local produce, the fairly priced food includes lunchtime filled baguettes and ploughman's, pâté with red onion chutney, marinated tiger prawns with thai chilli dip, lasagne, sausages with mash, gammon with cheese and pineapple, courgette, tomato and sweet potato bake topped with cheese, minted lamb burger topped with goats cheese with chips, bacon-wrapped chicken supreme stuffed with mushroom pâté with creamy white wine sauce, salmon fillet with cajun spices and raita dressing, daily specials and puddings. *Benchmark main dish: home-made beef in Guinness pie £9.25. Two-course evening meal £16.00.*

Punch ~ Lease Mandy Robinson ~ Real ale ~ (01822) 853892 ~ Open 11.30-2.30, 6.30-11; 11.30-11.30 Fri, Sat; 12-11 Sun ~ Bar food 12-2(2.30 weekends), 7-10(9.30 Sun) ~ Restaurant ~ Children in restaurant and area off main bar ~ Dogs allowed in bar ~ Bedrooms: /£90 ~ www.drakemanorinn.co.uk *Recommended by Maureen Wood, Suzy Miller, Di and Mike Gillam*

CLAYHIDON

Merry Harriers 🍷 🍺

ST1817 Map 1

3 miles from M5 junction 26: head towards Wellington; turn left at first roundabout signposted Ford Street and Hemyock, then after a mile turn left signposted Ford Street; at hilltop T-junction, turn left towards Chard – pub is 1.5 miles on right; at Forches Corner NE of the village itself; EX15 3TR

Bustling and friendly dining pub with several real ales and quite a few wines by the glass; sizeable garden

Handy for the M5, this extremely popular and well run pub is always packed with cheerful local customers. But even at its busiest, the hard-working, hands-on licensees and their staff offer all a warm welcome. Several small linked carpeted areas have comfortably cushioned pews and farmhouse chairs, a sofa beside a woodburning stove, candles in bottles, horse and hunting prints and local wildlife pictures. Two dining areas have a brighter feel with quarry tiles and lightly timbered white walls. Exmoor Ale and Antler, Otter Head and St Austell Trelawny on handpump, 14 wines by the glass, two local ciders, 25 malt whiskies and quite a choice of spirits; skittle alley, chess and solitaire. There are plenty of tables and chairs in the sizeable garden and on the terrace, and there's a wendy house and play equipment for children; good surrounding walks.

A wide choice of popular food (local suppliers are named on the menu) includes baguettes, pork and pistachio terrine with home-made fruit chutney, mussels in cider cream sauce, sweet potato and cashew nut green curry, organic pork and leek sausages on mustard mash, chicken braised in red wine with mushrooms and bacon lardons, supreme of guinea fowl on sweet potato mash with gravy, specials such as cornish hake on red onion potato cake with parsley sauce, and puddings like dark chocolate mousse with raspberry sauce and bakewell tart with clotted cream. *Benchmark main dish: scallop and smoked bacon salad with lemon cream sauce £11.00. Two-course evening meal £16.00.*

Free house ~ Licensees Peter and Angela Gatling ~ Real ale ~ (01823) 421270 ~ Open 12-3, 6.30-11; 12-3.30 Sun; closed Sun evening, Mon ~ Bar food 12-2(2.15 Sun), 6.30-9 ~ Restaurant ~ Children welcome ~ Dogs welcome ~ www.merryharriers.co.uk
Recommended by Bob and Margaret Holder, Peter Thornton, Michael and Maggie Betton, Richard Fox, John and Susan Miln, PLC, Bruce and Sharon Eden, Gerry and Rosemary Dobson, Mike Gorton, R T and J C Moggridge, Paul Humphreys, Paul Bonner

COCKWOOD   SX9780   Map 1
Anchor ♀ ◀

Off, but visible from, A379 Exeter–Torbay road, after Starcross; EX6 8RA

Busy dining pub specialising in seafood, with five real ales too

Even on a dreary day you must book in advance for this incredibly popular dining pub – there are often queues to get in at peak times. As well as an extension made up of mainly reclaimed timber and decorated with over 300 ship emblems, brass and copper lamps and nautical knick-knacks, there are several small, low-ceilinged, rambling rooms with black panelling and good-sized tables in various alcoves; the snug has a cheerful winter coal fire. Dartmoor Legend, Exmoor Ale, Otter Ale and Dark and St Austell Proper Job on handpump (beer festivals at Easter and Halloween), eight wines by the glass and 80 malt whiskies; background music, darts, cards and shove-ha'penny. From the tables on the sheltered verandah you can look across the road to the inlet (a pleasant spot for a wander).

A huge range of fish dishes includes 28 different ways of serving River Exe mussels, six ways of serving local scallops and five ways of serving oysters, as well as crab and brandy soup and various platters to share. Non-fishy dishes include sandwiches, steak in ale pie, pork sausages with onion gravy and mash, chicken wrapped in smoked bacon and stuffed with garlic and herb cheese, wild mushroom and spinach linguine, lamb cutlets with redcurrant and port jus, and puddings such as chocolate fudge crunch and treacle sponge and custard. *Benchmark main dish: mussels £14.95. Two-course evening meal £22.00.*

Heavitree ~ Lease Malcolm and Katherine Protheroe, Scott Hellier ~ Real ale ~ (01626) 890203 ~ Open 11-11; 11.30-10.30 Sun ~ Bar food all day ~ Restaurant ~ Children welcome if seated and away from bar ~ Dogs allowed in bar ~ www.anchorinncockwood.com *Recommended by Mr and Mrs A H Young, Col and Mrs Patrick Kaye, Dr A J and Mrs B A Tompsett, Adrian Johnson*

COLEFORD

SS7701   Map 1

New Inn 🍴 ♈ 🛏

Just off A377 Crediton–Barnstaple; EX17 5BZ

Ancient thatched inn with interestingly furnished areas, well liked food and real ales, and welcoming licensees; bedrooms

Many readers very much enjoy staying in this genuinely friendly 13th-c inn where there's quite a choice of bedrooms; breakfasts are particularly good. It's a U-shaped building with the servery in the 'angle' and interestingly furnished areas leading off it: ancient and modern settles, cushioned stone wall seats, some character tables – a pheasant worked into the grain of one – and carved dressers and chests. Also, paraffin lamps, antique prints on white walls, landscape plates on one beam and pewter tankards on another. Captain, the chatty parrot, may greet you with a 'hello' or even a 'goodbye'. Otter Ale, Sharps Doom Bar and a guest like Shepherd Neame Spitfire on handpump, local cider, 14 wines by the glass and a dozen malt whiskies; background music, darts and board games. There are chairs and tables on decking under a pruned willow tree by a babbling stream and more in a covered dining area.

 Sourcing local produce with great care, the interesting seasonal menu might include baguettes, local mussels in cider and crème fraîche, mushroom, spinach and sun-dried tomato risotto, slow-roasted lamb shank with tomato, red wine and butter bean sauce with chorizo, duck leg confit with bigarade orange and red wine sauce and apple savoy cabbage, chargrilled chilli chicken on red rice with manchego and yoghurt, grilled hake fillet on spring onion mash with soy butter sauce, and puddings such as strawberry cheesecake with raspberry coulis and cappuccino brûlée. *Benchmark main dish: home-made fish pie £12.95. Two-course evening meal £18.00.*

Free house ~ Licensees Carole and George Cowie ~ Real ale ~ (01363) 84242 ~ Open 12-3, 6-11(10.30 Sun) ~ Bar food 12-2, 6.30-9.30 ~ Restaurant ~ Children welcome ~ Dogs allowed in bar ~ Bedrooms: £67/£85 ~ www.thenewinncoleford.co.uk
Recommended by S G N Bennett, Michael Coleman, Pat and Tony Martin, Mrs P Sumner, Jan and Alan Summers, M A Borthwick, P and J Shapley, R Elliott

CULMSTOCK

ST1013   Map 1

Culm Valley 🍴 ♈ 🍺

B3391, off A38 E of M5 junction 27; EX15 3JJ

Quirky, friendly dining pub with imaginative food, interesting real ales and wines, lively atmosphere, and outside seats overlooking River Culm

'Always a pleasure to come here,' says one reader and it's clear from the crowds that many others agree. It's an unusual place – a touch eccentric, but all the better for that – and the landlord is slightly off-beat but quite charming. There's a good mix of chatty locals and visitors, a lively and informal atmosphere, and a bar with a hotch-potch of modern and unrenovated furnishings, horse racing-related paintings and other knick-knacks and a big fireplace. Further on is a dining room with a chalkboard menu, a small front conservatory and, leading off here, a little oak-floored room with views into the kitchen. A larger back room has paintings by local artists for sale. Board games and a portable TV for occasional rugby, rowing and racing events; the dogs are called Lady and Spoof. Six quickly changing ales tapped from the cask (they often have ten beers at weekends) might include Bays Top Sail, Branscombe

Vale Branoc, O'Hanlons Stormstay, Stonehenge Great Bustard and Yeovil Posh IPA and Somerset. The landlord and his brother import wines from smaller french vineyards, so you can count on a few of those as well as unusual french fruit liqueurs, somerset cider brandies, vintage rum, good sherries and madeira and local farm ciders. Outside, tables are very attractively positioned overlooking the bridge and the River Culm. The gents' is in an outside yard. The three bedrooms share two bathrooms.

They butcher their own meat and use local game and fish for the imaginative dishes (fairly priced for the quality): sandwiches, pickled herring, scallops with sweet chilli and crème fraîche, pasta with ricotta and spinach, home-made pork sausages with mash and onion gravy, trout and pollock fishcakes with home-made tartare sauce, sri lankan chicken and north indian lamb curries, greek-style goat, veal with sage and cream, and puddings such as honeycomb and vanilla cheesecake and crème brûlée. *Benchmark main dish: home-made venison burger £9.00. Two-course evening meal £20.00.*

Free house ~ Licensee Richard Hartley ~ Real ale ~ (01884) 840354 ~ Open 12-3, 6-11; 12-11 Fri, Sat; 12-10.30 Sun ~ Bar food 12-2, 7-9; not Sun evening ~ Restaurant ~ Children away from main bar ~ Dogs welcome ~ Impromptu piano or folk ~ Bedrooms: £40/£70 ~ www.culmvalleyinn.co.uk *Recommended by Steven King and Barbara Cameron, R T and J C Moggridge, J D O Carter, David and Sharon Collison, Hugo Jeune, Guy Vowles*

 DALWOOD   ST2400 Map 1
Tuckers Arms 🍴
Village signposted off A35 Axminster–Honiton; keep on past village; EX13 7EG

13th-c thatched inn with friendly, hard-working young licensees, real ales and interesting bar food

With fair prices for drinks and food, prompt and friendly service and a good mix of customers, it's no wonder that this pretty, thatched pub is so busy. The beamed and flagstoned bar has traditional furnishings including dining chairs, window seats and wall settles, a log fire in an inglenook fireplace with horsebrasses on the wall above, and a relaxed atmosphere. The back bar has an enormous collection of miniature bottles, and there's also a more formal dining room; lots of copper implements and platters. Branscombe Vale Branoc, Otter Bitter and a changing local guest beer on handpump, several wines by the glass and up to 20 malt whiskies; background music and a double skittle alley. In summer, the hanging baskets are pretty and there are seats in the garden. Apart from the church, this is the oldest building in the parish.

Good and often inventive, the food might include sandwiches, pork belly and pancetta in puff pastry with apricot, cider and raisin chutney, venison meatballs with mustard, tarragon and rosemary cream, spiced lamb burger with feta and mint relish, cajun potato wedges and beetroot coleslaw, lemon sole and crab lasagne with spicy tomato sauce, and puddings such as vanilla crème brûlée with home-made shortbread and ginger and toffee sponge with custard. *Benchmark main dish: pot-roast loin of pork £16.00. Two-course evening meal £22.50.*

Free house ~ Licensee Tracey Pearson ~ Real ale ~ (01404) 881342 ~ Open 11.30-3, 6.30-11.30 ~ Bar food 12-2, 6.30-9 ~ Restaurant ~ Children in restaurant but must be well behaved ~ Dogs allowed in bar ~ Bedrooms: £45/£69.50 ~ www.thetuckersarms.co.uk *Recommended by Peter Salmon, Dave Braisted, Mike and Jayne Bastin, Guy Vowles, Stephen and Jean Curtis, Patrick and Daphne Darley*

DARTMOUTH   SX8751 Map 1

Floating Bridge

Opposite Upper Ferry, use Dart Marina Hotel car park; Coombe Road (A379); TQ6 9PQ

Quayside pub with seats by the water and on roof terrace, some boating memorabilia and friendly staff

This bustling quayside pub has plenty of seats, including tables and chairs on the sizeable roof terrace and picnic-sets beside the River Dart and the little car ferry. The bar has lots of stools by the windows to make the most of the water view, oak chairs and tables, a few model boats and black and white photographs of local boating scenes, St Austell Tribute and Sharps Doom Bar on handpump and several wines by the glass; background music. The dining room on the left is lighter, with leather-backed dining chairs around a mix of wooden tables on bare boards and more black and white photographs. There's also a back family room with access to the roof terrace. The window boxes are pretty against the white-painted building.

 Tasty bar food includes sandwiches, chicken liver pâté, thai fishcakes with lemon and dill mayonnaise, lasagne, home-cooked ham and free-range eggs, mushroom linguine, chicken tikka masala, steak and kidney pie, roast lamb rump with honey and redcurrant gravy, daily fresh fish dishes and puddings. *Benchmark main dish: battered cod with chips £9.95. Two-course evening meal £18.00.*

Enterprise ~ Lease Alison Hogben ~ Real ale ~ (01803) 832354 ~ Open 11-11 ~ Bar food 12-9.30 ~ Restaurant ~ Children welcome ~ Dogs allowed in bar ~ www.thefloatingbridge.co.uk *Recommended by John and Fiona McIlwain, Alun and Jennifer Evans, Dave Webster, Sue Holland*

DARTMOUTH   SX8751 Map 1

Royal Castle Hotel 🛏

The Quay; TQ6 9PS

17th-c hotel with a lot of character in two quite different bars, a genuine mix of customers, real ales and good food; comfortable bedrooms

This thriving 350-year-old hotel, right at the heart of this lovely old town, is usefully open all day with bar food available. There are two ground-floor bars, each with its own identity. The traditional Galleon bar (on the right) has plenty of character, a Tudor fireplace, fine antiques and maritime pieces and quite a bit of copper and brass. The Harbour Bar (on the left of the flagstoned entrance hall) is contemporary and rather smart, with a big-screen TV and regular acoustic music. The more formal restaurant looks over the river. Dartmoor Jail Ale, Otter Amber and Sharps Doom Bar on handpump and several wines by the glass. The inn was originally two Tudor merchant houses (but the façade is Regency) and overlooks the inner harbour; they have their own secure parking.

 As well as breakfasts (for non-residents too), the wide choice of good food includes sandwiches, local mussels in creamy white wine sauce, potted chicken liver, port and tarragon parfait with local chutney, trio of honey-roast pork sausages with onion gravy, beer-battered cod with chips, pie of the week, seafood tagliatelle with dill and cherry vine tomatoes, chilli beef nachos with cheese, guacamole, sour cream and salsa, roasted rack of lamb with rosemary and red wine sauce, and puddings like vanilla bean crème brûlée with home-made walnut shortbread and sticky toffee pudding with butterscotch sauce. *Benchmark main dish: whole fresh crab £14.50. Two-course evening meal £21.25.*

Free house ~ Licensees Nigel and Anne Way ~ Real ale ~ (01803) 833033 ~ Open 8am-11pm(11.30 Sat) ~ Bar food 9am-11pm ~ Restaurant ~ Children welcome but not after 8pm in bar (can eat in restaurant then) ~ Dogs welcome ~ Live acoustic music Thurs evening, Sun afternoon ~ Bedrooms: £110/£160 ~ www.royalcastle.co.uk
Recommended by George Atkinson, Dave Webster, Sue Holland, Patrick and Daphne Darley

DODDISCOMBSLEIGH
SX8586 Map 1
Nobody Inn ♀
Off B3193; EX6 7PS

Busy old pub with plenty of character, a fine range of drinks, friendly staff and well liked bar food; bedrooms

There's a fantastic range of drinks in this 17th-c inn. As well as a beer named for the pub from Branscombe Vale and two changing guests such as Branscombe Vale Exe Valley Bitter and Dartmoor Legend on handpump, they keep 29 wines by the glass from a list of 200 wines, 262 whiskies and a farm cider. The two character rooms of the beamed lounge bar have handsomely carved antique settles, windsor and wheelback chairs, a mix of wooden tables, guns and hunting prints in a snug area by one of the big inglenook fireplaces and fresh flowers; service is friendly and helpful. The restaurant is more formal. There are picnic-sets in the pretty garden, with views of the surrounding wooded hill pastures. The medieval stained glass in the local church is some of the best in the west country.

Using produce from local growers and producers, the good, often inventive food might include sandwiches, potted brown shrimps, chicken liver parfait wrapped in prune butter with fig and grape chutney, ricotta, sun-blush tomato and basil roulade with beetroot three ways, beer-battered fish with tartare sauce, home-cooked ham with cider and cumin glaze and free-range eggs, slow-cooked pork belly with butternut squash purée and cider sauce, local mussels in white wine and cream with chips, duck breast with port and orange reduction and red wine sauce, and puddings like hot chocolate fondant with peanut butter centre and Horlicks ice-cream and mango parfait with mango coulis, fruit salsa and coconut sorbet. *Benchmark main dish: steak in ale pie £11.95. Two-course evening meal £21.00.*

Free house ~ Licensee Susan Burdge ~ Real ale ~ (01647) 252394 ~ Open 11-11; 12-10.30 Sun ~ Bar food 12-2, 6.30-9(9.30 Fri, Sat); 12-3, 7-9 Sun ~ Restaurant ~ Children welcome away from main bar; over-5s only in restaurant and bedrooms ~ Dogs allowed in bar ~ Bedrooms: £65/£90 ~ www.nobodyinn.co.uk
Recommended by W K Wood, Chris and Jan Swanwick, B J Thompson

EXMINSTER
SX9686 Map 1
Turf Hotel
Follow the signs to the Swan's Nest, signed from A379 S of village, then continue to end of track, by gates; park and walk along canal towpath for nearly a mile; EX6 8EE

Remote but very popular waterside pub with fine choice of drinks, super summer barbecues and lots of space in big garden

You can't get to this remote but charming family-run pub by car. You have to walk (about 20 minutes along the ship canal), cycle or catch a 60-seater boat down the Exe estuary from Topsham Quay (15-minute trip, adult £4.50, child £2); there's also a canal boat from Countess Wear Swing Bridge every lunchtime, and there's a large pontoon and several moorings for those arriving in their own boat. Arrive early in fine weather, when it's particularly popular. The end room has a slate floor, pine walls, built-in seats, a woodburning stove and lots of photographs of the pub; along a corridor (with a dining room to one side) is a simply furnished room with wood-plank seats around tables on a stripped wood floor. Exeter Avocet or Ferryman, Otter Ale and Bitter and O'Hanlons Yellowhammer on handpump, local cider and juices, ten wines by the glass (and local wines too) and jugs of Pimms. Plenty of picnic-sets are spread around the big garden; the sea and estuary birds are fun to watch at low tide.

As well as their own-grown vegetables and salad, the enterprising bar food includes sandwiches and toasties, crispy fried baby squid with sweet chilli dip, sticky jerk chicken wings with garlic mayonnaise dip, smoked haddock chowder topped with bacon, king prawn and parsley, pasta with aubergine, tomato and basil with mozzarella, greek beef stew with olives and sour cream, salmon fillet with lime, chilli and coriander butter and caribbean-style griddled aubergines, daily specials and puddings; they still do their smashing summer barbecues (and you can cook your own for a private party). *Benchmark main dish: beer-battered fish and chips £10.50. Two-course evening meal £16.50.*

Free house ~ Licensees Clive and Ginny Redfern ~ Real ale ~ (01392) 833128 ~ Open 11-11; 12-10.30 Sun; 11-3 in winter; closed Jan, Feb ~ Bar food 12-2.30(3 weekends), 6.30-9(9.30 Fri, Sat) ~ Restaurant ~ Children welcome ~ Dogs welcome ~ Bedrooms: £60/£80 ~ www.turfpub.net *Recommended by Comus and Sarah Elliott, J D O Carter, W K Wood, Rich Frith*

FROGMORE   SX7742 Map 1

Globe 🛏

A379 E of Kingsbridge; TQ7 2NR

Extended and neatly refurbished inn with a bar, several seating and dining areas, real ales and nice wines by the glass, helpful staff, popular food and seats outside; comfortable bedrooms

This white-painted inn with its lovely flowering window boxes is a nice place to stay: bedrooms are light, airy and well equipped and the wide choice at breakfast is much appreciated by readers. The neatly kept bar has a double-sided woodburner with horsebrass-decorated stone pillars on either side, another fireplace filled with logs, cushioned settles, chunky farmhouse chairs and built-in wall seating around a mix of tables on the wooden floor, and a copper diving helmet. Attentive staff serve Otter Bitter, Skinners Betty Stogs and South Hams Eddystone on handpump and several wines by the glass. The slate-floored games room has a pool table and darts, and there's also a comfortable lounge with an open fire, cushioned dining chairs and tables on red carpeting, a big leather sofa, a model yacht and a large yacht painting; spot the clever mural of a log pile. The back terrace has teak tables and chairs, with steps leading up to another level with picnic-sets.

Well liked food might include baguettes, baked potatoes, local pasty, chicken liver and bacon pâté with toasted brioche and red onion chutney, pigeon breast with beetroot dressing, pizzas with lots of toppings, steak burger with red onion marmalade, ham and egg, meat or vegetarian lasagne, lamb and apricot casserole, fish pie and puddings. *Benchmark main dish: steak in ale pie £8.95. Two-course evening meal £15.00.*

Free house ~ Licensees John and Lynda Horsley ~ Real ale ~ (01548) 531351 ~ Open 12-11; winter 12-2.30(3 Sun), 6-11(6.30-10.30 Sun) ~ Bar food 12-2, 6(6.30 Sun)-9 ~ Restaurant ~ Children in family room ~ Dogs allowed in bar and bedrooms ~ Live folk twice a month ~ Bedrooms: £50/£80 ~ www.theglobeinn.co.uk
Recommended by Dennis Jenkin, DHV, Keith Sale, B J Harding

GEORGEHAM   SS4639   Map 1
Rock 🍴 🍷

Rock Hill, above village; EX33 1JW

Beamed family pub with good food cooked by the landlord, five real ales on handpump, plenty of room inside and out and a relaxed atmosphere

Although a very popular dining pub, this neatly kept, cheerful place warmly welcomes drinkers too. It has plenty of heavy beams and a sizeable bar separated into two areas by a step. The pubby top part has half-planked walls, an open woodburning stove in a stone fireplace, and captain's and farmhouse chairs around wooden tables on quarry tiles; the lower bar has panelled wall seats, some built-in settles forming a cosy booth, old local photographs and ancient flat irons. Leading off here is a red-carpeted dining room with attractive black and white photographs of North Devon folk. Friendly young staff serve Exmoor Ale, Greene King Abbot, St Austell Tribute, Sharps Doom Bar and Timothy Taylors Landlord on handpump and around a dozen wines by the glass; background music and board games. The light, airy back dining conservatory has high-backed wooden or modern dining chairs around tables under a growing vine, with a little terrace beyond. There is wheelchair access. Next to the pretty hanging baskets and tubs in front of the pub are some picnic-sets.

🍴 Enterprising and well presented, the food might include sandwiches, salt and pepper chilli squid, warm shredded duck wrap with hoisin sauce, various deli boards, burger with cheese or bacon, tomato and chilli jam, coleslaw and chips, honey-glazed ham with free-range eggs and home-made piccalilli, butternut squash, sage and pine nut risotto, salmon and crayfish tagliatelle with tarragon, white wine and cream sauce, corn-fed chicken wrapped in pancetta with sweet potato purée, caramelised onions and caper jus, pressed pork belly with bubble and squeak cake and apple and grain mustard jus, and puddings like apple and rhubarb crumble and toasted marshmallow skewers with fresh fruit and chocolate fondue. *Benchmark main dish: fillet of wild line-caught bass £16.95. Two-course evening meal £19.00.*

Punch ~ Lease Darren Stocker and Daniel Craddock ~ Real ale ~ (01271) 890322 ~ Open 11-11; 12-11 Sun ~ Bar food 12-2.30, 6-9.30; 12-3, 6-9 Sun ~ Restaurant ~ Children welcome ~ Dogs welcome ~ www.therockgeorgeham.co.uk *Recommended by Bob and Margaret Holder, Ian Herdman, Paul and Penny Dawson, M and GR, Andrew Scott, Vanessa McGlade, Stephen Shepherd, Stephen and Judith Thomas*

HAYTOR VALE   SX7777   Map 1
Rock ★ 🍴 🛏

Haytor signposted off B3387 just W of Bovey Tracey, on good moorland road to Widecombe; TQ13 9XP

Civilised Dartmoor inn at its most informal at lunchtime; super food, real ales, and seats in pretty garden; comfortable bedrooms

Extremely good food, comfortable bedrooms and attentive, friendly staff continue to draw many readers to this civilised and very well run inn. It's at its most informal at lunchtime (good for walkers in Dartmoor National Park), when there's a fine value two- and three-course weekday set menu. Dartmoor IPA and Jail Ale on handpump, 15 wines (plus champagne and sparkling rosé) by the glass and 16 malt whiskies. The two neatly kept linked, partly panelled bar rooms have lots of dark wood and red plush, polished antique tables with candles and fresh flowers, old-fashioned prints and decorative plates, and warming winter log fires (the main fireplace has a fine Stuart fireback). There's a light and spacious dining room in the lower part of the inn and a residents' lounge. The large, pretty garden opposite has some seats, with more on the little terrace next to the pub. You can park at the back of the building. Some bedrooms are up steep stairs; breakfasts are excellent.

Naming local suppliers on the menu, the delicious food might include lunchtime sandwiches, tempura king prawns with home-made sweet chilli sauce, chicken liver parfait with red onion marmalade, pork and apple burger with mustard mayonnaise and chips, wild mushroom risotto, duck breast with celeriac purée and savoy cabbage with bacon, bass fillet with olive-crushed potatoes and tomato and olive dressing, guinea fowl supreme with roasted squash, truffled mash and wild mushroom and red wine sauce, and puddings such as vanilla panna cotta with stewed rhubarb and steamed chocolate pudding with clotted cream. *Benchmark main dish: lamb rump with asparagus, broad beans, new potatoes and olive and tomato dressing £16.50. Two-course evening meal £22.50.*

Free house ~ Licensee Christopher Graves ~ Real ale ~ (01364) 661305 ~ Open 11-11; 12-10.30 Sun ~ Bar food 12-2, 7-9 ~ Restaurant ~ Children welcome away from main bar ~ Dogs allowed in bedrooms ~ Bedrooms: £79/£110 ~ www.rock-inn.co.uk
Recommended by John and Gloria Isaacs, Hugh Tattersall, Mark O'Sullivan, Mike and Shirley Stratton, Steve Whalley, Robert Watt, Andrea Rampley, Philip Crawford

 HOLNE   SX7069   Map 1

Church House

Signed off B3357 W of Ashburton; TQ13 7SJ

Medieval inn on Dartmoor, plenty of surrounding walks, log fires, real ales and tasty bar food; bedrooms

In a lovely moorland village surrounded by good walks, this medieval inn was built as a resting place for visiting clergy and worshippers at the church (well worth a visit). The lower bar has stripped pine panelling and an 18th-c curved elm settle and is separated from the lounge bar by a 16th-c heavy oak partition; open log fires, candles and fresh flowers in both rooms. Dartmoor IPA, Jail Ale and Legend and St Austell Tribute on handpump, farm cider and several good wines by the glass; background music and board games. There are fine views from the pillared porch.

Tasty bar food includes sandwiches, smoked mackerel pâté, french onion soup, vegetarian homity pie, lasagne, lemon sole with lemon butter, venison stew, rib-eye steak, and puddings like apricot and apple crumble and chocolate brownie. *Benchmark main dish: 16oz T-bone steak £16.50. Two-course evening meal £16.00.*

Free house ~ Licensee Dave Binks ~ Real ale ~ (01364) 631208 ~ Open 12-3, 6-11; 12-4, 6.30-10.30 Sun; may open longer on summer weekends ~ Bar food 12-2.45, 6-8.45; not Sun evening ~ Children welcome ~ Dogs welcome ~ Monthly live band ~ Bedrooms: £40/£80 ~ www.dartmoorchurchhouseinn.co.uk *Recommended by Michael Coleman*

We say if we know a pub allows dogs.

HORNDON

SX5280 Map 1

Elephants Nest

If coming from Okehampton on A386, turn left at Mary Tavy Inn, then left after about 0.5 miles; pub signposted beside Mary Tavy Inn, then Horndon signposted; on the Ordnance Survey Outdoor Leisure Map it's named as the New Inn; PL19 9NQ

Isolated old inn surrounded by Dartmoor walks, some interesting original features, real ales and changing food; comfortable bedrooms

Run by a charming landlord, this is an isolated and cosy old pub surrounded by numerous walks. The main bar has lots of beer pump clips on the beams, high bar chairs by the bar counter, Dartmoor Jail Ale, Otter Ale, Palmers IPA and Tavy Nellis Best on handpump, a couple of farm ciders, several wines by the glass and 15 malt whiskies. Two other rooms have nice modern dark wood dining chairs around a mix of tables; throughout there are bare stone walls, flagstones and three woodburning stoves. The spreading, attractive garden (with an adult-only area) has picnic-sets under parasols, and looks over dry-stone walls to Dartmoor's lower pastured slopes and rougher moorland above. The bedrooms are attractively furnished and comfortable, and the breakfasts very good.

Enjoyable bar food includes baguettes, king prawns in lemon, garlic, chilli and parsley butter, portobello mushrooms topped with sun-dried tomatoes and blue cheese, cumberland sausages with mash and onion gravy, beer-battered fresh haddock with fries, pie of the day, pancetta-wrapped chicken breast stuffed with tallegio cheese and with light creamy sauce, roast pork loin with sage and onion stuffing, and puddings like bread and butter pudding with whisky and marmalade sauce and treacle tart with clotted cream. *Benchmark main dish: smoked haddock topped with welsh rarebit £13.95. Two-course evening meal £19.00.*

Free house ~ Licensee Hugh Cook ~ Real ale ~ (01822) 810273 ~ Open 12-3, 6.30-11 (10.30 Sun) ~ Bar food 12-2.15, 6.30-9 ~ Children welcome ~ Dogs welcome ~ Bedrooms: £77.50/£87.50 ~ www.elephantsnest.co.uk *Recommended by John and Bernadette Elliott, D P and M A Miles, Maurice Ricketts, M G Hart, P and J Shapley, Simon Lindsey, Rose Rogers*

IDDESLEIGH

SS5608 Map 1

Duke of York

B3217 Exbourne–Dolton; EX19 8BG

Unfussy and exceptionally friendly with simply furnished bars, popular food and a fair choice of drinks; charming bedrooms

This is a charming little local with a genuinely authentic and friendly atmosphere and plenty of regulars and visitors. The unspoilt bar has a lot of homely character: rocking chairs, cushioned benches built into the wall's black-painted wooden dado, stripped tables and other simple country furnishings, banknotes pinned to beams, and a large open fireplace. Adnams Broadside, Cotleigh Tawny and a changing guest beer like Bays Topsail tapped from the cask and quite a few wines by the glass. It can get pretty cramped at peak times. The dining room has a huge inglenook fireplace. Through a small coach arch is a little back garden with some picnic-sets. The timbered bedrooms have been upgraded.

Reasonably priced, honest food includes sandwiches, garlic mushrooms with crumbed stilton, scallops wrapped in crispy bacon with balsamic glaze, local sausages with mash, beer-battered fish and chips, red peppers with lemon and coriander couscous, chicken breast with asparagus in hollandaise sauce, lamb shank with mint and rosemary, pork and apple wellington with sweet potato mash and cider and mustard sauce, and home-made puddings. *Benchmark main dish: steak and kidney pudding £12.95. Two-course evening meal £17.50.*

Free house ~ Licensee John Pittam ~ Real ale ~ (01837) 810253 ~ Open 11am-midnight ~ Bar food all day ~ Restaurant ~ Children welcome ~ Dogs allowed in bar and bedrooms ~ Bedrooms: £40/£70 ~ www.dukeofyorkdevon.co.uk
Recommended by Peter Thornton, David Cheetham, Susan Manley, John Marsh, Anita French

KING'S NYMPTON
SS6819 Map 1

Grove 🍴 ◧

Off B3226 SW of South Molton; EX37 9ST

Thatched 17th-c pub in remote village, local beers, highly thought-of bar food and cheerful licensees

The particularly friendly landlord of this 17th-c thatched pub is careful to source his beers and the produce for his food as locally as possible. The low-beamed bar has bookmarks hanging from the ceiling, simple pubby furnishings on a flagstoned floor, bare stone walls, a winter log fire and Exmoor Ale, Forge Ascension, Sharps Own and a guest from Jollyboat on handpump; also, 26 wines (and champagne) by the glass, 60 malt whiskies, local cider, darts, shove-ha'penny and dominoes. They have a self-catering cottage and the pub is surrounded by quiet rolling and wooded countryside. This is a lovely conservation village.

🍴 From a thoughtful menu, the enjoyable food might include sandwiches, grilled goats cheese salad, trout with horseradish cream, tagine of seasonal vegetables with herby couscous, hog pudding with mash and onion gravy, all-day breakfast, venison burger with chunky chips, chicken breast stuffed with blue cheese, parma ham and thyme with dauphinoise potatoes, double lamb chop with rosemary bread sauce, beef wellington, and puddings like hot chocolate pudding with vanilla ice-cream and warm treacle tart with clotted cream. *Benchmark main dish: roast cod on potato and rapeseed mash with herb sauce £13.00. Two-course evening meal £18.00.*

Free house ~ Licensees Robert and Deborah Smallbone ~ Real ale ~ (01769) 580406 ~ Open 12-3, 6-11; 12-3, 7-10 Sun; closed Mon lunchtime except bank holidays ~ Bar food 12-2(3 Sun), 6.45-9 ~ Restaurant ~ Children welcome away from bar ~ Dogs welcome ~ www.thegroveinn.co.uk *Recommended by Robert Coleshill, Mark Flynn, Tony and Jill Radnor*

KINGSKERSWELL
SX8666 Map 1

Bickley Mill 🛏

Bickley Road, SW of Kingskerswell; TQ12 5LN

Friendly inn surrounded by lovely countryside with bustling bars, attractive furnishings and enjoyable food and drink; contemporary bedrooms

Tucked away in lovely countryside this former flour mill is doing particularly well under its friendly young licensees. The rambling beamed rooms have an appealing variety of seating, from rustic chairs and tables to settles to sofas piled with cushions and there are rugs on wooden floors, three open fires, black and white photos or modern art on the stone walls, and an easy-going atmosphere. Bays Devon Dumpling and Gold on handpump and 14 wines by the glass, served by helpful, courteous staff. Outside are seats on a big terrace and a sub-tropical hillside garden. The contemporary bedrooms are well equipped and comfortable.

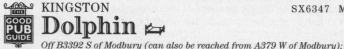

Enjoyable food includes lunchtime sandwiches, home-made fishcakes of the day, chicken liver parfait with red onion marmalade, pie of the day, seasonal vegetable tagliatelle with lemon, chives and crème fraîche, burger with gruyère, chutney and chips, thai red chicken curry, lamb shank with pea purée, spring onion and cheddar mash and madeira sauce, duck breast with celeriac rösti, white bean purée and juniper jus, and puddings such as white chocolate parfait with strawberries and steamed toffee, banana and pecan pudding with crème anglaise. *Benchmark main dish: fried monkfish with sweet potato fondant and sauce vierge £14.95. Two-course evening meal £18.50.*

Free house ~ Licensees Vanessa and James Woodleigh-Smith ~ Real ale ~ (01803) 873201 ~ Open 11-11 ~ Bar food 12-2.30, 6-8.45; 12-3, 6-9(8 Sun) Sat ~ Children welcome ~ Dogs allowed in bar ~ Bedrooms: £75/£90 ~ www.bickleymill.co.uk
Recommended by Mike and Mary Carter

KINGSTON
Dolphin 🛏   SX6347   Map 1

Off B3392 S of Modbury (can also be reached from A379 W of Modbury); TQ7 4QE

Peaceful old pub with walks down to the sea, cosy beamed rooms and enjoyable food and drink; bedrooms

This cosy and peaceful 16th-c inn is just a mile from the lovely Erme Estuary. Several knocked-through beamed rooms have wheelback chairs and built-in wooden wall seats with scatter cushions around dark tables on red patterned carpet, amusing drawings on stone walls, and an open fire and a woodburner in the inglenook fireplaces. Sharps Doom Bar and Timothy Taylors Landlord on handpump, wines by the glass and a farm cider are served by the friendly landlord and his brother. There are seats in the garden and pretty summer flowering tubs and window boxes. The comfortable bedrooms are in cottages opposite; plenty of surrounding tracks to explore.

Fair-priced tasty food includes sandwiches, deep-fried whitebait, duck liver and port parfait with sweet balsamic red onions, burger with onion rings and chips, battered chicken and orange skewers, a changing vegetarian dish, slow-roasted crispy pork belly with gravy and creamy mash, fresh fish of the day and puddings. *Benchmark main dish: steak in ale pie £9.95. Two-course evening meal £17.00.*

Punch ~ Lease Geoffrey Smith ~ Real ale ~ (01548) 810314 ~ Open 12-3, 6-11; 12-3, 7-10.30 Sun; closed some Sun evenings in winter ~ Bar food 12-2(3 Sun), 6-9 ~ Children welcome ~ Dogs welcome ~ Bedrooms: £45/£73.50 ~ www.dolphin-inn.co.uk
Recommended by B J Harding, Steve Whalley, Mrs A Taylor

LUSTLEIGH
Cleave   SX7881   Map 1

Off A382 Bovey Tracey–Moretonhampstead; TQ13 9TJ

In a popular beauty spot, so best to arrive early at this thatched pub with its roaring log fire and popular food and drink; pretty summer garden

Since the present landlord took over, we've had nothing but warm praise for this thatched 15th-c pub. In the hills of Dartmoor National Park at the heart of a pretty village, it's very popular with regulars, visitors and walkers. The low-ceilinged beamed bar has a roaring log fire, granite walls, attractive antique high-backed settles, cushioned wall seats and wheelback chairs around tables on red patterned carpet. Otter Ale and Bitter and a couple of guests such as Dartmoor Jail Ale and Skinners Betty Stogs on handpump, quite a few malt whiskies, several wines by the glass and local organic soft drinks. At the back – formerly the old station waiting room – is a light, airy bistro with pale wooden tables and chairs on a wood-strip floor, and candlelight; from here doors open to an outside eating area. The lovely sheltered garden has plenty of seats and lots of hanging baskets and flower beds.

🍴 Usefully serving some kind of food all day, the interesting, popular dishes might include half a rack of pork ribs, tandoori king prawns, beer-battered haddock and chips, sausages in ale gravy with bubble and squeak, vegetarian lasagne, chicken wrapped in parma ham with mushroom stuffing and palmier potatoes, pork in creamy apple sauce with fondant potatoes, duck breast in honey and five-spice with creamed celeriac, and puddings like vanilla panna cotta with rhubarb compote and banana cheesecake with toffee sauce. *Benchmark main dish: ligurian fish stew £10.95. Two-course evening meal £18.00.*

Heavitree ~ Tenant Ben Whitton ~ Real ale ~ (01647) 277223 ~ Open 11-11 ~ Bar food 11-9 ~ Restaurant ~ Children welcome ~ Dogs allowed in bar ~ www.thecleavelustleigh.com *Recommended by Geoffrey Medcalf, Jadzia Denselow, Mrs C Sleight, B J Harding, Julie and Bill Ryan*

LYDFORD
Dartmoor Inn 🍴 ♀ 🛏

SX5285   Map 1

Downton, A386; EX20 4AY

Welcoming restaurant-with-rooms with a cosy bar, several smart dining rooms, real ales and excellent food; comfortable bedrooms

Although this is more an attractive restaurant-with-rooms than a pub, it has a cheerful small bar with a log fire, Otter Ale and St Austell Tribute on handpump and good wines by the glass, and customers (often with their dogs) who drop in at lunchtime after a walk on the moors – the inn is on the edge of Dartmoor National Park – for a pint and an informal bar meal. Several interconnected, civilised and relaxed dining rooms are individually furnished, with stylish contemporary décor, upholstered high-backed chairs around white-clothed tables on wooden floors, gilt-edged mirrors and open fires. Each of the comfortable, well equipped, light and airy bedrooms has its own sitting area.

🍴 Excellent food using the best local produce might include (in the bar) sandwiches, chargrilled steak burger with chips, lambs liver and bacon with herb butter or scallops fritters with green mayonnaise; and in the dining rooms, pork cheek with potato purée and star anise sauce, crab mousseline with crab bisque sauce, fillet of duck with vanilla apple purée, prunes and toasted almonds, roasted rump of lamb with mini shepherd's pie and red wine sauce, lambs kidneys with bacon and herb butter, and puddings like chocolate and hazelnut torte and crème brûlée. *Benchmark main dish: slow-cooked beef rib tips £12.95. Two-course evening meal £22.00.*

Free house ~ Licensee Philip Burgess ~ Real ale ~ (01822) 820221 ~ Open 11.30-3, 6-11; 12-2.30 Sun; closed Sun evening, winter Mon evening ~ Bar food 12-2.30, 6.45-9.15 ~ Restaurant ~ Children welcome ~ Dogs allowed in bar ~ Bedrooms: /£110 ~ www.dartmoorinn.com *Recommended by R F Sawbridge, Isobel Mackinlay*

The knife-and-fork award 🍴 distinguishes pubs where the food is of exceptional quality.

MARLDON
SX8663 Map 1

Church House 🍴 ♀
Off A380 NW of Paignton; TQ3 1SL

Spreading bar plus several other rooms in this pleasant inn, particularly good food, fine choice of drinks, and seats on three terraces

To find this bustling, neatly kept and warmly welcoming pub, just head for the church. The attractively furnished, spreading bar with its woodburning stove has several areas radiating off the big semicircular bar counter: unusual windows, some beams, dark pine and other nice old dining chairs around solid tables, and yellow leather bar chairs. Leading off here is a cosy little candlelit room with four tables on bare boards, a dark wood dado and stone fireplace. There's also a restaurant with a large stone fireplace and, at the other end of the building, another interesting room split into two parts, with a stone floor in one and a wooden floor (and big woodburning stove) in the other. The old barn holds yet another restaurant with displays by local artists. Dartmoor Best, St Austell Tribute and Teignworthy Gun Dog on handpump, 15 wines by the glass and several malt whiskies; background music. There are picnic-sets on three carefully maintained grassy terraces behind the pub.

 Interesting and rather enticing, the food might include sandwiches, pork, sage and calvados pâté with apple and cider chutney, home-cured salmon gravadlax with dill, honey and mustard, fried whole mackerel with cajun slaw, lentil, leek and red pepper lasagne, corn-fed chicken filled with mozzarella mousse, tomato and bacon, steak and kidney pudding, tiger prawns with basil pesto, sunblush tomato and tagliatelle, and puddings such as spotted dick with home-made rum butter and custard. *Benchmark main dish: slow-roasted lamb shoulder with moroccan tagine £15.75. Two-course evening meal £20.50.*

Enterprise ~ Lease Julian Cook ~ Real ale ~ (01803) 558279 ~ Open 11.30-2.30, 5-11(5.30-11.30 Sat); 12-3, 5.30-10.30 Sun ~ Bar food 12-2(2.30 Sun), 6.30-9.30(9 Sun) ~ Restaurant ~ Children welcome ~ Dogs allowed in bar ~ www.churchhousemarldon.com
Recommended by Damian and Lucy Buxton, B J Harding

MORETONHAMPSTEAD
SX7586 Map 1

Horse
George Street; TQ13 8NF

Enthusiastic licensees for simply furnished town pub, a good choice of drinks, well liked food and mediterranean-style courtyard

Run with great energy and enthusiasm by the charming hands-on landlady – her husband is the chef – this is a simply furnished old pub with a friendly welcome for all. The bar has leather chesterfields and deep armchairs in front of a woodburning stove, all manner of wooden chairs, settles and tables on carpet or wooden floorboards, rustic tools and horse tack alongside military and hunting prints on the walls, a dresser offering home-made cakes and local cider and juice for sale, and stools by the green-planked counter where they serve Dartmoor IPA and Legend and Otter Ale on handpump, a dozen wines by the glass, ten malt whiskies and quite a few coffees. A long light room leads off here and a high-ceilinged barn-like back dining room too. The sheltered inner courtyard has metal tables and chairs – it's popular in warm weather. They hold monthly music events.

🍴 Cooked by the landlord – who also makes his own pastrami, salt beef and bresaola, smokes salmon and scallops and bakes bread daily – the popular food includes interesting sandwiches and paninis, various frittatas, antipasti, tempura cod cheeks with lemon caponata, moules frites, caesar salad with chicken or prawns, tuscan sausage pasta with tomatoes and red wine, chicken and tarragon pie, lamb cassoulet, vegetarian risotto, and puddings such as strawberry granita with white chocolate mousse, strawberry jelly, shortbread and mascarpone and warm chocolate fondant with kirsch cherries. *Benchmark main dish: thin-crust hand-rolled pizzas £10.00. Two-course evening meal £18.00.*

Free house ~ Licensees Nigel Hoyle and Malene Graulund ~ Real ale ~ (01647) 440242 ~ Open 12-midnight; 5-midnight Sun, Mon; closed Sun and Mon lunchtimes ~ Bar food 12.30-2.30, 6.30-9; pizzas only Sun and Mon evenings ~ Restaurant ~ Children welcome ~ Dogs allowed in bar ~ Live folk last Mon of month, blues second Thurs of month ~ www.thehorsedartmoor.co.uk *Recommended by Isobel Mackinlay, Emma Scofield*

PARKHAM
Bell 🍺
SS3821 Map 1

Rectory Lane; EX39 5PL

A proper village pub with chatty locals, welcoming landlord, neatly kept bars, four real ales and well liked food

If you're in need of a generous, pubby meal and a friendly welcome, head for this cheerful thatched village pub. Very much the heart of the community, its three connected rooms are spotlessly kept and full of chatty locals. There are beams and standing timbers hung with horsebrasses, a woodburning stove in the main bar and a small coal fire in the lower one, brass and copper jugs, nice old photos of the pub and the village, a grandfather clock and pubby tables and seats (mate's and other chairs and burgundy or green plush stools) on red patterned carpet. Model ships and lanterns hang above the bar, where there's Cotleigh Barn Owl, Country Life Old Appledore, Otter Ale and Sharps Doom Bar on handpump; darts. The covered back terrace has picnic-sets and fairy lights.

🍴 Honest food at fair prices includes seasonal soup, prawn and avocado salad, rice timbale topped with roast vegetables in tomato and cider sauce, slow-roasted lamb shoulder in red wine and rosemary, baked trout with lemon, turkey breast medallions wrapped in bacon with chestnut and pork stuffing and cranberry sauce, steak and kidney pie, chicken curry and puddings such as blackberry and apple crumble and home-made cheesecake. *Benchmark main dish: chicken breast with blue cheese and crispy bacon £10.95. Two-course evening meal £16.75.*

Free house ~ Licensees Michael and Rachel Sanders ~ Real ale ~ (01237) 451201 ~ Open 12-2.30, 5.30(5 Fri, 6 Sun)-11 ~ Bar food 12-1.30, 6-8.30 ~ Restaurant ~ Children welcome ~ Dogs allowed in bar ~ www.thebellinnparkham.co.uk *Recommended by Richard Tilbrook, Peter Thornton, M and GR, C and R Bromage*

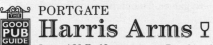

PORTGATE
Harris Arms ♀
SX4185 Map 1

Leave A30 E of Launceston at Broadwoodwidger turn-off (brown sign to Dingle Steam Village) and head S; Launceston Road (old A30 Lewdown–Lifton); EX20 4PZ

Enthusiastic, well travelled licensees in roadside pub with exceptional wine list and interesting food

In warm weather, try to bag a seat among the lavender pots on the heated back decking area – the views of rolling hills are very pretty; plenty of picnic-sets in the sloping garden too. One of the main reasons for coming here is for the carefully chosen wines. Mr and Mrs Whiteman are award-winning wine-makers and around 22 of their favourites are available by the glass with detailed, helpful notes; you can also buy to take home – and they're growing 24 of their own vines. The bar has a woodburning stove, fine photographs, burgundy end walls and cream ones in between, and afghan saddle-bag cushions scattered around a mix of dining chairs and along a red plush built-in wall banquette. On the left, steps lead down to the dining room with elegant beech dining chairs (and more afghan cushions) around stripped-wood tables, and some unusual paintings. Bays Topsail and Otter Bitter on handpump, local cider and Luscombe organic soft drinks; there may be a pile of country magazines.

Using local farmers and producers and artisan cheeses, the enjoyable food includes sandwiches, slow-cooked pork cheeks with sweet potato and mushroom hash with sage and cider sauce, prawns piri-piri, home-cooked ham and eggs, vegetarian shepherd's pie, beer-battered fish and chips, trio of local sausages with mash and onion gravy, fish of the day with creamy white wine sauce, roast breast and confit of duck with plum sauce, and puddings such as orange panna cotta with Cointreau cream and orange sorbet and dark chocolate truffle with pistachio ice-cream. *Benchmark main dish: 24-hour roasted pork £14.50. Two-course evening meal £17.00.*

Free house ~ Licensees Andy and Rowena Whiteman ~ Real ale ~ (01566) 783331 ~ Open 12-3, 6.30-11; 12-3 Sun; closed Sun evening, Mon ~ Bar food 12-2, 6.30-9 ~ Restaurant ~ Well behaved children welcome ~ Dogs allowed in bar ~ www.theharrisarms.co.uk *Recommended by David Jackman, Di and Mike Gillam, N R White, M G Hart*

POSTBRIDGE   SX6780 Map 1

Warren House

B3212 0.75 miles NE of Postbridge; PL20 6TA

Straightforward old pub, relaxing for a drink or meal after a Dartmoor hike

There's plenty of local character in this isolated Dartmoor pub – an invaluable refuge for walkers in poor weather and also something of a focus for the scattered moorland community. The cosy bar is straightforward, with easy chairs and settles under a beamed ochre ceiling, old pictures of the inn on partly panelled stone walls and dim lighting (powered by the pub's own generator); one fireplace is said to have been kept alight almost continuously since 1845. There's also a family room. Adnams Broadside, Otter Ale and Sharps Doom Bar and one or two guests on handpump, local farm cider and malt whiskies; background music, darts and board games. The picnic-sets on both sides of the road have moorland views.

Decent bar food includes sandwiches, pasties, deep-fried breaded king prawns with garlic dip, smoked haddock and spring onion fishcakes with chips, mushroom stroganoff, jumbo sausage and beans, low-braised lamb shank with red wine and rosemary gravy, steak in ale pie, gammon steak with pineapple, cajun chicken, and puddings like fruit crumble with clotted cream and toffee and pecan meringue roulade. *Benchmark main dish: home-made rabbit pie £11.95. Two-course evening meal £15.00.*

Free house ~ Licensee Peter Parsons ~ Real ale ~ (01822) 880208 ~ Open 11-11;
12-10.30 Sun; 11-5 winter Mon, Tues ~ Bar food 12-9(8.30 Sun); 12-4.30 winter Mon,
Tues ~ Restaurant ~ Children in family room only ~ Dogs allowed in bar ~
www.warrenhouseinn.co.uk *Recommended by Robert Watt, Christian Mole*

RATTERY   SX7461   Map 1
Church House
Village signposted from A385 W of Totnes, and A38 S of Buckfastleigh;
TQ10 9LD

**One of Britain's oldest pubs with plenty to look at, a friendly
landlord, good range of drinks and popular bar food; peaceful views**

Our readers enjoy this ancient pub very much, noting in particular
the friendly welcome, prompt service and good food and beer.
Some fine original features include the spiral stone steps behind a little
stone doorway (on your left as you come in), which date from about
1030. Rooms have plenty of character: massive oak beams and standing
timbers in the homely open-plan bar, large fireplaces (one with a cosy
nook partitioned off around it), traditional pubby chairs and tables on
patterned carpet, window seats, and prints and horsebrasses on plain
white walls. The dining room is separated by heavy curtains and there's
a lounge too. Dartmoor Jail Ale and Legend and a beer named for the
pub from Wells & Youngs on handpump, 15 malt whiskies and ten wines
by the glass. The garden has picnic-sets on the large hedged-in lawn,
and peaceful views of partly wooded hills. The original building here
probably housed the craftsmen who built the Norman church, and may
then have served as a hostel for monks.

Quite a choice of good food and nice specials might include up to a dozen
fresh fish dishes (plaice, megrim, bass, monkfish, tuna) as well as duck and
orange pâté, crab cakes with sweet chilli, leek and mushroom stroganoff, ham,
egg and chips, a fry-up, coq au vin, venison and stilton pie, lamb shanks cooked
in citrus and olives, and puddings like french apple tart and bread and butter
pudding. *Benchmark main dish: fresh fish dishes £14.00. Two-course evening
meal £16.00.*

Free house ~ Licensee Ray Hardy ~ Real ale ~ (01364) 642220 ~ Open 11-2.30, 6-11;
12-3, 6-10.30 Sun ~ Bar food 11.30-2, 6.30-9 ~ Restaurant ~ Children welcome ~ Dogs
allowed in bar ~ www.thechurchhouseinn.co.uk *Recommended by Dave Moor, David Eberlin,
B J Harding*

SANDFORD   SS8202   Map 1
Lamb
The Square; EX17 4LW

**Bustling, friendly 16th-c inn with beams and standing timbers, four
real ales and decent wines by the glass, very good food and seats in
garden; well equipped bedrooms**

Now with more emphasis on dining, this charming old village pub
seems more popular than ever and most people now book a table
in advance. It's not a big place and the beamed bar and dining area
are linked, which keeps the atmosphere easy-going and friendly. The
bar has a log fire in a stone fireplace with red leather sofas beside it,
cushioned window seats, a settle and various dining chairs around tables
on patterned carpet; towards the back there's a handsome carved chest,
a table of newspapers and magazines and a noticeboard of local news

and adverts. Dartmoor Jail Ale, Otter Bitter, O'Hanlons Yellowhammer and Teignworthy Reel Ale on handpump, lots of wines by the glass, cocktails and 20 malt whiskies. The dining side has a woodburning stove, a cushioned wall pew, all manner of nice old wooden dining chairs and tables (each with a church candle) and the same heavy beams; the landlord's wife created the large animal paintings (also in the bedrooms). There's also a simpler public bar and a skittle alley that doubles as a cinema. The jack russell is called Tiny, the collie Bob. The informal cobbled garden has fairy lights and simple seats and tables, and there are picnic-sets on grass beyond the hedge. The bedrooms are comfortable, modern and well equipped. Nearby parking is at a premium, but the village car park is a few minutes' walk up the small lane to the right.

They make their own bread and pasta and use some home-grown produce for the sensible short menu of imaginative food: duck liver parfait with red onion marmalade, pigeon spring roll, smoked mushrooms on toast with madeira jus, beef in ale pie, sausages with mash and onion gravy, mixed mushroom tart with goats cheese and roasted garlic purée, roast monkfish and serrano ham with vanilla butter sauce, roasted pheasant and crispy pork belly with butternut squash and pheasant jus, venison with spiced fig tart and celeriac purée, and puddings. *Benchmark main dish: leg and shoulder of lamb with shallot purée and lamb jus £14.50. Two-course evening meal £19.00.*

Free house ~ Licensee Mark Hildyard ~ Real ale ~ (01363) 773676 ~ Open 10.30(11 weekends)-midnight ~ Bar food 12.30-2.15(2.30 Sun), 6.30-9.15(9 Sun) ~ Restaurant ~ Children welcome ~ Dogs welcome ~ Bedrooms: £69/£125 ~ www.lambinnsandford.co.uk *Recommended by Peter Thornton, Michael Coleman, Charles Meade-King*

SIDBURY
Hare & Hounds ◖

SY1496 Map 1

3 miles N of Sidbury, at Putts Corner; A375 towards Honiton, crossroads with B3174; EX10 0QQ

Large, well run roadside pub with log fires, beams and attractive layout, popular daily carvery and a big garden

During high season, booking is essential here as the carvery is so popular. It's a big place with two log fires (and unusual wood-framed leather sofas, complete with pouffes), heavy beams and fresh flowers, red plush-cushioned dining chairs, window seats and leather sofas around plenty of tables on carpeting or bare boards. Otter Bitter and Ale and St Austell Tribute tapped from the cask and several wines by the glass. The newer dining extension, with its central open fire, opens out on to decking; seats here, and picnic-sets in the big garden, have marvellous views down the Sid Valley to the sea at Sidmouth.

As well as the daily carvery, the extensive menu includes sandwiches and baked potatoes, pâté of the day, home-made salmon, broccoli and lemon fishcake, beef or pork burgers with chips, trio of sausages with bubble and squeak and red wine and onion gravy, three-bean chilli, steak and kidney pudding, chicken breast in garlic, mushroom and creamy white wine sauce, fish or turkey and ham pie, curry of the day and puddings. *Benchmark main dish: carvery £9.95. Two-course evening meal £16.00.*

Heartstone Inns ~ Managers Graham Cole and Lindsey Chun ~ Real ale ~ (01404) 41760 ~ Open 10am-11pm ~ Bar food 12-9 ~ Children welcome ~ Dogs allowed in bar ~ www.hareandhounds-devon.co.uk *Recommended by Richard Wyld, George Atkinson, Geri Eld*

SLAPTON

SX8245 Map 1

Tower

Off A379 Dartmouth–Kingsbridge; TQ7 2PN

Bustling inn with friendly young owners, beams and log fires, good beers and wines, and pretty back garden; bedrooms

The picnic-sets on the neat lawn in the pretty garden behind this fine old inn are overlooked by the ivy-covered ruins of a 14th-c chantry. Inside, there's a good mix of customers (including a genuine core of chatty locals) and a relaxed, informal atmosphere. The low-ceilinged beamed bar has armchairs, low-backed settles and scrubbed oak tables on flagstones or bare boards, open log fires, Butcombe Bitter, Otter Bitter, St Austell Proper Job and Sharps Doom Bar on handpump and several wines by the glass; one reader said there was a photograph of a World War II airman who used the pub as his local. Next to the photograph was his cheque book, in a glass case – the last cheque he wrote was to the pub to clear his bar tab. The comfortable bedrooms are reached via an external staircase. The lane to the pub is very narrow, and parking can be tricky at peak times.

As well as lunchtime sandwiches, food includes chicken liver and foie gras parfait, flash-fried squid with tempura tentacles, chorizo and capers, twice-baked cheese soufflé, steak burger with onion relish, tomato, gherkin and fries, local mussels in cider cream broth with chips, bass fillets in vodka batter with tartare sauce, pork chop with black pudding, scotch egg, cassoulet and sauerkraut, and puddings. *Benchmark main dish: local rib of beef with roasted mushroom and tomato (for two) £45.00. Two-course evening meal £20.00.*

Free house ~ Licensee Dan Cheshire ~ Real ale ~ (01548) 580216 ~ Open 12-3, 6-11(10.30 Sun); closed Sun evening in winter ~ Bar food 12-2.30, 6.30-9.30 ~ Children welcome ~ Dogs welcome ~ Bedrooms: £60/£80 ~ www.thetowerinn.com
Recommended by Paul Humphreys

SOUTH POOL

SX7740 Map 1

Millbrook ⑪

Off A379 E of Kingsbridge; TQ7 2RW

Delightful village local by the Salcombe Estuary with local ales, very good food and a warm welcome for all

This charming little creekside pub has a genuinely warm welcome for both locals and visitors and several small beamed bars – all with a chatty, easy-going atmosphere. In the main room is a log fire in an inglenook fireplace, a couple of settles and a blanket box on turkey rugs, daily papers, and stools against the counter where they keep three ales on handpump – Red Rock, one named for the pub and a guest from Otter – and local farm cider. The dining area to the right has a woodburning stove, settles and wheelback chairs around scrubbed wooden tables, with maps, a few old pictures, a barometer and a brass clock on the stone and cream walls; this leads to another small dining area and there's also a simply furnished Top Bar for families. Outside, seats on the terrace overlook the water and there are mooring facilities for small boats. Be prepared for a bit of a squash at weekends. An honesty Veg Shed sells fresh vegetables and local sausages and bacon.

Using the best, local seasonal produce and with some french country dishes, the particularly good food includes potted crab, charcuterie plate, warm duck gizzards, smoked duck, black pudding and duck egg salad, a changing risotto, mixed fried fish, pheasant casserole, rump of lamb with smoked bacon, onion and cheese tartlet and red wine jus, pork tenderloin with chorizo and white haricot bean cassoulet with fresh sage jus, and puddings such as dark chocolate fondant with blueberries and plum and apple crumble with clotted cream; a good cheeseboard and a two- and three-course set lunch. *Benchmark main dish: bouillabaisse £18.00. Two-course evening meal £23.00.*

Free house ~ Licensees Ian Dent and Diana Hunt ~ Real ale ~ (01548) 531581 ~ Open 11-11(10.30 Sun) ~ Bar food 12-2(3 Sun), 7-9; no food winter Mon ~ Restaurant ~ Children welcome ~ Dogs welcome ~ Live jazz, check website for dates ~ www.millbrookinnsouthpool.co.uk *Recommended by Mark Davidson, Caroline Prescott*

 SOUTH ZEAL SX6593 Map 1

Oxenham Arms ⇔

Off A30/A382; EX20 2JT

Wonderful ancient inn with lots to look at, character bars, four real ales, enjoyable food and big garden; bedrooms

First licensed in 1477, this is a marvellous building that has grown up around the remains of a Norman monastery, built to combat the pagan power of the neolithic standing stone that still forms part of the wall in the room behind the bar (there's actually another 6 metres of stone below the floor). The heavily beamed, partly panelled front bar has elegant mullioned windows and Stuart fireplaces, all sorts of chairs and built-in wall seats with scatter cushions around low oak tables on bare floorboards, and stools against the counter where friendly staff serve Dartmoor IPA, Exmoor Fox, Teignworthy Gun Dog and a Red Rock beer named for the pub on handpump; also, wines by the glass and farm cider. A small room has beams, wheelback chairs around polished tables, decorative plates and another open fire. Imposing curved stone steps lead up to the four-acre garden, which has plenty of seats and fine views; there are also seats under parasols out in front. Charles Dickens, snowed up one winter, wrote a lot of *The Pickwick Papers* here. You can walk straight from the door on to the moor.

Good food includes toasted panini, breaded garlic mushrooms with sour cream and chive dip, smoked haddock, horseradish and dill fishcake with aioli, sharing platters, wild mushroom, stilton and pearl barley risotto, burgers (lamb, chicken, vegetarian) with fries, liver and bacon with mustard mash and red onion jus, ham and egg, venison steak with port and blueberry jus and dauphinoise potatoes, tiger prawn and clam linguine with tomato, chilli and rosemary sauce, and puddings; they also do takeaway fish and chips 6-9pm daily. *Benchmark main dish: beer-battered fish and chips £10.50. Two-course evening meal £16.00.*

Free house ~ Licensees Simon and Lyn Powell ~ Real ale ~ (01837) 840244 ~ Open 12-3, 6-11(10.30 Sun); 12-11 summer Sat ~ Bar food 12-3, 6-9 ~ Restaurant ~ Children welcome ~ Dogs allowed in bar ~ Regular live folk and jazz ~ Bedrooms: £105/£135 ~ www.theoxenhamarms.com *Recommended by David and Stella Martin*

Real ale to us means beer that has matured naturally in its cask – not pressurised or filtered. We name all real ales stocked. We usually name ales preserved under a light blanket of carbon dioxide too, though purists – pointing out that this stops the natural yeasts developing – would disagree (most people, including us, can't tell the difference!).

SPARKWELL

SX5857 Map 1

Treby Arms 🍴

Off A38 at Smithaleigh, W of Ivybridge, Sparkwell signed from village;
PL7 5DD

* *

Devon Dining Pub of the Year

Little village pub offering delicious food, real ales and a friendly welcome

Since the landlord Anton Piotrowski became *MasterChef* joint winner in 2012, this little village pub has really taken off – and the food is exceptional. On our visit, numerous customers dropped in hoping for a free table but without luck: you do need to book in advance. A small bar area (about to be extended as we went to press), used by locals for a pint and a chat, has stools against the counter, a woodburning stove in a stone fireplace flanked by shelves of cookery books and guidebooks, a built-in cushioned window seat, dining chairs around four tables, and tankards named for regulars hanging from a beam. Dartmoor Jail Ale and St Austell Tribute on handpump and several good wines by the glass from a list with helpful notes, served by friendly, competent staff. Off to the right is the dining room, with another woodburning stove, old glass and stone bottles on the mantelpiece and captain's and wheelback chairs around rustic tables; an upstairs carpeted dining area has similar furnishings. The sunny front terrace has seats and tables.

🍴 As well as nibbles such as mini fish and chips, the accomplished food includes summer sandwiches, black pudding scotch egg with onion purée, bacon popcorn and sun-dried tomatoes, smoked eel and white crab salad with chorizo jam and brown crab mayonnaise, baked brie with carrot purée, ale carrots, asparagus and wild garlic, white wine-battered haddock with chip-shop treats, stinging nettle and hazelnut-crusted john dory with pea purée and tartare hollandaise, pigeon with parsley root purée, game fritter with wild mushrooms and baby turnips, and puddings such as chocolate caramel, digestive biscuit, banana purée, banana parfait and yuzu (a japanese citrus fruit) foam and cardamom panna cotta with cinnamon ice-cream, coconut biscuit and tropical salsa. *Benchmark main dish: pork fillet wrapped in parma ham, black pudding scotch egg, slow-roasted pork belly and herby hogs pudding with apple sauce and mustard mash £22.00. Two-course evening meal £27.00.*

Free house ~ Licensees Anton and Clare Piotrowski ~ Real ale ~ (01752) 837363 ~ Open 12-3, 6-11; 12-11 Sat; 12-10.30 Sun; closed Mon ~ Bar food 12-2, 6-9; 12-2.30, 6-8 Sun ~ Restaurant ~ Children welcome ~ Dogs allowed in bar ~ www.thetrebyarms.co.uk
Recommended by Martin and Pauline Jennings, Brian and Maggie Woodford

SPREYTON

SX6996 Map 1

Tom Cobley 🍺

Dragdown Hill; W out of village; EX17 5AL

Huge range of quickly changing real ales and ciders in friendly and busy village pub; quite a choice of food too; bedrooms

The fantastic range of up to 14 real ales on handpump or tapped from the cask continues to draw lots of cheerful customers to this friendly, family-run village inn. Changing daily beers might include Country Life Black Boar, Dartmoor Jail Ale, Holsworthy Tamar Black, Otter Ale, St Austell Proper Job and Tribute and Skinners Betty Stogs, and they also keep up to 14 real ciders including perries and quite a range of malt whiskies. The comfortable little bar has straightforward pubby furnishings, an open fire and local photographs, country scenes and prints of Tom Cobley (who was born in the village) on the walls. There's also a large back dining room with beams and background music, and seats in the tree-shaded garden and by the quiet street in front. Some of the good value bedrooms have shared facilities.

🍴 A wide choice of popular food includes sandwiches, toasties, pasties, breaded garlic mushrooms with mayonnaise, pâté with hot buttered toast, omelettes, mushroom and red pepper stroganoff, thai cod and prawn fishcakes with sweet chilli sauce, ham, egg and chips, liver with bacon and onions, cumberland sausage with mash and onion gravy, steak and kidney pudding, southern fried chicken breasts with home-made coleslaw, lamb shank in red wine and rosemary sauce, half duck in orange sauce and puddings. *Benchmark main dish: home-made pies £9.95. Two-course evening meal £16.50.*

Free house ~ Licensees Roger and Carol Cudlip ~ Real ale ~ (01647) 231314 ~ Open 12-3, 6(6.30 Mon)-11(1am Fri, Sat); 12-4, 7-11 Sun; closed Mon lunchtime ~ Bar food 12-2, 7-9 ~ Restaurant ~ Children welcome ~ Dogs allowed in bar ~ Bedrooms: £40/£60 ~ www.tomcobleytavern.co.uk *Recommended by Peter Thornton, Mrs P Sumner, Dr A McCormick, Jeremy Whitehorn*

STAVERTON   SX7964   Map 1

Sea Trout 🍴 🛏

Village signposted from A384 NW of Totnes; TQ9 6PA

Hard-working, enthusiastic licensees in bustling village inn, real ales, enjoyable food and seats in garden; comfortable bedrooms

With lots to do and see nearby, it makes sense to stay in the well equipped and comfortable bedrooms at this very well run, partly 15th-c inn; rooms overlook the garden or the country lane, and the breakfasts are good. There's fishing on the nearby River Dart (packages for fishermen include accommodation and daily permits). The neatly kept and rambling beamed lounge bar has fishing flies and stuffed fish on the walls, and elegant wheelback armchairs around a mix of wooden tables on the part-carpeted, part-wooden floor. The simpler locals' bar has wooden wall and other seats, a stag's head, gun and horsebrasses on the walls, a large stuffed fish in a cabinet above a woodburning stove, and a cheerful mix of locals and visitors. Palmers Copper Ale, Dorset Gold and 200 on handpump and nine wines by the glass. The panelled restaurant and conservatory are both furnished with smart high-backed fabric-covered dining chairs around wooden tables. There are seats in the terraced garden, and they are kind to dogs with treats and water bowls dotted about.

🍴 The enjoyable, enterprising food might include lunchtime sandwiches, confit duck with sautéed sprouts, chestnuts and feta and port wine jus, stir-fried szechuan prawns and broccoli, wild mushroom and leek risotto, sausage and mash with shallot and smoked bacon sauce, lamb curry, confit pork belly, pork tenderloin stuffed with mushroom, sun-dried tomato and goats cheese and parsnip purée, brill fillet with warm salad of bacon, green beans, artichoke and new potatoes with salsa verde, and puddings such as lemon-topped panna cotta with home-made orange shortbread and warm chocolate brownie with warm chocolate sauce and vanilla ice-cream. *Benchmark main dish: salmon and mushroom wellington £13.95. Two-course evening meal £19.00.*

Palmers ~ Tenants Jason and Samantha Price ~ Real ale ~ (01803) 762274 ~ Open 8am-11pm ~ Bar food 12-2(2.30 Sat), 6-9(9.30 Fri, Sat); 12-3, 7-9 Sun ~ Restaurant ~

Children welcome ~ Dogs allowed in bar and bedrooms ~ Bedrooms: £65/£102 ~
www.seatroutinn.co.uk *Recommended by Michael Coleman, Lynda and Trevor Smith, Sara Fulton, Roger Baker, Richard and Patricia Jefferson, Will Palmer, David Jackman, Paul Humphreys*

TIPTON ST JOHN   SY0991   Map 1
Golden Lion
Pub signed off B3176 Sidmouth–Ottery St Mary; EX10 0AA

Friendly village pub with three real ales, well liked bar food, a good mix of customers and plenty of seats in an attractive garden

In warm weather, sitting outside this busy village pub is most enjoyable. There are seats on the terracotta-walled terrace with outside heaters and grapevines and more seats on the grass, edged by pretty flowering borders. There's a verandah for dog walkers and smokers, and jazz on Sunday evenings in summer. The interior is cheerful too. The main bar, split into two, has a comfortable, relaxed atmosphere, as does the back snug, and throughout are paintings by west country artists, art deco prints, Tiffany lamps and, hanging from the beams, hops, copper pots and kettles. A few tables are kept for those just wanting a pint and a chat. Bass and Otter Ale and Bitter on handpump and a dozen wines by the glass; maybe background music and cards.

 Popular food includes lunchtime sandwiches, moules marinière, home-smoked duck salad with onion marmalade, ham and egg, vegetable lasagne, beer-battered cod and chips, steak and kidney pudding, slow-braised lamb shank, chicken basque, steak frites, duck breast with oriental plum sauce and puddings. *Benchmark main dish: chunky fish soup £7.75. Two-course evening meal £20.50.*

Heavitree ~ Tenants François and Michelle Teissier ~ Real ale ~ (01404) 812881 ~ Open 12-2.30, 6-11; 12-3 Sun; closed Sun evening ~ Bar food 12-2, 6.30-8.30 ~ Children welcome ~ Live jazz summer evenings, check website for dates ~ www.goldenliontipton.co.uk *Recommended by George Atkinson, Gene and Tony Freemantle*

TORBRYAN   SX8266   Map 1
Old Church House
Pub signed off A381; TQ12 5UR

Ancient inn with original features in neat rooms, friendly service and popular food and beer

It's well worth negotiating the narrow lanes (plenty of passing places) to reach this warmly friendly 13th-c inn. The particularly attractive bar on the right is neatly kept and bustling, with benches built into the fine old panelling as well as a cushioned high-backed settle and leather-backed small seats around a big log fire. On the left is a series of comfortable and discreetly lit lounges, one with a splendid deep Tudor inglenook fireplace with a side bread oven; background music. Hunters Pheasant Plucker, Skinners Betty Stogs, St Austell Tribute and changing guest on handpump, several wines by the glass and around 35 malt whiskies; good service. There's live music on Thursday evenings. Some of the comfortable bedrooms have their own sitting room and one has a woodburning stove; breakfasts are good.

Using produce bought over the farm gate or from the local butcher, the fairly priced, tasty food includes sandwiches, garlic mushrooms with white wine and cream, salmon and prawn fishcakes with thai sweet chilli, lasagne, duck with black cherry and orange jus, haddock mornay with creamy cheese sauce, steak in ale pie, chicken with bacon, port and stilton cream sauce, pork escalope with onions, mushrooms and a brandy, madeira and cream sauce, and puddings; Tuesday is curry night. *Benchmark main dish: pork belly with star anise sauce £8.95. Two-course evening meal £15.00.*

Free house ~ Licensees Kane and Carolynne Clarke ~ Real ale ~ (01803) 812372 ~ Open 11-11 ~ Bar food 12-2, 7-9 ~ Restaurant ~ Children welcome away from bar ~ Live folk Sun evening and regular acoustic guitar ~ Bedrooms: £54/£89 ~ www.oldchurchhouseinn.co.uk *Recommended by David and Angela George, M G Hart*

TORQUAY   SX9265   Map 1

Cary Arms ⏍ ⇋

Beach Road: off B3199 Babbacombe Road, via Babbacombe Downs Road; turn steeply down near Babbacombe Theatre; TQ1 3LX

Interesting bar in secluded hotel with lovely sea views, plenty of outside seating, enjoyable if not cheap food, real ales and friendly service; sea-view bedrooms

The marvellous sea views over Babbacombe Bay and the surrounding cliffs can be enjoyed from picnic-sets on the terraces in front of this unusual and rather charming higgledy-piggledy place, from good quality teak chairs and tables on gravel, and from the big windows in the bar. Steps lead down to the quay, there's a little raised platform with just one table and a few chairs (much prized in good weather), an outside bar, a barbecue and a pizza oven. Inside, the beamed, grotto-effect bar has rough pink granite walls, alcoves, rustic hobbit-style red leather cushioned chairs around carved wooden tables on slate or bare boards, an open woodburning stove with a ship's wheel above, and some high bar chairs beside the stone bar counter. Bays Topsail and Otter Ale on handpump, local cider and decent wines by the glass; cheerful young staff. There's also a small, glass-enclosed entrance room with large ship lanterns and cleats; darts and board games. The civilised boutique-style hotel is a pretty special place to stay, and children and dogs are made extremely welcome; they also have four self-catering properties. There are six moorings and they can arrange a water taxi for guests arriving by boat. The lane down to the hotel is tortuously steep and not for the faint-hearted.

As well as interesting specials such as rabbit terrine with fig compote, local mussels in white wine, cream and shallots, cod fillet with pesto mash and mussel chowder or guinea fowl with chicken mousse and thyme and wild mushroom sauce, the inventive food might include goats cheese panna cotta with balsamic tomatoes, chicken, mushroom and tarragon terrine with red onion jam, crab salad with wholegrain mustard mayonnaise, baked risotto cake with brie, peppers, artichokes and cumberland dressing, and puddings like plum and almond tart with raspberry sorbet and iced white chocolate parfait. *Benchmark main dish: steak and mushroom in ale pie £14.95. Two-course evening meal £22.00.*

Free house ~ Licensee Matt Collins ~ Real ale ~ (01803) 327110 ~ Open 12-11 ~ Bar food 12-3, 6-9.30 ~ Children welcome ~ Dogs allowed in bar and bedrooms ~ Bedrooms: £175/£275 ~ www.caryarms.co.uk *Recommended by Comus and Sarah Elliott, Len Beattie, Dr and Mrs A K Clarke*

The price we give for a two-course evening meal in the featured entries is the mean (average of cheapest and most expensive) price of a starter and a main course – no drinks.

TOTNES
SX8059   Map 1

Steam Packet

St Peters Quay, on W bank (ie not on Steam Packet Quay); TQ9 5EW

Seats outside overlooking quay, attractive layout and décor inside, and well liked food and drink; bedrooms

After a walk along the riverbank, this popular place is perfect for a drink or a meal. It's interestingly laid out with bare stone walls, wooden flooring, an open log fire at one end, a squashy leather sofa with lots of cushions against a wall of books, a similar seat built into a small curved brick wall (which breaks up the room) and a TV. The main bar has built-in wall benches and plenty of stools and chairs around traditional pub tables, and another area has a coal fire and dark wood furniture. Dartmoor Jail Ale, Sharps Doom Bar and a guest from Hunters named for the pub on handpump and several wines by the glass. The conservatory restaurant has high-backed leather dining chairs around wooden tables, and smart window blinds. In warm weather, try to grab a seat on the front terrace overlooking the River Dart. If the little car park is full, there's a pay-and-display nearby.

Good quality food includes sandwiches, panini toasties, ham hock terrine with cider apple chutney, salmon and sweet chilli fishcakes with raita, gammon with free-range eggs, halloumi, roasted red pepper and tomato tagliatelle, steak burger with bacon, cheese and fries, beer-battered fish and chips, lamb rump with roasted garlic and red wine jus, and puddings such as lemon posset with shortbread and sticky toffee pudding with toffee sauce and clotted cream. *Benchmark main dish: slow-roasted belly pork with bubble and squeak and apple and cider gravy £12.95. Two-course evening meal £17.50.*

Buccaneer Holdings ~ Manager Richard Cockburn ~ Real ale ~ (01803) 863880 ~ Open 11-11; 12-10.30 Sun ~ Bar food 12-2.30(3 Sat), 6-9.30; 12-8 Sun ~ Restaurant ~ Children welcome ~ Dogs allowed in bar ~ Live folk Tues 9pm ~ Bedrooms: £75/£95 ~ www.steampacketinn.co.uk *Recommended by Gary Bloyce, Roger and Donna Huggins, Keith and Sandra Ross, Dave Webster, Sue Holland, N R White*

WIDECOMBE
SX7276   Map 1

Rugglestone

Village at end of B3387; pub just S – turn left at church and NT church house, OS Sheet 191 map reference 720765; TQ13 7TF

Unspoilt local near busy tourist village, with a couple of bars, cheerful customers, friendly staff, four real ales and traditional pub food

'A hidden gem' is how one reader describes this charming little pub – and it really is just that. It's up the road from the busy tourist village of Widecombe and in complete contrast to the busy comings and goings there. The unspoilt bar has just four tables, a few window and wall seats, a one-person pew built into the corner by a nice old stone fireplace (with a woodburner) and a good mix of customers. The rudimentary bar counter dispenses Butcombe Bitter, Dartmoor Legend and a couple of guests like Otter Bright and Teignworthy Gun Dog tapped from the cask; local farm cider and a decent small wine list. The room on the right is slightly bigger and lighter in feel, with beams, another stone fireplace, stripped-pine tables and a built-in wall bench; there's also a small dining room. There are seats in the field across a little moorland stream, and tables and chairs in the garden. A holiday cottage is for rent.

🍴 Generously served food includes sandwiches, chicken liver pâté, smoked duck with chutney and bread, cheese and spinach cannelloni, pasties, ham and eggs, beer-battered fresh haddock with chips, burger with cheese and bacon, beef in ale pie, baked trout with lemon and garlic, and puddings. *Benchmark main dish: fish pie £10.50. Two-course evening meal £16.00.*

Free house ~ Licensees Richard and Vicki Palmer ~ Real ale ~ (01364) 621327 ~ Open 11.30-3, 6-11.30(5-midnight Fri); 11.30am-midnight Sat; 12-11 Sun ~ Bar food 12-2, 6-9 ~ Restaurant ~ Children allowed away from bar area ~ Dogs welcome ~ www.rugglestoneinn.co.uk *Recommended by Michael Coleman, Andrea Rampley, Nigel and Sue Foster, John and Gloria Isaacs, Julie and Bill Ryan*

WINKLEIGH   SS6308   Map 1

Kings Arms

Fore Street; off B3220 Crediton–Torrington; EX19 8HQ

Friendly pub with woodburning stoves in beamed main bar, west country beers and popular food

This thatched village pub usefully serves food all day and there are always customers (locals and visitors) popping in and out. The cosy beamed main bar has the most character with its old-fashioned built-in wall settles and benches around scrubbed pine tables on flagstones, and a woodburning stove in a cavernous fireplace. Another woodburning stove separates the bar from the green- and red-painted dining rooms (one has military memorabilia and a glass-covered old mine shaft). Butcombe Bitter, Otter Bitter and Sharps Doom Bar on handpump and two local ciders; board games. There are seats in the garden.

🍴 Food might include sandwiches, afternoon cream teas, ham and egg, fish and chips, lambs liver and bacon, and puddings like lemon meringue roulade or sticky toffee pudding. *Two-course evening meal £20.00.*

Enterprise ~ Licensees Denis and Cheryl MacDonald ~ Real ale ~ (01837) 83384 ~ Open 11-11; 12-10.30 Sun ~ Bar food all day; may not serve food winter afternoons if quiet ~ Restaurant ~ Children welcome ~ Dogs allowed in bar ~ www. thekingsarmswinkleigh.co.uk *Recommended by John & Judy Phillips, Michael Coleman*

WOODBURY SALTERTON   SY0189   Map 1

Diggers Rest 🍴

3.5 miles from M5 junction 30: A3052 towards Sidmouth, village signposted on right about 0.5 miles after Clyst St Mary; also signposted from B3179 SE of Exeter; EX5 1PQ

Bustling village pub with real ales, well liked food, and country views from the terraced garden

In a quiet little village with many nearby walks around Woodbury Common, the Otter Valley and Sidmouth Hills coastline, this ancient thatched pub offers good beers and highly enjoyable food. The main bar has antique furniture, local art and a cosy seating area by an open fire. The light and airy modern extension opens on to the garden, which has contemporary garden furniture under canvas parasols on the terrace, and lovely countryside views. Bays Topsail and Otter Ale and Bitter on handpump, 13 wines by the glass and Weston's cider; service is attentive and efficient. Background music, darts, TV and board games. The window boxes and flowering baskets are pretty.

🍴 Using local seasonal (and often organic) produce, the enterprising food includes nice nibbles like cajun-spiced honey roast nuts and home-made pork scratchings, sandwiches and wraps, local mussels with garlic, white wine, shallots and cream, peking duck terrine with cucumber ribbons and spring onions, moroccan vegetable and chickpea tagine with spiced couscous and mint crème fraîche, chicken breast with confit wing, sweetcorn fritter, smoked bacon crumb and barbecue sauce, beer-battered fish and chips, pork belly and crispy rib with caramelised apple and confit new potatoes, and puddings such as lemon tart with lime, basil and blackcurrant sorbet and rhubarb sponge and custard. *Benchmark main dish: steak in ale pie £10.95. Two-course evening meal £18.50.*

Heartstone Inns ~ Licensee Ben Thomas ~ Real ale ~ (01395) 232375 ~ Open 11-3, 5.30-11; 12-3.30, 5.30-10.30 Sun ~ Bar food 12-2, 6-9(8.30 Sun) ~ Restaurant ~ Children welcome ~ Dogs allowed in bar ~ Live music, check website for dates ~ www.diggersrest.co.uk *Recommended by John Evans, Rich Frith*

Also Worth a Visit in Devon

Besides the fully inspected pubs, you might like to try these pubs that have been recommended to us and described by readers. Do tell us what you think of them: feedback@goodguides.com

ABBOTSKERSWELL   SX8568
Court Farm   (01626) 361866
Wilton Way; look for the church tower; TQ12 5NY Attractive neatly extended 17th-c longhouse tucked away in picturesque hamlet, various rooms off long beamed and paved main bar, good mix of furnishings, well priced popular food from sandwiches to steaks, friendly helpful staff, several ales including Bass and Otter, farm cider and decent wines, woodburners; background music, pool and darts; children welcome, picnic-sets in pretty lawned garden, open all day. *(Anon)*

APPLEDORE   SS4630
⚹ Beaver   (01237) 474822
Irsha Street; EX39 1RY Relaxed harbourside pub with good well priced food especially fresh local fish, nice home-made puddings too, prompt friendly service, good choice of west country ales, farm cider, decent house wines and great range of whiskies, lovely estuary view from popular raised dining area, some live music including jazz; pool in smaller games room, TV; children and dogs welcome, disabled access (but no nearby parking), tables on small sheltered water-view terrace. *(Derek and Sylvia Stephenson, Paul Bonner)*

ASHWATER   SX3895
Village Inn   (01409) 211200
Overlooking village green; EX21 5EY Roomy and well decorated slate-floored pub with relaxed friendly atmosphere, wide choice of good generous food from sandwiches up, efficient service, well kept Dartmoor and a guest, good sensibly priced wine, dining room, conservatory with venerable grapevine, pool room;

background music; children welcome, terrace tables. *(Garry Talbot, Carolyn Davies, John and Bernadette Elliott)*

BAMPTON   SS0520
⚹ Exeter Inn   (01398) 331345
A396 some way S, at B3227 roundabout; EX16 9DY Long low roadside pub, stone-built with several updated linked rooms, mainly flagstoned, two log fires and woodburner, large restaurant, wide choice of good generous food at sensible prices including plenty of fresh fish, friendly efficient service, up to six well kept ales tapped from the cask, decent coffee, daily papers; children and dogs welcome, disabled facilities, tables out in front, ten bedrooms, fairly handy for Knightshayes (NT), open all day. *(Anon)*

BAMPTON   SS9622
Quarrymans Rest   (01398) 331480
Briton Street; EX16 9LN Bustling village pub, sold as we went to press; beamed and carpeted main bar, leather sofas in front of woodburner in inglenook, dining chairs and some housekeeper's chairs around wooden tables, four west country ales, steps up to comfortable stripped-stone dining room with high-backed leather chairs and heavy pine tables; pool and games machines; children and dogs welcome, picnic-sets in pretty back garden, more seats in front, three bedrooms, open all day. *(Anon)*

BAMPTON   SS9522
Swan   (01398) 332248
Station Road; EX16 9NG Refurbished beamed village pub with spacious bare-boards bar, woodburners in two inglenooks, three changing local beers and good home-made food, efficient service; bedrooms. *(Anon)*

BANTHAM   SX6643
✳ **Sloop** (01548) 560489
Off A379/B3197 NW of Kingsbridge;
TQ7 3AJ Friendly 14th-c pub close to fine
beach and walks, good mix of customers
in black-beamed bar with stripped-stone
walls and flagstones, country chairs and
tables, woodburner, well kept St Austell and
a guest ale, enjoyable reasonably priced
food from good sandwiches to fresh fish,
efficient service even when busy, restaurant;
background music; children and dogs
welcome, seats out at back, five bedrooms,
open all day in summer. *(B J Harding, Lynda*
and Trevor Smith, Jane and Rowena Leverington,
Theocsbrian, Michael Doswell, Roy Hoing and
others)

BARNSTAPLE   SS5533
Panniers (01271) 329720
Boutport Street; EX31 1RX Centrally
placed Wetherspoons (close to Panniers
market), busy and reliable, with good range
of beers and decent food served by swift
pleasant staff; open all day. *(Derek and Sylvia*
Stephenson)

BEER   ST2289
Anchor (01297) 20386
Fore Street; EX12 3ET Friendly sea-view
dining pub with wide choice of enjoyable
food including good local fish, Greene King
and Otter, good value wines, coffee, rambling
open-plan layout with old local photographs,
large eating area; sports TV, background
music; children well looked after, lots of
tables in attractive clifftop garden over road,
delightful seaside village, reasonably priced
bedrooms. *(Simon Pyle)*

BEER   SY2289
Dolphin (01297) 20068
Fore Street; EX12 3EQ Hotel's comfortable
old-fashioned lounge bar with oak panelling
and interesting nooks, old distorting mirrors,
nautical bric-a-brac and antique boxing
prints, long public bar (open all day) with
darts, pool and machines, well kept ales
such as Bays, Cotleigh, Fullers and Skinners,
decent wine and coffee, enjoyable food
including fresh local fish (scallops and bacon
the signature dish), friendly service, large
back restaurant; background and some live
music; children and dogs welcome, sunny
back terrace, 22 bedrooms. *(Anon)*

BELSTONE ·   SX61293
Tors (01837) 840689
A mile off A30; EX20 1QZ Small family-
run Victorian granite pub-hotel in peaceful
Dartmoor-edge village, long carpeted bar
divided by settles, well kept ales such as
Dartmoor and Sharps, over 50 malt whiskies
and good choice of wines, enjoyable well
presented food from sandwiches to specials,
cheerful prompt service, restaurant; children
and dogs welcome, disabled access, seats

out on nearby grassy area overlooking valley,
good walks, bedrooms, open all day
in summer. *(Chris and Angela Buckell)*

BERE FERRERS   SX4563
Old Plough (01822) 840358
Long dead-end road off B3257 S of
Tavistock; PL20 7JL 16th-c pub with
stripped stone and panelling, low beam-and-
plank ceilings, slate flagstones and open
fires, enjoyable good value food, well kept
Sharps Doom Bar and a couple of guests,
farm cider, warm local atmosphere, steps
down to cosy restaurant; garden overlooking
estuary, secluded village. *(Michael Coleman)*

BERRYNARBOR   SS5546
Olde Globe (01271) 882465
Off A399 E of Ilfracombe; EX34 9SG
Rambling dimly lit rooms geared to family
visitors (cutlasses, swords, shields and rustic
oddments), good choice of reasonably priced
straightforward food, real ales, friendly
service, games area – and genuine age
behind the trimmings, with ancient walls
and flagstones, high-backed oak settles
and antique tables, lots of old pictures;
background music; children looked after
well, dogs welcome, paved front terrace, play
area, pretty village. *(Anon)*

BIDEFORD   SS4526
Kings Arms (01237) 475196
The Quay; EX39 2HW Cheerful old-
fashioned 16th-c pub with Victorian
harlequin floor tiles in alcovey front bar,
friendly staff, well kept west country ales
and reasonably priced pubby food all day,
back raised family area; background music;
dogs welcome, tables out on pavement, three
bedrooms, handy for Lundy ferry. *(Derek and*
Sylvia Stephenson)

BISHOP'S TAWTON   SS5629
✳ **Chichester Arms** (01271) 343945
Signed off A377 outside Barnstaple;
East Street; EX32 0DQ Friendly 15th-c
cob-and-thatch pub, good generous well
priced food from baguettes to fresh local fish
and seasonal game, quick obliging service
even when crowded, St Austell Tribute,
Wells & Youngs Bombardier and a guest,
decent wines, heavy low beams, large stone
fireplace, restaurant; children welcome,
disabled access not good but staff very
helpful, picnic-sets on front terrace and in
back garden, open all day. *(David Fletcher)*

BRANDIS CORNER   SS4103
Bickford Arms (01409) 221318
A3072 Hatherleigh–Holsworthy;
EX22 7XY Friendly 17th-c beamed village
pub restored after devastating 2003 fire;
wide choice of enjoyable locally sourced
food cooked to order, west country ales and
farm cider, log fires, restaurant; well
behaved children welcome if eating, garden
with circular picnic-sets, attractive

countryside, five comfortable bedrooms, good breakfast. *(J V Dadswell)*

BRAYFORD — SS7235
★ Poltimore Arms (01598) 710381
Yarde Down; 3 miles towards Simonsbath; EX36 3HA Unspoilt 17th-c beamed local – so remote it generates its own electricity – freshened up under present licensees, popular home-made food from local produce (best to book), well kept Skinners Betty Stogs and a guest tapped from the cask, basic traditional furnishings, fine woodburner in inglenook, interesting ornaments and murals, two attractive restaurant areas separated by another woodburner; children and dogs welcome, picnic-sets in side garden, closed Sun evening, Mon; up for sale as we went to press, so things may change. *(Andrew Scott)*

BRENDON — SS7648
Staghunters (01598) 741222
Leedford Lane; EX35 6PS Idyllically set family-run hotel with gardens by East Lyn river, good choice of enjoyable reasonably priced food, well kept Cotleigh and Exmoor ales, friendly efficient staff, bar with woodburner, restaurant; can get very busy, though quiet out of season; walkers and dogs welcome, riverside tables, 12 good value bedrooms. *(Peter Farman, Bob and Margaret Holder)*

BRIXHAM — SX9256
Blue Anchor (01803) 859373
Fore Street/King Street; TQ5 8AH Harbourside pub of some character, up to four well kept real ales, banquettes, plenty of nautical hardware, log fire, enjoyable food from good sandwiches to bargain Sun lunch in two small dining rooms (one a former chapel down steps) with interesting old photographs, friendly staff, regular live music; dogs welcome, open all day. *(Paul Humphreys)*

BRIXHAM — SX9256
Crown & Anchor (01803) 853570
The Quay; TQ5 8AW Cosy old fishermen's pub with good choice of local ales and two real ciders, lots of trawler pictures; dogs welcome, a few seats outside overlooking harbour. *(Eddie Edwards)*

BRIXHAM — SX9256
★ Maritime (01803) 853535
King Street (up steps from harbour – nearby parking virtually non-existent); TQ5 9TH Single bar packed with bric-a-brac, chamber-pots hanging from beams, hundreds of key fobs, cigarette cards, pre-war ensigns, toby jugs, mannequins, astronomical charts, even a binnacle by the door, friendly long-serving landlady, Bays Best and Hunters Half Bore and Pheasant Plucker, over 80 malt whiskies, no food or credit cards, lively terrier called George and Mr Tibbs the

parrot (watch your fingers); background music, small TV, darts and board games; well behaved children and dogs allowed, fine views over harbour, six bedrooms sharing bathroom, closed lunchtime. *(Anon)*

BROADCLYST — SX9997
New Inn (01392) 461312
Wimple Road; EX5 3BX Friendly former farmhouse with stripped bricks, boarded ceiling, low doorways and log fires, well cooked reasonably priced pubby food, local ales including Otter, small restaurant, skittle alley; children welcome, garden with play area. *(Cedric Robertshaw)*

BROADCLYST — SX9897
Red Lion (01392) 461271
B3121, by church; EX5 3EL Extended 16th-c pub with heavy beams, flagstones and log fires, four real ales, enjoyable traditional food including seasonal game in bar and carpeted restaurant, friendly service, stone-walled sun room; children welcome and dogs (menu for them), picnic-sets on front cobbles below wisteria, more in small enclosed garden across quiet lane, nice village and church, not far from Killerton (NT), six bedrooms, open all day weekends. *(David and Stella Martin)*

BROADHEMBURY — ST1004
Drewe Arms (01404) 841267
Off A373 Cullompton–Honiton; EX14 3NF Extended partly thatched family-run pub dating from the 15th c; carved beams and handsome stone-mullioned windows, woodburner and open fire, furniture perhaps not matching age of building, modernised dining room, four local real ales, pubby food including Thurs early-bird offer, skittle alley; terrace seats, more on lawn under trees, nice setting near church in pretty village, open all day. *(Dr Peter Crawshaw)*

BUCKFAST — SX7467
Abbey Inn (01364) 642343
Buckfast Road off B3380; TQ11 0EA On a sunny day, best to arrive early to get a terrace table overlooking the River Dart; partly panelled bar with woodburner, St Austell ales and local cider, decent reasonably priced food from sandwiches to blackboard specials, big dining room with more panelling and river views; background music; children and dogs welcome, bedrooms, open all day; for sale as we went to press. *(B J Harding)*

BUDLEIGH SALTERTON — SY0681
Feathers (01395) 442042
High Street; EX9 6LE Popular old town-centre pub with good mix of customers; long beamed room with nice bustling local atmosphere, well kept St Austell Tribute and three west country guests, good well presented/priced food (not Sun evening) from sandwiches up, more intimate softly lit

dining lounge, friendly hard-working staff; children and dogs welcome, four bedrooms, open all day. *(N R White, S Holder)*

BURGH ISLAND   SX6444
Pilchard   (01548) 810514

300 metres across tidal sands from Bigbury-on-Sea; walk, or summer Sea Tractor (unique bus on stilts) if tide's in; TQ7 4BG Sadly, the splendid beamed and flagstoned upper bar with its lanterns and roaring log fire is reserved for locals and guests at the associated flamboyantly art deco hotel, but the more utilitarian lower bar is still worth a visit for the unbeatable setting high above the sea swarming below this tidal island; well kept Sharps, Thwaites Lancaster Bomber and an ale brewed for the pub, local farm cider, good local oysters and lunchtime baguettes, Fri curry night; dogs welcome, tables outside, some down by beach. *(J F M and M West)*

BUTTERLEIGH   SS9708
Butterleigh Inn   (01884) 855433

Off A396 in Bickleigh; EX15 1PN Small-roomed heavy-beamed country pub, friendly and relaxed, with enjoyable reasonably priced food (not Mon) including Sun carvery, four real ales and good choice of wines, two big fireplaces, back dining room; children welcome, picnic-sets in large garden, four comfortable bedrooms, closed Mon lunchtime and winter Sun evening. *(John and Alison Hamilton, Jeremy Whitehorn)*

CADELEIGH   SS9107
✳ Cadeleigh Arms   (01884) 855238

Village signed off A3072 W of junction with A396 Tiverton–Exeter at Bickleigh; EX16 8HP Attractive old pub now owned by the local community, well kept Cotleigh, Dartmoor, St Austell and a guest, fresh locally sourced food (not Sun evening, Mon) from favourites up, Thurs curry night, carpeted room on left with bay-window seat and ornamental stove, flagstoned room to the right has high-backed settles and log fire in big fireplace, airy dining room down a couple of steps with valley views, local artwork, games room (pool and darts) and skittle alley; background music; children and dogs welcome, picnic-sets on gravel terrace with barbecue, more on gently sloping lawn, closed Mon lunchtime. *(Jeremy Whitehorn)*

CALIFORNIA CROSS   SX7053
California   (01548) 821449

Brown sign to pub off A3121 S of A38 junction; PL21 0SG Neatly modernised 18th-c or older dining pub with beams, panelling, stripped stone and log fire, wide choice of food from baguettes to steaks in dining bar and family area, restaurant menu, popular Sun lunch (best to book), sofa in small separate snug, St Austell Tribute, Sharps Doom Bar and a local guest, farm cider and decent wines by the glass;

background music; dogs welcome, attractive garden and back terrace, open all day. *(B J Harding, S Holder, M G Hart)*

CHAGFORD   SX7087
Ring o' Bells   (01647) 432466

Off A382; TQ13 8AH Welcoming old pub with beamed and panelled bar, four well kept ales including Dartmoor, traditional fairly priced home-made food, good friendly service, woodburner in big fireplace, some live music; dogs and well behaved children welcome, sunny walled garden, nearby moorland walks, four bedrooms, open all day. *(Anon)*

CHAGFORD   SX7087
Three Crowns   (01647) 433444

High Street; TQ13 8AJ Comfortably refurbished 13th-c stone and thatched inn (former manor house), big dimly lit bar with large fireplace, separate dining room, well kept St Austell ales, enjoyable food from sandwiches and good ploughman's up, efficient pleasant service; courtyard tables, bedrooms. *(Anon)*

CHALLACOMBE   SS6941
Black Venus   (01598) 763251

B3358 Blackmoor Gate–Simonsbath; EX31 4TT Low-beamed 16th-c pub with friendly helpful staff, two well kept changing ales, Thatcher's farm cider, enjoyable fairly priced food from sandwiches to popular Sun lunch, pews and comfortable chairs, woodburner and big fireplace, roomy and attractive dining area, games room with pool and darts; children welcome, garden tables, play area, lovely countryside and good walks from the door. *(Andrew Scott, Mrs P Abell)*

CHUDLEIGH   SX8679
Bishop Lacey   (01626) 854585

Fore Street, just off A38; TQ13 0HY Unpretentious and interesting partly 14th-c low-beamed church house, cheerful obliging staff and character locals, well kept St Austell Dartmoor and changing west country microbrews, farm cider, reasonably priced home-made food, log fires, dark décor, two bars and dining room; live bands in next-door offshoot; children welcome, garden tables, good value bedrooms, open all day. *(Anon)*

CHURCHSTOW   SX7145
Church House   (01548) 852237

A379 NW of Kingsbridge; TQ7 3QW Dating from the 13th c and well cared for by friendly licensees, heavy black beams and stripped stone, wide choice of enjoyable home-made food including popular evening carvery (Weds-Sat, booking advised), good local ales and decent wines, back conservatory with floodlit well; children welcome, dogs in certain areas, tables on big terrace. *(Tim and Joan Wright, B J Harding)*

CLAYHIDON ST1615

Half Moon (01823) 680291

On main road through village; EX15 3TJ
Attractive old village pub with warm friendly
atmosphere, wide choice of enjoyable home-
made food, well kept Otter and a couple of
guests, farm cider, good wine list, comfortable
bar with inglenook log fire, some live music;
children and dogs welcome, picnic-sets in
tiered garden over road, valley views. *(Anon)*

CLOVELLY SS3225

New Inn (01237) 431303

*High Street; car-free village, visitors
charged £6.50 (£4 children) to park and
enter; EX39 5TQ* Quaint peaceful 17th-c inn
halfway down steep cobbled street, arts-and-
crafts décor, simple lower bar with flagstones
and bric-a-brac (narrow front part has more
character than back eating room), well kept
Sharps Cornish Coaster and a beer brewed
for the pub by local Country Life, short choice
of good value bar food, upstairs restaurant;
great views, small garden behind, good
bedrooms. *(Anon)*

CLOVELLY SS3124

Red Lion (01237) 431237

The Quay; EX39 5TF Rambling 18th-c
building in lovely position on curving quay
below spectacular cliffs, beams, flagstones
and interesting local photographs in character
back bar (dogs on leads allowed here),
well kept ales such as Sharps Doom Bar,
bar food and upstairs restaurant; efficient
service; great views, 11 simple attractive
bedrooms. *(David and Gill Carrington)*

CLYST HYDON ST0201

Five Bells (01884) 277288

*W of village, just off B3176 not far from
M5 junction 28; EX15 2NT* Uncertain
plans for this popular thatched and beamed
pub after the licensees left and it was run
by a management company before closing;
big draw has been the immaculate cottagey
garden with its thousands of spring and
summer flowers and country views; inside
had several different seating areas, open fires
and lots of china, copper and brass; should
have reopened by the time you read this –
news please.

COCKINGTON SX8963

Drum (01803) 690264

Cockington Lane; TQ2 6XA Cheerfully
bustling Vintage Inn in thatched and
beamed tavern (designed by Lutyens to
match the quaintly touristy Torquay-edge
medieval village), Butcombe and St Austell,
good choice of wines by the glass, roomy
well divided wood-floor bar with open fires
and family eating areas, decent food, good
service; tables on terrace and in attractive
back garden by 500-acre park, open all day.
(Richard Hale)

COCKWOOD SX9780

★ Ship (01626) 890373

Off A379 N of Dawlish; EX6 8NU
Comfortable traditional 17th-c pub
overlooking estuary and harbour (gets
very busy in season); good value freshly
made food including good fish dishes and
puddings, Thurs pie night, Butcombe and
Sharps Doom Bar, friendly staff and locals,
partitioned beamed bar with big log fire and
ancient oven, decorative plates and seafaring
memorabilia, small restaurant; background
music; children and dogs welcome, nice
steep-sided garden. *(Adrian Johnson)*

COLYFORD SY2592

★ Wheelwright (01297) 552585

*Swan Hill Road (A3052 Sidmouth–
Lyme Regis); EX24 6QQ* Spacious 17th-c
thatched dining pub; bar with red leather
armchairs and a chesterfield, farmhouse
chairs and tables on stripped boards,
interesting knick-knacks, woodburner,
Badger ales and well liked seasonal food, two
dining rooms with high rafters and a snug
room just right for small group of friends, a
further big back dining area with chandelier
made of wine glasses, small gift shop;
children and dogs (in bar) welcome, plenty
of seats outside, open all day, sister pub to
the Harbour at Axmouth. *(Barry and Monica
Jones, Patrick and Daphne Darley)*

COMBE MARTIN SS5747

Dolphin (01271) 883424

Seaside; EX34 0AW Well placed one-room
pub with nice beach views, good friendly
staff, well kept Sharps Doom Bar and a
summer guest, freshly made tasty food, good
log fire, upstairs restaurant (not used out of
season); children and dogs welcome, back
terrace. *(Stephen and Judith Thomas)*

COMBE MARTIN SS5846

Pack o' Cards (01271) 882300

High Street; EX34 0ET Unusual 'house
of cards' building built in the late 17th c to
celebrate a big gambling win – four floors,
13 rooms and 52 windows; snug bar area
and various side rooms, St Austell, Sharps
and Timothy Taylors kept well, enjoyable
inexpensive pub food including children's
choices and good Sun roast, restaurant;
pretty riverside garden with play area,
six comfortable bedrooms, generous
breakfast. *(Ian Herdman)*

COMBEINTEIGNHEAD SX9071

★ Wild Goose (01626) 872241

*Off unclassified coast road Newton
Abbot–Shaldon, up hill in village;
TQ12 4RA* Rambling pub with up to seven
real ales in spacious back beamed lounge,
wheelbacks and red plush dining chairs,
agricultural bits and pieces, pubby food, front
bar with more beams, standing timbers and
some flagstones, step down to area with big

old fireplace and another cosy room with comfortable sofa and armchairs, bar billiards, darts and board games, delicatessen; background music (live Fri), games machine, TV; children in dining area only, dogs in bar, garden with nice country views. *(Comus and Sarah Elliott)*

COUNTISBURY   SS7449
Blue Ball 01598 741263
A39, E of Lynton; EX35 6NE Beautifully set rambling heavy-beamed pub, friendly licensees, good range of generous local food in bar and restaurant, three ales including one named for the pub, decent wines and proper ciders, handsome log fires; background music; children, dogs and walkers welcome, views from terrace tables, good nearby cliff walks (pub provides handouts of four circular routes), comfortable bedrooms, open all day. *(Lynda and Trevor Smith, Mr and Mrs D J Nash)*

CREDITON   SS8300
Crediton Inn (01363) 772882
Mill Street (follow Tiverton sign); EX17 1EZ Small friendly local with long-serving landlady, well kept O'Hanlons Yellow Hammer and up to nine quickly changing guests (Nov beer festival), cheap well prepared weekend food, home-made scotch eggs other times, back games room/skittle alley, open all day Mon-Sat. *(Anon)*

DARTINGTON   SX7861
Cott (01803) 863777
Cott signed off A385 W of Totnes, opposite A384 turn-off; TQ9 6HE Long 14th-c thatched pub with heavy beams, flagstones, nice mix of old furniture and two inglenooks (one with big woodburner), good home-made locally sourced food from traditional choices up in bar and restaurant, three ales including local Hunters and Greene King, Ashridge cider, nice wines by the glass, good service, live music Sat evening; children and dogs welcome, wheelchair access (with help into restaurant), picnic-sets in garden and on pretty terrace, five comfortable bedrooms, open all day. *(Charles Trevor-Roper, Paul Humphreys, John Evans)*

DARTMOUTH   SX8751
✴Cherub (01803) 832571
Higher Street; walk along river front, right into Hauley Road and up steps at end; TQ6 9RB Handsome timbered building (Dartmouth's oldest) with two heavily timbered upper floors jutting over the street and many original interior features, oak beams, leaded lights, tapestried seats and big stone fireplace with photo of pub ghost above; Otter, St Austell, Sharps Doom Bar and one or two guests in bustling bar, low-ceilinged upstairs restaurant, good food from pubby favourites to more imaginative dishes (not Mon or Tues evenings in winter),

efficient friendly service; background music, no children; dogs in bar, open all day in summer, closed winter afternoons Mon-Thurs. *(Steve and Liz Tilley, Alun and Jennifer Evans, Dave Webster, Sue Holland, Barrie Fischer, Roger and Donna Huggins, Simon Lindsey, Rose Rogers)*

DARTMOUTH   SX8751
Dartmouth Arms (01803) 832903
Lower Street, Bayard's Cove; TQ6 9AN Friendly local with tables out in prime harbour-wall spot overlooking estuary (Pilgrim Fathers set sail from here), well kept Otter and Sharps Doom Bar, enjoyable bar food, panelling and boating memorabilia, log fire; open all day. *(Dave Webster, Sue Holland)*

DARTMOUTH   SX8751
Dolphin (01803) 833698
Market Street; TQ6 9QE Interesting building in picturesque part of town, quirky and laid-back, with own Bridgetown beer (brewed in Totnes) and St Austell Tribute, good food including well priced fish platters, friendly staff; background and some live music; children and dogs welcome, open all day. *(Mrs Jo Rees, Bob and Margaret Holder)*

DAWLISH   SX9676
Smugglers (01626) 862301
A379 towards Teignmouth; EX7 0LA Roadside pub with views over the sea, decent choice of food including good daily carvery, St Austell and Sharps Doom Bar, friendly attentive staff; children welcome, open all day. *(Quentin and Carol Williamson)*

DITTISHAM   SX8654
Ferry Boat (01803) 722368
Manor Street; best to park in village car park and walk down; TQ6 0EX Cheerful riverside pub with lively mix of customers; beamed bar with log fires and straightforward pubby furniture, lots of boating bits and pieces, tide times chalked on wall, flags on ceiling, at least three ales such as Dorset, Otter and Sharps, a dozen wines by the glass, good range of home-made food including pie of the day and curries; background and some live music; children and dogs welcome, moorings for visiting boats on adjacent pontoon and bell to summon ferry, good walks, open all day. *(Lynda and Trevor Smith, Tim and Joan Wright, David and Sue Atkinson)*

DREWSTEIGNTON   SX7390
Drewe Arms (01647) 281224
Off A30 NW of Moretonhampstead; EX6 6QN This pretty thatched pub closed as we went to press – news please.

EAST ALLINGTON   SX7648
Fortescue Arms (01548) 521215
Village signed off A381 Totnes–Kingsbridge, S of A3122 junction; TQ9 7RA Pretty village pub under new

family management; two-room bar with mix of wooden tables and chairs on black slate floor, some brewery memorabilia, Dartmoor and a local guest ale, eight wines by the glass, restaurant with own bar, Farrow & Ball paintwork and high-backed dining chairs around painted tables, interesting well presented food from bar snacks up; background music; children and dogs welcome, seats at the front with more on sheltered terrace, open all day during school holidays (at other times open all day weekends, closed Mon). *(Anon)*

EAST PRAWLE   SX7836
Pigs Nose (01548) 511209
Prawle Green; TQ7 2BY Relaxed and quirky three-room 16th-c pub with low beams and flagstones, local ales tapped from the cask, farm ciders, enjoyable simple pubby food, lots of interesting bric-a-brac and pictures, mix of old furniture, jars of wild flowers and candles on tables, open fire, small family area with unusual toys, pool and darts, friendly dogs (others welcome – even a menu for them); unobtrusive background music, hall for live bands (friendly landlord was 1960s tour manager); tables outside, pleasant spot on village green. *(David Jackman)*

EXETER   SX9292
Chaucers (01392) 422365
Basement of Tesco Metro, High Street; EX4 3LR Steps down to this large, dimly lit olde-worlde-style pub-bistro-wine bar; beamed low ceiling and timber-framed walls, wood floors, several levels with booths and alcoves, comfortable furnishings, Marstons-related ales and well priced wines (plenty by the glass), cocktails, enjoyable good value food from snacks to specials, quick friendly service; background music, silent games machines, no under-14s; open all day (till 4pm Sun). *(George Atkinson, Jeremy King)*

EXETER   SX9390
Double Locks (01392) 256947
Canal Banks, Alphington, via Marsh Barton Industrial Estate; EX2 6LT Unchanging, unsmart and individual, by ship canal, remote yet busy, Wells & Youngs and guests, farm cider in summer, all-day bar food; background music, live at weekends; children and dogs welcome, seats out on grass or decking with distant view to city and cathedral (nice towpath walk out, or hire a canoe at the Quay), big play area, summer barbecues, camping, open all day. *(Anon)*

EXETER   SX9192
Fat Pig (01392) 437217
John Street; EX1 1BL Popular refurbished Victorian corner pub, welcoming and relaxed, with focus on dining, good food from daily changing blackboard menu using local produce (some from owner's farm), ales such as Exeter, decent ciders and good wine choice, light and airy stripped-pine interior with nice fire, small conservatory-style room, Mon quiz; tables in heated courtyard. *(Mike Gorton, Phil Bryant)*

EXETER   SX9193
Great Western (01392) 274039
St David's Hill; EX4 4NU Nine well kept changing ales, including some rarities, in this large commercial hotel's well worn-in plush-seated bar, friendly efficient staff, fresh good value pubby food from sandwiches up (kitchen also supplies hotel's restaurant), daily papers; may be background music, sports TV, pay parking; children and dogs welcome, 35 bedrooms, open all day. *(Peter Thornton)*

EXETER   SX9292
✳ Hour Glass (01392) 258722
Melbourne Street; off B3015 Topsham Road; EX2 4AU Old-fashioned corner local (notable for its unusual rounded shape) with enjoyable surprisingly inventive food including vegetarian, well kept ales such as Adnams, Exeter and St Austell, good range of wines by the glass, comfortable atmosphere (fine for meeting friends or a lone visit), beams and nice mix of furnishings, dark red walls, open fire in small brick fireplace; background music; children away from bar and dogs welcome (resident cats), open all day Fri-Sun, closed Mon lunchtime. *(Jeremy Whitehorn*

EXETER   SX9193
✳ Imperial (01392) 434050
New North Road (above St David's Station); EX4 4AH Impressive 19th-c mansion in own six-acre hillside park with sweeping drive, various areas including two clubby little side bars, fine old ballroom with elaborate plasterwork and gilding, light and airy former orangery with unusual mirrored end wall, interesting pictures, up to 14 real ales, standard good value Wetherspoons menu; can get very busy and popular with students; plenty of picnic-sets in grounds and elegant garden furniture in attractive cobbled courtyard, open all day. *(Dr and Mrs A K Clarke, Tony and Wendy Hobden)*

EXETER   SX9292
Old Fire House (01392) 277279
New North Road; EX4 4EP Compact relaxed city-centre pub in Georgian building behind high arched wrought-iron gates, up to eight ales including Otter (regular beer festivals), several real ciders and good choice of bottled beers and wines, bargain food including late evening pizzas, friendly efficient staff, dimly lit beamed rooms with simple furniture; background music, live folk and jazz weekends, popular with young crowd in evening; picnic-sets in front courtyard, open all day till late. *(Anon)*

EXETER SX9292
Prospect (01392) 273152
The Quay (left bank, near rowing club); EX2 4AN Early 19th-c pub in good quayside position, well kept ales such as Exmoor, Otter and St Austell, friendly efficient young staff, usual food, plenty of comfortable tables including raised river-view dining area, rather cavernous, sparsely furnished back part; background and live music; children welcome, tables out by historic ship-canal basin, open all day. *(Phil Bryant)*

EXETER SX9293
Rusty Bike (01392) 214440
Howell Road; EX4 4LZ Comfortably refurbished backstreet pub with bistro feel (same owners as Fat Pig in John Street), pine tables on stripped boards in large open bar, big black and white photographs, adjoining dining area, four changing ales, farm cider and good wine choice, well liked interesting blackboard food, good service, broad mix of customers including students; background music; walled beer garden with projector for live sport and film nights, limited parking. *(Mike Gorton, Jo McCreedie)*

EXETER SX9292
Ship (01392) 272040
Martins Lane, near cathedral; EX1 1EY Pretty 14th-c heavy-beamed building with olde-worlde city pub style, Greene King, St Austell and Sharps, popular bargain food all day, comfortable upstairs restaurant; background music and machines. *(P and J Shapley, Neil and Anita Christopher)*

EXETER SX9292
Well House (01392) 223611
Cathedral Yard (attached to Royal Clarence Hotel); EX1 1HB Good position with big windows looking across to cathedral in partly divided open-plan bar, good choice of west country ales, real cider, quick service, enjoyable food from hotel's kitchen, lots of Victorian prints, daily papers, Roman well below (can be viewed when pub not busy), live music (last Sun of month), beer/cider festivals; open all day. *(Phil and Jane Villiers)*

EXMOUTH SY9980
Grove (01395) 272101
Esplanade; EX8 1BJ Roomy Victorian pub set back from beach, traditional furnishings, caricatures and local prints, enjoyable pubby food all day including local fish specials, friendly staff, Wells & Youngs and guests kept well, decent house wines, attractive fireplace at back, sea views from appealing upstairs dining room and balcony; background music, live jazz first Sun of month; children

welcome, picnic-sets in front garden. *(Roger and Donna Huggins)*

EXTON SX9886
Puffing Billy (01392) 877888
Station Road/Exton Lane; EX3 0PR Well laid out brightly decorated dining pub, spacious and comfortable, with good modern cooking using local ingredients, beers such as Bath, Bays and Otter and good wine choice in bar extension, friendly service; gets busy weekends; tables out at front and in secluded garden, on the Topsham-Exmouth trail. *(Peter and Anne Hollindale, J D O Carter)*

GEORGEHAM SS4639
Kings Arms (01271) 890240
B3231 (Chapel Street) Croyde–Woolacombe; EX33 1JJ Welcoming comfortably updated pub with red walls, slate floors and some leather sofas by big woodburner, good freshly cooked food using local ingredients, efficient friendly service, St Austell ales and a guest from green-painted bar, good choice of wines, upstairs dining area with tables out on sunny balcony, some traditional pub games; background and live music; children and dogs welcome, small front terrace screened from road, open all day. *(Stephen Shepherd)*

HARTLAND SS2524
Hart 01237 441474
The Square; EX39 6BL Village pub with good freshly made food including nice fish and several vegetarian options, ales such as Sharps and Skinners, reasonably priced wines. *(Nick and Nikki Wright)*

HATHERLEIGH SS5404
George (01837) 810454
A386 N of Okehampton; Market Street; EX20 3JN Completely rebuilt after original 15th-c thatched and timbered pub burnt down in 2008; old-style interior with lots of reclaimed timbers and other old materials, mix of furniture (some new) on carpet, wood and tiled floors, open fires, good range of enjoyable home-made food, well kept beers and nice coffee, good friendly staff; bedrooms. *(Ryta Lyndley, John Marsh)*

HOLBETON SX6150
Dartmoor Union (01752) 395078
Off A379 W of A3121 junction; Fore Street; PL8 1NE Under new ownership; civilised and relaxed bare-boards bar with leather sofas and armchairs by open fire, nice food here or in back restaurant, beers such as Sharps Doom Bar, good friendly staff; dogs welcome in bar area, open all day Sun, closed Mon, lunchtime Tues. *(Lynda and Trevor Smith)*

Though we don't usually mention it in the text, most pubs
will now make coffee or tea – it's always worth asking.

HOLSWORTHY   SS3304
Rydon Inn (01409) 259444
Rydon (A3072 W); EX22 7HU
Comfortably extended dining pub under
newish family management, clean and
tidy, with enjoyable food and well kept ales
such as Dartmoor and Sharps, good service;
children welcome, disabled facilities, fine
country views from conservatory and well
tended garden. *(Ryta Lyndley)*

HONITON   ST1599
Heathfield (01404) 45321
Walnut Road; EX14 2UG Ancient
thatched and beamed pub in contrasting
residential area, well run and spacious,
with Greene King ales and good value
reliable food from varied menu including
the Heathfield Whopper (20oz rump steak),
Sun carvery, cheerful prompt service,
skittle alley; children welcome, seven
bedrooms. *(Bob and Margaret Holder)*

HONITON   SY1198
✳ Holt (01404) 47707
High Street, W end; EX14 1LA
Charming little pub run by two brothers,
relaxed and informal, with just one room
downstairs, chunky tables and chairs on slate
flooring, brown leather sofas, coal-effect
woodburner, shelves of books, shuttered
windows, the whole range of Otter beers (the
family founded the brewery), bigger brighter
upstairs dining room with similar furniture
on pale floorboards, attractive musician
prints, very good tapas and other inventive
food, friendly service; background music;
well behaved children welcome, dogs in bar,
music festival four times a year, closed Sun,
Mon. *(Comus and Sarah Elliott, Richard Wyld,
Chris Johnson, Guy Vowles)*

HOPE COVE   SX6740
Hope & Anchor (01548) 561294
Tucked away by car park; TQ7 3HQ
Bustling unpretentious inn, friendly and
comfortably unfussy, in lovely seaside spot,
good open fire, quick helpful service, good
value straightforward food including lots of
fish, well kept St Austell Dartmoor and a beer
named for the pub, reasonably priced wines,
flagstones and bare boards, dining room
views to Burgh Island, big separate family
room; background music; children and dogs
welcome, sea-view tables out on decking,
great coast walks, bedrooms, good breakfast,
open all day. *(Anon)*

HORNS CROSS   SS3823
✳ Hoops (01237) 451222
*A39 Clovelly–Bideford, W of village;
EX39 5DL* Pretty thatched inn with good
bustling atmosphere; traditionally furnished
bar has china hanging from beams, log fires
in sizeable fireplaces and some standing
timbers and partitioning, more formal
restaurant with attractive mix of tables

and chairs, some panelling, exposed stone
and another open fire, Hoops Bitter (from
Country Life) and Hoops Best and Light
(from Forge), over a dozen wines by the
glass, fairly straightforward locally sourced
food; may be background music; children and
dogs welcome, picnic-sets under parasols in
enclosed courtyard, more seats on terrace
and in two acres of gardens, well equipped
bedrooms, open all day. *(Richard and Penny
Gibbs, C and R Bromage)*

HORSEBRIDGE   SX4074
✳ Royal (01822) 870214
*Off A384 Tavistock–Launceston;
PL19 8PJ* Dimly lit ancient local with
dark half-panelling, log fires, slate floors,
scrubbed tables and interesting bric-a-
brac, good reasonably priced home-made
food including plenty of fish, friendly
landlord and staff, well kept Dartmoor, St
Austell and Skinners poured from the cask,
Rich's farm cider, café-style side room; no
children in evening; picnic-sets on front
and side terraces and in big garden, quiet
rustic spot by lovely old Tamar bridge,
popular with walkers and cyclists.
(Giles and Annie Francis, Peter Thornton)

IDE   SX8990
✳ Poachers (01392) 273847
*3 miles from M5 junction 31, via A30;
High Street; EX2 9RW* Nice beamed inn
in quaint village, good home-made food,
Branscombe Vale Branoc and four changing
west country guests from ornate curved
wooden bar, non-standard mix of old chairs
and sofas, big log fire, restaurant; tables
in pleasant garden with barbecue, three
comfortable bedrooms, open all day (till late
Fri, Sat). *(Anon)*

IDEFORD   SX8977
✳ Royal Oak (01626) 852274
2 miles off A380; TQ13 0AY
Unpretentious 16th-c thatched and
flagstoned village local, friendly helpful
service, Courage and guests, basic pub
snacks, navy theme including interesting
Nelson and Churchill memorabilia, beams,
panelling and big open fireplace; children
and dogs welcome, tables out at front and by
car park over road, closed Mon. *(Anon)*

ILFRACOMBE   SS5247
George & Dragon (01271) 863851
Fore Street; EX34 9ED Oldest pub here
(14th c), handy for harbour, clean and
comfortable with friendly local atmosphere,
ales such as Exmoor, Shepherd Neame and
Skinners, decent wines, traditional home-
made food including local fish, attractive
décor with stripped stone, beams, open
fireplaces, lots of ornaments, china etc, no
mobile phones; background music, quiz
nights, can get busy at weekends; dogs
welcome, open all day. *(Anon)*

ILFRACOMBE SS5247
Ship & Pilot (01271) 863562
Broad Street, off harbour; EX34 9EE
Bright yellow pub near harbour with friendly
mix of regulars and visitors, nine real ales
(six cask-tapped) including Exmoor, Otter
and Wizard, local cider and perry, no food
apart from rolls, traditional open-plan
interior with lots of old photos, darts and
juke box; a couple of TVs; tables outside,
open all day. *(N R White)*

ILSINGTON SX7876
Carpenters Arms (01364) 661629
Old Town Hill; TQ13 9RG Pretty, unspoilt
18th-c local next to church in quiet village,
beams and flagstones, county-style pine
furniture, brasses, woodburner, enjoyable
generous home-made food and well kept
changing ales, friendly atmosphere, darts;
children, well behaved dogs and muddy boots
welcome, tables out at front, good walks,
open all day weekends. *(David Jackman)*

INSTOW SS4730
Boat House (01271) 861292
Marine Parade; EX39 4JJ Airy modern
high-ceilinged place with huge tidal beach
just across lane and views to Appledore, well
kept ales and decent wines, wide choice of
good food including plenty of fish/seafood,
friendly prompt service, lively family bustle;
background music; roof terrace. *(Anon)*

INSTOW SS4730
Wayfarer (01271) 860342
Lane End; EX39 4LB Unpretentious
locals' pub tucked away near dunes and
beach, well kept ales tapped from the cask,
winter mulled wine, good choice of enjoyable
generous home-made food using local fish
and meat, quick cheerful service; children
and dogs welcome, enclosed garden behind,
six well presented bedrooms (some with sea
view), open all day. *(Anon)*

KILMINGTON SY2798
★Old Inn (01297) 32096
A35; EX13 7RB Thatched 16th-c pub,
beams and flagstones, welcoming licensees
and nice bustling atmosphere, enjoyable good
value food using local supplies, well kept
ales such as Butcombe, Cotleigh and Otter,
good choice of wines, small character front
bar with traditional games (also a skittle
alley), back lounge with leather armchairs by
inglenook log fire, small restaurant; children
welcome, beer gardens. *(C and R Bromage,
Robert Watt)*

KINGSBRIDGE SX7343
Crabshell (01548) 852345
*Embankment Road, edge of town;
TQ7 1JZ* Great waterside position,
charming when tide is in, with lovely views
from big windows and outside tables,
emphasis on food including good fish and

seafood, nice crab sandwiches too, friendly
staff, well kept local Quercus ales, feature
open fire; children welcome, open all day.
(Anon)

KINGSBRIDGE SX7344
Dodbrooke Inn (01548) 852068
*Church Street, Dodbrooke (parking some
way off); TQ7 1DB* Small terraced pub in
residential area with long-serving licensees,
traditional bar with décor to match – plush
stools, built-in cushioned stall seats, some
horse harnesses, old local photographs and
china jugs, log fire, Bass, Bath Gem and
Sharps Doom Bar, local cider, honest food in
simple dining room; some reader concerns
over housekeeping; children over 5 welcome,
dogs in bar, courtyard with covered eating
area, closed Mon and Tues lunchtimes.
(DHV, John and Gloria Isaacs)

KINGSWEAR SX8851
★Ship (01803) 752348
Higher Street; TQ6 0AG Attractive old
beamed local by the church, plenty of
atmosphere and kind friendly service, well
kept Adnams, Otter, Wadworths and guests
from horseshoe bar, farm cider, nice wines,
well liked food including good fresh fish (best
views from restaurant up steps), nautical
bric-a-brac and local photographs, tartan
carpets and two log fires, occasional live
music; big-screen sports TV; dogs welcome,
a couple of river-view tables outside, open
all day Fri-Sun and in summer (when it can
get very busy). *(D W Stokes, Alun and Jennifer
Evans, Dave Webster, Sue Holland, Nicky Lee,
David and Sue Atkinson)*

LAKE SX5288
★Bearslake (01837) 861334
A386 just S of Sourton; EX20 4HQ
Rambling low thatched stone pub, leather
sofas and high bar chairs on crazy-paved
slate floor at one end, three more smallish
rooms with woodburners, toby jugs, farm
tools and traps, stripped stone, well kept
Otter and Teignworthy, good range of spirits
and whiskies, decent wines and enjoyable
food, beamed restaurant; children allowed,
large sheltered streamside garden, Dartmoor
walks, six comfortably olde-worlde bedrooms,
generous breakfast. *(Anon)*

LANDSCOVE SX7766
Live & Let Live (01803) 762663
*SE end of village by Methodist church;
TQ13 7LZ* Friendly open-plan local
with good freshly made food, ales such
as Teignworthy Gun Dog, log fire; decked
terrace, more tables in small orchard across
lane, good walks, closed Mon. *(J D O Carter)*

LIFTON SX3885
★Arundell Arms (01566) 784666
Fore Street; PL16 0AA Good interesting
lunchtime food in substantial country-
house fishing hotel, warmly welcoming and

individual, with rich décor, nice staff and sophisticated service, good choice of wines by the glass, morning coffee with home-made biscuits, afternoon tea, restaurant; also adjacent Courthouse bar, complete with original cells, doing good fairly priced pubby food (not Mon evening), well kept St Austell Tribute and Dartmoor Jail; can arrange fishing tuition, also shooting, deer-stalking and riding; 21 refurbished bedrooms, useful A30 stop. (A E Forbes)

LITTLEHAM   SS4323
Crealock Arms (01237) 477065

W edge of village, signed; EX39 5HN
Friendly extended pub in lovely tucked-away village, good range of reasonably priced food and well kept beers, comfortably refurbished bar and dining room; pool, darts and TV; children welcome, disabled facilities, garden with nice views. (Ryta Lyndley)

LOWER ASHTON   SX8484
Manor Inn (01647) 252304

Ashton signposted off B3193 N of Chudleigh; EX6 7QL Well run country pub under friendly hard-working licensees, good quality sensibly priced food including lunchtime set menu, well kept ales such as Dartmoor and Teignworthy, good choice of wines, open fires in both bars, back restaurant in converted smithy; dogs welcome, disabled access, garden picnic-sets with nice rural outlook, open all day Sun, closed Mon. (Mike Gorton)

LUPPITT   ST1606
★ **Luppitt Inn** (01404) 891613

Back roads N of Honiton; EX14 4RT
Unspoilt basic farmhouse pub tucked away in lovely countryside, an amazing survivor, with chatty long-serving landlady, tiny room with corner bar and a table, another not much bigger with fireplace, cheap Otter tapped from the cask, intriguing metal puzzles made by a neighbour, no food or music, lavatories across the yard; closed lunchtime and Sun evening. (Anon)

LUTON   SX9076
★ **Elizabethan** (01626) 775425

Haldon Moor; TQ13 0BL Charming low-beamed dining pub once owned by Elizabeth I; wide choice of good well presented food including popular Sun lunch, five well kept ales and several reasonably priced wines by the glass, friendly efficient service, thriving atmosphere; pretty front garden. (Anon)

LYDFORD   SX5184
Castle Inn (01822) 820241

Off A386 Okehampton–Tavistock; EX20 4BH Tudor inn owned by St Austell, friendly helpful staff, traditional twin bars with big slate flagstones, bowed low beams and granite walls, four inglenook log fires, notable stained-glass door, good popular food (all day Thurs-Sun), restaurant; sheltered

beer garden, lovely nearby NT river gorge, open all day. (M G Hart)

LYMPSTONE   SX9884
Swan (01395) 272644

The Strand, by station entrance; EX8 5ET Well cared for pub with nice old-fashioned décor, split-level panelled dining area with leather sofas by big fire, good generously served home-made food including fresh local fish and Sun roasts, well kept ales such as Otter, Palmers, St Austell and Wadworths, short interesting wine list, may be winter mulled cider, welcoming helpful staff, games room with pool, Sun live music; children welcome, picnic-sets out at front, smokers' area, popular with cyclists (bike racks provided), open all day. (Andrew Abbott, J D O Carter, George Atkinson, Mrs Jo Rees, Christian Pilling, Peter Salmon and others)

LYNMOUTH   SS7249
Rising Sun (01598) 753223

Harbourside; EX35 6EG Wonderful position overlooking harbour; bustling beamed and stripped-stone bar, four Exmoor ales, popular food from comprehensive menu with emphasis on fish, good fire, upmarket hotel side with attractive restaurant; background music; dogs welcome, bedrooms in cottagey old thatched building stepped up hills, gardens behind, parking can be a problem – expensive by day, sparse at night. (Lynda and Trevor Smith, Taff Thomas)

MEAVY   SX5467
★ **Royal Oak** (01822) 852944

Off B3212 E of Yelverton; PL20 6PJ Partly 15th-c pub taking its name from 800-year-old oak tree on opposite village green; heavy-beamed L-shaped bar with church pews, red plush banquettes, old agricultural prints and church pictures, smaller locals' bar with flagstones and big open-hearth fireplace, separate dining room, well liked food using local beef and lamb, Dartmoor ales and guests, farm ciders, a dozen wines by the glass and several malt whiskies, cribbage and board games; background music; children in lounge bar only, dogs in bar, picnic-sets out in front and on green, pretty Dartmoor-edge village, open all day summer, all day weekends winter. (Martin Roberts)

MILTONCOMBE   SX4865
★ **Who'd A Thought It** (01822) 853313

Village signed off A386 S of Yelverton; PL20 6HP Attractive 16th-c whitewashed pub; black-panelled bar with interesting bric-a-brac, woodburner, barrel seats and high-backed winged settles, two separate dining areas, good home-made food from pub favourites up using local produce including own pork, friendly efficient staff, Sharps Doom Bar and three other west country ales, farm ciders, decent choice of wines; background music; children and dogs welcome, a few tables out in front, more in back beer garden with stream, flaming torches may light your way from the car park on summer nights, two bedrooms in converted hayloft, open all day weekends in summer (all day Sun winter). *(Jan Gould)*

MOLLAND   SS8028
London (01769) 550269
Village signed off B3227 E of South Molton; EX36 3NG A proper Exmoor inn, and at its busiest in the shooting season; two small linked rooms by old-fashioned central servery, local stag-hunting pictures, tough carpeting or rugs on flagstones, cushioned benches and plain chairs around rough stripped trestle tables, Exmoor Ale, attractive beamed room on left with famous stag story on wall, panelled dining room on right has big curved settle by fireplace (good hunting and gamebird prints), simple tasty food, small hall with stuffed birds and animals; fine Victorian lavatories; children and dogs welcome, picnic-sets in cottage garden, untouched early 18th-c box pews in church next door, bedrooms, closed Sun evening. *(Mike Gorton, Carolien Cornelisse, Jeremy Whitehorn)*

MORCHARD BISHOP   SS7607
London Inn (01363) 877222
Signed off A377 Crediton–Barnstaple; EX17 6NW Prettily placed 16th-c village coaching inn, helpful friendly service (mother and daughter licensees), good generous home-made food (best to book weekends), Fullers London Pride and a guest, low-beamed open-plan carpeted bar with woodburner in large fireplace, thriving local atmosphere, pool, darts and skittles, small dining room; children and dogs welcome. *(Mrs P Sumner)*

MORTEHOE   SS4545
Chichester Arms (01271) 870411
Off A361 Ilfracombe–Braunton; EX34 7DU Newish management and some refurbishment for this former 16th-c vicarage; enjoyable local food including good crab, well kept west country ales, quick friendly service, panelled lounge, dining room and pubby locals' bar with darts and pool, interesting old local photographs; skittle alley and games machines in summer children's room, dogs welcome in bar, tables out at front and in paved side garden, good coast walk, open all day. *(Dr D J and Mrs S C Walker)*

MORTEHOE   SS4545
Ship Aground (01271) 870856
Signed off A361 Ilfracombe–Braunton; EX34 7DT Large open-plan beamed village pub handy for coast walks, well kept beers such as Cotleigh, Exmoor and Sharps, decent wines, good choice of affordable food from

light meals up, big log fires, massive rustic furnishings, interesting nautical brassware, large back family room with games area; sheltered sunny terrace with good Bristol Channel views, by interesting church, open all day in season when popular with holidaymakers, limited parking. *(Stephen and Judith Thomas, Michael Tack)*

MUDDIFORD   SS5638
Muddiford Inn (01271) 850243
B3230 Barnstaple–Ilfracombe; EX31 4EY Family pub dating from the 16th c, plenty of character, enjoyable well priced food from landlord/chef (small helpings available), local real ale, open fire, pleasant restaurant with fancier menu, friendly helpful service; pool, car park over road; big garden with terrace, handy for Marwood Hill Garden. *(M and GR)*

NEWTON ABBOT   SX8671
☆ Olde Cider Bar (01626) 354221
East Street; TQ12 2LD Basic old-fashioned cider house, casks of interesting low-priced farm ciders (helpful long-serving landlord may give tasters), a couple of perries, more in bottles, good country wines from the cask too, baguettes and pasties etc, great atmosphere, dark stools made from cask staves, barrel seats and wall benches, flagstones and bare boards; small back games room with machines; terrace tables, open all day. *(Anon)*

NEWTON ABBOT   SX8671
Richard Hopkins (01626) 323930
Queen Street; TQ12 2EH Big partly divided open-plan Wetherspoons, busy and friendly, with ten real ales, proper cider and their usual good value food; covered tables out at front, open all day from 8am. *(Anon)*

NEWTON ABBOT   SX8468
Two Mile Oak (01803) 812411
A381 2 miles S, at Denbury/ Kingskerswell crossroads; TQ12 6DF Appealing beamed coaching inn, log fires, black panelling, traditional furnishings and candlelit alcoves, well kept Bass, Otter and guests tapped from the cask, enjoyable well priced pubby food from sandwiches and baked potatoes up, decent coffee, cheerful staff; background music, TV and games machine; children and dogs welcome, circular picnic-sets on terrace and lawn, open all day. *(George Atkinson)*

NEWTON FERRERS   SX5447
Dolphin (01752) 872007
Riverside Road East: Newton Hill off Church Park (B3186) then left; PL8 1AE Shuttered 18th-c pub in attractive setting and under newish management; L-shaped bar with a few low black beams, pews and

---

If you know a pub is ever open all day, please tell us.

benches on slate floors and some white plank panelling, open fire, three Badger ales, enjoyable traditional food including fresh specials, friendly staff; can get packed in summer, limited parking; children and dogs welcome, terraces over lane looking down on River Yealm and yachts, open all day in summer. *(M J Winterton)*

NEWTON ST CYRES   SX8798
Beer Engine (01392) 851282
Off A377 towards Thorverton; EX5 5AX Friendly former railway hotel brewing its own beers since the 1980s, wide choice of good home-made food including local fish and popular Sun lunch; children welcome, decked verandah, steps down to garden, open all day. *(Anon)*

NEWTON TRACEY   SS5226
Hunters (01271) 858339
B3232 Barnstaple–Torrington; EX31 3PL Extended 15th-c pub with massive low beams and two inglenooks, good reasonably priced food from pub standards up, two well kept St Austell ales and Jollyboat Mainbrace, decent wines, efficient friendly service; soft background music; children and dogs welcome, disabled access using ramp, skittle alley popular with locals, tables on small terrace behind, open all day. *(Dr D J and Mrs S C Walker, Mr and Mrs P R Thomas)*

NOMANSLAND   SS8313
Mount Pleasant (01884) 860271
B3137 Tiverton–South Molton; EX16 8NN Informal country local with good mix of customers, huge fireplaces in long low-beamed main bar, well kept ales such as Cotleigh, Exmoor and Sharps, several wines by the glass, Weston's cider, good freshly cooked hearty food all day from baguettes up, friendly attentive service, happy mismatch of simple well worn furniture including comfy old sofa, candles on tables, country pictures, daily papers, cosy dining room (former smithy with original forge), darts in public bar; background music; well behaved children and dogs welcome, picnic-sets in back garden. *(Jeremy Whitehorn)*

NORTH BOVEY   SX7483
⋆ Ring of Bells (01647) 440375
Off A382/B3212 SW of Moretonhampstead; TQ13 8RB Bulgy-walled thatched inn dating from the 13th c, low beams, flagstones, big log fire, sturdy rustic tables and winding staircases, good imaginative local food, well kept St Austell, Teignworthy and guests, plenty of wines by the glass from good list, friendly staff, carpeted dining room and overspill room; children and dogs welcome, garden by lovely tree-covered village green below Dartmoor, good walks, five big clean bedrooms, open all day. *(Julie and Bill Ryan, B J Harding)*

NOSS MAYO   SX5447
⋆ Ship (01752) 872387
Off A379 via B3186, E of Plymouth; PL8 1EW Charming setting overlooking inlet and visiting boats, thick-walled bars with bare boards and log fires, six well kept west country beers including local Summerskills, good choice of wines and malt whiskies, popular food all day from wide-ranging menu, friendly efficient service, lots of local pictures and charts, books, newspapers and board games, restaurant upstairs; can get crowded in good weather, parking restricted at high tide; children and dogs welcome, plenty of seats on heated waterside terrace. *(R T and J C Moggridge, Lynda and Trevor Smith, John Evans, Roy Hoing, Christian Mole and others)*

NOSS MAYO   SX5447
Swan (01752) 872392
Off B3186 at Junket Corner; PL8 1EE Small, blue-shuttered, two-room pub right on the creek with lovely harbour views; Sharps Doom Bar and guests, decent whisky choice, sensibly priced pubby food including fresh local fish, painted beams, scrubbed tables on stone floor, open fire, darts, Thurs quiz and other events; can get crowded and parking difficult, not good for disabled; children welcome, dogs on leads, two terraces (one down by jetty) facing the sunset. *(Martin and Pauline Jennings, M J Winterton)*

OTTERTON   SY0885
Kings Arms (01395) 568416
Fore Street; EX9 7HB Big open-plan carpeted pub handy for families from extensive nearby caravan site, enjoyable pubby food from baguettes up including good fresh fish, Sun carvery, fast friendly service even when busy, O'Hanlons and Otter, reasonable prices, restaurant; TV, darts, pool and good skittle alley doubling as family room; dogs welcome, beautiful evening view from attractive back garden with play area, also covered terrace, bedrooms, charming village, open all day. *(George Atkinson)*

PAIGNTON   SX8860
Isaac Merritt (01803) 556066
Torquay Road; TQ3 3AA Spacious well run Wetherspoons conversion of former shopping arcade, good range of ales (regular festivals) and usual low-priced food all day, friendly welcoming service, cosy alcoves, comfortable family dining area, air conditioning; good disabled access, open all day from 8am. *(Len Beattie)*

PARRACOMBE   SS6644
⋆ Fox & Goose (01598) 763239
Off A39 Blackmoor Gate–Lynton; EX31 4PE Popular rambling Victorian pub, hunting and farming memorabilia and interesting old photographs, well kept Cotleigh and Exmoor, farm cider, good choice of wines by the glass, generous well prepared

food from imaginative menu, friendly staff, log fire, separate dining room; children and dogs welcome, small front verandah, riverside terrace and garden room, three bedrooms, open all day in summer. *(M and R Ridge, M G Hart, Sheila Topham)*

PETER TAVY   SX5177
⋆ **Peter Tavy Inn** (01822) 810348
Off A386 near Mary Tavy, N of Tavistock; PL19 9NN Old stone village inn tucked away at end of little lane, bustling low-beamed bar with high-backed settles on black flagstones, stone-mullioned windows, good log fire in big stone fireplace, snug dining area with carved wooden chairs, hops on beams and plenty of pictures, up to five well kept west country ales, Winkleigh's cider, good wine and malt whisky choice, well liked food including vegetarian options, quick friendly service, separate restaurant; children and dogs welcome, picnic-sets in pretty garden, peaceful moorland views. *(Stephen Shepherd, Roy Hoing, Helen and Brian Edgeley, Christian Mole)*

PLYMOUTH
Bridge (01752) 403888
Shaw Way, Mount Batten; PL9 9XH Modern two-storey bar/restaurant with terrace and balcony overlooking busy Yacht Haven Marina, enjoyable food from sandwiches and pub favourites up including good value set menu, nice choice of wines by the glass, St Austell Tribute and Sharps Doom Bar, impressive fish tank upstairs; children welcome, well behaved dogs downstairs, open all day from 9am (8.30am weekends) for breakfast. *(Anon)*

PLYMOUTH   SX4854
China House (01752) 661592
Sutton Harbour, via Sutton Road off Exeter Street (A374); PL4 0DW Attractive Vintage Inns' conversion of Plymouth's oldest warehouse, lovely boaty views, dimly lit and inviting interior with beams and flagstones, bare slate and stone walls, two good log fires, interesting photographs, their usual food including good value set menu, Butcombe, St Austell Tribute and a guest, plenty of wines by the glass; background music, no dogs; children welcome, good parking and disabled access/facilities, tables out on waterside balconies, open all day. *(Anon)*

PLYMOUTH   SX4854
Dolphin (01752) 660876
Barbican; PL1 2LS Basic unchanging chatty local, good range of well kept cask-tapped ales including Bass and St Austell, woodburner and coal fire, Beryl Cook

paintings (even one of the friendly landlord), no food but can bring your own; open all day. *(Anon)*

PLYMOUTH   SX4555
Lounge (01752) 561330
Stopford Place, Stoke; PL1 4QT Old-fashioned panelled corner local with cheery landlord and chatty regulars, well kept Bass and guests, popular lunchtime food, busy on match days; open all day weekends, closed Mon lunchtime. *(Anon)*

PLYMOUTH   SX4853
Thistle Park (01752) 204890
Commercial Road; PL4 0LE Welcoming bare-boards pub near National Maritime Aquarium, full range of well kept South Hams ales (used to be brewed here), Thatcher's cider, lunchtime bar food and evening thai restaurant (upstairs), interesting décor, open fire, back pool room, juke box, live music at weekends; no children; dogs in bar, roof garden and smokers' shelter, open all day till late (very late Fri, Sat). *(Anon)*

PLYMTREE   ST0502
Blacksmiths Arms (01884) 277474
Near church; EX15 2JU Friendly 19th-c beamed and carpeted pub with reasonably priced home-made food (takeaways available), three well kept changing local ales, decent choice of wines by the glass, pool room and skittle alley; children welcome and dogs (theirs is called Jagermeister), garden with boules and play area, open all day Sat, till 4pm Sun, from 6pm weekdays. *(R J and D S Courtney)*

POUNDSGATE   SX7072
⋆ **Tavistock Inn** (01364) 631251
B3357 continuation; TQ13 7NY Friendly and picturesque old pub liked by walkers (plenty of nearby hikes), beams and other original features like narrow-stepped granite spiral staircase, original flagstones, ancient log fireplaces, Courage, Otter and Wychwood, traditional bar food (all day in summer); children and dogs welcome, tables on front terrace and in quiet back garden, pretty flower boxes, open all day in summer. *(Simon Lindsey, Rose Rogers)*

RINGMORE   SX6545
Journeys End (01548) 810205
Signed off B3392 at Pickwick Inn, St Anns Chapel, near Bigbury; best to park opposite church; TQ7 4HL Ancient village inn with friendly chatty licensees, character panelled lounge and other linked rooms, Sharps Doom Bar and local guests tapped from the cask, farm

---

Cribbage is a card game using a block of wood with holes for matchsticks or special pins to score with; regulars in cribbage pubs are usually happy to teach strangers how to play.

cider, decent wines, well executed nicely presented food from shortish menu (not Sun evening, best to book in summer), log fires, bar billiards (for over-16s), family dining conservatory with board games, folk night first Weds of month; pleasant big terraced garden with boules, attractive setting near thatched cottages and not far from the sea, open all day weekends. *(Christian Mole, MP)*

ROBOROUGH   SS5717
New Inn (01805) 603247
Off B3217 N of Winkleigh; EX19 8SY
Tucked-away 16th-c thatched village pub, family-run and friendly, with enjoyable freshly prepared blackboard food and well kept local beers such as Bays, beamed bar with woodburner, tiny back room leading up to dining room; seats on sunny front terrace. *(Ian Walton, Mark Flynn)*

ROCKBEARE   SY0195
★ Jack in the Green (01404) 822240
Signed from A30 bypass E of Exeter; EX5 2EE Neat welcoming dining pub run well by long-serving owner, flagstoned lounge bar with comfortable sofas, ales such as Butcombe, Otter and Sharps, local cider, a dozen wines by the glass (over 100 by the bottle), popular top notch food and emphasis on larger dining side with old hunting/shooting photographs and leather chesterfields by big woodburner, competent service; background music; well behaved children welcome, no dogs inside, disabled facilities, plenty of seats in courtyard, open all day Sun, closed 25 Dec-5 Jan, quite handy for M5. *(Comus and Sarah Elliott, Tracy Sheedy, Michael Coleman, John Evans, Cedric Robertshaw)*

SALCOMBE   SX7439
Fortescue 01548 842868
Union Street, end of Fore Street; TQ8 8BZ Good proper pub with five linked nautical-theme rooms, enjoyable food served promptly by cheerful helpful staff, well kept ales such as Bass, Courage and Otter, decent wines, good woodburner, old local black and white shipping pictures, big public bar with games, small dining room; children welcome, courtyard picnic-sets. *(Anon)*

SALCOMBE   SX7439
Kings Arms (01548) 842202
Fore Street; TQ8 8BU Enjoyable light and main meals, beers such as Dartmoor Jail; good smokers' area outside, separate upper deck with fine harbour views. *(B J Harding)*

SALCOMBE   SX7439
★ Victoria (01548) 842604
Fore Street; TQ8 8BU Attractive 19th-c pub opposite harbour car park, neat nautical décor, comfortable furnishings and big open fires, enjoyable sensibly priced home-made food, well kept St Austell ales, decent wines, friendly enthusiastic service, separate family area; background music, can get busy at

weekends; dogs welcome, large sheltered tiered garden behind with good play area and chickens, bedrooms. *(Simon Rodway, David and Sue Atkinson)*

SAMPFORD COURTENAY   SS6300
New Inn (01837) 82247
B3072 Crediton–Holsworthy; EX20 2TB Attractive 16th-c thatched restaurant and bar greatly improved under current management, nice choice of good interesting food from landlord/chef at reasonable prices, local ales and cider, relaxed atmosphere with candlelit tables, beams and log fires; garden picnic-sets, picturesque village. *(D P and M A Miles)*

SAMPFORD PEVERELL   ST0314
★ Globe (01884) 821214
A mile from M5 junction 27, village signed from Tiverton turn-off; Lower Town; EX16 7BJ Spacious and comfortable village pub backing on to Grand Western Canal; enjoyable good value home-made food from sandwiches to massive mixed grill and popular carvery (Fri, Sat evenings, all day Sun, Mon lunch), breakfast (8-11am), coffee and cream teas, seven well kept ales including Cotleigh, Exmoor and Otter (Nov beer festival), good wine choice, friendly efficient staff, cosy beamed lounge with boothed eating area, back restaurant; background music, sports TV in bar; children and dogs welcome, disabled facilities, courtyard and enclosed garden with play equipment, six bedrooms, open all day. *(Mr and Mrs Richard Osborne, Tina and David Woods-Taylor)*

SANDY PARK   SX7189
★ Sandy Park Inn (01647) 433267
A382 Whiddon Down– Moretonhampstead; TQ13 8JW Welcoming little thatched inn, beams and flagstones, varnished built-in wall settles around nice tables, high stools by counter, Dartmoor, Otter and a guest ale, good food from sensibly short menu including pizzas and vegetarian choices, small dining room on left, inner snug; open mike night third Sun of month; children and dogs welcome, big garden with fine views, smokers' shelter, five comfortable bedrooms, open all day. *(Anon)*

SCORRITON   SX7068
Tradesmans Arms (01364) 631206
Main road through village; TQ11 0JB Welcoming open-plan Dartmoor-edge pub, enjoyable locally sourced food, Dartmoor, Otter and guests, friendly service, wonderful rolling hill views from conservatory and garden; bedrooms, open all day Sun. *(Anon)*

SHALDON   SX9372
Clifford Arms (01626) 872311
Fore Street; TQ14 0DE Attractive, open-plan extended 18th-c pub on two levels, clean and bright, with good range of home-made blackboard food (not mid Jan), up to five

mainly local ales including Ringmore, eight wines by the glass, low beams and stone walls, wood or carpeted floors, log fire, live jazz Sun and Mon; front terrace and decked area at back with palms, pleasant seaside village. *(Comus and Sarah Elliott)*

SHALDON   SX9472
London Inn   (01626) 872453
Bank Street/The Green; TQ14 8AW
Popular bustling pub opposite bowling green in pretty waterside village, good generous reasonably priced food using local suppliers, Otter and St Austell ales, friendly service; pool, background music; children welcome, open all day. *(J D O Carter)*

SHALDON   SX9371
Ness House   (01626) 873480
Ness Drive; TQ14 0HP Updated Georgian hotel on Ness headland overlooking Teign estuary, comfortable nautical-theme bar, mixed furniture on bare boards, log fire, Badger ales and decent wines by the glass, young friendly well trained staff, quite pricey food in narrow beamed restaurant or small conservatory, afternoon tea; no dogs; children welcome, disabled facilities, terrace with lovely views, back garden picnic-sets, nine bedrooms, open all day. *(Ian and Jane Irving, Adrian Johnson)*

SHEBBEAR   SS4309
✶ Devils Stone Inn   (01409) 281210
Off A3072 or A388 NE of Holsworthy; EX21 5RU Neatly kept 17th-c beamed village pub reputed to be one of the most haunted in England; brown leather armchairs in front of open woodburner, long L-shaped pew and second smaller one, flagstone floors, old photographs of pupils from Shebbear school, bar counter with high-backed leather chairs, St Austell Tribute and three other west country beers, decent wines, enjoyable food in dining room across corridor, plain back games room with pool, darts, juke box and fruit machine; picnic-sets on front terrace and in garden behind, right by actual Devil's Stone (turned by villagers on 5 Nov to keep the devil at bay), eight bedrooms (steep stairs to some), open all day weekends. *(J V Dadswell)*

SHEEPWASH   SS4806
✶ Half Moon   (01409) 231376
Off A3072 Holsworthy–Hatherleigh at Highampton; EX21 5NE Ancient inn loved by anglers for its 12 miles of River Torridge fishing (salmon, sea trout and brown trout), small tackle shop and rod room with drying facilities; simply furnished main bar, lots of beams, log fire in big fireplace, well kept St Austell, Sharps and a local guest, several wines by the glass, wide choice of enjoyable food including blackboard specials, friendly service (may be slow at busy times), separate extended dining room, bar billiards; children and dogs welcome,

12 bedrooms (some in converted stables), generous breakfast, tiny Dartmoor village off the beaten track. *(John Spurgeon, Roy Hoing, J V Dadswell)*

SIDFORD   SY1389
✶ Blue Ball   (01395) 514062
A3052 just N of Sidmouth; EX10 9QL Handsome thatched pub run by same friendly family for over 100 years and restored after 2006 fire; happy mix of customers, central bar covers three main areas each with a log fire, pale beams, nice mix of wooden dining chairs around circular tables on patterned carpet, prints, horsebrasses and plenty of bric-a-brac, well kept Bass, Otter, St Austell Tribute and Sharps Doom Bar, popular bar food (chef happy to accommodate vegetarians), attentive service; chatty locals keep public bar lively, darts, board games, skittle alley; background music and games machine; children and dogs welcome, terrace and flower-filled garden, smokers' gazebo, coastal walks close by, bedrooms, open all day from 8am for breakfast. *(Dave Braisted, Dennis Jenkin, Dennis and Doreen Haward, Phil and Sally Gorton, Neil and Heather Cross)*

SIDMOUTH   ST1287
Anchor   (01395) 514129
Old Fore Street; EX10 8LP Welcoming open-plan pub popular for fresh fish and other good value food, well kept Caledonian ales including one named for them, good service; tables out in front, more in back beer garden, open all day. *(John and Gloria Isaacs, Roger and Donna Huggins)*

SIDMOUTH   SY1287
✶ Dukes   (01395) 513320
Esplanade; EX10 8AR More brasserie than pub, but long bar on left has Branscombe Vale, Otter and a guest beer, good food all day specialising in local fish (best to book in evening), efficient young staff, daily papers, linked areas including conservatory and flagstoned eating area (once a chapel), smart contemporary décor; big-screen TV, may be summer queues; children welcome, disabled facilities, prom-view terrace tables, bedrooms in adjoining Elizabeth Hotel, open all day. *(Dave Braisted, Guy Vowles)*

SIDMOUTH   SY1287
✶ Swan   (01395) 512849
York Street; EX10 8BY Cheerful old-fashioned town-centre local, well kept Wells & Youngs and good value food from splendid sandwiches up, helpful long-serving licensees, lounge bar with interesting pictures and memorabilia, darts and warm coal fire in bigger light and airy public bar with boarded walls and ceilings, daily newspapers, separate dining area; no credit cards; dogs welcome, nice little flower-filled garden with smokers' area. *(Phil and Sally Gorton)*

SILVERTON   SS9503
Lamb   (01392) 860272
Fore Street; EX5 4HZ Flagstoned local
run well by friendly landlord, Dartmoor, Exe
Valley, Otter and guests tapped from casks,
inexpensive home-made pubby food, separate
eating area, skittle alley; handy for Killerton
(NT), open all day weekends. *(Anon)*

SLAPTON   SX8245
⋆Queens Arms   (01548) 580216
*Sands Road corner, before church;
TQ7 2PN* Smartly kept one-room village
local with welcoming landlady, good
straightforward inexpensive food, ales such
as Dartmoor, Otter and Teignworthy, snug
comfortable corners, fascinating World War
II photos and scrapbooks, dominoes and
draughts; parking needs skill; children and
dogs welcome, lots of tables in lovely suntrap
stepped garden. *(Dave Webster, Sue Holland,
Steve Whalley)*

SOURTON   SX5390
⋆Highwayman   (01837) 861243
A386, S of junction with A30; EX20 4HN
A fantasy of dimly lit stonework and
flagstone-floored burrows and alcoves, all
sorts of things to look at, one room a make-
believe sailing galleon; a couple of local
ales and farm cider, organic wines, good
proper sandwiches or home-made pasties,
friendly chatty service, nostalgic background
music; children allowed in certain areas,
outside fairy-tale pumpkin house and an
old-lady-who-lived-in-the-shoe house, period
bedrooms with four-posters and half-testers,
bunkrooms for walkers/cyclists.
(M J Winterton)

SOUTH BRENT   SX6960
Oak   (01364) 72133
Station Road; TQ10 9BE Friendly village
pub with well priced traditional and modern
food, three well kept local ales, good choice
of wines by the glass, welcoming helpful
service, comfortable open-plan bar with
some leather sofas, restaurant, Weds folk
night; children and dogs welcome, small
courtyard, five bedrooms, limited parking
nearby. *(David Jackman)*

STICKLEPATH   SX6494
⋆Devonshire   (01837) 840626
*Off A30 at Whiddon Down or
Okehampton; EX20 2NW* Welcoming old-
fashioned 16th-c thatched village local next
to foundry museum (NT); low-beamed slate
floor bar with big log fire, longcase clock and
easy-going old furnishings, key collection,
sofa in small snug, well kept low-priced ales

tapped from the cask, farm cider, good value
sandwiches, soup and home-made pasties
from the Aga, games room, lively folk night
first Sun of month; dogs welcome (pub has
its own), wheelchair access from car park,
good walks, bedrooms, open all day Fri, Sat.
(Chris and Angela Buckell)

STOKE FLEMING   SX8648
Green Dragon   (01803) 770238
Church Street; TQ6 0PX Popular and
friendly village pub with yachtsman
landlord, well worn-in interior with beams
and flagstones, boat pictures, sleepy dogs
and cats, snug with sofas and armchairs,
grandfather clock and open fire, well
kept Otter ales, Addlestone's and Aspall's
ciders, good choice of wines by the glass,
bargain food; tables out on partly covered
heated terrace, lovely garden, handy for
coast path. *(Richard Tilbrook, Dave Webster,
Sue Holland)*

STOKE GABRIEL   SX8457
⋆Church House   (01803) 782384
*Off A385 just W of junction with A3022;
Church Walk; TQ9 6SD* Friendly and
popular early 14th-c pub; lounge bar with
fine medieval beam-and-plank ceiling, black
oak partition wall, window seats cut into
thick butter-coloured walls, woodburner in
huge fireplace, ancient mummified cat, well
kept Bass, Sharps Doom Bar and a guest,
enjoyable good value food, little locals'
bar; background music, no under-14s; dogs
welcome in bar, picnic-sets on small front
terrace, old stocks (can use them if you
wish), limited parking, open all day. *(Paul
Humphreys, Eddie Edwards)*

STOKENHAM   SX8042
⋆Church House   (01548) 580253
*Opposite church, N of A379 towards
Torcross; TQ7 2SZ* Attractive extended
old pub overlooking common, three spotless
open-plan areas, low beams, mix of seating
on flagstones and lots of knick-knacks,
Greene King, Otter and guests, local organic
cider, several wines by the glass, well liked
food from good sandwiches up using local
produce, pleasant helpful service, dining
conservatory, jazz Weds evening; children and
dogs welcome, picnic-sets on lawn with play
area, interesting church next door. *(Damian
and Lucy Buxton)*

STOKENHAM   SX8042
Tradesmans Arms   (01548) 580996
*Just off A379 Dartmouth–Kingsbridge;
TQ7 2SZ* Picturesque partly thatched
14th-c pub overlooking village green, good
attractively presented food using local

Please tell us if any pub deserves to be upgraded to a featured entry – and why:
feedback@goodguides.com, or (no stamp needed) The Good Pub Guide,
FREEPOST TN1569, Wadhurst, E Sussex TN5 7BR.

ingredients, sensible wine list and well kept local beers, traditional low-beamed cottagey interior, log fire, restaurant; children and dogs welcome, nice bedrooms. *(Simon Lindsey, Rose Rogers, Lynda and Trevor Smith)*

THORVERTON SS9202
Thorverton Arms (01392) 860205

Village signed off A396 Exeter–Tiverton; EX5 5NS Spacious 16th-c coaching inn with five adjoining areas including log-fire bar and restaurant, good well presented home-made food at reasonable prices, chatty landlord and friendly staff, three real ales, pool; wisteria-draped terrace and sunny garden, pleasant village, six comfortable bedrooms, nice breakfast. *(R T and J C Moggridge)*

THURLESTONE SX6743
Village Inn (01548) 563525

Part of Thurlestone Hotel; TQ7 3NN Small 16th-c pub attached to smart family-run hotel, good food from sandwiches to blackboard specials, well kept local beers, comfortable country-style furnishings, central fireplace with gas fire, some live music; children and dogs welcome, picnic-sets out at front, handy for coast path, open all day weekends and in high season. *(John and Gloria Isaacs, B J Harding)*

TOPSHAM SX9688
★ Bridge Inn (01392) 873862

2.5 miles from M5 junction 30: Topsham signposted from exit roundabout; in Topsham follow signpost (A376) Exmouth, on the Elmgrove Road, into Bridge Hill; EX3 0QQ Very special old drinkers' pub (16th-c former maltings) with up to nine well kept ales and in landlady's family for five generations; quite unchanging and completely unspoilt with friendly staff and locals, character small rooms and snugs, traditional furniture including a nice high-backed settle, woodburner, the 'bar' is landlady's front parlour (as notice on the door politely reminds customers), simple food, live folk and blues; no background music, mobile phones or credit cards; children and dogs welcome, picnic-sets overlooking weir. *(Peter Thornton, Chris Johnson)*

TOPSHAM SX9687
★ Globe (01392) 873471

Fore Street; 2 miles from M5 junction 30; EX3 0HR Substantial inn dating from the 16th c, recent refurbishment but keeping cosy traditional feel, heavy-beamed bow-windowed bar with open fire, daily newspapers, well kept St Austell ales, good interesting home-made food from sandwiches and snacks up, restaurant, nice relaxed atmosphere; children welcome, dogs in bar, 19 attractive bedrooms (some in courtyard), parking can be tricky, open all day. *(Phil and Sally Gorton)*

TOPSHAM SX9687
★ Lighter (01392) 875439

Fore Street; EX3 0HZ Big, busy well run pub looking out over quay, quickly served food from good sandwiches and light dishes to fresh fish, three Badger ales, nautical décor, old local photographs, panelling and large central log fire, friendly staff, good children's area; games machines, background music; lots of waterside tables – good bird views at half tide, handy for antiques centre but little nearby parking. *(George Atkinson, Dr A J and Mrs B A Tompsett)*

TOPSHAM SX9688
Passage House (01392) 873653

Ferry Road, off main street; EX3 0JN Relaxed 18th-c pub with traditional black-beamed bar and slate-floored lower dining area, good food from sandwiches to local fish, well kept ales and decent wines, friendly service; peaceful terrace looking over moorings and river (lovely at sunset) to nature reserve beyond. *(Mrs Jo Rees)*

TORCROSS SX8242
★ Start Bay (01548) 580553

A379 S of Dartmouth; TQ7 2TQ More fish and chip restaurant than pub but does sell Bass, Otter, local wine and cider; very much set out for eating and exceptionally busy at peak times with staff coping well, food is good and sensibly priced; wheelback chairs around dark tables, country pictures, some photographs of storms buffeting the pub, winter coal fire, small drinking area by counter, large family room; no dogs during food times; seats outside (highly prized) looking over pebble beach and wildlife lagoon, open all day. *(Damian and Lucy Buxton, John and Gloria Isaacs, Col and Mrs Patrick Kaye, Dave Webster, Sue Holland, Mark Lubienski)*

TORQUAY SX9166
Crown & Sceptre (01803) 328290

Petitor Road, St Marychurch; TQ1 4QA Two-bar local in 18th-c stone-built beamed coaching inn, five real ales including St Austell, Otter and Wells & Youngs, interesting naval memorabilia and chamber-pot collection, friendly long-serving licensees, basic good value lunchtime food, snacks any time, live jazz Tues, folk Fri; children and dogs welcome, two gardens; open all day Fri-Sun. *(Anon)*

TORQUAY SX9163
Hole in the Wall (01803) 200755

Park Lane, opposite clocktower; TQ1 2AU Ancient two-bar local near harbour, reasonably priced usual food including good fresh fish, several well kept ales such as Bays, Butcombe and Sharps, Blackawton cider, smooth cobbled floors, low beams and alcoves, lots of nautical brassware, ship models, old local

photographs, chamber-pots, restaurant/
function room (band nights); can get very
busy weekends; some seats out at front, open
all day. *(Dr and Mrs A K Clarke)*

TOTNES   SX8060
Albert (01803) 863214
Bridgetown; TQ9 5AD Unpretentious
roadside pub with small bar and two other
rooms, low beams, flagstones, panelling,
some old settles and lots of knick-knacks,
friendly landlord brewing own Bridgetown
ales, good local atmosphere; neat
garden. *(Sean Finnegan, David Jackman)*

TOTNES   SX7960
Bay Horse (01803) 862088
Cistern Street; TQ9 5SP Popular,
traditional two-bar inn dating from the
15th c, friendly community-spirited licensees,
four well kept changing local ales (regular
beer festivals), may be winter mulled cider,
lunchtime bar snacks such as pasties and
ploughman's; background and live music
including good Sun jazz; children and dogs
welcome, nice garden, two comfortable
bedrooms, good breakfast, open all day.
(Roger and Donna Huggins)

TOTNES   SX7960
Kingsbridge Inn (01803) 863324
Leechwell Street; TQ9 5SY Attractive
rambling 17th-c pub/restaurant, black beams,
timbering and white painted stone walls, big
woodburner, good variety of enjoyable freshly
cooked food including some interesting
choices, home-baked bread, a couple of real
ales and nice choice of wines, good attentive
service, occasional live music; open all
day. *(Roger and Donna Huggins)*

TOTNES   SX8060
★**Royal Seven Stars** (01803) 862125
Fore Street, The Plains; TQ9 5DD
Exemplary town-centre bar and coffee bar
in well run civilised old hotel, friendly and
easy-going, with well kept ales and enjoyable
good value food all day from breakfast on,
separate brasserie/grill room with adjoining
champagne bar; heated tables out in front,
river across busy main road, bedrooms.
(Dave Webster, Sue Holland)

TUCKENHAY   SX8156
★**Maltsters Arms** (01803) 732350
*Ashprington Road, off A381 from Totnes;
TQ9 7EQ* Popular old pub in lovely quiet
spot by wooded creek, good food from bar
snacks up, well kept west country ales and
farm ciders, great range of wines by the
glass, friendly service, creek-view restaurant;
children and dogs welcome, waterside
terrace with open-air bar and summer

barbecues, six pleasantly refurbished
bedrooms, open all day. *(Tim Maddison,
David and Sue Atkinson)*

TWO BRIDGES   SX6175
Two Bridges Hotel (01822) 890581
*B3357/B3212 across Dartmoor;
PL20 6SW* Rambling 18th-c hotel in
protected central Dartmoor hollow, popular
with walkers (boots and sticks left in porch),
good choice of beers and wines, good food in
bar and striking dining room, friendly helpful
staff. *(Rod Stoneman)*

UGBOROUGH   SX6755
Ship (01752) 892565
Off A3121 SE of Ivybridge; PL21 0NS
Friendly dining pub extended from cosy
16th-c flagstoned core, well divided open-
plan eating areas a step down from neat
bar, wide choice of good home-made food
including fresh fish and nice puddings,
willing pleasant service, well kept Palmers
and St Austell ales, good house wines;
background music; tables out in front. *(Neil
and Anita Christopher, John Evans, M G Hart,
David Jackman)*

UPOTTERY   ST2007
Sidmouth Arms (01404) 861252
Near the church; EX14 9PN Attractive
18th-c pub in pleasant village setting, roomy
and comfortable, with helpful staff, well
kept Otter beers and good value traditional
food. *(Patrick and Daphne Darley)*

WEARE GIFFARD   SS4722
Cyder Press (01237) 425517
Tavern Gardens; EX39 4QR Welcoming
local in pretty village overlooking River
Torridge, friendly licensees, three real ales
including Dartmoor and St Austell, local
ciders, enjoyable fairly standard food from
baguettes up, inglenook woodburner, darts
in public bar, separate dining area; children
welcome, garden with play area, beautiful
countryside and handy for Tarka Trail, two
bedrooms. *(Darren Hedden)*

WEMBURY   SX5349
Odd Wheel (01752) 863052
Knighton Hill; PL9 0ED Modernised
village pub with half a dozen well kept
west country ales, reasonably priced fairly
traditional food from sandwiches and panini
up, pool in bar, restaurant; children welcome,
seats out on decking, fenced play area, open
(and food) all day weekends. *(Hugh Roberts)*

WEMBWORTHY   SS6609
★**Lymington Arms** (01837) 83572
Lama Cross; EX18 7SA Large early
19th-c beamed dining pub in pleasant

If you report on a pub that's not a featured entry, please tell us any lunchtimes or
evenings when it doesn't serve bar food.

country setting, clean and bright, with wide choice of reliably good food including some interesting specials, good service from character landlady and friendly staff, well kept Sharps Doom Bar and Skinners Betty Stogs, Winkleigh farm cider, decent wines, comfortably plush seating and red tablecloths in partly stripped-stone bar, big back restaurant; children welcome, picnic-sets outside, closed Sun evening, Mon, Tues. *(Mrs P Sumner, Ron and Sheila Corbett)*

WESTLEIGH SS4728
Westleigh Inn (01271) 860867
0.5 miles off A39 Bideford–Instow; EX39 4NL Popular and comfortable beamed pub, well kept ales such as Sharps Doom Bar, enjoyable usual food from sandwiches and baguettes up, friendly prompt service, inglenook log fire, brass and knick-knacks, pool and darts; well behaved children and dogs welcome, play area in big garden overlooking Torridge estuary, Tarka Trail walks. *(Anon)*

WESTON ST1400
⋆ Otter (01404) 42594
Off A373, or A30 at W end of Honiton bypass; EX14 3NZ Big busy family pub with heavy low beams, enjoyable food (best to book) from light dishes up including lots of vegetarian options, good Sun carvery, OAP specials and other deals, cheerful helpful staff, well kept Cotleigh and Otter ales, good log fire; background music; disabled access, picnic-sets on big lawn leading to River Otter, play area, open all day. *(Bob and Margaret Holder, Alison Smith)*

WHIMPLE SY0497
New Fountain (01404) 822350
Off A30 Exeter–Honiton; Church Road; EX5 2TA Attractive two-bar beamed pub with friendly local atmosphere, good inexpensive home-made food (not Mon lunchtime), well kept changing beers including O'Hanlons brewed in the village, woodburner; well behaved dogs welcome. *(Anon)*

WONSON SX6789
⋆ Northmore Arms (01647) 231428
Between Throwleigh and Gidleigh; EX20 2JA Far from smart and a favourite with those who take to its idiosyncratic style (not everyone does); two simple old-fashioned rooms, log fire and woodburner, low beams and stripped stone, well kept ales such as Dartmoor tapped from the cask, farm cider and decent house wines, good honest home-made food (all day Mon-Sat), darts and board games; children and dogs welcome, picnic-sets outside, bedrooms, beautiful remote walking country, normally open all day. *(Anon)*

YEALMPTON SX5851
Rose & Crown (01752) 880223
A379 Kingsbridge–Plymouth; PL8 2EB Central bar counter, all dark wood and heavy brass, solid leather-seated stools, mix of furnishings, stripped-wood floor and open fire, carpeted dining areas, emphasis on enjoyable bar and restaurant food including good value lunchtime and early evening set menu, efficient service even at busy times, three St Austell ales, quite a few wines by the glass and nice coffee; children welcome, dogs in bar, tables in walled garden with pond, also a lawned area, open all day. *(Hugh Roberts, John Evans)*

LUNDY SS1344
⋆ Marisco (01271) 870870
Get there by ferry (Bideford and Ilfracombe) or helicopter (Hartland Point); EX39 2LY One of England's most isolated pubs (yet busy most nights), great setting, steep trudge up from landing stage, galleried interior with lifebelts and shipwreck salvage, two St Austell ales labelled for the island, its spring water on tap, good value house wines, welcoming staff, good basic food (all day from breakfast on) using Lundy produce and lots of fresh seafood, open fire; children welcome, tables outside, souvenir shop and doubles as general store for the island's few residents. *(Chas Bayfield, Stephen and Judith Thomas)*

Dorset

New entries this year include the Bull (a popular meeting place at any time of day) and Stable (amazing ciders and pizzas), both in Bridport and under the same ownership, Three Horseshoes in Burton Bradstock (very handy for the nearby beach), New Inn at Church Knowle (lots to look at in comfortable, traditionally furnished bars, and a cheerful landlord), Acorn in Evershot (enthusiastic hands-on licensees, plenty of character and pretty bedrooms), Museum in Farnham (delicious food in smart, civilised inn), Three Horseshoes at Powerstock (cosy, cheerful bar, impressive food, fine views), Rose & Crown in Trent (delightful little local with good food and drink, and friendly hands-on landlady) and Olive Branch in Wimborne Minster (handsome townhouse with bustling bar and spreading, contemporary dining areas). Other pubs doing well are the New Inn at Cerne Abbas (a lovely, beautifully refurbished place), Anchor (super position by a seaside cove) and George (the young licensees are making a big hit here), both in Chideock, Hunters Moon in Middlemarsh (an enjoyable all-rounder), Ship in Distress at Mudeford (cheerful place with amusing bric-a-brac), Marquis of Lorne in Nettlecombe (particularly good food), Brace of Pheasants in Plush (an especially enjoyable place to stay), Langton Arms in Tarrant Monkton (another comfortable place for a short break), West Bay in West Bay (interesting food and drinks), Red Lion in Weymouth (cheerful and lively with fair value food) and Green Man in Wimborne Minster (reasonably priced food and drink in a friendly local). Many of the pubs hold a Food Award, but the one that stands out most is the New Inn at Cerne Abbas, which is our Dorset Dining Pub 2014.

ASKERSWELL   SY5393 Map 2

Spyway £

Off A35 Bridport–Dorchester; DT2 9EP

Family-run country inn with friendly welcome, unspoilt décor, real ales, well liked food and fine views; bedrooms

You get marvellous views of the downs and coast from seats on the back terrace and in the garden behind this simple, family-run inn; there's a small children's play area too. Inside, the unspoilt little rooms are cosily filled with old-fashioned high-backed settles, cushioned wall and window seats and some tub chairs. Old photos of the pub and rustic scenes are displayed on the walls and jugs hang from the beams; the warm Rayburn is a bonus on chilly days. Otter Ale and Bitter and a guest such as Butcombe on handpump are served by friendly staff. The dining area has old oak beams and timber uprights, red-cushioned dining chairs around dark tables on patterned carpet, horse tack and horsebrasses on the walls, and a woodburning stove, with two smaller rooms leading off. The pub's steep lane continues up Eggardon Hill, one of the highest in the region. The bedrooms have valley views and the breakfasts are good.

Good value, enjoyable food includes sandwiches, smoked haddock topped with cider welsh rarebit, creamy baked mushrooms with home-baked bread, mixed bean chilli, wild boar sausages and mash, catch of the day with chips and peas, duck breast with five-spice sauce, pork belly with black pudding, and puddings. *Benchmark main dish: home-made pies £9.95. Two-course evening meal £16.00.*

Free house ~ Licensee Tim Wilkes ~ Real ale ~ (01308) 485250 ~ Open 12-3, 6-11 ~ Bar food 12-3, 6-9 ~ Restaurant ~ Children welcome ~ Bedrooms: £50/£80 ~ www.spyway-inn.co.uk *Recommended by Lois Dyer, Ragged Robin, Pete Flower, Itsguy*

BRIDPORT   SY4692 Map 1

Bull 🛏

East Street (B3162); DT6 3LF

Bustling inn with plenty of room to sit and chat, real ales, lots of coffees, very good food and helpful, friendly staff; bedrooms

This former coaching inn is in the centre of town and open all day, so customers are always popping in and out – the comfortable squashy armchairs and sofa by the open fire in the reception area seem much favoured by ladies chatting over morning coffee or afternoon tea. The bustling bar has another open fire, dark turquoise wall banquettes and white-painted dining chairs around dark tables on wooden floors, flowers and candlelight, and an unusual sculpture of a child lying on the back of a bellowing bull. Cheerful, helpful staff serve Otter Bitter and Ale on handpump, and good wines by the glass. French windows lead out to a sheltered courtyard with seats and benches under parasols and lots of pretty flowers. The relaxed, informal dining room is similarly furnished to the bar, and doubles as the breakfast room; it's incredibly popular in the evening, so booking is essential. Those in the know head upstairs to the tucked-away, cosy and candlelit Venner Bar, which is great fun: leather chesterfields, ornate gilt-edged period chairs, rugs on floorboards, big mirrors, a large central chandelier and a huge choice of cocktails enthusiastically concocted by the charming young barman. The bedrooms are well equipped and comfortable, and the extremely good breakfasts come with home-made breads and conserves.

🍴 Highly enjoyable and very popular, the food includes sandwiches, nibbles such as pork scratchings with apple sauce or pigs head croquette with piccalilli dipping sauce, scallops and brown shrimp risotto, pressed ham hock with celeriac remoulade, free-range chicken caesar salad, aubergine and pesto roulade with rosemary and cheese polenta, tempura-battered hake with chips, duck breast with cauliflower purée and redcurrant jus, and puddings. *Benchmark main dish: burger with cheese, gherkins, relish and fries £12.50. Two-course evening meal £22.00.*

Free house ~ Licensees Nikki and Richard Cooper ~ Real ale ~ (01308) 422878 ~ Open 8am-11pm ~ Bar food 8am-9.30pm ~ Restaurant ~ Children welcome ~ Dogs allowed in bar ~ Bedrooms: £75/£85 ~ www.thebullhotel.co.uk *Recommended by Ruth May, Harvey Brown*

BRIDPORT
SY4692 Map 1

Stable

At the back of the Bull Hotel; DT6 3LF

Lots of draught ciders and perry, big, freshly made pizzas, customers of all ages and friendly, helpful service in big, buzzy place

Tucked away behind the Bull Hotel on the High Street, this is a lively, cheerful and busy cider and pizza bar. It's not a proper pub but is great fun – you'd have to be a real curmudgeon not to enjoy yourself here a lot. The décor of the lofty barn-like room is rustic: rough planked walls and ceiling, some big steel columns, two long rows of pale wooden tables flanked by wide benches, hefty wooden candlesticks holding fat candles, and steps up to a raised end area with cushioned red wall benches and brass-studded red leather dining chairs around a few tables. They have Dorset Chesil and Durdle Door on handpump, around ten draught box ciders and perrys (these change frequently) plus lots of bottled choices, and six wines by the glass. It's the easy-going young-at-heart atmosphere, and music to match, that pulls it all together. An upstairs room (not always open) is similar in style. There's a sister Stable in Weymouth.

🍴 Very popular food includes a smashing choice of freshly made pizzas, a range of pies (beef and horseradish, spinach, pumpkin and feta cheese, pork, ham, cheese and chutney, free-range chicken with apricot), various big salads, and puddings such as apple crumble and chocolate brownie, both with clotted cream. *Benchmark main dish: roast lamb pizza £10.50. Two-course evening meal £15.00.*

Free house ~ Licensees Nikki and Richard Cooper ~ Real ale ~ (01308) 426876 ~ Open 5-11; 12-11 Sat, Sun; closed Mon-Fri lunchtimes ~ Bar food 5-9.30; all day weekends ~ Live music second Thurs of month; ukulele club Mon evening ~ www.thestabledorset.co.uk *Recommended by Ruth May*

BURTON BRADSTOCK
SY4889 Map 1

Three Horseshoes

Mill Street; DT6 4QZ

Well placed thatched village inn just a few minutes from the coast; traditional furnishings, a friendly welcome and popular food and drink

This traditional thatched pub is handy if you're visiting the long sandy beach nearby – and it's the honest welcome from both the landlady and the locals that makes newcomers feel at home. There are solid, cushioned pubby chairs and tables on a red patterned carpet, brocaded built-in wall seats, fresh flowers, and an open woodburning stove with horsebrasses on the mantelbeam. One table is made from an old bed with the headrest still intact, there are photographs of the pub on the walls, cacti in small glass cabinets on the window sills, and background music; there's also a neat little dining room. Palmers Best, Tally Ho!, 200 and Dorset Gold are on handpump. There are picnic-sets on grass at the back and a few seats out in front.

🍴 Well liked bar food includes sandwiches, mediterranean-style mushrooms, tiger prawns in garlic, ham, egg and chips, tortellini with stilton and rocket pesto, seafood gratin, baked bass with ginger and peppers, and puddings like brioche bread and butter pudding and chocolate truffle cheesecake. *Benchmark main dish: steak pie £12.90. Two-course evening meal £17.00.*

Palmers ~ Tenants William and Mandy Hay ~ Real ale ~ (01308) 897259 ~ Open 12-11 (10.30 Sun); 12-3, 6-11 in winter ~ Bar food 12-2, 6-9 ~ Restaurant ~ Children welcome ~ Dogs allowed in bar ~ www.3hsbb.co.uk *Recommended by Comus and Sarah Elliott, C and R Bromage*

CERNE ABBAS
ST6601   Map 2

New Inn 🍴 ⌕ 🛏

Long Street; DT2 7JF

Dorset Dining Pub of the Year

Carefully refurbished former coaching inn with character bar and two dining rooms, friendly licensees, local ales and inventive food; fine bedrooms

This is a lovely place to stay, with four of the smart, well equipped bedrooms in the charming 16th-c main building and eight in the newly converted stable block. This former coaching inn was sympathetically refurbished last year by its friendly, hands-on licensees, who have carefully kept many of its original features and much of its character. The bar has a solid oak counter, an attractive mix of nice old dining tables and chairs on slate or polished wooden floors, settles built into various nooks and crannies, and a woodburner in the opened-up Yorkstone fireplace; there are lovely mullioned windows and heavy oak beams throughout. Palmers Copper, Dorset Gold and IPA on handpump, a dozen wines by the glass, several malt whiskies and local cider. The two dining rooms are furnished in similar style. There are seats on a terrace and picnic-sets under mature fruit trees or parasols in the back garden. You can walk from the attractive stone-built village to the prehistoric Cerne Abbas Giant chalk carving and on to other villages.

🍴 Using the best local produce, the imaginative food includes sandwiches, warm braised brisket terrine with sweet mustard sauce, celeriac and capers, fresh crab and scallop chowder with sweetcorn and pancetta, ham terrine with egg and chips, burger with pickles and triple-cooked chips, baked fillet of hake with spiced lentils, duck breast with cauliflower purée and roasted peach, tranche of turbot with smoked haddock croquette, leeks and mustard cream, and puddings such as mango and orange parfait with mango sauce and white chocolate and passion-fruit panna cotta with coconut ice and pineapple salsa. *Benchmark main dish: slow-roast pork belly with champ potato and red cabbage £14.75. Two-course evening meal £23.50.*

Palmers ~ Tenant Jeremy Lee ~ Real ale ~ (01300) 341274 ~ Open 11-3, 6-11; 11-11 Sat, Sun ~ Bar food 12-2.15, 7-9 ~ Restaurant ~ Children welcome ~ Dogs welcome ~ Bedrooms: £75/£110 ~ www.thenewinncerneabbas.co.uk *Recommended by Alan Johnson*

 CHIDEOCK   SY4191   Map 1

Anchor £

Off A35 from Chideock; DT6 6JU

Dramatically set pub offering lovely sea and cliff views from large terrace, simple snug bars and fair value food

The position of this bustling old pub is pretty special – on its own by a seaside cove, close to the Dorset Coast Path and in front of the Golden Cap pinnacle, the signal station used by 17th-c smugglers. There are tables on the spacious front terrace, above a shallow stream bisecting the beach – but you must get there early in fine weather to bag one; the same goes for a parking space. In winter, when the sometimes overwhelming crowds have gone, the little bars feel especially snug, with white-planked low ceilings, roaring winter fires, some sea pictures, lots of interesting local photographs, a few fossils and shells, and simple but comfortable seats around neat tables. Friendly, efficient staff serve Palmers 200, IPA and Copper on handpump and there's a decent little wine list; background, mainly classical, music. Note that the pub will be closed in autumn 2013 for a major refurbishment.

Good value bar food includes sandwiches and baguettes, several ploughman's, crispy whitebait with herb aioli, antipasti plate, spiced squash, beetroot and goats cheese salad, sausages with mustard mash, caramelised onions and red wine gravy, home-cooked honey mustard glazed ham and egg, beer-battered fish and chips with minted peas and tartare sauce, and puddings. *Benchmark main dish: local whole plaice with smoked salmon, cider, samphire and clam sauce £13.95. Two-course evening meal £16.00.*

Palmers ~ Tenant Paul Wiscombe ~ Real ale ~ (01297) 489215 ~ Open 11-11; 11.30-10.30 Sun ~ Bar food 12-9; 12-2.30, 6-9 in winter ~ Children welcome ~ Dogs welcome ~ www.theanchorinnseatown.co.uk *Recommended by Peter Meister*

 CHIDEOCK   SY4292   Map 1

George

A35 Bridport–Lyme Regis; DT6 6JD

Comfortably traditional local with well liked food

Doing particularly well under its young licensees, this heavily thatched and bustling village pub makes a welcome break from the busy A35. The interior is nicely traditional, and the cosy low-ceilinged carpeted bar is just as you'd hope, with Palmers IPA, Copper, 200 and Tally Ho! on handpump and several wines by the glass served by attentive staff, log fires, and brassware and pewter tankards hanging from dark beams. There are wooden pews and long built-in tongue-and-groove banquettes, old tools on the cream walls and high shelves of bottles, plates and mugs; background music, TV, bar billiards, table skittles and board games. The garden room opens on to a pretty walled garden with a terrace and wood-fired oven.

Simply prepared and very well cooked, the short food menu might include sandwiches, chicken liver parfait, coley goujons with tartare sauce, home-cooked ham and eggs with piccalilli, burger with spicy tomato and caramelised onion chutney, cheese, bacon and chips, home-made basil linguine topped with goats cheese, black bream fillets with herby crab sauce, steak in ale stew, and puddings such as crème brûlée and chocolate brownie. *Benchmark main dish: beer-battered fish and chips £10.50. Two-course evening meal £16.50.*

Palmers ~ Tenants Mr and Mrs Steve Smith ~ Real ale ~ (01297) 489419 ~ Open 12-3, 6-11 ~ Bar food 12-2.30, 6-9.30 ~ Restaurant ~ Children welcome ~ Dogs allowed in bar ~ Live music Weds and Sat evenings in summer ~ www.georgeinnchideock.co.uk
Recommended by David and Sally Frost, George Atkinson

CHURCH KNOWLE
SY9381   Map 2

New Inn ♀

Village signed off A351 N of Corfe Castle; BH20 5NQ

Refurbished old inn with lots to look at, plenty of seating in various rooms, open fires, a thoughtful choice of drinks, good food and a cheerful landlord

The enthusiastic Mr Estop is only the fourth name on the licence of this partly thatched former farmhouse in 160 years. It's a characterful inn with lots of interesting collections in the connected bar rooms: brass and copper measuring jugs, bed-warmers, pots and pans and horse brasses, elderly board games and books, stone jars, china plates, a glass cabinet filled with household items from years ago, tilley lamps, the odd mangle and set of scales, a coastguard flag and an old diver's helmet. The main bar has an open fire in a stone fireplace, high-backed black leather dining chairs and cushioned wall settles around heavy rustic tables on the red-patterned carpet, and quite a few stools against the counter. They serve Butcombe Bitter, Dorset Jurassic and Sharps Doom Bar on handpump and Weston's Old Rosie cider; there's a wineshack from which you can choose your own wines, and also a wide choice of teas, coffees and local soft drinks. The dining room leads off here; it has similar furnishings, a serving counter with hotplates, two fireplaces (one with church candles, the other with a stove) and a dark red dado. Outside are picnic-sets on the lawn. The ruins of Corfe Castle are nearby.

As well as takeaway soups and fish and chips, and a popular carvery with two roasts using local farm meat, the careful choice of food includes their famous blue vinney soup, portuguese-style cornish sardines, trio of sausages with crispy onion rings, mash and red wine gravy, steak in ale pie, fishcakes (cod, hake, smoked haddock, salmon and tuna) with chips, saddle of venison on roasted vegetables, duck with parsnip mash and cherry port reduction, and puddings such as apple and black cherry crumble with custard and crème brûlée with gooseberry and elderflower ice-cream. *Benchmark main dish: carvery £9.95. Two-course evening meal £20.00.*

Punch ~ Tenants Maurice and Rosemary Estop ~ Real ale ~ (01929) 480357 ~ Open 11(12 Sun)-3, 6-11 ~ Bar food 12-2.15, 6-9.15 ~ Restaurant ~ Children welcome ~ www.newinn-churchknowle.co.uk *Recommended by David Eberlin, James A Waller, Nick and Sylvia Pascoe, George Atkinson*

EVERSHOT
ST5704   Map 2

Acorn ♀ 🛏

Off A37 S of Yeovil; DT2 0JW

400-year-old inn with plenty of character in several rooms, log fires, knick-knacks and friendly licensees, in a pretty village; bedrooms

Immortalised as the Sow & Acorn in Thomas Hardy's *Tess of the D'Urbervilles*, this is a prettily placed former coaching inn close to the church. It's very much the heart of the community, but there's a warm welcome for visitors too, and plenty of thoughtful touches. The public bar, with its chatty locals and cheerful atmosphere, has a log fire, lots of beer mats on beams, big flagstones, and high chairs against the counter – where they serve Otter Ale and Yeovil Star Gazer on handpump, 79 malt whiskies and home-made elderflower cordial; they keep dog biscuits behind the bar and there's a bowl of water too. A second bar has comfortable beige leather wall banquettes and little stools around tables set with fresh flowers, and a turkish rug on nice old quarry tiles. This leads to a bistro-style dining room with ladderback chairs around gingham and beige clothed tables; the slightly more formal restaurant is similarly furnished. There's also a comfortable lounge with armchairs, games, shelves of books and a skittle alley. Throughout are open fires, wood panelling, pretty knick-knacks, all manner of copper and brass items, water jugs, wall prints and photographs. The walled garden has picnic-sets under a fine beech tree, and there are lots of walks nearby. The attractive, individually decorated bedrooms have a Thomas Hardy theme.

🍴 Using free-range and other local produce, some own-grown salads and vegetables and game from local shoots, the enjoyable food includes sandwiches, twice-baked cheese soufflé with mushroom fricassée, potted shrimps with radish and cucumber salad, baked aubergine parmigiana, venison sausages with caramelised onion gravy, beer-battered fish of the day with triple-cooked chips, free-range chicken with onion and cheese potato cake and mustard and tarragon sauce, slow-braised pork belly with pearl onions and cider jus, and puddings such as tonka bean crème caramel with caramelised orange and date purée and warm treacle tart with salted caramel and pecan nut ice-cream. *Benchmark main dish: beer-battered fish and chips £12.75. Two-course evening meal £21.00.*

Free house ~ Licensee Alex Mackenzie ~ Real ale ~ (01935) 83228 ~ Open 11-11; 12-11 Sun ~ Bar food 12-2, 7-9 ~ Restaurant ~ Children welcome ~ Dogs allowed in bar and bedrooms ~ Bedrooms: £79/£100 ~ www.acorn-inn.co.uk *Recommended by A B Atkinson, Alan Johnson*

FARNHAM

Museum 🍴 ♟ 🛏

ST9515   Map 2

Village signposted off A354 Blandford Forum–Salisbury; DT11 8DE

Stylish civilised inn with appealing rooms including a bustling bar, inventive modern cooking, real ales and fine wines, and seats outside; lovely bedrooms

Although this rather smart 17th-c inn places much emphasis, not surprisingly, on the good inventive food, it also has a proper little bar with beams and flagstones, a big inglenook fireplace, a happy mismatch of dining chairs around plain or painted wooden tables, and bar stools against the counter. Friendly, helpful staff serve Fullers London Pride and Sixpenny Best Bitter on handpump, a fine choice of wines (including 22 by the glass) and some 30 malt whiskies. Leading off from here is a simply but attractively furnished dining room, with cushioned window seats, a long dark leather button-back wall seat, similar chairs and tables on bare floorboards and several photographs on patterned wallpaper; there's also a quiet lounge with armchairs around a low table in front of an open fire, books on shelves and board games. This leads to an outside terrace with cushioned seats and tables under parasols. The stylish, well equipped bedrooms are in the main building and converted stables, and there's also a self-catering cottage.

🍴 Using the best local, free-range and organic produce, the accomplished cooking might include dishes such as pigs cheek and ham hock terrine with smoked bacon popcorn, pork-scratching crumb and apple jelly, hand-dived scallops with devon crab risotto, tomato tart with sun-dried tomato tapenade and roasted vine tomatoes, steak and blue cheese pie, burger with pickled cucumber, cheese, bacon, mayonnaise and fries, local venison fillet with sour cherry and walnut sauce, sea bream fillet with tiger prawn, fennel and pink grapefruit salad and beetroot purée, and puddings such as lemon jelly with lime sorbet and citrus vodka and goats milk rice pudding with brandy-steeped prunes. *Benchmark main dish: slow-roasted pork belly with grain mustard mash, apple sauce and braised red cabbage £16.50. Two-course evening meal £22.00.*

Free house ~ Licensee Gary Brewer ~ Real ale ~ (01725) 516261 ~ Open 12-11 ~ Bar food 12-9(9.30 Fri-Sun) ~ Restaurant Fri and Sat evenings, Sun lunch ~ Children welcome ~ Dogs welcome ~ Bedrooms: £110/£120 ~ www.museuminn.co.uk
Recommended by Phyl and Jack Street, A B Atkinson, Bruce Jamieson

 MIDDLEMARSH   ST6607   Map 2

Hunters Moon 🛏

A352 Sherborne–Dorchester; DT9 5QN

Plenty of bric-a-brac in several linked areas, reasonably priced food and a good choice of drinks; comfortable bedrooms

A really good all-rounder and much enjoyed by our readers, this bustling former coaching inn has genuinely welcoming licensees and cheerful, helpful staff. The comfortably traditional beamed bar rooms are cosily filled with a great variety of tables and chairs on red patterned carpets, an array of ornamentation from horsebrasses up, and lighting in the form of converted oil lamps; the atmosphere is properly pubby. Booths are formed by some attractively cushioned settles, walls comprise exposed brick, stone and some panelling, and there are three log fires (one in a capacious inglenook); background music, children's books and toys, board games. Butcombe Bitter and a couple of guests such as Brains Reverend James and Ringwood Best on handpump, farm cider and 14 wines by the glass. A neat lawn has picnic-sets, including some circular ones.

🍴 Attractively served, the popular food includes sandwiches, mushrooms in ciabatta in stilton cream, local scallops with bacon and black pudding, braised vegetable wellington with tomato ragout, burgers with cheese and bacon, pie of the day, chicken topped with brie and bacon, game casserole, crispy duck in gooseberry sauce, and puddings. *Benchmark main dish: beer-battered cod with chips £11.75. Two-course evening meal £18.00.*

Enterprise ~ Lease Dean and Emma Mortimer ~ Real ale ~ (01963) 210966 ~ Open 10.30-2.30, 6-11; 10am-11pm Sat, Sun ~ Bar food 12-2, 6-9; all day weekends ~ Children welcome ~ Dogs welcome ~ Bedrooms: £65/£75 ~ www.hunters-moon.org.uk
Recommended by David Jackman, H J Reynolds, R J and G M Townson

 MUDEFORD   SZ1792   Map 2

Ship in Distress

Stanpit; off B3059 at roundabout; BH23 3NA

Wide choice of fish dishes, quirky nautical décor and friendly staff in a cheerful cottage pub

As cheerful as ever, this former smugglers' pub is much more fun inside than out. It's full of entertaining seaside bits and pieces, including brightly painted fish cutouts swimming across the walls, rope fancywork, brassware, lanterns, oars, an aquarium, model boats and the odd piratical figure; darts, games machine, board games, big-screen TV, background music and a winter woodburning stove. As well as several boat pictures, the room on the right has tables with masses of snapshots (beneath the glass tops) of locals caught up in various waterside japes. Ringwood Best and a guest or two such as Dartmoor Jail Ale are on handpump alongside several wines by the glass. A spreading and bustling two-room restaurant area has a fish tank, contemporary works by local artists for sale and a light-hearted mural giving the impression of a window opening on to a sunny boating scene. There are seats and tables on the suntrap back terrace and a covered heated area for chilly evenings. The pub is near Mudeford Quay and Stanpit Marsh Nature Reserve.

🍴 The speciality is good fresh fish dishes: shellfish bar with cockles, whelks, crevettes, green-lipped mussels and oysters, proper fish soup, whole local crab, tiger prawn stir-fry with oyster sauce, cod with chorizo and pesto, fillet of bass with saffron cream sauce and scottish salmon with dill mustard cream sauce. Non-fishy choices include sandwiches, duck and orange pâté, cottage pie, gammon with egg and chips, burger with fries and salad, and puddings such as lemon posset with raspberry coulis and crème brûlée. *Benchmark main dish: duo of bass and bream £15.50. Two-course evening meal £22.00.*

Punch ~ Lease Maggie Wheeler ~ Real ale ~ (01202) 485123 ~ Open 11-midnight (11 Sun) ~ Bar food 12-2.30, 6.30-9 ~ Restaurant ~ Children welcome ~ Dogs allowed in bar ~ www.ship-in-distress.co.uk *Recommended by Denise Flack*

NETTLECOMBE
SY5195   Map 2
Marquis of Lorne 🍷
Off A3066 Bridport–Beaminster, via West Milton; DT6 3SY

Attractive country pub with enjoyable food and drink, friendly licensees and seats in a large mature garden; bedrooms

Well worth negotiating the narrow lanes to find, this former farmhouse is in deep and unspoilt country within strolling distance of Eggardon Hill, one of Dorset's most evocative Iron Age hillfort sites. The comfortable, bustling main bar has a log fire, mahogany panelling and old prints and photographs around neatly matching chairs and tables. Two dining areas lead off, the smaller of which has another log fire. The wooden-floored snug (liked by locals) has board games, table skittles and background music, and there's Palmers IPA, Copper and 200 on handpump, with a dozen wines by the glass from a decent list. A lovely big mature garden has an array of pretty herbaceous borders, picnic-sets under apple trees and a rustic-style play area.

🍴 Using vegetables and salads grown in their own polytunnel and other local produce, the very good food includes sandwiches, duck liver pâté with spiced pears, sautéed soft herring roes with capers on fried home-made sourdough, grilled vegetable lasagne with lovage pesto, mustard- and sugar-baked ham with eggs and home-made piccalilli, sticky beef with indonesian-style salad, bass fillet with creamed prawn velouté on crushed new potatoes, pork wrapped in serrano ham on flageolet bean and spinach ragout with blue cheese mousse, and puddings such as triple-chocolate cheesecake and steamed lemon and lime sponge. *Benchmark main dish: roast half shoulder of local lamb with honey, mint and confit garlic £16.95. Two-course evening meal £19.50.*

Palmers ~ Tenants Stephen and Tracey Brady ~ Real ale ~ (01308) 485236 ~ Open 12-2.30, 6-11 ~ Bar food 12-2, 6-9 ~ Restaurant ~ Children welcome ~ Dogs allowed in bar ~ Bedrooms: £65/£90 ~ www.themarquisoflorne.co.uk *Recommended by Michael Bayne, Paul Goldman, David and Julie Glover*

PLUSH   ST7102 Map 2
Brace of Pheasants
Village signposted from B3143 N of Dorchester at Piddletrenthide; DT2 7RQ

16th-c thatched pub with friendly service, three real ales, lots of wines by the glass, generously served food and decent garden; good nearby walks; comfortable bedrooms

In a lovely position by Plush Brook and tucked into a fold of hills, this 16th-c thatched inn is a nice place to stay – the bedrooms, in a converted bowling alley, are nicely fitted out and comfortable and each has a little outside terrace. Attracting a mix of locals (some with dogs) and visitors, the welcoming beamed bar has windsor chairs around good solid tables on patterned carpet, a few standing timbers, a huge heavy-beamed inglenook at one end with cosy seating inside, and a good warming log fire at the other. Flack Manor Double Drop, Sharps Doom Bar and a guest such as Palmers Gold are tapped from the cask by the friendly licensees, and they offer a fine choice of wines with 18 by the glass, and two proper farm ciders. A decent-sized garden includes a terrace and a lawn sloping up towards a rockery. The pub is well placed for walks – an attractive bridleway behind the pub leads to the left of the woods and over to Church Hill.

Good, interesting food might include sandwiches, home-cured gravadlax with sweet pickled cucumber, seared diver-caught local scallops with black pudding and sweet chilli sauce, beer-battered fish of the day with tartare sauce, pine nut and goats cheese salad with herby sautéed potatoes, smoked chicken with orange and cornish brie cream sauce, garlic and herb-marinated local venison steak with red wine and madeira, thyme-stuffed gilt-head bream with herb butter, and puddings such as crystallised ginger cheesecake and chocolate and black cherry torte with clotted cream. *Benchmark main dish: slow-cooked faggots with mushy peas £12.25. Two-course evening meal £19.25.*

Free house ~ Licensees Phil and Carol Bennett ~ Real ale ~ (01300) 348357 ~ Open 12-3, 7-11(10.30 Sun) ~ Bar food 12-2, 7-9 ~ Children welcome ~ Dogs allowed in bar ~ Bedrooms: £105/£115 ~ www.braceofpheasants.co.uk *Recommended by A B Atkinson, Ron and Sheila Corbett, PLC, Barry Collett, Steve Whalley, R Elliott, M G Hart*

POWERSTOCK   SY5196 Map 2
Three Horseshoes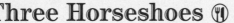
Off A3066 Beaminster–Bridport via West Milton; DT6 3TF

Carefully run, tucked-away inn with a friendly bar, real ales, enticing food and fine views from seats outside; simple but comfortable bedrooms

Tucked away down narrow lanes among steep valleys and with plenty of surrounding hikes, this Victorian inn has fine uninterrupted views from seats on the back terrace and in the big sloping garden, and from two of the comfortable bedrooms. You can expect a warm welcome from the helpful licensees, and the cosy bar has a cheerful atmosphere, some stripped panelling, open fires, mate's and elegant old windsor chairs around an assortment of tables on flagstones, and high wooden stools against the counter, where they serve Palmers IPA, Copper and 200 on handpump and eight wines by the glass. The slightly more formal dining room has local paintings for sale; background music and board games.

🍴 Using local seasonal produce and baking their own bread, the impressive food includes sandwiches, hand-dived scallops and crispy pigs head with cider and hazelnuts, welsh rarebit with wild boar scotch egg and ham and pickle salad, macaroni cheese with wild mushrooms, spinach, blue vinney and truffle, chicken, pheasant and ham hock pie with dripping chips, roast cod fillet with cod cheek scampi and triple-cooked chips, veal chop with devilled veal kidneys and mushrooms on toast, and puddings such as vanilla rice pudding with berries and condensed milk ice-cream and home-made profiteroles with salted caramel ice-cream and chocolate sauce. *Benchmark main dish: fresh fish dishes £14.00. Two-course evening meal £20.00.*

Palmers ~ Tenants Karl Bashford and Suzanna Prekopova ~ Real ale ~ (01308) 485328 ~ Open 12-2.30, 6.30-11; closed Mon lunchtime ~ Bar food 12-2.30, 6-9.30; not Mon ~ Children welcome ~ Dogs allowed in bar and bedrooms ~ Bedrooms: /£85 ~ www.threeshoesdorset.co.uk *Recommended by Caroline Prescott, Emma Scofield*

 SHERBORNE   ST6316   Map 2

Digby Tap 🍺 £

Cooks Lane; park in Digby Road and walk round corner; DT9 3NS

Regularly changing ales in simple alehouse, open all day with very inexpensive beer and food

Refreshingly unfussy and no-nonsense, this simple backstreet tavern changes little from year to year. It's the lively local atmosphere, friendly welcome and unspoilt interior that our readers enjoy so much. The simple flagstoned bar, with its cosy corners, is full of understated character; the small games room has a pool table and quiz machine, and there's a TV room. Bass, Otter Bitter, Teignworthy Neap Tide and a local guest on handpump, several wines by the glass and a choice of malt whiskies. There are some seats outside, and Sherborne Abbey is a stroll away.

🍴 Generous helpings of good value, straightforward lunchtime food includes sandwiches and toasties, soup, breaded plaice, burger, chilli con carne and a mixed grill. *Benchmark main dish: ham, egg and chips £4.80.*

Free house ~ Licensees Oliver Wilson and Nick Whigham ~ Real ale ~ No credit cards ~ (01935) 813148 ~ Open 11-11; 12-11 Sun ~ Bar food 12-2; not Sun ~ Children welcome ~ Dogs allowed in bar ~ www.digbytap.co.uk *Recommended by Roger Fox, Mr and Mrs P Wildman, Barrie and Mary Crees, Mark Flynn*

 SYDLING ST NICHOLAS   SY6399   Map 2

Greyhound 🍽 🍷 🛏

Off A37 N of Dorchester; High Street; DT2 9PD

Former coaching inn with a good balance of imaginative food, chatty drinkers and country décor; bedrooms

In a pretty village next to a stream, this neatly kept inn has a good local atmosphere in the beamed and flagstoned serving area, where drinkers gather for a pint and a chat. There are plenty of stools by the counter, and the carpeted bar has a comfortable mix of straightforward tables and chairs, some country decorations, and a warm fire in a handsome Portland stone fireplace. Butcombe Bitter, St Austell Dartmoor Best and a changing guest such as Dorset Fool Hardy on handpump and a farm cider. The cosy dining room is a little smarter, with fresh cream walls and white tablecloths; set into the floor is a glass-covered well, which coachmen used to provide buckets of water for their horses. A conservatory has attractive rustic furniture around scrubbed wooden tables, and a green leather chesterfield. The small front garden has picnic-sets and a play area.

🍴 Interesting food includes sandwiches, scallops with pea purée and black pudding, roasted figs with blue cheese and prosciutto, breaded and stuffed field mushroom with linguine and pine nuts, gilt-head bream with mussel broth, duck breast with orange jus and dauphinoise potatoes, open fish pie, and puddings such as white chocolate and cardamom mousse and chocolate brownie with vanilla-bean ice-cream. *Benchmark main dish: Sunday roast with all trimmings £12.50. Two-course evening meal £19.00.*

Free house ~ Licensee Alex Raybold ~ Real ale ~ (01300) 341303 ~ Open 12-3, 6-11; 12-3 Sun; closed Sun evening ~ Bar food 12-3, 6.30-9 ~ Restaurant ~ Children welcome ~ Dogs allowed in bar ~ Bedrooms: /£90 ~ www.dorsetgreyhound.co.uk *Recommended by Lois Dyer, Martin Roberts, Bruce Jamieson, David and Ruth Shillitoe, Phil and Jane Hodson*

TARRANT MONKTON   ST9408   Map 2
Langton Arms 🍴 🍺 🛏

Village signposted from A354, then head for church; DT11 8RX

Charming thatched pub in pretty village, with real ales in airy bars, good food, friendly staff and seats outside; bedrooms

This is a comfortable and enjoyable place to stay with six bedrooms in brick buildings around an attractive courtyard and four in the neighbouring cottage; breakfasts are lovely. It's very popular locally, but there's a welcome for visitors too. The beamed bar has wooden tables and chairs on flagstones, plenty of old black and white photos, a light oak counter with recessed lighting, and Ringwood Best and a guest like Dorset Piddle Jimmy Riddle on handpump; TV in the public bar. The restaurant and conservatory are in an attractively reworked stable and the skittle alley doubles as a family room during the day; background music and board games. In fine weather, you can sit out in front or at teak tables in the back garden; there's also a children's play area with woodchip. The pub is next to the church in a charming village with a ford.

🍴 Using their own home-grown vegetables, home-made bread, ice-cream and petits fours, and doing butchery on their own farm, the interesting food includes sandwiches, duck liver parfait with plum chutney, tiger prawn skewer marinated in lime, chilli and garlic with sweet chilli dip, several sharing platters, twice-baked cheese soufflé, home-cooked honey-glazed ham with free-range eggs, burger with mozzarella, onion rings and garlic bread, trio of home-made venison sausages with apple mash and red wine and onion gravy, chicken stuffed with leek and thyme, wrapped in bacon with white wine cream sauce, and puddings like apple and mixed berry crumble with custard and chocolate cake with chocolate sauce and vanilla ice-cream. *Benchmark main dish: steak in ale pie £15.50. Two-course evening meal £21.00.*

Free house ~ Licensee Barbara Cossins ~ Real ale ~ (01258) 830225 ~ Open 10(12 Sun) -midnight ~ Bar food 12-2.30, 6-9.30(10 Fri); all day weekends ~ Restaurant ~ Children welcome ~ Dogs allowed in bar and bedrooms ~ Bedrooms: £70/£90 ~ www.thelangtonarms.co.uk *Recommended by Michael Doswell, V A C Turnbull, James A Waller, Robert Watt, David Jackman, Leslie and Barbara Owen, Howard and Margaret Buchanan, Stewart Harvey*

It's very helpful if you let us know up-to-date food prices when you report on pubs.

TRENT　　　　　　　　　　　　　　　　ST5818　Map 2

Rose & Crown 🍴 🛏

Opposite the church; DT9 4SL

Character thatched pub in pretty rural position with friendly owners and staff, cosy rooms, open fires, a good choice of drinks and well thought-of food; bedrooms

---

Opposite a really lovely church and surrounded by attractive countryside, this partly thatched stone pub has a warmly friendly, easy-going atmosphere – all helped along by the hands-on landlady and her welcoming staff. The cosy little bar on the right has big, comfortable sofas and stools around a low table in front of an open fire (the logs are neatly piled on each side right to the ceiling), fresh flowers and candlelight. The bar opposite is liked by chatty locals (often with their dogs too) and is furnished with nice old wooden tables and chairs on quarry tiles, and stools against the counter where they serve Titanic First Class and Wadworths IPA on handpump; a room off here has similar wooden tables and chairs, built-in cushioned window seats and big church candles in a brick fireplace. An end room has settles and pews, a grandfather clock, pewter tankards hanging from a beam and more candles in yet another fireplace. Throughout are all kinds of pictures including Stuart prints commemorating the fact that Charles II sought refuge in the village after the Battle of Worcester. The simply furnished back dining room has doors leading to the garden, which has seats and tables and fine views (and sunsets); there are picnic-sets at the front. The pretty bedrooms are in a converted byre.

🍴 The inventive food cooked by the young chef includes sea trout ballotine with potato salad and vichyssoise, cod cheeks with shiitake mushrooms, almonds, lemon jelly and tomato essence, tarragon gnocchi with shallot jam, cauliflower velouté and mozzarella, seared pigeon with spring roll, pak choi, water chestnuts, spring onion jus and pigeon crackers, skate wing with mussel stew, clams and sorrel, duck breast and duck leg hash with charred pineapple, roast cashews and orange jus, and puddings like lemon millefeuille and dark chocolate soufflé with black cherry ice-cream and chocolate and cherry sauce. *Benchmark main dish: steak in ale pie £9.95. Two-course evening meal £20.50.*

Wadworths ~ Tenant Heather Kirk ~ Real ale ~ (01935) 850776 ~ Open 12-3, 6-11; 12-11 Sat; 12-9(5 in winter) Sun; closed winter Sun evening, Mon ~ Bar food 12-2.30, 6-9.30; 12-4 Sun ~ Restaurant ~ Live music Fri evening ~ Dogs welcome ~ Bedrooms: £65/£95 ~ www.roseandcrowntrent.co.uk *Recommended by Ruth May, Emma Scofield*

WEST BAY　　　　　　　　　　　　　　SY4690　Map 1

West Bay 🍴 🛏

Station Road; DT6 4EW

Relaxed seaside inn with emphasis on seafood; bedrooms

Doing particularly well under its present licensees, this is a bustling pub looking out to sea and within strolling distance of the little harbour. An island servery separates the fairly simple bare-boards front part (with coal-effect gas fire and a mix of sea and nostalgic prints) from a cosier carpeted dining area with more of a country kitchen feel; background music. Although it's so spacious that it never feels crowded, booking is virtually essential in season. Palmers 200, Best and Copper, and Dorset Gold are served on handpump alongside good house wines (with ten by the glass) and several malt whiskies. There are tables in the small side garden, with more in the large garden. Several local teams meet to play in the pub's 100-year-old skittle alley. The bedrooms are quiet and comfortable.

🍴 Fresh fish and seafood, caught from local boats, is listed on blackboards and might include seared hand-dived scallops with smoky bacon lardons and garlic butter, warm crab pâté, several ways of serving mussels, gilt-head bream fillet with oriental stir-fry, beer-battered local white fish, and lots of daily specials; also, non-fishy dishes such as lunchtime sandwiches, home-cooked honey-roast ham with free-range eggs, wild mushroom stroganoff, pork belly in creamy honey and wholegrain mustard sauce, beef stroganoff, and puddings. *Benchmark main dish: trio of fish with smoked bacon velouté and assorted shellfish £16.95. Two-course evening meal £21.50.*

Palmers ~ Tenants Paul and Tracy Crisp ~ Real ale ~ (01308) 422157 ~ Open 12-11(midnight Fri, Sat); 12-3, 6-11 weekdays in winter ~ Bar food 12-2, 6-9 ~ Children welcome till 8pm ~ Dogs allowed in bar ~ Bedrooms: £75/£100 ~ www.thewestbayhotel.co.uk *Recommended by Pat and Tony Martin, Dave Braiste*

WEST STOUR   ST7822   Map 2

Ship 🍷 🛏

A30 W of Shaftesbury; SP8 5RP

Civilised and pleasantly updated roadside dining inn, offering a wide range of food

Built in 1750, this neatly kept former coaching inn is run by a friendly, hands-on licensee. The smallish bar on the left is airy, with big sash windows looking beyond the road and car park to rolling pastures, and has cream décor and a mix of chunky farmhouse furniture on dark boards. The smaller flagstoned public bar has low ceilings and a good log fire. Dartmoor IPA and three guests from brewers such as Butcombe, Fullers and Sharps on handpump, good wines by the glass, a farm cider, elderflower pressé and organic apple juices. Their summer beer festival showcases a dozen beers and ten ciders, all from the West Country. On the right, two carpeted dining rooms with stripped pine dado, stone walls and shutters are similarly furnished in a pleasantly informal style, and have some attractive contemporary cow prints; TV, darts, lots of board games and background music. The bedlington terriers are called Douglas and Toby. The five bedrooms are attractive and comfortable.

🍴 Quite a choice of generously served food includes pâté of the day with gooseberry and coriander chutney, mussels in garlic, chilli and thai beer cream, sausage and mixed bean cassoulet, honey-baked ham and eggs, pumpkin, red onion, mushroom and blue cheese risotto, basil- and mozzarella-stuffed chicken wrapped in parma ham with tomato sauce, rabbit, smoked bacon and leek hotpot in grain mustard and cider gravy, venison haunch with sloe gin and blackberry sauce with leek and potato gratin, and puddings *Benchmark main dish: poached smoked haddock on spinach mash topped with poached egg and mornay sauce £11.95. Two-course evening meal £18.50.*

Free house ~ Licensee Gavin Griggs ~ Real ale ~ (01747) 838640 ~ Open 12-3, 6-11; 12-11 Sun ~ Bar food 12-2.30, 6-9; not Sun evening ~ Restaurant ~ Well behaved children in restaurant and lounge ~ Dogs allowed in bar ~ Bedrooms: £60/£90 ~ www.shipinn-dorset.com *Recommended by Comus and Sarah Elliott, Lois Dyer, Steve Jackson, Dennis Jenkin, S G N Bennett, S J and C C Davidson, Leslie and Barbara Owen*

You can send reports directly to us at feedback@goodguides.com

WEYMOUTH

Red Lion £

Hope Square; DT4 8TR

Cheery place with sunny terrace, great range of drinks including loads of whiskies and rums, and good value pubby food

Known locally as the lifeboat men's pub – it is the closest to the Weymouth RNLI – this lively place is a handsome Victorian building in the now pedestrianised Old Harbour. The refurbished bare-boards interior, kept cosy with candles, has all manner of wooden chairs and tables, cushioned wall seats, some unusual high, maroon-cushioned benches beside equally high tables, and lots of pictures and artefacts to do with the lifeboat crews and their boats and other bric-a-brac on stripped brick walls; some nice contemporary touches include the woven timber wall and loads of mirrors wittily overlapped. Tring Lifeboat, Dorset Jurassic, St Austell Proper Job and two guest beers on handpump, 14 wines by the glass, an impressive range of over 80 rums (with a rum 'bible' to explain them) and well over 100 whiskies; daily papers, board games and background music. There are plenty of seats outside that stay warmed by the sun well into the evening. This is part of the Cheshire Cat Pubs & Bars group, which also includes the Three Greyhounds in Allostock, Cholmondeley Arms at Bickley Moss and Bulls Head in Mobberley (all in Cheshire).

Fair value and very good, the food includes filled baps, duck liver pâté with tiny gherkins, seafood chowder, several sharing plates, steak in ale pie, burger with back bacon, cheese and caramelised onion chutney, homity pie with cheddar crust, fresh crab salad, breadcrumbed chicken with fresh tomato and basil sauce, bass, ginger and lime fishcakes with chilli sauce, and puddings like chocolate brownie and apple cake, both with ice-cream. *Benchmark main dish: fresh seafood sharing plate £12.95. Two-course evening meal £16.50.*

Free house ~ Licensee Brian McLaughlin ~ Real ale ~ (01305) 786940 ~ Open 11-11(midnight Sat); 12-10.30 Sun ~ Bar food 12-9; 12-3, 6-9 in winter ~ Children welcome until 7pm ~ Live music outside summer Sun afternoons ~ www.theredlionweymouth.co.uk *Recommended by Robin Manners*

WIMBORNE MINSTER

Green Man £

Victoria Road at junction with West Street (B3082/B3073); BH21 1EN

Cosy, warm-hearted town pub with simple food at bargain prices

In summer, the award-winning flowering tubs, hanging baskets and window boxes here are a fantastic sight; there are more on the heated back terrace. It's a cheerful local with regulars popping in and out throughout the day, but visitors get an equally warm welcome from the friendly landlord. The four small linked areas have red walls, maroon plush banquettes and polished dark pub tables, copper and brass ornaments, and Wadworths IPA, 6X and Bishops Tipple on handpump. One room has a log fire in a biggish brick fireplace, another has a coal-effect gas fire, and there are two dart boards, a silenced games machine, background music and TV; in summer the Barn houses a pool table. Their little border terrier is called Cooper.

As well as a popular breakfast, the bargain-priced traditional food includes jumbo rolls and sandwiches, beans on toast, thai-style prawn and cod cakes with chilli cakes, lasagne, meat or vegetarian burger, chilli con carne, and fish and chips. *Benchmark main dish: cottage pie £6.50. Two-course evening meal £11.50.*

Wadworths ~ Tenant Andrew Kiff ~ Real ale ~ (01202) 881021 ~ Open 10am-11.30pm(12.30 Sat) ~ Bar food 10-2 ~ Restaurant ~ Children welcome until 7.30pm ~ Dogs allowed in bar ~ Live music Fri-Sun evenings ~ www.greenmanwimborne.com
Recommended by Val and Alan Green, Dr and Mrs A K Clarke

 WIMBORNE MINSTER   SU0100   Map 2
Olive Branch
East Borough, just off Hanham Road (B3073, just E of the junction with B3078); good car park; BH21 1PF

Handsome spacious townhouse, contemporary décor, friendly staff, quite a choice of drinks and enjoyable food

Opened-up inside and extended, this is a handsome old townhouse with contemporary décor and a relaxed but civilised atmosphere. At the street end of the building is the bar, with some fine Jacobean panelling and handsome plasterwork, squishy sofas and leather stools around low tables beside a log fire, high chunky tables with matching stools and bar chairs, and a butcher's block with daily newspapers. Badger Best and Tanglefoot and a changing guest on handpump, alongside a good choice of wines by the glass; friendly, helpful service. The extensive dining room, divided into separate areas by partitions and standing timbers, has a high-pitched roof with heavy trusses, light brown leather or attractively cushioned high-backed wooden dining chairs around a mix of tables on wooden floors, and framed Penguin books on pale canary walls. There are lots of dog-latin mottoes, nightlights and church candles, and well designed lighting. A cosy side room, just right for a private party, has modern paintings on red or cream walls. The outside terrace has quite a few teak tables and chairs, and parking is easy.

 Interesting food includes sandwiches, eggs benedict, cornish sardines with sourdough toast and salsa verde, leek and tomato tart with beetroot and celery salad and sour cream dressing, poussin with roast garlic, anchovy mayonnaise and fries, burger with tomato, dill pickle, cheddar and crispy bacon, venison shank pie, cod on saffron risotto with red pepper sauce, and puddings such as chocolate and polenta cake with vanilla bean ice-cream and apple and blackberry crumble; they also offer a two-course weekday set menu until 7pm. *Benchmark main dish: honey-glazed duck with spiced orange chutney and red wine sauce £14.00. Two-course evening meal £22.00.*

Badger ~ Manager David Rushall ~ Real ale ~ (01202) 884686 ~ Open 9am-11pm(midnight Fri, Sat); 11-10.30 Sun ~ Bar food 12-3, 6-9.30(10 Fri, Sat);12-9 Sun ~ Restaurant ~ Children welcome in restaurant ~ Dogs allowed in bar ~ www.theolivebranchwimborne.co.uk *Recommended by Harvey Brown*

 WORTH MATRAVERS   SY9777   Map 2
Square & Compass ★
At fork of both roads signposted to village from B3069; BH19 3LF

Unchanging country tavern with masses of character, in the same family for many years; lovely sea views and fine walks nearby

From the benches of local stone in front of this 'quirky' and 'blissfully eccentric' pub, there's a fantastic view down over the village rooftops to the sea. The Newman family have been here for over 100 years – it's a basic, unchanging little place with simple offerings and no bar counter (it's not to everyone's taste). Palmers Copper, guests from brewers such as Frys, Otley and Wessex, and up to 15 ciders are tapped from a row of casks and passed through two serving hatches to customers in a drinking corridor; also about 20 malt whiskies. A couple of unspoilt rooms have simple furniture on flagstones, a woodburning stove, and a loyal crowd of friendly locals; darts and shove-ha'penny. There may be free-roaming chickens and other birds clucking around outside, and the small (free) museum exhibits local fossils and artefacts, mostly collected by the friendly landlord and his father. Wonderful walks lead to some exciting switchback sections of the coast path above St Aldhelm's Head and Chapman's Pool – you'll need to park in the public car park (£2 honesty box) 100 metres along the Corfe Castle road.

¶¶ Bar food is limited to home-made pasties and pies.

Free house ~ Licensees Charlie Newman and Kevin Hunt ~ Real ale ~ No credit cards ~ (01929) 439229 ~ Open 12-11; 12-3, 6-11 Mon-Thurs in winter ~ Bar food all day ~ Children welcome ~ Dogs welcome ~ Live music some Fri and Sat evenings, Sun lunchtime ~ www.squareandcompasspub.co.uk *Recommended by Mr Yeldahn, Michael Sargent, Tich Critchlow, Martin and Sue Day, Alan Johnson, Robert Watt, S J and C C Davidson*

Also Worth a Visit in Dorset

Besides the fully inspected pubs, you might like to try these pubs that have been recommended to us and described by readers. Do tell us what you think of them: feedback@goodguides.com

ALMER   SY9098
Worlds End (01929) 459671
B3075, just off A31 towards Wareham; DT11 9EW Handsome thatched family dining pub, plenty of individuality in long busy beamed and flagstoned bar with panelled alcoves, wide choice of enjoyable reasonably priced food all day, Badger ales, pleasant helpful staff; picnic-sets out in front and behind, play area. *(Richard Stanfield)*

BLANDFORD FORUM   ST8806
Crown (01258) 456626
West Street; DT11 7AJ Civilised red-brick Georgian hotel on edge of town, spacious bar area with Badger ales from nearby brewery, good choice of wines, teas and coffee, appetising food from sandwiches to daily specials, restaurant; children welcome, tables on big terrace with formal garden beyond, 32 bedrooms. *(Anon)*

BLANDFORD ST MARY   ST8805
Hall & Woodhouse (01258) 455481
Bournemouth Road; DT11 9LS Visitor centre for Badger brewery, their full range in top condition including interesting bottled beers, traditional lunchtime food from well filled baguettes up, friendly staff; spectacular chandelier made of beer bottles, lots of memorabilia in centre and upper gallery; popular tours of new brewery (not

Weds, Sun), open lunchtimes only, closed Sun. *(Anon)*

BOURNEMOUTH
Cricketers Arms (01202) 551589
Windham Road; BH1 4RN Well preserved Victorian pub near station, separate public and lounge bars, lots of dark wood, etched windows and stained glass, tiled fireplaces, Fullers London Pride and two quickly changing guests, food Sat and Sun lunchtimes only, Mon folk night; children and dogs welcome, picnic-sets out in front, open all day. *(Anon)*

BOURNEMOUTH   SZ0891
Goat & Tricycle (01202) 314220
West Hill Road; BH2 5PF Interesting two-level rambling Edwardian local (two former pubs knocked together); Wadworths and guest beers kept well from pillared bar's impressive rank of ten handpumps, farm cider, reasonably priced pubby food, friendly staff; no children; dogs welcome (Charlie is the resident jack russell), good disabled access, part-covered yard, open all day. *(Dr and Mrs A K Clarke)*

BOURTON   ST7731
★**White Lion** (01747) 840866
High Street, off old A303 E of Wincanton; SP8 5AT Popular 18th-c low-beamed dining pub with welcoming landlord, three smallish

opened-up rooms creating one well divided space, big flagstones, some stripped stone and half-panelling, bow-window seats and fine inglenook log fire, good well priced food here or in large restaurant, beers such as Otter and Sharps Doom Bar, Thatcher's cider and nice wines, neat friendly staff; picnic-sets on back paved area and sloping lawn, two bedrooms, open all day Fri-Sun. *(Anon)*

BRIDPORT   SY4692
Ropemakers (01308) 421255
West Street; DT6 3QP Welcoming town-centre local with well kept Palmers and very good value food, lots of pictures and memorabilia, live bands Fri, Sat; courtyard tables. *(Comus and Sarah Elliott)*

BRIDPORT   SY4692
Tiger (01308) 427543
Barrack Street, off South Street; DT6 3LY Cheerful open-plan Victorian beamed pub with well kept Sharps Doom Bar and three guests, real ciders, no food except breakfast for residents, skittle alley; sports TV; seats in heated courtyard, five bedrooms, open all day. *(Anon)*

BUCKHORN WESTON   ST7524
⋆**Stapleton Arms** (01963) 370396
Church Hill; off A30 Shaftesbury–Sherborne via Kington Magna; SP8 5HS Upmarket dining pub in handsome Georgian building, sizeable bar divided by glazed-in entrance lobby, farmhouse and pew chairs around scrubbed table on slate flagstones, comfortable sofas, log fire in fine stone fireplace, four real ales including Butcombe, Cheddar Valley cider, imaginative daily changing seasonal menu using locally sourced produce, dining room with mahogany tables on coir, church candles in fireplace; children welcome, dogs in bar, elegant metal tables and chairs out on York flagstones and gravel, good comfortable bedrooms, open all day weekends. *(Mr and Mrs Lynn)*

BUCKLAND NEWTON   ST6804
Gaggle of Geese (01300) 345249
Locketts Lane; E end of village; DT2 7BS Victorian country pub under newish owner-ship; enjoyable affordably priced home-made food, Ringwood, St Austell and guests, log fire in bar, dining room with mix of old and new furniture, skittle alley; children welcome and dogs (pub has its own), garden with terrace, orchard and pond, paddock with horses, may shut in winter Sun evening, Mon. *(Anon)*

CERNE ABBAS   ST6601
Royal Oak (01300) 341797
Long Street; DT2 7JG 16th-c thatched village-centre pub under new management; low beams, flagstones and rustic memorabilia, Badger ales, food from lunchtime sandwiches to daily specials; children and dogs welcome, small back garden. *(Mrs R Smith, Carol Wilson)*

CHARMOUTH   SY3693
Royal Oak (01297) 560277
Off A3052/A35 E of Lyme Regis; The Street; DT6 6PE Friendly three-room village local doing well under present welcoming couple, four Palmers ales, enjoyable food, quiz and music nights. *(Anon)*

CHEDINGTON   ST4805
Winyards Gap (01935) 891244
A356 Dorchester–Crewkerne; DT8 3HY Attractive dining pub surrounded by NT land with spectacular view over Parrett Valley and into Somerset; enjoyable good value food from sandwiches and ploughman's served on wooden boards to daily specials, nice choice of puddings, bargain OAP weekday lunch, four well kept beers including St Austell and Sharps Doom Bar, friendly staff and st bernard called Daisy, stylish dining room, skittle alley; children and dogs welcome, tables on front lawn under parasols, good walks, open all day weekends. *(Katie Collins)*

CHETNOLE   ST6008
⋆**Chetnole Inn** (01935) 872337
Village signed off A37 S of Yeovil; DT9 6NU Attractive inn with beams, huge flagstones and country kitchen décor, Sharps Doom Bar and guests, 16 malt whiskies, central woodburner and modern leather seats in minimalist snug, log fire and pale wood tables on stripped boards in dining room with fresh flowers, candles and linen napkins, well liked food, deli with small tearoom; dogs welcome in bar, picnic-sets out in front and in delightful back garden, three bedrooms overlooking old church, good breakfast, closed Sun evening, also Mon in winter. *(Anon)*

CHIDEOCK   SY4192
Clockhouse (01297) 489423
A35 W of Bridport; DT6 6JW Friendly family-run thatched village local, well kept Otter and guests, enjoyable straightforward food including bargain deals, long main bar and raised dining area, huge collection of clocks, skittle alley/games room; children welcome, dogs in bar. *(J V Dadswell)*

CHILD OKEFORD   ST8213
⋆**Saxon** (01258) 860310
Signed off A350 Blandford–Shaftesbury and A357 Blandford–Sherborne; Gold Hill; DT11 8HD Welcoming 17th-c village pub, quietly clubby snug bar with log fire, two dining rooms, Butcombe, Ringwood and guests, nice choice of wines, enjoyable reasonably priced home-made food including good Sun roast, efficient service; children welcome, dogs in bar, attractive back garden with wooden shelter, good walks on neolithic Hambledon Hill, four comfortable bedrooms. *(Robert Watt)*

CHRISTCHURCH
SZ1592
☆ **Olde George** (01202) 479383

Castle Street; BH23 1DT Bustling and cheerfully old-fashioned two-bar low-beamed pub dating from the 15th c, Dorset Piddle ales and a guest, real ciders and nice wine, enjoyable sensibly priced food all day using local suppliers, Sun carvery and different evening menu, friendly staff; dogs welcome (food for them), lots of teak seats and tables in heated character coachyard, open all day. *(Susan and Nigel Brookes)*

CHRISTCHURCH
SZ1593
Rising Sun (01202) 486122

Purewell; BH23 1EJ Sympathetically updated old pub specialising in authentic thai food, Flack Manor and Sharps Doom Bar from L-shaped bar, good choice of wines by the glass, pleasant helpful young staff; terrace with palms and black rattan-style furniture under large umbrellas. *(Mr and Mrs P D Titcomb)*

COLEHILL
SU0302
Barley Mow (01202) 882140

Colehill signed from A31/B3073 roundabout; Long Lane; BH21 7AH Refurbished part-thatched 16th-c pub under newish management; low-beamed main bar with brick inglenook, attractive oak panelling, library with tub chairs leading to restaurant and family area, three Badger ales, enjoyable freshly made food; background music, quiz first Weds of month; children and dogs welcome, tethering for horses, seats out at front and in garden behind with new deck, fenced part with kunekune pigs, also fields for various events such as farmers' market and lawnmower races, open all day weekends. *(Anon)*

CORFE CASTLE
SY9681
Castle Inn (01929) 480208

East Street; BH20 5EE Welcoming little two-room pub mentioned in Hardy's *The Hand of Ethelberta*, good fairly priced food using local suppliers including popular Fri fish night, competent service, Dorset and Ringwood ales, heavy black beams, exposed stone walls, flagstones and open fire; children welcome, back terrace and big sunny garden with mature trees. *(John and Joan Calvert, Malcolm and Maralyn Hinxman, M G Hart)*

CORFE CASTLE
SY9681
Fox (01929) 480449

West Street; BH20 5HD Old-fashioned take-us-as-you-find-us stone-built local, real ales such as Greene King Abbot and Wadworths 6X tapped from the cask, good log fire in early medieval stone fireplace, glassed-over well in second bar; dogs but not children allowed, informal castle-view garden. *(Tich Critchlow)*

CORFE CASTLE
SY9682
☆ **Greyhound** (01929) 480205

A351; The Square; BH20 5EZ Bustling picturesque old pub in centre of this tourist village, three small low-ceilinged panelled rooms, steps and corridors, well kept ales such as Ringwood and Sharps, local cider, wide choice of food from sandwiches and light dishes to good local seafood, traditional games including Purbeck longboard shove-ha'penny, family room; background music (live on Fri); garden with large decked area, great views of castle and countryside, pretty courtyard opening on to castle bridge, open all day weekends and in summer.
(Mr Yeldahn, Lesley and Peter Barrett, Dr and Mrs R E S Tanner)

CORFE MULLEN
SY9798
Coventry Arms (01258) 857284

Mill Street (A31 W of Wimborne); BH21 3RH Refurbished 15th-c pub under newish management; bar and four dining rooms, low ceilings, eclectic mix of furniture on flagstones or wood flooring, large central open fire, Ringwood, Timothy Taylors Landlord and one or two cask-tapped guests, generally well liked reasonably priced food from open kitchen, friendly helpful staff; mummified cat to ward off evil spirits; background and occasional live music; children and dogs welcome, big waterside garden with terrace, open all day. *(Fran Lane, John Dorricott, Richard Stanfield, Jenny and Brian Seller)*

CRANBORNE
SU0513
Inn at Cranborne (01725) 551249

Wimborne Street (B3078 N of Wimborne); BH21 5PP Attractive recently refurbished 17th-c inn; L-shaped bar/dining area with beams, flagstones and woodburners, Badger ales including Fleur named for the pub, several wines by the glass, food from sandwiches and pub favourites up, friendly hard-working staff; dogs welcome (the resident jack russel is Mikey), painted wooden furniture on gravel terrace, nice setting at edge of Cranborne Chase, eight good individually decorated bedrooms. *(Ian Herdman, Jane Hoskisson, Judith and Barry McCormick, David Guest)*

DORCHESTER
SY6990
☆ **Blue Raddle** (01305) 267762

Church Street, near central short-stay car park; DT1 1JN Cheery pubby atmosphere in long carpeted and partly panelled bar, well kept Butcombe, Fullers, Otter, St Austell and Sixpenny, local ciders, good wines and coffee, enjoyable simple home-made food at reasonable prices (not Sun, Mon or evenings Tues and Weds), coal-effect gas fires; background and live folk music (Weds fortnightly), no children; dogs welcome, good disabled access apart from one step, closed Mon lunchtime.
(Peter Thornton, David and Ruth Shillitoe)

EAST LULWORTH SY8581
Weld Arms (01929) 400211
B3070 SW of Wareham; BH20 5QQ
Thatched 17th-c cottage-row pub, civilised
log-fire bar with sofas, Isle of Purbeck,
Sharps and a guest ale, some nice wines by
the glass, well liked home-made food from
lunchtime sandwiches and baguettes up,
friendly helpful service, two dining rooms;
children and dogs welcome, picnic-sets out
in big back garden with play area, open
all day. *(Lawrence Pearse, Miles and Maxine
Wadeley, Peter and Anne Hollindale)*

EAST MORDEN SY9194
✶Cock & Bottle (01929) 459238
B3075 W of Poole; BH20 7DL Popular
dining pub with wide choice of good if not
cheap food (best to book), well kept Badger
ales, nice selection of wines by the glass,
efficient cheerful service, two dining areas
with heavy rough beams; children and dogs
allowed in certain areas, glassed-in terrace
area, garden and adjoining field, pleasant
pastoral outlook. *(Anon)*

EAST STOUR ST8123
Kings Arms (01747) 838325
*A30, 2 miles E of village; The Common;
SP8 5NB* Extended dining pub with popular
food from scottish landlord/chef including
bargain lunch menu and all-day Sun carvery
(best to book), Greene King IPA, St Austell
Tribute and Sharps Doom Bar, decent
wines and good selection of malt whiskies,
friendly efficient staff, open fire in bar,
airy dining area with light wood furniture,
scottish pictures and Burns quotes; gentle
background music; children welcome, dogs
in bar, good disabled access, picnic-sets in
big garden, bluebell walks nearby, three
bedrooms, open all day weekends. *(D M and
B K Moores, Anne de Gruchy, Paul Goldman,
Roy Hoing)*

FONTMELL MAGNA ST8616
✶Fontmell (01747) 811441
A350 S of Shaftesbury; SP7 0PA
Imposing, fully refurbished dining pub with
rooms, much emphasis on the enterprising
modern cooking, but also some more
straightforward reasonably priced dishes,
charming service, good wine list, local ales
including a house beer (Mallyshag) from
Keystone, small bar area with stripy stools,
comfy sofas and easy chairs, some bold
colours, restaurant with shelves of books
and wine bottles, windows overlooking fast
flowing stream that runs under the building;
tables on small terrace, six comfortable well
appointed bedrooms. *(Michael Doswell,
George Atkinson)*

GUSSAGE ALL SAINTS SU0010
✶Drovers (01258) 840084
8 miles N of Wimborne; BH21 5ET
Partly thatched pub with good proper home-
made food using local ingredients (some
home-grown), friendly service, Ringwood
ales and guests kept well, good wines by the
glass, log fire and pleasantly simple country
furnishings, public bar with piano and darts;
well behaved children and dogs welcome,
tables on pretty front lawn with views
across the Dorset hills, adjoining farm shop,
peaceful village. *(R Elliott)*

HIGHCLIFFE SZ2193
Galleon (01425) 279855
Lymington Road; BH23 5EA Fresh
contemporary refurbishment with leather
sofas, light wood floors and open fires,
well prepared food from snacks and pub
favourites up, local ales including Ringwood,
good service, conservatory opening on to
terrace and sunny garden; background music
(live weekends); children welcome, summer
barbecues, play area, open all day (till
midnight Fri, Sat). *(David M Cundy, Susan
Donkin, June Asher)*

HURN SZ1397
Avon Causeway (01202) 482714
*Village signed off A338, then follow
Avon, Sopley, Mutchams sign; BH23 6AS*
Roomy, civilised and comfortable hotel/
dining pub, food from well filled baguettes
and pub favourites up, Sun carvery, well kept
Wadworths ales, helpful welcoming staff,
interesting railway decorations, good disabled
access; Pullman-coach restaurant (breakfast
served here) by former 1870s station platform;
nice garden (some road noise), 12 bedrooms,
near Bournemouth Airport (2 weeks free
parking if you stay the night before you fly),
open all day. *(Val and Alan Green)*

IBBERTON ST7807
Crown (01258) 817448
*Village W of Blandford Forum;
DT11 0EN* Traditional village dining pub,
flagstones, toby jugs and comfortable seats
by inglenook woodburner, back eating area,
ales such as Butcombe and Palmers from
brick-faced bar, local cider, good variety of
freshly made food, friendly helpful staff; dogs
on leads in bar and in lovely garden, beautiful
spot under Bulbarrow Hill, good walks, closed
Mon. *(Peter Salmon)*

KINGSTON SY9579
✶Scott Arms (01929) 480270
West Street (B3069); BH20 5LH
Extensively modernised pub rambling
through several levels, some sofas and easy

If you stay overnight in an inn or hotel, they are allowed to serve you an alcoholic drink
at any hour of the day or night.

chairs, beams, stripped stone, bare boards and log fires, good reasonably priced local food including fresh fish, well kept Dorset, Ringwood and a couple of guests, decent wines, family dining area; dogs welcome, big attractive garden with outstanding views of Corfe Castle and the Purbeck Hills, summer barbecues, two well equipped bedrooms, good walks, open all day. *(John and Joan Calvert, M G Hart)*

LANGTON MATRAVERS   SZ0078
Ship (01929) 426910
B3069 near junction with A351; BH19 3EU Stone-built 18th-c pub with welcoming landlord, good choice of very enjoyable food from ciabattas to blackboard specials, Isle of Purbeck and Palmers ales, table skittles, Purbeck longboard shove-ha'penny and darts, Weds quiz, some live music; children welcome, disabled access and facilities, picnic-sets out behind under green parasols, handy for coastal path, three cosy bedrooms, open all day Fri-Sun. *(Mike and Jayne Bastin)*

LODERS   SY4994
Loders Arms (01308) 422431
Off A3066 just N of Bridport; DT6 3SA Unspoilt 17th-c stone-built pub in pretty thatched village, well kept Palmers ales, Thatcher's cider and good choice of wines by the glass, enjoyable home-made food, log fire, dining room, skittle alley; children and dogs welcome, pleasant views from picnic-sets in small garden behind, good surrounding walks, closed Sun evening winter. *(Anon)*

LYME REGIS   SY3391
Cobb Arms (01297) 443242
Marine Parade, Monmouth Beach; DT7 3JF Spacious place with well kept Palmers ales and decent wines, good choice of reasonably priced freshly cooked food (gluten-free options), cream teas, quick service, a couple of sofas, ship pictures and marine fish tank, open fire; pool, juke box, TVs; children and dogs welcome, disabled access (one step up from road), tables on small back terrace, next to harbour, beach and coastal walk, three bedrooms, open all day. *(Ian Cheal, Richard)*

LYME REGIS   SY3391
★Harbour Inn (01297) 442299
Marine Parade; DT7 3JF More eating than pubby with thriving family atmosphere, attentive young staff, good food from lunchtime sandwiches to local fish (not cheap), good choice of wines by the glass, well kept Otter and Town Mill, tea and coffee, clean-cut modern décor keeping original flagstones and stone walls (lively acoustic), paintings for sale, sea views from front windows; background music; dogs welcome, disabled access from street, verandah tables. *(Roger Fox, P Houldsworth, Michael Cooper, Martin and Sue Day, Guy Vowles)*

LYME REGIS   SY3492
★Pilot Boat (01297) 443157
Bridge Street; DT7 3QA Popular modern all-day family food place near waterfront, neatly cared for by long-serving licensees, friendly service even when busy, wide choice of good sensibly priced food including local fish, well kept Palmers ales and several wines by the glass, plenty of tables in cheery nautically themed areas, skittle alley; quiet background radio; dogs welcome, tables out on terrace. *(David and Julie Glover, George Atkinson)*

LYME REGIS   SY3391
★Royal Standard (01297) 442637
Marine Parade, The Cobb; DT7 3JF Right on broadest part of beach, properly pubby bar with log fire, fine built-in stripped high settles, local photographs and even old-fashioned ring-up tills, quieter eating area with stripped brick and pine, four well kept Palmers ales and good choice of wines by the glass, food from massive crab sandwiches up including local fish and good vegetarian choices, friendly helpful service; darts, prominent pool table, free wi-fi, background and some live music, gets very busy in season – may be long waits then; children and dogs welcome, good-sized suntrap courtyard with own servery and harbour views, open all day. *(Mrs P Abell, Henry Paulinski, Patrick and Daphne Darley)*

LYME REGIS   SY3492
Volunteer (01297) 442214
Top of Broad Street (A3052 towards Exeter); DT7 3QE Cosy old-fashioned unpretentious pub with long low-ceilinged bar, nice mix of customers (can get crowded), well kept changing west country ales (some tapped from the cask), farm cider, enjoyable modestly priced food in dining lounge (children allowed here), friendly young staff, roaring fires; dogs welcome, open all day. *(Roger Fox)*

LYTCHETT MINSTER   SY9593
Bakers Arms (01202) 622900
Dorchester Road; BH16 6JF Large, popular partly thatched Vintage Inn, modernised rambling interior with beams, timbers and log fires, their usual choice of food all day including good value fixed price menu (till 5pm) and enjoyable Sun roast, real ales such as Ringwood, efficient chatty staff; no dogs; children welcome, garden picnic-sets. *(Anon)*

LYTCHETT MINSTER   SY9693
★St Peters Finger (01202) 622275
Dorchester Road; BH16 6JE Well run two-part beamed roadhouse with cheerful efficient staff, popular sensibly priced food from sandwiches and baguettes up, small helpings available, Badger ales and several wines by the glass, welcoming end log fire,

cottagey mix of furnishings in different sections giving a cosy feel despite its size; good skittle alley, tables on big terrace, part covered and heated. (Leslie and Barbara Owen)

MANSTON ST8116
Plough (01258) 472484
B3091 Shaftesbury–Sturminster Newton, just N; DT10 1HB Welcoming, good-sized traditional country pub under newish management; Palmers ales and guests, fairly priced standard food, beams, richly decorated plasterwork, ceilings and bar front, red patterned carpets, dining conservatory, some live music; garden picnic-sets, adjacent caravan site. (Steve Jackson, Michael and Jenny Back)

MARNHULL ST7818
Crown (01258) 820224
About 3 miles N of Sturminster Newton; Crown Road; DT10 1LN Friendly part-thatched inn dating from the 16th c (the Pure Drop Inn in Hardy's Tess of the D'Urbervilles); linked rooms with oak beams, huge flagstones or bare boards, log fire in big stone hearth in oldest part, more modern furnishings and carpet elsewhere, Badger ales and enjoyable food, restaurant; peaceful enclosed garden, bedrooms. (S J and C C Davidson)

MARTINSTOWN SY6488
Brewers Arms (01305) 889361
Burnside (B3159); DT2 9LB Friendly village pub under newish family management, enjoyable reasonably priced food, Palmers Copper and Sharps Doom Bar, restaurant, live music including folk night third Tues of month, Weds quiz; children and dogs welcome, garden picnic-sets, good local walks, two bedrooms, closed Sun evening, Mon. (Ian and Rose Lock, Ann Salmon)

MELPLASH SY4897
✷ **Half Moon** (01308) 488321
A3066 Bridport–Beaminster; DT6 3UD Thatched and shuttered roadside dining pub, really good interesting food from landlord/chef with emphasis on fresh local produce, Palmers ales, friendly competent service, beams and log fire; children welcome, picnic-sets in front, more in well maintained back garden. (Bruce Jamieson)

MILTON ABBAS ST8001
Hambro Arms (01258) 880233
Signed off A354 SW of Blandford; DT11 0BP Refurbished pub in beautiful late 18th-c thatched landscaped village, two beamed bars and restaurant, well kept ales such as Dorset Piddle, Ringwood and Sharps Doom Bar, good food from ciabattas and panini up, prompt friendly service; children welcome, dogs in bar, tables on front terrace, four bedrooms, open all day weekends. (David and Ruth Shillitoe)

MORETON SY7789
Frampton Arms (01305) 852253
B3390 near station; DT2 8BB Neatly kept 19th-c railway inn, enjoyable generously served food, Dorset, Ringwood and Sharps Doom Bar, decent wines, good friendly service, steam railway pictures in lounge bar, Warmwell Aerodrome theme in public bar, conservatory restaurant, family room with pool and machines, skittle alley; disabled facilities, tables on front terrace and in garden with play equipment, bedrooms. (Eddie Edwards)

MOTCOMBE ST8426
Coppleridge (01747) 851980
Signed from The Street, follow to Mere/Gillingham; SP7 9HW Good food from sandwiches to speciality steaks and fresh fish, real ales including Butcombe, decent wines and welcoming service in former 18th-c farmhouse's bar and various dining rooms, some live music; children welcome, ten spacious courtyard bedrooms, 15-acre grounds, play area. (Anon)

MUDEFORD SZ1792
Nelson (01202) 485105
75 Mudeford; BH23 3NJ Friendly well run local, good service, six well kept ales including Ringwood, wide range of food from bar meals to authentic thai dishes (takeaways available, delivered locally on a tuk-tuk), bright modern back dining area; Thurs quiz, some live music including jazz, sports TV; pleasant back terrace, open all day. (Anon)

NORDEN HEATH SY94834
Halfway (01929) 480402
A351 Wareham–Corfe Castle; BH20 5DU Cosily laid out partly thatched pub with friendly staff, Badger beers, good wines by the glass, enjoyable food all day including children's choices, pitched-ceiling back serving bar where the locals congregate, front rooms with flagstones, log fires, stripped stonework, snug little side area; picnic-tables outside with play area, good nearby walks. (W Bowler)

OSMINGTON MILLS SY7381
✷ **Smugglers** (01305) 833125
Off A353 NE of Weymouth; DT3 6HF Bustling old partly thatched family-oriented inn, well extended, with cosy dimly lit timber-divided areas, woodburners, old local pictures, Badger ales and guests, several wines by the glass, good all-day food from varied well priced menu, friendly service; picnic sets on crazy paving by little stream, thatched summer bar, play area, useful for coast path, four bedrooms, parking charge refunded at bar. (Ann Salmon, Michael Coleman, Barrie and Mary Crees, Phil and Jane Hodson, Peter Salmon)

PAMPHILL ST9900
* **Vine** (01202) 882259
Off B3082 on NW edge of Wimborne: turn on to Cowgrove Hill at Cowgrove sign, then left up Vine Hill; BH21 4EE Simple old-fashioned place run by same family for three generations and part of Kingston Lacy estate (NT); two tiny bars with coal-effect gas fire, handful of tables and seats on lino floor, local photographs and notices on painted panelling, narrow wooden stairs up to room with darts, two changing ales, local cider and foreign bottled beers, lunchtime bar snacks; quiet background music, no credit cards, outside lavatories; children (away from bar) and dogs welcome, verandah with grapevine, sheltered gravel terrace and grassy area with picnic-sets. *(Anon)*

PIMPERNE ST9009
* **Anvil** (01258) 453431
Well back from A354; DT11 8UQ Attractive 16th-c thatched family pub with wide choice of food from generous lunchtime baguettes to substantial main dishes, well kept ales such as Fullers and local Waylands, cheerful efficient young staff, bays of plush seating in bright spacious bar, neat black-beamed dining areas; fruit machine, background music; dogs welcome in certain parts, good garden with fish pond and big weeping willow, 12 bedrooms, nice surroundings. *(George Atkinson, Leslie and Barbara Owen)*

POOLE SZ0391
Bermuda Triangle (01202) 748087
Parr Street, Lower Parkstone (just off A35 at Ashley Cross); BH14 0JY Old-fashioned bare-boards local with four interesting and particularly well kept changing ales, two or three good continental lagers on tap and many other beers from around the world, friendly landlady and staff, no food, dark panelling, snug old corners and lots of nautical and other bric-a-brac, cloudscape ceiling, back room with sports TV; too many steps for disabled access; pavement picnic-sets, open all day weekends. *(Charles Carter)*

POOLE SZ0391
Cow (01202) 749569
Station Road, Ashley Cross, Parkstone; beside Parkstone Station; BH14 8UD Interesting open-plan pub with airy bistro bar, squashy sofas, leather seating cubes and low tables on stripped-wood floors, open fire in exposed brick fireplace, good modern food (not Sun evening) from sensibly short menu, up to four real ales and a dozen wines by the glass from extensive list, friendly welcoming staff, evening dining room, board games and newspapers; background music, discreet TV; children welcome till 7.30pm, dogs in bar, enclosed heated terrace area, open all day. *(Anon)*

POOLE SZ0190
Poole Arms (01202) 673450
Town Quay; BH15 1HJ 17th-c waterfront pub looking across harbour to Brownsea Island, good fresh fish at reasonable prices, well kept Ringwood, one comfortably old-fashioned room with boarded ceiling and nautical prints, pleasant staff; outside gents'; picnic-sets in front of the handsome green-tiled façade, almost next door to the Portsmouth Hoy. *(Pat and Tony Martin, Tich Critchlow, D M and B K Moores)*

POOLE
Portsmouth Hoy (01202) 673517
The Quay; BH15 1HJ Harbourside pub with views to Brownsea Island, old-world atmosphere with dark wood, beams and bare boards, good value food including fresh fish and vegetarian choices, well kept Badger ales, friendly service, live music (jazz, blues, folk); children welcome, outside tables shared with the Poole Arms, open all day. *(David Hunt)*

PORTLAND SY6873
Cove House (01305) 820895
Follow Chiswell signposts – is at NW corner of Portland; DT5 1AW Low-beamed 18th-c pub in superb position effectively built into the sea defences just above the end of Chesil Beach, great views from three-room bar's bay windows, enjoyable reasonably priced pubby food (all-day weekends) including good crab sandwiches, Sharps Doom Bar and other well kept beers, friendly efficient service, Mon quiz; background music, steep steps down to gents'; picnic-sets out by seawall, open all day. *(Anon)*

PORTLAND SY6873
Royal Portland Arms
(01305) 862255 *Fortuneswell; DT5 1LZ* Friendly 18th-c stone-built local, homely and unfussy, with well kept quickly changing ales (some tapped from the cask), local ciders, bar snacks, live music Fri and winter Sun afternoon; open all day, till late Fri, Sat. *(Anon)*

PUDDLETOWN SY7594
Blue Vinney (01305) 848228
The Moor; DT2 8TE Popular well modernised village pub with beamed oak-floor bar and restaurant, enjoyable nicely

---

If you report on a pub that's not a featured entry, please tell us any lunchtimes or evenings when it doesn't serve bar food.

presented food (not Sun evening) from lunchtime baguettes and traditional choices to more elaborate dishes, good selection of well kept beers, ciders and wines, friendly service; children welcome, terrace overlooking garden with play area. *(Douglas and Ann Hare, Tim and Rosemary Wells, John and Sylvia Harrop)*

SANDFORD ORCAS ST6220
⋆ **Mitre** (01963) 220271
Off B3148 and B3145 N of Sherborne; DT9 4RU Thriving tucked-away country local with welcoming long-serving licensees, three well kept ales such as Ringwood, Sharps and Yeovil, wholesome home-made food (not Mon) from good soup and sandwiches up, flagstones, log fires and fresh flowers, small bar and larger pleasantly homely dining area; occasional open mike and quiz nights; children and dogs welcome, pretty back garden with terrace, closed Mon lunchtime. *(David Hudd, B J Thompson)*

SHAFTESBURY ST8622
Mitre (01747) 853002
High Street; SP7 8JE Imposing old sandstone building, unpretentious inside, with friendly efficient service, well kept Wells & Youngs ales and a couple of guests, good range of wines, decent pub food including well filled sandwiches, fine log fire, daily papers, varied mix of tables, Blackmore Vale views from back dining room and three-tier suntrap decking; background music; children and dogs welcome, open all day. *(Val and Alan Green)*

SHAPWICK ST9301
Anchor (01258) 857269
Off A350 Blandford–Poole; West Street; DT11 9LB Welcoming red-brick Victorian pub now owned by village consortium, popular freshly made food including set deals (booking advised), ales such as Palmers, Ringwood and Sharps, real cider, scrubbed pine tables on wood floors, pastel walls and open fires; children welcome, tables out in front, more in attractive garden with terrace behind, handy for Kingston Lacy (NT). *(Robert Watt)*

SHAVE CROSS SY4198
Shave Cross Inn (01308) 868358
On back lane Bridport–Marshwood, signposted locally; OS Sheet 193 map reference 415980; DT6 6HW Former medieval monks' lodging; small character timbered and flagstoned bar with huge inglenook, Branscombe Vale Branoc, Dorset Marshwood Vale and pub's own-label

4Ms, farm ciders, vintage rums, attractive restaurant with grandfather clock, pricey caribbean-influenced food (also more traditional bar menu), pleasant staff, ancient skittle alley with pool, darts and a juke box; background music; children and dogs welcome, sheltered pretty garden with thatched wishing-well, carp pool and play area, seven recently built boutique bedrooms, helipad, closed Mon. *(Kerry Law, Peter Thornton, Anita McCullough, Peter Meister, Pat and Tony Martin)*

SHROTON ST8512
Cricketers (01258) 860421
Off A350 N of Blandford (village also called Iwerne Courtney); follow signs; DT11 8QD Red-brick country pub on Wessex Ridgeway (leave muddy boots outside) overlooked by formidable grassy Iron Age ramparts of Hambledon Hill and cricket pitch; bright bar with mix of furniture, big stone fireplace, alcoves and cricketing memorabilia, Butcombe Bitter, St Austell Tribute, Sharps Doom Bar and guest from Isle of Purbeck, tasty food (not Sun evening in winter), comfortable back restaurant; background music; children welcome, secluded pretty garden with sturdy tables under parasols, well tended shrubs and herbs, open all day Sun. *(Anon)*

STOBOROUGH SY9286
Kings Arms (01929) 552705
B3075 S of Wareham; Corfe Road; BH20 5AB Part-thatched village pub with up to five well kept changing ales, Thatcher's cider, good choice of enjoyable reasonably priced food in bar and restaurant, live music Sat; children and dogs welcome, disabled access, views over marshes to River Frome from big terrace tables, open all day Fri-Sat. *(John Dorricott)*

STOKE ABBOTT ST4500
⋆ **New Inn** (01308) 868333
Off B3162 and B3163 2 miles W of Beaminster; DT8 3JW Spotless 17th-c thatched pub with friendly helpful staff, good nicely presented food from varied menu using local produce including own vegetables and herbs, well kept Palmers ales, woodburner in big inglenook, beams, brasses and copper, some handsome panelling, flagstoned dining room, fresh flowers on tables; occasional background music; children welcome, wheelchair access, two lovely gardens, unspoilt quiet thatched village with good surrounding walks, street fair third Sat in July, closed Sun evening, Mon. *(Councillor Stephen Chappell)*

Stars before the name of a pub show exceptional character and appeal.
They don't mean extra comfort. And they are nothing to do with food quality.
Even quite a basic pub can win stars, if it's individual enough.

STOURTON CAUNDLE ST7115
✴**Trooper** (01963) 362405
Village signed off A30 E of Milborne Port; The Square; DT10 2JW Pretty little stone-built pub in lovely village setting, friendly staff and atmosphere, good simple food and well kept changing beers including own microbrews, reasonable prices, spotless tiny low-ceilinged bar, stripped stone dining room, darts, dominoes and shove-ha'penny, skittle alley; background music, sports TV, outside gents'; children and dogs welcome, a few picnic-sets out in front, pleasant side garden with play area, camping, closed Mon lunchtime. *(Anon)*

STRATTON SY6593
Saxon Arms (01305) 260020
Off A37 NW of Dorchester; The Square; DT2 9WG Traditional but recently built flint and thatch local, open-plan, bright and spacious with light oak tables and comfortable settles on flagstones or carpet, open fire, well kept Ringwood, Timothy Taylors Landlord and two guests, good value wines, tasty generous food including good choice of specials and winter lunchtime set deal (Mon-Fri), large comfortable dining section on right, traditional games; background music; children and dogs welcome, terrace tables overlooking village green, open all day Fri-Sun. *(Anon)*

STUDLAND SZ0382
Bankes Arms (01929) 450225
Off B3351, Isle of Purbeck; Manor Road; BH19 3AU Very popular spot above fine beach, outstanding country, sea and cliff views from huge garden over road with lots of seating; comfortably basic big bar with raised drinking area, beams, flagstones and good log fire, well kept changing ales including own Isle of Purbeck, local cider, good wines by the glass, enjoyable all-day food, friendly efficient service, darts and pool in side area; background music, machines, sports TV, can get very busy on summer weekends and parking complicated (NT car park); over-8s and dogs welcome, just off coast path, big comfortable bedrooms. *(Lucy Johnstone, Lawrence Pearse, Alan Cowell, R Elliott, Jenny and Brian Seller, S J and C C Davidson)*

STURMINSTER MARSHALL SY9499
Black Horse (01258) 857217
A350; BH21 4AQ Welcoming pub with enjoyable good value food from nice sandwiches up, Badger ales, long comfortable beamed and panelled bar. *(Anon)*

STURMINSTER MARSHALL SY9500
Red Lion (01258) 857319
Opposite church; off A350 Blandford–Poole; BH21 4BU Attractive village pub opposite handsome church, bustling local atmosphere, wide variety of enjoyable food including set menu deal, special diets

catered for, well kept Badger ales and nice wines, old-fashioned roomy U-shaped bar with log fire, good-sized dining room in former skittle alley; background music; children and dogs welcome, disabled access, back garden with wicker furniture and picnic-sets, open all day Sun, closed Mon. *(Robert Watt)*

STURMINSTER NEWTON ST7813
✴**Bull** (01258) 472435
A357, S of centre; DT10 2BS Friendly thatched 16th-c country pub by River Stour, low beams, soft lighting and plenty of character, good home-made food, Badger ales; children welcome in compact eating area, roadside picnic-sets, more in secluded back garden. *(Sue Dean)*

SWANAGE SZ0278
Red Lion (01929) 423533
High Street; BH19 2LY Busy 17th-c low-beamed local, great choice of ciders and up to six well kept ales including Palmers, Ringwood, Sharps and Timothy Taylors, good value food from sandwiches and baked potatoes up; background and some live music, pool; children welcome, picnic-sets in garden with partly covered terrace, bedrooms in former back coach house, open all day. *(Tich Critchlow)*

SYMONDSBURY SY4493
Ilchester Arms (01308) 422600
Signed off A35 just W of Bridport; DT6 6HD Welcoming 16th-c thatched pub with rustic open-plan bar, low beams and a high-backed built-in settle by inglenook, three well kept Palmers ales, enjoyable traditional food from lunchtime sandwiches to fresh fish, pretty restaurant with another fire, pub games, skittle alley doubling as family room; dogs welcome in bar, level entrance (steps from car park), tables in nice brookside back garden with play area, peaceful village with good walks, three bedrooms, open all day weekends if busy. *(Anon)*

UPLODERS SY5093
Crown (01308) 485356
Signed off A35 E of Bridport; DT6 4NU Refurbished stone village pub, log fires, dark low beams, flagstones and mix of old furniture including stripped pine, traditional food, Palmers ales; background music; children and dogs welcome, tables in attractive two-tier garden. *(Anon)*

UPWEY SY6785
Old Ship (01305) 812522
Off A354; Ridgeway; DT3 5QQ Traditional 17th-c beamed pub (features in Hardy's *Under the Greenwood Tree*), alcoves and log fires, Ringwood and a couple of guests, enjoyable sensibly priced food served by friendly attentive staff, skittle alley; children welcome, picnic-sets in garden with

terrace, interesting walks nearby, open all day Fri, Sat. *(Terry Townsend)*

WAREHAM
SY9287

Kings Arms (01929) 552503

North Street (A351, N end of town); BH20 4AD Traditional stone and thatch town local, well kept Ringwood and guests, decent good value pubby food, friendly staff, back serving counter and two bars off flagstoned central corridor, beams and inglenook, darts; children and dogs welcome, garden behind with picnic-sets, open all day. *(S J and C C Davidson)*

WAREHAM
SY9287

Old Granary (01929) 552010

The Quay; BH20 4LP Fine old brick building with riverside terrace; emphasis on dining but two small beamed rooms by main door for drinkers, enjoyable fairly standard food, well kept Badger ales and good wines by the glass, neat efficient young staff, airy dining room with leather high-backed chairs and pews around pale wood tables, brick walls and new oak standing timbers, two further rooms with big photographs of the pub, woodburners, nice relaxed atmosphere; quiet background jazz; children welcome, boats for hire over bridge, open all day from 9am (10am Sun). *(Sue and Mike Todd, Hugh Roberts, Patrick and Daphne Darley, Peter Salmon)*

WAREHAM
SY9287

Quay Inn (01929) 552735

The Quay; BH20 4LP Comfortable 18th-c inn in great spot by the water, enjoyable food including pubby favourites and cook-your-own-meat on a hot stone, friendly attentive service, well kept Otter, Isle of Purbeck and Ringwood, reasonably priced wine list, flagstones and open fires; children welcome, terrace area and picnic-sets out on quay, boat trips, bedrooms, parking nearby can be difficult, market day Sat, open all day in summer. *(Anon)*

WAREHAM FOREST
SY9089

✴ Silent Woman (01929) 552909

Wareham–Bere Regis; Bere Road; BH20 7PA Long neatly kept dining pub divided by doorways and standing timbers, nice variety of enjoyable home-made food, Badger ales kept well including a seasonal one, country wines, traditional furnishings, farm tools and stripped masonry; background music, no children inside; dogs welcome, wheelchair access, plenty of picnic-sets outside including a covered area, walks nearby. *(R Elliott, Leslie and Barbara Owen)*

WAYTOWN
SY4797

Hare & Hounds (01308) 488203

Between B3162 and A3066 N of Bridport; DT6 5LQ Attractive 18th-c country local up and down steps, friendly caring staff, well kept Palmers tapped from the cask, local cider, enjoyable good value food generously served including popular Sun lunch, open fire, two small cottagey rooms and pretty dining room; children and dogs welcome, lovely Brit Valley views from sizeable and unusual garden with play area. *(Peter Thornton, Will Hancox)*

WEST BEXINGTON
SY5386

Manor Hotel (01308) 897660

Off B3157 SE of Bridport; Beach Road; DT2 9DF Relaxing quietly set hotel with long history and fine sea views – refurbishment by present owners; good choice of food in beamed cellar bar, flagstoned restaurant or Victorian-style conservatory, well kept Otter, Thatcher's cider and several wines by the glass; children welcome, dogs on leads (not in restaurant), charming well kept garden, close to Chesil Beach, 13 bedrooms. *(Pete Flower)*

WEST LULWORTH
SY8280

Castle Inn (01929) 400311

B3070 SW of Wareham; BH20 5RN Pretty 16th-c thatched inn in lovely spot near Lulworth Cove, good walks and lots of summer visitors; beamed flagstoned bar concentrating on wide choice of popular generously served food, well kept changing local ales, 12 ciders/perries, maze of booth seating divided by ledges, cosy more modern-feeling lounge bar, pleasant restaurant; background music; children and dogs welcome, front terrace, long attractive garden behind on several levels, boules and barbecues, 12 bedrooms. *(Lawrence Pearse, Ian and Sharon Shorthouse)*

WEST PARLEY
SZ0898

Curlew (01202) 594811

Christchurch Road; BH22 8SQ Vintage Inn in early 19th-c farmhouse; informal beamed areas around central bar, mixed furnishings, candles on tables, two log fires, emphasis on enjoyable food including good value fixed price menu (till 5pm), three well kept ales and plenty of wines by the glass, friendly courteous staff; picnic-sets in front garden. *(M J Potts, David and Sally Frost, Peter Salmon)*

WEST STAFFORD
SY7289

Wise Man (01305) 261970

Sgned off A352 Dorchester–Wareham; DT2 8AG 16th-c thatched and beamed pub near Hardy's cottage, open-plan interior with flagstone and wood floors, good well priced food from lunchtime ciabattas up including some interesting choices, Sun carvery, Butcombe Bitter, Dorset Jurassic, Ringwood Best and St Austell Proper Job from central bar, good choice of wines by the glass, friendly attentive staff; children and dogs welcome, disabled facilities, plenty of seats outside, lovely walks nearby, open all day weekends. *(Michael Coleman, Simon Rodway, Brian Boyland, R J and G M Townson)*

WEYMOUTH   SY6778
Boot 07809 440772
High West Street; DT4 8JH
Friendly unspoilt local dating from 1600s
near the harbour, well worn comfort with
beams, bare boards, panelling, hooded
stone-mullioned windows and coal fires, cosy
gently sloping snug, well kept Ringwood ales
and guests from five brass handpumps, real
cider and good selection of malt whiskies, no
food apart from pork pies and pickled eggs,
live music Tues, Weds quiz; disabled access,
pavement tables, open all day. *(Anon)*

WEYMOUTH   SY6878
Nothe Tavern (01305) 770935
Barrack Road; DT4 8TZ Roomy and
comfortable early 19th-c pub near Nothe
Fort, wide range of good food including fresh
local fish and good value Sun carvery, OAP
weekday deals too, friendly staff coping at
busy times, well kept ales such as Ringwood,
decent wines and good choice of malts,
lots of dark wood, whisky-water jugs on
ceiling, interesting prints and photographs,
restaurant with distant harbour glimpses;
may be quiet background music; children
and dogs welcome, more views from
terrace. *(Robin Manners, Leslie and
Barbara Owen)*

WEYMOUTH   SY6778
Ship (01305) 773879
Custom House Quay; DT4 8BE Neatly
modern extended waterfront pub with
several nautical-theme open-plan levels,
well kept Badger ales from long bar, several
wines by the glass, enjoyable good value
usual food (upstairs only in the evening)
from sandwiches and baguettes up, friendly
helpful staff; unobtrusive background music;
dogs welcome (biscuits for them), wheelchair
access downstairs, some quayside seating
and pleasant back terrace. *(Phil Bryant,
E J Palmer)*

WEYMOUTH   SY6778
Wellington Arms (01305) 786963
St Alban Street; DT4 8PY Friendly
backstreet pub with handsome 19th-c tiled
façade, panelled and carpeted interior with
banquettes, mirrors and lots of old local
photographs, well kept Ringwood and other
Marstons-related beers, good value pubby

food, some live music; children welcome in
back dining room, disabled access, open all
day. *(MLR)*

WIMBORNE MINSTER   SU0000
Kings Head (01202) 880101
The Square; BH21 1JG Imposing 18th-c
hotel (Old English Inn) with good choice of
enjoyable food in roomy bar or restaurant,
Greene King ales and some nice wines,
cheery helpful staff; children welcome,
comfortable reasonably priced bedrooms,
good breakfast, open all day. *(Sue and
Mike Todd)*

WIMBORNE ST GILES   SU0212
Bull (01725) 517300
Off B3078 N of Wimborne; BH21 5NF
Nicely refurbished open-plan Edwardian
dining inn, good if not particularly cheap
food using fresh local ingredients (organic
where possible), fine choice of wines by the
glass, Badger ales, good friendly service,
conservatory overlooking neatly kept garden;
children and dogs welcome, five stylish
bedrooms, closed Sun evening, Mon.
(Michael Doswell, Robert Watt)

WINKTON   SZ1696
Fishermans Haunt (01202) 477283
B3347 N of Christchurch; BH23 7AS
Comfortable big-windowed riverside inn on
fringes of New Forest, four well kept Fullers/
Gales beers, decent choice of food using
local produce such as venison, good helpful
service, two log fires, restaurant views of
River Avon; background music; children
welcome, dogs in bar, disabled facilities,
tables among shrubs in quiet back garden,
heaters in covered area, 12 comfortable
bedrooms, good breakfast, open all day.
(Sara Fulton, Roger Baker)

WINTERBORNE ZELSTON SY8997
Botany Bay (01929) 459227
A31 Wimborne–Dorchester; DT11 9ET
Spreading open-plan roadside dining pub,
front part divided into areas by partly glazed
partitions, back more restauranty, enjoyable
food from sandwiches through usual pubby
dishes to grills, Sun carvery, sensible prices
and good friendly service, well kept Badger
ales, decent house wines and coffee; children
welcome, tables on back terrace.
(R J and D S Courtney)

Post Office address codings confusingly give the impression that some pubs are in
Dorset, when they're really in Somerset (which is where we list them).

Essex

Quite a few pubs here hold regular summer beer festivals – the Hoop in Stock has been doing so for over 20 years. So for an interesting choice of ales, and pubs that hold a Beer Award, head to the Sun in Feering, Bell at Horndon-on-the-Hill, Crown in Little Walden, White Hart in Margaretting Tye, Viper in Mill Green and, of course, the Hoop in Stock. We've a good clutch of new entries this year: the Angel & Harp in Dunmow (nicely opened-up and relaxing, a wide choice of popular food and several ales), Square & Compasses at Fuller Street (neat country pub with nearby walks, thoughtful choice of drinks and good food), Pheasant in Gestingthorpe (civilised and easy-going with stylish bedrooms), Chequers at Goldhanger (cheerful village pub with half a dozen changing ales), Crown & Thistle in Great Chesterfield (interesting old place with some fine features), Rainbow & Dove at Hastingwood (good value food and handy for the M11), Compasses at Littley Green (classic country tavern owned by the Ridley brewing family), Rose in Peldon (handsome 15th-c coaching inn with popular cooking) and Bell at Wendens Ambo (a lively local with lots going on). There are some lovely old buildings that make a fine setting for a special meal. Pubs with a Food Award include the Axe & Compasses at Aythorpe Roding, Cricketers in Clavering, Bell in Horndon-on-the-Hill and Old Windmill at South Hanningfield. Our Essex Dining Pub 2014 is the Bell at Horndon-on-the-Hill.

 ARKESDEN   TL4834   Map 5

Axe & Compasses ♀

Off B1038; CB11 4EX

Comfortably traditional pub with Greene King beers and decent food

This rambling thatched pub in a particularly lovely village is popular locally and with its many visitors. The oldest part, which dates from the 17th c, is the traditionally carpeted lounge bar with its low-slung ceilings, polished upholstered oak and elm seats, sofas and a blazing fire. A smaller quirky public bar is uncarpeted, with built-in settles, and darts; throughout there are gleaming brasses and a relaxed welcoming atmosphere created by the pleasant licensees and their staff. Belhaven 80/-, Greene King IPA, H&H Olde Trip, St Austell Trelawny and Thwaites Wainwright on handpump, a very good wine list (with 15 by the glass) and around two dozen malt whiskies. There are seats on a side terrace with pretty hanging baskets. Parking is at the back.

Tasty bar food includes sandwiches, prawn and smoked mackerel roulade, chicken liver and bacon pâté, pancake filled with creamy mushrooms, cheddar-topped burger with home-made relish and chunky chips, chicken with lemon and tarragon, fresh grilled or battered cod, lambs liver and bacon, slow-roast pork belly on bubble and squeak, daily specials, and puddings. *Benchmark main dish: steak and kidney pie £13.95. Two-course evening meal £21.00.*

Greene King ~ Tenants Themis and Diane Christou ~ Real ale ~ (01799) 550272 ~ Open 11.30-2.30, 6-11; 12-3, 7-10.30 Sun ~ Bar food 12-2, 7-9; not winter Sun evening ~ Restaurant ~ Children welcome ~ www.axeandcompasses.co.uk *Recommended by Simon Watkins, David and Sue Smith, Alan Bulley*

AYTHORPE RODING
TL5915   Map 5

Axe & Compasses 🍴
B184 S of Dunmow; CM6 1PP

Appealing free house, nice balance of eating and drinking, and friendly welcome

Many customers at this pretty weatherboarded pub are here to enjoy the notably good food, but plenty of locals drop in for a chat and a pint of Sharps Doom Bar or three guests from local brewers such as Growler, Shepherd Neame and Wibblers on handpump or tapped from the cask; also, up to three Weston's farm ciders. Everything is neatly kept, warm and cosy, with bent old beams and timbers, stripped red-brick walls, comfortable bar chairs at the counter, leatherette settles and stools and dark country chairs around a few pub tables on pale boards and turkish rugs. The original part, on the left, has a two-way fireplace marking off a snug little raftered dining area with sentimental prints on dark masonry and a big open-faced clock; background music. The small back garden has stylish modern tables and chairs.

As well as serving breakfasts from 9am, the wide choice of enjoyable food includes sandwiches, mussels with white wine, garlic and cream, chicken liver and brandy with home-made chutney, an antipasti board, venison and wild boar sausages with wholegrain mustard mash and buttered leeks, butternut squash, chestnut and mushroom risotto, chicken breast with mushroom gnocchi, tasty pies such as rabbit in cider or feta, spinach and sweet potato or chicken and smoky bacon with vermouth, whole local plaice with lobster butter, and puddings like knickerbocker glory and spotted dick and custard. *Benchmark main dish: beer-battered fresh cod with chips £11.95. Two-course evening meal £17.00.*

Free house ~ Licensee David Hunt ~ Real ale ~ (01279) 876648 ~ Open 9am-11pm(midnight Fri, Sat); 12-10.30 Sun ~ Bar food 9-2.30, 6-9.30; 12-8 Sun ~ Restaurant ~ Children welcome ~ Dogs allowed in bar ~ www.theaxeandcompasses.co.uk *Recommended by R E Munn, Alan Just, N R White*

If a service charge is mentioned prominently on a menu or accommodation terms, you must pay it if service was satisfactory. If service is really bad, you are legally entitled to refuse to pay some or all of the service charge as compensation for not getting the service you might reasonably have expected.

CLAVERING

Cricketers

TL4832 Map 5

B1038 Newport–Buntingford; CB11 4QT

Busy dining pub with inventive food, real ales and a carefully chosen wine list; individually decorated bedrooms

Owned by Jamie Oliver's parents for many years, this neatly kept and carefully modernised pub has plenty of old-fashioned charm. The main area with its very low beams and big open fireplace has bays of deep purple button-backed banquettes and padded leather dining chairs on dark floorboards. The back part on the left is more obviously for eating: two fairly compact carpeted areas, with a step between them. The right side is similar, set more formally for dining, but still traditional with big copper and brass pans on dark beams and timbers; background music. Signed books by Jamie are on sale. Ales from Adnams, Nethergate and Saffron on handpump and 20 wines by the glass from a list with helpful notes. The attractive front terrace has wicker-look seats around teak tables among colourful flowering shrubs. They added six new bedrooms this year; the pub is handy for Stansted Airport.

As well as pizzas from the wood-fired oven (Friday-Sunday afternoons in warm weather) and using produce from Jamie's organic garden nearby, the tempting food includes sandwiches, home-cured gravadlax of organic salmon with creamy tarragon dressing, curried and creamy smoked haddock with free-range poached egg and toasted home-made sourdough, calves liver and bacon with shallot and madeira jus, fresh squid and chorizo with home-made linguine, trio of pork (chargrilled loin, slow-roast belly, crispy croquette) with crackling and apple and sage jus, 30-day-hung rib-eye with harissa sauce, and puddings. *Benchmark main dish: home-made pie of the day £14.50. Two-course evening meal £22.00.*

Free house ~ Licensee Trevor Oliver ~ Real ale ~ (01799) 550442 ~ Open 11-11 ~ Bar food 12-2(2.30 Sat), 6.30-9.30; 12-8 Sun ~ Children welcome ~ Live piano Sun afternoon ~ Bedrooms: £67.50/£95 ~ www.thecricketers.co.uk *Recommended by Tina and David Woods-Taylor, Mrs Margo Finlay, Jörg Kasprowski*

DUNMOW

Angel & Harp

TL6222 Map 5

Church Road, Church End; B1057 signposted to Finchingfield/The Bardfields, off B184 N of town; CM6 2AD

Comfortable and relaxing, a good place to drop in any time of day

Nicely opened up, this rambles about with a good choice of seating from armchairs, sofas and banquettes to more upright dining chairs – or, for a very pubby feel, the bar stools along each side of a free-standing zinc 'counter' that spans two structural uprights. The low-ceilinged main area has a substantial brick fireplace and some fine old floor tiling as well as carpet. The informal mood is heightened by the way the neatly dressed staff are as likely to be standing by the big espresso machine on a separate dresser as behind the bar – and by the broad hatch showing the gleaming kitchen at work. They have Adnams Lighthouse, Nethergate IPA and Wibblers Apprentice on handpump, a good choice of wines by the glass, and nostalgic background pop music. Up a few steps, an interesting raftered room has Perspex chairs around one huge table. A glass wall gives tables in the attractive L-shaped extension a view over the flagstoned courtyard with its wishing fountain, cushioned metal chairs under big canopies, and picnic-sets on the neat grass beyond.

As well as super breakfasts from 9am, the wide choice of popular food includes sandwiches with crisps and salad, several boards (meze, antipasti, fish), spicy chicken skewers with coriander and mint salad and lime yoghurt, broad bean and pea risotto, eight different pizzas, five different burgers, sausages with mash and onion gravy, half a free-range chicken with hickory barbecue sauce and home-made coleslaw, sea bream fillet with roasted red pepper dressing, artichokes and tomatoes, and puddings such as chocolate brownie with chocolate sauce and ice-cream and eton mess; Thursday is grill night. *Benchmark main dish: chargrilled burger with smoked bacon and cheese £10.95. Two-course evening meal £18.00.*

Free house ~ Licensee David Hunt ~ Real ale ~ (01371) 859259 ~ Open 9am-11pm(10pm Sun) ~ Bar food 9am-9.30pm ~ Restaurant ~ Live music third Fri of month ~ www.angelandharp.co.uk *Recommended by Ruth May, Caroline Prescott*

FEERING
TL8720   Map 5

Sun £

Just off A12 Kelvedon bypass; Feering Hill (B1024 just W of Feering proper); CO5 9NH

Striking timbered and jettied pub with good beer and food, and pleasant garden

With its handsome 16th-c frontage, this well run pub offers a warm welcome to all. The spreading carpeted bar is relaxed, unpretentious and civilised, with two big woodburning stoves, one in the huge central inglenook fireplace, another by an antique winged settle on the left. Throughout there are handsomely carved black beams and timbers galore, and attractive wildflower murals in a frieze above the central timber divider. Half a dozen Shepherd Neame ales on handpump – Bitter, Kents Best, Spitfire, Early Bird, Amber and Bishops Finger and monthly guests – and summer and winter beer festivals; cheerful service, daily papers, board games. A brick-paved back courtyard has tables, heaters and a shelter, and the garden beyond has tall trees shading picnic-sets.

At weekends they offer pizzas from a wood-fired oven, as well as serving sandwiches, potted crab with pickled cucumber salad, garlic- and rosemary-infused camembert with crusty bread, home-roasted ham and free-range eggs, aubergine and wild mushroom risotto, chicken kiev with green bean salad, sweet and sour pork belly with wilted pak choi, lambs liver and bacon with bubble and squeak, and puddings such as bakewell tart with home-made custard and a crumble of the day. *Benchmark main dish: home-made pie of the day £9.95. Two-course evening meal £16.00.*

Shepherd Neame ~ Tenant Andy Howard ~ Real ale ~ (01376) 570442 ~ Open 12-3, 5.30-11; 12-midnight Sat; 12-10.30 Sun ~ Bar food 12-2.30, 6-9.30; 12-8 Sun ~ Children welcome ~ Dogs welcome ~ www.suninnfeering.co.uk *Recommended by Mark Price, Steve Homer*

FULLER STREET
TL7416   Map 5

Square & Compasses

Back road Great Leighs–Hatfield Peverel; CM3 2BB

Neatly kept country pub, handy for walks, with two woodburning stoves, four ales and enjoyable food

In attractive countryside and handy for the Essex Way long-distance footpath, this is a small and well looked after country pub. The L-shaped beamed bar has two woodburning stoves in inglenook fireplaces, Dark Star Hophead, Farmers Ales A Drop of Nelsons Blood, a beer named for the pub and a changing guest on handpump, Weston's cider and 14 wines by the glass, served by friendly staff. The carpeted dining room has shelves of bottles and decanters against timbered walls and an appealing variety of dining chairs around dark wooden tables set with linen napkins; there's a small extension for walkers and dogs. Background jazz. Tables out in front on decking have gentle country views.

Using local produce where possible the good food includes sandwiches, cromer crab cake with lime, chilli, coriander and a chilli dipping sauce, baked goats cheese soufflé with salad and white truffle dressing, home-cooked ham with free-range eggs, cumberland herb sausage ring with spring onion mash and onion gravy, fresh fish pie, bacon-wrapped braised pheasant with parsnip purée, slow-cooked lamb shank with sweet potato mash and gravy, and puddings such as rhubarb and ginger crumble with ice-cream and iced banana and pistachio parfait with caramelised banana. *Benchmark main dish: steak in ale pie £11.95. Two-course evening meal £19.00.*

Free house ~ Licensee Victor Roome ~ Real ale ~ (01245) 361477 ~ Open 11.30-3, 5.30-11(11.30 Fri); 11.30am-midnight Sat; 12-11 Sun ~ Bar food 12-2(2.30 Sat), 6.30-9.30; 12-6 Sun ~ Restaurant ~ Well behaved children welcome ~ Dogs allowed in bar ~ www.thesquareandcompasses.co.uk *Recommended by Mrs Margo Finlay, Jörg Kasprowski*

GESTINGTHORPE   TL8138   Map 5
Pheasant 🛏
Off B1058; CO9 3AU

Civilised and easy-going inn with a good mix of customers, enjoyable food, a thoughtful range of drinks and seats outside; stylish bedrooms

Owned by a former garden designer and his wife – they grow their own fruit and vegetables and keep bees – this is a civilised country pub with plenty of lovely old-fashioned character. The small opened-up rooms have beamed low ceilings, woodburning stoves in nice old brick fireplaces, settles with big scatter cushions, an assortment of dining chairs around scrubbed or dark wooden tables on bare floorboards, a few hops here and there and shelves with books and china platters. Locals gather at the high bar chairs by the counter, where they serve Adnams Southwold, Crouch Vale Brewers Gold and a beer named for the pub on handpump, nine wines by the glass and a good choice of soft drinks. Outside on gravel are seats and stools, some under parasols, and views across the fields. The stylish bedrooms, named after historical local characters, are in the separate Coach House; breakfasts are good.

They hold regular themed evenings and use their smokehouse for the tempting food: sandwiches, crab and crayfish cake with thai green mayonnaise, melting goats cheese with beetroot, orange and walnut salad, trio of sausages with mash and onion gravy, sage-stuffed chicken breast with mashed swede and honey-roast carrots, pork belly with cider sauce, spring onion mash and crackling, confit duck with apple and red onion tarte tatin, and puddings such as raspberries in jelly with stem ginger ice-cream and sticky toffee pudding with caramel sauce and honeycomb ice-cream. *Benchmark main dish: pie of the day using meat from their own farm £12.50. Two-course evening meal £18.50.*

Free house ~ Licensees James and Diana Donoghue ~ Real ale ~ (01787) 461196 ~ Open 12-3, 6-11; 12-11.30 Sat, Sun; closed first two weeks of Jan ~ Bar food 12-2.30, 6.30-9 ~ Children welcome ~ Dogs allowed in bar ~ Bedrooms: /£80 ~ www.thepheasant.net *Recommended by Walter and Susan Rinaldi-Butcher*

GOLDHANGER TL9008 Map 5

Chequers

Church Street; off B1026 E of Heybridge; CM9 8AS

Cheerful and neatly kept pub with six real ales, traditional furnishings, friendly staff and tasty food

Overlooking a fine old church, this popular village pub keeps around half a dozen real ales on handpump, such as Adnams Ghost Ship, Crouch Vale Brewers Gold, Sharps Doom Bar, Woodfordes Wherry, Wells & Youngs Bitter and a guest like Hogs Back Englands Glory; they hold spring and autumn beer festivals. The nice old corridor with its red and black tiled floor leads to six rambling rooms, including a spacious lounge with dark beams, black panelling and a huge sash window overlooking the graveyard, a traditional dining room with bare boards and carpeting, and a games room with bar billiards; woodburning stove, open fires, TV and background music. There are picnic-sets under umbrellas in the courtyard with its grapevine.

Quite a choice of well liked bar food includes sandwiches, duck and port pâté with cumberland sauce, crispy cayenne whitebait with tartare sauce, ham with free-range eggs and chips, burger with bacon, cheese, coleslaw, barbecue relish and chips, courgette and almond crumble, smoked haddock and spring onion fishcakes with horseradish dip, chargrilled chicken breast with bacon and leeks in stilton and mushroom sauce, bass baked with fennel and thyme, and puddings like apple and cinnamon crumble and toffee and banana cheesecake. *Benchmark main dish: steak in stout pie £10.95. Two-course evening meal £15.00.*

Punch ~ Lease Philip Glover and Dominic Davies ~ Real ale ~ (01621) 788203 ~ Open 11-11; 12-10.30 Sun ~ Bar food 12-3, 6.30-9; not Sun evening or bank holiday Mon evening ~ Restaurant ~ Children welcome except in tap room ~ Dogs allowed in bar ~ www.thechequersgoldhanger.co.uk *Recommended by John Edwell*

GOSFIELD TL7829 Map 5

Kings Head £

The Street; CO9 1TP

Comfortable dining pub with proper public bar and good value food

Splashes of warm contemporary colour brighten the modernised interior of this old beamed pub. The softly lit beamed main bar, with red panelled dado and ceiling, has neat modern black leather armchairs, bucket chairs and a sofa, as well as sturdy pale wood dining chairs and tables on dark boards, and a log fire in a handsome old brick fireplace with big bellows. Black timbers mark off a dining area with red furnishings, carpets and walls that opens into a carpeted conservatory; background music, daily papers. Adnams Southwold, Sharps Doom Bar and Timothy Taylors Landlord on handpump, around a dozen wines by the glass (several english ones), organic soft drinks and an impressive list of 70 malt whiskies – the well supported whisky club meets four times a year for tastings. The good-sized, quite separate public bar, with a purple pool table, games machine, darts and TV, has its own partly covered terrace; the main terrace has circular picnic-sets.

Please tell us if the décor, atmosphere, food or drink at a pub is different from our description. We rely on readers' reports to keep us up to date: feedback@goodguides.com, or (no stamp needed) The Good Pub Guide, FREEPOST TN1569, Wadhurst, E Sussex TN5 7BR.

Neat, black-clad young staff serve the enterprising food: sandwiches, various sharing plates, chicken and asparagus terrine with onion chutney, portobello mushroom topped with cheddar wrapped in parma ham with red onion marmalade, burger with crispy bacon, cheddar, camembert or brie and chips, sweet potato and spinach tagliatelle with roquefort, trio of sausages with mash and onion gravy, chicken breast with crayfish and tarragon butter and spring onion potato cake, and puddings such as banoffi pie with honey and cinnamon twist and apple and ginger crumble with custard; there's also a two- and three-course set weekday menu and a Friday evening deal. *Benchmark main dish: pork loin with beetroot, dauphinoise potatoes and wilted spinach £11.95. Two-course evening meal £17.75.*

Enterprise ~ Lease Mark Bloomfield ~ Real ale ~ (01787) 474016 ~ Open 12-11 (1am Sat); 12-10.30 Sun ~ Bar food 12-2.30, 6.9.30; 12-5.30 Sun ~ Restaurant ~ Children welcome ~ Dogs allowed in bar ~ www.thekingsheadgosfield.co.uk
Recommended by Richard and Penny Gibbs

GREAT CHESTERFORD   TL5142   Map 5
Crown & Thistle
1.5 miles from M11 junction 9A; pub signposted off B184, in High Street; CB10 1PL

Interesting ancient pub with good home cooking and local ales

There's some attractive decorative plasterwork, inside and out, at this substantial village pub, particularly around the early 16th-c inglenook fireplace; look out for the lovely old wooden benches too. There's a low-ceilinged, carpeted area by the bar, and the long handsomely proportioned dining room has a striking photographic mural of the village. Ales on handpump come from breweries like Buntingford, Milton and Woodfordes and are served by friendly staff. The suntrap back courtyard has picnic-sets.

 The popular seasonal food includes sandwiches, potted crab and smoked salmon, garlic king prawns, wild mushroom and asparagus risotto, ham and eggs, sausage and mash, duck breast with plum sauce, grilled lemon sole with lemon and parsley, and puddings like chocolate sponge and cheesecake. *Benchmark main dish: steak and kidney pudding £12.95. Two-course evening meal £18.00.*

Free house ~ Licensee Simon Clark ~ Real ale ~ (01799) 530278 ~ Open 12-3, 6-midnight; 12-6 Sun; closed Sun evening, Mon ~ Bar food 12-2.30(3.30 Sun), 6.30-9.30 ~ Children welcome ~ Dogs allowed in bar   *Recommended by Ruth May, Harvey Brown, Mrs Margo Finlay, Jörg Kasprowski*

HASTINGWOOD   TL4807   Map 5
Rainbow & Dove £
0.5 miles from M11 junction 7; CM17 9JX

Pleasantly traditional low-beamed pub with good value food; handy for M11

This 16th-c cottage is just the place for a break from the nearby motorway. There's a warm welcome from the friendly licensees and the three small rooms have low beams, a woodburning stove in the original fireplace, built-in cushioned wall seats and mate's chairs around pubby tables, some stripped stone and cream or green paintwork, and golfing memorabilia. Adnams Broadside, Oakham Vagabond, Sharps Doom Bar and Timothy Taylors Landlord on handpump and 11 wines by the glass; background music and darts. There are seats and tables under parasols at the front with picnic-sets on grass, and country views.

🍴 Very fairly priced and using local produce, the food includes sandwiches and baguettes, port pâté with sweet piccalilli, crumbed whitebait with horseradish crème fraîche, garlic, broad bean and asparagus risotto, burger with bacon, tomato, onions and cheese, chicken curry, home-cured honey-glazed ham and free-range eggs, daily specials like baked mushroom rarebit, whole bass with rosemary and sea salt crust, game pie, and puddings such as steamed treacle sponge and custard and a cheesecake of the day. *Benchmark main dish: steak, kidney and ale pie £8.75. Two-course evening meal £14.50.*

Free house ~ Licensees Andrew and Kathryn Keep ~ Real ale ~ (01279) 415419 ~ Open 11.30-3, 6-11; 12-3.30, 6-11 Sat; 12-5 Sun; closed Sun evening ~ Bar food 12-2.30(3 Sat), 6-9(9.30 Sat); 12-4 Sun ~ Children welcome ~ Dogs welcome ~ www.rainbowanddove.com *Recommended by Charles and Pauline Stride, Roger and Pauline Pearce*

HATFIELD BROAD OAK
Dukes Head ♀

TL5416 Map 5

B183 Hatfield Heath–Takeley; High Street; CM22 7HH

Relaxed well run dining pub with enjoyable food, and nicely linked separate areas in attractive layout

Readers have particularly noted the kind and genuinely friendly staff in this comfortable village pub. Various intimate seating areas ramble pleasantly around the central-feature woodburner and side servery, and the atmosphere is relaxed and easy-going. Seating is mainly good solid wooden dining chairs around a variety of more or less chunky stripped tables, with a comfortable group of armchairs and a sofa at one end, and a slightly more formal area at the back on the right. Cheerful prints, and occasional magenta panels in the mainly cream décor, make for quite a buoyant mood. Greene King IPA, Sharps Doom Bar, Timothy Taylors Landlord and a guest like Hop Back Summer Lightning on handpump and 25 wines by the glass from a good list; background music and board games. Sam the dog welcomes other dogs, and there are always dog biscuits behind the bar. The back garden, with a sheltered terrace and wendy house, has chairs around teak tables under cocktail parasols; there are also some picnic-sets in the front angle of the building, which has some nice pargeting.

🍴 Good, popular food includes sandwiches, maple-smoked organic salmon and crab cake with chive bisque, bubble and squeak with oak-smoked bacon, free-range poached egg and hollandaise sauce, sweet potato and pumpkin gnocchi with sage and parsley pesto, sausages with mustard mash, slow-cooked beef cobbler with creamed cabbage and bacon, moroccan-spiced lamb shank with onion and herb tabbouleh and minted yoghurt, specials such as bass fillet with scallops, potato rösti and romano pepper sauce or moules marinière, and puddings. *Benchmark main dish: king prawn spaghetti £12.75. Two-course evening meal £19.00.*

Enterprise ~ Lease Liz Flodman ~ Real ale ~ (01279) 718598 ~ Open 11.30-11; 10.30am-11.30pm Sat; 11.30-11 Sun; 11.30-3, 5-11 Mon-Thurs in winter ~ Bar food 12-2.30, 6.30-9.30(10 Fri); 10.30-10 Sat; 12-9 Sun ~ Restaurant ~ Children welcome ~ Dogs allowed in bar ~ www.thedukeshead.co.uk *Recommended by David Jackman*

Real ale may be served from handpumps, electric pumps (not just the on-off switches used for keg beer) or – common in Scotland – tall taps called founts (pronounced 'fonts') where a separate pump pushes the beer up under air pressure.

HORNDON-ON-THE-HILL
Bell 🍴 🍷 ◀ 🛏

TQ6783 Map 3

M25 junction 30 into A13, then left on to B1007 after 7 miles, village signposted from here; SS17 8LD

Essex Dining Pub of the Year

Lovely historic pub with fine food and very good range of drinks; attractive bedrooms

To be sure of a table in this bustling Tudor inn, you need to arrive early or book in advance, and although emphasis is on the particularly good food, the heavily beamed bar maintains a strongly pubby appearance and stocks a great range of drinks. It's furnished with lovely high-backed antique settles and benches, with rugs on flagstones and highly polished oak floorboards. Look out for the curious collection of ossified hot cross buns hanging along a beam in the saloon bar. The first was put there some 90 years ago to mark the day (a Good Friday) that Jack Turnell became licensee; the tradition continues to this day, with the oldest available person in the village hanging the bun each year. The impressive range of drinks includes Bass (tapped from the cask), Crouch Vale Brewers Gold, Greene King IPA, Sharps Doom Bar and guests such as Batemans Hooker and Exmoor Antler on handpump, and over a hundred well chosen wines (16 by the glass). Two giant umbrellas cover the courtyard, which is very pretty in summer with hanging baskets.

🍴 Inventive and highly thought of (and now using home-grown herbs and vegetables), the food includes sandwiches, confit chicken croquette on chorizo and fried chicken livers, potted crab with hard-boiled egg and pickled cucumber, basil risotto balls with pine nut crust, oven-dried tomatoes and tomato jam, calves liver on bubble and squeak with pancetta, baby gem and mustard dressing, brill on ribboned vegetables with white wine velouté and crayfish, veal escalope with celeriac and chestnut purée and sultana jus, and puddings such as dark chocolate fondant with caramelised banana and pistachio ice-cream and mango and raspberry mousse. *Benchmark main dish: roast rack of lamb, confit shoulder, garlic jus and dauphinoise potatoes £19.95. Two-course evening meal £22.50.*

Free house ~ Licensee John Vereker ~ Real ale ~ (01375) 642463 ~ Open 11-3, 5.30-11; 12-4, 7-10.30 Sun ~ Bar food 12-1.45, 6.30-9.45; 12-2.15, 7-9.45 Sun ~ Restaurant ~ Children welcome in restaurant ~ Dogs allowed in bar and bedrooms ~ Bedrooms: /£93 ~ www.bell-inn.co.uk *Recommended by Bob and Tanya Ekers*

LITTLE WALDEN
Crown ◀ £

TL5441 Map 5

B1052 N of Saffron Walden; CB10 1XA

Bustling 18th-c cottage pub with a warming log fire, hearty food and bedrooms

The hub of the local community and popular with regulars and visitors, this homely place has good value, comfortable bedrooms and serves nice breakfasts. The licensees and their staff offer a genuinely warm welcome to all and the low-ceilinged rooms have a cosy atmosphere. Furnishings are traditional, with book-room-red walls, floral curtains, bare boards, navy carpeting, cosy warm fires and an unusual walk-through fireplace. A higgledy-piggledy mix of chairs ranges from high-backed pews to little cushioned armchairs spaced around a good variety of closely arranged tables, mostly big, some stripped. The small

red-tiled room on the right has two small tables. Four changing beers
are tapped straight from casks racked up behind the bar – normally
Adnams Best, Greene King IPA, Woodfordes Wherry and a guest such as
Nethergate; TV, disabled access. Tables out on the terrace take in views
of surrounding tranquil countryside.

🍴 Reasonably priced, the traditional choices on the menu include sandwiches
(the hot pork is very good), devilled whitebait, moussaka, liver and bacon,
lasagne, pork fillet in cajun sauce, king prawn curry, rib-eye steak, and puddings
such as apple crumb and rice pudding. *Benchmark main dish: steak in ale pie
£10.25. Two-course evening meal £13.00.*

Free house ~ Licensee Colin Hayling ~ Real ale ~ (01799) 522475 ~ Open 11.30-2.30
(3 Sat), 6-11; 12-10.30 Sun ~ Bar food 12-3, 7-9; 12-3 Sun; not Sun or Mon evenings ~
Restaurant ~ Children welcome ~ Dogs allowed in bar and bedrooms ~ Live jazz Weds
evenings ~ Bedrooms: /£75 ~ www.thecrownlittlewalden.co.uk *Recommended by Simon
Watkins, N R White, Mrs Margo Finlay, Jörg Kasprowski, Nick Clare, Sara Fulton, Roger Baker*

 LITTLEY GREEN   TL6917 Map 5

Compasses 🍺

*Village signposted off B1417 Felsted road in Hartoft End (opposite former
Ridleys Brewery), about a mile N of junction with B1008 – former A130; CM3 1BU*

**Classic East Anglian traditional country tavern – a prime example of
what is now an all too rare breed**

Owned by Jocelyn Ridley, this keeps the family brewing tradition alive
in its Bishop Nick Ridleys Rite – a smooth and slightly fruity easy-
drinking ale – brewed in Felsted by Joss's brother Nelion. On our visit
they also had Colchester Cream, Green Jack Trawlerboys and Golden
Best and Kirkby Lonsdale Stanleys, all tapped from casks in a back
cellar, as well as Fosseway and Tumpy Ground farm ciders, and perries
from Cornish Orchards and Gwynt y Ddraig. In summer and at Christmas
they run beer festivals, with a choice of dozens of ales, alongside
festivities that may include vintage ploughing in the field opposite. The
whisky range is pretty impressive too. At any time of year the bar is
a companionable place, highly traditional – brown-painted panelling
and wall benches, plain chairs and tables on quarry tiles, with chat and
laughter rather than background music, a piano, darts and board games
in one side room, decorative mugs hanging from beams in another. There
are picnic-sets out on the sheltered side grass and the garden behind,
with a couple of long tables on the front cobbles by the quiet lane. We
have not yet heard from readers using the newly built small bedroom
block, but would expect this to be a good overnight place.

🍴 A big blackboard shows the day's range of huffers: big rolls with a hearty
range of hot or cold fillings. They also do ploughman's, baked potatoes, and a
few sensibly priced hot dishes such as soup, gammon and egg, chicken curry, pork
medallions, scampi and rib-eye steak. *Benchmark main dish: big huffers £9.00.
Two-course evening meal £13.00.*

Free house ~ Licensee Jocelyn Ridley ~ Real ale ~ (01245) 362308 ~ Open 12-3, 5.30-
11.30; 12-11.30 Thurs-Sun ~ Bar food 12-2.30, 7-9.30; 12-9.30 Sat; 12-5, 7-9.30 Sun ~
Children welcome ~ Dogs welcome ~ Informal folk music monthly ~ Bedrooms: £75/£85
~ www.compasseslittleygreen.co.uk *Recommended by H Grace, Harvey Brown*

The 🍺 symbol shows pubs which keep their beer unusually well,
have a particularly good range or brew their own.

MARGARETTING TYE

TL6801   Map 5

White Hart 🍺 £ 🛏

From B1002 (just S of A12/A414 junction) follow Maldon Road for 1.3 miles, then turn right immediately after river bridge, into Swan Lane, keeping on for 0.7 miles; The Tye; CM4 9JX

Fine choice of ales tapped from the cask in cheery country pub, with good food and a family garden

Even when this deservedly popular pub is at its busiest, the hard-working and friendly staff manage to keep on top of things and offer a warm welcome to all. The open-plan but cottagey rooms have walls and wainscoting painted in chalky traditional colours that match well with the dark timbers and mix of old wooden chairs and tables; a stuffed deer head is mounted on the chimney breast above the woodburning stove. The neat carpeted back conservatory is similar in style, and the front lobby has a charity paperback table. There's an impressive range of eight real ales tapped from the cask, such as Adnams Best and Broadside, Mighty Oak IPA and Oscar Wilde and changing guests from breweries like Cottage, Franklins and Red Fox, a german wheat beer, interesting bottled beers and winter mulled wine; they hold beer festivals in June and October with around 60 different ales; darts, quiz machine, skittles, board games and background music. There are plenty of picnic-sets out on grass and terracing around the pub, with a sturdy play area, a fenced duck pond and pens of rabbits, guinea-pigs and a pygmy goat.

 Good food includes lunchtime sandwiches, baked mini camembert with dipping bread, smoked salmon, crab and king prawns with marie rose sauce, nut roast with sweet chilli sauce, lambs liver and bacon casserole, arbroath smokie fishcakes with chips, curry of the week, chicken with melted mozzarella, smoked bacon and barbecue sauce, and puddings like cheesecake of the week and sticky toffee pudding with custard. *Benchmark main dish: beef in ale pie with chunky chips £9.95. Two-course evening meal £16.00.*

Free house ~ Licensee Elizabeth Haines ~ Real ale ~ (01277) 840478 ~ Open 11.30-3, 6-midnight; 11.30-midnight Sat; 12-midnight Sun ~ Bar food 12-2(2.30 Sat, 4.30 Sun), 6.30-9(6-9.30 Fri, Sat, 6.30-8.30 Sun) ~ Well behaved children welcome in conservatory ~ Dogs allowed in bar ~ Bedrooms: /£80 ~ www.thewhitehart.uk.com *Recommended by Rob and Catherine Dunster, Paul Humphreys, N R White, John Saville, Ian Phillips*

MILL GREEN

TL6401   Map 5

Viper 🍺 £

The Common; from Fryerning (signposted off N-bound A12 Ingatestone bypass) follow Writtle signposts; CM4 0PT

Delightfully unpretentious, with local ales, simple pub food and no modern intrusions

Popular with a wide mix of customers – cyclists, families, walkers with their dogs – this is an unspoilt local tucked away in the woods. The cosy and unchanging rooms have spindleback and armed country kitchen chairs and tapestried wall seats around neat little old tables, and a log fire. The fairly basic tap room is more simply furnished with parquet floor, shiny wooden traditional wall seats and a coal fire, and beyond is another room with country kitchen chairs and sensibly placed darts. Nethergate Viper Vipa and Mighty Oak Jake the Snake (both brewed for the pub) and Oscar Wilde and a couple of quickly changing guests from brewers such as Crouch Vale and Mr Grundys on handpump, and Weston's scrumpy and perry. Live bands play during the Easter and

August beer festivals and morris men sometimes dance outside. The pub cat is called Millie and the west highland terrier Jimmy; dominoes and cribbage. Tables on the lawn overlook a beautifully tended cottage garden – a dazzling mass of colour in summer, further enhanced at the front by overflowing hanging baskets and window boxes.

🍴 Promptly served simple lunchtime food includes duck liver pâté, chicken curry with mango chutney, chilli con carne, meat or vegetarian lasagne, sausage and mash with onion gravy, and puddings such as apple crumble with custard and chocolate pudding. The tasty bread comes from the local baker just a mile away. *Benchmark main dish: steak in ale pie £6.95.*

Free house ~ Licensees Peter White and Donna Torris ~ Real ale ~ (01277) 352010 ~ Open 12-3, 6-11; 12-11(10.30 Sun) Sat ~ Bar food 12-2(3 Sat, Sun) ~ Children allowed ~ Dogs allowed in bar *Recommended by John Saville, Tina and David Woods-Taylor*

PELDON   TM0015 Map 5
Rose ♀

B1025 Colchester–Mersea (do not turn left to Peldon village); CO5 7QJ

Friendly old inn with a cosy bar, several dining rooms, real ales, enjoyable food and seats in spacious garden; bedrooms

This appealing old inn has been welcoming customers for around 500 years. The traditional interior has standing timbers supporting heavy low ceilings with dark bowed 17th-c oak beams, little leaded-light windows, an arched brick fireplace and some antique mahogany and padded leather wall banquettes. There's a cosy beamed restaurant, a smart airy garden room, stylish high-backed dining chairs around an attractive mix of tables, a two-way woodburner and views over the garden. Adnams Bitter, Greene King IPA and Woodfordes Wherry on handpump, 15 wines by the glass and Aspall's cider. The spacious garden has plenty of seats, and a pretty pond with ducks. The country-style bedrooms are comfortable.

🍴 Enjoyable food using seasonal, local ingredients includes lunchtime sandwiches, chicken and chorizo terrine with garlic aioli, beetroot-cured salmon with celeriac remoulade, burger with streaky bacon, cheddar, coleslaw and chips, thai-style vegetable linguine with coconut, chilli and coriander, lamb tagine with raita and pilaf rice, chicken wrapped in parma ham with creamed leeks and sage jus, slow-cooked duck leg in red wine and thyme with parsnip mash, a fish dish of the day, and puddings such as pear and apple tart with cider syrup and vanilla ice-cream and banoffi pie. *Benchmark main dish: beer-battered fish with mushy peas and home-made tartare sauce £10.95. Two-course evening meal £16.50.*

Free house ~ Licensee Adam Leydon ~ Real ale ~ (01206) 735248 ~ Open 11-11; 12-10.30(7 in winter) Sun ~ Bar food 12-2.30, 6.30-9(9.30 Fri, Sat); 12-6(10 July, Aug) Sun ~ Restaurant ~ Children welcome away from bar ~ Bedrooms: £50/£70 ~ www.thepeldonrose.co.uk *Recommended by Ryta Lyndley*

SOUTH HANNINGFIELD   TQ7497 Map 5
Old Windmill 🍴 ♀

Off A130 S of Chelmsford; CM3 8HT

Extensive but invitingly converted Brunning & Price pub with interesting food and good range of drinks

A pub since 1799, this rambling place has been carefully converted and knocked through – though the forest of stripped standing timbers and open doorways create lots of cosy areas. Décor is comfortably inviting, with an agreeable mix of highly polished old tables and chairs, frame-to-frame pictures on cream walls, woodburning stoves and homely pot plants. Deep green or dark red dado and a few old rugs dotted on the glowing wood floors provide splashes of colour; other areas are more subdued with beige carpeting. Phoenix Brunning & Price Original and five guests from brewers such as Crouch Vale, Mighty Oak, Timothy Taylor and Wibblers are on handpump, with 20 wines by the glass, farm cider, 70 malts and a good range of spirits; background music. A back terrace has tables and chairs, with picnic-sets on the lawn here and a few out in front.

Very good food includes sandwiches, pigeon breast with cauliflower purée and cumberland sauce, charcuterie plate for two, honey-roast ham with free-range eggs, steak burger topped with bacon and cheddar with coleslaw and chips, pea and gorgonzola risotto with tomato concasse, shellfish linguine, steak in ale pie, salmon fillet with wasabi and lime crust, asian stir-fry, and puddings like Amaretto cheesecake with belgian chocolate ice-cream and minted crème brûlée. *Benchmark main dish: duck breast with blackberry and madeira sauce and dauphinoise potatoes £15.95. Two-course evening meal £20.00.*

Brunning & Price ~ Manager Nick Clark ~ Real ale ~ (01268) 712280 ~ Open 11.30-11; 12-10.30 Sun ~ Bar food 12-10(9.30 Sun) ~ Restaurant ~ Children welcome ~ Dogs allowed in bar ~ www.oldwindmillpub.co.uk *Recommended by Richard and Penny Gibbs, Evelyn and Derek Walter, Tina and David Woods-Taylor*

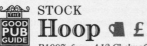

STOCK

Hoop ☜ £

TQ6999   Map 5

B1007; from A12 Chelmsford bypass take Galleywood, Billericay turn-off; CM4 9BD

Happy weatherboarded pub with interesting beers, nice food and a large garden

They've held an early summer beer festival here for over 20 years and can get through over 200 real ales and 80 ciders and perries; a hog roast and barbecue too. Adnams Southwold is regularly on handpump alongside three guests from brewers such as Crouch Vale, Mighty Oak and Wells & Youngs, plus around 20 wines by the glass. Simple fixtures and fittings, including stripped floors, wooden tables and brocaded wooden settles, keep the interior feeling appropriately down to earth and pubby – just the right setting for the cheery locals and visitors enjoying the happy bustle. Standing timbers and beams in the open-plan bar hint at the building's great age and its original layout as a row of three weavers' cottages. In winter, a warming fire burns in a big brick-walled fireplace. A restaurant up in the timbered eaves – very different in style, with a separate à la carte menu – is light and airy, with pale timbers in white walls and wood floors. Prettily bordered with flowers, the large sheltered back garden has picnic-sets and a covered seating area. Parking is limited, so it's worth getting here early.

Well thought-of food includes sandwiches, arbroath smokie on toast, curry-glazed scallops with cauliflower, dill and pine nuts, wild mushroom and chesnut risotto, roast rump of lamb with crisp belly, cumin-roasted squash purée and slow-roasted tomatoes, duck breast with turnip, caramel, raisin and spinach, specials like rabbit on toast, calves liver, bacon, home-cooked onion rings and gravy, a pie of the day, and puddings such as banana fritter with chocolate ganache, peanut and sea salt caramel ice-cream and tonka bean cream with redcurrant jelly, pistachio, honeycomb and meringue. *Benchmark main dish: toad in the hole £10.50. Two-course evening meal £22.00.*

Free house ~ Licensee Michelle Corrigan ~ Real ale ~ (01277) 841137 ~ Open 11-11; 12-10.30 Sun ~ Bar food 12-2.30, 6-9(9.30 Fri); 12-9 Sat; 12-8.30 Sun ~ Restaurant ~ Children welcome if eating ~ Dogs allowed in bar ~ www.thehoop.co.uk
Recommended by John Saville

WENDENS AMBO
TL5136   Map 5

Bell

B1039 W of village; CB11 4JY

Lively local with lots going on, good ales and ciders, pubby food and big garden

Very much the heart of the village, this small cottagey local is run by a cheerful, welcoming landlady who organises all sorts of events from jazz concerts to beer festivals, steam engine rallies and a weekly quiz. The bustling bars have low ceilings, brasses on ancient timbers, wheelback chairs at neat tables, a winter log fire and Oakhams JHB, Rudgate Ruby Mild, Sharps Doom Bar, Woodfordes Wherry and a beer named for the pub on handpump, up to seven farm ciders and perries, and a dozen good vodkas. There are seats under umbrellas on the paved terrace that overlooks the three acres of gardens, where there's a pond leading to the River Uttle, a woodland walk and children's timber playground.

Tasty bar food includes toasted ciabatta sandwiches, home-made scotch egg with haggis and whisky mustard, chicken liver pâté with fruit chutney, home-cooked ham and free-range eggs, sausages with mustard mash and red wine and onion gravy, caribbean chicken and fruit curry with rice, slow-roast gloucester old spot pork belly with apple mash and cider gravy, and puddings like warm chocolate brownie with ice-cream and apple and blackberry pie with custard. *Benchmark main dish: rare roast belted galloway beef with yorkshire pudding £10.50. Two-course evening meal £15.00.*

Free house ~ Licensee Anne Güney ~ Real ale ~ (01799) 540382 ~ Open 11.30(12 Sun)-midnight; 11.30-3, 5-midnight Mon in winter ~ Bar food 12-2.30(3 Sun), 6.30-9; not Sun evening or Mon ~ Restaurant ~ Children welcome ~ Dogs welcome ~ Regular live music ~ www.thebellatwenden.co.uk *Recommended by Caroline Prescott*

Also Worth a Visit in Essex

Besides the fully inspected pubs, you might like to try these pubs that have been recommended to us and described by readers. Do tell us what you think of them: feedback@goodguides.com

BELCHAMP ST PAUL   TL7942
Half Moon (01787) 277402
Cole Green; CO10 7DP Thatched 16th-c pub overlooking green, well kept Greene King IPA and guests, good choice of popular home-made food (not Sun evening), friendly staff, snug beamed interior with log fire, restaurant, Aug beer/music festival; no dogs inside; children welcome, tables out in front and in back garden, open all day weekends. *(Anon)*

BIRCHANGER   TL5122
Three Willows (01279) 815913
Under a mile from M11 junction 8: A120 towards Bishop's Stortford, then almost immediately right to Birchanger Village; don't be waylaid earlier by the Birchanger Services signpost; CM23 5QR Dining pub feeling nicely tucked away – some refurbishment from present owners; spacious carpeted bar with lots of cricketing memorabilia, Greene King ales, well furnished smaller lounge bar, good range

of popular, fairly traditional food including lots of fresh fish dishes; children welcome, dogs allowed in bar, picnic-sets out in front and on lawn behind (some motorway and Stansted Airport noise), good play area, closed Sun evening. *(Roy Hoing, Mrs Margo Finlay, Jörg Kasprowski)*

BOREHAM   TL7409
Lion (01245) 394900
Main Road; CM3 3JA Stylish bistro/bar with rooms, good well presented and affordably priced food (order at bar) from snacks to daily specials, several wines by the glass, bottled beers and well kept ales including one brewed for them, conservatory; children welcome. *(John Saville)*

BROOMFIELD   TL7010
Kings Arms (01245) 440258
Off A130 N of Chelmsford; CM1 7AU Attractive 15th-c timber-framed local improved under current management; knocked-through beamed bar, open fires, decent reasonably priced lunchtime food including Sun carvery, well kept Caledonian Deuchars IPA and Wibblers, dining room; pool, darts and sports TV, live bands Fri; children welcome, beer garden, open all day. *(Anon)*

BULMER TYE   TL8438
★ Bulmer Fox (01787) 312277/377505
A131 S of Sudbury; CO10 7EB Thriving dining pub with enjoyable fairly priced food, neatly laid tables with forms on which to write your order (or order at the bar), Adnams and Greene King IPA, help-yourself water fountain, friendly service, pastel colours and lively acoustics; bare boards (look out for one or two 'rugs' painted on them), quieter side room and intimate central snug, home-made chutneys, preserves etc for sale; children welcome, sheltered back terrace with arbour. *(Anon)*

BUMBLES GREEN   TL4105
King Harolds Head (01992) 893110
Nazeing Common; EN9 2RY Comfortable beamed and carpeted bar, separate dining room, reasonably priced food (all day Sun) from pub favourites to good fresh fish and vegetarian options, friendly attentive service, ales such as Courage Best, open fire; children welcome, terrace tables. *(Brian Glozier)*

BURNHAM-ON-CROUCH   TQ9495
★ White Harte (01621) 782106
The Quay; CM0 8AS Cosy old-fashioned hotel on water's edge with views from garden of yacht-filled River Crouch; partly carpeted bars with down-to-earth charm , assorted nautical bric-a-brac and hardware, other traditionally furnished high-ceilinged rooms with sea pictures on brown panelled or stripped-brick walls, cushioned seats around oak tables, enormous winter log fire, well kept Adnams and Crouch Vale, good food and

friendly efficient service; children and dogs welcome, bedrooms, open all day. *(Adrian Johnson, Gwyn Harries, N R White)*

BURTON END   TL5323
Ash (01279) 814841
Just N of Stansted Airport; CM24 8UQ Popular thatched country pub with dining extension, helpful cheerful staff, two or three real ales, enjoyable all-day food from lunchtime sandwiches and pubby choices up; tables outside on deck and grass, bedrooms in converted barn across lane. *(Mrs Margo Finlay, Jörg Kasprowski)*

CASTLE HEDINGHAM   TL7835
Bell (01787) 460350
B1058; CO9 3EJ Beamed and timbered three-bar pub dating from the 15th c, unpretentious and unspoilt (well run by same family for over 40 years), Adnams, Mighty Oak and guests served from the cask (July/Nov beer festivals), popular pubby food and turkish specials; background and some live music (lunchtime jazz last Sun of month); dogs welcome, children away from public bar, garden, handy for Hedingham Castle, open all day Fri-Sun. *(Peter Thornton)*

CHELMSFORD   TL7006
Orange Tree (01245) 262664
Lower Anchor Street; CM2 0AS Bargain lunchtime bar food in spacious local with good cheerful service, well kept Black Sheep, Dark Star, Mighty Oak and up to half a dozen changing guests (some tapped from the cask), Tues charity quiz, some live music; back terrace, open all day. *(Anon)*

CHELMSFORD   TL7006
★ Queens Head (01245) 265181
Lower Anchor Street; CM2 0AS Lively, well run Victorian corner local with very well kept Crouch Vale beers and interesting guests, summer farm cider, good value wines, friendly staff, bargain food weekday lunchtimes from baguettes up, winter log fires, Weds quiz; children welcome, picnic-sets in colourful courtyard, open all day. *(Anon)*

CHRISHALL   TL4439
Red Cow (01763) 838792
High Street; off B1039 Wendens Ambo–Great Chishill; SG8 8RN Popular refurbished 16th-c thatched pub with lots of atmosphere; timbers, low beams, wood floors and log fires, one half laid for dining, decent choice of enjoyable food from simple bar meals up including weekday set deals, well kept Adnams, Greene King IPA and a guest, interesting wine list, weekend newspapers, board games; children and dogs welcome, nice garden, old adjacent barn being developed as we went to press, handy for Icknield Way walkers, open all day weekends, closed Mon. *(Mrs Margo Finlay, Jörg Kasprowski)*

COGGESHALL TL8224
★**Compasses** (01376) 561322
*Pattiswick, signed off A120 W;
CM77 8BG* More country restaurant than
pub, enjoyable well presented food using
local produce from light lunches up, also
weekday set deals and children's meals,
two well kept ales such as Nethergate and
Woodfordes Wherry, good wine choice,
cheerful attentive young staff, neatly
comfortable spacious beamed bars, barn
restaurant, some live music; plenty of lawn
and orchard tables, rolling farmland beyond,
open all day. *(Charles Gysin, Steve Homer)*

COLCHESTER TM9824
Hospital Arms (01206) 542398
*Crouch Street (opposite hospital);
CO3 3HA* Friendly pub with several
small linked areas, good selection of well
kept Adnams ales and guests, enjoyable
inexpensive lunchtime food, quick cheerful
service; games machines; beer garden, open
all day. *(Anon)*

COLNE ENGAINE TL8530
Five Bells (01787) 224166
*Signed off A1124 (was A604) in Earls
Colne; Mill Lane; CO6 2HY* Welcoming
and popular old village pub, good home-made
food (all day weekends) using local produce,
own-baked breads, six well kept changing
ales including Adnams (Nov festival), friendly
efficient service, bare boards or carpeted
floors, woodburners, old photographs,
high-raftered dining area (former
slaughterhouse), public bar with pool and
sports TV, some live music; children and dogs
welcome, disabled facilities, attractive front
terrace with gentle Colne Valley views, open
all day Thurs-Sun. *(Evelyn and Derek Walter)*

COOPERSALE STREET TL4701
★**Theydon Oak** (01992) 572618
*Off B172 E of Theydon Bois; or follow
Hobbs Cross Open Farm brown sign off
B1393 at N end of Epping; CM16 7QJ*
Attractive old weatherboarded dining pub,
very popular for its good generous food (all
day Sun), Fullers London Pride, Greene
King IPA and a guest, friendly prompt
service, beams and masses of brass, copper
and old brewery mirrors, two woodburners;
background music, no dogs; children
welcome, tables on side terrace and in
fenced garden with small stream, lots of
hanging baskets, separate play area, open all
day. *(Anon)*

DANBURY TL7705
Griffin (01245) 222905
A414, top of Danbury Hill; CM3 4DH
Fully refurbished 16th-c pub; well divided
interior with beams and some carved
woodwork, mix of new and old furniture on
wood, stone or carpeted floors, log fires,
decent variety of food from deli boards and
pizzas to pub standards and up, changing
real ales and good choice of wines by the
glass; background music; children welcome,
terrace seating, views. *(Mrs Margo Finlay, Jörg
Kasprowski)*

DEDHAM TM0533
★**Sun** (01206) 323351
High Street (B2109); CO7 6DF
Stylish old Tudor coaching inn opposite
church; good italian-influenced food using
seasonal local produce, also cheaper set
menu (not Fri, Sat or Sun lunchtime),
impressive wine selection (over 20 by the
glass), well kept Adnams, Crouch Vale and
two guests, Aspall's cider, friendly efficient
young staff, historic panelled interior with
high carved beams, handsome furnishings
and splendid fireplaces; background music,
TV; children welcome, dogs in bar, picnic-
sets on quiet back lawn with mature trees,
characterful panelled bedrooms, good
Flatford Mill walk, open all day.
*(Roy Hoing, Keir Halliday, Steve Homer,
N R White and others)*

DUTON HILL TL6026
Three Horseshoes (01371) 870681
*Off B184 Dunmow–Thaxted, 3 miles N of
Dunmow; CM6 2DX* Friendly traditional
village local, well kept Mighty Oak and
guests (late May Bank Holiday beer festival),
central fire, aged armchairs by fireplace in
homely left-hand parlour, lots of interesting
memorabilia, darts and pool in small public
bar, no food, folk club third Thurs of month;
dogs welcome, old enamel signs out at front,
garden with pond and nice views, closed
lunchtimes Mon-Weds. *(Anon)*

EDNEY COMMON TL6504
Green Man (01245) 248076
Highwood Road; CM1 3QE Comfortable
country pub/restaurant with good well
presented food cooked by chef-owners
including some unusual choices, extensive
wine list (several by the glass), a couple of
real ales, friendly staff, carpeted interior with
black beams and timbers; tables out at front
and in garden, closed Sun evening, Mon.
(J B and M E Benson)

EPPING FOREST TL4501
Forest Gate (01992) 572312
Bell Common; CM16 4DZ Large friendly
open-plan pub dating from the 17th c, beams
and panelling, well kept Adnams, Nethergate
and guests from brick-faced bar, enjoyable
home-made food; tables on front lawn,
popular with walkers. *(Anon)*

FINCHINGFIELD   TL6832
Fox   (01371) 810151
The Green; CM7 4JX Splendidly pargeted
16th-c building with spacious beamed bar,
exposed brickwork and central fireplace,
four ales from Adnams and Nethergate, good
choice of wines by the glass, traditional
home-made food from sandwiches up;
background and monthly live music; children
and dogs welcome, picnic-sets in front
overlooking village duck pond, bedrooms,
open all day (closed Sun evening in
winter). *(S Holder)*

FINGRINGHOE   TM0220
Whalebone   (01206) 729307
*Off A134 just S of Colchester centre,
or B1025; CO5 7BG* Old pub geared for
dining, airy country-chic rooms with cream-
painted tables on oak floors, good local food
(not Sun evening) including some interesting
choices, nice sandwiches too, well kept
beers, friendly chatty staff, barn function
room; background music; children and
dogs welcome, charming back garden with
peaceful valley view, front terrace, handy
for Fingringhoe nature reserve, open all day
weekends. *(Anon)*

FYFIELD   TL5706
✳ Queens Head   (01277) 899231
*Corner of B184 and Queen Street;
CM5 0RY* Neat 16th-c pub with prettily
planted back garden down to sleepy River
Roding; half a dozen beers including Adnams,
Weston's Old Rosie cider and over a dozen
wines by the glass, good enterprising food
(not Sun evening), also pub favourites and
set menu (Tues-Thurs, lunchtimes Fri,
Sat), low-beamed, compact L-shaped bar,
exposed timbers, pretty lamps on sturdy elm
tables, comfortable seating from banquettes
to unusual high-backed chairs, snug little
side booth, open fires, more formal upstairs
restaurant; background music; children
welcome, closed Mon lunchtime, otherwise
open all day. *(Mrs Margo Finlay, Jörg
Kasprowski, John Saville, Rachel Heatley)*

GREAT BROMLEY   TM0923
Snooty Fox   (01206) 251065
Frating Road (B1029); CO7 7JW
Beamed country pub, clean and tidy,
with well kept real ales and popular
food (especially Sun lunch), friendly
service, separate dining area; garden with
decking. *(N R White)*

GREAT EASTON   TL6126
Green Man   (01371) 852285
*Mill End Green; pub signed 2 miles N
of Dunmow, off B184 towards Lindsell;
CM6 2DN* Popular dining pub with linked
beamed rooms, good food from varied
changing menu, four real ales including
Adnams Southwold and Woodfordes Wherry,
friendly helpful service; children welcome,
dogs in bar, good-sized attractive garden with
terrace, pleasant rural setting, closed Sun
evening, otherwise open all day. *(Mrs Margo
Finlay, Jörg Kasprowski)*

GREAT HENNY   TL8738
Henny Swan   (01787) 269238
Henny Street; CO10 7LS Welcoming
smartly refurbished dining pub in great
location on the River Stour (summer boat
trips); bar with open fire, more formal dining
room, well kept regularly changing ales, good
variety of food from bar snacks and pubby
choices to restaurant-style dishes, special
diets and vegetarians catered for, also weekday
OAP menu; children welcome, terrace and
waterside garden, play area, closed Sun
evening, otherwise open all day. *(Anon)*

GREAT STAMBRIDGE   TQ8991
Royal Oak   (01702) 258259
Stambridge Road; SS4 2AX Pleasant
country pub with enjoyable food in bar and
separate restaurant, Greene King IPA, Fullers
London Pride and a guest, several wines
by the glass, friendly staff; nice views from
big garden, nearby walk to river, open all
day. *(Bob and Tanya Ekers)*

GREAT TOTHAM   TL8511
Bull   (01621) 893385
B1022 N of Maldon; CM9 8NH
Modernised 16th-c coaching inn and
restaurant; bar with painted beams, wood or
stone floors and mix of seating including a
couple of booths, good range of well cooked
food from bar snacks up, weekday set lunch
deal, plenty of wines by the glass, monthly
quiz; background and some live music;
children welcome, lavender-filled garden
with fields beyond, four bedrooms in separate
cottage. *(Steve Homer)*

GREAT YELDHAM   TL7638
Waggon & Horses   (07000) 924466
High Street; CO9 4EX Cheerful 16th-c
timbered village inn with attractive L-shaped
beamed bar; well kept Greene King IPA and
three changing regional ales, local Delvin
End cider, good keenly priced fresh food from
baguettes to fish and steaks, friendly service,
popular restaurant, games room with pool,
darts and shove ha'penny; games machines;
children and dogs welcome, disabled access,
picnic sets on front terrace and in garden
behind, 16 bedrooms (most in modern back

extension), open all day. *(Adele Summers, Alan Black)*

HATFIELD HEATH   TL5115
Thatchers (01279) 730270
Stortford Road (A1005); CM22 7DU
16th-c thatched and weatherboarded dining pub at end of large green, good popular food (best to book weekends) from varied menu including set lunch Mon-Fri, well kept St Austell Tribute, Sharps Doom Bar and two guests from long counter, several wines by the glass, woodburners, beams, some copper and brass and old local photographs; background music, no dogs; children in back dining area, tables in front under parasols, open all day weekends. *(Anon)*

HEMPSTEAD   TL6337
Bluebell (01799) 599199
B1054 E of Saffron Walden; CB10 2PD
Comfortable and attractive beamed bar with two rooms off and a restaurant, enjoyable generous food including popular Sun roasts, Adnams, Woodfordes and guests, Aspall's cider, friendly service, log fires, folk music Tues evening, classic car meetings (first Sat of month); children and dogs welcome, terrace and garden seating, play area.
(Mrs Margo Finlay, Jörg Kasprowski)

HENHAM   TL5428
Cock (01279) 850347
Church End; CM22 6AN Welcoming old timbered place striking good balance between community local and dining pub, wide choice of well priced, nicely presented, home-made food using local suppliers, four ales including Saffron (brewed in the village), decent wines, good open fires, restaurant with leather-backed chairs on wood floor, sports TV in snug, live music last Sun of month; children welcome, dogs in bar, seats out at front and in tree-shaded garden. *(David and Gill Carrington, David Glynne-Jones)*

HERONGATE   TQ6491
★Olde Dog (01277) 810337
Billericay Road, off A128 Brentwood–Grays at big sign for Boars Head; CM13 3SD Welcoming weather-boarded country pub dating from the 16th c, long attractive dark-beamed bar and separate dining areas, well kept Greene King Abbot, a house beer from Crouch Vale and guests tapped from the cask, enjoyable food (all day weekends, Sun till 7pm); pleasant front terrace and neat sheltered side garden, open all day. *(John Murphy, N R White)*

HOCKLEY
Anchor (01702) 230777
Ferry Road; SS5 6ND Extensively refurbished riverside pub/restaurant, always busy but enough staff to cope well, good bar and restaurant food, plenty of wines by the glass including champagne,

real ales; children welcome, lots of seats outside overlooking River Crouch, summer barbecues, open all day.
(Bob and Tanya Ekers)

HOWE STREET   TL6914
Green Man (01245) 360203
Just off A130 N of Chelmsford; CM3 1BG Friendly newish management for this spacious heavily beamed and timbered 14th-c pub, enjoyable reasonably priced food, Greene King ales, log fire, some live music; children welcome, garden with decked area and adjoining paddock with small river. *(Anon)*

HOWLETT END   TL5834
White Hart (01799) 599030
Thaxted Road (B184 SE of Saffron Walden); CB10 2UZ Comfortable pub/restaurant with two smartly set modern dining rooms either side of small tiled-floor bar, good food from sandwiches and light dishes up, Greene King IPA and local dishes, nice choice of wines, friendly helpful service; children welcome, terrace and big garden, quiet spot. *(David Jackman)*

KELVEDON HATCH   TQ5798
Eagle (01277) 373472
Ongar Road (A128); CM15 0AA Friendly family local set back from the road, low-ceilinged bar area, good choice of food from sandwiches and baguettes to specials and Sun roasts, well kept ales such as Brentwood and Greene King, efficient service; background music, TV, quiz night Mon; covered seating area out at front, garden with play area, plenty of nearby walks, open all day (till 8pm Sun). *(Roxanne Chamberlain)*

LEIGH-ON-SEA   TQ8385
★Crooked Billet (01702) 480289
High Street; SS9 2EP Homely old pub with waterfront views from big bay windows, packed on busy summer days when service can be frantic but friendly, well kept Adnams, Nicholsons, Sharps and three changing guests including seasonals, enjoyable standard Nicholsons menu, log fires, beams, panelled dado and bare boards, local fishing pictures and bric-a-brac; background music; children allowed if eating, but no under-21s after 6pm, side garden and terrace, seawall seating over road shared with Osborne's good shellfish stall (plastic glasses for outside), pay-and-display parking by flyover, open all day. *(LM, N R White)*

LITTLE BRAXTED   TL8413
★Green Man (01621) 891659
Kelvedon Road; signed off B1389; OS Sheet 168 map reference 848133; CM8 3LB Homely place with cottagey feel, windsor chairs on patterned carpets, mugs hanging from beams and some 200 horse-brasses, open fire in traditional little lounge,

tiled public bar with darts and cribbage, Greene King ales and a guest, big helpings of good sensibly priced food, friendly helpful staff and nice chatty atmosphere; children till 8pm, dogs in bar, picnic-sets in pleasant sheltered garden, closed Sun evening. *(Charles and Pauline Stride, Claudia Ives)*

LITTLE TOTHAM · TL8811
Swan (01621) 892689
School Road; CM9 8LB Welcoming country local with up to a dozen cask-tapped ales, farm ciders and perry, straightforward good value lunchtime food, low 17th-c beams, log fire, back dining area, tiled games bar with darts, June beer festival; children, dogs and walkers welcome, disabled facilities, small terrace and informal front garden, camping, closed Mon and Tues till 4pm; currently for sale. *(Anon)*

LOUGHTON · TQ4296
Victoria (020) 8508 1779
Smarts Lane; IG10 4BP Welcoming flower-decked Victorian local with enjoyable home-made pubby food, good range of fairly mainstream beers including Adnms and Greene King, chatty panelled bare-boards bar with small raised end dining area; pleasant neatly kept front garden, Epping Forest walks. *(Phil Bryant)*

MALDON · TL8407
⋆Blue Boar (01621) 855888
Silver Street; car park behind; CM9 4QE Quirky cross between coaching inn and antiques or auction showroom, most showy in the main building's lounge and dining room, interesting antique furnishings and pictures also in the separate smallish dark-timbered bar and its spectacular raftered upper room, good Farmers ales brewed at the back, also Adnams Southwold and a guest, enjoyable food from bar snacks to daily specials, friendly helpful staff; tables outside, 22 bedrooms (some with four-posters), good breakfast, car park fee refunded at bar, open all day. *(Peter Thornton)*

MANNINGTREE · TM1031
Crown (01206) 396333
High Street; CO11 1AH Bare-boards bar on left with plenty of old local photographs and advertisements, low-ceilinged front public bar, estuary views from brightly carpeted or tiled two-level back area with more dining tables and nautical memorabilia under high pitched ceiling, full range of Greene King ales, usual reasonably priced food (all day weekends) from sandwiches and baked potatoes up, friendly service, live music Sun; children and dogs welcome

(menus for both), picnic-sets on back terrace overlooking water, attractively priced bedrooms, open all day. *(N R White)*

MORETON · TL5307
White Hart (01277) 890890
Off B184, just N of A414; CM5 0LF Traditional old village pub, spacious bar with leather sofas by woodburner, two other areas, well kept Adnams and Sharps Doom Bar, decent house wines, popular food from bar snacks up including good value set lunch, attractive small timbered dining room; background music, TV, pool, weekly quiz; children welcome, picnic-sets on smart decked terrace, garden, five bedrooms, open all day. *(Anon)*

MOUNT BURES · TL9031
⋆Thatchers Arms (01787) 227460
Off B1508; CO8 5AT Well run modernised pub with good local food (freshly prepared, so may be a wait), midweek meal deals, well kept ales such as Adnams Mild and Bitter and Crouch Vale Brewers Gold, cheerful efficient staff; background music; dogs welcome, plenty of picnic-sets out behind, peaceful Stour Valley views, open all day weekends, closed Mon. *(Alexandra Woolmore)*

MOUNTNESSING · TQ6297
George & Dragon (01277) 352461
Roman Road (B1002); CM15 0TZ Contemporary refurbishment blending with old beams and timbers, good choice of food all day in bar and restaurant including some mediterranean influences, weekday lunchtime and early evening set menu, real ales and plenty of wines by the glass, cocktails, colourful armchairs and stools on polished wood floors, open fires; modern wicker-style furniture outside under parasols, open all day. *(John Saville)*

PAGLESHAM · TQ9293
⋆Punchbowl (01702) 258376
Church End; SS4 2DP 16th-c former sailmaker's loft with low beams and stripped brickwork, pews, barrel chairs and lots of brass, lower room laid for dining, Adnams Southwold, Sharps Doom Bar and a couple of guests, straightforward fairly priced food including good OAP menu (Tues-Thurs), prompt friendly service, cribbage and darts; background music; children usually welcome but check first, lovely rural view from sunny front garden, open all day Sun. *(Gwyn Harries)*

RIDGEWELL · TL7340
White Horse (01440) 785532
Mill Road (A1017 Haverhill–Halstead); CO9 4SG Comfortable beamed village pub

---

The letters and figures after the name of each town are its Ordnance Survey map reference. *Using the Guide* at the beginning of the book explains how it helps you find a pub, in road atlases or large-scale maps as well as in our own maps.

with good range of well kept ales tapped from the cask, real ciders, good generous food from weekly changing bar and restaurant menus, friendly service; background music, no dogs; children welcome, tables out on terrace, modern bedroom block with good disabled access, closed lunchtimes Mon and Tues, otherwise open all day. *(Anon)*

ROXWELL   TL6508
Hare (01245) 248788
Bishops Stortford Road (A1060);
CM1 4LU Refurbished open-plan pub under new owners (Pie & Pint Inns); Golden Crust ales (brewed by Brentwood) and guests such as Adnams and Timothy Taylors, plenty of wines by the glass, good choice of traditional food with smaller helpings available, teas, coffee and home-made cakes, some timbers and log fire; children welcome, no dogs inside, terrace and garden with stream, farmland views, open all day. *(Anon)*

SAFFRON WALDEN   TL5338
Eight Bells (01799) 522790
Bridge Street; B184 towards Cambridge;
CB10 1BU Old refurbished beamed pub, open bar area with bare boards, leather arm-chairs and sofas, coal-effect gas fire in brick fireplace, back dining part in handsomely raftered and timbered 16th-barn with modern dark wood furniture and log-effect end wall, good home-made food from sandwiches and deli boards up, St Austell Tribute, Woodfordes Wherry and a guest, plenty of wines by the glass including champagne, helpful friendly staff; background music, DJ night last Fri of month; children welcome, dogs in bar, garden with raised deck, handy for Audley End, open all day. *(John Saville)*

SAFFRON WALDEN   TL5438
Old English Gentleman
(01799) 523595 *Gold Street; CB10 1EJ*
Busy 19th-c red-brick town pub with bare boards, panelling and log fires, four well kept beers such as Adnams Southwold and Woodfordes Wherry, plenty of wines by the glass, decent choice of lunchtime food from sandwiches up; background music; terrace tables, open all day (till 1am Fri, Sat). *(David Hawkes)*

STAPLEFORD TAWNEY   TL5001
✳ Mole Trap (01992) 522394
Tawney Common; signed off A113 N of M25 overpass – keep on; OS Sheet 167 map reference 500013; CM16 7PU
Popular unpretentious little country pub, carpeted beamed bar (mind your head as you go in) with brocaded wall seats and plain pub tables, steps down to similar area, warming fires, well kept Fullers London Pride and changing guests, pubby food (not Sun or Mon evenings); no credit cards, quiet background radio; plastic tables and chairs outside, along with various animals from rabbits and hens to goats and horses. *(Anon)*

STISTED   TL7923
Dolphin (01376) 321143
A120 E of Braintree, by village turn;
CM77 8EU Cheerful heavily beamed and timbered bar, good value straightforward fresh food (all day) cooked to order, Greene King and guest ales tapped from the cask, brasses, antlers and lots of small prints, newspapers, log fire, bright extended eating area on left; background music; children and dogs welcome, pretty back garden with heated covered area, nice hanging baskets, views over fields. *(Anon)*

STOCK   TQ6998
Bear (01277) 829100
Mill Road, just off B1007; CM4 9BH
Refurbished old village pub with emphasis on dining, civilised front bar with timbers, candles and woodburner, good varied choice of well presented food from bar snacks up, ales including Adnams, Greene King and Wells & Youngs, friendly efficient staff, restaurant, live music Sun; nice back garden overlooking pond. *(John Saville)*

STOW MARIES   TQ8399
✳ Prince of Wales (01621) 828971
B1012 between South Woodham Ferrers and Cold Norton Posters; CM3 6SA
Cheery atmosphere in several little low-ceilinged unspoilt rooms, bare boards and log fires, conservatory dining area, half a dozen widely sourced ales, bottled and draught belgian beers including fruit ones, enjoyable food (all day Sun) with some interesting specials, home-made pizzas (winter Thurs) from Victorian baker's oven, live jazz (third Fri of month); children in family room, terrace and garden tables, summer Sun barbecues, converted stable bedrooms, open all day. *(Anon)*

TENDRING   TM1523
Cherry Tree (01255) 830340
Off A120 E of Colchester; B1035 junction with Crow Lane, E of village centre;
CO16 9AP Extended and refurbished, heavy-beamed, red-brick dining pub, good sensibly priced country cooking (not Sun evening, booking advised weekends) including daily specials and set lunch (Tues-Sat), helpful friendly staff, high-backed black leather chairs around compact pub tables on broad polished boards, open fire, comfortable chairs by counter serving Adnams, Greene King and good value wines by the glass, two areas set with white linen, friendly tabby cat; disabled facilities, teak tables under parasols on sheltered back terrace, more tables on lawn behind tall hedge, closed Mon. *(N R White)*

THEYDON BOIS   TQ4598
Bull (01992) 812145
Station Approach; CM16 7HR Friendly beamed pub dating from the 17th c, polished wood and carpeted floors, log fire, three

well kept ales including Wells & Youngs Bombardier, enjoyable fairly standard food; sports TV; children welcome, dogs in bar, paved beer garden, open all day. *(Giles and Annie Francis)*

THEYDON BOIS   TQ4599
Queen Victoria (01992) 812392
Coppice Row (B172); CM16 7ES Nice spot on edge of green, cosy beamed and carpeted traditional lounge, roaring log fire, local pictures and mug collection, two further bars, popular good value food including children's menu, McMullens ales and decent house wines, friendly efficient young staff, end restaurant; background music; dogs welcome, picnic-sets on well laid out front terrace, open all day. *(John and Penelope Massey Stewart, Robert Lester, N R White)*

UPSHIRE   TL4100
Horseshoes (01992) 712745
Horseshoe Hill, E of Waltham Abbey; EN9 3SN Welcoming Victorian pub with small bar area and dining room, good freshly made food (not Sun evening, Mon) from chef/landlord with some emphasis on fish, well kept McMullens and guests, friendly helpful staff; children and dogs (in bar) welcome, garden overlooking Lea Valley, more tables out in front, good walks, open all day. *(Joel Calhoun)*

WICKHAM ST PAUL   TL8336
⋆Victory (01787) 269364
SW of Sudbury; The Green; CO9 2PT Attractive and spacious old dining pub,

interesting choice of good fresh food (not Sun evening), friendly efficient service, Adnams, Sharps Doom Bar and a guest from brick-fronted bar, beams and timbers, leather sofas and armchairs, inglenook woodburner; background music, pool and darts; children welcome, neat garden overlooking village cricket green, open all day. *(Anon)*

WIDDINGTON   TL5331
⋆Fleur de Lys (01799) 543280
Sgned off B1383 N of Stansted; CB11 3SG Welcoming unpretentious low-beamed and timbered village local, well prepared generous food (not Mon, evening Tues) in bar and dining room from sandwiches to Sun roasts, children's helpings, well kept Adnams, Sharps and two guests chosen by regulars, decent wines, dim lighting and inglenook log fire, pool and other games in back bar, Thurs quiz; dogs welcome, picnic-sets in pretty garden, open all day Fri-Sun. *(David and Gill Carrington)*

WRITTLE   TL6706
Wheatsheaf (01245) 420695
The Green; CM1 3DU Popular traditional two-room 19th-c local, friendly and chatty, with well kept Adnams, Farmers, Mighty Oak, Sharps, Wibblers and two guests, lunchtime baguettes and a couple of hot dishes (not Sun), free bar nibbles, folk night third Fri of month; terrace tables, open all day weekends. *(Bob Hibberd)*

Please keep sending us reports. We rely on readers for news of new discoveries, and particularly for news of changes – however slight – at the fully described pubs: feedback@goodguides.com, or (no stamp needed) The Good Pub Guide, FREEPOST TN1569, Wadhurst, E Sussex TN5 7BR.

Gloucestershire

We hope our readers enjoy these new entries as much as we did: Five Mile House at Duntisbourne Abbots (under friendly new owners), Ebrington Arms in Ebrington (hard-working licensees, six ales, interesting food and unusually decorated bedrooms), Bull in Fairford (smart old hotel in charming village with a cheery, bustling bar), Royal Oak in Gretton (golden stone inn, light and airy rooms, half a dozen beers and tasty food), Slaughters Country Inn at Lower Slaughter (civilised Cotswold-stone building, a clever blend of old and new, with thoughtful drinks and food and stylish bedrooms), Egypt Mill in Nailsworth (interesting restored watermill with waterside gardens) and Mount in Stanton (bustling inn with fine views and popular food). Other pubs doing well are the Queens Arms at Ashleworth (the hands-on south african licensees get consistent praise from our readers), Village Pub in Barnsley (civilised inn and delicious food), Kings Head at Bledington (top class all-rounder), Horse & Groom at Bourton-on-the-Hill (lovely old place), Eight Bells in Chipping Campden (open fires, candlelight and enjoyable food), Tunnel House at Coates (quirky, with a good choice of food and drink), Gloucester Old Spot at Coombe Hill (super pub, carefully restored by hands-on licensees, with inventive food), Green Dragon in Cowley (deservedly busy, attractive bars), Old Spot in Dursley (cheery atmosphere, enthusiastic landlord and 11 real ales), Hollow Bottom at Guiting Power (loved by the racing crowd and our readers), Royal Oak in Leighterton (buzzy atmosphere, inventive food and thoughtful drinks), Feathered Nest at Nether Westcote (civilised and special all-rounder), Ostrich in Newland (up to eight beers, popular food and a welcoming landlady), Bathurst Arms in North Cerney (super wines and food and friendly staff), Swan in Southrop (imaginative food using their own pigs, eggs and vegetables) and Horse & Groom at Upper Oddington (first-class landlord, popular food and local ales). Food in this county is top class, and many of the pubs here hold a Food Award. For its beautifully presented, exceptional food, our Gloucestershire Dining Pub 2014 is the Feathered Nest at Nether Westcote.

ASHLEWORTH

SO8125   Map 4

Queens Arms 🍴 ♈ 🍺

Village signposted off A417 at Hartpury; GL19 4HT

Neatly kept pub with friendly licensees, a civilised bar, highly rated food, thoughtful wines and sunny courtyard

Consistently well run and much enjoyed by our readers, this is a spic-and-span place with a warm welcome for all from the friendly, hands-on south african licensees. The civilised main bar has a happy mix of farmhouse and brocaded dining chairs around big oak and mahogany tables on green carpet, and all sorts of pictures and paintings on the faintly patterned wallpaper and washed red-ochre walls; at night, it's softly lit by candles and fringed wall lamps. A little art gallery displays work by local artists. Brains Rev James and guests like Adnams Bitter and Timothy Taylors Landlord on handpump, 15 wines by the glass including south african ones, 22 malt whiskies, winter mulled wine and summer home-made lemonade; background music, board games and (on request) a skittle alley. The friendly pub cat is called Talulah. The sunny courtyard has cast-iron chairs and tables and lovely flower beds in summer; two perfectly clipped mushroom-shaped yews dominate the front of the building.

 Promptly served and extremely good, the inventive food includes baguettes, moules marinière, baked field mushrooms with caramelised onions and goats cheese, south african spicy lamb stew, chicken breast stuffed with spinach and cream cheese with chive and white wine cream sauce, calves liver on bacon and onion mash with sage and port sauce, crab-stuffed red snapper with chilli, ginger and garlic dressing, roast partridge topped with game chips and juniper and red wine sauce, and puddings such as triple chocolate brownie and pecan nut and maple syrup pie. *Benchmark main dish: steak and kidney pie £11.95. Two-course evening meal £19.00.*

Free house ~ Licensees Tony and Gill Burreddu ~ Real ale ~ (01452) 700395 ~ Open 12-3, 7-11; 12-3 Sun; closed Sun evening, Mon ~ Bar food 12-2, 7-9 ~ Restaurant ~ Well behaved children allowed ~ www.queensarmsashleworth.co.uk
Recommended by Bernard Stradling, Ian Wilson, Chris and Angela Buckell

BARNSLEY

SP0705   Map 4

Village Pub 🍴 ♈ 🛏

B4425 Cirencester–Burford; GL7 5EF

Smart and enjoyable country pub with comfortable linked rooms, candles and open fires, excellent food and a good choice of drinks, and seats in the back courtyard; individually decorated bedrooms

This is an extremely comfortable and civilised place to stay, and the breakfasts are very good with local sausages, bacon and eggs and home-made bread and jam. The low-ceilinged bar rooms are smart and contemporary, with pale paintwork, flagstones and oak floorboards, heavy swagged curtains, oil paintings, plush chairs, stools and window settles around polished candlelit tables, three open fireplaces and country magazines and newspapers. There's always a cheerful mix of customers from regulars (often with a dog in tow) to diners out for a delicious meal. Butcombe Bitter, Hook Norton Old Hooky and a guest beer on handpump, and an extensive wine list with several by the glass. The sheltered back courtyard has good solid wooden furniture under parasols, outdoor heaters and its own outside servery.

🍴 Enticing contemporary food using the best local produce includes tasty nibbles like quail scotch eggs and mini chorizo and honey mustard sausages, as well as dorset crab with mayonnaise, potted pork and lemon with granary toast, baked sardine fillets with patatas bravas, wild mushroom linguine, shredded asian confit duck leg with chilli and coriander salad, chicken breast with savoy cabbage, artichoke, fried ceps and ham, smoked haddock fishcakes with poached egg, spinach and lemon butter sauce, braised lamb shoulder with root vegetables, mash and pickled red cabbage, and puddings such as baked rice pudding with jam and apple and treacle tart. *Benchmark main dish: whole plaice with parsley and caper nut butter £15.00. Two-course evening meal £21.50.*

Free house ~ Licensee Michael Mella ~ Real ale ~ (01285) 740421 ~ Open 11-3.30, 6-11; 11-11(10.30 Sun) Sat ~ Bar food 12-2.30(3 Sat), 6-9.30; 12-3, 6-9 Sun ~ Children welcome ~ Dogs welcome ~ Bedrooms: /£130 ~ www.thevillagepub.co.uk
Recommended by Michael Sargent, Caroline de Ville, Ellie Weld, David London

BLAISDON SO7016 Map 4
Red Hart 🍺

Village signposted off A4136 just SW of junction with A40 W of Gloucester; OS Sheet 162 map reference 703169; GL17 0AH

Village pub with interesting bric-a-brac in attractive rooms, popular bar food and several real ales

In a quiet village tucked away in the Forest of Dean, this bustling pub draws a good mix of locals and visitors. The flagstoned main bar has cushioned wall and window seats, traditional pub tables, a log fire, four real ales from breweries such as Bespoke, Stroud, Wells & Youngs and Wye Valley on handpump, several wines by the glass and local cider; background music and bar billiards. On the right is an attractive beamed restaurant with interesting prints and bric-a-brac; on the left is additional dining space for families. There are picnic-sets in the garden and a children's play area, and a terrace at the back for popular summer barbecues. The little church above the village is worth a visit.

🍴 Rearing their own pigs and using other local producers, the well liked food might include sandwiches, a tapas taster plate, scallops with black pudding and celeriac purée, game terrine with cumberland sauce, roasted vegetable gnocchi with spinach and parmesan, salmon and coriander fishcakes with hollandaise, gammon with egg or pineapple, specials such as rosemary and garlic chicken breast, herb-stuffed pork loin with crushed new potatoes and cider sauce or bacon-wrapped pheasant with boulangère potatoes, and puddings. *Benchmark main dish: slow-roast home-reared pork belly £12.75. Two-course evening meal £19.00.*

Free house ~ Licensee Sharon Hookings ~ Real ale ~ (01452) 830477 ~ Open 11.30-2.30(3 Sat), 6-11.30; 11.30-4, 7-10.30 Sun ~ Bar food 12-2, 7-9 ~ Restaurant ~ Children welcome ~ Dogs welcome ~ Quiz alternate Weds (not July/Aug) ~ www.redhartinn.co.uk
Recommended by Pete Flower, Paul and Sue Merrick

BLEDINGTON SP2422 Map 4
Kings Head 🍴 ♀ 🍺 🛏

B4450, OX7 0XQ

Beams and atmospheric furnishings in 16th-c former cider house, super wines by the glass, real ales and delicious food; smart bedrooms

Many customers are here to stay in the charming, elegantly simple bedrooms or to enjoy the excellent food, but the bar remains the focus, where both locals and visitors mix easily. The main bar is full of ancient beams and other atmospheric furnishings (high-backed wooden settles, gateleg or pedestal tables) and has a warming log fire in a stone inglenook with bellows and big black kettle; sporting memorabilia of rugby, racing, cricket and hunting. To the left, a drinking area has built-in wall benches, stools and dining chairs around wooden tables, rugs on bare boards and a woodburning stove. Hook Norton Best and guests from breweries such as Butcombe, Purity and Wye Valley on handpump, a super wine list with ten by the glass and 25 malt whiskies; background music and darts. There are seats out in front and more in the back courtyard garden; resident ducks and chickens. This is a pretty setting in a tranquil village, just back from the green with its brook. The same first class licensees also run the Swan at Swinbrook (Oxfordshire).

Imaginative food using free-range, organic and local produce might include sandwiches, chicken and lobster terrine with lobster emulsion, grilled field mushroom, spinach and double gloucester rarebit, roasted red pepper and wild mushroom risotto, beef stroganoff, fish pie with minted peas, grilled pork loin chop with black pudding mash and apple jus, fillet of salmon with samphire, peas and brown shrimps and hollandaise, duck breast, cassoulet of duck confit and toulouse sausage with herb crumb, and special Wednesday evening burgers using very local beef, roe deer or chicken. *Benchmark main dish: home-made chilli cheeseburger £12.50. Two-course evening meal £22.50.*

Free house ~ Licensees Nicola and Archie Orr-Ewing ~ Real ale ~ (01608) 658365 ~ Open 11(12 Sun)-11 ~ Bar food 12-2, 6.30-9 ~ Restaurant ~ Children welcome ~ Dogs allowed in bar ~ Bedrooms: £70/£95 ~ www.kingsheadinn.net
Recommended by Bernard Stradling, Ann Gray, Walter and Susan Rinaldi-Butcher, Jamie and Sue May, Jenny Smith, Richard Greaves, Jane McKenzie, Alun and Jennifer Evans, Maria Oakley, Sue Callard, Tracey and Stephen Groves

BOURTON-ON-THE-HILL SP1732 Map 4
Horse & Groom 🍴 ♟ 🛏
A44 W of Moreton-in-Marsh; GL56 9AQ

Handsome Georgian inn with a fine range of drinks, excellent food, friendly staff and lovely views from seats outside; smart bedrooms

Readers love this honey-coloured stone inn. Run by two brothers, it's a top class all-rounder with an excellent bustling atmosphere and the friendliest of welcomes. The light and airy pubby bar has a nice mix of wooden chairs and tables on bare boards, stripped-stone walls, a good log fire, Goffs Jouster and guests like Butcombe Rare Breed and Purity Mad Goose on handpump, Cotswold Brewing Company Lager, local cider, 20 wines by the glass and home-made lemonade and elderflower cordial. There are plenty of original features throughout. The large back garden has lots of seats under smart umbrellas and fine countryside views. Arrive early to be sure of a space in the smallish car park. This is a special place to stay, with individually styled bedrooms. Batsford Arboretum is not far away.

Stylishly presented, the interesting modern food includes cornish fish soup with rouille and gruyère, home-cured spiced salt beef with beetroot and horseradish relish and home-made foccacia, spinach, roast squash, lentil and mascarpone filo parcels with curried sauce, grilled salmon fillet with roasted beetroots and horseradish cream, pigeon breasts on creamed celeriac purée with chorizo and thyme jus, rare-breed pork chop with apple compote and green peppercorn sauce, and puddings such as vanilla gingernut cheesecake with spiced clementines and banana and pecan sponge pudding with butterscotch sauce. *Benchmark main dish: beer-battered cod with minted pea purée and tartare sauce £12.75. Two-course evening meal £20.00.*

Free house ~ Licensee Tom Greenstock ~ Real ale ~ (01386) 700413 ~ Open 11-2.30 (3 Sat), 6-11; 12-3.30 Sun; closed Sun evening ~ Bar food 12-2(2.30 Sun), 7-9.30 ~ Restaurant ~ Children welcome ~ Bedrooms: £80/£120 ~ www.horseandgroom.info
Recommended by Paul and Penny Dawson, Mads Rowsby, Richard Tilbrook, Andy and Jill Kassube, Simon Collett-Jones, Tracey and Stephen Groves, Di and Mike Gillam, Dr J J H Gilkes, Derek Thomas

BROAD CAMPDEN
SP1537   Map 4

Bakers Arms 🍺 £

Village signed from B4081 in Chipping Campden; GL55 6UR

Friendly village pub with five real ales, traditional food and a good mix of customers

This village pub (first licensed in 1724) has a good choice of real ales and a bustling, friendly feel. The tiny beamed bar has perhaps the most character, with a mix of seats and tables around the stripped-stone walls, an inglenook fireplace at one end, and Donnington BB, Wickwar Coopers, Bob and WPA and a couple of changing guest beers on handpump at the attractive oak counter; darts and board games. The simply furnished dining room has beams, exposed stone walls and a little open fire. There are picnic-sets under parasols on a terraced area, with more by flower tubs on other terraces and in the back garden. Plenty of nearby walks.

Tasty pubby food includes sandwiches, twice-baked cheese soufflé, whitebait with lemon, wild mushroom stroganoff, ham and egg, chicken, ham and leek pie, lamb shank with gratin potatoes, peppered salmon steak with chive cream sauce, slow-cooked pork belly, and puddings such as banana tarte tatin with bourbon vanilla ice-cream and apple charlotte with custard. *Benchmark main dish: beer-battered fresh cod or haddock with chips, peas and tartare sauce £9.95. Two-course evening meal £15.00.*

Free house ~ Licensees Lutti and Jess Bates ~ Real ale ~ (01386) 840515 ~ Open 11.30-2.30, 5.30-10.30; 11.30-11 Sat; 12-8 Sun; closed Mon lunchtime ~ Bar food 12-2, 6-8.30 (9 Fri, Sat); 12-3 Sun ~ Restaurant ~ Children welcome away from bar ~ Dogs welcome ~ www.bakersarmscampden.co.uk *Recommended by Andy and Jill Kassube*

BROCKHAMPTON
SP0322   Map 4

Craven Arms

Village signposted off A436 Andoversford–Naunton (look out for inn sign at head of lane in village; can also be reached from A40 Andoversford–Cheltenham via Whittington and Syreford; GL54 5XQ

Friendly village pub with tasty bar food, real ales, seats in a big garden and nice surrounding walks

Set in an attractive gentrified hillside village, this attractive old pub is much favoured by our readers after a walk. The bars have low beams, thick roughly coursed stone walls and some tiled flooring; although it's largely been opened out to give a sizeable eating area off the smaller bar servery, there's a feeling of several communicating rooms. The furniture is mainly pine with comfortable leather sofas, wall settles and tub chairs, and there are gin traps, various stuffed animal trophies and a warm log fire. Otter Bitter and a couple of changing guests like Cotswold Spring Stunner and Stroud Budding on handpump and several wines by the glass; board games. The dog is called Max and the cat Polly. There are plenty of seats in the large garden, and lovely views.

🍴 Well liked food includes chicken liver pâté with truffle butter and red onion marmalade, mussels with white wine, garlic and chilli cream, ham and free-range eggs, wild mushroom, apricot and goats cheese loaf, burger in a brioche bun with chips, steak in ale pie, beer-battered fish with creamed peas, sausages with onion gravy and mash, fried mackerel with samphire and green bean and caper salad, and puddings. *Benchmark main dish: slow-cooked lamb in mint and rosemary £16.95. Two-course evening meal £18.50.*

Free house ~ Licensees Barbara and Bob Price ~ Real ale ~ (01242) 820410 ~ Open 12-3, 6-11; 12-11 Sat; 12-6 Sun; closed Sun evening, Mon ~ Bar food 12-2, 7-9 ~ Restaurant ~ Children welcome ~ Dogs allowed in bar ~ www.thecravenarms.co.uk
Recommended by Guy Vowles, Geoffrey and Penny Hughes, David and Diane Young, Neil and Anita Christopher, Dr A J and Mrs B A Tompsett

CHELTENHAM
Royal Oak ♀ 🍺
SO9624   Map 4

Off B4348 just N; The Burgage, Prestbury; GL52 3DL

Bustling and friendly with popular food, several real ales and wine by the glass, and seats in a sheltered garden

Being the pub closest to Cheltenham Racecourse, this 16th-c inn gets pretty busy on race days. They hold regular festivals and theme nights throughout the year, so there's always a cheerful and friendly atmosphere. The congenial low-beamed bar has fresh flowers and polished brasses, a comfortable mix of seating including chapel chairs on the parquet flooring, some interesting pictures on the ochre walls and a woodburning stove in the stone fireplace. Dark Star Hophead, Harveys Best, Otley O1, Timothy Taylors Landlord and Wye Valley Bitter on handpump and several wines by the glass; efficient, helpful service. Dining room tables are nicely spaced, so that you don't feel crowded, and the skittle alley doubles as a function room. There are seats and tables under canopies on a heated terrace and in a sheltered garden.

🍴 Enjoyable food includes ciabattas, slow-braised pork ribs with celeriac remoulade, smoked eel and prawns with beetroot slaw and caper and mustard dressed salad, ham, tomato and free-range egg, courgette, celeriac and chickpea curry, smoked fish and seafood lasagne, pork belly with perry and apple sauce, red mullet fillet and prawns with sautéed chorizo, onions and aioli, lamb shank with garam masala and toasted almonds, and puddings. *Benchmark main dish: duck breast with rhubarb and berry sauce £16.50. Two-course evening meal £20.00.*

Free house ~ Licensees Simon and Kate Daws ~ Real ale ~ (01242) 522344 ~ Open 11-11 ~ Bar food 12-2, 6-9; all day Sun ~ Restaurant ~ Children welcome in dining room and before 7pm in bar ~ www.royal-oak-prestbury.co.uk *Recommended by Michael Sargent, Ian Herdman*

CHIPPING CAMPDEN
Eight Bells 🍺 🛏
SP1539   Map 4

Church Street (one-way – entrance off B4035); GL55 6JG

Handsome inn with massive timbers and beams, log fires, quite a choice of bar food, real ales and seats in a large terraced garden; bedrooms

This is a popular place to stay, with attractive, comfortable bedrooms – and well thought-of breakfasts. It's a lovely old building and the candlelit bars have heavy oak beams, massive timber supports and stripped-stone walls, with cushioned pews, sofas and solid dark wood furniture on broad flagstones, and log fires in up to three restored stone fireplaces. A glass panel in the dining room floor reveals the passage from the church by which Catholic priests could escape the Roundheads. Hook Norton Best, Goffs Jouster, Purity Mad Goose and a guest such as Wye Valley HPA on handpump from the fine oak bar counter, several wines by the glass and Weston's Old Rosie cider; background music and board games. The large terraced garden has plenty of seats, and striking views of the almshouses and church. The pub is handy for the Cotswold Way.

As well as a two- and three-course set weekday lunch, the good food includes lunchtime ciabattas, home-smoked sea trout pâté, deep-fried mature cheddar and chilli fritters with mustard sauce, pork sausages with mash, tagliatelle with goats cheese, roasted peppers and basil pesto, home-made lamb, garlic, rosemary and oregano burger with tzatziki and feta salad, chicken breast wrapped in parma ham on pasta with tomato, basil and red pepper sauce, and puddings like white chocolate and raspberry cheesecake and banana and walnut sponge with rum custard. *Benchmark main dish: beer-battered cod with home-made tartare sauce and pea purée £13.50. Two-course evening meal £22.00.*

Free house ~ Licensee Neil Hargreaves ~ Real ale ~ (01386) 840371 ~ Open 12-11; 12-10.30 Sun ~ Bar food 12-2, 6.30-9; 12-2.30, 6.30-9.30 Fri, Sat; all day Sun ~ Restaurant ~ Well behaved children welcome in dining room after 6pm ~ Dogs allowed in bar ~ Bedrooms: £60/£100 ~ www.eightbellsinn.co.uk *Recommended by Paul and Penny Dawson, Mike and Shirley Stratton, Dennis Jones, Brian and Ruth Young, Michael Carpenter, Jim Wolstenholme, K H Frostick, Bernard Stradling, J Trevor Roberts, Simon Collett-Jones, Jim and Maggie Cowell, Clive and Fran Dutson, Paul Humphreys*

CLIFFORD'S MESNE
Yew Tree ⑪ ♀ ◀   SO6922   Map 4

From A40 W of Huntley turn off at 'May Hill 1, Clifford's Mesne 2.5' signpost, then pub eventually signed up steep narrow lane on left; Clifford's Mesne also signposted off B4216 S of Newent, pub then signed on right; GL18 1JS

Unusual dining pub nicely tucked away on slopes of May Hill, with inventive food and wine bargains

Originally a cider press dating back centuries, this well run dining pub offers a remarkable choice of provincial french wines from small producers – all served by glass (three sizes), 500ml jug and bottle. A seating area in the small informal wine shop makes it a sort of wine bar with nibbles; if you buy a bottle with your meal, the mark-up is £6, which represents excellent value especially at the top end. Cottage DB5, Sharps Own and Wickwar Spring Ale on handpump, local farm cider and perry, 16 gins and good value winter mulled wine and cider; service is prompt and genial. The smallish two-room beamed bar has an attractive mix of small settles, a pew and character chairs around interesting tables including antiques, rugs on an unusual stone floor, and a warm woodburning stove. Up a few steps is a more formal carpeted dining room, and beyond a sofa by a big log fire; newspapers and unobtrusive nostalgic pop music. Teak tables on a side terrace have the best views, and there are steps down to a sturdy play area. Plenty of nearby walks.

🍴 Using their home-reared gloucester old spot pigs and other local produce, the interesting food includes nibbles and tapas, salmon and scallop terrine, goats cheese baked with spicy tomato sauce and rosemary crostini, butternut squash, roast garlic and stilton galette, salmon mousse-stuffed haddock fillets baked in seafood sauce, chicken and black pudding in creamy dijon sauce, rump of lamb with spinach and dauphinoise potatoes, and puddings such as chocolate and ginger torte and fresh pineapple crumble; they also offer light lunches and smaller helpings for under £8 (Weds-Sat lunchtimes). *Benchmark main dish: gloucester old spot loin steaks with chilli and ginger butter £15.00. Two-course evening meal £20.50.*

Free house ~ Licensees Mr and Mrs Philip Todd ~ Real ale ~ (01531) 820719 ~ Open 12-2.30, 6-11; 12-4 Sun; closed Sun evening, all Mon, Tues lunchtime ~ Bar food 12-2, 6-9; 12-4 Sun ~ Children welcome ~ Dogs welcome ~ www.yewtreeinn.com
Recommended by Guy Vowles, John and Sylvia Harrop, Eric and Mary Barrett

COATES
SO9600 Map 4

Tunnel House 🍺

Follow Tarlton signs (right then left) from village, pub up rough track on right after railway bridge; OS Sheet 163 map reference 965005; GL7 6PW

Friendly pub with interesting décor, lots of character, good food and drink, and seats in the sizeable garden; at entrance to derelict canal tunnel

It's really worth negotiating the rough track to reach this quirky bow-fronted stone house – for its character and its position. There are impressive views from the seats and tables on the front terrace and a big garden, which slopes down to the derelict entrance tunnel of the old Thames and Severn Canal. Inside, the atmosphere is cheerful and easy-going as it's especially popular with students from the Royal Agricultural College; readers enjoy their visits here very much. The rambling rooms have beams, flagstones, a mix of furnishings including massive rustic benches and seats built into the sunny windows, lots of enamel advertising signs, racing tickets and air travel labels, a stuffed wild boar's head and owl, plenty of copper and brass and an upside-down card table complete with cards and drinks fixed to the beams; there's a winter log fire with sofas beside (but you have to arrive early to grab them). The more conventional dining extension and back conservatory fill up quickly. Prescott Hill Climb, Sharps Doom Bar, Uley Bitter and a guest from Stroud on handpump, several wines by the glass and two draught ciders; background music. Good walks nearby; disabled lavatories.

🍴 Their proper tray-baked pies are popular, and they also serve sandwiches, thai fishcakes with sweet chilli sauce, seasonal vegetable risotto, gloucester old spot sausages with red onion marmalade, beer-battered cod and chips, slow-roast pork belly with wholegrain mustard potatoes and cider sauce, salmon fillet with dill sauce, and puddings like dark chocolate, apricot and whisky fudge cake and lemon cheesecake with lemon and raspberry coulis. *Benchmark main dish: burger with bacon, stilton or cheddar and skinny fries £10.95. Two-course evening meal £20.00.*

Free house ~ Licensee Michael Hughes ~ Real ale ~ (01285) 770280 ~ Open 12-midnight ~ Bar food 12-9.30 ~ Restaurant ~ Children welcome ~ Dogs welcome ~ www.tunnelhouse.com *Recommended by M G Hart, Ian Herdman, Neil and Anita Christopher*

Bedroom prices are for high summer. Even then you may get reductions for more than one night, or (outside tourist areas) weekends. Winter special rates are common, and many inns cut bedroom prices if you have a full evening meal.

COOMBE HILL   SO8926 Map 4
Gloucester Old Spot ★ ◀

A mile from M5 junction 10 (access only from southbound/to northbound carriageways); A4019 towards A38 Gloucester–Tewkesbury; GL51 9SY

The country local comes of age – a model for today's country pubs

Ten minutes from Cheltenham Racecourse and the town centre, this carefully restored country pub has a genuine welcome for all. The companionable quarry-tiled beamed bar has chapel chairs and other seats around mixed tables, one in a bow-windowed alcove, and opens into a lighter, partly panelled area with cushioned settles and stripped kitchen tables. They sometimes have their own-brewed cider or perry (Black Rat if not), as well as Gwynt y Ddraig Happy Daze, Hop Back GFB, Purity Mad Goose and Skinners Betty Stogs on handpump, and seven decent wines by the glass; young staff are friendly without being pushy. Decoration is in unobtrusive good taste, with winter log fires. A separate dining room, handsome with high stripped-brick walls, dark flagstones and candlelight, has similar country furniture. As we went to press, the garden was about to be redesigned. Sister pub is the Royal Oak in Cheltenham.

They make a particular feature of rare-breed pork and sausages; other food (strong on local seasonal produce) includes lunchtime cobs, potted smoked mackerel with mascarpone, horseradish and chives, braised rabbit and black pudding cannelloni in cider, mustard and cream, cauliflower and blue cheese risotto with poached egg, pork burger with barbecue sauce and celeriac and apple coleslaw, herb-crusted cod fillet with leek, spinach and moules marinière sauce, crispy pork belly with black pudding and mustard sauce, chicken breast with chorizo sausage with pesto and crème fraîche, and puddings. *Benchmark main dish: pork tenderloin with sautéed kidneys and mustard sauce £15.95. Two-course evening meal £19.50.*

Free house ~ Licensees Simon Daws and Hayley Cribb ~ Real ale ~ (01242) 680321 ~ Open 10.30am-11pm; 11-10.30 Sun ~ Bar food 12-2, 6-9; 12-6 Sun ~ Restaurant ~ Children welcome ~ Dogs welcome ~ Quiz first Thurs of month ~ www.thegloucesteroldspot.co.uk *Recommended by Di and Mike Gillam, Roger and Donna Huggins*

COWLEY   SO9714 Map 4
Green Dragon ⑪ ⇌

Off A435 S of Cheltenham at Elkstone, Cockleford sign; OS Sheet 163 map reference 970142; GL53 9NW

17th-c stone-fronted inn with plenty of character in beamed bars, two restaurants, popular food, real ales and seats on terraces; well appointed bedrooms

This is a particularly well run pub that our readers enjoy very much. It's an attractive stone-fronted place, smart yet characterful, and even when really busy – which it deservedly often is – the helpful and efficient staff offer a genuine welcome to all. The two beamed bars have a cosy, nicely old-fashioned feel with big flagstones and wooden floorboards, candlelit tables and winter log fires in two stone fireplaces. Hook Norton Old Hooky, Sharps Doom Bar and guests like Butcombe Bitter and Otter Bitter on handpump, and ten wines by the glass. The furniture, and the bar itself in the upper Mouse Bar, were made by Robert Thompson, and little mice run over the hand-carved tables, chairs and mantelpiece;

there's also a small upstairs restaurant. The bedrooms are comfortable and well appointed and the breakfasts generous. There are seats outside on terraces and this is good walking country.

🍴 Using local meat and cheeses, the good food includes sandwiches, minted lamb kofta meatballs with banana and coconut curry sauce, smoked trout, salmon, horseradish and dill pâté with tzatziki, wild mushroom and baby spinach risotto, burger with cheddar or stilton, caramelised onion and tomato chutney, slow-braised faggots with mash and onion gravy, steak and kidney pudding with minted mushy peas, hake steak in lemon, garlic and smoked salt with butter bean and chorizo cassoulet, venison haunch steak with honey-roast parsnips and port and redcurrant sauce, and puddings. *Benchmark main dish: leg of pork and sage casserole with glazed apples £15.95. Two-course evening meal £22.75.*

Buccaneer Holdings ~ Managers Simon and Nicky Haly ~ Real ale ~ (01242) 870271 ~ Open 11-11; 12-10.30 Sun ~ Bar food 12-2.30(3 Sat), 6-10; 12-3.30, 6-9 Sun ~ Restaurant ~ Children welcome ~ Dogs allowed in bar and bedrooms ~ Bedrooms: £70/£95 ~ www.green-dragon-inn.co.uk *Recommended by S G N Bennett, Barry and Monica Jones, Dave Braisted, Richard Tilbrook, Dr A J and Mrs B A Tompsett, Howard and Margaret Buchanan*

DUNTISBOURNE ABBOTS
SO9709 Map 4
Five Mile House 🍺
E of A417 on parallel old Main Road; GL7 7JR

Enthusiastic new landlord for bustling village pub with several character rooms, four ales, lots of bottled ciders and tasty food

After a lot of hard work, Mr Thomas has got this village pub back on its feet again – and our readers are delighted. It has plenty of original character. The front room has a companionable bare-boards drinking bar on the right, with wall seats around a big table in the bow window and pubby chairs around just one other table. On the left is a flagstoned hallway snug formed from two ancient high-backed settles placed beside a stove in the tall carefully exposed old fireplace; there's also a small cellar bar specialising in cider – there's always at least two on draught and up to 48 in bottles. The back restaurant is down steps and there's another room on the far side. Brakspears Oxford Gold, Church End What the Foxs Hat, Cotswold Spring Stunner and Hook Norton Cotswold Lion on handpump and 16 good wines by the glass. The gardens have nice country views, a very smart smokers' shelter and a summer marquee. The country lane was once Ermine Street, the main Roman road from Wales to London.

🍴 Well liked food includes sandwiches, grilled goats cheese with honey, smoked duck salad, vegetarian lasagne, pasta of the day, meatballs in tomato sauce, local sausages with mash and onion gravy, gammon with french fries, mussels with white wine and cream sauce, and puddings. *Benchmark main dish: mega-burger with bacon, cheese, caramelised onions and tomato topped with fried egg £12.00. Two-course evening meal £18.00.*

Free house ~ Licensee Martin Thomas ~ Real ale ~ (01285) 821432 ~ Open 12-11(10.30 Sun) ~ Bar food 12-9(4 Sun); phone to check Sun evening ~ Restaurant ~ Children welcome ~ Dogs allowed in bar ~ www.fivemilehouse.co.uk *Recommended by Guy Vowles, Pat Bunting, Nick and Meriel Cox, Richard Tilbrook, Giles and Annie Francis, R K Phillips, Tom McLean*

The details at the end of each featured entry start by saying whether the pub is a free house, or if it belongs to a brewery or pub group (which we name).

DURSLEY   ST7598 Map 4

Old Spot ◀ £

Hill Road; by bus station; GL11 4JQ

Unassuming and cheery town pub with up to 11 real ales and regular beer festivals, and good value lunchtime food

With a fantastic choice of up to 11 real ales on handpump, a genuinely happy atmosphere and a warm welcome from Mr Herbert and his staff, this notably well run town local is as much enjoyed by our readers as ever. There's always Uley Old Ric plus guests from breweries such as Bath Ales, Blue Bee, Butcombe, Felinfoel, Great Heck, Hereford, Hook Norton, Sarah Hughes, Thornbridge and Wickwar; they also hold four annual beer festivals and stock 40 malts too. The front door opens into a deep-pink small room with stools on shiny quarry tiles along a pine-boarded bar counter and old enamel beer advertisements on the walls and ceiling; there's a profusion of porcine paraphernalia. A small room leads off on the left, and the little dark wood-floored room to the right has a stone fireplace. A step goes down to a cosy Victorian tiled snug and (to the right) a meeting room. The heated and covered garden has seats. Wheelchair access.

 Good value lunchtime food (they offer Mon evening dishes too) includes doorstep sandwiches, a soup and salad deal (such as smoked salmon and prawn or chicken, bacon and avocado), cottage pie, seafood pancake, steak in ale pie, specials such as salmon, cheddar and leek crumble or butternut squash stuffed with roasted vegetables and goats cheese, and puddings like white chocolate cheesecake and lemon drizzle sponge. *Benchmark main dish: gloucester old spot pork belly on apple and sage mash with plum sauce £11.95.*

Free house ~ Licensee Steve Herbert ~ Real ale ~ (01453) 542870 ~ Open 11-11; 12-11 Sun ~ Bar food 12-3; 12-3, 6.30-9 Mon ~ Children in family room only (best to book) ~ Dogs welcome ~ www.oldspotinn.co.uk *Recommended by Mrs P Sumner, PL, Jim and Frances Gowers, Chris and Angela Buckell, Kerry Law, Dr and Mrs A K Clarke*

EBRINGTON   SP1839 Map 4

Ebrington Arms ⓨ ◀ ⇌

Off B4035 E of Chipping Campden or A429 N of Moreton-in-Marsh; GL55 6NH

17th-c village inn with enthusiastic young licensees, good choice of real ales, wines by the glass and interesting food; bedrooms

By the green at the heart of an attractive village and surrounded by good walks, this 17th-c Cotswold-stone pub is a delightful place with friendly, hard-working licensees and plenty of character and charm. The beamed bar has lots of cheerful locals, ladder-back chairs and cushioned settles around a mix of tables on the flagstoned floor, a fine inglenook fireplace, and seats built into an airy bow window. The similarly furnished beamed dining room has original ironwork in its inglenook fireplace. A fine choice of half a dozen real ales on handpump might include Crouch Vale Brewers Gold, North Cotswold Windrush Ale, Otter Amber, Prescott Hill Climb, Stroud Budding and Uley Bitter, and they keep nine wines by the glass and Weston's farm cider and perry. An arched stone wall shelters a terrace with picnic-table sets under parasols, with more on the lawn. The country-style bedrooms are well equipped and comfortable. The inn is handy for Hidcote (NT) and Kiftsgate gardens.

¶ As well as a £7 weekday lunchtime special and summer afternoon teas, the interesting food might include lunchtime sandwiches, inventive soups, potato gnocchi with cashew nuts, crispy pancetta and thyme vinaigrette, crispy slow-roasted pork shoulder with home-made black pudding and apple salad, vegetable filo parcel with caramelised cauliflower and rosemary sauce, steamed pollock with vegetable tagliatelle and lemon grass and ginger sauce, local venison loin, slow-cooked haunch and greens, and puddings such as Jaffa cake, orange jelly and white chocolate sorbet and apple tarte tatin with vanilla ice-cream. *Benchmark main dish: beer-battered fish and chips £12.00. Two-course evening meal £20.00.*

Free house ~ Licensees Claire and Jim Alexander ~ Real ale ~ (01386) 593223 ~ Open 9am-11pm ~ Bar food 12-2.30, 6-9(9.30 Fri, Sat); 12-3.30, 6-8.30 Sun ~ Restaurant ~ Children welcome but only in bedrooms by prior arrangement ~ Dogs allowed in bar ~ Acoustic/comedians Sun; monthly quiz and food night ~ Bedrooms: /£120 ~ www.theebringtonarms.co.uk *Recommended by Nigel and Sue Foster, Simon Collett-Jones, Martin and Pauline Jennings, Richard Tilbrook, Peter J and Avril Hanson*

FAIRFORD   SP1501   Map 4

Bull 🛏

Market Place; GL7 4AA

Rather smart old hotel with beams, timbers and pubby furnishings in relaxed bar, residents' lounge, and reasonably priced bar food

This is a rather smart and civilised hotel, but it also has a sizeable main bar with a bustling, chatty atmosphere and plenty of cheerful locals. The nicely laid out bar (being refurbished as we went to press) has comfortably old-fashioned pubby furnishings including dark pews and settles (try to sit at the big table in the bow window overlooking the market square), beams, timbers and an open fire. The long bar has Arkells 2B, 3B and Wiltshire Gold on handpump, and service is friendly. Up a few stone steps is a nice little residents' lounge, with attractive soft leather sofas and armchairs around a big stone fireplace, and fishing prints. The village is charming, and the church just along the street has Britain's only intact set of medieval stained-glass windows.

¶ Well liked food includes sandwiches, chicken liver parfait with home-made chutney, smoked salmon with capers, onion and crème fraîche, roasted pumpkin risotto, ham and eggs, pancetta-wrapped chicken with mushrooms and tarragon sauce, lambs liver and bacon, pie of the day, slow-braised beef, fresh fish of the day, and puddings such as triple chocolate terrine and fruit crumble; they have regular themed food evenings (pasta Monday, steak Wednesday, fish and chips Friday) and also a two-course menu (Sunday-Thursday). *Benchmark main dish: local sausages with mash and onion gravy £8.50. Two-course evening meal £15.00.*

Arkells ~ Tenant Ian Summers ~ Real ale ~ (01285) 712535 ~ Open 10am-11pm; 12-10.30 Sun ~ Bar food 12-2, 6.30-9.15 ~ Restaurant ~ Children welcome ~ Dogs allowed in bar and bedrooms ~ Bedrooms: £55/£85 ~ www.thebullhotelfairford.co.uk *Recommended by Harvey Brown, Emma Scofield*

FORD   SP0829   Map 4

Plough 🍴 🛏

B4077 Stow–Alderton; GL54 5RU

16th-c inn in horse racing country, with lots of horse talk, a bustling atmosphere, first class service, good food and well kept beer; bedrooms

Readers really enjoy their visits here – 'the place exudes friendliness,' says one. It has a lot of charm and character and a chatty atmosphere, all helped by the hands-on landlord and his courteous, efficient staff. The beamed and stripped-stone bar has racing prints and photos (many customers belong to the racing fraternity and a well known trainer's yard is opposite), old settles and benches around big tables on uneven flagstones, oak tables in a snug alcove, and open fires and woodburning stoves. Darts, TV (for the races) and background music. Donnington BB and SBA on handpump. There are picnic-sets under parasols and pretty hanging baskets at the front of the stone building, and a large back garden with a children's play fort. Cotswold Farm Park is nearby. Bedrooms are comfortable (the quietest ones are away from the pub) and there are views of the gallops. It gets packed on race days.

Using free-range meat and seasonal game, the good, popular food includes lunchtime baguettes, pigeon breast with wild mushroom and smoked bacon sauce, crispy coated whitebait with home-made tartare sauce, pasta with sunblush tomatoes, spinach, wild mushroom and parmesan, honey- and mustard-glazed ham with free-range eggs and chips, fillet of sea bream with morecambe bay shrimps on mushroom risotto, game casserole with dumplings, and puddings like passion-fruit crème brûlée with home-made shortbread and sticky toffee pudding with warm toffee sauce; they also serve breakfasts to non-residents from 9am. *Benchmark main dish: half roast gressingham duck with orange sauce £17.95. Two-course evening meal £19.00.*

Donnington ~ Tenant Craig Brown ~ Real ale ~ (01386) 584215 ~ Open 9am-11pm ~ Bar food 12-2, 6-9; all day Fri-Sun ~ Restaurant ~ Children welcome ~ Dogs welcome ~ Bedrooms: £60/£80 ~ www.theploughinnatford.co.uk *Recommended by Michael Sargent, Jamie and Sue May, Keith and Ann Arnold, Guy Vowles, K H Frostick, D L Frostick*

FOSSEBRIDGE
Fossebridge Inn ⑨ ⇔

SP0711　Map 4

A429 Cirencester to Stow-on-the-Wold; GL54 3JS

Handsome old inn with a proper bar, a good mix of customers, real ales, interesting food and seats in four acres of grounds; smart bedrooms

The original 15th-c heart of this partly Tudor and partly Georgian inn is the bustling bar, which has a relaxed, informal atmosphere, plenty of chatty regulars, North Cotswold Best, Otter Ale and St Austell Tribute on handpump, several wines by the glass and Stowford Press cider. The two rooms have beams and arches, stripped-stone walls and fine old flagstones, a happy mix of dining chairs, stools and wooden tables, copper implements, open fires, candles and fresh flowers. Two other dining rooms are rather grand. The pub is especially popular in summer as there are picnic-sets and other seats and tables under parasols on the terrace and four acres of lawned riverside gardens. The bedrooms are comfortable and there's a self-catering cottage. The National Trust Roman villa at Chedworth is nearby.

Good, popular food includes lunchtime sandwiches, duck scotch egg, game terrine with fig chutney and chargrilled soda bread, burgers with bacon, cheese and triple-cooked chips, fennel, spinach, tomato and olive lasagne, pollock with bubble and squeak and saffron and shellfish sauce, chicken breast stuffed with basil and sunblush tomatoes with savoy cabbage, bacon and thyme jus, and puddings like lavender crème brûlée with shortbread biscuits and spotted dick with banana custard. *Benchmark main dish: fishcakes with wilted spinach, poached free-range egg and hollandaise £14.50. Two-course evening meal £22.00.*

Free house ~ Licensee Samantha Jenkins ~ Real ale ~ (01285) 720721 ~ Open 12-midnight (11.30 Sun) ~ Bar food 12-2.30(3 Sat, 3.30 Sun), 6-9.30(9 in winter) ~ Restaurant ~ Children welcome ~ Dogs welcome ~ Bedrooms: £75/£85 ~ www.fossebridgeinn.co.uk *Recommended by Robert Wivell, John Holroyd, Richard Tilbrook*

GLOUCESTER
Café René ◀

SO8318 Map 4

Southgate Street; best to park in Blackfriars car park (Ladybellegate Street) and walk through passageway – pub entrance is just across road; GL1 1TP

Interesting and interestingly placed bar with good value food all day, and good choice of drinks

This bar is different to most places in the *Guide*: reached down a flagstoned passageway beside the partly Norman church of St Mary de Crypt, it dates from the 17th c, with some stripped brick and timbering. It has an internal floodlit well, with water trickling into its depths, and a very subterranean feel – no windows, black beams (with loads of beer mats), dim lighting – with a bustling atmosphere and helpful staff. The long bar counter is made of dozens of big casks; they have four changing real ales, tapped from the cask, from breweries like Blindmans, Freeminster, Stroud and Wickwar, plus farm ciders and a good choice of wines by the glass (decoration consists largely of great banks of empty wine bottles). One antique panelled high-backed settle joins the usual pub tables and wheelback chairs, on carpet, and there's a sizeable dining area on the right. Well reproduced background music, a silenced games machine and big-screen TV. There are plenty of picnic-sets under parasols by the churchyard. They hold a popular rhythm and blues festival in July and a Sunday night quiz.

Usefully served all day, the good value food includes sandwiches and wraps, baked potatoes, soup, organic chicken liver pâté with cranberry sauce, beer-battered cod and chips, steak in ale or fish pies, fresh tagliatelle with cream cheese, tomato and basil, trio of sausages with wholegrain mustard mash and red onion gravy, caribbean curried lamb, very popular chargrilled dishes such as whole rack of baby back ribs with barbecue sauce, cajun chicken, meat or vegetarian burgers and steaks, and puddings like lemon tart with raspberries and sticky toffee pudding with toffee sauce. *Benchmark main dish: chargrilled steaks £15.50. Two-course evening meal £18.00.*

Free house ~ Licensee Paul Soden ~ Real ale ~ (01452) 309340 ~ Open 11am-midnight (later Fri, Sat) ~ Bar food 11-10 ~ Restaurant ~ Well behaved children welcome ~ Live music Weds, Fri ~ www.caferene.co.uk *Recommended by Ruth May*

GREAT RISSINGTON
Lamb ♀ ⇔

SP1917 Map 4

Turn off A40 W of Burford to the Barringtons; keep straight on past Great Barrington until Great Rissington is signed on left; GL54 2LN

Pleasant old bar in Cotswold-stone pub with well liked bar food, changing real ales and seats in the sheltered garden; bedrooms

There are some interesting things to look out for in this 17th-c Cotswold-stone pub, such as parts of a propeller, artefacts in display cases and pictures of the canadian crew from the wellington bomber that crashed in the garden in October 1943. The two-roomed bar has high-backed leather and farmhouse chairs around polished tables on red carpet, a woodburning stove in the stone fireplace, and bar chairs at the counter where they serve Brakspears Bitter, Wychwood Hobgoblin and a guest such as Jennings Cumberland on handpump; also, several wines by the glass and quite a few malt whiskies. The restaurant has another woodburning stove and old agricultural tools on the walls; background music, TV, board games and books for sale (in aid of guide dogs for the blind). You can sit outside on the front terrace or in the sheltered, well kept hillside garden. A local circular walk takes in part of the idyllic village, church, River Windrush and stunning countryside surrounding the pub.

Interesting food includes sandwiches, ham hock terrine with home-made piccalilli and toasted brioche, dressed crab with celeriac and pickled apple, home-made gnocchi with butternut squash, truffle, chanterelles, chives and taleggio cheese, chicken and bacon pie, cod fillet with crushed potatoes, spinach, trompettes and chive butter, pork chop with bean and chorizo casserole and salsa verde, 30-day-aged rare-breed rib-eye with blue butter and watercress and radish salad, and puddings. *Benchmark main dish: beer-battered haddock with minted pea purée, crème fraîche tartare sauce and fat chips £13.00. Two-course evening meal £25.00.*

Free house ~ Licensees Paul and Jacqueline Gabriel ~ Real ale ~ (01451) 820388 ~ Open 12-11.30(midnight Sat, 11 Sun) ~ Bar food 12-2.30, 6.30-9.30 ~ Restaurant ~ Children welcome ~ Dogs allowed in bar ~ Bedrooms: £55/£80 ~ www.thelambinn.com
Recommended by Andrew Scott, Andrea Hughes, Neil and Angela Huxter

GRETTON
Royal Oak

SP0130   Map 4

Off B4077 E of Tewkesbury; GL54 5EP

Golden-stone pub with light, airy rooms, open fires, six real ales, popular food and friendly atmosphere; good surrounding walks

Once a pair of old stone-built cottages and surrounded by some fine walks, this refurbished pub has a light and airy feel and a wide mix of customers. The bar rooms have white-painted kitchen chairs and leather tub chairs around pale wood-topped tables on bare boards or flagstones, open fires, animal paintings and farm tools on pale walls above grey dados and an easy-going atmosphere. The dining room and conservatory are stylish, with high-backed chairs around large, chunky tables, antlers on one wall, a big central woodburning stove, and candelabras and evening candlelight. Brakspears Oxford Gold, Jennings Cocker Hoop, Malvern Hills Black Pearl, Ramsbury Pophams Pride and Wye Valley HPA and Dorothy Goodbodys Barrel of Laughs on handpump. The flower-filled terrace has plenty of seats and fine views across the village and valley to Dumbleton Hill and the Malverns; as well as a neat lawn, there's a children's play area and a bookable tennis court. In summer, steam trains from the Great Western Railway run along the bottom of the garden.

Well liked food includes sandwiches, mussels with garlic, shallots, wine and cream, a changing terrine with red onion marmalade and home-baked bread, gnocchi in tomato and chilli with parmesan, beer-battered haddock, slow-cooked lamb shoulder in red wine sauce, free-range pork belly and tenderloin with bacon and mustard sauce, and puddings. *Benchmark main dish: burger with spiced tomato relish, gherkins and chips £10.00. Two-course evening meal £20.00.*

Free house ~ Licensee Rob Owen ~ Real ale ~ (01242) 604999 ~ Open 12-11; 12-10 Sun ~ Bar food 12-2.30, 6-9; 12-3, 6-8 Sun ~ Restaurant ~ Children welcome ~ Dogs allowed in bar ~ www.royaloakgretton.co.uk *Recommended by Martin and Pauline Jennings*

GUITING POWER

SP0924   Map 4

Hollow Bottom

Village signposted off B4068 SW of Stow-on-the-Wold (still called A436 on many maps); GL54 5UX

Popular old inn with lots of racing memorabilia, a good bustling atmosphere, real ales and enjoyable food

Thanks to its affable licensees and warm welcome for all, our readers enjoy their visits here very much. It's a snug old stone cottage with many racing folk customers, live horse racing on TV and racing memorabilia in the comfortable beamed bar, including silks, tunics, photographs, badges, framed newspaper cuttings and horseshoes (their local horse won the Cheltenham Gold Cup in 2010 and an area of the bar is dedicated to him). There's a winter log fire in an unusual pillar-supported stone fireplace. The public bar has flagstones and stripped-stone masonry; newspapers, darts, board games and background music. Battledown Tipster, Donnington SBA and a beer named for the pub on handpump, several wines (including champagne) by the glass and a dozen malts. The pleasant garden behind the pub has views towards sloping fields; decent nearby walks.

 As well as particularly good baguettes, the fairly priced food includes soup, pâté with cumberland sauce, home-made burgers with cheese or bacon, ham and free-range eggs, pie or roast of the day, crispy battered fresh fish with chips, specials such as tiger prawns in garlic, chilli and parsley, local (grey) squirrel in white wine and herbs, stuffed red pepper with garlic mushrooms, venison haunch with roast banana shallots in red wine sauce, and puddings like banoffi pie or cheesecake. *Benchmark main dish: fresh smoked haddock in creamy cheese and chive sauce £15.95. Two-course evening meal £20.00.*

Free house ~ Licensees Hugh Kelly and Charles Pettigrew ~ Real ale ~ (01451) 850392 ~ Open 9am-midnight ~ Bar food all day ~ Restaurant ~ Children welcome ~ Dogs allowed in bar and bedrooms ~ Bedrooms: £75/£90 ~ www.hollowbottom.com
Recommended by Michael Sargent, Chris and Val Ramstedt, Michael and Jenny Back, Andrew Scott, Mrs S Watkins, Edna Jones, Colin McKerrow

KILCOT

SO6925   Map 4

Kilcot Inn

2.3 miles from M50 junction 3; B4221 towards Newent; GL18 1NG

Attractively reworked small country inn, kind staff, enjoyable local food and drink

Weston's the cider people own this carefully restored inn and keep Old Rosie, The Governor and Perry on handpump, with more by the bottle, as well as Marstons Pedigree and EPA and Wye Valley Butty Bach also on handpump, local wine and organic fruit juice; staff are courteous and friendly. It's open-plan, with stripped beams, bare boards and dark flagstones, sunny bay-window seats, homely armchairs by one of the two warm woodburning stoves, tables with padded dining chairs; daily papers, big-screen TV, may be background music. The front terrace has picnic-sets under parasols, with more out behind. Bedrooms are light, airy and comfortable, and good breakfasts include local bacon and free-range eggs. They have a smart bicycle shed.

As well as breakfast from 7am and afternoon tea, the good food includes lunchtime sandwiches, poached pear and goats cheese tartlet with red onion marmalade and port jus, smoked salmon and red onion with dill and lemon crème fraîche, fish and chips, medley of roast vegetables with tagliatelle and pesto cream sauce, chicken fillet with dauphinoise potatoes and wild mushroom and tomato compote, duck breast with noodles and soy and orange reduction, and puddings. *Benchmark main dish: welsh rarebit with Marmite £5.50. Two-course evening meal £20.00.*

Free house ~ Licensee Mark Lawrence ~ Real ale ~ (01989) 720707 ~ Open 8am-11pm ~ Bar food 12-3, 6-9; 12-3, 5-8 Sun; breakfast 7-11.30am; afternoon tea 3-5 ~ Restaurant ~ Children welcome ~ Dogs allowed in bar ~ Live music first Thurs of month ~ Bedrooms: /£80 ~ www.kilcotinn.com *Recommended by TB, P G Topp, Mike and Mary Carter*

 LEIGHTERTON ST8290   Map 2

Royal Oak

Village signposted off A46 S of Nailsworth; GL8 8UN

Handsome country pub elegantly refurbished, good choice of drinks, imaginative food and kind staff

'We left here feeling very cheered up on a miserable day,' says an enthusiastic reader about this well run, carefully refurbished rural inn. The rambling bar has plenty of nice touches, from the pair of log fireplaces facing each other (you have to look twice to be sure it's not a mirror) to the splendid heavy low-loading antique trolley holding the daily papers. Part parquet, part broad boards, with some stripped stone and some pastel paintwork, and carefully chosen furniture from stylish strung-seat dining chairs to soft sofas. There are interesting wines by the glass and local farm cider, as well as Bath Ales Gem Bitter, Hook Norton Old Hooky and Otter Bitter on handpump, and helpful, smartly dressed staff. Good disabled access. A sheltered side courtyard has mainly teak and metal tables and chairs, and there are walks near the quiet village, with Westonbirt Arboretum not far.

As well as a two- and three-course set menu and Wednesday steak night, the inventive food includes lunchtime sandwiches, soup, potted brown shrimps in myrtle butter, sourdough crisp and lemon and vanilla marmalade, charcuterie platter, pie of the week with red onion gravy, caramelised shallot, sprout top and brie tart with radicchio salad and pickled apricots, burger with home-made ketchup, hake with orange gnocchi, chestnuts and roasted garlic and rosemary oil and cranberry gel, game casserole with juniper berry dumplings and devils on horseback, and puddings like chocolate pecan pie with Baileys panna cotta and ginger and cinnamon sponge with warm poached apples. *Benchmark main dish: pie of the week £13.95. Two-course evening meal £19.50.*

Free house ~ Licensees Paul and Antonia Whitbread ~ Real ale ~ (01666) 890250 ~ Open 12-3, 5.30-11; 11-11 Sat; 12-9 Sun ~ Bar food 12-2.30, 6-9.30; 12-3 Sun ~ Restaurant ~ Children welcome ~ Dogs allowed in bar ~ www.royaloakleighterton.co.uk *Recommended by Guy Vowles, Chris and Angela Buckell, Mr and Mrs P R Thomas, Mike Longman, Dr and Mrs A K Clarke*

 LOWER SLAUGHTER SP1622   Map 4

Slaughters Country Inn

Village signposted off A429 Bourton-on-the-Water to Stow-on-the-Wold; GL54 2HS

Comfortable streamside inn in beautiful Cotswold village, enjoyable country food in attractive dining bar

Walkers and other visitors chat contentedly in the spreading bar of this much-extended stone inn. Several low-beamed linked rooms have well spaced tables on polished limestone flagstones, seats varying from simple chairs to heavy settles and soft sofas. Log fires, medieval-motif curtains for the mullioned windows, shelves of board games, a few carefully placed landscapes or stuffed fish on cream or puce walls add up to understated refinement, but what really sets the style of the place is the thoroughly professional, efficient service –where trays are balanced on fingertips, and your drink arrives almost before you've asked for it. There's Brakspears and Wychwood Hobgoblin on handpump and a good choice of wines by the glass. The carpeted and mirrored evening restaurant overlooks a sweep of lawn with sheep pasture beyond – birdsong out here, and the little River Eye flows slowly past the front of the inn and on through the village.

Using the best local, seasonal produce, the attractively presented and thoroughly enjoyable bar food includes nibbles like scotch egg and hand-made pork pie, good sandwiches, ham and (duck or hen) eggs, crab risotto, mussels in cider and bacon, fresh tagliatelle with cep cream and white truffle oil, burger with interesting cheeses, free-range chicken breast with leeks and wild mushrooms, salmon fillet, and puddings such as apple tart or raspberry and passion-fruit trifle. Wednesday is fish night, and there's a two-course winter weekday lunch deal. *Benchmark main dish: braised ox cheek £14.95. Two-course evening meal £23.00.*

Free house ~ Licensee Stuart Hodges ~ Real ale ~ (01451) 822143 ~ Open 12-11 ~ Bar food 12-3, 6.30-9(8.45 Sun); afternoon tea 3-5 ~ Restaurant ~ Children welcome ~ Dogs allowed in bar and bedrooms ~ Bedrooms: £85/£95 ~ www.theslaughtersinn.co.uk
Recommended by Richard Tilbrook

NAILSWORTH
Egypt Mill 🛏

ST8499 Map 4

Off A46; heading N towards Stroud, first right after roundabout, then left; GL6 0AE

Stylishly converted mill with lovely summer terrace and interesting split-level bar; bedrooms

This handsome 16th-c building is a fine conversion of a three-floored, stone-built mill still with working waterwheels and the millstream flowing through; the split-level bar with its brick and stone floor gives good views of the wheels. Stroud Budding and Wye Valley Bitter on handpump and several wines by the glass, served by cheerful, helpful staff. The comfortable carpeted lounge has lots of stripped beams along with some hefty yet elegant ironwork from the old machinery; background music and TV. In summer, there are plenty of seats and tables in the floodlit terraced garden overlooking the millpond. Some of the comfortable, well equipped bedrooms have wonderful beams and timbering.

Popular food includes sandwiches, free-range omelettes, local sausages with mash and onion gravy, gammon with free-range eggs, salmon and smoked haddock fishcakes, chicken with smoked bacon, gruyère, creamed leeks and dauphinoise potatoes, steak and kidney pie, skate wing with mushrooms, prawns, capers and lemon and chive butter, lamb noisettes with lamb wonton, rosemary-roasted lamb belly, cappuccino of white beans and madeira jus, and puddings such as chocolate and macadamia brownie with bitter chocolate sauce and treacle tart with toffee fudge ice-cream. *Benchmark main dish: beer-battered haddock and chips £11.50. Two-course evening meal £20.00.*

Free house ~ Licensees Stephen Webb and Rob Aldridge ~ Real ale ~ (01453) 833449 ~ Open 11-11(midnight Sat); 12-10.30 Sun ~ Bar food all day ~ Restaurant ~ Children

welcome ~ Dogs allowed in bedrooms ~ Bedrooms: $80/$100 ~ www.egyptmill.com
Recommended by Mr and Mrs W Mills, Dr A McCormick, Tom and Ruth Rees

NAILSWORTH   ST8699 Map 4
Weighbridge
B4014 towards Tetbury; GL6 9AL

Super two-in-one pies served in cosy old-fashioned bar rooms, a fine choice of drinks, friendly service and a sheltered garden

Many customers are here to enjoy the particularly good and extremely popular pies, but there's also a fine choice of ales and wines and a warm welcome from the helpful staff. The relaxed bar has three cosily old-fashioned rooms with open fires, stripped-stone walls and antique settles, country chairs and window seats. The black-beamed ceiling of the lounge bar is thickly festooned with black ironware – sheep shears, gin traps, lamps and a large collection of keys, many from the old Longfords Mill opposite the pub. Upstairs is a raftered hayloft with an engaging mix of rustic tables. No noisy games machines or background music. Uley Old Spot, Wadworths 6X and a couple of guest beers like Great Western Maiden Voyage and Timothy Taylors Landlord on handpump, 18 wines (and champagne and prosecco) by the glass, Weston's cider and 14 malt whiskies. A sheltered landscaped garden at the back has picnic-sets under umbrellas. Good disabled access and facilities.

The two-in-one pies (available to buy for home baking) come in a divided bowl: half contains the filling of your choice with a pastry topping, the other half has home-made cauliflower cheese (or broccoli mornay or root vegetables): fillings include pork, bacon and celery, salmon in creamy sauce, steak and mushroom, and root vegetables with pulses in spicy tomato sauce. Also, filled baguettes, soup, omelettes, home-cooked ham with free-range egg, spinach and mushroom lasagne, chicken kiev and puddings such as crème brûlée and banana crumble. *Benchmark main dish: two-in-one pies £11.40. Two-course evening meal £17.00.*

Free house ~ Licensee Howard Parker ~ Real ale ~ (01453) 832520 ~ Open 12-11 (10.30 Sun) ~ Bar food 12-9.30 ~ Restaurant ~ Children allowed away from the bars ~ Dogs welcome ~ www.2in1pub.co.uk *Recommended by Mrs P Sumner, Tom and Ruth Rees, Jack and Sandra Clarfelt*

NETHER WESTCOTE   SP2220 Map 4
Feathered Nest ★
Off A424 Burford to Stow-on-the-Wold; OX7 6SD

Gloucestershire Dining Pub of the Year

Caring service, a happy atmosphere, attractive surroundings, and beautifully presented, inventive food and drink; lovely bedrooms

This is a special place with interesting pubby rooms, really top notch service, delicious food and a neat garden with sweeping views; it's a lovely place to stay too, in individually decorated and well equipped rooms. The softly lit largely stripped-stone bar is companionable, with real saddles as bar stools (some of the best racehorse trainers live locally), a carved settle among other carefully chosen seats, dark flagstones and low beams. They have 19 wines by the glass from an impressive list, and a couple of beers on handpump such as North Cotswold Windrush Ale and Purity Mad Goose. The bar opens into an inner ochre-walled high-raftered room with deeply comfortable sofas by a vast log fire. Two attractively decorated dining rooms, both on two levels, have a pleasing mix of antique tables in varying sizes, and a lively up-to-date atmosphere. A flagstoned terrace and heated shelter have teak tables and wicker armchairs, and a spreading lawn bounded by floodlit trees has groups of rustic seats, with the Evenlode Valley beyond. If you stay in the lovely rooms, you'll get a very good breakfast.

🍴 Beautifully presented with real imagination, the exceptional food in the bar includes a two- and three-course set lunch (very fairly priced given the quality), as well as sandwiches, deep-fried whitebait with garlic mayonnaise, mussel chowder, burger with cheese or bacon and skinny chips, tagliatelle of roasted vegetables with basil oil and parmesan, beer-battered fish and chips, venison faggots with onion gravy and mash, sea bream with black bulgar wheat, pimento, fennel and bouillabaise sauce, rare-breed pork chop with mash, savoy cabbage, apple compote and onion and mustard sauce, and puddings such as caramel soufflé with orange sorbet and Grand Marnier and chocolate and saffron mousse, cashew nuts and waffle tuile; the restaurant menu is more elaborate (and more expensive). There's a Friday and Saturday afternoon tea menu too. *Benchmark main dish: seasonal suckling pig (pie, loin, head terrine, shoulder) with quinoa and calvados sauce £25.50. Two-course evening meal £23.00.*

Free house ~ Licensee Amanda Timmer ~ Real ale ~ (01993) 833030 ~ Open 11-11 (9 Sun); closed Mon except bank holidays ~ Bar food 12-2.30, 6.30-9.30; 12-3.30 Sun ~ Restaurant ~ Children welcome ~ Dogs allowed in bar ~ Bedrooms: £120/£175 ~ www.thefeatherednestinn.co.uk *Recommended by Liz Bell, Michael Doswell*

NEWLAND SO5509 Map 4
Ostrich 🍴 ♟ 🍺

Off B4228 in Coleford; or can be reached from the A466 in Redbrook, by turning off at the England–Wales border – keep bearing right; GL16 8NP

Liked by walkers and their dogs, with a friendly feel in spacious bar, great choice of beers, open fire, daily papers and smashing food

With up to eight real ales on handpump, a chatty, relaxed atmosphere and a warmly welcoming landlady, it's not surprising our readers enjoy their visits here so much. The low-ceilinged bar is spacious but cosily traditional with creaky floors, window shutters, candles in bottles on the tables, miners' lamps on the uneven walls and comfortable furnishings such as cushioned window seats, wall settles and country kitchen chairs. There's a big fireplace, newspapers, perhaps quiet background jazz and board games. Hook Norton Bitter, Otter Ale, Sharps Doom Bar, Timothy Taylors Landlord and Uley Pigs Ear on handpump, several wines by the glass and Weston's Old Rosie cider. The pub lurcher is called Alfie. There are picnic-sets in a walled garden behind and more out in front; the church, known as the Cathedral of the Forest, is worth a visit and the village is charmingly picturesque.

🍴 Interesting food might include chicken timbale of smoked salmon and salmon mousse with lemon crème fraîche, wild boar, stem ginger and dark rum pâté with blackcurrant jelly, steak in ale pie, wild mushroom risotto with white wine, truffle oil and crisp shallots, sausages with onion gravy, sizzling ribs in tangy sauce, foie gras-stuffed chicken breast with marsala sauce and rösti potatoes, plaice fillets and tiger prawns in lemon and parsley butter, lamb wellington with rosemary and redcurrant jus, and puddings. *Benchmark main dish: salmon and spinach fishcakes with parsley sauce £12.00. Two-course evening meal £20.00.*

Free house ~ Licensee Kathryn Horton ~ Real ale ~ (01594) 833260 ~ Open 12-3,
6.30-11; 12-3, 6-midnight Sat; 12-4, 6.30-10.30 Sun ~ Bar food 12-2.30, 6.30(6 Sat)-9.30 ~
Restaurant ~ Children welcome ~ Dogs allowed in bar ~ www.theostrichinn.com
Recommended by Tom and Ruth Rees, Carol Wilson, Phil and Augustine Sullivan

NORTH CERNEY   SP0208   Map 4
Bathurst Arms ♀ ⇌
A435 Cirencester–Cheltenham; GL7 7BZ

**Bustling inn with beamed bar, open fires, fine wines, real ales and
interesting food; comfortable bedrooms**

After enjoying one of the many surrounding walks, this handsome
17th-c inn is just the place to head for. The focus remains the
original beamed and panelled bar with its flagstones, good mix of old
tables, nicely faded chairs and old-fashioned window seats and fireplace
at each end – one is huge and houses an open woodburner. An oak-
floored room off here has country tables, winged high-backed settles
forming a few booths and background music; flat-screen TV and board
games. The restaurant has leather sofas and another woodburning
stove. Hook Norton Bitter and Lion and guests like Oxfordshire Ales
Marshmellow and Ramsbury Gold on handpump, and also a wine room
where you can choose your own bottle or one of the 20 by the glass; local
soft drinks and juices too. The pleasant riverside garden has picnic-
sets sheltered by trees and shrubs.The bedrooms are being carefully
refurbished this year. Cerney House Gardens are worth a visit.

 As well as a very good value two- and three-course set menu (before 7pm),
the enjoyable food includes lunchtime baguettes, confit duck and parma ham
terrine with spiced tomato chutney, grilled mackerel fillets with horseradish and
pickled vegetables, chicken and mushroom pie, pasta with roasted mediterranean
vegetables and tomato sauce, fresh beer-battered cod with chips, slow-cooked
gloucester old spot pork belly with mustard and cider sauce, roasted celeriac and
baby onions, chargrilled tuna on stir-fried vegetables with teriyaki dressing, and
puddings such as cinnamon panna cotta with poached apricots and mixed red
berry compote and banana and Baileys iced parfait with toffee curd and glazed
banana. *Benchmark main dish: burger with onion rings, bacon, cheese, gherkins
and chips £12.00. Two-course evening meal £20.00.*

Free house ~ Licensee James Walker ~ Real ale ~ (01285) 831281 ~ Open 12-11(10.30
Sun) ~ Bar food 12-2(2.30 Fri, Sat), 6-9(9.30 Fri, Sat); 12-2.30, 7-9 Sun ~ Restaurant ~
Children welcome ~ Dogs allowed in bar and bedrooms ~ Bedrooms: £65/£85 ~
www.bathurstarms.com *Recommended by Comus and Sarah Elliott, Brian and Carol Gold,
Tom and Ruth Rees, Peter and Heather Elliott, Steve Whalley, Di and Mike Gillam*

NORTHLEACH   SP1114   Map 4
Wheatsheaf ⑪ ♀ ⇌
*West End; the inn is on your left as you come in following the sign off A429,
just SW of the junction with A40; GL54 3EZ*

**17th-c stone inn with contemporary food, real ales, candles, fresh
flowers and a relaxed atmosphere; stylish bedrooms**

Cleverly managing to be both a pub and a restaurant, this 17th-c former
coaching inn is on a quiet street of similarly attractive buildings in
a lovely little town. The big-windowed, airy linked rooms have high
ceilings, antique and contemporary artwork, church candles and fresh
flowers, an attractive mix of dining chairs, big leather button-back settles

and stools around wooden tables, flagstones in the central bar, wooden floors laid with turkish rugs in the airy dining rooms and three open fires. Hook Norton Old Hooky, Sharps Doom Bar and a guest from Stroud on handpump, several wines by the glass from a fantastic list of around 300 and local cider; background music, TV and board games. There are seats in the pretty back garden and they can arrange fishing on the River Coln. This is an enjoyable place to stay but our readers suggest asking for the larger rooms. Dogs are genuinely welcomed – they keep a jar of pigs' ears behind the bar for them.

🍴 As well as breakfast for non-residents from 8am, afternoon tea and weekend brunch, the interesting modern food, using the best local, seasonal produce, includes devilled kidneys on toast, twice-baked cheddar soufflé with spinach and grain mustard, bouillabaise with gruyère, rouille and croutons, roast butternut squash with goats cheese, seeds and rocket, chicken breast with borlotti bean and vegetable broth and salsa verde, braised shin of beef with marrow bone, mash and peas, calves liver with sage and balsamic onions, and puddings like treacle tart with clotted cream ice-cream and crème brûlée. *Benchmark main dish: beer-battered fish with crushed peas, tartare sauce and fries £10.50. Two-course evening meal £19.00.*

Free house ~ Licensees Sam and Georgina Pearman ~ Real ale ~ (01451) 860244 ~ Open 9am-11pm ~ Bar food 12-3, 6-9(10 Fri, Sat); 12-3.30, 6-9 Sun; afternoon tea ~ Children welcome ~ Dogs allowed in bar and bedrooms ~ Bedrooms: /£156 ~ www.cotswoldswheatsheaf.com *Recommended by Martin and Pauline Jennings, Simon J Barber, Rod Stoneman*

OLDBURY-ON-SEVERN   ST6092   Map 2

Anchor ⏐ 🍺 £

Village signposted from B4061; BS35 1QA

Friendly country pub with tasty bar food, a fine choice of drinks and a pretty garden with hanging baskets

A favourite with many, this is a particularly well run and enjoyable pub with a happy mix of customers and welcoming, cheerful staff. The neatly kept lounge has modern beams and stonework, a variety of tables including an attractive oval oak gateleg, cushioned window seats, winged seats against the wall, oil paintings by a local artist and a big log fire. The bar has old photographs and farming and fishing bric-a-brac on the walls. Diners can eat in the lounge or bar area or in the back dining room (good for larger groups); the menu is the same everywhere. Bass, Butcombe Bitter, Otter Bitter and a changing guest like Great Western Maiden Voyage on handpump, well priced for the area; 80 malt whiskies (the tasting notes are really helpful) and a dozen wines by the glass. You can eat in the pretty garden in summer, when the hanging baskets and window boxes are lovely; boules. They have wheelchair access and a disabled lavatory. Plenty of walks to the River Severn and along numerous footpaths and bridleways; nearby St Arilda's church is interesting, on an odd little knoll with wild flowers (especially primroses and daffodils) among the gravestones.

🍴 Using produce from local farms and estates, the reasonably priced and well liked food includes ciabattas, warm goats cheese and chorizo salad, tempura king prawns with asian cucumber salad and sweet chilli and plum dipping sauce, home-baked ham with free-range eggs and bubble and squeak, kashmiri lamb curry, crab linguine with chilli, lime and coriander, smoked haddock and salmon pie in velouté sauce, butternut squash, cranberry and red onion tagine with tzatziki, and puddings such as raspberry pavlova with clotted cream and dark chocolate tart. *Benchmark main dish: beef and mushroom in ale pie £9.50. Two-course evening meal £16.00.*

Free house ~ Licensees Michael Dowdeswell and Mark Sorrell ~ Real ale ~ (01454) 413331 ~ Open 11.30-3, 6-11; 11.30am-midnight Fri, Sat; 12-11 Sun ~ Bar food 12-2 (3 Sun), 6-9 ~ Restaurant ~ Children in dining room only ~ Dogs allowed in bar ~ www.anchorinnoldbury.co.uk *Recommended by James Morrell, Roger and Donna Huggins, Chris and Angela Buckell, Alan Bulley, Barry and Monica Jones*

 SAPPERTON   SO9403   Map 4

Bell 🍴 🍺 🍺

Village signposted from A419 Stroud–Cirencester; OS Sheet 163 map reference 948033; GL7 6LE

Handsome pub with beamed cosy rooms, a good mix of customers, local ales and pretty outside dining areas

New licensees took over this 250-year-old pub as we went to press – we hope there won't be too many changes. The main bar has sofas, benches and armchairs where you can read the papers with a pint in front of the woodburning stove – Hook Norton Old Hooky, Otter Bitter, Stroud Budding and Uley Old Spot on handpump, 22 wines by the glass and carafe from a large and diverse wine list, 20 malt whiskies, farm cider and local soft drinks. The two other cosy rooms have beams, a nice mix of wooden tables and chairs, country prints on stripped-stone walls, one or two attractive rugs on flagstones, fresh flowers and open fires. There are armchairs and tables out on a small front terrace, with more in a mediterranean-style back courtyard garden with an old olive tree, herb-filled pots and a colourful, heated loggia. Horses have their own tethering rail (and bucket of water) and there are plenty of surrounding hacking trails and walks.

🍴 Enjoyable food includes lunchtime sandwiches with chips, goose liver and chicken terrine with golden raisin purée, lobster fishcakes with red onion and avocado salad, free-range scotch egg and pickles, caesar salad, vegetarian shepherd's pie, burger with bacon, cheese and relish, braised lamb shank with garlic sauce, monkfish in squid ink with saffron potatoes, bacon and cauliflower, and puddings such as floating island with vanilla custard and rhubarb eton mess. *Benchmark main dish: 36-hour confit pork belly with duck fat roasted potatoes £16.00. Two-course evening meal £20.00.*

Free house ~ Licensee Daniel Courtney ~ Real ale ~ (01285) 760298 ~ Open 11-3, 6.30-11; 12-10.30 Sun; closed Sun evening Jan, Feb, Mon all year ~ Bar food 12-2, 6-9.30; 12-3 Sun ~ Children welcome ~ Dogs welcome ~ www.bellsapperton.co.uk
Recommended by Bernard Stradling, Mrs P Bishop, Jack and Sandra Clarfelt, Mrs P Sumner, Betsy and Peter Little, David and Sue Atkinson

 SHEEPSCOMBE   SO8910   Map 4

Butchers Arms

Village signed off B4070 NE of Stroud; or A46 N of Painswick (but narrow lanes); GL6 7RH

Bustling country pub with enjoyable bar food, real ales, friendly young licensees and fine views

'The perfect place for lunch after a long dog walk,' is how one reader describes this friendly pub; walkers and cyclists can pre-book their food orders. There's an easy-going chatty atmosphere and the bustling lounge bar has beams, wheelback chairs, cushioned stools and other comfortable seats around simple wooden tables, built-in cushioned seats in big bay windows, interesting oddments like assorted blow lamps, irons and plates, and a woodburning stove. The restaurant has an open log fire. Otter Bitter, Ramsbury Gold and a guest like Wye Valley Dorothy Goodbody on handpump, several wines by the glass and Weston's cider or perry; darts, chess, cribbage and draughts. The view over the lovely surrounding steep beechwood valley is terrific and there are seats outside to make the most of it. It's thought this area was once a royal hunting ground for Henry VIII.

Consistently reliable food includes lunchtime sandwiches, chicken, thyme and bacon terrine with plum chutney, salmon, cod, lemon and dill fishcakes with lemon mayonnaise, sharing plates, ham and free-range eggs, pork, apple and sage sausages with wholegrain mustard mash and thyme gravy, sun-dried tomato and mixed pepper risotto with fresh basil pesto, beer-battered fish and chips, steak and mushroom in ale pie, daily specials and puddings. *Benchmark main dish: burger with home-made coleslaw and chips £10.50. Two-course evening meal £16.00.*

Free house ~ Licensees Mark and Sharon Tallents ~ Real ale ~ (01452) 812113 ~ Open 11.30-3, 6.30-11; 11.30-11.30 Sat; 12-10.30 Sun ~ Bar food 12-2.30, 6.30-9.30; all day weekends; no food after 6pm Sun Jan, Feb ~ Restaurant ~ Children welcome ~ Dogs allowed in bar ~ www.butchers-arms.co.uk *Recommended by Mr and Mrs W Mills, Dr and Mrs A K Clarke, GSB, B J Thompson, Mrs P Sumner, Tracey and Stephen Groves*

SOUTHROP
SP2003   Map 4

Swan 🍴 🍷
Off A361 Lechlade–Burford; GL7 3NU

Creeper-covered pub with proper village bar, two dining rooms, imaginative food and a fine choice of drinks

Even though the food in this creeper-covered old inn is excellent restaurant-standard, this does not detract from the chatty, informal atmosphere in the bar – which remains just the place for a pint and a natter. There are stools against the counter, simple tables and chairs, Hook Norton Hooky Bitter, St Austells Tribute, Sharps Doom Bar, Stroud Organic Ale and a guest like Wickwar Cotswold Way on handpump, 16 wines by the glass from a carefully chosen list and daily non-alcoholic cocktails. The low-ceilinged front dining rooms have open fires, all manner of leather dining chairs around a nice mix of old tables, cushions on settles, rugs on flagstones, nightlights, candles and lots of fresh flowers. There's a skittle alley and tables in the sheltered back garden. They have self-catering cottages to let.

Using their own eggs and pigs and much of their own vegetables as possible, the enticing food might include soup, salt and pepper squid with home-made chilli jam, home-cured gravadlax with dill mustard dressing and pickled courgette, chargrilled angus burger with skinny chips, butternut squash risotto with wensleydale and oregano, thai red seafood curry with jasmine rice, lamb rump with spinach and niçoise sauce, pork chop with calvados apples and mash, and puddings such as hot chocolate fondant with pistachio ice-cream and lime posset. *Benchmark main dish: guinea fowl with creamed leeks and garlic greens £16.50. Two-course evening meal £25.00.*

You can send reports directly to us at feedback@goodguides.com

Free house ~ Licensee Graham Williams ~ Real ale ~ (01367) 850205 ~ Open 12-3, 6.30-11; 12-4.30 Sun; closed Sun evening ~ Bar food 12-2.30(3 Sat), 6.30-9.30(10 Fri, Sat); 12-3.30 Sun ~ Restaurant ~ Children welcome ~ Dogs allowed in bar ~ www.theswanatsouthrop.co.uk *Recommended by Bernard Stradling, Mr and Mrs A H Young, Richard Tilbrook, Guy Vowles, Tom and Ruth Rees, Dennis and Doreen Haward, Elizabeth Stedman*

STANTON
Mount 🍴

SP0634   Map 4

Village signposted off B4632 SW of Broadway; keep on past village on no-through road up hill, bear left; WR12 7NE

Bustling pub in a lovely spot with fantastic views, friendly licensees and good, popular food

Just up a steep lane from a charming golden-stone village, this 17th-c pub is in a lovely spot with fantastic views over the Vale of Evesham and on towards the welsh mountains. There are seats on the terrace that make the most of this, more seats in the peaceful garden and a boules pitch. The friendly bars have low ceilings, heavy beams and flagstones and a big log fire in an inglenook fireplace. The restaurant has large picture windows overlooking the village. Donnington BB and SBA on handpump and a good choice of wines by the glass, served by cheerful staff; darts and board games and dog biscuits behind the bar. The pub is on the Cotswold Way.

 As well as good daily specials, the well liked food includes baguettes, fresh or lightly frittered oysters with shallot red wine vinegar or garlic mayonnaise, chicken liver foie gras parfait with red onion marmalade, a plate of cold meats and cheese with chutneys, vegetable curry, beer-battered fresh haddock with chips, gammon with free-range egg, slow-cooked beef with bacon and tomatoes, and puddings such as berry pavlova and lemon and lime cheesecake; they also offer a two- and three-course set menu. *Benchmark main dish: sausages with cheddar mash £11.00. Two-course evening meal £20.00.*

Donnington ~ Tenants Karl and Pip Baston ~ Real ale ~ (01386) 584316 ~ Open 12-3, 6-11 ~ Bar food 12-2, 6-9(8.30 Sun) ~ Restaurant ~ Well behaved children welcome ~ Dogs welcome ~ www.themountinn.co.uk *Recommended by Bernard Stradling, Dave Braisted, Rod Stoneman, Judith Lavender, Richard Tilbrook, R T and J C Moggridge, Paul and Claudia Dickinson, Clive and Fran Dutson, Dr A J and Mrs B A Tompsett, Dennis and Doreen Haward*

TETBURY
Gumstool 🍴 🍷 🛏

ST8494   Map 4

Part of Calcot Manor Hotel; A4135 W of town, just E of junction with A46; GL8 8YJ

Civilised bar with relaxed atmosphere, super choice of drinks and enjoyable food

Even on a wet Monday lunchtime, this place is buzzing. It's a bar-brasserie attached to the very smart Calcot Manor Hotel, rather than a proper pub, but they do keep up to four real ales on handpump and the atmosphere is informal and relaxed. The stylish layout is cleverly divided to give a feeling of intimacy without losing the overall sense of contented bustle: flagstones, elegant wooden dining chairs and tables, well chosen pictures and drawings on mushroom-coloured walls, and leather tub armchairs and stools in front of a big log fire. Butcombe Bitter, Blond, Gold and maybe Rare Breed, lots of interesting wines by the glass and quite a few malt whiskies; background music. Westonbirt Arboretum is not far.

Given the civilised setting, prices are fair and the food is first class: devilled lambs kidneys on toast, twice-baked arbroath smokie and montgomery cheddar soufflé, salmon and crab thai spiced fishcake with chilli salsa, free-range middle white pork sausages with creamy mash and onion gravy, steak and kidney pudding, calves liver, smoked bacon and caramelised shallots, corn-fed chicken with porcini mushroom sauce and sautéed potatoes, slow-braised lamb hotpot with root vegetables, seared scottish salmon with roasted red pepper and béarnaise sauce, venison steak with pepper sauce and rösti potato, and puddings. *Benchmark main dish: shredded confit of duck salad with sweet and sour dressing £12.50. Two-course evening meal £22.50.*

Free house ~ Licensees Paul Sadler and Richard Ball ~ Real ale ~ (01666) 890391 ~ Open 10am-11pm (10.30 Sun) ~ Bar food 12-2.30, 5.30-9.30; 12-4, 5.30-9 Sun ~ Children welcome ~ Bedrooms: £252/£280 ~ www.calcotmanor.co.uk *Recommended by Bernard Stradling, Mr and Mrs P R Thomas, Rod Stoneman, Gordon and Margaret Ormondroyd, Graham Lovis, Tom and Ruth Rees, Tracey and Stephen Groves, KC*

UPPER ODDINGTON
SP2225   Map 4

Horse & Groom 🍴 ♟

Village signposted from A436 E of Stow-on-the-Wold; GL56 0XH

Pretty 16th-c Cotswold inn with enterprising food, lots of wines by the glass, local beers and other local drinks, and comfortable, character bars; lovely bedrooms

'The warmth of the welcome more than compensated for the miserable cold and rainy weather' – this comment from one reader is as typically enthusiastic as many others about this very well run and attractive stone pub. Mr Jackson is a first class landlord who keeps good ales and offers inventive food – and it's is a lovely place to stay too. The bar has pale polished flagstones, a handsome antique oak box settle among other more modern seats, nice armchairs at one end, oak beams in the ochre ceiling, stripped-stone walls and a log fire in the inglenook fireplace; the comfortable lounge is similarly furnished. Box Steam Piston Broke, Prescott Hill Climb and Wye Valley Bitter on handpump, 25 wines (including champagne and pudding wines) by the glass, 20 malt whiskies, local apple juice and elderflower pressé, and cider and lager brewed by Cotswold. There are seats and tables under green parasols on the terrace and in the pretty garden.

Making everything in-house including bread and ice-cream, the imaginative food includes sandwiches, chicken liver pâté with cumberland sauce and apple salad, warm potato pancake with smoked salmon, chive crème fraîche and avruga caviar, home-cooked honey-roast ham with free-range eggs, trio of pork, apple and leek sausages with red onion marmalade gravy and mash, chestnut and mushroom risotto with thyme oil and parmesan crisp, corn-fed chicken breast with garlic and chive polenta, tarragon cream and parma ham crisp, grilled hake fillet with couscous, marinated aubergine, courgette and peppers and roast tomato coulis, and puddings like steamed pecan and maple syrup pudding with coffee ice-cream and ginger sauce and apple and cranberry crumble with sauce anglaise. *Benchmark main dish: pie of the day £12.95. Two-course evening meal £22.00.*

Free house ~ Licensees Simon and Sally Jackson ~ Real ale ~ (01451) 830584 ~ Open 12-3, 5.30-11; 12-3, 6-10.30 Sun ~ Bar food 12-2, 6.30 (7 Sun)-9 ~ Restaurant ~ Children welcome ~ Dogs welcome ~ Bedrooms: £79/£99 ~ www.horseandgroom.uk.com *Recommended by Michael Doswell, Bernard Stradling, Simon and Polly Alvin, Andy and Jill Kassube, Ian Wilson, M G Hart, Keith Moss, R T and J C Moggridge, Nigel and Sue Foster*

Also Worth a Visit in Gloucestershire

Besides the fully inspected pubs, you might like to try these pubs that have been recommended to us and described by readers. Do tell us what you think of them: feedback@goodguides.com

ALDERTON   SP9933
Gardeners Arms (01242) 620257
Beckford Road, off B4077 Tewkesbury–Stow; GL20 8NL Attractive thatched Tudor pub, well kept Greene King and guests, decent wines by the glass, enjoyable food from bar snacks and tapas up including weekday deals, breakfast from 9am, good welcoming service, some recent redecoration and changes to the bar area, informal restaurant, log fire; may be background music; children welcome, dogs in some areas, tables on sheltered terrace, good-sized well tended garden with boules. *(Paul and Claudia Dickinson, Dr A J and Mrs B A Tompsett)*

AMBERLEY   SO8401
Amberley Inn (01453) 872565
Steeply off A46 Stroud–Nailsworth – gentler approach from N Nailsworth; GL5 5AF Popular old stone inn with two comfortable bars and a snug, well kept Stroud ales, enjoyable food served by friendly helpful staff, beautiful views; children and dogs welcome, side terrace and back garden, good local walks, 11 bedrooms. *(Neil and Anita Christopher, Cath French)*

AMPNEY CRUCIS   SP0701
Crown of Crucis (01285) 851806
A417 E of Cirencester; GL7 5RS Refurbished roadside inn with spacious split-level bar, beams and log fires, good choice of food including competitively priced dish of the day (weekday lunchtimes), a beer brewed for them by Wickwar and a guest, decent house wines, pleasant efficient service; children and dogs welcome, disabled facilities, lots of tables out on grass by car park, quiet modern bedrooms around courtyard, good breakfast, cricket pitch over stream, open all day. *(Giles and Annie Francis, Neil and Anita Christopher)*

AMPNEY ST PETER   SP0801
⋆Red Lion (01285) 851596
A417, E of village; GL7 5SL This unspoilt and unchanging country pub has long been a monument to traditional hospitality under its welcoming veteran landlord – only the third in over a century; just two simple chatty little rooms, log fires, very well kept Timothy Taylors Landlord and Golden Best and maybe Hook Norton from the hatch, no food; outside lavatories; open from 6pm Mon-Sat, and Sun lunchtime. *(Mo and David Trudgill, Giles and Annie Francis, Tom McLean)*

AUST   ST5788
Boars Head (01454) 632278
0.5 miles from M48 junction 1, off Avonmouth Road; BS35 4AX 16th-c village pub handy for the 'old' Severn bridge, Marstons-related ales and nice house wines, decent choice of well priced food from good sandwiches and sharing boards up including weekday two-course deal, friendly service, linked rooms and alcoves, beams and some stripped stone, old prints and lots of bric-a-brac, huge log fire; background music; wheelchair access, children in eating area, dogs on leads in bar, attractive sheltered garden, covered area for smokers, open all day Sun with food till 4pm. *(Chris and Angela Buckell)*

AYLBURTON   SO6101
Cross (01594) 842823
High Street; GL15 6DE Decent choice of food from sandwiches and pub favourites to daily specials, changing ales such as Bath, Butcombe, Greene King and Wye Valley, several wines by the glass, welcoming helpful staff, open-plan layout with split-level flagstoned bar, beams, modern furniture alongside old high-backed settles, local photos and bric-a-brac, woodburners in large stone fireplaces, high-raftered dining room, some live music; children welcome, wheelchair access from car park, pleasant garden with play area, open all day weekends. *(Chris and Angela Buckell)*

AYLBURTON   SO6101
George (01594) 842163
High Street (A48); GL15 6DE Extended old inn with good choice of enjoyable reasonably priced food including Thurs curry night and Sun carvery, well kept regional ales such as Butcombe, friendly helpful staff, restaurant, Weds quiz; children welcome, beer garden and play area, bedrooms in adjacent lodge. *(Dave Braisted)*

BIBURY   SP1006
Catherine Wheel (01285) 740250
Arlington; B4425 NE of Cirencester; GL7 5ND Bright cheerful dining pub, enjoyable fresh food from sandwiches up, well kept Hook Norton, Sharps and a guest, friendly attentive service, open-plan main bar and smaller back rooms, low beams, stripped stone, log fires, raftered dining room; children welcome, picnic-sets out behind in good-sized garden, famously beautiful village, handy for country and riverside walks, four bedrooms, open all day. *(Bernard Stradling, George Atkinson)*

BIRDLIP
SO9214
Royal George (01452) 862506
B4070; GL4 8JH Welcoming two-level beamed bar beyond hotel reception, airy and open, with good value food from sandwiches up, Greene King ales and decent choice of wines, adjoining restaurant; background music, TVs; dogs welcome, decked terrace and fine grounds, 34 bedrooms, good breakfast. *(Neil and Anita Christopher)*

BISLEY
SO9006
★Bear (01452) 770265
Village signed off A419 E of Stroud; GL6 7BD Elegantly gothic 16th-c inn with bustling L-shaped bar, old oak settles, brass and copper implements around extremely wide stone fireplace, low ochre ceiling, well kept St Austell, Butcombe and Wells & Youngs, enjoyable pubby food, friendly staff, separate stripped-stone family area; dogs welcome, small flagstoned courtyard, stone mounting blocks in garden across quiet road, one bedroom, open all day Sun. *(Derek Hunt, Roger Smith)*

BLOCKLEY
SP1635
Great Western Arms
(01386) 700362 *Station Road (B4479); GL56 9DT* Nicely updated beamed pub with well kept Hook Norton and decent wines by the glass, enjoyable good value home-made food promptly served by friendly staff, dining room and public bar (dogs welcome here) with darts and TV; terrace seating, lovely valley view, attractive village, closed Mon lunchtime. *(Paul Humphreys, Guy Vowles)*

BOURTON-ON-THE-WATER
SP1620
Duke of Wellington (01451) 820539
Sherbourne Street; GL54 2BY Welcoming stone-built inn, relaxed open-plan carpeted bar with leather sofas, enjoyable fairly standard food all day, Sun carvery, Courage and Wells & Youngs ales, more formal back dining room, woodburner, darts; background and some live music, machines; children and dogs welcome, riverside decking under willows, five bedrooms, open all day. *(Will Raiment)*

BOX
SO8500
Halfway House (01453) 832631
By Minchinhampton Common; GL6 9AE Sadly, this well liked 300-year-old pub has closed. *(Giles and Annie Francis)*

BRIMPSFIELD
SO9413
Golden Heart (01242) 870261
Nettleton Bottom (not shown on road maps, so we list the pub instead under the name of the nearby village); on A417 N of the Brimpsfield turning northbound; GL4 8LA Traditional roadside inn with low-ceilinged bar divided into five cosy areas, log fire in huge inglenook, well worn built-in settles and other old-fashioned furnishings, exposed stone walls and wood panelling, brass items, typewriters and banknotes, parlour on right with decorative fireplace leading into further room, well kept Brakspears, Jennings, Otter and Ringwood, several wines by the glass, popular food from fairly extensive blackboard menu, friendly attentive staff; children and dogs welcome, seats and tables on suntrap terrace with pleasant valley views, nearby walks, bedrooms, open all day weekends and school holidays. *(Giles and Annie Francis, Richard Tilbrook, Ian Herdman, Dr A J and Mrs B A Tompsett, Guy Vowles)*

BROADWELL
SP2027
★Fox (01451) 870909
Off A429 2 miles N of Stow-on-the-Wold; GL56 0UF Family-run golden-stone pub above broad village green; traditional furnishings on flagstones in log-fire bar, stripped-stone walls, jugs hanging from beams, well kept Donnington BB and SBA, lots of rums, winter mulled wine, honest pubby food (not Sun evening) served by friendly staff, two carpeted dining areas, George the cat; background music, darts, board games; children welcome, dogs allowed in bar, picnic-sets on gravel in sizeable family-friendly back garden, paddock with horse called Herman, camping. *(Andy Dolan, Eddie Edwards, Alun and Jennifer Evans, John and Sarah Webb)*

BROCKWEIR
SO5301
Brockweir Inn (01291) 689548
Signed just off A466 Chepstow–Monmouth; NP16 7NG Welcoming country local near the Wye, beams, stripped stonework, quarry tiles, sturdy settles and woodburner, nice snug with parquet floor and open fire, well kept local Kingstone, Wye Valley and two guests, real ciders, enjoyable food from bar snacks up, friendly service, overflow dining room upstairs; children (in eating areas) and dogs welcome, small walled garden, good walks, open all day weekends. *(Neil and Anita Christopher)*

BROOKEND
SO6801
Lammastide (01453) 811337
New Brookend; GL13 9SF Small friendly 1930s pub in quiet roadside spot inland from Sharpness; linked carpeted rooms with roughcast walls and panelling, usual pubby furniture, brass, earthenware, old maps and cartoons, raised bare-boards area in bay window with faux-leather sofas, good choice of enjoyable food from baguettes through pub favourites to interesting specials, up to six ales including Bass, Marstons and Wye Valley, decent wines from short list and several malt whiskies, newspapers; fruit machine; children and dogs welcome, wheelchair access at side using ramp, picnic-sets on raised terrace, good views to Forest of Dean, play area. *(Chris and Angela Buckell)*

CAMP   SO9111
⋆ Fostons Ash (01452) 863262
B4070 Birdlip–Stroud, junction with Calf Way; GL6 7ES Popular open-plan dining pub, light and airy, with good food including interesting lunchtime sandwiches and imaginative light dishes, real ales such as Goffs, Greene King and Stroud, decent wines by the glass, neat welcoming staff, daily papers, one end with easy chairs and woodburner; background music; rustic tables in attractive garden with heated terrace and play area, good walks. *(Neil and Anita Christopher, Guy Vowles)*

CERNEY WICK   SU0796
Crown (01793) 750369
Village signed from A419; GL7 5QH Friendly old village inn with roomy modern lounge bar and comfortable conservatory dining extension, popular inexpensive food, well kept Wadworths 6X, Wells & Youngs Bombardier and a guest, good service, coal-effect gas fires, games in public bar; children welcome, good-sized garden with swings, ten bedrooms in motel-style extension. *(Neil and Anita Christopher)*

CHACELEY   SO8530
Yew Tree (01452) 780333
Stock Lane; GL19 4EQ Remote rambling country pub with spacious river-view dining room, good choice of reasonably priced pubby food (not Sun evening or Mon in winter) from bar snacks up, welcoming attentive staff, Hook Norton, Sharps and Wychwood, bar in original 16th-c core with log fire, quarry tiles and stripped-stone walls, second bar with pool, juke box and machines, skittle alley; children and dogs welcome, wheelchair access, terrace and attractive waterside lawns, summer barbecues and beer festival, own moorings, on Severn Way, open all day summer. *(Dave Braisted)*

CHARLTON KINGS   SO9620
Merry Fellow (01242) 525883
School Road/Church Street; GL53 8AU Refurbished 19th-c corner pub improved under current friendly licensees; enjoyable traditional food at bargain prices, well kept Sharps Doom Bar and three guests, cocktails (including own recipes), skittle alley/coffee lounge, live music or curry Fri night; children and dogs welcome (pub dog is Jess), paved back terrace, open all day. *(John Clancy)*

CHARLTON KINGS   SO9620
Royal (01242) 228937
Horsefair, opposite church; GL53 8JH Big 19th-c pub with clean modern décor, enjoyable realistically priced food (not Sun evening) in bar or dining conservatory, well kept real ales and decent wines, prompt service; children and dogs welcome, picnic-sets in garden overlooking church, open all day. *(Guy Vowles, John Coatsworth)*

CHEDWORTH   SP0608
Hare & Hounds (01285) 720288
Fosse Cross – A429 N of Cirencester, some way from village; GL54 4NN Rambling stone-built restauranty pub with good interesting food, lunchtime set menu, well kept Arkells and nice wines, efficient service, low beams and wood floors, soft lighting, cosy corners and little side rooms, two big log fires, small conservatory; children away from bar and dogs welcome, disabled facilities, ten courtyard bedrooms. *(John and Sharon Hancock, Helene Grygar, Tom and Ruth Rees)*

CHEDWORTH   SP0512
⋆ Seven Tuns
Village signposted off A429 NE of Cirencester; then take second signposted right turn and bear left towards church; GL54 4AE This popular 17th-c village pub closed shortly before we went to press, but should have reopened under new management by the time you read this – reports please.

CHELTENHAM
Bank House (01242) 240940
Clarence Street; GL50 3JL Newish Wetherspoons conversion on two floors, wide choice of real ales and usual well priced food, helpful staff; children welcome, open all day from 7am. *(Dave Braisted)*

CHELTENHAM   SO9421
Jolly Brewmaster (01242) 512176
Painswick Road; GL50 2EZ Popular convivial local with open-plan linked areas around big semicircular counter, fine range of changing ales and farm ciders, perhaps a perry, friendly obliging young staff, newspapers, log fires; dogs welcome, coachyard tables, open all day. *(Ian and Jane Irving)*

CHELTENHAM   SO9624
⋆ Plough (01242) 222180
Mill Street, Prestbury; GL52 3BG Unspoilt thatched village local tucked away behind the church; comfortable front lounge, service from corner corridor hatch in flagstoned back tap room, grandfather clock and big log fire, up to three well kept ales such as Hook Norton, Sharps and Wadworths, nice choice of ciders and perry, good traditional home-made food including blackboard specials, friendly service; lovely big flower-filled back garden (dogs on leads), some summer weekend barbecues, immaculate boules pitch, open all day. *(Ian and Jane Irving, John Coatsworth)*

CHELTENHAM   SO9321
Royal Union (01242) 224686
Hatherley Street; GL50 2TT Backstreet local with large bar and cosy snug up steps, half a dozen well kept ales, reasonably priced

wines, enjoyable good value food including nice steaks, may be Sun jazz; courtyard behind, open all day. *(Anon)*

CHIPPING CAMPDEN   SP1539

⋆ **Kings** (01386) 840256

High Street; GL55 6AW Fresh eclectic décor in 18th-c hotel's bar-brasserie and separate restaurant, cheery helpful service, good food from lunchtime sandwiches and baguettes to pubby dishes and more elaborate meals, well kept Hook Norton and a guest, good choice of wines by the glass, decent coffee, daily papers and nice log fire; secluded back garden with picnic-sets and terrace tables, 12 comfortable bedrooms, open all day Sat. *(Ryta Lyndley)*

CHIPPING CAMPDEN   SP1539

Noel Arms (01386) 840317

High Street; GL55 6AT Handsome 16th-c inn with refurbished beamed and stripped-stone bar, modern furniture, open fire, nice food from sandwiches to steaks, some good curries too from sri lankan chef, well kept Hook Norton and local guests, good choice of wines by the glass, coffee bar (from 9am), conservatory, restaurant, friendly efficient staff; children and dogs welcome, sunny courtyard tables, 27 well appointed bedrooms, good breakfast, open all day. *(Jim and Nancy Forbes)*

CIRENCESTER   SP0201

Bear (01285) 653472

Dyer Street; GL7 2PF Well refurbished Brains pub, beams and log fires, good food, well kept beers and friendly attentive staff; children welcome. *(Giles and Annie Francis)*

CIRENCESTER   SP0103

Drillmans Arms

Gloucester Road, Stratton; GL7 2JY Popular old two-room local, cheerful and welcoming, with well kept Sharps Doom Bar and quickly changing guests, usual food, low beams, woodburner, skittle alley doubling as eating area; tables out by small car park, open all day Sat. *(Richard Tilbrook)*

CIRENCESTER   SP0202

Fleece (01285) 658507

Market Place; GL7 2NZ Civilised, attractively revamped 17th-c hotel now owned by Thwaites, their ales kept well and enjoyable food from varied menu, good value wines, friendly competent service; terrace tables under parasols, 28 comfortably updated bedrooms, open all day. *(Comus and Sarah Elliott, Guy Vowles, Mrs Jo Rees)*

CLEEVE HILL   SO9826

Rising Sun (01242) 676281

B4632; GL52 3PX Hotel with splendid view over Cheltenham to the Malvern Hills from conservatory, covered terrace and lawn; large carpeted bar with friendly efficient

service, Greene King ales and a guest such as Goffs, decent wine choice, good value pubby food all day, lower eating area, restaurant beyond; sports TV, music and quiz nights; 24 affordable bedrooms, good breakfast. *(John Coatsworth)*

COBERLEY   SO9616

Seven Springs (01242) 870219

Andoversford, just SW of junction with A435 Cheltenham–Cirencester; GL53 9NG Spacious and airy Hungry Horse family dining pub, big helpings of competitively priced straightforward food, Greene King IPA, pleasant efficient service even when busy, very high ceiling, big windows, snugger side areas; background music; decking and sloping pondside garden. *(Neil and Anita Christopher)*

COLESBOURNE   SO9913

Colesbourne Inn (01242) 870376

A435 Cirencester–Cheltenham; GL53 9NP Civilised 19th-c grey-stone gabled coaching inn, good choice of enjoyable home-made food from baguettes and wraps up, friendly staff, well kept Wadworths ales and lots of wines by the glass, linked partly panelled rooms, log fires, soft lighting, comfortable mix of settles, softly padded seats and leather sofas, candlelit back dining room; TV above fireplace; dogs welcome, views from attractive back garden and terrace, nine bedrooms in converted stable block, good breakfast. *(Andrew Quinn, Neil and Anita Christopher)*

COLN ST ALDWYNS   SP1405

New Inn (01285) 750651

Back road Bibury–Fairford; Main Street; GL7 5AN Refurbished 16th-c creeper-covered hotel in peaceful village, dimly lit with low beams, some stripped stonework and tiled floor, enjoyable food from sandwiches and sharing boards up including seasonal game and tasting menus, good value weekday set lunch, ales such as Sharps, Wickwar and Wye Valley (cheaper 5-7pm Sun-Thurs), a dozen wines by the glass, dining rooms; provision for children and dogs, plenty of seats on split-level terrace, meadowside garden, 13 stylish bedrooms, open all day. *(Anon)*

COMPTON ABDALE   SP0717

⋆ **Garniche at the Puesdown**

(01451) 860262 *A40 outside village; GL54 4DN* Former Puesdown Inn under new ownership; spacious series of linked stylish bars and eating areas, mainly stripped-stone walls, rafter-effect or beamed ceilings, rugs on bare boards, log fire and woodburner, chesterfield sofas and armchairs and high-backed dining chairs around mix of tables, Hook Norton Old Hooky and Sharps Doom Bar, pubby lunchtime food with more elaborate evening choices, breakfast for non-residents, morning coffee and afternoon tea, gift shop; children welcome, no dogs inside, seats and tables in pretty back garden, comfortable ground-floor bedrooms, closed Sun and Mon evenings, otherwise open all day. *(Rod Stoneman, Guy Vowles)*

COOMBE HILL SO8827
Swan (01242) 680227

A38/A4019; GL19 4BA Light airy dining pub with several rooms, good generous fresh food from sandwiches up including deals, efficient friendly service, ales such as Battledown, Butcombe and Goffs, decent house wine, polished boards and panelling, red leather sofas; background music; large garden and own vineyard, nature reserve nearby, open all day Sun till 9pm. *(Dave Braisted, Rod Stoneman)*

CRANHAM SO8912
★ Black Horse (01452) 812217

Village signposted off A46 and B4070 N of Stroud; GL4 8HP Popular down-to-earth 17th-c local, cosy lounge, main bar with traditional furniture, window seats and log fire, well kept Hancocks HB, Sharps Doom Bar and a guest, real ciders, good value home-made blackboard food (not Sun evening, when pub opens at 8.30pm), two upstairs dining rooms (one with log fire); well behaved children and dogs welcome, tables out in front and to the side, good country views and walks, closed Mon. *(Neil and Anita Christopher, Guy Vowles, Alan Weedon)*

DIDMARTON ST8187
Kings Arms (01454) 238245

A433 Tetbury road; GL9 1DT Beamed 17th-c coaching inn recently reopened after major refurbishment – reports please.

DOYNTON ST7174
★ Cross House (0117) 937 2261

High Street; signed off A420 Bristol–Chippenham E of Wick; BS30 5TF Easy-going 18th-c village pub near fine walking country and Dyrham Park (NT), convivial landlord and staff, honest reasonably priced food, Bass, Bath, Courage, Sharps and Timothy Taylors, around 18 wines by the glass, softly lit carpeted bar with beams, some stripped stone, simple pub furniture and woodburner, cottagey candlelit dining room; background music, games machine, TV; children welcome, dogs in bar, picnic-sets out by the road, open all day Sun. *(Paul Humphreys, Mr and Mrs P R Thomas, Piotr Chodzko-Zajko, Stephen Shepherd)*

EASTINGTON SO7705
Old Badger (01453) 822892

Alkerton Road, a mile from M5 junction 13; GL10 3AT Traditionally refurbished sister pub to the Old Spot in Dursley; spacious split-level interior with two log fires, pubby furniture including settles on quarry-tiled or wood floors, various odds and ends such as old advertising signs, brewery mirrors, stone jars and a stuffed badger, good range of fresh food (not Sun evening) from sandwiches up including tapas, Moles, a house IPA (brewed by Marstons) and three guests, well chosen wines, cheerful chatty staff, weekly live music; sports TV in side alcove; children and friendly dogs welcome, wheelchair access to top bar, tables in pleasant little garden with covered terrace, open all day. *(Neil and Anita Christopher, Chris and Angela Buckell)*

EASTLEACH TURVILLE SP1905
★ Victoria (01367) 850277

Off A361 S of Burford; GL7 3NQ Open-plan low-ceilinged rooms around central servery, attractive built-in seats by log fire, unusual Queen Victoria pictures, well kept Arkells and several good value wines by the glass, shortish choice of sensibly priced pub food (not Sun evening) including baguettes, prompt friendly service; background music; children and dogs welcome, small pleasant front garden with picnic-sets overlooking picturesque village (famous for its spring daffodils), good walks, open all day Sat. *(R T and J C Moggridge, Guy Vowles)*

EDGE SO8409
★ Edgemoor (01452) 813576

Gloucester Road (A4173); GL6 6ND Tidy, modernised and spacious 19th-c dining pub with panoramic valley view across to Painswick from picture windows and pretty terrace, good food including deals, friendly efficient service, up to four well kept ales such as Stroud, Uley and Wickwar, nice coffee, restaurant; no dogs inside; children welcome, good walks nearby, closed Sun evening in winter. *(Lesley and Peter Barrett, Neil and Anita Christopher)*

ELKSTONE SO9610
★ Highwayman (01285) 821221

Beechpike; A417 6 miles N of Cirencester; GL53 9PL Interesting rambling 16th-c building, low beams, stripped stone and log fires, cosy alcoves, bric-a-brac, antique settles, armchairs and sofa among more usual furnishings, good value home-made food, Arkells beers and good house wines, friendly service, family room and big back eating area; dogs welcome, disabled access, outside play area. *(Anon)*

EWEN SU0097
★ Wild Duck (01285) 770310

Off A429 S of Cirencester; GL7 6BY Unchanging 16th-c inn with stylishly old-fashioned furnishings and pictures in high-beamed log-fire main bar, lounge with handsome Elizabethan fireplace and antique furnishings, some interesting if not cheap food, six real ales including Duck Pond badged for the pub, very good choice of wines by the glass; background music;

children welcome, tables in neatly kept heated courtyard (if you eat here they may ask to keep your credit card behind the bar), garden, 12 bedrooms, open all day. *(Ross Balaam)*

FORTHAMPTON SO8731
Lower Lode Inn (01684) 293224
At the end of Bishop's Walk by river; GL19 4RE Brick-built 15th-c coaching inn with River Severn moorings and plenty of waterside tables (prone to winter flooding), beams, flagstones, enormous log fire and traditional seating, enjoyable pubby food, friendly helpful staff, half a dozen well kept interesting beers, restaurant, back pool room; children and dogs welcome (lots of summer holiday families), disabled facilities, caravan site, four bedrooms, open all day. *(Ian Kirkwood)*

FRAMPTON COTTERELL ST6681
Globe (01454) 778286
Church Road; BS36 2AB Large knocked-through bar-dining area with black beams and some stripped stone, usual furniture on parquet or carpet, woodburner in old fireplace, well kept ales such as Butcombe, Fullers and Uley, real ciders, modest well chosen wine list, enjoyable pubby food and bar snacks, attentive friendly staff; background music; children welcome, dogs may get a treat, wheelchair access via side door, garden with play area and smokers' gazebo, church next door. *(Roger and Donna Huggins, Chris and Angela Buckell)*

FRAMPTON COTTERELL ST6681
Live & Let Live (01454) 772254
Off A432; Clyde Road; BS36 2EF Attractive chatty pub still serving Bath Ales (although no longer owned by them) and other beers including Timothy Taylors, real ciders and decent wines by the glass, enjoyable home-made food (not Sun evening) from shortish menu, helpful cheerful staff, linked rooms with carpeted bar and bare-boards dining areas; children and dogs welcome, disabled facilities, picnic-sets out in front and in big garden, play area, open all day. *(Chris and Angela Buckell)*

FRAMPTON MANSELL SO9202
★ Crown (01285) 760601
Brown sign to pub off A491 Cirencester–Stroud; GL6 8JG Welcoming licensees doing good choice of enjoyable hearty food including daily specials, well kept Butcombe Stroud, Uley and a guest, friendly young staff, heavy 17th-c beams, stripped stone and rugs on bare boards, two log fires and woodburner, restaurant; children and dogs welcome, disabled access, picnic-sets in sunny front garden, pretty outlook, 12 decent bedrooms

in separate block, open all day from midday. *(Ian and Melanie Henry, Stella and Geoffrey Harrison, Giles and Annie Francis, Tom and Ruth Rees, Alan Bulley, Di and Mike Gillam)*

FRAMPTON ON SEVERN SO7408
Bell (01452) 740346
The Green (B4071, handy for M5 junction 13, via A38); GL2 7EP Handsome creeper-covered Georgian inn attractively opened up, enjoyable good value food in extensive all-day family dining area, proper locals' bar with quarry tiles and flagstones, well kept ales such as Butcombe, Moles and Timothy Taylors, real cider, steps up to restaurant, skittle alley; background music; dogs welcome, plenty of seats outside (front and back), good play area and children's farm, stabling, village cricket green opposite, open all day. *(Neil and Anita Christopher, W K Wood)*

FRAMPTON ON SEVERN SO7407
Three Horseshoes (01452) 742100
The Green; GL2 7DY Cheerfully unpretentious 18th-c pub by splendid green, welcoming staff and locals, well kept beers and very good value home-made food; wheelchair access. *(Anon)*

GLASSHOUSE SO7121
★ Glasshouse Inn (01452) 830529
Off A40 just W of A4136; GL17 0NN Much-extended beamed red-brick pub with appealing old-fashioned and antique furnishings, cavernous black hearth, big flagstoned conservatory, well kept ales including Butcombe tapped from the cask, Stowford Press cider and reasonably priced wines, decent home-made food from sandwiches and basket meals to interesting specials (no bookings except Sun lunch), good service; background music, no under-14s in bars; good disabled access, neat garden with rustic furniture, interesting topiary, flower-decked cider presses and lovely hanging baskets, nearby paths up wooded May Hill, closed Sun evening. *(Paul and Sue Merrick, Carol Wilson)*

GLOUCESTER SO8318
Fountain (01452) 522562
Westgate Street; GL1 2NW Tucked-away 17th-c pub off pedestrianised street, well kept St Austell Tribute, Greene King Abbot and four mainly local guests, good reasonably priced pubby food from sandwiches to specials, quick helpful service, handsome stone fireplace, plush seats and built-in wall benches; background music; children welcome, disabled access, flower-filled courtyard, handy for cathedral, open all day. *(Dave Braisted, David Uren, Neil Griffins)*

If you report on a pub that's not a featured entry, please tell us any lunchtimes or evenings when it doesn't serve bar food.

GREAT BARRINGTON SP2013
⋆**Fox** (01451) 844385

Off A40 Burford–Northleach; pub towards Little Barrington; OX18 4TB 17th-c inn with stripped stone, simple country furnishings and low ceiling, well kept Donnington BB and SBA, farm cider and good apple juice, decent choice of quickly served food (all day weekends), big bare-boards river-view conservatory dining room with riverbank mural, traditional games, Aug 'Foxstock' folk festival; can get very busy, background music, TV; children and dogs welcome, two terraces by the Windrush (swans and private fishing), outside summer bar and barbecue, garden with orchard and ponds, seven bedrooms, open all day. *(Ian Herdman, Richard Tilbrook)*

GUITING POWER SP0924
⋆**Farmers Arms** (01451) 850358

Fosseway (A429); GL54 5TZ Nicely old-fashioned with stripped stone, flagstones, lots of pictures and warm log fire, well kept cheap Donnington BB and SBA, wide blackboard choice of enjoyable honest food cooked by landlord including good rabbit pie, welcoming prompt service, carpeted back dining part, games area with darts, dominoes, cribbage and pool, skittle alley; children welcome, garden with quoits, lovely village, good walks, bedrooms. *(Richard Tilbrook)*

HAM ST6898
Salutation (01453) 810284

On main road through village; GL13 9QH Unpretentious three-room local under new landlord; brasses on beams, horse and hunt pictures on Artex walls, pubby furniture including high-backed settles and bench seats, Butcombe Bitter and four well kept changing guests (plans for own microbrewery), eight ciders/perries, simple low-priced food lunchtime and early evening, occasional live music, skittle alley; no credit cards; wheelchair accessible, beer garden with views over the Severn, open all day weekends, closed Mon lunchtime. *(Chris and Angela Buckell)*

HAWKESBURY UPTON ST7786
⋆**Beaufort Arms** (01454) 238217

High Street; GL9 1AU Unpretentious 17th-c pub in historic village, welcoming landlord and friendly local atmosphere, well kept Wickwar ales and cider, guest beers, popular no-nonsense food (no starters, small helpings available), extended uncluttered dining lounge on right, darts in more spartan stripped-brick bare-boards bar, interesting local and brewery memorabilia, lots of pictures (some for sale), skittle alley; well behaved children allowed, dogs in bar, disabled access throughout and facilities, picnic-sets in smallish enclosed garden, on Cotswold Way, open all day. *(Chris and Angela Buckell)*

HILLESLEY ST7689
Fleece (01453) 520003

Hawkesbury Road/Chapel Lane; GL12 7RD Comfortably refurbished pub now owned by the local community; well kept ales such as Butcombe, Cotswold Spring, Severn Vale and Theakstons, real cider, enjoyable good value food including bargain two-course weekday lunch, carpeted main bar with steps down to dining room, snug with books and games, monthly live acoustic music; children, dogs and walkers welcome, back garden with play area, small village in lovely countryside near Cotswold Way, open all day. *(M G Hart, Martin and Margaret Thorpe)*

HINTON DYRHAM ST7376
⋆**Bull** (0117) 937 2332

2.4 miles from M4 junction 18; A46 towards Bath, then first right (opposite the Crown); SN14 8HG 17th-c stone pub in nice setting, main bar with two huge fireplaces, low beams, oak settles and pews on ancient flagstones, horsebrasses, stripped-stone back area and simply furnished carpeted restaurant (children allowed here till 7.30), food (all day weekends) from pub standards to specials including seasonal game, good value lunchtime and early evening set menu (not Fri evening), Wadworths and a guest; background music; dogs welcome in bar, wheelchair accessible with help, seats on front balcony and in sizeable sheltered upper garden with play equipment, open all day weekends, closed Mon lunchtime. *(Simon and Mandy King)*

HORSLEY ST8497
⋆**Tipputs** (01453) 832466

Just off A46 2 miles S of Nailsworth; Tiltups End; GL6 0QE Light and airy L-shaped bar with tall mullioned windows and raftered ceiling, panelling with arched bookshelves, boar's head above woodburner, interesting mix of good solid tables on broad boards, armchairs and chesterfield plus variety of dining chairs, enjoyable food including indian menu, Stroud ales, efficient staff, big back galleried restaurant with comfortable anteroom; background music; teak tables out behind on grass and decking, attractive countryside, open all day. *(Anon)*

KEMBLE ST9899
⋆**Thames Head** (01285) 770259

A433 Cirencester–Tetbury; GL7 6NZ Stripped stone, timberwork, intriguing little front alcove, pews in cottagey back area with log-effect gas fire in big fireplace, country-look dining room with another fire, good food from sandwiches and jacket potatoes to steaks, good value wines and well kept Arkells, friendly obliging staff, skittle alley; TV; children welcome, tables outside, four bedrooms in converted barn, good breakfast, walk (crossing railway line) to nearby

Thames source, open all day. *(Neil and Anita Christopher, KC, Heulwen and Neville Pinfield)*

KILKENNY   SP0118
Kilkeney Inn   (01242) 820341

A436, 1 mile W of Andoversford; GL54 4LN Reopened 2012 after long closure; refurbished spacious interior (originally six stone cottages) with extended beamed bar, stripped-stone walls and white plasterwork, wheelbacks around tables on quarry tiles or carpet, open fire and woodburner, airy conservatory, bar food including specials plus evening restaurant menu, Courage and Wells & Youngs ales, a dozen wines by the glass; background music; children welcome, dogs in bar, lovely Cotswold views from tables out in front, white wicker furniture in back garden, bedrooms, open all day. *(P and J Shapley)*

KINETON   SP0926
Halfway House   (01451) 850344

Signed from B4068 and B4077 W of Stow-on-the-Wold; GL54 5UG Simple and welcoming 17th-c beamed village pub, good nicely presented food (not Sun evening) from sandwiches up, well kept Donnington BB and SBA, farm cider and decent wines, restaurant, log fire; pool and darts; children welcome, picnic-sets in sheltered back garden, good walks, bedrooms, open all day weekends. *(Anon)*

KINGSCOTE   ST8196
✴ Hunters Hall   (01453) 860393

A4135 Dursley–Tetbury; GL8 8XZ Tudor beams, stripped stone, big log fires and plenty of character in individually furnished spotless linked rooms, some sofas and easy chairs, wide choice of good home-made food at reasonable prices, well kept Greene King and Uley, friendly attentive service, flagstoned back bar with darts, pool and TV; children and dogs welcome, big garden with good play area, 13 bedrooms, open all day. *(Peter and Margaret, Tom and Ruth Rees, Julian Cox)*

KNOCKDOWN   ST8388
Holford Arms   (01454) 238669

A433; GL8 8QY Spruced up under welcoming new owners, black beams and stripped-stone walls, flagstone or wood floors, cushioned wall/window seats, old dining tables with candles, flowers in bottles, some leather sofas and armchairs, woodburner in big old stone fireplace, ales such as Box Steam, Moles and Stonehenge, Sherston's cider, modest but good quality wine list, food from well filled baguettes up including good value Sun lunch, skittle alley; background and some live music; children and dogs welcome, disabled access, side garden, camping, handy for Westonbirt Arboretum. *(Chris and Angela Buckell)*

LECHLADE   SU2199
Crown   (01367) 252198

High Street; GL7 3AE Friendly old pub brewing its own Halfpenny ales (six on offer), busy bar with fire each end, back games room with pool and table football, no evening food, live music; children welcome, three bedrooms in separate block overlooking beer garden, open all day. *(Anon)*

LITTLE BARRINGTON   SP2012
Inn For All Seasons   (01451) 844324

A40 3 miles W of Burford; OX18 4TN Handsome old coaching inn with attractive comfortable lounge bar, low beams, stripped stone and flagstones, old prints, log fire, good food including fresh fish, Sharps Doom Bar and Wadworths 6X, lots of wines by the glass and malt whiskies, friendly service, restaurant and conservatory; background music; dogs welcome, garden with aunt sally, walks from door, bedrooms. *(Rhiannon Stevenson)*

LITTLETON-UPON-SEVERN ST5989
✴ White Hart   (01454) 412275

3.5 miles from M48 junction 1; BS35 1NR Former farmhouse with three main rooms, log fires and nice mix of country furnishings, loveseat in inglenook, flagstones at front, huge tiles at back, fine old White Hart Inn Simonds Ale sign, family room and snug, Wells & Youngs ales with guests such as Bath Gem, maybe cider from own apples, enjoyable fairly traditional food (all day Sun) plus some more adventurous specials; dogs welcome, wheelchair access with help, tables on front lawn, more behind by orchard, roaming chickens, walks from the door, open all day. *(Chris and Jenny Howland-Harris, Nigel and Sue Foster, Chris and Angela Buckell)*

LONGBOROUGH   SP1729
Coach & Horses   (01451) 830325

Ganborough Road; GL56 0QU Small, friendly 17th-c stone-built local, Donnington ales, Weston's cider and enjoyable wholesome food (not Sun evening, Mon), leather armchairs on flagstones, inglenook woodburner, darts, dominoes and cribbage; background music; children and dogs welcome, tables out at front looking down on stone cross and village, two simple clean bedrooms, open all day weekends, closed Mon evening. *(Eddie Edwards, Alan Weedon)*

LOWER ODDINGTON   SP2326
✴ Fox   (01451) 870555

Signed off A436; GL56 0UR Smart 16th-c creeper-covered inn with good mix of modern and traditional food, well kept Hook Norton and Sharps Doom Bar, little country-style flagstoned rooms with assorted chairs around pine tables, fresh flowers, hunting figures and pictures, inglenook fireplace, elegant red-walled dining room; children welcome, dogs in bar, white tables and chairs on heated terrace in cottagey garden, pretty village, three bedrooms. *(Bernard Stradling, Rod Stoneman, Neil Hardwick, Martin Smith, Ray Carter, Jenny Smith and others)*

MARSHFIELD   ST7773
✶ **Catherine Wheel** (01225) 892220

High Street; signed off A420 Bristol– Chippenham; SN14 8LR High-ceilinged stripped-stone front part with medley of settles, chairs and stripped tables, charming Georgian dining room with open fire in impressive fireplace, cottagey beamed back area warmed by woodburners, friendly staff and chatty locals, well kept ales such as Cotswold and Sharps, interesting wines and other drinks, enjoyable sensibly priced food (not Sun evening) from pub favourites up, darts and dominoes; dogs on leads and children welcome, wheelchair access with help, flower-decked backyard, unspoilt village, four bedrooms, open all day. *(John and Gloria Isaacs, Dr and Mrs A K Clarke)*

MEYSEY HAMPTON   SU1199
Masons Arms (01285) 850164

Just off A417 Cirencester–Lechlade; High Street; GL7 5JT 17th-c village local with enjoyable simple food and well kept Arkells, friendly considerate staff, longish open-plan beamed bar with big inglenook fire one end, restaurant; background music; tables out on green, pleasant compact bedrooms, good breakfast, parking may be a problem. *(Mr and Mrs Lynn)*

MINCHINHAMPTON   SO8500
Old Lodge (01453) 832047

Nailsworth–Brimscombe – on common, fork left at pub's sign; OS Sheet 162 map reference 853008; GL6 9AQ Food Club dining pub with civilised bistro feel, wood floors, stripped-stone walls, modern décor and furnishings, enjoyable food from pub favourites up, well kept beers and decent wines by the glass; children welcome, tables on neat lawn looking over NT common with grazing cows and horses, six bedrooms. *(David and Stella Martin)*

MINSTERWORTH   SO7716
Apple Tree (01452) 750345

A48 S of Gloucester; GL2 8JQ Refurbished dining pub extended around oak-beamed 17th-c farmhouse, wide choice of well priced generous food, OAP deal Weds, good service from friendly young staff, well kept ales, various eating areas including large barn-like room, inglenook log fires; children welcome, big garden with play area, lane beside pub leads to the Severn, closed Sun evening, Mon. *(Anon)*

MINSTERWORTH   SO7515
Severn Bore (01452) 750318

A48 2 miles SW; GL2 8JX In splendid Severn-side position, spotlessly clean open layout with central fireplace, usual pubby furniture, welcoming staff, ales such as Wickwar Severn Bore, Ashton's and Weston's cider, pubby food, skittle alley with pool table and darts; fruit machine, TV; wheelchair access (low step into bar), big riverside garden with superb views to the Cotswolds, play area, board giving times/heights of Severn Bore (open for breakfast on Bore days), handy for Westbury Court Garden (NT). *(Anon)*

MISERDEN   SO9308
Carpenters Arms (01285) 821283

Off B4070 NE of Stroud; GL6 7JA Country pub with open-plan low-beamed bar, stripped-stone walls, log fire and woodburner, friendly licensees, Wye Valley and a guest ale, good wine list, enjoyable reasonably priced food using local and home-grown produce including good vegetarian choices, charity quiz nights; children and dogs welcome, garden tables, popular with walkers and handy for Miserden Park, open all day. *(Giles and Annie Francis, Guy Vowles, Chris and Val Ramstedt)*

MORETON-IN-MARSH   SP2032
Black Bear (01608) 652992

High Street; GL56 0AX Unpretentious beamed and stripped-stone corner local with welcoming ex-footballer landlord, well kept local Donnington ales, good value generous pub food, large airy dining room, public bar with games and sports TVs; dogs welcome. *(Eddie Edwards)*

MORETON-IN-MARSH   SP2032
Inn on the Marsh (01608) 650709

Stow Road; GL56 0DW Interesting 19th-c beamed bar with warm layout including lovely curved sofa, quite a dutch flavour to the bric-a-brac, models, posters etc, dutch chef/landlady cooking national specialities alongside pubby favourites, four well kept Marstons-related ales, inglenook woodburner, modern conservatory restaurant; may be background music, quiz machine; children and dogs welcome, seats at front and in back garden, closed Mon lunchtime. *(JHBS)*

MORETON-IN-MARSH   SP2032
Redesdale Arms (01608) 650308

High Street; GL56 0AW Relaxed old hotel (17th-c coaching inn) with alcoves, sofas and big stone fireplace in solidly furnished comfortable panelled bar on right, darts in flagstoned public bar, log fires, stripped stone, Wickwar ales, decent wines and coffee,

---

Post Office address codings confusingly give the impression that some pubs are in Gloucestershire, when they're really in Warwickshire (which is where we list them).

enjoyable good value food, courteous helpful service, spacious child-friendly back brasserie and dining conservatory; background music, TVs, games machine; heated floodlit courtyard decking, 34 comfortable bedrooms (newer ones in mews), open all day from 8am. *(Tom and Ruth Rees, George Atkinson)*

MORETON-IN-MARSH   SP2032
White Hart Royal   (01608) 650731
High Street; GL56 0BA Refurbished 17th-c coaching inn with Charles I connection; cosy beamed quarry-tiled bar with fine inglenook and nice old furniture, adjacent smarter panelled room with Georgian feel, separate lounge and restaurant, Hook Norton and a guest ale, good choice of wines, well priced food from sandwiches and pub favourites up, friendly attentive service from smart staff; background music; courtyard tables, bedrooms. *(Eddie Edwards, Richard Tilbrook)*

NAILSWORTH   ST8499
Britannia   (01453) 832501
Cossack Square; GL6 0DG Large open-plan pub (part of the small Food Club chain) in former manor house, popular bistro food (best to book evenings), bargain weekday lunch menu, takeaway pizzas, friendly service, well kept Greene King IPA and a couple of local beers, good choice of wines by the glass, big log fire; picnic-sets in front garden, open all day. *(Tom and Ruth Rees)*

NAUNTON   SP1123
⋆**Black Horse**   (01451) 850565
Off B4068 W of Stow-on-the-Wold; GL54 3AD Friendly stripped-stone proper pub with well kept/priced Donnington BB and SBA, good fresh food from generously filled sandwiches and traditional favourites to specials including seasonal game, efficient service, plain tables with flowers, flagstones, black beams and log fire, darts, cribbage, dominoes, dining room; background music; children and dogs welcome, small seating area outside, charming village, fine Cotswold walks (walking groups asked to pre-order food). *(Ann Gray, Richard Tilbrook, Di and Mike Gillam and others)*

NORTH NIBLEY   ST7596
New Inn   (01453) 543659
E of village itself; Waterley Bottom; GL11 6EF Former cider house in secluded rural setting popular with walkers, well kept ales such as Cotleigh, Goffs, Wickwar and Wye Valley from antique pumps, five ciders (plenty more in bottles), basic bar food including good ploughman's, lounge bar with cushioned windsor chairs and high-backed settles, partly stripped-stone walls, simple cosy public bar with darts, beer and cider festivals; children and dogs welcome, tables on lawn and covered decked area with pool table, bedrooms, open all day weekends, closed Mon lunchtime. *(Guy Vowles)*

NYMPSFIELD   SO7900
Rose & Crown   (01453) 860240
The Cross; signed off B4066 Stroud–Dursley; GL10 3TU 17th-c stone-built inn with beamed front bar, pine tables, pews and old settles on bare boards, open fire and woodburner, large raftered back dining area, enjoyable sensibly priced food from pub favourites up, four local ales and decent wines, helpful staff; children welcome, dogs in bar, disabled access, picnic-sets in side yard and on sheltered lawn with play area, handy for Cotswold walks and Woodchester (NT), three bedrooms, open all day. *(J V Dadswell, Paul Rampton, Julie Harding)*

OAKRIDGE LYNCH   SO9103
Butchers Arms   (01285) 760371
Off Eastcombe–Bisley Road E of Stroud; GL6 7NZ Welcoming beamed pub refurbished under new licensees, emphasis on chef/landlord's good food, Wadworths ales, open fires, friendly relaxed atmosphere; tables on lawn overlooking valley, nice walks. *(David Butcher, David and Stella Martin)*

OLD DOWN   ST6187
⋆**Fox**   (01454) 412507
3.9 miles from M5 junction 15/16; A38 towards Gloucester, then Old Down signposted; turn left into Inner Down; BS32 4PR Popular low-beamed cottagey pub, pleasantly unassuming, with warm local atmosphere, seven real ales including Bath and Butcombe, farm cider and good choice of wines by the glass, good reasonably priced hearty food with some interesting specials (best to book), friendly efficient staff, mainly red-carpeted bar with log fire, chunky pine tables and traditional pub seating, snug stone-tiled family room; good disabled access, long verandah with grapevine, front and back gardens, play area. *(Nigel and Sue Foster, James Morrell)*

OLD SODBURY   ST7581
⋆**Dog**   (01454) 312006
3 miles from M4 junction 18, via A46 and A432; The Hill (a busy road); BS37 6LZ Welcoming and popular two-level bar with low beams, stripped stone and open fire, wide range of enjoyable food cooked to order including reasonably priced fish specials, friendly young staff, three well kept changing ales, good wine and soft drinks choice; children and dogs welcome, big garden with barbecue and good play area, bedrooms, open all day. *(Tom and Ruth Rees, Roger and Donna Huggins)*

PAINSWICK   SO8609
Falcon   (01452) 814222
New Street; GL6 6UN Sizeable old stone-built inn dating from the 16th c; sympathetically refurbished and comfortable open-plan layout with bar and two dining areas, popular above-average food, four

well kept beers including Sharps Doom Bar, friendly young staff, some live music; children and dogs welcome, 12 bedrooms, opposite churchyard famous for its 99 yews. *(Mark Sykes, Martin and Pauline Jennings, Neil and Anita Christopher)*

PAINSWICK   SO8609

Royal Oak   (01452) 813129

St Mary's Street; GL6 6QG Partly 16th-c two-room local reopened under enthusiastic new licensees; welcoming bustling atmosphere, well kept beers and enjoyable good value bar food, appealing nooks and crannies, cosy woodburner; suntrap back courtyard. *(Richard Tilbrook, Lesley and Peter Barrett, Neil and Anita Christopher)*

PARKEND   SO6107

Fountain   (01594) 562189

Just off B4234; GL15 4JD 18th-c village inn by terminus of restored Lydney–Parkend steam railway; three well kept ales including Wye Valley, Stowford Press cider, wines in glass-sized bottles, home-made traditional food including bargain OAP lunches (not Sun), welcoming helpful staff, coal fire, assorted chairs and settles in two linked rooms, old tools, bric-a-brac, photographs and framed local history information, quiz and live music nights; children and dogs welcome, wheelchair access, side garden, eight bedrooms and bunkhouse, open all day Sat. *(Chris and Angela Buckell)*

PARKEND   SO6308

Rising Sun   (01594) 562008

Off B4431; GL15 4HN Perched on wooded hillside and approached by roughish single-track drive – popular with walkers and cyclists; open-plan carpeted bar with modern pub furniture, Butcombe and a guest, real ciders, straightforward well priced generous food from sandwiches and baked potatoes up, friendly service, lounge/games area with pool and machines; children and dogs welcome, wheelchair access with help, balcony and terrace tables under umbrellas, big woodside garden with play area and pond, self-catering bedroom, open all day weekends in summer. *(Neil and Anita Christopher)*

PAXFORD   SP1837

✷ **Churchill Arms**   (01386) 594000

B4479, SE of Chipping Campden; GL55 6XH Smart dining pub with good well presented food from snacks up, Hook Norton Bitter, Sharps Doom Bar and Wadworths 6X, good blackboard wine list, pleasant staff, low ceilings and some timbering, flagstones, log fire, dining extension; children welcome, seats out on small front terrace and gravelled back area, four bedrooms, good

breakfast. *(Brian and Ruth Young, Caroline and Michael Abbey, Alan Weedon)*

PILNING   ST5684

Plough   (01454) 632556

Handy for M5 junction 17 via B4055 and Station Road; Pilning Street; BS35 4JJ Thriving local atmosphere under welcoming hard-working licensees, flagstones and bare boards, some faux beams, plates, country prints and repro adverts on dark cream/red dado walls, sofas and armchairs in small lounge area, newspapers in public bar, Wadworths ales and real ciders, good value bar food (some available all day), bargain OAP weekday lunch, cheerful efficient staff, live music; children welcome, disabled access to main areas, garden with large play area overlooking open country. *(Chris and Angela Buckell)*

POULTON   SP1001

Falcon   (01285) 850878

London Road; GL7 5HN Bistro feel with very good food from landlord/chef including set lunch, well kept local ales and nice wines by the glass, friendly unobtrusive service; well behaved children welcome, closed Sun evening, Mon. *(Nicky, Giles and Annie Francis)*

QUENINGTON   SP1404

Keepers Arms   (01285) 750349

Church Road; GL7 5BL Cosy and comfortable village local with stripped stone, low beams and log fires, amiable landlord, value for money food in bar and restaurant including good Sun lunch, well kept range of beers; dogs welcome, picnic-sets outside, bedrooms. *(Neil and Anita Christopher, Mo and David Trudgill, Tom McLean)*

SAPPERTON   SO9303

Daneway Inn   (01285) 760297

Daneway; off A419 Stroud–Cirencester; GL7 6LN Quiet tucked-away local in charming wooded countryside, flagstones and bare boards, woodburner in amazing floor-to-ceiling carved oak dutch fireplace, sporting prints, well kept Wadworths ales, farm ciders, generous simple food from filled baps up, long-serving landlord and friendly staff, small family room, traditional games in inglenook public bar, folk night Tues; no dogs, tricky wheelchair access; terrace tables and lovely sloping lawn, camping possible, good walks by disused canal with tunnel to Coates. *(Dr A Y Drummond)*

SHIPTON MOYNE   ST8989

Cat & Custard Pot   (01666) 880249

Off B4040 Malmesbury–Bristol; The Street; GL8 8PN Popular pub in picturesque village, good food from

Cribbage is a card game using a block of wood with holes for matchsticks or special pins to score with; regulars in cribbage pubs are usually happy to teach strangers how to play.

baguettes to restaurant dishes (booking recommended), efficient friendly service even when busy, well kept Flowers, Timothy Taylors and Wadworths, Thatcher's cider, well priced wines, deceptively spacious inside with several dining areas, beams and bric-a-brac, hunting prints, cosy back snug, chatty locals; walkers and dogs welcome, wheelchair access, tables out on lawn. *(Neil and Anita Christopher)*

SIDDINGTON   SU0399
Greyhound (01285) 653573
Ashton Road; village signed from A419 roundabout at Tesco; GL7 6HR
Refurbished beamed village pub, linked rooms with big log fires, enjoyable good value food, well kept Wadworths ales and plenty of wines by the glass; background music; children welcome, garden tables, open all day weekends. *(Anon)*

SLAD   SO8707
Woolpack (01452) 813429
B4070 Stroud–Birdlip; GL6 7QA
Friendly and unpretentiously old-fashioned hillside village local with lovely valley views, four little connecting rooms with Laurie Lee and other interesting photographs, some of his books for sale, log fire and nice tables, enjoyable pub food (not Sun evening) from sandwiches and baguettes up including generous Sun roast, home-baked bread, well kept Uley and guests, local farm ciders and perry, decent wines by the glass, good young staff, games and cards; children and dogs welcome, nice garden. *(Pete Flower)*

SNOWSHILL   SP0933
Snowshill Arms (01386) 852653
Opposite village green; WR12 7JU
Unpretentious country pub in honeypot village (so no shortage of customers); well kept Donnington ales and reasonably priced straightforward food from sandwiches up, prompt friendly service, log fire, stripped stone, neat array of tables, local photographs; skittle alley, charming village views from bow windows and big back garden with little stream and play area, children welcome if eating, handy for Snowshill Manor (NT), lavender farm and Cotswold Way walks. *(Roger and Ann King, Edna Jones)*

SOMERFORD KEYNES   SU0195
Bakers Arms (01285) 861298
On main street through village; GL7 6DN Pretty little 17th-c stone-built pub with catslide roof, four real ales including Butcombe and Stroud, Addlestone's cider, good house wine, traditional food and specials, friendly service, lots of pine tables in two linked stripped-stone areas, two log fires; children and dogs welcome, nice garden with play area, lovely village, handy for Cotswold Water Park. *(Anon)*

ST BRIAVELS   SO5504
★**George** (01594) 530228
High Street; GL15 6TA Old Wadworths pub with their beers and enjoyable sensibly priced pubby food including OAP weekday lunch deal, fast friendly service, rambling linked black-beamed rooms with attractive old-fashioned décor and big stone fireplace, restaurant; can get very busy weekends (booking advised); children and dogs welcome, flagstoned terrace over former moat of neighbouring Norman fortress, two bedrooms, open all day weekends. *(Bob and Margaret Holder, Lucien Perring)*

STAUNTON   SO7829
Swan (01452) 840323
Ledbury Road (A417); GL19 3QA Nice pubby atmosphere and good choice of enjoyable reasonably priced home-made food, friendly service, well kept ales (hundreds of pump clips on beams), interconnecting rooms including spacious restaurant, comfortable sofas by open fire, conservatory; background music; children and dogs welcome, disabled facilities, pretty garden, closed Sun and Mon evenings. *(Neil and Anita Christopher)*

STOW-ON-THE-WOLD   SP1729
★**Coach & Horses** (01451) 830208
Ganborough (on A424 about 2.5 miles N); GL56 0QZ Beamed and flagstoned country pub, bright and clean, with good reasonably priced local food from well filled baguettes up, special walkers' menu too, friendly prompt service, well kept Donnington ales and farm cider, decent wines by the glass, cheerful log fire, step up to compact dining area with high-backed settles on wood floor, black labrador (Pennell); children welcome, skittle alley, big garden with good new play area. *(Paul Humphreys, Guy Vowles, Helen Botterill)*

STOW-ON-THE-WOLD   SP1925
Eagle & Child (01451) 830670
Connected to Royalist Hotel, Digbeth Street; GL54 1BN Small bar attached to handsome old hotel; woodburner, flagstones and low beams, back conservatory, nice mix of tables, enjoyable food from pub favourites up, good wine and malt whisky choice, ales such as Brakspears Oxford Gold, charming service; background music; children and dogs welcome, a few picnic-sets in front, small courtyard behind, 14 good bedrooms, open all day. *(Richard Tilbrook)*

STOW-ON-THE-WOLD   SP1925
Kings Arms (01451) 830364
The Square; GL54 1AF Refurbished 16th-c coaching inn, black-beamed bar with wood floor, some blue-painted panelling and stripped stone, woodburner, Greene King ales, enjoyable food here or in upstairs Chophouse restaurant with saggy oak

floor, leopard-skin bar stools and ink-spot tables, friendly service; children welcome, ten bedrooms including three courtyard 'cottages', open all day. *(Richard Tilbrook)*

STOW-ON-THE-WOLD   SP1925
★ Queens Head   (01451) 830563
The Square; GL54 1AB Splendidly unpretentious for this upmarket town; well kept low-priced Donnington BB and SBA, good wines by the glass, good value sandwiches and basic pub meals including proper steak and kidney pudding, cheerful helpful service, bustling and chatty stripped-stone front lounge, heavily beamed and flagstoned back bar with high-backed settles, horse prints and coal-effect fire; children and dogs welcome, tables in attractive sunny back courtyard, open all day. *(Mitchell Cregor, Richard Tilbrook)*

TETBURY   ST8893
Priory   (01666) 502251
London Road; GL8 8JJ More civilised eating house than pub, with central log fire in comfortable if somewhat sombre high-raftered stone-built former stables, enjoyable food with emphasis on interesting local produce, even a local slant to the good wood-fired pizzas, cheerful service, well kept Stroud, Uley and a guest, three proper ciders and decent wines by the glass; comfortable coffee lounge, live music Sun; children very welcome, wheelchair access (staff helpful), roadside terrace picnic-sets, 14 good bedrooms, open all day. *(Alan Edwards)*

TETBURY   ST8993
★ Snooty Fox   (01666) 502436
Market Place; GL8 8DD High-ceilinged stripped-stone hotel lounge, unstuffy with well kept ales such as Butcombe, Moles and Wickwar, good house wines, friendly young staff, enjoyable all-day bar food from sandwiches up, leather sofas, brass ceiling fans and elegant fireplace, nice side room and anteroom, restaurant; unobtrusive background music, bar can get very busy weekend evenings; children and dogs welcome, large sheltered front terrace, 12 comfortable bedrooms. *(Anon)*

TETBURY   ST9195
★ Trouble House   (01666) 502206
A433 towards Cirencester, near Cherington turn; GL8 8SG Pretty 17th-c dining pub, simple and well looked after, with highly rated food, Wadworths ales from small saggy-beamed middle room, pleasant staff, big log fire, resident ghost; picnic-sets in back gravel courtyard, closed Sun evening, Mon. *(Mrs P Sumner, Paul and Jill Nash, Dr and Mrs A K Clarke, Derek Thomas, Nick and Sylvia Pascoe)*

TEWKESBURY   SO8931
★ Gupshill Manor   (01684) 292278
Gloucester Road (off A38 S edge of town); GL20 5SG Quaint old timbered building with Tardis-like series of lounge and dining areas, plenty of easy chairs and sofas on wood floors, beams and open fires, enjoyable well priced food (all day Sun) from pubby dishes up including lunchtime deals, friendly efficient staff, three well kept Greene King ales and a guest, decent wine list, good coffees; background music; children welcome, disabled access, teak tables on extensive heated terrace, open all day. *(J Chilver, Rod Stoneman)*

TEWKESBURY   SO8933
★ Olde Black Bear   (01684) 292202
High Street; GL20 5BJ County's oldest pub (early 14th c), well worth a look for its intricately rambling little rooms with ancient tiles, heavy timbering and low beams; up to five real ales, reasonably priced wines, cheap but decent pubby food, well worn furnishings, open fire; background music; children welcome, terrace and play area in nice riverside garden, open all day. *(Jeremy King)*

TEWKESBURY   SO8932
Royal Hop Pole   (01684) 278670
Church Street; GL20 5RT Wetherspoons conversion of old inn, original features, their usual value-minded all-day food and drink, good service; lovely garden leading down to river, bedrooms, open all day. *(Theocsbrian)*

TOCKINGTON   ST6086
Swan   (01454) 614800
Tockington Green; BS32 4NJ Spacious refurbished dining pub with good choice of reasonably priced popular food, Greene King ales and decent wines, log fire, beams and stripped stone walls; children welcome, tables in tree-shaded garden, open all day. *(Hugh Roberts, James Morrell)*

TODDINGTON   SP0432
Pheasant   (01242) 621271
A46 Broadway–Winchcombe, junction with A438 and B4077; GL54 5DT Extended stone-built roadside pub with enjoyable low-priced food from generously filled baguettes up, friendly helpful staff, well kept good value Stanway (brewed nearby), lots of railway prints – handy for preserved Gloucestershire Warwickshire Railway Station; no dogs while food is being served; bedrooms, breakfast for non-residents. *(R C Vincent, Chris and Angela Buckell)*

TODENHAM   SP2436
★ Farriers Arms   (01608) 650901
Between A3400 and A429 N of Moreton-in-Marsh; GL56 9PF Unspoilt and welcoming old pub with exposed stone and plastered walls in bar, hop-hung beams, polished flagstones by counter, woodburner in big inglenook, cosy room off with old books and photos, neat restaurant, Hook Norton and a couple of guests, several wines by the glass, well liked good value food, darts, board games; background music; children welcome,

dogs in bar, country views from walled garden, terrace overlooking quiet village road and church, aunt sally, good surrounding walks. *(Clive and Fran Dutson, Alun and Jennifer Evans, George Atkinson, Robert Wivell, Nick and Meriel Cox, Theocsbrian and others)*

TYTHERINGTON ST6788
Swan (01454) 412380
Duck Street, off A38 SE of Thornbury; GL12 8QB Friendly newish management for this sizeable 16th-c pub near church; low beams, bare stone and cream walls, parquet or carpeted floors, inglenook log fire, good value food including lunchtime deal, real ales such as Fullers London Pride and St Austell Tribute, games bar and skittle alley; children welcome, dogs in one part, wheelchair access from car park, enclosed garden, open all day Fri, Sat. *(David and Jenny Billington)*

ULEY ST7998
Old Crown (01453) 860502
The Green; GL11 5SN Recently refurbished 17th-c pub prettily set by village green just off Cotswold Way; long narrow room with settles and pews on bare boards, step up to partitioned-off lounge area, six well kept local ales including Uley, decent wines by the glass, enjoyable pubby food from baguettes up, friendly service, log fire; attractive garden behind, four bedrooms. *(Jim and Frances Gowers, M G Hart)*

UPTON CHEYNEY ST6969
Upton Inn (0117) 932 4489
Signed off A431 at Bitton; BS30 6LY 18th-c stone-built village pub, bar with old prints on stone and dark panelled walls, old tables and captain's chairs, step up to carpeted/bare-boards dining area with woodburner, good choice of home-made pubby food from sandwiches up, Sun carvery, well kept Badger ales, modern opulent mock-Regency restaurant with pictures of Bath, friendly helpful service; background music; children and dogs welcome, picnic-sets on terrace, picturesque spot with Avon Valley views, open all day. *(Anon)*

WESTON SUBEDGE SP1241
Seagrave Arms (01386) 840192
B4632; GL55 6QH Nicely refurbished Georgian country inn/restaurant, small log-fire bar, two dining rooms with mix of furniture on wood floors, good imaginative well presented food using seasonal local produce, Hook Norton and Purity ales, Hogan's cider, friendly efficient staff; large seating area outside, eight bedrooms, open (and food) all day weekends, closed Mon. *(Dennis and Doreen Haward)*

WESTONBIRT ST8690
Hare & Hounds (01666) 881000
A433 SW of Tetbury; GL8 8QL Substantial roadside hotel with separate entrance for pub, good choice of food from

snacks up, Cotswold Spring and Wickwar, lots of wines by the glass, interesting malts and english vodka, flagstoned bar with another panelled one to the left, series of interconnecting rooms with polished wood or sisal floors, woodburner in two-way fireplace, some leather sofas and banquettes, more formal restaurant; muddy boots and dogs welcome in bar, wheelchair access, shaded tables out on paved area, pleasant gardens, 42 bedrooms including some in annexe, handy for Arboretum, open all day. *(Chris and Angela Buckell)*

WHITECROFT SO6005
Miners Arms (01594) 562483
B4234 N of Lydney; GL15 4PE Friendly unpretentious local with up to five changing ales, farm ciders and perries, sensibly priced food from snacks up including some greek dishes (landlord is cypriot), attentive helpful service, two rooms on either side of bar, slate and parquet floors, pastel walls with old photographs, conservatory, skittle alley; background and some live music; children and dogs welcome, disabled access, good gardens front and back, one with stream, good local walks, handy for steam railway, self-catering cottage, open all day. *(Chris and Angela Buckell)*

WHITMINSTER SO7607
Fromebridge Mill (01452) 741796
Fromebridge Lane (A38 near M5 junction 13); GL2 7PD Comfortable mill-based dining pub handy for M5; interconnecting rooms, beams, brick walls, flagstone and carpeted floors, some tables overlooking river, well kept Greene King and guests, good choice of wines by the glass, food all day including lunchtime carvery (evenings too at weekends); can get very busy, no dogs inside; children welcome, wheelchair access, picnic-sets in big garden with play area, pretty waterside setting, footbridge from car park. *(Simon J Barber)*

WINCHCOMBE SP0228
Lion (01242) 603300
North Street; GL54 5PS Stylishly refurbished former coaching inn with plenty of rustic chic, good food in bar or restaurant, well kept ales such as Prescott and Ringwood, friendly helpful staff, newspapers, magazines and board games; background music turned down on request; children welcome, dogs in bar and snug, seven bedrooms, open all day. *(Richard Tilbrook)*

WINCHCOMBE SP0228
✱ Old Corner Cupboard
(01242) 602303 *Gloucester Street; GL54 5LX* Attractive old golden-stone pub continuing well under present landlord; wide range of good generous fair-priced food (booking advised weekends) in nice back dining room, well kept Fullers, Hook Norton and local Stanway, decent wines by the glass,

good service, comfortable stripped-stone lounge bar with heavy-beamed Tudor core, traditional hatch-service lobby, small side room with woodburner in massive stone fireplace, traditional games; children welcome, tables in back garden, open all day. *(Ellie Weld, David London, Dr A J and Mrs B A Tompsett)*

WINCHCOMBE SP0228

⋆**White Hart** (01242) 602359

High Street (B4632); GL54 5LJ Popular 16th-c inn with big windows looking out over village street, mix of chairs and small settles around pine tables, bare boards, grey-green paintwork, cricket memorabilia, well kept Goffs, Otter and Wickwar, wine shop at back (corkage added if you buy to drink on the premises), wide choice by the glass too, specialist sausage menu and other enjoyable food, courteous efficient service, separate restaurant; children welcome, dogs in bar and bedrooms, open all day from 9am (10am Sun). *(Ellie Weld, David London, Dr A J and Mrs B A Tompsett, Guy Vowles)*

WINTERBOURNE ST6678

Willy Wicket (0117) 956 7308

Wick Wick Close, handy for M4 junction 19 via M32, A4174 E; BS36 1DP Vintage Inn family dining pub on roundabout; popular generously served food all day including set menu (till 5pm), ales such as Butcombe and St Austell, friendly courteous service, two eating areas off big central bar, beams, timbers and stripped stone, picture windows, two log fires. *(Roger and Donna Huggins, David and Ruth Shillitoe)*

WITHINGTON SP0315

Kings Head (01242) 890216

Kings Head Lane; GL54 4BD Old-fashioned rural local (in same family for over 100 years – the friendly veteran landlady was born here), well kept Hook Norton and maybe Wickwar tapped from the cask, pickled eggs (can bring your own food), bar with woodburner, darts, shove-ha'penny, table skittles and pool, partly stripped-stone lounge bar, impromptu music sessions; children and dogs welcome (there's a pub dog), pleasant garden behind, open all day. *(Giles and Annie Francis)*

WITHINGTON SP0315

Mill Inn (01242) 890204

Off A436 or A40; GL54 4BE Idyllic streamside setting for mossy-roofed old stone inn, some refurbishment but keeping character with nice nooks and corners, beams, wood/flagstone floors, two inglenook log fires and a woodburner, Sam Smiths beers, reasonably priced food, two dining rooms; children and dogs welcome, big garden, splendid walks, open all day weekends. *(Anon)*

WOODCHESTER SO8403

⋆**Old Fleece** (01453) 872582

Rooksmoor; A46 a mile S of Stroud; GL5 5NB Old wisteria-clad roadside pub, part of the small Cotswold Food Club chain; good choice of well presented interesting food, friendly accommodating staff, well kept mostly local beers and good wines by the glass, bar, dining room and snug, big windows, bare boards and panelling, stripped-stone or dark salmon pink walls, modern paintings, large log fire, daily papers; children welcome, wheelchair access (except dining area – you can also eat in bar), two front terraces, open all day. *(Mike Burkinshaw, Tom and Ruth Rees)*

WOODCHESTER SO8302

Ram (01453) 873329

High Street, South Woodchester; off A46 S of Stroud; GL5 5EL Bustling country pub under new management; up to half a dozen well priced changing ales and three ciders, fairly standard home-made food, L-shaped beamed bar with bare boards and stripped stonework, nice mix of traditional furnishings including several cushioned antique panelled settles, open fires, maybe live acoustic music Sun afternoon; children and dogs welcome, spectacular valley views from terrace, open all day. *(Chris and Angela Buckell)*

WOODCHESTER SO8302

Royal Oak (01453) 872735

Off A46; Church Road, N Woodchester; GL5 5PQ 17th-c village pub under newish management; relaxing and comfortable low-beamed bar on right with oak tables, soft seats by huge fireplace next to old-fashioned stripped-stone area on left, locally sourced home-made food (not Sun evening, Mon or Tues), Stroud, Uley and a guest ale, nice views, regular live music; children and dogs welcome, some seating out front, more on back terrace, closed weekday lunchtimes, open all day weekends. *(Anon)*

YATE ST6983

Cross Keys (01454) 228314

Signed off B4059 Yate bypass at the Fox; North Road; BS37 7LQ Unpretentious two-bar beamed village local, good honest reasonably priced food (5-8pm, Sat lunchtime, not Sun, Mon) from sandwiches up including nice old-fashioned puddings, well kept Bass, Cotswold Spring, Courage and Sharps Doom Bar, cheerful chatty landlord, fires in both rooms, stripped stone and panelling, flagstones and carpet, mixed pubby furniture including pews and old dining tables, brasses and prints; background music, fruit machine and darts in public bar, Weds quiz; disabled access (a bit tricky for some wheelchairs), open all day Fri-Sun. *(Roger and Donna Huggins)*

Hampshire

This has always been an interesting county for pubs – there seems to be one for every mood and every occasion. New entries this year are the Wellington Arms in Baughurst (pretty little inn with delicious food cooked by the landlord), Northbrook Arms at East Stratton (unassuming country pub with local beers and courteous staff) and Angel & Blue Pig in Lymington (smart, newly refurbished place with stylish bedrooms and enjoyable food). Other pubs readers enjoy are the Oak at Bank (smashing New Forest spot, with enjoyable food and ales), Sun in Bentworth (cheerful pub with long-serving landlady and six beers), Three Tuns in Bransgore (inventive meals, a bustling feel and friendly landlord), Chestnut Horse in Easton (smart, cosy dining pub near the Itchen Valley), Royal Oak at Fritham (delightful country tavern in middle of the New Forest), Hogget in Hook (homely pub usefully open all day weekends), Plough in Longparish (accomplished food and handy for A303), Yew Tree at Lower Wield (run with care and thought by a lovely landlord), Mill House in North Warnborough (carefully restored mill house with bistro-style food and wide choice of drinks), White Horse near Petersfield (unchanging local with ten ales and character bars), Purefoy Arms in Preston Candover (enterprising, inventive food cooked by the landlord, carefully chosen wines and hand-made chocolates), Rose & Thistle at Rockbourne (first class landlady, warm welcome for all and tempting food), Plough at Sparsholt (courteous, hands-on landlord in very well run, popular pub), Harrow at Steep (unchanging little country gem) and Wykeham Arms in Winchester (historic pub with much character, lovely bedrooms and impressive food and drink). Our Hampshire Dining Pub 2014 is the Purefoy Arms at Preston Candover.

BANK
Oak

SU2806 Map 2

Signposted just off A35 SW of Lyndhurst; SO43 7FE

New Forest pub with a good mix of customers, well liked food and interesting décor

Readers thoroughly enjoy this very popular pub, tucked away in a quiet New Forest spot; it's just the place to visit after a walk. Even at its busiest, the efficient staff remain helpful and welcoming. The L-shaped bar has bay windows with built-in red-cushioned seats, and two or three little pine-panelled booths with small built-in tables and bench seats. The rest of the bare-boarded bar has low beams and joists, candles in brass holders on a row of stripped old and newer blond tables set against the wall and all manner of bric-a-brac: fishing rods, spears, a boomerang, old ski poles, brass platters, heavy knives and guns. There are cushioned milk churns along the counter and little red lanterns among hop bines above the bar. Fullers London Pride, Gales HSB and Seafarers and a changing guest on handpump and a dozen wines by the glass; background music. The pleasant side garden has picnic-sets and long tables and benches by big yew trees.

Good, well presented food includes doorstep sandwiches (the crab is popular), home-made ham hock terrine with piccalilli, fried chicken livers in brandy and sage cream, maple syrup-roasted ham with free-range eggs and pineapple chutney, beef and red onion burger with chips, wild mushroom and spinach linguine with truffle oil, chicken breast and bacon salad with free-range egg and mustard dressing, pie of the day, specials like local venison haunch with red wine sauce or crab gratin topped with prawn and cheese, and puddings. *Benchmark main dish: jumbo haddock and chips £14.50. Two-course evening meal £19.00.*

Fullers ~ Manager Martin Sliva ~ Real ale ~ (023) 8028 2350 ~ Open 11.30-11; 12-10.30 Sun; 11.30-3, 5.30-11 weekdays in winter ~ Bar food 12-2.30, 6-9.30; all day weekends ~ Children welcome, no under-5s after 6pm ~ Dogs welcome ~ www.oakinnlyndhurst.co.uk
Recommended by Adrian Johnson, Katharine Cowherd, Mr and Mrs P D Titcomb, Jane and Rowena Leverington, Mrs J Plante Cleall, Michael Butler, John Saville, H J Reynolds, Mrs J A Taylar, Martin and Karen Wake, N R White

BAUGHURST
Wellington Arms 🍴 🛏

SU5860 Map 2

Baughurst Road, S of village; RG26 5LP

Small pretty country pub with attractive little rooms, exceptional cooking and a friendly welcome; bedrooms

Run with enthusiasm and great care, this charming little country inn has a warm welcome for all. Rooms are simply and attractively decorated with an assortment of cushioned wooden dining chairs around a mix of tables on terracotta tiles, pretty blinds or curtains, brass candlesticks, flowers and shelves and window sills stacked with books. Two Cocks Roundhead and Cavalier on handpump and nine wines by the glass served by courteous, helpful staff; background music. Bedrooms (in a former hay store and scullery) have timbers, brickwork and underfloor-heated slate tiles, and are well equipped and comfortable.

Rearing sheep and pigs, keeping chickens and bees and growing vegetables, the licensees produce delicious food that includes terrine of rabbit, home-reared pork, pistachios and pancetta with spiced apple chutney, chargrilled diver-caught king scallops wrapped in bacon on crushed green peas and mint, potato gnocchi fried with garlic, caramelised butternut squash, purple sage and walnuts, beer-battered line-caught cod fillet with fat chips, moroccan free-range chicken kofta with red peppers, apricots, chickpeas and baked egg, pot pie of local venison with shallots and red wine, roast guinea fowl breast and confit leg on puy lentils with roast shallots and morel mushrooms, and puddings like flourless dark chocolate and walnut torte with caramel ice-cream and baked caramel custard with candied quinces and cinnamon bark; they also offer a two- and three-course set lunch. *Benchmark main dish: home-reared rack of pork with gourd apples and wilted leaves £14.50. Two-course evening meal £22.00.*

Free house ~ Licensees Simon Page and Jason King ~ Real ale ~ (0118) 982 0110 ~ Open 12-3, 6.30(6 Sat)-10.30; 12-4 Sun; closed Sun evening ~ Bar food 12-2, 7-9; 12-4 Sun ~ Children welcome ~ Dogs welcome ~ Bedrooms: /£130 ~ www.thewellingtonarms.com
Recommended by Harvey Brown, Caroline Prescott

 BENTWORTH   SU6740 Map 2

Sun 🍺

Sun Hill; from A339 from Alton, the first turning takes you there direct; or in village follow signpost 'Shalden 2¼, Alton 4¼'; GU34 5JT

Smashing choice of real ales, generously served food and welcoming landlady in popular country pub; nearby walks

With half a dozen real ales on handpump kept well by the long-serving landlady of this 17th-c pub, it's not surprising there are always so many cheerful customers: Andwell Resolute Bitter, Bowman Swift One, Fullers London Pride, Hook Norton Old Hooky, Itchen Valley Hampshire Rose and Sharps Doom Bar. The atmosphere is easy-going and chatty, and the two little traditional linked rooms have high-backed antique settles, pews and schoolroom chairs, olde-worlde prints and blacksmith's tools on the walls, and bare boards and scrubbed deal tables to the left; three big fireplaces with log fires make it especially snug in winter. An arch leads to a brick-floored room with another open fire. There are seats out in front and in the back garden; pleasant nearby walks.

🍴 Quite a choice of food might include deep-fried whitebait with tartare sauce, pork liver pâté with toast, mushroom stroganoff, steak and stilton pie, burger with a choice of toppings, beer-battered cod and chips, beef curry, calves liver and bacon with onion gravy, pork medallions in cider and apple sauce, bass with sweet chilli and crayfish sauce, and puddings like banoffi pie and sticky toffee pudding. *Benchmark main dish: steak in stilton pie £13.95. Two-course evening meal £19.00.*

Free house ~ Licensee Mary Holmes ~ Real ale ~ (01420) 562338 ~ Open 12-3, 6-11; 12-10.30 Sun ~ Bar food 12-2, 7-9.30 ~ Children welcome ~ Dogs welcome ~ www.thesuninnbentworth.co.uk *Recommended by Ann and Colin Hunt*

 BOLDRE   SZ3198 Map 2

Red Lion 🍴🍺

Off A337 N of Lymington; SO41 8NE

Friendly pub on the edge of the New Forest, lots of bygones in five beamed rooms, four real ales, interesting food and seats outside

On the edge of the New Forest in fine walking country, this well run pub has a warm, thriving atmosphere thanks largely to the friendly and efficient licensees. The five black-beamed rooms reveal an entertaining collection of bygones, with heavy-horse harness, gin traps, ferocious-looking man traps, copper and brass pans and rural landscapes, as well as a dainty collection of old bottles and glasses. Seating is on pews, sturdy cushioned dining chairs and tapestried stools. There's an old cooking range in the cosy little bar, and three good log fires. Brakspears Oxford Gold, Ringwood Best and Fortyniner and a guest like Wychwood Jester Jake on handpump and 16 wines by the glass. The pub is opposite the village green; in summer, there are seats outside among the flowering tubs and hanging baskets, with more tables in the back garden. A sunny self-catering apartment is for rent.

Using local, seasonal produce, the highly rated home-made food includes baguettes, prawn and smoked salmon cocktail, tempura-battered black pudding with caramelised apple, home-cooked ale and orange ham with free-range eggs, steak in ale pie, filo pastry parcel of spinach, asparagus and stilton with blue cheese sauce, free-range chicken with smoked bacon, cheese and barbecue sauce, lamb rump on sweet potato mash with creamy rosemary and mint sauce, deep-fried cod cheeks with pea purée, tartare sauce and chips, and puddings. *Benchmark main dish: pork duo on horseradish mash with red wine and garlic sauce and crackling £14.95. Two-course evening meal £17.00.*

Eldridge Pope ~ Lease Alan and Amanda Pountney ~ Real ale ~ (01590) 673177 ~ Open 11-3, 5.30-11; 11-11 Sat; 12-10.30 Sun; 11-3, 5.30-11 Sat in winter ~ Bar food 12-2.30, 6-9.30; all day Sun, summer Sat ~ Restaurant ~ Children welcome away from bar ~ Dogs allowed in bar ~ www.theredlionboldre.co.uk *Recommended by Phyl and Jack Street, Jules Seifert, Adrian Ballard, John and Hilary Murphy, Guy Vowles, Tim Rye*

BRANSGORE

SZ1997 Map 2

Three Tuns 🍴 🍺

Village signposted off A35 and off B3347 N of Christchurch; Ringwood Road, opposite church; BH23 8JH

Interesting food in pretty thatched pub with proper old-fashioned bar and good beers, as well as a civilised main dining area

Maintaining its high standards, this 17th-c thatched pub in the New Forest National Park offers a thoughtful choice of ales and food. There's plenty of cheerful customers, welcomed by the friendly landlord and his staff, and the roomy low-ceilinged and carpeted main area has a fireside 'codgers' corner', as well as a good mix of comfortably cushioned low chairs around a variety of dining tables. On the right is a separate traditional regulars' bar that seems taller than it is wide, with an impressive log-effect stove in a stripped-brick hearth, shiny black panelling and individually chosen pubby furnishings. Ringwood Best and Fortyniner and Timothy Taylors Landlord and guests like Otter Bitter and St Austell Tribute on handpump and nine wines by the glass. The Grade II-listed barn is popular for parties. In summer, the hanging baskets are lovely and there's an attractive, extensive shrub-sheltered terrace with picnic-sets; beyond are more tables on the grass looking over pony paddocks. They have a pétanque court.

Inventive and very good, the food might include sandwiches, beetroot and goats cheese salad with sugared walnuts and beetroot toast, mini pie of braised oxtail and snails, moules marinière, burger with cheese and bacon, grilled pineapple and coleslaw, calves liver and bacon with onion gravy, beer-battered hake, corn-fed chicken with local truffle and madeira jus, roasted wild duck with rhubarb, baby orange and dauphinoise potatoes, and puddings such as pumpkin cheesecake with orange marmalade and coconut, mango and passion-fruit surprise. *Benchmark main dish: venison pasty £9.95. Two-course evening meal £18.50.*

Enterprise ~ Lease Nigel Glenister ~ Real ale ~ (01425) 672232 ~ Open 11(11.30 weekends)-11(10.30 Sun) ~ Bar food 12-2.15, 6-9.15; all day weekends ~ Restaurant ~ Children welcome but not in lounge after 6pm ~ Dogs allowed in bar ~ www.threetunsinn.com *Recommended by Nigels, David Pollard, Phyl and Jack Street, Patrick and Daphne Darley, Colin McKerrow*

DROXFORD   SU6018   Map 2

Bakers Arms ⊕ ◀

High Street; A32 5 miles N of Wickham; SO32 3PA

Attractively opened-up and friendly pub with well kept beers, good interesting cooking and cosy corners

The highly thought-of food and impeccable service at this popular pub continue to please our readers, as does the warm welcome from the hands-on licensees. It's attractively laid-out with the central bar as the focus: Bowman Swift One and Wallops Wood on handpump, Stowford Press cider and a short carefully chosen list of wines by the glass. Well spaced tables on carpet or neat bare boards spread around the airy L-shaped open-plan bar, with low leather chesterfields and an assortment of comfortably cushioned chairs at one end; a dark panelled dado, dark beams and joists and a modicum of country oddments emphasise the freshness of the white paintwork; good log fire and board games. To one side, with a separate entrance, is the village post office. There are picnic-sets outside.

As well as a two-course set menu (Tuesday-Friday lunchtimes and Tuesday-Thursday evenings), the tasty food might include lambs kidneys on toast, bubble and squeak with soft poached egg and hollandaise, pork sausages with onion gravy, chicken with vegetable risotto and red wine sauce, fillet of hake with herb dressing and new potatoes, slow-cooked duck leg with sautéed potatoes and salsa verde, and puddings like caramelised rice pudding with clotted cream and chocolate fudge brownie with butterscotch ice-cream. *Benchmark main dish: grilled rib-eye steak with thyme, garlic and rosemary butter and chips £18.95. Two-course evening meal £26.00.*

Free house ~ Licensees Adam and Anna Cordery ~ Real ale ~ (01489) 877533 ~ Open 11.45-3, 6-11; 12-3 Sun; closed Sun evening, Mon ~ Bar food 12-2, 7-9 ~ Well behaved children welcome ~ Dogs allowed in bar ~ www.thebakersarmsdroxford.com *Recommended by Henry Fryer*

DROXFORD   SU6118   Map 2

Hurdles ⊕ ♟

Brockbridge, just outside Soberton; from A32 just N of Droxford, take B2150 towards Denmead; SO32 3QT

Roomy and smartly furnished country dining pub with enticing food and local ales

Surprisingly grand for such a tucked-away country pub, this is a handsome brick building that's been brought very suitably up to date. With an easy-going, friendly feel, it has dark grey leather chesterfields and armchairs by a log fire in one room with elegant columnar lamps in big windows; to the right, dining areas have stylish wallpaper, striped chairs around shiny modern tables, and glittering mirrors. High ceilings and stripped boards throughout. Attentive young staff serve Bowmans Swift One and Wallops Wood and a changing guest like Goddards Fuggle-Dee-Dum on handpump, decent wines by the glass and good coffee; unobtrusive piped pop music. It's a peaceful spot, with wooden and metal tables on neat terraces (one covered and heated) and a long flight of steps up to picnic-sets on a sloping lawn by tall trees.

As well as a two- and three-course set menu (not Friday evening or weekends), the interesting food includes baguettes, croque monsieur, crumbed crab cake with chilli, ginger and mint noodle salad, pork, apple and prune terrine with celeriac, apple and mustard rémoulade, smoked haddock and herb fishcake with leek and pancetta mash, spicy bean burger with harissa salsa, sweet potato fries and tzatziki, pheasant wellington with red cabbage and parsnip purée, duck breast with pancetta and thyme potato cake and roast beetroot, and puddings like Baileys profiteroles with chocolate sauce and sticky toffee pudding with toffee sauce and vanilla ice-cream. *Benchmark main dish: braised blade of beef with smoked mash and mushroom fricassée £14.25. Two-course evening meal £20.00.*

Enterprise ~ Lease Gareth and Sarah Cole ~ Real ale ~ (01489) 877451 ~ Open 11-11; 12-10 Sun ~ Bar food 12-3, 6-9.30; 12-7.30 Sun ~ Restaurant ~ Children welcome ~ Dogs allowed in bar ~ www.thehurdlesdroxford.co.uk *Recommended by Ian Herdman, Harvey Brown, Toby Jones*

EAST STRATTON   SU5339   Map 2
Northbrook Arms
Brown sign to pub off A33 4 miles S of A303 junction; SO21 3DU

Attractive brick pub with character bars, lots to look at, six real ales and enjoyable food; bedrooms

Just as welcoming if you want a meal or a chatty drink, this is a pleasantly unassuming pub with polite, hard-working staff. There's a relaxed traditional tiled-floor bar to the right, with Alfreds Saxon Bronze, Dorset Piddle Jimmy Riddle, Flack Manor Double Drop, Milk Street Mermaid, Otter Ale and Wyre Piddle April Showers on handpump and around ten wines by the glass. Also, a mix of pubby chairs around sturdy stripped-top tables, a big collection of horsebrasses and tack on beams and standing timbers and shelves of books; background music. On the left, it's carpeted, and progressively rather more formal, ending in a proper dining room beyond a little central hall. There are picnic-sets on the green across the quiet village road, with more in the pretty side garden; the former stables house the skittle alley. The bedrooms are clean, comfortable and quiet and breakfasts are good; fine nearby walks.

Enjoyable food includes sandwiches, crayfish and crab cocktail with lemon and lime mayonnaise, ham hock terrine with pineapple pickle, various deli boards, asparagus, pea and chive risotto, burger with bacon, tomato and red onion and chips, beer-battered cod with mushy peas, slow-roast duck confit with honeyed vegetables and fondant potatoes, venison steak in juniper, mushroom and red wine sauce with cauliflower purée, scallops with pea and mint purée, balsamic dressing and pea shoots, and puddings. *Benchmark main dish: pie of the day £13.95. Two-course evening meal £18.00.*

Free house ~ Licensees Jon Coward and Millie Spurr ~ Real ale ~ (01962) 774150 ~ Open 11-11(10.30 Sun) ~ Bar food 12-2.30, 6-9.30; 12-4 Sun ~ Restaurant ~ Children welcome ~ Dogs welcome ~ Bedrooms: £70/£80 ~ www.thenorthbrookarms.com *Recommended by Sara Fulton, Roger Baker*

EAST TYTHERLEY

SU2927 Map 2

Star ⇌

B3084 N of Romsey; turn off by railway crossing opposite Mill Arms,
Dundridge; SO51 0LW

New licensees for this pretty country pub with comfortable bars and
well liked food and drink; bedrooms

Close to good walks, this neatly kept pub has new licensees, who,
thankfully, don't plan to change too much (there's been some gentle
refurbishment). The bar has farmhouse and high-backed dining chairs
around pine or dark wood tables on bare boards, a log fire, and stools
against the counter where they keep Downton New Forest Ale, Flack
Manor Double Drop and Sharps Doom Bar on handpump, several wines
by the glass (including fizz), malt whiskies and Thatcher's rosé cider. The
restaurant is similarly furnished and there's another log fire; background
music and board games. There are picnic-sets out in front, and tables and
chairs on the back terrace. Bedrooms overlook the cricket pitch.

As well as daily specials, the bar food now includes panini and summer
sandwiches, deep-fried brie with redcurrant jelly, whitebait, ham and egg,
beer-battered cod and chips, chicken fajitas with guacamole, sour cream, salsa
and cheese, burger with stilton or cheddar, steak in ale pie, pasta in tomato sauce,
honey-baked salmon with lemon dressing, and puddings. *Benchmark main dish:*
pork medallions in creamy garlic sauce £10.95. Two-course evening meal £16.00.

Free house ~ Licensee Fay Wood ~ Real ale ~ (01794) 340225 ~ Open 12-3, 5-11; 12-11
(10 Sun) Sat; closed winter Mon (phone to check) ~ Bar food 12-2.30, 6-9; 12-4 Sun ~
Restaurant ~ Children welcome ~ Dogs welcome ~ Bedrooms: £50/£70 ~
www.thestarinn.co *Recommended by Dr and Mrs J D Abell, R Elliott*

EASTON

SU5132 Map 2

Chestnut Horse 🍴 ♀

3.6 miles from M3 junction 9: A33 towards Kings Worthy, then B3047
towards Itchen Abbas; Easton then signposted on right – bear left in village; SO21 1EG

Cosy dining pub with log fires, fresh flowers and candles, deservedly
popular food and friendly staff; Itchen Valley walks nearby

On Fridays and weekends, this smart 16th-c dining pub is open
all day, which is very useful for walkers from the nearby Itchen
Valley. The interior, although open-plan, has a pleasantly rustic and
intimate feel with a series of cosily separate areas and the snug décor
including candles and fresh flowers, log fires in cottagey fireplaces and
comfortable furnishings. The black beams and joists are hung with all
sorts of jugs, mugs and chamber-pots, and there are lots of attractive
pictures of wildlife and the local area. Badger K&B and Hopping Hare on
handpump, several wines by the glass and 30 malt whiskies; the landlady
and her staff are friendly and efficient. There are seats and tables on a
sheltered decked area with colourful flower tubs and baskets, and picnic-
sets in front. This is a pretty village of thatched cottages.

Good food using local produce includes sandwiches, confit duck terrine with
figs and griottine cherry dressing, seared pigeon breast with baked apple,
black pudding and port glaze, gnocchi with wild mushroom, artichoke and roasted
pepper sauté with watercress cream sauce, thai green chicken curry, slow-cooked
pork belly and seared scallops with pear and lychee purée and candied chilli
and ginger, bass fillet with kale and caper cream sauce, braised beef cheeks with

celeriac dauphinoise and veal jus, and puddings such as lemon and ginger sponge with custard and chocolate tart; there's also a two-course set menu (Monday-Saturday lunchtimes, Monday-Friday 6-7.30pm). *Benchmark main dish: beer-battered fresh cod fillet with minted pea purée and home-made tartare sauce £13.00. Two-course evening meal £20.00.*

Badger ~ Tenant Karen Wells ~ Real ale ~ (01962) 779257 ~ Open 12-3.30, 5.30-11; 12-11.30 Fri, Sat; 12-10.30 Sun ~ Bar food 12-2.30, 6(6.30 Sat)-9.30; 12-8 Sun ~ Restaurant ~ Children welcome ~ Dogs allowed in bar ~ www.thechestnuthorse.com
Recommended by Helen and Brian Edgeley, David and Sheila Pearcey, Anita McCullough, Michael Butler, Ann and Colin Hunt

EVERSLEY
SU7861   Map 2
Golden Pot
B3272; RG27 0NB

Bustling and friendly village pub with comfortable interlinked rooms, woodburning stoves, beers from smaller breweries, good food and seats outside

An inviting-looking little brick pub with tables and chairs at the front under colourful hanging baskets, more seats among flowering tubs at the back and a view over fields. Inside, the different spreading areas have a comfortable feel, with sofas and cushioned settles, mate's and farmhouse kitchen chairs around wooden tables on carpeting, brass implements, sizeable mirrors, fresh flowers and a two-sided woodburning stove. High chairs line the counter, where three quickly changing real ales on handpump come only from small local breweries such as Andwell, Bowman, Loddon, Rebellion and Windsor & Eton, and several wines by the glass; dog treats behind the bar. Monday evenings are fun with live music and a rösti menu.

As well as lunchtime baguettes (not Sunday), the enjoyable food includes seared scallops and tiger prawns with pea purée, crispy bacon and black pudding, terrine of the day, pumpkin and mascarpone cannelloni, smoked haddock kedgeree, calves liver, lambs kidney, bacon and gravy, venison and smoked bacon meatballs with parsnip mash and red onion gravy, roasted rack of lamb, and puddings such as chocolate assiette and walnut and date pudding with toffee sauce and custard. *Benchmark main dish: fillet of bass with tiger prawns, pak choi and asian noodle broth £16.75. Two-course evening meal £19.50.*

Free house ~ Licensee John Calder ~ Real ale ~ (0118) 973 2104 ~ Open 11.30-2.30, 5.30-10(11 Sat); 12-3.30 Sun; closed Sun evening ~ Bar food 12-2, 6-9; 12-3 Sun ~ Restaurant ~ Children welcome ~ Dogs allowed in bar ~ Live music Mon ~ www.golden-pot.co.uk *Recommended by Joan and Tony Walker, KC, Paul and Marion Watts*

FRITHAM
SU2314   Map 2
Royal Oak
Village signed from M27 J1; SO43 7HJ

Rural New Forest spot and part of a working farm; traditional rooms, log fires, seven real ales and simple lunchtime food

At weekends especially, this charming brick and cob thatched pub is packed with locals, walkers, cyclists, families and dogs. It's right in the middle of the New Forest and part of a working farm, so there are ponies and pigs on the green and plenty of livestock nearby. Three neatly kept straightforward black-beamed rooms are full of proper traditional character, with prints and pictures depicting local characters on the white walls, restored panelling, antique wheelback, spindleback and other old chairs and stools with colourful seats around solid tables on oak floors, and two roaring log fires. The chatty locals and hard-working staff are genuinely friendly. The back bar has several books; darts and board games. Up to seven real ales are tapped from the cask, including one named for the pub from Bowman, Flack Manor Double Drop, Keystone Large One, Ringwood Fortyniner, Sunny Republic Beach Blonde and Titanic Plum Porter. Also, ten wines by the glass, 14 country wines, local apple juice, a beer festival in September and mulled wine in winter. Summer barbecues may be held in the neatly kept big garden, which has a marquee and a pétanque pitch.

🍴 Good value, limited food at lunchtime only consists of wholesome soup, a particularly good pork pie, ploughman's, quiche and sausages. *Benchmark main dish: gammon and cheese ploughman's £7.50.*

Free house ~ Licensees Neil and Pauline McCulloch ~ Real ale ~ No credit cards ~ (023) 8081 2606 ~ Open 11-11; 12-10.30 Sun; 11-3, 5.30-11 weekdays in winter ~ Bar food 12-2.30(3 weekends) ~ Children welcome ~ Dogs welcome
Recommended by John and Annabel Hampshire, David and Judy Robison, Henry Paulinski, N R White, Nick Lawless

HOOK
SU7153   Map 2

Hogget 🍺
1.1 miles from M3 junction 5; A287 N, at junction with A30 (car park just before traffic lights); RG27 9JJ

Well run and accommodating, a proper pub moving with the times and giving good value

Usefully open all day at weekends and also serving food then (until 6pm on Sundays), this is a well run pub with plenty of cheerful customers. Rooms ramble round the central server and there's plenty of space for all; the lighting, wallpaper and carpet pattern, as well as the leather sofas and tub chairs at the back, give a friendly and homely feel – as do the several distinct smallish areas. Ringwood Best, Wychwood Hobgoblin and a guest beer on handpump, decent wines by three glass sizes, and plenty of staff in neat but informal black uniforms; daily papers, background music and wine bottles on shelves. A sizeable terrace has sturdy tables and chairs, with some in a heated covered area.

🍴 Enjoyable food includes nibbles (home-toasted nuts, pork scratchings) as well as pork belly with seared scallops and butternut purée, crispy duck salad with spring onions, toasted sesame seeds and hoisin vinaigrette, meze boards, ham and free-range eggs, wild mushroom tagliatelle, local sausages, colcannon mash and onion gravy, beer-battered hake and chips, braised ox cheek with spring onion mash and pickled baby carrots, and puddings. *Benchmark main dish: gourmet burger with triple-cooked chips, spiced mayonnaise and cheese or bacon toppings £11.00. Two-course evening meal £18.00.*

Marstons ~ Lease Tom Faulkner ~ Real ale ~ (01256) 763009 ~ Open 12-3, 5.30-11; 12-11(10.30 Sun) Sat ~ Bar food 12-2.30, 6.30-9; all day Sat; 12-6 Sun ~ Children welcome but not after 7pm Fri or Sat ~ Dogs allowed in bar ~ www.hogget.co.uk
Recommended by Mike and Jayne Bastin, Mark and Lia Chance, Simon Collett-Jones

---

If you're planning a long journey, it might help you to look at the list of pubs near motorway junctions at the end of the book.

HORDLE
SZ2996 Map 2

Mill at Gordleton 🍽 ♟ 🛏

Silver Street; SO41 6DJ

Charming tucked-away country inn with friendly bar, exceptional food and drink and delightful waterside gardens; comfortable bedrooms

On the edge of the New Forest, this very friendly and informal little hotel is run with love and care by its green-minded owners. The small main panelled bar on the right has casually dressed regulars (perhaps with their dogs), helpful staff, well kept Ringwood Best and a guest like Oakleaf Quercus Folium on handpump, good wines by the glass, a rack of daily papers, leather armchairs and Victorian-style mahogany dining chairs on the parquet floor, a little feature stove and a pretty corner china cupboard. This overflows into a cosy lounge, and there's a roomy second bar by the sizeable restaurant extension – an attractive beamed room with contemporary art and garden outlook. Bedrooms are comfortable and individual, with excellent breakfasts. The gardens are very special: an extensive series of interestingly planted areas looping about pools and a placid winding stream, dotted with intriguing art objects and with plenty of places to sit, from intimate pairs of seats to nicely lit teak or wrought-iron tables of the main waterside terrace. Plenty of walks nearby, and they also offer tours to local breweries.

🍽 Growing their own vegetables, keeping bees, using the best local producers and making absolutely everything in-house, the accomplished food includes ham hock and duck liver terrine with truffle mayonnaise and brioche soldiers, trio of smoked fish on lemon blini with chive crème fraîche and avruga caviar, butternut squash filled with spinach, goats cheese and red onion confit with spiced vegetable couscous, crab-crusted cod with braised fennel and shellfish bisque sauce, guinea fowl breast en croûte with mushrooms, red wine jus and duchesse potatoes, and puddings such as iced banana parfait with caramelised bananas and peanut butter ice-cream and Grand Marnier crêpe soufflé with orange syrup and vanilla seed ice-cream; they also offer a two- and three-course set lunch (very good value given the quality). *Benchmark main dish: home-cooked ham, egg and chips £10.95. Two-course evening meal £28.00.*

Free house ~ Licensee Liz Cottingham ~ Real ale ~ (01590) 682219 ~ Open 11-11; 12-10.30 Sun ~ Bar food 12-2, 7-9; 12-3, 6.15-8.15 Sun ~ Restaurant ~ Children welcome ~ Dogs allowed in bar ~ Bedrooms: £125/£150 ~ www.themillatgordleton.co.uk
Recommended by Richard and Penny Gibbs, Leslie and Barbara Owen, N R White

LISS
SU7826 Map 2

Jolly Drover 🛏

London Road, Hill Brow; B2070 S of town, near B3006 junction; GU33 7QL

Friendly, comfortable pub with plenty of locals and visitors, real ales, popular food and seats outside; good bedrooms

This well run traditional pub is deservedly busy, with cheerful customers keen to enjoy the real ales and generously served food. The hands-on landlord and his staff are friendly and helpful. The neatly carpeted low-beamed bar has leather tub chairs and a couple of sofas in front of an inglenook log fire, daily papers and board games, plus Fullers London Pride, Sharps Doom Bar and Timothy Taylors Landlord on handpump and ten wines by the glass. The several areas, with a gentle décor mainly in muted terracotta or pale ochre, include two back dining sections, one of which opens on to a sheltered terrace with teak furniture, and a lawn with picnic-sets beyond. The neat bedrooms are in a barn conversion.

🍴 Good traditional food includes baps and sandwiches, deep-fried whitebait, prawn cocktail, steak and kidney in ale pie, lasagne, sausages with onion gravy and mash, chicken in bacon and stilton sauce, roast of the day and puddings like treacle tart and fruit crumble; you can buy their jams and chutneys to take home. *Benchmark main dish: home-made pies £11.75. Two-course evening meal £18.00.*

Enterprise ~ Lease Barry and Anne Coe ~ Real ale ~ (01730) 893137 ~ Open 10.30-3, 5.30-11; 12-4 Sun; closed Sun evening ~ Bar food 12-2.15, 7-9.30; 12-2.30 Sun ~ Restaurant ~ Children welcome ~ Bedrooms: £70/£80 ~ www.thejollydrover.co.uk
Recommended by Tony and Wendy Hobden

 LONGPARISH SU4244 Map 2
Plough 🍴 ♀
B3048, off A303 just E of Andover; SP11 6PB

Bustling, upmarket dining pub with friendly staff, real ales, attractive bars, popular food and seats in garden

The Test Way passes through the car park here – and it's handy for the A303 – which makes this handsome brick inn the perfect place for a drink or meal. The various rooms, kept spic and span, have flagstones and oak flooring, elegant high-backed wooden dining chairs and pews around a mix of tables, some beams and standing timbers, contemporary paintwork and open fireplaces, one with a woodburning stove. The cosy snug has black leather bar chairs against the counter where they serve Ringwood Best, Sharps Doom Bar and Timothy Taylors Landlord on handpump and three ciders, and there's also a walk-in wine cellar (and several wines by the glass); background music.

🍴 Cooked by the landlord, the highly accomplished food ranges from sandwiches with home-made bread through nibbles like sausages with HP sauce and pubby choices such as cumberland sausage and mash, steak in ale pie with triple-cooked chips or angus burger with mature cheddar and onion relish to braised pork belly with rhubarb purée, black pudding croquettes and potato and egg hash, coq au vin free-range chicken leg with smoked bacon and baby onions and tarragon emulsion, fried bream with red pepper piperade, linguine, black olive purée and caper vinaigrette, and puddings. *Benchmark main dish: beer-battered haddock with mushy peas and triple-cooked chips £12.50. Two-course evening meal £23.00.*

Enterprise ~ Lease James Durrant ~ Real ale ~ (01264) 720358 ~ Open 12-11; 12-6 Sun; closed Sun evening ~ Bar food 12-2.30, 6-9.30; 12-4.30 Sun ~ Children welcome ~ Dogs allowed in bar ~ www.theploughinn.info *Recommended by Edward Mirzoeff, Dr and Mrs J D Abell, Phyl and Jack Street, Ann and Colin Hunt*

 LONGSTOCK SU3537 Map 2
Peat Spade 🍴 ♀
Off A30 on W edge of Stockbridge; SO20 6DR

Former coaching inn with boldly painted rooms, shooting and fishing themed décor, imaginative food and real ales; stylish bedrooms

Fishermen from far and wide come to this attractive, well run pub to try their luck in the River Test – famous for its fly fishing – which is just 100 metres away. And tired walkers on the Test Way are only too happy to rest with a pint and some food. This wide mix of customers helps create a cheerful, bustling atmosphere, and the hard-working landlady and her diligent young staff offer a warm welcome to all. The bars have a sporting feel with stuffed fish, lots of hunting pictures and prints on dark red or green walls and even a little fishing shop at the end of the garden (they can arrange fishing and shooting). Both the bar and dining room have pretty windows, an interesting mix of dining chairs around miscellaneous tables on bare boards, standard-lamps and candlelight, wine bottles, old stone bottles and soda siphons, a nice show of toby jugs and shelves of books. There's also an upstairs room with comfortable sofas and armchairs. Flowerpots Bitter, Marstons Double Drop and Ringwood Best on handpump and several wines by the glass; background music. The terrace and garden have plenty of seats, and the contemporary bedrooms are stylish and comfortable.

Tempting food includes sandwiches, crab mayonnaise, brown crab pâté, toasted chilli bread and avocado, cured venison with beetroot and orange chutney, tomato-stuffed red pepper with tomato coulis and goats cheese, steak in ale pie, hake fillet with scallops, parsley and tomato risotto and pepper oil, pigeon ballotine with crispy black cabbage, beetroot, capers and jus, whole plaice with brown butter and skinny chips, pork loin with black pudding, yellow carrots and haricot and chorizo cassoulet, and puddings. *Benchmark main dish: beer-battered haddock and triple-cooked chips £13.00. Two-course evening meal £19.50.*

Free house ~ Licensee Tracy Levett ~ Real ale ~ (01264) 810612 ~ Open 11-11; 12-4, 7-9 Sun ~ Bar food 12-2.30, 6.30-9.30; 12-4, 7-9 Sun ~ Well behaved children welcome ~ Dogs allowed in bar and bedrooms ~ Bedrooms: /£95 ~ www.peatspadeinn.co.uk
Recommended by Phyl and Jack Street, Graham and Toni Sanders

LOWER FROYLE
SU7643   Map 2

Anchor 🍽 🍷 🛏

Village signposted N of A31 W of Bentley; GU34 4NA

Civilised pub with lots to look at, real ales, good wines and imaginative bar food; comfortable bedrooms

Readers enjoy visiting this civilised yet informal old place, and it's a comfortable and stylish place to stay too, with first class breakfasts. The various rooms have a good, bustling atmosphere, blazing fires, candlelight, low beams and standing timbers, flagstones in the bar and stripped wood floors elsewhere, sofas and armchairs dotted about and a mix of nice old tables and dining chairs. Throughout are all sorts of interesting knick-knacks, books, lots of copper, horsebrasses, photographs (several of Charterhouse School) and all manner of pictures and prints; paint colours are fashionable, values are traditional, and at the counter, where there are high bar chairs, they keep Andwells Gold Muddler and Triple fff Altons Pride and Hallelujah on handpump, 11 wines by the glass (including fizz) and interesting pressés.

Imaginative and very popular, food includes sandwiches, guinea fowl, chicken and wild mushroom terrine with medjool date and thyme purée, roasted squid and chorizo with shaved fennel, capers and baked lemon dressing, pork faggots with buttery mash and red cabbage, liver and bacon with red onion marmalade, bass fillets with roasted gnocchi, spinach and wild mushroom ragout, venison four-ways with creamed sprouts, pancetta and parsnip purée, 28-day dry-aged steak with triple-cooked chips and watercress and pepper sauce, and puddings. *Benchmark main dish: pie of the day £13.00. Two-course evening meal £21.00.*

Free house ~ Licensee Tracy Levett ~ Real ale ~ (01420) 23261 ~ Open 11-11(10.30 Sun) ~ Bar food 12-2.30, 6.30-9.30; 12-4, 7-9 Sun ~ Restaurant ~ Children welcome ~

Dogs allowed in bar ~ Bedrooms: /$120 ~ www.anchorinnatlowerfroyle.co.uk
Recommended by John Branston, Martin and Karen Wake, Neil Hardwick, Tony and Jill Radnor

LOWER WIELD — SU6339 Map 2

Yew Tree 🍴 ⧖ £

Turn off A339 NW of Alton at 'Medstead, Bentworth 1' signpost, then follow village signposts; or off B3046 S of Basingstoke, signposted from Preston Candover; SO24 9RX

Bustling country pub with a hard-working, hands-on landlord, relaxed atmosphere and super choice of wines and food; sizeable garden and nearby walks

Unfailingly good service from the enthusiastic, charming landlord and his helpful staff, fair prices for the interesting ales and top quality food and an easy-going, friendly atmosphere – all contribute to our readers' enjoyment of this smashing little pub. A small flagstoned bar area on the left has pictures above a stripped-brick dado, a ticking clock and a log fire. Around to the right of the serving counter (with a couple of stylish wrought-iron bar chairs) it's carpeted; throughout there's a mix of tables, including quite small ones for two, and miscellaneous chairs. Twelve wines by the glass from a well chosen list (which may include summer rosé and Louis Jadot burgundies from a shipper based just along the lane), a changing ale from Cheriton and a beer from Triple fff named for the pub on handpump – and extremely reasonably priced for the area). There are solid tables and chunky seats on the front terrace, picnic-sets in a sizeable side garden, pleasant views and a cricket field across the quiet lane; nearby walks.

Interesting and extremely popular, food might include sandwiches, smoked haddock, spring onion and mozzarella fishcake with citrus tartare sauce, creamy garlic and blue cheese mushrooms on toasted ciabatta, mediterranean roasted vegetable tart with sun-dried tomatoes and mozzarella, local sausages with parsley mash and onion gravy, beef, smoked bacon, mushroom and thyme casserole with fried new potatoes, chinese ginger chicken breast with noodles and hoisin sauce, half a shoulder of lamb with rosemary and red wine jus and dauphinoise potatoes, and puddings like chocolate and orange truffle cake and rhubarb, apple and cherry crumble. *Benchmark main dish: pork belly with mustard, stilton and apricot cream sauce £11.95. Two-course evening meal £16.75.*

Free house ~ Licensee Tim Gray ~ Real ale ~ (01256) 389224 ~ Open 11-3, 6-11; 12-10.30 Sun; closed Mon, and first two weeks Jan ~ Bar food 12-2, 6.30-9(8.30 Sun) ~ Restaurant ~ Children welcome ~ Dogs allowed in bar ~ www.the-yewtree.org.uk
Recommended by David and Sheila Pearcey, Alan and Liz Haffenden, Phyl and Jack Street, Liz and Brian Barnard, Henry Paulinski, Ann and Colin Hunt, John Oates, Tony and Jill Radnor, R Elliott, Teddy O'Connor, Nick Duncan, Andrew Baker, N R White

LYMINGTON — SZ3295 Map 2

Angel & Blue Pig 🛏

High Street; SO41 9AP

Bustling and friendly inn with plenty of space in several connected rooms, four real ales, enjoyable food and helpful staff; bedrooms

Refurbished and reopened as we went to press, this busy place has several different seating areas radiating from the central bar – each with its own character. To the right of the door, the cosy front room has comfortable sofas and armchairs around a big chest, rugs on bare boards and an open fire; this leads into a pubby, flagstoned part with high tables and chairs and built-in leather wall seats. The two interconnected dining rooms to the left of the door – one carpeted, one with rugs on quarry tiles – have beams and timbers, dining chairs with zigzag backs and grey cushions around a variety of tables, an old range in a brick fireplace, a large boar's head, lots of books on shelves and a bookshelf mural; throughout are lots of hunting prints and porcine bits and pieces. At the back, overlooking the terrace with seats and tables under blue parasols, is yet another area, with some nice old leather armchairs beside a woodburning stove and the serving counter where they keep Ringwood Best, a beer named for them from Ringwood, Wychwood Hobgoblin and a changing guest on handpump and a good choice of wines, spirits and coffees; service is friendly and helpful. The stylish, modern bedrooms are comfortable and well equipped, and breakfasts are good.

Enjoyable food includes sandwiches, mussels in creamy shallot and white wine sauce, marinated duck skewers with cucumber and yoghurt, steak burger with onion, tomato, gherkin and special sauce, ham and free-range eggs, salmon and smoked salmon fishcakes with leeks, poached egg and hollandaise, vegetable tagine with butternut squash, parsnip and chickpeas, lemon and thyme chicken with potato and carrot rösti, bass fillet with parmentier potatoes, lardons, olives, spinach and a lemon butter sauce, 28-day dry-aged black angus charcoal steaks, and puddings. *Benchmark main dish: roasted half chicken with home-made coleslaw and chips £11.95. Two-course evening meal £18.00.*

Free house ~ Licensee Andrew Taylor ~ Real ale ~ (01590) 672050 ~ Open 8.30am-11.30pm(midnight Fri, Sat, 11 Sun) ~ Bar food 8.30am-10pm(9.30pm Sun) ~ Restaurant ~ Children welcome ~ Dogs allowed in bar ~ Bedrooms: £70/£95 ~ www.angel-lymington.com *Recommended by Ruth May, Harvey Brown*

NORTH WALTHAM   SU5645   Map 2
Fox 🍴 £

3 miles from M3 junction 7: A30 southwards, then turn right at second North Waltham turn, just after Wheatsheaf; pub also signed from village centre; RG25 2BE

Traditional flint country pub, very well run, with good food and drink, and nice garden

In a quiet country lane overlooking farmland, yet handy for the M3 and A30, this is a proper pub liked by both drinkers and diners. The low-ceilinged bar on the left has a chatty, relaxed atmosphere, Brakspears Bitter, Sharps Doom Bar, West Berkshire Good Old Boy and a guest beer on handpump, and lots of bottled ciders as well as Aspall's cider on draught; 14 wines by the glass, 22 malt whiskies and quite a collection of miniatures. The big woodburning stove, parquet floor, simple padded country kitchen chairs, poultry and 'Beer is Best' prints above the dark dado – all give a comfortably old-fashioned feel, in which perhaps the vital ingredient is the polite, friendly efficiency of the hands-on landlord; maybe faint background music. The separate dining room, with high-backed leather chairs on a blue tartan carpet, is larger. The garden, colourful in summer with its pergola walkway from the gate on the lane and with immaculate flower boxes and baskets, has picnic-sets under cocktail parasols in three separate areas. Walks include a pleasant one to Jane Austen's church at Steventon.

Good, tasty home-made food includes sandwiches, duck cake with mango and coriander salsa, deep-fried camembert with redcurrant jelly, pork sausages and mash with onion gravy, omelette and chips, mediterranean vegetable stack topped with melted brie on rösti, rack of barbecue ribs with triple-cooked chips, steak and venison pie, chicken breast topped with tomato sauce and melted cheese, pork tenderloin in brandy, wholegrain mustard and cream sauce, daily specials and puddings such as passion-fruit cheesecake and Malteser parfait. *Benchmark main dish: local vension with glazed shallots, field mushrooms and spinach with port glaze £16.00. Two-course evening meal £21.25.*

Free house ~ Licensees Rob and Izzy MacKenzie ~ Real ale ~ (01256) 397288 ~ Open 11-11(midnight Sat, 10.30 Sun) ~ Bar food 12-3, 6.30-9 ~ Restaurant ~ Children welcome ~ Dogs allowed in bar ~ www.thefox.org *Recommended by Jennifer Banks, Phyl and Jack Street, David Jackman*

NORTH WARNBOROUGH   SU7352   Map 2
Mill House 🍴 ♟ 🍺

A mile from M3 junction 5: A287 towards Farnham, then right (brown sign to pub) on to B3349 Hook Road; RG29 1ET

Converted mill with an attractive layout, inventive modern food, good choice of drinks and lovely waterside terraces

The extensive garden behind this raftered mill building makes a lovely break from the M3. There are lots of solid tables and chairs on terraces, even more picnic-sets on grass and attractive landscaping around the sizeable millpond; a couple of swings too. Inside, several linked areas on the main upper floor have heavy beams, plenty of well spaced tables in a variety of sizes and styles, rugs on polished boards or beige carpet, coal-effect gas fires in pretty fireplaces and a profusion of interesting pictures. A section of glass floor shows the rushing water and mill wheel below, and a galleried part on the left looks down into a dining room, given a more formal feel by panelling. The well stocked bar has an interesting changing range of malt whiskies and a good choice of wines, as well as Phoenix Brunning & Price Original, Flack Manor Double Drop, Hogs Back TEA, Three Castles Try Me and Upham Punter on handpump; the young staff are cheerful and effective, and the atmosphere relaxed and comfortable.

🍴 Tempting, highly popular food includes sandwiches, pink peppercorn and goats cheese panna cotta with pickled vegetables and parmesan crisp, charcuterie plate for two, tandoori grilled halloumi with toasted coconut, pineapple, lime and mint salad, burger with grilled bacon, cheese, coleslaw and chips, smoked haddock and salmon fishcakes, steak and kidney pie, duck breast with cabbage, bacon and a juniper and port sauce, trio of pork with black pudding croquette, red cabbage and crackling, and puddings such as iced chocolate parfait with raspberry coulis and lemon baked cheesecake with lemon curd cream. *Benchmark main dish: beer-battered haddock with mushy peas and tartare sauce £12.25. Two-course evening meal £19.50.*

Brunning & Price ~ Lease Philippa Powell ~ Real ale ~ (01256) 702953 ~ Open 11.30-11(10.30 Sun) ~ Bar food 12-10(9.30 Sun) ~ Restaurant ~ Children welcome ~ Dogs allowed in bar ~ www.millhouse-hook.co.uk *Recommended by Richard and Penny Gibbs, David Jackman, Edward Mirzoeff, Ian Herdman, Brian Glozier, M G Hart*

PETERSFIELD   SU7227   Map 2
Trooper 🍴 🍺 🛏

From A32 (look for staggered crossroads) take turning to Froxfield and Steep; pub 3 miles down on left in big dip; GU32 1BD

Charming landlord, popular food, decent drinks, and persian knick-knacks and local artists' work; comfortable bedrooms

This is a comfortable place to stay in neatly kept bedrooms with Hampshire down views and highly rated breakfasts. The bar has all sorts of cushioned dining chairs around dark wooden tables, old film-star photos, paintings by local artists (for sale), little persian knick-knacks here and there, several ogival mirrors, lit candles, fresh flowers and a log fire in a stone fireplace; a sun room has more lovely downland views, carefully chosen background music and newspapers and magazines to read. Bowman Swift One, Ringwood Best and a guest beer on handpump and several wines by the glass or carafe. The attractive raftered restaurant has french windows to a paved terrace with views across the open countryside, and there are lots of picnic-sets on an upper lawn. The horse rail in the car park is reserved 'for horses, camels and local livestock'. The inn backs on to Ashford Hangers nature reserve.

There are nibbles like calamari and whitebait, as well as a two- and three-course set menu (not Friday or Saturday evenings), plus sandwiches, mussels poached in coconut milk, lemon grass, shallot, chilli and coriander, free-range chicken breast skewers with spicy yoghurt dip, chilli con carne in taco shells with sour cream and peppers, red peppers stuffed with pine nuts and capers on lemon and saffron risotto, grilled fillet of bass with almond and raisin rice, carrot and onion seed salad and saffron sauce, and puddings. *Benchmark main dish: slow-roasted lamb shoulder in honey and mint £16.50. Two-course evening meal £21.00.*

Free house ~ Licensee Hassan Matini ~ Real ale ~ (01730) 827293 ~ Open 12-3, 6-11; 12-4 Sun; closed Sun evening, Mon lunchtime ~ Bar food 12-3, 6-9.30; 12-3.30 Sun ~ Restaurant ~ Children welcome ~ Dogs allowed in bar · Bedrooms. £69/£89 ~ www.trooperinn.com *Recommended by Martin and Karen Wake, Doug Kennedy*

PETERSFIELD

SU7129   Map 2

White Horse

Up on an old downs road about halfway between Steep and East Tisted, near Priors Dean – OS Sheet 186 or 197 map reference 715290; GU32 1DA

Unchanging and much loved old place with a great deal of simple character, friendly licensees and up to ten real ales

There's a reason this place is known as the Pub With No Name – keep your eyes skinned or you'll miss it. Nothing really changes here, which is just how the loyal customers would have it. The two parlour rooms remain charming and idiosyncratic, with open fires, oak settles, a mix of dark wooden dining chairs, nice old tables (including drop-leaf ones), various pictures, farm tools, rugs, a longcase clock, a couple of fireside rocking chairs and so forth. The beamed dining room is smarter, with lots more pictures on white or pink walls. A fine choice of up to ten ales includes two named for the pub, plus Butcombe Bitter, Fullers London Pride, Ringwood Best and Fortyniner and four quickly changing guests on handpump; lots of country wines. They hold a beer festival in June and a cider festival in September. There are rustic seats outside and camping facilities.

Using free-range local meat and eggs, food includes sandwiches, ploughman's, black pudding, pheasant and crispy bacon salad, home-cooked honey-glazed ham and egg, chestnut, cashew and ricotta tart on garlic and tomato sauce, burger with cheese, bacon and chips, lots of different sausages with caremlised onions, parsnip crisps and rich gravy, steak in ale or smoked fish pie, pork faggots braised in cider, duck breast with red cabbage and port, and puddings like dark chocolate terrine with white chocolate sauce and raspberry coulis and fruit crumble.

Benchmark main dish: steak pie with colcannon potatoes £11.95. Two-course evening meal £17.00.

Gales (Fullers) ~ Managers Georgie and Paul Stuart ~ Real ale ~ (01420) 588387 ~ Open 12-11.30 ~ Bar food 12-2.30, 6-9.30; all day weekends ~ Restaurant ~ Children welcome ~ Dogs allowed in bar ~ www.pubwithnoname.co.uk *Recommended by Ann and Colin Hunt, Geoff and Linda Payne*

 PORTSMOUTH   SZ6399   Map 2

Old Customs House 🍴 £

Vernon Buildings, Gunwharf Quays; follow brown signs to Gunwharf Quays car park; PO1 3TY

Handsome and well converted historic building in a prime waterfront development, with real ales and popular bar food

Helpfully open all day, this handsome brick building – once an 18th-c customs house – is very spacious, so even at peak times you can find somewhere to sit. Several big-windowed high-ceilinged rooms have bare boards, nautical prints and photographs on pastel walls, coal-effect gas fires, nice unobtrusive lighting and well padded chairs around sturdy tables in varying sizes; the sunny entrance area has leather sofas. Broad stairs lead up to a carpeted restaurant with similar décor. Fullers Discovery, ESB, HSB, London Pride and Seafarers and a changing guest on handpump, a decent range of wines by the glass and good coffees and teas. Staff are efficient, the background music well reproduced and the games machines silenced. Picnic-sets out in front are just yards from the water; the bar has disabled access and facilities. The pub is part of an extensive modern waterside shopping complex and just around the corner is the graceful Spinnaker Tower (165 metres tall with staggering views from its observation decks).

 All-day food includes breakfasts until midday, sandwiches, smoked salmon with horseradish and chive crème fraîche, chicken livers in madeira on toasted brioche, moules frites, sausages and mash with crispy onions and gravy, steak in ale pie, slow-roast pork belly with potato gratin and sticky red cabbage, salmon on crushed potatoes with herb butter, and puddings such as marmalade bread and butter pudding and double chocolate brownie. *Benchmark main dish: beer-battered cod or haddock with mushy peas and chips £8.95. Two-course evening meal £15.00.*

Fullers ~ Manager David Hughes ~ Real ale ~ (023) 9283 2333 ~ Open 9am-midnight (1.30am Sat, 11 Sun) ~ Bar food all day from 9am ~ Children allowed until 7.30pm ~ www.theoldcustomshouse.com *Recommended by John and Alison Hamilton, Peter Meister, Paul Rampton, Julie Harding*

PRESTON CANDOVER   SU6041   Map 2

Purefoy Arms 🍴 ♟

B3046 Basingstoke–Alresford; RG25 2EJ

Hampshire Dining Pub of the Year

First class food and wines in gently upmarket village pub

As both the landlady and landlord are passionate about food and wine, this smart and civilised dining pub has many loyal customers. Every Tuesday they hold a Wine Club evening, when for just £5 corkage diners can bring a special wine of their own to talk about with other interested customers. Two pairs of linked rooms have an easy-going, country pub feel. On the left, the airy front bar has chunky tables (including tall ones with bar stools) and a corner counter serving a fine changing choice of wines, as well as Andwell Spring Twist and Flack Manor Double Drop on handpump; this opens into a jute-floored back area with four dining tables and characterful mixed seats including old settles. The right-hand front room has red leather sofas and armchairs by a log fire, and leads back to a bare-boards area with some sturdy pale pine tables. The understated contemporary décor in grey and puce goes nicely with the informal friendliness of the service; maybe unobtrusive background music. Don't leave the pub empty-handed – the landlord's father makes delicious chocolates and truffles, and there are usually chutneys, ketchup and oils for sale too. The sizeable sloping garden has well spaced picnic-sets, a wendy house and sometimes a big hammock slung between trees; there are teak tables on a terrace sheltered by the pub. This is an attractive village, with nearby snowdrop walks in season.

Excellent, accomplished dishes cooked by the landlord include appetisers such as salt-cod scotch egg, grilled chorizo ibérico or manchego and membrillo, as well as ballotine of quail and foie gras with madeira jelly and spiced salt, seared hand-dived scallops with marsala sauce, spiced apples and baby spinach, gnocchi with roast pumpkin, mushrooms and aged pecorino, smoked haddock with colcannon potatoes and poached egg hollandaise, cider-cooked ham with duck eggs, ray wing with sea kale, brown shrimps and black butter, sage-marinated pork fillet with creamed spinach, apple rösti, wild mushrooms and cider sauce, and puddings like blackberry bakewell tart with spiced ice-cream and chocolate mousse with griottine cherries and salted caramel cookies; there's also a two- and three-course set lunch. *Benchmark main dish: rib of beef, dripping chips and roast marrow (for two) £49.00. Two-course evening meal £22.00.*

Free house ~ Licensees Andres and Marie-Louise Alemany ~ Real ale ~ (01256) 389777 ~ Open 12-3, 6-11; 12-4 Sun; closed Sun evening, Mon ~ Bar food 12-3, 6-10 ~ Well behaved children welcome until 7.30pm ~ Dogs allowed in bar ~ www.thepurefoyarms.co.uk
Recommended by Phyl and Jack Street

ROCKBOURNE   SU1118   Map 2

Rose & Thistle 🍴 ⚓

Signed off B3078 Fordingbridge–Cranborne; SP6 3NL

Pretty pub with hands-on landlady and friendly staff, informal bars, real ales, good food, and seats in garden

What stands out particularly here is the way the young landlady and her staff go out of their way to be helpful and friendly. Not surprisingly, the place is deservedly busy even on the most miserable of days; booking is essential to be sure of a table. It's all very warm and cosy – the bar has homely dining chairs, stools and benches around a mix of old pubby tables, Butcombe Best, Gold and Rare Breed and a guest such as Sharps Doom Bar on handpump, a dozen wines (and prosecco) by the glass and Black Rat and Weston's ciders; background music, dominoes and cards. The restaurant has a log fire in each of its two rooms (one in a big brick inglenook), old engravings and cricket prints, and an informal and relaxed atmosphere. There are benches and tables under pretty hanging baskets at the front, with picnic-sets under parasols on the grass; good nearby walks. This is a pretty village on the edge of the New Forest.

Good, tasty food using seasonal local produce includes sandwiches, rillette of pork with cucumber pickle, prawns in hot garlic butter, local sausages with wholegrain mustard mash and onion gravy, baked crêpes with spinach, mushrooms and gruyère, steak and kidney pudding, corn-fed chicken wrapped in bacon with sausage and leek stuffing on parsnip and rosemary purée, crispy confit pork belly with herb-crusted black pudding, apple sauce and crab apple gravy, and home-made puddings like spiced apple steamed syrup sponge and hot chocolate fondant. *Benchmark main dish: steak and kidney pudding £14.95. Two-course evening meal £20.00.*

Free house ~ Licensee Kerry Dutton ~ Real ale ~ (01725) 518236 ~ Open 11-3, 6-11; 11-11 Sat; 12-10.30(8 winter) Sun ~ Bar food 12-2.30, 7-9.30; not Sun evening ~ Restaurant ~ Children welcome ~ Dogs allowed in bar ~ www.roseandthistle.co.uk
Recommended by Ian Herdman, Richard and Sue Fewkes, David and Judy Robison, Mr and Mrs P R Thomas, Stewart Harvey

SPARSHOLT
SU4331 Map 2
Plough 🍽 🍷

Village signposted off B3049 (Winchester–Stockbridge), a little W of Winchester; SO21 2NW

Neat, well run dining pub with interesting furnishings, an extensive wine list and highly thought-of bar food; garden with children's play fort

'One of our favourite lunching places' and 'our pub of the year' are just two comments among many others from enthusiastic readers. This particularly well run country inn is always deservedly busy, so you must book a table in advance – and you can be sure of a genuine welcome from the courteous hands-on landlord and his staff. The main bar has an interesting mix of wooden tables and farmhouse or upholstered chairs, with farm tools, scythes and pitchforks attached to the ceiling; they keep Wadworths IPA, 6X, Bishops Tipple, Horizon and Swordfish on handpump and quite a few wines and champagne by the glass from an extensive list. The dining tables on the left look over fields and on to woodland. There are plenty of seats on the terrace and lawn, and a children's play fort; disabled access and facilities.

Reliably good and very popular, food includes sandwiches, warm pigeon salad with smoked bacon and mushrooms, salmon and crab fishcake with saffron and spinach, goats cheese, red onion and walnut tart with balsamic syrup and green beans, beer-battered fish and chips, chicken on rösti potatoes with wild mushrooms and shallot and tarragon cream, crab-crusted hake fillet with sweet potato gratin and hollandaise sauce, and puddings such as treacle tart with clotted cream and rhubarb and plum crumble. *Benchmark main dish: shoulder of lamb with mustard and mint jus and dauphinoise potatoes £16.95. Two-course evening meal £21.50.*

Wadworths ~ Tenant Richard Crawford ~ Real ale ~ (01962) 776353 ~ Open 11-3, 6-11; 11-11 Sun ~ Bar food 12-2, 6-9(9.30 Fri, Sat, 8.30 Sun, Mon) ~ Children welcome ~ Dogs welcome *Recommended by John and Annabel Hampshire, Tim Gray, John and Joan Calvert, Michael and Susanne Hart, Patrick and Daphne Darley, Peter and Andrea Jacobs*

STEEP
SU7525 Map 2
Harrow 🍽 £

Take Midhurst exit from Petersfield bypass, at exit roundabout take first left towards Midhurst, then first turning on left opposite garage, and left again at Sheet church; follow over dual carriageway bridge to pub; GU32 2DA

Unchanging, simple place with long-serving landladies, beers tapped from the cask, unfussy food and a big free-flowering garden; no children inside

Completely unpretentious and thankfully unchanging, this tiny little country gem of a pub is much loved by our readers – and by us too. It's been in the same family for 84 years and there's no pandering to modern methods – no credit cards, no waitress service, no restaurant, no music and rose-covered outside loos. Everything revolves around village chat and the friendly locals, who will probably draw you into light-hearted conversation. Adverts for logs sit next to calendars of local views (sold in support of local charities) and news of various quirky competitions. The little public bar has hops and dried flowers (replaced every year) hanging from the beams, built-in wall benches on the tiled floor, stripped-pine wallboards, a good log fire in a big inglenook, and wild flowers on the scrubbed deal tables; there might be bowls of seasonal walnuts and chestnuts, and dominoes. Bowman Swift One, Dark Star Hophead, Flack Manor Double Hop and Ringwood Best are tapped straight from casks behind the counter, and there's local wine and apple juice; staff are polite and friendly, even when under pressure. The big garden is left to flower freely, so that goldfinches can collect thistle seeds from the grass, but there are some seats on paved areas. The Petersfield bypass doesn't intrude on this idyll, though you will need to follow the directions above to find the pub. No children inside and dogs must be on leads.

🍴 Generously served home-made food includes own-made scotch eggs, sandwiches, hearty soup, ploughman's, quiches and puddings like treacle tart and seasonal fruit pie. *Benchmark main dish: split pea and ham soup £5.70.*

Free house ~ Licensees Claire and Denise McCutcheon ~ Real ale ~ No credit cards ~ (01730) 262685 ~ Open 12-2.30, 6-11; 11-3, 6-11 Sat; 12-3, 7-10.30 Sun; closed Sun evening in winter ~ Bar food 12-2, 7-9; not Sun evening ~ Dogs allowed in bar ~ www.harrow-inn.co.uk *Recommended by Greg Gregory, Tony and Jill Radnor, Philip and Susan Philcox, Ann and Colin Hunt, Jeremy Whitehorn*

🮲 SWANMORE   SU5815 Map 2

Rising Sun 🍷 🍺

Droxford Road; signed off A32 N of Wickham and B2177 S of Bishop's Waltham, at Hillpound E of village centre; SO32 2PS

Proper country pub with friendly staff, good beers and popular food

As the Kings Way long-distance path runs close to this friendly 17th-c coaching inn, it's a popular place with walkers. The low-beamed carpeted bar has easy chairs and a sofa by a good log fire and a few tables with pubby seats. Beyond the fireplace on the right is a pleasant, much roomier dining area (with similarly unpretentious furnishings) running back in an L past the bar; one part has stripped-brick barrel vaulting. Hop Back Summer Lightning, Palmers Copper Ale and Dorset Gold, and Sharps Doom Bar and Timothy Taylors Landlord on handpump and 13 wines by the glass. There are picnic-sets on the side grass with a play area.

🍴 As well as a two-course set menu (Tuesday-Thursday evening) and steak night (Friday), the wide choice of food might include sandwiches, devilled whitebait with home-made tartare sauce, chicken liver pâté with cumberland sauce, omelettes, home-cooked ham and free-range eggs, cottage pie, cheese, mushroom and tomato pasta, beer-battered fish and chips, lambs liver and bacon, chicken wrapped in smoked bacon and topped with cheese, delice of salmon with basil butter, and puddings. *Benchmark main dish: steak in ale pie with gravy and chips £11.95. Two-course evening meal £18.50.*

Free house ~ Licensees Mark and Sue Watts ~ Real ale ~ (01489) 896663 ~ Open 11.30-3, 5.30-11; 12-4, 5.30-10.30 Sun ~ Bar food 12-2(2.30 Sun), 6-9(8.30 Sun) ~ Restaurant ~ Children welcome ~ Dogs allowed in bar ~ www.risingsunswanmore.co.uk
Recommended by Jane and Rowena Leverington, mark watts, Val and Alan Green, Paul Sa

WEST MEON   SU6424 Map 2
Thomas Lord
High Street; GU32 1LN

Cricketing memorabilia in bar rooms of character, a smarter dining room, helpful staff, local beers, well thought-of food and a sizeable well kept garden

Named after the founder of Lord's Cricket Ground, this attractive place has plenty of character and appropriate memorabilia: cricket bats, gloves, balls, shoes, stumps, photographs and prints – even stuffed squirrels playing the game in a display cabinet above the counter. The relaxed, friendly bar has a leather chesterfield and armchairs beside a log fire, wooden chairs, animal-hide stools and corner settles on parquet flooring, Ringwood Best and a couple of guests from Upham on handpump, a dozen wines by the glass and farm cider served by chatty, helpful staff; a small room leads off here with similar furnishings, a brace of stuffed pheasant in the fireplace and antlers above; 1950s background music. The dining room is slightly more formal, with long wide tartan benches next to long tables, green cushioned chairs, a big clock above another fireplace, and ruched curtains; another little room has a large button-back banquette, tables and a rustic mural. There are candles everywhere – pretty in gloomy weather – in nice little teacups with saucers, in candlesticks, in silver glassware, in moroccan-style lanterns and in fireplaces. The sizeable garden has picnic-sets, herbaceous borders, outdoor pizza oven, barbecue area, chicken run and kitchen garden.

Using their own eggs, some home-grown produce and local free-range meat, the enterprising food includes sandwiches, rarebit on muffin with poached duck egg, smoked salmon, horseradish and celeriac remoulade, a good ploughman's, beer-battered hake with crushed peas and caper and parsley mayonnaise, sweet potato, leek, red onion and blue cheese pie with sautéed new potatoes, venison sausages with root vegetable dauphinoise and red onion gravy, guinea fowl breast and bacon-wrapped leg with duck fat roasted potatoes, charred leeks, golden raisins and marsala jus, skate wing with ox cheek hash, golden beetroot, celeriac and pickled shallot jus, and puddings such as apple and toffee parfait with salted popcorn and fudge cookie and chocolate tart with orange foam and jelly and brownie crumbs. *Benchmark main dish: dry-aged burger with truffle, tomato relish, parmesan, coleslaw and fries £11.50. Two-course evening meal £21.00.*

Free house ~ Licensee Clare Winterbottom ~ Real ale ~ (01730) 829244 ~ Open 12-11 (midnight Sat); 12-10.30 Sun ~ Bar food 12-2(3 Fri-Sun), 7-9(9.30 Fri, Sat); not Mon ~ Restaurant ~ Children welcome ~ Dogs allowed in bar ~ www.thethomaslord.co.uk
Recommended by Henry Fryer

WINCHESTER   SU4829 Map 2
Wykeham Arms
Kingsgate Street (Kingsgate Arch and College Street are now closed to traffic; there is access via Canon Street); SO23 9PE

Tucked-away pub with plenty to look at, several real ales, lots of wines by the glass and highly thought-of food; lovely bedrooms

This is a fine city pub, between the cathedral and the college, with much to look at, several real ales, good interesting food and welcoming staff. The series of bustling rooms have all sorts of interesting collections and three log fires – as well as 19th-c oak desks retired from Winchester College, a redundant pew from the same source, kitchen chairs and candlelit deal tables and big windows with swagged curtains. A snug room at the back, known as the Jameson Room (after the late landlord Graeme Jameson), is decorated with a set of Ronald Searle 'Winespeak' prints; another room is panelled. Fullers HSB, London Pride, Seafarers and a seasonal ale plus a guest such as Flowerpots Goodens Gold on handpump, lots of wines by the glass and several ports, sherries and malt whiskies; the tea list is pretty special. There are tables on a covered back terrace and more in a small courtyard. Some of the individually styled bedrooms have four-posters, and the two-level suite has its own sitting room.

Tempting and accomplished food includes ploughman's, confit duck leg terrine with cured duck breast, blood orange and celery, brown shrimp, mussels and clam bouillabaisse, leek and smoked ham hock pie with pea and bacon gravy, beer-battered haddock with triple-cooked chips, coq au vin with mash, poached egg with trompettes and truffle bulgar wheat, sweet pickled shallots and watercress, wild boar fillet with jerusalem artichoke, fondant potato and sage-roasted apple, and puddings like coffee panna cotta with white chocolate mousse, mocha macaroon, poached cherries and cocoa nibs and vanilla poached pear with warm coconut frangipane and tonka bean cream. *Benchmark main dish: beer-battered haddock and chips £13.00. Two-course evening meal £24.00.*

Fullers ~ Manager Jon Howard ~ Real ale ~ (01962) 853834 ~ Open 11-11; 12-11 Sun ~ Bar food 12-3(3.30 Sun), 6-9.30 ~ Restaurant ~ Children over 12 welcome ~ Dogs allowed in bar and bedrooms ~ Bedrooms: £82/£139 ~ www.wykehamarmswinchester.co.uk
Recommended by Martin and Karen Wake, John and Annabel Hampshire, Mark Sykes, Richard and Sissel Harris, Jane and Rowena Leverington, Ann and Colin Hunt, Stephen and Jean Curtis, Steve and Liz Tilley

Also Worth a Visit in Hampshire

Besides the fully inspected pubs, you might like to try these pubs that have been recommended to us and described by readers. Do tell us what you think of them: feedback@goodguides.com

ALRESFORD   SU5832
Bell (01962) 732429
West Street; SO24 9AT Comfortable and welcoming Georgian coaching inn, good popular food including weekday set menu, friendly helpful service, five well kept changing ales and good choice of wines, spic-and-span interior with bare boards, scrubbed tables and log fire, daily papers, smallish dining room; attractive sunny back courtyard, six bedrooms, open all day, closed Sun evening. *(Phyl and Jack Street, Neil Hardwick, John Oates, David and Judy Robison)*

ALRESFORD   SU5832
Running Horse (01962) 736506
Pound Hill; SO24 9BW Refurbished traditional country pub run by friendly young couple, good choice of well kept ales including Flowerpots (regular festivals), lots of wines by the glass, enjoyable modern pub food in bar or restaurant, cosy woodburner; children and dogs welcome, back terrace, closed Mon. *(Paul Granger)*

AMPFIELD   SU4023
⋆**White Horse** (01794) 368356
A3090 Winchester–Romsey; SO51 9BQ Snug low-beamed front bar with candles and soft lighting, inglenook log fire and comfortable country furnishings, far-spreading beamed dining area behind, well kept Greene King ales and guests, good food including all-day snacks, several nice wines by the glass, efficient service, locals' bar with another inglenook; background music; children and dogs welcome, high-hedged garden with plenty of picnic-sets, cricket green beyond, good walks in Ampfield Woods, handy for Hillier Gardens, open all day. *(Anon)*

BALL HILL   SU4263
Furze Bush (01635) 253228
*Leaving Newbury on A343 turn right
towards East Woodhay; RG20 0NQ* Clean
airy décor, pews and pine tables, log fire,
wide choice of good generous food promptly
served by friendly staff, well kept Greene
King ales and Fullers London Pride, decent
wines, reasonable prices, restaurant;
children welcome, dogs in back bar, tables
on terrace by good-sized sheltered lawn with
fenced play area. *(J V Dadswell)*

BARTON STACEY   SU4341
Swan (01962) 760470
Village signed off A303; SO21 3RL
Warm friendly atmosphere in beamed
former coaching inn, enjoyable food from
pubby choices up, well kept ales such as
Bowman, Fullers and Otter, good choice
of wines, little lounge area between front
log-fire bar and cosy dining part, restaurant
at back; background music; children and
dogs welcome, tables on front lawn and back
terrace, open all day Fri, Sat, closed Sun
evening. *(Anon)*

BASING   SU6653
Millstone (01256) 331153
*Bartons Lane, Old Basing; follow brown
signs to Basing House; RG24 8AE*
Busy pub with lots of picnic-sets by River
Loddon (ducks and swans) looking across
to former viaduct through scrubland, full
Wadworths range kept well, Weston's farm
cider and several wines by the glass, food
can be good, dark panelling, old prints and
etchings, sturdy pub furnishings; may be
faint background music; children and dogs
welcome, by ruins of Basing House, open all
day. *(Anon)*

BEAUWORTH   SU5624
Milbury's (01962) 771248
*Off A272 Winchester–Petersfield;
SO24 0PB* Attractive old tile-hung pub,
beams, panelling and stripped stone, massive
17th-c treadmill for much older, incredibly
deep well, galleried area, up to five changing
ales, straightforward reasonably priced food,
efficient service, skittle alley; children in
eating areas, garden with fine downland
views, good walks. *(Anon)*

BISHOP'S WALTHAM   SU5517
Barleycorn (01489) 892712
Lower Basingwell Street; SO32 1AJ
Buoyant 18th-c two-bar local, enjoyable
generously served pub food at sensible prices,
friendly efficient service, well kept Greene
King ales and a guest, decent wine, beams
and some low ceiling panelling, open fires;

children and dogs welcome, large garden with
back smokers' area, open all day. *(Stephen and
Jean Curtis, Ann and Colin Hunt)*

BISHOP'S WALTHAM   SU5517
⋆ Bunch of Grapes (01489) 892935
*St Peter's Street – near entrance to
central car park; SO32 1AD* Neat civilised
little pub in quiet medieval street, smartly
furnished keeping individuality and unspoilt
feel (run by same family for a century), good
chatty landlord and regulars, Goddards and
guests tapped from the cask, own wines
from nearby vineyard, no food; charming
walled back garden, opening times may
vary. *(Stephen and Jean Curtis)*

BISHOP'S WALTHAM   SU5517
Crown (01489) 893350
The Square; SO32 1AF Beamed 16th-c
coaching inn well refurbished by Fullers
after long closure; good range of their ales
including Gales HSB, popular food from
sandwiches and pub favourites up, helpful
staff, bare boards and log fires; courtyard
tables, opposite entrance to palace
ruins, eight bedrooms, open all day from
8.30am. *(Phil and Jane Villiers, Ann and Colin
Hunt, Val and Alan Green)*

BLACKNEST   SU7941
Jolly Farmer (01420) 22244
Binsted Road/Blacknest Road; GU34 4QD
Bright airy dining pub with nice relaxed
atmosphere, good food including some
unusual choices, beers such as Fullers
London Pride and HSB, friendly helpful staff,
log fire one end, family room; attractive
garden with sheltered terrace. *(I D Barnett)*

BRAISHFIELD   SU3725
Newport Inn (01794) 368225
*Newport Lane – from centre follow
Michelmersh, Timsbury signpost;
SO51 0PL* Plain old-fashioned two-bar brick
local, unchanging and in same family for 70
years, well kept Fullers/Gales ales, bargain
sandwiches or ploughman's, cribbage, piano
singalongs Sat night, maybe folk music
Thurs; informal and relaxing tree-shaded
garden. *(Andrea Rampley)*

BRAISHFIELD   SU3724
Wheatsheaf (01794) 367737
*Village signposted off A3090 on NW
edge of Romsey; SO51 0QE* Friendly
beamed pub with enjoyable home-made
food and well kept beers, cosy log fire, local
artwork for sale; background music, sports
TV and pool; children and dogs welcome,
garden with nice views, woodland walks
nearby, close to Hillier Gardens, open all
day Fri-Sun. *(Stuart Harvey)*

BRAMBRIDGE   SU4721
Dog & Crook   (01962) 712129
Near M3 junction 12, via B3335; Church Lane; SO50 6HZ Cheerful bustling 18th-c pub with beamed bar and cosy dining room, enjoyable traditional food, Fullers and Ringwood ales, several wines by the glass, friendly staff; background music, TV, regular events and summer music nights; dogs welcome, garden with decking and arbour, Itchen Way walks nearby. *(Anon)*

BRAMDEAN   SU6127
Fox   (01962) 771363
A272 Winchester–Petersfield; SO24 0LP 17th-c weatherboarded dining pub under friendly new italian family; open-plan bar, black beams, cushioned wall pews and wheelbacks, open fires, traditional pub food alongside italian dishes, ales such as Greene King and Marstons, fortnightly Mon quiz; children and dogs welcome, walled-in terraced area and spacious lawn under fruit trees, good surrounding walks. *(Helen and Brian Edgeley, Richard Tilbrook)*

BROOK   SU2713
⋆ Green Dragon   (023) 8081 2214
B3078 NW of Cadnam, just off M27 junction 1; SO43 7HE Immaculate thatched New Forest dining pub dating from 15th c, welcoming helpful staff, good fresh food including plenty of seasonal game and fish as well as pubby favourites, well kept Fullers and Ringwood, daily papers, bright linked areas with stripped pine and other pubby furnishings; disabled access from car park, attractive small terrace, garden with paddocks beyond, picturesque village, self-catering apartment. *(Janet de Lange, David and Sally Frost, Jennifer Bugg, PL)*

BROUGHTON   SU3032
Tally Ho   (01794) 301280
High Street, opposite church; signed off A30 Stockbridge–Salisbury; SO20 8AA Traditional pub reopened in 2012 after refurbishment, enjoyable food from pub favourites up (more elaborate evening choice), ales such as Ringwood, Sharps and Timothy Taylors, friendly service; children welcome, charming secluded back garden, good walks, open all day. *(Ann and Colin Hunt)*

BUCKLERS HARD   SU4000
⋆ Master Builders House
(01590) 616253 *M27 junction 2, follow signs to Beaulieu, turn left on to B3056, then left to Bucklers Hard; SO42 7XB* Sizeable hotel in lovely spot overlooking river; character main bar with heavy beams, log fire and simple furnishings, rugs on wooden floor, mullioned windows, interesting list of shipbuilders dating from 18th c, Ringwood Best and guests, stairs down to room with fireplace at each end, some sort

of food all day, afternoon teas; children welcome, small gate at bottom of garden for waterside walks, summer barbecues, 26 bedrooms, open all day. *(Barrie and Mary Crees, Guy Vowles)*

BURGHCLERE   SU4660
Carpenters Arms   (01635) 278251
Harts Lane, off A34; RG20 9JY Small unpretentious and well run, enjoyable sensibly priced home-made food (not Sun evening) from doorstep sandwiches up, Arkells and an occasional guest, friendly helpful staff, good country views (Watership Down) from dining extension and terrace picnic-sets, log fire; background music; children and dogs welcome, handy for Sandham Memorial Chapel (NT) and Highclere Castle, six comfortable annexe bedrooms, open all day. *(Pat and Graham Williamson)*

BURITON   SU7320
⋆ Five Bells   (01730) 263584
Off A3 S of Petersfield; GU31 5RX Low-beamed 17th-c pub, popular fresh pubby food (not Sun evening) from baguettes up, Badger ales and good wines by the glass, pleasant staff, big log fire, daily papers, flowers and church candles, some ancient stripped masonry and woodburner on public side; background music; children and dogs welcome, nice garden and sheltered terraces, pretty village, good walks, self-catering in converted stables, open all day. *(Ann and Colin Hunt)*

BURLEY   SU2202
White Buck   (01425) 402264
Bisterne Close; 0.7 miles E, OS Sheet 195 map reference 223028; BH24 4AZ Popular 19th-c mock-Tudor hotel owned by Fullers and due a refit as we went to press; their ales and a guest in long comfortably divided bar, lots of pictures, log fires each end, enjoyable sensibly priced food, pleasant dining room with tables out on decking, helpful friendly young staff; children and dogs welcome, front terrace and spacious lawn, lovely New Forest setting with superb walks towards Burley itself and over Mill Lawn, seven bedrooms (more being added), open all day. *(Sara Fulton, Roger Baker, Ian Herdman and others)*

BURSLEDON   SU4809
Fox & Hounds   (023) 8040 2784
Hungerford Bottom; 2 miles from M27 junction 8; SO31 8DE Popular rambling 16th-c Chef & Brewer of unusual character, ancient beams, flagstones and big log fires, linked by pleasant family conservatory area to ancient back barn, lantern-lit side stalls, lots of interesting farm equipment, well kept ales including Ringwood, good choice of wines, decent coffee, enjoyable reasonably priced food from sandwiches up with vegetarian choices, cheerful obliging

staff, daily papers; children allowed, tables outside. *(Phyl and Jack Street)*

BURSLEDON   SU4909
Jolly Sailor   (023) 8040 5557

Off A27 towards Bursledon Station, Lands End Road; handy for M27 junction 8; SO31 8DN Popular Badger dining pub in prime spot overlooking yachting inlet, food cooked to order (may be a wait), their usual ales and good wine choice, log fires; open all day. *(Ann and Colin Hunt)*

CADNAM   SU2913
Sir John Barleycorn
(023) 8081 2236   *Off Southampton Road; by M27 junction 1; SO40 2NP* Picturesque low-slung thatched dining pub extended from cosy beamed and timbered medieval core, fairly standard food including good value weekday two-course menu (till 6pm), friendly helpful service, Fullers ales, two log fires, modern décor and stripped wood flooring; background music; children welcome, no dogs inside, suntrap benches in front and out in colourful garden, open all day. *(R Aitken-Sykes)*

CADNAM   SU2913
White Hart   (023) 8081 2277

Old Romsey Road, handy for M27 junction 1; SO40 2NP Big rambling Home Counties family pub/restaurant, enjoyable food all day, ales from Flack Manor and Ringwood, plenty of wines by the glass, cheerful efficient service, mix of old table and chairs including pews on parquet, quarry tiles or bare boards, painted half-panelling, some stripped brickwork, lots of old prints, books and photographs, woodburner; background music, no dogs; disabled facilities, picnic-sets in garden with play area. *(Dr Elizabeth Fellows)*

CHALTON   SU7316
⋆Red Lion   (023) 9259 2246

Off A3 Petersfield–Horndean; PO8 0BG Largely extended thatched all-day dining pub with interesting 16th-c core around ancient inglenook fireplace, wide range of popular food from sandwiches and baguettes up, well kept Fullers/Gales ales and lots of country wines, helpful smart staff; children and dogs allowed, good disabled access and facilities, nice views from neat rows of picnic-sets on rectangular lawn by large car park, good walks, handy for Queen Elizabeth Country Park. *(Ann and Colin Hunt, Ian Phillips)*

CHARLTON DOWN   SU3549
Hare & Hounds   (01264) 735672

Hungerford Lane, off A343 N of Andover; SP11 0JA Tucked-away extended brick and flint country pub, neat and airy, with enjoyable food including fresh fish,

vegetarian dishes and popular Sun roasts, real ales, friendly staff, log fires; tables on pleasant terrace, good local walks, closed Sun evening, Mon. *(Phyl and Jack Street)*

CHAWTON   SU7037
⋆Greyfriar   (01420) 83841

Off A31/A32 S of Alton; Winchester Road; GU34 1SB Popular flower-decked beamed dining pub opposite Jane Austen's house; enjoyable food (till 7pm Sun) from lunchtime sandwiches and bar snacks up, Fullers ales, decent wines by the glass and good coffee, welcoming relaxed atmosphere with comfortable seating and sturdy pine tables in neat linked areas, open fire in restaurant end; background music; children welcome till 9pm, dogs in bar, small garden with terrace, good nearby walks, open all day. *(Anon)*

CHERITON   SU5828
⋆Flower Pots   (01962) 771318

Off B3046 towards Beauworth and Winchester; OS Sheet 185 map reference 581282; SO24 0QQ Unspoilt country local in same family for 45 years; three or four good value own-brewed beers tapped from casks (brewery tours by arrangement), standard food (not Sun evening or bank holiday evenings, possible restrictions during busy times), popular Weds curry night, extended plain public bar with covered well, another straightforward but homely room with country pictures on striped wallpaper and ornaments over small log fire; no credit cards or children; dogs welcome, seats on pretty front and back lawns, heated marquee, three bedrooms. *(John and Annabel Hampshire, Miss A E Dare, Val and Alan Green, Tony and Jill Radnor, R Elliott)*

CHILWORTH   SU4118
Chilworth Arms   (023) 8076 6247

Chilworth Road (A27 Southampton–Romsey); SO16 7JZ Stylish modern Mitchells & Butlers dining pub, popular food from sharing plates and home-made pizzas up, weekday set menu till 7pm, good wine choice, ales such as Robinsons and Sharps Doom Bar, cocktails, neat efficient young staff, chunky furniture including quite a lot of leather, log fires, conservatory-style back restaurant, chattier areas too; background music; children welcome, disabled facilities, large neat garden with terrace, open all day. *(Phyl and Jack Street)*

CHURCH CROOKHAM   SU8252
Foresters   (01252) 616503

Aldershot Road; GU52 9EP Restaurant-pub with good, often interesting food including Mon-Sat set menu (12-6.30), Sun carvery, pleasant if not always speedy service, ales such as Andwell, Otter and Sharps Doom Bar, two beamed areas, high-ceilinged

---

It's very helpful if you let us know up-to-date food prices when you report on pubs.

tiled-floor extension; french doors to garden, roadside verandah. *(Mike and Jayne Bastin, KC)*

CHURCH CROOKHAM SU8151
Tweseldown (01252) 613976
Beacon Hill Road; GU52 8DY Flower-decked 19th-c pub with public and lounge bars plus sizeable split-level barn restaurant, Courage, Fullers, Triple fff and a guest, good choice of wines by the glass, enjoyable home-cooked food from favourites to specials, cheerful service, horse racing décor (Tweseldown Racecourse nearby), log fires; pool, darts and fruit machine; children and dogs welcome, garden with heated smokers' shelter, open all day. *(KC)*

COLDEN COMMON SU4821
Fishers Pond (023) 8069 2209
Junction B3354/B2177 (Main Road), at Fishers Pond just S; SO50 7HG Big Vintage Inn in appealing position by peaceful woodside lake, various different areas and alcoves making most of waterside views, some painted brickwork, carpet or rugs on aged terracotta, dark leather built-in banquettes, heavy beams and log fires, brighter modern end section, ales such as Ringwood and Sharps Doom Bar, Aspall's cider, popular all-day food; background music, machines; children welcome, solid teak furniture on heated, partly covered lakeside terrace, handy for Marwell Zoo. *(Phyl and Jack Street, Ann and Colin Hunt)*

COLDEN COMMON SU4722
Rising Sun (01962) 711954
Spring Lane; SO21 1SB Refurbished 19th-c pub in residential street; reasonably priced tasty food including children's choices, well kept ales, bare boards, half-panelling and painted ceiling joists, leather sofas by open fire, some live music; a few picnic-sets in front behind picket fence, more in garden beyond car park. *(Hilary Kerr)*

CRAWLEY SU4234
✳ **Fox & Hounds** (01962) 776006
Village signed from A272 and B3420 NW of Winchester; SO21 2PR Attractive building with neat linked rooms, mix of wooden tables and chairs on polished floors, three log fires, traditional small bar with Ringwood, Wadworths and Wychwood, good choice of food from sandwiches up, cheerful service; children welcome, dogs in bar, picnic-sets in garden with play area, picturesque village, bedrooms in chalets named after species of duck, open all day Sat summer, till 8pm Sun (4pm winter). *(David and Ruth Hollands, Phyl and Jack Street, Mike and Lynn Robinson, R T and J C Moggridge, Mary Lincoln)*

CRONDALL SU7948
Plume of Feathers (01252) 850245
The Borough; GU10 5NT Attractive smallish 15th c village pub popular for good

range of home-made food from standards up, friendly helpful staff, well kept Greene King and some unusual guests, good wines by the glass, beams and dark wood, red carpet, prints on cream walls, restaurant with log fire in big brick fireplace; children welcome, picturesque village, three bedrooms. *(Anon)*

CROOKHAM SU7952
Exchequer (01252) 615336
Crondall Road; GU51 5SU Welcoming refurbished pub with enjoyable home-made food from lunchtime sandwiches to specials in bar and restaurant, four local ales and good choice of wines by the glass, daily papers, woodburner; terrace tables, near Basingstoke Canal, open all day weekends (Sun till 9pm). *(Anon)*

CURDRIDGE SU5314
Cricketers (023) 8078 4420
Curdridge Lane, off B3035 just under a mile NE of A334 junction; SO32 2BH Open-plan low-ceilinged Victorian village pub with cheery welcoming landlady, good well presented food, reasonably priced wines from short but varied list, well kept Greene King ales, friendly attentive service, lounge part with banquettes, traditional public area, dining section with large Beryl Cook-inspired mural of the locals, cricketing memorabilia; soft background music; tables on front lawn, pleasant walks. *(David M Smith, Ann and Colin Hunt)*

DENMEAD SU6211
Horse & Jockey (023) 9263 2728
Hipley; W on Southwick Road, right into Forest Road; PO7 4QY Lots of tables laid for the pub's good food but still room for drinkers, three well kept ales including Ringwood, cheerful service, beams and knick-knacks, open fire in bar area, central woodburner in restaurant. *(Ann and Colin Hunt)*

DUMMER SU5846
Queen (01256) 397367
Under a mile from M3 junction 7; take Dummer slip road; RG25 2AD Comfortable beamed pub, well divided with lots of softly lit alcoves, Courage Best, Fullers London Pride, John Smiths and a guest, decent choice of wines by the glass, popular food from lunchtime sandwiches and light dishes up, friendly service, big log fire, Queen and steeplechase prints, no mobile phones; background music; children welcome in restaurant; picnic-sets under parasols on terrace and in extended back garden, attractive village with ancient church. *(B J Thompson)*

DUNBRIDGE SU3126
✳ **Mill Arms** (01794) 340401
Barley Hill (B3084); SO51 0LF Much extended 18th-c coaching inn opposite station, friendly informal atmosphere in

spacious high-ceilinged rooms, scrubbed pine tables and farmhouse chairs on oak or flagstone floors, several sofas, two log fires, well kept Ringwood and guests, food (all day Sat) including grills and wood-fired pizzas, dinning conservatory, two skittle alleys; background music; children welcome, dogs in bar, big pretty garden, plenty of walks in surrounding Test Valley, six comfortable bedrooms, open till 4.30pm Sun, closed Mon. *(George Harrison)*

DUNDRIDGE   SU5718
★ **Hampshire Bowman**
(01489) 892940 *Off B3035 towards Droxford, Swanmore, then right at Bishop's Waltham signpost; SO32 1GD* Good chatty mix at this friendly relaxed country tavern, five well kept local ales tapped from the cask, summer farm cider, well liked good value food (all day Fri-Sun) from hearty pub dishes to specials using local produce, smart stable bar sitting comfortably alongside cosy and unassuming original one, some colourful paintings, no mobile phones (£1 fine in charity box); children (under-14s in stable bar) and dogs welcome, hitching post for horses, heated terrace, peaceful lawn, play equipment, open all day. *(Stephen and Jean Curtis, Henry Fryer, Audrey Dowsett)*

DURLEY   SU5116
Farmers Home   (01489) 860457
B3354 and B2177; Heathen Street/ Curdridge Road; SO32 2BT Comfortable beamed pub under newish management, spacious but cosy with two-bay dining area and restaurant, generous reasonably priced food including fresh fish, good friendly service, well kept Gales HSB and Ringwood, decent wines, log fire; children welcome, dogs in bar, big garden with good play area, nice walks, open all day. *(Stephen and Jean Curtis)*

DURLEY   SU5217
Robin Hood   (01489) 860229
Durley Street, just off B2177 Bishop's Waltham–Winchester – brown signs to pub; SO32 2AA Popular open-plan beamed pub with good food from varied blackboard menu (order at bar), Greene King and a guest, log fire and leather sofas in bare-boards bar, dining area with stone floors and mix of old pine tables and chairs, bookcase door to lavatories; background music; children and dogs welcome, disabled facilities, decked terrace with barbecue, garden with play area and nice country views, open all day Sun. *(Phyl and Jack Street, Graham Giles-Payne)*

EAST BOLDRE   SU3700
Turf Cutters Arms   (01590) 612331
Main Road; SO42 7WL Small dimly lit 18th-c New Forest local behind white picket fence, lots of beams and pictures, nicely worn-in furnishings on bare boards and

flagstones, log fire, enjoyable home-made food (worth booking in evening), well kept ales including Ringwood, friendly helpful staff and chatty relaxed atmosphere; children and dogs welcome, large garden, good heathland walks, bedrooms in nearby converted barn, open all day. *(N R White)*

EAST MEON   SU6822
Izaak Walton   (01730) 823252
High Street; GU32 1QA Friendly two-bar local in delightful village, cheerful helpful service, good value fresh food and well kept Wadworths; children welcome, stream at front, large back garden. *(Geoff and Linda Payne)*

EAST MEON   SU6822
★ **Olde George**   (01730) 823481
Church Street; signed off A272 W of Petersfield, and off A32 in West Meon; GU32 1NH Relaxing heavy-beamed rustic pub with enjoyable if not cheap bar and restaurant food, Badger ales, cosy areas around central bar counter, inglenook log fires; children and dogs welcome, nice back terrace, five comfortable bedrooms, pretty village with fine church, good walks, open all day Sun. *(Anon)*

EASTON   SU5132
Cricketers   (01962) 791044
Off B3047; SO21 1EJ Pleasantly smartened-up traditional local under newish licensees; well priced home-made pubby food in bar and smallish restaurant, three Marstons-related ales including Ringwood, friendly atmosphere, dark tables and chairs on carpet, bare-boards area with sports TV, fortnightly Sun quiz; background music; children and dogs welcome, front terrace with heated smokers' shelter, handy for Itchen Way walks, two bedrooms, open all day. *(John Jenkins, Ann and Colin Hunt)*

ELLISFIELD   SU6345
★ **Fox**   (01256) 381210
Green Lane; S of village off Northgate Lane; RG25 2QW Simple tucked-away place spruced up by present friendly owners; mixed collection of stripped tables, country chairs and cushioned wall benches on bare boards and old floor tiles, some stripped masonry, open fires in plain brick fireplaces, Sharps Doom Bar, Fullers London Pride and a guest or two, enjoyable sensibly priced home-made food; outside gents'; children and dogs welcome, picnic-sets in nice garden, good walking country near snowdrop and bluebell woods, open all day. *(Ann and Colin Hunt, Ian Webb, Tony and Jill Radnor)*

EMERY DOWN   SU2808
★ **New Forest**   (023) 8028 4690
Village signed off A35 just W of Lyndhurst; SO43 7DY Well run 18th-c weatherboarded pub in one of the best parts of the Forest for walking; good honest home-made food all day including local

venison, popular Sun roasts (should book), friendly attentive uniformed staff, ales such as Ringwood, real cider and good choice of wines by the glass, coffee and tea; attractive softly lit separate areas on varying levels, each with its own character, hunting prints, two log fires; background music; children and dogs welcome, covered heated terrace and pleasant little three-level garden, clean bedrooms, open all day and can get very busy weekends. *(Leslie and Barbara Owen, N R White)*

EMSWORTH SU7405
Blue Bell (01243) 373394
South Street; PO10 7EG Small timeless quayside pub with memorabilia everywhere, friendly busy atmosphere, good choice of popular no-nonsense food (not Sun evening) including local fish, should book weekends, Sharps Doom Bar and guest, live music; dogs welcome, terrace, Sun market in adjacent car park, open all day. *(Geoff and Linda Payne)*

EVERTON SZ2994
Crown (01590) 642655
Old Christchurch Road; pub signed just off A337 W of Lymington; SO41 0JJ Quietly set New Forest-edge restaurant-pub with enjoyable range of food, good service, Ringwood and guests, reliable wine choice, two attractive dining rooms off tiled-floor bar, log fires; picnic-sets on front terrace and in garden behind. *(Anon)*

EXTON SU6120
✴ Shoe (01489) 877526
Village signposted from A32 NE of Bishop's Waltham; SO32 3NT Popular brick-built country pub on South Downs Way, three linked rooms with log fires, good well presented food from traditional favourites to more imaginative restaurant-style dishes using own produce, Wadworths ales and a seasonal guest, good friendly service; children and dogs welcome, disabled facilities, seats under parasols at front, more in garden across lane overlooking River Meon. *(Nigel and Sue Foster, Dawn B, William Ruxton, Richard and Liz Dilnot)*

FACCOMBE SU3958
✴ Jack Russell (01264) 737315
Signed from A343 Newbury–Andover; SP11 0DS Light and airy, creeper-covered pub in village-green setting, opposite pond and by flint church, enjoyable fairly priced traditional food (not Sun evening) from snacks to popular Sun roasts, well kept ales including one named for the pub, nice wines, good cheerful service, carpeted bar with old farming tools and bric-a-brac, log fire, darts, conservatory restaurant (children welcome here); background music; disabled facilities, lawn by beech trees, good walks, three bedrooms, open all day Wed-Sat, closed Tues evening. *(Ian Herdman)*

FAREHAM SU5806
Golden Lion (01329) 234061
High Street; PO16 7AE Fullers town local, clean and welcoming, with their well kept ales and enjoyable fresh food from nice baguettes up, charity quiz Thurs; children and dogs welcome (resident retriever is Monty), open all day (till 3.30pm Sun, 9pm Mon). *(Val and Alan Green, Peter Meister)*

FAREHAM SU5206
Sir Joseph Paxton (01489) 572125
Hunts Pond Road; PO14 4PF Sizeable local on edge of estate; cosy beamed part with larger plainer area off, well kept ales including St Austell, good choice of low-priced bar food (all day weekends) including deals and Sun carvery, cheerful service, darts; children welcome, garden picnic-sets, open all day. *(Ann and Colin Hunt)*

FARNBOROUGH SU8756
✴ Prince of Wales (01252) 545578
Rectory Road, near station; GU14 8AL Up to ten good quickly changing ales in friendly Victorian local, exposed brickwork, carpet or wood floors, open fire, antiquey touches in three small linked areas, popular lunchtime pubby food (not Sun) including deals, good friendly service; terrace and smokers' gazebo, open all day Fri-Sun. *(Anon)*

FAWLEY SU4603
Jolly Sailor (023) 8089 1305
Ashlett Creek, off B3053; SO45 1DT Cottagey waterside pub near small boatyard and sailing club, straightforward good value bar food, Ringwood Best and a guest such as Flack Manor, cheerful service, raised log fire, mixed pubby furnishings on bare boards, second bar with darts and pool; children welcome, tables outside looking past creek's yachts and boats to busy shipping channel, good shore walks, handy for Rothschild rhododendron gardens at Exbury, open all day. *(Phil and Jane Villiers)*

FLEET SU8155
Heron on the Lake (01252) 812522
Old Cove Road (A3013); GU51 2RY By Fleet Pond, lots of beams, nooks and corners, two log fires, McMullens ales, decent reasonably priced food, efficient service coping well when busy; children welcome, decking over water, open all day. *(Mike and Jayne Bastin)*

FLEET SU8053
Oatsheaf (01252) 819508
Crookham Road/Reading Road; GU51 5DR Smartly refurbished Mitchells & Butlers dining pub with plenty of contemporary touches, usual good choice of enjoyable food, ales such as Timothy Taylors Landlord; tables on front terrace, garden behind, open all day. *(Mike and Jayne Bastin)*

GOODWORTH CLATFORD SU3642
Royal Oak (01264) 324105
Longstock Road; SP11 7QY Comfortably modern L-shaped bar with welcoming landlord and obliging staff, good carefully sourced food from pub staples up (maybe local buffalo), Flack Manor and Ringwood ales, good choice of wines by the glass, Weds quiz night; children welcome, sheltered and very pretty dell-like garden, large and neatly kept, attractive Test Valley village, good River Anton walks, closed Sun evening. *(Edward Leetham)*

GOSPORT SU6101
✳ **Jolly Roger** (023) 9258 2584
Priory Road, Hardway; PO12 4LQ Popular old beamed harbour-view pub with enjoyable home-made food and five real ales including Shepherd Neame, decent house wines, lots of bric-a-brac, log fire, attractive eating area including conservatory, efficient friendly service; open all day. *(Audrey Dowsett, Howard and Margaret Buchanan, Ann and Colin Hunt)*

GOSPORT SZ6100
Queens (023) 9258 2645
Queens Road; PO12 1LG Classic bare-boards local, long-serving landlady keeps Oakleaf, Palmers, Wells & Youngs and guests in top condition, beer festivals, quick service, three areas off bar with good log fire in interesting carved fireplace, sensibly placed darts, pub dog called Stanley; TV room (children welcome here daytime); closed lunchtimes Mon-Thurs, open all day Sat. *(Audrey Dowsett, Ann and Colin Hunt)*

GREYWELL SU7151
Fox & Goose (01256) 702062
Near M3 junction 5; A287 towards Odiham, then first right to village; RG29 1BY Traditional two-bar pub popular with locals and walkers, country kitchen furniture, open fire, enjoyable home-made pubby food from good lunchtime sandwiches up, Sun roast till 4pm, well kept ales including Sharps Doom Bar, friendly helpful service; children and dogs welcome, good-sized back garden, attractive village, Basingstoke Canal walks, open all day. *(Anon)*

HAMBLE SU4806
Bugle (023) 8045 3000
3 miles from M27 junction 8; SO31 4HA Chatty and bustling little 16th-c village pub by River Hamble, beamed and timbered rooms with flagstones and polished boards, church chairs, woodburner in fine brick fireplace, bar stools along herringbone-brick and timbered counter, ales such as Bowman and Ringwood, popular food (all day weekends); background music, TV; children welcome, dogs in bar, seats on terrace with view of boats, open all day. *(Anon)*

HAMBLE SU4806
King & Queen (023) 8045 4247
3 miles from M27 junction 8; High Street; SO31 4HA Simple pub with pine tables on bare boards, well kept real ales such as Sharps Doom Bar, generous helpings of low-priced food, friendly attentive service; background music; tables on front gravel. *(Ann and Colin Hunt, Mr and Mrs A Curry)*

HAMBLE SU4806
Olde Whyte Harte (023) 8045 2108
High Street; 3 miles from M27 junction 8; SO31 4JF Spotless old-fashioned village pub, locally popular, with big inglenook log fire and low dark 17th-c beams, small cottagey restaurant area, generous fresh pubby food all day along with specials, Fullers/Gales ales and a guest, good wines by the glass, friendly staff; background music; children and dogs welcome, small walled garden, handy for nature reserve, open all day. *(Ann and Colin Hunt)*

HAMBLE SU4806
Victory (023) 8045 3105
High Street; SO31 4HA 18th-c red-brick pub with four well kept ales and enjoyable reasonably priced bar food, cheerful welcoming staff, nautical theme including Battle of Trafalgar mural; children and dogs welcome, open all day. *(Ann and Colin Hunt)*

HAMBLEDON SU6716
✳ **Bat & Ball** (023) 9263 2692
Broadhalfpenny Down; about 2 miles E towards Clanfield; PO8 0UB Extended dining pub opposite historic cricket pitch and with plenty of cricketing memorabilia (the game's rules are said to have been written here), log fires and comfortable modern furnishings in three linked rooms, Fullers ales, enjoyable food from well priced snacks up, good friendly service, panelled restaurant; children and dogs welcome, tables on front terrace, garden behind with lovely downs views, good walks, open all day. *(Anon)*

HANNINGTON SU5455
Vine (01635) 298525
Signposted off A339; RG26 5TX Spacious 19th-c village pub with light bright décor, comfy leather sofas and woodburner, well kept ales such as Wadworths 6X and Wells & Youngs Bombardier, a dozen wines by the glass, popular fairly priced pubby food using home-grown produce, back dining conservatory; children and dogs welcome, big garden with terrace, nice spot up on downs, good walks, open all day Sat, closed evenings Sun and Mon. *(Ann and Colin Hunt)*

HAWKLEY SU7429
Hawkley Inn (01730) 827205
Off B3006 near A3 junction; Pococks Lane; GU33 6NE Small traditional village

pub with splendid range of well kept ales from central bar, farm ciders too (maybe a blackberry one), good home-made food from short changing menu, nice mix of customers, open fires (large moose head above one), bare boards, flagstones and well used carpet, old pine tables and assorted chairs; some live music; children and dogs welcome, covered seating area at front, big back garden, useful for walkers on Hangers Way, five clean comfortable bedrooms, good breakfast, open all day weekends. *(Geoff and Linda Payne, Tim Maddison, Stephen Sorby)*

HAYLING ISLAND SU7201
Maypole (023) 924 63670
Havant Road; PO11 0PS Sizeable two-bar 1930s roadside local, family-run and friendly, with generous reasonably priced pub food including good ploughman's (home-made pickles), fish night Fri, steaks Sat, well kept Fullers/Gales beers, parquet floors and polished panelling, plenty of good seating, open fires; darts, Thurs quiz; children and dogs welcome, garden picnic-sets and play equipment, closed Sun evening. *(Robert Brindle)*

HERRIARD SS6744
Fur & Feathers (01256) 384170
Pub signed just off A339 Basingstoke–Alton; RG25 2PN Victorian pub, clean, light and airy, with four changing ales and good choice of wines, nice coffee, popular home-made blackboard food served promptly by friendly staff, smallish bar area with stools along counter, dining areas either side, pine furniture on stripped-wood flooring, painted half-panelling, old photographs and farm tools, two woodburners; background music; garden behind, open all day Fri, Sat, closed Sun evening, Mon. *(Geoffrey and Penny Hughes, Comus and Sarah Elliott)*

HORSEBRIDGE SU3430
John o'Gaunt (01794) 388394
Off A3057 Romsey–Andover, just SW of Kings Somborne; SO20 6PU Traditional pub (spruced up by current management) in River Test village; good value generously served home-made food, three ales including Ringwood, real cider, friendly staff and locals, L-shaped log-fire bar and small back dining area; seats outside, popular with walkers. *(Dawn Harrison, Ann and Colin Hunt, Tony and Wendy Hobden)*

HOUGHTON SU3432
★ Boot (01794) 388310
Village signposted off A30 in Stockbridge; SO20 6LH Refurbished country pub with cheery log-fire bar and more formal dining room, well kept Flack Manor and Palmers, Weston's cider, enjoyable bar and restaurant food (not Sun evening), friendly helpful staff; picnic-sets out in front and in spacious tranquil garden by lovely (unfenced) stretch of River Test where they

have fishing rights, good walks, opposite Test Way cycle path. *(Edward Mirzoeff)*

HURSLEY SU4225
Kings Head (01962) 775208
A3090 Winchester–Romsey; SO21 2JW Substantial early 19th-c coaching inn, good local home-made food, five well kept changing ales such as Ringwood and Sharps Doom Bar, good choice of ciders, friendly staff, restaurant, skittle alley; children and dogs welcome, garden tables, eight comfortable bedrooms, open all day. *(June Kershaw)*

KEYHAVEN SZ3091
★ Gun (01590) 642391
Keyhaven Road; SO41 0TP Busy rambling 17th-c pub looking over boatyard and sea to Isle of Wight, low-beamed bar with nautical bric-a-brac and plenty of character (less in family rooms and conservatory), good reasonably priced local food including crab, Ringwood, Sharps, Timothy Taylors and Wells & Youngs tapped from the cask, Weston's cider, lots of malt whiskies, helpful young staff, bar billiards; background music; tables out in front and in big back garden with swings and fish pond, within walking distance of small harbour and Hurst Castle, open all day Sat, closed Sun evening. *(Barrie and Mary Crees, Neil and Angela Huxter, Stephen and Jean Curtis, David and Judy Robison)*

KING'S SOMBORNE SU3531
Crown (01794) 388360
Romsey Road (A3057); SO20 6PW Long low thatched pub opposite village church, friendly relaxed local atmosphere, good simple reasonably priced home-made food (not Sun evening), well kept Greene King Abbot, Ringwood Best, Wadworths 6X and Wychwood Hobgoblin, real ciders, good wines and decent coffee, several linked rooms, panelling, comfortable sofas, fresh flowers, woodburner; seats out in front and in garden behind, Test Way and Clarendon Way paths nearby, open all day Sun. *(Ann and Colin Hunt, David and Judy Robison)*

KINGSCLERE SU5160
Star (01635) 296241
A339 N of Kingsclere; RG20 4SY 19th-c beamed Vintage Inn with village pub atmosphere, central log-fire bar flanked by two simple dining areas, also restaurant part, Sharps Doom Bar, Wadworths 6X and a guest, enjoyable good value food including Fri fish day, efficient friendly service, Mon quiz; some picnic-sets on grass at front, open all day. *(KC)*

KINGSCLERE SU5258
Swan (01635) 298314
Swan Street; RG20 5PP 15th-c beamed village inn under welcoming long-serving licensees, Theakstons XB and four guests, enjoyable reasonably priced home-made

terrace, good walks, nine bedrooms. *(Anon)*

LANGSTONE SU7104
★ **Royal Oak** (023) 9248 3125

Off A3023 just before Hayling Island bridge; Langstone High Street; PO9 1RY Charmingly placed waterside dining pub overlooking tidal inlet and ancient wadeway to Hayling Island, boats at high tide, wading birds when it goes out; Greene King ales and good choice of wines by the glass, reasonably priced food with all-day sandwiches and snacks, spacious flagstoned bar and linked dining areas, log fire; nice garden and good coast paths nearby, open all day. *(Roger and Donna Huggins, David and Judy Robison, R Elliott)*

LINWOOD SU1910
High Corner (01425) 473973

Signed from A338 via Moyles Court, and from A31; keep on; BH24 3QY Big rambling pub very popular for its splendid New Forest position up a track, with extensive neatly kept wooded garden and lots for children to do; popular and welcoming with some character in original upper log-fire bar, big back extensions for the summer crowds, nicely partitioned restaurant, verandah lounge, interesting family rooms, wide choice of generous bar snacks and restaurant-style food, well kept Wadworths; welcomes dogs and horses (stables and paddock available), seven bedrooms, open all day summer and weekends. *(N R White)*

LINWOOD SU1809
Red Shoot (01425) 475792

Signed from A338 via Moyles Court, and from A31; go on up heath to junction with Toms Lane; BH24 3QT Edwardian pub in nice New Forest setting, big picture-window bar with attractive old tables, mixed chairs and rugs on bare boards, country pictures on puce walls, log fire, large back dining area, generous honest good value food (all day weekends), friendly helpful staff, well kept Wadworths and two or three ales brewed at the pub (beer festivals Apr and Oct); children, dogs and muddy boots welcome, some disabled access, sheltered side terrace, open all day summer, when it's very touristy (next to big campsite and caravan park). *(N R White)*

LITTLE LONDON SU6259
Plough (01256) 850628

Silchester Road, off A340 N of Basingstoke; RG26 5EP Tucked-away local, cosy and unspoilt, with log fires, low beams and mixed furnishings on brick and

bar billiards and darts; dogs welcome, attractive garden, handy for Pamber Forest and Calleva Roman remains. *(D Johnson)*

LITTLETON SU4532
★ **Running Horse** (01962) 880218

Main Road; village signed off B3049 NW of Winchester; SO22 6QS Popular dining pub refurbished in up-to-date style, enjoyable food from pubby to more elaborate dishes, good service, cushioned metal and wicker chairs at modern tables on polished boards, also some deep leather chairs, good colour photographs of Hampshire scenes, Sharps Doom Bar and a local guest served from marble and hardwood counter with swish bar stools, log fire, flagstoned back restaurant; background music; children welcome, dogs in bar, good disabled facilities, nice front and back terraces and garden, nine bedrooms, open all day. *(Phyl and Jack Street, Martin and Karen Wake, Robert Watt)*

LOCKERLEY SU3025
Kings Arms (01794) 340332

The Street; SO51 0JF Refurbished village pub with good food from bar snacks to more inventive restaurant dishes, interesting wine list, well kept ales, good service and thriving local atmosphere; landscaped back garden with heated dining cabins, summer barbecues, open all day. *(Phyl and Jack Street)*

LOCKS HEATH SU5006
Jolly Farmer (01489) 572500

Fleet End Road, not far from M27 junction 9; SO31 9JH Popular flower-decked pub with relaxing series of softly lit linked rooms, nice old scrubbed tables and masses of bric-a-brac and prints, emphasis on wide choice of enjoyable food (all day weekends), interesting long-serving landlord, Fullers/Gales ales, decent wines including country ones, coal-effect gas fires; two sheltered terraces (one with play area and children's lavatory), dogs allowed in some parts, nearby walks, five nice bedrooms, good breakfast, open all day. *(Ann and Colin Hunt, David and Gill Carrington)*

LONG SUTTON SU7447
Four Horseshoes (01256) 862488

Signed off B3349 S of Hook; RG29 1TA Welcoming unpretentious country local; open-plan with black beams and two log fires, long-serving landlord cooking uncomplicated bargain food like lancashire hotpot and fish and chips, friendly landlady serving good range of changing ales such as Palmers, decent wines and country wine, small glazed-in verandah, friendly resident

---

Real ale to us means beer that has matured naturally in its cask – not pressurised or filtered.

dalmatian; disabled access, lovely hanging
baskets, picnic-sets on grass over road,
boules and play area, three good value
bedrooms (bunk beds available for cyclists/
walkers). *(Simon Le Fort, Tony and Jill Radnor)*

LONGPARISH SU4344
Cricketers (01264) 720335
B3048, off A303 just E of Andover;
SP11 6PZ Cheerful homely village pub with
good chatty landlady, connecting rooms and
cosy corners, woodburner, wide choice of
carefully cooked food from light snacks to
popular Sun lunch, prompt service, well kept
Wadworths; sizeable back garden; closed
Mon. *(Sandra Ruddick)*

LYMINGTON SZ3295
Kings Head (01590) 672709
Quay Hill; SO41 3AR In steep cobbled
lane of smart small shops, friendly dimly lit
old local with well kept Fullers London Pride,
Ringwood, Timothy Taylors Landlord and a
couple of guests, several wines by the glass,
enjoyable home-made food from doorstep
sandwiches to specials, pleasant helpful staff,
nicely mixed old-fashioned furnishings in
rambling beamed and bare-boarded rooms
(some recent refurbishment), log fire and
woodburner, good classic yacht photographs,
daily papers; background music, can get very
busy; children and dogs welcome, nice little
sunny courtyard behind, open all day. *(Guy
Vowles, Steve and Liz Tilley)*

LYMINGTON SZ3295
★**Ship** (01590) 676903
Quay Road; SO41 3AY Lively pub with
popular quayside deck overlooking harbour,
light modern interior, lots of nautical bric-a-
brac, blue gingham and leather sofas, raised
log fire, Fullers and Wells & Youngs (plenty
of standing room by counter), enjoyable fair
value interesting food (all day), attractive
wall-planked restaurant with driftwood
decorations; some reader concerns over
service; children and dogs welcome, showers
for visiting sailors, open all day. *(Georgina
Blake, David Whitehead)*

LYNDHURST SU2908
Waterloo Arms (023) 8028 2113
Pikes Hill, just off A337 N; SO43 7AS
Thatched 17th-c New Forest pub with low
beams, stripped brick walls and log fire,
good choice of pubby food all day including
blackboard specials, two Ringwood beers and
Sharps Doom Bar, friendly staff, comfortable
bar and roomy back dining area, Tues quiz;
children welcome, terrace and nice big
garden, open all day. *(R G Stollery)*

MAPLEDURWELL SU6851
Gamekeepers (01256) 322038
*Off A30, not far from M3 junction 6;
RG25 2LU* Dark-beamed dining pub with
good upmarket food (not cheap and they add
a service charge) from interesting baguettes

up, welcoming landlord and friendly staff,
well kept Badger ales, good coffee, a few
sofas by flagstoned and panelled core,
well spaced tables in large dining room;
background music, TV; children welcome,
terrace and garden, lovely thatched village
with duck pond, good walks, open all
day. *(David Feldman)*

MARCHWOOD SU3809
Pilgrim (023) 8086 7752
*Hythe Road, off A326 at Twiggs Lane;
SO40 4WU* Popular picturesque thatched
pub (originally three cottages), good choice
of enjoyable sensibly priced food, well kept
Fullers ales and decent wines, open fires;
tree-lined garden with circular picnic-sets,
14 stylish bedrooms in building across car
park, open all day. *(Anon)*

MATTINGLEY SU7357
Leather Bottle (0118) 932 6371
*3 miles from M3 junction 5; in Hook,
turn right-and-left on to B3349 Reading
Road (former A32); RG27 8JU* Old red-
brick chain pub with enjoyable food from
varied menu, three local ales including
Andwell, plenty of wines by the glass, well
spaced tables in linked areas, black beams,
flagstones and bare boards, inglenook log
fire, extension opening on to covered terrace;
background music; children and dogs (in
bar) welcome, disabled facilities, two garden
areas, open all day. *(Bronwen Matthews-King)*

MEONSTOKE SU6120
Bucks Head (01489) 877313
*Village signed just off A32 N of
Droxford; SO32 3NA* Unassuming little
pub with partly panelled L-shaped dining
lounge looking over road to water meadows,
log fire, plush banquettes and bare boards,
popular food including Sun roasts, well kept
Greene King ales, friendly public bar (dogs
welcome) with another fire; small garden,
lovely village setting with ducks on pretty
little River Meon, good walks, five bedrooms,
hearty breakfast, open all day weekends.
(A and R MacDowall, Ann and Colin Hunt)

MILFORD-ON-SEA SZ2891
Beach House (01590) 643044
Park Lane; SO41 0PT Civilised well placed
Victorian hotel-dining pub recently bought
by Hall & Woodhouse, restored oak-panelled
interior, small bar with Badger First Gold and
Tanglefoot, enjoyable sensibly priced food
from baguettes and sharing boards up, also
good value lunchtime set deal, magnificent
views from dining room; grounds down to
the Solent looking out to the Needles, 14
bedrooms, open all day. *(David and Sally Frost)*

MINLEY MANOR SU8357
Crown & Cushion (01252) 545253
*A327, just N of M3 junction 4A;
GU17 9UA* Attractive little traditional pub
with enjoyable fairly priced food including

some thai choices, well kept Shepherd Neame ales, coal-effect gas fire; big separate raftered and flagstoned rustic 'meade hall' with huge log fire, very popular weekends when friendly staff cope well; children in eating area, heated terrace overlooking own cricket pitch, open all day. *(Anon)*

MINSTEAD SU2810
★ **Trusty Servant** (023) 8081 2137
Just off A31, not far from M27 junction 1; SO43 7FY Attractive 19th-c building in pretty New Forest hamlet with interesting church (Sir Arthur Conan Doyle buried here), wandering cattle and ponies, plenty of easy walks; two-room bar and big dining room, well kept ales and good reasonably priced food including local game, friendly helpful staff; dogs welcome, big sloping garden, open all day. *(Graham, Martin Gough, Revd Michael Vockins)*

NEW CHERITON SU5827
★ **Hinton Arms** (01962) 771252
A272 near B3046 junction; SO24 0NH Neatly kept popular country pub with cheerful accommodating landlord, three or four real ales including Bowman Wallops Wood and a house beer brewed by Hampshire, decent wines by the glass, good generous food from sandwiches to game specials, sporting pictures and memorabilia, relaxing atmosphere and friendly staff; TV lounge; terrace, big garden, very handy for Hinton Ampner House (NT). *(Stuart Paulley)*

ODIHAM SU7450
Bell (01256) 702282
The Bury; RG29 1LY Simple unspoilt two-bar local in pretty square opposite church and stocks, three well kept changing ales, good value straightforward lunchtime food, log fire; plenty of seats outside, open all day. *(Anon)*

ODIHAM SU7451
Water Witch (01256) 808778
Colt Hill – quiet no-through road signed off main street; RG29 1AL Olde-worlde décor in nicely kept Chef & Brewer pub by picturesque stretch of Basingstoke Canal (boat hire), big but cosily divided with more formal dining area at back, wide choice of food and three mainstream ales, friendly helpful staff; no dogs inside; children welcome, disabled access and parking, pretty hanging baskets in front, terrace with awning and dark raffia furniture, garden down to the water, open all day. *(Simon and Mandy King, Ian Phillips)*

OTTERBOURNE SU4522
Otter (023) 8025 2685
Boyatt Lane, off Winchester Road; SO21 2HW Unpretentious dining pub

opposite village green, enjoyable food from sandwiches and snacks up, Ringwood ales and Otter, good service, three-sided bar (one side set for dining), dark oak tables and chairs, banquettes; seats in garden. *(Anon)*

OVINGTON SU5631
★ **Bush** (01962) 732764
Off A31 W of Alresford; SO24 0RE Charming spot with streamside garden (lots of picnic-sets) and pergola dining terrace, appealing low-ceilinged bar with high-backed settles, pews and masses of old pictures, blazing fire, well kept Wadworths ales, good choice of wines by the glass, good if pricey food (not Sun evening); children and dogs welcome, nice walks, open all day summer holidays and can get very busy. *(Malcolm Derrick)*

PETERSFIELD SU7423
Good Intent (01730) 263838
College Street; GU31 4AF Homely 16th-c coaching inn, friendly and chatty, with five well kept Fullers/Gales beers and enjoyable fresh pubby food including range of O'Hagons sausages (some unusual choices like pheasant and springbok), low beams, pine tables and built-in upholstered benches, log fires; background music (live Sun), quiz Mon; children and dogs welcome, front terrace, three bedrooms. *(Val and Alan Green, Lucien Perring)*

PETERSFIELD SU7423
Old Drum (01730) 300544
Chapel Street; GU32 3DP Popular recently refurbished town-centre pub, good food in bar and separate dining area, five real ales including Bowman and Dark Star; children welcome if eating, bedrooms, closed Sun evening. *(Ann and Colin Hunt)*

PETERSFIELD SU7423
Red Lion (01730) 235160
College Street; GU31 4AE Wetherspoons in former coaching inn, usual good value food and beers; children welcome, open all day from 7am. *(Ann and Colin Hunt)*

PORTSMOUTH SZ6399
Bridge Tavern (023) 9275 2992
East Street, Camber Dock; PO1 2JJ Flagstones, bare boards and lots of dark wood, comfortable furnishings, maritime theme with good harbour views, Fullers ales, plenty of fish dishes; nice waterside terrace. *(Ann and Colin Hunt)*

PORTSMOUTH SU6402
Fountain (023) 9266 1636
London Road, North End; PO2 9AA Unchanging tiled pub with large bar and family room off, nicely polished brass,

interesting pictures of local pubs, mirrors each end, unusual ceiling lights, well kept beer including Gales HSB, no food; seats outside. *(Ann and Colin Hunt)*

PORTSMOUTH SZ6399
Pembroke (023) 9282 3961
Pembroke Road; PO1 2NR Traditional well run corner local with good buoyant atmosphere, comfortable and unspoilt under long-serving licensees, Bass, Fullers London Pride and Greene King Abbot from L-shaped bar, fresh rolls, coal-effect gas fire; open all day (except 5-7pm Sun). *(Ole Ponpey, Ann and Colin Hunt)*

PORTSMOUTH SZ6299
Still & West (023) 9282 1567
Bath Square, Old Portsmouth; PO1 2JL Great location with superb views of narrow harbour mouth and across to Isle of Wight, especially from glazed-in panoramic upper family area and waterfront terrace with lots of picnic-sets; nautical bar with fireside sofas and cosy colour scheme, Fullers ales, good choice of wines by the glass, enjoyable food all day including signature fish and chips; background music may be loud, nearby pay-and-display; children welcome, handy for Historic Dockyard. *(Anon)*

PORTSMOUTH SZ6399
Wellington (023) 9281 8965
High Street, off Grand Parade, Old Portsmouth; PO1 2LY Comfortable open-plan pub with large Georgian bay window, near seafront and historic square tower, enjoyable reasonably priced food including fresh fish, three real ales; open all day summer (all day Fri-Sun winter). *(Ann and Colin Hunt)*

ROCKFORD SU1608
Alice Lisle (01425) 474700
Follow sign on village green; BH24 3NA Big open-plan family dining pub (former school) attractively placed on green by New Forest, well laid out and can get very busy; large conservatory-style eating area, enjoyable choice of fresh food (all day weekends) from sandwiches to specials, Sun carvery, well kept Fullers ales and several wines by the glass, friendly efficient staff; baby-changing facilities, dogs welcome, big garden overlooking lake with ponies wandering nearby, play area, handy for Moyles Court, open all day. *(John Saville)*

ROMSEY SU3523
⋆ Dukes Head (01794) 514450
A3057 out towards Stockbridge; SO51 0HB Attractive 16th-c dining pub with warren of small comfortable linked rooms, big log fire, good varied choice of enjoyable food, well kept ales such as Fullers/Gales, Sharps and Wells & Youngs, decent wines and coffee, friendly staff and regulars; children welcome, colourful hanging baskets,

sheltered back terrace and pleasant garden, handy for Sir Harold Hillier Gardens, open all day. *(Ann and Colin Hunt, J V Dadswell, Martin and Karen Wake)*

ROMSEY SU3521
Old House At Home (01794) 513175
Love Lane; SO51 8DE Attractive 16th-c thatched pub surrounded by new development; friendly and bustling, with appealingly individual and old-fashioned décor, wide choice of freshly made, sensibly priced bar food including popular Sun lunch, well kept Fullers/Gales ales and guests, decent coffee, cheerful efficient service, good pubby atmosphere; children's play area. *(Ann and Colin Hunt, Colin and Peggy Wilshire)*

ROMSEY SU3520
Three Tuns (01794) 512639
Middlebridge Street (but car park signed straight off A27 bypass); SO51 8HL Old beamed and bow-windowed pub refurbished and continuing well under current owners, friendly buoyant atmosphere, well kept changing ales such as Flack Manor, Hop Back, Ringwood and Sharps, traditional pub food, open fire; children and dogs welcome, open all day. *(Phil and Jane Villiers, Natalie Tanner)*

ROTHERWICK SU7156
Coach & Horses (01256) 768976
Signed from B3349 N of Hook; also quite handy for M3 junction 5; RG27 9BG 17th-c pub with traditional beamed front rooms, good value locally sourced pubby food, well kept Badger ales, log fire and woodburners, newer back dining area; children, dogs and muddy boots welcome, tables out at front and on terrace behind, pretty flower tubs and baskets, good walks, open all day Sat, closed Sun evening, Mon. *(David and Judy Robison)*

SARISBURY SU5008
Bold Forester (01489) 576400
Handy for M27 junction 9; Bridge Road (A27), Sarisbury Green; SO31 7EL Roomy and well run with good choice of popular food from baguettes and sharing plates up, decent vegetarian options too, cheerful polite service, four real ales including Ringwood, pictures of this increasingly built-up area in its strawberry fields days; children welcome, pretty hanging baskets and tubs in front, large attractive garden behind, play area, open all day. *(Ann and Colin Hunt)*

SELBORNE SU7433
Queens (01420) 511454
High Street; GU34 3JJ Comfortably refurbished and welcoming, open fires, interesting local memorabilia, well kept Hogs Back TEA and Triple fff Alton Pride, food (not Sun evening) from sandwiches and pubby standards to french country

dishes, cream teas and nice coffee, cheerful smartly dressed staff, occasional jazz; children and dogs welcome, garden picnic-sets, eight bedrooms, very handy for Gilbert White's House, open all day. *(Ann and Colin Hunt)*

SHALDEN   SU7043
Golden Pot (01420) 80655
B3349 Odiham Road N of Alton; GU34 4DJ Airy décor with sage-green walls, bare boards and log fires, enjoyable sensibly priced food from baguettes up including themed nights, friendly service, beers such as Andwell and Otter, skittle alley; children welcome, some tables out on covered area at front, garden with play area. *(Martin and Karen Wake)*

SHEDFIELD   SU5513
Wheatsheaf (01329) 833024
A334 Wickham–Botley; SO32 2JG Busy friendly no-fuss local, well kept Flowerpots ales tapped from the cask, farm cider, short sensible choice of bargain bar lunches (evening food Tues and Weds), good service, regular live music; dogs welcome, garden, handy for Wickham Vineyard, open all day. *(Stephen and Jean Curtis)*

SHIPTON BELLINGER   SU2345
Boot (01980) 842279
High Street; SP9 7UF Village pub very popular for its huge range of enjoyable food including indian, chinese, thai, italian and mexican and traditional english dishes, friendly staff; children welcome, back garden with decked area, open all day weekends. *(Phil and Jane Hodson)*

SILCHESTER   SU6262
Calleva Arms (01734) 9700305
The Common; RG7 2PH Friendly bay-windowed pub facing the common, Fullers/ Gales and a guest beer, decent wines by the glass, wide range of food from baguettes up, roomy bar with lots of bric-a-brac, dining conservatory, pool area; handy for the Roman site, sizeable attractive garden, open all day Fri-Sun. *(Anon)*

SOPLEY   SZ1596
✱ Woolpack (01425) 672252
B3347 N of Christchurch; BH23 7AX Pretty thatched dining pub with rambling open-plan low-beamed bar, generous helpings of enjoyable traditional food (order at bar) including fish and chips served in newspaper, ales such as Ringwood and Sharps Doom Bar, Thatcher's cider, good choice of wines by the glass, modern dining conservatory overlooking weir; they may ask to keep a credit card if you run a tab; children in eating areas, dogs in certain parts, terrace and charming garden with weeping willows, duck stream and footbridges, open all day. *(Sue and Mike Todd)*

SOUTHAMPTON   SU4111
✱ Duke of Wellington (023) 8033 9222
Bugle Street (or walk along city wall from Bar Gate); SO14 2AH Striking ancient timber-framed building dating from 14th c, cellars even older, heavy beams and great log fire, well kept Wadworths ales, good choice of wines by the glass and good value traditional pub food (not Sun evening), friendly helpful service; background music (live Fri); children welcome, sunny streetside picnic-sets, handy for Tudor House Museum, open all day. *(Stephen and Jean Curtis, David Ellis, Val and Alan Green)*

SOUTHAMPTON   SU4213
White Star (023) 8082 1990
Oxford Street; SO14 3DJ Smart modern bar, banquettes and open fire, comfortable sofas and armchairs in secluded alcoves by south-facing windows, bistro-style dining area, good up-to-date food from interesting baguettes and light dishes up, efficient attentive service, Itchen Valley and Sharps ales, nice wines by the glass and lots of cocktails; they may try to keep your credit card while you eat; sunny pavement tables on pedestrianised street, 13 boutique bedrooms, open all day. *(Tracey and Stephen Groves)*

SOUTHSEA   SZ6699
Artillery Arms (023) 9273 3610
Hester Road; PO4 8HB Proper two-bar Victorian backstreet local, good choice of real ales including Bowmans Swift One, decent food, friendly busy atmosphere. *(Ann and Colin Hunt)*

SOUTHSEA   SZ6499
Eldon Arms (023) 9229 6374
Eldon Street/Norfolk Street; PO5 4BS Rambling backstreet pub under welcoming licensees, Fullers London Pride and three changing guests, Thatcher's cider, no food except good value Sun carvery, flowers on tables, old pictures and advertisements, attractive mirrors, bric-a-brac and shelves of books; background and occasional live acoustic music, sensibly placed darts, bar billiards, pool, fruit machine; children welcome, can bring dogs but best to ask (resident staffy is Bella); tables in back garden, open all day. *(Ann and Colin Hunt)*

SOUTHSEA   SZ6499
✱ Hole in the Wall (023) 9229 8085
Great Southsea Street; PO5 3BY Friendly unspoilt little local in old part of town, up to six well priced changing ales in good condition, Thatcher's cider, simple good value food including speciality local sausages and meat puddings, nicely worn boards, dark pews and panelling, old photographs and prints, over 700 pump clips on ceiling, little snug behind the bar, daily papers, quiz night Thurs, Oct beer festival; small outside tiled area at front

with benches, side garden, opens at 4pm (noon Fri, 2pm Sun). *(Ann and Colin Hunt)*

SOUTHSEA   SZ6499
King Street Tavern (023) 9287 3307
King Street; PO5 4EH Sympathetically refurbished corner pub in attractive conservation area, spectacular Victorian tiled façade, bare boards and original fittings, four well kept Wadworths ales and guests, real ciders, good value straightforward home-made food from short menu; background and live music including fortnightly Sat jazz; dogs welcome, courtyard tables, closed Mon-Weds lunchtimes. *(Ann and Colin Hunt)*

SOUTHSEA   SZ6698
Sir Loin of Beef (023) 9282 0115
Highland Road, Eastney; PO4 9NH Simple spic-and-span corner pub with up to eight well kept frequently changing ales (tasters offered), bottled beers, no food, helpful friendly staff and buoyant atmosphere, interesting ship photographs, parasols suspended from ceiling, monthly Sun jazz and Thurs quiz; open all day. *(Ann and Colin Hunt)*

SOUTHSEA   SZ6499
Wine Vaults (023) 9286 4712
Albert Road, opposite King's Theatre; PO5 2SF Bustling pub with eight changing ales including Fullers London Pride, ESB and London Porter, several chatty rooms on different floors, main panelled bar with long plain counter and pubby furniture, smarter restaurant area, limited choice of bar food but something available all day; background music, sports TV; children welcome, dogs in bar, smokers' roof terrace, open till 1am Fri, Sat. *(Ann and Colin Hunt, Jane and Rowena Leverington, Peter Meister)*

SOUTHWICK   SU6208
Golden Lion (023) 9221 0437
High Street; just off B2177 on Portsdown Hill; PO17 6EB Friendly two-bar 16th-c beamed pub refurbished without spoiling character (where Eisenhower and Montgomery came before D-Day); up to six local ales including two from Suthwyk using barley from surrounding fields, four ciders and a dozen wines by the glass, enjoyable locally sourced home-made food (not Sun and Mon evenings) from snacks up in bar and dining room, lounge bar with sofas and log fire, live music including Tues jazz; good outside lavatories; children and dogs welcome, picnic-sets on grass at side, picturesque estate village with scenic walks, open all day Sat, till 7pm Sun. *(Val and Alan Green)*

SOUTHWICK   SU6208
Red Lion (023) 9237 7223
High Street; PO17 6EF Neatly kept low-beamed village dining pub with good choice of popular food, Fullers/Gales and a guest ale, several wines by the glass, efficient friendly service from smartly dressed staff even when busy; children welcome, nice walks. *(Ann and Colin Hunt)*

ST MARY BOURNE   SU4250
Bourne Valley (01264) 738361
Upper Link (B3048); SP11 6BT Refurbished old red-brick inn under new management; lightened-up bar with central servery and log fire, separate raftered restaurant, enjoyable interesting food along with pubby choices, Upham Punter and three guests, lots of wines by the glass, deli counter; children and dogs welcome, terrace and nice garden backing on to stream, nine bedrooms, open all day. *(Jennifer Banks)*

STOCKBRIDGE   SU3535
Three Cups (01264) 810527
High Street; SO20 6HB Lovely low-beamed building dating from 1500, some emphasis on dining with lots of smartly set pine tables, but also high-backed settles, country bric-a-brac and four well kept ales such as Wells & Youngs, good interesting food along with more pubby choices, amiable service, nice wines by the glass, extended 'orangery' restaurant; children and dogs welcome, vine-covered verandah and charming cottage garden with streamside terrace, eight bedrooms, open all day. *(Conor McGaughey, Geoffrey Kemp)*

STOCKBRIDGE   SU3535
✳ White Hart (01264) 810663
High Street; A272/A3057 roundabout; SO20 6HF Thriving divided beamed bar, attractive décor with antique prints, oak pews and other seats, friendly helpful staff, enjoyable food from snacks to substantial daily specials, well kept Fullers/Gales beers, comfortable restaurant with blazing log fire (children allowed); dogs in bar, disabled facilities, terrace tables and nice garden, 14 good bedrooms, open all day. *(John and Joan Calvert, Val and Alan Green, Edward Mirzoeff)*

STUBBINGTON   SU5402
Crofton (01329) 314222
Crofton Lane; PO14 3QF Modern two-bar estate local, neat and airy, with five well kept ales including Sharps Doom Bar, good value wines and very popular generously served food at reasonable prices, friendly smartly dressed staff, skittle alley; children and dogs welcome. *(Ann and Colin Hunt)*

SWANMORE   SU5716
Brickmakers (01489) 890954
Church Road; SO32 2PA Friendly refurbished pub under newish management, four well kept ales including Bowman, decent wines and good interesting food all day (till 7pm Sun) from landlord-chef, leather sofas by log fire, dining area with local artwork, Tues quiz, some live music; children and dogs welcome, garden with raised deck, open all day. *(Val and Alan Green)*

SWANMORE   SU5816
Hunters (01489) 877214
Hillgrove; SO32 2PZ Popular rambling
old dining pub with friendly long-serving
licensees and nice staff, wide choice of
good honest freshly made food, home-baked
bread, well kept Bowman and a guest tapped
from the cask, lots of wines by the glass,
bank notes, carpentry and farm tools on
walls; background music; children and dogs
welcome, big garden with play area, nice
walks N of village, open all day weekends
(can be very busy then). *(Val and Alan Green)*

SWAY   SZ2898
Hare & Hounds (01590) 682404
*Durns Town, just off B3055 SW of
Brockenhurst; SO41 6AL* Bright, airy and
comfortable New Forest family dining pub,
popular generously served food, ales such
as Itchen Valley, Ringwood, St Austell and
Timothy Taylors, good helpful service even at
busy times, low beams and central log fire;
background music; dogs welcome, picnic-sets
and play frame in neatly kept garden, open
all day. *(D J and P M Taylor)*

THRUXTON   SU2945
White Horse (01264) 772401
*Mullens Pond, just off A303 eastbound;
SP11 8EE* Attractive old thatched pub
tucked below A303 embankment, comfortably
modernised, with emphasis on fresh food,
good friendly service, plenty of wines by
the glass, well kept ales such as Greene
King, woodburner, a couple of sofas, very
low beams, separate dining area; good-sized
garden and terrace, four bedrooms, closed
Sun evening. *(Anon)*

TICHBORNE   SU5730
★Tichborne Arms (01962) 733760
Signed off B3047; SO24 0NA Traditional
thatched pub with latticed windows,
panelling, antiques and stuffed animals,
open fire, Palmers and guests tapped from
the cask, local cider, food (not Sun evening)
from baguettes up, locals' bar, darts, board
games and shove-ha'penny; children and dogs
welcome, big garden in rolling countryside,
Wayfarers Walk and Itchen Way pass nearby,
closed Sun evening. *(R Elliott)*

TIMSBURY   SU3325
★Bear & Ragged Staff
(01794) 368602 *A3057 towards
Stockbridge; pub marked on OS Sheet
185 map reference 334254; SO51 0LB*
Reliable roadside dining pub with wide
choice of popular food including blackboard
specials, friendly efficient service, lots of
wines by the glass, Fullers, Hampshire,

Ringwood and Timothy Taylors, log fire, good-
sized beamed interior; children welcome in
eating part, tables in extended garden with
play area, handy for Mottisfont Abbey (NT),
good walks, open all day. *(Phyl and Jack Street,
Val and Alan Green)*

TITCHFIELD   SU5305
Bugle (01329) 841888
*The Square, off A27 near Fareham;
PO14 4AF* Roomy and comfortable 18th-c
coaching inn, popular good value food from
light meals up, friendly attentive service,
four well kept ales including Sharps Doom
Bar and a house beer from Tetleys, log fire,
old barn restaurant/function room behind;
no dogs; children welcome, attractive village
handy for Titchfield Haven nature reserve,
fine walk by former canal to coast, eight
bedrooms, open all day. *(Ann and Colin Hunt)*

TITCHFIELD   SU5406
Fishermans Rest (01329) 845065
*Mill Lane, off A27 at Titchfield Mill
pub; PO15 5RA* Refurbished dining pub
with good value popular food, well kept
Greene King ales; fine riverside position
opposite Titchfield Abbey, tables out behind
overlooking water. *(Ann and Colin Hunt)*

TITCHFIELD   SU5305
Queens Head (01329) 842154
*High Street; off A27 near Fareham;
PO14 4AQ* Ancient pub with good
straightforward home-made food and four
well kept ales including Wells & Youngs
Bombardier, cosy bar with old local pictures,
window seats and warm winter fire in central
brick fireplace, small attractive dining room;
picnic-sets in prettily planted back yard,
pleasant conservation village near nature
reserve and walks to coast. *(Ann and
Colin Hunt)*

TITCHFIELD   SU5405
Wheatsheaf (01329) 842965
*East Street; off A27 near Fareham;
PO14 4AD* Welcoming smartened-up old
place with well kept ales and good popular
food (not Mon) including lunchtime two-
course deal, bow-windowed front bar, side
snug and back dining extension, log fires;
background music; terrace, open all day
(afternoon break Mon). *(Ann and Colin Hunt,
David M Smith, Val and Alan Green)*

TOTFORD   SU5737
Woolpack (0845) 293 8066
B3046 Basingstoke–Alresford; SO24 9TJ
Nicely refurbished roadside inn, clean
and comfortable, with good food from bar
snacks to restaurant dishes, Palmers, an
ale brewed for the pub and a guest such as

We checked prices with the pubs as we went to press in summer 2013.
They should hold until around spring 2014.

Bowman, several wines by the glass including champagne, nice italian coffee, efficient service, raised open fire in bar, smart split-level dining room; pool; circular picnic-sets on gravel, lovely setting in good walking country, seven bedrooms, open all day. *(John and Anne Mackinnon)*

TWYFORD SU4824
★**Bugle** (01962) 714888
B3355/Park Lane; SO21 1QT Nicely done modern pub with good enterprising food served by attentive friendly young staff, well kept ales from Bowman, Flowerpots and Upham, woodburner; background music; attractive verandah seating area, good walks nearby, open all day. *(M and R Ridge, Phyl and Jack Street)*

TWYFORD SU4824
Phoenix (01962) 713322
High Street (B3335); SO21 1RF Cheerful open-plan local with raised dining area and big end inglenook, friendly long-serving landlord and attentive staff, eight real ales including Greene King, good value wines, traditional food (themed nights), side skittle alley; unobtrusive background music, sports TV; children allowed at one end lunchtime, garden with smokers' area, open all day Fri, Sat, till 7pm Sun. *(Anon)*

UPHAM SU5320
★**Brushmakers Arms** (01489) 860231
Shoe Lane; village signed from Winchester–Bishop's Waltham downs road, and from B2177; SO32 1JJ Plenty of regulars and weekend dog walkers at this cheery low-beamed village pub, L-shaped bar divided by central woodburner, cushioned settles and chairs around mix of tables, lots of brushes and related paraphernalia, little back snug, enjoyable home-made food including range of pies, Fullers, Ringwood, Upham and a guest, decent coffee, pub cats (Luna and Baxter); children and dogs welcome, big garden with picnic-sets on sheltered terrace and tree-shaded lawn, open all day Sun. *(Ann and Colin Hunt)*

UPPER CLATFORD SU3543
Crook & Shears (01264) 361543
Off A343 S of Andover, via Foundry Road; SP11 7QL Cosy 17th-c thatched pub with friendly relaxing atmosphere, several homely olde-worlde seating areas, bare boards and panelling, three good changing ales, decent reasonably priced food from doorstep sandwiches up, open fires and woodburner, small dining room, back skittle alley with own bar; pleasant secluded garden behind. *(Ann and Colin Hunt)*

UPPER FARRINGDON SU7135
Rose & Crown (01420) 588231
Off A32 S of Alton; Crows Lane – follow Church, Selborne, Liss signpost;

GU34 3ED Airy 19th-c village pub with L-shaped log-fire bar, several well kept ales including Triple fff, good reasonably priced food (all day Sun) with some interesting choices including vegetarian options, efficient friendly young staff, formal back dining room, jazz last Mon of month; well behaved children and dogs welcome, wide views from attractive back garden, open all day weekends. *(Anon)*

UPTON GREY SU6948
Hoddington Arms (01256) 862371
Signed off B3349 S of Hook; Bidden Road; RG25 2RL Nicely refurbished 18th-c beamed pub, good food from varied menu (sometimes themed), local ales such as Andwell and a beer named for them (Hodd), a dozen wines by the glass; children very welcome, big enclosed garden with terrace, quiet pretty village, good walking/cycling, open all day. *(Louise Richards)*

WALHAMPTON SZ3396
Walhampton Arms (01590) 673113
B3054 NE of Lymington; aka Walhampton Inn; SO41 5RE Large comfortable Georgian-style family roadhouse, popular well priced food including good carvery in raftered former stables and two adjoining areas, pleasant lounge, Ringwood ales and nice cider, cheerful helpful staff; attractive courtyard, good walks, open all day and handy for IOW ferry. *(Phyl and Jack Street, Barrie and Mary Crees, Penny and Peter Keevil)*

WALTHAM CHASE SU5614
Black Dog (01329) 832316
Winchester Road; SO32 2LX Old brick-built pub doing well under newish landlord, low-ceilinged front bar, three well kept Greene King ales and a guest, over a dozen wines by the glass, good choice of enjoyable home-made food including weekday lunch deal, back restaurant; children and dogs welcome, colourful hanging baskets, tables in good-sized neatly kept garden, open all day weekends in summer. *(Ann and Colin Hunt)*

WEST TYTHERLEY SU2730
Black Horse (01794) 340308
North Lane; SP5 1NF Compact unspoilt beamed village local, welcoming licensees and chatty regulars, traditional bar with a couple of long tables and big fireplace, nicely set dining area off, four real ales, enjoyable reasonably priced food including good Sun roasts, skittle alley; children and dogs welcome, closed Sun evening, Mon and Tues lunchtimes. *(Anon)*

WHERWELL SU3839
★**Mayfly** (01264) 860283
Testcombe (over by Fullerton, not in Wherwell itself); A3057 SE of Andover, between B3420 turn-off and Leckford where road crosses River Test; OS Sheet 185 map reference 382390; SO20 6AX

Well run busy pub with decking and conservatory overlooking fast-flowing River Test; spacious beamed and carpeted bar with fishing paraphernalia, rustic pub furnishings and woodburner, ales such as Adnams, Gales, Hop Back, Palmers and Wickwar, lots of wines by the glass, wide range of good popular bar food all day (must book for a good table), courteous well organised service; background music; well behaved children and dogs welcome. *(Helen and Brian Edgeley, Conor McGaughey, Martin and Karen Wake, Alan Wright, Mr and Mrs A Curry, Jeremy King and others)*

WHERWELL   SU3840
White Lion (01264) 860317
B3420; SP11 7JF Refurbished early 17th-c multi-level beamed village inn, good choice of enjoyable food including speciality pies, Ringwood, Sharps and three guests, several wines by the glass, very friendly helpful staff, open fire, comfy leather sofas and armchairs, dining rooms either side of bar; background music; dogs on leads and well behaved children welcome, sunny courtyard with good quality furniture, Test Way walks, six bedrooms, open all day from 7.30am (breakfast for non-residents). *(Michael and Jenny Back, N R White, Ann and Colin Hunt, Edward Mirzoeff, Graham Jerome and others)*

WICKHAM   SU5711
⋆Greens (01329) 833197
The Square, at junction with A334; PO17 5JQ Civilised dining place with clean-cut modern furnishings and décor, small bar with leather sofa and armchairs as well as bar stools, wide wine choice and a couple of real ales, efficient obliging young staff, step down to split-level balustraded dining areas, enjoyable food from typical bar lunches to imaginative water specials; pleasant lawn overlooking water meadows, closed Sun evening, Mon. *(Phyl and Jack Street)*

WINCHESTER   SU4828
⋆Black Boy (01962) 861754
B3403 off M3 junction 10 towards city, then left into Wharf Hill; no nearby daytime parking – 220 metres from car park on B3403; SO23 9NQ Splendidly eccentric décor at this chatty old-fashioned pub, floor-to-ceiling books, lots of big

clocks, mobiles made of wine bottles or spectacles, stuffed animals including a baboon and dachshund, two log fires, orange-painted room with big oriental rugs on red floorboards, barn room with open hayloft, five often local beers, straightforward food (not Sun evening, Mon, Tues lunchtime) including good doorstep sandwiches, friendly service, table football and board games; background music; supervised children and dogs welcome, slate tables out in front and seats on attractive secluded terrace, open all day. *(John and Annabel Hampshire, Mark Sykes, Dr Martin Owton, Ann and Colin Hunt, Val and Alan Green, Phil and Jane Villiers)*

WINCHESTER   SU4829
⋆Eclipse (01962) 865676
The Square, between High Street and cathedral; SO23 9EX Picturesque unspoilt 14th-c local with massive beams and timbers in its two small cheerful rooms, four ales such as Bath Gem and Otter, decent choice of wines by the glass, good value lunchtime food from nice ciabattas to popular Sun roasts, open fire, oak settles; children in back area, seats outside, very handy for cathedral. *(Val and Alan Green, Neil and Anita Christopher)*

WINCHESTER   SU4829
⋆Old Vine (01962) 854616
Great Minster Street; SO23 9HA Lively big-windowed town bar with well kept ales such as Bowman, Flowerpots, Ringwood and St Austell, high beams, worn oak boards, smarter and larger dining side with good choice of up-to-date food plus sandwiches and pub staples, modern conservatory; faint background music; by cathedral, with sheltered terrace, partly covered and heated, charming bedrooms, open all day. *(Neil and Anita Christopher)*

WOLVERTON   SU5658
George & Dragon (01635) 298292
Towns End; just N of A339 Newbury–Basingstoke; RG26 5ST Low-beamed and flagstoned pub in remote rolling country, long-serving licensees, linked cosy areas, log fire, good choice of enjoyable unpretentious food, beers such as Fullers, Greene King and Wadworths, decent wines, attentive service; children welcome, big garden with small terrace, ten bedrooms in separate block, good breakfast. *(Anon)*

Herefordshire

This is a lovely county with wonderful walks, and several of our pubs also have fantastic views. To make the most of this, why not stay for a couple of days at inns holding a Stay Award: the Cottage of Content at Carey (country furnishings, a nicely old-fashioned feel and good food), Feathers in Ledbury (an old favourite with a bustling bar in a civilised hotel), Kings Head in Ross-on-Wye (warmly friendly, super breakfasts and good value lunches), Saracens Head at Symonds Yat (riverside terraces and a chatty, bustling bar) and Stagg at Titley (an exceptional all-rounder). All these pubs, plus the Mill Race at Walford (smashing food using produce from their own farm), serve first class meals, but it is the wonderful Stagg at Titley that is our Herefordshire Dining Pub 2014.

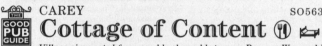

CAREY   SO5631   Map 4

Cottage of Content 🍴 🛏

Village signposted from good back road betweeen Ross-on-Wye and Hereford E of A49, through Hoarwithy; HR2 6NG

Country furnishings in a friendly rustic cottage, interesting food, real ales and seats on terraces; quiet bedrooms

In a tranquil spot near the River Wye, this medieval cottage is a lovely place to stay. Originally three labourers' cottages with an integral cider and ale parlour, the building has kept much of its old character. There's a multitude of beams and country furnishings including stripped-pine kitchen chairs, long pews by one big table and various old-fashioned tables on flagstones or bare boards. The friendly landlady serves Hobsons Best and Wye Valley Butty Bach on handpump, and a local cider in summer; background music. There are picnic-sets on the flower-filled front terrace and in the rural-feeling back garden.

Popular food includes chicken liver and pork pâté with caramelised red cabbage and crisp olive toasts, feta, olive and herb soufflé on baby spinach with tomato and basil sauce, griddled lamb steak with pea and mint pesto, bacon-wrapped roast hake on tomato and smoked paprika cassoulet, pork medallions on wilted spinach with creamy sage and cider sauce, rib-eye steak with mustard mash and green peppercorn sauce, and puddings like chocolate cheesecake and banoffi meringue. *Benchmark main dish: game crumble £13.25. Two-course evening meal £20.00.*

Free house ~ Licensees Richard and Helen Moore ~ Real ale ~ (01432) 840242 ~ Open 12-2.30(3 Sat), 6-11; 12-3 Sun; closed Sun evening, Mon, winter Tues, 1 week Feb,

two weeks Oct ~ Bar food 12-2, 6.30-9; 12-2 Sun ~ Restaurant ~ Children welcome ~
Dogs allowed in bar ~ Bedrooms: £65/£75 ~ www.cottageofcontent.co.uk
Recommended by Barry Collett, Mike and Mary Carter

EARDISLEY   SO3149   Map 6

Tram £

Corner of A4111 and Woodseaves Road; HR3 6PG

**Food is a growing focus in this character village pub, and the village
itself is a big draw too**

In a famous black and white village, this handsome old pub is doing
particularly well under its young licensees. The beamed bar on the left
has warm local character, especially in the cosy back section behind
sturdy standing timbers, where regulars congregate on the bare boards
by the counter, which serves Hobsons Best, Brecon Gold Beacons and
Wye Valley Butty Bach on handpump and local organic cider and perry.
Elsewhere, there are antique red and ochre floor tiles, a handful of
nicely worn tables and chairs, a pair of long cushioned pews flanking a
very long table, a high-backed settle, old country pictures and a couple
of pictorial Wye maps. There's a small pink-walled dining room on
the right, and a new games room with pool and darts in a converted
former brewhouse with an attached smokers' area; background music.
The outside gents' is one of the most stylish we've seen, and the neatly
planted sizeable garden has picnic-sets on a lawn; pétanque.

Popular food includes sandwiches, lightly spiced whitebait with sweet chilli
dip, quenelles of chicken and duck liver pâté with red onion marmalade,
tomato, olive and caper pasta, steak in ale pie, steak burger with bacon, cheddar,
onion rings, coleslaw and tomato relish, beer-battered hake, free-range chicken
with chorizo, mushroom and spinach stuffing on sunblush tomato risotto, and
puddings such as Baileys, hazelnut and chocolate cheesecake with chocolate ice-
cream and warm treacle tart with stem ginger ice-cream. *Benchmark main dish:
10oz 28-day-aged sirloin £15.50. Two-course evening meal £15.50.*

Free house ~ Licensees Mark and Kerry Vernon ~ Real ale ~ (01544) 327251 ~ Open
12-3, 6-midnight; 12-3, 7-11 Sun; closed Mon except spring and summer bank holidays ~
Bar food 12-3, 6-9; 12-3 Sun ~ Restaurant ~ Children welcome ~ Dogs allowed in bar ~
www.thetraminn.co.uk *Recommended by MLR, Tess White, John and Jennifer Spinks*

KILPECK   SO4430   Map 6

Kilpeck Inn ♀

Village and church signposted off A465 SW of Hereford; HR2 9DN

Imaginatively extended country inn in fascinating and peaceful village

Sensitively reworked a couple of years ago, this neat inn has a softly lit
dark beamed bar with dark slate flagstones. It rambles happily around
to give several tempting corners – one with an antique high-backed
settle, one with high stools around a matching chest-high table, and one
with a sheepskin thrown invitingly over a seat. This opens into three
cosily linked dining rooms on the left, with tall wainscoting. Throughout,
the mood is thoroughly up to date, with clean-cut décor and furnishings;
well reproduced background music. Wye Valley Butty Bach and HPA on
handpump, a good choice of wines by the glass and Weston's cider. The
neat back grass has picnic-sets (and there's a bicycle rack). The four
bedrooms, named after local rivers, look nice – they're very eco-minded,
with a biomass boiler and rainwater recycling system; we'd love to

hear from readers who have stayed here. The nearby castle ruins are intriguing and the unique romanesque church even more so.

🍴 Interesting food includes sandwiches, treacle-cured salmon with beetroot bavarois, rabbit and pistachio terrine with apricot chutney, warm pear, walnut and welsh blue cheese tart, ham and free-range eggs, field mushroom burger with tarragon mustard butter, pork sausages, mash and onion gravy, roast rack of lamb with lamb faggot and dauphinoise potatoes, venison loin with rosemary, goats cheese and redcurrant sauce, guinea fowl breast with confit leg, chestnut and pancetta sprouts and straw potatoes, and puddings such as warm chocolate fondant with pistachio ice-cream and lemoncello semifreddo with orange shortbread. *Benchmark main dish: beer-battered cod fillet with peas and tartare sauce £8.95. Two-course evening meal £20.00.*

Free house ~ Licensee Catherine Carleton-Smith ~ Real ale ~ (01981) 570464 ~ Open 12-2.30, 5.30-11; 12-5.30 Sun; closed Sun evening ~ Bar food 12-2, 7-9; 12.30-2.30 Sun ~ Restaurant ~ Children welcome ~ Dogs allowed in bar ~ Bedrooms: /£70 ~ www.kilpeckinn.com *Recommended by R and S Bentley, R K Phillips, R T and J C Moggridge*

LEDBURY
Feathers 🍴 ♟ 🛏
High Street (A417); HR8 1DS

SO7137 Map 4

Handsome old hotel with chatty relaxed bar, more decorous lounge, good food and friendly staff; comfortable bedrooms

We've known this strikingly timbered 16th-c hotel for many years and, thankfully, it remains as well run as ever. There's a civilised old-world atmosphere throughout. The convivial, carpeted back bar-brasserie has a chatty mix of drinkers at one end, with cosy leather easy chairs and sofas by the fire, and contented diners in the main section, with flowers and oil lamps on stripped-wood kitchen and other tables, and comfortable bays of banquettes and other seats. The long beams are a mass of hop bines, and small prints and antique sale notices decorate the stripped panelling. Fullers London Pride and a couple of guests such as Ledbury Gold and Prescott Hill Climb on handpump, good wines by the glass from an extensive list and 40 malt whiskies; first class staff. The sedate lounge is just right for afternoon tea, with high-sided armchairs and sofas in front of a big log fire, and daily papers. In summer, the sheltered back terrace has abundant pots and hanging baskets.

🍴 Well prepared and enjoyable food includes sandwiches, a tuscan platter, moules marinière, chicken liver parfait, foie gras en croûte and bramble and pear chutney, tomato and brie tartlets with basil-scented leeks and roast garlic and chilli dressing, moroccan lamb meatballs with aubergine, chickpea salad and minted yoghurt, beef and thyme burger with crispy smoked bacon, double gloucester cheese and spicy tomato relish, bass fillets with parsnip and potato mash, red wine shallots and rioja syrup, guinea fowl breast with colcannon potatoes, sautéed leeks and broad beans and madeira jus, and puddings. *Benchmark main dish: crispy beer-battered haddock with mushy peas and tartare sauce £13.50. Two-course evening meal £19.50.*

Free house ~ Licensee David Elliston ~ Real ale ~ (01531) 635266 ~ Open 11-11 (10.30 Sun) ~ Bar food 12-2(2.30 weekends), 6.30-9.30(10 weekends) ~ Restaurant ~ Children welcome ~ Dogs allowed in bar and bedrooms ~ Bedrooms: £97.50/£145 ~ www.feathers-ledbury.co.uk *Recommended by Guy Vowles, GSB, Mrs F Smith, Steve and Liz Tilley*

LITTLE COWARNE
Three Horseshoes ♀

SO6050 Map 4

Pub signposted off A465 SW of Bromyard; towards Ullingswick; HR7 4RQ

Long-serving licensees and friendly staff in bustling country pub with well liked food using home-grown produce; bedrooms

Having run this carefully kept place for over 20 years, the friendly licensees know many of their customers well, but you can be sure of an equally kindly welcome as a newcomer. The L-shaped middle bar has leather-seated bar stools, upholstered settles and dark brown kitchen chairs around sturdy tables, quarry tiles on the floor, old local photographs above the corner log fire and hop-draped beams. Opening off one side is a sun room with wicker armchairs around more tables; at the far end is a games room with darts, pool, juke box, games machine and cribbage. Wye Valley Bitter and Butty Bach and a guest beer on handpump, local Oliver's cider and perry, a dozen wines by the glass and a dozen malt whiskies. A popular Sunday lunchtime carvery is offered in the roomy and attractive restaurant extension with its rafters and stripped stone. There are well sited tables and chairs on the terrace and the neat, prettily planted lawn. Disabled access.

Cooked by the licensees' son, using own-grown and other local produce, the highly thought-of food includes sandwiches, salmon and lime fishcake, pork and pheasant pâté with pickled damsons, roasted butternut squash risotto, steak in ale pie, breast of chicken in perry sauce, salmon fillet with herb sauce, pheasant breast stuffed with spiced pear with elderberry sauce, cornish tuna with roasted vegetables and capers, and puddings. *Benchmark main dish: venison faggots on herb mash with damson gin gravy £11.50. Two-course evening meal £18.00.*

Free house ~ Licensees Norman and Janet Whittall ~ Real ale ~ (01885) 400276 ~ Open 11-3, 6.30-11.30; closed Tues, Sun evening in winter ~ Bar food 12-2, 7-9 ~ Restaurant ~ Children welcome ~ Bedrooms: £45/£80 ~ www.threehorseshoes.co.uk
Recommended by Martin and Sue Day, Ed and Glenda Buck

ROSS-ON-WYE
Kings Head £ 🛏

SO5924 Map 6

High Street (B4260); HR9 5HL

Welcoming bar in well run market-town hotel dating from 14th c; good bedrooms

At lunchtime, the enjoyable food here is very good value – hence our Bargain Award. The little beamed and panelled bar on the right has traditional pub furnishings on stripped floorboards, including comfortably padded bar seats and an antique cushioned box settle, and a couple of black leather armchairs by the log-effect fire; Wye Valley Butty Bach and a guest beer such as Sharps Doom Bar on handpump, sensibly priced wines by the glass, a farm cider and local apple juice. The beamed lounge bar on the left, also with bare boards, has some timbering, soft leather armchairs, padded wicker bucket seats and shelves of books. Friendly, efficient service, TV, unobtrusive background music. There's a big carpeted dining room, and the sheltered back courtyard has contemporary tables and chairs. They do a good breakfast for residents.

As well as a good value two-course lunch, the enjoyable food includes sandwiches, ham hock and smoked quails egg terrine with home-made piccalilli, cornish mussels with lemon grass, ginger, garlic and coriander, shepherd's pie, cauliflower, salsify and blue cheese tart with spinach and walnut pesto, local lambs liver and bacon, beer-battered fish, chicken breast with field mushrooms and tarragon and white wine velouté, slow-braised lamb shoulder with artichoke beignet and red wine and thyme jus, pigeon with black pudding fritter and pear and perry sauce, and puddings such as crème brûlée with lemon sable biscuit and sticky toffee pudding with butterscotch sauce. *Benchmark main dish: steak in ale pie £10.95. Two-course evening meal £18.00.*

Free house ~ Licensee James Vidler ~ Real ale ~ (01989) 763174 ~ Open 11-11; 12-10.30 Sun ~ Bar food 12-2.15(3 Sun), 6.30-9 ~ Restaurant ~ Children welcome ~ Dogs allowed in bar and bedrooms ~ Bedrooms: £56/£80 ~ www.kingshead.co.uk
Recommended by Neil and Anita Christopher, Howard and Margaret Buchanan, Lucien Perring

SYMONDS YAT   SO5616   Map 4
Saracens Head 🛏
Symonds Yat E; HR9 6JL

Friendly inn at a lovely riverside spot with a fine range of drinks, interesting food and seats on waterside terraces; comfortable bedrooms

One way to reach this 17th-c inn is by the hand ferry (pulled by one of the staff) that crosses the River Wye in front of the building. The waterside terraces have plenty of seats, though in fine weather it's best to arrive early to bag one. The bustling, flagstoned bar has a buoyant, welcoming atmosphere, plenty of chatty customers and cheerful staff who serve Bespoke Saved by the Bell, Kingstone 1503 Tudor Ale, Sharps Doom Bar and Wye Valley Butty Bach and HPA from handpump, 11 wines by the glass and Weston's cider. TV, background music and board games. There's also a cosy lounge and a modernised dining room with bare boards. Most of the bedrooms in the main building overlook the river; there are also two contemporary rooms in the boathouse annexe.

🍴 Popular food includes lunchtime sandwiches, crab and scallop gratin, local game ballotine with sweet pickles, sharing platters, burger with red cheddar, red onion, tomato and lettuce, mushroom and caramelised shallot pie, faggots with mash and mushy peas, corn-fed chicken with garlic and thyme mousse and vegetable pancake, fish stew with saffron and pernod, slow-braised rabbit with bitter chocolate jus, bass fillets with salsify, artichokes, braised lentils and chicory, daily specials such as pork and apple sausages with mash and red wine jus or maple-cured bacon and egg with crushed new potatoes, and puddings. *Benchmark main dish: pie of the day £10.95. Two-course evening meal £20.50.*

Free house ~ Licensees P K and C J Rollinson ~ Real ale ~ (01600) 890435 ~ Open 11-11 ~ Bar food 12-2.30, 6.30-9 ~ Restaurant ~ Children welcome ~ Dogs allowed in bar ~ Bedrooms: £59/£89 ~ www.saracensheadinn.co.uk *Recommended by MLR, Guy Vowles, Martin and Sue Radcliffe, Dave Webster, Sue Holland*

TILLINGTON   SO4645   Map 6
Bell 🍺
Off A4110 NW of Hereford; HR4 8LE

Friendly and relaxed, with snug character bar opening into civilised dining areas – good value

You can be sure of a friendly greeting from the hands-on landlord of this bustling pub – readers enjoy their visits here very much. The snug parquet-floored bar on the left has a variety of bucket armchairs around low chunky dark wood tables, brightly cushioned wall benches, team photographs and shelves of books; the black beams are strung with dried hops. Sharps Doom Bar, Wye Valley Bitter and a guest such as Mulberry Duck Amber Sparkle on handpump, cider made on site and locally produced spirits from Chase, all served by notably cheerful staff; daily papers, unobtrusive background music. The bar opens into a comfortable bare-boards dining lounge with stripy plush banquettes and a coal fire; beyond that is a pitched-ceiling restaurant area with more banquettes and big country prints; look through the slatted blinds to a sunken terrace with contemporary tables and a garden with teak tables, picnic-sets and a play area.

Using home-reared pigs and local produce, the enjoyable food includes sandwiches, salmon, crab and prawns with lemon and dill mayonnaise, chicken noodle salad with spicy peanut sauce, venison sausage with chorizo and butter bean casserole with rosemary and wild mushroom scone, home-baked honey-roast ham and fried egg, butternut squash and mediterranean vegetable bake topped with goats cheese, curries (lamb, prawn, vegetable, chicken), smoked haddock with welsh rarebit topping and chive mash, duck breast with sweet chilli and orange vegetable noodles and pineapple fritters, and puddings such as Mars Bar cheesecake and mulled cider-poached pear with orange sorbet; Wednesday is fish night. *Benchmark main dish: steak in ale pie £12.50. Two-course evening meal £18.00.*

Free house ~ Licensee Glenn Williams ~ Real ale ~ (01432) 760395 ~ Open 11-11; 12-10.30 Sun ~ Bar food 12-2.30, 6-9.15; all day Sat; 12-3 Sun ~ Restaurant ~ Children welcome ~ Dogs allowed in bar ~ www.thebelltillington.co.uk *Recommended by John and Jennifer Spinks, Revd Michael Vockins, Peter Cole*

TITLEY SO3359 Map 6

Stagg 🍴 🍷 🛏

B4355 N of Kington; HR5 3RL

Herefordshire Dining Pub of the Year

Terrific food using tip-top ingredients served in extensive dining rooms; real ales and a fine choice of other drinks, and seats in the two-acre garden; comfortable bedrooms

A first class all-rounder, this remains one of Britain's best dining pubs. It's as it's always been: a proper pub with genuinely welcoming and courteous staff and a really thoughtful choice of drinks. The little bar is comfortably hospitable with a civilised atmosphere, a fine collection of 200 jugs attached to the ceiling, Ludlow Stairway to Paradise and Wye Valley Butty Bach on handpump, nine house wines by the glass (plus a carefully chosen 100-strong bin list), Dunkerton's organic and Weston's ciders (lots of bottled cider and perry too), interesting local vodkas and gin from Chase, and quite a choice of spirits. The two-acre garden has seats on a terrace, and a croquet lawn. There are bedrooms above the pub and in a Georgian vicarage four minutes' walk away; super breakfasts. The inn is surrounded by good walking country and is handy for Offa's Dyke Path.

Using their own-made crisps, black pudding and other nice nibbles and growing their own vegetables and salads, the accomplished and delicious food includes snails with bacon, chestnuts and mushroom, baked pressed pigs head with pickled radish, potato gnocchi with charred leeks, mushroom duxelle, dill oil and spinach, home-made pork sausage and mash with onion rings, chicken breast with black pudding, pistachios, celeriac purée and sautéed potatoes, crispy duck leg with dauphinoise potatoes, cider, carrot and orange purée, ox cheek with smoked ox tongue and mash, slow-cooked pork belly with candied apple aubergine, little gem and noisette potatoes, and puddings such as apple, tapioca, oat crunch, apple sorbet and toffee apple and bread and butter pudding with beer caramel ice-cream; fantastic cheese list. *Benchmark main dish: local beef rump steak with béarnaise sauce and roast cherry tomatoes £16.90. Two-course evening meal £25.00.*

Free house ~ Licensees Steve and Nicola Reynolds ~ Real ale ~ (01544) 230221 ~ Open 12-3, 6.30-11(11.30 Sat); 12-3 Sun; closed Sun evening, Mon, two weeks Nov, one week Jan/Feb ~ Bar food 12-2, 6.30-9(9.30 Sat) ~ Restaurant ~ Children welcome ~ Dogs allowed in bar and bedrooms ~ Bedrooms: £80/£100 ~ www.thestagg.co.uk
Recommended by Chris Flynn, Wendy Jones, Steven King and Barbara Cameron, Peter Harrison, Jonathan Niccol, John Holroyd, Dr Kevan Tucker, Huw S Thomas

UPPER COLWALL   SO7643   Map 4

Chase

Chase Road, brown sign to pub off B4218 Malvern–Colwall, first left after hilltop on bend going W; WR13 6DJ

Cheerful country tavern with gorgeous sunset views from the garden, good drinks and cost-conscious food

Just the place for refreshment after enjoying one of the good surrounding walks, this is a traditional pub with fantastic views. Tables on the series of small, pretty, steep back terraces look right out over Herefordshire, and on a clear day as far as the Black Mountains and even the Brecon Beacons. Inside, it's chatty and companionable, with quite a pack of antique treadle sewing tables, a great variety of seats from a wooden-legged tractor seat to a carved pew, an old black kitchen range and plenty of decorations – china mugs, blue glass flasks, numerous small pictures. Half a dozen changing well kept ales on handpump such as Bathams Best, Brakspear Oxford Gold, St Georges Charger, Sharps Doom Bar and Woods Anniversary Ale and Shropshire Lad, and several wines by the glass; friendly, helpful staff. There may be free sandwiches in the early evening.

Under the new licensee, the food includes rolls and sandwiches, creamy garlic and parmesan mushrooms with basil toast, chicken, tarragon and ham hock terrine with red onion marmalade, smoked haddock and leek fishcakes with poached egg, butternut squash and thyme risotto, beer-battered fish and chips, chicken with garlic and thyme fondant potatoes and soubise sauce, king prawns in sweet chilli and garlic butter sauce with pak choi, coriander and prawn crackers, and puddings. *Benchmark main dish: beef bourguignon £12.80. Two-course evening meal £16.00.*

Free house ~ Licensee Phil Harrison ~ Real ale ~ (01684) 540276 ~ Open 12-3, 5-11; 12-11 Sat; 12-10.30 Sun ~ Bar food 12-2(2.30 weekends), 6.30-9 ~ Restaurant ~ Children welcome ~ Dogs allowed in bar ~ www.thechaseinnuppercolwall.co.uk
Recommended by Chris Flynn, Wendy Jones

A very few pubs try to make you leave a credit card at the bar, as a sort of deposit if you order food. They are not entitled to do this. The credit card firms and banks that issue them warn you not to let cards out of your sight. If someone behind the counter used your card fraudulently, the card company or bank could in theory hold you liable, because of your negligence in letting a stranger hang on to your card. Suggest instead that if they feel the need for security, they 'swipe' your card and give it back to you. And do name and shame the pub to us.

WALFORD

SO5820 Map 4

Mill Race 🍴 �

B4234 Ross-on-Wye to Lydney; HR9 5QS

Contemporary furnishings in uncluttered rooms, emphasis on good quality food ingredients, attentive staff, terrace tables and nearby walks

Although there's some emphasis in this pink-washed pub on the interesting food, the friendly landlord warmly welcomes drinkers too. A stylish, civilised place, it has a row of strikingly tall arched windows, comfortable leather armchairs and sofas on flagstones, and smaller chairs around broad pedestal tables. Walls are mainly cream or dark pink, with photographs of the local countryside, and there's good unobtrusive lighting. One wall, stripped back to the stonework, has a woodburning stove, which is open to the comfortable, compact dining area on the other side. The granite-topped modern bar counter has Butcombe Bitter, Wye Valley Bitter and a guest from St Georges on handpump, local ciders, 15 fairly priced wines by the glass, around 120 by the bottle and a dozen malt whiskies; background music. A terrace enjoys views towards Goodrich Castle and the garden has plenty of dining space. Leaflets detail pleasant nearby walks of an hour or so.

 Game, poultry, beef, fruit and vegetables from their own 1,000-acre farm and woodlands are used in the interesting food: sandwiches, pressed gammon terrine with fried quails egg, spiced pineapple pickle and mustard seed dressing, gloucester welsh rarebit with mussel beignets, pizzas from the outside oven, red onion, chilli and fennel tarte tatin with breaded goats cheese, burger with tomato relish, coleslaw and chips, beef cheeks with chanterelles, sloe gin-braised red cabbage and artichoke purée, chicken breast with butternut squash purée and truffled anna potatoes, and puddings. *Benchmark main dish: lamb hogget with stuffed cabbage, jerusalem artichoke purée, mint jelly and dauphinoise potatoes £18.95. Two-course evening meal £19.00.*

Free house ~ Licensee Luke Freeman ~ Real ale ~ (01989) 562891 ~ Open 11-3, 5-11; 10am-11pm Sat; 12-10.30 Sun ~ Bar food 12-2(2.30 Sat), 6-9.30; 12-9 Sun ~ Restaurant ~ Children welcome ~ www.millrace.info *Recommended by Mike and Mary Carter, Lucien Perring, Andy and Jill Kassube, GSB, R T and J C Moggridge*

WALTERSTONE

SO3424 Map 6

Carpenters Arms

Follow Walterstone signs off A465; HR2 0DX

Unchanging country tavern in the same family for many years

Though it takes some finding, this charming little unspoilt stone cottage on the edge of the Black Mountains is certainly worth the effort. It's been run by the charming Vera for many years since she took over from her mother, and the traditional rooms remain the same. Pewter mugs hang from beams, a fire roars in the gleaming black range (complete with hot water tap, bread oven and salt cupboard), ancient settles flank stripped-stone walls, and the broad polished flagstones are scattered with pieces of carpet. Breconshire Golden Valley, Wadworths 6X and a guest such as Breconshire County are tapped straight from the cask. The compact main dining room has mahogany tables, oak corner cupboards and maybe a big vase of flowers on the dresser. Another little dining area has old oak tables and church pews on flagstones. The outside lavatories are cold, but in character.

Straightforward food includes sandwiches, prawn cocktail, pâté, vegetarian lasagne, gammon with egg or pineapple, chicken with creamy mushroom sauce, baked fillet of salmon, daily specials and puddings. *Benchmark main dish: rump steak £14.95. Two-course evening meal £17.00.*

Free house ~ Licensee Vera Watkins ~ Real ale ~ No credit cards ~ (01873) 890353 ~ Open 12-11 ~ Bar food 12-2, 7-9 ~ Restaurant ~ Children welcome ~ www.thecarpentersarmswalterstone.com *Recommended by MLR*

WOOLHOPE SO6135 Map 4

Butchers Arms

Off B4224 in Fownhope; HR1 4RF

Pleasant country inn in peaceful setting, with an inviting garden, excellent food and a fine choice of real ales

'What was really exceptional was the warm welcome from the licensees and staff, who made us, and our dog, feel that they were really pleased to see us,' says one reader – and others echo the comments. The food and beer are really enjoyable too. The bar has very low beams (some hop-draped), red-cushioned built-in wall seats, farmhouse chairs and red-topped stools around a mix of old tables (some set for dining) on red-patterned carpet, hunting and horse pictures on cream walls, and an open fire in the big fireplace; the little beamed dining room is similarly furnished. Wye Valley Bitter and Butty Bach are kept on handpump alongside a couple of guests from brewers such as Breconshire, and there's a well annotated wine list, with several by the glass. There are picnic-sets beside a stream in the pretty garden, and the nearby countryside is lovely. To enjoy some of the surroundings, turn left as you come out of the pub and take the tiny left-hand road at the end of the car park; this becomes a track and then a path, and the view from the top of the hill is quite something.

Excellent food cooked by the landlord using rare-breed meat and other carefully sourced produce might include sandwiches, pheasant samosas with home-made piccalilli, potted crab with orange and cardamom, sformato (an italian soufflé) of spinach, parmesan and cream, chargrilled liver and bacon with crispy onion rings, chicken tagine with olives, preserved lemons and buttered quinoa, crispy duck breast with potato cake and lime compote, venison with rösti and juniper and chocolate sauce, and puddings such as brioche and butter marmalade pudding and blackberry eton mess. *Benchmark main dish: beer-battered cornish whiting with chips, peas and tartare sauce £10.50. Two-course evening meal £19.00.*

Free house ~ Licensee Stephen Bull ~ Real ale ~ (01432) 860281 ~ Open 12-3, 6-11; 12-3 Sun; closed Sun evening, Mon ~ Bar food 12-2, 7-9; 12-2.15 Sun ~ Children welcome ~ Dogs welcome ~ www.butchersarmswoolhope.com *Recommended by John and Jennifer Spinks, Victoria Sanders, Barry Collett, Chris and Val Ramstedt, Michael and Mary Smith, R T and J C Moggridge, David and Stella Martin*

WOOLHOPE SO6135 Map 4

Crown

Village signposted off B4224 in Fownhope; HR1 4QP

Cheery local with fine range of local ciders and perries, and tasty food

The enthusiastic landlord makes two of the farm ciders he serves and keeps another two guests; also 20 bottled ciders and perrys from within a 15-mile radius, and Hobsons Best Bitter, Wye Valley HPA and a changing guest on handpump. It's a busy, cheerful pub and the straightforwardly traditional bar has cream walls, standing timbers, patterned carpets, dark wood pubby furniture, plush built-in banquettes, cottagey curtained windows and a couple of woodburners; background music, darts, TV for sports events. There are marvellous views from the lovely big garden, which also has darts, quoits and cushions in the particularly comfortable smokers' shelter and a garden bar in summer; disabled access.

🍽 Well liked food includes lunchtime sandwiches, crispy chilli beef with coriander and spring onion salad, twiced-baked cheese soufflé with creamy garlic mushrooms, cider-braised ham with free-range eggs, grilled goats cheese with field mushrooms and red onion marmalade, beer-battered cod and chips, pheasant in cider pie, chicken curry with onion bhaji and pickles, and puddings. *Benchmark main dish: slow-braised pork belly with caramelised apple, perry reduction and crackling £13.00. Two-course evening meal £17.00.*

Free house ~ Licensees Matt and Annalisa Slocombe ~ Real ale ~ (01432) 860468 ~ Open 12-3, 6-11(midnight Fri); 12-midnight(11 Sun) Sat ~ Bar food 12-2.30(3.30 Sun), 6-9; 12-3, 6-9.30 Sat ~ Restaurant ~ Children welcome ~ www.crowninnwoolhope.co.uk
Recommended by Tim and Joan Wright, T M Griffiths, Martin and Sue Day, Guy Vowles

Also Worth a Visit in Herefordshire

Besides the fully inspected pubs, you might like to try these pubs that have been recommended to us and described by readers. Do tell us what you think of them: feedback@goodguides.com

ALMELEY   SO3351
Bell (01544) 327216
Off A480, A4111 or A4112 S of Kington; HR3 6LF Old country local with original jug-and-bottle entry lobby, carpeted beamed bar with woodburner, second bar recently converted to village shop/deli, Simpsons and another local ale, Stowford Press cider, food (not evenings) from sandwiches up, obliging landlord; children and dogs welcome, garden with decked area and boules, open all day. *(Guy Vowles)*

AYMESTREY   SO4265
✶ **Riverside Inn** (01568) 708440
A4110, at N end of village, W of Leominster; HR6 9ST Terrace and tree-sheltered garden making most of lovely waterside spot by ancient stone bridge over the Lugg; cosy rambling beamed interior with some antique furniture alongside stripped country kitchen tables, warm fires, well kept Hobsons, Wye Valley and a guest, local ciders, good lunchtime bar food and more expensive evening menu using rare-breed meat and own fruit and vegetables, friendly helpful landlord and efficient unobtrusive service; quiet background music; children welcome, dogs in bar, bedrooms (fly fishing for residents), nice breakfast, closed Sun evening, Mon lunchtime (all day Mon in winter). *(Steve Whalley, R T and J C Moggridge, Mel and May Mackie, Fiona Smith, Tim and Joan Wright)*

BISHOPS FROME   SO6648
✶ **Green Dragon** (01885) 490607
Just off B4214 Bromyard–Ledbury; WR6 5BP Half a dozen well kept ales such as Purple Moose, Timothy Taylors and Wye Valley, farm ciders, friendly licensees, traditional evening food (not Sun) including good steaks, four linked rooms with nice unspoilt rustic feel, beams, flagstones and log fires including fine inglenook; children and dogs welcome, tiered garden with smokers' shelter, on Herefordshire Trail, closed weekday lunchtimes, open all day Sat. *(Reg Fowle, Helen Rickwood, Roger and Diana Morgan, Guy Vowles)*

BODENHAM   SO5454
Englands Gate (01568) 797286
On A417 at Bodenham turn-off, about 6 miles S of Leominster; HR1 3HU Attractive black and white 16th-c coaching inn under newish management; beams and joists in low ochre ceilings around a vast central stone chimneypiece, sturdy timber props, well worn flagstones and one or two steps, lantern-style lighting, long table (just right for a party of eight) in cosy partly stripped-stone room, lighter upper area, Hobsons, Wye Valley and a guest, bar food; background music, TV; children welcome, dogs in bar, tables under parasols on terrace and in pleasant garden, smart modern bedrooms in converted coach house next door, open all day. *(Anon)*

BOSBURY   SO6943

Bell (01531) 640285

B4220 N of Ledbury; HR8 1PX
Traditional village pub with log fires in both
bars, five well kept ales and good choice
of wines by the glass, dining area serving
popular sensibly priced food (not Sun
evening, Mon) including home-made pizzas
and Sun carvery, friendly attentive staff; dogs
welcome, large garden with covered terrace,
open all day weekends, closed Mon and Tues
lunchtimes. *(Frank Krinks)*

BRINGSTY COMMON   SO6954

✳ Live & Let Live (01886) 821462

*Off A44 Knightwick–Bromyard 1.5
miles W of Whitbourne turn; take track
southwards at black cat inn sign,
bearing right at fork; WR6 5UW* Bustling
timbered and thatched 17th-c cottage; cosy
flagstoned bar with scrubbed or polished
tables, comfortably cushioned little chairs,
long stripped pew and high-backed winged
settle by log fire in cavernous stone fireplace,
earthenware jugs hanging from low beams,
old casks built into hop-hung bar counter,
Ludlow, Malvern Hills and Wye Valley, local
ciders and apple juice, well liked pubby
food, two dining rooms upstairs under
steep rafters; children and dogs welcome,
glass topped well and big wooden hogshead
as terrace tables, peaceful views from
picnic-sets in former orchard, handy for
Brockhampton Estate (NT), open all day
summer, closed Mon, winter afternoons Tues-
Thurs. *(Chris Flynn, Wendy Jones, Guy Vowles,
Susan Cook, Revd Michael Vockins)*

BROMYARD DOWNS   SO6755

✳ Royal Oak (01885) 482585

*Just NE of Bromyard; pub signed
off A44; HR7 4QP* Beautifully placed
low-beamed 18th-c pub with wide views;
open-plan carpeted and flagstoned bar, log
fire and woodburner, dining room with huge
bay window, enjoyable good value home-made
food from varied menu, well kept Malvern
Hills, Purity and Woods, real cider, friendly
service, pool and darts; background music;
children, walkers and dogs welcome, picnic-
sets on nice front terrace, swings, open all
day weekends in Aug. *(Anon)*

CANON PYON   SO4648

Nags Head (01432) 830725

A4110; HR4 8NY Old timbered roadside
pub with beamed log-fire bar, flagstoned
restaurant and overspill/function room,
popular good value food including blackboard
specials, friendly service; pool; children and
dogs welcome, extensive garden with play

area, open all day Sat, closed Sun evening,
Mon lunchtime. *(Anon)*

CLIFFORD   SO2445

Castlefields (01497) 831554

B4350 N of Hay-on-Wye; HR3 5HB
Newly rebuilt family pub, some old features
including a well, good popular fairly priced
food, Sharps Doom Bar and Wye Valley Butty
Bach, friendly helpful staff, woodburner in
two-way fireplace, restaurant; lovely country
views, camping, closed Mon, otherwise open
all day. *(Anon)*

CLODOCK   SO3227

Cornewall Arms

N of Walterstone; HR2 0PD Splendidly
old-fashioned and unchanging country local
in remote hamlet by historic church and
facing Black Mountains, stable-door bar
with a few mats and comfortable armchairs
on stone floor, lots of ornaments and knick-
knacks, photos of past village events, books
for sale, games including darts and Devil
Among the Tailors, bottled Wye Valley and
cider, no food or credit cards; erratic opening
times. *(Barry Collett)*

COLWALL   SO7440

Wellington (01684) 540269

A449 Malvern–Ledbury; WR13 6HW
Welcoming landlord and friendly staff, good
sensibly priced food from standards to more
imaginative dishes, well kept ales such as
Goffs, good wines by the glass, comfortably
lived-in two-level beamed bar with red
patterned carpet and nice fire, spacious
relaxed back dining area, newspapers and
magazines; children welcome, picnic-sets
on neat grass above car park, closed Sun
evening, Mon. *(Anon)*

DORSTONE   SO3141

✳ Pandy (01981) 550273

*Pub signed off B4348 E of Hay-on-Wye;
HR3 6AN* Ancient timbered inn by village
green, homely traditional rooms with low
hop-strung beams, stout timbers, upright
chairs on worn flagstones and in various
alcoves, vast open fireplace, locals by bar
with good range of beers including Wye
Valley, summer farm cider, quite a few malts
and irish whiskeys, good food from baguettes
and pubby choices to interesting specials,
friendly competent staff, board games;
background music; children welcome, dogs in
bar (resident red setter called Apache), neat
side garden with picnic-sets and play area,
five good bedrooms in purpose-built annexe,
open all day Sat, closed Mon lunchtime
except summer and bank holidays.
(Simon Le Fort, Mark Sykes, Martin and Sue Day)

Post Office address codings confusingly give the impression that a few pubs
are in Herefordshire when they're really in Gloucestershire or even Wales
(which is where we list them).

EWYAS HAROLD   SO3828
Dog (01981) 240598

In village centre; HR2 0EX Popular and friendly stone-built village pub, three well kept changing ales, reasonably priced home-made food including good Sun roasts, games room, some live music; dogs welcome (they have a cat), open all day. *(Reg Fowle, Helen Rickwood)*

FOWNHOPE   SO5734
Green Man (01432) 860243

B4224; HR1 4PE Striking 15th-c black and white inn, wall settles, window seats and leather chairs in one beamed bar, standing timbers dividing another, warm woodburners in old fireplaces, well presented imaginative food in bar and restaurant, friendly helpful service, three changing ales and Weston's cider, good wines, nice coffee; background music, no dogs; children welcome, attractive quiet garden, 11 bedrooms, open all day. *(John and Mary Ling, Michael and Mary Smith)*

GARWAY   SO4622
Garway Moon (01600) 750270

Centre of village, oppposite the green; HR2 8RQ Attractive good-sized 18th-c pub in pretty location overlooking common, friendly attentive service, good locally sourced food (some from own garden) including some unusual choices (best to book weekends), well kept regularly changing regional beers, woodburner, restaurant; children, dogs and muddy boots welcome, three bedrooms, open all day weekends, closed Mon and Weds lunchtimes, all day Tues. *(John Marsh, John and Nan Hurst)*

GORSLEY   SO6726
⋆ **Roadmaker** (01989) 720352

0.5 miles from M50 junction 3; village signposted from exit – B4221; HR9 7SW Popular 19th-c village pub run well by group of retired Gurkhas, large carpeted lounge bar with central log fire, very good nepalese food here and in evening restaurant, also Sun roasts, well kept Brains and Butcombe, efficient courteous service; no dogs; children welcome, terrace with water feature, open all day. *(Neil and Anita Christopher, LM)*

HAREWOOD END   SO5227
Harewood End Inn (01989) 730637

A49 Hereford to Ross-on-Wye; HR2 8JT Interesting old inn doing well under welcoming new management; comfortable panelled dining lounge and separate restaurant, good choice of enjoyable home-made food, well kept ales such as Black Sheep and Wychwood Hobgoblin, decent wines; nice garden and walks, five bedrooms, closed Mon. *(Anon)*

HEREFORD   SO5139
Barrels (01432) 274968

St Owen Street; HR1 2JQ Friendly 18th-c coaching inn and former home of the Wye Valley brewery, their very well kept keenly priced ales from barrel-built counter (end Aug beer festival), Thatcher's cider, no food, cheerful efficient staff and good mix of customers; pool room, big-screen sports TV, background and some live music; partly covered courtyard behind, open all day. *(Reg Fowle, Helen Rickwood)*

HEREFORD   SO5140
Kings Fee (01432) 373240

Commercial Road; HR1 2BP Wetherspoons supermarket conversion with half a dozen good value well kept ales plus local ciders, their usual food, cheerful attentive service, raised back section; no dogs; children till 8.30pm, sizeable back terrace with covered area, open all day from breakfast. *(Pat and Tony Martin, Reg Fowle, Helen Rickwood, Dave Braisted)*

HEREFORD   SO5039
⋆ **Lichfield Vaults** (01432) 266821

Church Street; HR1 2LR A pub since the 18th c (then called the Dog) in picturesque pedestrianised area near cathedral; dark panelling, some stripped brick and exposed joists, impressive plasterwork in big-windowed front room, traditionally furnished with dark pews, padded pub chairs and a couple of heavily padded benches, hot coal stove, charming greek landlord and friendly staff, well kept Adnams, Bass, Caledonian and Sharps, enjoyable food from sandwiches up including greek dishes, good Sun roasts, daily papers; faint background music, live blues/rock last Sun of month, games machines; children welcome, no dogs, picnic-sets in pleasant back courtyard. *(Michael Carpenter)*

HOARWITHY   SO5429
New Harp (01432) 840900

Off A49 Hereford to Ross-on-Wye; HR2 6QH Refurbished open-plan village dining pub with cheerful bustling atmosphere, good well presented local food from chef-landlord, friendly helpful service, Wye Valley ales and Weston's cider (maybe their own organic cider in summer), pine tables on slate tiles, two woodburners, darts; background and some live music; children, walkers and dogs welcome, pretty tree-sheltered garden with stream, picnic-sets and decked area, little shop and Mon morning post office, unusual italianate Victorian church, open all day Fri-Sun. *(Barry Collett, Dennis and Doreen Haward)*

KENTCHURCH   SO4125
Bridge Inn (01981) 240408

B4347 Pontrilas–Grosmont; HR2 0BY Ancient attractively refurbished rustic pub, big log fire, popular home-made food including weekday set lunch deal, up to four real ales including Otter, small pretty back restaurant overlooking River Monnow (two miles of trout fishing), friendly staff and collie called Freddie; waterside tables, handy for Herefordshire Trail, closed Mon lunchtime, Tues. *(Reg Fowle, Helen Rickwood)*

KINGSLAND   SO4461
Angel (01568) 709195
B4360; HR6 9QS 17th-c traditional beamed and timbered dining pub, enjoyable home-made food (not Mon or Tues lunchtimes) including deals, four well kept changing ales and a dozen wines by the glass, helpful friendly staff, comfortable open-plan interior with open fires, upstairs function/overspill area, summer live music (Fri); picnic-sets on front grass, garden behind, closed Sun evening in winter. *(Anon)*

KINGSLAND   SO4461
✶Corners (01568) 708385
B4360 NW of Leominster, corner of Lugg Green Road; HR6 9RY Comfortably updated, partly black and white 16th-c village inn with snug nooks and corners, log fires, low beams, dark red plasterwork and some stripped brick, comfortable bow-window seat, group of dark leather armchairs in softly lit carpeted bar, well kept Hobsons and a guest such as Wye Valley, decent selection of wines, airier big raftered side dining room in converted hay loft with huge window, enjoyable reasonably priced food from pubby choices up, cheerful attentive service; children welcome, no garden, comfortable bedrooms in new block behind. *(Mel and May Mackie, Peter and Heather Elliott, David M Smith)*

KINGTON   SO3056
✶Olde Tavern (01544) 239033
Victoria Road, just off A44 opposite B4355 – follow sign to Town Centre, Hospital, Cattle Market; pub on right opposite Elizabeth Road, no inn sign but Estd 1767 notice; HR5 3BX Gloriously old-fashioned with hatch-served side room opening off small plain parlour and public bar, plenty of dark brown woodwork, big windows, settles and other antique furniture on bare floors, gas fire, old local pictures, china, pewter and curios, four well kept mainly local beers, Weston's cider, beer festivals, no food (may have rolls and chocolate bars), friendly atmosphere; children and dogs welcome, little yard at back, closed weekday lunchtimes. *(MLR)*

KINGTON   SO2956
Oxford Arms (01544) 230322
Duke Street; HR5 3DR Well worn in (not to everyone's taste) with woodburners in main bar on left and dining area on right, smaller lounge with sofas and armchairs, well kept local ales such as Hereford and Mayfields, enjoyable reasonably priced food, good friendly service, pool; closed Mon and Tues lunchtimes. *(Reg Fowle, Helen Rickwood, MLR, Dave Braisted)*

KINGTON   SO2956
Royal Oak (01544) 230484
Church Street; HR5 3BE Cheerful two-bar pub serving enjoyable good value food including bargain OAP lunch, well kept Hereford, Ringwood and Sharps, welcoming caring landlord, two little open fires, old theatre posters and musical instruments in restaurant, darts and sports TV in public bar; children and dogs welcome, garden with terrace, three neat simple bedrooms, open all day summer, closed Mon-Fri lunchtimes in winter. *(R T and J C Moggridge)*

LEDBURY   SO7137
✶Prince of Wales (01531) 632250
Church Lane; narrow passage from Town Hall; HR8 1DL Friendly family-run local tucked prettily down narrow cobbled alley, seven well kept ales including Butcombe, Hobsons, Ledbury, Otter and Wye Valley, Weston's Bounds cider and foreign bottled beers, knowledgeable staff, simple very good value home-made food from sandwiches up, low beams, shelves of books, long back room; faint background music (live Weds and Sun); a couple of tables in flower-filled backyard, open all day. *(Brian and Anna Marsden, Ken Eames, Dave Braisted)*

LEDBURY   SO7137
Talbot (01531) 632963
New Street; HR8 2DX 16th-c black and white fronted coaching inn; log-fire bar with Wadworths ales and plenty of wines by the glass, good fairly traditional food from sharing boards and lunchtime sandwiches up, friendly efficient service, oak-panelled dining room; courtyard tables, bedrooms, open all day. *(John Evans, Dr A J and Mrs B A Tompsett)*

LEINTWARDINE   SO4073
Lion (01547) 540203
High Street; SY7 0JZ Nicely restored inn beautifully situated by packhorse bridge over River Teme; helpful efficient staff and friendly atmosphere, good well presented food from varied menu including some imaginative choices, popular two-room restaurant, well kept beer; children welcome, safely fenced riverside garden with play area, eight attractive bedrooms. *(Dr and Mrs James Harris, Warren Marsh)*

LEINTWARDINE   SO4073
✶Sun (01547) 540705
Rosemary Lane, just off A4113; SY7 0LP Fascinating 19th-c time warp; bare benches and farmhouse tables by coal fire in wallpapered brick-floored front bar (dogs welcome here), well kept Hobsons tapped from the cask and an occasional guest (Aug beer festival), another fire in snug carpeted parlour, pork pies and perhaps a lunchtime ploughman's (can bring food from adjacent fish and chip shop), friendly staff, open mike night last Fri of month; new pavilion-style

building with bar and garden room, closed Mon lunchtime. *(Reg Fowle, Helen Rickwood, Alun Jones, Peter Thornton)*

LEOMINSTER   SO4959
Grape Vaults (01568) 611404

Broad Street; HR6 8BS Compact well preserved two-room pub, friendly and popular, with well kept ales including Ludlow, good value pubby food, coal fire, beams and panelling, original dark high-backed settles, old local prints and posters, bottle collection, shelves of books in snug; tiny gents'; dogs welcome, open all day. *(Guy Vowles)*

LINTON   SO6525
Alma (01989) 720355

On main road through village; HR9 7RY Cheerful unspoilt local in small village, up to six well kept/priced changing ales such as Butcombe, Ludlow and Malvern Hills, no food (may be free Sun nibbles), homely carpeted front room with sleepy cats by good fire, small back room with pool, some live music including three-day summer charity music festival; children very welcome, good-sized garden behind with nice view, closed weekday lunchtimes. *(Reg Fowle, Helen Rickwood)*

LONGTOWN   SO3228
Crown (01873) 860217

South of village; HR2 0LT Welcoming old place in remote scenic spot, well kept changing ales such as Golden Valley and Wye Valley, enjoyable food from sandwiches to good value Sun lunch, woodburner in main beamed bar, restaurant, games room with pool; children welcome, garden, good walks (Offa's Dyke), seven bedrooms, open all day Fri-Sun. *(MLR)*

MICHAELCHURCH
ESCLEY   SO3133
★ Bridge Inn (01981) 510646

Off back road SE of Hay-on-Wye, along Escley Brook valley; HR2 0JW Black-beamed riverside inn restored by current hard-working licensees and delightfully tucked away in attractive valley; popular home-made food including some unusual choices, well kept Wye Valley beers and local farm cider, friendly atmosphere; children welcome, seats out on waterside terrace, field for camping (also a yurt), good walks, closed Mon lunchtime, otherwise open all day. *(Simon Daws, Neil Hogg, MJVK)*

MUCH DEWCHURCH   SO4831
Black Swan (01981) 540295

B4348 Ross-on-Wye to Hay-on-Wye; HR2 8DJ Roomy and attractive beamed and timbered local, partly 14th-c, with well kept Hook Norton ales, decent wines and enjoyable straightforward food, log fires in cosy well worn bar and lounge with eating area, welcoming helpful landlord; pool room with darts, TV, juke box, no credit cards; dogs welcome. *(Bob and Angie Farmer)*

MUCH MARCLE   SO6634
Royal Oak (01531) 660300

On A449 Ross-on-Wye to Ledbury; HR8 2ND Superb rural spot with magnificent views, pleasant lounge with open fire, good reasonably priced food using meat from local farms, friendly helpful service, well kept ales such as Jennings, Marstons and Wye Valley, large back dining area; garden, two bedrooms. *(Jason Bevan)*

ORLETON   SO4967
★ Boot (01568) 780228

Off B4362 W of Woofferton; SY8 4HN Popular pub with beams, timbering, even some 16th-c wattle and daub, inglenook fireplace in charming cosy traditional bar, steps up to further bar area, good-sized two-room dining part, varied choice of interesting well presented food, friendly quick service, Hobsons, Wye Valley and a local guest (July beer and music festival), real ciders; children and dogs welcome, seats in garden under huge ash tree, fenced-in play area, open all day weekends. *(Michael and Jenny Back, A N Bance, Dr P Brown, Ann and Tony Bennett-Hughes)*

PEMBRIDGE   SO3958
New Inn (01544) 388427

Market Square (A44); HR6 9DZ Timeless ancient inn overlooking small black and white town's church, unpretentious three-room bar with antique settles, beams, worn flagstones and impressive inglenook log fire, well kept changing ales, farm cider and big helpings of popular good value plain food, friendly service, traditional games, quiet little family dining room; downstairs lavatories; simple bedrooms. *(Anon)*

ROSS-ON-WYE   SO5924
Mail Rooms (01989) 760920

Gloucester Road; HR9 5BS Open modern Wetherspoons conversion of former post office, their usual well priced food and up to five real ales including Greene King, Weston's cider, friendly conscientious service; silent TV; children welcome till 8pm, decked back terrace, open all day from 8am. *(Reg Fowle, Helen Rickwood)*

ROSS-ON-WYE   SO6024
White Lion (01989) 562785

Wilton Lane; HR9 6AQ Friendly riverside pub dating from 1650, well kept Otter and Wye Valley, enjoyable traditional food plus specials at reasonable prices, good service, big fireplace in carpeted bar, stone-walled gaol restaurant (building once a police station), games room with pool and darts, Sun quiz; children welcome, lots of tables in garden and on covered terrace overlooking the Wye and historic bridge, bedrooms. *(Neil and Anita Christopher, Reg Fowle, Helen Rickwood)*

SELLACK SO5526
✳ **Lough Pool** (01989) 730888
Off A49; HR9 6LX Black and white
timbered cottage surrounded by bridleways
and walks, simple bars with beams and
standing timbers, flagstones, rustic furniture
and fires burning in two woodburners,
well kept Wye Valley ales and a guest, farm
ciders/perries and several wines by the
glass, enjoyable locally sourced home-made
food, restaurant with garden views; children
welcome, dogs allowed in bar, opening times
may vary according to season, best to check
first. *(Guy Vowles, Dr and Mrs R E S Tanner,
Lucien Perring, Peter Martin, Barry Collett
and others)*

ST OWEN'S CROSS SO5424
New Inn (01989) 730744
*Junction A4137 and B4521, W of Ross-
on-Wye; HR2 8LQ* Half-timbered 16th-c
dining pub with huge inglenook fireplaces,
dark beams and timbers, various nooks
and crannies, mix of furniture including
old pews, Marstons-related beers, food all
day (Sun till 6pm) in bar and restaurant;
background music; children welcome, dogs
in bar, spacious sheltered garden with play
things and views to Black Mountains, two
four-poster bedrooms. *(Anon)*

STAPLOW SO6941
Oak (01531) 640954
Bromyard Road (B4214); HR8 1NP
Popular roadside village pub, friendly bustle
in comfortable beamed bar, restaurant with
open kitchen producing enjoyable food from
sandwiches and sharing boards up, ales such
as Bathams, Brains and Wye Valley, Weston's
cider and good choice of wines, cheerful quick
service; bedrooms. *(John and Mary Ling)*

STIFFORDS BRIDGE SO7348
Red Lion (01886) 880318
*A4103 3 miles W of Great Malvern;
WR13 5NN* Refurbished beamed roadside
pub under new management; good choice of
enjoyable well priced pubby food (not Sun
evening), Greene King, Malvern Hills and
Wye Valley, real ciders; children welcome and
dogs (theirs is called Max), tables in nicely
kept garden, farmers' market first Sat of
month, open all day Fri-Sun. *(Anon)*

STOCKTON CROSS SO5161
✳ **Stockton Cross Inn** (01568) 612509
*Kimbolton; A4112, off A49 just N of
Leominster; HR6 0HD* Cosy half-
timbered coaching inn with heavily beamed
recently redecorated interior, huge log fire,
woodburner, handsome antique settle, old
leather chairs and brocaded stools, cast-iron-
framed tables, Wye Valley ales and a guest,
Robinson's cider, good choice of food cooked
by landlord including specials, friendly
service; background music, open mike night
(second Weds of month); children welcome,

pretty garden, handy for Berrington Hall
(NT), closed Sun evening, Mon except bank
holidays. *(Reg Fowle, Helen Rickwood,
R K Phillips)*

SUTTON ST NICHOLAS SO5345
Golden Cross (01432) 880274
Corner of Ridgeway Road; HR1 3AZ
Thriving modernised pub with enjoyable
food including deals, Wye Valley Butty Bach
and two regularly changing guests from
stone-fronted counter, good service, clean
décor, some breweriana, relaxed upstairs
restaurant, pool and darts, live music
Fri; children and dogs welcome, disabled
facilities, pretty village and good walks.
(Reg Fowle, Helen Rickwood)

SYMONDS YAT SO5515
Old Ferrie (01600) 890232
*Ferrie Lane, Symonds Yat West;
HR9 6BL* Unpretentious old inn in
picturesque spot by the River Wye with its
own hand-pulled ferry; enjoyable pub food,
Wye Valley ales and local cider, friendly
helpful staff, games room; riverside terrace,
canoeing and good walks, bedrooms and two
bunkhouses. *(David and Diane Young)*

TRUMPET SO6639
Trumpet Inn (01531) 670277
Corner A413 and A438; HR8 2RA
Modernised black and white timbered pub
dating from 15th c, well kept Wadworths ales,
good food (all day Fri-Sun) from sandwiches
to specials, efficient service, beams, stripped
brickwork and log fires, dining room, quiz
and live music nights; children welcome,
tables in big garden behind, campsite with
hard standings, open all day. *(David and
Julie Glover)*

UPTON BISHOP SO6326
Moody Cow (01989) 780470
B4221 E of Ross-on-Wye; HR9 7TT
Dining pub refurbished under present
friendly management, L-shaped bar with
sandstone walls, slate floor and fire, biggish
raftered restaurant and second more
intimate eating area, good freshly made food,
well kept ales and decent wines (including
local ones), cafetière coffee, friendly efficient
service; children, dogs and muddy boots
welcome, garden with new furniture and
fruit/vegetable beds, courtyard bedroom
up spiral staircase, closed Sun evening,
Mon. *(David and Anne Day, Guy Vowles)*

WELLINGTON SO4948
Wellington (01432) 830367
*Village signed off A49 N of Hereford;
HR4 8AT* Red-brick Victorian pub under
new management; big high-backed settles,
antique farm and garden tools, historical
photographs of the village, woodburner in
brick fireplace, Butcombe, Wye Valley and a
guest, traditional food, candlelit stable dining
room and conservatory, ladies' darts team;

background music; children welcome, dogs in bar, nice back garden, closed Mon. *(Anon)*

WEOBLEY SO4051

Salutation (01544) 318443

Off A4112 SW of Leominster; HR4 8SJ
Old beamed and timbered inn at top of delightful village green, good food cooked by chef-landlord from bar snacks up including set lunch, well kept ales such as Otter, Thwaites and Wye Valley, Robinson's cider, pleasant helpful service, two bars and restaurant, log fires; children welcome, sheltered back terrace, three bedrooms, good breakfast. *(R T and J C Moggridge, Reg Fowle, Helen Rickwood, R K Phillips)*

WHITNEY-ON-WYE SO2447

⋆**Rhydspence** (01497) 831262

A438 Hereford–Brecon; HR3 6EU New licensees for this splendid half-timbered inn (part dates from 1380) on the border with Wales; rambling rooms with heavy beams and timbers, attractive old-fashioned furnishings, log fire in fine big stone fireplace in central bar, well kept Bass, Otter and Robinsons, real cider, good wholesome food, restaurant; children welcome, no dogs while food is being served, garden with views to the Black Mountains, six bedrooms, open all day. *(Anon)*

YARPOLE SO4664

⋆**Bell** (01568) 780359

Just off B4361 N of Leominster; HR6 0BD Pleasant old black and white pub with basic tap room, comfortable beamed lounge with log fire, traditional furniture and some modern art, brass taps embedded in stone counter serving Wye Valley and a couple of guests, large high-raftered restaurant in former cider mill (the press and wheel remain), good well priced food from pub standards to more enterprising dishes, Sun night tapas, friendly atmosphere; background music; children welcome, dogs in bar, picnic-sets under green parasols in pretty gardens, handy for Croft Castle (NT), closed Mon. *(Neil and Anita Christopher, R K Phillips, Ann and Tony Bennett-Hughes)*

Hertfordshire

Real ales play a large part in our pubs here, with quite a few holding a Beer Award. For a fine choice, head to the Valiant Trooper in Aldbury (friendly small country pub with unpretentious bars), Holly Bush at Potters Crouch (immaculately kept and with a pretty garden), Red Lion in Preston (cheery local with fairly priced food), Cricketers at Redbourn (contemporary furnishings and good food) and Cricketers in Sarratt (half a dozen ales in cleverly converted cottages). Other pubs our readers are particularly enjoying include the Bricklayers Arms in Flaunden (excellent, attractively presented meals in civilised surroundings), Alford Arms in Frithsden (20 wines by the glass in pretty Victorian pub), College Arms at Hartford Heath (contemporary furnishings and interesting food), Sun in Northaw (a new entry, with pretty refurbished rooms and particularly good food using organic, free-range produce), Cock at Sarratt (well run and traditional with good value food), Bull in Watton-at-Stone (lots of cosy character and nice staff) and Fox at Willian (new to us this year, with five ales and inventive food). Several pubs serve exceptional food, but our Hertfordshire Dining Pub 2014 is the Alford Arms in Frithsden.

 ALDBURY　　　　　　　　　　　　　　　SP9612　Map 4
Valiant Trooper 🍺
Trooper Road (towards Aldbury Common); off B4506 N of Berkhamsted;
HP23 5RW

Cheery, traditional all-rounder with appealing interior, six real ales, generous helpings of pubby food, and garden

You can be sure of a warm welcome from the licensees and their helpful staff in this attractive little country pub. A relaxing place, it has an easy-going atmosphere through a series of unpretentious and appealing old rooms. The first, beamed and with red and black tiles, has built-in wall benches, a pew and small dining chairs around attractive country tables, and an inglenook fireplace. The middle bar has spindleback chairs around tables, a wooden floor and some exposed brickwork. The far room has nice country kitchen chairs around a mix of tables, and a woodburning stove, while the back barn has been converted

into a restaurant; dominoes, cribbage and bridge on Monday evenings.
Five well kept changing beers on handpump, such as Fullers London
Pride and Tring Side Pocket for a Toad, with guests from breweries like
Dark Star, Ridgeway and Vale, alongside local Millwhite's cider. The
enclosed garden has a wooden adventure playground, and the pub is well
placed for walks through the glorious beechwoods of the National Trust's
Ashridge Estate.

Promptly served food includes lunchtime sandwiches, spinach, feta and pine
nut filo parcel with sunblush tomatos and olives, venison patties with black
pudding croûton and cumberland dip, burger with coleslaw and chips, home-baked
ham with honey glaze and eggs, beer-battered fish and chips, smoked haddock
fishcakes with sorrel sauce, roasted beetroot risotto, goats cheese crumble, steak
in ale pie, venison goulash with mash and braised red cabbage, whole lemon sole
with lemon and caper butter, and puddings. *Benchmark main dish: sausage
with bubble and squeak and home-made baked beans £10.95. Two-course evening
meal £18.00.*

Free house ~ Licensee Wendy Greenall ~ Real ale ~ (01442) 851203 ~ Open 11-11;
12-10.30 Sun ~ Bar food 12-3, 6-9; 12-9 Sat; 12-4 Sun; not Sun and Mon evenings ~
Restaurant ~ Children welcome ~ Dogs allowed in bar ~ www.valianttrooper.co.uk
Recommended by Stephen Vincent, Dennis Jones

BARNET   TQ2599   Map 5

Duke of York ♀

Barnet Road (A1000); EN5 4SG

Big place with reasonably priced bistro-style food and nice garden

Once an important coaching inn on the main London-York route, this
sizeable place is rather grand. The interior has been cleverly and
attractively sectioned using stairs and open doorways, and big windows
and plenty of mirrors throughout keep it light and airy; there are some
cosy, more intimate areas too. As well as hundreds of prints and photos
on the cream walls, an eclectic mix of furniture on tiled or wooden floors
creates a relaxed atmosphere and table lamps, fireplaces, books, rugs,
fresh flowers and pot plants provide a homely air. There are stools at
the impressive bar counter, where friendly staff serve Phoenix Brunning
& Price Original and Tring Side Pocket on handpump alongside three
guests from brewers such as Adnams, Dark Star and Red Squirrel, 25
wines by the glass and about 80 whiskies; background music. The garden
is particularly attractive, with plenty of seats, tables and picnic-sets on a
tree-surrounded terrace and lawn, and a tractor in the fine play area.

Good, popular food includes sandwiches, baked camembert with rosemary
and garlic and tomato pickle, smoked mackerel pâté with fennel salad and
dill mayonnaise, butternut squash, spinach and goats cheese quiche, cajun chicken
burger with salsa and coleslaw, beer-battered haddock, braised lamb shoulder
with mustard mash and rosemary gravy, chicken breast with pasta in rocket and
parmesan pesto, and puddings such as hot waffle with banana ice-cream and toffee
sauce and chocolate brownie with white chocolate sauce. *Benchmark main dish:
cumberland sausage and mash with onion gravy £10.95. Two-course evening
meal £19.00.*

Brunning & Price ~ Manager Kit Lett ~ Real ale ~ (020) 8449 0297 ~ Open 11.30-11;
12-10.30 Sun ~ Bar food 11.30-10; 12-9.30 Sun ~ Children welcome ~ Dogs allowed in bar
~ www.brunningandprice.co.uk/dukeofyork *Recommended by Richard and Penny Gibbs*

EPPING GREEN   TL2906   Map 5

Beehive

Off B158 SW of Hertford, via Little Berkhamsted; back road towards Newgate Street and Cheshunt; SG13 8NB

Cheerful bustling country pub, popular for its good value food

Generous helpings of enjoyable fish dishes are quite a draw to this weatherboarded country pub. The traditional, low-ceilinged bar has been redecorated this year, but has kept its friendly informal atmosphere and the woodburning stove in a panelled corner – as well as Greene King IPA and Abbot and a changing guest on handpump, alongside a good range of wines by the glass; background music. Between the low building and quiet country road is a neat lawn and a decked area with plenty of tables; good woodland walks nearby.

With daily deliveries from Billingsgate, the fish dishes are good: skate with caper butter, cod with bacon and mushroom sauce, battered haddock, crab and mango salad and fresh tuna; there's also sandwiches, baguettes and daily specials. *Benchmark main dish: battered cod and chips £9.95. Two-course evening meal £16.99.*

Free house ~ Licensee Martin Squirrell ~ Real ale ~ (01707) 875959 ~ Open 11.30-3, 5.30-11; 12-10.30 Sun ~ Bar food 12-2.30, 6-9.30; 12-4, 6-8.30 Sun ~ Restaurant ~ Children welcome   *Recommended by Leanne Davey, John Branston, Ross Balaam*

FLAUNDEN   TL0101   Map 5

Bricklayers Arms 🍴 ♈

4 miles from M25 junction 18; village signposted off A41 – from village centre follow Boxmoor, Bovingdon road and turn right at Belsize, Watford signpost into Hogpits Bottom; HP3 0PH

Cosy country restaurant with fairly elaborate food; very good wine list

Most customers visit this tucked away country pub to enjoy excellent food in civilised surroundings, but the drinks are good too: Rebellion IPA, Fullers London Pride, a beer from Tring and a guest or two such as Sharps Doom Bar on handpump, plus an extensive wine list with 20 by the glass. Stubs of knocked-through oak-timbered wall indicate the original layout of the fairly open-plan interior, and the well refurbished low-beamed bar is snug and comfortable, with a roaring log fire in winter. This is a lovely peaceful spot in summer, when the terrace and beautifully kept old-fashioned garden with foxgloves against sheltering hedges come into their own. Just up the Belsize road, a path on the left leads through delightful woods to a forested area around Hollow Hedge.

Attractively presented dishes using their own-smoked meat and fish might include Sunday champagne breakfasts, as well as white crab with home-smoked salmon, blinis and chive cream, goose rillette with pear chutney, sausages with mash and onion gravy, duo of venison (haunch steak and slowly cooked shoulder) with cranberry jus, ox cheek in ale with spring onion and cabbage mash, chicken breast stuffed with rocket pesto with thyme, cream and mozzarella sauce, specials like suckling pig with apple compote and cider jus, and puddings such as chocolate fondant with pistachio ice-cream and lemon tart with panna cotta and raspberry ice-cream. *Benchmark main dish: guinea fowl with pheasant sausage and liver mousse feuilletée £17.95. Two-course evening meal £24.00.*

Free house ~ Licensee Alvin Michaels ~ Real ale ~ (01442) 833322 ~ Open 12-midnight (10.30 Sun) ~ Bar food 12-2.30(3.30 Sun); 6.30-9.30(8.30 Sun) ~ Restaurant ~ Children welcome ~ Dogs allowed in bar ~ www.bricklayersarms.com *Recommended by Mrs Margo Finlay, Jörg Kasprowski, Nicole Lambton*

FRITHSDEN   TL0109   Map 5

Alford Arms 🍴 ⛾

A4146 from Hemel Hempstead to Water End, second left (after Red Lion) signed Frithsden, left at T junction, then right after 0.25 miles; HP1 3DD

Hertfordshire Dining Pub of the Year

Thriving dining pub with a chic interior, good food from imaginative menu and a thoughtful wine list

The Ashridge Estate is on this pretty Victorian pub's doorstep and many customers combine a walk with a visit here for refreshment. The elegant, understated interior has simple prints on pale cream walls, with blocks picked out in rich Victorian green or dark red, and an appealing mix of good antique furniture (from Georgian chairs to old commode stands) on bare boards and patterned quarry tiles; it's all pulled together by luxuriously opulent curtains. Many people are here to eat, but they consider themselves a proper pub and you'll certainly find a few locals chatting at the bar. Sharps Doom Bar, Rebellion IPA and a guest such as Tring Side Pocket on handpump and 22 wines by the glass from a european list; background jazz. Plenty of tables outside.

 Using local, seasonal (and foraged) produce, the imaginative food includes confit rabbit and wild mushroom tart with pickled cucumber, potted salt beef with beetroot relish and chilli cornbread, bubble and squeak with oak-smoked bacon, free-range poached egg and hollandaise, chickpea, potato, spinach and coconut curry with red onion bhaji and chargrilled flatbread, home-smoked mackerel with kedgeree risotto and poached quails egg, hazelnut- and sage-crusted slow-roast pork belly with cider-potted cabbage, caramelised apple and crackling, and puddings like warm pecan, black treacle and bourbon tart with fudge ice-cream and orange rice pudding with nutmeg glaze. *Benchmark main dish: confit duck and jerusalem artichoke rösti £14.50. Two-course evening meal £20.50.*

Salisbury Pubs ~ Lease Darren Johnston ~ Real ale ~ (01442) 864480 ~ Open 11-11; 12-10.30 Sun ~ Bar food 12-2.30(4 Sun), 6.30-9.30; 12-3, 6.30-10 Sat ~ Restaurant ~ Children welcome ~ Dogs allowed in bar ~ www.alfordarmsfrithsden.co.uk *Recommended by Mrs Margo Finlay, Jörg Kasprowski, John and Joyce Snell*

HERTFORD HEATH   TL3510   Map 5

College Arms 🍴 ⛾

London Road; B1197; SG13 7PW

Light and airy rooms with contemporary furnishings, friendly service, good, interesting food and real ales; seats outside

'What a gem,' says a reader with enthusiasm – and many agree. A civilised place, run with care and attention to detail, it's light and airy throughout with comfortable contemporary furnishings. The bar has high chairs around high tables, long cushioned wall seats and pale leather dining chairs around tables on rugs or bare boards, and a modern bar counter where they serve Sharps Doom Bar and Woodfordes Wherry on handpump and 16 wines by the glass; background jazz. Another area has long button-back wall seating, an open fireplace piled with logs and a doorway that leads to a charming little room with leather armchairs, a couple of cushioned pews, a woodburning stove in an old brick fireplace, hunting-themed wallpaper and another rug on floorboards. The elegant, partly carpeted dining room contains a real mix of antique dining chairs and tables, and a couple of large house plants. There are tables, seats and a long wooden bench among flowering pots on the back terrace and a children's playhouse; dogs are welcome. It's on the edge of a village and backed by woodland – handy for walks.

As well as stone-baked pizzas and sandwiches, the highly thought-of food includes duck liver and orange parfait with rhubarb compote, king prawn tempura in sesame, soy and ginger marinade with sweet chilli, bubble and squeak with crispy bacon, duck egg and hollandaise, oyster mushroom, purple sprouting broccoli and stilton tagliatelle, beer-battered fish and chips, calves liver with english mustard mash, bacon and honey-mustard sauce, sea trout fillet with crab, leek and apple macaroni cheese and puddings like rhubarb and ginger trifle with ginger beer jelly and rhubarb custard and frozen white chocolate panna cotta with raspberry sorbet. *Benchmark main dish: crispy pork belly with black pudding purée, champ and savoy cabbage £15.95. Two-course evening meal £18.00.*

Punch ~ Lease Merissa Tharby ~ Real ale ~ (01992) 558856 ~ Open 12-11(10.30 Sun) ~ Bar food 12-3(5 Sat, 7 Sun), 6-10; not Sun evening ~ Restaurant ~ Children welcome ~ Dogs allowed in bar ~ www.thecollegearmshertfordheath.com *Recommended by Christopher Middleton, Tim Lightfoot, David Hunt*

NORTHAW
Sun ☏

TL2702   Map 5

B156; on green opposite the church; EN6 4NL

Appealing décor in several little rooms, local ales, helpful service and delicious food

On the village green overlooking the church, this civilised and attractively refurbished pub dates from the 16th c. The opened-up bar has a curved counter with a stained-glass gantry, green-painted panelling, an open fire in a little brick fireplace and big boxes of vegetables dotted about (it sounds odd but looks fun). Nethergate Growler Bitter and Red Squirrel Mr Squirrel on handpump, and several wines by the glass, served by friendly staff. The snug has another fireplace and the two dining rooms have exposed brick walls. Throughout is a happy mix of antique dining chairs and tables on bare boards or old brick floors, fresh flowers and various china items. The back terrace has picnic-sets under parasols, with more on the grass.

A food map on each table shows locations of the producers of the organic, biodynamic and outdoor-reared ingredients. There are nibbles like pork crackling with apple sauce, smoked sprats and horseradish or beer-battered cod cheeks with tartare sauce, as well as lunchtime sandwiches, fried duck egg with shrimps, black pudding and sea kale, chargrilled cuttlefish with shallots and aioli, rare-breed burger with cheddar and chips, lamb and mint sausages with cabbage mash and scrumpy fried onions, chicken and ham hock pie, bubble and squeak with broccoli, poached egg and hollandaise, chicken with wild garlic sauce, bass fillet with sea spinach, cockles and shrimps, and puddings such as Valrhona chocolate mousse and kirsch cherries and banana and caramel eton mess; they also offer a two- and three-course set lunch. *Benchmark main dish: saddle of hare with smoked bacon, peas and jerusalem artichokes £16.20. Two-course evening meal £24.00.*

Free house ~ Licensee Oliver Smith ~ Real ale ~ (01707) 655507 ~ Open 12-11; 12-6 Sun; closed Sun evening, Mon ~ Bar food 12-3, 6-10; 12-4 Sun; not Mon ~ Children welcome ~ Dogs allowed in bar ~ www.thesunatnorthaw.co.uk *Recommended by Harvey Brown, Tess White*

POTTERS CROUCH   TL1105 Map 5
Holly Bush 🍺 £

2.25 miles from M25 junction 21A: A405 towards St Albans, first left, after a mile turn left (away from Chiswell Green), then at T junction turn right into Blunts Lane; can also be reached fairly quickly, with a good map, from M1 junctions 6 and 8 (and even M10); AL2 3NN

Well tended cottage with gleaming furniture, fresh flowers and china, well kept Fullers beers, good value food and an attractive garden

On a warm day, the fenced-off back garden is a fine spot for a drink or a meal with plenty of sturdy picnic-sets on a lawn surrounded by handsome trees. This is an immaculately kept pub with highly polished dark wood furnishings, antique dressers (several filled with plates), a number of comfortably cushioned settles, a fox's mask, antlers, a fine old clock with a lovely chime, daily papers and, on the right as you enter, a big fireplace. In the evening, candles cast glimmering light over dark varnished tables, all sporting fresh flowers. The long, stepped bar has particularly well kept Fullers ESB, London Pride and a seasonal beer on handpump. Service is friendly and helpful, even when pushed. Although the pub seems to stand alone on a quiet little road, it's only a few minutes' drive from the centre of St Albans (or a pleasant 45-minute walk). Please note they don't allow children or dogs.

🍴 At lunchtime especially, prices are very fair for sandwiches, toasties, platters, prawn and egg mayonnaise, baked camembert with pickles and red onion marmalade, chicken or beef burger with tomato relish, cheddar, bacon and coleslaw, and chilli con carne with sour cream and tortilla chips; evening choices include trio of cumberland sausages with onion gravy and mash, mediterranean vegetable tartlet, lamb rump with redcurrant, orange and mint jus, baked salmon fillet on creamy basil sauce, and puddings. *Benchmark main dish: chicken and leek pie £11.00. Two-course evening meal £20.00.*

Fullers ~ Tenants Steven and Vanessa Williams ~ Real ale ~ (01727) 851792 ~ Open 12-2.30, 6-11; 12-3, 7-10.30 Sun ~ Bar food 12-2(2.30 Sun), 6-9; not Sun-Tues evenings ~ www.thehollybushpub.co.uk *Recommended by Sarah Bennett*

PRESTON   TL1824 Map 5
Red Lion 🍺 £

Village signposted off B656 S of Hitchin; The Green; SG4 7UD

Homely village local with changing beers, fairly priced food and neat colourful garden

On a warm day, the seats on the pergola-covered back terrace and the picnic-sets (with some shade from a tall ash tree) in the good-sized sheltered garden with its colourful herbaceous border are a fine place to enjoy a drink or meal. Inside, it's welcoming and cheery – it claims to be the first community-owned pub in the country. The main room on the left, with grey wainscot, has sturdy well varnished pub furnishings including padded country kitchen chairs and cast-iron-framed tables on patterned carpet, a generous window seat, a log fire in a brick fireplace and fox hunting prints. The somewhat smaller room on the right has steeplechase prints, varnished plank panelling, and brocaded bar stools on flagstones around the servery; darts and dominoes. Fullers London Pride and Wells & Youngs on handpump with guests such as Newby Wyke HMS Nelson, Oakhams Scarlet Macaw and Skinners Cornish Knocker; also farm cider and perry, several wines by the glass (including an english house wine) and winter mulled wine. A few picnic-sets on the front grass face lime trees on the peaceful village green.

Deserving a Bargain Award for fair prices, food includes sandwiches, stilton-stuffed mushrooms, chilli and garlic prawns, sausage and mash, spiced lentil moussaka, beer-battered cod and chips, rabbit and cider casserole, curries (chicken madras, lamb rogan josh), liver and bacon, pheasant in madeira sauce, plaice in caper butter, and puddings like chocolate fudge cake and crème brûlée. *Benchmark main dish: fish pie £9.95. Two-course evening meal £13.00.*

Free house ~ Licensee Raymond Lamb ~ Real ale ~ (01462) 459585 ~ Open 12-2.30 (3.30 Sat), 5.30-11(midnight Sat); 12-3.30, 7-10.30 Sun ~ Bar food 12-2, 7-8.30; not Sun evening, Mon ~ Children welcome ~ Dogs welcome ~ www.theredlionpreston.co.uk
Recommended by Peter and Jean Hoare, M J Daly, Andrew Jeeves, Carole Smart, George Atkinson, Ross Balaam

REDBOURN   TL1011   Map 5
Cricketers

3.2 miles from M1 junction 9; A5183 towards St Albans, bear right on to B487, first right into Chequer Lane, then third right into East Common; AL3 7ND

Good food and beer in a nicely placed and attractively updated pub

At the heart of the village and overlooking Redbourn Common, this is a well run pub with friendly, efficient staff and contemporary furnishings. The front bar, which was knocked into quite an unusual shape during the building's restyling, is cosily civilised with leather tub armchairs, plush banquettes and leather cube stools on pale carpet. It leads back to an attractive, comfortably modern dining room, also gaining from the unusual shape of the building. Greene King IPA on handpump and thoughtfully sourced guest beers from brewers such as Aylesbury, Church End, Tring and Sharps. They also serve local Millwhite's Rum Cask cider and about two dozen wines by the glass, along with decent coffees; well reproduced background music. There are picnic-sets on the side grass and sheltered benches by the front door; a map board beside the local museum next door describes interesting nearby walks.

Good food includes sandwiches (not weekends), haggis and spinach bonbons with spiced apple chutney, crayfish and chilli risotto, cheese burger with blue cheese, bacon and chips, sausages and mash with onion gravy, beetroot, goats cheese and cranberry parcels, guinea fowl with smoked sausage and butter bean cassoulet, chicken breast wrapped in parma ham and stuffed with mozzarella, poached turbot in saffron cream sauce with celeriac mash, and puddings like blood orange panna cotta with shortbread and white chocolate blondie with toasted macadamia nuts and caramel fudge ice-cream. *Benchmark main dish: venison rossini with rösti, braised red cabbage and red wine jus £20.95. Two-course evening meal £23.00.*

Free house ~ Licensees Colin Baxter and Andy Stuart ~ Real ale ~
(01582) 620612 ~ Open 12-11(midnight Sat, 10.30 Sun) ~ Bar food 12-3, 6-9
(10 Fri, Sat); 12-4 Sun ~ Restaurant ~ Children welcome ~ Dogs allowed in bar ~
www.thecricketersofredbourn.co.uk *Recommended by Ross Balaam*

SARRATT
Cock

TQ0498   Map 5

Church End: a very pretty approach is via North Hill, a lane N off A404, just under a mile W of A405; WD3 6HH

Plush pub with friendly staff and a wide choice of drinks and food including Badger beers; good for families outside on summer weekends

Even on a dreary rainy day, you'll find plenty of happy customers in this comfortably traditional and welcoming place. The latched back door opens straight into the homely tiled snug with its cluster of bar stools, vaulted ceiling and original bread oven. Through an archway, the partly oak-panelled cream-walled lounge has a lovely log fire in an inglenook, pretty Liberty-style curtains, red plush chairs at dark oak tables, lots of interesting artefacts and several namesake pictures of cockerels. Badger Best, Tanglefoot and a couple of guest beers on handpump; background music. The restaurant is in an attractively converted barn. In summer, children can enjoy the bouncy castle and play area, leaving parents to take in the open country views from picnic-sets on the pretty, sheltered lawn and terrace. More picnic-sets in front look across a quiet lane towards the churchyard.

Popular food includes chicken liver pâté with home-made chilli jam, tiger prawns in garlic butter, white wine, tomato and brandy, sweet potato and spinach curry, pork and leek sausages with mash and onion gravy, honey-glazed pork belly with cider and wholegrain mustard sauce, beer-battered fresh haddock with chips, gammon and eggs, curry of the day, steaks and puddings. *Benchmark main dish: steak in ale pie £12.45. Two-course evening meal £19.00.*

Badger ~ Tenants Brian and Marion Eccles ~ Real ale ~ (01923) 282908 ~ Open 12-11 (11.30 Sat, 9 Sun) ~ Bar food 12-2.30, 6-9; 12-5 Sun ~ Restaurant ~ Children welcome ~ Dogs allowed in bar ~ www.cockinn.net *Recommended by Roy Hoing, Paul Humphreys, Dr Kevan Tucker*

SARRATT
Cricketers ♀ ◀

TQ0499   Map 5

The Green; WD3 6AS

Charming pub by village green with lots to look at in rambling rooms, six real ales, nice wines, enjoyable food and friendly staff; seats outside

It's really worth wandering around this cleverly refurbished pub before you decide where to sit. It consists of three charming old cottages and the interlinked rooms have plenty of snugs and alcoves – perfect for a quiet drink – and several dining areas, connected or more private. Throughout there's plenty of cricketing memorabilia, fresh flowers, large plants and church candles, all manner of antique dining chairs and tables on rugs or stripped floorboards, comfortable armchairs or tub seats, cushioned pews and wall seats and two open fires in raised fireplaces. Phoenix Brunning & Price Original and guests like Fullers London Pride, Three Castles Saxon Archer, Tring Side Pocket for a Toad and Vale Red Kite on handpump, good wines by the glass and 50 whiskies; background music and board games. Several sets of french windows open on to the terrace where there are tables and chairs, with picnic-sets on grass next to a colourfully painted tractor.

As well as a two- and three-course weekday set menu, the interesting food includes sandwiches, south african-style lamb kekab with curried apricot sauce, smoked salmon on wholegrain pancake with sour cream, red pepper, mushroom and aubergine lasagne, corned beef hash with duck egg and red onion gravy, steak burger with bacon, cheese, gherkins, coleslaw and chips, mussel and prawn linguine with white wine, tomato and chilli, minted lamb shank with sweet potato dauphinoise, bass fillets with chorizo, cherry tomatoes and sautéed potatoes, and puddings such as strawberry eton mess and sticky toffee pudding with toffee sauce and vanilla ice-cream. *Benchmark main dish: beer-battered haddock and chips with mushy peas £12.25. Two-course evening meal £19.00.*

Brunning & Price ~ Licensee David Stowell ~ Real ale ~ (01923) 270877 ~ Open 11.30-11; 12-10.30 Sun ~ Bar food 12-10(9.30 Sun) ~ Restaurant ~ Children welcome ~ Dogs allowed in bar ~ www.cricketers-sarratt.co.uk *Recommended by John and Joyce Snell, Brian Glozier*

WATTON-AT-STONE
Bull
High Street; SG14 3SB

TL3019 Map 5

Bustling old pub, open all day, with much character in several rooms, candlelight and fresh flowers, real ales served by friendly staff and enjoyable food; seats outside

At the heart of this 15th-c pub is a huge inglenook fireplace with a log fire – the leather button-back chesterfield and armchairs in front of it are much prized in cold weather. The main bar has fresh flowers and a relaxed, friendly atmosphere, with interesting landscape-patterned wallpaper on one wall and a button-back leather banquette beside it, and solid dark wood dining chairs and plush-topped stools around a mix of tables on bare boards. Adnams Broadside, Sharps Doom Bar and Woodfordes Wherry on handpump, good wines by the glass and helpful service. Near the entrance are some high bar chairs along counters by the windows; from here, it's a step up to a charming little room with just four tables, wooden dining chairs with brown cushions, a wall banquette, decorative logs in the fireplace, books on shelves, board games and an old typewriter. At the other end of the building is an elegantly furnished dining room with both carpet and a slate floor. Paintwork throughout is contemporary. There are church chairs and tables on the covered terrace, picnic-sets on grass and a small, well equipped play area.

Good tempting food includes breakfasts and morning coffee as well as sandwiches, toasties, duck terrine with spiced plum chutney, mixed deli board to share, omelette arnold bennett, burger with beer-battered onion rings, cheese, bacon, free-range egg and chips, gloucester old spot pork chop with wholegrain mustard dressing and crushed new potatoes, wild mushroom, smoked cheddar and herb pancake with ratatouille and parmesan crisps, whole grilled fish of the day with confit fennel, lamb stew with pearl barley, swede and carrots, madeira jus and parsley dumplings, and puddings. *Benchmark main dish: chargrilled gammon with duck egg £9.95. Two-course evening meal £21.00.*

Punch ~ Lease Alastair and Anna Bramley ~ Real ale ~ (01920) 831032 ~ Open 9.30am-11pm; 12-6 Sun; closed Sun evening ~ Bar food 12-3, 6-10; 12-6 Sun ~ Restaurant ~ Children welcome ~ www.thebullwatton.co.uk *Recommended by Jason Campbell, Adam Jones, Alastair Bramley*

The ◖ symbol shows pubs which keep their beer unusually well, have a particularly good range or brew their own.

WILLIAN
Fox ⑪ ♀ ◖

TL2230   Map 5

A1(M) junction 9; A6141 W towards Letchworth, then first left; SG6 2AE

Civilised dining pub with a thoughtful range of drinks and imaginative food

This well run dining pub is fresh, clean-cut and contemporary in style. There are comfortable light wood chairs and tables on stripped boards or big ceramic tiles, with paintings by local artists on white or pastel walls. The modern bar counter – carefully lit, with contemporary grey wicker stools beside its pale blue frontage – has Adnams Bitter, Brancaster Oyster Catcher, Dark Star Hophead, Sharps Doom Bar and Woodfordes Wherry on handpump, a good wine list with 14 by the glass and a nice range of spirits, served by attentive, friendly young staff; unobtrusive TV. A side terrace has smart tables under cocktail parasols, and there are picnic-sets in the good-sized garden behind, below the handsome tower of the 14th-c All Saints church.

Using the best local, seasonal produce, the inventive food includes sandwiches, thai chicken and coriander ravioli with spiced consommé and crispy noodles, seared king scallop with smoked salmon, date purée and pear salsa, mushroom and truffle risotto with parsnip crisps, venison and beef burger with braised oxtail, cheddar and chips, chicken breast with pesto-crushed butter beans, fondant potato and red wine jus, roast rump of lamb and mini shepherd's pie with basil mash, confit tomatoes and red wine and mint jus, and puddings like Baileys panna cotta with chocolate sauce and vanilla and almond tuille and poached nectarine sundae with cherry sorbet, cranachan and lemon thyme mascarpone. *Benchmark main dish: pork tenderloin, pork and apple sausage roll, pork belly, black pudding, celeriac and apple remoulade £15.50. Two-course evening meal £19.00.*

Free house ~ Licensee Cliff Nye ~ Real ale ~ (01462) 480233 ~ Open 12-11(midnight Fri, Sat); 12-10.30 Sun ~ Bar food 12-2, 7-9(9.15 Fri, Sat); 12-3 Sun ~ Restaurant ~ Children welcome ~ Dogs allowed in bar ~ www.foxatwillian.co.uk
Recommended by Andy Lickfold, M and J White, Derek Thomas, Brian Glozier

Also Worth a Visit in Hertfordshire

Besides the fully inspected pubs, you might like to try these pubs that have been recommended to us and described by readers. Do tell us what you think of them: feedback@goodguides.com

ALDBURY   SP9612
✳ **Greyhound** (01442) 851228
Stocks Road; village signed from A4251 Tring–Berkhamsted, and from B4506; HP23 5RT Picturesque village pub with some signs of real age inside, copper-hooded inglenook in cosy traditional beamed bar, more contemporary area with leather chairs, airy oak-floored back restaurant with wicker chairs at big new tables, Badger ales, traditional food (all day weekends) from sandwiches up; children welcome, dogs in bar, front benches facing green with whipping post, stocks and duck pond, suntrap gravel courtyard, eight bedrooms (some in newer building behind), open all day. *(John Branston)*

ALDENHAM   TQ1498
Round Bush (01923) 855532
Roundbush Lane; WD25 8BG Cheery and bustling village pub with plenty of atmosphere, two front rooms and back restaurant, popular generously served food from baguettes to specials, five well kept ales including Black Sheep, friendly efficient staff, darts, live music and quiz (first Weds of month); children and dogs welcome, big garden, good walks. *(Ross Balaam)*

ARDELEY   TL3027
Jolly Waggoner (01438) 861350
Off B1037 NE of Stevenage; SG2 7AH Traditional beamed pub under newish management and back to its original

name (was briefly the Rabbits Foot); lots of nooks and corners, inglenook log fire, Buntingford Highwayman, Fullers London Pride and a guest ale, plenty of wines by the glass including some organic ones, fairly traditional food with much sourced from farm opposite (rare-breed meat), restaurant; children welcome, garden with terrace and pétanque, open all day. *(Anon)*

ASHWELL   TL2639
Rose & Crown (01462) 742420
High Street; SG7 5NP Friendly traditional local, Greene King ales and a guest, enjoyable home-made food (not Sun evening), good service, L-shaped bar with 16th-c beams and lovely log fire, candlelit restaurant; children welcome, big garden with play area and pétanque, open all day weekends. *(Simon Watkins, Eddie Edwards)*

ASHWELL   TL2739
Three Tuns (01462) 742107
Off A505 NE of Baldock; High Street; SG7 5NL New management for this comfortable gently old-fashioned red-brick hotel in charming village; cosy opulently Victorian lounge with panelling and dark green walls, lots of pictures, stuffed animals and antiques, relaxing chairs and big tables, open fire, more modern public bar with leather sofas on reclaimed oak flooring, Greene King ales and guests, good choice of wines, bar food (all day weekends); cribbage, dominoes, games machine and TV; children and dogs welcome, terrace and substantial garden with boules under apple trees, six bedrooms, open all day. *(Dennis Jones)*

AYOT GREEN   TL2213
Waggoners (01707) 324241
Off B197 S of Welwyn; AL6 9AA Former 17th-c coaching inn under french owners; good food from snacks and pubby choices in cosy low-beamed bar to more upmarket french cooking in comfortable restaurant extension, friendly attentive staff, good wine list, real ales; attractive and spacious suntrap back garden with sheltered terrace – some A1(M) noise, wooded walks nearby. *(James Luke)*

AYOT ST LAWRENCE   TL1916
Brocket Arms (01438) 820250
Off B651 N of St Albans; AL6 9BT Attractive 14th-c low-beamed inn under newish management; enjoyable interesting food (not Sun evening) in bar or restaurant, six real ales including Black Sheep, Greene King and one badged for the pub from Nethergate, wide choice of wines by the glass, inglenook log fires; children welcome, dogs in bar, nice suntrap walled garden with play area, handy for George Bernard Shaw's house (NT), six refurbished bedrooms, open all day. *(Anthony and Marie Lewis, Matthew Salisbury)*

BARKWAY   TL3834
⋆ Tally Ho (01763) 848389
London Road (B1368); SG8 8EX Quirky little local with inviting old sofa, armchairs, horsebrasses and log fire in relaxed cottagey bar, extraordinary range of drinks including 60 malt whiskies and over 200 other spirits, Buntingford, Rebellion and a guest ale (apparently tapped from big casks behind bar, but actually gently pumped), Aspall's cider, fresh flowers and silver candelabra, old-fashioned prints on brown ply panelling, another log fire in old-world dining area serving fairly traditional food; children welcome, dogs in bar, well spaced picnic-sets, weeping willow in garden behind car park, open all day except Sun evening. *(Simon Watkins, Jeremy Donaldson)*

BATFORD   TL1415
⋆ Gibraltar Castle (01582) 460005
Lower Luton Road; B653, S of B652 junction; AL5 5AH Traditional long carpeted bar with impressive military memorabilia (everything from rifles and swords to uniforms and medals – plenty of captions to read), also historical pictures of Gibraltar; area with low beams giving way to soaring rafters, comfortably cushioned wall benches, snug window alcoves and nice old fireplace, board games on piano, Fullers London Pride and ESB, popular food (not Sun evening, Mon); background music; children and dogs welcome, seats on front terrace looking across road to nature reserve, more tables behind on large decked area with lots of flowers, open all day. *(Ron and June Buckler, John Taylor)*

BENINGTON   TL3023
Bell (01438) 869270
Town Lane; just past Post Office, towards Stevenage; SG2 7LA Traditional 16th-c pub in very pretty village, well kept Greene King ales and enjoyable home-made food (not Sun evening, Mon) including monthly themed night, low beams, sloping walls and big inglenook, folk evening fourth Tues of month; big garden with country views, pétanque, handy for Benington Lordship Gardens, open all day Sun, closed Mon lunchtime. *(Mrs Margo Finlay, Jörg Kasprowski, Ian Burgess)*

BERKHAMSTED   SP9907
Rising Sun (01442) 864913
George Street; HP4 2EG Victorian canalside pub with five well kept ales including one badged for them by Tring, good range of ciders (three beer/cider festivals a year), interesting range of spirits, two very small traditional rooms with a few basic chairs and tables, coal fire, snuff and cigars for sale, no food apart from ploughman's, friendly service; background music; children and dogs welcome, chairs out by canal and well worn seating in covered side garden,

colourful hanging baskets, open all day in summer, closed Mon–Thurs lunchtimes in winter. *(Rick Nunn, Graeme Urwin, N R White)*

BOURNE END TL0206
★ **Three Horseshoes** (01442) 862585
Winkwell; just off A4251 Hemel–Berkhamsted; HP1 2RZ
Renovated 16th-c pub in charming setting by unusual swing bridge over Grand Union Canal, low-beamed three-room core with inglenooks, traditional furniture including settles, a few sofas, three well kept changing ales, straightforward reasonably priced food all day (they may ask to keep a credit card while you eat), efficient uniformed staff, bay-windowed extension overlooking canal; comedy and quiz nights; children welcome, picnic-sets out by the water. *(Dennis Jones)*

BRAUGHING TL3925
Axe & Compass (01920) 821610
Just off B1368; The Street; SG11 2QR
Nice country pub in pretty village with ford; enjoyable home-prepared food from traditional to more creative dishes, own-baked bread, well kept ales and several wines by the glass, friendly uniformed staff, mix of furnishings on wood floors in two roomy bars, log fires, restaurant; well behaved children and dogs welcome, garden overlooking playing field, outside bar. *(Mrs Margo Finlay, Jörg Kasprowski)*

BRAUGHING TL3925
Golden Fleece (01920) 823555
Green End (B1368); SG11 2PE
Refurbished 17th-c dining pub with good freshly made food (all day Sun till 6pm) including some imaginative choices, special diets catered for, Adnams and guests, plenty of wines by the glass including champagne, cheerful service, bare-boards bar and two dining rooms, beams and timbers, good log fire; circular picnic-sets out in front, back garden with metal furniture on paved terrace. *(Jeremy Donaldson)*

BUSHEY TQ1394
Horse & Chains (020) 8421 9907
High Street; WD23 1BL Comfortably modernised dining pub with woodburner in big inglenook, good choice of wines by the glass, real ales, enjoyable all-day bar food from sandwiches and sharing plates up, separate restaurant menu, view into kitchen from compact dining room; children welcome. *(Anon)*

CHANDLERS CROSS TQ0698
Clarendon (01923) 270009
M25 junction 20; A41 towards Watford, right at first traffic lights signed Sarratt, then into Redhall Lane; WD3 4LU
Stylish modern bar with tall swivelling chrome and leather chairs at long high dark wood counter, colourful contemporary artwork, side area with log fire and leather chesterfields, Tring ales and good choice of wines by the glass, dining part with open kitchen, grand upstairs restaurant, quite elaborate pricey food, cheerful well trained young staff; background music; children welcome, neatly landscaped terrace, open fire in substantial brick-built smokers' shelter, open all day. *(Anon)*

CHIPPERFIELD TL0401
Two Brewers (01923) 265266
The Common; WD4 9BS Attractive 18th-c country hotel housing bay-windowed Chef & Brewer, roomy linked areas with pretty décor and two log fires, enjoyable all-day food from sandwiches up including offers, good choice of wines by the glass, well kept ales such as Sharps Doom Bar, friendly efficient service; provision for children, disabled facilities, terrace seating, 20 comfortable bedrooms, lovely spot on common and handy for M25, walks nearby, open all day. *(Ross Balaam)*

CHORLEYWOOD TQ0395
★ **Black Horse** (01923) 282252
Dog Kennel Lane, The Common; WD3 5EG Welcoming old country pub popular for its good value generous food (smaller helpings available) from good sandwiches up, bargain OAP meals, well kept ales including Adnams, Wadworths and Wells & Youngs, decent wines, tea and coffee, good cheery service even when busy, low dark beams and two log fires in thoroughly traditional rambling bar, daily papers; big-screen TV; children, walkers and dogs welcome, picnic-sets overlooking common, open all day. *(Roy Hoing)*

CHORLEYWOOD TQ0294
★ **Land of Liberty Peace & Plenty** (01923) 282226
Long Lane, Heronsgate, just off M25 junction 17; WD3 5BS Well kept local Red Squirrel, Tring and interesting guest beers, Millwhite's and Weston's cider and perry, bottled belgian beers, decent coffee, enjoyable lunches including some imaginative dishes, snacks served all day, good friendly service, simple traditional layout, darts, skittles and board games; TV, no children inside; dogs welcome, covered deck with more picnic-sets in garden, open all day. *(N R White)*

CHORLEYWOOD TQ0295
Stag (01923) 282090
Long Lane/Heronsgate Road; WD3 5BT Spacious recently refurbished open-plan Edwardian dining pub, decent choice of food from sandwiches and light meals up, weekday set lunch, McMullens ales and good choice of wines by the glass, friendly attentive service, bar and eating areas extending into conservatory, woodburner in raised hearth; children welcome, tables on back lawn, closed Mon, otherwise open all day from 9am (10am weekends), Sun till 7pm. *(Anon)*

COLNEY HEATH TL2007
Plough (01727) 823720
Sleapshyde; handy for A1(M) junction 3; A414 towards Street Albans, double back at first roundabout then turn left; AL4 0SE Cosy 18th-c low-beamed thatched local, chatty atmosphere, good value generous home-made standard food (not Sun-Tues evenings) from lunchtime baguettes and baked potatoes up, well kept Greene King IPA and Abbot, St Austell Tribute and a guest, friendly efficient staff, big log fire, small brighter back dining area, charity quiz (first Tues of month); sports TV; children welcome, no dogs during food times, front and back terraces, picnic-sets on lawn overlooking fields, open all day weekends. *(Alan Weedon)*

COTTERED TL3229
Bull (01763) 281243
A507 W of Buntingford; SG9 9QP Friendly well run dining pub with airy low-beamed front lounge, good furniture on stripped wood floors, log fire, very well liked if not cheap food from sandwiches up, Greene King ales and decent wines; unobtrusive background music; no prams, no under-7s Mon-Sat, big garden with tables beneath majestic old trees, open all day Sun. *(Anon)*

ESSENDON TL2608
Candlestick (01707) 261322
West End Lane; AL9 6BA Peacefully located country pub under same ownership as the nearby Woodman at Wildhill; emphasis on dining but also well kept local beers and several wines by the glass, relaxed friendly atmosphere, good value freshly prepared bar and restaurant food, comfortable clean interior with faux black timbers, log fires; children and dogs welcome, plenty of seats outside, good walks, closed Mon, otherwise open all day (till 8pm Sun). *(Martin Gough)*

FLAUNDEN TL0100
Green Dragon (01442) 832269
Flaunden Hill; HP3 0PP Comfortable and chatty 17th-c beamed pub with partly panelled extended lounge, back restaurant and traditional little tap bar, log fire, popular good value thai food as well as pubby choices, Fullers, St Austell and Wells & Youngs, friendly service; background music; children and dogs welcome, well kept garden with smokers' shelter, pretty village, only a short diversion from Chess Valley Walk. *(Charles Harvey, N R White)*

GREAT HORMEAD TL4030
Three Tuns (01763) 289405
B1038/Horseshoe Hill; SG9 0NT Old thatched and timbered country pub in lovely surroundings, enjoyable good value food, Greene King IPA and a guest, small linked areas, huge inglenook with another great hearth behind, big back conservatory extension; children and dogs welcome, nice quiet garden, closed Sun evening. *(Anon)*

HARPENDEN TL1413
Carpenters Arms (01582) 460311
Cravells Road; AL5 1BD Compact and welcoming, with good value pubby food and well kept ales such as Adnams, Courage, Sharps and Timothy Taylors from corner bar, open fires, lovingly collected car memorabilia including models and overseas number-plates; side terrace, open all day Sat. *(Sean McNaboe)*

HARPENDEN TL1312
★ White Horse (01582) 469290
Redbourn Lane, Hatching Green (B487 just W of A1081 roundabout); AL5 2JP Thriving Peach dining pub with good range of enjoyable modern food from deli boards up, also breakfast (from 9.30am), daily roast and good value fixed-price menu, friendly young staff, Purity UBU, Timothy Taylors Landlord and a guest, a dozen wines by the glass, L-shaped flagstoned bar with logs either side of little brick fireplace, leather cushioned window seats, room off with armchairs and tub seats on stripped boards, attractive airy dining room, morning coffee and daily papers; children welcome, tables on large terrace, more on lawn, open all day. *(John and Joyce Snell)*

HEMEL HEMPSTEAD TL0411
★ Crown & Sceptre (01442) 234660
Bridens Camp; leaving on A4146, right at Flamstead/Markyate sign opposite Red Lion; HP2 6EY Traditional neatly refurbished rambling pub, welcoming and relaxed, with well kept Greene King ales and up to four guests such as Tring and Vale, local cider, good generous reasonably priced pubby food (not Sun evening), friendly efficient staff, dining room with woodburner, quiz nights and beer festivals; children welcome, outside bar/games room (dogs welcome here), picnic-sets out at front and in pleasant garden, good walks, open all day weekends. *(Peter and Jan Humphreys, Dennis Jones, Ross Balaam)*

HEMEL HEMPSTEAD TL0411
Paper Mill (01442) 288800
Stationers Place, Apsley; HP3 9RH Recently built canalside pub on site of former paper mill; spacious open-plan interior with upstairs restaurant, Fullers ales and a guest such as Red Squirrel,

sensibly priced food from sandwiches and light dishes up, basket meals too, friendly staff, candles on tables, log fire, comedy, quiz and live music nights; children welcome, tables out on balcony and by the water, open all day. *(Tony and Wendy Hobden)*

HERTFORD TL3008
Baker Arms (01992) 511235

Ashendene Road; SG13 8PX Nicely set village pub in row of former farm workers' cottages, traditionally refurbished with pubby furniture on wood floors, green wainscoting, enjoyable home-made food from daily changing menu, McMullens ales, helpful friendly staff, restaurant; children welcome, dogs in bar, garden with deck and play area, clean comfortable bedrooms, open all day in summer (till 6pm Sun, from 3pm Mon). *(Mrs Margo Finlay, Jörg Kasprowski)*

HIGH WYCH TL4714
Hand & Crown (01279) 725892

Signed off A1184 Harlow–Sawbridgeworth; CM21 0AY Nice interior with some interesting features including huge central fireplace dividing off restaurant area, good reasonably priced and generously served food (popular, so best to book), well kept Greene King IPA and Abbot, plenty of whiskies, attentive service; background music, no under-14s; open all day Weds-Sat, closed Sun evening. *(Stephen and Jean Curtis)*

HIGH WYCH TL4614
Rising Sun (01279) 724099

Signed off A1184 Harlow–Sawbridgeworth; CM21 0HZ Refurbished and opened up 19th-c red-brick local, well kept Courage Best, Oakham and up to four guests tapped from the cask, friendly staff and locals, woodburner, quiz second Tues of month; well behaved children and dogs welcome, small side garden. *(Anon)*

HITCHIN TL1828
Half Moon (01462) 452448

Queen Street; SG4 9TZ Tucked-away open-plan local, friendly and welcoming, with well kept Adnams, Wells & Youngs and interesting guests, real cider and perry, good choice of wines by the glass, traditional food (some themed nights), beer festivals; open all day Fri, Sat. *(Nicola Ridding, Ian Dunbar)*

HITCHIN TL1929
Radcliffe Arms (01462) 456111

Walsworth Road; SG4 9ST Busy modernised Victorian pub/restaurant with good freshly made food (some not particularly cheap), local Buntingford ales, extensive wine list with many by the glass,

decent coffee, friendly staff, conservatory; children welcome, terrace tables, open all day from 8am (9am weekends) for breakfast, closed Sun evening. *(M and J White)*

HUNSDON TL4114
Fox & Hounds (01279) 843999

High Street; SG12 8NJ Village dining pub with chef/landlord cooking good enterprising seasonal food (some quite pricey), friendly efficient service, Adnams, Red Squirrel, Saffron and a local guest, wide choice of wines by the glass, organic fruit juices, beams, panelling and fireside leather sofas, more formal restaurant with chandelier and period furniture, bookcase door to lavatories; children welcome, dogs in bar, heated covered terrace, closed Sun evening, Mon. *(Mrs Margo Finlay, Jörg Kasprowski)*

LITTLE GADDESDEN SP9913
Bridgewater Arms (01442) 842408

Nettleden Road, off B4506; HP4 1PD Pleasant well cared-for 19th-c dining pub, good value food from snacks up, well kept Greene King ales and good choice of wines by the glass, decent coffee, friendly attentive service, daily papers, tiled and carpeted bar, raftered restaurant, a couple of fires (one log-effect gas), games in small bare-boards public area; children welcome, garden tables, good walks from the door, open all day. *(N R White)*

LITTLE HADHAM TL4322
Nags Head (01279) 771555

Hadham Ford, towards Much Hadham; SG11 2AX Popular and welcoming 16th-c country dining pub with small linked heavily black-beamed rooms, enjoyable reasonably priced food from snacks up including good Sun roasts, small bar with three Greene King beers and decent wines, restaurant down a couple of steps; children in eating areas, tables in pleasant garden. *(Michael Domeney)*

LONG MARSTON SP8915
Queens Head (01296) 668368

Tring Road; HP23 4QL Refurnished beamed village local with well kept Fullers beers, Weston's cider and enjoyable traditional food including bargain two-course set weekday lunch, quiz and curry night Tues; dogs welcome, seats on terrace, good walks nearby, two bedrooms in separate annexe, open all day. *(Ron and June Buckler)*

MUCH HADHAM TL4219
✶ Bull (01279) 842668

High Street; SG10 6BU Neatly kept old dining pub with good home-made food changing daily, nice choice of wines by

---

We mention bottled beers and spirits only if there is something unusual about them – imported belgian real ales, say, or dozens of malt whiskies; so do please let us know about them in your reports.

the glass including champagne, well kept
Hancocks HB, cheerful efficient service even
at busy times, inglenook log fire in unspoilt
bar with locals and their dogs, attractive
pastel décor in roomy civilised dining lounge
and back dining room; children welcome,
good-sized garden, Henry Moore Foundation
nearby. *(Simon Watkins, Mrs Margo Finlay, Jörg
Kasprowski)*

NORTHAW   TL2802
Two Brewers (01707) 655557
Northaw Road W (B156); EN6 4NW
Popular village pub with several traditional
snug areas, nice dining room and garden
with view of ancient parish church, two well
kept ales such as Wells & Youngs Bombardier,
enjoyable generous food at reasonable prices,
friendly efficient staff. *(Ross Balaam)*

NUTHAMPSTEAD   TL4134
★ ## Woodman (01763) 848328
Off B1368 S of Barkway; SG8 8NB
Tucked-away thatched and weatherboarded
village pub with comfortable unspoilt core,
17th-c low beams/timbers and nice inglenook
log fire, plainer dining extension, good
home-made food (not Sun evening, Mon)
from traditional choices up, home-baked
bread, ales such as Adnams, Buntingford and
Greene King tapped from the cask, friendly
service, interesting USAF memorabilia
and outside memorial (near World War II
airfield); benches out overlooking tranquil
lane, two comfortable bedrooms, open all
day (Sun till 6.30pm, Mon 5-8pm). *(Mark
Farrington, Mrs Margo Finlay, Jörg Kasprowski)*

PERRY GREEN   TL4317
Hoops (01279) 843568
*Off B1004 Widford–Much Hadham;
SG10 6EF* Refurbished 19th-c pub-
restaurant in grounds of the Henry Moore
Foundation (the sculptor in evidence through
posters, photographs, prints and even the
cushion covers), airy open-plan interior with
beams and standing timbers, spindleback
chairs around rustic tables on tiled floor,
green banquettes, inglenook woodburner,
good reasonably priced locally sourced food
including some unusual choices, Adnams
Best; no dogs inside; children welcome,
garden with large covered terrace, open
all day Weds-Sat, Sun till 6pm, closed Mon,
evening Tues (winter hours may vary).
(Anon)

REDBOURN   TL1011
Hollybush (01582) 792423
Church End; AL3 7DU Picturesque
pub dating from the 16th c, black-beamed
lounge with big brick fireplace and heavy
wooden doors, larger area with some built-in
settles, well kept Brakspears and reasonably
priced food, good Thurs night folk club;
no children in bar, pleasant sunny garden
(distant M1 noise), pretty spot near medieval
church. *(Conor McGaughey)*

RICKMANSWORTH   TQ0594
Feathers (01923) 770081
Church Street; WD3 1DJ Quietly set off
the high street, beams, panelling and soft
lighting, well kept Fullers London Pride,
Tring and two guests, good wine list, varied
choice of freshly prepared seasonal food
(all day) from sandwiches up including
lunchtime deal, good friendly young staff
coping well when busy; children till 5pm,
picnic-sets out behind. *(Brian Glozier)*

RIDGE   TL2100
Old Guinea (01707) 660894
Crossoaks Lane; EN6 3LH
Welcoming country pub extensively
refurbished by present owners, pizzeria
alongside traditional bar with open fire,
enjoyable food all day at reasonable prices,
St Austell Tribute; children welcome, dogs
in bar, large garden with far-reaching
views. *(Anon)*

ROYSTON   TL3540
Old Bull (01763) 242003
High Street; SG8 9AW Chatty and
relaxed coaching inn dating from the 16th c
with bow-fronted Georgian façade; roomy
high-beamed bar, exposed timbers and
handsome fireplaces, wood flooring, easy
chairs, papers and magazines, dining area
with wall-sized photographs of old Royston,
decent choice of food from ciabattas up,
good value Sun carvery, Greene King ales
and a guest, several wines by the glass,
helpful pleasant service; background
music and monthly live folk; children
welcome, dogs in bar, suntrap courtyard,
11 bedrooms, open all day from 8am.
(Conor McGaughey, John Wooll)

SARRATT   TQ0499
Boot (01923) 262247
The Green; WD3 6BL Early 18th-c dining
pub continuing well under present licensees;
good food (all day Sat, not Sun evening) from
lunchtime sandwiches and sharing plates up,
weekend breakfast from 9.30am, also tapas
and pizzas Fri and Sat evenings, efficient
service from friendly young staff, well kept
ales and good choice of wines by the glass,
rambling bar with unusual inglenook,
restaurant extension; good-sized garden with
polytunnel growing own produce, pleasant
spot facing green, handy for Chess Valley
walks, open all day. *(N R White, Ross Balaam,
Jacquie Green)*

ST ALBANS   TL1407
Farriers Arms (01727) 851025
Lower Dagnall Street; AL3 4PT Plain
friendly two-bar backstreet local, well
kept McMullens and a guest ale, bar food
weekdays, lots of old pictures of the pub;
darts, sports TV; open all day weekends,
closed Mon lunchtime. *(Anon)*

ST ALBANS   TL1406
Garibaldi (01727) 894745
Albert Street; left turn down Holywell Hill past White Hart – car park left at end; AL1 1RT Busy little Victorian backstreet local with well kept Fullers/Gales beers and guests, good wines by the glass, reasonably priced food (all day weekends, till 7pm Sat, 5pm Sun), live music Sat; children welcome, garden tables, open all day. *(Nathan Gainford)*

ST ALBANS   TL1805
⋆ Plough (01727) 857777
Tyttenhanger Green, off A414 E; AL4 0RW 18th-c village pub with up to ten well kept ales including Fullers, friendly efficient staff, low-priced straightforward food (not Sun or Mon evenings) from filled pittas and panini up, good log fire and woodburner, interesting old beer bottles and mats, longcase clock, back conservatory, board games and daily newspapers; children welcome, tables on raised front terrace, big garden with play area, open all day Fri-Sun. *(Alan Weedon)*

ST ALBANS   TL1307
⋆ Six Bells (01727) 856945
St Michaels Street; AL3 4SH Well cared for rambling old pub popular for its good reasonably priced generous food, five well kept beers including Fullers London Pride and Timothy Taylors Landlord, cheerful helpful service, low beams and timbers, log fire, quieter panelled dining room, some live music; children welcome, occasional barbecues in small back garden, handy for Verulamium Museum, open all day. *(LM, Mike and Jennifer Marsh, Stephen and Jean Curtis, David and Sue Atkinson)*

ST ALBANS   TL1406
White Hart Tap (01727) 860974
Keyfield, round corner from Garibaldi; AL1 1QJ Friendly 19th-c corner local with half a dozen well kept ales (summer beer festivals), decent choice of wines by the glass, reasonably priced fresh food (all day Sat, not Sun evening) including good fish and chips Fri, some live music, Weds quiz; tables outside, open all day. *(Anon)*

ST ALBANS   TL1406
White Lion (01727) 850540
Sopwell Lane; AL1 1RN 16th-c local with good atmosphere in small friendly front bar and roomy linked lounge areas, enjoyable fairly priced food (not Sat or Sun evenings) from snacks to daily blackboard specials, up to eight well kept ales (spring and summer beer festivals), Weston's cider, darts, live music Tues; no children inside; dogs welcome (friendly three-legged pub dog called Sammy), big enclosed garden with pétanque and chickens, open all day. *(Stephen and Jean Curtis, Tony and Wendy Hobden)*

STAPLEFORD   TL3017
Woodhall Arms (01992) 535123
High Road; SG14 3NW Dining inn with good food in bar and spacious restaurant/conservatory, well kept Greene King, Wells & Youngs and guests; children welcome, ten comfortable reasonably priced bedrooms. *(Mike and Lynn Robinson)*

THERFIELD   TL3337
Fox & Duck (01763) 287246
Signed off A10 S of Royston; The Green; SG8 9PN Open-plan bow-windowed pub under newish management; country chairs and big stripped-top dark tables on stone flooring, enjoyable food (not Sun evening, Mon) from pub favourites up, Greene King and two guests, friendly helpful staff, smaller boarded area on left with darts, carpeted back restaurant; children welcome, garden behind with gate to park (play equipment), more picnic-sets out on front green, quiet village, pleasant walks nearby, open all day weekends. *(Simon Watkins)*

TRING   SP9211
Akeman (01442) 826027
Akeman Street; HP23 6AA Popular Oakman Inn (their first – opened 2007), good choice of interesting food with some mediterranean influences from bar snacks and sharing plates up, open kitchen, three well kept ales including Tring, plenty of wines by the glass, cocktails and good coffee, open-plan layout with leather sofas by log fire, afternoon acoustic music first Sun of month; children welcome, nice garden area, open all day from 8am (breakfast till midday). *(Taff Thomas)*

TRING   SP9211
⋆ Kings Arms (01442) 823318
King Street; by junction with Queen Street (which is off B4635 Western Road – continuation of High Street); HP23 6BE Delightful spic-and-span backstreet pub with lots of cheerful customers and relaxed atmosphere, well kept Wadworths 6X and four quickly changing guests such as Tring, Rosie's cider, hearty helpings of good value food including several spicy dishes, efficient service, cushioned pews and wooden tables, stools around cast-iron tables, carpeted floors, old brewery advertisements on green-painted or

---

Post Office address codings confusingly give the impression that some pubs are in Hertfordshire, when they're really in Bedfordshire, Buckinghamshire or Cambridgeshire (which is where we list them).

pine-panelled walls, two warm winter coal fires; dogs welcome, children till 8.30pm, tables and heaters in attractive side wagon yard. *(Alan Weedon, Malcolm and Sue Scott)*

TRING   SP9211
⋆ **Robin Hood** (01442) 824912
Brook Street (B486); HP23 5ED Welcoming traditional local with enjoyable good value pubby food (all day Sat, not Sun evening), half a dozen Fullers ales in good condition, homely atmosphere and genial service, several well cared for smallish linked areas, main bar has banquettes and standard pub chairs on bare boards or carpet, conservatory with vaulted ceiling and woodburner; background music; children welcome, dogs in bar (resident yorkshire terriers Buddy and Sugar), small back terrace, public car park nearby, open all day Fri-Sun. *(Anon)*

WARESIDE   TL3915
Chequers (01920) 467010
B1004; SG12 7QY Proper old-fashioned country local with down-to-earth landlady, three well kept ales including Buntingford, good straightforward home-made food at reasonable prices including vegetarian options, friendly staff, log fire; children, dogs and walkers welcome. *(Chris Allen)*

WATTON-AT-STONE   TL3019
George & Dragon (01920) 830285
High Street (B1001); SG14 3TA Appealing candlelit country dining pub; enjoyable food from sandwiches up using local produce (gluten-free diets catered for), Greene King and guests, interesting mix of antique and modern prints on partly timbered walls, big inglenook fireplace, daily papers; no dogs; children in eating areas, pretty shrub-screened garden with heaters, boules, open all day. *(N R White)*

WELWYN   TL2316
Wellington (01438) 714036
High Street, old village – not the Garden City; AL6 9EE Perhaps restaurant with rooms rather than pub; cushioned church and other dining chairs, window seats and copper-topped or wooden tables, lots of mirrors, standing timbers and open doorways, Greene King ales from zinc-topped counter, several wines by the glass, good coffee and teas, daily papers, light airy restaurant with stripped beams and central fire, glass wall looking on to High Street, popular food from traditional to more adventurous choices including good value fixed-price menu,

friendly efficient service; background music; terrace with modern wicker chairs, six good bedrooms, open all day. *(Anon)*

WHEATHAMPSTEAD   TL1713
Swan (01582) 833110
56 High Street; AL4 8AR Friendly busy village local, five well kept ales and good value pubby food, traditional furniture on patterned carpet, beams and inglenook, some live music; pool, sports TVs; dogs allowed in bar, open all day. *(John Taylor, Matthew Salisbury)*

WHEATHAMPSTEAD   TL1712
⋆ **Wicked Lady** (01582) 832128
Nomansland Common; B651 0.5 miles S; AL4 8EL Chain dining pub with clean contemporary décor, wide range of good well presented food including weekday fixed-price menu till 7pm, well kept Adnams, Fullers London Pride and Timothy Taylors Landlord, plenty of wines by the glass, cocktails, friendly attentive young staff, various rooms and alcoves, low beams and log fires, lots of stainless steel, conservatory; garden with pleasant terrace. *(David and Ruth Shillitoe)*

WIGGINTON   SP9310
Greyhound (01442) 824631
Just S of Tring; HP23 6EH Friendly village pub with four well kept ales including Tring, decent food from pubby choices to daily specials, restaurant; children and dogs welcome, back garden with fenced play area, good Ridgeway walks, three bedrooms, open all day. *(Ross Balaam)*

WILDHILL   TL2606
Woodman (01707) 642618
Off B158 Brookmans Park–Essendon; AL9 6EA Simple tucked-away country local with friendly staff and regulars, well kept Greene King and four guest ales, open-plan bar with log fire, two smaller back rooms (one with TV), enjoyable straightforward weekday bar lunches, darts; picnic-sets in big garden. *(David Hill)*

WILSTONE   SP9014
Half Moon (01442) 826410
Tring Road, off B489; HP23 4PD Traditional old village pub, clean and comfortable, with good value generous pubby food and well kept ales including Adnams, friendly efficient staff, big log fire, low beams, old local pictures and lots of brasses; may be background radio; handy for Grand Union Canal walks. *(John Kaye)*

Isle of Wight

This is a holiday island, so many of the pubs welcome families and provide facilities for children such as special menus and well equipped outdoor play areas. And several overlook the sea with plenty of seats on outside terraces with smashing views. Pubs that stand out this year include the White Lion at Arreton (run by a convivial landlord, with a good choice of ales), Crab & Lobster at Bembridge (delicious crab and lobster in well run pub), Horse & Groom in Ningwood (friendly, cosy and busy all year), Boathouse at Seaview (a light and contemporary interior and usefully serving food all day) and Crown in Shorwell (really nice pub with a pretty garden). With a new Food Award this year and lots of reader recommendations, our Isle of Wight Dining Pub 2014 is the Crab & Lobster at Bembridge – make sure you try the seafood.

ARRETON   SZ5386   Map 2

White Lion £

A3056 Newport–Sandown; PO30 3AA

Friendly local with good value pubby food

Our readers enjoy this comfortable white-painted village house, where the convivial landlord makes all his customers feel welcome. The neatly kept beamed lounge is old-fashioned and cosy, with dark pink walls or stripped brick above a stained pine dado, gleaming brass and horse tack and lots of cushioned wheelback chairs on patterned red carpet. The background music tends to be very quiet, and the public bar has a TV, games machine, darts and board games. Three changing real ales on handpump might be Greene King IPA, Sharps Doom Bar and Timothy Taylors Landlord; also a farm cider and draught pear cider. There's a separate restaurant (no children in here) and a family room. The pleasant garden has a small play area.

Quite a choice of well liked, reasonably priced food includes sandwiches, creamy garlic mushrooms with bacon and stilton, prawn cocktail, chicken, beef or vegetarian burgers with egg, cheese, bacon or fried onions, pie of the day, pork and ale sausages with mash and onion gravy, vegetable curry, smoked haddock and spring onion fishcakes, gammon with egg or pineapple, mixed grill and puddings. *Benchmark main dish: chicken breast with bacon and melted brie £10.95. Two-course evening meal £14.25.*

Enterprise ~ Lease Chris and Kate Cole ~ Real ale ~ (01983) 528479 ~ Open 11-11 ~ Bar food 12-9 ~ Children welcome except in restaurant ~ Dogs allowed in bar ~ www.white-lion-arreton.com *Recommended by A N Bance, Tom Evans, Michael Tack*

BEMBRIDGE
SZ6587   Map 2

Crab & Lobster 🍴

Foreland Fields Road, off Howgate Road (which is off B3395 via Hillway Road); PO35 5TR

Isle of Wight Dining Pub of the Year

Clifftop views from terrace and delicious seafood; bedrooms

Tucked away on a coastal bluff, this well run clifftop pub is not somewhere you'd stumble across by accident. And it's certainly worth searching out for the wonderful Solent views from seats on the terrace; the dining room and some bedrooms share the same aspect. In summer the picnic-sets are bagged pretty quickly, so do arrive early. Inside, it's roomier than you might expect and decorated in a parlour-like style, with lots of yachting memorabilia, old local photographs and a blazing winter fire; darts, dominoes and cribbage. Helpful, cheerful staff serve Goddards Fuggle-Dee-Dum, Greene King IPA and Sharps Doom Bar on handpump, a dozen wines by the glass, 16 malt whiskies and good coffee. The shore is just a stroll away.

As well as smashing seafood – crab and prawn cocktail, moules marinière, crab and lobster or hot seafood platters, seafood mixed grill – the good food includes lunchtime sandwiches and baguettes, ham and egg, pie and mash, all-day breakfast, mushroom, brie and redcurrant filo parcel, barbecue chicken, and puddings such as fruit pie or chocolate fudge cake. *Benchmark main dish: crab cakes £11.50. Two-course evening meal £17.50.*

Enterprise ~ Lease Caroline and Ian Quekett ~ Real ale ~ (01983) 872244 ~ Open 11-11; 12-10.30 Sun ~ Bar food 12-2.30, 6-9(9.30 Fri, Sat) with limited menu 2.30-5.30 weekends and holidays ~ Restaurant ~ Children welcome ~ Dogs allowed in bar ~ Bedrooms: £55/£80 ~ www.crabandlobsterinn.co.uk *Recommended by Tom Evans, Michael Tack*

FISHBOURNE
SZ5592   Map 2

Fishbourne Inn

From Portsmouth car ferry turn left into Fishbourne Lane (no through road); PO33 4EU

Attractively refurbished pub with a contemporary feel, several linked rooms, real ales, a good number of wines by the glass and all-day food; bedrooms

The attractive contemporary makeover in this half-timbered pub has settled in nicely. The open-plan rooms are connected by knocked-through doorways, and there's a mix of wooden and high-backed dining chairs around square tables on the slate floor, a red-painted area off the bar with a big model yacht and two leather sofas facing each other, and a woodburning stove in a brick fireplace with an ornate mirror above it. The smart dining room has leather high-backed chairs around circular tables on wood flooring and another model yacht on the window sill; one comfortable room has huge brown leather sofas, and throughout there are country pictures on the partly panelled walls. Goddards Fuggle-Dee-Dum and Sharps Doom Bar on handpump and a good list of wines. The inn is handy for the Wightlink ferry terminal, and is sister pub to the Boathouse in Seaview and New Inn at Shalfleet.

🍴 As well as breakfast from 9am (for non-residents too), the all-day food includes lunchtime sandwiches, sharing platters and deli boards, chicken caesar salad, ham and free-range eggs, trio of sausages with mash and gravy, broccoli, leek and goats cheese bake, pie of the day, rump steak with peppercorn sauce, whole crab salad, half or whole lobster salad, and puddings. *Benchmark main dish: beer-battered fish and chips £10.95. Two-course evening meal £17.00.*

Enterprise ~ Lease Richard Morey ~ Real ale ~ (01983) 882823 ~ Open 9am-11pm(10.30 Sun) ~ Bar food 12-9.30 ~ Children welcome ~ Dogs allowed in bar ~ Bedrooms: /£110 ~ www.thefishbourne.co.uk *Recommended by Richard and Penny Gibbs*

FRESHWATER   SZ3487   Map 2
Red Lion ♀

Church Place; from A3055 at E end of village by Freshwater Garage mini-roundabout follow Yarmouth signpost, then take first real right turn signed to Parish Church; PO40 9BP

Good mix of locals and visiting diners, good food, and composed atmosphere

In some choice walking country near the reedy Yar estuary and tucked well away, this red-brick pub has kept a genuine local atmosphere that visitors without small children tend to appreciate. The food is quite a draw, but you're likely to find a row of chatty regulars occupying stools along the counter, enjoying the Flowers Original, Goddards Fuggle-Dee-Dum, Otter Bitter and Sharps Doom Bar on handpump. The comfortably furnished open-plan bar has fires, low grey sofas and sturdy country kitchen furnishings on mainly flagstoned floors and bare boards. Outside, there are tables (some under cover) in a carefully tended garden beside the kitchen's herb and vegetable patch. A couple of picnic-sets in a quiet square at the front have pleasant views of the church.

🍴 Food, listed on blackboards behind the bar, includes a sensible cross-section of dishes such as field mushrooms with spinach and goats cheese, herring roes on toast, crispy duck salad, sharing platters, mushroom stroganoff, sausages, beans and chips, calves liver with bacon and onion gravy, chicken breast stuffed with brie and wrapped in bacon, beef curry, salmon fillet with dill sauce, and puddings such as jam roly-poly and raspberry and Grand Marnier brûlée. *Benchmark main dish: home-made fishcakes £11.50. Two-course evening meal £18.50.*

Enterprise ~ Lease Michael Mence ~ Real ale ~ (01983) 754925 ~ Open 11.30-3, 5.30-11; 11.30-4, 6-11 Sat; 12-3, 7-10.30 Sun ~ Bar food 12-2, 6-9 ~ Children under 10 at the landlord's discretion ~ Dogs welcome ~ www.redlion-freshwater.co.uk *Recommended by Tom Evans*

NINGWOOD   SZ3989   Map 2
Horse & Groom

A3054 Newport–Yarmouth, a mile W of Shalfleet; PO30 4NW

Spacious family dining pub with fairly priced all-day food, excellent play area and crazy golf

You can be sure of a friendly welcome from the licensee and his staff in this neatly kept and carefully extended pub, and with a winter log fire and a warm atmosphere, there are plenty of customers all year – both regulars and visitors. The roomy interior has been thoughtfully arranged with comfortable leather sofas grouped around low tables and a nice mix of sturdy tables and chairs, well spaced for a relaxing meal. Pale pink walls work nicely with the old flagstone flooring. Ringwood Best and a

couple of guests like Goddards Scrumdiggity Bitter and Sharps Doom
Bar on handpump and a dozen wines by the glass; background music,
games machine and board games. Families with children will find plenty
to keep them occupied outside, where there are ample tables in the
garden, a bouncy castle, crazy golf and a fully equipped play area.

🍴 Good value and enjoyable, the food might include sandwiches, deep-fried
prawns with garlic mayonnaise, home-cooked honey-roast ham with free-range
eggs, burgers with cheese or bacon, pasta topped with roast tomato sauce, goats
cheese and pesto, daily specials and puddings. *Benchmark main dish: steak in ale
pie £9.95. Two-course evening meal £15.00.*

Enterprise ~ Lease Steve Gilbert ~ Real ale ~ (01983) 760672 ~ Open 9am-11pm
(midnight Fri-Sun) ~ Bar food 9-9 ~ Children welcome ~ Dogs welcome ~
www.horse-and-groom.com *Recommended by Tom Evans, Penny and Peter Keevil,
Tonya Jayston*

 NITON   SZ5075   Map 2

Buddle 🍺

St Catherine's Road, Undercliff; off A3055 just S of village, towards
St Catherine's Point; PO38 2NE

**Stone pub with sea views from seats in clifftop garden, six real ales
and tasty food**

Now with a new landlady, this former smugglers' haunt is an attractive
stone cottage on a southerly cliff near St Catherine's Lighthouse;
the many picnic-sets on the stone terraces and on the grass in the neatly
kept garden look down to the sea. The traditional bar rooms have plenty
of character: heavy black beams, captain's chairs and wheelbacks or
cushioned wall seating around solid wooden tables on big flagstones
or carpet, and an open fire in a broad stone fireplace with a massive
black oak mantelbeam. A fine choice of six real ales on handpump might
include Fullers HSB, Otter Bitter, Sharps Doom Bar, Timothy Taylors
Landlord, Wells & Youngs Bombardier and a guest ale from Yates;
background music and bar billiards. The pub is surrounded by National
Trust land and is handy for the coast path. They keep dog treats behind
the bar.

🍴 Usefully serving some kind of food all day, there might be sandwiches,
mussels in cider and shallots, chicken liver pâté with home-made chutney,
curry of the day, pork and leek sausages with apple mash and onion gravy, roasted
vegetable tagliatelle, burgers with cheese, bacon or barbecue sauce, crab salad,
beef bourguignon, gammon and eggs, and puddings such as crème brûlée with
raspberries and warm chocolate and walnut brownie. *Benchmark main dish:
game, steak in ale or chicken pie £10.75. Two-course evening meal £15.00.*

Character Group ~ Lease Mandi O'Reilly ~ Real ale ~ (01983) 730243 ~ Open
11-11(midnight Fri, Sat); 12-10.30 Sun ~ Bar food 12-9 ~ Children allowed in Old Barn ~
Dogs welcome ~ Regular live jazz/blues/folk Weds, Fri, Sat evenings, Sun lunch ~
www.buddleinn.co.uk *Recommended by Tom Evans*

 SEAVIEW   SZ5992   Map 2

Boathouse

On B3330 Ryde–Seaview; PO34 5BW

**Contemporary décor in well run pub by the beach, real ales, quite
a choice of food, a friendly welcome and seats outside; bedrooms**

Usefully serving food all day at weekends (and every day from April to October), this extended blue-painted Victorian pub had an appealing and contemporary refurbishment recently. The bar has sturdy leather stools and blue tub-like chairs around circular wooden tables, a large model yacht on the mantelpiece above the open fire with a huge neat stack of logs beside it, fresh flowers and candles, and Ringwood Best and Sharps Doom bar on handpump from the pale wooden counter; another room has a dinghy with oars leaning against the wall. The dining room has elegant dining chairs, more wooden tables, portraits on pale blue walls and an ornate mirror over another open fire; background music. Throughout, the paintwork is light and fresh and there's a mix of polished bare boards, flagstones and carpet. Picnic-sets and white tables and chairs outside, some under parasols, look across to the sea – as do the double bedrooms. This is sister pub to the Fishbourne Inn at Fishbourne and the New Inn at Shalfleet.

Popular food includes sandwiches, smoked salmon cheesecake with croutons, prawn cocktail, ham and free-range eggs with home-made tomato relish, beef and vegetable pie, beer-battered fresh fish of the day, pheasant breast on thyme-roasted vegetables with cranberry jus, pangasius (a type of catfish) with stir-fried vegetables and red pesto sauce, and puddings such as warm chocolate brownie with chocolate sauce and turkish delight tart with chantilly cream. *Benchmark main dish: fillet of smoked haddock with prawn chowder £10.95. Two-course evening meal £16.00.*

Punch ~ Tenant Martin Bullock ~ Real ale ~ (01983) 810616 ~ Open 9am-11pm (10.30pm Sun) ~ Bar food 12-9.30; limited food 2.30-6 ~ Children welcome ~ Dogs allowed in bar ~ Bedrooms: /£110 ~ www.theboathouseiow.co.uk *Recommended by Richard and Penny Gibbs*

SHALFLEET
SZ4089 Map 2

New Inn 🍴 ♀

A3054 Newport–Yarmouth; PO30 4NS

Popular pub with seafood specialities, and good beers and wines

This 18th-c former fishermen's haunt is just a stroll from the quay at an inlet of the yacht-filled Newtown estuary. Its rambling rooms have plenty of character with warm fires, yachting photographs and pictures, boarded ceilings and scrubbed-pine tables on flagstone, carpet and slate floors. Sharps Doom Bar and a couple of guests such as Goddards Fuggle-Dee-Dum and Yates Golden on handpump, plus more than 60 wines; background music. There may be double sittings in summer; dogs are only allowed in areas with stone floors. This is sister pub to the Boathouse in Seaview and Fishbourne Inn at Fishbourne.

Bar food includes sandwiches, grilled black pudding with crispy bacon and soft cheese, crab and prawn ramekin with cream, butternut squash and shallots with walnuts, ham and eggs, fish or steak in ale pies, sharing platters of fresh and smoked fish and shellfish, and puddings. *Benchmark main dish: local pork belly with apple purée £13.95. Two-course evening meal £18.00.*

Enterprise ~ Lease Mr Bullock and Mr McDonald ~ Real ale ~ (01983) 531314 ~ Open 9am-11pm(10.30pm Sun) ~ Bar food 9am-11am, 12-2.30(3 Sun), 6-9.30; afternoon snacks 2.30-6 (not winter weekdays) ~ Children welcome ~ Dogs allowed in bar ~ www.thenew-inn.co.uk *Recommended by Tom Evans*

We say if we know a pub has background music.

SHORWELL

THE GOOD PUB GUIDE

Crown 🍺 £

SZ4582 Map 2

B3323 SW of Newport; PO30 3JZ

Popular pub with an appealing streamside garden and play area, pubby food and several real ales

This is a lovely pub with a friendly atmosphere; in good weather, the tree-sheltered garden with its little stream that broadens into a small trout-filled pool, is charming. There are plenty of closely spaced picnicsets and white garden chairs and tables on grass, and a decent children's play area. Inside, four opened-up rooms spread around a central bar, with carpet, tiles or flagstones, and chatty regulars lend local character. Adnams Broadside, Goddards Fuggle-Dee-Dum, St Austell Tribute and Sharps Doom Bar on handpump. The beamed knocked-through lounge has blue and white china on an attractive carved dresser, old country prints on stripped-stone walls and a winter log fire with a fancy tile-work surround. Black pews form bays around tables in a stripped-stone room to the left with another log fire; background music and board games.

🍴 Enjoyable food includes sandwiches and baguettes, pâté of the day, prawn cocktail, four-egg omelette, sausage and mash, ham and egg, vegetable curry, pizzas with various toppings, pie of the day, fisherman's platter for two, daily specials and puddings. *Benchmark main dish: beer-battered fish and chips £11.50. Two-course evening meal £16.00.*

Enterprise ~ Lease Nigel and Pam Wynn ~ Real ale · (01983) 740293 ~ Open 10.30am(11.30am Sun)-11pm ~ Bar food 12-9.30 ~ Children welcome ~ Dogs welcome ~ www.crowninnshorwell.co.uk *Recommended by Tom Evans, C and R Bromage, Susan Martin Jones*

Also Worth a Visit on the Isle of Wight

Besides the fully inspected pubs, you might like to try these pubs that have been recommended to us and described by readers. Do tell us what you think of them: feedback@goodguides.com

BEMBRIDGE SZ6488
Pilot Boat (01983) 872077
Station Road/Kings Road; PO35 5NN
Welcoming little harbourside pub with ship-like interior, good food from sandwiches to local seafood, well kept Goddards and guests; tables out overlooking water or in pleasant courtyard behind, well placed for coast walks, open all day. *(Stuart Williams, S Holder, A N Bance)*

BINSTEAD SZ5792
Fleming Arms (01983) 563415
Binstead Road; PO33 3RD Spacious family-friendly roadside pub with wide choice of good reasonably priced food, Flowers and Ringwood Best, attentive service; dogs welcome, garden. *(Tom Evans)*

BONCHURCH SZ5778
★ **Bonchurch Inn** (01983) 852611
Bonchurch Shute; from A3055 E of Ventnor turn down to Old Bonchurch;

opposite Leconfield Hotel; PO38 1NU
Quirky former stables with restaurant run by welcoming italian family; congenial bar with narrow-planked ship's decking and old-fashioned steamer-style seats, Courage ales tapped from the cask, bar food and good italian dishes, charming helpful service, fairly basic family room, darts, shove-ha'penny and other games; background music; dogs welcome, delightful continental-feel central courtyard (parking here can be tricky), holiday flat. *(S Holder, Tom Evans)*

CARISBROOKE SZ4687
★ **Blacksmiths Arms** (01983) 529263
B3401 1.5 miles W; PO30 5SS Quiet hillside pub with friendly landlord and staff, Fullers, Shepherd Neame and Yates, decent wines and cider, good well presented food including fresh fish, scrubbed tables in neat beamed and flagstoned front bars, superb Solent views from airy bare-boards family dining extension; dogs and walkers welcome, terrace tables and smallish back garden with

same view, play area, open all day. *(Tom Evans, Penny and Peter Keevil)*

COWES   SZ5092
⋆**Folly** (01983) 297171

Folly Lane signed off A3021 just S of Whippingham; PO32 6NB Glorious Medina estuary views from bar and waterside terrace of this cheery laid-back place, timbered ship-like interior with simple wood furnishings, wide range of sensibly priced hearty pub food from breakfast on, speedy service, Greene King, Goddards and possibly a guest; background and live music, TV, games machine and pool – can get very lively at weekends; children and dogs welcome, showers, long-term parking and weather forecasts for sailors, water taxi, open all day. *(Francis and Lyn Genever, Tom Evans)*

COWES   SZ4996
Union (01983) 293163

Watch House Lane, in pedestrian centre; PO31 7QH Old-town inn tucked back from the seafront and doing well under present management; good value freshly made food and well kept Fullers/Gales beers, friendly helpful young staff, log fire, cosy areas around central bar, dining room and conservatory; children and dogs welcome, tables outside, six comfortable clean bedrooms. *(Anon)*

GODSHILL   SZ5281
⋆**Taverners** (01983) 840707

High Street (A3020); PO38 3HZ Welcoming 17th-c pub with landlord/chef doing good seasonal food with emphasis on fresh local produce, children's menu and Sun roasts too, very popular weekends when booking advised, well kept Fullers London Pride, a house beer from Yates and a guest, good friendly service, spacious bar and two front dining areas, beams, bare boards and slate floors, woodburner; dogs welcome, garden with terrace and play area, own shop, limited parking, open all day, closed Sun evening (except bank/school summer holidays). *(Tom Evans)*

GURNARD   SZ4796
Woodvale (01983) 292037

Princes Esplanade; PO31 8LE Large 1930s inn with picture-window Solent views, friendly staff, good choice of real ales and plenty of wines by the glass, enjoyable food including good fish/seafood specials, weekend live music, Mon quiz; children welcome, garden with terrace and summer barbecues, bedrooms, open all day. *(Anon)*

HAVENSTREET   SZ5590
White Hart (01983) 883485

Off A3054 Newport–Ryde; Main Road; PO33 4DP Updated old red-brick village pub, good popular food (all day Sun) including daily specials, Ringwood and Goddards ales, cosy log-fire bar with locomotive prints, carpeted dining area;

children and dogs welcome, tables in secluded garden behind, open all day. *(Stuart Williams)*

HULVERSTONE   SZ3984
⋆**Sun** (01983) 741124

B3399; PO30 4EH Picture-book thatched country pub in charming peaceful setting with lovely views over the Channel, low-ceilinged bar, ales such as Adnams, Goddards, Ringwood and Timothy Taylors, nice mix of old furniture on flagstones and floorboards, brick and stone walls, horsebrasses and ironwork around fireplace, large windows in traditionally decorated newer dining area, all-day pubby food including local meat, darts and board games; background music (live Sat evening); dogs welcome in bar, children away from it, secluded split-level cottagey garden, open all day. *(Tom Evans)*

NEWCHURCH   SZ5685
⋆**Pointer** (01983) 865202

High Street; PO36 0NN Well run two-room pub by Norman church, enjoyable fairly priced food using local produce (booking advised in season), well kept Fullers and a guest ale, friendly service; children and dogs welcome, pleasant back garden, boules. *(S Holder, Tom Evans)*

NORTHWOOD   SZ4983
Travellers Joy (01983) 298024

Off B3325 S of Cowes; PO31 8LS Friendly real-ale pub with eight well kept beers including local brews (tasters offered), reasonably priced generous pubby food from sandwiches to daily specials, long bar with over 200 pump clips on the walls, conservatory, old pinball machine in games room, Sun quiz; background radio; children and dogs welcome, garden with pétanque and play area, open all day Fri, Sat. *(Tom Evans, Barrie and Mary Crees)*

SEAVIEW   SZ6291
⋆**Seaview Hotel** (01983) 612711

High Street; off B3330 Ryde–Bembridge; PO34 5EX Small gently civilised but relaxed hotel, traditional wood furnishings, seafaring paraphernalia and log fire in pubby bare-boards bar, comfortable more refined front bar, Goddards, Yates and a guest, good wine list including some local ones, good well presented pub food (smaller helpings available) and more elaborate restaurant menu using produce from their farm; may ask for a credit card if you run a tab, background music, TV; children welcome, dogs in bar, sea glimpses from tables on tiny front terrace, six nice bedrooms (some with sea views), open all day. *(Tom Evans)*

SHANKLIN   SZ5881
⋆**Fishermans Cottage** (01983) 863882

Bottom of Shanklin Chine; PO37 6BN Unchanging thatched cottage in terrific setting tucked into the cliffs on Appley beach, steep zigzag walk down beautiful chine; low-beamed little flagstoned rooms with stripped-stone walls, old local pictures and bric-a-brac, Goddards Fuggle-Dee-Dum, Island Yachtsman and Yates Undercliff, good value pub food including fish specials; background and some live music; wheelchair access, children and dogs welcome, sun-soaked terrace, lovely seaside walk to Luccombe, open all day, closed end Oct to early Mar. *(Tom Evans)*

SHANKLIN   SZ5881
Steamer (01983) 862641
Esplanade; PO37 6BS Nautical-theme bar, fun for holiday families, with good range of real ales, enjoyable fresh food including local seafood, cheery staff, live music most weekends; fine sea views from covered floodlit terrace, eight bedrooms, open all day. *(A N Bance)*

ST HELENS   SZ6289
Vine (01983) 872337
Upper Green Road; PO33 1UJ Family-run Victorian pub overlooking green, enjoyable range of food including stone-baked pizzas, good choice of well kept beers, friendly staff, live music Fri, quiz Sun; children welcome (play area across the road), open all day. *(A N Bance, N Jervis)*

VENTNOR   SZ5677
Perks (01983) 857446
High Street; PO38 1LT Little bar packed with interesting memorabilia behind shop-window front, well kept ales including Bass, good range of wines, popular well priced home-made food from sandwiches and baked potatoes up, bargain OAP two-course lunch, fast friendly service. *(Liz and John Soden)*

VENTNOR   SZ5677
★Spyglass (01983) 855338
Esplanade, SW end; road down is very steep and twisty, and parking nearby can be difficult – best to use pay-and-display (free in winter) about 100

metres up the road; PO38 1JX Perched above the beach with a fascinating jumble of seafaring memorabilia in snug quarry-tiled interior (anything from ship's wheels to wrecked rudders to stuffed seagulls), Ringwood ales and guests, popular food including fish dishes; background music, live bands every day in summer (Weds-Sun in winter); children welcome, dogs in bar, seawall terrace with lovely views, coast walk towards the Botanic Garden, heftier hikes on to St Boniface Down and towards the eerie shell of Appuldurcombe House, bedrooms, open all day. *(Francis and Lyn Genever, Tom Evans, Penny and Peter Keevil)*

WHITWELL   SZ5277
White Horse (01983) 730375
High Street; PO38 2PY Popular sympathetically restored old thatched pub, extensive range of good value generous food from pub staples up, several well kept ales including Goddards, good friendly service, large cheery high-ceilinged family dining area with small beamed bar and second area off; may be background music and quiz nights; dogs welcome, picnic-sets in big garden. *(Tom Evans)*

YARMOUTH   SZ3589
Kings Head (01983) 760351
Quay Street; PO41 0PB Cosy low-ceilinged traditional pub opposite car ferry, three well kept changing beers, food from sandwiches to local fish, friendly quick service, plush seats, old local pictures and good log fire; background music; children and dogs welcome, courtyard seats, open all day. *(Sally Matson)*

YARMOUTH   SZ3589
Wheatsheaf (01983) 760456
Bridge Road, near ferry; PO41 0PH Opened-up Victorian pub with enjoyable well priced food, cheerful service, Goddards, Ringwood and Shepherd Neame, glazed extension, pool; children and dogs welcome, handy for the harbour, open all day. *(D J and P M Taylor)*

If you stay overnight in an inn or hotel, they are allowed to serve you an alcoholic drink at any hour of the day or night.

Kent

Strong new entries this year include the George & Dragon in Chipstead (beamed 16th-c gastropub with carefully cooked food and a welcome for all), Windmill in Hollingbourne (excellent food, thoughtful drinks choice and attractive refurbishment) and Ferry at Stone in Oxney (warmly friendly cottage on the marshes, with popular food and drink). There are also some really good all-rounders: Three Chimneys in Biddenden (lovely food and charming staff), Hare in Langton Green (imaginative food and nice ales), Dering Arms in Pluckley (run by an enthusiastic landlord, with super fish dishes and comfortable bedrooms), White Hart in Sevenoaks (fine choice of drinks and interesting food), Plough near Stalisfield Green (deservedly popular old place), Tiger in Stowting (readers very much enjoy their visits) and Pepper Box in Ulcombe (friendly country pub with enjoyable food and beer). Food plays an important part, with nine main entries holding a Food Award, but the title of Kent Dining Pub 2014 goes to the Windmill in Hollingbourne.

BIDDENDEN   TQ8238   Map 3

Three Chimneys 🍴 ♀

A262, a mile W of village; TN27 8LW

Pubby beamed rooms of considerable individuality, log fires, imaginative food and pretty garden

Just the place to head to after a visit to nearby Sissinghurst Gardens (NT), this civilised and pretty place has top class food and four real ales. The small low-beamed rooms have plenty of character – they're simply done out with plain wooden furniture and old settles on flagstones and coir matting, some harness and sporting prints on stripped-brick walls and good log fires. The public bar on the left is quite down to earth, with darts, dominoes and cribbage. Well trained, attentive staff serve Adnams Best and Old and a guest from a brewer such as Franklins tapped from the cask, several wines by the glass, local Biddenden cider and apple juice and several malt whiskies. A candlelit bare-boards restaurant has rustic décor and french windows that open into a conservatory; seats in the garden.

🍴 Excellent, if not cheap, food might include baked field mushrooms topped with caramelised red onions and grilled goats cheese, salmon and smoked haddock fishcakes, fresh herb and pine nut pesto on couscous, grilled goats cheese on balsamic roasted vegetables and tomato sauce, pork and sage sausages with port and red onion gravy, sweet chilli fillet of salmon with roasted sweet potatoes and spicy aubergine and courgette ragout, roasted duck breast with roasted carrot and swede and parmentier potatoes, lamb rump with roasted butternut squash and dauphinoise potatoes, and puddings. *Benchmark main dish: smoked haddock on creamed leeks with parmesan-roasted potatoes and chive velouté £18.95. Two-course evening meal £23.50.*

Free house ~ Licensee Craig Smith ~ Real ale ~ (01580) 291472 ~ Open 11.30-3.30, 5.30-11; 12-4, 6-10.30 Sun ~ Bar food 12-2(2.30 Sat, Sun), 6.30-9(9.30 Sat) ~ Restaurant ~ Children welcome ~ Dogs allowed in bar ~ www.thethreechimneys.co.uk
Recommended by Bob and Margaret Holder, Jonathan and Ann Tross, Tony Swanson, Peter Chapman, M P Mackenzie, John Evans, Derek Thomas, Gordon and Margaret Ormondroyd, John Thompson, Mrs J Ekins-Daukes, J R Osborne

BROOKLAND
Woolpack £
TQ9724   Map 3

On A259 from Rye, about a mile before Brookland, take the first right turn signposted Midley where the main road bends sharp left, just after the expanse of Walland Marsh; OS Sheet 189 map reference 977244; TN29 9TJ

15th-c pub with simple furnishings, massive inglenook fireplace, big helpings of tasty food and large garden

With good nearby walks and not far from Camber Sands, this old inn was once the beacon keeper's house. The ancient entrance lobby has a lovely uneven brick floor and black-painted pine-panelled walls; to the right, the simple quarry-tiled main bar has basic cushioned plank seats in a massive inglenook fireplace and a painted wood-effect bar counter hung with lots of water jugs. Low-beamed ceilings incorporate some very early ships' timbers thought to come from local wrecks. A long elm table has shove-ha'penny carved into one end, and there are old and newer wall benches, chairs at mixed tables with flowers and candles, and photographs of locals on the walls. The two pub cats, Liquorice and Charlie Girl, are often warming themselves by the log fire. The traditional dining room to the left has carpets and dark wheelback chairs; background music and games machine. Shepherd Neame Master Brew and Spitfire and a seasonal brew on handpump. There are plenty of picnic-sets under parasols in the garden, which is nicely lit in the evening.

Good, popular food includes sandwiches, baked potatoes, soup, moules marinière, stilton and vegetable bake, spare ribs, battered fish and chips, mixed grill and puddings like eton mess and chocolate brownie. *Benchmark main dish: steak in ale pie £10.95. Two-course evening meal £20.00.*

Shepherd Neame ~ Tenant Scott Balcomb ~ Real ale ~ (01797) 344321 ~ Open 11-3, 6-11; 12-11 Sat, Sun, bank and school holidays ~ Bar food 12-2.30, 6-9; all day Sat, Sun, bank and school holidays ~ Restaurant ~ Children welcome ~ Dogs welcome
Recommended by Pat and Tony Martin, B and M Kendall, Conrad Freezer, Richard Tilbrook

CHIPSTEAD
George & Dragon
TQ5056   Map 3

Near M25 junction 5; TN13 2RW

Super food in popular village dining pub with three real ales, friendly, efficient service and seats in garden

At the heart of a pretty village, this 16th-c dining pub places much emphasis on its particularly good, interesting food – but they also have stools against the counter where they keep Westerham Goldings, Grasshopper and Georges Marvellous Medicine on handpump, good wines by the glass and a cocktail of the month. The opened-up bar has heavy black beams and standing timbers, grey-green panelling, framed articles on the walls about their suppliers, and an easy-going, friendly atmosphere. In the centre, a comfortable sofa and table sit in front of a log fire, with a tiny alcove to one side housing a built-in wall seat and just one table and chair. Up a step to each side are two small dining areas with more panelling, an attractive assortment of nice old dining chairs around various tables on bare floorboards and two more (unused) fireplaces. Upstairs is a sizeable timbered dining room with similar furnishings and a cosy room just right for a private party. The back garden has benches, modern chrome and wicker chairs and tables under parasols, as well as raised beds for flowers, herbs and vegetables.

Using organic and free-range meat and other seasonal local produce, the creative food includes lunchtime sandwiches and deli boards, shredded guinea fowl in rice-paper wrap with sesame and honey dip, tian of crab and prawn with harissa mayonnaise, roasted fennel tart with courgette ribbons and sun-dried tomatoes, burger with smoked cheddar, mustard mayonnaise and chips, gilt-head bream with brown shrimps, paprika and samphire, gremolata chicken with quinoa and lime and coriander crème fraîche, barbecue-spiced jacob's ladder with sweet potato wedges, and puddings such as toffee apple crumble with custard and chocolate and hazelnut praline with white chocolate ice-cream. *Benchmark main dish: steak sandwich with chips and béarnaise sauce £9.50. Two-course evening meal £22.00.*

Free house ~ Licensee Ben James ~ Real ale ~ (01732) 779019 ~ Open 11-11 ~ Bar food 12-3(4 weekends), 6-9.30(8.30 Sun) ~ Restaurant ~ Children welcome ~ Dogs allowed in bar ~ www.georgeanddragonchipstead.com *Recommended by Derek Thomas, Simon Pyle*

GOUDHURST   TQ7037 Map 3
Green Cross 🍴

East off A21 on to A262 (Station Road); TN17 1HA

Down-to-earth bar with real ales and more formal back restaurant

Although this place specialises in fresh seafood and fish, the little two-roomed front bar is relaxed and properly pubby. As well as Harveys Best on handpump, it has stripped wooden floors, dark wood furnishings, wine bottles on window sills, hop-draped beams, brass jugs on a mantelshelf above a fire and a few plush bar stools by the counter; background music. Attractive in an old-fashioned way, the back dining room is a little more formal with flowers on tables, dark beams in cream walls and country paintings for sale. You can sit out on a small side terrace.

Excellent fresh fish and shellfish might include proper fish soup, avocado and crab bake topped with cheddar, linguine with queen scallops, dry vermouth, fresh tarragon and cream, moules frites, cornish cock crab salad, skate wing with black butter and capers or seafood paella; they also offer non-fishy dishes such as baguettes, home-cooked ham and eggs, home-made sausages with mash and onion gravy, chicken pasta in creamy mushroom and tarragon sauce, and puddings such as chocolate tart with chocolate sauce and hokey pokey ice-cream and crème brûlée with mulberries. *Benchmark main dish: beer-battered fresh local fish and chips £13.00. Two-course evening meal £25.00.*

Free house ~ Licensees Lou and Caroline Lizzi ~ Real ale ~ (01580) 211200 ~ Open 12-3, 6-11; 11-3 Sun; closed Sun evening ~ Bar food 12-2.30, 7-9.30; 12-2.30 Sun ~ Restaurant ~ Children welcome ~ www.greencrossinn.co.uk *Recommended by Harvey Brown, Emma Scofield*

HOLLINGBOURNE

TQ8354   Map 3

Windmill 🍴

M20 junction 8: A20 towards Ashford then left into B2163 – Eyhorne Street; ME17 1TR

Kent Dining Pub of the Year

Delicious food and thoughtful drinks in professionally run dining pub, with friendly, helpful staff and a relaxed atmosphere

Most customers come to enjoy the excellent, beautifully presented food, but there's a proper little back bar for drinkers and they keep Harveys Best and Sharps Doom Bar on handpump and quite a few wines by the glass. The back bar has high tables and chairs to one side, low stools around a table in front of a woodburning stove, a cushioned settle and armchair, a few bar chairs beside the counter and distinctive red wallpaper patterned with gold stags' heads. The light and airy main room has white-painted beams, a log fire in a low inglenook fireplace with beribboned antlers above, a couple of armchairs and a table with daily papers, heavy settles with scatter cushions against one wall and a long red leather button-back banquette along the opposite one, dark wood dining chairs and tables and bare floorboards topped with an antelope skin. Up steps to the right is a small dining room with just four tables and logs piled into a brick fireplace. Leading off the main room at the other end is a second little room with pale blue wallpaper patterned with the same gold antlers, another brick fireplace with logs, and similar furnishings to the main room; various small deer skulls, a shelf of riding gear, candles and flowers here and there, background pop music. Service is attentive and friendly, and the atmosphere throughout relaxed and easy-going. A back terrace has wooden tables and chairs.

Using the best local, seasonal produce, the accomplished food includes nibbles such as pickled quails eggs with celery salt or pork scratchings with apple sauce, sandwiches, ballotine of rabbit in local wine with apple and pear chutney, pressed ham hock with piccalilli, poached smoked haddock with bubble and squeak, poached egg and grain mustard butter sauce, roast rump of 32-day aged beef with duck fat roast potatoes and red wine sauce, roast leg of lamb with red pepper ketchup, spiced aubergine and rosemary potatoes, and puddings such as dark chocolate pavé with hazelnut ice-cream and honeycomb and baked alaska with blood orange sorbet and citrus fruits; they also offer a two- and three-course set lunch. *Benchmark main dish: grilled calves liver with caramelised onions, creamed mash, devil sauce and crispy bacon £13.95. Two-course evening meal £20.00.*

Enterprise ~ Lease Richard Phillips ~ Real ale ~ (01622) 889000 ~ Open 12-11; 12-9 Sun ~ Bar food 12-2.30, 5.30-9.30; bar snacks all day; not Mon evening ~ Restaurant ~ Children welcome ~ Dogs allowed in bar ~ www.thewindmillbyrichardphillips.co.uk *Recommended by Jeff Roberts*

The price we give for a two-course evening meal in the featured entries
is the mean (average of cheapest and most expensive) price of a starter and
a main course – no drinks.

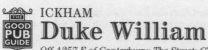

ICKHAM   TR2258 Map 3

Duke William

Off A257 E of Canterbury; The Street; CT3 1QP

Relaxing village pub under new owners with airy bar, enjoyable bar food, dining conservatory, and plenty of seats outside; bedrooms

You can be sure of a friendly welcome at this family-run pub – and the food is very good too. The big spreading bar has huge new oak beams and stripped joists, a fine mix of seats from settles to high-backed cushioned dining chairs, dark wheelback and bentwood chairs around all sorts of wooden tables on the stripped-wood floor, and a log fire with a couple of settles and a low barrel table in front of it. A central bar counter with high stools and brass coat-hooks offers Brains IPA and a guest such as Shepherd Neame Master Brew on handpump, served by chatty, attentive staff. A separate snug little area has one long table, black leather high-backed dining chairs, a flat-screen TV and a computer; daily papers, quiet background music, cheerful modern paintings and large hop bines. Off to the left is a low-ceilinged dining room with plenty of paintings and mirrors, and at the back an airy dining conservatory with interesting paintings, prints and heraldry. Doors lead from here to a big terrace with wooden and metal tables and chairs and a covered area to one side; picnic-sets on the lawn, swings and a slide.

Good, well liked food includes baguettes, chicken liver and brandy pâté with red onion chutney, field mushroom, walnut and stilton salad, beef in ale pie, mediterranean vegetables with goats cheese, calves liver in madeira and shallot jus with bacon lardons, bass fillets with lemon butter, pork medallions with apricot and brandy sauce, and puddings such as mixed berry crumble and banoffi pie. *Benchmark main dish: slow-roast pork belly with apple and sultana cider jus £13.95. Two-course evening meal £22.00.*

Free house ~ Licensees Kate & Ryan Coleman ~ Real ale ~ (01227) 721308 ~ Open 12-11(midnight Fri, Sat); 12-10 Sun ~ Restaurant ~ Children welcome ~ Dogs allowed in bar ~ Bedrooms: /£65 ~ www.dukewilliam.biz *Recommended by Sarah Flynn, Paul Goldman, John Saville, Sara Fulton, Roger Baker*

IVY HATCH   TQ5854 Map 3

Plough 🍴 🍷

High Cross Road; village signed off A227 N of Tonbridge; TN15 0NL

Country pub with landlord-cooked food, real ales and seats in landscaped garden

Our readers regularly return to this tile-hung village pub for the notably good food – booking is essential. The various rooms have light wooden flooring, leather chesterfields grouped around an open fire, a mix of cushioned dining chairs around assorted tables, and high bar chairs by the wooden-topped bar counter where they keep Long Man Best Bitter and Tonbridge Coppernob and Rustic on handpump and quite a few wines by the glass. There's also a conservatory; background music and board games. Seats in the landscaped garden are surrounded by cob trees – it's a shame they won't serve food out here. There are some very rewarding nearby walks through orchards and woodlands and along the greensand escarpment around One Tree Hill. Ightham Mote (National Trust) is close by.

Very good food, using the best local ingredients, includes sandwiches, smoked haddock and spring onion fishcake with wholegrain mustard sauce, ham hock and smoked chicken terrine with home-made brown pickle, mussels with pancetta, leeks and cider cream sauce, honey-roast ham and their own eggs, roast butternut squash, spinach and blue cheese tart, grey mullet fillet with kale and saffron sauce, guinea fowl breast and confit leg with soft polenta and redcurrant jus, and puddings like vanilla bean crème brûlée and warm chocolate fondant with mascarpone; they also offer a main course in the bar for £10. *Benchmark main dish: 6oz rump steak with wild mushrooms and chips £10.00. Two-course evening meal £19.25.*

Free house ~ Licensee Miles Medes ~ Real ale ~ (01732) 810100 ~ Open 9-3, 6-11; 10am-11pm Sat; 10-6 Sun; closed Sun evening ~ Bar food 12-2.45, 6-9.30; 12-5.30 Sun ~ Restaurant ~ Children welcome ~ www.theploughivyhatch.co.uk
Recommended by Bob and Margaret Holder, B and M Kendall, Derek Thomas, N R White, Mrs D Crew

LANGTON GREEN   TQ5439 Map 3
Hare 🍴 ♀
A264 W of Tunbridge Wells; TN3 0JA

Interestingly decorated Edwardian pub with a fine choice of drinks and imaginative, bistro-style food

With friendly, helpful staff and enjoyable food and drink, this roomy mock-Tudor place is as popular as ever. The high-ceilinged rooms have plenty of light flooding through large windows (especially in the front bar where drinkers tend to gather), dark-painted dados below light walls that are covered in old photographs and prints, 1930s oak furniture, light brown carpet and turkish-style rugs on stained wooden floors, old romantic pastels and a huge collection of chamber-pots hanging from beams. There's Greene King IPA and Abbot plus a couple of guests from brewers such as Titanic on handpump, two dozen wines by the glass, more than 60 whiskies and a fine choice of vodkas and other spirits; board games. French windows open on to a big terrace with pleasant views of the tree-ringed village green. Limited parking in front of the pub, but you can park in the side lane too.

🍴 Imaginative bistro-style food includes sandwiches, vegetable pakora with raita and coconut and mango salad, scallops with pork belly, pickled fennel and apple salad and rhubarb dressing, sharing platters, crispy beef salad with cashew nuts, sweet chilli and wasabi dressing, honey and mustard-roasted ham with free-range eggs, malaysian fish stew, five-spice duck breasts with stir-fried vegetables and crispy noodles, and puddings such as chocolate brownie with vanilla ice-cream and apple and pear crumble. *Benchmark main dish: beer-battered haddock with tartare sauce, mushy peas and chips £12.50. Two-course evening meal £18.00.*

Brunning & Price ~ Manager Tina Foster ~ Real ale ~ (01892) 862419 ~ Open 12-11(midnight Fri, Sat, 10.30 Sun) ~ Bar food 12-9.30(10 Fri, Sat, 9 Sun) ~ Restaurant ~ Children welcome ~ Dogs allowed in bar ~ www.hare-tunbridgewells.co.uk
Recommended by William Ruxton, Chris Flynn, Wendy Jones, Richard and Penny Gibbs, Alan Franck

NEWNHAM   TQ9557 Map 3
George
The Street; village signed from A2 W of Ospringe, outside Faversham; ME9 0LL

Old-world village pub with open-plan rooms, a fair choice of drinks and food, and seats in spacious garden

This tile-hung pub is in the same village where James Pimm was born (he invented the fruit cup Pimms). There's a series of spreading open-plan rooms with hop-strung beams, polished floorboards, stripped brickwork, candles and lamps on handsome tables, a mix of dining chairs and settles, and two inglenook fireplaces (one with a woodburning stove). Shepherd

Neame Master Brew and a seasonal beer on handpump and several wines by the glass. There are picnic-sets in the spacious tree-sheltered garden and good walks in this remote-feeling part of the North Downs.

🍴 Popular food includes sandwiches and baguettes, smoked fish and prawn medley with crème fraîche, chicken liver parfait with home-made onion chutney, pork and leek sausages with caramelised leek gravy, ham with free-range eggs, burger with bacon or cheese, spiced tomato mayonnaise and chips, chicken leg stuffed with mushroom and parsley mousse and dauphinoise potatoes, bass fillet with prawns on puy lentils and roasted vegetables, and puddings like warm chocolate brownie with toffee sauce and lemon posset with shortbread biscuits. *Benchmark main dish: pork belly braised in cider with champ and pickled red cabbage £14.25. Two-course evening meal £18.00.*

Shepherd Neame ~ Tenants Paul and Lisa Burton ~ Real ale ~ (01795) 890237 ~ Open 11.30-3, 6.30-11; 11.30-6.30 Sun; closed Sun evening ~ Bar food 12.30-2.30, 7-9.30; 12-4.30 Sun ~ Restaurant ~ Children welcome ~ Live music first Fri of month ~ www.georgeinnnewnham.co.uk *Recommended by Richard and Penny Gibbs, N R White*

PENSHURST   TQ5142   Map 3

THE GOOD PUB GUIDE
Bottle House 🍴 ♟

Coldharbour Lane; leaving Penshurst SW on B2188 turn right at Smarts Hill signpost, then bear right towards Chiddingstone and Cowden; keep straight on; TN11 8ET

Low-beamed, connected bars in country pub, friendly service, chatty atmosphere, real ales and decent wines, popular bar food and sunny terrace; nearby walks

This cottagey pub is consistently reliable, so readers tend to visit very regularly. The open-plan rooms are split into cosy areas by numerous standing timbers and there are all sorts of beams and joists (a couple of the especially low ones are leather padded), pine wall boards and bar stools ranged along the timber-clad copper-topped counter where they keep Harveys Best and Larkins Traditional on handpump, local apple juice and nearly a dozen wines by the glass from a good list. There's a nice hotchpotch of wooden tables with fresh flowers and candles, fairly tightly spaced chairs on dark boards or coir, and a woodburning stove; background music. Photographs of the pub and local scenes hang on the walls (some of which are stripped stone). The sunny, brick-paved terrace has teak chairs and tables under parasols and olive trees in white pots; parking is limited. Good surrounding walks in this charming area of rolling country.

🍴 Served all day, the reliably good food includes scallops with pea purée, black pudding and red pepper coulis, ham hock and green peppercorn terrine with home-made piccalilli, honey and mustard-roasted ham and eggs, moules frites, baked cannelloni stuffed with spinach and ricotta with herby tomato sauce, burger topped with smoked cheese and tomato chutney, parma ham-wrapped chicken stuffed with mozzarella with herb sauce, steak and kidney pudding, rack of lamb with port, redcurrant and rosemary, and puddings like chocolate mousse with hazelnut tuille and sticky toffee pudding with toffee sauce. *Benchmark main dish: slow-roast pork belly with creamed cabbage and bacon, butternut squash mash and apple and cider sauce £14.50. Two-course evening meal £19.00.*

Free house ~ Licensee Paul Hammond ~ Real ale ~ (01892) 870306 ~ Open 11-11(10.30 Sun) ~ Bar food 12-10(9 Sun) ~ Restaurant ~ Children welcome ~ Dogs allowed in bar ~ www.thebottlehouseinnpenshurst.co.uk *Recommended by Bob and Margaret Holder, Martin and Sue Day, Richard Tilbrook, Tina and David Woods-Taylor*

PLUCKLEY

Dering Arms ⑪ ♈ 🛏

TQ9243 Map 3

*Pluckley Station, which is signposted from B2077; or follow Station Road
(left turn off Smarden Road in centre of Pluckley) for about 1.3 miles S, through
Pluckley Thorne; TN27 0RR*

**Fine fish dishes plus other good food in handsome building,
stylish main bar, carefully chosen wines and roaring log fire;
comfortable bedrooms**

With excellent food and a friendly, enthusiastic landlord, this former
hunting lodge remains on top form. It's a striking building with its
imposing frontage, mullioned arched windows and dutch gables, and
the rooms have plenty of character. The high-ceilinged, stylishly plain
main bar has a solid country feel with a variety of wooden furniture on
flagstone floors, a roaring log fire in a great fireplace, country prints and
some fishing rods. The smaller half-panelled back bar has similar dark
wood furnishings, and an extension to this area has a woodburning
stove, comfortable armchairs, sofas and a grand piano; board games.
Though the emphasis tends to be on the food, the bar is characterful and
comfortable and they keep a beer named for the pub from Goachers on
handpump, as well as a very good wine list of around 100 wines; 50 malt
whiskies, 20 brandies and an occasional local cider. Classic car meetings
(the landlord James has a couple of classics) are held on the second
Sunday of the month. Readers very much enjoy staying overnight, and
the breakfasts are smashing.

Using local fish and their own herbs, the lovely dishes might include fish soup
with rouille and croutons, oysters, fillet of hake with crayfish and black butter,
smoked haddock fishcakes with mild curry sauce, whole crab salad, skate wing with
caper butter and a big fruits de mer (24 hours' notice); non-fishy dishes such as
duck rillettes with orange vinaigrette, all-day breakfast, pie of the day, coq au vin,
beef bourguignon, and puddings like rich chocolate truffle with brandy cream and
tiramisu parfait with coffee sauce. *Benchmark main dish: monkfish and bacon in
orange sauce £15.95. Two-course evening meal £19.00.*

Free house ~ Licensee James Buss ~ Real ale ~ (01233) 840371 ~ Open 11.30(11 Sat)
-3.30, 6-11; 12-4 Sun; closed Sun evening ~ Bar food 12-2.30, 6.30-9; 12-3 Sun ~
Restaurant ~ Children allowed away from the bar and at landlord's discretion ~ Dogs
allowed in bar ~ Bedrooms: £85/£95 ~ www.deringarms.com *Recommended by Stephen and
Jean Curtis, Richard Balkwill, Lee and Liz Potter, David and Ruth Hollands*

SEVENOAKS

White Hart ⑪ ♈

TQ5352 Map 3

Tonbridge Road (A225 S, past Knole); TN13 1SG

**Well run and bustling old coaching inn with a civilised atmosphere in
many bar rooms, a thoughtful choice of drinks, enjoyable modern food
and friendly, helpful staff**

A smashing all-rounder – our readers love it. A carefully refurbished
former coaching inn, it's run with friendly efficiency by the young
landlord and his staff. The many rooms are interconnected by open
doorways and steps and there are several open fires and woodburning
stoves. All manner of nice wooden dining chairs around tables of every
size sit on warming rugs or varnished bare floorboards, the cream
walls are hung with lots of prints and old photographs (many of local
scenes or schools) and there are fresh flowers and plants, daily papers

to read, board games and a bustling, chatty atmosphere. Brunning &
Price Original (brewed for the pub by Phoenix), Fullers London Pride,
Harveys Best, Old Dairy Blue Top and three guests from brewers such as
Belhaven, Sharps and Westerham on handpump, plus more than 25 good
wines by the glass, a fair choice of ciders and over 75 whiskies. It's all
very civilised. At the front of the building are picnic-sets under parasols.

 Interesting, popular food includes sandwiches, pulled and potted duck
with orange marmalade, moroccan-spiced chicken skewer with apricot
couscous and mint yoghurt, champ potato gnocchi with broad beans, red chard,
blue cheese and asparagus, roast ham with free-range eggs, sausages with mash,
green thai vegetable curry with griddled pineapple, steak burger with cheddar
and bacon, lambs liver with balsamic sauce, onion rings and crushed garlic
potatoes, grilled cajun salmon with citrus couscous and herb crème fraiche,
and puddings. *Benchmark main dish: malaysian fish stew £14.95. Two-course
evening meal £19.00.*

Brunning & Price ~ Manager Chris Little ~ Real ale ~ (01732) 452022 ~ Open 11.30-11;
12-10.30 Sun ~ Bar food 12-10(9 Sun) ~ Children welcome away from bar until 7pm ~
Dogs allowed in bar ~ www.bandp.co.uk/whitehart *Recommended by Tracy Collins, Martin
and Sue Day, Gordon and Margaret Ormondroyd, Mrs G Marlow, David Jackman, Mrs Margo
Finlay, Jörg Kasprowski, Colin McLachlan*

SPELDHURST   TQ5541   Map 3
George & Dragon 🍴 ▽
Village signed from A264 W of Tunbridge Wells; TN3 0NN

**Fine old pub, beams, flagstones and huge fireplaces, local beers,
good food and attractive outside seating areas**

It's worth coming here just to take in the distinguished half-timbered
building, which is based around a 13th-c manorial hall. Massive oak
beams were added during 'modernisation' in 1589, and it's not hard to
picture Kentish archers fresh from victory at Agincourt in 1415 resting
on the enormous flagstones. To the right of the splendid entrance
hall (where there's a water bowl for dogs), a half-panelled room is set
for dining with a mix of old wheelback and other dining chairs and a
cushioned wall pew around several tables, a few little pictures on the
walls, horsebrasses on one huge beam, a huge inglenook fireplace and
a sizeable bar counter with Brakspears Gold, Harveys Best and Larkins
Traditional Ale on handpump, 16 wines by the glass and local organic
cordials; friendly, efficient staff. A doorway leads to another dining room
with similar furnishings and another big inglenook. Those wanting a
drink and a chat tend to head to the room on the left of the entrance
(though people do eat here too), where there's a woodburning stove in
a small fireplace, high-winged cushioned settles and various wooden
tables and dining chairs on a wood-strip floor; background music. There's
also an aged-feeling upstairs restaurant. Teak tables, chairs and benches
sit on a nicely planted gravel terrace in front of the pub, while at the
back is a covered area with big church candles on wooden tables and a
lower terrace with seats around a 300-year-old olive tree; more attractive
planting here and some modern garden design.

 Enticing food includes sandwiches, seared pigeon breasts with puy lentils and
smoked bacon, hot smoked salmon and cornish crab tian with horseradish
crème fraîche, beer-battered cod and chips, roast beetroot and goats cheese
risotto, venison burger with onion beignet, chicken and preserved lemon salad
with pearl barley and pomegranate, calves liver and bacon with mash and

onion marmalade, pheasant breast and confit leg with pommes mousseline, and puddings. *Benchmark main dish: slow-roast pork belly £15.50. Two-course evening meal £19.00.*

Free house ~ Licensee Julian Leefe-Griffiths ~ Real ale ~ (01892) 863125 ~ Open 12-11(midnight Sat, 10.30 Sun) ~ Bar food 12-2.45(3 Sat), 7-9.30(10 Sat); 12-4 Sun ~ Restaurant ~ Children welcome ~ Dogs allowed in bar ~ www.speldhurst.com
Recommended by Jamie and Sue May, Gordon and Margaret Ormondroyd, Derek Thomas, N R White

STALISFIELD GREEN
Plough
Off A252 in Charing; ME13 0HY

TQ9552   Map 3

Ancient country pub with rambling rooms, open fires, interesting local ales, good bar food and friendly licensees

A lways deservedly popular, with a good mix of drinkers and diners and run by helpful, friendly people, this ancient country pub dates from 1350. The several hop-draped rooms are relaxed and easy-going, and ramble around, up and down, with open fires in brick fireplaces, interesting pictures, books on shelves, farmhouse and other nice old dining chairs around a mix of pine or dark wood tables on bare boards, and the odd milk churn. Dixie, the pub cat, likes to find a cosy lap to lie on. Beers come from kentish brewers such as Gadds, Goachers, Old Dairy and Whitstable and they stock kentish lagers, wines, water, fruit juices and cider. The pub appears to perch on its own amid downland farmland, and picnic-sets on a simple terrace overlook the village green below. There's a site for caravans.

Making their own sausages, bread, ice-cream and even ketchup, the interesting food includes pressed pigs head with piccalilli, potted brown shrimps with tomato compote, beer-battered fish and chips with pickled cucumber, preserved tomato and smoked cheese custard tart with nettles, veal burger with blue cheese, local chicken with smoked bacon, whole grilled plaice with anchovy butter, and puddings like treacle tart and rhubarb and ginger trifle; they also offer a midweek set menu. *Benchmark main dish: slow-cooked pork belly with crackling and apple sauce £13.95. Two-course evening meal £19.00.*

Free house ~ Licensees Robert and Amy Lloyd ~ Real ale ~ (01795) 890256 ~ Open 12-3, 6-11; 12-11.30 Sat; 12-6 Sun; closed Sun evening, Mon ~ Bar food 12-2(3 Sat), 6-9.30; 12-3 Sun ~ Restaurant ~ Children welcome away from main bar ~ Dogs welcome ~ Live music every two months ~ www.stalisfieldgreen.co.uk *Recommended by N R White, Mr and Mrs P R Thomas*

STONE IN OXNEY
Ferry
Appledore Road; N of Stone-cum-Ebony; TN30 7JY

TQ9428   Map 3

Bustling small cottage with character rooms, candlelight, open fires, real ales and popular food

A 17th-c former smugglers' haunt, this is a pretty little pub in a lovely marshland setting with tables and benches on a front terrace and more in a back garden that leads down to the river. Inside, it's all very easy-going and chatty. The main bar has hop-draped painted beams, a green dado, stools against the counter where they serve a beer named for the pub (from Westerham), Harveys Best, Sharps Doom Bar and

Spencers Galaxy on handpump, and a small eating area to the right
down a couple of steps: wheelback chairs and a banquette around a
few long tables, a log fire in an inglenook and candles in sconces on
the walls on each side. To the left of the main door is a dining area with
big blackboards on red walls, a woodburning stove beneath a large
bressumer beam and high-backed light wooden dining chairs around
assorted tables; up a couple of steps is another, smarter dining area
with modern chandeliers. Throughout are wooden floors, all sorts of
pictures and framed maps, a stuffed fish, beer flagons, an old musket
and various brasses.

Attractively presented food includes sautéed lambs kidneys in madeira
and peppercorn cream sauce, mussels and cockles in roast tomato sauce
with chorizo and shallots, charcuterie sharing plate, chestnut and herb pesto on
fettucine with mushrooms, cheese and white truffle oil, bacon steak with bubble
and squeak, eggs and cider sauce, burger with manchego, red pepper ketchup
and beef dripping chips, guinea fowl with wild mushroom and cream cheese pasta
topped with crispy shallots, and puddings. *Benchmark main dish: lamb and date
tagine with lemon couscous £14.95. Two-course evening meal £21.00.*

Free house ~ Licensee Paul Wither Green ~ Real ale ~ (01233) 758246 ~ Open 11-11 ~
Bar food 12-3, 6-9; 12-9 weekends ~ Restaurant ~ Live music regularly ~
www.oxneyferry.com *Recommended by Caroline Prescott, Tess White*

STOWTING
Tiger ◀   TR1241 Map 3

*3.7 miles from M20 junction 11; B2068 N, then left at Stowting signpost,
straight across crossroads, then fork left after 0.25 miles and pub is on right; coming
from N, follow Brabourne, Wye, Ashford signpost to right at fork, then turn left
towards Posting and Lyminge at T junction; TN25 6BA*

**Peaceful pub with helpful staff, traditional furnishings, well liked
food, several real ales and open fires; good walking country**

'We just love this pub for its great food and beer and really
helpful staff,' enthuses a reader and plenty of others agree. The
traditionally furnished bars, dating from the 17th c, have a happy mix of
wooden tables and chairs and built-in cushioned wall seats on wooden
floorboards, with warming woodburning stoves. There's an unpretentious
array of books, board games, candles in bottles, brewery memorabilia
and paintings, lots of hops and some faded rugs on the stone floor
towards the back of the pub. Shepherd Neame Master Brew and three or
four guests from local brewers such as Hot Fuzz and Old Dairy Brewery
on handpump, lots of malt whiskies, several wines by the glass, local
Biddenden cider and local fruit juice. Staff are helpful with wheelchairs.
On warmer days you can sit on the front terrace, and there are plenty of
nearby walks along the Wye Downs and North Downs Way.

Very good food includes king scallops, oak-smoked salmon and cheese gratin,
crab and king prawn tartlette on grilled local asparagus with organic egg
hollandaise, aberdeen angus burger with melted mozzarella, beef tomato and chips,
vintage parmesan soufflé with wild mushroom cream and baby leeks, dover sole
fillets with lemon velouté, and puddings such as white chocolate and raspberry
crème brûlée and trio of lemon curd. *Benchmark main dish: free-range local
pork belly on creamed smoked bacon and leek with caramelised apple £15.00.
Two-course evening meal £20.50.*

Free house ~ Licensees Emma Oliver and Benn Jarvis ~ Real ale ~ (01303) 862130 ~
Open 12-11; closed Mon lunchtime, Tues ~ Bar food 12-9(9.30 Fri, Sat, 8 Sun); 4-9 Mon ~

Restaurant ~ Children welcome ~ Dogs allowed in bar ~ www.tigerinn.co.uk
Recommended by Rob Jones, N R White, Rob and Catherine Dunster, Olly Tolhurst, Paul Goldman, Rob Newland, Evelyn and Derek Walter

TUNBRIDGE WELLS
Sankeys 🍴 � 🍺
TQ5839   Map 3

Mount Ephraim (A26 just N of junction with A267); TN4 8AA

Pubby street-level bar, informal downstairs brasserie (wonderful fish and shellfish), real ales and good wines, a chatty atmosphere and seats on sunny back terrace

As well as a changing beer from Goachers and guests such as Alpha State Poudrette.C, BrewDog Punk IPA and Dead Pony and Westerham Joeys Bite on handpump, the cheerful landlord also serves fruit beers and a good choice of american and british craft beers, plus several wines by the glass from a decent list. The relaxed street-level bar is light and airy with comfortably worn, informal leather sofas and pews around all sorts of tables on bare boards. There's also a fine collection of rare enamel signs and antique brewery mirrors, as well as old prints, framed cigarette cards and lots of old wine bottles and soda siphons; big flat-screen TV for sports (not football – it's very busy for major rugby matches) and background music. Downstairs is a chatty, informal fish restaurant with bistro-style décor; from here, french windows lead out to an inviting suntrap deck with wicker and chrome chairs around wooden tables.

The upstairs bar serves lunchtime sandwiches and baguettes, bangers and mustard mash with onion gravy, chilli con carne, a changing curry, mussels done several ways, cajun chicken or warm confit duck salads, beer-battered haddock and chips and smoked salmon risotto, and puddings; the excellent à la carte fish and shellfish menu is served downstairs only. *Benchmark main dish: whole cornish crab £18.50. Two-course evening meal £16.50.*

Free house ~ Licensee Matthew Sankey ~ Real ale ~ (01892) 511422 ~ Open 12-midnight(1am Thurs, 3am Fri, Sat, 11 Sun) ~ Bar food 12-3(4 Sun), 6-10 (8 Sun, Mon) ~ Restaurant ~ Children welcome before 6pm ~ Dogs allowed in bar ~ www.sankeys.co.uk *Recommended by Chris Flynn, Wendy Jones, Jamie and Sue May*

ULCOMBE
Pepper Box
TQ8550   Map 3

Fairbourne Heath; signposted from A20 in Harrietsham, or follow Ulcombe signpost from A20, then turn left at crossroads with sign to pub, then right at next minor crossroads; ME17 1LP

Friendly country pub with lovely log fire, well liked food, fair choice of drinks, and seats in a pretty garden

This popular pub was once used as a clearing house for smuggled spices – though its name refers to the pepperbox pistol, an early type of revolver with numerous barrels. The homely bar has standing timbers and a few low beams (some hung with hops), copper kettles and pans on window sills, and two leather sofas by the splendid inglenook fireplace (nice horsebrasses on the bressumer beam) with its lovely log fire. A side area, furnished more functionally for eating, extends into the opened-up beamed dining room with a range in another inglenook and more horsebrasses. The attentive and convivial licensees serve Shepherd Neame Master Brew and Spitfire and a seasonal beer on handpump, with local apple juice and several wines by the glass; background music. The two cats are called Murphy and Jim. There's a hop-covered terrace and a garden with shrubs and fine views. The village church is worth a look and the Greensand Way footpath runs nearby.

Good food includes sandwiches, beetroot and goats cheese stack with walnut dressing, home-made lamb samosas with hot chilli and mint and yoghurt dressing, potato gnocchi with rocket pesto, chicken curry, steak and kidney pudding, marinated lamb chops with minted pea purée and redcurrant sauce, salmon fillet with jerusalem artichoke purée and red wine sauce, and puddings such as vanilla and raspberry crème brûlée and salted caramel and chocolate tart with honeycomb ice-cream. *Benchmark main dish: slow-roasted pork belly in cider with sautéed savoy cabbage £13.00. Two-course evening meal £21.00.*

Shepherd Neame ~ Tenant Sarah Pemble ~ Real ale ~ (01622) 842558 ~ Open 11-3, 6-midnight; 11-midnight summer Sat; 12-5 Sun; closed Sun evening ~ Bar food 12-2.15 (3 Sun), 6.30-9.30 ~ Restaurant ~ Children allowed lunchtimes only (no babies) ~ Dogs allowed in bar ~ www.thepepperboxinn.co.uk *Recommended by Martin and Sue Day, Andrew White*

WHITSTABLE
TR1066   Map 3

Pearsons Arms

Sea Wall off Oxford Street after road splits into one-way system; public parking on left as road divides; CT5 1BT

Seaside pub with an emphasis on interesting food, several local ales and a good mix of customers

Many come to this weatherboarded pub to enjoy the interesting food and view across the pebble beach and out to sea – but it's also well liked as a place for a quiet pint and a newspaper. The two front bars, divided by a central chimney, have cushioned settles, captain's chairs and leather armchairs on a stripped-wood floor, driftwood walls and big flower arrangements on the bar counter where they serve Canterbury Ales The Pardoners Ale, Harveys Best, Ramsgate Gadds Common Conspiracy and Whitstable East India Pale Ale on handpump, several wines by the glass and an extensive choice of cocktails; background music. A cosy lower room has trompe l'oeil bookshelves, a couple of big chesterfields and dining chairs around plain tables on a stone floor. Up a couple of flights of stairs, the restaurant has sea views, mushroom paintwork, contemporary wallpaper, more driftwood, and church chairs and pine tables on nice wide floorboards.

The tempting food includes sandwiches, local foraged wild mushrooms on brioche toast with ham, fried duck egg and rosemary jus, salt and pepper squid with chilli, soy and miso, free-range chicken, gammon and leek pie, braised wild boar with apple purée, red wine jus and mash, confit duck leg with roast onion, haricot bean and mushroom ragout and madeira cream sauce, lemon sole with gravadlax salmon, cockles and parsley brown butter, and puddings such as arctic roll with caramelised clementines and chocolate, hazelnut and After Eight terrine with honeycomb ice-cream and caramel sauce. *Benchmark main dish: beer-battered fish and triple-cooked chips with tartare sauce £14.95. Two-course evening meal £20.50.*

Enterprise ~ Lease Jake Alder ~ Real ale ~ (01227) 773133 ~ Open 12-midnight (11 Sun) ~ Bar food 12-3.30, 6.30-10; not Mon, evening Tues ~ Restaurant ~ Children welcome ~ Dogs allowed in bar ~ Live music Tues and Sun evenings ~ www.pearsonsarmsbyrichardphillips.co.uk *Recommended by Adrian Johnson, Richard Mason, John Coatsworth, B and M Kendall*

Also Worth a Visit in Kent

Besides the fully inspected pubs, you might like to try these pubs that have been recommended to us and described by readers. Do tell us what you think of them: feedback@goodguides.com

ADDINGTON TQ6559
Angel (01732) 842117
Just off M20 junction 4; Addington Green; ME19 5BB 14th-c pub in classic village green setting, olde-worlde décor with beams, scrubbed tables and big fireplaces, enjoyable food from sandwiches/wraps and traditional things up including weekday set menus, fair choice of beers from barrel-fronted counter, lots of wines by the glass, good friendly service, stables restaurant, live music Fri; tables out at front and back, two bedrooms. *(Anon)*

BEARSTED TQ7956
Bell (01622) 738021
Ware Street; by railway bridge, W of centre; ME14 4PA Friendly local with well kept Greene King IPA and a guest, good range of enjoyable competitively priced food including blackboard specials; can get busy; garden and heated terrace. *(Michael Tack)*

BEARSTED TQ8055
Oak on the Green (01622) 737976
The Street; ME14 4EJ Two hop-festooned bar areas with bare boards and half-panelling, bustling friendly atmosphere, wide choice of home-made food all day including mexican dishes and tapas, children's menu too, a house beer from 1648, Fullers London Pride and two local guests, restaurant (they also own the smaller fish restaurant next door); disabled access, seats out at front under big umbrellas. *(Anon)*

BEKESBOURNE TR1856
Unicorn (01227) 830210
Bekesbourne Hill, off Station Road; village E of Canterbury; CT4 5ED Sadly, this simply furnished and friendly village pub has closed – please let us know if it reopens.

BENENDEN TQ8032
★ **Bull** (01580) 240054
The Street; by village green; TN17 4DE Relaxed informal atmosphere in rooms with bare boards or dark terracotta tiles, pleasing mix of furniture, church candles on tables, hops, fire in brick inglenook, friendly hands-on licensees, Dark Star, Harveys, Larkins and a guest from carved wooden counter, local cider too, smarter dining room with burgundy brocade dining chairs, tasty generously served food (not Sun evening) including various offers and popular Sun roasts; background jazz (live music most Sun afternoons), unobtrusive TV; children and dogs (in bar) welcome, picnic-sets by the

road, open all day except Mon lunchtime. *(N R White)*

BEXLEYHEATH TQ4875
Robin Hood & Little John
(020) 8303 1128 *Lion Road; DA6 8PF* Small 19th-c family-run local in residential area, welcoming and spotless, with eight well kept ales including Adnams Broadside, Fullers London Pride, Harveys Best and Sharps Doom Bar, popular bargain pubby food (mainly lunchtimes, not Sun) including an italian daily special (landlady is from Italy); garden. *(Casey Fleming)*

BODSHAM TR1045
Timber Batts (01233) 750237
Following Bodsham, Wye sign off B2068 keep right at unsigned fork after about 1.5 miles; TN25 5JQ Charming french owner-chef in cottagey country pub, traditional carpeted bar with Adnams Bitter, Woodfordes Wherry and a guest, good french wines by the glass (some from cousin's vineyard), informally rustic beamed dining area with happy mix of stripped-pine tables, pews, dark tables and dining chairs on carpet, french food including set lunch menu, some pubby dishes too; children and dogs welcome (resident labrador called Bounty), lovely views over wide-spreading valley from back garden, closed Sun evening, Mon. *(Anon)*

BOTOLPHS BRIDGE TR1233
Botolphs Bridge Inn
(01303) 267346 *W of Hythe; CT21 4NL* Edwardian red-brick country pub on edge of marshes; decent choice of good generous home-made food including fresh fish and Sun roasts, friendly service, well kept Greene King IPA, Sharps Doom Bar and a guest, airy and open-plan with tables laid for dining, two log fires; background music; children welcome, dogs in bar, nice little garden with marshland view, open all day till 10pm (11pm Fri, Sat), closed Mon. *(Eddie Edwards)*

BOUGH BEECH TQ4846
Wheatsheaf (01732) 700254
B2027, S of reservoir; TN8 7NU As we went to press this interesting old pub closed – news please.

BOUGHTON MONCHELSEA TQ7750
Cock
Heath Road; ME17 4JD Welcoming beamed pub with enjoyable freshly cooked food and good service, Shepherd Neame beers, log fires; dogs welcome. *(Olly Tolhurst, Richard and Gillian Fothergill)*

BOYDEN GATE TR2265
⁎**Gate Inn** (01227) 860498
*Off A299 Herne Bay–Ramsgate – follow
Chislet, Upstreet sign opposite Roman
Gallery; Chislet also signed off A28
Canterbury–Margate at Upstreet – after
turning right into Chislet main street,
keep right on to Boyden; CT3 4EB*
Delightfully unpretentious rustic pub with
comfortably worn traditional quarry-tiled
rooms, flowery-cushioned pews around tables
of considerable character, hop-strung beams,
attractively etched windows, inglenook
log fire, Shepherd Neame Master Brew,
Spitfire and a couple of guests from tap room
casks, interesting bottled beers, pubby food
lunchtime and evening; children and dogs
welcome, sheltered garden bounded by two
streams with tame ducks and geese. *(Anon)*

BRABOURNE TR1041
Five Bells (01303) 813334
East Brabourne; TN25 5LP Friendly
16th-c inn at foot of North Downs; opened-up
interior with hop-draped beams, standing
timbers and ancient brick walls, all manner
of dining chairs and tables on stripped
boards, wall seats here and there piled with
cushions, two log fires, quirky decorations
including candles in upturned bottles on
the walls and a garland-draped mermaid
figurehead, Dark Star, Goachers and
Redemption, selection of kentish wines, well
liked food from varied menu, shop selling
local produce, live music evenings and
monthly arts and crafts market; unisex loos;
children and dogs welcome, comfortable if
eccentric bedrooms, open all day from 9am
for breakfast. *(Richard Sparrow)*

BRASTED TQ4654
Stanhope Arms (01959) 564913
Church Road; TN16 1HZ Traditional
old pub in shadow of church and improved
under welcoming new licensees; well kept
Greene King London Glory, Old Golden
Hen, Tolly Cobbold and Timothy Taylors
Landlord, enjoyable food from sandwiches
and baguettes to blackboard specials, cosy
bar (plans to extend) with lots to look at,
homely log-fire dining room; well behaved
children and dogs welcome, back garden with
smokers' shelter, may be summer hog roasts
and jazz on Sun, open all day. *(Gwyn Jones)*

BRASTED TQ4755
White Hart (01959) 569457
High Street (A25); TN16 1JE Stylishly
refurbished Mitchells & Butlers Country
Pub & Eating House, wide choice of good
food including sharing plates, pizzas and
grills, weekday set menu till 7pm, real ales

and plenty of wines by the glass, cocktails,
conservatory; terrace and garden tables,
open all day. *(Derek Thomas, B J Harding)*

BRENCHLEY TQ6841
⁎**Halfway House** (01892) 722526
Horsmonden Road; TN12 7AX Beamed
18th-c inn with attractive mix of rustic and
traditional furnishings on bare boards, old
farm tools and other bric-a-brac, two log fires,
particularly friendly landlord and efficient
staff, up to a dozen well kept changing ales
tapped from the cask, enjoyable home-made
food including popular Sun roasts, two eating
areas; children and dogs welcome, picnic-
sets and play area in big garden, summer
barbecues and beer festivals, two bedrooms,
open all day (no food Sun evening).
(N R White, Alan Franck)

BROADSTAIRS TR3967
Charles Dickens (01843) 600160
Victoria Parade; CT10 1QS Refurbished
pub centrally placed with view of sea, big
busy bar with good selection of beers and
wines, wide choice of food including good fish
and chips, friendly efficient service, upstairs
restaurant, live music Sat; children welcome,
tables out overlooking Viking Bay, almost
next door to Dickens House Museum.
(Nigel and Jean Eames)

BROOKLAND TQ9825
Royal Oak (01797) 344025
*Just off A259 Rye–New Romney; High
Street; TN29 9QR* This civilised and very
popular old dining pub reopened after an
eight-month closure as we went to press -
news please.

BURHAM TQ7362
Robin Hood (01634) 861500
*Burham Common, just W of Blue Bell
Hill; not far from M2 junction 3;
ME5 9RJ* Cosy old pub deep in the woods
and downs; Fullers London Pride, Shepherd
Neame Master Brew and a guest, decent
choice of realistically priced food (all day
Fri-Sun) from sandwiches and baguettes
up, inglenook woodburner, conservatory
restaurant; list of rules on door such as no
baseball caps; good-sized garden with picnic-
sets, covered terrace, aviaries and play area,
open all day. *(N R White)*

BURMARSH TR1032
Shepherd & Crook (01303) 872336
Shear Way, next to church; TN29 0JJ
Traditional 16th-c local with smuggling
history in marshside village; well kept
Adnams and a guest beer, Weston's cider,
good straightforward home-made food at low
prices, prompt friendly service, interesting

Virtually all pubs in this book sell wine by the glass. We mention wines
if they are a cut above the average.

photographs and blow lamp collection, open
fire, bar games; children and dogs welcome,
seats on side terrace, closed Tues and Sun
evenings, otherwise open all day. *(Peter
Meister, Eddie Edwards)*

CANTERBURY TR1458
Dolphin *(01227) 455963*
St Radigunds Street; CT1 2AA
Modernised dining pub with enjoyable home-
made pubby food from baguettes up, Sharps
Doom Bar, Timothy Taylors Landlord and
a couple of guests, country wines, friendly
staff, bric-a-brac on delft shelf, board games,
flagstoned conservatory, pianist Sun evening,
quiz first Mon of month; no dogs; children
welcome, disabled access, good-sized back
garden with heaters, open all day. *(Anon)*

CANTERBURY TR1457
Foundry *(01227) 455899*
White Horse Lane; CT1 2RU Recently
opened pub in former 19th-c iron foundry,
light and airy interior on two floors, six
Canterbury Brewers beers from visible
microbrewery plus local guests such as
Ramsgate, enjoyable well presented pubby
food till 6pm including good sandwiches,
helpful cheerful staff; disabled access, small
courtyard area. *(John Coatsworth, Sue and Mike
Todd, Tony and Wendy Hobden)*

CANTERBURY TR1458
Millers Arms *(01227) 456057*
St Radigunds Street/Mill Lane; CT1 2AA
Shepherd Neame pub in quiet street near
river, enjoyable well priced food and good
wine choice, friendly helpful staff, flagstoned
front bar, bare-boards back area, traditional
solid furniture, newspapers and log fire,
small conservatory; unobtrusive background
music; good seating in attractive part-covered
courtyard, handy for Marlowe Theatre
and cathedral, 11 comfortable bedrooms,
ample breakfast, brunch till noon, open all
day. *(John Coatsworth, Ian Phillips)*

CANTERBURY TR1457
Parrot *(01227) 454170*
*Church Lane – the one off St Radigunds
Street, 100 metres E of St Radigunds car
park; CT1 2AG* Ancient pub with heavy
beams, wood and flagstone floors, stripped
masonry, dark panelling and big open fire,
Shepherd Neame ales and well liked food,
upstairs vaulted restaurant; nicely laid
out courtyard with central woodburning
barbecue, open all day. *(Anon)*

CAPEL TQ6444
Dovecote *(01892) 835966*
Alders Road; SE of Tonbridge; TN12 6SU
Cosy beamed pub with some stripped
brickwork and open fire, pitched-ceiling
dining end, enjoyable well priced food (not
Sun evening, Mon) from sandwiches to Sun
roasts, up to six ales tapped from the cask
including Gales and Harveys, farm ciders,

friendly helpful staff; lots of picnic-sets in
back garden with terrace and play area, nice
country surroundings, open all day Sun.
(N R White, Terry)

CHALLOCK TR0050
Half Way House *(01233) 740258*
Canterbury Road; TN25 4BB Large dining
pub by roundabout, popular generously served
food (best to book) from good baguettes up
with some emphasis on fish, beers such as
Adnams Broadside, Fullers London Pride
and Shepherd Neame Spitfire, polite friendly
service; children welcome, terrace and
garden tables, sizeable play area, open all day
weekends. *(Paul Rampton, Julie Harding)*

CHILHAM TR0653
☆White Horse *(01227) 730355*
The Square; CT4 8BY 15th-c pub in
picturesque village square; handsomely
carved ceiling beams and massive fireplace
with lancastrian rose carved on mantelbeam,
chunky light oak furniture on pale wooden
flooring and more traditional pubby furniture
on quarry tiles, bright paintings, horsebrasses
and a couple of stained-glass panels, four
well kept changing ales, good popular freshly
cooked food (not Sun evening) using local
produce, pleasant service; background music
and TV; children welcome, dogs in bar, handy
for the castle, open all day. *(N R White)*

CHILLENDEN TR2653
☆Griffins Head *(01304) 840325*
*SE end of village; 2 miles E of Aylesham;
CT3 1PS* Attractive beamed and timbered
14th-c pub with two bar rooms and flagstoned
back dining room, gently upscale local
atmosphere, big log fire, full range of
Shepherd Neame ales and decent choice
of popular home-made food, good wine list,
friendly attentive service; dogs welcome in
some parts, pretty garden surrounded by
wild roses, summer Sun barbecues, nice
countryside, open all day. *(N R White)*

CHIPSTEAD TQ4956
Bricklayers Arms *(01732) 743424*
Chevening Road; TN13 2RZ Attractive
busy place overlooking lake and green, wide
choice of good well priced pub food (not Sun
evening) served by cheerful helpful staff,
Harveys beers kept well and tapped from
casks behind long counter, relaxed chatty
atmosphere, heavily beamed bar with open
fire and fine racehorse painting, refurbished
larger back restaurant; seats out front, open
all day Fri-Sun. *(Stephen Funnell, Alan Cowell,
B J Harding, Pete Walker)*

COBHAM TQ6768
Leather Bottle *(01474) 814327*
*Handy for M2 junction 1; The Street;
DA12 3BZ* Old beamed and timbered pub,
much modernised, with interesting woodwork
and lots of Dickens memorabilia, Adnams,
Sharps and a couple of guests, enjoyable

traditional food including children's choices, restaurant and tea room, young staff; disabled access, picnic-sets on big back lawn with play area and fish pond, pretty village, five bedrooms, open all day. *(Dave Braisted)*

CONYER QUAY   TQ9664
Ship   (01795) 520881
Conyer Road; ME9 9HR Well renovated 18th-c creekside pub now owned by adjacent Swale Marina; bare boards and open fires, good home-cooked food including set lunch (Mon-Sat), weekend breakfast from 10am, Adnams Southwold, Shepherd Neame Master Brew and guests, live folk first and third Tues of month; children and dogs welcome, useful for boaters, walkers and birders, open all day weekends. *(Sarah Flynn)*

COWDEN   TQ4640
Fountain   (01342) 850528
Off A264 and B2026; High Street; TN8 7JG Good sensibly priced blackboard food in attractive tile-hung beamed village pub, steep steps up to unpretentious dark-panelled corner bar, well kept Harveys, decent wines, old photographs on cream walls, good log fire, mix of tables in adjoining room, woodburner in small back dining room with one big table; background music; walkers and dogs welcome, picnic-sets on small terrace and lawn, pretty village. *(Anon)*

COWDEN   TQ4642
✴ Queens Arms
Cowden Pound; junction B2026 with Markbeech Road; TN8 5NP Friendly two-room country pub like something from the 1930s, splendid veteran landlady still in attendance (pub known locally as Elsie's – she was born here), well kept Adnams Bitter, no lager, coal fire, darts, occasional folk music or morris dancers; dogs welcome, closed Mon-Sat lunchtimes, Sun evening. *(David Jackman)*

CROCKHAM HILL   TQ4450
Royal Oak   (01732) 866335
Main Road; TN8 6RD Cosy and chatty old village pub owned by Westerham brewery, their ales kept well, popular good value home-made food (best to book), friendly efficient staff, mix of furniture including comfy leather sofas on stripped-wood floor, painted panelling, original Tottering-by-Gently cartoons and old local photographs, quiz nights and live folk; walkers (remove muddy boots) and dogs welcome, small garden, handy for Chartwell (NT). *(N R White, Neil Hardwick, William Ruxton, Gwyn Jones, Pauline Fellows and Simon Robbins and others)*

DARGATE   TR0761
Dove   (01227) 751360
Village signposted from A299; ME13 9HB Tucked-away 18th-c restauranty pub with rambling rooms, very good food from landlord-chef (some quite expensive and

they add 10% service), nice wines, plenty of stripped-wood tables, log fire; children, walkers and dogs welcome, sheltered garden, open all day Fri, closed Sun evening to Tues lunchtime (no food Tues evening). *(Anon)*

DEAL   TR3751
Berry   (01304) 362411
Canada Road; CT14 7EQ Small friendly no-frills local opposite old Royal Marine barracks, welcoming enthusiastic landlord, well kept Dark Star, Harveys and several changing microbrews (tasting notes on slates, beer festivals), farm cider and perry, no food, L-shaped carpeted bar with coal fire, newspapers, quiz and darts teams, pool, live music Thurs; small vine-covered back terrace, open all day, closed Tues till 5.30pm. *(N R White)*

DEAL   TR3752
Bohemian   (01304) 361939
Beach Street opposite the pier; CT14 6HY Seafront bar reopened Nov 2012 after fire; five ales including Sharps Doom Bar, around 70 bottled beers and huge selection of spirits, home-made traditional food including Sun roasts, friendly helpful staff, L-shaped room with mismatched furniture (some découpage tables), polished wood floor, lots of pictures, mirrors, signs and other odds and ends (customers encouraged to donate items), weekend papers, similar décor in upstairs cocktail bar with good sea views; background music; children and dogs welcome, sunny split-level deck behind and heated smokers' gazebo, open all day (from 9am Sun). *(Alastair Knowles, N R White)*

DEAL   TR3752
Just Reproach   (07432) 413226
King Street; CT14 6HX Popular recently opened 'micropub' in former shop; simple drinking room with wooden tables, high chairs and wood floor, friendly knowledgeable service from father and daughter team, three changing small brewery ales from Kent and further afield poured from the cask, also local ciders and some organic wines, locally made cheese, friendly chatty atmosphere, no mobile phones; dogs welcome, closed Sun evening, Mon. *(N R White)*

DEAL   TR3753
Ship   (01304) 372222
Middle Street; CT14 6JZ Dimly lit traditional bare-boards local in historic maritime quarter; Ramsgate Gadds and changing guest ales, friendly landlord, lots of dark woodwork, stripped brick and local ship and wreck pictures, evening candles, woodburner, cosy back bar; dogs welcome, small pretty walled garden, open all day. *(N R White)*

DETLING   TQ7958
Cock Horse   (01622) 737092
The Street; ME14 3JT Popular tiled and

weatherboarded village pub, enjoyable freshly made food all day in bars and back dining room from baguettes to good value set menu (Mon-Thurs), well kept Greene King IPA, Thurs quiz; sports TV; children welcome, tables out behind, handy for M20 (junction 7), Kent Showground and North Downs Way. *(Michael Tack)*

DOVER TR3241
Blakes (01304) 202194
Castle Street; CT16 1PJ Small flagstoned cellar bar down steep steps, brick and flint walls, dim lighting, woodburner, Adnams Lighthouse and six changing guests, farm ciders and perries, over 50 malt whiskies, several wines by the glass, enjoyable lunchtime bar food from sandwiches up, panelled carpeted upstairs restaurant (food all day), friendly enthusiastic landlord, daily papers; well behaved children welcome, dogs in bar, side garden and suntrap back terrace, four bedrooms, open all day. *(N R White)*

DUNGENESS TR0916
Pilot (01797) 320314
Battery Road; TN29 9NJ Single-storey, mid 20th-c seaside café-bar by shingle beach, bustling and unaffected, with well kept Adnams, Courage, Harveys and a guest, decent choice of good value food from nice sandwiches to fish and chips, OAP lunch deal Mon, open-plan interior divided into three areas, dark plank panelling including slightly curved ceiling, lighter front part overlooking beach, prints and local memorabilia, books for sale (proceeds to RNLI), quick friendly service (even when packed); background music; picnic-sets in side garden, open all day till 10pm (9pm Sun). *(Paul Humphreys)*

DUNKS GREEN TQ6152
★ Kentish Rifleman (01732) 810727
Dunks Green Road; TN11 9RU Popular Tudor pub restored in modern rustic style, well kept ales such as Harveys and Westerham, enjoyable reasonably priced food (service charge added), efficient staff, bar and two dining areas, rifles on low beams, cosy log fire; children and dogs welcome, tables in pretty garden with well, good walks, open all day weekends (no food Sun evening). *(Bob and Margaret Holder, Gordon and Margaret Ormondroyd)*

EAST MALLING TQ7057
King & Queen (01732) 842752
New Road; N of station, back road between A20 at Larkfield and A26; ME19 6DD Welcoming 16th-c pub near church; big opened up low-ceilinged bar with pubby furniture on red carpet, woodburner in central brick fireplace, well liked imaginative food alongside pub standards, four ales such as Sharps and Westerham, a dozen wines by the glass, separate dining area, monthly quiz; tables in smallish garden, three

---

bedrooms in converted barn, open all day (Sun till 6.30pm). *(Anon)*

EAST PECKHAM TQ6649
Bush Blackbird & Thrush
(01622) 871349 *Bush Road; off A26/ B2016 near Hadlow; TN12 5LN* Refurbished old tile-hung country pub, well kept Shepherd Neame ales including seasonal ones tapped from the cask, wholesome good value local food, opened up beamed interior, bare-boards bar to the left with inglenook log fire, dining area to the right, warm welcoming atmosphere, some live music; children and dogs welcome, large garden with pergola, bat and trap and play area, regular classic car meetings, open all day Sun from noon, closed Mon lunchtime. *(Simon Bailey)*

EASTLING TQ9656
Carpenters Arms (01795) 890234
Off A251 S of M2 junction 6, via Painters Forstal; The Street; ME13 0AZ Cottagey, partly 14th-c pub with well kept Shepherd Neame ales and good freshly prepared food from bar snacks up, big log fires front and back, hop-strung beams, nice mix of old furniture including pews on bare boards, old photographs of the pub and surroundings, local art for sale, live music including jazz; children welcome, small garden with picnic-sets, open all day Sat, Sun till 8pm (food till 4pm), closed Mon and Tues lunchtimes. *(Marcel Veldhuyzen)*

EYNSFORD TQ5365
Malt Shovel (01322) 862164
Station Road; DA4 0ER Traditional dark-panelled pub near church, black beams, patterned carpet and copper kettles, well kept interesting changing ales, good choice of wines by the glass, reasonably priced nicely presented food (all day weekends) including plenty of daily specials, popular Sun lunch, prompt friendly service, restaurant; background radio, silent sports TV, no dogs; children welcome, a few tables out by the pavement, car park across busy road, handy for castles and Roman villa. *(Adrian Johnson, D P and M A Miles, A N Bance, N R White)*

FAVERSHAM TR0161
Anchor (01795) 536471
Abbey Street; ME13 7BP Two-bar character pub with chatty local atmosphere; good reasonably priced food from baguettes up, well kept Shepherd Neame range, friendly service, simple dimly lit bare-boards bar with log fire, ancient beams and dark panelling, frosted windows, boat pictures and models, small side room with pub games and books, restaurant; some live music; dogs welcome, tables in pretty enclosed garden with bat and trap, attractive 17th-c street near historic quay, open all day. *(N R White)*

FAVERSHAM TR0161
Bear (01795) 532668
Market Place; ME13 7AG Traditional
late Victorian Shepherd Neame pub (back
part from 16th c), their ales kept well and
occasional guests, locals' front bar, snug and
back dining lounge with open fire, all off side
corridor, pubby lunchtime food (evenings
Tues-Thurs), friendly service and relaxed
atmosphere; couple of pavement tables, open
all day. *(Anon)*

FAVERSHAM TR0160
Elephant (01795) 590157
The Mall; ME13 8JN Well run dimly lit
traditional town pub, friendly and chatty,
with four or five well kept changing ales,
belgian beers, Weston's cider, no food (can
bring your own), central log fire; juke box and
some live music, games machine; children
and dogs welcome, suntrap back garden
with pond, open all day weekends, from 3pm
weekdays. *(Graham Warner, N R White)*

FAVERSHAM TR0161
Phoenix (01795) 591462
Abbey Street; ME13 7BH Historic town
pub with heavy low beams and stripped
stone, six well kept beers including Harveys
and Timothy Taylors, food from pubby
choices up (all day Fri, Sat, not Sun evening),
friendly service, leather chesterfields by
inglenook log fire, restaurant, various events
including live music and poetry reading;
children and dogs welcome, back garden,
open all day. *(Anon)*

FAVERSHAM TR0161
Sun (01795) 535098
West Street; ME13 7JE Rambling old-world
15th-c pub in pedestrianised street, good
unpretentious atmosphere with small low-
ceilinged partly panelled rooms, scrubbed
tables and big inglenook, well kept Shepherd
Neame beers from nearby brewery, enjoyable
bar food, smart restaurant attached, friendly
efficient staff, unobtrusive background music;
wheelchair access possible (small step),
pleasant back courtyard, eight bedrooms,
open all day. *(Dr and Mrs A Pollock)*

FINGLESHAM TR3353
⋆ Crown (01304) 612555
*Just off A258 Sandwich–Deal; The Street;
CT14 0NA* Popular neatly kept low-beamed
country local dating from 16th c, good
value generous home-made food from usual
pub dishes to interesting specials, friendly
helpful service, well kept local ales such as
Ramsgate, Biddenden cider, softly lit carpeted
split-level bar with stripped stone and
inglenook log fire, two other attractive dining
rooms; children and dogs welcome, lovely big
garden with play area, bat and trap, field for
caravans, open all day Fri-Sun. *(Ian Coles)*

FRITTENDEN TQ8141
Bell & Jorrocks (01580) 852415
*Corner of Biddenden Road/The Street;
TN17 2EJ* Welcoming simple 18th-c tile-
hung and beamed local, well kept Harveys,
Woodfords and guests (Apr beer festival),
Weston's and Thatcher's ciders, good home-
made food (not Sun evening, Mon, Tues),
open fire with propeller from crashed plane
above, hops over bar, kentish darts, live
music and other events; sports TV; children
and dogs welcome, farmers' market third Sat
of month (breakfast available then), open all
day. *(Conor McGaughey)*

GOODNESTONE TR2554
⋆ Fitzwalter Arms (01304) 840303
*The Street; NB this is in E Kent, not the
other Goodnestone; CT3 1PJ*
Old lattice-windowed beamed village pub
under new enthusiastic young couple; rustic
bar with wood floor and open fire, Shepherd
Neame ales and local wine, carpeted dining
room with another fire, enjoyable reasonably
priced home-made food (Weds-Sun), shove-
ha'penny and bar billiards; well behaved
children and dogs welcome, terrace with
steps up to peaceful garden, lovely church
next door and close to Goodnestone Park
Gardens, open all day Fri-Sun, closed Mon,
lunchtime Tues. *(Rob and Catherine Dunster,
Alan Cowell, Keir Halliday)*

GOUDHURST TQ7237
Star & Eagle (01580) 211512
High Street; TN17 1AL Striking medieval
building, now a small hotel, next to the
church; settles and Jacobean-style seats in
heavily beamed open-plan areas, intriguing
smuggling-days history, log fires, good choice
of enjoyable food (some prices on the high
side), well kept Brakspears, Harveys and
Wychwood from fairly modern bar with lovely
views, friendly helpful staff, restaurant;
children welcome, no dogs inside, tables
out with same views, attractive village,
ten up-to-date character bedrooms, good
breakfast, open all day. *(Anon)*

GRAVESEND TQ6474
Rum Puncheon (01474) 353434
West Street; DA11 0BL Handsome
Georgian house by Tilbury ferry pier, eight
real ales and plenty of foreign beers, low-
priced home-made lunchtime food with
some emphasis on fish, tapas Fri and Sat
evenings, friendly staff, chandeliers and bare
boards, historic river prints and photographs;
background classical music or jazz; no under-
14s in bar after 6.30pm, tables on raised
river-view terrace with steps down to garden

Every entry includes a postcode for use with satnav devices.

area, open all day (till 9pm Sun and Mon in winter). *(A N Bance)*

GROOMBRIDGE — TQ5337
✳ **Crown** (01892) 864742

B2110; TN3 9QH Charming tile-hung wealden inn under newish management; snug low-beamed bar, old tables on worn flagstones, panelling, bric-a-brac, fire in sizeable brick inglenook, Harveys, Larkins and a guest, enjoyable fairly traditional food (all day Fri, Sat, till 6pm Sun), good service, newly decorated dining area; children welcome, dogs in bar, narrow old brick terrace overlooking steep green, plans for a play area in back garden, four bedrooms, handy for Groombridge Place Gardens, open all day. *(N R White, B J Harding)*

HAWKHURST — TQ7529
✳ **Black Pig** (01580) 752306

Moor Hill (A229); TN18 4PF Bustling pleasantly refurbished open-plan pub, L-shaped bar and eating areas on different levels, all manner of nice old dining chairs and tables, church candles, interesting old stove, lots of pictures on bare brick or painted walls, well kept Dark Star, Harveys, Larkins and a guest, decent wines by the glass, good food from lunchtime sandwiches up, friendly attentive service; plenty of seats in surprisingly big back garden.
(Peter Meister)

HAWKHURST — TQ7531
✳ **Great House** (01580) 753119

Gills Green; pub signed off A229 N; TN18 5EJ Busy, stylish, white weatherboarded restauranty pub (part of the Elite group), well liked if pricey food (all day weekends), ales such as Harveys, Old Dairy and Sharps from marble counter, polite efficient service, sofas, armchairs and bright scatter cushions in chatty bar, stools against the counter used by locals, dark wood dining tables and smartly upholstered chairs on slate floor beside log fire, steps down to airy dining room with attractive tables and chairs, working Aga (they do cook on it) and doors out to terrace with plenty of furniture; background music; children welcome, dogs in bar, open all day. *(Jamie and Sue May, Derek Thomas, Steve Holloway)*

HEAVERHAM — TQ5758
Chequers (01732) 763968

Watery Lane; TN15 6NP Attractive 15th-c beamed country pub under newish ownership; enjoyable well presented food (not Sun evening) from bar snacks up, well kept Shepherd Neame ales, a dozen wines by the glass, friendly locals' bar, inglenook woodburner in dining area, raftered barn restaurant with Cavalier ghost, some live music; children and dogs welcome, big garden with play area, nice local walks, open all day Fri, Sat, till 7pm Sun, closed Mon. *(Pauline Fellows and Simon Robbins)*

HERNE BAY — TR1768
Old Ship (01227) 366636

Central Parade; CT6 5HT Old white weatherboarded pub with window tables looking across road to sea, well kept beers such as Bass and Timothy Taylors, popular choice of food including good Sun roasts; children welcome till 6pm, sea-view deck. *(Michael Tack, N R White)*

HEVER — TQ4744
Henry VIII (01732) 862457

By gates of Hever Castle; TN8 7NH Predominantly 17th-c with some fine oak panelling, wide floorboards and heavy beams, inglenook fireplace, Henry VIII touches to décor, enjoyable mainly traditional food from baguettes up, well kept Shepherd Neame ales, friendly efficient staff, restaurant; no dogs even in garden; outside covered area with a couple of leather sofas, steps down to deck and pond-side lawn, very handy for Hever Castle, bedrooms, open all day. *(R and S Bentley)*

HODSOLL STREET — TQ6263
✳ **Green Man** (01732) 823575

Signed off A227 S of Meopham; turn right in village; TN15 7LE Bustling village pub with neatly arranged traditional furnishings in big airy carpeted rooms, friendly atmosphere, Greene King Old Speckled Hen, Harveys Bitter, Timothy Taylors Landlord and a guest, decent choice of enjoyable generously served food (all day Sun) including good baguettes and popular two-course weekday lunch deal; background music (live Sun), quiz Mon; children and dogs welcome, tables and climbing frame on well tended lawn, open (and food) all day Fri-Sun. *(Gordon and Margaret Ormondroyd, N R White, B and M Kendall, Martin and Sue Day, Dave Braisted and others)*

IDE HILL — TQ4851
Cock (01732) 750310

Off B2042 SW of Sevenoaks; TN14 6JN Pretty village-green local dating from 15th c, chatty, friendly and under newish management, two dimly lit bars with steps between, Greene King ales, enjoyable traditional food (not Sun, Mon or Tues evenings), cosy in winter with good inglenook log fire; well behaved children and dogs welcome, picnic-sets out at front, handy for Chartwell (NT) and nearby walks. *(N R White)*

IDE HILL — TQ4952
Woodman (01732) 750296

Whitley Row, Goathurst Common; B2042 N; TN14 6BU Large roadside pub with good choice of enjoyable food all day including dishes from South Africa (landlord's homeland), well kept beer and decent wine, young well trained staff; background music and live jazz; nice garden, good walks. *(Mrs Elizabeth Hough)*

IDEN GREEN TQ7437
Peacock (01580) 211233
A262 E of Goudhurst; TN17 2PB Village local dating from 14th c; blazing inglenook log fire in low-beamed main bar, quarry tiles and old sepia photographs, well priced enjoyable pubby food (all day Sat) from good baguettes up, very helpful service, well kept Shepherd Neame ales, pinky-red dining room and public bar with fire; well behaved children and dogs welcome, no muddy boots, attractive good-sized garden, closed Sun evening. *(Paul Humphreys)*

IDEN GREEN TQ8031
✱Woodcock (01580) 240009
Not the Iden Green near Goudhurst; village signed off A268 E of Hawkhurst and B2086 at W edge of Benenden; in village follow Standen Street sign, then fork left into Woodcock Lane; TN17 4HT Informal friendly little local with a couple of big standing timbers supporting very low ceilings, chatty regulars on high stools near corner counter, comfortable squashy sofa and low table by inglenook woodburner, concrete floor, brick walls hung with horsebrasses, Greene King Abbot, IPA, Morland Original and XX Mild plus seasonal guests, well liked/priced pubby food (not Sun evening), small panelled dining area with pine tables and chairs; children and dogs (in bar) welcome, back garden, open all day, closed Mon evening. *(Alan Weedon, Rob Newland)*

IGHTAM TQ5956
✱George & Dragon (01732) 882440
A227; TN15 9HH Ancient timbered pub, popular and stylish, with good reasonably priced food from generous snacks up (all day till 6.30pm, not Sun), plenty of friendly smartly dressed staff, well kept Shepherd Neame ales, decent wines, sofas among other furnishings in long sociable main bar, heavy-beamed end room, woodburner and open fires, restaurant; children and dogs welcome, back terrace, handy for Ightham Mote (NT), good walks, open all day. *(Bob and Margaret Holder, Martin and Sue Day)*

IGHTAM COMMON TQ5855
✱Harrow (01732) 885912
Signposted off A25 just W of Ightham; pub sign may be hard to spot; TN15 9EB Smart yet comfortably genial pub with emphasis on particularly good imaginative food from daily changing menu, Sunday roasts, relaxed cheerful bar area to the right with candles and fresh flowers, dining chairs on herringbone wood floor, winter fire, charming little antiquated

conservatory and more formal dining room, ales such as Gravesend Shrimpers and Loddon Hoppit; background music; children welcome (not in dining room on Sat evening), pretty little pergola-enclosed back terrace, handy for Ightham Mote (NT), closed Sun evening, Mon. *(Ian Scott-Thompson, Michael and Maggie Betton, Derek Thomas, Andrea Rampley, Nick Lawless)*

IGHTHAM COMMON TQ5955
Old House (01732) 882383
Redwell, S of village; OS Sheet 188 map reference 591559; TN15 9EE Basic two-room country local tucked down narrow lane, no inn sign, bare bricks and beams, huge inglenook, half a dozen interesting changing ales from tap room casks, no food, darts; closed weekday lunchtimes, opens 7pm and may shut early if quiet. *(Anon)*

KENNINGTON TR0245
Old Mill (01223) 737976
Mill Lane; TN25 4DZ Refurbished, much extended dining pub, reopened 2012 under same owners as the Oak on the Green at Bearstead; good choice of generously served food (some quite expensive), a house beer from 1648, Fullers London Pride and guests such as Goachers and Old Dairy; children welcome, plenty of terrace and garden seating, open all day. *(Tony and Wendy Hobden)*

KILNDOWN TQ7035
Globe & Rainbow (01892) 890803
Signed off A21 S of Lamberhurst; TN17 2SG Welcoming well cared for pub with small cheerful bar, Harveys and guests such as Westerham in good condition, decent wines, simple bare-boards dining room with imaginative attractively presented food (shorter lunchtime menu), some themed evenings, friendly young staff; background music; country views from decking out by cricket pitch, closed Mon, Tues, otherwise open all day (till 7pm Sun). *(Tom and Rosemary Hall, J Graveling, Conrad Freezer, Martin and Sue Day and others)*

KINGSDOWN TR3748
Kings Head (01304) 373915
Upper Street; CT14 8BJ Chatty tucked-away local with four small split-level rooms, black timbers, lots of old local photographs on faded cream walls, a few vintage amusement machines, woodburner, Greene King IPA and two mainly local guests, popular reasonably priced food, friendly landlord and staff, darts; soft background music; children (in family room) and dogs welcome, garden with skittle alley, open all day Sun, closed weekdays till 5pm. *(N R White)*

Half pints: by law, a pub should not charge more for half a pint than half the price of a full pint, unless it shows that half-pint price on its price list.

LADDINGFORD TQ6848
Chequers (01622) 871266
The Street; ME18 6BP Friendly old
beamed and weatherboarded village pub with
good sensibly priced food from sandwiches
and sharing boards up (restricted choice
Mon lunchtime), well kept Adnams Bitter
and three guests (Apr beer festival); children
and dogs welcome, big garden with play
area, shetland ponies in paddock, Medway
walks nearby, one bedroom, open all day
weekends. *(Roy Russell)*

LAMBERHURST TQ6735
⋆Vineyard (01892) 890222
*Lamberhurst Down; S of village
signed off A21; TN3 8EU* Pretty dining
pub (formerly the Swan) by green and
vineyards, now under same ownership as
the Great House in Hawkhurst; main bar
has most character with a few stools by
counter serving Harveys, Sharps and a
guest, log fire in brick fireplace with boar's
head above, wall banquette draped with
animal hide, cushioned leather armchairs
and mix of dining furniture on flagstones
or bare boards, enjoyable bistro-style food,
long narrow room off with similar tables
and chairs, equestrian pictures and antlers
over fireplace, large ham for carving,
sketched wallpaper of local landmarks,
more formal panelled restaurant; seats and
tables on terrace by car park, new bedroom
extension. *(Jamie and Sue May)*

LENHAM TQ8952
Red Lion (01622) 858531
The Square; ME17 2PG Well kept village
pub dating from the 14th c, Fullers, Harveys,
Shepherd Neame and guests, popular pubby
food, brasses, beams and timbers in divided
bar areas, patterned carpet and covered
seating with uniform tables, open fire,
pleasant chatty atmosphere; open all day.
(N R White)

LINTON TQ7550
Bull (01622) 743612
*Linton Hill (A229 S of Maidstone);
ME17 4AW* Comfortably modernised
17th-c dining pub; good choice of food
from sandwiches and light dishes to pub
favourites and grills, popular carvery (Sun,
Thurs evening), fine fireplace in nice old
beamed bar, carpeted restaurant area, well
kept Shepherd Neame ales, friendly attentive
staff; children welcome, dogs in bar, lovely
views from side garden and back decking,
two gazebos, open all day. *(Michael Tack,
N R White)*

LITTLE CHART TQ9446
Swan (01233) 840702
The Street; TN27 0QB Attractive 15th-c
beamed village pub with notable arched
Dering windows, open fires in simple
unspoilt front bar and good-sized dining area,
enjoyable fairly traditional food (smaller
appetites catered for), three well kept
beers and decent wines, friendly staff, pool;
children welcome, nice riverside garden,
closed Mon, Tues, otherwise open all day till
late (9pm Sun). *(Richard Mason)*

LOWER HARDRES TR1453
⋆Granville (01227) 700402
*Faussett Hill, Street End; B2068 S of
Canterbury; CT4 7AL* Spacious airy
interior with contemporary furnishings,
unusual central fire with large conical
hood and glimpses of kitchen, proper
public bar with farmhouse chairs, settles
and woodburner, good popular food (not
Sun evening – booking advised) including
cheaper weekday set lunch, fine choice of
wines from blackboard, Shepherd Neame
Master Brew and a seasonal beer, efficient
service, daily papers, artwork for sale;
background music; children and dogs
welcome, french windows to garden with
large spreading tree and small sunny terrace,
open all day Sun, closed Mon. *(Alan Cowell)*

LUDDESDOWNE TQ6667
⋆Cock (01474) 814208
*Henley Street, N of village – OS Sheet
177 map reference 664672; off A227 in
Meopham, or A228 in Cuxton; DA13 0XB*
Early 18th-c country pub with friendly long-
serving no-nonsense landlord, at least six ales
including Adnams, Goachers and Shepherd
Neame, sensibly priced all-day pubby food
(not Sun evening) from sandwiches up, rugs
on polished boards in pleasant bay-windowed
lounge, quarry-tiled locals' bar, woodburners,
pews and other miscellaneous furnishings,
aircraft pictures, masses of beer mats and
bric-a-brac such as stuffed animals, model
cars and beer can collections, bar billiards
and darts, back dining conservatory, Tues
quiz; no children in bar or part-covered
heated back terrace; dogs welcome, big
secure garden, good walks, open all day.
(N R White)

MAIDSTONE TQ7655
Rifle Volunteers (01622) 758891
Wyatt Street/Church Street; ME14 1EU
Quiet old-fashioned backstreet pub tied to
local Goachers, three of their ales and good
value simple home-made food, friendly
long-serving landlord, two gas fires, darts;
tables outside. *(Anon)*

MARGATE TR3570
Lifeboat 07837 024259
Market Street; CT9 1EU Corner ale and
cider house (opened 2010) with pleasant
cosy atmosphere, small front bar with
barrel tables on wood floor, dim lighting,
larger back room with open fire, a dozen
well kept local beers and proper ciders/
perries served from the cask, locally
sourced cheeses, sausages, pies and
seafood, friendly helpful service, live folk

Thurs, jazz Sun afternoon; handy for Turner Contemporary, open all day. *(N R White)*

MARSH GREEN   TQ4344
Wheatsheaf (01732) 864380

Marsh Green Road (B2028 SW of Edenbridge); TN8 5QL Unpretentious popular tile-hung pub with Harveys, Larkins and other well kept beers, Biddenden cider, good value fresh food from lunchtime sandwiches up, long-serving landlord and friendly helpful staff, simple linked bareboards areas with old photographs and wooden partitions, winter fire, roomy back conservatory; TV; tables out by road and in back garden, good local walks, open all day. *(N R White, R and S Bentley)*

MARTIN   TR3347
Old Lantern (01304) 852276

Off A258 Dover–Deal; The Street; CT15 5JL Pretty 17th-c pub (originally two farm worker cottages), low beams, stripped brick and cosy corners in small neat bar with dining tables, well cooked food from traditional choices up, friendly quick service, one or two Shepherd Neame ales and decent wines, soft lighting, open fire; quiet background music; children welcome, some tables out at front, more in good-sized back garden with big wendy house, beautiful setting, self-catering apartment, closed in winter Sun and Tue evenings, Mon. *(Paul Rampton, Julie Harding)*

MATFIELD   TQ6541
Wheelwrights Arms (01892) 722129

The Green; TN12 7JX Attractive old weatherboarded pub on edge of village green, well liked food cooked by landlord-chef from interesting varied menu, Shepherd Neame and guests, decent wine selection, friendly attentive service, hop-strung beams, bare boards and woodburner in brick fireplace; children and dogs welcome, picnic-sets out in front, open all day Fri-Sun. *(Mrs L McDermott, Colin Simpson)*

MERSHAM   TR0438
Farriers Arms (01233) 720444

The Forstal/Flood Street; TN25 6NU Large opened-up beamed pub owned by local consortium, good well presented fresh food from pub favourites to more innovative choices, beers from own microbrewery, friendly helpful staff, restaurant; pretty streamside garden behind, pleasant country views, open all day (from 9am Fri-Sun for breakfast). *(N R White)*

NEWENDEN   TQ8327
White Hart (01797) 252166

Rye Road (A268); TN18 5PN Popular 16th-c local; long low-beamed bar with big stone fireplace, dining areas off with enjoyable good value food including deals (Mon-Thurs), well kept Harveys and guests, friendly helpful young staff; back games

area with pool, sports TV, background music; children welcome, boules in large garden, near river (boat trips to Bodiam Castle), bedrooms. *(Peter Meister, Paul Humphreys, Conrad Freezer)*

NORTHBOURNE   TR3352
Hare & Hounds (01304) 365429

Off A256 or A258 near Dover; The Street; CT14 0LG Chatty village pub with several well kept ales including Harveys, good choice of popular generously served food (lamb from nearby farm), friendly efficient service, spacious modernised brick and wood interior, log fires; dogs welcome, terrace tables. *(N R White)*

OARE   TR0163
★Shipwrights Arms (01795) 590088

S shore of Oare Creek, E of village; signed from Oare Road/Ham Road junction in Faversham; ME13 7TU Remote and ancient marshland tavern with plenty of character, up to six kentish beers tapped from the cask (pewter tankards over counter), enjoyable traditional food (not Sun evening, Mon), three dark simple little bars separated by standing timbers, wood partitions and narrow door arches, medley of seats from tapestry-cushioned stools to black panelled built-in settles forming booths, flags and boating pennants on ceiling, wind gauge above main door (takes reading from chimney); background local radio; children (away from bar area) and dogs welcome, large garden, path along Oare Creek to Swale estuary, lots of surrounding bird life, closed Mon. *(Peter Chapman, Mrs G Marlow, Colin and Angela Boocock)*

OTFORD   TQ5259
Crown (01959) 522847

High Street, pond end; TN14 5PQ Well managed 16th-c two-bar local opposite village duck pond, pleasantly chatty beamed lounge with woodburner in old fireplace, well kept ales such as Harveys, Tonbridge and Westerham, cheerful landlord and staff, enjoyable locally sourced food (not Sun-Weds evenings) including bargain OAP lunch and good Sun roasts, frequent events including monthly folk club, darts; sports TV; back garden, walkers and dogs welcome, open all day. *(B and M Kendall, N R White)*

PENSHURST   TQ4943
★Rock (01892) 870296

Hoath Corner, Chiddingstone Hoath, on back road Chiddingstone–Cowden; OS Sheet 188 map reference 497431; TN8 7BS Tiny welcoming cottage under friendly newish licensees, undulating brick floor, simple furnishings and woodburner in fine brick inglenook, well kept Larkins and good simple food, large stuffed bull's head for ring the bull, up a step to smaller room with long wooden settle by nice table; walkers and dogs welcome, picnic-sets out in front and on back lawn. *(Gwyn Jones, Tina and David Woods-Taylor, Martin and Sue Day, Alan Franck)*

PENSHURST TQ5241
☀ Spotted Dog (01892) 870253
Smarts Hill, off B2188 S; TN11 8EP
Quaint old weatherboarded pub under welcoming family, heavy low beams and timbers, attractive moulded panelling, rugs and tiles, antique settles, inglenook log fire, Black Cat, Harveys, Larkins and a guest, local cider, good mostly traditional food (all day weekends) including weekday lunch deals, friendly caring service; children and dogs welcome, tiered back terrace (they may ask to keep your credit card while you eat), open all day (till 9pm Sun), closed Mon evening. *(Heather and Dick Martin, Malcolm, Alan Franck)*

PETTERIDGE TQ6640
Hopbine (01892) 722561
Petteridge Lane; NE of village; TN12 7NE
Small unspoilt cottage in quiet little hamlet, two small rooms with open fire between, traditional pubby furniture on red patterned carpet, hops and horsebrasses, well kept Badger ales, enjoyable good value home-made food, friendly staff, steps up to simple back part with piano and darts, flagons in brick fireplace; seats in side garden. *(Anon)*

PLAXTOL TQ6054
☀ Golding Hop (01732) 882150
Sheet Hill (0.5 miles S of Ightham, between A25 and A227); TN15 0PT
Secluded traditional country local with hands-on landlord who can be very welcoming; simple dimly lit two-level bar, cask-tapped Adnams and guests kept well, local farm ciders (sometimes their own), short choice of basic good value bar food (not Mon or Tues evenings), old photographs of the pub, woodburners, bar billiards; portable TV for big sports events; no children inside; suntrap streamside lawn and well fenced play area over lane, good walks, open all day Sat. *(Bob and Margaret Holder, Gwyn Jones, Alan Franck, Pete Walker)*

PLUCKLEY TQ9245
Black Horse
The Street; TN27 0QS Attractive medieval pub behind Georgian façade (Hare & Hounds in TV series *The Darling Buds of May;* five log fires including vast inglenook, bare boards, beams and flagstones, dark half-panelling, plenty to look at, Greene King IPA and Old Speckled Hen alongside Shepherd Neame Spitfire, traditional food from good baguettes up (just roasts on Sun), roomy carpeted dining areas, various ghosts; background and some live music; children

and dogs welcome, spacious informal garden by tall sycamores, play area, good walks, open all day. *(Paul Humphreys)*

ROCHESTER TQ7468
Coopers Arms (01634) 404298
St Margarets Street; ME1 1TL Jettied Tudor building behind cathedral, cosily unpretentious and quaint with good local atmosphere, two comfortable beamed bars, fairly priced pub food and well kept beers (range split between the bars), helpful cheery staff; tables in attractive courtyard. *(Richard Mason, Colin and Angela Boocock)*

ROLVENDEN TQ8431
Bull (01580) 241212
Regent Street; TN17 4PB Welcoming small tile-hung cottage with woodburner in fine brick inglenook, high-backed leather dining chairs around rustic tables on stripped boards, built-in panelled wall seats, fresh flowers, Harveys and a couple from Old Dairy, enjoyable food (not Sun evening in winter) from favourites up, pale oak tables in dining room, friendly helpful service; soft background music; children welcome, dogs allowed in bar, a few picnic-sets in front, more seats in sizeable back garden, open all day. *(Alec and Joan Laurence)*

ROMNEY STREET TQ5561
Fox & Hounds (01959) 525428
Back road Eynsford–Heaverham; TN15 6XR Tucked-away open-plan country pub with four well kept ales including Larkins and one badged for them by Goachers, enjoyable fairly priced mainly traditional food (not Sun evening), low beams, flagstones and woodburner creating a cosy atmosphere; background music; children, walkers and dogs welcome, tables out at front and in back garden, open all day. *(Gwyn Jones, John Webb)*

SANDWICH TR3358
George & Dragon (01304) 613106
Fisher Street; CT13 9EJ Open-plan 15th-c beamed dining pub in quiet backstreet location; enjoyable often interesting food from open-view kitchen, Wantsum, Shepherd Neame and a guest ale, good choice of wines by the glass, friendly obliging staff, warm fire; children and dogs allowed, pretty back terrace, open all day Sat, closed Sun evening. *(N R White, William and Ann Reid)*

SEASALTER TR0864
☀ Sportsman (01227) 273370
Faversham Road, off B2040; CT5 4BP
Restauranty dining pub just inside seawall and rather unprepossessing from outside;

We include some hotels with a good bar that offers facilities comparable to those of a pub.

imaginative contemporary cooking using plenty of seafood (not Sun evening or Mon, must book and not cheap), home-baked breads, good wine choice including english, a couple of well kept Shepherd Neame ales, friendly staff, two plain linked rooms and long conservatory, pine tables, wheelback and basket-weave dining chairs on wood floor, big film-star photographs; plastic glasses for outside; children welcome, open all day Sun. *(Jonathan and Ann Tross, Nicolas Roberts)*

SELLING
TR0455

⋆ **Rose & Crown** (01227) 752214

Follow Perry Wood signs; ME13 9RY Tucked-away 16th-c country pub, hop-strung beams and two inglenook log fires, well kept Adnams, Harveys and a guest, several ciders, generous pub food from sandwiches up, friendly service; background music, quiz first Weds of month; children welcome, dogs on leads in bar, cottagey back garden with play area and bat and trap, nice walks. *(N R White)*

SELLING
TR0356

White Lion (01227) 752211

Off A251 S of Faversham (or exit roundabout, M2 junction 7); The Street; ME13 9RQ 17th-c pub refurbished under new licensees, Shepherd Neame ales from unusual semicircular bar counter, locally sourced food cooked by landlord, main bar with log fire (working spit), another fire in small lower lounge, back restaurant; children and dogs welcome, tables out at front and in attractive side garden. *(N R White)*

SEVENOAKS
TQ5555

⋆ **Bucks Head** (01732) 761330

Godden Green, just E; TN15 0JJ Welcoming and relaxed flower-decked pub with neatly kept bar and restaurant area, good freshly cooked blackboard food from sandwiches up, roast on Sun, well kept Shepherd Neame and a guest, beams, panelling and splendid inglenooks; children and dogs welcome, front terrace overlooking informal green and duck pond, pretty back garden with mature trees, pergola and views over quiet country behind Knole (NT), popular with walkers. *(N R White)*

SEVENOAKS
TQ5055

Kings Head (01732) 452081

Bessels Green; A25 W, just off A21; TN13 2QA Village-green pub under new management, enjoyable french brasserie-style food including mussels cooked seven different ways, Sun carvery, ales such as Harveys, Sharps Doom Bar and Wells &

Youngs, Stowford Press cider, good wines by the glass from french list, two log fires, restaurant; children and dogs welcome, spacious back garden with play area, open all day, closed Sun evening. *(Taff Thomas)*

SHIPBOURNE
TQ5952

⋆ **Chaser** (01732) 810360

Stumble Hill (A227 N of Tonbridge); TN11 9PE Comfortably opened up with civilised linked rooms converging on large central island, stripped-wood floors, frame-to-frame pictures on deep red and cream walls, pine wainscoting, candles on mix of old solid wood tables, shelves of books, open fires, well kept Greene King ales, good wine and malt whisky choice, good popular food all day (breakfast Thurs, Sat, Sun), friendly well trained staff, dark panelling and high timber-vaulted ceiling in striking chapel-like restaurant; background music; children welcome, dogs in bar, courtyard and small side garden, good local walks, Thurs morning farmers' market, open all day. *(Gordon and Margaret Ormondroyd, B J Harding, Tina and David Woods-Taylor, Derek Thomas, Bob and Margaret Holder and others)*

SHOREHAM
TQ5162

Crown (01959) 522903

High Street; TN14 7TJ Friendly old-fashioned family-run village pub, three or more well kept ales such as Harveys and Sharps Doom Bar, good value food, two bars and separate dining areas, open fires; garden, walkers and dogs welcome. *(Anon)*

SHOREHAM
TQ5261

Olde George (01959) 522017

Church Street; TN14 7RY Refurbished 16th-c pub with low beams, uneven floors and a cosy fire, friendly staff, changing real ales, dining area; children and dogs welcome, picnic-sets by road with view of church, picturesque village. *(N R White)*

SHOREHAM
TQ5161

Two Brewers (01959) 522800

High Street; TN14 7TD Two softly lit refurbished beamed rooms, back part more restauranty, popular freshly made food from sandwiches up, well kept Greene King and Wells & Youngs, friendly helpful staff, snug areas with comfortable seating, two woodburners; handy for walkers, closed Mon, Tues. *(Pauline Fellows and Simon Robbins)*

SNARGATE
TQ9928

⋆ **Red Lion** (01797) 344648

B2080 Appledore–Brenzett; TN29 9UQ Little changed since 1890 and in the same

---

'Children welcome' means the pub says it lets children inside without any special restriction. If it allows them in, but to restricted areas such as an eating area or family room, we specify this. Some pubs may impose an evening time limit. We do not mention limits after 9pm as we assume children are home by then.

family for over 100 years, simple old-fashioned charm in three timeless little rooms with original cream wall panelling, heavy beams in sagging ceilings, dark pine Victorian farmhouse chairs on bare boards, an old piano stacked with books, coal fire, local cider and four or five ales including Goachers tapped from casks behind unusual free-standing marble-topped counter, no food, traditional games like toad in the hole, nine men's morris and table skittles; children in family room, dogs in bar, outdoor lavatories, cottage garden. (Anon)

ST MARGARET'S BAY   TR3744
✸ **Coastguard** (01304) 853176

Off A256 NE of Dover; keep on down through the village to the bottom of the bay, pub off on right by the beach; CT15 6DY Sea views from prettily planted balcony and beachside seating, nautical décor in carpeted wood-clad bar, four changing real ales, bottled continentals, over 40 whiskies and a carefully chosen wine list with some from Kent vineyards, good if not especially cheap food and more fine views from restaurant with close-set tables on wood-strip floor; background music, free wi-fi (mobile phones pick up french signal); children and dogs allowed in certain areas, good walks, open all day. (Michael Tack, Alastair Knowles, N R White)

STAPLEHURST   TQ7846
Lord Raglan (01622) 843747

About 1.5 miles from town centre towards Maidstone, turn right off A229 into Chart Hill Road opposite Chart Cars; OS Sheet 188 map reference 785472; TN12 0DE Country pub with cosy chatty area around narrow bar counter, hop-covered low beams, big log fire and woodburner, mix of comfortably worn dark wood furniture, enjoyable food from sandwiches up, Goachers, Harveys and a guest, farm cider and perry, good wine list; children and dogs welcome, reasonable wheelchair access, tables on terrace and in side orchard, closed Sun. (Ken and Marion Watson)

STODMARSH   TR2160
✸ **Red Lion** (01227) 721339

High Street; off A257 just E of Canterbury; CT3 4BA Quirky country pub with idiosyncratic landlord, all manner of bric-a-brac from life-size Tintin and Snowy to a tiger's head in hop-hung rooms, one wall covered in sheet music, empty wine bottles everywhere, green-painted cushioned mate's chairs around nice pine tables, candles, big log fire, good interesting food using prime local meat and seasonal produce, usually Greene King IPA and a couple of local beers tapped from the cask, nice wine, good summer Pimms and winter mulled wine/cider, dining conservatory; background jazz; children welcome, dogs in bar, pretty garden with roaming chickens and ducks, handy

for Stodmarsh National Nature Reserve, two bedrooms sharing bathroom, open all day Sat, closed Sun evening. (Adrian Johnson)

STONE IN OXNEY   TQ9327
✸ **Crown** (01233) 758302

Off B2082 Iden–Tenterden; TN30 7JN Smart country dining pub with friendly landlord and staff, very good food from landlady-chef including some imaginative dishes, also wood-fired pizzas Fri evening, Sat (takeaways available), well kept Larkins tapped from the cask, light airy open feel with lots of wood, red walls and big inglenook log fire; no under-12s in the evening, rustic furniture on terrace, two refurbished bedrooms. (Peter Meister, Toby Boyle, Alec and Joan Laurence)

THURNHAM   TQ8057
✸ **Black Horse** (01622) 737185

Not far from M20 junction 7; off A249 at Detling; ME14 3LD Large busy dining pub with enjoyable food all day, children's menu, three well kept ales including Westerham, farm ciders and country wines, friendly efficient uniformed staff, alcove seating, timbers and hop-strung beams, bare boards and log fires, back restaurant area; dogs and walkers welcome, pleasant garden with partly covered terrace, nice views, by Pilgrims Way, comfortable modern bedroom block, hearty breakfast. (Martin and Sue Day, Sara Fulton, Roger Baker, Lee and Liz Potter)

TOYS HILL   TQ4752
✸ **Fox & Hounds** (01732) 750328

Off A25 in Brasted, via Brasted Chart and The Chart; TN16 1QG Traditional country pub with plain tables and chairs on dark boards, leather sofa and easy chair by log fire, hunting prints, old photographs, plates and copper jugs, modern carpeted dining extension with big windows overlooking tree-sheltered garden, enjoyable well presented food (not Sun evening) including some interesting choices, well kept Greene King ales, several wines by the glass, traditional games, no mobile phones; background music; children and dogs welcome, roadside verandah used by smokers, good local walks and views, handy for Chartwell and Emmetts Garden (both NT), open all day weekends, closed Mon in winter. (Christian Mole)

TUNBRIDGE WELLS   TQ5638
Beacon (01892) 524252

Tea Garden Lane, Rusthall Common; TN3 9JH Cheery Victorian pub with Harveys, Timothy Taylors and Wells & Youngs, lots of wines by the glass, good coffee, airy interior with fireside sofas, stripped panelling, bare boards and ornate wall units, linked dining areas; children welcome, tables on decking with fine view, paths between lakes and springs, three bedrooms, open all day. (Anon)

UNDERRIVER   TQ5552
White Rock (01732) 833112
SE of Sevenoaks, off B245; TN15 0SB
Welcoming village pub, attractive and
relaxed, with good food from pubby choices
up (all day weekends, best to book), well
kept Harveys, Westerham and a guest, decent
wines, beams, bare boards and stripped
brickwork in cosy original part with adjacent
dining area, another bar in modern extension
with woodburner; background and some
live music; children welcome, dogs may
be allowed (ask first), small front garden,
back terrace and large lawn with boules
and bat and trap, pretty churchyard and
walks nearby, open all day in summer and
at weekends. *(P M Dodd, Martin and Sue Day,
Tina and David Woods-Taylor)*

WEST MALLING   TQ6857
Bull (01732) 842753
High Street; ME19 6QH Friendly old pub
with good selection of mainly local ales and
reasonably priced traditional home-made
food (not Sun-Weds evenings), hop-strung
beams, bare boards and big log fire,
refurbished restaurant, Mon quiz, live music
first Sat of month; open all day Fri-Sun.
(Ross Barnes)

WEST MALLING   TQ6857
Swan (01732) 521910
Swan Street; ME19 6JU Popular brasserie-
bar with good quality food (cheaper set menu
choices), nice wines, cocktails and beers
such as Chapel Down and Hepworth, airy
open-plan décor, end conservatory; children
welcome in restaurant, garden area with
stylish furniture and bar, open all day.
(Michael Tack)

WEST PECKHAM   TQ6452
Swan on the Green (01622) 812271
*Off A26/B2016 W of Maidstone;
ME18 5JW* Own-brewed Swan ales and
Biddenden cider in relaxed open-plan
beamed bar, stripped brickwork, bare boards
and mixed furnishings, good home-made food
(not Sun evening) including local venison,
friendly efficient service; well behaved
children and dogs welcome, charming village
green (great for a summer drink), interesting
part-Saxon church, open all day summer
weekends. *(Christian Mole, Martin and Sue Day,
Hugh Roberts)*

WESTGATE-ON-SEA   TR3270
Bake & Alehouse 07581 468797
*Off St Mildred's Road down alley by
cinema; CT8 8RE* Former bakery recently
converted to a 'micropub'; small simple

drinking room with a few tables (expect to
share when busy) on bare boards, collages
on walls, four interesting cask-poured ales
such as Wantsum, real ciders from the
barrel including a warmer winter one (Monks
Delight), kentish wines, local cheese,
sausage rolls and pork pies, friendly chatty
atmosphere; closed Sun evening, Mon.
(N R White)

WESTWELL   TQ9847
Wheel (01233) 712430
The Street; TN25 4LQ Traditional brick-
built village pub under newish management;
popular fairly pubby food from baguettes and
light dishes up, well kept Shepherd Neame
ales and decent choice of wines, efficient
cheery service, dining areas around bar
with stripped-pine tables and chairs, cosy
atmosphere; children welcome, dogs in bar
area, good-sized garden with metal furniture,
close to Pilgrims Way, open (and food) all day
weekends. *(Jan and Alan Summers, N R White)*

WHITSTABLE   TR1167
Continental (01227) 280280
Beach Walk; CT5 2BP Mix of 19th-c
seafront hotel, pub-café and brasserie
restaurant, full range of Whitstable ales,
friendly service, relaxed atmosphere, large
windows looking over Thames estuary (on a
clear day you can see Southend); children
welcome, metal tables and chairs outside,
23 bedrooms, more in converted fishermen's
huts. *(N R White)*

WHITSTABLE   TR1066
Old Neptune (01227) 272262
Marine Terrace; CT5 1EJ Great view
over Swale estuary from this unpretentious
weatherboarded pub set right on the beach
(rebuilt after being washed away in 1897
storm); reasonably priced lunchtime food
from shortish menu including seafood
specials, real ales, friendly helpful young
staff, weekend live music; children and dogs
welcome, picnic-sets on the shingle (plastic
glasses out here and occasional barbecues),
fine sunsets. *(Adrian Johnson, Mrs G Marlow,
Andrea Rampley, John Wooll)*

WHITSTABLE   TR1066
Royal Naval Reserve
(01227) 272068 *High Street; CT5 1BQ*
Friendly, comfortable and cosy, roomier
than it looks from outside, with well kept
Shepherd Neame ales, nice house wines,
good value home cooking including fresh
local fish and great steak and kidney
pudding, attractive upstairs dining room;
some tables under back awning, open all day
(till 7pm Sun). *(Dave Braisted)*

WICKHAMBREAUX TR2258
Rose (01227) 721763

The Green; CT3 1RQ Attractive 16th-c and partly older pub, good value traditional home-made food all day (not Sun evening), friendly helpful staff, Greene King IPA and a couple of guests, real ciders, small bare-boards bar with log fire in big fireplace, dining area beyond standing timbers with woodburner, beams, panelling and stripped brick, quiz second Weds of month, regular live music; children and dogs welcome (resident alsatian is Masy), garden and small courtyard, nice spot across green from church and watermill, open all day. *(Mr and Mrs Mike Pearson)*

WOODCHURCH TQ9434
Six Bells (01233) 860246

Front Road, opposite churchyard; TN26 3QQ Attractive weatherboarded pub, ales such as Fullers, Harveys, Old Dairy, Timothy Taylors and Wells & Youngs (regular beer festivals), real ciders, quieter bar on left opening to dining area, oak beams and log fires, friendly staff and good local atmosphere, quiz and music nights; dogs welcome, tables out in front under wisteria, big garden behind, open all day. *(Conor McGaughey)*

WORTH TR3356
☆ St Crispin (01304) 612081

Signed off A258 S of Sandwich; CT14 0DF Dating from 15th c with low beams, stripped brickwork and bare boards, welcoming landlady and friendly attentive staff, popular home-made food from good baguettes and pub staples to more adventurous choices in bar, restaurant and back conservatory (dogs allowed here), three changing ales (usually one from Shepherd Neame), belgian beers, local farm cider and well chosen wines, central log fire; children welcome away from bar, good bedrooms (including motel-style extension), charming big garden behind with terrace, bat and trap and play area, lovely village position. *(N R White)*

WROTHAM TQ6258
Moat (01732) 882263

London Road; TN15 7RR Well refurbished Badger family dining pub in Tudor-style building, flagstones, beams and stripped masonry, wide range of good value food, their usual ales kept well, friendly efficient staff; garden tables, great playground, open all day. *(Gordon and Margaret Ormondroyd)*

YALDING TQ6950
☆ Walnut Tree (01622) 814266

B2010 SW of Maidstone; ME18 6JB Timbered village pub with split-level main bar, fine old settles, a long cushioned mahogany bench and mix of dining chairs on brick or worn carpeted floors, chunky wooden tables with church candles, interesting old photographs on mustard walls, hops, big inglenook, Black Sheep, Harveys, Moorhouses and Skinners, good bar food and more inventive restaurant menu, attractive raftered dining room with high-backed leather dining chairs on parquet flooring, lots of local events; background and occasional live music, TV; a few picnic-sets out in front by road. *(Nigel and Jean Eames)*

Lancashire
with Greater Manchester and Merseyside

There's really somewhere for everyone here – from stylish up-to-date places with excellent food through to traditional pubs with a fine range of ales. Prices tend to be fair too. New finds this year are Britons Protection (235 whiskies, five beers and unspoilt little rooms) and the Wharf (huge two-level place with good modern cooking and five beers), both in Manchester, Millstone at Mellor (smart dining pub and stylish bedrooms) and Station Buffet in Stalybridge (Victorian railway platform bar with impressive ales and tasty, good value food). For smashing beers, head to the Eagle & Child at Bispham Green (half a dozen choices and interesting food), Ring o'Bells at Lathom (six ales and all-day food in antique-filled bars), Philharmonic in Liverpool (ten beers in magnificent Victorian gin palace), Taps in Lytham (eight ales and cheap snacks in unassuming, friendly town tavern), Church Inn at Uppermill (11 of their own-brew Saddleworth ales), Lower Buck in Waddington (five beers and good value food) and the Inn at Whitewell, Whitewell (five choices in civilised and beautifully set inn). Readers have particularly enjoyed the Three Fishes at Great Mitton (a favourite for many, with fantastic food), Dukes 92 in Manchester (always cheerful and busy, with three dozen cheeses), Clog & Billycock at Pleasington (reliably good all round), Waddington Arms in Waddington (lovely little place and very well run) and Inn at Whitewell (super place to stay). Five of the Main Entries hold a Food Award, but Lancashire Dining Pub 2014 goes to the Three Fishes at Great Mitton.

BASHALL EAVES   SD6943   Map 7
Red Pump 🍴
NW of Clitheroe, off B6478 or B6243; BB7 3DA

Beautifully placed country inn with cosy bar, changing beers, and good food in more contemporary dining rooms; bedrooms

In a quiet hamlet on the edge of the Forest of Bowland and with splendid views from the terraced gardens and comfortable bedrooms, this is a cheerfully run pub with a chatty, helpful landlord. As well as two pleasantly up-to-date dining rooms, there's now earthy coloured paintwork and a cosy, traditional central bar with bookshelves, cushioned settles, wheelbacks and other nice old chairs on flagstones, and a log fire; board games. The quickly changing three regional beers on handpump might include Hawkshead Windermere Pale, Moorhouses Blond Witch and Tirril Old Faithful; ten wines by the glass and a good range of malt whiskies. It's a good place to stay, with generous breakfasts and river fishing nearby for residents.

🍴 Using their own herbs and local meat and game, the enjoyable food includes sandwiches, hot smoked mackerel pâté with horseradish cream, pigeon breast with crispy black pudding and mustard dressing, linguine with pumpkin seed pesto and pecorino crisp, tempura-battered fish with twice-fried chips, chicken breast with white bean and chorizo sauce, honeyed gammon steak with poached egg, skinny chips and pineapple chutney, venison and pork burger with tomato and onion salad, and puddings such as blackcurrant sponge with liquorice ice-cream and spiced pear with home-made yoghurt parfait and cider toffee. *Benchmark main dish: rabbit hotpot with sweet pickled vegetables £10.50. Two-course evening meal £14.00.*

Free house ~ Licensees Jonathan and Martina Myerscough ~ Real ale ~ (01254) 826227 ~ Open 12-2.30, 5.45-11; 12-3, 5.30-11 Sat; 12-9 Sun; closed Mon, winter Tues, one week Jan ~ Bar food 12-2, 6-9(7 Sun) ~ Restaurant ~ Children welcome ~ Dogs allowed in bar ~ Bedrooms: £65/£95 ~ www.theredpumpinn.co.uk *Recommended by Steve Whalley, Dr Peter D Smart*

BISPHAM GREEN   SD4813 Map 7
Eagle & Child 🍴 ♀ 🍺
Maltkiln Lane (Parbold–Croston road, off B5246); L40 3SG

Successful all-rounder with antiques in stylishly simple interior, enterprising food, interesting range of beers and appealing rustic garden

Now under a new landlord, this striking red-brick pub facing the village green remains a civilised and friendly place. The largely open-plan bar is discerningly furnished with a lovely mix of small old oak chairs, an attractive oak coffer, several handsomely carved antique oak settles (the finest made in part, it seems, from a 16th-c wedding bedhead), old hunting prints and engravings and low hop-draped beams. Also, red walls, coir matting, oriental rugs on ancient flagstones in front of the fine old stone fireplace and counter; the pub's dogs are called Betty and Doris. Friendly young staff serve Thwaites Original on handpump alongside six guests from brewers such as AllGates, Copper Dragon, Derwent, Lancaster, Moorhouses and Southport, a farm cider, decent wines and around 30 malt whiskies. A popular beer festival is usually held on the early May Bank Holiday weekend. The spacious, gently rustic garden has a well tended but unconventional bowling green; beyond is a wild area that's home to crested newts and moorhens. The shop in the handsome side barn sells interesting wines and pottery and includes a proper butcher and deli. This is part of the Ainscoughs group.

🍴 Impressive food includes sandwiches, black pudding and bacon fritter with sage, cider and apple sauce, deep-fried fresh haddock goujons with tartare sauce, lancashire hotpot, chicken burger in caribbean chilli marinade with jalapeno relish and chips, wild mushroom and rosemary risotto, sausages with mash and onion gravy, duck breast with caramelised onion and potato cake, confit duck fritter and orange and madeira reduction, monkfish fillet in saffron, garlic and olive oil with lobster sauce, feathered game three-ways (wild duck wellington, pigeon rissole, pheasant breast with wild mushroom mousse) with bordelaise sauce, and puddings such as walnut and golden syrup tart with vanilla mascarpone and earl grey-infused sticky toffee pudding with salted caramel sauce. *Benchmark main dish: steak in ale pie £11.00. Two-course evening meal £17.50.*

Free house ~ Licensee Stuart Fletcher ~ Real ale ~ (01257) 462297 ~ Open 12-3, 5.30-11; 12-11 Fri, Sat; 12-10.30 Sun ~ Bar food 12-2, 5.30-8.30(9 Fri, Sat); 12-8.30 Sun ~ Children welcome ~ Dogs welcome ~ www.ainscoughs.co.uk *Recommended by Margaret Dickinson, Jane Green, Karen Eliot, Herbert and Susan Verity*

GREAT MITTON SD7139 Map 7

Three Fishes ⑪ 🍴 🍷 🍺

Mitton Road (B6246, off A59 NW of Whalley); BB7 9PQ

Lancashire Dining Pub of the Year

Contemporary and stylish pub with tremendous attention to detail, excellent regional food given a modern touch and interesting drinks

' A favourite place to meet friends,' says an enthusiastic reader. Thoughtfully and imaginatively converted, it's a cleverly laid out place with plenty of cosy corners despite its size. The areas closest to the bar are elegantly traditional with a couple of big stone fireplaces, rugs on polished floors and upholstered stools. A series of individually furnished and painted rooms with exposed stone walls, careful spotlighting and wooden slatted blinds end with another impressive fireplace. Write your name on a blackboard when you arrive and they'll find you when a table becomes free – the system works surprisingly well. Staff are young and friendly, and there's a good chatty atmosphere. The long bar counter (with elaborate floral displays) serves Lancaster Amber, Moorhouses White Witch and Thwaites Wainwright on handpump, a dozen wines by the glass and unusual soft drinks such as locally made sarsaparilla and dandelion and burdock. There are seats and tables on the terrace and in the garden, which overlooks the Ribble Valley.

Black and white photographs on the walls show the small local suppliers used, while their locations are on a map on the back of the menu: lunchtime (not Sunday) sandwiches, potted Morecambe Bay shrimps, corn-fed chicken liver pâté with blood orange marmalade and toasted home-made onion bread, various platters, beech- and juniper-smoked salmon with prawns, lemon and capers, lancashire hotpot, slow-cooked pigs cheeks in sticky sauce with champ and black pudding fritter, veal kidneys with bacon, roast garlic mash and mushroom sauce, and puddings like chocolate and orange pudding and lemon posset with candied lemon zest and shortbread biscuits. *Benchmark main dish: battered haddock with marrowfat peas, home-made tartare sauce and dripping chips £9.50. Two-course evening meal £15.00.*

Free house ~ Licensee Andy Morris ~ Real ale ~ (01254) 826888 ~ Open 12-11(10 Sun) ~ Bar food 12-8.30(9 Fri, Sat, 8 Sun) ~ Children welcome ~ www.thethreefishes.com *Recommended by Gordon and Margaret Ormondroyd, Rachel and Ross Gavin, John and Sylvia Harrop, Robert Wivell, Roger and Anne Newbury*

People named as recommenders after the full entries have told us that the pub should be included. But they have not written the report – we have, after anonymous on-the-spot inspection.

LATHOM
SD4510   Map 7

Ring o'Bells ✦ £

In Lathom, turn right into Ring o'Bells Lane; L40 5TE

Bustling family-friendly canalside pub, interconnected rooms with antique furniture, six real ales, some sort of food all day and children's play areas inside and out

With a warm welcome – particularly for children and dogs – this red-brick Victorian pub is beside the Leeds & Liverpool Canal. Handy for the M6, it usefully serves some sort of food all day, starting with morning coffee and cakes. Several interconnected rooms lead off from the handsome central bar counter with its pretty inlaid tiles; throughout are all manner of antique dining chairs and carved settles around lovely old tables, comfortable sofas, rugs on flagstones, lots of paintings and prints of the local area, sporting activities and plants, and large mirrors, brass lanterns and standard lamps; staffordshire dogs and decorative plates sit on mantelpieces above open fires. Cumbrian Legendary Loweswater Gold, George Wright Longboat, Prospect Nutty Slack and Silver Tally and Thwaites Langdale Tup and Wainwright on handpump, good wines by the glass and more than 25 whiskies; background music, TV, darts, board games. Downstairs is a more plainly furnished room and indoor and outdoor children's play areas. Plans for their four acres of land include a football pitch, vegetable garden, cider orchard – and, of course, seats and tables by the canal. This is part of the Ainscoughs group.

🍴 Using beef from their own organic farm and other local produce, the well liked food includes doorstep sandwiches, eggs benedict on toasted muffin, devilled kidneys, sausages with mash and gravy, mushroom tagliatelle, gammon, pineapple and egg, lambs liver with onions and bacon, pork belly with caramelised cauliflower and red wine jus, rib-eye steak with herb butter or peppercorn sauce, and puddings such as chocolate fondant with chocolate ice-cream and gooseberry crumble with custard. *Benchmark main dish: chargrilled organic burger and chips £8.95. Two-course evening meal £15.00.*

Free house ~ Licensee Amanda Roue ~ Real ale ~ (01704) 893157 ~ Open 11-11 (midnight Fri, Sat) ~ Bar food 12-2, 5-9; 12-9 Sat; 12-8 Sun ~ Restaurant ~ Children welcome ~ Dogs allowed in bar ~ www.ringobellspub.com *Recommended by Richard and Penny Gibbs, Emma Scofield*

LITTLE ECCLESTON
SD4240   Map 7

Cartford 🛏

Cartford Lane, off A586 Garstang–Blackpool, by toll bridge; PR3 0YP

Attractively refurbished 17th-c coaching inn in pretty position on riverbank

The tidal River Wyre flows beneath a toll bridge within yards of this former coaching inn, and seats and tables in the garden look over the water. Inside, the unusual four-level layout combines traditional and contemporary elements, with pinks and reds, and light wood floors and banquettes alongside oak beams and a log fire; background music, TV and board games. Hawkshead Lakeland Gold, Moorhouse Pride of Pendle, Theakston Old Peculier and a guest from Bowland on handpump alongside speciality bottled beers and Weston's cider; several wines by the glass.

🍴 Bar food includes sandwiches, confit duck leg with spiced braised red cabbage and orange sauce, beetroot tarte tatin with warm goats cheese, several platters, omelette arnold bennett, cumberland sausages on mash with caramelised red onion gravy, oxtail and beef in ale pudding, fresh hake korma with mango chutney, minted yoghurt and mini poppadums, lamb hotpot, chicken breast with wild mushrooms, cream and garlic potatoes, and puddings such as crème brûlée of the day and chocolate fondant with mascarpone cream. *Benchmark main dish: pork belly with sesame-roasted cabbage and noodles with ginger, chilli and teriyaki sauce £14.95. Two-course evening meal £18.00.*

Free house ~ Licensees Patrick and Julie Beaume ~ Real ale ~ (01995) 670166 ~ Open 12-11(11.30 Sat); 12-10 Sun; closed Mon lunchtime ~ Bar food 12-2, 5.30-9 (10 Fri, Sat); 12-8.30 Sun ~ Restaurant ~ Children welcome ~ Bedrooms: £70/£110 ~ www.thecartfordinn.co.uk *Recommended by Gordon and Margaret Ormondroyd*

LIVERPOOL
SJ3589   Map 7
Philharmonic Dining Rooms ★ ◗ £

36 Hope Street; corner of Hardman Street; L1 9BX

Beautifully preserved Victorian pub with superb period interior, up to ten real ales and sensibly priced food

Just right for a pre-concert meal and with a smashing choice of beers, this magnificent marble-fronted late Victorian building is filled with astonishing period details. The centrepiece is the mosaic-faced serving counter, from which heavily carved, polished mahogany partitions radiate beneath a high ceiling with intricate plasterwork. The echoing main hall has stained glass depicting Boer War heroes Baden-Powell and Lord Roberts, rich panelling, a huge mosaic floor, and copper panels of musicians in an alcove above the fireplace. More stained glass in one of the little lounges declares 'Music is the universal language of mankind' and backs this up with illustrations of musical instruments. Two side rooms are called Brahms and Liszt, and there's a couple of plushly comfortable sitting rooms. However, this is no museum piece and it can get very busy. The fine choice of around eight real ales on handpump might include Andwell Spring Magic, Dent Golden Fleece, Ilkley Wit Marie, Liverpool Organic 24 Carat Gold, Long Man Old Man, Moor Raw, Rudgate York Chocolate Stout and St Austell Nicholsons Pale Ale. Also, several malt whiskies and quite a few wines by the glass; quiz machine, fruit machine, background music. Don't miss the original 1890s Adamant gents' (all pink marble and mosaics); ladies are allowed a look if they ask first.

As well as breakfast (served till noon), the fairly priced food (available in the bar or by table service in the grand lounge dining room) includes sandwiches (until 5pm), sharing platters, piri-piri chicken wings with blue cheese dressing, gloucester old spot sausages, vegetable and brie pancakes with cheese sauce, various burgers, chicken breast with ginger beer and barbecue sauce, bacon and cheese, lamb shank pie, salmon steamed with herb oil and pak choi, and puddings such as double chocolate cheesecake with salted caramel suace and key lime tart. *Benchmark main dish: line-caught beer-battered cod and chips £10.75. Two-course evening meal £15.00.*

Mitchells & Butlers ~ Manager Nicola Hamilton-Coburn ~ Real ale ~ (0151) 707 2837 ~ Open 11am-midnight ~ Bar food 11-10 ~ Restaurant ~ Children welcome until 7pm ~ www.nicholsonspubs.co.uk *Recommended by Rob and Catherine Dunster, Mike and Wena Stevenson, Canon Michael Bourdeaux, C A Bryson, Susan and John Douglas*

If we know a pub has an outdoor play area for children, we mention it.

MANCHESTER   SJ8397   Map 7
Britons Protection £

Great Bridgewater Street, corner of Lower Mosley Street; M1 5LE

Lively city pub with a maze of unspoilt rooms, huge range of whiskies, five real ales and inexpensive lunchtime snacks; garden

Often busy with concert-goers and musicians from the Bridgewater Hall next door, this likeably unpretentious and rambling place has a fantastic range of around 330 malt whiskies and bourbons – as well as Coach House Innkeepers, Jennings Cumberland, Robinsons Unicorn and a beer named for the pub (from Tetleys) on handpump. One of the most notable features are the tiled murals depicting the Peterloo Massacre of 1819, which took place a few hundred yards away. The first of a series of unspoilt little rooms, the plush front bar has a fine chequered tile floor, glossy brown and russet wall tiles, solid woodwork and elaborate plastering. Two cosy inner lounges, both served by hatch, have attractive brass and etched-glass wall lamps, an art nouveau fireplace with coal-effect gas fire and mirror above, and good solidly comfortable furnishings. As something of a tribute to Manchester's notorious climate, the massive bar counter has a pair of heating pipes as a footrail. There are tables in the garden behind. It gets very busy at lunchtime and weekends, and in the evenings they sometimes host poetry readings, storytelling, silent film shows and acoustic gigs; note they may close early on match days.

🍴 Straightforward bar food includes lunchtime sandwiches, vegetable lasagne, various popular pies and daily specials such as roast pork with stuffing, apple sauce and cauliflower cheese. *Benchmark main dish: steak in Guinness pie £6.50.*

Punch ~ Lease Peter Barnett ~ Real ale ~ (0161) 236 5895 ~ Open 11-11 (midnight Fri, Sat); 12-10.30 Sun ~ Bar food 11-2 ~ Children allowed until 5pm ~ www.britonsprotection.co.uk *Recommended by Dave Webster, Sue Holland*

 MANCHESTER   SJ8397   Map 7
Dukes 92

Castle Street, below the bottom end of Deansgate; M3 4LZ

Waterside conversion with spacious interior, great range of cheeses and pizzas all day

What makes this cleverly converted, cavernous former stables stand out is its fine setting near locks and railway arches in the rejuvenated heart of old industrial Manchester; seats and tables on a big terrace (where they hold summer barbecues) overlook the canal basin, which opens into the bottom lock of the Rochdale Canal. Inside, the atmosphere is informal and cheerful, with well spaced old and modern furnishings, including comfortable chaises longues and deep armchairs on the ground floor, and boldly bare whitewashed or red walls hung with paintings and photographs. The stylish gallery bar, accessed by an elegant spiral staircase, looks over the canal. The handsome granite-topped counter serves three real ales on handpump such as BrewDog Punk IPA, Holts Two Hoots and Yorkshire Dales Witch Blonde Ale, as well as decent wines and a wide choice of spirits; background music.

🍴 Food includes an excellent range of cheeses, meats and pâtés with generous helpings of granary bread; also, hot and cold sandwiches, soup, salads, chicken wings, a good range of pizzas, caramel pecan brownie and ice-cream sundae; they also have a grill menu, available in one specific seating area. *Benchmark main dish: giant rack of ribs with coleslaw and chips £13.00. Two-course evening meal £16.00.*

Free house ~ Licensee James Ramsbottom ~ Real ale ~ (0161) 839 8642 ~ Open 11.30-11(1am Fri, Sat); 12-11 Sun ~ Bar food 12-10(10.30 Fri, 11 Sat) ~ Restaurant ~ Children welcome ~ www.dukes92.com *Recommended by Jeremy King*

MANCHESTER
SJ8297 Map 7

Wharf ♀ ◀

Blantyre Street/Slate Wharf; M15 4SW

Big wharf-like pub on two levels with large terrace overlooking the canal basin, all manner of furnishings and wall prints, six real ales and a fine choice of other drinks and good bistro-like food

In fine weather, head for the large front terrace of this wharf-like building (actually built in 1998 as a pub), where there's plenty of wood and chrome tables and chairs around a fountain, and picnic-sets overlooking the canal basin. It's a huge place, but has cosy alcoves and rooms away from the cheerful buzz of the main open-plan areas, and is on several levels: downstairs is more informal and pub-like, with groups of high tables and chairs; upstairs is restauranty with table service. Throughout there's an appealing variety of pre-war-style dining chairs around dark wooden tables on rugs and shiny floorboards, hundreds of interesting prints and posters on bare brick or painted walls, old stone bottles, church candles, house plants and fresh flowers on window sills and tables, bookshelves and armchairs here and there, and large mirrors over open fires. Despite the crowds of happy customers, staff remain unfailingly friendly and helpful. Phoenix Brunning & Price Original and guests from breweries like Beartown, Conwy, Thwaites, Titanic and Weetwood on handpump, 19 wines by the glass and lots of whiskies.

Appealing and attractively presented food includes sandwiches, potted ham hock with wholegrain mustard and beer soda bread, cured salmon with dill scones and black pepper crème fraîche, sharing platters, lancashire cheese and onion pie with smoked paprika butter beans, honey-roast ham with free-range eggs and chips, rare-breed pork sausages with onion gravy, moroccan-spiced chicken with pomegranate, date and mint couscous salad, duck breast with black pudding hash, balsamic shallots and Vimto sauce, salmon and smoked haddock fishcakes with tomato and spring onion salad, and puddings such as lemon tart with blueberry compote and bread and butter pudding with apricot sauce and clotted cream. *Benchmark main dish: lamb shoulder with dauphinoise potatoes and red wine and rosemary sauce £16.95. Two-course evening meal £19.00.*

Brunning & Price ~ Manager Siobhan Youngs ~ Real ale ~ (0161) 220 2960 ~ Open 11-11 (midnight Fri, Sat) ~ Bar food 12-10(9.30 Sun) ~ Restaurant ~ Children welcome ~ Dogs allowed in bar ~ Live acoustic music Fri ~ www.brunningandprice.co.uk/thewharf
Recommended by Mike and Wena Stevenson, Ruth May

MELLOR
SD6530 Map 7

Millstone ⊕ 🛏

The Mellor near Blackburn; Mellor Lane; BB2 7JR

Smart dining pub run by friendly chef-patron, stylish rooms, four real ales and impressive food; bedrooms

In a pretty Ribble Valley village, this is a smart former coaching inn run by an enthusiastic chef-patron. There's a beamed and panelled bar with a comfortable lounge to one side, a roaring log fire, attractive tables and chairs on carpet, and Thwaites Original, Lancaster Bomber, Wainwright and a guest beer on handpump, a dozen wines by the glass and a good choice of soft drinks. The stylish new dining room, decorated in cream and yellow, has another open fire, more panelling, a grandfather clock, big flower arrangements and comfortably cushioned chairs around polished tables on wooden floorboards; service is friendly and helpful. There are seats and tables under parasols on the terrace. Bedrooms are comfortable and well equipped and the breakfasts very good.

🍴 Using the best local, seasonal produce, the enterprising food includes nibbles like black pudding fritters and bacon-wrapped chipolata sausages with english mustard mayonnaise, as well as baps, duck spring rolls with plum sauce, chicken caesar salad, various deli boards, mushroom risotto with truffle oil and poached egg, beer-battered haddock and chips, chicken tandoori with bombay potatoes, slow-roast lamb shank with bubble and squeak and port and rosemary sauce, and puddings such as steamed rhubarb and stem ginger pudding with clotted cream and chocolate and salted caramel tart with peanut brittle. *Benchmark main dish: steak in ale pie £11.95. Two-course evening meal £16.50.*

Thwaites ~ Managers Anson and Sarah Bolton ~ Real ale ~ (01254) 813333 ~ Open 11-11(midnight Fri, Sat); 11-10.30 Sun ~ Bar food 12-9.30(9 Sun) ~ Restaurant ~ Children welcome ~ Bedrooms: £64/£76 ~ www.millstonehotel.co.uk
Recommended by Ben Williams, W K Wood, Dave Webster, Sue Holland

NETHER BURROW
Highwayman 🍴 ♀
SD6175 Map 7

A683 S of Kirkby Lonsdale; LA6 2RJ

Substantial and skilfully refurbished old stone house with country interior, serving carefully sourced food; lovely gardens

In the pretty Lune Valley, this 17th-c inn is a welcoming place serving extremely good food. Although large, the stylishly simple flagstoned interior is nicely divided into intimate corners, with a couple of big log fires and informal wooden furnishings. Black and white wall prints and placemats show the local farmers and producers used, with a map on the menu locating these 'regional food heroes'. Bowland Hen Harrier, Lancaster Amber, Moorhouses White Witch and Thwaites Wainwright on handpump, 14 wines by the glass, around a dozen whiskies and a particularly good range of soft drinks; service is friendly and efficient. French windows lead to a big terrace and lovely gardens.

🍴 Usefully serving some sort of food all day, the enticing choices include appetisers like leek and pea shoot croquettes with sour cream and chives or chipolatas (from free-range rare-breed pigs) with mustard mayonnaise, lunchtime sandwiches (not Sunday), potted Morecambe Bay shrimps, deep-fried spicy squid with spring onion and chilli salsa and roast garlic mayonnaise, various platters, cheese and onion pie with sour cream and pickled beetroot, rump burger with battered onion rings, bacon, cheese, spicy tomato relish and dripping chips, lancashire hotpot, ox cheek with horseradish mash and sticky sauce, and puddings such as lemon posset with candied lemon zest and shortbread biscuit and rhubarb and apple crumble. *Benchmark main dish: battered haddock and dripping chips with marrowfat peas £9.50. Two-course evening meal £17.50.*

Thwaites ~ Lease Andy Morris and Craig Bancroft ~ Real ale ~ (01254) 826888 ~ Open 12-11(10.30 Sun); closed Mon ~ Bar food 12-2, 5.30-8.30(8 Sun); reduced menu 2-5.30 ~ Children welcome ~ Dogs allowed in bar ~ www.highwaymaninn.co.uk *Recommended by Margaret Dickinson, J F M and M West, Ray and Winifred Halliday, Christine and Neil Townend*

PLEASINGTON

SD6528   Map 7

Clog & Billycock 🍴 ⚓

Village signposted off A677 Preston New Road on W edge of Blackburn; Billinge End Road; BB2 6QB

Carefully sourced local food in appealingly modernised stone-built village pub

A lways deservedly busy for its consistently good food, this extended and carefully modernised village pub is run by friendly and efficient licensees and attentive staff. With the feel of an upmarket barn conversion, it's light and airy with flagstoned floors and pale grey walls; a cosier room has high-backed settles and a fireplace at the end. The whole pub is packed with light wooden tables – even if they're full on arrival, such is the size of the place that you won't have to wait long in the little bar area for one to come free. Thwaites Original, Triple C and Wainwright on handpump and 15 wines by the glass. Some tables are outside, beside a small garden.

🍴 Good, often enterprising food includes lunchtime sandwiches (not Sunday), nibbles like bread with oil, treacle vinegar and black pea hummus or deep-fried cauliflower fritter with curried mayonnaise, corn-fed chicken liver pâté with blood orange marmalade and toasted home-made onion bread, potted Morecambe Bay shrimps, cheese and onion pie with sour cream and pickled beetroot, sweet-cured gloucester old spot bacon cutlet with grain mustard sauce, rump burger with battered onion rings, bacon, cheese, fried egg, tomato relish and dripping chips, lancashire hotpot, welfare-friendly veal kidneys with streaky bacon, roast garlic mash and mushroom sauce, and puddings such as rhubarb bakewell tart and double chocolate mousse with milk foam and warm chocolate sauce. *Benchmark main dish: battered line-caught haddock with marrowfat peas, tartare sauce and dripping chips £9.50. Two-course evening meal £17.50.*

Thwaites ~ Lease Andy Morris and Craig Bancroft ~ Real ale ~ (01254) 201163 ~ Open 12-11(10.30 Sun) ~ Bar food 12-2, 5.30-8.30(9 Fri, Sat); 12-8.30 Sun ~ Children welcome ~ Dogs allowed in bar ~ www.theclogandbillycock.com *Recommended by Rachel and Ross Gavin, W K Wood, Graham and Jane Bellfield*

SAWLEY

SD7746   Map 7

Spread Eagle

Village signed just off A59 NE of Clitheroe

Nicely refurbished pub with quite a choice of good food, four real ales and riverside restaurant

A lovely place for a drink or a meal, greatly enjoyed by our readers. An attractive former coaching inn, just across a country lane from the river, it has a lot of character with a pleasing mix of nice old and quirky modern furniture (from an old settle and pine tables to new low chairs upholstered in animal-print fabric), all set off well by the grey rustic stone floor. Low ceilings, cosy sectioning, a warming fire and cottagey windows keep it intimate. The dining areas are more formal, with modern stripes and, as a quip on the decorative trend for walls of unread books, a bookshelf mural (much easier to keep dust-free); background music. Dark Horse Hetton Pale Ale, Moorhouses Pride of Pendle and Thwaites Nutty Black and Wainwright on handpump and several wines by the glass. There are two smoking porches, and individually furnished, comfortable bedrooms. It's handy for exhilarating walks in the Forest of Bowland and near the substantial ruins of a 12th-c cistercian abbey.

🍴 Under the new licensees, the highly thought-of food includes nibbles like honey and mustard chipolatas with brown sauce or home-made pork pie with onion marmalade and pickled walnuts, sandwiches, various platters, spiced cauliflower and chickpea tagine with deep-fried falafel, honey-roast ham and eggs, battered haddock with chips, mussels with bacon in creamy white wine sauce and skinny fries, lambs liver with bacon, onions and red wine gravy, twice-cooked local pork belly with black pudding mash and mustard gravy, and puddings such as warm cherry bakewell tart with raspberry jam sauce and whipped cream and triple chocolate torte with hazelnut ice-cream and lime curd. *Benchmark main dish: fish pie with cheese topping £11.95. Two-course evening meal £20.00.*

Free house ~ Licensees Greg and Natalie Barns ~ Real ale ~ (01200) 441202 ~ Open 11-11(10.30 Sun) ~ Bar food 12-2, 5.30-9; 12-2, 6-9.30 Sat; 12-7.30 Sun ~ Restaurant ~ Children welcome ~ Dogs allowed in bar ~ Singer Fri nights, monthly live band, film club second Tues of month ~ www.spreadeaglesawley.co.uk *Recommended by Margaret Dickinson, John and Sylvia Harrop, Simon and Mandy King*

STALYBRIDGE
SJ9598 Map 7

Station Buffet 🍺 £

The Station, Rassbottom Street; SK15 1RF

Classic Victorian station buffet bar with eight quickly changing beers and a few cheap basic meals

A miraculous railway-age survival, this unpretentious Victorian platform bar has an impressive range of eight beers on handpump: Timothy Taylors and seven quickly rotating guests such as Buxton Dark Nights, Curious IPA, Liverpool Organic Kitty Wilkinson, Pure North Valley Gold, Sportsman Hops Cotch, and Thornbridge Kipling and Wild Swan. Busy with happy customers, the bar has a welcoming fire below an etched-glass mirror, period advertisements and photographs of the station and other railway memorabilia on cosy wood-panelled and red walls, and there's a conservatory. An extension leads into what was the ladies' waiting room and part of the stationmaster's quarters featuring original ornate ceilings and Victorian-style wallpaper. Picnic-sets outside are on sunny Platform 1 by the Manchester to Huddersfield line.

🍴 As well as crumpets that you can toast on the fire and Wednesday afternoon teas with home-made scones and cakes, the good value food includes sandwiches, swede and courgette cottage pie, corned beef hash with pickled cabbage, chilli with nachos and cheese, chicken, potato and mushroom curry and lamb and rosemary hotpot. *Benchmark main dish: home-made pie and peas £3.50. Two-course evening meal £8.00.*

Free house ~ Licensee Samantha Smith ~ Real ale ~ No credit cards ~ (0161) 303 0007 ~ Open 11-11; 12-10.30 Sun ~ Bar food 12-9 ~ Children welcome ~ Dogs welcome ~ Folk Sat evening ~ www.buffetbar.org *Recommended by John Fiander, Andy and Jill Kassube*

TUNSTALL
SD6073 Map 7

Lunesdale Arms 🍴 🍷

A683 S of Kirkby Lonsdale; LA6 2QN

Emphasis on good imaginative food, plus separate area with traditional games

The many loyal regulars in this cheerful, bustling dining pub make it sensible to book a table in advance – there's always a warm welcome for visitors too. The opened-up interior has bare boards throughout, and a white-walled area has a good mix of stripped dining tables and blue sofas facing one another across a low table (with daily papers) by a woodburning stove in a solid stone fireplace; background music. Another area has pews, armchairs and big unframed oil paintings (some for sale) and, to one end, an airy games section with pool, table football, board games and TV. A cosier little flagstoned back part has another woodburning stove. Black Sheep and a guest such as Cross Bay Pale Ale or Lancaster Blonde on handpump alongside a farm cider. The church in this Lune Valley village has Brontë associations.

Appealing food using very local produce (and their own summer herbs and leaves) and home-made bread includes sandwiches, ham hock terrine with fruit chutney, ceviche of queen scallops with fennel and bloody mary dressing, pork and leek sausages with red wine and onion gravy, tagine of vegetables with preserved lemons and spiced couscous, beer-battered haddock and chips, leg of lamb with spinach rice, raita and home-made chutney, poached salmon with prawns, free-range boiled egg and lemon mayonnaise, and puddings such as carpaccio of pineapple with mango sorbet and raspberry sauce and sticky toffee pudding with butterscotch sauce. *Benchmark main dish: steak in Guinness pie £13.95. Two-course evening meal £18.00.*

Free house ~ Licensee Emma Gillibrand ~ Real ale ~ (01524) 274203 ~ Open 11-3.30, 6-midnight; 12-4, 6-midnight Sun; closed Mon except bank holidays ~ Bar food 12-2(2.30 weekends, bank holidays), 6-9 ~ Restaurant ~ Children welcome ~ Dogs allowed in bar ~ Pianist most Thurs evenings ~ www.thelunesdale.co.uk *Recommended by Karen Eliot, Dr and Mrs Leach, Michael Doswell, John Evans*

UPPERMILL SD0006 Map 7
Church Inn ◧ £

From the main street (A607), look out for the sign for Saddleworth church, and turn off up this steep narrow lane – keep on up!; OL3 6LW

Lively, good value community pub with big range of own-brew beers at unbeatable bargain prices and good food; children very welcome

There's always something going on at this busy little pub. They hold a gurning (face-pulling) championship during the lively traditional Rush Cart Festival (usually August Bank Holiday) – the winner wears the horse-collar displayed on the wall of the bar. Local bellringers arrive on Wednesdays to practise with a set of handbells, and anyone can join the morris dancers on Thursdays. The big unspoilt L-shaped main bar has high beams and some stripped stone, settles, pews and a good mix of chairs, and lots of attractive prints and china on a high delft shelf, jugs, brasses and so forth. They brew up to 11 of their own Saddleworth beers (usually starting at just £1.90 a pint), though if the water levels from the spring aren't high enough for brewing, they bring in guest beers such as Black Sheep and Copper Dragon. Some of their seasonal ales are named after the licensee's children, only appearing around their birthdays; two home-brewed lagers on tap too. TV (when there's sport on) and unobtrusive background music. A conservatory opens on to the terrace. Children enjoy the animals, which include rabbits, chickens, dogs, ducks, geese, alpacas, horses, 14 peacocks in the next-door field and some cats that live in an adjacent barn; dogs are made to feel very welcome. It's next to an isolated church, with fine views down the valley.

Very reasonably priced, the food includes sandwiches, black pudding fritters with spiced chutney, creamy garlic mushrooms on garlic toast, steak and kidney pie, chicken jalfrezi, chilli con carne, chickpea tagine, specials like rabbit pie, pork stroganoff or lamb shank with red wine and rosemary sauce and puddings. *Benchmark main dish: beer-battered jumbo cod and chips £13.25. Two-course evening meal £15.00.*

Own brew ~ Licensee Christine Taylor ~ Real ale ~ (01457) 820902 ~ Open
12-midnight(1am Sat) ~ Bar food 12-2.30, 5.30-9; 12-9 Fri-Sun, bank holidays ~
Restaurant ~ Children welcome ~ Dogs allowed in bar ~ www.thechurchinn.co.uk
Recommended by Yvonne Hosker, John Fiander

WADDINGTON   SD7243 Map 7
Lower Buck £
Edisford Road; BB7 3HU

**Hospitable village pub with reasonably priced, tasty food and five
real ales**

With a good choice of ales and fair value food, this cosy, friendly little
18th-c pub always has plenty of chatty customers. The several small,
neatly kept cream-painted bars and dining rooms, each with a warming
coal fire, have good solid chairs and settles on carpet or stripped-wood
floors and lots of paintings on the walls. Welcoming staff serve up to
five real ales such as Bowland Hen Harrier, Moorhouses Premier Bitter
and White Witch and Timothy Taylors Landlord on handpump, around
a dozen malt whiskies and several wines by the glass; darts and pool.
There are picnic-sets on cobbles at the front and in the sunny back
garden, and the pub (tucked away behind the church) is handily placed
for Ribble Valley walks.

 Well liked food includes sandwiches, black pudding with wholegrain mustard
sauce, potted Morecambe Bay shrimps, stuffed peppers with rice, mushrooms
and tomatoes, gammon with free-range eggs and pineapple, 16oz steak and kidney
pudding, marinated chicken breast, and puddings like apple crumble and sticky
toffee pudding. *Benchmark main dish: steak, mushroom and Guinness pie
£10.95. Two-course evening meal £16.00.*

Free house ~ Licensee Andrew Warburton ~ Real ale ~ (01200) 423342 ~ Open
11-11(midnight Sat); 12-11 Sun ~ Bar food 12-2.30, 6-9; 12-9 Sat, Sun, bank holidays ~
Children welcome ~ Dogs allowed in bar ~ www.lowerbuckinn.co.uk
Recommended by Rachel and Ross Gavin

WADDINGTON   SD7243 Map 7
Waddington Arms ★ ♀ 🍴 🛏
Clitheroe Road (B6478 N of Clitheroe); BB7 3HP

**Classic *Guide* pub, good all round, with plenty of character,
interesting food, friendly service – and open all day; bedrooms**

This is a charming place to stay and, as it's on the edge of the Forest of
Bowland, there are good surrounding walks. Of the four linked bars,
the one on the left is snuggest in winter when a blazing woodburning
stove in the monumental fireplace puts real warmth into the ancient
flagstones. There's plenty to look at in the various low-beamed rooms,
including antique prints, an interesting series of vintage motor racing
posters, contemporary Laurie Williamson prints, an enlarged 19th-c
sporting print here and leather-bound-book wallpaper there. Furniture
also seems to have been carefully chosen, with fine antique oak settles and
chunky stripped-pine tables. As well as a house beer from Moorhouses
(The Waddy) and four guests on handpump from brewers such as
Bowland, Thwaites and Tirril, there's a good choice of wines by the glass
and a dozen malt whiskies. Wicker chairs on the sunny flagstoned front
terrace look across to this attractive village's church; more tables sit on
a two-level back terrace, with picnic-sets on a neat tree-sheltered lawn.

🍴 Under the new licensee, the enjoyable food includes sandwiches, cajun-spiced salmon fishcakes with garlic mayonnaise, black pudding with toasted crumpet, poached egg, bacon and chive hollandaise, seared tuna niçoise salad, sausages with mustard mash and onion gravy, cheese, potato and onion pie, beer-battered fish and chips, lancashire hotpot, bass with seafood risotto and crispy squid, and puddings. *Benchmark main dish: steak in ale pie £10.95. Two-course evening meal £17.00.*

Free house ~ Licensee Andrew Thompson ~ Real ale ~ (01200) 423262 ~ Open 11-11(midnight Sat) ~ Bar food 12-2.30, 6-9.30; 12-9.30(9 Sun) Sat ~ Children welcome ~ Dogs allowed in bar and bedrooms ~ Bedrooms: £60/£85 ~ www.waddingtonarms.co.uk
Recommended by Steve Whalley, Rachel and Ross Gavin, Gerry and Rosemary Dobson, David Heath

WHALLEY   SD7336 Map 7
Swan
King Street; BB7 9SN

Bustling old town inn with cheerful bar, lots of customers and good value food and drink; bedrooms

This friendly 17th-c former coaching inn usefully serves food all day. The cheerful bar, always with a good mix of customers, is big and nicely decorated in mushroom, beige and cream, with colourful blinds, some modern artwork and simple dark leather dining chairs around deco-look pedestal tables; Bowland Hen Harrier and Timothy Taylors Landlord on handpump and several wines by the glass. A quieter room leads off here with leather sofas and armchairs on neat bare boards; unobtrusive background music, games machine and maybe Wednesday quiz night; service is helpful and efficient. There are picnic-sets on a back terrace and on grass strips by the car park. The bedrooms are named after nearby rivers and attractions.

🍴 As well as breakfasts (also available to non-residents), the very reasonably priced food includes sandwiches, bacon and black pudding salad, port and stilton mushrooms, popular cheese and onion or steak and mushroom pies, gammon and eggs, chicken and brie wrapped in bacon, and puddings such as apple pie and sticky toffee pudding. *Benchmark main dish: beer-battered fish and chips £8.45. Two-course evening meal £15.00.*

Enterprise ~ Lease Louise Clough ~ Real ale ~ (01254) 822195 ~ Open 11.30am-midnight ~ Bar food 12-8.45(6.45 Sun) ~ Restaurant ~ Children welcome ~ Dogs allowed in bar ~ Bedrooms: £50/£78 ~ www.swanhotelwhalley.co.uk
Recommended by Gordon and Margaret Ormondroyd

WHITEWELL   SD6546 Map 7
Inn at Whitewell ★ 🍴 ⚗ 🛏
Most easily reached by B6246 from Whalley; road through Dunsop Bridge from B6478 is also good; BB7 3AT

Elegant manor house with smartly pubby atmosphere, good bar food and luxury bedrooms

As ever, our readers very much enjoy staying in the comfortable bedrooms in this civilised, elegant old manor house. It's in a fantastic spot with plenty of surrounding walks, and they own several miles of trout, salmon and sea trout fishing on the River Hodder; picnic hamper on request. Rooms have handsome old wood furnishings, including antique settles, oak gate-leg tables and sonorous clocks, set off beautifully against powder-blue walls neatly hung with big attractive prints. The pubby main bar has roaring log fires in attractive stone fireplaces, and heavy curtains on sturdy wooden rails; one area has newspapers, magazines, local maps and guidebooks. There's a piano for anyone who wants to play, and board games. Early evening sees a cheerful bustle that later settles to a more tranquil and relaxing atmosphere. Drinks include a good wine list of around 230 wines with 17 by the glass (reception has a good wine shop), organic ginger beer, lemonade and fruit juices and up to five real ales on handpump that might be from Bowland, Copper Dragon, Hawkshead, Moorhouses and Timothy Taylors. There's an idyllic view from the riverside bar and adjacent terrace.

Using game birds from local shoots and other top quality produce, the good, interesting food includes sandwiches, chicken liver pâté with toasted home-baked bread, potted cornish crab with cucumber pickle and avocado purée, grilled norfolk kipper with home-baked granary bread, cumberland sausages with champ and onion sauce, beer-battered haddock with chips, chicken thighs marinated in chilli, lime, ginger and coconut milk with sweet potato wedges and spicy peanut sauce, shoulder of lamb with hotpot potatoes, caramelised onions and carrot purée, seared salmon fillet with spinach, smoked haddock, potato chowder and pea purée, and puddings. *Benchmark main dish: fish pie with cheese topping £11.25. Two-course evening meal £20.00.*

Free house ~ Licensee Charles Bowman ~ Real ale ~ (01200) 448222 ~ Open 10am-midnight ~ Bar food 12-2, 7.30-9.30 ~ Restaurant ~ Children welcome ~ Dogs allowed in bar and bedrooms ~ Bedrooms: £117/£155 ~ www.innatwhitewell.com
Recommended by John and Sylvia Harrop, Karen Eliot, Rachel and Ross Gavin, Steve Whalley, Barry Collett, David and Sue Atkinson, W K Wood, Roger and Anne Newbury

Also Worth a Visit in Lancashire

Besides the fully inspected pubs, you might like to try these pubs that have been recommended to us and described by readers. Do tell us what you think of them: feedback@goodguides.com

ADLINGTON SD6114
Bay Horse (01257) 480309
Babylon Lane, Heath Charnock; PR6 9ER Friendly 18th-c country pub popular with walkers, simple well priced food from sandwiches and barm cakes to speciality pies, three well kept ales including Adnams and Jennings, log fires in cosy bar, events such as knitting (Tues), quiz (Weds) and acoustic music (Sun); children welcome, extensive crown bowling green behind, six bedrooms, open all day. *(Peter Heaton)*

APPLEY BRIDGE SD5210
Dicconson Arms (01257) 252733
B5375 (Appley Lane North)/A5209, handy for M6 junction 27; WN6 9DY Well run and civilised, with good nicely presented food (all day Sun till 8pm) including weekday set menu and blackboard specials, friendly attentive service, two or three well kept Marstons-related ales, uncluttered bar area with clubby chairs, dining room beyond, pine floors, woodburner; some seats outside, open all day. *(Anon)*

ARKHOLME SD5872
⋆**Redwell** (01524) 221240
B6254 Over Kellet–Arkholme; LA6 1BQ Nicely renovated 17th-c country pub-restaurant, spacious interior with wooden tables and chairs on flagstones, also some easy chairs, woodburners, newspapers and magazines, very good individual cooking from landlord-chef including ingredients from next-door smokehouse, home-baked bread, well kept real ales, friendly attentive service; background music; tables outside, closed Sun evening to Weds. *(paul gregory, Trevor Barber, Graham and Jane Bellfield, John and Sylvia Harrop, Diane Fairhall)*

BARLEY SD8240
Pendle (01282) 614808
Barley Lane; BB12 9JX Friendly 1930s stone pub in shadow of Pendle Hill, three cosy rooms, two log fires, six well kept regional ales, simple substantial food (all day weekends) using local produce including good sandwiches, conservatory; garden, lovely village and good walking country,

self-catering cottages, open all day Fri-Sun.
(Dr Kevan Tucker)

BARNSTON   SJ2783
⋆ **Fox & Hounds**   (0151) 648 7685
3 miles from M53 junction 3: A552
towards Woodchurch, then left on
A551; CH61 1BW Well run pub with
cheerful welcome, Brimstage, Theakstons
and guests, 60 malt whiskies and good
value traditional lunchtime food, roomy
carpeted bay-windowed lounge with built-in
banquettes and plush-cushioned captain's
chairs around solid tables, old local prints
and collection of police and other headgear,
charming old quarry-tiled corner with
antique range, copper kettles, built-in pine
kitchen cupboards, enamel food bins and
earthenware, small locals' bar (worth a look
for its highly traditional layout and collection
of horsebrasses and metal ashtrays), snug
where children allowed; dogs welcome in
bar, picnic-sets at back among colourful tubs
and hanging baskets, open all day. *(David
Jackman)*

BARROW   SD7337
Eagle   (01254) 825285
*Village signed off A59; Clitheroe Road
(A671 N of Whalley); BB7 9AQ* Stylish
dining pub with modern light leather chairs,
sofas and big low tables in bar, brasserie-style
dining room with busy open kitchen and
cabinet displaying their 35-day dry-aged
steaks, good varied choice of food (all day
Sun) from sandwiches and home-made
sausages to some imaginative dishes, up to
five well kept ales, nice wines, young
uniformed staff, back area with chandeliers
and big mirrors, clubby panelled piano bar,
deli; children welcome, tables outside
overlooking big car park, open all day.
(Rachel and Ross Gavin)

BAY HORSE   SD4952
⋆ **Bay Horse**   (01524) 791204
*1.2 miles from M6 junction 33: A6
southwards, then off on left; LA2 0HR*
Civilised country dining pub (useful
motorway stop); cosily pubby bar with good
log fire, cushioned wall banquettes and
fresh flowers, ales such as Black Sheep,
Lancaster and Moorhouses, 15 wines by the
glass, smarter restaurant with cosy corners,
another log fire and carefully presented
innovative food (not Sun evening and not
especially cheap), friendly efficient service;
children welcome, garden tables, two
bedrooms in converted barn over road,
closed Mon. *(Karen Eliot, Dave Braisted,
Mrs Anne Henley, Hugh Roberts)*

BELMONT   SD6715
⋆ **Black Dog**   (01204) 811218
Church Street (A675); BL7 8AB
Nicely set Holts pub with enjoyable good
value food all day (till 6pm Sun), well kept/
priced beers and friendly quick service,

---

cheery small-roomed traditional core,
coal and gas fires, picture-window dining
extension; children and dogs welcome, seats
outside with moorland views above village,
attractive part-covered smokers' area, good
walks, three decent well priced bedrooms,
open all day. *(Len Beattie)*

BLACKO   SD8641
Rising Sun   (01282) 612173
A682 towards Gisburn; BB9 6LS
Welcoming traditional village pub tied to
Moorhouses, four of their ales plus guests,
enjoyable low-priced pubby food including
local dish 'stew-and-hard', tiled entry, open
fires in three rooms off main bar; walkers and
dogs welcome, tables on front terrace with
Pendle Hill view, open all day Fri-Sun, from
5pm other days. *(Anon)*

BLACKPOOL   SD3035
Pump & Truncheon   (01253) 624099
Bonny Street; FY1 5AR Old real-ale pub
tucked away behind the Golden Mile opposite
police HQ; Moorhouses and guests, good
choice of bottled beers too, bargain food,
bare boards and coal fire; open all day.
(Sam White)

BLACKSTONE EDGE   SD9617
⋆ **White House**   (01706) 378456
*A58 Ripponden–Littleborough, just W
of B6138; OL15 0LG* Beautifully placed
moorland dining pub with remote views,
emphasis on good value hearty food from
sandwiches up (all day Sun), prompt friendly
service, Black Sheep, Theakstons and a
couple of regional guests, belgian bottled
beers, cheerful atmosphere, carpeted main
bar with hot fire, other areas off, most tables
used for food; children welcome. *(Brian and
Anna Marsden)*

BOLTON   SD7112
Brewery Tap   (01204) 302837
Belmont Road; BL1 7AN Tap for Bank
Top, their full range kept well and a guest,
knowledgeable friendly staff, no food; dogs
welcome, seats outside, open all day.
(Ben Williams)

BOLTON   SD6809
Victoria   (01204) 849944
Markland Hill; BL1 5AG Refurbished
and extended family-run pub known locally
as Fannys, good choice of enjoyable food
including regional dishes, plenty of wines
by the glass, well kept ales such as Jennings
Cumberland and Marstons Pedigree, good
service; children welcome, seats outside on
decking, open all day. *(W K Wood, David Heath)*

BOLTON   SD6913
Wilton Arms   (01204) 303307
Belmont Road, Horrocks Fold; BL1 7BT
Friendly roadside pub on edge of West
Pennine Moors, reasonably priced fresh food
and four well kept regional ales including

Bank Top Flat Cap, open fires, conservatory; children welcome, valley views and good walks, open all day. (Dr and Mrs A K Clarke, W K Wood)

BOLTON BY BOWLAND   SD7849
Coach & Horses (01200) 447202
Main Street; BB7 4NW Stone-built beamed pub-restaurant, strikingly modernised, with black chandeliers, bold fabric wall hangings and big mirrors, enjoyable food from pub favourites to more unusual choices, a couple of ales such as Bowland and Moorhouses, good choice of wines, open fires; children welcome, tables out at back, lovely streamside village with interesting church, three bedrooms, open all day weekends, closed Mon, Tues. (Steve Whalley, Phil Denton)

BRINDLE   SD5924
✷ Cavendish Arms (01254) 852912
3 miles from M6 junction 29, by A6 and B5256 (Sandy Lane); PR6 8NG Traditional village pub dating from the 15th c, welcoming and popular, with good inexpensive home-made food (all day weekends) from sandwiches up, Banks's, Marstons and two guest ales, beams, cosy snugs with open fires, stained-glass windows, carpets throughout; children welcome, dogs in tap room, heated canopied terrace with water feature, more tables in side garden, good walks, open all day. (Margaret Dickinson)

BROUGHTON   SD4838
✷ Plough at Eaves (01772) 690233
A6 N through Broughton, first left into Station Lane under a mile after traffic lights, then left after 1.5 miles, Eaves Lane; PR4 0BJ Pleasantly unpretentious old country tavern with two beamed homely bars, well kept Thwaites ales, good choice of enjoyable food (all day Sun), friendly service, lattice windows and traditional furnishings, old guns over woodburner in one room, Royal Doulton figurines above log fire in dining bar with conservatory; quiet background music, games machine; children welcome, front terrace and spacious side/back garden, well equipped play area, open all day weekends (till 1am Sat), closed Mon except bank holidays. (Michael Butler, Pauline and Derek Hodgkiss)

BURNLEY   SD8432
Bridge Bier Huis (01282) 411304
Bank Parade; BB11 1UH Open-plan town-centre pub with five well kept/priced ales including Moorhouses, lots of foreign beers on tap and by the bottle, real cider, bargain straightforward food till 7pm (5pm Sun), friendly atmosphere, Weds quiz and some live music; open all day (till 1am Fri, Sat), closed Mon, Tues. (Anon)

BURY   SD8313
Trackside (0161) 764 6461
East Lancashire Railway Station, Bolton Street; BL9 0EY Welcoming busy station bar by East Lancs steam railway, bright, airy and clean with nine changing ales, bottled imports, real ciders and great range of whiskies, enjoyable home-made food (not Mon, Tues), fine display of beer labels on ceiling; children welcome till 7.30pm, platform tables, open all day. (Anon)

CARNFORTH   SD5173
Longlands (01524) 781256
Tewitfield, about 2 miles N; A6070, off A6; LA6 1JH Family-run village inn with well liked food in bar and restaurant from pizzas and pub favourites up, four good local beers, friendly helpful staff, live music Mon; children and dogs welcome, bedrooms and self-catering cottages, Lancaster Canal nearby, open all day. (Anon)

CHEADLE HULME   SJ8785
Church Inn (0161) 485 1897
Ravenoak Road (A5149 SE); SK8 7EG Popular old family-run pub with good interesting food (Sun till 7.30pm) including deals, well kept Robinsons beers and nice selection of wines by the glass, gleaming brass on panelled walls, warming coal fire, friendly staff and locals, back restaurant, live music most Sun evenings; children welcome, seats outside (some under cover), car park across road, open all day. (G D K Fraser, Mike and Wena Stevenson)

CHIPPING   SD6141
✷ Dog & Partridge (01995) 61201
Hesketh Lane; crossroads Chipping–Longridge with Inglewhite–Clitheroe; PR3 2TH Comfortable old-fashioned and much altered 16th-c dining pub in grand countryside, enjoyable food (all day Sun) served by friendly staff, Tetleys ales, beams, exposed stone walls and good log fire, small armchairs around close-set tables in main lounge, smart casual dress for evening restaurant; children welcome, no dogs inside, open all day Sun, closed Mon. (Anon)

CHORLEY   SD5817
Yew Tree (01257) 480344
Dill Hall Brow, Heath Charnock – out past Limbrick towards the reservoirs; PR6 9HA Attractive tucked-away restauranty pub refurbished under newish management, good food from open kitchen including bar menu, Blackedge ales and a dozen wines by the glass; background music, no dogs inside; children welcome, picnic-sets out on decked area, open all day Sat, till 8.30pm Sun, closed Mon. (W K Wood)

Pubs close to motorway junctions are listed at the back of the book.

CHORLTON CUM HARDY   SJ8193
Horse & Jockey (0161) 860 7794
Chorlton Green; M21 9HS Refurbished low-beamed pub with mock-Tudor façade, own-brewed Bootleg ales and guests, knowledgeable chatty staff, all-day bar food, more restauranty menu in high-ceilinged evening/weekend dining room (part of former Victorian brewery), good mix of customers; children allowed till 9pm, dogs very welcome (even a non-alcoholic beer for them), picnic-sets on front terrace looking across to green, open all day. *(Anon)*

CLITHEROE   SD7441
Inn at the Station (01200) 425464
King Street; BB7 2EU Refurbished Victorian inn under same ownership as the Swan at Whalley; comfortable modern bar with well kept Thwaites beers, enjoyable home-made food including children's menu, friendly helpful staff; seven spotless bedrooms, good breakfast. *(Anon)*

COLNE   SD8939
Admiral Lord Rodney
(01282) 866565 *Mill Green; BB8 0TA*
Welcoming, chatty and unpretentious three-room local, up to six well kept changing ales from small breweries, bargain basic food (not Mon), open fire, live music including fortnightly folk night (Tues); children and dogs welcome, open all day weekends, closed weekday lunchtimes. *(Dr Kevan Tucker)*

COLNE   SD8940
Black Lane Ends (01282) 864235
Skipton Old Road, Foulridge; BB8 7EP Country pub in quiet lane with good sensibly priced food from large menu, well kept Copper Dragon and Timothy Taylors Landlord, cheerful landlord and staff, two massive fires, small restaurant; children welcome, garden with play area, good Pennine views, handy for canal and reservoir walks. *(M S Catling, John and Eleanor Holdsworth)*

CONDER GREEN   SD4556
Stork (01524) 751234
Just off A588; LA2 0AN Fine spot where River Conder joins the Lune estuary among bleak marshes, two blazing log fires in rambling dark-panelled rooms, good reasonably priced food with south african influences, friendly efficient staff, real ales such as Black Sheep and Lancaster; children welcome, handy for Glasson Dock, bedrooms, open all day. *(Michael Butler)*

CROSBY   SJ3100
Crows Nest (0151) 924 6953
Victoria Road, Great Crosby; L23 7XY Unspoilt character roadside local with cosy bar, snug and Victorian-style lounge, five well kept ales including Caledonian, friendly staff; tables outside, open all day. *(Anon)*

DENSHAW   SD9710
Printers Arms (01457) 874248
Oldham Road; OL3 5SN Above Oldham in shadow of Saddleworth Moor, modernised interior with small log-fire bar and three other rooms, popular good value food including OAP midweek deal, Timothy Taylors Golden Best and a beer brewed for them by Bazens, several wines by the glass, friendly efficient young staff. *(Michael Butler, Stuart Paulley)*

DENSHAW   SD9711
★ Rams Head (01457) 874802
2 miles from M62 junction 22; A672 towards Oldham, pub N of village; OL3 5UN Sweeping moorland views from inviting dining pub with four thick-walled traditional little rooms, good variety of food (all day Sun) including seasonal game and seafood, well kept Black Sheep and Timothy Taylors, efficient friendly service, beam-and-plank ceilings, panelling, oak settles and built-in benches, log fires, tea room and adjacent delicatessen selling local produce; soft background music; children welcome (not Sat evening), open all day Sun, closed Mon except bank holidays. *(Michael Butler)*

DENTON   SJ9395
Lowes Arms (0161) 336 3064
Hyde Road (A57); M34 3FF For now no longer brewing their own LAB ales, but serving good local Hornbeam and Phoenix, jovial community-spirited landlord and helpful friendly staff, wide choice of good bargain food including offers, bar with games, restaurant; tables outside, smoking shelter, open all day weekends. *(Dennis Jones, Stuart Paulley)*

DOBCROSS   SD9906
Swan (01457) 873451
The Square; OL3 5AA Unspoilt low-beamed pub sympathetically refurbished by present licensees, three areas off small central bar, all with open fires, flagstones and upholstered bench seating, five Marstons-related beers and enjoyable home-made food including specials, friendly atmosphere, folk and theatre evenings in upstairs function room; children and dogs welcome, tables out at front, attractive village below moors, open all day weekends, closed Mon lunchtime. *(Edward Atkinson)*

DOWNHAM   SD7844
★ Assheton Arms (01200) 441227
Off A59 NE of Clitheroe, via Chatburn; BB7 4BJ Well refurbished 18th-c dining pub in lovely village location with Pendle Hill view; cosy low-beamed L-shaped bar with pews, big oak tables and massive stone fireplace, separate split-level restaurant, good range of popular food (all day Sun) with emphasis on fish/seafood, efficient friendly service, ales such as Black Sheep, Timothy

Taylors and Thwaites, lots of wines by the glass; background music; children welcome, dogs in bar area, tables on front terrace, open all day. *(Rachel and Ross Gavin, John and Eleanor Holdsworth, John and Sylvia Harrop, Dr Kevan Tucker)*

ECCLESTON SD5117
Original Farmers Arms
(01257) 451594 *Towngate (B5250, off A581 Chorley–Southport); PR7 5QS* Long low-beamed pub-restaurant, good choice of enjoyable all-day food including bargain weekday set menu, six regularly changing ales (some special offers), several wines by the glass, efficient smartly dressed staff; background music and machines, parking can be tight when busy; children welcome, four comfortable good value bedrooms (one with own bathroom), open all day. *(Jim and Maggie Cowell)*

EGERTON SD7014
Thomas Egerton (01204) 301774
Blackburn Road; BL7 9SR Friendly village pub (part of the small Welcome Taverns group), freshly made traditional food (all day weekends, till 7pm Sun), good choice of wines and rotating ales including own Dunscar Bridge, efficient service, log fire, quiz Weds and live music Fri; landscaped garden, open all day. *(Sophie McManus)*

EUXTON SD5318
Travellers Rest (01257) 451184
Dawbers Lane (A581 W); PR7 6EG Refurbished old dining pub (most here to eat) with good varied range of popular food including daily specials, organised friendly staff, well kept Black Sheep and four guests; children welcome, dogs allowed in part of back bar, nice side garden, open all day, food all day weekends (till 6pm Sun). *(Anon)*

FENCE SD8237
⋆ Fence Gate (01282) 618101
2.6 miles from M65 junction 13; Wheatley Lane Road, just off A6068 W; BB12 9EE Imposing 17th-c building refurbished into smart pub-brasserie, Caledonian Deuchars IPA, Courage Directors, Theakstons Best and two changing guests, plenty of wines by the glass, teas and coffees, bar food and more expensive restaurant menu, carpeted bar divided into distinct areas with polished panelling, timbers, big fire, mix of wooden tables and chairs, sofas, sporting prints, contemporary brasserie with topiary; background music, TV; children welcome, open all day (till 1am Fri, Sat). *(Rachel and Ross Gavin)*

GARSTANG SD4945
⋆ Th'Owd Tithebarn (01995) 604486
Off Church Street; PR3 1PA Creeper-covered tithe barn with big terrace overlooking Lancaster Canal marina and narrow boats; linked high-raftered rooms

with red patterned carpet or flagstones, upholstered stools, armchairs and leather tub seats around assorted shiny tables, lots of cartwheels, rustic lamps, horse tack and a fine old kitchen range, ales from Coniston, Kirkby Lonsdale, Lancaster and York, fair value wines by the glass, popular all-day food served by friendly staff; children welcome, dogs in bar. *(Roger and Donna Huggins, Ben Williams, Tess White, Emma Scofield)*

GOOSNARGH SD5738
⋆ Horns (01772) 865230
On junction of Horns Lane and Inglewhite Road; pub signed off B5269, towards Chipping; PR3 2FJ Plush early 18th-c inn with relaxed atmosphere, neatly kept carpeted rooms with log fires, popular food from pub standards to local duck and pheasant, Bowland and guest ales, plenty of wines by the glass and good choice of malts, friendly helpful service; background music; children welcome, garden, six bedrooms (some with road noise), caravan park, not far from M6. *(Mark Woods Diabs, Rachel and Ross Gavin, Ray and Winifred Halliday, Yvonne Hosker)*

GREAT MITTON SD7138
Aspinall Arms (01254) 826223
B6246 NW of Whalley; BB7 9PQ Nicely situated pub dating from the 17th c, roomy bar with red plush wall banquettes, comfortable chairs and sofa by open fire, well kept ales such as Boland, Lancaster, Three B's and Tirril, enjoyable fairly traditional food from good cold or hot sandwiches to specials, small separate dining room, papers, books and magazines; background and live music including July Cloudspotting festival; children and dogs welcome, picnic-sets on flagstoned terrace and in big garden with play area, summer barbecues, just above River Ribble (fishing permits available), six bedrooms, open all day in summer. *(Richard and Karen Holt)*

GRINDLETON SD7545
⋆ Duke of York (01200) 441266
Off A59 NE of Clitheroe, either via Chatburn, or off A671 in W Bradford; Brow Top; BB7 4QR Welcoming chef-landlord and neat helpful staff in comfortable civilised dining pub, really good imaginative food with plenty of attention to detail, set deals too, nice wines and coffee, well kept Black Sheep and Copper Dragon, various areas (one with open fire), views over Ribble Valley to Pendle Hill; tables on raised decking and in garden behind, closed Mon. *(Margaret Dickinson, Steve Whalley, Peter Abbott)*

HAWKSHAW SD7515
Red Lion (01204) 856600
Ramsbottom Road; BL8 4JS Pub-hotel owned by Lees, their ales, enjoyable reasonably priced food and good service; children welcome, bedrooms, quiet spot by

River Irwell. *(Rachel and Ross Gavin, John and Sylvia Harrop)*

HAWKSHAW   SD7514
Waggon & Horses (01204) 882221
Bolton Road; BL8 4JL Good well priced home-made food using fresh local ingredients in bar and small restaurant, friendly service and well kept beers. *(Rachel and Ross Gavin)*

HESKIN GREEN   SD5315
Farmers Arms (01257) 451276
Wood Lane (B5250, N of M6 junction 27); PR7 5NP Popular country pub under long-serving family, good choice of well priced home-made food in two-level dining area, cheerful helpful staff, ales such as Jennings, Prospect, Timothy Taylors and Thwaites, heavy black beams, sparkling brasses, china and stuffed animals (some refurbishment planned as we went to press), darts in public bar, Thurs quiz; background music, Sky TV; children welcome, picnic-sets in big colourful garden, play area, more tables front and side, five good value bedrooms, open all day. *(Anon)*

HEST BANK   SD4766
★ Hest Bank Inn (01524) 824339
Hest Bank Lane; off A6 just N of Lancaster; LA2 6DN Good choice of enjoyable food in picturesque three-bar coaching inn, nice setting close to Morecambe Bay, well kept ales such as Black Sheep and Thwaites, decent wines, friendly helpful young staff, separate restaurant area with pleasant conservatory; children welcome, plenty of tables out by Lancaster Canal, open all day. *(Clive and Fran Dutson)*

HEYSHAM   SD4161
Royal (01524) 859298
Main Street; LA3 2RN Early 16th-c low-beamed pub in pretty fishing village; good choice of enjoyable well priced pubby food including weekday deals, Wells & Youngs, York and four guests, plenty of wines by the glass, quiz nights; children welcome, no dogs inside, a few benches out in front, raised sheltered terrace behind with covered area, great views from interesting church next door, open all day. *(Richard Cox)*

HORNBY   SD5868
Castle (015242) 21204
Main Street; LA2 8JT Nicely restored sizeable village inn; bar with sofas and open fires, bistro and restaurant, enjoyable food from sandwiches, pub favourites and pizzas up, Black Sheep, Bowland and guests, good selection of other drinks, friendly helpful staff; six bedrooms, open all day. *(Anon)*

HOYLAKE   SJ2189
Ship
Market Street; CH47 3BB Unpretentious local dating from 18th c, cosy and friendly, with several well kept ales and enjoyable

straightforward food, good service, maritime pictures and ship models, Thurs quiz. *(C A Bryson)*

HURST GREEN   SD6837
★ Shireburn Arms (01254) 826678
Whalley Road (B6243 Clitheroe–Goosnargh); BB7 9QJ Welcoming 17th-c hotel; peaceful Ribble Valley views from big light and airy restaurant and lovely neatly kept garden with attractive terrace, good food (all day weekends) from sandwiches to traditional dishes with a modern twist, armchairs, sofas and log fire in beamed and flagstoned lounge bar with linked dining area, well kept ales such as Moorhouses and Tirril, several wines by the glass, friendly helpful service, daily papers; children welcome, dogs too (may get a treat), pretty Tolkien walk from here, 22 comfortable bedrooms, open all day (from 9am for coffee). *(Steve Whalley)*

HYDE   SJ9495
Cheshire Ring (0161) 366 1840
Manchester Road (A57, between M67 junctions 2 and 3); SK14 2BJ Welcoming refurbished pub tied to Beartown brewery, their good value ales kept well, guest beers and imports on tap, farm ciders and perries, good house wines, Thurs curries and bargain Sun roasts; background music (live upstairs at weekends); open all day Sat, Sun, from 4pm Mon, Tues, from 1pm Weds-Fri. *(Dennis Jones)*

HYDE   SJ9493
Joshua Bradley (0161) 406 6776
Stockport Road, Gee Cross; SK14 5EZ Former mansion handsomely converted to pub-restaurant keeping panelling, moulded ceilings and imposing fireplaces, good range of well priced popular food, Hydes and a couple of guest beers in great condition, friendly efficient staff; children welcome, heated terrace, play area. *(Dennis Jones)*

HYDE   SJ9595
Sportsman (0161) 368 5000
Mottram Road; SK14 2NN Bright cheerful Victorian local, Rossendale Pennine ales and lots of changing guests (frequent beer festivals), welcoming licensees, bargain bar food, popular upstairs cuban restaurant, bare boards and open fires, pub games, full-size snooker table upstairs; children and dogs welcome, open all day. *(Dennis Jones)*

IRBY   SJ2586
Irby Mill (0151) 604 0194
Mill Lane, off Greasby Road; CH49 3NT Converted miller's cottage (original windmill demolished 1898), friendly and welcoming, with eight well kept ales and good choice of wines by the glass, popular reasonably priced food all day (till 6pm Sun) from generous sandwiches up, two low-beamed traditional flagstoned rooms and comfortable carpeted

lounge, log fire, interesting old photographs and history; tables on terraces and side grass, open all day. *(Tony Tollitt, Philip and Jane Hastain, Shirley and Clive Pickerill, Mark Delap)*

LANCASTER SD4761
⋇ **Borough** (01524) 64170

Dalton Square; LA1 1PP Popular city-centre pub, stylish and civilised, with chandeliers, dark leather sofas and armchairs, lamps on antique tables, high stools and elbow tables, seven ales including Bowland, Hawkshead and Lancaster, lots of bottled beers, big dining room with central tables and booths along one side, enjoyable all-day food with much emphasis on local suppliers, daily specials, good value two-course deal till 6.30pm (not Sun), jams and local produce for sale, upstairs comedy night Sun; children and dogs welcome, lovely tree-sheltered garden, open all day. *(Roger and Donna Huggins)*

LANCASTER SD4761
⋇ **Sun** (01524) 66006

Church Street; LA1 1ET Both traditional and comfortably contemporary, good range of customers, five well kept Lancaster ales and guests, plenty of continental beers, good choice of wines by the glass, enjoyable food from pub staples up using local suppliers, beamed bar with panelling, chunky modern tables, several fireplaces, conservatory, Tues quiz; background music and TV; children welcome away from bar, terrace, 16 comfortable bedrooms, open all day. *(David Aston)*

LANCASTER SD4761
⋇ **Water Witch** (01524) 63828

Parking in Aldcliffe Road behind Royal Lancaster Infirmary, off A6; LA1 1SU Attractive conversion of 18th-c canalside barge-horse stabling, flagstones, stripped stone, rafters and pitch-pine panelling, seven well kept changing ales (third-of-a-pint glasses available) from mirrored bar, enjoyable good value food all day including specials, prompt pleasant service, upstairs restaurant; children in eating areas, tables outside. *(Anon)*

LANESHAW BRIDGE SD9141
Alma (01282) 863447

Emmott Lane, off A6068 E of Colne; BB8 7EG Renovated pub with wide choice of good well priced food, real ales and several wines by the glass, friendly efficient service, large garden room extension; background music; clean comfortable bedrooms. *(Trevor Waddington, John and Eleanor Holdsworth)*

LIVERPOOL SD3489
⋇ **Baltic Fleet** (0151) 709 3116

Wapping, near Albert Dock; L1 8DQ Unusual bow-fronted pub with convivial local atmosphere, wide range of interesting beers including own good Wapping brews, several

wines by the glass, enjoyable straightforward well priced food (not Sat lunchtime) such as traditional scouse, weekend breakfasts, bare boards, big arched windows, simple mix of furnishings and nautical paraphernalia, newspapers, upstairs lounge; background music, TV; children welcome in eating areas, dogs in bar, back terrace, open all day. *(Claes Mauroy)*

LIVERPOOL SJ3589
Belvedere (0151) 709 0303

Sugnall Street; L7 7EB Unspoilt little two-room Victorian pub with friendly chatty atmosphere, original fittings including etched glass, coal fires, four changing ales, good pizzas, darts and other games; open all day. *(Anon)*

LIVERPOOL SJ3588
⋇ **Brewery Tap** (0151) 709 2129

Cains Brewery, Stanhope Street; L8 5XJ Victorian pub with full Cains range at reasonable prices, guest beers too, friendly efficient staff, good value food weekday lunchtimes, nicely understated clean décor, wooden floors, handsome bar, plush raised side snug, interesting old prints and breweriana, gas fire, daily papers; sports TV, no dogs; children welcome till 8pm, disabled access, brewery tours, open all day. *(Claes Mauroy)*

LIVERPOOL SJ3589
Cracke (0151) 709 4171

Rice Street; L1 9BB Friendly unsmart local popular with students; Liverpool Organic, Thwaites and several guests, farm cider, sandwiches till 6pm, small unspoilt bar with bare boards and bench seats, snug and bigger back room with unusual Beatles diorama, lots of posters for local events; juke box, sports TV; picnic-sets in sizeable back garden, open all day. *(Claes Mauroy)*

LIVERPOOL SJ3589
⋇ **Dispensary** (0151) 709 2160

Renshaw Street; L1 2SP Small busy central pub with up to ten well kept ales including Cains and other local brews, bottled imports, no food, bare boards and polished panelling, wonderful etched windows, comfortable raised back bar with coal fire, Victorian medical artefacts; background music, silent TVs; open all day. *(Claes Mauroy)*

LIVERPOOL SJ3490
⋇ **Doctor Duncan** (0151) 709 5100

St Johns Lane; L1 1HF Friendly Victorian pub with several rooms including impressive back area with pillared and vaulted tiled ceiling, full Cains range and guests kept well, belgian beers on tap, enjoyable good value food, pleasant helpful service, daily papers; may be background music, can get lively evenings and busy weekends; family room, open all day. *(Claes Mauroy)*

LIVERPOOL SJ3589
Fly in the Loaf (0151) 708 0817
Hardman Street; L1 9AS Former bakery
with smart gleaming bar serving Okells
and up to seven ales from smaller brewers,
foreign beers too, enjoyable simple home-
made food (not Mon) at low prices, friendly
service, long room with panelling, some
raised sections, even a pulpit; background
music, sports TV, upstairs lavatories, open all
day, till midnight weekends. *(Nicky McDowell,
Claes Mauroy)*

LIVERPOOL SJ3490
Globe (0151) 707 0067
Cases Street, opposite station; L1 1HW
Chatty traditional little local in busy
shopping area (can get packed), friendly
staff, good selection of well kept ales,
lunchtime cobs, sloping floor to quieter
cosy back room, prints of old Liverpool;
background music; open all day. *(Anon)*

LIVERPOOL SJ3490
Hole In Ye Wall (0151) 227 3809
Off Dale Street; L2 2AW Well restored
18th-c pub with thriving local atmosphere in
high-beamed panelled bar, seven changing
ales fed by gravity from upstairs (no cellar
as pub is on Quaker burial site), sandwiches
and basic food till 5pm, free chip butties Sun
when there's a traditional sing-along, friendly
staff, plenty of woodwork, stained glass and
old Liverpool photographs, coal-effect gas fire
in unusual brass-canopied fireplace; no dogs;
children allowed till 5pm, open all day.
(Claes Mauroy)

LIVERPOOL SJ3490
Hub (0151) 709 2401
Hanover Street; L1 4AA Busy recently
opened bow-fronted bar-bistro, light modern
bare-boards interior with big windows,
decent choice of food from sandwiches and
stone-baked pizzas up, reasonably priced
wines, five ales including Liverpool Organic;
children welcome, open all day. *(Robert W
Buckle)*

LIVERPOOL SJ3490
Lion (0151) 236 1734
Moorfields, off Tithebarn Street; L2 2BP
Beautifully preserved ornate Victorian
tavern, great changing beer choice, over 80
malt whiskies, friendly landlord interested
in pub's history, good value simple lunchtime
food including good home-made pork pies,
sparkling etched glass and serving hatches in
central bar, unusual wallpaper and matching
curtains, big mirrors, panelling and tilework,

two small back lounges, one with fine glass
dome, coal fire; silent fruit machine; open all
day. *(Claes Mauroy, C A Bryson)*

LIVERPOOL SJ3489
Monro (0151) 707 9933
Duke Street; L1 5AG Stylish gastropub,
popular comfortable and well run, with
good choice of interesting food including
vegetarian options, early evening deals (not
Sun), well kept Marstons and guests from
small bar, good friendly service; courtyard
tables, open all day. *(Colin Nicolson)*

LIVERPOOL SJ3589
Peter Kavanaghs (0151) 709 3443
*Egerton Street, off Catherine Street;
L8 7LY* Shuttered Victorian pub with
interesting décor in several small rooms
including old-world murals, stained glass
and lots of bric-a-brac (bicycle hanging
from ceiling), piano, wooden settles and
real fires, well kept Greene King Abbot and
guests, friendly licensees, popular with locals
and students; open all day (till 1am Fri,
Sat). *(Claes Mauroy)*

LIVERPOOL SJ3490
Richmond (0151) 709 2614
Williamson Street; L1 1EB Popular small
corner pub in pedestrianised area, changing
ales with support for smaller brewers such as
Burscough, Liverpool Organic, Southport and
George Wright, over 50 malt whiskies; sports
TVs; tables out in front, four bedrooms, open
all day. *(Anon)*

LIVERPOOL SJ3589
Roscoe Head (0151) 709 4365
Roscoe Street; L1 2SX Unassuming old
local with cosy bar, snug and two other
spotless unspoilt little rooms, friendly
long-serving landlady, well kept Jennings,
Tetleys and four guests, inexpensive home-
made lunches (not weekends), interesting
memorabilia, traditional games including
crib, quiz Tues and Thurs; open all day till
midnight. *(Claes Mauroy, C A Bryson)*

LIVERPOOL SJ3490
Ship & Mitre (0151) 236 0859
Dale Street; L2 2JH Friendly local with
fine art deco exterior and ship-like interior,
popular with university people, up to 12
changing unusual ales (many beer festivals),
over 70 bottled continentals, farm ciders,
good value basic food (all day Fri-Sun),
upstairs function room with original 1930s
décor; well behaved children (till 7pm) and
dogs welcome, open all day. *(Kerry Law,
C A Bryson)*

Post Office address codings confusingly give the impression that some pubs
are in Lancashire when they're really in Cumbria or Yorkshire
(which is where we list them).

LIVERPOOL SJ3589
Swan (0151) 709 5281
Wood Street; L1 4DQ Busy, unsmart three-floor pub with bare boards and dim lighting, up to eight beers including good value Hydes, bottled belgian beers, Weston's cider, well priced cobs and weekday lunches, friendly staff; loud rock juke box, silent fruit machine; open all day (till 2am Thurs-Sat). *(Anon)*

LIVERPOOL SJ3490
⋆ Thomas Rigbys (0151) 236 3269
Dale Street; L2 2EZ Spacious beamed and panelled Victorian pub with mosaic flooring, old tiles and etched glass, Okells and five changing guests, lots of bottled imports, impressively long bar, steps up to main area, table service from attentive staff, reasonably priced hearty home-made food (all day till 7pm) such as scouse; disabled access, seats in big courtyard, open all day. *(Claes Mauroy)*

LIVERPOOL SJ3197
Volunteer Canteen 07891 407464
East Street; L22 8QR Classic friendly old local with superb etched glass and wood panelling, busy bar, comfortable lounge (table service here), well kept Black Sheep and guests, newspapers; open all day (from 2pm Mon-Thurs). *(Anon)*

LIVERPOOL SJ3490
White Star (0151) 231 6861
Rainford Gardens, off Matthew Street; L2 6PT Lively traditional local dating to the 18th c, cosy bar, lots of woodwork, boxing photographs, White Star shipping line and Beatles memorabilia (they used to rehearse in back room), well kept ales including Bass, Bowland and Caledonian Deuchars IPA, basic lunchtime food, friendly staff; sports TVs; open all day. *(Claes Mauroy)*

LONGRIDGE SD6038
⋆ Derby Arms (01772) 782623
Chipping Road, Thornley; 1.5 miles N of Longridge on back road to Chipping; PR3 2NB Old stone-built country pub with comfortable red plush seats and hunting/fishing bric-a-brac in main bar, smaller bar with sporting mementoes and regimental tie collection, other rooms and converted barn beyond, Black Sheep and a guest like Thwaites, decent wines by the glass, good food including blackboard specials; background music, TV, darts and board games, gents' has dozens of riddles on the wall; children welcome, seats out in front, more behind car park with fine views, open all day weekends. *(Margaret Dickinson, Sarah Flynn, Steve Whalley)*

LYDGATE SD9704
⋆ White Hart (01457) 872566
Stockport Road; Lydgate not marked on some maps and not the one near Todmorden; take A669 Oldham– Saddleworth, right at brow of hill to A6050 after almost 2.5 miles; OL4 4JJ Smart up-to-date dining pub overlooking Pennine moors, mix of locals in bar or simpler end rooms and diners in elegant brasserie with smartly dressed staff, high quality (not cheap) food, Lees, Timothy Taylors and a guest beer, 16 wines by the glass, old beams and exposed stonework contrasting with deep red or purple walls and modern artwork, open fires, newspapers; TV in lounge; children welcome, dogs in bar, picnic-sets on back lawn making most of position, 12 bedrooms, open all day. *(W K Wood)*

LYDIATE SD3604
Scotch Piper (0151) 526 0503
Southport Road; A4157; L31 4HD Medieval thatched pub, well worn-in, with heavy low beams, flagstones, thick stone walls and dogs sprawled in front of roaring fires, Black Sheep and guests from tiny counter in main room, corridor to middle room with darts and back snug, no food; bikers' night Weds, outside lavatories; big garden, open all day. *(Anon)*

LYTHAM SD3627
⋆ Taps (01253) 736226
A584 S of Blackpool; Henry Street – in centre, one street in from West Beach; FY8 5LE Unassuming, cheerful town pub a couple of minutes from the beach; eight real ales (view-in cellar) including Greene King IPA and house beer from Titanic, country wines and farm cider, simple food (not Sun, no credit cards); open-plan Victorian-style bar with bare boards and stripped-brick walls, nice old chairs in bays around sides, open fires and a coal-effect gas fire between built-in bookcases, plenty of stained glass, rugby memorabilia, shove-ha'penny and dominoes; TV and machines; children allowed till 7.30pm, heated canopied area outside, parking nearby difficult, best to use West Beach car park on seafront (free Sun), open all day. *(Michael Butler, Dr Kevan Tucker)*

MANCHESTER SJ8498
Angel (0161) 833 4786
Angel Street, off Rochdale Road; M4 4BR Good value home-made food from pub standards to more upscale dishes, eight well kept changing ales including Bobs, bottled beers, farm cider and perry, bare-boards bar with piano, smaller upstairs restaurant with two log fires and local artwork; children and dogs welcome, back beer garden, open all day. *(Anon)*

MANCHESTER SJ8498
Bar Fringe (0161) 835 3815
Swan Street; M4 5JN Long bare-boards bar specialising in continental beers, also five changing ales from smaller breweries and real cider, friendly staff, basic snacks till 4pm (no food weekends), daily papers, shelves

of empty beer bottles, cartoons, posters, motorcycle hung above door, rock juke box; no children or dogs; tables out behind, open all day, till late Sat, Sun. *(Anon)*

MANCHESTER   SJ8498
Castle (0161) 237 9485
Oldham Street, about 200 metres from Piccadilly, on right; M4 1LE Restored 18th-c pub well run by former *Coronation Street* actor; simple traditional front bar, small snug, full Robinsons range plus guests from fine bank of handpumps, Weston's Old Rosie cider, back room for live music and other events, nice tilework outside; open all day till late. *(Dr and Mrs A K Clarke)*

MANCHESTER   SJ8497
Circus (0161) 236 5818
Portland Street; M1 4GX Traditional little bare-boards local with particularly well kept Tetleys from tiny corridor bar (or may be table service), friendly landlord and staff, walls covered with photos of regulars and local celebrities, football memorabilia, leatherette banquettes in panelled back room; often looks closed but normally open all day (you may have to knock), can get very busy. *(Martin and Sue Radcliffe)*

MANCHESTER   SJ8398
City Arms (0161) 236 4610
Kennedy Street, off St Peters Square; M2 4BQ Busy little pub with eight quickly changing real ales, belgian bottled beers and bargain bar lunches, friendly service, coal fires, bare boards and banquettes, prints, panelling and masses of pump clips, handsome tiled façade and corridor; background music, TV, games machine; wheelchair access but steps down to back lounge, open all day. *(Anon)*

MANCHESTER   SJ8298
Crescent (0161) 736 5600
Crescent (A6), opposite Salford University; M5 4PF Three areas off central servery with up to ten changing ales (quarterly beer festivals), many continental bottled beers and real ciders, buoyant local atmosphere (popular with university), low-priced lunchtime food, Weds curry night, bare boards and open fire, plenty of character, regular live music; small enclosed terrace, open all day. *(Anon)*

MANCHESTER   SJ8498
Hare & Hounds (0161) 832 4737
Shudehill, behind Arndale; M4 4AA Old-fashioned 18th-c local with long narrow bar linking front snug and comfortable back lounge, notable tilework, panelling and stained glass, cheap Holts beer, friendly staff; background music, TV; open all day. *(Anon)*

MANCHESTER   SJ8397
Knott (0161) 839 9229
Deansgate; M3 4LY Friendly modern

glass-fronted café-bar under railway arch by Castlefield heritage site; Manchester or Marble ales plus guests, lots of continental imports, good value all-day food with emphasis on greek dishes, upstairs smokers' balcony overlooking Rochdale Canal. *(Bob and Tanya Ekers)*

MANCHESTER   SJ8499
★**Marble Arch** (0161) 832 5914
Rochdale Road (A664), Ancoats; centre of Gould Street, just E of Victoria Station; M4 4HY Cheery own-brew pub with fine Victorian interior, magnificently restored lightly barrel-vaulted high ceiling, extensive marble and tiling, look out for sloping mosaic floor and frieze advertising various spirits, rustic furniture, their own good beers plus guests (brewery visible from windows in back dining room – tours by arrangement), enjoyable home-made food; background music, Laurel and Hardy Preservation Society meetings showing old films (third Weds of month); children welcome, small garden, open all day (till midnight Fri, Sat). *(Dr and Mrs A K Clarke, Nick Lawless)*

MANCHESTER   SJ8398
Mark Addy (0161) 832 4080
Stanley Street, off New Bailey Street, Salford; M3 5EJ Unusual converted waiting rooms for boat passengers, barrel-vaulted red sandstone bays with wide glassed-in brick arches, cast-iron pillars and flagstones, views over river, signature cheese and pâté board plus some good regionally influenced cooking, several real ales including local microbrews, lots of wines by the glass, brisk friendly service; background music, sports TV facing bar; flower-filled waterside courtyard. *(J F M and M West, Bob and Tanya Ekers)*

MANCHESTER   SJ8492
Metropolitan (0161) 438 2332
Lapwing Lane, Didsbury; M20 2WS Large gabled dining pub (former Victorian railway hotel) with good imaginative food alongside pub favourites, well kept Caledonian Deuchars IPA, Timothy Taylors Landlord and Thwaites Wainwright, extensive wine list, efficient service, numerous airy rooms with impressive period décor and open fires; children welcome, tables out on decking, open all day. *(Anon)*

MANCHESTER   SJ8398
★**Mr Thomas Chop House**
(0161) 832 2245 *Cross Street; M2 7AR* Interesting late 19th-c pub, tall and narrow, with well preserved features; good generous freshly made food including some unusual choices, friendly staff coping well when busy, ales such as Black Sheep, Holts, Lees and Robinsons, good wines by the glass, front bar with panelling, original gas lamp fittings and stools at wall and window shelves, back

green-tiled eating areas with rows of tables on black and white Victorian tiles, archways and high ceilings; seats out at back, open all day. *(Bob and Tanya Ekers)*

MANCHESTER   SJ8298
New Oxford (0161) 832 7082
Bexley Square, Salford; M3 6DB Up to 16 well kept changing ales plus a good range of draught and bottled continental beers, a couple of farm ciders too, friendly staff, light and airy café-style feel in small front bar and back room, coal fire, low-priced basic food till 6pm; background music; seats outside, open all day. *(Anon)*

MANCHESTER   SJ8284
Parkfield (0161) 766 3923
Park Lane; M45 7GT Recently refurbished dining pub with good variety of food from sandwiches and pub staples to restaurant choices, all-day Sun roasts, ales such as Jennings, Moorhouses and Timothy Taylors, freshly ground coffee, cocktails and good wine list; children welcome. *(Anon)*

MANCHESTER   SJ8397
★ Peveril of the Peak (0161) 236 6364
Great Bridgewater Street; M1 5JQ Vivid art nouveau external tilework and three sturdily furnished old-fashioned bare-boards rooms, interesting pictures, lots of mahogany, mirrors and stained or frosted glass, log fire, welcoming long-serving landlady, Caledonian Deuchars IPA, Copper Dragon, Everards and Jennings from central servery, cheap basic lunchtime food; pool, table football, background music, TV; children welcome, pavement tables, closed weekend lunchtimes. *(Dr and Mrs A K Clarke, Jeremy King)*

MANCHESTER   SJ8397
★ Rain Bar (0161) 235 6500
Great Bridgewater Street; M1 5JG Bare boards and lots of woodwork in former umbrella works, well kept Lees ales, plenty of wines by the glass, enjoyable good value pubby food all day, friendly efficient staff, relaxed atmosphere, nooks and corners, coal fire in small snug, large upstairs bar/function room, Weds quiz; background music may be loud and can be busy with young crowd in evenings; good back terrace overlooking spruced-up Rochdale Canal, handy for Bridgewater Hall, open all day. *(Giles and Annie Francis)*

MANCHESTER   SJ8398
Sams Chop House (0161) 834 3210
Back Pool Fold, Chapel Walks; M2 1HN Small thriving dining pub, offshoot from Mr

Thomas Chop House, with original Victorian décor, huge helpings of good plain english food including weekend brunch, formal waiters, well kept beers and good wine choice; open all day. *(Bob and Tanya Ekers)*

MANCHESTER   SJ8398
★ Sinclairs (0161) 834 0430
Cathedral Gates, off Exchange Square; M3 1SW Charming low-beamed and timbered 18th-c Sam Smiths pub (rebuilt here in redevelopment), all-day food including fresh oysters, brisk friendly service, bustling atmosphere, quieter upstairs bar with snugs and Jacobean fireplace; tables out in Shambles Square (plastic glasses), open all day. *(Anon)*

MARPLE   SJ9389
Hare & Hounds (0161) 427 0293
Dooley Lane (A627 W); SK6 7EJ Dining pub above River Goyt, modern layout and décor, decent choice of all-day food at reasonable prices, Hydes ales and three interesting guests from stainless servery, brisk friendly service; background and some live music, Weds quiz, sports TV, no dogs; well behaved children welcome, open all day. *(Peter Wilde, Dennis Jones)*

MARPLE   SJ9588
Ring o' Bells (0161) 427 2300
Church Lane; by Macclesfield Canal, Bridge 2; SK6 7AY Popular old-fashioned local with assorted memorabilia in four linked rooms, well kept Robinsons ales, decent food at reasonable prices, darts, quiz nights and some live music including brass bands in the waterside garden, own narrowboat, one bedroom, open all day. *(Anon)*

MARPLE BRIDGE   SJ9889
Hare & Hounds (01614) 274042
Mill Brow: from end of Town Street in centre, turn left up Hollins Lane and keep on uphill; SK6 5LW Comfortable and civilised stone-built country pub in lovely spot, smallish and can get crowded, good interesting local food (not Mon, Tues) from short menu, well kept Robinsons, log fires; garden behind, open all day weekends, closed Mon-Thurs lunchtimes. *(Anon)*

MELLOR   SJ9888
Devonshire Arms (0161) 427 2563
This is the Mellor near Marple, S of Manchester; heading out of Marple on the A626 towards Glossop, Mellor is the next road after the B6102, signposted off on the right at Marple Bridge; Longhurst Lane; SK6 5PP Carpeted front bar with

---

old leather-seated settles and open fire, two small back rooms with Victorian fireplaces, well kept Robinsons ales, enjoyable food, alternating live jazz/quiz Tues; children welcome, garden with waterfall tumbling into fish pond crossed by japanese bridge, large pergola, play area on small tree-sheltered lawn. *(Anon)*

MORECAMBE SD4264
Midland Grand Plaza
(01524) 424000 *Marine Road W; LA4 4BZ* Classic art deco hotel in splendid seafront position, comfortable if unorthodox contemporary furnishings in spacious sea-view Rotunda Bar, rather pricey but enjoyable food from interesting lancashire tapas to restaurant meals, good service; children welcome, 44 bedrooms, open all day. *(Anon)*

MORECAMBE SD4364
Palatine (01524) 410503
The Crescent; LA4 5BZ Comfortable Edwardian seafront pub, enjoyable reasonably priced food including deli boards, pizzas and pubby standards, four Lancaster ales and guests, good friendly staff, leather armchairs and some high tables with stools on wood floor, upstairs panelled sea-view dining lounge; seats out in front, open all day (till 1am Fri, Sat). *(Steve and Liz Tilley)*

NEWTON SD6950
Parkers Arms (01200) 446236
B6478 7 miles N of Clitheroe; BB7 3DY Friendly welcome from chatty landlord, good locally sourced food (suppliers listed) from lunchtime sandwiches to imaginative specials, available in bar or restaurant, four real ales including Bowland, good range of wines, nice coffee and afternoon tea, log fires; children welcome, garden with lovely views, four bedrooms, pretty spot. *(Peter G Jenkins, John and Sylvia Harrop)*

PARBOLD SD4911
Windmill (01257) 462935
Mill Lane; WN8 7NW Nicely modernised beamed pub with opened-up interior, good coal fire, mix of furniture including settles and some interesting carved chairs, candles on tables laid for popular well executed food (pub favourites to more adventurous specials), six well kept ales and eight wines by the glass, good friendly service from young staff; gents' down stairs; seats out in front and at back, next to village windmill and facing Leeds & Liverpool Canal, good local walks, open all day (food all day Sun). *(Herbert and Susan Verity, Clive and Fran Dutson, Mike and Wena Stevenson)*

PRESTON SD5329
Black Horse (01772) 204855
Friargate; PR1 2EJ Friendly pub in pedestrianised street, eight well kept Robinsons ales, unusual ornate curved and mosaic-tiled Victorian main bar, panelling, stained glass and old local photographs, two quiet cosy snugs, mirrored back area, upstairs bar serving inexpensive food; no children, open all day from 10.30am. *(Jim and Maggie Cowell)*

RABY SJ3179
⋆ Wheatsheaf (0151) 336 3416
Raby Mere Road, The Green; from A540 heading S from Heswall, turn left into Upper Raby Road, village about a mile further; CH63 4JH Up to nine well kept real ales in pretty thatched black and white pub, simply furnished rambling rooms with homely feel, cosy central bar and nice snug formed by antique settles around fine old fireplace, small coal fire in more spacious room, well liked reasonably priced bar food (not Sun and Mon evenings) including huge range of sandwiches, à la carte menu in large former cowshed restaurant (Tues-Sat evenings), conservatory; gets very busy at weekends; children welcome, dogs in bar, picnic-sets on terrace and in pleasant back garden, open all day. *(David Jackman, Claes Mauroy, Mike and Shirley Stratton, C A Bryson, Paul Humphreys)*

RAMSBOTTOM SD8016
Eagle & Child (01706) 557181
Whalley Road; BLO 0DL Friendly well run pub with good freshly made food using locally sourced produce including own vegetables (booking advised), well kept Thwaites ales, good service; children welcome, interesting recently revamped garden, open all day Fri and Sat, till 7pm Sun. *(Tom Hardcastle)*

RAMSBOTTOM SD8017
⋆ Fishermans Retreat
(01706) 825314 *Twine Valley Park/ Fishery signed off A56 N of Bury at Shuttleworth; Bye Road; BLO 0HH* Remote yet busy pub-restaurant, generous food all day using produce from surrounding estate and trout lakes (they can arrange fishing), also have own land where they raise cattle, mountain-lodge-feel bar with beams and bare stone walls, five well kept ales including Copper Dragon, Moorhouses, Timothy Taylors and Thwaites, over 500 malt whiskies (some sold in shop), good wine list, small family dining room and restaurant/ function room extension, helpful friendly staff; a few picnic-sets with lovely valley views, closed Mon, otherwise open all day. *(R T and J C Moggridge)*

RAMSBOTTOM SD7816
Shoulder of Mutton (01706) 822001
Lumb Carr Road (B6214), Holcombe; BL8 4LZ Refurbished 18th-c village dining pub with good well presented home-made food (all day Sun) in bar or more formal restaurant, four well kept beers including Timothy Taylors Landlord, friendly service, some live music; children, walkers and dogs

welcome, open all day. *(W K Wood, R T and J C Moggridge)*

RILEY GREEN   SD6225
★ Royal Oak (01254) 201445
A675/A6061; PR5 0SL Cosy low-beamed four-room pub (former coaching inn) extended under new owners; good freshly made food and friendly efficient service, four Thwaites ales and maybe a guest from long back bar, ancient stripped stone, open fires, seats from high-backed settles to red plush armchairs on carpet, lots of nooks and crannies, soft lighting, impressive woodwork and some bric-a-brac, comfortable dining rooms; children and dogs welcome, picnic-sets at front and in side beer garden, short walk from Leeds & Liverpool Canal, footpath to Hoghton Tower, open all day weekends. *(Anon)*

ROCHDALE   SD8913
Baum (01706) 352186
Toad Lane; OL12 0NU Plenty of old-fashioned charm, seven well kept changing ales and lots of bottled beers, good value food all day (Sun till 6pm) from sandwiches and tapas up including daily roast, bare boards, old advertising signs, conservatory; garden with pétanque, Co-op Museum next door, open all day. *(Anon)*

ROMILEY   SJ9390
Duke of York (0161) 430 2806
Stockport Road; SK6 3AN Popular old pub (former coaching inn) refurbished by newish licences but keeping character, five well kept beers including Thwaites and Wells & Youngs (Oct beer festival), good food at reasonable prices in beamed bar and upstairs restaurant, friendly efficient staff; seats out in front behind white picket fence. *(Dennis Jones, Alan Smith and others)*

ROMILEY   SJ9390
Platform 1 (0161) 406 8686
Stockport Road; SK6 4BN Recently revamped in modern/traditional style, open and airy with tiled floor, some high tables and chairs, six mostly local ales including a well priced house beer, enjoyable good value pubby food from sandwiches up, bargain OAP lunch, good friendly service, carpeted upstairs restaurant called Platform 2; small outside seating area, open all day. *(Dennis Jones)*

RUFFORD   SD4615
Hesketh Arms (01704) 821009
Junction of Liverpool Road (A59) and Holmeswood Road (B5246); L40 1SB Old beamed pub with modernised open-plan interior arranged into distinct areas, pictures and bric-a-brac, good choice of well kept ales from smaller local breweries, enjoyable predominantly pubby food (some with a modern twist) but also specials like scallops with pea risotto; short walk from Leeds &

Liverpool Canal, and handy for Rufford Old Hall (NT). *(Clive and Fran Dutson)*

SIMISTER   SD8305
Same Yet (0161) 653 1430
Simister Lane; M25 2SF Two-bar Lees local with their ales kept well, tasty attractively priced pub food all day, light and airy dining extension at back with good views over the moors, darts; children welcome, outside tables and play area. *(Gerry and Rosemary Dobson)*

SLAIDBURN   SD7152
Hark to Bounty (01200) 446246
B6478 N of Clitheroe; BB7 3EP Attractive old stone-built pub with homely linked rooms, enjoyable fresh food (all day Sun) from sandwiches and light dishes up, friendly young staff, four real ales including Theakstons, decent wines and whiskies, comfortable chairs by open fire, games room one end, restaurant the other; pleasant back garden, charming Forest of Bowland village, good walks, nine bedrooms, open all day. *(Anon)*

SOUTHPORT   SD3317
Sir Henry Segrave (01704) 530217
Lord Street; PR8 1RH Well placed comfortable Wetherspoons with a dozen well cared for beers and their usual good value food, efficient friendly service; children welcome, tables out on pavement, open all day from 8am. *(Anon)*

STALYBRIDGE   SJ9896
Waggon & Horses (01457) 764837
Mottram Road; SK15 2SU Popular family-run pub-restaurant with wide choice of enjoyable reasonably priced food, four well kept Robinsons ales and plenty of wines by the glass, Thurs quiz; children welcome. *(Dennis Jones)*

STANDISH   SD5711
Crown (08000) 686678
Not far from M6 junction 27; Platt Lane; WN1 2XF Multi-room country pub with comfortable panelled bar, eight changing ales kept in top condition by enthusiastic landlord (tasters offered, regular festivals), several bottled continentals, good choice of food all day including home-made pies and daily roast, various offers, airy dining extension and pleasant conservatory; children allowed away from bar, ten comfortable clean bedrooms. *(Simon J Barber)*

STOCKPORT   SJ8990
★ Arden Arms (0161) 480 2185
Millgate Street/Corporation Street, opposite pay car park; SK1 2LX Cheerful Victorian pub in handsome dark brick building, several well preserved high-ceilinged rooms off island bar (one tiny old-fashioned snug accessed through servery), tiling, panelling and two coal fires,

good sensibly priced food (not Mon and Tues evenings) from lunchtime sandwiches to interesting specials, half a dozen well kept Robinsons ales, friendly efficient service; background music; tables in sheltered courtyard with much-used smokers' shelter, open all day. *(Dennis Jones, Brian and Anna Marsden, Steve Hampson)*

STOCKPORT   SJ8990
Crown   (0161) 429 0549
Heaton Lane, Heaton Norris; SK4 1AR Partly open-plan Victorian pub popular for its well kept changing ales (minimum of 12), also bottled beers and real cider, three cosy lounge areas off bar, spotless stylish décor, wholesome bargain lunches, darts; frequent live music; tables in cobbled courtyard, huge viaduct above. *(G D K Fraser, Dennis Jones)*

STOCKPORT   SJ8890
Magnet   (0161) 429 6287
Wellington Road North; SK4 1HJ Over half a dozen well kept ales including own Cellar Rat beers, pool and juke box in one of the five rooms, regular events including comedy and quiz nights; open all day Fri-Sun, from 4pm other days. *(Dennis Jones, Helen McGlasson)*

STOCKPORT   SJ8890
Nursery   (0161) 432 2044
Green Lane, Heaton Norris; off A6; SK4 2NA Popular 1930s pub on narrow cobbled lane (E end of N part of Green Lane), enjoyable straightforward lunchtime food from kitchen servery on right, friendly efficient service, well kept Hydes, big bays of banquettes in panelled stained-glass front lounge, brocaded wall banquettes in back one; children welcome if eating, immaculate bowling green behind, open all day. *(Anon)*

STOCKPORT   SJ8990
Queens Head   (0161) 480 0725
Little Underbank (can be reached by steps from St Petersgate); SK1 1JT Splendid Victorian restoration, long and narrow, with charming separate snug and back dining area, rare brass cordials fountain, double bank of spirits taps and old spirit lamps, old posters and adverts, reasonably priced lunchtime snacks, bargain Sam Smiths, daily papers, good friendly bustle, bench seating and bare boards; famous tiny gents' upstairs; open all day, till 7pm Sun. *(Anon)*

STOCKPORT   SJ8990
Railway   (0161) 429 6062
Avenue Street (just off M63 junction 13, via A560); SK1 2BZ Bright and airy L-shaped bar with up to 15 real ales (always a mild), lots of foreign beers, farm cider, friendly staff, no food, old Stockport and railway photographs, bar billiards; tables out behind, open all day. *(Dennis Jones)*

STOCKPORT   SJ8990
★ Red Bull   (0161) 480 1286
Middle Hillgate; SK1 3AY Steps up to friendly well run pub, beamed bar with dark panelling and wood floor, various areas off, well kept Robinsons ales from traditional island servery, good value home-cooked food; background and some live music, Weds quiz; four bedrooms, open all day. *(Anon)*

STOCKPORT   SJ8990
Swan With Two Necks
(0161) 480 2341   *Princes Street; SK1 1RY* Traditional narrow pub with welcoming local atmosphere, front panelled bar, back room with button-back wall benches, stone fireplace and skylight, drinking corridor, lunchtime food (not Sun, Mon) from sandwiches up, Robinsons ales; small outside area, open all day till 7pm (6pm Sun). *(Anon)*

STRINES   SJ9686
Sportsmans Arms   (0161) 427 2888
B6101 Marple–New Mills; SK6 7GE Well cared for roadside local with panoramic Goyt Valley view from picture-window lounge bar, good changing ale range, enjoyable well priced home-made food including specials board, small separate bar, log fire, some live music; children and dogs welcome, tables out on side decking, heated smokers' shelter, open all day weekends. *(Anon)*

TATHAM   SD6169
Tatham Bridge Inn   (01524) 221326
B6480, off A683 Lancaster–Kirkby Lonsdale; LA2 8NL Busy old pub with cosy low-beamed bar, well kept ales and good range of enjoyable food, friendly staff, dining room along corridor; bedrooms. *(Vicki Trowler)*

TYLDESLEY   SD6902
Mort Arms   (01942) 883481
Elliott Street; M29 8DG Holts ales in two-room 1930s pub, etched glass and polished panelling, comfortable lounge with old local photographs, friendly staff and regulars, darts and dominoes; nice back terrace, open all day. *(Simon Minshall)*

WEST KIRBY   SJ2186
White Lion   (0151) 625 9037
Grange Road (A540); CH48 4EE Friendly proper pub in interesting 18th-c sandstone building, several small beamed areas on different levels, Black Sheep, Courage Director and a couple of quickly changing guests, good value simple bar lunches (not Sun), coal stove; no children; attractive secluded back garden up steep

---

We say if we know a pub allows dogs.

stone steps, fish pond, open all day.
(MLR, C A Bryson)

WHEATLEY LANE   SD8338

✶**Sparrowhawk** (01282) 603034

Wheatley Lane Road; towards E end of village road, which runs N of and parallel to A6068; one way of reaching it is to follow 'Fence, Newchurch 1¾' signpost, then turn off at 'Barrowford ¾' signpost; BB12 9QG Comfortably civilised 1930s feel in imposing black and white pub with quirky domed stained-glass skylight, oak panelling, parquet flooring and leather tub chairs, well kept Bass, Greene King, Thwaites and a couple of guests, draught Fransizkaner wheat beer and nice wines by the glass from cushioned leatherette counter, good imaginative bar food (all day weekends), friendly if not always speedy service from smart young staff, daily papers and board games; background music, TV; children welcome, dogs in bar, heavy wooden tables on spacious front terrace with good views to the moors beyond Nelson and Colne, open all day. *(John and Eleanor Holdsworth, Dr Kevan Tucker, Rachel and Ross Gavin)*

WHEELTON   SD6021

✶**Dressers Arms** (01254) 830041

Briers Brow; off A674, 2.1 miles from M61 junction 8; PR6 8HD Traditional pub in converted cottage, eight real ales, popular pubby food (all day weekends, Sun carvery), snug low-beamed rooms with simple furnishings on patterned carpets, handsome woodburner, newspapers and magazines, restaurant; background music, games machine, TV and pool; children welcome till 9pm, dogs allowed in bar, picnic-sets under large umbrella on heated front terrace, open all day till 12.30am (midnight Sun). *(Anon)*

WHEELTON   SD5921

Top Lock (01257) 263376

Copthurst Lane, by canal; PR6 8LS Picturesque spot by Leeds & Liverpool Canal; well kept Coniston Bluebird and eight guest ales (beer festivals), enjoyable inexpensive food all day including Tues curry night, prompt friendly service, canal-related décor, upstairs ice-cream parlour, live music Thurs; children welcome, no dogs inside, seats out in front and behind. *(Anon)*

WISWELL   SD7437

✶**Freemasons Arms** (01254) 822218

Village signposted off A671 and A59 NE of Whalley; pub on Vicarage Fold, a gravelled pedestrian passage between Pendleton Road and Old Back Lane in village centre (don't expect to park very close); BB7 9DF Civilised dining place with informal feel of an upmarket pub; rugs on polished flagstones, carved oak settles and attractive mix of chairs around handsome stripped or salvaged tables (all beautifully laid), lots of sporting antique prints on cream

or pastel walls, open fires and woodburner, more rooms upstairs, really good food from lunchtime sandwiches to restaurant dishes (not Sun evening, Mon), competent service from neatly uniformed young staff, well kept ales such as Bank Top, Moorhouses and Tirril, excellent choice of wines by the glass from good list; dogs allowed in bar, candlelit tables under awning on heated front terrace, open all day weekends, closed first two weeks of Jan. *(Dr Kevan Tucker, W K Wood)*

WORSLEY   SD7500

Barton Arms (0161) 728 6157

Stablefold; just off Barton Road (B5211, handy for M60 junction 13); M28 2ED Bright clean Ember Inn, popular and friendly, with good value food, well kept Black Sheep, Timothy Taylors Landlord and guests; children welcome in dining areas, open all day. *(Gerry and Rosemary Dobson)*

WRIGHTINGTON   SD5011

✶**Rigbye Arms** (01257) 462354

3 miles from M6 junction 27; off A5209 via Robin Hood Lane and left into High Moor Lane; WN6 9QB 17th-c dining pub in attractive moorland setting, welcoming and relaxed, with wide choice of good sensibly priced food (all day Sun) including game menu, hot and cold sandwiches too, friendly prompt service even when busy, well kept Black Sheep, Tetleys and Timothy Taylors, decent wines, several carpeted rooms including cosy tap room, open fires, separate evening restaurant (Weds-Sat); children welcome, garden, bowling green, regular car club meetings, open all day Sun. *(David Heath, Will Hancox)*

WRIGHTINGTON BAR   SD5313

✶**Corner House** (01257) 451400

B5250, N of M6 junction 27; WN6 9SE Light, airy and well maintained restaurant pub, very good food (all day weekends) from traditional to more upscale choices, light lunch and early-bird menus too, a couple of real ales and good quality wines, plenty of tables in different refurbished areas; children welcome, seats outside. *(Margaret and Jeff Graham)*

YEALAND CONYERS   SD5074

New Inn (01524) 732938

3 miles from M6 junction 35; village signed off A6; LA5 9SJ Welcoming ivy-covered 17th-c village pub; traditionally furnished cosy beamed bar, log fire, Robinsons ales and a guest, good choice of malt whiskies, two communicating dining rooms serving enjoyable good value pubby food; children welcome, dogs in bar, picnic-sets in enclosed garden, smokers' shelter, usefully positioned for walks through Leighton Moss RSPB reserve and up Warton Crag, open all day. *(Brian and Anna Marsden, Tony and Maggie Harwood, Richard Cox)*

Leicestershire
and Rutland

There are plenty of really good, well run pubs here, often in handsome buildings and with first class food too. Our readers have particularly enjoyed the Three Horse Shoes at Breedon on the Hill (super food and their own farm shop), Olive Branch in Clipsham (an exceptional all-rounder), George in Coleorton (open nearly all day and handy for the M1), Fox & Hounds in Exton (civilised and with food cooked by the italian landlord), Marquess of Exeter at Lyddington (stylish and popular with landlord-cooked food), Grainstore in Oakham (ten own-brewed ales), Lord Nelson in Oakham (lots to look at, super value pizzas and five real ales), White Swan in Sileby (long-serving landlord and tasty, homely food), Red Lion in Stathern (sister pub to the Olive Branch and a first class place), Griffin in Swithland (always something going on, plus weekend breakfasts and all-day Sunday roasts), Kings Arms in Wing (own-made bread and ice-creams and have their own smokehouse) and Wheatsheaf in Woodhouse Eaves (cheerful and friendly with interesting flying memorabilia). New finds include the Cow & Plough in Oadby (extraordinary breweriana and fine choice of ales) and Star at Thrussington (notably well run and neatly refurbished). The very special Olive Branch in Clipsham (with sister pub the Red Lion in Stathern snapping at its heels) is our Leicestershire Dining Pub 2014.

 BREEDON ON THE HILL   SK4022   Map 7
Three Horse Shoes
Main Street (A453); DE73 8AN

Comfortable pub with friendly licensees and emphasis on popular food

This thoroughly enjoyable and thoughtfully run 18th-c dining pub began life as a farriers. It's been nicely restored and decorated to make the best of its attractive structure. The clean-cut central bar has a stylishly simple feel with heavy worn flagstones, green walls and ceilings, a log fire, pubby tables and a dark wood counter, Marstons Pedigree on handpump, 30 malt whiskies and decent house wines; staff are chatty and helpful. Beyond is a dining room with maroon walls, dark pews and tables. The two-room dining area on the right has a comfortably civilised chatty feel, with big antique tables set quite closely together on seagrass matting and colourful modern country prints and antique engravings on canary yellow walls. Even at lunchtime there are lit candles in elegant modern holders. The farm shop sells their own and other local produce – eggs, jams, meat, smoked foods, chocolates. Look out for the quaint conical village lock-up opposite.

Interesting food includes sandwiches, rabbit terrine with cumberland sauce, mushroom stroganoff, sausages with mash and onion gravy, creamy pork and cider casserole, beef hotpot with yorkshire pudding, duck breast with cabbage and whisky, lamb shank in rosemary gravy with parsnip mash, salmon with sweet potato curry, and puddings like chocolate whisky trifle and bread and butter pudding. *Benchmark main dish: beer-battered fish and chips £10.75. Two-course evening meal £22.00.*

Free house ~ Licensees Ian Davison, Jennie Ison and Stuart Marson ~ Real ale ~ (01332) 695129 ~ Open 11.30-2.30, 5.30-11; 12-3 Sun; closed Sun evening ~ Bar food 12-2, 5.30-9; 12-3 Sun ~ Restaurant ~ Children welcome ~ Dogs allowed in bar ~ www.thehorseshoes.com *Recommended by David and Sue Atkinson, Dr Brian and Mrs Anne Hamilton, Mike and Mary Carter, GSB, Peter J and Avril Hanson, R T and J C Moggridge*

BUCKMINSTER   SK8822 Map 7

Tollemache Arms 🍴 £

B676 Colsterworth–Melton Mowbray; Main Street; NG33 5SA

Emphasis on good food in stylishly updated pub run by two enthusiastic young couples

Just a few miles from the A1 and handy for a lunchtime stop, this stone and brick building – surprisingly stately for a village pub – serves interesting, good value food. One elegant corner room has comfortable easy chairs around a log fire, and quite a library of books. Other linked areas contain a dark leather chesterfield by a low table of magazines and newspapers in another fireside corner, and otherwise there's a mix of wheelback, dining and stripped kitchen chairs and some nice specially made small pews around tables set on floorboards; table lamps and standard lamps, big bunches of flowers and board games add a homely touch, and they don't turn up their noses at dogs or muddy boots. There's a good choice of wines by the glass and Oakham JHB and Tring Jack O'Legs on handpump; perhaps discreet nostalgic background music. On the back grass, by a clump of sycamores, are plenty of teak tables; beyond is a small herb and salad garden and a swing.

As well as tasty nibbles, pie nights and a takeaway menu, the popular food might include sandwiches, pigeon breast, parma ham, poached fruit and peanut salad, moules marinière, butternut, spinach and goats cheese open ravioli, toulouse sausage and wholegrain mustard mash, salmon en croûte with garlic and lemon potatoes, duck breast with sweet potato chips and beetroot salad, and puddings such as ginger beer roulade and rhubarb compote and chocolate mousse with honeycomb and marshmallow. *Benchmark main dish: fish and chips with smashed peas and tartare sauce £9.95. Two-course evening meal £18.00.*

Free house ~ Licensees Matt and Amanda Wrisdale ~ Real ale ~ (01476) 860477 ~ Open 12-3, 6-11; 12-4 Sun; closed Sun evening, Mon ~ Bar food 12-2, 6.30-9; 12-2.30 Sun ~ Restaurant ~ Children welcome ~ Dogs allowed in bar ~ www.tollemache-arms.co.uk *Recommended by Martin Jones*

CLIPSHAM
SK9716 Map 8

Olive Branch ★

Take B668/Stretton exit off A1 N of Stamford; Clipsham signposted E from exit roundabout; LE15 7SH

Leicestershire Dining Pub of the Year

An exceptional place for a drink, a meal or an overnight stay

'It deserves all its awards' and 'the ultimate pub experience' are just two of the enthusiastic reports we've had from readers recently. A first class all-rounder and a special place to stay, too – breakfasts are delicious and the bedrooms extremely comfortable. The various small charmingly attractive rooms have a relaxed country cottage atmosphere, with dark joists and beams, rustic furniture, an interesting mix of pictures (some by local artists), candles on tables and a cosy log fire in a stone inglenook fireplace. Many of the books dotted around (sometimes for sale) were bought at antiques fairs; background music. A carefully chosen range of drinks includes a beer named for the pub and a couple of guests from Sharps or Timothy Taylors on handpump, an enticing wine list (with 16 by the glass), a thoughtful choice of spirits and cocktails, and several different british and continental bottled beers. Outside, there are tables, chairs and big plant pots on a pretty little terrace, with more on the neat lawn, sheltered in the L of its two low buildings. It can get busy at peak times.

Served by smiling, efficient staff, the outstanding food includes a two- and three-course set lunch as well as lunchtime sandwiches, twice-baked cheese soufflé with pear and walnut salad, seared pigeon with jerusalem artichoke mousse and braised puy lentils, wild mushroom and truffle risotto, local sausages with english mustard mash, smoked haddock with bubble and squeak cake, poached egg and parsley sauce, honey-roast duck breast with confit leg boulangère and turnip fondant, slow-roasted pork shoulder with beef dripping roast potatoes, apple sauce and crackling and puddings such as chocolate and hazelnut mousse with caramelised bananas and steamed seville orange marmalade pudding with liquorice ice-cream. *Benchmark main dish: honey-roast pork belly with cider and fondant potatoes £16.50. Two-course evening meal £22.50.*

Free house ~ Licensees Sean Hope and Ben Jones ~ Real ale ~ (01780) 410355 ~ Open 12-3, 6-11; 12-11 Sat; 12-4, 6-10.30 Sun ~ Bar food 12-2(2.15 Sat), 6.30(7 Sat)-9.30; 12-2.45, 7-9 Sun ~ Restaurant ~ Children welcome ~ Dogs allowed in bar and bedrooms ~ Bedrooms: £112.50/£135 ~ www.theolivebranchpub.com *Recommended by Michael Sargent, Jamie and Sue May, Gordon and Margaret Ormondroyd, Hugo Jeune, Michael Doswell, M and GR, Bob and Tanya Ekers*

COLEORTON
SK4117 Map 7

George
Loughborough Road (A512 E); LE67 8HF

Attractively traditional homely pub with dining area, honest food and drink and large garden

This comfortable pub is open all day (except for a couple of hours in the afternoon), so it's ideal for a break from the M1; do book at peak times as it's very popular. There's a good welcoming atmosphere, and the bar on the right is nicely laid out to give the feel of varied smallish separate areas: a dark leather sofa and tub chairs by a woodburning stove in front, scatter-cushioned pews and mixed chairs below shelves of books in one corner and mixed seating elsewhere. This room has lots of local photographs on ochre or dove-grey walls, black beams and joists and a dark-panelled dado. A bigger room on the left, broadly similar and also with plenty to look at, has another woodburning stove and more of a dining-room feel. Black Sheep, Burton Bridge Bitter and Marstons Pedigree on handpump, served by cheerful, efficient staff. The spreading garden behind has sturdy wooden furniture among sizeable trees, and a play area.

 Honest and fair-priced food includes panini, chicken liver pâté with onion marmalade, devilled whitebait, butternut squash, chilli and coconut curry, chicken with barbecue sauce, bacon and cheddar cheese, fresh fish and chips, lambs liver and bacon with shallot and red wine gravy, whole lemon sole with creamy leek and white wine sauce, and puddings. *Benchmark main dish: steak in ale pie £10.95. Two-course evening meal £17.00.*

Free house ~ Licensees Mark and Janice Wilkinson ~ Real ale ~ (01530) 834639 ~ Open 12-3, 5.30-11; 12-11 Fri, Sat; 12-4 Sun; closed Sun evening, Mon ~ Bar food 12-2.30, 6-9(9.30 Fri, Sat); 12-3 Sun ~ Restaurant ~ Well behaved supervised children welcome ~ Dogs allowed in bar ~ www.georgeinncoleorton.co.uk *Recommended by Lucien Perring*

COTTESMORE
Sun 🍴 £
SK9013   Map 7

B668 NE of Oakham; LE15 7DH

Nice village pub with friendly staff and reasonably priced food

A comfortable and attractive 17th-c thatched and white-painted village pub popular for its reasonably priced food and drink. Décor is simple and homely, with stripped pine and plush stools on flagstones, an inglenook fire and lots of pictures and ornaments. The carpeted back restaurant has white walls and dark wheelback chairs. Friendly staff serve Bath Golden Hare, Everards Beacon, Brunswick Triple Hop and Shardlow Reverend Eatons Ale on handpump, six wines by the glass and ten malt whiskies; background music. There are picnic-sets in front of the building with more in the large garden.

 As well as a two- and three-course set menu, the fairly priced food (several main courses cost under £10) includes baps and baguettes, smoked duck and pork terrine with sweet chilli jam, smoked salmon and prawns in marie rose sauce, wild mushroom risotto with balsamic syrup, burger with gherkins, cheese, bacon and chips, local sausages in red wine and onion gravy with yorkshire pudding, beer-battered haddock, lamb and chickpea curry, pies (venison or chicken and leek), and puddings such as profiteroles with hot chocolate sauce and pear and ginger pudding with custard. *Benchmark main dish: steak and mushroom in ale pie £9.50. Two-course evening meal £14.00.*

Everards ~ Tenants Neil and Karen Hornsby ~ Real ale ~ (01572) 812321 ~ Open 11.30-11(10 Sun) ~ Bar food 12-2, 6-9; 12-3, 6-8 Sun ~ Restaurant ~ Children welcome ~ Dogs allowed in bar ~ www.everards.co.uk *Recommended by Barry Collett, Pat and Stewart Gordon*

EXTON
Fox & Hounds 🍴 🛏
SK9211   Map 7

The Green; signed off A606 Stamford–Oakham; LE15 8AP

Well run, friendly inn with comfortable lounge bar, real ales, popular food and quiet garden; bedrooms

The licensees here – Mrs Floris is front of house and Mr Floris is the chef – are warmly friendly and their staff helpful and polite. The handsome inn, by the village green, has a genteel atmosphere, and the comfortable high-ceilinged lounge bar is traditionally civilised with dark red plush easy chairs and wheelback seats around lots of pine tables, maps and hunting prints on the walls, fresh flowers and a winter log fire in a large stone fireplace. Grainstore Ten Fifty, Greene King IPA and a changing guest beer on handpump, and several wines by the glass; TV and background music. The lovely sheltered walled garden has seats among large rose beds overlooking pretty paddocks. If you stay in the spotlessly clean bedrooms, the breakfasts are very good. It's handy for Rutland Water and the gardens at Barnsdale.

Cooked by the landlord, the highly thought-of food includes sandwiches, avocado and crayfish salad, chicken liver pâté with chutney, deli boards to share, lots of pizzas, home-made tagliatelle with bolognese sauce, local sausages with creamy mash and onion gravy, beer-battered fresh cod and fries, gammon with pineapple and egg, slow-cooked pork belly with wholegrain mustard mash and red cabbage, and puddings. *Benchmark main dish: coq au vin £13.95. Two-course evening meal £18.00.*

Free house ~ Licensees Valter and Sandra Floris ~ Real ale ~ (01572) 812403 ~ Open 11-3, 6-11; 11-11 Sat, Sun ~ Bar food 12-2, 6.30-9; all day weekends ~ Restaurant ~ Children welcome ~ Dogs allowed in bar and bedrooms ~ Bedrooms: £55/£80 ~ www.foxandhoundsrutland.co.uk *Recommended by Marcus Mann, Barry Collett, Mike Proctor, M Mossman, Mrs S Hewitt, Lois Dyer, Dr A J and Mrs B A Tompsett*

LEICESTER

Rutland & Derby Arms £

SK5804 Map 4

Millstone Lane; nearby metered parking; LE1 5JN

Neatly kept modern town bar with interesting food, impressive drinks range and sheltered courtyard

With four real ales on handpump and bottled beers from all over the world, this city tavern has a good bustling atmosphere: Adnams Broadside, three beers from Everards and a guest such as Wells & Youngs Bombardier on handpump, a farm cider, 20 wines by the glass, 20 whiskies and an impressive array of spirits and cocktails, served by bright, pleasant staff. The open-plan interior has a pleasing clean-cut modernity, with comfortable bar chairs by the long counter, padded high seats including an unusual high banquette by chunky tall tables, a few small prints of classic film posters; apart from some stripped brick, décor is in shades of ochre and coffee. Well reproduced background music and a games machine. The neat cream-walled courtyard shelters sunny picnic-sets, with more on an upper terrace.

Usefully served all day, the much liked food includes tapas such as salt cod croquettes with wasabi dip or sticky chicken wings, baguettes, popular pizzas with various toppings, burger with barbecue relish and fries, chicken katsu curry with pickled ginger, asparagus, broad bean and roasted garlic risotto and rib-eye steak with herb butter and chips. *Benchmark main dish: flatbread pizza with chorizo and smoked applewood cheese £8.95. Two-course evening meal £13.95.*

Everards ~ Tenant Samuel Hagger ~ Real ale ~ (0116) 2623299 ~ Open 12-11; closed Sun ~ Bar food 12-9 ~ Children welcome ~ Acoustic music last Fri of month ~ www.therutlandandderby.co.uk *Recommended by Emma Scofield, Harvey Brown*

Half pints: by law, a pub should not charge more for half a pint than half the price of a full pint, unless it shows that half-pint price on its price list.

LYDDINGTON

SP8797 Map 4

Marquess of Exeter 🍴 ℗

Main Street; LE15 9LT

Stone inn with contemporary décor, real ales and excellent food cooked by the landlord

Booking is essential at this handsome place as it's so very popular. The spacious open-plan areas are laid out with understated stylish furnishings – the fine flagstone floors, thick walls, beams and exposed stonework are left to speak for themselves. There's a mix of old tables and chairs, smart fabrics, leather sofas, pine chests and old barrels that might always have been here. In winter, the place is warmed by several open fires – one a quite striking structure in dark iron. Brakspears Bitter and Marstons Pedigree on handpump and around a dozen wines by the glass. There are seats on a terrace and picnic-sets in tree-sheltered gardens that seem to merge with the countryside beyond. The pub is named after the Burghley family, which has long owned this charming village (Burghley House is about 15 miles away).

Impressive food includes sandwiches, crispy salt and chilli squid, chicken liver parfait with fig chutney, king prawn, spinach and chilli linguine, lemon chicken with grilled aubergines and crispy fennel, pea, summer greens and parmesan risotto, calves liver with shallots and lemon and sage dressing, grilled rib of beef with béarnaise sauce (for two) and puddings such as dark chocolate tart with poached pears and white chocolate ice-cream and apricot upside-down cake with vanilla ice-cream. *Benchmark main dish: flat-iron steak with frites £15.95. Two-course evening meal £22.00.*

Marstons ~ Lease Brian Baker ~ Real ale ~ (01572) 822477 ~ Open 10am-11pm (10.30pm Sun) ~ Bar food 12-6(3 Sun), 6.30-9.30(9 Sun) ~ Restaurant ~ Well behaved children welcome ~ Dogs allowed in bar and bedrooms ~ Live music last Sun of month ~ Bedrooms: £70.50/£99.50 ~ www.marquessexeter.co.uk *Recommended by Mike and Margaret Banks, Dr A J and Mrs B A Tompsett*

OADBY

SK6202 Map 4

Cow & Plough

Gartree Road (B667 N of centre); LE2 2FB

Fantastic collection of brewery memorabilia, seven real ales and good bar food

Converted from an old farm and dairy buildings about 20 years ago, this interesting place has a few original individual rooms and an extensive long, light front extension with flagstones. Two of the original dark back rooms, known as the Vaults, contain an extraordinary collection of brewery memorabilia (almost every piece has a story behind it): enamel signs and mirrors advertising long-forgotten brews, an aged brass cash register, and furnishings and fittings salvaged from pubs and even churches (there's some splendid stained glass behind the counter). One section has descriptions of all Leicester's pubs. The front extension has plenty of plants and fresh flowers, a piano, beams liberally covered with hops, and a real mix of traditionally pubby tables and chairs with lots of green leatherette sofas and small circular cast-iron tables. The conservatory also has a fine collection of brewery and pub signs and the like, and a very eclectic mix of chairs and tables. An excellent range of seven real ales on handpump includes Steamin' Billy Bitter and Skydiver plus guest beers from breweries such as Abbeydale,

Dark Horse, Great Heck, Oakham and Powerhouse – as well as a dozen country wines, several wines by the glass and up to six ciders. TV, darts, board games and background music. There are picnic-sets outside in the old yard.

🍴 Using local produce, the popular food includes sandwiches, duck liver parfait with apricot chutney, quail scotch egg with pigs head croquettes and wholegrain mustard mayonnaise, sausages with mash and onion gravy, pie of the day, honey-roast ham and eggs, chargrilled vegetable tarte tatin with vine tomato confit, beer-battered cod with chips, chicken and wild mushrooms in cream and tarragon port sauce, bacon-wrapped saddle of rabbit with honey and mustard sauce, and puddings like chocolate brownie with chocolate sauce and cheesecake of the day. *Benchmark main dish: Thursday evening pie night for two £16.00. Two-course evening meal £21.00.*

Free house ~ Licensee Barry Lount ~ Real ale ~ (0116) 272 0852 ~ Open 12-11 ~ Bar food 12-2, 6-9; 12-4 Sun ~ Restaurant ~ Children welcome ~ Dogs welcome ~ Live jazz Weds lunchtime ~ www.steamin-billy.co.uk *Recommended by Barry Collett*

OAKHAM
Grainstore 🍺 £
SK8509   Map 4

Station Road, off A606; LE15 6RE

Super own-brewed beers in a converted railway grain warehouse, cheerful customers and pubby food

The Grainstore Brewery tours here are popular, but must be booked ahead. It's an interesting place – a former Victorian grain store – and most customers are here to try the own-brewed beers; the staff will usually let you taste a sample or two before you decide. There are ten beers – served traditionally at the left end of the bar counter, and through swan necks with sparklers on the right. As per the traditional tower system of production, the beer is brewed on the upper floors of the building directly above the down-to-earth bar; during working hours, you'll hear the busy noises of the brewery rumbling overhead. Takeaways are offered and there's a beer festival with over 80 real ales and live music during the August Bank Holiday weekend. Décor is plain and functional, with wide well worn floorboards, bare ceiling boards above massive joists supported by red metal pillars, a long brick-built bar counter with cast-iron bar stools, tall cask tables and simple elm chairs; games machine, darts, board games, giant Jenga and bottle-walking. In summer, the huge glass doors are pulled back, opening on to a terrace with picnic-sets (and often stacked with barrels). Disabled access.

🍴 Tasty, straightforward food (including weekend breakfasts 9-11.30am) includes sandwiches and rolls, devilled crispy whitebait, ham hock and black pudding terrine, beef or chicken burgers, mediterranean vegetable lasagne, steak, stout and stilton pie, cajun salmon with crushed new potatoes, sausages with mustard mash and onion gravy, hot and spicy chicken wings and legs and a Wednesday evening pie-and-pint deal. *Benchmark main dish: beef and mushroom in ale pie £8.45.*

Own brew ~ Licensee Peter Atkinson ~ Real ale ~ (01572) 770065 ~ Open 11-11 (midnight Fri); 9am-midnight Sat; 9am-10.30pm Sun ~ Bar food 11.30(9 weekends)-3; no evening food except Weds ~ Children welcome till 8pm ~ Dogs welcome ~ Live music twice a month ~ www.grainstorebrewery.com *Recommended by Jim Farmer, Barry Collett, Andy Lickfold, David Jackman, J F M and M West*

It's very helpful if you let us know up-to-date food prices when you report on pubs.

OAKHAM

SK8608 Map 4

Lord Nelson ★ ♀ ◀

Market Place; LE15 6DT

Splendidly restored as proper relaxed grown-up pub, full of interest; open all day from 9am and with excellent pizzas

Look round this handsome old building before you decide where to sit as there are over half a dozen rooms spread over two floors, giving plenty of companionable places for chatty relaxation. Choose from cushioned church pews, leather elbow chairs, long oak settles, sofas, armchairs – or, to watch the passing scene, a big bow window seat. Floors are carpet, bare boards or ancient red and black tiles; walls come in soft shades of ochre, canary yellow, sage or pink paintwork, or William Morris wallpaper. There's plenty to look at, from intriguing antique Police News and other prints – plenty of Nelson, of course – to the collections of Mullers, copper kettles and other homely bric-a-brac in the heavy-beamed former kitchen with its Aga. But the key thing is the easy-going, good-natured atmosphere. Fullers London Pride, Harveys Best and guests like Abbeydale Daily Bread and Faith Book and Hambleton Final Furlong on handpump; also Weston's farm cider and a good changing choice of wines by the glass. Staff are helpful, efficient and clearly love working here. The resident king charles spaniel is called Buzz.

Proper stone-cooked pizzas are the focus and you can choose your own toppings; also, focaccia sandwiches, sharing antipasti and cheese boards, smoked haddock rarebit, pork steak and chickpea cassoulet, roasted pepper and pesto quiche, roasted salmon niçoise salad, beef pie with horseradish bubble and squeak, barbecue plate (pork ribs, lamb chop, sausages, rump steak) with roasted sweetcorn, coleslaw and potato salad, and puddings. *Benchmark main dish: pizza with duck, hoisin sauce, spring onion and mozzarella £9.50. Two-course evening meal £16.00.*

Free house ~ Licensee Adam Dale ~ Real ale ~ (01572) 868340 ~ Open 10am-11pm(midnight Fri, Sat); 12-11 Sun ~ Bar food 12-2.30, 6-9; not Sun evening ~ Restaurant ~ Over-4s allowed till 8pm away from bar; no pushchairs ~ Dogs allowed in bar ~ Live jazz every other Sun ~ www.thelordnelsonoakham.com
Recommended by G Jennings, J F M and M West, John and Sylvia Harrop

PEGGS GREEN

SK4117 Map 7

New Inn £

Signposted off A512 Ashby–Shepshed at roundabout, then turn immediately left down Zion Hill towards Newbold; pub is 100 metres down on the right, with car park opposite; LE67 8JE

Intriguing bric-a-brac in unspoilt pub, friendly welcome, good value food and drinks; cottagey garden

Quirky, with genial irish licensees and chatty customers, this is a simple and unspoilt little pub. The two cosy tiled front rooms contain a diverting collection of old bric-a-brac that covers almost every inch of the walls and ceilings. The little room on the left, a bit like an old kitchen parlour (called the Cabin), has china on the mantelpiece, lots of prints and photographs and sundry collections, three old cast-iron tables, wooden stools and a small stripped kitchen table. The room to the right has nice stripped panelling and another lot of appealing bric-a-brac. The small back 'Best' room, with stripped-wood floor, has a touching display of old local photographs including colliery ones. Bass, Marstons Pedigree and a guest beer on handpump; background music and board games. There are plenty of seats out in front, with more in the peaceful back garden. Do note the unusual opening times.

🍴 Unbelievably cheap food includes hot and cold cobs, baked potatoes, ham and eggs, omelettes, corned beef hash, sausages in onion gravy, steak pie and daily specials. *Benchmark main dish: faggots and peas £4.95.*

Enterprise ~ Lease Maria Christina Kell ~ Real ale ~ (01530) 222293 ~ Open 12-2.30, 5.30-11; 12-3, 6.30-11 Sat 12-3, 7-10.30 Sun; closed Tues-Thurs lunchtimes ~ Bar food 12-2, 6-8 Mon; 12-2 Fri, Sat; filled rolls might be available at other times ~ Well behaved children only ~ Dogs welcome ~ www.thenewinnpeggsgreen.co.uk *Recommended by Michael Butler*

SILEBY   SK6015   Map 7
White Swan £

Off A6 or A607 N of Leicester; in centre turn into King Street (opposite church), then after mini-roundabout turn right at Post Office signpost into Swan Street; LE12 7NW

Exemplary town local, a boon to its chatty regulars, with good honest home cooking luring others from further afield

What sets this solidly built red-brick pub above thousands of other good locals is the can-do attitude of the helpful staff, and the very popular, good value food. Run by the same licensees for nearly 30 years, it has all the touches that marked the best of between-the-wars estate pub design, such as an art deco-tiled lobby, polychrome-tiled fireplaces, shiny red Anaglypta ceiling and the comfortable layout of linked but separate areas including a small restaurant (now lined with books). Packed with bric-a-brac from bizarre hats to decorative plates and lots of prints, it quickly draws you in with its genuinely bright and cheerful welcome. Fullers London Pride is on handpump, and they stock good value house wines.

🍴 The homely bar food uses carefully chosen ingredients and includes rolls (they bake their own bread), breaded mushrooms with garlic mayonnaise, prawn cocktail, cheese, tomato and mushroom pasta, chicken with barbecue sauce, cheese and bacon, beef and mushroom in ale pie, gammon with egg or pineapple, prawn linguine with chilli and ginger, roast leg of lamb with mediterranean vegetables, and puddings; they also offer a two-course set menu and a weekday light lunch main course for £5. *Benchmark main dish: beef cobbler £10.95. Two-course evening meal £14.00.*

Free house ~ Licensee Theresa Miller ~ Real ale ~ (01509) 814832 ~ Open 12-2, 6-11; 12-3 Sun; closed Mon, lunchtimes Tues, Sat, evening Sun ~ Bar food 12-1.30, 6-8.30 ~ Children welcome ~ www.whiteswansileby.co.uk *Recommended by Rob and Catherine Dunster*

STATHERN   SK7731   Map 7
Red Lion 🍴 ☆ 🍺

Off A52 W of Grantham via the brown-signed Belvoir road (keep on towards Harby – Stathern signposted on left); or off A606 Nottingham–Melton Mowbray via Long Clawson and Harby; LE14 4HS

Fine range of drinks and popular food in country-style dining pub with open fires and good garden with a play area; own shop too

'What a truly special pub,' enthuses one of our more discerning readers. There's a lovely welcoming and informal atmosphere created by the dedicated staff and it's decorated in a charming rustic style. The yellow room on the right, with its collection of wooden spoons and lambing chairs, has a simple country-pub feel. The lounge bar has sofas, an open fire and a big table with books, newspapers and magazines. It leads to a smaller, more traditional flagstoned bar, with terracotta walls, another fireplace with a log pile and lots of beams and hops. A little room with tables set for eating leads to the long, narrow, main dining room, and out to a nicely arranged suntrap lawn and terrace with good hardwood furnishings; background music. Red Lion Ale (from Grainstore) and guests such as Brewsters Belly Dancer, Fullers London Price and Oldershaw Heavenly Blonde on handpump, with a lager from Brewsters, lots of bottled craft beers, cocktails and 16 wines by the glass. There's an unusually big play area behind the car park with swings and climbing frames. Sister pub is the top class Olive Branch in Clipsham.

Using own-grown produce and other carefully sourced ingredients, and with fish and chips on Friday and two- and three-course set menus, the delicious food might include sandwiches, rabbit ballotine with smoked eel and carrots, salad of braised octopus, cannellini beans, olives, chorizo and piquillo peppers, wild mushroom and truffle risotto, local sausages with mash and onions, fish pie, rolled pork belly with rhubarb and turnip gratin, lamb loin with parsnip and raspberry purée, and puddings such as bakewell tart with almond cream and cappuccino mousse with chocolate ice-cream. *Benchmark main dish: 28-day aged rib-eye steak £20.50. Two-course evening meal £20.00.*

Free house ~ Licensees Sean Hope and Ben Jones ~ Real ale ~ (01949) 860868 ~ Open 12-3, 6-11; 12-11 Sat; 12-7.30 Sun; closed Mon ~ Bar food 12-2(3 Sun), 6.30-9 (7-9.30 Sat) ~ Children welcome ~ Dogs allowed in bar ~ Live jazz last Fri of month ~ www.theredlioninn.co.uk *Recommended by Daz Smith, Vivienne Stott, Comus and Sarah Elliott, David Glynne-Jones, Michael Doswell*

STRETTON
Jackson Stops
SK9415 Map 8

Rookery Lane; a mile or less off A1, at B668 (Oakham) exit; follow village sign, turning off Clipsham Road into Manor Road, pub on left; LE15 7RA

Attractive thatched former farmhouse with good food, just off the A1

There are always plenty of happy customers in this 16th-c stone inn – all made welcome by the licensee and his helpful staff. It's a place of great character with meandering rooms filled with lots of lovely period features. The black-beamed country bar on the left has wall timbering, a couple of bar stools, a cushioned wall pew and an elderly settle on the worn tile and brick floor, and a coal fire in one corner. Grainstore Ten Fifty and Cooking on handpump alongside several wines by the glass. The smarter main room on the right is light and airy with a nice mix of ancient and modern tables on dark blue carpet, and a coal fire in a stone corner fireplace. Past the bar is the dining room with stripped-stone walls, a tiled floor and an old open cooking range, and there's a second smaller dining room; background music. The pub has one of the only two nurdling benches (a game involving old pennies) left in Britain.

Good, reasonably priced food includes a two-course set lunch, baguettes, chicken liver parfait with earl grey red onion marmalade, timbale of prawns, trout and lobster with marie rose sauce, beer-battered haddock with chips, cauliflower purée and baby vegetable panache, slow-roasted pork belly, monkfish, mussels and tiger prawn marinière, and puddings such as almond crumble with apple, rhubarb and crème anglaise and sticky toffee pudding with caramel ice-cream. *Benchmark main dish: burgundy beef pie £14.95. Two-course evening meal £19.50.*

Free house ~ Licensee Robert Reid ~ Real ale ~ (01780) 410237 ~ Open 12-3, 6-10.30 (11 Fri, Sat); 12-4 Sun; closed Sun evening, Mon ~ Bar food 12-2.30, 6.30-9(9.30 Fri, Sat) ~ Restaurant ~ Children welcome ~ Dogs allowed in bar ~ www.thejacksonstops.com
Recommended by Arthur Pickering, Pat and Stewart Gordon, Peter and Heather Elliott, Barry Collett, Andy Lickfold, Mike and Margaret Banks, G Jennings, John and Sylvia Harrop

SWITHLAND
Griffin ⌐ SK5512   Map 7

Main Street; between A6 and B5330, between Loughborough and Leicester; LE12 8TJ

A good mix of cheerful customers, well liked food in a well run, busy pub

This is a friendly place where the staff work really hard to please their customers. The three beamed communicating rooms are cosy and traditional, with some panelling, leather armchairs and sofas, cushioned wall seating, a woodburner, a nice mix of wooden tables and chairs, and stools at the counter where Adnams Bitter, Everards Original and Tiger and guests like Holdens Golden Glow and Wells & Youngs Bombardier are kept on handpump, plus a couple of farm ciders, several malt whiskies and wines by the glass from a good list; background music and skittle alley. There are wicker seats on the terrace screened by plants, more seats in the streamside garden overlooking open fields and painted picnic-sets outside the Old Stables. The pub is in a quiet tucked-away village in the heart of Charnwood Forest and is handy for walks in Bradgate Park & Swithland Wood Country Park. Good wheelchair access and disabled facilities.

The highly thought-of food includes sandwiches, tempura king prawns, baked camembert with toasted onion bread and red onion chutney, ham and eggs, battered haddock with chips, mushroom, spinach and tomato frittata, local sausages with rich gravy, moroccan-style lamb tagine with lemon couscous, specials like pork belly with borlotti beans and red wine and shallot jus or beef and venison stew with chive mash and roasted root vegetables, and puddings. *Benchmark main dish: chicken ballotine stuffed with sunblush tomatoes, basil and mozzarella with dauphinoise potatoes £12.95. Two-course evening meal £21.00.*

Everards ~ Tenant John Cooledge ~ Real ale ~ (01509) 890535 ~ Open 9am-11pm (10.30 Sun) ~ Bar food 12-2.30, 5.30-9; 12-2, 6-8.30 Mon; all day Fri-Sun ~ Restaurant ~ Children welcome ~ www.griffininnswithland.co.uk *Recommended by SAB and MJW, Simon and Mandy King, Comus and Sarah Elliott*

THRUSSINGTON
Star ⌐ SK6415   Map 7

Village signposted off A46 N of Syston; The Green; LE7 4UH

Neatly refurbished 18th-c inn overlooking small village green, usefully open all day from breakfast; comfortable new bedrooms

Heavy low stripped beams and broad floorboards show the age of the friendly L-shaped bar, but it's thoroughly up to date on the comfort side, with careful LED lighting, well reproduced relaxing music and stylish contemporary versions of those good-pub staples, the inglenook fireplace and the high-backed settle. There are two cast-iron stoves (one with an inn-side horse print above by the early 19th-c sporting painter John Ferneley, who was born nearby), and a couple of hunting cartoons on the cream walls. They have a well kept house beer on handpump, as well as Mr Grundy's Red Baron and Timothy Taylors Landlord; welcoming efficient staff. The skylit dining room, up a few steps from the bar (with separate level access too), is similar in mood and décor; there are tables under cocktail parasols in the side garden, which has a flagstoned terrace.

Using carefully sourced local produce, the popular food includes sandwiches, chicken and pistachio terrine with fruit chutney, stilton panna cotta with pickled walnuts and roasted plums, honey-roast ham and eggs, local sausages with mash and onion gravy, creamy mushroom pasta, bacon and cheese burger with home-made tomato relish, corn-fed chicken breast with butterbean and chorizo cassoulet, blade of beef with garlic mash and bourguignon sauce, and puddings such as cheesecake or chocolate fondant with pistachio ice-cream; pie night is Monday, fish and chips night Tuesday, steak night Wednesday. *Benchmark main dish: burger with home-made tomato relish, bacon, cheese and chips £9.95. Two-course evening meal £19.00.*

Free house ~ Licensee Robert Smith ~ Real ale ~ (01664) 424220 ~ Open 8am-11pm(midnight Fri, Sat); 9am-11.30pm Sun ~ Bar food 12-2, 6.30-9.30; breakfast 8am-10am; 12-8 Sun ~ Restaurant ~ No children after 8.30pm in bar (but allowed in restaurant) ~ Dogs allowed in bar ~ Bedrooms: £65/£86 ~ www.thestarinn1744.co.uk
Recommended by Paul McQueen, U Dunton, Comus and Sarah Elliott, Tess White, Emma Scofield

 WING   SK8902   Map 4

Kings Arms 🍴 ♀ 🛏

Village signposted off A6003 S of Oakham; Top Street; LE15 8SE

Nicely kept old pub, big log fires, super choice of wines by the glass, good modern cooking and smokehouse

This former farmhouse is an understated civilised place for an enjoyable drink or a meal, but you'll need to book in advance. Long and narrow, the neatly kept, attractive bar is warm and inviting with two large log fires (one in a copper-canopied central hearth), various nooks and crannies, nice old low beams and stripped stone and flagstone or wood-strip floors. Friendly, helpful staff serve nearly three dozen wines by the glass, as well as Grainstore Cooking, a seasonal Grainstore ale and Marstons Pedigree on handpump, several grappas and malt whiskies and a local cider; board games. There are seats out in front, and in the sunny yew-sheltered garden; the car park is spacious. There's a medieval turf maze just up the road, and we're told it's just a couple of miles to one of England's two osprey hotspots.

Making their own bread, biscuits and ice-cream and using their smokehouse for anything from charcuterie to nuts (produce is for sale), the interesting food includes sandwiches, air-dried wild boar with melon, pine nuts and goats cheese, pancake stuffed with chinese-style duck wing, plum sauce, cucumber and spring onions, frittata with a choice of cheese, burger with home-smoked bacon, cheese, sweet chilli ketchup and beef dripping chips, honey and cider ham with free-range eggs, rabbit in pancetta with confit leg and potato croquette, seared monkfish with scallops, tempura pak choi and coconut lime cream, and puddings such as vanilla crème brûlée with berry compote and pistachio cookies and fruit crumble with cinnamon yoghurt ice-cream. *Benchmark main dish: saddle of roe deer with celeriac purée, pancetta crisps and red wine and cranberry jus £16.50. Two-course evening meal £25.00.*

Free house ~ Licensee David Goss ~ Real ale ~ (01572) 737634 ~ Open 12-3, 6.30-11; closed Sun evening, Mon lunchtime; in winter all Mon, Tues lunchtime ~ Bar food 12-2, 6.30-8.30(9 Fri, Sat) ~ Restaurant ~ Children welcome away from bar ~ Dogs allowed in bar and bedrooms ~ Bedrooms: £77.50/£100 ~ www.thekingsarms-wing.co.uk
Recommended by Michael Sargent, O K Smyth, Trevor Single, Alan Johnson, Colin McKerrow

WOODHOUSE EAVES   SK5313   Map 7
Wheatsheaf 🛏

Brand Hill; turn right into Main Street, off B591 S of Loughborough; LE12 8SS

Bustling and friendly country pub, with interesting things to look at, good bistro-type food and a fair choice of drinks; well equipped bedrooms

Readers very much enjoy their visits to this particularly well run and hospitable pub, and the friendly, hands-on licensees manage to strike an easy balance between all aspects – food, beers and bedrooms. The beamed bar areas have a good pubby feel, are traditionally furnished (wooden pews, log fires, daily papers) and full of interesting motor racing and family RAF and flying memorabilia; the cosy dining area (The Mess) even has an RAF Hurricane propeller. It's all very cheerful and chatty, and the kind staff will help with wheelchair access. Adnams Bitter and Broadside, Marstons Pedigree, Thwaites Wainwright and Timothy Taylors Landlord on handpump and around 17 wines by the glass, including champagne, from a thoughtfully compiled list. The floodlit heated terrace has plenty of seating. There's a disabled parking space in the car park.

Enjoyable food includes sandwiches, stilton cheese fondue with walnut bread and pear, prawn cocktail with marie rose sauce, burger with stilton, bacon, dill pickle, onion rings and fries, mixed root vegetable bake with goats cheese, fresh salmon fishcakes with herb sauce, gammon and eggs, spit-roast chicken (plain, garlic, herb, piri-piri) with coleslaw and fries, tuna steak with oriental vegetables and sweet chilli dressing, and puddings. *Benchmark main dish: arbroath smokies with chips £11.95. Two-course evening meal £18.00.*

Free house ~ Licensees Richard and Bridget Dimblebee ~ Real ale ~ (01509) 890320 ~ Open 12-3, 6-11; 12-11 Sat; 12-4 Sun; closed Sun evening ~ Bar food 12-2.30, 6.30-9.30; 12-3 Sun ~ Restaurant ~ Children welcome ~ Dogs allowed in bar and bedrooms ~ Bedrooms: £60/£80 ~ www.wheatsheafinn.net *Recommended by Andy Lickfold, Barry and Anne, Dr Martin Owton, Peter Ridley, Roger and Ann King, Andy and Jill Kassube, Phil and Jane Villiers, SAB and MJW, David Jackman, Michelle Gallagher, Simon and Mandy King*

WYMONDHAM   SK8518   Map 7
Berkeley Arms

Main Street; LE14 2AG

Pleasant village pub with interesting food and sunny terrace

In a pretty village surrounded by footpaths and walkways, this is a friendly golden stone inn dating from the 16th c. There's a welcoming, relaxed feel, helped by all the knick-knacks, magazines, table lamps and cushions. At one end, two wing chairs are set on patterned carpet beside a low coffee table and a cosy log fire. The red-tiled dining area, dense with sripped beams and standing timbers, is furnished kitchen-style with light wood tables and red-cushioned chunky chairs; there's also a smarter dining area with dark leather chairs. Greene King IPA, Marstons Pedigree and a guest such as Banks's Sunbeam on handpump, ten wines by the glass and local cider. Outside in front, on small terraces to either side of the entrance, picnic-sets benefit from the sun nearly all day.

🍴 Good bar food includes sandwiches, twice-baked cheese soufflé, curried scallops with cauliflower purée and cauliflower fritters, local sausages with mash and onion gravy, pasta with artichokes, sun-dried tomatoes and olives, beer-battered pollack and chips, chicken, pancetta and butternut squash risotto, rack of lamb and braised shoulder with potato gratin and ratatouille, venison loin with caramelised walnuts and poached pear, and puddings such as warm chocolate sponge with chocolate sauce and vanilla ice-cream and honey parfait with caramelised poached pear and pear sorbet. *Benchmark main dish: loin of local rabbit wrapped in spinach and parma ham £14.95. Two-course evening meal £21.00.*

Free house ~ Licensee Louise Hitchen ~ Real ale ~ (01572) 787587 ~ Open 12-3 (5 Sun), 6-11; closed Sun evening, Mon, first two weeks Jan, ten days Aug ~ Bar food 12-1.45(3 Sun), 6.30-9 ~ Restaurant ~ Children welcome ~ Dogs allowed in bar ~ www.theberkeleyarms.co.uk *Recommended by M and GR, R L Borthwick*

Also Worth a Visit in Leicestershire

Besides the fully inspected pubs, you might like to try these pubs that have been recommended to us and described by readers. Do tell us what you think of them: feedback@goodguides.com

AB KETTLEBY SK7519
Sugar Loaf (01664) 822473
Nottingham Road (A606 NW of Melton); LE14 3JB Beamed pub with comfortably modernised open-plan carpeted bar, country prints and big photographs of Shipstones brewery dray horses, bare-boards end with coal-effect gas fire, good reasonably priced all-day food, well kept Bass, Marstons Pedigree and guests, decent coffee, friendly attentive staff, dining conservatory; quiet juke box, games machine; children welcome if eating, picnic-sets out by road and car park, open all day. *(Ryta Lyndley)*

BILLESDON SK7102
Queens Head (0116) 259 6352
Church Street; LE7 9AE Beamed and thatched pub near village square, friendly helpful landlord and staff, well kept Everards and good choice of wines by the glass, generous reasonably priced food, carpeted lounge bar with log fire, bare-boards public bar with stripped-pine tables, small conservatory; children welcome, pretty stone village. *(R L Borthwick)*

BOTCHESTON SK4804
Greyhound (01455) 822355
Main Street, off B5380 E of Desford; LE9 9FF Beamed village pub popular for its freshly cooked generous food including some

unusual dishes (should book), bargain OAP weekday lunch and other deals, pine tables in two light and airy dining rooms, three well kept changing ales; children welcome, garden with play area. *(Anon)*

BRANSTON SK8129
⋆**Wheel** (01476) 870376
Main Street; NG32 1RU Refurbished 18th-c stone-built beamed village pub with stylishly simple open-plan décor, friendly attentive service from smartly dressed staff, chef-landlord cooking good country food such as crispy pigs cheek salad and pheasant, bacon and prune pie, three well kept changing ales from central servery (could be Batemans, Brewsters and Oldershaws – festival early Sept), woodburner and open fires; background and occasional live music; children welcome, dogs in bar, attractive garden, next to church, splendid countryside near Belvoir Castle, closed Mon. *(Derek and Sylvia Stephenson, David Glynne-Jones, Ian Johnson)*

BRAUNSTON SK8306
Blue Ball (01572) 722135
Off A606 in Oakham; Cedar Street; LE15 8QS Pretty thatched and beamed dining pub with good food (not Sun evening) including weekday set lunch, well kept Marstons-related ales, decent wines, log fire, leather furniture and country pine in linked

rooms including small conservatory, local art for sale, monthly Sun lunchtime jazz; children welcome, tables outside, attractive village, open all day weekends. *(R L Borthwick, Nick and Elaine Hall, Barry Collett)*

BRUNTINGTHORPE SP6089
⋆ **Joiners Arms** (0116) 247 8258
Off A5199 S of Leicester: Church Walk/ Cross Street; LE17 5QH More restaurant than pub with most of the two beamed rooms set for eating, drinkers have area by small light-oak bar with open fire; an ale such as Greene King or Sharps, plenty of wines by the glass including champagne, first-class imaginative food served by friendly efficient staff, candles on tables, elegant dining chairs, big flower arrangements, civilised but relaxed atmosphere; picnic-sets in front, closed Sun evening, Mon. *(Rob and Catherine Dunster, SAB and MJW, Keith and Sandra Ross)*

BURTON OVERY SP6797
Bell (0116) 259 2365
Main Street; LE8 9DL Good interesting choice of food from lunchtime sandwiches up in L-shaped open-plan bar and dining room (used mainly for larger parties), log fire, comfortable sofas, ales such as Langton and Timothy Taylors Landlord, effective service; children welcome, nice garden, lovely village, open all day weekends. *(Duncan Cloud)*

CALDECOTT SP8693
Plough (01536) 770284
Main Street; LE16 8RS Welcoming pub in attractive ironstone village; carpeted bar with banquettes and small tables leading to spacious eating area, well kept Langton and a guest, wide range of enjoyable inexpensive food including blackboard specials, prompt service; children welcome, garden at back. *(Sue Kidd)*

CASTLE DONINGTON SK4427
Jolly Potters (01332) 811912
Hillside; DE74 2NH Genuine unspoilt town local, basic and friendly, with pews on flagstones, hanging tankards and jugs, framed beer mats, good coal fire, well kept Bass, Fullers, Marstons, Timothy Taylors and guests, back room with darts and juke box; open all day. *(Anon)*

CHURCH LANGTON SP7293
Langton Arms (01858) 545181
B6047 about 3 miles N of Market Harborough; just off A6; LE16 7SY Extended old village dining pub with enjoyable sensibly priced home-made food (Sun till 7pm) including specials, well kept Greene King ales and decent wines by the glass, friendly helpful service, bar to the left, small eating area on right with open fire, restaurant behind; background music, TV; children welcome, garden with heated shelter and maybe summer bouncy castle, open all day Fri-Sun. *(Veronica Brown)*

COLEORTON SK4016
Kings Arms (01530) 815435
The Moor (off A512); LE67 8GD Refurbished village pub with its own Tap House ales along with Bass and a changing guest, enjoyable reasonably priced food (not Sun evening, Mon) including daily carvery, friendly staff, pool room with TV, live music last Sun of month; children and dogs welcome, garden with pétanque and play area, open all day. *(Ian and Jane Irving)*

DADLINGTON SP4097
Dog & Hedgehog (01455) 213151
The Green, opposite church; CV13 6JB Welcoming red-brick village dining pub with generally well liked food, friendly efficient service, local ales; children welcome. *(Mike and Margaret Banks)*

EAST LANGTON SP7292
Bell (01858) 545278
Off B6047; Main Street; LE16 7TW Appealing creeper-clad beamed country inn buzzing with locals and families, well kept Fullers, Greene King, Langton and a guest, nice wines, good well presented food including daily specials and popular Sun carvery, friendly efficient staff, long low-ceilinged stripped-stone bar, spacious restaurant, modern pine furniture, log fires; picnic-sets on sloping front lawn, bedrooms. *(John Saville, Gerry and Rosemary Dobson)*

FOXTON SP6989
⋆ **Foxton Locks** (0116) 279 1515
Foxton Locks, off A6 3 miles NW of Market Harborough (park by bridge 60/62 and walk); LE16 7RA Popular place in great canalside setting at foot of spectacular flight of locks; large comfortably reworked L-shaped bar, pubby food including winter set menu, converted boathouse does snacks, friendly service (may be slow at busy times), half a dozen well kept ales such as Caledonian Deuchars IPA, Fullers London Pride and Theakstons; children welcome, large raised terrace and covered decking, steps down to fenced waterside lawn, good walks. *(Rob and Catherine Dunster, Martin Smith, Veronica Brown, Gerry and Rosemary Dobson, Dr Kevan Tucker)*

GADDESBY SK6813
Cheney Arms (01664) 840260
Rearsby Lane; LE7 4XE Refurbished red-brick village pub, bar with bare-boards and terracotta-tiled floor, well kept Everards and a guest from brick-faced servery, open fires including inglenook in more formal dining room, enjoyable fairly pubby food from good lunchtime baguettes up, Weds pie night; children welcome, walled back garden with smokers' shelter, lovely medieval church, four bedrooms. *(Clark Thornton, R T and J C Moggridge)*

GILMORTON · SP5787

Grey Goose (01455) 552555

Lutterworth Road; LE17 5PN Busy
bar-restaurant with good range of enjoyable
freshly made food from lunchtime
sandwiches up, early-bird weekday deals, Sun
carvery, real ales such as Grainstore, several
wines by the glass including champagne,
good friendly service, light contemporary
décor, stylish wood and metal bar stools
mixing with comfortable sofas and armchairs,
woodburner in stripped-brick fireplace with
logs stacked beside; modern furniture on
terrace. *(Anon)*

GREAT CASTERTON SK9909

★ Plough (01780) 762178

*B1081, just off A1 N of Stamford
(coming from the S or returning to A1
southbound, use A606 junction instead);
Main Street; PE9 4AA* New licensees were
meant to be taking over this homely pub
(a previous Main Entry) as we went to press
– news please.

GREETHAM SK9314

★ Wheatsheaf (01572) 812325

B668 Stretton–Cottesmore; LE15 7NP
Attractive old stone-built pub with linked,
recently refurbished L-shaped rooms;
really good food (must book) from regularly
changing menu, everything home-made
including bread and ice-cream, things
for sale such as pickles, chutneys and
chocolates, friendly welcoming service, well
kept ales like Great Oakley, Greene King and
Oldershaws, good choice of wines, log fire
and blazing open stove, games room with
darts, pool and sports TV; soft background
music; children welcome, dogs in bar
(resident labradoodle and dachshund),
wheelchair access using ramp, front lawn,
back terrace by pretty stream with duck
house, open all day weekends, closed Mon,
no food Sun evening and first two weeks of
Jan. *(Michael and Jenny Back, Colin McKerrow
and others)*

GRIMSTON SK6821

Black Horse (01664) 812358

*Off A6006 W of Melton Mowbray; Main
Street; LE14 3BZ* Popular village-green
pub with interesting interior, welcoming
licensees and friendly locals, well kept
Everards, Marstons and guests, decent
wines, fairly priced wholesome food served
promptly, darts; attractive village with stocks
and 13th-c church. *(Robert Holmes, Comus and
Sarah Elliott)*

GUMLEY SP6890

Bell (0116) 279 2476

*NW of Market Harborough; Main Street;
LE16 7RU* Neatly kept beamed village pub
with wide choice of popular good value food
including bargain over-50s lunch (Tues-Sat),
four well kept changing ales, traditional
country décor, lots of hunting prints, small
log fire, darts, cribbage and dominoes, border
collie called Bailey, Weds quiz; no mobile
phones, muddy boots, dogs or young children;
pond in pretty terrace garden, closed Sun
evening, Mon. *(Edward Leetham, Gerry and
Rosemary Dobson)*

HALLATON SP7896

Bewicke Arms (01858) 555217

*On Eastgate, opposite village sign;
LE16 8UB* Attractive thatched pub dating
from the 16th c, Greene King, Langton and
Timothy Taylors, enjoyable well priced food
from baguettes to grills including bargain
set deals, two bar dining areas, restaurant
of small linked areas, scrubbed pine tables
and two log fires, memorabilia from ancient
inter-village bottle-kicking match (still
held on Easter Mon), darts; background
music; children allowed in eating areas,
dogs on leads, disabled facilities, big terrace
overlooking paddock and lake with play area,
tea room and three bedrooms in converted
stables, open all day weekends (no food Sun
evening). *(Jim Farmer)*

HATHERN SK5021

Dew Drop (01509) 842438

Loughborough Road (A6); LE12 5HY
Unspoilt two-room beamed local, welcoming
landlord and friendly regulars, well kept
Greene King and guests, lots of malt
whiskies, coal fire in larger room, good
lunchtime cobs, darts and dominoes; tables
outside. *(Anon)*

HOBY SK6717

Blue Bell (01664) 434247

Main Street; LE14 3DT Attractive rebuilt
thatched pub, well run, with good range of
enjoyable realistically priced food (all day
weekends – best to book), small helpings
available, friendly attentive uniformed staff,
up to six well kept ales, good choice of wines
by the glass and teas/coffees, open-plan and
airy with beams, comfortable traditional
furniture, old local photographs, skittle
alley, darts; background music; children
and dogs welcome, valley-view garden with
picnic-sets and boules, open all day.
(Phil and Jane Hodson)

Please keep sending us reports. We rely on readers for news of new discoveries,
and particularly for news of changes – however slight – at the fully described pubs:
feedback@goodguides.com, or (no stamp needed) The Good Pub Guide,
FREEPOST TN1569, Wadhurst, E Sussex TN5 7BR.

HOSE
SK7329

Rose & Crown (01949) 869458

Bolton Lane; LE14 4JE Modernised 200-year-old beamed village pub, good selection of well kept beers, real cider and several wines by the glass, interesting nicely presented food (all day Sat, not Sun evening, Mon or Tues), pub staples too, small raised dining area and steps up to intimate restaurant; tables on back decking, open all day weekends, closed Mon and Tues lunchtimes. *(David Glynne-Jones)*

HOTON
SK5722

Packe Arms (01509) 889106

Rempstone Road (A60); LE12 5SJ Spacious old Vintage Inn with sturdy beams and open fires, their usual choice of enjoyable food including good value set menu, well kept ales such as Batemans, Black Sheep and Everards, realistically priced wines, prompt friendly service from uniformed staff; children welcome, tables outside, open all day. *(Phil and Jane Hodson, Mike and Mary Carter)*

HOUGHTON ON THE HILL SK6703

Old Black Horse (0116) 241 3486

Main Street (just off A47 Leicester–Uppingham); LE7 9GD Lively and comfortable, with above-average home-made food (no hot food Mon lunchtime), welcoming helpful staff, Everards and a guest beer, good wines by the glass, reasonable prices, bare-boards dining area with lots of panelling; background music; big attractive garden. *(Barry Collett)*

HUNGARTON
SK6907

Black Boy (0116) 259 5410

Main Street; LE7 9JR Large open-plan partly divided restauranty bar with minimal decoration and open fire, good well priced food cooked to order by landlord-chef (weekend booking advised), changing ales such as Greene King, Fullers and Wells & Youngs, cheerful welcoming staff; background music; picnic-sets out on deck, closed Sun evening, Mon. *(R L Borthwick, Jim Farmer)*

ILLSTON ON THE HILL
SP7099

⋆**Fox & Goose** (0116) 259 6340

Main Street, off B6047 Market Harborough–Melton Mowbray; LE7 9EG Individual two-bar local, simple, comfortable and friendly, with hunting pictures and assorted oddments including stuffed animals, woodburner and good coal fire, well kept Everards and a guest, home-made food (Wed-Sat); children and dogs welcome, closed weekday lunchtimes, open all day weekends. *(Jim Farmer)*

KEGWORTH
SK4826

Cap & Stocking (01509) 672018

Handy for M1 junction 24, via A6; Borough Street; DE74 2FF Nicely old-fashioned three-room pub under newish landlord; etched windows, button-back bench seats and traditional furniture on carpet or old tiles, coal fire and woodburner, Bass (from the jug), Castle Rock Harvest Pale, Sharps Doom Bar, Wells & Youngs Bombardier and a guest, no food yet, darts and dominoes, back room opening to secluded two-tier garden with pétanque; juke box (occasional live music) and quiz machine; children and dogs welcome, open all day. *(Anon)*

KILBY
SP6295

Dog & Gun (0116) 240 2398

Main Street, off A5199 S of Leicester; LE18 3TD Much extended cleanly kept pub, locally popular for its good straightforward well priced food, friendly helpful service, ales including Greene King, coal fire, side restaurant with grandfather clock; disabled access and parking, colourful back garden with terrace and pergola, open all day. *(Anon)*

KILBY BRIDGE
SP6197

Navigation (0116) 288 2280

Welford Road (A5199 S of Leicester); LE18 3TE Fine canalside position with waterside garden, nice old tiled-floor front bar, big dining area, four real ales and generous well priced lunchtime food (all day weekends); background music; children welcome. *(Veronica Brown)*

KIRBY MUXLOE
SK5104

Royal Oak (0116) 239 3166

Main Street; LE9 2AN Comfortable modernish pub (don't be put off by the plain exterior) with good food from sandwiches and snacks through pub favourites to more inventive choices including tapas, early-bird deals, pleasant prompt service, Adnams, Everards and a guest ale, good wine choice, sizeable restaurant, some live jazz, Mon quiz; disabled facilities, picnic-sets outside, nearby 15th-c castle ruins, open all day weekends. *(Anon)*

KNIPTON
SK8231

Manners Arms (01476) 879222

Signed off A607 Grantham–Melton Mowbray; Croxton Road; NG32 1RH Handsome Georgian hunting lodge beautifully renovated by Duke and Duchess of Rutland as upscale country inn, hunting prints and furniture from Belvoir Castle, log fire, well kept Belvoir and other ales, good choice of wines by the glass, enjoyable food including game from the estate, sizeable restaurant with attractive conservatory, sumptuous lounge; background music; terrace with ornamental pool, lovely views over pretty village, ten comfortable individually furnished bedrooms, open all day. *(Jonathan Peel)*

KNOSSINGTON
SK8008
Fox & Hounds (01664) 452129
*Off A606 W of Oakham; Somerby Road;
LE15 8LY* Attractive 18th-c ivy-covered
village dining pub refurbished by present
landlady, beamed bar with log fire, cosy
dining areas, good food from traditional
choices to blackboard specials, Fullers
London Pride; no children under 8; dogs
welcome, big back garden, closed Mon,
lunchtimes Tues-Thurs, evening Sun.
(R L Borthwick, SAB and MJW)

LEICESTER
SK5804
Ale Wagon (0116) 262 3330
Rutland Street/Charles Street; LE1 1RE
Basic 1930s two-room corner local with
nine real ales including its own Hoskins
Brothers beers, a traditional cider, no food
apart from baps, coal fire, upstairs function
room; background music; handy for Curve
Theatre and station, open all day, closed Sun
lunchtime. *(Anon)*

LEICESTER
SK5804
Cradock Arms (0116) 270 6680
*Knighton Road/Newmarket Street;
LE2 3TT* Substantial beamed and partly
thatched Everards pub, good choice of
enjoyable well priced food all day (till 4pm
Sun) from open kitchen including weekday
lunch deal, Tues quiz; children welcome,
disabled facilities, beer garden with terrace,
open all day. *(Nigel Siesage, Veronica Brown)*

LEICESTER
SK5804
Criterion (0116) 262 5418
Millstone Lane; LE1 5JN 1960s building
with dark wood and carpeted main room,
Oakham ales and up to ten guests at
weekends, 100 bottled beers and a couple of
real ciders, good value stone-baked pizzas
(not Sun) plus some other food, room on
left with games and old-fashioned juke box,
regular live music and quiz nights, annual
comedy festival; picnic-sets outside, open
all day. *(Anon)*

LEICESTER
SK5804
⋆Globe (0116) 253 9492
Silver Street; LE1 5EU Refurbished but
keeping original character, lots of woodwork
in partitioned areas off central bar, bare
boards and some Victorian mosaic floor tiles,
mirrors and working gas lamps, four Everards
ales along with three guests, two real ciders
and over a dozen wines by the glass, friendly
staff, enjoyable well priced food (till 6pm
Sun) from bar snacks up, good upstairs
evening bistro (Thurs-Sat); background
music (not in snug); children and dogs
welcome, metal café-style tables out in front,
open all day. *(Val and Alan Green)*

LEICESTER
SK5803
Kings Head (0116) 254 8240
King Street; LE1 6RL Drinkers pub with

good atmosphere and helpful friendly staff,
three well kept Black Country ales and five
regularly changing guests, proper cider, can
bring your own food, log fire; no children or
dogs, raised back terrace, open all day.
(Andrew Bosi)

LEICESTER
SK5803
⋆Swan & Rushes (0116) 233 9167
Oxford Street/Infirmary Square; LE1 5WR
Triangular-shaped pub with up to nine well
kept ales including Batemans and Oakham,
over 100 bottled beers, real cider, welcoming
staff and thriving local atmosphere in two
rooms with big oak tables, low-priced home-
made food (not Sun) including stone-baked
pizzas, bar billiards and darts, themed beer
and cider festivals, Thurs quiz, maybe Sat
live music; very busy on match days; dogs
welcome, sunny back terrace, open all day.
(Anon)

LEICESTER
SK5804
Tom Hoskins (0116) 266 9659
*Beaumanor Road; off Abbey Lane
(A5131), right fork S from A6 at Red
Hill Circle; LE4 5QE* Friendly two-room
backstreet local with up to six real ales
including Black Sheep, Brains and Greene
King, bar snacks such as cobs, darts, Sun
quiz and some live music; children welcome,
beer garden and small play area, open all
day. *(Phil and Jane Hodson)*

LOUGHBOROUGH
SK5319
⋆Swan in the Rushes (01509) 217014
The Rushes (A6); LE11 5BE Bare-boards
town local with three smallish high-ceilinged
rooms, good value Castle Rock and plenty of
interesting changing guests, foreign bottled
beers and real cider, well priced chip-free
food (not Sun evenings), open fire and daily
papers, good juke box, live music and theatre
nights in upstairs skittle alley/function room;
children welcome in eating areas, tables
outside, four bedrooms, open all day. *(Anon)*

LOUGHBOROUGH
SK5319
Tap & Mallet (01509) 210028
Nottingham Road; LE11 1EU Basic
friendly pub with well kept Abbeydale,
Oakham and interesting microbrews, also
foreign beers and Weston's cider, coal fire,
darts and pool, juke box; children welcome,
walled back garden with play area and pets
corner, open all day Sat, closed lunchtimes
other days. *(Anon)*

LYDDINGTON
SP8796
⋆Old White Hart (01572) 821703
*Village signed off A6003 N of Corby;
LE15 9LR* Popular welcoming old pub,
softly lit front bar with heavy beams in low
ceiling, just a few tables, glass-shielded
log fire, Greene King and Timothy Taylors
Landlord, good food (not Sun evening in
winter) including own sausages and cured
meats (landlord is a butcher), efficient

obliging service, attractive restaurant, further tiled-floor room with rugs, lots of fine hunting prints and woodburner; children welcome, seats by heaters in pretty walled garden, eight floodlit boules pitches, handy for Bede House and good nearby walks, bedrooms. *(John and Sylvia Harrop, Tracey and Stephen Groves, Howard and Margaret Buchanan)*

MANTON   SK8704

Horse & Jockey (01572) 737335

St Mary's Road; LE15 8SU Welcoming early 19th-c stone pub with updated low-beamed interior, modern furniture on wood or stone floors, woodburner, well kept ales such as Grainstore and Greene King plus a house beer (Fall at the First), decent fairly priced food from baguettes to blackboard specials, good service; background music; children and dogs welcome, colourful tubs and hanging baskets, terrace picnic-sets, maybe the Rutland Morris Men, nice location – on Rutland Water cycle route (bike racks provided), open all day in summer (all day Fri, Sat, till 7pm Sun in winter). *(Lois Dyer, Barry Collett)*

MARKET HARBOROUGH   SP7387

Sugar Loaf (01858) 469231

High Street; LE16 7NJ Popular Wetherspoons, smaller than many, attracting an eclectic mix of customers, half a dozen well priced ales (frequent beer festivals), usual good value food all day; children welcome. *(Gerry and Rosemary Dobson)*

MARKET HARBOROUGH   SP7387

★ Three Swans (01858) 466644

High Street; LE16 7NJ Comfortable banquettes and plush-cushioned library chairs in traditional bay-windowed front bar of Best Western conference hotel, well kept Langton and guests such as Adnams and St Austell, decent wines, good spread of enjoyable well presented pubby food from sandwiches up, good value set deals, friendly uniformed staff, flame-effect fires (one in grand coaching-era inglenook), flagstoned back area, corridor to popular conservatory bistro (Mon-Sat evenings), pricier more formal upstairs restaurant; background music; attractive suntrap courtyard, useful parking, good bedrooms, open all day from 9.30am. *(Gerry and Rosemary Dobson)*

MARKET OVERTON   SK8816

Black Bull (01572) 767677

Opposite the church; LE15 7PW Attractive thatched and low-beamed stone-built pub (dates from 17th c) in pretty village well placed for Rutland Water, welcoming licensees and staff, good home-made food (booking advised) from pub staples up in long carpeted bar and two separate dining areas, well kept Batemans, Black Sheep, Greene King and Theakstons, woodburner, banquettes and sofas, newspapers; some background and live music; children and

dogs welcome, tables out in front by small carp pool, five bedrooms (two ensuite), open all day Sun till 6pm, closed Mon. *(D and D G Humpherson, Phil and Jane Hodson)*

MEDBOURNE   SP7992

★ Nevill Arms (01858) 565288

B664 Market Harborough–Uppingham; LE16 8EE Handsome stone-built Victorian inn nicely located by stream and footbridge, wide range of good bar and restaurant food including vegetarian choices, pleasant helpful uniformed staff, well kept ales such as Bass, Fullers London Pride and Sharps Doom Bar, beams and mullion windows, log fires, modern artwork, stylish restaurant; no dogs; back terrace with stable-conversion café (8am-4pm), streamside picnic-sets, 11 refurbished bedrooms, good breakfast, open all day. *(Rob and Catherine Dunster, Robin and Jasmine Marson, Barry Collett)*

MELTON MOWBRAY   SK7519

Anne of Cleves (01664) 481336

Burton Street, by St Mary's Church; LE13 1AE Monks' chantry dating from the 14th c and gifted to Anne of Cleves by Henry VIII; chunky tables, character chairs and settles on flagstones, heavy beams and latticed mullioned windows, tapestries on burnt orange walls, well kept Everards and guests, decent wines and above average food, small end dining room; background music; tables in pretty little walled garden with flagstoned terrace, open all day. *(Comus and Sarah Elliott)*

MELTON MOWBRAY   SK7518

Boat (01664) 500969

Burton Street; LE13 1AF Chatty and welcoming one-room local with four real ales and lots of malt whiskies, no food, panelling and open fire, darts; open all day Fri, Sat. *(Glenn Upton)*

MOUNTSORREL   SK5715

Swan (0116) 230 2340

Loughborough Road, off A6; LE12 7AT Log fires, old flagstones and stripped stone, friendly staff and locals, enjoyable well priced food from baguettes and light dishes to generous full meals (best to book evenings), well kept ales including Theakstons, Stowford Press cider and good choice of wines, pine tables and gingham cloths in neat dining area and restaurant; dogs welcome in bar, pretty walled back garden down to canalised River Soar, self-contained accommodation, open all day weekends. *(Jim Farmer)*

MOWSLEY   SP6488

Staff of Life (0116) 240 2359

Village signposted off A5199 S of Leicester; Main Street; LE17 6NT Some recent refurbishment at this well run high-gabled little village pub; roomy fairly traditional bar, high-backed settles on flagstones, wicker chairs on shiny wood floor and stools lined up along unusual circular counter, woodburner, Sharps Doom Bar, Shepherd Neame Spitfire and guests, half a dozen wines by the glass, well liked interesting mid-priced food (not Sun or Mon evenings), good service; background music; well behaved children over 12 welcome weekdays, seats out in front and on nice leaf-shaded deck, open all day Sun, closed Mon-Fri lunchtimes. *(Michael Sargent, Rob and Catherine Dunster, Mark Bernstein, SAB and MJW, Nigel and Sue Foster)*

NARBOROUGH   SP5397
Narborough Arms (0116) 284 8212
Coventry Road; LE19 2GR 17th-c inn now part of the John Barras chain; generous bargain food all day, well kept ales such as Wadworths 6X and reasonably priced wines by the glass, popular with young people and busy at weekends; sports TV; children welcome, eight bedrooms, pay car park (money refunded at bar). *(Howard and Margaret Buchanan)*

OADBY   SP6399
Grange Farm (0116) 281 5600
Off Glen Road (A6); LE2 4RH Popular roomy Vintage Inn based on early 19th-c farmhouse, smart welcoming young staff, wide choice of generous reasonably priced food, Batemans, Black Sheep and Everards, good range of wines and spirits, log fires, old local photographs, daily papers; no dogs; well behaved children welcome, tables out in front, open all day. *(Anon)*

OAKHAM   SK8508
Admiral Hornblower
(01572) 723004 *High Street; LE15 6AS* Former 17th-c farmhouse with several differently decorated areas, three log fires, enjoyable food including good value early-bird menu (Mon-Thurs 6-7.15pm) and generous Sun carvery with plenty of fresh vegetables, three well kept ales, good service, conservatory; country-feel garden, ten comfortable bedrooms. *(R C Vincent)*

OLD DALBY   SK6723
Crown (01664) 823134
Debdale Hill; LE14 3LF Creeper-clad early 16th-c pub under new management; intimate farmhouse rooms up and down steps, black beams, antique oak settles among other seats, rustic prints and open fires, five real ales including Belvoir and plenty of wines by the glass, enjoyable well presented food from traditional choices up (not Sun evening, Mon), extended dining room opening on to terrace; background music; children and dogs welcome, disabled facilities, attractive

garden with boules, open all day weekends, closed Mon lunchtime. *(Anon)*

REDMILE   SK7935
★ ## Windmill (01949) 842281
Off A52 Grantham–Nottingham; Main Street; NG13 0GA Snug low-beamed bar with sofas, easy chairs and log fire in capacious hearth, comfortable roomier dining areas with woodburners, wide choice of good generous home-made food from sandwiches and tapas to game from local Belvoir estate, meal deals and Sun roasts too, well kept Adnams and Timothy Taylors Landlord, good wines by the glass, local cordials, neat friendly young staff; children welcome, sizeable well furnished front courtyard, open all day. *(Anon)*

ROTHLEY   SK5812
Woodmans Stroke (0116) 230 2785
Church Street; LE7 7PD Immaculate family-run thatched pub with good value weekday lunchtime bar food from sandwiches up, well kept changing ales, good wines by the glass including champagne, friendly service, beams and settles in front rooms, open fire, old local photographs plus rugby and cricket memorabilia; sports TV; pretty front hanging baskets, cast-iron tables in attractive garden with heaters, pétanque, open all day Sat. *(Anon)*

RYHALL   TF0310
Wicked Witch (01780) 763649
Bridge Street; PE9 4HH Refurbished dining pub with good upmarket food including set deals, main bar, lounge and restaurant; children welcome, tables in back garden. *(Mike and Margaret Banks)*

SHAWELL   SP5480
White Swan (01788) 860357
Main Street; village signed down declassified road (ex A427) off A5/A426 roundabout – turn right in village; not far from M6 junction 1; LE17 6AG Attractive little beamed 17th-c dining pub given clean modern refurbishment by new owners; interesting food (all day, till 6pm Sun) from landlord-chef along with some pub staples, Adnams and local Dow Bridge ales, lots of wines by the glass, restaurant; children welcome, open all day. *(Anon)*

SHEARSBY   SP6290
Chandlers Arms (0116) 247 8384
Fenny Lane, off A50 Leicester–Northampton; LE17 6PL Comfortable old creeper-clad pub in attractive village, four well kept ales including Dow Bridge (tasting trays, July beer festival), good value pubby food (not Sun evening, Mon), wall seats and

---

We include some hotels with a good bar that offers facilities comparable to those of a pub.

wheelback chairs, table skittles; background music, Weds quiz night; tables in secluded raised garden overlooking green, open all day Sun, closed Mon lunchtime. *(Jim Farmer)*

SIBSON   SK3500
Cock (01827) 880357

A444 N of Nuneaton; Twycross Road; CV13 6LB Picturesque old black and white thatched pub with Dick Turpin connection, Bass and Hook Norton, a dozen wines by the glass, decent if pricey food, cheerful quick service, low doorways, heavy black beams and genuine latticed windows, immense inglenook; background music, games machine; children welcome, tables in courtyard and small garden, handy for Bosworth Field. *(Joan and Tony Walker, Mike and Margaret Banks)*

SILEBY   SK6015
Horse & Trumpet (01509) 812549

Barrow Road, opposite church; LE12 7LP Beamed village pub recently renovated by the Steamin' Billy Brewing Co, their beers and guests, a real cider, fresh cobs, curry evening last Thurs of month, darts; well behaved dogs welcome, terrace picnic-sets. *(Mike and Mary Carter)*

SOMERBY   SK7710
⋆ Stilton Cheese (01664) 454394

High Street; off A606 Oakham–Melton Mowbray, via Cold Overton, or Leesthorpe and Pickwell; LE14 2QB Friendly staff in enjoyable ironstone pub with comfortable beamed and hop-strung bar/lounge, comfortable furnishings on red patterned carpets, country prints, copper pots and a stuffed badger, Grainstore, Marstons, Tetleys and guests, 30 malt whiskies, reasonably priced pubby food and some interesting daily specials, restaurant; children welcome, seats on terrace, peaceful setting on edge of pretty village, bedrooms. *(Jim Farmer, Mike and Margaret Banks)*

SOUTH CROXTON   SK6810
Golden Fleece (01664) 840275

Main Street; LE7 3RL Restaurant more than pub; clean minimalist feel with comfortable modern furniture, friendly helpful staff, good choice of popular food including cheaper weekday lunchtime/early evening set menu, Sun carvery, ales such as Adnams and Wells & Youngs, good house wine, log fire; lovely area. *(O K Smyth, SAB and MJW)*

SOUTH LUFFENHAM   SK9401
⋆ Coach House (01780) 720166

Stamford Road (A6121); LE15 8NT Nicely reworked old inn with flagstoned bar, stripped timber or terracotta walls, bright scatter cushions on small pews, church candles and log fire, Adnams, Greene King and Timothy Taylors, decent wines by the glass, good well priced food served by friendly efficient staff, neat built-in seating in

separate snug, smarter more modern-feeling back dining room; children welcome, dogs in bar, small deck behind, seven bedrooms, closed Sun evening, Mon lunchtime. *(Mike and Mary Carter)*

SPROXTON   SK8524
Crown (01476) 860035

Coston Road; LE14 4QB Friendly 19th-c stone-built inn with spotless well laid-out interior, good reasonably priced food from bar snacks to restaurant dishes, well kept Greene King ales, good wines and coffee, light airy bar with woodburner, restaurant with big glassed-off wine store; children welcome, dogs in bar (there's a pub dog), lovely sunny courtyard, attractive village and nice local walks, three bedrooms, closed Sun evening, Mon. *(Phil and Jane Hodson)*

SWINFORD   SP5779
Chequers (01788) 860318

Handy for M1/M6/A14 interchange; High Street, opposite church; LE17 6BL Long pub with bare-boards bar and carpeted dining areas, well kept beers including Tetleys Mild, decent choice of enjoyable food (not Sun evening) from standards to pizzas and curries, some pine panelling and old local photographs, traditional games including table skittles, library, Sun quiz; children welcome, garden with terrace and play area, Shrove Tues pancake race, St George's Day worm-charming championship, closed Mon lunchtime. *(R C Vincent)*

THORPE LANGTON   SP7492
⋆ Bakers Arms (01858) 545201

Off B6047 N of Market Harborough; LE16 7TS Civilised restaurant with bar rather than pub, consistently good imaginative food from regularly changing menu (must book), cottagey beamed linked areas and stylishly simple country décor, well kept local Langton ale, good choice of wines by the glass, friendly efficient staff, maybe a pianist; no under-12s; garden picnic-sets, closed weekday lunchtimes, Sun evening, Mon. *(R L Borthwick, Phil and Jane Hodson, SAB and MJW)*

UPPER HAMBLETON   SK8907
⋆ Finchs Arms (01572) 756575

Off A606; Oakham Road; LE15 8TL Friendly 17th-c stone inn with outstanding views over Rutland Water, four log fires, beamed and flagstoned bar, Black Sheep, Timothy Taylors Landlord and a guest, several wines by the glass including champagne, afternoon teas, elegant restaurant with decorative bay trees and modern seating, second newly built dining room, well liked food including set menus; no dogs; children welcome, suntrap hillside terrace, good surrounding walks, ten bedrooms, open all day. *(Jim Farmer, Nichola Hanman, Caro Millington, Mike and Mary Carter, Colin McKerrow)*

UPPINGHAM SP8699
Crown (01572) 822302
High Street East; LE15 9PY Clean, honest 18th-c town inn, half a dozen or so well kept ales including Everards (beer festivals), decent reasonably priced home-made food (not Sun evening) including range of pies, back restaurant; background and some live music; bedrooms, open all day. *(D Goodger)*

UPPINGHAM SP8699
Falcon (01572) 823535
High Street East; LE15 9PY Old coaching inn, relaxed and quietly refined, with oak-panelled bar and spacious nicely furnished lounge with roaring fire and big windows overlooking market square, enjoyable food (not Sun evening) from bar snacks up, three Grainstore ales, good smiling service; children welcome, dogs in bar, back garden with terrace, bedrooms, open all day.
(R C Vincent, Michael Doswell)

UPPINGHAM SP8699
Vaults (01572) 823259
Market Place; LE15 9QH Attractive old pub next to church, enjoyable reasonably priced traditional food, friendly helpful staff, Adnams Broadside, Marstons Pedigree, house beer from Grainstore and a guest, several wines by the glass, comfortable banquettes, pleasant upstairs dining room; background music, sports TVs; children and dogs welcome, some tables out overlooking picturesque square, four bedrooms (bookings from nearby Falcon Hotel), open all day.
(Barry Collett)

WHITWELL SK9208
Noel at Whitwell (01780) 460334
Main Road (A606); LE15 8BW Smart spacious bistro-pub handy for Rutland Water, wide choice of food including good value set lunch, friendly young staff, well kept local ales, decent wines by the glass and good coffee, live music; children welcome, suntrap tables outside, play area, bedrooms.
(Colin McKerrow)

WHITWICK SK4316
Three Horseshoes (01530) 837311
Leicester Road; LE67 5GN Unpretentious unchanging local with long quarry-tiled bar, old wooden benches and open fires, tiny snug to the right, well kept Bass and Marstons Pedigree, piano, darts, dominoes and cards, newspapers, no food; outdoor lavatories, no proper pub sign so easy to miss. *(Anon)*

WOODHOUSE EAVES SK5214
Curzon Arms (01509) 890377
Maplewell Road; LE12 8QZ Welcoming old beamed pub with enjoyable food (not Sun evening) from lunchtime sandwiches and pub favourites up, also good value weekday set menu, Adnams Bitter, Marstons EPA, Sharps Doom Bar and a guest, good service, attractive up-to-date décor, interesting collection of wall clocks, carpeted dining room; background music; children and dogs welcome, ramp for disabled access, good-sized front lawn and terrace, open all day weekends. *(Barry and Anne)*

WOODHOUSE EAVES SK5214
Old Bulls Head (01509) 890255
Main Street; LE12 8RZ Big open-plan contemporary Mitchells & Butlers dining pub, clean and tidy, with good choice of food including pizzas, pasta and grills, set menu (lunchtime till 7pm weekdays), good wine list and well kept ales such as Timothy Taylors Landlord, friendly staff in black; well behaved children welcome, outside tables, nice village setting and handy for Charnwood Forest and Bardon Hill, open all day.
(Phil and Jane Hodson)

WYMESWOLD SK6023
Three Crowns (01509) 880153
Far Street (A6006); LE12 6TZ Snug chatty 18th-c local in attractive village, good friendly staff, four real ales including Adnams and Marstons, decent reasonably priced pubby food, pleasant character furnishings in beamed bar and lounge, open fire, lots of atmosphere; picnic-sets out on decking, open all day. *(Comus and Sarah Elliott)*

WYMESWOLD SK6023
Windmill (01509) 881313
Brook Street; LE12 6TT Bustling side-street village pub refurbished under newish owners; enjoyable good value home-made food from lunchtime snacks up, ales such as Castle Rock, Langton and Sharps Doom Bar, friendly hard-working staff; children welcome, dogs in bar, back garden, open all day weekends. *(Mike and Mary Carter, Comus and Sarah Elliott)*

Post Office address codings confusingly give the impression that some pubs are in Leicestershire, when they're really in Cambridgeshire (which is where we list them).

Lincolnshire

Food plays a major part in the pubs here, with more than half our Main Entries holding a Food Award. So there's a fine choice for a special meal out: the Ship at Barnoldby le Beck (a refined dining pub with Victorian and Edwardian bric-a-brac), Chequers in Gedney Dyke (stylish dining pub and new to us this year), Brownlow Arms in Hough-on-the-Hill (smashing food in civilised surroundings), Inn on the Green at Ingham (nicely modernised with a chatty atmosphere) and Chequers at Woolsthorpe (a former coaching inn with castle views). Other pubs that are particularly pleasing to readers are the Wheatsheaf at Dry Doddington (very well run by hands-on licensees), Butcher & Beast in Heighington (six real ales, a cheerful atmosphere and hard-working landlord and landlady) and the Queens Head in Kirkby la Thorpe (much loved by our readers). Our Lincolnshire Dining Pub 2014 is the Chequers in Woolsthorpe.

BARNOLDBY LE BECK   TA2303   Map 8

Ship ⏸ ♟

Village signposted off A18 Louth–Grimsby; DN37 0BG

Tranquil refined dining pub with Edwardian and Victorian bric-a-brac

The good, popular food in this charming little dining pub obviously draws in most customers – but drinkers do pop in, and the helpful staff keep Black Sheep and Tom Woods on handpump, up to a dozen malt whiskies and wines by the glass from a good list. It's all neatly kept, with a friendly welcome and an appealing collection of Edwardian and Victorian bric-a-brac: stand-up telephones, violins, a horn gramophone, bowler and top hats, old racquets, crops and hockey sticks. Heavy drapes swathe the windows, with plants in ornate china bowls on the sills. Furnishings include comfortable dark green wall benches with lots of pretty cushions, heavily stuffed green plush Victorian-looking chairs on a green fleur de lys carpet, and a warming winter coal fire; background music. A fenced-off sunny area behind has hanging baskets and a few picnic-sets under parasols.

🍴 Attractively presented, with interesting daily specials, food might include sandwiches, smoked haddock with poached egg, spinach and mornay sauce, shredded duck with caramelised kumquat salad and hoisin sauce, camembert and fig filo parcel with tomato and basil sauce, braised lamb shank with bubble and squeak cake and red wine and redcurrant reduction, salmon fillet with crushed chive potatoes and smoked mussel and white wine sauce, and puddings such as bakewell tart and custard and chocolate and Amaretto cheesecake. *Benchmark main dish: skate wing with caper butter £16.50. Two-course evening meal £20.00.*

Free house ~ Licensee Michele Hancock ~ Real ale ~ (01472) 822308 ~ Open 12-3, 6-11(midnight Sat); 12-5 Sun; closed Sun evening ~ Bar food 12-2(5 Sun), 6-9 ~ Restaurant ~ Children welcome ~ www.the-shipinn.com *Recommended by Kay and Alistair Butler, J F M and M West*

DRY DODDINGTON
SK8546 Map 8
Wheatsheaf
Main Street; 1.5 miles off A1 N of Grantham; NG23 5HU

Happy, bustling pub with good food cooked by chef-patron; handy for A1

'We wished we lived nearer,' says one reader wistfully – we know others feel the same. It's spotlessly kept by an enthusiastic young couple (he does the cooking), with a genuinely warm welcome for both regulars and visitors. The front bar is basically two rooms, with a woodburning stove, a variety of settles and chairs enlivened by bold-patterned scatter cushions, and tables in the windows facing across to the green and lovely 14th-c church with its crooked tower. The serving bar on the right has Batemans XB, Greene King Abbot, Timothy Taylors Landlord and a guest on handpump, and a nice choice of over a dozen wines by the glass. A slight slope leads down to the extended dining room, which is comfortable with a thick carpet, sparkling glassware and napery. Once a cow byre, this part is older than the rest of the building, perhaps dating from the 13th c; background music. The front terrace has neat tables under cocktail parasols among tubs of flowers; disabled access at the side.

Attractively presented and very good, the food includes sandwiches, crispy whitebait with tartare sauce, black pudding and poached egg salad, honey-baked ham and egg, steak burger in rosemary bun with cheese, pickles and frites, toad in the hole with mash, beer-battered haddock with twice-baked chips, chicken breast with wild mushroom sauce and sautéed potatoes, salmon fillet with beetroot and orange oil dressing, and puddings such as baked alaska and vanilla panna cotta. *Benchmark main dish: rack of lamb with bordelaise sauce and dauphinoise potatoes £14.95. Two-course evening meal £18.00.*

Free house ~ Licensees Dan and Kate Bland ~ Real ale ~ (01400) 281458 ~ Open 12-2.30, 5-11; 12-11 Sat, Sun; closed Mon ~ Bar food 12-2, 7-9 ~ Restaurant ~ Children welcome ~ Dogs allowed in bar ~ www.wheatsheaf-pub.co.uk *Recommended by B and M Kendall, Michael and Jenny Back, M Mossman, Jim McRobert, Ryta Lyndley, Michael Doswell*

GEDNEY DYKE
TF4125 Map 8
Chequers
Off A17 Holbeach–Kings Lynn; PE12 0AJ

Smart dining pub with small bar, stylish restaurant rooms and imaginative food

Opened in 2012 after a careful refurbishment, this stylish and friendly fenland village pub is popular with both drinkers and diners. The beamed bar has an open fire, several high chairs around high tables on wooden floors, and seats against the counter where they serve Tydd Steam Barn Ale on handpump and quite a few wines by the glass. The smart, interconnected and carpeted dining rooms and conservatory have high-backed cream or black dining chairs around white-clothed tables, and throughout there's some bare brick and good lighting; service is helpful and courteous. There's seating on the back terrace and in the fenced-off garden.

Using carefully sourced local produce, the extremely good food includes brown shrimp, leek and chive risotto, ham hock terrine with home-made piccalilli, chicken with celery and truffled cream sauce, pork fillet wrapped in parma ham with black pudding, apple, shallot and cider juices, corn-fed duck breast with buttered vegetables, gilt-head bream fillet with coconut and ginger sauce and sweet and sour peppers, and puddings such as blood orange trifle and glazed white chocolate and passion-fruit crème brûlée. *Benchmark main dish: pork fillet with black pudding, creamed savoy cabbage, fondant potato and roasting juices £14.95. Two-course evening meal £20.00.*

Free house ~ Licensee Gareth Franklin ~ Real ale ~ (01406) 366700 ~ Open 12-2, 7-11; 12-8 Sun; closed Mon, Tues ~ Bar food 12-2.30, 6-9; 12-3 Sun ~ Restaurant ~ Children welcome ~ www.the-chequers.co.uk *Recommended by Ken Marshall*

HEIGHINGTON
Butcher & Beast ◖ £
High Street; LN4 1JS

TF0369   Map 8

Traditional village pub with terrific range of drinks, pubby food and a pretty streamside garden

There's always something going on at this cheerful village pub and the hard-working licensees are very hands-on: Mr Gray is front of house and Mrs Gray runs the kitchen. They hold weekly themed food evenings, quizzes and beer festivals and keep half a dozen real ales on handpump such as Batemans XB, XXXB, Dark Mild, GHA Pale and Salem Porter, with a guest from breweries such as Theakstons, Thornbridge and Welbeck Abbey; also two farm ciders, eight wines by the glass, 25 gins and 24 malt whiskies. The simply furnished bar has button-back wall banquettes, pubby furnishings and stools along the counter; occasional TV. The Snug has red-cushioned wall settles and high-backed wooden dining chairs, and the beamed dining room is neatly set with proper tablecloths and napkins; throughout, the cream walls are hung with old village photos and country pictures. There are picnic-sets on a lawn that runs down to a stream and the award-winning hanging baskets and tubs are very pretty in summer.

Tasty, good value bar food includes sandwiches, creamy garlic mushrooms, mushroom and pepper stroganoff, chilli con carne, burgers with different toppings, chicken breast topped with barbecue sauce, bacon and melted cheese, specials like home-baked ham with pork pie, pickles and chips and fillet of pork stuffed with black pudding with home-grown roasted rhubarb, and puddings. *Benchmark main dish: steak in ale pie £9.25. Two-course evening meal £15.00.*

Batemans ~ Tenants Mal and Diane Gray ~ Real ale ~ (01522) 790386 ~ Open 12-11 ~ Bar food 12-2, 5.30-8; 12-3 Sun ~ Restaurant ~ Children welcome away from bar area ~ Dogs allowed in bar ~ www.butcherandbeast.co.uk *Recommended by Chris Johnson, Paul Strange*

HOUGH-ON-THE-HILL
Brownlow Arms ⊕♀
High Road; NG32 2AZ

SK9246   Map 8

Refined country house with beamed bar, real ales, imaginative food and graceful terrace; bedrooms

Timothy Taylors Landlord and a guest such as Black Sheep on handpump are served by impeccably polite staff in this smart old stone inn – though most customers are here for the sophisticated dining experience. The beamed bar is comfortable and welcoming, with plenty of panelling, exposed brickwork, local prints and scenes, a large mirror, and a pile of logs beside the big fireplace. Seating is on elegant, stylishly mismatched upholstered armchairs, and the carefully arranged furnishings give the impression of several separate cosy areas. Several wines by the glass and a good choice of malt whiskies; easy-listening background music. The well equipped bedrooms are attractive, and breakfasts hearty. Do check the limited opening times – and note you'll probably need to book a table in advance.

Highly rated and often inventive, the food might include juniper and citrus confit salmon with pickled vegetables, goats cheese with port-poached fig, chicory, orange marmalade and toasted pine nuts, corn-fed chicken, ham hock and creamed leek pithiviers, rack of lamb with rosemary jus and dauphinoise potatoes, duck breast with french-style peas and madeira jus, and puddings such as citrus fruit jelly with gin and tonic sorbet, confit zest and lemon cream and steamed treacle sponge with vanilla crème anglaise and stem ginger ice-cream. *Benchmark main dish: slow-cooked pork belly with crushed root vegetables, quince and apple compote and red wine jus £16.95. Two-course evening meal £25.25.*

Free house ~ Licensee Paul L Willoughby ~ Real ale ~ (01400) 250234 ~ Open 6-11; 12-4 Sun; closed Sun evening, Mon, lunchtimes Tues-Sat ~ Bar food 6.30-9 (9.30 Fri, Sat); 12-2.30 Sun; see opening hours ~ Restaurant ~ Bedrooms: £65/£98 ~ www.thebrownlowarms.com *Recommended by Kay and Alistair Butler, Lisa Robertson, William and Ann Reid*

INGHAM SK9483 Map 8

Inn on the Green 🍴

The Green; LN1 2XT

Nicely modernised place serving thoughtfully prepared food; chatty atmosphere

If it's just a drink and a chat beside the log fire that you want, head for the opened-up locals' bar at this friendly dining pub. It has attractive village-green views and a relaxed, pubby feel, although several tables will probably be occupied by people here for the tasty good value food. The beamed and timbered dining room is spread over two floors with lots of exposed brickwork, brasses and copper, local prints and a warm winter fire; the lounge between these rooms has leather sofas and background music, and you can buy home-made jams, marmalade and chutney from the bar counter; Sharps Doom Bar and two guests like Oldershaw Regal Blonde and Wold Top Gold on handpump and nine wines by the glass. Service is good.

With own-made bread and ice-cream and using some home-grown produce, the popular food includes chicken liver pâté with red onion marmalade, tapas, sausages and gravy, chicken and leek pie, thai vegetable curry, free-range gammon and egg, salmon with bubble and squeak and herb dressing, specials like treacle-marinated pork fillet with mustard mash, black pudding and cider jus, lightly curried monkfish with chickpeas, saffron and celeriac, and puddings such as marinated pineapple carpaccio and lime and fromage frais sorbet and treacle tart with cinnamon crème anglaise and advocaat ice-cream. *Benchmark main dish: braised lamb shoulder with spring onion mash £13.00. Two-course evening meal £17.50.*

Free house ~ Licensees Andrew Cafferkey and Sarah Sharpe ~ Real ale ~ (01522) 730354 ~ Open 11.30-3, 6(5 Fri in summer)-11; 11.30-11 Sat (11.30-3, 6-11 in winter); 12-10.30 Sun; closed Mon ~ Bar food 12-2(4 Sun), 6-9 ~ Restaurant ~ Children welcome ~ www.innonthegreeningham.co.uk *Recommended by Geoffrey and Tina Robinson, Tony and Maggie Harwood, Paul Humphreys*

KIRKBY LA THORPE   TF0945 Map 8
Queens Head 🍴

Village and pub signposted off A17, just E of Sleaford, then turn right into Boston Road cul-de-sac; NG34 9NU

Reliable dining pub very popular for its good food and helpful, efficient service

Readers really enjoy visiting this well organised pub – 'it ticks all the right boxes,' says one. Neatly comfortable and gently traditional – and being refurbished as we went to press – it has plenty of dark-waistcoated staff, open woodburning stoves and huge elaborate flower arrangements. You can choose almost any degree of formality (and fresh air), from teak tables and chairs in a lantern-lit back arbour with a glazed canopy, through a sizeable brightly carpeted bar with stools along the counter, button-back banquettes and sofas, and dining chairs around shiny dark tables, to a verdant light and airy conservatory with informal dining tables, or – beyond heavily swagged curtains – a smart linen-set beamed restaurant. Nice decorative touches include thoughtful lighting, big prints and five handsome longcase clocks (it's quite something when they all chime at midday). Batemans XB and a guest or two like Copper Dragon Golden Pippin and 8 Sail Merry Miller on handpump, and in summer there's home-made lemonade; easy disabled access; background music.

 As well as an early- and late-bird menu, Thursday night steaks and Friday night fish suppers, the highly thought-of food includes popular specials (only £8.95 at lunchtime) such as rabbit stew with sage, baby onions and mushrooms, whole plaice grilled in lemon butter with capers or venison pie, as well as scottish scallops and smoked pancetta with lemon and white wine vinaigrette, twice-baked soufflé with cheese on caramelised onions, slow-braised lamb shank with sweet potato mash and mint and redcurrant gravy, good steaks with a choice of sauces, and puddings like baked banana and toffee cheesecake with toffee sauce and plum bread and butter pudding with home-made cinnamon ice-cream. *Benchmark main dish: steak and kidney pudding £13.95. Two-course evening meal £24.00.*

Free house ~ Licensee John Clark ~ Real ale ~ (01529) 305743 ~ Open 12-3, 6-11; 12-10.30 Sun ~ Bar food 12-2.30, 6-9.30; 12-8.30 Sun ~ Restaurant ~ Children welcome ~ www.thequeensheadinn.com *Recommended by Dr and Mrs R G J Telfer, Maurice and Janet Thorpe, Mark, Amanda, Luke and Jake Sheard, Mrs P Bishop, WAH, David Jackman, James Stretton*

WOOLSTHORPE   SK8334 Map 8
Chequers 🍴 �

Woolsthorpe near Belvoir, signposted off A52 or A607 W of Grantham; NG32 1LU

Lincolnshire Dining Pub of the Year

Interesting food at comfortably relaxed inn with good drinks and appealing castle views from outside tables

The heavy-beamed main bar in this 17th-c former coaching inn has two big tables (one a massive oak construction), a comfortable mix of seating including some handsome leather chairs and banquettes, and a huge boar's head above a good log fire in a big brick fireplace. Among cartoons on the wall are some of the illustrated claret bottle labels from the series commissioned from famous artists. There are more leather seats in a dining area on the left, in what was once the village bakery. A corridor leads off to the light and airy main restaurant, with contemporary pictures, and another bar; background music and board games. Friendly licensees and their cheerful staff serve Grainstore Cooking, Sharps Doom Bar, Skinners Cornish Trawler and Timothy Taylors Landlord on handpump, around 35 wines by the glass, 50 malt whiskies, 20 gins and local Belvoir fruit pressé. There are good quality teak tables, chairs and benches outside and, beyond these, picnic-sets on the edge of the pub's cricket field, with views of Belvoir Castle.

Excellent food using local, seasonal produce includes sandwiches, seared scallops with curried parsnip purée, chicken and parma ham terrine with tomato and roasted red pepper chutney, sausages and mash with onion gravy, burger with goats cheese, pancetta, tomato and rocket, open lasagne of basil pasta with spiced vegetables, tomato compote and goats cheese cream, chicken breast with chorizo and red wine sauce, braised oxtail with white turnip purée, mash and onion gravy, salmon, cod and seafood curry with garlic and coriander flatbread, and puddings like cinnamon rice pudding with caramel glaze and hazelnut and white chocolate millefeuille. *Benchmark main dish: rib of beef with pepper sauce, garlic mushrooms and chips (for two) £29.00. Two-course evening meal £21.50.*

Free house ~ Licensee Justin Chad ~ Real ale ~ (01476) 870701 ~ Open 12-11 (midnight Sat); 12-10.30 Sun ~ Bar food 12-2.30(4 Sun), 6-9.30(8.30 Sun) ~ Restaurant ~ Children welcome ~ Dogs allowed in bar and bedrooms ~ Bedrooms: £50/£70 ~ www.chequersinn.net *Recommended by Philip and Susan Philcox, M Mossman, Howard and Margaret Buchanan*

Also Worth a Visit in Lincolnshire

Besides the fully inspected pubs, you might like to try these pubs that have been recommended to us and described by readers. Do tell us what you think of them: feedback@goodguides.com

ALLINGTON   SK8540
⋆ **Welby Arms** (01400) 281361
The Green; off A1 at N end of Grantham bypass; NG32 2EA Friendly, well run and well liked inn with helpful staff, large simply furnished bar divided by stone archway, beams and joists, log fires (one in an attractive arched brick fireplace), comfortable plush wall banquettes and stools, up to six changing ales, over 20 wines by the glass and plenty of malt whiskies, good popular bar food including blackboard specials, civilised back dining lounge; background music; children welcome, tables in walled courtyard with pretty flower baskets, picnic-sets on front lawn, comfortable bedrooms, open all day Sun. *(Terry and Barbara, Pat and Stewart Gordon, Michael and Jenny Back, Roger and Pauline Pearce, Mrs P Bishop and others)*

ASLACKBY   TF0830
Robin Hood & Little John
(01778) 440681 *A15 Bourne–Sleaford; NG34 0HL* Nicely renovated timbered village pub, split-level bar with woodburners, mix of seating including a chesterfield in former inglenook, good choice of food (not Sun evening) from pub favourites up, ales such as Batemans, Greene King and Oldershaws, friendly staff, separate more modern oak-floored restaurant; discreet background music; three-level terrace with pergola and smokers' shelter, closed Mon. *(Tony and Maggie Harwood, R and S Bentley)*

BASSINGHAM   SK9160
Five Bells (01522) 788269
High Street; LN5 9JZ Cheerful old country pub with good choice of real ales and well liked fairly traditional food including good value set menu, bare-boards interior with hop-adorned beams and lots of brass and

bric-a-brac, some quotations on the walls, cosy log fires, even a well in one part; children and dogs welcome, open all day Sun till 7pm. *(Tony and Maggie Harwood)*

BECKINGHAM   SK8753
Pack Horse
Sleaford Road, off A17; LN5 0RF
Welcoming village local with enjoyable home-made food and four well kept ales, open fires; pleasant beer garden. *(Anon)*

BELCHFORD   TF2975
✱ Blue Bell (01507) 533602
Village signed off A153 Horncastle–Louth; LN9 6LQ 18th-c dining pub with cosy comfortable bar, Batemans, Worthington and guests, Thatcher's cider, good traditional and modern food, efficient friendly service, restaurant; children and dogs welcome, picnic-sets in terraced back garden, good base for Wolds walks and Viking Way (remove muddy boots), closed second and third weeks in Jan. *(Mr and Mrs D Mackenzie)*

BILLINGBOROUGH   TF1134
✱ Fortescue Arms (01529) 240228
B1177, off A52 Grantham–Boston; NG34 0QB Popular country local with old stonework, exposed brick, wood panelling, beams and big see-through fireplace in carpeted rooms, well kept Adnams, Everards, Greene King and Timothy Taylors, pubby food (all day Sun), good friendly service, Victorian prints, brass and copper, stuffed badger and pheasant, fresh flowers and pot plants, attractive flagstoned dining rooms each end and another fire; children welcome, picnic-sets on side lawn, more in sheltered courtyard with flowering tubs, open all day weekends. *(Anon)*

BURTON COGGLES   SK9725
Cholmeley Arms (01476) 550225
Village Street; NG33 4JS Well kept ales such as Fullers London Pride, Greene King Abbot and Grainstore in small beamed pubby bar with warm fire, generous helpings of good reasonably priced home-made food (not Sun evening), friendly efficient service, restaurant; farm shop, handy for A1, open all day weekends, closed lunchtimes Mon and Tues. *(Anon)*

CAYTHORPE   SK9348
Red Lion (01400) 272632
Signed just off A607 N of Grantham; High Street; NG32 3DN Refurbished village pub with good fairly traditional home-made food (booking advisable), friendly staff, well kept Adnams and Everards, good sensibly priced wine, bare-boards bar with light wood counter, black beams and open

fire, carpeted restaurant; back terrace by car park. *(David Howe)*

CLAYPOLE   SK8449
Five Bells (01636) 626561
Main Street; NG23 5BJ Brick-built village pub with good-sized beamed bar and smaller dining area beyond servery, four real ales, good choice of home-made food, pool and darts; grassy back garden with play area, four bedrooms, closed Mon lunchtime, otherwise open all day. *(Anon)*

CLEETHORPES   TA3009
No 2 Refreshment Room
07905 375587 *Station Approach; DN35 8AX* Comfortably refurbished carpeted platform bar, friendly staff, well kept Hancocks HB, M&B Mild, Sharps Doom Bar and three guests (June beer festival), real cider, interesting old pictures of the station, historical books on trains and the local area, no food but a free Sun night buffet, Thurs quiz; tables out under heaters, open all day from 7.30am. *(Lisa Robertson)*

CLEETHORPES   TA3108
✱ Willys (01472) 602145
Highcliff Road; south promenade; DN35 8RQ Popular open-plan bistro-style seafront pub with panoramic Humber views, café tables, tiled floor and painted brick walls; visibly brews its own good ales, also changing guests and belgian beers, good home-made bargain bar lunches (evening food Mon-Thurs), friendly fast service, nice mix of customers from young and trendy to weather-beaten fishermen; quiet juke box; a few tables out on the promenade, open all day (till late Fri, Sat). *(John Honnor)*

CONINGSBY   TF2458
Lea Gate Inn (01526) 342370
Leagate Road (B1192 southwards, off A153 E); LN4 4RS Heavy-beamed 16th-c Fenland pub with three cosy linked rooms, medley of furnishings including high-backed settles around the biggest of the three log fires, dim lighting, ancient oak panelling, attractive dining room, even a priest hole, food (all day Sun) from extensive menu, Adnams, Batemans and Wells & Youngs; children welcome, dogs in bar, pleasant garden, site of old gallows at front, eight motel bedrooms, open all day Sun. *(Mrs P Bishop)*

FOSDYKE   TF3132
Ship (01205) 260764
Moulton Washway; A17; PE12 6LH Refurbished roadside pub (a useful stop) with reasonably priced food from varied menu, Sun carvery, two Adnams beers and

---

Post Office address codings confusingly give the impression that a few pubs are in Lincolnshire, when they're really in Cambridgeshire (which is where we list them).

Batemans XB, friendly staff, simple pine and quarry-tile decor, woodburner; children welcome, garden tables. *(John Honnor, Derek and Sylvia Stephenson)*

FULBECK SK9450
Hare & Hounds (01400) 272322
The Green (A607 Leadenham–Grantham); NG32 3JJ Converted 17th-c maltings with modernised linked areas, log fire, good food from ciabattas and pub favourites up, well kept ales such as Brakspears and Marstons Pedigree, efficient well dressed staff, raftered upstairs function room; terrace seating, nice village, ridge views, eight bedrooms in adjacent barn conversion, closed Sun evening.
(Maurice and Janet Thorpe)

GAINSBOROUGH SK8189
Eight Jolly Brewers (01427) 611022
Ship Court, Silver Street; DN21 2DW Small drinkers' pub in former warehouse, eight interesting real ales, traditional cider and plenty of bottled beers, friendly staff and locals, beams and bare brick, may be more room upstairs and live music Thurs; seats outside, open all day. *(Anon)*

GRANTHAM SK9136
Blue Pig (01476) 563704
Vine Street; NG31 6RQ Cosy three-bar Tudor pub, well kept Timothy Taylors Landlord and changing guests, Weston's cider and perry, cheerful staff, low beams, panelling, stripped stone and flagstones, open fire, daily papers, lots of pig ornaments, prints and bric-a-brac, no food; juke box, games machines; dogs welcome; tables out behind, open all day (till 1.30am Fri, Sat). *(Anon)*

GRIMSTHORPE TF0423
Black Horse (01778) 591093
A151 W of Bourne; PE10 0LY Extensive, handsome grey-stone coaching inn, light and airy long narrowish bar, eclectic mix of furniture, open fires, well kept Batemans and a guest, good food including weekend carvery, friendly local atmosphere; children welcome lunchtime only, garden picnic-sets, three bedrooms, closed Sun evening, Mon.
(Tony and Maggie Harwood)

HORNCASTLE TF2669
Red Lion (01507) 523338
Bull Ring; LE9 5HT Big busy market-town pub (former coaching inn), good Oakwell beers and enjoyable down-to-earth food (not Mon), reasonable prices, pool room, theatre in converted outbuildings; side courtyard, three good value bedrooms, open all day (till 1am Fri, Sat). *(Val and Alan Green)*

IRNHAM TF0226
Griffin (01476) 550201
Bulby Road; NG33 4JG Welcoming old stone-built inn with generous home-made

food including good value set lunch, ales such as Batemans and Oakham, three rooms (two for dining), log fires, warm friendly atmosphere; background music; children welcome, classic car meetings first Weds of month (spring/summer), four bedrooms, nice village setting. *(Tony and Maggie Harwood)*

KIRKBY ON BAIN TF2462
⋆Ebrington Arms (01526) 354560
Main Street; LN10 6YT Popular village pub with good value traditional food (booking advised), half a dozen well kept changing ales, friendly service, beer mats on low 16th-c beams, carpets and banquettes, open fire, restaurant behind; background music, darts; children and dogs welcome, wheelchair access, tables out in front by road, lawn to the side with play equipment, campsite next door, closed Mon lunchtime. *(Kay and Alistair Butler)*

LINCOLN SK9871
Green Dragon (01522) 567155
Waterside North/Broadgate; LN2 5DH Revamped waterside Tudor building on three floors with handsome carved façade; downstairs bar with character timbers, beams, flagstones and stripped brickwork, lounge bar above and restaurant on top floor with fine canal views, enjoyable food including good value Sun carvery, four interesting real ales, good service; plenty of terrace seating. *(George Atkinson)*

LINCOLN SK9771
Jolly Brewer (01522) 528583
Broadgate; LN2 5AQ Popular pub (good mix of customers) with art deco interior, well kept mainly local ales and several ciders, no food, open fire, regular live music; can be crowded weekend evenings; tables outside, open all day. *(Chris Johnson)*

LINCOLN SK9871
Morning Star (01522) 527079
Greetwell Gate; LN2 4AW Friendly traditional local handy for the cathedral, enjoyable good value lunches (not Sun), well kept reasonably priced mainstream ales, helpful service, two bar areas and comfortable snug, aircraft paintings, coal fire, some live music (piano often played); nice covered outside area, open all day. *(the Didler)*

LINCOLN SK9771
Strugglers (01522) 535023
Westgate; LN1 3BG Cosily worn-in beer lovers' haunt, half a dozen or more well kept ales including Bass and Timothy Taylors, lots of knick-knacks and beer mats, coal-effect fire in back snug, some live music; no children inside; dogs welcome, steps down to sunny back courtyard with heated canopy, open all day (till 1am Thurs-Sat).
(Richard Stanfield)

LINCOLN SK9771

★**Victoria** (01522) 541000

Union Road; LN1 3BJ Main draw to this old-fashioned backstreet local are the eight real ales (including Batemans), foreign draught and bottled beers and farm cider (summer and Halloween beer festivals); simply furnished tiled front lounge with pictures of Queen Victoria, coal fire, basic lunchtime food, friendly staff and good mix of customers (gets especially busy lunchtime and later in evening); children and dogs welcome, seats on heated terrace, castle views, open all day till midnight (1am Fri, Sat). *(Chris Johnson, Peter Meister, Richard Luck, John Honnor, Sean Finnegan)*

LINCOLN SK9771

Widow Cullens Well (01522) 523020

Steep Hill; LN2 1LU Ancient simply revamped building on two floors, cheap Sam Smiths beers and bar food, chatty mix of customers, good service; back terrace. *(Michael Butler, Tony and Maggie Harwood)*

LINCOLN SK9771

★**Wig & Mitre** (01522) 535190

Steep Hill; just below cathedral; LN2 1LU Civilised café-style dining pub with plenty of character and attractive period features over two floors; big-windowed downstairs bar, beams and exposed stone walls, pews and Gothic furniture on oak boards, comfortable sofas in carpeted back area, quieter upstairs dining room with views of castle walls and cathedral, antique prints and caricatures of lawyers/clerics, all-day food from breakfast on including good value set menus and some interesting seasonal dishes, extensive choice of wines by the glass from good list, well kept Black Sheep, Everards and Oakham; children and dogs welcome, open 8am-midnight. *(Tom and Ruth Rees, Tony and Maggie Harwood, Dr and Mrs A K Clarke, Val and Alan Green, Ryta Lyndley)*

LONG BENNINGTON SK8344

★**Reindeer** (01400) 281382

Just off A1 N of Grantham – S end of village, opposite school; NG23 5DJ Thriving atmosphere in attractively traditional low-beamed pub with popular long-serving landlady, consistently good if not always cheap food from sandwiches up in bar and more formal restaurant, John Smiths, Timothy Taylors Landlord and one or two guests, nice wines, good friendly service, coal-effect stove in stone fireplace; background music not too obtrusive; picnic-sets under parasols in small front courtyard, closed Sun evening, Mon. *(Gordon and Margaret Ormondroyd, Tony and Maggie Harwood, Brian and Janet Ainscough)*

LONG BENNINGTON SK8344

Royal Oak (01400) 281332

Main Road; just off A1 N of Grantham;

NG23 5DJ Popular local with enthusiastic welcoming licensees; good-sized bar serving well kept Marstons and Mansfield ales, several wines by the glass, good home-made food including specials, friendly helpful staff; children welcome, seats out in front and in big back garden with play area, path for customers to river, open all day. *(Tony and Maggie Harwood, Adrian Finn)*

LOUTH TF3287

Wheatsheaf (01507) 606262

Westgate; LN11 9YD Cheerful 17th-c low-beamed pub under welcoming new landlady; coal fires in all three bars, old photographs, good changing ales and inexpensive food; can get busy; tables outside. *(Liz Bell)*

MINTING TF1873

Sebastopol (01507) 578577

Off A158 Lincoln–Horncastle; LN9 5RT Refurbished 19th-c red-brick village pub; good home-made food from traditional choices up using Lincolnshire suppliers, well kept local ales such as Batemans and Brewsters, nine wines by the glass, friendly staff, quiz first Weds of month; children welcome, picnic-sets on front terrace, self-catering barn conversion, closed Sun evening. *(Andy Brown, John F Knutton)*

NORTH THORESBY TF2998

New Inn (01472) 840270

Station Road; DN36 5QS Popular and friendly village pub, good reliable home-made food, well kept Marstons Pedigree, Theakstons and guests, nice fire in bar, roomy restaurant; disabled facilities, terrace. *(Anon)*

NORTON DISNEY SK8859

Green Man (01522) 789804

Main Street, off A46 Newark–Lincoln; LN6 9JU Old beamed village pub-restaurant with opened-up modernised interior; enjoyable food from sandwiches and traditional dishes up including some interesting specials, three well kept ales from central bar, friendly young staff, high-backed dining chairs on wood floor; TV; tables out behind. *(Paul Humphreys)*

PINCHBECK TF2326

Ship (01775) 766800

Northgate; PE11 3SE Old thatched and beamed riverside pub refurbished under newish licensees; carpeted front bar and extended back restaurant, good choice of enjoyable food (not Sun or Mon evenings) from snacks and pub favourites up, breakfasts and packed lunches for fishermen by arrangement, Fullers London Pride and maybe a guest (July beer festival with live music and tug-of-war), nostalgic odds and ends, Chicku the parrot; children welcome, no dogs inside, terrace tables and garden with play equipment, open all day summer weekends. *(Michael and Jenny Back)*

SCAMPTON SK9579
Dambusters (01522) 731333
High Street; LN1 2SD Several beamed
rooms around central bar with masses
of interesting Dambusters and other
RAF memorabilia, reasonably priced
straightforward food (not Sun evening),
also home-made chutneys, pâté and biscuits
for sale, five interesting real ales (ceiling
covered in beer mats from past guests), a
couple of sofas on wood floor, log fire in big
brick fireplace, more formal seating at back;
very near Red Arrows runway viewpoint, open
all day Fri, Sat, till 6pm Sun, closed Mon
lunchtime. *(Paul Humphreys)*

SOUTH RAUCEBY TF0245
Bustard (01529) 488250
Main Street; NG34 8QG Modernised
19th-c stone-built pub with good food from
varied menu, well kept ales and plenty of
wines by the glass, friendly staff, restaurant;
children welcome, attractive sheltered
garden, closed Sun evening, Mon. *(Sarah
Flynn)*

STAMFORD TF0207
All Saints Brewery – Melbourn Brothers (01780) 7521865
All Saints Street; PE9 2PA Nicely
reworked old building (core is a medieval
hall) with warren of rooms on three floors;
friendly enthusiastic licensees (took over
2012), upstairs bar serving bottled fruit
beers from adjacent early 19th-c brewery and
low-priced Sam Smiths on handpump, food
from pub favourites up including set deals,
ground-floor dining area with log fire and
woodburner, top floor with leather sofas and
wing chairs, board games; children and dogs
welcome, picnic-sets in cobbled courtyard,
brewery tours, open all day. *(John Coatsworth)*

STAMFORD TF0306
Bull & Swan (01780) 766412
High Street, St Martins; PE9 2LJ
Traditional old inn refurbished under newish
management; three low-beamed connecting
rooms, log fires, enjoyable food from
sandwiches and sharing plates up, Adnams,
Grainstore and Oakham ales, plenty of wines
by the glass; children and dogs welcome,
tables out in former back coachyard,
seven individually styled bedrooms named
after animals (some road noise), open all
day. *(John Coatsworth, Richard and Penny
Gibbs)*

STAMFORD TF0207
⋆Crown (01780) 763136
All Saints Place; PE9 2AG Well
modernised stone-built hotel with emphasis
on good seasonal country cooking using
local produce (some from their own farm),
friendly helpful staff, well kept ales such as
Adnams, decent wines, whiskies and coffee,
spacious main bar, long leather-cushioned

counter, substantial pillars, step up to more
traditional flagstoned area with stripped
stone and lots of leather sofas and armchairs,
civilised dining room; back courtyard,
28 comfortable bedrooms, good breakfast,
open all day. *(Gerry and Rosemary Dobson,
Les and Sandra Brown)*

STAMFORD TF0306
⋆George of Stamford (01780) 750750
*High Street, St Martins (B1081 S of
centre, not the quite different central
pedestrianised High Street); PE9 2LB*
Grand old coaching inn with civilised but
informal atmosphere and many carefully
preserved features; York Bar is properly
pubby with traditional furniture, Adnams
Broadside, Grainstore Triple B and a guest,
excellent choice of wines (many are italian)
with around 17 by the glass, striking central
lounge with sturdy beams and timbers,
broad flagstones and substantial stonework,
formal oak-panelled restaurant (jacket or tie
required, no under-8s), less formal Garden
Room Restaurant with central tropical
planting, some other comfortable areas
with interesting furnishings, very good if not
cheap food (bar snacks are fair), impeccable
service; dogs welcome in bar, charming
cobbled courtyard surrounded by ancient
stone buildings, immaculately kept walled
garden with sunken lawn, bedrooms, open
all day. *(Michael Sargent, Andy Lickfold, Mrs P
Bishop, Colin Chambers, Tom Carver and others)*

STAMFORD TF0207
Jolly Brewer (01780) 755141
Foundry Road; PE9 2PP Welcoming
19th-c stone-built pub with half a dozen well
kept ales, traditional ciders/perries and wide
range of interesting whiskies (some from
India and Japan), low-priced simple food,
regular beer festivals and quiz & curry nights,
pub games, nice open fire; sports TV, open
all day. *(Anon)*

STAMFORD TF0207
St Marys Vaults (01780) 764305
St Marys Street; PE9 2DG Spacious late
medieval timber-framed pub in centre of
conservation area; cheap well kept Sam
Smiths beers, good choice of enjoyable
food at bargain prices, cosy back dining
part; wheelchair access but lavatories
(and games room) upstairs, flower-filled
courtyard. *(Michael Tack, David and Ruth
Hollands)*

STAMFORD TF0307
⋆Tobie Norris (01780) 753800
St Pauls Street; PE9 2BE Great fun,
centuries old and full of character;
beautifully restored making the most of
its age with worn flagstones, meticulously
stripped stonework and huge hearth for
woodburning stove, several linked rooms
including handsomely panelled shrine
to Nelson and Battle of Trafalgar, also

an upstairs room with steeply pitched rafters, Ufford White Hart from owner's microbrewery along with Adnams and three guest beers, Weston's cider, lots of 'compile your own' pizzas and other food (not Sun evening), relaxed easy-going atmosphere; children over 10 allowed at lunchtime, dogs in bar (resident labradoodles Fraggle and Sprocket), open all day. *(Andy Lickfold, Michael Doswell, John Coatsworth)*

STOW   SK8881
★ Cross Keys (01427) 788314
Stow Park Road; B1241 NW of Lincoln; LN1 2DD Cosy carpeted bar in traditional pub with big woodburner, straightforward furnishings, some wood panelling, decorative china and country prints, five changing ales such as Castle Rock, Batemans and Theakstons, quite a range of bar food in neatly laid dining areas, good service; background music, no dogs inside; children welcome, near interesting Saxon minster church, open all day Sun till 8.30pm, closed Mon lunchtime. *(Paul Humphreys)*

SURFLEET   TF2528
Mermaid (01775) 680275
B1356 (Gosberton Road), just off A16 N of Spalding; PE11 4AB Welcoming and traditional with two high-ceilinged carpeted rooms, huge sash windows, banquettes, captain's chairs and spindlebacks, four changing real ales, good choice of fairly straightforward food including a monthly themed night, friendly fast service, restaurant; background music; pretty terraced garden with bar and seats under thatched parasols, children's play area walled from River Glen, moorings, four bedrooms, open all day Sat in summer, closed Sun evening. *(Colin McIlwain)*

SURFLEET SEAS END   TF2729
★ Ship (01775) 680547
Reservoir Road; off A16 N of Spalding; PE11 4DH Immaculately rebuilt pub just below seawall; woodburner, chesterfields and handsomely made seating in good-sized civilised bar with old scrubbed tables in open bays, enjoyable reasonably priced food including OAP deal, changing well kept ales such as Elgoods and Slaters, helpful friendly service, upstairs overflow restaurant; tables on front terrace, boating-view benching and picnic-sets on embankment across lane, four good value bedrooms. *(Tony and Maggie Harwood, M J Daly)*

TATTERSHALL THORPE   TF2159
Blue Bell (01526) 342206
Thorpe Road; B1192 Coningsby–Woodhall Spa; LN4 4PE Ancient low-beamed pub (said to date from the 13th c) with friendly cosy atmosphere, RAF memorabilia including airmen's signatures on the ceiling (pub was used by the Dambusters), big open fire, four well kept ales, some nice wines and enjoyable well priced pubby food, small dining room; garden tables, bedrooms. *(Pat and Stewart Gordon)*

THEDDLETHORPE ALL SAINTS   TF4787
★ Kings Head (01507) 339798
Pub signposted off A1031 N of Mablethorpe; Mill Road; LN12 1PB Long 16th-c thatched building, carpeted two-room front lounge with lowest ceiling we've found in any pub, brass platters on timbered walls, antique dining chairs and tables, easy chairs by log fire, central bar (more low beams) with well kept Batemans XB, a seasonal ale and Skidbrooke local cider, shelves of books, coal fire with side oven, stuffed owls and country pictures, long dining room with colourful mugs and jugs hanging from black joists, good local food including steaks and fresh Grimsby fish, Sun carvery, cheerful helpful landlord; one or two picnic-sets in prettily planted front area, more on lawn, open all day Sat, closed Sun evening, Mon. *(Anon)*

THREEKINGHAM   TF0836
Three Kings (01529) 240249
Just off A52 12 miles E of Grantham; Saltersway; NG34 0AU Big entrance hall (former coaching inn), beamed and dark panelled bar with coal fire and pubby furniture including banquettes, compact restaurant plus bigger dining/function room, good choice of enjoyable home-made food from baguettes up, Bass, Timothy Taylors Landlord and guests such as Cottage and Tom Woods, friendly efficient staff; children and dogs welcome, terrace with covered smokers' area, closed Mon. *(Nigel and Jean Eames)*

WAINFLEET   TF5058
★ Batemans Brewery (01754) 882009
Mill Lane, off A52 via B1195; PE24 4JE Circular bar in brewery's ivy-covered windmill tower, Batemans ales in top condition, czech and belgian beers on tap, ground-floor dining area with cheap food including baguettes and a few pubby dishes, plenty of old pub games (more outside), lots of brewery memorabilia and plenty for families to enjoy; entertaining brewery tours and shop, tables on terrace and grass, open 11.30am-4pm (2.30pm in winter), closed Mon, Tues. *(J F M and M West)*

WEST DEEPING   TF1009
Red Lion (01778) 347190
King Street; PE6 9HP Welcoming stone-built family-run pub with long low-beamed bar, half a dozen well kept interesting beers, popular food including OAP weekday lunch and early-bird deal, back dining extension, stripped stone and open fire, live music including monthly folk club; children welcome, tables in back garden with fenced play area. *(Phil and Jane Hodson)*

Norfolk

With so much to look at, places to visit and vast empty beaches, this is a very popular holiday county. New entries – or pubs back in these pages – include the Kings Head in Bawburgh (bustling and cheerful, with five ales and interesting food), Jolly Sailors in Brancaster Staithe (own-brew beers and popular food in seaside pub), Kings Head at Great Bircham (Edwardian hotel with busy bar and four real ales), Bank House in King's Lynn (civilised bar-brasserie by quay) and Wildebeest Arms at Stoke Holy Cross (enterprising food). Other pubs our readers enjoy are the Hoste Arms in Burnham Market (civilised hotel with a proper bar), Saracens Head in Erpingham (easy-going atmosphere and a nice place to stay), Swan at Ingham (a clever mix of old and new furnishings, landlord-cooked food, comfortable bedrooms), Fat Cat in Norwich (a mecca for real ale lovers), Dun Cow at Salthouse (much enjoyed and overlooking the salt marshes), King William IV at Sedgeford (hands-on licensees in well run pub, with good food and beer), Rose & Crown in Snettisham (very special all-rounder), Red Lion at Stiffkey (popular, with well liked meals and drinks), Orange Tree in Thornham (amazingly inventive, delicious food and a warm welcome), Bell in Wiveton (smashing mix of customers and impressive food) and Fur & Feather in Woodbastwick (full range of Woodfordes ales from next-door brewery and generous food). For sheer enjoyment mixed with exciting dishes, our Norfolk Dining Pub 2014 is the Orange Tree in Thornham.

BAWBURGH
TG1508   Map 5

Kings Head ♀ ◀

Harts Lane; A47 just W of Norwich then B1108; NR9 3LS

Busy small-roomed pub, open fire and woodburners, five real ales, good wines by the glass, interesting food and friendly service

Opposite a little green, this bustling 17th-c pub has a cheerful atmosphere and a good mix of customers. The small rooms have low beams and standing timbers, leather sofas and an attractive assortment of old dining chairs and tables on wood-strip floors, a knocked-through open fire and a couple of woodburning stoves in the restaurant areas.

Adnams Bitter and Broadside, Woodfordes Wherry and guest beers like Humpty Dumpty Swallow Tail and Theakstons Lightfoot Bitter on handpump, 11 wines by the glass and 14 malt whiskies; friendly and helpful service. There are seats in the garden.

🍴 Tempting food includes sandwiches, smoked salmon with pea mousse, soft boiled egg and watercress, ham hock terrine with piccalilli and apple chutney, crispy polenta with sun-dried tomato and feta risotto balls and roasted pepper jus, poached chicken breast stuffed with wild mushrooms with chicken consommé, beef and horseradish suet pudding, duck breast with plum and port jelly, pork belly, chorizo, paprika and bean cassoulet, and puddings such as coconut parfait, pineapple and mango salsa and shortbread crumbs and rhubarb and custard panna cotta with bubble gum ice-cream, chocolate and honeycomb. *Benchmark main dish: fish and chips with minted mushy peas and home-made tartare sauce £12.00. Two-course evening meal £19.00.*

Free house ~ Licensee Anton Wimmer ~ Real ale ~ (01603) 744977 ~ Open 12-11; 12-6 Sun in winter ~ Bar food 12-2, 5.30-9; 12-9 Sun ~ Restaurant ~ Children welcome ~ Dogs allowed in bar ~ www.kingshead-bawburgh.co.uk *Recommended by Alan Bulley, Chris Price*

BLAKENEY
White Horse ♀

TG0243   Map 8

Off A149 W of Sheringham; High Street; NR25 7AL

Cheerful small hotel with popular dining conservatory, interesting food and drinks and helpful staff; bedrooms

Just a stroll from the small tidal harbour, this is a bustling former coaching inn with lots of bird-watching, walking and sailing all around; it's also great fun to take a boat to see the local common and grey seal colony. The informal long bar has cream-coloured walls above a pale grey dado hung with fine-art equestrian prints and paintings from a local gallery, high-backed brown leather dining and other chairs around light oak tables on a new black and white striped carpet, and natural linen window blinds; Adnams Bitter, Broadside, Explorer and a seasonal guest on handpump and a dozen wines by the glass. There's also an airy conservatory. The suntrap courtyard and pleasant paved garden have plenty of tables.

🍴 Attractively presented food includes baguettes, ham hock and mustard terrine with piccalilli, pigeon breast with confit shallot, parsnip purée and brandy jus, basil pesto tagliatelle with home-made garlic dough balls, pie of the day, burger with blue cheese, bacon, mushrooms, coleslaw and fries, chicken with pumpkin and squash purée, celeriac remoulade and chicken and bacon mousse, braised brisket with horseradish mash, wild mushrooms and red wine jus, cod fillet with brown shrimps, crab bisque and dauphinoise potatoes, and puddings such as gooseberry jam crème brûlée and triple chocolate brownie with Baileys sundae and mint ice-cream. *Benchmark main dish: portuguese stew of chicken, squid and olives £15.95. Two-course evening meal £22.00.*

Free house ~ Licensee Francis Guildea ~ Real ale ~ (01263) 740574 ~ Open 11-11 ~ Bar food 12-2, 6-9; 12-2.30, 6.30-8.30 Sun ~ Restaurant ~ Children welcome ~ Dogs allowed in bar ~ Bedrooms: /£110 ~ www.blakeneywhitehorse.co.uk
Recommended by Tracey and Stephen Groves, David Eberlin, David Carr, W K Wood, Mike and Shirley Stratton, Revd Michael Vockins

---

If we know a featured-entry pub does sandwiches, we always say so – if they're not mentioned, you'll have to assume you can't get one.

BRANCASTER STAITHE

Jolly Sailors

TF7944 Map 8

Main Road (A149); PE31 8BJ

Bustling pub with own-brewed beers, traditional food, friendly staff and plenty of seats in sizeable garden; great for bird-watching

Run with cheerful enthusiasm, this happily unpretentious pub has own-brewed beers and a peaceful garden with plenty of seats – all much enjoyed by our readers. The main bar has a mix of wheelback, cushioned captain's and other dark wooden dining chairs around pubby tables on red quarry tiles, a log fire in a brick fireplace, stripped stone walls and Brancaster Best, Grain Oak and Redwood, and Wolf Lupus Lupus on handpump and a dozen wines by the glass; there's a serving hatch to the outside terraced seating area. Two snug areas have local books, board games and views to the harbour; darts. The dining lounge has old-fashioned comfortable furnishings, easy chairs by an open fire and scrub-top tables; a further room, facing the garden, has pool and TV. In summer, there's a beach-themed ice-cream hut. This is prime bird-watching territory – the pub is on the edge of thousands of acres of National Trust dunes and salt flats.

 As well as stone-baked pizzas (also available for takeaway) and local fish and shellfish, the popular food includes sandwiches, whitebait, nachos with sour cream and guacamole, stilton, mushroom and spinach tagliatelle, steak in ale pie, chicken curry, hickory barbecue burger with coleslaw and chips, bass with bacon, mint fricassée, pork steak with peppercorn sauce, and puddings such as chocolate tart with mint choc chip ice-cream and sticky toffee pudding with toffee sauce. *Benchmark main dish: local moules marinière £9.95. Two-course evening meal £16.00.*

Free house ~ Licensees Cliff and James Nye ~ Real ale ~ (01485) 210314 ~ Open 12-11 (10.30 Sun) ~ Bar food 12-9; 12-2, 6-9 in winter ~ Children welcome ~ Dogs welcome ~ www.jollysailorsbrancaster.co.uk *Recommended by Mike and Linda Hudson, Tracey and Stephen Groves, Derek and Sylvia Stephenson*

BURNHAM MARKET

Hoste Arms

TF8342 Map 8

The Green (B1155); PE31 8HD

Civilised and stylish with excellent food and drinks, a proper bar, several lounge areas and dining rooms, and a lovely garden; elaborately decorated bedrooms

Most emphasis at this smart and civilised 17th-c former coaching inn is on the hotel and restaurant side, but at its heart there remains a bustling front bar with the feel of a proper village pub and a good mix of chatty drinkers. This is panelled, with a log fire, watercolours showing scenes from local walks, and Adnams Broadside, Woodfordes Wherry and a changing guest beer on handpump. The extensive and carefully chosen wine list has helpful notes and around 19 wines (including champagne and sparkling) by the glass; lots of whiskies and liqueurs. There's a conservatory with leather armchairs and sofas, a lounge for afternoon tea and several restaurants (best to book to be sure of a table). The lovely walled garden has plenty of seats and a big awning over the moroccan-style dining area.

Using the best local, seasonal produce, the sophisticated modern – if not cheap – food includes tian of crab with piquillo peppers, cucumber noodles and white tomato sorbet, blue cheese crème brûlée with pecan and poached pear salad and olive biscotti, corn-fed chicken caesar salad, thai green vegetable curry, burger with cheese, bacon, gherkin and chips, steak and kidney pudding, seafood, chorizo and chive risotto, pork belly with sage and onion gnocchi, apple purée and crackling, seared lambs liver with pancetta and horseradish and chive mash, and puddings such as trifle with seasonal fruits and treacle tart with orange clotted cream. *Benchmark main dish: sesame-crusted fillet of bass with oriental vegetable stir-fry, sweet chilli potatoes and coriander £20.00. Two-course evening meal £25.00.*

Free house ~ Licensee Emma Tagg ~ Real ale ~ (01328) 738777 ~ Open 11-11(10.30 Sun) ~ Bar food 12-2, 6-9 ~ Restaurant ~ Children welcome ~ Dogs allowed in bar and bedrooms ~ Bedrooms: £122/£149 ~ www.thehoste.com *Recommended by Michael Sargent, Simon Rodway, Michael and Maggie Betton, Mike and Linda Hudson, Derek Thomas, Roy Hoing, James Stretton, W K Wood, David Carr*

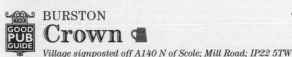

BURSTON
TM1383 Map 8

Crown

Village signposted off A140 N of Scole; Mill Road; IP22 5TW

Friendly, relaxed village pub usefully open all day, with a warm welcome, real ales and well liked bar food

This is the sort of village pub where even visitors will feel immediately at home – you can be sure of a friendly welcome. Locals tend to gather near the bar counter, with its high bar chairs, where they serve Adnams Bitter, Greene King Abbot and guests from breweries like Growlers and Woodfordes on handpump or tapped from the cask, a farm cider and half a dozen wines by the glass. In cold weather, the best spot in this heavy-beamed, quarry-tiled room is on the comfortably cushioned sofas in front of the woodburning stove in the huge brick fireplace, and there are also stools by a low chunky wooden table; newspapers and magazines. The public bar on the left has a nice long table and panelled settle on an old brick floor in one alcove, straightforward tables and chairs on carpet by the pool table, games machine and juke box, and, up a step, more tables and chairs. Both of these cream-painted rooms are hung with cheerful naive local character paintings; background music and board games. The simply furnished, beamed dining room has another big brick fireplace. Outside, there's a smokers' shelter, a couple of picnic-sets in front of the old brick building and more seats in a hedged-off area with a barbecue.

Quite a choice of popular food includes sandwiches, crayfish cocktail, chicken liver parfait with red onion marmalade, thai yellow chicken curry, burger with chips, spinach and cream cheese pancakes, beef, mushroom and Guinness pie, lambs liver and gravy, braised beef cheeks with pear, chocolate and celeriac mash, pigeon with juniper berries, dauphinoise potatoes and port and rhubarb sauce, and puddings. *Benchmark main dish: rib-eye steak with café de paris butter £17.90. Two-course evening meal £19.50.*

Free house ~ Licensees Bev and Steve Kembery and Jonathan Piers-Hall ~ Real ale ~ (01379) 741257 ~ Open 12-11(10.30 Sun) ~ Bar food 12-2, 6.30-9; 12-4 Sun; not Mon ~ Restaurant ~ Children welcome ~ Dogs allowed in bar ~ Buskers night Thurs, live music every other Sun ~ www.burstoncrown.com *Recommended by Ruth May, Evelyn and Derek Walter*

 CASTLE ACRE   TF8115   Map 8

Ostrich

Stocks Green; PE32 2AE

Friendly old village pub with original features, fine old fireplaces, real ales and tasty food

Informal and friendly, this handsome old former coaching inn has a warm atmosphere in its various rooms and a good mix of locals and visitors. Although largely rebuilt in the 18th c, some of the original masonry, beams and trusses are visible in the lofty ceilings; the L-shaped low-ceilinged front bar (on two levels) has a woodburning stove in a huge old fireplace, lots of wheelback chairs and cushioned pews around pubby tables on a wood-strip floor and gold patterned wallpaper. A step leads up to an area in front of the bar counter where there are similar seats and tables and a log fire in a brick fireplace. Greene King IPA, Abbot and Old Speckled Hen and a seasonal guest beer on handpump, around a dozen wines by the glass and several malt whiskies. A separate dining room has another brick fireplace. The sheltered garden has picnic-sets under parasols and the inn faces the tree-lined village green; the village has the remains of a Norman castle and a Cluniac monastery.

 Well liked food in generous helpings includes sandwiches and panini, wild mushroom and truffle pâté, salt cod fritters with sweet chilli dip, gammon with egg, butternut squash and sage linguine with pine nuts, toad in the hole with mash and gravy, tuna steak with spring onion, ginger and chilli noodles, chicken breast with tarragon and mustard sauce and colcannon mash, venison stew and dumplings, and puddings. *Benchmark main dish: steak burger with bacon, cheese, onions and chips £13.95. Two-course evening meal £19.00.*

Greene King ~ Tenant Tiffany Turner ~ Real ale ~ (01760) 755398 ~ Open 10am-11pm (12.30am Sat, 11.30 Sun) ~ Bar food 12-3, 6-9 ~ Restaurant ~ Children welcome ~ Dogs allowed in bar ~ Bedrooms: £70/£80 ~ www.ostrichcastleacre.com
Recommended by Colin and Louise English, Dr and Mrs R G J Telfer, Colin McKerrow, Maureen Wood, Nigel and Sue Foster

CLEY NEXT THE SEA   TG0443   Map 8

George ♀ 🛏

Off A149 W of Sheringham; High Street; NR25 7RN

Pubby bar and two dining rooms in sizeable inn, real ales, good choice of wines and popular food; bedrooms

If staying in the comfortable bedrooms here, try to get one overlooking the salt marshes – a focal bird-watching point for many years; the little garden, just across a small lane, backs on to them too. Inside, the small public bar has photographs of Norfolk wherries and other local scenes on cream walls, a long leather settle and sturdy dark wooden chairs by a couple of green-topped tables on carpet, a huge candle in a big glass jar on one window sill, a table of newspapers and a stained-glass window showing St George and the dragon. Adnams Broadside, Woodfordes Wherry and Yetmans Red on handpump and lots of wines by the glass. The dining rooms are similarly furnished with pale wooden cushioned dining chairs around a mix of tables, prints of Frank Brangwyn's drawings on the walls and evening candlelight. This is a charming and peaceful brick and flint village.

Making good use of the smokehouse just a few doors away, the well liked food includes sandwiches, curried potted prawns, terrine of the day with home-made chutney, pear, spinach and goats cheese parcel, moules marinière, lamb and mint pie, venison sausages with dauphinoise potatoes and red wine gravy, pork chop with chorizo, chickpea and pepper casserole, salmon with caper butter sauce and herb-crushed new potatoes, and puddings such as star anise panna cotta with rhubarb and ginger sorbet and black forest mess; Thursday is curry night. *Benchmark main dish: beer-battered haddock with peas and home-made tartare sauce £12.95. Two-course evening meal £19.00.*

Free house ~ Licensee Martin Panter ~ Real ale ~ (01263) 740652 ~ Open 11-11 ~ Bar food 12-2.15, 6.30-9; 12.30-2.30, 6.30-8.30 Sun ~ Restaurant ~ Children welcome ~ Dogs allowed in bar and bedrooms ~ Bedrooms: /£90 ~ www.thegeorgehotelatcley.co.uk
Recommended by Philip Lane, David and Judy Robison, Pauline Fellows and Simon Robbins, R C Vincent, John Evans

GREAT BIRCHAM   TF7632   Map 8
Kings Head

B1155, S end of village (called and signed Bircham locally); PE31 6RJ

Cheerful little bar in relaxed hotel, comfortable seating areas, four real ales, enjoyable food and seats outside; bedrooms

Although this handsome Edwardian place is more a hotel than a straightforward pub, the attractively contemporary small bar has plenty of regulars and up to four real ales on handpump: Greene King Old Speckled Hen, Humpty Dumpty Ale, Woodfordes Wherry and a changing guest. Also, several good wines by the glass and over 50 gins. There are comfortable sofas and tub chairs, a few high chairs against the counter and a log fire, as well as lounge areas and a light, airy modern restaurant; staff are friendly and helpful. Outside, front and back, are plenty of tables and chairs, with country views. The bedrooms are comfortable and breakfasts good.

The varied food includes sandwiches, scotched quails eggs with celery salt and spiced tomato sauce, a meze plate, mushroom, spinach and parmesan linguine with truffle-foam velouté, sausages with red onion gravy and mash, beer-battered fish and chips, chicken stuffed with apricots, pistachios and spinach with potato mousseline, lamb rump with leek and onion tartlet and tarragon and tomato jus, and puddings such as salted caramel cheesecake with espresso milkshake and mascarpone ice-cream and a little pot of cream with hot sugared doughnuts. *Benchmark main dish: fillet of bass with lardons, glazed spring onions and white bordelaise foam butter sauce £15.95. Two-course evening meal £20.00.*

Free house ~ Licensee Charles Campbell ~ Real ale ~ (01485) 578265 ~ Open 11-2.30, 6.30-11 ~ Bar food 12-3, 6-9; cream teas 3-6 ~ Restaurant ~ Children welcome ~ Dogs welcome ~ Bedrooms: £90/£100 ~ www.the-kings-head-bircham.co.uk
Recommended by Tess White, Toby Jones

GREAT MASSINGHAM   TF7922   Map 8
Dabbling Duck

Off A148 King's Lynn–Fakenham; Abbey Road; PE32 2HN

Unassuming from the outside but with a friendly atmosphere, character bars and warm fires, real ales and interesting food; comfortable bedrooms

To find this bustling, well run pub, just head for the village church. The attractively furnished, relaxed bars have leather sofas and armchairs by woodburning stoves (three in all), a mix of antique wooden dining tables and chairs on flagstones or stripped-wood floors, a very high-backed settle, 18th- and 19th-c quirky prints and cartoons, and plenty of beams and standing timbers. At the back of the pub is the Blenheim room, just right for a private group, and there's also a candlelit dining room. Adnams Broadside, Beestons Worth the Wait, Greene King IPA, Woodfordes Wherry and a guest beer like Timothy Taylors Landlord on handpump, from a bar counter made of great slabs of polished tree trunk; background music, darts and board games. There are tables and chairs on a front terrace overlooking the sizeable village green with its big duck ponds, and more seats in the enclosed back garden with a play area. The bedrooms are named after famous local sportsmen and airmen from the World War II air base in Massingham.

🍴 Popular food includes sandwiches, crispy-skin mackerel with asian-style salad, chicken liver and port pâté with apple chutney, smoked haddock with cheddar and herb crust and creamy pesto leeks, wild mushroom risotto, battered haddock and chips, pie of the day, confit duck leg with celeriac dauphinoise and sweet and sour beetroot purée, and puddings such as rhubarb and turkish delight and coconut cheesecake with spiced pineapple salsa and guava purée. *Benchmark main dish: rump burger with bacon, gruyère, tomato relish and coleslaw £12.00. Two-course evening meal £17.50.*

Free house ~ Licensee Dominic Symington ~ Real ale ~ (01485) 520827 ~ Open 12-11.30 ~ Bar food 12-2.30, 6.30-9.30 ~ Restaurant ~ Children welcome ~ Dogs allowed in bar ~ Bedrooms: £65/£90 ~ www.thedabblingduck.co.uk *Recommended by R C Vincent, Philip and Susan Philcox, Anthony Barnes, George Atkinson, F and M Pryor, Derek and Sylvia Stephenson, Mike and Shelley Woodroffe, Nigel and Sue Foster*

KING'S LYNN   TF6119   Map 8
Bank House ♀ 🛏

Kings Staithe Square via Boat Street and along the quay in one-way system; PE30 1RD

Georgian bar-brasserie with plenty of history and character, airy rooms, real ales and some sort of interesting food all day; bedrooms

In the 1780s, Mr Gurney, one of the founding fathers of Barclays Bank, set up his first bank in this handsome building on a splendid quayside spot. The big-windowed airy bar, once the bank manager's office, is now civilised and elegant, with pastel paintwork, sofas, armchairs and some dining tables; there's also a restaurant with fine antique chairs and tables on bare boards and a light brasserie with modern metalwork chairs around dark tables on pale wooden floors and a big brick fireplace. The atmosphere throughout is bustling and friendly, with customers popping in all day; service is helpful and courteous. Adnams Bitter and Woodfordes Wherry on handpump, ten wines by the glass, farm cider and cocktails. There are seats on the west-facing riverside terrace. Bedrooms mostly look over the river and are stylish and thoughtfully decorated. It's on the quayside, next to the Corn Exchange theatre and arts centre. Sister pub is the Rose & Crown in Snettisham.

🍴 As well as breakfasts and proper afternoon teas, and using the best local seasonal produce, the impressive food includes sandwiches, smoked rabbit, radicchio, orange and fennel salad, chive scrambled eggs with smoked salmon, local mussels with shallots, thyme and cider, battered haddock and chips, confit duck leg with mango and coriander salad, lamb tagine with couscous, chicken breast with shepherdess pie and red wine gravy, hake fillet with shellfish and vegetable en papillote, and puddings. *Benchmark main dish: chargrilled steak burger with cheese, onion rings, gherkins and barbecue sauce £10.75. Two-course evening meal £17.25.*

Free house ~ Licensee Anthony Goodrich ~ Real ale ~ (01553) 660492 ~ Open 11-11 ~ Bar food 12-2.30, 6-9(9.30 Fri, Sat); 12-5.30, 6-9.30 weekends; breakfast 8.30-11am; afternoon tea 2.30-5.30 ~ Restaurant ~ Children welcome ~ Live jazz fourth Sun of month 4-7pm ~ Bedrooms: £90/£110 ~ www.thebankhouse.co.uk
Recommended by R C Vincent, John Wooll

LARLING   TL9889   Map 5
Angel 🍺 🛏
From A11 Thetford–Attleborough, take B1111 turn-off and follow pub signs; NR16 2QU

Good-natured chatty atmosphere in busy pub, several real ales and tasty bar food; bedrooms

This well run inn is open all day – and serves food then too – so it's always busy with customers keen on the surrounding fine walks and bird-watching; they also have secure cycle storage. The comfortable 1930s-style lounge on the right has cushioned wheelback chairs, a nice long cushioned and panelled corner settle, some good solid tables for eating and squared panelling; plus a collection of whisky-water jugs on a delft shelf over the big brick fireplace, a woodburning stove, a couple of copper kettles and some hunting prints. The same friendly family have run the place since 1913 – they still have the original visitors' books dating from 1897 to 1909. Adnams Bitter and four guests from breweries such as Crouch Vale, Hook Norton, Hop Back and Orkney on handpump, 110 malt whiskies and ten wines by the glass; they hold an August beer festival with over 100 real ales and ciders, live music and barbecues. The quarry-tiled black-beamed public bar has a good local feel with darts, juke box, games machine, board games and background music. A neat grass area behind the car park has picnic-sets around a big apple tree covered in fairy lights, and a fenced play area. The four-acre meadow becomes a caravan and camping site from March to October.

Well liked food includes sandwiches and toasties, creamy mushroom and bacon pot, breadcrumbed king prawns with sweet chilli sauce, omelettes, sausage, egg and chips, burger with cheese, bacon or garlic mushrooms, sweet pepper lasagne, pork in wild mushroom, basil, tomato and red wine sauce, chicken with bacon, cheese and barbecue sauce, salmon and prawn pasta with creamy white wine and dill sauce, and puddings. *Benchmark main dish: steak and kidney pie £10.95. Two-course evening meal £17.50.*

Free house ~ Licensee Andrew Stammers ~ Real ale ~ (01953) 717963 ~ Open 10am-midnight ~ Bar food 12-9.30(10 Fri, Sat) ~ Restaurant ~ Children welcome ~ Bedrooms: £50/£80 ~ www.angel-larling.co.uk
Recommended by Ruth May, Emma Scofield, J F M and M West, R C Vincent

MORSTON   TG0043 Map 8
Anchor
A149 Salthouse–Stiffkey; The Street; NR2 7AA

Quite a choice of rooms filled with bric-a-brac and prints, real ales and some sort of food served all day

There's a warm welcome for all from the friendly young licensees, and the atmosphere is bustling and easy-going. On the right are three traditional rooms with pubby seating and tables on original wooden floors, coal fires, local 1950s beach photographs and lots of prints and bric-a-brac. Adnams Bitter, local Winters Golden and Woodfordes Wherry on handpump, 18 wines by the glass. The contemporary airy extension on the left has comfortable benches and tables and leads into the more formal restaurant where local art is displayed on the walls. You can sit outside at the front. Seal-spotting trips can be booked from here and the surrounding area is wonderful for bird-watching and walking. If parking is tricky at the pub, there's an off-road overflow area around the corner and a National Trust car park five minutes' walk away.

Popular food cooked by one of the landlords includes local oysters, home-made smoked mackerel pâté, ham and egg, rosemary-infused polenta with mushrooms, vine tomatoes and parmesan, burger with cheese or bacon and chips, locally caught fish of the day, venison and other game from nearby estates, and puddings such as vanilla crème brûlée with honeycomb ice-cream and baked toffee and chocolate cheesecake. *Benchmark main dish: local mussels £12.00. Two-course evening meal £17.50.*

Free house ~ Licensees Harry Farrow and Rowan Glennie ~ Real ale ~ (01263) 741392 ~ Open 9am-11pm(10.30 Sun) ~ Bar food 12-3, 6-9(8.30 Sun) ~ Restaurant ~ Children welcome ~ Dogs allowed in bar ~ www.morstonanchor.co.uk
Recommended by David and Judy Robison, David Jackman, R C Vincent, David Carr

NORTH CREAKE   TF8538   Map 8
Jolly Farmers
Burnham Road; NR21 9JW

Friendly village local with three cosy rooms, open fires and woodburners, well liked food and several real ales

A former coaching inn in a charming flintstone village, this is a friendly place where nothing is too much trouble for the cheerful licensees. There are three cosy, relaxed rooms; the main bar has a large open fire in a brick fireplace, a mix of pine farmhouse and high-backed leather dining chairs around scrubbed pine tables on quarry tiles, and pale yellow walls. Beside the wooden bar counter are high bar chairs, and they keep Woodfordes Nelsons Revenge and Wherry and a guest like Adnams Southwold on handpump or tapped from the cask, 11 wines by the glass and a dozen malt whiskies. There's also a cabinet of model cars. A smaller bar has pews and a woodburning stove, while the red-walled dining room has similar furniture to the bar and another woodburner. There are seats outside on a terrace.

Tasty food cooked by the landlady includes pigeon breast and bacon in sweet dressing, baked crab pot topped with cheddar, local mussels served several ways, creamy stilton, walnut and tomato pasta, honey-roast ham and egg, slow-cooked lamb breast with mint and redcurrant glaze and dauphinoise potatoes, haddock and tiger prawns in spinach sauce with cheesy crumble topping, specials like lambs liver and bacon in red wine gravy or monkfish and chorizo stew, and puddings such as apple and berry crumble and whisky and banana flummery. *Benchmark main dish: steak and kidney pie £12.00. Two-course evening meal £17.00.*

Free house ~ Licensees Adrian and Heather Sanders ~ Real ale ~ (01328) 738185 ~ Open 12-2.30, 7-11; 12-3, 7-10.30 Sun; closed Mon, Tues ~ Bar food 12-2, 7-9 ~ Children welcome ~ Dogs allowed in bar ~ www.jollyfarmersnorfolk.co.uk *Recommended by R L Borthwick, Linda Miller and Derek Greentree, Derek and Sylvia Stephenson*

NORWICH
Eagle
TG2207   Map 5

Newmarket Road (A11, between A140 and A147 ring roads); NR2 2HN

Popular pub with a variety of seating areas for both drinking and dining, real ales, lots of coffees, wines by the glass and quite a choice of fairly priced food

With plenty of room inside and out, this sizeable Georgian pub copes well with the cheerful crowd of customers at peak times. The main bar has comfortable sofas and armchairs by an open fire in an ornate fireplace, white-painted chairs around pine tables on tiled or stripped-wood floors, cream paintwork above a red dado and more sofas and straightforward pubby seating in a cosy end room. There's also a low-ceilinged dining room and a spiral staircase in the bar leading to another dining room with high-backed brown leather chairs around various tables on pale floorboards. Sharps Doom Bar, Wolf Edith Cavell and a house beer from Bass called Eagles Nest on handpump and decent wines; background music. A 'conservatory' with chrome and bentwood chairs and wooden tables leads on to a sunny terrace with picnic-sets and a smart barbecue, and there are more seats on grass.

Popular food includes baguettes, sticky barbecue chicken wings, crab pâté, croque monsieur, nachos with chilli, cheese sauce, guacamole and crème fraîche, ham and duck eggs, mushroom, brie, cranberry and wilted spinach wellington, baked trout stuffed with couscous with provençale sauce, lamb leg steak on greek salad, mixed grill, confit duck leg with plum sauce and dauphinoise potatoes, and puddings. *Benchmark main dish: pork belly with apple and cider relish and jus £12.50. Two-course evening meal £18.00.*

Free house ~ Licensee Nigel Booty ~ Real ale ~ (01603) 624173 ~ Open 11-11 ~ Bar food 12-2.30, 6-9; 12-4 Sun ~ Restaurant ~ Children welcome ~ Dogs allowed in bar ~ www.theeaglepub.co.uk *Recommended by Emma Scofield, Ruth May*

NORWICH
Fat Cat
TG2109   Map 5

West End Street; NR2 4NA

A place of pilgrimage for beer lovers and open all day; lunchtime rolls and pies

The knowledgeable landlord and his helpful staff cope well with the lively and cheerful crowd of customers keen to enjoy the fantastic range of up to 31 quickly changing real ales. On handpump or tapped from the cask in a still room behind the bar – big windows reveal all – are their own beers, Fat Cat Brewery Tap Bitter, Cougar, Hell Cat, Honey Ale, Marmalade Cat and Wild Cat, as well as Adnams Bitter, Crouch Vale Yakima Gold, Dark Star American Pale Ale, Oakham Bishops Farewell, Timothy Taylors Landlord, Woodfordes Once Bittern and guests from breweries like BrewDog, Castle Rock, Felinfoel, Fullers, Green Jack, Kelham Island and Thornbridge. You'll also find imported draught beers and lagers, over 50 bottled beers from around the world plus ciders and perries. The no-nonsense furnishings include plain scrubbed pine tables and simple solid seats, lots of brewery memorabilia, bric-a-brac and stained glass. There are tables outside.

Bar food consists of rolls and good pies at lunchtime (not Sunday).

Own brew ~ Licensee Colin Keatley ~ Real ale ~ No credit cards ~ (01603) 624364 ~
Open 12-11; 11-midnight Sat ~ Bar food available until sold out; not Sun ~ Children
allowed until 6pm ~ Dogs allowed in bar ~ www.fatcatpub.co.uk
Recommended by the Didler, Colin and Ruth Munro

SALTHOUSE
TG0743 Map 8
Dun Cow 🍴 🍺
*A149 Blakeney–Sheringham (Purdy Street, junction with Bard Hill);
NR25 7XA*

Relaxed seaside pub, a good all-rounder and with enterprising food

Readers really enjoy their visits to this bustling pub and come back
again and again. The flint-walled bar consists of a pair of high-
raftered rooms opened up into one area, with stone tiles in the back half
where regulars congregate by the serving counter, carpet at the front.
There are log fireplaces at each end, scrubbed tables, a very high-backed
settle, country kitchen chairs and elegant little red-padded dining chairs,
and big prints of sailing ships. With Adnams Southwold, Greene King
IPA and Woodfordes Wherry on handpump, and quick service by friendly
helpful staff, the place has a good relaxed atmosphere. There's a separate
games room with pool. Picnic-sets on the front grass look across the
bird-filled salt marshes towards the sea, and there are more tables in
a sheltered back courtyard and an orchard garden beyond. The bedrooms
are self-catering.

 Helpfully served all day, the thoughtful and interesting choice of food
includes sandwiches (until 6pm), nibbles like venison and juniper scotch
egg with cumberland dipping sauce or home-made sausage roll laced with black
pudding, plus curried potted prawns and shrimps, ham hock terrine, four ways
of serving local mussels, cheese, onion and leek or game pies, sausages with
grain mustard and white onion sauce, fresh tuna niçoise, chargrilled guinea fowl
with wild mushrooms, artichokes and bay leaf cream, and puddings such as hot
chocolate brownie with ice-cream and blood orange posset with home-made
shortbread. *Benchmark main dish: grilled garlic lobster with fries and salad
£14.00. Two-course evening meal £18.00.*

Punch ~ Lease Daniel Goff ~ Real ale ~ (01263) 740467 ~ Open 11-11 ~ Bar food 12-9
~ Children welcome ~ Dogs welcome ~ www.salthouseduncow.com *Recommended by
Philip and Susan Philcox, DF and NF, carolyn newman, Fren Ewing, Brian Glozier, Neil and Angela
Huxter, Linda Miller and Derek Greentree*

SEDGEFORD
TF7036 Map 8
King William IV 🍷 🛏
B1454, off A149 Kings Lynn–Hunstanton; PE36 5LU

**Carefully run inn with enthusiastic owners, plenty of space inside,
a wide choice of bar food, four real ales, several wines by the glass
and attractive covered outdoor dining area; bedrooms**

Readers really enjoy staying in the immaculate and comfortable
bedrooms in this well run inn, and the enthusiastic, hands-on
licensees make their guests feel special; they have family- and dog-
friendly rooms too and the breakfasts are delicious. There's a relaxed,
homely bar, and several different dining areas that are decorated with
paintings of the north Norfolk coast and bird life, with high-backed
dark leather dining chairs around a mix of pine tables on slate tiles,
log fires, Adnams Bitter, Greene King Abbot and Old Speckled Hen and

Woodfordes Nelsons Revenge or Wherry on handpump and ten good wines by the glass; friendly obliging staff. There are seats on the terrace and picnic-sets under parasols on the grass, as well as an attractive covered dining area surrounded by flowering tubs. Several beaches are just a few miles away, the bird-watching is fantastic and you'll find plenty to do nearby.

🍴 As well as lunchtime paninis and toasties and Tuesday curry night, the highly enjoyable food includes shredded confit of duck leg with hoisin sauce, liver pâté with red onion marmalade, roasted mediterranean vegetables with pasta, local crab salad, steak burger with blue cheese, fried onions and fries, guinea fowl stuffed with pork and sage sausage meat in port sauce, moroccan-style lamb shank with spicy couscous, lobster ravioli in light shellfish sauce, and puddings such as treacle sponge with custard and chocolate tart. *Benchmark main dish: steak in ale pie £10.95. Two-course evening meal £19.00.*

Free house ~ Licensee Nick Skerritt ~ Real ale ~ (01485) 571765 ~ Open 11.30-11(6-11 Mon); 12-10.30 Sun; closed Mon lunchtime except bank holidays ~ Bar food 12-2(2.30 Sun), 6-9(8.30 Sun) ~ Restaurant ~ Children welcome but no under-4s in main restaurant after 6.30pm ~ Dogs allowed in bar and bedrooms ~ Bedrooms: £65/£105 ~ www.thekingwilliamsedgeford.co.uk *Recommended by R C Vincent, David Jackman*

SNETTISHAM TF6834 Map 8
Rose & Crown 🍴 ♟ 🛏

Village signposted from A149 King's Lynn–Hunstanton just N of Sandringham; coming in on the B1440 from the roundabout just N of village, take first left turn into Old Church Road; PE31 7LX

Particularly well run old pub with log fires and interesting furnishings, imaginative food, a fine range of drinks and stylish seating on heated terrace; well equipped bedrooms

A lways busy and with consistently high standards, this first class pub continues to please its many contented customers. The smallest of the three bars is pale grey in colour with coir flooring and old prints of King's Lynn and Sandringham. Each of the other two bars has a distinct character: an old-fashioned beamed front room with black settles on a tiled floor and a big log fire, and a back bar with another large log fire and the landlord's sporting trophies, old sports equipment and the pub's cricket team photos. There's also the Garden Room with inviting wicker-based wooden chairs, careful lighting and a quote by Dr Johnson in old-fashioned rolling script on a huge wallboard, and a residents' lounge (liked by non-residents too) with squashy armchairs and sofas, rugs, newspapers, magazines, jigsaws and board games. Adnams Bitter, Fullers London Pride, Greene King Abbot and Woodfordes Wherry on handpump, ten wines by the glass (a Master of Wine is employed part-time to teach the staff) and local cider and fruit juices; staff are neatly dressed and courteous. Two of the comfortable bedrooms are downstairs and there are disabled lavatories and wheelchair ramps. The garden is lovely in warm weather, with stylish café-like blue chairs and tables under cream parasols on a terrace, outdoor heaters and colourful herbaceous borders; there's also a wooden galleon-shaped climbing frame for children. Sister pub the Bank House in King's Lynn is also worth a visit.

🍴 Using very carefully sourced local produce, the impressive and highly enjoyable food might include sandwiches, sardine escabeche with noodle salad, pork belly and pistachio terrine with rhubarb chutney, spiced chickpea and fennel salad with pomegranate molasses, sausage and mash with beer gravy, beer-battered haddock with mushy peas, barbecued king ribs with coleslaw and fries, crispy-skin salmon with smoked haddock and clam chowder, pigeon breast with game jus and forestier potatoes, and puddings such as chocolate fondant with vanilla ice-cream and lemon tart with clotted cream and zabaglione ice-cream. *Benchmark main dish: local steak burger with bacon, emmenthal, red pepper relish and fries £11.75. Two-course evening meal £19.50.*

Free house ~ Licensee Anthony Goodrich ~ Real ale ~ (01485) 541382 ~ Open 11-11 ~ Bar food 12-2, 6-9; 12-5.30, 6-9.30(9 Sun) Sat ~ Restaurant ~ Children welcome ~ Dogs welcome ~ Bedrooms: £70/£90 ~ www.roseandcrownsnettisham.co.uk
Recommended by Pat and Graham Williamson, Tracey and Stephen Groves, David Eberlin, John Wooll, R C Vincent, Pauline Fellows and Simon Robbins, Sally Anne and Peter Goodale, Mike and Shirley Stratton, M J Daly, Dr Peter Crawshaw, Sara Fulton, Roger Baker

 STANHOE   TF8037   Map 8

Duck 🍴 🛏

B1155 Docking–Burnham Market; PE31 8QD

Smart candlelit country dining pub, good food (especially fish), appealing layout and attentive staff; bedrooms

Handy for the beaches of Brancaster and Holkham, this smart, neatly kept dining pub is set in quiet farmland. The charming and atmospheric original bar forms three cosy dining areas with beams, country kitchen chairs and pews around wooden tables on bare boards or black slate flooring, a couple of woodburning stoves and original oil paintings by local artists. Elgoods Cambridge, EPA and a guest like Golden Newt on handpump from a fine slab-topped counter and several wines by the glass; good service. There's also a garden room, and seats under apple trees in the pretty garden; well appointed bedrooms and caravan site. This is sister pub to the Bell in Wiveton.

As well as a winter offer of a main dish and a pint/glass of wine for £9.99, the interesting food includes sandwiches, goats cheese, marinated beetroot salad and rocket, braised pig cheeks with celeriac purée and wild mushrooms, honey-roast ham with free-range eggs, courgette, pea and mint risotto, caramelised fillet of cod with crayfish, lemon and fennel, pork rib-eye with crispy pig head torchon, duck fat roast potatoes and apple and vanilla purée, and puddings such as pistachio, lemon and olive oil cake and plum and almond tart with clotted cream. *Benchmark main dish: duck breast, confit leg and potato terrine, crispy liver beignets and duck jus £17.95. Two-course evening meal £22.00.*

Elgoods ~ Tenants Sarah and Ben Handley ~ (01485) 518330 ~ Open 11-11 ~ Bar food 12-2.30, 6.30-9; 12-8 Sun ~ Restaurant ~ Children welcome ~ Dogs allowed in bar ~ Bedrooms: /£95 ~ www.duckinn.co.uk *Recommended by Paul Clarke-Scholes, David and Sue Medcalf*

 STIFFKEY   TF9643   Map 8

Red Lion 🍷 £ 🛏

A149 Wells–Blakeney; NR23 1AJ

Appealing layout, perky atmosphere and good staff; comfortable bedrooms

'A cracking pub,' says one reader – and many others agree. It's an interesting place with a friendly atmosphere and plenty of cheerful customers. The front bar has a tiled floor, big log fireplace, cushioned pews and other pubby seats, local landscape photographs and shelves of books. A room off here has high-backed stripped settles brightened up with scatter cushions and more standard seats around informal candlelit tables; in another room there's dark panelling, maroon paintwork, lots more photographs and a splendid curved and winged settle. There's also a pair of back dining rooms, one of them flint-walled and almost a conservatory. They serve good wines by the glass, a couple of dozen malt whiskies, and Greene King IPA Gold and Ale Fresco and Woodfordes Wherry and Nelsons Revenge on handpump. A big gravelled courtyard, sheltered and partly canopied, has picnic-sets and heaters, with more tables on a covered heated deck. Bedrooms have their own balconies or terraces, and there are good coastal walks nearby.

🍴 They offer several ways of serving fresh local crab and lobster, as well as popular choices like sandwiches, potted brown shrimps with toast, thai vegetable spring rolls with sweet chilli sauce, honey and mustard-roasted ham and eggs, burger topped with bacon and blue cheese, beer-battered cod, specials like bass fillet with beetroot salad or chargrilled lemon chicken, and puddings such as apple crumble and chocolate brownie. *Benchmark main dish: fish pie with beetroot and green salad £11.00. Two-course evening meal £19.00.*

Free house ~ Licensee Stephen Franklin ~ Real ale ~ (01328) 830552 ~ Open 11-11 ~ Bar food 12-2.30, 6-9; 12-9 Sun ~ Restaurant ~ Children welcome ~ Dogs welcome ~ Bedrooms: £99/£119 ~ www.stiffkey.com *Recommended by Chris Johnson, Jim Farmer, David and Judy Robison, David Carr, W K Wood, Pauline Fellows and Simon Robbins, Roy Hoing, John Wooll, David Jackman, Ian Herdman*

STOKE HOLY CROSS
TG2302   Map 5

Wildebeest Arms

Village signposted off A140 S of Norwich; turn left in village; NR14 8QJ

Stylish restaurant pub with good enterprising food, thriving relaxed atmosphere and attractive terrace

A lthough all the inside tables are set for dining, you can drop in for just a drink – there are several bar stools by the sleek semicircular bar, and a few casual chairs and outside tables. The long room has an understated african theme with carefully placed carvings and hangings on the dark sandy walls. Unusual dark leather chairs are grouped on polished boards around striking tables consisting of heavy slabs of nicely grained wood on elegant wrought-iron supports. The atmosphere is a cheerful blend of expectation and contentment, depending on what stage of their meal people are at; the neatly dressed staff are helpful and efficient. Woodfordes Wherry on handpump and quite a few wines by the glass. The subtly lit front terrace is a great asset, well sheltered from the road by tall woven willow hurdles, with comfortable wicker armchairs or cushioned benches around glass-topped tables, most under big heated canvas parasols.

🍴 As well as a two- and three-course set lunch, the highly thought-of food includes goats cheese cake with confit red onions, sun-dried tomato and basil beignet and roasted pepper coulis, a seafood plate, seared salmon fillet with leek and mushroom fricassée and mussel cream sauce, corn-fed chicken breast with bubble and squeak and tarragon jus, venison with cep mushroom purée, sautéed wild mushrooms and potato terrine, and puddings such as dark chocolate marquise with kirsch cherries and white chocolate sauce and apple, pear and rhubarb crumble with honey ice-cream. *Benchmark main dish: pork three-ways with sage gnocchi and vanilla apple purée £15.25. Two-course evening meal £20.00.*

Animal Inns ~ Manager Ben Gibbins ~ Real ale ~ (01508) 492497 ~ Open 10am-11pm(midnight Fri, Sat); 10-10 Sun ~ Bar food 12-2.30, 6.30-9.30; 12-8 Sun ~ Restaurant ~ Children welcome ~ Dogs welcome ~ www.thewildebeest.co.uk *Recommended by Toby Jones, Isobel Mackinlay*

SWANTON MORLEY
TG0217 Map 8

Darbys ◧ £

B1147 NE of Dereham; NR20 4NY

Unspoilt country local with six real ales, plenty of farming knick-knacks, tasty bar food and children's play area

The six real ales on offer in this creeper-covered brick pub continue to draw in lots of happy customers – and all get a warm welcome. The long bare-boarded country-style bar has a comfortable lived-in feel, with big stripped-pine tables and chairs, lots of gin traps and farming memorabilia, a log fire (with the original bread oven alongside) and tractor seats lining the long, attractive serving counter. Adnams Bitter and Broadside and Woodfordes Wherry plus guests like Beeston Afternoon Delight and Humpty Dumpty Ale tapped from the cask, several wines by the glass and quite a few coffees; good, efficient service. A step up through a doorway by the fireplace leads to a pleasant dining room with neat dark tables and chairs on a wooden floor; the children's room has a toy box and a glassed-over well, floodlit from inside. TV and board games. There are picnic-sets and a children's play area in the back garden. There's plenty to do locally as the family also owns the adjoining 720-acre estate. B&B is available in carefully converted farm buildings nearby, and they have a well equipped camping site.

Reasonably priced food with several dishes costing under £10 (hence our Bargain Award) might include sandwiches, smoked haddock and spinach spring rolls with lemon and chervil mayonnaise, chorizo and mixed bean chilli pot, beef or lamb burger with chips, lemon and thyme-baked mushroom, goats cheese and pine nut rice pilaf, steak in ale pudding, stir-fried calamari, octopus, prawns and mussel pasta in a rich tomato and garlic sauce, venison steak in orange, honey and ginger with chive mash, and puddings such as baked orange marmalade and whisky pudding and chocolate and chilli mousse with ginger honeycomb pieces. *Benchmark main dish: pork belly with cider sauce £10.95. Two-course evening meal £16.00.*

Free house ~ Licensees John Carrick and Louise Battle ~ Real ale ~ (01362) 637647 ~ Open 11.30-3, 6-11; 11.30-11 Fri, Sat; 12-10.30 Sun ~ Bar food 12-2.15, 6.30-9; all day weekends ~ Restaurant ~ Children welcome ~ Dogs allowed in bar ~ www.darbysfreehouse.com *Recommended by Roy Hoing, Richard and Penny Gibbs, John Staples*

THORNHAM
TF7343 Map 8

Lifeboat ◧ ⇐

A149 by Kings Head, then first left; PE36 6LT

Good mix of customers and lots of character in traditional inn, real ales and super surrounding walks; bedrooms

Looking very neat with its whitewashed walls and grey-painted windows, this carefully run dining pub faces half a mile of coastal salt marshes, where there are lots of walks. The rambling rooms – mainly set for eating – have a great deal of character with heavy beams, quite a mix of seating including low settles and pews, wooden and more ornate dining chairs and cushioned window seats, on rugs or tiles, and open fires and woodburning stoves. Throughout are reed-slashers and other antique farm tools, an array of traps and yokes, oars and paddles, lighting from antique paraffin lamps, fresh flowers and candles. Adnams Bitter, Greene King Abbot and IPA, Woodfordes Wherry and The Governor (named for chef Marco Pierre White) on handpump, ten wines by the glass and several malt whiskies; one bench has an antique penny-in-the-hole game. Up some steps from the conservatory with its ancient vine is a sunny terrace with seats; at the front of the building there are modern grey seats and tables and picnic-sets under parasols.

Attractively presented, the tempting food includes sandwiches, kipper pâté with whisky, corned beef hash with poached duck egg and béarnaise sauce, wild mushroom risotto with truffle oil, burger with cheese, smoked bacon, barbecue sauce and chips, corn-fed chicken with wild mushrooms and madeira jus, yellow-fin tuna with roast cherry tomatoes, capers and olives, roast rump of lamb with dauphinoise potatoes, fish platter, and puddings such as sherry trifle and knickerbocker glory. *Benchmark main dish: fish pie £11.95. Two-course evening meal £19.00.*

Free house ~ Licensee Helen Stafford ~ Real ale ~ (01485) 512236 ~ Open 11-11(midnight Sat) ~ Bar food 12-2.30, 6.30-9.30; lighter meals 3-5.30 ~ Restaurant ~ Children welcome ~ Dogs allowed in bar and bedrooms ~ Bedrooms: $90/$130 ~ www.lifeboatinnthornham.com *Recommended by the Didler, Tracey and Stephen Groves, David Brown, David and Ruth Hollands, Marianne and Peter Stevens, James Stretton, Derek and Sylvia Stephenson*

THORNHAM   TF7343   Map 8
Orange Tree
Church Street/A149; PE36 6LY

Norfolk Dining Pub of the Year

Nice combination of friendly bar and good contemporary dining

You must book ahead to guarantee a table – this genuinely welcoming inn is extremely and deservedly popular. There are stripped beams and a low ceiling, a log fire, comfortable leather and basket-weave chairs on a tiled floor, Adnams Bitter, Woodfordes Wherry and a guest like Wychwood Tight Head on handpump, 27 wines by the glass and good courteous service; their labrador is called Poppy. A similarly relaxed feel runs through the more extensive two-part dining area, which is cheerfully contemporary in style, partly carpeted, with colourful neat modern seating around plain tables, and artworks above a dark grey dado; this area may have background music. The main garden, shaded by tall sycamores, has picnic-sets under white canvas parasols, and a round smokers' shelter in one discreet corner; a second area has safely enclosed play things. The courtyard bedrooms make a good base for this lovely stretch of coast, and the breakfasts are very good. They are kind to dogs and offer a doggie menu and snacks.

Using the best local, seasonal produce, the innovative, delicious food might include lunchtime sandwiches (not Sunday), confit octopus and grilled squid with rose harissa and lime and parsley salad, potted pigs cheek with lemon grass and pineapple jelly and beer-pickled shallots, seafood spaghetti with chilli and lemon oil, rare-breed burger with smoked onion, cheddar and thyme and mustard coleslaw, free-range chicken and wild mushroom pie, pheasant kiev with stuffed roast parsnip, chorizo and pearl barley risotto and rum and clove jus, wild sea trout with smoked salmon and parma ham gratin and mussel and leek velouté, and puddings like three-chocolate mousse with chocolate sorbet and chocolate sauce and a 'fairground' to share (candyfloss, bubblegum panna cotta, popcorn, toffee apple, marshmallow, doughnuts, screwball and brandy snap). *Benchmark main dish: chargrilled free-range chicken and wild mushroom pie with smoked pancetta mash and chicken gravy £14.75. Two-course evening meal £20.00.*

Punch ~ Lease Mark Goode ~ Real ale ~ (01485) 512213 ~ Open 11-11(midnight Sat); 11-10.30 Sun ~ Bar food 12-9.30 ~ Restaurant ~ Children welcome ~ Dogs allowed in bar and bedrooms ~ Bedrooms: /£85 ~ www.theorangetreethornham.co.uk
Recommended by John F Knutton, David Jackman, Derek and Sylvia Stephenson

THORPE MARKET   TG2434   Map 8
Gunton Arms ⑪
Cromer Road; NR11 8TZ

Impressive place with an easy-going atmosphere, open fires and antiques in bar and dining rooms, real ales, interesting food and friendly staff; bedrooms

This stylish place – surrounded by a 1,000-acre deer park – is both grand and interesting. The large entrance hall sets the scene; throughout, the atmosphere is informal and relaxed but definitely gently upmarket. The simply furnished bar has dark pubby chairs and tables on a wooden floor, a log fire, a long settle beside a pool table, and high stools against the mahogany counter where they serve Adnams Bitter, St Peters Mild, Woodfordes Wherry and Yetmans Red on handpump, several wines by the glass and apple juice made on the estate; staff are chatty and friendly. Heavy curtains line the open doorway that leads into a dining room with vast antlers on the wall above the big log fire (they often cook over this) and straightforward chairs around scrubbed tables on stone tiles. There's also a lounge with comfortable old leather armchairs and a sofa on a fine rug in front of yet another log fire, some genuine antiques, big house plants and standard lamps, a more formal restaurant with candles and napery, and two homely sitting rooms for residents. Many of the walls are painted dark red and hung with assorted artwork and big mirrors. The bedrooms have many original fittings, but no TV or tea-making facilities.

Hearty food – served all day – using their own venison, local fish and shellfish, foraged plants and seashore vegetables includes nibbles like venison sausage roll and pork crackling with apple sauce, sandwiches (until 5pm), home-smoked salmon with irish soda bread, lamb sweetbreads with wild garlic and creamed spelt, venison burger with coleslaw and chips, pollack fish fingers with mushy peas, rack of lamb with spiced aubergine and slow-roasted tomatoes, red deer haunch steak with pickled red cabbage, and puddings such as rice pudding with poached pears and hazelnut and white chocolate cheesecake. *Benchmark main dish: venison mixed grill with redcurrant jelly £17.50. Two-course evening meal £25.00.*

Free house ~ Licensee Simone Baker ~ Real ale ~ (01263) 832010 ~ Open 12-11(10.30 Sun) ~ Bar food all day ~ Restaurant ~ Children welcome ~ Dogs allowed in bar and bedrooms ~ Bedrooms: £85/£120 ~ www.theguntonarms.co.uk
Recommended by Richard and Penny Gibbs

Please tell us if the décor, atmosphere, food or drink at a pub is different from our description. We rely on readers' reports to keep us up to date: feedback@goodguides.com, or (no stamp needed) The Good Pub Guide, FREEPOST TN1569, Wadhurst, E Sussex TN5 7BR.

WEST BECKHAM
Wheatsheaf

TG1439 Map 8

Church Road; off A148 Holt–Cromer; NR25 6NX

Traditional pub with several real ales, proper home cooking and seats in the garden

All – including dogs – are welcome at this friendly brick-built pub in a quiet village. The bars have beams, standing timbers, cottagey doors, lots of horsebrasses and a roaring winter log fire, and furnishings are pleasantly traditional with plenty of wheelback chairs, settles and comfortably cushioned wall seats around dark wood pubby tables. Woodfordes Nelsons Revenge and Wherry on handpump and quite a few wines by the glass. The charming garden and terrace have plenty of tables and seats.

As well as takeaway fish and chips on Tuesday-Thursday evenings, the well liked food includes baguettes, breaded whitebait with home-made tartare sauce, garlic mushrooms, lasagne, burger and chips, broccoli and stilton pasta bake, sausages of the week, chicken carbonara, specials like gammon, egg and chips or swordfish steak topped with garlic and herb butter, and puddings such as cheesecake of the week and bread and butter pudding. *Benchmark main dish: pie of the day £10.95. Two-course evening meal £17.25.*

Free house ~ Licensee Matt Lock ~ Real ale ~ (01263) 822110 ~ Open 12-3, 6-11; 12-6 Sun; closed Sun evening, Mon ~ Bar food 12-2, 6-9; 12-5 Sun ~ Restaurant ~ Children welcome ~ Dogs allowed in bar ~ www.thewheatsheafwestbeckham.co.uk
Recommended by Tony Middis, Philip and Susan Philcox

WIVETON
Wiveton Bell

TG0442 Map 8

Blakeney Road; NR25 7TL

Busy open-plan dining pub, drinkers welcomed too, local beers, consistently enjoyable food and seats outside; bedrooms

Always busy with a wide mix of customers, this well run dining pub has a cheerful atmosphere and a fine choice of both drinks and food. Mainly open-plan, it has some fine old beams, an attractive mix of dining chairs around wooden tables on a stripped-wood floor, a log fire and prints on yellow walls. The sizeable conservatory has smart beige dining chairs around wooden tables on coir flooring, and the atmosphere is chatty and relaxed. Norfolk Brewhouse Moon Gazer Amber Ale, Woodfordes Wherry and Yetmans Blue on handpump, and several wines by the glass; service is attentive and friendly. Outside, at the front, picnic-sets on grass look across to the church; at the back, stylish wicker tables and chairs on several decked areas are set among decorative box hedging. The bedrooms are comfortable, and they also have a self-catering cottage.

Attractively presented and imaginative, and using the best, very local seasonal produce, the food might include free Friday early-evening nibbles like scotch eggs and sausage rolls, pigeon breast with apple, pomegranate and chicory salad, rabbit and guinea fowl terrine with home-made fig and grape chutney, steak burger with smoked cheese, onion rings, home-made relish and chips, roasted beetroot, fennel and saffron risotto with sage and mascarpone, prosciutto-wrapped chicken filled with cheese and sun-dried tomato and béarnaise sauce, cod steak with chorizo and butter bean cassoulet and red pepper velouté, and puddings such as passion-fruit mousse with blueberry ice-cream and chocolate and hazelnut parfait with honeycomb and raspberry coulis; in winter they offer a main dish and a pint or glass of wine for £9.99. *Benchmark main dish: slow-braised local pork belly with smoked bacon mash and apple and calvados jus £15.45. Two-course evening meal £19.00.*

Free house ~ Licensee Berni Morritt ~ Real ale ~ (01263) 740101 ~ Open 12-11 (10.30 Sun) ~ Bar food 12-2.15, 6-9.15 ~ Children welcome ~ Dogs allowed in bar ~ Bedrooms: /£95 ~ www.wivetonbell.co.uk *Recommended by Michael Sargent, Roy Hoing, Peter and Eleanor Kenyon, Simon Rodway, Revd Michael Vockins, Roger and Gillian Holmes, John Wooll, Barrie Fischer, Neil and Angela Huxter, Brian Glozier, David Carr, John Millwood, Derek and Sylvia Stephenson, R L Borthwick*

WOLTERTON
Saracens Head 🛏

TG1732 Map 8

Wolterton; Erpingham signed off A140 N of Aylsham, on through Calthorpe; NR11 7LZ

Remote inn with stylish bars and dining room and seats in courtyard; good bedrooms

Tucked away down country lanes, this Georgian inn is a civilised place with an easy-going atmosphere. The two-room bar is simple but stylish with high ceilings, pale terracotta walls and cream and gold curtains at tall windows – all lending a feeling of space, though it's not very large. There's a mix of seats from built-in wall settles to wicker fireside chairs as well as log fires and flowers, and the windows look on to a charming old-fashioned gravel stableyard with plenty of chairs, benches and tables. A pretty six-table parlour on the right has a big log fire. Woodfordes Wherry and a summer guest on handpump, several wines by the glass and local soft drinks. Bedrooms are comfortable and up to date.

As well as a two- and three-course set lunch (Wednesday-Saturday), the tempting food includes summer lunchtime sandwiches, mussels with shallots, bacon and tomatoes, pigeon breast with black pudding and apple, leek and carrot tarte tatin, pork stir-fry with chilli, ginger, soy and shiitake mushrooms, whole lemon sole with crayfish tails, fennel, baby capers and lemon, local venison with red wine jus and parsnip crisps, and puddings such as chocolate nemesis with pistachio ice-cream and treacle tart with cream. *Benchmark main dish: slow-cooked pork belly with mustard mash £14.50. Two-course evening meal £21.00.*

Free house ~ Licensees Tim and Janie Elwes ~ Real ale ~ (01263) 768909 ~ Open 11.30-2.30, 6-11; 12-2, 6.30-9 Sun; closed Mon except bank holidays, Oct-June Tues lunchtime ~ Bar food 12-2(2.30 summer), 6.30-8.30(9 summer); not Mon ~ Restaurant ~ Children welcome ~ Dogs allowed in bar and bedrooms ~ Bedrooms: £65/£90 ~ www.saracenshead-norfolk.co.uk *Recommended by Diana Owen, W K Wood*

WOODBASTWICK
Fur & Feather 🍺

TG3214 Map 8

Off B1140 E of Norwich; NR13 6HQ

Full range of first class beers from next-door Woodfordes brewery, friendly service and popular bar food

Bustling and cheerful with efficient and helpful staff keeping everything running smoothly, this thatched cottagey pub is next door to the Woodfordes brewery. Their beers are notably well kept and tapped from the cask: Bure Gold, Headcracker, Ketts Rebellion, Mardlers, Nelsons Revenge, Norfolk Nog, Once Bittern, Sundew and Wherry; you can also visit the brewery shop. A dozen wines by the glass and around a dozen malt whiskies. The style and atmosphere are not what you'd expect of a brewery tap – it's more like a comfortable and roomy dining pub with wooden chairs and tables on bare boards, and sofas and armchairs; background music. There are seats and tables in a pleasant garden. This is a lovely estate village.

🍴 Generous helpings of reliably good food include breakfasts (10-11.30am), baps and panini, garlic mushrooms with blue cheese, chilli and garlic king prawn skewers, honey-roast ham and egg, beef and triple-cheese lasagne, roasted vegetable pasta in basil creamy sauce, burgers with various toppings, eight different pies (such as rabbit and bacon, venison in red wine, salmon en croûte) and puddings such as panna cotta with berry compote and cherry bakewell tart with custard. *Benchmark main dish: steak and kidney pudding £12.95. Two-course evening meal £17.00.*

Woodfordes ~ Tenant Tim Ridley ~ Real ale ~ (01603) 720003 ~ Open 10-10 (9.30 Sun) ~ Bar food 10-9 ~ Restaurant ~ Well behaved children welcome ~ www.thefurandfeatherinn.co.uk *Recommended by Roy Hoing, Mrs D Barrett, Mrs Margo Finlay, Jörg Kasprowski, Tracey and Stephen Groves, N R White*

Also Worth a Visit in Norfolk

Besides the fully inspected pubs, you might like to try these pubs that have been recommended to us and described by readers. Do tell us what you think of them: feedback@goodguides.com

AYLMERTON   TG1840
Roman Camp (01263) 838291
Holt Road (A148); NR11 8QD
Large late Victorian inn with comfortable panelled bar, cosy sitting room off with warm fire, and light airy dining room, good choice of enjoyable fairly priced food, well kept mainstream ales, helpful staff; children welcome, attractive sheltered garden behind with terrace and pond, 15 bedrooms. *(Judith and David Salter, David Carr)*

AYLSHAM   TG1926
✱ **Black Boys** (01263) 732122
Market Place; off B1145; NR11 6EH
Small hotel with imposing Georgian façade and informal open-plan bar, well liked generously served food (all day) from snacks up including good value Sun roasts, Adnams and guests such as Timothy Taylors Landlord, Woodfordes Wherry and Wychwood Hobgoblin, decent wines in three glass sizes, comfortable seats, plenty of tables, high beams, part carpet, part bare boards, helpful young uniformed staff coping well at busy times; children and dogs welcome, modern seats in front by marketplace and more behind, bedrooms, open all day. *(John Wooll, Dr and Mrs R G J Telfer, David Carr, Mike Proctor)*

BANNINGHAM   TG2129
Crown (01263) 733534
Colby Road; NR11 7DY Welcoming 17th-c beamed pub, good choice of enjoyable sensibly priced food (they're helpful with gluten-free diets), well kept Greene King and local guests, decent wines, good quick service; children and dogs welcome, garden, jazz festival Aug, open all day Sun. *(Julie Hobday)*

BINHAM   TF9839
Chequers (01328) 830297
B1388 SW of Blakeney; NR21 0AL
Long low-beamed 17th-c local with coal fires at each end, sturdy plush seats, nice old local prints and photographs, own-brewed Front Street beers plus changing guests, lots of bottled imports and decent house wines, pubby food; children welcome, picnic-sets in front and on back grass, interesting village with huge priory church. *(Chris Johnson, John Millwood)*

BLAKENEY   TG0243
Kings Arms (01263) 740341
West Gate Street; NR25 7NQ A stroll from the harbour, friendly and chatty, with Adnams, Greene King Old Speckled Hen,

---

If you know a pub is ever open all day, please tell us.

Marstons Pedigree and guests, decent pub food all day from breakfast on, three simple linked low-ceilinged rooms and airy garden room; children and dogs welcome, big garden, bedrooms. *(Mr and Mrs D J Nash, David Carr)*

BLICKLING TG1728
Buckinghamshire Arms
(01263) 732133 *B1354 NW of Aylsham; NR11 6NF* New owners (Colchester Inns) and some refurbishment for this handsome Jacobean inn – reports please; small proper bar, lounge set for eating with woodburner, smarter more formal dining room with another woodburner, local ales and good choice of wines by the glass; background music; children and dogs welcome, tables on lawn, well placed by gates to Blickling Hall (NT), lovely walks nearby, three bedrooms. *(Anon)*

BRANCASTER TF7743
✶ Ship (01485) 210333
London Street (A149); PE31 8AP 18th-c roadside inn (part of the small Flying Kiwi Inns chain) in traditional fishing village; elegant bar with contemporary paintwork and built-in cushioned and planked wall seats, dining area with woodburner, pale settles and nice mix of other furniture on rugs and bare boards, restaurant has unusual Norfolk map wallpaper, plates on a dresser, bookcases, shipping memorabilia and lots of prints, good modern food, Adnams Bitter and Jo C's Norfolk Ale, nice wines by the glass, daily papers; background music, TV; children and dogs welcome, gravelled seating area with circular picnic-sets by car park, attractive well equipped bedrooms, open all day. *(Michael and Maggie Betton, Derek Thomas, David Jackman)*

BRANCASTER STAITHE TF8044
✶ White Horse (01485) 210262
A149 E of Hunstanton; PE31 8BY Very popular place – not a pub but does have proper informal front locals' bar; three Brancaster ales and Woodfordes, lots of wines by the glass, log fire, pine furniture, historical photographs and bar billiards, middle area with comfortable sofas and newspapers, big airy dining conservatory overlooking tidal marshes, enjoyable all-day bar and restaurant food including 'tapas' and plenty of fish, they ask to keep a credit card when you run a tab; children welcome, dogs in bar, seats on sun deck with fine views, more under cover on heated terrace, nicely seasidey bedrooms, coast path at bottom of garden. *(Chris Johnson, Jim Farmer, Colin and Louise English, Susan and Nigel Brookes, John Honnor, W K Wood and others)*

BROOME TM3591
Artichoke (01986) 893325
Yarmouth Road; NR35 2NZ Unpretentious split-level roadside pub with up to eight well kept ales (some from tap room casks) including Adnams and Elgoods, belgian fruit beers and excellent selection of whiskies, enjoyable traditional home-made food in bar or dining room, friendly helpful staff, wood and flagstone floors, inglenook log fire; dogs welcome, garden picnic-sets, smokers' shelter, closed Mon otherwise open all day. *(Anon)*

BURNHAM MARKET TF8342
Nelson (01328) 738321
Creake Road; PE31 8EN Restyled dining pub with nice food from shortish menu including interesting vegetarian dishes in bar and restaurant, pleasant efficient uniformed staff, Woodfordes Wherry and guests, extensive wine list, local artwork for sale; children and dogs (in bar) welcome, terrace picnic-sets, four attractive bedrooms (two in former outbuilding). *(Mike and Linda Hudson, John Wooll, David Carr)*

BURNHAM OVERY STAITHE TF8444
Hero (01328) 738334
A149; PE31 8JE Modernised spacious pub with good variety of well liked and fairly priced food from baguettes up, cheerful young staff, good value wines by the glass, Adnams and Woodfordes, comfortable pastel décor, woodburner, two dining areas; children welcome, no dogs inside, picnic-sets out on gravel. *(N R White, Mike and Linda Hudson)*

BURNHAM THORPE TF8541
✶ Lord Nelson (01328) 738241
Off B1155 or B1355, near Burnham Market; PE31 8HL Neatly kept 17th-c pub with lots of Nelson memorabilia (he was born in this sleepy village), antique high-backed settles on worn red tiles in small bar, smoke ovens in original fireplace, little snug leading off, two dining rooms one with flagstones and open fire, good bar food, Greene King, Woodfordes and a guest tapped from the cask, several wines by the glass, secret rum-based recipes (Nelson's Blood and Lady Hamilton's Nip); children and dogs welcome, good-sized play area and pétanque in big garden, open all day in summer, closed Mon evening except school/bank holidays. *(the Didler, Mike and Linda Hudson, John Honnor, Rita Scarratt, Sheila Topham, David Carr)*

CATFIELD TG3821
Crown (01692) 580128
The Street; NR29 5AA Immaculate homely village local with warmly welcoming landlady, good choice of changing ales, real ciders and enjoyable food from italian landlord-chef; bedrooms, not far from Hickling Broad, closed Mon except bank holidays (when closed Tues). *(Roy Hoing)*

CAWSTON TG1422
Ratcatchers (01603) 871430
Off B1145; Eastgate, S of village; NR10 4HA Popular beamed dining pub

with old chairs and fine mix of walnut, beech, elm and oak tables, nooks and crannies, quieter candlelit dining room on right, good well priced food cooked to order, Adnams and Woodfordes, quite a few malt whiskies, friendly attentive service, conservatory; background and some live music; children welcome, dogs in designated area, tables on heated terrace, open all day Sun. *(R C Vincent)*

CHEDGRAVE   TM3699
White Horse (01508) 520250
Norwich Road; NR14 6ND Welcoming pub with Timothy Taylors Landlord and four other well kept ales (festivals Apr and Nov), decent wines by the glass, good choice of enjoyable sensibly priced food from lunchtime baguettes up, friendly attentive service, log fire and sofas in bar, restaurant, regular events including monthly quiz, pool, darts; children and dogs welcome, garden picnic-sets. *(Richard Ball)*

CLEY NEXT THE SEA   TG0443
✻ **Three Swallows** (01263) 740526
Holt Road off A149; NR25 7TT Busy recently refurbished local, log fires in bar and dining room, stripped-pine tables, enjoyable reasonably priced pubby food (all day Sun) from sandwiches up, well kept Adnams, Greene King and Woodfordes from unusual richly carved bar, cheerful hard-working staff; children and dogs welcome, disabled access, metal tables and chairs out at front facing green, big garden with surprisingly grandiose fountain, aviary and heated smokers' shelter, four annexe bedrooms, good breakfast, handy for the salt marshes, open all day. *(Neil and Angela Huxter)*

COCKLEY CLEY   TF7904
Twenty Churchwardens
(01760) 721439 *Off A1065 S of Swaffham; PE37 8AN* Friendly nicely informal pub in converted former school next to church, three linked beamed rooms, good open fire, popular home-made food and well kept Adnams Southwold; no credit cards; children and dogs welcome, tiny unspoilt village. *(Anon)*

COLKIRK   TF9226
Crown (01328) 862172
Village signposted off B1146 S of Fakenham, and off A1065; Crown Road; NR21 7AA Unpretentious red-brick local under welcoming newish licensees; chatty bar and left-hand dining room, comfortable and cosy with solid furniture on rugs and tiles, lots to look at, open fires, Greene King ales and a guest, enjoyable fairly traditional food; children welcome, dogs in bar,

picnic-sets on suntrap terrace and in pleasant garden. *(Mike Proctor, Steve Short)*

COLTISHALL   TG2719
Kings Head (01603) 737426
Wroxham Road (B1354); NR12 7EA Popular dining pub close to River Bure and moorings, imaginative food from owner-chef (especially fish/seafood), also bar snacks and lunchtime set menu, well kept Adnams, nice wines by the glass, open fire, fishing nets and stuffed fish including a monster pike, also the bill from a marlin caught recently by the landlord, cookery school; background music; seats outside (noisy road), four bedrooms. *(David and Sue Atkinson, Philip and Susan Philcox)*

CONGHAM   TF7123
Anvil (01485) 600625
St Andrews Lane; PE32 1DU Tucked-away modern country pub with welcoming licensees, wide choice of enjoyable home-made food from light choices up, quick friendly service, three well kept ales such as Batemans, reasonable prices, live music and quiz nights; children welcome, picnic-sets in small walled front garden. *(R C Vincent)*

CROMER   TG2242
Red Lion (01263) 514964
Off A149; Tucker Street/Brook Street; NR27 9HD Substantial refurbished Victorian hotel with elevated sea views, original features including panelling and open fires, five well kept ales in bare-boards flint-walled bar, enjoyable food from sandwiches and ciabattas up including nice local mussels, good friendly service, restaurant and conservatory; background music; children and dogs welcome, disabled facilities, tables in back courtyard, 14 bedrooms, open all day. *(N R White, Anna Parrott, Anthony Barnes, David Carr, Adrian Johnson)*

DERSINGHAM   TF6930
Feathers (01485) 540768
B1440 towards Sandringham; Manor Road; PE31 6LN Refurbished Jacobean carrstone inn once part of the Sandringham Estate; two adjoining bars (main one with big open fire), Adnams, Woodfordes and a guest, enjoyable traditional home-made food, back dining room, function room in converted stables; background music; children and dogs welcome, large garden with play area, five bedrooms, open all day. *(Anon)*

DOWNHAM MARKET   TF6003
Railway Arms (01366) 386636
At railway station, Railway Road; PE38 9EN Cosy station bar with tiny

---

If you report on a pub that's not a featured entry, please tell us any lunchtimes or evenings when it doesn't serve bar food.

adjoining rooms, one with glowing coal fire, another with second-hand bookshop, real ales tapped from the cask, tea, coffee and some snacky food, model train sometimes running around; best to check opening times. *(Anon)*

EAST BARSHAM   TF9133
White Horse (01328) 820645
B1105 3 miles N of Fakenham; NR21 0LH Extended 17th-c inn refurbished under new management, big log fire in beamed bar with adjoining dining area, step up to more formal restaurant, good range of well liked home-made food, Greene King ales, friendly helpful staff; children and dogs (in bar) welcome, new decked area out behind with barbecue, three updated bedrooms and two self-catering cottages, open all day. *(R C Vincent)*

EAST RUDHAM   TF8228
✳ Crown (01485) 528530
A148 W of Fakenham; The Green; PE31 8RD Contemporary and open-plan with several distinct areas, brown leather and wood dining chairs around mix of tables, rugs on stripped boards, log fire in modern brick fireplace, their own Jo C's Norfolk Kiwi and Adnams from slate-topped counter, several wines by the glass, more informal end with attractive seats and tables, bookshelves by fireplace and 1950/60s actor prints, also pubby part with cushioned built-in seats and cosy lower area with leather sofas and armchairs, interesting well presented food, can also eat in upstairs pitched-ceiling dining room; TV; children welcome, neat picnic-sets on front gravel, bedrooms, open all day. *(Derek Thomas, Mr and Mrs D J Nash)*

EAST WINCH   TF6916
Carpenters Arms (01553) 841228
Lynn Road (A47); PE32 1NP Useful roadside pub with good value generous home-made food in bar and restaurant, several beers and ciders, friendly service; children welcome, no dogs inside, open all day. *(R C Vincent)*

EDGEFIELD   TG0934
✳ Pigs (01263) 587634
Norwich Road; B1149 S of Holt; NR24 2RL Friendly bustling pub with carpeted bar, Adnams, Greene King, Woodfordes and a house beer from Wolf tapped from casks, arches through to simply furnished area with mixed chairs and pews on broad pine boards, airy dining extension in similar style split into stall areas by standing timbers and low brick walls, nice mix of good quality food including Norfolk tapas, games room with bar billiards, also children's playroom; background music; dogs allowed in bar, good wheelchair access, rustic seats and tables on big covered front terrace, adventure playground, boules, ten bedrooms (some with spa facilities), open (and food)

all day Sun. *(Dr and Mrs R G J Telfer, Jim Farmer, Roy Hoing)*

ERPINGHAM   TG1931
Erpingham Arms (01263) 761591
Eagle Road; NR11 7QA Refurbished 18th-c brick-built pub with good choice of local beers including Woodfordes, enjoyable food from bar and restaurant menus, lunchtime set deal (not Sun, OAP discount Thurs); children and dogs welcome, disabled facilities, front terrace, garden behind with play area, open all day weekends. *(Anthony Barnes)*

FAKENHAM   TF9229
Limes (01328) 850050
Bridge Street; NR21 9AZ New Wetherspoons, clean, light and spacious, with good choice of beers, enjoyable food and usual value, separate coffee corner; plenty of seats outside, open all day from 8am. *(Edna Jones)*

FAKENHAM   TF9129
Oak (01328) 855077
Oak Street; NR21 9DX Welcoming pub-restaurant (busy market day lunchtime) with enjoyable good value food from traditional choices up cooked by landlord-chef, efficient service, ales such as Winters and Woodfordes, plenty of wines by the glass, modernised open-plan bar with leather sofas by gas woodburner, upstairs dining room and evening cellar restaurant; no dogs inside, children welcome, disabled facilities, a few pavement tables, more under parasols on back terrace, open all day summer weekends, closed Sun evening in winter. *(John Wooll, Alan Weedon)*

GAYTON   TF7219
Crown (01553) 636252
Lynn Road (B1145/B1153); opposite church; PE32 1PA Low-beamed village pub with plenty of character, unusual old features and charming snug as well as three main areas, good choice of popular sensibly priced food from sandwiches up, Greene King ales, friendly service, sofas and good log fire, games room; dogs welcome in bar, tables in attractive sheltered garden, four bedrooms. *(Anon)*

GELDESTON   TM3990
✳ Locks (01508) 518414
Off A143/A146 NW of Beccles; off Station Road S of village, obscurely signed down long rough track; NR34 0HW Remote candlelit pub at navigable head of River Waveney; ancient tiled-floor core with beams and big log fire, good Green Jack ales and guests tapped from casks, enjoyable food including burgers, vegetarian dishes and Fri curry night, large extension for summer crowds, regular live music; no credit cards; children welcome, riverside garden, moorings, open all day in summer, closed Mon-Weds in winter. *(the Didler, Mrs D Barrett)*

GELDESTON   TM3991
Wherry   (01508) 518371
The Street; NR34 0LB Welcoming,
extended red-brick local, enjoyable home-
made food including good value Sun roast
and monthly themed night, well kept Adnams
and some interesting wines by the glass;
pleasant garden. *(Anon)*

GREAT CRESSINGHAM   TF8401
✳**Windmill**   (01760) 756232
*Village signed off A1065 S of Swaffham;
Water End; IP25 6NN* Interesting pictures
and bric-a-brac in warren of rambling linked
rooms, plenty of cosy corners, good value
fresh bar food from baguettes to steak and
Sun roasts, half a dozen ales including
Adnams, Greene King and a house beer
called Windy Miller Quixote, decent wines,
60 malt whiskies and good coffee, cheery
staff, well lit pool room, pub games;
background music (live country & western
Tues), big sports TV in side snug; children
and dogs welcome, large garden with picnic-
sets and good play area, caravan parking,
bedroom extension. *(Anthony Barnes)*

GREAT RYBURGH   TF9627
Blue Boar   (01328) 829212
Station Road; NR21 0DX Rambling 17th-c
beamed pub in nice setting opposite church,
good locally sourced food from landlord-
chef, can eat in bar or restaurant, a house
beer from Winters along with guests such as
Yetmans Red, inglenook woodburner;
children welcome, garden with enclosed play
area, pleasant local walks, five bedrooms,
closed Tues, lunchtimes Mon, Weds, Sat.
(George Atkinson)

GREAT YARMOUTH   TG5207
St Johns Head   (01493) 843443
North Quay; NR30 1JB Friendly
traditional flintstone pub, real ales including
bargain Elgoods; pool; sports TV; open all day.
(the Didler, David Carr)

HARLESTON   TM2483
J D Young   (01379) 852822
Market Place; IP20 9AD Hotel-pub
(former coaching inn) with convivial bar,
three local ales, enjoyable good value fresh
food all day from breakfast on, friendly
efficient staff, comfortable spacious
library-feel dining room with lamps on well
spaced tables, open fire; sports TV; children
welcome, disabled facilities, 11 bedrooms.
(Paul Baxter)

HARPLEY   TF7825
Rose & Crown   (01485) 521807
*Off A148 Fakenham–Kings Lynn;
Nethergate Street; PE31 6TW* Old village
pub saved from developers and doing well
under present welcoming licensees; above
average pub food, ales such as Adnams
and Woodfordes Wherry, Aspall's cider,

modernised interior with open fires; children
welcome, garden. *(Anon)*

HEACHAM   TF6737
Fox & Hounds   (01485) 570345
Station Road; PE31 7EX Unpretentious
open-plan pub brewing its own good Fox
beers, also well kept guests and Saxon farm
cider (regular beer festivals), cheery chatty
service, good generous home-made food
(not Sun evening) in comfortable bar and
spotless light and airy dining area; live music
Tues, pool; small garden, open all day.
(Alan Weedon)

HEYDON   TG1127
✳**Earle Arms**   (01263) 587376
Off B1149; NR11 6AD Nice old dutch-
gabled pub overlooking green and church in
delightfully unspoilt estate village; well kept
Adnams, Woodfordes and a guest, enjoyable
food from varied if not extensive menu using
local fish and meat (gluten-free choices
marked), decent wine list, friendly efficient
service, racing prints, some stuffed animals
and good log fire in old-fashioned candlelit
bar, more formal dining room; children
welcome, dogs on leads in bar, picnic-sets
in small cottagey back garden, open all day
Sun (no evening food then), closed Mon.
(John Beeken, John Wooll)

HICKLING   TG4123
Greyhound   (01692) 598306
The Green; NR12 0YA Small busy pub
with welcoming open fire, good choice of
enjoyable food in bar and neat restaurant,
well kept ales including Woodfordes Wherry,
local cider, friendly long-serving landlord;
well behaved children welcome, pretty
back garden with terrace tables, bedroom
annexe. *(Simon Watkins, Roy Hoing)*

HINGHAM   TG0202
✳**White Hart**   (01953) 850214
*Market Place, just off B1108 W of
Norwich; NR9 4AF* Friendly and civilised
Flying Kiwi Inn with character rooms
arranged over two floors, beams and standing
timbers, stripped floorboards with oriental
rugs, attractive mix of furniture including
comfortable sofas in quiet corners, lots of
prints and photographs on mushroom walls,
several woodburners, galleried long room
up steps from main bar with egyptian frieze,
own-brewed Jo C's Norfolk Kiwi plus Adnams
Bitter, lots of wines by glass, good interesting
food; children and dogs (in bar) welcome,
modern benches and seats in gravelled
courtyard, pretty village, open all day.
(Emma Jay, Evelyn and Derek Walter)

HOLKHAM   TF8943
✳**Victoria**   (01328) 711008
A149 near Holkham Hall; NR23 1RG
Upmarket but informal small hotel (owned by
Holkham Estate), eclectic mix of furnishings
including deep low sofas, lit candles in heavy

sticks, big log fire, well kept Adnams Bitter, Woodfordes Wherry and a guest, nice wines and coffee, good local seasonal food, friendly service, anglo-indian décor in linked dining rooms (best to book); background music; children welcome, dogs in bar, sheltered courtyard with retractable awning, walks to nature-reserve salt marshes and sea, ten stylish bedrooms, open all day. *(Michael Sargent, John Honnor, Mike Proctor, David Carr)*

HOLME-NEXT-THE-SEA   TF7043
White Horse   (01485) 525512
Kirkgate Street; PE36 6LH Attractive old-fashioned place, cosy and rambling, with warm log fires, ample choice of food including local fish and Sun roasts, reasonable prices, friendly helpful service, Adnams beers and decent wine; children and dogs welcome (they have two friendly dogs and a cat), small back garden, seats out in front and on lawn opposite. *(Anon)*

HOLT   TG0738
Feathers   (01263) 712318
Market Place; NR25 6BW Unpretentious hotel with popular locals' bar comfortably extended around original panelled area, open fire, antiques in attractive entrance/ reception area, good choice of enjoyable fairly priced food, quick friendly service, Greene King ales and decent wines, good coffee, restaurant and dining conservatory; background music, no dogs; children welcome, 15 comfortable bedrooms, open all day. *(David Carr, John Wooll)*

HOLT   TG0738
Kings Head   (01263) 712543
High Street/Bull Street; NR25 6BN Bustling rustic public bar, two roomy back bars and conservatory, enjoyable food including charcoal-grilled steaks, prompt friendly service, beers such as Adnams, Humpty Dumpty and Woodfordes, fair choice of wines; some live music, sports TV, pool; children welcome, back terrace with heated smokers' shelter, good-sized garden, three stylish bedrooms, open all day. *(Simon Watkins, N R White)*

HORNING   TG3417
Swan   (01692) 630316
Lower Street; NR12 8AA Popular mock-Tudor Vintage Inn with lovely Broads views, enjoyable generous food including set menu till 5pm (not Sun), Adnams and Fullers ales, beams and log fire in split-level carpeted interior; background music; disabled facilities, picnic-sets on splendid riverside terrace, eight bedrooms, open all day. *(Paul and Corinna Goldman)*

HORSTEAD   TG2619
Recruiting Sergeant   (01603) 737077
B1150 just S of Coltishall; NR12 7EE Light, airy and roomily set out roadside pub, enjoyable generously served food from fresh

panini and wraps up including good fish choice, efficient friendly service even when busy, up to half a dozen changing ales such as Adnams, Greene King, Timothy Taylors and Woodfordes, plenty of wines by the glass, big open fire; children welcome, terrace and garden tables, new bedrooms, open all day. *(John Wooll)*

HUNSTANTON   TF6740
Waterside   (01485) 535810
Beach Terrace Road; PE36 5BQ Former station buffet just above prom, now bar-restaurant with great sea views from popular conservatory (children welcome here), Adnams, Greene King and good value wines, straightforward inexpensive tasty food all day from sandwiches up, quick service by friendly uniformed staff, Fri quiz; dogs allowed on lead. *(John Honnor, John Wooll)*

HUNWORTH   TG0735
⭐ Hunny Bell   (01263) 712300
Signed off B roads S of Holt; NR24 2AA Welcoming carefully furnished 18th-c pub, neat bar with nice mix of cushioned dining chairs around wooden tables, stone floor and woodburner, cosy snug with homely furniture on old tiles, some original stripped-brick walls throughout, another woodburner in high-raftered dining room, good variety of popular well presented food, Adnams, Greene King, Woodfordes and a guest, good informal service from young staff; children and dogs welcome, picnic-sets on terrace overlooking village green, more seats in garden among fruit trees. *(Robert Watt, Brian Glozier, David Carr)*

INGHAM   TG3926
⭐ Swan   (01692) 581099
Off A149 SE of North Walsham; signed from Stalham; NR12 9AB Smart 14th-c thatched dining pub nicely placed for Broads and coast; rustic main area divided by massive chimneybreast with woodburner on each side, low beams and hefty standing timbers, bare boards or parquet, some old farm tools, quieter small brick-floored part with leather sofas, good well presented restaurant-style food including cheaper lunchtime set menu, home-baked bread, Woodfordes ales and local cider; children welcome, picnic-sets on sunny back terrace, more at side, five bedrooms in converted stables, good breakfast. *(N R White, Roy Hoing, David Carr)*

ITTERINGHAM   TG1430
⭐ Walpole Arms   (01263) 587258
Village signposted off B1354 NW of Aylsham; NR11 7AR Beamed 18th-c pub close to Blickling Hall (NT) and under newish ownership; good modern cooking using fresh local ingredients (some from own farm) along with more traditional choices, efficient friendly service, well kept Adnams and Woodfordes, nice wines by the glass,

sizeable open-plan bar with woodburner, stripped-brick walls and dark wood dining tables on red carpet, light airy restaurant opening on to vine-covered terrace, Weds quiz; children welcome, dogs in bar, two-acre landscaped garden open all day Sat, closed Sun evening. *(Anthony Barnes, Mike Proctor, Paul and Linda Aquilina, Paul McIntyre)*

KING'S LYNN   TF6120

Crown & Mitre   (01553) 774669

Ferry Street; PE30 1LJ Old-fashioned pub in great riverside spot, lots of interesting naval and nautical memorabilia, up to six well kept beers such as Cambridge and Humpty Dumpty (the long-serving no-nonsense landlord may have started brewing his own beers by the time you read this), good value straightforward home-made food, river-view back conservatory; no credit cards; well behaved children and dogs welcome, quayside tables. *(John Wooll, Pete Walker)*

KING'S LYNN   TF6120

Dukes Head   (01553) 774996

Tuesday Market Place; PE30 1JS Imposing early 18th-c hotel with comfortable bar, elegant restaurant and smaller front bistro (open till 6pm), good range of enjoyable food (restaurant quite pricey), Adnams ales and nice selection of wines, cheerful attentive service; children welcome, good bedrooms, open all day. *(John Wooll)*

KING'S LYNN   TF6220

Lattice House   (01553) 769585

Corner of Market Lane, off Tuesday Market Place; PE30 1EG Old beamed and raftered Wetherspoons with good choice of ales, reasonably priced food and friendly speedy service, several well divided areas including upstairs bar; children welcome, open all day from 9am (till 1am Fri, Sat). *(Pete Walker)*

LETHERINGSETT   TG0638

⋆**Kings Head**   (01263) 712691

A148 (Holt Road) W of Holt; NR25 7AR Civilised country house-style pub (Flying Kiwi Inns); small bar on right, main bar to the left with big leather armchairs and sofas, rugs on quarry tiles, hunting and coaching prints on mushroom-painted walls, daily papers and open fire, own-brewed Jo C's Norfolk Kiwi plus Adnams Best, several wines by the glass and decent coffee, very good modern food served by friendly attentive young staff, dining room with built-in cushioned wall seats and mix of tables and chairs on bare boards, some old farm tools, back area with painted rafters and more leather sofas; TV; children welcome, dogs in bar, picnic-sets under parasols on front gravel, more on side lawn, play fort, open all day. *(Philip and Susan Philcox, R L Borthwick, R C Vincent, Derek Thomas, Brian Glozier)*

MARSHAM   TG1924

Plough   (01263) 735000

Old Norwich Road; NR10 5PS 18th-c pub with split-level open-plan bar, enjoyable food using local produce including good value set lunch, Adnams and Greene King, friendly helpful staff; comfortable bedrooms, open all day in summer. *(David Carr)*

MUNDFORD   TL8093

Crown   (01842) 878233

Off A1065 Thetford–Swaffham; Crown Road; IP26 5HQ Unassuming old pub, warmly welcoming, with heavy beams and huge fireplace, interesting local memorabilia, Courage Directors and one or two guests, over 50 malt whiskies, enjoyable generously served food at sensible prices, spiral iron stairs to two restaurant areas (larger one has separate entrance accessible to wheelchairs), locals' bar with sports TV; children and dogs welcome, back terrace and garden with wishing well, Harley-Davidson meeting first Sun of month, bedrooms (some in adjoining building), self-catering property, open all day. *(Anon)*

NECTON   TF8709

Windmill   (01760) 722057

Mill Street; PE37 8EN Family-run village pub with black-beamed carpeted bar and clean modern restaurant, wide choice of well cooked food (not Sun evening) including good value two-course lunch, friendly competent young staff, well kept ales such as Beeston and Greene King, monthly quiz, pool and darts; children welcome. *(B R and M F Arnold, Mr and Mrs D G Waller)*

NORTHREPPS   TG2439

Foundry Arms   (01263) 579256

Church Street; NR27 0AA Welcoming village pub with enjoyable, reasonably priced traditional food (not Sun evening, Mon), well kept Adnams and Woodfordes, decent choice of wines, woodburner, smallish restaurant; pool and darts; children and dogs welcome, picnic-sets in back garden, open all day. *(David and Gill Carrington)*

NORWICH   TG2309

⋆**Adam & Eve**   (01603) 667423

Bishopgate; follow Palace Street from Tombland, N of cathedral; NR3 1RZ Ancient pub dating from at least 1241 when used by workmen building the cathedral, has Saxon well beneath the lower bar floor and striking dutch gables (added in 14th and 15th c); old-fashioned small bars with tiled or parquet floors, cushioned benches built into partly panelled walls and some antique high-backed settles, Adnams, Theakstons Old Peculier, Wells & Youngs Bombardier and a guest, Aspall's cider and 40 malt whiskies, traditional pubby food (not Sun evening); background music; children allowed in snug till 7pm, outside seating with award-winning tubs and hanging baskets, open all day, closed 25, 26 Dec, 1 Jan. *(Jane and Alan Bush, the Didler, John Honnor, David Carr, Marianne and Peter Stevens)*

NORWICH TG2408
Coach & Horses (01603) 477077
Thorpe Road; NR1 1BA Light and airy tap for Chalk Hill brewery, friendly staff, generous inexpensive home-made food including all-day breakfast, bare-boards L-shaped bar with open fire, dark wood, posters and prints, pleasant back dining area; sports TVs, gets very busy on home match days; disabled access possible (not to lavatories), front terrace, open all day. *(the Didler, David Carr)*

NORWICH TG2210
Duke of Wellington (01603) 441182
Waterloo Road; NR3 1EG Friendly rambling local with up to 21 well kept quickly changing ales including Oakham and Wolf, many served from tap room casks, foreign bottled beers too, no food except sausage rolls and pies (can bring your own), real fire, traditional games, folk music Tues, beer festival Aug; nice back terrace, open all day. *(the Didler)*

NORWICH TG2310
Fat Cat Brewery Tap
(01603) 413153 *Lawson Road; NR3 4LF* 1970s shed-like building home of the Fat Cat brewery (and sister to the Fat Cat – see Main Entries); their beers and up to 12 guests along with draught continentals, 30 bottled beers and eight or more local ciders/perries, no food apart from rolls and pork pies, live music Fri night, Sun afternoon; children (till 6pm) and dogs welcome, seats out in front and behind, open all day. *(the Didler)*

NORWICH TG2307
Kings Arms (01603) 766361
Hall Road; NR1 3HQ Busy Batemans local with plenty of changing guest beers, good whisky and wine choice, friendly atmosphere, food Sun lunchtime and match days (can bring your own at other times), garden room overlooking courtyard; sports TV, poker nights and monthly quiz; open all day. *(the Didler)*

NORWICH TG2309
✶ **Kings Head** (01603) 620468
Magdalen Street; NR3 1JE Traditional Victorian local with friendly licensees and good atmosphere in two simply furnished bare-boards bars, up to 18 very well kept changing regional ales, good choice of imported beers and a local cider, no food except pork pies, bar billiards in bigger back bar; open all day. *(the Didler)*

NORWICH TG2208
Plough (01603) 661384
St Benedicts Street; NR2 4AR Friendly little city-centre pub owned by Grain, their ales and guests kept well, good wines, knowledgeable staff, comfortable seating and open fire; good beer garden behind, open all day. *(Anon)*

NORWICH TG2308
Ribs of Beef (01603) 619517
Wensum Street, S side of Fye Bridge; NR3 1HY Welcoming and comfortable with nine real ales including Adnams, Fullers, Wolfs and Woodfordes, traditional cider and good wine choice, deep leather sofas and small tables upstairs, attractive smaller downstairs room with river view, generous well priced pubby food (till 5pm weekends), quick cheerful service, monthly quiz; children welcome, tables out on narrow waterside walkway, open all day. *(the Didler)*

NORWICH TG2308
Take Five (01603) 763099
Opposite cathedral gate; NR3 1HF Old black and white timber-fronted building, a mix of wine bar, pub and restaurant; four mainly local real ales and decent wines, enjoyable well priced home-made food with good vegetarian choice, friendly efficient service from aproned staff, good open fire; children welcome, closed Sun. *(John Wooll)*

NORWICH TG2309
Wig & Pen (01603) 625891
St Martins.Palace Plain; NR3 1RN Friendly and relaxed 17th-c beamed pub opposite cathedral close, lawyer and judge prints, woodburner, good value generous food with regularly changing specials, prompt service, six ales including Adnams, Fullers and local brews, good value wines; background music, sports TV; tables out at front, closed Sun evening, otherwise open all day. *(the Didler)*

OLD BUCKENHAM TM0691
✶ **Gamekeeper** (01953) 860397
B1077 S of Attleborough; The Green; NR17 1RE Pretty 16th-c pub with civilised beamed bar, leather armchairs and sofa in front of big inglenook woodburner, nice mix of old wooden seats and tables on fine flagstones or wood floor, local watercolours and unusual interior bow window, well kept Adnams Bitter and Woodfordes Wherry, Aspall's cider, quite a few wines by glass and several malt whiskies, well liked food including excellent (if pricey) ploughman's, comfortable main back dining area plus a small room for private dining; children welcome away from bar, dogs allowed, sunny

---

Though we don't usually mention it in the text, most pubs will now make coffee or tea – it's always worth asking.

back garden with terrace, closed Sun evening. *(Helena Reis, Sheila Topham, Tony Middis)*

OVERSTRAND TG2440
Sea Marge (01263) 579579
High Street; NR27 0AB Substantial sea-view hotel (former Edwardian country house) with separate entrance to spacious bar area, enjoyable food from ciabattas up, restaurant; five-acre grounds with terraced lawns down to coast path and beach, 25 comfortable bedrooms. *(David Carr)*

OVERSTRAND TG2440
White Horse (01263) 579237
High Street; NR27 0AB Light fresh refurbishment, comfortable and stylish, with good choice of enjoyable food in bar, dining room or barn restaurant, at least three well kept local ales, friendly staff, pool room; background music, silent sports TV; children and dogs welcome, picnic-sets in front, more in garden behind with play equipment, eight bedrooms, open all day from 8am. *(David and Gill Carrington, John Millwood)*

OXBOROUGH TF7401
Bedingfeld Arms (01366) 328300
Opposite church; PE33 9PS Comfortably refurbished late 18th-c coaching inn peacefully set opposite Oxburgh Hall (NT); good food (not Mon) from bar and restaurant menus, well kept Wells & Youngs and a guest such as Adnams Broadside, Weston's and Aspall's ciders, friendly helpful staff; background music, TV for major sporting events; children welcome, dogs on the lead in bar, garden with terrace, nine bedrooms (five in separate coach house), open all day. *(Colin McKerrow, Chris Price, Rita Scarratt)*

RINGSTEAD TF7040
★Gin Trap (01485) 525264
Village signed off A149 near Hunstanton; OS Sheet 132 map reference 707403; PE36 5JU Attractive well run 17th-c coaching inn with friendly helpful licensees, two bar areas, original part with beams, woodburner and pubby furniture, Adnams and Woodfordes ales, generous helpings of enjoyable home-made food from changing blackboard menu, airy dining conservatory; background and monthly live acoustic music; children and dogs welcome, tables in walled garden, art gallery next-door, Peddars Way walks, three bedrooms, open all day in summer when it can get very busy. *(Philip and June Caunt, John Wooll, David and Ruth Hollands, Roy Hoing, Linda Miller and Derek Greentree and others)*

SALHOUSE TG3014
Bell (01603) 721141
Lower Street; NR13 6RW Welcoming village local with tasty home-cooked food and well kept ales such as Copper Dragon, darts, Weds quiz, weekend live music; dogs welcome, pick-up service for boaters on Salhouse Broad. *(R C Vincent)*

SCULTHORPE TF8930
Hourglass (01328) 856744
The Street; NR21 9QD Restauranty place with long open room combining light modern style with some dark beams, good choice of enjoyable fairly priced food including OAP lunch deal (Mon, Tues), Adnams Broadside and Woodfordes Wherry, quick friendly service. *(M and J White, John Wooll, George Atkinson)*

SCULTHORPE TF8930
★Sculthorpe Mill (01328) 856161
Inn signed off A148 W of Fakenham, opposite village; NR21 9QG Welcoming dining pub in rebuilt 18th-c mill, appealing riverside setting, seats out under weeping willows and in attractive garden behind; light, airy and relaxed with leather sofas and sturdy tables in bar/dining area, well liked reasonably priced food from sandwiches to daily specials, Greene King ales and good house wines, upstairs restaurant; background music; six comfortable bedrooms, open all day weekends and in summer. *(Roy Hoing, John Wooll)*

SHERINGHAM TG1543
Lobster (01263) 822716
High Street; NR26 8JP Busy pub almost on seafront, friendly panelled bar with old sewing-machine tables and warm fire, seafaring décor, wide range of well kept changing ales (bank holiday festivals), bottled belgian beers and real ciders, decent well priced wines by the glass, good value generous bar meals quickly served, restaurant with seafood including fresh lobster (get there early) and good crab, games in public bar including pool, maybe live music Weds; dogs welcome, two courtyards, heated marquee, open all day. *(Tracey and Stephen Groves, N R White, Barry Collett, Mr and Mrs D J Nash, Adrian Johnson)*

SHERINGHAM TG1543
Two Lifeboats (01263) 823144
Promenade/High Street; NR26 8JR Cleanly refurbished open-plan seafront inn, enjoyable well priced pubby food from baguettes up, Adnams, Nethergate and Woodfordes, friendly staff; background music; children welcome, no dogs in summer, picnic-sets on small terrace overlooking beach, six refurbished bedrooms (some with sea view). *(David Carr)*

SHERINGHAM TG1543
Windham Arms (01263) 822609
Wyndham Street; NR26 8BA Dutch-gabled brick and cobble pub with well kept Woodfordes and other ales, enjoyable sensibly priced food (not Sun) with greek influences (chef is greek), friendly efficient service,

woodburner and tightly packed dining tables in carpeted beamed lounge, separate public bar, pool; dogs welcome, picnic-sets outside, sizeable car park (useful here), open all day but may not serve food weekday lunchtimes out of season. *(Adrian Johnson)*

SMALLBURGH   TG3324
✳ **Crown**   (01692) 536314
A149 Yarmouth Road; NR12 9AD
Thatched and beamed village inn dating from the 15th c, friendly proper landlord and nice old-fashioned pub atmosphere, well kept Adnams, Greene King, Woodfordes and guests, good choice of wines by the glass, enjoyable home-made pub food in bar and upstairs dining room, prompt service, log fire, daily papers, darts; no dogs or children inside; picnic-sets in pretty back garden, bedrooms, closed Sun evening, Mon lunchtime. *(Roy Hoing)*

SOUTH CREAKE   TF8635
Ostrich   (01328) 823320
B1355 Burnham Market–Fakenham; NR21 9PB Well kept ales including Woodfordes Wherry in cosy unpretentious village pub, plenty of tables on bare boards, shelves of books, enjoyable pub food from sandwiches up, helpful young staff, woodburner; children and dogs welcome, back terrace, three bedrooms, open all day weekends. *(Linda Miller and Derek Greentree)*

SOUTH LOPHAM   TM0481
White Horse   (01379) 688579
A1066 Diss–Thetford; The Street; IP22 2LH Beamed village pub under friendly new management, well kept Buffys Mucky Duck, Greene King IPA and Woodfordes Wherry, enjoyable food including deals and Sun carvery, log fires; big garden with play area, handy for Bressingham Gardens. *(Anon)*

SOUTH WOOTTON   TF6622
Farmers Arms   (01553) 675566
Part of Knights Hill Hotel, Grimston Road (off A148/A149); PE30 3HQ Hotel complex's olde-worlde barn and stables conversion, popular food all day including good value lunchtime carvery (not Sat), Adnams and guests, good wines and abundant coffee, pleasant helpful service, stripped brick and timbers, quiet snugs and corners, hayloft with snooker; may be background music, sports TV, machines, no dogs; children welcome, tables and play area outside, 79 comfortable bedrooms, open all day. *(R C Vincent, John Wooll)*

SOUTH WOOTTON   TF6422
Swan   (01553) 672084
Nursery Lane; PE30 3NG Friendly local overlooking village green, duck pond and bowling green, popular reasonably priced food (not Sun or Mon evenings – booking advised) in lounge bar and conservatory

restaurant, Thurs curry night, well kept Greene King and a couple of guests, quieter public bar to the side; children welcome, small enclosed garden. *(R C Vincent, John Wooll)*

SOUTHREPPS   TG2536
✳ **Vernon Arms**   (01263) 833355
Church Street; NR11 8NP Popular old-fashioned village pub, welcoming and relaxed, with good food (not Mon evening) running up to steaks and well priced crab and lobster specials (must book weekend evenings), friendly helpful young staff, well kept ales such as Adnams, Black Sheep, Timothy Taylors and Wells & Youngs, good choice of wines and malt whiskies, big log fire; darts and pool; tables outside, children, dogs and muddy walkers welcome. *(Jim Farmer, Mike Proctor)*

SPOONER ROW   TM0997
Boars   (01953) 605851
Just off A11 SW of Wymondham; NR18 9LL 1920s pub-restaurant in tiny village, enjoyable locally sourced food from light meals to more expensive (though not pretentious) choices including good vegetarian options, well kept Adnams and nice range of wines (three glass sizes), friendly service, amazing collection of food and wine books; tables in well tended garden. *(N R White)*

SPORLE   TF8411
Peddars Inn   (01760) 788101
The Street; PE32 2DR Refurbished beamed pub (was the Squirrels Drey); log-fire bar, dining room and little conservatory, good sensibly priced pubby food, Adnams and a local guest such as Beeston, Aspall's cider, quiz third Sun of month, some live music; children and dogs welcome, garden with play area, well placed for Peddars Way walkers, open all day Sat, closed Sun evening, Mon and Tues lunchtimes. *(Anon)*

STOW BARDOLPH   TF6205
Hare Arms   (01366) 382229
Just off A10 N of Downham Market; PE34 3HT Cheerful bustling village pub under long-serving licensees; bar with traditional pub furnishings and some interesting bric-a-brac suspended from ceiling, log fire, Greene King ales and a couple of guests, nine wines by glass and several malt whiskies, well liked food (all day Sun), family conservatory; plenty of seats in front and back gardens, maybe some wandering fowl, Church Farm Rare Breeds Centre nearby. *(John Saville, David and Sharon Collison, John Honnor, John Wooll)*

TACOLNESTON   TM1495
✳ **Pelican**   (01508) 489521
Norwich Road (B1113 SW of city); NR16 1AL Chatty timbered bar with relaxed, comfortable atmosphere, good log fire, sofas, armchairs and old stripped settle,

candles and flowers on tables, some booth seating, four well kept ales including one badged for them from Brandon, Aspall's cider and 36 malt whiskies, restaurant area with high-backed leather chairs around oak tables, good choice of food (not weekday lunchtimes) from pub favourites up, friendly service, shop selling local produce and bottled Norfolk/Suffolk ales; background music; plenty of tables on decking behind, sheltered lawn beyond, three bedrooms, open all day weekends in summer. *(Anthony Barnes, N R White)*

THETFORD   TL8782
Dolphin (01842) 762406
Old Market Street; IP24 2EQ Recently refurbished 17th-c beamed pub with good food including signature steaks (not cheap), Adnams, Sharps, Wells & Youngs and a house beer from Tetleys, Aspall's cider, friendly staff; children welcome, nice walled garden with gate to Castle Park, open all day. *(Anon)*

THOMPSON   TL9296
Chequers (01953) 483360
Griston Road, off A1075 S of Watton; IP24 1PX Long, low and picturesque 16th-c thatched dining pub tucked away in attractive spot, enjoyable food including bargain weekday lunch offer, real ales, helpful staff and friendly atmosphere, series of quaint rooms with low beams, inglenooks and some stripped brickwork; children welcome, dogs allowed in bar, good-sized garden with play equipment, bedroom block. *(Anon)*

TITCHWELL   TF7543
Briarfields (01485) 210742
Main Road (A149); PE31 8BB Hotel in converted roadside farm buildings with modern bar and restaurant, good food especially fish and seafood, Fri sushi night, Norfolk Brewhouse Moon Gazer and some nice wines, friendly service; children welcome, dogs in bar, sunny inner courtyard with pond, deck overlooking salt marshes to the sea, play area, 23 comfortable well appointed bedrooms, open all day. *(Tracey and Stephen Groves, Linda Miller and Derek Greentree)*

WALSINGHAM   TF9336
Bull (01328) 820333
Common Place/Shire Hall Plain; NR22 6BP Unpretentious rather quirky pub in pilgrimage village; bar's darkly ancient walls covered with clerical visiting cards and pictures of archbishops, various odds and ends including a half-size statue of Charlie Chaplin, typewriter in snug, welcoming landlord and friendly efficient staff, three well kept changing ales, tasty food (not Sat and Sun evenings) from shortish inexpensive menu, log fire, old-fashioned cash register in gents'; children welcome, dovecote

above entrance stuffed with plastic lobsters and crabs, picnic-sets in courtyard and on attractive flowery terrace by village square, outside games room, snowdrop walk in nearby abbey garden, open all day. *(John Wooll)*

WARHAM   TF9441
★**Three Horseshoes** (01328) 710547
Warham All Saints; village signed from A149 Wells-next-the-Sea to Blakeney, and from B1105 S of Wells; NR23 1NL Old-fashioned pub with gas lighting in simple rooms looking unchanged since the 1920s (parts date from 1720); stripped-deal or mahogany tables (one marked for shove-ha'penny) on stone floor, red leatherette settles built around partly panelled walls of public bar, royalist photographs, old working american one-arm bandit, longcase clock with clear piping strike, twister on ceiling to show who gets the next round, open fires in Victorian fireplaces, well kept Greene King, Woodfordes and guests (some cask tapped), local cider and good home-made lemonade, generous helpings of pubby food, friendly if unhurried service, gramophone museum opened on request; children away from bar and dogs welcome, seats in courtyard garden with flower tubs and well, bedrooms. *(the Didler, Chris Johnson, Jim Farmer, Barry Collett, David Eberlin, Linda Miller and Derek Greentree and others)*

WEASENHAM ST PETER   TF8522
Fox & Hounds (01328) 838868
A1065 Fakenham–Swaffham; The Green; PE32 2TD Traditional 18th-c beamed local with bar and two dining areas (one with inglenook woodburner), spotless and well run by friendly family, three changing ales, good honest home-made food at reasonable prices including Sun roasts, pubby furniture and carpets throughout, lots of military prints; children welcome, big well kept garden and terrace, closed Mon. *(Anon)*

WELLS-NEXT-THE-SEA   TF9143
Albatros 07979 087228
The Quay; NR23 1AT Bar on 1899 quayside clipper, charts and other nautical memorabilia, Woodfordes beers served from the cask, speciality pancakes, good views of harbour and tidal marshes, live weekend music; children and dogs welcome, not good for disabled, cabin accommodation with shared showers, open all day. *(Chris Johnson, John Millwood)*

WELLS-NEXT-THE-SEA   TF9143
★**Globe** (01328) 710206
The Buttlands; NR23 1EU Handsome Georgian inn a short walk from the quay; plenty of space in opened-up contemporary rooms, tables on oak boards, comfortable sofas and armchairs, walls in grey and cream hung with quirky driftwood artwork, three big bow windows, Adnams beers, thoughtful wine choice and enjoyable food, evening jazz third

Sun of month; background music, TV, board games; children and dogs welcome, attractive heated courtyard with green cast-iron furniture on pale flagstones, bedrooms, open all day. *(Chris Johnson, David Carr, W K Wood, Mr and Mrs D J Nash)*

WEST ACRE   TF7815
Stag (01760) 755395
Low Road; PE32 1TR Small family-run local with three or more well kept changing ales in appealing unpretentious bar, obliging cheerful staff, good value home-made food, neat dining room; attractive spot in quiet village, closed Mon. *(Dr and Mrs R G J Telfer)*

WEYBOURNE   TG1143
Ship (01263) 588721
A149 W of Sheringham; The Street; NR25 7SZ Popular village pub refurbished under new management; Woodfordes Wherry and two local guests such as Grain and Humpty Dumpty, big bar with pubby furniture and woodburner, two dining rooms, good reasonably priced home-made food (not Mon, should book weekends), pleasant service; background music; well behaved children welcome, dogs in bar, seats out at front and in nice side garden handy for Muckleburgh Military Vehicle Museum, open all day in season. *(Anon)*

WYMONDHAM   TG1001
★Green Dragon (01953) 607907
Church Street; NR18 0PH Picturesque heavily timbered 14th-c inn, simple beamed back bar with log fire under Tudor mantelpiece, interesting pictures, bigger dining area, friendly helpful staff, four well kept ales including Adnams, popular good value food; children and dogs welcome, beer garden behind, modest bedrooms, near glorious 12th-c abbey church, open all day. *(Rita Scarratt, Lucien Perring, N R White)*

Post Office address codings confusingly give the impression that a few pubs are in Norfolk, when they're really in Cambridgeshire or Suffolk (which is where we list them).

Northamptonshire

Four of the Main Entry pubs here hold a Bargain Award, which means you can find several proper main courses for under £10. Beer prices are fair too; for a fantastic choice, head to the Queens Head in Bulwick (cheerful, well run and with interesting food,), Kings Arms in Farthingstone (pleasant pub with a tranquil garden), Althorp Coaching Inn at Great Brington (nine beers and lots of cheery locals), Olde Sun in Nether Heyford (fantastic bric-a-brac), Malt Shovel in Northampton (an amazing 13 ales on handpump) and Ship in Oundle (down-to-earth town pub with friendly people). New entries include the Olde Coach House at Ashby St Ledgers (carefully modernised old place with new boutique bedrooms and original features mixing with contemporary touches), Snooty Fox in Lowick (refurbished village pub with lots of space in beamed bars and tasty food), Star in Sulgrave (creeper-covered former farmhouse with good beers and popular food) and Narrow Boat at Weedon (next to the Grand Union Canal, with water-view bedrooms, heated terraces and wide choice of food). For a special meal out, the Falcon in Fotheringhay is our Northamptonshire Dining Pub 2014.

ASHBY ST LEDGERS   SP5768   Map 4

Olde Coach House 🛏

Main Street; 4 miles from M1 junction 18; A5 S to Kilsby, then A361
S towards Daventry; village also signed off A5 N of Weedon; CV23 8UN

Carefully modernised former farmhouse with lots of different seating areas, real ales and good wines, friendly staff and plenty of outside seating; bedrooms

As we went to press, 11 new boutique bedrooms had been added to this handsome creeper-clad inn. There's an opened-up bar on the right with some original charm, Wadworths Bishops Tipple and Wells & Youngs Bitter and Bombardier on handpump and eight wines by the glass, plus several dining areas, all very relaxed, that take in paintwork ranging from white and light beige to purple and flooring that includes stripped wooden boards, original red and white tiles and beige carpeting. All manner of pale wooden tables are surrounded by church chairs, high-backed leather dining chairs and armchairs, with comfortable squashy leather sofas and stools in front of a log fire. Also, hunting pictures, large mirrors, an original old stove and fresh flowers; background music and TV. There are picnic-sets in the back garden among shrubs and trees, modern tables and chairs out in front under pretty hanging baskets, and a dining courtyard. The nearby church is interesting.

Well liked food includes sandwiches, chicken liver parfait with red onion marmalade, thai-scented crab balls with lime chilli dressing, grazing boards, pizzas (available for takeaway too), chicken caesar salad, mushroom and spinach risotto, burger (steak and coriander, lamb and mint) with chips, lambs liver and bacon with red wine and baby onions, twice-cooked pork belly with apple sauce, king prawn and salmon with lemon and dill crème fraîche, and puddings such as warm chocolate brownie with chocolate ice-cream and lemon and sultana sponge with custard; they also offer a two-course set menu (Monday-Thursday before 7.30pm, Friday lunchtime). *Benchmark main dish: steak in ale pie £11.95. Two-course evening meal £17.00.*

Quicksilver Management ~ Manager Mark Butler ~ Real ale ~ (01788) 890349 ~ Open 12-11 ~ Bar food 12-2.30, 6-9.30 ~ Restaurant ~ Children welcome ~ Dogs allowed in bar ~ Bedrooms: /£65 ~ www.oldecoachhouse.co.uk *Recommended by George Atkinson*

BULWICK   SP9694   Map 4

Queens Head 🍺
Off A43 Kettering–Duddington; NN17 3DY

Honey-coloured 17th-c stone pub with five ales, good interesting food and friendly licensees

Very popular locally, and also offering a genuinely warm welcome for visitors (and their dogs, who get a bowl of water), this is a pretty old stone cottage with cheerful licensees. The beamed bar has exposed stone walls, contemporary paintwork, cushioned wall seats and wooden dining chairs, stone floors, a woodburning stove and a traditional feel; the bellringers pop in after their Wednesday practice and the place is liked by local clubs. The dining room has high-backed black or brown leather dining chairs around light wooden tables on floor tiles, another fireplace and interesting little knick-knacks. Digfield Barnwell, Oakham JHB, Shepherd Neame Spitfire and a couple of guest beers such as Great Oakley Gobble and Whistling Kite Wet your Whistle on handpump. Outside, there are rattan tables and chairs under a pergola and on the terrace, and a pizza oven; it's a lovely spot, with the summer sounds of swallows and house martins, sheep in the adjacent field and bells ringing in the nearby church.

Interesting food might include sandwiches, smoked leg of local rabbit, chorizo and vegetable ragout, mackerel three-ways (soused, home-smoked, grilled), crab and chilli linguine, free-range sausages with patatas bravas, salted ox tongue with puy lentils, salsa verde and bacon jam, confit duck leg with beetroot marmalade and blood orange and watercress salad, breast of local pigeon with cauliflower cream, sautéed potatoes and café de paris butter, and puddings such as vanilla crème brûlée and steamed chocolate pudding with custard. *Benchmark main dish: beer-battered haddock with peas and tartare sauce £10.50. Two-course evening meal £17.00.*

Free house ~ Licensees Julie Barclay and Robert Windeler ~ Real ale ~ (01780) 450272 ~ Open 12-3, 6-11; 12-7 Sun; closed Mon ~ Bar food 12-2, 6-9; 12-3 Sun ~ Restaurant ~ Children welcome ~ Dogs allowed in bar ~ www.thequeensheadbulwick.co.uk
Recommended by Maurice and Janet Thorpe, Michael and Jenny Back, Howard and Margaret Buchanan, M Ross-Thomas, Michael Doswell

FARTHINGHOE

Fox

SP5339   Map 4

Just off A422 Brackley–Banbury; Baker Street; NN13 5PH

Golden-stone pub, carefully spruced up, with popular food and well kept ales

As this lichened golden-stone pub is very popular, it's best to book a table in advance. Carefully restored, it has small landscape pictures, old country photographs and framed period advertisements on pastel walls, and a striking triptych of a prowling fox. Seating ranges from dark leather tub chairs, green padded seats, banquettes and neatly built-in traditional wall seats to well cushioned ladder-back and other dining chairs in the eating area, which has quite a low plank-panelled ceiling in one part. The dark-beamed front bar has a log fire in a great stripped-stone fireplace with a side salt cupboard. Lighting is sympathetic, and flooring includes attractively coloured slate tiles. Courage Directors and Wells & Youngs Bitter and Bombardier on handpump, and several good wines by the glass; background music. Behind is a sheltered terrace with teak tables, with picnic-sets under cocktail parasols in the neatly kept garden beyond. The comfortable bedrooms are in the adjoining barn conversion.

Well liked food includes sandwiches and wraps, sharing boards, smoked salmon blinis with horseradish cream and caper butter, breaded mushrooms with garlic mayonnaise, barbecue ribs with coleslaw and chips, mushroom and spinach linguine, angus burger with cheese and bacon, kedgeree with poached egg, chicken breast with peppercorn, stilton or red wine sauce, pork loin with black pudding mash, bacon and shallot and cider sauce, and puddings; curry night is Tuesday, ladies evening is Wednesday, seafood specials on Thursday and Friday (also happy hour Friday 5-7pm) and coffee morning on the first Friday of the month. *Benchmark main dish: caesar chicken and bacon salad £12.00. Two-course evening meal £20.00.*

Charles Wells ~ Lease Mark Higgs ~ Real ale ~ (01295) 713965 ~ Open 12-3, 6-11; 12-11(10 Sun) Sat ~ Bar food 12-2.30, 6-9.30; 12-4, 6-8 Sun ~ Restaurant ~ Children welcome ~ Bedrooms: /£60 ~ www.foxatfarthinghoe.co.uk *Recommended by Phil and Jane Hodson, Donna Burton-Wilcock, M G Hart, Martin and Karen Wake, Ian Herdman*

FARTHINGSTONE

Kings Arms ◧ £

SP6155   Map 4

Off A5 SE of Daventry; village signed from Litchborough; NN12 8EZ

Individual place with cosy traditional interior, carefully prepared food using own produce and lovely gardens

In summer, the tranquil terrace at this quirky gargoyle-embellished country pub has seats among hanging baskets, flower and herb pots, plant-filled painted tractor tyres and recycled art. Inside, the cosy flagstoned bar has a cheerful, bustling atmosphere with plenty of customers, a huge log fire, comfortable homely sofas and armchairs

'Children welcome' means the pub says it lets children inside without any special restriction. If it allows them in, but to restricted areas such as an eating area or family room, we specify this. Places with separate restaurants often let children use them, and hotels usually let children into public areas such as lounges. Some pubs impose an evening time limit – let us know if you find one earlier than 9pm.

near the entrance, whisky-water jugs hanging from oak beams and lots of pictures and decorative plates on the walls. A games room at the far end has darts, dominoes, cribbage, table skittles and board games. Black Sheep, Skinners Betty Stogs and Wadworth 6X on handpump and a short but decent wine list. Look out for the interesting newspaper-influenced décor in the outside gents'. This is a picturesque village and good walks nearby include the Knightley Way. It's worth ringing in advance to check the opening and food serving times.

🍴 Using some home-grown produce, the food includes sandwiches, home-made soup, fish or cheese platters, pork cassoulet, chicken with feta and red peppers, salmon fishcakes, game casserole, and puddings like hot gingerbread with maple syrup and raspberry meringue. *Benchmark main dish: yorkshire pudding filled with steak and kidney £8.25. Two-course evening meal £14.25.*

Free house ~ Licensees Paul and Denise Egerton ~ Real ale ~ (01327) 361604 ~ Open 7-11.30(6.30-midnight Fri); 12-4, 7-11.30 Sat; 12-4, 9-11 Sun; closed Mon and weekday lunchtimes ~ Bar food 12-2.15 Sat, Sun; 7.15-9.15 last Fri of month ~ Children welcome ~ Dogs allowed in bar *Recommended by Richard and Penny Gibbs, George Atkinson*

FOTHERINGHAY   TL0593   Map 5
Falcon 🍴 ♀

Village signposted off A605 on Peterborough side of Oundle; PE8 5HZ

Northamptonshire Dining Pub of the Year

Upmarket dining pub with good range of drinks and interesting food from snacks up, and attractive garden

This lovely village has plentiful River Nene moorings and isn't far from the ruins of Fotheringhay Castle, where Mary, Queen of Scots was executed. Everything in this civilised pub is neatly turned out, and the staff serving the good, attractively presented food are polite and friendly. There are cushioned slat-back arm and bucket chairs and comfortably cushioned window seats on bare floorboards, fresh flowers and warming winter log fires in stone fireplaces. The new Orangery restaurant opens on to a charming lavender-surrounded terrace with lovely views of the vast church behind and the attractively planted garden; plenty of seats under parasols. Surprisingly, given the emphasis on dining, there's a thriving little locals' tap bar and a darts team, and a fine choice of drinks including Digfield Fools Nook, Fullers London Pride and Greene King IPA on handpump, 16 good wines by the glass and several malt whiskies.

🍴 As well as a two- and three-course set menu, the interesting food includes sandwiches, sesame seed-crusted tuna with noodles, chilli, coriander and ginger dressing, rabbit rillette with prune and Armagnac chutney, chicken caesar salad, orzo pasta with squash, girolles, courgettes and salsa verde, steak in ale pie, poussin with fondant potato, broad beans and wild mushroom jus, lamb rump with celeriac dauphinoise, confit garlic cabbage and rosemary jus, bass with lemon-crushed potatoes, pak choi and salsa rossa, and puddings such as white and dark chocolate cheesecake with pistachio ice-cream and raspberry crème brûlée. *Benchmark main dish: salmon and crab fishcakes with tartare sauce £9.95. Two-course evening meal £15.00.*

Free house ~ Licensee Sally Facer ~ Real ale ~ (01832) 226254 ~ Open 12-11(10 Sun); closed Sun evening Jan-late May ~ Bar food 12-2, 6-9; 12-4, 6-8 Sun ~ Restaurant ~ Children welcome ~ Dogs allowed in bar ~ www.thefalcon-inn.co.uk *Recommended by Michael Sargent, Clive and Fran Dutson, Phil and Jane Hodson, Ryta Lyndley, James Stretton, Derek and Sylvia Stephenson, Tracey and Stephen Groves*

GREAT BRINGTON   SP6664   Map 4

Althorp Coaching Inn

Off A428 NW of Northampton, near Althorp Hall; until recently known as the Fox & Hounds; NN7 4JA

Friendly golden-stone thatched pub with a great choice of real ales, tasty popular food and sheltered garden

Deservedly popular with a good mix of customers, this lovely old inn scores highly for both ales and food. Cheerful staff serve nine or so beers on handpump: Butcombe Gold, Byatts XK Dark, Fullers London Pride, Greene King IPA, Hook Norton Old Hooky, Hopping Mad Fruitcase, Potbelly Old Barsteward, Skinners Cornish Trawler and Wadworths St George & the Dragon. The extended dining area gives views of the 30 or so casks racked in the cellar; also, eight wines by the glass and a dozen malt whiskies. The ancient bar has all the traditional features you'd wish for, from a dog or two sprawled out by the huge log fire, to old beams, sagging joists and an attractive mix of country chairs and tables (maybe with fresh flowers) on broad flagstones and bare boards. There are snug alcoves and nooks with some stripped-pine shutters and panelling, two fine log fires and a medley of bric-a-brac from farming implements to an old clocking-in machine and country pictures. Next to a converted stable block – now a function room – is a lovely cobbled and paved courtyard (also accessible by the old coaching entrance) with sheltered tables and tubs of flowers; more seating in the lovely garden.

 Quite a choice of good food includes sandwiches, mushrooms in pepper sauce, moules marinière, gloucester old spot chop topped with mustard and cheddar on colcannon mash, pasta with leeks in creamy cheese sauce, pie of the day, sausages with mash and onion gravy, chicken breast with chestnut stuffing wrapped in smoked bacon with creamy stilton sauce, salmon with orange and cranberry sauce, slow-cooked venison in chestnut, mushroom and red wine sauce, and puddings such as warm chocolate brownie with vanilla ice-cream and fruit crumble with custard. *Benchmark main dish: pork fillet stuffed with apricot and sage with cider and apple sauce £12.95. Two-course evening meal £19.00.*

Free house ~ Licensee Michael Krempels ~ Real ale ~ (01604) 770651 ~ Open 11am-midnight; 12-11 Sun ~ Bar food 12-3, 6.30-9.30(10 Fri, Sat); 12-4, 6-8 Sun ~ Restaurant ~ Children welcome ~ Dogs allowed in bar ~ Live music Tues evening ~ www.althorp-coaching-inn.co.uk *Recommended by Michael Butler, George Atkinson, Clive and Fran Dutson, Patrick and Daphne Darley, Gerry and Rosemary Dobson, Jim and Nancy Forbes, Ron and Sheila Corbett*

LOWICK   SP9780   Map 4

Snooty Fox

Off A6116 Corby–Raunds; NN14 3BH

Bustling village pub with plenty of seating, real ales, quite a choice of food and friendly staff

Dating from the 16th c, this solidly built traditional pub is at the heart of a peaceful village. The spacious lounge bar has handsomely moulded dark oak beams, leather sofas, stools and bucket armchairs on big terracotta tiles, stripped stonework and a woodburning stove in the sizeable fireplace. A formidable carved counter serves Nene Valley BSA and Oakham JHB on handpump and several wines by the glass. The more formal dining rooms have high-backed leather and other dining chairs around a choice of chunky tables on pale wooden floorboards; background music. There are picnic-sets under parasols on the front grass and a play area.

Popular food includes sandwiches, potted mackerel with lemon mayonnaise, mushrooms in cream and stilton, beer-battered cod with peas and tartare sauce, gammon with egg and chips, linguine with red onions, olives and spicy tomato sauce, sausages with mash and onion gravy, sea trout on spinach with shellfish bisque and tempura-coated samphire, duck breast with glazed shallots and raspberry sauce, and puddings such as blackberry and apple crumble with crème anglaise and banana butterscotch pudding with vanilla ice-cream. *Benchmark main dish: rack of salt marsh lamb with redcurrant and mint sauce, chilli and garlic asparagus £18.95. Two-course evening meal £20.00.*

Free house ~ Licensee Aran Biris ~ Real ale ~ (01832) 733434 ~ Open 12-3, 5-11; 12-11 Sat, Sun; closed Mon ~ Bar food 12-2, 6-9(9.30 Sat); 12-9 Sun ~ Restaurant ~ Children welcome ~ Dogs allowed in bar ~ www.thesnootyfoxlowick.com
Recommended by Alan Sutton

NETHER HEYFORD
Olde Sun ♨ £

SP6658 Map 4

1.75 miles from M1 junction 16: village signposted left off A45 W; Middle Street; NN7 3LL

Unpretentious place with diverting bric-a-brac, reasonably priced pubby bar food and garden with play area

With fair value, tasty food and well kept ales, this golden-stone pub makes a good break from the M1. The several small linked rooms have all manner of entertaining bric-a-brac hanging from the ceilings and packed into nooks and crannies, including brassware (one fireplace is a grotto of large brass animals), colourful relief plates, 1930s cigarette cards, railway memorabilia and advertising signs, World War II posters and rope fancywork. The nice old cash till on one of the two counters is wishfully stuck at one and a ha'penny. Banks's Bitter, Greene King Ruddles, Marstons Pedigree and a guest such as Ringwood Best on handpump. Most of the furnishings are properly pubby. There are beams and low ceilings (one painted with a fine sunburst), partly glazed dividing panels, steps between some areas, rugs on parquet, red tiles or flagstones, a big inglenook log fire and, up on the left, a room with full-sized hood skittles, games machine, darts, Sky TV, cribbage and dominoes; background music. The garden has antiquated hand-operated farm machines (some with plants in their hoppers) you can't miss the row of bright blue grain kibblers by the front terrace (with fairy lights and picnic-sets).

Good value food includes sandwiches, deep-fried spicy chicken goujons with garlic mayonnaise, soup of the day, lasagne, gammon with pineapple, smoked haddock, spring onion and cheese fishcakes, vegetarian risotto, and puddings such as jam sponge with custard and profiteroles. *Benchmark main dish: ham, egg and chips £7.95. Two-course evening meal £15.00.*

Free house ~ Licensees P Yates and Alan Ford ~ Real ale ~ (01327) 340164 ~ Open 12-2.30, 5-11; 12-midnight Fri, Sat; 12-11 Sun ~ Bar food 12-2, 7-9; 12-4 Sun ~ Restaurant ~ Children welcome ~ Dogs welcome *Recommended by Andy Dolan, Nigel and Sue Foster, Gerry and Rosemary Dobson, Brian and Anna Marsden, Paul Humphreys, George Atkinson*

You can send reports directly to us at feedback@goodguides.com

NORTHAMPTON
Malt Shovel ◖ £

SP7559 Map 4

Bridge Street (approach road from M1 junction 15); no parking in nearby street, best to park in Morrisons central car park, far end – passage past Europcar straight to back entrance; NN1 1QF

Friendly, well run real ale pub with bargain lunches and over a dozen varied beers

Mecca for the real ale enthusiast, this bustling tavern serves up to 13 real ales from a battery of handpumps lined up on the long counter – and even more during beer festivals. As well as regulars from both Great Oakley and Frog Island, there might be guests like Cotleigh Nutcracker, Elland Lock Keeper, Fullers London Pride, Goffs Black Knight, Mallinsons Citra, Mayfields Festival Ale, Oakham Bishops Farewell and JHB and RCH Firebox; also, belgian draught and bottled beers, over 40 malt whiskies, english country wines and Rich's farm cider. There's quite an extensive collection of carefully chosen brewing memorabilia, some from Phipps Northampton Brewery Company (which was once across the road – the site is now occupied by Phipps Brewery). Look out for the rare Phipps Northampton Brewery Company star, displayed outside the pub, and some high-mounted ancient beer engines from the Carlsberg Brewery. Staff are cheery and helpful; darts, daily papers, background music and disabled facilities. The secluded backyard has tables and chairs, a smokers' shelter and occasional barbecues.

Bargain lunchtime-only food includes rolls, breaded lemon and black pepper cod goujons, spinach and ricotta cannelloni, gammon and egg, lambs liver and bacon casserole with mash and onion gravy, and braised pork belly with spring onion mash, red cabbage and parsnip chips. *Benchmark main dish: thai green chicken curry £6.00.*

Free house ~ Licensee Mike Evans ~ Real ale ~ (01604) 234212 ~ Open 11.30-3, 5-11 (11.30 Fri, Sat); 12-10.30 Sun ~ Bar food 12-2; not Sun ~ Well behaved children welcome in bar ~ Dogs allowed in bar ~ Blues Weds evening ~ www.maltshoveltavern.com
Recommended by George Atkinson, Dr J Barrie Jones

OUNDLE
Ship ◖ £

TL0388 Map 5

West Street; PE8 4EF

Bustling down-to-earth town pub with interesting beers and good value pubby food

The constant comings and goings of local characters and the buzz of happy chat fill the rooms of this easy-going community pub. To the left of the central corridor, the heavily beamed lounge (watch your head if you're tall) consists of three cosy areas with a mix of leather and other seats, sturdy tables and a warming log fire in a stone inglenook. A charming little panelled snug at one end has built-in button-back leather seats. The wood-floored public bar (refurbished this year) has poker evenings on Wednesdays, while the terrace bar has pool and table football; background music. Friendly staff serve Brewsters Hophead, Nene Valley DXB, Phipps NBC India Pale Ale, Sharps Doom Bar and Timothy Taylors Landlord on handpump, plus a good range of malt whiskies, and cocktails on Thursday and Friday evenings. Midnight, the sleepy black and white pub cat, seems oblivious to all the cheery bustle. The wooden tables and chairs out on the series of small sunny covered terraces are lit at night.

As well as Tuesday pie night, Wednesday evening curries, Thursday evening burgers and Friday night fish and chips, the cheap pubby food includes sandwiches, breaded whitebait, haddock and chips, sausage and mash and daily specials. *Benchmark main dish: home-cooked ham, egg and chips £9.95. Two-course evening meal £17.00.*

Free house ~ Licensees Andrew and Robert Langridge ~ Real ale ~ (01832) 273918 ~ Open 11am(12 Sun)-midnight ~ Bar food 12-3, 6-9; 12-9 Sat, Sun ~ Children welcome ~ Dogs welcome ~ Live bands monthly Sat ~ Bedrooms: £39/£69 ~ www.theshipinn-oundle.co.uk *Recommended by Richard and Penny Gibbs*

SULGRAVE
SP5545   Map 4

Star

Manor Road; E of Banbury, signed off B4525; OX17 2SA

Pleasant country pub with popular food and nice gardens

Just a short walk from Sulgrave Manor (the ancestral home of George Washington) is this lovely creeper-covered former farmhouse. The little bar is furnished with cushioned window seats and wall benches, with polished flagstones by the inglenook and carpet elsewhere. Hook Norton Bitter and Old Hooky and a guest beer on handpump from the tiny counter and several wines by the glass. The dining room has an assortment of cushioned wooden dining chairs around big tables (one covered with pin-up girls from the 1920s). In summer, you can eat outside beneath a vine-covered trellis, and there are benches out front and in the back garden.

 Tasty food includes sandwiches, marinated sardines with rocket and balsamic dressing, bacon and goats cheese salad, ham and egg, parsnip and apple bake, duck breast with port, orange and redcurrant reduction, whole sea bream with chilli, garlic and lime, and puddings such as rhubarb tart with ginger cream and chocolate brioche pudding. *Benchmark main dish: fresh tuna steak on asparagus £14.50. Two-course evening meal £18.00.*

Hook Norton ~ Tenant Sue Hilton ~ Real ale ~ (01295) 760389 ~ Open 12-midnight ~ Bar food 12-9.30 ~ Restaurant ~ Children welcome ~ Dogs welcome ~ Bedrooms: £49/£69 ~ www.thestarinnsulgrave.co.uk *Recommended by Alan Sutton, Philip and Susan Philcox*

WEEDON
SP6458   Map 4

Narrow Boat

3.9 miles from M1 junction 16: A45 towards Daventry, left on to A5, pub then on left after canal, at Stowe Hill – junction Watling Street/Heyford Lane; NN7 4RZ

Canalside dining pub, comfortably updated, with pleasant conservatory, outside tables and new bedroom block

Soft lighting and a dusky ceiling give the rambling bar a relaxing feel even at busy times, helped along by unobtrusive piped pop music, comfortable dark banquettes and padded chairs around neat tables, and a woodburning stove in one side area. A new carpeted conservatory has heavy curtains for cooler nights, and there are plenty of tables outside: comfortable armchairs on heated covered decking, picnic-sets on flagstones and on the grass that slopes down towards the Grand Union Canal with its colourful narrowboats. They have a summer bar out there and a children's play trail. Wells & Youngs Eagle and Bombardier on handpump, a good choice of wines by the glass; efficient interested service, disabled facilities. We haven't yet heard from readers using the new back bedroom block, but it certainly looks comfortable.

🍴 Using local produce, the popular food includes sandwiches, pork and black pudding scotch egg with sweet pickle mayonnaise, ham hock terrine with boiled egg and piccalilli, sharing platters, stone-baked pizzas, squid ink and crab risotto, ham and eggs, pork burger with spicy barbecue sauce, coleslaw and chips, curried cauliflower in coconut cream with cashews, pineapple and onion flatbread, specials like slow-braised pigs cheeks with wild boar salami, mash, buttered cabbage and leeks or cajun yellow-fin tuna on beetroot mash with cucumber raita, and puddings such as chocolate and praline tart with vanilla ice-cream. *Benchmark main dish: beer-battered fish and chips £11.95. Two-course evening meal £18.75.*

Wells & Youngs ~ Lease Karen and Richard Bray ~ Real ale ~ (01327) 340333 ~ Open 12-11(10.30 Sun) ~ Bar food 12-2.30, 6-9.30; 12-10 Sat; 12-8 Sun ~ Restaurant ~ Children welcome ~ Dogs allowed in bar ~ Bedrooms: /£75 ~ www.narrowboatatweedon.co.uk *Recommended by Gerry and Rosemary Dobson, Dr Kevan Tucker, Brian and Anna Marsden, Mike and Margaret Banks, George Atkinson*

Also Worth a Visit in Northamptonshire

Besides the fully inspected pubs, you might like to try these pubs that have been recommended to us and described by readers. Do tell us what you think of them: feedback@goodguides.com

ABTHORPE   SP6446
✶ **New Inn** (01327) 857306
Signed from A43 at first roundabout S of A5; Silver Street; NN12 8QR Traditional partly thatched country local run by cheery farming family, fairly basic rambling bar with dining area down a couple of steps, four well kept Hook Norton beers and Stowford Press cider, good pubby food (not Sun evening) using their own meat and home-grown herbs, beams, stripped stone and inglenook woodburner, darts and table skittles; juke box, TV; children and dogs welcome, garden tables, bedrooms in converted barn (short walk across fields), open all day Sun, closed Mon, lunchtime Tues. *(Dr D J and Mrs S C Walker, George Atkinson)*

AYNHO   SP5133
Cartwright (01869) 811885
Croughton Road (B4100); OX17 3BE 16th-c coaching inn with linked areas, contemporary furniture on wood or tiled floors, some exposed stone walls, leather sofas by big log fire in small bar, ales such as Black Sheep, nice wines and coffee, good well presented food including set deals, efficient uniformed staff, daily papers; background music, TV; children welcome, a few seats in pretty corner of former coachyard, pleasant village with apricot trees growing against old cottage walls, 21 bedrooms, good breakfast, open all day. *(M G Hart, George Atkinson)*

AYNHO   SP4932
✶ **Great Western Arms** (01869) 338288
On B4031 1.5 miles E of Deddington, 0.75 miles W of Aynho, adjacent to Oxford Canal and Old Aynho station;
OX17 3BP Attractive old pub with series of linked cosy rooms, fine solid country tables on broad flagstones, golden stripped-stone walls, warm cream and deep red plasterwork, fresh flowers and candles, log fires, well kept Hook Norton and guests, good wines by the glass, enjoyable all-day pubby food served by friendly attentive young staff who cope well at busy times, elegant dining area on right, daily papers and magazines, extensive GWR collection including lots of steam locomotive photographs, pool, skittle alley; background music; children and dogs welcome, white cast-iron furniture in back former stable courtyard, moorings on Oxford Canal and nearby marina, bedrooms (may ask for payment on arrival). *(Malcolm and Jo Hart, Ian Herdman, John and Anne Mackinnon, M O S Hawkins, Mike and Margaret Banks, Tony Hobden)*

BADBY   SP5558
Windmill (01327) 311070
Village signposted off A361 Daventry–Banbury; NN11 3AN Attractive refurbished 18th-c thatched and beamed pub, flagstoned bar area with woodburner in huge inglenook, up to four changing ales, enjoyable varied choice of good value home-made food from lunchtime sandwiches up, friendly serving staff, restaurant extension; background and occasional live music; children and dogs welcome, terrace out by pretty village green, nice walks, eight good bedrooms, open all day. *(George Atkinson)*

BARNWELL   TL0584
Montagu Arms (01832) 273726
Off A605 S of Oundle, then fork right at

Thurning, Hemington sign; PE8 5PH
Attractive old stone-built pub with Adnams,
Digfield (brewed in village) and guests,
decent ciders, good range of well priced food,
cheerful staff, log fire, low beams, flagstones
or tile and brick floors, back dining room and
conservatory; children welcome, big garden
with play area, pleasant streamside village,
nice walks. *(Anon)*

BRACKLEY   SP5836
Crown   (01280) 702210
Market Place; NN13 7DP Smartly
refurbished Georgian inn with open fire
and stripped masonry in comfortable
carpeted bar overlooking market square,
lots of motor racing memorabilia (not far
from Silverstone), well kept beers such
as Bass and Hook Norton from carved
counter, friendly competent service, popular
reasonably priced food including good Sun
carvery, more formal dining room and small
lounge; children welcome, dogs in bar (not
at food times), back courtyard leading to
antiques centre, 29 bedrooms, open all day.
(Michael Tack)

BRAUNSTON   SP5465
Admiral Nelson   (01788) 891900
*Dark Lane, Little Braunston, overlooking
Lock 3 just N of Grand Union Canal
tunnel; NN11 7HJ* 18th-c ex-farmhouse in
peaceful setting by Grand Union Canal Lock
3 and hump bridge, good range of sensibly
priced food (not Sun evening, Mon) from
sandwiches and baguettes up, four changing
ales, canal pictures, smallish log-fire bar,
carpeted restaurant area with fairly modern
pastel décor and brick pillars, games part
with hood skittles and darts, some live music
including Aug festival; well behaved children
and dogs welcome, lots of waterside picnic-
sets, closed Mon lunchtime, otherwise open
all day. *(G Jennings, George Atkinson)*

BRAYBROOKE   SP7684
Swan   (01858) 462754
Griffin Road; LE16 8LH Nicely kept
thatched pub with good drinks choice
including Everards ales, popular sensibly
priced food (all day Sat), friendly staff,
fireside sofas, soft lighting, beams and
some exposed brickwork, restaurant; quiet
background music, silent fruit machine;
children and dogs welcome, disabled
facilities, attractive hedged garden with
covered terrace, open all day weekends.
(Carl Stasiak)

BRIXWORTH   SP7470
Coach & Horses   (01604) 880329
*Harborough Road, just off A508 N of
Northampton; NN6 9BX* Welcoming 17th-c
stone-built beamed pub, generous helpings of
enjoyable good value food including popular
Sun lunch, some interesting pricier specials
including seasonal game, Greene King and
Marstons ales, good attentive service, log-fire

bar with small dining area off, back lounge;
tables on gravelled terrace behind, bedrooms
in converted outbuildings, attractive village
with famous Saxon church. *(Justin Maeers,
George Atkinson, Gerry and Rosemary Dobson)*

BROUGHTON   SP8375
Red Lion   (01536) 790239
High Street; NN14 1NF Large welcoming
stone-built village local with half a dozen
well kept ales, farm cider and good choice of
wines by the glass from central bar, enjoyable
competitively priced home-made food (not
Sun evening, Mon lunchtime), bargain
OAP lunch Tues and Thurs, Sun carvery,
good attentive service, comfortable lounge
and dining room, plainer public bar with
games, events including beer festivals, live
music, poker and quiz nights; background
music; children welcome, small pleasant
garden with water feature, open all day
weekends. *(Paul Gordon)*

BUCKBY WHARF   SP6066
New Inn   (01327) 844747
A5 N of Weedon; NN6 7PW New owners
and some refurbishment for this canalside
pub; traditional pubby food from baguettes
and baked potatoes up, Marstons-related
beers, several rooms radiating from central
servery including a small dining room with
fire, games area with table skittles; children
welcome, dogs outside only, pleasant terrace
by busy Grand Union Canal Lock 7, popular
with boaters, open all day. *(Anon)*

BUGBROOKE   SP6756
Wharf Inn   (01604) 832585
The Wharf; off A5 S of Weedon; NN7 3QB
Super spot by Grand Union Canal, plenty
of tables on big lawn with moorings, large
beamed water-view restaurant, bar/lounge
with small informal raised eating area either
side, lots of stripped brickwork, good food
from fairly imaginative menu using local
organic produce, prompt cheerful service,
three well kept ales, lots of wines by the
glass, woodburner; background music;
children welcome, dogs in garden only,
disabled facilities, heated smokers' shelter,
open all day. *(R K Phillips, Dr Kevan Tucker,
George Atkinson)*

CHACOMBE   SP4943
George & Dragon   (01295) 711500
*Handy for M40 junction 11, via A361;
Silver Street; OX17 2JR* Welcoming
pub dating from the 17th c with beams,
flagstones, panelling and bare stone walls,
two inglenook woodburners, even a deep
glass-covered well, good popular food (not
Sun evening) in three dining areas from
lunchtime sandwiches and traditional
choices up, vegetarian options, good service,
Everards and a couple of guests from brass-
topped counter, several wines by the glass,
decent coffee, darts; background music;
children welcome, dogs in bar, picnic-sets

on suntrap terrace, pretty village with interesting church, open all day. *(George Atkinson, Ian and Suzy Masser)*

CHAPEL BRAMPTON   SP7366
⋆ **Brampton Halt** (01604) 842676
Pitsford Road, off A5199 N of Northampton; NN6 8BA Well laid out McManus pub on Northampton & Lamport Railway (which is open some weekends) in much extended former station master's house, large restaurant, railway memorabilia and train theme throughout, wide choice of enjoyable generous food (smaller helpings available) from sandwiches up, meal deals Mon-Fri, well kept ales such as Phipps IPA, St Austell Tribute and Sharps Doom Bar, good wine choice, cheerful attentive service even when busy, games and TV in bar; background music; children welcome, lots of tables in big garden with awnings and heaters, summer barbecues and maybe marquee, pretty views over small lake, Nene Way walks. *(George Atkinson, Gerry and Rosemary Dobson)*

CHAPEL BRAMPTON   SP7366
Spencer Arms (01604) 842237
Northampton Road; NN6 8AE Comfortable Chef & Brewer family dining pub, plenty of stripped tables in long timber-divided L-shaped bar, good choice of sensibly priced food all day, well kept Adnams, Fullers, Greene King and a guest ale, several wines by the glass, friendly generally efficient service, beams, two log fires, knick-knacks, daily papers; soft background music; tables outside. *(Gerry and Rosemary Dobson)*

CHAPEL BRAMPTON   SP7266
Windhover (01604) 847859
Welford Road (A5199)/Pitsford Road; NN6 8AA Roomy Vintage Inn dining pub with well kept changing ales and good choice of wines, their usual all-day food including competitively priced set menu (weekdays till 5pm), friendly efficient service, open-plan interior with some nooks and crannies, log fires; background music; children welcome, disabled access and facilities, tables in good-sized front garden with terrace and old-fashioned lamp posts, pleasant Brampton Valley Way walks. *(Gerry and Rosemary Dobson, George Atkinson)*

CHARLTON   SP5235
Rose & Crown (01295) 811317
Main Street; OX17 3DP Cosy well run 17th-c thatched pub in nice village, enjoyable home-made food using local suppliers, changing ales, friendly prompt service, beams and stripped stone, well spaced pale wood tables and chairs, inglenook log fire; well behaved children welcome (no pushchairs),

back garden with picnic-sets and wisteria arbour, closed Mon lunchtime. *(Anon)*

CLIPSTON   SP7181
Bulls Head (01858) 525268
B4036 S of Market Harborough; LE16 9RT Welcoming bustling village pub with enjoyable good value food including tapas, Everards ales and five guests, log fire and heavy beams – coins in the cracks put there by World War II airmen who sadly never made it back for their next drink; background music, TV, Tues quiz; children and dogs welcome, terrace tables, three comfortable bedrooms, open all day weekends. *(Peter Hallinan, Mike and Margaret Banks)*

COLLYWESTON   SK9902
⋆ **Collyweston Slater** (01780) 444288
The Drove (A43); PE9 3PQ Roomy, recently redecorated 17th-c inn on main road; enjoyable generously served pub food (all day Sun, when can get very busy), well kept Everards ales and decent wines, friendly service, surprisingly contemporary with brown leather easy chairs and sofas, smart modern two-part dining room (log fire) and two or three more informal areas, one with a raised stove in dividing wall, beams, stripped stone and mix of dark flagstones, bare boards and carpeting; background music, darts; children welcome, teak seats on flagstoned terrace, boules, three bedrooms, open all day. *(R T and J C Moggridge, Brian and Janet Ainscough)*

COSGROVE   SP7942
Barley Mow (01908) 562957
The Stocks; MK19 7JD Friendly new management for this old village pub by Grand Union Canal, well kept Everards ales and enjoyable reasonably priced home-made food, lounge/dining area with dark furniture, small public bar, pool and skittles; children welcome, tables on terrace and lawn down to canal, open all day. *(Stuart and Jasmine Kelly)*

CRICK   SP5872
⋆ **Red Lion** (01788) 822342
1 mile from M1 junction 18; in centre of village off A428; NN6 7TX Nicely worn-in, family-run, stone and thatch coaching inn with jovial long-serving landlord, traditional low-ceilinged bar with lots of old horsebrasses (some rare) and tiny log stove in big inglenook, generous helpings of straightforward good value lunchtime food, more elaborate evening menu (not Sun) including popular steaks, bargain Sun roast, plenty for vegetarians too, well kept Adnams Southwold, Greene King Old Speckled Hen, Wells & Youngs Bombardier and a guest, good service; children allowed (under-12s at

---

If you have to cancel a reservation for a bedroom or restaurant, please telephone or write to warn them. You may lose your deposit if you've paid one.

lunchtime only), dogs welcome, picnic-sets on terrace and in Perspex-covered coachyard with pretty hanging baskets. *(Andrew Jeeves, Carole Smart, George Atkinson, Ted George)*

DENTON SP8358
Red Lion (01604) 890510
Main Street; village off A428; NN7 1DQ Old refurbished pub up steps opposite small green, good well priced pubby food (not Sun evening) and blackboard specials, Wells & Youngs ales, good choice of wines; tables out at front under parasols, closed Mon and lunchtime Tues. *(Alan Sutton)*

EAST HADDON SP6668
✶Red Lion (01604) 770223
High Street; village signposted off A428 (turn right in village) and off A50 N of Northampton; NN6 8BU Substantial and elegant golden-stone thatched hotel with sizeable dining room, log-fire lounge and bar, emphasis on well presented imaginative food and most tables set for dining, but they do keep Wells & Youngs ales in good condition and over a dozen wines by the glass, efficient friendly service; background music; children welcome, attractive grounds including walled side garden, cookery school, seven comfortable bedrooms and two-bed cottage, good breakfast, closed Sun evening. *(Clifford Blakemore, David and Sue Atkinson, Ron and Sheila Corbett)*

EASTON ON THE HILL TF0104
✶Exeter Arms (01780) 756321
Stamford Road (A43); PE9 3NS Nicely renovated 18th-c pub well run by brother and sister team; snug candlelit country-feel bar with traditional furniture on stone floor, hops, well kept ales such as Black Sheep and Oakham, Aspall's cider, plenty of wines by the glass, wide choice of good food (must book weekends) from sandwiches, pizzas and pub favourites to more enterprising dishes using fresh local ingredients including seasonal game, swift smiling service, restaurant and new orangery with modern wicker furniture; background music; sunny split-level terrace, paddock, five bedrooms, open all day, closed Sun evening. *(G Jennings, Michael Doswell)*

EYDON SP5450
✶Royal Oak (01327) 263167
Lime Avenue; village signed off A361 Daventry–Banbury, and from B4525; NN11 3PG Interestingly laid-out 300-year-old ironstone inn, some lovely period features including fine flagstone floors and leaded windows, cosy snug on right with cushioned benches built into alcoves, seats in bow window, cottagey pictures and inglenook log fire, long corridor-like central bar linking three other small characterful rooms, four real ales including Fullers, Hook Norton and Timothy Taylors Landlord, good food (takeaway only Mon evening), friendly staff, table skittles in old stable; background music;

children and dogs welcome, terrace seating (some under cover), open all day weekends, closed Mon lunchtime. *(Mick Coles)*

FLORE SP6460
White Hart (01327) 341748
A45 W of M1 junction 16; NN7 4LW Welcoming modernised dining pub with good well presented food (not Sun evening, Mon) including set deals Tues-Thurs, St Austell Tribute, Sharps Doom Bar and a guest such as Jennings Sneck Lifter, largish front bar/dining lounge, other carpeted eating areas to the back and side; tables out on screened deck, open all day weekends, closed Mon lunchtime. *(George Atkinson)*

GRAFTON REGIS SP7546
✶White Hart (01908) 542123
A508 S of Northampton; NN12 7SR Thatched dining pub with several linked rooms, good pubby food (not Sun evening) including range of home-made soups and popular well priced Sun roasts using local meat, Greene King ales and Aspall's cider, good wines by the glass, friendly helpful staff coping well when busy, african grey parrot (can be very vocal), restaurant with open fire and separate menu; background music; terrace tables and gazebo in good-sized garden, closed Mon. *(George Atkinson)*

GREAT BILLING SP8162
Elwes Arms (01604) 407521
High Street; NN3 9DT Thatched stone-built 16th-c village pub, two bars (steps between rooms), whole choice of good value tasty food (all day Fri and Sat, not Sun evening), Black Sheep, Wadworths 6X and Shepherd Neame Spitfire, pleasant dining room (children allowed), darts, quiz Thurs and Sun; background music, TVs, no dogs; garden tables and nice covered decked terrace, play area, open all day Wed-Sun. *(Alan and Shirley Sawden)*

GREAT DODDINGTON SP8864
Stags Head (01933) 222316
High Street (B573 S of Wellingborough); NN29 7TQ Old stone-built pub with pleasant bar and split-level lounge/dining room, Black Sheep and a house beer from Caledonian, nice wines and good soft drinks range, varied choice of fairly priced food from sandwiches up, special diets catered for, smart cheery service, also separate barn restaurant extension, public bar with pool and games; background music; children and dogs welcome, picnic-sets out in front and in garden, open all day Sun. *(Anon)*

GREAT EVERDON SP5957
Plough (01327) 361606
Next to church; NN11 3BL Small fairly simple bare-boards pub in tucked-away village; bar with a couple of steps down to lounge/dining area, open fire and woodburner, Sharps Doom Bar and a guest

such as Gun Dog Jack's Spaniels, short choice of enjoyable reasonably priced food cooked by landlady, fortnightly quiz Tues; seats out in front and in spacious garden behind, shop selling vintage furniture, collectables and plants, good walks nearby. *(George Atkinson)*

GREAT HOUGHTON   SP7959
Old Cherry Tree   (01604) 761399
Cherry Tree Lane; no through road off A428 just below White Hart; NN4 7AT
Thatched village pub under new licensees; low beams, stripped stone, panelling and open fires, traditional food from lunchtime snacks up, prompt friendly service, Wells & Youngs and a couple of guests, steps up to restaurant; well behaved children and dogs welcome, tables in back garden, open all day Sun till 7pm. *(Anon)*

GREAT OXENDON   SP7383
✶ George   (01858) 465205
A508 S of Market Harborough; LE16 8NA Elegant 16th-c dining inn with comfortable convivial bar, well kept Adnams and Timothy Taylors, lots of wines by the glass, good reasonably priced food from light choices up, friendly attentive staff, green leatherette bucket chairs around small tables, brown panelled dado with wallpaper or dark painted walls above, big log fire, tiled-floor entrance lobby with easy chairs and former inn sign, carpeted conservatory; background music; children welcome, big shrub-sheltered garden, bedrooms, closed Sun evening; up for sale, so may be changes. *(Jamie and Sue May, Gerry and Rosemary Dobson, Fergus Munro, George Atkinson, Henry Paulinski, R T and J C Moggridge and others)*

GREENS NORTON   SP6649
Butchers Arms   (01327) 350488
High Street; NN12 8BA Comfortable welcoming village pub with enjoyable straightforward food from sandwiches and pizzas up, lunchtime carvery Weds and Sun, reasonable prices, Hook Norton, St Austell, Sharps and a guest, bar and games room with pool, darts and skittles, Sun quiz; piped and some live music; children (till 9pm) and dogs allowed, disabled access, picnic-sets and play area outside, pretty village near Grafton Way walks, closed lunchtimes Mon and Tues. *(Anon)*

GUILSBOROUGH   SP6772
Ward Arms   (01604) 740265
High Street; NN6 8PY Small 17th-c thatched and beamed pub in historic village, entrance lobby with stained-glass panels, bar and lounge/dining area with open fire, Nobbys ales (brewed in adjacent stables) and guests, hearty good value food (more extensive evening choice), friendly chatty staff, pool, darts and table skittles; tables outside, open all day Fri-Sun, closed Mon lunchtime. *(George Atkinson)*

HACKLETON   SP8054
White Hart   (01604) 870271
B526 SE of Northampton; NN7 2AD Comfortably traditional 18th-c country pub; wide choice of enjoyable generous food (smaller helpings available) from sandwiches up including early-evening bargains, good friendly staff, Fullers London Pride, Greene King IPA and a guest, decent choice of wines and other drinks, nice coffee, dining area up steps with flame-effect fire, stripped stone, beamery and brickwork, illuminated well, brasses and artefacts, split-level flagstoned bar with log fire, pool and hood skittles, curry/quiz night Tues; quiet background music; children (not in bar after 5pm) and dogs welcome, disabled access, sunny garden with picnic-sets and goal posts, open all day. *(George Atkinson)*

HARRINGTON   SP7780
✶ Tollemache Arms   (01536) 710469
High Street; off A508 S of Market Harborough; NN6 9NU Pretty thatched Tudor pub in lovely quiet ironstone village; very low ceilings in compact bar with log fire and in pleasant partly stripped-stone dining room, enjoyable generous food from sandwiches up, well kept ales such as Elgoods, Grainstore, Great Oakley and Wells & Youngs, friendly efficient staff, table skittles; children welcome, nice back garden with country views. *(Simon Chandler, Gerry and Rosemary Dobson)*

HELLIDON   SP5158
Red Lion   (01327) 261200
Stockwell Lane, off A425 W of Daventry; NN11 6LG Welcoming wisteria-covered inn, bar with woodburner, cosy lounge, softly lit low-ceilinged stripped-stone dining area with lots of hunting prints, ales such as Hook Norton, Shepherd Neame and Timothy Taylors, enjoyable home-made food served by helpful friendly staff, hood skittles and pool in back games room; children and dogs welcome, picnic-sets out in front, beautiful setting by unspoilt village's green, Windmill Vineyard and pleasant walks nearby, four bedrooms, open all day weekends. *(Mark Englert)*

HINTON-IN-THE-HEDGES   SP5536
Crewe Arms   (01280) 705801
Off A43 W of Brackley; NN13 5NF Welcoming 17th-c extended stone-built village pub, well kept Hook Norton and guests, decent home-made food (Sun till 6pm); two bothy bedrooms, closed weekday lunchtimes, open all day weekends. *(Mick Furn)*

KETTERING   SP8778
Alexandra Arms   (01536) 522730
Victoria Street; NN16 0BU Friendly backstreet real ale pub with a dozen or so changing quickly, hundreds each year, also Julian Church beers brewed in the cellar,

pump clips covering walls and ceiling, games bar with darts and hood skittles; back terrace, open all day (from 2pm weekdays). *(Anon)*

KILSBY SP5671
✶ George (01788) 822229
2.5 miles from M1 junction 18: A428 towards Daventry, left on to A5 – pub off on right at roundabout; CV23 8YE Popular pub (handy for motorway) with friendly hard-working landlady, proper old-fashioned public bar, wood-panelled lounge with plush banquettes and coal-effect gas stove opening into smarter area with solidly comfortable furnishings, well kept Adnams, Fullers, Timothy Taylors and a guest, splendid range of malt whiskies, enjoyable good value pubby food, speedy service; live jazz first Sun of month, quiz nights, darts, free-play pool tables, TV; children welcome if dining, dogs in bar, garden picnic-sets, six bedrooms. *(Rob and Catherine Dunster, Ted George, Andy and Jill Kassube, Dr Martin Owton)*

KISLINGBURY SP6959
✶ Cromwell Cottage (01604) 830288
High Street; NN7 4AG Sizeable Mitchells & Butlers family dining pub tucked away near River Nene; bar/lounge with open fire and some beams, smart bistro dining area with candles on tables, good popular food from snacks to set choices and specials, Wells & Youngs and a couple of guests, nice wines, efficient service from neat cheerful staff; no dogs; terrace tables, open all day. *(G Jennings, Gerry and Rosemary Dobson, Mike and Margaret Banks, Jim and Nancy Forbes, George Atkinson)*

KISLINGBURY SP6959
Olde Red Lion (01604) 830219
High Street, off A45 W of Northampton; NN7 4AQ Roomy renovated 19th-c stone-fronted pub, good freshly cooked bar and restaurant food, decent wine list, well kept Timothy Taylors ales and a guest, friendly helpful service, beams, woodburners and open fire, events including summer beer festival; background and some live music, TV, no dogs; suntrap back terrace with marquee, barbecues, two bedrooms, closed Sun evening, Mon, lunchtime Tues. *(Jim and Nancy Forbes)*

LITTLE BRINGTON SP6663
✶ Saracens Head (01604) 770640
4.5 miles from M1 junction 16, first right off A45 to Daventry; also signed off A428; Main Street; NN7 4HS Friendly old pub with good sensibly priced food (not Sun evening, Mon) from interesting menu (smaller helpings available), well kept Greene King IPA, Timothy Taylors Landlord and a guest such as Hoggleys, several wines by the glass, roomy U-shaped beamed lounge with woodburner, flagstones, chesterfields and lots of old prints, book-lined dining

room (proper napkins); gentle background music; plenty of tables out on gravel/paved area, handy for Althorp House and Holdenby House. *(D Broughton, Gerry and Rosemary Dobson, Sue Kidd, George Atkinson and others)*

LITTLE HARROWDEN SP8671
Lamb (01933) 673300
Orlingbury Road/Kings Lane – off A509 or A43 S of Kettering; NN9 5BH Popular pub in delightful village, split-level carpeted lounge with log fire and brasses on 17th-c beams, dining area, good promptly served bargain food, Wells & Youngs Eagle and a couple of guests, short sensibly priced wine list, good coffee, games bar with darts, hood skittles and machines, resident cocker spaniel called Rio; background music; children welcome, small raised terrace and garden, open all day weekends. *(Howard and Margaret Buchanan, Gerry and Rosemary Dobson)*

LITTLE HOUGHTON SP8059
Four Pears (01604) 890900
Bedford Road, off A428 E of Northampton; NN7 1AB Popular pub refurbished in contemporary style, three well kept local ales and several wines by the glass, fresh coffee, food (not Sun evening) from light dishes up, friendly service, good-sized bar, comfortable lounge with woodburner and separate restaurant; children and dogs welcome, spacious outside area, open all day fron noon. *(Gerry and Rosemary Dobson, Mr and Mrs D J Nash)*

MAIDWELL SP7477
✶ Stags Head (01604) 686700
Harborough Road (A508 N of Northampton); a mile from A14 junction 2; NN6 9JA Comfortable dining pub with woodburner in pubby part by bar, extensive eating areas, good value traditional food including set lunchtime/early evening menu, helpful friendly staff and cheery locals, well kept Black Sheep and guests, good choice of other drinks; background and some live music; disabled facilities, picnic-sets on back terrace (dogs on leads allowed here), good-sized sheltered sloping garden beyond, bedrooms, not far from splendid Palladian Kelmarsh Hall and park. *(Gerry and Rosemary Dobson, Michael Tack, Mike and Margaret Banks)*

MOULTON SP7866
Telegraph (01604) 648228
West Street; NN3 7SB Friendly old stone-built village pub with good value food (not Sun evening) and real ales such as Fullers London Pride, log fire in bar, restaurant extension; open all day Fri-Sun. *(G Jennings)*

NASSINGTON TL0696
Queens Head (01780) 784006
Station Road; PE8 6QB Refurbished stone dining inn, softly lit beamed bar with mix of old tables and chairs, large oriental rug in front of roaring fire, good reasonably

priced food from traditional choices to imaginative restaurant dishes using local ingredients, pleasant helpful uniformed staff, nice choice of wines by the glass, ales such as Greene King IPA and Oakham, good coffee, separate restaurant; pretty garden by River Nene, delightful village, nine chalet bedrooms. *(Michael Doswell)*

NORTHAMPTON   SP7560
Eastgate   (01604) 633535
Abington Street; NN1 2BP Wetherspoons conversion with eight real ales from central servery, their usual good value food, lots of local photos around the walls, upstairs bar with smokers' balcony, friendly staff; open all day from 9am. *(George Atkinson)*

NORTHAMPTON   SP7560
Wig & Pen   (01604) 622178
St Giles Street; NN1 1JA L-shaped beamed pub with well kept Greene King IPA, Fullers London Pride and eight interesting guest ales, good choice of bottled beers too, enjoyable food (not weekend evenings) from sandwiches and deli boards up, live music; sports TV; attractive split-level walled garden, open all day. *(Paul Humphreys)*

RUSHDEN   SP9566
Station Bar   (01933) 318988
Station Approach; NN10 0AW Not a pub, part of station HQ of Rushden Historical Transport Society (non-members can sign in), restored in 1940s/60s style with gas lighting, enamel signs and old-fangled furnishings, Oakham, Phipps and guests, tea and coffee, filled rolls and perhaps some hot food, friendly staff; authentic waiting room with piano, also museum and summer steam-ups; open all day weekends, closed weekday lunchtimes. *(Anon)*

RUSHTON   SP8483
Thornhill Arms   (01536) 710251
Station Road; NN14 1RL Rambling family-run dining pub opposite attractive village's cricket green, popular food including keenly priced set menu (weekday evenings, Sat lunchtime) and carvery (Sun, Mon evening), prompt friendly service, usually three well kept ales such as Fullers, Hook Norton and Shepherd Neame, several neatly laid out dining areas including smart high-beamed back restaurant, open fire; children welcome, garden with decked area, bedrooms, open all day Sun. *(Gerry and Rosemary Dobson)*

SLIPTON   SP9579
✶ Samuel Pepys   (01832) 731739
Off A6116 at first roundabout N of A14 junction, towards Twywell and Slipton; NN14 3AR Old reworked stone pub with long gently modern bar, heavy low beams and log fire, great central pillar, area with squashy leather seats around low tables, five changing ales including local Digfield, interesting reasonably priced wines, good

choice of enjoyable food from thick-cut sandwiches and tapas up (booking advised), friendly prompt service, dining room extending into roomy conservatory with country views; background music; children welcome, dogs in bar, wheelchair access from car park using ramp, well laid-out sheltered garden with heated terrace, open all day weekends. *(Peter Travis, Ryta Lyndley, Michael and Jenny Back and others)*

STAVERTON   SP5461
Countryman   (01327) 311815
Daventry Road (A425); NN11 6JH Beamed and carpeted dining pub under enthusiastic licensees, popular food including good value weekday two-course menu, Wells & Youngs Bombardier and a couple of local ales such as Potbelly, good friendly service even when busy; background music; children welcome, disabled access, some tables outside and in small garden. *(George Atkinson)*

STOKE BRUERNE   SP7449
Boat   (01604) 862428
3.5 miles from M1 junction 15 – A508 towards Stony Stratford, then signed on right; Bridge Road; NN12 7SB Old-world flagstoned bar in picturesque canalside spot by restored lock, more modern central-pillared back bar and bistro, half a dozen Marstons-related ales and local Frog Island, Thatcher's cider, fairly standard food from baguettes up including OAP lunch deal, friendly efficient young staff, comfortable upstairs bookable restaurant with more elaborate menu, shop for boaters (nice ice-creams); background music, can get busy in summer especially weekends and parking nearby difficult; welcomes dogs and children (local school in for lunch from midday), disabled facilities, tables out by towpath opposite British Waterways Museum, canal trips on own narrowboat, open all day. *(George Atkinson)*

STOKE BRUERNE   SP7449
Navigation   (01604) 864988
E side of bridge; NN12 7SD Large canalside pub with changing range of well kept Marstons beers, quite a few wines by the glass and wide choice of good fairly priced pubby food including blackboard specials, friendly busy young staff, several levels and cosy corners, sturdy wood furniture, separate family room, pub games; background music (outside too) and some live jazz; wheelchair access, plenty of tables out overlooking the water, big play area, towpath walks, open all day. *(Michael Tack)*

STOKE DOYLE   TL0286
✶ Shuckburgh Arms   (01832) 272339
Village signed (down Stoke Hill) from SW edge of Oundle; PE8 5TG Attractively reworked relaxed 17th-c pub in quiet hamlet, four traditional rooms with some modern

touches, low black beams in bowed ceilings, pictures on pastel walls, lots of pale tables on wood or carpeted floors, stylish art deco seats and elegant dining chairs, stove in inglenook, Digfield and Timothy Taylors from granite-top bar, well selected wines, good food served by competent staff; faint background music; children welcome, garden with decked area and play frame, bedrooms in separate modern block, closed Sun evening. *(Howard and Margaret Buchanan)*

SUDBOROUGH   SP9682
Vane Arms (01832) 730033
Off A6116; Main Street; NN14 3BX Refurbished thatched pub with low beams, stripped stonework and inglenook fires, enjoyable freshly cooked food, well kept Everards and guests, friendly staff, restaurant; tables out on terrace, pretty village. *(Ryta Lyndley)*

THORNBY   SP6675
Red Lion (01604) 740238
Welford Road; A5199 Northampton–Leicester; NN6 8SJ Popular old country pub with interesting range of well kept changing ales and enjoyable reasonably priced home-made food (not Mon) from standards up, prompt friendly service, beams and log fire, back dining area; children and dogs welcome, garden picnic-sets, open all day weekends when it can be busy. *(Gerry and Rosemary Dobson, C A Bryson)*

THORPE MANDEVILLE   SP5344
⋆Three Conies (01295) 711025
Off B4525 E of Banbury; OX17 2EX Attractive and welcoming 17th-c pub with wide choice of enjoyable food from good value sandwiches up, well kept Hook Norton ales and a guest, beamed bare-boards bar with some stripped stone, mix of old dining tables, three good log fires, large dining room, pub cat called Pepper; background and some live music; children and dogs welcome, disabled facilities, tables out in front and behind on decking and lawn, open all day (from 10am for breakfast). *(Michael Butler)*

THORPE WATERVILLE   TL0281
Fox (01832) 720274
A605 Thrapston–Oundle; NN14 3ED Extended stone-built pub with emphasis on chef-landlord's good food, well kept Wells & Youngs ales from central bar, several wines by the glass, friendly attentive staff, nice fire, light modern dining area; background music; children welcome, small garden with play area, open all day. *(Guy and Caroline Howard)*

TOWCESTER   SP6948
Saracens Head (01327) 350414
Watling Street W; NN12 6BX Recently revamped coaching inn with interesting *Pickwick Papers* connection; split-level interior with range of seating including sofas, open fire, emphasis on enjoyable good value food (order at the bar), Greene King ales; children welcome, well equipped bedrooms. *(George Atkinson)*

TURWESTON   SP6037
Stratton Arms (01280) 704956
E of crossroads in village; pub itself just inside Buckinghamshire; NN13 5JX Friendly chatty local in picturesque village, well kept Courage, Shepherd Neame, John Smiths, Timothy Taylors and a guest, good choice of other drinks, enjoyable reasonably priced traditional food (not Sun evening, Mon, Tues), low ceilings and two log fires, small restaurant; background music, sports TV; children and dogs welcome, big garden by Great Ouse with barbecue and play area, camping, open all day. *(Anon)*

TWYWELL   SP9578
Old Friar (01832) 732625
Lower Street, off A14 W of Thrapston; NN14 3AH Well run popular pub with enjoyable good value food including deals, Sun carvery, beers such as Fullers, Langton and Oakham, cheerful attentive service, beams and exposed stonework, some live music; children welcome, garden with good play area, open all day weekends. *(Guy and Caroline Howard, George Atkinson)*

WADENHOE   TL0183
⋆Kings Head (01832) 720024
Church Street; village signposted (in small print) off A605 S of Oundle; PE8 5ST Beautifully placed 17th-c country pub with picnic-sets on sun terrace and among trees on grassy stretch by River Nene (moorings); uncluttered partly stripped-stone bar with woodburner in fine inglenook, pale pine furniture and a couple of cushioned wall seats, simple bare-boards public bar, games room with darts, dominoes and table skittles, and attractive little beamed dining room with more pine furniture, beers from Digfield and perhaps three changing guests from other local brewers, good well presented food (all day Sat), friendly efficient service; children and dogs welcome, open all day weekends (closed Sun evening in winter). *(Ryta Lyndley, John Wooll, Clive and Fran Dutson, Philip Lane and others)*

Real ale to us means beer that has matured naturally in its cask – not pressurised or filtered. We name all real ales stocked. We usually name ales preserved under a light blanket of carbon dioxide too, though purists – pointing out that this stops the natural yeasts developing – would disagree (most people, including us, can't tell the difference!).

WALGRAVE SP8072
Royal Oak (01604) 781248
*Zion Hill, off A43 Northampton–
Kettering; NN6 9PN* Welcoming old stone-
built village local, Adnams, Greene King
and three interesting guests, decent wines,
well priced food usually including a good
choice of fish dishes, friendly prompt service,
long three-part carpeted beamed bar, small
lounge, restaurant extension behind; children
welcome, small garden with play area, open all
day Sun. *(Gerry and Rosemary Dobson)*

WELFORD SP6480
Wharf Inn (01858) 575075
*Pub just over Leicestershire border;
NN6 6JQ* Castellated Georgian folly in
delightful setting by two Grand Union Canal
marinas, Marstons and three changing guests
in unpretentious bar, popular straightforward
pubby food, pleasant dining section; children
welcome, big waterside garden, open all day.
(Dr Kevan Tucker)

WOODNEWTON TL0394
White Swan (01780) 470944
Main Street; PE8 5EB Modernised village
pub-restaurant with good food including
competitively priced set lunch, pleasant
service, Digfield beers; children welcome,
open all day weekends in summer. *(Anon)*

YARDLEY HASTINGS SP8656
∗Rose & Crown (01604) 696276
*Just off A428 Bedford–Northampton;
NN7 1EX* Spacious and popular 18th-c pub
in pretty village, flagstones, beams, stripped
stonework and quiet corners, step up to big
comfortable family dining room, flowers on
tables, good reliable food served by friendly
staff, six real ales, four ciders, decent
range of wines and soft drinks, newspapers;
background and some live music; dogs
welcome, picnic-sets in small courtyard and
good-sized garden, open from 5pm Mon-
Thurs, all day Fri, Sat, closed Sun evening.
(S Holder, Alan Sutton, G Jennings)

Northumbria

(County Durham, Northumberland and Tyneside)

They really care about real ales in this lovely county, with 13 of our top pubs holding a Beer Award; several places brew their own. There's the Rat in Anick (very relaxed, with interesting food), County at Aycliffe (super all-rounder), Manor House Inn at Carterway Heads (nice meals and Derwent Valley walks), Dipton Mill Inn at Diptonmill (six smashing own-brews and homely food), Victoria in Durham (tucked-away gem, in the same family for 30 years), Feathers at Hedley on the Hill (delicious food, nice welcome and knowledgeable staff), Crown Posada in Newcastle upon Tyne (the city's oldest pub with grand architecture), Shiremoor Farm at New York (incredibly busy and very well run), Keelman in Newburn (eight own-brews and a wide mix of customers), Ship in Newton-by-the-Sea (harbourside inn with their own ales), Olde Ship at Seahouses (fantastic seafaring memorabilia and in the same family for over a century) and Battlesteads in Wark (most enjoyable and run on 'green' ideals). The friendliness of the licensees stands out too, for both visitors and regulars – as our readers have commented warmly. And with such fantastic produce, you can be sure of an enjoyable meal, often at very fair prices. For a special occasion, try the Rat at Anick, County at Aycliffe, Feathers at Hedley on the Hill and Rose & Crown in Romaldkirk. Our Northumbria Dining Pub 2014 is the County in Aycliffe.

ANICK   NY9565   Map 10

Rat 🍴 🍷 🍺

Village signposted NE of A69/A695 Hexham junction; NE46 4LN

Views over Tyne Valley from terrace and garden, refurbished bar and lounge, lots of interesting knick-knacks, half a dozen mainly local real ales and interesting bar food

The conservatory has pleasant views and the garden is quite charming with its dovecote, statues, pretty flower beds and North Tyne Valley views from seats on the terrace. Inside, the traditional bar is snug and welcoming with a coal fire in a blackened kitchen range, lots of cottagey knick-knacks from antique floral chamber-pots hanging from the beams to china and glassware on a delft shelf, and little curtained windows that let in a soft and gentle light; background music, daily papers and magazines. The enthusiastic licensees keep Cumberland Corby, Timothy Taylors Landlord and four changing guests on handpump from mostly local brewers such as Gundog, Hexhamshire, High House Farm and Wylam (and an unpasteurised, unfiltered craft ale from them too), a dozen wines by the glass (including champagne), a local gin and farm cider. Parking is limited, but you can park by the village green.

Using local seasonal produce and other carefully sourced ingredients, the consistently good food includes sandwiches, local game terrine with fig chutney, kipper rillettes with potato and horseradish salad and home-made soda bread, sausage, leek and potato cake with onion gravy, pan haggerty of parsnips and wild mushrooms topped with cheese, braised beef in ale, coley with creamed samphire, lemon and capers, confit duck leg with dauphinoise potatoes, rib of beef for two with chips and béarnaise sauce, and puddings such as apple and blueberry crème brûlée and ginger sponge with jersey cream ice-cream. *Benchmark main dish: rump steak, roasted tomatoes, watercress and chips £13.50. Two-course evening meal £18.50.*

Free house ~ Licensees Phil Mason and Karen Errington ~ Real ale ~ (01434) 602814 ~ Open 12-11(10.30 Sun) ~ Bar food 12-2, 6-9; 12-3 Sun; not Mon except bank holidays ~ Restaurant ~ Children welcome ~ www.theratinn.com *Recommended by Comus and Sarah Elliott, Michael Doswell*

AYCLIFFE
NZ2822 Map 10

County

The Green, Aycliffe; just off A1(M) junction 59, by A167; DL5 6LX

Northumbria Dining Pub of the Year

Friendly, well run pub with four real ales, good wines and popular, interesting food; bedrooms

A perfect break from the A1, this friendly, very well run and smart place is on the village green – therefore easy to find. Many customers are here to enjoy the top quality food, but locals like to pop in for a chat at one of the high bar chairs by the counter, where they keep Hawkshead Bitter, Just A Minute IPA, Wychwood Hobgoblin and Yard of Ale 400 Yards of Ale on handpump and ten wines by the glass. More or less open-plan, it's warmly decorated with pastel blue, green and yellow paintwork, some red carpeting, local art and careful lighting. The wood-floored bar has attractive solid pine dining chairs and cushioned settles around pine tables, while the carpeted lounge has a woodburning stove in a brick fireplace with candles in brass candlesticks on either side, a second fireplace, similar furniture to the bar and painted ceiling joists; background music. The wood-floored restaurant is minimalist with high-backed black leather dining chairs and dark window blinds. There are some metal tables and chairs out in front. Bedrooms are individually designed and attractive.

Delicious food includes sandwiches, duck pâté with fig chutney, warm caramelised red onion and feta cheese tartlet, wild mushroom risotto with pine nuts, cheese and tarragon, beer-battered cod, braised lamb shank on minted mash with rosemary and port jus, chicken with black trumpet mushrooms, smoked bacon and cheese shavings on tagliatelle, crispy pork belly with black pudding, chorizo and spinach and cider cream, and puddings such as vanilla panna cotta with poached rhubarb and chocolate and toffee tart with peanut brittle ice-cream. *Benchmark main dish: steak in ale pie £11.25. Two-course evening meal £19.00.*

Free house ~ Licensee Colette Farrell ~ Real ale ~ (01325) 312273 ~ Open 11.30-3, 5-11; 11.30-11 Sun ~ Bar food 12-2, 5.30-9; 12-9 Sun ~ Restaurant ~ Children welcome ~ Bedrooms: £49/£70 ~ www.thecountyaycliffevillage.com *Recommended by Rob and Catherine Dunster, Michael Doswell, Pat and Tony Martin*

CARTERWAY HEADS
Manor House Inn

NZ0452 Map 10

A68 just N of B6278, near Derwent Reservoir; DH8 9LX

Handy after a walk, with a simple bar and more comfortable lounge, bar food and five real ales; bedrooms

This simple slate-roofed stone house is very popular for miles around for its friendly welcome, well kept ales and enjoyable food. The heartwarming locals' bar is just right if you've worked up a thirst in the nearby Derwent Valley. Homely and old-fashioned, it has an original boarded ceiling, pine tables, chairs and stools, old oak pews and a mahogany counter. The carpeted lounge bar (warmed by a woodburning stove) and restaurant are comfortably pubby, with wheelback chairs, stripped-stone walls and picture windows that make the most of the lovely setting. Black Sheep Golden Sheep, Greene King Old Speckled Hen, Northumberland Castles and Wells & Youngs London Gold on handpump alongside 15 wines by the glass, 20 malt whiskies and Weston's Old Rosie cider; TV, darts, board games and background music. There are stunning views over the Derwent Reservoir and beyond from picnic-sets on the terrace.

Helpfully served all day and featuring locally caught game, the good food includes sandwiches, tempura-battered king prawns with sweet chilli dip, seasonal pâté with red onion marmalade, free-range omelettes, pasta dish of the day, cumberland sausages with rich onion gravy, wild mushroom risotto with pesto, chicken breast on lyonnaise potatoes with café au lait sauce, rolled lamb shoulder with rich redcurrant jus, beer-battered haddock with chips, and puddings. *Benchmark main dish: slow-roasted pork belly with braised red cabbage, honey parsnip purée and redcurrant jus £12.95. Two-course evening meal £18.00.*

Enterprise ~ Licensee Chris Baxter ~ Real ale ~ (01207) 255268 ~ Open 12-11; 12-10.30 Sun ~ Bar food 12-9(8 Sun) ~ Restaurant ~ Children welcome ~ Dogs allowed in bar and bedrooms ~ Bedrooms: £55/£75 ~ www.themanorhouseinn.com *Recommended by Simon Le Fort*

COTHERSTONE
Fox & Hounds

NZ0119 Map 10

B6277; DL12 9PF

Bustling 18th-c inn with cheerful beamed bar, good bar food and quite a few wines by the glass; bedrooms

The hospitable landlord of this mid 18th-c country inn offers tasty home-made food and well kept ales to his many customers – and it's a popular place to stay too. The cheerful, simply furnished beamed bar has a partly wooden floor (elsewhere it's carpeted), a good log fire, thickly cushioned wall seats, and local photographs and country pictures in its various alcoves and recesses. Black Sheep Best and Rudgates

Battleaxe on handpump alongside several malt whiskies from smaller distilleries; efficient service from friendly staff. Don't be surprised by the unusual loo attendant – an african grey parrot called Reva. Seats outside on a terrace and quoits. The inn makes an excellent focal point for walks along the dramatic wooded Tees Valley from Barnard Castle.

 Generously served, the well liked food includes sandwiches, cheese and hazelnut pâté with onion relish, vegetable bake, gammon with tomato and cheese melt and chunky chips, beer-battered fresh haddock with minted mushy peas, salad of local cheese, prawns and roast beef, lambs liver with mustard mash, bacon and rich gravy, cheese-filled chicken in creamy leek sauce, and puddings. *Benchmark main dish: home-made smoked mackerel, prawn and salmon fishcakes £10.60. Two-course evening meal £15.50.*

Free house ~ Licensee Ian Swinburn ~ Real ale ~ (01833) 650241 ~ Open 12-3, 5-11(10.30 Sun) ~ Bar food 12-2, 6(5 Tues)-8.30 ~ Restaurant ~ Children welcome ~ Dogs allowed in bedrooms ~ Bedrooms: £47.50/£75 ~ www.cotherstonefox.co.uk
Recommended by John H Smith, Lucien Perring, Michael Doswell

 DIPTONMILL   NY9261   Map 10
Dipton Mill Inn ♀ ◖ £
S of Hexham; off B6306 at Slaley; NE46 1YA

Own-brew beers, good value bar food and waterside terrace

'A pub to be snowed up in' is how one reader describes this quaint little isolated pub. The neatly kept snug bar has genuine character, dark ply panelling, low ceilings, red furnishings, a dark red carpet and newspapers by two welcoming open fires. All six of the nicely named beers from the family-owned Hexhamshire Brewery are well kept on handpump: Blackhall English Stout, Devils Elbow, Devils Water, Old Humbug, Shire Bitter and Whapweasel. Also, 14 wines by the glass, 20 malt whiskies, Weston's Old Rosie and a guest cider. The peaceful, pretty garden has a sunken crazy-paved terrace by a restored mill stream and attractive planting; Hexham Racecourse is not far.

 Reasonably priced, homely food includes an interesting choice of cheeses, sandwiches, soup, ratatouille and couscous, steak and kidney pie, haddock with tomato and basil, chicken in sherry sauce, lamb leg steak in wine and mustard sauce, and puddings such as apple and pear crumble and syrup sponge and custard. *Benchmark main dish: mince and dumplings £7.50. Two-course evening meal £10.00.*

Own brew ~ Licensee Geoff Brooker ~ Real ale ~ No credit cards ~ (01434) 606577 ~ Open 12-2.30, 6-11; 12-3 Sun; closed Sun evening ~ Bar food 12-2, 6.30-8.30; 12-2 Sun ~ Children welcome ~ www.diptonmill.co.uk
Recommended by the Didler, LC, Claes Mauroy, Dr Kevan Tucker, Andy and Jill Kassube

DURHAM   NZ2742   Map 10
Victoria ◖
Hallgarth Street (A177, near Dunelm House); DH1 3AS

Unchanging, neatly kept Victorian pub with royal memorabilia, cheerful locals and well kept regional ales; bedrooms

This little gem is extremely popular locally. It's been run by the same friendly family for well over 30 years, and has changed little since it was built. Three little rooms lead off a central bar, with typical Victorian décor that takes in mahogany, etched and cut glass and mirrors, colourful William Morris wallpaper over a high panelled dado, maroon plush seats in little booths, leatherette wall seats and long narrow drinkers' tables. Also, coal fires in handsome iron and tile fireplaces, photographs and articles showing a real pride in the pub, lots of period prints and engravings of Queen Victoria, and staffordshire figurines of her and the Prince Consort. Coniston Bluebird Bitter, Big Lamp Bitter, Hadrian & Border Tyneside Blonde, Orkney Red MacGregor and guest beers on handpump, over 30 irish whiskeys and cheap house wines; dominoes. Credit cards are accepted only for accommodation. No food.

Free house ~ Licensee Michael Webster ~ Real ale ~ No credit cards ~ (0191) 386 5269 ~ Open 11.45-3, 6-11; 12-3, 7-11 Sun ~ Children welcome ~ Dogs welcome ~ Bedrooms: £52/£72 ~ www.victoriainn-durhamcity.co.uk *Recommended by the Didler, Comus and Sarah Elliott, Peter F Marshall, Richard Tilbrook, Roger and Donna Huggins, Alan and Jane Shaw, Eric Larkham, Edward Leetham*

 HALTWHISTLE   NY7166   Map 10
Milecastle Inn £
Military Road; B6318 NE – OS Sheet 86 map reference 715660; NE49 9NN

Close to Hadrian's Wall and some wild scenery, with straightforward bar food and cosy little rooms warmed by winter log fires; fine views and walled garden

Despite the remote situation – on a moorland road running alongside Hadrian's Wall – this sturdy stone-built pub can get very busy at peak times. The snug little rooms of the beamed bar have two log fires and are decorated with brasses, horsey and local landscape prints and attractive fresh flowers; at lunchtime, the small, comfortable restaurant is used as an overflow. Big Lamp Prince Bishop Ale, Black Sheep and Cumberland Corby Blonde on handpump and several malt whiskies. The big sheltered walled garden has tables and benches, a dovecote and rather stunning views; two self-catering cottages and a large car park.

Pubby food includes sandwiches, game pâté, prawn cocktail, lasagne, beer-battered haddock, wild boar and duck pie, gammon with egg and chips, and steaks. *Benchmark main dish: slow-cooked pork belly £10.25. Two-course evening meal £16.00.*

Free house ~ Licensees Clare and Kevin Hind ~ Real ale ~ (01434) 321372 ~ Open 12-midnight; 12-3, 6-11 in winter ~ Bar food 12-8.45; 12-2.30, 6-8.30 in winter ~ Restaurant ~ Children welcome ~ www.milecastle-inn.co.uk *Recommended by Martin Jones*

 HEDLEY ON THE HILL   NZ0759   Map 10
Feathers
Village signposted from New Ridley, which is signposted from B6309 N of Consett; OS Sheet 88 map reference 078592; NE43 7SW

Imaginative food, interesting beers from small breweries and friendly welcome in a quaint tavern

Tiny, very well run and welcoming, this 200-year-old hilltop tavern is much enjoyed by our readers. The three neat, homely bars are properly pubby, with open fires, tankard-hung beams, stripped stonework, solid furniture including settles, and old black and white photographs of local places and farm and country workers. Friendly knowledgeable staff serve quickly changing local beers such as Allendale Wagtail Ale, Cumberland Corby Ale and Consett Ale Works Red Dust on handpump, as well as six farm ciders, 23 wines by the glass and 30 malt whiskies. They hold an Easter beer and food festival with over two dozen real ales, a barrel race on Easter Monday and other traditional events; darts and dominoes. Picnic-sets in front are a nice place to sit and watch the world drift by.

🍴 Excellent food using the best local produce (rare-breed beef, game from local shoots, carefully sourced fish) might include sandwiches, potted pigs cheeks with pickles, black pudding with free-range poached egg and devilled gravy, vegetarian meze plate, pheasant and rabbit pie, red-leg partridge with braised white cabbage and sausage and rösti potatoes, mussel and smoked haddock chowder, twice-cooked duck legs with apple sauce and real ale gravy, venison shoulder with glazed onions and hotpot potatoes, and puddings such as marmalade bakewell tart with clotted cream and sticky toffee pudding with spiced ice-cream and butterscotch sauce. *Benchmark main dish: beer-battered fish and chips £12.00. Two-course evening meal £18.00.*

Free house ~ Licensees Rhian Cradock and Helen Greer ~ Real ale ~ (01661) 843607 ~ Open 12-11(10.30 Sun); closed Mon lunchtime except bank holidays, lunchtimes first two weeks Jan ~ Bar food 12-2, 6-8.30; 12-2.30 Sun; not Mon ~ Children welcome ~ www.thefeathers.net *Recommended by Comus and Sarah Elliott, Dr Kevan Tucker, Peter and Eleanor Kenyon*

NEW YORK NZ3269 Map 10
Shiremoor Farm 🍺

Middle Engine Lane; at W end of New York A191 bypass, turn S into Norham Road, then first right (pub signed); NE29 8DZ

Large dining pub with interesting furnishings and décor, popular food all day, decent drinks and covered heated terrace

Even when this interesting dining pub is absolutely packed – which it often is, with a wide mix of customers of all ages – the efficient friendly staff keep things running smoothly. A successful transformation of some derelict agricultural buildings, the several well divided, spacious areas have beams and joists (including the conical rafters of a former gin-gan), broad flagstones, several kilims, a mix of unusual and comfortable furniture, and farm tools, shields, swords and country pictures on the walls. The bar is quieter and more relaxed, with up to six quickly changing real ales on handpump such as Batemans XXXB, Cullercoats Jack the Devil and Lovely Nelly, Hadrian & Border Tyneside Blonde, Marstons Pedigree and Timothy Taylors Landlord, and several wines by the glass. There are seats out on the covered, heated terrace.

🍴 Now open from 10am (for breakfast snacks), the wide choice of very reasonably priced, popular food includes sandwiches, seared king scallops on black pudding fritters with sliced radishes, pea shoots and cider vinaigrette, pork fillet and gammon terrine with sun-dried tomato ciabatta and piccalilli, aubergine, goats cheese and tomato stack with herby tomato coulis, beer-battered haddock, chargrilled chicken on champ potato with madeira jus, roast of the day, fish dish of the day, kebab of the day, and puddings such as raspberry tart alaska and chocolate and pistachio cheesecake; the cheese platter is very popular. *Benchmark main dish: steak and mushroom in ale casserole £8.95. Two-course evening meal £17.00.*

Sir John Fitzgerald ~ Manager C W Kerridge ~ Real ale ~ (0191) 257 6302 ~ Open 10am-11pm ~ Bar food 10-10 ~ Restaurant ~ Children welcome ~ www.sjf.co.uk *Recommended by Toby Jones, Harvey Brown*

> The 🍺 symbol shows pubs which keep their beer unusually well, have a sparticularly good range or brew their own.

NEWCASTLE UPON TYNE NZ2563 Map 10

Crown Posada

The Side; off Dean Street, between and below the two high central bridges (A6125 and A6127); NE1 3JE

Busy city-centre pub with grand architecture, lots of locals in long narrow bar, tip-top beers and a warm welcome

This is the city's oldest pub and it hasn't changed for decades. Fascinating architecturally, it's certainly worth a visit to see the elaborate coffered ceiling, stained glass in the counter screens and the line of gilt mirrors, each with a tulip lamp on a curly brass mount matching the great ceiling candelabra. It's a long narrow room, with quite a bottleneck by the serving counter where they keep Anarchy Citra St*r, Hadrian & Border Black Gate Bitter and Tyneside Blonde, Loch Ness Light Ness, Rat Cherry Stout and Wylam Gold Tankard on handpump. A long green built-in leather wall seat is flanked by narrow tables, low-level heating pipes make a popular footrest when the east wind brings the rain off the North Sea and an old record player in a wooden cabinet provides mellow background music. During the week, regulars read papers in the front snug, but at weekends it's often packed. It's a short stroll to the castle. No food.

Sir John Fitzgerald ~ Licensee Andrew Nicholson ~ Real ale ~ No credit cards ~ (0191) 232 1269 ~ Open 12-11.30; 12-midnight Sat; 7-10.30 Sun ~ www.crownposadanewcastle.co.uk *Recommended by the Didler, Susan and Nigel Brookes, Dave Webster, Sue Holland*

NEWTON-BY-THE-SEA NU2424 Map 10

Ship

Village signed off B1339 N of Alnwick; NE66 3EL

In a charming square of fishermen's cottages close to the beach, good simple food and own-brew beers; best to check winter opening times

After a walk along the massive stretch of empty, beautiful beach with views all the way to Dunstanburgh Castle (NT), head to this row of converted fishermen's cottages for a pint of their own-brewed Ship Inn ales; dogs on a lead are very welcome. There are usually five ales at any one time from a choice of 20 – see their website for choices. The plainly furnished but cosy bare-boards bar on the right has nautical charts on dark pink walls, while another simple room on the left has beams, hop bines, bright modern pictures on stripped-stone walls and a woodburning stove in a stone fireplace; darts, dominoes. It can get extremely busy at peak times, so it's best to book in advance – and there might be a queue for the bar. Tables outside look across the sloping village green to the beach. No nearby parking from 1 May to 30 September, but there's a car park up the hill.

Generous helpings of simple lunchtime food (phone to check if and when they're doing evening meals) includes delicious local crab stotties, local kipper pâté, quite a choice of other sandwiches and ciabattas, potted crab with chilli and garlic, sausages and onions with mash and cabbage, undyed smoked haddock with spring onion mash and creamed spinach, moroccan-spiced lentil and chickpea stew with couscous, and puddings such as chocolate espresso pudding with mixed berries. *Benchmark main dish: crab sandwich £6.75. Two-course evening meal £13.00.*

Own brew ~ Licensee Christine Forsyth ~ Real ale ~ No credit cards ~ (01665) 576262
~ Open 11-11; 12-10.30 Sun; phone for winter opening hours ~ Bar food 12-2.30, 7-8 (but
check evening times) ~ Children welcome ~ Dogs welcome ~ Folk last Mon of month ~
www.shipinnnewton.co.uk *Recommended by the Didler, Comus and Sarah Elliott, Pat and Tony
Martin, David Eberlin, Penny and Peter Keevil, Sheila Topham*

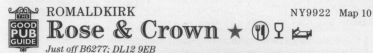

ROMALDKIRK NY9922 Map 10
Rose & Crown ★ ⑪ ♀ ⇐

Just off B6277; DL12 9EB

**A civilised base for the area, with accomplished cooking, attentive
service and a fine choice of drinks; lovely bedrooms**

Although a new licensee has taken over this handsome 18th-c inn, all
the staff are staying on and no major changes are planned. Indeed,
recent reports from readers have confirmed that they found 'pub
perfection' here. The cosily traditional beamed bar has lots of brass and
copper, old-fashioned seats facing a warming log fire, a Jacobean oak
settle, a grandfather clock, and gin traps, old farm tools and black and
white pictures of Romaldkirk on the walls. Black Sheep and Thwaites
Original on handpump, ten wines by the glass, organic fruit juices and
pressed vegetable juices. The smart brasserie-style Crown Room (bar
food is served here too) has large cartoons of french waiters, big old
wine bottles and high-backed dining chairs. The hall has farm tools,
wine maps and other interesting prints, along with a photograph (taken
by a customer) of the Hale-Bopp comet over the interesting old village
church. There's also an oak-panelled restaurant. Pleasantly positioned
tables outside look over the village green with its original stocks and
water pump. The exceptional Bowes Museum and High Force waterfall
are nearby and the owners provide an in-house local guide and a *Walking
in Teesdale* book. This is a lovely place to stay.

As well as light bar lunches that include sandwiches with salad and potato
crisps, smoked salmon and scrambled eggs on wholemeal toast or smoked
mackerel, warm fennel and baby potato salad with lime and caper dressing, the
excellent food includes cheese and spinach soufflé, smoked haddock kedgeree
with prawns, quails egg and parmesan, roasted butternut squash, pine nut and
rocket risotto, steak and mushroom in ale pie, chargrilled venison rump and
chips, slow-cooked pork with apple mash, black pudding and grain mustard sauce,
and puddings such as rhubarb and apple brown betty with vanilla ice-cream and
caramel panna cotta with ginger bread; they also offer a two- and three-course set
lunch and a four-course set dinner (in the restaurant). *Benchmark main dish: hot
ham hock terrine with poached egg, crushed peas and triple-cooked chips £14.00.
Two-course evening meal £20.00.*

Free house ~ Licensee Cheryl Robinson ~ Real ale ~ (01833) 650213 ~ Open 11.30-11
(10.30 Sun) ~ Bar food 12-1.45, 6.30-9.30 ~ Restaurant ~ Children welcome, must
be over 6 in restaurant ~ Dogs allowed in bar and bedrooms ~ Bedrooms: £95/£150 ~
www.rose-and-crown.co.uk *Recommended by Ben and Ruth Levy, Ian Malone, Pat and Stewart
Gordon, Mr and Mrs P R Thomas, Gordon and Margaret Ormondroyd, Comus and Sarah Elliott*

SEAHOUSES NU2232 Map 10
Olde Ship ★ ◧ £ ⇐

Just off B1340, towards harbour; NE68 7RD

**Lots of atmosphere and maritime memorabilia in busy little inn;
views across harbour to Farne Islands; bedrooms**

The same friendly family have been running this harbourside stone inn since it was first licensed in 1812 to serve visiting herring fishermen. The old-fashioned bar has seen a rich assemblage of nautical bits and pieces growing ever since – even the floor is made of scrubbed ship's decking. There's lots of shiny brass fittings, ship's instruments, a knotted anchor made by local fishermen, sea pictures and model ships, including fine ones of the North Sunderland lifeboat and the Seahouses' Grace Darling lifeboat. There's also a model of the *Forfarshire*, the paddle steamer that local heroine Grace Darling went to rescue in 1838 (you can read more of the story in the pub), and even the ship's nameboard. An anemometer takes wind-speed readings from the top of the chimney. It's all gently lit by stained-glass sea-picture windows, lantern lights and an open fire in winter. Simple furnishings include built-in leatherette pews, stools and cast-iron tables. Black Sheep Best, Courage Directors, Greene King Old Speckled Hen and Ruddles and Hadrian & Border Farne Island Pale Ale on handpump, a good wine list and several malt whiskies; background music and TV. The battlemented side terrace (you'll find fishing memorabilia out here too) and one window in the sun lounge look across the harbour to the Farne Islands – if you're here as dusk falls, the light of the Longstones lighthouse shining across the fading evening sky is a charming sight. It's not really suitable for children, though there is a little family room and they're welcome on the terrace (as are walkers). You can book boat trips to the Farne Islands at the harbour, and there are bracing coastal walks, particularly to Bamburgh, Grace Darling's birthplace.

As well as generous sandwiches, the short choice of reasonably priced food includes venison and pork terrine with caramelised red onion marmalade, prawn and pineapple mayonnaise, gammon and egg, vegetable lasagne, fresh crab salad, barbecue spare ribs with chips, steak in ale pie, chicken and mushroom casserole, trio of mixed grilled fish, and puddings such as rhubarb and ginger tart and banana and chocolate bread and butter pudding. *Benchmark main dish: smoked fish chowder £10.50. Two-course evening meal £15.00.*

Free house ~ Licensees Judith Glen and David Swan ~ Real ale ~ (01665) 720200 ~ Open 11-11; 12-11 Sun ~ Bar food 12-2.30, 7-8.30; no evening food Dec-late Jan ~ Restaurant ~ Children allowed in lounge and dining room if eating, but must be over 10 if staying ~ Bedrooms: £47/£110 ~ www.seahouses.co.uk *Recommended by the Didler, Comus and Sarah Elliott, D Crook, Pat and Tony Martin, Penny and Peter Keevil, Dr Kevan Tucker, Derek and Sylvia Stephenson*

 STANNERSBURN   NY7286   Map 10

Pheasant £ 🛏

Kielder Water road signposted off B6320 in Bellingham; NE48 1DD

Friendly village local close to Kielder Water, with quite a mix of customers and homely bar food; streamside garden; bedrooms

Near Kielder Water and in a quiet valley surrounded by forests, this nice old farmhouse has picnic-sets in a streamside garden, and a pony paddock too. Inside, it's cosy and traditional; the comfortable low-beamed lounge (being refurbished as we went to press) has ranks of

---

Stars after the name of a pub show exceptional character and appeal.
They don't mean extra comfort. And they are nothing to do with food quality,
for which there's a separate knife-and-fork symbol. Even quite a basic pub can
win stars, if it's individual enough.

old local photographs on stripped stone and panelling, brightly polished surfaces, shiny brasses, dark wooden pubby tables and chairs on red patterned carpet, upholstered stools ranged along the counter, and several open fires. A separate public bar is simpler and opens into a snug seating area with beams and panelling; background music. The friendly licensees and courteous staff serve Timothy Taylors Landlord and Wylam Dognobbler and Gold Tankard on handpump and 50 malt whiskies.

🍴 Using home-grown and other local produce, the good seasonal food might include sandwiches, chicken liver parfait with apple and ginger chutney, twice-baked cheese soufflé, game and mushroom pie, lasagne, stilton and vegetable crumble, fresh crab salad, confit duck leg with braised red cabbage and berry sauce, salmon with hot pepper marmalade and crème fraîche, and puddings such as lemon and lime cheesecake and bakewell tart. *Benchmark main dish: slow-roasted local lamb with rosemary and redcurrant jus £13.95. Two-course evening meal £17.70.*

Free house ~ Licensees Walter and Robin Kershaw ~ Real ale ~ (01434) 240382 ~ Open 11-3, 6-11; closed Mon and Tues Nov-Mar ~ Bar food 12-2.30, 6.30-8.30 ~ Restaurant ~ Children welcome ~ Dogs allowed in bedrooms ~ Bedrooms: £65/£95 ~ www.thepheasantinn.com *Recommended by Pat and Stewart Gordon*

WARK
NY8676   Map 10

Battlesteads 🍴 🛏

B6320 N of Hexham; NE48 3LS

Eco pub with good local ales, fair value interesting food and a relaxed atmosphere; comfortable bedrooms

The licensees in this well run 18th-c stone inn go to great lengths to encourage wildlife into their neatly kept garden, and have binoculars on window sills for bird-watching. They also have a biomass boiler, a charging point in the car park for electric cars and grow their own produce; they've won several national awards for their green credentials. It's a warmly welcoming place with excellent staff; the nicely restored carpeted bar has a woodburning stove with a traditional oak surround, low beams, comfortable seats including deep leather sofas and easy chairs, and old *Punch* country life cartoons on terracotta walls above a dark dado. As well as a dozen or so wines by the glass, they keep five good changing local ales such as Allendale Wagtail Ale, Durham Magus, Gundog Fox, Hadrian & Border Tyneside Blonde and Wylam Spring Thing on handpump at the heavily carved dark oak counter. The bar leads to a restaurant and spacious conservatory; background music. There are tables on a terrace, disabled access to some of the ground-floor bedrooms and they're licensed to hold civil marriages.

🍴 Using own-grown produce and other carefully sourced ingredients, the very good food includes sandwiches, ham hock terrine with home-made piccalilli, own-made salmon gravadlax with dill cream, lasagne, beer-battered hake and chips, wild mushroom and halloumi stack with chilli and ginger oil, pork, leek and lager sausages with bubble and squeak, cajun-spiced chicken with bacon, prawns and cream sauce, pork loin with black pudding mash, confit duck leg with pea and ham jus, and puddings such as cheesecake of the day and chocolate brownie with warm chocolate sauce. *Benchmark main dish: blackened cajun salmon with sautéed potatoes and sweet chilli sauce £11.50. Two-course evening meal £18.50.*

Free house ~ Licensees Richard and Dee Slade ~ Real ale ~ (01434) 230209 ~ Open 11-11 ~ Bar food 12-3, 6.30-9 ~ Children welcome ~ Dogs allowed in bar ~ Bedrooms: £60/£115 ~ www.battlesteads.com *Recommended by R L Borthwick, LC*

WELDON BRIDGE

NZ1398 Map 10

Anglers Arms 🛏

B6344, just off A697; village signposted with Rothbury off A1 N of Morpeth;
NE65 8AX

**Large helpings of food in appealing bar or converted railway dining
car, real ales and a friendly welcome; fishing on River Coquet;
bedrooms**

Even when this traditional former coaching inn is at its busiest –
which it deservedly often is – the welcoming staff cope efficiently
and professionally. The bar is divided into two parts: cream walls
on the right; oak panelling, shiny black beams hung with copper
pans, a mantelpiece with staffordshire cats on the left. There's also
a grandfather clock, a sofa beside a coal fire, old fishing and country
prints, a profusion of fishing memorabilia and some taxidermy. Some
tables are lower than you'd expect for eating, but the chairs have short
legs to match – different and rather engaging; background music.
Greene King Old Speckled Hen, Timothy Taylors Landlord and a
changing guest on handpump, with around 30 malt whiskies and decent
wines. You can feel very Agatha Christie in the restaurant in the former
railway dining car, which is set with crisp white linen and a red carpet.
The attractive garden has tables and a good play area with an assault
course. The pub is beside a bridge over the River Coquet and they have
fishing rights to a mile of riverbank. The bedrooms are comfortable.

Very well cooked and generously served food includes mushrooms in chilli
and bacon cream sauce topped with cheese, duck and chicken liver pâté
with plum sauce, chicken caesar salad, home-baked ham with free-range eggs,
vegetarian pasta of the day, steak in ale pie, pork and leek sausages on mash with
vegetable sauce, lime and ginger grilled bass fillets with saffron rice, chicken
stuffed with leek and stilton and wrapped in bacon with diane sauce, mixed grill,
and puddings. *Benchmark main dish: cod and chips £10.95. Two-course evening
meal £17.00.*

Enterprise ~ Lease John Young ~ Real ale ~ (01665) 570271 ~ Open 11-11; 12-10.30
Sun ~ Bar food 12-9.30 ~ Restaurant ~ Children welcome ~ Dogs allowed in bar and
bedrooms ~ Bedrooms: £49.50/£95 ~ www.anglersarms.com *Recommended by Dr Peter D
Smart, Dave Braisted, Rob and Catherine Dunster, J F M and M West, Lee and Liz Potter, Gordon and
Margaret Ormondroyd, WAH, Ian Herdman, Pat and Tony Martin*

Also Worth a Visit in Northumbria

Besides the fully inspected pubs, you might like to try these pubs that
have been recommended to us and described by readers. Do tell us what
you think of them: feedback@goodguides.com

ACOMB NY9366
Miners Arms (01434) 603909
Main Street; NE46 4PW Friendly little
18th-c village pub under newish family
ownership, at least three real ales such as
Black Sheep, Wylam and Yates, very good
value traditional food including popular
Sun roasts, comfortable settles in carpeted
bar, huge fire in stone fireplace, back dining
area, folk night first Mon of month, quiz last
Thurs of month; children and dogs welcome,

a couple of tables out in front , more in back
courtyard, open all day weekends, closed
lunchtimes Mon and Tues. *(Claes Mauroy,
Comus and Sarah Elliott)*

ALLENDALE NY8355
Golden Lion (01434) 683225
Market Place; NE47 9BD Friendly 18th-c
two-room pub with enjoyable good value
traditional food, well kept Wylam, Timothy
Taylors and three guests, games area with
pool and darts, upstairs weekend restaurant,

occasional live music; children and dogs welcome, Allendale Fair first weekend June, New Year's Eve flaming barrel procession, open all day. *(Comus and Sarah Elliott)*

ALNMOUTH   NU2410
⋆ **Red Lion** (01665) 830584
Northumberland Street; NE66 2RJ
Friendly 18th-c coaching inn with seats in neat sheltered garden and on raised deck giving wide view over Aln estuary; bar with heavy black beams, scatter cushions brightening up classic leather wall banquettes and window seats, old local photographs on dark mahogany brown panelling, cheerful fires, relaxed atmosphere and friendly staff, ales like Allendale, Black Sheep and Tempest, mainly new world wines by the glass, unpretentious stripped-brick restaurant with high-backed leather dining chairs around polished tables on stone floor, enjoyable fairly pubby food; quiet background music; children welcome, well equipped, comfortable bedrooms, open all day from 9.30am for coffee and breakfast. *(Comus and Sarah Elliott, Dr Kevan Tucker)*

ALNWICK   NU1911
Hogs Head (01665) 606576
Hawfinch Drive; turn right at BP petrol station; NE66 2BF Newly built pub-hotel (opened 2012) just off the A1 south of Alnwick; large open-plan high-ceilinged interior with exposed brickwork and restful colours, mix of dark wood tables and chairs on light wood floor, some easy chairs and banquettes, plants dotted about, enjoyable fairly traditional food (all day from 7.30am) including specials, children's menu and Sun carvery, well kept local beers such as Hadrian & Border Tyneside Blonde, good attentive young staff; spacious terrace with teak tables under large white parasols, 53 bedrooms. *(Michael Doswell)*

ALNWICK   NU1813
John Bull (01665) 602055
Howick Street; NE66 1UY Popular chatty drinkers' pub, essentially front room of early 19th-c terraced house, good selection of well kept changing ales, real cider, extensive choice of bottled belgian beers and well over 100 malt whiskies; closed weekday lunchtimes. *(the Didler, Laura Greenaway)*

ALNWICK   NU1813
Plough (01665) 602395
Bondgate Without; NE66 1PN Smart contemporary pub-boutique hotel in Victorian stone building (was Blackmores), well kept Black Sheep and Caledonian Deuchars IPA in lively front bar, several wines by the glass, consistently good food all day in bar, bistro or upstairs restaurant from snacky things up, bargain OAP weekday lunch, traditional set menu on Sun, friendly helpful service; pleasant street-side raised terrace, 13 bedrooms. *(Lee and Liz Potter, Pat and Tony Martin)*

ALNWICK   NU1813
Tanners Arms (01665) 602553
Hotspur Place; NE66 1QF Welcoming little drinkers' pub with well kept local ales and decent glasses of wine, flagstones and stripped stone, warm woodburner, plush stools and wall benches, small tree in the centre of the room; juke box and some live acoustic music, TV; closed lunchtimes. *(John Cook)*

AMBLE   NU2604
Wellwood Arms ´(01665) 714646
High Street, off A1068; NE65 0LD Stylishly refurbished bistro-feel dining pub with pleasant welcoming staff, carefully prepared good value food including local fish/seafood, a house ale brewed by Tetleys along with some well chosen wines, cocktails and good coffee, separate nicely laid-out restaurant area with own bar; children welcome, bedrooms planned, open all day. *(Jane Dargue, Michael Doswell)*

BAMBURGH   NU1834
⋆ **Castle** (01668) 214616
Front Street; NE69 7BW Clean comfortably old-fashioned pub with friendly landlord and staff, well kept ales such as Hadrian & Border, decent house wines, winter mulled wine, wide choice of enjoyable reasonably priced food all day including good Craster kippers and nice fish and chips, expanded dining area to cope with summer visitors, open fires; big courtyard, garden. *(Comus and Sarah Elliott, Clifford Blakemore, Robin Constable, Derek and Sylvia Stephenson, Dennis Jones)*

BAMBURGH   NU1834
Lord Crewe Arms (01668) 214243
Front Street; NE69 7BL Small early 17th-c hotel prettily set in charming coastal village dominated by Norman castle; refurbished bar and restaurant (Wynding Inn) with painted joists and panelling, bare stone walls and light wood floor, warm woodburner, beers from Northumberland and Wells & Youngs, good food from varied menu including some interesting choices; sheltered garden with castle view, short walk from splendid sandy beach, 17 comfortable bedrooms, good breakfast. *(Barry Collett, Comus and Sarah Elliott)*

Please tell us if any pub deserves to be upgraded to a featured entry – and why: feedback@goodguides.com, or (no stamp needed) The Good Pub Guide, FREEPOST TN1569, Wadhurst, E Sussex TN5 7BR.

BAMBURGH
NU1734
Mizen Head (01668) 214254
Lucker Road; NE69 7BS Smartly
refurbished hotel (sister inn to the nearby
Castle), light airy bar with open fire,
enjoyable locally sourced food including
good seafood, ales such as Black Sheep,
nice affordably priced house wines, friendly
staff; children and dogs welcome, good
bedrooms. *(Comus and Sarah Elliott, Clifford
Blakemore, Janet and Peter Race, Marianne and
Peter Stevens, Penny and Peter Keevil)*

BAMBURGH
NU1834
✷ Victoria (01668) 214431
Front Street; NE69 7BP Substantial
Victorian hotel with sofas in mildly
contemporary, partly divided bar, chunky
tables and chairs in dining area, good food
all day from sandwiches up, Black Sheep
and Caledonian Deuchars IPA, nice wines
by the glass, competent friendly service,
refurbished restaurant; children welcome,
nice setting with seats out in front, more in
garden behind with play area, 36 comfortable
bedrooms. *(W K Wood, Gordon and Margaret
Ormondroyd)*

BARRASFORD
NY9173
✷ Barrasford Arms (01434) 681237
*Village signposted off A6079 N of
Hexham; NE48 4AA* Good country cooking
at this bustling sandstone inn using carefully
sourced local ingredients, nice staff and
genuinely local atmosphere, traditional
log-fire bar with old local photographs and
bric-a-brac from horsebrasses to antlers,
ales such as Caledonian, Hadrian & Border
and Wylam, two dining rooms, one with
wheelback chairs around neat tables and
stone chimneybreast hung with guns and
copper pans, the second with comfortably
upholstered dining chairs; background
music, TV, darts; children welcome, plenty
of nearby walks and handy for Hadrian's
Wall, 11 bedrooms and a well equipped
bunkhouse, open all day weekends, closed
Mon lunchtime. *(LC)*

BEADNELL
NU2229
Beadnell Towers (01665) 721211
The Wynding, off B1340; NE67 5AY
Large slightly old-fashioned pub-hotel with
unusual mix of furnishings, good food in bar
or restaurant including local game and fish,
well kept ales such as Allendale and Hadrian
& Border, reasonably priced wines by the
glass, nice coffee, some live music; can get
more touristy in summer; seats outside,
ten bedrooms. *(Comus and Sarah Elliott,
W K Wood, Derek and Sylvia Stephenson, John
and Sylvia Harrop)*

BEADNELL
NU2229
Craster Arms (01665) 720272
The Wynding, off B1340; NE67 5AX
Roomy neatly kept old building with modern

fittings, red banquettes, stripped-brick
and stone walls, popular pubby food and
blackboard specials including local fish, well
kept Black Sheep and a local guest, friendly
efficient staff, pictures for sale, live music
including Aug 'Crastonbury' festival, July
beer festival; background music, TV; children
welcome, dogs in one area, picnic-sets and
decking in big enclosed garden, three
good bedrooms, open all day in summer.
(Derek and Sylvia Stephenson)

BEAMISH
NZ2154
Beamish Hall (01207) 233733
NE of Stanley, off A6076; DH9 0YB
Converted stone-built stables in courtyard
at back of hotel, popular and family friendly
(can get crowded), five or six good beers
from own microbrewery, decent wines, well
liked food all day including some interesting
choices and good value Sun roast, efficient
service from friendly uniformed staff; plenty
of seats outside, big play area, open all day.
*(Rob Weeks, Gerry and Rosemary Dobson, Penny
and Peter Keevil)*

BEAMISH
NZ2153
✷ Beamish Mary (0191) 370 0237
*Off A693 signed No Place and
Cooperative Villas, S of museum;
DH9 0QH* Friendly down-to-earth former
pit village inn, eight well kept mainly
local ales (May beer festival), farm cider,
good home-made pubby food at bargain
prices, coal fires, two bars with 1960s-feel
mix of furnishings, bric-a-brac, 1920s/30s
memorabilia and Aga with pots and pans,
regular live music in converted stables;
sports TV; children till early evening,
bedrooms. *(Anon)*

BEAMISH
NZ2055
Black Horse (01207) 232569
*Red Row (off Beamishburn Road NW,
near A6076); OS Sheet 88 map reference
205541; DH9 0RW* Late 17th-c country
pub reworked as stylish dining place,
contemporary/rustic interior in heritage
colours with beams, flagstones and some
exposed stonework, well kept Wells & Youngs
Bombardier and a guest, nice wines, friendly
attentive staff, cosy fire-warmed front room
extending to light spacious dining area with
central bar, another dining room upstairs,
food can be good; children welcome, restful
views from big paved terrace, picnic-sets on
grass, open all day. *(John Coatsworth)*

BELFORD
NU1033
Blue Bell (01668) 213543
*Off A1 S of Berwick; Market Place;
NE70 7NE* Substantial old coaching inn
– hotel rather than pub, but with a friendly
pubby bar; Black Sheep and a guest, good
choice of wines and whiskies, food can be
very good in bar or garden-view restaurant,
sensible prices, impressive upstairs ballroom;
popular quiz every other Sun, background

music; children welcome, 16 good value bedrooms, open all day. *(Gordon and Margaret Ormondroyd)*

BERWICK-UPON-TWEED   NT9952
Barrels (01289) 308013
Bridge Street; TD15 1ES Small friendly pub with interesting collection of pop memorabilia and other bric-a-brac, eccentric furniture including barber's chair in bareboards bar, red banquettes in back room, well kept Jarrow Rivet Catcher and four guests, foreign bottled beers, live music (Fri) and DJs (Sat) in basement bar, good quality background music; open all day, from 2pm Jan, Feb. *(Anon)*

BOULMER   NU2614
Fishing Boat (01665) 577750
Beach View; NE66 3BP Worth knowing for its position, with conservatory dining room and decking overlooking sea; light and airy inside with interesting nautical memorabilia, good value food, real ales such as Black Sheep and Tetleys; dogs welcome, self-catering apartment. *(Anon)*

CATTON   NY8257
★ Crown (01434) 683447
B6295, off A686 S of Haydon Bridge; NE47 9QS Friendly 19th-c pub in good walking country; inner bar with stripped stone and bare boards, dark tables, mate's chairs and a traditional settle, coloured lanterns and good log fire, well kept Allendale Golden Plover and Wagtail Ale, reasonably priced food (not Sun evening) served by efficient staff, partly carpeted, lighter extension, interesting local photographs; children and dogs (in bar) welcome, picnic-sets on side terrace and neat small lawn, open all day Fri-Sun, closed Mon. *(Comus and Sarah Elliott, Marcus Byron, John Coatsworth, Michael Doswell)*

CORBRIDGE   NY9964
★ Angel (01434) 632119
Main Street; NE45 5LA Imposing coaching inn at end of a broad street facing handsome bridge over the Tyne; sizeable modernised main bar with plain light wood tables and chairs and a few prints on pastel walls, carpeted lounge also with modern feel, strongly patterned wallpaper, some tall metal-framed café-bar seats and leather bucket armchairs, Hadrian & Border, Timothy Taylors and Wylam, Weston's cider, a dozen wines by the glass and 30 malts, popular food (not Sun evening), separate lounge with button-back armchairs, sofa, oak panelling and big stone fireplace, daily papers, stripped masonry and local artwork in small raftered restaurant; children welcome, seats on front cobbles below wall sundial, fine 17th-c arched doorway in left-hand porch, bedrooms, open all day. *(Dr Peter D Smart, R T and J C Moggridge, Comus and Sarah Elliott, Eric Larkham)*

CORBRIDGE   NY9864
★ Black Bull (01434) 632261
Middle Street; NE45 5AT Rambling 18th-c beamed pub with four linked rooms, mix of traditional pub furniture including leather banquettes, wood, flagstone or carpeted floors, log fires (one in open hearth with gleaming copper canopy), enjoyable pubby food, three Greene King ales and a guest such as Black Sheep, good choice of wines by the glass, efficient friendly service; children welcome, seats out on two-level terrace, open all day. *(W K Wood, Peter and Eleanor Kenyon, Comus and Sarah Elliott)*

CORBRIDGE   NY9868
★ Errington Arms (01434) 672250
About 3 miles N of town; B6318, on A68 roundabout; NE45 5QB Busy 18th-c stone-built pub by Hadrian's Wall attracting good mix of diners and walkers, beamed bars with pine panelling, stone and burgundy walls, farmhouse and other chairs around pine tables on strip-wood flooring, log fire and woodburner, good well presented fresh food including interesting sandwiches, Jennings and Wylam ales, decent choice of wines by the glass, friendly helpful staff; background music; children welcome, a few picnic-sets out in front, closed Sun evening, Mon. *(Pat and Stewart Gordon)*

CRAMLINGTON   NZ2373
Snowy Owl (01670) 736111
Just off A1/A19 junction via A1068; Blagdon Lane; NE23 8AU Large Vintage Inn, relaxed and comfortable, with their usual all-day food, friendly efficient young staff, Black Sheep and a couple of guests, beams, flagstones, stripped stone, soft lighting and an interesting mix of furnishings and decorations, three log fires; background music; disabled access, bedrooms in adjoining Innkeepers Lodge. *(Comus and Sarah Elliott, Dr Peter D Smart, Paul and Sue Merrick, Michael Doswell)*

CRASTER   NU2519
★ Jolly Fisherman (01665) 576461
Off B1339, NE of Alnwick; NE66 3TR Recently refurbished under welcoming newish management; great spot, long a favourite for its lovely sea and coast views, good food with emphasis on fish/seafood including local crab and good value mixed fishboard, also produce from smokehouse opposite, well kept Black Sheep, Mordue, Timothy Taylors and a guest, good wine list, friendly if not always attentive service, main bar area with nice open fire, snug, steps up to extended restaurant with picture-window views and seats out on balcony; children and dogs welcome, disabled facilities, beer garden, open all day. *(John and Sylvia Harrop, Comus and Sarah Elliott, GSB, Barry Collett, Michael Doswell and others)*

DARLINGTON NZ2814
Number Twenty 2 (01325) 354590
Coniscliffe Road; DL3 7RG Long
Victorian pub with bistro feel, high ceiling,
bare boards and exposed brickwork, 14
quickly changing ales including own Village
Brewer range (supplied by Hambleton),
draught continentals too, decent food (not
Fri and Sat evenings) in compact panelled
back room, good friendly service; closed Sun,
otherwise open all day. *(WAH)*

DURHAM NZ2642
Colpitts (0191) 386 9913
*Colpitts Terrace/Hawthorn Terrace;
DH1 4EG* Comfortable two-bar traditional
backstreet pub, friendly landlady and locals,
cheap well kept Sam Smiths, open fires and
original Victorian fittings, back pool room,
seats in yard, open all day (from 2pm
Mon-Wed). *(the Didler, Eric Larkham)*

DURHAM NZ2742
Court (0191) 384 7350
Court Lane; DH1 3AW Comfortable 19th-c
town pub near law courts; good home-made
food all day (till 10.20pm) from sandwiches
and sharing plates to steaks and blackboard
specials, two changing ales from smaller
local brewers (not cheap), friendly helpful
staff, extensive stripped-brick eating area, no
mobile phones; background music; children
and dogs welcome, seats outside, smokers'
shelter, open all day. *(Roger and Donna
Huggins, Alan and Jane Shaw, Eric Larkham)*

DURHAM NZ2742
⋆ Dun Cow (0191) 386 9219
Old Elvet; DH1 3HN Unchanging
backstreet pub in pretty 16th-c black and
white timbered cottage, cheerful licensees,
tiny chatty front bar with wall benches,
corridor to long narrow back lounge with
banquettes, machines etc (can be packed
with students), particularly well kept
Camerons and other ales, good value basic
lunchtime snacks, decent coffee; background
music; children welcome, open all day except
Sun in winter. *(the Didler, Eric Larkham)*

DURHAM NZ2742
Market Tavern (0191) 386 2069
Market Place; DH1 3NJ Recently
refurbished Taylor Walker pub; decent choice
of pubby food, six changing real ales and
a proper cider, friendly efficient service,
popular with students (university folk night
Weds); looks out on market place at front
and to indoor market at back, open all day.
*(Roger and Donna Huggins, Alan and Jane Shaw,
Dennis Jones)*

DURHAM NZ2642
Old Elm Tree (0191) 386 4621
Crossgate; DH1 4PS Comfortable friendly
old pub on steep hill across from castle,
two-room main bar and small lounge, four

well kept ales (occasional beer festivals),
reasonably priced home-made food, open
fires, folk and quiz nights; dogs welcome,
small back terrace, open all day. *(Richard
Tilbrook, Eric Larkham)*

EGGLESCLIFFE NZ4213
Pot & Glass (01642) 651009
Church Road; TS16 9DQ Friendly
little village pub with Bass, Black Sheep,
Caledonian Deuchars IPA and a couple of
guests kept well by enthusiastic landlord,
good value straightforward food, folk club
and quiz nights; tables on terrace, lovely
setting behind church. *(Taff Thomas,
Craig Buckingham)*

EGLINGHAM NU1019
⋆ Tankerville Arms (01665) 578444
B6346 Alnwick–Wooler; NE66 2TX
Traditional pub with contemporary touches,
cosy friendly atmosphere, beams, bare
boards, some stripped stone, banquettes and
warm fires, a couple of well kept local ales
like Hadrian & Border and Mordue, good
wines, imaginative nicely presented food
from shortish changing menu, raftered split-
level restaurant; children and dogs welcome,
country views from garden, three bedrooms,
attractive village. *(Comus and Sarah Elliott,
Dr and Mrs P Truelove, John and Sylvia Harrop
and others)*

EMBLETON NU2322
Greys (01665) 576983
*Stanley Terrace off W T Stead Road,
turn at the Blue Bell; NE66 3UY* Warmly
welcoming pub with carpeted main front
bar, more lived-in part with old photographs
and cuttings, cottagey back dining room,
open fires, well priced home-made food from
sandwiches to local fish, interesting choice
of well kept local ales; dogs welcome, small
walled back garden, raised decking with
village views, open all day. *(David Eberlin,
Derek and Sylvia Stephenson)*

FALSTONE NY7287
Blackcock Country Inn
(01434) 240200 *E of Yarrow and Kielder
Water; NE48 1AA* Cosy, clean and friendly
17th-c inn, homely bar with beams and open
fires, well kept ales including one badged
for them, Weston's cider, bottled beers and
50 malt whiskies, enjoyable food in bar and
restaurant with good vegetarian choice,
pool room; quiet juke box; children allowed,
dogs very welcome (own menu), garden
with covered smokers' area, six bedrooms,
handy for Kielder Water, closed Wed evening,
weekday lunchtimes in winter. *(Anon)*

FROSTERLEY NZ0236
⋆ Black Bull (01388) 527784
Just off A689 W of centre; DL13 2SL
The only pub to have its own peal of
bells (licensee is a campanologist); great
atmosphere in three interesting traditional

beamed and flagstoned rooms with coal fires, landlord's own fine photographs and three grandfather clocks, four well kept local ales, farm cider and perry, carefully chosen wines and malt whiskies, good food using local and organic ingredients (best to book evenings), popular Sun lunch, occasional acoustic live music; well behaved children and dogs welcome, attractive no-smoking terrace with wood-fired bread oven and old railway furnishings (opposite steam station), closed Sun lunch, Mon, Tues, otherwise open all day. *(Dr Peter D Smart, Duncan Walker, John Coatsworth)*

GATESHEAD   NZ2563
Central (0191) 478 2543
Half Moon Lane; NE8 2AN Large multi-room pub renovated by the Head of Steam chain, great choice of changing local ales, lots of bottled beers, real ciders, low-priced food including themed evenings, roof terrace, live music; open all day (till 1am Fri, Sat). *(Eric Larkham, Dave Webster, Sue Holland)*

GREAT WHITTINGTON   NZ0070
⋆ Queens Head (01434) 672267
Village signed off A68 and B6018 N of Corbridge; NE19 2HP Handsome golden-stone pub with dark leather chairs around sturdy tables, one or two good pictures on stripped-stone or grey-green walls, soft lighting, nice hunting mural above old fireplace in long narrow bar, Allendale, Hadrian & Border and Wylam, several malt whiskies, much emphasis on good interesting food (not Sun evening) in tartan-carpeted dining areas with modern furnishings, friendly efficient staff; background music; children welcome, dogs in bar, picnic-sets under parasols on little front lawn, closed Mon, Tues, otherwise open all day. *(LC, Michael Doswell)*

GRETA BRIDGE   NZ0813
⋆ Morritt Arms (01833) 627232
Hotel signposted off A66 W of Scotch Corner; DL12 9SE Striking 17th-c country house hotel popular for weddings and the like; properly pubby bar with big windsor armchairs and sturdy oak settles around traditional cast-iron-framed tables, open fires and remarkable 1946 mural of Dickensian characters by JTY Gilroy (known for Guinness advertisements), big windows looking on to extensive lawn, Thwaites Major Morritt (brewed for them) and Timothy Taylors Landlord, 19 wines by the glass from extensive list, good tasty food, friendly knowledgeable staff, restaurant; background music; children welcome, dogs allowed in bar and bedrooms, attractively laid-out

garden with teak tables and play area, open all day. *(Comus and Sarah Elliott, Barry Collett, GSB)*

HAYDON BRIDGE   NY8364
⋆ General Havelock (01434) 684376
A69 Corbridge–Haltwhistle; NE47 6ER Old stone pub – a short stroll downstream from Haydon Bridge itself; best part of L-shaped bar is the back with interestingly shaped mahogany-topped tables, long pine benches with colourful cushions and pine chest of drawers topped with bric-a-brac, good wildlife photographs, ales from Geltsdale and High House Farm, nine wines by the glass, traditional food (not Sun evening), board games, table football and hockey, stripped-stone barn dining room and terrace with fine South Tyne river views; children welcome, dogs in bar, closed Mon. *(Marcus Byron)*

HOLWICK   NY9126
Strathmore Arms (01833) 640362
Back Road up Teesdale from Middleton; DL12 0NJ Attractive old stone-built country pub in beautiful scenery just off Pennine Way, welcoming newish licensees, real ales including a house beer (Strathmore Gold) brewed by Allendale, low-priced traditional food all day, home-baked bread, flagstones and open fire, live music Fri, quiz first Weds of month; well behaved dogs welcome, popular with walkers, four bedrooms and campsite, closed Tues. *(Roxanne Chamberlain)*

HOLY ISLAND   NU1241
Crown & Anchor (01289) 389215
Causeway passable only at low tide, check times (01289) 330733; TD15 2RX Comfortably unpretentious pub-restaurant by the priory, enjoyable fairly traditional home-made food including vegetarian choices, Wells & Youngs Bombardier and Caledonian Deuchars IPA, welcoming helpful staff, compact bar with open fire, roomy modern back dining room; children and dogs welcome, garden with lovely views (may ask to keep a credit card while you eat here), four bedrooms. *(John and Sylvia Harrop, Barry Collett)*

HORSLEY   NZ0965
Lion & Lamb (01661) 852952
B6528, just off A69 Newcastle–Hexham; NE15 0NS 18th-c former coaching inn; main bar with scrubbed tables, stripped stone, flagstones and panelling, five changing ales including local ones, maybe a blackberry cider, decent choice of good mainly pubby food, attentive service, bare-boards restaurant; Tyne views from attractive garden

---

with roomy terrace, good adventure play area, open all day. *(Comus and Sarah Elliott)*

HURWORTH-ON-TEES NZ2814
⭐ Bay Horse (01325) 720663
Church Row; DL2 2AQ Popular dining pub (best to book, particularly weekends) with top notch imaginative food, quite pricey but they also do a set lunch, children's choices too, three changing ales, smiling efficient young staff, sizeable bar with good open fire, restaurant; seats on back terrace and in well tended walled garden beyond, charming village by River Tees, open all day. *(Jill and Julian Tasker, Rory Hutchison)*

HURWORTH-ON-TEES NZ3110
Otter & Fish (01325) 720019
Off A167 S of Darlington; Strait Lane; DL2 2AH Pleasantly up-to-date open-plan layout with comfortable armchairs and sofas by bar, nice mix of dining furniture, some wall banquettes, flagstones and stripped wood, good fresh local food (wise to book, especially weekends) including set deals, good wine selection, well kept ales such as Black Sheep, open fires and church candles; closed Sun evening. *(Richard Tilbrook)*

KENTON BANKFOOT NZ2068
Twin Farms (0191) 286 1263
Main Road; NE13 8AB Good roomy Fitzgerald pub in elegant period-rustic style, recycled stone, timbers etc, real fires, several pleasant softly lit areas off central bar, decent food from good value sandwiches to some imaginative specials, well kept changing ales including local ones, good selection of wines by the glass, quick friendly service, Mon quiz; background music may be obtrusive, machines; children welcome, disabled facilities, garden and terrace, open all day. *(Michael Doswell)*

KNARSDALE NY6754
Kirkstyle (01434) 381559
A689 Alston–Brampton, just N of Slaggyford; CA8 7PB Friendly pub in lovely setting, enjoyable good value food and well kept local ales; children welcome, good walks along nearby South Tyne Trail. *(Marcus Byron)*

LANGDON BECK NY8531
Langdon Beck Hotel
(01833) 622267 *B6277 Middleton–Alston; DL12 0XP* Isolated unpretentious inn with two cosy bars and spacious lounge, well placed for walks and Pennine Way, Jarrow and a guest ale (late May beer festival), good choice of enjoyable generous food including local teesdale beef and lamb, decent coffee, friendly helpful staff, 'geology room' with interesting rock collection; wonderful fell views from garden, seven bedrooms, open all day, closed Mon in winter. *(John H Smith, Roxanne Chamberlain, Comus and Sarah Elliott)*

LANGLEY ON TYNE NY8160
Carts Bog Inn (01434) 684338
A686 S, junction B6305; NE47 5NW Isolated moorside pub with heavy beams and stripped stone walls, old photographs, lovely open fire, good range of reasonably priced generous food from sandwiches up including popular Sun lunch (best to book), two or three well kept local ales, friendly efficient young staff, games room with pool and darts; children and dogs welcome, picnic-sets in big garden with views, quoits, open all day weekends. *(Lucien Perring, Sara Fulton, Roger Baker)*

LESBURY NU2311
Coach (01665) 830865
B1339; NE66 3PP Picturesque stone pub at heart of pretty village; contemporary paintwork throughout the low-beamed rooms, pubby tables and chairs on tartan carpet, dark leather stools by counter serving Black Sheep Best and Golden Sheep, part off to left with sofas and armchairs, small dining room and a further seating area with woodburner and tub-like chairs; background music, TV; children welcome in dining areas till 7.30pm, seats out in front and on neat terrace, pretty flowering tubs and baskets, handy for Alnwick Castle, open all day. *(Comus and Sarah Elliott, Dr Peter D Smart)*

LONGFRAMLINGTON NU1301
Village Inn (01665) 570268
Just off A697; Front Street; NE65 8AD 18th-c stone inn arranged into three distinct areas; tasty freshly prepared pub food including good Sun carvery, own-brewed VIP beer along with local guests, good coffee, some live music, Mon quiz; bedrooms, open all day. *(Michael Doswell)*

LONGHORSLEY NZ1494
Shoulder of Mutton (01670) 788236
East Road; A697 N of Morpeth; NE65 8SY Comfortable bar and restaurant with welcoming staff, good choice of generously served food from lunchtime baguettes through pub favourites to some imaginative dishes, popular Sun carvery (must book), Courage Directors, Caledonian Deuchars IPA and a guest such as Everards Tiger, good selection of other drinks; background music; children and dogs (in bar) welcome, picnic-sets in back garden, three bedrooms, open all day. *(Michael Doswell)*

LUCKER NU1530
Apple (01668) 213450
Off A1 N of Morpeth; NE70 7JH Refurbished old stone-built pub in tiny village, good locally sourced food from rather upmarket menu, Allendale and Hadrian & Border ales, good value wines, friendly welcoming staff, woodburner in bar's large fireplace, roomy big-windowed side dining

area; children and dogs welcome, open all day weekends. *(Janet and Peter Race)*

MICKLETON NY9724

Crown (01833) 640381

B6277; DL12 0JZ Cleanly refurbished bar area with woodburner and view into kitchen, popular well priced food all day including specials, four real ales and good wines by the glass; children welcome, garden tables, small campsite. *(Comus and Sarah Elliott)*

MIDDLETON-IN-TEESDALE NY9425

Teesdale (01833) 640264

Market Place; DL12 0QG Welcoming family-owned hotel (18th-c coaching inn), comfortable and homely, with good value food from sandwiches to daily specials, well kept beers and decent wines, friendly helpful service, carpeted log-fire bar and restaurant; background music; children welcome, a few tables outside, 15 bedrooms, open all day. *(Comus and Sarah Elliott)*

MILBOURNE NZ1275

Waggon (01661) 881872

Higham Dykes; A696 NW of Ponteland; NE20 0DH Popular, comfortably traditional open-plan bar with adjoining restaurant area, soft lighting, beams, stripped stone and panelling, fire each end, good generously served home-made food, well kept ales and decent choice of wines by the glass, friendly staff, quiz first Mon of month; children welcome, side garden with picnic-sets, open all day. *(James and Judith Buchanan, Geoff and Olive Charnock)*

MILFIELD NT9333

Red Lion (01668) 216224

Main Road (A697 Wooler–Cornhill); NE71 6JD Welcoming 17th-c coaching inn with good fairly priced food including popular Sun carvery, well kept ales such as Black Sheep, helpful service; pretty garden by car park at back, two bedrooms. *(M Mossman, Comus and Sarah Elliott)*

MORPETH NZ1986

★ Tap & Spile (01670) 513894

Manchester Street; NE61 1BH Consistently welcoming, cosy and easy-going two-room pub, up to seven ales such as Caledonian, Everards, Hadrian & Border and Mordue, Weston's Old Rosie cider and country wines, limited choice of good value lunchtime food Fri and Sat, traditional pub furniture and interesting old photographs, quieter back lounge (children allowed here) with coal-effect gas fire, board and other games, good local folk music Sun afternoon, Mon quiz night; unobtrusive background music, sports TV and quiz machine; dogs welcome in front bar, open all day Fri-Sun. *(Eric Larkham)*

NETHERTON NT9807

Star (01669) 630238

Off B6341 at Thropton, or A697 via Whittingham; NE65 7HD Simple unchanging village local under charming long-serving landlady (licence has been in her family since 1917), friendly regulars, a changing ale served by jug from hatch in small entrance lobby, only bottled beers in winter, large high-ceilinged room with wall benches, many original features; no food, music, children or dogs; open evenings only from 7.30pm, closed Mon, Thurs. *(the Didler)*

NEWBIGGIN-BY-THE-SEA NZ3188

Queens Head (01670) 817293

High Street; NE64 6AT Unchanging Edwardian pub with good friendly landlord and thriving local atmosphere, high-ceilinged rooms and cosy back snug, well kept low-priced ales (pump clips on display from previous guests), original features including curved bar, mosaic floors and etched windows, lots of old local photographs, dominoes; dogs allowed in some parts, open all day 9.45am-midnight. *(the Didler)*

NEWBURN NZ1665

★ Keelman (0191) 267 0772

Grange Road: follow Riverside Country Park brown signs off A6085; NE15 8ND Former 19th-c pumping station with eight well kept Big Lamp beers from on-site brewery, good mix of customers of all ages and nice relaxed atmosphere, high-ceilinged airy bar with lofty arched windows, more tables in upper gallery, fair value traditional food served by friendly efficient staff, modern dining conservatory contrasting stylishly with original building; unobtrusive background music; children welcome, plenty of seating on spacious terraces among tubs and shrub beds, adventure playground, comfortable bedrooms, open all day. *(GSB, Eric Larkham, David Heath)*

NEWCASTLE UPON TYNE NZ2464

★ Bacchus (0191) 261 1008

High Bridge E, between Pilgrim Street and Grey Street; NE1 6BX Smart, spacious and comfortable with ocean liner look, ship and shipbuilding photographs, good value lunchtime food from sandwiches and panini to a few pubby main meals, Sun roasts, nine very well kept changing ales (beer festivals), plenty of bottled imports, farm cider and decent coffee, friendly helpful staff, can get very busy; background music; disabled facilities, handy for Theatre Royal,

---

With the iPhone *Good Pub Guide* App, you can use the iPhone's camera to send us pictures of pubs you visit – outside or inside.

open all day. *(the Didler, R T and J C Moggridge, GSB, Comus and Sarah Elliott, Eric Larkham, Gordon)*

NEWCASTLE UPON TYNE NZ2464
Bodega (0191) 221 1552
Westgate Road; NE1 4AG Majestic Edwardian drinking hall next to Tyne Theatre; Big Lamp, Durham and six guest ales, real cider, friendly service, colourful walls and ceiling, bare boards, snug front cubicles, spacious back area with two magnificent stained-glass cupolas; background music, machines, big-screen TV, very busy on match days; open all day. *(Eric Larkham)*

NEWCASTLE UPON TYNE NZ2563
★ Bridge Hotel (0191) 232 6400
Castle Square, next to high-level bridge; NE1 1RQ Big, well divided, high-ceilinged bar around servery with replica slatted snob screens, Black Sheep, Caledonian Deuchars IPA and seven guests kept well, real cider, friendly staff, bargain generous lunchtime food (not weekends), magnificent fireplace, great river and bridge views from raised back area, live music upstairs including long-standing Mon folk club; background music, sports TV, games machines; flagstoned back terrace overlooking part of old town wall, open all day. *(the Didler, Eric Larkham, Derek Wason)*

NEWCASTLE UPON TYNE NZ2563
Broad Chare (0191) 211 2144
Broad Chare, just off quayside opposite law courts; NE1 3DQ Traditional feel although only recently converted to a pub (was a café), british-leaning food (not Sun evening) from bar snacks such as crispy pigs ears and Lindisfarne oysters to spicy blood pudding and steaks, four real ales including a house beer from Wylam (Writer's Block), good choice of bottled beers, wines and whiskies, ground-floor bare-boards bar and snug, old local photographs, upstairs dining room; background music; children welcome in bar till 7pm (later upstairs), no dogs, theatre next door, open all day. *(Comus and Sarah Elliott, Peter Smith and Judith Brown, Michael Doswell, Eric Larkham, Andy and Jill Kassube)*

NEWCASTLE UPON TYNE NZ2464
Centurion (0191) 261 6611
Central Station, Neville Street; NE1 5HL Glorious high-ceilinged Victorian décor with tilework and columns in former first-class waiting room, well restored with comfortable leather seats giving club-like feel, Black Sheep, Caledonian Deuchars IPA , Jarrow Rivet Catcher and a couple of guests, farm cider, friendly staff; background music, big-screen sports TV; useful deli next-door, open all day. *(Tony and Wendy Hobden, Eric Larkham)*

NEWCASTLE UPON TYNE NZ2664
★ Cluny (0191) 230 4474
Lime Street; NE1 2PQ Trendy bar-café in interesting 19th-c mill/warehouse, striking setting below Metro bridge, good value home-made food all day from massive sandwiches up, cheerful staff, up to eight well kept ales, some exotic beers and rums, sofas in comfortable raised area with daily papers and art magazines, back gallery with artwork from studios in same complex; background and regular live music; children welcome till 7pm, picnic-sets out on green, parking nearby can be difficult, open all day. *(Comus and Sarah Elliott, Eric Larkham)*

NEWCASTLE UPON TYNE NZ2664
Cumberland Arms (0191) 265 6151
James Place Street; NE6 1LD Friendly, unspoilt and traditional, seven particularly well kept mainly local ales including a house beer from Wylam, six farm ciders/perries, two annual beer festivals, limited choice of good value pubby food, obliging staff, open fires, events most nights including live music (regular ukulele band); dogs welcome, tables out overlooking Ouseburn Valley, four bedrooms, open all day weekends, from 3pm other days. *(the Didler, R T and J C Moggridge, Eric Larkham)*

NEWCASTLE UPON TYNE NZ2470
Falcons Nest (0191) 236 7078
Rotary Way, Gosforth (handy for racecourse); NE3 5EH Roomy Vintage Inn with comfortable traditional-style linked rooms, their usual food from sandwiches up including good value weekday set menu till 5pm, pleasant staff, good choice of wines by the glass, well kept Black Sheep and a couple of guests; children welcome, tables out on terrace and lawn, open all day. *(Gerry and Rosemary Dobson)*

NEWCASTLE UPON TYNE NZ2664
Free Trade (0191) 265 5764
St Lawrence Road, off Walker Road (A186); NE6 1AP Splendidly basic proper pub with outstanding views up river from big windows, terrace tables and seats on grass, fine choice of beers including Mordue, real ciders, good sandwiches, original Formica tables and coal fire, free juke box, warm friendly atmosphere; steps down to back room and lavatories; open all day. *(Eric Larkham)*

NEWCASTLE UPON TYNE NZ2464
Newcastle Arms (0191) 221 2519
St Andrews Street; NE1 5SE Open-plan drinkers' pub on fringe of Chinatown; Caledonian Deuchars IPA and five quickly changing guests including a porter or stout (beer festivals), farm ciders and perries, friendly staff, interesting old local photographs; background music, big-screen sports TV, can

get very busy especially on match days; open all day. *(Eric Larkham, Gordon)*

NEWCASTLE UPON TYNE NZ2463
Town Wall (0191) 232 3000
Pink Lane; across from Central Station; NE1 5HX Recently opened pub in handsome listed building, warm friendly welcome, spacious bare-boards interior with dark walls, button-back banquettes and mix of well spaced tables and chairs, pictures in heavy gilt frames, up to 12 ales including one badged for them, good choice of bottled beers and wines by the glass, fairly simple well priced food including burgers and pub favourites, all day brunch, overspill basement dining area; background music; well behaved children and dogs welcome, open all day (till 1am Fri, Sat). *(Denise McGuire, Eric Larkham, Andy and Jill Kassube)*

NEWTON NZ0364
Duke of Wellington (01661) 844446
Off A69 E of Corbridge; NE43 7UL Extensively refurbished old stone inn in attractive farming hamlet, good nicely presented food from interesting menu, well kept local ales and comprehensive wine list, efficient service from friendly uniformed young staff, large L-shaped bar/dining area with wood or flagstone floors, comfortable mix of modern and traditional furnishings, sofas and armchairs in one corner, wood-burner, daily papers, darts; dogs welcome in bar area, back terrace with lovely views, seven bedrooms. *(GSB, Michael Doswell, Pat and Stewart Gordon, Andy and Jill Kassube)*

NEWTON ON THE MOOR NU1705
☆ Cook & Barker Arms
(01665) 575234 *Village signed from A1 Alnwick–Felton; NE65 9JY* Nicely traditional stone-built country inn, beamed bar with stripped-stone and partly panelled walls, broad-seated settles around oak-topped tables, horsebrasses, coal fires, Black Sheep, Timothy Taylors and a guest beer, extensive wine list, good popular food using meat from own farm (set deals Mon, Tues lunchtime and early evenings Weds and Thurs), friendly staff, separate restaurant with french windows opening on to terrace; background music, TV, no dogs; children welcome, 18 comfortably refurbished bedrooms, Boxing Day hunt starts here, open all day. *(Comus and Sarah Elliott, Tony and Edwina Bayley, Tony Baldwin, Paul and Sue Merrick, Barry and Monica Jones, Les and Sandra Brown and others)*

NEWTON-BY-THE-SEA NU2325
Joiners Arms (01665) 576112
In village by turning to Linkhouse; NE66 3EA Stylishly refurbished open-plan pub-restaurant run by enthusiastic couple, good imaginative well presented food all day from interesting sandwiches and sharing plates up, takeaway fish and chips too, real

ales such as Hadrian & Border and Mordue plus carefully chosen wines, good service; children welcome, sturdy furniture on terrace overlooking village green, bedrooms. *(John Woodman, Michael Doswell, Frances Gill, Comus and Sarah Elliott, GSB)*

NORTH SHIELDS NZ3568
Quay Taphouse (0191) 259 2023
Bell Street; NE30 1HF Refurbished quayside pub, clean and airy, with good value tapas, sandwiches and home-made cakes, Sun roasts too, Maxim Wards and a guest ale such as Wylam, nice coffee, quick friendly service; children welcome, open all day. *(Comus and Sarah Elliott, Eric Larkham)*

PIERCEBRIDGE NZ2115
George (01325) 374576
B6275 just S of village, over bridge; DL2 3SW Old refurbished riverside pub-hotel under newish management; enjoyable bar food from sandwiches up, well kept Black Sheep, Mithril and guest, efficient service, river-view dining room; children and dogs welcome, decked terrace and attractive garden with bridge to small island (not easy for disabled people), 36 bedrooms, open all day. *(John H Smith)*

PONTELAND NZ1771
Badger (01661) 867931
Street Houses; A696 SE, by garden centre; NE20 9BT Recently refurbished early 18th-c Vintage Inn with warren of rooms and alcoves, good log fire, well kept beers such as Black Sheep and Timothy Taylors, decent range of wines by the glass, their usual all-day food; background music; children welcome. *(Dr Peter D Smart, Peter and Eleanor Kenyon, Gerry and Rosemary Dobson, Michael Doswell)*

RENNINGTON NU2118
☆ Horseshoes (01665) 577665
B1340; NE66 3RS Comfortable family-run pub with nice local feel (may be horses in car park), well kept ales including Hadrian & Border and decent wines by the glass, ample helpings of enjoyable locally sourced food, friendly efficient service, simple neat bar with flagstones and woodburner, carpeted restaurant, darts; children welcome, tables out in front, attractive quiet village near coast, Aug scarecrow competition, closed Mon. *(Peter Veness)*

RENNINGTON NU2118
Masons Arms (01665) 577275
Stamford Cott; B1340 N; NE66 3RX Stone-built former coaching inn with long beamed bar divided by woodburner, tables set for dining on tartan carpet, enjoyable food including several vegetarian options, a couple of well kept local ales such as Hadrian & Border and High House Farm, good malt whisky range, smiling relaxed service, brassware, flintlock pistols etc; roadside

terrace, more picnic-sets behind, llamas and rare-breed pigs, 14 comfortable bedrooms in converted outbuildings. *(W K Wood, GSB)*

SHINCLIFFE NZ2941
Rose Tree (0191) 386 8512

Lower Shincliffe, A177 S of Durham; DH1 2LY Comfortable local by River Wear with wide range of good value food (till 6pm Sun) including bargain weekday two-course deal, well kept ales and several wines by the glass, friendly caring staff; children welcome, tables outside, open all day weekends. *(Mr and Mrs R Duys)*

SLAGGYFORD NY6754
Kirkstyle (01434) 381559

Just N, signed off A689 at Knarsdale; CA8 7PB Spotlessly clean little 18th-c country pub in lovely spot looking over South Tyne Valley to hills beyond; friendly staff and locals, good straightforward food (not Mon, Tues) plus some interesting specials, a couple of well kept ales from Geltsdale and Yates, board games, darts and pool area, dining room; dogs very welcome, quoits team, handy for Pennine Way, Cycle Way and South Tyneside Railway (Lintley terminus), closed Sun evening, lunchtimes Mon and Tues, and may close early from 9pm if quiet. *(Dr Kevan Tucker)*

SLALEY NY9658
⋆**Travellers Rest** (01434) 673231

B6306 S of Hexham (and N of village); NE46 1TT Attractive and busy stone-built country pub, spaciously opened up, with farmhouse-style décor, beams, flagstones and polished wood floors, huge fireplace, comfortable high-backed settles forming discrete areas, friendly uniformed staff, popular generously served food (not Sun evening) in bar or quieter dining room, good children's menu, real ales such as Allendale, Black Sheep and Wylam; dogs welcome, tables outside with well equipped adventure play area on grass behind, three good value bedrooms, open all day. *(WAH, Andy and Jill Kassube)*

SOUTH SHIELDS NZ3567
Alum Ale House (0191) 427 7245

Ferry Street (B1344); NE33 1JR Welcoming 18th-c pub handy for ferry, good choice of well kept ales, bare boards, coal fire in old inglenook range, no food; open all day. *(R T and J C Moggridge, Eric Larkham)*

SOUTH SHIELDS NZ3666
Maltings (0191) 427 7147

Claypath Road; NE33 4PG Former dairy now home to Jarrow brewery, their full range

and guest ales from upstairs bar (showpiece staircase), food served; open all day. *(Eric Larkham)*

SOUTH SHIELDS NZ3566
Steamboat (0191) 454 0134

Mill Dam/Coronation Street; NE33 1EQ Very friendly 19th-c corner pub with eight well kept changing ales, lots of nautical bric-a-brac, bar ceiling covered in flags, raised seating area and separate lounge; open all day, near river and marketplace. *(Roger and Donna Huggins, Alan and Jane Shaw)*

STAMFORDHAM NZ0772
⋆**Bay Horse** (01661) 855489

Off B6309; NE18 0PB Refurbished beamed and stone-built dining pub at end of green in attractive village; good competently cooked generous food from new owners (both chefs) with emphasis on local produce including own lamb and seasonal game, afternoon tea, well kept Wylam ales and well chosen wines from shortish list (most offered by the glass), attentive efficient service, clean uncluttered interior, bar, comfortable lounge with woodburner, restaurant; children welcome, six good value bedrooms, open all day (food till 5pm on Sun). *(Michael Doswell, Comus and Sarah Elliott)*

STANLEY NZ2054
South Causey (01207) 235555

South Causey Farm; DH9 0LS Stone-built inn by riding school in 100-acre grounds, beams, oak floors, open fires and eclectic mix of old furniture, wide choice of popular food all day including very good value weekday lunchtime carvery, Wells & Youngs Bombardier and two local ales kept well, good service; children welcome, dogs allowed in one area, picnic-sets outside, small farm with alpacas, goats etc, 28 bedrooms. *(John Coatsworth)*

STANNINGTON NZ2179
⋆**Ridley Arms** (01670) 789216

Village signed off A1 S of Morpeth; NE61 6EL Attractive extended 18th-c stone pub with several linked rooms, each with slightly different mood and style, proper front bar with log fire and stools along counter, Black Sheep, Caledonian and two guests, beamed dining areas with comfortable bucket chairs around dark tables on bare boards or carpet, cartoons and portraits on cream, panelled or stripped-stone walls, well cooked reasonably priced pubby food (not Sun evening) from sandwiches up, pleasant staff, busy but relaxed atmosphere; background music, fruit machine, no dogs; children welcome, good disabled access,

---

'Children welcome' means the pub says it lets children inside without any special restriction; some may impose an evening time limit earlier than 9pm – please tell us if you find this.

front picnic-sets by road, more on back terrace, open all day. *(Comus and Sarah Elliott, Dr Peter D Smart, GSB, Derek and Sylvia Stephenson and others)*

TYNEMOUTH   NZ3669
Hugos at the Coast (0191) 257 8956
Front Street; NE30 4DZ Well refurbished chain pub with open-plan split-level interior, four real ales and good choice of wines, bar food from sandwiches and wraps up, modest prices; open all day. *(Comus and Sarah Elliott, Eric Larkham)*

TYNEMOUTH   NZ3669
Priory (0191) 257 8302
Front Street; NE30 4DX Good friendly atmosphere in this rather quirky place describing itself as 'shabbily comfortable', mismatching furniture including union-jack sofas on bare boards, lots of pictures on grey and red walls, various odds and ends including the front of a Mini (working headlights) suspended above the entrance, Black Sheep, Mordue and a house beer from Jarrow, pubby food from sandwiches and baked potatoes up, very cheap prices, weekend live music, quiz night Tues; dogs welcome (treats for good ones), café-style pavement tables, open all day, till 1am Fri, Sat. *(Comus and Sarah Elliott)*

WARENFORD   NU1429
White Swan (01668) 213453
Off A1 S of Belford; NE70 7HY Simply decorated friendly bar with changing ales such as Adnams and Black Sheep, steps down to cosy restaurant with imaginative carefully presented food (good value set lunch), efficient helpful service, warm fires; dogs welcome. *(Nick Pickard, Janet and Peter Race)*

WARKWORTH   NU2406
Masons Arms (01665) 711398
Dial Place; NE65 0UR Welcoming village pub in shadow of castle; enjoyable food including daily specials and Sun carvery in comfortable bar or separate dining area, four changing ales, friendly staff; Tues night quiz, sports TV; children and dogs welcome, disabled facilities, back flagstoned courtyard, appealing village not far from the sea, open all day. *(Clive Flynn, Michael Doswell)*

WEST BOLDON   NZ3460
Red Lion (0191) 536 4197
Redcar Terrace; NE36 0PZ Bow-windowed and flower-decked family-run pub, hop-strung beamed bar with open fire, ales such as Black Sheep from ornate wood counter, separate snug and conservatory dining room, good choice of well priced pubby food, friendly smiling service; seats out on back decking, open all day. *(Roger and Donna Huggins)*

WHITLEY BAY   NZ3473
Briar Dene (0191) 252 0926
The Links; NE26 1UE Smart brightly decorated two-room pub, fine sea-view spot, with up to eight interesting changing ales, good value pubby food till 3pm (4pm weekends) from sandwiches up, friendly efficient staff; children welcome, seats outside, open all day. *(Dr Peter D Smart, Adrian Johnson, Eric Larkham)*

WINSTON   NZ1416
Bridgewater Arms (01325) 730302
B6274, just off A67 Darlington–Barnard Castle; DL2 3RN Converted Victorian school house with high-ceilinged log-fire bar and separate restaurant, top notch cooking from chef-owner with some emphasis on fish/seafood but also traditional choices on cheaper lunchtime/early evening menu, cheerful well trained staff, ales such as Greene King IPA and Timothy Taylors Landlord, nice wines; tables outside, closed Sun and Mon. *(Graham Stevens)*

WOLSINGHAM   NZ0737
Black Bull (01388) 527332
Market Place; DL13 3AB Old beamed inn with well kept beers and generous helpings of enjoyable modestly priced food, friendly staff, pubby furnishings including button-back wall benches, bare boards and carpet, some exposed stonework, open fire; children welcome, picnic-sets on part-covered back terrace, four bedrooms (two sharing bathroom), open all day. *(Comus and Sarah Elliott)*

WYLAM   NZ1164
⋆ Boathouse (01661) 853431
Station Road, handy for Newcastle–Carlisle railway line; across Tyne from village (and Stephenson's birthplace); NE41 8HR Thriving convivial pub with a dozen real ales, 15 ciders (some tapped from cellar) and good choice of malt whiskies, bargain food Fri-Sun till 4pm, snacks available other times, polite helpful young staff, open stove in bright low-beamed bar, dining room; children and dogs welcome, seats outside, close to station and river, open all day. *(the Didler, Eric Larkham)*

Nottinghamshire

A couple of new pubs, or places back in these pages after a break, include the Full Moon at Morton (stylish pub in a remote hamlet with newly refurbished bars, five ales and enjoyable food) and Olde Trip to Jerusalem in Nottingham (unique – built into the rock below the castle – with nine ales and good value nibbles and meals). The Black Horse in Caythorpe (own-brews in charming little local run by the same family for three generations) and Martins Arms in Colston Basset (delicious food, seven real ales and a civilised interior) are strongly supported by our readers. The Martins Arms in Colston Basset is our Nottinghamshire Dining Pub 2014.

CAYTHORPE
SK6845   Map 7
Black Horse ◀ £

Turn off A6097 0.25 miles SE of roundabout junction with A612, NE of Nottingham; into Gunthorpe Road, then right into Caythorpe Road and keep on; NG14 7ED

Quaintly old-fashioned little pub brewing its own beer, with simple interior and enjoyable homely food; no children or credit cards

Many customers come to enjoy the good value food cooked by the long-serving landlady in this 300-year-old country local – it's been run by the same friendly family for three generations. The uncluttered carpeted bar has just five tables, brocaded wall banquettes and settles, decorative plates on a delft shelf, a few horsebrasses on the ceiling joists, and a coal fire. Cheerful regulars might occupy the few bar stools to enjoy the Caythorpe Bitter and One Swallow that are brewed in outbuildings and served alongside a couple of guests like Fullers London Pride and Wentworth Full Malty on handpump. Off the front corridor is a part-panelled inner room with a wall bench running around three unusual long copper-topped tables, plus several old local photographs; darts and board games. An end room has just one huge round table. There are some seats outside, and the River Trent is fairly close for waterside walks.

Book a table in advance to enjoy the good value, landlady-cooked food: sandwiches, home-made soup, lambs kidneys in cream sauce, omelettes, local sausages with mash and onion gravy, grilled lamb chops with potatoes, seafood salad, and puddings such as apple pie and sticky toffee pudding with walnuts. *Benchmark main dish: fried fillets of fish with mushy peas and chips £9.00. Two-course evening meal £14.00.*

Own brew ~ Licensee Sharron Andrews ~ Real ale ~ No credit cards ~ (0115) 966 3520 ~ Open 12-2.30, 5.30-11.30; 12-5, 8-11.30 Sun; closed Mon except bank holidays ~

Bar food 12-2, 6-9; not Sat evening, Sun ~ Restaurant ~ Dogs allowed in bar ~
www.caythorpebrewery.co.uk/the_black_horse *Recommended by David Eberlin, David and Sue Atkinson*

COLSTON BASSETT   SK6933 Map 7

Martins Arms 🍴 🍷 🍺

Village signposted off A46 E of Nottingham; School Lane, near market cross in village centre; NG12 3FD

Nottinghamshire Dining Pub of the Year

Smart dining pub with impressive food, good range of drinks including seven real ales and attractive grounds

A civilised interior and imaginatively presented, first class food continue to draw many customers to this lovely country pub. There's a comfortably relaxed atmosphere, warm log fires in Jacobean fireplaces, fresh flowers and candlelight – and smart decoration with period fabrics and colours, antique furniture and hunting prints. If you're dining in the elegant restaurant, you may be welcomed by Salvatore, the friendly front-of-house manager. Neatly uniformed staff serve Bass, Fullers Seafarers, Greene King IPA, Marstons Pedigree, Ringwood Best, Timothy Taylors Landlord and a couple of guests from brewers such as Black Dog and Castle Rock on handpump, as well as 19 wines by the glass (including prosecco, champagne and sweet wines), Belvoir organic ginger beer and ten malt whiskies; cribbage, dominoes and board games. The lawned garden (summer croquet here) backs on to National Trust parkland and readers recommend visiting the church opposite and Colston Bassett Dairy, which sells its own stilton cheese, and is just outside the village.

🍴 Using the best locally sourced produce and game, the enticing food might include sandwiches, duck liver parfait with pear and cinnamon chutney and sourdough, poached egg royale with smoked salmon, hollandaise and toasted muffins, burger with bacon, stilton and triple-cooked chips, jerusalem artichoke risotto with crunchy salad and truffle vinaigrette, smoked haddock with poached egg and parsley sauce, pork belly with black pudding purée, hash brown, apple sauce and crackling, corn-fed chicken with dauphinoise potatoes and swiss chard, and puddings such as golden syrup sponge with custard and chocolate torte with frothy hot chocolate mocha. *Benchmark main dish: chargrilled steak sandwich with stilton, onion jam, coleslaw and chips £11.50. Two-course evening meal £20.00.*

Free house ~ Licensees Lynne Strafford Bryan and Salvatore Inguanta ~ Real ale ~ (01949) 81361 ~ Open 12-3, 6-11; 12-5, 7-10.30 Sun ~ Bar food 12-2, 6-9; 12-3 Sun ~ Restaurant ~ Children welcome ~ www.themartinsarms.co.uk *Recommended by Jack and Sandra Clarfelt, O K Smyth, Mike Proctor, David Glynne-Jones, Mike and Mary Carter*

MORTON   SK7251 Map 7

Full Moon 🍺

Pub and village signed off Bleasby–Fiskerton back road, SE of Southwell; NG25 0UT

Five real ales and good food at stylish village local, with play area in nice garden

T his attractive old brick pub is tucked away in a remote hamlet not far from the River Trent. It's been refurbished this year with pale cream paintwork and smart new carpeting, and the simple furnishings are an eclectic mix of tables and chairs, with high-backed wooden or upholstered dining chairs around wooden tables in the restaurant; there are also comfortable armchairs and two roaring log fires. Timothy Taylors Landlord and guests such as Acorn Barnsley Bitter, Greene King IPA, and Navigation Golden and Traditional on handpump and several wines by the glass; background music and board games. There are picnic-sets at the front and on a peaceful back terrace, as well as a sizeable lawn and sturdy play equipment.

Enjoyable food includes lunchtime sandwiches, smoked salmon and chive roulade with watercress salad, deep-fried risotto balls with sweet chilli dip, steak in Guinness pie, ricotta dumplings with aubergines and tomato and basil sauce, slow-cooked beef with mustard mash and jus, bass with garlic new potatoes, and puddings such as lemon tart with raspberry sorbet and vanilla cheesecake. *Benchmark main dish: beer-battered fish with minted pea purée and skinny chips £10.95. Two-course evening meal £14.00.*

Free house ~ Licensee David Newby ~ Real ale ~ (01636) 830251 ~ Open 11-3, 6-11.30; 10-midnight Sat; 10-10 Sun ~ Bar food 12-2.30, 6-9; 12-9 Sat; 12-4 Sun ~ Children welcome ~ Dogs allowed in bar ~ www.thefullmoonmorton.co.uk
Recommended by Derek and Sylvia Stephenson, M Mossman, David Glynne-Jones, R and M Tait

NOTTINGHAM
SK5739 Map 7

Olde Trip to Jerusalem ♠ £

Brewhouse Yard; from inner ring road follow The North, A6005 Long Eaton signpost until in Castle Boulevard, then right into Castle Road; pub is on the left; NG1 6AD

Unusual pub partly built into sandstone caves, good range of real ales and reasonably priced pubby food

Although this unusual pub is mainly 17th c, its cavern may have served as cellarage for an early medieval brewhouse that stood here. Carved into the rock, the friendly downstairs bar has leatherette-cushioned settles built into dark panelling, tables on flagstones and snug banquettes built into low-ceilinged rocky alcoves. Staff cope efficiently with the busy mix of tourists, chatting locals and students, serving Greene King IPA, Abbot, H&H Olde Trip and Old Speckled Hen and Nottingham Rock Ale Bitter, Mild and Extra Pale Ale and a couple of beers named for the pub on handpump. There are seats in a snug courtyard; ring the bull. The pub's name refers to the 12th-c crusaders who used to meet nearby on their way to the Holy Land; the little souvenir shop with its panelled walls soaring into the dark cavernous heights is very popular.

As well as sandwiches, the very good value food includes tapas-style nibbles such as pork scotch egg with HP sauce, gloucester old spot sausages with beer, mustard and honey dip or breaded haddock goujons with lime and coriander dip, several sharing boards, honey-roast ham and eggs, sausage and mash, steak in ale pie, chicken with bacon, gruyère and provençale sauce, and puddings such as marmalade and ginger biscuit cheesecake and apple tarte tatin with toffee sauce. *Benchmark main dish: fish and chips £9.45. Two-course evening meal £15.00.*

Greene King ~ Manager Carl Gibson ~ Real ale ~ (0115) 947 3171 ~ Open 11-11(midnight Fri, Sat) ~ Bar food 11-10 ~ Children welcome till 10pm ~ www.triptojerusalem.com *Recommended by Andy Lickfold, Richard Tilbrook*

Also Worth a Visit in Nottinghamshire

Besides the fully inspected pubs, you might like to try these pubs that have been recommended to us and described by readers. Do tell us what you think of them: feedback@goodguides.com

AWSWORTH   SK4844
Gate (0115) 932 9821
Main Street, via A6096 off A610 Nuthall–Eastwood bypass; NG16 2RN Friendly Victorian free house with six well kept ales (usually Blue Monkey and Burton Bridge), cosy bar, coal fire in lounge, small pool room, some snacks, refurbished skittle alley; children welcome till 8pm, dogs in bar, disabled facilities, picnic-sets out in front, near site of once-famous railway viaduct, open all day (till 1am Fri, Sat). *(Fiona Coupland)*

BAGTHORPE   SK4751
Dixies Arms (01773) 810505
A608 towards Eastwood off M1 junction 27, right on B600 via Sandhill Road, left into School Road; Lower Bagthorpe; NG16 5HF Friendly unspoilt 18th-c beamed and tiled-floor local with D H Lawrence connections, well kept Greene King Abbot, Theakstons Best and a guest, no food, fine fireplace in small part-panelled parlour, entrance bar with tiny snug, longer narrow room with toby jugs, darts and dominoes, live music Sat, quiz Sun; children and dogs (on leads) welcome, good big garden with play area and football pitch, open all day. *(Anon)*

BEESTON   SK5236
Crown (0115) 925 4738
Church Street; NG9 1FY Owned and sensitively restored by Everards, real ale enthusiast landlord serving up to 14 (some keenly priced), also real ciders, perry and good choice of bottled beers (regular beer festivals), no hot food but fresh cobs and other snacks; front snug and bar with quarry-tiled floor, carpeted parlour with padded wall seats, Victorian décor and new polished bar in lounge, beams, panelling, bric-a-brac, old red telephone box; terrace tables, open all day. *(Steve Bakewell, Andrew Abbott, Johnston and Maureen Anderson)*

BEESTON   SK5336
✱**Victoria** (0115) 925 4049
Dovecote Lane, backing on to railway station; NG9 1JG Genuine down-to-earth all-rounder attracting good mix of customers, up to 15 real ales (regular beer festivals), two farm ciders, 120 malt whiskies and 30 wines by the glass, good value interesting food (half the menu is vegetarian), friendly efficient service, three fairly simple unfussy rooms with original long narrow layout, solid furnishings, bare boards and stripped woodwork, stained-glass windows, open fires, newspapers and board games, live music (Sun, Mon evening Oct-May); children welcome till 8pm, dogs in bar, seats out on covered heated area overlooking platform (trains pass just a few feet away), limited parking, open all day. *(Ian and Helen Stafford, Johnston and Maureen Anderson, David and Sue Atkinson, John and Hazel Sarkanen, David Hunt, Derek and Sylvia Stephenson)*

BINGHAM   SK7039
✱**Horse & Plough** (01949) 839313
Off A52; Long Acre; NG13 8AF Former 1818 Methodist chapel with low beams, flagstones and stripped brick, prints and old brewery memorabilia, comfortable open-plan seating including pews, well kept Caledonian Deuchars IPA, Thwaites Wainwright and four guests (tasters offered), real cider, good wine choice, enjoyable reasonably priced home-made weekday bar food, popular upstairs grill room (Tues-Sat evenings, all day Sun) with polished boards, hand-painted murals and open kitchen; background music; children and dogs welcome, disabled facilities, open all day. *(Anon)*

BLEASBY   SK7149
Waggon & Horses (01636) 830283
Gypsy Lane; NG14 7GG Popular early 19th-c pub with six real ales including Blue Monkey, carpeted lounge/dining room, character bar, snug with leather sofas and armchairs, good value home-made pub food (not Sun evening, Mon, Tues); background music, darts; children, dogs and muddy boots welcome, tables on front terrace and in back garden, good local walks, open all day weekends, closed lunchtimes Mon-Weds. *(Steve Homer)*

BRAMCOTE   SK5037
White Lion (0115) 925 5413
Just off A52 W of Nottingham; Town Street; NG9 3HH Small and homely 18th-c pub, well kept Greene King ales from bar serving two split-level adjoining rooms, low-priced pubby food including Weds curry and Sun roasts, darts and dominoes, quiz nights; children welcome, tables in attractive garden behind, open all day. *(Anon)*

BUNNY   SK5829
Rancliffe Arms (0115) 984 4727
Loughborough Road (A60 S of Nottingham); NG11 6QT Substantial early 18th-c former coaching inn reworked with emphasis on linked dining areas, upscale food from enterprising sandwich range to adventurous dishes, popular carvery (Mon evening, Weds, Sat, Sun), prompt friendly service, chunky country chairs around

mixed tables on flagstones or carpet, well kept Marstons-related ales in comfortable log-fire bar with sofas and armchairs; children welcome, decking outside, open all Fri-Sun. *(Gerry and Rosemary Dobson)*

CAR COLSTON   SK7242
Royal Oak (01949) 20247
The Green, off Tenman Lane (off A46 not far from A6097 junction); NG13 8JE Good well priced traditional food (not Sun evening) in biggish 19th-c pub opposite one of England's largest village greens, four well kept ales including Marstons and Brakspears, decent choice of wines by the glass, woodburner in lounge bar with tables set for eating, public bar with unusual barrel-vaulted brick ceiling, spotless housekeeping; children welcome, picnic-sets on spacious back lawn, heated smokers' den, camping, open all day Fri-Sun. *(Anon)*

CAUNTON   SK7459
⋆ Caunton Beck (01636) 636793
Newark Road; NG23 6AE Cleverly reconstructed low-beamed dining pub made to look old using original timbers and reclaimed oak; scrubbed pine tables and country-kitchen chairs, rag-finished paintwork, some clever lighting, open fire, three ales such as Black Sheep, Derby and Everards, over two dozen wines by the glass, enjoyable popular food from breakfast on, decent coffee and daily papers, friendly caring staff; children welcome, dogs in bar, seats on flowery terrace, open all day from 8.30am, handy for A1. *(B and M Kendall, Rob Winstanley, James Stretton, David and Ruth Hollands, G Jennings, W J Taylor)*

COLLINGHAM   SK8361
Kings Head (01636) 892341
High Street; NG23 7LA Gently upscale modern pub-restaurant behind unpretentious Georgian façade, two well kept changing ales from long steel bar, courteous helpful staff, food from baguettes to good restaurant dishes with unusual touches, light and airy dining area with pine furniture on polished boards; children welcome, no dogs, disabled access, garden tables, open all day Sun. *(Tom Carver)*

CROPWELL BUTLER   SK6837
Plough (0115) 933 3124
Main Street; NG12 3AB Honest village pub serving very good value home-made food (not Sun evening) and well kept ales, log-fire bar, comfortable restaurant, back conservatory, books sold for charity, pool; children welcome, well looked after garden, good walks nearby, open all day Fri-Sun, closed Mon lunchtime. *(MP)*

EDWINSTOWE   SK6266
Forest Lodge (01623) 824443
Church Street; NG21 9QA Friendly 18th-c inn with enjoyable home-made food in

pubby bar or restaurant, good service, well kept Wells & Youngs Bombardier and four regularly changing guests, log fire; children welcome, 13 bedrooms, handy for Sherwood Forest. *(Anon)*

FARNDON   SK7652
⋆ Boathouse (01636) 676578
Off A46 SW of Newark; keep on towards river – pub off Wyke Lane, just past the Riverside pub; NG24 3SX Big-windowed contemporary bar-restaurant overlooking the Trent, emphasis on food but Greene King IPA and a guest served from stylish counter, good choice of wines, main area indeed reminiscent of a boathouse with high ceiling trusses supporting bare ducting and scant modern decoration, second dining area broadly similar, modern cooking along with some pubby dishes, neat young staff; background and live music (Sun); children welcome, wicker chairs around teak tables on terrace, own moorings, open all day. *(David Hunt)*

GRANBY   SK7436
⋆ Marquis of Granby (01949) 859517
Off A52 E of Nottingham; Dragon Street; NG13 9PN Popular, stylish and friendly 18th-c pub in attractive Vale of Belvoir village, tap for Brewsters with their ales and interesting guests from chunky yew bar counter, decent home-made food from Fri evening (fish and chips) to Sun lunchtime, two small comfortable rooms with broad flagstones, some low beams and striking wallpaper, open fire; children and dogs welcome, open from 4pm Mon-Fri, all day weekends. *(Anon)*

HALAM   SK6754
Waggon & Horses (01636) 813109
Off A612 in Southwell centre, via Halam Road; NG22 8AE More pubby with less emphasis on dining under current management; low-ceilinged open-plan interior with several cosy areas formed by layout of original 17th-c building, wood or tiled floors, three Thwaites beers and enjoyable straightforward food; pool; a few roadside picnic-sets. *(Derek and Sylvia Stephenson)*

HARBY   SK8870
⋆ Bottle & Glass (01522) 703438
High Street; village signed off A57 W of Lincoln; NG23 7EB Civilised dining pub with pair of bay-windowed front bars, attractive pubby furnishings, lots of bright cushions on built-in wall benches, arts-and-crafts chairs, dark flagstones and red walls, log fire, splendid range of wines (big vineyard map of Côte de Beaune in left-hand bar), Black Sheep and Titanic beers, good country cooking all day including set menu, friendly attentive service, small area with squashy sofas and armchairs and more formal restaurant; children welcome, dogs allowed

in bar, modern wrought-iron furniture on back terrace, picnic-sets on grass beyond. *(Pauline Fellows and Simon Robbins)*

HOVERINGHAM   SK6946
Reindeer (0115) 966 3629
Main Street; NG14 7GR Beamed pub with intimate bar and busy restaurant (best to book), good home-made food (not Sun evening) from standards to more enterprising dishes, good value lunchtime set menu, Black Sheep, Castle Rock Harvest Pale and two guests, good wines by the glass, log fire; children welcome, seats outside overlooking cricket pitch, open all day weekends, closed lunchtimes Mon, Tues. *(Anon)*

KIMBERLEY   SK4944
✶ **Nelson & Railway** (0115) 938 2177
Station Road; handy for M1 junction 26 via A610; NG16 2NR Comfortable beamed Victorian pub in same family for 43 years; well kept Greene King ales and guests, mix of Edwardian-looking furniture, brewery prints (was tap for defunct H&H Brewery) and railway signs, dining extension, traditional games including alley and table skittles; juke box, games machine; children and dogs allowed, nice front and back gardens, 11 good value bedrooms, open all day. *(Comus and Sarah Elliott)*

KIMBERLEY   SK5044
Stag (0115) 938 3151
Nottingham Road; NG16 2NB Friendly 18th-c traditional local spotlessly kept by devoted landlady, two cosy rooms, small central counter and corridor, low beams, dark panelling and settles, working vintage slot machines, old Shipstones Brewery photographs, well kept Adnams, Timothy Taylors Landlord and three guests (May beer festival), no food; children and dogs welcome, attractive back garden with play area, opens 5pm (1.30 Sat, 12 Sun). *(Anon)*

LAMBLEY   SK6345
Woodlark (0115) 931 2535
Church Street; NG4 4QB Welcoming and interestingly laid-out village local, neatly furnished bare-brick beamed bar, careful extension into next house giving comfortable lounge/dining area, popular good value freshly made food, downstairs steak bar (Fri, Sat evenings), well kept Castle Rock, Sam Smiths, Timothy Taylors Landlord and a guest, open fire; children and dogs welcome, tables on side terrace, open all day. *(Anon)*

LAXTON   SK7266
✶ **Dovecote** (01777) 871586
Off A6075 E of Ollerton; NG22 0NU Red-brick pub handy for A1; cosy country atmosphere in three traditionally furnished dining areas, nice food including good value Sun lunch, Batemans XB, Timothy Taylor Landlord and guests, farm cider and several

wines by the glass, friendly efficient staff; background music; children welcome, small front terrace and sloping garden with views towards church, interesting village that still strip farms, bedrooms, open all day Sun. *(Michele Summers, R and M Tait, Chris Lowe, David and Ruth Hollands)*

MANSFIELD   SK5561
Il Rosso (01623) 623031
Nottingham Road (A60); NG18 4AF Refurbished restauranty pub with enjoyable italian-influenced food including good fresh fish, takeaway pizza too, up to five well kept changing ales, good service, regular live acoustic music (jazz Mon); no dogs inside; children welcome, terraces front and back, open all day from 8.30am for breakfast. *(Anon)*

MANSFIELD   SK5363
Railway Inn (01623) 623086
Station Street; best approached by viaduct from near Market Place; NG18 1EF Friendly traditional local with long-serving landlady, three changing ales, real cider and good bottled beer choice, bargain home-made food (till 5pm Sun), two little front rooms leading to main bar, another cosy room at back, laminate flooring throughout; children and dogs welcome, small courtyard and beer garden, handy for Robin Hood Line station, open all day. *(Anon)*

MANSFIELD WOODHOUSE SK5463
Greyhound (01623) 464403
High Street; NG19 8BD Friendly 17th-c village local with up to half a dozen well kept ales including Adnams and Caledonian Deuchars IPA (beer festivals), cosy lounge, darts, dominoes and pool in busy bar, no food; dogs welcome, open all day. *(Anon)*

MAPLEBECK   SK7160
✶ **Beehive**
Signed down pretty country lanes from A616 Newark–Ollerton and from A617 Newark–Mansfield; NG22 0BS Relaxing beamed country tavern in nice spot, chatty landlady, tiny front bar, slightly bigger side room, traditional furnishings and antiques, open fire, well kept Maypole and guests, no food; tables on small terrace with flower tubs and grassy bank running down to a stream, summer barbecues, play area, may be closed weekday lunchtimes in winter, very busy weekends and bank holidays. *(David and Ruth Hollands)*

NEWARK   SK8053
Fox & Crown (01636) 605820
Appleton Gate; NG24 1JY Open-plan bare-boards Castle Rock pub with their well priced ales and four or more guests from central servery, Weston's cider, dozens of whiskies, vodkas and other spirits, good tea, coffee and decent wines by the glass, friendly obliging staff, inexpensive food from rolls and baked

potatoes up, several side areas; background music (live Fri); children in dining room and dogs welcome, good wheelchair access, open all day. *(Andy Lickfold)*

NEWARK SK7953
Just Beer 07983 993747
Swan & Salmon Yard, off Castle Gate (B6166); NG24 1BG Small welcoming one-room pub (opened 2010), four or five interesting quickly changing microbrewery ales from brick bar, real cider and perry served from cellar, no other alcoholic drinks or food, bright airy minimalist décor with some brewery memorabilia, half a dozen tables on stone floor, eclectic mix of customers; open all day (from 1pm weekdays). *(Tony and Maggie Harwood)*

NEWARK SK7953
Prince Rupert (01636) 918121
Stodman Street, off Castle Gate; NG24 1AW Ancient renovated timber-framed pub near market, several small rooms on two floors, beams, exposed brickwork and many original features (some previously covered up), nice old furniture including high-backed settles, conservatory, five real ales such as Blue Monkey, Oakham and Thornbridge, Weston's cider, blackboard choice of wines by the glass, pubby food plus speciality pizzas with some unusual toppings and other imaginative food, friendly staff, live music most weekends; courtyard with old enamel signs, open all day (till 1am Fri, Sat). *(Tony and Maggie Harwood, David and Ruth Hollands)*

NORMANTON ON THE WOLDS SK6232
Plough (0115) 937 2401
Off A606 5 miles S of Nottingham; NG12 5NN Ivy-clad pub on edge of village, enjoyable freshly made food from extensive menu including particularly good steaks, friendly uniformed staff, five real ales such as Fullers London Pride, Theakstons Best and Wells & Youngs Bombardier, fires in bar and restaurant; soft background music; children welcome, big garden with play area and summer barbecues. *(David and Sue Atkinson, Phil and Jane Hodson)*

NORTH MUSKHAM SK7958
Muskham Ferry (01636) 704943
Ferry Lane, handy for A1 (which has small sign to pub); NG23 6HB Traditional well furnished panelled pub in splendid location on River Trent, relaxing views from bar-restaurant, fairly priced food including children's meals and Sun roast, four well kept real ales including Greene King Abbot and Sharps Doom Bar, good wine and soft drinks choice, friendly chatty staff; piped radio, games machine, pool; dogs welcome, terrace overlooking water, moorings, open all day. *(John and Alison Hamilton)*

NOTTINGHAM SK5739
★ **Bell** (0115) 947 5241
Angel Row; off Market Square; NG1 6HL Deceptively large pub with late Georgian frontage concealing two 500-year-old timber-framed buildings; front Tudor Bar with café feel in summer when french windows open to pavement tables, bright blue walls with glass panels protecting patches of 300-year-old wallpaper; larger low-beamed Elizabethan Bar with half-panelled walls, maple parquet flooring and upstairs Belfry with more heavy panelling and 15th-c crown post; up to a dozen real ales from remarkable deep sandstone cellar, ten wines by the glass, reasonably priced straightforward bar food, welcoming staff; piped and regular live music including trad jazz, TV, silent fruit machine; children welcome in some parts, open all day (till 1am Sat). *(Richard Tilbrook, David Hunt)*

NOTTINGHAM SK5843
Bread & Bitter (0115) 960 7541
Woodthorpe Drive; NG3 5JL In former suburban bakery still showing ovens, three bright and airy bare-boarded rooms, around a dozen well kept ales including Castle Rock, farm cider, decent wine choice, reasonably priced wholesome food all day from cobs up, defunct brewery memorabilia, some live music; well behaved children and dogs welcome. *(Tony and Maggie Harwood)*

NOTTINGHAM SK5639
Browns (0115) 958 8183
Park Row; NG1 6GR Stylish bar-brasserie opened 2012; real ales, good choice of wine and cocktails, enjoyable food from bar snacks up; service variable; handy for the Playhouse Theatre, open all day. *(David Hunt)*

NOTTINGHAM SK5739
★ **Canal House** (0115) 955 5060
Canal Street; NG1 7EH Converted wharf building, bridge over indoors canal spur complete with narrowboat, lots of bare brick and varnished wood, huge joists on steel beams, long bar with well kept Castle Rock and three guests, 80 or so bottled beers and good choice of wines, enjoyable sensibly priced pubby food (not Sun evening), efficient service; background music; masses of tables out on attractive waterside terrace, open all day. *(David Hunt)*

NOTTINGHAM SK5639
Cast Bar (0115) 852 3898
Wellington Circus; NG1 5AL Adjoining Playhouse Theatre and more wine bar-restaurant than pub, lots of chrome and glass, good range of wines by the glass, local ales from handpumps hidden below counter, good food including light choices, pre-theatre menu and more adventurous restaurant meals, integral all-day deli serving coffee and snacks (8.30am-4.30pm, not Sun); children welcome, plenty of tables out on notable

courtyard terrace by huge Anish Kapoor *Sky Mirror* sculpture, open all day. *(David Hunt)*

NOTTINGHAM   SK5739
Cock & Hoop (0115) 852 3231
High Pavement; NG1 1HF Tiny bareboards front bar with fireside armchairs and flagstoned cellar bar attached to decent hotel; characterful décor, reasonably priced fairly traditional food including good Sun roasts, well kept ales such as Amber, Blue Monkey, Flipside and Magpie, attentive friendly service; background music, live jazz last Thurs of month; children and dogs welcome, disabled facilities, smart bedrooms (ones by the street can be noisy at weekends), open all day. *(Anon)*

NOTTINGHAM   SK5739
★Cross Keys (0115) 941 7898
Byard Lane; NG1 2GJ Restored Victorian city-centre pub on two levels, lower carpeted part with leather banquettes, panelling and chandeliers, upper area with old wooden chairs and tables on polished boards, interesting prints and pictures and more chandeliers, seven well kept ales including Batemans and Navigation, good home-made food from breakfast on, friendly service, upstairs weekend restaurant; sports TV; seats outside, open all day from 9am. *(George Atkinson)*

NOTTINGHAM   SK5542
Fox & Crown (0115) 942 2002
Church Street/Lincoln Street, Old Basford; NG6 0GA Range of good Alcazar beers brewed behind this refurbished open-plan pub (window shows the brewery, Sat tours), also guest ales, continentals and good choice of wines, enjoyable thai food; background music, games machines and big-screen sports TV; disabled access, tables on back terrace, beer shop next door, open all day. *(David Hunt)*

NOTTINGHAM   SK5642
Gladstone (0115) 912 9994
Loscoe Road, Carrington; NG5 2AW Welcoming backstreet local with half a dozen well kept ales including Castle Rock, Fullers, Nottingham, Oakham and Timothy Taylors, good range of malt whiskies, comfortable lounge with reading matter, basic bar with old sports memorabilia and darts, upstairs folk club Weds, quiz Thurs; background music and sports TV; tables in back garden among colourful tubs and hanging baskets, closed weekday lunchtimes, open all day weekends. *(David Hunt)*

NOTTINGHAM   SK5640
Hand & Heart (0115) 958 2456
Derby Road; NG1 5BA Unexceptional exterior but unusual inside with bar and dining areas cut deep into back sandstone, a house beer from Dancing Duck, Maypole and six guests, two real ciders and good range of whiskies, enjoyable fairly priced traditional food from sandwiches and snacks up, friendly helpful service, upstairs area with glassed-in part overlooking street; background and interesting live music Thurs (jazz, world, klezmer); children welcome till 7pm if eating, dogs in bar, open all day (late licence Fri, Sat). *(Andrew Cooper)*

NOTTINGHAM   SK5542
Horse & Groom (0115) 970 3777
Radford Road, New Basford; NG7 7EA Eight good changing ales and a real cider in well run open-plan local by former Shipstones Brewery, still with their name and other memorabilia, good value fresh straightforward food from sandwiches to Sun lunch, nice snug, some live music; open all day (from 4pm Mon–Weds). *(Anon)*

NOTTINGHAM   SK5739
★Kean's Head (0115) 947 4052
St Mary's Gate; NG1 1QA Cheery pub in attractive Lace Market area; fairly functional single room with simple wooden café furnishings on wooden boards, some exposed brickwork and red tiling, low sofa by big windows overlooking street, stools by wood counter and small fireplace, Castle Rock and three guests, draught belgian and interesting bottled beers, 20 wines by the glass, around 60 malt whiskies and lots of teas/coffees, tasty fairly traditional food (not Sun evening), friendly service, daily papers; background music; children welcome till 7pm, church next door worth a look, open all day. *(Andrew Abbott)*

NOTTINGHAM   SK5539
King William IV (0115) 958 9864
Manvers Street/Eyre Street, Sneinton; NG2 4PB Two-room Victorian corner local with plenty of character, Oakham and six guests from circular bar, Weston's Old Rosie cider, good fresh cobs, friendly staff, fine tankard collection, pool upstairs, irish music Thurs; silenced sports TV; heated smokers' shelter, handy for cricket, football and rugby grounds, open all day. *(Anon)*

NOTTINGHAM   SK5740
★Lincolnshire Poacher
(0115) 941 1584 *Mansfield Road; up hill from Victoria Centre; NG1 3FR* Impressive range of drinks at this popular down-to-earth pub (attracting younger evening crowd), ten or so real ales, continental draught and bottled beers, farm cider and over 70 malt whiskies, above average all-day food at reasonable prices; big simple traditional front bar with wall settles, wooden tables and breweriana,

plain but lively room on left and corridor to chatty panelled back snug with newspapers and board games, conservatory overlooking tables on large heated back area, live music Sun evening; children (till 8pm) and dogs welcome, open all day (till midnight Sat). *(David Hunt)*

NOTTINGHAM SK5541

⋆ **Lion** (0115) 970 3506

Lower Mosley Street, New Basford; NG7 7FQ Ten ales including regulars Batemans and Mallards from one of the city's deepest cellars (glass viewing panel – can be visited at quiet times), farm ciders, ten wines by the glass and good value home-made food all day including doorstep sandwiches, quick service; well fabricated feel of separate areas, bare bricks and polished dark oak boards, old brewery pictures and posters, open fires, daily papers, weekend live music including Sun lunchtime jazz, beer festivals; children welcome till 8pm, disabled facilities, garden with terrace and smokers' shelter, summer barbecues. *(David Hunt)*

NOTTINGHAM SK5739

News House (0115) 952 3061

Canal Street; NG1 7HB Friendly two-room 1950s Castle Rock pub with notable blue exterior tiling, their ales and half a dozen changing guests, belgian and czech imports, decent fresh lunchtime food (Mon-Sat), mix of bare boards and carpet, local newspaper and radio memorabilia, darts, table skittles and bar billiards, Thurs quiz; big-screen sports TV; a few tables out at front, open all day. *(Anon)*

NOTTINGHAM SK5540

Plough (0115) 942 2649

St Peters Street, Radford; NG7 3EN Friendly 19th-c local brewing its own good value Nottingham ales at the back, also guest beers and farm cider, weekday sandwiches, mosaic floors, old tables and chairs, two coal fires, traditional games and skittle alley, Thurs quiz with free food; dogs welcome (may get a chew), covered smokers' area, open all day. *(Anon)*

NOTTINGHAM SK5739

Salutation (0115) 947 6580

Hounds Gate/Maid Marian Way; NG1 7AA Proper pub, low beams, flagstones, ochre walls and cosy corners including two small quiet rooms in ancient lower back part, plusher modern front lounge, up to six real ales and good choice of draught/bottled ciders, quickly served food till 8pm (6pm Sun), helpful friendly staff (ask them to show you the haunted caves below the pub); background music (live rock upstairs); open all day (till 3am Fri, Sat). *(Anon)*

NOTTINGHAM SK5640

Sir John Borlase Warren

(0115) 947 4247 *Ilkeston Road/Canning*

Circus (A52 towards Derby); NG7 3GD Roadside pub with four comfortable linked rooms, interesting Victorian decorations, enjoyable good value food all day, friendly staff, Everards and three or four guests, Weston's cider, good mix of customers including students; children welcome, tables in nicely lit back garden with raised deck. *(David Hunt)*

NOTTINGHAM SK5739

⋆ **Vat & Fiddle** (0115) 985 0611

Queens Bridge Road; alongside Sheriffs Way (near multistorey car park); NG2 1NB Plain open-plan brick pub acting as tap for next door Castle Rock Brewery; unspoilt 1930s feel, varnished pine tables, bentwood chairs and stools on parquet or terrazzo flooring, some brewery memorabilia and interesting photographs of demolished local pubs, a dozen real ales including guests, bottled continentals, farm ciders and 60 malt whiskies, fresh cobs, nice chatty atmosphere; no credit cards; children and dogs welcome, picnic-sets out front by road, open all day (till midnight Fri, Sat). *(David Hunt)*

ORSTON SK7741

Durham Ox (01949) 850059

Church Street; NG13 9NS Comfortable village pub opposite church; four well kept mainstream ales and a guest, traditional pub food, open-plan split-level bar, old local photographs, small dining room with coal fire; background and some live music; children and dogs welcome, tables out at front and in big back garden with four heated summer houses, hitching rails for horses and ferrets, pleasant countryside, open all day weekends. *(Anon)*

RADCLIFFE ON TRENT SK6439

Horse Chestnut (0115) 933 1994

Main Road; NG12 2BE Smart pub with plenty of Victorian features, well kept Black Sheep, Castle Rock, Fullers London Pride and three guests, sensibly priced home-made food including good value Sun roasts (12-4pm), competent service, two-level main bar, panelling, parquet, polished brass and woodwork and impressive lamps, handsome leather seating, books by fireplace; background music; disabled access, attractive terrace, open all day (afternoon break Mon). *(M Mossman)*

RADCLIFFE ON TRENT SK6439

Manvers Arms (0115) 933 2404

Main Road, opposite church; NG12 2AA Early 19th-c village pub with good nicely presented food (till 7pm Sun) including set menus, prompt friendly service, well kept Caledonian, Castle Rock, Jennings, St Austell and two guests, fairly priced wines, spotless opened-up interior keeping original fireplaces and other features, assorted pubby furniture, some cosy areas with banquettes, pictures and ornaments, chandeliers and potted palms, an old harmonium; mellow background music, live folk/jazz Thurs, quiz Tues and Sun; well behaved children and dogs welcome, plenty of seats in large back garden with trees and shrubs, open all day. *(M Mossman, Tony and Maggie Harwood, David Glynne-Jones)*

RADCLIFFE ON TRENT   SK6439
Royal Oak   (0115) 933 5659
Main Road; NG12 2FD Opened-up beamed village-centre pub (part of the small Moleface group); good bar/restaurant food from open kitchen including weekend breakfast (10am on), efficient friendly service, plenty of wines by the glass, Castle Rock, Sharps Doom Bar and a guest, live music and quiz nights; children welcome, open all day. *(M Mossman, David Glynne-Jones)*

ROLLESTON   SK7452
Crown   (01636) 819000
Staythorpe Road; NG23 5SG Smartly modernised pub with good well priced food including vegetarian menu and early evening deal (Mon-Thurs), real ales, friendly efficient service; small garden, five bedrooms, handy for Southwell Racecourse, open all day, Sun till 9.30pm (food till 4pm). *(Barry Morrison)*

RUDDINGTON   SK5733
Three Crowns   (0115) 921 3226
Easthorpe Street; NG11 6LB Open-plan village pub with well kept Fullers, Nottingham and guest ales, indian food in back evening restaurant, June beer festival; open all day weekends, closed lunchtimes Mon, Tues. *(Anon)*

SELSTON   SK4553
★ Horse & Jockey   (01773) 781012
Handy for M1 junctions 27/28; Church Lane; NG16 6FB Dating from the 17th c, intelligently renovated with interesting 18th- and 19th-c survivals and good carving, different levels, low heavy beams, dark flagstones, individual furnishings and good log fire in cast-iron range, friendly staff, Greene King Abbot, Timothy Taylors Landlord (poured from jug) and some unusual guests, real cider, no food, folk night Weds; games area with darts and pool; dogs welcome, terrace with smokers' shelter, pleasant rolling country. *(Anon)*

SOUTHWELL   SK7054
★ Final Whistle   (01636) 814953
Station Road; NG25 0ET Railway themed pub commemorating the long defunct Southwell line; ten mainly local ales including Everards and Leatherbritches (beer festivals), real ciders and perries, foreign bottled beers and good range of wines, snacky food, traditional opened-up bar area with tiled or wood floor, settles and armchairs in quieter carpeted room, corridor drinking area, two open fires, panelling, lots of railway memorabilia and

other odds and ends; some live music, Tues quiz; children and dogs welcome, back garden with wonderful mock-up of 1920s platform complete with track and buffers, open all day. *(Derek and Sylvia Stephenson, Tony and Maggie Harwood, Dr Brian and Mrs Anne Hamilton)*

SOUTHWELL   SK7053
Hearty Goodfellow   (01636) 919176
Church Street (A612); NG25 0HQ Traditional open-plan pub under welcoming new management, Everards Tiger and seven guests including Mallards, good range of house wines, enjoyable fairly straightforward food at reasonable prices (now evenings too), friendly young staff, lots of polished wood, two brick fireplaces; background and some live music, sport TVs; children and dogs welcome, covered terrace and nice big tree-shaded garden beyond car park, play area, handy for Southwell Workhouse (NT) and Minster, open all day Fri-Sun, closed Mon lunchtime. *(Tony and Rosemary Swainson, Pat and Tony Martin, Derek and Sylvia Stephenson)*

THURGARTON   SK6949
Red Lion   (01636) 830351
Southwell Road (A612); NG14 7GP Cheery 16th-c pub with split-level beamed bars and restaurant, ales such as Black Sheep and Marstons from dark-panelled bar, nice range of enjoyable reasonably priced food (all day weekends and bank holidays), good service, comfortable banquettes and other seating on patterned carpets, lots of nooks and crannies, grandfather clock, open fires, big windows to attractive good-sized back garden on two levels (dogs on leads allowed here); children welcome. *(Derek and Sylvia Stephenson, Margaret Wilson)*

UNDERWOOD   SK4751
★ Red Lion   (01773) 810482
Off A608/B600, near M1 junction 27; Church Lane, nearly in Bagthorpe; NG16 5HD Welcoming 18th-c split-level beamed village pub, enjoyable sensibly priced food including set lunch (Mon-Fri), other bargains and good fresh fish (best to book weekends), Jennings Cumberland, Marstons Pedigree and a couple of guests, good soft drinks choice, pleasant helpful service, open-plan quarry-tiled bar with dining area, some cushioned settles, coal-effect gas fire; background music, games machine in lobby; children till 7pm away from bar, dogs welcome, play area in big woodside garden with terrace, barbecues, good nearby walks, open all day Fri-Sun. *(GSB)*

UPTON   SK7354
★ Cross Keys   (01636) 813269
A612; NG23 5SY 17th-c pub in fine spot with rambling, heavy-beamed bar, several alcoves, log fire in brick fireplace, some brass and copper, dark wooden cushioned dining chairs around mix of tables on red and white

floor tiles, Greene King, Wells & Youngs and a guest, tasty bar food (not Mon evening), back extension with long carved pew, live music Sun and Mon; children and dogs (in bar) welcome, plenty of seats on decked terrace, British Horological Institute opposite, open all day Sun. *(Anon)*

WATNALL CHAWORTH   SK5046
★ **Queens Head** (0115) 938 9395

3 miles from M1 junction 26; A610 towards Nottingham, left on B600, then keep right; Main Road; NG16 1HT
Reasonably priced pubby food including good fish and chips (Fri night) in extended 18th-c roadside pub, well kept Adnams, Everards, Greene King, Wells & Youngs and guests, efficient staff, beams and stripped pine, old photographs, grandfather clock, woodburner, intimate snug, plank-ceilinged dining lounge; background and some live music, Mon quiz; children welcome, dogs in bar, flower tubs and a few picnic-sets at front, more tables on back lawn with marquee and play area, beer festivals and barbecues, open all day. *(David and Sue Atkinson)*

WEST BRIDGFORD   SK5838
Larwood & Voce (0115) 981 9960

Fox Road; NG2 6AJ Well run open-plan dining pub (part of the small Moleface group); good locally sourced home-made food in bar and restaurant area including some imaginative choices, plenty of wines by the glass, cocktail menu and three well kept real ales, cheerful staff; sports TV; children welcome away from bar, seats out on raised deck with heaters, on the edge of the cricket ground and handy for Nottingham Forest FC, open all day, from 9am weekends for breakfast. *(David Hunt)*

WEST BRIDGFORD   SK5837
★ **Stratford Haven** (0115) 982 5981

Stratford Road, Trent Bridge; NG2 6BA
Good Tynemill pub; bare-boards front bar leading to linked areas including airy skylit back part with relaxed local atmosphere, their well kept Castle Rock ales plus

Batemans, Everards and six changing guests (monthly brewery nights), exotic bottled beers, farm ciders, ample whiskies and wines, wide range of good value home-made food all day, fast friendly service, daily papers, some live music (nothing loud); dogs welcome, tables outside, handy for cricket ground and Nottingham Forest FC (busy on match days), open all day from 10.30am (midday Sun). *(Andrew Bosi)*

WEST LEAKE   SK5126
Star (01509) 856480

Melton Lane, off A6006; LE12 5RQ
Welcoming old country pub reopened 2012 after major refurbishment but keeping character; good choice of popular food (all day Sat, till 5pm Sun) in opened-up bar or restaurant, well kept Marstons EPA and Pedigree along with Sharps Doom Bar, lots of wines by the glass; children and dogs welcome, picnic-sets out in front, garden behind, open all day. *(Frank Swann)*

WEST STOCKWITH   SK7994
White Hart (01427) 892672

Main Street; DN10 4EY Small recently refurbished country pub at junction of Chesterfield Canal with River Trent, its own good Idle ales from next door brewery, enjoyable good value traditional food, friendly atmosphere, games area with pool, live music Fri; sports TV; children and dogs welcome, garden overlooking water, open all day. *(Anon)*

WYSALL   SK6027
Plough (01509) 880339

Keyworth Road; off A60 at Costock, or A6006 at Wymeswold; NG12 5QQ
Attractive 17th-c beamed village local; popular good value lunchtime food from shortish menu, cheerful staff, Bass, Greene King Abbot, Timothy Taylors Landlord and three guests, rooms either side of bar with nice mix of furnishings, soft lighting, big log fire; french doors to pretty terrace with flower tubs and baskets, open all day. *(Nigel and Sue Foster)*

Post Office address codings confusingly give the impression that a few pubs are in Nottinghamshire, when they're really in Derbyshire (which is where we list them).

Oxfordshire

Strong new entries or places back after some changes include the Plough at Alvescot (tasty food and beers and country garden), Red Lion in Brightwell Salome (interesting food and drinks and a warm welcome), Saye & Sele Arms at Broughton (run by a popular chef-patron), Highway in Burford (comfortable old pub with enjoyable wines and food), Five Alls in Filkins (creative food, attractive bedrooms and friendly staff) and Plough in West Hanney (friendly new licensee for thatched village pub). Pubs our readers feel are on top form include the Olde Reindeer (fine original features in bustling town tavern), Lord Nelson in Brightwell Baldwin (relaxed atmosphere and highly rated drinks and meals), Chequers in Chipping Norton (eight beers and tasty food), Eyston Arms at East Hendred (inventive food and appealing bar areas), Plough in Kingham (accomplished cooking and easy-going atmosphere), Oxford Arms in Kirtlington (super food and an informal atmosphere), Blue Boar at Longworth (cheerful crowd and very popular food), Crown in Pishill (run by caring professional people), Royal Oak in Ramsden (unpretentious, with long-serving owners), Rose & Crown in Shilton (well run all-rounder), Baskerville at Shiplake (consistently enjoyable and a nice place to stay), Masons Arms in Swerford (popular fish and shellfish), Trout at Tadpole Bridge (Thames-side spot with delicious food) and Kings Arms in Woodstock (top class staff, bedrooms and meals). The Trout at Tadpole Bridge is Oxfordshire Dining Pub 2014.

ALVESCOT   SP2704   Map 4

Plough

B4020 Carterton–Clanfield, SW of Witney; OX18 2PU

Neatly kept bar with Wadworths ales, well liked food and colourful hanging baskets

In summer, this pretty stone pub is festooned with hanging baskets and window tubs and there are picnic-sets on the back terrace, a children's play area in the country garden and aunt sally. You'll get a friendly welcome in the neatly kept bar, which has some aircraft and cottagey

prints and pictures, a large poster of Concorde's last flight, house plants
and a woodburning stove. Comfortable seating includes cream, red and
green cushioned dark wooden chairs around dark wooden tables, some
cushioned settles and bar stools (bagged by chatty regulars in the early
evening). Wadworths IPA, 6X and a seasonal beer on handpump. There's
a proper public bar with TV, darts, board games and background music;
skittle alley.

 Tasty food includes sandwiches, trio of fish (salmon mousse, mackerel fillets,
smoked salmon) with potato salad, soup, ham and egg, chicken breast with
stilton, wild mushrooms, bacon and sautéed potatoes, greek salad, beer-battered
fish and chips, and puddings such as eton mess with mixed berries and warm fruit
cake with whisky cream. *Benchmark main dish: chicken and asparagus pie £9.95.
Two-course evening meal £17.00.*

Wadworths ~ Tenants Ian and Liz Summers ~ Real ale ~ (01993) 842281 ~ Open
12-midnight(10.30 Sun) ~ Bar food 12-2.30, 5-8.30; 12-9 Fri-Sun ~ Children welcome ~
Dogs allowed in bar *Recommended by Isobel Mackinlay, Caroline Prescott*

BANBURY   SP4540   Map 4
Olde Reindeer 🍺 £
Parsons Street, off Market Place; OX16 5NA

**Interesting town pub with fine original features, plenty of shoppers
and regulars, real ales and simple food**

There's always a good, bustling atmosphere and plenty of cheerful
customers in this unpretentious town tavern – and the friendly
landlord offers a genuine welcome to all. The front bar has heavy 16th c
beams, very broad polished oak floorboards, a magnificent carved
overmantel for one of the two roaring log fires and traditional solid
furnishings; some interesting breweriana too. It's worth looking at the
handsomely proportioned Globe Room used by Oliver Cromwell as his
base during the Civil War. Quite a sight, it still has very fine carved 17th-c
dark oak panelling. Hook Norton Hooky Bitter, Hooky Dark, Old Hooky,
Hooky Mild and a changing guest beer on handpump, wines by the glass
and several malt whiskies; maybe background music. The little back
courtyard has tables and benches under parasols, aunt sally and pretty
flowering baskets.

 Honest, fair value food includes sandwiches, pâté, whitebait, venison burger
with chips and salad, beer-battered fish, vegetable lasagne, steak in ale pie,
cumberland sausages with gravy in a big yorkshire pudding, daily specials like
chicken kiev with brie, and pudding. *Benchmark main dish: ham, egg and bubble
and squeak £6.95. Two-course evening meal £14.00.*

Hook Norton ~ Tenant Jeremy Money ~ Real ale ~ (01295) 264031 ~ Open 11-11
(midnight Fri, Sat); 12-11 Sun ~ Bar food 11-4, 6-9 ~ Children welcome ~ Dogs welcome
~ www.yeoldereindeer.co.uk *Recommended by Andy Dolan, Clive and Fran Dutson, Andy
Lickfold, Ben Weedon, Richard Stanfield*

BESSELS LEIGH   SP4501   Map 4
Greyhound 🍴 🍺
A420 Faringdon–Botley; OX13 5PX

**Handsome 400-year-old stone pub with knocked-through rooms,
plenty of character and interest, half a dozen real ales, lots of wines
by the glass and enjoyable interesting food**

There's always a cheerful crowd of both locals and visitors in this 400-year-old Cotswold-stone inn, and all are warmly welcomed by the efficient and friendly staff. The knocked-through rooms create plenty of space and the half-panelled walls are covered in all manner of old photographs and pictures. The individually chosen cushioned dining chairs, leather-topped stools and dark wooden tables are grouped on carpeting or rug-covered floorboards, and there are books on shelves, glass and stone bottles on window sills, big gilt mirrors, three fireplaces (one with a woodburning stove) and sizeable pot plants. Wooden bar stools sit against the counter where they serve Phoenix Brunning & Price Original, Hook Norton Hooky Bitter, White Horse Wayland Smithy and guest beers such as Hook Norton Cotswold Lion and Three Castles Barbury Castle and Wilder & Milder on handpump, 15 wines by the glass and 80 malt whiskies. By the back dining extension there's a white picket fence-enclosed garden with picnic-sets under green parasols.

Popular and extremely good, the food includes sandwiches, pork, apricot and pistachio terrine with apple, celery and grape salad, scallops with saffron cauliflower purée, crispy bacon, tempura samphire and rhubarb dressing, bouillabaisse, sausages with mash and red wine and onion gravy, mediterranean vegetable lasagne, irish lamb stew with rosemary dumplings, chicken breast with wild mushroom and tarragon tagliatelle, orange and rosemary-marinated duck breast with fondant potatoes and cherry and port sauce, plum- and cider-braised pig cheeks with honey-roast parsnips, and puddings such as raspberry cheesecake with mixed berry compote and spiced ginger pudding with custard. *Benchmark main dish: beer-battered haddock and chips £10.95. Two-course evening meal £20.00.*

Brunning & Price ~ Manager Peter Palfi ~ Real ale ~ (01865) 862110 ~ Open 12-11 (10.30 Sun) ~ Bar food 12-10(9.30 Sun) ~ Children welcome ~ Dogs allowed in bar ~ www.greyhound-besselsleigh.co.uk *Recommended by David Jackman, Taff Thomas, Derek Goldrei, N R White, William Goodhart, Paul Humphreys*

BRIGHTWELL BALDWIN   SU6594 Map 4
Lord Nelson 🍴 ♀

Off B480 Chalgrove–Watlington, or B4009 Benson–Watlington; OX49 5NP

Attractive inn with several different character bars, real ales, good wines by the glass and enjoyable well thought-of food; bedrooms

'Sunday wouldn't be Sunday without a trip here,' one loyal reader tells us. Although the emphasis is on the particularly good food, the relaxed atmosphere makes this 300-year-old inn just as popular for a drink and a chat. There are wheelback and other dining chairs around a mix of dark tables, candles and fresh flowers, wine bottles on window sills, horsebrasses on standing timbers, lots of paintings on the white or red walls and a big brick inglenook fireplace. One cosy room has cushions on comfortable sofas, little lamps on dark furniture, ornate mirrors and portraits in gilt frames; background music. Black Sheep, Rebellion IPA and Sharps Doom Bar on handpump, around 14 wines (including champagne) by the glass and winter mulled wine. The back terrace has seats and tables with more in the willow-draped garden; the village church is opposite.

Using fresh local produce, the good food includes sandwiches, chicken liver and pistachio parfait with chutney, haddock and crab fishcakes on pea purée, free-range pork sausages on wholegrain mustard mash with red onion gravy, wild mushroom, squash and blue cheese bake, calves liver and bacon on champ mash with red wine sauce, beer-battered fresh haddock with triple-cooked chips, pork medallions on glazed apples with madeira sauce, and puddings such as chocolate and nut brownie and apple, sultana and cinnamon crumble. *Benchmark main dish: half roast duck with spiced plum sauce £18.95. Two-course evening meal £23.00.*

Free house ~ Licensees Roger and Carole Shippey ~ Real ale ~ (01491) 612497 ~ Open 12-3, 6-11; 12-10.30 Sun ~ Bar food 12-2.30, 6-10; 12-4, 7-9.30 Sun ~ Restaurant ~ Children welcome ~ Dogs allowed in bar ~ Bedrooms: £70/£90 ~ www.lordnelson-inn.co.uk
Recommended by Dave Braisted, Richard Endacott, Roy Hoing, Torrens Lyster

BRITWELL SALOME
Red Lion 🍴

SU6793   Map 4

B4009 Watlington–Benson; OX49 5LG

Interesting landlord-cooked food in handsome village pub, thoughtful choice of drinks and friendly welcome

Run by extremely good, hands-on licensees, this brick and flint pub has been recently refurbished. They've created an easy-going, friendly atmosphere that attracts drinkers and diners from the village and further afield. The bar has comfortable sofas, pews with scatter cushions and all sorts of dining chairs around various tables and they keep West Berkshire Mr Chubbs and Gundog Jack's Spaniels on handpump, 13 wines by the glass, unusual gins and seasonal cordials; two dining rooms lead off and there are red-painted walls, open fires (one with antlers above the mantelpiece) and lots of church candles throughout. There are seats in a courtyard garden.

 Using local seasonal produce and cooked by the landlord, the interesting food includes sandwiches, enterprising nibbles such as black pudding scotch egg and lincolnshire poacher with chilli pineapple, and meals such as trout with grapefruit, cucumber and fennel, couscous with feta, pickled vegetables and mint yoghurt, duck hearts with balsamic vinegar and truffle oil, allium tart with roasted red peppers and rocket, beer-battered fish and chips, grilled lemon sole with caper butter, pork T-bone with carrot and rosemary purée and hispi cabbage, daily specials, and puddings; they also offer a £10 weekday lunch. *Benchmark main dish: local mutton burger with chilli and mint and cumin chips £13.50. Two-course evening meal £20.00.*

Free house ~ Licensees Eilidh Ferguson and Andrew Hill ~ Real ale ~ (01491) 613140 ~ Open 12-3, 6(5.30 Sat)-11; 12-5 Sun; closed Sun evening, Mon, Tues lunchtime ~ Bar food 12-2, 6-9; 12-3 Sun ~ Restaurant ~ Children welcome ~ Dogs welcome ~ www.theredlionbritwellsalome.co.uk *Recommended by Jane Taylor and David Dutton, Jackie Martin and Andy Norris, David and Stella Martin, Torrens Lyster, David Lamb*

BROUGHTON
Saye & Sele Arms 🍺

SP4238   Map 4

B4035 SW of Banbury; OX15 5ED

Smartly furnished golden stone pub with attentive service, four ales, good food cooked by the landlord and seats in the pretty garden

Handy for Broughton Castle, which is just five minutes away, this 16th-c pub has been recently redecorated. The sizeable bar has polished flagstones, cushioned window seats, dark wooden furnishings and a few brasses, plus Adnams Bitter, North Cotswold Windrush, Sharps Doom Bar and a guest beer on handpump, nine wines by the glass and a dozen malt whiskies; friendly service. The two carpeted dining rooms have exposed stone walls, open fires, over 240 ornate water jugs hanging from the beams, and blue-cushioned mate's chairs around tables set with neat napkins. There are picnic-sets and hanging baskets on the terrace, tables and chairs under parasols on the neat lawn and a pergola and smokers' shelter; aunt sally.

🍴 Cooked by the landlord, the popular food includes lunchtime sandwiches, deep-fried whitebait with tartare sauce, chicken liver and port pâté, roasted vegetable lasagne, ham and eggs, jumbo sausages with mash and onion gravy, poached salmon with shallot, white wine, tarragon and mushroom sauce, specials like confit duckling on apple mash with green peppercorn sauce or bass fillet on tomato and herb concasse with lemon and garlic butter, and puddings such as baked alaska and bread and butter pudding; Wednesday is steak night. *Benchmark main dish: home-made pies £13.95. Two-course evening meal £20.50.*

Free house ~ Licensees Danny and Liz McGeehan ~ Real ale ~ (01295) 263348 ~ Open 10.30-2.30(3 Sat), 7-11; 12-5 Sun; closed Sun evening ~ Bar food 12-2, 7-9; 12-3 Sun ~ Restaurant ~ Children welcome ~ www.sayeandselearms.co.uk
Recommended by P and J Shapley, Martin Jones

BURFORD   SP2512 Map 4
Highway 🛏
High Street (A361); OX18 4RG

Comfortable old inn overlooking this honeypot village's main street, a good choice of wines and well liked bar food; bedrooms

The main feature in the bar of this 15th-c inn is the pair of big windows overlooking the bustle of the High Street; each is made up of several dozen panes of old float glass and has a long cushioned window seat. There are all sorts of other interesting touches too, such as the stag candlesticks set on tables on well worn floorboards, the neat modern dark leather chairs, the Cecil Aldin hunting prints, the careful balance of ancient stripped stone with black and pale blue filigree wallpaper and the nice old station clock above a big log fire in the attractively simple stone fireplace. A small corner counter has Hook Norton Best and a guest such as Wye Valley Dorothy Goodbodys Golden Ale on handpump and a dozen wines including champagne and sparkling wines by the glass; background music and board games. On the right, a second bar room, with another big window seat, is carpeted but otherwise similar in style; there's also a cellar restaurant. There are picnic-sets under parasols on the front pavement.

🍴 Making their own bread and marmalade, the popular food includes lunchtime sandwiches, potted cornish crab with melba toast, fricassée of wild mushrooms with garlic cream, beer-battered fish and chips, braised beef with smoked bacon dumplings, risotto of the day, slow-cooked smoked pork belly with roast garlic mash, spinach and apple jus, fish dish of the day, confit duck with dauphinoise potatoes, pak choi, crispy leeks and balsamic onions, and puddings such as spiced apple and walnut crumble and warm chocolate and hazelnut brownie with rum and raisin ice-cream. *Benchmark main dish: rack of ribs with barbecue sauce, coleslaw and chips £16.50. Two-course evening meal £20.00.*

Free house ~ Licensees Scott and Tally Nelson ~ Real ale ~ (01993) 823661 ~ Open 12-11 ~ Bar food 12-2.30(3 Sun), 6.30-9(9.30 Fri, Sat) ~ Restaurant ~ Children welcome ~ Dogs allowed in bar and bedrooms ~ Bedrooms: £85/£89 ~ www.thehighwayinn.co.uk
Recommended by Martin Jones, Caroline Prescott

BURFORD

Lamb 🍴 🍺 🛏️

SP2412　Map 4

Village signposted off A40 W of Oxford; Sheep Street (B4425, off A361); OX18 4LR

Proper pubby bar in civilised inn, with real ales, an extensive wine list, interesting bar and restaurant food and pretty gardens; bedrooms

Thankfully, the cosy bar in this lovely 15th-c inn remains the heart of the place, and the atmosphere is civilised but relaxed and friendly. There are high-backed settles and old chairs on flagstones in front of a log fire, Hook Norton Hooky Bitter and Wickwar Cotswold Way on handpump, an extensive wine list with 20 by the glass and 15 malt whiskies; background music. The roomy beamed main lounge is charmingly traditional, with distinguished old seats including a chintzy high-winged settle, ancient cushioned wooden armchairs, and seats built into stone-mullioned windows; fresh flowers on polished oak and elm tables, rugs on wide flagstones and polished oak floorboards, a winter log fire under a fine mantelpiece, and plenty of antiques and other decorations including a grandfather clock. Service is impeccable. A pretty terrace with teak furniture leads down to small neatly kept lawns surrounded by flowers, shrubs and small trees. The garden is a real suntrap, enclosed by the warm stone of the surrounding buildings.

🍴 Quite a choice of enjoyable food includes open sandwiches, deli boards, eggs benedict, scallops and black pudding, chicken caesar salad, steak burger topped with blue cheese, sausages with mash and onion gravy, pasta with ratatouille sauce, game pie with confit red onion, bass with saffron risotto and pesto cream, and puddings such as chocolate tart with coffee ice-cream and apple and cinnamon crumble with custard; they also offer a two- and three-course set menu and afternoon tea. *Benchmark main dish: slow-cooked confit duck leg with sautéed potatoes £14.95. Two-course evening meal £20.50.*

Cotswold Inns & Hotels ~ Manager Bill Ramsay ~ Real ale ~ (01993) 823155 ~ Open 11-11 ~ Bar food 12-9.30 ~ Restaurant ~ Children welcome ~ Dogs welcome ~ Bedrooms: £150/£160 ~ www.cotswold-inns-hotels.co.uk/lamb *Recommended by Alistair Forsyth, D L Frostick, George Atkinson, David Glynne-Jones, David Carr*

CAULCOTT

Horse & Groom 🍺

SP5024　Map 4

Lower Heyford Road (B4030); OX25 4ND

Obliging licensee for small cottagey pub, three local ales and a choice of bar food

Thatched and pretty, this is a 16th-c cottage with a french chef-patron. It's not huge – an L-shaped red-carpeted room angles around the servery, with a blazing fire in a big inglenook (brassware under its long bressumer beam) and plush-cushioned settles, chairs and stools around a few dark tables at the low-ceilinged bar end. White Horse Bitter and a couple of guest ales on handpump and decent house wines; shove-ha'penny and board games. The far end, up a shallow step, is set for dining and has lots of decorative jugs hanging on black joists, china plates and attractive watercolours and original drawings. There's a small sun lounge to the side, and picnic-sets under cocktail parasols on the neat lawn.

As well as a dozen different sausages, the food includes baguettes, rabbit terrine with baby onion chutney, grilled sardines with peppercorn dressing, omelettes made with free-range eggs, burgers with bacon and cheese, trio of cheese with risotto, rump of local lamb with red wine and olive sauce, seared beef fillet with rossini sauce, and puddings such as crème brûlée and ginger pudding with caramelised bananas and toffee ice-cream. *Benchmark main dish: speciality sausages £9.95. Two-course evening meal £19.00.*

Free house ~ Licensee Jerome Prigent ~ Real ale ~ (01869) 343257 ~ Open 12-3, 6-11; 12-3, 7-10.30 Sun; closed Mon evening ~ Bar food 12-2, 7-9; not Sun evening or Mon ~ Children must be over 5 and well behaved ~ www.horseandgroomcaulcott.co.uk
Recommended by John Taylor, R J Herd, David Lamb, Dave Braisted, Tony Hobden

 CHIPPING NORTON   SP3127   Map 4
Chequers ★
Goddards Lane; OX7 5NP

Busy, friendly town pub open all day with several real ales, tasty bar food, a cheerful mix of customers and simple bars

Although this cheerful town pub is a proper local, the friendly licensees extend a genuine welcome to visitors too. The three softly lit beamed rooms have no frills, but are clean and comfortable with low ochre ceilings, a blazing log fire and lots of character. Efficient staff serve up to eight real ales on handpump: Fullers Chiswick, Discovery, ESB, HSB, London Pride and Seafarers Ale, and a couple of changing seasonal guest beers. They also have good house wines, and 15 by the glass. The light and airy conservatory restaurant is used for more formal dining. The town's theatre is next door.

 As well as efficiently served pre-theatre suppers, the popular bar food includes sandwiches, mini crab cakes with chilli and lime dressing, black pudding and bacon salad with roast tomato vinaigrette, chilli con carne, wild mushroom risotto, honey and cider-roast ham with free-range eggs, sausages with mash and onion gravy, burger with home-made relish, cheese and chips, pie of the day, chicken breast with white wine and tarragon sauce, and puddings such as chocolate coconut brownie and lemon cheesecake. *Benchmark main dish: beer-battered haddock with peas and tartare sauce £10.00. Two-course evening meal £15.00.*

Fullers ~ Lease Jim Hopcroft ~ Real ale ~ (01608) 644717 ~ Open 11-11(midnight Sat); 11.30-11 Sun ~ Bar food 12-2.30, 6-9.30; 12-4 Sun ~ Restaurant ~ Children welcome ~ Dogs allowed in bar ~ www.chequers-pub.com *Recommended by Guy Vowles, Richard Tilbrook, P and J Shapley,*

 CLIFTON   SP4931   Map 4
Duke of Cumberlands Head
B4031 Deddington–Aynho; OX15 0PE

Cosy bars with beams, a big log fire, good food and a short walk to canal; cosy good value bedrooms

Readers enjoy staying overnight at this thatched, golden-stone former coaching inn where the bedrooms are very reasonably priced; breakfasts are continental. A friendly place with an easy-going atmosphere, it has beams in low ceilings, rugs on bare boards, an attractive mix of dining chairs and settles around nice old tables, church candles, paintings on exposed stone walls and a good log fire in a vast inglenook fireplace. Hook Norton Hooky Bitter and guests like Ramsbury Gold and Sharps Doom Bar on handpump and several wines by the glass; background music. There are a couple of picnic-sets out in front, good quality seats and tables under parasols on the sunny back terrace, and the Oxford Canal is close by.

Good, popular food includes sandwiches, ham hock terrine with apple and cider chutney, prawn and shrimp cocktail, vegetable ragout linguine, pie of the day, chicken supreme with pea risotto, beer-battered fish and chips, duo of duck with black cherry liqueur sauce, pork chops with black pudding mash and cider and apple jus, grilled monkfish with carrot purée and cauliflower almond butter, and puddings such as crumble of the day and lemon pistachio cake with pistachio ice-cream. *Benchmark main dish: braised brisket of beef with bourguignon sauce £14.95. Two-course evening meal £19.50.*

Free house ~ Licensee Alan Newman ~ Real ale ~ (01869) 338534 ~ Open 12-11 ~ Bar food 12-2.30(3 weekends), 6.30-9.30(6-9 Sun) ~ Restaurant ~ Children welcome ~ Dogs welcome ~ Bedrooms: /£45 ~ www.cliftonduke.com *Recommended by David Jackman*

EAST HENDRED   SU4588 Map 2
Eyston Arms 🍴
Village signposted off A417 E of Wantage; High Street; OX12 8JY

Attractive bar areas with low beams, flagstones, log fires and candles, imaginative food and helpful service

Although it's the inventive food that draws most customers to this well run dining pub, there are a few tables for drinkers and seats at the bar and locals do pop in for a chat and a pint of Hook Norton Hooky Bitter or Wadworths 6X on handpump; several wines by the glass too. A busy, welcoming place, it has several separate-seeming areas with contemporary paintwork and modern country-style furnishings. Also, low ceilings and beams, stripped timbers, the occasional standing timber, an inglenook fireplace, nice tables and chairs on flagstones and carpet, some cushioned wall seats and candlelight; background music. Picnic-sets outside overlook the pretty lane and there are seats in the back courtyard garden.

Imaginative food includes sandwiches, chicken and black pudding terrine with pickled mushrooms, wild garlic pesto and smoked salmon fettuccine with toasted pine nuts, oxford blue and leek bread and butter pudding with apple, walnut and fennel salad, crispy rosemary and chilli-salted poussin with aioli and string chips, lamb rump with potato tartlet, spinach purée and warm broad bean, artichoke and cherry tomato dressing, and puddings such as elderflower and berry jelly with mint mascarpone and caramel custard with home-made gingerbread. *Benchmark main dish: scallop and king prawn spaghetti with bouillabaisse sauce £19.95. Two-course evening meal £22.00.*

Free house ~ Licensees George Dailey and Daisy Barton ~ Real ale ~ (01235) 833320 ~ Open 12-3, 6-11; 12-11 Fri, Sat; 11.30-11 Sun ~ Bar food 12-2, 7-9; 12-9 Fri, Sat; 11.30-3 Sun ~ Restaurant ~ Children over 8 welcome ~ Dogs allowed in bar ~ www.eystonarms.co.uk *Recommended by Dan Rooms, Caroline Prescott*

> Stars after the name of a pub show exceptional quality. One star means most people (after reading the report to see just why the star has been won) would think a special trip worthwhile. Two stars mean that the pub is really outstanding – for its particular qualities it could hardly be bettered.

FILKINS
Five Alls ⛨

SP2304   Map 4

Signed off A361 Lechlade–Burford; GL7 3JQ

**Carefully refurbished inn with creative food, thoughtful choice
of drinks, friendly welcome and seats outside; bedrooms**

Under its present landlord, this partly creeper-covered stone inn is
going from strength to strength. The cosy beamed bar has leather
chesterfields around a low rustic table in front of an open fire, church
candles in glass jars, a cushioned window seat and Brakspears Bitter
and Oxford Gold, Wychwood Hobgoblin and a beer named for the pub
on handpump, 16 wines by the glass, a dozen malt whiskies and
cocktails; service is warmly friendly and helpful. The dining rooms have
stripped-stone walls or half-panelling, an appealing variety of dining
chairs around tables on flagstones or floorboards and a chandelier;
background music and board games. There are chunky tables and chairs
under parasols on a back terrace, and a few picnic-sets at the front.
Bedrooms are comfortable and well equipped.

🍴 Using local, seasonal produce and cooked by the landlord, the impressive
food includes sandwiches, carpaccio of line-caught tuna with avocado, ginger,
lime and coriander dressing, a sharing plate of antipasti and cured meats, gruyère,
caramelised onion and sage tart, cassoulet of toulouse sausage and confit duck,
steak and kidney pie, guinea fowl two-ways with wild mushrooms, garlic leaves,
broad beans and rösti potato, stuffed saddle of rabbit en croûte with black pudding
and apple, and puddings such as chocolate, honeycomb and Grand Marnier mousse
and chargrilled banana with butterscotch and vanilla ice-cream. *Benchmark main
dish: cracked pork with fricassée of mushrooms and jerusalem artichokes £16.00.
Two-course evening meal £22.00.*

Free house ~ Licensee Sebastian Snow ~ Real ale ~ (01367) 860875 ~ Open 12-11; 12-9
Sun ~ Bar food 12-2.30, 6-9.30(10 Sat); 12-3 Sun ~ Restaurant ~ Children welcome ~
Dogs welcome ~ Bedrooms: £95/£110 ~ www.thefiveallsfilkins.co.uk
Recommended by Mr and Mrs A H Young

HEADINGTON
Black Boy

SP5407   Map 4

*Old High Street/St Andrews Road; off A420 at traffic lights opposite B4495;
OX3 9HT*

**Stylish and enterprising dining pub with good, enjoyable food,
and useful summer garden**

This modern dining pub has a cool contemporary look with black
leather seating on dark parquet, big mirrors, silvery patterned
wallpaper, nightlights in tall opaque cylinders and glittering bottles
behind a long bar counter. It's light and airy, particularly the two tables
in the big bay window; just to the side is an open fire, with softer lower
seats by it. Crisp white tablecloths and bold black and white wallpaper
lend the area on the left a touch of formality. Changing weekly, the
beers might include Everards Tiger and a guest from Greene King on
handpump, and there's a good choice of wines by the glass and several

People named as recommenders after the full entries have told us that the pub
should be included. But they have not written the report – we have, after anonymous
on-the-spot inspection.

coffees and teas. The appealing back terrace has picnic-sets beneath alternating black or white parasols on smart pale stone chippings, and a central seat encircling an ash tree.

🍴 Interesting food includes lunchtime sandwiches, chicken liver and foie gras parfait with chutney, beer-battered fish and chips, gnocchi with roasted tomato and basil sauce, seafood linguine with creamy white wine sauce, sausage and mash with beer and onion gravy, chicken stuffed with creamed leeks and mushroom mousse with sautéed potatoes, specials like braised lamb shoulder with red wine jus or bass with lemon and parsley butter, and puddings such as bakewell tart with blueberry filling and home-made blueberry ice-cream and dark chocolate brownie with chocolate ganache and mint chocolate ice-cream. *Benchmark main dish: chicken kiev with chips £14.95. Two-course evening meal £20.00.*

Greene King ~ Lease Abi Rose and Chris Bentham ~ Real ale ~ (01865) 741137 ~ Open 12-3, 5-11 ~ Bar food 12-2.45, 6-9.15 ~ Children welcome ~ www.theblackboy.uk.com
Recommended by Richard and Penny Gibbs, David Bull

KINGHAM   SP2624   Map 4

Plough 🍴 ♀ 🛏

Village signposted off B4450 E of Bledington; or turn S off A436 at staggered crossroads a mile SW of A44 junction – or take signed Daylesford turn off A436 and keep on; The Green; OX7 6YD

Friendly dining pub combining an informal pub atmosphere with upmarket food; bedrooms

This bustling place is more of a dining pub-with-rooms, but it does offer snacks as well as top class restaurant meals, and has a properly pubby bar too. The latter has nice old high-backed settles and brightly cushioned chapel chairs on broad dark boards, candles on stripped tables and cheerful farmyard animal and country prints; at one end is a big log fire, at the other (by an unusual cricket table) a woodburning stove. There's a piano in one corner and a snug one-table area opposite the servery, which has Butcombe Bitter and Hook Norton Hooky Bitter on handpump, good wines by the glass, home-made cordials, local cider and some interesting liqueurs. The fairly spacious and raftered two-part dining room is up a few steps. The bedrooms are comfortable and the breakfasts very good. There's a heated smokers' shelter at the back.

🍴 Headed by chef-owner Emily Watkins and using local, seasonal produce, the accomplished food might include snacks (such as home-made venison salami with pickled onions or snails and mushrooms on toast) as well as cornish clam and white bean stew with tomato and wild garlic, smoked pig cheeks with asparagus and poached pheasant egg, hereford burger with cheese, triple-cooked chips and home-made ketchup, steak and mushroom in ale pie, lamb wellington with baby carrots, cod with scotch salt cod egg, asparagus and morels with hollandaise, steak of the day such as skirt with bone marrow butter and onion rings, and puddings like rhubarb lardy cake with rhubarb ice-cream and milk chocolate and salted caramel pot with peanut butter ice-cream; also, good local cheeses with home-made apple jelly, oatcakes and hazelnut fruit bread. *Benchmark main dish: steak of the day £19.00. Two-course evening meal £26.00.*

Free house ~ Licensees Emily Watkins and Miles Lampson ~ Real ale ~ (01608) 658327 ~ Open 12-11(midnight Sat, 10.30 Sun) ~ Bar food 12-2, 6.30-9 (light snacks all day); 12-3, 6-9 Sat; only light snacks Sun evening ~ Restaurant ~ Children welcome ~ Dogs allowed in bar and bedrooms ~ Bedrooms: /£90 ~ www.thekinghamplough.co.uk
Recommended by David Glynne-Jones, Jenny Smith, William Goodhart, Andy and Jill Kassube, Bernard Stradling

KINGSTON LISLE

SU3287 Map 4

Blowing Stone 🍴 ♀ 🍺

Village signposted off B4507 W of Wantage; OX12 9QL

Easy-going chatty country pub with up-to-date blend of simple comfort and good interesting food and drink

Close to the Ridgeway and Uffington White Horse, this friendly village pub is just the place to head for after a walk. This is racehorse country, so you'll find the *Racing Post* alongside other daily papers, lots of photographs of racehorses on the pale sage walls, often spectacularly coming to grief over jumps, and broad tiles by the log fire which suit the muddy riding boots of the cheerful young people in from nearby training stables. Several separate areas radiate off from the central bar, most of them carpeted, quite small and snug, though a back dining conservatory is more spacious. Apart from a couple of high-backed winged settles, the furniture is mainly an unfussy mix of country dining tables each with its own set of matching chairs, either padded or generously cushioned. Greene King Morland Original, Ramsbury Bitter and Sharps Doom Bar on handpump and ten decent wines by the glass; service is attentive and there may be unobtrusive background music. The pretty front terrace has a couple of picnic-sets under cocktail parasols, with more on the back lawn by a rockery.

 As well as a very good value two-course weekday set lunch and Sunday evening pizzas from a wood-fired oven, the enjoyable food includes sandwiches, fresh crab with tomato salad and curried mayonnaise, sautéed lambs kidneys with wild mushrooms on toast, antipasti and meze platters, vegetable and mixed bean chilli with cheese nachos, beer-battered haddock and chips, steak burger with cheese, bacon and onion rings, pork fillet with apricot and almond sauce and lemon and herb couscous, salmon with pink ginger and cream tagliatelle, specials such as cornish seafood medley with bisque sauce and crab or king prawn and chilli linguine, and puddings such as raspberry crème brûlée and profiteroles with chocolate sauce. *Benchmark main dish: prosciutto-wrapped chicken breast stuffed with sunblush tomato and pesto butter with ratatouille £14.95. Two-course evening meal £21.50.*

Free house ~ Licensees Angus and Steph Tucker ~ Real ale ~ (01367) 820288 ~ Open 12-midnight(11pm Sun) ~ Bar food 12-2, 6.30-9; not Sun evening (except summer Sun for freshly made pizzas) ~ Restaurant ~ Children welcome ~ Dogs allowed in bar ~ www.theblowingstone.co.uk *Recommended by Emma Scofield, Martin Jones*

KIRTLINGTON

SP4919 Map 4

Oxford Arms 🍴 ♀

Troy Lane, junction with A4095 W of Bicester; OX5 3HA

Civilised and friendly stripped-stone pub with enjoyable food using local produce and good wine choice

Next to the post office in a lovely village, this is a neatly kept and deservedly popular stone pub, where you can be sure of a friendly welcome from the chef-landlord and his courteous staff. A long line of linked rooms is divided by a central stone hearth with a great round stove, and by the servery itself – where you'll find Brakspears Oxford Gold and St Austell Tribute on handpump, an interesting range of 16 wines in two glass sizes, 15 malt whiskies, farm cider and organic soft drinks. Past the bar area with its cushioned wall pews, creaky beamed ceiling and age-darkened floor tiles, dining tables on parquet have neat red chairs, and beyond that leather sofas cluster round a log fire at the end; also, church candles, fresh flowers and plenty of stripped stone. A sheltered back terrace has teak tables under giant parasols with heaters, and beyond are picnic-sets on pale gravel; the geranium-filled window boxes are pretty.

Highly enjoyable and well prepared using local produce, the food might include lunchtime sandwiches, potted shrimps, devilled lambs kidneys on toast, salmon and prawn fishcakes with sweet chilli sauce, wild mushroom tagliatelle with parmesan and truffle oil, warm pigeon, black pudding and bacon salad, salmon and prawn fishcakes with sweet chilli sauce, breaded plaice fillets with tartare sauce, pork belly with black pudding and puy lentils, lamb and vegetable pie with champ, 28-day aged sirloin steak and triple-cooked chips with mustard and horseradish butter, and puddings such as chocolate Grand Marnier mousse with raspberries and warm treacle tart with white chocolate ice-cream. *Benchmark main dish: venison burger with triple-cooked chips and chutney £13.00. Two-course evening meal £20.00.*

Punch ~ Lease Bryn Jones ~ Real ale ~ (01869) 350208 ~ Open 12-3, 6-11; 12-3 Sun; closed Sun evening ~ Bar food 12-2.30, 6.30-9.30; 12-2.30 Sun ~ Restaurant ~ Well behaved children welcome ~ Dogs allowed in bar ~ www.oxford-arms.co.uk
Recommended by Veronica Hall, Jamie and Sue May, Simon Thomas, Ian Herdman, Val and Alan Green, Ian Wilson, N R White, John Evans, Tony Hobden

LANGFORD
Bell 🍴 🍷 ☕   SP2402   Map 4

Village signposted off A361 N of Lechlade, then pub signed; GL7 3LF

Civilised pub with beams, flagstones and log fire, friendly service, well chosen wines and beer and extremely good food

New licensees took over this bustling pub as we went to press and are planning some refurbishments. The main bar has just six sanded-down tables on grass matting, a variety of chairs, three nice cushioned window seats, an attractive carved oak settle, polished broad flagstones by a big stone inglenook fireplace with a good log fire, low beams and butter-coloured walls with two or three antique engravings. A second smaller room on the right is similar in character; daily papers on a little corner table. Hook Norton Hooky Bitter, Sharps Cornish Coaster and St Austell Tribute on handpump and 11 wines by the glass. The bearded collie is called Madison. There are two or three picnic-sets in the small garden with a play house; aunt sally. The village is quiet and charming.

Good food has included sandwiches, pigeon breast with gnocchi and apple, sage and onion dressing, seared king scallops with chorizo and pancetta, steak and kidney pie, calves liver with bacon, bubble and squeak and spinach, nut roast with tomato and basil sauce, slow-cooked pork belly with root vegetables and swede mash, cornish cod with tomatoes, mushrooms and lemon and pesto dressing, and puddings such as iced mango parfait with caramelised bananas and passion-fruit and mango salsa and treacle tart with ice-cream. *Benchmark main dish: smoked haddock with poached egg, spinach and mustard and leek mash £13.95. Two-course evening meal £19.50.*

Free house ~ Licensees David Kyte and Nicholas Brentnall ~ Real ale ~ (01367) 860249 ~ Open 12-3, 7-11(6-midnight Fri); 12-3, 7-11.30 Sat; 12-3.30 Sun; closed Sun evening, Mon ~ Bar food 12-1.45, 7-9; not Sun evening ~ Restaurant ~ Children welcome but no under-4s after 7pm ~ Dogs allowed in bar ~ www.bellatlangford.co.uk *Recommended by D C T and E A Frewer, Bernard Stradling, Sue Callard, Chris Fagence, Mrs Dawn Dunleavy*

LONGWORTH

SU3899 Map 4

Blue Boar 🍴

Tucks Lane; OX13 5ET

Smashing old pub with a friendly welcome for all, good wines and beer, and fairly priced reliable food; Thames-side walks nearby

Locals dropping in for a chat and a drink, weekend family groups and plenty of visitors – all help create a bustling, easy-going atmosphere in this well run village pub. The three low-beamed, characterful small rooms are properly traditional with well worn fixtures and furnishings and two blazing log fires (the one by the bar is noteworthy). Brasses, hops and assorted knick-knacks such as skis and an old clocking-in machine line the ceilings and walls, there are fresh flowers on the bar, and scrubbed wooden tables and faded rugs on the tiled floor; benches are wooden, not upholstered. The red-painted room at the end is the main eating area, but there's a quieter restaurant extension too. Brakspears Bitter, Sharps Doom Bar and a guest ale on handpump, 20 malt whiskies and a dozen wines by the glass. There are tables out in front and on the back terrace, and the Thames is a short walk away.

🍴 Popular food includes all-day pizzas, lunchtime sandwiches, haggis fritters with beetroot relish, smoked salmon and prawn terrine with cucumber yoghurt, chargrilled herb polenta, toasted goats cheese, confit tomatoes and beetroot pesto, steak, kidney and Guinness stew with sage and onion dumplings, mixed seafood and chilli linguine, malaysian chicken curry, vanilla-glazed duck breast with crispy leg, carrot and anise purée and rosemary-roasted plums, and puddings. *Benchmark main dish: burger with bacon, choice of cheese and string fries £10.95. Two-course evening meal £19.50.*

Free house ~ Licensee Paul Dailey ~ Real ale ~ (01865) 820494 ~ Open 11.30-11 (midnight Sat); 12-11 Sun ~ Bar food 12-2.30, 6.30-9.30(10 Fri, Sat); 12-3, 6.30-9 Sun; limited menu in afternoon ~ Restaurant ~ Children welcome ~ Dogs allowed in bar ~ www.blueboarlongworth.co.uk *Recommended by Franklyn Roberts, David Fowler, Tim Maddison, Dick and Madeleine Brown*

MINSTER LOVELL

SP3211 Map 4

Old Swan & Minster Mill 🍴 🍷 🛏

Just N of B4047 Witney–Burford; OX29 0RN

Carefully restored ancient inn with old-fashioned bar, real ales, a fine wine list, pubby and more elaborate food and acres of gardens and grounds; exceptional bedrooms

The emphasis at this lovely ancient inn is on the hotel and restaurant side – but at its heart is an unchanging and restful little bar, which has stools at an old wooden counter: Brakspears Bitter and Oxford Gold and Wychwood Hobgoblin on handpump, several wines by the glass from a fine list, 23 malt whiskies and quite a choice of teas and coffees. Leading off here are several attractive low-beamed rooms with big log fires in huge fireplaces, red and green leather tub chairs, all manner of comfortable armchairs, sofas, dining chairs and wooden tables, rugs on bare boards or ancient flagstones, antiques, prints and lots of horsebrasses, bed-warming pans, swords, hunting horns and even a suit of armour; fresh flowers everywhere. Seats are dotted around the 65 acres of grounds (the white metal ones beside the water are much prized) and they have a mile of fishing on the River Windrush, tennis courts, boules and croquet. The bedrooms have plenty of character and some are luxurious.

🍴 Using produce from their kitchen garden and other local, seasonal ingredients, the excellent food might include doorstep sandwiches, duck terrine with aged port dressing, king scallops with white pudding and watercress sauce, chicken caesar salad, butternut squash and sage risotto with truffle oil, steak in ale pie, trio of local sausages with mash and onion gravy, burger with bacon, cheese, triple-cooked chips and home-made relish, rack of lamb with wild garlic, rosemary and redcurrant jus, and puddings such as baked alaska with berry coulis and warm chocolate fondant with hot chocolate sauce. *Benchmark main dish: beer-battered haddock with triple-cooked chips, minted mushy peas and home-made tartare sauce £16.00. Two-course evening meal £24.00.*

Free house ~ Licensee Ian Solkin ~ Real ale ~ (01993) 774441 ~ Open 12-3, 6.30-11 ~ Bar food 12.30-3, 6.30-9 ~ Restaurant ~ Children welcome ~ Dogs allowed in bar and bedrooms ~ Live jazz first Sun of month ~ Bedrooms: £135/£155 ~ www.oldswanandminstermill.com *Recommended by Richard and Penny Gibbs, Bernard Stradling, David Carr, Simon and Mandy King*

 OXFORD   SP5106 Map 4
Bear 🍺
Alfred Street/Wheatsheaf Alley; OX1 4EH

Delightful pub with friendly staff, two cosy rooms, six real ales and well liked bar food

L ow-key and rather charming, this little local is the oldest pub in the city. There are two small low-ceilinged, beamed and partly panelled rooms, not over-smart and often packed with students, with a bustling chatty atmosphere, winter coal fires, thousands of vintage ties on the walls and up to six real ales from handpumps on the fine pewter bar counter: Fullers Chiswick, ESB, HSB and London Pride and a couple of guests beers from Butcombe or Prospect. Staff are friendly and helpful. There are seats under parasols in the terraced back garden where summer barbecues are held.

🍴 Bar food includes sandwiches, nibbles like olives and hummus with local bread, a proper ploughman's, various burgers including a vegetarian one, steak in ale pie, sausages with mash and onion gravy, barbecue chicken, and puddings such as treacle sponge and chocolate fudge cake. *Benchmark main dish: beer-battered fish and chips £8.95. Two-course evening meal £15.00.*

Fullers ~ Manager James Vernede ~ Real ale ~ (01865) 728164 ~ Open 11-11(midnight Sat); 11.30-10.30 Sun ~ Bar food 12-9 ~ Children welcome ~ Dogs allowed in bar ~ www.bearoxford.co.uk *Recommended by Andy Dolan, Simon Watkins, David Carr*

 OXFORD   SP5005 Map 4
Punter
South Street, Osney (off A420 Botley Road via Bridge Street); OX2 0BE

Friendly, relaxed pub overlooking the water with lots of character and enjoyable modern food

W ith a cheerful welcome for all – dogs included – from the enthusiastic young landlord and his staff, this Thames-side pub has a bustling and easy-going atmosphere and is usefully open all day. The lower area has attractive rugs on flagstones and an open fire, while the upper room has more rugs on floorboards and a single big table surrounded by oil paintings – just right for a private party. Throughout are all manner of nice old dining chairs around an interesting mix of tables, affordable art on whitewashed walls and one rather fine stained-glass window. Greene King Old Golden Hen, Timothy Taylors Golden Best and Wadworths St George & the Dragon on handpump from the tiled counter, several wines by the glass and friendly service; board games. This is sister pub to the Punter in Cambridge.

As well as three daily dishes on a weekday £5 lunch board, the good, modern food includes rabbit rillettes with spicy beetroot chutney, potted salmon with pickled cucumber salad, pork and leek sausages with mash and gravy, roasted fennel and courgette gnocchi with basil butter, whole mackerel with herb and citrus couscous, burger with cheese, red onion relish and chips, onglet steak with horseradish crème fraîche and frites, and puddings. *Benchmark main dish: venison haunch with red cabbage and dauphinoise potatoes £12.00. Two-course evening meal £16.00.*

Greene King ~ Lease Tom Rainey ~ Real ale ~ (01865) 248832 ~ Open 12-midnight ~ Bar food 12-3, 6-10; all day weekends ~ Children welcome ~ Dogs welcome ~ www.thepunteroxford.com *Recommended by Richard and Penny Gibbs, Susan Loppert, Jane Caplan*

OXFORD   SP5107   Map 4

Rose & Crown ◀

North Parade Avenue; very narrow, so best to park in a nearby street; OX2 6LX

Long-serving licensees in lively friendly local with a good mix of customers, fine choice of drinks and proper home cooking

For 30 years, the licensees have given a great deal of atmosphere and originality to this neighbourhood pub and offered a warm welcome to their mixed customers of undergraduates, locals and more mature drinkers. The front door opens on to a passage with a small counter and bookshelves of reference books for crossword buffs. This leads to two rooms: a cosy front one looking on to the street and a panelled back room housing the main bar and traditional pub furnishings. Adnams Bitter, Hook Norton Old Hooky, Shotover Scholar and a guest beer on handpump, around 30 malt whiskies and quite a choice of wines by the glass (including champagne and sparkling wine). The pleasant walled and heated back courtyard can be covered with a huge awning; at the far end is a 12-seater dining/meeting room. The lavatories are basic.

Traditional but enjoyable food at honest prices includes sandwiches and baguettes, ploughman's, omelettes, ham, egg and beans, beer-battered fish and chips, sausages with mash and gravy, steaks, and puddings such as apple pie and a changing hot pudding with custard; popular Sunday roast from September to June. *Benchmark main dish: sausage, mash and onion gravy £8.45. Two-course evening meal £11.50.*

Free house ~ Licensees Andrew and Debbie Hall ~ Real ale ~ No credit cards ~ (01865) 510551 ~ Open 11am-midnight(11 Sun); closed afternoons Aug-early Sept ~ Bar food 12-2.15(3 Sun) ~ Well behaved and accompanied children may sit in courtyard until 5pm ~ Occasional live music, see website ~ www.rose-n-crown.com *Recommended by Chris Glasson*

We checked prices with the pubs as we went to press in summer 2013.
They should hold until around spring 2014.

 PISHILL   SU7190   Map 2

Crown

B480 Nettlebed–Watlington; RG9 6HH

Fine old inn with attractive beamed bars, winter fires, real ales, several wines by the glass and popular food

In a peaceful valley, this red brick and flint pub dates mainly from the 15th century, but there was a monastic building here at least 400 years earlier. It's particularly well run by warmly friendly, professional licensees who ensure their customers of all ages really enjoy their visits. The partly panelled walls in the beamed bars are hung with old local photographs and maps, there are nice old chairs around a mix of wooden tables, candles everywhere, Brakspears Bitter and Rebellion IPA on handpump and nine wines by the glass. There are standing oak timbers in the knocked-through back area and three roaring log fires in winter; the priest's hole is said to be one of the largest in the country. The beautiful thatched barn is used for parties, and the pretty garden has plenty of seats and tables under neat blue parasols; nearby walks. The self-catering cottage can be rented by the night and breakfast can be provided.

 Enjoyable food includes lunchtime sandwiches, smoked salmon and scrambled eggs with hollandaise, pork rillettes with apple compote, baby gherkins and tarragon mustard, honey-glazed ham with free-range eggs, steak burger with red onion, bacon, cheese, spiced relish and chips, trio of sausages with mash and onion gravy, pollack and crayfish in creamy white sauce with leek-wrapped saffron risotto cake, guinea fowl coq au vin, and puddings such as apple, raisin and cinnamon crumble and lemon tart with raspberry coulis. *Benchmark main dish: fish pie topped with leek mash with celeriac purée £11.50. Two-course evening meal £16.50.*

Free house ~ Licensee Lucas Wood ~ Real ale ~ (01491) 638364 ~ Open 12-3, 6-11; 12-3.30, 7-10 Sun ~ Bar food 12-2.30(3 Sun), 6.30-9(9.30 Fri, Sat) ~ Children welcome ~ Dogs allowed in bar ~ www.thecrowninnpishill.co.uk *Recommended by Nigel Henbest, Robert Polatajko, R T and J C Moggridge, John and Jackie Chalcraft, Susan and John Douglas*

RAMSDEN   SP3515   Map 4

Royal Oak 🍽 🍺

Village signposted off B4022 Witney–Charlbury; OX7 3AU

Busy pub with long-serving licensees, large helpings of varied food, carefully chosen wines and seats outside; bedrooms

Opposite the village church, this 17th-c Cotswold-stone pub has been run by the same enthusiastic licensees for 26 years. It's a friendly, relaxed place with no background music; the unpretentious rooms have all manner of wooden tables, chairs and settles, cushioned window seats, exposed stone walls, bookcases with past and current copies of *Country Life* and, when the weather gets cold, a cheerful log fire. Butts Barbus Barbus, Hook Norton Old Hooky, Stonehenge Spire Ale and Wye Valley Dorothy Goodbodys Blissful Brown Ale on handpump, 30 wines by the glass from a carefully chosen list and three farm ciders. There are tables and chairs out in front and on the terrace behind the restaurant (folding doors give easy access). The bedrooms are in separate cottages and there are fine surrounding walks.

🍴 Quite a choice of food includes sandwiches, devilled lambs kidneys in dijon mustard sauce, chicken liver parfait, chilli con carne, pie of the week, fresh pasta with wild mushroom and truffle sauce, bass with fennel sauce and leek ribbons, venison in piquant orange sauce, specials such as french-style fish stew or free-range poussin with sweet peppers and tomato and chorizo sauce, and puddings. *Benchmark main dish: steak and kidney pudding £14.50. Two-course evening meal £20.00.*

Free house ~ Licensee Jon Oldham ~ Real ale ~ (01993) 868213 ~ Open 11.30-3, 6.30-11; 11.30-11(10.30 Sun) Sat ~ Bar food 12-2, 7-10; all day weekends ~ Restaurant ~ Children welcome ~ Dogs allowed in bar ~ Bedrooms: £60/£80 ~ www.royaloakramsden.com
Recommended by Malcolm and Jo Hart, Chris Glasson, David and Sue Atkinson

ROTHERFIELD GREYS SU7282 Map 2
Maltsters Arms ♀

Can be reached off A4155 in Henley, via Greys Road passing Southfields long-stay car park; or follow Greys Church signpost off B481 N of Sonning Common; RG9 4QD

Well run, civilised country pub in the Chilterns with well liked, fairly priced food, nice scenery and walks

You'll quickly be made at home by the friendly, helpful staff in this civilised pub. It's just the place to head for after a walk, with two good footpaths nearby. The maroon-carpeted front room has comfortable wall banquettes and lots of horsebrasses on black beams, Brakspears Bitter and Oxford Gold on handpump, a dozen wines by the glass and decent coffee; there's a warm winter open fire and maybe soft background music. Beyond the serving area, which has hop bines and pewter tankards hanging from its joists, a back room has cricketing prints on dark red walls over a shiny panelled dado, and a mix of furnishings from pink-cushioned pale wooden dining chairs to a pair of leatherette banquettes forming a corner booth. The chocolate labrador has been here as long as the licensees – 15 years. Terrace tables under a big heated canopy are set with linen for meals, and the grass behind has picnic-sets under green parasols, looking over paddocks to rolling woodland. Greys Court (National Trust) is not far away.

🍴 Popular food includes paninis, crispy salt and pepper calamari with aioli, devilled whitebait, leek, mushroom and cherry tomato cottage pie, honey-roast ham, egg and chips, smoked haddock rarebit on colcannon mash, bacon-wrapped pheasant stuffed with pâté with cumberland sauce, steak and kidney pudding (Tuesdays only October-March), daily specials and puddings. *Benchmark main dish: chicken and mushroom pancake £9.25. Two-course evening meal £18.25.*

Brakspears ~ Tenants Peter and Helen Bland ~ Real ale ~ (01491) 628400 ~ Open 11.45-3, 6-11(midnight Sat); 12-9(6 winter) Sun ~ Bar food 12-2.15, 6.15-9.15; not Sun evening ~ Children welcome ~ Dogs allowed in bar ~ www.maltsters.co.uk
Recommended by David and Sue Smith, Paul Humphreys, Roy Hoing, Penny and Peter Keevil, DHV

SHILTON SP2608 Map 4
Rose & Crown

Just off B4020 SE of Burford; OX18 4AB

Simple and appealing little village pub, with a relaxed civilised atmosphere, real ales and good food

This pretty 17th-c stone pub in a lovely village is enjoyed by our readers in both summer and winter, and you can be sure of a warm welcome from the hands-on licensee and his staff. The small front bar has an unassuming but civilised feel, low beams, timbers, exposed stone walls, a log fire in a big fireplace and half a dozen or so kitchen chairs and tables on a red tiled floor. There are usually a few locals at the planked counter, where they serve Hook Norton Cotswold Lion, Wells & Youngs Bitter and Wye Valley Butty Bach on handpump, along with nine wines by the glass; big cafetières of coffee. A second room, similar but bigger, is used mainly for eating, with flowers on the tables and another fireplace. The attractive side garden has picnic-sets.

Cooked by the landlord, the enjoyable food includes ciabattas, game terrine with red onion marmalade, gravadlax with dill and mustard sauce, aubergine parmigiana, ham and egg, smoked haddock, prawn and salmon pie, pheasant breast with bacon and cabbage, liver with swede purée and sage brown butter, and puddings such as plum tart with crème fraîche and steamed apple pudding with blackberry coulis. *Benchmark main dish: steak and mushroom in ale pie £12.50. Two-course evening meal £19.00.*

Free house ~ Licensee Martin Coldicott ~ Real ale ~ (01993) 842280 ~ Open 11.30-3, 6-11; 11.30-11 Fri, Sat; 12-10 Sun ~ Bar food 12-2(2.45 weekends and bank holidays), 7-9 ~ Well behaved children welcome lunchtime only ~ Dogs allowed in bar ~ www.roseandcrownshilton.com *Recommended by Andy Dolan, C A Hall, Dennis and Doreen Haward, Richard Willis, R K Phillips, David Handforth*

SHIPLAKE   SU7779   Map 2

Baskerville ① ♀ ◧ ⇖

Station Road, Lower Shiplake (off A4155 just S of Henley); RG9 3NY

Emphasis on imaginative food but a proper public bar too; real ales, several wines by the glass, interesting sporting memorabilia and a pretty garden; bedrooms

Readers always enjoy their visits to this consistently well run pub – while most customers are there to enjoy the impressive food, there's a fine choice of drinks too. Served by neat uniformed staff, these might include Fullers London Pride, Loddon Hoppit, Sharps Doom Bar and Timothy Taylors Landlord on handpump, a dozen wines by the glass from a thoughtfully chosen list and 40 malt whiskies; to support WaterAid, they charge 50p for a jug of iced water and have so far raised £3,600. There are bar chairs around the light modern counter (used by the chatty locals), a few beams, pale wooden dining chairs and tables on floors of light wood or patterned carpet, plush red banquettes by the windows and a couple of log fires in brick fireplaces. The red walls are hung with sporting memorabilia and pictures, especially old rowing photos (Henley is nearby) and signed rugby shirts and photos (the pub has its own rugby club), along with Thames maps, and flowers and large house plants are dotted about. It feels quite homely in a smart way, with chintzy touches such as a shelf of china cow jugs; there's a separate dining room and a small room for private parties. The pretty garden has a covered barbecue area, smart teak furniture under huge parasols, some rather fun statues made from box hedges, and a timber play frame. The bedrooms are well equipped and comfortable and the breakfasts extremely good.

Using very carefully sourced produce, the imaginative food includes open sandwiches, rope-grown mussels in coriander, chilli, ginger and coconut, goats cheese panna cotta with parma ham-wrapped fig and sage and walnut bread, omelettes, mushroom linguine with truffle oil, steak and kidney in ale pie, seafood linguine in spicy tomato sauce, honey and orange-glazed duck with sweet potato and ginger mash and vegetable dumpling, and puddings such as triple-chocolate orange brownie with home-made vanilla pod ice-cream and sticky toffee pudding with toffee sauce; they also offer a daily changing set menu Monday-Thursday (January-March, October, November). *Benchmark main dish: slow-cooked pork belly with apple confit and star anise and orange sauce £15.95. Two-course evening meal £22.50.*

Free house ~ Licensee Allan Hannah ~ Real ale ~ (0118) 940 3332 ~ Open 11-11; 12-10.30 Sun ~ Bar food 12-9.30(10 Fri, Sat); 12-3.30 Sun ~ Restaurant ~ Children welcome except in restaurant after 7pm Fri, Sat ~ Dogs allowed in bar and bedrooms ~ Bedrooms: £89/£99 ~ www.thebaskerville.com *Recommended by Dr D J and Mrs S C Walker, Paul Humphreys*

STANFORD IN THE VALE
SU3393 Map 4

Horse & Jockey 🍴 £

A417 Faringdon–Wantage; Faringdon Road; SN7 8NN

Friendly traditional village local with real character, highly thought-of, good value food and well chosen wines

The friendly, hard-working landlord has managed to keep several of his main courses at around £10 in this bustling pub – not easy to do in these tough times. As this is racehorse training country (and given the pub's name) there are big Alfred Munnings' racecourse prints, card collections of Grand National winners and other horse and jockey pictures, and the atmosphere is easy-going and comfortably welcoming. Greene King Morlands Original and Old Speckled Hen and St Austell Trelawny on handpump, carefully chosen wines in a sensible choice of glass sizes and a dozen malt whiskies. The main area, with flagstones, a low ochre ceiling and a woodburning stove in a big fireplace, has several old high-backed settles and a couple of bucket armchairs. On the right is a carpeted area with a lofty raftered ceiling, a lattice-windowed inner gallery and some stripped stone; at the back is a spacious bare-boards dining room. As well as tables under a heated courtyard canopy, there's a separate enclosed and informal family garden with a play area and picnic-sets on grass; aunt sally. The bedrooms are comfortable.

🍴 The highly thought-of food includes sandwiches and baguettes, whole baked camembert with red onion marmalade, salt, pepper and chilli-battered calamari with sweet chilli dipping sauce, sharing platters, chicken caesar salad, ham and free-range eggs, vegetable pie, curry of the day, beer-battered fish and chips, steaks, and puddings. *Benchmark main dish: burger with home-made sauce and onion rings, cheese, bacon and chips £8.95. Two-course evening meal £17.00.*

Greene King ~ Lease Charles and Anna Gaunt ~ Real ale ~ (01367) 710302 ~ Open 11-2.30, 5-midnight; 11am-12.30am Sat; 12-midnight Sun ~ Bar food 12-2.30, 6.30-9(9.30 Fri); 12-2.30 Sun ~ Restaurant ~ Children welcome ~ Dogs allowed in bar ~ Open mike first Weds of month ~ Bedrooms: £55/£65 ~ www.horseandjockey.org
Recommended by R K Phillips, Cliff Sparkes

STONESFIELD
SP3917 Map 4

White Horse

Village signposted off B4437 Charlbury–Woodstock; Stonesfield Riding; OX29 8EA

Attractively upgraded small country pub with tasty food using local produce and a relaxed atmosphere

Opening times are restricted here, so it's best to phone ahead to be sure. There are contemporary artworks, restful colours (duck-egg blue in the snug little bar, dark pink over a grey dado in the dining room) and nicely chosen furniture. One of the best touches is the little inner room with just a pair of sheraton-style chairs around a single mahogany table. The corner bar counter, with padded stools, has Ringwood Best on handpump; woodburning stove, daily papers, quiet background music. French windows in the dining room open on to a neat walled garden with picnic-sets, and there's a skittle alley in a separate stone barn. Good walks nearby as the pub is on the Oxfordshire Way, and it's not far to the North Leigh Roman Villa (English Heritage).

 As well as sandwiches, the well liked food includes smoked salmon pâté, mushroom risotto with lemon and sage butter, pork steak with parma ham and apple and cream sauce with dauphinoise potatoes, bass with lemon grass dressing and crushed new potatoes, sirloin steak with french fries, and puddings such as rhubarb crumble and strawberry and kiwi pavlova. *Benchmark main dish: chicken and leek pie £10.95. Two-course evening meal £15.50.*

Free house ~ Licensees John and Angela Lloyd ~ Real ale ~ (01993) 891063 ~ Open 5-11; 12-3, 6(5 Fri)-11 Sat; 12-3 Sun; closed Mon, lunchtimes Tues-Thurs, evening Sun ~ Bar food 12-2, 6-9; 12-2.30 Sun ~ Restaurant ~ Children welcome ~ Dogs allowed in bar
Recommended by Richard and Penny Gibbs, Dennis and Doreen Haward

SWERFORD
SP3830   Map 4

Masons Arms ⊕ ♀

A361 Banbury–Chipping Norton; OX7 4AP

Attractive dining pub with well liked food, a fair choice of drinks, a relaxed atmosphere and country views from outside tables

In warm weather, the picnic-sets in the neat garden with views over the Oxfordshire countryside are just the place to enjoy a drink or meal. It's a pretty brick dining pub, and the bar has rugs on pale wooden floors, a big brown leather sofa facing a couple of armchairs in front of a log fire in a stone fireplace, Brakspears Bitter and Jennings Cumberland on handpump and several wines by the glass. The light and airy dining extension has pastel-painted dining chairs around nice old tables on beige carpet, and steps lead down to a cream-painted room with chunky tables and contemporary pictures. Round the other side of the bar is another spacious dining room with great views by day, candles at night and a civilised feel.

By popular demand, the specials are focused on fish and seafood: tiger prawns with chilli and chorizo on pak choi, ginger and spring onions, scallops with pea purée, black butter broad beans and parma ham crisp, cornish crab with dill mayonnaise, megrim with lemon and caper butter or red mullet and samphire linguine. Also, sandwiches, duck confit with red plum chutney, honey-roast ham and eggs, butternut squash, spinach and goats cheese puff pastry parcel with mushroom sauce, coq au vin, venison wellington with port and juniper jus, and puddings such as chocolate toffee brownies and apple and mulled berry crumble. *Benchmark main dish: braised beef cobbler with root vegetables and horseradish dumpling £9.00. Two-course evening meal £17.00.*

Free house ~ Licensee Louise Davies ~ Real ale ~ (01608) 683212 ~ Open 11-3, 6-11; 12-10 Sun ~ Bar food 12-2, 6-9; 12-8 Sun ~ Restaurant ~ Children welcome ~ www.masons-arms.com *Recommended by Clare Tagg, Richard Tilbrook, Ian Herdman*

SWINBROOK SP2812 Map 4
Swan ⓘ ♀ 🛏

Back road a mile N of A40, 2 miles E of Burford; OX18 4DY

Rather smart old pub with handsome oak garden rooms, antique-filled bars, local beers and contemporary food using local and organic produce; bedrooms

Handy for the A40, this civilised 17th-c pub is in a lovely spot by a bridge over the River Windrush, with seats and circular picnic-sets making the best of the view. It's owned by the Dowager Duchess of Devonshire (the last of the Mitford sisters, who grew up in the village) and there are lots of interesting Mitford family photographs on the walls. The little bar has simple antique furnishings, settles and benches, an open fire and (in an alcove) a stuffed swan; locals drop in here for a pint and a chat. A small dining room leads off from the bar to the right of the entrance, and there are also two green-painted oak garden rooms with high-backed beige and green dining chairs around pale wood tables, and views over the garden and orchard. Hook Norton Hooky Bitter and guests such as Oxfordshire Churchill and Wye Valley Bitter on handpump, ten wines by the glass and Weston's organic cider. The bedrooms are in a smartly converted stone barn beside the pub. The Kings Head in Bledington (Gloucestershire) is run by the same first class licensees.

🍴 Using produce from the family farm, other nearby farms and local game, the delicious food includes sandwiches, home-cured bresaola with rocket, parmesan and croutons, antipasti plate for two, saffron risotto with sunblush tomatoes, corn-fed chicken breast with walnut pesto, artichoke, tomatoes and olives, chorizo sausage with sweetcorn pancake and fried egg, whole plaice with shrimp, dill and lemon butter, shredded venison confit with black pudding and haricot beans, button onions and thyme, and puddings. *Benchmark main dish: beer-battered haddock and chips £12.00. Two-course evening meal £22.00.*

Free house ~ Licensees Archie and Nicola Orr-Ewing ~ Real ale ~ (01993) 823339 ~ Open 11(12 Sun)-11; 11-3, 6-11 in winter ~ Bar food 12-2, 7-9 ~ Restaurant ~ Children welcome ~ Dogs allowed in bar ~ Bedrooms: £90/£120 ~ www.theswanswinbrook.co.uk
Recommended by Andy Dolan, Bernard Stradling, Stuart Turner, Malcolm and Jo Hart, Di and Mike Gillam, C A Hall, David Glynne-Jones, Dr and Mrs S G Barber, Mike and Mary Carter

TADPOLE BRIDGE SP3200 Map 4
Trout ⓘ ♀ 🛏

Back road Bampton–Buckland, 4 miles NE of Faringdon; SN7 8RF

Oxfordshire Dining Pub of the Year

Busy country inn by the River Thames with a fine choice of drinks, popular modern food, and seats in the waterside garden; bedrooms

'An excellent all-rounder' is how one reader describes this notably well run inn – and many agree. Very civilised and friendly, it has an L-shaped bar with attractive green- and red-checked chairs around a mix of nice wooden tables, rugs on flagstones, green paintwork behind a modern wooden bar counter, fresh flowers, two woodburning stoves and a large stuffed trout. The airy restaurant is appealingly candlelit in the evenings. Ramsbury Bitter, Loose Cannon Abingdon Bridge, Wells & Youngs Bitter and White Horse Wayland Smithy on handpump, 12 wines by the glass from a wide-ranging and carefully chosen list and 14 malt whiskies. This is a peaceful and picturesque spot by the Thames and there are good quality teak chairs and tables under blue parasols in the pretty garden; arrived early in fine weather as it can get packed. You can hire punts with champagne hampers and there are moorings (book in advance) for six boats.

The enticing food includes specials such as mussels in garlic and cream, ham hock and rhubarb terrine with pear chutney, beer-battered haddock and chips or roast suckling pig with spinach and dauphinoise potatoes, as well as scallops, razor clams, crispy parma ham and celeriac purée, sunblush tomato and feta risotto, whole dressed crab with citrus mayonnaise, rack of lamb with rosemary crust, fondant potatoes and faggots, duck breast with pear and potato cake and beetroot and ginger purée, and puddings. *Benchmark main dish: trio of pork with parsnip dauphinoise and apple jelly £15.25. Two-course evening meal £23.00.*

Free house ~ Licensees Gareth and Helen Pugh ~ Real ale ~ (01367) 870382 ~ Open 11.30-11; 12-10 Sun; 11.30-3, 6-11 Mon-Fri in winter ~ Bar food 12-2, 7-9; some food all day at weekends ~ Children welcome ~ Dogs welcome ~ Bedrooms: £85/£130 ~ www.troutinn.co.uk *Recommended by Richard Tilbrook, M and J White, Ross Balaam, Derek Thomas, Charles Gysin, R K Phillips, Tony Hobden*

WEST HANNEY   SU4092 Map 2
Plough
Just off A338 N of Wantage; Church Street; OX12 0LN

Thatched village pub with tasty popular food, a good choice of drinks and plenty of seats outside

Under a friendly new licensee as we went to press, this is a pretty and neatly thatched, early 16th-c village pub. Happily, not too much has changed: the comfortable simply furnished bar has horsebrasses on beams, bar stools, wheelback chairs around wooden tables, a log fire in a stone fireplace and lots of photographs of the pub on the walls. Sharps Doom Bar and Timothy Taylors Landlord plus a couple of changing local ales on handpump, half a dozen wines by the glass and a farm cider. There's a separate dining room. Outside is a covered seating area, more tables and chairs on a back terrace overlooking the walled garden and plenty of picnic-sets on the grass; aunt sally. Good walks start with a village path right by the pub.

Popular bar food includes baguettes, home-made pâté with chutney, moules marinière, wild mushroom risotto, home-made steak burger with cheese, bacon and chips, steak in ale pie, seafood risotto, rack of lamb, parma ham-wrapped chicken breast, daily specials, and puddings such as apple and mango crumble and sticky toffee pudding. *Benchmark main dish: liver, bacon and mash with rich onion gravy £9.95. Two-course evening meal £17.00.*

Free house ~ Licensee Steve Cadogan ~ Real ale ~ (01235) 868674 ~ Open 12-3, 6-11; 12-midnight Fri-Sun; closed Mon lunchtime ~ Bar food 12-2.30, 6-9.30; 12-9 Fri, Sat; 12-8 Sun; not Mon ~ Restaurant ~ Children welcome ~ Dogs allowed in bar ~ www.theploughwesthanney.co.uk *Recommended by D C T and E A Frewer, Dennis and Doreen Haward, Evelyn and Derek Walter*

Real ale to us means beer that has matured naturally in its cask – not pressurised or filtered. We name all real ales stocked. We usually name ales preserved under a light blanket of carbon dioxide too, though purists – pointing out that this stops the natural yeasts developing – would disagree (most people, including us, can't tell the difference!).

WOODSTOCK   SP4416   Map 4

Kings Arms 🍴 £ 🛏

Market Street/Park Lane (A44); OX20 1SU

**Stylish town-centre hotel with well liked food, a wide choice of drinks
and an enjoyable atmosphere; comfortable bedrooms**

Readers love this particularly well run and stylish town-centre inn. It's
a comfortable place to stay, with smashing breakfasts, the welcome
from the efficient but charming staff is genuine and the food tempting
and highly popular. A good mix of customers in the unfussy bar creates
a relaxed and informal atmosphere, and there's an appealing variety
of old and new furnishings including brown leather furniture on the
stripped-wood floor, smart blinds and black and white photographs; at
the front is an old wooden settle and an interesting little woodburner.
The bar leading to the brasserie-style dining room has an unusual
stained-glass structure used for newspapers and magazines, and the
attractive restaurant has a fine old fireplace. Brakspears Oxford Gold,
Hook Norton Hooky Bitter and Wychwood Hobgoblin on handpump,
good coffees, 11 wines plus champagne by the glass and 30 malt
whiskies. There are seats and tables on the street outside.

Snacks and cream teas are served all day, while the interesting main menu
includes game terrine with pear chutney, devilled chicken livers, pumpkin
and cheese gateau with toasted seed salad, ham and free-range eggs, smoked
haddock fishcake with butter sauce, burger with stilton, bacon and horseradish
coleslaw, free-range chicken with mushroom pâté, chestnuts and braised leeks,
duck leg in rich plum sauce with celeriac dauphinoise, daily specials like bass fillet
with crayfish butter and samphire or venison steak with peppercorn sauce, and
puddings such as chocolate quartet and treacle and walnut tart. *Benchmark main
dish: lamb shank with shallot sauce and honeyed parsnips £14.75. Two-course
evening meal £19.00.*

Free house ~ Licensees David and Sara Sykes ~ Real ale ~ (01993) 813636 ~ Open
11am-11.30pm(11pm Sun) ~ Bar food 12-2, 6.30-9; some snacks all day ~ Restaurant ~
Children welcome in bar and restaurant but no under-12s in bedrooms ~ Dogs allowed in
bar ~ Bedrooms: $80/$150 ~ www.kings-hotel-woodstock.co.uk *Recommended by Martin
and Pauline Jennings, Mike and Shirley Stratton, John Branston, Neil and Angela Huxter,
Mr and Mrs P R Thomas, Richard Tilbrook*

Also Worth a Visit in Oxfordshire

Besides the fully inspected pubs, you might like to try these pubs that
have been recommended to us and described by readers. Do tell us what
you think of them: feedback@goodguides.com

ABINGDON   SU4997
Brewery Tap (01235) 521655
Ock Street; OX14 5BZ Former tap for
defunct Morland Brewery (now flats) but
still serving Original along with five changing
guests, proper ciders and good choice of
wines, well priced lunchtime food including
popular Sun roasts, stone floors and panelled
walls, two log fires; background and some live
music; children and dogs welcome, enclosed
courtyard with aunt sally, three bedrooms,
open all day (till 1am Fri, Sat).
(Kenny Moore)

ADDERBURY   SP4735
⋆**Red Lion** (01295) 810269
*The Green; off A4260 S of Banbury;
OX17 3NG* Attractive 17th-c stone coaching
inn with good choice of enjoyable well
priced food (all day weekends) including
deals, helpful friendly staff, Greene King
ales, good wine range and coffee, linked bar
rooms with high stripped beams, panelling
and stonework, big inglenook log fire, old
books and Victorian/Edwardian pictures,
daily papers, games area, more modern back
restaurant extension; background music;

children in eating areas, picnic-sets on roadside terrace, 12 character bedrooms, good breakfast, open all day in summer. *(George Atkinson, M G Hart)*

ASHBURY SU2685
Rose & Crown (01793) 710222
B4507/B4000; High Street; SN6 8NA
16th-c coaching inn under new management, roomy open-plan beamed bar with three well kept Arkells beers and good range of wines by the glass, enjoyable food from pub favourites up, polished woodwork, traditional pictures, chesterfields and pews, raised section with further oak tables and chairs, games room with table tennis, pool and darts, separate restaurant; background and occasional live music; children and dogs welcome, disabled facilities, tables out at front and in garden behind, lovely view down pretty village street of thatched cottages, handy for Ridgeway walks, eight bedrooms, open all day. *(David Lamb)*

ASTON TIRROLD SU5586
⋆**Sweet Olive** (01235) 851272
Aka Chequers; Fullers Road; village signed off A417 Streatley–Wantage; OX11 9EN Has atmosphere of a rustic french restaurant rather than village pub, but people do pop in for just a drink; main room with wall settles, mate's chairs, a few sturdy tables, grass matting over quarry tiles, small fireplace, good fresh bistro-style food including daily specials, nice french wines by the glass (wine box ends decorate the back of the servery), Brakspears and Fullers beers, friendly service, smaller room more formally set as restaurant with restrained décor; background music; children welcome, dogs in bar, picnic-sets under parasols in small cottagey garden, aunt sally, closed Sun evening, Weds, all Feb, two weeks in July. *(Rob Winstanley, Colin McLachlan, D C T and E A Frewer)*

BECKLEY SP5611
⋆**Abingdon Arms** (01865) 351311
Signed off B4027; High Street; OX3 9UU
Old dining pub in attractive unspoilt village; comfortably modernised simple lounge, smaller public bar with antique carved settles, open fires, well kept Brakspears and guests, fair range of good reasonably priced wines, enjoyable home-made food from pub favourites up including good Sun roasts, friendly attentive service; background and some live music; children and dogs welcome, big garden dropping away from floodlit terrace to trees, summer house, superb views over RSPB Otmoor reserve – good walks, open all day weekends. *(Stephen and Jean Curtis, Mr and Mrs Lynn)*

BEGBROKE SP4713
Royal Sun (01865) 374718
A44 Oxford–Woodstock; OX5 1RZ
Welcoming old stone-built pub with

modernised bare-boards interior, wide choice of good value food from snacks to Sun carvery, well kept Hook Norton and a guest, good friendly service, free monkey nuts on the bar; may be background music, big-screen sports TV; children welcome, tables on terrace and in small garden, open all day from 8.30am for breakfast. *(Anon)*

BERRICK SALOME SU6294
Chequers (01865) 891118
Towards Berrick Prior; OX10 6JN
Large family-run 18th-c brick and flint village pub; popular home-made food and Brakspears ales, friendly atmosphere, darts and board games, fortnightly quiz Tues; children welcome, garden with play area and aunt sally, open all day Sat, closed Sun evening, Mon. *(Anon)*

BINFIELD HEATH SU7479
Bottle & Glass (01491) 575755
Off A4155 at Shiplake; between village and Harpsden; RG9 4JT Chocolate-box thatched black and white Tudor cottage – a popular choice with readers but for sale as we went to press and under temporary management: sensibly priced pubby food, two Brakspears ales and a guest, ten wines by the glass, bleached pine tables, low beams and flagstones, dark squared panelling, old local photographs on pastel walls, old stove (converted to gas) in fine fireplace, board games and dominoes; children and dogs welcome, nice big garden with picnic-sets (some under little thatched roofs), aunt sally, open all day. *(Anon)*

BLADON SP4414
White House (01993) 811582
Park Street (A4095); OX20 1RW Smartly refurbished pub opposite church where Churchill is buried; good sensibly priced food (not Sun evening) from sandwiches up, three Greene King ales, friendly staff; children welcome, secluded split-level back garden, handy for back gate of Blenheim Park (beautiful right-of-way walk), open all day. *(Anon)*

BLEWBURY SU5385
Red Lion (01235) 850403
Nottingham Fee – narrow turning N from A417; OX11 9PQ Attractive and welcoming downland village pub, enjoyable home-made food from generous ploughman's and sharing plates up, well kept Brakspears and a guest, good service, beams, tiled floor and big log fire, restaurant; children welcome, terrace tables in peaceful back garden, pretty surroundings. *(Baz Manning)*

BLOXHAM SP4235
⋆**Joiners Arms** (01295) 720223
Old Bridge Road, off A361; OX15 4LY
Golden-stone 16th-c inn with rambling rooms, white dining chairs around pale tables on wood floor, plenty of exposed stone, open

fires, ales such as Brakspears and Marstons, enjoyable traditional food including deals, old well in raftered room off bar; children and dogs welcome, pretty window boxes, seats out under parasols on various levels – most popular down steps by stream (play house there too), open all day. *(David Jackman, R T and J C Moggridge, Alan Weedon)*

BOARS HILL SP4901
Fox (01865) 735131
Between A34 and B4017; Fox Lane; OX1 5DR Spacious comfortable Chef & Brewer in pretty wooded countryside, interesting rambling rooms on different levels, beams and substantial log fireplaces, good all-day food, decent wines by the glass and a couple of well kept ales; may be background music; children welcome, pleasant raised verandah, charming big sloping garden with fish pond, open all day. *(William Goodhart)*

BRIGHTWELL SU5890
Red Lion (01491) 837373
Signed off A4130 2 miles W of Wallingford; OX10 0RT Welcoming community-spirited village pub, five well kept ales including Appleford, Loddon and West Berkshire, wines from nearby vineyard, enjoyable good value home-made food, two-part bar with snug seating by log fire, dining extension; dogs welcome, seats out at front and in back garden, open all day Sun till 9pm. *(Franklyn Roberts)*

BUCKLAND SU3497
★ **Lamb** (01367) 870484
Off A420 NE of Faringdon; SN7 8QN 18th-c stone-built dining pub with good value interesting seasonal food in bar or restaurant, Loose Cannon Abingdon Bridge and a local guest, good choice of wines by the glass; well behaved children and dogs welcome (resident cocker called Oats), pleasant tree-shaded garden, good walks nearby, three comfortable bedrooms, closed Sun evening, Mon. *(William Goodhart)*

BUCKNELL SP5525
Trigger Pond (01869) 252817
Handy for M40 junction 10; Bicester Road; OX27 7NE Stone-built beamed pub opposite pond; small bar with dining areas either side, inglenook woodburner, conservatory, Wadworths ales and enjoyable food from baguettes and pub favourites up; children welcome, colourful terrace and garden, open all day. *(Anon)*

BURFORD SP2512
★ **Angel** (01993) 822714
Witney Street; OX18 4SN Long heavy-beamed dining pub in attractive ancient building, warmly welcoming with roaring log fire, popular well cooked brasserie food including set lunch, good range of drinks; big secluded garden,

three comfortable bedrooms, closed Sun evening, Mon. *(Di and Mike Gillam)*

BURFORD SP2512
Golden Pheasant (01993) 823223
High Street; OX18 4QA Small early 18th-c hotel's flagstoned split-level bar, civilised yet relaxed and pubby, sofas, armchairs and well spaced tables, woodburner, enjoyable food including pizzas and grills, well kept Greene King ales, good house wines, back dining room down steps, weekend live music; children welcome, pleasant terrace behind, ten bedrooms, open all day. *(Anon)*

BURFORD SP2512
★ **Mermaid** (01993) 822193
High Street; OX18 4QF Handsome old dining pub with beams, flagstones, panelling, stripped stone and nice log fire, good food (all day weekends) at sensible prices including local free-range meat and fresh fish, friendly efficient service, well kept Greene King ales and a guest, bay window seating at front, further airy back dining room and upstairs restaurant; background music; children welcome, tables out at front and in courtyard behind, open all day. *(Anon)*

CHADLINGTON SP3222
Tite (01608) 676910
Off A361 S of Chipping Norton; Mill End; OX7 3NY Friendly renovated 17th-c country pub; bar with small eating areas either side, beams and stripped stone, pubby furniture including spindleback chairs and settles, flagstones and bare boards, woodburner in large fireplace, three real ales and fairly traditional food; split-level terrace and attractive shrub-filled garden with stream (runs under the pub), good walks nearby. *(Richard Stanfield, J C Burgis)*

CHALGROVE SU6397
Red Lion (01865) 890625
High Street (B480 Watlington–Stadhampton); OX44 7SS Attractive and popular beamed village pub, owned by local church trust since 1637; good home-made seasonal food (not Sun evening) from interesting menu, well kept Butcombe, Fullers London Pride, Rebellion Mild and two guests, friendly helpful staff, separate restaurant; nice front and back gardens, open all day Sun. *(Torrens Lyster)*

CHARLBURY SP3519
Bull (01608) 810689
Sheep Street; OX7 3RR Comfortable beamed stripped-stone bistro-style dining pub, restaurant on left with inglenook log fire, another in dining bar on right with rattan chairs, interesting food from sandwiches up, a house bitter brewed by Goffs and two guests, good choice of wines by the glass; no dogs; children welcome, attractive sunny back terrace, four bedrooms, closed Sun evening, Mon. *(Geoff Clifford)*

CHARLBURY
SP3519

Rose & Crown (01608) 810103

Market Street; OX7 3PL Welcoming
town-centre pub with strong following for its
seven particularly well kept beers including
Ramsbury, real ciders and perry too, simple
split-level interior with proper pubby feel, no
food except rolls, pool, weekend live music;
tables out behind, open all day (till late Fri,
Sat). *(Geoff Clifford, Andy and Jill Kassube)*

CHARNEY BASSETT
SU3794

Chequers (01235) 868642

Chapel Lane off Main Street; OX12 0EX
18th-c village-green pub with spacious
modernised interior, Brakspears ales, fairly
priced food from lunchtime sandwiches and
baguettes to steaks; picnic-sets in small
garden, three bedrooms. *(Helene Grygar,
R K Phillips)*

CHECKENDON
SU6684

✷ Black Horse (01491) 680418

*Village signed off A4074 Reading–
Wallingford; RG8 0TE* Charmingly
old-fashioned country tavern (tucked into
woodland away from main village) kept by
the same family for 108 years; relaxing and
unchanging series of rooms, back one with
West Berkshire and White Horse tapped from
the cask, one with bar counter has some tent
pegs above fireplace (a reminder they used
to be made here), homely side lounge with
some splendidly unfashionable 1950s-style
armchairs and another room beyond that,
only baguettes and pickled eggs; no credit
cards; children allowed but must be well
behaved, seats on verandah and in garden,
popular with walkers and cyclists. *(Anon)*

CHECKENDON
SU6682

Four Horseshoes (01491) 680325

*Off A4074 Reading–Wallingford;
RG8 0QS* Attractive partly thatched two-
bar pub refurbished under newish licensees;
black beams, wood floors and some bare-
brick walls, leather sofas by open fires,
high-backed dining chairs around light wood
tables, some carved bar stools, Brakspears
ales, enjoyable well priced traditional
food, friendly helpful service, bar billiards;
children and dogs welcome, big garden with
play area and summer barbecues, good walks,
open all day Sat, closed Sun evening, Mon.
(Paul Humphreys, Roy Hoing)

CHISLEHAMPTON
SU5998

Coach & Horses (01865) 890255

*B480 Oxford–Watlington, opposite
B4015 to Abingdon; OX44 7UX*
Extended 16th-c coaching inn, two homely
and civilised beamed bars, big log fire,
sizeable restaurant with polished oak tables
and wall banquettes, good choice of well
prepared food (not Sun evening), friendly
attentive service, three well kept ales usually
including Hook Norton; background music;
neat terraced gardens overlooking fields
by River Thame, some tables out in front,
bedrooms in courtyard block, open all day,
closed 3-7pm Sun. *(Roy Hoing, Mike and
Mary Carter)*

CHURCH ENSTONE
SP3725

✷ Crown (01608) 677262

*Mill Lane; from A44 take B4030
turn-off at Enstone; OX7 4NN* Pleasant
uncluttered bar in beamed country pub,
straightforward furniture, country pictures
on stone walls, some horsebrasses, log
fire in large fireplace, well kept Hook
Norton and guests, consistently good food
from pub favourites up, friendly efficient
service, carpeted dining room with red
walls, slate-floored conservatory with
farmhouse furniture; children welcome,
dogs in bar, white metal tables and chairs
on front terrace overlooking lane, picnic-
sets in sheltered back garden, closed Sun
evening. *(Stuart Turner, Malcolm and Jo Hart,
Martin and Pauline Jennings, Ian Herdman,
Dr Nigel Bowles, Guy Vowles and others)*

CHURCHILL
SP2824

✷ Chequers (01608) 659393

*Church Road; B4450 Chipping Norton
to Stow-on-the-Wold (and village signed
off A361 Chipping Norton–Burford);
OX7 6NJ* Golden-stone village pub
refurbished under new management (same
owners as the Wheatsheaf in Northleach
– see Gloucestershire); front bar with
modern oak furnishings on light flagstoned
floor, some old timbers and country prints,
exposed stone walls around big inglenook
log fire, Hook Norton and five guests, some
craft lagers, Dunkerton's organic cider and
a dozen wines by the glass, good choice of
enjoyable food including chargrills, big back
extension with soaring rafters and cosy
upstairs dining area; background music;
children and dogs welcome, impressive
church opposite, open all day from 9am.
*(Bernard Stradling, Stuart Turner, R I Howe,
Jane and Alan Bush, Guy Vowles, Martin and
Pauline Jennings and others)*

COLESHILL
SU2393

✷ Radnor Arms (01793) 861575

*B4019 Faringdon–Highworth; village
signposted off A417 in Faringdon and
A361 in Highworth; SN6 7PR* Pub and
village owned by NT; bar with cushioned
settles, plush carver chairs and woodburner,
back alcove with more tables, steps down to
main dining area, once a blacksmiths' forge
with lofty beamed ceiling, log fire, dozens of
tools and smiths' gear on walls, Old Forge
ales brewed on site (tasting trays available),
shortish choice of good well priced home-
made food (not Sun evening); children and
dogs welcome, garden with aunt sally and
play area, open all day. *(Tom McLean)*

CRAWLEY SP3412
Lamb (01993) 703753
Steep Hill; just NW of Witney; OX29 9TW
18th-c stone-built dining pub with good
imaginative food (daily changing menu)
from owner-chef, friendly attentive service,
Brakspears ales, simple beamed bar with
polished boards and lovely fireplace, steps
up to dining room; views from tables on back
terrace and lawn, pretty village, good walks
(on Palladian Way), closed Sun evening, Mon,
otherwise open all day. *(Anon)*

CUMNOR SP4503
Bear & Ragged Staff
(01865) 862329 *Signed from A420;*
Appleton Road; OX2 9QH Extensive
restaurant-pub dating from 16th c,
contemporary décor in linked rooms
with wood floors, good food from shared
charcuterie and meze plates through pizzas
and pub standards up, friendly efficient
service, flagstoned bar with log fire, well
kept Greene King ales and good wine choice,
airy garden room, some events including
live music; children welcome, decked terrace
and fenced play area, nine bedrooms, open
all day. *(David Handforth)*

DEDDINGTON SP4631
★ Deddington Arms (01869) 338364
Off A4260 (B4031) Banbury–Oxford;
Horse Fair; OX15 0SH Beamed and
timbered hotel with emphasis on sizeable
contemporary back dining room doing very
good food including set lunch, comfortable
bar with mullioned windows, flagstones and
log fire, good food here too, Adnams, Black
Sheep and a guest, plenty of wines by the
glass, attentive friendly service; unobtrusive
background music; children welcome,
attractive village with lots of antiques
shops and good farmers' market fourth Sat
of month, nice walks, comfortable chalet
bedrooms around courtyard, good breakfast,
open all day. *(Michael Sargent, George Atkinson)*

DEDDINGTON SP4631
Unicorn (01869) 338838
Market Place; OX15 0SE 17th-c inn
now under same management as the Boat
at Thrupp; beamed L-shaped bar, cosy
snug with inglenook log fire, candlelit
restaurant, sensibly priced pubby food (not
Sun evening, Mon), Hook Norton and Wells
& Youngs ales, good choice of wines by the
glass, friendly service; background music;
well behaved children and dogs welcome,
cobbled courtyard leading to long walled
back garden, seven bedrooms, open all day
(from 9am for good farmers' market on last
Sat of month). *(Anon)*

DENCHWORTH SU3891
Fox (01235) 868258
Off A338 or A417 N of Wantage; Hyde
Road; OX12 0DX Comfortable 17th-c

thatched and beamed pub in pretty village,
enjoyable sensibly priced food from extensive
menu, good Sun carvery (best to book),
friendly efficient staff, well kept Greene King
ales, good choice of reasonably priced wines,
two log fires and plush seats in low-ceilinged
connecting areas, old prints and paintings,
airy dining extension; children and dogs
welcome, tables under umbrellas in pleasant
sheltered garden. *(D C T and E A Frewer, Lesley*
and Peter Barrett, N R White, Cliff Sparkes)

DORCHESTER SU5794
Fleur de Lys (01865) 340502
Just off A4074 Maidenhead–Oxford;
High Street; OX10 7HH Former 16th-c
coaching inn opposite abbey, traditional
two-level interior with interesting old
photographs of the pub, open fire and
woodburner, some good creative cooking
from chef-landlord (more pubby choices at
lunchtime), efficient service, Brakspears,
St Austell Tribute and a guest (spring and
summer beer festivals); children (away from
bar) and dogs welcome, picnic-sets on front
terrace and in back garden with play area
and aunt sally, four bedrooms, open till 6pm
Sun, closed Mon. *(Anon)*

DORCHESTER SU5794
George (01865) 340404
Just off A4074 Maidenhead–Oxford;
High Street; OX10 7HH Handsome 15th-c
timbered hotel in lovely village, roaring
log fire and charming furnishings in smart
beamed bar, enjoyable attractively presented
(if not over generous) food from lunchtime
baguettes up, ales such as Brakspears, Hook
Norton and Wadworths, cheerful efficient
uniformed staff, restaurant; background
music; children welcome, 17 bedrooms, open
all day. *(R L Borthwick, Simon Collett-Jones)*

DUCKLINGTON SP3507
Bell (01993) 700341
Off A415, a mile SE of Witney; Standlake
Road; OX29 7UP Pretty thatched and
beamed local with good value traditional
home-made food including OAP lunchtime
deal (not Sun), Greene King ales, friendly
service, big stripped-stone and flagstoned
bar with scrubbed tables, log fires, glass-
covered well, old local photographs and
farm tools, hatch-served public bar, roomy
back restaurant, its beams festooned with
bells; cards and dominoes, background
music; children welcome, seats outside
and play area, four bedrooms, open all day
Fri-Sun. *(Anon)*

EAST HENDRED SU4588
Plough (01235) 833213
Off A417 E of Wantage; Orchard Lane;
OX12 8JW 16th-c village pub with good
choice of home-made food (till 7pm Sun)
from traditional choices to specials including
good fresh fish/seafood, Greene King-
related ales, 11 wines by the glass including

champagne, efficient friendly service, lofty raftered main room with interesting farming memorabilia, side dining area; background music, sports TV; children and dogs welcome, nice enclosed back garden, attractive village, open all day Fri-Sun, closed Mon. *(Anon)*

EATON   SP4403
Eight Bells (01865) 862261
Signed off B4017 SW of Oxford; OX13 5PR Cosy unpretentious old pub with relaxed local atmosphere, two small low-beamed bars with open fires and a dining area, well kept Loose Cannon ales, traditional low-priced food served by friendly helpful staff; pleasant garden, nice walks, open all day Fri-Sun, closed Mon. *(Tony Hobden)*

EWELME   SU6491
Shepherds Hut (01491) 835661
Off B4009 about 6 miles SW of M40 junction 6; High Street; OX10 6HQ Cleanly refurbished and extended village pub, beams and bare boards, woodburner, decent home-made food, Greene King ales; children welcome, terrace picnic-sets with steps up to lawn and play area. *(Daniel Wall)*

EXLADE STREET   SU6582
✶ Highwayman (01491) 682020
Just off A4074 Reading–Wallingford; RG8 0UA Two beamed bar rooms, mainly 17th-c (parts older), with interesting rambling layout and mix of furniture, consistently good food from landlord-chef with plenty of variety, some pricey but also good value deals, friendly efficient service, well kept Fullers London Pride and Loddon Hoppit, lots of wines by the glass, airy conservatory dining room; soft background music; children and dogs welcome, terrace and garden with fine views, closed Sun evening, Mon. *(Richard Endacott, Mrs R Somers, Colin and Bernardine Perry)*

FERNHAM   SU2991
✶ Woodman (01367) 820643
A420 SW of Oxford, then left into B4508 after about 11 miles; village another 6 miles on; SN7 7NX Friendly 17th-c country pub with heavily beamed character main rooms, various odds and ends such as milkmaids' yokes, leather tack, coach horns and an old screw press, original oil paintings and old photographs, cushioned benches, pews and windsor chairs, candlelit tables made from casks and a big open fire, also some comfortable newer areas, Greene King, Oakham, Sharps, Timothy Taylors, Wadworths and White Horse tapped from the cask, several malt whiskies and decent choice of wines by the glass, well thought-of food; background music; children and dogs (in bar) welcome, disabled facilities, terrace seats, good walks below the downs, open all day. *(Barry and Anne, M J Daly, Dave Braisted, Brian Glozier)*

FIFIELD   SP2318
Merrymouth (01993) 831652
A424 Burford–Stow; OX7 6HR Simple but comfortable stone inn dating from 13th c, L-shaped bar with bay-window seats, flagstones and low beams, some walls stripped back to old masonry, warm stove, quite dark in places, generous food from good baguettes to blackboard fish specials, well kept Hook Norton and a couple of other ales, decent choice of wines, friendly landlord and staff; background music; children and dogs welcome, tables on terrace and in back garden, nine stable-block bedrooms. *(Anon)*

FINSTOCK   SP3616
✶ Plough (01993) 868333
Just off B4022 N of Witney; High Street; OX7 3BY Thatched low-beamed village pub nicely split up by partitions and alcoves, long rambling bar with leather sofas by massive stone inglenook, some unusual horsebrasses and historical documents to do with the pub, roomy dining room with candles and fresh flowers on stripped-pine tables, good food cooked by landlord (best to book), two or three well kept ales including Adnams Broadside, traditional cider, several wines by the glass and 20 malt whiskies, bar billiards, board games; children at discretion of licensees, dogs allowed in bar (pub has two cats), seats in neatly kept garden, aunt sally, walks in woodland and along River Evenlode, open all day Sat, closed Sun evening, Mon, two weeks in Feb. *(Dr Nigel Bowles, P and J Shapley)*

FYFIELD   SU4298
✶ White Hart (01865) 390585
Main Road; off A420 8 miles SW of Oxford; OX13 5LW Grand medieval hall with soaring eaves, huge stone-flanked window embrasures and minstrel's gallery, contrasting cosy low-beamed side bar with large inglenook, fresh flowers and evening candles throughout, civilised friendly atmosphere and full of history; good imaginative modern food (best to book) cooked by licensee using home-grown produce, Hook Norton, Loddon, Rebellion and Sharps Doom Bar (festivals May and Aug bank holidays), around 16 wines by the glass (including champagne), several malt whiskies and home-made summer elderflower pressé; background music; well behaved children welcome, elegant furniture under umbrellas on spacious heated terrace, lovely gardens, good Thames-side walks, open all day weekends, closed Mon. *(David Handforth, William Goodhart)*

GALLOWSTREE COMMON SU6980
Reformation (0118) 972 3126
Horsepond Road; RG4 9BP Friendly black-beamed village local with good value home-made food from nice lunchtime baguettes up, special diets catered for,

bargain OAP menu Tues-Sat, a couple of Brakspears ales, open fires, conservatory; events like tractor runs and log-splitting competitions; children very welcome, dogs allowed (but ask first as they have their own), garden with 'shipwreck' play area, open all day Fri and Sat, till 5pm Sun, closed Mon lunchtime. *(Anon)*

GODSTOW SP4809
★ **Trout** (01865) 510930

Off A40/A44 roundabout via Wolvercote; OX2 8PN Pretty 17th-c Mitchells & Butlers dining pub in lovely riverside location (gets packed in fine weather); bistro-style food all day (booking essential at busy times), four beamed linked rooms with contemporary furnishings, flagstones and bare boards, log fires in three huge hearths, Adnams and Timothy Taylors Landlord, several wines by the glass; background music; children welcome till 7pm, plenty of terrace seats under big parasols (dogs allowed here), footbridge to island (may be closed), abbey ruins opposite, pay car park with fee redeemed at bar, open all day. *(Martin and Pauline Jennings, Simon Watkins, Conor McGaughey, Martin and Alison Stainsby, David Handforth)*

GORING SU5980
★ **Catherine Wheel** (01491) 872379

Station Road; RG8 9HB Friendly 18th-c village pub doing well under newish licensees; two neat and cosily traditional bar areas, especially the more individual lower room with its low beams and big inglenook log fire, popular home-made food (not Sun evening) including good value midweek roasts, well kept Brakspears and guests, Thatcher's cider, back restaurant, notable doors to lavatories; children and dogs welcome, sunny garden and terrace, handy for Thames Path, open all day. *(Anon)*

GOZZARD'S FORD SU4698
★ **Black Horse** (01865) 390530

Off B4017 NW of Abingdon; N of A415 by Marcham–Cothill Road; OX13 6JH Ancient traditional pub in tiny hamlet, good fresh food (all day Sun) especially fish and seafood, well kept Greene King ales and guests, some nice wines, cheerful efficient service, carpeted beamed main bar partly divided by stout timbers and low steps, end woodburner, separate plainer public bar with darts and pool; children welcome, pleasant garden, open all day. *(T M Griffiths, Karen Aplin, William Goodhart)*

GREAT TEW SP3929
★ **Falkland Arms** (01608) 683653

The Green; off B4022 about 5 miles E of Chipping Norton; OX7 4DB Golden-stone thatched cottage in lovely village, unspoilt partly panelled bar with high-backed settles, diversity of stools and plain tables on flagstones or bare boards, one-,

two- and three-handled mugs hanging from beam-and-boards ceiling, dim converted oil lamps, shutters for stone-mullioned latticed windows and open fire in fine inglenook, Wadworths and guests, Weston's cider, country wines and 30 malt whiskies, snuff for sale, straightforward good value food, friendly service, separate dining room, live folk Sun evening; children and dogs welcome, tables out at front and under parasols in back garden, small fair value bedrooms (no under-16s), open all day. *(Andy Dolan, Guy Vowles, D L Frostick, Paul Humphreys, Nancy Weber, Richard Stanfield)*

HAILEY SU6485
★ **King William IV** (01491) 681845

The Hailey near Ipsden, off A4074 or A4130 SE of Wallingford; OX10 6AD Fine old pub in lovely countryside, beamed bar with good sturdy furniture on tiles in front of big log fire, three other cosy seating areas opening off, enjoyable reasonably priced food from baguettes to specials, Brakspears and guests tapped from the cask, helpful friendly staff; children and dogs welcome, terrace and large garden enjoying wide-ranging peaceful views, may be red kites overhead, good walking (Chiltern Way and Ridgeway), leave muddy boots in porch, open all day. *(Mrs Margo Finlay, Jörg Kasprowski, Linda Fawke, Brian Patterson, Paul Humphreys)*

HENLEY SU7682
Angel on the Bridge (01491) 410678

Thames-side, by the bridge; RG9 1BH 17th c and worth knowing for its prime Thames-side position; small front bar with log fire, downstairs back bar and adjacent restaurant, beams, uneven floors and dim lighting, Brakspears ales and good choice of wines by the glass, enjoyable food from sandwiches and pubby choices up, friendly well organised staff; nice waterside deck (plastic glasses here), moorings for two boats, open all day in summer. *(N R White, Dr D J and Mrs S C Walker)*

HENLEY SU7882
Row Barge (01491) 572649

West Street; RG9 2ED Unpretentious Brakspears local with cosy low-beamed bar dropping down the hill in steps, their ales kept well, tasty good value pubby food from sandwiches up, nice cafetière coffee, good helpful service; sizeable garden. *(Paul Humphreys)*

HENLEY SU7582
★ **Three Tuns** (01491) 410138

Market Place; RG9 2AA Doing well under present licensees and some refurbishment; small heavy-beamed front bar with fire, well kept Brakspears and guests such as Ringwood, good attractively presented food from imaginative menu including own-cured salmon, set menu, nice wines, friendly helpful service, panelled back dining area with painted timbers and wood floor; monthly comedy and music nights; tables in small attractive back courtyard, closed Mon, otherwise open all day (bar snacks only Sun evening). *(Paul Humphreys)*

HIGHMOOR　　　　　　　　　SU6984
★ **Rising Sun**　(01491) 640856
Witheridge Hill, signposted off B481; OS Sheet 175 map reference 697841; RG9 5PF Friendly licensee in pretty 17th-c village pub in heart of the Chilterns; bar with tiled or stripped-wood floor, cream and terracotta walls, woodburner in big brick inglenook, main area spreading back from here has shiny bare boards and swathe of carpeting with well spaced tables, Brakspears ales, Weston's cider and ten wines by the glass, good food from sandwiches and tapas up; background music; children under strict supervision in dining areas only, dogs in bar, pleasant back garden with boules, plenty of surrounding walks, open all day weekends (till 10pm Sun). *(Bob and Margaret Holder, Richard Endacott, Simon Rodway, David and Sue Smith and others)*

HOOK NORTON　　　　　　　SP3534
★ **Gate Hangs High**　(01608) 737387
N towards Sibford, at Banbury–Rollright crossroads; OX15 5DF Snug tucked-away family-run pub, low-ceilinged bar with traditional furniture on bare boards, attractive inglenook, good reasonably priced home-made food from bar snacks up, well kept Hook Norton ales and a guest, decent wines, friendly helpful service, side dining extension (booking advised); background music; pretty courtyard and country garden, four bedrooms, good breakfast, quite near Rollright Stones, open all day. *(K H Frostick)*

HORNTON　　　　　　　　　SP3945
Dun Cow　(01295) 670524
West End; OX15 6DA Traditional 17th-c thatch and ironstone village pub, friendly and relaxed, with sensibly short choice of good fresh food (not Sun or Mon evenings) from lunchtime sandwiches up using local suppliers, Hook Norton, XT and Wells & Youngs, a dozen wines by the glass; children and dogs welcome, attractive small garden behind, open all day weekends, closed lunchtimes Mon, Tues (in winter lunchtimes Mon-Thurs). *(Guy Vowles)*

KELMSCOTT　　　　　　　　SU2499
★ **Plough**　(01367) 253543
NW of Faringdon, off B4449 between A417 and A4095; GL7 3HG Refurbished country pub with ancient flagstones, stripped stone and log fire, wide choice of good food (more restauranty in the evening), well kept beers such as Hook Norton, Vale, Wickwar and Wye Valley, real cider, helpful friendly staff; children, dogs and boots welcome, tables out in covered area and garden, lovely spot near upper Thames (good moorings

a few minutes away), eight comfortable bedrooms, good breakfast, no car park, handy for Kelmscott Manor (open Weds, Sat), pub open all day. *(R K Phillips, W M Lien, David and Stella Martin, Tony Hobden)*

KIDMORE END　　　　　　　SU6979
New Inn　(01189) 723115
Chalkhouse Green Road; signed from B481 in Sonning Common; RG4 9AU Extended black and white pub by village church; beams and big log fire, enjoyable freshly made food, well kept Brakspears ales and decent wines by the glass, pleasant restaurant; children welcome, tables in large sheltered garden with pond, six bedrooms, open all day Thurs-Sat, closed Sun evening. *(Tony and Gill Powell, Richard Endacott)*

LAUNTON　　　　　　　　　SP6022
Bull　(01869) 240176
Just E of Bicester; OX26 5DQ Modernised part-thatched 17th-c village pub, welcoming and well managed, with enjoyable food (not Sun evening) including OAP lunchtime discount (Mon-Fri), two well kept Greene King ales and a guest, Sun quiz; background music; children allowed away from bar, dogs on leads, wheelchair access from car park, disabled facilities, garden with terrace, open all day. *(Anon)*

LEWKNOR　　　　　　　　　SU7197
★ **Olde Leathern Bottel**
(01844) 351482　*Under a mile from M40 junction 6; off B4009 towards Watlington; OX49 5TH* Popular and friendly family-run place, two heavy beamed bars with understated décor and rustic furnishings, open fires, well kept Brakspears and Marstons, several wines by the glass, tasty pub food and specials served quickly, family room separated by standing timbers; dogs welcome, splendid garden with plenty of picnic-sets under parasols, play area and boules, handy for walks on Chiltern escarpment. *(Mike Horgan, Di Wright, Nigel and Sue Foster, Dr A J and Mrs B A Tompsett, R K Phillips, Dave Braisted)*

LONG HANBOROUGH　　　　SP4214
★ **George & Dragon**　(01993) 881362
A4095 Bladon–Witney; Main Road; OX29 8JX Substantial pub with original two-room bar (17th-c or older), stripped stone, low beams and two woodburners, Courage and Wells & Youngs ales, Weston's cider and good range of wines, roomy thatched restaurant extension with comfortably padded dining chairs around sturdy tables on floorboards, plenty of pictures on deep pink walls, decorative plates on beams, wide choice of well liked food (not Sun evening) served by neat, uniformed staff; background music; children and dogs (in bar) welcome, peaceful back garden with picnic-sets among attractive shrubs,

tables beneath canopy on separate sheltered terrace, and further areas with rabbits and guinea pigs. *(Anon)*

LONG WITTENHAM   SU5493
Plough (01865) 407738
High Street; OX14 4QH Friendly local under new management; low beams, inglenook fires and lots of brass, three real ales including Butcombe, good choice of well priced traditional food from sandwiches up, dining room, games in public bar; Thames moorings at bottom of nice spacious garden with aunt sally. *(David Lamb)*

LOWER HEYFORD   SP4824
★ **Bell** (01869) 347176
Market Square; OX25 5NY Charming creeper-clad building in small thatched village square, popular with locals and boaters on nearby Oxford Canal, enjoyable fresh food from baguettes to specials, well kept interesting beers including one named for them, good coffee, cheerful quick service, uncluttered pleasantly refurbished rooms around central beamed bar; children welcome, disabled facilities, nice long walled garden with gazebo and aunt sally, canal walks and handy for Rousham Garden. *(Edward Mirzoeff, Tony Hobden)*

MAIDENSGROVE   SU7288
Five Horseshoes (01491) 641282
Off B480 and B481, W of village; RG9 6EX 16th-c dining pub set high in the Chilterns, rambling bar with low ceiling and log fire, enjoyable food (not Sun evening) including home-smoked salmon and local game, weekday set menu, friendly service, well kept Brakspears and good choice of wines by the glass, airy conservatory restaurant; children and dogs welcome, plenty of garden tables and lovely views, wood-fired pizzas on summer weekends, good walks, open all day Sat, Sun, closed Mon evening. *(Sharon Oldham)*

MARSH BALDON   SU5699
Seven Stars (01865) 343337
The Baldons; signed off A4074 N of Dorchester; OX44 9LP Small refurbished beamed village-green pub now owned by the village; two bar areas and snug dining room, leather sofas and armchairs by corner fire, fairly traditional food and ales such as Brakspears and Timothy Taylors Landlord; open all day (till late Fri, Sat). *(Katie Jayson-Morgan)*

MARSTON   SP5209
Victoria Arms (01865) 241382
Mill Lane; OX3 0PZ Much extended old pub in idyllic location by the Cherwell; well kept Wadworths ales and enjoyable food from ciabattas up, good service with a smile, plainly furnished main room with smaller ones off, log fires; background music; children and dogs allowed, spacious

waterside terrace, play area, punt moorings, open all day. *(Paul Humphreys)*

MURCOTT   SP5815
★ **Nut Tree** (01865) 331253
Off B4027 NE of Oxford, via Islip and Charlton-on-Otmoor; OX5 2RE Beamed and thatched 15th-c dining pub, good imaginative cooking (not cheap) using own produce including home-reared pigs, neat friendly young staff, Vale and two guests, carefully chosen wines; background music; children and dogs (in bar) welcome, terrace and pretty garden, unusual gargoyles on front wall (modelled loosely on local characters), closed Sun evening, Mon. *(Dennis and Doreen Haward, David and Sue Atkinson, Phil and Helen Holt)*

NORTH MORETON   SU5689
Bear at Home (01235) 811311
Off A4130 Didcot–Wallingford; High Street; OX11 9AT Dating from the 15th c with traditional beamed areas, cosy fireside areas and dining part with stripped-pine furniture, enjoyable reasonably priced home-made food, friendly service, Timothy Taylors, a beer for the pub from West Berkshire and a couple of local guests (July beer festival), Weston's cider, several wines by the glass; attractive garden overlooking cricket pitch, aunt sally, pretty village, open all day Sat. *(Franklyn Roberts)*

NUFFIELD   SU6787
Crown (01491) 641335
A4130/B481; RG9 5SJ Friendly new management at this attractive little brick and flint country pub; enjoyable home-made food, good service and well kept Brakspears ales, bare boards and inglenook log fire in beamed lounge bar; children and dogs in small garden room, disabled access, tables at front and in enclosed back garden, good walks nearby, closed Sun evening, Mon. *(Ross Balaam)*

OXFORD   SP5106
Chequers (01865) 727463
Off High Street; OX1 4DH Narrow 16th-c courtyard pub with several areas on three floors, interesting architectural features, beams, panelling and stained glass, wide choice of rotating ales and of enjoyable well priced pubby food (sausage specialities), quick friendly service, games room with balcony; walled garden. *(Simon Watkins, Roger and Donna Huggins, George Atkinson)*

OXFORD   SP5106
★ **Eagle & Child** (01865) 302925
St Giles; OX1 3LU Long narrow Nicholsons pub dating from the 16th c with two charmingly old-fashioned panelled front rooms, well kept Brakspears, Hook Norton and interesting guests, wide range of food all day from sandwiches to Sun roasts, friendly service and bustling atmosphere, stripped-brick back dining extension

and conservatory, Tolkien and C S Lewis connections; games machine; children allowed in back till 8pm. *(Stuart Doughty, N R White)*

OXFORD   SP5106
Far From the Madding Crowd
(01865) 240900 *Friars Entry; OX1 2BY*
Busy open-plan free house with six quickly changing ales, regular beer and cider festivals, straightforward well priced food, quiz and live music nights, 'Ox Factor' talent show; children and dogs welcome, disabled access, open all day (till midnight Thurs-Sat). *(Anon)*

OXFORD   SP5105
Head of the River (01865) 721600
Folly Bridge; between St Aldates and Christ Church Meadow; OX1 4LB
Civilised well renovated pub by river, boats for hire and nearby walks; spacious split-level downstairs bar with dividing brick arches, flagstones and bare boards, Fullers/Gales beers, good choice of wines by the glass, popular pubby food from sandwiches up, good service, daily papers; background music; tables on stepped heated waterside terrace, 12 bedrooms, open all day. *(Dave Braisted)*

OXFORD   SP5203
Isis Farmhouse (01865) 247006
Off Donnington Bridge Road; no car access; OX4 4EL Charming waterside spot for early 19th-c former farmhouse (accessible only to walkers/cyclists), relaxed lived-in interior with two woodburners, short choice of home-made locally sourced food (sensible prices), Appleford and a guest such as Shotover, nice wines and interesting soft drinks, afternoon teas with wonderful home-baked cakes; picnic-sets on terrace and in garden, aunt sally by arrangement, canoe hire, short walk to Iffley Lock and nearby lavishly decorated early Norman church, open all day Thurs-Sat in summer (Fri-Sun in winter) and all bank holidays including Christmas. *(Martin and Alison Stainsby)*

OXFORD   SP5106
★ **Kings Arms** (01865) 242369
Holywell Street; OX1 3SP Dating from the early 17th c, convivial, relaxed and popular with locals and students, quick helpful service, well kept Wells & Youngs range and four guests, fine choice of wines by the glass, eating area with counter servery doing good variety of reasonably priced food all day, cosy rooms up and down steps, lots of panelling and pictures, daily papers; downstairs lavatories; a few tables outside, open from 10.30am. *(George Atkinson)*

OXFORD   SP5106
Lamb & Flag (01865) 515787
St Giles/Banbury Road; OX1 3JS
Old pub owned by nearby college, modern airy front room with light wood panelling and

big windows over street, more atmosphere in back rooms with stripped stonework and low-boarded ceilings, a beer by Palmers for the pub (L&F Gold), Shepherd Neame Spitfire, Skinners Betty Stogs and guests, some lunchtime food including sandwiches and tasty home-made pies, Thomas Hardy *Jude the Obscure* connection; open all day. *(Anon)*

OXFORD   SP5006
Old Bookbinders (01865) 553549
Victor Street; OX2 6BT Dark and mellow family-run local tucked away in the Jericho area; friendly and unpretentious, with old fittings and lots of interesting bric-a-brac, Greene King ales and three guests, decent choice of whiskies, enjoyable french-leaning food (not Sun) including speciality crêpes and some bargain main dishes, board games and shove-ha'penny, concealed bookcase door to lavatories, Tues quiz, live music; children, dogs and students welcome, open all day, closed Mon. *(Anon)*

OXFORD   SP4907
Perch (01865) 728891
Binsey Lane, on right after river bridge leaving city on A420; OX2 0NG
Beautifully set 17th-c thatched limestone building in tiny riverside hamlet, more restaurant than pub and efficiently run by french team, imaginative modern cooking, not particularly cheap but they also do a good value weekday set lunch, prompt friendly service, well kept real ales and good wine list, décor successfully blending new with old beams, flagstones and log fire, Lewis Carroll connection; lovely garden running down to Thames Path, river cruises, closed Sun evening, Mon, Tues, otherwise open all day. *(Giles and Annie Francis, Jeremy Whitehorn)*

OXFORD   SP5105
Royal Blenheim (01865) 242355
Ebbes Street; OX1 1PT Popular airy 19th-c corner pub, opened by Queen Victoria during her Golden Jubilee, and now the tap for the White Horse Brewery; their range and many interesting guests, good value straightforward food (all day weekends), single room with original tiled floor, raised perimeter booth seating; big-screen sports TV, Weds quiz, Mon knitting club; open all day (till midnight Fri, Sat). *(Peter Martin, Roger and Donna Huggins, Tony Hobden)*

OXFORD   SP5106
★ **Turf Tavern** (01865) 243235
Bath Place; via St Helen's Passage, between Holywell Street and New College Lane; OX1 3SU Interesting character pub hidden away behind high walls, two small dark-beamed bars with lots of snug areas, always packed, but run efficiently by knowledgeable young staff; up to a dozen constantly changing real ales (spring and summer festivals) including Greene King,

also Weston's Old Rosie cider and winter mulled wine, enjoyable reasonably priced food (booking advised); children and dogs welcome, three walled-in courtyards (one with own bar), coal braziers to roast chestnuts, open all day. *(Andy Dolan, Simon Watkins, G Jennings, Jane and Rowena Leverington, Stuart Doughty, Brian Glozier and others)*

OXFORD   SP5106
⋆ White Horse   (01865) 204801

Broad Street; OX1 3BB Bustling and studenty, squeezed between bits of Blackwells bookshop, small narrow bar with snug one-table raised back alcove, low beams and timbers, ochre ceiling, beautiful view of the Clarendon Building and the Sheldonian, good choice of ales including Hook Norton, St Austell and Shotover, friendly staff, good value simple food; open all day. *(Paul Humphreys)*

PLAY HATCH   SU7477
Shoulder of Mutton   (0118) 947 3908

W of Henley Road (A4155) roundabout; RG4 9QU Dining pub with low-ceilinged log-fire bar and large conservatory restaurant, good generous food including signature mutton dishes, well kept Greene King and guests such as Loddon, good value house wines, friendly efficient service; children welcome, picnic-sets in carefully tended walled garden with well, closed Sun evening. *(Paul Humphreys)*

ROKE   SU6293
Home Sweet Home   (01491) 838249

Off B4009 Benson–Watlington; OX10 6JD Wadworths pub with two smallish bars, heavy stripped beams, big log fire and traditional furniture, carpeted room on right leading to restaurant area, enjoyable food served by friendly staff; background music; children welcome and dogs (they have one), low-walled front garden. *(Sharon Oldham)*

ROTHERFIELD PEPPARD   SU7081
Unicorn   (01491) 628674

Colmore Lane; RG9 5LX Attractive country pub in the Chilterns, run by same people as the Little Angel, Henley and Cherry Tree, Stoke Row; bustling bar with open fire, real ales and good wines, dining room with high-backed chairs around mix of tables on stripped boards, well liked interesting food including lunchtime sandwiches and daily specials, friendly service; seats out in front and in pretty back garden. *(Anon)*

SANDFORD-ON-THAMES   SP5301
Kings Arms   (01865) 777095

Church Road; OX4 4YB Delightful lockside spot on Thames with tables on waterside terrace; usual Chef & Brewer menu, well kept ales and good choice of wines by the glass; can get very busy and

may be queues; children welcome, moorings, open all day. *(Martin and Alison Stainsby)*

SHENINGTON   SP3742
⋆ Bell   (01295) 670274

Off A422 NW of Banbury; OX15 6NQ Good wholesome home cooking in hospitable 17th-c two-room village pub, nice sandwiches too, well kept Flowers and Hook Norton, decent wine choice, friendly informal service and long-serving licensees, heavy beams, some flagstones, stripped stone and pine panelling, two woodburners; children in eating areas and dogs in bar, picnic-sets out at front, charming quiet village with good walks, three simple bedrooms, generous breakfast, closed Sun evening, Mon. *(Peter J and Avril Hanson, D L Frostick)*

SHIPLAKE   SU7476
Flowing Spring   (0118) 969 9878

A4155 towards Play Hatch and Reading; RG4 9RB Roadside pub built on bank (all on first floor with slight slope front to back), warm open fires in small two-room bar, assorted bric-a-brac, good value home-made food (not Sun or Mon evenings) from sandwiches, wraps and pizzas up, special diets catered for, Fullers ales, Aspall's cider, modern dining room with floor-to-ceiling windows, tables out on covered balcony, various events including astronomy nights and occasional live music; children and dogs welcome, lawned garden bordered by streams, summer marquee and barbecues, open all day. *(Paul Humphreys)*

SHIPTON-UNDER-WYCHWOOD   SP2717
⋆ Lamb   (01993) 830465

High Street; off A361 to Burford; OX7 6DQ Mother-and-son team at this handsome stone inn, beamed bar with oak-panelled settle, farmhouse chairs and polished tables on wood-block flooring, stripped-stone walls, church candles and log fire, three changing beers, plenty of wines by the glass and well liked food, restaurant area; children welcome, dogs allowed in bar (there are two pub dogs), wheelchair access, garden with modern furniture on terrace, five themed bedrooms, open all day. *(Andy Dolan, Bernard Stradling, David Jackman, E Clark, R K Phillips and others)*

SHIPTON-UNDER-WYCHWOOD   SP2717
Shaven Crown   (01993) 830330

High Street (A361); OX7 6BA Ancient monastic building with magnificent lofty medieval rafters and imposing double stairway in hotel part's hall, separate more down-to-earth back bar with beams, panelling and booth seating, lovely log fires, good helpings of enjoyable food, Hook Norton and a couple of guests, several wines by the glass, helpful friendly service, restaurant; background music; children and dogs welcome, peaceful central courtyard with heaters, bowling green, eight bedrooms (one in former chapel). *(Christine Murphy, Richard Stanfield, N R White)*

SIBFORD GOWER   SP3537
★**Wykham Arms** (01295) 788808

Signed off B4035 Banbury–Shipston on Stour; Temple Mill Road; OX15 5RX Cottagey 17th-c thatched and flagstoned dining pub, good food from light lunchtime menu up, friendly attentive staff, two well kept changing ales, plenty of wines by the glass, comfortable open-plan interior with low beams and stripped stone, glass-covered well, inglenook; children and dogs welcome, country views from big garden, lovely manor house opposite, open all day Sun, closed Mon. *(Anon)*

SOULDERN   SP5231
Fox (01869) 345284

Off B4100; Fox Lane; OX27 7JW Pretty pub set in delightful village, comfortable open-plan beamed layout with settles and chairs around oak tables, big log fire, enjoyable fairly priced food including the Fox Sandwich (roast beef between two yorkshire puddings), well kept Hook Norton and two guests (July beer/music festival), good choice of wines by the glass, quiz nights; dogs welcome (they have one), garden and terrace, aunt sally, four bedrooms, open all day Sat, till 4pm Sun. *(Andy Dolan)*

SOUTH NEWINGTON   SP4033
Duck on the Pond (01295) 721166

A361; OX15 4JE Dining pub with tidy modern-rustic décor in small flagstoned bar and linked carpeted eating areas up a step, enjoyable food from light dishes to steak and family Sun lunch, Hook Norton and a couple of guests, decent coffee, cheerful landlord and friendly young staff, woodburner; background music, no dogs; spacious grounds with tables on deck and lawn, aunt sally, pond with waterfowl, walk down to River Swere, open all day weekends. *(George Atkinson)*

SOUTH STOKE   SU5983
Perch & Pike (01491) 872415

Off B4009 2 miles N of Goring; RG8 0JS Friendly family-run brick and flint pub just a field away from the Thames, cottagey low-beamed bar with open fire, well kept beer and enjoyable home-made food, sizeable timbered restaurant extension where children allowed; may be background music; tables on terrace and flower-bordered lawn, four bedrooms. *(Anon)*

SPARSHOLT   SU3487
Star (01235) 751873

Watery Lane; OX12 9PL Compact 16th-c beamed country pub greatly improved by present owners; very good upmarket modern food along with cheaper bar menu, friendly welcoming service, beers such as Sharps

Doom Bar; dogs allowed, back garden, pretty village (snowdrops fill churchyard in spring), eight refurbished bedrooms in converted barn, open all day Fri-Sun, closed Mon. *(David Lamb, Terry Miller, Andrew Loudon)*

STANTON ST JOHN   SP5709
Star (01865) 351277

Pub signed off B4027; village signed off A40 E of Oxford; OX33 1EX Pleasant old Wadworths pub tucked away at end of village and under newish management (sister pub to Abingdon Arms, Beckley); two small low-beamed rooms, one with ancient brick floor, other with close-set tables, up stairs to attractive flagstoned extension (on same level as car park – wheelchair access using ramp) with old-fashioned dining chairs around dark oak or elm tables, bookshelves either side of inglenook log fire, family conservatory, reasonably priced traditional food; background music; dogs welcome, seats in walled garden with play area, open all day weekends, closed Mon. *(Anon)*

STANTON ST JOHN   SP5709
★**Talk House** (01865) 351648

Middle Road/Wheatley Road (B4027 just outside village); OX33 1EX Attractive part-thatched dining pub; older part on left with steeply pitched rafters soaring above stripped-stone walls, mix of old dining chairs and big stripped tables, large rugs on flagstones; rest of building converted more recently but in similar style with massive beams, flagstones or stoneware tiles, and log fires below low mantelbeams, well liked food, three Fullers ales and several wines by the glass; children welcome, dogs in bar, inner courtyard with teak tables and chairs, a few picnic-sets on side grass, bedrooms, open all day; new management taking over as we went to press. *(Brenda Keogh, V A C Turnbull, Martin and Pauline Jennings, David Jackman)*

STEEPLE ASTON   SP4725
★**Red Lion** (01869) 340225

Off A4260 12 miles N of Oxford; OX25 4RY Cheerful village pub with neatly kept beamed and partly panelled bar, antique settle and other good furnishings, well kept Hook Norton ales and good choice of wines by the glass, enjoyable food from shortish menu including pizzas served by obliging young staff, back conservatory-style dining extension; well behaved children welcome lunchtime and until 7pm, dogs in bar, suntrap front garden with lovely flowers and shrubs, parking may be awkward, open all day Fri, Sat, till 5pm Sun. *(Ian Herdman, Roy Hoing, M S and M Imhoff)*

STEVENTON   SU4691
North Star

Stocks Lane, The Causeway, central westward turn off B4017; OX13 6SG Traditional little village pub through yew tree gateway, tiled entrance corridor, main area with ancient high-backed settles around central table, well kept Greene King Morland and guests from side tap room, hatch service to another room with plain seating, a couple of tables and good coal fire, simple lunchtime food, friendly staff; background music; dogs welcome, tables on front grass, open all day weekends, closed weekday lunchtimes. *(Anon)*

STOKE LYNE   SP5628
Peyton Arms
From minor road off B4110 N of Bicester fork left into village; OX27 8SD
Beautifully situated and largely unspoilt one-room stone-built alehouse, character landlord (Mick the Hat) and loyal regulars, very well kept Hook Norton from casks behind small corner bar, filled rolls, inglenook fire, tiled floor and lots of memorabilia, games area with darts and pool; no children or dogs; pleasant garden with aunt sally, open all day Sat, closed Sun evening, Mon. *(Anon)*

STOKE ROW   SU6884
Cherry Tree (01491) 680430
Off B481 at Highmoor; RG9 5QA
Refurbished pub-restaurant with good up-to-date food including lunchtime set deal, well kept Brakspears ales, ten wines by the glass, four linked rooms with stripped wood, heavy low beams and some flagstones, helpful friendly staff; background music, TV in bar; well behaved children and dogs welcome, lots of tables in attractive garden, nearby walks, four good bedrooms in converted barn, open all day (Sun till 5pm). *(Paul Humphreys)*

STOKE ROW   SU6884
★ **Crooked Billet** (01491) 681048
Nottwood Lane, off B491 N of Reading – OS Sheet 175 map reference 684844; RG9 5PU Very nice place, but more restaurant than pub; charming rustic layout with heavy beams, flagstones, antique pubby furnishings and great inglenook log fire, crimson Victorian-style dining room, wide choice of competently cooked interesting food (all day weekends) using local produce, cheaper set lunches Mon-Fri, helpful friendly staff, Brakspears Oxford Gold, tapped from the cask (no counter), good wines, relaxed homely atmosphere; children very welcome, weekly live music, big garden by Chilterns beechwoods, open all day. *(Judi Sutherland)*

STONOR   SU7388
Quince Tree (01491) 639039
B480, off A4130 NW of Henley; RG9 6HE
Extensive and stylish revamp of former hotel (shut for many years); bar in modern country style with bleached wood furniture, well kept changing local ales, good food here and in back restaurant (not cheap), friendly prompt service from young staff; children welcome, dogs in bar, landscaped garden and terrace, new barn-like building housing a café on

two floors and farm shop/deli, closed Sun evening. *(Susan and John Douglas)*

SUNNINGWELL   SP4900
Flowing Well (01865) 735846
Just N of Abingdon; OX13 6RB
Recently refurbished timbered pub (built as a rectory in the early 19th c) with bistro feel; popular home-made food (discount Mon night) from pizzas and pub favourites up, Greene King and guest ales, good choice of wines, Weds quiz; children welcome, large heated raised terrace, more seats in garden with small well, open all day. *(William Goodhart, Baz Manning)*

SWINFORD   SP4308
Talbot (01865) 881348
B4044 just S of Eynsham; OX29 4BT
Roomy and comfortable 17th-c beamed pub, well kept Arkells direct from cooled cask, good choice of wines and soft drinks, enjoyable reasonably priced pubby food, friendly staff, long attractive flagstoned bar with some stripped stone, cheerful log-effect gas fire, occasional live jazz; may be background music; children and dogs welcome, garden with decked area overlooking Wharf Stream, pleasant walk along lovely stretch of the Thames towpath, moorings quite nearby, 11 bedrooms. *(Anon)*

SYDENHAM   SP7201
Crown (01844) 351634
Off B4445 Chinnor–Thame; OX39 4NB
Friendly low-beamed pub in picturesque village, good food cooked by landlord, Brakspears, Fullers London Pride and a guest, nice wines, open fires in long narrow bar; children welcome, small garden, views of lovely church, open all day Sat, closed Sun evening, Mon. *(Anon)*

THAME   SP7105
Cross Keys (01844) 212147
Park Street/East Street; OX9 3HP
One-bar 19th-c local with wide range of well kept ales including own Thame beers (tasting trays available), friendly atmosphere, no food but can bring your own; courtyard garden. *$(Doug Kennedy)*

THAME   SP7005
James Figg (01844) 260166
Cornmarket; OX9 2BL Friendly coaching inn, clean and well furnished, with four well kept ales including Purity and Vale, Addlestone's and Aspall's ciders, ten wines by the glass, enjoyable straightforward locally sourced food from sandwiches up, open fire below portrait of James Figg (local 18th-c boxer), converted stables with own bar for music/functions; busier and noisier evenings; children and dogs welcome, back garden, open all day. *(Richard and Liz Thorne, Tim and Ann Newell)*

THAME SP7005
Swan (01844) 260399
Upper High Street; OX9 3ER Recently
refurbished heavily beamed 16th-c inn;
three Rebellion ales and guests, food in bar
and upstairs evening restaurant with its
painted medieval ceiling; background and
some live music; children and dogs welcome,
bedrooms, open all day. *(Anon)*

THRUPP SP4815
⋆Boat (01865) 374279
*Brown sign to pub off A4260 just N of
Kidlington; OX5 1JY* Attractive 16th-c
stone pub set back from the Southern Oxford
Canal (moorings), low ceilings, bare boards
and some ancient floor tiles, log fires and old
coal stove, enjoyable well priced home-made
food (all day weekends) including vegetarian
options, specials and Sun carvery, friendly
service, Greene King ales and decent wines;
gets busy in summer; children and dogs
welcome, fenced garden behind with plenty
of tables, open all day. *(Tony Hobden)*

TOOT BALDON SP5600
Mole (01865) 340001
*Between A4074 and B480 SE of Oxford;
OX44 9NG* Light open-plan restauranty
dining pub with very good if not cheap food
(booking advisable), nice wines by the glass,
Hook Norton and a guest, leather sofas by
bar, neat country furniture or more formal
leather dining chairs in linked eating areas
including conservatory, stripped 18th-c
beams and big open fire; background music;
children welcome, no dogs inside, garden
tables, open all day. *(Susan Loppert, Jane
Caplan)*

WANTAGE SU3988
Lamb (01235) 766768
*Mill Street, past square and Bell; down
hill then bend to left; OX12 9AB* Popular
17th-c thatched pub with low beams, log fire
and cosy corners, well kept ales including
Fullers London Pride from brick-faced bar,
good straightforward food at reasonable
prices; children welcome, disabled facilities,
garden with play area, open all day. *(D C T
and E A Frewer, Cliff Sparkes)*

WANTAGE SU3987
⋆Royal Oak (01235) 763129
Newbury Street; OX12 8DF Popular
two-bar corner local with a dozen well
kept ales including Wadworths and West
Berkshire, good choice of ciders and perries
too, friendly knowledgeable landlord, lots
of pump clips, old ship photographs, darts;
bedrooms, closed weekday lunchtimes.
(Anon)

WANTAGE SU3987
Shoulder of Mutton 07870 577742
Wallingford Street; OX12 8AX Victorian
pub renovated by enthusiastic landlord

keeping character in bar, dining lounge
and snug, ten well kept changing mainly
local ales including own Betjeman brews
(beer festivals), good cider/perry choice,
vegetarian food, regular folk music and other
events (even belly dancing classes); children
welcome, dogs allowed in bar, back terrace
with hop-covered pergola, four bedrooms,
open all day till midnight. *(Anon)*

WARBOROUGH SU6093
⋆Six Bells (01865) 858265
*The Green S; just E of A329, 4 miles
N of Wallingford; OX10 7DN* Thatched
16th-c pub opposite village cricket green,
well kept Brakspears ales and wide choice of
good interesting food, friendly attentive staff,
attractive country furnishings in small linked
areas off bar, low beams, stripped stone
and big log fire; tables in pleasant orchard
garden. *(Barry Collett, John and Pauline Young)*

WESTCOTT BARTON SP4325
Fox (01869) 340338
*Enstone Road; B4030 off A44 NW of
Woodstock; OX7 7BL* Spacious 18th-c
stone-built village pub, low beams and
flagstones, pews and high-backed settles,
five well kept beers including Hook Norton,
food from baguettes to pub standards and
pizzas, log fire, small restaurant; background
music and regular live bands, steps down
to lavatories; children and dogs welcome,
pleasant garden with play area and aunt sally,
peaceful view, open all day Sat. *(Ryan Bass)*

WESTON-ON-THE-GREEN SP5318
Ben Jonson (01869) 351153
B430 near M40 junction 9; OX25 3RA
Ancient stone and thatch country pub with
long beamed bar and three dining areas,
open log fire and inglenook woodburner,
well kept changing ales such as Brakspears,
Hook Norton and Wychwood, good choice of
wines including local Brightwell, enjoyable
food all day using locally sourced ingredients
(some home-grown), friendly helpful service;
children and dogs welcome, picnic-sets
out in front, rustic smokers' shelter, garden.
(Val and Alan Green)

WESTON-ON-THE-GREEN SP5318
Chequers (01869) 351743
*Handy for M40 junction 9, via A34;
Northampton Road (B430); OX25 3QH*
Extended thatched village pub with three
areas off large semicircular raftered bar, fair
choice of food from traditional favourites up,
well kept Fullers and a guest, nice wines by
the glass; children welcome, tables under
parasols in attractive garden, open all day
Sat, till 6pm Sun. *(G Jonnings)*

WHITCHURCH SU6377
Greyhound (0118) 984 4800
*High Street, just over toll bridge from
Pangbourne; RG8 7EL* A friendly welcome
at this pretty former ferryman's cottage, cosy

low-beamed bar with fire, well kept ales such as Black Sheep and Shepherd Neame, good value tasty pub food from baguettes up; small sheltered back garden, attractive village on Thames Path, open all day weekends. *(Ross Balaam, Paul Humphreys)*

WHITCHURCH HILL SU6378
Sun (01189) 842260
Hill Bottom; signed from B471; RG8 7PG Friendly unassuming brick-built pub in sleepy village, homely L-shaped bar with carpet and bare boards, white textured walls, dark woodwork, plush chairs and wall benches, enjoyable reasonably priced home-made food including vegetarian choices, Brakspears, Hook Norton, Ringwood and a guest; children and dogs welcome, couple of picnic-sets out at front, small side terrace, back lawn with play area, open all day Fri-Sun. *(Richard Endacott, Paul Humphreys, Richard and Stephanie Foskett)*

WITNEY SP3509
Angel (01993) 703238
Market Square; OX28 6AL Wide choice of well priced food from good sandwiches up in unpretentious 17th-c town local, a house beer from Wychwood along with Hobgoblin, Brakspears, Marstons and occasional guest, quick friendly service even when packed, daily papers, hot coal fire; background music, big-screen sports TV, pool; lovely hanging baskets, back terrace with smokers' shelter, parking nearby can be difficult, open all day. *(George Atkinson)*

WITNEY SP3509
Fleece (01993) 892270
Church Green; OX28 4AZ Smart civilised town pub (part of the Peach group), popular for its wide choice of good often imaginative food from sandwiches and deli boards up, weekday fixed-price menu till 7pm, friendly attentive service, Greene King and a couple of guests, leather armchairs on wood floors, daily papers, restaurant; background music; children welcome, café-style tables out at front overlooking green, ten affordable bedrooms, open all day from 9am. *(J A Snell, Jane Taylor and David Dutton, R K Phillips)*

WITNEY SP3510
✳ Horseshoes (01993) 703086
Corn Street, junction with Holloway Road; OX28 6BS Attractive 16th-c modernised stone-built pub, wide choice of good home-made food from pubby choices to more imaginative restauranty dishes, Wychwood Hobgoblin and two local guests, decent house wines, friendly accommodating staff, heavy beams, flagstones and

comfortable old furniture, log fires, separate back dining room; tables on sunny terrace, open all day. *(Ian Herdman)*

WOLVERCOTE SP4909
Plough (01865) 556969
First Turn/Wolvercote Green; OX2 8AH Comfortably worn-in pubby linked areas, armchairs and Victorian-style carpeted bays in main lounge, well kept Greene King ales, farm cider and decent wines by the glass, friendly helpful staff and bustling atmosphere, enjoyable good value usual food in flagstoned former stables dining room and library (children allowed here), traditional snug, woodburner; picnic-sets on front decking looking over rough meadow to canal and woods, open all day weekends. *(Anon)*

WOODSTOCK SP4417
Black Prince (01993) 811530
Manor Road (A44 N); OX20 1XJ Old pub with one modernised low-ceilinged bar, timbers and stripped stone, suit of armour, log fire one end, good value home-made food from sandwiches to specials, four well kept ales including Vale, friendly service, some live music; outside lavatories; children walkers and dogs welcome, tables in attractive garden by small River Glyme, nearby right of way into Blenheim parkland, open all day. *(Geoff Clifford, Andy and Jill Kassube)*

WOODSTOCK SP4416
Star (01993) 811373
Market Place; OX20 1TA Sizeable old inn with light and airy front part, big windows, high ceiling and bare boards, tall black chairs around high tables, lower ceilinged area with pale stripped stone and comfortable seats on mulberry carpet, back part has a profusion of beams, coal-effect stove and unusually wide antique settle; interesting food (cheaper lunchtime), good variety of wines by the glass, Courage Directors and three Wells & Youngs ales, helpful proficient service; background music; sheltered flagstoned courtyard behind with stylish metal furniture and one or two cask tables, more seats in front, bedrooms, open all day from 8am. *(Anon)*

WOODSTOCK SP4416
Woodstock Arms (01993) 811251
Market Street; OX20 1SX Welcoming 16th-c heavy-beamed stripped-stone pub, enjoyable home-made food (not Sun evening), four well kept Greene King ales and good wine choice, prompt helpful service, log fire in splendid stone fireplace, long narrow bar with end eating area; background music

and occasional live jazz; children and dogs welcome, courtyard tables, open all day. *(Tony and Glenys Dyer, John and Sarah Webb)*

WOOLSTONE   SU2987
White Horse   (01367) 820726
Off B4507; SN7 7QL Appealing partly thatched pub with Victorian gables and latticed windows, plush furnishings, spacious beamed and part-panelled bar, two big open fires, Arkells ales and enjoyable good value food from lunchtime sandwiches up, prompt friendly staff even when busy, restaurant; well behaved children allowed, plenty of seats in front and back gardens, secluded interesting village handy for White Horse and Ridgeway, six bedrooms, open all day. *(Guy Vowles, R K Phillips, Cliff Sparkes)*

WOOTTON   SP4320
Killingworth Castle   (01993) 811401
Glympton Road; B4027 N of Woodstock; OX20 1EJ Under same ownership as the Ebrington Arms in Gloucestershire (see Main Entries); striking three-storey 17th-c

coaching inn with simply furnished candlelit rooms, built-in wall seats and mix of chairs around farmhouse tables on bare boards, woodburner and another fire, well kept Oxfordshire, Prescott, Shotover and Uley, farm cider, english lager and locally made vodka and gin, interesting food (themed evenings), enthusiastic staff, live acoustic music and comedy evenings; revamped garden, open all day. *(Martin and Pauline Jennings)*

WYTHAM   SP4708
White Hart   (01865) 244372
Off A34 Oxford ring road; OX2 8QA Refurbished 15th-c country pub, several areas with log fires including converted stables, some settles, handsome panelling and uneven flagstones, fairly traditional sensibly priced food, cosy bar with well kept Wadworths ales and lots of wines by the glass, conservatory; children and dogs welcome, courtyard tables, unspoilt preserved village, open all day. *(Franklyn Roberts, Jeremy Whitehorn)*

Shropshire

Good new entries this year are the Castle Hotel in Bishop's Castle (substantial 18th-c inn with interesting bars, popular food and ales and comfortable bedrooms), Woodbridge in Coalport (handsomely reworked Brunning & Price place in super riverside spot), Golden Ball at Ironbridge (friendly new landlord for unassuming Elizabethan pub with good value meals and drinks) and Hundred House in Norton (in the same friendly family for over 25 years, with enjoyable food and beers and a lovely herb garden). Other pubs doing especially well include the Fox in Chetwynd Aston (a Brunning & Price establishment with a fine choice of drinks, good bistro-style food and a buzzy atmosphere), Jolly Frog in Leintwardine (smashing pub with a cheerful bar and informal restaurant), Navigation in Maesbury Marsh (lots to look at and interesting food), George & Dragon in Much Wenlock (a genuinely welcoming town pub) and Armoury in Shrewsbury (another Brunning & Price pub, in an impressive riverside warehouse). A good choice of well kept real ales can also be found at the Old Castle in Bridgnorth, White Horse in Clun and Church Inn at Ludlow. Our Shropshire Dining Pub 2014 is the Fox at Chetwynd Aston.

BISHOP'S CASTLE   SO3288   Map 6

Castle Hotel 🛏

Market Square, just off B4385; SY9 5BN

Substantial coaching inn with bags of old-fashioned charm; bedrooms

At the top of a lovely market town, this fine old place has been offering sustenance to travellers since 1719. The clubby little beamed and panelled bar is neatly kept and attractively furnished, with a warm log fire, hunting prints and sturdy leather chairs on a muted carpet. It opens into a much bigger room, with maroon plush wall seats and stools, big Victorian engravings and another log fire in a cast-iron fireplace. The lighting in both rooms is gentle and relaxing, and the pub tables have unusually elaborate cast-iron frames; darts, background music and board games. Clun Pale Ale, Hobsons Best, Six Bells Big Nevs and Three Tuns Stirling on handpump, ten wines by the glass, 30 malt whiskies and farm cider; there's also a handsome panelled dining room. The bedrooms are spacious and full of period character, and breakfasts are good. In summer the pub is festooned with pretty hanging baskets, and the back garden has terraces with seats and tables on either side of a large raised fish pond, pergolas, climbing plants and stone walls; it looks out over rooftops to gentle countryside; disabled access. Plenty of surrounding walks.

❚❚ Good popular food includes sandwiches, chicken liver and chorizo pâté with home-made chutney, grilled goats cheese, bacon and pine nuts, green thai vegetable curry, honey-baked ham and eggs, lamb, mint and honey burger with cheese, onion rings and chips, seafood linguine, chicken in leek and stilton sauce with almond croquette potatoes, hake with tomatoes, olives and mascarpone, and puddings such as apricot and almond tart and lemon cheesecake with orange curd. *Benchmark main dish: rack of local lamb with celeriac purée and mustard and tarragon sauce £15.95. Two-course evening meal £17.50.*

Free house ~ Licensees Henry and Rebecca Bex ~ Real ale ~ (01588) 638403 ~ Open 11-11; 12-10.30 Sun ~ Bar food 12-2.30, 6.30-9 ~ Restaurant ~ Children welcome ~ Dogs welcome ~ Bedrooms: £65/£100 ~ www.thecastlehotelbishopscastle.co.uk
Recommended by Pat and Tony Martin

BRIDGNORTH
SO7192 Map 4

Old Castle £

West Castle Street; WV16 4AB

Traditional town pub, relaxed and friendly, with generous helpings of good value pubby food, well kept ales and good-sized suntrap terrace

A big plus at this little town pub is the sunny back terrace with its picnic-sets, lovely hanging baskets, big pots of flowers and shrub borders, and decking at the far end giving an elevated view over the west side of town; children's playthings. This was once two knocked-together cottages, as is evident from the outside. The low-beamed open-plan bar is properly pubby with genuine character: there are tiles and bare boards, cushioned wall banquettes and settles around cast-iron-framed tables, and bar stools arranged by the counter where the friendly landlord and his cheery staff serve Hobsons Town Crier, Sharps Doom Bar, Timothy Taylors Landlord and Wye Valley HPA on handpump. A conservatory extension at the back has darts and pool; background music, big-screen TV for sports. Do walk up the street to the ruined castle - its 20-metre Norman tower tilts at such an extraordinary angle that it makes the leaning tower of Pisa look like a model of rectitude.

❚❚ Generous helpings of good value pubby food include peppers stuffed with cheese and barbecue sauce, beetroot risotto, battered cod and chips, spicy meatballs with linguine, liver and bacon with mustard mash, lamb shank, chicken stuffed with haggis, specials like 10oz horse steak, chilli king prawns with vodka and noodles, and puddings such as fruit crumble and chocolate bread and butter pudding. *Benchmark main dish: steak in ale pie £8.50. Two-course evening meal £13.00.*

Punch ~ Tenants Bryn Charles Masterman and Kerry Senior ~ Real ale ~ (01746) 711420 ~ Open 11.30-11.30(midnight Sat) ~ Bar food 12-3, 6.30-8.30 ~ Children welcome ~ Dogs welcome ~ www.oldcastlebridgnorth.co.uk *Recommended by Ian Herdman, Jim and Frances Gowers, Jean and Douglas Troup, David Bennott, David and Katharine Cooke, Brian and Anna Marsden*

If you're planning a long journey, it might help you to look at the list of pubs near motorway junctions at the end of the book.

CARDINGTON

SO5095   Map 4

Royal Oak

*Village signposted off B4371 Church Stretton–Much Wenlock, pub behind
church; also reached via narrow lanes from A49; SY6 7JZ*

Lovely country spot, heaps of character inside and seasonal bar food

Tucked away in a rural spot, this unchanging ancient place is said to
be Shropshire's oldest continuously licensed pub. The rambling low-
beamed bar, gently frayed around the edges, has a roaring winter log fire,
a cauldron, black kettle and pewter jugs in a vast inglenook fireplace, the
aged standing timbers from a knocked-through wall, and red and green
tapestry seats solidly capped in elm; shove-ha'penny and dominoes.
Ludlow Best, Sharps Doom Bar, Three Tuns XXX and Salopian Hop
Twister on handpump. A comfortable dining area has exposed old beams
and studwork. This is glorious country for walks (such as to the summit
of Caer Caradoc, a couple of miles to the west – ask for directions at the
pub), and the front courtyard makes the most of its beautiful position.

 Using local, seasonal produce, the generously served bar food includes
baguettes, fried black pudding and bacon with pepper sauce, caramelised
red onion and tomato tart, mushroom stroganoff, battered cod and chips, lamb
steak with redcurrant, rosemary and red wine jus, salmon with lemon and
parsley sauce, specials such as honey and chilli pork belly and game pie, and
puddings. *Benchmark main dish: fidget pie (gammon in cider with apples)
£10.65. Two-course evening meal £18.00.*

Free house ~ Licensees Steve and Eira Oldham ~ Real ale ~ (01694) 771266 ~
Open 12-2.30, 6.30-11(midnight Sat); 12-3.30; 7-11 Sun; closed Mon ~ Bar food 12-2,
6.30-9; 12-2.30, 7-9 Sun ~ Restaurant ~ Children welcome ~ Dogs allowed in bar ~
www.at-the-oak.com *Recommended by Mark O'Sullivan, S and R Dowdy*

CHETWYND ASTON

SJ7517   Map 7

Fox ⑪ ♀ ◀

Village signposted off A41 and A518 just S of Newport; TF10 9LQ

Shropshire Dining Pub of the Year

**Civilised dining pub with generous helpings of well liked food and
a fine array of drinks served by ever-attentive staff**

'What a delight' and 'what a splendid pub' are just two comments
from readers on this handsome, spotlessly kept 1920s pub. It's big
and usually busy (with some cosy corners too), but the friendly staff
cope well. A series of linked areas, one with a broad arched ceiling,
has plenty of tables in all shapes and sizes, some quite elegant, and a
loosely matching diversity of comfortable chairs, all laid out in a way
that's fine for eating but works equally well for drinking and chatting.
There are masses of attractive prints, three open fires and a few oriental
rugs on polished parquet, boards or attractive tiles; big windows and
careful lighting contribute to the relaxed atmosphere; board games.
The handsome bar counter, with a decent complement of bar stools,
serves an excellent changing range of about 18 wines by the glass,
50 malt whiskies and Phoenix Brunning & Price Original, Three Tuns
XXX, Woods Shropshire Lad and three guests like Goffs Tournament,
Lymestone Stone Cutter and Purple Moose Snowdonia Ale on handpump;
good disabled access. The spreading garden is lovely, with a sunny
terrace, picnic-sets tucked into the shade of mature trees and extensive
views across quiet fields.

Good, enjoyable food from an extensive menu includes sandwiches, duck liver pâté with red onion jam, pork and black pudding croquettes with tarragon dressing, aubergine parmigiana, pork sausages with mash and onion gravy, crab linguine with ginger, chilli and coriander, chicken with wild mushroom pasta, braised pork belly on rice noodles with teriyaki glaze, slow-cooked rose veal with chive and saffron risotto, lamb rump with greek salad, and puddings such as treacle tart with mascarpone and raspberries and waffle with butterscotch sauce and vanilla ice-cream. *Benchmark main dish: beer-battered haddock and chips £12.25. Two-course evening meal £18.00.*

Brunning & Price ~ Manager Samantha Forrest ~ Real ale ~ (01952) 815940 ~ Open 12-11(10.30 Sun) ~ Bar food 12-10(9.30 Sun) ~ Children welcome ~ Dogs allowed in bar ~ www.fox-newport.co.uk *Recommended by Henry Pursehouse-Tranter, M G Hart, Brian and Anna Marsden, Ian Herdman, Dave Webster, Sue Holland, Brian and Jacky Wilson*

CLUN   SO3080   Map 6
White Horse 🍺 £
The Square; SY7 8JA

Cheery local with seven real ales and good value traditional food

As well as two or three of their own Clun beers (brewed behind the pub), attentive staff serve four or five changing guests, usually from local brewers such as Hobsons, Salopian, Three Tuns and Wye Valley; also Weston's farm cider and a good range of bottled beers. The cheery low-beamed front bar is cosy and friendly and warmed in winter by an inglenook woodburning stove. From the bar, a door leads into a separate little dining room with a rare plank and muntin screen. In the back games room you'll find a TV, games machine, darts, pool, juke box and board games; small garden.

 Traditional, tasty bar food using local produce includes baguettes, smoked mackerel and horseradish pâté, battered brie with redcurrant jelly, mushroom stroganoff, sausages with baked beans and chips, gammon with egg or pineapple, cajun chicken with salsa and cheese, mixed grill and puddings. *Benchmark main dish: regularly changing suet puddings £9.95. Two-course evening meal £15.50.*

Own brew ~ Licensee Jack Limond ~ Real ale ~ No credit cards ~ (01588) 640305 ~ Open 12-midnight ~ Bar food 12-2, 6.30-8.30; 12-2.30, 6.30-9 Sun ~ Children welcome ~ Dogs allowed in bar and bedrooms ~ Bedrooms: $35/$60 ~ www.whi-clun.co.uk *Recommended by Brian and Anna Marsden, MLR, David Heath*

COALPORT   SJ7002   Map 4
Woodbridge 🍷 🍺
Village signposted off A442 1.5 miles S of A4169 Telford roundabout; down in valley, turn left across narrow bridge into Coalport Road, pub then on left; TF8 7JF

Superb Ironbridge Gorge site for extensive and handsomely reworked pub, an all-round success

Numerous mainly 18th- and 19th-c prints – the signature Brunning & Price design feature – decorate this spreading series of linked rooms; the pictures, often of local scenes, are well worth a look. It's comfortable and civilised throughout, with log fires and Coalport-style stoves, rugs on broad boards, tiles or carpet, black beams in the central part, plenty of polished tables, cosy armchair corners – all relaxed and chatty. Big windows look out on a choice section of the wooded gorge, and there are lots of good tables outside, some under cocktail parasols, on a long mainly flagstoned terrace high above the River Severn, and the 1799 iron bridge, the world's second-oldest. Handpumps dispense a splendid array of well kept real ales such as Phoenix Brunning & Price Original, Hobsons Twisted Spire, Ironbridge Gold, Joules Slumbering Monk, Ludlow Black Knight and Sadlers JPA, a good choice of interesting wines by the glass; daily papers. Service is quick and friendly.

Imaginative food includes sandwiches, smoked salmon, apple and celeriac salad with horseradish crème fraîche, pigeon and thyme wellington with parsnip purée and redcurrant and juniper jus, red mullet and garlic risotto with samphire, honey-roast ham and free-range eggs, pork sausages with mash and onion gravy, steak and kidney pudding with grain mustard mash, hake with chorizo and caper-crushed new potatoes with tomato and butter bean cassoulet, slow-braised rabbit, chicken and prune hotpot with cider-pickled cabbage, and puddings such as passion-fruit tart with coconut ice-cream and crème brûlée with shortbread. *Benchmark main dish: steak burger with bacon, cheese, coleslaw and chips £11.95. Two-course evening meal £18.50.*

Brunning & Price ~ Manager Vrata Krist ~ Real ale ~ (01952) 882054 ~ Open 11.30-11(midnight Fri, Sat); 11.30-10.30 Sun ~ Bar food 12-10(9.30 Sun) ~ Restaurant ~ Children welcome ~ Dogs allowed in bar ~ www.brunningandprice.co.uk/woodbridge
Recommended by Nick Jenkins

IRONBRIDGE
SJ6703   Map 4

Golden Ball ◗ 🛏

Brown sign to pub off Madeley Road (B4373) above village centre –
pub behind Horse & Jockey, car park beyond on left; TF8 7BA

Low-beamed partly Elizabethan pub, good value, with bedrooms too

Tucked away in a steep little hamlet of other ancient buildings, this feels very 'old Ironbridge' – the sort of place it's easy to imagine being used by the local people who started the Industrial Revolution. It's unassuming inside, with worn boards, red cushioned pews, one or two black beams, a dresser of decorative china and a woodburning stove. Everards Tiger and Wye Valley HPA with guests such as Greene King Abbot, Ringwood Boondoggle and Timothy Taylors Landlord on handpump and Weston's Old Rosie farm cider; TV, piped music. There's a pretty pergola path with fairy lights to the door, and a sheltered side courtyard with tables under cocktail parasols. You can walk down to the river, and beyond – but it's a steep climb back up.

As well as a very good value two- and three-course set lunch, the tasty food includes smoked mackerel mousse, chicken liver pâté, aubergine filled with feta, olives and cherry tomatoes, pork loin steak with mushrooms and white wine, salmon fillet with cream and white wine, chicken in stilton sauce, beef wellington with marsala sauce, and puddings such as ginger sponge and caramel sauce and berry crème patisserie tart. *Benchmark main dish: steak and onion ciabatta with home-made coleslaw and chips £6.95. Two-course evening meal £17.50.*

Enterprise ~ Lease Helen Pickerill ~ Real ale ~ (01952) 432179 ~ Open 12-3, 5-11 Mon-Weds; 12-11 Thurs-Sat; 12-10.30 Sun ~ Bar food 12-2.30, 6-9; all day weekends ~ Restaurant ~ Children welcome ~ Dogs allowed in bar ~ Live acoustic music second Sun of month ~ Bedrooms: £55/£60 ~ www.goldenballinn.com *Recommended by Paul Colley, Mrs Blethyn Elliott*

Bedroom prices are for high summer. Even then you may get reductions for more than one night, or (outside tourist areas) weekends. Winter special rates are common, and many inns cut bedroom prices if you have a full evening meal.

LEINTWARDINE
SO4175   Map 6

Jolly Frog

A4113 Ludlow–Knighton, E edge of village; The Toddings; SY7 0LX

Friendly, cheerful bar and good bistro restaurant specialising in fish

'A real treasure' is how one reader describes this extremely nice pub – and we agree. The front bar has just a few tables on its light oak boards, with red- or blue-check covers, and red leatherette dining chairs with lion's-head knobs. In addition to good wines by the glass (including two champagnes and a prosecco) or in 50cl pitchers, they have Hobsons Town Crier, Three Tuns 1642 and Wye Valley Butty Bach on handpump, and do good coffees; unobtrusive well reproduced jazz. There's a woodburning stove at each end and light-heartedly frenchified décor – kepis and other hats hanging from stripped beams, street signs from Paris, a metro map. The dining room, up a few steps, is similarly furnished and decorated; and we liked the frog-embroidered hand towels in the lavatories. Staff are friendly and professional. There are a couple of tables under a sail canopy in an inner courtyard, and more wicker chairs and tables on an upper deck with wide and peaceful pastoral views.

 Using only the best seasonal produce and baking bread daily, the popular food includes chicken liver parfait with chutney, twice-baked gruyère and tarragon soufflé, cannellini bean stew with pork belly or confit duck leg, meatballs in tomato sauce with tagliatelle, chicken breast stuffed with wild mushroom farce, celeriac rösti and madeira jus, various fish dishes (megrim, plaice, salmon), and puddings like lemon posset with blackcurrant sorbet and mint chocolate crème brûlée. *Benchmark main dish: 'seafood extravaganza' £40.00. Two-course evening meal £22.00.*

Free house ~ Licensee Kelvin Woodfield ~ Real ale ~ (01547) 540298 ~ Open 12-3, 6-11; closed Mon ~ Bar food 12-2, 6-9 ~ Restaurant ~ Children welcome ~ www.thejollyfrog.co.uk *Recommended by David Aston*

LUDLOW
SO5174   Map 4

Church Inn £

Church Street, behind Butter Cross; SY8 1AW

Splendid range of real ales in characterful town-centre inn

There are always plenty of cheerful customers in this lively town-centre pub – all keen to try the fine range of regularly changing ten real ales on handpump. There might be Hobsons Town Crier and Mild, Ludlow Boiling Well and Gold, and Wye Valley Bitter and HPA, with guests from brewers such as Brains, Clun, Sarah Hughes, Montys, Salopian, Three Tuns and Woods. They also serve several malt whiskies and mulled cider. The ground floor is divided into three appealingly decorated areas, with hops hanging from heavy beams, comfortable banquettes in cosy alcoves off the island counter (part of it is a pulpit) and pews and stripped stonework from the nearby church. There are displays of old photographic equipment, plants on window sills and church prints in the side room. A long central area has a fine stone fireplace (good winter fires) and old black and white photos of the town; daily papers, background music. The civilised upstairs lounge bar has good views of the church and countryside, vaulted ceilings, a display case of glass, china and old bottles, and musical instruments on the walls. The bedrooms are simple but comfortable and one reader told us their dog was welcomed with dog treats and a bowl of water.

🍴 As well as up to 40 different pies, the reasonably priced food includes sandwiches and paninis, chicken liver pâté with onion marmalade, garlic mushrooms, salads and platters, vegetable frittata, beer-battered cod and chips, faggots and mash, salmon and seafood pasta in creamy sauce, and puddings such as pecan and treacle pie and toffee and caramel bonanza. *Benchmark main dish: beef in ale pie £7.95. Two-course evening meal £14.00.*

Free house ~ Licensee Graham Willson-Lloyd ~ Real ale ~ (01584) 872174 ~ Open 10am(11am Sun)-midnight(1am Fri, Sat) ~ Bar food 12-2.30, 6.30-9(8.30 Sun) ~ Restaurant ~ Children welcome ~ Dogs allowed in bar ~ Live musicians every second Weds of month ~ Bedrooms: £50/£80 ~ www.thechurchinn.com *Recommended by Derek and Sylvia Stephenson, Theocsbrian, Michelle and Graeme Voss, Edward Leetham*

MAESBURY MARSH
SJ3125   Map 6
Navigation
Follow Maesbury Road off A483 S of Oswestry; by canal bridge; SY10 8JB

Versatile and friendly canalside pub with cosy bar and enjoyable food using local seasonal produce in a choice of dining areas

Splendid hosts run this friendly place – and both the food and beer are very good indeed. The quarry-tiled bar on the left has squishy brown leather sofas by a traditional black range blazing in a big red fireplace, little upholstered cask seats around three small tables, and dozens of watches (wrist and pocket) hanging from the beams. A couple of steps lead up to a carpeted area beyond a balustrade, with dining chairs around a few more tables, and a piano; off to the left is another dining area with cheerful prints. The main beamed dining room, with some stripped stone, is beyond another small bar with a coal fire – and an amazing row of cushioned carved choir stalls complete with misericord seats. Stonehouse Station and a local guest beer on handpump, ten wines by the glass and Weston's cider; very quiet background music.
The terrace has picnic-sets under cocktail parasols, safely fenced off from a restored stretch of the Montgomery Canal. There's also a book exchange, a shop where you can buy fresh local produce and a two-pint takeaway beer service.

🍴 Using free-range and seasonal produce, the interesting and very popular food might include a two- and three-course set menu (not Sunday) and an early-bird offer (6-7pm, not Saturday), lunchtime sandwiches, free-range chicken wings in honey and soy, moules marinière, macaroni cheese, burger with cheese, bacon and chips, open crab and prawn lasagne, chicken chasseur, baked outdoor-reared ham with parsley sauce, lamb rump with butternut squash purée, roasted red onions and salsa verde, and puddings such as crème brûlée and rocky road pavlova with chocolate chip cookies and home-made marshmallow; Tuesday is steak night and Friday brings fish and chips. *Benchmark main dish: trio of sausages with bubble and squeak £9.95. Two-course evening meal £17.00.*

Free house ~ Licensees Brent Ellis and Mark Baggett ~ Real ale ~ (01691) 672958 ~ Open 12-2, 6-11; 12-6 Sun; closed Sun evening, Mon and Tues lunchtimes, first two weeks Jan ~ Bar food 12-2, 6-8.15 ~ Restaurant ~ Children welcome ~ Dogs allowed in bar ~ www.thenavigation.co.uk *Recommended by Julia and Richard Tredgett, Pat and Tony Martin*

If a service charge is mentioned prominently on a menu or accommodation terms, you must pay it if service was satisfactory. If service is really bad, you are legally entitled to refuse to pay some or all of the service charge as compensation for not getting the service you might reasonably have expected.

MUCH WENLOCK SO6299 Map 4
George & Dragon ◧ £
High Street (A458); TF13 6AA

**Bustling and atmospheric with plenty to look at, reasonably priced
food and good beer selection; usefully open all day**

You'll be made to feel most welcome in this pubby little place, and
the five real ales and simple but well executed food are an added
bonus. It's filled with a fascinating collection of pub paraphernalia such
as old brewery and cigarette advertisements, bottle labels, beer trays and
George and the Dragon pictures, as well as 200 jugs hanging from the
beams. The front door leads straight into a beamed and quarry-tiled room
with wooden chairs and tables and antique settles around the walls, and
there are a couple of open fires in attractive Victorian fireplaces. At the
back is a timbered dining room. Greene King Abbot and Twisted Wheel,
Hobsons Best, Lancaster Blonde and St Austell Tribute on handpump,
a wide choice of wines by the glass and 14 decent malt whiskies; one
reader says the pork scratchings are outstanding. Background music,
dominoes, cards, board games and daily newspapers. There's a pay-and-
display car park behind the pub.

 Good tasty food includes baguettes and sandwiches, duck, orange and cognac
pâté, deep-fried breaded brie with redcurrant sauce, faggots with gravy, jumbo
sausages with egg, chips and peas, cottage or fish pies, gammon with free-range
eggs or pineapple, bacon-wrapped chicken stuffed with garlic mushrooms and
cheese sauce, daily specials and puddings. *Benchmark main dish: beef in ale pie
£8.95. Two-course evening meal £14.50.*

Punch ~ Tenant James Scott ~ Real ale ~ (01952) 727312 ~ Open 12-11(midnight Sat)
~ Bar food 12-2.30, 6-9; not Weds or Sun evenings ~ Restaurant ~ Children welcome ~
Dogs allowed in bar ~ www.thegeorgedragon.co.uk *Recommended by Mike Proctor, James
Stretton, Mike and Wena Stevenson, David Bennett, C A Bryson*

NORTON SJ7200 Map 4
Hundred House ⚑ ⇌
A442 Telford–Bridgnorth; TF11 9EE

**Family-run inn with rambling rooms, open fires, lots of fresh and
dried flowers, quite a choice of drinks and good food; comfortable
large bedrooms with antique beds**

Always busy with returning customers, this carefully kept place has
been run by the same family for 25 years. The rambling rooms have
log fires in handsome fireplaces (one has a great Jacobean arch with
fine old black cooking pots), a variety of interesting chairs and settles
with long colourful patchwork leather cushions around sewing-machine
tables. Hops and huge bunches of dried flowers and herbs hang from
beams, and bunches of fresh flowers brighten the tables and counter
in the neatly kept bar. Steps lead up past a little balustrade to a partly
panelled eating area, where the stripped brickwork looks older than it
does elsewhere. Heritage Ales Northgate Ale, Ironbridge Gold and Three
Tuns Rantipole and Stout on handpump. The garden is lovely with its
old-fashioned roses, herbaceous plants and big working herb garden
(with over 100 varieties) that supplies the kitchen. The bedrooms
have antique four-posters or half-testers, Victorian-style baths and rain
showers, and a trademark velvet-cushioned swing.

🍴 Enjoyable, attractively presented food might include sandwiches, chicken liver pâté with onion chutney, crayfish, prawn and guacamole cocktail with tomato salsa, spiced broccoli loaf with feta and aubergine rolls and red pepper coulis, free-range chicken stuffed with tarragon mousse and tomato and wild mushroom sauce, chump of lamb with leek, parsnip and lamb cake, sautéed kidneys and rosemary jus, game pudding with mash and juniper sauce, duck leg with pork sausage, braised leeks, mash and mustard cream sauce, and puddings such as blueberry crème brûlée and steamed lemon sponge with custard. *Benchmark main dish: jacob's ladder beef with goats cheese tortellini and roasted pepper sauce £22.95. Two-course evening meal £22.00.*

Free house ~ Licensees Henry, Stuart and David Phillips ~ Real ale ~ (01952) 730353 ~ Open 8.30am-11pm ~ Bar food 12-2.30, 6-9.30; 12-9 Sun ~ Restaurant ~ Children welcome ~ Dogs allowed in bar ~ Bedrooms: £75/£90 ~ www.hundredhouse.co.uk
Recommended by Adrian Ballard, Titia Ketelaar

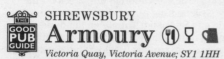

SHREWSBURY
SJ4812   Map 6

Armoury 🍴 🍷 🎒
Victoria Quay, Victoria Avenue; SY1 1HH

Vibrant atmosphere in interestingly converted riverside warehouse, enthusiastic young staff, good tempting food all day and excellent drinks selection

The spacious open-plan interior of this 18th-c former warehouse, with its long runs of big arched windows and views across the broad River Severn, makes quite an impression. It's light and airy, but the eclectic décor, furniture layout and lively bustle give a personal feel. Mixed wood tables and chairs are grouped on stripped-wood floors, huge brick walls display floor-to-ceiling books or masses of old prints mounted edge to edge, and there's a grand stone fireplace at one end. Colonial-style fans whirr away on the ceilings, which are supported by some green-painted columns, and small glass wall-cabinets display smoking pipes. The long bar counter has a terrific choice of drinks including Phoenix Brunning & Price, Hobsons Twisted Spire and Salopian Shropshire Gold with guests such as Ludlow Gold, Montys Mojo, Weetwood Cheshire Cat Blonde Ale, Woods Shropshire Lad and Wye Valley HPA on handpump, a great wine list (with 16 by the glass), around 50 malt whiskies, a dozen gins, lots of rums and vodkas, a variety of brandies and some unusual liqueurs. Hanging baskets and smart coach lights decorate the massive red-brick frontage. The pub doesn't have its own car park, but there are plenty of places to park nearby.

🍴 Good, interesting food includes sandwiches, lime-cured sea trout with wasabi crème fraîche and sesame shrimp toast, rabbit faggot with split peas and wild mushrooms, crab, dill and asparagus quiche with lemon, caper and samphire salad, sharing platters, honey-roast ham and free-range eggs, steak in ale pie, smoked haddock and salmon fishcakes, oriental crispy beef salad with sweet chilli dressing, lamb shoulder with new potatoes, and puddings such as lemon tart with mixed berry coulis and dark chocolate and praline marquise with raspberry sorbet. *Benchmark main dish: beer-battered haddock and chips £11.95. Two-course evening meal £17.50.*

Brunning & Price ~ Manager Emily Waring ~ Real ale ~ (01743) 340525 ~ Open 12-11 (10.30 Sun) ~ Bar food 12-10 (9.30 Sun) ~ Children welcome ~ Dogs allowed in bar ~ www.armoury-shrewsbury.co.uk *Recommended by Richard J Holloway, David Aston, David Bennett, John Oates*

Also Worth a Visit in Shropshire

Besides the fully inspected pubs, you might like to try these pubs that have been recommended to us and described by readers. Do tell us what you think of them: feedback@goodguides.com

BISHOP'S CASTLE   SO3288
Boars Head (01588) 638521
Church Street; SY9 5AE Comfortable beamed and stripped-stone bar with mix of furniture including pews, settles and sofas, fire in big inglenook, welcoming efficient young staff, well kept Courage, Joules and Theakstons, enjoyable good value pub food served all day, family room with TV; no dogs inside; picnic-sets on back terrace, three good roomy high-raftered bedrooms in converted barn. *(Anon)*

BISHOP'S CASTLE   SO3288
✶**Six Bells** (01588) 630144
Church Street; SY9 5AA 17th-c pub with own-brew beers the main draw (brewery tours available); smallish no-frills bar with mix of well worn furniture, old local photographs and prints, bigger room with stripped-stone walls, benches around plain tables on bare boards and inglenook woodburner, country wines and summer farm cider, July beer festival, basic food (not evenings Sun-Tues); no credit cards; children and dogs welcome, open all day Sat, closed Mon lunchtime. *(MLR, Dr Peter Crawshaw)*

BISHOP'S CASTLE   SO3288
✶**Three Tuns** (01588) 638797
Salop Street; SY9 5BW Extended and updated old pub adjacent to unique four-storey Victorian brewhouse (a brewery said to have existed here since 1642), busy chatty atmosphere in public, lounge and snug bars, Three Tuns beers (including 1642) from old-fashioned handpumps (cheaper 5-7pm Fri), several wines by the glass, tasty good value food (not Sun evening) from sandwiches to venison, friendly young staff, modernised dining room done out in smart oak and glass; lots going on including film club, live jazz, local rugby club events, July beer festival and maybe morris men or a brass band in the garden; children and dogs welcome, open all day. *(Mike and Eleanor Anderson, Dr Peter Crawshaw, Mike and Mary Carter, Pat and Tony Martin)*

BRIDGES   SO3996
Bridges (01588) 650260
Bridges, W of Ratlinghope; SY5 0ST Old beamed country pub now the Three Tuns brewery tap and returned to its pre-1860 name (was the Horseshoe); their well kept range of ales and enjoyable fairly traditional home-made food (not Sun evening, winter Mon), helpful staff, regular live music; tables (some on raised deck) out by little River Onny, bedrooms, also camping

and youth hostel nearby, open all day. *(Dr Peter Crawshaw, C A Bryson)*

BRIDGNORTH   SO6890
✶**Down** (01746) 789539
The Down; B4364 Ludlow Road 3 miles S; WV16 6UA Good value roadside dining pub overlooking rolling countryside, enjoyable food including popular daily carvery, efficient service, a house beer (Down & Out) from Three Tuns and a couple of local guests; background music; children welcome, nine comfortable bedrooms, open all day. *(David Aston)*

BRIDGNORTH   SO7193
Kings Head (01746) 762141
Whitburn Street; WV16 4QN Well restored 17th-c timbered coaching inn with high-raftered back stable bar, enjoyable food here from 5pm (all day weekends) or in all-day restaurant with separate menu, Hobsons, Wye Valley and several changing guests, friendly staff, log fires, beams and flagstones, pretty leaded windows; children and dogs welcome, courtyard picnic-sets, open all day. *(Anon)*

BRIDGNORTH   SO7192
✶**Railwaymans Arms** (01746) 764361
Severn Valley Station, Hollybush Road (off A458 towards Stourbridge); WV16 5DT Bathams, Hobsons and plenty of other good value local ales kept well in chatty old-fashioned converted waiting room at Severn Valley steam railway terminus, bustling on summer days, coal fire, old station signs and train nameplates, superb mirror over fireplace, may be simple summer snacks, annual beer festival; children welcome, wheelchair access with help, tables out on platform – the train to Kidderminster (station bar there too) has an all-day bar and bookable Sun lunches, open all day Fri-Sun. *(Henry Pursehouse-Tranter)*

BROCKTON   SO5793
✶**Feathers** (01746) 785202
B4378; TF13 6JR Stylish restauranty country dining pub with good interesting food including lunchtime and early evening deals, efficient friendly service, well kept changing ales such as Hobsons and Three Tuns, comfortable seats in attractively decorated beamed rooms, conservatory gift shop; children allowed, closed Mon (no food Tues lunchtime). *(Anon)*

BROMFIELD   SO4877
✶**Clive** (01584) 856565
A49 2 miles NW of Ludlow; SY8 2JR Sophisticated minimalist bar-restaurant

taking its name from Clive of India who once lived here; emphasis mainly on imaginative modern food but also Hobsons and Ludlow ales, several wines by the glass and various teas and coffees, also lunchtime sandwiches, efficient welcoming staff, dining room with light wood tables, door to sparsely furnished bar with metal chairs, glass-topped tables and sleek counter, step down to room with woodburner in huge fireplace, soaring beams and rafters, exposed stonework and well worn sofas, fresh flowers, daily papers; piped jazz; children welcome, tables under parasols on secluded terrace, fish pond, 15 stylish bedrooms, good breakfast, open all day. *(Mike and Shirley Stratton, Michael Rugman, Mike and Mary Carter)*

BURLTON SJ4526

✱ **Burlton Inn** (01939) 270284

A528 Shrewsbury–Ellesmere, near B4397 junction; SY4 5TB Attractively refurbished 18th-c pub with wide choice of good popular food including early evening set deal (Mon-Fri), well kept Robinsons ales, friendly helpful staff, beams, timbers and log fires, comfortable snug, restaurant with garden room; children welcome, disabled facilities, teak furniture on pleasant terrace, comfortable well equipped bedrooms, good breakfast. *(J S Burn)*

BURWARTON SO6185

✱ **Boyne Arms** (01746) 787214

B4364 Bridgnorth–Ludlow; WV16 6QH Handsome Georgian coaching inn with welcoming cheerful staff, enjoyable generous food (not Sun evening, Mon) including good value deals, three Hobsons ales and a guest, Robinson's cider, decent coffee, separate restaurant and public bar (dogs allowed here), function room with pool and other games; children welcome, good timber adventure playground in large garden, hitching rail for horses, open all day weekends, closed Mon lunchtime. *(Anon)*

CHURCH STRETTON SO4593

Bucks Head (01694) 722898

High Street; SY6 6BX Old town pub with several good-sized modernised areas including restaurant, four well kept Marstons ales, decent good value pubby food plus vegetarian options, friendly attentive staff, black beams and timbers, mixed dark wood tables and chairs; four bedrooms, open all day. *(David Aston)*

CHURCH STRETTON SO4593

Housmans (01694) 724441

High Street; SY6 6BX Buzzing and welcoming restaurant-bar with two well kept ales from Three Tuns and good wine and cocktail lists, food mainly tapas-style sharing plates but also good value two-course weekday lunch deal, local art on walls, occasional jazz and acoustic music; children welcome, open all day weekends. *(Kim Skuse)*

CLEE HILL SO5975

Kremlin (01584) 890950

Track up hill off A4117 Bewdley–Cleobury, by Victoria Inn; SY8 3NB Shropshire's highest pub (former quarrymaster's house), enjoyable good value straightforward food including children's menu, friendly service, well kept Hobsons and guests, farm cider; splendid view from garden and terrace, play area, open all day weekends (till 8pm Sun), closed Mon, lunchtime Tues. *(Anon)*

CLEOBURY MORTIMER SO6775

Kings Arms (01299) 271954

A4117 Bewdley–Ludlow; DY14 8BS Refurbished 15th-c beamed inn opposite the church, open-plan bar with good log fire, four well kept Hobsons ales and a guest, good value straightforward lunchtime food, friendly staff; dogs welcome, four well fitted bedrooms, open all day. *(Anon)*

CLUN SO3080

Sun (01588) 640559

High Street; SY7 8JB Beamed and timbered 15th-c pub under newish friendly landlady; enormous open fire in traditional flagstoned public bar (dogs welcome here) with old clock and simple seating, darts, cards and dominoes, larger carpeted lounge bar, enjoyable home-made food (not Sun evening) from lunchtime sandwiches up, four well kept Marstons-related beers, occasional acoustic music; children allowed, terrace tables in back garden, peaceful village and lovely rolling countryside, nice bedrooms (some in converted outbuildings), open all day. *(Mike and Eleanor Anderson, A N Bance)*

CLUNTON SO3381

Crown (01588) 660265

B4368; SY7 0HU Cosy old country local, welcoming and friendly, with good choice of well kept changing ales and enjoyable generous food (Thurs-Sat evenings), also Weds fish and chips and good value Sun lunch, log fire in small flagstoned bar, dining room, games room, folk night third Weds of month; open all day Fri-Sun, closed lunchtimes other days. *(Anon)*

COALPORT SJ6902

Shakespeare (01952) 580675

High Street; TF8 7HT Relaxing early 19th-c inn by pretty Severn gorge park, timbering, bare stone walls and tiled floors, well kept Everards, Hobsons, Ludlow and guests, good value food from sandwiches through pub standards to mexican specialities; children welcome, picnic-sets in tiered garden with play area, handy for China Museum, four bedrooms, open all day weekends, closed weekday lunchtimes. *(Anon)*

CORFTON   SO4985

✶ **Sun** (01584) 861239

*B4368 Much Wenlock–Craven Arms;
SY7 9DF* Lived-in unchanging three-
room country local, own good Corvedale
ales (including an unfined beer), friendly
long-serving landlord (often busy in back
brewery), decent well presented pubby food
from baguettes to steaks, lots of breweriana,
basic quarry-tiled public bar with darts
and pool, quieter carpeted lounge, dining
room with covered well, tourist information;
children welcome, dogs in bar, good
wheelchair access throughout and disabled
lavatories, tables on terrace and in large
garden with good play area. *(MLR)*

CRESSAGE   SJ5704

✶ **Riverside** (01952) 510900

A458 NW, near Cound; SY5 6AF
Spacious pub-hotel, neat, light and airy,
with good well presented food from snacks
up, efficient cheerful staff, well kept ales
including a house beer brewed by Coors,
lovely Severn views from roomy conservatory,
bar with central woodburner (dogs
welcome here); big terraced garden, seven
comfortable bedrooms, good breakfast, open
all day weekends in summer. *(Mark Sykes,
Mr and Mrs D Hummond)*

DORRINGTON   SJ4703

Bridge Inn (01743) 718209

A49 N; SY5 7ED Popular streamside
dining pub with well prepared food including
good value deals, daily roast, a beer from
Jennings or Greene King, cheerful helpful
staff, roomy bar/dining area with wood floor,
conservatory restaurant; background music,
no dogs; children welcome, garden tables.
(T M Griffiths)

ELLESMERE   SJ3934

✶ **Black Lion** (01691) 622418

*Scotland Street; back car park on A495;
SY12 0EG* Welcoming former coaching
inn, good simple substantial food at bargain
prices (pay at bar in advance), friendly
helpful staff, two well kept Marstons-related
beers, relaxed beamed bar with interesting
décor and unusual features such as
traditional wood-and-glass screen along tiled
entrance corridor, comfortable roomy dining
room; background music; children welcome,
some covered tables outside, handy car park,
not far from canal wharf, bedrooms. *(Andrew
Jeeves, Carole Smart, Mike and Wena Stevenson)*

GRINDLEY BROOK   SJ5242

Horse & Jockey (01948) 662723

A41; SY13 4QJ Extended 19th-c pub
with enjoyable good value food all day from
varied menu, friendly helpful service, eight
well kept ales including a house beer from
Phoenix named after the pub dog (Blaze),
teas and coffees, well divided open-plan
interior with old pine furniture on wood

floors, some interesting bits and pieces,
woodburners; sports TV, pool; children and
dogs welcome, big play area, handy for
Sandstone Trail and Llangollen Canal, open
all day. *(Mike and Wena Stevenson, Ann and
Tony Bennett-Hughes)*

GRINSHILL   SJ5223

✶ **Inn at Grinshill** (01939) 220410

Off A49 N of Shrewsbury; SY4 3BL
Civilised early Georgian country inn with
comfortable 19th-c log-fire bar, Greene King
beers and a local guest, spacious modern
restaurant with view into open kitchen, good
well coked food including set menu choices,
cafetière coffee, friendly competent young
staff; background music, TV; children and
dogs welcome, pleasant back garden with
plenty of tables and chairs, comfortable
clean bedrooms, closed Sun evening, Mon.
*(Steve Whalley, Mrs Debbie Tether, R T and J C
Moggridge)*

HIGHLEY   SO7483

Ship (01746) 861219

Severnside; WV16 6NU Refurbished 18th-c
inn in lovely riverside location, good choice
of enjoyable food (although not much for
vegetarians), bargain OAP weekday lunch
and early-bird deals, Sun carvery, real ales
including one named for the pub; children
welcome, tables on raised front deck, handy
for Severn Way walks (and Severn Valley
Railway), fishing rights, bedrooms. *(Anon)*

HINDFORD   SJ3333

Jack Mytton (01691) 679861

*Village and pub signed from A495;
SY11 4NL* Pleasant rustic bar with log fire,
four changing ales kept well by character
landlord, food from bar snacks up, airy
raftered dining room; children and dogs
welcome, picnic-sets in attractive canalside
garden, good-sized courtyard with summer
bar and carved bear (pub is named after
an eccentric squire who rode a bear),
moorings. *(Mike and Wena Stevenson)*

HOPE   SJ3401

Stables (01743) 891344

*Just off A488 3 miles S of Minsterley;
SY5 0EP* Hidden-away little 17th-c beamed
country pub, a couple of ales such as Six Bells
and Wye Valley Butty Bach, enjoyable home-
made food evenings and weekday lunchtimes,
newspapers, log fires; fine views from garden,
two bedrooms. *(Gerry Price)*

HOPTON WAFERS   SO6376

✶ **Crown** (01299) 270372

A4117; DY14 0NB Attractive 16th-c
creeper-covered inn, light comfortable
décor and furnishings, beams and big
inglenook, enjoyable variety of food (all day
Sun) in three separate dining areas, well
kept Hereford, Hobsons and Wye Valley
Butty Bach, good choice of wines, relaxed
atmosphere and friendly efficient staff;

children and dogs welcome, inviting garden with terraces, duck pond and stream, 18 bedrooms (11 in new adjoining building), open all day. *(Dave Braisted)*

IRONBRIDGE   SJ6603
✷**Malthouse** (01952) 433712

The Wharfage (bottom road alongside Severn); TF8 7NH Converted 18th-c malthouse wonderfully located in historic gorge, spacious bar with iron pillars supporting heavy pine beams, lounge/ dining area, up to three well kept changing ales, good reasonably priced food all day from baguettes up, live music Fri, Sat; children and dogs welcome, terrace tables, 11 individually styled bedrooms and self-catering cottage. *(Peter and Jean Hoare, David Bennett)*

LEEBOTWOOD   SO4798
✷**Pound** (01694) 751477

A49 Church Stretton–Shrewsbury; SY6 6ND Thatched cruck-framed building dating from 1458 (thought to be oldest in the village); bar rooms are stylishly modern with minimalist fixtures and wooden furnishings, Fullers and changing guest such as Salopian Shropshire Gold, decent wines by the glass, good bar food including deals, friendly efficient service; background music; seats on flagstoned terrace; disabled parking spaces (level access to bar), closed Sun evening, Mon. *(Mr and Mrs A H Young, Neil and Anita Christopher)*

LITTLE STRETTON   SO4491
Green Dragon (01694) 722925

Village well signed off A49 S of Church Stretton; Ludlow Road; SY6 6RE Refurbished village pub at the foot of Long Mynd; popular good value food in bar or adjacent dining area (well behaved children allowed here), Wye Valley ales and a guest, efficient service, warm woodburner; tables outside and play area, handy for Cardingmill Valley (NT). *(T M Griffiths, Susan and Neil McLean, David Aston, S and R Dowdy)*

LITTLE STRETTON   SO4492
✷**Ragleth** (01694) 722711

Village well signed off A49 S of Church Stretton; Ludlow Road; SY6 6RB Characterful attractively opened-up 17th-c dining pub; light and airy bay-windowed front bar with eclectic mix of old tables and chairs, some exposed brick and timber work, huge inglenook in heavily beamed brick- and tile-floored public bar, four mainly local beers, good generous bar food, cheerful attentive owners and staff; background music, TV, darts and board games; children welcome, dogs in bar, lovely garden with tulip tree-shaded lawn and good play area, thatched and timbered church and fine hill walks nearby, open all day Sat (summer) and Sun. *(Michael Rugman, Ray and Winifred Halliday, Bernard Stradling, David Aston, Clive Watkin, John Oates and others)*

LONGDON UPON TERN   SJ6215
Tayleur Arms (01952) 770335

Long Waste (B5063); TF6 6LJ Family-run pub-restaurant with enjoyable sensibly priced food including popular Sun carvery, Jennings ales; children welcome, garden picnic-sets and maybe bouncy castle, nine bedrooms in separate building, open all day Sat, till 6pm Sun. *(Ken Richards)*

LOPPINGTON   SJ4729
Dickin Arms (01939) 233471

B4397; SY4 5SR Cheerful two-bar country local, comfortably plush banquettes, open fire, shallow steps to neat back dining room with good value generous food including landlady's speciality curries, lunchtime OAP deals, well kept Bass and interesting guests, good friendly service; pool; children welcome, play area, pretty village. *(Tim Williams)*

LUDLOW   SO5174
✷**Charlton Arms** (01584) 872813

Ludford Bridge, B4361 Overton Road; SY8 1PJ Big comfortably extended inn in superb position by massive medieval bridge over the Teme; open-plan red-carpeted lounge overlooking the water some 10 metres below with the interesting town spreading uphill on far side, high-backed dining chairs around polished dark tables, some leather armchairs and sofas, adjoining dining room with same view, more pubby back area with two-way woodburner, Hobsons, Ludlow and Wye Valley, good food, cheerfully old-fashioned service; seats on three or four terraces and decks on varying levels, comfortable bedrooms. *(T M Griffiths)*

LUDLOW   SO5174
Queens (01584) 879177

Lower Galdeford; SY8 1RU Family-run 19th-c pub with good food concentrating heavily on fresh local produce, five well kept ales including Ludlow, Hobsons and bargain Three Tuns 1642, long narrow oak-floor bar, pine tables in vaulted-ceiling dining area, good friendly service and nice pub dog, popular monthly charity quiz, some live music; children welcome (not in bar after 6pm), no dogs inside at food times, open all day. *(Roy Payne, Dave Braisted)*

LUDLOW   SO5174
Rose & Crown (01584) 872098

Off Church Street, behind Buttercross; SY8 1AP Small unpretentious pub with 13th-c origins, enjoyable bargain food all day, Hobsons and a guest ale, clean comfortably lived-in L-shaped bar with hop-strung beams and open brick fireplace, separate dining area, friendly staff; approached through passageway with a few courtyard seats at front, pretty spot, bedrooms. *(Dave Braisted, Mr and Mrs A H Young)*

LUDLOW   SO5174
Wheatsheaf (01584) 872980
Lower Broad Street; SY8 1PQ
Traditional 17th-c beamed pub spectacularly
built into medieval town gate, good value
pubby food, Sun carvery, well kept Marstons-
related ales, efficient cheerful staff; children
welcome, no dogs inside, a few seats out
in front, five comfortable bedrooms, open
all day. *(Anon)*

MARKET DRAYTON   SJ6734
Red Lion (01630) 652602
Great Hales Street; TF9 1JP Extended
17th-c coaching inn now tap for the
new Joules Brewery; back entrance into
attractive modern bar with light wood floor
and substantial oak timbers, traditional
dark-beamed part to the right, updated
but keeping original features, with pubby
furniture on flagstones, brewery mirrors
and signs, woodburner, more breweriana in
dining/function room to left featuring Robert
'Mousey' Thompson carved oak panelling
and fireplace; Joules Pale Ale, Blonde and
Slumbering Monk, maybe a trial brew, good
selection of wines, fairly straightforward food
including pies and Sun carvery till 4pm, some
live music; picnic-sets outside, brewery tours
first Weds of month, open all day. *(Clive and
Fran Dutson)*

MARTON   SJ2802
⋆**Sun** (01938) 561211
B4386 NE of Chirbury; SY21 8JP Warmly
inclusive family-run pub with well liked
food including seasonal game and good
fresh fish, light and airy black-beamed
bar with comfortable sofa and traditional
pub furnishings, woodburner in big stone
fireplace, Hobsons Best and a guest, chunky
pale tables and tall ladder-back chairs in
restaurant; children welcome, dogs in bar
(but ask first), front terrace, closed Sun
evening, Mon, lunchtime Tues. *(Mike Walker)*

MUCH WENLOCK   SO6299
Gaskell Arms (01952) 727212
High Street (A458); TF13 6AQ 17th-c
coaching inn with comfortable old-fashioned
lounge divided by brass-canopied log fire,
enjoyable straightforward bar food at fair
prices, friendly attentive service, three well
kept ales such as Stonehouse, Woods and Wye
Valley, brasses and prints, civilised beamed
restaurant, locals' public bar; background
music; no dogs; well behaved children
allowed, disabled facilities, roomy neat
back garden with terrace, 16 bedrooms,
open all day. *(Jean and Douglas Troup)*

MUCH WENLOCK   SO6299
Talbot (01952) 727077
High Street (A458); TF13 6AA Friendly
unspoilt medieval inn with several cosy
traditional areas, low ceilings, red tapestry
button-back wall banquettes, art deco-style

lamps, local pictures and cottagey plates,
some gleaming brasses, well kept Bass and
a guest, several wines and whiskies, fair-
priced bar food with more elaborate evening
choices including good value set menu,
cheerful prompt service; background music,
TV; children welcome, seats in courtyard,
characterful bedrooms, open all day (till 2am
if busy). *(A N Bance, Mrs Blethyn Elliott,
T M Griffiths, Mike and Wena Stevenson)*

MUNSLOW   SO5287
⋆**Crown** (01584) 841205
*B4368 Much Wenlock–Craven Arms;
SY7 9ET* Former courthouse with imposing
exterior and pretty back façade showing
Tudor origins; lots of nooks and crannies,
split-level lounge bar with old-fashioned
mix of furnishings on broad flagstones,
old bottles, country pictures, bread oven
by log fire, traditional snug with another
fire, eating area with tables around central
oven chimney, more beams, flagstones and
stripped stone, enjoyable imaginative food
(local suppliers listed), ales such as Holdens,
Ludlow, Salopian and Six Bells, local bottled
cider, good wines, helpful efficient staff and
friendly bustling atmosphere; background
music; children welcome, level wheelchair
access to bar only, bedrooms, closed Sun
evening, Mon. *(David and Katharine Cooke)*

NESSCLIFFE   SJ3819
Old Three Pigeons (01743) 741279
*Off A5 Shrewsbury–Oswestry
(now bypassed); SY4 1DB* Friendly 16th-c
beamed pub with quaint and appealing
dining area, good fairly priced food including
fresh fish, well kept ales such as Salopian
and Stonehouse, nice wines by the glass,
warm log fires, two bar areas; children and
dogs welcome, some tables outside, opposite
Kynaston Cave, good cliff walks, open all
day Sun, closed Mon lunchtime. *(Julia and
Richard Tredgett)*

PICKLESCOTT   SO4399
Bottle & Glass (01694) 751252
Off A49 N of Church Stretton; SY6 6NR
Remote 17th-c rambling country pub
reopened under new licensees; plenty of
character in quarry-tiled bar and lounge/
dining areas, low black beams, oak panelling
and log fires, assortment of old tables and
chairs, traditional home-made food (not Sun
evening) from baps up, well kept ales such as
Hobsons and Woods; TV; children welcome,
seats out on raised front area, bedrooms,
open all day weekends (till 7pm Sun). *(Anon)*

QUEENS HEAD   SJ3326
Queens Head (01691) 610255
*Just off A5 SE of Oswestry, towards
Nesscliffe; SY11 4EB* Emphasis on wide
choice of generous fairly priced food (all
day) from sandwiches and pizzas up, good
vegetarian options too, well kept Stonehouse,
Theakstons and a guest, decent wines by the

glass, two dining areas with coal fires, roomy conservatory overlooking Montgomery Canal; children welcome, picnic-sets under parasols in suntrap waterside garden, country walks. *(Deanna Hughes)*

RUYTON XI TOWNS   SJ3922
Talbot (01939) 262882
Church Street; SY4 1LA Old refurbished black and white pub with good selection of wines and local beers, enjoyable well presented food from lunchtime sandwiches up, friendly service, bar and separate eating areas with well spaced tables, log fires; dogs welcome, three bedrooms, open all day weekends. *(Mrs Angela Davies)*

SHIFNAL   SJ7407
Odfellows (01952) 461517
Market Place; TF11 9AU Friendly bistro-style pub with good choice of sensibly priced food in linked rooms, four well kept ales including Salopian and good wine choice, conservatory, regular live music; tables outside, seven bedrooms, open all day. *(R Anderson)*

SHIFNAL   SJ74508
White Hart (01952) 461161
High Street; TF11 8BH Seven well kept interesting ales in chatty 17th-c timbered pub, quaint and old-fashioned with separate bar and lounge, good home-made lunchtime food (not Sun), several wines by the glass, welcoming staff; couple of steep steps at front door, back terrace and beer garden, open all day. *(John Oates)*

SHREWSBURY   SJ4912
Admiral Benbow (01743) 244423
Swan Hill; SY1 1NF Great choice of mainly local ales including one named for them from Six Bells, bottled belgians, also real ciders and perry; no children; closed lunchtimes apart from Sat. *(David Aston)*

SHREWSBURY   SJ4812
Boat House Inn (01743) 231658
New Street/Quarry Park; leaving centre via Welsh Bridge/A488, turn into Port Hill Road; SY3 8JQ Recently refurbished pub in lovely position by footbridge to Severn park, river views from long lounge bar and terrace tables, well kept ales and enjoyable food including grills, friendly staff; background music; children welcome, no dogs inside, open all day. *(Duncan Kirkby)*

SHREWSBURY   SO4912
Coach & Horses (01743) 365661
Swan Hill/Cross Hill; SY1 1NF Friendly and relaxed Victorian local with panelled main bar, cosy little side room and back dining lounge, enjoyable fresh food, Salopian

Shropshire Gold, Stonehouse and guests, real cider, happy hour (5-7pm Mon-Fri, 7-10pm Sun), prompt helpful service, interesting Guinness prints; background music; children allowed in dining room, dogs in bar, disabled facilities, smokers' roof terrace, open all day. *(Anon)*

SHREWSBURY   SJ4912
Loggerheads (01743) 355457
Church Street; SY1 1UG Chatty old-fashioned local with panelled back room, flagstones, scrubbed-top tables, high-backed settles and coal fire, three other rooms with lots of prints, bare boards and more flagstones, quaint linking corridor and hatch service of five Marstons-related ales, short choice of bargain pub food, friendly prompt service; open all day. *(David Bennett)*

SHREWSBURY   SJ4912
Nags Head (01743) 362455
Wyle Cop; SY1 1XB Attractive old two-room pub, small, unpretentious and welcoming, with changing ales such as Brakspears Oxford Gold, Salopian Shropshire Gold, Sharps Doom Bar, Stonehouse Station Bitter and Timothy Taylors Landlord; silent TV; area for smokers at back, open all day (till 1am Fri, Sat). *(Kerry Law)*

SHREWSBURY   SO4812
Olde Bucks Head (01743) 369392
Frankwell; SY3 8JR Quietly placed 17th-c inn with traditional bar and restaurant, cheerful staff, enjoyable inexpensive pub food, Salopian and a couple of other well kept ales; dogs welcome, flower-decked raised terrace and nice secluded little garden, ten good value bedrooms, open all day Sat. *(Anon)*

SHREWSBURY   SJ4911
Prince of Wales (01743) 343301
Bynner Street; SY3 7NZ Traditional backstreet pub popular for its good range of well kept ales (always a mild), friendly atmosphere, Shrewsbury Town FC memorabilia, darts; sunny back deck overlooking own bowling green, open all day Fri-Sun when lunchtime food is served, from 5pm other days. *(John Neal)*

SHREWSBURY   SJ4912
Salopian Bar (01743) 351505
Smithfield Road; SY1 1PW Comfortable modern refurbishment facing the river; eight well kept ales such as Bathams, Dark Star, Oakham, Salopian and Stonehouse, good choice of belgian beers and real ciders (regular beer and cider festivals), cheap sandwiches and pies, friendly staff, local artwork for sale; sports TV, open mike and quiz nights; open all day. *(David Aston, D Weston, David Bennett)*

Post Office address codings confusingly give the impression that some pubs are in Shropshire, when they're really in Cheshire (which is where we list them).

SHREWSBURY   SJ4912
⋆ Three Fishes (01743) 344793
Fish Street; SY1 1UR Well run timbered
and heavily beamed 16th-c pub in quiet
cobbled street, small tables around three
sides of central bar, flagstones, old pictures,
half a dozen changing beers from mainstream
and smaller breweries like Stonehouse, good
value wines, fairly priced food (not Sun)
including blackboard specials ordered from
separate servery, good friendly service even if
busy, no mobiles; open all day Fri, Sat. *(Anon)*

STIPERSTONES   SJ3600
⋆ Stiperstones Inn (01743) 791327
*Village signed off A488 S of Minsterley;
SY5 0LZ* Cosy traditional pub useful for a
drink after walking (some stunning hikes
on Long Mynd or up dramatic quartzite
ridge of the Stiperstones); small modernised
lounge with comfortable leatherette wall
banquettes and lots of brassware on ply-
panelled walls, plainer public bar with TV,
games machine and darts, a couple of real
ales such as Hobsons and Three Tuns, good
value bar food usefully served all day, friendly
service; background music; children and dogs
welcome, two comfortable bedrooms, open
all day (till 2am Fri, Sat). *(Rob and Catherine
Dunster)*

STOTTESDON   SO6782
Fighting Cocks (01746) 718270
High Street; DY14 8TZ Welcoming old
half-timbered community pub in unspoilt
countryside, low ceilings and log fire, good
hearty home-made food using local produce,
well kept Hobsons and three guests, live
music and occasional quiz nights; small
shop behind; nice views from garden tables,
good walks, open all day weekends, closed
weekday lunchtimes. *(Anon)*

TELFORD   SJ6910
Crown (01952) 610888
*Market Street, Oakengates (off A442,
handy for M54 junction 5); TF2 6EA*
Bright 19th-c local (list of licensees to 1835),
Hobsons Best and many changing guests,
May and Oct beer festivals with up to 60
ales, draught continentals and lots of foreign
bottled beers, a real cider or perry, helpful
knowledgeable staff, simple snacky food
(can bring your own), bustling bare-boards
front bar with woodburner, small sky-lit side
room and quarry-tiled back room; regular live
music and comedy nights; suntrap courtyard,
handy for station, open all day. *(Anon)*

TILLEY   SJ5027
Raven (01939) 234419
*Tilley Road, right at T junction;
SY4 5HE* Modernised bare-boards dining
pub in pretty 18th-c building, good choice
of traditional locally sourced food including
low-priced smaller meals till 7pm, Hobsons,

Three Tuns and a couple of guests, Gwynt
y Ddraig cider, friendly service, live music
Fri; metal café-style tables out in front, teak
furniture on heated terrace, beautiful village,
open all day. *(David Aston)*

WELLINGTON   SJ6511
Cock (01952) 244954
*Holyhead Road (B5061 – former A5);
TF1 2DL* Former 18th-c coaching inn
popular for its friendly real ale bar, Hobsons
and five well kept quickly changing guests
usually from small breweries, farm cider,
separate bar specialising in belgian beers,
friendly knowledgeable staff, big fireplace;
beer garden with covered area, bedrooms,
closed lunchtime Mon-Weds, open all day
Thurs-Sat. *(Mark Sykes, D Weston)*

WELLINGTON   SJ6410
Old Orleton (01952) 255011
*Holyhead Road (B5061, off M54
junction 7); TF1 2HA* Sympathetically
modernised old coaching inn with restaurant
and bar, good interesting attractively
presented food, two well kept Hobsons beers,
Weston's cider; nice view of the Wrekin, ten
bedrooms. *(Nick Jenkins)*

WELLINGTON   SJ6511
William Withering (01952) 642800
New Street; TF1 1LU Comfortable
Wetherspoons named after 18th-c local
physician, half a dozen real ales, usual
good value food till 10pm, friendly landlord
and staff, interesting pictures of historic
Wellington. *(Nick Jenkins, J F M and M West,
D Weston)*

WHITCHURCH   SJ5345
Willey Moor Lock (01948) 663274
*Tarporley Road; signed off A49 just
under 2 miles N; SY13 4HF* Large
opened-up pub in picturesque spot by
Llangollen Canal; two log fires, low beams
and countless teapots, cheerful chatty
atmosphere, half a dozen changing local
ales and around 30 malt whiskies, enjoyable
good value quickly served pub food from
sandwiches up; background music, games
machine, no credit cards (debit cards
accepted), no dogs inside; children welcome
away from bar, terrace tables, secure garden
with big play area. *(Dr Kevan Tucker, Mike and
Wena Stevenson)*

WHITTINGTON   SJ3231
White Lion (01691) 662361
Castle Street; SY11 4DF Sizeable
refurbished pub just below castle, tasty good
value food including early-bird deal, cheerful
attentive young staff, two well kept ales
and decent wines by the glass, light wood
tables in front bar, smaller area with leather
sofas, dining room and conservatory beyond;
children welcome, plenty of tables in good
outdoor space. *(Anon)*

Somerset

We're delighted with our new entries this year: the Old Green Tree (tiny unspoilt tavern with six ales) and Star (the brewery tap for Abbey Ales, with a real sense of the past) both in Bath, Luttrell Arms in Dunster (handsome old hotel with character bar and well thought-of food), Rose & Crown at Hinton Charterhouse (friendly 18th-c village pub with good food), Holcombe Inn in Holcombe (cosy bars, a wide choice of drinks and interesting meals), Talbot in Mells (carefully refurbished coaching inn, easy-going with super food and drinks and lovely bedrooms), Hope & Anchor in Midford (long-serving owners in spacious civilised pub, with smashing food), Masons Arms at Odcombe (own-brewed beers and tasty food in thatched cottage), and Swan in Wedmore (bustling place serving interesting food from 9am, thoughtful choice of drinks and friendly staff). This is a big county with some particularly good pubs – on top form according to our readers are the Square & Compass at Ashill (traditional country pub with fair prices and long-serving owners), Red Lion at Babcary (well run and popular, with new dining room and well equipped bedrooms), Candlelight in Bishopswood (neatly furnished dining pub, handy for the A303), Kings Arms in Charlton Horethorne (highly rated all-rounder in imposing Edwardian building), Wheatsheaf in Combe Hay (exceptional food in smart but easy-going place), Queens Arms in Corton Denham (excellent food, fine range of drinks and stylish bedrooms), Woods in Dulverton (amazing wines, charming staff and lovely food), Lord Poulett Arms in Hinton St George (really special inn, with top class food, drinks and bedrooms), Halfway House in Pitney (ten ales and unspoilt atmosphere in honest village tavern), Carpenters Arms at Stanton Wick (warm welcome, quiet bedrooms and interesting meals) and Plough at Wrington (popular and very well run; handy for the Cheddar Gorge). So many places serve fantastic food, but our Somerset Dining Pub 2014 is the Lord Poulett Arms in Hinton St George.

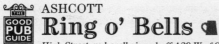

ASHCOTT   ST4337   Map 1
Ring o' Bells ▄

High Street; pub well signed off A39 W of Street; TA7 9PZ

Friendly village pub with traditional décor in several bars, separate restaurant, tasty bar food and changing local ales

The same friendly family have run this 18th-c pub for some years now and our readers enjoy the place very much. The three main bars, on different levels, are all comfortable: maroon plush-topped stools, cushioned mate's chairs and dark wooden pubby tables on patterned carpet, horsebrasses on the bressumer beam above the big stone fireplace and a growing collection of hand bells. Ordnance City Detonator and Summerskills Tamar on handpump, eight wines by the glass and local farm and bottled cider. There's also a separate restaurant, a skittle alley/function room and plenty of picnic-sets on the terrace and in the garden. The pub is handy for the RSPB Ham Wall nature reserve.

Good reasonably priced food includes sandwiches, deep-fried mushrooms stuffed with stilton, fresh grilled sardines, celery, almond and cashew nut roast with cheese sauce, lasagne, chicken breast with bacon, mozzarella and barbecue sauce, pork escalope with apricot and brandy sauce, hake florentine, and puddings that include ice-cream sundaes. *Benchmark main dish: ham, egg and chips £10.20. Two-course evening meal £14.00.*

Free house ~ Licensees John and Elaine Foreman and John Sharman ~ Real ale ~ (01458) 210232 ~ Open 12-3, 7-11(10.30 Sun) ~ Bar food 12-2, 7-10 ~ Restaurant ~ Children welcome ~ Dogs welcome ~ Live folk music twice a month ~ www.ringobells.com *Recommended by Warren Marsh, Chris and Angela Buckell, R L Borthwick, John and Nan Hurst, M G Hart, Jenny and Brian Seller*

ASHILL   ST3116   Map 1
Square & Compass £ ⇌

Windmill Hill; off A358 between Ilminster and Taunton; up Wood Road for a mile behind Stewley Cross service station; OS Sheet 193 map reference 310166; TA19 9NX

Friendly simple pub with local ales, tasty food and good regular live music in separate sound-proofed barn; comfortable bedrooms

The long-serving helpful owners offer such a genuine welcome to their customers at this traditional country pub that most return again and again. It's tucked away in the Blackdown Hills and the little beamed bar has a chatty feel, upholstered window seats that take in the fine view over rolling pastures, heavy hand-made furniture, an open winter fire – look out for the pub cat, Lily. Exmoor Ale, St Austell Tribute and a guest or two such as St Austell Trelawny and Stocklinch Ramblers Gold on handpump and good house wines by the glass. The background music is often classical. There's a garden with picnic-sets and a large glass-covered walled terrace. The bedrooms are spacious and comfortable and two have full disabled facilities. The sound-proofed barn, rural-theme in style, is popular for weddings, parties and live music events.

Generously served and good value, the food includes several dishes under £10, meaning it qualifies for a Value Award: sandwiches, breaded mushrooms with garlic mayonnaise, moules marinière, omelettes, mushroom stroganoff, beer-battered cod and chips, ham and egg, beef curry, lasagne, chicken in stilton and bacon sauce, pork tenderloin in mushroom and madeira sauce, and puddings such as banoffi pie and apple crumble. *Benchmark main dish: steak and kidney pie £9.95. Two-course evening meal £15.00.*

Free house ~ Licensees Chris, Janet and Beth Slow ~ Real ale ~ (01823) 480467 ~ Open 12-3, 6.30(7 Sun)-11.30; closed Tues-Thurs lunchtimes ~ Bar food 12-2, 7-9.30 ~ Children welcome ~ Dogs welcome ~ Country music events held regularly in barn ~ Bedrooms: £65/£85 ~ www.squareandcompasspub.com *Recommended by Roy Hoing, Nick and Sylvia Pascoe*

BABCARY ST5628 Map 2
Red Lion 🍴 ♟ 🛏

Off A37 S of Shepton Mallett; 2 miles or so N of roundabout where A37 meets A303 and A372; TA11 7ED

Thatched pub with informal atmosphere in comfortable rambling rooms, interesting daily changing food and local beers; bedrooms

A smart new building, The Den, has opened in the pretty courtyard here – it has light modern furnishings, a wood-fired pizza oven (open at weekends) and a brasserie-style menu and will double as a party, wedding and conference venue. The main stone-built thatched inn remains as popular as ever with readers. Several distinct areas work their way around the carefully refurbished bar; to the left of the entrance is a longish room with dark red walls, a squashy leather sofa and two housekeeper's chairs around a low table by a woodburning stove, and a few well spaced tables and captain's chairs. There are elegant rustic wall lights, clay pipes in a cabinet, local papers or magazines to read and board games. Leading off here is a more dimly lit public bar with lovely dark flagstones, a panelled dado, a high-backed old settle and other more straightforward chairs; table skittles and background music. The good-sized dining room has a large stone lion's head on a plinth above the open fire (and a huge stack of logs to one side), a big rug on polished boards and formally set tables. Otter Bright, Teignworthy Reel Ale and a guest like Bays Best on handpump, about ten wines by the glass and two farm ciders. The long informal garden has picnic-sets and a play area. The bedrooms are comfortable and well equipped, and the pub is handy for the Fleet Air Arm Museum at Yeovilton, the newly expanded Haynes Motor Museum in Sparkford and for shopping at Clarks Village in Street. Wheelchair access.

🍴 From a well thought-out menu, the good popular food includes sandwiches, warm goats cheese cheesecake with roasted red pepper, basil pesto and chorizo jam, smoked haddock kedgeree topped with a poached egg, wild mushroom pappardelle with parmesan, burger with smoked cheese, bacon and chips, sausages with bean cassoulet, pollock fillet with crisp polenta and minted pea purée, braised beef with horseradish mash and red wine jus, and puddings such as vanilla panna cotta with blood orange jelly and lemon curd and hot chocolate fondant with red wine-poached cherries and vanilla mascarpone. *Benchmark main dish: slow-cooked pork belly with braised red cabbage and mustard mash £14.75. Two-course evening meal £19.50.*

Free house ~ Licensee Charles Garrard ~ Real ale ~ (01458) 223230 ~ Open 12-2.30 (3 Sat), 6-midnight; 12-3, 6-11 Sun ~ Bar food 12-2, 7-9 ~ Restaurant ~ Children welcome ~ Dogs allowed in bar ~ Bedrooms: £90/£110 ~ www.redlionbabcary.co.uk *Recommended by Bob and Margaret Holder, John and Fiona McIlwain, Guy Vowles, John and Philippa Cadge, M G Hart, Chris and Angela Buckell, D and K*

BATCOMBE
ST6839 Map 2

Three Horseshoes

Village signposted off A359 Bruton–Frome; BA4 6HE

Handsome old inn with smart bar rooms, enjoyable well presented food, local ales and friendly owners; comfortable bedrooms

In a gentrified village and next door to a lovely church, this honey-coloured old inn has plenty of character and a warm welcome for all. The long, rather narrow main room is smartly traditional, with beams, local pictures, built-in cushioned window seats, solid chairs around a nice mix of old tables; at one end is a woodburning stove, at the other a big open fire. There's also a pretty stripped-stone dining room – best to book to be sure of a table, especially at weekends. Exmoor Gold, Plain Ales Innocence and Wild Beer Scarlet Fever on handpump, around a dozen wines by the glass and several malt whiskies. This is a nice place to stay and the bedrooms are delightful; they sell local honey.

Using small producers for their seasonal, local ingredients, the interesting food includes lunchtime sandwiches, antipasti plate, chicken liver pâté with home-made tomato chutney, butternut squash and pea risotto with parmesan crisps, cumberland sausages with mash and red onion marmalade, ham and free-range eggs, slow-cooked pork belly with apple sauce and crackling, chicken with sautéed potatoes and tarragon cream sauce, cod fillet with braised chicory, roasted fennel and caper butter, and puddings. *Benchmark main dish: burger with local cheese, spicy tomato chutney, onions and skinny fries £12.00. Two-course evening meal £16.00.*

Free house ~ Licensee Kav Javvi ~ Real ale ~ (01749) 850359 ~ Open 11-3, 6-11; 11-11 Sat; 12-10.30 Sun ~ Bar food 12-2.30, 6-9.30(9 Sun) ~ Restaurant ~ Children welcome ~ Dogs welcome ~ Open mike last Thurs of month ~ Bedrooms: £60/£85 ~ www.thethreehorseshoesinn.co.uk *Recommended by Mr and Mrs J Davis, Chris and Angela Buckell, S G N Bennett*

BATH
ST7564 Map 2

Old Green Tree

Green Street; BA1 2JZ

Tiny, unspoilt local with six real ales and lots of cheerful customers

Unspoilt and unchanging, this tiny bustling 18th-c tavern has an easy-going atmosphere and a cheerful mix of locals and visitors – all welcomed by the efficient and helpful staff. The three small rooms, with oak panelling and low wood and plaster ceilings, include a comfortable lounge on the left as you go in, its walls decorated with wartime aircraft pictures (in winter) and local artists' work (in spring and summer), and a back bar; the big skylight lightens things up attractively. Green Tree Bitter (named for the pub by Blindmans Brewery), Butcombe Bitter and RCH Pitchfork, with guests such as Cotswold Spring Old Sodbury Mild, Cottage Waterloo and Stonehenge Danish Dynamite, on handpump, a dozen wines by the glass from a nice little list with helpful notes and 35 malt whiskies. The gents' is basic and down steep steps. No children.

Lunchtime sandwiches and soup.

Free house ~ Licensees Nick Luke and Tim Bethune ~ Real ale ~ No credit cards ~ (01225) 448259 ~ Open 11am-11.30pm; 12-10.30 (12-4.30 in summer) Sun ~ Bar food 12-2.30; not evenings, not Sun, Mon *Recommended by M G Hart, Taff Thomas, N R White*

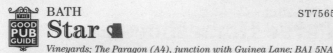

BATH

Star 🍺

ST7565   Map 2

Vineyards; The Paragon (A4), junction with Guinea Lane; BA1 5NA

Quietly chatty and unchanging old town local, the brewery tap for Abbey Ales; filled rolls only

The brewery tap for Abbey Ales, this unspoilt city-centre pub has Bellringer and Salvation plus guests such as Bass, Lancaster Black and St Austell Tribute on handpump, several wines by the glass, quite a few malt whiskies and Cheddar Valley cider. You get a real sense of the past in the four small linked rooms (served from a single bar) and the many original features include traditional wall benches (one is known as Death Row), panelling, dim lighting and open fires; darts, shove-ha'penny, board games – and complimentary snuff. It gets particularly busy at weekends. Food is filled rolls only.

Punch ~ Lease Paul Waters and Alan Morgan ~ Real ale ~ (01225) 425072 ~ Open 12-2.30, 5.30-midnight(1am Fri); noon-1am Sat; 12-midnight Sun ~ Children welcome ~ Dogs welcome ~ Live folk Fri, trad singing Sun ~ www.star-inn-bath.co.uk
Recommended by Dr and Mrs A K Clarke

BISHOPSWOOD

Candlelight 🍴 🍺

ST2512   Map 1

Off A303/B3170 S of Taunton; TA20 3RS

Friendly, hard-working licensees in neatly refurbished dining pub, candlelight and fresh flowers, real ales and farm cider, enjoyable imaginative food and seats in garden

If you fancy a break from the A303, just head for this neatly refurbished and warmly friendly pub. Inside, it's more or less open-plan though separated into different areas by standing stone pillars and open doorways, and the atmosphere throughout is relaxed and informal. The beamed bar has high chairs by the counter where they serve Bass, Branscombe Vale Summa That, Otter Bitter and Skinners Cornish Knocker Ale tapped from the cask, nice wines by the glass, a couple of farm ciders and winter drinks like hot Pimms, whisky toddies and hot chocolate; also, captain's chairs, pews and cushioned window seats around a mix of wooden tables on newly sanded boards and a small ornate fireplace. To the left is a comfortable area with a button-back sofa beside a big woodburner, wheelback chairs and cushioned settles around wooden tables set for dining, country pictures, photos, a hunting horn and bugles on the granite walls; background music and shove-ha' penny. To the other side of the bar is a similarly furnished dining room. Outside, a decked area has picnic-sets and a neatly landscaped garden has a paved path winding through low walls set with plants.

🍴 Imaginative food includes sandwiches, smoked salmon terrine wrapped in home-smoked trout with lemon and black pepper syrup, ballotine of foie gras with sauternes jelly, roast butternut squash risotto, chicken supreme stuffed with sun-dried tomato mousse with basil cream sauce, chargrilled black bream with sauce vierge and herb roast new potatoes, duck leg bourguignon with bacon, shallots and garlic mash, and puddings such as prune and Armagnac tart with chantilly cream and dark chocolate fondant with clotted cream. *Benchmark main dish: pork tenderloin wellington with honey-roasted carrots and sage and red wine jus £15.00. Two-course evening meal £22.00.*

Free house ~ Licensees Tom Warren and Debbie Lush ~ Real ale ~ (01460) 234476 ~ Open 12-3, 6-11; 12-11 Sun; closed Mon ~ Bar food 12-2(2.30 weekends), 7-9(9.30 Fri, Sat) ~ Well behaved children welcome ~ Dogs allowed in bar ~ www.candlelight-inn.co.uk *Recommended by Bob and Margaret Holder, Cath Hine, Ian Herdman*

BRISTOL ST5873 Map 2
Highbury Vaults 🍺 £
St Michael's Hill, Cotham; BS2 8DE

Cheerful town pub with up to eight real ales, good value tasty bar food and friendly atmosphere

Eight real ales on handpump and a location near the university almost guarantees a constant stream of customers to this friendly and unpretentious pub. The little front bar, with a corridor beside it, leads through to a series of small rooms with wooden floors, green and cream paintwork and old-fashioned furniture and prints, including lots of period royal family engravings and lithographs in the front room. A model railway runs on a shelf the full length of the pub, with tunnels through the walls. Wells & Youngs Bitter, Bombardier and Highbury Gold plus guests such as Bath Ales Gem, Box Steam Funnel Blower, Cotswold Spring Stunner, Courage Directors and St Austell Tribute on handpump and several malt whiskies. The attractive back terrace has tables built into a partly covered flowery arbour. In early Georgian times the pub was used as the gaol where condemned men ate their last meal – the bars can still be seen on some windows.

Good value food includes rolls and baked potatoes, vegetarian and meat nachos with sour cream, salsa and melted cheese, lasagne, warm quiche of the day, burgers with cheddar, brie or stilton, bacon and coleslaw, fish pie, and puddings such as sticky toffee or chocolate puddle puddings with custard or ice-cream. *Benchmark main dish: chilli con carne £5.95. Two-course evening meal £11.00.*

Youngs ~ Manager Bradd Francis ~ Real ale ~ No credit cards ~ (0117) 973 3203 ~ Open 12-midnight(11 Sun) ~ Bar food 12-2(2.30 Fri, Sat, 3 Sun), 5.30-8.30 ~ Children welcome ~ www.highburyvaults.co.uk *Recommended by Warren Marsh, Roger and Donna Huggins, Barry Collett, Taff Thomas*

CHARLTON HORETHORNE ST6623 Map 2
Kings Arms 🍽 🛏
B3145 Wincanton–Sherborne; DT9 4NL

Bustling inn with relaxed bars and more formal restaurant, plenty of drinkers and diners, a good choice of ales and wines and enjoyable food using local produce; comfortable bedrooms

A thoroughly good all-rounder, this is a carefully furnished and rather smart Edwardian inn with a cheerful mix of drinkers and diners. The main bar has an appealing assortment of local art (all for sale) on dark mulberry or cream walls, nice old carved wooden dining chairs and pine pews around a mix of tables on a slate floor, and a woodburning stove. Leading off here is a cosy room with sofas and newspapers on low tables. Butcombe Bitter, Sharps Doom Bar and a changing guest such as Wadworths St George & the Dragon on handpump are served from a fine granite bar counter, and they keep 13 wines by the glass, nine malt whiskies and local draught cider. To the left of the main door is an informal dining room with Jacobean-style chairs and tables on a pale wooden floor and more local artwork. The back restaurant (you have to walk past the open kitchen, which is fun to peek into) has decorative wood and glass mirrors, wicker or black leather high-backed dining chairs around chunky polished pale wooden tables on coir carpeting, and handsome striped curtains. At the back of the building, there's an attractive courtyard with chrome and wicker chairs around teak tables under green parasols, and a smokers' shelter overlooking a croquet lawn. The contemporary bedrooms are comfortable and well equipped.

Baking their own bread and making pasta and ice-cream, the high quality food includes twice-baked goats cheese soufflé with beetroot and horseradish chutney, duck liver parfait with seville orange marmalade, steak and kidney pudding, free-range chicken with pancetta and butternut squash salad and tarragon and mushroom cream sauce, moroccan-style pork with roast sweet potatoes, pak choi and sherry vinegar jus, cod with coconut rice, thai vegetables and crab cream sauce, and puddings such as earl grey panna cotta with macerated strawberries and chocolate clafoutis with praline ice-cream. *Benchmark main dish: salmon fishcakes with red onion and mango salsa and chips £14.50. Two-course evening meal £23.00.*

Free house ~ Licensee Tony Lethbridge ~ Real ale ~ (01963) 220281 ~ Open 11am-11.30pm ~ Bar food 12-2.30, 7-9.30(9 Sun) ~ Restaurant ~ Children welcome ~ Dogs allowed in bar ~ Bedrooms: /£125 ~ www.thekingsarms.co.uk *Recommended by Harvey Brown, B J Thompson*

CHURCHILL
Crown 🍺 £

ST4459 Map 1

The Batch; in village, turn off A368 into Skinners Lane at Nelson Arms; BS25 5PP

Unspoilt and unchanging small cottage with friendly customers and staff, super range of real ales and homely lunchtime food

Now under a new landlord, this is a simple pub with an untouched interior. The small and rather local-feeling stone-floored and cross-beamed room on the right has a wooden window seat, an unusually sturdy settle, built-in wall benches, a log fire and chatty, friendly customers. The left-hand room has a slate floor, and steps past the big log fire in a large stone fireplace that lead to more sitting space. No noise from music or games (except perhaps dominoes) and nine real ales tapped from the cask: Bath Ales Gem, Bass, Butcombe Bitter, Palmers Best, RCH Hewish IPA and PG Steam, St Austell Tribute and changing guest beers. Several wines by the glass and local ciders. Outside lavatories are basic. There are garden tables at the front with more seats on the back lawn and hill views; the Mendip morris men visit in summer. There's no pub sign but no one seems to have a problem finding it. Some of the best walking on the Mendips is nearby.

Using beef from the field next door, the straightforward and reasonably priced lunchtime bar food includes sandwiches (the rare roast beef is popular), cauliflower cheese, lasagne, chilli con carne and tasty beef casserole. *Benchmark main dish: rare roast beef sandwich £5.25.*

Free house ~ Licensee Brian Clements ~ Real ale ~ No credit cards ~ (01934) 852995 ~ Open 11(12 Sun)-11 ~ Bar food 12-2.30 ~ Children welcome away from bar ~ Dogs allowed in bar *Recommended by Bob and Margaret Holder, Taff Thomas, Dr and Mrs A K Clarke, Debs Kelly, Adrian Johnson*

CLAPTON-IN-GORDANO

ST4773   Map 1

Black Horse 🍺 £

4 miles from M5 junction 19; A369 towards Portishead, then B3124 towards Clevedon; in North Weston opposite school, turn left signposted Clapton, then in village take second right, may be signed Clevedon, Clapton Wick; BS20 7RH

Old-fashioned pub with lots of cheerful customers, friendly service, real ales and cider, and simple lunchtime food; pretty garden

Readers have enjoyed this unspoilt local for many years and are happy that its old-fashioned charm and atmosphere never changes. The partly flagstoned, partly red-tiled main room has winged settles and built-in wall benches around narrow, dark wooden tables, window seats, a big log fire with stirrups and bits on the mantelbeam, and amusing cartoons and photographs of the pub. A window in an inner snug retains bars from the days when this room was the petty sessions gaol; also, high-backed settles – one with a marvellous carved and canopied creature, another with an art nouveau copper insert reading 'East, West, Hame's Best' – lots of mugs hanging from black beams and plenty of little prints and photographs. There's also a simply furnished room, which is the only place families are allowed; darts. Butcombe Bitter, Courage Best, Otter Ale, Shepherd Neame Spitfire and Wadworths 6X on handpump or tapped from the cask, several wines by the glass and two farm ciders. There are old rustic tables and benches in the garden, with more to one side of the car park – the summer flowers are quite a sight. Paths from the pub lead up Naish Hill or to Cadbury Camp and there's access to local cycle routes.

🍴 Traditional lunchtime-only food includes baguettes and baps with hot and cold fillings, pork in cider, lamb tagine, lasagne and paprika chicken. *Benchmark main dish: beef stew £8.50.*

Enterprise ~ Lease Nicholas Evans ~ Real ale ~ (01275) 842105 ~ Open 11-11; 12-10 Sun ~ Bar food 12-2; not Sun ~ Children in family room only ~ Dogs allowed in bar ~ Live music Mon evening ~ www.thekicker.co.uk *Recommended by Bob and Margaret Holder, Tom Evans, Pat Bunting, Taff Thomas, Roy Hoing, Paul Humphreys, Dr and Mrs A K Clarke, Guy Vowles*

COMBE FLOREY

ST1531   Map 1

Farmers Arms 🍺

Off A358 Taunton–Williton, just N of main village turn-off; TA4 3HZ

Pretty pub with delightful garden, open fire and real ales in cosy bar, popular food using local produce in little dining room and friendly landladies

In warm weather, the charming cottagey garden is a big draw with its picnic-sets under white parasols and lovely flowering tubs and beds, and you may hear the whistle of a steam train as the Taunton-Minehead line runs close by. A pretty thatched place, run by a mother-and-daughter team, it's so popular (especially at weekends) that you'd be wise to book in advance. The little bar has a log fire in a big stone fireplace with lanterns on either side, cushioned pubby chairs and a settle around wooden tables on flagstones, and stools against the bar where they serve Cotleigh Tawny Owl, Exmoor Ale and Gold and St Austell HSD on handpump and several wines by the glass. Off here is the cosy dining room with traditional seats and tables on red patterned carpet and heavy beams. Evelyn Waugh lived in the village, as did his son Auberon.

🍴 Good, highly thought-of food includes sandwiches, whitebait with home-made tartare sauce, meze plate, ham with free-range eggs and chips, vegetarian and meat lasagne, a changing curry, lambs liver, bacon, sage and onions, salmon and smoked haddock fishcakes with tarragon mayonnaise, specials like all-day breakfast or king prawns in chorizo, tomato and basil sauce, and puddings such as chocolate brownie with ice-cream and treacle tart with clotted cream. *Benchmark main dish: fish pie £9.95. Two-course evening meal £20.00.*

Free house ~ Licensee Patricia Vincent ~ Real ale ~ (01823) 432267 ~ Open 12-11 ~ Bar food 12-2.30, 6.30-9; only curry or chilli on Sun quiz evening ~ Restaurant ~ Children welcome ~ Dogs allowed in bar ~ www.farmersarmsatcombeflorey.co.uk
Recommended by Bob and Margaret Holder, Christine and Neil Townend, Richard and Penny Gibbs

COMBE HAY
ST7359   Map 2

Wheatsheaf 🍴 ♟ 🛏
Village signposted off A367 or B3110 S of Bath; BA2 7EG

Smart and cheerful country dining pub with first class food using game and fish caught by the landlord and locally foraged produce; attractive bedrooms

Perched on the side of a steep wooded valley, this is an especially well run dining pub where most of the space is devoted to eating; the exception is a central area by a big fireplace, which has sofas on dark flagstones, with daily papers and current issues of *The Field* and *Country Life* on a low table. Other parts all have stylish high-backed grey wicker dining chairs around chunky modern dining tables, on parquet or coir matting. It's fresh and bright, with block-mounted photo-prints, contemporary artwork and mirrors with colourful ceramic mosaic frames (many for sale) on white-painted stonework or robin's egg blue plaster walls. The sills of the many shuttered windows house anything from old soda siphons to a stuffed kingfisher and a Great Lakes model tugboat, and glinting glass wall chandeliers (as well as nightlights in entertaining holders) supplement the ceiling spotlights. There's a very good if not cheap choice of wines, and Butcombe Bitter, Adam Hensons Rare Breed and a seasonal ale on handpump; staff are friendly and informal, the background music faint enough and the cheerful springer is called Brie. Picnic-sets in the two-level front garden have a fine view over the church and valley; you can walk from the pub. Bedrooms are stylishly simple and spacious.

🍴 As well as a two- and three-course set menu, the accomplished dishes might include lunchtime sandwiches, black pudding scotch egg with griddled asparagus, salt and pepper squid with aioli, lasagne of veal with caesar salad, duck breast with chorizo, red pepper and confit duck leg, whole plaice with brown shrimp and caper butter, venison loin with beetroot fondant and smoked cherry jus, 21-day aged 10oz ribeye steak with duck egg and wild garlic butter, and puddings such as dark chocolate and hazelnut brownie and treacle tart with lemon curd ice-cream. *Benchmark main dish: lamb rump with potato gallette and minted peas £18.00. Two-course evening meal £25.00.*

Free house ~ Licensee Ian Barton ~ Real ale ~ (01225) 833504 ~ Open 10.30-3, 6-11; closed Sun evening, Mon except bank holidays ~ Bar food 12-2, 7-9 ~ Restaurant ~ Children welcome ~ Dogs welcome ~ Bedrooms: /£120 ~ www.wheatsheafcombehay.co.uk
Recommended by M P Mackenzie, Taff Thomas

Virtually all pubs in this book sell wine by the glass. We mention wines if they are a cut above the average.

CORTON DENHAM

ST6322   Map 2

Queens Arms

Village signposted off B3145 N of Sherborne; DT9 4LR

Civilised stone inn with super choice of drinks, interesting food and a sunny garden; comfortable, stylish bedrooms

A new dining room has been added to this particularly well run 18th-c inn with cushioned wall seating and chunky leather chairs around dark wooden tables and mirrors along one side giving the impression of even more space; a drop-down screen here is used for cinema showings on the second Wednesday of the month. The bustling, high-beamed bar has a woodburning stove in an inglenook at one end, with rugs on flagstones and two big armchairs in front of the open fire at the other, some old pews, barrel seats and a sofa, church candles and big bowls of flowers; there's also a separate restaurant. Bath Golden Hare, Moor Nor'Hop and Revival and Timothy Taylors Landlord on handpump, 16 wines (including champagne) by the glass from a carefully chosen list, 53 whiskies, six ciders, unusual bottled beers from Belgium, Germany and the US and eight local apple juices. A south-facing back terrace has teak tables and chairs under parasols (or heaters if it's cool), with colourful flower tubs. The comfortable bedrooms have lovely country views and the breakfasts are delicious; fine surrounding walks.

Using home-reared pork, their own eggs and carefully sourced local produce, the excellent food includes sandwiches, rabbit, ham hock, black pudding and roasted shallot terrine with beetroot chutney, king scallops with pancetta, sage and onion purée and squid ink essence, butter bean, ricotta and sage cannelloni with creamed leeks and black olive tapenade, corn-fed chicken with wild mushrooms and crayfish tails, crispy rösti and tarragon reduction, lemon sole with garlic and caper butter, and puddings such as coconut, chilli and vanilla rice pudding with caramelised banana and mango and apple tart with caramel and honeycomb ice-cream and crème anglaise. *Benchmark main dish: fish and chips £10.95. Two-course evening meal £22.50.*

Free house ~ Licensees Jeanette and Gordon Reid ~ Real ale ~ (01963) 220317 ~ Open 10am-11pm(10.30pm Sun) ~ Bar food 12-3, 6-10 ~ Restaurant ~ Children welcome ~ Dogs allowed in bar ~ Fortnightly film nights ~ Bedrooms: £80/£110 ~ www.thequeensarms.com *Recommended by David Hudd, David and Sue Smith, Edward Mirzoeff, Amber Cotton, M G Hart, Mr and Mrs Lynn, S G N Bennett*

CROSCOMBE

ST5844   Map 2

George

Long Street (A371 Wells–Shepton Mallet); BA5 3QH

Carefully renovated, warmly welcoming, family-run coaching inn with informative canadian landlord, enjoyable food, good local beers and attractive garden; bedrooms

The genuine welcome from the first class landlord in this family-run 16th-c inn is second to none – this, combined with popular food, well kept ales and a lively atmosphere, is what draws readers back on a regular basis. The main bar has stripped stone, dark wooden tables and chairs and more comfortable seats, a new settle by one of the log fires in inglenook fireplaces, and the family's grandfather clock; a snug area has a woodburning stove. The attractive dining room has more stripped stone, local artwork and family photographs on burgundy walls and high-backed cushioned dining chairs around a mix of tables. The back bar has canadian timber and a pew reclaimed from the local church, and there's a family room with games and books for children. King George the Thirst (named for them by Blindmans), Arbor Hoptical Illusion, Butcombe Bitter, Cheddar Ales Potholer, Moor Old Freddy Walker and St Austell Proper Job on handpump or tapped from the cask, four farm ciders, ten wines by the glass and home-made elderflower cordial. Darts, bar billiards, a skittle alley, board games, shove-ha'penny and a canadian wooden table game called crokinole. The friendly pub dog is called Tessa and the cats DJ and Cookie. The attractive, sizeable garden has seats on a heated covered terrace, flower borders, a grassed area, a new wood-fired pizza oven (used at weekends) and chickens; children's swings. The bedrooms are comfortable.

Cooked by the landlady and using home-grown and other local produce, the highly thought-of food includes baguettes, smoked mackerel pâté, goats cheese and caramelised red onion tart, home-cooked ham and eggs, local bangers and mash with onion gravy, vegetable lasagne, monkfish, scallop and king prawn skewers with lemon and dill oil dressing, pork and prosciutto ravioli in sage cream sauce, specials such as coq au vin, local venison medallions in port reduction and bass en papillote with ginger, lemon grass and garlic, and puddings such as chocolate truffle mousse and plum and apple crumble; steak night is Wednesday and curry night is the last Thursday of the month. *Benchmark main dish: steak in ale pie £10.95. Two-course evening meal £19.00.*

Free house ~ Licensees Peter and Veryan Graham ~ Real ale ~ (01749) 342306 ~ Open 12-3(3.30 Sun), 6-11 ~ Bar food 12-2.30, 6-9(8 Sun) ~ Restaurant ~ Children welcome ~ Dogs allowed in bar ~ Bedrooms: £45/£80 ~ www.thegeorgeinn.co.uk
Recommended by Dr J Barrie Jones, David and Sue Atkinson, Michael Butler, Mrs P Bishop, Jenny and Brian Seller, Kim Skuse

DULVERTON SS9127 Map 1

Woods ★

Bank Square; TA22 9BU

Smartly informal place with exceptional wines, real ales, first rate food and a good mix of customers

'Why can't every pub get it this right?' asks one of our readers, while another says: 'always a very special occasion to come here, even if that occasion is just for a pint and a chat.' Still run by the charming Mr Groves and his helpful, courteous staff, it continues to attract a wide mix of customers and you must book to be sure of a table. Many are here for the top class food but they keep local beers and, in particular, exceptional wines – if you want just a glass, they'll open any of their 400 wines from an extraordinarily good list, and there's also an unlisted collection of about 500 well aged, new world wines that the landlord will happily chat about. St Austell Dartmoor Best and HSD and a guest from Red Rock tapped from the cask, a farm cider, many sherries and some unusual spirits. The pub is on the edge of Exmoor, so there are plenty of sporting prints on the salmon pink walls, antlers and other hunting trophies, stuffed birds and a couple of salmon rods. There are bare boards on the left by the bar counter, daily papers, tables partly separated by stable-style timbering and masonry dividers, and a carpeted area on the right with a woodburning stove in a big fireplace; maybe unobjectionable background music. Big windows look on to the quiet town centre (or you can sit on the pavement at a couple of metal tables) and a small suntrap back courtyard has a few picnic-sets.

🍴 Delicious food using their home-bred meat includes ciabatta rolls, chicken liver and foie gras parfait with pickled wild mushrooms, quail egg and port wine syrup, bresaola with parmesan, olives, sunblush tomatoes and mustard ice-cream, omelette arnold bennett, burger with serrano ham, mozzarella, tomato chutney and chips, guinea fowl supreme on puy lentils with confit garlic and red wine sauce, bass with razor clam and seared scallop, truffle purée and sauce vierge, and puddings such as chocolate brownie with coffee ice-cream and lemon tart with blood orange posset, iced lime parfait and Pimms and elderflower sorbet. *Benchmark main dish: slow-roast pork shoulder and tenderloin with black pudding, apple jam and cider sauce £16.50. Two-course evening meal £19.00.*

Free house ~ Licensee Patrick Groves ~ Real ale ~ (01398) 324007 ~ Open 11-3, 6-midnight; 12-3, 7-11 Sun ~ Bar food 12-2, 7-9.30 ~ Restaurant ~ Children welcome ~ Dogs welcome ~ www.woodsdulverton.co.uk *Recommended by Guy Vowles, Mr and Mrs P D Titcomb, Lynda and Trevor Smith, Gerry Price, Mike Gorton, Sheila Topham, Bob and Margaret Holder, Jeremy Whitehorn, Richard and Penny Gibbs*

DUNSTER   SS9943   Map 1
Luttrell Arms 🛏

High Street; A396; TA24 6SG

Fine old stone building with a great deal of character in several bar rooms, good choice of drinks, enjoyable food and seats in courtyard and garden; bedrooms

Based around a great hall built for the Abbot of Cleeve some 500 years ago, this is a civilised hotel with a proper old back bar at its heart. This room has plenty of character – it's got the old workings of the former kitchen, meat hooks on a beamed ceiling, a huge log fire and bread oven and high chairs at the counter where they keep Exmoor Ale, Otter Bitter and Sharps Doom Bar on handpump and several good wines by the glass. Locals enjoy the simpler front bar; the comfortable lounge has armchairs, sofas, a cushioned window seat and a woodburning stove, and throughout are panelled and cushioned wall seats, old settles and handsome carved dining chairs around an assortment of wooden tables, rugs on tiles and ancient timber uprights. Plenty of seats in the back garden and metalwork chairs and tables in a galleried courtyard. Bedrooms are well equipped and comfortable; some have antique four-poster beds. The town, on the edge of Exmoor National Park, is pretty and full of interest.

🍴 Enjoyable food includes sandwiches and baguettes, sharing platters, smoked salmon and crayfish cocktail with bloody mary sauce, deep-fried soft shell crab in light vodka batter with pepper compote, honey-glazed home-cooked ham and eggs, mushroom, pine nut and parmesan linguine, steak and kidney pie, rack of ribs in barbecue sauce, curry of the day, duck breast with champ mash and walnut and orange butter, local lamb in rosemary, redcurrant and port jus with dauphinoise potatoes, and puddings. *Benchmark main dish: burger with stilton, cheddar, bacon or barbecue sauce and chips £11.75. Two-course evening meal £19.00.*

Free house ~ Licensee Tim Waldren ~ Real ale ~ (01643) 821555 ~ Open 11-11 ~ Bar food 12-3, 7-9; all day summer; breakfast 7.30-10.30am ~ Restaurant ~ Children welcome in family area and restaurant only ~ Dogs allowed in bar ~ Bedrooms: £100/£130 ~ www.luttrellarms.co.uk *Recommended by Mr and Mrs P D Titcomb*

We say if we know a pub allows dogs.

HINTON CHARTERHOUSE

ST7758   Map 2

Rose & Crown

B3110 about 4 miles S of Bath; BA2 7SN

Friendly 18th-c village pub with well kept ales, tasty food and seats outside; bedrooms

The window boxes in front of this stone-built 18th-c pub are pretty in summer, and the terraced garden has picnic-sets under parasols. The partly divided bar has some fine panelling, cushioned wall seats and bar stools, a mix of dark wooden chairs around chunky tables on red patterned carpet and a woodburning stove in an ornate carved stone fireplace; there's a second small brick fireplace on the other side, Butcombe Bitter and a seasonal guest and Fullers London Pride on handpump and several wines by the glass; TV and background music. The long dining room, with steps down to a lower area, has an unusual beamed ceiling.

Quite a choice of well liked food includes potted ham hock terrine with home-made chutney, creamy garlic mushrooms, pasta with spicy tomato and pepper sauce, ham with free-range eggs, beer-battered haddock and chips, liver and bacon casserole with mash, pie of the day, cajun salmon with basil oil dressing, pork loin in creamy cider sauce with caramelised apple, mixed grill, and puddings. *Benchmark main dish: chicken with pancetta, mushrooms and cream £9.95. Two-course evening meal £14.00.*

Butcombe ~ Manager Shane Smith ~ Real ale ~ (01225) 722153 ~ Open 11-3, 5-midnight; 11-midnight Weds-Sun ~ Bar food 12-3, 6-9.30; 12-9.30 Fri-Sun; afternoon tea 2-5 Weds-Sat ~ Restaurant ~ Children welcome ~ Dogs welcome ~ Monthly summer live music and barbecue ~ Bedrooms: £49/£63 ~ www.roseandcrown.butcombe.com
Recommended by Dave Braisted

HINTON ST GEORGE

ST4212   Map 1

Lord Poulett Arms ⏹ ♀ ⇌

Off A30 W of Crewkerne and off Merriott road (declassified – former A356, off B3165) N of Crewkerne; TA17 8SE

Somerset Dining Pub of the Year

Thatched 17th-c stone inn with antique-filled rooms, top class food using home-grown vegetables, good choice of drinks and a pretty garden; attractive bedrooms

Our readers love all aspects of this genuinely friendly and civilised inn. The bedrooms are pretty and cottagey, the food first class, the choice of drinks interesting and thoughtful and the service exemplary. Several attractive and cosy linked areas have rugs on bare boards or flagstones, open fires (one in an inglenook and another in a raised fireplace that separates two rooms), walls of honey-coloured stone or painted in bold Farrow & Ball colours, hop-draped beams, antique brass candelabra, fresh flowers and candles and some lovely old farmhouse, windsor and ladder-back chairs around fine oak or elm tables. Branscombe Branoc, Otter Ale and a guest such as Cotleigh Tawny Owl on handpump, ten wines by the glass, jugs of Pimms and home-made cordial, some interesting whiskies and local bottled cider and perry; the pub cat is called Honey. Outside, under a wisteria-clad pergola, are white metalwork tables and chairs in a mediterranean-style lavender-edged gravelled area, and picnic-sets in a wild flower meadow; boules. This is a peaceful, pretty village with nice surrounding walks.

🍴 Using home-grown and other organic local produce, the enticing food includes lunchtime sandwiches, blue vinney cheesecake with watercress and bacon salad, hot smoked salmon with trio of beetroot and horseradish cream, wild boar meatloaf with smoked tomato sauce, pork bath chap (cheek) fritters with fried duck egg and chips, spelt spaetzle with sprouting broccoli pesto and mozzarella, brisket of beef chilli with corn bread, sour cream and coriander, tandoori-dusted brill with sweet potato, curry oil and cauliflower bhaji, delicious specials, and puddings such as coconut crème brûlée with rum syrup and roasted pineapple and chocolate and salt caramel tart with toffee ice-cream. *Benchmark main dish: cider-battered fish and triple-cooked chips £14.00. Two-course evening meal £20.00.*

Free house ~ Licensees Steve Hill and Michelle Paynton ~ Real ale ~ (01460) 73149 ~ Open 12-11 ~ Bar food 12-2.30(3.45 Sun), 7-9.15; reduced menu 3 6.30 ~ Restaurant ~ Children welcome ~ Dogs allowed in bar ~ Live music summer Sun 4-7pm ~ Bedrooms: £60/£85 ~ www.lordpoulettarms.com *Recommended by Simon Pyle, Hilary Kerr, R T and J C Moggridge*

HOLCOMBE   ST6649   Map 2
Holcombe Inn 🛏

Off A367; Stratton Road; BA3 5EB

Friendly inn with far-reaching views, cosy bars, open woodburners, a wide choice of drinks and enjoyable food; comfortable bedrooms

There are peaceful farmland views to Downside Abbey's school from picnic-sets on the terrace and side lawn, and the sunsets can be stunning. Inside, a cosy room to the right has sofas around a central table and an open woodburning stove; to the left is the bar with fine old flagstones, window seats and chunky captain's chairs around pine-topped tables (each with a little bucket of primroses) and a carved wooden counter where they serve Bath Ales Gem and Otter Bitter on handpump, 20 wines and champagne by the glass, 25 malt whiskies, cocktails and a thoughtful choice of local drinks (cider, vodka, sloe gin and various juices); service is friendly and chatty. A two-way woodburning stove also warms the dining room, which is partly carpeted and partly flagstoned with partitioning creating snugger seating areas, a mix of high-backed patterned or brass-studded leather dining chairs around all sorts of tables, and daily newspapers; a little sitting area with a TV leads off here. The refurbished bedrooms are individually decorated and comfortable.

🍴 Using home-grown herbs, the highly thought-of food includes sandwiches, grilled sardines on toast with tomato fondue and olive tapenade, smoked duck salad with apple, walnuts and raspberry jus vinaigrette, pie of the day, breaded goats cheese bonbons with polenta chips and slow-roasted tomatoes, trio of sausages with herb mash and red wine gravy, lager-battered haddock with mushy peas, loin of rabbit with confit leg, pine nuts, raisins and hotpot potatoes, teriyaki-marinated salmon on stir-fried noodles and vegetables, chicken breast stuffed with mushroom duxelles with wild mushroom and madeira jus, and puddings. *Benchmark main dish: pork tenderloin wrapped in parma ham and spinach with sausage and sage sauce £16.95. Two-course evening meal £21.00.*

Free house ~ Licensee Julie Berry ~ Real ale ~ (01761) 232478 ~ Open 12-3, 6-11; 12-11 Sat, Sun ~ Bar food 12-2.30, 6-9; 12-9 Fri-Sun ~ Restaurant ~ Children welcome ~ Dogs allowed in bar ~ Bedrooms: £65/£100 ~ www.holcombeinn.co.uk *Recommended by Isobel Mackinlay, Martin Jones*

HUISH EPISCOPI ST4326 Map 1

Rose & Crown £

Off A372 E of Langport; TA10 9QT

17th-c pub in the same family for over a century, local cider and real ales, simple food and a friendly welcome

Known locally as Eli's (after the present licensee's grandfather), this quite unspoilt village inn has been in the same friendly family for more than 140 years. There's no bar as such, just a central flagstoned still room where drinks are served: Teignworthy Reel Ale and a couple of guests such as Hop Back Crop Circle and Glastonbury Ales Mystery Tor, local Burrow Hill farm cider and Somerset cider brandy. The casual little front parlours, with their unusual pointed arch windows, have family photographs, books, cribbage, dominoes, shove-ha'penny and bagatelle and attract a good mix of locals and visitors. A much more orthodox big back extension has pool, games machine and a juke box. There are plenty of seats and tables in the big outdoor eating area and two lawns – one is enclosed and has a play area; you can camp (free by arrangement to pub customers) on the adjoining paddock. Separate skittle alley and big car park. Every Friday (4.30-7pm), they host an organic co-operative, where you can buy free-range eggs, local produce and freshly made bread. Summer morris men; fine river walks and the site of the Battle of Langport (1645) are nearby.

The reasonably priced home-made food might include sandwiches, two different daily soups, ploughman's, pork, apple and cider cobbler, chicken in tarragon sauce, stilton and broccoli tart, and puddings such as apple crumble and bread and butter pudding. *Benchmark main dish: steak in ale pie £7.95. Two-course evening meal £11.00.*

Free house ~ Licensees Maureen Pittard, Stephen Pittard, Patricia O'Malley ~ Real ale ~ No credit cards ~ (01458) 250494 ~ Open 11.30-3, 5.30-11; 11.30-11.30 Fri, Sat; 12-10.30 Sun ~ Bar food 12-2, 5.30-7.30; not Sun evening ~ Children welcome ~ Dogs allowed in bar ~ Music and quiz evenings; phone for details *Recommended by Paul Humphreys, Mr Yeldahn*

MELLS ST7249 Map 2

Talbot

W of Frome, off A362 or A361; BA11 3PN

Substantial, careful refurbishments for interesting old coaching inn, real ales and good wines, enticing food and seats in courtyard; lovely bedrooms

Now run by the same people as the first class Beckford Arms at Fonthill Gifford (in our Wiltshire chapter), this former coaching inn has had a thoughtful recent refurbishment. The bustling candlelit bar is nicely informal with various wooden tables and chairs on big quarry tiles, a woodburning stove in a stone fireplace, and stools (much used by locals) against the counter where friendly, helpful staff serve Butcombe Bitter, a changing seasonal ale and one named for the pub on handpump and several good wines by the glass. The two linked dining rooms have brass-studded leather chairs around more wooden tables, a log fire with candles in fine clay cups on the mantelpiece above and lots of coaching prints on the walls; quiet background music. The courtyard with its pale green wire-work chairs and tables has a mediterranean feel; off from here, in separate buildings, are the enjoyable, rustic-feeling sitting room with sofas, chairs and tables, smart magazines, a huge mural and vast glass bottles (free films or popular TV programmes are shown on Sunday evenings), and the grill room where food is cooked simply on a big open fire and served at shared refectory tables looked down on by 18th-c portraits. The bedrooms are stylish, comfortable and well equipped and the breakfasts very good. This is an interestingly preserved feudal village with a lovely church where Siegfried Sassoon is buried. Do wander into the walled gardens opposite the pub.

Imaginative food might include lunchtime sandwiches, smoked haddock and crayfish terrine with sour cream, celery, cucumber, dill and sourdough, hog's pudding with soft boiled egg, bath chaps (pig cheeks), baby gherkins and mustard cream, burger with bacon, cheddar, pickles and chips, crispy goats curd, artichoke and spinach roll with radishes and lentil vinaigrette, loin of venison with roasted garlic and mash, salmon with roasted beetroots, cauliflower purée, sorrel and hazelnut butter, and puddings such as dark chocolate mousse with vanilla ice-cream and caramelised hazelnuts and vanilla rice pudding with blackberry jam and nutmeg. *Benchmark main dish: beer-battered fish and chips £11.50. Two-course evening meal £19.00.*

Free house ~ Licensee Matt Greenlees ~ Real ale ~ (01373) 812254 ~ Open 11-11(10.30 Sun) ~ Bar food 12-3, 6-9.30; breakfast 8-10am ~ Restaurant ~ Children welcome ~ Dogs allowed in bar ~ Bedrooms: /£95 ~ www.talbotinn.com *Recommended by Lois Dyer, Ruth May*

MIDFORD
Hope & Anchor
ST7660   Map 2

Bath Road (B3110); BA2 7DD

Friendly long-serving owners in partly 17th-c pub, handy for Bath; popular food and several real ales

At the heart of the Cam Valley and with walks nearby on the disused Somerset and Dorset rail track, this neat, open-plan dining pub is run by friendly, long-serving owners. There's a civilised bar, a heavy-beamed restaurant with a long cushioned settle against red patterned wallpaper, a mix of dark wooden dining chairs and tables on flagstones and a woodburning stove. The back conservatory is stylish and modern, and popular with families. Box Steam Tunnel Vision, Sharps Doom Bar, Wadworths IPA on handpump and several wines by the glass. There are seats outside on the sheltered back terrace with an upper tier beyond. The pub is on the newish Colliers Way cycle path.

Well liked food includes lunchtime sandwiches (not Sunday), pork and sage dumpling parcels with onions, bacon and sour cream, fish soup with rouille and croûte, feta and goats cheese strudel with pesto, tomato and pine nuts, home-cooked ham and eggs, lasagne, cajun chicken with mango mayonnaise and fries, salmon fillet with prawns and chilli cream sauce, duck breast with stir-fried vegetables and plum sauce on chinese noodles, daily specials and puddings. *Benchmark main dish: steak and mushroom in ale pie £11.50. Two-course evening meal £15.00.*

Free house ~ Licensee Richard Smolarek ~ Real ale ~ (01225) 832296 ~ Open 10.30-3, 6-11; 10.30-11 Sat, Sun ~ Bar food 12-2, 6-9.30; all day weekends ~ Restaurant ~ Children welcome ~ www.hopeandanchormidford.co.uk *Recommended by Harvey Brown, Tess White*

There are report forms at the back of the book.

ODCOMBE
ST5015 Map 2

Masons Arms 🍺 🛏

Off A3088 or A30 just W of Yeovil; Lower Odcombe; BA22 8TX

Own-brew beers and tasty food in pretty thatched cottage; bedrooms

---

Well worth a diversion from the A303 or A30, this pretty thatched cottage has a genuinely cheerful atmosphere and a good mix of customers. The homely little bar has joists and a couple of standing timbers, a mix of cushioned dining chairs around all sorts of tables on a cream and blue patterned carpet and a couple of tub chairs and a table in the former inglenook fireplace. Up a step is a similar area, while more steps lead down to a dining room with a squashy brown sofa and a couple of cushioned dining chairs in front of a woodburning stove; the sandstone walls are hung with black and white local photographs and country prints. Friendly, chatty staff serve their own-brewed Odcombe No 1, Roly Poly and seasonal beers on handpump, 11 wines by the glass and farm cider; they also make their own sloe and elderflower cordials. There's a thatched smokers' shelter and picnic-sets in the garden, plus a vegetable patch and chicken coop at the bottom. Bedrooms are well equipped and comfortable, and breakfasts good and hearty; they also have a campsite.

 Using some home-grown produce and their own eggs, the well liked food includes ciabattas, scallops with black pudding and pea purée, smoked duck breast with pomegranate sauce and tomato salsa, ham, free-range duck egg and chips, pie of the day, beetroot and caramelised onion tart with crushed garlic potatoes, lambs liver and bacon with bubble and squeak and gravy, chicken stuffed with chorizo and spinach, and puddings such as bakewell tart with strawberry ice-cream and peanut butter crème brûlée. *Benchmark main dish: fishcakes with sweet chilli sauce £10.75. Two-course evening meal £20.00.*

Own brew ~ Licensees Drew Read and Paula Tennyson ~ Real ale ~ (01935) 862591 ~ Open 10-3.30, 6-midnight ~ Bar food 12-2, 6.30-9.30 ~ Children welcome ~ Dogs welcome ~ Bedrooms: £55/£85 ~ www.masonsarmsodcombe.co.uk *Recommended by Mike and Mary Carter, Michelle Power*

PITNEY
ST4527 Map 1

Halfway House 🍺 £

Just off B3153 W of Somerton; TA10 9AB

Bustling, friendly local with up to ten real ales, local ciders and good simple food

---

This is such a firm favourite with many that it always has a cheerful, chatty atmosphere and remains an unchanging, reliably idiosyncratic village local. A good mix of people are usually found at the communal tables in the three old-fashioned rooms, all with roaring log fires, and the homely feel is underlined by a profusion of books, maps and newspapers. The fine range of up to ten regularly changing beers tapped from the cask might include Butcombe Bitter, Cheddar Ales Totty Pot, Dark Star Hophead, Dorset Yachtsman, Hop Back Crop Circle and Summer Lightning, Otter Bright, Pitchfork IPA, Quantock Wills Neck and Teignworthy Reel Ale; also, five farm ciders, a dozen malt whiskies and several wines by the glass; board games. There are tables outside.

 As well as lunchtime sandwiches, simple food served in generous helpings includes baked potatoes, french onion tart, sausage and mash with onion gravy, lamb, chicken or beef curry, and pork in cider casserole, and puddings. *Benchmark main dish: beer-battered fish and chips £8.50. Two-course evening meal £15.00.*

Free house ~ Licensee Mark Phillips ~ Real ale ~ (01458) 252513 ~ Open 11.30-3, 5.30-11(midnight Sat); 12-11 Sun ~ Bar food 12-2.30, 7-9.30; some sort of food all day Sun ~ Children welcome ~ Dogs welcome ~ www.thehalfwayhouse.co.uk
Recommended by Edward Mirzoeff, Patrick and Daphne Darley, Bob and Margaret Holder, Richard and Penny Gibbs

PRIDDY
Queen Victoria £
Village signed off B3135; Pelting Drove; BA5 3BA

ST5250   Map 2

Stone-built country pub with lots of interconnecting rooms, open fires and woodburners, a friendly atmosphere and staff, real ales and honest food; seats outside

After walking in the Mendip Hills, this creeper-clad stone pub is just the place to relax, with its two woodburning stoves – and dogs are very welcome. The various dimly lit rooms and alcoves have a lot of character and plenty of original features. One room leading off the main bar has a log fire in a big old stone fireplace with a huge cauldron to one side, and there are flagstoned or slate floors, bare stone walls (though the smarter dining room is half-panelled, half-painted), Queen Victoria photographs, horse tack, farm tools and chatty, cheerful customers. Furniture is traditional: cushioned wall settles, farmhouse and other solid chairs around all manner of wooden tables, one nice old pew beside a screen settle making a cosy alcove, and high chairs beside the bar counter where they serve Butcombe Bitter and guests such as Belvoir Rare Breed and Fullers London Pride on handpump, two farm ciders, 20 malt whiskies and eight wines by the glass. There are seats in the front courtyard and more across the lane where there's a children's playground. Five bedrooms are planned.

As well as baguettes, the fairly priced food includes chicken liver and bacon pâté, creamy garlic mushrooms, ham and eggs, vegetarian or meat burgers with chips, chicken breast with barbecue sauce, curry of the day, fish pie, steaks and puddings. *Benchmark main dish: beef in ale pie £9.75. Two-course evening meal £13.00.*

Butcombe ~ Manager Mark Walton ~ Real ale ~ (01749) 676385 ~ Open 12-midnight(10.30 Sun) ~ Bar food 12-2, 6-9; 12-9 Sat; 12-4 Sun; all day all week June-Sept ~ Children welcome ~ Dogs welcome ~ www.queenvictoria.butcombe.com
Recommended by Paul Humphreys, Taff Thomas, Mr and Mrs P R Thomas

STANTON WICK
Carpenters Arms 🍽 ♀ 🛏
Village signposted off A368, just W of junction with A37 S of Bristol; BS39 4BX

ST6162   Map 2

Bustling, warm-hearted dining pub in country setting with enjoyable food, friendly staff and fine choice of drinks; comfortable bedrooms

Readers greatly enjoy their visits to this attractive little stone inn and return on a regular basis. The bedrooms are comfortable and quiet, the food good and interesting and the landlord and his staff friendly and helpful; country walks nearby too. Coopers Parlour on the right has a couple of beams, seats around heavy tables on a tartan carpet and attractive curtains and window plants; at the angle between here and the bar area is a wide woodburning stove in an opened-through corner fireplace. The bar has wood-backed wall settles with cushions, stripped-stone walls and a big log fire in an inglenook. There's also a snug inner room (brightened by mirrors in arched recesses) and a restaurant with leather sofas and easy chairs with a lounge area at one end. Butcombe Bitter and Sharps Doom Bar and a seasonal ale on handpump, ten wines by the glass (plus some interesting bin ends) and several malt whiskies; TV in the snug. There are picnic-sets on the front terrace and pretty flower beds, hanging baskets and tubs.

The good, popular food includes sandwiches, tian of prawns with lime and chilli crème fraîche, asparagus, pancetta and black pudding salad topped with poached egg and tomato and chive dressing, courgette, butternut squash and red pepper risotto with goats cheese, beer-battered haddock with chips, steak and mushroom pudding, trout fillet on linguine with prawn, tomato and dill cream sauce, duck confit with pancetta, broad beans and red wine sauce, and puddings such as chocolate and hazelnut brownie with vanilla ice-cream and bakewell tart with clotted cream. *Benchmark main dish: chicken wrapped in parma ham with creamy mushroom sauce £14.95. Two-course evening meal £19.45.*

Free house ~ Licensee Simon Pledge ~ Real ale ~ (01761) 490202 ~ Open 11-11; 12-10.30 Sun ~ Bar food 12-2.30, 6-9.30(10 Fri, Sat); 12-9 Sun; sandwiches all afternoon Sat ~ Restaurant ~ Children welcome ~ Dogs allowed in bar ~ Bedrooms: £72.50/£105 ~ www.the-carpenters-arms.co.uk *Recommended by Chris and Val Ramstedt, Tania Harris, Steve and Liz Tilley, Alan Bowker, Lindsay White, Warren Marsh, David Jackman, Dr and Mrs A K Clarke, Julian and Jennifer Clapham, Mike and Mary Carter, Hugh Roberts, M G Hart*

STOKE ST GREGORY   ST3527 Map 1
Rose & Crown ⑪ ♀ ⇌

Woodhill; follow North Curry signpost off A378 by junction with A358 – keep on to Stoke, bearing right in centre, passing church and follow lane for 0.5 miles; TA3 6EW

Friendly, family-run pub with quite a choice of popular food and a fine range of drinks; comfortable bedrooms

Several readers stop at this highly enjoyable pub for a meal or an overnight stay on their way to and from the west country, and consistently send us positive feedback; it's been run by the same friendly, hands-on family for over 33 years. The interior is more or less open-plan, and the bar area has wooden stools by a curved brick and pale wood-topped counter with Exmoor Ale and Otter Bright on handpump, local farm cider and several wines by the glass. This leads into a long, airy dining room with all manner of light and dark wooden dining chairs and pews around a mix of tables under a high-raftered ceiling. There are two other beamed dining rooms, with similar furnishings and photographs of the village and of the recent fire damage to the pub; one room has a woodburning stove, another has an 18th-c glass-covered well in a corner. Throughout are flagstoned or wooden floors. The sheltered front terrace has plenty of seats. They have three ensuite bedrooms, one of which can connect to make a family room.

Good and very highly regarded, the food includes sandwiches, mussels in local cider, cream and garlic, deep-fried local brie with warm cranberry sauce, stilton and mushroom vol au vent, tandoori chicken with sweet peppers and onions, crispy half-duck with orange and Grand Marnier sauce, lamb rump with redcurrant sauce, specials such as whole kipper with lemon and horseradish mayonnaise or lamb shank with root vegetables in red wine, and puddings such as profiteroles in warm chocolate sauce and vanilla panna cotta. *Benchmark main dish: pork tenderloin in somerset brandy and wholegrain mustard sauce £13.95. Two-course evening meal £19.50.*

Free house ~ Licensees Stephen, Sally, Richard and Leonie Browning ~ Real ale ~ (01823) 490296 ~ Open 11-3, 6-11; 12-3, 6.30-10.30 Sun ~ Bar food 12-2, 7-9 ~ Restaurant ~ Children welcome ~ Dogs allowed in bar ~ Bedrooms: £55/£85 ~ www.browningpubs.com
Recommended by Bob and Margaret Holder, Damian and Lucy Buxton, Richard and Liz Thorne, Richard and Judy Winn, Adrian Johnson, Mrs Wendda Knapp

 WATERROW   ST0525   Map 1
Rock 🍺
A361 Wiveliscombe–Bampton; TA4 2AX

Handsome inn with local ales, interesting food and a nice mix of customers; comfortable bedrooms

On the edge of Exmoor National Park, this is a striking timbered inn with a good mix of locals and visitors, and friendly licensees. The relaxed and informal bar area has a dark brown leather sofa and a low table with newspapers and books in front of a log fire in a stone fireplace, a mix of dining chairs and wooden tables on the partly wood and partly red-carpeted floor, a few high-backed bar chairs and a couple of built-in cushioned window seats. Cotleigh Tawny Owl and Barn Owl and Exmoor Gold on handpump, several wines by the glass and farm cider. The heavily beamed restaurant is up some steps from the bar; there's also a private dining room. Seats under umbrellas out in front.

🍴 Highly thought-of, the food might include ham hock terrine with fig chutney, camembert fondant with spinach and beetroot salad, filo parcel of leeks, wild mushrooms and goats cheese with yellow pepper sauce, beer-battered haddock and chips, calves liver with caramelised onions on bubble and squeak, chicken with herb stuffing, wild mushrooms and spinach on rösti potato, salmon steak in chive butter sauce, and puddings such as vanilla panna cotta with rhubarb compote and dark chocolate marquise with frosted walnuts and coffee sauce. *Benchmark main dish: pig cheeks braised in cider with black pudding £14.50. Two-course evening meal £23.00.*

Free house ~ Licensees Darren and Ruth Barclay ~ Real ale ~ (01984) 623293 ~ Open 12-3, 6-11; closed Mon lunchtime except bank holidays, Tues lunchtime after bank holiday Mon ~ Bar food 12-2, 6-9(9.30 Fri, Sat) ~ Restaurant ~ Children welcome ~ Dogs allowed in bar ~ Bedrooms: £60/£85 ~ www.rockinn.co.uk *Recommended by John and Fiona McIlwain, Patrick and Daphne Darley, Bob and Margaret Holder, Kim Skuse*

 WEDMORE   ST4348   Map 1
Swan 🍷
Cheddar Road, opposite Church Street; BS28 4EQ

Bustling place with a friendly, informal atmosphere, lots of customers, efficient service and enjoyable food and drinks

With people dropping in and out all day, this bustling place has a really good buoyant atmosphere. It feels more like a café than a traditional pub, but they do keep Bath Ales Gem, Cheddar Ales Potholer, Milk Street March Madness and Otter Bitter on handpump, as well as nine good wines by the glass, cocktail specials on the third Thursday of the month, several coffees and teas and hot chocolate;

service is quick and friendly. The layout is open-plan – mirrors everywhere give the feeling of even more space – and the main bar has all sorts of wooden tables and chairs on polished floorboards, a wall seat with attractive scatter cushions, a woodburning stove, suede stools against the panelled counter and a rustic central table with daily papers. At one end, a step leads down to an area with rugs on huge flagstones, a leather chesterfield sofa, armchairs and brass-studded leather chairs, then down another step to more sofas and armchairs. The airy dining room has high-backed pretty chairs, tables set with candles in glass jars and another woodburner, and this leads to the former skittle alley. There are plenty of seats and tables on the terrace and lawn, and at the front of the building the metal furniture among flowering tubs gives a continental feel. The contemporary bedrooms are well equipped and comfortable.

They bake their own bread, cakes and biscuits with organic flour and use local, seasonal produce for the enjoyable food: sandwiches, potted pig with piccalilli and malted toast, chargrilled organic burger with cheddar, rémoulade and chips, smoked cheese-stuffed portabello mushroom with ratatouille and wholegrain spelt, pollack fillet with potatoes, beetroot and anchovy and lemon butter, slow-cooked beef rib with bubble and squeak cake, spiced lamb shoulder slow-cooked in the wood oven with tabbouleh and mint yoghurt, and puddings such as vanilla panna cotta with home-made rhubarb sorbet and warm chocolate pudding with home-made vanilla ice-cream and salted pralines. *Benchmark main dish: pork belly with herb gnocchi and cider sauce £16.00. Two-course evening meal £20.00.*

Free house ~ Licensee Cassia Stevens ~ Real ale ~ (01934) 710337 ~ Open 9am-11pm(10.30pm Sun) ~ Bar food 12-3, 6-10; breakfast 9-11.30am ~ Restaurant ~ Children welcome ~ Dogs allowed in bar ~ Bedrooms: /£100 ~ www.theswanwedmore.com
Recommended by Hugo Jeune, John and Gloria Isaacs, Michael Doswell, Mr Yeldahn

WELLS
ST5546   Map 2
Fountain
St Thomas Street; BA5 2UU

Friendly and attractive small pub in town centre, with plenty of room and a bustling atmosphere

'We've known this pub for 60 years and it's never been better than now,' says one of our more discerning readers. An attractive little pub with blue shutters and pretty window boxes, it was built in the 18th c to house builders working on the nearby cathedral. There are always lots of customers popping in and out, but there's plenty of space in the big comfortable bar with its large open fire, interesting bric-a-brac, Butcombe Bitter and Sharps Doom Bar on handpump and several wines by the glass; unobtrusive background music and board games. There's an upstairs restaurant too, called Boxers.

As well as a good value two- and three-course set menu and a popular over-60s' lunch club, the well liked food includes sandwiches, pork and apricot terrine with red onion, apple and balsamic jam, ham and eggs, salad niçoise, sausages with onion gravy, quiche of the day, mediterranean ratatouille pasta topped with goats cheese, duck breast with orange and honey jus, and puddings. *Benchmark main dish: steak with mustard and onion butter, beer-battered onion rings and chips £15.50. Two-course evening meal £19.00.*

Punch ~ Tenants Adrian and Sarah Lawrence ~ Real ale ~ (01749) 672317 ~ Open 12-2.30, 6-11; 12-2.30, 7-10.30 Sun ~ Bar food 12-2, 7-9.30 ~ Restaurant ~ Children welcome ~ www.fountaininn.co.uk *Recommended by Paul Humphreys, R K Phillips, Jenny and Brian Seller*

WRINGTON
Plough
ST4762 Map 2

2.5 miles off A370 Bristol–Weston, from bottom of Rhodiate Hill; BS40 5QA

Welcoming, popular pub with bustling bar and two dining rooms, good food using local produce and well kept beer, and seats outside

A lways deservedly busy with a good mix of locals and visitors, this particularly well run and neatly kept pub offers a friendly welcome to all; it's handy for both the Cheddar Gorge and Bristol Airport. There's a chatty bar with stools by the counter where they serve Butcombe Bitter (the brewery is in the village), St Austell Tribute and Wells & Youngs Bitter on handpump and 18 wines by the glass, and two distinct dining rooms – the one at the back has lots of big windows overlooking the gazebo and garden. Open doorways link the rooms, and throughout you'll find (three) winter fires, slate or wooden floors, beams and standing timbers, plenty of pictures on the planked, red or yellow walls and all manner of high-backed leather or wooden dining or farmhouse chairs around many different sizes of table; fresh flowers, a games chest, table skittles and helpful service. There are picnic-sets at the front and on the back grass; boules. They hold a farmers' market on the second Friday of the month. This is sister pub to the Rattlebone at Sherston (Wiltshire).

Quite a range of popular food includes lunchtime sandwiches and ciabattas, pigeon breast with cauliflower purée, curried almonds and apricots, warm blini with smoked salmon, crème fraîche, capers and red onion, savoury bread and butter pudding with goats cheese, olives and tomato sauce, sausages with grain mustard mash and onion gravy, gammon, free-range eggs and bubble and squeak, burger with cheese, bacon, coleslaw and chips, chicken breast and confit drumstick with wild mushroom sauce and fondant potato, calves liver with bacon, rosemary mash and onion gravy, and puddings such as key lime pie and raspberry sorbet and dark chocolate and caramel tart with coffee cream. *Benchmark main dish: smoked haddock with spinach, poached egg and local cheddar £11.95. Two-course evening meal £16.00.*

Youngs ~ Tenant Jason Read ~ Real ale ~ (01934) 862871 ~ Open 12-3, 5-11; 12-midnight Fri, Sat; 12-11 Sun ~ Bar food 12-2.30, 6-9.30; 12-5 (roasts), 7-9 (burgers) Sun ~ Restaurant ~ Children welcome ~ Dogs allowed in bar ~ Live irish and folk music monthly ~ www.theploughatwrington.co.uk *Recommended by Bob and Margaret Holder, Robin Manners, John and Gloria Isaacs, Dr and Mrs A K Clarke, Taff Thomas, M G Hart*

Also Worth a Visit in Somerset

Besides the fully inspected pubs, you might like to try these pubs that have been recommended to us and described by readers. Do tell us what you think of them: feedback@goodguides.com

APPLEY   ST0721
★ **Globe** (01823) 672327
Hamlet signposted from the network of back roads between A361 and A38, W of B3187 and W of Milverton and Wellington; OS Sheet 181 map reference 072215; TA21 0HJ New friendly licensees for this unspoilt 15th-c pub liked by walkers and cyclists; entrance corridor with serving hatch, simple pubby furnishings in beamed front room, second room with Great Western Railway bench and 1930s railway posters and further room with easy chairs, Sharps Doom Bar and a guest, local cider, good value straightforward locally sourced food; children welcome, no dogs inside, seats in garden, path opposite leading to River Tone, closed Mon (and Sun evening in winter). *(Bob and Margaret Holder, Peter Thornton, S G N Bennett and others)*

AXBRIDGE ST4354
⭑ Lamb (01934) 732253
The Square; off A371 Cheddar–Winscombe; BS26 2AP Big rambling carpeted pub with heavy 15th-c beams and timbers, stone and roughcast walls, large stone fireplaces, old settles, unusual bar front with old bottles set in plaster, Butcombe and guests, well chosen wine and good coffee, enjoyable food including vegetarian and children's, OAP lunch deals (Tues, Thurs), friendly service, board games, table skittles and alley; they may ask for a credit card if you run a tab; dogs allowed, pretty and sheltered small back garden, medieval King John's Hunting Lodge (NT) opposite, open all day Thurs-Sun. *(Paul Humphreys, Steve and Claire Harvey)*

BACKWELL ST4969
George (01275) 462770
Farleigh Road; A370 W of Bristol; BS48 3PG Modernised main road dining pub, former coaching inn, under relatively new management, popular food in bar and restaurant from sandwiches and sharing boards up, Bath Gem, Butcombe and Dartmoor ales, good choice of wines, friendly staff; children welcome, gravel terrace and grass behind, open all day. *(Taff Thomas, Steve and Liz Tilley)*

BARROW GURNEY ST5367
Princes Motto (01458) 850451
B3130, just off A370/A38; BS48 3RY Cosy and welcoming, with unpretentious local feel in traditional tap room, long lounge/dining area up behind, Butcombe and Wadworths ales, good value weekday lunchtime food, log fire, some panelling, cricket team photographs, jugs and china; pleasant garden with terrace, open all day. *(Taff Thomas)*

BARTON ST DAVID ST5432
Barton Inn (01458) 850451
Main Street; TA11 6BZ Unpretentious lived-in and locally well loved brick pub, open-plan bar with bare boards and quarry tiles, old pews and battered tables, rough pine panelling, well kept constantly changing cask-tapped ales, real ciders, simple food such as pizzas and baguettes (no menu), lots of pictures, posters and bric-a-brac, live music and movie nights; big-screen TV for rugby; wet dogs and muddy walkers welcome, wheelchair accessible (friendly locals may also lend a hand), pub sign in mirror writing, events such as frog racing and worm charming, open all day weekends, from 5pm other days; for sale as we went to press, so may change. *(Anon)*

BATH ST7565
Bell (01225) 460426
Walcot Street; BA1 5BW Nine real ales from local independent brewers and farm cider in long narrow split-level pub, lots of pump clips and gig notices, some basic good value food, a couple of fires (one gas), bar billiards and table football; packed and lively evenings with regular live music and DJ sets; canopied garden, open all day. *(Dr and Mrs A K Clarke)*

BATH ST7165
Boathouse (01225) 482584
Newbridge Road; BA1 3NB Large light and airy pub in nice riverside spot near Kennet & Avon marina, good value food from club sandwiches and sharing boards up, efficient courteous young staff, well kept Brains and guests, decent house wines, rugs on wooden floor, conservatory on lower level, newspapers; children very welcome, boat views from garden tables and deck, nine bedrooms some with balconies overlooking the river, open all day. *(Ian Phillips)*

BATH ST7465
Chequers (01225) 360017
Rivers Street; BA1 2QA Renovated pub with enjoyable food including set deals, real ales and decent wines by the glass, upstairs restaurant, friendly service. *(S Chaudhuri, Dr and Mrs A K Clarke)*

BATH ST7564
⭑ Coeur de Lion (01225) 463568
Northumberland Place, off High Street by W H Smith; BA1 5AR Tiny stained-glass-fronted single-room pub, perhaps Bath's prettiest, simple, cosy and jolly, with candles and log-effect gas fire, well kept Abbey ales and guests, good well priced food from huge baps to roasts (vegetarian options too), good Christmas mulled wine; may be background music, stairs to lavatories; tables out in charming flower-filled flagstoned pedestrian alley, open all day. *(Dr and Mrs A K Clarke, Taff Thomas)*

BATH ST7564
Crystal Palace (01225) 482666
Abbey Green; BA1 1NW Good spacious two-room pub with dark panelling and tiled floors, enjoyable sensibly priced home-made food all day, speedy friendly service, well kept Fullers ales, log fire, family room and conservatory; background music; sheltered heated courtyard, handy for Roman Baths and main shopping areas. *(Roger and Donna Huggins, Dr and Mrs A K Clarke)*

BATH ST7464
⭑ Garricks Head (01225) 318368
St Johns Place/Westgate, beside Theatre Royal; BA1 1ET Civilised relaxed place with high-windowed bar, gingham-covered wooden armchairs by gas-effect coal fire, church candles on mantelpiece and fine silver meat domes on wall above, wheelback and other dining chairs around wooden tables on bare boards, big black squashy sofa and more armchairs at far end, sizeable

brass chandeliers, ales such as Palmers, Otter and Stonehenge, real ciders and decent wines by the glass, proper cocktails, good food including pre-theatre set meals, separate smartly set dining room; may be soft background jazz; children welcome, dogs in bar, pavement tables, open all day. *(S Chaudhuri, Mr and Mrs A H Young, Dr and Mrs A K Clarke)*

BATH   ST7766
George   (01225) 425079
Bathampton, E of Bath centre, off A36 or (via toll bridge) off A4; Mill Lane; BA2 6TR Beautifully placed old canalside Chef & Brewer, popular well priced food all day including offers, Bath Spa, Wells & Youngs Bombardier and three guests, good choice of wines by the glass, well organised young uniformed staff, good-sized bar opening into rambling beamed rooms with three log fires, contemporary décor and furnishings; background music; children welcome, no dogs inside, wheelchair access, enclosed suntrap terrace and waterside tables. *(Phil Bryant, Ian and Rose Lock)*

BATH   ST7564
Graze   (01225) 429392
Behind Bath Spa station; BA1 1SX Spacious new Bath Ales bar-restaurant (part of the city's Vaults development) arranged over upper floor and served by lift; modern steel and glass construction with leather chairs and benches on wood-strip flooring, slatted ceiling with exposed air conditioning and pendant lighting, good selection of beers (some from onsite microbrewery) and extensive range of wines and spirits, enjoyable food including dry-aged steaks and good value weekday set lunch, helpful cheery staff; children welcome, two sizeable terraces overlooking Bath one side, the station the other, life-size models of cows, pigs and chickens, open all day from 8am (9am Sun) for breakfast. *(Dr and Mrs A K Clarke, Chris and Angela Buckell)*

BATH   ST7465
Hall & Woodhouse   (01225) 469259
Old King Street; BA1 2JW 2010 conversion of stone-fronted warehouse/auction rooms; big open-plan interior on two floors, steel girders and glass, palms and chandeliers, mix of modern and traditional furniture including old-fashioned iron-framed tables with large candles and some simple bench seating, parquet and slate floors, Badger ales from full-length servery on the right with fresh flowers, sweeping stairs up to another bar and eating area (disabled access via lift), roof terrace, decent choice of food from pub favourites to specials, helpful

chatty staff, but service can be slow when busy (standing room only early evening after work). *(Chris and Angela Buckell)*

BATH   ST7467
Hare & Hounds   (01225) 482682
Lansdown Road, Lansdown Hill; BA1 5TJ Popular recently refurbished stone pub with superb views from big garden and terrace; open-plan bar with wood floor and blue half-panelling, real ales and plenty of wines by the glass from old carved oak counter, good if not cheap food all day including pub favourites, friendly efficient staff, leaded lights in mullioned windows, conservatory; children welcome, open all day from 8.30am for breakfast. *(Mr and Mrs A H Young, Dr and Mrs A K Clarke)*

BATH   ST7465
✴ Hop Pole   (01225) 446327
Albion Buildings, Upper Bristol Road; BA1 3AR Bustling family-friendly Bath Ales pub, well kept guest beers and decent wines by the glass, good food (not Sun evening or Mon lunchtime) from traditional favourites up in bar and former skittle alley restaurant, settles and other pub furniture on bare boards in four tastefully reworked linked areas, lots of black woodwork, ochre walls, some bric-a-brac, board games and daily papers; Mon quiz night, background music, discreet sports TV; wheelchair access, attractive two-level back courtyard with boules, fairy-lit vine arbour and heated summerhouses, opposite Victoria Park with its great play area, open all day. *(Phil Bryant, Chris and Angela Buckell, Taff Thomas, Dr and Mrs A K Clarke)*

BATH   ST7565
King William   (01225) 428096
Thomas Street/A4 London Road; BA1 5NN Small corner dining pub with chunky old tables on bare boards, a few lighted church candles and perhaps a big bunch of flowers on counter, well cooked food from short daily changing menu, four local ales and good choice of wines by the glass, steep stairs up to simple attractive dining room; background music; children and dogs welcome, open all day weekends. *(Bernard Sulzmann)*

BATH   ST7465
Marlborough   (01225) 423731
Marlborough Buildings; BA1 2LY Interesting well cooked local food including good value weekday set lunch (limited menu Sun evening), nice wines, real ales, cocktails, attentive pleasant service, busy at weekends; tables in courtyard garden. *(Richard Mason, Bernard Sulzmann, Dr and Mrs A K Clarke)*

We can always use photos of pubs on our website – why not e-mail us one – feedback@thegoodpubguide.co.uk

BATH ST7565
Pig & Fiddle (01225) 460868
Saracen Street; BA1 5BR Lively, not
smart, with half a dozen good sensibly priced
local ales, friendly staff, two big open fires,
bare boards and bright paintwork, clocks
on different time zones, steps up to darker
bustling servery and little dining area,
games part and several TVs for sport; lots of
students at night; picnic-sets on big heated
front terrace, open all day. *(Taff Thomas,
Dr and Mrs A K Clarke)*

BATH ST7565
Pulteney Arms (01225) 463923
Daniel Street/Sutton Street; BA2 6ND
Cosy and cheerful 18th-c pub, Fullers
London Pride, Timothy Taylors Landlord,
Wells & Youngs and guests, Thatcher's cider,
enjoyable well priced fresh food including
Fri fish night, lots of Bath RFC memorabilia,
traditional furniture on wooden floors, gas
lamps, woodburner; background music,
sports TV; pavement tables and small back
terrace, handy for Holburne Museum, open
all day Fri-Sun. *(Taff Thomas, Dr and Mrs A K
Clarke)*

BATH ST7464
Raven (01225) 425045
Queen Street; BA1 1HE Small buoyant
city-centre local, two well kept ales for the
pub from Blindmans and local guests, a
changing farm cider, limited food including
good reasonably priced pies, quick friendly
service, bare boards, some stripped stone and
an open fire, newspapers, upstairs area, live
acoustic music; open all day. *(Andy Lickfold,
Taff Thomas, Tony and Wendy Hobden, Dr and
Mrs A K Clarke)*

BATH ST7364
Royal Oak (01225) 481409
Lower Bristol Road; BA2 3BW Friendly
bare-boards pub with Butts ales and guests,
four ciders, local artwork, regular live music
including Weds folk night; popular with Bath
Rugby supporters – busy on match days;
open all day Fri-Sun, from 4pm other days.
(Taff Thomas)

BATH ST7464
Salamander (01225) 428889
John Street; BA1 2JL Busy city local tied
to Bath Ales, their full range and guests kept
well, good choice of wines by the glass, bare
boards, black woodwork and dark ochre
walls, popular food including some unusual
choices, friendly young staff, two rooms
downstairs, open-kitchen restaurant upstairs,

daily papers, Sun quiz; background music, no
dogs; children till 8pm, open all day. *(Steve
Jackson, Taff Thomas, Steve and Liz Tilley, Richard
Mason, Dr and Mrs A K Clarke)*

BATH ST7564
Sam Weller (01225) 474910
Upper Borough Walls; BA1 1RH Fairly
simple pub with Bath Ales and decent choice
of wines by the glass, sensibly priced food,
friendly service, small and cosy with big
window for watching the world go by.
(Roger and Donna Huggins)

BATH ST7564
Volunteer Riflemans Arms
(01225) 425210 *New Bond Street Place;
BA1 1BH* Friendly little pub-café with
leather sofas and just four close-set tables,
wartime posters, open fire, well kept ales
including a beer named for them, a couple of
draught ciders, upstairs restaurant and roof
terrace; pavement tables. *(Roger and Donna
Huggins, Dr and Mrs A K Clarke, Andrew Gardner)*

BATH ST7564
White Hart (01225) 313985
Widcombe Hill; BA2 6AA Bare-boards
bistro-style pub popular for its food, quick
friendly service even when busy, well kept
Butcombe from attractive panelled bar,
farm cider, fresh flowers; pretty beer garden,
bedrooms and self-catering hostel.
(Dr and Mrs A K Clarke)

BATHFORD ST7866
Crown (01225) 852426
*Bathford Hill, towards Bradford-on-
Avon, by Batheaston roundabout and
bridge; BA1 7SL* Welcoming bistro pub
with good blackboard food including weekday
set deals, ales such as Bath and Timothy
Taylors Landlord, nice wines, charming
french landlady; children and dogs welcome,
tables out in front and in back garden with
pétanque, open all day. *(John and Gloria
Isaacs, Dr and Mrs A K Clarke, Taff Thomas)*

BECKINGTON ST8051
★Woolpack (01373) 831244
*Warminster Road, off A36 bypass;
BA11 6SP* Civilised old inn with welcoming
helpful staff, enjoyable home-made food
from sandwiches up, Greene King ales and
a guest, real cider and decent wines, big log
fire and chunky candlelit tables in flagstoned
bar, attractive oak-panelled dining room
(separate menu), conservatory; can get very
busy Sat night; children and dogs welcome,
terrace tables, 11 appealing period bedrooms,
open all day. *(Carole Tagg, Taff Thomas)*

Stars before the name of a pub show exceptional character and appeal.
They don't mean extra comfort. And they are nothing to do with food quality, for which
there's a separate knife-and-fork symbol. Even quite a basic pub can win stars,
if it's individual enough.

BICKNOLLER ST1139
Bicknoller Inn (01984) 656234
Church Lane; TA4 4EW New management for this old thatched pub nestling below the Quantocks, traditional flagstoned front bar, refurbished side room and large back restaurant with open kitchen, food from pub favourites up, Palmers ales, skittle alley; children and dogs (in bar) welcome, courtyard and good-sized garden, boules, attractive village. *(Richard and Penny Gibbs)*

BLAGDON ST5058
✶New Inn (01761) 462475
Signed off A368; Park Lane/Church Street; BS40 7SB Lovely view over Blagdon Lake (where they get their trout) from seats in front of this friendly pub; well kept Wadworths and guests, tasty reasonably priced home-made food, cheerful service, bustling bars with two inglenook log fires, heavy beams hung with horsebrasses and tankards, comfortable antique settles and mate's chairs among more modern furnishings, old prints and photographs, plainer side bar; children (over 10) and dogs welcome, wheelchair access best from front. *(Dennis Jenkin, R T and J C Moggridge, Warren Marsh, Dr and Mrs A K Clarke, Taff Thomas)*

BLAGDON HILL ST2118
Lamb & Flag (01823) 421736
4 miles S of Taunton; TA3 7SL Atmospheric country pub with 16th-c beams, mixed traditional furniture, woodburner in double-sided fireplace and unusual red and green colour scheme, four well kept west country ales, good value traditional food (not Mon lunchtime), small helpings available, games room/skittle alley, some live music; children and dogs welcome, picnic-sets in nice garden with Taunton Vale views, shop and post office, open all day Fri-Sun, closed Sun evening. *(Patrick and Daphne Darley, Mr Yeldahn)*

BLEADON ST3457
✶Queens Arms (01934) 812080
Just off A370 S of Weston; Celtic Way; BS24 0NF Popular 16th-c village pub with informal chatty atmosphere in carefully divided areas, candles on sturdy tables flanked by winged settles, solid fuel stove, old hunting prints, generous reasonably priced food (not Sun evening) from lunchtime baguettes to steaks, friendly service, well kept Butcombe and guests tapped from the cask, local cider, several wines by the glass, flagstoned restaurant and stripped-stone back bar with woodburner, darts, clean lavatories (mind the steps); children (away from bar) and dogs (away from diners) welcome, picnic-sets on pretty heated terrace, open all day. *(Michael Mellers, Barry and Anne, Dr Martin Owton, Taff Thomas)*

BRADFORD-ON-TONE ST1721
Worlds End (01823) 462928
S of village, towards Silver Street; on A38 NE of Wellington; TA4 1ET Neat, comfortable and spacious roadside pub, Badger ales, wide choice of decent good value food including set lunch deal, friendly staff, interesting artefacts inside and out; children welcome. *(Dennis and Doreen Haward)*

BRISTOL ST5773
✶Albion (0117) 973 3522
Boyce's Avenue, Clifton; BS8 4AA Bustling 18th-c dining pub down cobbled alley in Clifton Village; entrance with open kitchen, jars of pickles/chutneys on dresser for sale, L-shaped bar with chapel chairs around oak tables on wood floor, leather armchairs in front of woodburner, end room up a step with long high-backed settle; all-day tapas and other imaginative if not cheap food, friendly service, St Austell ales and guests such as Dartmouth and Otter, decent wines by the glass, 30 whiskies; children welcome, dogs allowed in bar, picnic-sets under fairy lights on covered and heated front terrace, open all day, closed Mon till 5pm. *(Peter Meister, Taff Thomas)*

BRISTOL ST5773
Alma (0117) 973 5171
Alma Vale Road, Clifton; BS8 2HY Two-bar pub with good choice of real ales, proper cider and several wines by the glass, well priced food from lunchtime sandwiches up, sofas and armchairs as well as plain tables and chairs, thriving upstairs theatre Tues-Sat; background music, popular with students evenings; wheelchair access, small back terrace (not late evening), open all day. *(Taff Thomas)*

BRISTOL ST5873
Bank (0117) 930 4691
John Street; BS1 2HR Small proper single-bar pub, centrally placed (but off the beaten track) and popular with office workers; four changing local ales (may include a porter), real ciders, standard well priced food till 4pm such as good beef and ale casserole, comfortable bench seats, newspapers, books on shelf above fireplace, blackboard for quirky stuff like 'phobia of the month' and 'chemical reaction of the month'; gentle background music; dogs welcome, wheelchair access, tables under umbrellas in paved courtyard, open all day. *(Jeremy King)*

BRISTOL ST5972
Barley Mow (0117) 930 4709
Barton Road; The Dings; BS2 0LF 19th-c Bristol Beer Factory pub in the old industrial area close to floating harbour; their ales and guests, proper ciders, slightly limited choice of other drinks, good filling pub food (not Sun evening) from shortish

but well thought-out menu, cheerful chatty landlord, wood floors, off-white walls with dark green pine-panelled dados, cushioned wall seats and pubby furniture, tables with fresh flowers in old beer bottles, some old photographs of the pub, open fire in brick fireplace; sports TV; disabled access, open all day Fri, Sat, till 8pm Sun. *(Chris and Angela Buckell)*

BRISTOL ST5774
Blackboy (0117) 973 5233
Whiteladies Road; BS8 2RY Refurbished dining pub with good uncomplicated food from chef-owner, relaxed friendly atmosphere, dining room with light furniture, small front bar with armchairs and open fire, Butcombe Bitter, St Austell Tribute and Timothy Taylors Landlord, several draught continental lagers. *(Geof Cox)*

BRISTOL ST5872
BrewDog (0117) 927 9258
Baldwin Street, opposite church; BS1 1QW Revamped corner bar now owned by BrewDog with their beers such as Dead Pony Club, Tactical Nuclear Penguin and Sink the Bismarck along with guests from other craft breweries (draught and bottled), limited but interesting selection of substantial bar snacks, happy willing young staff, starkly modern feel with exposed brick, stainless-steel furniture and granite surfaces; can get noisily busy; wheelchair access, open all day. *(Chris and Angela Buckell, Taff Thomas)*

BRISTOL ST5773
Clifton (0117) 974 1967
Regent Street; BS8 4HG Relaxed Clifton Village pub with four changing ales and good choice of wines, enjoyable food (sandwiches to some unusual dishes) from open kitchen in larger back bar, eclectic mix of seating including retro leather armchairs and sofas on bare boards, local artwork; events such as quiz, magic, film and music nights, TVs; dogs welcome, children till 7pm, open all day. *(Roger and Donna Huggins)*

BRISTOL ST5873
Colston Yard (0117) 376 3232
Upper Maudlin Street/Colston Street; BS1 5BD Popular nicely updated Butcombe pub (site of the old Smiles Brewery), their ales and guests kept well, interesting bottled beers and good choice of wines and spirits, bare-boards front bar split into two, leather stools and banquettes, brewery mirrors, newspapers and board games, larger dining room, good quality pub food from lunchtime sandwiches to grills and evening restaurant menu, friendly staff; background music; children welcome, disabled facilities (other lavatories downstairs), a few pavement tables, open all day (till 1am Fri, Sat). *(Phil Bryant, Taff Thomas, Jeremy King, Chris and Angela Buckell, Roger and Donna Huggins)*

BRISTOL ST5872
Commercial Rooms (0117) 927 9681
Corn Street; BS1 1HT Spacious colonnaded Wetherspoons conversion (former merchants' club) with lofty stained-glass domed ceiling, gas lighting, comfortable quieter back room with ornate balcony; wide changing choice of real ales, nice chatty bustle (busiest weekend evenings), their usual food all day and low prices; ladies' with chesterfields and open fire; children welcome, no dogs, side wheelchair access and disabled facilities, good location, open all day from 8am and till late Fri-Sun. *(Anon)*

BRISTOL ST5872
Cornubia (0117) 925 4415
Temple Street; BS1 6EN 18th-c backstreet real ale pub with good range including Hidden and several recherché regional guests, interesting bottled beers, farm cider and perry, limited weekday pubby food till 7.30pm (Sun till 6pm), friendly service, nicely worn-in with small woody seating areas; can be crowded evenings, not for wheelchairs; picnic-sets on cobbles outside. *(Warren Marsh, Dr and Mrs A K Clarke)*

BRISTOL ST5772
Cottage (0117) 921 5256
Baltic Wharf, Cumberland Road; BS1 6XG Converted stone-built panelled harbour master's office near Maritime Heritage Centre, comfortable, roomy and civilised with fine views of Georgian landmarks and Clifton suspension bridge, popular generous pub food from sandwiches up at reasonable prices, well kept Butcombe ales and a guest, real cider and nice wines, good cheery service even when busy; background music; children welcome, portable ramps for wheelchairs, waterside terrace tables, access through sailing club, on foot along waterfront, or by round-harbour ferry, neighbouring camp/caravan site, open all day. *(Phil Bryant, Stuart and Jasmine Kelly, Ian Herdman, Peter Meister, Taff Thomas)*

BRISTOL ST5772
Grain Barge (0117) 929 9347
Hotwell Road; BS8 4RU Floating 100-foot barge owned by Bristol Beer Factory, their ales kept well, good freshly made food at fair prices including Sun roasts, friendly staff, seats out on top deck, sofas and tables on wood floor below, art exhibitions, live music Fri night; open all day. *(Roger and Donna Huggins, Taff Thomas, Tony and Wendy Hobden, Peter Meister)*

BRISTOL ST5872
Graze Bar & Chophouse
(0177) 929 0700 *Queen Square; BS1 4JZ* Stylish big-windowed restauranty pub owned by Bath Ales, their beers kept well and imaginative good value food all day from open kitchen including vegetarian options,

cheerful efficient staff, light wood tables, benches and chairs, cow wallpaper and bull's head over green-tiled bar, comfortable raised seating areas, suspended modern lighting; wheelchair access through side door, open all day and from 9am weekends. *(Anon)*

BRISTOL ST5772

★**Hope & Anchor** (0117) 929 2987

Jacobs Wells Road, Clifton; BS8 1DR
Friendly 18th-c pub with half a dozen good changing ales from central bar, nice wines and good choice of malts, tables of various sizes (some shaped to fit corners) on bare boards, darker back area, flowers and candles, sensibly priced hearty food all day – very popular lunchtime, friendly staff; soft background music (occasional live), can get crowded late evening; children welcome, disabled access, barbecues in good-sized tiered back garden with interesting niches, parking nearby can be tricky, open all day. *(Anon)*

BRISTOL ST5977

Inn on the Green (0117) 952 1391

Filton Road (A38), Horfield; BS7 0PA
Busy open-plan pub improved under current landlord, up to 12 changing real ales and half a dozen ciders/perries, good selection of malt whiskies and gins, some interesting food served by helpful staff, wood or slate floors, lots of mirrors and old prints, modern pub furniture along with sofas and armchairs, more screened seating areas in former skittle alley dining area; disabled access and facilities, beer garden. *(Nigel and Sue Foster, Chris and Angela Buckell)*

BRISTOL ST5874

Kensington Arms (0117) 944 6444

Stanley Road; BS6 6NP Dining pub in the centre of Redland with well liked if not particularly cheap food from light lunches up, nice relaxed atmosphere and cheerful accommodating staff, well kept Greene King ales and a guest, good choice of wines by the glass; may be background music; children and dogs welcome, disabled facilities and access (not to dining rooms, but can eat in bar), heated terrace, open all day. *(Anon)*

BRISTOL ST5972

★**Kings Head** (0117) 927 7860

Victoria Street; BS1 6DE Friendly relaxed 17th-c pub with big front window and splendid mirrored bar-back, corridor to cosy panelled snug with serving hatch, four well kept ales including Butcombe and Sharps Doom Bar, toby jugs on joists, old-fashioned local prints and photographs, reasonably priced wholesome food weekday lunchtimes (get there early for a seat); background music, no credit cards; pavement tables, open all day (closed Sun afternoon). *(Dr and Mrs A K Clarke)*

BRISTOL ST5976

Lazy Dog (0117) 924 4809

Ashley Down Road; BS7 9JR Popular local with two refurbished bar areas (one upstairs), ales such as Bath, Bristol Beer Factory and Wye Valley, local ciders/perries, good choice of wines, gins and malt whiskies, well priced food all day from snacks and sharing plates to blackboard specials, bargain weekday lunch deal, dark green interior with wood panelled alcoves, white marble-effect bar counter, leather wall benches, sofas and armchairs on light wood floors, lots of mirrors, family room with metal furniture (children till 7pm), vintage juke box, Tues quiz; dogs welcome, wheelchair access, seats out at front and in partly decked back garden. *(Chris and Angela Buckell)*

BRISTOL ST5673

Mall (0117) 974 5318

The Mall, Clifton; BS8 4JG Laid-back corner pub with well kept changing local ales, interesting continental beers and lots of wines by the glass, pubby food, tall windows, ornate ceiling, some panelling and mix of old furniture on wood floors, downstairs bar; small garden behind, open all day. *(Roger and Donna Huggins)*

BRISTOL ST5772

Merchants Arms (0117) 904 0037

Merchants Road, Hotwells; BS8 4PZ
Tiny two-room pub close to historic dockside, welcoming landlord and friendly locals, well kept Bath Ales and their Bounders cider, modest choice of well chosen wines, limited food, open fire; popular Thurs quiz, sing-alongs/karaoke; sports TV; wheelchair access with help (narrow door and steps). *(Taff Thomas, Chris and Angela Buckell)*

BRISTOL ST5772

Nova Scotia (0117) 929 7994

Baltic Wharf, Cumberland Basin; BS1 6XJ Unreconstructed old local on south side of floating harbour, views to Clifton and Avon Gorge; Courage Best and guests, a real cider and generous helpings of enjoyable pub food, four linked areas, snob screen, mahogany and mirrors, nautical charts as wallpaper, welcoming atmosphere and friendly regulars; wheelchair access with help through snug's door, plenty of tables out by water, bedrooms share bathroom. *(Warren Marsh, Taff Thomas, Chris and Angela Buckell, Peter Meister and others)*

BRISTOL ST5872

Old Duke (0117) 927 7137

King Street; BS1 4ER Duke Ellington, that is – inside festooned with jazz posters, plus one or two instruments, good bands nightly and Sun lunchtime, usual pub furnishings, real ales and simple food; in attractive cobbled area between docks and Bristol

Old Vic, gets packed evenings, open all day.
(Taff Thomas)

BRISTOL   ST5772
Orchard (0117) 926 2678
Hanover Place, Spike Island; BS1 6XT
Friendly unpretentious one-room local; half
a dozen well kept ales from stillage behind
bar and great choice of ciders (perhaps a
winter mulled one), good sandwiches (hot
lunchtime food Weds-Fri); sports TV (pub
gets busy on match days); tables out in front,
handy for SS *Great Britain*, open all day.
(Taff Thomas)

BRISTOL   ST5774
Penny Farthing (0117) 973 3539
Whiteladies Road, Clifton; BS8 2PB
Bright panelled ex-bank with full Wadworths
range racked behind bar, late Victorian
bric-a-brac including penny-farthing (and
photographs of them), armchairs opposite
bar, lots of table seating, good value pubby
food; can get very busy evenings; pavement
tables. *(Comus and Sarah Elliott)*

BRISTOL   ST5672
Portcullis (0117) 908 5536
Wellington Terrace; BS8 4LE Compact
two-storey pub in Georgian building with
spectacular views, well kept Dawkins and
several changing guests, farm ciders, fine
range of wines by the glass and spirits, simple
food, good friendly staff, flame-effect gas
fire, dark wood and usual pubby furniture;
tricky wheelchair access, closed weekday
lunchtimes, open all day weekends. *(Phil
Bryant, Roger and Donna Huggins)*

BRISTOL   ST5772
Pump House (0117) 927 2229
Merchants Road; BS8 4PZ Spacious
attractively converted dockside building
(former 19th-c pumping station); charcoal-
grey brickwork, tiled floors and high ceilings,
good food in bar and smart candlelit
mezzanine restaurant, ales such as Bath,
Butcombe and St Austell, decent wines
from comprehensive list, friendly staff and
cheerful atmosphere; waterside tables.
(Taff Thomas)

BRISTOL   ST5975
Robin Hoods Retreat
(0117) 924 8639 *Gloucester Road,
Bishopston; BS7 8BG* Relaxed place with
up to eight real ales, good wines by the glass
and cocktails, good food including tapas, set
lunch and evening tasting menu, cheerful
young staff. *(Tom and Ruth Rees)*

BRISTOL   ST5672
Rose of Denmark 07709 832626
Dowry Place; BS8 4QL Friendly
welcoming atmosphere, good value
interesting bar food from lunchtime
sandwiches up, several well kept ales tapped
from the cask, stripped pine, candles and

leather sofas, open fires, evening cellar
brasserie (Thurs-Sat), Mon quiz, Thurs live
jazz and folk; open all day Fri-Sun, closed
Mon lunchtime. *(Taff Thomas)*

BRISTOL   ST5972
Seven Stars (0117) 927 2845
Thomas Lane; BS1 6JG Unpretentious
one-room real ale pub near harbour (and
associated with Thomas Clarkson and slave
trade abolition), much enjoyed by students
and local office workers, eight well kept
changing ales (20 from a featured county on
first Mon-Weds of month), some interesting
malts and bourbons, dark wood and bare
boards, old local prints and photographs, no
food but can bring in takeaways, weekend
folk music; juke box, pool, games machine;
disabled access (but narrow alley with
uneven cobbles and cast-iron kerbs).
*(Taff Thomas, Chris and Angela Buckell,
Dr Kevan Tucker)*

BRISTOL   ST5771
Spotted Cow (0117) 963 4433
North Street; BS3 1EZ Modernised early
19th-c pub with open-plan split-level bar,
beers from Bath and Butcombe, good choice
of sensibly priced food including popular Sun
lunch with live jazz (suckling pig first Sun of
month); DJ and open mike nights; good-sized
enclosed garden behind, open all day (till
1am Thurs-Sat). *(Taff Thomas)*

BRISTOL   ST5873
Zero Degrees (0117) 925 2706
Colston Street; BS1 5BA Converted
Victorian tramshed, austere stone exterior
giving way to big contemporary industrial-
style bar popular with young people, own
low-priced beers brewed behind glass walls,
up-to-date food from open kitchen including
wood-fired pizzas and mussel dishes, cheerful
helpful staff, upper gallery; loud background
music; good disabled facilities, rooftop
Bristol views from terrace tables, open all
day. *(Taff Thomas, Kathrine Haddrell)*

BUCKLAND DINHAM   ST7551
⋆ **Bell** (01373) 462956
*High Street (A362 Frome–Radstock);
BA11 2QT* Friendly 16th-c pub with great
atmosphere and interesting décor in narrow
beamed main bar, pine furnishings including
booth settles, woodburner in huge inglenook,
food from speciality local sausages and pies
to a vast 74oz steak (free if you can eat
all of it), Butcombe and two guests, farm
ciders, several malt whiskies, two-level
dining room (a remote control helicopter
may direct you to your table), antiques for
sale, dominoes and board games, beer/cider
festivals; background and some live music,
cinema in attached barn; children and
dogs welcome, pet (and human) weddings,
difficult wheelchair access, walled garden
with side terraces, campsite, closed Mon,
Tues lunchtimes. *(Taff Thomas)*

CHEW MAGNA ST5763
Bear & Swan (01275) 331100
B3130 (South Parade); BS40 8SL
Open-plan Fullers pub under new
management; still plenty of emphasis on
food from traditional choices up, their ales
and guests, good choice of wines, friendly
staff, mix of pine tables, pews and big log
fire, L-shaped dining room with stripped
stone, bare boards and woodburner;
background music; children and dogs
welcome, wheelchair access from small car
park (street parking not easy), secluded beer
garden, cheerful tubs and hanging baskets,
open all day. *(Hugo Jeune, Meg and Colin
Hamilton)*

CHEW MAGNA ST5763
Pelican (01275) 331777
South Parade; BS40 8SL Refurbished
village pub with friendly welcome and buzzy
atmosphere; opened-up modern interior with
polished wood flooring, candles on chunky
tables, some high-backed settles and old pew
chairs, leather armchairs by woodburners
in stone fireplaces, fresh flowers, changing
ales such as Butcombe, Otter and St Austell,
good choice of wines by the glass, enjoyable
food (some served on wooden boards)
including daily specials; children and dogs
welcome, wheelchair access from courtyard,
grassy beer garden, open all day, closed Sun
evening. *(Taff Thomas, Chris and Angela Buckell,
Dr and Mrs A K Clarke)*

CHEW MAGNA ST5861
⋆ Pony & Trap (01275) 332627
*Knowle Hill, New Town; from B3130
in village, follow Bishop Sutton, Bath
signpost; BS40 8TQ* Dining pub in nice
rural spot near Chew Valley Lake, very good
imaginative food from sandwiches through
to restaurant dishes (best to book), efficient
friendly service, Butcombe, Sharps and a
guest, front bar with cushioned wall seats
and built-in benches on parquet, snug area
on left with old range, dark plank panelling
and housekeeper's chair in corner, lovely
pasture views from two-level back dining area
with rush-seated chairs around white tables
on slate flagstones; children welcome, dogs
in bar, modern furniture on back terrace,
picnic-sets on grass with chickens in runs
below, front smokers' shelter, good walks,
closed Mon (except Dec). *(Michael Doswell,
Paul Humphreys, Pat Bunting, David and Jenny
Billington, Taff Thomas and others)*

CHILCOMPTON ST6451
Somerset Wagon (01761) 232732
B3139; Broadway; BA3 4JW Cosy and

welcoming Wadworths pub with well liked
fairly priced food, good service even when
packed, pleasant olde-worlde areas off
central bar, lots of settles, newspapers,
log fire; children welcome, small front
garden. *(Ian Phillips, Richard and Judy Winn)*

CHISELBOROUGH ST4614
Cat Head (01935) 881231
*Cat Street; leave A303 on A356 towards
Crewkerne; take the third left (at 1.4
miles) signed Chiselborough, then
left after 0.2 miles; TA14 6TT* 16th-c
hamstone pub refurbished under new
family owners; bar and three dining
areas, flagstones and mullioned windows,
woodburner in fine fireplace, home-cooked
food from lunchtime sandwiches up,
Butcombe, Otter and a guest, Ashton's
cider and nine wines by the glass, skittle
alley; background music; children and dogs
welcome (three pub dogs), seats on terrace
and in pretty garden, open all day Sat, closed
Sun evening, Tues. *(Anon)*

CLEVEDON ST4071
⋆ Old Inn (01275) 340440
*Walton Road (B3124 on outskirts);
BS21 6AE* Friendly mix of regulars and
visitors in neatly extended beamed pub,
good value food (not Mon lunchtime) from
baguettes to Sun roasts, well kept changing
ales and half a dozen wines by the glass,
seating from cushioned settles and stools
to sofas, carpeted floors; background
music, silent TV; children welcome,
pleasant secluded back garden with boules,
bedrooms. *(R T and J C Moggridge, Robin
Manners)*

COMPTON DANDO ST6464
Compton Inn (01761) 490321
Court Hill; BS39 4JZ Welcoming
two-bar stone-built village pub in lovely
setting; enjoyable food from sandwiches
up (not particularly cheap), well kept
Bath, Butcombe and Sharps, open fire;
garden. *(Taff Thomas)*

COMPTON MARTIN ST5457
Ring o' Bells (01761) 221284
A368 Bath–Weston; BS40 6JE Country
pub in attractive spot and under newish
owners; traditional flagstoned front part,
inglenook log fire, steps up to spacious
back area, stripped stone, Butcombe and
a guest, Ashton's and Thatcher's ciders,
decent choice of malt whiskies, enjoyable
fairly priced home-made food, good friendly
service, pub games, folk night first Thurs of
month; children and dogs welcome, charming
big garden with play area, two bedrooms,

Real ale may be served from handpumps, electric pumps (not just the on-off switches
used for keg beer) or – common in Scotland – tall taps called founts (pronounced
'fonts') where a separate pump pushes the beer up under air pressure.

open all day weekends. *(Warren Marsh, Stuart Paulley, Zoe Garside, Edward Mirzoeff)*

CORFE ST2319
White Hart (01823) 421388
B3170 S of Taunton; TA3 7BU
Friendly 17th-c village pub with enjoyable reasonably priced food and well kept ales. *(Bob and Margaret Holder, Patrick and Daphne Darley)*

CRANMORE ST6643
Strode Arms (01749) 880450
West Cranmore; signed with pub off A361 Frome–Shepton Mallet; BA4 4QJ
Pretty dining pub (former 15th-c farmhouse) under new management; rambling rooms with country furnishings, grandfather clock on flagstones, brasses on beams, remarkable old locomotive engineering drawings and big black and white steam train murals in central lobby, local art for sale, log fires in handsome fireplaces, pub food with a twist including weekday set deal (early evenings, all day Mon), Wadworths ales and a dozen wines by the glass, daily papers, monthly comedy and quiz nights; children and dogs welcome, front terrace, more seats in back garden with play area, vintage car meetings first Tues of month, handy for East Somerset Railway. *(Martin and Pauline Jennings, Justin Pumfrey, Pat Crabb, M G Hart, Graham Bennett)*

CROWCOMBE ST1336
Carew Arms (01984) 618631
Just off A358 Taunton–Minehead; TA4 4AD
Interesting 17th-c beamed inn with hunting trophies, huge flagstones and good inglenook log fire in small unspoilt front bar, well kept Exmoor, Otter and guests, farm cider, popular fairly traditional home-made food served by friendly staff, dining room allowing children, skittle alley; dogs, walkers and cyclists welcome, garden tables, six bedrooms, open all day summer weekends. *(N R White, Richard and Penny Gibbs)*

CULBONE HILL SS8247
Culbone (01643) 862259
Culbone Hill; A39 W of Porlock, opposite Porlock Weir Toll Road; TA24 8JW
More restaurant-with-rooms than pub, set high on the moors and refurbished by present owner; good food all day including themed nights and reasonably priced set lunches, a couple of well kept beers and decent choice of malt whiskies, good friendly service, events such as star-gazing, cookery school; children welcome, terrace with wonderful views over Lorna Doone valley, five well appointed bedrooms. *(Dave Snowden, Richard and Penny Gibbs)*

DINNINGTON ST4013
Dinnington Docks (01460) 52397
NE of village; Fosse Way; TA17 8SX
Good cheery atmosphere in large old-fashioned country local, unspoilt and unfussy, with good choice of inexpensive genuine home cooking including fresh fish Fri, well kept Butcombe and guests, farm ciders, log fire, friendly attentive staff, memorabilia to bolster the myth that there was once a railway line and dock here, sofas in family room, skittle alley in adjoining building, some live music; large garden behind, good walks, open all day Fri-Mon. *(Peter Thornton)*

DITCHEAT ST6236
⋆ Manor House (01749) 860276
Signed off A37 and A371 S of Shepton Mallet; BA4 6RB
Pretty 17th-c red-brick village inn, buoyant atmosphere and popular with jockeys from nearby racing stables, enjoyable home-made food from sandwiches and pubby bar meals to more sophisticated choices, Butcombe and guests, unusual arched doorways linking big flagstoned bar to comfortable lounge and restaurant, open fires, skittle alley; children welcome, tables on back grass, handy for Royal Bath & West showground, three mews bedrooms, open all day. *(Anon)*

DOWLISH WAKE ST3712
New Inn (01460) 52413
Off A3037 S of Ilminster, via Kingstone; TA19 0NZ
Comfortable and welcoming dark-beamed village pub, decent home-made food using fresh local produce, well kept Butcombe and Otter, local farm cider, woodburners in stone inglenooks, pleasant dining room; attractive garden and village, Perry's cider mill and shop nearby, four bedrooms. *(Tony and Gill Powell)*

DULVERTON SS9127
Bridge Inn (01398) 324130
Bridge Street; TA22 9HJ
Welcoming unpretentious pub redecorated after recent floods, well prepared reasonably priced food using local suppliers, up to four ales including Exmoor and St Austell, some unusual imported beers, Addlestone's cider and 30 malt whiskies, comfortable sofas, log fires, folk night third Sat of month, fortnightly quiz Sun; children and dogs welcome (pub dogs Milly and Molly), riverside terrace, open all day summer (all day Fri-Sun, closed Mon evening winter). *(Peter Thornton, Richard and Penny Gibbs, Peter and Teresa Blackburn)*

DUNSTER SS9843
⋆ Stags Head (01643) 821229
West Street (A396); TA24 6SN
Friendly helpful staff and lively atmosphere in unassuming 15th-c roadside inn, good value food, Exmoor and a guest ale, candles, beams, timbers and inglenook log fire, steps up to small back dining room; dogs welcome, comfortable simple bedrooms, good breakfast, closed Weds lunchtime. *(John and Alison Hamilton, Michael Butler)*

EAST COKER   ST5412
Helyar Arms (01935) 862332
*Village signposted off A37 or A30 SW of
Yeovil; Moor Lane; BA22 9JR* Old pub in
charming village with comfortable big bar,
high-backed settles and leather sofas in front
of log fire, chairs around candlelit tables,
lots of hunting and other country pictures,
brass and copper, daily papers, steps up to
high-raftered back dining room, Butcombe,
Dorset and a guest ale, several wines by the
glass, enjoyable food (cooked by landlord),
skittle alley; background music; children
and dogs welcome, picnic-sets on neat
lawn, six bedrooms, open all day summer
weekends. *(M G Hart)*

EAST HARPTREE   ST5453
Castle of Comfort (01761) 221321
*B3134, SW on Old Bristol Road;
BS40 6DD* New family management and
refurbishment for this former coaching inn
set high in the Mendips (last stop before
the gallows for some past visitors); hefty
timbers and exposed stonework, pubby
furniture including cushioned settles on
carpet, log fires, Butcombe and two guests,
good choice of reasonably priced traditional
food including nice steaks, friendly staff;
children (away from bar) and dogs welcome,
wheelchair access, big garden with raised
deck and play area, fine walks nearby.
(Chris and Angela Buckell, Taff Thomas)

EAST HARPTREE   ST5655
Waldegrave Arms (01761) 221429
Church Lane; BS40 6BD Welcoming old
pub keeping local feel although largely set
out for chef-landlord's good food (not Sun
evening, Mon), cheerful young staff, well
kept Butcombe and guests, small beamed
bar and two dining areas, eclectic mix of
furniture and plenty of things to look at, log
fires; children and dogs welcome, picnic-sets
in attractive sheltered garden, delightful
village, closed Mon lunchtime. *(Tina Hunt,
Ian and Rose Lock, Taff Thomas)*

EAST LAMBROOK   ST4218
Rose & Crown (01460) 240433
Silver Street; TA13 5HF New owners and
some refurbishment; stone-built dining pub
spreading extensively from compact 17th-c
core with inglenook log fire, friendly staff and
relaxed atmosphere, decent choice of freshly
made food using local supplies, Palmers
ales and nine wines by the glass, restaurant
extension with old glass-covered wall, skittle
alley; picnic-sets on neat lawn, opposite East
Lambrook Manor Garden, closed Sun and
Mon evenings. *(Peter Salmon, Stan Lea)*

EAST WOODLANDS   ST7944
✻ Horse & Groom (01373) 462802
Off A361/B3092 junction; BA11 5LY
Small pretty pub tucked away down country
lanes, enjoyable well priced fresh food (not

Sun evening), friendly service, Butcombe and
a couple of quickly changing guests tapped
from the cask, pews and settles in flagstoned
bar, woodburner in comfortable lounge, big
dining conservatory, traditional games; dogs
welcome away from restaurant, children in
eating areas, disabled access, tables out in
nice front garden with more seats behind,
handy for Longleat. *(Anon)*

ENMORE   ST2434
Tynte Arms (01278) 671351
Enmore Road; TA5 2DP
Open-plan low-beamed pub with wide choice
of good generous food including lots of
fish, home-made puddings and good value
set menus, friendly service, west country
ales from long bar, plenty of dining tables,
chesterfields and settles, end inglenook,
china collection; no dogs; car park over road,
good walking country. *(Bob and Margaret
Holder)*

EVERCREECH   ST6538
Bell (01749) 830287
Bruton Road (B3081); BA4 6HY
Spacious stone-built former coaching inn now
strongly involved with the local community;
good choice of enjoyable home-made food
including OAP deal Thurs and Sun carvery,
well kept ales such as Butcombe, Sharps and
Yeovil, maybe local Heck's cider, clean high-
ceilinged linked rooms, open fires, skittle
alley; disabled facilities, courtyard and open-
view garden, quiet village handy for Royal
Bath & West showground, three bedrooms,
open all day. *(M G Hart)*

EVERCREECH   ST6336
Natterjack (01749) 860253
*A371 Shepton Mallet–Castle Cary;
BA4 6NA* Former Victorian station hotel
(line closed 1966), good choice of popular
generous food at reasonable prices,
Butcombe and a couple of guests, real cider
and good range of wines, welcoming landlord
and cheerful efficient staff, long bar with
eating areas off; lots of tables under parasols
in big neatly kept garden, five bedrooms in
restored cider house. *(Col and Mrs Patrick Kaye,
Mrs D Lush)*

EXEBRIDGE   SS9324
Anchor (01398) 323433
*B3222 S of Dulverton; pub itself actually
over the river, in Devon; TA22 9AZ*
Newish management and refurbishment
for this idyllically placed Exmoor-edge inn,
good food using local suppliers with some
emphasis on fresh fish/shellfish, friendly
service, Exmoor and Greene King ales,
Thatcher's cider, seven wines by the glass,
spacious lounge/restaurant area; children
welcome, dogs in bar, nice big riverside
garden with plenty of tables, six bedrooms
(fishing rights for residents), open (and
food) all day weekends. *(Anon)*

EXFORD
SS8538
★White Horse (01643) 831229
B3224; TA24 7PY Popular and welcoming
three-storey creeper-clad inn, more or less
open-plan bar, high-backed antique settle
among more conventional seats, scrubbed
deal tables, hunting prints and local
photographs, good log fire, Exmoor ales and
Sharps Doom Bar, over 100 malt whiskies,
Thatcher's cider, enjoyable hearty food
from sandwiches to good value Sun carvery;
children and dogs welcome, play area and
outside tables, pretty village, Land Rover
Exmoor safaris, comfortable bedrooms, open
all day from 8am. *(Andrew Scott, Lynda and
Trevor Smith, N R White)*

FAILAND
ST5171
Failand Inn (01275) 392220
B3128 Bristol–Clevedon; BS8 3TU
Welcoming old coaching inn with wide choice
of popular generously served pub food, well
kept Butcombe, Courage and Sharps, good
wines by the glass, large bright dining areas
either side of entrance, two bars, low beams,
toby jugs, decorative plates and brasses;
gentle background music, they ask to keep
a credit card while you run a tab; children
and dogs welcome, garden with decking and
heated smokers' shelter, open all day. *(John
and Gloria Isaacs, Tom Evans, Taff Thomas)*

FAULKLAND
ST7555
★Tuckers Grave (01373) 834230
A366 E of village; BA3 5XF Unspoilt,
unchanging and absolutely tiny cider house
with friendly locals and charming licensees,
flagstoned entrance opening into simple
room with casks of Butcombe, Fullers
London Pride and Thatcher's Cheddar Valley
cider in alcove on left, perhaps lunchtime
sandwiches, two high-backed settles facing
each other across a single table on right, side
room with shove-ha'penny, open fires, daily
papers, skittle alley; children welcome in one
area, lots of tables and chairs on attractive
back lawn, good views, closed Mon lunchtime
except bank holidays. *(Taff Thomas, Chris and
Angela Buckell)*

FRESHFORD
ST7960
Inn at Freshford (01225) 722250
Off A36 or B3108; BA2 7WG Roomy
beamed stone-built pub in attractive spot
near river, enjoyable food from lunchtime
sandwiches up, more evening choice, well
kept Box Steam ales and guests, real ciders/
perries, decent wines by the glass and good
choice of gins and malts, helpful attentive
staff; wheelchair access from car park, pretty
hillside garden. *(Chris and Angela Buckell, Taff
Thomas)*

FROME
ST7748
Griffin (01373) 467766
Milk Street; BA11 3DB Unpretentious
bare-boards bar with etched glass and open
fires, long counter serving good Milk Street
beers brewed here by the friendly landlord,
hot food Sun, easy-going mixed crowd, quiz
and live music nights; small garden, closed
lunchtimes, open till 1am Fri, Sat, 1-9pm
Sun. *(Tessa Clist)*

HALLATROW
ST6357
★Old Station (01761) 452228
A39 S of Bristol; BS39 6EN Friendly
former station hotel with extraordinary
collection of bric-a-brac including railway
memorabilia, musical instruments, china
cows, post boxes from sailing boats, even
half an old Citroen, wide mix of furnishings,
Brains Rev James and Butcombe Bitter,
popular food, Pullman carriage restaurant;
children and dogs (in bar) welcome, modern
furniture on decking, picnic-sets on grass,
bedrooms in converted outbuilding (no
breakfast), open all day Fri-Sun. *(Dave
Braisted, Stuart Paulley)*

HARDWAY
ST7234
★Bull (01749) 812200
*Off B3081 Bruton–Wincanton at brown
sign for Stourhead and King Alfred's
Tower; Hardway; BA10 0LN* Charming
beamed 17th-c country dining pub popular
locally, especially with older people weekday
lunchtimes, good food (not Sun evening,
Mon) in comfortable bar and character
dining rooms, good informal service, well
kept Butcombe and Otter, farm cider, nice
wines by the glass, log fire; unobtrusive
background music; tables and barbecues in
garden behind, more seats in rose garden
over road. *(Anon)*

HINTON BLEWETT
ST5956
★Ring o' Bells (01761) 452239
Signed off A37 in Clutton; BS39 5AN
Charming low-beamed stone-built country
local opposite village green, old-fashioned bar
with solid furniture including pews, log fire,
good value food cooked by landlady including
walkers' menu, obliging service, Butcombe
and guests, good wines by the glass, dining
room; children and dogs welcome, pleasant
view from tables in sheltered front yard, open
all day weekends. *(Taff Thomas)*

HOLCOMBE
ST6648
Duke of Cumberland
(01761) 233731 *Edford Hill; BA3 5HQ*
Popular modernised pub with good
competitively priced food including
home-made pizzas, local ales such as Bath,

All *Guide* inspections are anonymous. Anyone claiming to be a *Good Pub Guide*
inspector is a fraud. Please let us know.

Butcombe and Milk Street, ciders from Ashton Press and Thatcher's, friendly helpful staff, log fires, skittle alley; background and some live music; children and dogs welcome, riverside garden with picnic-sets, open all day from 9am (weekend breakfasts). *(Ian Phillips)*

HOLTON ST6826
★ Old Inn (01963) 32002
Off A303 W of Wincanton; BA9 8AR Refurbished and extended 16th-c dining pub; good imaginative cooking using top quality ingredients (some from own farm), well kept local beers, good attentive service, oak beams, ancient flagstones and big woodburner, lots of button-back leather banquettes, raftered evening restaurant with pale green and cherry pink walls; picnic-sets in front, sheltered garden up steps, closed Sun evening. *(Michael Doswell, Ian Jenkins)*

HORTON ST3214
Five Dials (01460) 55359
Hanning Road; off A303; TA19 9QH Cleanly refurbished pub run by friendly helpful young couple, popular reasonably priced home-made food including good steaks, Otter, Sharps Doom Bar and a guest, local ciders and good choice of wines by the glass, restaurant; children and dogs welcome, five bedrooms, open all day Fri-Sun, closed Mon. *(Evelyn and Derek Walter, Patrick and Daphne Darley)*

KELSTON ST7067
★ Old Crown (01225) 423032
Bitton Road; A431 W of Bath; BA1 9AQ Four small traditional rooms with beams and polished flagstones, carved settles and cask tables, logs burning in ancient open range, two more coal-effect fires, well kept ales including Butcombe, Thatcher's cider, good choice of wines and whiskies, friendly helpful staff, good fairly priced food (not Mon evenings) in bar and small restaurant; children welcome, dogs in bar, wheelchair access with help, picnic-sets under apple trees in sheltered sunny back garden, four bedrooms in converted outbuildings, open all day. *(Roger and Donna Huggins, Dr and Mrs A K Clarke, Ian and Rose Lock)*

KEYNSHAM ST6669
★ Lock-Keeper (0117) 986 2383
Keynsham Road (A4175 NE of town); BS31 2DD Friendly riverside pub with plenty of character, bare boards and relaxed worn-in feel, simple left-hand bar with big painted settle, cushioned wall benches, trophy cabinet and old local photographs, two more little rooms with assorted cushioned dining chairs, more photographs and rustic prints, Wells & Youngs and guests, good choice of wines and coffees, popular reasonably priced bar food, cheerful young staff, light modern conservatory (quite different in style), live music Fri, Sat;

children welcome, dogs in bar, disabled facilities, teak furniture under giant parasols on big heated decked terrace overlooking water, steps down to picnic-sets on grass, outside bar and barbecue, pétanque, open all day. *(Michael Doswell, Lucy Fey, Taff Thomas, Chris and Angela Buckell, Dr and Mrs A K Clarke and others)*

KEYNSHAM ST6568
Ship (0117) 986 9841
Temple Street; BS31 1ER Unpretentious 17th-c local with long low main bar, well kept Marstons-related beers, pubby food and friendly service, darts; nice views from back garden. *(Dr and Mrs A K Clarke)*

KILMERSDON ST6952
Jolliffe Arms (01761) 436699
High Street; BA3 5TD Large attractive stone-built Georgian local overlooking pretty churchyard, Butcombe and Sharps Doom Bar, good wines by the glass, enjoyable home-made pub food, friendly staff and charismatic landlord, four linked areas (three mainly for dining) reminiscent of unpretentious farmhouse parlour, some huge black flagstones, interesting old local photographs, curtained-off skittle alley; background music; front picnic-sets, Jack & Jill Hill walk close by, open all day Sat, till 4pm Sun. *(Ian Phillips)*

KILVE ST1442
Hood Arms (01278) 741210
A39 E of Williton; TA5 1EA Welcoming neatly kept beamed 18th-c country pub, well kept Otter, Palmers and guest ales, good interesting food from bar snacks up including popular Sun lunch, cosy plush lounge, warm woodburner in bar, restaurant, skittle alley; children and dogs welcome, well tended back garden with tables on sheltered terrace, play area, 12 bedrooms (two in back lodge). *(David Jackman, Steve and Liz Tilley, Ian Kirkwood, Mrs Jo Rees)*

KINGSDON ST5126
Kingsdon Inn (01935) 840543
Off B3151; TA11 7LG Pretty 18th-c thatched dining pub, busy friendly atmosphere in attractively decorated beamed rooms, open fires, enjoyable food (more evening choice), well kept local ales, good service; children and dogs welcome, picnic-sets on front grass, three bedrooms and holiday cottage, handy for Lytes Cary Manor (NT) and Fleet Air Arm Museum. *(Stan Lea)*

KINGSTON ST MARY ST2229
Swan (01823) 451383
Lodes Lane, in centre of village; TA2 8HW Cosy 17th-c roadside pub, very neat and tidy, with long knocked-through panelled bar, modern furniture on carpets, rough plastered walls with local artwork for sale and lots of signed cricket bats, fresh flowers, big stone fireplaces, home-made mostly pubby food (not Sun

evening), well kept ales such as Otter and Wadworths, Thatcher's cider, well priced wines; unobtrusive jazz-based background music; children and dogs welcome, disabled access, garden with play area, handy for Hestercombe Gardens. *(Alan Weedon, Giles and Annie Francis)*

KNAPP   ST3025
Rising Sun (01823) 491027
Village W of North Curry (pub signed from here); TA3 6BG Tucked-away 15th-c longhouse surrounded by lovely countryside; handsome beams, flagstones and two inglenooks with woodburners, Exmoor Gold and Sharps Doom Bar, proper cider, good food with emphasis on fish/seafood, seasonal game too, friendly helpful staff; children and dogs welcome, sunny little front terrace, open all day Sat, closed Sun evening (except first Sun of month when there's a quiz) and Mon. *(Kerry Law, Jo Furley, Mr Yeldahn)*

LANGFORD BUDVILLE   ST1122
⋆ Martlet (01823) 400262
Off B3187 NW of Wellington; TA21 0QZ Cosy, comfortable and cottagey with friendly landlady and staff, good generously served food popular at lunchtime with older diners, well kept ales including Exmoor, inglenook, beams and flagstones, central woodburner, steps up to carpeted lounge with another woodburner; skittle alley. *(Anon)*

LANGLEY MARSH   ST0729
Three Horseshoes (01984) 623763
Just N of Wiveliscombe; TA4 2UL Traditional red sandstone pub with well kept beers tapped from the cask and enjoyable pubby food in bar and dining area, low modern settles in back bar, stone fireplace; background music; seats on verandah and in sloping back garden, monthly vintage car meetings, closed Mon, best to check other opening/food times. *(Richard and Penny Gibbs)*

LANGPORT   ST4625
⋆ Devonshire Arms (01458) 241271
B3165 Somerton–Martock, off A372 E of Langport; TA10 9LP Handsome gabled inn (former hunting lodge) with civilised atmosphere; simple back bar with modern metal and leather bar stools, rush-seated high-backed chairs around dark tables on flagstones, west country ales tapped from the cask, local cider brandy and several wines by the glass, stylish main room with comfortable leather sofas and glass-topped log table by fire, scatter cushions on long wall bench, church candles, elegant dining room with brown wicker chairs around pale wood tables on broad boards, good interesting food (local suppliers listed) from lunchtime

sandwiches up, charming efficient service, evening pianist; wheelchair access from car park, teak furniture out at front, pretty box-enclosed courtyard with unusual water-ball feature, more seats on raised terraces, nice bedrooms, good breakfast. *(Comus and Sarah Elliott, Mr and Mrs P D Titcomb, Chris and Angela Buckell, Hugh Roberts, M G Hart, Ian Herdman and others)*

LITTON   ST5954
Kings Arms (01761) 241301
B3114, NW of Chewton Mendip; BA3 4PW Refurbished partly 15th-c dining pub, flagstones, low heavy beams and log fires, enjoyable food from open kitchen including home-made pizzas, pub favourites and more expensive upscale dishes, well kept Butcombe and Greene King, plenty of wines by the glass, friendly service; terrace overlooking River Chew, circular picnic-sets on sloping lawn, good reservoir walks nearby, open all day. *(Jim and Frances Gowers, Taff Thomas)*

LONG ASHTON   ST5370
Bird in Hand (01275) 395222
Weston Road; BS41 9LA Refurbished stone-built dining pub with good locally sourced food (not Sun evening) from bar meals to restaurant dishes, well kept Bath, Butcombe, St Austell, Sharps and a guest, Ashton Press cider, nice wines, spindleback chairs and blue-painted pine tables on wood floors, open fire and woodburner; children and dogs welcome, side terrace, parking may be tricky, open all day. *(John and Gloria Isaacs)*

LONG ASHTON   ST5370
Miners Rest (01275) 393449
Providence Lane; BS41 9DJ Welcoming three-room country pub, comfortable and unpretentious, with well kept Butcombe, Fullers London Pride and a guest tapped from casks, three or four good farm ciders, inexpensive simple food, local mining memorabilia, log fire, darts; no credit cards; children and dogs welcome, vine-covered verandah and suntrap terrace with picnic-sets, open all day. *(Taff Thomas)*

LOVINGTON   ST5831
⋆ Pilgrims (01963) 240597
B3153 Castle Cary–Keinton Mandeville; BA7 7PT More restaurant but does have a pubby corner serving a local ale, farm cider and plenty of wines by the glass, good imaginative food (not cheap) using local produce, efficient friendly service, cosy flagstoned inner area with modern prints, bookshelves, china and some sofas by big fireplace, compact eating area with candles

---

If you report on a pub that's not a featured entry, please tell us any lunchtimes or evenings when it doesn't serve bar food.

on tables and more formal carpeted dining room; children welcome, dogs in bar, decked terrace in enclosed garden, car park exit has own traffic lights, bedrooms (no children), closed Sun evening, Mon, lunchtime Tues. *(Anon)*

LOWER GODNEY ST4742
Sheppey Inn (01458) 831594
Tilleys Drove; BA5 1RZ Recently revamped place attracting good mix of customers; at least six local ciders tapped from the barrel along with ales such as Milk Street and Theakstons Old Peculier, imaginative choice of food, some cooked in charcoal oven, black beams, bare boards and open fire, some stripped-stone walls, brightly coloured wallpaper and stuffed animals, long simply furnished pitched-ceilinged dining area, art exhibitions and live music; children welcome, seats on deck overlooking small river. *(Peter Meister)*

LUXBOROUGH SS9837
Royal Oak (01984) 640319
Kingsbridge; S of Dunster on minor roads into Brendon Hills – OS Sheet 181 map reference 983378; TA23 0SH Sadly, as we went to press, this old favourite had closed – news please.

MARK ST3747
Pack Horse (01278) 641209
B3139 Wedmore–Highbridge; Church Street; TA9 4NF Attractive traditional 16th-c village pub run by welcoming greek-cypriot family, good choice of enjoyable home-made food including Sun roasts and fresh Brixham fish (prices can be on the high side), well kept Butcombe and guests, good friendly service, log fire; next to church. *(Richard Wyld)*

MILVERTON ST1225
Globe (01823) 400534
Fore Street; TA4 1JX Popular smartly reworked coaching inn – more restaurant than pub now; much liked mainly local food from interesting lunchtime baguettes and ciabattas up, good value Sun roasts and occasional themed nights, well kept Otter and nice choice of wines by the glass, friendly helpful staff, local art for sale; children welcome, terrace tables, bedrooms. *(Bob and Margaret Holder, Giles and Annie Francis)*

MONKTON COMBE ST7761
Wheelwrights Arms (01225) 722287
Just off A36 S of Bath; Church Cottages; BA2 7HB Compact old stone-built pub with clean modern uncluttered feel, competently prepared food including sharing plates and good value lunchtime set menu (Mon-Thurs), quick friendly service, well kept Butcombe and Sharps Doom Bar from high green-painted wood counter, good choice of wines, some stripped-stone walls, ladder-back chairs around modern tables, an old settle, wood or

carpeted floors, log fire in big stone fireplace; children welcome, attractively expanded garden with valley view, seven good annexe bedrooms. *(Mr and Mrs A H Young, Taff Thomas)*

MONTACUTE ST4916
Phelips Arms (01935) 822557
The Borough; off A3088 W of Yeovil; TA15 6XB 18th-c stone pub in pretty square next to Montacute House (NT), part-carpeted open-plan bar with well kept Palmers, Thatcher's cider and good choice of wines by the glass, reasonably priced traditional home-made food, nice fireplace with woodburner, homely old-fashioned décor, restaurant area, darts and skittle alley; background music; children and dogs welcome, attractive walled garden behind, bedrooms, closed Sun evening. *(Anon)*

NAILSEA ST4469
Blue Flame (01275) 856910
Netherton Wood Lane, West End; BS48 4DE Small friendly 19th-c farmers' local taken over by daughter of former long-serving landlord; two unchanging lived-in rooms, coal fire, well kept ales from casks behind bar, Thatcher's cider, fresh rolls, pub games; outside lavatories including roofless gents', limited parking (may be filled with Land Rovers and tractors); children's room, sizeable informal garden, best to phone about opening times. *(Taff Thomas)*

NETHER STOWEY ST1939
Rose & Crown (01278) 732265
St Mary Street; TA5 1LJ Friendly former 16th-c posting inn, good value straightforward home-made food, well kept ales such as Jennings, Marstons and Ringwood, Thatcher's cider, decent wines, cosy log-fire bar with interesting old local photographs and memorabilia, back bar with pool, darts and TV, restaurant, folk music and quiz nights; children and dogs welcome, tables in walled garden with play area, comfortable bedrooms, good breakfast, open all day. *(Richard and Liz Thorne, Neil Hardwick)*

NEWTON ST LOE ST7065
Globe (01225) 872891
A4/A36 roundabout; BA2 9BB Popular 17th-c Vintage Inn, large and rambling, with pleasant décor and dark wood partitions, pillars and timbers giving secluded feel, their usual food all day including set menu (Mon-Sat till 5pm), well kept Butcombe, St Austell Tribute and a guest, prompt friendly service by uniformed staff, good atmosphere; children welcome, nice back terrace. *(M G Hart, Richard and Judy Winn)*

NORTH CURRY ST3125
Bird in Hand (01823) 490248
Queens Square; off A378 (or A358) E of Taunton; TA3 6LT Friendly village pub, cosy main bar with old pews, settles, benches

and yew tables on flagstones, some original beams and timbers, locally woven willow work, cricket memorabilia, good inglenook log fire, well kept real ales and decent wines by the glass, enjoyable food; background music; children, dogs and muddy boots welcome, open all day Sun. *(Bob and Margaret Holder, PLC, Tony German, Barry Collett)*

NORTON ST PHILIP   ST7755
George (01373) 834224
A366; BA2 7LH Wonderful building full of history and interest (an inn for over 700 years); big heavy beams, timbering, stonework and panelling, vast open fires, distinctive furnishings, plenty of 18th-c pictures, fine pewter and heraldic shields, Wadworths ales, fairly straightforward food; children welcome, dogs in bar, appealing flagstoned courtyard, atmospheric bedrooms (some reached by Norman turret), worth strolling over meadow to attractive churchyard, open all day. *(Taff Thomas, Andrea Rampley, David Heath)*

OAKHILL   ST6347
Oakhill Inn (01749) 840442
A367 Shepton Mallet–Radstock; BA3 5HU Dining pub with sofas and easy chairs among candlelit tables around bar, friendly atmosphere and welcoming staff, decent if not particularly cheap food including some interesting choices, ales such as Butcombe, dining extension in former skittle alley, rugs on bare boards, wall of clocks, log fires; background music; nice views from garden, five bedrooms, open all day weekends. *(Anon)*

PITMINSTER   ST2219
Queens Arms (01823) 421529
Off B3170 S of Taunton (or reached direct); near church; TA3 7AZ Friendly village pub improved under new management, good imaginative food, well kept Otter and a guest, decent wines, pleasant service. *(Patrick and Daphne Darley, Kerry Law)*

PORLOCK   SS8846
⋆**Ship** (01643) 862507
High Street; TA24 8QD Picturesque old thatched pub with beams, flagstones and big inglenook log fires, enjoyable food from sandwiches up, well kept ales such as Cotleigh, Exmoor, Otter and St Austell, good friendly service, back dining room, small locals' front bar with games; children welcome, attractive split-level sunny garden with decking and play area, nearby nature trail to Dunkery Beacon, five bedrooms, open all day; known as the Top Ship to distinguish it from the Ship at Porlock Weir. *(Anon)*

PORLOCK WEIR   SS8846
⋆**Ship** (01643) 863288
Porlock Hill (A39); TA24 8PB
Unpretentious thatched bar in wonderful spot by peaceful harbour (so can get packed), long and narrow with dark low beams, flagstones and stripped stone, simple pub furniture, woodburner, west country ales including Exmoor, real ciders and a perry, good whisky and soft drinks choice, friendly prompt service, pubby food, games rooms across small backyard, tea room; background music and big-screen TV, little free parking but pay & display opposite; children and dogs welcome, sturdy picnic-sets in front and at side, good coast walks, three decent bedrooms; calls itself the Bottom Ship to avoid confusion with the Ship at Porlock. *(Mr and Mrs D J Nash, Neil Hardwick, Taff Thomas)*

PORTBURY   ST4975
⋆**Priory** (01275) 376307
Station Road, 0.5 miles from A369 (just S of M5 junction 19); BS20 7TN Spreading early 19th-c Vintage Inn dining pub, lots of linked beamed areas, appealing mix of comfortable furnishings in alcoves, tartan carpets, log fire, well kept Butcombe, St Austell and a guest, good range of wines by the glass, popular sensibly priced food all day till 10pm (9.30pm Sun) including specials, friendly prompt service; background music; children welcome, no dogs inside, pleasant front and back gardens. *(Bob and Margaret Holder)*

PORTISHEAD   ST4675
Albion (01275) 817906
Old Bristol Road; BS20 6PZ Greene King family pub with plenty of good value food all day including sharing plates and flame grills, bargain meal deals Mon-Sat, monthly live music; seats outside. *(Tom Evans)*

PORTISHEAD   ST4776
Hall & Woodhouse (01275) 848685
Chandlery Square, Portishead Quays Marina; BS20 7DF Striking new H&W pub overlooking marina slipway, unusual steel and glass construction incorporating shipping containers; main entrance with old admiralty charts, bar with floor-to-ceiling glass, exposed utilities and suspended copper-shaded lights, long benched wooden tables, some low coffee tables and easy chairs, bookshelves one end with old radios, ships telegraph etc, woodburner, Badger ales and Stowford Press cider from panelled bar, food from baguettes and sharing plates up, more elaborate menu (must book) in upstairs restaurant (lift) with reclaimed wood floors and open kitchen, helpful cheerful staff; children welcome, dogs in bar, disabled access and facilities, covered seating area outside, open all day from 9am for breakfast. *(Chris and Angela Buckell)*

PORTISHEAD   ST4576
⋆**Windmill** (01275) 843677
M5 junction 19; A369 into town, then follow Sea Front sign and into Nore Road; BS20 6JZ Busy dining pub making

most of terrific panorama over Bristol Channel; completely restyled with curving glass frontage rising two storeys (adjacent windmill remains untouched), contemporary furnishings, Bass, Butcombe, Courage and local guests, traditional bar food (may be early-evening deal), efficient service; children welcome in lower family floor, dogs allowed in bar, disabled access including lift, picnic-sets on tiered lantern-lit terraces and decking, open all day. *(Steve and Claire Harvey, Pat Bunting, Dave Braisted, R T and J C Moggridge, Dr and Mrs A K Clarke)*

PRIDDY ST5450

★**Hunters Lodge** (01749) 672275

From Wells on A39 pass hill with TV mast on left, then next left; BA5 3AR Welcoming and unchanging farmers', walkers' and potholers' pub above Ice Age cavern, in same family for generations, well kept local beers tapped from casks behind bar, Thatcher's and Wilkin's ciders, simple cheap food, log fires in huge fireplaces, low beams, flagstones and panelling, old lead mining photographs, perhaps live folk music; no mobiles or credit cards; children and dogs in family room, wheelchair access, garden picnic-sets. *(Chris and Angela Buckell, Taff Thomas)*

PRISTON ST6960

Ring o' Bells (01761) 471467

Village SW of Bath; BA2 9EE Unpretentious old stone pub with large knocked-through bar, good reasonably priced traditional food cooked by licensees using nearby farm produce, real ales from small local brewers including a house beer from Blindmans, quick friendly service, flagstones, beams and good open fire, skittle alley; children, dogs and muddy boots welcome, benches out at front overlooking little village green (maypole here on May Day), good walks, two bedrooms, closed Mon lunchtime. *(Guy Vowles)*

PURITON ST3141

Puriton Inn (01278) 683464

Just off M5 junction 23; Puriton Hill; TA7 8AF Character pub well screened from motorway, clean and tidy, with ample straightforward food and well kept ales, warmly welcoming service even when busy, pool; children allowed, good disabled access, front terrace and back garden with play area. *(Robert Smith, MP)*

RICKFORD ST4859

Plume of Feathers (01761) 462682

Very sharp turn off A368; BS40 7AH Cottagey 17th-c local with enjoyable reasonably priced home-made food in bar and dining room, friendly service, well kept

Butcombe and guests, local cider and good choice of wines, black beams and half-panelling, mix of furniture including cast-iron tables and settles, log fires, table skittles, darts and pool; well behaved children and dogs welcome, rustic tables on narrow front terrace, pretty streamside hamlet, bedrooms, open all day. *(Taff Thomas)*

ROWBERROW ST4458

★**Swan** (01934) 852371

Off A38 S of A368 junction; BS25 1QL Neat and spacious dining pub opposite pond, olde-worlde beamery and so forth, good log fires, friendly atmosphere especially in nicely unsophisticated old bar part, good reasonably priced food (small helpings available), prompt pleasant service, well kept Butcombe ales and a guest like Wadworths 6X, Thatcher's cider, decent choice of wines by the glass, live music first Sun of month; children welcome, good-sized garden over road, open all day weekends. *(Hugh Roberts, Taff Thomas)*

RUMWELL ST1923

Crown (01823) 461662

A38 Taunton–Wellington, just past Stonegallows; TA4 1EL Roomy roadside pub with old beams, cosy corners and roaring log fire, good choice of enjoyable fairly priced food including daily carvery, well kept ales such as Otter, friendly landlord and staff, family room; tables in nice garden, handy for Sheppy's Cider, closed Sun evening. *(Peter Salmon, Shirley and Bob Gibbs, Christine and Neil Townend, Bob and Margaret Holder, Tina and David Woods-Taylor)*

SALTFORD ST6867

Bird in Hand (01225) 873335

High Street; BS31 3EJ Comfortable and friendly, with lively front bar, well kept beers such as Butcombe, Courage, Otter and Sharps, farm cider, attractive back conservatory dining area, good choice of popular fairly priced food from well filled fresh rolls up, midweek lunch offer, prompt cheerful service, pubby furniture including settles, carpets throughout, lots of bird pictures and old plates, small family area; live entertainment, fruit machine; wheelchair access at front (not from car park), picnic-sets down towards river, handy for Bristol and Bath Railway Path. *(M G Hart, Dr and Mrs A K Clarke)*

SALTFORD ST6968

★**Jolly Sailor** (01225) 873002

Off A4 Bath–Keynsham; Mead Lane; BS31 3ER Great spot by lock and weir on River Avon, with dozens of picnic-sets, garden heaters and own island between lock and pub; enjoyable generous pubby food all day,

---

Pubs close to motorway junctions are listed at the back of the book.

Wadworths ales with guests like Butcombe and Sharps, flagstones, low beams and two log fires, daily papers, conservatory dining room; background music; children allowed, disabled facilities. *(Dr and Mrs A K Clarke, David Crook)*

SHEPTON MONTAGUE ST6731
⋆**Montague Inn** (01749) 813213
Village signed off A359 Bruton–Castle Cary; BA9 8JW Simply but tastefully furnished dining pub with welcoming licensees, popular for a civilised meal or just a drink, stripped-wood tables and kitchen chairs, inglenook log fire, interesting well presented food from lunchtime ciabattas up, good value 'simple suppers' menu, well kept Bath Ales, Wadworths and local guest tapped from the cask, farm ciders, good wine (three glass sizes) and whisky choice, friendly service, bright spacious restaurant extension; children welcome, dogs in bar, garden and big terrace with teak furniture, maybe summer Sun jazz, peaceful farmland views, closed Sun evening. *(Hugh Stafford, Edward Mirzoeff, Mrs Blethyn Elliott, Hugh Roberts)*

SIMONSBATH SS7739
⋆**Exmoor Forest Inn** (01643) 831341
B3223/B3358; TA24 7SH Beautifully placed in remote countryside and run by friendly licensees; circular tables by the bar counter, larger area with cushioned settles, upholstered stools and mate's chairs around mix of dark tables, hunting trophies, antlers and horse tack, woodburner, good reasonably priced traditional food alongside more imaginative choices including local game, well kept ales such as Cotleigh, Dartmoor and Exmoor, real cider, good choice of wines by the glass and malt whiskies, residents' lounge, airy dining room; children and dogs welcome, seats in front garden, fine walks along River Barle, own trout and salmon fishing, ten comfortable bedrooms, open all day in high season. *(Andrew Scott, Guy Vowles, Richard and Penny Gibbs)*

STAPLE FITZPAINE ST2618
⋆**Greyhound** (01823) 480227
Off A358 or B3170 S of Taunton; TA3 5SP Light rambling country pub with good food from nicely varied menu (best to book evenings), well kept changing ales and good wines by the glass, welcoming attentive staff, flagstones and inglenooks, pleasant mix of settles and chairs, olde-worlde pictures, farm tools and so forth; children and dogs welcome, comfortable well equipped bedrooms, good breakfast. *(Bob and Margaret Holder, Sara Fulton, Roger Baker and others)*

STOGUMBER ST0937
White Horse (01984) 656277
Off A358 at Crowcombe; TA4 3TA Friendly old village local with well kept ever-changing west country ales, food can be good especially home-made steak and

kidney pudding, carpeted beamed bar with raised end section, old local photographs, log fire, separate restaurant, games room with pool; quiet back terrace, two bedrooms accessed by external staircase, open all day (discounted drinks weekday afternoons). *(Michael Coleman, Richard and Penny Gibbs, Bob and Margaret Holder)*

TARR SS8632
⋆**Tarr Farm** (01643) 851507
Tarr Steps – narrow road off B3223 N of Dulverton; deep ford if you approach from the W (inn is on E bank); TA22 9PY Lovely Exmoor setting above River Barle's medieval clapper bridge for this 16th-c inn; compact unpretentious bar rooms with good views, stall seating, wall seats and leather chairs around slabby rustic tables, game bird pictures on wood-clad walls, three woodburners, Exmoor ales and several wines by the glass, good food, residents' end with smart evening restaurant (mix of bar or restaurant choices using local produce), friendly service, pleasant log-fire lounge with dark leather armchairs and sofas; children and dogs welcome, slate-topped stone tables outside making most of setting, extensive grounds, good bedrooms (no under-10s), open all day but closed 1-10 Feb. *(Lynda and Trevor Smith, Mr and Mrs D J Nash, Christine and Neil Townend, Bob and Margaret Holder)*

TAUNTON ST2525
⋆**Hankridge Arms** (01823) 444405
Hankridge Way, Deane Gate (near Sainsbury's); just off M5 junction 25 – A358 towards city, then right at roundabout, right at next roundabout; TA1 2LR Well appointed Badger dining pub based on 16th-c former farmhouse – splendid contrast to the modern shopping complex around it; different-sized linked areas, big log fire, popular generous food from interesting sandwiches through pubby things to restaurant dishes, set lunch deal, well kept ales and decent wines by the glass, quick friendly young staff; background music; dogs welcome, plenty of tables in pleasant outside area. *(Warren Marsh, R T and J C Moggridge, Bob and Margaret Holder)*

TAUNTON ST2225
Plough (01823) 324404
Station Road; TA1 1PB Small, homely and welcoming with eight well kept local ales tapped from the cask and up to ten racked ciders, good choice of wines by the glass, simple food all day till 10pm including unusual pies, bare boards, panelling, candles on tables, cosy nooks, open fire, hidden door to lavatories, friendly pub dog (others welcome), live music Sun night, popular quiz Tues, board games; open all day till late (3am Fri, Sat). *(John and Fiona McIlwain, Kerry Law, Simon Matthews)*

TAUNTON ST2223
Vivary Arms (01823) 272563
Wilton Street; across Vivary Park from centre; TA1 3JR Popular low-beamed 18th-c local (Taunton's oldest), good value fresh food from light lunches up in snug plush lounge and small dining room, friendly helpful young staff, well kept ales including Butcombe, decent wines, interesting collection of drink-related items; lovely hanging baskets and flowers. *(Bob and Margaret Holder)*

THURLOXTON ST2729
Maypole (01823) 412286
A38 Taunton–Bridgwater, between M5 junctions 24 and 25; TA2 8RF Spacious but cosy beamed pub with several traditional areas, welcoming staff, locally sourced food including good two-course deal and Sun carvery, well kept ales such as Exmoor, Quantock and Otter, local cider, well chosen wines and some interesting malt whiskies, good service, pubby furniture on carpet, shelves of jugs and plates, old local photographs, log fire, skittle alley, eggs and preserves for sale at the bar; no dogs; children welcome, wheelchair access (portable ramp to bar), enclosed garden with play area, surrounding paddock, peaceful village, closed Sun evening. *(Chris and Angela Buckell, Mrs Wendda Knapp)*

TIMBERSCOMBE SS9542
Lion (01643) 841243
Church Street; TA24 7TP Exmoor-edge coaching inn dating from 15th c, thriving village pub atmosphere in flagstoned main bar with rooms off, scrubbed pine tables in dining area, enjoyable pub food (not Sun evening, Mon) from good fresh ciabattas up, Thurs OAP lunch, friendly efficient service, well kept Exmoor and guests tapped from the cask, nice wines, woodburner and open fire; children and dogs welcome, closed Mon lunchtime. *(Mark Flynn)*

TINTINHULL ST5019
*Crown & Victoria (01935) 823341
Farm Street, village signed off A303; BA22 8PZ Handsome golden-stone inn, carpeted throughout, with high bar chairs by new oak counter, well kept Butcombe, Cheddar Ales, Sharps and Yeovil, farmhouse furniture and big woodburner, good popular food (best to book weekends) including blackboard specials, efficient friendly service, dining room with more pine tables and chairs, former skittle alley also used for dining, end conservatory; children welcome, disabled facilities, big garden with play area, five bedrooms, handy for Tintinhull Garden (NT). *(Charles A Hey, Roger Fox, Mrs T A Bizat)*

TRISCOMBE ST1535
*Blue Ball (01984) 618242
Village signed off A358 Crowcombe–

Bagborough; turn off opposite sign to youth hostel; OS Sheet 181 map reference 155355; TA4 3HE* Smartly refurbished old thatched inn tucked beneath the Quantocks and under newish management; first floor of original stables sloping down gently on three levels, each with own fire and cleverly divided by hand-cut beech partitions, Cotleigh and two guests, local farm cider and several wines by the glass, food can be very good; background music; children and dogs welcome, chair lift to bar-restaurant area for disabled customers, decking at top of woodside terraced garden making most of views, bedrooms, closed Sun evening, Mon lunchtime. *(Christine and Neil Townend, Rich Frith)*

TRULL ST2122
Winchester Arms (01823) 284723
Church Road; TA3 7LG Cosy streamside village pub with good value food including popular Sun lunch, west country ales and ciders, friendly attentive staff, small dining room, skittle alley; garden with decked area, six bedrooms. *(Neil and Heather Cross)*

UPTON ST0129
Lowtrow Cross Inn (01398) 371220
A3190 E of Upton; TA4 2DB Welcoming old pub under newish management; character low-beamed bar with log fire and woodburner, bare boards and flagstones, two carpeted country kitchen dining areas, one with enormous inglenook, traditional home-made food (not Mon, lunchtime Tues), Cotleigh Tawny and two guests, good mix of locals and diners; children and dogs welcome, attractive surroundings, camping nearby, closed Mon lunchtime. *(Anon)*

VOBSTER ST7049
*Vobster Inn (01373) 812920
Lower Vobster; BA3 5RJ Roomy old stone-built dining pub with good reasonably priced food including some spanish dishes (chef-landlord is from Spain) and fresh fish daily from Cornwall, good service, Butcombe and a Blindmans seasonal ale, Ashton Press cider, good wines by the glass, three comfortable open-plan areas with antique furniture, plenty of room for just a drink; dogs allowed in bar, side lawn, peaceful views, boules, adventure playground and chickens behind, four bedrooms, closed Sun evening and Mon. *(Anon)*

WAMBROOK ST2907
Cotley Inn (01460) 62348
Off A30 W of Chard; don't follow the small signs to Cotley itself; TA20 3EN Recently reopened and refurbished old stone-built pub under welcoming new licensees; light and airy beamed bar with flagstones and double-sided woodburner, carpeted dining areas off, two further fires, Otter ales and a guest tapped from the cask, enjoyable reasonably priced traditional food, evening linen napkins, friendly attentive service,

skittle alley; background music; children and dogs welcome, lovely view from terrace tables, nice garden below, quiet spot with plenty of surrounding walks, tethering for horses, closed Sun evening, Mon lunchtime. *(PLC)*

WASHFORD ST0440
White Horse (01984) 640415
Abbey Road/Torre Rocks; TA23 0JZ Welcoming and popular old local, good selection of real ales and enjoyable pubby food including daily specials and deals, can eat in bar or separate restaurant area, log fires; large smokers' pavilion over road next to trout stream, bedrooms, good traditional breakfast. *(Richard and Penny Gibbs, Robert Ensor)*

WATCHET ST0643
Star (01984) 631367
Mill Lane (B3191); TA23 0BZ Late 18th-c pub near seafront, main flagstoned bar with other low-beamed side rooms and nooks and crannies, pubby furniture including oak settles, window seats, lots of bric-a-brac, ornate fireplace with woodburner, enjoyable food cooked to order (seafood a speciality), four well kept mainly local ales, Thatcher's cider, some interesting whiskies, cheerful efficient staff; children and dogs welcome, wheelchair access, picnic-sets out in front and in beer garden behind. *(John and Alison Hamilton, Michael Butler)*

WELLOW ST7358
Fox & Badger (01225) 832293
Signed off A367 SW of Bath; BA2 8QG Opened-up village pub, flagstones one end, bare boards the other, some snug corners, woodburner in massive hearth, Butcombe, Fullers, Greene King and Sharps, four ciders including Thatcher's, wide range of enjoyable bar food from doorstep sandwiches and generous ploughman's up, good Sun lunch, friendly service; children and dogs welcome, picnic-sets in covered courtyard, open all day Fri, Sat. *(Meg and Colin Hamilton)*

WELLS ST5445
★ City Arms (01749) 673916
High Street; BA5 2AG Bustling town-centre pub with up to seven well kept ales, three ciders and decent reasonably priced food from breakfast on; main bar with leather sofas and chairs around assorted tables, plenty of prints and paintings, gas-effect log fire, upstairs restaurant with vaulted ceiling, red walls and chandeliers; background music; children and dogs welcome, cobbled courtyard and some reminders that the building was once a jail, first-floor terrace, open all day. *(R T and J C Moggridge, Paul Humphreys, Chris and Angela Buckell)*

WELLS ST5445
Crown (01749) 673457
Market Place; BA5 2RF Former 15th-c coaching inn overlooked by cathedral, various bustling areas with light wooden flooring, plenty of matching chairs and cushioned wall benches, Butcombe and Sharps Doom Bar, enjoyable good value food from sandwiches up in bar and bistro including early-evening deal, competent helpful service; background music, TV and games machine; no dogs; children until 8pm, small heated courtyard, 15 bedrooms, open all day. *(Michael Butler, David Carr, Stan Lea)*

WEST BAGBOROUGH ST1733
★ Rising Sun (01823) 432575
Village signed off A358 NW of Taunton; TA4 3EF Charming village pub lit up with evening candles; small flagstoned bar to right of massive main door with settles and carved dining chairs around polished tables, daily papers on old-fashioned child's desk, fresh flowers and quirky ornaments dotted about, well kept west country ales, good if not cheap food, friendly service, smart cosy dining room with attractive mix of chippendale and other chairs around a few dark wood tables, big modern photographs and coal-effect gas fire in attractive back snug, upstairs room with trusses in high-pitched ceiling, refectory tables and oriental rug on wood floor, large prints of cathedral cities; children and dogs welcome, teak seats outside by lane, two bedrooms, closed Sun evening (and Mon in winter). *(M and R Ridge, Bob and Margaret Holder, Dr Nigel Bowles)*

WEST HUNTSPILL ST3145
Crossways (01278) 783756
A38, between M5 junctions 22 and 23; TA9 3RA Rambling 17th-c tile-hung pub, six well kept ales, good choice of enjoyable generously served food at reasonable prices, friendly efficient staff, split-level carpeted areas with beams and log fires, skittle alley; pool, TV; children and dogs welcome, disabled facilities, garden with play area and heated smokers' shelter, seven bedrooms, open all day. *(R K Phillips, Martin Peters, Richard Tilbrook, Robert Ravenscroft)*

WEST MONKTON ST2628
Monkton (01823) 412414
Blundells Lane; signed from A3259; TA2 8NP Welcoming village dining pub refurbished under newish licensees, good choice of freshly made food including some south african influences (best to book weekends), bare-boards bar with central woodburner, snug off, separate carpeted restaurant, Exmoor, Otter and Sharps Doom Bar, Aspall's and Thatcher's ciders, wines in

---

If we know a pub has an outdoor play area for children, we mention it.

three glass sizes, good service; children and dogs welcome, wheelchair access from car park, lots of tables in big garden bounded by stream, play area. (*M G Hart*)

WEST PENNARD ST5438
Lion (01458) 832941

A361 E of Glastonbury; Newtown; BA6 8NH Traditional stone-built 16th-c village inn; bar and dining areas off small flagstoned black-beamed core, enjoyable pubby food plus daily specials board, Butcombe, Otter and Sharps Doom Bar, inglenook woodburner and open fires; background music; children and dogs welcome, tables on big forecourt, good nearby walks, seven bedrooms in converted side barn. (*Alan Todesco-Bond*)

WHEDDON CROSS SS9238
Rest & Be Thankful (01643) 841222

A396/B3224, S of Minehead; TA24 7DR Good choice of reasonably priced uncomplicated food from sandwiches up including Sun carvery, Butcombe, Exmoor and guest ales, three real ciders, good friendly service, comfortable twin-room bar with back-to-back fires, wooden tables and chairs, leather sofas and huge jug collection hanging from beams, restaurant, flagstoned games area with darts and pool, skittle alley; background music; children and clean dogs welcome, tables out in back courtyard adjoining Exmoor public car park (with disabled lavatory), good walks, five clean good value bedrooms, nice breakfast. (*Winifred Maynard, Mrs Brenda Southill*)

WINCANTON ST7028
Nog (01963) 32998

South Street; BA9 9DL Welcoming pub with Otter, Sharps and guests, real cider and continental beers, reasonably priced traditional food from lunchtime sandwiches and baked potatoes up, Sun carvery, bare boards, carpet and flagstones, lots of old photographs, open fires, pool and darts, charity quiz (last Thurs of month); well behaved children and dogs welcome, pleasant back garden with heated smokers' shelter, open all day. (*Anon*)

WINFORD ST5262
Crown (01275) 472388

Crown Hill, off Regil Road; BS40 8AY Old pub in deep country with linked beamed rooms, mix of pubby furniture including settles on flagstones or quarry tiles, old pictures and photographs on rough walls, copper and brass, leather sofas in front of big open fire, enjoyable generous home-made food (all day Sun) at very reasonable prices, Butcombe, Wadworths 6X and a guest, good choice of wines by the glass, friendly new landlord and staff, table skittles and skittle alley; children and dogs welcome, wheelchair access with help, tables out in front and in back garden, closed Mon lunchtime,

otherwise open all day. (*David and Bridget Mackwood, Taff Thomas*)

WINSCOMBE ST4257
Woodborough (01934) 844167

Sandford Road; BS25 1HD Big 1930s mock-Tudor village dining pub, smart, comfortable and busy, with wide choice of good generous local food, Butcombe and Sharps Doom Bar, good wine choice, helpful friendly staff, large public bar, skittle alley; disabled access, bedrooms. (*Susan and Nigel Brookes*)

WINSFORD SS9034
Royal Oak (01643) 851455

Off A396 about 10 miles S of Dunster; TA24 7JE Prettily placed thatched and beamed Exmoor inn, good choice of fresh food, Exmoor ales and Addlestone's cider, friendly helpful staff, lounge bar with big stone fireplace and large bay window seat looking across towards village green and foot and packhorse bridges over River Winn, more eating space in second bar, several comfortable lounges; children welcome and dogs, disabled facilities, good bedrooms. (*Geof Cox*)

WITHAM FRIARY ST7440
★ Seymour Arms (01749) 850742

Signed from B3092 S of Frome; BA11 5HF Well worn-in unchanging flagstoned country tavern, in same friendly family since 1952; two simple rooms off 19th-c hatch-service lobby, one with darts and bar billiards, other with central table skittles, well kept Cheddar Ales Potholer and an occasional guest, Rich's local cider tapped from back room, low prices, open fires, panelled benches, cards and dominoes, no food (can bring your own); children and dogs welcome, garden by main rail line, cricket pitch over the road. (*Anon*)

WITHYPOOL SS8435
★ Royal Oak (01643) 831506

Village signed off B3233; TA24 7QP Well run prettily placed country inn – where R D Blackmore stayed while writing *Lorna Doone*; lounge with raised working fireplace, comfortably cushioned wall seats and slat-backed chairs, sporting trophies, paintings and copper/brass ornaments, good food here and in restaurant, well kept Exmoor ales, friendly helpful service, character locals' bar; children in eating areas, walkers and dogs welcome (leave muddy boots in porch), wooden benches on terrace, attractive riverside village with lovely walks, grand views from Winsford Hill just up the road, eight bedrooms (twisting staircase to top-floor ones), open all day. (*Andrew Scott, Mr and Mrs P D Titcomb, Lynda and Trevor Smith, Guy Vowles, R J and D S Courtney and others*)

WIVELISCOMBE   ST0827
Bear   (01984) 623537
North Street; TA4 2JY Friendly and popular old community pub, well kept Otter Amber, Sharps Doom Bar and guests such as local Cotleigh and Exmoor, farm cider, generous home-made food; sports TV, games machines; children and dogs welcome, terrace with play area, five good value bedrooms, open all day. *(Peter Thornton, Giles and Annie Francis)*

WOOKEY   ST5245
⋆Burcott   (01749) 673874
B3139 W of Wells; BA5 1NJ Cheerful beamed roadside pub with two simply furnished old-fashioned front bar rooms, flagstones, some exposed stonework and half-panelling, lantern wall lights, old prints, woodburner, three changing ales, Addlestone's cider, enjoyable food (not evenings Sun and Mon, or Mon lunchtime in winter) from snacks up in bar and restaurant (children allowed here), OAP lunch deal, good service, small games room with built-in wall seats; soft background music, no dogs; wheelchair access, front window boxes and tubs, picnic-sets in sizeable garden with Mendip Hills views, four self-catering units in converted stables. *(Chris and Angela Buckell)*

WOOKEY HOLE   ST5347
Wookey Hole Inn   (01749) 676677
High Street; BA5 1BP Usefully placed open-plan family pub, welcoming and relaxed, with idiosyncratic contemporary décor, two eating areas and bar, wood floors and good log fire, three changing local ales, several belgian beers, ciders and perry, good generous innovative food using lots of local ingredients, tables with paper cloths for drawing on (crayons provided), efficient friendly staff; background music; dogs allowed in bar, pleasant garden with various sculptures, five individually styled bedrooms, open all day except Sun evening. *(Anon)*

WRAXALL   ST4971
Battleaxes   (01275) 857473
Bristol Road (B3130), E of Nailsea; BS48 1LQ Interesting stone-built

Victorian pub nicely refurbished by the small Flatcappers group; well kept local ales including one badged for them by Three Castles, good choice of wines and other drinks, imaginative food from snacks up as well as pub favourites (they may ask for a credit card if you run a tab), spacious interior split into two main areas, polished boards, painted panelling and good mix of old furniture; children and dogs welcome, wheelchair access using ramps, six bedrooms, handy for Tyntesfield (NT), open all day. *(Steve and Liz Tilley, Warren Marsh, Chris and Angela Buckell, Taff Thomas)*

WRAXALL   ST4971
⋆Old Barn   (01275) 819011
Just off Bristol Road (B3130) in grounds of Wraxall House; BS48 1LQ Idiosyncratic gabled barn conversion, scrubbed tables, school benches and soft sofas under oak rafters, stripped boards and flagstones, welcoming atmosphere and friendly service, well kept Butcombe, Fullers, Otter, Sharps and a guest tapped from the cask, farm ciders, good wines by the glass, simple sandwiches, unusual board games; occasional background music and sports TV; children and dogs welcome, nice garden with terrace barbecue (bring your own meat), smokers' shelter, closed Mon lunchtime, otherwise open all day. *(Mike Burkinshaw, Taff Thomas, Steve and Liz Tilley)*

YARLINGTON   ST6529
Stags Head   (01963) 440393
Pound Lane; BA9 8DG Old low-ceilinged and flagstoned country pub tucked away in rustic hamlet, Bass, Greene King IPA and a local guest from small central bar, woodburner, chapel chairs and mixed pine tables on left, carpeted dining area on right with big log fire, modern landscape prints and feature cider-press table, second dining room with doors on to terrace, enjoyable food from traditional choices up including OAP lunch menu, good service; background music; well behaved children welcome, dogs in bar, picnic-sets in sheltered back garden, maybe summer morris men, three bedrooms, closed Sun evening. *(Stan Lea, M G Hart, John and Gloria Isaacs)*

Staffordshire

For sheer character and great interest, Alan East's Yew Tree at Cauldon is the only pub in this book with two stars – everyone should visit it at least once to see the extraordinary collection of curios. Other Main Entries are the Queens at Freehay in Cheadle (neatly kept, family-run dining pub), Holly Bush in Salt (chocolate box-pretty in summer and very popular with readers) and Hand & Trumpet at Wrinehill (under the Brunning & Price umbrella, light and airy, with a fantastic choice of drinks and interesting and appealing food). Our Staffordshire Dining Pub 2014 is the Hand & Trumpet at Wrinehill.

 CAULDON   SK0749   Map 7
Yew Tree ★ ★ £
Village signposted from A523 and A52 about 8 miles W of Ashbourne;
ST10 3EJ

Treasure-trove of fascinating antiques and dusty bric-a-brac, simple good value snacks and bargain beer; very eccentric

---

Like an Aladdin's cave, the unassuming exterior of this roadside local gives no hint to the museum's worth of curiosities inside. Run by jovial Alan East for over 50 years (though he is now helped by his stepson, Dan), it's much loved for its unusual charm (it's been affectionately described as a junk shop with a bar). The most impressive pieces are perhaps the working polyphons and symphonions – 19th-c developments of the musical box, some taller than a person, each with quite a repertoire of tunes and elaborate sound-effects. But there are also two pairs of Queen Victoria's stockings, an amazing collection of ceramics and pottery including a Grecian urn dating back almost 3,000 years, penny-farthing and boneshaker bicycle and the infamous Acme Dog Carrier. Soggily sprung sofas mingle with 18th-c settles, plenty of little wooden tables and a four-person oak church choir seat with carved heads that came from St Mary's church in Stafford. As well as all this, there's an array of musical instruments ranging from a one-string violin (phonofiddle) through pianos and sousaphone to the aptly named Serpent. Drinks are very reasonably priced, so it's no wonder the place is popular with locals. You'll find Burton Bridge Bitter, Rudgate Ruby Mild and a guest or two on handpump, along with about a dozen interesting malt whiskies; darts, table skittles, dominoes and cribbage. When you arrive, don't be put off by the plain exterior, or the fact that the pub is tucked unpromisingly between enormous cement works and quarries and almost hidden by a towering yew tree.

🍴 Available during opening hours, the simple good value tasty snacks include cornish pasties, large sausage rolls, pies like steak in ale or meat and potato, and puddings such as apple crumble and chocolate pudding.

Free house ~ Licensee Alan East ~ Real ale ~ No credit cards ~ (01538) 309876 ~ Open 12-3.30, 6-midnight; 12-midnight Sat; 12-11 Sun; may be closed Mon-Weds lunchtimes, phone to check ~ Bar food available when open ~ Children allowed in polyphon room ~ Dogs welcome ~ Folk music first Tues of month; ukulele first and third Mon of month ~ www.yewtreeinncauldon.co.uk *Recommended by Emma Scofield, Paul Goldman*

CHEADLE SK0342 Map 7
Queens at Freehay

A mile SE of Cheadle; take Rakeway Road off A522 (via Park Avenue or Mills Road), then after 1 mile turn into Counslow Road; ST10 1RF

Friendly dining pub with a couple of local beers and a decent garden

The emphasis at this well managed family-run dining pub is on the enjoyable food, but they do keep Marstons Pedigree, Ringwood Fortyniner and Peakstones Rock Alton Abbey on handpump and seating is set aside for those who want just a drink and a chat. The neatly kept interior has a few cottagey touches that blend well with the modern refurbishments, and the atmosphere is relaxed and friendly. The comfortable lounge bar has pale wood tables on stripped wood floors, small country pictures and curtains with matching cushions, and opens through an arch into a simple light and airy dining area with elegant chairs and tables on light blue carpet. Service is helpful and welcoming; background music. The attractive little back garden with its mature shrubs and picnic-sets is kept in immaculate condition.

🍴 Attractively presented and popular, the good food includes sandwiches, tiger prawns in garlic butter and parsley, chicken liver and bacon pâté, sausage, egg and chips, red pepper stuffed with garlic mushroom risotto and basil pesto dressing, burger with cheese, gherkins and coleslaw, chicken breast in creamy blue cheese sauce, duck with egg noodles, stir-fried vegetables and hoisin sauce, lamb tagine, battered cod and chips, and puddings. *Benchmark main dish: beef in red wine pie £11.95. Two-course evening meal £17.50.*

Free house ~ Licensee Adrian Rock ~ Real ale ~ (01538) 722383 ~ Open 12-3, 6-11; 12-3, 6.30-10.30 Sun ~ Bar food 12-2, 6-9.30; 12-2.30, 6.30-9.30 Sun ~ Restaurant ~ Children welcome ~ www.queensatfreehay.co.uk *Recommended by Richard and Penny Gibbs, Mr and Mrs J Morris*

SALT SJ9527 Map 7
Holly Bush £

Village signposted off A51 S of Stone (and A518 NE of Stafford); ST18 0BX

Delightful medieval pub offering all-day food

Decked with brightly coloured flowers in summer, this thatched pub is in a pretty village. Inside, several cosy areas spread off from the standing-only serving section, with high-backed cushioned pews, old tables and more conventional seats. The oldest part has a heavy-beamed and planked ceiling (some of the beams are attractively carved), a woodburning stove and a salt cupboard built into a big inglenook, with other nice old-fashioned touches such as copper utensils, horsebrasses and an ancient pair of riding boots on the mantelpiece. A modern back extension, with beams, stripped brickwork and a small coal fire, blends in well. Adnams Bitter, Marstons Pedigree and a guest such as Greene

King Ruddles Best on handpump, alongside a dozen wines by the glass; service is helpful and efficient. The back of the pub is beautifully tended and filled with flowers, with rustic picnic-sets on a big lawn. It can get busy, so arrive early for a table. They operate a secure locker system for credit cards, which they will ask to keep if you are running a tab.

Fair value, hearty food includes hot and cold sandwiches, breaded mushrooms with garlic dip, baked camembert with apricot preserve, home-made pasty with horseradish mash and gravy, corned beef hash with spinach and poached egg, burger with coleslaw and chips, venison casserole, free-range bacon-wrapped chicken breast stuffed with spiced pork and Guinness gravy, mixed grill, and puddings. *Benchmark main dish: steak in ale pie £9.95. Two-course evening meal £15.00.*

Admiral Taverns ~ Licensees Geoffrey and Joseph Holland ~ Real ale ~ (01889) 508234 ~ Open 12-11(11.30 Sat); 12-10.30 Sun ~ Bar food 12-9.30(9 Sun) ~ Children welcome ~ www.hollybushinn.co.uk *Recommended by Andy Dolan, Henry Pursehouse-Tranter, Brian and Anna Marsden, Dennis Jones*

WRINEHILL   SJ7547 Map 7
Hand & Trumpet 🍴 ♟ ◧
A531 Newcastle–Nantwich; CW3 9BJ

Staffordshire Dining Pub of the Year

Big attractive dining pub with good food all day, professional service, nice range of real ales and wines; pleasant garden

Consistently well run by knowledgeable staff, this is a substantial dining pub done out in an attractive open-plan style. The spreading, interconnected rooms have a gentle mix of dining chairs and sturdy tables on polished tiles or stripped-oak boards, and several warming oriental rugs that soften the acoustics. There are lots of nicely lit prints and mirrors on cream walls between mainly dark dado, plenty of house plants, open fires and deep red ceilings. Original bow windows and, in one area, a large skylight keep it light and airy, and french windows open on to a spacious balustraded deck from where teak tables and chairs look down over ducks swimming on a big pond in the sizeable garden, which has plenty of trees. At the heart of the pub is a long, solidly built counter, where friendly attentive staff serve Caledonian Deuchars IPA, Phoenix Brunning & Price Original, Salopian Oracle and guests such as Slaters Black IPA, Tatton Gold and Woods Parish Bitter on handpump, as well as 16 wines by the glass and about 70 whiskies; good disabled access and facilities; board games.

Good interesting food includes sandwiches, brown shrimp and prawn salad with lemon and dill crème fraîche, potted duck with foie gras and blood orange jelly, ham with free-range eggs, tandoori chicken salad with minted pea cakes, beer-battered haddock with chips, duck breast with sloe-glazed plums and pink peppercorn sauce, slow-cooked pork with black pudding and ham hock hash and cider and mustard gravy, and puddings such as dark chocolate tart with boozy cherries and pistachio ice-cream and steamed lemon sponge with raspberry compote and vanilla custard. *Benchmark main dish: lamb shoulder with redcurrant and red wine gravy and dauphinoise potatoes £16.95. Two-course evening meal £19.00.*

Brunning & Price ~ Manager John Unsworth ~ Real ale ~ (01270) 820048 ~ Open 11.30-11(10.30 Sun) ~ Bar food 12-10(9.30 Sun) ~ Children welcome ~ Dogs allowed in bar ~ www.handandtrumpet-wrinehill.co.uk *Recommended by Mike Horgan, Di Wright, Paul and Gail Betteley, Rachel and Ross Gavin, Dave Webster, Sue Holland, Mrs G Marlow, Steve and Liz Tilley*

Also Worth a Visit in Staffordshire

Besides the fully inspected pubs, you might like to try these pubs that have been recommended to us and described by readers. Do tell us what you think of them: feedback@goodguides.com

ABBOTS BROMLEY   SK0824
Coach & Horses (01283) 840256
High Street; WS15 3BN Refurbished village pub with good choice of enjoyable home-made food including weekday tapas, beamed bar with stone floor, carpeted restaurant, log fire, three or four mainstream ales and several wines by the glass, friendly helpful staff; children and dogs (in bar) welcome, pleasant garden with circular picnic-sets, open all day Sun (food till 7pm), closed Mon lunchtime. *(Anon)*

ABBOTS BROMLEY   SK0824
★**Goats Head** (01283) 840254
Market Place; WS15 3BP Beamed and timbered village pub with friendly local atmosphere, Greene King, Marstons, St Austell, Timothy Taylors and two guests (May beer festival), lots of wines by the glass, enjoyable home-made food (not Sun evening) served by attentive helpful staff, opened-up cream-painted interior, unpretentious but comfortable, with oak floors, traditional furnishings and fire in big inglenook; juke box and TV; children and dogs welcome, teak furniture on sheltered lawn looking up to church tower, open all day. *(Richard and Jean Green, Tony W Dickinson, Simon Le Fort)*

ALSAGERS BANK   SJ8048
Gresley Arms (01782) 722469
High Street; ST7 8BQ At the top of Alsagers Bank with wonderful far-reaching views; eight or more interesting ales from smaller breweries and several real ciders, good value pubby food (not lunchtimes except Sun), traditional slate-floor bar with beams and open fire, comfortable lounge, picture-window dining room taking in the view, and a lower family room, monthly folk night and regular beer festivals; children, dogs and walkers welcome, garden tables, open all day Thurs-Sun, from 3pm other days. *(Dave Webster, Sue Holland)*

ALSTONEFIELD   SK1355
★**George** (01335) 310205
Village signed from A515 Ashbourne–Buxton; DE6 2FX Stone-built pub overlooking small village green, straightforward bar with low beams, old Peak District photographs and pictures, warming fire, well kept Marstons-related beers from copper-topped counter, a dozen wines by the glass, farmhouse furniture and woodburner in neat dining room, good locally sourced food cooked to order from shortish menu (some prices on the high side); children welcome, dogs in bar, seats out in front or in big sheltered back stableyard, open all day Fri-Sun. *(Ann and Colin Hunt, Stuart Paulley, J and E Dakin)*

ALSTONEFIELD   SK1255
Watts Russell Arms (01335) 310126
Hopedale; DE6 2GD Nicely placed 18th-c stone-built beamed pub, three well kept Thornbridge ales, fairly short menu including lunchtime wraps and perhaps lobby (a local stew), tapas Fri and Sun evenings, two lived-in carpeted rooms with pubby furniture and banquettes, stone fireplace; children and dogs welcome (Hector is the large pub dog), picnic-sets on sheltered tiered terrace and in garden, open all day, closed Mon evening. *(Dennis Jones, Ian Phillips)*

BARTON-UNDER-NEEDWOOD   SK1818
Shoulder of Mutton (01283) 712568
Main Street; DE13 8AA Modernised 17th-c village pub under new landlord; low beams, panelling and open fire, Bass, Marstons Pedigree and a guest, food from pub favourites up, pool in public bar (dogs allowed here), maybe live music Fri; children welcome, seats out at front and in back garden with covered terrace, four bedrooms with showers, open all day. *(Anon)*

BARTON-UNDER-NEEDWOOD   SK2018
Waterfront (01283) 711500
Barton Marina, Barton Turns; DE13 8DZ Huge pub, new but cleverly done to look long-established, part of marina complex; wide choice of enjoyable quickly served food including pubby favourites (light dishes all day), two good value house beers from local Blythe, Marstons Pedigree, St Austell Tribute and three guests, good friendly service, thriving atmosphere, weekend live music; children welcome until early evening, no dogs inside, seats out overlooking water, open all day (till 2am Fri, Sat). *(Anon)*

BLACKBROOK   SJ7638
Swan With Two Necks
(01782) 680343 *Nantwich Road (A51);*

If you stay overnight in an inn or hotel, they are allowed to serve you an alcoholic drink at any hour of the day or night.

ST5 5EH Smart contemporary décor in civilised open-plan dining areas, efficient friendly service, good well presented food (all day), nice wines by the glass; they ask to keep a credit card while running a tab; comfortable tables out on decking. *(Chris Brammeld)*

BLITHBURY SK0819
Bull & Spectacles (01889) 504201
Uttoxeter Road (B5014 S of Abbots Bromley); WS15 3HY 17th-c pub with obliging friendly service, wide choice of homely food including popular bargain lunchtime Hot Table (half a dozen or so generous main dishes with help-yourself vegetables, and some puddings), an ale from Greene King; children welcome, open all day Sun. *(David Green)*

BOBBINGTON SO8190
Red Lion (01384) 221237
Six Ashes Road, off A458 Stourbridge–Bridgnorth; DY7 5DU Friendly family-run pub popular for its good choice of enjoyable food and well kept ales (Enville, Hobsons, Holdens and Wye Valley), drinking and eating areas well separated, games part with darts, table football and pool; children welcome, good-sized garden with robust play area, 17 comfortable bedrooms in modern block, good breakfast, open all day weekends. *(David Heath)*

BREWOOD SJ8808
Swan (01902) 850330
Market Place; ST19 9BS Former coaching inn with two low-beamed bars, Caledonian, Courage, Theakstons and some more local beers, good selection of whiskies, no food except lunchtime baguettes, inglenook log fire, upstairs skittle alley; open all day. *(Tony and Wendy Hobden)*

BURTON UPON TRENT SK2523
✴ Burton Bridge Inn (01283) 536596
Bridge Street (A50); DE14 1SY Genuinely friendly down-to-earth local with own good Burton Bridge ales from brewery across old-fashioned brick yard; simple little front area leading into adjacent bar with pews, plain walls hung with notices, awards and brewery memorabilia, 20 malt whiskies and lots of country wines, small beamed and oak-panelled lounge with simple furniture and flame-effect fire, panelled upstairs dining room, simple but hearty food (lunchtimes only, not Sun); no credit cards; children welcome, dogs in bar, skittle alley, open all day Fri, Sat. *(John Honnor, David H Bennett)*

BURTON UPON TRENT SK2423
✴ Coopers Tavern (01283) 532551
Cross Street; DE14 1EG Old-fashioned 19th-c backstreet local tied to Joules – was tap for the Bass brewery and still has some glorious ephemera including mirrors and glazed adverts; homely and warm with coal fire, straightforward front parlour with pleasant jumble of furniture, back bar doubling as tap room, up to half a dozen guest ales including Bass, good selection of ciders/perries, friendly landlady, pork pies only but can bring your own food (or take beer to next-door curry house); children and dogs welcome, small back garden, open all day Fri-Sun, closed lunchtimes Mon and Tues. *(Andy Dolan, John Honnor, David H Bennett)*

BURTON UPON TRENT SK2423
Old Cottage Tavern (01283) 511615
Rangemoor Street/Byrkley Street; DE14 2EG Friendly local owned by Burton Old Cottage, their well kept ales and guests, two bars, snug and compact back restaurant, upstairs games room with skittle alley; three bedrooms, open all day. *(Anon)*

BUTTERTON SK0756
Black Lion (01538) 304232
Off B5053; ST13 7SP Nicely placed traditional 18th-c low-beamed stone-built inn, logs blazing in inner room's kitchen range, good-humoured efficient service, enjoyable food from rolls up including two-for-one deal on main courses, up to five changing often unusual ales, pool room with darts; background music; no dogs inside; children welcome, back terrace tables, three tidy bedrooms, closed weekday lunchtimes in winter, Mon and Tues lunchtimes in summer, open all day Sun. *(Mike Proctor)*

CODSALL SJ8603
Codsall Station (01902) 847061
Chapel Lane/Station Road; WV8 1BY Simply restored vintage waiting room and ticket office of working station, comfortable and welcoming, with well kept Holdens ales and a guest like Enville, good value food (sandwiches only Sun) including blackboard specials, lots of railway memorabilia, open fire, conservatory; terrace seating, open all day Fri-Sun. *(Tony Hobden)*

CONSALL SK0049
✴ Black Lion (01782) 550294
Consall Forge, OS Sheet 118 map reference 000491; best approach from Nature Park, off A522, using car park 0.5 miles past Nature Centre; ST9 0AJ Traditional take-us-as-you-find-us local tucked away in rustic old-fashioned canalside settlement by restored steam railway station, generous helpings of enjoyable unpretentious food made by landlord (may be only baps midweek), wide range of well kept mostly local ales (tasting trays available), several ciders, flagstones and good coal fire; background music, can get very busy weekend lunchtimes but staff cope well; seats outside among roaming chickens, good walking area. *(Mike Proctor, Brian and Anna Marsden)*

DRAYCOTT IN THE MOORS SJ9840
Draycott Arms (01782) 395595
Cheadle Road; ST11 9RQ Recently
reopened village pub under local ownership;
traditional bar and snug with original floor
tiles and woodwork, a beer for them from
Marstons (Draycott Crusader) along with
Pedigree and well kept guests, good food in
restaurant including meat from own farm,
friendly staff. *(George Peacock)*

ELLASTONE SK1143
Duncombe Arms (01335) 324275
Main Road; DE6 2GZ Refurbished
village dining pub with good food in bar and
restaurant including lunchtime/evening set
deal (Mon-Thurs), Marstons Pedigree, a
house beer brewed by Banks's and guests,
friendly staff; garden bar. *(Damian Chase)*

ENVILLE SO8286
Cat (01384) 872209
*A458 W of Stourbridge (Bridgnorth
Road); DY7 5HA* Ancient beamed village
pub on Staffordshire Way; two appealingly
old-fashioned log-fire rooms on one side of
servery, plush banquettes on the other, local
Enville ales and guests, good choice of well
priced home-made food (not Mon), garden
room and upstairs function room; children
and dogs welcome, pretty courtyard sheltered
by massive estate wall, open all day Sat,
closed Sun evening, Mon lunchtime.
(Julian Cox)

FLASH SK0267
Travellers Rest/Knights Table
(01298) 236695 *A53 Buxton–Leek;
SK17 0SN* Isolated main-road pub and one
of the highest in Britain, clean and friendly,
with good reasonably priced traditional food
including nice home-made cakes, four well
kept ales and good selection of wines, beams,
bare stone walls and open fires, medieval
knights' theme, live music Sat, Weds quiz;
children welcome, great Peak District views
from back terrace, open all day (till 1.30am
Sat). *(Kevin Upton, Clive Dennis)*

FRADLEY SK1414
✳ **White Swan** (01283) 790330
Fradley Junction; DE13 7DN Perfect
canalside location at Trent & Mersey and
Coventry junction, well kept Black Sheep,
Greene King Abbot, Marstons Pedigree
and three guests, cheery traditional public
bar with two fires, quieter plusher lounge
and lower vaulted room (former stable),
food including Sun carvery, cribbage and
dominoes, Thurs folk night, open mike Sun;
children (not in bar) and dogs welcome,
waterside tables, classic car/motorbike
meetings, open all day. *(S J and C C Davidson)*

GAILEY SJ9010
Spread Eagle (01902) 790212
A5/A449; ST19 5PN Spacious Marstons
roadhouse, variety of separate areas
including relaxing sofas and family part with
toys, good value usual food, daily carvery,
efficient helpful service; good disabled access
and facilities, big terrace, lawn with play
area, open all day. *(Paul Nickson)*

GNOSALL SJ8120
Navigation (01785) 822327
Newport Road; ST20 0EQ Relaxed
two-bar pub with dining conservatory and
terrace overlooking Shropshire Union Canal
(moorings), good friendly service, popular
reasonably priced traditional food and
specials, well kept Banks's ales, good value
wines, live music Thurs, pool and darts;
children welcome, dogs in bar, disabled
facilities. *(Anon)*

HANLEY SJ8847
Coachmakers Arms (01782) 262158
Lichfield Street; ST1 3EA Chatty
traditional 19th-c town local with four small
rooms and drinking corridor, Bass and half
a dozen good changing ales, farm cider,
darts, cards and dominoes, original seating
and local tilework, open fire; children
welcome, open all day (but under threat of
demolition). *(Dave Webster, Sue Holland)*

HAUGHTON SJ8620
Bell (01785) 780301
A518 Stafford–Newport; ST18 9EX
19th-c village pub with good value popular
pub food (not Sun or Mon evenings, best to
book), well kept Banks's, Marstons, Timothy
Taylors and a guest, friendly attentive service
even when busy; sports TV in bar, no dogs
inside; children welcome, picnic-sets in back
garden, open all day Fri-Sun. *(Anon)*

HIGH OFFLEY SJ7725
Anchor (01785) 284569
*Off A519 Eccleshall–Newport; towards
High Lea, by Shropshire Union Canal
Bridge 42; Peggs Lane; ST20 0NG* Real
boaters' pub on Shropshire Union Canal,
little changed in the century or more this
family have run it; two small simple front
rooms, Marstons Pedigree and Wadworths
6X, Weston's farm cider, sandwiches on
request, owners' sitting room behind bar,
occasional weekend sing-alongs; no children
inside; outbuilding with semi-open lavatories
(swallows may fly through), lovely garden
with great hanging baskets and notable
topiary anchor, caravan/campsite, closed
Mon-Thurs in winter. *(Peter Stevenson, S J and
C C Davidson)*

HIMLEY SO8990
✳ **Crooked House** (01384) 238583
*Signed down long lane from B4176
Gornalwood–Himley, OS Sheet 139 map
reference 896908; DY3 4DA* Extraordinary
sight, building thrown wildly out of kilter
(mining subsidence), slopes so weird things
look as if they roll up not down them; public

bar (dogs allowed here) with grandfather clock and hatch serving Banks's and other Marstons-related ales, lounge bar, good food from bar snacks and pub standards to more unusual creative choices, efficient cheery service, some local antiques in level extension, conservatory; children in eating areas, big outside terrace, closed Mon, otherwise open all day (till 8pm Sun). *(Simon Le Fort, Sue Partridge)*

HOAR CROSS   SK1323
Meynell Ingram Arms
(01283) 575202 *Abbots Bromley Road, off A515 Yoxall–Sudbury; DE13 8RB* This 17th-c country dining pub was closed for major refurbishment as we went to press – news please.

HOPWAS   SK1704
Tame Otter (01827) 53361
Hints Road (A51 Tamworth–Lichfield); B78 3AT Popular Vintage Inn by Birmingham & Fazeley Canal (moorings), refurbished beamed interior on different levels, cosy corners, their usual fairly priced food all day, Adnams, Everards and Marstons, decent choice of wines, nice mixed furnishings, old photographs and canalia, three fires; children welcome, large garden with plenty of seating. *(David Green, Mike and Mary Carter)*

IVETSEY BANK   SJ8311
Bradford Arms (01785) 840297
A5 Telford–Cannock, 5 miles from M6 junction 12; ST19 9QT Large partly flagstoned dining pub, substantial helpings of straightforward wholesome food at affordable prices, three well kept ales, Fri folk club upstairs; disabled access, big garden with play area, campsite. *(Robert W Buckle)*

KIDSGROVE   SJ8354
⋆ Blue Bell (01782) 774052
Hardings Wood; off A50 NW edge of town; ST7 1EG Simple friendly pub (looks more like a house) with half a dozen thoughtfully chosen and constantly changing ales from smaller breweries, around 30 bottled continentals, up to three draught farm ciders and a perry, filled rolls at weekends only; four small, carpeted rooms, unfussy and straightforward, with blue upholstered benches, basic pub furniture, gas-effect coal fire; may be background music, no credit cards; dogs and well behaved children welcome, tables in front and on little back lawn, open all day Sun, closed Mon and weekday lunchtimes. *(Dave Webster, Sue Holland)*

KINVER   SO8582
Whittington Inn (01384) 872110
A449 between Kidderminster and Wall Heath, by Staffordshire & Worcestershire Canal; DY7 6NY Striking half-timbered house dating from 14th c, genuine Dick Whittington connection and a priest hole upstairs, interesting old-fashioned bar, roaring fire, lots of 18th-c panelling, little nooks and corners, low doorways, passages and wall paintings, conservatory, well kept Banks's, Marstons Pedigree and a guest, decent wines, good value food all day, friendly young staff; background music; attractive garden with fountain. *(Iain Clark)*

KNIGHTON   SJ7240
White Lion (01630) 647300
B5415 Woore–Market Drayton; TF9 4HJ Welcoming unpretentious local with well kept changing ales and enjoyable traditional food (not Sun or Mon evenings), some good deals like Sat set lunch and midweek pie and pint, nice bar areas with open fires, more formal conservatory restaurant; open all day weekends, closed weekday lunchtimes. *(Richard and Penny Gibbs)*

LEEK   SJ9856
Den Engel (01538) 373751
Stanley Street; ST13 5HG Relaxed belgian-style bar in high-ceilinged Jacobean building, great selection of bottled and draught continental beers, three dozen genevers, plus three or four changing real ales, knowledgeable landlord, enjoyable food in upstairs restaurant; background classical music, can get packed weekends; dogs welcome, tables on back terrace, closed lunchtimes, open all day weekends. *(Anon)*

LEEK   SJ9856
⋆ Wilkes Head (01538) 383616
St Edward Street; ST13 5DS Friendly three-room local dating from the 18th c (still has back coaching stables), owned by Whim with their ales and interesting guests, farm cider and good choice of whiskies, filled rolls, gas fire and lots of pump clips, pub games, juke box in back room, Mon music night; children allowed in one room (not really a family pub), dogs welcome but ask first (resident staffy), fair disabled access, tables outside, open all day except Mon lunchtime. *(Anon)*

LICHFIELD   SK0705
⋆ Boat (01543) 361692
3.8 miles from M6 toll junction 6; head E on A5, turn right at first roundabout into B4155, then left on to A461 Walsall Road; leaving pub, keep straight on to rejoin A5 at Muckley Corner roundabout; WS14 0BU Efficiently run dining pub, handy break for a meal off M6 toll; most emphasis on food with huge floor-to-ceiling menu boards, views into kitchen and dishes ranging from lunchtime sandwiches through light snacks to interesting main choices, cheery café atmosphere, bright plastic flooring, striking photo-prints, leather club chairs and sofas around coffee tables and potted palms, more conventional and comfortable dining

areas with sturdy modern pine furniture on carpet and views of disused canal, three well kept changing ales, ten wines by the glass; background music; children welcome, good wheelchair access, seats on raised decking, open (and food) all day Sun. *(Caro Davies, Clifford Blakemore, David Green)*

LICHFIELD
Horse & Jockey (01543) 410033
SK1308

Tamworth Road (A51 Lichfield–Tamworth); WS14 9JE Small old-fashioned pub with half a dozen ales including Fullers, Holdens, Marstons and Timothy Taylors Landlord, wide range of popular freshly prepared food (booking advisable), good helpful service, four linked rooms; Sky Sports, darts; open all day. *(David Green)*

LITTLE BRIDGEFORD
Mill (01785) 282710
SJ8727

Worston Lane; near M6 junction 14; turn right off A5013 at Little Bridgeford; ST18 9QA Useful sensibly priced dining pub in attractive 1814 watermill, enjoyable food in bar and restaurant including Sun carvery, ales such as Greene King and Marstons, good friendly service, Thurs quiz; children welcome, attractive grounds with adventure playground and nature trail (lakes, islands etc); open all day. *(Brenda Keogh, Stuart Paulley)*

LONGNOR
Old Cheshire Cheese (01298) 83218
SK0965

High Street; SK17 0NS Welcoming 17th-c village pub, hearty helpings of good value straightforward food, well kept Robinsons ales, open fire, bric-a-brac and pictures in traditional main bar, two dining rooms, pool and TV in separate rooms; children, walkers and dogs welcome, tables out in front, four bedrooms in converted stables over road, open all day (may close Mon in winter). *(Michael Butler)*

MEERBROOK
Lazy Trout (01538) 300385
SJ9960

Centre of village; ST13 8SN Welcoming country pub with good generously served food from imaginative menu, attentive friendly service, four ales such as Banks's, Wincle and Wychwood Hobgoblin, cosily old-fashioned bar, comfortable lounge with log fire and dining area; children welcome, dogs and muddy boots in bar, pleasant garden behind, attractive setting and good walks. *(Dr D J and Mrs S C Walker, Michael Mellers)*

ONECOTE
Jervis Arms (01538) 304206
SK0455

B5053; ST13 7RU Busy country pub, black-beamed main bar with inglenook woodburner, well kept Titanic, Wadworths 6X and three or four changing guests, friendly staff, reasonably priced food, separate dining and family rooms; dogs welcome in bar, attractive streamside garden with footbridge to car park, play area, open all day

in summer, all day Sun in winter. *(Brian and Anna Marsden)*

PENKRIDGE
Littleton Arms (01785) 716300
SJ9214

St Michaels Square/A449 – M6 detour between junctions 12 and 13; ST19 5AL Busy Mitchells & Butlers dining pub-hotel (former coaching inn) with contemporary layout, varied choice of enjoyable good value food including lunchtime deals, several wines by the glass, ales such as Salopian, Wells & Youngs and Wye Valley, friendly young staff; background music; children welcome, ten bedrooms, open all day. *(Stuart Paulley)*

SEIGHFORD
Holly Bush (01785) 281644
SJ8725

3 miles from M6 junction 14 via A5013/B5405; ST18 9PQ Recently refurbished beamed pub (was an indian restaurant) now owned by the village and leased to Titanic, their ales and guests, good value locally sourced pubby food (all day Fri, Sat and till 7pm Sun) from lunchtime sandwiches and light choices up; beer garden. *(Mike Walker)*

SHEEN
Staffordshire Knot (01298) 84329
SK1160

Off B5054 at Hulme End; SK17 0ET Welcoming traditional 17th-c stone-built village pub, nice mix of old furniture on flagstones or red and black tiles, stag's head and hunting prints, two log fires in hefty stone fireplaces, good interesting food cooked by landlady including deals, well kept local Whim Hartington, good value wines, friendly helpful staff; closed Mon. *(Nick and Clare Kendall)*

STAFFORD
Radford Bank (01785) 242825
SJ9321

Radford Bank (A34); ST17 4PG Very child-friendly with bargain all-day carvery in large downstairs lounge (easy wheelchair access), well kept Marstons Pedigree and EPA, cheerful staff; nice outdoor seating and play area, canal walks nearby, open all day. *(Henry Pursehouse-Tranter)*

STOKE-ON-TRENT
Glebe (01782) 860670
SJ8745

35 Glebe Street, by the Civic Centre; ST4 1HG Well restored 19th-c Joules corner pub, their ales and good choice of ciders and wines from central mahogany counter, William Morris leaded windows, bare boards and panelling, some civic portraits and big fireplace with coat of arms above, wholesome bar food (not Sun, Mon evening), friendly staff, live music; quite handy for station, open all day. *(Lucy Garner, Susan and Nigel Brookes)*

STONE
Wayfarer (01785) 811023
SJ8933

The Fillybrooks (A34 just N); ST15 0NB Fresh contemporary refurbishment (sister pub to the Swan With Two Necks at

Blackbrook), good food from varied menu including sharing plates and stone-baked pizzas, beers such as Fullers, Sharps and Timothy Taylors, lots of wines by the glass, friendly staff; terrace seating, open all day. *(Susan and Nigel Brookes, Dave Webster, Sue Holland)*

STOWE   SK0027

⋆**Cock** (01889) 270237

Off A518 Stafford–Uttoxeter; ST18 0LF Popular bistro-style conversion of old village pub (calls itself Bistro le Coq), good competently cooked french food (not Sun evening) from sensibly short fixed-price menus, some reasonably priced wines, small bar area serving real ale, friendly efficient service; well behaved children welcome, closed Mon lunchtime. *(Susan and Nigel Brookes)*

TRYSULL   SO8594

Bell (01902) 892871

Bell Road; WV5 7JB Extended 19th-c village local next to church, cosy bar, inglenook lounge and large back dining area with conservatory, well kept/priced Holdens, Bathams and a guest, popular good value food from cobs up including meal deals, friendly service; dogs welcome, front terrace, open all day weekends. *(Andy Dolan, Tony Hobden, Robert Parker)*

TUTBURY   SK2128

Olde Dog & Partridge

(01283) 813030 *High Street; off A50 N of Burton; DE13 9LS* Chef & Brewer in handsome Tudor inn, rambling extensively back with heavy beams, timbers, various small rooms, nooks and corners, good choice of ales and plenty of wines by the glass, their usual all-day food including deals and children's meals, prompt friendly service, good log fire; nine comfortable bedrooms. *(John Saville)*

WETTON   SK1055

⋆**Olde Royal Oak** (01335) 310287

Village signed off Hulme End–Alstonefield road, between B5054 and A515; DE6 2AF Welcoming old stone-built pub in lovely NT countryside – a popular stop for walkers; traditional bar with white ceiling boards above black beams, small dining chairs around rustic tables, oak corner cupboard, open fire in stone fireplace, more modern-feeling area leading to carpeted sun lounge overlooking small garden, four changing ales and 30 malt whiskies, well cooked good value pubby food, darts and shove-ha'penny; background music, TV; children and dogs welcome, picnic-sets in shaded garden, self-catering cottage and paddock for caravans/tents, closed Mon, Tues. *(Dennis Jones, R L Borthwick, MP)*

WHITTINGTON   SK1608

Dog (01543) 432601

The one near Lichfield; Main Street; WS14 9JU Beamed 18th-c village inn with good freshly made food (not Sun evening, Mon) from sensibly short menu, three well kept ales including Black Sheep and decent choice of wines by the glass, pleasant efficient service; small terrace, bedrooms, open all day Fri-Sun, closed Mon lunchtime. *(Clive and Fran Dutson)*

YARLET   SJ9129

Greyhound (01889) 508480

Stone Road (A34) Popular mock-Tudor dining pub on dual carriageway (access from both sides), good selection of reasonably priced food, Wells & Youngs ales and decent wines, friendly efficient young staff, large dining conservatory at back; children welcome, open all day Sun till 8pm, closed Mon. *(Susan and Nigel Brookes)*

YOXALL   SK1418

Golden Cup (01543) 472295

Main Street (A515); DE13 8NQ Friendly well run village inn dating from the early 18th c, reasonably priced traditional home-made food from sandwiches to good value three-course Sun lunch, well kept Marstons Pedigree and a guest, lounge bar, games and sports TV in public bar; cheery window boxes and hanging baskets, nice garden down to small river, reasonably priced bedrooms, open all day weekends. *(Anon)*

Post Office address codings confusingly give the impression that some pubs are in Staffordshire, when they're really in Cheshire or Derbyshire (which is where we list them).

Suffolk

New pubs – or those back here after a break – include the Queens Head in Bramfield (beamed village pub with bustling atmosphere and pretty garden), Black Lion at Long Melford (civilised hotel with chatty bar, interesting food and bedrooms), Greyhound in Pettistree (tasty food cooked by the landlady and four real ales), Brewers Arms in Rattlesden (open all day, with inventive food cooked by the enthusiastic landlord) and St Peters Hall at South Elmham (beautiful old manor house with its own brewery). Pubs doing especially well are the Ship in Dunwich (warm welcome and enjoyable food and drink), Eels Foot in Eastbridge (beside the marshes with tasty simple meals), Dog in Grundisburgh (popular locally for food and beer), Fat Cat in Ipswich (16 or so beers in cheery, well run tavern), White Horse at Sibton (super all-rounder with an easy-going atmosphere), Crown (first class inn with mass appeal), Harbour Inn (nautical décor and good fish dishes) and Lord Nelson (always packed, well run and friendly) all in Southwold, Crown in Stoke-by-Nayland (excellent food and drink), Bell in Walberswick (charming bar, sea-view bedrooms and inventive food), Crown in Westleton (sophisticated cooking and mixed customers) and White Horse in Whepstead (smashing country pub with highly thought-of food and a tuck shop). With so much tempting food available, choosing an award-winner is not easy – but our choice for Suffolk Dining Pub 2014 is the Crown in Southwold.

ALDEBURGH
Cross Keys

TM4656 Map 5

Crabbe Street; IP15 5BN

16th-c pub with seats outside near the beach, chatty atmosphere, friendly licensee and local beers; bedrooms

Given its position on the seafront, this old pub gets busy at weekends and in high season – there are views across the promenade and shingle to the water from seats on the sheltered back terrace. The low-ceilinged interconnecting bars have antique and other pubby furniture, miscellaneous paintings and log fires in two inglenook fireplaces. Adnams Bitter, Broadside and Ghost Ship on handpump, Aspall's cider, decent wines by the glass and several malt whiskies; background music and board games. The bedrooms are attractively furnished.

As well as local fresh fish, the traditional bar food includes sandwiches, pâté with toast, moules marinière, tomato and goats cheese tart, trout stuffed with prawns, steak and kidney pie, mixed grill, and puddings such as sticky toffee pudding and treacle tart. *Benchmark main dish: fresh fish of the day £10.50. Two-course evening meal £21.00.*

Adnams ~ Tenants Mike and Janet Clement ~ Real ale ~ (01728) 452637 ~ Open 11(12 Sun)-midnight ~ Bar food 12-2(3 weekends), 7-9; no food Sun evening ~ Children welcome ~ Dogs allowed in bar ~ Bedrooms: $55/$89.50 ~ www.aldeburgh-crosskeys.co.uk
Recommended by Mr and Mrs A Curry, Andrew Gardner, Sheila Topham, C A Bryson

BOXFORD
Fleece ★ ◖

TL9640   Map 5

Broad Street (A1071 Sudbury–Ipswich); CO10 5DX

Attractively restored partly 15th-c pub flourishing under new ownership, with good food and splendid beer range

With its chatty companionable atmosphere, the Corder Room is very special – and it's for this room (on the right-hand side) that we gave the pub a star last year. It's beautifully done out, with dark panelled wainscoting, handsome William Morris wallpaper under a high delft shelf, sweeping heavy red curtains and a handful of attractive period dining tables with good chairs and a built-in wall settle. The beamed bar on the left has a woodburning stove in the terracotta-tiled front part, a big fireplace under a wall-hanging at the back, a couple of rugs on the boards there, and a mix of seats including pews and a winged settle around old stripped tables. Centre of attraction is the serving counter, with local farm cider, and changing ales on handpump: their own Mill Green White Horse Bitter plus Red Barn, Tornado Smith, Horsecroft Organic and Strong Ale and guests such as Mauldons Mid-Winter Gold and Mighty Oak Kings. Sister pub is the White Horse, Edwardstone (also in Suffolk).

Very good food includes sandwiches, pigeon salad with stilton, walnuts, bacon and pear chutney, crispy calamari with chilli mayonnaise, dry-cured ham and free-range eggs, wild mushroom, spinach and pea risotto, steak burger with bacon, cheese, coleslaw and skinny fries, beef stew with horseradish dumplings, free-range chicken with potato pancakes and champagne cream sauce, and puddings. *Benchmark main dish: slow-roasted pork belly with ale chutney £12.50. Two-course evening meal £17.00.*

Free house ~ Licensees Jarred and Clare Harris ~ Real ale ~ (01787) 211183 ~ Open 12-3, 5-11; 12-midnight Fri, Sat; 12-11 Sun ~ Bar food 12-2(2.30 weekends), 6-9; not Sun evening, Mon ~ Restaurant ~ Children welcome away from bar ~ Dogs welcome ~ Live folk several times a month ~ www.boxfordfleece.com *Recommended by Giles and Annie Francis, Mrs Margo Finlay, Jörg Kasprowski*

'Children welcome' means the pub says it lets children inside without any special restriction. If it allows them in, but to restricted areas such as an eating area or family room, we specify this. Places with separate restaurants often let children use them, and hotels usually let children into public areas such as lounges. Some pubs impose an evening time limit – let us know if you find one earlier than 9pm.

BRAMFIELD
Queens Head

TM3973 Map 5

The Street; A144 S of Halesworth; IP19 9HT

Popular pub with pretty garden, well liked food and a decent choice of drinks

Next door to an interesting and rather lovely church, this bustling village pub has plenty of picnic-sets under parasols in the tiered garden. The various rooms have heavy beams and timbering, some exposed brickwork, country kitchen-style tables (each with a church candle) and chairs on carpeting and work by local artists on the walls. The high-raftered lounge has a good log fire in an impressive fireplace and a new bar has winter fires in brick fireplaces. Adnams Bitter, Broadside and Ghost Ship on handpump, several wines by the glass and friendly service.

Using local, seasonal produce, the food includes lunchtime sandwiches, baguettes and ciabattas, bacon-wrapped dates in mustard and cream sauce, chicken liver pâté, sausages with mash and onion sauce, peppered mushroom and stilton pie, chilli con carne, steak, mushroom and kidney pie, wild rabbit casserole, monkfish in a parcel with dill, ginger, fish sauce and rice wine, and puddings such as clementine crème brûlée and chocolate and brandy pot. *Benchmark main dish: steaks from local farms £14.95. Two-course evening meal £18.00.*

Adnams ~ Tenant Stewart Jackson-Cox ~ Real ale ~ (01986) 784214 ~ Open 11-2.30, 6.30-11; 12-3, 7-10.30 Sun ~ Bar food 12-2(2.30 Sun), 6.30-9.15; no food winter Sun evenings ~ Children welcome away from main bar area ~ Dogs welcome ~ Regular live music, phone for details ~ www.queensheadbramfield.co.uk
Recommended by Caroline Prescott

BURY ST EDMUNDS
Old Cannon

TL8564 Map 5

Cannon Street, just off A134/A1101 roundabout at N end of town; IP33 1JR

Busy own-brew town pub with local drinks and interesting bar food

As well as being a comfortable place to stay, with bedrooms in the former brewhouse across the courtyard, this Victorian townhouse now has its brewery in the bar. There are two huge gleaming stainless-steel brewing vessels and views up to a steel-balustraded open-plan malt floor above the ochre-painted counter, where they serve their own-brewed Old Cannon Best, Gunner's Daughter and Blonde Bombshell alongside guests such as Adnams Bitter and Oyster and Fullers London Pride on handpump, plus a dozen wines by the glass and carefully chosen spirits. Chunky old bar stools line the counter, and there's an appealing assortment of old and new chairs and tables and upholstered banquettes on well worn bare boards; background music. Behind, through the old side coach arch, is a good-sized cobbled courtyard with hanging baskets and stylish metal tables and chairs.

Popular and highly thought-of food includes baguettes, moules marinière, warm chicken liver and chorizo salad, sausages with colcannon mash, onion gravy and beer batter pudding, pasta with ham, chestnuts and wild mushrooms in madeira and parmesan sauce (vegetarian option too), slow pot-roasted ham hock with apple, cider and mustard sauce, steak and kidney pie, thai red chicken curry, and puddings such as apple and passion-fruit crumble and dark chocolate brownie in stout and chocolate sauce. *Benchmark main dish: fish and chips £11.95. Two-course evening meal £18.00.*

Own brew ~ Licensee Garry Clark ~ Real ale ~ (01284) 768769 ~ Open 12-11(10.30 Sun) ~ Bar food 12-9; 12-3 Sun ~ Restaurant ~ Children in restaurant and only if eating ~ Bedrooms: £85/£110 ~ www.oldcannonbrewery.co.uk *Recommended by Bruce M Drew, PL*

CHELMONDISTON
Butt & Oyster
TM2037   Map 5

Pin Mill; signposted from B1456 SE of Ipswich, continue to bottom of road; IP9 1JW

Chatty old riverside pub with pleasant views, good food and drink and seats on the terrace

Named for the flounders and oysters that used to be caught here, this simple old bargeman's pub has fine views over the bustling River Orwell from seats on the terrace or by the windows in the bar. The half-panelled little smoke room, pleasantly worn and unfussy, has high-backed and other old-fashioned settles on a tiled floor. There's also a two-level dining room with country kitchen furniture on bare boards, and pictures and artefacts relating to boats and the water on the walls. Adnams Bitter, Ghost Ship and two changing guests tapped from the cask by friendly, efficient staff, several wines by the glass and local cider; board games. The annual Thames Barge Race (end June/early July) is fun. The car park can fill up pretty quickly.

Using local fish and meat, the good food includes sandwiches, crispy squid with green peppercorn and chilli dressing, stuffed vine leaves with hummus and pitta bread, vegetarian pasta bake, ham and free-range eggs, burger with home-made relish and chips, rice noodle salad with king prawns and thai dressing, sticky Guinness and marmalade lamb shank, and puddings such as eton mess and lemon tart with clotted cream. *Benchmark main dish: beer-battered fresh cod and chips £10.95. Two-course evening meal £17.00.*

Adnams ~ Lease Steve Lomas ~ Real ale ~ (01473) 780764 ~ Open 10am-11pm ~ Bar food 10-9.30 ~ Restaurant ~ Children welcome in dining rooms ~ Dogs allowed in bar ~ www.debeninns.co.uk/buttandoyster *Recommended by the Didler, Mike and Mary Carter, Mrs Carolyn Dixon, Roger and Anne Newbury*

DUNWICH
Ship
TM4770   Map 5
St James Street; IP17 3DT

Friendly, well run and pleasantly traditional pub in a coastal village, tasty bar food and local ales; bedrooms

'This never disappoints,' says one reader and many others agree. Just a stone's throw from the sea, it"s handy for some of the best coast paths in Suffolk. Inside, the atmosphere is informal and relaxed and you can be sure of a warm welcome from the licensee and his friendly staff; dogs are given a treat and a bowl of water. The traditionally furnished main bar has benches, pews, captain's chairs and wooden tables on a tiled floor, a woodburning stove (left open in cold weather) and lots of sea prints. From the handsomely panelled bar counter they serve Adnams Bitter and a couple of guests like Cliff Quay Bitter and Earl Soham Albert Ale from antique handpumps and several wines by the glass; board games. A simple conservatory looks on to a back terrace, and the large garden is very pleasant, with well spaced picnic-sets, two large anchors and an enormous fig tree – they may have Shakespeare performances here in August. Readers enjoy staying here and the

breakfasts are hearty. The RSPB Minsmere reserve and Dunwich
Museum are worth visiting and there's more walking in Dunwich Forest.

 Popular food includes mackerel pâté with cucumber relish, twice-baked
stilton soufflé with pear and endive salad, beetroot and red onion tart with
honey-glazed goats cheese, home-baked ham with free-range eggs and pineapple
relish, steak and kidney pudding, slow-cooked pork belly with date and apple purée,
fish pie, and puddings such as treacle tart and sticky toffee pudding. *Benchmark
main dish: beer-battered fish and chips £11.95. Two-course evening meal £20.00.*

Free house ~ Licensee Matt Goodwin ~ Real ale ~ (01728) 648219 ~ Open 11-11;
12-10.30 Sun ~ Bar food 12-3, 6-9 ~ Restaurant evening only ~ Children welcome away from
bar ~ Dogs allowed in bar and bedrooms ~ Bedrooms: £75/£95 ~ www.shipatdunwich.co.uk
*Recommended by Andrew and Ruth Triggs, Nigel Long, Ann and Colin Hunt, Sara Fulton, Roger
Baker, Derek and Sylvia Stephenson, George Atkinson, David and Judy Robison*

EARL SOHAM
Victoria ◀ £

TM2263 Map 5

A1120 Yoxford–Stowmarket; IP13 7RL

**Friendly informal local with beers from across the road and
simple food**

The three beers on handpump in this simple pub are brewed across
the road at the Earl Soham brewery: Victoria Bitter, Brandeston
Gold and Sir Rogers Porter. Fairly basic and definitely well worn, the
bar is sparsely furnished with kitchen chairs and pews, plank-topped
trestle sewing machine tables and other simple scrubbed-pine country
tables. It also has stripped panelling, tiled or board floors, open fires and
an interesting range of pictures of Queen Victoria and her reign; board
games. There are seats on a raised back lawn, with more out in front.
The pub is quite close to a wild fritillary meadow at Framlingham and
a working windmill at Saxtead.

 Food includes sandwiches, salads, casseroles and curries. *Benchmark main
dish: beef in ale casserole £10.95. Two-course evening meal £15.00.*

Earl Soham ~ Licensee Paul Hooper ~ Real ale ~ (01728) 685758 ~ Open 11.30-3, 6-11;
12-3, 7-10.30 Sun ~ Bar food 12-2, 7-10 ~ Children welcome ~ Dogs allowed in bar
Recommended by Ann and Colin Hunt

EASTBRIDGE
Eels Foot 🛏

TM4566 Map 5

Off B1122 N of Leiston; IP16 4SN

**Country local with hospitable atmosphere, fair value food using their
own eggs and Thursday evening folk sessions; bedrooms**

Handy for RSPB Minsmere, this hospitable inn also borders the
freshwater marshes where there's an abundance of birds and
butterflies; a footpath leads directly to the sea. It's a friendly, simple
pub: the upper and lower parts of the bar have light modern furnishings
on stripped wood floors, a warming fire and Adnams Bitter, Broadside,
Ghost Ship and a changing guest on handpump, around a dozen wines
by the glass and several malt whiskies; darts in a side area, board games,
cribbage and a neat back dining room. There are seats on the terrace
and benches in the lovely big back garden. The bedrooms (one with
wheelchair access) in the newish building are comfortable and attractive.
It does get busy in summer.

🍴 The good choice of food includes baguettes, mushroom and stilton pot, beer-battered line-caught cod and chips, spinach and ricotta cannelloni in creamy cheese sauce, local sausages with mash and gravy, smoked haddock, mozzarella and spring onion fishcakes, and puddings such as rhubarb crumble and sticky toffee pudding. *Benchmark main dish: steak in ale pie £11.50. Two-course evening meal £15.00.*

Adnams ~ Tenants Julian and Alex Wallis ~ Real ale ~ (01728) 830154 ~ Open 12-3, 6-11; 12-11 Fri; 11.30-11 Sat; 12-10.30 Sun ~ Bar food 12-2.30, 7-9(6.30-8.30 Thurs) ~ Children welcome ~ Dogs welcome ~ Live folk music Thurs evening, last Sun of month ~ Bedrooms: £80/£99 ~ www.theeelsfootinn.co.uk *Recommended by Charles and Pauline Stride, Mr and Mrs A Curry, Alan Weedon, Anthony Barnes, Roy Hoing*

EDWARDSTONE
White Horse 🍺

TL9542   Map 5

Mill Green, just E; village signed off A1071 in Boxford; CO10 5PX

Own-brew pub, traditional furnishings in simple rooms, hearty food, self-catering and a campsite

Under a new licensee, this unpretentious village local serves its own-brewed ales from the on-site Mill Green brewery. On handpump or tapped from the cask, these might include White Horse Bitter, Green Goose, Hopped Down Under, Horsecroft and Tasmanian Hop Devil with a guest such as Adnams Broadside; also, local farm cider and organic fruit juices. There are several bar rooms of various sizes, including a tiny one with just one table and lots of beer mats on the walls. The floors are bare boards throughout, cream walls above a pink dado are hung with rustic prints and photographs, there's a mix of second-hand tables and chairs including an old steamer bench and panelled settle, and both a woodburner and open fire; background music, darts, bar billiards, ring the bull, quoits, dominoes, cards and board games. There are sturdy teak tables and seats on an end terrace, an attractive smokers' shelter with green-panelled seating and some makeshift picnic-sets on a grassy area. The self-catering 'cottages' are rather scandinavian in style, and there's also a campsite.

🍴 As well as a good value two-course set lunch, the popular food includes ham hock terrine with piccalilli, goats cheese bonbons with apricot and ginger chutney, beer-battered haddock and chips, ham and free-range eggs, sausages with mash and onion gravy, slow-cooked lamb shoulder with red wine sauce, pork belly with chorizo and three-bean cassoulet, and puddings such as lemon posset and ginger sponge pudding with ginger compote. *Benchmark main dish: burger (beef, boar, lamb, vegetarian) with coleslaw and chips £8.95. Two-course evening meal £15.00.*

Own brew ~ Licensee Natasha Long ~ Real ale ~ (01787) 211211 ~ Open 12-midnight (11 Sun, Mon); 12-3, 5-11 Mon-Thurs in winter ~ Bar food 12-2.30(3.30 Sun), 6-9; not Sun evening, Mon except bank holidays; all day summer Sun ~ Restaurant ~ Children welcome in bar until 6pm ~ Dogs welcome ~ Open mike night, jazz or folk Weds, live band last Sat of month ~ Bedrooms: /£90 ~ www.edwardstonewhitehorse.co.uk *Recommended by Tim Woodward*

Stars after the name of a pub show exceptional quality. One star means most people (after reading the report to see just why the star has been won) would think a special trip worthwhile. Two stars mean that the pub is really outstanding – for its particular qualities it could hardly be bettered.

GRUNDISBURGH

TM2250   Map 5

Dog ❦❢❢ ♀ ◖

The Green; off A12 via B1079 from Woodbridge bypass; IP13 6TA

Civilised, friendly pub with enjoyable food, fine choice of drinks and a log fire; garden with play area

There's always a friendly crowd of locals in this pink-washed pub – and a consistently warm welcome for visitors too. Nicely villagey, the public bar (on the left) has an open log fire, oak settles and dark wooden carvers around a mix of tables on a tiled floor, and Adnams Bitter, Earl Soham Victoria Bitter, Woodfordes Wherry and a changing guest on handpump and half a dozen wines by the glass; good coffee too. The softly lit and relaxing carpeted lounge bar has comfortable seating around dark oak tables; it links with a similar bare-boards dining room, with some attractive antique oak settles. Several picnic-sets are out in front by flowering tubs and the wicker-fenced back garden has a mediterranean feel with kitchen herbs, an olive tree, a grapevine and comfortable seats under white parasols; there's also a play area.

 As well as a two- and three-course set lunch (not Sunday) and using local game and meat, the consistently good, interesting food includes sandwiches, goats cheese panna cotta with beetroot dressing, ham hock terrine with piccalilli, beer-battered haddock with mushy peas, burger with onion rings, cheese, bacon, coleslaw and fries, roast vegetable lasagne, chicken with thyme and bacon sauce, honey-roast carrots and fondant potato, pork tenderloin with oyster mushrooms, spinach and wellington potatoes, and puddings such as raspberry cheesecake and chocolate fondant with chantilly cream. *Benchmark main dish: rump of lamb with rosemary jus and dauphinoise potatoes £13.95. Two-course evening meal £15.00.*

Free house ~ Licensees Charles and Eilir Rogers ~ Real ale ~ (01473) 735267 ~ Open 12-3, 5.30-11; 12-11 Fri, Sat; 12-10.30 Sun; closed Mon ~ Bar food 12-2, 5.30-9 ~ Restaurant ~ Children welcome ~ Dogs allowed in bar ~ www.grundisburghdog.co.uk
Recommended by J F M and M West, Roger White, Charles and Pauline Stride

IPSWICH

TM1844   Map 5

Fat Cat ◖

Spring Road, opposite junction with Nelson Road (best bet for parking); IP4 5NL

Fantastic range of changing real ales in a well run town pub; garden

As ever, the fantastic range of up to 16 real ales on handpump or tapped from the cask in this friendly, cheerful town pub continues to draw the crowds. Coming from all over the country, the ales might include Abbeydale Alchemy, Adnams Kristal White, Castle Rock Bouncing Bomb, Cotleigh Lemon Ale, Crouch Vale Brewers Gold and Yakima Gold, Elgoods Black Dog Mild and Saturday Night Beaver, Fat Cat Honey Cat, Fullers London Pride, Hop Back Summer Lightning, Oakham Inferno and Woodfordes Wherry. They also stock quite a few belgian bottled beers, Aspall's cider and local lager. The bare-boarded bars have a mix of café and bar stools, unpadded wall benches and cushioned seats around cast-iron and wooden pub tables, and lots of enamel brewery signs and posters on canary yellow walls. Often to be seen perched on a pub stool are the pub cat Dave or the sausage dog Stanley. There's also a spacious back conservatory and several picnic-sets on the terrace and lawn. Very little nearby parking.

There's no kitchen, but they keep a supply of scotch eggs, pasties, pies and (sometimes) baguettes in the fridge and are happy for you to bring in takeaways (not Friday or Saturday).

Free house ~ Licensees John and Ann Keatley ~ Real ale ~ (01473) 726524 ~ Open 12-11(midnight Fri, Sat) ~ Bar food all day ~ www.fatcatipswich.co.uk
Recommended by the Didler, Richard and Penny Gibbs

LAVENHAM TL9149 Map 5
Angel ♀ 🛏
Market Place; CO10 9QZ

Handsome old inn with emphasis on dining, imaginative food, a wide range of drinks, character rooms and sizeable back garden; comfortable bedrooms

As we went to press some gentle refurbishment was planned for the restaurant areas of this lovely Tudor building. The emphasis is firmly on dining, but there's a proper bar and they keep a beer named for Marco Pierre White from Lees, Adnams Bitter and two changing guests on handpump; also, quite a few wines by the glass and several malt whiskies. Light and airy, the long bar area has a big inglenook log fire under a heavy mantelbeam and some attractive 16th-c ceiling plasterwork (and even more elaborate pargeting in the residents' sitting room upstairs). Other dining areas have elegant dark wooden dining chairs around white-clothed tables, more heavy beams and panelling, and cartoons and David Bailey celebrity photographs on the walls. There are seats and tables in the large sheltered back garden, and picnic-sets in front make the most of the setting in the former market square of this delightful small town. A good base for the area.

As well as a two- and three-course set menu, the interesting food includes lunchtime sandwiches, potted jellied ham with home-made piccalilli, soft roes on toast with lemon and caper butter, cumberland sausages with onion gravy, fried haddock and triple-cooked chips, caramelised honey-roast pork belly with honey spice and butter beans, peppered venison with braised red cabbage and Armagnac, and puddings such as sherry trifle and rice pudding with hot red fruit compote. *Benchmark main dish: fish pie £15.50. Two-course evening meal £19.00.*

Free house ~ Licensee Rob Jackson ~ Real ale ~ (01787) 247388 ~ Open 11am-11.30pm ~ Bar food 12-2.30(3.30 Sun), 6-9.30 ~ Children welcome ~ Dogs allowed in bar ~ Bedrooms: £70/£115 ~ www.wheelersangel.com *Recommended by Toby Jones, Emma Scofield*

LINDSEY TYE TL9846 Map 5
Red Rose
Village signposted off A1141 NW of Hadleigh; IP7 6PP

15th-c hall house with a couple of neat bars, enjoyable popular food, real ales and plenty of outside seating

Consistently well run and enjoyable, this handsome hall house offers a warm welcome to all. The neatly kept main bar has low beams and some standing timbers, an assortment of wooden tables and chairs, red-painted walls and dried teasels in glass jugs on the window sills. In front of a splendid log fire in an old brick fireplace are a couple of squashy red leather sofas, a low table and some brass measuring jugs. A second room, again with a big brick fireplace, is furnished in the same way but is much simpler in feel and perhaps quieter; background music. Adnams Bitter and Mauldons Mole Trap on handpump and ten wines by the glass.

There are flowering tubs and a few picnic-sets in front, with more picnic-sets at the back, where there's also a play area, a football pitch and an animal pen with chickens and sheep.

Using their own meat and other local ingredients, the good food includes sandwiches, smoked salmon, eggs benedict and hollandaise, goats cheese tempura with chilli jam, vegetable stir-fry with coriander omelette, beer-battered haddock and chips, slow-roasted pork belly with apple and black pudding croquettes, celeriac purée and sage mash, lamb shepherd's pie, and puddings such as warm chocolate brownie with ice-cream and lemon posset with home-made shortbread; they also offer a two- and three-course weekday set lunch. *Benchmark main dish: rare-breed burger with blue cheese, bacon and chips £12.00. Two-course evening meal £20.00.*

Free house ~ Licensee Peter Miller ~ Real ale ~ (01449) 741424 ~ Open 11-3, 5.30-11; 11-11 Sun ~ Bar food 12-2.30, 6.30-9.30; 12-3, 7-9 Sun; not winter Sun evening ~ Children welcome ~ Dogs welcome ~ www.thelindseyrose.co.uk *Recommended by Steve Stagg, Mrs Carolyn Dixon*

LONG MELFORD   TL8646 Map 5
Black Lion 🍴 � 🛏
Church Walk; CO10 9DN

Well appointed hotel with relaxed and comfortable bar, modern bar food, attentive staff and seats in pretty garden; comfortable bedrooms

This is a civilised and comfortable hotel rather than a straightforward pub, but customers do drop in for just a drink and a chat, and it's the back bar that locals head for with its two comfortable sofas and leather winged armchairs, open fire and Adnams Bitter and sometimes Broadside on handpump; around 15 wines by the glass too. The red-walled dining room has attractive chairs around handsome candlelit tables on a tartan carpet, another open fire and heavy swagged curtains; the windows look over the village green. You can take afternoon tea in the appealing Victorian walled garden and our readers enjoy staying in the individually decorated bedrooms; breakfasts are particularly good.

Impressive food includes sandwiches, open raviolo of rabbit, garlic greens and morel mushrooms, scottish smoked salmon with lobster aspic, sea fennel, avruga, brown shrimps and black butter, crispy tempura vegetable fritti with baked polenta, asparagus and crème fraîche dressing, free-range chicken with black pudding masala, cumin potato and curried lentils, slow-cooked shin of beef with pommes purée and cavolo nero, gilt-head bream with seaweed, violet potato and citrus fruit dressing, and puddings such as dark chocolate and vanilla brownie and caramel sauce and hazelnut meringue millefeuille; they also offer a two- and three-course set menu. *Benchmark main dish: beer-battered cod and chips £14.00. Two-course evening meal £24.00.*

Ravenwood Group ~ Licensee Craig Jarvis ~ Real ale ~ (01787) 312356 ~ Open 7.30am(8.30 weekends)-11pm ~ Bar food 12-2, 7-9.30 ~ Restaurant ~ Children welcome ~ Dogs allowed in bar and bedrooms ~ Bedrooms: £102/£125 ~ www.blacklionhotel.net *Recommended by Annette and John Derbyshire, Paul and Marion Watts, Mrs Carolyn Dixon*

MIDDLETON   TM4267 Map 5
Bell 🍺 £
Off A12 in Yoxford via B1122 towards Leiston, also signposted off B1125 Leiston–Westleton; The Street; IP17 3NN

Thatch and low beams, friendly chef-landlord, good beer and popular good value food – a peaceful spot

There's always a cheerful bustle in this popular pub and the character landlord is friendly and welcoming. On the left, the traditional bar has a log fire in a big hearth, old local photographs, a low plank-panelling ceiling, bar stools and pew seating, Adnams Bitter, Broadside and a seasonal ale tapped from the cask and darts. On the right, an informal two-room carpeted lounge/dining area has padded mate's and library chairs around dark tables below low black beams, with pews by a big woodburning stove, and modern seaside brewery prints. Dogs are welcomed with treats and a bowl of water. It's a pretty cream-washed building, with picnic-sets under cocktail parasols out in front, and camping available in the broad meadow behind. Coast walks and the RSPB Minsmere reserve are nearby.

Using local, seasonal ingredients, the generous helpings of good value food includes sandwiches, ham and egg, liver and bacon, a couple of vegetarian choices, sausages and mash, specials such as grilled salmon, bass and mackerel paupiette with lemon and cucumber dressing, and chicken supreme with chicken and stilton mousse and garlic cream, and puddings. *Benchmark main dish: stuffed pork belly on mash £10.95. Two-course evening meal £15.50.*

Adnams ~ Tenants Nicholas and Trish Musgrove ~ Real ale ~ (01728) 648286 ~ Open 12-3, 6-11; 12-midnight(10.30 Sun) Sat; closed Mon lunchtime ~ Bar food 12-2.15, 6-9.15; 12-5 Sun; not Mon except bank holidays ~ Restaurant ~ Well behaved children allowed away from bar ~ Dogs allowed in bar *Recommended by B R and M F Arnold, Stephen and Jean Curtis, Charles and Pauline Stride, Paul Humphreys, R L Borthwick*

PETTISTREE
Greyhound

TM2954 Map 5

The Street; brown sign to pub off B1438 S of Wickham Market, 0.5 miles N of A12; IP13 0HP

Neatly kept village pub with enjoyable food and drink

In a peaceful setting next to the church, this friendly pub has just two smallish rooms – so it's worth booking in advance to be sure of a table. There are open fires, some rather low beams, chunky farmhouse chairs and cushioned settles around dark wooden tables on bare floorboards and candlelight. Earl Soham Victoria Bitter and guests like Adnams Ghost Ship and Earl Soham Brandeston Gold on handpump, and several wines by the glass. The well kept side garden has picnic-sets under parasols, with more beside the front gravel car park.

Cooked by the landlady using local, seasonal produce, the well thought-of food includes sandwiches, confit duck and orange salad with honey mustard dressing, sticky pork belly with raisins, cod and salmon fishcake with creamed leeks and chips, gnocchi with roasted red peppers and herb pesto, haggis-stuffed chicken breast with whisky cream, and puddings. *Benchmark main dish: slow-roasted pork belly in cider with black pudding and red cabbage £12.95. Two-course evening meal £15.00.*

Free house ~ Licensees Stewart and Louise McKenzie ~ Real ale ~ (01728) 746451 ~ Open 12-3, 6-11; 12-4, 7-10.30 Sun; closed Mon except evening second Mon of month ~ Bar food 12-3, 6-9; 12-4 Sun ~ Restaurant ~ Children welcome ~ Dogs allowed in bar ~ Live folk evening second Mon of month ~ www.greyhoundinnpettistree.co.uk
Recommended by Roger White

RATTLESDEN
TL9758   Map 5

Brewers Arms

Lower Road; off B1115 via Buxhall or A45 via Woolpit, W of Stowmarket; IP30 0RJ

Friendly staff and interesting, generously served food at attractively decorated village pub

Usefully open all day, this 16th-c village pub places quite an emphasis on its food – though the traditionally furnished bar on the right, with its modern paintwork and stools on flagstones against the counter, does keep three Greene King beers on handpump: an ale named for the pub, Ruddles Best and St Edmunds. The lounge bar on the left winds back through standing timbers to the restaurant area, which is partly flint-walled and has a magnificent old bread oven; background music. French windows open on to the walled garden where there are plenty of seats.

Cooked by the landlord, the interesting food includes brunch (smoked ham with croissant and gruyère, smoked salmon with scrambled eggs, sausage sandwich with melted onions), devilled sprats with aioli, crayfish caesar salad, beer-battered haddock and chips, pork and fennel sausages with borlotti beans, calves liver with bubble and squeak and devils on horseback, swordfish with chickpeas, preserved lemon, harissa and mint, rare-breed steak with snail butter, and puddings such as double chocolate brownie with chocolate ice-cream and Alder Tree ice-cream with a waffle cone. *Benchmark main dish: tagliatelle with veal ragout £9.50. Two-course evening meal £19.00.*

Greene King ~ Tenant Rebekkah Scalco ~ Real ale ~ (01449) 736377 ~ Open 10am-11pm ~ Bar food 12-3(4 Sat), 6-9.30(10 Fri, Sat); 12-4, 6-9 Sun ~ Children welcome ~ Dogs allowed in bar ~ www.brewersarms-rattlesden.com *Recommended by Olly Headey*

SIBTON
TM3570   Map 5

White Horse

Halesworth Road/Hubbard`s Hill, N of Peasenhall; IP17 2JJ

Particularly well run inn with nicely old-fashioned bar, good mix of customers, real ales and imaginative food using produce from their own kitchen garden; comfortable bedrooms

The warmly friendly, hands-on licensees have created an easy-going village atmosphere with lots of chatty locals – as well as offering first class food and appealing bedrooms. The comfortable bar has horsebrasses and tack on the walls, old settles and pews and a large inglenook fireplace with a roaring log fire. Adnams Bitter, Woodfordes Wherry and a guest such as Green Jack Trawlerboys Best Bitter on handpump (they hold a June beer festival with around 16 ales), several wines by the glass and a dozen malt whiskies are served from the old oak-panelled counter; a viewing panel shows the working cellar with its Roman floor. Steps lead past an ancient partly knocked-through timbered wall into a carpeted gallery, and there's a smart dining room too. The big garden has plenty of seats.

Using their own kitchen garden vegetables and eggs and other local, seasonal produce, the excellent food includes a two- and three-course set lunch (not Sunday), sandwiches, rabbit and wild duck terrine with apple, sultana and apricot chutney, crayfish and lemon risotto, brie, courgette and cherry tomato tarte tatin with roast potatoes and fennel, lamb rump and crispy breast with apricot and coriander couscous, tagine sauce and curry oil, bass fillets with lemon and thyme crushed potatoes and ratatouille, and puddings such as stem ginger crème brûlée with spiced plum compote and warm chocolate brownie with orange ice-cream and mandarin gel. *Benchmark main dish: beer-battered haddock with chips and mushy peas £10.50. Two-course evening meal £21.00.*

Free house ~ Licensees Neil and Gill Mason ~ Real ale ~ (01728) 660337 ~ Open 12-2.30, 6.30(6 Sat)-11; 12-4, 7-10.30 Sun; closed Mon lunchtime ~ Bar food 12-2, 6.30-9; 12-2.30, 7-8.30 Sun ~ Restaurant ~ Well behaved children welcome but must be over 6 in evening and over 13 for accommodation ~ Dogs allowed in bar ~ Bedrooms: /£90 ~ www.sibtonwhitehorseinn.co.uk *Recommended by Lois Dyer, Ann and Colin Hunt, Mark Barker, R L Borthwick, M and J White*

SNAPE
Golden Key
TM4058 Map 5

Priory Lane; IP17 1SA

Traditionally furnished village pub with Adnams beers and changing bar food

Just a few minutes' walk from the Maltings, this 16th-c pub is friendly and well run. The traditional low-beamed lounge bar has an old-fashioned settle curving around a couple of venerable stripped tables on a chequerboard tiled floor, a winter open fire and a mix of pubby tables and chairs; there's also a small snug. The two dining rooms have open fireplaces, settles and scrubbed pine tables. Adnams Bitter, Broadside and Ghost Ship on handpump, around a dozen wines by the glass and local cider. Outside are two terraces (one good for early in the morning, the other an evening suntrap) – both with pretty hanging baskets and seats under large parasols. There are plenty of surrounding walks and the inn makes a good base for exploring the area.

Good food includes lunchtime sandwiches, chicken liver pâté with home-made chutney, smoked haddock and smoked cheese gratin, vegetable hotpot with goats cheese and sage crumble topping, sausages with creamed leeks and ale gravy, lamb curry with tomato and coriander salad, free-range chicken and ham pie, line-caught cod with chips, and puddings such as rhubarb crème brûlée and baked vanilla cheesecake. *Benchmark main dish: steak and kidney pudding £11.00. Two-course evening meal £17.50.*

Adnams ~ Tenant Inga Haselmann ~ Real ale ~ (01728) 688510 ~ Open 12-3, 6-11 ~ Bar food 12-2.45, 6-9 ~ Restaurant ~ Children welcome ~ Dogs welcome ~ Bedrooms: /£75 ~ www.goldenkeysnape.co.uk *Recommended by Hazel Morgan, Bernard Patrick, Simon Rodway, Anthony Barnes*

SOUTH ELMHAM
St Peters Hall
TM3385 Map 5

St Peter South Elmham; off B1062 SW of Bungay; NR35 1NQ

Lovely manor dating from the 13th c with some fine original features, own-brew beers and popular food

Dating from the late 13th c, this fine manor house was much extended in 1539 using materials from the then recently dissolved Flixton Priory. It's simply but beautifully decorated, with antique tapestries and furnishings that are completely in keeping with the building. In addition to the bar, there's a particularly dramatic high-ceilinged dining hall with elaborate woodwork, a big flagstoned floor, an imposing chandelier, and candles and fresh flowers on crisp white-clothed dining tables with smart dining chairs. A couple of appealing old rooms are reached up steepish stairs. The brewery buildings are laid out around a courtyard and the beers are made using water from a 100-metre bore hole. Over 90% of their real ale is bottled (available to buy in the shop), the remainder being used for cask beer which they keep on one (in high season, two) handpumps. Regularly changing, these might be St Peters Best Bitter, Organic Best Bitter, Ruby Red, Suffolk Gold and Mild. Also, Aspall's cider and good wines by the glass. Outside, tables overlook the original moat.

Using fresh local produce, the tasty food includes pork and cider terrine with beetroot relish, hot smoked salmon and crayfish tails with horseradish dressing, sausages with wholegrain mustard mash, goats cheese, red onion and thyme tart, beer-battered plaice or haddock with minted mushy peas, burger topped with cheddar, bacon and tomato relish, slow-braised lamb shank with puy lentils, bacon and red wine gravy, and puddings such as stem ginger crème brûlée and rum and banana bread and butter pudding with custard. *Benchmark main dish: smoked haddock with wholegrain mustard sauce £13.00. Two-course evening meal £16.00.*

Own brew ~ Licensee Colin Candy ~ Real ale ~ (01986) 782288 ~ Open 11-4(3 Thurs), 6-11; 11-11 Fri, Sat; 12-4 Sun; closed Mon, evenings Sun, Tues, Weds ~ Bar food 12-2.30, 6-9; see opening hours ~ Restaurant ~ Children welcome ~ Dogs allowed in bar ~ www.stpetershall.co.uk *Recommended by Isobel Mackinlay, Martin Jones*

SOUTHWOLD
Crown 🏵 ♈ 🍺 🛏
High Street; IP18 6DP

TM5076   Map 5

Suffolk Dining Pub of the Year

Comfortable hotel with relaxed bars, a fine choice of drinks, excellent imaginative food, papers to read and seats outside; lovely bedrooms

Whether you want a morning coffee, a pint and a chat, some excellent food or a relaxing and comfortable overnight stay, this smart and civilised hotel ticks all the boxes. It's a friendly place with courteous, welcoming staff and, although there are plenty of seating areas, our readers are very fond of the cosy, oak-panelled back locals' bar (reserved for drinkers and where dogs are allowed), which has a proper pubby atmosphere, red leatherette wall benches on red carpeting, Adnams Bitter, Broadside, Ghost Ship and Kristal White on handpump, 20 wines by the glass from a splendid list, over 20 malt whiskies and several hand-crafted spirits. The elegant beamed front bar has a relaxed, informal atmosphere, a stripped curved high-backed settle and other dark varnished settles, kitchen and other chairs, and a carefully restored, rather fine carved wooden fireplace; maybe newspapers to read. The tables out in a sunny sheltered corner are very pleasant.

Accomplished and highly enjoyable, the food might include sandwiches, duck and parma ham roulade with sautéed duck livers, ginger-spiced cookies and raisin chutney, cured pork fillet with pea purée, chips and fried quail egg, spiced lamb burger with feta, apricot and red onion chutney, tzatziki and chips, chicken breast with confit leg, goats cheese, beetroot and watercress, fillet of bass with chorizo, spinach, capers, almonds, saffron and red pepper purée, and puddings such as molten chocolate pudding with white chocolate ripple ice-cream and iced lime parfait with passion-fruit curd, coconut ice and sorbet. *Benchmark main dish: sirloin steak with rustic chips and peppercorn sauce £19.95. Two-course evening meal £22.50.*

Adnams ~ Manager Lukasz Juszczak ~ Real ale ~ (01502) 722275 ~ Open 8am-11pm(10.30 Sun) ~ Bar food 12-2(2.30 Sat), 6.30(6 Sat and in summer)-9 ~ Children welcome ~ Dogs allowed in bar ~ Bedrooms: £140/£185 ~ www.adnams.co.uk/stay-with-us/the-crown *Recommended by Martin and Pauline Jennings, Andrew and Ruth Triggs, N R White, Stephen Funnell, Sheila Topham, Roger and Lesloy Everett, Pat and Tony Martin, Derek Thomas, George Atkinson, Colin McLachlan, W K Wood, David Carr, Roger Fox, M and GR*

 SOUTHWOLD TM4975 Map 5

Harbour Inn ♀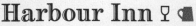

Blackshore, by the boats; from A1095, turn right at the Kings Head, and keep on past the golf course and water tower; IP18 6TA

Great spot down by the boats, lots of outside tables – interesting inside too; popular food with emphasis on local seafood

As popular locally as it is with visitors, this old fisherman's pub is in a fine spot overlooking the boats on the Blyth estuary; picnic-sets on the front terrace, by a big cannon, make the most of this view and there are more seats and tables out behind looking over the marshy commons to the town. The back bar is nicely nautical, with dark panelling and built-in wall seats around scrubbed tables, a low ceiling draped with ensigns, signal flags, pennants and a string of ancient dried fish, plus a quaint old stove, rope fancywork, a plethora of local fishing photographs and even portholes with water bubbling behind them. Cheerful staff serve a good choice of wines by the glass, along with Adnams Bitter, Broadside, Ghost Ship and Old Ale on handpump. They have their own weather station for walkers and sailors. The lower front bar, also panelled and with a tile floor, is broadly similar, while the large, elevated dining room has panoramic views of the harbour, lighthouse, brewery and churches beyond the marshes. A couple of readers have suggested walking from here along the estuary to Walberswick (where the Bell is under the same good management as this pub) via a footbridge and returning by the one-man ferry.

As well as fresh fish dishes such as clam, king prawn and smoked haddock chowder, butterflied mackerel fillet, chorizo and rocket burger, mussels in cider, cream and bacon with chips and skate wing with caper and almond butter, the highly thought-of food includes little plates of potted shrimps, flaked smoked haddock in cheese sauce and herring milts plus sandwiches, vegetable lasagne, steak, Guinness and mushroom pudding with onion gravy, moroccan-style lamb curry, and puddings such as toffee-baked cheesecake and lemon tart with raspberry coulis. *Benchmark main dish: battered plaice, haddock or rock eel with minted peas and chips £10.00. Two-course evening meal £15.50.*

Adnams ~ Tenant Nick Attfield ~ Real ale ~ (01502) 722381 ~ Open 11-11 ~ Bar food 12-9 ~ Children welcome away from top bar ~ Dogs allowed in bar ~ Regular folk evenings ~ www.harbourinnsouthwold.co.uk *Recommended by Martin and Pauline Jennings, Simon Rodway, Ann and Colin Hunt, N R White, Rita Scarratt*

 SOUTHWOLD TM5076 Map 5

Lord Nelson ◪ £

East Street, off High Street (A1095); IP18 6EJ

Bow-windowed town pub with long-serving owners, well liked pubby food and a good choice of drinks; seats outside

Always packed out with a cheerful crowd of customers (often with their dogs), this is a well run pub with efficient, friendly staff. The partly panelled traditional bar and its two small side rooms are kept spotless, with good lighting, a small but extremely hot coal fire, light wood furniture on a tiled floor, lamps in nice nooks and corners and some interesting Nelson memorabilia including attractive nautical prints and a fine model of HMS *Victory*. They serve the whole range of Adnams beers alongside Aspall's cider and several good wines by the glass; board games. There are seats out in front with a sidelong view to the sea and more in a sheltered and heated back garden, with the Adnams brewery visible (and often the appetising fragrance of brewing in progress). Disabled access is not perfect, but is possible.

Very fairly priced, the traditional food includes sandwiches, cod fishcakes with lemon and herb crust and sun-dried tomato mayonnaise, chicken liver pâté with redcurrant jam, greek salad, rump burger with bacon, cheese and chips, chicken or vegetable thai green curry, chilli con carne, and puddings. *Benchmark main dish: beer-battered fish and chips £9.95. Two-course evening meal £14.50.*

Adnams ~ Tenants David and Gemma Sanchez ~ Real ale ~ (01502) 722079 ~ Open 10.30am-11pm; 12-10.30 Sun ~ Bar food 12-2, 7-9 ~ Children welcome in snug and family room ~ Dogs welcome ~ www.thelordnelsonsouthwold.co.uk *Recommended by the Didler, Giles and Annie Francis, Sheila Topham, Lloyd Johnson, Pat and Tony Martin, Howard and Margaret Buchanan, R J Herd, Conrad Freezer, David Carr, C A Bryson, Richard Symonds, Barry Collett, Roger and Anne Newbury, Rita Scarratt*

STOKE-BY-NAYLAND
TL9836   Map 5

Crown ★ ⑪ ♀ ⇌
Park Street (B1068); CO6 4SE

Smart dining pub with attractive modern furnishings, imaginative food using local produce, real ales and a great wine choice; good bedrooms

After a walk around the pretty village, head to this civilised and chatty place for a drink or a meal. Readers enjoy their visits very much and the place is very popular, so it's worth booking a table in advance. The extensive open-plan dining bar is well laid out to give several distinct-feeling areas: a sofa and easy chairs on flagstones near the serving counter, a couple of armchairs under heavy beams by a big woodburning stove, one sizeable table tucked nicely into a three-sided built-in seat, a lower side room with more beams and cheerful floral wallpaper. Tables are mostly stripped veterans, with high-backed dining chairs, but there are more modern chunky pine tables at the back; contemporary artworks (most for sale) and daily papers. Friendly informally dressed staff bustle happily about, and they have Aspall's cider as well as Adnams Bitter, Crouch Vale Brewers Gold, Woodfordes Wherry and a guest beer on handpump. Wine is a big plus, with more than three dozen by the glass and hundreds more from the glass-walled 'cellar shop' – where you can buy to take away too. Disabled access is good. The sheltered flagstoned back terrace has comfortable teak furniture, heaters, big terracotta-coloured parasols and a peaceful view over lightly wooded rolling countryside. Beyond is the very well equipped separate bedroom block (breakfasts are first class).

Using the best local produce, the attractively presented, high quality food includes potted crab with rustic toast, ham hock terrine with pink peppercorns and plum chutney, chicken caesar salad, moules frites, ricotta gnocchi with lemon and thyme cream, chicken kiev with wild garlic butter, confit duck leg cassoulet with chorizo, pancetta and haricot beans, lamb with crushed jersey royals and salsa verde, mixed grill, and puddings such as nectarine melba with nectarine and cinnamon ice-cream and chocolate tart with kumquat and marmalade ice-cream. *Benchmark main dish: beer-battered haddock and chips £12.95. Two-course evening meal £20.00.*

Free house ~ Licensee Richard Sunderland ~ Real ale ~ (01206) 262001 ~ Open 11-11; 12-10.30 Sun ~ Bar food 12-2.30, 6-9.30(10 Fri, Sat); all day Sun ~ Children welcome ~ Dogs allowed in bar ~ Bedrooms: £120/£155 ~ www.crowninn.net *Recommended by Bruce and Sharon Eden, Donna Jenkins, Anthony Barnes, J F M and M West, N R White, Mrs Carolyn Dixon, Gerry and Rosemary Dobson*

THORPENESS   TM4759   Map 5

Dolphin

Just off B1353; Old Homes Road; village signposted from Aldeburgh; IP16 4FE

Neatly kept, extended pub in an interesting village, popular food, local ales and plenty of outside seating; bedrooms

This neatly kept pub is at the heart of a quaint seaside holiday village (purpose-built in the early 1900s). The main bar is a light room with a scandinavian feel: well spaced, pale wooden tables and an attractive assortment of old chairs on broad modern quarry tiles, a built-in cushioned seat in a sizeable bay window, a warming log fire and Adnams Bitter, Broadside and Ghost Ship, Woodfordes Wherry and a guest beer on handpump, quite a few wines by the glass and a good choice of whiskies and bourbons; TV, background music and board games. The public bar to the left of the door is more traditional, with pubby furniture on a stripped wooden floor, built-in cushioned wall seats with open 'windows' to the bar and fine old photographs of long-ago sporting teams, villagers and local scenes on bottle-green planked walls; there's also a small area with a few high bar stools. The airy dining room has wide strips of coir matting on light wooden flooring, country kitchen-style tables and chairs and seaside prints. French windows open on to a terrace with teak furniture; beyond are picnic-sets on an extensive stretch of grass. You can hire electric bikes.

Good bar food includes sandwiches, grilled whole sardines with capers and cherry tomatoes, chicken liver pâté with red onion chutney, mussels with smoked bacon, thyme, garlic and cider, wild mushroom and parmesan risotto, chicken breast with sweet potato mash, lamb shank with red cabbage and parsnip mash, and puddings such as warm chocolate brownie with chocolate sauce and apple and rhubarb crumble with custard. *Benchmark main dish: grilled local cod with chips £11.50. Two-course evening meal £19.00.*

Free house ~ Licensee David James ~ Real ale ~ (01728) 454994 ~ Open 11-3, 6-11 (11-11 July/Aug); 11-11 Sat; 11-10.30 Sun; Jan/Feb closed Sun evening, Mon ~ Bar food 12-2(2.30 Sun), 7-9 ~ Restaurant ~ Children welcome ~ Dogs allowed in bar and bedrooms ~ Bedrooms: £65/£95 ~ www.thorpenessdolphin.com *Recommended by Simon Rodway, Mrs Margo Finlay, Jörg Kasprowski, George Atkinson, Mike and Linda Hudson, Anthony Barnes, J F M and M West*

WALBERSWICK   TM4974   Map 5

Bell

Just off B1387; IP18 6TN

Interesting and thriving 16th-c inn with good food and drinks choice, friendly atmosphere and nice garden; cosy bedrooms

Readers enjoy staying in the attractively decorated bedrooms here – some with sea or harbour views – and the freshly cooked breakfasts are good. The charming rambling bar has antique curved settles, cushioned pews, window seats, scrubbed tables and two huge fireplaces (one with an elderly woodburning stove watched over by a pair of staffordshire china dogs); fine old flooring ranges from sagging ancient bricks through broad boards or flagstones to black and red tiles. Friendly staff serve a good choice of wines by the glass, and Adnams Bitter, Broadside, Ghost Ship, Sole Star and Spindrift on handpump; background music. Don't miss the classic *New Yorker* wine cartoons in the lavatories. The Barn Café is open during school holidays for light snacks, cakes, teas and so forth. A big neatly planted sheltered garden behind has blue picnic-sets and solid old teak furniture, with a view over the dunes to the sea; the rowing-boat ferry to Southwold is nearby (there's a footbridge a bit further away). Sister pub is the Harbour Inn in Southwold.

🍴 Impressive food using local fish and free-range meat might include sandwiches, shredded sticky pork belly with apples and raisins, home-cured gravadlax with dill crème fraîche, lemon and garlic-marinated halloumi with pea and herb couscous, sausages braised in cider with bacon, apples and juniper, garlic and parmesan chicken schnitzel with minted pea purée, tagliatelle with hot smoked salmon, capers and chives in creamy white wine sauce, confit duck leg on flageolet beans with smoked bacon, garlic and thyme, and puddings such as baked alaska with pistachio ice-cream and espresso crème brûlée. *Benchmark main dish: battered fresh cod with minted peas and chips £12.00. Two-course evening meal £19.00.*

Adnams ~ Tenant Nick Attfield ~ Real ale ~ (01502) 723109 ~ Open 11-11 ~ Bar food 12-2.30, 6-9 ~ Children welcome away from bar ~ Dogs allowed in bar and bedrooms ~ Bedrooms: £90/£100 ~ www.bellinnwalberswick.co.uk *Recommended by Andrew and Ruth Triggs, Lois Dyer, Conrad Freezer, R L Borthwick*

WALDRINGFIELD
Maybush £

TM2844   Map 5

Off A12 S of Martlesham; The Quay, Cliff Road; IP12 4QL

Busy pub with tables outside by the riverbank; nautical décor, a fair choice of drinks and traditional good value bar food

The many seats and tables outside this busy family pub make the most of the lovely view over the River Deben; alternatively, if you arrive early enough, you might bag a window table inside. The spacious knocked-through bar is divided into separate areas by fireplaces or steps. There's a nautical theme, with an elaborate ship's model in a glass case and a few more in a light, high-ceilinged extension – as well as lots of old lanterns, pistols and aerial photographs; background music and board games. Adnams Bitter, Ghost Ship and a changing guest on handpump and a fair choice of wines by the glass. River cruises are available nearby but you have to pre-book; the area is a haven for bird-watchers and ramblers.

🍴 Fair value and popular, the traditional food might include sandwiches, breaded garlic mushrooms with garlic mayonnaise, prawn and crayfish cocktail, meat or vegetarian lasagne, barbecue chicken with cheddar and bacon, gammon and egg, lamb shank with redcurrant gravy, and puddings such as chocolate brownies and bread and butter pudding with custard. *Benchmark main dish: fresh cod and chips £10.95. Two-course evening meal £17.00.*

Adnams ~ Lease Steve and Louise Lomas ~ Real ale ~ (01473) 736215 ~ Open 9am-11pm ~ Bar food 9am-9.30pm ~ Restaurant ~ Children welcome ~ Dogs allowed in bar ~ www.debeninns.co.uk/maybush *Recommended by Charles and Pauline Stride, Colin and Louise English*

WESTLETON
Crown 🍽 🍷 🛏
B1125 Blythburgh–Leiston; IP17 3AD

TM4469   Map 5

Bustling old inn with a cosy chatty bar, plenty of dining areas, carefully chosen drinks and interesting food; comfortable modern bedrooms

A t the heart of this comfortably stylish old coaching inn is an attractive little bar with a lovely log fire and plenty of original features. Locals drop in here for a pint and a chat, which keeps the atmosphere informal and relaxed, and they serve Adnams Bitter, Brandon Rusty Bucket and Nethergate Hogwash on handpump and a thoughtfully chosen wine list; background music and board games. There's also a parlour, a dining room and conservatory, all manner of wooden dining chairs and tables, and old photographs on some fine old bare-brick walls. The charming terraced garden has plenty of seats and the spotless, comfortable bedrooms are either in the main inn itself (some up steep stairs) or in converted stables and cottages.

🍴 Imaginative and well presented, the food includes sandwiches, terrine of minced pork, smoked bacon and toulouse sausage with sweetcorn and red pepper chutney and boiled quail eggs, escabeche of red mullet with tapenade croûte and tarragon and tomato oil, goats cheese, mixed pepper and pesto spring roll with tomato, olive, shallot and artichoke salad, beer-battered fish and chips, slow-braised duck leg with pearl barley, smoked bacon and vegetable broth, daily specials like bass with cockle, lobster and dill risotto with crispy leeks, and puddings such as steamed syrup sponge with vanilla custard and chocolate and salted caramel tart with pistachio cream and yoghurt sauce. *Benchmark main dish: beef and mushroom pudding with chive mash £13.95. Two-course evening meal £21.50.*

Free house ~ Licensee Gareth Clarke ~ Real ale ~ (01728) 648777 ~ Open 11-11; 12-10.30 Sun ~ Bar food 12-2.30, 6.30-9.30 ~ Restaurant ~ Children welcome ~ Dogs allowed in bar and bedrooms ~ Bedrooms: £90/£120 ~ www.westletoncrown.co.uk *Recommended by Andrew and Ruth Triggs, Mr and Mrs A Curry, Paul Humphreys, Derek and Sylvia Stephenson, R L Borthwick, Richard Seal*

WHEPSTEAD
White Horse 🍽 🍷
Off B1066 S of Bury; Rede Road; IP29 4SS

TL8258   Map 5

Charmingly reworked country pub with attractively furnished rooms and well liked food and drink

O ne reader describes this well run place as 'restaurant in style but staying nicely on the pub side' – we thought this rather apt. There's plenty of space for a drink or a meal in the several Victorian additions to what was originally a 17th-c building. The dark-beamed bar has a woodburning stove in a low fireplace, little stools around pubby tables on a tiled floor, and wallboards listing the menu. Linked rooms have sturdy, country kitchen tables and chairs on striped carpeting or antique floor tiles, with some attractively cushioned traditional wall seats and rather fine old farmhouse chairs. Oil paintings of food by a local artist (for sale) and old prints decorate walls painted in Farrow & Ball burnt orange; the bookshelves have books that are actually worth reading. Adnams Bitter and Broadside or Ghost Ship on handpump and eight wines by the glass, served by attentive, friendly staff. A tuck shop sells sweets, chocolates and ice-creams; the resident westie is called Skye. A neat sheltered back terrace is brightened by colourful oilcloth tablecloths, and at the picnic-sets on the grass, birdsong emphasises what a peaceful spot this is.

Interesting and very good, the food includes venison and cranberry terrine, flash-fried squid with ginger and toasted pine nuts, steak burger with local cheese, chilli jam and chips, tagliatelle with blue cheese, spinach and herb pesto, salt beef casserole with chunky vegetables, duck breast with marmalade gravy, halibut with tomato and red pepper purée and saffron potatoes, and puddings such as date and walnut tart with sauce anglaise and chilled rice pudding brûlée with fruit compote. *Benchmark main dish: smoked haddock florentine £12.95. Two-course evening meal £19.00.*

Free house ~ Licensees Gary and Di Kingshott ~ Real ale ~ (01284) 735760 ~ Open 11-3, 7-11; 12-2 Sun ~ Bar food 12-2, 7-9.30 ~ Children welcome ~ Dogs allowed in bar ~ www.whitehorsewhepstead.co.uk *Recommended by Jane and Alan Bush, J F M and M West, George Atkinson, Lucien Perring*

Also Worth a Visit in Suffolk

Besides the fully inspected pubs, you might like to try these pubs that have been recommended to us and described by readers. Do tell us what you think of them: feedback@goodguides.com

ALDRINGHAM TM4461
Parrot & Punchbowl
(01728) 830221 *B1122/B1353 S
of Leiston; IP16 4PY* Attractive and
welcoming beamed country pub with good
fairly priced standard food (not Sun evening),
well kept Greene King and Woodfordes, two-
level restaurant; nice sheltered garden, also
family garden with adventure play area.
(George Atkinson)

BADINGHAM TM3068
White Horse (01728) 638280
A1120 S of village; IP13 8JR Welcoming
and relaxed 16th-c low-beamed pub,
enjoyable reasonably priced traditional
food including vegetarian options, three
well kept Adnams beers, longcase clock by
big fireplace with woodburner, two other
fires; occasional live bands in public bar;
children and dogs welcome, neat bowling
green and nice rambling garden, closed
Sun evening, Tues and winter weekday
lunchtimes. *(Anon)*

BARHAM TM1251
Sorrel Horse (01473) 830327
Old Norwich Road; IP6 0PG Friendly
open-plan country inn with good log fire
in central chimneybreast, dark beams and
timbers, well kept real ales and popular
food; children and dogs welcome, disabled
facilities, picnic-sets on side grass with big

play area, bedrooms in converted barn, open
all day Weds-Sun. *(Anon)*

BILDESTON TL9949
Crown (01449) 740510
B1115 SW of Stowmarket; IP7 7EB
Good upmarket food (not cheap) in this
picturesque and impressively refurbished
15th-c timbered country inn, smart beamed
main bar with leather armchairs and
inglenook log fire, more intimate back area
with contemporary art, ales such as Greene
King and Mauldons, good choice of wines by
the glass, dining room; children welcome,
disabled access and parking, tables laid for
dining in attractive central courtyard, more
in large beautifully kept garden with decking,
quiet comfortable bedrooms. *(Mrs Margo
Finlay, Jörg Kasprowski)*

BILDESTON TL9949
Kings Head (01449) 741434
High Street; IP7 7ED Small beamed
16th-c village pub brewing its own good
beers (brewery tours), also a local small
brewery guest, well priced home-made food
(Fri evening, Sat, Sun lunchtime), pleasant
chatty staff, wood floor bar with inglenook
woodburner, darts; children welcome, back
garden with terrace and play equipment,
open all day weekends, closed Mon, Tues,
lunchtimes Weds-Fri. *(Jeremy King,
Iain Lister)*

BLAXHALL   TM3656
Ship (01728) 688316
Off B1069 S of Snape; can be reached
from A12 via Little Glemham; IP12 2DY
Attractive country setting for this popular
and friendly low-beamed 18th-c pub;
good traditional home-made food in bar
and restaurant, well kept Adnams Bitter,
Woodfordes Wherry and guests, some live
music including folk; children in eating
areas, dogs in bar, eight chalet bedrooms
and good breakfast, open all day weekends.
(Mike Proctor, R J Herd)

BLYFORD   TM4276
Queens Head (01502) 478404
B1123 Blythburgh–Halesworth; IP19 9JY
Attractive and popular 15th-c thatched pub,
good food, well kept Adnams ales and cheery
staff, very low beams, some antique settles,
huge fireplace; tables outside. *(John Lunniss,*
R L Borthwick)

BRENT ELEIGH   TL9348
★**Cock** (01787) 247371
A1141 SE of Lavenham; CO10 9PB
Timeless and friendly thatched country pub,
Adnams, Greene King Abbot and a guest,
organic farm cider, enjoyable traditional food
cooked by landlady, cosy ochre-walled snug
and second small room, antique floor tiles,
lovely coal fire, old photographs of village
(church well worth a look), darts, shove-
ha'penny and toad in the hole; well behaved
children and dogs welcome, picnic-sets up
on side grass with summer hatch service, one
bedroom, open all day Fri-Sun. *(the Didler)*

BROCKLEY GREEN   TL7247
★**Plough** (01440) 786789
Hundon Road; CO10 8DT Friendly, neatly
kept knocked-through bar, beams, timbers
and stripped brick, scrubbed tables and open
fire, good food from lunchtime sandwiches to
some enterprising dishes and nice puddings,
Tues steak night, cheerful efficient staff,
Greene King IPA, Woodfordes Wherry and
a guest, good choice of wines by the glass
and malt whiskies, restaurant; children
and dogs welcome, extensive attractive
grounds, peaceful country views, comfortable
bedrooms. *(Adele Summers, Alan Black,*
G M Hollington, Robert Turnham)

BROMESWELL   TM3050
British Larder (01394) 460310
Orford Road, Bromeswell Heath;
IP12 2PU Neat beamed restauranty pub
with good if not cheap food from chef-
licensees using local seasonal produce,
well kept ales such as Woodfordes Wherry
and nice wines by the glass in separate
bar, pleasant service, home-made jams etc
for sale (they've also written a cookbook);
children welcome, plenty of tables outside,
big play area, open all day weekends.
(J F M and M West)

BUNGAY   TM3389
Castle (01986) 892283
Earsham Street; NR35 1AF Pleasantly
informal 16th-c dining inn with good
interesting food from chef-owner;
opened-up beamed interior with restaurant
part at front, two open fires, friendly
efficient staff, Earl Soham Victoria Bitter
and a guest like Cliff Quay Sea Dog, Aspall's
cider, nice choice of wines by the glass,
afternoon teas, french windows to pretty
courtyard garden, live acoustic music every
other Sun; children welcome, dogs in bar
area, four comfortable bedrooms, open all
day in summer. *(Anon)*

BURY ST EDMUNDS   TL8463
Dove (01284) 702787
Hospital Road; IP33 3JU 19th-c alehouse
with rustic bare-boards bar and separate
parlour, half a dozen well kept mostly local
beers, quiz, folk and comedy nights, no food;
closed weekday lunchtimes. *(Anon)*

BURY ST EDMUNDS   TL8564
Fox (01284) 705562
Eastgate Street; IP33 1XX Attractive
ancient beamed pub with informal bustling
atmosphere, enjoyable locally sourced food
from good sandwiches up, well kept Greene
King ales, plenty of wines by the glass,
cocktails, efficient friendly staff, Sun evening
jazz; bedrooms in converted barn behind,
open all day from 7am (breakfast for non-
residents). *(John Saville)*

BURY ST EDMUNDS   TL8564
★**Nutshell** (01284) 764867
The Traverse, central pedestrian link
off Abbeygate Street; IP33 1BJ Tiny
simple local with timeless interior (can be
a crush at busy times), lots of interest such
as a mummified cat (found walled up here)
hanging from dark brown ceiling along with
companion rat, bits of a skeleton, vintage
bank notes, cigarette packets, military and
other badges, spears and a great metal
halberd, one short wooden bench along
shopfront corner windows, a cut-down
sewing-machine table and an elbow rest
running along a rather battered country,
Greene King ales, no food; background
music, steep narrow stairs up to lavatories;
children (till 7pm) and dogs welcome, open
all day. *(the Didler)*

BURY ST EDMUNDS   TL8563
★**Rose & Crown** (01284) 755934
Whiting Street; IP33 1NP Cheerful
black-beamed corner local with long-serving
affable licensees, bargain simple lunchtime
home cooking (not Sun), particularly well
kept Greene King ales (including XX Mild)
and guests, pleasant lounge with lots of
piggy pictures and bric-a-brac, good games-
oriented public bar, rare separate off-sales
counter; piped radio, no credit cards or

under-14s; pretty back courtyard, open all day weekdays. *(Anon)*

BUXHALL   TM9957
Crown (01449) 736521

Off B1115 W of Stowmarket; Mill Road; IP14 3DW Cosy and welcoming low-beamed bar with inglenook woodburner, well kept Greene King ales and nice choice of wines by the glass, good well presented food (not especially cheap), airy dining room; children and dogs welcome, plenty of tables on terrace with views over open country (ignore the pylons), herb garden, closed Sun evening, Mon. *(J F M and M West)*

CAVENDISH   TL8046
Bull (01787) 280245

A1092 Long Melford–Clare; CO10 8AX Spotless old inn with heavy beams, timbers and fine fireplaces, Adnams ales and good choice of food, reasonable prices, attentive friendly service; children in eating areas, garden tables, car park (useful in this honeypot village), bedrooms, closed Sun evening, Mon, Tues. *(Marianne and Peter Stevens, N R White)*

CAVENDISH   TL8046
✶ George (01787) 280248

A1092; The Green; CO10 8BA 16th-c dining inn with contemporary feel in two bow-windowed front areas, beams and timbers, big woodburner in stripped-brick fireplace, good food from interesting varied menu including set deals, Nethergate ales and plenty of wines by the glass, back servery and further eating area, friendly helpful staff, daily newspapers; children welcome, stylish furniture on sheltered back terrace, tree-shaded garden with lovely village church behind, five good bedrooms up rather steep staircase, open all day except Sun evening. *(P Waterman, Sadie Clayton, Marianne and Peter Stevens)*

CHELSWORTH   TL9848
Peacock (01449) 740758

B1115 Sudbury–Needham Market; IP7 7HU Attractive and prettily set old dining pub with lots of Tudor brickwork and exposed beams, separate pubby bar with big inglenook log fire, real ales and fairly standard food, friendly service; attractive small garden and village. *(Christopher Sewell, Mrs Carolyn Dixon)*

CHILLESFORD   TM3852
✶ Froize (01394) 450282

B1084 E of Woodbridge; IP12 3PU Restaurant rather than pub (open only when they serve food, so not Mon or evenings Sun–Weds), pleasant bar and restaurant, reliably good if not cheap buffet-style food from chef-owner using carefully sourced local produce including game, nice wines by the glass and well kept Adnams, warmly welcoming service, little deli next to bar; no dogs inside. *(Mike and Linda Hudson)*

DENNINGTON   TM2867
✶ Queens Head (01728) 638241

A1120; The Square; IP13 8AB Well refurbished beamed and timbered Tudor pub prettily placed by church, L-shaped main bar, Adnams and maybe a guest, local cider, enjoyable food (best to book weekends) including some unusual choices, friendly service; background music; children in family room, side lawn by noble lime trees, pond at back with ducks and carp, backs on to Dennington Park with swings etc. *(R and M Tait)*

EASTON   TM2858
✶ White Horse (01728) 746456

N of Wickham Market on back road to Earl Soham and Framlingham; IP13 0ED Pretty 16th-c pub with newish landlord and some refurbishment; three smartly simple rooms, country kitchen chairs, good small settles, cushioned stripped pews and stools, open fires, Adnams and two local guests, ten wines by the glass, good choice of bar food using local produce, restaurant; background music; children and dogs welcome, seats out at front and in back garden, good local walks, open (and food) all day weekends. *(Charles and Pauline Stride, Ann and Colin Hunt, Hayley Roche, Anthony Barnes)*

FELIXSTOWE FERRY   TM3237
Ferry Boat (01394) 284203

Off Ferry Road, on the green; IP11 9RZ Much modernised 17th-c pub tucked between golf links and dunes near harbour, martello tower and summer rowing-boat ferry; enjoyable fair value pub food including good fish and chips, friendly efficient service, well kept Adnams, decent coffee, warm log fire; background music, busy on summer weekends, they may ask to keep a credit card while you eat; dogs welcome, tables out in front, on green opposite and in fenced garden, good coast walks. *(Ryta Lyndley, N R White)*

FORWARD GREEN   TM0959
✶ Shepherd & Dog (01449) 711361

A1120 E of Stowmarket; IP14 5HN Smart dining pub with attractive pastel décor, comfortable dining tables and some sofas, good interesting food (not particularly cheap) in contemporary bar and restaurant including upmarket burgers from local wagyu herd (must order these in advance), well kept Greene King IPA and Fullers London Pride, good wines by the glass and coffee, helpful pleasant young staff; disabled access, terrace tables, closed Sun evening, Mon. *(J F M and M West, R A P Cross)*

FRAMLINGHAM   TM2863
Crown (01728) 723521

Market Hill; IP13 9AP Stylishly refurbished 16th-c beamed coaching inn doing well under new management; good food and service, Greene King and guest ales, several wines by the glass, open fires; background and occasional live acoustic music; children and dogs welcome, tables in back courtyard, 14 bedrooms, open all day. *(David and Sue Atkinson)*

FRAMLINGHAM TM2862
Station Hotel (01728) 723455
Station Road (B1116 S); IP13 9EE
Simple high-ceilinged big-windowed bar with scrubbed tables on stripped boards, candles in bottles, well kept Earl Soham ales and good choice of house wines, popular freshly cooked food from interesting menu, friendly staff and relaxed atmosphere, back snug with tiled floor; children and dogs welcome, picnic-sets in pleasant garden. *(J F M and M West)*

FRESSINGFIELD TM2677
★ Fox & Goose (01379) 586247
Church Street; B1116 N of Framlingham; IP21 5PB Relaxed dining pub in beautifully timbered 16th-c building next to church, very good food in cosy informal heavy-beamed rooms with log fire, upstairs restaurant, good wines by the glass, Adnams and a guest tapped from the cask in side bar; faint background music; children welcome, downstairs disabled facilities, tables out by duck pond, closed Mon. *(Lois Dyer, W K Wood)*

GREAT BRICETT TM0450
Red Lion (01473) 657799
B1078, E of Bildeston; IP7 7DD Old extended beamed pub serving really good interesting vegetarian and vegan food at competitive prices (nothing for meat eaters), children's menu and takeaways too; dogs welcome in bar, garden with deck and play equipment, closed Mon. *(Maggie Woolley)*

GREAT WRATTING TL6848
Red Lion (01440) 783237
School Road; CB9 7HA Welcoming, popular country pub with a couple of ancient whale bones flanking the front door; well kept Adnams in log-fire bar, restaurant serving good generous home-made food at closely set tables, some bargain prices and very friendly service; children welcome – huge garden for them to play in, open all day Sat. *(Adele Summers, Alan Black)*

HAUGHLEY TM0262
Kings Arms (01449) 614462
Off A45/B1113 N of Stowmarket; Old Street; IP14 3NT 16th-c extended timbered pub, horsebrasses and other bits and pieces, big brick fireplace, enjoyable fairly traditional pub food cooked to order, well kept Greene King (their Abbot ale was named here by a landlord in 1950), good choice of wines by the glass, busy public bar with pool, darts and trophies above TV; background music, no dogs inside;

children welcome, tables in back garden with play area, nice village, open all day Fri-Sun. *(Jeremy King)*

HAWKEDON TL7953
★ Queens Head (01284) 789218
Off A143 at Wickham Street, NE of Haverhill; and off B1066; IP29 4NN Flint Tudor pub in pretty setting looking down broad peaceful green to interesting largely Norman village church; quarry-tiled bar with dark beams and ochre walls, plenty of pews and chapel chairs around scrubbed tables, elderly armchairs by antique woodburner in huge fireplace, cheerful young landlady, Adnams, Woodfordes and guests, farm cider and perry, nice choice of wines, good popular food using home-reared meat, dining area stretching back with country prints and a couple of tusky boars' heads on the walls, some live music; picnic-sets out in front, more on back terrace overlooking rolling country, little shop (Fri and Sat mornings) selling carefully chosen meats as well as their own bacon, pies, casseroles etc; tables out front and back, closed Mon-Thurs lunchtimes. *(Susan Cook, Lucien Perring)*

HITCHAM TL9851
White Horse (01449) 740981
The Street (B1115 Sudbury–Stowmarket); IP7 7NQ Friendly 16th-c village pub, a former staging post for travellers between London and Norfolk, two bars with ales from Adnams, Brandon, St Peters and Woodfordes, log fire, beams and timbering, dark wooden chairs around clothed tables in restaurant, honest pubby dishes plus more elaborate evening choices, obliging service; children and dogs welcome, nice bedrooms in separate barn conversion. *(Sarah Pawsley)*

HOXNE TM1877
★ Swan (01379) 668275
Low Street; off B1118, signed off A140 S of Diss; IP21 5AS Timber-framed 15th-c building with pubby bar, two solid oak counters, broad oak floorboards and deep-set inglenook, Adnams, Woodfordes and a guest tapped from the cask (beer festivals May and Nov), Aspall's cider and several wines by the glass, good well presented bar food, friendly staff, restaurant; children and dogs welcome, seats under parasols on two sheltered terraces and in attractive spacious garden extending to stream, boules, nearby is tree to which King Edmund was tied at his execution, open all day Sun. *(Ian Herdman, KC, Sheila Topham, Pat and Tony Martin, Martin and Pauline Jennings, Alan Weedon)*

IPSWICH TM1644
Dove Street (01473) 211270
St Helen's Street; IP4 2LA Over 20 well kept quickly changing ales including their own brews (regular beer festivals), farm ciders, bottled beers and good selection of

whiskies, low priced simple home-made food, hot drinks, friendly staff, bare-boards bar, carpeted snug and back conservatory; dogs welcome, children till 7pm, terrace seating, two bedrooms and brewery shop across the road, open all day. *(Anon)*

IPSWICH TM1645
Greyhound (01473) 252862
Henley Road/Anglesea Road; IP1 3SE Popular 19th-c pub close to Christchurch Park; cosy front bar, corridor to larger lounge/dining area, five well kept Adnams ales and a couple of guests, good substantial home cooking including bargain weekday lunch, quick service; sports TV; children welcome, picnic-sets under parasols on back terrace, open all day Fri-Sun (breakfast from 10am Sun). *(the Didler, Giles and Annie Francis)*

KENTFORD TL7066
Cock (01638) 750360
Bury Road, just off A14; CB8 7PR Comfortable and attractive Greene King pub, inglenook log fire and beautiful carved beams, good food (all day but not Sun or Mon evenings) from bar snacks and light set lunch up, friendly service, airy restaurant; neat garden behind, open all day (Sun till 10pm). *(M and GR)*

KESGRAVE TM2346
Kesgrave Hall (01473) 333741
Hall Road; IP5 2PU Country hotel with Greene King ales in comfortably contemporary bare-boards bar, popular imaginative food all day in open-kitchen bistro (no booking so best to arrive early), efficient young staff; children and dogs welcome, attractive heated terrace with huge retractable awning, 23 stylish bedrooms. *(J F M and M West)*

LAVENHAM TL9149
Greyhound (01787) 247475
High Street; CO10 9PZ Traditional and unpretentious 14th-c local under new management; Greene King IPA and Abbot plus a weekend guest, good value generously served pubby food, friendly service, public bar, lounge with woodburner and back snug; background and some live music including Sun afternoon folk; children and dogs welcome, seats in yard behind, open all day. *(Jeremy King)*

LAVENHAM TL9149
Swan (01787) 247477
High Street; CO10 9QA Smart, well equipped and by no means cheap hotel incorporating handsome medieval buildings, well worth a look for its appealing network of beamed and timbered alcoves and more open areas, including peaceful little tiled-floor inner bar with leather chairs and memorabilia of its days as the local for US 48th Bomber Group, well kept Adnams and a guest beer, wide choice of food from good

sandwiches up, efficient young staff, informal eating area as well as lavishly timbered restaurant; children and dogs welcome, sheltered courtyard garden, 45 bedrooms, open all day. *(Mrs Carolyn Dixon)*

LAXFIELD TM2972
★ Kings Head (01986) 798395
Gorams Mill Lane, behind church; IP13 8DW Unspoilt thatched pub with no bar counter – instead, Adnams range and a guest poured in tap room; interesting little chequer-tiled front room dominated by a three-sided booth of high-backed settles in front of old range fire, two other equally unspoilt rooms with pews, old seats and scrubbed deal tables, well liked tasty bar food including good home-made pies served by friendly helpful staff; children and dogs welcome, neatly kept garden with colourful borders, arbour with hops and grapevine, small pavilion for cooler evenings, boules, bedrooms and self-catering apartment, open all day in summer. *(the Didler, Nigel Long, Sheila Topham, Ann and Colin Hunt, Tim Maddison, R and M Tait and others)*

LEVINGTON TM2339
Ship (01473) 659573
Gun Hill; from A14/A12 Bucklesham roundabout, take A1156 exit, then first sharp left into Felixstowe Road, then after nearly a mile turn right into Bridge Road at Levington signpost, bearing left into Church Lane; IP10 0LQ This charming old Adnams pub (a previous Main Entry) shut as we went to press – we're hoping it will have reopened by the time you read this; plenty of nautical trappings and character, settles and built-in wall benches, big black round stove, flagstoned dining room with more nautical bric-a-brac; beside little lime-washed church and has views (if a little obscured) over River Orwell estuary.

LONG MELFORD TL8645
★ Bull (01787) 378494
Hall Street (B1064); CO10 9JG Small 15th-c hotel in good location and full of character; old-fashioned timbered front lounge with beautifully carved beams, antique furnishings, log fire in huge fireplace, more spacious back bar with sporting prints, well kept Greene King ales and a guest, Aspall's cider, decent wines, reasonably priced standard Old English Inns menu, good helpful service from cheerful staff, daily papers, restaurant; children welcome, tables in attractive courtyard, comfortable bedrooms and substantial breakfast, open all day weekends. *(Ian Herdman, Ron and Sheila Corbett)*

LOWESTOFT TM5593
Triangle (01502) 582711
St Peter's Street; NR32 1QA Popular two-bar tap for Green Jack ales, guest beers too and real cider, regular beer festivals,

breweriana, open fire; pool and TV in back bar, live music Fri; open all day (till 1am Fri, Sat). *(Anon)*

MONKS ELEIGH   TL9647
⋆ Swan (01449) 741391
A1141 NW of Hadleigh; IP7 7AU Gently upmarket dining pub but has informal side too; long pleasantly bright bar with high-backed leather-seated dining chairs around light wood tables on pale oak floor, red walls hung with Jack Vettriano prints and cheerful country landscapes, good imaginative food including set lunch menu, efficient helpful service, open fire in small brick fireplace in high-ceilinged end room, fresh flowers on cream-painted wooden-topped bar counter, Adnams and a guest, good choice of wines by the glass; children welcome, village post office in car park, closed Sun evening, Mon and a week in July (best to phone). *(Stephen and Jean Curtis, Ian Wilson, Mrs Carolyn Dixon)*

NAYLAND   TL9734
⋆ Anchor (01206) 262313
Court Street; just off A134 – turn-off S of signposted B1087 main village turn; CO6 4JL Friendly pub by River Stour under same ownership as the Angel at Stoke-by-Nayland; bare-boards bar with assorted wooden dining chairs and tables, big gilt mirror on silvery wallpaper one end, another mirror above pretty fireplace at the other, five changing ales and several wines by the glass, interesting food (some home-smoked) along with more standard dishes, two other rooms behind and steep stairs up to cosy restaurant; children welcome, dogs in bar, terrace tables overlooking river, open all day (no food Sun evening). *(Simon and Mandy King, Brian and Anna Marsden)*

NEWBOURNE   TM2743
⋆ Fox (01473) 736307
Off A12 at roundabout 1.7 miles N of A14 junction; The Street; IP12 4NY Pink-washed 16th-c pub, low-beamed bar with slabby elm and other dark tables on tiled floor, stuffed fox in inglenook, comfortable carpeted dining room with modern artwork and antique mirrors, ales such as Adnams, Brains, Purity and Sharps, decent wines by the glass, good variety of well liked food (all day weekends) including reasonably priced Sun roasts, good service; background music; children welcome, dogs in bar, wheelchair access, attractive grounds with rose garden and pond, open all day. *(George Atkinson)*

ORFORD   TM4249
Crown & Castle (01394) 450205
Castle Terrace; IP12 2LJ Hotel-restaurant rather than pub; good food from pubby standards up (smaller helpings available), evening food more upscale and expensive, compact smartly minimalist bar used largely for pre-meal drinks with well kept

Adnams and wide choice of wines by the glass including champagne; children (no under-8s in the evening) and dogs welcome, tables outside, residents' garden, 19 good bedrooms. *(Edward Mirzoeff, Richard Tilbrook)*

ORFORD   TM4249
⋆ Jolly Sailor (01394) 450243
Quay Street; IP12 2NU Friendly pub liked by walkers and bird-watchers and built mainly from wrecked ships' timbers, several snug rooms with lots of exposed brickwork, boating pictures and shipping charts celebrating the river, four Adnams beers served from counters and hatches in old-fashioned central cubicle, popular food from doorstep sandwiches up, unusual spiral staircase in corner of flagstoned main bar with horsebrasses, local photographs, two cushioned pews and long antique stripped deal table, woodburner in big brick fireplace; picnic-sets on back grass with views over marshes, play tower, can camp in the orchard. *(M P Mackenzie, Stephen Funnell, Charles and Pauline Stride, George Atkinson)*

ORFORD   TM4249
Kings Head (01394) 450271
Front Street; IP12 2LW This likeable old pub (a popular Main Entry) was closed and in the process of being taken over as we went to press – news please.

REDE   TL8055
⋆ Plough (01284) 789208
Village signposted off A143 Bury St Edmunds–Haverhill; IP29 4BE Pretty thatched pub in tucked-away village, traditional low-beamed bar with comfortable seating, solid fuel stove in brick fireplace, popular food (not Sun evening) from quickly changing menu, three real ales; children welcome till 8pm, picnic-sets in sheltered cottage garden and in front near village green. *(Mrs Margo Finlay, Jörg Kasprowski)*

RENDHAM   TM3564
White Horse (01728) 663497
B1119 Framlingham–Saxmundham; IP17 2AF Partly divided open-plan pub with good reasonably priced home-made food using local suppliers, ales including Earl Soham and Mauldons, friendly service, two open fires, quiz and folk nights; well behaved dogs welcome, garden tables, lovely spot opposite 14th-c church, good local walks, closed weekday lunchtimes. *(Anon)*

REYDON   TM4977
⋆ Randolph (01502) 723603
Wangford Road (B1126 just NW of Southwold); IP18 6PZ Stylish inn with quite an emphasis on dining and bedroom side; bar with high-backed leather dining chairs around chunky wooden tables on parquet floor, sofa and a couple of comfortable armchairs, prints of pub from 1910 and photographs of Southwold beach,

Adnams beers, dining room with more high-backed chairs on red carpet, pretty little Victorian fireplace filled with candles, nicely varied menu including children's choices, pleasant staff; background music, TV, games machine; dogs welcome in small back bar, wheelchair access, picnic-sets on decked area and grass, ten bedrooms, good breakfast, open all day. *(Anon)*

ROUGHAM   TL9063
⋆ **Ravenwood Hall**   (01359) 270345
Off A14 E of Bury St Edmunds;
IP30 9JA Country-house hotel with two compact bar rooms, tall ceilings, patterned wallpaper and big heavily draped windows overlooking sweeping lawn with stately cedar, back area set for eating with upholstered settles and dining chairs, sporting prints and log fire, very good well presented bar food (own smoked meats and fish), well kept Adnams, good choice of wines and malts, comfortable lounge area with horse pictures, a few moulded beams and early Tudor wall decoration above big inglenook, separate more formal restaurant; background music; children and dogs welcome, teak furniture in garden, swimming pool, croquet, geese and pygmy goats in big enclosures, 14 bedrooms, open 9am-midnight. *(Ryta Lyndley, J F M and M West, R and S Bentley, Mr and Mrs M Walker)*

SHOTTISHAM   TM3244
Sorrel Horse   (01394) 411617
Hollesley Road; IP12 3HD Charming 15th-c thatched community-owned local; ales such as Greene King and Woodfordes Wherry tapped from the cask, decent choice of home-made traditional food including deals, attentive helpful staff, good log fire in tiled-floor bar with games area (bar billiards), woodburner in attractive dining room, fortnightly quiz Weds; children and dogs welcome, tables out on sloping front lawn and in small garden behind, open all day weekends. *(the Didler, Brian and Anna Marsden)*

SNAPE   TM3958
⋆ **Crown**   (01728) 688324
Bridge Road (B1069); IP17 1SL Small, well laid out 15th-c beamed pub with brick floors, inglenook log fire and fine double suffolk settle, well kept Adnams ales, good fresh food using local ingredients including own meat (reared behind the pub), reasonable prices, efficient friendly young staff, folk night last Thurs of month, darts; children and dogs welcome, garden. *(Edward Mirzoeff, Simon Rodway, R J Herd, Conrad Freezer and others)*

SNAPE   TM3957
⋆ **Plough & Sail**   (01728) 688413
The Maltings, Snape Bridge (B1069 S); IP17 1SR Nicely placed dining pub (part of the Maltings complex) airily extended

around original 16th-c core, mostly open-plan with a clever blend of traditional and modern furnishings, Adnams Bitter, Woodfordes Wherry and guests, a dozen wines by the glass including champagne, good bistro-style food (pre- and post-concert menus), spacious dining room and upstairs restaurant; background music; children and dogs (in bar) welcome, teak furniture on flower-filled terrace, picnic-sets at front, open all day. *(George Atkinson)*

SOUTHWOLD   TM5076
⋆ **Red Lion**   (01502) 722385
South Green; IP18 6ET Cheerful pubby front bar with big windows looking over green towards the sea, sturdy wall benches and bentwood bar stools on flagstones, well kept Adnams including seasonals, quieter back room with mate's chairs, cushioned pews and polished dark tables on pale woodstrip flooring, seaside cartoons by Giles, Mac and the like, good range of popular reasonably priced food, friendly neatly dressed staff, three linked dining rooms; maybe nostalgic background music; tables out in front and in small sheltered back courtyard, right by the Adnams retail shop. *(Gwyn and Anne Wake, Ann and Colin Hunt, Ryta Lyndley, Barry Collett)*

SOUTHWOLD   TM5076
Sole Bay   (01502) 723736
East Green; IP18 6JN Busy pub near Adnams Brewery, their full range kept well and good wine choice, cheerful efficient staff, enjoyable reasonably priced simple food (not Sun evening) including good fish and chips, airy interior with well spaced tables, conservatory; sports TV; children and dogs welcome, disabled facilities, picnic-sets outside, moments from sea and lighthouse, open all day. *(Gwyn and Anne Wake, Pat and Tony Martin, W K Wood)*

SOUTHWOLD   TM5076
⋆ **Swan**   (01502) 722186
Market Place; IP18 6EG Relaxed comfortable back bar in smart Adnams-owned hotel, their full range and bottled beers, fine wines and malt whiskies, good bar food including lunchtime set menu (Mon-Sat), cheerful competent staff, coffee and teas in luxurious chintzy front lounge, restaurant; nice garden, 42 bedrooms – some in separate block where (by arrangement) dogs can stay too, good breakfast. *(George Atkinson, Richard Symonds)*

STOKE ASH   TM1170
White Horse   (01379) 678222
A140/Workhouse Road; IP23 7ET Popular 17th-c beamed coaching inn, welcoming helpful young staff, enjoyable reasonably priced pub food all day from 8am, well kept Adnams; annexe bedrooms. *(J F M and M West, Mr and Mrs M Walker)*

STOKE-BY-NAYLAND   TL9836
⋆**Angel** (01206) 263245

B1068 Sudbury–East Bergholt; CO6 4SA
Elegant and comfortable 17th-c inn, lounge
with handsome beams, timbers and stripped
brickwork, leather chesterfields and wing
armchairs around low tables, pictures of local
scenes, more formal room with deep glass-
covered well, chatty bar with straightforward
furniture on red tiles, well kept ales such as
Greene King, Hellhound and Nethergate, ten
wines by the glass, wide range of enterprising
food (all day weekends) served promptly by
friendly uniformed staff; children and dogs
(in bar) welcome, seats on sheltered terrace,
six individually styled bedrooms, open all day
from 8am (noon Sun). *(John Prescott, Brian
and Anna Marsden, MDN, Gerry and Rosemary
Dobson)*

STUTTON   TM1434
Gardeners Arms (01473) 328868

*Manningtree Road, Upper Street
(B1080); IP9 2TG* Cottagey roadside pub
on edge of small village, well kept Adnams
and guests, enjoyable home-made food
including daily specials and OAP meals,
friendly helpful landlord, cosy L-shaped bar
with log fire, side dining room and larger
area stretching to the back, lots of bric-a-
brac, film posters and musical instruments;
children and dogs (on lead) welcome,
two-tier back garden with pond, open all day
weekends. *(N R White)*

SUDBURY   TL8741
Brewery Tap (01787) 370876

East Street; CO10 2TP Corner tap for
Mauldons brewery, their range and guests
kept well, good choice of malt whiskies,
bare boards and scrubbed tables, some food
(can bring your own), darts, cribbage and
bar billiards, live music including jazz; dogs
welcome, open all day. *(John Prescott)*

SWILLAND   TM1852
Moon & Mushroom (01473) 785320

Off B1078; IP6 9LR Old-fashioned country
local with well kept East Anglian beers from
racked casks behind long counter, old tables
and chairs on quarry tiles, log fire, good value
home-made food such as venison pudding
and rabbit pie; children and dogs welcome,
heated terrace with grapevines and roses,
closed Sun evening, Mon. *(the Didler, David
M Smith)*

THORNHAM MAGNA   TM1070
Four Horseshoes (01379) 678777

*Off A140 S of Diss; Wickham Road;
IP23 8HD* Extensive thatched dining pub
dating from 12th c, dimly lit rambling well
divided bar, Greene King ales, good choice
of wines and whiskies, enjoyable reasonably
priced food including popular Sun carvery,
friendly helpful staff, very low heavy black
beams, plush banquettes, country pictures

and brass, big log fireplaces, interior
well; background music; children and
dogs welcome, disabled access, handy for
Thornham Walks and interesting thatched
church, picnic-sets on big sheltered lawn,
seven comfortable bedrooms, good breakfast,
open all day. *(Mr and Mrs M Walker)*

THURSTON   TL9165
Fox & Hounds (01359) 232228

Barton Road; IP31 3QT Quite an imposing
building, welcoming inside, with well kept
Adnams Bitter, Greene King IPA and guests
such as Woodfordes, pubby furnishings in
neatly kept carpeted lounge (back part set
for dining), lots of pump clips, ceiling fans,
big helpings of reasonably priced pubby
food (not Sun evening or Mon), bare-boards
public bar with pool, darts and machines;
background music and quiz nights; dogs
welcome, picnic-sets in garden and on
small covered side terrace, pretty village,
two bedrooms, open all day Fri-Sun.
(Jeremy King)

TUDDENHAM   TM1948
⋆**Fountain** (01473) 785377

*The Street; village signed off B1077 N of
Ipswich; IP6 9BT* Buzzy well run dining
pub in nice village, several linked café-style
rooms (minimal décor) with heavy beams
and timbering, stripped floors, wooden dining
chairs around light tables, open fire, lots of
prints (some by cartoonist Giles who spent
time here after Second World War), nice
choice of well cooked food (all day Sun till
7pm) including set menus, Adnams Bitter
and good selection of wines by the glass,
decent coffee, pleasant helpful service;
background music; no under-10s in bar after
6.30pm, wicker and metal chairs on covered
heated terrace, more seats under huge
parasols on sizeable lawn, closed first
week Jan. *(J F M and M West, Nick Clare)*

UFFORD   TM2952
White Lion (01394) 460770

*Lower Street (off B1438, towards Eyke);
IP13 6DW* Home to the Uffa Brewery with
Gold, Tipple, Pride and Punch plus guests
from Adnams, Earl Soham and Woodfordes in
16th-c village pub near quiet stretch of River
Deben; captain's chairs and wheelbacks
around simple tables, central woodburning
stove, enjoyable generous home-made food
(they raise their own pigs, free-range hens
and bees) and a shop/deli with pies, tarts and
quiches (two days' notice); nice views from
outside tables, may be summer barbecues,
closed Mon lunchtime, Sun evening. *(Brian
and Anna Marsden)*

WALBERSWICK   TM4974
⋆**Anchor** (01502) 722112

*The Street (B1387); village signed off
A12; IP18 6UA* More restaurant-with-bar
than pub, and food highly rated (best to
book); simply furnished front bar divided

into snug halves by two-way open fire, big windows, heavy stripped tables on original oak flooring, sturdy built-in green leather wall seats and nicely framed black and white photographs of fishermen on colourwashed panelling, good range of Adnams and Meantime ales, over 40 bottled beers and fine choice of wines by the glass, extensive dining area stretching back from small more modern-feeling lounge, good friendly service; young children (not in bar) and dogs welcome, bar serving flagstoned terrace, attractive gardens, coast path and pleasant walk across to Southwold (may be summer pedestrian ferry), good bedrooms (some in chalets), open all day. *(Simon Rodway, Stephen Funnell, Sheila Topham, Alan Cowell, M S Catling, Barry Collett and others)*

WANGFORD   TM4679
Angel (01502) 578636
Signed just off A12 by B1126 junction; High Street; NR34 8RL Handsome old village coaching inn with light airy bar, enjoyable good value food from sandwiches up, pleasant efficient service, Adnams, Black Sheep, Brakspears and Greene King, decent wines, family dining room; seven comfortable bedrooms (the church clock sounds on the quarter), good breakfast. *(Charles and Pauline Stride, Annamstorey)*

WESTLETON   TM4469
White Horse (01728) 648222
Darsham Road, off B1125 Blythburgh– Leiston; IP17 3AH Comfortable, friendly traditional pub with generous straightforward food (not Tues) including good value Sun roasts, four well kept Adnams ales, unassuming high-ceilinged bar with central fire, steps down to stone-floored back dining room; children welcome, picnic-sets in cottagey garden with climbing frame, more out by village duck pond, four bedrooms, good breakfast, open all day Fri, Sat, closed Tues lunchtime. *(Stephen and Jean Curtis, George Atkinson)*

WITNESHAM   TM1850
Barley Mow (01473) 785395
Mow Hill; IP6 9EH Friendly old two-bar beamed local with well kept ales such as Woodfordes Wherry, reasonably priced tasty pub food (not Mon, Sat lunchtime, Sun evening) including specials, Giles cartoons dotted about (he used to drink here); quiz, bingo and music nights; children and dogs welcome, back garden, open all day except Mon lunchtime. *(Paul Rampton, Julie Harding)*

WOODBRIDGE   TM2648
Cherry Tree (01394) 384627
Opposite Notcutts Nursery, off A12; Cumberland Street; IP12 4AG 17th-c open-plan pub (bigger than it looks) with well kept Adnams and guests, good wines by the glass and popular reasonably priced pubby food including specials, friendly service, beams and two log fires, mix of pine furniture, old local photographs; children welcome, dogs in bar, garden with play area, three bedrooms in converted barn, good breakfast (for non-residents too), open all day. *(Pat and Tony Martin)*

WOODBRIDGE   TM2748
Crown (01394) 384242
Thoroughfare/Quay Street; IP12 1AD Stylishly refurbished 17th-c dining inn, well kept Adnams and Meantime from glass-roofed bar (boat suspended above counter), lots of wines by the glass, good imaginative food including set menu, pleasant young staff, various eating areas with contemporary furnishings, live jazz last Thurs of month; courtyard tables, ten well appointed bedrooms. *(J F M and M West)*

WOODBRIDGE   TM2749
Olde Bell & Steelyard
(01394) 382933 *New Street, off Market Square; IP12 1DZ* Ancient and unpretentious timber-framed pub with two smallish beamed bars and compact dining room, lots of brassware, log fire, Greene King ales and guests from canopied servery, real ciders, enjoyable home-made food from bar snacks up, friendly welcoming staff, traditional games including bar billiards, live music; well behaved children and dogs welcome, back terrace, steelyard still overhanging street, open till late Fri, Sat. *(Anon)*

WOOLPIT   TL9762
Swan (01359) 240482
The Street; IP30 9QN Welcoming old coaching house pleasantly situated in village square, heavy beams and painted panelling, mixed tables and chairs on carpet, roaring log fire one end, very good inventive food from daily changing blackboard menu, prompt friendly service, well kept Adnams from slate-top counter and lots of wines by the glass; soft background music; walled garden behind, four bedrooms in converted stables. *(J F M and M West, Michael and Mary Smith)*

Post Office address codings confusingly give the impression that some pubs are in Suffolk, when they're really in Cambridgeshire, Essex or Norfolk (which is where we list them).

Surrey

If you're a lover of fine wines, this county is for you. Nearly half our Main Entry pubs hold a Wine Award, including the Jolly Farmer in Bramley (comfortable and cosy, with super beers too), White Hart in Chipstead (civilised and stylish, smashing food and 80 whiskies), Seven Stars in Leigh (extremely well run, with tasty, popular food), Running Horses in Mickleham (deservedly busy, friendly and excellent food), Refectory in Milford (beautiful building, a huge range of drinks and bistro-style food) and Inn at West End in West End (their own wine shop, speciality drinks from Portugal and Spain and a revamped menu). Food tends not to be cheap, but quality is always high. Good new entries are the Foley in Claygate (carefully refurbished Youngs pub with a wide choice of drinks and food), Mill at Elstead (converted watermill in lovely spot with Fullers beers), Bell in Outwood (extended country pub with pretty garden), Flower Pot in Sunbury (new refurbishment for handsome old coaching inn) and Olde Swan at Thames Ditton (seats by the water and plenty of character in ancient rooms). Special places for a meal are the Jolly Farmers in Buckland, White Hart in Chipstead, Running Horses in Mickleham, Three Horseshoes in Thursley (nice little pub and handy after a walk) and Inn at West End in West End. Our Surrey Dining Pub 2014 is the Running Horses at Mickleham.

BRAMLEY   TQ0044   Map 3

Jolly Farmer ♀ ◀

High Street; GU5 0HB

Relaxed village inn near Surrey Hills with great selection of beers

On a cold bleak day, this family-run pub is comfortably warm and welcoming. The traditional interior is filled with a homely miscellany of wooden tables and chairs, with collections of plates, enamel advertising signs, sewing machines, antique bottles, prints and old tools filling the walls and surfaces. Timbered semi-partitions, a mix of brick and timbering and an open fireplace give it a snug cosy feel. Handpumps serve W J King Horsham Best alongside up to seven guests – they can get through 20 different ales a week – such as Hammerpot HPA and Double Helix, Irving Illustrious and Type 42, Nottingham Dreadnought, Pilgrim Luperc Alia and Wells & Youngs Bitter. They also keep six imported draught lagers, two ciders and around 15 wines by the glass; background music and board games. There are tables out by the car park, and the village is handy for Winkworth Arboretum (National Trust) and walks up St Martha's Hill.

As well as sandwiches, the food might include devilled whitebait with home-made tartare sauce, half rack of barbecue ribs, honey and mustard-glazed home-cooked ham and eggs, chicken with chilli, red peppers, cheese and cream, cod and chips, beef in ale pie, smoked salmon and scallop risotto, and puddings such as chocolate brownie with home-made vanilla ice-cream and treacle tart with custard. *Benchmark main dish: home-made burger with chips £10.00. Two-course evening meal £18.00.*

Free house ~ Licensees Steve and Chris Hardstone ~ Real ale ~ (01483) 893355 ~ Open 11-11(11.30 Sat); 12-11 Sun ~ Bar food 12-2.30, 6(7 Sun)-9.30 ~ Restaurant ~ Children welcome ~ Dogs allowed in bar and bedrooms ~ Bedrooms: £65/£75 ~ www.jollyfarmer.co.uk *Recommended by Tim Chandler*

BUCKLAND
Jolly Farmers

TQ2250 Map 3

Reigate Road (A25 W of Reigate); RH3 7BG

Unusual place that sells and serves a wide range of local produce; fun to eat or shop in, and atmospheric too

' A pub eatery and farm shop' is how this unusual place describes itself. It's now been extended to create a larger dining area and an open kitchen, a children's play area, a kitchen garden and a bigger car park. They open early in the morning for breakfast and carry on serving some sort of food through morning coffee, lunch, afternoon tea and supper. The flagstoned bar is beamed and timbered with an informal, relaxed atmosphere, brown leather sofas and armchairs, Hogs Back TEA and Pilgrim Surrey Bitter on handpump, local wines and home-made cordials. A little brick fireplace separates the bar from the (now bigger) wooden-floored dining room. The expanded and revamped shop stretches across three little rooms and stocks fresh vegetables, deli meats, cheeses, cakes, chocolates and their own range of preserves; they hold a weekly food market with stalls outside (Saturdays 9am-3pm) and organise several food festivals and events throughout the year. Tables out on a back terrace overlook the car park.

As well as breakfast from 9am, the imaginative food includes sandwiches, home-cured salmon with garlic and caper dressing and lemon crème fraîche, slow-roast pork belly and black pudding lollipops with apple salad and honey and mustard dip, various platters, butternut squash, celeriac and spinach wellington with roasted tomato and potato ragout, day-boat beer-battered fresh cod and chips, burgers with mozzarella, mushrooms, cheese, bacon and free-range egg, steak and kidney pudding with thyme and rosemary gravy, king prawn, bacon, saffron and cognac pasta, and puddings. *Benchmark main dish: salmon, cod and smoked haddock in herb cream pie £11.50. Two-course evening meal £17.50.*

Free house ~ Licensees Jon and Paula Briscoe ~ Real ale ~ (01737) 221355 ~ Open 9am-11.30pm ~ Bar food 12-11.30; 9-11.15am breakfast ~ Restaurant ~ Children welcome ~ Dogs allowed in bar ~ www.thejollyfarmersreigate.co.uk
Recommended by M G Hart, Gordon and Margaret Ormondroyd, Derek Thomas, John Faircloth

CHIDDINGFOLD

SU9635   Map 2

Crown 🍺 🛏️

The Green (A283); GU8 4TX

Lovely old inn by village green with several bars and dining rooms, fine old woodwork and stained-glass windows, five real ales and enjoyable, fairly priced food; well equipped and comfortable bedrooms

In 1552, Edward VI and a vast retinue stayed in this lovely 700-year-old timbered building – today, the bedrooms are well equipped but still have a great deal of character, with sloping floors and heavy beams, and several have four-posters. It's the oldest licensed house in Surrey and one of the oldest in the country, so the sense of history is strong. The bar and connected dining rooms (just the right size for a private party) have massive beams – some over 2-ft thick – oak panelling, a magnificently carved inglenook fireplace and huge chimneys; note the lovely stained-glass windows. There are mate's and other pubby chairs, comfortable cushioned wall seats, leather dining chairs with wooden barley-twist arms around fine antique tables, and lots of portraits. The simple, two-level back public bar has an open fire; there's also a play room with toys. Fullers London Pride, Hogs Back TEA, Ringwood Bitter and Sharps Doom Bar on handpump and several wines by the glass; service is helpful and friendly. Seats outside look across the village green to the interesting church, with more tables in a sheltered central courtyard.

 As well as snacks, sandwiches and sharing platters, the often interesting food includes sandwiches, salt and pepper squid with chilli and lime, potted chicken liver pâté with grape chutney, vegetable stack with goats cheese, provençale sauce and polenta chips, smoked haddock on creamed mash with spinach, poached egg and chive cream, curry and pie of the day, roast chicken with fries and aioli, and puddings. *Benchmark main dish: beer-battered fish and chips with mushy peas £12.00. Two-course evening meal £20.50.*

Free house ~ Licensee Daniel Hall ~ Real ale ~ (01428) 682255 ~ Open 7am-11pm; 8am-11pm(10.30 Sun) Sat ~ Bar food 12-2.30, 6.30-10; all day weekends; breakfast 7 (8 weekends)-11am ~ Restaurant ~ Children welcome ~ Dogs allowed in bar ~ Bedrooms: £100/£135 ~ www.thecrownchiddingfold.com *Recommended by Richard and Penny Gibbs, David H T Dimock*

CHIPSTEAD

TQ2757   Map 3

White Hart 🍽️ 🍷

Hazelwood Lane; CR5 3QW

Neatly kept 18th-c pub with antique tables and chairs in open-plan rooms, lots to look at, real ales and several wines by the glass, good bistro-style food and friendly staff

Although less than 20 minutes from the hustle and bustle of Croydon, this nicely kept pub feels like a country retreat – it's opposite rugby fields and has distant views. The open-plan rooms have an informal, friendly feel, with a raftered dining room to the right, elegant metal chandeliers, rough-plastered walls, an open fire in a brick fireplace and a couple of carved metal standing uprights. The central bar has stools by the panelled counter where helpful, friendly staff serve Phoenix Brunning & Price Original, Pilgrim Surrey, Sharps Doom Bar and guests such as By the Horns Lambeth Walk and Surrey Hills Shere Drop on handpump, around 16 good wines by the glass and up to 80 malt whiskies; background music. The long room to the left is light and airy with lots of windows overlooking the seats on the terrace, wall panelling at one end and a woodburning stove. Throughout, there's a fine mix of antique dining chairs and settles around all sorts of tables (each set with a church candle), rugs on bare boards or flagstones, hundreds of interesting cartoons, country pictures, cricketing prints and rugby team photographs, large ornate mirrors and, on the window sills and mantelpieces, old glass and stone bottles, clocks, books and plants.

As well as good sandwiches, the excellent food includes pigeon breast with figs, watercress and walnuts with honey mustard dressing, grilled sardines with pink grapefruit and rocket salad, chilli con carne, smoked haddock kedgeree with poached egg, steak burger with bacon, cheese, coleslaw, relish and chips, chicken tikka masala, pheasant kiev with chestnut and thyme butter and sweet potato fondant, and puddings such as raspberry crème brûlée and warm chocolate brownie with boozy cherries and chocolate ice-cream. *Benchmark main dish: steak in ale pie with chips £13.95. Two-course evening meal £19.00.*

Brunning & Price ~ Manager Damian Mann ~ Real ale ~ (01737) 554455 ~ Open 11.30-11; 12-10.30 Sun ~ Bar food 12-10(9.30 Sun) ~ Children welcome ~ Dogs allowed in bar ~ www.brunningandprice.co.uk/whitehartchipstead *Recommended by Rob Hudson, Nick Kounoupias, Fiona Smith*

CLAYGATE
Foley ♀

TQ1563   Map 3

Hare Lane; KT10 0LZ

Carefully refurbished spreading place with lots of interesting drinking and dining areas, a thoughtful choice of drinks, wide range of snacks and full meals and efficient service; attractive bedrooms

Named for the Foley family who once owned much of the surrounding land, this has been a Youngs pub since 1888. They've done a magnificent job of restoring and updating the huge spreading place, and the 17 bedrooms are well equipped and comfortably contemporary. The most pubby part is at the front with an assortment of wooden dining chairs and tables on bare boards, stools against the counter and leather armchairs and sofas by a Victorian fireplace: Wells & Youngs Bitter, Bombardier, London Gold and Special on handpump, lots of wines by the glass, interesting spirits and quite a choice of coffees and teas. Leading off here are lots of interconnected but separate sitting and dining areas, with more armchairs and sofas, settles, long cushioned wall benches, an appealing variety of upholstered and wooden dining chairs around every size and style of table on floorboards or slate tiles, a glass-fronted, two-way open fire, candles in glass jars and plenty of modern artwork; it's fun to watch the action in the open kitchen. Background music, board games and daily papers. There's a lot of space for drinking and dining on the two-level terraces.

As well as croissants, cakes and snacks such as sausage rolls and scotch eggs, the thoughtful food includes sandwiches, duck terrine with spicy pear chutney, box-baked camembert with pickles and crusty bread, sausages with battered onion rings, mash and caramelised onion jus, wild mushroom risotto, honey and mustard-roasted ham with duck eggs, burger with cheddar and bacon, chicken supreme with red wine jus and gratin potatoes, venison medallions with peppercorn sauce, and puddings. *Benchmark main dish: bass with coconut rice and sweet and sour chilli dressing £13.95. Two-course evening meal £18.50.*

Wells & Youngs ~ Manager Laura Bugbee ~ Real ale ~ (01372) 462021 ~ Open 11-11;
12-10.30 Sun ~ Bar food 12-3, 6-9.45; 12-9.45(9 Sun) Sat; snacks all day ~ Restaurant ~
Children welcome ~ Dogs allowed in bar ~ Bedrooms: £110/£120 ~ www.thefoley.co.uk
Recommended by Caroline Prescott, Martin Jones

CRANLEIGH   TQ0539 Map 3

Richard Onslow 🍺

High Street; GU6 8AU

**Busy pub with a good mix of customers in several bar rooms,
four real ales and interesting all-day food; bedrooms**

A s this bustling place is right in the centre of town, there are always
people popping in and out, which creates a lively atmosphere.
The little public bar has stools by the counter, leather tub chairs,
a built-in sofa and a slate-floored drinking area where they keep
Adnams Lighthouse, Hogs Back TEA, Sharps Doom Bar and Surrey
Hills Shere Drop on handpump, several wines by the glass and home-
made summer lemonade and fresh lime soda. Two dining rooms have
a mix of tartan tub chairs around wooden tables, a rather fine long
leather-cushioned church pew, local photographs on mainly pale
paintwork and a couple of open fires, one in a nice brick fireplace.
The sizeable restaurant, with pale wooden tables and chairs on
a wooden floor and modern flowery wallpaper, has big windows
overlooking the street; background music and board games. There are
a few tables and chairs in the back terraced garden and a few on the
front pavement. Bedrooms are smart and well equipped.

Starting with breakfasts at 7am, the imaginative food might include
sandwiches, rabbit and ham terrine with prune chutney, beef carpaccio with
crispy shallots and parmesan, sharing deli boards, carrot, leek and goats cheese
fritters with apple salsa, free-range sausages and mash with onion gravy, pigeon
kiev with bacon and pomegranate salad, roast of the day, lamb medallions with
bombay potatoes, pea bhaji and yoghurt dressing, and puddings such as Valrhona
chocolate tart with orange jelly and steamed ginger pudding with orange crisp and
custard. *Benchmark main dish: 28-day aged rump steak with garlic butter
and chips £19.00. Two-course evening meal £20.00.*

Peach Pub Company ~ Licensee John Taylor ~ Real ale ~ (01483) 274922 ~ Open
12-midnight(11 Sun) ~ Bar food 7am(7.30am weekends)-10pm ~ Restaurant ~ Children
welcome ~ Dogs allowed in bar and bedrooms ~ Live music monthly, see website ~
Bedrooms: /£85 ~ www.therichardonslow.co.uk *Recommended by Justin Thomas*

ELSTEAD   SU9044 Map 2

Mill at Elstead

*Farnham Road (B3001 just W of village, which is itself between Farnham
and Milford); GU8 6LE*

**Fascinating building, big attractive waterside garden, Fullers beers
and well liked food**

T his largely 18th-c four-storey watermill has a rather special setting
above the prettily banked River Wey. Plenty of picnic-sets are dotted
around by the water with its lovely millpond, swans and weeping willows
– the entire area is nicely floodlit at night. Big windows throughout
the sensitively converted building make the most of the charming
surroundings. A series of rambling linked bar areas on the spacious
ground floor, and a restaurant upstairs, change in mood from one part

to the next. You'll find brown leather armchairs and antique engravings by a longcase clock, neat modern tables and dining chairs on dark woodstrip flooring, big country tables on broad ceramic tiles, iron pillars and stripped masonry, and a log fire in a huge inglenook. Fullers London Pride, ESB and Seafarers on handpump and a good range of wines by the glass; background music, board games.

🍴 Popular food includes sandwiches, smoked salmon with pickled cucumber and horseradish crème fraîche, sautéed wild mushrooms with tarragon cream and toasted brioche, sharing boards, tagliatelle with roasted squash, spinach, garlic cream and toasted pine nuts, sausages with mustard mash and red wine and thyme gravy, roasted trout with lemon and herb butter and toasted almonds, half roast lemon chicken with aioli and chips, and puddings such as chocolate brownie with honeycomb ice-cream and baked lemon tart with honeyed mascarpone. *Benchmark main dish: beer-battered haddock with chips and mushy peas £9.95. Two-course evening meal £16.00.*

Fullers ~ Managers Jeff and Georgia Watts ~ Real ale ~ (01252) 703333 ~ Open 11-11; 11.30-10.30 Sun ~ Bar food 12-9(8 Sun) ~ Restaurant ~ Children welcome ~ Dogs allowed in bar ~ www.millelstead.co.uk *Recommended by Ian Wilson, P G Topp, John Beeken*

🍺 ESHER   TQ1566   Map 3
Marneys £
Alma Road (one-way), Weston Green; heading N on A309 from A307 roundabout, after Lamb & Star pub turn left into Lime Tree Avenue (signposted to All Saints Parish Church), then left at T junction into Chestnut Avenue; KT10 8JN

Country-feeling pub with good value traditional food and attractive garden

' A rural idyll in the heart of suburbia' is how a reader aptly described this charming little pub – it's certainly popular with walkers and their dogs. The front terrace has wooden tables and views over the wooded common, village church and duck pond, and there are more seats on the decked area in the pleasantly planted and sheltered garden. Inside, there are just two rooms. The small snug bar has a low-beamed ceiling, Fullers London Pride, Sharps Doom Bar and Wells & Youngs Bitter on handpump, about a dozen wines by the glass and perhaps horse racing on the unobtrusive corner TV. To the left, past a little cast-iron woodburning stove, the dining area has big pine tables, pews, pale country kitchen chairs and cottagey blue-curtained windows; background music. The pub is only a mile from Hampton Court Palace.

🍴 As well as sandwiches and baguettes, the reasonably priced traditional food includes deep-fried whitebait with tartare sauce, box-baked camembert with redcurrant chutney, wild boar and apple sausages with mustard mash and red onion gravy, slow-roasted tomato and brie tartlet with coleslaw and fries, lamb burger with goats cheese and caramelised onions, thai-style salmon fishcakes with sweet chilli sauce, and puddings such as crème brûlée and warm chocolate fudge cake. *Benchmark main dish: steak in ale pie £10.95. Two-course evening meal £16.00.*

Free house ~ Licensee Thomas Duxberry ~ Real ale ~ (020) 8398 4444 ~ Open 11am-11.30pm; 12-11 Sun ~ Bar food 12-2.30(3 Sun), 6-9; not Fri-Sun evenings ~ Restaurant ~ Children welcome away from bar ~ Dogs allowed in bar ~ www.marneys.com
Recommended by Jenny Smith, Simon Rodway, Ian Phillips, C and R Bromage

---

There are report forms at the back of the book.

 LEIGH   TQ2147   Map 3

Seven Stars ♀

Dawes Green, S of A25 Dorking–Reigate; RH2 8NP

Popular country dining pub with enjoyable food and good wines

This pretty tile-hung pub is all neatly kept and homely with plenty of traditional atmosphere. The comfortable saloon bar has fine flagstones, beams, a 1633 inglenook fireback showing a royal coat of arms and dark wheelback chairs. The public bar is plainer, with Fullers London Pride, Hogs Back TEA, Sharps Doom Bar and Wells & Youngs Bitter on handpump from the glowing copper counter, alongside decent wines including about a dozen by the glass. The sympathetic restaurant extension at the side incorporates 17th-c floor timbers from a granary. Outside, there's plenty of room in the front beer garden, on the terrace and in the side garden.

 Good quality food from a nicely varied menu includes sandwiches, pheasant pâté, king scallop and black pudding salad, leek and gruyère tart, honey-glazed gammon with duck egg, confit duck leg with champ mash and rosemary jus, fillet of hoki, prawn, coconut and coriander risotto with tomato and chilli jam, roast half shoulder of lamb with sweet potato and parsnip gratin, and puddings such as vanilla-poached pear with marshmallow and steamed chocolate pudding with orange chocolate sauce. *Benchmark main dish: calves liver and bacon with mustard mash and shallot and red wine jus £16.00. Two-course evening meal £20.00.*

Punch ~ Lease James Slayford ~ Real ale ~ (01306) 611254 ~ Open 12-11(10.30 Sun) ~ Bar food 12-2.30, 6-9; 12-3, 6.30-9.30 Fri, Sat; 12-6 Sun ~ Restaurant ~ Children welcome in restaurant only ~ Dogs allowed in bar ~ Live jazz every other month ~ www.7starsleigh.co.uk *Recommended by M G Hart, LM, Mr and Mrs Price, Nick Lawless, Michael and Margaret Cross, John Saville, R K Phillips*

MICKLEHAM   TQ1753   Map 3

Running Horses ❢ ♀ ⇌

Old London Road (B2209); RH5 6DU

Surrey Dining Pub of the Year

Upmarket pub with elegant restaurant and comfortable bar, and food from sandwiches through to very imaginative smart dining

This particularly well run place is so popular you must arrive early – even if it's just a drink and a chat that you want – as tables get snapped up quickly, especially at weekends. But despite being pretty pushed at times, staff remain efficient and welcoming. The spacious bar is stylish, with a cheerfully smart atmosphere, hunting pictures, racing cartoons and Hogarth prints, lots of race tickets hanging from a beam, fresh flowers or a fire in an inglenook at one end, cushioned wall settles and other dining chairs around straightforward pubby tables and bar stools. Brakspears Bitter, Fullers London Pride and Ringwood Best and Boondoggle on handpump alongside good wines by the glass from a serious wine list; background music. The extensive restaurant is open to the bar and, although set out fairly formally with crisp white cloths and candles on each table, shares the same relaxing atmosphere. The front terrace with picnic-sets and lovely flowering tubs and hanging baskets takes in a peaceful view of the old church with its strange stubby steeple. Parking is in a narrow lane (or on the main road). A notice by the door asks walkers to remove or cover their boots; dogs are welcome.

As well as lunchtime sandwiches, the first class food might include devilled lambs kidneys with crispy shallot rings, scallops with parsnip purée, pancetta and truffle, cheese, cep and caramelised onion filo pie with root vegetable mash, pie of the week, herb-crusted pollock with spinach, mussels and clams marinière, cumberland sausages with caramelised red onion gravy, corn-fed chicken with poached leeks and mustard sauce, twice-cooked pork belly with garlic and herb mash and cider sauce, and puddings. *Benchmark main dish: 10oz scottish burger with applewood cheddar, spicy tomato chutney and chips £12.50. Two-course evening meal £23.00.*

Free house ~ Licensees Steve and Josie Slayford ~ Real ale ~ (01372) 372279 ~ Open 12-11.30(10.30 Sun) ~ Bar food 12-2.30(3 Sat), 7-9.30; 12-3, 6-9 Sun ~ Restaurant ~ Children welcome but must be over 10 in bar area ~ Dogs allowed in bar ~ Bedrooms: £95/£110 ~ www.therunninghorses.co.uk *Recommended by Guy Vowles, Karen Eliot, Sheila Topham*

MILFORD SU9542 Map 2

Refectory 🍴 ♦

Portsmouth Road; GU8 5HJ

Handsome building with plenty of interest inside – beams, timbering, fine stone fireplaces and so forth – lots of space, real ales and well liked food

This is a first class all-rounder – and our readers love it. Previously a cattle barn and then a tea and antiques shop, it's a lovely golden-stone and timbered building. The L-shaped, mainly open-plan rooms are spacious and extremely interesting: there are strikingly heavy beams, lots of timbering, exposed stone walls, stalling and standing timbers creating separate seating areas and a couple of big log fires in handsome stone fireplaces. A two-tiered balconied part at one end has a wall covered with huge brass platters; the rest of the walls are hung with nice old photographs and a variety of paintings. Dining chairs and dark wooden tables are grouped on wooden, quarry-tiled or carpeted flooring, and there are also rugs, bookshelves, big pot plants, stone bottles on window sills and fresh flowers. High wooden bar stools line the long counter where they serve Phoenix Brunning & Price Original, Hogsback TEA, Dark Star Hophead and guests from breweries such as Andwell and Tillingbourne on handpump, 16 wines by the glass, around 80 malt whiskies and three farm ciders. There are teak tables and chairs in the back courtyard adjacent to the characterful pigeonry. Facilities for wheelchair users are outstandingly good and there are disabled parking spaces.

As well as sandwiches, the extremely good, interesting food includes red pepper panna cotta, seared scallops with griddled asparagus and white wine sauce, mediterranean vegetable wellington with basil couscous and tomato sauce, chicken carbonara with pasta and courgette ribbons, steak and kidney pie, pork and leek sausages with bubble and squeak and caramelised onion gravy, slow-roasted rolled lamb breast with shallot cake and minted red wine jus, and puddings such as almond meringue with nut brittle cream and mixed fruit berry compote and banana cheesecake with maple walnuts and bitter chocolate sauce. *Benchmark main dish: beer-battered fish and chips with mushy peas £12.25. Two-course evening meal £19.00.*

Brunning & Price ~ Manager Katie Dallyn ~ Real ale ~ (01483) 413820 ~ Open 12-11; 12-10.30 Sun ~ Bar food 12-10(9.30 Sun) ~ Restaurant ~ Children welcome ~ Dogs welcome ~ Occasional live jazz Sun ~ www.brunningandprice.co.uk/refectory *Recommended by Richard and Penny Gibbs, Simon and Mandy King*

 OUTWOOD　　　　　　　　　　　　　　TQ3246　Map 3
Bell
Outwood Common, just E of village; off A23 S of Redhill; RH1 5PN

Enjoyable pub with Fullers beers, tasty food and nice garden

There is indeed a bell here – an enormous one in a bar alcove. This is an attractive, extended 17th-c dining pub on the outskirts of a village and our readers enjoy their visits here very much. The softly lit, smartly rustic beamed bar is warm and cosy, with oak and elm tables and chairs (some Jacobean in style), low beams and a vast stone inglenook fireplace. If you want to eat, it's best to book in advance, especially in the evening (when drinking-only space is limited too). Fullers London Pride, ESB and Brewers Bragg on handpump with good wines by the glass and a large range of spirits; background music. The well managed garden has a play area in summer; it's a peaceful place to sit among flowers and shrubs on the sheltered lawn, looking past pine trees to woods and rolling fields.

Good food includes sandwiches, breaded whitebait with lemon aioli, crispy oriental pork salad, sharing boards, blue cheese mushroom burger with salad, gherkins, onion rings and egg, pie of the day, mozzarella and sun-dried tomato-stuffed chicken with sautéed potatoes, sea trout fillet with warm fennel and samphire salad, potato gnocchi and butter sauce, calves liver with bacon, onions and madeira cream sauce, half roast duck with spiced clementine sauce, and puddings such as chocolate brownie with salted caramel ice-cream. *Benchmark main dish: selection of breaded fish in tortilla basket with chips £14.50. Two-course evening meal £18.00.*

Fullers ~ Managers Jason and Sian Smith ~ Real ale ~ (01342) 842989 ~ Open 12-11 (10.30 Sun) ~ Bar food 12-2.30, 6-9.30; 12-9 Sun ~ Restaurant ~ Children welcome ~ Dogs allowed in bar ~ www.belloutwood.co.uk *Recommended by Chris Bell, Geoffrey Kemp*

 SHAMLEY GREEN　　　　　　　　　　　TQ0343　Map 3
Red Lion
The Green; GU5 0UB

Pleasant dining pub with popular tasty food and nice gardens

This is just the place in warm weather as there are plenty of hand-made rustic tables and benches – both at the front of this friendly pub, overlooking the village green and cricket pitch, and at the back, which is more secluded with seats on a heated, covered terrace overlooking a pond, and grassed dining areas. Inside, it's fairly traditional with real fires in the two connected bars, a mix of new and old wooden tables, chairs and cushioned settles on bare boards and red carpet, stripped standing timbers, fresh white walls and deep red ceilings; background music. Wells & Youngs IPA and a couple of guests such as Hogs Back TEA and Sharps Doom Bar on handpump, and over a dozen wines by the glass.

As well as sandwiches, the well liked food includes crispy duck salad with oranges, watercress and hoisin dressing, warm bacon and scallop salad, wild mushroom lasagne, chilli con carne, sausage and mash with onion gravy, calves liver with pancetta and onions, chicken with broad beans, asparagus and cider sauce, specials such as smoked haddock with spinach, cheese sauce and poached egg or veal schnitzel in lemon garlic butter with fries and egg, and puddings. *Benchmark main dish: steak in ale pie £12.95. Two-course evening meal £22.00.*

Punch ~ Lease Debbie Ersser ~ Real ale ~ (01483) 892202 ~ Open 11.30-11; 12-10
(8 in winter) Sun ~ Bar food 12-2.30(3 Sat), 6.30-9.30; 12-3, 6.30-8.30 Sun; not winter
Sun evening ~ Restaurant ~ Children welcome ~ Dogs allowed in bar ~
www.redlionshamleygreen.com *Recommended by Richard and Penny Gibbs, Emma Scofield*

SUNBURY   TQ1068   Map 3

Flower Pot 🛏

*1.6 miles from M3 junction 1; follow Lower Sunbury sign from exit
roundabout, then at Thames Street turn right; pub on next corner, with Green Street;
TW16 6AA*

**Newly refurbished former coaching inn with attractive, contemporary
bar and dining room, real ales and all-day food; bedrooms**

Although it's not actually on the river, this pub – with its attractive
façade and elegant wrought-iron balconies – is just across the road
from an attractive reach of the Thames, in quite a villagey area with
waterside walks. It's been carefully refurbished using contemporary
paintwork and the airy bar now has leather tub chairs around copper-
topped tables, high chairs upholstered in brown and beige tartan
around equally high, light wooden tables, stools against the counter and
attractive flagstones; there's also a couple of comfortably plush burgundy
armchairs. The bar leads to the dining area with duck egg blue-painted
and dark wooden cushioned dining chairs around an assortment of partly
painted tables on wooden flooring, all manner of artwork on wallpapered
walls and a large gilt-edged mirror over the open fireplace; candles in
glass jars, fresh flowers and newspapers to read. Brakspears Oxford
Gold and Ringwood Fortyniner on handpump and several wines by the
glass. There are wood and metal tables and chairs on a side terrace. The
bedrooms are smart and comfortable.

🍴 As well as breakfast (from 7am), the well liked food includes sandwiches,
duck and pork pâté with chutney, baked camembert with garlic and
rosemary, broccoli, mushroom and blue cheese pasta, stone-baked pizzas, beer-
battered hake and chips, pork and leek sausages with caramelised onion gravy,
pie of the day, chicken kiev with creamy mushroom and spinach linguine, and
puddings. *Benchmark main dish: chicken piri-piri £12.95. Two-course evening
meal £16.50.*

Brakspears ~ Tenant Simon Bailey ~ Real ale ~ (01932) 780741 ~ Open 7am-11pm;
8am-11.30pm(11pm Sun) Sat ~ Bar food 12-3, 6-9(10 Fri); 12-10 Sat; 12-9 Sun ~
Restaurant ~ Children welcome ~ Dogs allowed in bar ~ Bedrooms: /£109 ~
www.theflowerpothotel.co.uk *Recommended by Martin Jones, Isobel Mackinlay*

THAMES DITTON   TQ1667   Map 12

Olde Swan

Summer Road; KT7 0QQ

**Fine spot by the Thames with outside terraced seating, character
bars, plenty of space inside, several ales and tasty pubby food**

Dating from the 13th c, this big refurbished pub has smart wooden
tables and chairs under blue parasols overlooking a quiet Thames
backwater and across to Ditton Island – it's a lovely spot on a warm
day. Inside, the long bar area has wood and flagstone flooring, dark
farmhouse and other dining chairs around all sorts of tables, and
comfortable leather sofas in front of an open log fire in a big brick
fireplace. Greene King IPA, Abbot and Old Speckled Hen with guests

such as Morlands Original, Ruddles County and Hydes Manchester's Finest on handpump and several wines by the glass. The carpeted dining rooms are similarly furnished and also have open fires (one in a Tudor fireplace), standing timbers, bare brick (or interestingly wallpapered) walls and various prints and paintings. Arrive early to be sure of finding a parking space just down the road.

 As well as themed evenings, the tasty food includes sandwiches and wraps, king prawn cocktail, crispy chicken wings with citrus mayonnaise, lasagne, vegetable and cashew nut paella, burgers with cheese, bacon, battered onion rings and chips, steak in ale pie, half roast chicken with barbecue sauce, mixed grill, and puddings. *Benchmark main dish: battered haddock with mushy peas and chips £8.49. Two-course evening meal £14.00.*

Greene King ~ Manager Mike Dandy ~ Real ale ~ (020) 8398 1814 ~ Open 11-11 ~ Bar food 11-10; 12-9 Sun ~ Restaurant ~ Children welcome ~ Dogs allowed in bar ~ Live jazz third Sun of month ~ www.yeoldeswan-thames-ditton.co.uk
Recommended by Richard and Sissel Harris

THURSLEY   SU9039   Map 2

Three Horseshoes 🍴 🍺

Dye House Road, just off A3 SW of Godalming; GU8 6QD

Civilised country village pub with a broad range of good food

It's very pleasant to have an early lunch here and then do a circular walk across the vast common; they keep walking maps by the bar. A pretty tile-hung pub owned by a consortium of villagers who rescued it from closure, it has the feel of a gently upmarket country local. The convivial beamed front bar has a winter log fire, Hogs Back TEA and guests such as Dark Star Hophead and Tillingbourne Bitter Gem on handpump, a farm cider and perry; background music. The art on the dining room walls is for sale. Tables in the attractive two-acre garden take in pleasant views over Thursley Common and the 1,000-year-old Saxon church. On the terrace are smart comfortable chairs around tables with parasols. A separate area has a big play fort, a barbecue and a charcoal spit-roast that is used on bank holidays. Visiting dogs and horses might get offered a biscuit or carrot.

 Using local produce, the superior food includes sandwiches, terrine of rabbit, pigeon, wild mushrooms and bacon with piccalilli and red onion relish, trout with brown shrimp, capers, seaweed potato salad, shallots, horseradish and raspberry vinegar, free-range omelette with bacon and chips, pork and leek sausages with onions and mash, salmon and smoked haddock fishcakes with dill mayonnaise, confit duck leg with black pudding, goose fat beans and dauphinoise potatoes, and puddings such as treacle tart with triple jersey cream and steamed spotted dick with golden syrup. *Benchmark main dish: ham, egg and chips £9.50. Two-course evening meal £21.50.*

Free house ~ Licensees David Alders and Sandra Proni ~ Real ale ~ (01252) 703268 ~ Open 12-3, 5.30-11; 12-11 Sat; 12-8 Sun ~ Bar food 12.30-2.15, 7-9.15; 12-3 Sun ~ Restaurant ~ Well behaved children welcome ~ Dogs allowed in bar ~ www.threehorseshoesthursley.com *Recommended by Hunter and Christine Wright, Nicky Lee, N R White*

People named as recommenders after the full entries have told us that the pub should be included. But they have not written the report – we have, after anonymous on-the-spot inspection.

WEST END   SU9461   Map 2

Inn at West End 🍴 ♑

Just under 2.5 miles from M3 junction 3; A322 S, on right; GU24 9PW

Clean-cut dining pub with prompt friendly service, excellent wines, popular inventive food using village-reared pork, game shot by the landlord and their own vegetables, and pretty terrace

The hard-working and enthusiastic licencees here have bought the freehold from Enterprise and made some changes. The cellar and bar have been revamped, they have a new menu with lighter options and customers can bring in wines from the pub's own wine shop with little or no corkage. There are around 500 wines, mostly from Spain and Portugal, with 16 served in three sizes of glass and quite a few sherries, sweet wines and ports too; regular wine tastings. The pub is open-plan and café-like with bare boards, attractive modern prints on canary yellow walls above a red dado; on the left is a row of dining tables with crisp white linen over pale yellow tablecloths. The bar counter, with Fullers London Pride and guests such as Flack Manor Double Drop Exmoor Ale and Fullers Seafarers on handpump, and around 30 whiskies, is straight ahead as you come in, with chatting regulars perched on the comfortable bar stools. The area on the right has a pleasant relaxed atmosphere, with blue-cushioned wall benches and dining chairs around solid pale wood tables, broadsheet daily papers, magazines and a row of reference books on the brick chimneybreast above an open fire. This leads into a garden room, which in turn opens on to a terrace shaded by a grape- and clematis-covered pergola and a very pleasant garden; boules.

🍴 The attractively presented and very good food (using village-reared pork and lamb that they butcher themselves, game from local shoots and their own vegetables) might include sandwiches, hot smoked salmon with wasabi mayonnaise and pickled cucumber, crispy pork fritters with apple sauce and black pudding, mushrooms on toast, cumberland sausages with mash and caramelised onion gravy, butternut squash, red onion and sage risotto with infused oil, fresh fish with smoked salmon and chive beurre blanc, parma ham-wrapped corn-fed chicken stuffed with wild mushrooms and pistachios with garlic and herb sauce, and puddings such as south african vinegar pudding with boozy raisins and crème anglaise and warm chocolate brownie with iced peanut butter parfait and toffee sauce. *Benchmark main dish: kedgeree £11.75. Two-course evening meal £25.00.*

Free house ~ Licensees Gerry and Ann Price ~ Real ale ~ (01276) 858652 ~ Open 11-3, 5-11; 11-11 Sat; 12-10.30 Sun ~ Bar food 12-2.30, 6-9.30 ~ Restaurant ~ Children over 5 welcome if seated and dining ~ Dogs allowed in bar ~ www.the-inn.co.uk
Recommended by David and Sue Smith, Peter Veness, David and Ruth Shillitoe, David and Katharine Cooke, Ian Wilson, Edward Mirzoeff

Also Worth a Visit in Surrey

Besides the fully inspected pubs, you might like to try these pubs that have been recommended to us and described by readers. Do tell us what you think of them: feedback@goodguides.com

ABINGER COMMON   TQ1146
Abinger Hatch (01306) 730737
Off A25 W of Dorking, towards Abinger Hammer; RH5 6HZ New owners as we went to press for this modernised dining pub in beautiful woodland spot; spacious interior with heavy beams and flagstones, log fires, plainer extension, food has been very popular; some disabled access, picnic-sets in side garden with boules, summer barbecues, near pretty church and pond. *(R G Glover, R C Vincent)*

ALBURY   TQ0447
Drummond Arms   (01483) 202039
Off A248 SE of Guildford; The Street;
GU5 9AG Smartened-up pub in pretty
village; Adnams, Courage, Fullers and a
guest like Hogs Back TEA, good choice of
wines, food from sandwiches and light dishes
up, good welcoming service, opened-up
bar with leather chesterfields, log fire
and newspapers, parquet-floored dining
room, conservatory; pretty back garden
by little River Tillingbourne, duck island,
summer barbecues and hog roasts, pleasant
walks nearby, nine bedrooms, open all day
weekends. *(Ian Phillips)*

ALBURY HEATH   TQ0646
William IV   (01483) 202685
Little London, off A25 Guildford–
Dorking; OS Sheet 187 map reference
065468; GU5 9DG 16th-c local with rustic
low-beamed bar, high-backed settles and
chunky tables on flagstones, inglenook log
fire, daily newspapers, good straightforward
food (not Sun evening) using local produce
including landlord's free-range pork, four or
five well kept ales such as Hogs Back, Surrey
Hills and Wells & Youngs, restaurant area up
steps; well behaved children welcome, dogs
in bar, picnic-sets in small front garden, good
walks, open all day weekends. *(Ian Phillips,*
Alan and Shirley Sawden)

ALFOLD   TQ0435
Alfold Barn   (01403) 752288
Horsham Road, A281; GU6 8JE
Beautifully preserved 16th-c building with
bar and restaurant, good locally sourced food
including weekday lunch deal, good friendly
service, up to three well kept ales from
nearby breweries, beams and rafters, mixed
furniture on flagstones or carpet, warming
log fires; children welcome, garden with play
area and animals including a goat called
Rosie, closed Sun evening, Mon. *(Tony and*
Wendy Hobden, Lois Dyer)

ALFOLD   TQ0334
Three Compasses   (01483) 275729
Dunsfold Road; GU6 8HY Refurbished
200-year-old pub on back lane to former
Dunsfold Aerodrome (now Dunsfold Park,
home to *Top Gear*'s test track); well kept Hop
Back Summer Lightning, Sharps Doom Bar
and Surrey Hills Shere Drop, freshly made
food at reasonable prices, log-fire bar with
large bay window, separate games room and
back dining room; good-sized garden, near
Wey & Arun Canal, open all day. *(Tony and*
Wendy Hobden)

ASH VALE   SU8952
Swan   (01252) 325212
Hutton Road, off Ash Vale Road (B3411)
via Heathvale Bridge Road; GU12 5HA
Welcoming three-room Chef & Brewer on
Basingstoke Canal, wide choice of popular

well priced food all day including specials,
prompt smiling service, ales such as Fullers
London Pride and Surrey Hills Shere
Drop, good value wines by the glass, mix
of furniture on tiles or carpet, large log
fires; background music; children welcome,
attractive garden, neat heated terraces and
window boxes, open all day. *(KC)*

BANSTEAD   TQ2659
Mint   (01737) 362785
Park Road, off High Street towards
Kingswood; SM7 3DS Rambling Vintage
Inn, low beams and flagstones, dimly lit cosy
areas, their usual food cooked well including
weekday set menu till 5pm, real ales such as
Fullers, Harveys and Shepherd Neame, good
choice of wines by the glass; background
music may be intrusive; children welcome,
open all day. *(Maureen and Keith Gimson)*

BANSTEAD   TQ2559
Woolpack   (01737) 354560
High Street; SM7 2NZ Busy open-plan pub
with well kept Shepherd Neame ales and a
couple of guests, enjoyable home-made food
from standard dishes up (some available in
smaller helpings), pleasant helpful service,
Thurs quiz, live music including afternoon
trad jazz (first Tues of month); plenty of seats
in big garden, open all day. *(C and R Bromage,*
Conor McGaughey, Sue and Mike Todd)

BATTS CORNER   SU8140
Blue Bell   (01252) 792801
Batts Corner; GU10 4EX New
management and refurbishment for this
tucked-way country pub; light fresh décor
in linked stone-floored rooms with mix of
furniture including sofas by log fire, Hogs
Back TEA, Triple fff Moondance and two
guests, enjoyable good value home-made food
from short menu, friendly staff; big garden
with rolling views, handy for Alice Holt
Forest, open all day weekends. *(Anon)*

BETCHWORTH   TQ1950
Arkle Manor   (01737) 842110
Reigate Road; RH3 7HB Smart Mitchells
& Butlers restauranty pub with variety of
enjoyable food from pizzas and pub staples
to more upscale choices, good value weekday
set menu too, attentive friendly service,
attractive rambling layout with easy chairs
and so forth, real ales and lots of wines by the
glass, cocktails; may ask to keep a credit card
while running a tab; children welcome, steps
up to back terrace and leafy garden, open
all day. *(John Evans and others)*

BETCHWORTH   TQ2149
Dolphin   (01737) 842288
Off A25 W of Reigate; The Street;
RH3 7DW 16th-c village pub on Greensand
Way, plain tables on ancient flagstones
in neat front bar with inglenook log fire,
snug and a further panelled bar with
chiming grandfather clock, nice old local

photographs, well kept Wells & Youngs ales and enjoyable fairly priced traditional food (all day weekends), friendly helpful service, restaurant; children and dogs welcome, front and side terraces, back garden, picturesque village (fine Pre-Raphaelite pulpit in church), open all day. *(M G Hart, Conor McGaughey)*

BLETCHINGLEY TQ3250
Red Lion (01883) 743342
Castle Street (A25), Redhill side; RH1 4NU Old beamed village dining pub with fresh modern décor, mix of tables and chairs, lots of racing prints, good reasonably priced mainly traditional food all day (till 8pm Sun), friendly helpful staff, well kept Greene King ales and good choice of wines by the glass; monthly quiz, some live music including tribute bands; children welcome (under-10s till 7pm), tables on heated terrace by car park, secret garden, open all day. *(Geoffrey Kemp, R K Phillips, David Jackman)*

BLINDLEY HEATH TQ3645
✱ Red Barn (01342) 830820
Tandridge Lane, just off B2029, which is off A22; RH7 6LL Splendid farmhouse/barn conversion; contemporary furnishings mixing with 17th-c beams and timbers, central glass-sided woodburner (its flue soaring up into the roof), large model plane hanging from rafters, one wall with shelves of books, another hung with antlers, clever partitioning creating cosier areas too; red cooking range and big wooden tables in farmhouse-style room, adjacent bar with sofas by large fireplace, bar billiards, one or two real ales and good wine list, well liked food efficiently served by smart staff; background and some live music; children welcome, dogs in bar, solid granite tables on lawn, farmer's market first Sat of month, open all day. *(N R White, Peter Loader, Derek Thomas)*

BROCKHAM TQ1949
Inn on the Green (01737) 845101
Brockham Green; RH3 7JS Comfortably refurbished dining pub facing village green, enjoyable if not cheap food from traditional choices up including steaks cooked on a hot stone, well kept Adnams, Black Sheep and Fullers London Pride, conservatory; children welcome, picnic-sets out at front, garden behind. *(C and R Bromage)*

BROCKHAM TQ1949
Royal Oak (01737) 843241
Brockham Green; RH3 7JS Nice spot opposite fine church on charming village green below North Downs, refurbished bare-boards bar and expanded dining area, well kept Sharps and Wells & Youngs, enjoyable freshly cooked pub food, good service from genuinely friendly staff; children and dogs welcome, garden, handy for Greensand Way. *(Peter Hailey)*

BYFLEET TQ0661
Plough (01932) 354895
High Road; KT14 7QT Small friendly local under new management and closing for refurbishment as we went to press; eight real ales including Sharps Doom Bar and Wells & Youngs Bombardier, traditional food, beams, two open fires, rustic furnishings, farm tools, brass and copper, more modern back area, crib and dominoes, charity quiz second Tues of month; children (away from bar) and dogs welcome, terrace and small shady back garden, open all day. *(Ian Phillips)*

CARSHALTON TQ2764
Hope (020) 8240 1255
West Street; SM5 2PR Friendly community pub saved from closure by local consortium; well kept Kings, Windsor & Eton and five guests (regular festivals), real ciders and perry, generous low-priced pubby food (limited evening choice), 1950s feel with a room either side of bar, open fire, larger back room with bar billiards, some live mainly acoustic music; garden, open all day. *(Mark Franks, Leslie Button, Conor McGaughey, Tony Hobden)*

CATERHAM TQ3254
Harrow (01883) 343260
Stanstead Road, Whitehill; CR3 6AJ Beamed 16th-c pub high up in open country by North Downs Way; L-shaped bare-boards bar and carpeted back dining area, several real ales (sometimes straight from the cask), enjoyable food (not Sun evening) including daily specials, good local atmosphere and friendly service; children and dogs welcome, garden picnic-sets, popular with walkers and cyclists, open all day. *(Tim Everitt)*

CHARLESHILL SU8844
Donkey (01252) 702124
B3001 Milford–Farnham near Tilford; coming from Elstead, turn left as soon as you see pub sign; GU10 2AU Old-fashioned beamed dining pub with nice landlady and prompt friendly service, enjoyable home-made food, well kept ales such as Fullers, Greene King and Harveys, good choice of wines by the glass, conservatory restaurant, traditional games; children and dogs welcome, attractive garden with wendy house, two much-loved donkeys, good walks, open all day Sun. *(Sally Kerr, Mrs P Sumner, Tony and Jill Radnor)*

CHERTSEY TQ0566
Kingfisher (01932) 579811
Chertsey Bridge Road (Shepperton side of river); KT16 8LF Big Vintage Inn in delightful spot by Thames lock; repro period décor and furnishings in spreading series of small intimate areas, Fullers, Sharps and Wadworths ales, good choice of wines by the glass, their usual menus from sandwiches up including fixed-price offer till 5pm, log fires,

daily papers, large-scale map for walkers, interesting old pictures; soft background music; families welcome if eating, roadside garden, open all day. *(Ian Phillips)*

CHERTSEY   TQ0466
Thyme at the Tavern
(01932) 429667 *London Street; KT16 8AA* Busy local with Courage Best, Shepherd Neame Spitfire and two guests from nearby breweries (regular festivals), well priced pubby food (not Mon) from sandwiches and sharing plates up, popular Sun lunch (must book), live music Fri; dogs welcome, bedrooms, closed Sat lunchtime, open all day Sun. *(Hunter and Christine Wright)*

CHILWORTH   TQ0347
Percy Arms (01483) 561765
Dorking Road; GU4 8NP Refurbished partly 18th-c inn with south african influences in décor and food, good choice of wines by the glass, Greene King ales and a beer named for the pub, front bar and lounge with steps down to dining area, efficient service despite being busy, newspapers and cool background jazz; children welcome, garden tables with pretty views over Vale of Chilworth to St Martha's Hill, good walks, five bedrooms. *(Anon)*

CHIPSTEAD   TQ2757
Ramblers Rest (01737) 552661
Outwood Lane (B2032); CR5 3NP Mitchells & Butlers country dining pub with contemporary furnishings and cocktail bar décor in partly 14th-c rambling building, low beams (old and new), flagstones, panelling and log fires, enjoyable up-to-date and more traditional food including popular Sun lunch, real ales and interesting continental beers, Aspall's cider, good value wines by the glass, young friendly staff (may be a wait at busy times), daily papers; children and dogs welcome, disabled access (from front) and facilities, big pleasant garden with terrace, attractive views, good walks, open (and food) all day. *(Sheila Topham, Maureen and Keith Gimson, C and R Bromage, N R White)*

CHIPSTEAD   TQ2555
Well House (01737) 830640
Chipstead signed with Mugswell off A217, N of M25 junction 8; CR5 3SQ Cottagey and comfortable 16th-c pub with log fires in all three rooms, well kept Adnams, Fullers, Surrey Hills and local guests, Millwhite's cider, food from baguettes up (not Sun evening), friendly staff, bric-a-brac above bar, pewter tankards hanging from ceiling, conservatory, resident ghost called Harry the Monk; dogs allowed (they have cats), large

attractive hillside garden with ancient well (reputed to be mentioned in the Domesday Book), delightful setting, open all day. *(Conor McGaughey, N R White)*

CHURT   SU8538
Crossways (01428) 714323
Corner of A287 and Hale House Lane; GU10 2JE Friendly down-to-earth local, quarry-tiled public bar and carpeted saloon with panelling and plush banquettes, busy evenings for great changing beer range at reasonable prices, also four or more real ciders, good well priced home-made pub lunches (not Sun) including nice pies, evening food Weds only, cheerful young staff; TVs and machines; dogs welcome, garden, open all day Fri, Sat. *(Phil Bryant, Emily Murphy)*

CLAYGATE   TQ1663
Griffin (01372) 463799
Common Road; KT10 0HW Properly old-fashioned Victorian village local, well kept ales including Fullers London Pride, some interesting dishes along with usual pub food freshly cooked and reasonably priced. *(Gordon Stevenson)*

CLAYGATE   TQ1563
Hare & Hounds (01372) 465149
The Green; KT10 0JL Renovated flower-decked Victorian/Edwardian village pub with small restaurant, good sensibly priced french food, nice wines and competent service; outside seating at front and in small back garden. *(Anon)*

COBHAM   TQ1058
Cricketers (01932) 862105
Downside Common; 3.75 miles from M25 junction 10; A3 towards Cobham, first right on to A245, right at Downside signpost into Downside Bridge Road, follow road into right fork (away from Cobham Park) at second turn after bridge, then eventually turn into the pub's own lane, immediately before Common crossroads; KT11 3NX Worth visiting for idyllic views from terrace across village green; open-plan areas with crooked standing timbers, low oak beams (some with crash pads), wide ceiling boards and ancient plastering laths, log fire, well kept Fullers London Pride, Sharps Doom Bar and Surrey Hills Shere Drop, service and food can be good, dining room recently refurbished; background music, nostalgic DJ Sat; children and dogs welcome, modern furniture in neatly kept garden (AstroTurf at front), pretty hanging baskets, open all day (till 1am Fri, Sat). *(Ian Phillips, Colin McKerrow, Geoffrey Kemp)*

We include some hotels with a good bar that offers facilities comparable to those of a pub.

COBHAM
TQ1159
Running Mare (01932) 862007
Tilt Road; KT11 3EZ Attractive old pub overlooking the green, can get very busy; well kept Fullers, Hogs Back and Wells & Youngs, good food including popular Sun lunch, efficient friendly service, two timbered bars and restaurant, some refurbishment; children very welcome, a few tables out at front and on rose-covered back terrace. *(Shirley Mackenzie)*

COMPTON
SU9546
Harrow (01483) 810594
B3000 towards Godalming off A3; GU3 1EG Refurbished 18th-c roadside pub with emphasis on enjoyable good value pub food (not Sun evening), three real ales and good choice of wines by the glass, friendly attentive service, split-level bar with log fire, beamed dining area; children welcome, back terrace and streamside garden, open all day. *(Anon)*

COMPTON
SU9646
✶ Withies (01483) 421158
Withies Lane; pub signed from B3000; GU3 1JA Carefully altered 16th-c pub, charmingly civilised and gently old-fashioned, with low-beamed bar, some 17th-c carved panels between windows, splendid art nouveau settle among old sewing-machine tables, log fire in massive inglenook, well kept Adnams, Greene King IPA, Hogs Back TEA and Sharps Doom Bar, popular (not cheap) bar food served by efficient, helpful, bow-tied staff; children welcome, seats on terrace, under apple trees and creeper-hung arbour, flower-edged neat front lawn, on edge of Loseley Park and close to Watts Gallery, closed Sun evening. *(Helen and Brian Edgeley, Conor McGaughey, Colin McKerrow, D J and P M Taylor and others)*

DORMANSLAND
TQ4042
Old House At Home (01342) 836828
West Street; RH7 6QP Country pub under newish ownership; beamed bar with traditional furniture on parquet floor, horsebrasses above unusual barrel-fronted counter serving Shepherd Neame ales, good sensibly priced food (all day Sat, not Sun evening) cooked by landlady-chef from pub standards up, carpeted restaurant and plainer room with darts and TV, weekend live music; children and dogs welcome, a few picnic-sets in front, beer garden behind. *(Tony Hobden)*

DORMANSLAND
TQ4042
Plough (01342) 832933
Plough Road, off B2028 NE; RH7 6PS Friendly traditional old pub in quiet village, well kept Fullers, Harveys and Sharps, Weston's cider, decent wines, good choice of enjoyable bar food including specials board, thai restaurant, log fires and original features; children welcome, disabled facilities, good-sized garden. *(Mark Kingsley-Monks)*

DUNSFOLD
TQ0036
Sun (01483) 200242
Off B2130 S of Godalming; GU8 4LE Elegantly double-fronted pub with four rooms (brighter at the front), beams and some exposed brickwork, scrubbed pine furniture and inglenook log fire, ales such as Adnams, Harveys and Sharps, decent wines, enjoyable home-made pub food at reasonable prices, friendly busy staff; seats out on terrace and overlooking quiet village green. *(Robert A Watson)*

EASHING
SU9543
✶ Stag (01483) 421568
Lower Eashing, just off A3 southbound; GU7 2QG Civilised, gently upmarket riverside pub with Georgian façade masking much older interior; attractively opened-up rooms including charming old-fashioned locals' bar with armchairs on red and black quarry tiles, cosy log-fire snug beyond, Hogs Back TEA, a house beer from Marstons and two guests, Hazy Hog cider, good choice of enjoyable food served by attentive courteous staff, several linked dining areas including river room up a couple of steps looking out on to mature trees by millstream; dogs allowed in bar, extensive terrace with wicker or wooden furniture under parasols (some by weir), picnic-sets on grass, seven bedrooms, open all day. *(Martin and Karen Wake, Sheila Topham)*

EAST CLANDON
TQ0551
✶ Queens Head (01483) 222332
Just off A246 Guildford–Leatherhead; The Street; GU4 7RY Refurbished dining pub in same small group as Duke of Cambridge at Tilford and Stag at Eashing, good food from light dishes up including set deals (Mon-Thurs), well kept Hogs Back, Ringwood and Surrey Hills from fine elm-topped counter, also Hazy Hog cider, good friendly service, comfortable linked rooms, log fire in big inglenook; children welcome, tables out in front and on new side terrace, handy for Clandon Park and Hatchlands (both NT), open all day Fri, Sat, till 9pm Sun. *(John Evans, John Allman, John Saville and others)*

EFFINGHAM
TQ1153
✶ Plough (01372) 458121
Orestan Lane; KT24 5SW Popular recently refurbished Youngs pub with well kept ales from traditional bar, good food including Sun roasts, plenty of wines by the glass, friendly efficient staff, two coal-effect gas fires, beams and panelling in long lounge; plenty of tables on forecourt and in attractive garden with fruit trees, disabled parking, handy for Polesden Lacey (NT). *(P G Topp, Shirley Mackenzie, Alan and Shirley Sawden)*

ENGLEFIELD GREEN SU9771
Sun (01784) 432515
Wick Lane, Bishopsgate; TW20 0UF Friendly beamed local with well kept Courage Best, Greene King and Sharps Doom Bar, good blackboard wine choice, generous inexpensive pubby food from sandwiches up, small wooden tables with banquettes and low stools, lots of pub bric-a-brac including interesting beer bottle collection, colourful photographs, open fire, conservatory; soft background music and silent games machine; children welcome, biscuits and water for dogs, a few tables out at front and in quiet little garden, handy for Savill Garden and Windsor Great Park. *(Ian Phillips)*

EPSOM TQ2160
Rising Sun (01372) 740809
Heathcote Road; KT18 5DX Friendly well restored Victorian town pub, Wells & Youngs and a couple of mainstream guests, enjoyable food including good Sun lunch, log fire; nice garden. *(Stephen O'Neill)*

EPSOM TQ2158
Rubbing House (01372) 745050
Langley Vale Road (on Epsom racecourse); KT18 5LJ Restauranty dining pub popular for its fantastic racecourse views, can get very busy but staff cope well; attractive modern décor, good value promptly served food including children's menu, tables perhaps a little too close together, Greene King and Sharps ales, serious wine list, upper balcony for Derby days; background music; seating out by course, open all day. *(Maureen and Keith Gimson, P and J Shapley, David Jackman, C and R Bromage)*

ESHER TQ1364
Bear (01372) 469786
High Street; KT10 9RQ Youngs pub with two landmark life-size bears behind roof parapet; their well kept ales and a couple of guests, good choice of wines by the glass, prompt friendly service, popular reasonably priced food in bar and dining end, high tables and chairs, big leather sofas; sports TV; paved seating area outside, seven comfortable bedrooms, open all day. *(Ian Phillips)*

ESHER TQ1264
Prince of Wales (01372) 465483
West End Lane; off A244 towards Hersham, by Princess Alice Hospice; KT10 8LA Busy Chef & Brewer dining pub in nice village setting on edge of green; wide choice of reasonably priced food all day including children's menu, well kept Adnams, Fullers London Pride and two from Rebellion, good wine choice, friendly efficient service, log fires and newspapers; background music; disabled access, big garden, old brewery building next door (now staff accommodation), open all day. *(Ian Wilson, Geoffrey Kemp, Tom and Ruth Rees, Ian Phillips)*

FARNHAM SU8547
Shepherd & Flock (01252) 716675
Moor Park Lane, on A31/A324/A325 roundabout; GU9 9JB Flower-decked pub on Britain's largest inhabited roundabout; seven interesting changing ales kept well, enjoyable food from baguettes to good Sun roasts, efficient friendly service, simple up-to-date décor; picnic-sets out in front and in pleasant enclosed back garden with barbecue, open all day weekends. *(Anon)*

FICKLESHOLE TQ3960
White Bear (01959) 573166
Featherbed Lane/Fairchildes Lane; off A2022 Purley Road just S of A212 roundabout; CR6 9PH 16th-c country dining pub popular for its good value generous food (all day Fri, Sat, best to book weekends), lots of small rooms, beams, flagstones and open fires, friendly prompt service, Brakspears, Pilgrim and a couple of guests; children and well behaved dogs welcome, picnic-sets sharing front terrace with stone bear, sizeable back garden, open all day, from 9am Fri, Sat for breakfast. *(Mrs Elizabeth Hough, C and R Bromage)*

FOREST GREEN TQ1241
⋆ Parrot (01306) 621339
B2127 just W of junction with B2126, SW of Dorking; RH5 5RZ Cheerful old tile-hung village pub, heavy beams, timbers, flagstones and nooks and crannies, inglenook log fire, popular food (not Sun evening) using produce from own farm, five well kept changing ales including Ringwood, 16 wines by the glass, local fruit juices, efficient friendly service; shop selling own meat, cheeses, cured hams, pies and so forth; dogs welcome in bar, disabled facilities, attractive gardens with lovely country views, good walks nearby, open all day (till midnight Sat). *(Sheila Topham, Guy Vowles, Peter Loader, Steve Tilley)*

GODALMING SU9643
Star (01483) 417717
Church Street; GU7 1EL Friendly 17th-c local in cobbled pedestrian street, cosy low-beamed and panelled L-shaped bar, eight well kept changing ales (four tapped from the cask) including Greene King, farm ciders/perries, lunchtime bar food, more modern function room; heated back terrace, open all day. *(Tony Hobden, George Batty)*

If you're planning a long journey, it might help you to look at the list of pubs near motorway junctions at the end of the book.

GODSTONE TQ3551

Bell (01883) 743216

Under a mile from M25 junction 6, via B2236; RH9 8DX Handsome old Mitchells & Butlers family dining pub, comfortable modern furnishings and lighting in heavily beamed open-plan areas including small conservatory, good up-to-date and more traditional food, weekday set menu (till 7pm), well kept ales and decent choice of wines by the glass, efficient friendly service, three open fires; children welcome, terrace and garden seating, open all day. *(Geoffrey Kemp)*

GOMSHALL TQ0847

Compasses (01483) 202506

Station Road (A25); GU5 9LA Popular village pub with plain bar and much bigger comfortable dining room, good value home-made food (all day except Sun evening), well kept Surrey Hills ales, decent wines by the glass, friendly helpful service; background music (live Fri) – also Aug 'Gomstock' festival; children welcome, pretty garden sloping down to roadside millstream. *(N R White, Alan and Shirley Sawden)*

GRAYSWOOD SU9134

Wheatsheaf (01428) 644440

Grayswood Road (A286 NE of Haslemere); GU27 2DE Welcoming family-run dining pub with light airy décor, enjoyable freshly made food in bar and restaurant, good range of well kept beers, friendly helpful staff; front verandah, side terrace, seven bedrooms in extension, good breakfast. *(Anon)*

GUILDFORD SU9949

Kings Head (01483) 575004

Quarry Street; GU1 3XQ Dating from the 16th c with lots of beams and stripped brickwork, cosy corners with armchairs, stylish oval tables, inglenook log fire, well kept Hogs Back and guests, decent wines, enjoyable reasonably priced food (not Sun evening) including variety of burgers and pizzas, quiz-and-curry night Mon, friendly young staff; background music (live Weds, Sun), fruit machine, sports TV, no dogs inside; picnic-sets in pleasant back courtyard with roof terrace giving castle views, open all day (till 3am Fri, Sat). *(Phil and Jane Villiers)*

GUILDFORD SU9948

Olde Ship (01483) 575731

Portsmouth Road (St Catherine's, A3100 S); GU2 4EB Three cosy areas around central bar, ancient beams, bare boards and flagstones, roaring log fire in big fireplace, woodburner at the other end, comfortable mix of furniture, enjoyable food including good wood-fired pizzas, well kept Greene King ales and a guest, decent wines, friendly service, open all day weekends. *(Ian Phillips)*

GUILDFORD SU9949

Three Pigeons (01483) 575728

High Street; GU1 3AJ Nicholsons pub with good beer range, pleasant panelled décor, spiral stairs to upper bar; background music; open all day (till midnight Fri, Sat). *(Phil and Jane Villiers)*

HAMBLEDON SU9639

Merry Harriers (01428) 682883

Off A283; just N of village; GU8 4DR Popular beamed 16th-c country local with huge inglenook log fire and pine tables on bare boards, five well kept ales and decent wines, good generous pub food from sandwiches up, all home-made and sourced locally, friendly staff, occasional live music and beer festivals; children welcome, seats out in front and in big garden with boules, llamas and wandering chickens, attractive walking country near Greensand Way, three bedrooms in converted barn, campsite, open all day weekends. *(N R White)*

HASCOMBE TQ0039

White Horse (01483) 208258

B2130 S of Godalming; GU8 4JA Spacious pub under new management; 16th-c origins with beams and small-windowed alcoves, well kept ales including Hogs Back, Otter and Sharps, nice wines by the glass, good choice of popular food from sandwiches and sharing plates up, friendly young staff, bar on right with scrubbed tables and pews on wood floor, carpeted lounge on left with dining areas off, woodburner; children and dogs welcome, small front terrace, picnic-sets on sloping back lawn, pretty village with duck pond, good walks and handy for Winkworth Arboretum (NT), open all day. *(N R White, Mr and Mrs A H Young)*

HORSELL SU9859

Cricketers (01483) 762363

Horsell Birch; GU21 4XB Country pub popular for its good sensibly priced food including Sun carvery, cheerful efficient service, Shepherd Neame ales and plenty of wines by the glass, quietly comfortable sections and extended back eating area, log fires, newspapers, live jazz Mon; no dogs inside; children welcome, wheelchair access, picnic-sets out at front overlooking Horsell Common, big back garden with barbecue and play area. *(Ian Phillips)*

HORSELL SU9959

Plough (01483) 714105

Off South Road; Cheapside; GU21 4JL Small friendly local overlooking wooded heath, relaxed atmosphere, up to six well kept changing ales, three ciders and good choice of wines and malt whiskies, reasonably priced fresh food (not evenings Sat-Mon) including fine range of home-made pies, L-shaped bar with woodburner, newspapers; TV, games machine; children and dogs welcome, tables in pretty garden with play area, open all day. *(Harry Roy, Ian Phillips)*

HORSELL ⭐Red Lion SU9959 (01483) 768497

High Street; GU21 4SS Large and very popular with light airy feel, split-level bar with comfortable sofas and easy chairs, clusters of pictures on cream-painted walls, Fullers London Pride, St Austell Tribute and a guest from long wooden servery, a dozen wines by the glass, dining room with exposed brick walls, old pews and blackboards listing the good bistro-style food, efficient service; children allowed till early evening, ivy-clad passage to garden and comfortable tree-sheltered terrace, good walks, open all day. *(Ian Phillips, Nigel and Sue Foster, Simon Collett-Jones)*

HORSELL COMMON ⭐Sands at Bleak House TQ0160 (01483) 756988 *Chertsey Road, The Anthonys; A320 Woking–Ottershaw; GU21 5NL* Smart contemporary restauranty pub, grey split sandstone for floor and face of bar counter, brown leather sofas and cushioned stools, two dining rooms with dark wood furniture, good if not cheap food, Andwell, Hogs Back and Sharps, fresh juices, friendly attentive uniformed staff, woodburners, daily newspapers; background jazz, TV, lively acoustics; smokers' marquee in courtyard with picnic-sets, good shortish walks to sandpits which inspired H G Wells's *The War of the Worlds*, seven bedrooms, open all day, till 6pm Sun. *(Harry Roy, Ian Phillips)*

IRONS BOTTOM Three Horseshoes TQ2546 (01293) 862315 *Sidlow Bridge, off A217; RH2 8PT* Welcoming roadside pub with good reasonably priced home-made food from pub favourites up, well kept Fullers, Harveys, Wells & Youngs and three interesting guests, quick friendly service, traditional furnishings including upholstered banquettes, dark wood and patterned carpet, some barrel tables, darts; tables outside, summer barbecues, handy for Gatwick Airport. *(LM, C and R Bromage)*

KNAPHILL Hunters Lodge SU9557 (01483) 474602 *Bagshot Road; GU21 2RP* Spotless 18th-c Vintage Inn with comfortable linked beamed rooms, good log fires, assorted tables and chairs, their usual food including good value weekday set menu (till 5pm) and children's choices, Fullers London Pride, Sharps Doom Bar and a summer guest, plenty of wines by the glass, helpful friendly service, daily papers; disabled facilities, tables in pleasant

well established garden with decked area, open all day. *(Ian Phillips)*

LALEHAM ⭐Three Horseshoes TQ0568 (01784) 455014 *Shepperton Road (B376); TW18 1SE* Spacious airy bar with white walls and contrasting deep-blue woodwork, easy-going mix of furniture on bare boards, well kept Fullers/Gales beers, over a dozen wines by the glass, smarter dining areas with grey woodwork and caramel leather chairs, popular food all day, efficient young staff (they ask to keep a credit card while you eat); background music (live first Fri of month); children welcome in restaurant till 7pm, tables on flagstoned terrace, picnic-sets on grass, near pleasant stretch of the Thames. *(Hunter and Christine Wright, Nigel and Sue Foster, Simon Collett-Jones, Ian Phillips, Ron and Sheila Corbett and others)*

LIMPSFIELD CHART Carpenters Arms TQ4251 (01883) 722209 *Tally Road; RH8 0TG* Friendly open-plan pub recently taken over and refurbished by Westerham, their full range kept well (tasting trays available), enjoyable home-made food including good sandwiches, friendly helpful staff; nice little garden, delightful setting by village common, lovely walks and handy for Chartwell (NT). *(John Branston, Nick Lawless)*

LINGFIELD ⭐Hare & Hounds TQ3844 (01342) 832351 *Turn off B2029 N at the Crowhurst/ Edenbridge signpost; RH7 6BZ* Smallish open-plan bar with bare boards and flagstones, mixed seating including leather chesterfield, dining area, very good food from wide ranging menu cooked and beautifully presented by french landlord (sometimes 'daringly innovative' says one reader), efficient friendly service, well kept Harveys and Sharps Doom Bar, good wines by the glass; children and dogs welcome, tables in pleasant split-level garden with decking, nice walking country, open all day, closed Sun evening. *(Paul Nash and Colin Rugless, Peter and Michael Lee, David Alexander)*

MICKLEHAM King William IV TQ1753 (01372) 372590 *Just off A24 Leatherhead–Dorking; Byttom Hill; RH5 6EL* Steps up to small nicely placed country pub, well kept Hogs Back TEA, Surrey Hills Shere Drop and Triple fff Alton's Pride, wide choice of enjoyable food including blackboard specials and good vegetarian options, friendly attentive service, pleasant outlook from snug plank-panelled front bar; background music, outside gents'; children welcome, plenty of tables (some in heated open-sided timber shelters) in lovely

---

We say if we know a pub allows dogs.

terraced garden with great valley views, closed evenings Sun and Mon. (Jack and Sandra Clarfelt, John Coatsworth, Matthew Salisbury)

NEWDIGATE   TQ2043
✶ Surrey Oaks (01306) 631200
Off A24 S of Dorking, via Beare Green; Parkgate Road; RH5 5DZ Friendly village pub (known as the Soaks), well kept Harveys, Surrey Hills and three guests from smaller brewers (beer festivals May and Aug), bottled continentals and farm cider/perry, well liked reasonably priced bar food (not evenings Sun or Mon), open fire in snug beamed room, standing area with large flagstones and inglenook woodburner, rustic tables in light airy main lounge, separate games room with pool, skittle alley; maybe classical background music, TV and machines; children and dogs welcome, garden with terrace, rockery (pools and waterfall), play area and two boules pitches, open all day Sun till 9pm. (Graham and Elizabeth Hargreaves, D P and M A Miles, C and R Bromage)

OCKLEY   TQ1440
Inn on the Green (01306) 711032
Billingshurst Road (A29); RH5 5TD Welcoming 17th-c beamed coaching inn on green of charming village, good fresh traditional food, well kept Greene King and a guest like Kings, cheerful attentive service, slightly dated décor with usual pubby furniture and a few sofas, steps up to quiet eating area and dining conservatory; children welcome, tables in secluded garden with play area, six comfortable bedrooms, good breakfast. (Steve Tilley, Patricia Walker)

OCKLEY   TQ1337
✶ Punchbowl (01306) 627249
Oakwood Hill, signed off A29 S; RH5 5PU Attractive 16th-c tile-hung country pub with horsham slab roof; friendly landlord and welcoming relaxed atmosphere, wide choice of good value generously served food (all day weekends), Badger ales, central bar with huge inglenook, polished flagstones and low beams, collections of brass spiles, horsebrasses and cigarette lighters, restaurant area to left and another bar to right with sofas, armchairs and TV, daily papers; children welcome and dogs (water bowl and biscuits), picnic-sets in pretty garden, smokers' awning, quiet spot with good walks including Sussex Border Path, open all day (till 6.30pm Sun). (Pam Adsley, C and R Bromage)

OTTERSHAW   TQ0263
✶ Castle (01932) 872373
Brox Road, off A320 not far from M25 junction 11; KT16 0LW Friendly two-bar early Victorian local with big crackling log fires, country paraphernalia on black ceiling joists and walls, well kept Courage, Harveys, Hogs Back and Sharps, Addlestone's cider, enjoyable bar food (not Sun evening); background music, TV; children welcome in conservatory till 7pm, dogs in bar, tables on terrace and grass, open all day. (Ian Phillips)

OUTWOOD   TQ3146
Dog & Duck (01342) 842964
Prince of Wales Road; turn off A23 at station sign in Salfords, S of Redhill – OS Sheet 187 map reference 312460; RH1 5QU Unhurried beamed country pub with good fairly priced home-made food in bar or restaurant, friendly service, well kept Badger ales from brick-faced bar, decent wines, warm winter fires, monthly quiz and live music nights; children welcome, garden with duck pond and play area. (Richard Tilbrook)

OXTED   TQ3852
Old Bell (01883) 712181
High Street, Old Oxted; RH8 9LP Large beamed and panelled Chef & Brewer, good choice of popular well priced food, ales such as Sharps Doom Bar; children welcome, good wheelchair access, disabled facilities, garden. (Conor McGaughey, Neil Hardwick)

OXTED   TQ4048
Royal Oak (01883) 722207
Caterfield Lane, Staffhurst Wood, S of town; RH8 0RR Popular well managed pub, cheerful and comfortable, with good range of beers including Adnams, Harveys and Larkins, Biddenden cider, good value house wines, enjoyable locally sourced food including some imaginative dishes, back dining room; dogs welcome, nice garden with lovely views across fields, open all day weekends. (Simon Rodway, N R White, David Jackman)

PUTTENHAM   SU9347
Good Intent (01483) 810387
Signed off B3000 just S of A31 junction; The Street/Seale Lane; GU3 1AR Well worn-in convivial beamed village local, good choice of well kept changing ales alongside Otter, Sharps and Timothy Taylors, popular reasonably priced traditional food (not Sun, Mon), log fire in cosy front bar with alcove seating, newspapers, old photographs of the pub, simple dining area; well behaved children and dogs welcome, small sunny garden, good walks, open all day weekends. (N R White, John Mitchell)

PYRFORD LOCK   TQ0559
Anchor (01932) 342507
3 miles from M25 junction 10 – S on A3, then take Wisley slip road and go on past RHS Wisley garden; GU23 6QW Light and airy Badger family dining pub (can get very busy), food all day with small helpings available, lunchtime sandwiches too, simple tables on bare boards, quieter more comfortable panelled back area, narrowboat memorabilia, pleasant oak-framed

conservatory, daily papers; dogs allowed in part, splendid terrace in lovely spot by bridge and locks on River Wey Navigation, fenced-off play area, large car park across road, handy for RHS Wisley. *(Mervyn Granshaw, Ian Phillips, Susan and John Douglas)*

REDHILL TQ2850
Home Cottage (01737) 762771
Redstone Hill; RH1 4AW Stylishly refurbished 19th-c Youngs pub with their ales and guests, good variety of enjoyable food all day in bar and restaurant; seats outside including raised deck. *(Anon)*

REIGATE HEATH TQ2349
Skimmington Castle (01737) 243100
Off A25 Reigate–Dorking via Flanchford Road and Bonny's Road; RH2 8RL Nicely located small country pub, emphasis on enjoyable home-made food, ales such as Black Sheep, Harveys, Hogs Back and St Austell, friendly service, panelled beamed rooms, big working fireplace; children, dogs and muddy boots welcome. *(C and R Bromage, Ian Phillips)*

RIPLEY TQ0455
Jovial Sailor (01483) 224360
Portsmouth Road; GU23 6EZ Large Chef & Brewer, popular and cheerfully run, with decent reasonably priced food, four well kept changing ales and good wine choice, reconstructed well divided interior with standing timbers, beams, stripped brickwork and log fires including inglenook, country bric-a-brac, daily papers; background music; good-sized garden, handy for Wisley. *(Ian Phillips)*

RIPLEY TQ0456
Seven Stars (01483) 225128
Newark Lane (B367); GU23 6DL Neat 1930s family-run pub, enjoyable food from extensive menu, Brakspears, Fullers, Sharps and Shepherd Neame, good wines and coffee, snug areas, red patterned carpet, gleaming brasses and open fire; quiet background music; picnic-sets and heated wooden booths in tidy garden, river and canalside walks, closed Sun evening. *(Ian Phillips, Gordon Stevenson)*

SEND TQ0156
New Inn (01483) 762736
Send Road, Cartbridge; GU23 7EN Well placed old pub by River Wey Navigation, long bar decorated to suit, Adnams, Fullers, Greene King, Ringwood and a weekly guest, friendly informed service, good choice of well presented generous food from sandwiches to blackboard specials, beams and log-effect gas fires; large waterside garden with moorings and smokers' shelter. *(Anon)*

SEND MARSH TQ0455
★ Saddlers Arms (01483) 224209
Send Marsh Road; GU23 6JQ Genial and attentive licensees in unpretentious low-beamed local, homely and warm, with Fullers London Pride, Sharps Doom Bar and a couple of guests, good value generous home-made food (Sun till 4pm) from sandwiches to pizzas and pubby favourites, log-effect gas fire, sparkling brassware, toby jugs etc, live music and quiz nights; children and dogs welcome, picnic-sets out in front and behind, open all day. *(Ian Phillips)*

SHALFORD TQ0047
★ Seahorse (01483) 514350
A281 S of Guildford; The Street; GU4 8BU Gently upmarket Mitchells & Butlers dining pub with wide range of food from simple to more sophisticated choices, popular set menu (weekday lunchtimes, early evenings), friendly well trained young staff, Adnams and Sharps Doom Bar, good choice of wines and other drinks, contemporary furniture and artwork, double-sided log fire, smart dining room, comfortable part near entrance with sofas and huge window; picnic-sets in big lawned garden, covered terrace, handy for Shalford Mill (NT), open all day. *(Mr and Mrs A H Young, Ian Phillips)*

SHEPPERTON TQ0765
Thames Court (01932) 221957
Shepperton Lock, Ferry Lane; turn left off B375 towards Chertsey, 100 metres from Square; TW17 9LJ Huge Vintage Inn dining pub in great location by the Thames; plenty of wines by the glass, well kept ales such as Fullers, Purity and Sharps, their usual food all day from sandwiches to good Sun roasts, friendly efficient service, galleried central atrium with attractive panelled areas up and down stairs, two good log fires, daily papers; can get very busy weekends; children welcome, large attractive tree-shaded terrace with heaters, open all day. *(Brian Glozier, Ian Phillips, Ross Balaam)*

STAINES TQ0371
Bells (01784) 454240
Church Street; TW18 4ZB Sociable Youngs pub in old part of town, comfortable and well looked after, with good, promptly served fresh food (special diets catered for), their well kept ales and a guest, decent choice of wines, central fireplace; tables in nice back garden with heated terrace, limited roadside parking, open all day Fri-Sun (no food Sun evening). *(Ron and Sheila Corbett)*

STAINES TQ0371
Swan (01784) 452494
The Hythe; south bank, over Staines Bridge; TW18 3JB Splendid Thames-side setting, with moorings, good tables on riverside verandah and terrace, big conservatory, several distinctly different areas including river-view upstairs restaurant, enjoyable food from sandwiches up, prompt friendly service, well kept Fullers ales; can be very busy Sun lunchtime and on

summer evenings; 11 comfortable bedrooms, open all day. *(Ross Balaam)*

STOKE D'ABERNON TQ1259
Old Plough (01932) 862244
Station Road, off A245; KT11 3BN
Nicely refurbished 300-year-old pub under same ownership as the Red Lion at Horsell and Three Horseshoes at Laleham; good all-day food, Fullers and a guest like Surrey Hills, plenty of wines by the glass, competent friendly staff; children welcome in restaurant till 7.30pm, dogs in bar, seats out under pergola and in attractive garden. *(Lorry Spooner, Shirley Mackenzie)*

SUTTON ABINGER TQ1045
Volunteer (01306) 730798
Water Lane; just off B2126 via Raikes Lane, 1.5 miles S of Abinger Hammer; RH5 6PR Picturesque family-run pub in attractive setting above clear stream, low-ceilinged linked rooms, log fires, Badger ales, enjoyable standard food from sandwiches up, good friendly service, restaurant; terrace and suntrap lawns stepped up behind, nice walks. *(John Ecklin, Gill Hancock, Tom and Ruth Rees)*

SUTTON GREEN TQ0054
☆ Olive Tree (01483) 729999
Sutton Green Road; GU4 7QD
Big rambling dining pub in quiet countryside, good fresh food including fish and seafood, cheaper bar menu, well kept Ringwood, Sharps Doom Bar and Timothy Taylors Landlord, a dozen wines by the glass, pleasant helpful staff, bare boards and clean-cut pastel décor, fireside leather sofas, relaxing back dining room; terrace tables, closed Sun and Mon evenings. *(Ian Phillips)*

TADWORTH TQ2355
☆ Dukes Head (01737) 812173
Dorking Road (B2032 opposite common and woods); KT20 5SL Roomy and comfortably refurbished 19th-c pub, popular for its good varied choice of well priced food (all day except Sun evening) from generous sandwiches up, five well kept ales including a house beer (KT20) brewed by Morlands, Aspall's cider, good choice of wines by the glass, helpful cheery staff, three dining areas and two big inglenook log fires; background music, Weds quiz; lots of hanging baskets and plenty of tables in well looked after back garden, open all day (till 8pm Sun). *(Gwyn Harries, C and R Bromage, John Branston)*

TANDRIDGE TQ3750
Barley Mow (01883) 713770
Tandridge Lane, off A25 W of Oxted; RH8 9NJ Three decent sized bars, front

ones carpeted, beams, exposed brick and stonework, enjoyable food all day with fresh fish specials alongside pub staples, well kept Badger ales, good wines by the glass, friendly helpful service; background and Fri live music including jazz; children welcome till 9pm, dogs in bar, pleasant garden (summer barbecues) with heated smokers' shelter, three bedrooms, good breakfast. *(N R White, Ross Balaam)*

THAMES DITTON TQ1567
Albany (020) 8972 9163
Queens Road, signed off Summer Road; KT7 0QY Mitchells & Butlers bar-with-restaurant in lovely Thames-side position, light airy modern feel, with good variety of food from sharing plates and pizzas to more upscale dishes, weekday set menu lunchtime and early evening, good choice of wines by the glass, cocktails, a couple of beers such as Sharps Doom Bar and Timothy Taylors Landlord, log fire, river pictures, daily papers; nice balconies and river-view terrace, moorings, open all day. *(Tom and Ruth Rees)*

THAMES DITTON TQ1666
Ferry (020) 8398 1581
Portsmouth Road; KT7 0XY Welcoming and relaxed bistro-style dining pub with good reasonably priced food from chef-landlord, well kept ales; some tables out at front. *(Tom and Ruth Rees)*

THAMES DITTON TQ1667
Red Lion (020) 8398 8662
High Street; KT7 0SF Recently revamped (not smart) and extended, enjoyable home-made food from regularly changing menu, decent wines and coffee, ales such as Surrey Hills and Twickenham from servery clad with reclaimed doors, cheerful young staff; children welcome, seats on split-level terrace with Lego wall, open all day. *(Tom and Ruth Rees)*

THORPE TQ0268
Rose & Crown (01344) 845154
Sandhills Lane, Thorpe Green; TW20 8QL Part of the small Barons group, spacious with discrete nooks and crannies, Greene King, Sharps Doom Bar and Timothy Taylors Landlord, good variety of fairly priced food, friendly efficient staff; children welcome, smart outside eating area, garden play area. *(Ian Phillips, Gerry and Rosemary Dobson)*

TILFORD SU8742
Duke of Cambridge (01252) 792236
Tilford Road; GU10 2DD Civilised smartly done pub in same small local group as Queens Head at East Clandon and Stag

---

Though we don't usually mention it in the text, most pubs will now make coffee or tea – it's always worth asking.

at Eashing; enjoyable food with emphasis on local ingredients from varied interesting menu, children's meals too, good choice of wines, ales such as Hogs Back TEA and Surrey Hills Shere Drop, helpful service; terrace and garden with picnic-sets, good play area, open all day weekends. *(Mike and Jayne Bastin)*

VIRGINIA WATER SU9968
Rose & Olive Branch
(01344) 843713 *Callow Hill; GU25 4LH* Small unpretentious red-brick pub, with good choice of popular food including speciality pies, gluten-free and children's choices too, three Greene King ales, decent wines, friendly busy staff; background music; tables on front terrace and in garden behind, good walks. *(D J and P M Taylor)*

VIRGINIA WATER TQ9768
Wheatsheaf (01344) 842057
London Road; A30; GU25 4QF Several linked areas in large 18th-c inn (Chef & Brewer), reasonably priced food, real ales such as Hogs Back TEA and Sharps Doom Bar; children welcome, garden tables (traffic noise), by wooded entry to lake area, bedrooms, open all day. *(Ian Phillips)*

WALLISWOOD TQ1138
Scarlett Arms (01306) 627243
Signed from Ewhurst–Rowhook back road, or off A29 S of Ockley; RH5 5RD Cottagey 16th-c village pub with low beams, flagstones, simple furniture and two log fires (one in big inglenook), Badger ales, well priced traditional food plus some good malaysian dishes, friendly helpful staff, dining room behind; background music; children and dogs welcome, tables out at front and in garden under parasols, good walks, closed Sun evening, Mon. *(Anon)*

WALTON-ON-THAMES TQ1068
Weir (01932) 784530
Towpath, Waterside Drive, off Sunbury Lane; KT12 2JB Edwardian pub in nice Thames-side spot with big terrace overlooking river and weir (and steel walkway), decent choice of food all day (till 7.30pm Sun) from snacks up, ales such as Greene King, Sharps and Woodfordes, traditional décor, river pictures, newspapers; children and dogs welcome, lovely towpath walks, six bedrooms. *(Ian Phillips)*

WARLINGHAM TQ3955
Botley Hill Farmhouse
(01959) 577154 *S on Limpsfield Road (B269); CR6 9QH* Busy country pub dating from the 16th c with low-ceilinged linked rooms up and down steps, enjoyable reasonably priced food (till 6.30pm Sun) from standards up, well kept Greene King Abbot and local guests, decent choice of wines by the glass, good friendly staff, soft lighting, spreading carpet, quite close-set tables, big log fireplace in one attractive flagstoned room; marquee for weekend entertainment including tribute bands and discos; children and dogs welcome, disabled access, side and back terraces, neat garden with fine view, play area and aviary, open all day. *(Anon)*

WEST CLANDON TQ0451
⋆ Bulls Head (01483) 222444
A247 SE of Woking; GU4 7ST Comfortable, spotless and unchanging, based on 1540s timbered hall house, popular especially with older people at lunchtime for good value straightforward food (not Sun evening) including proper home-made pies, friendly helpful staff, ales such as Sharps, Surrey Hills and Wells & Youngs, good coffee, small lantern-lit beamed front bar with open fire and some stripped brick, old local prints and bric-a-brac, hops, simple raised back inglenook dining area, games room with darts and pool; children and dogs on leads welcome, disabled access from car park, good play area in neat garden, nice walks, handy for Clandon Park. *(Ian Phillips, Ron and Sheila Corbett, Richard and Sissel Harris)*

WEST CLANDON TQ0452
Onslow Arms (01483) 222447
A247 SE of Woking; GU4 7TE Fully refurbished, partly 17th-c beamed country pub (same owners as Red Lion at Horsell and Three Horseshoes at Laleham); good popular food from traditional choices up, well kept ales such as Harveys, Hop Back and Ringwood, friendly efficient service, leather sofas by big log fire, live music Weds; children (till early evening) and dogs welcome, terrace and garden seating. *(Geoffrey Kemp, Ian Phillips, Phil Bryant, Gordon and Margaret Ormondroyd, Alan Bowker)*

WEST HORSLEY TQ0853
⋆ Barley Mow (01483) 282693
Off A246 Leatherhead–Guildford at Bell & Colvill garage roundabout; The Street; KT24 6HR Welcoming tree-shaded traditional pub, low beams, mix of flagstones, bare boards and carpet, two log fires, well kept ales such as Fullers London Pride, Surrey Hills and Wells & Youngs, decent wines, enjoyable traditional food (not Sun evening) and thai menu (not Sun lunchtime), barn function room; background music; children welcome, dogs on leads, picnic-sets in good-sized garden, open all day. *(Anon)*

WEYBRIDGE TQ0763
Hand & Spear (01932) 828063
Old Heath Road/Station Road; KT13 8TX Big popular Youngs pub (former station hotel) with several different areas, enjoyable generous food including some unusual choices, their ales and a guest, good friendly staff; seats outside. *(Anne Rowe, Ian Phillips, John Coatsworth)*

WEYBRIDGE TQ0765
Minnow (01932) 831672
Thames Street/Walton Lane; KT13 8NG
Busy bay-windowed Mitchells & Butlers
dining pub, contemporary pastel décor and
unusual decorative panels, chunky tables and
chairs on gleaming flagstones, some sofas
and armchairs, two-way log fire in raised
hearth, popular well presented food from
pizzas and pasta up, set menu weekdays till
7pm, ales such as Fullers, Timothy Taylors
and Wells & Youngs, good wines by the glass,
friendly service; children welcome, big front
terrace with heaters, open all day. *(Ron and
Sheila Corbett)*

WEYBRIDGE TQ0965
Oatlands Chaser (01932) 253277
Oatlands Chase; KT13 9RW Big
attractively modernised building in quiet
residential road, rambling bar with stylish
contemporary décor, pastels and unusual
wallpaper, glazed panels, flagstones and
painted boards, feature central fireplace,
carefully mismatched furnishings mainly laid
out for the wide range of good all-day food
from sharing plates and light lunches to
Sun roasts and proper children's meals,
three well kept changing ales, good wine
choice, newspapers; disabled access, lots
of tables out at front (some under trees),
19 bedrooms. *(Ian Phillips, Minda and
Stanley Alexander)*

WEYBRIDGE TQ0765
✱ Old Crown (01932) 842844
Thames Street; KT13 8LP Comfortably
old-fashioned three-bar pub dating from
the 16th c, good value traditional food (not
Sun-Tues evenings) from sandwiches to
fresh fish, well kept Courage and Wells &
Youngs, good choice of wines by the glass,
friendly efficient service, family lounge and
conservatory, coal-effect gas fire; may be sports
TV in back bar with Lions RFC photographs,
silent fruit machine; children welcome,
secluded terrace, smokers' shelter, steps down
to suntrap garden overlooking Wey/Thames
confluence, mooring for small boats.
(Ian Phillips, James Barratt, John Millwood)

WEYBRIDGE TQ0865
Prince of Wales (01932) 852082
*Cross Road/Anderson Road, off Oatlands
Drive; KT13 9NX* Flower-decked mid
19th-c local with bargain pubby lunchtime
food in its three bars and back restaurant
(children allowed here), beers from Adnams,
Fullers and Wells & Youngs plus one badged
for the pub (Old Tosser) featuring a picture
of the landlord, several wines by the glass,
friendly relaxed atmosphere, open fire, tribal
mask collection and other bits and pieces,
daily papers; big-screen TV for major sports
events, live music Thurs; dogs welcome,
small pretty garden with sheltered area for
smokers, open all day. *(Ian Phillips)*

WEYBRIDGE TQ0664
Queens Head (01932) 839820
Bridge Road; KT13 8XS Refurbished
18th-c pub owned by Raymond Blanc's White
Brasserie Company, emphasis on dining but
also a proper bar serving Fullers and Sharps,
friendly staff; children under 8 eat free, open
all day. *(Ian Phillips, John Millwood)*

WINDLESHAM SU9464
Brickmakers (01276) 472267
*Chertsey Road (B386, W of B383
roundabout); GU20 6HT* Refurbished
red-brick dining pub, linked areas with pastel
and more vibrant colour schemes, light wood
furniture on flagstone or wood floors, two-way
woodburner, enjoyable freshly prepared
food (all day Fri-Sun), Courage Best, Fullers
London Pride and Sharps Doom Bar, good
choice of wines by the glass and decent
coffee, friendly helpful service, conservatory;
well behaved children allowed, attractive
garden with pergola, open all day from 9am
for breakfast. *(Anon)*

WOKING TQ0058
Herbert Wells (01483) 722818
Chertsey Road; GU21 5AJ Wetherspoons
named after H G Wells, busy with shoppers
yet with lots of cosy areas and side snugs,
ten well kept ales, three ciders and their
usual competitively priced all-day food,
friendly helpful staff, daily papers, old local
pictures; open from 8am. *(Harry Roy, Ian
Phillips)*

WOOD STREET SU9550
Royal Oak (01483) 235137
Oak Hill; GU3 3DA Popular 1920s village
local, comfortably unpretentious, with well
kept Courage, Surrey Hills Shere Drop and
four guests, local cider, good value traditional
home-cooked lunchtime food, friendly staff;
dogs welcome, good-sized garden. *(Ian Phillips)*

WOOD STREET SU9550
White Hart (01483) 235939
*White Hart Lane; off A323 just
W of Guildford; GU3 3DZ* Smartly
modernised 17th-c country dining pub,
good choice of well cooked food from open
kitchen including stone-baked pizzas,
several wines by the glass, friendly service,
sofas in beamed bar area with gas fire,
restaurant, buzzy atmosphere; a couple
of picnic-sets out at front, peaceful spot
tucked away off green, open all day.
(Richard Chinn, Martin and Karen Wake)

WORPLESDON SU9854
Jolly Farmer (01483) 234658
*Burdenshott Road, off A320 Guildford–
Woking, not in village; GU3 3RN* Old pub
in pleasant country setting, dark-beamed
bar with small log fire, Fullers/Gales beers,
stripped-brick dining extension with rugs
on bare boards, enjoyable traditional food

from lunchtime sandwiches up (they may ask to swipe your credit card if running a tab); background music; children and dogs welcome, garden tables under parasols and pergola, open all day. *(Anon)*

WOTTON   TQ1247
Wotton Hatch (01306) 887694
A25 Dorking–Guildford; RH5 6QQ
Stylish modern Mitchells & Butlers roadside dining pub, real ales, continental beers and good choice of wines and cocktails from zinc-topped bar, good popular food including pizzas, pasta and grills, weekday set menu till 7pm, attentive friendly service, log fire in 17th-c core, daily papers, conservatory; no dogs; children welcome, neat garden with impressive views, good local walks, open all day. *(Guy Vowles, Paul Rampton, Julie Harding)*

WRECCLESHAM   SU8344
Bat & Ball (01252) 792108
Bat & Ball Lane, South Farnham; approach from Sandrock Hill and Upper Bourne Lane, then narrow steep lane to pub; GU10 4SA Neatly refurbished pub tucked away in hidden valley, wide range of pubby and more upmarket food (small helpings available) including good puddings display, well kept Bowman, Hogs Back and

four guests (June beer festival), good choice of wines by the glass, friendly efficient staff, some live music; children and dogs welcome, disabled facilities, tables out on attractive heated terrace with vine arbour and in garden with substantial play fort, open all day. *(Anon)*

WRECCLESHAM   SU8244
Royal Oak (01252) 728319
The Street; GU10 4QS Black beamed 17th-c village pub with enjoyable fairly straightforward home-made food (smaller helpings available), friendly helpful staff, log fire, Sun quiz; children and dogs welcome, big garden with play area, open all day. *(R K Phillips, Patric Curwen)*

WRECCLESHAM   SU8344
Sandrock (01252) 715865
Sandrock Hill Road; GU10 4NS Two-bar pub with chunky furniture on bare boards, eight well kept changing ales and ten wines by the glass, friendly staff, enjoyable pubby evening food (not Sun – lunchtime roasts then) including range of good home-made pies, open fires; dogs welcome, a few seats in front, more on pleasant back terrace, open all day except Mon lunchtime. *(Tony and Jill Radnor)*

Post Office address codings confusingly give the impression that some pubs are in Surrey when they're really in Hampshire or London (which is where we list them). And there's further confusion from the way the Post Office still talks about Middlesex – which disappeared in local government reorganisation nearly 50 years ago.

Sussex

New to these pages, or back after a gap, are the Angel at Petworth (handsome inn with a long wine list, enterprising seasonal menu and pretty bedrooms), Blackboys Inn in Blackboys (newly refurbished, with local beers, good food and plenty of outside seating), Rose & Crown in Mayfield (weatherboarded pub in a beautiful village, with a new chef and menu), Gribble Inn at Oving (eight home-brew beers and tasty food using some foraged ingredients), Green Man in Partridge Green (upmarket but chatty dining pub using local ingredients) and Lamb at Wartling (newly refurbished country pub on the Pevensey Levels). Pubs our readers feel are doing very well include the Rose Cottage at Alciston (nice pub food and a great spot for South Downs walks), Coach and Horses at Danehill (busy dining pub with welcoming staff), Jolly Sportsman at East Chiltington (super upmarket food, smashing wines, seats in pleasant garden and rural location), Tiger at East Dean (lovely village-green spot, beers from adjacent brewery and near some of the South-east's finest coastal walks), Griffin at Fletching (as good as ever, with excellent food and four real ales), Horse Guards at Tillington (impressive food, comfortable bedrooms and thoughtful choice of drinks) and Cat in West Hoathly (extremely good food and in a charming Wealden village). Our Sussex Dining Pub 2014 is the Jolly Sportsman at East Chiltington.

ALCISTON
Rose Cottage
TQ5005   Map 3

Village signposted off A27 Polegate–Lewes; BN26 6UW

Old-fashioned cottage with cosy fires and country bric-a-brac, several wines by the glass, well liked food and local beers; bedrooms

You can walk straight to the South Downs from here, along the village street, which winds past a huge, ancient tithe barn and comes out beneath the steep escarpment. There are half a dozen tables with cushioned pews, winter log fires and quite a forest of harnesses, traps, a thatcher's blade and lots of other black ironware; more bric-a-brac on the shelves above the stripped pine dado or in the etched-glass windows and look out for Jasper the parrot (only at lunchtimes – he gets too noisy in the evenings). The restaurant area has a lunchtime overflow area as they don't take bookings in the bar then. Dark Star Hophead and Harveys Best on handpump and several wines by the glass. There are heaters outside for cooler evenings, and the small paddock in the garden has ducks and chickens. Nearby fishing and shooting. They take self-catering bedroom bookings for a minimum of two nights.

Good food might include ploughman's, various salads, smoked salmon cornet filled with prawns, pâté of the day with red onion relish, local pork sausages with onion gravy and mash, beer-battered cod and chips, steak and ale pie, cheddar and asapargus quiche, casserole of local wild rabbit with Harveys ale and orange, cheesy-topped garlic mussels, roast breast of free-range chicken with cajun seasoning, and puddings. *Benchmark main dish: fish pie £11.50. Two-course evening meal £17.50.*

Free house ~ Licensee Ian Lewis ~ Real ale ~ (01323) 870377 ~ Open 11.30-3, 6.30-11; 12-3, 6.30-10.30 Sun ~ Bar food 12-2, 6.30-9.30(9 Sun) ~ Restaurant ~ Children 10 and over welcome ~ Dogs allowed in bar ~ Bedrooms: /£60 ~ www.therosecottageinn.co.uk
Recommended by R and S Bentley, Peter and Jan Humphreys, Richard Tilbrook

ALFRISTON
George ♀

TQ5203   Map 3

High Street; BN26 5SY

Venerable 14th-c timbered inn in lovely village with comfortable, heavily beamed bars, good wines and several real ales; fine nearby walks; bedrooms

Just a few steps away from the bucolic village green, thatched Clergy House (National Trust) and a footbridge over the serenely beautiful Cuckmere River, this fine old inn has a spacious flint-walled garden with seats. The long bar has massive hop-hung low beams, appropriately soft lighting and a log fire (or summer flower arrangement) in a huge stone inglenook fireplace that dominates the room, with lots of copper and brass around it. Settles and chairs surround sturdy stripped tables; Greene King Abbot, Hardys & Hansons Old Trip and a guest like Dark Star Hophead on handpump, decent wines including champagne and several others by the glass, board games and background music; good service. The lounge has comfortable sofas, standing timbers and rugs on a wooden floor, and the restaurant is cosy and candlelit. Two long-distance paths, the South Downs Way and Vanguard Way, cross here. The beamed bedrooms are comfortable; they don't have a car park but there's parking a couple of minutes away.

Served all day, the well liked food includes lunchtime sandwiches, crayfish, crab and salmon tian, chicken and spinach roulade wrapped in parma ham, sharing boards (seafood, charcuterie), roasted rump of lamb with puy lentils and roasted beetroot, venison casserole, mediterranean stuffed aubergine, grilled sardines with rocket, red pepper and tomato salad, and puddings such as chocolate and walnut brownie or apple mousse with apple crisps and blackcurrant sorbet. *Benchmark main dish: linguine with king prawns, squid, mussels, spinach, chilli and tomatoes £14.50. Two-course evening meal £21.50.*

Greene King ~ Lease Roland and Cate Couch ~ Real ale ~ (01323) 870319 ~ Open 11(12 Sat, Sun)-11 ~ Bar food 12-9 ~ Restaurant ~ Children welcome ~ Dogs welcome ~ Bedrooms: £70/£140 ~ www.thegeorge-alfriston.com *Recommended by Brian and Anna Marsden, Richard Tilbrook*

ASHURST
Fountain ♀

TQ1816   Map 3

B2135 S of Partridge Green; BN44 3AP

**16th-c country pub with beams, flagstones and open fires,
good enjoyable food and drink and seats outside**

With plenty of character inside, this welcoming old tavern is an inviting spot for a drink or a meal. The neatly kept and charmingly rustic tap room on the right has a couple of high-backed wooden cottagey armchairs by a log fire in a brick inglenook, country dining chairs around polished wooden tables, a few bar stools on fine old flagstones and horsebrasses on the bressumer beam. The opened-up snug has wonky walls, more flagstones, heavy beams, simple furniture and its own inglenook fireplace; an oak-beamed skittle alley doubles as a function room. Harveys Best and three guests such as Courage Directors and Sharps Cornish Knocker on handpump, and several wines by the glass; service is friendly and attentive. The garden is prettily planted, there are seats on the front brick terrace, raised herb beds at the back, a young orchard and a duck pond.

Food includes sandwiches, confit duck with rhubarb, beer-battered fish and chips, calves liver and bacon, fish pie, butternut squash and blue cheese risotto, and puddings such as blood orange cheesecake and spiced tarte tatin. *Benchmark main dish: burger with tomato, red onion and fries £10.00. Two-course evening meal £16.00.*

Free house ~ Licensee Alex Tipping ~ Real ale ~ (01403) 710219 ~ Open 11-11; 12-10.30 Sun ~ Bar food 12-2.30, 6-9.30; 12-9.30 Sat; 12-8 Sun ~ Restaurant ~ Children welcome except in front bar ~ Dogs allowed in bar ~ www.fountainashurst.co.uk
Recommended by Emma Scofield, Steve Homer, Pete Walker

BLACKBOYS
Blackboys Inn

TQ5220   Map 3

B2192, S edge of village; TN22 5LG

**Weatherboarded and tile-hung 14th-c pub with a bustling locals' bar,
nice dining rooms, good choice of drinks and food and plenty of seats
in an attractive garden**

Set back from the road beyond a lawn, this conspicuously attractive pub is a pleasant place for sitting outside, with seating areas beneath trees to the front, plenty of contemporary tables and chairs on a terrace and more under cover beside a sizeable duck pond; up a step, a side lawn has yet more seats and a pretty gazebo. Inside, parquet flooring runs through the rooms, with the beamed locals' bar to the left having a good, chatty atmosphere and lots of bric-a-brac, while, to the right, the main bar has beams, timbers, dark wooden furniture and a winter log fire in a brick fireplace. The restaurant has a cream colour scheme with panelled walls and wooden chairs and tables, framed prints and knick-knacks, and another dining area has cream walls and panelling and green and purple padded chairs and curtains. Harveys Best and a couple of seasonal Harveys brews on handpump and several wines by the glass; background music. The Vanguard Way passes the pub, the Wealdway goes close by and there's a woodland walk opposite.

Food includes sandwiches, tomato and roast pepper soup, prawn and crayfish cocktail, chicken breast wrapped in parma ham with mushroom stuffing, steak and ale pie, sausage and mash, rib-eye steak, tuna steak with chilli and lime glaze, and leek and butter bean risotto, and puddings. *Benchmark main dish: Sussex smokie £10.95. Two-course evening meal £16.50.*

Harveys ~ Tenant Nick Pearce ~ Real ale ~ (01825) 890283 ~ Open 12-midnight(10.30 Sun) ~ Bar food 12-2.30(3 Fri), 6-9.30; 12-9 Sat; 12-7 Sun ~ Restaurant ~ Children welcome ~ Dogs allowed in bar ~ Live music fortnightly ~ www.theblackboys.co.uk
Recommended by Isobel Mackinlay

CHARLTON

SU8812 Map 2

Fox Goes Free

Village signposted off A286 Chichester–Midhurst in Singleton, also from Chichester–Petworth via East Dean; PO18 0HU

Comfortable old pub with beamed bars, popular food and drink and big garden; bedrooms

On a delightfully unspoilt village street and not far from Goodwood, this place is popular with both walkers and race-goers. In fine weather, you can sit at a picnic-set under the apple trees in the attractive back garden with the downs as a backdrop, or at the rustic benches and tables on the gravelled front terrace. Inside, the bar is the first of a dark, cosy series of separate rooms: old irish settles, tables and chapel chairs and an open fire. Standing timbers divide a larger beamed bar, which has a huge brick fireplace with a woodburning stove and old local photographs on the walls. A dining area with hunting prints overlooks the garden. The family extension is a clever conversion from horse boxes and the stables where the 1926 Goodwood winner was housed; darts, TV, games machine, background music and board games. Ballards Best, Otter Bitter, a beer named for the pub brewed by Arundel and a guest such as Sharps Doom Bar on handpump, several wines by the glass and Addlestone's cider. You can walk up to Levin Down nature reserve or stroll around the Iron Age hillfort on the Trundle, with huge views to the Isle of Wight; the Weald & Downland Open Air Museum and West Dean Gardens are nearby too.

Food includes ciabattas, soup, smoked salmon and anchovy salad, scallop and prawn risotto, pie of the day, tomato and onion tart with halloumi and sweet chilli sauce, rib-eye steak, and puddings. *Benchmark main dish: home-made pie £12.50. Two-course evening meal £22.50.*

Free house ~ Licensee David Coxon ~ Real ale ~ (01243) 811461 ~ Open 11am-11.30pm; 12-10.30 Sun ~ Bar food 12-2.30, 6.15-9.30; 12-10 weekends ~ Restaurant ~ Children welcome ~ Dogs allowed in bar ~ Live music Weds ~ Bedrooms: £65/£90 ~ www.thefoxgoesfree.com *Recommended by Roy Hoing, J A Snell, Steve Homer, C and R Bromage*

CHIDDINGLY

TQ5414 Map 3

Six Bells £

Village signed off A22 Uckfield–Hailsham; BN8 6HE

Lively, unpretentious village local with good weekend live music, bargain bar food and a friendly long-serving landlord

It's distinctly lively here at weekends, when bands play, but even at busy times the place ticks along very well. There's plenty of unpretentious character in the many small interconnected bars with their interesting bric-a-brac, local pictures, photographs and posters – as well as solid old wood pews, antique chairs and tables and cushioned window seats;

log fires too. A sensitive extension provides some much-needed family space; board games. Courage Directors, Harveys Best and a guest beer such as Theakstons Double Cross IPA on handpump and decent wines by the glass. Outside at the back there are tables beyond a big raised goldfish pond and a boules pitch; the church opposite has the interesting Jefferay Monument. Popular weekend live music, and vintage and kit car meetings outside the pub every month. This is a pleasant area for walks.

Exceptionally good value and well liked, the food includes rolls, french onion soup, green-lipped mussels, ham hock, large yorkshire pudding filled with roast beef, stilton and walnut pie, spicy prawns mexicano on rice, and puddings such as raspberry pavlova and chocolate sponge pudding. *Benchmark main dish: steak and kidney pie £4.80. Two-course evening meal £9.00.*

Free house ~ Licensee Paul Newman ~ Real ale ~ (01825) 872227 ~ Open 11-3, 6-11; 11am-midnight Fri, Sat; 12-10.30 Sun ~ Bar food 12-2.15, 6-9.30; all day Fri-Sun ~ Children allowed away from main bar ~ Dogs allowed in one bar only ~ Live music Fri-Sun evenings, Sun lunchtime *Recommended by Dr A J and Mrs B A Tompsett, Jason Caulkin, Ann and Colin Hunt*

CHILGROVE
Royal Oak £
SU8116   Map 2

Off B2141 Petersfield–Chichester, signed Hooksway; PO18 9JZ

Unchanging and peaceful country pub with welcoming licensees, honest food and big pretty garden

Well tucked away in a wooded location amid the South Downs, this isolated pub is a lovely place to visit during a country walk. The two simple, cosy bars have huge log fires, plain country kitchen tables and chairs, and Sharps Doom Bar and three guests such as Exmoor Beast, Fullers HSB and Gales HSB on handpump. There's also a cottagey dining room with a woodburning stove and a plainer family room; background music, cribbage, dominoes and shut the box. Twiglet and Amber are the pub staffies and there's a parrot called Gilbert. The large pretty garden has picnic-sets under parasols.

Satisfying, unpretentious food includes sandwiches, pâté and toast with cranberry sauce, creamy garlic mushrooms, mixed grill, rump steak with stilton or au poivre sauce, salmon fillet, chicken curry, home-made pies, tuna pasta bake, vegetable lasagne, slow-cooked pork hock with apple and cider sauce and venison steak with mulled wine and redcurrant jelly, and puddings. *Benchmark main dish: venison pie £10.95. Two-course evening meal £15.00.*

Free house ~ Licensee Dave Jeffery ~ Real ale ~ (01243) 535257 ~ Open 11.30-2.30, 6-11; 12-3 Sun; closed Sun evening, Mon, first two weeks Nov ~ Bar food 12-2, 7-9 ~ Restaurant ~ Children allowed in family room ~ Dogs allowed in bar ~ Live country and western music second Fri evening of month ~ www.royaloakhooksway.co.uk
Recommended by Ann and Colin Hunt

DANEHILL
Coach & Horses ⦿ ♀
TQ4128   Map 3

Off A275, via School Lane towards Chelwood Common; RH17 7JF

Well run dining pub with bustling bars, welcoming staff, very good food and ales and a big garden

This pub on the fringes of the Ashdown Forest continues its winning ways, serving enjoyable food and giving a friendly welcome. A little

bar to the right has half-panelled walls, simple furniture on polished
floorboards, a small woodburner in a brick fireplace and a big hatch
to the bar counter. Harveys Best and a guest such as Dark Star Best on
handpump, local Black Pig farmhouse cider and several wines by the glass
including prosecco and Bluebell sparkling wine from Sussex. A couple of
steps lead down to a half-panelled area with a mix of dining chairs around
characterful wooden tables (set with flowers and candles) on a fine brick
floor, and artwork on the walls that changes every couple of months;
cribbage, dominoes and cards. Down another step is a dining area with
stone walls, beams, flagstones and a woodburning stove. There's an adult-
only terrace under a huge maple tree, and picnic-sets and a play area in the
big garden, which has fine views of the South Downs.

🍴 Using local produce, the enjoyable food might include sandwiches, butternut
squash and chilli soup, fennel-cured roast salmon with pickled rhubarb,
confit duck leg with roast garlic potato gratin, rib-eye steak, beer-battered fish and
chips, chicken and ham pie, specials such as roasted veal sirloin with braised oxtail
parcel or smoked bacon and blue cheese risotto with crispy shallots and sorrel,
and puddings. *Benchmark main dish: roast haunch of local venison £14.00.
Two-course evening meal £19.00.*

Free house ~ Licensee Ian Philpots ~ Real ale ~ (01825) 740369 ~ Open 12-3, 5-11;
12-11 Sat; 12-10.30 Sun ~ Bar food 12-2(2.30 Sat), 7-9(9.30 Fri, Sat); 12-3 Sun ~
Restaurant ~ Well behaved children welcome except on adult terrace ~ Dogs allowed
in bar ~ www.coachandhorses.danehill.biz *Recommended by David Jackman, N R White,
Steve Homer, Alan Bowker, R and S Bentley, Pete Walker*

DIAL POST
Crown

TQ1519 Map 3

Worthing Road (off A24 S of Horsham); RH13 8NH

**Tile-hung village pub with interesting food and a good mix of drinkers
and diners**

Run by very friendly staff, this extended, pleasantly spacious village
pub is much liked for its food. The beamed bar has a couple of
standing timbers, brown squashy sofas and pine tables and chairs on
a stone floor, a small woodburning stove in a brick fireplace, and Harveys
Best and two changing guest beers from breweries such as Bedlam
and Downlands on handpump from the attractive herringbone brick
counter; several wines by the glass. The pub dog is called Chops. The
straightforwardly furnished dining conservatory, facing the village green,
is light and airy. To the right of the bar, the restaurant (with more beams)
has an ornamental woodburner in a brick fireplace, a few photographs,
chunky pine tables, chairs and a couple of cushioned pews and a shelf of
books; steps lead down to a further dining room; background music and
board games. There are picnic-sets on grass behind the pub.

🍴 Using local, seasonal produce, the extremely popular food might include
lunchtime sandwiches, chicken liver pâté, ham and free-range egg, natural
smoked haddock in fish velouté sauce on spinach topped with prawns, breaded
veal escalope, beer-battered fish and chips, fregola pasta with tomatoes and mixed
beans, and puddings such as seasonal fruit crumble and home-made ice-creams
and sorbets. *Benchmark main dish: steak burger £10.50. Two-course evening
meal £19.50.*

Free house ~ Licensees James and Penny Middleton-Burn ~ Real ale ~ (01403) 710902
~ Open 11.30-3, 6-11; 12-10 Sat; 12-4 Sun; closed Sun evening ~ Bar food 12-2.15, 6-9
(9.30 Fri, Sat); not Sun evening ~ Restaurant ~ Children welcome but must be dining

after 7pm ~ Dogs allowed in bar and bedrooms ~ www.crowninndialpost.co.uk
Recommended by Simon and Mandy King, Pat and Stewart Gordon, Geoffrey Taylor, Ron and Sheila Corbett, Sara Fulton, Roger Baker, Tony and Wendy Hobden, Tracey and Stephen Groves

DUNCTON
Cricketers

SU9517 Map 3

Set back from A285; GU28 0LB

Charming old coaching inn near Goodwood, with friendly licensees, real ales, popular food and suntrap back garden

The inn here dates from at least the 1600s, and its present name was given by its 19th-c owner John Wisden, the cricketer who published the famous *Wisden Cricketers' Almanack*. Accordingly, there's a display of cricketing memorabilia in the friendly traditional bar, which has a few standing timbers, simple seating and an open woodburning stove in an inglenook fireplace. Steps lead down to a dining room simply furnished with wooden tables and chairs. Gribble Fuzzy Duck, Kings Horsham Best Bitter and Triple fff Moondance alongside a guest such as Bowman Quiver on handpump, several wines by the glass and Thatcher's cider. There are picnic-sets out in front beneath flowering window boxes and more on decked areas and under parasols on the grass in the picturesque back garden, which makes the most of the pub's position in the Goodwood Hills.

 Food includes lunchtime sandwiches (not Sunday), chicken liver pâté with chutney, crab, prawn and leek gratin, ham and eggs, chicken caesar salad, toad in the hole with onion gravy, pie of the day, beer-battered fresh haddock, steamed steak and kidney pudding, field mushroom burger topped with goats cheese and vine tomatoes, and puddings. *Benchmark main dish: steak, ale and mushroom pie £10.95. Two-course evening meal £16.00.*

Inn Company ~ Lease Martin Boult ~ Real ale ~ (01798) 342473 ~ Open 11-11; 12-10.30 Sun ~ Bar food 12-2.30, 6-9; 12-9 weekends and summer holidays ~ Restaurant ~ Children welcome ~ Dogs allowed in bar ~ www.thecricketersduncton.co.uk
Recommended by John and Anne Mackinnon, Martin and Karen Wake, Steve Homer

EAST CHILTINGTON
Jolly Sportsman 🍴 ♟

TQ3715 Map 3

2 miles N of B2116; Chapel Lane – follow sign to 13th-c church; BN7 3BA

Sussex Dining Pub of the Year

Excellent modern food in civilised, rather smart place, small bar for drinkers, contemporary furnishings, fine wine list and huge range of malt whiskies; pleasant garden

Getting consistently good reports for many years, this is an accomplished dining pub that does things with considerable flair. The bar may be small but it's light and full of character, with a roaring winter fire, a mix of furniture on stripped-wood floors and Dark Star Hophead and Harveys Best tapped from the cask. They also have a remarkably good wine list with around a dozen by the glass, over 100 malt whiskies, a good choice of ciders (including from France), an extensive list of cognacs, Armagnacs and grappa and quite a choice of bottled belgian beers. The larger restaurant is smart but cosy and welcoming, with contemporary light wood furniture and modern landscapes on coffee-coloured walls; there's also a garden room.

The cottagey front garden is inviting, with rustic tables and benches under gnarled trees on the terrace and front bricked area, and more on a large back lawn; views extend towards the downs and there's a play area. From here, you can stroll or cycle past the church and through the trees along an unmade track (following the course of a Roman road).

¶ Exceptional food includes lunchtime sandwiches and ploughman's, mussel and oyster chowder, pigs head terrine with pork rillettes and celeriac remoulade, oysters, fillet of gurnard with ratatouille and bouillabaisse sauce, barbary duck breast with puy lentils, cashew nut roast with grilled peppers and asparagus, and puddings. *Benchmark main dish: rump of lamb with dauphinoise potatoes £16.95. Two-course evening meal £20.00.*

Free house ~ Licensee Bruce Wass ~ Real ale ~ (01273) 890400 ~ Open 12-3, 6-11; 12-11 Sat; 12-4 Sun ~ Bar food 12-2.30(3 Sat), 6.30-9.30; 12-3.30 Sun ~ Restaurant ~ Children welcome ~ Dogs allowed in bar ~ www.thejollysportsman.com
Recommended by Jason Woodford, Kim Turner, Steve Homer, N R White, Nick Lawless

EAST DEAN TV5597 Map 3
Tiger ♀ 🛏
Off A259 Eastbourne–Seaford; BN20 0DA

Charming old pub by cottage-lined village green, two little bars and a dining room, and an informal and friendly atmosphere; bedrooms

Well positioned for walks to the coast and along the clifftops of the Seven Sisters and up to Belle Tout Lighthouse and Beachy Head, this inn has a picture-perfect location, with customers sitting out on the village green. As popular with drinkers as it is with diners, the atmosphere is always chatty and relaxed and the staff are welcoming and attentive, though it can get busy – it does pay to arrive early to be sure of a seat. The focal point of the little beamed main bar is the open woodburning stove in a brick inglenook surrounded by polished horsebrasses; there are just a few rustic tables with benches, simple wooden chairs, a window seat and a long cushioned wall bench. The walls are hung with fish prints and a stuffed tiger's head, with a couple of hunting horns above the long bar counter. Harveys Best and their own-brewed Beachy Head Legless Rambler, Lighthouse and a seasonal brew are available on handpump (brewery tours available on request), and several wines by the glass. Down a step on the right is a small room with an exceptionally fine high-backed curved settle and a couple of other old settles, nice old chairs and wooden tables on coir carpeting, and an ancient map of Eastbourne and Beachy Head and photographs of the pub on the walls; the dining room to the left of the main bar has a cream woodburner and hunting prints. There are picnic-sets on the terrace among window boxes and flowering climbers. The bedrooms are comfortable and the breakfasts good.

¶ Using some of their own-grown salad and vegetables, the much liked food includes soup, pâté of the day, goats cheese mousse with mediterranean vegetables, beer-battered cod and chips, fried duck breast, pork loin steak with champ mash and caramelised apples, sausage and mash, risotto of the day, and puddings such as steamed pudding of the day and cheesecake. *Benchmark main dish: Tiger burger £10.95. Two-course evening meal £18.50.*

Free house ~ Licensee Jacques Pienaar ~ Real ale ~ (01323) 423209 ~ Open 11am-11.30pm(12.30am Sat) ~ Bar food 12-3, 6-9 ~ Children welcome ~ Dogs allowed in bar ~ Bedrooms: /£110 ~ www.beachyhead.org.uk *Recommended by MP, David Hill, Jason Caulkin, Ron and Sheila Corbett, Steve Homer, Pete Walker*

EAST LAVANT   SU8608 Map 2
Royal Oak 🍴 ♀ 🛏
Pook Lane, off A286; PO18 0AX

Bustling and friendly dining pub with proper drinking area, excellent food, extensive wine list and real ales; super bedrooms

In a quiet village beneath the downs, and run by attentive staff, this attractive pub puts an emphasis on food, but still welcomes those coming in for just a drink. It's open-plan with low beams and exposed brickwork, crooked timbers, winter log fires and church candles. The much used drinking area at the front has wall seats and sofas, Arundel Gold and Sharps Doom Bar tapped from the cask, 20 wines by the glass from an extensive list and a friendly welcome from attentive staff. The attached seating area is focused on dining and sensitively furnished with brown suede and leather dining chairs around scrubbed pine tables, with pictures of motor sport and local scenes on the walls; background music. Outside are cushioned seats and tables under green parasols on a flagstoned front terrace offering far-reaching views to the downs; rambling around the side and back are terraced, brick and grass areas with more seats and attractive flowering tubs and baskets. Bedrooms are stylish and well equipped and they also have self-catering cottages. The car park is across the road.

 The innovative modern menu typically includes sandwiches, ham hock and parsley terrine, breast of woodpigeon with apple tarte tatin, steaks, vegetable risotto, roast breast of guinea fowl with prune terrine and blackcurrant jus, roast fillet of monkfish wrapped in nori seaweed and parma ham, and puddings. *Benchmark main dish: assiette of pork with confit belly pork and pork shoulder gallette £16.90. Two-course evening meal £22.50.*

Free house ~ Licensee Charles Ullmann ~ Real ale ~ (01243) 527434 ~ Open 11-11 (midnight Sat); 12-11 Sun ~ Bar food 12-2.30, 6-9(9.30 Fri, Sat); 12-3, 6.30-9 Sun ~ Restaurant ~ Children welcome ~ Dogs allowed in bar ~ Bedrooms: £95/£125 ~ www.royaloakeastlavant.co.uk *Recommended by John Evans, Tony and Jill Radnor*

ERIDGE GREEN   TQ5535 Map 3
Nevill Crest & Gun ♀
A26 Tunbridge Wells–Crowborough; TN3 9JR

Handsome 16th-c former farmhouse with lots of character, beams and standing timbers, hundreds of pictures and photographs, six real ales, enjoyable modern food and friendly efficient staff

The good choice of drinks at this efficiently run Brunning & Price pub features Adnams, Groombridge Black Cat, Harveys, Larkins Original and Phoenix Brunning & Price alongside a guest such as Kings Spring Ale on handpump, two farmhouse ciders including Biddenden and good wines by the glass. The 500-year-old building has been carefully and cleverly opened up with standing timbers and doorways keeping some sense of separate rooms; the atmosphere is civilised but informal, with

---

'Children welcome' means the pub says it lets children inside without any special restriction. If it allows them in, but to restricted areas such as an eating area or family room, we specify this. Some pubs may impose an evening time limit. We do not mention limits after 9pm as we assume children are home by then.

a happy mix of customers of all ages. Throughout are heavy beams (some carved), panelling, rugs on wooden floors, woodburning stoves and an open fire in three fireplaces (the linenfold carved bressumer above one is worth seeking out), all manner of individual dining chairs around dark wood or copper-topped tables and lots of pictures, maps and photographs, many of them local to the area. The window sills are full of toby jugs, stone and glass bottles and plants; daily papers, board games and background music. There are a few picnic-sets out in front, as well as teak furniture on a back terrace, beside the more recent dining extension with its large windows, light oak rafters, beams and coir flooring.

From a bistro-style menu, the popular food might include sandwiches, beetroot-cured trout with avocado crème fraîche and pickled ginger, pulled pork and black pudding croquette, beer-battered haddock, sausage and mash, gnocchi with roasted butternut squash, and puddings such as dark chocolate brownie and poached rhubarb, apple and ginger crumble. *Benchmark main dish: braised shoulder of lamb with dauphinoise potatoes £16.50. Two-course evening meal £20.00.*

Brunning & Price ~ Manager Adam Holland ~ Real ale ~ (01892) 864209 ~ Open 12-11 (10.30 Sun) ~ Bar food 12-9,30(9 Sun) ~ Children welcome ~ Dogs allowed in bar ~ www.nevillcrestandgun.co.uk *Recommended by Richard and Penny Gibbs, Nigel and Jean Eames*

EWHURST GREEN   TQ7924   Map 3
White Dog
Turn off A21 to Bodiam at S end of Hurst Green, cross B2244, pass Bodiam Castle, cross river then bear left uphill at Ewhurst Green sign; TN32 5TD

Welcoming village pub with a nice little bar, several real ales and popular food

The garden behind this friendly family-run pub has plenty of picnic-sets and views of Bodiam Castle (National Trust), making it a lovely place to sit out on a summer's day. The bar on the left has a fine inglenook fireplace, hop-draped beams, wood-panelled walls, farm implements, horsebrasses and just a few tables with high-backed, rush-seated dining chairs and red plush bar stools on the old brick or flagstoned floor. There's also a high-backed cushioned settle by the counter; Harveys Best and a Long Man ale alongside two guest beers from breweries such as Hastings and Old Dairy on handpump and several wines by the glass. To the right of the entrance is the dining room with murals of the local area, and sturdy wooden tables and chairs on more flagstones; background music. A games room has darts, pool and board games.

Making the most of local, seasonal produce, the well liked food could feature baguettes, goats cheese and tomato tart, steamed scallops or seared pigeon breasts, a catch of the day, roasted glazed rack of lamb, mushroom risotto, free-range chicken escalope, and puddings. *Benchmark main dish: chargrilled chump of lamb with rosemary and garlic oil £15.50. Two-course evening meal £20.00.*

Free house ~ Licensees Harriet and Dale Skinner ~ Real ale ~ (01580) 830264 ~ Open 12-3, 5-11; 12-11 Fri, Sun; 12-11.30 Sat ~ Bar food 12-2.30, 6.30-9; 12-3 Sun ~ Restaurant ~ Children welcome ~ Dogs allowed in bar and bedrooms ~ Live music monthly ~ Bedrooms: /£85 ~ www.thewhitedogewhurst.co.uk *Recommended by Tom and Rosemary Hall, Conrad Freezer, Rob Newland, Mrs Blethyn Elliott, B and M Kendall*

FLETCHING
TQ4223 Map 3

Griffin 🍴 🍷 🛏

Village signposted off A272 W of Uckfield; TN22 3SS

Busy, gently upmarket inn with a fine wine list, bistro-style bar food, real ales and big garden with far-reaching views; bedrooms

The high standards at this civilised, well run inn have been much appreciated by readers over the years. The beamed and quaintly panelled bar rooms have blazing log fires, old photographs and hunting prints, straightforward close-set furniture including some captain's chairs, and china on a delft shelf. There's a small bare-boards serving area off to one side and a snug separate bar with sofas and a TV. Harveys Best, Hogs Back TEA, Kings Horsham Best and a guest beer on handpump, a fine wine list with about 20 by the glass (including champagne and dessert wine) and farm cider. The bright, airy bedrooms are comfortable and the breakfasts good. There are ramps for wheelchairs. An appealing and very spacious two-acre back garden has plenty of seats for diners on the sandstone terrace and grass, as well as lovely views towards Sheffield Park Garden (National Trust); regular summer Sunday barbecues.

 Using local and organic produce, the well rounded menu might include ciabattas, wild garlic soup, home-cured gravadlax, rib-eye steak, fresh crab linguine, baby leek, white onion and taleggio tart, roast rack of romney marsh lamb with butternut squash and borlotti bean stew, and puddings such as home-made mint sorbet, cardamom custard tart with chocolate sauce and sticky toffee pudding; children's menu. *Benchmark main dish: beer-battered cod and hand-cut chips £13.50. Two-course evening meal £21.50.*

Free house ~ Licensees James Pullan and Samantha Barlow ~ Real ale ~ (01825) 722890 ~ Open 11.30am-1am; 11.30am-1.30am Sat; 12-midnight Sun ~ Bar food 12-2.30 (3 Sat, Sun), 7-9.30 ~ Restaurant ~ Children welcome ~ Dogs allowed in bar ~ Bedrooms: £80/£85 ~ www.thegriffininn.co.uk *Recommended by Nigel and Jean Eames, Tom and Ruth Rees, Mrs J Ekins-Daukes, Nick Lawless*

HEATHFIELD
TQ5920 Map 3

Star 🍺

Church Street, Old Heathfield, off A265/B2096 E; TN21 9AH

Pleasant old pub with bustling, friendly atmosphere, good mix of locals and visitors, well liked food and decent choice of drinks; pretty garden

This character-laden, charmingly unchanged old building dates from the 14th c, when it was built as a resting place for pilgrims on their way across the Weald to Canterbury. It has ancient heavy beams, built-in wall settles and window seats, panelling, inglenook fireplaces and a roaring winter log fire; a doorway leads to a similarly decorated room more set up for eating with wooden tables and chairs and a woodburning stove. An upstairs dining room has a striking barrel-vaulted ceiling (built as a dormitory for masons working on the reconstruction of the church after a fire in 1348). Harveys Best and three changing guest ales on handpump and an extensive wine list including several by the glass; friendly, helpful staff and background music. The garden is very prettily planted, with rustic furniture under smart umbrellas and lovely views of rolling oak-lined sheep pastures.

Popular food includes tiger prawns in garlic and ginger, stuffed baked mushroom with goats cheese, lasagne, beer-battered fish and chips, home-cooked ham and eggs, local sausages, seasonal game and fish dishes, specials such as fillet of hake, asparagus and wild garlic risotto or free-range pork fillet stuffed with sun-dried tomatoes, and puddings such as knickerbocker glory and citrus ginger crunch. *Benchmark main dish: rib-eye steak £11.95. Two-course evening meal £19.00.*

Free house ~ Licensees Mike and Sue Chappell ~ Real ale ~ (01435) 863570 ~ Open 11-11; 12-10 Sun ~ Bar food 12-2.30, 6.30-9; 12-3, 6-8.30 Sun ~ Restaurant ~ Children welcome ~ Dogs welcome ~ www.starinnoldheathfield.co.uk *Recommended by Nick Lawless, Mrs Blethyn Elliott*

HORSHAM
TQ1730   Map 3

Black Jug ♀
North Street; RH12 1RJ

Bustling town pub with wide choice of drinks, efficient staff and freshly produced bar food

Part of the excellent Brunning & Price chain, this well run pub has an impressive range of drinks including Caledonian Deuchars IPA, Harveys Best and three guests such as Theakstons on handpump, 20 wines by the glass, around 100 malt whiskies and farmhouse cider. The one large open-plan turn-of-the-century room has a long central bar, a nice collection of sizeable dark wood tables and comfortable chairs on a stripped-wood floor, board games, bookcases and interesting old prints and photographs above a dark wood-panelled dado on the cream walls. A spacious, bright conservatory has similar furniture and lots of hanging baskets. The pretty flower-filled back terrace has plenty of garden furniture. The small car park is for staff and deliveries only, but you can park next door in the council car park.

...................andwiches, the well liked food from a frequently changing menu ....ilton cheesecake with walnut and biscuit base and ....ed haddock and salmon fishcake with tomato ....e, braised shoulder of lamb with gratin potato and ....k breast with avocado and mango salad, and puddings ....ramelised apple tart with toffee sauce. *Benchmark* ....ddock with chips £12.25. Two-course evening

.........: Alastair Craig ~ Real ale ~ (01403) 253526 ~ Open 10.30am-.........r food 12-10(9.30 Sun) ~ Children welcome till 5pm ~ Dogs ....lackjug-horsham.co.uk *Recommended by Emma Scofield*

......ORTH
SU9321   Map 2

H...lfway Bridge Inn ⑪ ♀ ⇐
Just before village, on A272 Midhurst–Petworth; GU28 9BP

Restauranty coaching inn with contemporary décor in several dining areas, log fires, local real ales and interesting modern food using local produce; lovely bedrooms

Nicely intimate in character, this thoughtfully decorated inn has plenty of little corners, and although the emphasis is on the very good food, with most of the tables set for eating, it is a place where regulars do still pop in for a pint and a chat. The various bar rooms are carefully furnished with good oak chairs and an individual mix of tables; one of the log fires is in a well polished kitchen range. The interconnecting restaurant rooms have beams, wooden floors and a cosy atmosphere. Ales from Langham, Long Man and Sharps Doom Bar on handpump and 27 wines by the glass; background music and board games. There are seats on a small back terrace. This is an appealing place to stay, with stylish and comfortable bedrooms in a former stableyard and good breakfasts too.

Using local produce, the well presented and interesting food includes lunchtime sandwiches, crispy sweet and sour pork on oriental-style salad, ham hock terrine with truffle-scented brioche, calves liver, monkfish and tiger prawn thai green curry, sausage and mash, moroccan-style vegetable tagine, roasted rump of lamb with dauphinoise potatoes, and puddings such as spotted dick and spiced poached pear in brandy basket topped with curd cheese; they also offer a two- and three-course set menu. *Benchmark main dish: twice-cooked belly of pork £16.50. Two-course evening meal £25.50.*

Free house ~ Licensee Sam Bakose ~ Real ale ~ (01798) 861281 ~ Open 11-11 ~ Bar food 12-2.30, 6-9.30; 12-10 Sat; 12-9 Sun ~ Restaurant ~ Children welcome ~ Dogs allowed in bar ~ Bedrooms: £80/£120 ~ www.halfwaybridge.co.uk *Recommended by Diana Blake, Peter Loader*

LODSWORTH
SU9223   Map 2
Hollist Arms
Off A272 Midhurst–Petworth; GU28 9BZ

Friendly and smart 200-year-old village pub with local beers, good choice of wines, well liked bar food and seats outside

Open all day and beautifully placed by the village green, this civilised village pub is nicely laid out for eating or drinking. A small snug room on the right has a sofa and two tables by an open fire – just right for a cosy drink. The public bar area on the left has stools against a pale wooden counter, more around a few tables and a comfortable built-in window seat. Langham Hip Hop, Skinner  Timothy Taylors Landlord on handpump and a de background music. The L-shaped dining room has a c squidgy sofas facing each other in front of an inglenook fi plenty of elegant dining chairs and wheelbacks around tables wood-strip floor; the pale blue walls are completely covered with genuinely interesting prints and paintings. In fine weather, you can sit on picnic-sets on the terrace in the cottagey back garden or underneath the huge horse chestnut tree on the green.

Popular food typically includes duck rillette with golden beetroot marmalade, salt beef brisket with spiced cannellini beans, grilled marinated chicken thigh with tahini sauce, courgette and roquefort fritters, osso bucco (veal shanks) cassoulet, and puddings such as french bread and butter pudding and home-made ice-cream. *Benchmark main dish: steak and ale pie £12.50. Two-course evening meal £17.00.*

Free house ~ Licensee Sally Hossack ~ Real ale ~ (01798) 861310 ~ Open 11-11(10.30 Sun) ~ Bar food 12-3, 6-9; not Sun evening, Mon ~ Children welcome ~ Dogs allowed in bar ~ www.thehollistarms.com *Recommended by Colin McKerrow, Ann and Colin Hunt, Martin and Karen Wake*

We checked prices with the pubs as we went to press in summer 2013.
They should hold until around spring 2014.

 LURGASHALL   SU9327   Map 2

Noahs Ark

Off A283 N of Petworth; GU28 9ET

Busy old pub in nice spot with neatly kept rooms, real ales and pleasing food using local produce

Idyllically placed by the village green, with cricketers downing pints before a game, this spotlessly kept old place has a restaurant that one reader likened to 'eating in someone's very upmarket living room'. The simple traditional bar – popular locally – has leather-topped bar stools by the counter where they serve Greene King IPA and Abbot and a guest such as St Austell Trelawny on handpump, several wines by the glass, including local Upperton Nebula sparkling wine, and Gospel Green farm cider. Beams, a mix of wooden chairs and tables on parquet flooring, and an inglenook fireplace are also features. Open right up to its apex, the dining room is spacious and airy with church candles and fresh flowers on light wood tables; a couple of comfortable sofas face each other in front of an open woodburning stove; background music. The pub border terrier is called Gillie and visiting dogs may get a dog biscuit. Picnic-sets make the most of the location, overlooked by Blackdown Hill and with views of the village green and cricket pitch; there are more tables in the large side garden.

From a sensibly short menu, the enjoyable food using local produce might include sandwiches (not Sunday), haddock and smoked salmon terrine, blue cheese rarebit, rib-eye steak, beer-battered haddock, pearl barley risotto with roasted pumpkin, fried fillet of salmon and chorizo in mussel broth, and puddings. *Benchmark main dish: burger with cheese, bacon and mushroom £11.95. Two-course evening meal £21.00.*

Greene King ~ Lease Henry Coghlan and Amy Whitmore ~ Real ale ~ (01428) 707346 ~ Open 11-11(midnight Sat); 12-10.30(8 in winter) Sun ~ Bar food 12-2.30, 7-9.30; 12-3 Sun ~ Restaurant ~ Children welcome ~ Dogs allowed in bar ~ www.noahsarkinn.co.uk
Recommended by Richard Tilbrook, Tony and Rachel Schendel

 MAYFIELD   TQ5927   Map 3

Rose & Crown

Fletching Street; TN20 6TE

Pretty weatherboarded cottage with unspoilt bars, relaxed atmosphere, local beers and popular bar food

In one of the most beautiful villages of the Weald, this gracious old 16th-c weatherboarded pub was once a brewhouse. Several bars wander round the little central servery, but the two cosy small front rooms have the most character: low ceiling boards with coins embedded in the glossy paintwork, bench seats built into the partly panelled walls, pewter tankards hanging above the bar and along a beam, and a mix of simple dining chairs around wooden tables on stripped floorboards. There are candles in the first brick fireplace, a big log fire in the inglenook, Harveys Best and a changing guest on handpump and ten wines by the glass. Down some steps to the left is a larger carpeted room with a couple of big comfortable cushioned sofas, similar tables and chairs, a woodburning stove and several mirrors; steps at the far end lead up to a less used back area. There are picnic-sets beneath parasols on the front terrace.

Food includes sandwiches, chicken liver pâté, prawns and chorizo, beefburger, gammon with egg and hand-cut chips, sausage (vegetarian or meat) and mash, specials like cod fillet wrapped in parma ham, and puddings such as fruit crumble and crème brûlée. *Benchmark main dish: beer-battered haddock and chips £9.90. Two-course evening meal £15.00.*

Free house ~ Licensee Liz Maltman ~ Real ale ~ (01435) 872200 ~ Open 11-11(midnight Sat); 12-10.30 Sun ~ Bar food 12-9(9.30 Fri, Sat; 8 Sun) ~ Children welcome ~ Dogs welcome ~ Live music Sat, first Thurs of month ~ www.roseandcrownmayfield.co.uk
Recommended by Isobel Mackinlay

 OVING   SU9005   Map 2
Gribble Inn
Between A27 and A259 E of Chichester; PO20 2BP

Own-brewed beers in bustling 16th-c thatched pub with beamed and timbered linked rooms, well liked bar food and pretty garden

Eight own-brew beers on handpump are on offer at this thatched pub. You have a choice of Fuzzy Duck, Gribble Ale, Pig's Ear, Plucking Pheasant, Reg's Tipple and three seasonal ales, such as CHI.P.A, Sussex Quad Hopper or the strong Wobbler Ale. The chatty bar has lots of heavy beams and timbering, old country kitchen furnishings and pews, and the linked rooms have a cottagey feel and huge winter log fires. Also, board games and a skittle alley with its own bar. There are seats outside under cover and more chairs and tables in the pretty, recently tidied-up garden with its apple and pear trees. Inside the pub are a village shop, selling organic produce, and a coffee shop.

Using yeast from the brewery for home-baked bread, and featuring foraged mushrooms, watercress and other vegetables, the seasonally changing menu might include sandwiches, poached pheasant egg with black pudding, game terrine, beer-battered haddock and chips, venison burger, roulade of spinach, wild mushroom and parmesan, and puddings such as home-made ice-cream and vanilla crème brûlée. *Benchmark main dish: slow-roasted pork belly £13.95. Two-course evening meal £17.00.*

Badger ~ Licensees Simon Wood and Nicola Tester ~ Real ale ~ (01243) 786893 ~ Open 11-11; 12-10 Sun ~ Bar food 12-2(2.30 Sat), 6-9; 12-3 Sun ~ Restaurant ~ Children in family room ~ Dogs allowed in bar ~ Jazz first Tues of month ~ www.gribbleinn.co.uk
Recommended by John Beeken, Nigel and Sue Foster

 PETWORTH   SU9721   Map 2
Angel
Angel Street; GU28 0BG

Medieval building with an 18th-c façade, a chatty atmosphere in opened-up beamed bars, log fires, friendly service and good, interesting food; newly refurbished bedrooms

Run by top class licensees whom we have known for many years, this is a carefully renovated inn just 300 metres from the central square of a market town famed for its antiques shops. Many original features have been kept in the opened-up, interconnected rooms and the atmosphere throughout is easy-going and friendly. The front bar has beams, a log fire in an inglenook fireplace and an appealing variety of old wooden and cushioned dining chairs and tables on wide floorboards. This leads through to the main room with high chairs by the counter where they keep Langham Best alongside a couple of guests from breweries such as Andwell, Dark Star and Hop Back on handpump, 25 wines by the glass from an extensive list and a good array of malt whiskies. There are also high-backed brown leather and antique chairs and tables on pale wooden flooring, the odd milk churn and french windows to a sizeable three-level back garden. The cosy and popular back bar is similarly furnished, with a second log fire.

Using locally sourced ingredients, the changing menu might include goats cheese crème brûlée, eggs benedict, beer-battered haddock and chips, roasted cherry tomato, asparagus and pappardelle pasta in parmesan and nutmeg cream sauce, steak burger with pesto-drizzled bun, bacon, gruyère and tomato and chipotle mayonnaise, seafood linguine, steak and kidney pudding, braised shoulder of lamb, and puddings such as chocolate brownie with hot fudge sauce and blueberry buttermilk pancakes. *Benchmark main dish: beer-battered fresh haddock and chips £11.75. Two-course evening meal £21.00.*

Free house ~ Licensee Murray Inglis ~ Real ale ~ (01798) 342153 ~ Open 10.30am-11pm; 11.30-10.30 Sun ~ Bar food 12-3.30, 6.30-9.30; Sun 12-2.30, 6-9 ~ Children welcome ~ Dogs allowed in bar and bedrooms ~ Bedrooms: £85/£95 ~ www.angelinnpetworth.co.uk *Recommended by Martin Jones, Toby Jones*

RINGMER
TQ4313   Map 3

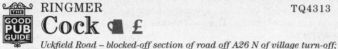

Cock 🍺 £

Uckfield Road – blocked-off section of road off A26 N of village turn-off;
BN8 5RX

16th-c country pub with a wide choice of popular bar food, real ales in character bar, and plenty of seats in the garden

Tucked well away from the main road, this 16th-c weatherboarded tavern is a welcoming place at which to arrive, with a log fire blazing away in winter. The unspoilt bar has traditional pubby furniture on flagstones, heavy beams, Harveys Best and a couple of guests from breweries like Hammerpot and Hogs Back on handpump, 11 wines by the glass and 12 malt whiskies. There are also three dining areas; background music. Outside on the terrace and in the garden are lots of picnic-sets with views across open fields to the South Downs. Visiting dogs are offered a bowl of water and a chew, and the owners' dogs are called Bailey and Tally. Atmosphere and service are good.

A big choice of popular food using locally sourced produce and seasonal game, with several dishes priced at under £10, typically includes lunchtime sandwiches and ploughman's, egg and prawn mayonnaise, deep-fried camembert with cranberry sauce, cajun chicken, sausage and chips, chicken curry and rice, venison burger, beer-battered cod and chips, lamb chops, mushroom and red pepper stroganoff, steaks and puddings. *Benchmark main dish: steak and ale pie £10.75. Two-course evening meal £17.00.*

Free house ~ Licensees Ian, Val, Nick and Matt Ridley ~ Real ale ~ (01273) 812040 ~ Open 11-3, 6-11.30; 11-11.30 Sun ~ Bar food 12-2.15(2.30 Sat), 6-9.30; all day Sun ~ Restaurant ~ Well behaved children welcome away from bar ~ Dogs allowed in bar ~ www.cockpub.co.uk *Recommended by Tony and Wendy Hobden, N R White*

Bedroom prices are for high summer. Even then you may get reductions for more than one night, or (outside tourist areas) weekends. Winter special rates are common, and many inns cut bedroom prices if you have a full evening meal.

ROBERTSBRIDGE
George 🛏

TQ7323   Map 3

High Street; TN32 5AW

Friendly former coaching inn with local beers in bustling bar, good food using seasonal produce in dining room and seats outside; good bedrooms

'We received a friendly, cheerful welcome and the service throughout our stay lived up to its beginning,' remarked one reader of this immaculately kept village pub. There's a log fire in a handsome brick inglenook fireplace with a leather sofa and a couple of armchairs in front of it – just right for a quiet pint and a chat – high bar stools by the counter where they serve Harveys Best, Sharps Doom Bar and a guest from a brewer such as Rother Valley on handpump and 20 wines by the glass including several local ones. Staff are friendly and the atmosphere is easy-going; Stanley the basset hound may appear but please don't feed him. The dining area leads off here with elegant high-backed pale wooden chairs around a mix of tables (each with fresh flowers and a nightlight) on stripped floorboards, photographs or block paintings of local scenes, and big church candles in a small fireplace; background music. In warm weather, there are plenty of seats and tables outside on the back terrace. The bedrooms are comfortable and the breakfasts good.

Using local, seasonal produce, the well-liked food has some innovative little touches and might include lunchtime baguettes, carpaccio-style marinated beef, beer-battered cod and chips, hand-made sausages with bubble and squeak, moroccan marinated lamb saddle chop, roasted beetroot with marinated feta cheese and rocket salad, and roasted chicken breast stuffed with fresh lemon and thyme, and puddings. *Benchmark main dish: slow-roasted free-range pork belly with apple rösti £13.00. Two-course evening meal £19.00.*

Free house ~ Licensees John and Jane Turner ~ Real ale ~ (01580) 880315 ~ Open 11-11; 12-8 Sun; closed Mon ~ Bar food 12-2.30, 6.30-9; 12-3 Sun ~ Children welcome but must be with adults at all times ~ Dogs allowed in bar ~ Live music last Sun of month (not summer) ~ www.thegeorgerobertsbridge.co.uk   *Recommended by John and Elspeth Howell, B and M Kendall, Pete Walker*

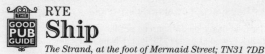

RYE
Ship

TQ9120   Map 3

The Strand, at the foot of Mermaid Street; TN31 7DB

Informal and prettily set old inn with a relaxed atmosphere, straightforward furnishings, local ales and often inventive food; bedrooms

A successful blend of quirkiness and comfort, this is an inviting place for a meal or a drink. There's a comfortable, easy-going atmosphere and a friendly welcome from the pleasant staff. The ground floor is all opened up, from the sunny big-windowed front part to a snugger section at the back, with a log fire in the stripped-brick fireplace below a stuffed boar's head. Flooring varies from one area to the next: composition, stripped boards, flagstones, a bit of carpet in the armchair corner. There are beams and timbers, a mixed bag of rather second-hand-feeling furnishings – a cosy group of overstuffed leather armchairs and sofa, random stripped or Formica-topped tables and various café chairs – that suit it nicely, as do the utilitarian bulkhead wall lamps. Harveys Best and

mint risotto, gnocchi, fish and chips, beefburger with cheese, rib-eye steak with béarnaise sauce, and puddings such as custard tart and chocolate soufflé. There is also a two- and three-course set lunch on weekdays. *Benchmark main dish: smoked haddock with poached egg and mustard sauce £14.75. Two-course evening meal £20.50.*

Free house ~ Licensee Jhonnie de Oliveira ~ Real ale ~ (01580) 200234 ~ Open 9am-11pm(10.30 Sat, 10 Sun) ~ Bar food 12-3, 6-9.30(9 Sun) ~ Restaurant ~ Children welcome ~ Dogs allowed in bar and bedrooms ~ Live music last Sun of month ~ Bedrooms: £90/£120 ~ www.thebellintichurst.com *Recommended by Jamie and Sue May, Richard and Penny Gibbs, Charles and Gillian Van Der Lande*

 TILLINGTON   SU9621   Map 2

Horse Guards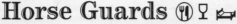

Off A272 Midhurst–Petworth; GU28 9AF

300-year-old inn with beams, panelling and open fires in rambling rooms, inventive food and thoughtful choice of drinks; cottagey bedrooms

Beside a medieval church with an unusual spire painted by both Constable and Turner, this 18th-c inn has won much praise from readers for its food and friendly service, and attracts a good blend of locals and visitors. The neatly kept and cosy beamed front bar has some good country furniture on bare boards, a chesterfield in one corner, a log fire and a lovely view beyond the village to the Rother Valley from a seat in the big black-panelled bow window. High bar chairs line the counter where they keep Harveys Best and a guest beer such as Otter Bitter on handpump, 15 wines by the glass, home-made sloe gin and local farm juices. Other rambling beamed rooms have similar furniture on brick floors, rugs, more open fires and original panelling, and throughout there are fresh flowers and a relaxed, gently civilised atmosphere. There's a terrace outside and more tables and chairs in a sheltered garden behind. The cosy country bedrooms are comfortable and our readers enjoy staying here.

Growing some of their own vegetables and salads and using other local, seasonal produce, the excellent food might include sandwiches, parsnip soup, dorset snails, organic 28-day-hung steaks with peppercorn or wild garlic sauce, fish and shellfish bouillabaisse, organic chicken stew, black bean chilli with sour cream and cherry tomato salsa, fried bream with salsa verde, and puddings such as marmalade sponge with Drambuie custard and lemon posset. *Benchmark main dish: South Downs venison £17.00. Two-course evening meal £20.50.*

Enterprise ~ Lease Sam Beard ~ Real ale ~ (01798) 342332 ~ Open 12-midnight ~ Bar food 12-2.30(3.30 Sun), 6.30(6 Fri)-9; 12-3, 6-9 Sat ~ Children welcome ~ Dogs welcome ~ Bedrooms: /£105 ~ www.thehorseguardsinn.co.uk *Recommended by Karen Pearson, Richard Tilbrook, Ann and Colin Hunt, Tracey and Stephen Groves, John Evans, Derek Thomas*

 WARNINGLID   TQ2425   Map 3

Half Moon

B2115 off A23 S of Handcross or off B2110 Handcross–Lower Beeding; RH17 5TR

Good modern cooking in simply furnished pub with an informal chatty atmosphere, real ales, lots of wines by the glass and seats in sizeable garden

Efficiently run and with a proper pubby atmosphere, this fills with the chat of happy diners and drinkers. The lively locals' bar has straightforward wooden furniture on bare boards and a small victorian fireplace and a room just off here has oak beams and flagstones. A couple of steps lead down to the dining areas with a happy mix of wooden chairs, cushioned wall settles and nice old tables on floorboards, plank panelling and bare brick, and old photographs of the village; there's also another open fire and a glass-covered well. Dark Star American Pale, Greene King Old Speckled Hen, Harveys Best and a guest beer on handpump and around 20 wines by the glass. There are quite a few picnic-sets outside on the lawn in the sheltered, sizeable garden, which has a most spectacular avenue of trees, with uplighters that glow at night.

Attractively presented, the carefully sourced bar food might include ciabattas, oriental crispy pork balls with smoked apple purée, potato gnocchi with wild mushroom and herb cream sauce, thai green chicken curry, rib-eye steak, beer-battered cod and chips, burgers, beer-battered halloumi with tomato fondue, seared bass with beetroot and orange compote, trio of pork with black pudding and sweet corn fritters, and puddings such as warm bakewell tart. *Benchmark main dish: calves liver with smoked bacon £16.00. Two-course evening meal £18.50.*

Free house ~ Licensees Jonny Lea and James Amico ~ Real ale ~ (01444) 461227 ~ Open 11.30-3, 5.30-11; 11.30-11 Sat; 12-9 Sun ~ Bar food 12-2, 6-9.30; not Sun evening ~ Restaurant ~ Children welcome ~ Dogs allowed in bar ~ www.thehalfmoonwarninglid.co.uk
Recommended by Conor McGaughey, Michael Rugman, Donna Jenkins, Guy Vowles, Derek Thomas

WARTLING
TQ6509 Map 3

Lamb ♀

Village signed with Herstmonceux Castle off A271 Herstmonceux–Battle; BN27 1RY

Friendly family-owned country pub, comfortable seating areas, cosy little bar, changing real ales, good food and seats on pretty back terrace; bedrooms

On a gentle rise above the fen-like beauty of the Pevensey Levels, this is an easy-going, rather civilised place with plenty of room for a drink and a chat or an enjoyable meal. The little entrance bar on the right has a few dining chairs with arms around a rustic circular table on wide floorboards, an open fireplace, grey-green paintwork and tapestry curtains. A two-level beamed and timbered dining room leads off here with similar furnishings on more wide boards, a couple of armchairs in front of a woodburning stove in an inglenook fireplace and a handsome settle against a panelled end wall; plenty of candles in brass sticks. At the back is a larger bustling bar with sheepskins draped over built-in panelled and cushioned benches on a raised area, another woodburner fronted by armchairs and a sofa, and french windows to steps that lead up to the terraced garden where there are chunky green-painted seats and benches among flowering tubs. Harveys Best, 1648 ales (brewed at the Kings Head in East Hoathly) and a guest from Dark Star on handpump and ten wines by the glass. The sizeable restaurant right at the back of the building has animal and country paintings on the walls, antiques and large flower arrangements. The sussex spaniel is called Maude.

Tempting food includes black pudding scotch egg, smoked mackerel and horseradish pâté, risotto of the day, burger with bacon, cheese, coleslaw and chips, pie of the day, pigeon breast salad with croutons and parmesan, monkfish with salsa verde and rosemary roast potatoes, 40-day dry-aged steaks, daily specials, and puddings such as chocolate and orange fondant with hazelnut cracknel and black gingerbread pudding. *Benchmark main dish: haddock and leek fishcakes £12.00. Two-course evening meal £18.50.*

Free house ~ Licensee Charlie Braxton ~ Real ale ~ (01323) 832116 ~ Open 11.30-11 (5 Sun); closed Sun evening ~ Bar food 12-3.30, 6-9.30 ~ Children welcome ~ Dogs allowed in bar ~ Bedrooms: /£95 ~ www.lambinnwartling.co.uk *Recommended by Caroline Prescott, Isobel Mackinlay*

WEST HOATHLY   TQ3632   Map 3

Cat 🍴 🛏

Village signposted from A22 and B2028 S of East Grinstead; North Lane; RH19 4PP

Popular 16th-c inn with old-fashioned bar, airy dining rooms, local real ales, good food and seats outside; lovely bedrooms

'What a fabulous place to stay – our idea of a perfect pub, we really couldn't fault it,' remarked one reader of this village inn, where the styles are a thoughtful mix of old and new. There's a lovely old bar with beams, proper pubby tables and chairs on the old wooden floor, and a fine log fire in the inglenook fireplace. The focus is on local breweries, so Harveys Best and Larkins Traditional Ale are available alongside a couple of guests such as Black Cat and a seasonal Harveys on handpump, as well as local cider and apple juice, and several wines by the glass; look out for a glass cover over the 23-metre well. The dining rooms are light and airy with a nice mix of wooden dining chairs and tables on the pale wood-strip flooring, and throughout there are hops, china platters, brass and copper ornaments. The atmosphere is gently upmarket. The contemporary-style garden room has glass doors that open on to a terrace with teak furniture. This is a comfortable and enjoyable place to stay (some of the pleasant rooms overlook the church), with coffee machines in bedrooms and goose-down duvets and the breakfasts are very good. The cocker spaniel is called Harvey. The Bluebell Railway is nearby, and the Priest House in the village is a fascinating museum within a cottage endowed with an extraordinary array of ancient anti-witch symbols. Parking is limited.

🍴 The very highly thought-of food, using local, seasonal produce and including first rate vegetarian options, might include lunchtime sandwiches and ploughman's, home-made black pudding duck scotch egg, stuffed portobello mushroom with blue cheese and tomato, spiced moroccan pulled lamb and kofta, beer-battered fish and chips, steak and ale pie, guinea fowl supreme stuffed with pork and chestnuts, sweet miso and mirin-glazed aubergine with japanese stir-fry vegetables and soba noodles, fillet of hake, and puddings such as steamed ginger sponge and chocolate and peanut tart. *Benchmark main dish: steak, mushroom and ale pie £13.25. Two-course evening meal £22.00.*

Free house ~ Licensee Andrew Russell ~ Real ale ~ (01342) 810369 ~ Open 12-11.30 (3.30 Sun); closed Sun evening ~ Bar food 12-2(2.30 Fri, Sat), 6-9(9.30 Fri, Sat); 12-2.30 Sun ~ Children welcome if over 7 ~ Dogs allowed in bar and bedrooms ~ Pianist last Fri evening of month ~ Bedrooms: £90/£110 ~ www.catinn.co.uk *Recommended by B J Harding, Chris Flynn, Wendy Jones, Peter Loader, Keir Halliday, Nick Lawless, Bernard Stradling, Grahame Brooks, Martin and Karen Wake, Steve Homer, Hunter and Christine Wright*

Also Worth a Visit in Sussex

Besides the fully inspected pubs, you might like to try these pubs that have been recommended to us and described by readers. Do tell us what you think of them: feedback@goodguides.com

---

ALFOLD BARS TQ0333
Sir Roger Tichborne
(01403) 751873 *B2133 N of Loxwood;*
RH14 0QS Renovated and extended beamed country pub keeping original nooks and crannies, good well presented food (not Sun evening) from varied reasonably priced menu, friendly prompt service, five real ales including Dark Star, Tillingbourne and Wells & Youngs, flagstones and log fires; children and dogs welcome, back terrace and sloping lawn with lovely rural views, good walks, open all day. *(Shirley Mackenzie, Allister Hambly, Ian Phillips, Tony and Wendy Hobden)*

ALFRISTON TQ5203
Olde Smugglers
(01323) 870241
Waterloo Square; BN26 5UE Charming 14th-c inn, low beams and panelling, brick floor, sofas by huge inglenook, masses of bric-a-brac and smuggling mementoes, various nooks and crannies, wide range of popular bar food from sandwiches to specials, Harveys and guests, real cider and good choice of wines by the glass; background music, can get crowded (lovely village draws many visitors); children in eating area and conservatory, dogs welcome, tables on well planted back suntrap terrace and lawn, three bedrooms, open all day. *(Dr A J and Mrs B A Tompsett)*

ALFRISTON TQ5203
Star
(01323) 870495
High Street; BN26 5TA Fine painted medieval carvings outside, heavy-beamed old-fashioned bar with some interesting features including a sanctuary post, antique furnishings and big log fire in Tudor fireplace, comfortable lounge with easy chairs, more space behind for eating, bar and pricey restaurant food, ales such as Beachy Head; children welcome, dogs allowed in bar and most of the 37 bedrooms in up-to-date part behind, open all day summer. *(Brian and Anna Marsden, John Warner)*

AMBERLEY TQ0211
Bridge
(01798) 831619
Houghton Bridge, off B2139; BN18 9LR Popular and welcoming open-plan dining pub, comfortable and relaxed even when busy, pleasant bar and two-room dining area, candles on tables, log fire, wide range of reasonably priced generous food (not Sun evening) from good sandwiches up, well kept ales including Harveys, cheerful efficient service; children and dogs welcome, seats out in front, more tables in enclosed side garden, handy for station, open all day.

(J A Snell, Julie and Bill Ryan, N R White, Ann and Colin Hunt)

AMBERLEY TQ0313
★ Sportsmans
(01798) 831787
Crossgates; Rackham Road, off B2139; BN18 9NR Popular pub with good fairly priced food and well kept ales such as Harveys, Hammerpot, Kings and Langhams (Aug festival), friendly efficient young staff, three bars including brick-floored one with darts, great views over Amberley Wild Brooks from pretty back conservatory restaurant and tables outside; dogs welcome, good walks, neat bedrooms. *(Tony and Wendy Hobden, N R White, Pete Walker)*

ANGMERING TQ0704
Spotted Cow
(01903) 783919
High Street; BN16 4AW Six well kept ales including Fullers, Harveys, Skinners and Timothy Taylors, decent wines by the glass, smallish bar on left, long dining extension with large conservatory on right, popular food from sandwiches up, good friendly service, two fires, sporting caricatures, smuggling history; children welcome, disabled access, big garden with boules and play area, lovely walk to Highdown Hill fort, open all day weekends. *(Peter Meister)*

ARDINGLY TQ3430
★ Gardeners Arms
(01444) 892328
B2028 2 miles N; RH17 6TJ Reliable food from sandwiches and pub favourites up in old linked rooms, Badger beers, pleasant efficient service, standing timbers and inglenooks, scrubbed pine on flagstones and broad boards, old local photographs, mural in back part, good relaxed atmosphere; children and dogs welcome, disabled facilities, café-style furniture on pretty terrace and in side garden, opposite South of England showground and handy for Borde Hill and Wakehurst Place (NT), open all day. *(C and R Bromage, Grahame Brooks)*

ARLINGTON TQ5507
★ Old Oak
(01323) 482072
Caneheath; off A22 or A27 NW of Polegate; BN26 6SJ 17th-c former almshouse with open-plan L-shaped bar, beams, log fires and comfortable seating, well kept Harveys and a guest tapped from the cask, traditional bar food (all day weekends), toad in the hole (old Sussex coin game), played here; background music; children and dogs welcome, circular picnic-sets in quiet garden, play area, walks in nearby Abbots Wood, open all day. *(Fr Robert Marsh, Alan Weedon)*

ARUNDEL   TQ0208
★ **Black Rabbit** (01903) 882828

Mill Road, Offham; keep on and don't give up!; BN18 9PB Recently refurbished riverside pub, in lovely spot near wildfowl reserve with timeless views of water meadows and castle – well organised for families and can get very busy; long bar with eating areas at either end, enjoyable fairly priced food all day from baguettes and sharing boards up, well kept Badger ales, several decent wines by the glass, log fires, newspapers; background music; dogs welcome, covered tables and pretty hanging baskets out at front, extensive terrace across road overlooking river, play area, boat trips and good walks. *(Brian and Anna Marsden, Phyl and Jack Street, Julie and Bill Ryan, Peter Meister)*

ARUNDEL   TQ0107
★ **Swan** (01903) 882314

High Street; BN18 9AG Smart but comfortably relaxed open-plan L-shaped bar with attractive woodwork and matching fittings, friendly efficient young staff, well kept Fullers ales, good tea and coffee, enjoyable fairly priced food from baguettes to blackboard specials, sporting bric-a-brac and old photographs, open fire, restaurant, live jazz (third Sun of month from 5pm); 15 bedrooms, no car park (pay-and-display opposite), open all day. *(John and Alison Hamilton, Nigel and Sue Foster, Alan Bulley)*

BALLS CROSS   SU9826
★ **Stag** (01403) 820241

Village signed off A283 at N edge of Petworth; GU28 9JP Unchanging and cheery 17th-c country pub, fishing rods and country knick-knacks, tiny flagstoned bar with log fire in huge inglenook, a few seats and bar stools, Badger beers, summer cider and several wines by the glass, second tiny room and appealing old-fashioned restaurant with horse pictures, pubby food (not Sun evening), bar skittles, darts and board games in separate carpeted room; veteran outside lavatories; well behaved children allowed away from main bar, dogs welcome, seats in front under parasols, more in good-sized back garden divided by shrubbery, bedrooms. *(Anon)*

BARCOMBE CROSS   TQ4212
Royal Oak (01273) 400418

Off A275 N of Lewes; BN8 5BA Refurbished red-brick village pub much improved under present friendly licensees; good value food cooked by landlord-chef from bar snacks up, three well kept Harveys ales, reasonably priced wine list, skittle alley;

a few tables out in front and in small tree-shaded garden, open all day. *(John Beeken)*

BARNS GREEN   TQ1227
Queens Head (01403) 730436

Chapel Road; RH13 0PS Welcoming traditional village pub, extensive blackboard choice of good generous home-made food, Kings ales along with Fullers London Pride and Sharps Doom Bar, a couple of real ciders, reasonable prices, regular quiz nights; children welcome, tables out at front and in back garden with play area. *(Tony and Wendy Hobden)*

BEPTON   SU8620
Country Inn (01730) 813466

Severals Road; GU29 0LR Popular old-fashioned country local, well kept Sharps, Wells & Youngs and Weltons, hearty helpings of good value bar food (not Sun evening), friendly helpful staff, heavy beams, stripped brickwork and log fire, darts, quiz nights; background music, TV; children welcome, tables out at front and in big garden with shady trees and play area, quiet spot, open all day Fri-Sun. *(Peter Long, Ann and Colin Hunt, John Beeken)*

BERWICK   TQ5105
★ **Cricketers Arms** (01323) 870469

Lower Road, S of A27; BN26 6SP Charming local with three small unpretentious bars, huge supporting beam in each low ceiling, simple country furnishings on quarry tiles, cricketing pictures and bats, two log fires, friendly staff, four Harveys ales tapped from the cask, country wines, good coffee, well liked bar food (all day weekends and summer weekdays), toad in the hole; children in family room only, dogs welcome, delightful cottagey front garden with picnic-sets among small brick paths, more seats behind, Bloomsbury Group wall paintings in nearby church, good South Downs walks. *(MP, Alec and Joan Laurence, Mrs S Watkins, Alan Cowell, John Beeken and others)*

BILLINGSHURST   TQ0830
Blue Ship (01403) 822709

The Haven; hamlet signposted off A29 just N of junction with A264, then follow signpost left towards Garlands and Okehurst; RH14 9BS Unspoilt pub in quiet country spot, beamed and brick-floored front bar, scrubbed tables and wall benches, inglenook woodburner, Badger ales served from hatch, traditional home-made food (not Mon), two small carpeted back rooms, darts, bar billiards, shove-ha'penny, cribbage and dominoes; children and dogs welcome, tables out at front and in side garden with play area, local produce for sale, closed Sun evening, Mon lunchtime. *(N R White)*

With the iPhone *Good Pub Guide* App, you can use the iPhone's camera to send us pictures of pubs you visit – outside or inside.

BILLINGSHURST TQ0725
Limeburners (01403) 782311
*Lordings Road, Newbridge (B2133/
A272 W); RH14 9JA* Friendly characterful
pub in converted row of cottages, Fullers
ales, enjoyable well priced food (not
Sun evening) from snacks up, good
friendly service, open fires; TV in bar
providing background music; children
welcome, pleasant front garden, play area
behind. *(John and Joyce Snell, Richard Luck,
Tony and Wendy Hobden, Ian Phillips)*

BOGNOR REGIS SZ9201
Royal Oak (01243) 821002
*A259 Chichester Road, North Bersted;
PO21 5JF* Old-fashioned two-bar beamed
local (aka the Pink Pub), well kept Long
Man, food till 6.30pm (not Sun evening),
pleasant service; bar billiards, darts, sports
TV; children and dogs welcome (pub boxer is
called Alfie). *(Eddie Edwards)*

BOLNEY TQ2623
Bolney Stage (01444) 881200
*London Road, off old A23 just N of A272;
RH17 5RL* Sizeable well refurbished 16th-c
timbered dining pub (part of the Home
Counties group), enjoyable varied choice
of food all day, three or four changing ales
(usually local Bedlam) and good selection
of wines by the glass, friendly service, low
beams and polished flagstones, nice mix of
old furniture, woodburner and big two-way
log fire; children welcome, dogs in main bar,
disabled facilities, tables on terrace and
lawn, play area, handy for Sheffield Park
(NT) and Bluebell Railway. *(Anon)*

BOLNEY TQ2622
Eight Bells (01444) 881396
The Street; RH17 5QW Well managed
village pub with wide food choice from
ciabattas and light dishes to enjoyable
specials, bargain OAP lunch Tues and Weds,
efficient friendly service, well kept Harveys
and guests such as Downlands and Kings,
local wines from Bookers vineyard, brick-
floor bar with eight handbells suspended
from ceiling, good log fire, timbered dining
extension; tables under big umbrellas on
outside decking with neatly lit steps, pram
race Easter Mon, three bedrooms. *(Tony and
Wendy Hobden)*

BOSHAM SU8003
★ Anchor Bleu (01243) 573956
High Street; PO18 8LS Waterside inn
overlooking Chichester Harbour; two
simple bars with some beams in low ochre
ceilings, worn flagstones and exposed
timbered brickwork, lots of nautical
bric-a-brac, robust furniture (some tables
very close together), up to six real ales
and popular bar food; they ask for a credit
card if you run a tab; children and dogs
welcome, seats on back terrace looking
out over ducks and boats on sheltered
inlet, massive wheel-operated bulkhead
door wards off high tides, church up lane
figures in Bayeux Tapestry, village and
shore are worth exploring, open all day in
summer. *(Val and Alan Green, Roy Hoing,
Shirley King, J A Snell, Bob Wiggins and others)*

BOSHAM SU8105
White Swan (01243) 578917
*A259 roundabout; Station Road;
PO18 8NG* Refurbished dining pub with
enjoyable sensibly priced food (not Sun
evening) including offers and themed nights,
three well kept ales such as Dark Star, Hop
Back and Langhams, good-sized bar area
with bucket chairs on flagstones, restaurant
beyond, darts in snug, regular quiz; open all
day. *(J A Snell, Ann and Colin Hunt, Tony and
Wendy Hobden)*

BREDE TQ8218
Red Lion (01424) 882188
A28 opposite church; TN31 6EJ Relaxed
beamed village pub with plain tables and
chairs on bare boards, candles, inglenook
log fire, good reasonably priced food
including local fish, Sun carvery (should
book), well kept Sharps Doom Bar, Wells &
Youngs and two local guests, friendly helpful
staff, back dining area decorated with
sheet music and musical instruments, pub
sheepdog called Billy (other dogs welcome);
a few picnic-sets out at front, garden behind
with roaming chickens (eggs for sale),
narrow entrance to car park, open all day
weekends. *(V Brogden)*

BRIGHTON TQ3104
★ Basketmakers Arms (01273) 689006
*Gloucester Road – the E end, near
Cheltenham Place; off Marlborough Place
(A23) via Gloucester Street; BN1 4AD*
Cheerful bustling backstreet local with
eight pumps serving Fullers/Gales beers
and guests, decent wines by the glass, over
100 malt whiskies and quite a choice of
other spirits, enjoyable very good value bar
food all day (till 6pm weekends), two small
low-ceilinged rooms, lots of interesting old
tins, cigarette cards on one beam, whisky
labels on another, also beer mats, old
advertisements, photographs and posters;
background music; children welcome till
8pm, dogs on leads, a few pavement tables,
open all day (till midnight Fri, Sat). *(Brian
and Anna Marsden, Rob and Catherine Dunster,
Tony and Wendy Hobden, Pete Walker)*

By law, pubs must show a price list of their drinks. Let us know if you are
inconvenienced by any breach of this law.

BRIGHTON TQ3104
Colonnade (01273) 328728
New Road, off North Street; by Theatre Royal; BN1 1UF Small richly restored Edwardian bar, with red plush banquettes, velvet swags, shining brass and mahogany, gleaming mirrors, interesting pre-war playbills and signed theatrical photographs, well kept Fullers London Pride and Harveys Best, lots of lagers, bar snacks, daily papers; tiny front terrace overlooking Pavilion gardens. *(Anon)*

BRIGHTON TQ3004
Craft Beer Company
Upper North Street; BN1 3FG Corner pub refurbished by this small growing company (their first outside London); simple L-shaped bar with raised back section, fine choice of interesting draught and bottled beers from UK and international brewers, friendly knowledgeable staff, food limited to pork pies and scotch eggs; open all day. *(N R White)*

BRIGHTON TQ3104
✷Cricketers (01273) 329472
Black Lion Street; BN1 1ND Proper town pub, friendly bustle at busy times, nice relaxed atmosphere when quieter, cosy and darkly Victorian with lots of interesting bric-a-brac including a stuffed bear, well kept Fullers, Kings, Theakstons and Wells & Youngs tapped from the cask, decent coffee, well priced pubby food (till 8pm weekends) from sandwiches up, attentive service, tables in covered former stables courtyard, upstairs bar with Graham Greene memorabilia (pub features in *Brighton Rock*); background and live music; children allowed till 8pm, tall tables out in front, open all day. *(Pete Walker)*

BRIGHTON TQ3004
✷Evening Star (01273) 328931
Surrey Street; BN1 3PB Popular chatty drinkers' pub with good mix of customers, simple pale wood furniture on bare boards, up to four well kept Dark Star ales (originally brewed here) and lots of changing guest beers including continentals (in bottles too), farm ciders and perries, country wines, lunchtime baguettes, friendly staff coping well when busy; background and some live music; pavement tables, open all day. *(N R White, Pete Walker)*

BRIGHTON TQ2804
Ginger Pig (01273) 736123
Hove Street; BN3 2TR Large friendly place with Harveys Best and a guest, good choice of wines, enjoyable interesting food including short set menu (weekday lunchtime and early evening); children welcome, outside seating. *(Val and Alan Green)*

BRIGHTON TQ3104
Prince George (01273) 681055
Trafalgar Street; BN1 4EQ Three linked rooms (front ones are best) off main bar, mix of furnishings on stripped floor, several big mirrors, six well kept changing local ales and lots of wines by the glass, inexpensive popular organic and vegetarian/vegan food all day, friendly helpful staff; children and dogs welcome, small heated back courtyard. *(Rob and Catherine Dunster)*

BRIGHTON TQ3004
Pub du Vin (01273) 718588
Ship Street; BN1 1AD Next to Hotel du Vin; long narrow stripped-boards bar with comfortable wall seating one end, bay window the other, soft lighting and local photographs, five well kept ales including Arundel and Dark Star from ornate pewter counter, good choice of wines by the glass, enjoyable pubby food served by friendly staff, modern leather-seated bar chairs and light oak tables, flame-effect fire, small cosy coir-carpeted room opposite with squashy black armchairs and sofas; splendid gents' with original marble fittings; 11 comfortable bedrooms, open all day. *(N R White)*

BRIGHTON TQ2904
Sussex Cricketer (01273) 771645
Eaton Road, Hove, by cricket ground; BN3 3AF Comfortable Ember Inn with eight interesting well kept ales, decent wines by the glass and good value food all day including bargain set menu till 5pm (not Sun), friendly efficient young staff; children welcome in dining area. *(Matt Crowther, Tony and Wendy Hobden)*

BROWNBREAD STREET TQ6714
Ash Tree (01424) 892104
Off A271 (was B2204) W of Battle; 1st northward road W of Ashburnham Place, then 1st fork left, then bear right into Brownbread Street; TN33 9NX Tranquil 17th-c country local tucked away in isolated hamlet, enjoyable affordably priced home-made food, good choice of wines and well kept ales including Harveys Best, cheerful service, cosy beamed bars (some refurbishment) with nice old settles and chairs, stripped brickwork, interesting dining areas with timbered dividers, good inglenook log fires, quiz first Tues of month; children allowed in eating area, pretty garden, open all day. *(R D Skibinski)*

BURPHAM TQ0308
✷George (01903) 883131
Off A27 near Warningcamp; BN18 9RR Popular recently refurbished 17th-c pub under new local ownership – reports please.

BURWASH TQ6724
Rose & Crown (01435) 882600
Inn sign on A265; TN19 7ER Low-beamed timbered local tucked away down lane in pretty village, enjoyable food, well kept Harveys and decent wines, inglenook log fire in bar, pleasant restaurant

area with woodburner, glass-covered well just inside front door; tables out in small quiet garden, bedrooms. *(Colin McKerrow)*

BURY   TQ0013
Squire & Horse (01798) 831343
Bury Common; A29 Fontwell–Pulborough; RH20 1NS Smart roadside dining pub with good imaginative food from australian chef (highish prices), friendly efficient service, well kept Harveys and a guest, good choice of wines, several attractive partly divided beamed areas, plush wall seats, hunting prints and ornaments, log fire; no dogs; children welcome, pleasant garden and pretty terrace (some road noise), open all day Sun. *(Ann and Colin Hunt)*

BYWORTH   SU9821
★ Black Horse (01798) 342424
Off A283; GU28 0HL Popular and chatty country pub with smart simply furnished bar, pews and scrubbed tables on bare boards, pictures and old photographs, daily papers and open fires, four ales such as Arundel, Flowerpots, Wells & Youngs and Weltons, decent food (not winter Sun evening) from light lunchtime dishes up, children's menu, nooks and crannies in back restaurant, spiral staircase to heavily beamed function/dining room, games room with pool; dogs allowed in bar, attractive garden with tables on steep grassy terraces, lovely downs views, open all day. *(Tony and Wendy Hobden)*

CHAILEY   TQ3919
Horns Lodge (01273) 400422
A275; BN8 4BD Traditional former coaching inn, heavily timbered inside, with settles, horsebrasses and local prints, log fires at each end of longish front bar, well kept Dark Star, Harveys and two guests, real cider, good range of fairly priced bar food (not Tues) from sandwiches up, obliging staff, brick-floored restaurant, games area with bar billiards, darts and toad in the hole, cribbage, dominoes and board games too; background music; children and dogs welcome, tables in garden with sandpit, bedrooms, open all day weekends; for sale (but business as usual) as we went to press. *(John Beeken, Steve Homer)*

CHALVINGTON   TQ5209
Yew Tree Inn (01323) 811326
Chalvington Road, between Chalvington and Golden Cross; BN27 3TB Isolated 17th-c country pub with low beams, stripped brick, flagstones and inglenook, enjoyable keenly priced home-made food (not Sun evening) from lunchtime baguettes and ciabattas up, Harveys ales with guests such as Long Man and Wells & Youngs, conservatory; children and dogs welcome, good-sized terrace, extensive grounds with play area, own cricket pitch and camping, good walks, open all day (till 6pm Sun). *(Anon)*

CHELWOOD GATE   TQ4130
Red Lion (01825) 740265
A275, S of Forest Row junction with A22; RH17 7DE Roomy open-plan dining pub with good choice of enjoyable food, well kept Shepherd Neame ales and nice range of wines, cosy bar area with comfortable sofas by open fire; can get very busy; dogs welcome, big sheltered side garden, handy for Ashdown Forest walks, closed Mon. *(Neil Hardwick, Steve Homer)*

CHICHESTER   SU8605
Chichester Inn (01243) 783185
West Street; PO19 1RP Georgian pub with half a dozen local ales such as Dark Star, Irving and Langhams, bargain pubby food all day from snacks up, smallish front lounge with plain wooden tables and chairs, sofas by open fire, larger back public bar, live music Weds, Fri, Sat; pool and sports TV; courtyard garden with smokers' shelter, two bedrooms, open all day summer, all day Fri-Sun winter. *(Tony and Wendy Hobden)*

CHICHESTER   SU8504
Fountain (01243) 781352
Southgate; PO19 1ES Attractive two-room front bar with beams, painted panelling, stone floor and open fire, dining room behind incorporating part of Roman wall, enjoyable sensibly priced food from pub standards to some more adventurous choices, Badger ales, friendly helpful staff, live music and quiz nights; children and dogs welcome, tables in side courtyard, open all day. *(John and Alison Hamilton, Nigel and Sue Foster)*

CHIDHAM   SU7804
Old House At Home (01243) 572477
Off A259 at Barleycorn pub in Nutbourne; Cot Lane; PO18 8SU Neat cottagey pub in remote unspoilt farm-hamlet; wide choice of popular food including local fish and a very good steak and ale pie, good friendly service, five real ales including Otter and Sharps, decent wines, low beams and timbering, log fire; children allowed in eating areas, tables in nice garden, nearby walks by Chichester Harbour, open all day. *(R L Borthwick, J A Snell)*

CLAPHAM   TQ1105
Coach & Horses (01903) 692721
Arundel Road (A27 Worthing–Arundel); BN13 3UA Friendly 18th-c former coaching inn with well priced generous food including some south african dishes, well kept ales such as Harveys Best and Wychwood Hobgoblin, wooden tables and chairs, sofas and armchairs on wood or stone floors, log fire; background music, live jazz every other Thurs, quiz last Mon of month; children welcome, tables on sundeck, play area, open all day Fri, Sat, till 7pm Sun, closed Mon. *(Anon)*

CLIMPING TQ0001
Black Horse (01903) 715175
Climping Street; BN17 5RL Extended
18th-c country pub under new management;
enjoyable food from snacks up, well kept
ales such as Arundel and Sharps Doom Bar,
decent wines by the glass, good smiling
service, log fires, skittle alley; children
welcome, tables out in front and on back
decking, short walk to the beach.
(Axel F Bengsch, Colin McKerrow)

COCKING SU8717
Blue Bell (01730) 810200
A286 S of Midhurst; GU29 0HN Calls
itself a restaurant with rooms, although still
quite pubby; eating areas around bar, mix
of traditional and more restaurant food
including some japanese choices, generously
filled sandwiches too, reasonably priced wine
list with several by the glass, good friendly
service, log fire; nice walks – just off South
Downs Way, five bedrooms. *(John Evans)*

COCKING CAUSEWAY SU8819
Greyhound (01730) 814425
A286 Cocking–Midhurst; GU29 9QH
Pretty 18th-c tile-hung pub, enjoyable
good value home-made food (should book
weekends), Sharps Doom Bar and three
sussex beers such as Anchor Springs,
Downlands and Long Man, friendly prompt
service, cosy beamed and panelled bar,
log fire, pine furniture in big new dining
conservatory; children welcome, grassed area
at front with picnic-sets and huge eucalyptus,
sizeable garden and play area behind, open
all day Sun. *(John Beeken, Ann and Colin Hunt,
Tony and Wendy Hobden)*

COLEMANS HATCH TQ4533
★ Hatch (01342) 822363
*Signed off B2026, or off B2110 opposite
church; TN7 4EJ* Quaint and attractive
little weatherboarded Ashdown Forest pub
dating from 1430, big log fire in quickly
filling beamed bar, small back dining room
with another fire, very wide choice of good
generous home-made food, well kept Harveys,
Larkins and one or two guest beers, quick
service from friendly young staff, good mix
of customers including families and dogs;
not much parking so arrive early; picnic-sets
on front terrace and in beautifully kept
big garden, open all day Sun, and Sat in
summer. *(N R White, Pete Walker)*

COMPTON SU7714
Coach & Horses (02392) 631228
B2146 S of Petersfield; PO18 9HA
Welcoming 16th-c two-bar local in charming
downland village, not far from Uppark (NT),
beams, panelling, shuttered windows and
log fires, up to five changing ales, good pub
food cooked by chef-landlord including some
interesting dishes, bar billiards; children and
dogs welcome, tables out by village square,

nice surrounding walks. *(John and Alison
Hamilton, Geoff and Linda Payne)*

COOKSBRIDGE TQ4014
Rainbow (01273) 400334
*Junction A275 with Cooksbridge and
Newick Road; BN8 4SS* Attractive 18th-c
flint dining pub with good locally sourced
food from snacks to specials, helpful friendly
service, good choice of wines and sussex ales,
small bar well used by locals, restaurant, log
fires; children welcome, tables out under
parasols, open all day weekends (Sun till
6pm), closed Mon. *(Anon)*

COOLHAM TQ1423
George & Dragon (01403) 741320
*Dragons Green, Dragons Lane; pub
signed off A272; RH13 8GE* Newish
local owners and some refurbishment for
this tile-hung cottage; cosy chatty bar,
massive unusually low black beams (see if
you can decide whether the date cut into
one is 1677 or 1577), timbered walls and
log fire in big inglenook, Harveys, Kings,
Sharps and a guest, enjoyable food from pub
standards up, friendly staff, smaller back
bar, separate restaurant; children welcome,
picnic-sets in pretty orchard garden with
play area. *(Anon)*

COOTHAM TQ0714
Crown (01903) 742625
Pulborough Road (A283); RH20 4JN
Extended village pub with L-shaped bar
on two levels, well kept Bass, Harveys
and Wychwood Hobgoblin, wide choice of
food from bar snacks up (smaller helpings
available), also set menus, friendly efficient
service, two open fires, large back dining
area, games room (darts and pool); children
and dogs welcome, large back garden with
play area and goats, handy for Parham House,
open all day. *(Tony and Wendy Hobden,
John Beeken)*

COUSLEY WOOD TQ6533
★ Old Vine (01892) 782271
B2100 Wadhurst–Lamberhurst; TN5 6ER
Popular 16th-c weatherboarded pub with
linked, uncluttered rooms, heavy beams and
open timbering, church candles on attractive
old pine tables surrounded by farmhouse
chairs, several settles (one by big log fire
has an especially high back), bare boards
or parquet flooring (restaurant area is
carpeted), well kept Harveys Best and a guest
from attractively painted servery, several
good wines by the glass, tasty food served
by friendly helpful staff; dogs welcome,
picnic-sets on front terrace, open all day
weekends. *(N R White, Alec and Joan Laurence)*

COWBEECH TQ6114
★ Merrie Harriers (01323) 833108
Off A271; BN27 4JQ White clapboarded
16th-c village local, beamed public bar
with inglenook log fire, high-backed settle

and mixed tables and chairs, old local photographs, carpeted dining lounge with small open fire, well kept Harveys Best and a guest, winter mulled wine, good food from nice bar snacks up, friendly service, brick-walled back restaurant; occasional background music; rustic seats in terraced garden with country views, open all day Fri-Sun. *(Anon)*

COWFOLD   TQ2122
Hare & Hounds (01403) 865354
Henfield Road (A281 S); RH13 8DR Small friendly village pub, well kept Dark Star, Harveys and Shepherd Neame (July beer festival), good value traditional home-made food including Thurs OAP lunch deal, bar with log fire, little room off to the right, dining room to the left, some flagstones and bric-a-brac; a couple of picnic-sets out in front, back terrace, open all day weekends. *(Tony and Wendy Hobden)*

CRAWLEY DOWN   TQ3437
Dukes Head (01342) 712431
A264/A2028 by roundabout; RH10 4HH Big refurbished place with emphasis on eating, large lounge bar and three differently styled dining areas, log fires, good choice of well liked food all day including set menu and popular Sun roasts, decent wines, ales such as Fullers London Pride and Harveys, quick service from nice staff; can get very busy weekends; seats out at the front, handy for Gatwick Airport. *(Richard Mason, Gene and Tony Freemantle)*

CUCKFIELD   TQ3024
Talbot (01444) 455898
High Street; RH17 5JX Thriving pub under same management as the Half Moon at Warninglid (see Main Entries); light airy feel, imaginative food in bar and upstairs restaurant, real ales, good service; parking may be dificult; open all day. *(Anon)*

DALLINGTON   TQ6619
⋆Swan (01424) 838242
Woods Corner, B2096 E; TN21 9LB Popular old local with cheerful chatty atmosphere, well kept Harveys and a guest, decent wines by the glass, enjoyable blackboard food including deals, takeaway fish and chips (Tues), efficient friendly service, bare-boards bar divided by standing timbers, mixed furniture including cushioned settle and high-backed pew, candles in bottles and fresh flowers, big woodburner, simple back restaurant with far-reaching views to the coast; background music; children and dogs welcome, steps down to lavatories and garden. *(Anon)*

DELL QUAY   SU8302
Crown & Anchor (01243) 781712
Off A286 S of Chichester – look out for small sign; PO20 7EE Modernised 19th/20th-c beamed pub in splendid spot overlooking Chichester Harbour – best at high tide and quiet times (can be packed on sunny days and parking difficult); comfortable bow-windowed lounge bar, panelled public bar (dogs welcome), two log fires, well kept Wells & Youngs ales and a guest, lots of wines by the glass, enjoyable food all day including specials (maybe Selsey crab), friendly young staff who cope well at busy times; children welcome, views from large terrace, nice walks. *(J A Snell, Colin McKerrow, Nigel and Sue Foster, John Beeken)*

DENTON   TQ4502
Flying Fish (01273) 515440
Denton Road; BN9 0QB Welcoming new landlady and refurbishment for this 17th-c flint village pub; enjoyable food from baguettes up, well kept Shepherd Neame ales, friendly helpful staff; picnic-sets in front and on back decking looking up to sloping garden, by South Downs Way, open all day. *(Anon)*

DEVILS DYKE   TQ2511
Devils Dyke (01273) 857256
Devils Dyke Road; BN1 8YJ Vintage Inn set alone on downs above Brighton and worth visiting for the spectacular views night and day; their usual food, well kept ales such as Harveys Best, Shepherd Neame Spitfire and Timothy Taylors Landlord, helpful friendly staff; children welcome, tables outside, NT pay car park, open all day. *(Dave Snowden)*

DITCHLING   TQ3215
⋆Bull (01273) 843147
High Street (B2112); BN6 8TA Handsome rambling old building, beams, old wooden furniture on bare boards, fire, well kept Harveys, Timothy Taylors Landlord and two guests, home-made food from sandwiches up including good Sun roasts, nicely furnished dining rooms with mellow décor and candles, snug area with chesterfields; background music; children welcome, dogs in bar, tricky for wheelchairs (lots of steps), attractive big garden and suntrap terrace, barbecue, four nice bedrooms, good breakfast, open all day. *(Anon)*

EARTHAM   SU9309
⋆George (01243) 814340
Signed off A285 Chichester–Petworth, from Fontwell off A27, from Slindon off A29; PO18 0LT Welcoming village pub

---

Anyone claiming to arrange, or prevent, inclusion of a pub in the *Guide* is a fraud. Pubs are included only if recommended by genuine readers and if our own anonymous inspection confirms that they are suitable.

with enjoyable locally sourced food, up to
five real ales and decent wines including
good selection of English ones, log fires in
comfortable lounge and flagstoned public
bar (dogs allowed on leads), restaurant and
café; background music; children welcome
in eating areas, easy disabled access, large
garden, attractive surroundings and lovely
walks, closed Mon, otherwise open all day.
(David H T Dimock)

EAST ASHLING   SU8207
⋆ **Horse & Groom** (01243) 575339
B2178; PO18 9AX Busy country pub with
well kept Hop Back Summer Lightning,
Sharps Doom Bar and Wells & Youngs Bitter,
decent choice of wines by the glass, bar
food from good sandwiches up, reasonable
prices and helpful service, unchanging
front drinkers' bar with old pale flagstones
and inglenook woodburner, carpeted area
with scrubbed trestle tables, fresh and airy
extension with solid pale country kitchen
furniture on neat bare boards; children and
dogs allowed in some parts, garden with
picnic-sets under umbrellas, 11 bedrooms,
open all day Sat, closed Sun evening.
(Ann and Colin Hunt, J A Snell)

EAST DEAN   SU9012
Star & Garter (01243) 811318
*Village signed with Charlton off A286
in Singleton; also signed off A285;
PO18 0JG* Airy dining pub in peaceful
village-green position; attractive bar and
restaurant with panelling, exposed brickwork
and oak floors, furnishings from sturdy
stripped tables and country kitchen chairs
through chunky modern to some antique
carved settles, Arundel ales tapped from the
cask, several wines by the glass, food pricey
and can be very good especially the fresh fish,
pleasant service; background music; children
welcome, dogs in bar, teak furniture on
heated terrace, smokers' shelter, steps down
to walled lawn with picnic-sets, near South
Downs Way, bedrooms, open all day weekends
(food all day then too). *(Ann and Colin Hunt,
Martin and Karen Wake, M and GR)*

EAST GRINSTEAD   TQ3936
⋆ **Old Mill** (01342) 326341
*Dunnings Road, S towards Saint Hill;
RH19 4AT* Interesting 16th-c mill cottage
over stream reworked as spacious informal
Whiting & Hammond dining pub; lots of
panelling, old photographs and pictures,
carpeted main dining area with mix of old
tables (each with church candle), steps
down to ancient very low-ceilinged part with
fine timbers and inglenook woodburner,
sizeable bar with long curved counter, library
dining area off, enjoyable hearty fresh food
all day, good choice of wines by the glass,
Harveys ales including seasonal, friendly
efficient service; background music; children
welcome, picnic-sets in front garden, covered
deck next to working waterwheel, handy

for Standen (NT), open all day from 9am
(breakfast Fri-Sun). *(Anon)*

EAST HOATHLY   TQ5216
⋆ **Kings Head** (01825) 840238
High Street/Mill Lane; BN8 6DR Well
kept 1648 ales (brewed here) and Harveys
Best in long comfortably worn-in open-plan
bar, some dark panelling and stripped brick,
upholstered settles, old local photographs,
log fire, wide choice of enjoyable generously
served food at sensible prices, friendly staff
and locals, daily papers, restaurant; TV; steps
up to back garden safe for children. *(John
Beeken, Ann and Colin Hunt)*

EASTERGATE   SU9405
Wilkes Head (01243) 543380
*Just off A29 Fontwell–Bognor; Church
Lane; PO20 3UT* Small friendly red-
brick local with two bars and back dining
extension, flagstones and inglenook log fire,
enjoyable reasonably priced blackboard food
from sandwiches up, Adnams and four guest
ales, proper cider, darts; tables in big garden
with covered smokers' area, open all day
weekends. *(Nigel and Sue Foster, Tony Hobden)*

ELSTED   SU8320
Elsted Inn (01730) 813662
Elsted Marsh; GU29 0JT Attractive
Victorian country pub, enjoyable reasonably
priced food from shortish menu, real ales
such as Gales and Otter, friendly efficient
service, two log fires, nice country furniture
on bare boards, old Goodwood racing photos
(both horses and cars), dining area at back;
plenty of seating in lovely enclosed downs-
view garden with big terrace, four bedrooms,
open all day summer. *(John Beeken)*

ELSTED   SU8119
⋆ **Three Horseshoes** (01730) 825746
*Village signed from B2141 Chichester–
Petersfield; from A272 about 2 miles W of
Midhurst, turn left heading W; GU29 0JY*
A congenial bustle at this pretty white-
painted old pub, beamed rooms, log fires
and candlelight, ancient flooring, antique
furnishings, fresh flowers and attractive
prints and photographs, four changing ales
tapped from the cask, summer cider, really
good freshly made food including some
interesting choices, friendly service; well
behaved children allowed, dogs in bar, two
delightful connecting gardens with plenty of
seats and fine views of South Downs, good
surrounding walks. *(John Beeken, Martin and
Karen Wake, Tony and Jill Radnor, Stephen and
Jean Curtis and others)*

ERIDGE STATION   TQ5434
⋆ **Huntsman** (01892) 864258
*Signed off A26 S of Fridge Green;
TN3 9LE* Country local with two opened-up
rooms, pubby furniture on bare boards,
some tables with carved/painted board
games including own 'Eridgeopoly', hunting

pictures, three Badger ales, over a dozen wines by the glass, popular bar food (not Sun evening, Mon) including fresh fish, seasonal game and home-grown produce, friendly staff; children and dogs welcome, picnic-sets and heaters on decking, outside bar, more seats on lawn among weeping willows, open all day weekends, closed Mon lunchtime. *(Pete Christie, Terry and Barbara, Claire Millar)*

FERNHURST   SU9028

Red Lion   (01428) 643112

The Green, off A286 via Church Lane; GU27 3HY Friendly wisteria-covered 16th-c pub tucked quietly away by green and cricket pitch near church, heavy beams and timbers, attractive furnishings, enjoyable food from sandwiches and snacks up, well kept Fullers ales and a guest, good wines, cheerful helpful service, restaurant; children welcome, seats out in front and in pretty back garden, open all day Sun. *(Martin and Karen Wake)*

FERRING   TQ0903

Henty Arms   (01903) 241254

Ferring Lane; BN12 6QY Six well kept changing ales, generous attractively priced food (can get busy, so best to book), breakfast from 9am Tues-Fri, neat friendly staff, opened-up lounge/dining area, log fire, separate bar with games and TV; garden tables. *(Tony and Wendy Hobden)*

FINDON   TQ1208

Gun   (01903) 873206

High Street; BN14 0TA Low-beamed rambling pub with good range of enjoyable reasonably priced food, three well kept beers; children welcome, large sheltered garden, pretty village below Cissbury Ring (NT), Sept sheep fair. *(J A Snell)*

FINDON   TQ1208

Village House   (01903) 873350

High Street; off A24 N of Worthing; BN14 0TE Converted 16th-c coach house, panelling, pictures and big open fire in large L-shaped bar, restaurant beyond, enjoyable good value pubby food (not Sun evening) including blackboard specials and thai menu Mon evening, Fullers London Pride, Harveys Best, Sharps Cornish Coaster and a guest, regular live music, monthly quiz; small attractive walled garden, six comfortable bedrooms, handy for Cissbury Ring (NT) and downland walks. *(Tony and Wendy Hobden)*

FIRLE   TQ4607

⋆ Ram   (01273) 858222

Village signed off A27 Lewes–Polegate; BN8 6NS Refurbished 16th-c village pub geared for dining but welcoming drinkers, locally sourced restauranty food (not particularly cheap) including good Sun roasts, well kept Harveys with guests such as Hop Back and Sharps, real cider and plenty of wines, friendly staff, three main areas with log fires, rustic furniture on

wood floors, soft lighting; children and dogs welcome, picnic-sets out in front, big walled garden behind with fruit trees, play area, good walks, four stylish bedrooms, open all day. *(Pete Walker)*

FISHBOURNE   SU8304

Bulls Head   (01243) 839895

Fishbourne Road (A259 Chichester–Emsworth); PO19 3JP Former 17th-c farmhouse, thoroughly traditional with copper pans on black beams, some stripped brick and panelling, good log fire, well kept Fullers/Gales ales, popular good value food (not Sun evening) from varied menu, efficient staff, newspapers; unobtrusive background music; children welcome, tables on heated covered deck, four bedrooms in former skittle alley, handy for Roman villa. *(J A Snell, David H T Dimock, John Beeken and others)*

FULKING   TQ2411

Shepherd & Dog   (01273) 857382

Off A281 N of Brighton, via Poynings; BN5 9LU 17th-c bay-windowed pub in beautiful spot below downs, low beams, panelling and inglenook, their own Downland beers (brewed a couple of miles away) and guests, traditional food from baguettes up (fish on Fri), friendly efficient service; children and dogs welcome, terrace and pretty streamside garden, straightforward climb to Devils Dyke, open all day till 10.30pm (8pm Sun). *(John Beeken)*

FUNTINGTON   SU7908

⋆ Fox & Hounds   (01243) 575246

Common Road (B2146); PO18 9LL Old bay-windowed pub with updated beamed rooms in grey/green shades, welcoming log fires, good adventurous food from open sandwiches and snacks up, popular all-day Sun carvery, booking advised weekends, well kept Harveys, Timothy Taylors and guests, lots of wines by the glass and good coffee, comfortable spacious dining extension; children welcome, tables out in front and in walled garden behind, pair of inn signs (one a pack of hounds, the other a family of foxes), open all day from 8am. *(Lawrence Pearse, Tim and Joan Wright, Nigel and Sue Foster, J A Snell)*

GLYNDE   TQ4508

Trevor Arms   (01273) 858208

Over railway bridge, S of village; BN8 6SS Fine downland views from this brick and flint village pub now under same management as the Ram at Firle; impressive dining area with mix of high-backed settles, pews and cushioned chairs around assorted tables, games part with toad in the hole and darts, through to opened-up bar with Glyndebourne pictures, old photos of the pub, two boars' heads, piano and large woodburner, popular fairly traditional home-made food (all day weekends) including range of pies, Harveys and local guests;

children and dogs welcome, big back garden with downs backdrop, popular with walkers, station next door, open all day. *(Ann and Colin Hunt)*

GORING-BY-SEA   TQ1002
Bulls Head (01903) 247622
Goring Street; BN12 5AR Chef & Brewer with several small beamed rooms and dining conservatory at back, good choice of reasonably priced pubby food all day including deals, friendly efficient staff, well kept Fullers London Pride and Harveys Best, decent wine selection; background music; children and dogs welcome, large walled garden. *(Tony and Wendy Hobden)*

GRAFFHAM   SU9218
Foresters Arms (01798) 867202
Village off A285; GU28 0QA 16th-c pub doing well under present licensees; heavy beams, log fire in huge brick fireplace, pews, wheelback and old-fashioned school chairs around antique pine tables, two other areas, ales such as Dark Star and Harveys, good food from ciabattas up including weekday set lunch, friendly attentive service, monthly live jazz; children and dogs welcome, attractive sunny back garden and good local walks, some classic car meetings, three bedrooms. *(Roger and Val)*

GUN HILL   TQ5614
★ Gun (01825) 872361
Off A22 NW of Hailsham, or off A267; TN21 0JU Big 15th-c country dining pub, large central bar with nice old brick floor, stools against counter, Aga in corner, Harveys and Sharps on handpump, decent wines by glass, efficient, friendly service, background jazz; good, popular bistro-style food; small grey-panelled room leads off with rugs on bare boards, animal skins on cushioned wall benches, logs piled into tall fireplace, nice mix of scrubbed and dark tables with all sorts of dining chairs; cosy and cottagey two-room restaurant, close-set tables and chairs, old glass bottles and glasses along gantry, gun prints and other country prints, beams and log fires, children welcome, picnic-sets on lantern-lit front terrace and more in garden; right on Wealden Way, open all day Sun. *(Dr A J and Mrs B A Tompsett)*

HALNAKER   SU9008
★ Anglesey Arms (01243) 773474
A285 Chichester–Petworth; PO18 0NQ Georgian pub belonging to the Goodwood Estate; bare boards, settles and log fire, well kept Black Sheep, Wells & Youngs and a couple of guests, decent wines, good varied if not particularly cheap food including local organic produce and Selsey fish, friendly accommodating service, simple but smart L-shaped dining room (children allowed) with woodburners, stripped pine and some flagstones, traditional games; dogs welcome in bar, tables in big tree-lined

garden, good nearby walks, open all day Fri, Sat. *(Howard and Margaret Buchanan)*

HAMMERPOT   TQ0605
★ Woodmans Arms (01903) 871240
On N (eastbound) side of A27; BN16 4EU Well kept pretty thatched pub rebuilt after 2004 fire, beams and timbers, good choice of enjoyable food from sandwiches up (smaller helpings available) including popular Sun lunch, four well kept Fullers/Gales beers and a guest, nice wines by the glass, efficient service from friendly neat staff, inglenook woodburner; no dogs inside; children welcome if eating, tables in nice garden, open all day, closed Sun evening. *(Peter Meister, Ann and Colin Hunt, Val and Alan Green)*

HASSOCKS   TQ3016
Friars Oak (01273) 847801
London Road (A273 N); BN6 9NA Big 19th-c Vintage Inn with their usual food including good value weekday set menu till 5pm, plenty of wines by the glass, well kept Harveys Best, Shepherd Neame Spitfire and Timothy Taylors Landlord, friendly efficient service, several areas (some made to look older than they are), log fires; background music; pleasant garden, open all day. *(A N Bance)*

HENLEY   SU8925
★ Duke of Cumberland Arms
(01428) 652280 *Off A286 S of Fernhurst; GU27 3HQ* Wisteria-clad 15th-c stone-built pub with log fires in two small rooms, low ceilings, scrubbed oak furniture on brick or flagstoned floors, rustic decorations, well kept Harveys and a couple of guests tapped from the cask, very good food (not Sun or Mon evenings) from well executed pub favourites to interesting restaurant-style dishes, separate tiled-floor dining room with more modern feel, friendly attentive staff; well behaved children and dogs welcome, deck with lovely hill views, charming sloping garden and trout ponds, open all day. *(Conor McGaughey, Matthew Cramer)*

HERMITAGE   SU7505
★ Sussex Brewery (01243) 371533
A259 just W of Emsworth; PO10 8AU Bustling, welcoming and interesting, with small bare-boards (and maybe sawdust) bar, good fire in brick inglenook, simple furniture, little flagstoned snug, Wells & Youngs and four guest ales, ten wines by the glass, hearty food including speciality sausages (even vegetarian ones), small upstairs restaurant; children and dogs welcome, picnic-sets in small back courtyard, open all day. *(Andy Rhodes, Miss J F Reay)*

HOOE   TQ6910
Red Lion (01424) 892371
Denbigh Road; TN33 9EW Attractive old local behind screen of pollarded lime trees,

plenty of original features including two big inglenooks, enjoyable home-cooked food and well kept ales such as Harveys, good friendly service, main bar and back snug, overflow function room and further eating space upstairs; children and dogs welcome, open all day weekends. *(Anon)*

HOUGHTON   TQ0111
★ **George & Dragon** (01798) 831559
B2139 W of Storrington; BN18 9LW
13th-c beams and timbers in attractive spic and span bar rambling up and down steps, note the elephant photograph above the fireplace, good Arun Valley views from back extension, well liked reasonably priced food and good friendly service, Marstons-related ales, decent wines by the glass; background music; children and dogs welcome, seats on decked terrace and in charming sloping garden, good walks, open all day Fri-Sun. *(Colin McKerrow, Julie and Bill Ryan, Ann and Colin Hunt, Mrs T A Bizat)*

HUNSTON   SU8601
Spotted Cow (01243) 786718
B2145 S of Chichester; PO20 1PD
Flagstoned pub with friendly staff and locals, wide choice of enjoyable food, chilled Fullers/Gales beers, big fires and up-to-date décor, small front bar, roomier side lounge with armchairs, sofas and low tables as anteroom for airy high-ceilinged restaurant; may be background music; good disabled access, children welcome if eating, big pretty garden, handy for towpath walkers. *(David H T Dimock)*

HURST GREEN   TQ7326
★ **White Horse** (01580) 860235
Silverhill (A21); TN19 7PU Friendly well run pub with enjoyable food and well kept Harveys, bare-boards bar with leather armchairs and white-painted dining chairs around various wooden tables, game trophies, prints and photographs on the walls, open fire, second bar area with built-in leather wall seats, elegant dining room with oil paintings, chandeliers and panelling, monthly live jazz; children welcome, dogs allowed in bar, seats in garden, open all day Sun till 8pm. *(Anon)*

HURSTPIERPOINT   TQ2816
★ **New Inn** (01273) 834608
High Street; BN6 9RQ Popular 16th-c beamed pub under same management as Bull in Ditchling, well kept ales including Harveys, good wines by the glass, enjoyable food with plenty for vegetarians, efficient friendly young staff, contrasting linked areas including dimly lit oak-panelled back part (children allowed here) with bric-a-brac

and open fire, and smart apple-green dining room; sports TV; dogs welcome, garden tables, open all day. *(Conor McGaughey)*

ICKLESHAM   TQ8716
★ **Queens Head** (01424) 814552
Off A259 Rye–Hastings; TN36 4BL
Friendly well run country pub, extremely popular locally (and at weekends with cyclists and walkers), open-plan areas around big counter, high timbered walls, vaulted roof, shelves of bottles, plenty of farming implements and animal traps, pubby furniture on brown pattered carpet, other areas with inglenooks and a back room with old bicycle memorabilia, Greene King, Harveys and a couple of guests, local cider, several wines by the glass, good choice of reasonably priced home-made food (all day weekends); background jazz and blues (live 4-6pm Sun); well behaved children allowed away from bar till 8.30pm, dogs welcome in bar, picnic-sets, boules and play area in peaceful garden with fine Brede Valley views, you can walk to Winchelsea, open all day. *(Andrea Rampley, Martin and Sue Day, Lucien Perring)*

ICKLESHAM   TQ8716
★ **Robin Hood** (01424) 814277
Main Road; TN36 4BD Friendly no-frills beamed pub with enthusiastic landlord and cheerful attentive staff, great local atmosphere, good value unpretentious home-made food including blackboard specials, nine well kept changing ales and three real ciders, hops overhead, lots of copper bric-a-brac, log fire, games area with pool, back dining extension; big garden with Brede Valley views. *(Anon)*

ISFIELD   TQ4417
Laughing Fish (01825) 750349
Station Road; TN22 5XB Nicely old-fashioned opened-up Victorian local with jovial landlord and friendly staff, good value home-made bar food (not Sun evening) including specials board and some good vegetarian dishes, well kept Greene King with guests such as Dark Star and Elgoods, open fire, train pictures, bar billiards and other traditional games, events including entertaining beer race Easter Mon; children and dogs welcome, disabled access, small pleasantly shaded walled garden with enclosed play area, field for camping, right by Lavender Line (pub was station hotel), open all day. *(John Beeken, Ann and Colin Hunt)*

KINGSTON   TQ3908
★ **Juggs** (01273) 472523
Village signed off A27 by roundabout W of Lewes; BN7 3NT Popular tile-hung

---

All *Guide* inspections are anonymous. Anyone claiming to be a *Good Pub Guide* inspector is a fraud. Please let us know.

village pub with heavy 15th-c beams and very low front door, lots of neatly stripped masonry, sturdy wooden furniture on bare boards and stone slabs, log fires, smaller eating areas including a family room, variety of enjoyable food from sandwiches and pub standards up with some interesting choices, well kept Shepherd Neame ales, good coffee and wine list, friendly helpful staff; background music; dogs welcome, disabled facilities, tables outside including covered area with heaters (they ask to swipe your credit card if you eat out here), lots of tubs and hanging baskets, play area, nice walks, open all day. *(Tony and Wendy Hobden, PL, Conor McGaughey)*

LEWES TQ4210

Gardeners Arms (01273) 474808

Cliffe High Street; BN7 2AN Welcoming unpretentious little local opposite brewery, light and airy, with plain scrubbed tables on bare boards around three narrow sides of bar, well kept Harveys and interesting changing guests, farm ciders, some lunchtime food including good pies, bar nibbles on Sun, newspapers and magazines, toad in the hole played here; no children; open all day. *(Anon)*

LEWES TQ4210

John Harvey (01273) 479880

Bear Yard, just off Cliffe High Street; BN7 2AN Bustling no-nonsense tap for nearby Harveys brewery, four of their beers including seasonals kept perfectly, some tapped from the cask, good well priced food (not Sun evening) from huge lunchtime sandwiches, baked potatoes and ciabattas up, friendly efficient young staff, basic dark flagstoned bar with one great vat halved to make two towering 'snugs' for several people, lighter room on left, newspapers, woodburner; background and occasional live music, machines; a few tables outside, open all day, breakfast from 10am. *(Martin and Oliver Wright, Tony and Wendy Hobden, Ann and Colin Hunt, Pete Walker)*

LEWES TQ4110

⋆ Lewes Arms (01273) 473152

Castle Ditch Lane/Mount Place – tucked behind castle ruins; BN7 1YH Cheerful unpretentious little local with half a dozen well kept ales, 30 malt whiskies and plenty of wines by the glass, very good reasonably priced bar food (all day Sat, not Sun evening), tiny front bar on right with stools along nicely curved counter and bench window seats, two other simple rooms hung with photographs and information about the famous Lewes bonfire night, beer mats pinned over doorways, poetry and folk evenings; children (not in front bar) and dogs welcome, picnic-sets on attractive two-level back terrace, open all day (till midnight Fri, Sat). *(MP, Pat and Tony Martin, Conor McGaughey, Gene and Kitty Rankin)*

LEWES TQ4110

⋆ Pelham Arms (01273) 476149

At top of High Street; BN7 1XL Popular 17th-c beamed pub, good well presented food (booking advised) including some interesting vegetarian choices, friendly staff, three Badger ales, character rambling interior with inglenook, live music Thurs from flamenco to jazz; children till 8pm, dogs in bar areas, small courtyard garden, open all day. *(Anon)*

LEWES TQ4210

⋆ Snowdrop (01273) 471018

South Street; BN7 2BU Welcoming pub tucked below the cliffs, narrowboat theme with brightly painted servery and colourful jugs, lanterns etc hanging from planked ceiling, buoyant atmosphere, well kept ales such as Dark Star, Harveys, Hogs Back and Rectory, hearty helpings of enjoyable good value local food including good vegetarian choice, friendly efficient service; background music (live jazz Mon); they may ask to keep your credit card while running a tab; dogs very welcome (menu for them), small garden and terrace, open all day. *(MP, John Beeken, Mrs G Marlow, Ann and Colin Hunt, Steve Homer)*

LITTLEHAMPTON TQ0202

⋆ Arun View (01903) 722335

Wharf Road; W towards Chichester; BN17 5DD Airy attractive 18th-c pub in lovely harbour spot with busy waterway directly below windows, very popular lunchtimes with older people (younger crowd in evenings) for enjoyable interesting food (all day Sun) from sandwiches to good fresh fish, well kept Arundel, Fullers London Pride and Ringwood, 20 wines by the glass, cheerful helpful staff, lots of drawings, caricatures and nautical collectables, flagstoned and panelled back bar with banquettes and dark wood tables, large conservatory; background and some live music, TVs, pool; disabled facilities, flower-filled terrace, summer barbecues, interesting waterside walkway to coast, four bedrooms, open all day. *(S Holder)*

LITTLEHAMPTON TQ0202

Crown (01903) 719842

High Street; BN17 5EG Town-centre pub with six well kept changing ales including Anchor Springs, low-priced pubby food, daily carvery (maybe upstairs on Sun), regular live music; children and dogs welcome, open all day from 9am (till 2am Thurs-Sat). *(Tony and Wendy Hobden)*

LOWER BEEDING TQ2225

Crabtree (01403) 892666

Brighton Road; RH13 6PT Family-run pub with Victorian façade but much older inside with Tudor beams and huge inglenook (dated 1537), simple light modern décor, dining room in converted barn, good interesting food using genuinely local seasonal produce including daily changing set lunch, service with a smile, well kept Badger beers and good selection of wines by the glass (including english); children welcome, dogs in bar, landscaped garden, with fine country views, handy for Nymans (NT), open all day. *(R J and D S Courtney, Martin and Karen Wake, Tony and Wendy Hobden, Alan Cowell)*

LOXWOOD TQ0331
Onslow Arms (01403) 752452
B2133 NW of Billingshurst; RH14 0RD Comfortable and welcoming with popular food (not Mon evening) from doorstep sandwiches up, three Badger ales, good house wines, coffees and teas, daily papers and lovely log fires, quiz and music nights; dogs welcome, picnic-sets in good-sized garden sloping to river and nearby restored Wey & Arun Canal, good walks and boat trips, open all day. *(Tony and Wendy Hobden, Ian Phillips)*

LYMINSTER TQ0204
Six Bells (01903) 713639
Lyminster Road (A284), Wick; BN17 7PS Unassuming 18th-c flint pub with enjoyable nicely presented food from weekday soup-and-sandwich and daily roast bargains to some interesting specials (best to book weekends), well kept Fullers London Pride and Greene King Abbot, good house wine, low black beams and big inglenook, pubby furnishings; dogs on leads welcome, terrace and garden seating. *(Tony and Wendy Hobden, Dr and Mrs R E S Tanner)*

MAYFIELD TQ5826
Middle House (01435) 872146
High Street; TN20 6AB Handsome 16th-c timbered inn, L-shaped beamed bar with massive fireplace, several well kept ales including Harveys, local cider, decent wines, quiet lounge area with leather chesterfields around log fire in ornate carved fireplace, good choice of food, panelled restaurant; background music; children welcome, terraced back garden with lovely views, five bedrooms, open all day. *(Anon)*

MID LAVANT SU8508
Earl of March (01243) 533993
A286 Lavant Road; PO18 0BQ Updated and extended with emphasis on eating but seats for drinkers in flagstoned log-fire bar serving well kept ales such as Ballards, Harveys and Hop Back, good if pricey food with much sourced locally, nice wines including nearby Tinwood (sparkling) and other english choices, plush dining area and conservatory with seafood bar, polite efficient staff; delightful location with view up to Goodwood from neatly kept garden, local walks. *(John Ecklin, Tracey and Stephen Groves)*

MILLAND SU8328
Rising Sun (01428) 741347
Iping Road junction with main road through village; GU30 7NA Three linked rooms including cheery log-fire bar and bare-boards restaurant, Fullers/Gales beers, good variety of well cooked nicely presented food including some interesting specials, attentive amiable staff, live music first Mon of month; children welcome (popular with families at weekends), garden with heated terrace and smokers' gazebo, good walking area, open all day weekends. *(KC, John Evans, J R Evans)*

MILTON STREET TQ5304
✩ Sussex Ox (01323) 870840
Off A27 just under a mile E of Alfriston roundabout; BN26 5RL Extended country pub (originally a 1900s slaughterhouse) with magnificent downs views; bar area with a couple of high tables and chairs on bare boards, old local photographs, Dark Star, Hammerpot and Harveys, good choice of wines by the glass, lower brick-floored room with farmhouse furniture and woodburner, similarly furnished hop-draped dining room (children allowed here), further two-room front dining area with high-backed rush-seated chairs, popular bistro-style food, friendly service; dogs welcome in bar, teak seating on raised back deck taking in the view, picnic-sets in garden below and more under parasols at front, closed Sun evening in winter and between Christmas and New Year. *(Dr Nigel Bowles, John Beeken)*

NEWHAVEN TQ4500
Hope (01273) 515389
Follow West Beach signs from A259 westbound; BN9 9DN Big-windowed pub overlooking busy harbour entrance, long bar with raised area, open fires and comfy sofas, upstairs dining conservatory and breezy balcony tables with even better view towards Seaford Head, well kept ales such as Harveys and Hop Head, good choice of generous bar food, friendly new landlord and pub dog (Pip); waterside terrace. *(Peter Meister, John Beeken)*

NEWICK TQ4121
Royal Oak 0800 0236085
Church Road; BN8 4JU White weather-boarded pub on edge of lovely village green, neat and comfortable, with enjoyable good value food, Fullers London Pride and Harveys Best, friendly service, open fire; children and dogs welcome, tables out in front, open all day. *(SRK)*

NUTBOURNE TQ071
Rising Sun (01798) 812191
Off A283 E of Pulborough; The Street;

It's very helpful if you let us know up-to-date food prices when you report on pubs.

RH20 2HE Unspoilt creeper-clad village pub dating partly from the 16th c, beams, bare boards and scrubbed tables, friendly helpful licensees (same family ownership for over 30 years), well kept Fullers London Pride and guests, good range of bar food and blackboard specials, big log fire, daily papers, enamel signs and 1920s fashion and dance posters, cosy snug, attractive back family room, some live music; dogs welcome, garden with small back terrace under apple tree, smokers' shelter, listed outside lavatory. *(N R White)*

OFFHAM TQ3912
* **Blacksmiths Arms** (01273) 472971
A275 N of Lewes; BN7 3QD Civilised open-plan dining pub, comfortable and welcoming, with good food from chef-owner including seafood and some nice vegetarian choices, well kept Harveys Best and a seasonal beer, good wines, efficient friendly service from uniformed staff, huge end inglenook; french windows to terrace with picnic-sets, four bedrooms. *(Christine and Andy Farley)*

OFFHAM TQ4011
* **Chalk Pit** (01273) 471124
Offham Road (A275 N of Lewes); BN7 3QF Former late 18th-c chalk pit building on three levels, well kept Harveys and a guest, decent wines by the glass, great choice of popular home-made food including OAP bargains, attentive cheerful staff, neat restaurant extension, skittle alley, toad in the hole played Mon nights; children welcome, garden with terrace seating, smokers' shelter with pool table, three bedrooms, open (and usually food) all day Fri-Sun. *(John Beeken, Ann and Colin Hunt)*

PARTRIDGE GREEN TQ1819
* **Green Man** (01403) 710250
Off A24 just under a mile S of A272 junction – take B2135 at West Grinstead signpost; pub at Jolesfield, N of Partridge Green; RH13 8JT Relaxed gently upmarket dining pub with popular enterprising food, several champagnes by the glass and other good wines, Dark Star and Harveys Best, truly helpful service; unassuming front area by counter with bentwood bar chairs, stools and library chairs around one or two low tables, old curved high-back settle, main eating area widening into back part with pretty enamelled stove and pitched ceiling on left, more self-contained room on right with stag's head, minimal decoration but plenty of atmosphere; cast-iron seats and picnic-sets under parasols in neat back garden. *(N R White, Val and Alan Green)*

PARTRIDGE GREEN TQ1819
Partridge (01403) 710391
Church Road/High Street; RH13 8JS Spaciously renovated village pub acting as tap for Dark Star, their full range with at least one guest, real cider, enjoyable home-made food at sensible prices, friendly atmosphere; children and dogs welcome, garden with play equipment and large terrace, open from 10am weekends for breakfast. *(Colin Gooch)*

PATCHING TQ0705
Fox (01903) 871299
Arundel Road; signed off A27 eastbound just W of Worthing; BN13 3UJ Generous good value home-made food including popular Sun roasts (best to book), quick friendly service even at busy times, well kept Harveys Best and Shepherd Neame Spitfire, good wine choice, large dining area off roomy panelled bar, hunting pictures; quiet background music; children and dogs welcome, disabled access, nice tree-shaded garden with play area. *(Tony and Wendy Hobden, John Beeken)*

PETT TQ8713
Royal Oak (01424) 812515
Pett Road; TN35 4HG Refurbished and under same ownership as the Queens Head at Icklesham, roomy main bar with big open fire, Harveys and a couple of changing guests, good popular home-made food including plenty of fish, two dining areas, efficient friendly service, monthly live music and quiz nights; small garden behind, open all day. *(Peter Meister, Mr and Mrs Price, Lucien Perring)*

PETT TQ8613
Two Sawyers (01424) 812255
Pett Road, off A259; TN35 4HB Meandering low-beamed rooms including bare-boards bar with stripped tables, tiny snug, passage sloping down to restaurant allowing children, popular good value freshly made food, friendly service, well kept Harveys with guests like Dark Star, Ringwood and Wells & Youngs, local farm cider and perry, wide range of wines; background music; dogs allowed in bar, suntrap front courtyard, back garden with shady trees and well spaced tables, three bedrooms, open all day. *(Peter Meister, Lucien Perring)*

PETWORTH SU9721
Star (01798) 342569
Market Square; GU28 0AH Airy open-plan pub in centre with seats out in front, well kept Fullers ales and decent wines, enjoyable reasonably priced food, good coffee, leather armchairs and sofa by open fire, friendly atmosphere. *(Ann and Colin Hunt)*

PETWORTH SU9921
* **Welldiggers Arms** (01798) 342287
Low Heath; A283 E; GU28 0HG Nicely opened up L-shaped bar with low beams and log fire, pictures on ochre walls, long rustic settles and well spaced tables to match (made by present landlord's father), good local food (not always cheap) including

excellent rib of beef Sun lunchtime, Wells & Youngs in good condition, decent wines; well behaved children and dogs allowed, plenty of tables on attractive lawns and terrace, nice views, closed Sun evening, Mon. *(Richard Tilbrook, Colin McKerrow)*

PLAYDEN   TQ9121
Playden Oasts (01797) 223502
Rye Road; TN31 7UL Converted three-roundel oast house with comfortable bar and restaurant, helpful chatty landlord, enjoyable food from well filled baguettes up, Harveys Best, friendly homely atmosphere; eight bedrooms. *(Paul Humphreys)*

PLUMPTON   TQ3613
★ Half Moon (01273) 890253
Ditchling Road (B2116); BN7 3AF Enlarged beamed and timbered dining pub with good interesting home-made food using local produce including midweek set lunch, also children's menu and traditional Sun roasts, local ales and wines (even an organic Sussex lager), good friendly service, log fire with unusual flint chimneybreast; background music (live Thurs); dogs welcome in bar, tables in wisteria-clad front courtyard and on back terrace, big downs-view garden with picnic area, summer family days (last Sun of July and Aug) with face painting and bouncy castle, good walks, open all day. *(Steve Homer, Roger and Val)*

PLUMPTON GREEN   TQ3617
Plough (01273) 890311
South Road/Station Road; BN7 3DF 1950s pub with well kept Harveys ales and good selection of sensibly priced traditional food, log fires in both bars, striking Spitfire and Hurricane pictures (there's a pilots' memorial outside), shelves of books, bar billiards, monthly quiz; children and dogs welcome, covered terrace and large downs-view garden with play area, open all day. *(John Beeken)*

POYNINGS   TQ2611
Royal Oak (01273) 857389
The Street; BN45 7AQ Well run 19th-c pub with large beamed bar, good food from sandwiches and sharing plates up, helpful efficient service, real ales including Harveys from three-sided servery, leather sofas and traditional furnishing, woodburner; children and dogs welcome, big attractive garden with country/downs views. *(Helene Grygar, R Anderson)*

RINGMER   TQ4512
Green Man (01273) 812422
Lewes Road; BN8 5NA Improved under present landlord, busy friendly bar with six real ales from brick-faced counter, log fire, ample helpings of reasonably priced hearty food, good service, restaurant area; children and dogs welcome, picnic-sets on lawn under trees, play area. *(John Beeken)*

ROGATE   SU8023
★ White Horse (01730) 821333
East Street; A272 Midhurst–Petersfield; GU31 5EA Rambling heavy-beamed local in front of village cricket field, friendly relaxed atmosphere, with Harveys full range kept particularly well, flagstones, stripped stone, timbers and big log fire, attractive candlelit sunken dining area, good range of enjoyable reasonably priced food (not Sun evening) served by helpful staff, traditional games (and quite a collection of trophy cups), quiz last Sun of month; may be background Radio 2; children welcome, some tables on back terrace, open all day. *(John Evans)*

ROWHOOK   TQ1234
★ Chequers (01403) 790480
Off A29 NW of Horsham; RH12 3PY Attractive welcoming 16th-c pub, relaxing beamed and flagstoned front bar with portraits and inglenook log fire, step up to low-beamed lounge, well kept Harveys and guests, decent wines by the glass, good cooking from chef-landlord using local ingredients including home-grown vegetables, separate restaurant; background music; children and dogs welcome, tables out on front terraces and in pretty garden behind with good play area, attractive surroundings, closed Sun evening. *(Gerald and Gabrielle Culliford)*

RUDGWICK   TQ0934
Kings Head (01403) 822200
Off A281; Church Street (B2128); RH12 3EB Beamed 13th-c pub by fine old church in pretty village, well kept Harveys Best and Fullers London Pride, good italian cooking and lots of seafood, reasonable prices; flower-decked seating area at front, more seats behind. *(John Beeken)*

RUSHLAKE GREEN   TQ6218
★ Horse & Groom (01435) 830320
Off B2096 Heathfield–Battle; TN21 9QE Cheerful little village-green pub under new licensees, L-shaped low-beamed bar with brick fireplace and local pictures, small room down a step with horsey décor and local artwork, simple beamed restaurant, good food cooked by chef-landlord from pub favourites to more elaborate daily changing choices, Harveys and Shepherd Neame, a dozen wines by the glass; children and dogs welcome, attractive cottagey garden with pretty country views, nice walks, open all day weekends. *(J H Bell)*

RUSPER   TQ1836
★ Royal Oak (01293) 871393
Friday Street, towards Warnham – back road N of Horsham, E of A24 (OS Sheet 187 map reference 185369); RH12 4QA Old-fashioned and well worn-in tile-hung pub in very rural spot on Sussex Border Path, small carpeted top bar with leather

sofas and armchairs, log fire, steps down to long beamed main bar with plush wall seats, pine tables and chairs and homely knick-knacks, well kept Surrey Hills Ranmore and six changing guests, farm ciders and perries, short choice of enjoyable low-priced lunchtime food (evenings and Sun lunch by prearrangement), local farm produce for sale, plain games/family room with darts; a few picnic-sets on grass by road and in streamside garden beyond car park, roaming chickens, open all day Sat, till 9pm Sun. *(Ian Phillips)*

RUSPER TQ2037
Star (01293) 871264
Off A264 S of Crawley; RH12 4RA Several linked rooms in rambling 15th-c beamed coaching inn, friendly helpful staff, cosy atmosphere, Fullers London Pride, Greene King Abbot and Ringwood Best, good choice of popular food from sandwiches and light meals up, wood floors, old tools on walls, fine brick inglenook; dogs welcome, picnic-sets on small back terrace. *(Ian Phillips)*

RYE TQ9220
★**George** (01797) 222114
High Street; TN31 7JT Busy, sizeable hotel with popular beamed bar, bare boards and log fire, quite an assortment of wooden dining chairs and settles around a mix of tables, ales such as Dark Star, Franklins, Harveys and Old Dairy, continental beers on tap, good, friendly service from neat staff, interesting bistro-style food, big spreading restaurant to right of main door; background jazz, attractive bedrooms, open all day; children and dogs welcome. *(M P Mackenzie, Phil Bryant)*

RYE TQ9220
★**Mermaid** (01797) 223065
Mermaid Street; TN31 7EY Lovely old timbered hotel on famous cobbled street with civilised antiques-filled bar, Victorian gothick carved chairs, older but plainer oak seats, huge working inglenook with massive bressumer, Fullers, Greene King and Harveys, good selection of wines and malt whiskies, short bar menu, more elaborate and expensive restaurant choices, good friendly service; background music; children welcome, seats on small back terrace, bedrooms (most with four-posters), open all day. *(Phil Bryant, Richard Tilbrook, Pete Walker)*

RYE TQ9220
Queens Head (01797) 222181
Landgate; TN31 7LH Friendly recently refurbished old pub with good selection of changing ales and ciders, enjoyable home-made food including fresh local fish, bar billiards and pool, live weekend music; grassed area at back, open all day. *(Anon)*

RYE HARBOUR TQ9419
Inkerman Arms (01797) 222464
Rye Harbour Road; TN31 7TQ Friendly plain pub near nature reserve and under newish management, enjoyable food including good fish and chips, Harveys and guests; tables out in small sheltered back area. *(Rob Newland)*

SCAYNES HILL TQ3824
Sloop (01444) 831219
Sloop Lane, Freshfield Lock; RH17 7NP Improved under present welcoming owners, main bar with wood floors, painted panelling and wood burner, fresh flowers and daily papers, linked dining area to the right and public bar with old photographs, good fairly standard food (not Sun evening) including a weekday lunchtime menu for smaller appetites, well kept Harveys and a guest like Hammerpot, several wines by the glass, friendly staff, Sun live acoustic music; picnic-sets in sheltered garden, open all day. *(Martin and Oliver Wright, Steve Homer)*

SEDLESCOMBE TQ7817
Queens Head (01424) 870228
The Green; TN33 0QA Attractive heavily beamed tile-hung village-green pub refurbished under new management; main bar on right with mixed tables and wheelback chairs on wood floor, church candles and fresh flowers, a huge cartwheel and some farming odds and ends, Harveys and Sharps Doom Bar from plank-fronted servery, side room laid for dining with brick fireplace, sofas in back lounge, another dining room to left of entrance with sisal flooring and huge working inglenook, good popular food (best to book) from shortish menu; quiet background music; children and dogs welcome, garden picnic-sets. *(Anon)*

SELHAM SU9320
Three Moles (01798) 861303
Village signed off A272 Petworth–Midhurst; GU28 0PN Small, quiet and relaxing pub tucked away in woodland village with tiny late Saxon church; steep steps up to bar with well kept ales and farm cider, tasty lunchtime food from short menu, church furniture and blazing coal fires, friendly atmosphere; garden tables, good walks nearby, open all day weekends, closed Thurs. *(Anon)*

SHOREHAM-BY-SEA TQ2005
Fly Inn (01273) 452300
Shoreham Airport, signed off A27, A259; BN43 5FF Not a pub, but this small bar is worth knowing for its interesting 1930s art deco airport building and uninterrupted downs views with plenty of light aircraft action; Shepherd Neame ales, simple

---

If we know a pub has an outdoor play area for children, we mention it.

well priced food served by cheerful staff; background music; children welcome, picnic-sets on large terrace, small airport museum. *(John Beeken)*

SHOREHAM-BY-SEA   TQ2105
Red Lion (01273) 453171
Upper Shoreham Road; BN43 5TE
Modest dimly lit low-beamed and timbered 16th-c pub with settles in snug alcoves, wide choice of good value pubby food including speciality pies, half a dozen well kept changing ales such as local Adur, Arundel and Hepworths (Easter beer festival), farm cider, decent wines, friendly staff, log fire in unusual fireplace, another open fire in dining room, further bar with covered terrace; pretty sheltered garden behind, old bridge and lovely Norman church opposite, good downs views and walks. *(John Coatsworth)*

SIDLESHAM   SZ8697
⋆ Crab & Lobster (01243) 641233
Mill Lane; off B2145 S of Chichester; PO20 7NB Restaurant-with-rooms rather than pub but walkers and bird-watchers welcome in small flagstoned bar for light meal, Harveys and Sharps, 17 wines by the glass including champagne (also interesting selection of 50cl carafes), stylish, upmarket restaurant with good imaginative (and pricey) food including local fish, friendly young staff; background music; children welcome, tables on back terrace overlooking marshes, smart bedrooms, self-catering cottage, open all day (food all day weekends). *(M J Daly, Colin McKerrow, Richard Tilbrook)*

SINGLETON   SU8713
⋆ Partridge (01243) 811251
Just off A286 Midhurst–Chichester; PO18 0EY Pretty 16th-c pub handy for Weald & Downland Open Air Museum; all sorts of light and dark wood tables and dining chairs on polished wooden floors, flagstones or carpet, some country knick-knacks, daily papers, open fires and woodburner, Fullers London Pride, Harveys Best and a summer guest, several wines by the glass, well liked food from good lunchtime sandwiches up, board games, maybe summer table tennis; background music; children welcome, plenty of seats under parasols on terrace and in walled garden. *(Martin and Karen Wake, Richard Tilbrook, Val and Alan Green)*

SLINDON   SU9708
Spur (01243) 814216
Slindon Common; A29 towards Bognor; BN18 0NE Roomy 17th-c pub with welcoming licensees and efficient friendly staff, wide choice of popular carefully cooked food from bar snacks to more upmarket (but good value) restaurant dishes, Courage

Directors and Sharps Doom Bar, pine tables and two big log fires, large panelled restaurant with linen table cloths, games room with darts and pool, skittle alley; children welcome, pretty garden (traffic noise), good local walks, open all day Sun. *(David H T Dimock, M G Hart, Nigel and Sue Foster)*

SMALL DOLE   TQ2112
Fox (01273) 491196
Henfield Road; BN5 9XE Popular open-plan village local on busy road, good choice of reasonably priced bar food from sandwiches and light meals up, set menu choices too (not weekends), well kept Fullers London Pride and Harveys Best, friendly staff coping well at busy times, raised dining areas; background music; tables on small front terrace, handy for downland walks, open all day weekends. *(Tony and Wendy Hobden)*

SOUTH HARTING   SU7819
White Hart (01730) 825355
B2146 SE of Petersfield; GU31 5QB Welcoming 16th-c beamed pub with well spaced tables on polished wood floor, lounge and lower level bar area, three well kept beers and good sensibly priced interesting food, inglenook restaurant; background music; children, dogs and walkers welcome, nice walled garden with spectacular downs views, handy for Uppark (NT), open all day. *(Anon)*

SOUTHWATER   TQ1528
Bax Castle (01403) 730369
Two Mile Ash, a mile or so NW; RH13 0LA Early 19th-c country pub spruced up under new management; well liked traditional home-made food including popular Sun roasts, three Marstons-related ales, friendly staff, sofas next to big log fire, barn restaurant; background music (live Fri); children and dogs welcome, pleasant garden with play area, near Downs Link path on former rail track, open all day (till 9pm Sun). *(Mike Thorne)*

STAPLEFIELD   TQ2728
Jolly Tanners (01444) 400335
Handcross Road, just off A23; RH17 6EF Neatly kept split-level local by cricket green, welcoming landlord and pub dogs, two good log fires, padded settles, lots of china, brasses and old photographs, well kept Fullers London Pride, Harveys and guests (three beer festivals), real ciders, pubby food including good Sun roasts, friendly chatty atmosphere; background and weekends live music including jazz; children welcome and dogs (may be a treat), attractive suntrap garden, quite handy for Nymans (NT), open all day Fri-Sun. *(Alan Weedon, Mike and Eleanor Anderson)*

We list pubs that serve food all day on at least some days at the end of the book.

STAPLEFIELD
TQ2728

Victory (01444) 400463

Warninglid Road; RH17 6EU Pretty little shuttered dining pub overlooking cricket green (and Brighton veteran car run, first weekend in Nov), friendly staff, good choice of popular home-made food, smaller helpings for children, well kept Harveys Best from zinc-topped counter, local cider and decent wines, beams and woodburner; nice tree-shaded garden with play area. *(C and R Bromage, N R White, Philip Holloway and others)*

STEDHAM
SU8522

Hamilton Arms (01730) 812555

School Lane (off A272); GU29 0NZ Proper english local but decorated with thai artefacts and run by friendly thai family, basic pub food as well as good thai bar snacks and restaurant dishes (you can buy ingredients in the little shop), good value Sun buffet, reasonably priced wines and four or more well kept ales; unobtrusive background music, muted TV; pretty hanging baskets, tables out by green and quiet lane, good walks nearby, closed Mon. *(J A Snell)*

STEYNING
TQ1711

Chequer (01903) 814437

High Street; BN44 3RE Rambling low-beamed Tudor coaching inn, five or so well kept ales such as Cottage, Dark Star, Gales, Harveys and Timothy Taylors, good choice of wines, enjoyable well priced usual food (not Sun evening) from sandwiches up including breakfast from 10am, log fire, antique snooker table, large painting featuring the locals, some live music; smokers' shelter, bedrooms, open all day. *(Pete Walker)*

STOPHAM
TQ0318

★**White Hart** (01798) 873321

Off A283 E of village, W of Pulborough; RH20 1DS Fine old pub by medieval River Arun bridge, heavy beams, timbers and panelling, log fire and sofas in one of its three snug rooms, well kept ales such as Arundel, Langhams and Kings, good generous food (all day weekends) from baguettes and pizzas up, friendly efficient service, some interesting bric-a-brac, Thurs quiz night; children welcome, waterside tables, some under cover, open all day. *(Tony and Wendy Hobden, Jay Marsh)*

STORRINGTON
TQ0814

Moon (01903) 744773

High Street; RH20 4DR Split-level interior (children allowed in lower part) with mix of furniture on wood or carpeted floors, wide choice of fairly priced food from lunchtime ciabattas to grills, Sun carvery till 4pm, takeaway pizzas, well kept Arundel, Otter and Sharps, blackboard wine list, friendly staff, live music and quiz nights; TV and fruit machine; children and dogs welcome, terrace tables, open all day. *(Tony and Wendy Hobden)*

STOUGHTON
SU8011

Hare & Hounds (023) 9263 1433

Signed off B2146 Petersfield–Emsworth; PO18 9JQ Airy pine-clad country dining pub with simple contemporary décor, good reasonably priced fresh food including doorstep sandwiches and Sun roasts (till 4pm), up to six well kept ales and two real ciders, good helpful service, big open fires, public bar with darts, quiz nights; children in eating areas, dogs welcome, tables on pretty front terrace and on grass behind, lovely setting near Saxon church, good local walks, open all day Fri-Sun. *(Geoff and Linda Payne)*

SUTTON
SU9715

★**White Horse** (01798) 869221

The Street; RH20 1PS Opened-up country inn close to Bignor Roman Villa; bar with open brick fireplaces at each end, nightlights on mantelpieces, cushioned high bar chairs, Wadworths 6X and a guest, good wines by the glass, two-room barrel-vaulted dining area with minimalist contemporary décor and another little fire, well thought-of food, friendly young staff; children welcome, dogs in bar, steps up to lawn with plenty of picnic-sets, more seats in front, good surrounding walks, bedrooms, closed Sun evening, Mon. *(Colin and Louise English, Glenwys and Alan Lawrence)*

THAKEHAM
TQ1017

White Lion (01798) 813141

Off B2139 N of Storrington; The Street; RH20 3EP Tile-hung 16th-c two-bar village pub, good food (not Sun evening) from open kitchen, friendly informal service, real ales such as Arundel, Fullers, Harveys and St Austell, good choice of wines by the glass, heavy beams, panelling, bare boards and traditional furnishings including settles, pleasant dining room with inglenook woodburner, fresh flowers, newspapers; dogs welcome, sunny terrace tables, more on small lawn, pretty village, open all day. *(Anon)*

TICEHURST
TQ6831

Bull (01580) 200586

Three Legged Cross; off B2099 towards Wadhurst; TN5 7HH Attractive 14th-c pub with big log fires in two heavy-beamed old-fashioned bars, well kept Harveys and a guest, contemporary furnishings and flooring in light airy dining extension serving enjoyable food; charming front garden (busy in summer), bigger back one with play area. *(Tim Loryman)*

TROTTON
SU8322

★**Keepers Arms** (01730) 813724

A272 Midhurst–Petersfield; GU31 5ER Pretty cottage above River Rother with beamed and timbered L-shaped bar, comfortable sofas and old winged-back leather armchairs around big log fire, simple rustic tables on oak flooring, other interesting old furniture, two dining rooms, one with elegant oak tables and woodburner, well liked food, Ballards, Dark Star and a guest, comprehensive wine list, good friendly service; children welcome (no babies or toddlers in evening), dogs allowed in bar, seats on sunny terrace, closed Sun evening, Mon. *(Matthew Cramer, Richard and Judy Winn)*

TURNERS HILL   TQ3435
★ **Red Lion** (01342) 715416
Lion Lane, just off B2028; RH10 4NU
Old-fashioned, unpretentious and welcoming country local, snug parquet-floored bar with plush wall benches, homely memorabilia and small open fire, steps up to carpeted area with inglenook log fire, cushioned pews and settles forming booths, well kept Harveys ales, generous straightforward home-made food, daily papers; background and some live music in summer, fruit machine; children (away from bar) and dogs welcome, picnic-sets on side grass overlooking village, open all day, Sun till 10pm (8pm winter). *(William Ruxton, Nick Lawless, Pete Walker, Mrs P R Sykes)*

UPPER BEEDING   TQ1910
Kings Head (01903) 812196
High Street; BN44 3HZ Old pub opened up but keeping some intimate seating areas, more formal dining part at one end, well kept Fullers London Pride and Harveys Best, enjoyable pubby food, good service, warming log fire; rather basic gents'; children, dogs and walkers welcome, back garden with beautiful downland views, play area and access to River Adur. *(David Jackman)*

VINES CROSS   TQ5917
Brewers Arms (01435) 812435
Vines Cross Road off B2203 then left at T junction; 1 mile E of Horam; TN21 9EN
Red-brick Victorian country pub under new local management (former licensees of the Horse & Groom, Rushlake Green); sizeable public bar, stools by counter, mix of dining chairs, benches and settles around wooden tables on stripped boards, three similarly furnished connecting rooms, one with open fire, another with woodburner, Harveys, Long Man and a house beer brewed by Shepherd Neame, several wines by the glass, enjoyable food (all day Sun); children and dogs welcome, some picnic-sets in front and to the side, open all day. *(Brian Farley)*

WALDERTON   SU7910
Barley Mow (02392) 631321
Stoughton Road, just off B2146 Chichester–Petersfield; PO18 9ED
Country pub with good value generous food from lunchtime sandwiches up including Sun carvery, well kept ales such as Arundel, Harveys and Ringwood, good wine choice, friendly service even on busy weekends, two log fires and rustic bric-a-brac in U-shaped bar with roomy dining areas, live jazz suppers (third Tues of month), popular skittle alley;

children welcome, big pleasant streamside back garden, good walks (Kingley Vale nearby), handy for Stansted House. *(J A Snell, Ann and Colin Hunt, Lawrence Pearse, Tim and Joan Wright)*

WALDRON   TQ5419
Star (01435) 812495
Blackboys–Horam side road; TN21 0RA
Big inglenook log fire in candlelit, beamed and panelled bar, padded window seat and nice mix of furniture including small settle on bare boards and quarry tiles, old prints and photographs, snug off to left, well kept Harveys and a guest such as 1648 or Bass, locally pressed apple juice, good if not cheap food from lunchtime sandwiches up, friendly prompt service, separate back dining room, quiz last Mon of month; picnic-sets in pleasant garden, a couple more at front overlooking pretty village, wassailing in Jan, small café and shop next door. *(Mike and Eleanor Anderson, PL)*

WARBLETON   TQ6018
★ **Black Duck** (01435) 830636
S of B2096 SE of Heathfield; TN21 9BD
Friendly licensees at this small recently renovated pub tucked down from church; L-shaped main room with pale oak flooring, cushioned leather sofas in front of roaring inglenook, beams and walls hung with horsebrasses, tankards, musical instruments, farm tools, even an old typewriter, high-backed dining chairs around mix of tables, enjoyable pubby food and good daily specials, bar area up a step with stools along counter, Harveys, Sharps Doom Bar and nice wines by the glass, cabinet of books and board games, perky pub dog; background music; picnic-sets in back garden with sweeping valley views, more on front grass. *(Chris Bell, J H Bell)*

WEST ASHLING   SU8007
Richmond Arms (01243) 572046
Just off B2146; Mill Road; PO18 8EA
Village dining pub in quiet pretty setting near big millpond with ducks and geese, good interesting food (quite pricey), Harveys ales and plenty of wines by the glass, competent staff; no dogs; children welcome, two nice bedrooms, closed Sun evening, Mon and Tues. *(Ann and Colin Hunt)*

WEST WITTERING   SZ8099
Lamb (01243) 511105
Chichester Road; B2179/A286 towards Birdham; PO20 8QA Welcoming 18th-c tile-hung country pub, enjoyable range of food including blackboard specials, Badger ales, good service even during busy summer months, rugs and mix of furniture on wood floor, blazing fire; children and dogs welcome, tables out in front and in small sheltered back garden with terrace. *(David H T Dimock, Nigel and Sue Foster)*

WILMINGTON   TQ5404
⋆ Giants Rest (01323) 870207

Just off A27; BN26 5SQ Busy country
pub under new management, long wood-
floored bar, adjacent open areas with
simple furniture, log fire, well kept Harveys,
Hop Back and Timothy Taylors, enjoyable
food from french chef-landlord, wooden
puzzles and board games; children and
dogs welcome, lots of seats in front garden,
surrounded by South Downs walks and village
famous for chalk-carved Long Man, two
comfortable bedrooms up narrow stairs with
shared bathroom. *(John Warner, John Beeken)*

WINCHELSEA   TQ9017
New Inn (01797) 226252

German Street; just off A259; TN36 4EN
Attractive pub with L-shaped front bar
mainly laid for dining, good fair-value food
and well kept Greene King ales, friendly
helpful staff, some slate flagstones and
log fire, separate back bar with darts and
TV; background music; children welcome,
pleasant walled garden, delightful setting
opposite church (Spike Milligan buried
here), comfortable bedrooms, good
breakfast. *(Lucien Perring)*

WINEHAM   TQ2320
⋆ Royal Oak (01444) 881252

*Village signposted from A272 and
B2116; BN5 9AY* Splendidly old-fashioned
local with log fire in enormous inglenook,
Harveys Best and guests tapped from casks
in still room, enjoyable seasonal food (not
Sun evening), jugs and ancient corkscrews on
very low beams, collection of cigarette boxes,
a stuffed stoat and crocodile, more bric-
a-brac in back parlour with views of quiet
countryside; children away from bar and
dogs welcome (resident bearded collie called
Bella), picnic sets outside, closed evenings
25 and 26 Dec, 1 Jan. *(Peter and Heather
Elliott, Tony and Wendy Hobden)*

WITHYHAM   TQ4935
⋆ Dorset Arms (01892) 770278

B2110; TN7 4BD Unpretentious 16th-c pub
handy for Forest Way walks, friendly service,

well kept Harveys ales and decent wines,
good choice of enjoyable fairly priced food
including specials, sturdy tables and simple
country seats on wide oak boards, roaring
fire in Tudor fireplace, darts, dominoes,
shove-ha'penny and cribbage, restaurant;
background music; dogs welcome, tables on
brick terrace by small green. *(Chris Bell)*

WOODMANCOTE   SU7707
Woodmancote (01243) 371019

*The one near Emsworth; Woodmancote
Lane; PO10 8RD* Village pub saved from
developers and given major revamp – quite
contemporary with some quirky touches;
good choice of enjoyable fairly priced food
from doorstep sandwiches and sharing
boards up (smaller helpings available), ales
such as Brains, Courage and Hogs Back,
several wines by the glass, restaurant;
outside seating, open all day. *(Mrs Wendda
Knapp)*

WORTHING   TQ1502
Selden Arms (01903) 234854

*Lyndhurst Road, between Waitrose
and hospital; BN11 2DB* Friendly chatty
backstreet local opposite the gasworks,
welcoming long-serving licensees, well kept
Dark Star Hophead and several changing
guests, several continental bottled beers
and farm cider, bargain lunchtime food
(not Sun) including doorstep sandwiches,
comfortably worn interior with lots of old
local photographs, log fire, occasional live
music; dogs welcome, open all day.
(Tony and Wendy Hobden, N R White)

WORTHING   TQ1502
Swan (01903) 232923

High Street; BN11 1DN Villagey
atmosphere with good mix of customers in
U-shaped bar, four well kept ales including
Harveys and Sharps Doom Bar, reasonably
priced pubby lunchtime food, friendly
welcoming staff, old-fashioned carpeted
interior with lots of odds and ends hanging
from beams, some stained glass, bar billiards,
live music and quiz nights; small back terrace
used by smokers, handy for hospital, open
all day. *(Tony and Wendy Hobden)*

Warwickshire

with Birmingham and West Midlands

From the little villages of Warwickshire and the North Cotswolds countryside to the big West Midlands towns, there's a wide range of pubs to suit every mood. Pubs doing particularly well are the Bell in Alderminster (contemporary décor mixes well here with original features, plus good modern food), Malt Shovel in Barston (run with care by a hands-on landlady, and delicious food), Malt Shovel at Gaydon (enjoyable food cooked by the landlord, in a neatly kept pub), Red Lion in Long Compton (charmingly furnished, with a thoughtful choice of drinks and interesting food), Crabmill in Preston Bagot (reliably well run, a cheery atmosphere and much liked food and drink), Bear in Stratford-upon-Avon (part of a smart hotel, with a bustling bar and eight ales) and Bell in Welford-on-Avon (really caring licensees, five ales and well thought-of food from a comprehensive menu). New entries are the Holly Bush in Alcester (unpretentious 17th-c pub with hard-working landlady, eight real ales and tasty food) and Howard Arms in Ilmington (civilised golden-stone inn with smart rooms and tempting food and drink). The particularly well run Malt Shovel at Barston is our Warwickshire Dining Pub 2014.

ALCESTER SP0957 Map 4

Holly Bush ◀

Henley Street (continuation of High Street towards B4089; not much nearby parking); B49 5QX

Traditional inn with timeless appeal, eight real ales and well liked food

---

They keep a fine choice of eight real ales on handpump at this unpretentious 17th-c pub: Black Sheep, Hobsons Town Crier, Purity Pure Gold, Greene King Ruddles County, Hook Norton Cotswold Lion, Ossett Silver Shadow, Rat Brown Rat and Timothy Taylors Landlord. Also, wines by the glass, quite a few whiskies and farm cider. Several small rooms have a variety of simple furniture on bare boards or flagstones, stripped masonry and dark board panelling, some antique prints and open fires. The chatty heart of the place is at the back on the left, with a few big Victorian lithographs and a woodburning stove in a capacious fireplace. The hard-working landlady is helped by friendly staff. Outside, there are seats in a pretty little garden with a sheltered side terrace; good disabled access.

As well as pub classics such as omelettes and a pasta of the day for £6 (6-7pm, not Fri-Sun), the tasty food includes sandwiches, home-potted shrimps, chicken and asparagus terrine with apple and pear chutney, lamb or free-range chicken burger with fries, salad and coleslaw, risotto of the day, pork fillet with sage mash, caramelised apple and wholegrain mustard jus, fish specials such as whole dressed brixham crab or blackened salmon with cajun potatoes, fennel purée and citrus sauce, and puddings. *Benchmark main dish: beer-battered haddock and chips £9.00. Two-course evening meal £16.00.*

Free house ~ Licensee Teej Deffley ~ Real ale ~ (01789) 762482 ~ Open 12-11.30 (midnight Sat) ~ Bar food 12-2.30, 6-9(9.30 Fri, Sat); 12-3 Sun; not Mon ~ Restaurant ~ Children welcome ~ Dogs allowed in bar ~ Occasional acoustic duo ~ www.thehollybushalcester.co.uk *Recommended by Ian and Jane Irving*

ALDERMINSTER
SP2348 Map 4

Bell ①♀🛏
A3400 Oxford–Stratford; CV37 8NY

Handsome coaching inn with contemporary décor mixing easily with original features, real ales, a good choice of wines, excellent modern cooking and helpful service; individually decorated bedrooms

In a middle of an attractive village, this smart 18th-c former coaching inn is decorated in contemporary style while carefully keeping plenty of original features. The layout is open-plan with beams, standing timbers, flagstoned or wooden floors and fresh flowers, and the atmosphere is easy-going and friendly. A small, bustling bar – with Alscot Ale (from the Warwickshire Beer Co) and Byatts Phoenix Gold on handpump, a dozen wines by the glass and proper cocktails (including a special bloody mary) – has comfortable brown leather armchairs in front of an open fire, high bar chairs by the blue-painted counter and daily papers; background music. The restaurant, with an eclectic mix of furniture including painted dining chairs and tables, leads into the conservatory, which shares the same Stour Valley views as the modern chairs and tables in the attractive courtyard. The nine boutique-style bedrooms are comfortable and individually decorated.

Using local, seasonal produce – much coming from the Alscot Estate – the good interesting food might include crab and prawn cake with thai red curry sauce, potted duck liver and orange pâté, spinach, squash and smoked almond pasta with white wine and cream, parmesan and rosemary-crumbed chicken schnitzel with cajun-roasted potatoes and tomato relish, ginger and lemon grass salmon fillet with sweet and sour sauce and sesame prawn toast, slow-cooked pork belly stuffed with pepperoni and sage with smoked bacon and pearl barley risotto, and puddings such as bitter red berry and white chocolate crème brûlée with mini double chocolate cookies and steamed upside-down caramelised pineapple cake with blood orange syrup and mango ice-cream; they also offer a two- and three-course weekday set menu. *Benchmark main dish: sea bream and scallop bouillabaisse £14.95. Two-course evening meal £18.50.*

Free house ~ Licensee Emma Holman-West ~ Real ale ~ (01789) 450414 ~ Open 9-3, 5.30-11; 9.30am-11pm Fri-Sun ~ Bar food 12-2, 6.30-9; 12-3, 6.30-9.30 Fri-Sun (light snacks all afternoon) ~ Restaurant ~ Children welcome ~ Dogs allowed in bar ~ Live acoustic guitarist monthly ~ Bedrooms: /£120 ~ www.thebellald.co.uk
Recommended by R J Herd, David and Sue Atkinson

ARDENS GRAFTON   SP1153 Map 4

Golden Cross

Off A46 or B439 W of Stratford, corner Wixford Road/Grafton Lane; B50 4LG

Friendly relaxed beamed bar and attractive dining room in bustling country dining pub with well thought-of food

With excellent, friendly service from helpful staff, this pub has a nice, comfortable feeling and is popular for its good, pleasing food. There are character seats among the chapel chairs around country kitchen tables, rugs on ancient dark flagstones, buff-coloured walls hung with contemporary local photographs and a woodburning stove in the large old fireplace. Wells & Youngs IPA and Bombardier and a couple of guests such as Hook Norton Old Hooky and Purity UBU on handpump, ten wines by the glass and – by a fine antique curved-back settle – a table of daily papers including the *Racing Post*. The carpeted dining room has local prints, an unusual coffered ceiling and a big mullioned bay window. The good-sized, neatly planted back garden has picnic-sets, with big canopied heaters on the terrace and a pleasant country outlook.

A thoughtful choice of food includes chicken liver pâté with onion marmalade, bacon and black pudding hash with poached egg and hollandaise, thai green vegetable curry, barbecue pork ribs with sour cream, chives and tomato and pepper relish, faggots with mash and mushy peas, burger with shilton, cheddar or bacon toppings, specials such as bass fillet with spring onion mash and citrus cream, slow-cooked lamb shank with rosemary gravy, and puddings; Friday is fish and chip night. *Benchmark main dish: ham with bubble and squeak, roasted root vegetables, poached egg and parsley sauce £12.95. Two-course evening meal £17.50.*

Charles Wells ~ Lease Debbie Honychurch ~ Real ale ~ (01789) 772420 ~ Open 12-2.30, 5-midnight; 12-midnight Sat, Sun ~ Bar food 12-2.30, 5-9; 12-9(8 Sun) Sat ~ Restaurant ~ Children welcome ~ Dogs allowed in bar ~ Live acoustic music Thurs evenings ~ www.thegoldencross.net *Recommended by Edward Whittle, Martin and Pauline Jennings, Clive and Fran Dutson, Dave Braisted, Mrs Blethyn Elliott*

BARSTON   SP1978 Map 4

Malt Shovel ❢ ♀

3 miles from M42 junction 5; A4141 towards Knowle, then first left into Jacobean Lane/Barston Lane; B92 0JP

Warwickshire Dining Pub of the Year

Well run country dining pub full of happy eaters enjoying the delicious carefully prepared food, attractive layout and good service

With bright, welcoming décor, imaginative food and a friendly, hands-on landlady, this well run dining pub is always deservedly busy. The light and airy bar, its big terracotta tiles neatly offset by dark grouting, rambles extensively around the zinc-topped central counter, which is painted blue to match the dado and other panelling, and has a dozen wines by the glass and Black Sheep, Oakham Inferno and Sharps Doom Bar on handpump. It's comfortably furnished, with informal dining chairs and scatter-cushioned pews around stripped-top tables of varying types and sizes. Cheerful fruit and vegetable paintings decorate the cream walls and, at one end, brown slatted blinds give a glimpse of the kitchen; efficient service by neat young staff. There are picnic-sets in the sheltered back garden with its weeping willow, and the teak seats for the terrace and verandah tables have cushions in summer.

🍴 Plenty of delicious fish dishes on the daily specials board might include scottish scallops on pea purée with black pudding and bacon, seared peppered tuna with celeriac, horseradish and enoki mushrooms or cornish wild turbot with mussels, crayfish, samphire and saffron broth; other inventive menu choices might be lamb kofta and lemon grass skewer with tzatziki and flatbread, butternut squash and sage tortellini with white wine cream, steak in ale pudding, smoked gammon hock with parsley and mustard cream, duck breast wrapped in bacon and sage with gremolata potatoes and jus, and puddings such as toffee fudge cheesecake with banana cream and brandy snap millefeuille with honey-roast blackberry and blueberry jam. *Benchmark main dish: salmon fishcakes on spinach with poached egg and tarragon hollandaise £13.95. Two-course evening meal £20.50.*

Free house ~ Licensee Helen Somerfield ~ Real ale ~ (01675) 443223 ~ Open 12-11.30 ~ Bar food 12-2.30, 6-9.30; 12-4 Sun ~ Restaurant ~ Children welcome ~ Dogs allowed in bar ~ www.themaltshovelatbarston.com *Recommended by Martin Smith, Susan and John Douglas, Ian Herdman, Di and Mike Gillam, P A Rowe*

BIRMINGHAM
Old Joint Stock 🍺 £

SP0686 Map 4

Temple Row West; B2 5NY

Big bustling Fullers pie-and-ale pub with impressive Victorian façade and interior, and a small back terrace

The sober exterior of this romanesque building gives little indication of the impressive flamboyance within – which is extraordinary. Chandeliers hang from the soaring pink and gilt ceiling, gently illuminated busts line the top of the ornately plastered walls and there's a splendid, if well worn, cupola above the centre of the room. Big portraits and smart long curtains create an air of unexpected elegance. Around the walls are plenty of tables and chairs, some in cosy corners, with more on a big dining balcony that overlooks the bar and is reached by a grand staircase. A separate room, with panelling and a fireplace, has a more intimate, clubby feel. As far as we know, this is the northernmost venue to be owned by London-based brewer Fullers – they keep the full range of Fullers beers on handpump alongside up to four local guests such as Beer Geek Great White Geek, Hobsons Mild and Merry Miner Cap Lamp and Davys Lamp, a dozen wines by the glass and a decent range of malt whiskies, all served from a handsome dark wood island bar counter; daily papers, background music and board games. Most nights there's something on in the smart purpose-built little theatre on the first floor. A small back terrace has cast-iron tables and chairs, and wall-mounted heaters. The cathedral is opposite.

🍴 The reasonably priced food includes sandwiches, creamed mushrooms and shallots on toast, smoked salmon with capers and lemon, sharing boards, broad bean and tomato tart, pork and apple sausages with mustard mash and red onion gravy, bacon and smoked cheddar burger with chips, chicken and sweetcorn pie, and puddings such as chocolate brownie and eton mess. *Benchmark main dish: steak in ale pie £10.25. Two-course evening meal £16.00.*

Fullers ~ Manager Paul Bancroft ~ Real ale ~ (0121) 200 1892 ~ Open 11-11; 12-5 Sun; closed Sun evening ~ Bar food 12-10; 12-4 Sun ~ Restaurant ~ Children welcome in dining area only ~ Jazz in the bar Sun, last Weds of month ~ www.oldjointstocktheatre.co.uk *Recommended by Andy Dolan, Andy and Jill Kassube, Richard Tilbrook, Dave Webster, Sue Holland, Susan and John Douglas, Alan Johnson*

FARNBOROUGH
SP4349   Map 4

Inn at Farnborough
Off A423 N of Banbury; OX17 1DZ

Snug bar in civilised dining pub with wide choice of enjoyable food, both traditional and more elaborate

Tucked away in a village and with some interesting National Trust properties nearby, this golden-stone house is a popular place for a drink or a meal. The cosy bar on the right has dark beams and flagstones, some honey-coloured stripped stone, bucket armchairs with scatter cushions and matching window seats, racing car pictures and a log fire in a big stone fireplace. They serve Purity Gold and Mad Goose on handpump, local Chase vodka and gin, about 18 wines by the glass and enterprising bar nibbles – charcuterie, whitebait and crayfish tails, for example; background music and board games. A second fireplace, open on two sides, with a built-in seat around it, divides off a compact two-room dining area with sturdy stripped kitchen tables and high-backed leather chairs; the carpeted inner room has wallpaper imitating shelves of books. There are blue picnic-sets and other seats in the neat sloping garden, which has a big yew tree and a canopied deck. Not a lot of nearby parking.

 Naming their local producers, the enjoyable, interesting food includes nibbles like little pots of honey and mustard sausages or crayfish tails, sandwiches, duck pâté with pear and perry chutney, seared king scallops with cashews, apple and curry dressing, salmon fishcakes with hollandaise, steak burger with blue cheese and parma ham, chicken curry with lime and coriander rice, grilled free-range pork fillet, slow-cooked cheek and black pudding mash with scrumpy apple sauce, and puddings such as spiced plum and hazelnut crumble with pistachio ice-cream and dark chocolate and cherry cheesecake with Baileys and white chocolate milkshake; also, a two- and three-course set menu. *Benchmark main dish: slow-cooked beef with parsnip purée, peppercorn and cognac sauce and dauphinoise potatoes £16.95. Two-course evening meal £21.50.*

Free house ~ Licensees Anthony and Jo Robinson ~ Real ale ~ (01295) 690615 ~ Open 10-3, 6-11; 10-midnight Sat; 10-10.30 Sun ~ Bar food 12-3, 6-10; 12-10 Sun ~ Restaurant ~ Children welcome ~ Dogs allowed in bar ~ www.innatfarnborough.co.uk
Recommended by Della Young, Michael Tack

GAYDON
SP3654   Map 4

Malt Shovel
Under a mile from M40 junction 12; B4451 into village, then over roundabout and across B4100; Church Road; CV35 0ET

Bustling pub in a quiet village with a nice mix of pubby bar and smarter restaurant, tasty food cooked by the chef-landlord and four real ales

'The perfect break from the delights of the M40,' says one reader and quite a few others back up the sentiment. You can be sure of a cheerful welcome from the landlady, who keeps her pub spotless and offers a fine range of drinks: Black Sheep, Fullers London Pride, Greene King Old Speckled Hen and Wye Valley Bitter, along with a dozen or so wines by the glass. Varnished mahogany boards through to bright carpeting link the entrance, the bar counter on the right and the woodburning stove on the left. The central area has a high-pitched ceiling, milk churns and earthenware containers in a loft above the bar.

Three steps lead up to a little space with comfortable sofas overlooked by a big stained-glass window, with reproductions of classic posters on the walls. A busy eating area has fresh flowers on a mix of kitchen, pub and dining tables; background music, darts. The jack russell is called Mollie.

 Cooked by the landlord, the popular food includes sandwiches, interesting soups, smoked haddock welsh rarebit, three-egg omelettes, wild boar and apple sausages in calvados and cider with mustard mash, steak and kidney pudding, specials such as three-cheese vegetable lasagne, chicken tagine with cashews and apricots or halibut with lentils and provençale sauce, and puddings such as ginger and rhubarb cheesecake and chocolate bread and butter pudding. *Benchmark main dish: home-made pies £9.95. Two-course evening meal £17.50.*

Enterprise ~ Lease Richard and Debi Morisot ~ Real ale ~ (01926) 641221 ~ Open 11-3, 5-11; 11-11 Sat; 12-10.30 Sun ~ Bar food 12-2, 6.30-9 ~ Restaurant ~ Children welcome ~ Dogs allowed in bar ~ www.maltshovelgaydon.co.uk *Recommended by Dr D J and Mrs S C Walker, George Atkinson, Piotr Chodzko-Zajko, Paul Humphreys*

HAMPTON-IN-ARDEN   SP2080   Map 4
White Lion
High Street; handy for M42 junction 6; B92 0AA

Useful village local and five real ales; bedrooms

Customers tend to return to this former farmhouse on a regular basis. The carpeted bar is nice and relaxed, with a mix of furniture trimly laid out, neatly curtained small windows, low-beamed ceilings and some local memorabilia on the fresh cream walls. Banks's Sunbeam, Hobsons Best and Town Crier, M&B Brew XI and Sharps Doom Bar on handpump from the timber-planked bar; background music, TV and board games. The modern dining areas are fresh and airy with light wood and cane chairs on stripped floorboards. The pub is in an attractive village, opposite a church mentioned in the Domesday Book, and is handy for the NEC. The bedrooms are quiet and comfortable and the breakfasts good.

 Tasty food includes sandwiches, eggs mayonnaise, tiger prawns and scallop tempura, tomato, garlic and basil pasta, smoked salmon and pea risotto, sausage and mash with gravy, jamaican jerk chicken, calves liver and bacon with onion gravy, battered fish and chips, daily specials and puddings. *Benchmark main dish: 10oz rib-eye steak £16.95. Two-course evening meal £17.00.*

Punch ~ Tenant Chris Roach ~ Real ale ~ (01675) 442833 ~ Open 12-11(11.30 Sat); 12-10.30 Sun ~ Bar food 12-2.30, 6.30-9.30; 12-4 Sun ~ Restaurant ~ Children welcome ~ Dogs welcome ~ Bedrooms: £70/£85 ~ www.thewhitelioninn.com *Recommended by Martin Smith, Sara Fulton, Roger Baker, Dr and Mrs A K Clarke, Dr D J and Mrs S C Walker*

ILMINGTON   SP2143   Map 4
Howard Arms
Village signed with Wimpstone off A3400 S of Stratford; CV36 4LT

Lovely mellow-toned interior, lots to look at and enjoyable food and drink; attractive bedrooms

Usefully open all day – there are lovely walks on the nearby hills – this golden-stone inn is beside the village green. The attractive rooms have an appealing variety of furniture ranging from hardwood pews through old church chairs and wheelbacks to leather dining chairs around all manner of tables on worn flagstones, rugs and bare boards. Also, quite a few prints on golden walls, shelves of books, candles and a log fire in a huge stone inglenook. Several high stools and chairs line the counter where they keep Hook Norton Old Hooky, Purity Pure Gold and a guest beer on handpump and several wines by the glass; background music. The garden is particularly charming with fruit trees sheltering the lawn, a colourful herbaceous border and a handful of tables on a neat York-stone terrace; the window boxes are pretty in summer. The bedrooms are comfortable and the breakfasts good.

Good, popular food includes lunchtime sandwiches, potted duck liver pâté with red onion jam, smoked haddock and salmon fishcake with aioli, sharing boards, herb-roasted ham with free-range eggs, pineapple chutney and chips, pie of the day, battered fish and chips, gloucester old spot pork and apple sausages with bubble and squeak cake, specials such as teriyaki-marinated grilled black bream fillet with stir-fried pak choi and noodles, confit duck leg with spinach and puy lentils with plum sauce, and puddings like frangipane and pear tart with custard and glazed rice pudding with honeycomb ice-cream and butterscotch sauce. *Benchmark main dish: calves liver and bacon with shallot jus £14.50. Two-course evening meal £17.50.*

Free house ~ Licensee Emma O'Connell ~ Real ale ~ (01608) 682226 ~ Open 11-11; 12-10.30 Sun ~ Bar food 12-2.30, 6.30-9.30; 12-3, 4.30-9.30(9 Sun) Sat ~ Restaurant ~ Children welcome ~ Dogs allowed in bar ~ Live music last Sun of month ~ Bedrooms: £85/£135 ~ www.howardarms.com *Recommended by Clive and Fran Dutson, N R White*

LONG COMPTON SP2832 Map 4

Red Lion 🛏

A3400 S of Shipston-on-Stour; CV36 5JS

Traditional character and contemporary touches in comfortably refurbished coaching inn; bedrooms

With a warm welcome, a good choice of drinks and enjoyable food, it's not surprising that our readers keep returning to this lovely old coaching inn. The roomy and charmingly furnished lounge bar has some exposed stone and beams and nice rambling corners with cushioned settles among pleasantly assorted and comfortable seats and leather armchairs; there are tables on flagstones and carpets, warm paintwork and both an open fire and a woodburning stove. Hook Norton Hooky Bitter and a guest such as Wickwar Cotswold Way on handpump and a dozen wines by the glass. The simple public bar has darts, pool and TV; background music. There are tables out in the big back garden and a play area; they sell pig's ears for dogs.

As well as sandwiches and a weekday set menu (not after 7pm), the interesting, popular food includes ham hock, grain mustard and leek terrine with home-made piccalilli, goats cheese tart with spiced red onion, figs and watercress and apple salad, butternut squash, caramelised onion and spinach filo parcel with curry cream sauce, slow-braised shin of beef with creamed parsnips, shiitake mushrooms and madeira jus, pancetta-wrapped chicken stuffed with dolcelatte and leek cream sauce, salmon and prawn brochette with chilli, spring onions, horseradish and soy noodles, daily specials and puddings. *Benchmark main dish: battered cod fillet with chips and mushy peas £13.95. Two-course evening meal £20.00.*

Cropthorne Inns ~ Manager Lisa Phipps ~ Real ale ~ (01608) 684221 ~ Open 10-2.30, 6-11; 1-11 Fri-Sun ~ Bar food 12-2.30, 6-9; 12-9.30(9 Sun) Fri, Sat ~ Restaurant ~ Children welcome ~ Dogs welcome ~ Bedrooms: £60/£90 ~ www.redlion-longcompton.co.uk

Recommended by David Gunn, R I Howe, Chris Glasson, Sara Fulton, Roger Baker, Alun and Jennifer Evans, Bernard Stradling, Barry Collett, J R and P D Holt, K H Frostick

PRESTON BAGOT SP1765 Map 4
Crabmill ⊛ ♈

A4189 Henley-in-Arden to Warwick; B95 5EE

Cider mill conversion with comfortable décor, relaxed atmosphere, a good choice of drinks and smart food

Consistently enjoyable and well run, this is a rambling old cider mill with cheerful staff and imaginative food. It's attractively decorated with contemporary furnishings and warm colour combinations; the smart two-level lounge area has comfortable sofas and chairs, low tables, big table lamps and one or two rugs on bare boards. The elegant, low-beamed dining area is spacious with caramel leather banquettes and chairs at pine tables, and a beamed and flagstoned bar area has stripped-pine country tables and chairs and snug corners. From the gleaming metal bar they serve Fullers London Pride, Greene King Abbot and Purity Pure Gold on handpump and 14 wines by the glass; background music is well chosen and well reproduced. There are lots of tables (some under cover) in the large, attractive, decked garden.

 The wide-ranging choice of inventive food might include sandwiches, lamb kofta, pomegranate, feta and pistachio tabbouleh, mint yoghurt and flatbread, prawn, crayfish and crab caesar salad, roast pumpkin, chilli, feta and spinach risotto, steak and mushroom in ale pie, pork tenderloin with confit potatoes, chorizo, broad beans and apple and thyme compote, specials such as smoked chicken, black pudding and poached egg salad with honey and mustard dressing or roast cod loin with chargrilled vegetable antipasti and red pepper coulis, and puddings. *Benchmark main dish: duck platter with confit leg, seared breast and croquette with apple and blackberry compote £17.50. Two-course evening meal £21.00.*

Free house ~ Licensee Sally Coll ~ Real ale ~ (01926) 843342 ~ Open 11-11; 12-6 Sun; closed Sun evening ~ Bar food 12-2.30, 6.30-9.30, sandwiches till 5pm; 12-4 Sun ~ Restaurant ~ Children welcome ~ Dogs allowed in bar ~ www.thecrabmill.co.uk
Recommended by Dennis and Doreen Haward, Rob and Catherine Dunster, Martin Smith, Paul and Anita Brannan, S Holder, Dr Brian Hands, Clive and Fran Dutson, Mrs Blethyn Elliott

STRATFORD-UPON-AVON SP2055 Map 4
Bear ♈ ▥ ⛉

Swan's Nest Hotel, just off A3400 Banbury Road, by bridge; CV37 7LT

Great real ale choice in properly pubby bar of large comfortable riverside hotel

In the Swan's Nest hotel complex, this cosy and friendly place has a fine choice of ales from an impressive row of handpumps on the pewter-topped counter. As well as Bear Bitter (named for them by North Cotswold) there might be Birds Natural Blonde, Castle Rock Harvest Pale, Everards Sunchaser, Hook Norton Old Hooky and Cotswold Lion, Purity Pure UBU and Wye Valley Butty Bach; also, good wines by the glass. The two linked rooms are thoroughly traditional with china and other bric-a-brac on a delft shelf above panelling, a couple of wing armchairs by the fire, a variety of other carefully chosen seats including sofas and scatter-cushioned banquettes, a character settle and a splendid long bench with baluster legs. Big windows look out to the swans on a reach of river between two bridges, and in summer there are teak tables out on a waterside lawn, beyond the service road. Service is thoroughly professional.

Good value and much liked, the food includes sandwiches, pâté of the week, devilled lambs kidneys, a sharing platter, chicken caesar salad, curry and pie of the week, burger with pickles, relish and cheese with skinny fries, and puddings such as lemon posset and dark chocolate fondant. *Benchmark main dish: beer-battered fish of the day with chips and mushy peas £8.50. Two-course evening meal £13.00.*

Free house ~ Licensee Simon Taylor ~ Real ale ~ (01789) 265540 ~ Open 10-11 (midnight Fri, Sat) ~ Bar food 12-3, 5-10; all day weekends and school holidays ~ Restaurant ~ Children welcome ~ Dogs welcome ~ Bedrooms: /£129 ~ www.thebearfreehouse.co.uk *Recommended by Val and Alan Green, Alan Johnson, N R White, JHBS*

STRATFORD-UPON-AVON SP2054 Map 4
Encore
Bridge Street; CV37 6AB

Well run relaxed modern bar with enjoyable food all day, and good river views from upstairs dining room

Inside, this is more modern bar than traditional pub – but customers of all ages enjoy it very much, thanks partly to the efficient, pleasantly informal staff. The main area has well spaced, scrubbed-top cast-iron tables with bucket armchairs or fat soft square stools, stripped beams, broad oak boards or polished pale flagstones, big windows on two sides and big charcoal sketches of local sights on the butter-coloured walls. A softly lit dark-walled back area with barrel and other rustic tables has stairs up to a long comfortable dining room, which looks across the road to the river. They have good coffees and plenty of wines by the glass, as well as Purity UBU, Robinsons Hoptimus Prime and Sharps Doom Bar on handpump; log fire, well reproduced background music. It can get pretty busy at weekends.

Popular food includes a two- and three-course weekday set menu as well as sandwiches, box-baked camembert with white grape and onion jam, a sticky platter of pork ribs, chicken wings, lamb koftas and salad, wood-fired pizzas, cannelloni with butternut squash, spinach, ricotta and tomato sauce, salmon, dill and coarse-grain mustard fishcakes with orange, fennel and rocket salad, gammon with free-range eggs, lamb rump with chorizo dauphinoise and soubise sauce, and puddings. *Benchmark main dish: beer-battered haddock with mushy peas and chips £11.95. Two-course evening meal £16.00.*

Mitchells & Butlers ~ Manager Jack Butler ~ Real ale ~ (01789) 269462 ~ Open 9am-11pm(midnight Fri, Sat, 10.30 Sun) ~ Bar food 9.30am-10pm ~ Restaurant ~ Children welcome ~ Dogs allowed in bar ~ www.theencorestratford.co.uk *Recommended by N R White*

WELFORD-ON-AVON SP1452 Map 4
Bell ⑪ ♀ 🍴
Off B439 W of Stratford; High Street; CV37 8EB

Enjoyably civilised pub with appealing ancient interior, good carefully sourced food, a great range of drinks and seats on pretty terrace

The charming licensees and their staff in this 17th-c pub are really attentive and welcoming, managing to cater for all their customers' needs – whatever their age and whatever the occasion. The attractive interior, with plenty of signs of the building's venerable age, is divided into five comfortable areas, each with its own character, from the cosy terracotta-painted bar to a light and airy gallery room with antique wood panelling, solid oak floor and contemporary Lloyd Loom chairs. Flagstone floors, stripped or well polished antique or period-style furniture and three good fires (one in an inglenook) add warmth and cosiness. Hobsons Best, Purity Pure Gold and UBU and a guest such as Greene King IPA on handpump and 18 wines (including prosecco and champagne) by the glass; background music. In summer, the virginia creeper-covered exterior is festooned with colourful hanging baskets. Lots of thought has gone into the garden with its solid teak furniture, vine-covered terrace, water features and gentle lighting. This riverside village has an appealing church and pretty thatched black and white cottages.

🍴 Using the best local producers (listed on the menu), the impressive food includes sandwiches, black pudding, boiled egg and crispy bacon salad with maple syrup, crayfish, prawn and melon cocktail, brunch (not Sunday), squash with blue cheese and pine nut stuffing with turnip dauphinoise, pork and leek sausages with redcurrant and rosemary gravy, chicken supreme stuffed with sausage meat on creamy garlic and bacon sauce, pancetta-wrapped salmon fillet on wild mushroom risotto, and puddings such as orange, ginger and cinnamon rice pudding with brûlée topping and rich pot au chocolat with amaretti biscuits; also, themed evenings such as indian, St George's Day, Burns Night and so forth. *Benchmark main dish: pie of the day £13.75. Two-course evening meal £19.00.*

Laurel (Enterprise) ~ Lease Colin and Teresa Ombler ~ Real ale ~ (01789) 750353 ~ Open 11.30-3, 6-11; 11.30-11.30 Sat; 11.45-10.30 Sun ~ Bar food 11.45-2.30, 6-9.30 (10 Fri); 11.45-10 Sat; noon-9.30 Sun ~ Children welcome ~ www.thebellwelford.co.uk
Recommended by Mrs A M Sabin, Martin Smith, Theocsbrian, K H Frostick, Mike and Mary Carter, Sarah Everson, Mrs D L Wilson, Beryl Chisholm, P B Smith

Also Worth a Visit in Warwickshire

Besides the fully inspected pubs, you might like to try these pubs that have been recommended to us and described by readers. Do tell us what you think of them: feedback@goodguides.com

ALVECOTE   SK2404
Samuel Barlows (01827) 898175
Robeys Lane; B78 1AS Modern canalside pub by Alvecote Marina, popular good value food cooked by australian landlord, three or four well kept ales, friendly staff and dog, lift to first-floor function room with balcony overlooking water; moorings, closed Mon, otherwise open all day. *(Alan Champion, David M Smith, Paul and Karen Cornock)*

ALVESTON   SP2356
Ferry (01789) 269883
Ferry Lane; end of village, off B4086 Stratford–Wellesbourne; CV37 7QX Comfortable and stylish beamed dining pub, good imaginative food along with pub favourites, reasonable prices, ales such as

Hook Norton, Sharps and Wells & Youngs, friendly staff; nice spot with seats out in front, open all day Sat, closed Sun evening, first Mon of month. *(Mark Sykes, R J Herd)*

ASTON CANTLOW   SP1360
Kings Head (01789) 488242
Village signed off A3400 NW of Stratford; B95 6HY Wisteria-covered Tudor pub under newish ownership; low-beamed bar on right, old settles on flagstones and log fire in big inglenook, chatty quarry-tiled main room with attractive window seats and big country oak tables, ales from Greene King and Purity, real ciders, several wines by the glass, enjoyable food from sandwiches and sharing boards up; background music (outside too); children welcome, dogs in bar, seats in lovely garden with big chestnut tree and pretty

summer hanging baskets, open all day.
(Martin and Pauline Jennings)

AVON DASSETT   SP4049
Avon Inn (01295) 690270

Off B4100 Banbury–Warwick; CV47 2AS
Traditional double-fronted mellow-stone pub
with pleasant décor and relaxing atmosphere,
welcoming helpful staff, enjoyable good
value pubby food including dozens of pies
and bargain two-course weekday offer, well
kept Fullers London Pride and Timothy
Taylors Landlord, several wines by the
glass, flagstones and bare boards, stools and
cushioned wall benches around simple pub
tables, carpeted area with padded dining
chairs; unobtrusive background music (live
Fri), TV; children and dogs welcome, picnic-
sets out in front by quiet road, small side
garden, attractive village on slopes of Burton
Dassett Hills Country Park, open all day
weekends. *(Martin and Pauline Jennings)*

BAGINTON   SP3474
Oak (024) 7630 1187

Coventry Road; CV8 3AU Sizeable pub by
Coventry Airport and handy for Midland Air
Museum; large bar area with beams, arches
and open fire, some old pictures and model
planes, four well kept ales including Greene
King Abbot, eclectic menu from all-day
breakfast and pub staples to caribbean
dishes, also bargain weekday set lunch,
restaurant; well behaved children and dogs
welcome, garden with play area, 13 bedrooms
in back annexe. *(Lee Fraser)*

BALSALL COMMON   SP2377
Old Saracens Head (01676) 533862

Balsall Street; CV7 7AS Welcoming dining
pub reopened after major refurbishment;
spacious beamed interior, Marstons ales
and a beer named for the pub, good choice
of wines by the glass, ample helpings of
enjoyable food from ciabattas to steaks (not
cheap) cooked in a charcoal oven; children
welcome, large terrace, open all day.
(Ian Herdman)

BARFORD   SP2660
⋆ Granville (01926) 624236

*1.7 miles from M40 junction 15; A429 S
(Wellesbourne Road); CV35 8DS*
Attractive gently up-to-date décor with sage
green paintwork, pale wooden tables and
chairs on floorboards, art deco-style leather
sofas by fire, berber-pattern hangings on end
walls and contemporary lighting, more formal
raftered and stripped-brick restaurant, well
kept Hook Norton and Purity, decent wines
by the glass, impressive food (all day Sat, not
Sun evening) including good value set menu,
friendly staff; background music, sports
TV; children and dogs (in bar) welcome,
disabled parking (wheelchair access from
side entrance), floodlit back terrace with
smart rattan chairs and loungers under huge
retractable awnings, rustic play area, open

all day weekends. *(Rob and Catherine Dunster,
Ian Herdman, R L Borthwick, David M Smith,
Simon and Mandy King)*

BARNT GREEN   SP0074
Barnt Green Inn (0121) 445 4949

*3 miles from M42 junction 2; A441
towards Birmingham, then first left on
to B4120; Kendal End Road; B45 8PZ*
Large Elizabethan dining pub (Mitchells &
Butlers) with their usual good choice of food
from shared meze through wood-fired pizzas
to grills, weekday set menu till 7pm, Purity,
Sharps and a guest ale, plenty of wines
by the glass, friendly if not always speedy
service, relaxed atmosphere, comfortable
contemporary décor, log fire, clubby seating
in panelled front bar, large brasserie area;
can get very busy; tables outside, handy for
Lickey Hills walks, open all day. *(Anon)*

BARSTON   SP2078
⋆ Bulls Head (01675) 442830

*From M42 junction 5, A4141 towards
Warwick, first left, then signed down
Barston Lane; B92 0JU* Unassuming and
unspoilt partly Tudor village pub, well kept
Adnams, Hook Norton, Purity and a guest,
popular traditional home-made food from
sandwiches to specials, friendly helpful staff,
log fires, comfortable lounge with pictures
and plates, oak-beamed bar and separate
dining room; children and dogs allowed,
good-sized secluded garden alongside pub
and barn, open all day Fri-Sun. *(Martin Smith,
Clive and Fran Dutson, Don Bryan)*

BINLEY WOODS   SP3977
Roseycombe (024) 7654 1022

Rugby Road; CV3 2AY Warm and friendly
1930s pub with wide choice of bargain home-
made food, Bass and Theakstons, Weds quiz
night, some live music; children welcome,
big garden. *(Alan Johnson)*

BIRMINGHAM   SP0788
⋆ Bartons Arms (0121) 333 5988

High Street, Aston (A34); B6 4UP
Magnificent Edwardian landmark, an oasis
in a rather daunting area, impressive linked
richly decorated rooms from the palatial to
the snug, original tilework murals, stained
glass and mahogany, decorative fireplaces,
sweeping stairs to handsome upstairs rooms,
well kept Oakham and guest ales from ornate
island bar with snob screens in one section,
interesting imported bottled beers and
frequent mini beer festivals, nice choice of
well priced thai food (not Mon), good young
staff; open all day. *(Andy Dolan)*

BIRMINGHAM   SP0686
Brasshouse (0121) 633 3383

Broad Street; B1 2HP Handsome bank
conversion with lots of dark oak and brass,
enjoyable reasonably priced food from
sandwiches up, well kept ales including
Marstons and Timothy Taylors, good quick

service, attractive dining area (children welcome here till 6pm); canalside seats, handy for National Sea Life Centre and convention centre, open all day. *(Colin Gooch, Tony Hobden, Dr and Mrs A K Clarke)*

BIRMINGHAM SP0688
Lord Clifden (0121) 523 7515
Great Hampton Street (Jewellery Quarter); B18 6AA Fairly traditional with leather banquettes and padded stools around dimpled copper-top tables, bustling atmosphere, wide choice of good value generous food from sandwiches to daily specials, Wye Valley and guests, continental beers, prompt friendly service, interesting collection of street art including by Banksy, darts in front bare-boards part; sports TVs (outside too), Thurs quiz night and weekend DJs; plenty of seats in enclosed part-covered beer garden with table tennis and table football, open all day (till late Fri, Sat). *(Anon)*

BIRMINGHAM SP0786
Old Contemptibles (0121) 236 5264
Edmund Street; B3 2HB Spacious well restored Edwardian corner pub with lofty ceiling and lots of woodwork, decent choice of real ales (customers vote for guest beers), enjoyable well priced food including range of sausages and pies, friendly efficient young staff; upstairs lavatories, no children; handy central location, so popular at lunchtime with office workers, open all day (till 6pm Sun). *(Andy Dolan, Tony Hobden, Alan Johnson)*

BIRMINGHAM SP0686
Pennyblacks (0121) 632 1460
Mailbox shopping mall, Wharfside Street; B1 1RQ Good atmosphere and service in well run spacious pub with mix of contemporary and old furnishings on wood or slate floors, appealing up-to-date décor, enjoyable food, up to seven real ales including Church End, Hook Norton and St Austell (third of a pint glasses available), extensive wine range; DJ Thurs-Sat nights, Sky Sports, free wi-fi; good spot by the canal, open all day. *(Andy Dolan)*

BIRMINGHAM SP0586
Prince of Wales (0121) 643 9460
Cambridge Street; B1 2NP Traditional pub behind the repertory theatre and symphony hall; L-shaped bar with friendly mix of customers, half a dozen or more well kept beers such as Everards, Timothy Taylors and Wells & Youngs, bargain straightforward lunchtime food including good baguettes, fast friendly service; may be background music; popular with Grand Union Canal users in summer. *(Chris Evans, Stephen and Jean Curtis)*

BIRMINGHAM SP0687
Pub du Vin (0121) 200 0600
Church Street; B3 2NR Arched slate-floor cellar bar with island servery, comfortable

seating and some unusual artwork, well kept Kinver, Purity and Silhill, simple food, walk-in humidor/whisky room; background music and sports TV; another bar and 66 good bedrooms in hotel upstairs; open all day, closed Sun. *(Tony Hobden, Andy Dolan, Dr and Mrs A K Clarke)*

BIRMINGHAM SP0687
Rose Villa (0121) 236 7910
By clock in Jewellery Quarter (Warstone Lane/Vyse Street); B18 6JW Listed 1920s building with panelled front saloon leading through to small but magnificent bar, floor-to-ceiling green tiles and superb massive tiled arch over fireplace, original parquet flooring and impressive stained glass, quirky touches like antler chandeliers and a red phone box, four or five well kept ales including Sharps Doom Bar, cocktails, reasonably priced food from sandwiches and burgers up; live music and DJs Fri, Sat till late – can get very busy; open all day, from 11am weekends for brunch. *(Anon)*

BIRMINGHAM SP0686
✶**Wellington** (0121) 200 3115
Bennetts Hill; B2 5SN Old-fashioned high-ceilinged pub with superb range of changing beers (listed on TV screens – order by number), most from small breweries and always one from Black Country Ales, also farm ciders, experienced landlord, friendly staff and nice pub cat, no food but plates and cutlery if you bring your own, regular beer festivals and quiz nights, can get very busy; tables out behind, open all day. *(Tony Hobden, Andy Dolan, Eddie Gallacher, Dr and Mrs A K Clarke, Dave Webster, Sue Holland)*

BLOXWICH SJ9902
✶**Turf** (01922) 407745
Wolverhampton Road, off A34 just S of A4124; WS3 2EZ Utterly uncontrived, unchanging terraced pub in side street and run by the same family for nearly 140 years; entrance hall like a 1930s home, public bar through door on right (reminiscent of a waiting room) with wooden slatted wall benches and three small tables on fine tiled floor, William Morris curtains and wallpaper and simple fireplace, more comfortable old smoking room and tiny back parlour, friendly landladies and chatty locals, Oakham, Otter, RCH and a couple of guests, no food; no-frills lavatories outside at end of simple garden; best to check opening hours before setting out. *(Anon)*

BRIERLEY HILL SO9286
✶**Vine** (01384) 78293
B4172 between A461 and (nearer) A4100; straight after the turn into Delph Road; DY5 2TN Popular Black Country pub offering a true taste of the West Midlands; down-to-earth welcome and friendly chatty locals in meandering series of rooms, each different in character, traditional front bar

with wall benches and simple leatherette-topped oak stools, comfortable extended snug with solidly built red plush seats, tartan-decorated back bar with brass chandeliers, well kept and priced Bathams from brewery next door, a couple of simple, very cheap lunchtime dishes (no credit cards); TV, games machine; children and dogs welcome, tables in backyard, open all day. *(Anon)*

CLAVERDON   SP2064
✶ **Red Lion** (01926) 842291

Station Road; B4095 towards Warwick; CV35 8PE Beamed Tudor dining pub with good food (all day Sun) from pub favourites up, friendly attentive service, decent wines and well kept Purity Mad Goose, log fires, linked rooms including back dining area with country views over sheltered heated deck and gardens; open all day. *(Martin Smith, Ian Herdman)*

COVENTRY   SP3279
Old Windmill (024) 7625 1717

Spon Street; CV1 3BA Timber-framed 15th-c pub (known as Ma Brown's locally) with lots of tiny rooms, exposed beams in uneven ceilings, carved oak seats on flagstones, inglenook woodburner, half a dozen real ales, often farm cider, pubby food till 6pm (not Sun, Mon); popular with students and busy at weekends, games machines and juke box, darts, no credit cards; open all day, closed Mon lunchtime. *(Anon)*

COVENTRY   SP3379
Town Wall (024) 7622 0963

Bond Street, among car parks behind Belgrade Theatre; CV1 4AH Busy Victorian city-centre local with half a dozen real ales including Bass in top condition, farm cider, food from lunchtime doorstep sandwiches to hearty pub dishes, unspoilt basic front bar and tiny snug, engraved windows, bigger back lounge with actor/playwright photographs and pictures of old Coventry, open fires; big-screen sports TV; open all day (till 6pm Sun). *(Alan Johnson, Howard and Margaret Buchanan)*

COVENTRY   SP3378
✶ **Whitefriars** (024) 7625 1655

Gosford Street; CV1 5DL Pair of well preserved medieval townhouses, three old-fashioned rooms on both floors, lots of ancient beams, timbers and furniture, flagstones, cobbles and coal fire, nine well kept changing ales (more during beer festivals), daily papers, bar lunches; some live music, no children inside unless eating; smokers' shelter on good-sized terrace behind, open all day. *(Alan Johnson)*

DUDLEY   SO9591
✶ **Bottle & Glass**

Black Country Museum, Tipton Road; DY1 4SQ Reconstructed alehouse moved here as were other buildings in this extensive open-air working museum (well worth a visit for its re-created period village complete with shops, fairground, school, barge wharf and tram system); friendly staff in costume, three well kept local beers, chunky filled rolls, front parlour and back room with piano, wall benches, sawdust on old boards, two fires. *(George Atkinson)*

DUNCHURCH   SP4871
Green Man (01788) 810210

Daventry Road; CV22 6NS Small beamed village local with enjoyable food and several well kept beers including Greene King IPA and Wells & Youngs Bombardier, good helpful service; bedrooms. *(P M Newsome)*

EASENHALL   SP4679
✶ **Golden Lion** (01788) 833577

Main Street; CV23 0JA Spotless bar in 16th-c part of busy comfortable hotel, low beams, dark panelling, settles and inglenook log fire, changing real ales, enjoyable food including Sun carvery, friendly helpful service; background music; children welcome, disabled access, tables out at side and on spacious lawn, 20 well equipped bedrooms, attractive village, open all day. *(Susan and John Douglas)*

EDGE HILL   SP3747
✶ **Castle** (01295) 670255

Off A422; OX15 6DJ Curious crenellated octagonal tower built 1749 as gothic folly (marks where Charles I raised his standard at start of Battle of Edgehill); lots of interest in museum-like interior, eight-walled lounge bar decorated with maps, swords, pistols, photographs of re-enactments and a collection of Civil War memorabilia, arched doorways, open fire, decent bar food including good sandwiches, Hook Norton ales, 25 malt whiskies, friendly helpful service; background music, TV; children and dogs welcome, seats on terrace and in attractive big garden with outstanding views (once leaves have fallen), beautiful Compton Wynyates nearby, four bedrooms, open all day. *(Susan and John Douglas, Dr A J and Mrs B A Tompsett)*

ETTINGTON   SP2748
Chequers (01789) 740387

Banbury Road (A422); CV37 7SR Nicely refurbished and popular locally for its enterprising well presented food, ales such as Fullers, Greene King and St Austell, good

---

Places with gardens or terraces usually let children sit there – we note in the text the very few exceptions that don't.

wines, efficient friendly service, log fire in drinkers area at front, steps up to dining part with painted tables and matching upholstered chairs; big back garden with raised section, closed Sun evening, Mon. *(Pat and Graham Williamson, David and Jenny Billington)*

FENNY COMPTON   SP4152
Merrie Lion (01295) 771134
Brook Street; CV47 2YH Early 18th-c beamed pub saved from development by the village and recently refurbished; three well kept beers and decent range of wines, good freshly made food from pubby choices up, friendly welcoming atmosphere; tables outside, handy for Burton Dassett country park. *(Miles and Tracey Forsyth, John and Sharon Hancock)*

FIVE WAYS   SP2270
★Case is Altered (01926) 484206
Follow Rowington signs at junction roundabout off A4177/A4141 N of Warwick, then right into Case Lane; CV35 7JD Convivial unspoilt old cottage licensed for over three centuries; Old Pie Factory ales and three guests served by friendly landlady, no food, simple small main bar with fine old poster of Lucas, Blackwell & Arkwright Brewery (now flats), clock with hours spelling out Thornleys Ale (another defunct brewery) and just a few sturdy old-fashioned tables and couple of stout leather-covered settles facing each other over spotless tiles, modest little back room with old bar billiards table (it takes pre-decimal sixpences); no children, dogs or mobiles; full disabled access, stone table on little brick courtyard. *(Martin Smith, Kerry Law)*

FLECKNOE   SP5163
Old Olive Bush (01788) 891134
Off A425 W of Daventry; CV23 8AT Character unspoilt Edwardian pub in quiet photogenic village, friendly chatty atmosphere, enjoyable traditional food cooked by landlady, well kept changing ales and decent wines, open fire in bar with stripped-wood floor, steps up to games room with table skittles, small dining room with etched glass windows and another fire; attractive garden, closed Mon, weekday lunchtimes. *(George Atkinson)*

FRANKTON   SP4270
Friendly (01926) 632430
Just over a mile S of B4453 Leamington Spa–Rugby; Main Street; CV23 9NY Popular old low-ceilinged village pub with good food and four real ales, wines in mini bottles, two neat rooms, open fire, welcoming friendly atmosphere. *(Rob and Catherine Dunster, Ted George)*

GREAT WOLFORD   SP2434
★Fox & Hounds (01608) 674220
Village signed on right on A3400,

---

3 miles S of Shipston-on-Stour; CV36 5NQ Delightful unspoilt 16th-c inn with helpful friendly staff, inglenook log fire with bread oven, low hop-strung beams, appealing collection of old furniture including tall pews on flagstones, motley assortment of antique hunting prints, vintage photographs and so on, Hook Norton, Purity and a guest from old-fashioned tap room, much enjoyed creative cooking using local ingredients (not Sun evening, two weeks in Jan), home-baked bread; children and dogs welcome, terrace with solid wooden furniture and a well, three bedrooms, open all day Sun, closed Mon. *(Paul and Penny Dawson, David Gunn, M Mossman)*

HALFORD   SP2645
Halford (01789) 748217
A429 Fosse Way; CV36 5BN Cotswold-stone inn handy if walking Fosse Way; pastel-walled bar on right of cobbled entry with lattice-decorated dining chairs around chunky tables, bay window seats and leather sofa by woodburner, Hook Norton Old Hooky and St Austell Tribute, decent generously served food, unusual rustic benches and table in back room, partly flagstoned restaurant on left with dark wooden tables and chairs and another fire; background music; teak furniture in spacious old coach yard, water feature and contemporary ironwork, 11 comfortable modern bedrooms, open all day. *(Martin Smith, George Atkinson, Richard Tilbrook)*

HAMPTON LUCY   SP2557
Boars Head (01789) 840533
Church Street, E of Stratford; CV35 8BE Roomy two-bar local next to lovely church, changing real ales and enjoyable good value pubby food, friendly service, low beams and log fire; soft background music; secluded back garden, pretty village near Charlcote House (NT). *(Anon)*

HARBORNE   SP0384
Plough (0121) 427 3678
High Street; B17 9NT Popular quirky place with enjoyable pubby food including stone-baked pizzas, lots of deals, well kept Purity, Wye Valley and a guest ale, quiz Tues, live music Thurs; well behaved children welcome, garden with covered area, open all day. *(Rupert Kenefeck)*

HARBOROUGH MAGNA   SP4779
Old Lion (01788) 833238
3 miles from M6 junction 1; B4122; CV23 0HL Welcoming village pub stylishly refurbished under new management with emphasis on good food, friendly attentive staff, Greene King ales; open all day. *(Anon)*

HATTON   SP2367
★Falcon (01926) 484281
Birmingham Road, Haseley (A4177, not far from M40 junction 15); CV35 7HA

Smartly refurbished dining pub with relaxing rooms around island bar, lots of stripped brickwork and low beams, tiled and oak-planked floors, good moderately priced food (not Sun evening) from sandwiches and pub favourites up, friendly service, nice choice of wines by the glass, well kept Marstons-related ales, barn-style back restaurant; children welcome, disabled facilities, garden (dogs allowed here) with heated covered terrace, eight bedrooms in converted barn, open all day. *(Andy Dolan, Nigel and Sue Foster)*

HENLEY-IN-ARDEN   SP1566
✶ **Bluebell** (01564) 793049
High Street (A3400, M40 junction 16); B95 5AT Impressive timber-framed dining pub with fine coach entrance, emphasis on imaginative food (not Sun evening) from sandwiches to restaurant-style dishes, cheaper lunchtime/early evening set menu (Tues-Fri), rambling old beamed and flagstoned interior with contemporary furnishings creating a stylish but relaxed atmosphere, big fireplace, well kept ales such as Church End and Purity, 20 wines by the glass, good coffee and afternoon teas, friendly helpful staff, daily papers; may be background music; children welcome if eating, dogs allowed, tables on back decking, closed Mon, otherwise open all day. *(Corienne Reed, George Atkinson, R J Herd)*

HUNNINGHAM   SP3768
✶ **Red Lion** (01926) 632715
Village signposted off B4453 Leamington–Rugby just E of Weston, and off B4455 Fosse Way 2.5 miles SW of A423 junction; CV33 9DY Enthusiastic landlord with passion for vintage comics (320 examples on the walls); light and airy open-plan yet cleverly sectioned layout with easy-going mix of old and new, Greene King ales and a couple of guests, impressive range of wines by the glass and lots of malt whiskies, enjoyable food from sandwiches up; background music, board games and maybe a house magician; children welcome (no prams or pushchairs), dogs in bar, attractive riverside spot by arched 14th-c bridge, picnic-sets on lawn and a 1948 tractor to play on, open all day. *(Andy Dolan, Rob and Catherine Dunster, G Jennings, George Atkinson, Martin and Pauline Jennings and others)*

ILMINGTON   SP2143
Red Lion (01608) 682366
Front Street; CV36 4LX Popular stone-built village pub, flagstoned bar with fire on one side of central servery, dining room the other, well kept Hook Norton, enjoyable good value food cooked by landlady; secluded garden. *(K H Frostick)*

KENILWORTH   SP2872
Clarendon Arms (01926) 852017
Castle Hill; CV8 1NB Busy pub opposite castle and under same ownership as next

door Harringtons restaurant; well kept Hook Norton, Sharps, Wye Valley and a local guest, generous reasonably priced pub food including good fish and chips, several rooms off long bare-boards bustling bar (dogs allowed here), largish peaceful upstairs dining room, cheerful enthusiastic young staff; children welcome, metal tables on small raised terrace, daytime car park fee deducted from food bill, open all day Fri-Sun. *(Ian Herdman, Alan Johnson, Andy Dolan)*

KENILWORTH   SP2871
Queen & Castle (01926) 852661
Castle Green; CV8 1ND Old dining pub (Mitchells & Butlers) opposite castle, modernised beamed interior, good range of enjoyable food including set weekday menu (till 7pm); children welcome, open all day. *(Dr D J and Mrs S C Walker)*

KENILWORTH   SP2872
✶ **Virgins & Castle** (01926) 853737
High Street; CV8 1LY Maze of intimate rooms off inner servery, small snugs by entrance corridor, flagstones, heavy beams, lots of woodwork including booth seating, coal fire, four well kept Everards ales and a couple of guests, good food at reasonable prices, friendly service, games bar upstairs, restaurant; children in eating areas, disabled facilities, tables in sheltered garden, open all day. *(R J Herd, Roger and Donna Huggins, Dr D J and Mrs S C Walker)*

KNOWLE   SP1875
Herons Nest (01564) 771177
A4110 (Warwick Road) about a mile S; B93 0EE Popular beamed Vintage Inn dining pub, updated but keeping character, their usual range of all-day food cooked well including good value weekday set menu till 5pm, three real ales and plenty of good value wines by the glass, open fires, interesting décor, some flagstones and high-backed settles, big dining room overlooking Grand Union Canal; lots of tables out by the water, moorings, 11 Innkeepers Lodge bedrooms, open all day. *(Rob Bray, Martin Smith, David Green)*

LADBROKE   SP4158
Bell (01926) 813562
Signed off A423 S of Southam; CV47 2BY Beamed country pub set back from the road, smallish bar area with leather sofas and tub chairs, log fire in little brick fireplace, Fullers London Pride, Hook Norton Old Hooky and St Austell Tribute, airy restaurant with light oak furniture and flooring, enjoyable generously served traditional food including bargain weekday set lunch, well priced house wines; children welcome, picnic-sets in side garden, pleasant surroundings, closed Mon, otherwise open all day (till late Fri, Sat). *(Anon)*

LAPWORTH SP1871
★ Boot (01564) 782464
Old Warwick Road; B4439 Hockley Heath–Warwick – 2.8 miles from M40 junction 1, but from southbound carriageway only, and return only to northbound; B94 6JU Popular upmarket dining pub near Stratford Canal, good contemporary brasserie menu from panini and interesting light dishes up, efficient cheerful young staff, upscale wines (big glasses), Purity UBU and St Austell Tribute, stripped beams and dark panelling, big antique hunting prints, cushioned pews and bucket chairs on ancient quarry tiles and bare boards, warm fire, charming low-raftered upstairs dining room; background music; children and good-natured dogs welcome, teak tables, some under extendable canopy on side terrace, and picnic-sets on grass beyond, nice walks, open all day. *(Mark Sykes, Martin Smith, W M Lien)*

LAPWORTH SP1970
Navigation (01564) 783337
Old Warwick Road (B4439 SE); B94 6NA Clean up-to-date refurbishment for this beamed pub by the Grand Union Canal, slate floor bar with woodburner, bare-boards snug and restaurant, well kept ales such as Banks's, Byatts, Purity, Timothy Taylors and Wadworths, unusually Guinness also on handpump, enjoyable food (all day Fri-Sun) from sandwiches and other bar choices up; children welcome, dogs in bar, covered terrace and waterside garden, handy for Packwood House and Baddesley Clinton (both NT), open all day. *(Anon)*

LAPWORTH SP1872
★ Punch Bowl (01564) 784564
Not far from M42 junction 4, off old Warwick–Hockley Heath Road; B94 6HR Completely reconstructed using old beams etc, most emphasis on dining with good range of well presented interesting food from lunchtime sandwiches and light dishes up, stools along bar for drinkers, Greene King IPA and Wells & Youngs Bombardier, friendly efficient staff; garden picnic-sets, open all day. *(R L Borthwick, R J Herd)*

LEAMINGTON SPA SP3165
Cricketers Arms (01926) 881293
Archery Road; CV31 3PT Friendly town local opposite bowling greens; fairly priced generous food using meat from good local butcher, popular Sun roasts (till 6pm), also nice home-made sausage rolls and scotch eggs, well kept Slaughterhouse and guests from central bar, comfortable banquettes, some panelling and open fires; darts, sports TV, fortnightly quiz Mon; children and dogs welcome, heated back terrace, open all day. *(David Barras, Lee Fraser, Geoffrey and Penny Hughes)*

LEEK WOOTTON SP2868
Anchor (01926) 853355
Warwick Road; CV35 7QX Neat and well run dining lounge popular for enjoyable fresh food including good fish specials, well kept Bass, Hook Norton Old Hooky and two guests, good selection of affordably priced wines and soft drinks, attentive friendly service, lots of close-set tables, smaller overflow dining area; background music, sports TV; children welcome, no dogs inside, long garden behind with play area, open all day Sun. *(Keith and Ann Arnold)*

LIGHTHORNE SP3455
Antelope (01926) 651188
Old School Lane, Bishops Hill; a mile SW of B4100 N of Banbury; CV35 0AU Attractive early 18th-c stone-built pub in pretty village setting, two neatly kept comfortable bars (one old, one newer), separate dining area, well kept ales and enjoyable food including good sandwiches; children welcome, little waterfall in banked garden. *(John and Sharon Hancock)*

LITTLE COMPTON SP2530
★ Red Lion (01608) 674397
Off A44 Moreton-in-Marsh to Chipping Norton; GL56 0RT Low-beamed 16th-c Cotswold-stone inn, enjoyable good value food cooked by landlady from pubby choices up, Donnington ales, good choice of wines by the glass, snug alcoves, inglenook woodburner, darts and pool in public bar; well behaved children and dogs welcome, pretty side garden with aunt sally, two nice bedrooms. *(Bernard Stradling, R K Phillips, Grahame Brooks)*

LONG ITCHINGTON SP4165
Blue Lias (01926) 812249
Stockton Road, off A423; CV47 8LD Pretty flower-decked pub by the Grand Union Canal, spic and span, with well kept ales including Adnams and Greene King (up to six in the summer), pubby food, snug booth seating in eating area, friendly staff; children welcome, disabled facilities, plenty of tables in waterside grounds (dogs allowed here), marquee for functions, plenty at weekends and may stay open all day if busy. *(John Clancy, Adrian Johnson)*

LONG ITCHINGTON SP4165
Buck & Bell (01926) 811177
A423 N of Southam; The Green; CV47 9PH Friendly, attractively laid-out dining pub, plenty of character in several linked rambling areas, good choice of food including lunchtime set menu, decent wines by the glass and well kept ales such as Banks's, Church End, Hook Norton and Marstons, big log fireplaces, hunting prints and interesting variety of seating around cast-iron-framed tables, elegantly furnished flagstoned restaurant, stairs up to carpeted

gallery; background music; tables on back verandah, more in front looking across village green and rookery, open all day. (Andy Dolan, Rob and Catherine Dunster, Clive and Fran Dutson, Dr Kevan Tucker)

LOWER BRAILES   SP3139
★ George (01608) 685223
B4035 Shipston–Banbury; OX15 5HN Handsome old stone-built inn with roomy front bar, dark oak tables on flagstones, inglenook log fire, beamed and panelled back bar, good food cooked by chef-landlord from bar snacks and pub favourites to imaginative restaurant-style dishes, also good value set lunch, well kept Hook Norton ales, restaurant, some live music; children and dogs welcome, aunt sally in sizeable, neatly kept sheltered garden with terrace and covered area, lovely village and interesting church, good walks, four comfortable bedrooms, open from 9am and all day weekends. (Clive and Fran Dutson, JHBS)

LOWER GORNAL   SO9191
Fountain (01384) 242777
Temple Street; DY3 2PE Lively two-room local with friendly helpful staff, nine changing ales including Greene King, Hobsons and RCH, draught continentals, real ciders and country wines, enjoyable inexpensive food (not Sun evening), back dining area, pigs-and-pen skittles; background music; garden behind, open all day. (Anon)

LYE   SO9284
★ Windsor Castle (01384) 895230
Stourbridge Road (corner A458/A4036; car park in Pedmore Road just above traffic lights – don't be tempted to use the next-door restaurant's parking!); DY9 7DG Focus on the interesting well kept beers from impressive row of ten handpumps including own Sadlers ales (brewery tours available); central flagstoned part is functionally furnished with bar stools by counter and by cask table, a tall tripod table and a window shelf overlooking the road, several snugger rooms off with bare boards or carpet, some brewing memorabilia, enjoyable food (not Sun evening) using free-range and local produce; children welcome, disabled facilities, picnic-sets on side terrace plus some verandah seating, handy for Lye station, open all day. (Anon)

MONKS KIRBY   SP4682
Bell (01788) 832352
Just off B4027 W of Pailton; CV23 0QY Popular pub run by hospitable long-serving spanish landlord, lived-in interior with dark beams, timber dividers, flagstones and cobbles, wide choice of good spanish food including starters doubling as tapas, fine range of spanish wines and of brandies and malt whiskies, two well kept Greene King ales, relaxed informal service; appropriate background music; children and dogs

welcome, streamside back terrace with country view, closed Mon. (Jill and Julian Tasker, Susan and John Douglas)

NETHER WHITACRE   SP2292
Gate (01675) 481292
Gate Lane; B46 2DS Warmly welcoming traditional community pub with six well kept Marstons-related ales and good honest local food, different rooms reflecting generations of expansion and change, conservatory, games room with pool; no credit cards; children welcome, garden picnic-sets, open all day. (David M Smith)

NETHERTON   SO9488
★ Old Swan (01384) 253075
Halesowen Road (A459 just S of centre); DY2 9PY Victorian tavern full of traditional character and known locally as Ma Pardoe's after a former long-serving landlady; wonderfully unspoilt front bar with big swan centrepiece in patterned enamel ceiling, engraved mirrors, traditional furnishings and old-fashioned cylinder stove, other rooms including cosy back snug and more modern lounge, good value own-brewed ales, wholesome bar food (not Sun evening), upstairs restaurant; no under 16s; dogs allowed in bar, open all day (Sun break 4-7pm). (Tony Hobden)

NEWBOLD ON STOUR   SP2446
White Hart (01789) 450205
A3400 S of Stratford; CV37 8TS Welcoming dining pub in same family for many years, proper pubby atmosphere, with good varied home-made food (not Sun evening) including specials board, Adnams Southwold and Purity Mad Goose, long airy beamed bar with good log fire in large stone fireplace, flagstones and big bay windows, roomy back bar and separate dining room, ring the bull; children and dogs welcome, picnic-sets out at front and on back lawned area, open all day weekends. (JHBS)

NUNEATON   SP3790
Attleborough Arms (024) 7638 3231
Highfield Road, Attleborough; CV11 4PL Large fairly recently rebuilt pub, attractively open, modern and comfortable, with wide choice of enjoyable low-priced food, good range of Marstons-related beers and a dozen wines by the glass, helpful attentive service; disabled access, open all day. (David Green)

OFFCHURCH   SP3665
★ Stag (01926) 425801
N of Welsh Road, off A425 at Radford Semele; CV33 9AQ Refurbished 16th-c thatched and beamed village pub, oak-floored bar with log fires and buoyant atmosphere, Purity and Warwickshire ales, about a dozen wines by the glass, good interesting food served by friendly efficient young staff, more formal cosy restaurant areas with bold wallpaper, striking fabrics, animal heads

and big mirrors; children and dogs (in bar) welcome, garden with black furniture on terrace, open all day. *(Clive and Fran Dutson, Anna Field, W M Lien)*

OXHILL SP3149

★ **Peacock** (01295) 688060

Off A422 Stratford–Banbury; CV35 0QU Popular pleasantly upgraded stone-built country pub, good varied menu including special offers, friendly attentive young staff, well kept Marstons and Sharps Doom Bar (May, Aug beer festivals), good selection of wines by the glass, cosy character bar, half-panelled bare-boards dining room; light background music; children welcome, dogs in bar (friendly resident retriever), nice back garden, pretty village, open all day. *(George Atkinson, JHBS, K H Frostick)*

PRINCETHORPE SP4070

Three Horseshoes (01926) 632345

High Town; junction A423/B4453; CV23 9PR Friendly old beamed village pub with Marstons EPA, Pedigree and Wells & Youngs Bombardier, enjoyable traditional food, decorative plates, pictures, comfortable settles and chairs, two restaurant areas; TV projector; big garden with terrace and play area, five bedrooms, open all day Fri-Sun. *(Alan Johnson)*

PRIORS MARSTON SP4857

Holly Bush (01327) 260934

Off A361 S of Daventry; Holly Bush Lane; CV47 7RW Clean and smart with beams, flagstones and lots of stripped stone in rambling linked rooms, log fire and woodburners, above-average well presented food, ales such as Hook Norton, friendly efficient young staff; children welcome, terrace and sheltered garden, four bedrooms, open all day weekends. *(Di and Mike Gillam, Alan Johnson, Andy Dolan)*

RATLEY SP3847

★ **Rose & Crown** (01295) 678148

Off A422 NW of Banbury; OX15 6DS Ancient golden-stone beamed village pub, cosy and charming, well kept Wells & Youngs ales along with Purity Mad Goose, enjoyable good value straightforward food from sandwiches up, friendly helpful staff, daily papers, woodburners in flagstoned area on left and in right carpeted part with wall seats, small back restaurant; children and dogs welcome, tables in sunny gravel garden,

near lovely church in sleepy village. *(Clive and Fran Dutson)*

RUGBY SP5075

Merchants (01788) 571119

Little Church Street; CV21 3AN Open-plan pub tucked away near main shopping area, cheerfully busy, with nine quickly changing ales, real ciders and lots of continental bottled beers (regular beer/cider festivals), low priced pubby food and pizzas, quite dark inside with flagstones, beams and lots of breweriana, live music Tues; sports TVs; open all day, till 1am Fri, Sat. *(Clive and Fran Dutson, Andy Dolan, George Atkinson)*

SALFORD PRIORS SP0751

Bell (01789) 772112

Evesham Road (B439); WR11 8UU Welcoming modernised roadside pub, bucket chairs and leather sofas in log-fire bar, separate dining room, changing choice of enjoyable freshly cooked food including good value lunchtime set menu, special diets catered for and local suppliers listed, well kept Sharps Doom Bar, Wickwar BOB and Wye Valley HPA, real cider and decent wines, friendly service, Sun quiz; outside eating and drinking areas, self-catering apartment, open all day. *(Martin and Pauline Jennings, Clive and Fran Dutson)*

SAMBOURNE SP0561

Green Dragon (01527) 892465

Village signed off A448; B96 6NU Family-run 18th-c pub opposite village green, low-beamed rooms with flagstones and open fires, enjoyable fairly straightforward food (not Sun evening) including weekday lunchtime deal, well kept Adnams, Hobsons and Purity; children welcome, seats in courtyard, six bedrooms. *(Dave Braisted, Clive and Fran Dutson)*

SEDGLEY SO9293

★ **Beacon** (01902) 883380

Bilston Street; A463, off A4123 Wolverhampton–Dudley; DY3 1JE Plain old brick pub with own highly thought-of Sarah Hughes ales from traditional Victorian tower brewery behind; cheery locals in simple quarry-tiled drinking corridor, little snug on left with wall settles, imposing green-tiled marble fireplace and glazed serving hatch, old-fashioned furnishings like velvet and net curtains, mahogany tables on patterned carpet, small

---

A very few pubs try to make you leave a credit card at the bar, as a sort of deposit if you order food. They are not entitled to do this. The credit card firms and banks that issue them warn you not to let cards out of your sight. If someone behind the counter used your card fraudulently, the card company or bank could in theory hold you liable, because of your negligence in letting a stranger hang on to your card. Suggest instead that if they feel the need for security, they 'swipe' your card and give it back to you. And do name and shame the pub to us.

landscape prints, sparse tap room on right with blackened range, dark-panelled lounge with sturdy red leather wall settles and big dramatic sea prints, plant-filled conservatory (no seats), little food apart from cobs; no credit cards; children allowed in some parts including garden with play area. *(Anon)*

SHIPSTON-ON-STOUR   SP2540
Black Horse   (01608) 238489
Station Road (off A3400); CV36 4BT
Ancient thatched pub doing well under newish management, ales including Purity and Wye Valley, authentic thai food, low-beamed rooms off central entrance passage, inglenook log fire; enclosed back garden. *(JHBS)*

SHIPSTON-ON-STOUR   SP2540
★ Horseshoe   (01608) 662190
Church Street; CV36 4AP Pretty 17th-c timbered coaching inn, friendly and relaxed, with open-plan carpeted bar, big fireplace, refurbished restaurant, three ales such as Lancaster, Sharps and Wye Valley, Hogan's cider, enjoyable reasonably priced food (not Sun evening), pub games including aunt sally, live folk second Tues of month; free wi-fi; children and dogs welcome, sunny back terrace with heated smokers' shelter, open all day. *(JHBS)*

SHUSTOKE   SP2290
★ Griffin   (01675) 481205
Church End, a mile E of village; 5 miles from M6 junction 4; A446 towards Tamworth, then right on to B4114 straight through Coleshill; B46 2LB
Unpretentious country local with a dozen changing ales including own Griffin (brewed in next-door barn), farm cider and country wines, may be winter mulled wine, standard lunchtime bar food (not Sun); cheery low-beamed bar with log fires in two stone fireplaces (one a big inglenook), fairly simple décor, cushioned café seats, elm-topped sewing trestles and a nice old-fashioned settle, beer mats on ceiling, conservatory (children allowed here); games machine, no credit cards, dogs welcome, old-fashioned seats on back grass with distant views of Birmingham, large terrace, play area, marquee (live music), camping field. *(Martin Smith, Frank Swann, Alan Bulley, M S and M Imhoff)*

STRATFORD-UPON-AVON   SP2054
Dirty Duck   (01789) 297312
Waterside; CV37 6BA Bustling 16th-c Greene King Old English Inn near the Memorial Theatre; their ales and good choice of wines, well presented fairly priced food all day from sandwiches up (allow plenty of time for a pre-theatre meal), friendly helpful staff, wood floors and panelling, lots of signed RSC photographs, open fire, modern conservatory restaurant (best to book weekends); children allowed in dining area, dogs in bar, attractive small terrace looking over riverside public gardens which tend to act as a summer overflow. *(Edward Mirzoeff, George Atkinson, N R White, Dr D J and Mrs S C Walker)*

STRATFORD-UPON-AVON   SP2054
★ Garrick   (01789) 292186
High Street; CV37 6AU Bustling ancient pub with heavy beams and timbers, odd-shaped rooms and simple furnishings on bare boards or flagstones, friendly helpful staff, enjoyable fairly priced food all day from sandwiches and light dishes up, well kept Greene King ales, decent wines by the glass, small air-conditioned back dining area; background music, TV, games machine; children welcome. *(George Atkinson, Alan Johnson, N R White)*

STRATFORD-UPON-AVON   SP1955
Old Thatch   (01789) 295216
Rother Street/Greenhill Street; CV37 6LE Cosy and welcoming thatched pub dating from the 15th c on corner of market square, well kept Fullers ales, nice wines, popular fairly priced food including Sun carvery, rustic décor, beams, slate or wood floors, sofas and log fire, back dining area; covered tables outside. *(Alan Johnson, Val and Alan Green, N R White)*

STRATFORD-UPON-AVON   SP1954
Windmill   (01789) 297687
Church Street; CV37 6HB Ancient black and white pub (with town's oldest licence) beyond the attractive Guild Chapel, very low beams, panelling, mainly stone floors, big fireplace (gas fire), enjoyable good value food (till 8pm) from varied menu including deals, friendly efficient staff, Greene King, Purity UBU and guests; background music, sports TV, games machines; courtyard tables, open all day. *(George Atkinson)*

STRETTON-ON-FOSSE   SP2238
★ Plough   (01608) 661053
Just off A429; GL56 9QX Popular unpretentious 17th-c village local, central servery separating small bar and snug candlelit dining area, good food from pubby choices up including Sun spit roasts in winter, friendly fast service, Ansells, Hook Norton and interesting guests, stripped brick/stone walls and some flagstones, low oak beams, inglenook log fire, dominoes and cribbage; no dogs; children welcome, a few tables outside, smokers' shelter, closed Sun evening, Mon lunchtime. *(David Gunn, Guy Vowles, JHBS)*

TANWORTH-IN-ARDEN   SP1170
★ Bell   (01564) 742212
The Green; B94 5AL Restauranty pub with contemporary bar-style décor, nice food from light dishes including 'tapas' to full meals, good choice of wines by the glass and a couple of well kept ales, friendly staff; children in eating areas, outlook on pretty

village's green and lovely 14th-c church, back terrace with alloy planters, nine stylish modern bedrooms (good base for walks), also has a post office, open all day. *(Dave Braisted, Andy Dolan)*

TANWORTH-IN-ARDEN SP1071
Warwickshire Lad (01564) 742346
Broad Lane; B94 5DP Beamed country pub with good reasonably priced home-made food (all day Fri, Sat, till 7.30pm Sun), lunchtime bargains, local Whitworths ales including one specially brewed for the pub; popular with walkers, open all day. *(Dave Braisted)*

TEMPLE GRAFTON SP1355
Blue Boar (01789) 750010
1 mile E, towards Binton; off A422 W of Stratford; B49 6NR Welcoming stone-built dining pub with good choice of enjoyable food from bar snacks up, four well kept ales, beams, stripped stonework and log fires, glass-covered well with goldfish, smarter dining room up a couple of steps; big-screen TVs; children and dogs welcome, picnic-sets outside, comfortable bedrooms. *(Martin and Pauline Jennings, Martin Smith, Grahame Brooks)*

TIPTON SO9492
Pie Factory (0121) 557 1402
Hurst Lane, Dudley Road towards Wednesbury; A457/A4037; DY4 9AB Mildly zany décor and quirky food – the mixed grill comes on a shovel, and you're awarded a certificate if you finish their massive Desperate Dan Cow Pie – other pies and good value food including Sun carvery, well kept Lump Hammer house ales brewed by Enville plus a guest; background music (live weekends), TV; children welcome, bedrooms. *(Anon)*

UPPER BRAILES SP3039
Gate (01608) 685212
B4035 Shipston-on-Stour to Banbury; OX15 5AX Traditional low-beamed village local, well kept Hook Norton and a guest, enjoyable food (not Sun evening, Mon) including good fish and chips, efficient friendly service, coal fire; TV; children welcome, tables in extensive back garden with play area and aunt sally, pretty hillside spot with lovely walks, newly refurbished bedrooms, closed Mon lunchtime. *(Stephen and Jean Curtis, JHBS)*

UPPER GORNAL SO9292
⋆ Britannia (01902) 883253
Kent Street (A459); DY3 1UX Popular old-fashioned 19th-c local with friendly chatty atmosphere (known locally as Sally's after former landlady), particularly well kept Bathams Best and Mild (bargain prices),

---

tiled floors, coal fires in front bar and time-trapped little back room with wonderful handpumps, some bar snacks including good local pork pies; sports TV; nice flower-filled backyard, open all day. *(Anon)*

WARMINGTON SP4147
Plough (01295) 690666
Just off B4100 N of Banbury; OX17 1BX Attractive and welcoming old stone-built pub under new brother-and-sister team, some refurbishment but keeping character and good local atmosphere, low heavy beams, comfortable chairs by inglenook woodburner, well kept Greene King and guests, enjoyable home-made food (not Mon), extended dining room; background music; children welcome, tables on back terrace, delightful village with interesting church, closed Sun evening. *(Anon)*

WARWICK SP2864
⋆ Rose & Crown (01926) 411117
Market Place; CV34 4SH Up-to-date uncluttered décor, bustling and friendly, with big leather sofas and low tables by open fire, dining area with large modern photographs, good choice of sensibly priced interesting food all day, well kept Purity and Sharps Doom Bar, plenty of fancy keg dispensers, good wines and coffee, cheerful efficient service, newspapers; background music; tables out under parasols, comfortable good-sized bedrooms, open all day from 8am for breakfast. *(Rob and Catherine Dunster, Alan Johnson)*

WARWICK SP2967
⋆ Saxon Mill (01926) 492255
Guys Cliffe, A429 just N; CV34 5YN Well run Mitchells & Butlers dining pub in charmingly set converted mill; beams and log fire, smart contemporary chairs and tables on polished boards and flagstones, cosy corners with leather armchairs and big rugs, mill race and turning wheel behind glass, friendly attentive service, enjoyable good value food in bar and (best to book) upstairs family restaurant, good choice of wines by the glass, M&B and local beers; background music; tables out on terraces by broad willow-flanked river, more over bridge, delightful views across to Guys Cliffe House ruins, open all day. *(Iain Clark, Ian Herdman, Susan and John Douglas, Stephen and Jean Curtis, Nigel and Sue Foster)*

WARWICK SP2864
⋆ Zetland Arms (01926) 491974
Church Street; CV34 4AB Cosy town pub with good sensibly priced traditional food (not weekend evenings) including nice sandwiches and set menu deals, friendly quick service even when busy, Adnams, Black

---

Sheep and Marstons, decent wines, small panelled front bar with toby jug collection, comfortable larger L-shaped back eating area with small conservatory, pictures of old Warwick; sports TV; children welcome, sheltered garden, bedrooms sharing bathroom. *(Alan Johnson, Andy Dolan)*

WHICHFORD   SP3134
Norman Knight (01608) 684621
Ascott Road, opposite village green; CV36 5PE Sympathetically extended beamed and flagstoned pub, good Patriot ales from own microbrewery and changing guests, traditional ciders and perry, enjoyable freshly made food (not Sun and Mon evenings) from favourites up, friendly helpful service, live music including monthly folk club; children and dogs welcome (resident pugs – beer named after them), tables out by attractive village green, aunt sally, site at back for five caravans, good walks, classic car/bike meetings third Thurs of month in summer, open all day weekends. *(Clive and Fran Dutson)*

WILLEY   SP4885
Wood Farm (01788) 833469
Coalpit Lane; CV23 0SL Visitor centre attached (and with views into) the Wood Farm Brewery, eight of their ales and occasional guests, enjoyable reasonably priced food including Sun carvery, upstairs function/overflow room; children and well behaved dogs welcome, picnic-sets outside, camping, brewery tours (must pre-book, not Sun), open all day from 9am (midday Sun). *(Alan Johnson)*

WILLOUGHBY   SP5267
Rose (01788) 891180
Just off A45 E of Dunchurch; Main Street; CV23 8BH Neatly decorated old beamed and thatched pub with wood or tiled floors, some panelling and inglenook woodburner, good range of food cooked well by italian chef, Adnams, friendly attentive service; children and dogs welcome, disabled facilities, seating in side garden with gate to park and play area. *(George Atkinson, M C and S Jeanes, Liane)*

WOLVERHAMPTON   SO9298
☀ Great Western (01902) 351090
Corn Hill/Sun Street, behind railway station; WV10 0DG Cheerful pub hidden away in cobbled lane down from mainline station; Holdens and guest beers kept well, real cider, bargain home-made food (not Sun – bar nibbles then), helpful friendly staff, traditional front bar, other rooms including neat dining conservatory, interesting railway memorabilia, open fires; background radio, TV; children and dogs welcome, yard with barbecues, open all day. *(Anon)*

Please tell us if any pub deserves to be upgraded to a featured entry – and why: feedback@goodguides.com, or (no stamp needed) The Good Pub Guide, FREEPOST TN1569, Wadhurst, E Sussex TN5 7BR.

Wiltshire

There are so many lovely pubs in this big county that it's hard to mention just a few here. We're delighted with our new entries, which include the Methuen Arms in Corsham (handsome town pub with first class licensees, a civilised atmosphere, delicious food and comfortable bedrooms), White Hart in Ford (lovely trout-stream spot, with attractively refurbished rooms and interesting food), Three Tuns in Great Bedwyn (simple village inn run by a hard-working chef-owner and his wife, with enjoyable food), Old Spotted Cow at Marston Meysey (cheerful country inn with lots of cow bric-a-brac and popular meals), Weighbridge Brewhouse in Swindon (stunningly converted building with stylish modern décor, own-brewed beers and creative cooking), King John at Tollard Royal (gently upmarket and elegantly furnished with accomplished food and pretty bedrooms) and Prince Leopold in Upton Lovell (neatly modernised and tucked away country pub with charming licensees, cheerful locals and highly thought-of food). Places our readers have found particularly rewarding this year are the Compasses at Chicksgrove (loved as a smashing all-rounder), Red Lion at Cricklade (a special place for both locals and visitors, now with own-brewed ales), Potting Shed in Crudwell (top class pub with creative food, thoughtful choice of drinks and exceptional staff), Beckford Arms at Fonthill Gifford (civilised but informal and friendly, with excellent food, drink and bedrooms), Hatchet at Lower Chute (bustling country pub with a convivial landlord and cheerful atmosphere), Malet Arms at Newton Tony (charming, enthusiastic landlord in highly popular country pub with interesting food and ales), Vine Tree in Norton (enormously popular locally, enterprising food and fantastic wines), Raven in Poulshott (consistently enjoyable, neatly kept and with tasty landlord-cooked food) and Longs Arms at South Wraxall (lots of character, convivial atmosphere and inventive food). Creative chefs and delicious accomplished food means that half the Main Entries hold a Food Award – but our Wiltshire Dining Pub 2014 is the Potting Shed at Crudwell.

BERWICK ST JOHN
ST9422   Map 2

Talbot

Village signed from A30 E of Shaftesbury; SP7 0HA

Unspoilt and friendly pub in attractive village, with simple furnishings and fairly priced food using local produce

In a village with pretty thatched houses, this unspoilt village pub continues to offer reasonably priced food. The heavily beamed bar has plenty of character, a huge inglenook fireplace with a good iron fireback and bread ovens, and simple furnishings such as solid wall and window seats, spindleback chairs and a high-backed built-in settle at one end. Ringwood Best, Wadworths 6X and a guest like Sixpenny IPA on handpump and several wines by the glass; darts. There are seats outside and the pub is well placed for choice walks southwards through the deep countryside of Cranborne Chase and towards Tollard Royal.

Quite a choice of tasty food includes lunchtime sandwiches and baguettes, deep-fried whitebait with tartare sauce, garlic mushrooms, omelettes, mediterranean vegetable lasagne, ham and egg, sausages with mash and onion gravy, cajun chicken with creole salad, mixed grill, and puddings such as syrup sponge with custard and seasonal fruit crumble. *Benchmark main dish: chicken with mushroom and tarragon sauce and sautéed potatoes £12.50. Two-course evening meal £22.00.*

Free house ~ Licensee Venetia Whale ~ Real ale ~ (01747) 828222 ~ Open 12-2.30, 6.30-11; 12-5 Sun; closed Sun evening, Mon ~ Bar food 12-2, 6.30-9 ~ Restaurant ~ Children welcome ~ Dogs welcome ~ www.talbotinnberwickstjohn.co.uk *Recommended by Tess White, Toby Jones*

BROAD HINTON
SU1176   Map 2

Barbury ♀

A4361 Swindon–Devizes; SN4 9PF

Friendly roadside pub with an easy-going atmosphere, enjoyable food, comfortable and contemporary furnishings and a good balance between eating and drinking

With an easy-going and friendly atmosphere, this well run roadside pub is welcoming to all, dogs included – there are dog treats on the bar and champagne buckets full of fresh water. The long bar room has a comfortable sofa and two stumpy armchairs in pale brown leather beside a woodburner at one end, a few high-backed wicker armchairs around a couple of tables on bare boards, and game, hunting, shooting and fishing prints. The area around the dark grey-painted counter has regency-striped modern armchairs and tables and stools used by cheerful locals: Otter Bitter, St Austell Trelawny and guest beers on handpump, good wines by the glass and helpful, willing service. Beside the second woodburner at the other end of the room are leather-cushioned chairs around polished tables (set for dining); a step leads up to a carpeted dining room with high-backed black wicker or wooden dining chairs around a mix of tables. Throughout there are cream altar candles, basket-weave lamp shades, ornate mirrors and planked ceilings; daily papers and background music. There are seats and tables on a partly covered back terrace.

As well as their well liked Sunday brunch and afternoon teas, the good, popular food includes sandwiches, ham hock and parsley terrine with home-made piccalilli, smoked haddock fishcake with curried egg mayonnaise, home-baked ham with free-range eggs, asparagus, pea and mint risotto with poached egg and parmesan, moroccan-spiced lamb with olive and tomato couscous and mint and cucumber yoghurt, fillet of scottish salmon with grain mustard and honey dressing and sweet potatoes, and puddings such as rosewater and vanilla panna cotta with lemon shortbread and dark chocolate and chestnut brownie with clotted cream ice-cream. *Benchmark main dish: 8oz rump steak, fried duck egg and chips £14.50. Two-course evening meal £17.00.*

Free house ~ Licensees Charles Walker and Tiggi Wood ~ Real ale ~ (01793) 731510 ~ Open 11-11(midnight Fri, Sat); 10.15am-10.30pm Sun ~ Bar food 12.30-2.30, 6.30-9; 10.30-4 Sun ~ Children welcome ~ Dogs welcome ~ www.thebarburyinn.co.uk
Recommended by Isobel Mackinlay, Martin Jones

 BROUGHTON GIFFORD   ST8763 Map 2

Fox

Village signposted off A365 to B3107 W of Melksham; The Street; SN12 8PN

Comfortably stylish pub with good, interesting food, real ales and several wines by the glass, and a nice garden

Readers enjoy this civilised pub a great deal – much of this is down to the genuinely friendly welcome from the landlord and his helpful, courteous staff. Each of the interconnected areas has a chatty atmosphere, and the big bird and plant prints, attractive table lamps and white-painted beams contrast nicely with the broad dark flagstones. You can sink into sofas or armchairs by a table of daily papers or another with magazines and board games, take one of the padded stools by the pink-painted bar counter, or go for the mix of gently old-fashioned dining chairs around the unmatched stripped dining tables, which have candles in brass sticks; there's also a warm log fire in a stone fireplace. Bath Ales Gem Bitter, Butcombe Bitter, Fullers London Pride and Otter Bitter on handpump, lots of wines by the glass, 24 malt whiskies and a good choice of spirits. The terrace behind has picnic-sets, and leads on to a good-sized sheltered lawn. They have biscuits behind the bar for dogs.

Raising their own pigs, using produce from their kitchen garden and baking bread daily, the extremely popular food includes lunchtime sandwiches, chicken liver parfait with home-made chutney, fishcakes with lemon mayonnaise, wild mushroom risotto, cornish fish and chips, venison pie, pork belly with mustard mash, braised local mutton with baby root vegetables, and puddings such as chocolate and peanut butter pudding with toffee nuts and honeycomb ice-cream and vanilla rice pudding with rhubarb compote; they also offer a two- and three-course weekday set menu. *Benchmark main dish: 8oz fillet steak with chips and salad £24.95. Two-course evening meal £25.00.*

Free house ~ Licensee Derek Geneen ~ Real ale ~ (01225) 782949 ~ Open 12-midnight; 5-11 Mon; 12-10 Sun; closed Mon lunchtime ~ Bar food 12-2.30(3 Sat), 6-9.30; 12-5.30 Sun ~ Restaurant ~ Children welcome ~ Dogs welcome ~ www.thefox-broughtongifford.co.uk
Recommended by Michael Doswell, Guy Vowles, Alan Sutton, Colin and Peggy Wilshire, Mr and Mrs A H Young, Mr and Mrs P R Thomas

CHICKSGROVE   ST9729 Map 2

Compasses ★ 🍴 ♀ 🛏

From A30 5.5 miles W of B3089 junction, take lane on N side signposted Sutton Mandeville, Sutton Row, then first left fork (small signs point the way to the pub, in Lower Chicksgrove; look out for the car park); can also be reached off B3089 W of Dinton, passing the glorious spire of Teffont Evias church; SP3 6NB

An excellent all-rounder with enjoyable food, a genuine welcome, four real ales and seats in the quiet garden; comfortable bedrooms

'A really lovely place' and 'a gem' are just two examples of readers' comments on their thoroughly enjoyable visits to this 14th-c thatched inn. The landlord and his staff go out of their way to ensure customers are happy – whether just dropping in for a pint or staying overnight in the comfortable bedrooms. The unchanging bar has plenty of real character: old bottles and jugs hanging from beams above the roughly timbered counter, farm tools and traps on the partly stripped stone walls, high-backed wooden settles forming snug booths around tables on the mainly flagstoned floor and a log fire. Butcombe Bitter, Plain Inntrigue and Sixpenny Best Bitter on handpump, eight wines by the glass and several malt whiskies. There are plenty of seats in the quiet garden and on the terraces and flagstoned courtyard. Good walks in the surrounding countryside.

The highly thought-of food includes sandwiches, beetroot-cured salmon with celeriac remoulade and crème fraîche, duck liver parfait with white onion and orange marmalade, beer-battered haddock with chips, roasted mediterranean vegetable and goats cheese tart, free-range chicken breast stuffed with smoked cheese mouse with provençale vegetables and spinach mousse, hake fillet with lemon, pea and tiger prawn risotto and smoked paprika oil, daily specials, and puddings such as whisky bread and butter pudding with marmalade ice-cream and apple crumble with toffee ice-cream. *Benchmark main dish: slow-cooked pork belly with apricot and chestnut stuffing and apple and leek mash £15.50. Two-course evening meal £21.00.*

Free house ~ Licensee Alan Stoneham ~ Real ale ~ (01722) 714318 ~ Open 12-3, 6-11; 12-3, 7-10.30 Sun ~ Bar food 12-2, 7-9 ~ Children welcome ~ Dogs welcome ~ Bedrooms: £65/£85 ~ www.thecompassesinn.com *Recommended by M and R Ridge, Helen and Brian Edgeley, Dr A McCormick, Martin Warne, Andrea Rampley, Simon Lindsey, Rose Rogers, Phil and Jane Hodson*

COMPTON BASSETT
SU0372   Map 2
White Horse 🍴 ♈

At N end of village; SN11 8RG

Bustling, refurbished village pub with four ales, good wines by the glass, inventive food and seats in big garden; bedrooms

After enjoying one of the good surrounding walks, this 18th-c village pub is just the place for a drink or meal. The simply furnished, friendly bar has some homely upholstered chairs and a carved settle around assorted tables on parquet flooring, a woodburning stove, and bar stools against the counter where they keep Bath Ales Gem Bitter, Sharps Doom Bar, Wadworths 6X and Wells & Youngs Bombardier on handpump, ten wines by the glass and farm cider. The dining room is red-walled and carpeted at one end and has bare floorboards and pale paintwork at the other, and throughout there are beams, joists and miscellaneous antique tables and chairs; another woodburning stove here too. The large garden has picnic-sets and other seats and a boules pitch, and the paddock holds pigs, sheep and geese. The comfortable bedrooms are in a separate building and look over the grounds.

Popular enterprising food includes sandwiches, scallops with sweetcorn purée and potato and truffle millefeuille, cornish crab with crème fraîche, beetroot jelly and peppered pastry, home-made tagliatelle with olive tapenade and grilled mozzarella, cheese burger with coleslaw and chips, steak and kidney pudding, seared scotch salmon with creamy mash, lettuce and fresh tomato dressing, rack of lamb with leeks and redcurrant jus, duck breast with creamed cabbage, roasted beetroot and raspberry jus, and puddings such as crème brûlée and chocolate cup filled with coffee sabayon and petits fours. *Benchmark main dish: home-reared sausages with mash and red wine and shallot jus £11.95. Two-course evening meal £19.00.*

Free house ~ Licensees Danny and Tara Adams ~ Real ale ~ (01249) 813118 ~ Open 12-11; 12-4 Sun; closed Sun evening, Mon ~ Bar food 12-2.30, 6-9; teas all afternoon; 12-2 Sun ~ Restaurant ~ Children welcome ~ Dogs allowed in bar ~ Bedrooms: £75/£95 ~ www.whitehorse-comptonbassett.co.uk *Recommended by Bridget Scott, Alastair Muir*

CORSHAM
Methuen Arms 🍴 🛏
ST8670 Map 2

High Street; SN13 0HB

Easy-going and civilised hotel with character bars, friendly staff, imaginative food, good wines and ales and seats outside; comfortable bedrooms

In a bustling market town, this handsome Georgian inn is run by professional licensees and their warmly friendly staff. It's a civilised but informal place and the little front bar is cosy and much favoured locally. There's a log fire, a big old clock under a sizeable mirror, an assortment of antique dining chairs and tables, rugs on elm floorboards, Butcombe Bitter, Otter Ale and Palmers Dorset Gold on handpump, 14 wines by the glass and ten malt whiskies. Across the green-painted bar counter is a second small bar, which has similar furnishings on bare boards and rugs and a couple of armchairs. The dining room has a carved and a plain settle, high-backed wooden dining chairs with arms around old sewing machine treadle tables, an open fire with nightlights, fine black and white photographs of large local houses on pale sage green paintwork, and swagged curtains on poles leading into a further room. The back restaurant, with a penny farthing in one corner, is to have french windows installed, which will add much more light; two other rooms are often used for private parties or meetings. The side garden has seats and tables. The bedrooms are well equipped and comfortable.

🍴 Accomplished cooking using local, seasonal ingredients might include nibbles like beer-battered prawns and saffron and goats cheese arancini, sandwiches, mackerel, leek and pink fur apple potato terrine, sauté of prawns with chilli, garlic and parsley butter, wild mushroom and ricotta crêpe gratin with soft poached egg and parsley pesto, line-caught cod with clam chowder, spinach and saffron new potatoes, confit duck leg, sweet and sour butternut squash and lyonnaise potatoes, pot-roasted beef cheek with spelt and beetroot risotto and roasted carrots, and puddings such as crème caramel with roasted spiced plums and dark chocolate and espresso pot with walnut and orange biscotti. *Benchmark main dish: chargrilled rump steak with roasted portobello mushrooms, hand-cut chips and béarnaise sauce £19.00. Two-course evening meal £22.50.*

Free house ~ Licensees Martin and Debbie Still ~ Real ale ~ (01249) 717060 ~ Open 7am-midnight; 8am-1am Sat; 8am-midnight Sun ~ Bar food 12-3, 6-10 ~ Restaurant ~ Children welcome ~ Dogs allowed in bar ~ Bedrooms: £85/£120 ~ www.themethuenarms.com *Recommended by Mr and Mrs P R Thomas*

The knife-and-fork award 🍴 distinguishes pubs where the food is of exceptional quality.

CRICKLADE

SU1093 Map 4

Red Lion 🍴 🍺 🛏

Off A419 Swindon–Cirencester; High Street; SN6 6DD

16th-c inn with imaginative food in two dining rooms, ten real ales (some now own-brew), lots of bottled beers and several wines by the glass, friendly, relaxed atmosphere and big garden; bedrooms

Their own-brewed ales (from the microbrewery in the garden) are now on offer at this very well run former coaching inn: Hop Kettle Adders Tongue, Blizzard, East Side of Providence and North Wall. They also offer quickly changing guests such as Arbor Down Deeperer, Blue Monkey BG Sips, Butcombe Bitter, Flying Dog Big Black Wit, Hop Back Summer Lightning, Otter Seville Bitter and Ramsbury Bitter on handpump; 70 bottled beers, local cider, eight wines by the glass and 13 gins during gin hour (5.30-6.30, not Sunday). The bar has a good community atmosphere, stools by the nice old counter, wheelbacks and other chairs around dark wooden tables on red-patterned carpet, an open fire and all sorts of bric-a-brac including stuffed fish and animal heads and old street signs on the stone walls. You can eat here or in the slightly more formal dining room, which has pale wooden farmhouse chairs and tables, beige carpeting and a woodburning stove in a brick fireplace. There are plenty of picnic-sets in the big back garden. This is a popular place to stay – the bedrooms are attractive and comfortable and the breakfasts good. You can walk along the nearby Thames Path or through the attractive historic town.

Using home-reared pigs, making their own butter and bread and name-checking the best local suppliers, the good, interesting food includes lunchtime sandwiches, mussels in parsley, garlic, white wine and shallot cream, home-cured air-dried ham with crispy free-range egg and pickle salad, macaroni cheese with jerusalem artichokes, portobello mushroom, spinach and cheddar duck egg omelette, free-range chicken breast with crushed carrot and swede and tarragon potato rösti, confit cornish pollock with squid ink, mussels and cider butter sauce, and puddings such as treacle tart with clotted cream ice-cream and lemon and vanilla cheesecake with cherry plum jam. *Benchmark main dish: beer-battered haddock with triple-cooked chips £9.95. Two-course evening meal £14.00.*

Free house ~ Licensee Tom Gee ~ Real ale ~ (01793) 750776 ~ Open 12-11(midnight Sat); 12-10.30 Sun ~ Bar food 12-2.30, 6.30-9(9.30 Fri, Sat), 12-3 Sun ~ Restaurant ~ Children welcome ~ Dogs welcome ~ Bedrooms: /£80 ~ www.theredlioncricklade.co.uk
Recommended by Sue Bastone, Evelyn and Derek Walter, John Clancy, Dr A J and Mrs B A Tompsett, Simon Daws, Michael Doswell, Ian Herdman, Paul Moss, Mrs Margo Finlay, Jörg Kasprowski, Giles and Annie Francis, Lesley Dick, Simon Collett-Jones

CRUDWELL

ST9592 Map 4

Potting Shed 🍴 🍷 🍺

A429 N of Malmesbury; The Street; SN16 9EW

Wiltshire Dining Pub of the Year

Civilised but relaxed dining pub with low-beamed rambling rooms, friendly, helpful staff, an interesting range of drinks and creative cooking; seats in the big garden

What really stands out among all the highly enthusiastic reports on this first class pub is the warmth of the genuine welcome from the friendly, courteous staff – and this extends to dogs too, who may meet Barney, Rubble and Tilly (the pub dogs) and be offered a biscuit.

Low-beamed rooms ramble around the bar with mixed plain tables and chairs on pale flagstones, log fires (one in a big worn stone fireplace), some homely armchairs in one corner and daily papers. Four steps take you up into a high-raftered area with coir carpeting, and there's a smaller separate room ideal for a lunch or dinner party. The quirky, rustic decorations are not overdone: a garden-fork door handle, garden-tool beer pumps, rather witty big black and white photographs. A fine range of drinks includes Bath Ales Gem Bitter, Butcombe Gold, Sharps Doom Bar and Timothy Taylors Landlord on handpump, as well as an excellent range of 21 wines and champagne by the glass, home-made seasonal cocktails using local or home-grown fruit, local fruit liqueurs, good coffees and popular winter mulled cider; well chosen background music and board games. There are sturdy teak seats around cask tables as well as picnic-sets out on the side grass among weeping willows. The pub's two acres of gardens supply a lot of ingredients used in the kitchen; they've also donated ten raised beds to the village and these are pleasant to wander through. Good access for those in need of extra assistance. They also own the hotel across the road.

Using home-grown and other top quality local, seasonal produce, the imaginative food includes sandwiches, arbroath smokies on toast with soft poached egg and hollandaise, galantine of quail with raisin, spinach and walnut salad, quince, chestnut and roquefort risotto with poached pear, stuffed oxtail with mash and red wine jus, pork loin and parmesan with sweetcorn fritters, spinach and smoked pepper jus, fallow deer stew with chard and tarragon dumplings, sea bream with samphire and vegetable verde broth, and puddings such as chocolate and cherry jam roulade with dark chocolate ice-cream and cherry and kirsch purée and rum baba with lime syrup and rum and raisin ice-cream. *Benchmark main dish: lamb and harissa burger with mesclun salad, mint yoghurt and triple-cooked chips £14.50. Two-course evening meal £20.00.*

Enterprise ~ Lease Jonathan Barry and Julian Muggridge ~ Real ale ~ (01666) 577833 ~ Open 11am-midnight(11 Sun) ~ Bar food 12-2.30, 7-9.30; 12-3, 7-9 Sun ~ Restaurant ~ Children welcome ~ Dogs welcome ~ www.thepottingshedpub.com
Recommended by Michael Sargent, Di and Mike Gillam, Malcolm and Jo Hart, M G Hart, Mrs Blethyn Elliott, Paul Goldman, R J Herd, Mr and Mrs A H Young, KC, Michael Doswell, Maureen Wood, Mr and Mrs P R Thomas, Dr and Mrs A K Clarke, Leslie and Barbara Owen

EAST CHISENBURY   SU1352   Map 2
Red Lion ⑪ ♀ 🛏

At S end of village; SN9 6AQ

Thatched country inn run by hard-working chef-owners, contemporary décor, an informal atmosphere and delicious food; bedrooms

The owners of this thatched dining inn have just opened five well equipped, lovely bedrooms in their Troutbeck boutique guesthouse across the road; the breakfasts are delicious (and the bloody marys and bucks fizz are complimentary). Two top chefs run the pub and so, of course, the emphasis is on the exceptional food – but they do keep a couple of local beers from breweries like Plain Ales and Three Castles on handpump, ten wines by the glass, farm cider, home-made cordial and some interesting spirits – and make a fine bloody mary. It's basically one long room split into different areas by brick and green-planked timbers. One end has a big woodburner in a brick inglenook, the other a comfortable black leather sofa and armchairs; in between are painted or wooden dining chairs around chunky pale oak tables on bare boards or stone, and wine bottles and candles on the window sills. Drinkers tend to congregate at the high chairs by the bar counter. There's a further dining room too. Décor includes a huge string of chillis and country and other pictures on the walls; background music, table skittles. Outside, there are picnic-sets on a terrace and tables and chairs on grass above; you can also go into the upper garden where they keep chickens. They make their own dog treats.

Using their own bread, sausages, smoked meats and home-grown vegetables, the accomplished food includes sandwiches, warm crab tart, chicken liver pâté with madeira jelly, a charcuterie plate, wild garlic risotto with roasted jerusalem artichokes and pine nut pesto, cornish cod with braised gem lettuce, mussels and chive beurre blanc, lamb rump with charred leeks, potato gratin, anchovy beignet and red wine, and puddings such as blood orange salad with blood orange sorbet, coffee cream and japonaise and Valrhona chocolate cremeux with cocoa crumbs and sea salt. *Benchmark main dish: roast rib of beef for two people with béarnaise sauce and hand-cut chips £55.00. Two-course evening meal £27.00.*

Free house ~ Licensees Britt and Guy Manning ~ Real ale ~ (01980) 671124 ~ Open 12-3, 6-11; 12-midnight(11 Sun) Sat ~ Bar food 12-2.30, 6.30-9.30; 12-3.30, 6.30-8.30 Sun ~ Children welcome ~ Dogs allowed in bar and bedrooms ~ Bedrooms: /£120 ~ www.redlionfreehouse.com *Recommended by Michael Doswell*

EAST KNOYLE
ST8731 Map 2
Fox & Hounds ♨ ♟

Village signposted off A350 S of A303; The Green (named on some road atlases), a mile NW at OS Sheet 183 map reference 872313; or follow signpost off B3089, about 0.5 miles E of A303 junction near Little Chef; SP3 6BN

Beautiful thatched village pub with splendid views, welcoming service, good beers and popular enjoyable food

In a charming setting overlooking Blackmore Vale, this is a reliably well run village pub where you can be sure of a friendly welcome from the landlord, his staff and the chatty locals. The three linked areas are on different levels around the central horseshoe-shaped servery and have big log fires, plentiful oak woodwork and flagstones, comfortably padded dining chairs around big scrubbed tables with vases of flowers, and a couple of leather sofas; the furnishings are very individual and uncluttered. There's also a small light-painted conservatory restaurant. Hop Back Summer Lightning, Plain Ales Sheep Dip and a guest or two on handpump, 14 well-chosen wines by the glass and farm cider. Background music, board games and skittle alley. The nearby woods are good for a stroll and the Wiltshire Cycleway passes through the village.

Consistently enjoyable food using the best local produce includes pigeon and foie gras terrine with chutney, mixed seafood salad, chicken caesar salad, pizzas from their clay oven, lasagne, steak and kidney pudding, duck breast in port and redcurrant sauce, pork belly with cider and apples, monkfish fillet with crab risotto, and puddings such as dark chocolate and raspberry tart and sticky toffee pudding. *Benchmark main dish: fresh fish of the day £12.00. Two-course evening meal £19.00.*

Free house ~ Licensee Murray Seator ~ Real ale ~ (01747) 830573 ~ Open 11.30-3, 5.30-11(10 Sun) ~ Bar food 12-2.30, 6-9.30 ~ Children welcome ~ Dogs welcome ~ www.foxandhounds-eastknoyle.co.uk *Recommended by David and Judy Robison, Edward Mirzoeff, Paul Goldman, Roy Hoing, Mr and Mrs J Davis, Ian Herdman*

We say if we know a pub has background music.

FONTHILL GIFFORD

ST9231 Map 2

Beckford Arms ⊕ ♀ ⇔

Off B3089 W at Fonthill Bishop; SP3 6PX

18th-c coaching inn with character bar and restaurant, unfailingly excellent interesting food, thoughtful drinks choice and an informal but civilised atmosphere; bedrooms

On the edge of the lovely rolling parkland of the Fonthill Estate is this elegant Georgian coaching inn – much loved by locals and visitors alike – and just the place for a civilised break from the A303; do book a table in advance. The main bar has a huge fireplace, bar stools beside the counter, various old wooden dining chairs and tables on parquet flooring, Butcombe Bitter, Keystone Phoenix (brewed especially for them) and a changing guest on handpump, 15 wines by the glass, winter mulled wine and cider and cocktails such as a bellini using locally produced peach liqueur and a bloody mary using home-grown horseradish; service is friendly and helpful. The stylish but cosy sitting room has comfortable sofas facing each other across a low table of newspapers, a nice built-in window seat and other chairs and tables, and an open fire in a stone fireplace with candles in brass candlesticks and fresh flowers on the mantelpiece. There's also a separate restaurant and charming private dining room. Much of the artwork on the walls is by local artists. They host film nights on occasional Sundays and will provide water and bones for dogs (the pub dog is called Elsa). The mature rambling garden has seats on a brick terrace, hammocks under trees, games for children, a dog bath and boules. This is a lovely place to stay and the breakfasts are very good.

Using local, seasonal produce (some home-grown) and making their own chutneys and jams, the inventive food includes sandwiches, confit rabbit terrine with spiced pear and vanilla chutney, scallops with beetroot, quail egg, samphire and salmon roe vinaigrette, burger with bacon, cheddar, coleslaw and chips, ox cheek pie, creamed lentils with poached egg, oyster and chestnut mushrooms and jerusalem artichokes, lambs liver with bacon, mash and red wine gravy, fillet of bass with braised fennel, toasted almonds and anchovy dressing, and puddings such as rhubarb and ginger nut fool and dark chocolate fondant with honeycomb, vanilla ice-cream caramel and salted peanuts. *Benchmark main dish: lambs liver with smoked bacon, chilli greens, sautéed potatoes and red wine sauce £13.50. Two-course evening meal £21.00.*

Free house ~ Licensees Dan Brod and Charlie Luxton ~ Real ale ~ (01747) 870385 ~ Open 11-11 ~ Bar food 12-2.30(3 weekends), 6-9.30 ~ Restaurant ~ Children welcome ~ Dogs welcome ~ Bedrooms: /£95 ~ www.beckfordarms.com *Recommended by Douglas and Ann Hare, Edward Mirzoeff, Alex Talbot, Tony and Caroline Elwood, Anne de Gruchy, Dave Braisted, B J Thompson, Richard and Penny Gibbs*

FORD

ST8474 Map 2

White Hart ⇔

Off A420 Chippenham–Bristol; SN14 8RP

16th-c inn with attractively refurbished rooms, good choice of food and drink, helpful staff and seats beside trout stream; bedrooms

On the Palladian Way trail, this handsome stone-built country inn has plenty of tables and chairs under parasols in the front courtyard and on a terrace and picnic-sets beside the trout stream by a small stone bridge. Inside, the refurbished beamed rooms are painted in bold, contemporary colours, there's an appealing variety of dining and tub chairs, cushioned wall seats, leather-padded benches, button-back sofas and both high and low stools around all sizes of wooden tables on bare floorboards or quarry tiles, lots of wall prints, candles in glass lanterns, books on shelves and both a woodburning stove and an open log fire. The atmosphere is friendly and relaxed and the staff are helpful and efficient. Banks's Serial Thriller, Bath Ales Gem Bitter, Ringwood Boondoggle and a beer named for the pub (from Ringwood) on handpump and several wines by the glass. The bedrooms are comfortable and the breakfasts good.

In addition to their well known steaks, the imaginative food includes lunchtime sandwiches, crispy crab, salmon and chilli cake with avocado and sweetcorn salsa and spicy yoghurt dressing, stilton and hazelnut-stuffed mushrooms with grape, endive and chive salad, gloucester old spot sausages with mash and bacon and onion gravy, ham with poached and fried egg, piccalilli and chips, butternut squash, parsnip and chickpea tagine, seafood and chorizo linguine, corn-fed free-range half chicken with honey and mustard glaze and coleslaw, and puddings such as lemon posset with home-made shortbread and butterscotch and apple crumble. *Benchmark main dish: steak burger with bacon, a choice of cheeses, burger sauce and chips £10.95. Two-course evening meal £16.00.*

Marstons ~ Manager Adam Ford ~ Real ale ~ (01249) 782213 ~ Open 8am-11pm ~ Bar food 8am-10pm ~ Restaurant ~ Children welcome ~ Dogs allowed in bar ~ Bedrooms: /£85 ~ www.whitehart-ford.com *Recommended by John and Gloria Isaacs, Jim and Maggie Cowell*

GREAT BEDWYN   SU2764   Map 2

Three Tuns

Village signposted off A338 S of Hungerford, or off A4 W of Hungerford via Little Bedwyn; High Street; SN8 3NU

Carefully refurbished village pub with simple furnishings and original features, a friendly welcome, three real ales and highly thought-of food

Gently refurbished by the enthusiastic chef-owner and his wife, this 18th-c village pub was once a bakery – you can still see the bread oven. The beamed front bar remains traditional and simply furnished with pubby chairs and stools on bare floorboards, an open fire, and Butcombe Bitter, Otter Bitter and Ramsbury Gold on handpump, 11 wines by the glass, local soft drinks and several malt whiskies; they've carefully kept plenty of the original features. The back dining room now has french windows into the garden, which has also been smartened up and has plenty of tables and chairs. They hope to renovate a barn to create guest bedrooms.

Cooked by the landlord and with everything from bread to ice-cream made in-house, the good food includes snacks such as chorizo scotch egg and pork and fennel salami, foie gras and duck ballotine, a british charcuterie plate, wild mushroom pasta with aged pecorino, oxtail, hock and kidney pie, pollock with truffled leeks and mussels, pigeon with black pudding, roast potatoes and cauliflower cheese, chicken kiev, confit duck leg with duck croquette, sticky red cabbage and celeriac purée, and puddings such as apple and blackberry crumble and custard and chocolate fondant with cookie dough ice-cream. *Benchmark main dish: crispy chicken thighs with peas, bacon and girolles £12.00. Two-course evening meal £21.50.*

Free house ~ Licensees James and Ashley Wilsey ~ Real ale ~ (01672) 870280 ~ Open 10am-11pm(9pm summer Sun, 6pm winter Sun); closed Mon, winter Sun evening ~

Bar food 12.30-2.30, 6-9.30; bar snacks all day ~ Restaurant ~ Children welcome ~
Dogs welcome ~ Live jazz last Sun of month ~ www.threetunsbedwyn.co.uk
Recommended by John Griffiths, Mr and Mrs P R Thomas

GRITTLETON
ST8680 Map 2

Neeld Arms 🍺 🛏️

*From M4 junction 17, follow A429 to Cirencester and immediately left,
signed Stanton St Quinton and Grittleton; SN14 6AP*

**Bustling village pub with popular food and beer and friendly staff;
comfortable bedrooms**

Our readers come back to this charming village pub on a regular basis
for the genuine welcome, friendly atmosphere and enjoyable food.
Dating from the 17th c, it's now largely open-plan with Cotswold-stone
walls, contemporary colours on wood panelling and a pleasant mix of
seating including bar stools, a traditional settle, window seats and pale
wooden dining chairs around an assortment of tables – each set with
fresh flowers. The little brick fireplace houses a woodburning stove and
there's an inglenook fireplace on the right. Wadworths IPA and 6X and
guests such as Three Castles Barbury Castle and Otter Ale on handpump,
served from the blue-painted panelled and oak-topped bar counter. The
back dining area has another inglenook with a big woodburning stove;
even back here, you still feel thoroughly part of the action. There's an
outdoor terrace with a pergola. The comfortable bedrooms have a lot
of character.

Reasonably priced and very good, the food includes lunchtime ciabatta
sandwiches, moules marinière, pigeon breast with raspberry vinaigrette, ham
and egg, wild mushroom stroganoff, local sausages and mash, pork medallions with
apple and calvados sauce, lambs kidneys with dijon mustard, grilled whole bass
with butter and parsley sauce, and puddings such as fresh mango crème brûlée and
lemon tart with mango and passion-fruit sorbet. *Benchmark main dish: pie of the
day £10.50. Two-course evening meal £18.00.*

Free house ~ Licensees Charlie and Boo West ~ Real ale ~ (01249) 782470 ~ Open 12-3,
5.30(7 Sun)-11.30 ~ Bar food 12-2, 6.30-9.30; 12-2.30, 7-9 Sun ~ Children welcome ~
Dogs welcome ~ Bedrooms: £50/£80 ~ www.neeldarms.co.uk
*Recommended by Michael Doswell, Nick Jerman, P M Newsome, Mike and Mary Carter, Sara Fulton,
Roger Baker*

LACOCK
ST9367 Map 2

Rising Sun 🍺

*Bewley Common, Bowden Hill – out towards Sandy Lane, up hill past abbey;
OS Sheet 173 map reference 935679; SN15 2PP*

**Unassuming stone pub with welcoming atmosphere, well liked food
and great views from garden**

Well worth the journey out of the touristy village, this cosy pub is
nestled on the side of a hill with a stunning 25-mile view over the
Avon Valley; plenty of modern steel and wood tables and chairs on
the big two-level terrace make the most of this, and the sunsets can
be glorious. Inside, three welcoming little rooms have been knocked
together to form one simply furnished area with a mix of wooden chairs
and tables on stone floors, country pictures and open fires; there's also
a conservatory with the same fantastic view as the terrace. Moles Best
Bitter, Barleymole and Mole Catcher on handpump, several wines by the

glass and maybe farm cider; friendly, helpful service and background music. Disabled access is tricky.

🍴 Well liked food includes ciabatta sandwiches, chicken livers on toast, smoked salmon with lemon and dill dressing, burger with relish and chips, sweet potato, spinach and broad bean risotto, sausage and mash with red onion gravy, chicken on bacon mash with garlic and mushroom sauce, and puddings. *Benchmark main dish: local ham, free-range eggs and chips £9.95. Two-course evening meal £17.00.*

Moles ~ Managers Julie & Chris Haslett ~ Real ale ~ (01249) 730363 ~ Open 12-3, 5-11; 12-11 Fri-Sun ~ Bar food 12-2.30(2 Sun), 5-9(7 Sun); 12-9 Fri, Sat, bank holidays ~ Restaurant ~ Children welcome ~ Dogs allowed in bar ~ www.therisingsunlacock.co.uk
Recommended by Lois Dyer, Chris and Angela Buckell, Simon and Mandy King, Mrs M Chater

LOWER CHUTE   SU3153 Map 2
Hatchet 🍺 🛏
The Chutes well signposted via Appleshaw off A342, 2.5 miles W of Andover; SP11 9DX

Unchanging and neatly kept old country inn with a friendly welcome for all, four beers and enjoyable food; comfortable bedrooms

Even though this thatched 13th-c cottage is tucked away down narrow lanes, there's always a chatty friendly atmosphere, plenty of locals and visitors and a warm welcome from the convivial landlord. The very low-beamed bar has a splendid 16th-c fireback in the huge fireplace (and a roaring winter log fire), a mix of captain's chairs and cushioned wheelbacks around oak tables and a peaceful local feel; there's also an extensive restaurant. Bowmans Swift One, Otter Bitter, Sharps Doom Bar and Timothy Taylors Landlord on handpump, a dozen wines by the glass, 25 malt whiskies and several farm ciders; board games, cribbage and background music. There are seats out on a terrace and on the side grass and a safe play area for children. The snug bedrooms make this a fine place to stay overnight (dogs are welcome in one bedroom); breakfasts are hearty.

🍴 Good popular food includes deep-fried whitebait with tartare sauce, chicken liver pâté with apricot chutney, spinach and red pepper lasagne, ham, egg and chips, lamb shanks in redcurrant and rosemary sauce, chicken in bacon, leek and stilton sauce, liver and bacon with onion gravy, salmon supreme in tarragon sauce, and puddings. *Benchmark main dish: steak in ale pie £9.95. Two-course evening meal £17.00.*

Free house ~ Licensee Jeremy McKay ~ Real ale ~ (01264) 730229 ~ Open 11.30-3, 6-11; 12-4, 7-10.30 Sun ~ Bar food 12-2.15, 6.30-9.45; 12-3, 7-9.30 Sun ~ Restaurant ~ Children welcome ~ Dogs welcome ~ Bedrooms: £70/£90 ~ www.thehatchetinn.com
Recommended by Ian Herdman, N R White

MANTON   SU1768 Map 2
Outside Chance ♀
Village (and pub) signposted off A4 just W of Marlborough; High Street; SN8 4HW

Popular dining pub, civilised and traditional, nicely reworked with sporting theme; interesting modern food

This is a charming country pub in a quiet village just outside Marlborough. The three small linked rooms have flagstones or bare boards, hops on beams, and mainly plain pub furnishings such as chapel chairs and a long-cushioned pew; one room has a more cosseted feel, with panelling and a comfortable banquette. The décor celebrates unlikely winners, such as 100-1 Grand National winners Coughoo and Fuinavon, Mr Spooner's Only Dreams (a 100-1 winner at Leicester in 2007) or the odd-gaited little Seabiscuit who cheered many thousands of Americans with his dogged pursuit of victory during the Depression years. There's a splendid log fire in the big main fireplace and maybe fresh flowers and candlelight; background music and board games. Wadworths IPA and 6X and a guest like Horizon on handpump, quite a few good wines by the glass, nicely served coffees and neatly dressed young staff. A suntrap side terrace has contemporary metal-framed granite-topped tables and the good-sized garden has sturdy rustic tables and benches under ash trees; they have private access to the local playing fields and children's play area.

Good interesting food includes eggs benedict, piquillo pepper and black pudding stack with fried egg, meze and charcuterie boards, cajun chicken in creamy dressing, potato gnocchi with tomato and chilli sauce, beer-battered fresh fish and chips, barbary duck breast with rosemary mash, smoked pancetta and baby onions, lamb rump with chorizo, pepper and chickpea stew, and puddings such as warm chocolate brownie and apple crumble with home-made vanilla custard. *Benchmark main dish: burger with smoked bacon, cheddar, salad, home-made coleslaw and chips £12.95. Two-course evening meal £20.50.*

Wadworths ~ Tenant Howard Spooner ~ Real ale ~ (01672) 512352 ~ Open 12-3, 5.30-11; 12-11 Sat, Sun ~ Bar food 12-2.30(3 weekends), 6(7 Sun)-9 ~ Children welcome ~ Dogs welcome ~ www.theoutsidechance.co.uk *Recommended by Mr and Mrs P R Thomas*

MARLBOROUGH   SU1869   Map 2

Lamb £

The Parade; SN8 1NE

Friendly former coaching inn with big helpings of popular food, real ales, plenty of customers and traditional pubby furnishings; comfortable bedrooms

Dating from the 17th c, this tucked away, traditional local always has plenty of customers. There's a friendly atmosphere and the L-shaped bar has lots of hop bines, wall banquette seating and wheelback chairs around cast-iron-framed pubby tables on parquet flooring, Cecil Aldin prints on red walls, candles in bottles and a two-way log-effect gas fire; the easy-going bulldog may be poddling about. Wadworths 6X and a guest tapped from the cask and several wines by the glass; games machine, juke box, darts and TV. There are green picnic-sets and modern alloy and wicker seats and tables in the attractive back courtyard. The bedrooms are light and cottagey (some are in the former stable block) and the breakfasts hearty. The summer window boxes are very pretty.

Cooked by the landlady, the generous helpings of popular food includes lunchtime sandwiches and toasties, eggs benedict, seared squid, chorizo and feta salad, corned beef hash with fried egg and pickle, all-day breakfast, steak and kidney in ale pie, thai coconut, sweet potato, chickpea and spinach curry, battered cod and chips, free-range pork sausages with bubble and squeak and pickled red cabbage, and puddings such as sticky toffee pudding and gooseberry and elderflower crumble. *Benchmark main dish: slow-cooked pork belly £11.00. Two-course evening meal £16.00.*

Wadworths ~ Tenant Vyv Scott ~ Real ale ~ (01672) 512668 ~ Open 11-11(11.30 Sat);
12-10.30 Sun ~ Bar food 12-2.30, 6-9; not Fri-Sun evenings ~ Children welcome ~ Dogs
allowed in bar ~ Live music monthly ~ Bedrooms: /£70 ~ www.thelambinnmarlborough.com
Recommended by Tony Baldwin, Ian Herdman, D and M T Ayres-Regan

MARSTON MEYSEY
SU1297   Map 2
Old Spotted Cow
Off A419 Swindon–Cirencester; SN6 6LQ

**An easy-going atmosphere in cottagey bar rooms, friendly young staff,
lots to look at, well kept ales and enjoyable food**

There are cows of some sort all around this cheerfully run stone pub:
paintings, drawings and postcards, all manner and colour of china
ones – some actually are spotted – and embroidery and toy ones too; they
also have lots of beer mats and bank notes pinned to beams. The main
bar has high-backed cushioned dining chairs around chunky pine tables
on wooden floorboards or parquet, a few rugs here and there, an open
fire at each end of the room (comfortable sofas in front of one), fresh
flowers and candles in brass candlesticks and Butcombe Gold, Moles Tap
and St Austell Tribute on handpump, eight wines by the glass, farm cider,
a proper bloody mary and home-made cordials served by warmly friendly
young staff. Two cottagey dining rooms lead off here with similar tables
and chairs, a couple of long pews and a big bookshelf. There are seats
and picnic-sets on the front grass and a children's play area beyond a big
willow tree. The bedrooms will be ready by Christmas 2013.

 From a varied menu, the good food includes sandwiches, crispy duck salad
with soy and sesame dressing, smoked salmon and spring onion pancakes with
wasabi, mussels and bacon in cider with chips, black bean, chilli and chocolate
burritos with salsa and avocado, megrim sole in lemon and butter with garlic mash,
chicken holstein with warm potato, celery and fennel salad, lemon and parsley
lamb burger in pitta bread with feta, cucumber and chilli, rib-eye steak with
roasted vine tomatoes, rocket and parmesan, and puddings. *Benchmark main
dish: bubble and squeak with bacon, mustard cream and poached free-range egg
£8.00. Two-course evening meal £18.50.*

Free house ~ Licensee Anna Langley-Poole ~ Real ale ~ (01285) 810264 ~ Open 11-11
(9.30 Sun); 11-6 Sun in winter ~ Bar food 12-2(3 Sun), 7-9 ~ Children welcome but must
be over 10 in bar ~ Dogs allowed in bar ~ www.theoldspottedcow.co.uk
Recommended by Gavin May, Isobel Mackinlay

NEWTON TONY
SU2140   Map 2
Malet Arms 🍴 🍺
Village signposted off A338 Swindon–Salisbury; SP4 0HF

**Smashing village pub with no pretensions, a good choice of local beers
and highly thought-of food**

As ever, our readers enjoy this river-fronted old coaching inn very
much for its cheerful informality and unpretentious charm – all
helped along by the friendly, enthusiastic landlord. The low-beamed
interconnecting rooms have nice furnishings, including a mix of tables
of different sizes with high-winged wall settles, carved pews, chapel
and carver chairs, and lots of pictures, mainly from imperial days. The
main front windows are said to be made from the stern of a ship, and
there's a log and coal fire in a huge fireplace. The snug is noteworthy for
its fantastic collection of photographs and prints celebrating the local

aviation history of Boscombe Down, together with archive photographs of Stonehenge festivals of the 1970s and '80s. At the back is a homely dining room. Four real ales on handpump come from breweries such as Andwell, Butcombe, Fullers, Itchen Valley, Ramsbury, Salisbury, Stonehenge and Triple fff and they also keep 40 malt whiskies, eight wines by the glass and Weston's Old Rosie cider. There are seats on the small front terrace with more on grass and in the back garden. Getting to the pub takes you through a ford and it may be best to use an alternative route in winter, as the water can be quite deep. There's an all-weather cricket pitch on the village green.

Using seasonal game from local shoots (bagged by the landlord), lamb raised in the surrounding fields, free-range local pork and baking their own bread, the enjoyable and interesting food might include pancetta and avocado salad with honey and mustard dressing, salt and pepper squid with spring onions and chilli, steak and mushroom pie, whole plaice with gremolata and crushed new potatoes, venison stew with chilli, garlic and peanuts, creamy fish pie, good changing curries, crispy pork belly with bramley apple sauce and vegetables, and puddings such as rhubarb crumble tart with fig and honey ice-cream and devon fudge cheesecake. *Benchmark main dish: game pie £11.75. Two-course evening meal £17.50.*

Free house ~ Licensees Noel and Annie Cardew ~ Real ale ~ (01980) 629279 ~ Open 11-3, 6-11; 12-3, 7-10.30 Sun ~ Bar food 12-2.30, 6.30-10 (6-9 Sun) ~ Restaurant ~ Children only in restaurant or snug ~ Dogs allowed in bar ~ www.maletarms.com
Recommended by Andre Peathey-Johns, Phyl and Jack Street, Pat and Tony Martin, Chris and Jan Swanwick, James Bedforth, Mr and Mrs P R Thomas, Tony and Rachel Schendel, S G N Bennett, Howard and Margaret Buchanan

NORTON
ST8884 Map 2
Vine Tree ⏃ ♈
4 miles from M4 junction 17; A429 towards Malmesbury, then left at Hullavington, Sherston signpost, then follow Norton signposts; in village turn right at Foxley signpost, which takes you into Honey Lane; SN16 0JP

Civilised dining pub with beams and candlelight, big choice of first class seasonal food, super wines and a sizeable garden

With plenty to do and see nearby – as well as good walks and the county's official cycle route – this civilised and friendly place is always buzzing with visitors and loyal locals; it's best to book a table in advance. Three neatly kept small rooms open into one other, with aged beams, some old settles and unvarnished wooden tables on flagstone floors, big cream church altar candles, a woodburning stove at one end of the restaurant and a large open fireplace in the central bar, and limited edition and sporting prints; look out for Clementine, the friendly and docile black labrador. St Austell Trelawny and Tribute, Stonehenge Pigswill and a guest like Otter Bitter on handpump, 48 wines by the glass including sparkling wines and champagne, and quite a choice of malt whiskies and Armagnacs, as well as mulled wine in the winter and award-winning bloody marys year-round. There are picnic-sets and a children's play area in a two-acre garden, plus a pretty suntrap terrace with teak furniture under big cream umbrellas, and an attractive smokers' shelter. Pets (including horses!) are welcomed and provided for. Look out for the two ghosts that some visitors have spotted. The licensees also run the Barbury at Broad Hinton.

As well as a Tuesday lunch club, a moules frites night on Wednesdays and a special fish and seafood menu on Friday evenings, the first class food continues to use the best local produce (particularly game) available: hearty sandwiches, salt and pepper squid with garlic saffron mayonnaise, chicken liver parfait with apple chutney, vegetarian antipasti board or charcuterie platter, organic chicken kiev with bacon, shallots, parsley and paprika, lamb two-ways (herb-crusted rack and crispy breast) with rosemary olive oil-infused sweet potatoes, seasonal ratatouille and red wine jus, luxury fish stew, venison steak in juniper oil with turnip, hazelnuts and greens and port game sauce, and puddings such as pear tarte tatin with toffee sauce and chocolate nemesis with warm chocolate sauce and chantilly cream. *Benchmark main dish: moules frites with home-made mayonnaise £9.95. Two-course evening meal £18.95.*

Free house ~ Licensees Charles Walker and Tiggi Wood ~ Real ale ~ (01666) 837654 ~ Open 12-3, 6-midnight; 12-midnight Sat, Sun; closed winter Sun evenings ~ Bar food 12-2.30(3.30 Sun), 7-9.30(10 Fri, Sat) ~ Restaurant ~ Children welcome ~ Dogs welcome ~ www.thevinetree.co.uk *Recommended by Roger and Anne Mallard, Rod Stoneman, James Morrell, David Jackman*

PITTON   SU2131   Map 2
Silver Plough ♀ ⇔

Village signed from A30 E of Salisbury (follow brown signs); SP5 1DU

Bustling country dining pub with popular, reasonably priced bar food, good drinks and nearby walks; bedrooms

Being warmly welcoming and cheerful themselves, the licensees here have created a lively, bustling atmosphere and the place is always packed with happy customers. The comfortable and neatly kept front bar has plenty to look at as the black beams are strung with hundreds of antique boot-warmers and stretchers, pewter and china tankards, copper kettles, toby jugs, earthenware and glass rolling pins and so forth. Seats include half a dozen cushioned antique oak settles (one elaborately carved, beside a very fine reproduction of an Elizabethan oak table) around rustic pine tables; they keep Badger Bitter, First Gold and Tanglefoot on handpump and 13 wines by the glass served from a bar made from a hand-carved Elizabethan overmantel. The back bar is simpler, but still has a big winged high-backed settle, cases of antique guns and some substantial pictures; there are two woodburning stoves for winter warmth; background music. The skittle alley is for private use only. The quiet south-facing lawn has picnic-sets and other tables under cocktail parasols and there are more seats on a heated terrace; occasional barbecues. If you stay overnight and don't have breakfast, prices will be cheaper than those given below. They keep dog biscuits on the bar in the snug bar. There are plenty of walks in the surrounding woodland and on downland paths.

As well as a two- and three-course set lunch (Monday-Thursday in autumn), the popular food includes sandwiches, chicken liver pâté, garlic king prawns, beer-battered fish and chips, chilli con carne with sour cream and nachos, vegetable lasagne, sausage and mash with onion gravy, half rack of ribs with Jack Daniels barbecue sauce, salmon fillet with herby rösti potatoes and garlic and lemon butter sauce, chicken and mushrooms in white wine, cream and tarragon sauce, and puddings. *Benchmark main dish: steak in ale pie £10.95. Two-course evening meal £16.00.*

Badger ~ Tenants Stephen and Susan Keyes ~ Real ale ~ (01722) 712266 ~ Open 12-3, 6-11(10.30 Mon); 12-9.30 Sun ~ Bar food 12-2, 6-9; 12-8 Sun ~ Restaurant ~ Children welcome ~ Dogs allowed in bar ~ Bedrooms: £60/£70 ~ www.silverplough-pitton.co.uk
Recommended by Phyl and Jack Street, Conor McGaughey, Malcolm and Maralyn Hinxman, Edward Mirzoeff, George Atkinson, N R White

POULSHOT

Raven
Off A361; SN10 1RW

ST9760 Map 2

Pretty village pub with friendly licensees, enjoyable beer and food (cooked by the landlord) and seats in a walled back garden

With a reliably warm welcome and enjoyable food, this pretty half-timbered pub receives enthusiastic praise from our readers. The welcoming licensees take great care of both their pub and their customers, and the two cosy black-beamed rooms are spotlessly kept with comfortable banquettes, pubby chairs and tables and an open fire. Wadworths IPA and 6X plus a weekend guest beer tapped from the cask; background music in the dining room only. The jack russell is called Faith and the doberman, Harvey. There are picnic-sets under parasols in the walled back garden and the pub is just across from the village green.

Cooked by the landlord, the highly thought-of food includes baguettes, chicken liver pâté with spiced apple chutney, devilled whitebait with tartare sauce, chicken caesar salad, beer-battered haddock and chips, butternut squash and spinach cannelloni, burger with roasted red onions, cheese, bacon, coleslaw and garlic mayonnaise, gammon with pineapple or egg, liver and bacon with red wine gravy, mutton and sweet potato curry, and puddings such as gooseberry flapjack tart and sticky toffee pudding with toffee sauce. *Benchmark main dish: steak and kidney pie £11.50. Two-course evening meal £17.50.*

Wadworths ~ Tenants Jeremy and Nathalie Edwards ~ Real ale ~ (01380) 828271 ~ Open 11.30-3, 6.30-11; 12-3, 7-10.30 Sun; closed Mon, winter Sun evening ~ Bar food 12-2(2.30 Sun), 6-9 ~ Restaurant ~ Children welcome ~ Dogs allowed in bar ~ www.ravenpoulshot.co.uk *Recommended by Bridget Scott, Mr and Mrs P R Thomas*

SALISBURY
Haunch of Venison £
Minster Street, opposite Market Cross; SP1 1TB

SU1429 Map 2

Ancient pub oozing history, with tiny beamed rooms, unique fittings and a famous mummified hand

This ancient pub is really worth exploring while enjoying a pint of Courage Best, Hop Back GFB and Summer Lightning and Salisbury English Ale on handpump from a unique pewter bar counter – there's also a rare set of antique taps for gravity-fed spirits and liqueurs, 60 malt whiskies and several wines by the glass. Both the tiny downstairs rooms have a great deal of character and atmosphere, and date from 1320 when the place was used by craftsmen working on the cathedral spire. There are massive beams in the white ceiling, stout oak benches built into the timbered walls, black and white floor tiles and an open fire. A tiny snug (popular with locals, but historically said to be where the ladies drank) opens off the entrance lobby. Halfway up the stairs is a panelled room they call the House of Lords, which has a small-paned window looking down on to the main bar and a splendid fireplace that dates back to the building's early years; behind glass in a small wall slit is the smoke-preserved mummified hand of an 18th-c card sharp still clutching his cards.

Bar food includes creamy garlic mushrooms on toast, spiced ham hock terrine with piccalilli, creamy wild mushrooms and soft cheese puff pastry, venison and redcurrant sausages with red wine and onion gravy, smoked haddock, salmon and spring onion fishcake, free-range chicken with lemon and thyme butter, crackled pork belly with cider mustard sauce and spring onion mash, bass fillet with vegetable spaghetti and basil pesto, and puddings. *Benchmark main dish: venison and bacon casserole £11.95. Two-course evening meal £18.50.*

Scottish Courage ~ Lease Alex Marshall ~ Real ale ~ (01722) 411313 ~ Open 11-11(midnight Sat); 12-10 Sun ~ Bar food 12-2.30, 5-9 ~ Restaurant ~ Children welcome ~ Dogs allowed in bar ~ www.haunchofvenison.uk.com
Recommended by Ann and Colin Hunt, Howard and Margaret Buchanan, Andrea Rampley, Giles and Annie Francis, Paul Humphreys

SANDY LANE
George
A342 Devizes–Chippenham; SN15 2PX

ST9668 Map 2

Friendly licensees at immaculately kept old pub with open fires, Wadworths ales and well liked tasty food

Overlooking the small green in a charming village of thatched houses, this handsome Georgian pub looks more like a manor house than a pub. Run by friendly and helpful licensees, it has a neatly kept and cosy bar area with an open fire, plush stools and a mix of chairs around pubby tables on wooden flooring, Wadworths IPA and 6X and a guest such as Thwaites Nutty Black on handpump and 14 wines by the glass. There's also a back dining room with local artwork and a wooden-framed conservatory with farmhouse and other dining chairs around all sorts of tables on more pale floorboards. Outside, the terrace has rattan furniture and picnic-sets, with more seats on the lawn and pretty flower beds.

 Tasty food includes chicken and ham terrine with chutney, home-cured salmon gravadlax with celeriac remoulade, wild mushroom and garlic risotto cake with wild garlic and walnut pesto, home-cooked ham with bubble and squeak and free-range fried egg, lambs liver, smoked bacon, parsley mash and mint and madeira cream, rainbow trout with samphire, cherry tomatoes, mussels and dill, and puddings such as fruit crumble with custard and dark chocolate and pecan nut brownie with marmalade sauce and honeycomb ice-cream; they also serve afternoon cream teas. *Benchmark main dish: beer-battered daily fresh fish with tartare sauce and chips £12.50. Two-course evening meal £17.50.*

Wadworths ~ Tenants Mark and Harriet Jenkinson ~ Real ale ~ (01380) 850403 ~ Open 12-10.30(11 Sat); 12-3.30 Sun; closed Sun evening, Mon except bank holiday lunchtimes ~ Bar food 12-9(9.30 Fri, Sat); 12-2.30 Sun ~ Restaurant ~ Children welcome ~ Dogs allowed in bar ~ www.georgeinnsandylane.co.uk *Recommended by Michael Doswell, David Crook*

SHERSTON
Rattlebone ♀
Church Street; B4040 Malmesbury–Chipping Sodbury; SN16 0LR

ST8585 Map 2

Village pub with lots of atmosphere in rambling rooms, good bar food using local and free-range produce, and real ales; friendly staff

It's thought that the name Rattlebone comes from the Saxon habit of warrior-farmers wearing bags of bones around their necks – armour was just too expensive. This is a pub of great character with a bustling atmosphere in its softly lit rambling rooms. The public bar has a good mix of locals and visitors, there's a long back dining room and throughout you'll find beams, standing timbers and flagstones, pews, settles and country kitchen chairs around a mix of tables, armchairs and sofas and roaring fires. Purity Pure Gold, St Austell Tribute and Wells & Youngs Bitter on handpump, 16 wines by the glass from a thoughtful list, local cider and home-made lemonade; background music, board games, TV and games machine. Outside there's a skittle alley and three boules pitches, often in use by one of the many pub teams; a boules festival is held in July and mangold hurling (similar to boules but using cattle-feed turnips), as well as other events. The two pretty gardens include an extended terrace where they hold barbecues and spit roasts. Wheelchair access.

Using the best local, seasonal produce, the good food includes sandwiches, smoked salmon fishcake with hollandaise and poached egg, confit of chicken terrine with apple and brandy chutney and sweet pickled carrots, spinach and mushroom tortellini with roast tomato sauce, ham with free-range eggs, charcuterie board, pie of the day, trio of sausages with onion gravy, burger with onion rings, cheese, bacon and skinny fries, pancetta-wrapped free-range chicken breast with stilton mousse, thai fish curry, and puddings such as blackcurrant and frangipane tart with clotted cream and dark chocolate pot with blood orange marmalade and tangerine sorbet. *Benchmark main dish: wild boar ragout on fresh pasta £9.95. Two-course evening meal £10.50.*

Youngs ~ Tenant Jason Read ~ Real ale ~ (01666) 840871 ~ Open 12-3, 5-11 (midnight Fri); 12-midnight(11 Sun) Sat ~ Bar food 12-2.30, 6-9.30 ~ Restaurant ~ Children welcome ~ Dogs allowed in bar ~ Acoustic music evenings monthly ~ www.therattlebone.co.uk *Recommended by Michael Doswell, John and Gloria Isaacs, Tom and Ruth Rees, David Jackman, Michael Snelgrove*

SOUTH WRAXALL
Longs Arms 🍴

ST8364   Map 2

Upper South Wraxall, off B3109 N of Bradford-on-Avon; BA15 2SB

Friendly licensees at well run old stone inn with plenty of character, real ales and first class food using local seasonal produce

Our readers enjoy their visits to this handsome stone inn – you can be sure of a genuinely warm welcome and some excellent food. The bar has windsor and other pubby chairs around wooden tables on flagstones, a woodburning stove in the fireplace and high chairs by the counter where they keep Wadworths IPA and 6X and maybe a guest beer on handpump and nine wines by the glass. Another room has cushioned and other dining chairs, a nice old settle and a wall banquette around a mix of tables on carpeting, fresh flowers and lots of prints and paintings; a further room has attractive boxy settles and other seats on pale oak flooring. There are tables and chairs in the pretty little walled back garden, where they have raised beds and a greenhouse for salad leaves and herbs. They keep dog biscuits behind the bar.

As well as having a smoke house, baking their own bread and using local, seasonal produce, everything is made in-house (salami, ham, black pudding, haggis, ice-creams and sorbets, jams and chutneys). Also, lunchtime sandwiches, smoked salmon with pickled cucumber, lamb sweetbreads with white asparagus and truffle butter, twice-baked cheese soufflé, muntjac burger with chips, smoked pollack with spelt risotto and leeks, lamb shoulder with wild garlic, lobster and crab with samphire, and puddings such as bramley apple and cider crumble and chocolate tart with vanilla ice-cream. *Benchmark main dish: muntjac loin and salami with home-made medlar jelly and asparagus £16.50. Two-course evening meal £22.50.*

Wadworths ~ Tenants Rob and Liz Allcock ~ Real ale ~ (01225) 864450 ~ Open 12-3,
5.30-11; 12-11 Fri-Sun ~ Bar food 12-3, 5.30-9.30; 12-9.30 Fri, Sat; 12-4.30 Sun; not Mon ~
Restaurant ~ Children welcome ~ Dogs allowed in bar ~ www.thelongsarms.com
Recommended by Alan Sutton, Gareth Davies, D P and M A Miles, R L Borthwick, Pete Flower

SWINDON   SU1384   Map 2
Weighbridge Brewhouse ◧
Penzance Drive; SN5 7JL

**Stunning building with stylish modern décor, their own microbrewery
ales, a huge wine list, a big range of popular food and helpful staff**

There is indeed a brewhouse in this fantastic building (you can peek
through a glass viewing panel to see all the equipment) and they
serve six own-brewed ales at any one time: Weighbridge Brewhouse
Brinkworth Village, Dam Buster, Pooleys Golden, South Island,
Trainspotter and Weighbridge Best. Also, an enormous choice of wines
by the glass. It's a huge place with a steel-tensioned high-raftered roof
– the big central skylight adds even more light – and a bar area with
comfortable brown leather chesterfields and wood and leather armchairs
around a few tables on a dark flagstoned floor, much used blue bar chairs
against the long dimpled and polished steel counter and a sizeable carved
wooden eagle on a stand. The airy and stylish dining area has attractive
striped high-backed chairs and long wall banquettes, bare brick walls,
candles in red glass jars on the window sills and an end glass cabinet
displaying about 1,000 bottled beers from around the world. Metal stairs
lead up to an area with big sofas and chairs beside a glass piano that
overlooks the dining room below; there's also a room up here for smaller
parties and private functions. There are seats on an outside terrace.

Popular and very good – if not cheap – the wide choice of food includes home-
made faggots with red wine gravy and pepper mash, peppers, cherry tomatoes
and button mushrooms with fresh egg tagliatelle in a light sweet chilli and coconut
cream sauce, bubble and squeak with fried eggs and crispy bacon, sausages with
spring onion mash and onion gravy, bass fillets with scallops, prawns and scampi,
savoury butters and balsamic and raspberry dressing, half a crispy duck with cherry
wine and redcurrant sauce, and puddings such as banoffi pie and white chocolate
and raspberry brûlée. *Benchmark main dish: venison, wild boar and crocodile
with black pudding and wild mushrooms flambéed in cherry wine £24.00.
Two-course evening meal £29.00.*

Free house ~ Licensees Anthony and Allyson Windle ~ Real ale ~ (01793) 881500 ~
Open 11-11; 12-10.30 Sun ~ Bar food 12-2, 6-9.30; 12-8 Sun ~ Restaurant ~ Children
welcome before 8pm ~ Regular piano playing ~ www.weighbridgebrewhouse.co.uk
Recommended by Ruth May, Emma Scofield

TOLLARD ROYAL   ST9317   Map 2
King John 🍽 ⌷ ⛏
B3081 Shaftesbury–Sixpenny Handley; SP5 5PS

**Pleasing contemporary furnishings in carefully opened-up pub,
courteous helpful service, a good choice of drinks and excellent food;
pretty bedrooms**

On a bitterly cold and wet lunchtime inspection visit to this elegantly
furnished pub, we were warmly welcomed by the friendly staff and
an open log fire. L-shaped and opened up, it has an easy-going, civilised
feel and nice little touches such as a rosemary plant and tiny metal

buckets of salt and pepper on the scrubbed kitchen tables, dog-motif cushions, a screen made of wine box sides, a methuselah of wine on the counter and candles in big glass jars. An attractive mix of seats takes in spindlebacks, captain's and chapel chairs (some built into the bow windows) plus the odd cushioned settle, and there are big terracotta floor tiles, hound, hunting and a couple of blown-up antique spoon and knife photographs, a master of hounds picture and prints of early 19th-c scientists, and lantern-style wall lights. A second log fire has fender seats to each side and leather chesterfields in front, and there's a stuffed heron and grouse and daily papers. Butcombe Bitter, Fullers London Pride, Ramsbury Gold on handpump and good wines by the glass; you can buy wine from the shop too. At the front of the building are seats and tables under parasols with more up steps in the raised garden, where there's also an outdoor kitchen pavilion. The bedrooms are comfortable and pretty and there's a self-catering cottage opposite.

Delicious food using the best local, seasonal produce includes lunchtime sandwiches, rabbit and gherkins on toast, beetroot and dandelion salad with crottin de chavignol cheese, beer-battered line-caught fish and chips, twice-baked cheddar cheese soufflé, venison and steak haché with fried egg, wild garlic chicken kiev with slaw, merguez sausage with pommes purée and wine sauce, black bream fillet with smoked eel chowder, and puddings such as apple doughnuts with toffee sauce and mulled cider and hot chocolate toasted sandwich with vanilla ice-cream. *Benchmark main dish: 28-day aged rump steak with béarnaise sauce and chips £21.95. Two-course evening meal £24.00.*

Free house ~ Licensees Alex and Gretchen Booj ~ Real ale ~ (01725) 516207 ~ Open 12-3, 6-midnight ~ Bar food 12-2, 7-9 ~ Restaurant ~ Children welcome ~ Dogs welcome ~ Bedrooms: /£120 ~ www.kingjohninn.co.uk
Recommended by Mr and Mrs Lynn, Mr and Mrs J J A Davis

UPTON LOVELL
ST9441   Map 2
Prince Leopold
Up Street, village signed from A36; BA12 0JP

Snug little rooms, a friendly atmosphere, welcoming licensees and enjoyable food and drink; bedrooms

This is a prettily tucked away and neatly modernised Victorian pub that's made special by the charming and genuinely welcoming licensees; on our visit, they were taking round complimentary nibbles and dips and making sure all their customers were happy. The simply furnished bar – with lots of chatty, cheerful locals – has two farmhouse tables with sturdy chairs, well used bar stools against the hand-crafted elm counter and Butcombe Bitter, Fullers London Pride and Plain Ales Arty Farty on handpump and interesting wines by the glass. A cosy little dining room to the right of the door has bookshelves on either side of the open fire, candlelit tables, rugs on floorboards and an easy-going atmosphere. Two linked rooms lead off the bar with a mix of high-backed leather or wooden dining chairs, more rugs on floorboards and some country prints on pale green panelled walls; the second room has comfortable sofas around a table with daily papers and a few settles with tapestry and other cushions. The more formal restaurant overlooks the river. There are water bowls for dogs and seats in the terraced riverside garden. The cottagey bedrooms are comfortable and well equipped.

Using free-range and other carefully chosen local produce, the tempting food includes popular grazing boards, terrine of local game with chutney, hake and smoked salmon fishcakes with ribbon vegetables and sweet chilli, butternut squash and cumin filo pie with seasoned yoghurt, sausage, mash and onion gravy, slow-roast pork belly with smoked bacon, cider sauce and dauphinoise potatoes, venison haunch with juniper jus, and puddings such as vanilla panna cotta with berry compote and chocolate brownie with chocolate sauce and vanilla ice-cream. *Benchmark main dish: salmon with watercress butter and sautéed new potatoes £12.50. Two-course evening meal £22.00.*

Free house ~ Licensee Jayne Duff ~ Real ale ~ (01985) 850460 ~ Open 12-3, 6-11(midnight Fri, Sat); 12-3, 6-10 Sun ~ Bar food 12-2.30, 6.30-9.30; 12-3 Sun; not Sun evening except for residents ~ Restaurant ~ Children welcome ~ Dogs welcome ~ Bedrooms: £60/£75 ~ www.princeleopoldinn.co.uk *Recommended by Michael Levy, Edward Mirzoeff, Richard Zambuni, John and June Freeman*

WEST LAVINGTON   SU0052   Map 2
Bridge Inn
Church Street (A360); SN10 4LD

Friendly village pub with good bar food cooked by the landlord, real ales and a light, comfortable bar

With quite an emphasis on the enterprising food, this is a quietly civilised and easy-going dining pub. The comfortable spacious bar mixes contemporary features with firmly traditional fixtures such as the enormous brick inglenook with its roaring log fire; at the opposite end is a smaller modern fireplace, in an area set mostly for eating. The cream-painted or exposed brick walls are hung with local pictures of the Lavingtons and there are fresh flowers and evening candlelight; timbers and the occasional step divide the various areas. Sharps Doom Bar and Wadworths IPA on handpump, ten wines by the glass and half a dozen malt whiskies; background music. A raised lawn at the back makes a pleasant place to spend a summer's afternoon and there are large vegetable patches for home-grown produce and chickens; boules.

Cooked by the landlord, the interesting food includes a two- and three-course set lunch (Tuesday-Friday) as well as lunchtime sandwiches, fried foie gras with black pudding and poached rhubarb, chargrilled sardines with watercress and lemon salad and salsa verde, burger with red onion marmalade, onion rings and fries, seasonal vegetable risotto with buffalo mozzarella, black bream fillet with niçoise vegetables and romesco sauce, pork loin with potato cannelloni and air-dried tomato, and puddings. *Benchmark main dish: trio of lamb with fondant potato and mint and caper jus £16.50. Two-course evening meal £20.50.*

Enterprise ~ Lease Emily Robinson and James Stewart ~ Real ale ~ (01380) 813213 ~ Open 12-3, 6-10; 12-6.30(4.30 in winter) Sun; closed Sun evening, Mon ~ Bar food 12-2.30, 6.30-9; 12-4 Sun ~ Children welcome ~ Dogs allowed in bar ~ www.the-bridge-inn.co.uk *Recommended by Verity Wills, Mrs Blethyn Elliott*

WINSLEY   ST7960   Map 2
Seven Stars 🍴 🍺
Off B3108 bypass W of Bradford-on-Avon (pub just over Wiltshire border); BA15 2LQ

Attractive old stone pub with neatly kept bars, imaginative food, good real ales and friendly staff; seats outside

Partly dating from the early 18th c, this well run and handsome inn is at the heart of a pretty village. There's obviously quite a bit of emphasis on the interesting food, but plenty of jovial banter from locals enjoying their Bath Ales Gem Bitter, Skinners Knocker and Betty Stogs and Wadworths 6X creates a warm and informal atmosphere. The low-beamed linked areas have stripped-stone walls and light pastel paintwork, candlelight, farmhouse chairs and wooden tables on flagstones and carpeting and a woodburning stove in a stone fireplace; several wines by the glass, background music and board games. Outside, there are lots of picnic-sets and tables and chairs under parasols on the terrace or on neat grassy surrounds with flowering borders looking across to the bowling green opposite.

Making their own ice-cream and sorbets, jams, chutneys and pickles and baking their own bread, the tempting food includes ciabatta sandwiches, scallops on tempura calamari with lemon sauce, free-range chicken liver parfait with fruit chutney, ratatouille and fontina cheese strudel with basil cream and garlic potatoes, mussels with chilli, lemon grass and coconut broth, pie of the day, braised duck leg with white bean and sausage cassoulet, and puddings such as white chocolate and orange cheesecake with berry compote and treacle tart with clotted cream. *Benchmark main dish: fish and seafood pot in garlic and white wine with fries £13.90. Two-course evening meal £17.00.*

Free house ~ Licensee Alan Appleby ~ Real ale ~ (01225) 722204 ~ Open 12-2.30(3 Sat), 6-10.30(11 Sat); 12-3.30 Sun; closed Sun evening ~ Bar food 12-2, 6-9; 12-2.30 Sun ~ Children welcome ~ Dogs allowed in bar ~ www.sevenstarswinsley.co.uk
Recommended by Michael Doswell, Mr and Mrs P R Thomas, Taff Thomas

Also Worth a Visit in Wiltshire

Besides the fully inspected pubs, you might like to try these pubs that have been recommended to us and described by readers. Do tell us what you think of them: feedback@goodguides.com

ALDBOURNE SU2675
Blue Boar (01672) 540237
The Green (off B4192 in centre); SN8 2EN New licensees as we went to press for this popular village pub; left-hand bar is homely, with pubby seats around rustic tables on bare boards or flagstones, lots of low black beams in ochre ceiling, boar's head above bigger of two log fires, darts, board games, Wadworths ales, separate more modern dining bar on right; children and dogs have been welcome, picnic-sets in front overlooking pretty green, has opened all day weekends – reports please. *(Anon)*

ALDBOURNE SU2675
Crown (01672) 540214
The Square; SN8 2DU Old local overlooking pretty village's pond, good value straightforward food including pizzas and Sun carvery, Sharps Doom Bar, Shepherd Neame Spitfire and guests, friendly helpful staff, comfortable two-part beamed lounge with sofas by log fire in huge brick inglenook

linking to public bar, old tables and bare boards, small nicely laid out dining room, darts, Tues quiz; background and some live music; children and dogs welcome, courtyard tables, Early English church nearby, four bedrooms. *(Neil and Anita Christopher)*

ALVEDISTON ST9723
Crown (01722) 780335
Off A30 W of Salisbury; SP5 5JY Refurbished 15th-c thatched inn, three cosy very low-beamed partly panelled rooms, two inglenooks, good choice of enjoyable fairly priced home-made food, well kept ales such as Plain and Sixpenny, Wessex cider, pleasant service; children and dogs welcome, pretty views from attractive garden with terrace, good local walks, three bedrooms, open all day weekends (till 9pm Sun). *(David and Judy Robison)*

AVEBURY SU1069
Red Lion (01672) 539266
High Street (A361); SN8 1RF Greene King pub substantially extended from pretty thatched front part, in tourist hotspot so

If you know a pub is ever open all day, please tell us.

can be very busy, good choice of reasonably priced food, plenty of wines by the glass, open fires; may be background music; children welcome, open all day. *(Jenny and Brian Seller)*

BADBURY   SU1980
⋆**Plough** (01793) 740342

A346 (Marlborough Road) just S of M4 junction 15; SN4 0EP Country pub well placed for M4 with good choice of enjoyable fairly priced food (all day weekends), friendly helpful staff, well kept Arkells and decent wines, large rambling bar with log fire, light airy dining room; background music; children and dogs welcome, tree-shaded garden with downs views, open all day. *(Pat Crabb)*

BARFORD ST MARTIN   SU0531
⋆**Barford Inn** (01722) 742242

B3089 W of Salisbury (Grovely Road), just off A30; SP3 4AB Welcoming 16th-c coaching inn, dark panelled front bar with big log fire, other interlinking rooms, old utensils and farming tools, beamed bare-brick restaurant, wide choice of enjoyable fairly priced food including deals, prompt friendly service, well kept Badger ales and decent wines by the glass; children welcome, dogs in bar, disabled access (not to bar) and facilities, terrace tables, more in back garden, four comfortable annexe bedrooms, good walks, open all day. *(Dennis Jenkin)*

BECKHAMPTON   SU0868
⋆**Waggon & Horses** (01672) 539418

A4 Marlborough–Calne; SN8 1QJ Handsome stone and thatch former coaching inn; generous fairly priced home-made food from varied menu in open-plan beamed bar or separate dining area, well kept Wadworths ales, cheerful service; background music; children and dogs welcome, pleasant raised garden with play area, handy for Avebury, open all day. *(Sheila and Robert Robinson, P A Rowe, David Crook)*

BERWICK ST JAMES   SU0739
⋆**Boot** (01722) 790243

High Street (B3083); SP3 4TN Welcoming flint and stone pub not far from Stonehenge, good locally sourced food from daily changing blackboard menu, friendly efficient staff, well kept Wadworths ales and a guest, huge log fire in inglenook at one end, sporting prints over brick fireplace at other, lit candles, small back dining room with collection of celebrity boots; children and dogs welcome, sheltered side lawn. *(Fr Robert Marsh, N R White, Gavin McLauchlan)*

BIDDESTONE   ST8673
Biddestone Arms (01249) 714377

Off A420 W of Chippenham; The Green; SN14 7DG Welcoming spacious pub mostly set up for its well liked food from standards to specials, good vegetarian options and Sun carvery too, friendly helpful service,

well kept ales such as Wadworths, games in compact public bar, nice open fire; children and dogs (in bar) allowed, tables in pretty back garden, attractive village with lovely pond. *(Cane family, Jenny Hughes)*

BISHOPSTONE   SU2483
Royal Oak (01793) 790481

Cues Lane; near Swindon; at first exit roundabout from A419 N of M4 junction 15, follow Wanborough sign, then keep on to Bishopstone, at small sign to pub turn right; SN6 8PP Informal dining pub run by local farmers using seasonal produce including properly hung home-reared steaks (farm shop too) for their good daily changing menu; mainly scrubbed-wood furnishings on bare boards or parquet, animal pictures for sale, log fire on left and little maze of dark pews, Arkells beers, organic wines, over 30 malt whiskies and good choice of gins, maybe home-made elderflower cordial, charity shelves and window sills of paperbacks; children and dogs welcome, picnic-sets on grass and among trees, smarter modern tables on front deck, cheap serviceable bedrooms in back cabins, pretty village below Ridgeway and White Horse, closed Sun evening. *(David Jackman, R T and J C Moggridge, Alistair Forsyth, Brian Glozier)*

BOX   ST8168
Northey Arms (01225) 742333

A4, Bath side; SN13 8AE Stone-built 19th-c dining pub with good choice of enjoyable food all day, Wadworths ales, decent wines by the glass, fresh contemporary décor with chunky modern tables and high-backed rattan chairs; background music; children welcome, garden tables, five new bedrooms, open all day from 8am for breakfast. *(Mr and Mrs P R Thomas)*

BOX   ST8369
⋆**Quarrymans Arms** (01225) 743569

Box Hill; from Bath on A4 right into Bargates 50 metres before railway bridge, left up Quarry Hill at T junction, left again at grassy triangle; from Corsham, left after Rudloe Park Hotel into Beech Road, third left on to Barnetts Hill, and right at top of hill; OS Sheet 173 map reference 834694; SN13 8HN Enjoyable unpretentious pub with friendly staff and informal relaxed atmosphere, comfortable rather than overly smart (even mildly untidy in parts), plenty of mining-related photographs and memorabilia dotted around (once the local of Bath-stone miners – licensees run interesting guided trips down mine itself), one modernised room with open fire set aside for drinking, Butcombe, Moles, Wadworths and guests, 60 malt whiskies, several wines by the glass, tasty bar food at fair prices; children and dogs welcome, picnic-sets on terrace with sweeping views, popular with walkers and potholers, bedrooms, open all day. *(Guy Vowles, Ian*

Herdman, Peter Salmon, Mr and Mrs A H Young, MJVK, Dr and Mrs A K Clarke)

BRADFORD LEIGH ST8362
Plough (01225) 862037
B3109 N of Bradford-on-Avon; BA15 2RW Welcoming family-run pub with enjoyable reasonably priced food including fresh fish in extended dining area, well kept Otter, Sharps and guests, good friendly service, cheery public bar with fire; children welcome, play area in big garden, bedrooms. *(Bernard Sulzmann, R L Borthwick)*

BRADFORD-ON-AVON ST8260
Barge (01225) 863403
Frome Road; BA15 2EA Large modernised open-plan pub set down from canal, well kept ales such as Brakspears, Fullers, Marstons and Ringwood, good wines by the glass, enjoyable pub food including children's choices, stripped stone and flagstones, solid furniture, woodburners; wheelchair access, garden with smokers' pavilion, steps up to canalside picnic-sets, moorings, bedrooms. *(Chris and Angela Buckell, Phil Bryant, J D O Carter)*

BRADFORD-ON-AVON ST8261
☀ Castle (01225) 865657
Mount Pleasant, by junction with A363, N edge of town; extremely limited pub parking, spaces in nearby streets; BA15 1SJ Friendly young landlady and cheerful staff at this imposing stone pub; unspoilt bar with individual atmosphere, wide range of seating on dark flagstones, church candles, daily papers and good log fire, Abbey, Exmoor, Glastonbury, Milk Street and Three Castles, farm cider and nice wines, good all-day food from breakfast on, bare-boards rooms on right similar in style; background music, board games; children welcome, long tables and benches on sunny front terrace with sweeping town views, comfortable bedrooms, open all day. *(Dr and Mrs A K Clarke, Mike and Mary Carter, Chris and Angela Buckell, Mr and Mrs P R Thomas)*

BRADFORD-ON-AVON ST8060
Cross Guns (01225) 862335
Avoncliff, 2 miles W; OS Sheet 173 map reference 805600; BA15 2HB Congenial bustle on summer days with swarms of people in floodlit partly concreted areas steeply terraced above the bridges, aqueducts and river; appealingly quaint at quieter times, with stripped-stone low-beamed bar, 16th-c inglenook, full Box Steam range kept well and a guest, several ciders, lots of malt whiskies and interesting wines by the glass including country ones, comprehensive choice of enjoyable food from baguettes up, good friendly service, upstairs river-view restaurant; children and dogs welcome, wheelchair accessible, bedrooms, open all day. *(Peter Salmon, Alan Sutton, Paul Humphreys, Don Bryan)*

BRADFORD-ON-AVON ST8161
Dog & Fox (01225) 862137
Ashley Road; BA15 1RT Traditional pub under welcoming new licensees; three well kept ales and three good ciders, enjoyable straightforward low-priced food (not Sun or Mon evenings); children welcome, garden with play area, open all day weekends. *(Taff Thomas)*

BRINKWORTH SU0184
Three Crowns (01666) 510366
The Street; B4042 Wootton Bassett– Malmesbury; SN15 5AF Dining pub but with traditional bar (some refurbishment under newish management), horsebrasses on dark beams, tapestry-upholstered pews and log fire, Fullers London Pride, Sharps Doom Bar and guests, a dozen wines by the glass, food from pub favourites up including good steaks, most people eat in conservatory or airy garden room; background music; children and dogs (in bar) welcome, heated terrace, more tables in garden looking across to church and farmland, open all day. *(Tom and Ruth Rees, Ian Herdman, Kristin Warry)*

BROMHAM ST9665
Greyhound (01380) 850241
Off A342; High Street; SN15 2HA Popular old beamed dining pub with light modern décor, comfortable sofas and log fires, walk-across well in back bar, wide choice of good reasonably priced home-made food (all day) including weekday set lunch, efficient friendly service, particularly well kept Wadworths ales, wide choice of wines, upstairs skittle alley/restaurant; children welcome, pretty hanging baskets in front, big enclosed garden (dogs allowed here) with decking and boules. *(Sue Vince)*

BULKINGTON ST9458
☀ Well (01380) 828287
High Street; SN10 1SJ Roomy and attractively modernised open-plan pub, good value competently cooked food from traditional favourites to interesting well presented restaurant-style dishes, good Sun roasts too, efficient friendly service, ales such as Butcombe, Sharps, Timothy Taylors and Wadworths, well priced wines. *(Steve Price, Paul Humphreys)*

BURCOMBE SU0631
☀ Ship (01722) 743182
Burcombe Lane; brown sign to pub off A30 W of Salisbury, then turn right; SP2 0EJ Busy pub and most customers here for the food – pubby dishes through to elaborate pricey restaurant-style meals; area by entrance with log fire, beams and leather-cushioned wall and window seats on dark slate tiles, steps up to spreading area of pale wood dining chairs around bleached tables on neat dark brown wood-strip floor, more beams (one supporting a splendid

chandelier), small modern pictures and big church candles, Butcombe, Ringwood and Wadworths, good choice of wines by the glass and whiskies; background music; children welcome, dogs in bar, picnic-sets in informal back garden sloping down to willows by safely fenced-off River Nadder. *(Andre Dugas, Col and Mrs Patrick Kaye)*

BURTON   ST8179
Old House At Home   (01454) 218227
B4039 Chippenham–Chipping Sodbury; SN14 7LT Spacious ivy-clad stone dining pub, popular food including fresh fish and game, friendly efficient service, a couple of well kept ales and good choice of wines by the glass, log fire; open all day serving food from breakfast on. *(Roger and Donna Huggins)*

CASTLE COMBE   ST8477
Castle Inn   (01249) 783030
Off A420; SN14 7HN Handsome inn in remarkably preserved Cotswold village, beamed bar with big inglenook, padded bar stools and fine old settle, hunting and vintage motor racing pictures, Butcombe and Great Western, decent wines by the glass, well liked bar food and more restaurant evening menu, friendly attentive service, two snug sitting rooms, formal dining rooms and big upstairs eating area opening on to charming little roof terrace; no dogs; children welcome, tables out at front looking down idyllic main street, fascinating medieval church clock, 11 bedrooms, limited parking, open all day. *(Anon)*

CHARLTON   ST9688
Horse & Groom   (01666) 823904
B4040 towards Cricklade; SN16 9DL Smartly refurbished stone-built village inn under Marco Pierre White's Wheeler's of St James's brand; flagstones and log fire in proper bar (dogs welcome), interlinked dining areas with stylish décor, well liked food from pub standards to upscale modern cooking, polished friendly service, ales including a house beer from Lees, good choice of wines by the glass; tables out under trees, play area, five well appointed bedrooms, good breakfast, open all day. *(Anon)*

CHILMARK   ST9732
Black Dog   (01722) 716344
B3089 Salisbury–Hindon; SP3 5AH Comfortable 15th-c beamed village pub with several cosy linked areas, cushioned window seats, inglenook woodburner, enjoyable well priced food including sandwiches and pizzas, prompt courteous service, Wadworths ales; good-sized roadside garden. *(B and F A Hannam, Muriel and John Hobbs, John and Alison Hamilton, Mr and Mrs J Davis)*

CHIRTON   SU0757
Wiltshire Yeoman   (01380) 840665
Andover Road (A342 SE of Devizes); SN10 3QN Red-brick 19th-c roadside pub

under new management, traditional pub food with a twist, Wadworths ales, proper bar with log fire, separate carpeted dining room, skittle alley/function area; background music; children and dogs welcome, back garden with heated gazebo, has closed Sun evening, Mon. *(Anon)*

CHITTERNE   ST9843
Kings Head   (01985) 850770
B390 Heytesbury–Shrewton; BA12 0LJ Attractive traditional pub under friendly management, slate-floor bar with wood burner, two dining areas, well kept Flowers and Plain (brewed in the village), home-made pubby food (Tues-Sat evenings, Sun lunchtime); children and dogs welcome, side garden, pretty village, handy for Salisbury Plain walks. *(Hugh Roberts)*

CORSHAM   ST8770
Flemish Weaver   (01249) 701929
High Street; SN13 0EZ Welcoming town pub in attractive 17th-c building, three main areas mostly set for good value popular food, Bath Gem, Sharps Doom Bar and a couple of guests; children and dogs welcome, tables in back courtyard, open all day. *(Elizabeth Stedman, Dr and Mrs A K Clarke)*

CORSHAM   ST8670
★ Two Pigs   (01249) 712515
Pickwick (A4); SN13 0HY Friendly and cheerfully eccentric little beer-lovers' pub run by individualistic landlord – most lively on Mon evenings when there's live music; zany collection of bric-a-brac in narrow dimly lit flagstoned bar, enamel signs on wood-clad walls, pig-theme ornaments and old radios, Stonehenge ales including Pigswill and a couple of guests, no food; background blues, no under-21s; covered yard outside called the Sty, closed lunchtimes except Sun. *(Dr and Mrs A K Clarke, Roger and Donna Huggins)*

CORTON   ST9340
★ Dove   (01985) 850109
Off A36 at Upton Lovell, SE of Warminster; BA12 0SZ Popular food from ciabattas and pub favourites to more enterprising dishes, good service, up to five well kept ales and nice wines by the glass, renovated linked rooms with flagstones and oak boards, woodburner in bar, flowers on dining room tables, conservatory; can get very busy; children and dogs welcome, wheelchair access, rustic furniture in garden, lovely valley, five comfortable courtyard bedrooms, open all day Sun. *(Chris and Angela Buckell)*

CROCKERTON   ST8642
★ Bath Arms   (01985) 212262
Off A350 Warminster–Blandford; BA12 8AJ Welcoming old dining pub, bar with plush banquettes and matching chairs, well spaced tables on parquet, beams in

whitewashed ceiling, crackling log fire, three Wessex ales, real cider and several wines by the glass, well liked food including some interesting modern dishes, cheerful staff, two formal dining rooms with chunky pine furniture; background music; children and dogs welcome, several garden areas with plenty of picnic-sets, gets crowded during school holidays (Longleat close by), bedrooms, open all day weekends. *(Michael Doswell, Mr and Mrs A H Young, Taff Thomas, Mrs P Bishop)*

DEVIZES   SU0061
Bear (01380) 722444
Market Place; SN10 1HS Refurbished ancient coaching inn, big carpeted main bar with log fires, winged wall settles and upholstered bucket armchairs, steps up to room named after portrait painter Thomas Lawrence with oak-panelled walls and big open fireplace, well kept Wadworths and extensive choice of wines by the glass, enjoyable food from sandwiches and light dishes up, Bear Grills bistro, cellar bar with live music (Fri) and comedy night (first Thurs of month); children welcome, dogs in front bar, wheelchair access throughout, mediterranean-style courtyard, 25 bedrooms, open all day. *(Theocsbrian)*

DEVIZES   SU0061
British Lion (01380) 720665
A361 Swindon roundabout; SN10 1LQ Chatty bare-boards beer-lover's pub with good choice of well kept changing ales, brewery posters and mirrors, gas fire, back bar with darts, no food; garden behind, open all day. *(Theocsbrian)*

DEVIZES   SU0262
Hourglass (01380) 727313
Horton Avenue; follow boat brown sign off A361 roundabout, N edge of town; SN10 2RH Modern pub featuring sturdy beams, broad bare boards, cream and terracotta décor, wall of windows looking across canalside terrace to fields beyond, enjoyable food from pub favourites to more enterprising dishes including blackboard specials, well kept Marstons-related ales, good coffees and wine list, daily papers; unobtrusive background music; children welcome, open all day. *(M J Winterton)*

DONHEAD ST ANDREW   ST9124
⋆**Forester** (01747) 828038
Village signposted off A30 E of Shaftesbury, just E of Ludwell; Lower Street; SP7 9EE Attractive 14th-c thatched dining pub in charming village; relaxed atmosphere in nice bar, stripped tables on

wood floors, log fire in inglenook, alcove with sofa and magazines, Butcombe Bitter and a guest, 15 wines by the glass including champagne, very good well presented food from bar tapas up with much emphasis on fresh fish/seafood, comfortable main dining room with country kitchen tables, second cosier dining room; children and dogs welcome, seats outside on good-sized terrace with country views, can walk up White Sheet Hill and past the old and 'new' Wardour castles, closed Sun evening. *(Edward Mirzoeff)*

EBBESBOURNE WAKE   ST9924
⋆**Horseshoe** (01722) 780474
On A354 S of Salisbury, right at signpost at Coombe Bissett; village about 8 miles further; SP5 5JF Unspoilt country pub in pretty village with plenty of regular customers, welcoming long-serving licensees and friendly staff, well kept Bowman, Otter, Palmers and guests tapped from the cask, farm cider, good traditional bar food (not Mon), neatly kept and comfortable character bar, collection of farm tools and bric-a-brac on beams, conservatory extension and small restaurant; children (away from bar) and dogs welcome, seats in pretty little garden with views over River Ebble valley, chickens and a goat in paddock, good nearby walks, bedrooms, closed Sun evening, Mon lunchtime. *(Phil and Jane Villiers, Ian Herdman)*

EDINGTON   ST9353
Three Daggers (01380) 830940
Westbury Road (B3098); BA13 4PG Refurbished heavily beamed open-plan village pub, own-brewed beers along with Wadworths and other local guests, Weston's cider, nice choice of wines by the glass, good home-made food from bar snacks up including notable fish pie, friendly efficient young staff, sofas and assorted old pine furniture on slate floor, two open fires, modern conservatory dining area, upstairs raftered function/overspill room; background and occasional live music; children and dogs welcome, garden tables (access to pretty village's play area beyond), farm shop, great views and good walks, three bedrooms, open all day from breakfast on. *(Taff Thomas, Michael Doswell, N R White)*

ENFORD   SU14351
Swan (01980) 670338
Long Street, off A345; SN9 6DD Attractive thatched village pub with comfortable beamed interior, good range of beers and enjoyable well presented food including daily specials; seats out on small front terrace. *(David Wiltshire)*

'Children welcome' means the pub says it lets children inside without any special restriction; some may impose an evening time limit earlier than 9pm – please tell us if you find this.

FARLEIGH WICK ST8063
Fox & Hounds (01225) 863122
A363 NW of Bradford-on-Avon;
BA15 2PU Rambling low-beamed 18th-c
pub, welcoming and clean, with enjoyable
food including good value lunchtime set deal
(Tues-Sat), six wines by the glass and Bath
Gem, log fire in big oak-floored dining area;
children welcome, area for dogs, attractive
garden, closed Mon. *(Anon)*

FOXHAM ST9777
Foxham Inn (01249) 740665
NE of Chippenham; SN15 4NQ Small
remote country dining pub with simple
traditional décor, enterprising food strong on
local produce along with more straightforward
bar meals, well kept ales such as Bath and
Wadworths, good choice of wines by the
glass and nice coffee, woodburner, more
contemporary back restaurant, own bread,
chutneys, jams etc for sale; children and
dogs welcome, disabled access and facilities,
terrace tables with pergola, extensive views
from front, peaceful village, two bedrooms,
closed Mon. *(Alastair Muir)*

FROXFIELD SU2968
Pelican (01488) 682479
Off A4; SN8 3JY Modernised 17th-c
coaching inn, good choice of enjoyable
home-made food served by helpful friendly
young staff, local ales, comfortable relaxed
atmosphere; pleasant streamside garden with
terrace and duck pond, Kennet & Avon Canal
walks, bedrooms, open all day. *(David and
Judy Robison)*

HAMPTWORTH SU2419
Cuckoo (01794) 390302
Hamptworth Road; SP5 2DU 17th-c
thatched New Forest pub, peaceful and
unspoilt, with welcoming landlord, friendly
mix of customers from farmers to families
in four compact rooms around tiny servery,
well kept Bowman, Hop Back, Ringwood
and guests tapped from the cask (June and
September beer festivals), five real ciders,
simple food like pasties and pies, mugs and
jugs hanging from ceiling, beer memorabilia,
basic wooden furniture, open fire; big garden
(adults' area with view of golf course), open
all day Fri-Sun. *(Anon)*

HANNINGTON SU1793
Jolly Tar (01793) 762245
*Off B4019 W of Highworth; Queens
Road; SN6 7RP* Relaxing beamed bar
with big log fire, steps up to flagstoned
and stripped-stone dining area, good
straightforward food from baguettes up,
well kept Arkells ales, reasonable prices,
friendly helpful service; children welcome,
picnic-sets on front terrace and in big garden
with play area, four comfortable bedrooms,
good breakfast, pretty village. *(Neil and Anita
Christopher, Ross Balaam)*

HEDDINGTON ST9966
Ivy (01380) 859652
Off A3102 S of Calne; SN11 0PL
Picturesque thatched 17th-c village local
under welcoming new licensees; good
inglenook log fire in L-shaped bar, heavy low
beams, timbered walls, assorted furnishings
on parquet floor, cask-tapped Wadworths
ales, pubby food (not Sun evening, Mon),
back family dining room; disabled access,
front garden, open all day Fri-Sun, closed
Mon lunchtime. *(Anon)*

HEYTESBURY ST9242
Angel (01985) 840330
*Just off A36 E of Warminster; High
Street; BA12 0ED* In quiet village
just below Salisbury Plain, spacious
and comfortable, with good food from
sandwiches up, friendly helpful staff, Greene
King ales, log fire, restaurant; children
welcome. *(Edward Mirzoeff)*

HINDON ST9032
Angel (01747) 820696
B3089 Wilton–Mere; SP3 6DJ Modernised
dining pub with big log fire, flagstones and
other coaching-inn survivals, enjoyable food
from pub favourites through grills to specials,
good friendly service, nice choice of wines,
ales such as Otter, Sharps and Timothy
Taylors; children welcome, dogs in bar,
courtyard tables, nine comfortable bedrooms
(named after game birds), open all day.
(Lisa Barratt)

HINDON ST9132
Lamb (01747) 820573
B3089 Wilton–Mere; SP3 6DP Smart,
attractive old hotel with long roomy log-fire
bar, two flagstoned lower sections with very
long polished table, high-backed pews and
settles, up steps to a third, bigger area, well
kept Butcombe, St Austell Tribute and Wells
& Youngs Best, several wines by the glass
and around 100 malt whiskies, cuban cigars,
enjoyable bar and restaurant food, polite
friendly service from smartly dressed staff;
can get very busy, 10% service charge added
to bill; children and dogs welcome, tables on
roadside terrace and in garden across road
with boules, 19 bedrooms, good breakfast,
open all day from 7.30am. *(Anon)*

HOLT ST8561
Toll Gate (01225) 782326
*Ham Green; B3107 W of Melksham;
BA14 6PX* Appealing individual décor and
furnishings in comfortable bar, welcoming
newish licensees and good friendly service,
four real ales, lots of wines by the glass,
enjoyable home-made food from lunchtime
sandwiches up, log fire, another in more
sedate high-raftered former chapel
restaurant up steps; background music;
children welcome, wheelchair access to main
bar only, pretty terrace and fenced garden

with gazebo, shop in barn selling local produce, four bedrooms, closed Sun evening, Mon. *(Anon)*

HONEYSTREET SU1061
Barge (01672) 851705
Off A345 W of Pewsey; SN9 5PS Early 19th-c stone pub in nice setting by Kennet & Avon Canal, open-plan bar with wood floor and dark walls, good Honeystreet beers (brewed by Stonehenge) including 1810, Croppie and Alien Abduction, traditional cider, tasty reasonably priced traditional food, friendly service, pool room with painted ceiling of local area, occasional magic shows, live music Sat; children, dogs, crop-circle and UFO enthusiasts welcome, waterside picnic-sets, camping field, good walks, open all day summer. *(Pat and Tony Martin, N R White)*

HOOK SU0785
Bolingbroke Arms (01793) 852357
B4041, off A420 just W of M4 junction 16; SN4 8DZ Airy bare-boards bar with lots of light pine, lounge, and pleasantly decorated restaurant popular with older lunchers, enjoyable freshly prepared food from sandwiches up, good service, well kept Arkells beers; background music; children welcome, garden with pond and fountain, bedrooms, closed Sun evening. *(Fr Robert Marsh)*

HORNINGSHAM ST8041
Bath Arms (01985) 844308
By entrance to Longleat House; BA12 7LY Handsome old stone-built inn on pretty village's sloping green, stylishly opened up as welcoming dining pub with several linked areas including a proper bar, polished wood floors and open fires, good generous local food, well kept Wessex ales and a guest, local cider, good choice of wines and other drinks, charming efficient staff, side restaurant and conservatory; can get very busy; wheelchair access to bars via side door, attractive garden with neat terraces, smokers' gazebo, 15 bedrooms. *(Lois Dyer, Chris and Angela Buckell, Mark Flynn)*

HORTON SU0363
Bridge Inn (01380) 860273
Horton Road; village signed off A361 London road, NE of Devizes; SN10 2JS Former flour mill and bakery by Kennet & Avon Canal, carpeted log-fire area on left with tables set for dining, more pubby part to right of bar with some stripped brickwork and country kitchen furniture on reconstituted flagstones, old bargee photographs and rural pictures, Wadworths ales, food and service can be good; background music, TV; well behaved children welcome, dogs in bar, disabled facilities, safely fenced garden with picnic-sets, original grinding wheel, canal walks and moorings, bedrooms, closed Mon. *(Anon)*

KILMINGTON ST7835
Red Lion (01985) 844263
B3092 Mere–Frome, 2.5 miles S of Maiden Bradley; 3 miles from A303 Mere turn-off; BA12 6RP NT-owned country pub with low-beamed flagstoned bar, cushioned wall and window seats, curved high-backed settle, log fires in big fireplaces (fine iron fireback in one), Butcombe, Butts and a guest, Thatcher's cider, lunchtime bar food and more elaborate evening menu, newer big-windowed dining area with modern country feel; children and dogs (in bar) welcome, picnic-sets in large attractive garden with smokers' shelter, White Sheet Hill (hang-gliding) and Stourhead gardens (NT) nearby. *(Edward Mirzoeff, Chris and Angela Buckell, Pete Walker)*

LACOCK ST9268
Bell (01249) 730308
E of village; SN15 2PJ Extended cottagey pub with warm welcome, well kept ales such as Bath, Palmers, Plain and Great Western (beer festivals), traditional ciders, decent wines by the glass and lots of malt whiskies, good choice of popular food, linked rooms off bar including pretty restaurant, conservatory; children welcome away from bar, disabled access, sheltered well tended garden with smokers' shelter, open (and food) all day weekends. *(MLR, Chris and Angela Buckell, Dr and Mrs A K Clarke, N R White)*

LACOCK ST9168
★George (01249) 730263
West Street; village signed off A350 S of Chippenham; SN15 2LH Newish management (more reports please) for this rambling inn at centre of busy NT tourist village; low-beamed bar with upright timbers creating cosy corners, armchairs and windsor chairs around close-set tables, seats in stone-mullioned windows, some flagstones, dog treadwheel in outer breast of central fireplace, lots of old pictures and bric-a-brac, souvenirs from filming *Cranford* and *Harry Potter* in the village, Wadworths beers and Weston's cider, bar food from snacks up; background music; children and dogs welcome, tricky wheelchair access, picnic-sets on grass and in attractive courtyard with pillory and well, open all day in summer. *(Mr and Mrs A Curry, Roger and Donna Huggins, Chris and Angela Buckell)*

LACOCK ST9168
★Red Lion (01249) 730456
High Street; SN15 2LQ Popular NT-owned Georgian inn, sizeable bar with log fire, heavy tables and oriental rugs on flagstones, cosy snug with leather armchairs, well kept Wadworths ales, good choice of enjoyable food (all day weekends) from nice sandwiches and baguettes up, pleasant service (may be slow at very busy times); background music; children and dogs

welcome, seats outside, bedrooms, open all day. *(Ian Phillips, Mr and Mrs A H Young, Paul Humphreys, J D O Carter, Steve Whalley)*

LIDDINGTON   SU2081
Village Inn (01793) 790314
Handy for M4 junction 15, via A419 and B4192; Bell Lane; SN4 0HE Comfortable and welcoming with enjoyable good value food from varied menu including early-bird bargains and popular Sun roasts, well kept Arkells ales, linked bar areas, stripped-stone and raftered back dining extension, conservatory, log fire in splendid fireplace; well behaved children over 8 allowed in restaurant area, disabled facilities, terrace tables. *(KC, Ian Herdman)*

LIMPLEY STOKE   ST7861
Hop Pole (01225) 723134
Off A36 and B3108 S of Bath; at foot of Limpley Stoke Hotel drive; BA2 7FS Largely panelled 16th-c stone-built pub, warmly welcoming, with well kept Bath Gem, Sharps Doom Bar and a guest, generous fairly priced traditional food including OAP weekday lunch, log fire; background music TV; children in eating areas, dogs in bar, disabled access with help, valley views from nice garden behind. *(Meg and Colin Hamilton)*

LITTLE SOMERFORD   ST9784
Somerford Arms (01666) 826535
Signed off B4042 Malmesbury–Brinkworth; SN15 5JP Modernised village pub saved from housing development by the local community; good welcoming atmosphere with easy chairs in front of bar's woodburner, green-painted half-panelling and stone flooring, linked restaurant with good food – all home-made including some inventive dishes, well kept changing ales and lots of wines by the glass, pub dog (boxer called Nutmeg) and parrot; children, other dogs and muddy boots welcome, open all day. *(MJVK)*

LONGBRIDGE DEVERILL   ST8640
George (01985) 840396
A350/B3095; BA12 7DG Friendly extended roadside inn with well kept ales including Deverill Advocate named for them, reasonably priced usual food, popular Sun carvery, good coffee; children welcome, big riverside garden with play area, 12 bedrooms, open all day. *(George Atkinson)*

LOWER WOODFORD   SU1235
✱**Wheatsheaf** (01722) 782203
Signed off A360 just N of Salisbury; SP4 6NQ Refurbished and extended 18th-c Badger dining pub, open airy feel,

with good choice of fairly priced traditional food from sharing boards up, well kept beers, good wines and coffee, well trained genial staff, beams, mix of old furniture, log fire and woodburner; background music; children welcome, dogs in bar, disabled access and parking, tree-lined fenced garden with play area, pretty setting, open all day. *(Anon)*

LUCKINGTON   ST8384
✱**Old Royal Ship** (01666) 840222
Off B4040 SW of Malmesbury; SN14 6PA Friendly pub by village green, opened up inside with one long bar divided into three areas, Bass, Stonehenge, Wadworths and Wickwar from central servery, also farm cider and several wines by the glass, good range of well liked food including vegetarian, decent coffee, neat tables, spindleback chairs and small cushioned settles on dark boards, some stripped masonry and small open fire, skittle alley; background music (live jazz second Weds of month), games machine; children welcome, garden (beyond car park) with boules, play area and plenty of seats, Badminton House close by, open all day Sat. *(Michael Doswell, Hugh Thomas, John and Gloria Isaacs)*

MALMESBURY   ST9287
Smoking Dog (01666) 825823
High Street; SN16 9AT Old mid-terrace stone local with two cosy flagstoned front bars, well kept ales and several wines by the glass, decent choice of food in back dining area, log fire; children and dogs welcome, small secluded garden up steep steps, spring sausage and beer festival, bedrooms, open all day. *(David Eberlin, MLR, Jim and Maggie Cowell)*

MARLBOROUGH   SU1869
Castle & Ball (01672) 515201
High Street; SN8 1LZ Popular fully refurbished coaching inn dating from the 15th c (Greene King Old English Inn); spacious interior with lounge bar and restaurant, wide choice of enjoyable food including deals, their ales and nice range of well listed wines by the glass, good attentive service; background music; children and dogs (in bar) welcome, seats out under projecting colonnade and in back walled garden, 37 bedrooms, open all day. *(George Atkinson, Susan and Nigel Brookes)*

MERE   ST8132
✱**Old Ship** (01747) 860258
Castle Street; BA12 6JE Handsome old stone coaching inn still with its 18th-c wrought-iron sign, cosy panelled Cabin

---

The letters and figures after the name of each town are its Ordnance Survey map reference. *Using the Guide* at the beginning of the book explains how it helps you find a pub, in road atlases or large-scale maps as well as in our own maps.

Bar (just four tables on bare boards) with imposing Jacobean carved fireplace framing portrait of Charles II, adjacent brighter restaurant, more spacious public bar across cobbled coach entry with back pool room, Exmoor and Otter ales, local cider, enjoyable sensibly priced food from sandwiches and sharing boards up, good considerate service; children welcome, a few picnic-sets out behind, picturesque village, nine bedrooms. *(Anon)*

MONKTON FARLEIGH   ST8065
Muddy Duck (01225) 858705
Signed off A363 Bradford–Bath; BA15 2QH Refurbishment and new name (was the Kings Arms) for this imposing 17th-c stone building; bare-boards bar with leather armchairs by inglenook woodburner, Butcombe, St Austell and a guest from zinc-topped counter, good wine and whisky choice, parquet-floored restaurant with low pendant lighting and open fire, good variety of enjoyable food (all day weekends, till 7.30pm Sun), efficient friendly service; background music; children welcome, dogs in bar, seats in front courtyard and two-tier back garden with country views , lovely village, five bedrooms (three with log fires), open all day. *(Alan Sutton, Taff Thomas)*

NESTON
Neston Country Inn (01225) 811694
Pool Green; SN13 9SN Welcoming village pub with good reasonably priced food cooked to order from varied menu, well kept ales such as Fullers, Milk Street and Plain, friendly helpful staff; four bedrooms, open all day weekends (till 9pm Sun), closed Mon lunchtime (and Tues lunchtime after bank holiday). *(Jenny and Brian Seller)*

NETHERHAMPTON   SU1129
★ Victoria & Albert (01722) 743174
Just off A3094 W of Salisbury; SP2 8PU Cosy black-beamed bar in simple thatched cottage, good generous food from nicely presented sandwiches up, sensible prices and local supplies, three well kept changing ales, farm cider, decent wines, friendly helpful staff, nicely cushioned old-fashioned wall settles on ancient floor tiles, restaurant; children and dogs welcome, hatch service for sizeable terrace and garden behind, handy for Wilton House and Nadder Valley walks. *(Anon)*

OGBOURNE ST ANDREW   SU1871
Silks on the Downs (01672) 841229
A345 N of Marlborough; SN8 1RZ Civilised restauranty pub with horse racing theme, good variety of enjoyable food, ales such as Adnams, Ramsbury and Wadworths, decent wines by the glass, good friendly service, stylish décor with mix of dining tables on polished wood floors, some good prints and photographs as well as framed racing silks; well behaved children allowed,

small decked area and garden, closed Sun evening. *(Jan and Roger Ferris, Ross Balaam)*

PEWSEY   SU1561
French Horn (01672) 562443
A345 towards Marlborough; Pewsey Wharf; SN9 5NT Pleasant red-brick roadside pub; two-part back bar with steps down to more formal front dining area (children allowed here), flagstones and log fires, wide choice of enjoyable fairly priced home-made food, well kept Wadworths ales, good attentive service; background music; dogs welcome in bar, picnic-sets out behind, walks by Kennet & Avon Canal below, closed Tues. *(Kristin Warry, Sheila and Robert Robinson)*

RAMSBURY   SU2771
Bell (01672) 520230
Off B4192 NW of Hungerford, or A4 W; SN8 2PE Stylishly refurbished former coaching inn, light and airy despite lots of small eating areas, enjoyable reasonably priced local food (some from own garden), Ramsbury and a guest ale, pleasant understated service, bar, lounge and restaurant, log fires, café at back; nine good bedrooms. *(Michael Patterson, Maureen Wood)*

REDLYNCH   SU2021
Kings Head (01725) 510420
Off A338 via B3080; The Row; SP5 2JT Refurbished early 18th-c low-ceilinged pub on edge of New Forest; four well kept ales including Ringwood Best, decent house wines and coffee, good value food including evening deal for two Weds evening, two bays, one a small conservatory, off beamed and flagstoned main bar, woodburner in large brick fireplace, Thurs quiz; children, dogs and muddy boots welcome, picnic-sets out in front and in side garden, nice Pepper Box Hill walks nearby, shuts 3-6pm. *(Anon)*

REDLYNCH   SU1920
Woodfalls Inn (01725) 513222
The Ridge; SP5 2LN Friendly 19th-c family-run village inn with good mix of customers, enjoyable home-made food and well kept beers, conservatory restuarant, function room/skittle alley; children welcome, terrace picnic-sets under parasols, 11 bedrooms, handy for New Forest. *(Jeremy Siderfin, Mrs A W Johns)*

ROWDE   ST9762
★ George & Dragon (01380) 723053
A342 Devizes–Chippenham; SN10 2PN Lots of character in this welcoming and well run 16th-c coaching inn, two low-beamed rooms with large open fireplaces, wooden dining chairs around candlelit tables, antique rugs and walls covered with old pictures and portraits, Butcombe and guests, good food including plenty of fresh fish, not cheap but they do offer a good value set menu; background music; children and dogs

welcome, seats in pretty back garden, Kennet & Avon Canal nearby, three bedrooms, closed Sun evening. *(Ari, Richard and Patricia Jefferson, Patrick Hunt)*

SALISBURY SU1430
Avon Brewery (01722) 416184
Castle Street; SP1 3SP Long narrow city bar with frosted and engraved bow window, dark mahogany and two open fires, friendly staff and regulars, well kept Ringwood Best and a couple of other Marstons-related beers, reasonably priced pubby food from sandwiches up, small back dining room; sheltered courtyard garden overlooking river, open all day (till 5pm Sun). *(Paul Humphreys)*

SALISBURY SU1429
Kings Head (01722) 342050
Bridge Street; SP1 2ND Corner Wetherspoons in nice spot by river (site of former hotel), variety of seating in large relaxed bar with separate TV area, upstairs gallery, regularly changing real ales, low-priced menu including breakfast, log fire; good value bedrooms, open all day from 7am (till 1am Thurs-Sat). *(Jim and Maggie Cowell)*

SALISBURY SU1429
New Inn (01722) 326662
New Street; SP1 2PH Much extended old building with massive beams and timbers, good choice of home-made food from pub staples up, well kept Badger ales and decent house wines, cheerful but not always speedy service, flagstones, floorboards and carpet, quiet cosy alcoves, inglenook log fire; children welcome, attractive walled garden with striking view of nearby cathedral spire, three bedrooms, open all day. *(Paul Humphreys)*

SALISBURY SU1329
★ Old Mill (01722) 327517
Town Path, West Harnham; SP2 8EU Charming 17th-c pub-hotel in tranquil setting, unpretentious beamed bars with prized window tables, decent good value food from sandwiches up, well kept local ales, good wines and malt whiskies, efficient friendly service, attractive restaurant showing mill race; children welcome, small floodlit garden by duck-filled millpond, delightful stroll across water meadows from cathedral (classic view of it from bridge beyond garden), 11 bedrooms, open all day. *(Paul Wilson, Mr and Mrs J J A Davis, Paul Humphreys)*

SALISBURY SU1429
Village (01722) 329707
Wilton Road; SP2 7EF Friendly corner pub popular for its interesting range of real ales, railway memorabilia (near the station); sports TV; open all day (from 3pm Mon-Thurs). *(Steve Curtis)*

SALISBURY SU1430
Wyndham Arms (01722) 331026
Estcourt Road; SP1 3AS Corner local with unpretentious modern decor, popular and friendly, with full Hop Back range (brewery was based here) and a guest such as Downton, bottled beers and country wines, no food, small front and side rooms, longer main bar, darts and board games; children and dogs welcome, open all day Thurs-Sun, from 4.30pm other days. *(N R White)*

SEEND ST9361
★ Barge (01380) 828230
Seend Cleeve; signed off A361 Devizes–Trowbridge; SN12 6QB Busy place with plenty of seats in garden making most of boating activity on Kennet & Avon Canal, unusual seating in bar including milk churns, an upturned canoe and high-backed chairs made from old boat parts, small oak settle among the rugs on parquet floor, well stocked aquarium, pretty Victorian fireplace, Wadworths ales and 30 wines by the glass, decent choice of food, good service; background music; children and dogs welcome, summer barbecues, open all day. *(Alan Sutton, Meg and Colin Hamilton, J D O Carter)*

SEMINGTON ST9259
★ Lamb (01380) 870263
The Strand; A361 Devizes–Trowbridge; BA14 6LL Refurbished dining pub with various eating areas including wood strip-floor bar with log fire, enjoyable food from pub favourites to specials, Wiltshire tapas too, beers from Bath and Box Steam, efficient friendly staff; background music; children and dogs welcome, pleasant garden with views to the Bowood Estate, closed Sun evening. *(E Clark, Mark O'Sullivan, Paul Humphreys)*

SHALBOURNE SU3162
Plough (01672) 870295
Off A338; SN8 3QF Low-beamed traditional village pub on green, good choice of enjoyable fairly priced blackboard food including vegetarian options, Butcombe and Wadworths, friendly helpful landlady, neat tiled-floor bar with sofa and armchairs in snug; disabled access, small garden with play area. *(E A Sclater, R Elliott)*

SHAW ST8765
Golden Fleece (01225) 702050
Folly Lane (A365 towards Atworth); SN12 8HB Attractive former coaching inn, bright and clean, with low-ceilinged L-shaped bar and long front dining extension, good fresh food from shortish reasonably priced menu along with blackboard specials, OAP lunch Tues, well kept Box Steam, Fullers London Pride, Moles and a guest, pleasant welcoming staff, charity quiz first Tues of

month; background music; children and dogs welcome, back terrace with steps up to lawn, open all day weekends, closed Mon lunchtime. *(Maureen Wood)*

STAPLEFORD   SU0636
Pelican (01722) 792642

Warminster Road (A36); SP3 4LT Long carpeted bar and spacious restaurant, beams and open fires, Marstons-related ales, good choice of enjoyable well priced food from lunchtime sandwiches and baked potatoes up, friendly helpful staff; children and dogs welcome, big riverside garden with play area, five bedrooms in separate block. *(David Hunt, E J Palmer)*

STEEPLE ASHTON   ST9056
Longs Arms (01380) 870245

High Street; BA14 6EU 17th-c renovated coaching inn with friendly local atmosphere, well kept Wadworths and guests, food locally sourced and can be good, open fire; children and dogs welcome, big garden with play area, adjoining self-catering cottage, delightful village, open all day weekends if busy. *(Paul Humphreys)*

STOCKTON   ST9738
Carriers

Just off A36 Salisbury–Warminster, or follow Wylye sign off A303 then turn right; BA12 0SQ In quiet Wylye Valley thatched village and doing well under newish management; enjoyable good value food cooked by landlady, well kept ales, decent wines and coffee, good friendly service, open-plan carpeted interior with modern pubby furniture, soft lighting and huge log fire; children and dogs welcome, disabled access (not to bedrooms), a few roadside seats, picnic-sets in pleasant back garden. *(Chris and Angela Buckell)*

STOURTON   ST7733
★ **Spread Eagle** (01747) 840587

Church Lawn; follow Stourhead brown signs off B3092, N of junction with A303 W of Mere; BA12 6QE Georgian inn, always packed as at entrance to Stourhead Estate; old-fashioned, rather civilised interior with antique panel-back settles, new and old solid tables and chairs, sporting prints, log fires in handsome fireplaces, room by entrance with armchairs, longcase clock and corner china cupboard, well kept Butcombe and a guest, interesting wines by the glass, well liked home-made food (must book), cream teas, restaurant, good helpful service; background music; children welcome, wheelchair access (step down to dining areas), smart back courtyard, bedrooms (guests can wander

freely around famous NT gardens outside normal hours), open all day. *(Phyl and Jack Street, Tom and Ruth Rees, Mr and Mrs A Curry, Sheila Topham, Di and Mike Gillam, S J and C C Davidson and others)*

STUDLEY   ST9671
Soho (01249) 812408

New Road (A4 W of Calne); SN11 9LX Pleasantly revamped former coaching inn, well kept Wadworths and nice variety of enjoyable food including good value weekday set lunch, friendly service, airy dining conservatory; picnic-sets in hedged back garden. *(Anon)*

SUTTON BENGER   ST9478
Wellesley Arms (01249) 721721

Handy for M4 junction 17, via B4122 and B4069; High Street; SN15 4RD Beamed 15th-c Cotswold-stone pub with pleasant bar areas and restaurant, good pubby food (not Sun evening) including lunchtime set menu, Wadworths ales, efficient friendly service; background music, TV; children and dogs welcome, garden with play area, paddock, open all day weekends, closed Mon lunchtime. *(David Crook)*

SUTTON VENY   ST8941
Woolpack (01985) 840834

High Street; BA12 7AW Small well run village local pleasantly refurbished by present licensees, good blackboard food including some inventive dishes cooked by landlord-chef (best to book), Marstons and Ringwood ales, sensibly priced wines by the glass, charming service, compact side dining area. *(Edward Mirzoeff)*

TISBURY   ST9429
Boot (01747) 870363

High Street; SP3 6PS Ancient unpretentious village local with long-serving welcoming licensees, up to four well kept changing ales tapped from the cask, cider/perry, good range of pizzas and reasonably priced pubby food, notable fireplace; tables in good-sized back garden, closed Sun evening, Tues lunchtime. *(Maureen Wood)*

UPAVON   SU1355
Ship (01980) 630313

High Street; SN9 6EA Large thatched pub with good local atmosphere, enjoyable home-made food including nice steak and kidney pie and Sun roasts, brisk friendly service, well kept Sharps, Stonehenge and Wadworths, two farm ciders, decent range of wines and whiskies, interesting nautical memorabilia, some gentle live music; parking can be tricky; dogs welcome (may

---

Half pints: by law, a pub should not charge more for half a pint than half the price of a full pint, unless it shows that half-pint price on its price list.

get a treat after Sun lunch), picnic-sets in front and on small side terrace. *(Michael Doswell, John and Nan Hurst)*

UPTON SCUDAMORE ST8647
★ **Angel** (01985) 213225
Off A350 N of Warminster; BA12 0AG Stylish contemporary dining pub in former 16th-c coaching inn, airy upper part leading down to bar area with sofas and armchairs by open fire, mixed traditional pine furniture on wood floor, good choice of popular modern food (not particularly cheap) served by competent friendly staff, well kept ales including Butcombe, decent wines by the glass; background music; children welcome, dogs on leads in bar, sheltered back terrace, ten bedrooms in house across car park. *(Mrs P Bishop, N R White)*

WARMINSTER ST8745
Organ (01985) 211777
49 High Street; BA12 9AQ Sympathetic restoration of former 18th-c inn (shut in 1913), front bar, snug and traditional games room, delightful owners and chatty regulars, local beers including one named for the pub, real ciders/perries, good cheap lunchtime cheeseboard, skittle alley, local art in upstairs gallery; no under 21s, open 4-midnight, all day Sat. *(Anon)*

WARMINSTER ST8745
★ **Weymouth Arms** (01985) 216995
Emwell Street; BA12 8JA Charming backstreet pub with snug panelled entrance bar, log fire in fine stone fireplace, ancient books on mantelpiece, leather tub chairs around walnut and satinwood table, more seats against the walls, daily papers, Butcombe and Wadworths 6X, nice wines by the glass, second heavily panelled room with wide floorboards and smaller fireplace, candles in brass sticks, split-level dining room stretching back to open kitchen, good interesting food, friendly service; children welcome, dogs in bar, seats in flower-filled back courtyard, well equipped comfortable bedrooms, closed Mon lunchtime. *(Michael Sargent)*

WEST OVERTON SU1368
Bell (01672) 861099
A4 Marlborough–Calne; SN8 1QD Refurbished former coaching inn with good fresh food (not Sun evenings) from sandwiches and traditional choices to imaginative more expensive dishes, set lunch too, bar with woodburner and spacious restaurant beyond, Wadworths and local guests, attentive friendly uniformed staff; background music; disabled access, nice secluded back garden with terrace and own bar, country views, good walks nearby,

open all day Sat, closed Mon, Tues. *(Michael Doswell, P A Rowe, Mr and Mrs P R Thomas)*

WESTWOOD ST8159
★ **New Inn** (01225) 863123
Off B3109 S of Bradford-on-Avon; BA15 2AE Traditional 18th-c country pub under friendly newish management, several linked rooms, beams and stripped stone, scrubbed tables on slate floor, lots of pictures, imaginative good value food (not Sun evening) cooked by chef-owner together with pub staples, generous Sun lunch and a monthly themed night, well kept Wadworths, buzzy atmosphere; children and dogs welcome, tables in paved garden behind, pretty village with good surrounding walks, Westwood Manor (NT) opposite. *(Michael Doswell, Mark Flynn)*

WHITLEY ST8866
★ **Pear Tree** (01225) 709131
Off B3353 S of Corsham; SN12 8QX Attractive and civilised dining pub under Marco Pierre White's Wheeler's of St James's brand; charming front bar with stripped shutters, open fire and stools around pubby tables on flagstones, a beer for them from Lees and changing guests, several wines by the glass, enjoyable inventive food, big back formal restaurant and airy garden room; children welcome, dogs in bar, terrace with good teak furniture and views over nice garden, eight well equipped bedrooms, open all day. *(Taff Thomas, Mrs Blethyn Elliott, Dr and Mrs A K Clarke)*

WILTON SU2661
Swan (01672) 870274
The village S of Great Bedwyn; SN8 3SS Light and airy 1930s pub, good food including fresh fish (not Sun evening), efficient friendly service, reasonably priced wines, two Ramsbury ales and a local guest, farm ciders, stripped pine tables, high-backed settles, pews and a woodburner; children and dogs welcome, disabled access, front garden with picnic-sets, picturesque village with windmill, open all day weekends. *(Anon)*

WINGFIELD ST8256
★ **Poplars** (01225) 752426
B3109 S of Bradford-on-Avon (Shop Lane); BA14 9LN Attractive country pub with beams and log fires, very popular (especially with older people at lunchtime) for its sensibly priced food from pub staples to interesting specials, Wadworths ales and Weston's cider, friendly fast service even when busy, warm atmosphere, light and airy family dining extension; nice garden, own cricket pitch. *(Mrs P Bishop, Taff Thomas)*

We accept no free drinks or meals and inspections are anonymous.

WINTERBOURNE BASSETT   SU1075
White Horse (01793) 731257

Off A4361 S of Swindon; SN4 9QB
Roadside dining pub with gently old-fashioned feel, carpeted bar with plenty of wood, wrought-iron plush-topped stools and cushioned dining chairs, Wadworths ales and quite a few wines by the glass, uncomplicated food, dining rooms with country kitchen furniture on light wood floors, old prints and paintings, woodburner in little brick fireplace, conservatory; background music; children welcome, tables on good-sized lawn, closed Sun evening, Mon and Tues. *(Tony Baldwin)*

WOOTTON RIVERS   SU1963
Royal Oak (01672) 810322

Off A346, A345 or B3087; SN8 4NQ
Cosy 16th-c beamed and thatched pub, good food from lunchtime sandwiches to nice fish dishes, ales such as Ramsbury and Wadworths 6X, plenty of wines by the glass, friendly competent service, comfortable L-shaped dining lounge with woodburner, timbered bar and small games area; children and dogs welcome, tables out in yard, pleasant village, bedrooms in adjoining house. *(David and Judy Robison, Audrey Dowsett)*

WYLYE   SU0037
Bell (01985) 248338

Just off A303/A36; High Street; BA12 0QP Welcoming newish management for this partly 14th-c former coaching inn prettily set in peaceful village; black beams, sturdy rustic furnishings, stripped stone and herringbone brickwork, inglenook log fire, Salisbury and guest ales, enjoyable fairly standard food cooked by landlord, OAP lunch Weds; children welcome, a few picnic-sets out in front, walled terrace and back garden attractively flanked by church's clipped yews, good riverside and downland walks nearby. *(Anon)*

ZEALS   ST7831
Bell & Crown (01747) 840404

A303; BA12 6NJ Nicely laid out beamed dining pub, warm and friendly, with good freshly made food, efficient service, ales such as Wadworths 6X, big log fire in bar, restaurant. *(Hugo Jeune)*

Worcestershire

From cheerful town locals through historic buildings to smart dining pubs, this county is rich in interesting places. Readers have particularly enjoyed the Fleece at Bretforton (a wonderful building to wander around with a pint), Crown & Trumpet in Broadway (bustling backstreet tavern with good value food and ales), Bell & Cross at Holy Cross (impressive food and drink served by courteous staff in original little bars), Nags Head in Malvern (smashing place, with 15 real ales and other fine drinks served by friendly, professional staff; enjoyable food too) and Talbot in Tenbury Wells (new to us this year – thoughtfully refurbished inn with much character, lovely bedrooms and rewarding food). For its consistently first class food and thoughtful attitude to its customers, the Bell & Cross at Holy Cross is our Worcestershire Dining Pub 2014.

BEWDLEY SO7875 Map 4

Little Pack Horse

High Street; no nearby parking – best to use main car park, then cross B4190 (Cleobury Road), and keep walking on down narrowing High Street; DY12 2DH

Friendly town pub tucked away in side street, with a bustling atmosphere, decent beer and tasty bar food

In a quiet riverside town full of attractive buildings, this characterful pub is tucked away from the crowds. Much bigger than its unassuming exterior suggests, it's nicely timbered inside with reclaimed oak panelling and floorboards, some memorabilia on the walls, a warming woodburning stove and friendly, chatty staff. As well as Bewdley Worcestershire Way, they keep guests such as Hobsons Town Crier, Holdens Golden Glow and Wye Valley Butty Bach on handpump, a selection of bottled ciders and perries and just under two dozen wines; background music and TV. An area outside has heaters. No parking.

Tasty food includes potted shrimps on toasted brioche, warm pear and walnut tartlet topped with blue cheese, several platters, moroccan vegetable tagine, lambs liver and bacon with rich gravy, fish pie, venison, cranberry and stilton pudding, slow-cooked lamb shank with garlic, honey and rosemary, and puddings such as crumble of the day and whisky and orange bread and butter pudding. *Benchmark main dish: beef in ale pie with pastry horns £8.95. Two-course evening meal £15.00.*

Punch ~ Tenant Mark Payne ~ Real ale ~ No credit cards ~ (01299) 403762 ~ Open 12-3, 6-11; 12-midnight Sat; 12-11 Sun ~ Bar food 12-2, 6-9; 12-4, 6-9.30 Sat; 12-4,

5.30-8 Sun ~ Restaurant ~ Children welcome ~ Dogs allowed in bar ~ Live music last Fri
of month ~ www.littlepackhorse.co.uk *Recommended by Save Dore, Pat Crabb*

 BRANSFORD SO8052 Map 4

Bear & Ragged Staff

Off A4103 SW of Worcester; Station Road; WR6 5JH

**Cheerfully run dining pub with pleasant places to sit both inside
and out; well liked food using their own vegetables**

In a hamlet in the Teme Valley, this is a civilised and warmly friendly
dining pub with hard-working licensees. The relaxed bar has Hobsons
Twisted Spire and Sharps Doom Bar on handpump, a dozen wines by
the glass, lots of malt whiskies and quite a few brandies and liqueurs.
The restaurant is more formal with upholstered dining chairs, proper
tablecloths and linen napkins, and these interconnecting rooms give fine
views of attractive rolling country (as do the pretty garden and terrace)
and in winter there's a warming open fire; background music and darts.
Good disabled access and facilities.

Using the best local produce, including some own-grown fruit, vegetables and
salads and making everything in-house from scratch, the highly thought-of
food includes sandwiches, crab and crayfish in ginger, chilli and lime crème fraîche
wrapped in lettuce, camomile tea-smoked duck on spinach, orange and watercress
salad with passion-fruit dressing, home honey-baked ham with eggs, burger with
salad, relish and chips, filo pastry filled with spinach, pine nuts, aubergine, tomato,
tarragon and ricotta cheese with caper and butter sauce, lamb shoulder cooked
three-ways on vegetable couscous, fillet of red bream with yellow pepper velouté
and black olive tapenade, and puddings. *Benchmark main dish: beer-battered
fresh fish and chips with mushy peas and home-made tartare sauce £12.95.
Two-course evening meal £21.00.*

Free house ~ Licensee Lynda Williams ~ Real ale ~ (01886) 833399 ~ Open 11.30-2,
6-11; 12-2.30 Sun; closed Sun evening ~ Bar food 12-2, 6-9; 12-2.30 Sun ~ Restaurant ~
Children welcome ~ Dogs allowed in bar ~ www.bear.uk.com *Recommended by R T and
J C Moggridge, Vivienne Howard, Dave de Santis, Melanie Dawson, Tricia Rawlings, Norman and
Barbara Kay*

BRETFORTON SP0943 Map 4

Fleece £

*B4035 E of Evesham: turn S off this road into village; pub is in central
square by church; there's a sizeable car park at one side of the church; WR11 7JE*

Marvellously unspoilt medieval pub owned by the National Trust

This is a wonderful place to wander around with your pint. It's been
a pub for more than 160 years, but before that it was owned by the
same family for nearly 500 years, and many of the furnishings, such as
the great oak dresser that holds a priceless 48-piece set of Stuart pewter,
are heirlooms passed down through the generations. The little rooms are
atmospherically dim with massive beams, exposed timbers and marks
scored on the worn and crazed flagstones to keep out demons. There are
two fine grandfather clocks, ancient kitchen chairs, curved high-backed
settles, a rocking chair, a rack of heavy pointed iron shafts (probably for
spit roasting) in one of the huge inglenook fireplaces and two other log
fires. Plenty of oddities include a great cheese-press and set of cheese
moulds and a rare dough-proving table; a leaflet details the more bizarre
items. They keep Uley Pigs Ear, Wye Valley Bitter and three changing

guest beers on handpump, two farm ciders (one made by the landlord), local apple juices, german wheat beer and fruit wines, and ten wines by the glass; darts. They hold an asparagus auction at the end of May as part of the Vale of Evesham British Asparagus Festival, and also host the village fête on August Bank Holiday Monday. The calendar of events includes morris dancing and the village silver band plays here regularly too. The lawn, with fruit trees around a beautifully restored thatched and timbered barn, is a lovely place to sit, and there are more picnic-sets and a stone pump-trough in the front courtyard. If you're visiting to enjoy the famous historic interior, best to go midweek as it can be very busy at weekends.

Bar food includes sandwiches, smoked haddock and spinach fishcake with cheese sauce, sharing platter of the day, ham and egg, potato gnocchi in tomato sauce, pie of the day, chicken curry, lamb, pea and mint hotpot, pork belly with white and black pudding, mustard mash and apple and brandy sauce, and puddings; pie and pint deal is Wednesday evening and takeaway fish and chips is available during food service hours. *Benchmark main dish: trio of local sausages with red onion marmalade and mustard mash £8.75. Two-course evening meal £15.00.*

Free house ~ Licensee Nigel Smith ~ Real ale ~ (01386) 831173 ~ Open 11-11; 11-3, 6-11 Mon and Tues in winter ~ Bar food 12-2.30, 6.30-9; 12-4, 6.30-8.30 Sun ~ Restaurant ~ Children welcome ~ Dogs allowed in bar ~ Bedrooms: /£97.50 ~ www.thefleeceinn.co.uk
Recommended by David Gunn, Dennis Jones, Tom Evans, Torrens Lyster

BROADWAY SP0937 Map 4
Crown & Trumpet ◀ £
Church Street; WR12 7AE

Unreconstructed honest local with good real ale and decent food

In a lovely little town, this cosy, old-fashioned local is hidden away in a side street. With a cheerful, easy-going atmosphere and a friendly welcome for all, the bustling beamed and timbered bar has antique dark high-backed settles, large solid tables and a blazing log fire. Cotswold Spring Codrington Codger, a seasonal brew from local Stanway, Stroud Tom Long and a guest such as Butcombe Bitter on handpump, alongside local farm cider, nine wines by the glass, hot toddies, mulled wine and a good range of soft drinks. An assortment of pub games includes darts, shove-ha'penny, cribbage, shut the box, dominoes, bar skittles and ring the bull, as well as a quiz machine, TV and background music. The hardwood tables and chairs outside, among flowers on a slightly raised front terrace, are popular with walkers, even in adverse weather.

Extremely good value food includes lunchtime baguettes, deep-fried brie with cranberry sauce, devilled whitebait with cayenne pepper and mayonnaise, cheese omelette, vegetable lasagne, faggots with chips and mushy peas, steak and kidney pie, chicken breast in mushroom sauce, and puddings such as spotted dick and custard and treacle tart; they offer a midweek early-evening pie and pudding deal too. *Benchmark main dish: duck and apricot sausages with mash and plum sauce £6.95. Two-course evening meal £17.00.*

Laurel (Enterprise) ~ Lease Andrew Scott ~ Real ale ~ (01386) 853202 ~ Open 11-3, 5-11; 11am-midnight Fri, Sat; 11-11 Sun ~ Bar food 12-2.30, 5.45-9.30; 12-9.30 weekends ~ Children welcome ~ Dogs allowed in bar ~ Bedrooms: /£75 ~ www.cotswoldholidays.co.uk
Recommended by Roger and Ann King, Canon Michael Bourdeaux, Ian and Jane Irving, Lucien Perring

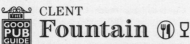

CLENT   SO9279   Map 4
Fountain 🍴 ♀

*Adams Hill/Odnall Lane; off A491 at Holy Cross/Clent exit roundabout,
via Violet Lane, then right at T junction; DY9 9PU*

**Restauranty pub often packed to overflowing, serving imaginative
dishes and good choice of drinks**

Most customers are here to enjoy the good, interesting food – it's
best to book in advance; attentive uniformed staff will lead you
to your seat. The long, carpeted dining bar (three knocked-together
areas) is fairly traditional, with teak chairs, pedestal tables and some
comfortably cushioned brocaded wall seats. There are nicely framed
local photographs on the rag-rolled pinkish walls above a dark panelled
dado, pretty wall lights and candles on the tables (flowers in summer).
The changing real ales include Banks's EPA, Brakspears Oxford Gold,
Crouch Vale Amarillo and Rudgate Battleaxe Bitter on handpump and
most of their 36 wines are served by the glass; also speciality teas, good
coffees and freshly squeezed orange juice. Background music and alley
skittles. There are tables out on a decked area.

 As well as lunchtime sandwiches, the highly popular food includes crispy pork
belly on sweet thai salad with spicy sweet and sour sauce, duck liver pâté with
apricot and ginger chutney, battered fresh haddock with mushy peas, calves liver
with spring onion and smoked bacon mash and red wine sauce, breadcrumbed veal
on spicy tomato sauce with red-hot chilli and parmesan, free-range chicken breast
with a choice of toppings, and puddings such as white chocolate crème brûlée and
sticky toffee pudding with toffee sauce. *Benchmark main dish: lamb pot roast in
rich sauce with potatoes of the day £14.95. Two-course evening meal £20.00.*

Marstons ~ Lease Richard and Jacque Macey ~ Real ale ~ (01562) 883286 ~
Open 11-11; 12-8 Sun ~ Bar food 12-2, 6-9(9.30 Fri, Sat); 12-6 Sun ~ Children welcome ~
www.thefountainatclent.co.uk *Recommended by Emma Scofield*

HOLY CROSS   SO9278   Map 4
Bell & Cross ★ 🍴 ♀

*4 miles from M5 junction 4: A491 towards Stourbridge, then follow Clent
signpost off on left; DY9 9QL*

Worcestershire Dining Pub of the Year

**Super well liked food, staff with a can-do attitude, delightful
old interior and pretty garden**

'A real winner' and 'a pity this is so far from my home' are just two
comments from readers about this charming dining pub; it's quite
handy for a break from the M5 too. Smart and very attractive, with
neatly dressed, courteous staff, the unspoilt early 19th-c layout has five
beautifully decorated little rooms and a kitchen opening off a central
corridor with a black and white tiled floor. Rooms offer a choice of
carpet, bare boards, lino or nice old quarry tiles, a variety of moods
from snug and chatty to bright and airy, and individual décor: theatrical
engravings on red walls, nice sporting prints on pale green walls, and
racing and gundog pictures above a black panelled dado. Most of the
rooms have coal fires and two have small serving bars, with Banks's
Bitter, Everards Tiger, Timothy Taylors Landlord and Wye Valley HPA
on handpump, 14 wines by the glass from a good list, organic soft drinks
and a range of coffees; daily papers and background music. The lovely
garden has a spacious lawn, and the terrace offers pleasant views.

Impressive food includes lunchtime sandwiches, pork and cep terrine with apple and calvados compote, vietnamese chicken with lemon grass, coconut and chilli salad, ham and free-range eggs, burger with cheese, bacon, relish and fries, porcini mushroom, spinach, squash and parmesan lasagne, pie of the day, malaysian chicken curry, barbecued lamb koftas with marinated aubergine and harissa tzatziki, slow-cooked pork belly with smashed apples and cider sauce, and puddings such as white chocolate and passion-fruit cheesecake with chocolate chip ice-cream and treacle tart with orange confit and clotted cream. *Benchmark main dish: slow-cooked lamb shoulder with chorizo and sweet potato dauphinoise and pea and mint purée £16.75. Two-course evening meal £18.75.*

Enterprise ~ Tenants Roger and Jo Narbett ~ Real ale ~ (01562) 730319 ~ Open 12-3, 6-11; 12-9 Sun ~ Bar food 12-2, 6.30-9(9.15 Fri, Sat); 12-7 Sun ~ Restaurant ~ Children welcome ~ Dogs allowed in bar ~ www.bellandcrossclent.co.uk *Recommended by Bernard Stradling, Simon Le Fort, David Jackman, Lynda and Trevor Smith, Brian and Maggie Woodford, Susan and John Douglas, Michael Butler, Dave and Pauline Powers, John and Gloria Isaacs, Andy Dolan, David Heath, Dr D J and Mrs S C Walker, Steve Whalley, Dennis and Doreen Haward, David and Katharine Cooke*

KNIGHTWICK
SO7355 Map 4

Talbot 🍴 🍷 🍺 🛏

Knightsford Bridge; B4197 just off A44 Worcester–Bromyard; WR6 5PH

Interesting old coaching inn with good beer from its own brewery, and riverside garden

In warm weather, it's lovely to sit at the seats and tables across the lane on a lawn beside the River Teme (they serve out here too) or you can sit out in front of the building on old-fashioned seats. A rambling country hotel with long-serving licensees, it draws a good mix of visitors and locals keen to enjoy the own-brew beers and inventive food. Their Teme Valley microbrewery uses locally grown hops to produce the That, This, T'Other and the seasonal ale that are served alongside Hobsons Best, a farm cider, a dozen wines by the glass and a number of malt whiskies; they hold regular beer festivals. The heavily beamed and extended traditional lounge bar has a warm winter log fire, a variety of seats from small carved or leatherette armchairs to winged settles by the windows, and a vast stove in a big central stone hearth. The bar opens on to a terrace and arbour with summer roses and clematis. The well furnished back public bar has pool on a raised side area, TV, games machine, darts, juke box and cribbage. In contrast, the dining room is a sedate place for a quiet meal. A farmers' market takes place here on the second Sunday of the month.

Rearing their own pigs, growing vegetables and salad leaves and making bread, pickles and jams in-house – as well as supporting local producers – the food includes pigs head brawn with honey and mustard dressing, salt-cured duck breast with red onion marmalade, wild brown trout with wild garlic gnocchi, wild mushroom timbales with herby couscous, fillet of brill with stir-fried greens, lamb stuffed with crab, lava bread, rice and spinach in ginger wine on mung bean dahl, and puddings such as chocolate truffle cake with rum filling and apple and cider syrup cake with home-made lemon and honey ice-cream. *Benchmark main dish: raised pork and game pie with chips £12.00. Two-course evening meal £20.00.*

Own brew ~ Licensee Annie Clift ~ Real ale ~ (01886) 821235 ~ Open 10(12 Sun)-11 ~ Bar food 12-9 ~ Restaurant ~ Children welcome ~ Dogs allowed in bar ~ Bedrooms: £60/£100 ~ www.the-talbot.co.uk *Recommended by J R Simmons, Hilary Adams, David Jackman, Pat and Tony Martin, Clare Tagg*

MALVERN

 SO7845 Map 4

Nags Head

Bottom end of Bank Street, steep turn down off A449; WR14 2JG

Remarkable range of real ales, delightfully eclectic layout and décor, tasty lunchtime bar food and warmly welcoming atmosphere

This has just about everything a good pub should have – an extraordinary choice of ales, cheerful, professional staff, chatty customers and enjoyable food. If you struggle to choose from the 15 beers on handpump, you will be offered a taster. House ales are Banks's Bitter, Bathams Best Bitter, St Georges Charger, Dragons Blood and Friar Tuck, Sharps Doom Bar, Woods Shropshire Lad and Wychwood Hobgoblin, and they have seven changing guests. Also, two farm ciders, more than two dozen malt whiskies and ten gins. A series of snug individually decorated rooms, with one or two steps between and two open fires, have an easy-going chatty atmosphere. Each is filled with all sorts of chairs from leather armchairs to pews sometimes arranged as booths and a mix of tables with sturdy ones stained different colours; bare boards here, flagstones there, carpet elsewhere and plenty of interesting pictures and homely touches such as house plants, shelves of well thumbed books and broadsheet newspapers; board games. The front terrace and garden have picnic-sets, benches and rustic tables as well as parasols and heaters.

 Popular lunchtime food includes sandwiches, ham, eggs and chips, vegetable lasagne, venison in ale pie and moroccan lamb and apricot with lemon zest rice; evening meals are served in the barn extension dining room only and might include ham hock, apple and thyme terrine with caramelised red onion jam, steamed mussels in curried coconut cream sauce, braised pork shoulder with apple mash, cider and parsnips, cajun monkfish with roasted sweet potato and squash and sun-dried tomato pesto, 10oz fillet steak with a choice of sauces, and puddings. *Benchmark main dish: platter of pork pie, black pudding, ham, sausages, pickles and crusty bread £9.90. Two-course evening meal £17.00.*

Free house ~ Licensees Clare Keane and Alex Whistance ~ Real ale ~ (01684) 574373 ~ Open 11am-11.15pm(11.30pm Sat); 12-11 Sun ~ Bar food 12-2, 6.30-8.30; 12-2.30, 7-8.30 Sun ~ Restaurant ~ Children welcome ~ Dogs welcome ~ www.nagsheadmalvern.co.uk
Recommended by Brian and Anna Marsden, Chris Flynn, Wendy Jones, Steve Tilley, Barry Collett, Paul Humphreys, Torrens Lyster, Jean and Douglas Troup

NEWLAND

SO7948 Map 4

Swan

Worcester Road (set well back from A449 just NW of Malvern); WR13 5AY

Popular, interesting pub with six real ales and seats in the big garden

There's a lot of character in this attractive, creeper-clad place and our readers enjoy visiting it very much. The dimly lit bar is quite traditional, with dark beams and a forest canopy of hops, whisky-water jugs, beakers and tankards. Several of the comfortable and clearly individually chosen seats are worth a close look for their carving, and the wall tapestries are interesting. The carved counter has St Georges Dragons Blood and Friar Tuck plus Sharps Doom Bar, Wychwood Hobgoblin and a couple of guests such as Crouch Vale Amarillo and Otter Bright on handpump. On the right is a broadly similar red-carpeted dining room, and beyond it, in complete contrast, an ultra-modern glass garden room; background music, bar billiards and board games.

The garden is as individual as the pub, with a cluster of huge casks topped with flowers – even a piano doing flower-tub duty – and a set of stocks on the pretty front terrace.

🍴 Enjoyable food includes lunchtime sandwiches, chicken liver pâté with red onion marmalade, smoked salmon, parmesan and beetroot salad, wild mushroom risotto, honey-baked ham and free-range eggs, chilli con carne, smoked haddock and leek macaroni, venison sausage casserole, cajun chicken with stir-fried chilli greens, bass fillets filled with crab, slow-roasted pork belly with colcannon and cider vinegar caramel, and puddings. *Benchmark main dish: chicken, ham and leek pie £9.50. Two-course evening meal £16.00.*

Free house ~ Licensee Nick Taylor ~ Real ale ~ (01886) 832224 ~ Open 12-11 ~ Bar food 12-2.30, 6.30-9; 12-3, 7-9 Sun ~ Restaurant ~ Children welcome ~ Dogs allowed in bar ~ www.theswaninnmalvern.co.uk *Recommended by Lynette Willey, Denys Gueroult, Noel Thomas, Paul Humphreys*

TENBURY WELLS
SO6468   Map 4

Talbot 🍴 🛏
Newnham Bridge; A456; WR15 8JF

Carefully refurbished Victorian coaching inn with a lot of character in bar and dining rooms, real ales and good wines and highly thought-of food; bedrooms

In lovely Teme Valley countryside, this interesting 19th-c inn has been stylishly refurbished while keeping as much original character as possible. The friendly landlord and his staff offer a warm welcome to both locals and visitors and the atmosphere throughout is civilised but informal; it gets pretty busy at weekends when it's essential to book a table in advance. There are nice old red and black and original quarry tiles, bare floorboards, open fires and candlelight, and the bar and dining rooms are quite different in style: an assortment of chairs – some dark and pubby, some high-backed in painted wood and some comfortably upholstered – around an assortment of tables, with leather tub chairs and sofas here and there, bookshelves, old photographs of the area, table lights and standard lamps, some elegant antiques and pretty fresh flower arrangements. Hobsons Best Bitter, Otter Ale, Teme Valley Talbot Blond and Wye Valley HPA on handpump, local cider and several wines by the glass from a good list. The bedrooms are thoughtfully decorated and well equipped.

🍴 Using the best local, seasonal produce, the rewarding food includes sandwiches, cornish crab and prawn tart with avocado purée, bubble and squeak with bacon, poached egg and hollandaise, rare-breed sausages with creamed cabbage and bacon, wild mushroom and leek gnocchi with pesto dressing, free-range chicken breast with creamed peas, bacon and potato fritters, cod fillet with fennel mash, roasted cherry tomatoes and citrus beurre blanc, gressingham duck breast with parsnip purée and celeriac gratin, and puddings. *Benchmark main dish: assiette of gloucester old spot pork £16.95. Two-course evening meal £20.50.*

Free house ~ Licensee Ian Dowling ~ Real ale ~ (01584) 781941 ~ Open 11.30-11(11.30 Sat); 12-7 Sun ~ Bar food 12-3, 6-9.30; 12-5.30 Sun ~ Restaurant ~ Children welcome ~ Dogs allowed in bar ~ Bedrooms: £75/£85 ~ www.talbotinnnewnhambridge.co.uk *Recommended by Gavin May, Isobel Mackinlay*

If we don't specify bar meal times for a featured entry, these are normally 12-2 and 7-9; we do show times if they are markedly different.

Also Worth a Visit in Worcestershire

Besides the fully inspected pubs, you might like to try these pubs that have been recommended to us and described by readers. Do tell us what you think of them: feedback@goodguides.com

ABBERLEY   SO7567
Manor Arms   (01299) 896507
Netherton Lane; WR6 6BN Good value comfortable country inn nicely tucked away in quiet village backwater opposite fine Norman church, façade emblazoned with coats of arms, warm welcome, quick friendly service, six ales including Wye Valley, good carefully prepared food from baguettes up, lunchtime bargains, two bars and restaurant, interesting toby jug collection; ten bedrooms. *(Peter and Jean Hoare)*

ALVECHURCH   SP0172
Weighbridge   (0121) 445 5111
Scarfield Wharf; B48 7SQ Converted little house by Worcester & Birmingham Canal marina, bar and a couple of small rooms, well kept ales such as Kinver Bargees Bitter and Weatheroaks Tillerman's Tipple, simple low-priced food (not Tues, Weds); tables outside. *(Tony Hobden)*

ASTON FIELDS   SO9669
Ladybird Inn   (01527) 878014
Finstall Road (B184 just S of Bromsgrove); B60 2DZ Light and airy red-brick Edwardian pub adjoining hotel (next to station), panelled bar and comfortable lounge, reasonably priced pub food along with separate italian restaurant, well kept Birds and guests such as Bathams and Wye Valley, good service; children welcome, open all day. *(Tony Hobden, Dave Braisted)*

BARNARDS GREEN   SO7945
Blue Bell   (01684) 575031
Junction B4211 to Rhydd Green with B4208 to Malvern Show Ground; WR14 3QP Chain dining pub in pleasant setting, comfortable and reliable, with good choice of enjoyable well priced food, Marstons-related ales, friendly efficient service even when busy, quiz first Weds of month; children welcome, disabled facilities, nice garden. *(Chris Evans, Paul Humphreys)*

BELBROUGHTON   SO9177
Queens   (01562) 730276
Queens Hill (B4188 E of Kidderminster); DY9 0DU Old refurbished red-brick pub by Belne Brook, several linked areas including beamed bar with slate floor, good modern food alongside pub standards, also set menu choices, three well kept beers and nice selection of wines, friendly staff coping at busy times; disabled facilities, small roadside terrace, pleasant village and handy for M5 (junction 4), open all day weekends. *(Eric Thomas Yarwood, W M Lien)*

BERROW   SO7835
Duke of York   (01684) 833449
Junction A438/B4208; WR13 6JQ Warmly welcoming old country pub under newish landlord; two spic and span linked rooms, beams, nooks and crannies and log fire, enjoyable food from baguettes up including daily fresh fish (crab recommended), Wye Valley and a guest ale, good service, restaurant; big garden behind, handy for Malvern Hills. *(Geoffrey and Penny Hughes)*

BERROW GREEN   SO7458
⋆Admiral Rodney   (01886) 821375
B4197, off A44 W of Worcester; WR6 6PL Light and roomy high-beamed 17th-c dining pub, big stripped kitchen tables and two woodburners, popular reasonably priced food from varied menu (should book Fri, Sat evenings), friendly fast service, well kept Birds, Wye Valley and guests, real cider/perry, charming end restaurant in rebuilt barn, folk music third Weds of month, skittle alley; well behaved children and dogs welcome, disabled facilities, tables outside with pretty view and heated covered terrace, good walks, three bedrooms, closed Mon lunchtime, open all day weekends. *(Neil and Anita Christopher)*

BEWDLEY   SO7875
Mug House   (01299) 402543
Severn Side North; DY12 2EE 18th-c bay-windowed pub in charming spot by River Severn, enjoyable traditional food, five well kept ales including Bewdley, Timothy Taylors and Wye Valley, friendly helpful service, log fire, restaurant with lobster tank; dogs welcome, disabled access, glass-covered terrace behind, seven river-view bedrooms, open all day. *(Derek and Sylvia Stephenson, Michael Coleman)*

BIRLINGHAM   SO9343
Swan   (01386) 750485
Church Street; off A4104 S of Pershore, via B4080 Eckington Road, turn off at sign to Birlingham with integral 'The Swan Inn' brown sign (not the 'Birlingham (village only)' road), then left; WR10 3AQ Pretty thatched and timbered cottage, beamed quarry-tiled bar with copper-topped tables, darts, woodburner in big stone fireplace, snug inner carpeted area by smallish counter, Wye Valley Bitter and three guests, real ciders, beer festival May and Sept, cribbage, dominoes, poker; simple back dining conservatory, reasonably priced straightforward food (not Sun evening), may be a wait when busy; children

welcome, dogs in bar, pretty back garden
divided by shrubs, seats and tables under
parasols. *(Roger and Gillian Holmes)*

BIRTSMORTON SO7936
Farmers Arms (01684) 833308
Birts Street, off B4208 W; WR13 6AP
Timbered village local, pubbily
straightforward, with well kept Hook Norton
and two changing guests, simple cheap
bar food including good pies, friendly staff,
gently old-fashioned room on right with low
dark beams and some standing timbers,
spindleback chairs and flowery-panelled
cushioned settles on big flagstones, large
inglenook, lower-beamed room on left (even
cosier), cribbage and darts teams; children
and dogs welcome, seats and swings on lovely
big lawn with Malvern Hills view, plenty of
surrounding walks. *(Dave Braisted)*

BREDON SO9236
✳ **Fox & Hounds** (01684) 772377
*4.5 miles from M5 junction 9; A438
to Northway, left at B4079, in Bredon
follow sign to church; GL20 7LA* Cottagey
16th-c thatched pub with open-plan carpeted
bar, low beams, stone pillars and stripped
timbers, central woodburner, traditional
furnishings including upholstered settles, a
variety of wheelback, tub and kitchen chairs
around handsome mahogany and cast-iron-
framed tables, elegant wall lamps, smaller
side bar, Banks's Bitter, Greene King Old
Speckled Hen and a guest, nice wines by the
glass, wide choice of food; background music;
children welcome, dogs in bar, outside picnic-
sets (some under cover), handy M5 break.
*(J V Dadswell, Dr A J and Mrs B A Tompsett,
R J Herd)*

BROADWAS-ON-TEME SO7555
Royal Oak (01886) 821353
A44; WR6 5NE Red-brick roadside pub
with relaxed lounge bar and dining area,
unusual lofty-raftered medieval-style dining
hall, and separate public bar with pool, well
kept Jennings and Marstons ales, decent
wines by the glass, popular food (all day
weekends) including good value lunchtime
carvery, friendly helpful service; they may ask
for a credit card if running a tab; children
welcome, terrace picnic-sets, open all day
weekends. *(Denys Gueroult, Martin and Pauline
Jennings)*

BROADWAY SP0937
Swan (01386) 852278
The Green (B4362); WR12 7AA
Sizeable reworked Mitchells & Butlers dining
pub with several linked areas, imaginative
décor, good sensibly priced food and wine,
three well kept changing ales, polite friendly
young staff; café-style tables on small
front terrace looking over road to village
green. *(Steve and Julie Buckingham, Glenwys
and Alan Lawrence)*

CALLOW END SO8349
Blue Bell (01905) 830261
Upton Road; WR2 4TY Marstons local
with two bars and dining area, wide variety of
enjoyable food including lots of specials, good
vegetarian options and cheap OAP lunch
deal, well kept beers, friendly welcoming
staff, open fire; children allowed, dogs in
garden only, open all day weekends.
(Dave Braisted)

CALLOW HILL SO7473
Royal Forester (01299) 266286
*Near Wyre Forest visitors' centre;
DY14 9XW* Dining pub dating in part from
the 15th c, good food and friendly helpful
service, relaxed lounge bar with two well
kept ales such as Wye Valley, Robinson's
cider, restaurant; children and dogs welcome,
seats outside, seven contemporary bedrooms,
open all day. *(Michael Coleman)*

CAUNSALL SO8480
Anchor (01562) 850254
Caunsall Road, off A449; DY11 5YL
Traditional unchanging two-room pub (in
same family since 1927), friendly atmosphere
and can get busy, well kept Hobsons, Ludlow,
Wye Valley and a guest, good filled cobs,
friendly efficient service; dogs welcome,
tables outside, near canal. *(Tony Hobden)*

CHILDSWICKHAM SP0738
✳ **Childswickham Inn** (01386) 852461
Off A44 NW of Broadway; WR12 7HP
Restauranty dining pub with big rugs on
boards or terracotta tiles, contemporary
artwork on part-timbered walls, woodburner,
good food from pubby choices to pricier
brasserie food, friendly attentive staff, locals'
lounge bar with leather sofas and armchairs
(dogs allowed here), good choice of wines,
beers such as Brakspears, Hook Norton and
Greene King; background music, TV; children
and dogs welcome, disabled facilities,
garden with decked area, barbecue, open
all day Sun. *(Bernard Stradling, Dr A J and
Mrs B A Tompsett)*

CLAINES SO8558
Mug House (01905) 456649
*Claines Lane, off A449 3 miles W of M5
junction 3; WR3 7RN* Fine views from
ancient country tavern in unique churchyard
setting by fields below the Malvern Hills;
several small rooms around central bar, low
doorways and heavy oak beams, well kept
Banks's and other Marstons-related beers,
simple lunchtime pub food (not Sun); no
credit cards, outside lavatories; children
allowed away from servery, open all day
weekends. *(Tony Hobden)*

COOKLEY SO8479
Island Pool (01562) 850311
Wolverhampton Road; DY10 3RX
Large open-plan pub popular for its bargain

food including all-you-can-eat breakfast and daily carvery, helpful polite staff, well priced beers such as Sharps Doom Bar and Wye Valley; children welcome, outside tables. *(Phil and Jane Hodson)*

CROWLE   SO9256
Old Chequers (01905) 381275
Crowle Green, not far from M5 junction 6; WR7 4AA Civilised 17th-c dining pub mixing traditional and contemporary décor; oak beams and log fires, leather sofas, modern tables and chairs in bar and restaurant, friendly prompt service, good variety of enjoyable home-made food from pub favourites up including set menu, three real ales and nice choice of wines by the glass, baby grand piano, some live jazz; children welcome, dogs in bar, disabled facilities, picnic-sets in garden behind, open all day, closed Sun evening. *(Alan Weedon, Martin and Pauline Jennings)*

CUTNALL GREEN   SO8868
Chequers (01299) 851292
Kidderminster Road; WR9 0PJ Comfortable and stylish beamed country dining pub with enjoyable food from pubby lunchtime snacks and sandwiches to more elaborate dishes, good wine choice, three well kept ales such as Marstons, Sharps and Wye Valley, friendly staff; children and dogs (in bar) welcome, open all day. *(Dave Braisted)*

DEFFORD   SO9042
★ Monkey House (01386) 750234
A4104, after passing Oak pub on right, it's the last of a small group of cottages; WR8 9BW Tiny black and white cider house, a wonderful time warp and in the same family for 150 years; drinks limited to cider and a perry tapped from barrels into pottery mugs and served by landlady from a hatch, no food (can bring your own); children welcome, no dogs (resident rottweilers), garden with caravans, sheds and Mandy the horse, small spartan outbuilding with a couple of plain tables, settle and fireplace, open Fri and Sun lunchtimes, Weds and Sat evenings. *(Anon)*

DEFFORD   SO9042
Oak (01386) 750327
Woodmancote (A4104); WR8 9BW Refurbished 17th-c beamed country inn with two front bars and back restaurant, well kept Sharps Doom Bar and Wye Valley ales, Thatcher's cider, enjoyable fairly priced food from ciabattas up, friendly staff and resident black labrador; children welcome, vine-covered front pergola, garden with chickens and orchard, bedrooms and camping. *(Brian and Maggie Woodford, Dave Braisted, Paul Humphreys)*

DRAYTON   SO9075
Robin Hood (01562) 730526
Off B4188; DY9 0BW Refurbished early 19th-c dining pub, inglenook log fire, low

beams and lovely stained glass in large lounge, good food from sensibly priced menu, also themed evenings such as seafood and japanese, well kept Enville, Holdens and Wye Valley, Thatcher's cider; can get very busy weekends; children welcome, terrace and garden tables, play area, attractive surroundings and good walks, open all day. *(Dave Braisted)*

DROITWICH   SO9063
Hop Pole (01905) 770155
Friar Street; WR9 8ED Heavy-beamed local with panelled rooms on different levels, friendly staff, well kept Wye Valley ales and guests such as Enville and Malvern Hills, bargain home-made lunchtime food including doorstep sandwiches, dominoes, darts and pool, live music first Sun of month; children welcome, partly canopied back garden, open all day. *(Dave Braisted, Chris Evans, Tony Hobden, Alan Weedon and others)*

ELDERSFIELD   SO8131
★ Butchers Arms (01452) 840381
Village signposted from B4211; Lime Street (coming from A417, go past the Eldersfield turn and take the next one), OS Sheet 150 map reference 815314; also signposted from B4208 N of Staunton; GL19 4NX Pretty cottage with deliberately simple unspoilt little locals' bar, ales such as St Austell, Wickwar and Wye Valley tapped from the cask, a farm cider and short but well chosen wine list, just a dozen seats in candlelit dining room, carefully prepared, well presented food (not cheap) using ingredients from named local farms, booking essential lunchtime and advisable evening; no under-10s, garden picnic-sets, nice surroundings, closed Sun evening, Mon, ten days Jan and the latter part of Aug, lunchtime food served Fri-Sun, evening Tues-Sat. *(Rod Stoneman, Chris Marshall)*

EVESHAM   SP0344
Evesham Hotel (01386) 765566
Coopers Lane; WR11 1DA Idiosyncratic hotel's busy bar with amazing range of malt whiskies and spirits, a beer from Teme Valley and good if quirky wine list, interesting menu including good value lunchtime buffet (no tips or service charge), elegant dining room; remarkable lavatories with talking mirrors; children welcome, indoor swimming pool, 39 bedrooms, open all day. *(Denys Gueroult)*

FECKENHAM   SP0061
Lygon Arms (01527) 893495
B4090 Droitwich–Alcester; B96 6JE Welcoming village pub freshened up under new management; enjoyable well priced food including Sun carvery, Fullers, Shepherd Neame and Wye Valley ales, traditional slate-floored bar, airy dining conservatory; pool, fortnightly quiz; children welcome, metal furniture on part-covered terrace. *(Dave Braisted)*

FLADBURY   SO9946

Chequers (01386) 860276

Chequers Lane; WR10 2PZ Refurbished dining pub dating from the 14th c, huge old-fashioned range with log fire at end of long beamed bar, good food including three or four daily specials, ales such as Black Sheep and Sharps Doom Bar, timbered back restaurant with conservatory; children welcome, steps up to walled terrace, play area on lawn, peaceful pretty village, bedroom extension. *(Dave Braisted)*

FORHILL   SP0575

⋆ **Peacock** (01564) 757307

Handy for M42 junctions 2 and 3; pub at junction of Lea End Lane and Icknield Street; B38 0EH Attractive, quietly placed and well run Chef & Brewer with wide range of enjoyable food all day, plenty of tables in comfortably fitted knocked-through beamed rooms, woodburner in big inglenook, Greene King, Highgates, Hobsons, Wells & Youngs and guest ales, friendly helpful service; background music; children and dogs welcome, disabled facilities, picnic-sets on back terrace and front grass, other heated covered areas. *(Anon)*

GRIMLEY   SO8359

Camp House (01905) 640288

A443 5 miles N from Worcester, right to Grimley, right at village T junction; WR2 6LX Unspoilt old character pub in same family since 1939, pleasant Severn-side setting with own landing stage, generous home-made food at bargain prices, well kept Bathams and guests, Thatcher's and Robinson's ciders; no credit cards; children and well behaved dogs welcome, attractive lawns with wandering peacocks, small campsite, open all day. *(Chris Evans)*

GUARLFORD   SO8245

Plough & Harrow (01684) 310453

B4211 E of village; WR13 6NY Country dining pub reopened under new management; contemporary feel despite low beams in bar, airy two-level restaurant; children welcome, hedged back garden, closed Wed. *(Anon)*

HADLEY   SO8662

Bowling Green (01905) 620294

Hadley Heath; off A4133 Droitwich–Ombersley; WR9 0AR Friendly 16th-c inn with beams and big log fire, sofas in back lounge, well kept Wadworths range and decent wines by the glass, enjoyable food from sandwiches up, attractive restaurant; children welcome, tables out overlooking its bowling green (UK's oldest), eight

comfortable bedrooms, nice walks (footpath starts from car park). *(M Ross-Thomas)*

HAGLEY   SO9180

Lyttleton Arms (01562) 882213

Park Road/Bromsgrove Road; DY9 9LJ Civilised place with comfortable contemporary décor, good choice of food all day including weekday set menu (till 7pm), efficient young staff, wide range of wines by the glass, cocktail list; children welcome, tables on sizeable terrace. *(D M and B K Moores)*

HANBURY   SO9662

Vernon (01527) 821236

Droitwich Road (B4090); B60 4DB 18th-c former coaching inn reopened after major contemporary refurbishment, calls itself a country restaurant with rooms but still serves real ales such as Wye Valley and Sharps in beamed bar with woodburner, nice food from light choices to more enterprising restaurant-style dishes, good value set menu too; modern terrace seating, five stylish bedrooms, open all day. *(Dave Braisted)*

HANLEY CASTLE   SO8342

⋆ **Three Kings** (01684) 592686

Church End, off B4211 N of Upton upon Severn; WR8 0BL Timeless, hospitable and by no means smart (a favourite for those who put unspoilt character and individuality first); cheerful, homely tiled-floor tap room separated from entrance corridor by monumental built-in settle, equally vast inglenook fireplace, room on left with darts and board games, separate entrance to timbered lounge with second inglenook and neatly blacked kitchen range, leatherette armchairs, spindleback chairs and antique winged settle, well kept Butcombe, Hobsons and three guests from smaller brewers, farm cider and around 75 malt whiskies, simple snacks; old-fashioned wood and iron seats on front terrace looking across to great cedar shading tiny green. *(Joan and Tony Walker)*

HANLEY SWAN   SO8142

Swan (01684) 311870

B4209 Malvern–Upton; WR8 0EA Contemporary rustic décor and furnishings blending well with old low beams, bare boards and log fire, extended back part set for dining, enjoyable fairly standard food including good steaks and Sun carvery, friendly helpful service, well kept St Austell Tribute, Shepherd Neame Spitfire and Wells & Youngs Bombardier, good wines by the glass, lively atmosphere; background music and some live; children welcome, disabled facilities, good-sized side lawn with play area, nice spot facing green and big duck pond, five comfortable bedrooms (one

Post Office address codings confusingly give the impression that some pubs are in Worcestershire, when they're really in Gloucestershire, Herefordshire, Shropshire or Warwickshire (which is where we list them).

over kitchen can be noisy), open all day weekends. *(Joan and Tony Walker)*

HARTLEBURY   SO8470
Old Ticket Office   (01299) 253275
Station Road; DY11 7YJ Recently converted station buildings (a few trains still stop here), four well priced Attwoods beers from adjacent brewery, enjoyable food in bar and restaurant including carvery (not Mon or Sat); sports TV; open all day. *(Dave Braisted)*

KEMPSEY   SO8548
Walter de Cantelupe
(01905) 820572 *3.7 miles from M5 junction 7: A44 towards Worcester, left on to A4440, then left on A38 at roundabout; Main Road; WR5 3NA* Traditional carpeted bar with inglenook log fire, ales such as Cannon Royall, Cotleigh and Timothy Taylors, summer farm cider and maybe locally pressed apple juice, enjoyable home-made food, table skittles; background music, sports TV; children in dining area till 8.15pm, dogs in bar and bedrooms, pretty suntrap walled garden, closed Mon. *(Anon)*

KIDDERMINSTER   SO8376
★ King & Castle   (01562) 747505
Railway Station, Comberton Hill; DY10 1QX Bustling and neatly re-created Edwardian refreshment room suiting its setting in Severn Valley Railway terminus, steam trains outside and railway memorabilia and photographs inside, simple furnishings, Bathams, very good value Wyre Piddle and guests, reasonably priced straightforward food in adjacent dining room (9am-3pm), cheerful staff coping well on busy bank holidays and railway gala days; little museum close by, open all day. *(Anon)*

LULSLEY   SO7354
Fox & Hounds   (01886) 821228
Signed a mile off A44 Worcester–Bromyard; WR6 5QT Pleasant tucked-away country pub with well kept Greene King, Hobsons, Otter and a guest (May beer festival), Robinson's cider and nice wines, good choice of enjoyable reasonably priced food (not evenings Sun, Mon, Weds), friendly staff and locals, smallish parquet-floored bar with open fire, steps down to lounge area, sizeable dining conservatory, Tues jazz night; children welcome, dogs in bar, colourful side rose garden and separate enclosed play area, nice walks (near Worcestershire Way), open all day Fri-Sun. *(Anon)*

MALVERN   SO7746
Foley Arms   (01684) 573397
Worcester Road, WR14 4QS Substantial Georgian hotel taken over by Wetherspoons, usual good value; splendid views from sunny terrace and back bedrooms, open all day from 7am. *(Dave Braisted, Torrens Lyster, Alan Weedon)*

MALVERN   SO7746
Red Lion   (01684) 564787
St Ann's Road; WR14 4RG Enjoyable food (all day weekends) from substantial sandwiches and baguettes up, also adjacent thai restaurant (asian-fusion buffet Sun), well kept Marstons-related ales, cheerful prompt service, airy modern décor with stripped pine, bare boards, flagstones and pastel colours; background and live music; attractive partly covered front terrace, well placed for walks. *(Paul Humphreys)*

OMBERSLEY   SO8463
★ Cross Keys   (01905) 620588
Just off A449; Main Road (A4133, Kidderminster end); WR9 0DS Carpeted bar with easy-going atmosphere, archways opening into several separate areas – nicest on left with attractive Bob Lofthouse animal etchings, hop-strung beams and some horse tack on dark-varnished country panelling, Timothy Taylors Landlord and Wye Valley HPA, good value wines by the glass and decent coffee, comfortable back room with softly upholstered sofas and armchairs leading to dining conservatory, nice food including enterprising daily specials (good fish choice), friendly service; unobtrusive background music; children welcome if eating, terrace with alloy furniture under big heated canopy. *(Dave Braisted, Eric Thomas Yarwood, M and GR)*

OMBERSLEY   SO8463
★ Kings Arms   (01905) 620142
Main Road (A4133); WR9 0EW Imposing beamed and timbered Tudor pub, spotless rambling rooms with nooks and crannies, three splendid fireplaces, low-ceilinged quarry-tiled bar with dark wood pew and stools around cast-iron tables, three dining areas, one room with Charles II coat of arms decorating its ceiling, ales such as Jennings and Marstons, well liked food; background music; children and dogs welcome, seats on tree-sheltered courtyard, colourful hanging baskets and tubs, open all day. *(Chris Flynn, Wendy Jones, Stuart Paulley, Dr and Mrs A K Clarke, E Clark)*

PENSAX   SO7368
★ Bell   (01299) 896677
B4202 Abberley–Clows Top, Snead Common part of village; WR6 6AE Mock-Tudor roadside pub with good local atmosphere and welcoming landlord, half a dozen changing ales such as Hobsons (festival last weekend of June), also cider and perry, tasty bar food (not Sun evening) including generous sandwiches, L-shaped main bar with traditional décor, cushioned pews and pubby tables on bare boards, vintage beer ads and wartime newspaper front pages, two open fires and woodburner, dining room with french windows opening on to deck; children welcome, dogs in bar,

country-view garden, open all day summer weekends, closed Mon. *(R T and J C Moggridge, Kerry Law)*

PEOPLETON   SO9350
Crown (01905) 840222
Village and pub signed off A44 at Allens Hill; WR10 2EE Cosy village pub with good mix of drinkers and diners, beamed bar with big inglenook, well laid out eating area, good generous food (must book) from sandwiches up including set deals, Fullers and Hook Norton ales, nice wines by the glass, efficient friendly service; surcharge added if paying by card; flower-filled back garden. *(Martin and Pauline Jennings)*

PERSHORE   SO9545
★ Brandy Cask (01386) 552602
Bridge Street; WR10 1AJ Plain high-ceilinged bow-windowed bar, own good ales from courtyard brewery and guests, friendly helpful service, coal fire, reasonably priced generous food from sandwiches to steaks, quaintly decorated dining room; well behaved children allowed, no dogs inside, terrace and koi pond in long attractive garden down to river (watch the kids). *(Joan and Tony Walker)*

RYALL   SO8640
Blue Bell (01684) 594624
Grove Crescent; WR8 0PP Refurbished main-road pub with good range of food including light lunch menu, well kept Wye Valley and other beers, several wines by the glass, good service. *(Dr A J and Mrs B A Tompsett, Dave Braisted)*

SEVERN STOKE   SO8544
Rose & Crown (01905) 371249
A38 S of Worcester; WR8 9JQ Attractive 16th-c black and white pub, low beams, knick-knacks and good fire in character bar, some cushioned wall seats and high-backed settles among more modern pub furniture, well kept Marstons-related ales, decent choice of enjoyable sensibly priced food (all day) including vegetarian, good friendly service, carpeted back restaurant, music and quiz nights; dogs welcome, wheelchair access with help, picnic-sets in big garden with play area, Malvern Hills views and good walks. *(Brian Yates, R L Borthwick)*

SHATTERFORD   SO7981
★ Bellmans Cross (01299) 861322
Bridgnorth Road (A442); DY12 1RN Welcoming french-mood dining pub with good well presented food from sandwiches up including set choices, smart tasteful restaurant with kitchen view, french chefs and bar staff, pleasant deft service, real ales and good choice of wines from neat timber-

effect bar, teas and coffees; picnic-sets outside, handy for Severn Woods walks, open all day weekends. *(Anon)*

SNEACHILL   SO9053
Nightingale (01905) 344901
A44, E of Spetchley; WR5 1RR Roomy Vintage Inn with some character, their usual food well prepared and pleasantly served by efficient staff, ales such as Sharps Doom Bar and decent wines by the glass, inglenook log fire; can get busy lunchtime; children welcome, open all day. *(David Green, Martin and Pauline Jennings, Mike and Mary Carter)*

STOCK GREEN   SO9959
Bird in Hand (01386) 793158
Stockwood Lane; B96 6SX Proper old-fashioned rural pub with Banks's, Wadworths and Wye Valley, no food apart from lunchtime baps, photos of prize bulls. *(Dave Braisted)*

STOKE WORKS   SO9365
Boat & Railway (01527) 831065
Shaw Lane, by Bridge 42 of Worcester & Birmingham Canal; B60 4EQ Friendly unpretentious pub with enjoyable food and Marstons-related ales, attentive helpful staff; covered canalside terrace. *(Dave Braisted)*

STOKE WORKS   SO9365
Bowling Green (01527) 861291
A mile from M5 junction 5, via Stoke Lane; handy for Worcester & Birmingham Canal; B60 4BH Friendly comfortable pub, bargain traditional food, Banks's and Marstons EPA, polished fireplace; big garden with neat bowling green. *(Dave Braisted)*

TIBBERTON   SO9057
Bridge Inn (01905) 345874
Plough Road; WR9 7NQ By Bridge 25 of Worcester & Birmingham Canal; two comfortable dining sections with central fireplace, separate public bar, enjoyable reasonably priced traditional food, Banks's ales and a Marstons guest, friendly staff, some live music; children, dogs and muddy boots welcome, picnic-sets by water and in garden with secure play area, moorings, open all day. *(Tony Hobden, Dave Braisted)*

UPHAMPTON   SO8464
Fruiterers Arms (01905) 620305
Off A449 N of Ombersley; WR9 0JW Homely country local (looks like a private house, and has been in the same family for over 160 years), good value Cannon Royall ales (brewed at back of pub) and guests, farm cider, simple rustic Jacobean panelled bar and lounge with comfortable armchairs, beamery, log fire, lots of photographs and memorabilia, filled rolls (Fri-Sun);

If you report on a pub that's not a featured entry, please tell us any lunchtimes or evenings when it doesn't serve bar food.

back terrace and some seats out in front, open all day. *(Anon)*

✳ Coach & Horses (01564) 823386
WEATHEROAK HILL   SP0574

Icknield Street – coming S on A435 from Wythall roundabout, filter right off dual carriageway a mile S, then in village turn left towards Alvechurch; not far from M42, junction 3; B48 7EA Roomy country pub (in same family since 1968) brewing its own good Weatheroak beers, well kept guests too and farm ciders, enjoyable choice of fairly priced home-cooked food (not Sun evening); proper old-fashioned tiled-floor bar with log fire (dogs allowed here), lounge bar with steps up to comfortably furnished high-raftered room with another fire, modern barn-style restaurant; children welcome, plenty of seats out on lawns and terrace, open all day. *(Anon)*

✳ Brewers Arms (01684) 568147
WEST MALVERN   SO7645

The Dingle, signed off B4232; WR14 4BQ Attractive and friendly little two-bar beamed country local down steep path, Malvern Hills, Marstons, Wye Valley and up to four guests (Oct beer festival), good value food including bargain OAP weekday lunches, neat airy dining room; children, walkers and dogs welcome, glorious view from small garden, smokers' folly, open all day Fri-Sun. *(Anon)*

New Inn (01386) 853226
WILLERSEY   SP1039

Main Street; WR12 7PJ Friendly and attractive old stone-built local in lovely village, generous good value pub food all day from sandwiches up, prompt service, well kept Donnington ales, ancient flagstones, darts and raised end area in traditional main bar with woodburner, pool in separate public bar, skittle alley; background music, TV; tables outside, good local walks, open all day. *(Alan Weedon)*

Crown (0121) 445 2300
WITHYBED GREEN   SP0172

Near Bridge 61 of Worcester & Birmingham Canal; B48 7PN Tucked-away pub in row of former canal workers' cottages overlooking fields, simple low-priced food (not Sun evening), Greene King Abbot and a couple of guests, two open fires; no dogs inside; children welcome; picnic-sets out in front and on terrace, open all day. *(Tony Hobden, Dave Braisted)*

Alma (01905) 28103
WORCESTER   SO8456

Droitwich Road (A38); WR3 7HT Well kept ales and good value hearty food including OAP deals. *(Alan Weedon)*

Dragon (01905) 25845
WORCESTER   SO8455

The Tything; WR1 1JT Simply furnished

open-plan alehouse with six well kept interesting beers from smaller brewers, bottled belgians and Thatcher's cider too, friendly staff; dogs welcome, partly covered back terrace, open all day Fri, Sat (lunchtime food then), closed Mon and Tues lunchtimes. *(Giles and Annie Francis)*

✳ Marwood (01905) 330460
WORCESTER   SO8455

The Tything (A38); some nearby parking; WR1 1JL Easy to miss this old building, quirky and civilised with a long narrow series of small linked areas, dark flagstones and broad old floorboards, stripped or cast-iron-framed tables, the odd chandelier, a few italian deco posters, open fires, upstairs room looking across to Law Courts, well kept Butcombe, Purity, Sharps Doom Bar and guests, enjoyable food (not Sun evening) from sandwiches and tapas up, friendly service; background music; children (in bar till 7.30pm) and dogs welcome, sunny flagstoned courtyard, open all day (till late Sat). *(Anon)*

Plough (01905) 21381
WORCESTER   SO8555

Fish Street; WR1 2HN Traditional corner pub with two simple rooms off entrance lobby, six interesting ales usually including Hobsons and Malvern Hills, farm cider and perry, good whisky choice, coal-effect gas fire; outside lavatories; small back terrace with cathedral view, open all day, closed Thurs lunchtime. *(Anon)*

Postal Order (01905) 22373
WORCESTER   SO8455

Foregate Street; WR1 1DN Popular Wetherspoons in former sorting office, wide range of well kept beers, Weston's cider and their usual good value food; open all day from 8am. *(Tony Hobden)*

Swan With Two Nicks
WORCESTER   SO8554

(01905) 28190 *New Street/Friar Street; WR1 2DP* Rambling town pub dating from the 16th c, plenty of character in bare-boards low-ceilinged front rooms, four well kept changing local ales and some interesting bottled ciders, good value lunchtime food including specials, friendly atmosphere, other areas (one for Fri live music); open all day except Sun evening. *(Robert W Buckle)*

Anchor (01386) 554114
WYRE PIDDLE   SO9647

Off A4538 WNW of Evesham; WR10 2JB Great position by River Avon, with moorings, decking on three levels, floodlit lawn and view from big airy back dining bar, enjoyable food (not Sun evening) with emphasis on fish/seafood, beers such as Courage and Wye Valley, good friendly service; children and dogs welcome, open all day. *(Dave Braisted)*

Yorkshire

What shines through in all our Main Entry pubs in this large county – from simple walkers' taverns to smart bars in civilised inns and hotels – is the warmth of the welcome from the landlords and landladies. And this follows through to our new pubs too: the Fox & Rabbit in Lockton (handy for North York Moors National Park and with enjoyable food and drink), Black Sheep Brewery in Masham (unusual bistro-style place plus a brewery tour and shop), Kelham Island Tavern in Sheffield (tucked away in a backstreet with 13 real ales), Ring o' Bells in Thornton (long-serving owners and reliably good food in hilltop dining pub) and Maltings in York (jovial landlord, seven beers and exceptionally good value food). Readers have also much enjoyed the Fleece at Addingham (smart and civilised, with thoughtful drinks and super modern food), Malt Shovel at Brearton (family-run with good food and live opera), Wyvill Arms in Constable Burton (smashing place to stay and dine), Durham Ox in Crayke (excellent all-rounder), Blue Lion at East Witton (delicious food and warm welcome for all), General Tarleton in Ferrensby (beautifully presented food, spotless bedrooms and friendly atmosphere), Grantley Arms in Grantley (lovely welcome, super food and a local feel), Shibden Mill at Halifax (restored mill with high quality food, fine wine list and individually decorated bedrooms), Chequers in Ledsham (lovely landlord, well kept ales and interesting food), Horseshoe in Levisham (friendly, traditional and run by two brothers), Sandpiper in Leyburn (excellent landlord-cooked food and a nice place to stay), White Swan in Pickering (charming little bar, fine drinks choice and super food), Nags Head in Pickhill (long-serving landlord who keeps everything top notch), Crown at Roecliffe (fabulous food, drink, atmosphere and bedrooms), Pipe & Glass at South Dalton (delicious meals and stylish bedrooms) and Buck at Thornton Watless (run for 27 years by charming hands-on licensees). With over half the Main Entry pubs holding a Food Award and with some extraordinarily gifted chefs, it's no easy task to choose a winner – but the Pipe & Glass in South Dalton is Yorkshire Dining Pub 2014.

ADDINGHAM
Fleece 🍴 ♀

SE0749   Map 7

Main Street (B6160, off A65); LS29 0LY

Enterprising management with strong sense of style; good food cooked by the landlord and his team, using local produce

They keep a carefully chosen list of drinks in this creeper-covered stone-built inn: four real ales on handpump such as Black Sheep Best, Ilkley Gold, Timothy Taylors Landlord and Wharfedale Tether, and over 28 wines (including champagne and rosé) by the glass. The smart bar on the right has a cool décor of dark flagstones, polished floorboards, crisp cream paintwork and some wallpaper based on antique fish prints above a charcoal-grey high dado. A pair of grey plaid tub armchairs stand by a great arched stone fireplace, and down a few steps is the civilised dining room (occasionally given over to their cookery classes). The interesting black-beamed village bar on the left has a good log fire in its high-manteled fireplace, comfortably worn easy chairs as well as well cushioned wall benches and window seats, and some most unusual substantial tables on its broad floorboards. Nicely framed local photographs include a series devoted to former landlord 'Heapy', hero survivor of a 1944 torpedoing. The flagstoned front terrace has neat tables under giant parasols, and a further dining terrace looks out over the garden. They have a cookery school and a deli next door.

 They bake their own bread twice daily and use the best local, seasonal produce for the enticing, landlord-cooked food: sandwiches, queenie scallops with garlic butter and gruyère, crispy duck egg with devil sauce and chorizo and bacon salad, gnocchi with leeks, cheese and wholegrain mustard cream, burger with coleslaw, relish and chips, ham and chicken pie, smoked haddock with samphire, poached egg and chervil hollandaise, specials such as moules marinière or lobster risotto with mature cheddar and bisque sauce, and puddings; they also offer a two- and three-course weekday set menu (lunchtime, 6-7pm). *Benchmark main dish: slow-cooked pork belly, cheek, black pudding, parma ham-wrapped fillet, apple purée and red wine jus £16.00. Two-course evening meal £19.50.*

Punch ~ Lease Craig Minto ~ Real ale ~ (01943) 830491 ~ Open 12-11(midnight Sat, 10 Sun) ~ Bar food 12-2, 6(5 Fri, Sat)-9; 12-8 Sun ~ Restaurant ~ Children welcome ~ Dogs allowed in bar ~ fleeceinnaddingham.co.uk *Recommended by Gordon and Margaret Ormondroyd, Dave Braisted, Tina and David Woods-Taylor*

AMPLEFORTH
White Swan

SE5878   Map 10

Off A170 W of Helmsley; East End; YO62 4DA

Quite a choice of seating areas in this attractive pub, attentive service, enjoyable food and real ales; seats on back terrace

People tend to return to this extremely well run pub again and again. As it's close to Ampleforth College and Abbey, many of the customers are visitors and parents – but there's a warm welcome for all and it's nearly always busy. The beamed lounge has plum-coloured décor, sporting prints, slate or carpeted flooring and a double-sided woodburning stove. The more conventional beamed front bar, popular with locals, has a blazing log fire, red patterned wall seating, standing timbers and a comfortable seating area at the end with big soft red cushions; there's also a more formal dining area with plush furnishings and tables covered in crisp white linen. Black Sheep Best and

Theakstons Best on handpump, good wines by the glass and ten malt whiskies; background music, pool, darts and dominoes. At the back of the pub is a large, attractive terrace with plenty of seats and tables and views over the valley.

🍴 A good choice of generously served food might include sandwiches and toasties, twice-baked crab and gruyère cheese soufflé, crayfish tails and parma ham salad, field mushroom, pecorino and herb wellington with madeira and shallot cream sauce, steak in ale pie, gammon with onion rings and egg, curried tempura tiger prawns with lime and coriander yoghurt, chicken in mushoom and bacon sauce, lambs liver and bacon with onion gravy, half gressingham duckling with orange sauce, and puddings. *Benchmark main dish: deep-fried fresh haddock with mushy peas and chips £13.30. Two-course evening meal £18.75.*

Free house ~ Licensees Mr and Mrs R Thompson ~ Real ale ~ (01439) 788239 ~ Open 12-3, 5.30-11; 12-1am Sat; 12-11 Sun ~ Bar food 12-2, 6-9 ~ Restaurant ~ Children welcome ~ www.thewhiteswan-ampleforth.co.uk *Recommended by Pat and Stewart Gordon*

ASENBY
SE3975   Map 7

Crab & Lobster 🍴 ♟ 🛏

Dishforth Road; village signed off A168 – handy for A1; YO7 3QL

Interesting furnishings and décor in rambling bar, inventive restauranty food, good drinks choice and seats on an attractive terrace; smart bedrooms

Handy for the A1, this is a smart, handsome place with much emphasis on the hotel and restaurant side – though the rambling L-shaped bar still attracts customers dropping in for a drink and a chat, and they keep Copper Dragon Golden Pippin and Hambleton Bitter on handpump and lots of wines by the glass. The bustling bar has an interesting jumble of seats from antique high-backed and other settles through sofas and wing armchairs heaped with cushions to tall and rather theatrical corner seats; the tables are almost as much of a mix, and the walls and available surfaces are quite a jungle of bric-a-brac including lots of race tickets, with standard and table lamps and candles keeping the lighting pleasantly informal. There's also a cosy main restaurant and a dining pavilion with big tropical plants, nautical bits and pieces and Edwardian sofas; background music. The gardens have bamboo and palm trees lining the paths, which lead to a gazebo; there are seats on a mediterranean-style terrace. The opulent bedrooms (based on famous hotels around the world) are in the nearby Crab Manor, which has seven acres of mature gardens and a 180-metre golf hole with full practice facilities.

🍴 Enticing – if not cheap – food includes sandwiches, pot of salmon three-ways with lemon and dill butter and horseradish soldiers, sticky pork ribs with orange, ginger and five spice, Jack Daniels and treacle, beer-battered fresh fish with proper chips, free-range chicken with cheese, ham, herb breadcrumbs and cream, local venison with smoked bacon, rösti potatoes, pink grapefruit, ginger jelly and game gravy, tandoori tiger and king prawns with cucumber yoghurt and naan bread, and puddings such as triple belgian chocolate cheesecake with sweet wine-poached pears and chilled stem ginger custard and date and banana toffee pudding with maple butterscotch sauce and double vanilla ice-cream. *Benchmark main dish: half lobster thermidor with scallops and prawns £22.00. Two-course evening meal £33.00.*

Vimac Leisure ~ Licensee Mark Spenceley ~ Real ale ~ (01845) 577286 ~ Open 11am-11.30pm ~ Bar food 12-2, 7(6.30 Sat)-9 ~ Restaurant ~ Children welcome ~ Live jazz

Sun lunchtime, Weds evening ~ Bedrooms: /£160 ~ www.crabandlobster.co.uk
Recommended by Marcus Mann, Taff Thomas

BLAKEY RIDGE
SE6799 Map 10
Lion 🍺 🛏

*From A171 Guisborough–Whitby follow Castleton, Hutton le Hole signposts;
from A170 Kirkby Moorside–Pickering follow Keldholm, Hutton le Hole, Castleton
signposts; OS Sheet 100 map reference 679996; YO62 7LQ*

**Extended pub in fine scenery and open all day; popular food;
bedrooms**

Miles from anywhere and very useful for thirsty and hungry walkers
(especially those walking the Coast to Coast path), this extended
pub has breathtaking views over the valleys of Rosedale and Farndale.
The low-beamed and rambling bars have warm open fires, a few big
high-backed rustic settles around cast-iron-framed tables, lots of
small dining chairs, a nice leather sofa and stone walls hung with old
engravings and photographs of the pub under snow (it can easily get
cut off in winter – 40 days is the record so far). A fine choice of beers
might include Black Sheep Best, Copper Dragon Golden Pippin, Hook
Norton Cotswold Lion, Theakstons Best, Old Peculier and Paradise Ale
and Thwaites Wainwright on handpump; background music and games
machine. If you're thinking of staying, you must book well in advance;
they offer good value midweek winter deals. This is a regular stop-off
for coach parties.

Popular food includes lunchtime sandwiches, giant yorkshire pudding with
gravy, chicken goujons with barbecue dip, home-cooked ham and egg, burger
with chilli, sweetcorn and onion relish, vegetable lasagne, beef or chicken curry,
beer-battered haddock with chips and peas, specials such as chicken kiev and duck
breast in cointreau and orange sauce, and puddings such as jam roly-poly with
custard and chocolate nut sundae. *Benchmark main dish: steak and mushroom
pie £11.50. Two-course evening meal £16.00.*

Free house ~ Licensees Barry, Diana, Paul and David Crossland ~ Real ale ~ (01751)
417320 ~ Open 10am-11pm(midnight Sat) ~ Bar food 12-10 ~ Restaurant ~ Children
welcome ~ Dogs allowed in bar ~ Bedrooms: £45.50/£80 ~ www.lionblakey.co.uk
Recommended by Dr J Barrie Jones, G Jennings, WAH, Stephen Funnell

BOROUGHBRIDGE
SE3966 Map 7
Black Bull ♀ £

St James Square; B6265, just off A1(M); YO51 9AR

**Bustling town pub with real ales, several wines by the glass and
traditional bar food; bedrooms**

This attractive village inn is a quiet respite from the A1 and has been
looking after travellers between England and Scotland for centuries.
There are lots of separate drinking and eating areas where plenty of
cheerful locals drop in regularly for a pint and a chat. The main bar
area has a big stone fireplace and comfortable seats and is served
through an old-fashioned hatch; there's also a cosy snug with traditional
wall settles, and a tap room, lounge bar and restaurant. John Smiths,
Timothy Taylors Best and a changing guest such as Theakstons Best on
handpump, six wines by the glass and 17 malt whiskies; dominoes. The
borzoi dog is called Spot and the two cats Kia and Mershka. The hanging
baskets are lovely.

🍴 As well as hot and cold sandwiches, the very fair-priced bar snacks include mince and onion pie, battered haddock with mushy peas and chips, and thai beef strips with noodles and stri-fried vegetables in hot and sour sauce; also, chicken liver pâté with cumberland sauce, duck salad with hoisin sauce, pork tenderloin in pink peppercorn and calvados sauce, salmon steak with chips and salad, and pudding such as chocolate fudge cake and baked jam sponge with custard. *Benchmark main dish: pie of the day £8.25. Two-course evening meal £19.00.*

Free house ~ Licensee Anthony Burgess ~ Real ale ~ (01423) 322413 ~ Open 11-11 (midnight Sat); 12-11 Sun ~ Bar food 12-2, 6-9(9.30 Fri, Sat ~ Restaurant ~ Children welcome ~ Dogs welcome ~ Bedrooms: £48/£72 ~ www.blackbullboroughbridge.co.uk
Recommended by Michael Butler, Barry Collett, Roger and Donna Huggins, Martin and Sue Day, John and Eleanor Holdsworth

BRADFIELD
SK2290   Map 7
Strines Inn £ 🛏

From A57 heading E of junction with A6013 (Ladybower Reservoir), take first left turn (signposted with Bradfield) then bear left; with a map can also be reached more circuitously from Strines signpost on A616 at head of Underbank Reservoir, W of Stocksbridge; S6 6JE

Surrounded by fine scenery with quite a mix of customers and traditional beer and bar food; bedrooms

If you stay here, the bedrooms have four-poster beds and a dining table (they serve breakfast in your room); the front room overlooks the reservoir. The inn is on the edge of the Peak District National Park, so the surrounding scenery is superb and walkers and their dogs are most welcome. The main bar has black beams liberally decked with copper kettles and so forth, quite a menagerie of stuffed animals, homely red plush-cushioned traditional wooden wall benches and small chairs, and a coal fire in a rather grand stone fireplace. Two other rooms to the right and left are similarly furnished. Bradfield Farmers Blonde, Jennings Cocker Hoop and Marstons Pedigree on handpump and several wines by the glass; background music. There are plenty of picnic-sets outside, as well as swings and a play area and peacocks, geese and chickens.

🍴 Food includes sandwiches, game and port pâté, prawn cocktail, macaroni cheese, chilli in a giant yorkshire pudding, liver and onions with gravy, big mixed grill, specials like chicken breast in mushroom and white wine sauce or duck in port and cranberry sauce, and puddings such as apple and rhubarb crumble and bread and butter pudding. *Benchmark main dish: steak in ale pie £9.30. Two-course evening meal £13.00.*

Free house ~ Licensee Bruce Howarth ~ Real ale ~ (0114) 285 1247 ~ Open 10.30am-11pm; 10.30-3, 5.30-11 weekdays in winter ~ Bar food 12-9; 12-2.30, 5.30-9 weekdays in winter ~ Children welcome ~ Dogs welcome ~ Bedrooms: £60/£80 ~ www.thestrinesinn.webs.com *Recommended by Brian and Janet Ainscough*

BREARTON
SE3260   Map 7
Malt Shovel 🍴 ♗

Village signposted off A61 N of Harrogate; HG3 3BX

Friendly, family-run dining pub with imaginative food and good choice of drinks in heavily beamed rooms; airy conservatory

Our readers enjoy their visits to this bustling dining pub and the friendly Bleiker family and their staff are sure to make you welcome.

The heavily beamed rooms have a cosy atmosphere helped by the two fires in original fireplaces and the woodburning stove, and radiate from the attractive linenfold oak bar counter (made from old church panelling). There's an attractive mix of wooden dining chairs around tables on wood or slate floors and some partitioning that separates several candlelit dining areas. Black Sheep Best, Timothy Taylors Landlord and a guest like Daleside Blonde on handpump, 21 wines by the glass from a very good list and ten malt whiskies. The conservatory is light and airy with a piano (used for Sunday jazz); they also hold occasional live opera evenings. There are seats and tables under parasols in the garden and pretty summer hanging baskets. The family are also associated with Bleiker's Smokehouse near Harrogate.

🍴 They bake their own bread and rear their own pigs for the highly popular food: sandwiches, salt and chilli squid with salad, black pudding scotch egg with celeriac remoulade and crispy bacon, mushroom and spinach wellington, chicken breast with serrano ham, chorizo and herb gnocchi, wienerschnitzel with dauphinoise potatoes and anchovy and caper garnish, specials like queenie scallops with gruyère or turbot fillet with lobster, turbot quenelle and beurre blanc, and puddings such as crème brûlée and chocolate fondant tart with hot boozy chocolate sauce; there's also a good cheese board and they offer a three-course set menu. *Benchmark main dish: slow-cooked pork belly with boulangère potatoes, red cabbage and crackling £16.95. Two-course evening meal £21.00.*

Free house ~ Licensee Jurg Bleiker ~ Real ale ~ (01423) 862929 ~ Open 12-3, 5.30-11; 12-4.30 Sun; closed Sun evening, Mon ~ Bar food 12-2, 7-9; 12-4 Sun ~ Restaurant ~ Children welcome ~ Jazz pianist Sun, occasional opera evenings with dinner ~ www.themaltshovelbrearton.co.uk *Recommended by Anthony Stoker, Comus and Sarah Elliott, Ryan Green, Dennis Jones, Derek and Sylvia Stephenson*

BROUGHTON
Bull 🍴 ♀

SD9450   Map 7

A59; BD23 3AE

Handsome, carefully refurbished inn making good use of pale oak and contemporary paintwork, good choice of drinks and enjoyable bar food

This handsome stone inn overlooks the grounds of Broughton Hall and you can walk through the Estate's 3,000 acres of beautiful countryside and parkland. The various carefully furnished rooms have lots of pale oak, handsome flagstones, exposed stone walls, built-in wall seats and a mix of dining chairs around polished tables, contemporary paintwork hung with photographs of local suppliers, and open log fires. Copper Dragon Golden Pippin, Dark Horse Hetton Pale Ale, Settle Signal Main Line and Thwaites Original on handpump, several malt whiskies and around a dozen wines (including champagne) by the glass. Outside, there are solid benches and tables on an attractive terrace.

🍴 Under the newish landlord, the very good food now includes sandwiches, pressed terrine of gammon with fried quail egg and spiced pineapple pickle, welsh rarebit with mussel beignets, sharing platters, honey-roast ham with free-range eggs, pork and chive sausages with onion marmalade gravy, pie of the day, gnocchi with wild mushrooms, shallots, truffle and butternut squash, burger with tomato relish, coleslaw and chips, fish pie, slow-cooked ox cheek with horseradish mash, and puddings such as chocolate cake with salted hazelnuts and milk chocolate ice-cream and baked alaska. *Benchmark main dish: battered fish of the day with home-made tartare sauce and chips £11.50. Two-course evening meal £17.50.*

Ribble Valley Inns ~ Manager Craig Bancroft ~ Real ale ~ (01756) 792065 ~ Open
12-11(10 Sun); closed Mon ~ Bar food 12-2, 5.30-8.30(9 Fri, Sat); 12-8.30 Sun ~
Children welcome ~ Dogs allowed in bar ~ www.thebullatbroughton.com
Recommended by Graham and Jane Bellfield

 CONSTABLE BURTON   SE1690   Map 10

Wyvill Arms 🍽 ♀ 🍺 🛏

A684 E of Leyburn; DL8 5LH

**Well run, friendly dining pub with interesting food, a dozen wines
by the glass, real ales and efficient helpful service; comfortable
bedrooms**

After enjoying the popular food in this well run 18th-c former
farmhouse, do pay a visit to the Constable Burton Hall Gardens
opposite. The small bar area has a mix of seating, a finely worked plaster
ceiling with the Wyvill family's coat of arms and an elaborate stone
fireplace with a warm winter fire. The second bar has a lower ceiling
with fans, leather seating, old oak tables, various alcoves and a model
train on a railway track running around the room; the reception area
includes a huge leather sofa that can seat up to eight people, another
carved stone fireplace and an old leaded church stained-glass window
partition. Both rooms are hung with pictures of local scenes. The three
real ales on handpump are Rudgate Ruby Mild, Theakstons Best and
Wensleydale Coverdale Gamekeeper and they have a dozen wines by the
glass and ten malt whiskies; chess, backgammon and dominoes. There
are several large wooden benches under large white parasols for outdoor
dining and picnic-sets by a well. This is a comfortable place to stay with
hearty breakfasts.

 Using their own-grown produce and naming local suppliers, the attractively
presented food includes lunchtime sandwiches, duck liver pâté, pigeon breast
with smoked venison, black pudding and bacon with blackcurrant jus, battered
fresh fish and chips, wild mushroom risotto, sea beam on stir-fried vegetables
with pesto, pork medallions with caper, mustard and cream sauce, venison on
roast vegetable purée with cranberry and cassis jus, and puddings such as vanilla
panna cotta with strawberry sauce and mascarpone cheesecake with lemon curd
topping. *Benchmark main dish: fillet of cod with scallops and prawns in chorizo
cream sauce £15.75. Two-course evening meal £19.50.*

Free house ~ Licensee Nigel Stevens ~ Real ale ~ (01677) 450581 ~ Open 11-3, 5.30
(6 Sun)-11; closed Mon ~ Bar food 12-2, 5.30(6 Sun)-9 ~ Restaurant ~ Children welcome
until 8.30pm ~ Dogs allowed in bar ~ Bedrooms: £60/£85 ~ www.thewyvillarms.co.uk
*Recommended by Ed and Anna Fraser, Noel Thomas, Donna Jenkins, Jill and Julian Tasker,
John and Sylvia Harrop, Janet and Peter Race, Michael Doswell*

COXWOLD   SE5377   Map 7

Fauconberg Arms 🍽 ♀ 🛏

Off A170 Thirsk–Helmsley, via Kilburn or Wass; easily found off A19 too;
YO61 4AD

**Family-run inn with highly popular food, a good range of drinks
and seats in the back garden; comfortable bedrooms**

A thoroughly good all-rounder, this is a family-run, nicely updated
17th-c inn and an attractive place to stay – super breakfasts too.
The heavily beamed and flagstoned bar has log fires in both linked
areas (one in an unusual arched fireplace in a broad low inglenook),

muted contemporary colours, some attractive oak chairs by local craftsmen alongside more usual pub furnishings, carefully chosen old local photographs and other pictures, and copper implements and china. Rudgate Jorvik Blonde, John Smiths and Theakstons Best on handpump, a thoughtful choice of wines by the glass, farm cider and 28 malt whiskies. The pub dogs are called Peggy, Bramble and Phoebe. The candlelit dining room is quietly elegant, with a gently upmarket yet relaxed atmosphere. The garden behind the inn has seats and tables on a terrace and views across fields to Byland Abbey; picnic-sets and teak benches on the front cobbles look along this charming village's broad tree-lined verges, bright with flower tubs. They have a shop selling home-baked bread, their own cheese and other groceries. The inn is named after Lord Fauconberg, who married Oliver Cromwell's daughter Mary.

Cooked by the landlord and his daughters using local, seasonal produce and game, the much enjoyed food includes sandwiches, black pudding, smoked bacon and red onion salad, prawn cocktail, various sharing platters, ham and eggs, burger with smoked bacon, cheese, coleslaw and chips, pie of the day, rabbit in champagne with wild mushrooms, duck breast in honey, Cointreau and fresh orange juice, and puddings such as caramelised rice pudding and seasonal fruit crumble. *Benchmark main dish: beer-battered haddock and chips £11.50. Two-course evening meal £18.50.*

Free house ~ Licensee Simon Rheinberg ~ Real ale ~ (01347) 868214 ~ Open 11-11 ~ Bar food 12-2.30(3 weekends), 6.30(6 Sun)-9(8 Sun) ~ Restaurant ~ Children welcome ~ Dogs allowed in bar ~ Live music twice a month; check website for details ~ Bedrooms: /£105 ~ www.fauconbergarms.com *Recommended by Pat and Tony Martin, John Oates*

CRAYKE

SE5670   Map 7

Durham Ox 🍴 � 🛏

Off B1363 at Brandsby, towards Easingwold; West Way; YO61 4TE

Highly enjoyable and well run inn with interesting décor in old-fashioned, relaxing rooms, fine drinks and smashing food; lovely views and comfortable bedrooms

Always friendly and busy, this is a particularly well run inn that seems to have the best of all worlds. The old-fashioned lounge bar has an enormous inglenook fireplace, pictures and photographs on the dark red walls, interesting satirical carvings in the panelling (Victorian copies of medieval pew ends), polished copper and brass, and venerable tables, antique seats and settles on the flagstones. In the bottom bar is a framed illustrated account of the local history (some of it gruesome) dating back to the 12th c, and a large framed print of the original famous Durham Ox, which weighed 171 stone. The Burns Bar has a woodburning stove, exposed brickwork and large french windows that open on to a balcony area. Black Sheep Best, Timothy Taylors Landlord and a changing guest like Rudgate Blonde on handpump, ten wines by the glass and several malt whiskies; background music. There are seats in the courtyard garden and fantastic views over the Vale of York on three sides; on the fourth is a charming view up the hill to the medieval church – the tale is that this is the hill up which the Grand Old Duke of York marched his men. They hold interesting regular events such as a Meet the Brewers evening hosted by Timothy Taylors and cookery demonstrations from the head chef. The bedrooms in renovated farm cottages (dogs allowed here) or in the main building, are well equipped, spacious and comfortable;

breakfasts are very good. The nearby A19 leads straight to a Park & Ride for York. The pub is part of Provenance Inns.

🍴 With their own-made bread and petits fours, the imaginative food includes sandwiches, salmon gravadlax with citrus fennel and candied lemon, ham hock terrine with quail egg and pineapple relish, spicy and sticky pork ribs with spicy beans, chickpea burger with aubergine and onion rings, braised lamb shoulder with sweet red cabbage and rosemary mash, pancetta-wrapped corn-fed chicken breast with tomato and olive dressing and fondant potato, specials like potted kippers with cucumber pickle or confit duck leg cassoulet, and puddings such as dark chocolate and pecan pie with rum and raisin ice-cream and baked orange and vanilla cheesecake with orange jelly. *Benchmark main dish: rib-eye steak with béarnaise sauce and skinny fries £19.95. Two-course evening meal £21.00.*

Free house ~ Licensee Michael Ibbotson ~ Real ale ~ (01347) 821506 ~ Open 11-11 ~ Bar food 12-2.30, 5.30-9.30 ~ Restaurant ~ Children welcome ~ Dogs allowed in bar and bedrooms ~ Bedrooms: £80/£100 ~ www.thedurhamox.com *Recommended by Liz Bell, S and D Hunter, Roger and Diana Morgan, Ian Malone, Neil Ingoe, John and Sylvia Harrop, David Jackman, Janet and Peter Race, Walter and Susan Rinaldi-Butcher*

 CROPTON SE7588 Map 10

New Inn 🍺

Village signposted off A170 W of Pickering; YO18 8HH

Genuinely warm welcome in a modernised village pub with own-brew beers, traditional furnishings and brewery tours; bedrooms

Brewery tours here are fun and the £6 fee includes a pint of their own-brew beers. They usually have six on handpump at any one time, such as Cropton Blackout, Endeavour, Honey Gold, Monkmans Slaughter, Two Pints and Yorkshire Moors; also, craft lagers, a dozen malt whiskies and seven wines by the glass. The traditional village bar has wood panelling, plush seating, lots of brass and a small fire. A local artist has designed the historical posters lining the downstairs conservatory, which doubles as a visitor centre at busy times. The elegant restaurant has locally made furniture and paintings by local artists; background music, TV, games machine, darts, pool and a juke box. There's a neat terrace, a garden with a pond and a brewery shop.

🍴 Food includes lunchtime sandwiches, chicken liver pâté with tomato chutney, oak-roast salmon with lemon and chive dressing, roasted vegetable and tomato bake, bacon, black pudding and blue cheese salad, burger with bacon, cheddar, tomato relish and chips, beer-battered cod and tartare sauce, chicken breast with wild mushroom and red wine jus, and puddings such as orange panna cotta with mixed berry compote and sticky toffee pudding with butterscotch sauce. *Benchmark main dish: steak in ale pie with chips £9.95. Two-course evening meal £15.00.*

Own brew ~ Licensee Philip Lee ~ Real ale ~ (01751) 417330 ~ Open 11-11(midnight Sat) ~ Bar food 12-2(2.30 Sun), 5.30-8.30 ~ Restaurant ~ Well behaved children welcome ~ Dogs allowed in bar ~ Bedrooms: £60/£85 ~ www.croptonbrewery.com *Recommended by Derek and Sylvia Stephenson, David and Lin Short, P Dawn*

The price we give for a two-course evening meal in the featured entries is the mean (average of cheapest and most expensive) price of a starter and a main course – no drinks.

DOWNHOLME
SE1197 Map 10

Bolton Arms

Village signposted just off A6108 Leyburn–Richmond; DL11 6AE

Tasty food in unusual village's cosy country pub; bedrooms

In a largely unspoilt swathe of Swaledale, this is a welcoming little place with magnificent views. The softly lit black-beamed and carpeted bar is down a few steps and has two smallish linked areas off the servery where they keep Black Sheep Best and Timothy Taylors Landlord on handpump, eight wines by the glass at fair prices and ten malt whiskies. There are comfortable plush wall banquettes, a log fire in a neat fireplace, quite a lot of gleaming brass, a few small country pictures and drinks' advertisements on pinkish rough-plastered walls. Background music and dominoes. The tidy garden, on the same level as the dining room (and up steps from the front), shares the same view – as does the back conservatory; there are also some lower picnic-sets and benches, and quoits.

The landlord cooks the tasty food, which might include baked goats cheese on watercress and pear salad, king prawns in garlic butter, cumberland sausage ring with mash and onion gravy, spinach and ricotta pancakes, steak and mushroom pie, duck breast with honey, orange and ginger sauce, thai beef stir-fry, salmon fillet in creamy prawn sauce, guinea fowl stuffed with black pudding with mushroom and shallot sauce, and puddings; they also offer an early bird menu (6-7pm Mon-Thurs). *Benchmark main dish: slow-cooked lamb shoulder with mint and redcurrant gravy £14.95. Two-course evening meal £20.00.*

Free house ~ Licensees Steve and Nicola Ross ~ Real ale ~ (01748) 823716 ~ Open 10.30-3, 6-midnight; closed Tues lunchtime ~ Bar food 12-2, 6-9.30 ~ Restaurant ~ Children welcome ~ Dogs allowed in bedrooms ~ Bedrooms: £45/£60 ~ www.boltonarmsdownholme.com *Recommended by WAH, Ryta Lyndley*

EAST WITTON
SE1486 Map 10

Blue Lion 🍴 ♗ 🛏

A6108 Leyburn–Ripon; DL8 4SN

Civilised dining pub with interesting rooms, daily papers, real ales, delicious food and courteous service; comfortable bedrooms

Once again we've had nothing but praise from our many readers for this first class 18th-c former coaching inn. It manages to be all things to all people – a tricky thing to pull off, but the long-serving landlord and his charming, courteous staff seem to manage it with ease. Whether you're after just a drink and a chat, a leisurely meal (the food is excellent) or an overnight stay in the extremely comfortable bedrooms, you'll be made equally welcome; they're kind to dogs too. The big squarish bar is civilised but informal with soft lighting, high-backed antique settles and old windsor chairs on turkish rugs and flagstones, ham-hooks in the high ceiling decorated with dried wheat, teazles and so forth, a delft shelf filled with bric-a-brac, plus several prints, sporting caricatures and other pictures, a log fire and daily papers. Black Sheep Best and Golden Sheep and Theakstons Best on handpump, an impressive list of wines with a dozen (plus champagne) by the glass and 17 malt whiskies. Picnic-sets on the gravel outside look beyond the stone houses on the far side of the village green to Witton Fell, and there's a big, pretty back garden.

🍴 Imaginative – if not cheap – food might include lunchtime sandwiches, king scallops with herb gnocchi, smoked chicken and chive sauce, mild curried crab cakes with cucumber ribbons and mango chutney, home-made tagliatelle with pancetta, wild mushrooms, cream and truffle oil, rabbit and chicken ballotine, rabbit leg pie and tarragon cream, steak and kidney pudding with red wine gravy, stone bass with parsnip, red wine-braised salsify, pearl onions and samphire, and puddings such as honey-roast plum crumble with lemon thyme ice-cream and liquorice arctic roll with roasted pineapple and caramel; they also offer a two- and three-course set lunch (not Sunday). *Benchmark main dish: slow-roasted honey-glazed duckling with apple gravy (evenings only) £21.00. Two-course evening meal £25.00.*

Free house ~ Licensee Paul Klein ~ Real ale ~ (01969) 624273 ~ Open 11-11 ~ Bar food 12-2, 7-9 ~ Restaurant ~ Children welcome ~ Dogs allowed in bar and bedrooms ~ Bedrooms: £69.50/£94 ~ www.thebluelion.co.uk *Recommended by Comus and Sarah Elliott, Mrs W Montague, Rod Stoneman, Lynda and Trevor Smith, Neil and Angela Huxter, John and Dinah Waters, Rob and Catherine Dunster, Dr Kevan Tucker, Janet and Peter Race, J R Wildon*

ELSLACK SD9249 Map 7
Tempest Arms 🍴 ♀ 🍺 🛏
Just off A56 Earby–Skipton; BD23 3AY

Friendly inn with three log fires in stylish rooms, six real ales, good wines and popular food; bedrooms

Being so close to the fantastic walks and scenery of the Yorkshire Dales, it does make sense to stay overnight in the well equipped and warm bedrooms in this 18th-c stone pub. There's always a wide mix of customers coming and going, from families to diners and walkers with their dogs, and everyone is made to feel welcome and relaxed. It's stylish but understated and cosy with plenty of character in the bar and surrounding dining areas: cushioned armchairs, built-in wall seats with comfortable cushions, stools and lots of tables and three log fires – one greets you at the entrance and divides the bar and restaurant. There's quite a bit of exposed stonework, amusing prints on cream walls, half a dozen real ales such as Dark Horse Hetton Pale Ale, Ilkley Mary Jane, Theakstons Best, Thwaites Wainwright and a beer named for the pub on handpump, 16 wines by the glass and up to 14 malt whiskies; limited background music. The tables outside are largely screened from the road by a raised bank.

🍴 From a wide-ranging menu, the good, generously served food might include lunchtime sandwiches, interesting nibbles, smoked duck, tiger prawn and crispy pancetta on caesar salad, goats cheese and red pepper pancake on watercress sauce, minced steak and onion pudding, toad-in-the-hole with onion gravy, roasted vegetable lasagne topped with goats cheese, lamb curry, salmon and crab fishcakes with lime and dill tartare sauce, duck breast with apple and sage and red wine gravy, venison steak with smoked bacon and shallot sauce, and puddings. *Benchmark main dish: slow-cooked lamb shoulder on roasted vegetables with redcurrant and mint sauce £13.95. Two-course evening meal £18.75.*

Free house ~ Licensees Martin and Veronica Clarkson ~ Real ale ~ (01282) 842450 ~ Open 11-11; 12-10.30 Sun ~ Bar food 12-2.30, 6-9(9.30 Fri, Sat); 12-7.30 Sun ~ Restaurant ~ Children welcome ~ Dogs allowed in bar and bedrooms ~ Bedrooms: £85/£110 ~ www.tempestarms.co.uk *Recommended by Gordon and Margaret Ormondroyd, Ian Malone, Bruce and Sharon Eden, Brian and Janet Ainscough, Steve Whalley, S Holder, Glenn Foard, Claes Mauroy, Les and Sandra Brown, Christopher Mobbs*

FELIXKIRK

SE4684 Map 10

Carpenters Arms 🍴 ♟

Village signed off A170 E of Thirsk; YO7 2DP

Pretty village pub, carefully refurbished, with opened-up rooms, beams and candlelight, friendly service, real ales and highly thought-of food; lodge-style bedrooms

The ultra-modern and well equipped bedrooms, arranged around the landscaped garden behind this friendly inn, come with a drying wardrobe for wet days and a log-effect gas fire; dogs are welcome. The spacious opened-up bars have a pubby feel and a warm welcome for both drinkers and diners, with dark beams and joists, candlelight and fresh flowers, stools against the panelled counter where they keep Black Sheep Best, Rudgate Viking and Timothy Taylors Landlord on handpump, 19 wines by the glass and 18 malt whiskies, and a mix of chairs and tables on big flagstones; there's also a snug seating area with tartan armchairs in front of a double-sided woodburning stove. The red-walled dining room has a mix of antique and country kitchen chairs around scrubbed tables; throughout, the walls are hung with traditional prints, local pictures and maps; background music. The front of the pub enjoys all-day sunshine and is a fine spot in warm weather. The pub is part of Provenance Inns.

🍴 Enjoyable food includes sandwiches, baked queenie scallops with gruyère and garlic butter, tian of Whitby crab with avocado, citrus and herb crème fraîche, eggs benedict, various sharing platters, beer-battered fish and chips, venison burger with spring onion, sour cream and chips, smoked haddock, salmon and prawn pie with dill cream, chicken breast with potato and thyme rösti, braised chicory and pancetta broth, specials like beef carpaccio or mixed grill, and puddings such as dark chocolate tart with orange sorbet and praline and steamed treacle sponge with vanilla custard. *Benchmark main dish: venison cutlet with mini venison cottage pie, dauphinoise potatoes and red wine jus £18.95. Two-course evening meal £22.50.*

Free house ~ Licensee Michael Ibbotson ~ Real ale ~ (01845) 537369 ~ Open 12-11 ~ Bar food 12-2.30, 5.30(6 Sat)-9.30; 12-3, 5.30-8.30 Sun ~ Children welcome ~ Dogs allowed in bar and bedrooms ~ Bedrooms: £165/£185 ~ www.thecarpentersarmsfelixkirk.com
Recommended by Jill and Julian Tasker, Ray and Rita Bannon, Clive and Fran Dutson

FERRENSBY

SE3660 Map 7

General Tarleton 🍴 ♟ 🛏

A655 N of Knaresborough; HG5 0PZ

Stylish coaching inn with enterprising restauranty food, lots of wines by the glass, courteous service and a relaxed atmosphere; comfortable bedrooms

This is a carefully renovated, 18th-c former coaching inn with high standards of service and pretty country views. Although many customers are here to stay overnight in the spotlessly kept and individually decorated bedrooms (the breakfasts are excellent too) or for an exceptional meal, they do keep Black Sheep Best and Timothy Taylors Landlord on handpump and a dozen good wines by the glass, and service is friendly and helpful. You can enjoy a drink in the more informal bar area with its comfortable sofas and woodburning stove; the rest of the rambling open-plan rooms have low beams, brick pillars creating cosy alcoves, some exposed stonework, dark leather high-backed dining chairs grouped around wooden tables, and plenty of prints on cream walls. A door leads to a pleasant tree-lined garden – there are seats here as well as in a covered courtyard.

🍴 Cooked by the chef-patron, the exquisitely presented and delicious food might include warm confit duck salad, seafood in a crisp pastry bag with lobster sauce, angus burger with pancetta, cheese and triple-cooked chips, tagliatelle with mushrooms, spinach, truffle oil and pesto, rabbit loin, best end, herb-stuffed leg wrapped in bacon, mini rabbit pie, celeriac purée and girolles, bass fillet with crisp vine tomato tart and pesto, specials like crab bake, cocktail and spring roll (all made with white crab meat) or confit lamb shoulder with spinach and thyme jus, and puddings such as dark chocolate fondant with orange curd, orange jelly and vanilla ice-cream and sticky toffee pudding with caramel sauce; there's also a two- and three-course set menu. *Benchmark main dish: pork loin, braised shoulder, slow-cooked belly, black pudding and pancetta-wrapped prunes £18.95. Two-course evening meal £22.50.*

Free house ~ Licensee John Topham ~ Real ale ~ (01423) 340284 ~ Open 12-3, 6-11(10.30 Sun) ~ Bar food 12-2, 5.30-9.15(8.30 Sun) ~ Children welcome ~ Bedrooms: $85/$129 ~ www.generaltarleton.co.uk *Recommended by J F M and M West, Janet and Peter Race*

GRANTLEY SE2369 Map 7
Grantley Arms 🍴 ♀
Village signposted off B6265 W of Ripon; HG4 3PJ

Relaxed and interesting dining pub with good food

With a lovely welcome, plenty of local atmosphere and excellent food, this creeper-clad 17th-c country inn comes in for high praise from our readers. The front bar has a huge fireplace built of massive stone blocks and housing a woodburning stove, brown beams supporting shiny cream ceiling planks, and traditional furnishings: green wall banquettes, comfortable dining chairs, nightlights on polished tables (some cast-iron-framed) and a flowery carpet, with some of the landlady's own paintings of ponies and dogs above the green dado. The back dining room has crisp linen tablecloths, decorative plates and more paintings, mainly landscapes. Great Newsome Pricky Back Otchan and Theakstons Best on handpump, well chosen wines and attentive friendly service. Teak tables and chairs on the flagstoned front terrace have a pleasant outlook, and Fountains Abbey and Studley Royal are nearby.

🍴 As well as a two- and three-course set lunch (not Sunday), the highly enjoyable food includes open sandwiches, prawns in lemon mayonnaise with avocado purée and lime and cucumber sorbet, warm pork and ham rillette with grilled pineapple and fried egg, omelettes, beer-battered fresh haddock with triple-cooked chips, pie of the week, fresh pasta with tomato, peas, asparagus and parmesan, confit lamb breast with onion purée, black olives, tomatoes and red wine sauce, fish pie with cream and dill, and puddings such as baked white chocolate and vanilla cheesecake with caramelised banana and apple crumble tart with egg custard. *Benchmark main dish: rare-breed confit pork belly with apple compote and red wine sauce £14.95. Two-course evening meal £18.95.*

Free house ~ Licensees Valerie and Eric Sails ~ Real ale ~ (01765) 620227 ~ Open 12-3, 5.30-10.30; 12-10.30 Sun; closed Mon except bank holidays ~ Bar food 12-2, 5.30-9; 12-3.30, 5.30-8 Sun ~ Restaurant ~ Well behaved children welcome ~ Music first Sat evening of month ~ www.grantleyarms.com *Recommended by Mrs Blethyn Elliott, James Naylor, Michael Doswell, Janet and Peter Race, Walter and Susan Rinaldi-Butcher*

GRINTON

Bridge Inn 🍺 🛏

B6270 W of Richmond; DL11 6HH

SE0498 Map 10

Bustling pub with traditional comfortable bars, log fires, several real ales and malt whiskies, and tasty bar food; neat bedrooms

Walkers and their dogs get a warm welcome here, and there are some lovely walks in and around this pretty Swaledale village. A former coaching inn with a relaxing, comfortable atmosphere, it has bow-window seats and a pair of stripped traditional settles among more usual pub seats (all well cushioned), a good log fire, and Arbor Single Hop, Bank's EPA, Jennings Cumberland and a guest like Wychwood Dirty Tackle on handpump; also, eight wines by the glass and 30 malt whiskies. On the right, a few steps lead down into a room with darts and ring the bull. On the left, past leather armchairs and a sofa by a second log fire (and a glass chess set) is an extensive two-part dining room. The décor is in cream and shades of brown, with a modicum of fishing memorabilia. The bedrooms are simple, neat and comfortable, and the breakfasts good. The inn is opposite a lovely church known as the Cathedral of the Dales, and there are picnic-sets outside.

 Curing their own bacon, making their own black pudding and using their own smokehouse, they serve food all day. Dishes might include baguettes, black pudding scotch egg with mustard dressing, lamb koftas with tomato, onion and mint salad and roast garlic dip, courgette and chickpea curry, beer and dill-battered cod and chips, lambs liver with bacon, onion, mash and red wine gravy, free-range chicken breast with chorizo on tomato, pepper and mixed bean stew, pork belly in soy and five-spice with pak choi and sweet chilli sauce, and puddings. *Benchmark main dish: steak in ale pie £9.95. Two-course evening meal £17.00.*

Jennings (Marstons) ~ Lease Andrew Atkin ~ Real ale ~ (01748) 884224 ~ Open 12-11 (midnight Sat) ~ Bar food 12-9 ~ Restaurant ~ Children welcome ~ Dogs allowed in bar and bedrooms ~ Live music Thurs evening ~ Bedrooms: £51/£82 ~ www.bridgeinngrinton.co.uk *Recommended by Comus and Sarah Elliott*

HALIFAX
Shibden Mill 🍽 ♟ 🍺

Off A58 into Kell Lane at Stump Cross Inn, near A6036 junction; keep on, pub signposted from Kell Lane on left; HX3 7UL

SE1027 Map 7

Tucked away 300-year-old mill with cosy rambling bar, four real ales and inventive, highly thought-of bar food; comfortable bedrooms

In a lovely valley with nearby walks, this is a 17th-c restored mill with interesting local ales and top class food using local game and meat. There's always a good mix of both locals and visitors, and the rambling bar, full of nooks and crannies, has a bustling atmosphere. Some cosy side areas have banquettes heaped with cushions and rugs, well spaced attractive old tables and chairs, and the candles in elegant iron holders give a feeling of real intimacy; also, old hunting prints, country landscapes and so forth and a couple of big log fires. A beer named for them (from Moorhouses), Black Sheep Best, Castle Rock Harvest Pale, Copper Dragon Golden Pippin and Little Valley Withens IPA on handpump and 20 wines by the glass from a wide list. There's also an upstairs restaurant; background music and TV. Outside on the attractive heated terrace, there are plenty of seats and tables, and the building is prettily floodlit at night. Bedrooms are well equipped and individually decorated.

🍴 Impressive and highly enjoyable, the food might include sandwiches, duck and foie gras terrine with game and sherry tea and duck breast pastrami, chicken liver parfait with madeira jelly and onion brioche, red onion tarte tatin with pear and walnut salad, burger with crispy onion rings, home-made ketchup, garlic mayonnaise, bacon, cheese and chips, rope-grown mussels with white wine, saffron, aioli and fries, rabbit with air-dried ham, pearl barley and morel mushroom risotto, prunes and leg shepherd's pie, and puddings such as caramelised lemon tart with passion fruit and fondant brownie pudding with chocolate sauce and vanilla milkshake. *Benchmark main dish: venison with pigeon pâté, crispy bacon, dock pudding, braised cabbage and madeira jus £19.00. Two-course evening meal £26.00.*

Free house ~ Licensee Glen Pearson ~ Real ale ~ (01422) 365840 ~ Open 12-2.30, 5.30-11; 12-11(10.30 Sun) Sat ~ Bar food 12-2(2.30 Fri, Sat), 6-9.30; 12-7.30 Sun ~ Restaurant ~ Children welcome ~ Dogs allowed in bar ~ Bedrooms: £90/£111 ~ www.shibdenmillinn.com *Recommended by Michael Butler, Gordon and Margaret Ormondroyd, Dr Kevan Tucker, Stanley and Annie Matthews*

HARTSHEAD   SE1822   Map 7
Gray Ox 🍴 ♟

3.5 miles from M62 junction 25; A644 towards Dewsbury, left on to A62, next left on to B6119, then first left on to Fall Lane; left into Hartshead Lane; pub on right; WF15 8AL

Attractive dining pub with cosy beamed bars, inventive cooking, real ales, several wines by the glass and fine views

At lunchtime particularly, most customers are here to enjoy the very good food – it makes a fine stop when travelling the M62 too. The main bar has beams and flagstones, bentwood chairs, leather stools around stripped-pine tables and a roaring log fire. Comfortable carpeted dining areas with bold paintwork and leather dining chairs around polished tables lead off; the hunting-theme wallpaper is interesting and unusual. They now have a private dining room. Jennings Cumberland, Cocker Hoop and Sneck Lifter and a changing guest on handpump, 15 wines by the glass and two champagnes and a new cocktail menu; background music. There are picnic-sets outside and fine views through the latticed pub windows across the Calder Valley to the distant outskirts of Huddersfield – the lights are pretty at night.

🍴 As well as a two- and three-course menu (12-2, 6-7; not weekends), the very high standard of good, popular food includes lunchtime sandwiches, goats cheese with sloe gin syrup, roasted golden beetroots and candied walnuts, pigeon breast with braised celeriac, pickled chanterelles and pear and vanilla purée, sweet potato, chickpea and vegetable thai curry with coconut rice, free-range chicken breast stuffed with haggis, neeps and tatties with whisky cream, smoked haddock with wilted spinach, soft poached egg, chive-crushed potatoes and mustard cream, specials like whole lemon sole with cashew beurre noisette, and puddings such as dark chocolate and cherry tiramisu and bread and butter pudding with crème anglaise. *Benchmark main dish: pork loin, belly, cheek and black pudding with apple purée and red wine jus £16.00. Two-course evening meal £22.00.*

Banks's (Marstons) ~ Lease Bernadette McCarron ~ Real ale ~ (01274) 872845 ~ Open 12-3, 6-midnight; 12-midnight Sat; 12-11 Sun ~ Bar food 12-2, 6-9(9.30 Sat); 12-7 Sun ~ Children welcome ~ www.grayoxinn.co.uk *Recommended by Gordon and Margaret Ormondroyd, Glenwys and Alan Lawrence, Pat and Tony Martin, Keith Moss*

It's very helpful if you let us know up-to-date food prices when you report on pubs.

HEATH

SE3520 Map 7

Kings Arms ◖£

Village signposted from A655 Wakefield–Normanton – or, more directly, turn left opposite the Horse & Groom; WF1 5SL

Old-fashioned gas-lit pub in interesting location with dark-panelled original bar and up to 11 real ales; seats outside

Something of a surprise being so close to industrial Wakefield, this is an old-fashioned pub that makes the most of its setting opposite the village green, surrounded by 19th-c stone merchants' houses. It has a lot of genuine character; the original bar has gas lighting, giving it a cosy feel, a fire burning in an old black range (with a long row of smoothing irons on the mantelpiece), plain elm stools, oak settles built into the walls and dark panelling. A more comfortable extension has carefully preserved the original style, down to good wood-pegged oak panelling (two panels embossed with royal arms) and a high shelf of plates; there are also two other small flagstoned rooms and a conservatory that opens on to the garden. Clarks Traditional Bitter, Ossett Silver King and Yorkshire Blonde and a beer named for the pub from Ossett, as well as Coach House Gunpowder Strong Mild, Coastal Short & Stout and Oldershaw Great Expectations on handpump. There are sunny benches facing the green and picnic-sets on a side lawn and in the nice walled garden.

As well as a two- and three-course set menu (Monday-Thursday), the food includes braised rabbit and apricot terrine with raspberry vinaigrette, smoked salmon roulade filled with herby cream cheese, spinach and ricotta stack with tomato sauce, chicken breast with chorizo, moroccan-style lamb with curried chickpeas and red pepper sauce, braised oxtail and wild mushroom pudding with red wine jus, and puddings such as chocolate and walnut tart and mixed berry fool. *Benchmark main dish: steak and treacle stout pie with dripping chips £10.95. Two-course evening meal £17.50.*

Ossett ~ Manager Angela Cromack ~ Real ale ~ (01924) 377527 ~ Open 12-11.30 ~ Bar food 12-2, 5-9; 12-9 Fri, Sat; 12.30-5 Sun ~ Restaurant ~ Children welcome ~ Dogs allowed in bar ~ Summer folk events ~ www.thekingsarmsheath.co.uk
Recommended by Malcolm Gillett, John and Eleanor Holdsworth, Michael Butler, Derek and Sylvia Stephenson

HELPERBY

SE4370 Map 7

Oak Tree ⑪ ♈ ⇔

Raskelf Road; YO61 2PH

Attractive pub, carefully renovated, with real ales in friendly bar, fine food in elegant dining rooms, bold paintwork and seats on terrace; comfortable bedrooms

Much of the original character has been kept during the renovation of this pretty brick pub – they've been careful to use slate, oak and weathered brick. The informal bar has bold red walls, open fires, church chairs and elegant wooden dining chairs around a mix of wooden tables on old quarry tiles, flagstones and oak floorboards, and stools against the counter where they keep Black Sheep Best, Rudgate Jorvik Blonde and Timothy Taylors Golden Best and Landlord on handpump and a dozen wines by the glass served by helpful staff. The main dining room has a large woodburner in a huge brick fireplace, a big central flower arrangement, high-backed burgundy and elegant wooden chairs around nice old tables on oak flooring, ornate mirrors and some striking artwork on the turquoise or exposed brick walls. French windows lead on to the terrace where there are plenty of seats and tables for summer dining. Upstairs, a private dining room has a two-way woodburner, a sitting room and doors to a terrace. The bedrooms are comfortable and well equipped. The pub is part of Provenance Inns.

As well as light snacks from 8am, the thoughtful choice of good food includes sandwiches, eggs benedict, ham hock terrine with home-made piccalilli, home-made black pudding with poached egg and bacon salad, sharing platters, spinach and vegetable cannelloni, burger with cheese, bacon, onion rings and chips, chicken breast with mushroom fricassée and fondant potato, lamb rump with mini shepherd's pie, braised red cabbage and mint gravy, gremolata-crusted cod with parsley butter sauce, and puddings such as treacle sponge with custard and warm chocolate fondant. *Benchmark main dish: spicy, sticky pork ribs with coleslaw and skinny fries £14.95. Two-course evening meal £20.00.*

Free house ~ Licensee Michael Ibbotson ~ Real ale ~ (01423) 789189 ~ Open 11-11 ~ Bar food 12-2.30, 5.30-9.30; 12-3, 5.30-8.30 Sun ~ Restaurant ~ Children welcome ~ Dogs allowed in bar and bedrooms ~ Bedrooms: /£120 ~ www.theoaktreehelperby.com
Recommended by Ed and Anna Fraser, Walter and Susan Rinaldi-Butcher

 KIRKBY FLEETHAM   SE2894   Map 10
Black Horse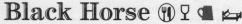
Village signposted off A1 S of Catterick; Lumley Lane; DL7 0SH

Attractively reworked country inn with good enterprising food, cheerful atmosphere and stylish comfortable bedrooms

With plenty of antique charm, the bedrooms here are comfortable and stylish and the breakfasts excellent; they don't start till 9am, but if you can't wait you can get good continental hampers. The long softly lit beamed and flagstoned bar on the right has cosy little settles and high-backed dining chairs by the log fire at one end (blazing even at breakfast time), and at the other wrought-iron chairs that are a good deal more comfortable than they look. They have a good choice of wines by the glass, and Black Sheep Best, Ossett Yorkshire Blonde and Timothy Taylors Landlord on handpump; plenty of local regulars congregate at the counter's leather bar stools. The dining room on the right is light and open, with big bow windows each side and a casual contemporary look: loose-covered dining chairs or pastel garden settles with scatter cushions around tables painted pale green. There is also a dark and intimate private dining room. Service is friendly and very attentive; maybe background pop music. Teak tables on a flagstoned side terrace include one with a couple of toffs dressed for a country outing – you have to look twice to see that they're models. A neat sheltered back lawn has a guinea pig hutch.

Enjoyable and rewarding, the food includes sandwiches, black pudding, dry-cured bacon and poached egg salad, potted crab with wasabi and prawn toasts, steak in ale pie, gammon with duck egg and chips, chicken breast with goats cheese, parma ham and wild mushroom risotto, cod with mussel and clam mouclade, calves liver with bubble and squeak and tomato and thyme jus, and puddings such as passion-fruit crème brûlée and banana and walnut cake with banana crisp and honeycomb ice-cream. *Benchmark main dish: confit pork belly, roast fillet, sticky cheek, black pudding and vanilla mayonnaise £16.95. Two-course evening meal £20.00.*

Free house ~ Licensee Philip Barker ~ Real ale ~ (01609) 749011 ~ Open 11-11 (10.30 Sun) ~ Bar food 12-2, 6-9; 12-7 Sun ~ Restaurant ~ Children welcome ~

Dogs allowed in bar ~ Bedrooms: /£120 ~ www.blackhorsekirkbyfleetham.com
Recommended by Jill and Julian Tasker

LEDSHAM SE4529 Map 7

Chequers 🍴 ☗

*1.5 miles from A1(M) junction 42: follow Leeds signs, then Ledsham
signposted; Claypit Lane; LS25 5LP*

**Friendly village pub, handy for the A1, with hands-on landlord, log
fires in several beamed rooms, real ales and interesting very popular
food; pretty back terrace**

Our readers love this 16th-c stone inn and this year many have said
that 'it's as good as ever'. You can be sure of a friendly welcome
from the landlord and his helpful staff, the beer is well kept and fairly
priced and the food is very popular. There's also plenty of character in
the several small, individually decorated rooms with low beams, lots of
cosy alcoves, toby jugs and all sorts of knick-knacks on the walls and
ceilings (cricketing enthusiasts will be interested to see a large photo in
one room of four yorkshire heroes) and log fires. From the old-fashioned
little central panelled-in servery, they offer beers from breweries such as
Brown Cow, John Smiths, Theakstons and Timothy Taylors and a dozen
wines by the glass. A lovely sheltered two-level terrace at the back has
plenty of tables among roses, and the hanging baskets and flowers are
very pretty. RSPB Fairburn Ings reserve is nearby and the ancient village
church is worth a visit.

From a varied menu, the good, interesting food includes lunchtime
sandwiches, crab and smoked salmon blinis with basil mayonnaise, scallops
with sautéed wild mushrooms and crisp pancetta, vegetable moussaka, gammon
with duck egg, caramelised onion sausage with mash and gravy, corn-fed chorizo-
stuffed chicken with sweet potato wedges, duck confit, toulouse sausage and bean
cassoulet, hake loin with potted shrimps, specials such as tian of smoked salmon,
trout and mackerel with lime mayonnaise or venison steak with sweet potato mash
and redcurrant jus, and puddings. *Benchmark main dish: steak and mushroom
pie £10.95. Two-course evening meal £22.00.*

Free house ~ Licensee Chris Wraith ~ Real ale ~ (01977) 683135 ~ Open 11-11; 12-6 Sun
~ Bar food 12-9; 12-6 Sun ~ Restaurant ~ Children until 8pm ~ Dogs allowed in bar ~
www.thechequersinn.f9.co.uk *Recommended by Dr D J and Mrs S C Walker, Piotr Chodzko-
Zajko, Paul Goldman, Robert Wivell, M and A H, John and Anne Mackinnon, R C Vincent, Tony
Middis, Michael Butler, Pat and Stewart Gordon*

LEVISHAM SE8390 Map 10

Horseshoe 🍴

Off A169 N of Pickering; YO18 7NL

**Friendly village pub run by two brothers, neat rooms, real ales,
very good food cooked by one of the landlords and seats on the
village green; bedrooms**

It's really worth making the most of this warmly friendly, traditional pub
by staying in the smart, comfortable bedrooms; you can then explore
the pretty village and nearby North York Moors National Park. The bars
have beams, blue banquettes, wheelback and captain's chairs around a
variety of tables on polished wooden floors, vibrant landscapes by a local
artist on the walls and a log fire in the stone fireplace; an adjoining snug
has a woodburning stove, comfortable leather sofas and old photographs

of the pub and the village. Black Sheep Best and a couple of guests like Cropton Endeavour Ale and Wold Top Gold on handpump, home-made elderflower cordial, and 20 malt whiskies; board games and background music. There are seats on the attractive green, with more in the back garden. The ancient church is worth a visit.

🍴 Cooked by one of the landlords, the generously served and very good food might include lunchtime sandwiches, crab and smoked salmon terrine, pigeon breast on creamed potato and black pudding stack with red wine sauce, nut roast with tomato and basil sauce, sausage and mash with onion gravy, deep-fried whitby haddock with chips, chicken breast wrapped in bacon on creamed leeks, beef stroganoff, duck breast on sweet potato mash with port and red wine sauce, and puddings. *Benchmark main dish: guinea fowl breast with mustard mash, lemon and thyme mousse and white wine sauce £13.95. Two-course evening meal £17.50.*

Free house ~ Licensees Toby and Charles Wood ~ Real ale ~ (01751) 460240 ~ Open 10am-11.30pm(10.30pm Sun) ~ Bar food 12-2, 6-8.30 ~ Children welcome ~ Dogs allowed in bar ~ Bedrooms: /£80 ~ www.horseshoelevisham.co.uk
Recommended by Derek and Sylvia Stephenson, Dr Kevan Tucker, B R Merritt, David and Lin Short, Simon and Mandy King, Comus and Sarah Elliott, Peter and Anne Hollindale

LEYBURN   SE1190   Map 10

Sandpiper 🍴 ☂ 🛏

Just off Market Place; DL8 5AT

Appealing food and cosy bar for drinkers in 17th-c cottage; real ales and impressive choice of whisky; bedrooms

Of course, the excellent food in this attractive 17th-c pub is a big draw, but it's also liked by locals for a drink and a chat, which keeps the atmosphere relaxed and informal – and the friendly landlord offers a warm welcome to all. The cosy bar has a log fire, a couple of black beams in the low ceiling and wooden or cushioned built-in wall seats around a few tables; the back snug, up three steps, has lovely Dales photographs – get here early to be sure of a seat. There are photographs and a woodburning stove in a stone fireplace by the linenfold panelled bar counter; to the left is the attractive restaurant, with dark wooden tables and chairs on bare boards and fresh flowers. Black Sheep Best and a guest from breweries like Copper Dragon, Rudgate and Yorkshire Dales on handpump, up to 100 malt whiskies and a decent wine list with several by the glass; background music. In good weather, you can enjoy a drink on the front terrace among the pretty hanging baskets and flowering climbers. This is a fine place to stay, with charming bedrooms.

🍴 The landlord cooks the excellent food, and also makes his own bread and ice-creams: lunchtime sandwiches, caramelised pork belly with scallops and cauliflower purée, fishcakes on herb and caviar sauce, omelette arnold bennett, mixed mushroom risotto, rib burger with onions, tomato relish and thin fries, coq au vin, slow-cooked lamb with smoked garlic, wilted greens and potato gnocchi, venison on pearl barley and vegetable risotto with chestnut mushrooms, bass with a shellfish sausage with a light curry and apple sauce, and puddings. *Benchmark main dish: duck breast with dauphinoise potatoes and sherry and thyme sauce £17.75. Two-course evening meal £24.50.*

Free house ~ Licensee Jonathan Harrison ~ Real ale ~ (01969) 622206 ~ Open 11.30-3, 6.30-11(10.30 Sun); closed Mon, some winter Tues ~ Bar food 12-2.30, 6.30-9 ~ Restaurant ~ Children welcome ~ Dogs allowed in bar and bedrooms ~ Bedrooms: £75/£85 ~ www.sandpiperinn.co.uk *Recommended by Andy Lickfold, M and J White, Comus and Sarah Elliott, Robert Wivell, Penny and Peter Keevil, J R Wildon, Simon Hand*

 LINTON IN CRAVEN   SD9962   Map 7

Fountaine ◄

Off B6265 Skipton–Grassington; BD23 5HJ

Neatly kept pub in charming village, attractive furnishings, open fires, five real ales and popular food; bedrooms

This neatly kept and civilised inn is so popular that you must book in advance to guarantee a table. There are beams and white-painted joists in the low ceilings, log fires (one in a beautifully carved heavy wooden fireplace), attractive built-in cushioned wall benches and stools around a mix of copper-topped tables, little wall lamps and quite a few prints on the pale walls. As well as a beer named for the pub from Cuerden, there might be a seasonal ale from Dark Horse, John Smiths, Tetleys Bitter and Thwaites Original on handpump and 14 wines by the glass served by efficient staff; background music, darts and board games. There are teak benches and tables under green parasols on the terrace – looking over to the duck pond across the road – and attractive hanging baskets; this is a pretty hamlet. The bedrooms are in a converted barn behind the pub – we'd love to hear about readers staying here; fine surrounding walks in the lovely Dales countryside.

 As well as a very good value two-course menu (not weekends), the wide choice of much liked food includes sandwiches, lightly battered black pudding and haggis on smoked bacon and sesame seed savoy cabbage, king prawns in white wine, chilli and tomato, roast pepper and cheese quiche, gammon and eggs, cumberland sausage curl with mash and gravy, steak in ale pasty, local game casserole, lamb shank hotpot, and puddings. *Benchmark main dish: brisket of beef with yorkshire pudding, mash and gravy £11.95. Two-course evening meal £17.00.*

Individual Inns ~ Manager Christopher Gregson ~ Real ale ~ (01756) 752210 ~ Open 11-11; 12-10.30 Sun ~ Bar food 12-9 ~ Restaurant ~ Children welcome ~ Dogs allowed in bar ~ Bedrooms: /£99 ~ www.individualinns.co.uk *Recommended by Tim and Joan Wright, Robert Wivell, Lynda and Trevor Smith, B and M Kendall, Gavin Dingley, John and Eleanor Holdsworth*

LOCKTON   SE8488   Map 10

Fox & Rabbit

A169 N of Pickering; YO18 7NQ

Neatly kept pub with fine views, a friendly atmosphere in bars and restaurant, real ales, popular food and seats outside; pretty bedrooms

On the edge of Dalby Forest in the North York Moors National Park, this neatly kept and attractive pub is just the place to head for after a walk. The interconnected rooms have beams and panelling, some exposed stonework, wall settles and banquettes, dark pubby chairs and tables on the red-patterned carpet, a log fire and a warm inviting atmosphere; fresh flowers, brasses, china plates, prints and old local photographs too. The locals' bar is busy and cheerful and the views from the comfortable restaurant are panoramic – it's worth arriving early to bag a window seat. Black Sheep, Cropton Yorkshire Moors and Marstons Pedigree on handpump and several wines by the glass. The bedrooms are pretty and they have a field for caravans. Outside, there are seats under parasols and some picnic-sets. This is sister pub to the Horseshoe in Levisham.

 Naming their local suppliers on the menu, the popular food includes sandwiches, ham hock terrine with home-made piccallili, smoked and flaky salmon with rocket and potato salad, sausages and mash with onion gravy, deep-fried haddock and chips, chicken and chorizo pasta with mozzarella, gammon with egg and pineapple, honey-glazed duck breast with black pudding, champ mash and port and cherry sauce, winter game dishes, and puddings such as glazed lemon tart with red berries and mascarpone and warm chocolate cake with cherries and vanilla ice-cream. *Benchmark main dish: steak and mushroom in ale pie and chips £11.50. Two-course evening meal £19.00.*

Free house ~ Licensees Charles and Toby Wood ~ Real ale ~ (01751) 460213 ~ Open 10am-11.30pm(10.30pm Sun) ~ Bar food 12-2(4 Fri-Sun), 5-8.30 ~ Restaurant ~ Children welcome ~ Dogs allowed in bar ~ www.foxandrabbit.co.uk
Recommended by Comus and Sarah Elliott

LOW CATTON
SE7053 Map 7
Gold Cup
Village signposted with High Catton off A166 in Stamford Bridge or A1079 at Kexby Bridge; YO41 1EA

Friendly, pleasant pub with attractive bars, real ales, decent dependable food, seats in garden and ponies in paddock

At weekends, this proper village pub is usefully open - and serves food – all day. The neatly kept beamed bars have a bustling atmosphere and chatty locals, plenty of smart tables and chairs on the stripped wooden floors, quite a few pictures, an open fire at one end opposite a woodburning stove, and coach lights on the rustic-looking walls. The spacious restaurant has solid wooden pews and tables (said to be made from a single oak tree) and pleasant views of the surrounding fields. Theakstons Black Bull on handpump; background music and pool. The garden has a grassed area for children and the back paddock houses two ponies, Cinderella and Polly. The pub has fishing rights on the adjoining River Derwent.

 The wide choice of tasty food includes lunchtime sandwiches, breaded brie wedges with orange and cranberry dip, chicken liver pâté with onion marmalade, three-egg omelette, vegetable stroganoff, cajun chicken with mint yoghurt dip, steak in ale pie, gammon with pineapple and cheese, salmon fillet with asparagus and lemon hollandaise, half duck with cherry brandy sauce, and puddings. *Benchmark main dish: lamb rump with port and redcurrant gravy £13.95. Two-course evening meal £18.00.*

Free house ~ Licensees Pat and Ray Hales ~ Real ale ~ (01759) 371354 ~ Open 12-2.30, 6-11; 12-11(10.30 Sun) Sat; closed Mon lunchtime ~ Bar food 12-2, 6-9; all day weekends ~ Restaurant ~ Children welcome ~ Dogs allowed in bar ~ www.goldcuplowcatton.com
Recommended by Peter and Anne Hollindale, Gordon and Margaret Ormondroyd

MARTON CUM GRAFTON
SE4263 Map 7
Punch Bowl 🍴 ♟
Signed off A1 3 miles N of A59; YO51 9QY

Refurbished 16th-c inn in lovely village, with beams and standing timbers, character bar and dining rooms, real ales, interesting food using seasonal local produce and seats outside

The cosy rooms in this handsome inn have been carefully renovated without stripping away their original character, and the atmosphere throughout is relaxed and easy-going. The main bar is beamed and timbered with a built-in window seat at one end, lots of red leather-topped stools, cushioned settles and church chairs around pubby tables on flagstones or bare floorboards, Black Sheep Best, Great Yorkshire Classic, Rudgate Viking and Timothy Taylors Landlord on handpump, 23 wines by the glass and a dozen malt whiskies served by friendly staff. Open doorways lead to five separate dining areas, each with an open fire, heavy beams, red walls covered with photographs of vintage car races and racing drivers, sporting cartoons and old photographs of the pub and village, and an attractive mix of cushioned wall seats and wooden or high-backed red dining chairs around antique tables on oak floors. Up a swirling staircase is a coffee loft and a private dining room. There are seats and tables in the back courtyard where they hold summer barbecues. The pub is part of Provenance Inns.

🍴 Using carefully sourced local produce, the very good, interesting food might include lunchtime sandwiches, rabbit terrine with celeriac remoulade, cured apple and pickled wild mushrooms, queenie scallops with garlic and parsley butter, eggs benedict, chickpea burger with chips, spicy and sticky pork ribs with skinny fries, seafood linguine, chicken supreme with fennel and potato rösti, tomato concasse and herb sauce, lamb with pancetta, pea purée and rosemary jus, and puddings such as dark chocolate brownie parfait with vanilla ice-cream and warm carrot and orange cake with cardamom ice-cream and orange syrup. *Benchmark main dish: burger with cheese, bacon, onion rings and chunky chips £11.95. Two-course evening meal £20.00.*

Free house ~ Licensee Michael Ibbotson ~ Real ale ~ (01423) 322519 ~ Open 12-11 ~ Bar food 12-2.30(3 Sun), 5.30-9.30(8.30 Sun) ~ Restaurant ~ Children welcome ~ Dogs allowed in bar ~ www.thepunchbowlmartoncumgrafton.com
Recommended by John and Eleanor Holdsworth, Walter and Susan Rinaldi-Butcher

MASHAM   SE2281   Map 10
Black Sheep Brewery 🍺
Brewery signed off Leyburn Road A6108; HG4 4EN

Lively place with friendly staff, quite a mix of customers, unusual décor in big warehouse room, well kept beers (brewery tours and shop) and popular food

With a bustling atmosphere and a wide range of customers, this is an extremely popular and different place – more of a bistro than a pub – but of course the beers are very well kept. A huge upper warehouse room has a bar serving Black Sheep Best, Ale, Golden Sheep, Riggwelter and a changing guest beer such as All Creatures on handpump, several wines by the glass and a fair choice of soft drinks. Most of the good-sized tables have cheery gingham tablecloths and brightly cushioned green café chairs, but there are some modern pubbier tables near the bar. There's a good deal of bare woodwork, with some rough stonework painted cream and also green-painted steel girders and pillars. This big area is partly divided up by free-standing partitions; background music and friendly service. There are interesting brewery tours and a shop selling beers and mainly beer-related items from pub games and T-shirts to pottery and fudge. A glass wall lets you see into the brewing exhibition centre. Picnic-sets out on the grass.

🍴 As well as sandwiches, ciabattas and toasties, the popular lunchtime food includes chicken liver pâté with sweet onion marmalade, burger with battered onion rings and chips, vegetable tower with tomato sauce, fish pie topped with cheese, and ale-cured gammon and egg. More elaborate evening choices include prawns in creamy brandy and mustard sauce, beer-braised lamb shank, poached salmon fillet in puff pastry with spinach and fish velouté sauce, pork medallions in cider and apple brandy sauce, and puddings. *Benchmark main dish: beer-battered fresh haddock with chips and mushy peas £11.95. Two-course evening meal £18.00.*

Free house ~ Licensee Paul Theakston ~ Real ale ~ (01765) 680100 ~ Open 10.30-4.30 Mon-Weds, Sun; 10.30am-11pm Thurs-Sat ~ Bar food 12-2.30 daily; 6.30-8.45 Thurs-Sat; no evening food Mon-Weds, Sun ~ Children welcome ~ www.blacksheepbrewery.co.uk
Recommended by Gavin May, Isobel Mackinlay

PICKERING
SE7984   Map 10

White Swan ⑪ ⏲ 🛏

Market Place, just off A170; YO18 7AA

Relaxed little bar in civilised coaching inn with several smart lounges, an attractive restaurant, real ales, an excellent wine list and first class food; lovely bedrooms

Of course this is a smart and civilised 16th-c coaching inn, but at its heart is a cosy, properly pubby bar that our readers enjoy enormously. There's a genuinely warm welcome from the attentive staff, a relaxed atmosphere, sofas and a few tables, wood panelling, a log fire, Black Sheep Best and Theakstons Best on handpump, a dozen wines by the glass from an extensive list that includes fine old St Emilions and pudding wines, and ten malt whiskies. Opposite, a bare-boards room with a few more tables has another fire in a handsome art nouveau iron fireplace, a big bow window and pear prints on plum-coloured walls. The restaurant has flagstones, yet another open fire, comfortable settles and gothic screens, and the residents' lounge is in a converted beamed barn. The old coach entry to the car park is narrow. This is a fine place to stay, with luxurious bedrooms and delicious breakfasts; do visit their next-door Feast deli. The inn is just a stone's throw from the North York Moors Railway and on the edge of the North York Moors National Park.

As well as lunchtime sandwiches (their soup and sandwich deal is popular), the delicious food using the best local, seasonal produce might include potted shrimps with toast, fig and parma ham salad with local cheese, moules frites, home-made corned beef and bacon hash with béarnaise sauce and fried egg, aubergine, courgette and green bean curry with paneer and saffron rice, whitby haddock and chips, lamb rump with spinach, puy lentils and watercress, sea bream with smoked paprika mayonnaise and straw potatoes, venison saddle with beetroot and berry sauce, and puddings such as a plate of chocolate (panna cotta, white chocolate ice-cream, warm brownie and chocolate sauce) and sticky toffee pudding with toffee sauce. *Benchmark main dish: slow-cooked pork belly with braised red cabbage, bramley apple sauce and mash £16.95. Two-course evening meal £25.00.*

Free house ~ Licensees Marion and Victor Buchanan ~ Real ale ~ (01751) 472288 ~ Open 7.30am-11pm ~ Bar food 12-2, 7-9 ~ Restaurant ~ Children welcome ~ Dogs allowed in bar ~ Bedrooms: $105/$139 ~ www.white-swan.co.uk
Recommended by Peter Burton, John and Dinah Waters, Mrs G Marlow, Glenwys and Alan Lawrence, Dr D J and Mrs S C Walker, Comus and Sarah Elliott, Barbara and Peter Kelly, Janet and Peter Race

---

The details at the end of each featured entry start by saying whether the pub is a free house, or if it belongs to a brewery or pub group (which we name).

PICKHILL
Nags Head 🍴 ⅋ ⇌

SE3483 Map 10

A1 junction 50 (northbound) or junction 51 (southbound), village signed off A6055, Street Lane; YO7 4JG

Neatly kept dining pub with consistently good food, a fine choice of carefully chosen drinks, a tap room, smarter lounge and friendly service; comfortable bedrooms

'Ayorkshire gem and everything an english inn should be,' says one of our more discerning readers after another enjoyable visit to this excellent place. All aspects are top class – thanks to the hard-working and hands-on licensee Mr Boynton, who's been here for over 40 years. Most of the tables are laid for eating, so if it's just a drink you're after head for the bustling tap room on the left: beams hung with jugs, coach horns, ale-yards and so forth, and masses of ties hanging as a frieze from a rail around the red ceiling. The smarter lounge bar has deep green plush banquettes on a matching carpet, pictures for sale on neat cream walls and an open fire. There's also a library-themed restaurant. Black Sheep Best, Rudgate Viking, Theakstons Best and a guest beer on handpump, a good choice of malt whiskies, vintage Armagnacs and a carefully chosen wine list with several by the glass. One table is inset with a chessboard; darts, TV and background music. There's a front verandah, a boules and quoits pitch and a nine-hole putting green. The bedrooms are comfortable and well equipped and the buffet-style breakfasts are lovely.

🍴 Using fresh, seasonal produce, the enticing and extremely popular food includes lunchtime sandwiches, pigeon breast and chestnut risotto with beetroot and thyme purée, smoked ham hock terrine with apple and sultana chutney, red lentil and coconut dhal with naan, pickle and chutney, pork sausages with mash and onion gravy, tiger prawn caesar salad, free-range chicken breast with braised baby gem, wild mushrooms and red onions, salmon fillet with potato and chive blini and wild garlic velouté, and puddings such as dark chocolate griottine cherry pave with liquorice ice-cream and coconut and cardamom crème brûlée with pineapple compote and lime biscotti. *Benchmark main dish: steak, kidney and Guinness pie £12.95. Two-course evening meal £17.00.*

Free house ~ Licensee Edward Boynton ~ Real ale ~ (01845) 567391 ~ Open 11-11 (10.30 Sun) ~ Bar food 12-2, 6-9.30; 12-3, 5.30-8 Sun ~ Restaurant ~ Well behaved children welcome until 7.30pm (after that in dining room only) ~ Dogs allowed in bedrooms ~ Bedrooms: £55/£80 ~ www.nagsheadpickhill.co.uk
Recommended by Ian Malone, Edward Atkinson, Jill and Julian Tasker, Les and Sandra Brown

RIPPONDEN
Old Bridge ⅋ ◗

SE0419 Map 7

From A58, best approach is Elland Road (opposite the Golden Lion), park opposite the church in pub's car park and walk back over ancient hump-back bridge; HX6 4DF

Pleasant old pub by medieval bridge with relaxed communicating rooms and well-liked food

They cleverly manage to combine being both a local and a dining pub at this fine 14th-c inn. It's run by the third generation of the same family, who are always happy to chat and welcome all their customers with genuine friendliness. The three communicating rooms, each on a slightly different level, have a relaxed atmosphere, oak settles built into the window recesses of the thick stone walls, antique oak tables, rush-seated chairs and comfortably cushioned free-standing settles, a few well chosen pictures and prints on the panelled or painted walls and a big woodburning stove. Timothy Taylors Best, Dark Mild, Golden Best and Landlord and a couple of guests such as Burton Bridge Bitter and Oates Summit on handpump, quite a few foreign bottled beers, a dozen wines by the glass and 30 malt whiskies. The pub is by a beautiful medieval packhorse bridge over the little River Ryburn and there are seats in the pub garden overlooking the water. If you have trouble finding the pub (there's no pub sign outside), just head for the church.

Making everything in-house (except for the award-winning pork pies and the ice-cream) and using the best local, seasonal produce, the good lunchtime food includes only sandwiches and soup and the popular help-yourself salad carvery; in the evening and at weekends there might be king scallops with black pudding fritters and apple purée, crab cake with herb mayonnaise, smoked haddock and spinach pancakes topped with cream and parmesan, confit duck leg with oriental sauce, chicken kiev with wild garlic mayonnaise and chips, lamb hotpot with braised red cabbage, and puddings such as chocolate and orange brownie and fruit crumble. *Benchmark main dish: steak in ale pie with pickled red cabbage £10.00. Two-course evening meal £15.00.*

Free house ~ Licensees Tim and Lindsay Eaton Walker ~ Real ale ~ (01422) 822595 ~ Open 12-3, 5.30-11; 12-11 Fri, Sat; 12-10.30 Sun ~ Bar food 12-2, 6.30-9.30; 12-4 Sun ~ Children allowed until 8pm but must be seated away from bar ~ www.theoldbridgeinn.co.uk *Recommended by Mike Samuels, Dr Kevan Tucker*

 ROBIN HOOD'S BAY   NZ9505   Map 10
Laurel
Bay Bank; village signed off A171 S of Whitby; YO22 4SE

Charming little pub in unspoilt fishing village, with neat friendly bar and real ales; no food

At the bottom of a row of fishermen's cottages at the heart of one of the prettiest and most unspoilt fishing villages on the north-east coast, this little local remains quite unchanging and unspoilt. The charming landlord is welcoming to all his customers, and the beamed main bar is neatly kept and decorated with old local photographs, Victorian prints and brasses and lager bottles from all over the world. There's an open fire and Adnams Best and Theakstons Best and Old Peculier on handpump; darts, board games and background music. In summer, the hanging baskets and window boxes are lovely. They have a self-contained apartment for two people.

No food, but you can bring in sandwiches from the tea shop next door and eat them in the pub.

Free house ~ Licensee Brian Catling ~ Real ale ~ No credit cards ~ (01947) 880400 ~ Open 12-11(10.30 Sun); 3-11 Mon-Thurs in winter ~ Children in snug bar only ~ Dogs welcome *Recommended by Harvey Brown, Toby Jones*

 ROECLIFFE   SE3765   Map 7
Crown 🍴 🍷 🛡 🛏
Off A168 just W of Boroughbridge; handy for A1(M) junction 48; YO51 9LY

Smartly updated and attractively placed pub with a civilised bar, excellent enterprising food and a fine choice of drinks; lovely bedrooms

A wonderful place that has everything a good pub should have, this is run by the friendly and hard-working Mainey family and deservedly popular with both regulars and visitors. The bar has a contemporary colour scheme of dark reds and near whites with pleasant prints carefully grouped and lit; one area has chunky pine tables on flagstones, while another part, with a log fire, has dark tables on plaid carpet. Rudgate Battleaxe, Theakstons Best, Timothy Taylors Landlord and a changing guest beer on handpump, 30 wines by the glass and ten malt whiskies. For meals, you have a choice between a small candlelit olive green bistro with nice tables, a longcase clock and a couple of paintings, and a more formal restaurant. This is a very nice place to stay, with cosy, country-style bedrooms. The village green is opposite.

Using only small local suppliers and making their own bread, jams and chutneys, the first class, imaginative food includes lunchtime sandwiches, small rabbit pie over madeira jus with parsnip crisps, queenie scallops with gruyère, garlic and parsley, home-made beef in ale sausages with caramelised onion mash and white onion sauce, smoked trout fishcakes with tartare sauce and chips, steak in ale pudding, free-range chicken breast with wild mushroom and tarragon risotto and pancetta crisp, venison on port-mulled pears and fried jerusalem artichokes, and puddings such as melting chocolate fondant pudding with honey and almond tuille and vanilla pod crème brûlée with home-made ginger snaps, brandy-soaked oranges and caramel snaps. *Benchmark main dish: salmon, smoked haddock, king prawn and mussel pie £13.95. Two-course evening meal £20.50.*

Free house ~ Licensee Karl Mainey ~ Real ale ~ (01423) 322300 ~ Open 12-3.30, 5-11; 12-11 Sat; 12-8 Sun ~ Bar food 12-2.30, 6-9.30; 12-7 Sun ~ Restaurant ~ Children welcome ~ Dogs allowed in bar ~ Bedrooms: £82/£97 ~ www.crowninnroecliffe.com
Recommended by Peter Hacker, Ian Malone, Donna Jenkins, Martin Cawley, Gordon and Margaret Ormondroyd, Les and Sandra Brown, David Jackman, Janet and Peter Race

SANDHUTTON
Kings Arms ◖

SE3882 Map 10

A167, 1 mile N of A61 Thirsk–Ripon; YO7 4RW

Good chef-landlord in cheerful pub with friendly service, interesting food and beer and comfortable furnishings; bedrooms

Still the hub of the village, as it has been for 200 years, this is a charming inn with a traditional pubby atmosphere but also a strong emphasis on its appealing food. The bustling bar has an unusual circular woodburner in one corner, a high central table with four equally high stools, high-backed brown leather-seated dining chairs around light pine tables, a couple of cushioned wicker armchairs, some attractive modern bar stools and photographs of the pub in years gone by. Black Sheep Best, Rudgate Jorvik Blonde and Viking and Village Brewer White Boar Bitter on handpump, nine wines by the glass and efficient, friendly service. The two connecting dining rooms have similar furnishings to the bar (though there's also a nice big table with smart high-backed dining chairs), arty flower photographs on cream walls and a shelf above a small woodburning stove with more knick-knacks and some candles; background music, darts, board games and TV. They have a shop selling their own ready meals as well as sausages, pies and sandwiches.

Cooked by the landlord using local produce, the lunchtime food includes sandwiches, salmon, cod and prawn fishcake, beef and game pie, halloumi cheese and red pepper spring rolls with spicy beetroot chutney, chilli con carne and tandoori chicken; in the evening, customers can chat with the chef who will help them choose meat and fish from the display cabinet and then cook it as they want it, with their own choice of ingredients. *Benchmark main dish: deep-fried large scampi with chunky chips £11.50. Two-course evening meal £16.00.*

Free house ~ Licensees Raymond and Alexander Boynton ~ Real ale ~ (01845) 587887 ~ Open 12-midnight(10 Sun) ~ Bar food 12-2.30, 5.30-9; 12-5 Sun ~ Restaurant ~ Children welcome ~ Bedrooms: £55/£70 ~ www.thekingsarmssandhutton.co.uk
Recommended by Ian Wilson, Janet and Peter Race

SHEFFIELD   SK4086 Map 7
Kelham Island Tavern £
Kelham Island; S3 8RY

Busy little local with 13 changing real ales, basic but decent lunchtime pub food, a friendly welcome and pretty back garden

It's a bit like being at a permanent beer festival here, with up to 13 interesting ales on handpump (there's always a mild and a stout or porter) served by well organised, knowledgeable and friendly staff. Their regulars are Abbeydale Deception, Acorn Barnsley Bitter, Bradfield Farmers Blonde and Pictish Brewers Gold with guests from breweries such as Black Sheep, North Riding, Rudgate, Thwaites, Wentworth, Wold Top and Yorkshire Dales. It's a busy backstreet local with a wide mix of cheerful customers and pubby furnishings. The flower-filled and unusual back courtyard garden has plenty of seats and tables and a woodburning stove for chilly evenings. The front window boxes regularly win awards.

Served lunchtimes only, the tasty and very good value pubby food includes sandwiches and toasties, burgers with chips, liver and onions, chilli prawns, mushroom and red pepper stroganoff, and lamb curry. *Benchmark main dish: steak pie £5.50.*

Free house ~ Licensee Trevor Wraith ~ Real ale ~ (0114) 272 2482 ~ Open 12-midnight ~ Bar food 12-3.30; not Sun ~ Dogs welcome ~ Live folk Sun evenings ~ www.kelhamislandtavern.co.uk *Recommended by Toby Jones*

SOUTH DALTON   SE9645 Map 8
Pipe & Glass ⏰🍴 ♀ 🛏
West End; brown sign to pub off B1248 NW of Beverley; HU17 7PN

Yorkshire Dining Pub of the Year

Attractive dining pub with a proper bar area, real ales, interesting modern cooking, good service, garden and front terrace; stylish bedrooms

The exceptional food in this attractive whitewashed dining pub continues to draw in many customers – but there's a proper bustling bar area too and a fine choice of drinks: Black Sheep Best, Cropton Two Chefs (named for them), Wold Top Gold and a guest from York on handpump, ten wines by the glass, over 50 malt whiskies and draught cider; service is prompt and friendly. The beamed and bow-windowed bar has copper pans hanging above a log fire in the sizeable fireplace, some old prints, and cushioned window seats, high-backed settles and traditional pubby chairs around a mix of tables (each set with a church candle). Beyond that, all is airy and comfortably contemporary, angling around past some soft modern dark leather chesterfields into a light restaurant area overlooking Dalton Park, with high-backed stylish dining chairs around well spaced country tables on bare boards. The decorations – a row of serious cookery books and framed big-name restaurant menus – show how high the licensee aims; background music. There are tables on the garden's peaceful lawn and picnic-sets on the front terrace; the yew tree is said to be some 500 years old. The two suites are stylish and well equipped and have views over Dalton Park. The village is charming and its elegant Victorian church spire, 204ft tall, is visible for miles around.

🍴 Using the best local, seasonal produce and cooked by the landlord, the creative food might include lunchtime sandwiches, potted gloucester old spot pork with sticky apple and crackling salad, tartare of salmon with hot smoked salmon scotch egg, crowdie, pickled samphire and fennel pollen, pork sausages with bubble and squeak and ale and onion gravy, three-onion, goats cheese and oregano tart with honey-roast beets and soubise cream, free-range chicken breast with wild garlic forcemeat, peas, morel mushrooms, champ potatoes, nettles and mint, beef fillet with salt beef and potato pasty and beer mustard hollandaise, and puddings such as ginger crème brûlée with stewed rhubarb and sugar cakes and warm pistachio and raspberry bakewell tart with raspberry, lime and basil sorbet; they do takeaway dishes too, with a week's notice. *Benchmark main dish: lamb rump with vegetable hotch potch and crispy mutton belly £19.95. Two-course evening meal £28.00.*

Free house ~ Licensees Kate and James Mackenzie ~ Real ale ~ (01430) 810246 ~ Open 12-11(10.30 Sun); closed Mon except bank holidays ~ Bar food 12-2, 6-9.30; 12-4 Sun ~ Restaurant ~ Children welcome ~ Bedrooms: /£160 ~ www.pipeandglass.co.uk
Recommended by Huw Jones, G Jennings, Dr Kevan Tucker

THORNTON
Ring o' Bells
SE0933   Map 7

Hill Top Road, W of village and N of B6145; BD13 3QL

Particularly well run, cosy dining pub with long-serving owners and highly thought-of food

This is a thoroughly reliable hilltop dining pub with long-serving owners and staff and a friendly, chatty atmosphere. The cosy series of linked rooms have dark beams and panelling, plush seating for the glass-topped tables on red carpeting and old local photographs at one end, and an elegant and more modern linen-set restaurant at the other. Black Sheep Best, Copper Dragon Golden Pippin and Saltaire Blonde on handpump and several wines by the glass; background music. The high position gives long views towards Shipley and Bingley.

🍴 As well as a lunchtime and early evening two- and three-course set menu, the consistently popular food includes sandwiches, rare-breed pork and cox apple terrine with fruit chutney, potted prawns and white crab with brown crab mayonnaise and marinated cucumbers, seasonal pie of the day, beer-battered whitby haddock and chips, wild mushroom, beetroot and stilton ravioli with nut brown butter and pickled mushrooms, cumberland sausage ring with bacon, herb mash and red onion gravy, 12-hour braised lamb shoulder with faggot, thyme mash, squash and red wine sauce, and puddings such as lemon crème brûlée with home-made biscotti and sticky toffee pudding with butterscotch sauce. *Benchmark main dish: slow-cooked rare-breed pork belly with sage and onion rösti, parsnip purée and home-made black pudding £13.95. Two-course evening meal £16.00.*

Enterprise ~ Lease Ann and Clive Preston ~ Real ale ~ (01274) 832296 ~ Open 11.30-3.30, 5.30-11; 11.30-5, 6.15-10.30 Sun ~ Bar food 12-2, 5.30-9; 12-2, 6.15-9.30(8.30 Sun) Sat ~ Restaurant ~ Children welcome ~ Dogs welcome ~ www.theringobells.com
Recommended by John and Eleanor Holdsworth

THORNTON WATLASS

SE2385 Map 10

Buck ♦ ⌂

Village signposted off B6268 Bedale–Masham; HG4 4AH

Honest village pub with five real ales, traditional bars, well-liked food, and popular Sunday jazz

This is a welcoming place to stay: the bedrooms are clean and comfortable and the breakfasts excellent, and the hard-working and hands-on licensees, Michael and Margaret Fox, have been here for 27 years. The pleasantly traditional bar on the right has upholstered old-fashioned wall settles on carpet, a fine mahogany bar counter, a high shelf packed with ancient bottles, several mounted fox masks and brushes and a brick fireplace. The Long Room (which overlooks the cricket green) has large prints of old Thornton Watlass cricket teams, signed bats, cricket balls and so forth. Black Sheep Best, Theakstons Best and guests like Black Sheep All Creatures, Durham Cloister and Rudgate Ruby Mild on handpump, several wines by the glass, their famous bloody mary and over 40 interesting malt whiskies; darts and board games. The sheltered garden has a children's play area and summer barbecues, and they have their own cricket team; quoits.

 Good, popular food includes sandwiches, chicken liver parfait with red onion marmalade, creamy garlic mushrooms with smoked bacon, omelettes, burger with blue cheese or mozzarella, bacon, mushrooms, relish and chips, chicken breast with banana, sultana and almond curry cream, steak in ale pie, lambs liver and bacon with caramelised onion gravy, gammon with egg or pineapple, daily specials, and puddings. *Benchmark main dish: beer-battered fish and chips with home-made tartare sauce £9.95. Two-course evening meal £16.50.*

Free house ~ Licensees Michael and Margaret Fox ~ Real ale ~ (01677) 422461 ~ Open 11-11(11.30 Sat) ~ Bar food 12-2, 6-9; 12-3, 6-8.30 Sun ~ Restaurant ~ Children welcome ~ Dogs allowed in bedrooms ~ Trad jazz Sun lunchtimes ~ Bedrooms: £65/£90 ~ www.thebuckinn.net *Recommended by Richard and Penny Gibbs, David and Ruth Hollands, Brian and Audrey Goodson*

WASS

SE5579 Map 7

Wombwell Arms ⌂

Back road W of Ampleforth; or follow brown sign for Byland Abbey off A170 Thirsk–Helmsley; YO61 4BE

Consistently enjoyable village pub with a friendly atmosphere, good mix of locals and visitors, interesting bar food and real ales; bedrooms

As this bustling 17th-c place is handy for Byland Abbey it does get busy at lunchtimes, so you must book a table in advance; good nearby walks too. The two neatly kept bars have plenty of simple character, pine farmhouse chairs and tables, some exposed stone walls and log fires; the walls of the Poacher's Bar (dogs are welcome here) are hung with brewery memorabilia. From the panelled bar counter, the friendly staff serve Black Sheep Best, Timothy Taylors Landlord and a guest from Marston Moor on handpump, ten wines by the glass (quite a few from Mrs Walker's native South Africa) and several malt whiskies; darts. The two restaurants are incorporated into a former granary and there are seats outside.

🍴 As well as their fantastic value three-course menu (Monday-Thursday lunchtimes), the highly thought-of food includes sandwiches, trio of smoked fish, black pudding, smoked bacon and chive breadcrumbed balls with chutney, butternut squash, chickpea, mushroom and blue cheese pie, beer-battered haddock and chips, pork and apple sausages with mash and gravy, lemon sole with white wine, cucumber and mint sauce, duck breast with stilton, grapefruit and watercress sauce, bobotie (traditional south african curry), and puddings such as coffee and Tia Maria crème brûlée with coffee and chocolate macaroons and apple and cinnamon cake with custard. *Benchmark main dish: steak in Guinness pie £11.95. Two-course evening meal £17.00.*

Free house ~ Licensees Ian and Eunice Walker ~ Real ale ~ (01347) 868280 ~ Open 12-3, 6-11; 12-11 Sat; 12-10.30 Sun ~ Bar food 12-2(2.30 Sat), 6-8.30(9 Fri, Sat); 12-3, 6-8 Sun ~ Restaurant ~ Children welcome ~ Dogs allowed in bar ~ Folk music Thurs evening ~ Bedrooms: £69/£89 ~ www.wombwellarms.co.uk *Recommended by Keith Moss, Dr and Mrs R G J Telfer, Dr D J and Mrs S C Walker*

🏅 WIDDOP   SD9531   Map 7

Pack Horse 🍺 £

The Ridge; from A646 on W side of Hebden Bridge, turn off at Heptonstall signpost (as it's a sharp turn, coming out of Hebden Bridge the road signs direct you around a turning circle), then follow Slack and Widdop signposts; can also be reached from Nelson and Colne, on high pretty road; OS Sheet 103 map reference 952317; HX7 7AT

Friendly pub high up on the moors and liked by walkers for generous, tasty honest food, five real ales and lots of malt whiskies; bedrooms

After a wet moorland walk, this isolated traditional pub is a cosy haven. The bar has welcoming winter fires, window seats cut into the partly panelled stripped-stone walls that take in the beautiful views, sturdy furnishings and horsey mementoes. Black Sheep, Copper Dragon Golden Pippin, Thwaites Bitter and a guest like Worsthorne Old Trout on handpump, 140 single malt whiskies and some irish ones as well, and a dozen wines by the glass. The friendly golden retrievers are called Padge and Purdey and the alsatian is Holly. There are seats outside in the cobblestoned beer garden and pretty summer hanging baskets. As well as comfortable bedrooms (the breakfasts are very good), they also offer a smart self-catering apartment.

🍴 Substantial helpings of honest food include sandwiches, garlic mushrooms topped with stilton, pâté of the day, chilli con carne, mushroom stroganoff, gammon and eggs, lambs liver and bacon, fish pie, seasonal pheasant dishes, and puddings. *Benchmark main dish: rack of lamb with mint sauce £14.95. Two-course evening meal £15.00.*

Free house ~ Licensee Andrew Hollinrake ~ Real ale ~ (01422) 842803 ~ Open 12-3, 7-11; 12-10 Sun; closed Mon, in winter lunchtimes Tues-Fri ~ Bar food 12-2, 7-9; 12-7 Sun ~ Children in eating area of bar ~ Dogs allowed in bar ~ Bedrooms: £43/£69 ~ www.thepackhorse.org *Recommended by Emma Scofield, Toby Jones*

🏅 YORK   SE5951   Map 7

Maltings 🍺 £

Tanners Moat/Wellington Row, below Lendal Bridge; YO1 6HU

Bustling, friendly city pub with cheerful landlord, interesting real ales and other drinks plus good value standard food

The jovial landlord of this lively pub, tucked away by the river, keeps seven real ales on handpump including Black Sheep Bitter, one each from Roosters and York and four that change daily. He also has six continental beers on tap, two craft beers, lots of bottled beers, four farm ciders, 15 country wines and 25 whiskies from all over the world. The tricksy décor is entirely contrived and strong on salvaged, somewhat quirky junk: old doors for the bar front and much of the ceiling, a marvellous collection of railway signs and amusing notices, an old chocolate dispensing machine, cigarette and tobacco advertisements alongside cough and chest remedies, what looks like a suburban front door for the entrance to the ladies', partly stripped orange brick walls and even a lavatory pan in one corner; games machine. The day's papers are framed in the gents'; live music on Mondays and Tuesdays. Nearby parking is difficult; the pub is very handy for the National Railway Museum and the station. Please note that dogs are allowed in only after food has stopped being served.

🍴 Incredibly good value pubby food served lunchtime only includes sandwiches and toasties, chips done all sort of ways with lots of different dips, baked potatoes, vegetarian lasagne, ham and eggs, sausage and beans, and beef in ale pie. *Benchmark main dish: boozy beef pie £6.75.*

Free house ~ Licensee Shaun Collinge ~ Real ale ~ No credit cards ~ (01904) 655387 ~ Open 11-11; 12-10.30 Sun ~ Bar food 12-2 weekdays; 12-4 weekends ~ Children allowed only during meal times ~ Dogs allowed in bar ~ www.maltings.co.uk
Recommended by Nigel Hartle, Pat and Graham Williamson, David H Bennett, Ryta Lyndley, Eric Larkham, G Jennings

Also Worth a Visit in Yorkshire

Besides the fully inspected pubs, you might like to try these pubs that have been recommended to us and described by readers. Do tell us what you think of them: feedback@goodguides.com

ADDINGHAM SE0749
Swan (01943) 831999
Main Street; LS29 0NS Unspoilt and atmospheric, with open fires in comfortably worn linked rooms around central servery, flagstones and ancient iron range, well kept changing ales and good value simple food (not Mon, Tues, Thurs), also tapas (Weds and Fri evenings), live music and quiz nights; open all day weekends, closed Mon-Thurs lunchtimes. *(Claes Mauroy)*

AINTHORPE NZ7007
Fox & Hounds (01287) 660218
Brook Lane; YO21 2LD Traditional beamed moorland inn with wonderful views, nice open fire in unusual stone fireplace, comfortable seating, well kept Theakstons ales and good choice of wines by the glass, generous fairly priced food including good vegetarian options, friendly staff, restaurant, games room; great walks from the door, seven bedrooms and a self-catering cottage attached to the pub. *(Dr Kevan Tucker, Paul and Karen Cornock)*

ALDBOROUGH SE4166
Ship (01423) 322749
Off B6265 just S of Boroughbridge, close to A1; YO51 9ER Attractive 14th-c beamed village dining pub, good food from sandwiches and pub standards up, cheerful service, well kept ales including Theakstons, extensive wine list, some old-fashioned seats around cast-iron-framed tables, lots of copper and brass, inglenook fire, restaurant; children welcome, a few picnic-sets outside, handy for Roman remains and museum, bedrooms, open all day Sun, closed Mon lunchtime. *(Paul Smurthwaite, John and Eleanor Holdsworth)*

ALLERTHORPE SE7847
Plough (01759) 302349
Main Street; YO42 4RW Airy two-room lounge bar, popular and cheerful, with wide daily changing choice of good sensibly priced food including local game, well kept Black Sheep, John Smiths and two guests, decent house wines, snug alcoves, hunting prints, World War II RAF and RCAF photographs, open fires, restaurant, games extension with pool; background music; tables out in

pleasant garden, handy for Burnby Hall, open all day weekends. *(Roger A Bellingham)*

APPLETON-LE-MOORS   SE7388
✷ **Moors**   (01751) 417435

N of A170, just under 1.5 miles E of Kirkby Moorside; YO62 6TF Traditional stone-built village pub, beamed bar with built-in high-backed settle next to old kitchen fireplace, plenty of other seating, some sparse decorations (a few copper pans, earthenware mugs, country ironwork), Black Sheep and two guests, over 50 malt whiskies, generous good value home-made food (something all day) using vegetables from own allotment, darts; background music; children and dogs welcome, tables in lovely walled garden with quiet country views, walks to Rosedale Abbey or Hartoft End, seven bedrooms, open all day. *(Richard and Karen Holt, Shirley and Clive Pickerill)*

APPLETREEWICK   SE0560
✷ **Craven Arms**   (01756) 720270

Off B6160 Burnsall–Bolton Abbey; BD23 6DA Character creeper-covered 17th-c beamed pub, comfortably down-to-earth settles and rugs on flagstones, oak panelling, fire in old range, good welcoming service, up to eight well kept ales including a house beer from Dark Horse, good choice of wines by the glass, home-made food from baguettes up, small dining room and splendid thatched and raftered cruck barn with gallery; children, dogs and boots welcome (plenty of surrounding walks), wheelchair access, nice country views from front picnic-sets, more seats in back garden, open all day Weds-Sun. *(Jeremy Ward, Lynda and Trevor Smith, Claes Mauroy, Simon and Mandy King, Lawrence Pearse)*

APPLETREEWICK   SE0560
New Inn   (01756) 720252

W end of main village; BD23 6DA Unpretentious warmly welcoming country local with lovely views, six well kept ales including Black Sheep and Daleside, good choice of continental bottled beers, generous tasty home cooking, distinctive décor and interesting old local photographs; children and dogs welcome, three garden areas, good walks, five bedrooms and nearby camping, open all day. *(Claes Mauroy)*

ARNCLIFFE   SD9371
✷ **Falcon**   (01756) 770205

Off B6160 N of Grassington; BD23 5QE Basic no-frills country tavern in same family for generations; lovely setting on moorland village green, coal fire in small bar with elderly furnishings, well kept Timothy Taylors Landlord tapped from cask into stoneware jugs in central hatch-style servery, low-priced simple lunchtime and early evening food from old family kitchen, cheerful service, attractive watercolours, sepia photographs and humorous sporting prints, back sunroom

(dogs allowed here) overlooking pleasant garden; no credit cards; children welcome till 9pm, four miles of trout fishing (free for residents), nice walks, five bedrooms (two with own bathroom), good breakfast and evening meal. *(Neil and Angela Huxter, B and M Kendall, Claes Mauroy)*

ASKRIGG   SD9491
Kings Arms   (01969) 650113

Signed from A684 Leyburn–Sedbergh in Bainbridge; DL8 3HQ 18th-c coaching inn (the Drovers in TVs All Creatures Great and Small) and under same ownership as the Charles Bathurst at Langthwaite; flagstoned high-ceilinged main bar with good log fire, traditional furnishings and décor, well kept Black Sheep, Theakstons, a house beer from Yorkshire Dales and two guests, 13 wines by the glass, enjoyable reasonably priced food and friendly efficient service, restaurant with inglenook, games room in former barrel-vaulted beer cellar; background music; children welcome, pleasant side courtyard, bedrooms run separately as part of Holiday Property Bond complex behind. *(Gerry and Rosemary Dobson, Janet and Peter Race)*

ASKRIGG   SD9491
White Rose   (01969) 650515

Main Street; DL8 3HG Refurbished 19th-c hotel with well presented reasonably priced food in carpeted bar, dining room or conservatory, efficient staff, well kept John Smiths, Theakstons and Yorkshire Dales (brewed behind), good choice of wines by the glass, pool room; suntrap back garden, 12 comfortable bedrooms, open all day. *(Gerry and Rosemary Dobson, Simon and Mandy King)*

AUSTWICK   SD7668
✷ **Game Cock**   (01524) 251226

Just off A65 Settle–Kirkby Lonsdale; LA2 8BB Quaint civilised place in pretty spot below Three Peaks, good log fire in old-fashioned beamed bare-boards back bar, cheerful efficient staff and friendly locals, well kept Thwaites and a guest, winter mulled wine, nice coffee, most space devoted to the food side, with good fairly priced choice from french chef-landlord, pizzas and children's meals as well, two dining rooms and modern front conservatory-type extension; walkers and dogs welcome, tables out in front with play area, four neat bedrooms, closed Mon, otherwise open all day (till 1am if busy). *(Pat and Graham Williamson, Christopher Mobbs)*

BARKISLAND   SE0419
Fleece   (01422) 820687

B6113 towards Ripponden; HX4 0DJ Refurbished 18th-c beamed moorland dining pub, good choice of enjoyable fairly priced food (all day, till 7pm Sun), efficient friendly service from uniformed staff, well kept ales; children welcome, Pennine views from first-floor terrace and garden, five bedrooms, handy for M62. *(Gordon and Margaret Ormondroyd)*

BARMBY ON THE MARSH SE6828
Kings Head (01757) 630705
High Street; DN14 7HT Early 19th-c refurbished and extended beamed village pub, good locally sourced home-made food with some interesting choices, Yorkshire tapas, four real ales, bar, lounge and restaurant, deli (home-baked bread to order); children welcome, disabled facilities, open all day weekends, closed Mon and Tues lunchtimes. *(John and Eleanor Holdsworth)*

BECK HOLE NZ8202
★ Birch Hall (01947) 896245
Off A169 SW of Whitby, from top of Sleights Moor; YO22 5LE Tiny pub-cum-village-shop in stunning surroundings, two unchanging rooms (shop sells postcards, sweets and ice-creams), simple furnishings, built-in cushioned wall seats, wooden tables (one embedded with 136 pennies), flagstones or composition flooring, unusual items like french breakfast cereal boxes, tube of toothpaste priced 1/3d and model train running around head-height shelf, well kept ales such as Black Sheep and North Yorkshire, bar snacks including local pies and cakes, exceptionally friendly service, dominoes and quoits; no credit cards; children in small family room, dogs welcome, old painting of river valley outside and benches, streamside garden, self-catering cottage, good walks (one along disused railway), open all day summer, closed Mon evening, Tues winter. *(Eddie Cullen, Dr Kevan Tucker, Roger and Ann King, John and Dinah Waters, P Dawn)*

BEDALE SE2688
Old Black Swan (01677) 422973
Market Place; DL8 1ED Thriving old pub with attractive façade, welcoming efficient staff, generous helpings of good value straightforward food, wide choice of well kept ales including Theakstons Old Peculier, log fire, darts, pool; sports TV; children welcome, disabled facilities, small back terrace, Tues market, open all day. *(Janet and Peter Race)*

BEVERLEY TA0339
White Horse (01482) 861973
Hengate, off North Bar; HU17 8BN Carefully preserved Victorian interior with basic little rooms huddled around central bar, brown leatherette seats (high-backed settles in one little snug) and plain chairs and benches on bare boards, antique cartoons and sentimental engravings, gas-lit chandelier, open fires, games room, upstairs family room, bargain Sam Smiths and guest beers, basic food; children till 7pm, open all day. *(Anon)*

BINGLEY SE1039
Brown Cow (01274) 564345
Ireland Bridge; B6429 just W of junction with A650; BD16 2QX Comfortable open-plan pub in pleasant spot by the river, Timothy Taylors range and good choice of enjoyable food including burgers and stone-baked pizzas, popular live music Sat, quiz Tues; children and dogs welcome, tables on sheltered terrace, open all day Fri-Sun. *(Anon)*

BINGLEY SE1242
Dick Hudsons (01274) 552121
Otley Road, High Eldwick; BD16 3BA Good Vintage Inn family dining pub, Black Sheep, Marstons and Timothy Taylors, lots of wines by the glass, their usual food done well, quick service; tables out by cricket field, great views, open all day. *(Pat and Graham Williamson)*

BIRSTWITH SE2459
Station Hotel (01423) 770254
Off B6165 W of Ripley; HG3 3AG Welcoming stone-built Dales pub with bar, log-fire restaurant and new garden room, good well priced home-made food including lunchtime/early evening set deal, well kept local ales and decent choice of wines by the glass; tables in relandscaped garden with heated smokers' shelter, picturesque valley, four bedrooms, open all day. *(Anon)*

BRADFORD SE1533
Fighting Cock (01274) 726907
Preston Street (off B6145); BD7 1JE Busy bare-boards alehouse by industrial estate, a dozen well kept changing ales, foreign draught/bottled beers and real ciders, friendly staff and lively atmosphere, all-day doorstep sandwiches plus good simple lunchtime hot dishes (not Sun), may be free bread and dripping on the bar, low prices, coal fires; open all day. *(Anon)*

BRADFORD SE1533
New Beehive (01274) 721784
Westgate; BD1 3AA Robustly old-fashioned five-room Edwardian inn, plenty of period features including gas lighting, big mirrors, interesting paintings and coal fires, changing ales (mostly from smaller brewers) along with continental bottled beers, welcoming staff and friendly atmosphere, good pool room, weekend live music in cellar bar; children welcome, nice back courtyard, 17 bedrooms, open all day (till 1am Fri, Sat), from 6pm Sun. *(Anon)*

BRADFORD SE1633
Sparrow Bier Café (01677) 470411
North Parade; BD1 3HZ Bare-boards bar with great selection of bottled beers, draught continentals and local real ales, friendly knowledgeable staff, good deli platters and pies, local artwork, more tables in cellar bar;

background music; open all day,
closed Sun. *(Pat and Tony Martin)*

BRAMHAM   SE4242
Swan (01937) 843570
Just off A1 2 miles N of A64; LS23 6QA
Civilised and unspoilt three-room local
with engaging long-serving landlady, good
mix of customers, well kept Black Sheep,
Hambleton and Leeds Pale. *(Les and
Sandra Brown)*

BRAYTON   SE6030
Swan (01757) 703870
Doncaster Road; YO8 9EG Simple
traditional pub with good friendly
atmosphere, well liked uncomplicated food
including notable fish and chips, prompt
service, well kept ales. *(Hilary Forrest)*

BRIGHOUSE   SE1320
Clough House (01484) 512120
*Clough Lane, A6107 towards Fixby;
HD6 3QL* Well worn-in pub with bar and
two dining areas, clean and comfortable,
with good popular food including set-menu
choices (best to book), well kept Bass and
two other beers, pleasant chatty service,
roaring winter fire; impressive hanging
baskets. *(Gordon and Margaret Ormondroyd,
Andy and Jill Kassube and others)*

BURN   SE5928
⋆**Wheatsheaf** (01757) 270614
*Main Road (A19 Selby–Doncaster);
YO8 8LJ* Welcoming busy mock-Tudor
roadside pub, comfortable seats and tables
in partly divided open-plan bar with masses
to look at – gleaming copper kettles, black
dagging shears, polished buffalo horns,
cases of model vans and lorries, decorative
mugs above one bow-window seat, a drying
rack over the log fire; John Smiths, Timothy
Taylors and guests, 20 malt whiskies, good
value straightforward food (not Sun-Weds
evenings), roasts only on Sun; pool table,
games machine, TV and may be unobtrusive
background music; children and dogs
welcome, picnic-sets on heated terrace
in small back garden, open all day till
midnight. *(John and Eleanor Holdsworth)*

BURNSALL   SE0361
⋆**Red Lion** (01756) 720204
B6160 S of Grassington; BD23 6BU
Family-run 16th-c inn in lovely spot by River
Wharfe, looking across village green to
Burnsall Fell, tables out on front cobbles and
on big back terrace; attractively panelled,
sturdily furnished front dining rooms with
log fire, more basic back public bar, good
imaginative food (all day weekends), well
kept such as Copper Dragon and Timothy
Taylors, nice wines, efficient friendly service,
conservatory; children welcome, comfortable
bedrooms (dogs allowed in some and in bar),
fishing permits available, open all day.
(John Urquhart, M J Daly)

BURTON LEONARD   SE3263
⋆**Hare & Hounds** (01765) 677355
*Off A61 Ripon–Harrogate, handy for
A1(M) exit 48; HG3 3SG* Civilised and
welcoming country dining pub, good popular
food served promptly, well kept ales such as
Black Sheep and Timothy Taylors from long
counter, large carpeted main area divided by
log fire, traditional furnishings, bright little
side room; children in eating areas, pretty
back garden. *(Robert Wivell)*

BURYTHORPE   SE7964
Bay Horse (01653) 658302
*Off A64 8.5 miles NE of York ring road,
via Kirkham and Westow; 5 miles S of
Malton, by Welham Road; YO17 9LJ*
Welcoming dining pub with linked rooms,
good choice of reasonably priced food from
blackboard menu, Black Sheep, Copper
Dragon and several wines by the glass, main
bar has carved antique pews and old hunting
prints, end dining room with attractive
farmyard animal paintings, also a snug with
sofa and log fire and red-walled room with
rugs on flagstones; unobtrusive background
music; children welcome, dogs in bar, flat
disabled access from car park, contemporary
furniture on terrace under parasols, nice
Wolds-edge village with fine surrounding
walks, open all day Sun, closed Mon.
(Simon and Mandy King)

CARLTON HUSTHWAITE   SE4976
Carlton Inn (01845) 501265
Butt Lane; YO7 2BW Cosy modernised
beamed dining pub under newish
management; nice food cooked by landlady
including lunchtime/early evening set menu,
cheerful helpful service, John Smiths and
Theakstons, local cider, mix of country
furniture including some old settles, open
fire; children welcome, dogs in back bar area,
garden picnic-sets, open all day Sun, closed
Mon. *(Walter and Susan Rinaldi-Butcher)*

CARTHORPE   SE3083
⋆**Fox & Hounds** (01845) 567433
*Village signed from A1 N of Ripon, via
B6285; DL8 2LG* Welcoming neatly kept
dining pub with emphasis on good well
presented food, attractive high-raftered
restaurant with lots of farm and smithy tools,
Black Sheep and Worthington in L-shaped
bar with two log fires, plush seating, plates
on stripped beams and evocative Victorian
photographs of Whitby, some theatrical
memorabilia in corridors, good friendly
service; background classical music; children
welcome, handy for A1, closed Mon and first
week Jan. *(Michael and Maggie Betton, M and
J White, P A Rowe)*

CATTAL   SE4455
Victoria (01423) 330249
Station Road; YO26 8EB Bustling
Victorian-themed dining pub, good food

(should book) from extensive menu including specials, friendly attentive service, well kept ales including one named for the landlord from local Rudgate, good value wines; children welcome, picnic-sets in gravelled back garden, closed lunchtime (except Sun) and all day Mon. *(Les and Sandra Brown)*

CAWOOD SE5737
Ferry (01757) 268515
King Street (B1222 NW of Selby), by Ouse swing bridge; YO8 3TL Interesting 16th-c inn with several comfortable areas, enjoyable unpretentious food and well kept ales, cheerful efficient sevice, log fire in massive inglenook, low beams, stripped brickwork and bare boards; nice flagstone terrace and lawn down to river, bedrooms, open all day (from 3pm Mon). *(Pat and Graham Williamson)*

CHAPEL LE DALE SD7477
★ **Hill Inn** (01524) 241256
B5655 Ingleton–Hawes, 3 miles N of Ingleton; LA6 3AR Former farmhouse with fantastic views to Ingleborough and Whernside, a haven for weary walkers (wonderful remote surrounding walks); relaxed, chatty atmosphere, beams, log fires, straightforward furniture on stripped wooden floors, nice pictures, bare-stone recesses, Black Sheep, Dent and Theakstons, enjoyable bar food, separate dining room and well worn-in sun lounge; children welcome, dogs in bar, bedrooms, open all day Sat, closed Mon. *(David Heath)*

CLIFTON SE1622
★ **Black Horse** (01484) 713862
Westgate/Coalpit Lane; signed off Brighouse Road from M62 junction 25; HD6 4HJ Friendly 17th-c inn-restaurant, pleasant décor, front dining rooms with good interesting food including a few pubby dishes, can be pricey, efficient uniformed service, open fire in back bar with beam-and-plank ceiling, well kept Timothy Taylors Landlord and a house beer brewed by Brass Monkey, decent wines; nice courtyard, 21 comfortable bedrooms, pleasant village, open all day. *(John and Eleanor Holdsworth, Michael Butler)*

CLOUGHTON NEWLANDS TA0195
Bryherstones (01723) 870744
Newlands Road, off A171 in Cloughton; YO13 0AR Traditional stone pub back under licensees from 15 years ago; several interconnecting rooms including dining room up on right and flagstoned stable-theme room on left, lighter bare-boards back room with open fire, enjoyable popular food using locally sourced meat, Timothy Taylors and a house beer from Wold Top, games room with pool and darts; children and dogs welcome, picnic-sets and play area in sheltered back garden, closed lunchtimes Mon-Weds. *(Peter Hargreaves, Robin Constable)*

COLTON SE5444
★ **Old Sun** (01904) 744261
Off A64 York–Tadcaster; LS24 8EP Top-notch cooking at this refurbished and extended 18th-c beamed dining pub, good wine list with plenty available by the glass, well kept Black Sheep and Cropton (proper bar area), friendly competent staff; cookery demonstrations and little shop selling home-made and local produce; children welcome, seats out on front terrace, bedrooms in separate building, open all day Sun (food till 7pm then). *(Gordon and Margaret Ormondroyd)*

CONEYTHORPE SE3958
★ **Tiger** (01423) 863632
2.3 miles from A1(M), junction 47; A59 towards York, then village (and brown sign to Tiger Inn) signposted; bear left at brown sign in Flaxby; HG5 0RY Spreading red-carpeted bar with hundreds of pewter tankards hanging from ochre-painted joists, olde-worlde prints, china figurines in one arched alcove, padded grey wall seats, pews and settles around sturdy scrubbed tables, open fire, more formal dining area at back, sensibly priced food from lunchtime sandwiches through pubby favourites, also set menu deals, Black Sheep, Copper Dragon and Timothy Taylors Landlord, friendly helpful staff; nostalgic background music; picnic-sets on front gravel terrace and on small green opposite, open all day. *(Malcolm Bond)*

CRAY SD9479
★ **White Lion** (01756) 760262
B6160 N of Kettlewell; BD23 5JB Highest Wharfedale pub (under new licensees) in lovely countryside and popular with walkers; simple bar with open fire and flagstones, hearty well priced food, up to five local ales in the summer, back room, original bull 'ook game; children and dogs welcome, picnic-sets above quiet steep lane or can sit on flat limestone slabs in shallow stream opposite, nine bedrooms. *(Lawrence Pearse)*

CROSS HILLS SE0045
Old White Bear (01535) 632115
Keighley Road; BD20 7RN Cheery 17th-c local with five well kept Naylors ales (brewed nearby), good choice of affordably priced home-made food including OAP lunch deal, five rooms off central bar, beams and open fires, pub games such as ring the bull, Thurs quiz; sports TV; garden behind, open all day. *(Anon)*

CULLINGWORTH SE0636
George (01535) 275566
Station Road; BD13 5HN Under newish local management, own Old Spot beers brewed in the village, enjoyable reasonably priced home-made food from light lunchtime choices up, good service; children welcome

till 9pm, open all day. *(John and Eleanor Holdsworth)*

DACRE BANKS   SE1961
✳ Royal Oak (01423) 780200
B6451 S of Pateley Bridge; HG3 4EN
Popular solidly comfortable 18th-c pub with Nidderdale views, traditional food done very well, attentive friendly staff, well kept ales including Rudgate, good wine choice, beams and panelling, log-fire dining room, games room with darts, dominoes and pool; TV, background music; children in eating areas, terrace tables, informal back garden, three character bedrooms, good breakfast, open all day. *(Claes Mauroy)*

DARLEY   SE1961
Wellington Arms (01423) 780362
B6451; HG3 2QQ Roadside stone inn with fine Nidderdale views, beams and big open fire, good freshly made food (same menu lunchtime and evening), well kept Black Sheep, Copper Dragon, Timothy Taylors and Tetleys, helpful friendly staff; children welcome, seats on large grassed area, bedrooms, good breakfast, open all day. *(Stanley and Annie Matthews)*

DEWSBURY   SE2622
Huntsman (01924) 275700
Walker Cottages, Chidswell Lane, Shaw Cross – pub signed; WF12 7SW Cosy low-beamed converted cottages alongside urban-fringe farm, long-serving amiable landlord and friendly locals, lots of agricultural bric-a-brac, blazing log fire, small front extension, a well kept house beer (Chidswell) along with Black Sheep and Timothy Taylors Landlord, decent home-made food (not lunchtimes Sun, Mon or evenings except Thurs, Fri), quiet relaxed atmosphere. *(Michael Butler)*

DEWSBURY   SE2420
Leggers (01924) 502846
Robinsons Boat Yard, Savile Town Wharf, Mill Street East (SE of B6409); WF12 9BD Hayloft conversion above former stables by Calder & Hebble Navigation marina, well kept Everards Tiger and five guests, bottled belgian beers, real cider and perry, good value straightforward food, friendly staff, assorted memorabilia, pool; picnic-sets outside, boat trips, open all day. *(Anon)*

DEWSBURY   SE2421
✳ West Riding Licensed Refreshment Rooms (01924) 459193
Station, Wellington Road; WF13 1HF Convivial three-room early Victorian station bar, eight well kept changing ales such as Black Sheep, Oakham, Timothy Taylors and Sportsman (brewed at their sister pub in Huddersfield), foreign bottled beers and farm ciders, bargain generous lunchtime food on scrubbed tables, popular pie night Tues, curry night Weds and Yorkshire tapas night

Thurs, good weekend breakfast too, friendly staff, lots of steam memorabilia including paintings by local artists, coal fire, daily papers, impressive juke box, some live music; children till 6pm in two end rooms, disabled access, open all day. *(Andy Lickfold, Andy and Jill Kassube)*

DONCASTER   SE5702
Corner Pin (01302) 340670
St Sepulchre Gate West, Cleveland Street; DN1 3AH Plush beamed lounge with old local pub prints, welsh dresser and china, York and interesting guests kept well (beer festivals), good value traditional food from fine hot sandwiches to Sun roasts, friendly landlady, cheery public bar with darts, games machine and TV; back decking, open all day. *(P Dawn)*

DONCASTER   SK6299
Hare & Tortoise (01302) 867329
Parrots Corner, Bawtry Road, Bessacarr (A638); DN4 7PB Popular Vintage Inn all-day dining pub, ales such as Black Sheep, Leeds and Marstons, friendly young staff, several small rooms off central bar, log fire; background music; children welcome. *(Stephen Woad)*

DONCASTER   SE5703
Plough (01302) 738310
West Laith Gate, by Frenchgate shopping centre; DN1 1SF Small old-fashioned local with friendly long-serving licensees and chatty regulars, Acorn Barnsley Bitter and guests, bustling front room with darts, dominoes and sports TV, old town maps, quieter back lounge; tiny central courtyard, open all day (Sun afternoon break). *(Peter F Marshall, P Dawn)*

DONCASTER   SE5703
Tut 'n' Shive (01302) 360300
West Laith Gate; DN1 1SF Well kept Abbeydale, Black Sheep, Greene King and guests, Aspall's cider, bargain food all day, eccentric décor with old doors acting as wall/ceiling coverings, flagstones lots of pump clips, dim lighting; good rock juke box, big-screen sports TVs, games machines; open all day. *(P Dawn)*

DUNNINGTON   SE6751
Windmill (01904) 481898
Hull Road (A1079); YO19 5LP Welcoming dining pub, large and fairly modern, with popular home-made food served by friendly staff, good range of beers, back conservatory, quieter small raised dining area; ten bedrooms, open all day Sun. *(David H Bennett)*

EASINGWOLD   SE5270
✳ George (01347) 821698
Market Place; YO61 3AD Neat, bright and airy market town hotel (former 18th-c coaching inn), quiet corners even when

busy, helpful cheerful service, well kept Black Sheep, Moorhouses and a guest, good sensibly priced food in bar and restaurant, beams, horsebrasses and warm log fires, slightly old-fashioned feel and popular with older customers; pleasant bedrooms, good breakfast. *(Roger A Bellingham, Robert Turnham)*

EAST MARTON   SD9050
Cross Keys   (01282) 844326
A59 Gisburn–Skipton; BD23 3LP
Comfortable and welcoming 18th-c pub behind small green near Leeds & Liverpool Canal (and Pennine Way), heavy beams and big open fire, good freshly cooked food (all day Sun) from shortish menu supplemented by interesting blackboard specials, well kept Copper Dragon and Theakstons, friendly caring service, more restauranty dining room; background music; children and dogs welcome, tables on front deck, open all day. *(Pat and Graham Williamson, John and Hazel Sarkanen, Richard and Karen Holt, Brian and Janet Ainscough)*

EAST MORTON   SE0941
Busfeild Arms   (01274) 563169
Main Road; BD20 5SP Attractive 19th-c stone-built village pub (originally a school), traditionally furnished beamed and flagstoned bar with woodburner, four ales including Tetleys and Timothy Taylors Landlord, good range of enjoyable well priced food including weekday early-bird deal (5.30-6.30pm), cheerful service, restaurant; quiz Thurs, live music Sat, TV; children welcome, picnic-sets on front terrace, open all day. *(John and Eleanor Holdsworth)*

EAST WITTON   SE1487
✶ Cover Bridge Inn   (01969) 623250
A6108 out towards Middleham; DL8 4SQ
Cosy and welcoming 16th-c flagstoned country local, good choice of well kept Yorkshire ales, enjoyable generous pub food, sensible prices, small restaurant, roaring fires; children and dogs welcome, riverside garden with play area, three bedrooms, open all day. *(Anon)*

EASTBURN   SE0144
Nightingale   (01535) 653000
Main Road; BD20 7SN Popular pub close to Airedale Hospital, enjoyable good value food including lunchtime set menu, efficient friendly service; children welcome. *(John and Eleanor Holdsworth)*

EGTON   NZ8006
Wheatsheaf   (01947) 895271
Village centre; YO21 1TZ Village pub of real character, interesting paintings and prints in small bar with open fire, good generously served inexpensive food, friendly service, Black Sheep, John Smiths and guests, several wines by the glass, restaurant; six bedrooms, open

all day weekends. *(Gordon and Margaret Ormondroyd, P Dawn)*

EGTON BRIDGE   NZ8005
Horseshoe   (01947) 895245
Village signed off A171 W of Whitby; YO21 1XE Attractively placed 18th-c stone inn with some refurbishment under present landlord; open fire, high-backed built-in winged settles, wall seats and spindleback chairs, various odds and ends including a big stuffed trout (caught nearby in 1913), Theakstons, Black Sheep, Copper Dragon and a guest, traditional food; background music; children welcome, dogs in some areas, seats on quiet terrace in attractive mature garden bordering small river Esk, good walks (on coast-to-coast path), six bedrooms, open all day weekends. *(Sara Fulton, Roger Baker, Phil and Jane Villiers, P Dawn)*

EGTON BRIDGE   NZ8005
✶ Postgate   (01947) 895241
Village signed off A171 W of Whitby; YO21 1UX Moorland village pub with good imaginative fairly priced food, friendly staff, well kept Black Sheep and a guest, traditional quarry-tiled panelled bar with beams, panelled dado and coal fire in antique range, elegant restaurant; children and dogs welcome, garden picnic-sets, three nice bedrooms. *(Dr and Mrs R G J Telfer, Mrs Grace Smith, P Dawn)*

EMBSAY   SE0053
Elm Tree   (01756) 790717
Elm Tree Square; BD23 6RB Good value open-plan beamed village pub, hearty popular food from tasty sandwiches up, good range of well kept ales, friendly young staff, settles and old-fashioned prints, log-effect gas fire, dining room, games area; busy weekends especially evenings; comfortable bedrooms, handy for steam railway. *(Anon)*

ETTON   SE9743
Light Dragoon   (01430) 810282
3.5 miles N of Beverley, off B1248; Main Street; HU17 7PQ Roomy country local under newish landlord-chef, enjoyable food including good reasonably priced Sun lunch, two real ales and several wines by the glass, cheerful staff, inglenook fireplace; children welcome, back garden with swings and slide, nice village on Wolds cycle route, open all day Sun, closed Mon lunchtime. *(Dr Kevan Tucker, C A Hall)*

FARNLEY TYAS   SE1612
Golden Cock   (01484) 664863
Signed off A629 Huddersfield–Sheffield; HD4 6UD Spacious dining pub well refurbished under new owners, front bar, dining room and further large restaurant, good variety of enjoyable food served by friendly helpful staff, well kept Copper Dragon and several wines by the glass; pleasant hill village, open all day. *(Gordon and Margaret Ormondroyd)*

FILEY TA1180
Bonhommes (01723) 514054
The Crescent; YO14 9JH Friendly busy
bar with several well kept ales including one
badged for them, live music and quiz nights;
open all day till late. *(Brian Daley)*

FINGHALL SE1889
✱ Queens Head (01677) 450259
Off A684 E of Leyburn; DL8 5ND
Welcoming comfortable dining pub, log fires
either end of tidy low-beamed bar, settles
making stalls around big tables, Theakstons
and guests, good food from sandwiches,
deli boards and traditional favourites up,
midweek deals and Sat brunch, extended
back Wensleydale-view dining room; children
and dogs welcome, disabled facilities, back
garden with decking sharing same view,
three bedrooms. *(Anon)*

FIXBY SE1119
Nags Head (01727) 871100
*New Hey Road, by M62 junction 24
south side, past Hilton; HD2 2EA*
Spacious ivy-covered chain dining pub,
attractive outside and comfortable in, pubby
bar with four well kept ales, enjoyable fairly
priced food including carvery and OAP deals,
friendly helpful service, linked areas with
wood and slate floors, restaurant on two
levels; garden tables, bedrooms in adjoining
Premier Inn, open all day. *(Brenda Keogh,
Gordon and Margaret Ormondroyd and others)*

FLOCKTON SE2314
Sun (01924) 848603
*Off A642 Wakefield–Huddersfield at
Blacksmiths Arms; WF4 4DW* Old
beamed pub much improved under present
management; warm welcome, open fires
in bar and dining area, good reasonably
priced food (nothing too elaborate), prompt
efficient service, well kept real ales; children
welcome, garden tables with lovely views
towards Emley Moor, open all day. *(Michael
Butler, Carl Rahn Griffith)*

GIGGLESWICK SD8164
✱ Black Horse (01729) 822506
*Church Street – take care with the car
park; BD24 0BE* Hospitable licensees in
17th-c village pub prettily set by church; cosy
bar with gleaming brass, copper and bric-a-
brac, coal-effect fire, good value generous
food, well kept Timothy Taylors, Tetleys
and guests, intimate dining room, good
service, piano (often played), monthly quiz;
children welcome till 9pm, no dogs, sheltered
heated back terrace, smokers' shelter, three
reasonably priced comfortable bedrooms,
good breakfast, open all day weekends;

for sale as we went to press but business as
usual. *(Dr and Mrs Leach)*

GIGGLESWICK SD8164
Craven Arms (01729) 825627
*Just off A65 W of village at junction
with Brackenber Lane, opposite station;
BD24 0EB* Modern refurbishment and
interesting well presented food including
meat from licensee's organic farm (good
vegetarian options too), moderate prices,
well kept ales such as Black Sheep, Copper
Dragon and Tetleys, attentive friendly
service, restaurant; children welcome,
disabled access, seven bedrooms, closed Mon.
(Canon Graham Bettridge)

GIGGLESWICK SD8164
Harts Head (01729) 822086
Belle Hill; BD24 0BA Cheerful bustling
18th-c village inn, comfortable carpeted
bar/lounge with well kept Copper Dragon,
Tetleys and guests, good choice of enjoyable
reasonably priced food, restaurant, resident's
snooker room; Sky TV; picnic-sets on sloping
lawn, ten bedrooms, open all day Fri-Sun,
closed lunchtimes Tues, Thurs. *(Anon)*

GILLAMOOR SE6890
✱ Royal Oak (01751) 431414
Off A170 in Kirkbymoorside; YO62 7HX
Stone-built 18th-c dining pub with interesting
local food including seasonal game at fair
prices (can get busy), friendly staff, ales
such as Black Sheep and Copper Dragon,
reasonably priced wines, roomy bar with
heavy dark beams, log fires in two tall stone
fireplaces (one with old kitchen range),
overspill dining room (dogs allowed here);
children welcome, eight comfortable modern
bedrooms, good breakfast, attractive village
handy for Barnsdale Moor walks. *(David and
Lin Short, Stanley and Annie Matthews)*

GILLING EAST SE6176
✱ Fairfax Arms (01439) 788212
*Main Street (B1363, off A170 via
Oswaldkirk); YO62 4JH* Smartly
refurbished country inn, beamed bar with
bare boards by handsome oak counter,
carpeted area with woodburner, Black Sheep,
Tetleys and some interesting wines by the
glass, daily newspapers, two-part carpeted
dining room with big hunting prints on red
walls, nicely old-fashioned floral curtains
and some padded oak settles, enjoyable
modern food plus pub favourites, friendly
black-aproned staff; picnic-sets out in
front by floodlit roadside stream, pleasant
village well placed for Howardian Hills and
North York Moors, comfortably up-to-date
bedrooms, good breakfast, open all day
weekends. *(Anon)*

Virtually all pubs in this book sell wine by the glass. We mention wines
if they are a cut above the average.

GOATHLAND NZ8200
Mallyan Spout Hotel
(01947) 896486 *Opposite church;*
YO22 5AN Old creeper-clad stone hotel
with three spacious lounges and traditional
bar, open fires and fine views, good fairly
priced bar lunches and Sun carvery, three
real ales, good malt whiskies and wines,
friendly helpful staff, smart restaurant; well
behaved children in eating areas, handy for
namesake waterfall, comfortable bedrooms
and good buffet breakfast, usually open all
day. *(Comus and Sarah Elliott)*

GOODMANHAM SE8943
★Goodmanham Arms (01430) 873849
Main Street; YO43 3JA Welcoming little
red-brick country pub with three traditional
linked areas, beam-and-plank ceilings,
some red and black floor tiles, good mix of
furniture and plenty of odds and ends, even a
Harley Davidson, good wholesome food from
italian chef-owner (no starters) including a
winter casserole cooked over the open fire,
evening meals served 5-7pm Mon and Fri
only, seven real ales – three from on-site All
Hallows microbrewery, reasonable prices,
occasional acoustic music; children and dogs
welcome, good walks (on Wolds Way), open
all day. *(Pat and Graham Williamson, John and
Eleanor Holdsworth, David Heath, P Dawn)*

GRANGE MOOR SE2215
Kaye Arms (01924) 848385
Wakefield Road (A642); WF4 4BG
Smartly refurbished dining pub with good
popular food including set menus, efficient
service, ales such as Black Sheep, Ossett and
Timothy Taylors; handy for Mining Museum,
closed Sun evening, Mon. *(Gordon and
Margaret Ormondroyd)*

GRASSINGTON SE0064
★Devonshire (01756) 752525
The Square; BD23 5AD Small handsome
reliably run hotel, good window seats and
tables outside overlooking sloping village
square, decent food from substantial
sandwiches up, Fri fish night, well kept
ales such as Black Sheep and Moorhouses,
interesting pictures and ornaments,
beams and open fires, pleasant family
room, spacious restaurant, prompt service
and cheerful relaxed atmosphere; seven
comfortable bedrooms, open all day Sun.
(B and M Kendall, Michael Butler)

GRASSINGTON SE0064
Foresters Arms (01756) 752349
Main Street; BD23 5AA Comfortable
opened-up old coaching inn with friendly
bustling atmosphere, good reasonably priced
generous food, well kept ales including Black
Sheep, cheerful efficient service, log fires,
dining room off on right, pool and sports TV
on left, popular Mon quiz; children welcome,
outside tables, 14 affordable bedrooms (ones

over bar noisy), nice breakfast, good walking
country, open all day. *(Michael Butler)*

GREAT BROUGHTON NZ5405
Bay Horse (01642) 712319
High Street; TS9 7HA Big creeper-clad
dining pub in attractive village, wide choice
of food including blackboard specials like
Whitby crab and good value set lunch,
friendly attentive service, real ales such as
Camerons and Jennings, restaurant; children
welcome, seats outside. *(Stephen Funnell)*

GREAT HABTON SE7576
★Grapes (01653) 669166
*Corner of Habton Lane and Kirby
Misperton Lane; YO17 6TU*
Traditionally refurbished beamed dining
pub in small village, homely and cosy, with
good cooking including fresh local fish and
game, home-baked bread, Marstons-related
ales, open fire, small public bar with darts
and TV; background music; a few roadside
picnic-sets (water for dogs), nice walks,
open all day Sun, closed Tues lunchtime
and Mon. *(Anon)*

GREAT OUSEBURN SE4461
Crown (01423) 330013
*Off B6265 SE of Boroughbridge;
YO26 9RF* Welcoming 18th-c pub with some
refurbishment under new owner, enjoyable
food from traditional choices up, good value
early-bird menu, Black Sheep, Copper Dragon
and Timothy Taylors Landlord, various areas
including back dining extension; children
and dogs welcome, garden with terrace
tables, open all day. *(Anon)*

GUISELEY SE1941
Coopers (01943) 878835
Otley Road; LS20 8AH Market Town
Taverns conversion of former Co-operative
store, open-plan bare-boards bar with good
range of food from lunchtime sandwiches up,
eight real ales including Black Sheep and
Timothy Taylors, music nights in upstairs
function/dining room; open all day. *(Anon)*

HALIFAX SE0924
Dirty Dicks (07887) 510354
Clare Road; HX1 2HX Interesting 1930s
listed building with eight well kept ales
including one named for them; open all
day. *(Eric Larkham)*

HALIFAX SE0924
Three Pigeons (01422) 347001
*Sun Fold, South Parade; off Church
Street; HX1 2LX* Carefully restored,
four-room 1930s pub (Grade II listed), art
deco fittings, ceiling painting in octagonal
main area, original flooring, panelling and
tiled fireplaces with log fires, up to six well
kept Ossett ales and local guests, friendly
chatty staff; tables outside, handy for Eureka!
Museum and Shay Stadium, open all day
Fri-Sun, from 3pm other days. *(Eric Larkham)*

HARDROW SD8691
★**Green Dragon** (01969) 667392
Village signed off A684; DL8 3LZ
Friendly traditional Dales pub dating from
13th c and full of character; stripped stone,
antique settles on flagstones, lots of bric-a-
brac, low-beamed snug with fire in old iron
range, another in big main bar, five well
kept ales including one badged for them by
Yorkshire Dales, enjoyable generous food,
small neat restaurant, annual brass band
competition; children and dogs welcome,
bedrooms, next to Hardraw Force – England's
highest single-drop waterfall. *(David and
Jenny Billington, M and J White, Rob and
Catherine Dunster, Comus and Sarah Elliott)*

HAROME SE6482
★**Star** (01439) 770397
*High Street; village signed S of A170,
E of Helmsley; YO62 5JE* Restaurant-
with-rooms (need to book well in advance
for both) in pretty 14th-c thatched building,
but bar does have informal feel, bowed
beam-and-plank ceiling, plenty of bric-a-brac,
interesting furniture including 'Mousey'
Thompson pieces, log fire and well polished
tiled kitchen range, three changing ales
and 18 wines by the glass, home-made fruit
liqueurs, snacks served in cocktail bar,
popular coffee loft in the eaves, inventive
ambitious cooking (not cheap), well trained
staff; background music; children welcome,
seats on sheltered front terrace, more
in garden, open all day Sun, closed Mon
lunchtime. *(Dr Kevan Tucker, John and Dinah
Waters, G Jennings, Ryta Lyndley, Barbara and
Peter Kelly)*

HARPHAM TA0961
St Quintin Arms (01262) 490329
Main Street; YO25 4QY Comfortable old
village pub with enjoyable reasonably priced
home-made food including good mixed grill,
well kept Tetleys and Wold Top, friendly
landlord and staff, small dining room;
sheltered garden with pond, on National
Cycle Route 1, three bedrooms. *(C A Hall,
Dr Kevan Tucker)*

HARROGATE SE3155
Coach & Horses (01423) 561802
West Park; HG1 1BJ Very friendly bustling
pub with half a dozen good Yorkshire ales and
over 80 malt whiskies, enjoyable lunchtime
food at bargain prices, obliging service,
nice interior with booth seating; open all
day. *(David and Susan Nobbs)*

HARROGATE SE2955
★**Hales** (01423) 725570
Crescent Road; HG1 2RS Classic Victorian
décor in 18th-c gas-lit local close to Pump

Rooms, leather seats in alcoves, stuffed birds,
comfortable saloon and tiny snug, seven real
ales including Daleside, simple good value
lunchtime food, friendly helpful staff; can get
lively weekend evenings. *(Martin Cawley)*

HARROGATE SE2955
★**Old Bell** (01423) 507930
Royal Parade; HG1 2SZ Thriving
Market Town Taverns pub with eight mainly
Yorkshire beers from handsome counter,
lots of bottled continentals and impressive
choice of wines by the glass, friendly
helpful staff, lunchtime snacks including
sandwiches (interesting choice of breads),
more elaborate evening meals upstairs,
newspapers, panelling, old sweet shop ads
and breweriana; no children; open all day.
(Anon)

HARROGATE SE3055
Swan on the Stray (01423) 524587
*Corner Devonshire Place and A59;
HG1 4AA* Refurbished Market Town Tavern,
enjoyable reasonably priced food from
shortish menu plus a few specials including
game, free coffee if you order a lunchtime
main course (Mon-Fri), five mostly local
ales, ciders and perry, good range of bottled
imports, cheerful efficient service, daily
newspapers. *(Brian and Janet Ainscough,
Pat and Tony Martin)*

HARROGATE SE3155
Winter Gardens (01423) 877010
Royal Baths, Crescent Road; HG1 2RR
Interesting Wetherspoons transformation of
former ballroom in landmark building, well
kept ales, generous usual good value food,
many original features, comfortable sofas
in lofty hall, upper gallery; very busy late
evening; attractive terrace, open all day.
*(S Holder, Ryta Lyndley, B and M Kendall,
Brian and Anna Marsden)*

HAWNBY SE5489
Inn at Hawnby (01439) 798202
*Aka Hawnby Hotel; off B1257 NW of
Helmsley; YO62 5QS* Attractively
situated inn with good local food including
some interesting choices, helpful
welcoming service, Black Sheep, Great
Newsome and Timothy Taylors, good choice
of wines by the glass; children welcome,
lovely views from restaurant and garden
tables, pretty village in walking country
(packed lunches available), nine bedrooms
(three in converted stables), open all day
Fri-Sun. *(Dr Nigel Bowles)*

HEADINGLEY SE2736
Arcadia (0113) 274 5599
Arndale Centre; LS6 2UE Small Market
Town Tavern in former bank, good choice

of changing Yorkshire ales kept well, lots of continental bottled beers and good range of wines, knowledgeable staff, bar food (Thurs-Sun), stairs to mezzanine; no children; open all day. *(Daniel Lezcano)*

HEBDEN   SE0263
Clarendon (01756) 752446
B6265; BD23 5DE Pleasant spic and span pub in nice location close to good moorland walks; bar, snug and dining area, open fire, well kept Thwaites and good variety of enjoyable plentiful food, friendly service; children welcome, three updated bedrooms, open all day weekends. *(Gordon and Margaret Ormondroyd, Claes Mauroy, Robert Wivell)*

HEBDEN BRIDGE   SD9827
Stubbings Wharf (01422) 844107
About a mile W; HX7 6LU Friendly pub in good spot by Rochdale Canal with adjacent moorings, popular good value food (all day weekends, booking advised) from sandwiches and light meals up, half a dozen well kept regional ales, proper ciders; children and dogs welcome, boat trips, open all day. *(Martin Smith)*

HEBDEN BRIDGE   SD9927
★ White Lion (01422) 842197
Bridge Gate; HX7 8EX Solid stone-built 17th-c inn with spacious refurbished interior, good choice of enjoyable sensibly priced food (all day) from sandwiches and deli boards up, five well kept ales including Black Sheep and Timothy Taylors, friendly service; children welcome, dogs in snug, disabled facilities, attractive secluded riverside garden, ten good bedrooms (four in courtyard). *(Brian and Anna Marsden, Martin Smith, Michael Butler, David Heath)*

HELMSLEY   SE6183
Feathers (01439) 770275
Market Place; YO62 5BH Substantial stone inn with sensibly priced generous food from sandwiches to good seasonal crab, popular Sun carvery, well kept Black Sheep, Tetleys and a guest, good friendly service, several rooms with comfortable seats, oak and walnut tables (some by Robert 'Mouseman' Thompson – as is the bar counter), flagstones or tartan carpet, heavy medieval beams and huge inglenook log fire, panelled corridors; children welcome in eating area, tables out in front, 22 clean comfortable bedrooms, open all day. *(Ben and Ruth Levy, Glenwys and Alan Lawrence, David and Lin Short)*

HETTON   SD9658
★ Angel (01756) 730263
Off B6265 Skipton–Grassington; BD23 6LT Busy dining pub with three neatly kept timbered and panelled rooms mainly set for their highly rated imaginative food (all day Sun), good friendly service, main bar with farmhouse range in stone fireplace, well kept Black Sheep, Dark Horse and a guest, 20 wines by the glass, lots of nooks and alcoves, country-kitchen and smart dining chairs, plush seats, all sorts of tables, Ronald Searle wine-snob cartoons along with older engravings and photographs, log fires; children welcome, smart furniture on two covered terraces, nice bedrooms, closed Jan. *(Rod Stoneman, John and Sharon Hancock, John and Sylvia Harrop, M J Daly, B and M Kendall)*

HOLMFIRTH   SD1408
Nook (01484) 681568
Victoria Square/South Lane; HD9 2DN Tucked-away basic 18th-c brew pub (aka Rose & Crown) with own-brew beers and guests, home-made pubby food all day and adjoining tapas bar, low beams, flagstones and big open fire, pool, some live music; heated streamside terrace, open all day. *(Anon)*

HORBURY   SE2918
Boons (01924) 277267
Queen Street; WF4 6LP Lively, chatty and comfortably unpretentious flagstone local, Clarkes, John Smiths, Timothy Taylors Landlord and up to four quickly changing guests, pleasant young staff, no food, rugby league memorabilia, warm fire, back tap room with pool; TV, no children; courtyard tables, open all day Fri-Sun. *(Michael Butler)*

HORBURY   SE2917
Bulls Head (01924) 265526
Southfield Lane; WF4 5AR Large well divided pub very popular locally for its food, smart attentive staff, Black Sheep and Tetleys, lots of wines by the glass, panelling and wood floors, relaxing linked rooms including snug, library and more formal restaurant; front picnic-sets. *(Michael Butler)*

HORBURY   SE2918
Cricketers (01924) 267032
Cluntergate; WF4 5AG Welcoming refurbished Edwardian pub, Black Sheep, Timothy Taylors and several local guests such as Five Towns, Tigertops and Sportsman (brewed at it sister pub in Huddersfield), real cider and good selection of spirits, reasonably priced cheeseboards and meze platters, regular beer festivals, Weds quiz and monthly acoustic night; open all day Fri-Sun, from 4pm other days. *(Andy and Jill Kassube)*

HORSFORTH   SE2438
Town Street Tavern (0113) 281 9996
Town Street; LS18 4RJ Market Town Tavern with eight well kept ales and lots of draught/bottled continental beers, good generous food including some south african dishes in small bare-boards bar and upstairs evening bistro (closed Sun), good service; children and dogs welcome, small terrace, open all day. *(Pat and Tony Martin)*

HUBBERHOLME
SD9278
⋆ **George** (01756) 760223
Dubbs Lane; BD23 5JE Small beautifully
placed ancient Dales inn with River Wharfe
fishing rights, heavy beams, flagstones and
stripped stone, quick simple enjoyable food,
well kept ales including Black Sheep and
Copper Dragon, good log fire, perpetual
candle on bar; no dogs, outside lavatories;
children allowed in dining area, terrace, six
comfortable bedrooms (three in annexe),
closed Mon. *(Mark, Amanda, Luke and Jake
Sheard, M J Daly)*

HUDDERSFIELD
SE1416
Grove (01484) 430113
Spring Grove Street; HD1 4BP Lots
of exotic bottled beers, well kept Timothy
Taylors, Thornbridge and 16 interesting
changing guest ales at sensible prices,
120 malt whiskies and 60 vodkas, also real
cider, friendly knowledgeable staff, no food
but choice of snacks from dried crickets
to biltong, traditional irish music (Thurs
evening), art gallery; children and dogs
welcome, back terrace, open all day.
(Pat and Tony Martin)

HUDDERSFIELD
SE1416
Head of Steam (01484) 454533
*St Georges Square, part of the station
(direct access to platform 1); HD1 1JF*
Railway memorabilia and old advertising
signs, model trains, cars, buses and planes
for sale, long bar with up to ten changing
ales, lots of bottled beers, farm ciders and
perry, good choice of enjoyable well priced
food, black leather easy chairs and sofas, hot
coal fire, back buffet, some live jazz and blues
nights in lounge; unobtrusive background
music, can be very busy; open all day.
(Pat and Tony Martin)

HUDDERSFIELD
SE1520
High Park (01484) 534226
Bradley Road, Bradley; HD2 1PX Neatly
kept modern dining pub, attractively done
and spacious keeping plenty of room for
drinking and chatting, Greene King ales,
wide choice of good value popular pub food
including deals, friendly attentive service;
children welcome (good inside play area),
disabled facilities, outside seating, open
all day. *(Gordon and Margaret Ormondroyd)*

HUDDERSFIELD
SE1416
Kings Head (01484) 511058
Station, St Georges Square; HD1 1JF
Victorian station building housing friendly
well run pub (perhaps more utilitarian
than the alternative Head of Steam); large
open-plan room with original tiled floor, two
smaller rooms off, ten well kept beers, good
sandwiches and cobs, some live afternoon/
evening music, Jimi Hendrix pub sign;
disabled access via platform 1, open all day.
(Anon)

HUDDERSFIELD
SE1416
Rat & Ratchet (01484) 542400
Chapel Hill; HD1 3EB Split-level flagstone
and bare-boards local with its own-brew
beers and several guests such as Fullers,
Pictish and Ossett, farm ciders/perries, pork
pies and sausage rolls, friendly staff, some
brewery memorabilia and music posters;
open all day Fri-Sun, from 3pm other days.
(Anon)

HUDDERSFIELD
SE1417
Slubbers Arms (01484) 429032
Halifax Old Road; HD1 6HW Friendly
V-shaped traditional three-room pub, good
range of beers including Timothy Taylors, pie-
and-peas menu, black and white photographs
and old wartime posters; terrace for smokers,
open all day. *(Jeremy King)*

HUDDERSFIELD
SE1417
Sportsman 07766 131123
St Johns Road; HD1 5AY Same owners
as the West Riding Licensed Refreshment
Rooms at Dewsbury; eight real ales including
Black Sheep, Timothy Taylors and their own
beers (brewed here), regular beer festivals,
good value food such as meat and cheese
boards, hot lunchtime food Fri-Sun (bargain
roast), comfortable lounge and two cosy side
rooms; handy for station, open all day.
(Andy and Jill Kassube)

HUDDERSFIELD
SE1415
Star (01484) 545443
Albert Street, Lockwood; HD1 3PJ
Unpretentious friendly local with excellent
range of competitively priced ales kept
well by enthusiastic landlady, continental
beers and farm cider, beer festivals in back
marquee, open fire; closed Mon, lunchtimes
Tues-Fri, open all day weekends. *(Anon)*

HUDSWELL
NZ1400
George & Dragon (01748) 518373
Hudswell Lane; DL11 6BL Popular
community pub with good choice of well
priced food (must book) including vegetarian
options and early-bird menu, Black Sheep
and guests, friendly atmosphere; children
and dogs welcome, panoramic Swaledale
views from back terrace, open all day
weekends, closed Mon lunchtime.
(Ms S Young)

HUGGATE
SE8855
Wolds Inn (01377) 288217
Driffield Road; YO42 1YH Traditional
16th-c village pub cheerfully blending locals'
bar and games room with civilised and
comfortable panelled dining room, wide
range of enjoyable food including substantial
mixed grill, well kept Timothy Taylors, John
Smiths and a guest ale, good range of wines;
benches out in front, pleasant garden behind
with delightful views, lovely village and good
walks, handy for Wolds Way, three bedrooms,

open all day Sun till 9pm (8pm in winter), closed Mon. *(C A Hall)*

HULL TA0929

Hop & Vine 07500 543199

Albion Street; HU1 3TG Small basement bar with three interesting changing ales, bottled belgians, farm ciders and perries, friendly knowledgeable staff, good sandwiches (home-baked breads) and bargain basic specials; closed Sun evening, Mon, Tues lunchtime, otherwise open all day. *(Anon)*

HULL TA1028

★ Olde White Harte (01482) 326363

Passage off Silver Street; HU1 1JG Ancient pub with Civil War history, carved heavy beams, attractive stained glass, two big inglenooks with frieze of delft tiles, well kept Caledonian, Theakstons and guests from copper-topped counter, 80 or so malt whiskies, bargain pubby food; children welcome in upstairs restaurant, dogs in bar, heated courtyard, open all day. *(G Jennings)*

HULL TA0929

Whalebone (01482) 226648

Wincolmlee; HU2 0PA Friendly local brewing its own good value ales such as Neckoil, also Copper Dragon, Tetley, Timothy Taylors Landlord and other guests, real ciders and perry, no food, old-fashioned décor and plenty of memorabilia including Hull City AFC and black and white photos of closed local pubs; open all day. *(Anon)*

HUTTON-LE-HOLE SE7089

Crown (01751) 417343

The Green; YO62 6UA Overlooking pretty village green with wandering sheep in classic coach-trip country; enjoyable home-made pubby food (not Sun evening), Black Sheep, Tetleys and a guest, decent wines by the glass, cheerful efficient service, opened-up bar with varnished woodwork, dining area; children and clean dogs welcome, small site for caravans behind, Ryedale Folk Museum next door and handy for Farndale walks, open all day weekends, closed winter Mon, Tues. *(Glenwys and Alan Lawrence)*

ILKLEY SE1346

Cow & Calf (01943) 607335

Hangingstone Road (moors road towards Hawksworth); LS29 8BT Vintage Inn in stunning spot with lovely views over Ilkley and Wharfedale, their usual food cooked well including good value set menu till 5pm (not Sun), ales such as Black Sheep, Greene King and Shepherd Neame, lots of wines by the glass, efficient young staff, log fires and old-world décor; children welcome, outside tables popular on sunny days, 13 bedrooms, open all day. *(Gordon and Margaret Ormondroyd)*

ILKLEY SE1048

Riverside (01943) 607338

Nesfield Road; LS29 0BE Friendly family-run hotel in good position by River Wharfe, cosy with nice open fire, well kept Copper Dragon, Ilkley, Tetleys and Timothy Taylors Landlord, good home-cooking all day (till early evening in winter); handy for start of Dales Way, 13 bedrooms, open from 10am. *(James Stretton)*

ILKLEY SE1347

Wheatley Arms (01943) 816496

Wheatley Lane, Ben Rhydding; LS29 8PP Nice Ilkley Moor location and part of the small Individual Inns group, stylish lounge/dining areas and garden room, open log fires, locals' bar, good food (very popular weekends) from varied menu including blackboard specials, set choices and children's menu, efficient cheerful service; outside tables, 12 good bedrooms, open all day. *(Gordon and Margaret Ormondroyd)*

KEIGHLEY SE0641

Boltmakers Arms (01535) 661936

East Parade; BD21 5HX Small open-plan split-level character local, friendly and bustling, with full Timothy Taylors range and a guest kept well, keen prices, limited food, lots to look at including brewing pictures and celebrity photos, coal fire; Tues quiz, Weds live music, sports TV; short walk from Keighley & Worth Valley Railway, open all day. *(Anon)*

KEIGHLEY SE0641

Cricketers Arms (01535) 669912

Coney Lane; BD21 5JE Opened-up bar with Moorhouses, Yates and guests, selection of bottled beers, cellar bar, weekend live music and monthly comedy club; sports TV; open all day. *(Anon)*

KELD NY8900

Keld Lodge (01748) 886259

Butthouse Rigg (B6270); DL11 6LL Remote former youth hostel now serving as village inn, three well kept Black Sheep ales and tasty sensibly priced food, good service, various rooms including conservatory-style restaurant with superb Swaledale views; children and dogs welcome, popular with coast-to-coast walkers, 11 bedrooms, open all day. *(Ian Collyer, Stephen Funnell)*

KETTLESING SE2257

★ Queens Head (01423) 770263

Village signposted off A59 W of Harrogate; HG3 2LB Welcoming stone pub with enjoyable good value traditional food, L-shaped carpeted main bar with lots of close-set cushioned dining chairs and tables, open fires, little heraldic shields on walls, 19th-c song sheet covers and lithographs of Queen Victoria, delft shelf of blue and white china, smaller bar on left with built-in red banquettes and cricketing prints, life-size portrait of Elizabeth I in lobby, Black Sheep, Roosters and Theakstons, good service; background radio; children welcome, seats in neatly kept suntrap back garden, benches in front by lane, eight bedrooms, open all day Sun. *(Anon)*

KETTLEWELL   SD9672
Blue Bell   (01756) 760230
Middle Lane; BD23 5QX Roomy knocked-through 17th-c coaching inn, Copper Dragon ales kept well, home-made food all day using local ingredients, low beams and snug simple furnishings, old country photographs, daily newspapers, woodburner, restaurant; Sun quiz, TV and free wi-fi; children welcome, shaded picnic-sets on cobbles facing bridge over the Wharfe, six annexe bedrooms. *(M J Daly)*

KETTLEWELL   SD9672
★Racehorses   (01756) 760233
B6160 N of Skipton; BD23 5QZ Comfortable, civilised and friendly two-bar inn with dining area, enjoyable sensibly priced food, well kept Timothy Taylors ales, good log fire; children welcome, dogs in bar areas, front and back terrace seating, pretty village well placed for Wharfedale walks, parking can be difficult, 13 good bedrooms, open all day. *(B and M Kendall, Jeremy King)*

KILBURN   SE5179
Forresters Arms   (01347) 868386
Between A170 and A19 SW of Thirsk; YO61 4AH Welcoming inn next to Robert Thompson furniture workshops (early examples of his work in both bars); roaring fires, well kept local ales and good choice of food including home-made ice-cream and cakes, lounge and restaurant; background music, TV; children and dogs (in some areas) welcome, suntrap seats out in front, smoker's shelter at back, ten refurbished bedrooms, open all day. *(Dr D J and Mrs S C Walker)*

KILDWICK   SE0145
White Lion   (01535) 632265
A629 Keighley–Skipton; BD20 9BH Old two-bar stone pub near Leeds & Liverpool Canal, enjoyable food (not Sun evening) including good value theme nights, Copper Dragon, Ilkley, Tetleys and Timothy Taylors; children and dogs welcome, next to ancient church in attractive village, nice walks, two refurbished bedrooms, open all day. *(Pat and Graham Williamson, Dr Kevan Tucker)*

KIRKBY OVERBLOW   SE3249
Shoulder of Mutton   (01423) 871205
Main Street; HG3 1HD 19th-c shuttered village pub, three linked areas with bare boards or flagstones, comfortable banquettes, two open fires, well kept local ales and plenty of wines by the glass, good freshly prepared food including early-bird menu, friendly attentive service, Sun quiz;

picnic-sets in back garden, shop, closed Mon. *(Howard and Margaret Buchanan)*

KIRKBYMOORSIDE   SE6986
George & Dragon   (01751) 433334
Market Place; YO62 6AA 17th-c coaching inn, front bar with beams and panelling, tubs seats around wooden tables on carpet or stripped wood, log fire, good choice of well kept ales, several malt whiskies, enjoyable generous bar food including good value lunchtime set deal and Sun carvery, afternoon teas, also a snug, bistro and more formal restaurant; background music; children welcome, seats and heaters on front and back terraces, 20 bedrooms, Weds market day, open all day. *(Derek and Sylvia Stephenson, I D Barnett, John and Dinah Waters)*

KNARESBOROUGH   SE3556
★Blind Jacks   (01423) 869148
Market Place; HG5 8AL Simply done multi-floor tavern in 18th-c building (pub since 1990s), old-fashioned traditional character with low beams, bare brick and floorboards, cast-iron-framed tables, pews and stools, brewery mirrors, etc, well kept ales including Black Sheep, Marple, Village Brewer and some from on-site microbrewery, continental draught beers, friendly helpful staff, limited food (cheese and pâté), two small downstairs rooms, quieter upstairs; well behaved children allowed away from bar, dogs welcome, open all day Fri-Sun, from 4pm other days; shop next door sells all sorts of rare bottled beers. *(Paul Smurthwaite)*

KNARESBOROUGH   SE3457
Mitre   (01423) 868948
Station Road; HG5 9AA Refurbished Market Town Tavern by the station, friendly helpful service, up to eight regional ales including Black Sheep, Copper Dragon, Roosters and Thwaites, interesting continental beers, decent choice of enjoyable sensibly priced food (not Sun evening) in bar and evening brasserie (Fri, Sat); background music (live Sun evening); children and dogs welcome, terrace tables under parasols, four bedrooms, open all day. *(Doug Learmonth, Pat and Tony Martin, B and M Kendall)*

KNARESBOROUGH   SE3556
Old Royal Oak   (01423) 865880
Market Place; HG5 8AL Friendly bustling 18th-c pub with three well kept Theakstons ales, decent home-made food all day (limited choice Sun), good service; six bedrooms. *(Brian and Anna Marsden)*

LANGTHWAITE   NY0002
★Charles Bathurst   (01748) 884567
Arkengarthdale, a mile N towards Tan Hill; DL11 6EN Welcoming busy country inn (worth checking no corporate events/weddings on your visit) with strong emphasis on dining and bedrooms, but pubby feel in long bar; scrubbed pine tables and country

chairs on stripped floors, snug alcoves, open fire, some stools by counter, Black Sheep, Theakstons and Timothy Taylors, several wines by the glass, popular often interesting food, dining room with views of Scar House, Robert 'Mouseman' Thompson furniture, several other dining areas; background music, TV, pool, darts and other games; children welcome, lovely walks from door and views over village and Arkengarthdale, smart bedrooms (best not above dining room), open all day. *(Anthony Barnes, Jill and Julian Tasker, Canon Michael Bourdeaux, WAH, David and Ruth Hollands)*

LANGTHWAITE   NZ0002
✶ **Red Lion** (01748) 884218
Just off Reeth–Brough Arkengarthdale Road; DL11 6RE Proper pub dating from 17th c, homely and relaxing, in beguiling Dales village with ancient bridge; friendly and welcoming with character landlady, lunchtime sandwiches, pasties and sausage rolls, well kept Black Sheep, Thatcher's cider, country wines, tea and coffee, well behaved children allowed lunchtime in low-ceilinged side snug, newspapers and postcards; the ladies' is a genuine bathroom; seats outside, good walks including circular ones from the pub (maps and guides for sale), open all day. *(Anthony Barnes, Comus and Sarah Elliott)*

LASTINGHAM   SE7290
✶ **Blacksmiths Arms** (01751) 417247
Off A170 W of Pickering; YO62 6TL Popular old beamed pub opposite beautiful Saxon church in attractive village, log fire in open range, traditional furnishings, Theakstons and other regional ales, several wines by the glass, good generously served home-made food (not Sun evening), friendly prompt service, darts, board games; background music; children and walkers welcome, seats in back garden, three bedrooms, open all day in summer. *(W M Hogg, M and A H, Shirley and Clive Pickerill)*

LEALHOLM   NZ7607
✶ **Board** (01947) 897279
Off A171 W of Whitby; YO21 2AJ In wonderful moorland village spot by wide pool of River Esk; homely bare-boards bar on right with squishy old sofa and armchairs by big black stove, local landscape photographs on stripped-stone or maroon walls, china cabinet and piano, left-hand bar with another fire, traditional pub furniture, darts and a stuffed otter, carpeted dining room, four well kept changing ales, five ciders (maybe a raspberry one) and dozens of whiskies, good seasonal food using meat from own farm and other local produce, friendly helpful staff; children, dogs and muddy boots welcome, secluded waterside garden with decking,

bedrooms and self-catering cottage, open all day. *(James McLean, Susan and Neil McLean, Comus and Sarah Elliott)*

LEAVENING   SE7863
Jolly Farmers (01653) 658276
Main Street; YO17 9SA Bustling village local, friendly and welcoming, with four changing ales and enjoyable good value food (not Mon, Tues), front bar with eating area behind, separate dining room, some live music; open all day weekends, closed weekday lunchtimes. *(Anon)*

LEEDS   SE2932
Cross Keys (0113) 243 3711
Water Lane, Holbeck; LS11 5WD Revamped early 19th-c pub; flagstones and bare boards, stripped brick, original tiling and timbers, old prints and photographs, a collection of clocks in one part, four interesting Yorkshire ales and imported bottled beers, shortish choice of good well prepared food (not Sun evening), winding stairs up to function/dining room, newspapers and board games; children welcome, tables under big parasols in sheltered back courtyard, open all day. *(David and Sue Smith, Jeremy King)*

LEEDS   SE3131
Garden Gate (0113) 277 7705
Whitfield Place, Hunslet; LS10 2QB Impressive Edwardian pub (Grade II★ listed) owned by Leeds Brewery, their well kept ales from rare curved ceramic counter, a wealth of other period features in rooms off central drinking corridor including intricate glass and woodwork, art nouveau tiling, moulded ceilings and mosaic floors, hearty pub food (not Tues evening); tables out in front, open all day weekends (till 9pm Sun). *(Anon)*

LEEDS   SE2932
✶ **Grove** (0113) 243 9254
Back Row, Holbeck; LS11 5PL Unspoilt and lived-in 1930s-feel local overshadowed by towering office blocks, tables and stools in main bar with marble floor, panelling and original fireplace, large back room and snug off drinking corridor, good choice of well kept ales including Daleside and Moorhouses, Weston's cider, lunchtime food (not Sat), friendly staff and pub dog, regular live music; open all day. *(Anon)*

LEEDS   SE2932
Midnight Bell (0113) 244 5044
Water Lane, Holbeck; LS11 5QN Leeds Brewery pub on two floors in Holbeck Urban Village, three of their ales kept well and enjoyable home-made food (all day weekends), friendly staff, light contemporary décor mixing with original beams and

---

We list pubs that serve food all day on at least some days at the end of the book.

stripped brickwork; families welcome, beer garden, open all day. (Dr Kevan Tucker, Jeremy King)

LEEDS   SE3037
Mustard Pot (0113) 269 5699
Strainbeck Lane, Chapel Allerton; LS7 3QY Friendly management in relaxed easy-going dining pub, enjoyable interesting food (all day Sun till 8pm) including lunchtime sandwiches, Marstons-related ales, decent wines by the glass, mix of furniture from farmhouse tables and chairs to comfortable banquettes and leather chesterfields, half-panelling and pastel paintwork, open fire; background music; children welcome, pleasant front garden, open all day. (Anon)

LEEDS   SE2236
Palace (0113) 244 5882
Kirkgate; LS2 7DJ Traditional Nicholsons pub with stripped boards and polished panelling, friendly helpful staff, good choice of reasonably priced food, Bass, Fullers, Tetleys and seven guests; tables out in front and in small back courtyard, open all day. (Anon)

LEEDS   SE2933
Pour House 07816 481492
Canal Wharf, Holbeck; LS11 5PS Refurbished canalside pub with good value food all day from sandwiches and sharing plates up, friendly service, two Wharfedale ales and good choice of bottled beers and gins, seating on two levels. (Andy and Jill Kassube)

LEEDS   SE2236
Railway Hotel (0113) 257 6603
Calverley Bridge, Rodley; off A6120 Horsforth ring road; LS13 1NR Friendly straightforward pub by Leeds & Liverpool Canal, enjoyable simple food, well kept Leeds ales; children and dogs welcome, towpath walks/cycling. (Dr Kevan Tucker)

LEEDS   SE3033
Victoria (0113) 245 1386
Great George Street; LS1 3DL Opulent early Victorian pub with grand cut and etched mirrors, impressive globe lamps extending from majestic bar, carved beams, leather-seat booths with working snob-screens, smaller rooms off, eight real ales, friendly efficient service, standard Nicholsons food in separate room with serving hatch; open all day. (Andy Lickfold)

LEEDS   SE3033
✱ Whitelocks (0113) 245 3950
Turks Head Yard, off Briggate; LS1 6HB Classic Victorian pub (unspoilt but some signs of wear) with long narrow old-fashioned bar, tiled counter, grand mirrors, mahogany and glass screens, heavy copper-topped tables and red leather, well kept Theakstons

ales, enjoyable generous all-day food, friendly hard-working young staff; crowded at lunchtime; children welcome, tables in narrow courtyard, open all day. (Eric Larkham)

LEYBURN   SE1190
Black Swan (01969) 623131
Market Place; DL8 5AS Attractive old creeper-clad hotel with chatty locals and character landlord in cheerful open-plan bar, decent range of food including popular Sun carvery, quick service, well kept Black Sheep, Timothy Taylors, Theakstons and a guest, good wines by the glass; no credit cards; children welcome, dogs before 6pm, disabled access, tables on cobbled terrace, seven bedrooms, open all day. (M and J White)

LEYBURN   SE1190
Bolton Arms (01969) 623327
Market Place; DL8 5BW Substantial stone-built inn at top of market place, varied choice of well priced generous home-made food including good Sun carvery, ales such as Black Sheep, good mix of customers; seats outside, bedrooms. (Barry Collett, Robert Wivell)

LINTHWAITE   SE1014
✱ Sair (01484) 842370
Lane Top, Hoyle Ing, off A62; HD7 5SG Old-fashioned four-room pub brewing its own good value Linfit beers, pews and chairs on rough flagstones or wood floors, log-burning ranges, dominoes, cribbage and shove-ha'penny, piano and vintage rock juke box; no food or credit cards; dogs welcome, children till 8pm, plenty of tables out in front with fine Colne Valley views, restored Huddersfield Narrow Canal nearby, open all day weekends, from 5pm weekdays. (Anon)

LINTON   SE3846
✱ Windmill (01937) 582209
Off A661 W of Wetherby; LS22 4HT Welcoming upmarket pub on different levels, beams, stripped stone, antique settles around copper-topped tables, log fires, enjoyable food including lunchtime bargains, more expensive evening menu (not Sun), John Smiths, Theakstons Best and guests, several wines by the glass, friendly service, restaurant and conservatory; background music; children and dogs welcome, sunny back terrace and sheltered garden with pear tree raised from seed brought back from Napoleonic Wars, open all day weekends. (Peter and Anne Hollindale)

LITTON   SD9074
Queens Arms (01756) 770006
Off B6160 N of Grassington; BD23 5QJ Beautifully placed Dales pub refurbished under newish owner; main bar with coal fire, rough stone walls, beam-and-plank ceiling, stools around cast-iron-framed tables on

stone floor, carpeted dining room with woodburner and pictures of local scenes, Black Sheep, Goose Eye and Thwaites (maybe own brews for 2014), enjoyable freshly made food from baguettes up (something available all day, till 7pm Sun), friendly staff; children and dogs welcome, plenty of seats in two-tier garden, good surrounding walks, six bedrooms, open all day. *(Robert Wivell)*

LOFTHOUSE SE1073

Crown (01423) 755206

Pub signed from main road; Nidderdale; HG3 5RZ Prettily placed Dales pub, friendly and relaxed, with hearty simple food from good proper sandwiches up, well kept Black Sheep, decent coffee, small public bar, eating extension where children allowed, two well behaved pub dogs; no credit cards, outside gents'; good walks from the door, bedrooms. *(B and M Kendall)*

LONG PRESTON SD8358

Maypole (01729) 840219

A65 Settle–Skipton; BD23 4PH As we went to press the long-serving licensees left this gently old-fashioned pub (a popular previous Main Entry) – news please.

LOW BRADFIELD SK2691

★ Plough (0114) 285 1280

Village signposted off B6077 and B6076 NW of Sheffield; New Road; S6 6HW Warm-hearted traditional pub ideally placed for some of South Yorkshire's finest scenery; cosy carpeted L-shaped bar with dark stone walls, comfortable wall banquettes and captain's chairs, lots of gleaming copper and brass, big arched inglenook coal fire, well kept local Bradfield ales and a guest, very good value food from hearty sandwiches and light dishes to generous honest meals, afternoon cakes too, cheerful, efficient staff; unobtrusive background music; children welcome, seats on fairy-lit back verandah, gravel terrace and lawn with slide, good walks, Damflask and Agden Reservoirs close by. *(Peter F Marshall)*

LOW ROW SD9898

★ Punch Bowl (01748) 886233

B6270 Reeth–Muker; DL11 6PF 17th-c country inn under same ownership as the Charles Bathurst at Langthwaite; long bare-boards bar with peaceful view over Swaledale, stripped kitchen tables and a variety of seats, armchairs and sofa by woodburner at one end, pastel walls, good food (menu on huge mirror) including some interesting choices, nice wines by the glass, well kept Black Sheep ales with a guest like Theakstons, cheerful efficient staff, separate dining room similar in style – even an identical giant clock permanently stuck on 12; wide views from front terrace set above road, comfortable bedrooms, good breakfast, open all day. *(P A Rowe, John Coatsworth,*

Comus and Sarah Elliott, Michael Doswell, Derek and Sylvia Stephenson)

LUND SE9748

★ Wellington (01377) 217294

Off B1248 SW of Driffield; YO25 9TE Smart busy pub with cosy Farmers Bar, beams, well polished wooden banquettes and square tables, quirky fireplace, plainer side room with flagstones and wine-theme décor, Yorkstone walkway to room with village's Britain in Bloom awards, highly rated well presented food (not Sun evening and not cheap) in restaurant and bistro dining area, Copper Dragon, Timothy Taylors Landlord and a guest, good wine list, 25 malt whiskies, friendly efficient staff; background music, TV; children welcome, benches in pretty little back courtyard, open all day Sun, closed Mon lunchtime. *(Derek and Sylvia Stephenson, Michael Butler, Pat and Stewart Gordon, P Dawn, Roger A Bellingham, Dr Kevan Tucker)*

MALHAM SD9062

Lister Arms (01729) 830330

Off A65 NW of Skipton; BD23 4DB Friendly creeper-clad stone-built inn tied to Thwaites, their well kept ales (tasting trays available) and lots of bottled imports, enjoyable food including lunchtime sandwiches, deli boards and daily specials, steps down to bare-boards dining room with stripped-pine tables, woodburners; children and dogs welcome, seats out overlooking small green, more in back garden, lovely spot by river and good walking country, nine comfortable clean bedrooms, open all day. *(Comus and Sarah Elliott)*

MANFIELD NZ2213

Crown (01325) 374243

Vicars Lane; DL2 2RF Traditional unpretentious village local, friendly and welcoming, with eight interesting regularly changing ales including own Village Brewer beers (brewed by Hambleton), enjoyable simple home-made food, two bars and games room with pool; dogs welcome, garden, good walks nearby. *(D G Collinson)*

MANKINHOLES SD9523

Top Brink Inn (01706) 812616

Lumbutts Lane; signed from Lumbutts Road; OL14 6JB Family-owned moorland village pub with extensive range of well cooked food including good specials board, efficient friendly young staff, good choice of changing ales, large open-plan bar area with panelled and bare-stone walls, family room at back; fine views from conservatory and terrace tables, quite close to Pennine Way and nice walks to nearby monument on Stoodley Pike. *(Lucien Perring)*

MARSDEN SE0411

★ Riverhead Brewery Tap

(01484) 841270 *Peel Street, next to Co-op; just off A62 Huddersfield–*

Oldham; HD7 6BR Owned by Ossett with up to ten well kept ales including Riverhead range (microbrewery visible from bare-boards bar), bustling friendly atmosphere, airy upstairs beamed restaurant with stripped tables (moors view from some) and open kitchen, good choice of enjoyable food including set menu; unobtrusive background music; dogs welcome, wheelchair access, some riverside tables, open all day. *(Brian and Anna Marsden)*

MASHAM   SE2280
Kings Head (01765) 689295
Market Place; HG4 4EF Handsome 18th-c stone inn (Chef & Brewer), two modernised linked bars with stone fireplaces, well kept Black Sheep and Theakstons, nice choice of wines, good food served by friendly helpful staff, part-panelled restaurant; background music, TV; children welcome, tables out at front and in sunny back courtyard, 27 bedrooms, open all day. *(JJW, CMW, Dr and Mrs R G J Telfer)*

MASHAM   SE2281
White Bear (01765) 689227
Wellgarth, Crosshills; signed off A6108 opposite turn into town; HG4 4EN Comfortably updated stone-built beamed inn, small public bar with full range of Theakstons ales kept well, larger lounge with welcoming coal fire, good choice of enjoyable food from sandwiches up (not Sun evening), decent wines by the glass, friendly efficient staff, restaurant extension; background music; children and dogs welcome, terrace tables, 14 bedrooms, open all day. *(Mark, Amanda, Luke and Jake Sheard, Janet and Peter Race)*

MENSTON   SE1744
Fox (01943) 873024
Bradford Road (A65/A6038); LS29 6EB Contemporary Mitchells & Butlers dining pub in former coaching inn on busy junction, good choice of popular fairly priced food, efficient friendly staff, Black Sheep, Timothy Taylors Landlord and a guest, Aspall's cider, big fireplace, flagstones and polished boards in one part; background music; two terraces looking beyond car park to cricket field, open all day. *(Gordon and Margaret Ormondroyd, Lucien Perring)*

MIDDLEHAM   SE1287
✱White Swan (01969) 622093
Market Place; DL8 4PE Extended coaching inn opposite cobbled market town square, beamed and flagstoned entrance bar with built-in window pew and pubby furniture, open woodburner, well kept Theakstons ales, several wines by the glass and malt whiskies, enjoyable bistro-style food, friendly efficient staff, modern spacious dining room, large fireplace and small area with contemporary leather seats and sofa, more dining space in back room; background

music; children welcome, comfortable bedrooms. *(Anon)*

MIDDLETON TYAS   NZ2205
Shoulder of Mutton (01325) 377271
Just E of A1 Scotch Corner roundabout; DL10 6QX Welcoming old pub with three low ceilinged rooms on different levels, good freshly made food from snacks up, well kept ales including Black Sheep, prompt friendly service. *(Gerry and Rosemary Dobson, Lawrence Pearse, M W Graham)*

MILLINGTON   SE8351
Gait (01759) 302045
Main Street; YO42 1TX Friendly and popular 16th-c beamed local, good straightforward food, five well kept ales including York, nice mix of old and newer furnishings, large map of Yorkshire on ceiling, big inglenook log fire; children welcome, garden picnic-sets, appealing village in good Wolds walking country, closed Mon-Thurs lunchtimes, open all day Sun. *(Robert Wivell)*

MIRFIELD   SE2017
Hare & Hounds (01924) 481021
Liley Lane (B6118 2 miles S); WF14 8EE Popular well cared for Vintage Inn, attractive open-plan interior with several distinct areas, their usual good choice of reasonably priced food all day including set menu till 5pm (not Sun), well kept ales such as Black Sheep and Timothy Taylors, efficient cheerful staff, roaring fire; children welcome, tables outside with good Pennine views. *(Gordon and Margaret Ormondroyd)*

MUKER   SD9097
✱Farmers Arms (01748) 886297
B6270 W of Reeth; DL11 6QG Small unpretentious walkers' pub in beautiful valley village, four well kept local ales, wines, teas and coffees, enjoyable straightforward good value food, warm fire, simple modern pine furniture, flagstones and panelling, darts and dominoes; soft background music; children and dogs welcome, hill views from terrace tables, stream across road, open all day. *(David and Jenny Billington, JJW, CMW)*

MYTHOLMROYD   SD9922
Hinchcliffe Arms (01422) 883256
Off B6138 S at Cragg Vale; HX7 5TA Tucked-away old stone-built pub with really good food from traditional choices to more enterprising restaurant dishes (everything home-made), four well kept ales including a house beer from Ilkley, friendly staff, open fires; well behaved dogs allowed in bar, attractive setting near village church on road leading only to reservoir, popular with walkers, open all day weekends (Sun till 9pm), closed Mon, lunchtime Tues. *(John and Eleanor Holdsworth)*

NAFFERTON
Cross Keys   TA0559

North Street; YO25 4JW Friendly corner
pub in pretty Wolds village, enjoyable food
including pub standards, pizzas, pasta and
a few greek dishes (owner is from greece),
well kept John Smiths and Wold Top, some
live music; children welcome, on National
Cycle Route 1, open all day (from 3.30pm
Mon). *(Dr Kevan Tucker)*

NEWTON-ON-OUSE
Dawnay Arms (01347) 848345   SE5160

Off A19 N of York; YO30 2BR 18th-c
with two bars and airy river-view dining
room, low beams, stripped masonry, open
fire and inglenook woodburner, chunky
pine tables and old pews on bare boards
and flagstones, fishing memorabilia,
competently cooked food (till 6pm Sun)
from lunchtime sandwiches (home-baked
bread) up including vegetarian and
children's choices, ales such as Tetleys and
Timothy Taylors, good range of wines by the
glass, friendly efficient service; terrace
tables, lawn running down to Ouse
moorings, handy for Beningbrough Hall
(NT), closed Mon. *(Roger and Lesley Everett)*

NORLAND
Moorcock (01422) 832103   SE0521

Moor Bottom Lane; HX6 3RP Pleasantly
modernised old building with fairly simple
L-shaped bar and beamed restaurant, good
blackboard food including competitively
priced lunch (weekends only) and more
sophisticated evening choices (Tues to Sat),
friendly easy-going service, well kept Timothy
Taylors and Thwaites; children welcome,
fine valley views from village, popular
scarecrow festival early Sept. *(Mike Proctor,
Pat and Tony Martin)*

NORTH RIGTON
Square & Compass (01423) 733031 SE2749

Hall Green Lane/Rigton Hill; LS17 ODJ
Substantial stone building recently reopened
after refurbishment; beamed bar with Copper
Dragon, Leeds and Theakstons, plenty of
wines by the glass, good choice of food from
sandwiches and sharing boards up, pleasant
service by aproned staff, restaurant; well
behaved children welcome, tables on tiered
terrace, peaceful village, open all day from
10am. *(D W Stokes)*

NORTHALLERTON
Tithe Bar (01609) 778482   SE3794

Friarage Street; DL6 1DP Market Town
Tavern with half a dozen good mainly
Yorkshire ales changing quickly, plenty of
continental beers, friendly staff, tasty food
including set deals, three traditional bar
areas with tables and chairs, settle and
armchairs, bare boards and brewery posters,
upstairs evening brasserie; children and dogs
welcome, open all day. *(Pat and Tony Martin)*

NORWOOD GREEN
⋆ **Old White Beare** (01274) 676645   SE1326

*Signed off A641 in Wyke, or off A58
Halifax–Leeds just W of Wyke; Village
Street; HX3 8QG* Nicely renovated and
extended 16th-c pub named after ship
whose timbers it incorporates; well kept
Copper Dragon, Timothy Taylors and a guest,
good variety of enjoyable well presented
food (all day weekends) including set
menu, friendly service, bar with steps up to
dining area, small character snug, imposing
galleried flagstoned barn restaurant, some
live music; children and dogs welcome,
a few tables out in front and in back garden,
Calderdale Way and Brontë Way pass
the door, open all day. *(John and Eleanor
Holdsworth, Michael Butler, Gordon
and Margaret Ormondroyd)*

NUNNINGTON
⋆ **Royal Oak** (01439) 748271   SE6679

*Church Street; at back of village, which
is signposted from A170 and B1257;
YO62 5US* Reliable neatly kept old pub,
bar with high black beams strung with
earthenware flagons, copper jugs and lots
of antique keys, fine collection of old farm
tools on a bare-stone wall, carefully chosen
furniture, dining area linked to bar by
double-sided woodburner, enjoyable food
cooked to order including local game, well
kept Black Sheep and Wold Top, ten wines by
the glass and several malt whiskies, friendly
service; background music; children and
dogs welcome, terrace seating, handy for
Nunnington Hall (NT), closed Mon.
*(Peter Burton, Richard Cole, David Jackman,
Robert Wivell)*

OAKWORTH
Grouse (01535) 643073   SE0138

*Harehills, Oldfield; 2 miles towards
Colne; BD22 0RX* Comfortable old pub
back under previous long-serving licensees,
enjoyable food all day including blackboard
specials, well kept Timothy Taylors ales,
friendly service; children and dogs (in
snug) welcome, undisturbed hamlet in
fine moorland surroundings, picnic-sets on
terrace with good Pennine views. *(Anon)*

OLDSTEAD
⋆ **Black Swan** (01347) 868387   SE5380

*Village signed off Thirsk Bank,
W of Coxwold; YO61 4BL* Tucked away
16th-c restaurant with rooms in beautiful
surroundings; bar with beams, flagstones
and 'Mousey' Thompson furniture, log fire,
lots of wines by the glass, Black Sheep Best,
attractive back dining rooms serving first
class food (not cheap, but bar food and
sandwiches available lunchtime), friendly
attentive staff; children welcome, picnic-sets
out in front, four comfortable well equipped
bedrooms with own terrace, good breakfast,
fine surrounding walks, closed Mon-Weds

lunchtimes, two weeks in Jan. *(Andrew and Ruth Triggs, Hunter and Christine Wright)*

OSMOTHERLEY SE4597
⋆ **Golden Lion** (01609) 883526
The Green, West End; off A19 N of Thirsk; DL6 3AA Attractive busy old stone pub with friendly welcome, Timothy Taylors and guests, around 50 malt whiskies, roomy beamed bar on left with old pews and a few decorations, similarly unpretentious well worn-in eating area on right, weekend dining room, well liked pubby food and good service; background music; children welcome, dogs in bar, seats in covered courtyard, benches out front looking across village green, 44-mile Lyke Wake walk starts here and coast-to-coast walk nearby, comfortable bedrooms, closed Mon and Tues lunchtimes, otherwise open all day. *(Andy and Jill Kassube, Peter Thompson)*

OSSETT SE2719
⋆ **Brewers Pride** (01924) 273865
Low Mill Road/Healey Lane (long cul-de-sac by railway sidings, off B6128); WF5 8ND Friendly local with Bobs White Lion (brewed at back of pub), Rudgate Ruby Mild and seven guests, cosy front rooms and flagstoned bar, open fires, brewery memorabilia, good well priced food (not Sun evening), dining extension and small games room, live music first Sun of month; well behaved children welcome, big back garden, near Calder & Hebble Navigation, open all day. *(Michael Butler)*

OSSETT SE2719
Tap (01924) 272215
The Green; WF5 8JS Basic décor with flagstones and open fire, pleasant relaxed atmosphere, Ossett ales and guests (usually Fullers London Pride), decent wines by the glass, friendly service and locals, photos of other Ossett pubs; small car park and parking nearby can be difficult; open all day Thurs-Sun, from 3pm other days. *(Michael Butler)*

OTLEY SE2045
Chevin (01943) 876109
West Chevin Road, off A660; LS29 6BE Well maintained pub largely rebuilt after fire, good home-made food including seasonal game and early evening deal, Timothy Taylors Landlord and a guest, friendly young staff; children and dogs welcome, garden with splendid Wharfedale views, open (and food) all day. *(John and Eleanor Holdsworth, Gordon and Margaret Ormondroyd)*

OTLEY SE2045
Horse & Farrier (01943) 468400
Bridge Street; LS21 1BQ Modernised Market Town Tavern with five real ales and enjoyable reasonably priced food from sandwiches (hot and cold) up, most main courses available in smaller helpings, friendly young staff; disabled facilities,

four bedrooms, nice outside seating area. *(Pat and Tony Martin)*

OXENHOPE SE0434
⋆ **Dog & Gun** (01535) 643159
Off B6141 towards Denholme; BD22 9SN Beautifully placed roomy 17th-c moorland pub, smartly extended and comfortable, with good varied food from sandwiches to lots of fish and Sun roasts (worth booking then), thriving atmosphere, ebullient landlord and attentive friendly staff, full Timothy Taylors range kept well, good choice of malts, beamery, copper, brasses, plates and jugs, big log fire each end, padded settles and stools, glass-covered well in one dining area, wonderful views; five bedrooms in adjoining hotel. *(John and Eleanor Holdsworth, Gordon and Margaret Ormondroyd and others)*

PENISTONE SE2402
Cubley Hall (01226) 766086
Mortimer Road, out towards Stocksbridge; S36 9DF Rambling centre for functions, weddings and so forth as well as family meals and drinks; early 18th c with panelling, elaborate plasterwork, mosaic tiling and pubby furnishings, conservatory extension, wide choice of bar food all day including home-made pizzas, Sun carvery, well kept ales such as Adnams, Black Sheep and Hook Norton, decent wines; background music, fruit machine, TV; big garden with plenty of tables and good distant views, play area, 12 bedrooms. *(Anon)*

POOL SE2445
White Hart (0113) 2037862
Just off A658 S of Harrogate, A659 E of Otley; LS21 1LH Smart and airy Mitchells & Butlers dining pub (bigger inside than it looks), well liked food all day including sharing plates, pizzas and more restauranty dishes with some mediterranean influences, set menu too, good service from friendly young staff, nice choice of wines by the glass, Leeds and Timothy Taylors, stylishly simple bistro eating areas, armchairs and sofas on bar's flagstones and bare boards; plenty of tables outside, open all day. *(Colin Woodward, Michael Butler)*

POTTO NZ4703
Dog & Gun (01642) 700232
Cooper Lane; DL6 3HQ Tucked-away modern bar-restaurant-hotel, clean contemporary décor, enjoyable food (not Sun evening) from shortish menu including some interesting choices, well kept Captain Cook ales (brewed at sister pub, the White Swan at Stokesley) and a local guest, friendly attentive staff; tables under parasols on front decking, five bedrooms, open all day weekends, closed Mon. *(Anon)*

PUDSEY SE2037
Thornhill Arms (0113) 256 5492
Town Gate; LS28 5NF Comfortably modernised old pub with good affordably

priced home-made food, real ales, two lounges; TV and darts; seats outside. *(John and Eleanor Holdsworth)*

RAMSGILL SE1171
✳ **Yorke Arms** (01423) 755243
Centre of village; Nidderdale; HG3 5RL Upmarket 18th-c creeper-clad hotel (not a pub), small smart bar with some heavy Jacobean furniture and log fires, Black Sheep Best, a fine wine list, good choice of spirits and fresh juices, Michelin-starred restaurant; background music, no under-12s; seats outside (snack menu), comfortable bedrooms, good quiet moorland and reservoir walks. *(Anon)*

REDMIRE SE0491
Bolton Arms (01969) 624336
Hargill Lane; DL8 4EA Village pub under welcoming licensees, popular promptly served food, well kept Black Sheep, Wensleydale and a guest, comfortable carpeted bar, attractive dining room; disabled facilities, small garden, handy for Wensleydale Railway and Bolton Castle, good walks, three courtyard bedrooms. *(Donna Jenkins)*

REETH SE0499
Buck (01748) 884210
Arkengarthdale Road/Silver Street; DL11 6SW Beamed 18th-c coaching inn by village green, Black Sheep, Caledonian, Copper Dragon, Timothy Taylors and a guest, pizzas and other enjoyable home made food, regular live music including name bands; children welcome, dogs in bar, a few tables out in front, also a secret walled garden, good walking country, ten bedrooms, open all day. *(Stephen Funnell)*

RIBBLEHEAD SD7678
Station Inn (01524) 241274
B6255 Ingleton–Hawes; LA6 3AS Great spot up on the moors by Ribblehead Viaduct (Settle to Carlisle trains), friendly licensees doing varied food from snacks up (all day weekends), half a dozen well kept ales such as Black Sheep, Copper Dragon, Dent and Timothy Taylors, good value wines, tea and coffee, simple public bar with woodburner, dining room with open fire, viaduct and train pictures (some you can buy); background music, TV, darts and pool; children welcome, muddy boots and paws in bar, picnic-sets outside, five bedrooms (some sharing bath), bunkhouse, open all day. *(Ian and Helen Stafford, Claes Mauroy)*

RICHMOND NZ1701
Black Lion (01748) 826217
Finkle Street; DL10 4QB Family-run Georgian coaching inn with enjoyable good value food including lunchtime sandwiches/ light meals and weekday early-bird deal (5-7pm), can eat in bar or upstairs restaurant, well kept Black Sheep, St Austell

Tribute and Timothy Taylors Landlord, good friendly service, log fires; TV; comfortable reasonably priced bedrooms. *(Derek and Sylvia Stephenson)*

RICHMOND NZ1700
Kings Head (01748) 850220
Market Place; DL10 4HS Civilised and chatty lounge bar in friendly Best Western hotel overlooking square, enjoyable well presented food including all-day snacks, Theakstons and decent wines by the glass, helpful service, comfortable bistro; seats out in front under parasols, 30 bedrooms. *(David and Ruth Hollands)*

RIPLEY SE2860
✳ **Boars Head** (01423) 771888
Off A61 Harrogate–Ripon; HG3 3AY Smart old hotel with informal relaxed atmosphere, long bar-bistro with nice mix of dining chairs and tables, warm yellow walls hung with golf clubs, cricket bats, some jolly cricketing/hunting drawings, a boars head and an interesting religious carving, Black Sheep Best, Daleside and Theakstons, 20 wines by the glass and several malt whiskies, popular food (all day Sun) using produce from the Estate (the Ingilby family have lived in next door Ripley Castle for over 650 years); children welcome, dogs in bar and bedrooms, pleasant little garden, open all day summer. *(Gerry and Rosemary Dobson, Janet and Peter Race)*

RIPON SE3171
✳ **One-Eyed Rat** (01765) 607704
Allhallowgate; HG4 1LQ Friendly little bare-boards pub with numerous well kept ales (occasional festivals), farm cider, lots of bottled beers and country wines, long narrow bar with roaring fire, cigarette cards, framed beer mats, bank notes and old pictures, no food but may be free black pudding, pool; children welcome, pleasant outside area, open all day Sat, closed weekday lunchtimes. *(Anon)*

RIPON SE3171
Royal Oak (01765) 602284
Kirkgate; HG4 1PB Centrally placed coaching inn owned by Timothy Taylors, their ales kept well and good choice of wines, comfortable modernised interior with rooms off L-shaped bar, enjoyable food (all day weekends) from doorstep lunchtime sandwiches and pub standards to more imaginative choices; no dogs inside; children welcome, courtyard tables, six bedrooms, open all day. *(Ed and Anna Fraser)*

RIPON SE3170
Water Rat (01765) 602251
Bondgate Green, off B6265; HG4 1QW Small pub on two levels, prettily set by footbridge over River Skell and near restored canal basin; well kept ales including Black

Sheep, a real cider and keenly priced wines, reliable straightforward food, friendly service, conservatory; charming view of cathedral, ducks and weir from riverside terrace. *(Liz Bell, Dr Kevan Tucker, M and J White)*

RIPPONDEN SE0319
Fox (01422) 825880
Oldham Road; just off M62 junction 22; HX6 4DP Modern pub restaurant with wide choice of good food cooked by landlord-chef including fresh fish/seafood, some two-for-one offers, efficient service, well kept Copper Dragon Golden Pippin and Thwaites Wainwright; children welcome, seats outside, closed Mon-Thurs lunchtime. *(Pat and Tony Martin)*

RISHWORTH SE0316
Booth Wood (01422) 825600
Oldham Road (A672); HX6 4QU Newly refurbished beamed pub (former Old Bore); local Oates beers and guests, good range of enjoyable well priced food from sandwiches to blackboard specials, lunchtime/early evening deal, friendly staff, some leather sofas and wing-back chairs, woodburners; children welcome, picnic-sets outside, open all day (from 9.30 Sun for breakfast). *(Jim and Sheila Wilson)*

ROBIN HOOD'S BAY NZ9504
Bay Hotel (01947) 880278
The Dock, Bay Town; YO22 4SJ Friendly old village inn at end of the 191-mile coast-to-coast path (so popular with walkers); fine sea views from cosy picture-window upstairs bar (Wainwright bar downstairs open too if busy), Caledonian Deuchars IPA, Courage Directors and Theakstons, reasonably priced home-made food in bar and separate dining area from good sandwiches up, young staff coping well, log fires; background music; lots of tables outside, cosy bedrooms, steep road down and no parking at bottom, open all day. *(Stephen Funnell, Barbara and Peter Kelly)*

ROBIN HOOD'S BAY NZ9505
Victoria (01947) 880205
Station Road; YO22 4RL Clifftop Victorian hotel with great bay views, good choice of beers from curved counter in traditional carpeted bar, enjoyable fresh food here, in restaurant or large family room, also a coffee shop/tearoom; dogs welcome, useful car park, play area in big garden overlooking sea and village, tidy comfortable bedrooms, good breakfast. *(Stephen Funnell)*

ROSEDALE ABBEY SE7295
Coach House (01751) 417208
Alder Carr Lane; YO18 8SD Friendly pub with good value generous food and ales such as Black Sheep and Wold Top, modern dining room on left of central bar, games room to the right; children welcome, caravan site opposite. *(Anon)*

ROSEDALE ABBEY SE7295
White Horse Farm Inn
(01751) 417239 *300 metres up Rosedale Chimney Bank – entering village, first left after Coach House Inn; YO18 8SE* Welcoming 16th-c stone-built inn with rambling log-fire bar and dining room on left, good value well cooked pub food, ales such as Theakstons and Black Sheep in good condition, reasonably priced wines by the glass; wonderful dale views from terrace (and from restaurant and bedrooms), good walks. *(Graham Lovis, Glenwys and Alan Lawrence, Mike and Jayne Bastin)*

SALTBURN-BY-THE-SEA NZ6621
Ship (01287) 622361
A174 towards Whitby; TS12 1HF Beautiful setting among beached fishing boats, sea views from nautical-style black-beamed bars and big dining lounge, well kept Tetleys and good choice of wines by the glass, wide range of inexpensive generous food including fresh fish, friendly helpful service, restaurant and family room; busy at holiday times; tables outside, open all day summer. *(Barbara and Peter Kelly)*

SANCTON SE9039
Star (01430) 827269
King Street (A1034 S of Market Weighton); YO43 4QP Neatly modernised and extended village dining pub, competently cooked food (local produce including own vegetables), vegetarian and children's menus, extensive wine list, well kept ales such as Black Sheep, good friendly service; lovely surrounding countryside, open all day Sun, closed Mon. *(John and Eleanor Holdsworth)*

SAWDON TA9484
✳ Anvil (01723) 859896
Main Street; YO13 9DY Pretty high-raftered former smithy with good locally sourced food from chef-landlord, well kept Black Sheep and guests, nice range of wines, friendly attentive staff and immaculate housekeeping, feature smith's hearth, anvil and old tools, woodburner, lower-ceilinged second bar leading through to small neat dining room; terrace seating, two self-catering cottages, closed Mon, Tues. *(Peter Burton, Stanley and Annie Matthews)*

SCAWTON SE5483
✳ Hare (01845) 597769
Off A170 Thirsk–Helmsley; YO7 2HG Attractive quietly placed dining pub under new owners (previously at the Crown at Great Ouseburn), really good imaginative cooking (not cheap) from landlord-chef, nice wines by the glass and well kept ales such as Black Sheep, stripped-pine tables, heavy beams and some flagstones, open fire and woodburner, pub ghost called Bob; children and dogs (in bar) welcome, garden tables,

closed Sun evening, Mon. *(Ben and Ruth Levy, Graham Lovis, Dr Nigel Bowles, M and A H)*

SCORTON NZ2500
Farmers Arms (01748) 812533
Northside; DL10 6DW Comfortably refurbished little pub in terrace of old cottages overlooking green, well kept Black Sheep, Copper Dragon and Courage Directors, enjoyable good value food including popular Sun lunch (till 3pm), friendly staff, bar with open fire, restaurant, darts and dominoes, fortnightly quiz; background music; children and dogs welcome, open all day Fri-Sun, closed Mon lunchtime. *(Pat and Stewart Gordon, Dr Brian Hands)*

SETTLE SD8163
✶ Lion (01729) 822203
B6480 (main road through town), off A65 bypass; BD24 0HB Refurbished market-town inn with grand staircase sweeping down into baronial-style high-beamed hall bar, lovely log fire, second bar with bare boards and dark half-panelling, lots of old local photographs and another open fire, enjoyable all-day food including deli boards and specials, well kept Thwaites and occasional guests like Fullers, decent wines by the glass, helpful welcoming staff, restaurant; monthly quiz, silent TV and games machine; children and dogs welcome, courtyard tables, 14 bedrooms. *(Karen Eliot)*

SHEFFIELD SK3487
Bath (0114) 249 5151
Victoria Street, off Glossop Road; S3 7QL Victorian corner pub with well restored 1930s interior, two rooms and a drinking corridor, friendly staff, well kept Thornbridge and guests, simple lunchtime bar food (sandwiches only Sat), live music Sun and Weds with some emphasis on jazz/blues; open all day (from 4pm Sun). *(Anon)*

SHEFFIELD SK3687
Beauchief (0114) 262 0500
Abbeydale Road South; S7 2QW Former railway hotel with good all-day food in bar and brasserie including Sun carvery, Thornbridge ales and nice choice of wines, friendly service; children welcome (under-8s eat free), large garden, six bedrooms, open all day from 7am (happy hour 5-7pm). *(Tom and Ruth Rees)*

SHEFFIELD SK3687
✶ Fat Cat (0114) 249 4801
23 Alma Street; S3 8SA Deservedly busy town local with own Kelham Island ales and plenty of changing guests, draught and bottled belgian beers, real cider/perry and country wines, low-priced mainly vegetarian bar food (not Sun evening), friendly staff, two small downstairs rooms with coal fires, simple wooden tables and cushioned seats, brewery-related prints, jugs, bottles and advertising mirrors, upstairs overspill room; children welcome away from main bar, dogs allowed, picnic-sets in back courtyard with heated smokers' shelter, new brewery shop/visitor centre (book tours on 0114 249 4804), open all day. *(Anon)*

SHEFFIELD SK3687
Gardeners Rest (0114) 272 4978
Neepsend Lane; S3 8AT Welcoming beer-enthusiast landlord serving his own good Sheffield ales from light wood counter, also several changing guests tapped from the cask, farm cider and continental beers, no food, old brewery memorabilia, changing local artwork, daily papers, games including bar billiards, live music, popular Sun quiz; well behaved children (till 9pm) and dogs welcome, disabled facilities, back conservatory and tables out overlooking River Don, open all day Thurs-Sun, from 3pm other days. *(Anon)*

SHEFFIELD SK3588
Harlequin (0114) 275 8195
Nursery Street; S3 8GG Welcoming open-plan corner pub owned by nearby Brew Company, their well kept ales and great selection of changing guests, also bottled imports and real ciders/perries, straightforward cheap lunchtime food including Sun roasts, beer festivals, weekend live music, Weds quiz; children till 7pm and dogs welcome, outside seating, open all day. *(Anon)*

SHEFFIELD SK3687
✶ Hillsborough (0114) 232 2100
Langsett Road/Wood Street; by Primrose View tram stop; S6 2UB Chatty and friendly pub-in-hotel, own microbrews along with four quickly changing guests, good choice of wines and soft drinks, generous well priced food including Sun roasts, daily papers, open fire, bare-boards bar, lounge, views to ski slope from attractive back conservatory and terrace tables; silent TV; children and dogs welcome, six good value bedrooms, covered parking, open all day. *(Anon)*

SHEFFIELD SK3290
✶ New Barrack (0114) 234 9148
601 Penistone Road, Hillsborough; S6 2GA Friendly lively pub with nine ales including Castle Rock and lots of bottled belgian beers, good choice of whiskies too, tasty good value bar food (Fri, Sat light suppers till midnight), Sun carvery, comfortable front lounge with log fire and upholstered seats on old pine floors, tap room with another fire, back room for small functions, daily papers, bar billiards, regular events including chess club, live music and comedy nights; TV; children (till 9pm) and dogs welcome, attractive little walled garden, difficult local parking, closed lunchtimes Mon, Tues, otherwise open all day. *(Anon)*

SHEFFIELD   SK3186
Ranmoor (0114) 230 1325
Fulwood Road (across from church);
S10 3GD Comfortable and neat open-plan
Victorian local, five well kept ales including
Abbeydale and Bradfield, good value home
cooking (not Sun, Mon), leather sofas
by etched bay windows, big mirrors and
period fireplaces, well varnished tables,
china display cabinet, piano (often played),
newspapers; dogs welcome, two outside
seating areas, open all day. *(Jeremy King)*

SHEFFIELD   SK3487
Red Deer (0114) 272 2890
Pitt Street; S1 4DD Friendly backstreet
local among university buildings, seven well
kept changing ales (some at bargain prices)
and a real cider from central bar, big
helpings of good value simple food (all day
weekends), Tues quiz, live music; tables
outside, open all day (till 1am Fri, Sat).
(Sarah Hawley, Brian and Anna Marsden)

SHEFFIELD   SK3185
Rising Sun (0114) 230 3855
Fulwood Road; S10 3QA Friendly drinkers'
pub with 13 ales including five or more from
Abbeydale (July beer festival), bottled beers,
simple lunchtime food, two rooms one with
raised back area, some leather sofas and
well worn furniture, prints and black and
white photos, shelves of books; background
music (live Mon), quiz Weds and Sun; dogs
welcome, a few tables out in front, more on
back terrace, open all day. *(Jeremy King)*

SHEFFIELD   SK3586
Sheffield Tap (0114) 273 7558
Station, Platform 1B; S1 2BP Busy
station bar in restored Edwardian
refreshment room, popular for its huge
choice of world beers on tap and in bottles,
also four Thornbridge ales and half a dozen
guests, knowledgeable helpful staff, snacky
food, tiled interior with vaulted roof; open all
day. *(Andy Lickfold, Tony and Wendy Hobden)*

SHEFFIELD   SK3687
∗ Wellington (0114) 249 2295
*Henry Street; Shalesmoor tram stop
outside; S3 7EQ* Unpretentious relaxed
corner pub with up to ten changing beers
including own bargain Little Ale Cart brews,
bottled imports, real cider, coal fire in lounge,
photographs of old Sheffield, daily papers and
pub games, friendly staff; tables out behind, open
all day with afternoon break on Sun. *(Anon)*

SHELLEY   SE2112
∗ Three Acres (01484) 602606
*Roydhouse (not signed); from B6116
towards Skelmanthorpe, turn left in
Shelley (signposted Flockton, Elmley,
Elmley Moor), go up lane for 2 miles
towards radio mast; HD8 8LR* Civilised
former coaching inn with emphasis on

hotel and dining side; roomy lounge with
leather chesterfields, old prints and so forth,
tankards hanging from main beam, well kept
Copper Dragon, 40 malt whiskies and up to 17
wines by the glass from serious (not cheap)
list, several formal dining rooms, wide choice
of good if expensive food from lunchtime
sandwiches up, competent friendly service;
conferences, weddings and events; children
welcome, fine moorland setting and lovely
views, smart well equipped bedrooms. *(Colin
McKerrow, Gordon and Margaret Ormondroyd)*

SHEPLEY   SE1809
Farmers Boy (01484) 605355
*Marsh Lane, W of village – off A629 at
Black Bull (leads on past pub to A635);
HD8 8AP* Smart stone-built dining pub,
small traditional beamed public bar on right,
Black Sheep, Bradfield and Copper Dragon,
bare-boards area on left with coal fire and
sturdy country tables, carpeted part rambling
back through plenty of neat linen-set dining
tables, barn restaurant with own terrace,
popular often imaginative food, not cheap
but good value early-bird menu (Mon-
Thurs, 6-7pm), friendly service; unobtrusive
background music; picnic-sets out in front,
open all day. *(Anon)*

SHERBURN IN ELMET   SE4933
Oddfellows Arms (01977) 682368
Low Street; LS25 6BA Traditional village
pub with enjoyable well priced food and
friendly staff, John Smiths and decent house
wine; background music. *(John and Eleanor
Holdsworth)*

SHIPLEY   SE1437
Fannys Ale House (01274) 591419
Saltaire Road; BD18 3JN Cosy and
friendly bare-boards alehouse on two floors,
gas lighting, log fire and woodburner, brewery
memorabilia, up to ten real ales including
Timothy Taylors and Theakstons in top
condition, bottled beers and farm ciders,
back extension; can be crowded weekend
evenings; dogs welcome, open all day, closed
Mon lunchtime. *(James Stretton)*

SINNINGTON   SE7485
∗ Fox & Hounds (01751) 431577
Off A170 W of Pickering; YO62 6SQ
Pretty village's popular 18th-c coaching
inn, carpeted beamed bar with woodburner,
various pictures and old artefacts,
comfortable seats, imaginative well
presented food, particularly friendly and
helpful staff, well kept ales such as Black
Sheep, Copper Dragon and Wold Top, several
wines by the glass, a few rare whiskies,
lounge and smart separate restaurant;
background music; children and dogs
welcome, picnic-sets in front, more in garden,
ten good comfortable bedrooms. *(Derek and
Sylvia Stephenson, I D Barnett, Bruce and Sharon
Eden, Janet and Peter Race, Susan Hornby, Shirley
and Clive Pickerill and others)*

SKIPTON SD9849
Copper Dragon Brewery
(01756) 7045560 *Snaygill Industrial Estate, Keighley Road; BD23 2QR* Visitor centre's modern bar/bistro across road from brewery, perhaps more canteeny than pubby, with full range of Copper Dragon ales, good plentiful food at realistic prices including daily specials, friendly efficient staff; brewery tours and shop, open all day Thurs-Sat, till 6pm Sun, 4pm other days. *(John and Eleanor Holdsworth, Gordon and Margaret Ormondroyd)*

SKIPTON SD9851
⋆**Narrow Boat** (01756) 797922
Victoria Street; pub signed down alley off Coach Street; BD23 1JE Lively extended pub down cobbled alley, eight well kept real ales, draught and bottled continental beers, farm cider and perry, church pews, dining chairs and stools around wooden tables, old brewery posters, mirrors decorated with beer advertisements, upstairs gallery area with interesting canal mural, decent reasonably priced bar food (not Sun evening) including sausage menu, folk club Mon evening; children allowed if eating, dogs welcome, picnic-sets under front colonnade; Leeds & Liverpool Canal nearby, open all day. *(Pat and Tony Martin, John and Dinah Waters, David Jackman)*

SKIPTON SD9851
Woolly Sheep (01756) 700966
Sheep Street; BD23 1HY Big bustling pub with full Timothy Taylors range kept well and a guest, prompt friendly enthusiastic service, two beamed bars off flagstoned passage, exposed brickwork, stone fireplace, lots of sheep prints and bric-a-brac, daily papers, attractive and comfortable raised lunchtime dining area, good value and variety of enjoyable food (plenty for children); wheelchair access with help, enclosed terrace garden behind, six good value bedrooms, good breakfast, open all day. *(John and Hazel Sarkanen, John and Dinah Waters, Gary Simcoe, Simon and Mandy King, B and M Kendall)*

SLEDMERE SE9364
⋆**Triton** (01377) 236078
B1252/B1253 junction, NW of Great Driffield; YO25 3XQ Handsome old inn by Sledmere House, open-plan bar with old-fashioned atmosphere, dark wooden furniture on red patterned carpet, 15 clocks ranging from grandfather to cuckoo, lots of willow pattern plates, all manner of paintings and pictures, open fire, Greene King, Timothy Taylors, Tetleys and Wold Top, 50 different gins, well liked freshly cooked food (only take bookings in separate restaurant),

friendly helpful staff; children welcome till 8pm, five good bedrooms, massive breakfast, open all day Sun till 9pm, closed winter Mon lunchtime. *(Dennis Jones, Pat Bunting, Roger A Bellingham, Dr D Jeary and others)*

SNAITH SE6422
Brewers Arms (01405) 862404
Pontefract Road; DN14 9JS Georgian inn tied to local Old Mill brewery, their distinctive range from brick and timber-fronted servery, decent home-made food including weekend fish/seafood, friendly helpful staff, open-plan carpeted interior, old well complete with skeleton; children welcome in eating areas, bedrooms. *(Michael Butler)*

SNAPE SE2684
⋆**Castle Arms** (01677) 470270
Off B6268 Masham–Bedale; DL8 2TB Neat homely pub in pretty village, flagstoned bar with open fire, horsebrasses on beams, straightforward pubby furniture, Banks's, Jennings and Marstons, well liked bar food, dining room (also flagstoned) with another fire and plenty of dark tables and chairs; children and dogs welcome, picnic-sets out at front and in courtyard, fine walks in Yorkshire Dales and on North York Moors, nine bedrooms. *(John and Eleanor Holdsworth)*

SOWERBY BRIDGE SE0623
Jubilee Refreshment Rooms
(01422) 648285 *Sowerby Bridge Station; HX6 3AB* Refurbished 19th-c station building run by two railway-enthusiast brothers, up to six real ales, bottled continentals, ciders and perries, simple food including breakfast, good pies and home-made cakes, railway memorabilia, old enamel signs, art deco ceiling lamps and feature jeweller's clock; open all day from 9.30am (12 Sun). *(Pat and Tony Martin)*

SOWERBY BRIDGE SE0523
Works (01422) 834821
Hollins Mill Lane, off A58; HX6 2QG Big airy bare-boards pub in converted joinery workshop by Rochdale Canal, seating from pews to comfortable sofas, nine well kept ales and a couple of ciders, good bargain home-made food from sandwiches and pub favourites to vegetarian choices, Weds curry night, Sun brunch, comedy and folk night in big upstairs room; children and dogs welcome, backyard (covered in poor weather), disabled facilities, open all day. *(Herbert and Susan Verity)*

STAMFORD BRIDGE SE7055
⋆**Three Cups** (01759) 375901
A166 W of town; YO41 1AX Recently redecorated Vintage Inn family dining pub,

---

Tipping is not normal for bar meals, and not usually expected.

popular food all day including set menu, plenty of wines by the glass, ales such as Black Sheep and Leeds, friendly helpful staff, pleasant rustic décor with two blazing fires, glass-topped well in bar; disabled access, play area behind, river walks nearby. *(Pat and Graham Williamson, David Carr, Margaret and Jeff Graham, Roger A Bellingham, Michael Butler)*

STANBURY   SE0037
Old Silent (01535) 647437

Hob Lane; BD22 0HW Friendly moorland dining pub near Ponden Reservoir, good reasonably priced fresh food, Timothy Taylors Landlord, Theakstons Old Peculier and guests, attentive helpful service, character linked rooms with beams, flagstones, mullioned windows and open fires, games room, restaurant and conservatory; children and dogs welcome, bedrooms, open all day. *(Anon)*

STAVELEY   SE3662
Royal Oak (01423) 340267

Signed off A6055 Knaresborough– Boroughbridge; HG5 9LD Popular welcoming pub in village conservation area; beams and panelling, open fires, broad bow window overlooking front lawn, well kept Black Sheep, Timothy Taylors and a guest, several wines by the glass, good choice of enjoyable food in bar and restaurant. *(Michael Coleman, David Battle)*

STILLINGTON   SE5867
✴ **Bay Tree** (01347) 811394

Main Street; leave York on outer ring road (A1237) to Scarborough, first exit on left signposted B1363 to Helmsley; YO61 1JU Cottagey pub in pretty village's main street, contemporary bar areas with civilised chatty atmosphere, comfortable cushioned wall seats and leather/bamboo tub chairs around mix of tables, church candles and lanterns, basketwork and attractive prints on cream walls, central gas-effect coal fire, enjoyable bistro-style food (all day Sun till 6pm), good sandwiches too, Black Sheep, Moorhouses and fair-priced wines, friendly helpful staff, steps up to cosy dining area, larger conservatory-style back restaurant; background music; seats in garden and a couple of picnic-sets at front, two new self-catering cottages, closed Mon. *(Michael Butler)*

STOKESLEY   NZ5208
✴ **White Swan** (01642) 710263

West End; TS9 5BL Good Captain Cook ales brewed in attractive flower-clad pub, L-shaped bar with three relaxing seating areas, log fire, lots of brass on elegant dark panelling, lovely bar counter carving, assorted memorabilia and unusual clock, good lunchtime ploughman's (Weds-Sat), live music, beer festivals; no children; open all day. *(Anon)*

SUTTON UPON DERWENT   SE7047
✴ **St Vincent Arms** (01904) 608349

Main Street (B1228 SE of York); YO41 4BN Enjoyable cheerful pub with Fullers and up to seven guests, lots of wines by the glass, good popular bar food (more elaborate evening meals), bustling parlour-style front bar with panelling, traditional high-backed settles, windsor chairs, cushioned bow-window seat and gas-effect coal fire, another lounge and separate dining room open off here; children welcome, dogs in bar, garden tables, handy for Yorkshire Air Museum. *(Anon)*

TAN HILL   NY8906
Tan Hill Inn (01833) 628246

Arkengarthdale Road Reeth–Brough, at junction Keld/West Stonesdale Road; DL11 6ED Basic old pub (Britain's highest) in wonderful bleak setting on Pennine Way, full of bric-a-brac and interesting photographs, simple sturdy furniture, flagstones, ever-burning big log fire (with prized stone side seats), chatty atmosphere, five well kept ales including one badged for them from Dent, good cheap pubby food, family room, live music at weekends; can get overcrowded, often snowbound; children and dogs welcome, seven bedrooms, bunk rooms and camping, ducks and chickens, Swaledale sheep show here last Thurs in May, open all day. *(Comus and Sarah Elliott)*

THIRSK   SE4282
Golden Fleece (01845) 523108

Market Place; YO7 1LL Comfortable bustling old coaching inn with enjoyable generous bar food, Black Sheep ales, friendly competent service, restaurant, view across marketplace from bay windows; dogs welcome, 23 bedrooms, good breakfast. *(Janet and Peter Race, Dr D J and Mrs S C Walker)*

THIXENDALE   SE8461
Cross Keys (01377) 288272

Off A166 3 miles N of Fridaythorpe; YO17 9TG Unspoilt welcoming country pub in deep valley below the rolling Wolds and popular with walkers; cosy L-shaped bar with fitted wall seats, relaxed atmosphere, ales such as Rudgate, Tetleys and Titanic, sensible home-made blackboard food; large pleasant garden behind with nice views, handy for Wharram Percy earthworks, comfortable bedrooms, good breakfast. *(Brian and Anna Marsden)*

THORNTON-LE-CLAY   SE6865
✴ **White Swan** (01653) 618286

Off A64 SW of Malton, via Foston; Low Street; YO60 7TG Welcoming early 19th-c family-run pub set in two acres of landscaped gardens; snug L-shaped beamed bar, comfortably cushioned and red carpeted, with plenty of ornaments, books, board games and toys on shelves and arched recesses, daily papers, changing ales such as Copper Dragon and Moorhouses, decent wines by the glass and good coffee, well cooked pub food at reasonable prices; maybe piped music; children welcome, neat grounds with terrace, ornamental shrubs, fruit trees and pond, summerhouse and penthouse, vegetable/herb garden and donkey paddock, attractive countryside nearby and Castle Howard. *(Mr and Mrs R J Oliver, Gordon and Margaret Ormondroyd)*

THORPE ARCH — SE4346
Pax (01937) 843183

The Village; LS23 7AR 19th-c village pub improved under present welcoming licensees, enjoyable home-made food (notable steak and ale pie) at sensible prices, two or three changing ales such as Black Sheep, Moorhouses and Roosters, friendly helpful service, two bar areas, open fire, plans to turn function room at back into restaurant/grill; children and dogs welcome, useful for A1, open all day weekends, closed Mon. *(Les and Sandra Brown)*

THRESHFIELD — SD9863
Old Hall Inn (01756) 752441

B6160/B6265 just outside Grassington; BD23 5HB Popular place under newish owners; well cooked attractively presented food form landlord-chef, good choice of beers and wines, linked rooms including smart dining room, log fires, high beam-and-plank ceiling, cushioned wall pews and a fine blacked kitchen range; neat garden, comfortable bedrooms and self-catering cottage, open all day. *(Pat and Stewart Gordon)*

TIMBLE — SE1852
⋆ Timble Inn (01943) 880530

Off Otley–Blubberhouses moors road; LS21 2NN Smartly restored 18th-c inn tucked away in quiet farmland hamlet, good food from pub favourites up including well aged Nidderdale beef (not Mon-Weds lunchtime – booking advised), Timothy Taylors Landlord, Theakstons and a guest; children welcome, dogs outside of food times, good walks from the door, seven well appointed bedrooms. *(Robert Wivell, Janet and Peter Race)*

TOCKWITH — SE4652
Spotted Ox (01423) 358387

Westfield Road, off B1224; YO26 7PY Traditional beamed village local, friendly and relaxed, with well served ales including Tetleys, good choice of enjoyable sensibly priced home-made food, attentive staff, three areas off central bar, interesting local history; open all day Fri-Sun. *(Les and Sandra Brown)*

TOTLEY — SK3080
Cricket (0114) 236 5256

Signed from A621; Penny Lane; S17 3AZ Tucked-away stone-built pub opposite rustic cricket field, much focus on dining but still a friendly local atmosphere, pews, mixed chairs and pine tables on bare boards and flagstones, good-quality blackboard food (all day weekends) from sandwiches and pubby staples to some interesting imaginative cooking, cheaper lunchtime, early-evening set menu (Mon-Fri), friendly service, Thornbridge ales, log fires; children and dogs welcome, tables outside, good Peak District views, open all day. *(W K Wood)*

TOTLEY — SK3079
Cross Scythes (0114) 236 0204

A621 (Baslow Road); S17 4AE Smartly refurbished dining pub with good freshly prepared food from sandwiches using home-baked bread up, well kept ales such as Peak, efficient friendly staff; children welcome, four bedrooms (three with balconies), substantial breakfast, open all day from 8.30am. *(David and Ruth Hollands)*

TOWTON — SE4839
Rockingham Arms (01937) 530948

A162 Tadcaster–Ferrybridge; LS24 9PB Comfortably refurbished under new management, enjoyable range of home-made food including popular Sun lunch, friendly attentive service, ales such as Black Sheep and Theakstons, back conservatory; garden tables, handy for Towton Battlefield, closed Sun evening, Mon. *(Robert Wivell)*

WAKEFIELD — SE3320
Bull & Fairhouse (01924) 362930

George Street; WF1 1DL Welcoming chatty 19th-c pub, well kept Bobs White Lion, Great Heck Golden Bull and four other changing ales (beer festivals), bare-boards bar with comfortable rooms off, open fire, no food, live music weekends, quiz Thurs; children welcome till 8pm, dogs on leads, open all day Fri-Sun, from 4pm other days. *(Anon)*

WAKEFIELD — SE3417
Castle (01924) 256981

Barnsley Road, Sandal; WF2 6AS Popular refurbished dining pub with good attractively priced food cooked to order, well kept beers such as York, friendly staff and pleasant relaxed atmosphere; unobtrusive background music. *(Michael Butler, John and Eleanor Holdsworth)*

WAKEFIELD — SE3320
Fernandes Brewery Tap

(01924) 291709 *Avison Yard, Kirkgate; WF1 1UA* Owned by Ossett but still brewing Fernandes ales in cellar, interesting guest beers, bottled imports and traditional ciders, newish ground-floor bar with flagstones, bare brick and panelling, original raftered top-floor bar with unusual breweriana; dogs welcome, open all day Fri-Sun when some lunchtime food available, from 4pm other days. *(Anon)*

WAKEFIELD SE3220
Harrys Bar (01924) 373773
Westgate; WF1 1EL Cheery little one-room local, well kept Leeds, Ossett and guests, stripped-brick walls, open fire, live music Wed; small back garden, open all day Sun, closed lunchtime other days. *(Anon)*

WALKINGTON SE9937
Dog & Duck (01482) 423026
B1230, East End; HU17 8RX Comfortably modernised pub with enjoyable competitively priced food, four well kept beers including Jennings and Marstons; sports TV; garden and terrace with pizza oven and barbecue, charming village. *(Michael Butler)*

WALKINGTON SE9937
Ferguson-Fawsitt Arms
(01482) 882665 *East End; B1230 W of Beverley; HU17 8RX* Named after two important local families and known as the 'Fergie'; wide choice of popular reasonably priced food including carvery (all day Sun), good friendly service, real ales and decent wines, interesting mock-Tudor bars; children welcome, tables out on terrace, ten good value bedrooms in modern annexe, delightful village. *(Michael Butler)*

WALTON SE4447
Fox & Hounds (01937) 842192
Hall Park Road, off back road Wetherby–Tadcaster; LS23 7DQ Welcoming dining pub with enjoyable reasonably priced food from good sandwiches to specials (should book Sun lunch), well kept Black Sheep, John Smiths and a guest, friendly thriving atmosphere; children welcome, handy A1 stop. *(Michael Doswell, Robert Wivell, Malcolm and Pauline Pellatt)*

WATH SE3277
George (01765) 641324
Main Street; village N of Ripon; HG4 5EN Friendly refurbished village pub with good range of enjoyable traditional food (not Sun evening), Rudgate, Theakstons and a guest, decent choice of wines; five comfortable bedrooms, open all day weekends, closed lunchtimes Mon, Tues. *(Andy and Jill Kassube)*

WATH IN NIDDERDALE SE1467
✶ Sportsmans Arms (01423) 711306
Nidderdale road, off B6265 in Pateley Bridge; village and pub signposted over hump-back bridge on right after a couple of miles; HG3 5PP Civilised, beautifully located restaurant with rooms run by long-serving owner, most emphasis on the excellent food and bedrooms but has proper welcoming bar with open fire (a highly rated ploughman's here), Black Sheep and Timothy Taylors Landlord, Thatcher's cider, 20 wines by the glass from extensive list and 40 malt whiskies, helpful hospitable staff;

background music; children welcome, dogs in bar, benches and tables outside and seats in pretty garden with croquet, own fishing on River Nidd. *(Walter and Susan Rinaldi-Butcher, John and Sharon Hancock, Lynda and Trevor Smith, Jill and Julian Tasker, Janet and Peter Race, Stephen Woad and others)*

WEAVERTHORPE SE9670
Blue Bell (01944) 738204
Main Road; YO17 8EX Upscale country dining pub, quite ornate in parts, with good attractively presented food and fine choice of wines (many by the glass including champagne), well kept Tetleys and Timothy Taylors Landlord, cosy cheerful bar with unusual collection of bottles and packaging, open fire, intimate back restaurant, friendly attentive staff; 12 bedrooms (six in annexe), interesting village, closed Sun evening, Mon. *(R G Stollery)*

WELBURY NZ3902
Duke of Wellington (01609) 882464
Centre of village; DL6 2SG Friendly relaxed pub in small village, generous helpings of good value food including early-bird deals, up to five mainly local ales; darts, TV and juke box; tables out at front, five new bedroom in courtyard annexe behind, open all day Sun (food then till 3.30pm). *(Tim and Ann Newell)*

WENSLEY SE0989
Three Horseshoes (01969) 622327
A684; DL8 4HJ Three nicely refurbished simple flagstoned rooms, friendly staff and regulars, warm woodburner, good selection of local ales and tasty straightforward food; spotless outside lavatories; dogs welcome, lovely views from garden, popular with walkers, open all day. *(Anon)*

WEST TANFIELD SE2678
Bruce Arms (01677) 470325
Main Street (A6108 N of Ripon); HG4 5JJ Comfortable and welcoming with good affordably priced food from landlord-chef, well kept Black Sheep and Copper Dragon, nice wines, flagstones and log fires; two bedrooms, good breakfast, closed Mon. *(John and Eleanor Holdsworth, Alan English)*

WEST TANFIELD SE2678
Bull (01677) 470678
Church Street (A6108 N of Ripon); HG4 5JQ Open-plan with slightly raised dining area to the left and flagstoned bar on right, popular fairly standard food (all day Sat, not Sun evening), well kept Black Sheep and Theakstons, friendly service; background and occasional live music; children (away from bar) and dogs welcome, tables on terraces in attractive garden sloping steeply to River Ure and its old bridge, five bedrooms, open all day weekends, closed Tues. *(Anon)*

WESTOW
SE7565
Blacksmiths Arms (01653) 619606
Off A64 York–Malton; Main Street;
YO60 7NE Refurbished 18th-c pub with
attractive beamed bar, woodburner in brick
inglenook, original bread oven, beers such
as Copper Dragon, Tetleys and Thwaites,
home-made food from sandwiches and pub
favourites up, restaurant; picnic-sets on
side terrace, closed Mon, otherwise open all
day. *(Michael Butler)*

WETHERBY
SE4048
Muse (01937) 580201
Bank Street; LS22 6NQ Popular single-
storey bistro-bar (Market Town Tavern) with
good brasserie/pub food, friendly helpful
young staff, well kept regional ales and good
choice of continental beers, decent wines
and coffee, simple smart décor; children
welcome, dogs allowed in bar and outside
seating area, open all day. *(Brian and Janet
Ainscough, Stuart Paulley)*

WHITBY
NZ9011
Black Horse (01947) 602906
Church Street; YO22 4BH Small
traditional two-room pub, much older than
its Victorian frontage, and previously a
funeral parlour and brothel; friendly and
down to earth with well kept Adnams, Black
Dog, Timothy Taylors and a couple of guests,
Yorkshire tapas, tins of snuff for sale; dogs
welcome, four cosy bedrooms open all day.
(Sarah Marriott)

WHITBY
NZ9011
★ Duke of York (01947) 600324
Church Street, Harbour East Side;
YO22 4DE Busy pub in fine harbourside
position, good views and handy for the
famous 199 steps leading up to abbey;
comfortable beamed lounge bar with fishing
memorabilia, Black Sheep, Caledonian and
three guests, decent wines and several malt
whiskies, enjoyable straightforward bar food
all day, attentive service; background music,
TV, games machine; children welcome,
bedrooms overlooking water, no nearby
parking. *(Pat and Graham Williamson,
Comus and Sarah Elliott)*

WHITBY
NZ8911
Station Inn (01947) 603937
New Quay Road; YO21 1DH Friendly
three-room bare-boards drinkers' pub, clean
and comfortable, with good mix of customers,
eight well kept ales, Weston's cider and
good wines by the glass, traditional games;
background and live music; dogs welcome,
open all day. *(Sara Fulton, Roger Baker)*

WIGGLESWORTH
SD8056
Plough (01729) 840243
B6478, off A65 S of Settle; BD23 4RJ
Light, airy and comfortable old inn with good
elegantly presented modern food (all day Sun

till 7pm), friendly efficient service, local ales
and decent wines by the glass, cosy log fire,
panoramic Dales views; bedrooms. *(John and
Sylvia Harrop)*

WIGHILL
SE4746
White Swan (01937) 832217
Main Street; LS24 8BQ Updated fairly
modern village pub with two cosy front
rooms and larger side extension, enjoyable
traditional home-cooked food, well kept
Black Sheep, a house brew from Moorhouses
and a guest, tea room; children welcome,
no dogs inside, wheelchair access with help
(steps down to lavatories), picnic-sets on
side lawn, closed Mon, Tues. *(Simon and
Mandy King)*

YORK
SE5951
Ackhorne (01904) 671421
St Martins Lane, Micklegate; YO1 6LN
Proper unspoilt pub under newish
management, friendly and welcoming, with
good choice of ales including Caledonian
Deuchars IPA and Roosters Yankee, Weston's
Old Rosie cider, enjoyable pubby food
(weekday lunchtimes, till 7pm weekends),
beams, bare boards and panelling, leather
wall seats, stained glass, Civil War prints,
bottles and jugs, old range and open fire,
carpeted snug, traditional games, some live
music; suntrap back terrace with smokers'
shelter, open all day. *(Eric Larkham)*

YORK
SE6051
★ Black Swan (01904) 686910
Peasholme Green (inner ring road);
YO1 7PR Striking timbered and jettied
Tudor building, compact panelled front bar,
crooked-floored central hall with fine period
staircase, vast inglenook in black-beamed
back bar, good choice of real ales, decent
wines and reasonably priced pubby food from
sandwiches up; background music; children
welcome, useful car park behind, bedrooms,
open all day. *(Anon)*

YORK
SE6051
★ Blue Bell (01904) 654904
Fossgate; YO1 9TF Delightfully old-
fashioned little Edwardian pub, very friendly
and chatty, with well kept Black Sheep,
Roosters, Timothy Taylors Landlord and
three guests (a mild always available), good
value lunchtime sandwiches (not Sun), daily
papers, tiny tiled-floor front bar with roaring
fire, panelled ceiling, stained glass, bar pots
and decanters, corridor to small back room,
hatch service, lamps and candles, pub games;
soft background music; no children; dogs
welcome, open all day. *(Kerry Law, David H
Bennett, Eric Larkham)*

YORK
SE5951
★ Brigantes (01904) 675355
Micklegate; YO1 6JX Comfortably
traditional Market Town Taverns bar-
bistro, eight well kept mainly Yorkshire

ales, good range of bottled beers, decent wines and coffee, enjoyable unpretentious brasserie food all day including snacks and sandwiches, quick cheerful service, upstairs dining room, simple pleasant décor. *(Pat and Tony Martin, Eric Larkham)*

YORK   SE6051
Golden Ball   (01904) 652211
Cromwell Road/Victor Street; YO1 6DU
Friendly well preserved four-room Edwardian corner pub, enjoyable straightforward weekday lunchtime food, five well kept changing ales, bar billiards, cards and dominoes; TV, live music Thurs; lovely small walled garden, closed weekday lunchtimes, open all day weekends. *(Simon and Mandy King)*

YORK   SE6051
Golden Fleece   (01904) 625171
Pavement; YO1 9UP Popular little city-centre pub with good value generously served food, beers from Copper Dragon, Timothy Taylors, Theakstons and Wychwood, long corridor from bar to comfortable back dining room (beware the sloping floors – it dates from 1503), interesting décor with quite a library, lots of pictures and ghost stories; background music and occasional folk evenings; children allowed if eating, no dogs, four bedrooms, open all day. *(Chris and Jenny Howland-Harris, Robert Lester)*

YORK   SE6052
Golden Slipper   (01904) 651235
Goodramgate; YO1 7LG Dating from 15th c with unpretentious bar and three comfortably old-fashioned small rooms, one lined with books, cheerful efficient staff, good cheap plain lunchtime food from sandwiches up including an OAP special, John Smiths and up to three other beers; TV; tables in back courtyard. *(Pete Coxon, Eric Larkham)*

YORK   SE6052
Guy Fawkes   (01904) 466674
High Petergate; YO1 7HP Friendly pub in splendid spot next to York Minster, dark panelled interior with small bar to the left, half a dozen real ales including a house beer from Great Heck, enjoyable sensibly priced food (not Sun evening) from shortish menu plus blackboard specials, dining rooms lit by gas wall-lights and candles, open fires; 13 bedrooms, open all day. *(Brian and Janet Ainscough, Eric Larkham, M and J White)*

YORK   SE6052
Lamb & Lion   (01904) 612078
High Petergate; YO1 7EH Sparse furnishings and low lighting including candles giving a spartan Georgian feel,

friendly helpful service, four well kept ales including Black Sheep and a locally brewed house beer, enjoyable simple bar food plus more elaborate evening set menu (Tues-Sat), no food Sun evening, compact rooms off dark corridors; steep steps up to small attractive garden below city wall and looking up to the Minster, 12 bedrooms, open all day. *(Eric Larkham)*

YORK   SE6051
Lendal Cellars   (01904) 623121
Lendal; YO1 8AA Split-level ale house in broad-vaulted 17th-c cellars, stripped brickwork, stone floor, linked rooms and alcoves, good choice of changing ales and wines by the glass, foreign bottled beers, farm cider, decent coffee, enjoyable generous pub food all day, friendly helpful staff; background music; no dogs; children allowed if eating. *(Eric Larkham)*

YORK   SE5952
Minster Inn   (01904) 624499
Marygate; YO30 7BH Multi-roomed Edwardian local, bric-a-brac and dark old settles, fires and woodburners, corridor to distinctive back room, friendly staff, well kept changing Marstons-related ales, sandwiches, table games; children welcome, seats out behind, open all day Fri-Sat, from 2pm Mon-Thurs. *(Eric Larkham)*

YORK   SE6052
Old White Swan   (01904) 540911
Goodramgate; YO1 7LF Bustling spacious pub with Victorian, Georgian and Tudor-themed bars, popular lunchtime food including nine types of sausage, Black Sheep and several other well kept ales, good whisky choice, central glass-covered courtyard good for families; background and frequent live music, big-screen sports TV, games machines, Mon quiz; open all day. *(R K Phillips, Eric Larkham)*

YORK   SE6051
Phoenix   (01904) 656401
George Street; YO1 9PT Friendly, well restored little pub next to city walls, proper front public bar and comfortable back horseshoe-shaped lounge, fresh flowers and candles, five well kept Yorkshire ales, good wines, simple food, live jazz two or three times a week, bar billiards; beer garden, handy for Barbican, open all day Sat, closed lunchtimes other days. *(Anon)*

YORK   SE6051
Punch Bowl   (01904) 615491
Stonegate; YO1 8AN Bustling old black and white fronted pub, friendly helpful service, wide range of generous bargain food

---

If you report on a pub that's not a featured entry, please tell us any lunchtimes or evenings when it doesn't serve bar food.

all day, small panelled rooms off corridor, TV in beamed one on left of food servery, well kept ales such as Black Sheep Leeds, John Smiths and Thornbridge, good wine choice; background music, games machines, regular quiz nights; open all day. *(Eric Larkham)*

YORK SE6151
Rook & Gaskill (01904) 674067
Lawrence Street; YO10 3WP Traditional Castle Rock pub with up to a dozen ales, enjoyable food (not Sun), dark wood tables, banquettes, chairs and high stools, conservatory; open all day. *(Eric Larkham)*

YORK SE6051
Swan (01904) 634968
Bishopgate Street, Clementhorpe; YO23 1JH Unspoilt 1930s pub (Grade II listed), hatch service to lobby for two small rooms off main bar, several changing ales and ciders, friendly knowledgeable staff may offer tasters; busy with young people weekends; small pleasant walled garden, near city walls, open all day weekends, closed weekday lunchtimes. *(Anon)*

YORK SE6052
✶ Three Legged Mare (01904) 638246
High Petergate; YO1 7EN Bustling light and airy modern café-bar with York Brewery's full range and guests kept well (12 handpumps), plenty of belgian beers, quick friendly young staff, interesting sandwiches and some basic lunchtime hot food, low prices, back conservatory; no children; disabled facilities (other lavatories down spiral stairs), back garden with replica gallows after which pub is named, open all day till midnight (11pm Sun). *(Kerry Law, Eric Larkham)*

YORK SE5951
✶ York Brewery Tap (01904) 621162
Toft Green, Micklegate; YO1 6JT Members only for York Brewery's upstairs lounge (annual fee unless you go on brewery tour), their own full cask range in top condition, also bottled beers, nice clubby atmosphere with friendly staff happy to talk about the beers, lots of breweriana and view of brewing plant, comfortable sofas and armchairs, magazines and daily papers, brewery shop; no food; children allowed during the day, open all day except Sun evening. *(Eric Larkham)*

YORK SE5951
York Tap (01904) 659009
Station Road; YO24 1AB Restored Edwardian bar at York Station, high ceiling with feature stained-glass dome, columns and iron fretwork, bentwood chairs and stools on terrazzo floor, button-back banquettes, period fireplaces, great selection of real ales from circular counter with brass footrail, also bottled beers, good pork pies (three types); open all day from 10am. *(David Heath)*

London

A great many of the capital's pubs are full of ancient history and character and you could spend a happy day (or two) dropping in and out of a few of the best; many have not changed for years. Really interesting places in Central London include the Dog & Duck (tiny Soho pub with bags of character), Lamb (almost the same as it was in Victorian times), Lamb & Flag (Dickens and Dryden were regular visitors) and Olde Mitre (a gem with – unusually for London – proper hands-on licensees); in East London, the Gun (two character bars and first class food); in North London, the Holly Bush (a village feel with a dignified old-fashioned atmosphere); in South London, the Royal Oak (you'd never know it had been so painstakingly restored); and in West London, the Dove (in the Guinness World Records for having the smallest bar room). Don't miss the beautifully converted former bank, the Old Bank of England, with its quite astonishing décor. For a surprisingly wide choice of real ales in Central London, head to the Harp (delightful, with eight beers and nine farm ciders), Lamb & Flag (Fullers ales plus changing guests), Old Bank of England (the full range of Fullers ales) and Olde Mitre (a choice of eight beers); in South London, the Greenwich Union (one of only two taps for the Meantime Brewery plus visiting guests) and Royal Oak (with the full range of Harveys beers); and in West London, the White Horse (a quickly changing choice of eight beers plus top class food) and Windsor Castle (quite unspoilt, with a lovely garden and ten beers). If you want to eat, the pub food here is surprisingly good value – though for a special meal, try the Gun in East London and Duke of Sussex, Old Orchard and White Horse in West London. Our London Dining Pub 2014 is the Gun in East London.

CENTRAL LONDON   Map 13

Bountiful Cow

Eagle Street; ✪ *Holborn; WC1R 4AP*

Bustling and informal place popular with those wanting either a chat at the bar or a meaty meal

Concentrating on, as one reader described it, 'bovine bountifulness', this is cheerful part pub/part grill house serving excellent monster burgers and steaks – though they do keep Adnams Best and Dark Star Hophead on handpump and offer several wines by the glass (they import wine from France). The informal street-level bar has chrome and beige leather bar stools against the counter – grabbed quickly by those wanting a chat and a pint – a raised area by the windows with booth seating, and a smallish upper room with red wicker dining chairs around oak tables on stripped wooden floorboards, beef-related prints and posters on the painted brick walls and a mixture of happy chat and piped jazz; helpful, quick service. There's also a larger downstairs dining room with red-painted walls and cow prints. The licensees also run the Seven Stars.

As well as first class burgers and steaks, the good food includes rillettes of duck, garlic-fried prawns, a charcuterie plate, linguine with artichoke hearts and peas, corn-fed chicken on couscous, home-made sausages with mash, chargrilled sea bream with chips, and puddings such as crème brûlée and apple tart with vanilla ice-cream. *Benchmark main dish: 11oz rib-eye steak with chips £19.50. Two-course evening meal £21.00.*

Free house ~ Licensee Roxy Beaujolais ~ Real ale ~ (020) 7404 0200 ~ Open 11-11; closed Sun ~ Bar food 12-10.30 ~ Children welcome ~ www.thebountifulcow.co.uk
Recommended by Richard and Penny Gibbs, David Jackman, Ian Phillips, Phil Bryant

CENTRAL LONDON   Map 13

Dog & Duck 🕭 £

Bateman Street/Frith Street; ✪ *Leicester Square, Tottenham Court Road; W1D 3AJ*

Tiny Soho pub with unusual old tiles and mosaics, good beers and a warmly welcoming atmosphere

This tiny Soho pub manages to squeeze bags of character into its little rooms – it gets packed in the evenings when people spill on to the street. Probably the best time to visit is the afternoon when you can fully appreciate the décor, which has some interesting details and individual touches. On the floor near the door is an engaging mosaic showing a dog with its tongue out in hot pursuit of a duck; the same theme is embossed on some of the shiny tiles that frame the heavy old advertising mirrors. There are high stools by the ledge along the back wall, further seats in a slightly roomier area at one end and a fire in winter; the background music is usually drowned out by good-natured chatter. There's also a rather cosy upstairs bar, which often has some free space. Fullers London Pride and guests from breweries such as Jack Black, Lancaster, Sharps, Stonehenge, Strathaven and Thornbridge from the unusual little bar counter and quite a few wines by the glass.

Tasty food includes sandwiches, crayfish cocktail, breadcrumbed brie with redcurrant jelly, baked vegetable pancakes with cheese sauce, venison sausages with mash and onion rings, quite a choice of burgers, beef in ale pie, gammon and free-range eggs, half lemon and garlic chicken with rich gravy, slow-roast pork belly with ginger beer glaze and pak choi, and puddings such as chocolate orange pot and apple crumble. *Benchmark main dish: beer-battered cod and chips with mushy peas £11.75. Two-course evening meal £12.50.*

Mitchells & Butlers ~ Manager Natalie Hubbard ~ Real ale ~ (020) 7494 0697 ~ Open 11-11(11.30 Fri, Sat); 12-10.30 Sun ~ Bar food 11-10(9 Sun) ~ Restaurant ~ Children allowed in dining room ~ Dogs allowed in bar ~ www.nicholsonspubs.co.uk/ thedogandducksoholondon *Recommended by Mike Gorton, Richard Endacott, Richard and Penny Gibbs*

 CENTRAL LONDON   Map 13

Harp

47 Chandos Place; ⊖ *Leicester Square* ⊖ ⇄ *Charing Cross; WC2N 4HS*

Narrow little pub with eight real ales, friendly service, a cheerful atmosphere and nice sausage baguettes

'What a lovely little pub,' say many of our readers – and we agree. It's run with real friendliness and efficiency by the cheerful, long-serving landlady and her attentive staff – but can get packed as it's so central and handy for the theatres; at peak times, customers are happy to spill out on to the pavement or into the back alley. It pretty much consists of one long narrow, very traditional bar, with lots of high bar stools along the wall counter and around elbow tables, big mirrors on red walls, some lovely stained glass and loads of interesting, quirkily executed celebrity portraits. If you're very lucky, you may be able to get one of the prized seats looking out through the front windows. A little room upstairs is much quieter, with comfortable furniture and a window looking to the road below. The eight real ales on handpump are particularly well kept and quickly changing: usually three from Dark Star, one from Harveys, two from Sambrooks and one or two widely sourced guests – maybe from Ascot, Burton Bridge, Redemption, Red Squirrel, Twickenham or Windsor & Eton; up to nine farm ciders and three perries and quite a few malt whiskies.

Lunchtime food consists of good changing sausages in baguettes with lots of fried onions: wild boar, duck, venison, pork and ale or pork with garlic, beef and Guinness, and flavours like italian, spanish, mexican and american smokey. These are served until they run out. *Benchmark main dish: sausage in toasted baguette £3.50.*

Free house ~ Licensee Bridget Walsh ~ Real ale ~ (020) 7836 0291 ~ Open 10am-11.30pm; 12-10.30 Sun ~ Bar food 12-3 ~ www.harpcoventgarden.com
Recommended by Mike Gorton, Richard Endacott, Dr and Mrs A K Clarke, David Jackman, Brian and Anna Marsden, Comus and Sarah Elliott, Pete Walker, N R White

 CENTRAL LONDON   Map 13

Lamb & Flag 🍺 £

Rose Street, off Garrick Street; ⊖ *Covent Garden, Leicester Square; WC2E 9EB*

Historic yet unpretentious, full of character and atmosphere and with eight real ales and pubby food; especially busy in the evening

In Regency times, this cheerful, tucked-away pub was known as the Bucket of Blood thanks to the bare-knuckle prize-fights held here; the eight real ales and friendly efficient service tend to be the main draw now. It's an unspoilt and, in places, rather basic old tavern – the more spartan front room leads into a cosy atmospheric low-ceilinged back bar with high-backed black settles and an open fire. As the pub is owned by Fullers, they keep around half a dozen of their beers plus guests like Butcombe Bitter and Redemption Pale Ale on handpump, as well as ten wines by the glass and 16 malt whiskies. The pub cat is called Beautiful. The upstairs Dryden Room is often less crowded and has more seats (though fewer beers). The pub has a lively and well documented history: Dryden was nearly beaten to death by hired thugs outside, and Dickens made fun of the Middle Temple lawyers who frequented it when he was working in nearby Catherine Street.

The tasty food is served upstairs and includes sandwiches, salt and pepper calamari with smoked paprika mayonnaise, mussels in white wine, burger with cheese, bacon, pickled cucumber and chips, tagliatelle with asparagus, peas, broad beans, garlic and parmesan, shepherd's pie, cumberland sausages with mash and red wine and onion gravy, stuffed chicken breast with red pepper and almond salsa, and puddings such as lemon and mint cheesecake and apple crumble and custard. *Benchmark main dish: beer-battered cod and chips £10.50. Two-course evening meal £15.50.*

Fullers ~ Manager Christopher Buckley ~ Real ale ~ (020) 7497 9504 ~ Open 11-11; 12-10.30 Sun ~ Bar food 12-7(5 Fri, Sat); 12-8 Sun ~ Restaurant ~ Children in upstairs dining room only ~ Dogs allowed in bar ~ Live jazz Sun evening ~ www.lambandflagcoventgarden.co.uk *Recommended by Andrea Rampley, Pete Walker*

CENTRAL LONDON
Old Bank of England ♀

Map 13

Fleet Street; ⊖ *Chancery Lane (not Sundays), Temple (not Sundays)* ⇌ *Blackfriars; EC4A 2LT*

Dramatically converted former bank building, with gleaming chandeliers in impressive, soaring bar, well kept Fullers beers and good pies

A former subsidiary branch of the Bank of England and with a quite astounding interior, this is a Grade I-listed Italianate building – visitors never fail to be amazed. The soaring, spacious bar has three gleaming chandeliers hanging from an exquisitely plastered ceiling, high above an unusually tall island bar counter, crowned with a clock. The end wall has huge paintings and murals that look like 18th-c depictions of Justice, but in fact feature members of the Fuller, Smith and Turner families, who run the brewery that owns the pub. There are well polished dark wooden furnishings, luxurious curtains swagging massive windows, plenty of framed prints and, despite the grandeur, some surprisingly cosy corners, with screens between tables creating an unexpectedly intimate feel. Tables in a quieter galleried section upstairs offer a bird's-eye view of the action, and some smaller rooms (used mainly for functions) open off. Seven Fullers beers are on handpump alongside a good choice of malt whiskies and a dozen wines by the glass. At lunchtimes the background music is generally classical or easy listening; it's louder and livelier in the evenings. There's also a garden with seats (one of the few pubs in the area to have one).

Pies have a long if rather dubious pedigree in this area: it was in the vaults and tunnels below the Old Bank and the surrounding buildings that Sweeney Todd butchered the clients destined to provide the fillings for his mistress Mrs Lovett's nearby pie shop. Well, somehow or other, good home-made pies have become a speciality on the menu here too: ham and leek, chicken and sweetcorn, brie and sweet potato, and fish. Also, sandwiches, sharing boards, pork and apple sausages with mustard mash and red onion gravy, burger with bacon and smoked cheddar, beer-battered hake and chips, and puddings such as apple crumble and custard and Baileys bread and butter pudding. *Benchmark main dish: steak in ale pie £10.25. Two-course evening meal £15.00.*

Fullers ~ Manager Jo Farquhar ~ Real ale ~ (020) 7430 2255 ~ Open 11-11; closed weekends and bank holidays ~ Bar food 12-9 ~ Children welcome until 5pm ~ www.oldbankofengland.co.uk *Recommended by David Jackman, David Carr, Dr and Mrs A K Clarke, Barry Collett, Conor McGaughey*

CENTRAL LONDON   Map 13

Olde Mitre ⬤ £

Ely Place; the easiest way to find it is from the narrow passageway beside 8 Hatton Garden; ⊖ *Chancery Lane (not Sundays)* ⊖ ⇄ *Farringdon; EC1N 6SJ*

Hard to find but well worth it – an unspoilt old pub with a lovely atmosphere, unusual guest beers and bargain toasted sandwiches

'A rare gem' say readers – and it's true. With its nice homely atmosphere and proper hands-on licensees, it can be hard to believe you're so close to Holborn and the edge of the City. The cosy small rooms have lots of dark panelling as well as antique settles and – particularly in the popular back room, where there are more seats – old local pictures and so forth. It gets good-naturedly packed with the City suited-and-booted between 12.30 and 2.15pm, filling up again in the early evening, but in the early afternoon and by around 8pm is a good deal more tranquil. An upstairs room, mainly used for functions, may double as an overflow at peak periods. Adnams Broadside and Fullers London Pride and Seafarer with guests like Abbeydale Prophecy, Caledonian Deuchars IPA, Dark Star Hophead and Phoenix Arizona on handpump, and they hold three beer festivals a year. No music, TV or machines – the only games here are board games. There's some space for outside drinking by the pot plants and jasmine in the narrow yard between the pub and St Ethelreda's church (which is worth a look). Note the pub doesn't open weekends or bank holidays. The iron gates that guard one entrance to Ely Place are a reminder of the days when the law in this district was administered by the Bishops of Ely. The best approach is from Hatton Garden, walking up the right-hand side away from Chancery Lane; an easily missed sign on a lamp post points the way down a narrow alley. No children.

Served all day, bar snacks are limited to scotch eggs, pork pies, sausage rolls and really good value toasted sandwiches with cheese, ham, pickle or tomato.

Fullers ~ Managers Eamon and Kathy Scott ~ Real ale ~ (020) 7405 4751 ~ Open 11-11; closed weekends and bank holidays ~ Bar food 11.30-9.30 ~ www.yeoldemitreholburn.co.uk *Recommended by Dr and Mrs A K Clarke, Martin and Sue Radcliffe, Conor McGaughey*

CENTRAL LONDON   Map 13

Seven Stars ⬤

Carey Street; ⊖ *Chancery Lane (not Sundays), Temple (not Sundays), Holborn; WC2A 2JB*

Quirky pub with cheerful staff, an interesting mix of customers and a good choice of drinks and food

This cosy and unchanging little pub faces the back of the Law Courts and is a favourite with lawyers, Church of England music directors and choir singers; there are plenty of caricatures of barristers and judges on the red-painted walls of the two main rooms. Also, posters of legal-themed british films, big ceiling fans and a relaxed, intimate atmosphere; checked tablecloths add a quirky, almost continental touch. A third area is in what was formerly a legal-wig shop next door – it still retains the original frontage, with a neat display of wigs in the window. It's worth getting here early as they don't take bookings and tables get snapped up quickly. Adnams Best and Broadside and a couple of guests such as Sambrooks Wandle and Sharps Cornish Coaster on handpump, wines by the glass (they import wine from France) and they do a particularly good dry martini. On busy evenings there's an overflow of customers on to the quiet road in front; things generally calm down after 8pm and there can be a nice, sleepy atmosphere some afternoons. The Elizabethan stairs up to the lavatories are rather steep, but there's a good strong handrail. The pub cat is called Ray Brown and wears a ruff. The licensees also run the Bountiful Cow near Holborn tube station. No children.

🍴 Cooked according to the landlady's fancy, the good, interesting food includes house terrine on toast, a charcuterie plate, various frittata, vegetarian chinese stir-fry, beef and potato or lamb pie, napoli sausages and mash, corn-fed chicken with creamed spinach, linguine with oysters and pancetta, and puddings. *Benchmark main dish: home-made sausages with potato salad £11.00. Two-course evening meal £16.00.*

Free house ~ Licensee Roxy Beaujolais ~ Real ale ~ (020) 7242 8521 ~ Open 11 (12 Sat)-11; 12-10.30 Sun; closed some bank holidays ~ Bar food 12(1 weekends)-9.30 ~ www.thesevenstars1602.co.uk *Recommended by N R White, Tracey and Stephen Groves, Andrea Rampley, Conor McGaughey, Phil Bryant*

CENTRAL LONDON   Map 13
THE GOOD PUB GUIDE
Star 🍺
Belgrave Mews West, behind the German Embassy, off Belgrave Square;
⊖ *Knightsbridge, Hyde Park Corner; SW1X 8HT*

Bustling local with restful bar, upstairs dining room, Fullers ales, well liked bar food and colourful hanging baskets

Outside peak times, this popular pub has a restful local feel, tucked away in cobbled mews – and it's said that this is where the Great Train Robbery was planned. The small bar is a pleasant place with sash windows, a winter fire, stools by the counter on the wooden floor, and Fullers ESB, Seafarers and Summer Ale with a guest such as Redemption Pale Ale on handpump, good wines by the glass and 35 malt whiskies. An arch leads to the main seating area with well polished tables and chairs and good lighting; there's also an upstairs dining room. In summer, the pub is covered with an astonishing array of hanging baskets and flowering tubs.

🍴 Popular food includes sandwiches, deep-fried soft shell crab with citrus and thyme salt and aioli, chicken and bacon terrine, chargrilled burger with onions, bacon, cheddar and chips, fresh pasta with asparagus, peas and artichokes topped with parmesan, corn-fed chicken breast with elderberry wine sauce and sautéed potatoes, john dory fillet with potato and chickpea curry, and puddings such as chocolate marquise and ginger and rhubarb fool. *Benchmark main dish: beer-battered haddock and chips with mushy peas £9.80. Two-course evening meal £15.00.*

Fullers ~ Managers Jason and Karen Tinklin ~ Real ale ~ (020) 7235 3019 ~ Open 11(12 Sat)-11; 12-10.30 Sun ~ Bar food 12-4, 5-9; 12-7 Sat; 12-5 Sun ~ Restaurant ~

Children welcome ~ Dogs welcome ~ www.star-tavern-belgravia.co.uk
Recommended by Dr and Mrs A K Clarke, N R White, Susan and John Douglas, Mike and Jayne Bastin, Phil Bryant

EAST LONDON

Map 12

Gun

27 Coldharbour; ⊖ Blackwall on the DLR is probably closest, although the slightly longer walk from Canary Wharf has splendid Dockland views; E14 9NS

London Dining Pub of the Year

Top notch gastropub, pricey but worth it, great views from the riverside terrace, plenty of character and history, well chosen wines

Even on cooler or wet days (there are heaters and huge umbrellas) you can make the most of the seats and tables on the long narrow terrace behind this busy riverside pub with its uninterrupted views of the 02 Centre across a broad sweep of the Thames. The two rooms nearest the terrace are the nicest: a busy flagstoned bar for drinkers with antique guns on the wall and no tables – just a large barrel in the centre of the room – that shares a log fire with the cosy red-painted room next door, with its comfy leather sofas and armchairs, a stuffed boar's head, some modern prints, well stocked bookshelves and views on to the terrace. Crisp white walls and smart white tablecloths and napkins on tables at one end of the main bar contrast strikingly with dark wood floors and the black wood counter at the other. Adnams Bitter and guests from Botonist, Dark Star and Late Knights on handpump and several wines by the glass served by neatly aproned staff; background music. They may occasionally close the pub on Saturdays for weddings, and will keep your credit card if you are sitting on the terrace and want to run a tab.

Delicious and contemporary – if not cheap – the constantly changing dishes might include sandwiches, oysters (sold by the half dozen), roast quail, white onion purée, hazelnut, bacon and cherry jus, cured sea trout with caviar, crème friache potatoes and pickled cucumber, burger with cheddar and hand-cut chips, a lunchtime pie of the day, saddle of rabbit with peas, asparagus, duck fat potatoes and grain mustard jus, lamb rump with truffled polenta and thyme jus, and puddings such as lemoncello parfait with blueberry compote and praline and dark chocolate mousse with mango sorbet. *Benchmark main dish: bass fillets with queen scallop, crisp squid and sorrel risotto £18.00. Two-course evening meal £25.00.*

Free house ~ Licensees Ed and Tom Martin ~ Real ale ~ (020) 7515 5222 ~ Open 11am-midnight(11pm Sun) ~ Bar food 12-3(4 Sat), 6-10.30; 12-4, 6.30-9.30 Sun ~ Restaurant ~ children welcome until 8pm ~ www.thegundocklands.com *Recommended by Martin Frowde, Stuart Doughty, Dave Snowden*

NORTH LONDON

Map 13

Drapers Arms ♀

Far west end of Barnsbury Street; ⊖ ⇌ Highbury & Islington; N1 1ER

Streamlined place with good mix of customers, a thoughtful choice of drinks, imaginative modern food and seats in an attractive back garden

In warm weather, the very attractive back terrace here is a real bonus with its white or green benches and chairs around zinc-topped tables (each set with a church candle in a hurricane lamp), flagstones and large parasols. But, of course, the year-round draw is the first class modern cooking. It's a simply furnished Georgian townhouse and the spreading bar has a mix of elegant dark wooden tables and dining chairs on bare boards, an arresting bright green-painted counter contrasting with soft duck-egg walls, gilt mirrors over smart fireplaces, a sofa and some comfortable chairs. Harveys Best and guests such as Dark Star Hophead and Windsor & Eton Kohinoor on handpump, 21 carefully chosen wines by the glass and british draught lagers. The stylish upstairs dining room has similar tables and chairs on a striking chequerboard-painted wood floor; background music and board games.

🍴 Changing daily and using carefully sourced seasonal produce, the enticing food might include nibbles like haggis sausage roll, pork pie and ham hock croquettes as well as sandwiches, black pudding, gloucester old spot bacon, chard and mustard dressing, devilled sand eels with mayonnaise, wild garlic and potato dumplings with broad beans, hispi cabbage, crème fraîche and mint, shepherd's pie, grilled quail, baby gem, bacon, crouton and anchovy salad, pork chop with chorizo, chickpeas and aioli, confit duck leg with spring onions, peas and green sauce, and puddings such as chocolate brownie sundae and pear and buttermilk pudding with shortbread. *Benchmark main dish: beef and oyster pie £12.50. Two-course evening meal £22.00.*

Free house ~ Licensee Nick Gibson ~ Real ale ~ (020) 7619 0348 ~ Open 12-11 ~ Bar food 12-3, 6-10.30; 12-4, 7-10.30 Sat; 12-8.30 Sun ~ Restaurant ~ Children welcome but must be seated and dining after 6pm ~ Dogs allowed in bar ~ www.thedrapersarms.com
Recommended by Richard and Penny Gibbs, Fr Robert Marsh

NORTH LONDON

Holly Bush 🍷 🍺

Map 12

Holly Mount; ⊖ Hampstead; NW3 6SG

Unique village local with good food and drinks and lovely unspoilt feel

With plenty of atmosphere even when quiet, this is a proper local that wears its charm with dignity. You can be sure of a warm welcome too. The old-fashioned front bar has a dark sagging ceiling, brown and cream panelled walls (decorated with old advertisements and a few plates), open fires, bare boards and secretive bays formed by partly glazed partitions. The slightly more intimate back room, named after the painter George Romney, has an embossed red ceiling, panelled and etched glass alcoves and ochre-painted brick walls covered with small prints; lots of board and card games. Fullers London Pride, Seafarers, Summer Ale and Wild River and a guest such as Butcombe Bitter on handpump, as well as 23 whiskies and 16 wines by the glass from a good wine list. The upstairs dining room has table service at the weekend, as does the rest of the pub on a Sunday. There are benches on the pavement outside.

🍴 Well liked food might include ham hock terrine, quinoa with roasted peppers, sun-dried tomatoes and grilled sheeps cheese, beef in ale pie, marinated chicken breast with pancetta, peas and broad beans, pork loin and black cabbage with mustard sauce, confit duck leg with wild berry jus, and puddings such as panna cotta with strawberry compote and chocolate brownie with earl grey ice-cream. *Benchmark main dish: fish pie £14.00. Two-course evening meal £20.00.*

Fullers ~ Manager Hannah Borkulak ~ Real ale ~ (020) 7435 2892 ~ Open 12-11 (10.30 Sun) ~ Bar food 12-3(4 Sat), 6-10; 12-5, 6-9 Sun ~ Restaurant ~ Children welcome till 7pm ~ Dogs welcome ~ www.hollybushhampstead.co.uk
Recommended by Jim Craig-Gray, N R White, Phil Bryant

SOUTH LONDON   Map 12

Greenwich Union ◖

Royal Hill; ⊖ ⇌ *Greenwich; SE10 8RT*

Enterprising pub with distinctive beers from small local Meantime Brewery, plus other unusual drinks and good popular food

They choose their interesting drinks meticulously here and try to shy away from the usual big-name brands. It's still just one of two taps for the small Meantime Brewery, stocking all their distinctive unpasteurised beers. The range includes a traditional pale ale (served cool, under pressure), a mix of proper pilsners, lagers and wheat beers, one a deliciously refreshing raspberry flavour, and a stout; the knowledgeable, helpful staff will usually offer small tasters to help you choose. They also have Hawkshead Cumbrian Five Hop and Dark Star American Pale Ale and Hophead on handpump and a draught cider, as well as a helpfully annotated list of around 150 bottled beers. There's also a good choice of unusual spirits, a thoughtful wine list, carefully chosen teas and coffees and daily squeezed fresh orange juice. Perhaps feeling a little more like a bar than a pub, the long, narrow stone-flagged room has several different parts: a simple area at the front with a few wooden chairs and tables, a stove and newspapers, then, past the counter with its headings recalling the branding of the brewery's first beers, several brown leather cushioned pews and armchairs under framed editions of Picture Post on yellow walls; background music, TV. Beyond here a much lighter, more modern-feeling conservatory has comfortable brown leather wall benches, a few original pictures and paintings, and white fairy lights under the glass roof; it leads out to an appealing terrace with green picnic-sets and a couple of old-fashioned lamp posts. The fence at the end is painted to resemble a poppy field, and the one at the side a wheat field. Though there are plenty of tables out here, it can get busy in summer (as can the whole pub on weekday evenings). In front a couple of tables overlook the street. The pub is slightly removed from Greenwich's many attractions and there's a particularly good traditional cheese shop as you walk towards the pub.

🍴 Seasonally changing and very popular, the food might include sandwiches, lunchtime nibbles such as ham hock with english mustard, whitebait with tartare sauce and home-made sausage rolls, as well as lamb burger with feta and harissa, crumbed cod fillet with chips, mussels with wild garlic mayonnaise and chips, chargrilled angus rump steak with peppercorn butter, and puddings such as panna cotta with strawberry coulis and sticky toffee pudding with vanilla ice-cream. *Benchmark main dish: angus burger with coleslaw and home-made chips £11.30. Two-course evening meal £17.50.*

Free house ~ Licensee Daniel Persson ~ Real ale ~ (020) 8692 6258 ~ Open 12-11; 11-11 Sat; 12-10.30 Sun ~ Bar food 12-10(9 Sun); 11-10 Sat ~ Children welcome ~ Dogs allowed in bar ~ www.greenwichunion.com *Recommended by Ian Phillips, Simon Pyle*

SOUTH LONDON   Map 13

Royal Oak ◖

Tabard Street/Nebraska Street; ⊖ *Borough* ⊖ ⇌ *London Bridge; SE1 4JU*

Old-fashioned corner house with particularly well kept beers and honest food

This enjoyable corner house is always packed with customers of all ages – all keen to enjoy the full range of Harveys ales, plus a guest

from Fullers on handpump and Thatcher's cider. This was the first
London pub belonging to the Sussex brewer, who have transformed
it (they now also run the Cats Back in Wandsworth), painstakingly re-
creating the look and feel of a traditional London alehouse; you'd never
imagine it hadn't been like this all along. The two busy little L-shaped
rooms meander around the central wooden servery, which has a fine
old clock in the middle. They're done out in a cosy traditional style with
patterned rugs on the wooden floors, plates running along a delft shelf,
black and white scenes or period sheet music on the red-painted walls,
and an assortment of wooden tables and chairs. There's a disabled ramp
at the Nebraska Street entrance.

🍴 Wholesome pub grub includes sandwiches, duck liver pâté, deep-fried
whitebait, courgette cake with salad, venison pie, half a roast duck, and
puddings such as lemon tart and fruit crumble. *Benchmark main dish: steak in
ale pie £10.45. Two-course evening meal £15.50.*

Harveys ~ Tenants John Porteous, Frank Taylor ~ Real ale ~ (020) 7357 7173 ~ Open
11-11; 12-9 Sun ~ Bar food 12-2.30, 5-9.15; 12-8 Sun ~ Children welcome until 9pm ~
Dogs welcome ~ www.harveys.org.uk *Recommended by Mike Gorton, Giles and Annie Francis,
Comus and Sarah Elliott, Pete Walker*

WEST LONDON   TQ1370   Map 3
Bell
Thames Street, Hampton; 🚉 *Hampton; TW12 2EA*

**Bustling pub by the Thames with seats outside, real ales, popular food
and friendly service**

Opposite the Thames, this refurbished pub has plenty of seats and
tables in the partly covered courtyard garden, where they hold
barbecues in warm weather. Inside, the interconnected rooms have
wooden dining and tub chairs around copper-topped or chunky wooden
tables, comfortably upholstered wall seats with scatter cushions, mirrors
and old photographs and plenty of church candles. From the long
panelled counter they serve Binghams Space Hoppy IPA, Sambrooks
Wandle and Sharps Doom Bar on handpump, several wines by the glass
and speciality teas and coffees. Service is helpful and friendly.

🍴 Using local, seasonal produce the popular food includes sandwiches, chicken
liver pâté with crab apple and grape jam, five-spice pork belly with ginger
and apple purée, various sharing boards, a pie of the day, aubergine, feta and herb
croquette stack with tomato sauce, indian-spiced lamb burger with cucumber and
coriander raita and rosemary flatbread, slow-cooked lamb shank with mint and
rosemary broth and sweet potato mash, and puddings such as knickerbocker glory
and apple and rhubarb crumble with custard. *Benchmark main dish: piri-piri
chicken £12.95. Two-course evening meal £18.50.*

Absolute Pubs ~ Lease Simon Bailey ~ Real ale ~ (020) 8941 9799 ~ Open 11am-
midnight(11 Sun) ~ Bar food 12-3, 6-10; 12-10 Sat; 12-9 Sun ~ Restaurant ~ Children
welcome ~ Dogs allowed in bar ~ Live acoustic music Sat, comedy first Weds of month ~
www.thebellinnhampton.co.uk *Recommended by Emma Scofield, Caroline Prescott*

Please keep sending us reports. We rely on readers for news of new discoveries,
and particularly for news of changes – however slight – at the fully described pubs:
feedback@goodguides.com, or (no stamp needed) The Good Pub Guide,
FREEPOST TN1569, Wadhurst, E Sussex TN5 7BR.

Churchill Arms ♀ ◧ £

Kensington Church Street; ⊖ Notting Hill Gate, Kensington High Street;
W8 7LN

**Cheery irish landlord at bustling and friendly local with very well
kept beers and popular thai food; even at its most crowded, it stays
relaxed and welcoming**

The façade of this bustling local is quite a sight in summer as it almost
disappears behind the glorious display of 85 window boxes and
42 hanging baskets. It's been run by the same enthusiastic and friendly
irish landlord for 29 years and there's always a warm welcome for both
locals and visitors. Mr O'Brien is a great collector and loves butterflies –
you'll see a variety of prints and books on the subject dotted around the
bar. He doesn't stop there, though: the pub is also filled with countless
lamps, miners' lights, horse tack, bedpans and brasses hanging from the
ceiling, a couple of interesting carved figures and statuettes behind the
central bar counter, prints of american presidents and lots of Churchill
memorabilia. Well kept Fullers Chiswick, ESB, London Pride and Fullers
seasonal beers on handpump and two dozen wines by the glass. The
spacious and rather smart plant-filled dining conservatory may be used
for hatching butterflies, but is better known for its big choice of excellent
thai food. They have their own cricket and football teams and hold
regular special events. There can be quite an overspill on to the street,
where there are some chrome tables and chairs.

Splendid value thai food ranges from a proper thai curry to various rice, noodle
and stir-fry dishes. At lunchtimes they usually also have a very few traditional
dishes such as fish and chips or sausage and chips, and they do a good value Sunday
roast. *Benchmark main dish: pad thai noodles (peanuts, bean sprouts, spring
onion, chilli and egg) £7.50. Two-course evening meal £19.00.*

Fullers ~ Manager Gerry O'Brien ~ Real ale ~ (020) 7727 4242 ~ Open 11-11(midnight
Thurs-Sat); 12-10.30 Sun ~ Bar food 12-10(9.30 Sun) ~ Restaurant ~ Children welcome
~ Dogs welcome ~ www.churchillarmskensington.co.uk *Recommended by LM, N R White*

Dove ◧

Upper Mall; ⊖ Ravenscourt Park; W6 9TA

**One of London's best-known pubs with a lovely riverside terrace,
cosily traditional front bar and an interesting history**

This 17th-c riverside pub is in the Guinness World Records for having
the smallest bar room – the front snug is a mere 1.3 metres by
2.4 metres. This little room is cosy, traditional and unchanging with
black panelling and red leatherette cushioned built-in wall settles and
stools around assorted tables; it leads to a bigger, similarly furnished
back room that's more geared to eating ,which in turn leads to a
conservatory. There's also a verandah, down some steps, with highly
prized tables looking over the low river wall to the Thames reach just
above Hammersmith Bridge. A tiny exclusive area can be reached
up a spiral staircase – a prime spot for watching the rowing crews
out on the water. Fullers ESB and London Pride plus guests such as
Summer Ale and Wild River on handpump and lots of wines by the glass
including champagne and sparkling wine. The pub has played host
to many writers, actors and artists over the years and there's a rather

fascinating framed list of them all on a wall. This is said to be where 'Rule Britannia' was composed and it was a favourite with Turner (who painted the view of the Thames from the delightful back terrace) and also Graham Greene. The street itself is associated with the foundation of the arts and crafts movement – William Morris's old residence (Kelmscott House, open certain afternoons) is nearby.

🍴 Tasty food includes pork terrine with piccalilli, king scallops with roasted beets, brown butter and chervil, goats cheese salad, sausages with caramelised onion jus and mash, honey-glazed corn-fed chicken breast with artichoke and watercress, burger with bacon, cheddar, onions, gherkins, coleslaw and chips, sea trout with fennel and radish salad, and puddings such as profiteroles with chocolate sauce and glazed lemon tart. *Benchmark main dish: beer-battered haddock and chips with minted mushy peas and home-made tartare sauce £11.50. Two-course evening meal £21.00.*

Fullers ~ Manager Matthew England ~ Real ale ~ (020) 8748 9474 ~ Open 11-11; 12-10.30 Sun ~ Bar food 12-10(8 Sun) ~ Dogs welcome ~ Live irish folk Mon evenings ~ www.dovehammersmith.co.uk *Recommended by Rob and Catherine Dunster, N R White*

WEST LONDON   Map 12
Duke of Sussex 🍴 🍷 🍺
South Parade; ⊖ Chiswick Park ⇌ South Acton; W4 5LF

Attractively restored Victorian local with interesting bar food, a good choice of drinks and a lovely big garden

The garden at the back of this sizeable Victorian pub is quite a surprise – it's unexpectedly big. There are plenty of tables under parasols, nicely laid out plants, heaters and carefully positioned lighting – it's a real oasis, though it can get packed on sunny days. Once through the intriguing entrance lobbies with their cut-glass, mahogany and mosaics, you enter the classy, simply furnished bar. This has some original etched glass, chapel and farmhouse chairs around scrubbed pine and dark wood tables and huge windows overlooking Acton Green. New floorboards and a big horseshoe-shaped counter lined with high bar stools is where they serve St Austells Proper Job, Sharps Cornish Coaster and Twickenham Naked Ladies on handpump and several wines by the glass. Leading off is a dining room, again with plenty of simple wooden furnishings on parquet, but also six-seater booths, chandeliers, antique lamps and a splendid skylight framed by colourfully painted cherubs; there are a couple of big mirrors, one above a small tiled fireplace. At the very back the room opens on to the garden.

🍴 Likeable and interesting, the food includes lots of tapas such as razor clams with chorizo, garlic and chilli, salt cod fritters and spanish cured meats plus more substantial choices such as galician fish stew, rabbit paella, fish and chips, lamb rump with tabbouleh and harissa, half a pig's head (for two people) with quince aioli, and puddings such as dulce de leche ice-cream and lemon meringue pie. *Benchmark main dish: seafood paella £14.00. Two-course evening meal £20.00.*

Greene King ~ Manager Claude Levi ~ Real ale ~ (020) 8742 8801 ~ Open 12-11(11.30 Sat, 10.30 Sun) ~ Bar food 12-10.30(9.30 Sun) ~ Restaurant ~ Children welcome ~ Dogs allowed in bar ~ www.thedukeofsussex.co.uk *Recommended by N R White, Simon Rodway*

The knife-and-fork award 🍴 distinguishes pubs
where the food is of exceptional quality.

Old Orchard 🍴 ♟

Off Park Lane; Harefield; UB9 6HJ

Wonderful views from the garden in front of this Edwardian house, a good choice of drinks, friendly staff and well liked, interesting brasserie-type food

We've had nothing but warm, enthusiastic praise from readers for this particularly well run former country house. Of course, one of the main draws in warm weather is its position. Tables on the front terrace have a stunning view down over the narrowboats on the canal and on to the lakes that make up a conservation area known as the Colne Valley Regional Park; it's a haven for wildlife. Seats from the gazebo and picnic-sets in the garden have the same fantastic view. Inside, the knocked-through open-plan rooms have an attractive mix of cushioned dining chairs around all sizes and shapes of dark wooden tables, lots of prints, maps and pictures covering the walls, books on shelves, old glass bottles on window sills and rugs on wood or parquet flooring. One room is hung with a sizeable rug and some tapestries. There are daily papers to read, three cosy coal fires, big pot plants and fresh flowers. Half a dozen real ales on handpump served by top notch staff include Phoenix Brunning & Price Original, Mighty Oak Oscar Wilde and Tring Side Pocket for a Toad, alongside guests such as Binghams Smiled, Lymestone Pounamu and Triple fff Ramble Tamble; also about two dozen wines by the glass and more than 100 whiskies. The atmosphere is civilised and easy-going.

 Popular brasserie-type food includes sandwiches, piri-piri king prawns on harissa couscous with red pepper and yoghurt relish, chicken liver parfait with plum and ginger chutney, smoked haddock kedgeree with poached egg and parsley sauce, halloumi and vegetable kebabs with sweet chilli and puy lentils, lamb, rosemary and redcurrant pie, pork and leek sausages with mash and red wine gravy, steak burger topped with bacon and cheddar with coleslaw and chips, grey mullet fillet with crab potato cake, red pepper coulis and chicory salad, and puddings such as dark chocolate mousse with basil jelly and blackcurrant sorbet. *Benchmark main dish: sesame-crusted pork belly with five-spice carrots, sticky cabbage, noodles and cider sauce £13.95. Two-course evening meal £18.00.*

Brunning & Price ~ Manager Dan Redfern ~ Real ale ~ (01895) 822631 ~ Open 11.30-11; 12-10.30 Sun ~ Bar food 12-10(9.30 Sun) ~ Children welcome ~ Dogs welcome ~ www.oldorchard-harefield.co.uk *Recommended by Richard and Penny Gibbs, Dave Hoare, Mark Strathdee, Nicole Strathdee, M J Daly, Ross Balaam, David Jackman*

Portobello Gold ♟

95 Portobello Road; ✆ Notting Hill Gate; W11 2QB

Engaging combination of pub, hotel and restaurant with a relaxed atmosphere, enjoyable food (especially in attractive dining conservatory) and excellent range of drinks; bedrooms

Usefully opening early for morning coffee, pastries and the papers, this is an enterprising and almost bohemian place with a monthly art and photographic exhibition and regular live music. Our favourite part is the exotic-seeming dining room with its big tropical plants, photographs of famous singers and bands on the red or green walls, contemporary high-backed wicker dining chairs around all sizes of polished wooden tables and a cage of vocal canaries adding to the outdoor effect – in summer, they open the sliding roof. The smaller front bar has a nice old fireplace, cushioned banquettes and, more unusually, several internet terminals (which disappear in the evening). It's all very relaxed, cheerful and informal, though things can get a bit rushed when they're busy in the evening. Brakspears Oxford Gold and Harveys Best on handpump, 18 wines by the glass from a thoughtfully chosen list, 'as many quality tequilas as are imported into the UK' and classic cocktails. They also have a cigar menu, an eclectic choice of background music, TV, chess and backgammon. The back garden has seats and tables for dining, and there are one or two tables and chairs on the pretty street outside. Some bedrooms are small but there's a spacious apartment with a rooftop terrace and putting green. Parking nearby is restricted, but you can usually find a space (not so easily on Saturdays).

The modern british and mediterranean menu (and lots of fish specials) might include all-day dips and nibbles, sandwiches, fajitas, salmon, prawn and dill fishcakes, pea and wild garlic spelt tart, burger with cheese, bacon and fries, vegetarian shepherd's pie, wild boar and apple sausages with parsley mash and gravy, butterflied cajun jumbo shrimps, pork chop with cider sauce and aubergine and new potato salad, bavette steak with green peppercorn sauce and fries, seafood platter to share, and puddings. *Benchmark main dish: moules marinière (or thai-style) £9.20. Two-course evening meal £20.00.*

Enterprise ~ Lease Michael Bell and Linda Johnson-Bell ~ Real ale ~ (020) 7460 4910 ~ Open 10am-11.30pm; 9am-12.30am Sat; 10am-10.30pm Sun ~ Bar food 12-10; 12-5, 7-10 Sat; 10-9 Sun ~ Restaurant ~ Children welcome ~ Dogs allowed in bar ~ Live music Sun evening ~ Bedrooms: /£75 ~ www.portobellogold.com *Recommended by Martin Jones, Harvey Brown*

 WEST LONDON   Map 12

White Horse 🍴 🍷 🍺

Parsons Green; ❸ Parsons Green; SW6 4UL

Cheerfully relaxed local with big terrace, an excellent range of carefully sourced drinks and imaginative food

On summer evenings and weekends, the front terrace of this much loved pub – which overlooks the green – has something of a continental feel with its many seats and tables; they hold barbecues out here most sunny evenings. Inside, the stylishly modernised U-shaped bar has a gently upmarket and chatty atmosphere, plenty of chesterfield leather sofas and wooden tables, huge windows with slatted wooden blinds, wood and flagstone floors and winter coal and log fires – one in an elegant marble fireplace. There's also an upstairs dining room with its own bar. An impressive range of drinks takes in regular real ales like Adnams Broadside, Hobsons Best, Oakham JHB and guests such as Late Knights Crack of Dawn Pale Ale, Moorhouses Black Cat, Portobello Market Porter and Tiny Rebel Flux on handpump, imported keg beers from overseas (usually belgian and german but occasionally from further afield), six of the seven trappist beers, around 140 other

---

'Children welcome' means the pub says it lets children inside without any special restriction. If it allows them in, but to restricted areas such as an eating area or family room, we specify this. Places with separate restaurants often let children use them, and hotels usually let children into public areas such as lounges. Some pubs impose an evening time limit – let us know if you find one earlier than 9pm.

foreign bottled beers, several malt whiskies and 20 good wines by the glass. They hold quarterly beer festivals, often spotlighting regional breweries. The well trained and friendly staff remain as efficient as ever – even when really pushed.

🍴 Good rewarding food includes sandwiches, ham hock and broad bean terrine, crab, avocado, celeriac and apple coleslaw, gloucester old spot sausages with mash and cider gravy, gnocchi with quinoa, chestnut mushrooms and truffled cream, beer-battered haddock and chips, full english breakfast, pie of the day, braised duck leg with sweet potato mash, lamb rump with samphire, broad beans and parmesan suet crumble, and puddings. *Benchmark main dish: rib-eye and chuck steak with marrow bone burger, bacon jam, relish and chips £18.00. Two-course evening meal £21.00.*

Mitchells & Butlers ~ Manager Jez Manterfield ~ Real ale ~ (020) 7736 2115 ~ Open 9.30am-11.30pm(midnight Thurs-Sat) ~ Bar food 9.30am-10.30pm; brunch 9.30-12 ~ Restaurant ~ Children welcome ~ Dogs allowed in bar ~ www.whitehorsesw6.com
Recommended by Phil Bryant

WEST LONDON   Map 12

Windsor Castle 🍺

Campden Hill Road; ⊖ Notting Hill Gate; W8 7AR

Genuinely unspoilt, with lots of atmosphere in tiny dark rooms and lovely summer garden; good beers and reliable food

After some recent refurbishment (moving the loos upstairs and adding a new kitchen), there's now a new panelled and wood-floored dining room at the back overlooking one of London's best pub gardens. This has quite a secluded feel thanks to the high ivy-covered sheltering walls, and there's a summer bar as well as heaters for cooler days and lots of tables and chairs on the flagstones. Inside has a lot of character and genuine old-fashioned charm, with a wealth of dark oak furnishings, high-backed sturdy built-in elm benches, time-smoked ceilings, soft lighting and a coal-effect fire. Three of the tiny unspoilt rooms have their own entrance from the street, but it's much more fun trying to navigate through the minuscule doors between them inside. Usually fairly quiet at lunchtime, it tends to be packed most evenings. Portobello VPA, Timothy Taylors Landlord and Windsor & Eton Knight of the Garter on handpump alongside guests from breweries such as Batemans, Ilkley, Sambrooks, Shepherd Neame and Triple fff, farm ciders, decent house wines and malt whiskies and jugs of Pimms.

🍴 Interesting food includes sandwiches, chargrilled cuttlefish with peas, lardons and mint, ham hock terrine with piccalilli, gnocchi with quinoa, chestnut mushrooms and truffled cream, gloucester old spot sausages and mash with cider gravy, cheese burger with chips, chicken hotpot with bacon, ale and pickled onions, bass with chickpeas, chorizo and cuttlefish, and puddings such as potted custard caramel with lavender shortbread and apple and blackberry pistachio and thyme crumble with vanilla cream. *Benchmark main dish: confit pork belly with shallot purée £18.00. Two-course evening meal £24.00.*

Mitchells & Butlers ~ Manager Suzanne Grantham ~ Real ale ~ (020) 7243 8797 ~ Open 9am-11pm; 12-10.30 Sun ~ Bar food 12-10(9 Sun) ~ Restaurant ~ Children welcome till 7pm ~ Dogs welcome ~ www.thewindsorcastlekensington.co.uk
Recommended by John Best, Ian Phillips, Conor McGaughey

Also Worth a Visit in London

Besides the fully inspected pubs, you might like to try these pubs that have been recommended to us and described by readers. Do tell us what you think of them: feedback@goodguides.com

CENTRAL LONDON

EC1

⋆ **Bishops Finger** (020) 7248 2341
West Smithfield; EC1A 9JR Smartly civilised little pub close to Smithfield Market, friendly welcoming atmosphere, well laid-out bar with cushioned chairs on polished boards, framed market prints on cream walls, big windows, fresh flowers, Shepherd Neame ales including seasonal brews, a fine range of sausages plus other dishes in bar or upstairs restaurant, efficient service; children welcome, outside seating, closed weekends and bank holidays, otherwise open all day. *(John and Gloria Isaacs, Dr and Mrs A K Clarke)*

Butchers Hook & Cleaver
(020) 7600 9181 *West Smithfield; EC1A 9DY* Fullers bank conversion with friendly helpful staff and pleasant relaxed atmosphere, their full range kept well, enjoyable all-day pubby food (good choice of pies), breakfast from 7.30am, daily papers, nice mix of chairs including some button-back leather armchairs, wrought-iron spiral stairs to mezzanine; background music, big-screen sports TV; open all day, closed weekends. *(Dr and Mrs A K Clarke, John and Gloria Isaacs)*

Craft Beer Company
Leather Lane; EC1N 7TR Old corner pub transformed into drinking hall with 16 real ales and great selection of other beers including over 300 in bottles (some rarities), good selection of wines and spirits too, high stools and tables on bare-boards, big chandelier hanging from mirrored ceiling, can get very busy but service remains efficient and friendly, food limited to snacks, upstairs room; open all day. *(N R White)*

⋆ **Eagle** (020) 7837 1353
Farringdon Road; EC1R 3AL Original gastropub and still popular – arrive early as dishes run out or change quickly; one bare-boards room dominated by the giant cooking range and too busy, noisy and scruffy for some, basic well worn school chairs, assorted tables and a sofa, modern art (gallery upstairs too), Wells & Youngs and a guest, good wines by the glass and decent coffee; background music sometimes loud, not ideal for a quiet dinner (weekends quieter); children and dogs welcome, closed Sun evening, bank holidays and for a week at Christmas, otherwise open all day. *(John and Gloria Isaacs)*

Fox & Anchor (020) 7250 1300
Charterhouse Street; EC1M 6AA Beautifully restored late Victorian pub by Smithfield Market, welcoming staff, long slender bar with unusual pewter-topped counter, lots of mahogany, green leather and etched glass, small back snugs, ales such as Adnams, Harviestoun and Purity served in pewter tankards plus a house beer from Nethergate, oyster bar and good range of freshly cooked food including popular home-made pies and a daily roast carved at your table, tempting traditional puddings too; six individual well appointed bedrooms, open all day from 7am (8.30am weekends). *(N R White)*

Gunmakers (020) 7278 1022
Eyre Street Hill; EC1R 5ET Popular two-room Victorian pub with four interesting changing ales, friendly knowledgeable landlord, enjoyable and often individual food from daily blackboard, back conservatory; dogs welcome, open all day weekdays, closed weekends. *(Anon)*

⋆ **Hand & Shears** (020) 7600 0257
Middle Street; EC1A 7JA Traditional panelled Smithfield pub dating from 16th c, three basic bright rooms and small snug off central servery, bustling at lunchtime, quiet evenings, six changing real ales, friendly service, interesting prints and old photographs; maybe background jazz/blues; open all day, closed weekends. *(Anon)*

⋆ **Jerusalem Tavern** (020) 7490 4281
Britton Street; EC1M 5UQ Convincing and atmospheric re-creation of a dark 18th-c tavern (1720 merchant's house with shopfront added 1810), tiny dimly lit bar, simple wood furnishings on bare boards, some remarkable old wall tiles, coal fires and candlelight, stairs to a precarious-feeling (though perfectly secure) balcony, plainer back room, St Peters beers tapped from the cask, short choice of lunchtime food, friendly attentive young staff; can get very crowded at peak times, no children; dogs welcome, seats out on pavement, open all day during the week, closed weekends, bank holidays, 24 Dec-2 Jan. *(Mike Gorton, Andy Lickfold, Giles and Annie Francis, Phil Bryant, Roger and Donna Huggins, Tom McLean)*

Old Fountain (020) 7253 2970
Baldwin Street; EC1V 9NU Popular traditional old pub in same family since 1964; long bar serving two rooms, up to eight real ales chalked up on board including Fullers

London Pride, pubby food from sandwiches up, main carpeted part with wooden tables and chairs, padded stools and fish tank, darts, roof terrace and function room for live music; open all day. *(Roger and Donna Huggins, Dave G)*

Old Red Cow (020) 7726 2595

Long Lane; EC1A 9EJ Cheerful little corner pub with five changing ales form smaller brewers and a good range of other draught and bottled beers, nice food from home-made pies to steak tartare, Sun roasts, second bar upstairs; open all day. *(John and Gloria Isaacs)*

EC2

⋆**Dirty Dicks** (020) 7283 5888

Bishopsgate; EC2M 4NR Olde-worlde re-creation of traditional City tavern, busy and fun for foreign visitors, booths, barrel tables, exposed brick and low beams, interesting old prints, Wells & Youngs ales, good variety of enjoyable well priced food from sandwiches up, pleasant service, calmer cellar wine bar with wine racks overhead in brick barrel-vaulted ceiling, further upstairs area too; background music, games machines and TV; closed weekends. *(Phil Bryant)*

Fox (020) 7729 5708

Paul Street; EC2A 4LB Relaxed friendly atmosphere in this high-ceilinged bare-boards corner pub, well kept Harveys, Sharps Doom Bar and a guest from central servery, several wines by the glass, good food from bar snacks up, dining room upstairs with coal-effect gas fire and canopied roof terrace; gets busy lunchtime and early evening with local office workers; dogs welcome, open all day (till 5pm Sun). *(Jamie and Sue May)*

Hamilton Hall (020) 7247 3579

Bishopsgate; also entrance from Liverpool Street Station; EC2M 7PY Showpiece Wetherspoons with flamboyant Victorian baroque décor, plaster nudes and fruit mouldings, chandeliers, mirrors, good-sized comfortable mezzanine, food all day, lots of real ales including interesting guests, decent wines and coffee, good prices and friendly staff; silenced machines, can get very crowded after work; good disabled access, tables outside, open all day. *(Claes Mauroy)*

Lord Aberconway (020) 7929 1743

Old Broad Street; EC2M 1QT Victorian feel with high moulded ceiling, dark panelling and some red leather bench seats, six well kept ales such as Adnams, Fullers and Lancaster, reasonably priced food from sandwiches up, wrought-iron railed upper dining gallery; silent fruit machine, gets busy with after-work drinkers; handy for Liverpool Street Station. *(Jeremy King)*

EC3

East India Arms (020) 7265 5121

Fenchurch Street; EC3M 4BR Standing-room Victorian corner pub popular with City workers, well kept Shepherd Neame ales, good service, single room with wooden floor, old local photographs and brewery mirrors; tables outside, closed weekends. *(Anon)*

Hoop & Grapes (020) 7481 4583

Aldgate High Street; EC3N 1AL Originally 17th-c (dismantled and rebuilt 1983) and much bigger inside than it looks; long partitioned bare-boards bar with beams, timbers and panelling, furniture more modern including sofas, good range of real ales and standard Nicholsons menu (very popular lunchtime); a few seats in front, closed weekends, otherwise open all day. *(Phil Bryant)*

Jamaica Wine House

(020) 79296972 *St Michael's Alley, Cornhill; EC3V 9DS* 19th-c pub on the site of London's first coffee house in a warren of small alleys; traditional Victorian décor with ornate ceilings, oak-panelled bar, booths and bare boards, Shepherd Neame ales and wide choice of wines, food in downstairs lunchtime dining area, friendly helpful service, bustling atmosphere (quietens after 8pm); closed weekends. *(Ross Balaam)*

Lamb (020) 7626 2454

Leadenhall Market; EC3V 1LR Well run stand-up bar, staff always polite and efficient even when very busy with sharp City lads, Wells & Youngs ales, good choice of wines by the glass, panelling, engraved glass, plenty of ledges and shelves, spiral stairs up to tables and seating in small light and airy carpeted gallery overlooking market's central crossing, corner servery doing lunchtime carvery and other food, separate stairs to nice bright dining room (not cheap), also basement bar with shiny wall tiling and own entrance; tables out under splendid Victorian market roof (crowds here in warmer months), open all day, closed weekends. *(N R White)*

Minories (020) 7702 1658

Minories, next to Tower Gateway Station; EC3N 1JL In railway arches near Tower of London; surprisingly spacious with lots of separate seating areas, ales such as Banks's, Brakspears, Marstons and Wells & Youngs, plenty of well priced food; sports TVs; tree-shaded tables outside, open all day from 8am. *(Ian Phillips)*

Ship (020) 7929 3903

Talbot Court, off Eastcheap; EC3V 0BP Interesting pub tucked down alleyway; busy bare-boards bar with soft lighting and ornate decor, quieter upstairs carpeted bar usually set for dining, friendly efficient staff, several well kept ales including a house beer from St Austell, good value Nicholsons food; open all day weekdays, closed weekends. *(N R White)*

Simpsons Tavern (020) 762 69985

Just off Cornhill; EC3V 9DR Pleasingly old-fashioned place founded in 1757; rather clubby small panelled bar serving Bass, Harveys and a couple of guests, stairs down to another bar with snacks, traditional chophouse with upright stall seating (expect to share a table) and similar upstairs restaurant, good value food such as braised oxtail stew, steak and kidney pie and lancashire hotpot; open weekday lunchtimes and from 8am Tues-Fri for breakfast. *(Anon)*

Swan (020) 7929 6550

Ship Tavern Passage, off Gracechurch Street; EC3V 1LY Traditional Fullers pub with bustling narrow flagstoned bar, their ales kept well, generous lunchtime sandwiches and snacks, friendly efficient service, neatly kept Victorian panelled décor, low lighting, larger more ordinary carpeted bar upstairs; silent corner TV; covered alley used by smokers, open all day Mon-Fri (may be closed by 8.30pm), shut at weekends. *(N R White)*

EC4

✴Black Friar (020) 7236 5474

Queen Victoria Street; EC4V 4EG An architectural gem (some of the best Edwardian bronze and marble art nouveau work to be found anywhere) and built on site of 13th-c Dominican Priory; inner back room (the Grotto) with low vaulted mosaic ceiling, big bas-relief friezes of jolly monks set into richly coloured florentine marble walls, gleaming mirrors, seats built into golden marble recesses and an opulent pillared inglenook, tongue-in-cheek verbal embellishments such as Silence is Golden and Finery is Foolish, and try to spot the opium-smoking hints modelled into the front room's fireplace; ales including Fullers, Sharps and St Austell Nicholsons, plenty of wines by the glass, sound traditional all-day food (speciality pies); children welcome if quiet, plenty of room on wide forecourt, handy for new Blackfriars Station. *(Sue and Mike Todd, Stuart Doughty, N R White, Phil Bryant, G Jennings and others)*

Centre Page (020) 7236 3614

Aka the Horn; Knightrider Street near Millennium Bridge; EC4V 5BH Modernised pub with window booths or 'traps' in narrow entrance room, more space beyond, traditional style with panelling and subdued lighting, chatty atmosphere, mix of after-work drinkers and tourists, friendly efficient young staff, simple reasonably priced bar menu (from 9am for breakfast), downstairs dining room, well kept Fullers

ales, tea and coffee; background music; tables outside with good view of St Pauls. *(N R White)*

Old Bell (020) 7583 0216

Fleet Street, near Ludgate Circus; EC4Y 1DH Dimly lit 17th-c tavern backing on to St Brides, heavy black beams, bareboards and flagstones, stained-glass bow window, brass-topped tables, half a dozen or more well kept changing ales from island servery (can try before you buy, and tasting trays available), friendly efficient young staff, usual Nicholsons food, various seating nooks and coal fire, cheerful atmosphere; background music; covered and heated outside area, open all day (may close early weekend evenings). *(N R White, Conor McGaughey, David M Smith)*

✴Olde Cheshire Cheese

(020) 7353 6170 *Wine Office Court, off 145 Fleet Street; EC4A 2BU* Best to visit this 17th-c former chophouse outside peak times (early evening especially) when packed and staff may struggle; soaked in history with warmly old-fashioned unpretentious rooms, high beams, bare boards, old built-in black benches, Victorian paintings on dark brown walls, big open fires, tiny snug and steep stone steps down to unexpected series of cosy areas and secluded alcoves, Sam Smiths, all-day pubby food; look out for the famous parrot (now stuffed), which entertained princes and other distinguished guests for over 40 years; children allowed in eating area lunchtime only, closed Sun evening. *(David Carr, Dr and Mrs A K Clarke)*

Olde Watling (020) 7248 8935

Watling Street; EC4M 9BR Heavy-beamed and timbered post-blitz replica of pub built by Wren in 1668; interesting choice of well kept beers, standard Nicholsons menu, good service, quieter back bar and upstairs dining room; open all day. *(Phil Bryant)*

SW1

✴Albert (020) 7222 5577

Victoria Street; SW1H 0NP Busy open-plan airy bar with cut and etched windows, gleaming mahogany, ornate ceiling, solid comfortable furnishings, enjoyable pubby food all day from sandwiches up, well kept Fullers London Pride, Wells & Youngs Bombardier and guests, 24 wines by the glass, efficient cheerful service, handsome staircase lined with portraits of prime ministers leading up to carvery/dining room; background music, games machine, lavatories down steep stairs; children welcome if eating, open all day from 8am (breakfast till noon). *(Simon and Mandy King)*

✴Buckingham Arms (020) 7222 3386

Petty France; SW1H 9EU Welcoming and relaxed bow-windowed early 19th-c local, good value pubby food from back open kitchen, Wells & Youngs ales and a guest such as Sambrooks from long curved bar, good range of wines by the glass, elegant mirrors and dark woodwork, stained-glass screens, stools at modern high tables, some armchairs and upholstered banquettes, unusual side corridor with elbow ledge for drinkers; TV; dogs welcome, handy for Buckingham Palace, Westminster Abbey and St James's Park, open all day, till 6pm weekends. *(Dr and Mrs A K Clarke, Conor McGaughey, Phil Bryant)*

Cask & Glass (020) 7834 7630

Palace Street; SW1E 5HN Snug one-room traditional pub with good range of Shepherd Neame ales, friendly staff and atmosphere, good value lunchtime sandwiches, old prints and shiny black panelling; quiet corner TV; hanging baskets and a few tables outside, handy for Queen's Gallery, open all day, till 8pm Sat, closed Sun. *(Simon and Mandy King)*

Cask Pub & Kitchen

(020) 7630 7225 *Charlwood Street/Tachbrook Street; SW1V 2EE* Modern and spacious with simple furnishings, eight well kept frequently changing ales from far and wide, 14 foreign draught beers and over 500 in bottles, decent range of wines too, friendly knowledgeable staff, enjoyable food including sharing plates and good burgers, chatty atmosphere – can get packed evenings and noisy, regular beer related events like 'Meet the Brewer'; downstairs gents'; some outside seating, open all day. *(Dave Butler, Jack Sutcliffe, N R White, Richard Tilbrook, Brad W Morley)*

Clarence (020) 7930 4808

Whitehall; SW1A 2HP Civilised beamed corner pub (Geronimo Inn), Wells & Youngs and guests, decent wines by the glass, friendly chatty staff, well spaced tables and varied seating including tub chairs and banquettes, popular food all day from snacks up, upstairs dining area; pavement tables. *(Si Young)*

✶ Fox & Hounds (020) 7730 6367

Passmore Street/Graham Terrace; SW1W 8HR Small convivial Wells & Youngs local, warm red décor with big hunting prints, old sepia photographs and toby jugs, wall benches and sofas, book-lined back room, hanging plants under attractive skylight, coal-effect gas fire, some low-priced pubby food; can get crowded with after-work drinkers. *(Claes Mauroy)*

✶ Grenadier (020) 7235 3074

Wilton Row; the turning off Wilton Crescent looks prohibitive, but the barrier and watchman are there to keep out cars; SW1X 7NR Steps up to cosy old mews pub with lots of character and military history, but not much space (avoid

5-7pm); simple unfussy panelled bar, stools and wooden benches, changing ales such as Fullers, Timothy Taylors, Wells & Youngs and Woodfordes from rare pewter-topped counter, famous bloody marys, bar food on blackboard, intimate back restaurant, no mobiles or photography; children over 8 and dogs allowed, sentry box and single table outside, open all day. *(Conor McGaughey, Barry and Anne, Richard Tilbrook, Ian Phillips, Phil Bryant)*

Jugged Hare (020) 7828 1543

Vauxhall Bridge Road/Rochester Row; SW1V 1DX Popular Fullers Ale & Pie pub in former colonnaded bank; pillars, dark wood, balustraded balcony, large chandelier, busts and sepia London photographs, smaller back dining room, six well kept ales, reasonably priced food from sandwiches up including pie range, good friendly service; background music, TVs, silent fruit machine; open all day. *(Nigel and Sue Foster, N R White)*

✶ Lord Moon of the Mall

(020) 7839 7701 *Whitehall; SW1A 2DY* Wetherspoons bank conversion with elegant main room, big arched windows looking over Whitehall, old prints and a large painting of Tim Martin (founder of the chain), through an arch style is more recognisably Wetherspoons with neatly tiled areas, bookshelves opposite long bar, up to nine real ales and their good value food; silenced fruit machines, cash machine; children allowed if eating, dogs welcome, open all day from 9am (till midnight Fri, Sat). *(Andy Lickfold, Dr and Mrs A K Clarke, Pete Walker)*

Morpeth Arms (020) 7834 6442

Millbank; SW1P 4RW Victorian pub facing Thames, roomy and comfortable, with fine view across river from upstairs room, some etched and cut glass, lots of mirrors, paintings, prints and old photographs, well kept Wells & Youngs and a guest, decent choice of wines, enjoyable good value food served all day, welcoming staff, reputedly haunted (built on site of Millbank Prison, some cells remain below); background music; seats outside (a lot of traffic), handy for Tate Britain and Thames Path walkers. *(George and Marion Anderson)*

✶ Nags Head (020) 7235 1135

Kinnerton Street; SW1X 8ED Unspoilt little mews pub, low-ceilinged panelled front room with unusual sunken counter, log-effect gas fire in old range, narrow passage down to even smaller bar, Adnams from 19th-c handpumps, all-day no-frills food, theatrical mementoes, old what-the-butler-saw machine and one-armed bandit, no mobiles; individual background music; well behaved children and dogs allowed, a few seats outside, open all day. *(Conor McGaughey, John and Gloria Isaacs, Ole Ponpey, Mike Buckingham, Claes Mauroy)*

Orange (020) 7881 9844

Pimlico Road; SW1W 8NE Popular
gastropub with good choice of enjoyable food
including wood-fired pizzas, friendly attentive
staff, real ales such as Adnams, linked light
and airy rooms with rustic furniture and
relaxed weathered feel; children welcome,
four bedrooms, open all day from 8am.
(Richard Tilbrook)

Red Lion (020) 7930 5826

Parliament Street; SW1A 2NH Congenial
pub by Houses of Parliament, used by
Foreign Office staff and MPs, soft lighting,
parliamentary cartoons and prints, Fullers/
Gales beers and decent wines from long bar,
good range of food, efficient staff, also cellar
bar and small narrow upstairs dining room;
outside seating. *(Dr and Mrs A K Clarke)*

✳ Red Lion (020) 7321 0782

Duke of York Street; SW1Y 6JP Pretty
little Victorian pub, remarkably preserved
and packed with customers often spilling
out on to pavement by mass of foliage and
flowers; series of small rooms with lots of
polished mahogany, a gleaming profusion of
mirrors, cut/etched windows and chandeliers,
striking ornamental plaster ceiling, Fullers/
Gales beers, simple good value bar food (all
day weekdays, snacks evening, diners have
priority over a few of the front tables);
no children; dogs welcome, closed Sun
and bank holidays, otherwise open all day.
(Stuart Doughty, James Stretton, Ian Phillips)

Speaker (020) 7222 1749

Great Peter Street; SW1P 2HA Bustling
chatty atmosphere in unpretentious smallish
corner pub (can get packed at peak times),
well kept Timothy Taylors, Wells & Youngs
and guests, bottled beers and lots of whiskies,
limited simple food, friendly staff, panelling,
political cartoons and prints, no mobiles or
background music; open all day weekdays,
closed Sat, Sun. *(Nigel and Sue Foster)*

✳ St Stephens Tavern (020) 7925 2286

Parliament Street; SW1A 2JR Victorian
pub opposite Houses of Parliament and
Big Ben (so quite touristy), lofty ceilings
with brass chandeliers, tall windows with
etched glass and swagged curtains, gleaming
mahogany, charming upper gallery bar
(may be reserved for functions), four well
kept Badger ales from handsome counter
with pedestal lamps, friendly efficient staff,
enjoyable good value food from baguettes
up, Division Bell for MPs and lots of
parliamentary memorabilia; open
all day. *(Ross Balaam, Dave Braisted)*

SW3

✳ Coopers Arms (020) 7376 3120

Flood Street; SW3 5TB Useful bolthole
for Kings Road shoppers (so can get busy);
comfortable dark-walled open-plan bar with

mix of good-sized tables on floorboards,
pre-war sideboard and dresser, railway
clock, moose head, Wells & Youngs ales and
good all-day bar food; well behaved children
till 7pm, dogs in bar, seats in courtyard
garden. *(Richard and Penny Gibbs)*

Crown (020) 7352 9505

Dovehouse Street; SW3 6LB Little 19th-c
corner pub (part of the small Shannon
group) with decent food and well kept
beers such as Fullers and Marstons, friendly
service; pavement tables, open all day.
(Colin McKerrow)

Pigs Ear (020) 7352 2908

Old Church Street; SW3 5BS Civilised
L-shaped corner pub, friendly and relaxed,
with short interesting bar food choice and
more elaborate evening menu, lots of wines
by the glass including champagne and good
Ridge View english sparkling wine, three
changing ales such as Caledonian Deuchars
IPA, Sambrooks Junction and Uley Pigs Ear,
good coffee and service, tables and benches
on wood floors, butterflies and 1960s posters
on grey/green panelling, large mirrors and
huge windows, open fire, upstairs restaurant;
background music; children and dogs (in
bar) welcome, open all day. *(Richard and
Penny Gibbs)*

Surprise (020) 7351 6954

Christchurch Terrace; SW3 4AJ
Late Victorian Chelsea pub revamped
by Geronimo Inns and popular with well
heeled locals, Wells & Youngs, Sharps and
a house beer (HMS Surprise) from light
wood servery, champagne and plenty of
other wines by the glass, interesting food
including british tapas-style choices and
canapé boards, friendly service, soft grey
décor and comfortable furnishings with floral
sofas and armchairs on sturdy floorboards,
stained glass partitioning, upstairs dining
room, daily papers; open all day. *(Susan and
John Douglas)*

W1

Albany (020) 7387 0221

Great Portland Street; W1W 5QU Single
room pub with raised section in one corner,
eclectic mix of furnishings including some
big sofas and large tables, bare boards,
unusual lamps (quite low lighting), dramatic
patterned ceiling, three well kept real ales
from long bar, good choice of other beers
(some fruit ones), decent food including
interesting snacks, pleasant service.
(Jeremy King)

✳ Argyll Arms (020) 7734 6117

Argyll Street; W1F 7TP Popular and
unexpectedly individual pub with three
interesting little front cubicle rooms
(essentially unchanged since 1860s),
wooden partitions and impressive frosted

and engraved glass, mirrored corridor to spacious back room, Brains, Fullers, St Austell, Sharps and four guests, well liked all-day food in bar or upstairs dining room overlooking pedestrianised street, theatrical photographs; background music, fruit machine; children welcome till 8pm. *(Ross Balaam)*

⋆**Audley** (020) 7499 1843
Mount Street; W1K 2RX Classic late Victorian Mayfair pub, opulent red plush, mahogany panelling and engraved glass, chandelier and clock hanging in lovely carved wood bracket from ornately corniced ceiling, Fullers London Pride, Greene King IPA, Wells & Youngs Bombardier and guests from long polished bar, good choice of all-day pub food (reasonably priced for the area), friendly efficient service, upstairs panelled dining room; quiet background music, TV, pool; children till 6pm, pavement tables. *(Anon)*

Crown & Two Chairmen
(020) 7437 8192 *Bateman Street/Dean Street; W1D 3SB* Large main room with smaller area off to the right, different height tables on bare boards, Sharps Doom Bar and three other ales, decent food from bar snacks up including set menu, upstairs dining room, gets busy after work with mixed crowd. *(Jeremy King)*

French House (020) 7437 2477
Dean Street; W1D 5BG Character pub with impressive range of wines and bottled beers, other unusual drinks, some draught beers (no real ales or pint glasses), lively chatty atmosphere – mainly standing room, windows keeping good eye on passers-by, theatre memorabilia, efficient staff, good french-leaning food in upstairs restaurant; can get very busy evenings; open all day. *(Jeremy King)*

⋆**Grapes** (020) 7493 4216
Shepherd Market; W1J 7QQ Genuinely old-fashioned pub with dimly lit bar, plenty of well worn plush red furnishings, stuffed birds and fish in display cases, wood floors, panelling, coal fire and snug back alcove, six ales including Fullers, Sharps and a house beer from Brains, good choice of authentic thai food (not Sun evening), english food too, lots of customers (especially early evening) often spilling out on to square; children till 6pm weekdays (anytime weekends), open all day. *(Ian Phillips, Dr Matt Burleigh)*

⋆**Guinea** (020) 7409 1728
Bruton Place; W1J 6NL Lovely hanging baskets and chatty customers outside this tiny 17th-c mews pub, standing room only at peak times, appealingly simple with a few cushioned wooden seats and tables tucked to left of entrance, more in snug back area (most people prop themselves against the little side shelf), bare boards, old-fashioned

prints, red planked ceiling with raj fans, famous steak and kidney pie, grills and some sandwiches (no food weekends), Wells & Youngs and a guest from striking counter; very easy to walk into smart Guinea Grill (uniformed doormen will politely redirect you); no children; closed Sat lunchtime, Sun and bank holidays. *(Stuart Doughty, Dr Matt Burleigh)*

Three Greyhounds (020) 7494 0953
Greek Street; W1D 5DD Busy black and white timber-fronted pub in the heart of Soho, good range of beers and wines, Nicholsons menu; open all day. *(John and Gloria Isaacs)*

Three Tuns (020) 7408 0330
Portman Mews S; W1H 6HP Large bare-boards front bar and sizeable lounge/dining area with beams and nooks and crannies, Greene King, Timothy Taylors and Wells & Youngs, enjoyable reasonably priced pubby food, good friendly staff and vibrant atmosphere; street benches. *(Ian Phillips, Phil and Jane Hodson)*

Tottenham (020) 7636 8324
Oxford Street, near junction with Tottenham Court Road; W1D 1AZ Ornate late Victorian pub with long narrow bar, old tiling, mirrors mahogany fittings and so forth, also three notable murals behind glass of voluptuous nymphs, dark floorboards and leather banquettes, extensive range of reasonably priced beers, enjoyable all-day food from Nicholsons menu, friendly service, dining room downstairs; background music and fruit machine; can get very busy lunchtime. *(Susan and John Douglas, Comus and Sarah Elliott)*

W2

Mad Bishop & Bear
(020) 7402 2441 *Paddington Station; W2 1HB* Up escalators from concourse, full Fullers range kept well and a guest beer, good wine choice, reasonably priced standard food quickly served including breakfast from 8am (10am Sun), ornate plasterwork, etched mirrors and fancy lamps, parquet, tiles and carpet, booths with leather banquettes, lots of wood and prints, train departures screen; background music, TVs, games machine; tables out overlooking station, open all day till 11 (10.30 Sun). *(Dr and Mrs A K Clarke, Pete Walker)*

⋆**Victoria** (020) 7724 1191
Strathearn Place; W2 2NH Well run pub with lots of Victorian pictures and memorabilia, cast-iron fireplaces, gilded mirrors and mahogany panelling, brass mock-gas lamps above attractive horseshoe bar, bare boards and banquettes, relaxed chatty atmosphere, good friendly service, Fullers ales along with guests from smaller

breweries, several wines by the glass and good choice of reasonably priced popular food; upstairs has leather club chairs in small library/snug, and (mostly for private functions now) replica of Gaiety Theatre bar, all gilt and red plush; quiet background music, TV; pavement picnic-sets, open all day. *(Conor McGaughey, Ian Herdman, Dr and Mrs A K Clarke, Phil Bryant)*

WC1

⋆**Cittie of Yorke** (020) 7242 7670
High Holborn; WC1V 6BN Splendid back bar rather like a baronial hall with extraordinarily extended bar counter, 1,000-gallon wine vats resting above gantry, big bulbous lights hanging from soaring raftered roof, intimate ornately carved booths, triangular fireplace with grates on all three sides, smaller comfortable panelled room with lots of little prints of York, cheap Sam Smiths beers, bar food, lots of students, lawyers and City types but plenty of space to absorb crowds; fruit machine; children welcome, open all day, closed Sun. *(Stuart Doughty, Barry Collett, Pete Walker)*

⋆**Lamb** (020) 7405 0713
Lamb's Conduit Street; WC1N 3LZ Famously unspoilt Victorian pub with bank of cut-glass swivelling snob-screens around U-shaped counter, sepia photographs of 1890s actresses on ochre panelled walls, traditional cast-iron-framed tables, snug little back room, Wells & Youngs and guests, good choice of malt whiskies, straightforward pubby food; children welcome till 5pm, slatted wooden seats out in front, more in small courtyard, Foundling Museum nearby, open all day (till midnight Thurs-Sat). *(John and Gloria Isaacs, David Carr, Roy Hoing)*

Museum Tavern (020) 7242 8987
Museum Street/Great Russell Street; WC1B 3BA Traditional high-ceilinged ornate Victorian pub facing British Museum, busy lunchtime and early evening, but can be quite peaceful other times, seven well kept beers including some unusual ones, Weston's cider, several wines by the glass and good hot drinks, straightforward food, friendly helpful staff; one or two tables out under gas lamps, open all day. *(Eric Larkham)*

Norfolk Arms (020) 7388 3937
Leigh Street; WC1H 9EP Atmospheric tile-fronted pub with ornate ceilig and other high-Victorian features; real ales, nice wines and good tapas, friendly service; handy for British Museum. *(Richard Tilbrook)*

Penderels Oak (020) 7242 5669
High Holborn; WC1V 7HJ Vast Wetherspoons with attractive décor and woodwork, lots of books, pew seating around central tables, their well priced food and fine choice of good value real ales, efficient

friendly staff, cellar bar; pavement seating, open all day from 8am. *(Anon)*

Plough (020) 3582 3812
Museum Street/Little Russell Street; WC1A 1LH Popular and welcoming Bloomsbury local, with longish bar and upstairs drinking/dining room, well kept ales such as Greene King Abbot, enjoyable fairly priced food from short menu, quick service; a few tables out in front. *(John Wooll, Eric Larkham)*

⋆**Princess Louise** (020) 7405 8816
High Holborn; WC1V 7EP Splendid Victorian gin palace with extravagant décor – even the gents' has its own preservation order; gloriously opulent main bar with wood and glass partitions, fine etched and gilt mirrors, brightly coloured and fruit-shaped tiles, slender Portland stone columns soaring towards the lofty and deeply moulded plaster ceiling, open fire, cheap Sam Smiths from long counter, competitively priced pubby food (not Fri-Sun) in quieter upstairs room; gets crowded early weekday evenings, no children; open all day. *(Barry Collett, Ian Phillips, Giles and Annie Francis, Phil Bryant)*

Queens Larder (020) 7837 5627
Queen Square; WC1N 3AR Small character pub on corner of traffic-free square and cobbled Cosmo Place, also known as Queen Charlotte (where she stored goodies for her mad husband George III who was being cared for nearby); circular cast-iron tables, wall benches and stools around attractive U-shaped bar, theatre posters on dark panelled walls, Greene King ales, decent choice of fairly priced food including vegetarian dishes, upstairs function room; background jazz; dogs welcome, picnic-sets and heater outside. *(John Wooll, Phil Bryant)*

⋆**Skinners Arms** (020) 7837 5621
Judd Street; WC1H 9NT Richly decorated, with glorious woodwork, marble pillars, high ceilings and ornate windows, lots of London prints, interesting layout including comfortable back seating area, Greene King Abbot and guests from attractive long bar, decent home-made food; unobtrusive background music, muted corner TV; pavement picnic-sets, handy for British Library, open all day, closed Sun. *(Andy Lickfold)*

WC2

⋆**Chandos** (020) 7836 1401
St Martins Lane; WC2N 4ER Busy bare-boards bar (can get packed early evening) with snug cubicles, lots of theatre memorabilia on stairs up to smarter more comfortable lounge with opera photographs, low wooden tables, panelling, leather sofas and coloured windows, cheap Sam Smiths and reasonably priced food; background

music and games machines; children upstairs till 6pm, note the automaton on the roof (working 10am-2pm, 4-9pm), open all day from 9am (for breakfast). *(G Jennings)*

Coal Hole (020) 7379 9883

Strand; WC2R 0DW Well preserved Edwardian pub adjacent to the Savoy; original leaded windows, classical wall reliefs, mock-baronial high ceiling and raised back gallery, ten changing ales from central servery, standard Nicholsons menu, wine bar downstairs; sports TV; open all day. *(Dr and Mrs A K Clarke)*

✶ Cross Keys (020) 7836 5185

Endell Street/Betterton Street; WC2H 9EB Relaxed and friendly, quick service even at busy times, good lunchtime sandwiches and a few bargain hot dishes, three well kept Brodies ales and couple of guests (usually smaller London brewers), decent wines by the glass, masses of photographs and posters including Beatles memorabilia, brassware and tasteful bric-a-brac; fruit machine, gents' downstairs; sheltered outside cobbled area with flower tubs, open all day. *(John and Gloria Isaacs, Dr and Mrs A K Clarke)*

Edgar Wallace (020) 7353 3120

Essex Street; WC2R 3JE Simple spacious open-plan pub dating from 18th c, eight well kept ales including some unusual ones and a beer badged for them from Nethergate, enjoyable good value food all day including doorstep sandwiches, friendly efficient service, half-panelled walls and red ceilings, interesting Edgar Wallace memorabilia (pub renamed 1975 to mark his centenary) and lots of old beer and cigarette adverts, upstairs dining room; a few high tables in side alleyway, closed weekends. *(LM, Andy and Jill Kassube)*

George (020) 7353 9638

Strand; WC2R 1AP Timbered pub near the law courts, long narrow bare-boards bar, nine real ales and a dozen wines by the glass, lunchtime food from sandwiches to good value weekday carvery in upstairs bar, separate evening menu, comedy club Sat night; sports TVs; open all day. *(Anon)*

Knights Templar (020) 7831 2660

Chancery Lane; WC2A 1DT Reliable Wetherspoons in big-windowed former bank, marble pillars, handsome fittings and plasterwork, good bustling atmosphere on two levels, some interesting real ales at bargain prices, good wine choice and usual well priced food, friendly staff; remarkably handsome lavatories; open all day Mon-Fri, till 7pm Sat, closed Sun. *(Tracey and Stephen Groves, Andy and Jill Kassube, Ian Herdman)*

Lady Ottoline (020) 7831 0008

Northington Street; WC1N 2JF Restored Bloomsbury pub with enjoyable food from

short menu, four real ales and good wines, friendly service, upstairs dining rooms; peaceful atmosphere despite TV; open all day. *(Tom and Ruth Rees)*

Porterhouse (020) 7379 7917

Maiden Lane; WC2E 7NA Good daytime pub (can be packed evenings), London outpost of Dublin's Porterhouse microbrewery, their interesting beers along with guests and lots of bottled imports, good choice of wines by the glass, reasonably priced food from sandwiches up, shiny three-level labyrinth of stairs (lifts for disabled), galleries and copper ducting and piping, some nice design touches, sonorous openwork clock, neatly cased bottled beer displays; background and live music, sports TV (repeated in gents'); tables on front terrace, open all day. *(James Longridge)*

Salisbury (020) 7836 5863

St Martins Lane; WC2N 4AP Gleaming Victorian pub in the heart of the West End, a wealth of cut glass and mahogany, curved upholstered wall seat creating impression of several distinct areas, wonderfully ornate bronze light fittings, lots of mirrors, back room popular with diners (can be closed for private functions) and separate small side room, some interesting photographs including Dylan Thomas enjoying a drink here in 1941, lots of theatre posters, up to six well kept ales, bar food all day, coffees and cheerful staff; steep stairs down to lavatories; children allowed till 5pm, fine details on building exterior, seats in pedestrianised side alley, open till midnight Fri, Sat. *(Mike Gorton, Tracey and Stephen Groves, Colin and Ruth Munro, Michael Butler, B and M Kendall and others)*

✶ Ship & Shovell (020) 7839 1311

Craven Passage, off Craven Street; WC2N 5PH Well kept Badger ales and a guest, good friendly staff, decent reasonably priced food including wide range of baguettes etc; brightly lit with dark wood, etched mirrors and interesting mainly naval pictures, plenty of tables, open fire, compact back section, separate partitioned bar across Underneath the Arches alley; TV; open all day, closed Sun. *(Taff Thomas, Andy and Jill Kassube)*

EAST LONDON

E1

✶ Prospect of Whitby (020) 3603 4041

Wapping Wall; E1W 3SH Claims to be oldest pub on Thames dating from 1520 (although largely rebuilt after much later fire), was known as the Devil's Tavern and has a colourful history (Pepys and Dickens used it regularly and Turner came for weeks at a time to study the river views) – tourists love it; L-shaped bar has plenty of beams, bare boards, flagstones and panelling, ales such as Adnams, Fullers, Wells & Youngs and Woodfordes from fine pewter counter, good choice of wines by the glass, bar food from sandwiches up, more formal restaurant upstairs; children welcome (only if eating after 5.30pm), unbeatable views towards Docklands from tables on waterfront courtyard, open all day. *(Paul Rampton, Julie Harding, Phil Bryant, N R White, Phil and Jane Hodson and others)*

Town of Ramsgate (020) 7481 8000

Wapping High Street; E1W 2PN Interesting old-London Thames-side setting affording a restricted but evocative river view from small back floodlit terrace with mock gallows (hanging dock was nearby), long narrow chatty bar with squared oak panelling, ales such as Bath, Fullers London Pride and Sharps Doom Bar, friendly helpful service, good choice of generous standard food and daily specials, various deals; background music, Mon quiz; open all day. *(Brian and Anna Marsden)*

Water Poet (020) 7426 0495

Folgate Street; E1 6BX Big rambling Spitalfields pub with bohemian feel, enjoyable food in bar and dining room including good Sun roasts, real ales such as Dark Star, London Fields, Meantime and Trumans, decent wines, friendly staff and good mix of customers, comfortable leather sofas and armchairs on wood floor, basement bar/function room, comedy club, separate pool room with two tables; sports TV; big enclosed outside area with 'barn' room and barbecue, open all day. *(Tom and Ruth Rees)*

E3

✳ Crown (020) 8880 7261

Grove Road/Old Ford Road; E3 5SN Stylish dining pub (Geronimo Inn) with relaxed welcoming bar, faux animal hide stools and chunky pine tables on polished boards, big bay window with comfortable scatter cushion seating area, books etc on open shelves, well kept Wells & Youngs and guests, good choice of wines by the glass, friendly chatty young staff, three individually decorated upstairs dining areas overlooking Victoria Park, imaginative well priced food (all day Sun); background music; children and dogs welcome, open all day. *(Paul Sherfield)*

E10

King William IV (020) 8556 2460

High Road Leyton; E10 6AE Imposing flower-decked Victorian building, home to Brodies brewery; up to 20 well kept low-priced ales including guests, beer festivals, enjoyable bargain food, darts and bar billiards; big-screen sports TV; eight bedrooms. *(Anon)*

E11

George (020) 8989 2921

High Street Wanstead; E11 2RL Large popular Wetherspoons in former 18th-c coaching inn, their usual good value food and real ales, plenty of books to read, pictures of famous Georges down the ages, friendly atmosphere. *(Robert Lester)*

Red Lion (020) 8988 2929

High Road Leytonstone; E11 3AA Large friendly 19th-c corner pub revamped by the Antic group with plenty of quirky character, high-ceilinged open-plan interior with lots of pictures, mirrors, books and general bric-a-brac, ten changing ales, real ciders, enjoyable good value pubby food, bar billiards and table football; weekend DJs and live music; children welcome, back garden, open all day. *(John and Annabel Hampshire, Robert Person, Phil Bryant)*

E14

✳ Grapes (020) 7987 4396

Narrow Street; E14 8BP Relatively unchanged since Charles Dickens used it as a model for his Six Jolly Fellowship Porters in *Our Mutual Friend*; a proper traditional tavern with friendly atmosphere and good mix of customers, partly panelled bar with lots of prints of actors, old local maps and the pub itself, elaborately etched windows, plates along a shelf, daily papers, larger back area leading to small deck with views over river towards Canary Wharf, Adnams, Marstons, Timothy Taylors and a guest, good value tasty food, upstairs fish restaurant with fine views; no children, dogs on lead welcome, can catch Canary Wharf ferry and enter pub via steps from foreshore, open all day. *(Mike Gorton, Ross Balaam, John and Gloria Isaacs, Claes Mauroy, John Wooll and others)*

Narrow (020) 7592 7950

Narrow Street; E14 8DJ Popular stylish dining pub (owned by Gordon Ramsay) with great Thames views from window seats and covered terrace, simple but smart bar with white walls and blue woodwork, mosaic-tiled fireplaces and colourfully striped armchairs, Adnams, Greene King and a guest, good wines, food from bar snacks to pricier restaurant meals, dining room also white with matching furnishings, local maps and prints, and a boat complete with oars; background and some live music; children welcome, open all day. *(Anon)*

NORTH LONDON

N1

Albion (020) 7607 7450

Thornhill Road; N1 1HW Charming wisteria-clad Georgian building in Islington conservation area; attractive bare-boards interior with minimalist front bar and spacious back lounge/dining room, interesting choice of enjoyable mid-priced home-made food, a couple of well kept ales such as Caledonian Deuchars IPA and Ringwood Best, helpful cheerful service, Victorian gents'; tables out at front and in impressive walled back garden with pergola, open all day. *(Phil Bryant)*

Charles Lamb (020) 7837 5040

Elia Street; N1 8DE Small friendly backstreet pub with four well kept ales including Dark Star, interesting bottled beers and decent choice of wines by the glass including own-label, good blackboard food (french and english), big windows, polished boards and simple traditional furniture; background jazz; tables outside, closed Mon and Tues lunchtimes, otherwise open all day. *(Anon)*

Crown (020) 7837 7107

Cloudesley Road; N1 0EB Good food and bustling atmosphere in Victorian Fullers pub, their ales from impressive island bar with snob screens, scrubbed boards, plenty of light oak panelling and cut and etched glass, helpful friendly staff; dogs welcome, tables out on small railed front terrace, quiet tree-lined street. *(Anon)*

✶ Duke of Cambridge (020) 7359 3066

St Peters Street; N1 8JT Warmly inviting and was London's first organic pub, simply decorated busy main room with chunky wooden tables, pews and benches on bare boards, corridor past open kitchen to more formal dining room and conservatory Little Valley Tod's Blonde and Withens Pale Ale, St Peters Best Bitter and a guest from Pitfield, also organic draught lagers, ciders, spirits and wines, interesting bar food using seasonal produce, teas and coffees; children welcome, dogs in bar, open all day. *(LM, Mary Shaw, Adrian Scott)*

Eagle (020) 7250 0507

Shepherdess Walk/City Road; N1 7LB On site of the Eagle referred to in Pop Goes the Weasel – 'Up and down the City Road, In and out the Eagle...' ; bare-boards Edwardian pub with original features including tiling and sturdy iron pillars, mix of furniture from leather benches to sofas (some well worn), Fullers London Pride, Sharps Doom Bar and guests from panelled central servery, enjoyable home-made food including sandwiches and blackboard specials, fixed price menu too; busy at lunchtime; fine for wheelchairs (once over entrance threshold), seats outside, open all day from noon (11am Sun) and till 1am Fri, Sat. *(Simon and Mandy King, Roger and Donna Huggins)*

Earl of Essex (020) 7424 5828

Danbury Street; N1 8LE Recently reopened one-room Islington pub now brewing its own Earl ales on site, great choice of other beers too on draught and in bottles, straightforward home-made food with beer recommendations listed on menu; back walled garden, open all day (from 3pm Mon). *(Anon)*

Fellow (020) 7837 3001

York Way; N1 9AA Contemporary pub-restaurant by King's Cross Station, gets very busy and booking advised, well liked unusual food, real ales and good choice of wines, friendly staff coping well, upstairs cocktail bar; background music; roof terrace. *(Pauline Fellows and Simon Robbins)*

Hemingford Arms (020) 7607 3303

Hemingford Road; N1 1DF Ivy-clad Capital pub filled with bric-a-brac, good choice of real ales from central servery, traditional food alongside good evening thai menu, open fire, upstairs bar, live music and Weds quiz night; sports TV, machines; picnic-sets outside. *(Perry Benson)*

✶ Island Queen (020) 7354 8741

Noel Road; N1 8HD Fine high-ceilinged Victorian pub handy for Camden Passage antiques area, Fullers London Pride, a guest ale, lots of imported beers and good value wines from island bar, sensibly short choice of fresh often unusual food, pleasant staff and laid-back atmosphere, dark wood and big decorative mirrors, intimate back area, upstairs room; popular weekend evenings with young crowd; children welcome, café-style pavement tables, open all day. *(John Wooll)*

✶ Parcel Yard (020) 7713 7258

King's Cross Station, N end of new concourse, up stairs (or lift); N1C 4AH Impressive restoration of listed Victorian parcel sorting office, lots of interesting bare-boards rooms off corridors around airy central atrium, pleasing old-fashioned feel with exposed pipework and ducting adding to the effect, back bar serving full range of Fullers beers plus guests from long modern counter, plenty of wines by the glass, similar upstairs area with old and new furniture including comfortable sofas, railway memorabilia and some nice touches like Victorian envelope wallpaper, good imaginative food from bar snacks up, breakfast till 11.45am, prompt smiling service, power points to recharge phones/laptops, platform views; open all day from 8am (9am Sun). *(Susan and John Douglas, David and Sue Smith, Peter Wright, Pete Walker)*

N6

✶ Flask (020) 8348 7346

Highgate West Hill; N6 6BU Comfortable traditional Georgian pub owned by Fullers; intriguing up-and-down layout, sash-windowed bar hatch, panelling and high-backed carved settle in snug lower area with log fire, enjoyable food from pub favourites to more elaborate dishes, efficient friendly service; picnic-sets out in front courtyard, handy for strolls around Highgate village or Hampstead Heath, open all day. *(John Wooll, John and Gloria Isaacs, Phil Bryant, N R White, Roger and Donna Huggins)*

Prince of Wales (020) 8340 0445

Highgate High Street; N6 5JX Small unpretentious bare-boards local, said to be haunted, bench seats, stools and old wooden tables, two coal-effect gas fires, well kept Butcombe and up to three guests from horseshoe bar, decent choice of blackboard wines, food from thai dishes to Sun roasts, friendly prompt service; background music, TV, Tues quiz; tables on small terrace behind, open all day. *(John and Sarah Webb)*

Victoria (020) 8340 4609

North Hill; N6 4QA Tucked-away traditional Victorian pub in tree-lined street, Harveys, Timothy Taylors Landlord and Wells & Youngs, good food including popular Sun lunch, themed nights, Mon quiz; children and dogs welcome. *(Anon)*

N8

Kings Head (020) 8340 1028

Crouch End Hill/Broadway; N8 8AA Victorian corner pub with well kept ales such as Sambrooks and Sharps, good choice of other drinks, enjoyable food including set menu, friendly helpful staff, downstairs comedy club; background music, TV; open all day (till 2am Fri, Sat). *(John Wooll)*

N19   TQ3086

Landseer (020) 7263 4658

Landseer Road; N19 4JU Popular family dining pub with big windows overlooking small square, scrubbed pine tables and some leather sofas, lots of pot plants, enjoyable food including tapas, ales such as Harveys Best and Wells & Youngs Bombardier, daily newspapers, Mon quiz; background and some live music; pavement tables. *(Jeremy King)*

NW1

Albert (020) 7722 1886

Princess Road; NW1 8JR Welcoming split-level Victorian corner pub tucked away in residential street; partly green-tiled exterior, roomy U-shaped bar with corniced ceiling, bare boards and cast-iron fireplace, some old photographs, decent selection of fairly priced pubby food from panini and baked potatoes up including good fish and chips, well kept Greene King and Timothy Taylors Landlord, obliging friendly staff, conservatory, live music and quiz nights; children welcome, attractive back garden. *(Phil Bryant)*

☆ Chapel (020) 7402 9220

Chapel Street; NW1 5DP Busy and noisy in the evening (quieter during the day) this dining pub attracts an equal share of drinkers, spacious cream-painted rooms dominated by open kitchen, smart but simple furnishings, sofas at lounge end by big fireplace, Adnams and Greene King ales, good choice of wines by the glass, several coffees and teas, well liked food from shortish blackboard menu, prompt service; children and dogs welcome, picnic-sets in sizeable back garden, more seats on decking under heated parasols, covered smokers' area, open all day. *(Michael Rugman, Jeremy King)*

☆ Doric Arch (020) 7388 2221

Eversholt Street; NW1 2DN Virtually part of Euston Station, up stairs from bus terminus with raised back part overlooking it, well kept Fullers ales and guests, Weston's cider, friendly prompt service (even when busy), enjoyable well priced pubby food lunchtime and from 4pm weekdays (12-5pm weekends), pleasantly nostalgic atmosphere and some quiet corners, intriguing train and other transport memorabilia including big clock at entrance, downstairs restaurant; discreet sports TV, machines, lavatories on combination lock; open all day. *(Tony and Wendy Hobden, Dr and Mrs A K Clarke, Dennis Jones, N R White, Eric Larkham and others)*

Edinboro Castle (020) 7255 9651

Mornington Terrace/Delancy Street; NW1 7RU Open-plan bare-boards pub with reasonably priced all-day food from open kitchen including set menu choices, lots of wines by the glass, ales such as Sharps Doom Bar and Timothy Taylors Landlord, raised skylit back area with small fireplace; background music may be loud, and can get very busy with young evening crowd; children welcome, big enclosed sunny garden with bar, summer barbecues. *(Jeremy King)*

Engineer (020) 7483 1890

Gloucester Avenue; NW1 8JH Refurbished Mitchells & Butlers pub with L-shaped panelled bar, dining area and individual more ornate rooms upstairs, good choice of popular food, Sharps Doom Bar and a couple of guests, plenty of wines by the glass, good service; TV for major sporting events; children welcome, attractive secluded garden (some tables set for dining), handy for Primrose Hill, open all day from 9am for breakfast. *(Taff Thomas, Jeremy King)*

Euston Flyer (020) 7383 0856

Euston Road, opposite British Library; NW1 2RA Big welcoming open-plan pub, Fullers/Gales beers, good choice of standard food all day, relaxed lunchtime atmosphere, plenty of light wood, mix of furniture on carpet or boarded floors, mirrors, photographs of old London, smaller raised areas and private corners, big doors open to street in warm weather; background music, Sky TV, silent games machine, can get packed evenings; open all day, till 8.30pm Sun. *(Dr and Mrs A K Clarke, Eric Larkham, Pete Walker)*

Euston Tap (020) 3137 8837

Euston Road; NW1 2EF Small gatehouse-type building in front of Euston Station, good selection of ever-changing real ales and other beers from around the world including a huge bottled range; identical building opposite is dedicated to ciders/perries. *(Clive Connor, Eric Larkham)*

Lansdowne (020) 7483 0409

Gloucester Avenue; NW1 8HX Tile-fronted 19th-c corner pub, dark Anaglypta ceiling and dado, wooden tables and chairs on varnished boards, open fire with picture of the pub above, candles on shelves, ales such as Wells & Youngs Bombardier, enjoyable mediterranean-influenced food from open kitchen, pizzas and snacks available all day, also weekend breakfasts; children welcome, street tables. *(Jeremy King)*

Metropolitan (020) 7486 3489

Baker Street Station, Marylebone Road; NW1 5LA Wetherspoons in impressively ornate Victorian hall, large with lots of tables on one side, very long bar the other, leather sofas and some elbow tables, ten or more real ales, good coffee, their usual inexpensive food; games machines; family area, open all day. *(Tony Hobden)*

Pembroke Castle (020) 7483 2927

Gloucester Avenue; NW1 8JA Popular split-level bare-boards pub, Brakspears and Sharps Doom Bar, decent quickly served food including pizzas, short wine list (but most by the glass), newspapers, upstairs dining/function room; background music, TV, Mon quiz; children welcome, spacious terrace. *(Jeremy King)*

✶ Queens Head & Artichoke

(020) 7916 6206 *Albany Street; NW1 4EA* Corner pub-restaurant near Regent's Park with good sensibly priced modern food (all day Sun) including tapas, blackboard sherries and good choice of wines by the glass, well kept Adnams, Marstons, Sharps and Timothy Taylors from Edwardian counter, bare boards and panelling, large leaded windows, upstairs dining room; may be background music; pavement picnic-sets under awning. *(Jeremy King)*

NW3

✶ Flask (020) 7435 4580

Flask Walk; NW3 1HE Bustling local (popular haunt of Hampstead artists, actors and local characters), unassuming old-fashioned bar, unique Victorian screen

dividing it from cosy lounge with smart banquettes, panelling, lots of little prints and attractive fireplace, Wells & Youngs and a guest like Sambrooks, 30 wines by the glass and maybe winter mulled wine, popular all-day food, good friendly service, redecorated dining conservatory; background music, TV; children (till 8pm) and dogs welcome, seats and tables in alley, open all day. *(B J Harding, Tom McLean, N R White)*

Magdala (020) 7435 2503

South Hill Park; NW3 2SB Where Ruth Ellis (the last woman to be hanged in England) shot her lover – the bullet holes are still visible outside; bar with minimal decoration and a piano, three real ales, dining lounge with leather chesterfields and open fire, second more formal dining room, good variety of food from sharing plates up, bar snacks including home-made crisps, friendly staff; open all day. *(Roger and Donna Huggins, Tom McLean)*

✶ Spaniards Inn (020) 8731 8406

Spaniards Lane; NW3 7JJ Busy 16th-c pub right next to Heath with charming big garden split up into areas by careful planting, flagstoned walk among roses, side arbour with climbing plants and plenty of seats on crazy-paved terrace (arrive early weekends as popular with dog walkers and families); attractive and characterful low-ceilinged rooms with oak panelling, antique winged settles, snug alcoves and open fires, up to five real ales, two ciders, continental draught lagers and several wines by glass, popular all-day pubby food with a few twists, upstairs dining room; car park fills fast and nearby parking is difficult. *(Barry and Anne, James White, Phil Bryant, N R White and others)*

NW5   TQ2886

✶ Bull & Last (020) 7267 8955

Highgate Road; NW5 1QS Traditional décor with a stylish twist and liked by customers of all ages; single room with big windows, colonial-style fans in planked ceiling, collection of tankards, faded map of London, stuffed bulls' heads and pheasants, good imaginative food (not cheap), takeaway tubs of home-made ice-cream and picnic hampers for Hampstead Heath, four well kept changing ales, nice selection of wines and plenty of whiskies and gins (maybe own sloe gin), friendly enthusiastic staff; quiz Sun evening; children (away from bar) and dogs welcome, hanging baskets and picnic-sets by street, open all day. *(Tim Maddison, Gerry Price)*

Junction Tavern (020) 7485 9400

Fortess Road; NW5 1AG Victorian corner pub with good fresh food (service charge added) including some enterprising dishes in bar, dining room and back conservatory, modern décor, St Austell, Sambrooks, Shepherd Neame and Thwaites (beer festivals), good choice of wines by the glass, friendly staff; background music; no children after 7pm, garden tables, open all day Fri-Sun, closed lunchtimes Mon-Thurs. *(Phil Bryant)*

Southampton Arms
Highgate Road; NW5 1LE Nicely restored, well run little pub with impressive range of small-brewery beers, ciders and perries, snacky food including good rolls and scotch eggs, can get crowded. *(Tim Maddison, Gerry Price)*

NW7

Adam & Eve (020) 8959 1553
The Ridgeway; NW7 1RL Nicely revamped Edwardian dining pub in Mill Hill village area, good food from eclectic menu including set menu choices, up to six fairly mainstream ales, decent wines and coffee, dining rooms upstairs, winter log fires, some live music and monthly quiz; children and dogs welcome, walled garden behind, open all day. *(Anon)*

NW8

Clifton (020) 7624 5233
Clifton Hill; NW8 0JT Attractive bare-boards rooms around ornate central servery, stripped pine and Victorian-style wallpaper, conservatory, enjoyable varied choice of food and well kept ales; children welcome, leafy front terrace with big umbrellas and heaters. *(Anon)*

SOUTH LONDON

SE1

Anchor (020) 7407 1577
Bankside; SE1 9EF In great Thames-side spot with river views from upper floors and roof terrace, beams, stripped brickwork and old-world corners, well kept Fullers London Pride and Wells & Youngs, good choice of wines by the glass, popular fish and chip bar including takeaways, other good value all-day food as well as breakfast and tearoom; can get very busy and service may suffer; background music; provision for children, disabled access, more tables under big parasols on raised riverside terrace, bedrooms in friendly quiet Premier Inn behind. *(N R White, Pete Walker)*

Anchor & Hope (020) 7928 9898
The Cut; SE1 8LP Informal bare-boards gastropub, food from changing menu can be good (and prices can be high), well kept

Wells & Youngs and guests, sensibly priced wines by tumbler or carafe, plain bar with big windows and mix of furniture including elbow tables, curtained-off dining part with small open kitchen, tight-packed scrubbed tables and contemporary art; children and dogs welcome, closed Sun evening and Mon lunchtime, otherwise open all day. *(Tim Maddison, John Saville, Gerry Price)*

Doggetts Coat & Badge
(020) 7633 9081 *By Blackfriars Bridge; SE1 9UD* Modern Nicholsons pub on four floors with great Thames views, ten well kept interesting beers, pleasant service, their usual menu including children's choices; TVs; nice outside drinking area by the river, open all day. *(Dave Braisted, Ian Phillips)*

Fire Station (020) 7620 2226
Waterloo Road; SE1 8SB Unusual fire station conversion, busy and noisy, with two huge knocked-through tiled rooms, lots of wooden tables and mix of chairs, pews and worn leather armchairs, distinctive box-shaped floral lampshades, sizeable plants, back bar with red fire buckets on shelf, smarter dining room, good modern all-day food, real ales and plenty of wines by the glass including champagne, prices on the high side; background music; children welcome, tables out in front, picnic-sets in scruffy side alley, handy for Old Vic, open all day from 9am for breakfast. *(Simon Collett-Jones, Ian Phillips)*

✴ Founders Arms (020) 7928 1899
Hopton Street; SE1 9JH Modern building with glass walls in superb location – outstanding terrace views along Thames and handy for South Bank attractions; plenty of customers (City types, tourists, theatre- and gallery-goers) spilling on to pavement and river walls, Wells & Youngs and a guest, lots of wines by glass, good choice of well priced bar food all day (weekend breakfasts from 9am), tea and coffee from separate servery, cheerful service; background music; children welcome away from bar, open till midnight Fri, Sat. *(Val and Alan Green, David Carr, Robert Lester, Pete Walker, Jeremy King)*

✴ George (020) 7407 2056
Off 77 Borough High Street; SE1 1NH Tucked-away 16th-c coaching inn (mentioned in Little Dorrit), now owned by National Trust and beautifully preserved; lots of tables in bustling cobbled courtyard with views of the tiered exterior galleries, series of no-frills ground-floor rooms with black beams, square-latticed windows and some panelling, plain oak or elm tables on bare boards, old-fashioned built-in settles, dimpled glass

---

If you report on a pub that's not a featured entry, please tell us any lunchtimes or evenings when it doesn't serve bar food.

lanterns and a 1797 Act of Parliament clock, impressive central staircase up to series of dining-rooms and balcony, well kept Greene King ales plus a beer for the pub, good value traditional food all day (not Sun evening), friendly staff; children welcome away from bar, open all day. *(Michael Butler, B and M Kendall, Pete Walker)*

Horniman (020) 7407 1991

Hays Galleria, off Battlebridge Lane; SE1 2HD Spacious, bright and airy Thames-side drinking hall with lots of polished wood, comfortable seating including a few sofas, upstairs seating, several real ales with unusual guests (may offer tasters), lunchtime food from soup and sandwiches up, snacks other times, efficient bar staff coping with large numbers after work; unobtrusive background music; fine river views from picnic-sets outside, open all day. *(Anon)*

⋆ Kings Arms (020) 7207 0784

Roupell Street; SE1 8TB Proper corner local, bustling and friendly, with curved servery dividing traditional bar and lounge, bare boards and attractive local prints, well kept changing ales, good wine and malt whisky choice, welcoming efficient staff, enjoyable food from thai dishes to Sun roasts, big back extension with conservatory/courtyard dining area; background music; open all day. *(Richard Endacott, Stephen and Jean Curtis)*

Mad Hatter (020) 7401 9222

Stamford Street, Blackfriars Road end; SE1 9NY Fullers pub-hotel in former hat factory; smartly Edwardianised bar with booth seating, etched glass, lots of prints and interesting hat collection, traditional food including pies, four well kept beers and fine choice of whiskies, helpful staff; clean bedrooms, open all day. *(Claes Mauroy)*

⋆ Market Porter (020) 7407 2495

Stoney Street; SE1 9AA Properly pubby no-frills place opening at 6am weekdays for workers at neighbouring market, up to ten unusual real ales (over 60 guests a week) often from far-flung brewers and in top condition, particularly helpful friendly service, bare boards and open fire, beams with beer barrels balanced on them, simple furnishings, food in bar and upstairs lunchtime restaurant; background music; children allowed weekends till 7pm, dogs welcome, drinkers often spill out on to street, open all day. *(Mike Gorton, N R White, Neil Hardwick, Comus and Sarah Elliott, Pete Walker, Jeremy King)*

Rake (020) 7407 0557

Winchester Walk; SE1 9AG Tiny discreetly modern Borough Market bar with amazing bottled beer range in wall-wide cooler, also half a dozen continental lagers on tap and three real ales, good friendly service;

fair-sized covered and heated outside area. *(N R White, Comus and Sarah Elliott, Jeremy King)*

Wheatsheaf (020) 7407 9934

Southwark Street; SE1 1TY In cellars beneath the Hop Exchange, brick vaulted ceilings and iron pillars, great range of well kept changing beers, decent pubby food; sports TV; open all day. *(Pete Walker)*

Wheatsheaf (020) 7940 3880

Stoney Street; opposite Borough Market main entrance under new railway bridge; SE1 9AA Recently reopened Youngs pub (had been shut for three years) with comfortably refurbished interior, three of their well kept beers and a guest, 'street food with style' from side campervan kitchen; open all day from 9am (midday Sun). *(Comus and Sarah Elliott)*

White Hart (020) 7928 9190

Cornwall Road/Whittlesey Street; SE1 8TJ Backstreet corner local near Waterloo Station, friendly community bustle, comfortable sofas, stripped boards and so forth, Fullers London Pride, Sharps Doom Bar and two guests, several belgian beers including fruit ones, good range of ciders and wines, sensibly priced up-to-date blackboard food as well as pub standards, helpful efficient staff; background music; open all day. *(Phil Bryant, Adam Gordon)*

SE5

⋆ Crooked Well (020) 7252 7798

Grove Lane; SE5 8SY Popular early 19th-c restauranty pub with really good imaginative food (not especially cheap), nice wines and cocktails, Sharps Doom Bar, welcoming helpful staff; seats outside, closed Mon lunchtime, otherwise open all day. *(Jeremy Bennett, John Saville, Matthew Read)*

SE8

Dog & Bell (020) 8692 5664

Prince Street; SE8 3JD Friendly old-fashioned tucked-away local on Thames Path, wood benches around bright, cheerfully decorated L-shaped bar, half a dozen well kept ales including Fullers, bottled belgians, prompt friendly service, reasonably priced pub food including good sandwiches, dining room, bar billiards; TV; tables in yard, open all day. *(Anon)*

SE10

Cutty Sark (020) 8858 3146

Ballast Quay, off Lassell Street; SE10 9PD Great Thames views from this early 19th-c Greenwich tavern, genuinely unspoilt old-fashioned bar, dark flagstones, simple furnishings including barrel seats, open fires, narrow openings to tiny side snugs, upstairs room (reached by winding staircase) with ship deck-feel and prized seat in big bow window, up to five changing ales, organic wines, malt whiskies, all-day bar food; background music; children and dogs welcome, busy riverside terrace across narrow cobbled lane, limited parking (but free if you get a space). *(John Saville)*

SE12   TQ3974

Lord Northbrook (020) 8318 1127
Burnt Ash Road; SE12 8PU Recently refurbished and opened up Victorian corner pub, welcoming friendly staff, enjoyable food from sharing plates up, five interesting ales; open all day. *(Jason Wollington, Kath Butler)*

SE15   TQ3475

Old Nuns Head (020) 7639 4007
Nunhead Green; SE15 3QQ Open-plan 1930s brick and timber pub on edge of small green, four well kept changing ales and enjoyable food from standards up including some interesting choices, roasts only on Sun, cheerful efficient staff, Thurs quiz; children welcome, back garden and a few seats out in front, handy for the fascinating Nunhead Cemetery. *(John Wooll)*

SE16

★ Mayflower (020) 7237 4088
Rotherhithe Street; SE16 4NF Unchanging cosy old riverside pub in unusual street with lovely early 18th-c church; good generous bar food including more upmarket daily specials, Greene King and guests, good value wines and decent coffee, obliging service, black beams, panelling, nautical bric-a-brac, high-backed settles and coal fires, good Thames views from upstairs evening restaurant; background music; children welcome, fun jetty/terrace over water (barbecues), open all day. *(Phil Bryant)*

SE19   TQ3370

Westow House (020) 8670 0654
Westow Hill; SE19 1TX Character local with eight well kept beers and good if limited all-day food, busy convivial atmosphere. *(Brian and Anna Marsden)*

SE21

Crown & Greyhound
(020) 8299 4976 *Dulwich Village; SE21 7BJ* Big busy (especially evenings) Victorian pub with cosy period interior, traditional upholstered settles and stripped kitchen tables on bare boards, big back dining room, conservatory, Fullers London

Pride, Harveys and a couple of guests (Easter beer festival and summer cider festival), just under two dozen wines by the glass, straightforward bar food (all day), popular Sun carvery, service can be slow; background music; children and dogs welcome, summer barbecues in pleasant back garden. *(Christine Murphy, Giles and Annie Francis)*

SE24

Florence (020) 7326 4987
Dulwich Road; SE24 0NG Tile-fronted Victorian pub visibly brewing its own ales, guest beers and farm cider available too, enjoyable sensibly priced food including Sun roasts, friendly busy atmosphere, contemporary décor with comfortable booth seating, open fire, conservatory; children's play room, a few tables out in front under awning, more on back terrace, open all day (till 1am Fri, Sat). *(Anon)*

SE26

Dulwich Wood House
(020) 8693 5666 *Sydenham Hill; SE26 6RS* Extended well refurbished Youngs pub in Victorian lodge gatehouse complete with turret, nice local atmosphere, friendly service, good food cooked to order; steps up to entrance; children welcome, picnic-sets in big back garden with covered seating area, summer barbecues, handy for Dulwich Wood. *(Anon)*

SW4

Windmill (020) 8673 4578
Clapham Common South Side; SW4 9DE Big bustling pub by the common, contemporary front bar, quite a few original Victorian features, pillared dining room leading through to conservatory-style eating area, good varied choice of food all day, Wells & Youngs ales and decent wines by the glass, background music, Sun quiz; children welcome, bar, tables under red umbrellas along front, also seats in side garden area, good bedrooms, open all day. *(Giles and Annie Francis)*

SW11

Eagle Ale House (020) 7228 2328
Chatham Road; SW11 6HG Attractive unpretentious backstreet local, seven changing ales including southern brewers like Harveys, Surrey Hills and Westerham, welcoming efficient service, worn leather chesterfield in fireside corner of L-shaped bar; big-screen sports TV; dogs welcome, back terrace with heated marquee, small front terrace too, open all day weekends, from 3pm other days. *(Anon)*

★**Fox & Hounds** (020) 7924 5483
Latchmere Road; SW11 2JU Victorian
local with particularly good mediterranean
cooking (all day Sun, not Mon-Thurs
lunchtimes), four real ales and several
wines by glass, spacious straightforward
bar with big windows overlooking street,
bare boards, mismatched tables and chairs,
photographs on walls, fresh flowers, daily
papers, view of kitchen behind, two rooms
off; background music, TV; children (till
7pm) and dogs welcome, garden seats under
big parasols, open all day Fri-Sun, closed Mon
lunchtime. *(Anon)*

Prince Albert (020) 7228 0923
Albert Bridge Road; SW11 4PF Large
modernised Victorian pub (Geronimo
Inn) popular with young professionals,
good range of beers, decent pub food and
efficient friendly staff; regular backgammon
tournaments; seats and heaters out in
front overlooking Battersea Park, garden
behind. *(Richard and Penny Gibbs)*

Westbridge (020) 7228 6482
Battersea Bridge Road; SW11 3AG
Interesting ever-changing choice of real ales
and ciders, above average food from open
kitchen particularly steaks, can eat in bar or
back restaurant, friendly staff; background
music may be loud, popular with art
students early evening; seats for smokers
out at front and back, open all day. *(Richard
and Penny Gibbs)*

Woodman (020) 7228 2968
Battersea High Street; SW11 3HX
Sensitively refurbished and well run by nice
young couple (he's the chef), good food from
bar snacks up, Badger ales and Stowford
Press cider, friendly service, has village
local-feel and can get busy in summer; dogs
welcome, garden. *(Richard and Penny Gibbs)*

SW12

3 Monkeys (020) 8673 4447
Fernlea Road; SW12 9RT Balham cocktail
bar with concoctions such as Monkey
Nuts, Chocolate Chimp and King Kiwi from
extensive list, two-for-one deal before 8pm
and all day Sun, regular events including
comedy and 80s nights, cocktail school and
popular basement karaoke complete with
smoke machine and mirror ball, friendly
welcoming staff; open all day from 4.30pm
(till 1am Fri, Sat), closed Mon. *(Adam
Hempenstall, Nelly Whaley)*

Avalon (020) 8675 8613
Balham Hill; SW12 9EB Part of the
Renaissance group of S London pubs, popular
food including some interesting takes on
traditional cooking, well kept changing ales
and good choice of wines by the glass, plenty
of room in split-level bar and dining area,
big murals and stuffed animals, coal fires;

children welcome, front terrace and nice
sunny back garden, open all day (till 1am
Fri, Sat). *(Anon)*

★**Nightingale** (020) 8673 1637
Nightingale Lane; SW12 8NX Cosy and
civilised early Victorian local, small woody
front bar opening into larger back area and
attractive family conservatory, well kept Wells
& Youngs ales, enjoyable sensibly priced bar
food, friendly service, board games; sports TV;
small secluded back garden with smokers'
shelter. *(Giles and Annie Francis)*

SW14

Victoria (020) 8876 4238
West Temple Sheen; SW14 7RT
Contemporary styling with emphasis
on conservatory restaurant, good if
not particularly cheap food including
breakfast from 8.30am (not Sun), friendly
service, well kept Fullers London Pride
and Timothy Taylors Landlord in small
wood-floored bar with leather sofas and
woodburners; background music; children
and dogs welcome, play area in nice
garden, barbecues, comfortable bedrooms,
open all day. *(Simon Rodway, Gerry and
Rosemary Dobson)*

SW15

Dukes Head (020) 8788 2552
*Lower Richmond Road, near Putney
Bridge; SW15 1JN* Smart Victorian pub
with comfortable furnishings in knocked-
together front bars, good range of pubby
food all day including sharing plates and
snacks, Wells & Youngs ales, lots of wines
by the glass, friendly service, light and
airy back dining room with great river
views, downstairs bar in disused skittle
alley; plastic glasses for outside terrace
or riverside pavement; children welcome
(high chairs and smaller helpings), open
all day. *(Anon)*

Kings Head (020) 8789 1539
Roehampton High Street; SW15 4HL
Major refurbishment for this weatherboarded
former coaching inn, various individually
styled rooms and spaces, decent choice of
food from open kitchen with its rotisserie
and charcoal grill, Wells & Youngs ales and
guests such as Meantime and Sambrooks, lots
of wines by the glass; terrace tables under
parasols, open all day. *(Anon)*

★**Telegraph** (020) 8788 2011
Telegraph Road; SW15 3TU Big pub on
Putney Heath, two attractively modernised
rooms with bold décor, leather armchairs
and sofas, rugs on polished wood, grand
dining table, six real ales including house
Semaphore brewed by Weltons, bistro-style
food all day, newspapers and board games;
background music and live blues/jazz

nights, sports TV, occasional quiz; children and dogs welcome, great garden with rural feel, busy outside with families and dogs in summer. *(Colin McKerrow)*

SW16

Earl Ferrers (020) 8835 8333

Ellora Road; SW16 6JF Opened-up Streatham corner local, Sambrooks and several other well kept ales (tasters offered), some interesting food as well as pub favourites, good friendly service, mixed tables and chairs, sofas, old photographs; music Mon, Thurs, quiz Weds, book and knitting clubs, pool and darts; children welcome, some tables outside with tractor-seat stools, open all day weekends, from 5pm weekdays. *(Anon)*

SW18 TQ2575

Cats Back (020) 8874 7277

Point Pleasant; SW18 1NN Traditionally refurbished 19th-c pub, Harveys first in SW London – news please.

Ship (020) 8870 9667

Jews Row; SW18 1TB Popular riverside pub by Wandsworth Bridge; light and airy conservatory-style decor, mix of furnishings on bare boards, basic public bar, well kept Wells & Youngs, Sambrooks and a guest, freshly cooked interesting bistro food (not especially cheap) in extended restaurant with own garden; children and dogs welcome, good-sized terrace with barbecue and outside bar, open all day. *(Anon)*

SW19

Alexandra (020) 8947 7691

Wimbledon Hill Road; SW19 7NE Busy Youngs pub with well kept beers including guests from central bar, good wine choice, enjoyable well priced food from sandwiches to good Sun roasts, friendly alert service, comfortably up-to-date décor in linked rooms; sports TVs; tables out in mews and on attractive roof terrace. *(Colin McKerrow)*

Fox & Grapes (020) 8619 1300

Camp Road; SW19 4UN Busy 18th-c dining pub by Wimbledon Common; modern bistro feel but keeping some original features in two linked areas (step between), some adventurous cooking from french chef-owner alongside more traditional dishes (not cheap and they add a service charge), view into kitchen from high-ceilinged upper room with its unusual chandeliers, well chosen wines by the glass, Sharps Doom Bar and guest from central servery, relaxed atmosphere; children and dogs welcome, three bedrooms, open all day, food all day Sun. *(John Coatsworth, Susan and John Douglas)*

Hand in Hand (020) 8946 5720

Crooked Billet; SW19 4RQ Friendly Youngs local on edge of Wimbledon Common, their ales and guests kept well, enjoyable home-made pubby food, several areas off central bar including family room with games, log fire; front courtyard, benches out by common, open all day. *(Paul Bonner)*

Sultan (020) 8544 9323

Norman Road; SW19 1BN Red-brick 1930s drinkers' pub owned by Hop Back and hidden in a tangle of suburban roads; their ales and maybe a guest in top condition, friendly locals, big scrubbed tables, darts in public bar; nice walled beer garden with summer barbecues, open all day. *(John Coatsworth)*

WEST LONDON

SW6

★Atlas (020) 7385 9129

Seagrave Road; SW6 1RX Busy tucked-away pub with long simple bar, plenty of panelling and dark wall benches, mix of old tables and chairs, brick fireplaces, good italian-leaning food (all day Sun), well kept Fullers, St Austell, Sharps and a guest, lots of wines by the glass and decent coffee, friendly service; they may ask for a credit card while you run a tab, background music; children (till 7pm) and dogs welcome, seats under awning on heated and attractively planted side terrace, open all day. *(Fr Robert Marsh, Alistair Forsyth)*

Harwood Arms (020) 7386 1847

Walham Grove; SW6 1QP Bare-boards gastropub with good food from bar snacks to enterprising pricey full meals, extensive wine list, a couple of well kept changing ales, bar area with leather sofas, young lively atmosphere; closed Mon lunchtime, otherwise open all day. *(Anon)*

Sands End (020) 7731 7823

Stephendale Road; SW6 2PR Fulham dining pub with modern british food, real ales such as Black Sheep, Hook Norton and Sharps Doom Bar, simple country furnishings and open fire; attracts upmarket crowd and can be very busy. *(Richard Tilbrook, Susan and John Douglas)*

SW7

★Anglesea Arms (020) 7373 7960

Selwood Terrace; SW7 3QG Very busy Victorian pub, well run and friendly, with mix of cast-iron tables on wood-strip floor, central elbow tables, panelling and heavy portraits, large brass chandeliers hanging from dark ceilings, big windows with swagged curtains, several booths at one end with partly glazed screens, half a dozen ales including Adnams, Fullers London Pride and Sambrooks, around 20 malt whiskies and 30 wines by the glass, interesting bar food, steps down to refurbished dining room; children welcome, dogs in bar, heated front terrace, open all day. *(Phil Bryant, B and M Kendall)*

Queens Arms (020) 7823 9293

Queens Gate Mews; SW7 5QL Popular Victorian corner pub with open-plan bareboards bar, generous helpings of enjoyable good value home-made food, decent wines by the glass, beers including Adnams and Fullers, good thoughtful service; TV; disabled facilities, handy for Albert Hall, open all day. *(John Branston)*

SW10

Chelsea Ram (020) 7351 4008

Burnaby Street; SW10 0PL Refurbished corner Geronimo Inn, mix of furniture on bare boards or stripy carpet including farmhouse tables, padded stools around an old workbench, cushioned wall seats, shelves of books and some striking artwork, Victorian fireplace, Wells & Youngs and guests, good food including daily specials, friendly service, board games; pavement picnic-sets, open all day. *(Neil Edmundson)*

W4

★ Bell & Crown (020) 8994 4164

Strand on the Green; W4 3PF Well run Fullers local, good friendly staff, enjoyable sensibly priced food, panelling and log fire, great Thames views from back bar and conservatory, lots of atmosphere, daily newspapers; can get very busy weekends; dogs welcome, terrace and towpath area, good walks, open all day. *(Ian Phillips, Ian Herdman, Phil Bryant)*

★ Bulls Head (020) 8994 1204

Strand on the Green; W4 3PQ Renovated old Thames-side pub (served as Cromwell's HQ during Civil War), seats by windows overlooking the water in beamed rooms, steps up and down, ales such as Fullers and Wells & Youngs, several wines by the glass, decent all-day pubby food served by friendly helpful staff; background music, games machine; seats out by river, pretty hanging baskets, part of Chef & Brewer chain. *(Ross Balaam)*

City Barge (020) 8994 2148

Strand on the Green; W4 3PH Small panelled riverside bars with some nice original features in picturesque front part, airy newer back section done out with maritime signs and bird prints, conservatory, all-day food from sandwiches to popular Sun roasts, Greene King ales, open fire;

noticeable background music, TV, Tues quiz; well behaved children and dogs welcome, waterside picnic-sets facing Oliver's Island, nice spot to watch sun set over Kew Bridge. *(Jeremy King)*

Roebuck (020) 8995 4392

Chiswick High Road; W4 1PU Popular relaxed Victorian dining pub with high ceilings and bare boards, front bar and roomy back dining area opening on to delightful paved garden, enjoyable well presented food (all day Sun) from daily changing menu, open kitchen, four real ales and good choice of wines by the glass; dogs welcome, open all day. *(Simon Rodway, N R White)*

Swan (020) 8994 8262

Evershed Walk, Acton Lane; W4 5HH Cosy well supported 19th-c local with good mix of customers and convivial atmosphere, nice food (all day Sun) including some interesting choices, friendly staff, a dozen or so wines by the glass, Sharps Doom Bar and guests, two bars with wood floors and panelling, leather chesterfields by open fire; dogs very welcome, children till 7.30, good spacious terrace, open all day weekends, from 5pm other days. *(N R White, Simon Rodway)*

Tabard (020) 8994 3492

Bath Road; W4 1LW Roomy Chiswick pub built in 1880, pleasant chatty atmosphere, up to ten changing ales, decent choice of wines and all-day pubby food, friendly efficient staff, arts & crafts interior with lots of nooks and corners, period mirrors and high frieze of William de Morgan tiles, fringe theatre upstairs; well behaved children welcome, disabled access, terrace tables by busy road, open all day. *(N R White)*

W6

★ Anglesea Arms (020) 8749 1291

Wingate Road; W6 0UR Good interesting food including weekday set lunches in homely bustling pub, welcoming staff, good choice of wines by the glass and several real ales, close-set tables in dining room facing kitchen, roaring fire in simply decorated panelled bar; children welcome, tables out by quiet street, open all day. *(Michael Rugman)*

Black Lion (020) 8748 2639

South Black Lion Lane; W6 9TJ Welcoming old pub set back from the river; helpful friendly staff, well kept Thwaites, Wells & Youngs Bombardier and three guests, good choice of wines by the glass and nice coffee, enjoyable food including some New Zealand influences and tapas, refurbished L-shaped interior, pastel shades and bare boards, some high tables and stools, skittle alley; children and dogs welcome, tables on heated terrace with table tennis, garden, open all day. *(Michael Butler, Phil Bryant, Simon Rodway)*

Blue Anchor (020) 8748 5774
Lower Mall; W6 9DJ Refurbished pub right on the Thames (first licensed 1722), a short walk from Hammersmith Bridge; two traditional linked areas with oak floors and panelling, good value enjoyable bar lunches including daily specials, a house beer from Nelsons along with guests such as Andwell, Otter and Skinners, friendly helpful service, pleasant river-view room upstairs; busy at weekends; disabled facilities, waterside tables. *(Phil Bryant, N R White)*

Carpenters Arms (020) 8741 8386
Black Lion Lane; W6 9BG Good imaginative cooking at this relaxed corner dining pub, fine for just a drink too with plenty of wines by the glass and Adnams Bitter, friendly staff, simple bare-boards interior with open fire; attractive garden, open all day. *(Simon Rodway)*

Queens Head (020) 7603 3174
Brook Green; W6 7BL Big Fullers pub dating from early 18th c with cosy linked rooms, beams, fires, country furniture and pictures in keeping with period, fairly interesting reasonably priced menu from sandwiches up, well kept beers and nice wines, attentive service; tables out in front overlooking green with tennis courts, pleasant garden behind. *(Edward Mirzoeff)*

W7

Fox (020) 8567 4021
Green Lane; W7 2PJ Friendly open-plan 19th-c local in quiet cul-de-sac near Grand Union Canal, several real ales and decent wines, well priced food including popular Sun lunch, panelling and stained glass, farm tools hung from ceiling; dogs welcome, small side garden, horse and donkey in pub's field across road, food/crafts market last Sat of month, towpath walks, open all day. *(Susan and John Douglas)*

W8

Britannia (020) 7937 6905
Allen Street, off Kensington High Street; W8 6UX Welcoming refurbished Wells & Youngs pub, decent-sized traditional front bar with pastel shades contrasting dark panelling, patterned rugs on bare boards, banquettes, leather tub and high-backed chairs, steps down to back area with wall-sized photograph of the old Britannia Brewery (now demolished), dining conservatory beyond, enjoyable freshly prepared food including pub staples; background music, sports TV; open all day. *(Phil Bryant)*

Scarsdale (020) 7937 1811
Edwardes Square; W8 6HE Busy Georgian pub in lovely leafy square, stripped-wood floors, good coal-effect gas fires, various knick-knacks, well kept Fullers/Gales ales from ornate counter, enjoyable good value pubby food, friendly helpful service; nice front terrace, open all day. *(Anon)*

★ Uxbridge Arms (020) 7727 7326
Uxbridge Street; W8 7TQ Friendly and cottagey backstreet local with three brightly furnished linked areas, well kept ales including Fullers and Harveys, good choice of bottled beers, china, prints and photographs; sports TV; open all day. *(Anon)*

W9

Prince Alfred (020) 7286 3287
Formosa Street; W9 1EE Well preserved austerely ornate Victorian pub with five separate bars, snob-screens and duck-through doors, beautiful etched-glass bow window, Wells & Youngs ales, enjoyable food including some imaginative choices in airy modern dining room with large centre skylight, cellar function rooms; background music; open all day. *(Anon)*

W12

★ Princess Victoria (020) 8749 5886
Uxbridge Road; W12 9DH Imposing Victorian gin palace with carefully restored rather grand bar, oil paintings on slate-coloured walls, a couple of stuffed animal heads, comfortable leather wall seats, parquet flooring, small fireplace, Fullers and Timothy Taylors, 36 wines by the glass and lots of spirits from handsome marble-topped horseshoe counter, imaginative modern bar food, large dining room with plenty of original features and more paintings, wine and cigar shop; children allowed if eating, dogs in bar, white wrought-iron furniture on pretty terrace, popular artisan market in front (Sat), open all day. *(Anon)*

W14   TQ2477

★ Colton Arms (020) 7385 6956
Greyhound Road; W14 9SD Unspoilt little gem, like an old-fashioned country tavern and in same family for over 40 years; main U-shaped front bar with log fire, polished brasses, fox mask, hunting crops and hunting-scene plates, fine collection of handsomely carved antique oak furniture, two tiny back rooms with own serving counters (ring bell for service), Fullers London Pride, Sharps Doom Bar and a guest, old-fashioned brass till; no food or credit cards; children (over 4) till 7pm, dogs allowed in bar, charming back terrace with neat rose arbour, next to the Queens Club tennis courts and gardens. *(Emma Scofield)*

★**Havelock Tavern** (020) 7603 5374
Masbro Road; W14 0LS Popular gastropub
in former shop, light airy L-shaped bar with
plain unfussy décor, second small room with
pews, good imaginative freshly prepared
food from daily changing menu, home-baked
bread, Sambrooks Wandle, Sharps Doom Bar
and guests, wide choice of interesting wines
by the glass, swift friendly service; free wi-fi;
children and dogs welcome, picnic-sets on
small paved terrace, open all day. *(John and
Annabel Hampshire, Martin and Karen Wake)*

OUTER LONDON

BECKENHAM   TQ3769
Jolly Woodman (020) 8663 1031
Chancery Lane; BR3 6NR Welcoming
old-fashioned local in conservation area,
cosy chatty atmosphere in L-shaped bar
with woodburner, five or so well kept
changing ales such as Harveys and Timothy
Taylors Landlord, good choice of whiskies,
reasonably priced home-made food (weekday
lunchtimes only) including sandwiches; dogs
welcome, flower-filled sunny back courtyard
and pavement tables, open all day (from 4pm
Mon). *(N R White)*

BIGGIN HILL   TQ4359
★**Old Jail** (01959) 572979
*Jail Lane; (E off A233 S of airport and
industrial estate, towards Berry's Hill
and Cudham); TN16 3AX* Big family
garden with picnic-sets, substantial trees
and good play area for this popular country
pub (on fringe of London); traditional
beamed and low-ceilinged rooms with RAF
memorabilia, two cosy small areas to right
divided by timbers, one with big inglenook,
other with cabinet of Battle of Britain plates,
Fullers, Harveys and Shepherd Neame,
standard fairly priced food (not Sun evening)
from sandwiches up, friendly service, step
up to dining room with more wartime
prints/plates and small open fire; discreet
background music; dogs welcome, nice
hanging baskets, open all day weekends.
(N R White, Alan Weedon, Pete Walker)

BROMLEY BR1   TQ4069
Red Lion (020) 8460 2691
North Road; BR1 3LG Chatty well
managed backstreet local in conservation
area, traditional dimly lit interior with wood
floor, tiling, green velvet drapes and shelves
of books, well kept Greene King, Harveys and
guests, lunchtime food, good friendly service;
tables out in front, open all day. *(N R White)*

BROMLEY BR2   TQ4265
Two Doves (020) 8462 1627
Oakley Road (A233); BR2 8HD Popular,
comfortable and unpretentious, and notable
for its lovely garden; friendly staff and locals,
well kept St Austell Tribute, Wells & Youngs
and a guest, no hot food but ploughman's and
snacks, modern back conservatory, open all
day Fri-Sun. *(N R White)*

CHELSFIELD   TQ4864
Five Bells (01689) 821044
*Church Road; just off A224 Orpington
bypass; BR6 7RE* Chatty 17th-c white
weatherboarded village local, two separate
bars and dining area, settle by inglenook,
friendly staff, well kept Courage, Harveys and
guests, reasonably priced food from snacks
up (evening food Thurs-Sat only), live music
including jazz, Tues quiz; sports TV; children
welcome, picnic-sets among flowers out in
front, open all day. *(Conor McGaughey)*

EASTCOTE   TQ1089
Case is Altered (020) 8866 0476
High Road/Southill Lane; HA5 2EW
Attractive 17th-c pub in quiet setting
adjacent to cricket ground; main bar,
flagstoned snug and barn dining area,
Brakspears, Sharps Doom Bar and three
guests, good choice of tasty generously served
food all day (Sun till 6pm), friendly efficient
staff; children and dogs welcome, nice front
garden (very popular in fine weather), handy
for Eastcote House Gardens. *(Brian Glozier)*

ENFIELD   TQ3599
Pied Bull (01992) 710619
*Bulls Cross, Bullsmoor Lane W of A10;
handy for M25 junction 25; EN2 9HE*
Friendly modernised 17th-c pub, low beam-
and-plank ceilings, lots of comfortable little
rooms and extensions, well kept ales and
decent choice of wines, well priced all-day
food including deals, good prompt service,
conservatory; dogs welcome, pleasant
terrace. *(Ron and June Buckler)*

HAMPTON COURT   TQ1668
★**Kings Arms** (020) 8977 1729
*Hampton Court Road, by Lion Gate;
KT8 9DD* Civilised well run pub by
Hampton Court itself (so popular with
tourists), comfortable furnishings including
sofas in back area, attractive Farrow &
Ball colours, good open fires, lots of oak
panelling, beams and some stained glass,

If you report on a pub that's not a featured entry, please tell us any lunchtimes or
evenings when it doesn't serve bar food.

well kept Badger beers, good choice of wines by the glass, friendly service, sensibly priced pubby food from sandwiches up, restaurant too; background music; children and dogs welcome, picnic-sets on roadside front terrace, limited parking, 13 bedrooms, open all day. *(Anon)*

HARROW TQ1587

Castle (020) 8422 3155

West Street; HA1 3EF Edwardian Fullers pub in picturesque area, their ales and enjoyable food from lunchtime sandwiches up, several rooms around central servery, open fires, rugs on bare boards and lots of panelling, collection of clocks in cheery front bar, more sedate back lounge; children welcome, steps up from street, nice garden behind. *(Linda Miller and Derek Greentree, Phil Bryant)*

ISLEWORTH TQ1675

London Apprentice (020) 8560 1915

Church Street; TW7 6BG Large Thames-side Taylor Walker pub, reasonably priced food from sandwiches up, well kept ales such as Adnams, Fullers, Hook Norton, Sharps and Wells & Youngs, good wine choice, log fire, pleasant friendly service, upstairs river-view restaurant; may be background music; children welcome, attractive riverside terrace, open all day. *(Susan and John Douglas)*

KEW TQ1877

Botanist (020) 8948 4838

Kew Green; TW9 3AA Own-brew pub handy for Kew Gardens and attracting a good cross-section of customers, ales such as Humulus Lupulus and Kew Green, also lots of UK and foreign bottled beers and affordable cocktails, food from sandwiches and sharing plates up, friendly helpful service, wood floors, comfortable leather bench seats and eclectic mix of other furnishings, Weds quiz; prominent background music; children welcome, small back terrace. *(Jeremy King)*

KEW TQ1977

Coach & Horses (020) 8940 1208

Kew Green; TW9 3BH Recently refurbished coaching inn overlooking green, Wells & Youngs ales and a guest, enjoyable food from sandwiches and traditional choices up, friendly young staff, relaxed open-plan interior with armchairs, sofas and log fire, shelves of books, restaurant with kitchen view; background music, sports TV; children and dogs welcome, teak tables on front terrace, secret garden behind with chickens, nice setting handy for Kew Gardens and National Archive, 31 bedrooms, buffet breakfast, open all day. *(Susan and John Douglas)*

KINGSTON KT1 TQ1769

Bishop Out of Residence

(020) 8546 4965 *Bishops Hall, down alley off Thames Street; KT1 1PY* Thames-side pub with spacious open-plan bar, sumptuous modern décor, river views from upstairs lounge, Wells & Youngs and a guest, over 20 wines by the glass and various cocktails, food all day including sandwiches, sharing plates and stone-baked pizzas; children and dogs welcome (not upstairs), waterside terrace. *(Anon)*

KINGSTON KT2 TQ1869

Boaters (020) 8541 4672

Canbury Gardens (park in Lower Ham Road if you can); KT2 5AU Family-friendly pub by Thames, half a dozen real ales such as Twickenham, good wines from reasonably priced list, well prepared and nicely presented food including weekend breakfast from 10am, efficient staff, comfortable banquettes in charming bar, newspapers, Sun evening jazz, quiz Mon; smart riverside terrace, in small park, ideal for children in summer, parking nearby can be difficult, open all day. *(Sue and Mike Todd, David and Sally Frost)*

Canbury Arms (020) 8255 9129

Canbury Park Road; KT2 6LQ Open-plan pub with simple contemporary décor, bare boards and big windows, relaxed friendly atmosphere, good up-to-date food including breakfast from 9am (10am Sun), helpful young staff, five well kept ales and good wine choice, nice coffee, stone-floor side conservatory, regular events; children and dogs welcome, tables out at front under parasols, open all day. *(Tom Gardner, Geoffrey and Penny Hughes, Meg and Colin Hamilton)*

ORPINGTON TQ4963

★ Bo-Peep (01959) 534457

Hewitts Road, Chelsfield; 1.7 miles from M25 junction 4; BR6 7QL Useful M25 country-feel dining pub, old low beams and enormous inglenook in carpeted bar, two cosy candlelit dining rooms, airy side room overlooking lane, Sharps Doom Bar, Wells & Youngs Bombardier and a changing beer from Westerham, cheerful service, pubby food (all day Sat, not Sun evening) as well as some more interesting choices; background music; children welcome, dogs in bar, picnic-sets on big brick terrace, open all day. *(Pete Walker)*

PINNER TQ1289

Queens Head (020) 8868 4607

High Street; HA5 5PJ Traditional beamed and panelled local dating from the 16th c, welcoming bustle and interesting décor, well kept Adnams, Greene King, Wells & Youngs Bombardier and two guests, simple good value lunchtime bar food; no children inside; dogs welcome (not during lunch), small back terrace for evening sun, open all day. *(Jonathan Peel, Brian Glozier)*

RICHMOND   TQ1877

Princes Head (020) 8940 1572
The Green; TW9 1LX Large open-plan pub overlooking cricket green near theatre, clean and well run, with low-ceilinged panelled areas off big island bar, well kept Fullers ales, popular sensibly priced pub food, friendly young staff and chatty locals, coal-effect fire; over-21s only, dogs welcome, circular picnic-sets outside, open all day. *(N R White)*

Watermans Arms (020) 8940 2893
Water Lane; TW9 1TJ Friendly old-fashioned Youngs local with well kept ales and enjoyable thai food, traditional layout with open fire, pub games; handy for the Thames. *(Claes Mauroy)*

✹ White Cross (020) 8940 6844
Water Lane; TW9 1TH Very pleasant garden with terrific Thames views, seats on paved area, outside bar and boats to Kingston and Hampton Court; two recently redecorated chatty main rooms, local prints and photographs, three log fires (one unusually below a window), well kept Wells & Youngs and guests from old-fashioned island servery, a dozen wines by the glass, decent bar food all day, bright and airy upstairs room (children welcome here till 6pm) with pretty cast-iron balcony for splendid river view, good mix of customers; background music, TV; dogs welcome, tides can reach the pub entrance (wellies provided). *(Ross Balaam, Mrs Margo Finlay, Jörg Kasprowski, N R White, Simon Collett-Jones)*

White Swan (020) 8940 0959
Old Palace Lane; TW9 1PG Small 18th-c cottagey pub, civilised and relaxed, with rustic dark-beamed open-plan bar, good friendly service, well kept Sambrooks, Otter, Sharps and Timothy Taylors, popular freshly made food (must book weekends), coal-effect fires, back dining conservatory and popular upstairs restaurant; background music; children allowed in back conservatory, some seats on narrow paved area at front, more in pretty walled back terrace below railway, open all day. *(Claes Mauroy, N R White)*

ROMFORD   TQ5188

Ship (01708) 741571
Main Road; RM2 5EL Recently refurbished 17th-c black and white pub, panelling, low beams and woodburner in fine brick fireplace, Adnams, Courage, Fullers, Sharps and guests, all-day food (till 5pm Fri-Sun) from sandwiches and sharing boards up, live weekend music; children welcome, beer garden. *(Robert Lester)*

TEDDINGTON   TQ1671

Anglers (020) 8977 7475
Broom Road; TW11 9NR Large Fullers pub in good spot on Thames at Teddington Lock, lots of different seating areas, decent food including fresh fish, friendly attentive service; children welcome, spacious garden popular summer evenings and weekends with adult-only areas, well placed for footpath walk from Hampton Court. *(Eddie Davies)*

Lion (020) 8977 4779
Wick Road; TW11 9DN Refurbished backstreet pub extended to include french restaurant, good food including well priced set choices, nice selection of wines and well kept beers such as Fullers and Sharps; outside seating, open all day. *(Hunter and Christine Wright)*

TWICKENHAM TW1   TQ1673

Crown (020) 8892 5896
Richmond Road, St Margarets; TW1 2NH Recent major refurbishment, emphasis on good food (several large dining areas), but also well kept real ales, friendly efficient staff. *(Hunter and Christine Wright)*

White Swan (020) 8892 2166
Riverside; TW1 3DN Refurbished 17th-c Thames-side pub up steep anti-flood steps, bare-boards L-shaped bar with cosy log fire, river views from prized bay-window, changing ales such as Hogs Back, Sambrooks, Sharps and Twickenham, enjoyable food (all day weekends) including some good value deals, friendly local atmosphere, board games; children welcome, tranquil setting opposite Eel Pie Island with well used balcony and waterside terrace across quiet lane, open all day. *(Helen Freeman, N R White, Charles Meade-King, Phil Bryant)*

TWICKENHAM TW2   TQ1572

Sussex Arms (020) 8894 7468
Staines Road; TW2 5BG Traditional bare-boards pub with a dozen real ales and six ciders from long counter, plenty in bottles too, simple food including good home-made pies, walls and ceilings covered in beer mats and pump clips, open fire, some live acoustic music; large back garden with boules, open all day. *(Steve Derbyshire, Mark Percy, Lesley Mayoh)*

With the iPhone *Good Pub Guide* App, you can use the iPhone's camera to send us pictures of pubs you visit – outside or inside.

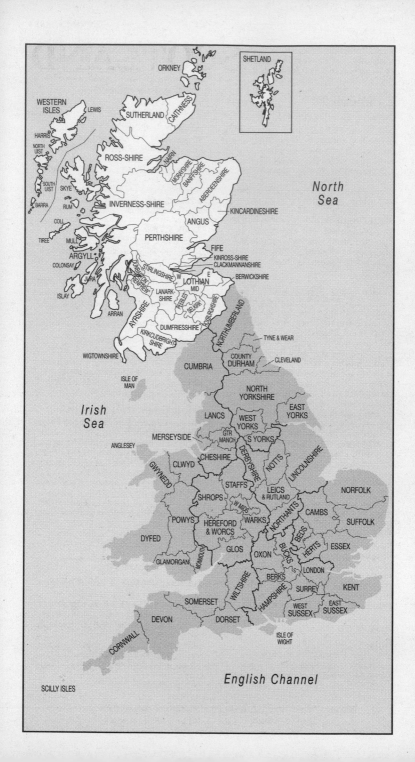

SCOTLAND

Returning to these pages after a gap is the Clachaig at Glencoe (popular with the mountaineering fraternity, with a tremendous range of drinks that includes more than 300 malts and around 15 real ales). We continue to receive encouraging reviews of the Plockton Hotel at Plockton (by the row of palm trees on the waterfront of a very attractive highland village, with plenty of fish dishes on the menu, and attractive bedrooms), Abbotsford in Edinburgh (fine Edwardian pub with a decent choice of drinks and bar food), Applecross Inn at Applecross (a jaw-dropping drive to get there, among extremely wild landscapes; much liked seafood and fish), Burts Hotel in Melrose (comfortable hotel keeping up good standards for food and accommodation) and Guildford Arms in Edinburgh (making impressive efforts with its choice of real ales, and readers much enjoy the opulent interior). Some pubs stand out for their drinks selection, such as the Bow Bar in Edinburgh and the Bon Accord in Glasgow, both of which have big selections of real ales and several hundred malts; the Old Inn at Gairloch, Houston Inn at Houston and Moulin at Pitlochry, all of which have own-brewed beers; and the stunningly located Sligachan Hotel at Sligachan, which has own-brews as well as some 350 malts. Others worth a special mention for their waterside location are the Steam Packet at Isle of Whithorn (pleasantly modernised inn at the southern tip of the Machars peninsula), the Tigh an Eilean Hotel at Shieldaig (marvellously placed by Loch Shieldaig beneath the Torridon Hills), Plockton Hotel in Plockton (lovely views from family-run lochside hotel, great food and comfortable bedrooms) and the Stein Inn at Stein (fine setting on the Isle of Skye, with lots of character inside, very reasonably priced food and pleasant bedrooms). For its delicious fresh local fish and seafood, our Scotland Dining Pub 2014 is the Plockton Hotel in Plockton.

APPLECROSS
NG7144 Map 11

Applecross Inn ★ 🛏
Off A896 S of Shieldaig; IV54 8LR

Wonderfully remote pub on famously scenic route on west coast; particularly friendly welcome, real ales and good seafood; bedrooms

Driving through miles of spectacularly wild, unpopulated scenery and over the famous pass of the cattle (Beallach na Ba), you may get a surprise at the number of visitors who beat a path to this remote inn, looking across the water to the Cuillin Hills on Skye. The no-nonsense, welcoming bar has a woodburning stove, exposed stone walls and upholstered pine furnishings on a stone floor; An Teallach Beallach na Ba and Isle of Skye Young Pretender on handpump and over 50 malt whiskies; pool (winter only), TV, and board games; some disabled facilities. The tables in the shoreside garden enjoy magnificent views. If you wish to stay overnight, you might have to book well in advance. The alternative route here, along the single-track lane winding round the coast from just south of Shieldaig, has equally glorious sea loch and then sea views nearly all the way.

With an emphasis on top quality local fish and seafood – peeled prawns in garlic butter, squat lobsters, oysters, seafood platter, king scallops and dressed crab with smoked salmon – the menu also includes dishes such as haggis, chicken liver parfait, sirloin steak, gammon with eggs and chips, haddock and chips with home-made tartare sauce, pork fillet topped with apple and stilton on bubble and squeak, and puddings such as raspberry cranachan on meringue topped with praline and sticky toffee pudding. *Benchmark main dish: Applecross Bay prawns £18.50. Two-course evening meal £17.50.*

Free house ~ Licensee Judith Fish ~ Real ale ~ (01520) 744262 ~ Open 11am-11.30pm (midnight Sat); 12-11 Sun ~ Bar food 12-9 ~ Restaurant ~ Children welcome until 8.30pm ~ Dogs welcome ~ Occasional live traditional music ~ Bedrooms: £80/£120 ~ www.applecross.uk.com *Recommended by the Dutchman, Barry Collett, Tom Jensen, Richard and Penny Gibbs, John and Pauline Cope*

CARBOST
NG3731 Map 11

Old Inn 🍺 £
B8009; IV47 8SR

Little changed, unpretentious waterside pub with stunning views, well positioned for walkers and climbers; bedrooms and bunkhouse

The blue-painted picnic-sets on the terrace here are right by Loch Harport and look across the water to the Cuillin Hills; the bedrooms in the Lodge share the same lovely water views – as does the family chalet and the popular bunkhouse. The simply furnished chatty bar has exposed stone walls, plush wall seats, cushioned stools, wooden chairs and benches around pine tables on bare floorboards or tiling, an open fire and Cuillin Pinnacle, Skye Ale and a guest beer on handpump, farm cider and quite a few malt whiskies served by friendly staff. Background music, darts, pool and board games. The Talisker distillery is close by.

A small choice of good, reasonably priced bar meals might include sandwiches, venison liver pâté, baked camembert, sharing platter, burgers with cheese, bacon or black pudding, battered haddock and chips, pesto pasta with onion and mushrooms, chicken and leek pie, fish specials, and puddings such as crumble of the day and sticky toffee pudding with Drambuie toffee sauce and honeycomb ice-cream. *Benchmark main dish: haggis strudel £9.95. Two-course evening meal £16.00.*

Free house ~ Licensees Angus Cooper and Spencer Smith ~ Real ale ~ (01478) 640205 ~ Open 11am-1am(12.30 Sat); 12.30-11 Sun; closed afternoons in winter ~ Bar food 12-9 ~ Restaurant ~ Children welcome ~ Dogs welcome ~ Open jam session Fri evenings ~ Bedrooms: £48/£76 ~ www.theoldinnskye.co.uk *Recommended by David and Sue Atkinson*

EDINBURGH
NT2574 Map 11

Abbotsford ◖ £

Rose Street; E end, beside South St David Street; EH2 2PR

Lively city pub with period features, six changing beers and bar and restaurant food

Little altered in over 100 years, this splendid Edwardian pub has a fine choice of beers. Perched at its centre, on red flooring, is a hefty highly polished Victorian island bar ornately carved from dark spanish mahogany, serving up to six changing real ales (on handpump and air pressure) from independent Scottish brewers such as Alechemy, Fyne, Highland, Isle of Skye, Stewart and Tryst, plus a selection of bottled american craft beers and around 70 malt whiskies. At lunchtime you'll usually find an eclectic mix of business people and locals occupying stools around the bar and long wooden tables and leatherette benches running the length of the dark wooden high-panelled walls. Above all is a rather handsome green and gold plaster-moulded high ceiling. The smarter upstairs restaurant, with its white tablecloths, black walls and high ornate white ceilings, looks impressive too.

Food includes smoked haddock soup, chargrilled mediterranean vegetables, baked cod wrapped in virginia cured bacon, chicken cassoulet with chorizo, steaks, venison casserole, steak and ale pie, tomato, caramelised shallot and basil risotto, duck breast and sweet potato, and puddings such as sticky date and ginger sponge. *Benchmark main dish: fish and chips £8.95. Two-course evening meal £16.00.*

Stewart ~ Licensee Daniel Jackson ~ Real ale ~ (0131) 225 5276 ~ Open 11-11 (midnight Fri, Sat); 12.30-11 Sun ~ Bar food 12(12.30 Sun)-10 ~ Restaurant 12-2.15, 5.30-9.30 ~ Children over 5 allowed in restaurant ~ www.theabbotsford.com
Recommended by David and Sue Smith, John Beeken, Eric Larkham

EDINBURGH
NT2574 Map 11

Bow Bar ◖

West Bow; EH1 2HH

Cosy, enjoyably unpretentious backstreet pub with an excellent choice of well kept beers

A classic unchanged city drinking room, this is a memorable place for a drink. Its rectangular bar has an impressive carved mahogany gantry, and from the tall 1920s founts on the bar counter, knowledgeable staff dispense eight well kept real ales such as Stewart Edinburgh No 3 Premium Scotch Ale and guests like Fyne Hurricane Jack, Highland Orkney Best, Hornbeam Black Coral Stout, Tempest Re-Wired and Tryst Raj IPA; regular beer festivals. Also on offer are some 220 malts, including five 'malts of the moment', a good choice of rums, 40 international bottled beers and 20 gins. The walls are covered with a fine collection of enamel advertising signs and handsome antique brewery mirrors, and there are sturdy leatherette wall seats and café-style bar seats around heavy narrow tables on the wooden floor; free wi-fi.

🍴 Food is limited to lunchtime pies and soup.

Free house ~ Licensee Mike Smith ~ Real ale ~ (0131) 226 7667 ~ Open 12-midnight; 12.30-11 Sun ~ Bar food 12-3 ~ Dogs welcome *Recommended by Sophie Holborow*

EDINBURGH

NT2574 Map 11

Guildford Arms 🍺 £

West Register Street; EH2 2AA

Busy and friendly, with spectacular Victorian décor, a marvellous range of real ales and good food

Well worth seeking out for its wonderful interior, this bustling and sumptuously fitted pub hosts regular beer festivals. The opulently excessive décor features ornate painted plasterwork on the lofty ceiling, heavy swagged velvet curtains, heavy dark mahogany fittings and a busy patterned carpet. Tables and stools are lined up along the towering arched windows opposite the bar where knowledgeable, efficient staff may offer a taste before you select fromm the fine range of ten quickly changing beers, including Caledonian Deuchars IPA, Fyne Jarl, Harviestoun Bitter & Twisted, Orkney Dark Gold and quickly changing guests from brewers such as Bath Ales, Dark Star, Leeds, Magic Rock and Raw. Also over a dozen wines by the glass, about 40 malt whiskies, a dozen rums and a dozen gins; board games, TV and background music. The snug little upstairs gallery restaurant, with strongly contrasting modern décor, gives a fine dress-circle view of the main bar (notice the lovely old mirror decorated with two tigers on the way up).

🍴 Tasty food includes lunchtime open sandwiches, fish chowder, mussels, haggis with neeps and tatties, broccoli, potato and cheese sauce puff pastry pie, sausage and mash, steaks, fillet of salmon with wild mushroom cream sauce, chicken fillet with sweet chilli glaze, and puddings. *Benchmark main dish: steak and ale pie £9.95. Two-course evening meal £18.50.*

Stewart ~ Lease Steve Jackson ~ Real ale ~ (0131) 556 4312 ~ Open 11-11(midnight Fri, Sat); 12.30-11 Sun ~ Bar food 12-9.30(10 Fri, Sat) ~ Restaurant 12(12.30 Sun)-2.30, 6-9.30(10 Fri, Sat) ~ Children welcome in upstairs gallery if dining ~ Dogs allowed in bar ~ Live music nightly during the Edinburgh Festival ~ www.guildfordarms.com
Recommended by David Hunt, Roger and Donna Huggins, John Beeken, Janet and Peter Race

EDINBURGH

NT2574 Map 11

Kays Bar 🍺 £

Jamaica Street West; off India Street; EH3 6HF

Cosy, enjoyably chatty backstreet pub with good value lunchtime food and an excellent choice of well kept beers

'No trip to Edinburgh would be complete without a call here,' remarked a reader of this thoroughly convivial tavern. Inside, it's unpretentious and warmly welcoming, with long well worn curving red plush wall banquettes and stools around cast-iron tables on red carpets, and red pillars supporting a red ceiling. It's simply decorated with big casks and vats arranged along the walls, old wine and spirits merchant notices and gas-type lamps. A quiet panelled back room (a bit like a library) leads off, with a narrow plank-panelled pitched ceiling and a collection of books ranging from dictionaries to ancient steam-train books for boys; lovely warming coal fire in winter. The seven real ales include Caledonian Deuchars IPA and Theakstons Best, plus guests Alechemy Amarillo Burst, Caledonian Dry Dock Stout, Greene King Old Speckled Hen and Wells & Youngs Bitter on handpump; they also stock more than 70 malt whiskies aged between eight and 50 years, and ten blended whiskies; board games. In days past, the pub was owned by John Kay, a whisky and wine merchant – wine barrels were hoisted up to the first floor and dispensed through pipes attached to nipples visible around the light rose.

🍴 Very reasonably priced food includes lunchtime open sandwiches, soup, steak pie, prawn salad, beef or chicken curry and a platter of cold meats. *Benchmark main dish: chilli, mince and potatoes £4.50.*

Free house ~ Licensee Fraser Gillespie ~ Real ale ~ (0131) 225 1858 ~ Open 11-midnight(1am Fri, Sat); 12.30-11 Sun ~ Bar food 12-2.30; not Sun ~ Children welcome ~ Dogs welcome ~ www.kaysbar.co.uk *Recommended by John and Annabel Hampshire, Roger and Donna Huggins, Peter F Marshall*

GAIRLOCH
Old Inn 🍷 🍺

NG8075 Map 11

Just off A832/B8021; IV21 2BD

Quietly positioned old inn specialising in local fish and seafood; good beers

Idyllically placed overlooking an old stone bridge over the stream at the bottom of Flowerdale Glen, this long-established drovers' inn is tucked comfortably away from the modern waterside road, with picnic-sets prettily placed by the trees. A fine selection of beers includes their own-brew Blind Piper, Erradale, Flowerdale and Slattadale, in addition to beers from An Teallach, Atlas, Cairngorm and Orkney breweries. There are also quite a few fairly priced wines by the glass and around 20 malt whiskies. The relaxed public bar is popular with chatty locals and is quite traditional, with paintings, murals on exposed stone walls, stools lined up along the counter and a warming woodburner; board games, background music, TV, fruit machine and juke box. Credit (but not debit) cards incur a surcharge of £1.50.

🍴 They have their own smokery producing smoked meats, fish and cheese and bake their own bread. As well as fresh local fish and game, such as scallops, mussels, haddock, crab, lobster, pheasant and venison, the tasty food includes sandwiches, cullen skink, vegetable tagine, braised pork belly on puy lentil broth, several pies and pizzas, tagliatelle with clams and garlic, chicken breast whisky roulade stuffed with haggis, and puddings such as vanilla cheesecake, clootie dumpling and double chocolate crêpe. *Benchmark main dish: fried scallops £16.95. Two-course evening meal £19.00.*

Own brew ~ Licensees Alastair and Ute Pearson ~ Real ale ~ (01445) 712006 ~ Open 11am-1am; 12-11 Sun ~ Bar food 12-2.30, 5-9 ~ Restaurant ~ Children welcome ~ Dogs welcome ~ Live music Fri evening ~ Bedrooms: £60/£104 ~ www.theoldinn.net *Recommended by Richard and Penny Gibbs*

The letters and figures after the name of each town are its Ordnance Survey map reference. *Using the Guide* at the beginning of the book explains how it helps you find a pub, in road atlases or large-scale maps as well as in our own maps.

GLASGOW
Babbity Bowster 🍴 ♀

NS5965 Map 11

Blackfriars Street; G1 1PE

Very much a Glasgow institution: friendly, comfortable and sometimes lively mix of traditional and modern, with something of a continental feel too; very reasonably priced bar food

Extremely popular and with a thoroughly convivial atmosphere, this city-centre pub has a good mix of locals and visitors. The simply decorated light interior has fine tall windows, well lit photographs and big pen-and-wash drawings of the city, its people and musicians, dark grey stools and wall seats around dark grey tables on stripped wooden boards, and a peat fire. The bar opens on to a pleasant terrace with tables under cocktail parasols, trellised vines and shrubs; they may have barbecues out here in summer. Caledonian Deuchars IPA and a couple of guests such as Fyne Jarl and Williams May Bee on air-pressure tall fount, and a remarkably sound collection of wines and malt whiskies; good tea and coffee too. On Saturday evenings, the pub has live traditional scottish music, while at other times you may find games of boules in progress outside. Note the bedroom price is for the room only.

🍴 Enjoyable food at fair prices from a short bar menu includes sandwiches, mussels, haggis, neeps and tatties, pie of the day, vegetarian lasagne, daily specials, and puddings such as steamed sponge with citrus syrup and strawberry compote; the more elaborate choice in the airy upstairs restaurant might include cullen skink, puff pastry goats cheese tart with confit tomatoes, roasted herb-crusted rack of lamb, butternut squash risotto, slow-cooked loin of pork stuffed with black pudding and apple, and puddings like caramelised lemon tart. *Benchmark main dish: haunch of venison £15.25. Two-course evening meal £20.00.*

Free house ~ Licensee Fraser Laurie ~ Real ale ~ (0141) 552 5055 ~ Open 11am (12.30 Sun)-midnight ~ Bar food 12-10 ~ Restaurant ~ Children welcome if eating ~ Live traditional music Sat ~ Bedrooms: £45/£60 ~ www.babbitybowster.com
Recommended by Peter F Marshall, Theocsbrian, Comus and Sarah Elliott

GLASGOW
Bon Accord 🍺 £

NS5965 Map 11

North Street; G3 7DA

Remarkable choice of drinks with an impressive range of whiskies and real ales, a good welcome and bargain food

With its happy mix of customers, this neatly kept pub leads the way among the city's real ale haunts. Alongside Caledonian Deuchars they have eight daily changing beers (they can get through around 1,000 a year), sourced from breweries around Britain and served from swan-necked handpumps. They also have continental bottled beers, a farm cider and, in a remarkable display behind the counter, 350 malt whiskies and lots of gins, vodkas and rums. Staff are knowledgeable, so do ask for help if you need it. The several linked traditional bars are warmly understated with cream or terracotta walls, a mix of chairs and tables, a leather sofa and plenty of bar stools on polished bare boards or carpeting; TV, background music and board games. There are circular picnic-sets on a small terrace with modern tables and chairs out in front.

🍴 Astonishingly good value bar food includes baguettes, soup, cod goujons, peppered mushrooms, fish and chips, scampi, cajun chicken, macaroni cheese, steaks, giant yorkshire pudding, burgers, and puddings such as apple pie and clootie dumpling. *Benchmark main dish: fish and chips £6.95. Two-course evening meal £9.50.*

Free house ~ Licensee Paul McDonagh ~ Real ale ~ (0141) 248 4427 ~ Open 11am(12.30 Sun)-midnight ~ Bar food 12(12.30 Sun)-8 ~ Children welcome until 8pm ~ Live band Sat ~ www.bonaccordweb.co.uk *Recommended by Barry Collett, Dr and Mrs A K Clarke*

GLENCOE
NN1058 Map 11
Clachaig
Old Glencoe Road, behind NTS Visitor Centre; PH49 4HX

Climbers' and walkers' haunt with a broad selection of scottish beers and malts

Right in the hub of the majestic mountain scenery of Glencoe, this is a popular target for walkers, climbers and mountain bikers to relax over a pint by the log fire in the Boots Bar, which hosts live bands on Saturday nights. There's also a whisky barrel-panelled, slate-floored snug and a lounge with a mix of dining chairs and leather sofas, and with walls hung with photos signed by famous climbers. Up to 15 scottish real ales on handpump from a frequently changing selection could include An Teallach Ale, Cairngorm Black Gold, Fraoch Heather Ale and Williams Kelpie; also, Williams alcoholic ginger beer, around 300 malt whiskies and some unusual scottish lagers; background music, TV and pool. We imagine this would be a useful base and would welcome reports from readers who stay here; the pub also runs self-catering properties in the area.

Food includes lunchtime rolls, soup, black pudding with oatcakes, haggis, neeps and tatties, venison casserole, mixed bean chilli, and puddings. *Benchmark main dish: steak and ale pie £10.95. Two-course evening meal £16.00.*

Free house ~ Licensees Guy and Edward Daynes ~ Real ale ~ (01855) 811252 ~ Open 11(12.30 Sun)-11(11.30 Sat); closed 24-26 Dec ~ Bar food 12-9 ~ Children allowed in lounge ~ Dogs allowed in bar and bedrooms ~ Live music Sat night ~ Bedrooms: $50/$100 ~ www.clachaig.com *Recommended by Tess White*

HOUSTON
NS4066 Map 11
Fox & Hounds ♀ ◀
South Street at junction with Main Street (B789, off B790 at Langbank signpost E of Bridge of Weir); PA6 7EN

Popular 18th-c pub with beers from own brewery, fine range of other drinks and tasty food

Inside the bar of this village pub you can peer through a window to see the small brewery where their distinctive beers are produced. The seven constantly changing ales include a guest beer plus their own Barochan, Houston Mild, Killellan, Peters Well and Sweet Stout; the pub holds a couple of Best of Scotland beer festivals during the summer. You can try a fantastic choice of other drinks too, such as 87 malt whiskies, a dozen wines by the glass, 12 rums and 12 gins. The clean, plush, hunting-theme lounge has beams, comfortable seats by a fire and polished brass and copper; background music. Popular with a younger crowd, the lively downstairs bar has a large-screen TV, pool, juke box and fruit machines. At the back is a covered and heated area with decking.

Served upstairs (downstairs only substantial sandwiches are served), the food might include mussels with white wine and garlic, peppered goats cheese salad with sesame and red onion jam, beer-battered haddock and chips, beefburger, apple, celery and mushroom stroganoff, medallion of venison with caramelised black cherry and onion jus, and puddings like apple and seasonal berry crumble or chocolate fudge cake. *Benchmark main dish: rib-eye steak £18.50. Two-course evening meal £17.00.*

Own brew ~ Licensee Debbie Anderson ~ Real ale ~ (01505) 612448 ~ Open 11am-midnight(1am Fri, Sat); 12-midnight Sun ~ Bar food 12-10(9 Sun) ~ Restaurant ~ Children welcome ~ Dogs welcome ~ www.foxandhoundshouston.co.uk
Recommended by Martin and Sue Day, Barry Collett

ISLE OF WHITHORN   NX4736 Map 9
Steam Packet ♀ 🛏
Harbour Row; DG8 8LL

Waterside views from this friendly family-run inn with five real ales and tasty pubby food; bedrooms

The setting makes this a tempting spot to linger, with views out of the picture windows and from several bedrooms over an assortment of boats in a harbour at the southernmost tip of the Machars peninsula. It's a welcoming, family-run place with a comfortable low-ceilinged bar that's split into two: on the right, plush button-back banquettes and boat pictures, and on the left, green leatherette stools around cast-iron-framed tables on big stone tiles, and a woodburning stove in the bare stone wall. Bar food can be served in the lower beamed dining room, which has excellent colour wildlife photographs, rugs on a wooden floor and a solid fuel stove, and there's also a small eating area off the lounge bar, as well as a conservatory. Timothy Taylors Landlord and guest beers from brewers such as Houston or Orkney on handpump, quite a few malt whiskies and a good wine list; TV, dominoes and pool. There are white tables and chairs in the garden. You can walk from here up to the remains of St Ninian's kirk, on a headland behind the village.

Food typically includes lunchtime sandwiches, baguettes and baked potatoes, garlic mushrooms, smoked salmon and nachos, beer-battered haddock and chips, steak pie, steaks, chicken curry, mussels in cream and white wine sauce, lamb shank with root vegetables, and puddings. *Benchmark main dish: fish and chips £10.95. Two-course evening meal £19.00.*

Free house ~ Licensee Alastair Scoular ~ Real ale ~ (01988) 500334 ~ Open 11 (12 Sun)-11(midnight Sat); 12-midnight Sun; 11-3, 6-11 Mon-Thurs in winter ~ Bar food 12-2, 6.30-9 ~ Restaurant ~ Children welcome except in public bar ~ Dogs allowed in bar and bedrooms ~ Bedrooms: /£40 ~ www.steampacketinn.biz
Recommended by the Didler, John and Sylvia Harrop

KIPPEN   NS6594 Map 11
Cross Keys 🛏
Main Street; village signposted off A811 W of Stirling; FK8 3DN

Cosy 18th-c inn with obliging staff, enjoyable food and views of the Trossachs

With a nice mix of locals and visitors, this civilised village inn dates from 1707 and is a pleasant place to stay. Its bar has a timeless quality, with attractive bare stone walls and subdued lighting. A straightforward lounge has a good log fire, and there's a coal fire in the attractive family dining room. On handpump are 1703 Archies Amber (brewed for the pub by Fallen) and a guest such as Fallen Blackhouse Smoked Porter, several malts and wines by the glass; background music. Tables in the garden have good views towards the Trossachs.

Along with lunchtime sandwiches, the tasty food might include smoked pheasant and chicken terrine, haddock and chips, sausage and mash, spinach and garlic mushroom pie, venison and beetroot baked casserole with herb dumplings, mediterranean fish stew, and puddings like apple and winter fruit crumble. *Benchmark main dish: steak pie £12.00. Two-course evening meal £16.00.*

Free house ~ Licensees Debby McGregor and Brian Horsburgh ~ Real ale ~ (01786) 870293 ~ Open 12-3, 5-11(midnight Fri); 12pm-1am Sat; 12-11 Sun; closed Mon ~ Bar food 12-2.30, 5-9; 12-9 Sat; 12-8 Sun ~ Children welcome till 9pm ~ Dogs welcome ~ Open folk music session twice monthly ~ Bedrooms: £55/£70 ~ www.kippencrosskeys.com
Recommended by J F M and M West

MELROSE
NT5433   Map 9
Burts Hotel 🍴 🛏
B6374, Market Square; TD6 9PL

Comfortable town-centre hotel with imaginative food and a fine array of malt whiskies

Right in the middle of a beautifully unspoilt small town and a stroll from the abbey ruins, this carefully kept and very comfortable hotel has been in the same family for many years. Neat public areas are maintained with attention to detail. The welcoming red carpeted bar has tidy pub tables between cushioned wall seats and windsor armchairs, a warming fire, scottish prints on pale green walls and a long dark wood counter serving Scottish Borders Game Bird, Timothy Taylors Landlord and a guest such as Scottish Borders Gold Dust on handpump, several wines by the glass from a good wine list, a farm cider and around 80 malt whiskies. The elegant restaurant with its swagged curtains, dark blue wallpaper and tables laid with white linen offers a smarter dining experience. Service here is particularly helpful and polite, with staff well led by the hands-on licensees. The bedrooms, though quite small, are immaculate and comfortably decorated, and the breakfasts are good too. In summer you can sit out in the well tended garden.

Good food includes lunchtime sandwiches, soup, vegetable and chickpea fritters with mint and cucumber yoghurt, salad of crisp pork with black pudding and caramelised apple, home-made beefburger, roast red pepper and vegetable bake, seared salmon with chorizo and pea risotto, steaks, roast haunch of venison with red onion tarte tatin, and puddings such as passion-fruit mousse or a trio of chocolate. *Benchmark main dish: braised shoulder of lamb £13.95. Two-course evening meal £19.50.*

Free house ~ Licensees Graham and Nick Henderson ~ Real ale ~ (01896) 822285 ~ Open 11-2.30, 5-11; 12-2.30, 6-11 Sun; closed 6-13 Jan ~ Bar food 12-2, 6-9.30 (10 Fri, Sat) ~ Restaurant ~ Children welcome ~ Dogs allowed in bar and bedrooms ~ Bedrooms: £72/£133 ~ www.burtshotel.co.uk *Recommended by Donna Jenkins, Gordon and Margaret Ormondroyd, J F M and M West, Comus and Sarah Elliott*

The ◖ symbol shows pubs which keep their beer unusually well, have a particularly good range or brew their own.

PITLOCHRY

NN9459 Map 11

Moulin ◧ £

Kirkmichael Road, Moulin; A924 NE of Pitlochry centre; PH16 5EH

Attractive inn with own-brewed beers, reasonably priced food and a nicely pubby bar, open all day; comfortable bedrooms

A particular draw of this characterful, flower-bedecked 17th-c inn is the range of home-brewed Moulin beers (Ale of Atholl, Braveheart, Light and the stronger Old Remedial), brewed in the little stables across the street and served on handpump. They also keep around 45 malt whiskies and a good choice of wines by the glass and carafe. Although much extended over the years, the lively bar, in the oldest part of the building, still seems an entity in itself, nicely down to earth and pubby and with plenty of traditional character. Above the fireplace in the smaller bare-boarded room is an interesting painting of the village before the road was built (Moulin used to be a bustling market town, far busier than upstart Pitlochry), while the bigger carpeted area has a good few tables and cushioned banquettes in little booths divided by stained-glass country scenes, another big fireplace, some exposed stonework, fresh flowers, antique golf clubs, and local and sporting prints around the walls; bar billiards and a 1960s one-arm bandit; there's also a restaurant. Outside on a gravelled area and surrounded by tubs of flowers, picnic-sets look across to the village kirk and there are excellent walks nearby.

 Reasonably priced food includes lunchtime sandwiches, tomato and aubergine tartlet, mussels, venison terrine, fish and chips, batter pudding filled with beef and vegetable stew, steak and ale pie, seafood pancake, vegetarian haggis, game casserole, and puddings such as bread and butter pudding and raspberry crumble. *Benchmark main dish: haggis and neeps £9.50. Two-course evening meal £16.50.*

Own brew ~ Licensee Heather Reeves ~ Real ale ~ (01796) 472196 ~ Open 11-11 (11.45 Sat) ~ Bar food 12-9.30 ~ Restaurant ~ Children welcome ~ Dogs allowed in bar ~ Bedrooms: £62/£72 ~ www.moulinhotel.co.uk *Recommended by Pat and Stewart Gordon, Brian and Anna Marsden, David and Sue Atkinson, Pete Walker*

PLOCKTON

NG8033 Map 11

Plockton Hotel ★ ⑪ ⇌

Village signposted from A87 near Kyle of Lochalsh; IV52 8TN

Scotland Dining Pub of the Year

Lovely views from this family-run lochside hotel; real ales and very good food with emphasis on local seafood; bedrooms

Readers report this wonderfully sited waterside hotel is very much keeping up standards: 'friendly, nicely low key, with quality service'. In a lovely village owned by the National Trust for Scotland and forming part of a long, low terrace of stone-built houses, it's a great place for a break (it's worth booking well ahead, with most of the comfortable bedrooms in an adjacent building). Half the bedrooms have extraordinary views over the loch; the others, some with balconies, look over the hillside garden – and the breakfasts are good. The welcoming, comfortably furnished lounge bar has window seats looking out to the boats on the water, as well as antiqued dark red leather seating around neat regency-style tables on a tartan carpet, three model ships set into the woodwork and partly panelled stone walls. The separate public bar has pool, board games, TV, a games machine and background music. Four real ales feature Cromarty Happy Chappy and three guests such as Highland Island Hopping or Orkney Blast and Windswept Blonde on handpump, 30 malt whiskies and several wines by the glass. Tables in the front garden look out past the village's trademark palm trees and colourfully flowering shrub-lined shore, across the sheltered anchorage to the rugged mountainous surrounds of Loch Carron; a stream runs down the hill into a pond in the attractive back garden. There's a hotel nearby called the Plockton, so don't get the two confused.

Especially strong on fresh local seafood, the menu includes lunchtime toasted paninis and warm bloomers, cream of smoked fish soup, haggis and a tot of whisky, beer-battered fish and chips, venison casserole, steak, vegetarian dish of the day, chargrilled local prawns, baked fillet of monkfish wrapped in streaky bacon, seafood platter, and puddings. *Benchmark main dish: chargrilled hand-dived scallops £16.95. Two-course evening meal £20.00.*

Free house ~ Licensee Alan Pearson ~ Real ale ~ (01599) 544274 ~ Open 11-12 (11.30 Sat); 12.30-11 Sun ~ Bar food 12-2.15, 6-9 ~ Restaurant ~ Children welcome ~ Dogs allowed in bar ~ Local musicians Weds evening ~ Bedrooms: £55/£130 ~ www.plocktonhotel.co.uk *Recommended by Walter and Susan Rinaldi-Butcher, Dr Peter Crawshaw, M J Winterton, Les and Sandra Brown, Pete Walker*

SHIELDAIG NG8153 Map 11
Tigh an Eilean Hotel 🛏
Village signposted just off A896 Lochcarron–Gairloch; IV54 8XN

Separate, contemporary hotel bar memorably placed beneath formidable peaks; real ales and enjoyable food; tranquil bedrooms

The setting here is really exceptional, beneath the Torridon summits and looking down Loch Shieldaig, a haunt of otters and sea eagles. It's all very bright and attractive. The bar, separate from the hotel, is on two storeys with an open staircase; there's dining on the first floor and a decked balcony with a magnificent view of the loch and village. It's gently contemporary and nicely relaxed with timbered floors, timber-boarded walls, shiny bolts through exposed timber roof beams, and an open kitchen. An Teallach Ale and a guest such as An Teallach Suilven on handpump (although sometimes in January there may be no real ale on offer) and up to a dozen wines by the glass. Next door, the bedrooms are comfortable and peaceful. Tables outside are in a sheltered little courtyard and well placed to enjoy the gorgeous position.

In addition to more elaborate restaurant menus that make much use of fish and seafood, the bar food includes sandwiches, seafood chowder, haggis, neeps and tatties, venison sausages with mustard mash, beer-battered haddock and chips, broccoli and cheese crumble, seafood pizza, and puddings such as clootie dumpling. *Benchmark main dish: langoustine, scampi and chips £15.95. Two-course evening meal £16.00.*

Free house ~ Licensee Cathryn Field ~ Real ale ~ (01520) 755251 ~ Open 11-11 (midnight Fri, 1am Sat) ~ Bar food 12-9; 12-2.30, 6-9 in winter ~ Restaurant ~ Children welcome till 10pm ~ Dogs allowed in bar ~ Traditional live folk music some weekends and holidays ~ Bedrooms: £75/£150 ~ www.tighaneilean.co.uk *Recommended by the Dutchman, Steve Homer*

The details at the end of each featured entry start by saying whether the pub is a free house, or if it belongs to a brewery or pub group (which we name).

SLIGACHAN
NG4930 Map 11

Sligachan Hotel 🍺 🛏

A87 Broadford–Portree, junction with A863; IV47 8SW

**Summer-opening mountain hotel with spectacular setting on
the Isle of Skye, with walkers' bar and plusher side, food all day,
impressive range of whiskies and useful children's play area**

'As a walkers' retreat this is hard to beat, with its stunning location
at the foot of the Cuillins,' remarked one reader of this memorably
placed hotel. The huge modern pine-clad main bar, falling somewhere
between an original basic climbers' bar and the plusher more sedate
hotel side, is spaciously open to its ceiling rafters and has geometrically
laid out dark tables and chairs on neat carpets; pool. There is a
restaurant within the hotel. On handpump are their own Cuillin Black
Face, Eagle, Glamaig, Pinnacle and Skye, and a guest from another
scottish brewery, and the splendid range of 350 malt whiskies makes
a most impressive display behind the bar counter at one end. It can
get quite lively in here some nights, but there's also a more sedate
lounge bar with leather bucket armchairs on plush carpets and a coal
fire; background highland and islands music. A feature here is the
little museum charting the history of the island, and children should be
delighted with the big play area which can be watched from the bar. There
are tables out in a garden, and as well as self-catering accommodation they
have a campsite with caravan hook-ups across the road. Dogs are only
allowed in the main bar, not in the hotel's cocktail bar.

🍴 As well as sandwiches, the hearty food might include cullen skink, scallops
and black pudding, curry of the day, grilled mackerel fillet, burgers, vegetarian
cottage pie, lamb shanks, and puddings such as cranachan and sticky toffee
pudding. *Benchmark main dish: beer-battered fish and chips £10.00. Two-course
evening meal £16.00.*

Own brew ~ Licensee Sandy Coghill ~ Real ale ~ (01478) 650204 ~ Open 8am-midnight;
11-11 Sun; closed Nov-Feb (hotel side); the separate attached pubby bar is closed
beginning Oct-some time in May, best to phone ~ Bar food 8am-9pm ~ Restaurant ~
Children welcome ~ Dogs allowed in bar and bedrooms ~ Bedrooms: £65/£130 ~
www.sligachan.co.uk *Recommended by Phil Bryant, Dave Braisted*

STEIN
NG2656 Map 11

Stein Inn 🛏

*End of B886 N of Dunvegan in Waternish, off A850 Dunvegan–Portree;
OS Sheet 23 map reference 263564; IV55 8GA*

**Lovely setting on northern corner of Skye, welcoming 18th-c inn with
good, simple food and lots of whiskies; a rewarding place to stay**

A drink from the benches outside this inn, in a tiny waterside hamlet
on the west side of the island's Waternish peninsula, gets classic
Hebridean views across Loch Dunvegan. On inclement days, the
unpretentious original public bar makes a particularly inviting retreat
from the elements, with great character in its sturdy country furnishings,
flagstones, beam-and-plank ceiling, partly panelled stripped-stone walls
and warming double-sided stove between the two rooms. There's a
games area with pool table, darts, board games, dominoes and cribbage,
and maybe background music. Caledonian Deuchars IPA and a couple of
local guests such as Harviestoun Bitter & Twisted and Orkney Corncrake
on handpump, a dozen wines by the glass and more than 125 malt

whiskies. Good service from smartly uniformed staff. There's a lively children's indoor play area and showers for yachtsmen. All the bedrooms look out to sea and breakfasts are good – if you stay, it's well worth pre-ordering the tasty smoked kippers.

🍴 Using local fish and highland meat, the short choice of good, simple and very sensibly priced food might include sandwiches, peat-smoked salmon, black pudding with whisky and mustard dressing, venison burger, scampi, macaroni cheese, langoustines, and puddings such as blueberry cranachan and rhubarb crumble. *Benchmark main dish: beer-battered haddock and chips £10.50. Two-course evening meal £15.00.*

Free house ~ Licensees Angus and Teresa Mcghie ~ Real ale ~ (01470) 592362 ~ Open 11-midnight; 11.30-11 Sun; 12-11 winter weekdays; 12-midnight winter Sat; 12.30-11 winter Sun ~ Bar food 12-4, 6-9.30; 12.30-4, 6-9 Sun ~ Children welcome ~ Dogs allowed in bar and bedrooms ~ Bedrooms: £43/£74 ~ www.steininn.co.uk *Recommended by Phil Bryant, Walter and Susan Rinaldi-Butcher, Jane and Alan Bush, David and Sue Atkinson*

SWINTON
NT8347 Map 10

Wheatsheaf ♀ 🛏

A6112 N of Coldstream; TD11 3JJ

Civilised place with small bar for drinkers, comfortable lounges, quite a choice of food and drinks, professional service; comfortable bedrooms

Run by attentive staff, this restaurant-with-rooms stands in a Borders village a few miles from the River Tweed. The emphasis is on accommodation and food, but it does have a little bar and informal lounges, with Belhaven IPA and Broughton The Ghillie on handpump alongside 40 malt whiskies and several wines by the glass. There are comfortable plush armchairs and sofas, several nice old oak settles with cushions, a little open fire, sporting prints and china plates on the bottle-green walls in the bar, and small agricultural prints and a fishing-theme décor on the painted or bare stone walls in the lounges. You'll also find cushioned bamboo and barley-twist dining chairs around pale wood tables on carpeting and fresh flowers on the tables in the dining room and front conservatory with its vaulted pine ceiling, and black leather high-backed dining chairs around clothed tables in the more formal restaurant; background music. The bedrooms are well equipped and comfortable.

🍴 Along with sandwiches and wraps, and a good value two- and three-course set weekend lunch, the menu and specials are strong on fish and seafood, and might include grilled langoustines, game terrine, sausage and mash, beer-battered haddock goujons, steaks, various salads, seared halibut, roast lamb rump, and puddings like warm choclate brownie. *Benchmark main dish: 8oz 33-day matured sirloin steak £21.95. Two-course evening meal £21.00.*

Free house ~ Licensees Chris and Jan Winson ~ Real ale ~ (01890) 860257 ~ Open 4-11; 11-midnight Sat; 11-11 Sun; closed weekday lunchtimes ~ Bar food 6-9 weekdays; 12-3, 6-9 Sat; 12-4, 6-9 Sun ~ Restaurant ~ Young children allowed in restaurant 6-7pm ~ Dogs allowed in bar ~ Live music most Fri nights ~ Bedrooms: £89/£119 ~ www.wheatsheaf-swinton.co.uk *Recommended by Martin Jones*

Please let us know what you think of a pub's bedrooms: feedback@goodguides.com or (no stamp needed) The Good Pub Guide, FREEPOST TN1569, Wadhurst, E Sussex TN5 7BR.

THORNHILL   NS6699   Map 11

Lion & Unicorn

Main Street (A873); FK8 3PJ

Busy, interesting pub with emphasis on its home-made food; friendly staff

Run by welcoming staff and warmed by blazing fires, this 17th-c inn has an invitingly pubby character, although the accent is on dining. The bar at the back has some exposed stone walls, a wooden floor and stools lined along the counter. It opens to a games room with a pool table, juke box, fruit machine, darts, TV and board games. The more restauranty-feeling carpeted front room has pub furniture, usually set for dining, a beamed ceiling and – as evidence of the building's 17th-c origins – an original massive fireplace with a log fire in a high brazier, almost big enough to drive a car into. A couple of real ales such as Belhaven IPA and Ruddles Best are on handpump, and they have a good choice of malt whiskies; background music. Outside are benches in a gravelled garden and a play area on the lawn.

Food might include warm goats cheese salad, thai spiced mussels, steak burger, chicken, leek and mushroom puff pastry pie, leek with field mushroom and parsnip crumble, steaks, and puddings. *Benchmark main dish: steak and ale pie £10.25. Two-course evening meal £20.00.*

Free house ~ Licensees Bobby and Fiona Stevenson ~ Real ale ~ (01786) 850204 ~ Open 11am(12.30 Sun)-midnight (1am Sat) ~ Bar food 12(12.30 Sun)-9 ~ Restaurant ~ Children welcome until 9pm ~ Bedrooms: £55/£75 ~ www.lion-unicorn.co.uk
Recommended by Caroline Prescott

WEEM   NN8449   Map 11

Ailean Chraggan ♀

B846; PH15 2LD

Changing range of seasonal food in homely, family-run hotel

With welcoming owners, this inviting and beautifully placed hotel has a simple bar with chatty locals, a couple of beers from the local Inveralmond Brewery on handpump, more than 100 malt whiskies and a very good wine list. There's also an adjoining neatly old-fashioned dining room. Winter darts; the bedrooms are pleasantly presented. There are great views from the two flower-filled front terraces to the mountains beyond the Tay and up to Ben Lawers (the highest peak in this part of Scotland); the owners can arrange fishing nearby.

As well as lunchtime sandwiches, the changing menu (served in either the comfortably carpeted modern lounge or the dining room) includes items such as cullen skink, venison and prune terrine, mixed grill, scallops with broad bean risotto, roast pepper and ricotta cannelloni, slow-braised pork belly and sausage meat roulade, and puddings such as peach and blueberry trifle with mango jelly and chocolate and whisky truffle torte. *Benchmark main dish: seafood platter £21.50. Two-course evening meal £18.00.*

Free house ~ Licensee Alastair Gillespie ~ Real ale ~ (01887) 820346 ~ Open 11-11 ~ Bar food 12-2, 5.30-8.30(9 Sat, Sun) ~ Restaurant ~ Children welcome ~ Dogs allowed in bar and bedrooms ~ Bedrooms: £53.75/£107.50 ~ www.aileanchraggan.co.uk
Recommended by Roger and Gill Walker, Susan and John Douglas

Also Worth a Visit in Scotland

Besides the fully inspected pubs, you might like to try these pubs that have been recommended to us and described by readers. Do tell us what you think of them: feedback@goodguides.com

ABERDEENSHIRE

ABERDEEN   NJ9305
Grill (01224) 573530
Union Street; AB11 6BA Don't be put off by the exterior of this 19th-c granite building – the remodelled 1920s interior is well worth a look; long wood-floored bar with fine moulded ceiling, mahogany panelling and original button-back leather wall benches, ornate servery with glazed cabinets housing some of the 500 or so whiskies (a few distilled in the 1930s), five well kept ales including Caledonian 80/- and Harviestoun Bitter & Twisted, basic snacks; no children or dogs; open all day (till 1am Fri, Sat). *(Anon)*

ABERDEEN   NJ9406
Old Blackfriars (01224) 581922
Castle Street; AB11 5BB Welcoming and cosy ancient building on two levels, plenty of character, several well kept mainly scottish beers, good value pubby food; open all day. *(Anon)*

ABERDEEN   NJ9406
★ **Prince of Wales** (01224) 640597
St Nicholas Lane; AB10 1HF Individual and convivial old tavern with eight changing ales from very long counter, bargain hearty food, painted floorboards, flagstones or carpet, pews and screened booths, original tiled spitoon running length of bar; games machines; children over 5 welcome if eating, open all day from 10am (11am Sun). *(Pete Walker)*

ABOYNE   NO5298
★ **Boat** (01339) 886137
Charlestown Road (B968, just off A93); AB34 5EL Friendly country inn with fine views across River Dee, partly carpeted bar with model train chugging its way around just below ceiling height, scottish pictures, brasses and woodburner in stone fireplace, games in public-bar end, spiral stairs up to roomy additional dining area, three well kept ales such as Belhaven, Deeside and Inveralmond, decent wine and some 30 malts, tasty bar food from sandwiches up, more elaborate seasonal evening menu; background music, games machine; children welcome, dogs in bar, six comfortable well equipped bedrooms, open all day. *(the Dutchman, Michael and Maggie Betton, J F M and M West)*

OLDMELDRUM   NJ8127
Redgarth (01651) 872353
Kirk Brae, off A957; AB51 0DJ Good-sized comfortable lounge with traditional décor and subdued lighting, three well kept real ales, good range of malt whiskies, popular reasonably priced food, pleasant attentive service, restaurant; lovely views to Bennachie, bedrooms (get booked quickly). *(David and Betty Gittins)*

ANGUS

BROUGHTY FERRY   NO4630
★ **Fishermans Tavern** (01382) 775941
Fort Street; turning off shore road; DD5 2AD Once a row of fishermen's cottages, this friendly pub is just steps from the beach, six well kept changing ales (May beer festival) and good range of malt whiskies, secluded lounge area with coal fire, small carpeted snug with basket-weave wall panels, another fire in back bar popular with diners for the reasonably priced pubby food, fiddle music Thurs night, quiz every other Mon; TV, fruit machine; children and dogs welcome, disabled facilities, tables on front pavement, more in secluded little walled garden, 12 bedrooms, open all day (till 1am Thurs-Sat). *(Christine and Neil Townend, Susan and John Douglas)*

ARGYLL

BRIDGE OF ORCHY   NN2939
★ **Bridge of Orchy Hotel**
(01838) 400208 *A82 Tyndrum–Glencoe; PA36 4AB* Spectacular spot on West Highland Way, very welcoming with good fairly priced food in bar and restaurant, decent choice of well kept ales, house wines and malt whiskies, interesting mountain photographs; ten good bedrooms, more in newly built riverside annexe. *(Anon)*

CONNEL   NM9034
Oyster (01631) 710666
A85, W of Connel Bridge; PA37 1PJ 18th-c pub opposite former ferry slipway, lovely view across the water (especially at sunset), decent-sized bar with friendly Highland atmosphere, log fire in stone fireplace, enjoyable food including good local seafood, Caledonian Deuchars IPA,

We say if we know a pub allows dogs.

good range of wines and malts, attentive service; sports TV, pool and darts; modern hotel part next door with separate evening restaurant. *(Richard J Holloway)*

INVERARAY   NN0908
⭑ **George**   (01499) 302111
Main Street East; PA32 8TT Very popular Georgian hotel (packed during holiday times) at hub of this appealing small town; bustling pubby bar with exposed joists, bare stone walls, old tiles and big flagstones, antique settles, carved wooden benches and cushioned stone slabs along the walls, four log fires, ales such as Belhaven, 100 malt whiskies, nice food in bar and smarter restaurant, live entertainment Fri, Sat; children and dogs welcome, well laid-out terraces with plenty of seats, bedrooms, Inveraray Castle and walks close by, open all day till 1am. *(Roger and Gill Walker)*

OBAN   NM8530
Cuan Mor   (01631) 565078
George Street; PA34 5SD Contemporary quayside bar-restaurant with good choice of competitively priced food all day, real ales including their own brews, friendly service; children welcome, some seats outside. *(Dave Braisted)*

OBAN   NM8529
Lorne   (01631) 570020
Stevenson Street; PA34 5NA Nice Victorian décor including tiles and island bar with ornate brasswork, well kept Oban Bay ales, reasonably priced food from ciabattas and wraps through pizzas to local fish, good service, live music and DJs at weekends; children welcome, sheltered beer garden, open all day till late. *(Carola and Brian Groom)*

OTTER FERRY   NR9384
Oystercatcher   (01700) 821229
B8000, by the water; PA21 2DH Friendly family-run pub-restaurant in old building in outstanding spot overlooking Loch Fyne, good locally sourced food, well kept ales including Fyne from pine-clad bar, decent wine list; lots of tables out on spit, free moorings, open all day. *(Lindsay White)*

TARBERT   NR8365
West Loch Hotel   (01880) 820283
A83 a mile S; PA29 6YF Friendly 18th-c family-run inn overlooking sea loch, comfortably updated, with enjoyable reasonably priced local food (try the Iron Bru ice-cream), Belhaven and good selection of whiskies and gins, helpful cheerful service; children and dogs welcome, eight bedrooms – some with loch views, handy for ferry terminal. *(Dave Braisted)*

LOCH ECK   NS1491
Coylet   (01369) 840426
A815, E shore; PA23 8SG Beautiful lochside setting and under friendly new management, good food, Fyne Highlander on draught; three bedrooms. *(Dave Braisted)*

AYRSHIRE

DUNURE   NS2515
Dunure   (01292) 500549
Just off A719 SW of Ayr; KA7 4LN Welcoming place attractively set by harbourside ruined castle; updated bar, lounge and restaurant, good food including fresh fish/seafood, nice wines; no real ales; courtyard tables, bedrooms and two cottages, not far from Culzean Castle. *(Paul Bromley)*

SYMINGTON   NS3831
Wheatsheaf   (01563) 830307
Just off A77 Ayr–Kilmarnock; Main Street; KA1 5QB Single-storey former 17th-c posting inn, charming and cosy, with wide choice of good well priced food (must book weekends) including lunchtime/early evening set menu, efficient friendly service, log fire; keg beers; children welcome, tables outside, quiet pretty village, open (and food) all day. *(Anon)*

BERWICKSHIRE

ALLANTON   NT8654
Allanton Inn   (01890) 818260
B6347 S of Chirnside; TD11 3JZ Pretty stone-built village inn, light and airy, with welcoming owners, good fairly priced food including fresh fish from daily changing menu, a couple of real ales, good wine list, log fire in small attractive side dining room; children welcome, sheltered garden behind, six bedrooms, open all day. *(Simon Daws, Comus and Sarah Elliott)*

AUCHENCROW   NT8560
Craw   (01890) 761253
B6438 NE of Duns; pub signed off A1; TD14 5LS Attractive little 18th-c pub in row of cream-washed slate-roofed cottages, friendly and welcoming, with good well presented food including fresh fish and seafood, changing ales from smaller brewers, good wines by the glass, beams decorated with hundreds of beer mats, pictures on panelled walls, woodburner, more formal back restaurant; children welcome, tables on decking behind and out on village green, three bedrooms, open all day weekends. *(GSB)*

CAITHNESS

MEY   ND2872
Castle Arms   (01847) 851244
A836; KW14 8XH 19th-c former coaching inn refurbished under welcoming new owners; enjoyable home-made food and

friendly helpful service, plenty of malt whiskies, views of Dunnet Head and across Pentland Firth to the Orkneys; pool; seven comfortable bedrooms in back extension, well placed for N coast of Caithness, Gills Bay ferry and Castle of Mey. *(Dave Braisted)*

DUMFRIESSHIRE

BARGRENNAN   NX3576
House O'Hill (01671) 840243
Off A714, road opposite church;
DG8 6RN Small refurbished pub on edge of Galloway Forest, interesting well cooked/priced food (best to book), a couple of real ales and good wine list, friendly helpful staff; two bedrooms (good breakfast) and self-catering cottage, open all day.
(Dr Peter D Smart)

DUMFRIES   NX9776
✷ **Cavens Arms** (01387) 252896
Buccleuch Street; DG1 2AH Good home-made food all day (not Mon) from pubby standards up, seven well kept interesting ales, Aspall's and Stowford Press cider, fine choice of malts, friendly landlord and good helpful staff, civilised front part with lots of wood, drinkers' area at back with bar stools, banquettes and traditional cast-iron tables, recently added lounge areas; can get very busy, discreet TV, no under-14s or dogs; disabled facilities, small terrace at back, open all day. *(Eric Larkham, Dr J Barrie Jones)*

DUMFRIES   NX9775
Globe (01387) 252335
High Street; DG1 2JA Proper town pub with strong Burns connections, especially in old-fashioned dark-panelled 17th-century snug and little museum of a room beyond; main part more modern in feel, ales such as Caledonian Deuchars IPA and Sulwath The Grace, plenty of whiskies, good value food (evening by arrangement), friendly service; children welcome in eating areas, terrace seating, open all day. *(the Didler)*

MOFFAT   NT0805
Annandale Arms (01683) 220013
High Street; DG10 9HF 18th-c hotel's pleasant oak-panelled bar, local Broughton ales, Weston's cider and around 50 malt whiskies (also a breakfast one), nice food served by friendly staff, restauarant; 16 bedrooms. *(Johnston and Maureen Anderson)*

MOFFAT   NT0805
Black Bull (01683) 220206
Churchgate; DG10 9EG Attractive small hotel (former coaching inn), comfortable dimly lit bar with Burns memorabilia, well kept Caledonian Deuchars IPA and several dozen malts, enjoyable food including steaks and grills, simply furnished carpeted dining room, friendly public bar across courtyard with railway memorabilia, pool, darts and

big-screen sports TV; background and live acoustic music; children and dogs welcome, tables in courtyard, seven small bedrooms in annexe, hearty breakfast, no car park, open all day. *(Johnston and Maureen Anderson)*

MOFFAT   NT0805
Buccleuch Arms (01683) 220003
High Street; DG10 9ET Friendly rather old-fashioned Georgian coaching inn with roomy carpeted bar and lounge areas, open fire, good popular food using local produce (suppliers listed), informal upstairs restaurant, polite quick service, interesting wines by the glass, good choice of malts and bottled beers, cocktails; soft background music, Sky TV; dogs welcome, garden, 16 bedrooms, open all day. *(Anon)*

DUNBARTONSHIRE

ARROCHAR   NN2903
Village Inn (01301) 702279
A814, just off A83 W of Loch Lomond;
G83 7AX Friendly, cosy and interesting with well kept ales such as Caledonian and Fyne, enjoyable home-made hearty food in simple all-day dining area (can get booked up) with heavy beams, bare boards, some panelling and roaring fire, steps down to unpretentious bar, several dozen malts, good coffee, fine sea and hill views; background music, juke box, can be noisy on busy summer weekends; children welcome in eating areas till 8pm, no dogs, tables out on deck and lawn, comfortable bedrooms including spacious ones in former back barn, good breakfast, open all day.
(Eric Larkham, David and Sue Atkinson)

EAST LOTHIAN

DUNBAR   NT6779
Rocks (01368) 862287
Marine Road; EH42 1AR Atmospheric 19th-c clifftop hotel with great sea views, well liked food including local fish, real ales, welcoming staff; 12 bedrooms. *(Sarah Flynn)*

GULLANE   NT4882
✷ **Old Clubhouse** (01620) 842008
East Links Road; EH31 2AF Single-storey building with bar and more formal dining room, Victorian pictures and cartoons, stuffed birds, pre-war sheet music, golfing and other memorabilia, open fires, good sensibly priced pubby food and specials, four ales including Belhaven and Caledonian, nice house wines, fast friendly service, views over golf links to Lammermuirs; children and dogs welcome, open all day. *(Comus and Sarah Elliott, GSB)*

HADDINGTON   NT5173
Victoria (01620) 823332
Court Street; EH41 3JD Popular

refurbished bar-restaurant with good imaginative local food cooked by chef-landlord, a couple of changing real ales, short but decent wine list, prompt friendly service; five bedrooms, open all day. *(Ian Wilson, Comus and Sarah Elliott)*

HADDINGTON   NT5173
Waterside (01620) 825674
Waterside; just off A6093, over pedestrian bridge at E end of town; EH41 4AT Attractively set riverside dining pub next to historic bridge, spacious modernised interior with some stylish touches, enjoyable food including set lunch, three real ales from smaller brewers, good wine choice, pleasant friendly staff; children welcome (family room with toys), picnic-sets out overlooking the Tyne. *(Comus and Sarah Elliott)*

FIFE

CUPAR   NO3714
Boudingait (01334) 654681
Bonnygate; KY15 4BU Revamped former Drookit Dug; friendly attentive staff, good variety of reasonably priced home-made food (something available all day), live folk and quiz nights; children welcome. *(Anon)*

ELIE   NO4999
⋆**Ship** (01333) 330246
The Toft, off A917 (High Street) towards harbour; KY9 1DT Pleasant seaside inn, very much part of the community, and in good position for enjoying a drink overlooking the sandy bay and on towards the stone pier and old granary; unspoilt beamed nautical-feel bar with old prints and maps on partly panelled walls, coal fires, Caledonian Deuchars IPA, a few malt whiskies, decent bar food, simple carpeted back room with board games (children welcome here); dogs allowed in bar, open all day (till 1am Fri, Sat). *(John and Alison Hamilton, Susan and John Douglas, Pat and Stewart Gordon)*

ST ANDREWS   NO5116
Central (01334) 478296
Market Street; KY16 9NU Traditional Victorian town-centre pub (Taylor Walker) with good choice of english and scottish beers from island servery, knowledgeable friendly staff, fair-priced pubby food, friendly mix of customers; pavement tables, open all day. *(Pat and Tony Martin, E Dawson)*

INVERNESS-SHIRE

MALLAIG   NM6796
Steam (01687) 462002
Davies Brae; PH41 4PU Refurbished Victorian inn run by mother and daughter, good choice of food from bar snacks to freshly landed fish, speedy service, bar with open

fire and pool, split-level restaurant, live music including traditional; children and dogs welcome, tables in back garden, five bedrooms. *(Mike and Mary Carter)*

AVIEMORE   NH8612
Cairngorm (01479) 810233
Grampian Road (A9); PH22 1PE Large flagstoned bar in traditional hotel, lively and friendly, with prompt helpful service, good value food from wide-ranging menu using local produce, Cairngorm ales, good choice of other drinks, informal dining lounge/conservatory; some live music, sports TV; children welcome, comfortable bedrooms. *(Christine and Neil Townend)*

CARRBRIDGE   NH9022
Cairn (01479) 841212
Main Road; PH23 3AS Welcoming tartan-carpeted hotel bar, enjoyable pubby food and well kept ales such as Black Isle, Cairngorm and Highland, old local pictures, warm coal fire, separate more formal dining room; pool and sports TV; children and dogs welcome, seven comfortable bedrooms, open all day. *(Johnston and Maureen Anderson, Brian and Anna Marsden)*

FORT WILLIAM   NN1073
Ben Nevis Bar (01397) 702295
High Street; PH33 6DG Comfortable wood-floor bar with several real ales, enjoyable food, harbour views from upstairs restaurant; no dogs. *(Dave Braisted)*

FORT WILLIAM   NN1274
Ben Nevis Inn (01397) 701227
N off A82: Achintee; PH33 6TE Roomy, well converted, raftered stone barn in stunning spot by path up to Ben Nevis, good mainly straightforward food (lots of walkers so best to book), ales such as Cairngorm Nessies Monster Mash, prompt cheery service, bare-boards dining area with steps up to bar, live music; seats out at front and back, bunkhouse below, open all day Apr-Oct, otherwise closed Mon-Weds. *(Phil Bryant, Michael Peters, M J Winterton)*

GLEN SHIEL   NH0711
⋆**Cluanie Inn** (01320) 340238
A87 Invergarry–Kyle of Lochalsh, on Loch Cluanie; IV63 7YW Welcoming inn in lovely isolated setting by Loch Cluanie, stunning views, friendly table service for drinks including well kept Isle of Skye, fine malt range, big helpings of enjoyable food (good local venison) in three knocked-together rooms with dining chairs around polished tables, overspill into restaurant, warm log fire, chatty parrots in lobby – watch your fingers; children allowed, dogs too (owners have several of their own), big comfortable pine-furnished modern bedrooms, bunkhouse, great breakfasts (non-residents welcome). *(Dave Braisted)*

GLENUIG
NM6576
Glenuig Inn (01687) 470219
*A861 SW of Lochailort, off A830 Fort
William–Mallaig; PH38 4NG* Friendly
refurbished bar on picturesque bay, enjoyable
locally sourced food including some from
next-door smokery, well kept Cairngorm
ales and a scottish cider on tap, lots of
bottled beers and good range of whiskies,
woodburner in dining room; dogs welcome,
bedrooms in adjoining block, also bunkhouse
popular with walkers and divers, moorings for
visiting yachts, open all day. *(David and Sue
Atkinson, Dave Braisted)*

INVERIE
NG7500
★ Old Forge (01687) 462267
Park in Mallaig for ferry; PH41 4PL
Utterly remote waterside stone pub with
fabulous views; comfortable mix of old
furnishings, lots of charts and sailing
prints, open fire, buoyant atmosphere, good
reasonably priced bar food including fresh
seafood, two well kept changing ales in
season, lots of whiskies and good wine choice,
restaurant extension, occasional live music
and ceilidhs (instruments provided); the
snag is getting there – boat (jetty moorings
and new pier), Mallaig foot ferry three days a
week (five days a week in summer) or 15-mile
walk through Knoydart from nearest road;
children and dogs welcome, open all day
summer. *(Dave Braisted)*

INVERMORISTON
NH4216
Glenmoriston Arms (01320) 51206
A82/A887; IV63 7YA Small civilised hotel
dating in part from 1740 when it was a
drovers' inn, tartan-carpeted bar with open
fire, neatly laid out restaurant, well kept beer
and over 100 malt whiskies, enjoyable food
from lunchtime sandwiches up, friendly staff;
handy for Loch Ness, 11 bedrooms (three in
converted outbuilding). *(Theocsbrian)*

INVERNESS
NH6645
Number 27 (01463) 241999
Castle Street; IV2 3DU Busy pub opposite
the castle, cheery welcoming staff, plenty
of draught and bottled beers, good choice
of well prepared food at reasonable prices,
restaurant at back; open all day. *(A J Holland,
the Dutchman)*

ROY BRIDGE
NN2781
Stronlossit Inn (01397) 712253
off A86; PH31 4AG Village inn three well
kept changing ales and over 80 malts, good
choice of enjoyable sensibly price food all
day, decent coffee, open fire; good disabled
access, ten bedrooms. *(M J Winterton)*

KINCARDINESHIRE

FETTERCAIRN
NO6573
Ramsay Arms (01561) 340334
Burnside Road; AB30 1XX Hotel with
enjoyable food in tartan-carpeted bar and
smart oak-panelled restaurant, friendly
service, well kept ales and several malts
including the local Fettercairn; children
welcome, garden tables, attractive village
(liked by Queen Victoria who stayed at the
hotel), 12 bedrooms, good breakfast. *(Anon)*

STONEHAVEN
NO8785
Marine Hotel (01569) 762155
Shore Head; AB39 2JY Popular
harbourside pub with six well kept ales
including own Dunnottar brews, over 170
bottled belgian beers and good choice of
whiskies, nice food especially local fish,
large stripped-stone bar with log fire in cosy
side room, upstairs sea-view restaurant;
children welcome, pavement tables, updated
bedrooms, open all day (till 1am Fri, Sat).
(Stuart Sim)

KIRKCUDBRIGHTSHIRE

GATEHOUSE OF FLEET
NX6056
Masonic Arms (01557) 814335
Ann Street; off B727; DG7 2HU Spacious
dining pub with comfortable two-room
pubby bar, traditional seating, pictures on
timbered walls, plates on delft shelf, stuffed
fish above brick fireplace, real ales and
good choice of malts, enjoyable food in bar
and contemporary restaurant, attractive
terracotta-tiled conservatory with cane
furniture; background music (live Thurs),
quiz Weds; children and dogs welcome,
picnic-sets under parasols in neatly kept
sheltered garden, more seats in front, open
all day. *(Anon)*

GATEHOUSE OF FLEET
NX5956
Ship (01557) 814217
Fleet Street; DG7 2JT Late Victorian
village inn on the banks of the River Fleet,
enjoyable popular food, Belhaven beers
and good choice of malt whiskies, neatly
kept refurbished interior with woodburner,
welcoming service, restaurant; waterside
garden, bedrooms, Dorothy Sayers wrote
Five Red Herrings while staying here in
the 1930s. *(Phil and Jane Hodson)*

HAUGH OF URR
NX8066
★ Laurie Arms (01556) 660246
*B794 N of Dalbeattie; Main Street;
DG7 3YA* Neatly kept and attractively

Anyone claiming to arrange, or prevent, inclusion of a pub in the *Guide* is a fraud.
Pubs are included only if recommended by genuine readers and if our own anonymous
inspection confirms that they are suitable.

decorated 19th-c pub with good local atmosphere, a few tables in log-fire bar with steps up to similar area, decent food from bar snacks to steaks, good changing real ales and decent wines by the glass, welcoming attentive service, restaurant, games room with darts, pool and juke box, splendid Bamforth comic postcards in the gents'; tables out at front and on sheltered terrace behind, open all day weekends. *(Douglas Johnson, R J Herd)*

KIRKCUDBRIGHT   NX6850
⋆**Selkirk Arms**   (01557) 330402

High Street; DG6 4JG Comfortable, well run 18th-c hotel in pleasant spot by mouth of the Dee, simple locals' front bar (own street entrance), partitioned high-ceilinged lounge with upholstered armchairs, wall banquettes and paintings for sale, ales including a house beer from local Sulwath, generous food in bistro and restaurant from pub standards up, good helpful service; background music, TV; children (not in bar) and dogs welcome, smart wooden furniture under blue parasols in neat garden with 15th-c font, 17 comfortable bedrooms, open all day. *(the Didler, J F M and M West, Christine and Neil Townend, Steve Whalley)*

LANARKSHIRE

BALMAHA   NS4290
Oak Tree   (01360) 870357

B837; G63 0JQ Recently built slate-clad inn on Loch Lomond's quiet side, beams, timbers and panelling, pubby bar with lots of old photographs, farm tools and collection of grandfather clocks, log fire, good choice of enjoyable food from sandwiches and snacks up, scottish ales (own brew-house planned), good whisky selection, restaurant; children welcome, plenty of tables out around ancient oak tree, popular with West Highland Way walkers, seven bedrooms, two bunkhouse and four cottages. *(Laurence Smith)*

GLASGOW   NS5965
Counting House   (0141) 225 0160

Corner of St Vincent Place and George Square; G1 2DH Impressive Wetherspoons bank conversion, imposing interior rising into lofty richly decorated coffered ceiling culminating in great central dome, big windows, decorative glasswork, wall-safes, several areas with solidly comfortable seating, smaller rooms (once managers' offices) around perimeter, one like a well stocked library, a few themed with pictures and prints of historical characters, real ales from far and wide, bottled beers and lots of malt whiskies, usual good value food all day; children welcome if eating, open 8am-midnight. *(Theocsbrian, Comus and Sarah Elliott)*

GLASGOW   NS5865
Drum & Monkey   (0141) 221 6636

St Vincent Street; G2 5TF Nicholsons bank conversion with ornate ceiling, granite pillars and lots of carved mahogany, Caledonian and other beers from island bar, decent range of wines and good value food, pleasant staff, quieter back area; open all day. *(Jeremy King)*

GLASGOW   NS5865
Pot Still   (0141) 333 0980

Hope Street; G2 2TH Comfortable and welcoming little pub with hundreds of malt whiskies, traditional bare-boards interior with dark panelling, etched and stained glass, columns up to ornately corniced ceiling, button-back leather bench seats, raised area at the back, four changing real ales and interesting bottled beers from nice old-fashioned servery, knowledgeable friendly staff; silent fruit machine; open all day. *(Jeremy King)*

GLASGOW   NS5965
⋆**Sloans**   (0141) 221 8886

Argyle Arcade; G2 8BG Restored Grade A listed building over three floors, many original features including a fine mahogany staircase, etched glass, ornate woodwork and moulded ceilings, Caledonian Deuchars IPA and Kelburn, good choice of food from sandwiches up in ground-floor bar-bistro and upstairs restaurant, friendly staff, events in impressive barrel-vaulted parquet-floored ballroom; children welcome, tables in courtyard, Sun market, open all day (till late Fri, Sat). *(Comus and Sarah Elliott, Dr and Mrs A K Clarke)*

GLASGOW   NS5865
State   (0141) 332 2159

Holland Street; G2 4NG High-ceilinged bar with marble pillars, lots of carved wood including handsome oak island servery, half a dozen or so well kept changing ales, bargain basic lunchtime food from sandwiches up, some areas set for dining, good atmosphere and friendly staff, armchairs among other comfortable seats, coal-effect gas fire in big wooden fireplace, old prints and theatrical posters; background music (live weekends), silent sports TVs, games machine. *(Jeremy King)*

GLASGOW   NS5666
Tennents   (0141) 339 7203

Byres Road; G12 8TN Big busy high-ceilinged Victorian corner pub near university, ornate plasterwork, panelling and paintings, a dozen well kept ales, wide range of good value food from sandwiches and baked potatoes up including bargain offers, basement bar for weekend DJs and Mon quiz; sports TVs; open all day. *(Dr and Mrs A K Clarke)*

GLASGOW NS5666

Three Judges (0141) 337 3055

Dumbarton Road, opposite Byres Road; G11 6PR Traditional corner bar with up to nine quickly changing real ales from small breweries far and wide (they get through several hundred a year), pump clips on walls, friendly staff and locals, live jazz Sun afternoons, no food; dogs welcome, open all day. *(Dr and Mrs A K Clarke)*

MIDLOTHIAN

DALKEITH NR3264

Sun (0131) 663 2456

A7 S; EH22 4TR Refurbished dining pub and boutique hotel with good quality local food, early-bird deals Mon-Thurs, changing real ales and extensive range of wines by the glass including champagne; courtyard garden, five individually styled bedrooms, good generous breakfast, open all day. *(Anon)*

EDINBURGH NT2574

⋆**Café Royal** (0131) 556 1884

West Register Street; EH2 2AA Opulent building with dazzling Victorian baroque interior, floors and stairway laid with marble, chandeliers hanging from magnificent plasterwork ceilings, superb series of Doulton tilework portraits of historical innovators (Watt, Faraday, Stephenson, Caxton, Benjamin Franklin and Robert Peel), substantial island bar serving Caledonian Deuchars IPA and three guests, several wines by the glass and 25 malts, well liked food, good friendly service, the restaurant's stained glass is also worth seeing (children welcome here); background music and games machine; open all day (till 1am Fri, Sat); can get very busy. *(Comus and Sarah Elliott, Michael Butler, Christine and Neil Townend, Barry Collett, David and Sue Smith and others)*

EDINBURGH NT2471

⋆**Canny Man's** (0131) 447 1484

Morningside Road; aka Volunteer Arms; EH10 4QU Utterly individual and distinctive, saloon, lounge and snug with fascinating bric-a-brac, ceiling papered with sheet music, huge range of appetising open sandwiches, very efficient friendly service, lots of whiskies, good wines and well kept ales such as Caledonian and Timothy Taylors Landlord, cheap children's drinks, no credit cards, mobile phones or backpackers; courtyard tables. *(John and Anne Mackinnon, Pat and Stewart Gordon)*

EDINBURGH NT2573

Deacon Brodies (0131) 225 6531

Lawnmarket; EH1 2NT Entertainingly commemorating the notorious highwayman town councillor who was eventually hanged on the scaffold he'd designed; bustling ornately high-ceilinged city bar, well kept Belhaven and Caledonian from long counter, decent whisky selection, good choice of reasonably priced food in upstairs dining lounge, service may struggle at busy times; background music, TV; pavement seating. *(John Beeken)*

EDINBURGH NT2573

Ensign Ewart (0131) 225 7440

Lawnmarket, Royal Mile; last pub on right before castle; EH1 2PE Charming dimly lit old-world pub handy for castle (so gets busy), beams peppered with brasses, huge painting of Ewart at Waterloo capturing french banner, assorted furniture including elbow tables, friendly efficient staff, well kept Caledonian ales and plenty of whiskies, simple enjoyable food; background music, games machine, keypad entry to lavatories; open all day. *(Peter F Marshall)*

EDINBURGH NT2573

⋆**Halfway House** (0131) 225 7101

Fleshmarket Close (steps between Cockburn Street and Market Street, opposite Waverley Station); EH1 1BX Tiny one-room pub off steep steps, part carpeted, part tiled, with a few small tables and high-backed settles, lots of prints (some golf and railway themes), four well kept scottish ales (third-of-a-pint glasses available), good range of malt whiskies, short choice of decent cheap food all day; TV turned up for racing; dogs welcome, open all day. *(Derek Wason)*

EDINBURGH NT2676

Kings Wark (0131) 554 9260

The Shore, Leith; EH6 6QU Old bare-boards pub on Leith's restored waterfront; plenty of atmosphere in stripped-stone candlelit interior, good selection of well kept ales, nice food and good value wines; open all day. *(David Hunt)*

EDINBURGH NT2473

Oxford (0131) 539 7119

Young Street; EH2 4JB Welcoming no-frills local with two built-in wall settles in tiny bustling bar, rugby memorabilia, steps up to quieter back room, lino floor, well kept Caledonian Deuchars IPA and guests, a good range of whiskies, cheap filled cobs; no children; dogs welcome, links with scottish writers and artists, open all day. *(David and Sue Smith)*

EDINBURGH NT2872

Sheep Heid (0131) 661 7974

The Causeway, Duddingston; EH15 3QA Comfortably refurbished coaching inn (part of the Village Pub & Kitchen chain) in lovely spot near King Arthur's Seat, long history, fine rounded bar counter in main room, well kept beers and above average food (all day) including children's menu, friendly young staff, skittle alley; courtyard tables. *(Anthony Jones)*

EDINBURGH   NT2574
Standing Order (0131) 225 4460
George Street; EH2 2JP Grand
Wetherspoons bank conversion in three
elegant Georgian houses, imposing columns,
enormous main room with elaborate
colourful ceiling, lots of tables, smaller side
booths, other rooms including two with floor-
to-ceiling bookshelves, comfortable clubby
seats, Adam fireplace and portraits, wide
range of real ales from long counter, bar food;
sports TV, weekend live music, gets very busy
particularly on Sat night; disabled facilities,
open all day till 1am. *(John Beeken)*

EDINBURGH   NT2574
★ Starbank (0131) 552 4141
*Laverockbank Road, off Starbank Road,
just off A901 Granton–Leith; EH5 3BZ*
Cheerful pub in a fine spot with terrific views
over the Firth of Forth, long light and airy
bare-boards bar, some leather bench seats,
up to eight well kept ales and good choice
of malt whiskies, reasonably priced food in
conservatory restaurant; background and
some live music, sports TV, fruit machine;
children welcome till 9pm if dining, dogs on
leads, sheltered back terrace, parking on
adjacent hilly street, open all day. *(John and
Annabel Hampshire, the Dutchman)*

RATHO   NT1470
Bridge (0131) 333 1320
Baird Road; EH28 8RA Extended 18th-c
pub with good food (all day) from varied
menu using local produce including some
of their own, changing scottish ales such as
Cairngorm, Inveralmond and Orkney, good
malt whisky choice, friendly staff; children
very welcome, garden by Union Canal with
wandering ducks, trips on own canal boats,
four bedrooms. *(Anon)*

PEEBLESSHIRE
INNERLEITHEN   NT3336
★ Traquair Arms (01896) 830229
*B709, just off A72 Peebles–Galashiels;
follow signs for Traquair House;
EH44 6PD* Modernised inn at heart of
pretty Borders village, one of the few places
serving Traquair ale (produced in original
oak vessels in 18th-c brewhouse at nearby
Traquair House), also Caledonian Deuchars
IPA and Timothy Taylors Landlord, 40 malt
whiskies, enjoyable italian-influenced
food (all day weekends), main bar with
warm open fire, another in relaxed bistro-
style restaurant, good mix of customers;
background music, TV; children welcome,
dogs in bar, picnic-sets on neat back lawn,
bedrooms and self-catering cottages, open
all day. *(the Didler)*

PERTHSHIRE
BLAIR ATHOLL   NN8765
★ Atholl Arms (01796) 481205
B8079; PH18 5SG Sizeable hotel's cosy
stable-themed Bothy Bar in lovely setting
near the castle, four local Moulin ales, good
well priced food all day from sandwiches
to interesting dishes, local meat and wild
salmon, quick friendly service, open fire;
31 good value bedrooms. *(Lucien Perring)*

BRIG O' TURK   NN5306
★ Byre (01877) 376292
*A821 Callander–Trossachs, just outside
village; FK17 8HT* Beautifully placed
byre conversion with flagstoned log-fire bar
and roomier high-raftered restaurant area,
popular food including local trout and some
imaginative dishes (best to book), friendly
helpful staff; tables out on extensive decking,
boules piste, good walks, open all day, closed
Jan. *(David and Katharine Cooke)*

DUNBLANE   NN7801
Tappit Hen (01786) 825226
Kirk Street; FK15 0AL Across close from
cathedral, small drinkers' pub with five
changing ales and good range of other drinks,
friendly busy atmosphere, traditional music
Tues; open all day. *(David McCullagh)*

DUNKELD   NO0243
Atholl Arms (01350) 727219
Atholl Street (A923); PH8 0AQ
Comfortably furnished smallish hotel
bar, good choice of well kept ales such as
Inveralmond, enjoyable food from varied
menu including cullen skink and beef stovies,
friendly service; 17 bedrooms (some with
River Tay views). *(Pat and Tony Martin)*

DUNNING   NO0114
Kirkstyle (01764) 684248
*B9141, off A9 S of Perth; Kirkstyle
Square; PH2 0RR* Unpretentious 18th-c
streamside pub with chatty regulars, log fire
in snug bar, up to three real ales and good
choice of whiskies, enjoyable good value
home-made food including some interesting
specials (book in season), attentive friendly
service, split-level stripped-stone back
restaurant; background music; children
welcome, dogs allowed in garden only, open
all day weekends, closed Mon and Tues
lunchtimes. *(Anon)*

KENMORE   NN7745
★ Kenmore Hotel (01887) 830205
A827 W of Aberfeldy; PH15 2NU Civilised
small hotel dating from the 16th c in pretty
Loch Tay village; comfortable traditional
front lounge with warm log fire and poem
pencilled by Burns himself on the chimney

---

breast, dozens of malts helpfully arranged alphabetically, polite uniformed staff, modern restaurant with balcony; back public bar and terrace overlooking River Tay with enjoyable food from lunchtime soup and sandwiches up, Inveralmond Ossian, decent wines by the glass; pool and winter darts, juke box, TV, fruit machine; children and dogs welcome, 40 good bedrooms, open all day. *(Anon)*

KILMAHOG   NN6008

⋆**Lade** (01877) 330152

A84 just NW of Callander, by A821 junction; FK17 8HD Lively place with a strong scottish theme – traditional weekend music, real ale shop with over 190 bottled beers from regional microbreweries and their own-brewed WayLade ales; plenty of character in several cosy beamed areas with panelling and stripped stone, Highland prints and works by local artists, 40 malt whiskies, enjoyable home-made food from bar snacks up, big-windowed restaurant, friendly staff; background music; children and dogs (in bar) welcome, terrace tables, pleasant garden with fish ponds, open all day (till 1am Fri, Sat). *(Pat and Stewart Gordon)*

LOCH TUMMEL   NN8160

⋆**Loch Tummel Inn** (01882) 634272

B8019 4 miles E of Tummel Bridge; PH16 5RP Beautifully placed traditional lochside inn renovated by present owners, great views over water to Schiehallion, cosy bar area with woodburner, good fresh seasonal food, two changing ales such as Inveralmond and Orkney, converted hayloft restaurant; children and dogs welcome, lots of walks and wildlife, six bedrooms, closed Mon (and Tues Nov-Mar), shut early Jan to early Feb. *(Anon)*

MEIKLEOUR   NO1539

⋆**Meikleour Hotel** (01250) 883206

A984 W of Coupar Angus; PH2 6EB Early 19th-c creeper-covered inn, well run and a good base for rural Perthshire; main lounge bar is basically two rooms (one carpeted, the other with stone floor), comfortable seating, some angling equipment and fishing/shooting pictures, oil-burning fires, Inveralmond ales including one brewed for the pub, good food from lunchtime snacks to local fish and game, attentive friendly service, elegant panelled restaurant; background music; children welcome, seats on small colonnaded verandah and sloping lawn with distant Highland view, spectacular nearby beech hedge planted over 250 years ago, comfortable bedrooms, good breakfast, open all day weekends. *(David and Betty*

Gittins, Susan and John Douglas, Les and Sandra Brown)

PITLOCHRY   NN9163

⋆**Killiecrankie Hotel** (01796) 473220

Killiecrankie, off A9 N; PH16 5LG Comfortable splendidly placed country hotel with attractive panelled bar and airy conservatory, good nicely varied and reasonably priced food, friendly efficient service, well kept ales and good choice of wines, restaurant; children in eating areas, extensive peaceful grounds with dramatic views, ten bedrooms. *(Anon)*

ROSS-SHIRE

BADACHRO   NG7873

⋆**Badachro Inn** (01445) 741255

2.5 miles S of Gairloch village turn off A832 on to B8056, then after another 3.25 miles turn right in Badachro to the quay and inn; IV21 2AA Superbly positioned by Loch Gairloch with terrific views from decking down to water's edge, popular (especially in summer) with happy mix of sailing visitors (free moorings) and chatty locals; welcoming bar with interesting photographs, An Teallach, Caledonian and a guest ale, about 30 malt whiskies and eight wines by the glass, quieter eating area with big log fire, dining conservatory overlooking bay, good reasonably priced food including locally smoked fish and seafood; background music; children and dogs welcome, one bedroom, open all day. *(Kate Vogelsang)*

FORTROSE   NH7256

⋆**Anderson** (01381) 620236

Union Street, off A832; IV10 8TD Friendly enthusiastic american licensees at this seaside hotel with vast selection of international beers (one of the largest collections of bottled belgians in the UK), also two or three well kept changing ales, Addlestone's cider and 250 malt whiskies, quite a few wines too, good food in homely bar and light airy dining room with open fire, board and puzzle-type games; background and live traditional music (every other Sun), knitting club and monthly quiz; children welcome, dogs in bar (resident dog and cat), seats out behind on gravel, nine bedrooms, open from 4pm (3pm Sun). *(Charles and Pauline Stride, Brian and Anna Marsden)*

MELVAIG   NG7485

Melvaig (01445) 771212

Aultgrishan (B8021); IV21 2DZ Remotely placed down long track leading to Rua Reidh lighthouse, and with wonderful

---

'Children welcome' means the pub says it lets children inside without any special restriction; some may impose an evening time limit earlier than 9pm – please tell us if you find this.

views across to Skye; reminiscent of a pebble-dashed bungalow and eccentrically packed with memorabilia including thousands of records (landlord had connection with Pink Floyd), 1960s juke box, old car parts, even a mannequin sitting at a piano, surprisingly good food particularly fish, An Teallach ales, open fire, pool and darts; closed Mon, only open weekends in winter; for sale as we went to press. *(Dave Braisted, Richard and Penny Gibbs)*

PLOCKTON   NG8033
★ **Plockton Inn**   (01599) 544222

Innes Street; unconnected to Plockton Hotel; IV52 8TW Close to the harbour in this lovely village, congenial bustling atmosphere even in winter, good well priced food with emphasis on local fish/seafood (some from back smokery), friendly efficient service, well kept changing beers and good range of malts, lively public bar with regular traditional music; seats out on decking, 14 bedrooms (seven in annexe over road), good breakfast. *(Dave Braisted, Martin and Sue Day, Dr Peter Crawshaw, Pete Walker)*

SHIEL BRIDGE   NG9319
Kintail Lodge   (01599) 511275

A87, N of Sheil Bridge; IV40 8HL Lots of varnished wood in large plain bar adjoining hotel, convivial bustle in season, Isle of Skye Red Cuillin and plenty of malt whiskies, particularly good food from same kitchen as attractive conservatory restaurant with magnificent view down Loch Duich to Skye, local game, wild salmon and own smokings, also children's helpings, friendly efficient service, occasional traditional music; 12 comfortable bedrooms, bunkhouse, good breakfast. *(Anon)*

ROXBURGHSHIRE

KELSO   NT7234
Cobbles   (01573) 223548

Bowmont Street; TD5 7JH Small comfortably refurbished 19th-c dining pub just off the main square, friendly and well run with good range of food from pub standards to more enterprising dishes, local Tempest ales, decent wines and malts from end bar, wall banquettes and panelling, welcoming fire, overspill dining room upstairs, folk music Fri till late; children welcome, disabled facilities, open all day. *(Anon)*

KIRK YETHOLM   NT8328
Border   (01573) 420237

Village signposted off B6352/B6401 crossroads, SE of Kelso; The Green; TD5 8PQ Change of ownership as we went to press for this well liked comfortable hotel (previous Main Entry); unpretentious bar with beams, flagstones and log fire, snug side rooms, beers have included Broughton and Scottish Borders, spacious dining room with fishing theme, lounge with another fire

and neat conservatory; background music; has allowed children (away from bar) and dogs (in bar and bedrooms), sheltered back terrace. *(Anon)*

ST BOSWELLS   NT5930
Buccleuch Arms   (01835) 822243

A68 just S of Newtown St Boswells; TD6 0EW Civilised 19th-c sandstone hotel with bar, comfortable lounge and new bistro, good popular food served by prompt friendly staff, real ale, open fires; children and dogs welcome, tables in attractive garden behind, 19 bedrooms. *(Adele Summers, Alan Black)*

SELKIRKSHIRE

MOUNTBENGER   NT3324
Gordon Arms   (01750) 82222

A708/B709; TD7 5LE Nice old pub reopened after long closure and sensitively restored by enthusiastic licensees – an oasis in these empty moorlands; public bar with winter fire, one real ale, good value food, live music; open all day. *(Comus and Sarah Elliott)*

STIRLINGSHIRE

DRYMEN   NS4788
Winnock   01360 660245

Just off A811; The Square; G63 0BL Big Best Western's modern split-level stripped-stone and beamed lounge bar, blazing log fires, leather sofas and easy chairs, well kept Caledonian Deuchars IPA and good choice of malt whiskies, popular fairly priced food, quick service from neat helpful young staff, steps down to restaurant area; background music; big garden, 48 bedrooms. *(Lucien Perring)*

SUTHERLAND

LAIRG   NC5224
★ **Crask Inn**   (01549) 411 241

A836 13 miles N towards Altnaharra; IV27 4AB Remote homely inn on single-track road through peaceful moorland, good simple food cooked by landlady including own lamb (the friendly hard-working licensees keep sheep on this working croft), comfortably basic bar with large peat stove to dry the sheepdogs (other dogs welcome), a summer real ale, Black Isle bottled beers in winter, interesting books, piano, pleasant separate dining room; three bedrooms (lights out when generator goes off), simple nearby bunkhouse. *(Dr Peter Crawshaw, Les and Sandra Brown)*

LOCHINVER   NC0922
Caberfeidh   (01571) 844321

Culag Road (A837); IV27 4JY Delightful lochside position with lovely views, cosy bar, conservatory and more formal restaurant, shortish menu with emphasis on local seafood, well kept beers including Caledonian, charming landlord and staff; dogs welcome, small harbourside garden, open all day in summer. *(George Atkinson)*

WEST LOTHIAN

LINLITHGOW   NS0077

⋆ **Four Marys** (01506) 842171

High Street; 2 miles from M9 junction 3 (and little further from junction 4) – town signposted; EH49 7ED Evocative 16th-c place – named after Mary, Queen of Scots' four ladies-in-waiting – and filled with mementoes of the ill-fated queen including pictures and written records, pieces of bed curtain and clothing, even a facsimile of her death-mask; neatly kept L-shaped room with mahogany dining chairs around stripped period and antique tables, attractive old corner cupboards, elaborate Victorian dresser serving as part of the bar, mainly stripped-stone walls with some remarkable masonry in the inner area, up to nine real ales (May and Oct beer festivals), good range of malt whiskies, fair value food including good cullen skink, cheery landlord and courteous staff; background music; children in dining area until 9.30pm, heated outdoor smoking area, difficult parking, open all day (till 1am Fri, Sat). *(Peter F Marshall)*

WIGTOWNSHIRE

BLADNOCH   NX4254

Bladnoch Inn (01988) 402200

Corner of A714 and B7005; DG8 9AB Cheerful bar, neat and bright, with eating area, enjoyable well prepared pubby food from sandwiches up, a beer such as St Andrews, friendly obliging service, restaurant; background music; children and dogs welcome, picturesque riverside setting across from Bladnoch distillery (tours), four good value bedrooms (two share bathroom), open all day. *(Anon)*

PORTPATRICK   NW9954

Crown (01776) 810261

North Crescent; DG9 8SX Popular seafront hotel in delightful harbourside village, enjoyable reasonably priced food all day including notable seafood, friendly prompt service, several dozen malts, decent wines by the glass, warm fire in rambling traditional bar with cosy corners, sewing machine tables, old photographs and posters, attractively decorated early 20th-c dining room opening through quiet conservatory into sheltered back garden; background music, TV; children and dogs welcome, tables out in front. *(John and Sylvia Harrop, R J Herd, Desmond Hall)*

SCOTTISH ISLANDS

ARRAN

CATACOL   NR9049

Catacol Bay (01770) 830231

A841; KA27 8HN Unpretentious hotel rather than pub run by same family for 30 years and in wonderful setting yards from the sea, with bay window looking across to Kintyre – cosy when gales blow; simple bar, ales from Belhaven, Houston and Timothy Taylors, pool, good food and hearty breakfasts; tables outside, simple bedrooms with washbasins (the ones at the front have the view); own mooring. *(Dave Braisted)*

BARRA

CASTLEBAY   NL6698

Castlebay Hotel (01871) 810223

By aeroplane from Glasgow or ferry from Oban; HS9 5XD Big but cosy and lively bar – once popular with those in the herring trade – next to hotel, good meeting place, regular local musicians and comedians, comfortable seating, restaurant with great harbour view, enjoyable food, pleasant young staff; decent bedrooms (dogs allowed). *(Steve Homer)*

BUTE

PORT BANNATYNE   NS0767

Port Royal (01700) 505073

Marine Road; PA20 0LW Cheerful stone-built inn looking across sea to Argyll, interior reworked as pre-revolution russian tavern with bare boards, painted timbers and tapestries, all-day food including russian dishes and good seafood, choice of russian beers and vodkas as well as real ales tapped from the cask, open fire, candles and wild flowers; right by beach, deer on golf course behind, five annexe bedrooms (some sharing bath), substantial breakfast. *(Eric Von Willegen)*

COLONSAY

SCALASAIG   NR3893

⋆ **Colonsay** (01951) 200316

W on B8086; PA61 7YP Stylish 18th-c hotel, a haven for ramblers and birders, with log fires, interesting old islander pictures, pastel walls and polished painted boards, bar with sofas and board games, enjoyable food from lunchtime doorstep sandwiches to fresh seafood and game, good local Colonsay ale, lots of malt whiskies, informal restaurant; children and dogs welcome, pleasant views from gardens, comfortable bedrooms. *(Anon)*

HARRIS

TARBERT   NB1500

★ **Harris Hotel** (01859) 502154

Scott Road; HS3 3DL Large hotel in same
family for over a century, nice small panelled
bar with welcoming feel, local Hebridean
ales, rare malt whiskies, interesting food
with modern touches using best local meat
and shellfish and ranging from lunchtime
baguettes through afternoon teas and
up, smart but relaxed airy restaurant;
comfortably refurbished bedrooms with
sea views. *(Dave Braisted)*

ISLAY

BOWMORE   NR3159

★ **Harbour Inn** (01496) 810330

The Square; PA43 7JR Fine inn with
traditional local bar and plenty of regulars,
lovely harbour and loch views from attractive
dining room, good local fish and seafood,
proper afternoon teas, pleasant service, nice
choice of wines and local malts including
attractively priced rare ones, warmly
welcoming service; good value bedrooms
with views. *(Richard J Holloway)*

PORT ASKAIG   NR4369

Port Askaig 01496 840245

A846, by port; PA46 7RD On shores of
Sound of Islay and overlooking ferry pier,
snug, tartan-carpeted original bar with
good range of malt whiskies, local bottled
ales, popular bar food all day, neat bistro
restaurant overlooking water, traditional
residents' lounge; dogs in public bar, plenty
of picnic-sets on grass, eight neat clean
bedrooms, open all day. *(Dave Braisted)*

PORT CHARLOTTE   NR2558

★ **Port Charlotte Hotel**

(01496) 850360 *Main Street;
PA48 7TU* Most beautiful of Islay's
Georgian villages and in lovely position with
sweeping views over Loch Indaal, exceptional
collection of about 150 Islay malts including
rare ones, two changing local ales, decent
wines by the glass, good food using local
meat, game and seafood, civilised bare-
boards pubby bar with padded wall seats,
open fire and modern art, comfortable back
bar, neatly kept separate restaurant and
roomy conservatory (overlooking beach),
regular traditional live music; children (not
in bar after 10pm) and well behaved dogs
(not in public areas) welcome, garden tables,
near sandy beach, ten bedrooms (nine with
sea view), open all day till 1am. *(Richard J
Holloway)*

PORTNAHAVEN   NN1652

An Tighe Seinnse (01496) 860224

Queen Street; PA47 7SJ Friendly little
end-of-terrace harbourside pub tucked away

in this remote attractive fishing village, cosy
bar with room off, open fire, fair-priced tasty
food including local seafood, Belhaven keg
beer and bottled Islay ales, good choice of
malts; sports TV and occasional live music;
can get crowded, open all day. *(Anon)*

JURA

CRAIGHOUSE   NR5266

Jura Hotel (01496) 820243

A846, opposite distillery; PA60 7XU
Family-run and in superb setting with view
over the Small Isles to the mainland, bar
and restaurant; garden down to water's edge,
17 bedrooms, most with sea view. *(Anon)*

MULL

DERVAIG   NM4251

★ **Bellachroy** (01688) 400314

B8073; PA75 6QW Island's oldest inn
dating from 1608, enjoyable pub and
restaurant food including local seafood and
plenty of other fresh produce, afternoon teas,
generous helpings, local ales, good choice of
whiskies and wine, traditional bar with darts,
attractive dining area, comfortable residents'
lounge with games and TV; children and dogs
welcome, covered outside area plus plenty
of picnic-sets, nice spot in sleepy lochside
village, six comfortable bedrooms, open all
year. *(Michael Butler, Dave Braisted)*

TOBERMORY   NM5055

Macdonald Arms (01688) 302011

Main Street; PA75 6NT Seafront hotel
very popular for its tasty low-priced food,
well kept Belhaven Best, basic décor and
furnishings. *(Michael Butler)*

TOBERMORY   NM5055

Mishnish (01688) 302500

*Main Street – the yellow building;
PA75 6NU* Popular lively place right on
the bay, dimly lit two-room bar with cask
tables, lots of old photographs and nautical/
fishing bric-a-brac, woodburner, little snugs,
well kept Belhaven, nice food in Mishdish
restaurant next door; background and live
music; pool; beer garden behind, refurbished
bedrooms (some with sea views), good
breakfast. *(Richard and Penny Gibbs)*

NORTH UIST

CLADDACH KIRKIBOST   NF7766

Westford (01876) 580653

A865; HS6 5EP Bright cheerful place run
by young landlady from Kent, welcoming and
cosy with woodburner, enjoyable home-made
food from shortish menu, well kept Isle of
Skye along with bottled beers, lovely scenery
and white beaches; dogs welcome, cottage
accommodation. *(Mr and Mrs M Wall)*

ORKNEY

DOUNBY
HY3001

Merkister (01856) 771366

Russland Road, by Harray Loch;
KW17 2LF Fishing hotel in great location
on the loch shore, bar dominated by prize
catches, good food here and in pricey
restaurant including hand-dived scallops and
local aberdeen angus steaks, Belhaven and
McEwans ales; 16 bedrooms. *(Dave Braisted)*

ST MARY'S
HY4700

Commodore (01856) 781788

A961; KW17 2RU Modern single-storey
building with stunning views over Scapa
Flow, bar with well kept Orkney beers, pool
and darts, enjoyable food using local produce
in popular restaurant; open all day. *(Anon)*

STROMNESS
HY2509

Ferry Inn (01856) 850280

John Street; KW16 3AD Busy place
opposite ferry terminal with enjoyable
quickly served decent food and several
Orkney ales; bedrooms. *(Brian and Anna
Marsden)*

WESTRAY
HY4348

Pierowall Hotel (01857) 677472

Centre of Pierowall village, B9066;
KW17 2BZ Comfortable pub-hotel near
ferry, friendly main bar largely given over to
eating, from sandwiches and light snacks up
including good freshly landed fish, bottled
Orkney beers and good choice of malts, pool
room and separate dining area; nine spacious
bedrooms with bay or hill views. *(Dave
Braisted)*

SKYE

ARDVASAR
NG6303

Ardvasar Hotel (01471) 844223

*A851 at S of island, near Armadale
pier; IV45 8RS* Lovely sea and mountain
views from comfortable white stone inn in
peaceful, very pretty spot, charming owner
and friendly efficient staff, good home-made

food including local fish and meat (children
welcome in eating areas), lots of malt
whiskies, real ales including Isle of Skye, two
bars and games room; TV, background music;
tables outside, bedrooms, good walks, open
all day. *(Walter and Susan Rinaldi-Butcher)*

DUNVEGAN
NG2547

Dunvegan (01470) 521497

A850/A863; IV55 8WA Early 19th-c
inn on the Duirnish peninsula; plenty of
tables in airy lounge bar, good reasonably
priced home-cooked food from baguettes up
including local seafood, evening restaurant,
conservatory with superb loch and mountain
views, friendly service, live music in cellar
bar with pool and snooker; waterfront
garden, six bedrooms and bunkhouse.
(M J Winterton)

ISLE ORNSAY
NG7012

⋆ Eilean Iarmain (01471) 833332

Off A851 Broadford–Armadale;
IV43 8QR Small traditional bar at smartly
old-fashioned hotel in beautiful location,
friendly locals and staff, bar food most of the
day from same kitchen as charming sea-view
restaurant, an Isle of Skye real ale, good
choice of vatted (blended) malt whiskies
including their own Gaelic Whisky Collection,
banquettes, open fire; traditional background
music; children welcome, outside tables
with spectacular views, 16 very comfortable
bedrooms, open all day. *(Anon)*

SOUTH UIST

LOCH CARNAN
NF8144

Orasay Inn (01870) 610298

Signed off A865 S of Creagorry;
HS8 5PD Lovely remote spot overlooking
sea, wonderful sunsets, friendly service,
tempting local fish/seafood and beef
from own herd in comfortable modern
lounge and conservatory, pleasant public
bar; seats outside on raised decked area,
compact comfortable bedrooms – two
with own terrace, open all day (at least in
summer). *(Linda Miller and Derek Greentree)*

WALES

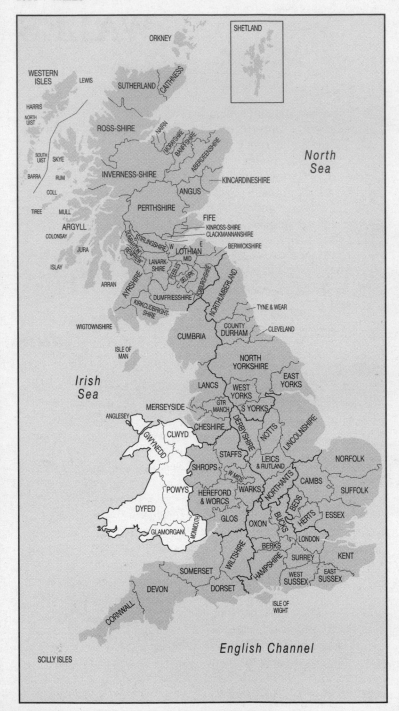

Two pubs appear as Main Entries for the first time – the Anchor at Tintern (medieval building beautifully placed by the abbey ruins) and Tudor Lodge in Jameston (a promising all-rounder, run by the same licensees as the Carew Inn at Carew – itself a chatty, unpretentious waterside pub that's back in these pages after a break). Other reinstated pubs include the Nantyffin Cider Mill at Crickhowell (an old drovers' inn and under new owners), Harbourmaster at Aberaeron (lovely waterside position, and good food and bedrooms) and Queens Head at Llandudno Junction (efficient staff, excellent wine list). Many places are worth visiting for their position or character alone. There's the Pen-y-Gwryd at Llanberis in the heart of Snowdonia (a character-laden mountaineers' haunt), Harp at Old Radnor and Hand at Llanarmon Dyffryn Ceiriog (both well run inns scenically placed in hill country with comfortable rooms), Old Point House at Angle (unpretentious, with much nautical character), Stackpole Inn at Stackpole (near the Bosherston Lily Ponds and a superb beach) and two character-laden pub buildings: the thatched Blue Anchor at East Aberthaw (good value food too) and the ancient, massively thick-walled Plough & Harrow at Monknash.

Pubs particularly getting things right are the Pen-y-Bryn at Colwyn Bay (friendly staff, enjoyable food and eight real ales), Bear at Crickhowell (nicely unchanging inn that copes admirably; readers very much enjoy staying here), Griffin at Felinfach (continuing to get praise for its food), Pant-yr-Ochain at Gresford (remarkable drinks range), Corn Mill at Llangollen (fine drinks and readers love its waterside position), Golden Lion at Newport (welcoming all-rounder with good accommodation), Crown at Pantygelli (good service and useful for the southern Black Mountains), Riverside at Pennal (pleasant young staff, bedrooms and good food), Bunch of Grapes in Pontypridd (carefully sourced food, its own deli and plenty of real ales) and Nags Head in Usk (run by the ever-welcoming Key family for many years). For a civilised and very special meal out, our Wales Dining Pub 2014 is the Griffin in Felinfach.

ABERAERON
Harbourmaster 🍴 🍷 🛏

SN4562 Map 6

Harbour Lane; SA46 0BA

Thriving waterside dining pub-hotel, interesting food and wines and up-to-date bedrooms

Stylish and chic, this hotel has an enticing setting by a yacht-filled harbour lined with colour-washed buildings. The freshly turned out bar has blue walls, a zinc-clad counter, an assortment of leather sofas, a stuffed albatross reputed to have collided with a ship belonging to the owner's great-grandfather and french windows. A large minimalist dining area has modern light wood furniture on light wood floors against aqua blue walls, amd there's also a four-seater cwtch, or snug, within the former porch; TV in the bar for rugby matches. Purple Moose Glaslyn and a beer brewed by them for the pub alongside a guest from a brewer such as Otley on handpump, and a good wine list, with 15 sold by the glass. The owners are chatty and welcoming, the bedrooms comfortable and the breakfasts good; disabled access. You can sit outside on a bench near the road and take in the view.

 Tasty food features prawn and crab cocktail, welsh rarebit with home-cured bacon, beefburger with skinny chips, steaks, salmon and haddock fish pie, pizzas, leek and cheese tartlet, and puddings such as white chocolate and raspberry crème brûlée and lemon tart with meringue and raspberry sorbet. There's also a more expensive restaurant menu. *Benchmark main dish: burger with skinny chips £10.00. Two-course evening meal £18.00.*

Free house ~ Licensees Glyn and Menna Heulyn ~ Real ale ~ (01545) 570755 ~ Open 10am-11.30pm ~ Bar food 12-2.30, 6-9 ~ Restaurant ~ Children over 5 if staying ~ Bedrooms: £65/£110 ~ www.harbour-master.com
Recommended by Bob and Tanya Ekers, Mr and Mrs P R Thomas

ANGLE
Old Point House £

SM8703 Map 6

Signed off B4320 in village, along long rough waterside track; SA71 5AS

Thoroughly unpretentious, welcoming seafarers' pub on the Pembrokeshire Coast Path, with quite a choice of food and waterside tables

Efficient even when busy, this simple place, known in the area as the 'lifeboatman's local' ever since the neighbouring lifeboat station opened in 1868, has a memorable location on the Pembrokeshire Coast Path, overlooking Milford Haven. Some of the snug little windows, and the picnic-sets on the big gravelled terrace, give charming views across the water. Run by a friendly landlord and his staff, it has stacks of seafaring character with plenty of photographs and charts. Until the 1980s the tiny spartan snug bar was the only public room. It has a small length of bar in one corner serving Felinfoel Single Dragon and a guest such as Felinfoel IPA, farm cider, wines by the glass and cheap soft drinks; also, a concrete floor, two simple wood settles and a warming fire in a lovely old fireplace. There's also a lounge bar and a dining room; outside lavatories. It's reached from Angle by an unmade road, which gets cut off about four times a year for a couple of hours by spring tides. From here you can walk west round the peninsula to the beach at West Angle Bay.

🍴 Likeable pubby food might include sandwiches, fish chowder, chicken liver and bacon pâté, half a rack of barbecue pork ribs, lasagne, sweet potato and mushroom risotto, west coast chicken, fresh fish dishes, rib-eye steak with tarragon butter, and puddings like bread and butter pudding with custard and chocolate fudge cake. *Benchmark main dish: fish and chips £9.00. Two-course evening meal £16.00.*

Free house ~ Licensee Robert Noble ~ Real ale ~ (01646) 641205 ~ Open 12-10(11 Sat); 12-3, 6-10 Weds-Sun in winter; closed Mon, Tues in winter, Nov, Jan ~ Bar food 12.30-2.30, 6.30-8.15; no food except to residents Mon-Thurs Nov-Feb ~ Restaurant ~ Children welcome ~ Dogs allowed in bar and bedrooms ~ Bedrooms: £43/£90
Recommended by David and Susan Nobbs, Pauline Fellows and Simon Robbins, Stephen and Jean Curtis, David Jackman, DHV, Barry Collett

BEAUMARIS
SH6076   Map 6
Olde Bulls Head 🍷 🛏
Castle Street; LL58 8AP

Interesting historic inn of many faces including a rambling bar, stylish brasserie and restaurant; well equipped bedrooms

Dating from 1472 and near the castle, this inn was variously visited by the likes of Samuel Johnson and Charles Dickens. The cosy bar has reminders of the town's past: a rare 17th-c brass water clock, a bloodthirsty crew of cutlasses and even an oak ducking stool tucked among the snug alcoves. There are lots of copper and china jugs, comfortable low-seated settles, leather-cushioned window seats, and a good log fire. Kindly staff serve Bass, Hancocks and a guest such as Shenstone Doctor J on handpump. In contrast, the busy brasserie behind is lively and stylishly modern, with a wine list that includes around 20 by the glass, and the exceptionally good upstairs restaurant is elegantly smart for a more formal meal and a wine list that runs to 120 bottles; background music. The entrance to the pretty courtyard is closed by a huge simple-hinged door that's an astonishing 3.3 metres feet wide and 4 metres high. Named after characters in Dickens's novels, the bedrooms are very well equipped; some are traditional, others more contemporary in style. There are more bedrooms in the Townhouse, an adjacent property with disabled access.

🍴 Soup and sandwiches are served in the bar at lunchtime. The much enjoyed brasserie menu typically includes sandwiches, tapas, duck rillette, breadcrumbed haddock and chips, rib-eye steak, baked field mushrooms with caerphilly mash and tomato sauce, sea-reared trout fillet, asian-spiced chicken with noodles, and puddings such as mango crème brûlée and belgian white chocolate and raspberry cheesecake. *Benchmark main dish: slow-cooked lamb shoulder £14.50. Two-course evening meal £20.00.*

Free house ~ Licensee David Robertson ~ Real ale ~ (01248) 810329 ~ Open 11-11; 12-10.30 Sun ~ Bar food 12-2(3 Sun), 6-9 ~ Restaurant ~ Children welcome till 9pm in China Bar only ~ Bedrooms: £87.50/£105 ~ www.bullsheadinn.co.uk
Recommended by Karen Eliot, Jonathan Bamford, Stuart Doughty

Real ale to us means beer that has matured naturally in its cask – not pressurised or filtered. We name all real ales stocked. We usually name ales preserved under a light blanket of carbon dioxide too, though purists – pointing out that this stops the natural yeasts developing – would disagree (most people, including us, can't tell the difference!).

CAREW
Carew Inn

SN0403 Map 6

A4075 off A477; SA70 8SL

Stone-built pub with appealing cottagey atmosphere, interesting views from pleasant gardens and good pubby food

A popular place to stop in summer, when the only restored tide mill in Wales and the ruins of Carew Castle are open, this cheerful riverside pub has good views from its gardens. Run by the same owner-managers for over 21 years, it has open fires in winter and the landlady is chatty and attentive. The little panelled public bar is unpretentious and welcoming, with nice old bentwood stools at the curved counter and mixed tables and chairs on bare boards; there's a small dining area and a lounge bar with low tables. The two upstairs dining rooms have been freshly decorated and have black leather chairs at black tables (with little vases of flowers) on bare boards. Beers include Brains Rev James, Sharps Doom Bar, Worthington and a guest beer on handpump; background music and darts. The back garden is safely enclosed for small children to play, with a colourful plastic wendy house, climbing frame, slide and other toys. Nearby is a remarkable 9th-c Celtic cross.

 In addition to lunchtime sandwiches, the pubby food might include smoked mackerel pâté, nachos topped with chilli con carne and melted cheese, steaks, lasagne, steak and ale pie, curry, chicken breast in creamy garlic sauce, roasted salmon fillet, goats cheese and red pepper quiche, chorizo pork tenderloin with chorizo sausage in spicy tomato sauce, and puddings. *Benchmark main dish: chicken breast stuffed with onion, bacon and mushrooms, in puff pastry £14.75. Two-course evening meal £17.00.*

Free house ~ Licensee Mandy Scourfield ~ Real ale ~ (01646) 651267 ~ Open 11-11 ~ Bar food 12-2, 6-9 ~ Restaurant ~ Children welcome ~ Dogs allowed in bar ~ www.carewinn.co.uk *Recommended by Andrew and Vanessa Thomas, Pauline Fellows and Simon Robbins*

COLWYN BAY
Pen-y-Bryn 🍴 ♀ 🍺

SH8478 Map 6

B5113 Llanwrst Road, on southern outskirts; when you see the pub, turn off into Wentworth Avenue for the car park; LL29 6DD

Spacious open-plan modern bungalow overlooking the bay, with reliable food all day, good range of drinks and obliging staff

Much liked for its friendly, welcoming staff, excellent choice of beers and changing menu, this has tremendous views from inside and out. Extending around the three long sides of the bar counter, the mix of seating and well spaced tables, oriental rugs on pale stripped boards, shelves of books, welcoming coal fires, the profusion of pictures, big pot plants, careful lighting and dark green school radiators are all typical of the pubs in this small, well received chain. Interested young staff serve Phoenix Brunning & Price, Purple Moose Snowdonia and half a dozen changing guests from brewers such as Derby, Rudgate, North Star, Tatton, Three Tuns and Woodlands on handpump, well chosen good

---

The price we give for a two-course evening meal in the featured entries is the mean (average of cheapest and most expensive) price of a starter and a main course – no drinks.

value wines including 20 by the glass and more than 60 malts; board games and background music. Outside are sturdy tables and chairs on a side terrace and on a lower one by a lawn with picnic-sets.

🍴 Served all day, reliable food from the changing menu might include substantial sandwiches, vegetable pakora with indian spiced yogurt, seared scallops and crispy pork belly with pickled mushrooms, beer-battered haddock and chips, steak burger, roast topside of beef with yorkshire pudding, gnocchi with goats cheese and peppers, grilled bass fillets with bacon, and puddings such as chocolate brownie and sticky toffee pudding. *Benchmark main dish: braised shoulder of lamb £16.95. Two-course evening meal £18.00.*

Brunning & Price ~ Managers Andrew Grant and Graham Price ~ Real ale ~ (01492) 533360 ~ Open 11.30-11; 12-10.30 Sun ~ Bar food 12-9.30(9 Sun) ~ Children welcome ~ www.penybryn-colwynbay.co.uk *Recommended by Dr D A Gidlow, Stuart and Jasmine Kelly, Mike Proctor, Clive Watkin, John and Sylvia Harrop*

CRICKHOWELL

Bear ★ ♀ 🛏

SO2118   Map 6

Brecon Road; A40; NP8 1BW

Convivial, interesting and bustling inn with splendid, old-fashioned bar area warmed by a log fire and enjoyable food; comfortable bedrooms

'It really is so very good, and nothing changes,' enthused one reader about this efficiently run and thoroughly welcoming inn at the heart of an appealing small town. The heavily beamed lounge has fresh flowers on tables, lots of little plush-seated bentwood armchairs and handsome cushioned antique settles, and a window seat that looks down on the market square. Next to the great roaring log fire, a big sofa and leather easy chairs are on rugs on oak parquet flooring. Other antiques include a fine oak dresser filled with pewter mugs and brassware, a longcase clock and interesting prints. Brains Rev James, Hancocks HB, Wye Valley Butty Bach and a frequently changing guest such as Theakstons Old Peculier are on handpump, alongside 50 malt whiskies, local ciders, vintage and late-bottled ports, unusual wines (with several by the glass); disabled lavatories. This is a particularly appealing place to stay: older bedrooms in the main building have antiques, while some of the refurbished ones are in a country style, some with jacuzzis and four-poster beds; breakfast is excellent. Reception rooms, ably hosted by patient staff, are comfortably furnished. There's a small garden.

🍴 Much liked food from a changing menu (with sandwiches and baguettes) might include potato gnocchi with chorizo and tomato, ham hock and parsley terrine, beer-battered fish and chips, beef lasagne, chicken and leek pie, sausage and mash, mushroom and potato tart with vegetables and ragu sauce, roast chicken supreme with wild mushroom, marsala and peppercorn sauce, and puddings such as triple chocolate brownie and fruit crumble. *Benchmark main dish: slow-roasted pork belly with chinese five-spice, apple and potato purée and black pudding £14.95. Two-course evening meal £17.50.*

Free house ~ Licensee Judy Hindmarsh ~ Real ale ~ (01873) 810408 ~ Open 10.30-11; 11-10.30 Sun ~ Bar food 12-2, 6-10; 12-2, 7-9 Sun ~ Restaurant ~ Children welcome ~ Dogs allowed in bar and bedrooms ~ Bedrooms: £77/£95 ~ www.bearhotel.co.uk *Recommended by Guy Vowles, Adrian Johnson, LM, David and Sue Atkinson, Tom and Ruth Rees, Michael Carpenter, R T and J C Moggridge, Bob and Margaret Holder, Ron and Sheila Corbett, Dave Webster, Sue Holland, Mike and Mary Carter*

CRICKHOWELL
Nantyffin Cider Mill
SO1919 Map 6

A40/A479 NW; NP8 1LP

Former drovers' inn in the Black Mountains, interesting drinks and food, and a friendly welcome

Run by efficient staff, this pink L-shaped dining pub on a main road by the River Usk, beneath the Black Mountains and close to Tretower Court and Castle, is a civilised spot place for a meal or drink. The bar has good, solid wooden chairs and tables on tiles or carpeting, a big woodburning stove with a large wood basket beside it in the big, broad fireplace and Gower Gold on handpump, two farm ciders from Weston's and several wines by the glass including dessert wines; background music. The open-plan main area has a few beams and standing timbers, similar solid tables and chairs and an open fire in the grey stonework wall. The striking, high-raftered restaurant has an old cider press and a mix of wooden furniture, with a large rug on pale stripped wooden flooring. Tables on the lawn make the most of the rural river views.

The menu includes free-range chicken liver and brandy parfait, baked welsh goats cheese on toasted crouton, sausages and mash, steak burger, tempura-battered fish and chips, mixed vegetarian platter, steaks, scallopini of free-range chicken supreme, and puddings such as bakewell tart and lemon chiffon and kumquat pie. *Benchmark main dish: Grilled whole lemon sole with garlic parsley and lemon butter £15.50. Two-course evening meal £22.00.*

Free house ~ Licensees Glyn & Jess Bridgeman ~ Real ale ~ (01873) 810775 ~ Open 11.45-3, 5.45-11 Weds-Fri; 12-11 Sat, Sun; closed Mon except bank holidays, Tues ~ Bar food 12-2.30, 6-9.30 ~ Children welcome ~ Dogs welcome ~ www.cidermill.co.uk
Recommended by Mike and Mary Carter, Tom and Ruth Rees

EAST ABERTHAW
Blue Anchor £
ST0366 Map 6

Village signed off B4265; CF62 3DD

Character-laden thatched pub with cosy range of low-beamed little rooms, making a memorable spot for a drink

Dating from 1380, this massive-walled thatched building is one of the oldest pubs in Wales. Its series of low-beamed rooms have tiny doorways, with open fires everywhere, including one in an inglenook with antique oak seats built into the stripped stonework; Brains Bitter, Theakstons Old Peculier, Wadworths 6X and Wye Valley Hereford Pale Ale on handpump, as well as Gwynt y Ddraig farm cider. Other seats and tables are worked into a series of chatty little alcoves, and the more open front bar still has an ancient lime-ash floor. Rustic seats shelter peacefully among tubs and troughs of flowers outside, with stone tables on a newer terrace. The pub can get very full in the evenings and on summer weekends, and is used as a base by a couple of local motorbike clubs. A path from here leads to the shingly flats of the estuary.

Good value bar food includes baguettes, salmon and prawn fishcakes, goats cheese soufflé, steaks, thai green chicken curry, steak and kidney pudding, deep-fried haddock with home-cut chips, chestnut mushroom and spinach lasagne, herb-stuffed baked bass with preserved lemon and braised fennel, and puddings. *Benchmark main dish: fried fillet of hake with crayfish, mussel and tiger prawn linguine £10.50. Two-course evening meal £15.50.*

Free house ~ Licensee Jeremy Coleman ~ Real ale ~ (01446) 750329 ~ Open 11-11; 12-10.30 Sun ~ Bar food 12-2, 6-9.30; not Sun evening ~ Restaurant ~ Children welcome ~ Dogs allowed in bar ~ www.blueanchoraberthaw.com *Recommended by Richard and Penny Gibbs, Daz Smith, Heulwen and Neville Pinfield*

FELINFACH
Griffin 🍴🍷🍺🛏

SO0933 Map 6

A470 NE of Brecon; LD3 0UB

Wales Dining Pub of the Year

Highly thought-of dining pub with home-grown vegetables among its carefully sourced ingredients and fine range of drinks; upbeat rustic décor, inviting bedrooms

A commendably relaxed place to dine, stay and drink, this pub continues to strike the right balance. Efficient staff serve a fine array of drinks, many from smaller, independent suppliers, including a thoughtful choice of wines that varies through the seasons (with 20 by the glass and carafe), welsh spirits, cocktails, local bottled cider, locally sourced apple juice, non-alcoholic cocktails made with produce from their garden, unusual continental and local bottled beers, a fine range of sherries and four real ales from Brecon, Montys, Otley and Wye Valley on handpump. The back bar is quite pubby in an up-to-date way: four leather sofas sit around a low table on pitted quarry tiles, by a high slate hearth with a log fire, and behind them mixed stripped seats around scrubbed kitchen tables on bare boards, and a bright blue and ochre colour scheme, with some modern prints. The acoustics are pretty lively thanks to so much bare flooring and uncurtained windows; background music, board games and plenty of books. The two smallish front dining rooms that link through to the back bar are attractive: on the left, mixed dining chairs around mainly stripped tables on flagstones and white-painted rough stone walls, with a cream-coloured Aga in a big stripped-stone embrasure; on the right, similar furniture on bare boards, big modern prints on terracotta walls and smart dark curtains. This is a lovely place to stay, with nothing missed. Bedrooms are comfortable and tastefully decorated and the hearty breakfasts nicely informal: you make your own toast and help yourself to home-made marmalade and jam. Children can play with the landlady's dog and visit the chickens in the henhouse and dogs may sit with owners at certain tables while dining. Good wheelchair access, and outside tables.

🍽 Using carefully sourced seasonal ingredients and organic produce from the pub's own organically certified kitchen garden (the surplus is often for sale), as well as game from local shoots and produce from nearby farms, the consistently good food from a sensibly short, thoughtful menu might include ploughman's with caerphilly, pickles and soda bread, jerusalem artichoke velouté with poached egg, portland crab with pickled cucumber, grapes and crème fraîche, egg pappardelle with cauliflower and pecorino, salmon fishcake with lemon mayonnaise, pheasant with pearl barley bourguignon, braised ox cheek with horseradish risotto, cod fillet with garlic pommes purée and puy lentils, and puddings. *Benchmark main dish: rib-eye of welsh beef £20.00. Two-course evening meal £25.00.*

Free house ~ Licensees Charles and Edmund Inkin and Julie Bell ~ Real ale ~ (01874) 620111 ~ Open 11-11(10.30 Sun) ~ Bar food 12-2.30, 6-9(9.30 Fri, Sat) ~ Children welcome ~ Dogs allowed in bar and bedrooms ~ Acoustic session lunchtime first and third Sun of month ~ Bedrooms: £105/£122.50 ~ www.eatdrinksleep.ltd.uk
Recommended by Bernard Stradling, Karen Eliot, B and M Kendall, Taff Thomas, David and Susan Nobbs, Warren Marsh, David Jackman

GRESFORD SJ3453 Map 6
Pant-yr-Ochain 🍴 ⛾ 🦪

Off A483 on N edge of Wrexham: at roundabout take A5156 (A534) towards Nantwich, then first left towards the Flash; LL12 8TY

Thoughtfully run, gently refined dining pub in the Brunning & Price chain, good food all day, very wide range of drinks and pretty lakeside garden

The impressive line-up of drinks in this well run dining pub in the Brunning & Price chain features Flowers Original, Phoenix Brunning & Price Original, Purple Moose Snowdonia and three to five guest ales from brewers such as Hawkshead, Titanic and Tatton on handpump, Weston's farm cider, a good range of decent wines (strong on upfront new world ones), with 15 by the glass, and around 100 malt whiskies. Within the elaborately gabled former manor house, the light and airy rooms are stylishly decorated, with a wide range of interesting prints and bric-a-brac, and a good mix of individually chosen country furnishings including comfortable seats for relaxing as well as more upright ones for eating. There's a recently rebuilt conservatory as well as a good open fire; one area is set out as a library, with floor-to-ceiling bookshelves. The enchanting garden has herbaceous borders, mature trees and thriving box-edged herb beds; solid wooden furniture overlooks a lake frequented by waterfowl. Service is exemplary and disabled access is good.

🍴 The well balanced daily changing menu features thoughtfully prepared food and includes sandwiches and ploughman's, along with changing dishes such as asparagus with poached egg and hollandaise sauce, salt and pepper squid with chilli, noodles and pak choi, lamb and leek pie, sausages and mash, smoked haddock and salmon fishcakes with tomato salad, spiced mediterranean vegetable stew with tempura courgettes, whole baked bass with crab and saffron butter, and puddings such as chocolate marquise with raspberry coulis and belgian waffle with butterscotch sauce. *Benchmark main dish: steak burger topped with grilled bacon and cheddar £11.95. Two-course evening meal £16.50.*

Brunning & Price ~ Licensee James Meakin ~ Real ale ~ (01978) 853525 ~ Open 11.30-11; 12-10.30 Sun ~ Bar food 12-9.30(9 Sun) ~ Children welcome ~ Dogs allowed in bar ~ www.brunningandprice.co.uk/pantyrochain/ *Recommended by David Jackman, Bruce and Sharon Eden, Dr D A Gidlow, Di and Mike Gillam, Clive Watkin, Roger and Anne Newbury*

JAMESTON SS0699 Map 6
Tudor Lodge 🛏

A4139, E of Jameston; SA70 7SS

Friendly family-run inn, close to the coast, with character bars, airy dining rooms, enjoyable food and beer and comfortable bedrooms

Just a few minutes' drive from the coast at Manorbier, this family-run inn has been carefully refurbished. There are two bars, each with either an open fire or a woodburning stove, lots of fresh flowers, leather armchairs with scatter cushions and sizeable leather pouffes around various tables, and high bar chairs or stools against the counter where they keep Sharps Doom Bar and a guest (perhaps from Evan Evans) on handpump and several wines by the glass, served by friendly staff. The airy main dining room has pale beams, more fresh flowers and chunky wooden high-backed and leather-seated chairs around sturdy tables on carpeting; there's also a second dining room with modern art on the walls. In warm weather, the garden has plenty of picnic-sets and there's a children's play area. The contemporary bedrooms are comfortable and well equipped, and the breakfasts good.

🍴 Food includes lunchtime sandwiches, mushroom bruschetta in creamy garlic sauce, whitebait, mixed grill, steaks, scampi, curry, lamb chops, butternut squash tortellini, and puddings such as lemon cheesecake and apple and cinnamon crumble. They have themed nights such as curry night on Tuesday and steak night on Thursday. *Benchmark main dish: chicken breast stuffed with stilton and wrapped in bacon £15.50. Two-course evening meal £19.00.*

Free house ~ Licensee Mandy Scourfield ~ Real ale ~ (01834) 871212 ~ Open 11-11; 11-3, 5-11 in winter ~ Bar food 12-2(5 Sun), 6-9; Sat 12-9 ~ Restaurant ~ Children welcome ~ Bedrooms: £70/£85 ~ www.tudorlodgejameston.co.uk *Recommended by Isabel MacKinley, Harvey Brown*

LLANARMON DYFFRYN CEIRIOG   SJ1532   Map 6
Hand 🛏
B4500 from Chirk; LL20 7LD

Comfortable rural hotel in a remote valley with cosy low-beamed bar area; good bedrooms

At the crossing of tranquil country lanes beneath the Berwyn Mountains, this inviting inn sets a welcoming note as soon as you enter. The black-beamed, carpeted bar on the left of the broad-flagstoned entrance hall has a hearty log fire in an inglenook fireplace, a mix of chairs and settles, old prints on cream walls and bar stools along the modern bar counter, which has Weetwood Cheshire Cat and a guest from a brewery such as Conwy on handpump, several malt whiskies and reasonably priced wines by the glass. Round the corner is the largely stripped-stone dining room, with a woodburning stove and carpeted floor; darts, dominoes and pool in a games room. Bedrooms are attractive and spacious, and breakfasts are very satisfying; the residents' lounge on the right is comfortable and attractive. There are tables out on a crazy-paved front terrace, with more in the garden, which has flowerbeds around another sheltered terrace.

🍴 As well as lunchtime sandwiches and ploughman's, items from a seasonally changing menu using named local suppliers might include pork and black pudding terrine with basil jam, beetroot and horseradish brûlée, gammon steak with eggs and chips, beefburger with dry-cured bacon and mature welsh cheddar cheese, chestnut mushrooms with chargrilled courgettes and local cheese, braised neck of welsh lamb with tuscan bean ragout and beetroot mash, and puddings such as caramel syrup poached pear with orange sorbet and sticky toffee pudding. *Benchmark main dish: slow-braised welsh lamb £17.00. Two-course evening meal £18.00.*

Free house ~ Licensees Gaynor and Martin de Luchi ~ (01691) 600666 ~ Open 11 (12 Sun)-11(midnight Sat) ~ Bar food 12-2.15, 6.30–8.45; 12.30-2.45, 6.30-8.45 Sun ~ Restaurant ~ No children in dining room after 7.30pm ~ Dogs allowed in bar and bedrooms ~ Bedrooms: £45/£90 ~ www.thehandhotel.co.uk *Recommended by Kim Skuse*

LLANBERIS   SH6655   Map 6
Pen-y-Gwryd 🛏
Nant Gwynant; at junction of A498 and A4086, ie across mountains from Llanberis – OS Sheet 115 map reference 660558; LL55 4NT

Atmospheric and cheerfully unchanged mountaineers' haunt in the wilds of Snowdonia, run by the same family since 1947

With views across a striking mountain landscape, this much loved Snowdonia institution is packed with items left by the climbing fraternity over the years. You can still make out the fading signatures scrawled on the ceiling by the 1953 Everest team, who used this as a training base, and on display is the very rope that connected Hillary and Tenzing on top of the mountain. One snug little room in the homely slate-floored log cabin bar has built-in wall benches and sturdy country chairs. From here you can look out on to precipitous Moel Siabod beyond the lake opposite. A smaller room has a worthy collection of illustrious boots from famous climbs, and a cosy panelled smoke room has more fascinating climbing mementoes and equipment; darts, pool, board games, skittles, bar billiards and table tennis. Purple Moose Glaslyn and Madogs are on handpump and they have several malts. Staying in the comfortable but basic bedrooms can be quite an experience, and the excellent traditional breakfast is served between 8.30 and 9am (they may serve earlier); dogs £2 a night. The inn has its own chapel (built for the millennium and dedicated by the Archbishop of Wales), sauna and outdoor natural pool, and the garden overlooks a lake.

The short choice of simple, good-value but carefully sourced home-made lunchtime bar food (you order through a hatch) includes rolls, ploughman's, pies, salads and quiche of the day, as well as daily specials like roast beef. The three- or five-course hearty set meal in the evening restaurant is signalled by a gong at 7.30pm (if you're late, you'll miss it): maybe chicken liver pâté or smoked salmon salad followed by beef and Guinness pie, roast loin of pork, chargrilled mediterranean vegetables with halloumi, and sticky toffee pudding. *Benchmark main dish: roast lamb with redcurrant gravy £8.95. Three-course evening meal £25.00.*

Free house ~ Licensee Jane Pullee ~ Real ale ~ (01286) 870211 ~ Open 11-11(10.30 Sun); closed all Nov, Dec, midweek in Jan and Feb ~ Bar food 12-2, evening meal 7.30pm ~ Restaurant ~ Children welcome ~ Dogs allowed in bar and bedrooms ~ Bedrooms: /£100 ~ www.pyg.co.uk *Recommended by Earl and Chris Pick*

LLANDUDNO JUNCTION
SH8180 Map 6
Queens Head 🍴 �

Glanwydden; heading towards Llandudno on B5115 from Colwyn Bay, turn left into Llanrhos Road at roundabout as you enter the Penrhyn Bay speed limit; Glanwydden is signed as the first left turn; LL31 9JP

Consistently good food served all day at comfortably modern dining pub

Unassuming from the outside, this whitewashed dining pub is run by attentive staff and draws people from some distance for its food, although you're equally welcomed if you just want to come in for a drink. Adnams and Great Orme Best are on handpump, alongside decent wines (including 14 by the glass), several malt whiskies and good coffee. The spacious modern lounge bar – partly divided by a white wall of broad arches – has brown plush wall banquettes and windsor chairs around neat black tables, and there's a little public bar; unobtrusive background music. An outdoor seating area is available for smokers. Northern Snowdonia is in easy reach, and you can rent the pretty stone cottage (which sleeps two) across the road.

The enjoyable food might include lunchtime sandwiches, fish soup, crispy confit duck leg, steak and ale pie, chicken curry, seared bass fillet, spinach and ricotta cannelloni, braised lamb shank with white bean cassoulet, steamed halibut steak with seared king scallops, king prawn and butter sauce, and puddings. *Benchmark main dish: baked cod fillet topped with welsh rarebit £13.50. Two-course evening meal £20.00.*

Free house ~ Licensees Robert and Sally Cureton ~ Real ale ~ (01492) 546570 ~ Open 11-10.30 ~ Bar food 12-9 ~ Restaurant ~ Children welcome ~ www.queensheadglanwydden.co.uk *Recommended by John and Sylvia Harrop, Mike and Mary Carter*

LLANGOLLEN
Corn Mill ⬤ ⅋ ◧

SJ2142   Map 6

Dee Lane, very narrow lane off Castle Street (A539) just S of bridge; nearby parking can be tricky, may be best to use public car park on Parade Street/East Street and walk; LL20 8PN

Excellent on all counts, with personable young staff, super food all day, good beers and in a fascinating riverside building with fine views

This bustling, chatty, converted watermill makes a fascinating place for a drink or a meal, with quite a lot of the old machinery still in place, including the huge waterwheel (often turning). From here you look across the River Dee to the Llangollen Canal. A long narrow deck along one side of the building juts out over the water, while the interior has been interestingly refitted with pale pine flooring on stout beams, a striking open stairway with gleaming timber and tensioned steel rails, and mainly stripped-stone walls. Pleasant young staff give quick service, and there are good-sized dining tables, big rugs, thoughtfully chosen pictures (many to do with water) and lots of pot plants. One of the two serving bars, away from the water, has a much more local feel, with regulars sitting on the bar stools, pews on dark slate flagstones and daily papers. As well as Phoenix Brunning & Price and Facers DHB, they have a great range of drinks, with three guests from brewers such as Boggart, Brains and Caledonian, farm cider, around 50 sensibly priced malt whiskies and a decent wine choice with around a dozen by the glass.

The pub can get busy, so it's best to book if you're planning to eat. In addition to lunchtime sandwiches and ploughman's, good food from a daily changing menu might include seared scallops with pea purée, pigeon breast with wild mushroom sausage and beetroot fondant, ham with eggs and chips, chicken and ham hock pie, fish pie, beer-battered haddock and chips, tagliatelle with tomatoes, artichokes and peppers, braised shoulder of lamb, and puddings such as apple and blackberry crumble and chocolate nut brownie. *Benchmark main dish: pork belly with dauphinoise potatoes £12.95. Two-course evening meal £18.00.*

Brunning & Price ~ Manager Andrew Barker ~ Real ale ~ (01978) 869555 ~ Open 12-11(10.30 Sun) ~ Bar food 12-9.30(9 Sun) ~ Children welcome but no high chairs available ~ www.brunningandprice.co.uk/cornmill/ *Recommended by Mike and Mary Carter, Bob and Margaret Holder, Claes Mauroy, Clive Watkin, R Anderson*

MOLD
Glasfryn ⬤ ⅋ ◧

SJ2465   Map 6

N of the centre on Raikes Lane (parallel to the A5119), just past the well signposted Theatr Clwyd; CH7 6LR

Lively open-plan bistro-style pub with inventive, well prepared upmarket food available all day, nice décor and wide choice of drinks

Popular with theatre-goers and families, this friendly open-plan dining pub has a cheery bustle, helped along by its enthusiastic staff. Decorated in the Brunning & Price chain's trademark successful style, its interior is cleverly laid out to create plenty of nice quiet corners. It has a mix of informal attractive country furnishings, turkey-style rugs on bare boards, deep red ceilings(some high), a warming fire and plenty of homely close-hung pictures; background music. As well as 30 wines by the glass, local apple juice, farm cider and around 70 malt whiskies, they've got a wide choice of beers on handpump, with Flowers Original, Phoenix Brunning & Price Original and Purple Moose Snowdonia alongside several swiftly changing guests such as Phoenix Arizona, Roosters Yankee, Timothy Taylors Landlord and Wells & Young Bombardier. On warm days, the large terrace with wooden tables in front of the pub is an idyllic place to sit, with sweeping views of the Clwydian Hills.

🍴 From a daily changing menu, the full choice of good, well prepared food might include sandwiches and ploughman's, spicy crab spring roll with avocado, tomato and coriander salsa, red onion and cherry tomato tarte tatin with black peppered goats cheese, thai green chicken curry, haddock and salmon fishcakes, beer-battered haddock and chips, sausage and mash, butternut, parsnip, spinach and bean goulash, slow-roasted pork belly with black pudding and ham hock croquette, and puddings. *Benchmark main dish: braised shoulder of lamb £16.95. Two-course evening meal £19.00.*

Brunning & Price ~ Manager Graham Arathoon ~ Real ale ~ (01352) 750500 ~ Open 11.30-11; 12-10.30 Sun ~ Bar food 12-9.30(9 Sun) ~ Children welcome ~ Dogs allowed in bar ~ www.glasfryn-mold.co.uk *Recommended by Chris Flynn, Wendy Jones, David Jackman, Clive Watkin, C A Bryson*

MONKNASH   SS9170   Map 6
Plough & Harrow 🍺 £
Signposted Marcross, Broughton off B4265 St Brides Major–Llantwit Major – turn left at end of Water Street; OS Sheet 170 map reference 920706; CF71 7QQ

Old building full of history and character, with a huge log fire and a good choice of real ales

This character-laden building dating back some 900 years originated as part of a monastic grange, the ruins of which can be seen in adjacent fields. The unspoilt main bar, with its massively thick stone walls, used to be the scriptures room and mortuary, and has ancient ham hooks in the heavily beamed ceiling, an intriguing arched doorway to the back and a comfortably informal mix of furnishings that includes three fine stripped-pine settles on the broad flagstones. There's a log fire in a huge fireplace with a side bread oven large enough to feed a village. The room on the left has background music. Up to eight real ales on handpump or tapped from the cask might include Bass, Hancocks HB, Wye Valley HPA and four changing guests from brewers such as Brecon, Gower and Sharps; they hold beer festivals in June and September. They also have a good range of local farm cider and welsh and scottish malt whiskies. There are picnic-sets in the front garden; dogs are welcome in the bar, but not while food is being served. A path leads from the pub through the wooded valley of Cwm Nash to the coast, revealing a spectacular stretch of coastal cliffs around Nash Point.

🍴 Food includes baguettes, chicken liver pâté, prawns in marie rose sauce, cheese and leek sausages with garlic and herb mayonnaise, home-made welsh cawl, steak and ale pie, butternut squash balti, rump steak, and puddings like apple crumble and bread and butter pudding. *Benchmark main dish: steak and ale pie £8.25. Two-course evening meal £16.50.*

Free house ~ Licensce Paula Jones ~ Real ale ~ (01656) 890209 ~ Open 12-11 ~ Bar food 12-2.30(5 Sat), 6-9; 12-5 Sun ~ Restaurant ~ No children in bar after 7pm ~ Live music Sat evening ~ www.ploughandharrow.org *Recommended by Harvey Brown, Ruth May*

NEWPORT   SN0539   Map 6
Golden Lion 🛏

East Street (A487); SA42 0SY

Nicely redone, friendly local, with tasty food, pleasant staff and well appointed bedrooms

In a coastal village making a good base for exploring northern Pembrokeshire, this is a fine all-rounder for drinking and dining, and its bedrooms are good value too. Some of the cosy series of beamed rooms have distinctive old settles, and on offer are three changing beers from brewers such as Gwaun Valley, Hook Norton, Sharps and St Austell on handpump, as well as several malt whiskies, wines by the glass and Gwynt y Ddraig cider; pool, juke box, darts, board games, dominoes and a games machine. The dining room has elegant light wood oak furniture, whitewashed walls and potted plants; service is efficient and friendly. There are tables outside at the front and in a side garden; good disabled access and facilities.

 Enjoyable, carefully presented food includes lunchtime sandwiches and ploughman's, vegetable spring rolls, smoked peppered mackerel pâté with soda bread, beefburger with bacon and cheese, lamb chops, fish of the day, steak and Guinness stew with puff pastry lid, roasted mediterranean vegetable lasagne, haddock in coriander tempura batter with sweet chilli dip, and puddings like eton mess and sticky toffe and date pudding. *Benchmark main dish: hake fillets with fresh herb and brioche crust, vine cherry tomato confit and samphire £15.95. Two-course evening meal £17.50.*

Free house ~ Licensee Daron Paish ~ Real ale ~ (01239) 820321 ~ Open 12pm-2am ~ Bar food 12-2.30, 6.30-9 ~ Restaurant ~ Children welcome ~ Dogs allowed in bar and bedrooms ~ Live music weekends in winter ~ Bedrooms: £70/£90 ~ www.goldenlionpembrokeshire.co.uk *Recommended by R T and J C Moggridge, Jen Llywelyn, Tim Arnold and Jim Wingate, David Jackman, Geoff and Linda Payne*

OLD RADNOR   SO2459   Map 6
Harp 🍴 🛏

Village signposted off A44 Kington–New Radnor in Walton; LD8 2RH

Delightfully placed with cottagey bar, tasty food and comfortable bedrooms

The friendly licensees at this beautifully placed pub overlooking Radnor Forest make locals and tourists feel very welcome, and readers enjoy staying here. The warmly characterful public bar has high-backed settles, an antique reader's chair and other elderly chairs around a log fire; board games, cribbage, darts and quoits. The snug slate-floored lounge has a handsome curved antique settle, a log fire in a fine inglenook and lots of local books and guides for residents; a quieter dining area is off to the right, extending into another dining room with a wood-burning stove. They have a couple of changing real ales from brewers such as Hobsons and Three Tuns, as well as Dunkerton's and Ralph's cider, local cassis and several malt whiskies, and they hold a beer, cider and perry festival in June. Tables outside make the most of the view. The impressive village church is worth a look for its early organ case (Britain's oldest), fine rood screen and ancient font.

The sensibly short menu features produce from the publicans' own garden and other carefully sourced seasonal ingredients; as well as sandwiches, there might be oriental duck salad, home-cured gravadlax, ham, eggs and chips, fish and chips, wild mushroom fricassée with basmati rice, lemon and honey roast poussin, roast fillet of bass, and puddings like rhubarb crumble. *Benchmark main dish: welsh black rump steak £14.00. Two-course evening meal £20.00.*

Free house ~ Licensees Chris Ireland and Angela Lyne ~ Real ale ~ (01544) 350655 ~ Open 6-11; 12-3, 6-11 Sat; 12-3, 6-10.30 Sun; closed Mon, weekday lunchtimes ~ Bar food 12-2.30, 6-9 Sat; 12-2.30, 6-8 Sun; not Sun evening in winter ~ Children welcome ~ Dogs allowed in bar and bedrooms ~ Bedrooms: £55/£90 ~ www.harpinnradnor.co.uk
Recommended by Steve Whalley, Kim Skuse, Ann and Colin Hunt

OVERTON BRIDGE
SJ3542 Map 6
Cross Foxes 🍴 ♟
A539 W of Overton, near Erbistock; LL13 0DR

Terrific river views from well run 18th-c coaching inn with good carefully prepared bar food and extensive drinks range

Views of the River Dee are a particular feature here, and oak chairs and tables on a raised terrace make the most of the riverside position; picnic-sets down on a lawn are even closer to the water. The ancient low-beamed bar, with its red-tiled floor, dark timbers, warm fire in a big inglenook and built-in old pews, is more traditional than most pubs in the Brunning & Price group, though the characteristic turkey rugs and frame-to-frame pictures are present, as they are in the dining areas; board games and newspapers. Big windows all round the walls of the airy dining room give a great view. Friendly, competent staff serve Brakspear and a guest from Marstons from handpumps, a farm cider, 50 malts, an excellent range of Armagnacs and a changing choice of around 15 wines by the glass.

As well as sandwiches and ploughman's, carefully prepared food from a tempting changing menu might include fried scallops with black pudding and cauliflower purée, braised ox cheeks with colcannon cake and crispy bacon, king prawn and chorizo linguine, beer-battered haddock and chips, sausages and mash, chargrilled spiced halloumi with coconut, pineapple, lime and mint salad, fried duck breast with creamed cabbage and chestnut, and puddings such as fruits of the forest cheesecake and crème brûlée. *Benchmark main dish: braised pork belly with apples and chorizo, dauphinoise potatoes and calvados sauce £12.95. Two-course evening meal £18.50.*

Brunning & Price ~ Manager Ian Pritchard-Jones ~ Real ale ~ (01978) 780380 ~ Open 12-11(10.30 Sun) ~ Bar food 12-9.30(9 Sun) ~ Children welcome ~ Dogs allowed in bar ~ www.crossfoxes-erbistock.co.uk
Recommended by Peter and Josie Fawcett

People named as recommenders after the full entries have told us that the pub should be included. But they have not written the report – we have, after anonymous on-the-spot inspection.

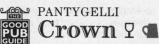

PANTYGELLI

SO3017   Map 6

Crown ♀ 🍺

Old Hereford Road N of Abergavenny; off A40 by war memorial via Pen Y Pound, passing leisure centre; Pantygelli also signposted from A465; NP7 7HR

Prettily placed country pub, attractive inside and out, with good food and drinks

At the foot of the slopes of the Sugar Loaf, this well run country pub has had consistent reports over the years for its friendly service, hands-on owners and imaginative food. The dark flagstoned bar, with sturdy timber props and beams, has a piano at the back, darts opposite, a log fire in the stone fireplace and – from its slate-roofed counter – well kept Bass, Rhymney Best, Wye Valley HPA and a guest such as Mayfields Auntie Myrtle on handpump, Gwatkin's farm cider, good wines by the glass, local organic apple juice and good coffees. On the left are four smallish, linked, carpeted dining rooms, the front pair separated by a massive stone chimneybreast; thoughtfully chosen individual furnishings and lots of attractive prints by local artists make it all thoroughly civilised. Background music, darts and board games. Comfortable wrought-iron and wicker chairs on the flower-filled front terrace look up from this lush valley to the hills; a smaller back terrace is surrounded by lavender.

🍴 Food includes baguettes and pubby standards like sausages and mash and rib-eye steak, with additional daily specials such as smoked duck with beetroot and plum chutney, seared king scallops wrapped in sage and smoked bacon, roast cod steak on hand-made pasta, wild mushroom, blue cheese and broad bean risotto, venison loin medallions, and puddings such as rhubarb crème brûlée and mango and lime fool. *Benchmark main dish: welsh black beef with bubble and squeak £10.25. Two-course evening meal £17.00.*

Free house ~ Licensees Steve and Cherrie Chadwick ~ Real ale ~ (01873) 853314 ~ Open 12-2.30(3 weekends), 6-11(10.30 Sun); closed Mon lunchtime ~ Bar food 12-2, 7-9; not Sun evening or Mon except bank holidays ~ Restaurant ~ Children welcome ~ Dogs allowed in bar ~ www.thecrownatpantygelli.com *Recommended by R T and J C Moggridge, John Edwell, Trevor Swindells*

PENNAL

SH6900   Map 6

Riverside

A493; opposite church; SY20 9DW

Fresh refurbishment with tasty food and local beers, and efficient young staff

In the Dovey Valley just inside the southern boundary of Snowdonia National Park, this village pub has a good mix of customers, with diners as well as hikers. It's been neatly refurbished with fresh green and white walls, slate floor tiles, a woodburning stove, modern light wood dining furniture and some funky fabrics. High-backed stools are lined up along the stone-fronted counter where they serve three changing beers such as Blue Monkey Infinity, Purple Moose Snowdonia and Salopian Oracle, several malts and around a dozen wines by the glass; background music, TV and garden.

🍴 In addition to lunchtime sandwiches, tasty food includes warm duck salad, welsh rarebit, beef and ale pie, lamb steak, fish stew, stuffed pepper with mushroom risotto, fried fillet of bass and king prawns, and puddings like passion-fruit possett with kir royale and lemon and lime cheesecake. *Benchmark main dish: fried fillet of bass with king prawns £14.95. Two-course evening meal £19.50.*

Free house ~ Licensees Glyn and Corina Davies ~ Real ale ~ (01654) 791285 ~ Open 12-3, 6-11.30; 12-midnight Sat; 12-11 Sun; closed two weeks Jan ~ Bar food 12-2.30, 6-9.30 ~ Restaurant ~ Children welcome ~ Dogs allowed in bar ~ Bedrooms: £60/£70 ~ www.riversidehotel-pennal.co.uk *Recommended by Mike and Mary Carter, Mrs F Smith, Phil and Helen Holt*

 PONTYPRIDD   ST0790   Map 6

Bunch of Grapes

Off A4054; Ynysangharad Road; CF37 4DA

Refurbished pub with a fine choice of drinks in friendly, relaxed bar, delicious inventive food and a warm welcome for all

In addition to its excellent food, a great attraction at this 18th-c pub by the defunct Glamorganshire Canal is the terrific range of drinks, with Otley Croeso and three guests plus another four quickly changing guest beers from breweries far and wide (such as Crouch Vale, Dark Star and Milestone) on handpump, and four or five beer festivals with music each year. They also serve continental and american ales on draught or in bottles, a couple of local ciders or perrys, seven wines by the glass and good coffee. Service is knowledgeable, friendly and efficient. The cosy bar has an informal relaxed atmosphere, comfortable leather sofas, wooden chairs and tables, a roaring log fire, newspapers to read and background music. There's also a restaurant with elegant high-backed wooden dining chairs around a mix of tables, and prints on pale contemporary paintwork; some seats outside on decking. The pub also has a deli with home-baked bread, chutneys, home-cooked ham, local eggs, quite a choice of welsh cheeses and so forth, and holds cookery classes and regular themed evenings.

Inventive food from an ever-changing menu that uses the best local, seasonal produce might include sandwiches, devilled lambs kidneys with toasted focaccia, tempura of asparagus, spring onion and samphire, various burgers, chargrilled gammon steak with egg and chips, mushroom risotto with celeric and smoked cerwyn cheese, ballottine of chicken breast with smoked paprika and chorizo butter, braised brisket of beef, and puddings such as blackberry cheesecake and lavender crème brûlée. *Benchmark main dish: Otley ale braised rabbit with black pudding and charred asparagus £16.00. Two-course evening meal £21.00.*

Free house ~ Licensee Nick Otley ~ Real ale ~ (01443) 402934 ~ Open 11am-11.30pm; 12-11 Sun ~ Bar food 12-9.30; 12-3.30 Sun ~ Restaurant ~ No children after 8pm unless dining in restaurant ~ Dogs allowed in bar ~ www.bunchofgrapes.org.uk *Recommended by James Morris, Taff Thomas*

 RAGLAN   SO3609   Map 6

Clytha Arms

Clytha, off Abergavenny road – former A40, now declassified; NP7 9BW

Fine setting in spacious grounds, a relaxing spot for enjoying good food and an impressive range of drinks; comfortable bedrooms

Beautifully placed in parkland and within strolling distance of the riverside path along the Usk, this country inn is an inviting place for a drink or a meal, and the bedrooms are comfortable, with good welsh breakfasts. The notable array of drinks features well kept Kite

Carmarthen Pale Ale, Rhymney Bitter, Wye Valley and three swiftly changing guests, an extensive wine list with about a dozen or so by the glass, over 20 malt whiskies, about three farm ciders, their own perry and various continental beers; it hosts occasional cider and beer festivals. With long heated verandahs and diamond-paned windows, it's comfortable, light and airy, with scrubbed wood floors, pine settles, big faux fur cushions on the window seats, a good mix of old country furniture and a couple of warming fires, and there's a contemporary linen-set restaurant; darts, bar skittles, boules, large-screen TV for rugby matches and board games. The pub has its own labrador and collie.

As well as a tapas menu (part welsh, part spanish) and sandwiches, the enjoyable menu might include soup, leek and laverbread rissoles with beetroot chutney, pie and mash, wild boar sausages with potato pancakes, rump steak, lentil moussaka with greek salad, loin of lamb with wild garlic crust and potato gratin, and puddings like treacle pudding and rhubarb and ginger cheesecake. *Benchmark main dish: wild boar and duck cassoulet £14.00. Two-course evening meal £22.00.*

Free house ~ Licensees Andrew and Beverley Canning ~ Real ale ~ (01873) 840206 ~ Open 12-3, 6-12; 12-midnight Fri, Sat; 12-11 Sun; closed Mon lunchtime ~ Bar food 12.30-2.15, 7-9.30; not Sun evening ~ Restaurant ~ Children welcome ~ Dogs allowed in bar and bedrooms ~ Bedrooms: £60/£90 ~ www.clytha-arms.com *Recommended by R T and J C Moggridge, David Jackman*

ROSEBUSH
SN0729   Map 6

Tafarn Sinc

B4329 Haverfordwest–Cardigan; SA66 7QU

Unique 19th-c curio, a slice of social and industrial history by abandoned slate quarries

Wonderfully unconventional, this maroon-painted corrugated structure is an extraordinary relic. It originated in 1876 as a hotel on a long-defunct railway serving the nearby abandoned slate quarries, which now form a dramatic landscape. The halt itself has been more or less re-created, even down to life-size dummy passengers waiting out on the platform; the sizeable garden is periodically enlivened by the sounds of steam trains chuffing through – actually broadcast from a replica signal box. Inside, it's like a museum of local history, with sawdust on the floor, hams, washing and goodness knows what else hung from the ceiling, and an appealingly buoyant atmosphere. You'll hear Welsh spoken here. The bar has plank panelling, an informal mix of old chairs and pews and a woodburner, and Cwrw Tafarn Sinc (brewed locally for the pub) and Sharps Doom Bar on handpump; background music, darts, games machine, board games and TV.

Basic food includes gammon steak with pineapple, vegetable lasagne, lamb burgers, steaks, and puddings; no starters. *Benchmark main dish: faggots and mushy peas £10.50. Two-course evening meal £15.00.*

Free house ~ Licensee Hafwen Davies ~ Real ale ~ (01437) 532214 ~ Open 12-11 (midnight Sun); closed Mon exceot bank holidays and in Aug ~ Bar food 12-2, 6-9 ~ Restaurant ~ Children welcome ~ www.tafarnsinc.co.uk *Recommended by Pete Flower, Mike and Eleanor Anderson, Jen Llywelyn, Tom Arnold and Jim Wingate, Stephen and Jean Curtis, David Jackman*

We say if we know a pub has background music.

SKENFRITH

SO4520 Map 6

Bell 🍴 🍷 🛏

Just off B4521, NE of Abergavenny and N of Monmouth; NP7 8UH

Elegant but relaxed, generally much praised for classy food and excellent accommodation

This upmarket, rather smart country inn almost adjacent to the imposing medieval ruin of Skenfrith Castle (National Trust) is a thoroughly civilised place for a special meal. It's the little details, like the set of leaflets describing walks from the pub and their immaculate kitchen garden that make all the difference. For a special occasion, head for the big bare-boards dining area at the back. Neat, light and airy, it has dark country kitchen and rush-seated dining chairs, church candles and flowers on dark tables, canary walls and brocaded curtains on sturdy big-ring rails. The flagstoned bar on the left has rather similar décor, with old local and school photographs, a couple of pews plus tables and café chairs; board games. From an attractive bleached oak bar counter, Wye Valley Bitter and Hereford Pale Ale are served on handpump, plus bottled local cider and perry. The impressive wine list has 13 wines by the glass and half bottle, local sparkling wine, early-landed cognacs and a good range of malts. The lounge bar on the right, opening into the dining area, has a nice Jacobean-style carved settle and a housekeeper's chair by a log fire in the big fireplace. There are good solid tables on the terrace, with steps up to a sloping lawn. Disabled access is good.

 Food is prepared using named local suppliers of carefully chosen fresh ingredients, vegetables, soft fruit and herbs from the pub's kitchen garden (you're welcome to look around), pork from their own-reared saddleback pigs and game from local shoots. As well as lunchtime sandwiches, the changing menu might include scallops, garden beetroot with orange dressing and goats cheese bon bon, fillet of pollack or line-caught bass, thyme and lemon roasted chicken breast, roasted ratatouille on spring onion rösti, and puddings such as glazed lemon tart and vanilla rice pudding. *Benchmark main dish: sirloin of beef with miniature cottage pie £21.50. Two-course evening meal £24.00.*

Free house ~ Licensees William and Janet Hutchings ~ Real ale ~ (01600) 750235 ~ Open 11-11; 12-10 Sun; closed Tues Nov-March ~ Bar food 12-2.30, 7-9.30(9 Sun) ~ Restaurant ~ Children over 8 welcome in restaurant in evening ~ Dogs allowed in bar and bedrooms ~ Bedrooms: £75/£110 ~ www.skenfrith.co.uk *Recommended by Lucien Perring, Christopher Vallely*

STACKPOLE

SR9896 Map 6

Stackpole Inn 🍴 🛏

village signed off B4319 S of Pembroke; SA71 5DF

Enjoyable food, good accommodation, friendly service and usefully placed for exploring the Pembrokeshire Coast Path and Bosherston Lily Ponds

On the Stackpole Estate, this thoughtfully run dining pub with rooms is within strolling distance of the coast path and an idyllically secluded beach. One area around the bar has pine tables and chairs, but the major part of the pub, L-shaped on four different levels, is given over to diners, with neat light oak furnishings and ash beams and low ceilings to match; background music and board games. Brains Rev James, Felinfoel Best and Double Dragon and a guest from a brewer such as Rhymney are on handpump, with several wines by the glass and farm cider. The attractive gardens feature colourful flowerbeds and mature trees, while the spotless bedrooms are comfortable and the breakfasts enjoyable.

|▌| The impressive food might include ciabattas, ploughman's, pressed ham hock terrine, prawn cocktail, shepherd's pie, grilled fillet of haddock with chips, faggots with welsh stout and red onion gravy, creamy wild mushroom linguine with teifi cheese, slow-roasted pork belly with celeriac and pear mash and cider gravy, very good fish specials, and puddings such as lemon tart and chocolate brownie. *Benchmark main dish: hake fillet baked with black olive tapenade and tomato sauce £16.50. Two-course evening meal £21.00.*

Free house ~ Licensees Gary and Becky Evans ~ Real ale ~ (01646) 672324 ~ Open 12-3, 6-11; 12-11 Sat, Sun ~ Bar food 12-2(2.30 Sun), 6.30-9 ~ Restaurant ~ Children welcome ~ Dogs allowed in bar ~ Bedrooms: $60/$90 ~ www.stackpoleinn.co.uk
Recommended by Diane Dallyn, David and Susan Nobbs, Pauline Fellows and Simon Robbins, R T and J C Moggridge, Barry Collett

TINTREN   SO5300   Map 6
Anchor
Off A466 at brown sign for abbey; NP16 6TE

Medieval building next to magnificent abbey ruins, an enjoyable mix of old and modern; good range of drinks including local ciders

Standing adjacent to the gracious ruin of Tintern Abbey, this character-laden pub is in a super position in the very heart of the lower Wye Valley, with a big choice of walks along the river and high up along the wooded slopes either side. The bar was originally the abbey's cider mill and has bare stone walls and a low beamed ceiling; Bath Ales Gem, Otter Amber, Wye Valley Bitter and a guest such as Sharps Spring Ale, a wide range of farm and local bottled ciders as well as several wines by the glass; background music. The airy garden room, set out with brightly painted chairs around wooden tables, has picture windows making the most of the views of the abbey, which is floodlit at night. There's also a restaurant within the former ferryman's cottage.

|▌| With reasonably priced pub favourites as well as more expensive dinner dishes, the food includes sandwiches, tea-smoked duck breast and orange salad, home-cured salmon infused with dill and lemon, burgers, beer-battered hake and chips, steaks, thai green vegetable curry, braised shank of lamb with rosemary jus, fried snapper supreme, trio of pork, and puddings like mulled poached pear or chocolate croissant bread and butter pudding. *Benchmark main dish: beef, mushroom and ale pie £9.95. Two-course evening meal £17.50.*

Free house ~ Licensee Geoff Dawe ~ Real ale ~ (01291) 689582 ~ Open 9am-11pm ~ Bar food 12-3, 6-9; Sun 12-4, 5.30-7.30 ~ Restaurant ~ Children welcome ~ Dogs allowed in bar ~ www.theanchortintern.co.uk   *Recommended by Harvey Brown, Tess White*

TRESAITH   SN2751   Map 6
Ship 🛏
Off A487 E of Cardigan; bear right in village and keep on down – pub's car park fills quickly; SA43 2JL

Memorable position right beside a broad sandy surfing beach, nice terrace and seaview bedrooms

A fine place to contemplate the view and look out for peregrine falcons and even the occasional dolphin, this seaside pub is right by the cliffs. Teak tables and chairs under a glass canopy on heated front decking and unusual picnic-sets on a two-level terrace make the most of the position, and picture windows open the views to the front dining area too. Behind here is a winter log fire, with some chunky pine tables, tub armchairs and sofas in the carpeted part on the right, and large attractive local photographs. They have Brains Rev James and SA on handpump, and a good choice of wines by the glass and other drinks. Two back rooms – possibly a quieter escape in summer – are appealing, especially the one on the right with its striking blue and red décor, bright flooring tiles, old-fashioned range stove and snug alcove with a shelf of board games; background music and TV. As well as water sports, there are good coast walks from this steep little village.

🍴 With an accent on fresh fish, the menu might include sandwiches, pork rillettes with sweet mustard pickle, asparagus with hollandaise sauce, sausage and mash, lasagne, beer-battered cod and chips, caramelised red onion and fennel tarte tatin, slow-roasted pork belly, chicken stuffed with brie and tomatoes, and puddings like apple pie and baked white chcolate and raspberry cheesecake. *Benchmark main dish: salmon fillet, dill vinaigrette, samphire and crushed potatoes £10.25. Two-course evening meal £16.50.*

Brains ~ Manager Adam Baynton ~ Real ale ~ (01239) 811816 ~ Open 12-3, 6-9(8 Sun) ~ Bar food 8-11am, 12-3, 5-9; 12-9 in summer ~ Restaurant ~ Children welcome ~ Bedrooms: /£69.95 ~ www.shiptresaith.co.uk *Recommended by Mr and Mrs A Burton, R T and J C Moggridge, D Crook, Simon Rodway*

TY'N-Y-GROES
Groes 🍴 🛏
B5106 N of village; LL32 8TN

SH7773   Map 6

Stacks of character in gracious, antique-laden 15th-c Snowdonia hotel, local beer and lovely garden

Beautifully placed in the Vale of Conwy on the east side of Snowdonia National Park, this welcoming hotel serves Groes Ale (brewed for the pub) from the family's own Great Orme brewery, a couple of miles away, alongside a guest such as Sharps Doom Bar on handpump, several bottled Great Orme beers and 17 wines by the glass. Past the hot woodburning stove in the entrance area, the rambling, low-beamed and thick-walled rooms are nicely decorated with antique settles and an old sofa, old clocks, portraits, hats and tins hanging from the walls and fresh flowers. A fine antique fireback is built into one wall, perhaps originally from the formidable fireplace in the back bar, which houses a collection of stone cats as well as cheerful winter log fires; background music. You might find a harpist playing here on certain days. Several options for dining include an airy conservatory and a smart white-linen dining restaurant. Well equipped bedroom suites (some with terraces or balconies) have gorgeous views, and the hotel also rents out a well appointed wooden cabin, and a cottage in the historic centre of Conwy. The idyllic back garden has flower-filled hayracks and an enchantingly verdant outlook, and there are more seats on a narrow flower-decked roadside terrace.

🍴 Using local lamb, salmon and game, and herbs from the hotel garden, food might include sandwiches, haddock and prawn smokie with creamy sauce, cheese and tomato tartlet, beer-battered cod and chips, cottage pie, sausages and mash, vegetable burger, parma ham-wrapped chicken breast with tarragon white wine sauce, venison pie, steaks, and puddings such as apple and blackberry crumble and spiced orange and cranberry parfait. *Benchmark main dish: beefburger £13.10. Two-course evening meal £18.00.*

Free house ~ Licensee Dawn Humphreys ~ Real ale ~ (01492) 650545 ~ Open 12-3, 6-11 ~ Bar food 12-2, 6.30-9 ~ Restaurant ~ Children welcome ~ Dogs allowed in bar and bedrooms ~ Bedrooms: £90/£130 ~ www.groesinn.com *Recommended by Mike and Shirley Stratton, David and Sue Atkinson, R and S Bentley, Steve Whalley, Mike and Mary Carter, Mr and Mrs J S Heathcote, Mike Proctor, Dr and Mrs P Truelove*

USK   SO3700   Map 6

Nags Head ♀

The Square; NP15 1BH

Spotlessly kept by the same family for 46 years, traditional in style with hearty welcome, and good food and drinks

The Key family continue to give a warm welcome as they have for many years at this beautifully kept coaching inn. The traditional main bar is cheerily chatty and cosy, with lots of well polished tables and chairs packed under its beams (some with farming tools), lanterns or horsebrasses and harness attached, as well as leatherette wall benches, and various sets of sporting prints and local pictures – look out for the original deeds to the pub. Tucked away at the front is an intimate little corner with some african masks, while on the other side of the room a passageway leads to a new dining area converted from the old coffee bar; background music. There may be prints for sale, and perhaps a group of sociable locals. They do several wines by the glass, along with Brains Arms Park, Rev James and SA, and a guest such as Sharps Doom Bar on handpump. The church is well worth a look. The pub has no parking and nearby street parking can be limited.

Huge helpings of reasonably priced popular food includes sandwiches, leek and welsh cheddar soup, grilled sardines, faggots and gravy, steak pie, sausage and mash, a brace of quails, fresh salmon, glamorgan sausage, white partridge stuffed with apricots, and puddings such as sticky toffee pudding and treacle and walnut tart. *Benchmark main dish: rabbit pie £10.00. Two-course evening meal £17.00.*

Free house ~ Licensee Key family ~ Real ale ~ (01291) 672820 ~ Open 10.30-2.30, 5-11 ~ Bar food 12-2, 5.30-9.30 ~ Restaurant ~ Children welcome ~ Dogs allowed in bar *Recommended by R T and J C Moggridge, Lucien Perring, Sue and Ken Le Prevost, Maurice Potts, Eryl and Keith Dykes*

Also Worth a Visit in Wales

Besides the fully inspected pubs, you might like to try these pubs that have been recommended to us and described by readers. Do tell us what you think of them: feedback@goodguides.com

ANGLESEY

BEAUMARIS   SH6076

White Lion (01248) 810589

Castle Street; LL58 8DA Welcoming and cleanly refurbished 19th-c family-run hotel overlooking Castle Square, two bars, one with open fire, well kept ales including Marstons Pedigree, good locally sourced food from proprietor-chef, restaurant; children welcome, dogs in bar, tables out at front and in sheltered beer garden behind,

nine bedrooms with castle or Menai Strait views. *(Nick Coleman, Chris and Val Ramstedt)*

RED WHARF BAY   SH5281

✻**Ship** (01248) 852568

Village signed off B5025 N of Pentraeth; LL75 8RJ Whitewashed old pub worth visiting for position right on Anglesey's east coast (arrive early for a seat with fantastic views of miles of tidal sands); big old-fashioned rooms either side of bar counter, nautical bric-a-brac, long varnished wall pews, cast-iron-framed tables and open fires, three real ales including Adnams, 50 malt whiskies and decent choice of wines, enjoyable food and friendly service; if you run a tab they lock your card in a numbered box and hand you the key, background Classic FM in lounge; children welcome in room on left, dogs in bar, disabled access, open all day. *(Philip and Jane Hastain, Gordon and Margaret Ormondroyd, Alan Sutton)*

RHOSCOLYN   SH2675
⋆**White Eagle** (01407) 860267
Off B4545 S of Holyhead; LL65 2NJ
Remote place rebuilt almost from scratch on site of an old pub; airy modern feel in neatly kept rooms, relaxed atmosphere and nice winter fire, Cobblers Ale (brewed for the pub by Thornbridge), Marstons, Weetwood and a guest from smart oak counter, several wines by the glass, extensive choice of good locally sourced food (all day Sun, and school holidays, best to book), friendly helpful service, restaurant; children welcome, dogs in bar, terrific sea views from decking and picnic-sets in good-sized garden, lane down to beach, open all day. *(Gordon and Margaret Ormondroyd, Alan Sutton, Chris and Val Ramstedt, Howard Drake)*

CEREDIGION

ABERAERON   SN4562
Castle (01545) 570205
Market Street; SA46 0AU Red-painted early 19th-c building with popular contemporary café-bar and elegant upstairs restaurant, good friendly service, wide choice of enjoyable home-cooked food and sensibly priced wine list, ales such as Evan Evans and Tomos Watkins; welsh whisky; six comfortable bedrooms. *(Peter Hacker)*

CLWYD

CARROG   SJ1143
Grouse (01490) 430272
B5436, signed off A5 Llangollen–Corwen; LL21 9AT Small unpretentious pub with superb views over River Dee and beyond from bay window and balcony, Lees ales, enjoyable food all day from sandwiches up, reasonable prices, friendly helpful staff, local pictures, pool in games room; background music; children welcome, wheelchair access (side door a bit narrow), tables in pretty walled garden, covered terrace for smokers, narrow turn into car park, handy for Llangollen steam railway. *(Anon)*

COLWYN BAY   SH8479
Picture House (01492) 535286
Princes Drive; LL29 8LA Interesting Wetherspoons conversion of 1914 cinema, good range of beers and their usual competitively priced food, seating areas on different levels, efficient service; open all day from 8am. *(Andrew Bosi)*

GRAIG FECHAN   SJ1454
Three Pigeons (01824) 703178
Signed off B5429 S of Ruthin; LL15 2EU
Extended largely 18th-c pub with enjoyable inexpensive food from sandwiches up, friendly licensees, good range of real ales and plenty of wines by the glass, various nooks and corners, interesting mix of furniture and some old signs on the walls, great country views from restaurant; children allowed if eating, big garden with terrace and same views, good walks. *(Mike and Wena Stevenson)*

**LLANARMON DYFFRYN
CEIRIOG**   SJ1532
⋆**West Arms** (01691) 600665
End of B4500 W of Chirk; LL20 7LD
16th-c beamed and timbered inn in lovely surroundings, cosy atmosphere in picturesque upmarket lounge bar full of antique settles, sofas, even an elaborately carved confessional stall, good original bar food strong on local produce, friendly staff, good range of wines, malt whiskies and three well kept local ales, more sofas in old-fashioned entrance hall, comfortable back bar too, roaring log fires, good restaurant; children welcome, disabled access, pretty lawn running down to River Ceiriog (fishing for residents), good walks, 16 comfortable character bedrooms. *(Peter and Josie Fawcett, Edward Leetham)*

LLANELIAN-YN-RHOS   SH8676
White Lion (01492) 515807
Signed off A5830 (shown as B5383 on some maps) and B5381, S of Colwyn Bay; LL29 8YA Cosy village pub tucked away in rolling country above Colwyn Bay; two distinct parts each with own personality and linked by steps, at top is neat spacious dining area, at other end is traditional old bar with antique high-backed settles around big fireplace, off to the left is another dining room with jugs hanging from beams and teapots above window, Marstons ales and a guest, nice choice of wines, food can be good; background and live music (jazz Tues, bluegrass Weds); children welcome, tables in attractive courtyard (also used for parking), open all day Sun, closed Mon. *(C A Bryson, Mr and Mrs J J A Davis,)*

LLANFERRES   SJ1860
⋆**Druid** (01352) 810225
A494 Mold–Ruthin; CH7 5SN Extended 17th-c whitewashed inn set in fine walking country along the Alyn Valley towards Loggerheads Country Park, or up Offa's Dyke Path to Moel Famau; views from broad bay window in civilised plush lounge and from bigger beamed back bar with two handsome antique oak settles, pleasant mix of more modern furnishings, quarry-tiled area by log fire, and maybe three-legged cat called Chu.

Marstons-related ales, 30 malt whiskies, decent reasonably priced food, games room with darts and pool, board games; background music, TV; children welcome, dogs in bar and bedroom, stables outside at the front, open all day Fri, Sat till 10pm Sun. *(David Jackman, David and Katharine Cooke, Neil and Anita Christopher)*

RUABON SJ3043
Bridge End (01978) 810881
Bridge Street; LL14 6DA Proper old-fashioned pub owned by McGivern, their ales (brewed here) and guests, decent wines, enthusiastic staff, basic home-made food, black beams and open fires, Tues quiz, folk music Weds evening; open all day weekends and from 5pm weekdays (4pm Fri).
(Claes Mauroy)

DYFED

ABERCYCH SN2539
★ **Nags Head** (01239) 841200
Off B4332 Cenarth–Boncath; SA37 0HJ
Tucked-away riverside pub with dimly lit beamed and flagstoned bar, big fireplace, stripped wood tables, clocks showing time around the world, piano, hundreds of beer bottles, photographs of locals and a coracle on brick and stone walls, even a large stuffed rat, own-brewed Cych Valley beers, two sizeable dining areas; background music; children welcome and dogs (pub yorkie called Scrappy), benches in garden overlooking river (fishing rights), play area with wooden castle, barbecues, three bedrooms, open all day weekends, closed Mon lunchtime. *(Anon)*

ABERGORLECH SN5833
★ **Black Lion** (01558) 685271
B4310; SA32 7SN Friendly old coaching inn in fine rural position; traditionally furnished stripped-stone bar with flagstones, coal stove, oak furniture and high-backed black settles, copper pans on beams, old jugs on shelves, local paintings and fresh flowers, dining extension with french windows opening on to enclosed garden, Rhymney and a guest beer, local cider, good varied choice of inexpensive home-cooked food; background music; children and dogs welcome, lovely views of Cothi Valley from riverside garden, self-catering cottage, open all day weekends, closed Mon. *(Anon)*

ABERYSTWYTH SN5882
Ship & Castle 07773 778785
High Street; SY23 1JG Friendly drinkers' pub with well kept Wye Valley HPA and Butty Bach plus three changing guests, welsh cider; pool and sports TV; open from 2pm. *(R T and J C Moggridge)*

BROAD HAVEN SM8614
★ **Druidstone Hotel** (01437) 781221
N on coast road, bear left for about 1.5 miles then follow sign left to Druidstone Haven; SA62 3NE Cheerfully informal country house in grand spot above the sea, individualistic, relaxed and with terrific views, inventive cooking using fresh often organic ingredients (best to book) including good value 'feast evening' Tues, helpful efficient service, cellar bar with local ale tapped from the cask, country wines and other drinks, ceilidhs and folk events, friendly pub dogs (others welcome), all sorts of sporting activities from boules to sand-yachting; attractive high-walled garden, spacious homely bedrooms, even an eco-friendly chalet and apartment built into a hill, closed Jan, Nov, restaurant closed Sun evening. *(Pete Flower, John and Fiona McIlwain, Geoff and Linda Payne)*

CAIO SN6739
Brunant Arms (01558) 650483
Off A482 Llanwrda–Lampeter; SA19 8RD Unpretentious and interestingly furnished village pub, comfortable and friendly, with nice log fire, a couple of local ales, enjoyable regularly changing home-made food from baguettes up, stripped-stone public bar with games including pool, some live music; sports TV; children and dogs welcome, small Perspex-roofed verandah and lower terrace, handy for Dolaucothi Gold Mines (NT), open all day. *(John Crellin)*

CILYCWM SN7540
Neuadd Fawr Arms (01550) 721644
By church entrance; SA20 0ST
Former 18th-c drovers' inn, restored by present owners, eclectic mix of old furniture on huge slate flagstones, woodburners, one or two changing local ales, good seasonal home-made food with a modern twist in bar or smaller dining room, friendly helpful service; children and dogs welcome, good spot by churchyard above River Gwenlais, among lanes to Llyn Brianne, open all day weekends, closed weekday lunchtimes in winter. *(Anon)*

COSHESTON SN0003
Brewery Inn (01646) 686678
Signed E from village crossroads; SA72 4UD Welcoming 17th-c village pub with three well kept ales, good reasonably priced food (not Sun evening, Mon) freshly cooked by landlord, helpful friendly service, quiz and curry Weds; five self-catering apartments at back. *(Bob Butterworth, David Hughes, R Page, Jon Rowlands)*

Half pints: by law, a pub should not charge more for half a pint than half the price of a full pint, unless it shows that half-pint price on its price list.

CRESSWELL QUAY   SN0506
✴ Cresselly Arms   (01646) 651210
Village signed from A4075; SA68 OTE
Simple unchanging alehouse overlooking tidal creek, plenty of local customers in two old-fashioned linked rooms, built-in wall benches, kitchen chairs and plain tables on red and black tiles, open fire in one room, Aga in the other with lots of pictorial china hanging from high beam-and-plank ceiling, a third more conventionally furnished red-carpeted room, Worthington and a winter guest ale served from glass jugs, no food apart from rolls on Sat; no children; seats outside making most of view, you can arrive by boat if tide is right, open all day weekends. *(David and Susan Nobbs)*

CWM GWAUN   SN0333
✴ Dyffryn Arms   (01348) 881305
Cwm Gwaun and Pontfaen signed off B4313 E of Fishguard; SA65 9SE
Classic rural time warp, virtually the social centre for this lush green valley, very relaxed, basic and idiosyncratic, with much-loved veteran landlady (her farming family have run it since 1840, and she's been in charge for well over a third of that time); 1920s front parlour with plain deal furniture and draughts boards inlaid into tables, coal fire, well kept Bass served by jug through sliding hatch, low prices, World War I prints and posters, large collection of banknotes, darts, duck eggs for sale; lovely outside view, open more or less all day (may close if no customers). *(Giles and Annie Francis, R T and J C Moggridge)*

DALE   SM8105
Griffin   (01646) 636227
B4327, by sea on one-way system; SA62 3RB Old waterside pub run by friendly couple, two imaginatively decorated cosy rooms, open fires, well kept Brains, Evan Evans and a local guest, nice wines, popular food including good local fish/seafood specials, pleasant attentive service; children welcome, lovely estuary views (can sit out on seawall), open all day summer. *(Pete Flower, Alan Bulley, Geoff and Linda Payne)*

DINAS   SN0139
Old Sailors   (01348) 811491
Pwllgwaelod; from A487 in Dinas Cross follow Bryn-henllan signpost; SA42 0SE
Shack-like building in superb position, snugged down into the sand by isolated cove below Dinas Head with its bracing walks; specialising in fresh local seafood including crab and lobster, also good snacks, coffee and summer cream teas, well kept Felinfoel Double Dragon, decent wine, maritime bric-a-brac; children welcome, no dogs inside, picnic-sets on grass overlooking beach, closed Mon, open all day rest of week (Tues till 6pm), shut Jan. *(Anon)*

FISHGUARD   SM9537
✴ Fishguard Arms   (01348) 872763
Main Street (A487); SA65 9HJ
Tiny unspoilt bay-windowed pub; front bar with well priced cask-tapped Bass from unusually high counter, chatty character landlord and friendly atmosphere, open fire, rugby photographs, woodburner and traditional games in back snug, no food; sports TV; smokers' area out at back, open all day, closed Weds evening. *(Giles and Annie Francis)*

FISHGUARD   SM9637
Ship   (01348) 87403
Newport Road, Lower Town; SA65 9ND
Cheerful atmosphere and seafaring locals in dimly lit 18th-c pub near old harbour, friendly licensees and well kept ales including Theakstons tapped from the cask, homely food from sandwiches and cawl up, coal fire, lots of boat pictures, model ships, photos of Richard Burton, piano; children welcome, toys provided. *(Giles and Annie Francis)*

GOGINAN   SN6881
Druid   (01970) 880650
A44 E of Aberystwyth; SY23 3NT
Welcoming roadside pub with well kept Wye Valley Butty Bach and enjoyable food. *(Anon)*

LITTLE HAVEN   SM8512
✴ Castle Inn   (01437) 781445
Grove Place; SA62 3UF Welcoming pub well placed by green looking over sandy bay (lovely sunsets), popular food including pizzas and good local fish, Marstons-related ales, decent choice of wines by the glass, tea and cafetière coffee, bare-boards bar and carpeted dining area with big oak tables, beams, some stripped stone, castle prints, pool in back area; children welcome, picnic-sets out in front, New Year's Day charity swim, open all day. *(Pete Flower, John and Fiona McIlwain, Geoff and Linda Payne)*

LITTLE HAVEN   SM8512
St Brides Inn   (01437) 781266
St Brides Road; SA62 3UN Just 20 metres from Pembrokeshire Coast Path; neat stripped-stone bar and linked carpeted dining area, log fire, interesting well in back corner grotto thought to be partly Roman, Banks's, Marstons and a guest, enjoyable bar food; background music and TV; children welcome, dogs in bar, seats in sheltered suntrap terrace garden across road, two bedrooms, open all day summer. *(Pete Flower, Paul and Sue Merrick, Stephen and Jean Curtis)*

LLANDDAROG   SN5016
✴ Butchers Arms   (01267) 275330
On back road by church; SA32 8NS
Ancient heavily black-beamed local with three intimate eating areas off small central bar, welcoming staff, enjoyable generous home-made food, cask-tapped Felinfoel ales

and good wines by the glass, conventional pub furniture, gleaming brass, candles in bottles, open woodburner in biggish fireplace; background music; children welcome, tables outside, nice window boxes, bedroom in converted stables, closed Sun and Mon. *(Anon)*

LLANDDAROG SN5016
White Hart (01267) 275395

Off A48 E of Carmarthen, via B4310; aka Yr Hydd Gwyn; SA32 8NT Ancient thatched pub with own-brew beers using water from 300ft borehole, also own ciders and may start distilling soon; comfortable lived-in beamed rooms with lots of engaging bric-a-brac and antiques including a suit of armour, 17th-c carved settles by huge log fire, interestingly furnished high-raftered dining room, generous if not cheap food, home-made jams, chutneys and honey for sale; cash or debit cards only, background music, no dogs inside; children welcome, disabled access (ramps provided), picnic-sets on front terrace and in back garden with play area, small farmyard, closed Weds. *(David and Susan Nobbs, Taff Thomas)*

LLANDOVERY SN7634
Castle (01550) 720343

Kings Road; SA20 0AP Welcoming hotel next to castle ruins, good food from sandwiches and deli boards to charcoal grills and fresh fish specials, courteous efficient service, well kept Brains, Kite and Evan Evans; comfortable bedrooms. *(Brian and Anna Marsden, Gareth Davies, Mo and David Trudgill, Hugh Davies)*

LLANDOVERY SN7634
Kings Head (01550) 720393

Market Square; SA20 0AB Refurbished early 18th-c beamed coaching inn, enjoyable food from bar and restaurant menus, three well kept changing ales, attentive friendly service; 14 bedrooms, open all day. *(Brian and Anna Marsden)*

LLANDOVERY SN7634
Red Lion (01550) 720813

2 Market Square (no pub sign); SA20 0AA One basic welcoming room with no bar, good changing ales tapped from the cask, long-serving jovial landlord (pub has been in his family for 100 years), no food; restricted opening – may be just Fri and Sat evenings. *(Giles and Annie Francis)*

LLANFALLTEG SN1519
Plash (01437) 563472

Vilage NE of Whitland; SA34 0UN Small mid-terrace village local with a warm welcome, beamed bar with piano and open fire, well kept ales such as Black Sheep, Gwaun Valley and Wye Valley (plans for own microbrewery), Stowford Press cider, some low-priced bar food along with pizzas; children and dogs welcome, garden tables,

self-catering cottage, closed lunchtimes Mon and Tues, otherwise open all day. *(Brian Yates, C Johnstone, Steve Goymer, David and Julie Glover)*

LLANFIHANGEL-Y-CREUDDYN SN6676
Y Ffarmers (01974) 261275

Village signed of A4120 W of Pisgah; SY23 4LA Nicely refurbished family-run village pub, good locally sourced seasonal food cooked by landlord-chef, well kept Felinfoel with guests such as Purple Moose, friendly helpful service, traditional bar with oak boards and woodburner; children welcome, closed Sun evening, all Mon, Tues lunchtime. *(Anon)*

NEWCHAPEL SN2239
Ffynnone Arms (01239) 841800

B4332; SA37 0EH Refurbished 18th-c beamed pub, friendly and welcoming, with home-made food in restaurant (Weds evening to Sun lunchtime) including carvery, Evan Evans and guests, local ciders, afternoon teas in season, two woodburners, darts, pool and table skittles; disabled facilities, picnic-sets in small garden, open all day weekends, closed weekday lunchtimes. *(Barry and Lyn Davis)*

NEWPORT SN0539
Royal Oak (01239) 820632

West Street (A487); SA42 0TA Sizeable pub with good food including lunchtime light dishes, local lamb and lots of authentic curries, Felinfoel Double Dragon and Sharps Doom Bar, friendly helpful staff, children welcome in lounge with eating areas, separate stone and slate bar with pool and games, upstairs dining room; some tables outside, easy walk to beach and coast path, open all day. *(Heulwen and Neville Pinfield)*

PEMBROKE DOCK SM9603
Shipwright (01646) 682090

Front Street; SA72 6JX Little waterfront pub overlooking estuary, good choice of enjoyable food including authentic thai dishes, well kept Sharps Doom Bar, friendly efficient service; five minutes from Ireland ferry terminal. *(Pauline Fellows and Simon Robbins)*

PENRHIWLLAN SN3641
Daffodil (01559) 370343

A475 Newcastle Emlyn–Lampeter; SA44 5NG Smart contemporary open-plan dining pub with comfortable welcoming bar (though most there to eat), scatter-cushion sofas and leather tub chairs on pale limestone floor, woodburner, bar chairs by granite-panelled counter serving well kept Evan Evans and Greene King, two lower-ceilinged end rooms with big oriental rugs, steps down to two airy dining rooms, one with picture windows by open kitchen, food can be very good; background music; children welcome, nicely furnished decked area outside with valley views. *(Anon)*

PONTRHYDFENDIGAID   SN7366
Black Lion   (01974) 831624
Off B4343 Tregaron–Devils Bridge; SY25 6BE Relaxed country inn under new ownership; smallish main bar with dark beams and floorboards, lots of stripped stone, old country furniture, woodburner and big pot-irons in vast fireplace, copper, brass and so forth on mantelpiece, historical photographs, Felinfoel Double Dragon and a local guest (plans for microbrewery), seven wines by the glass, home-cooked food including vegetarian/vegan options, quarry-tiled back dining room, small games room with pool and darts; background music; children and dogs (away from diners) welcome, back courtyard and tree-shaded garden, seven bedrooms (five in converted stables), good walking/cycling country and not far from Strata Florida Abbey, open all day. *(Anon)*

PORTHGAIN   SM8132
✶ Sloop   (01348) 831449
Off A487 St Davids–Fishguard; SA62 5BN Busy tavern (especially holiday times) snuggled down in cove wedged tightly between headlands on Pembrokeshire Coast Path – fine walks in either direction; plank-ceilinged bar with lots of lobster pots and fishing nets, ship clocks and lanterns and even relics from local wrecks, decent-sized eating area with simple furnishings and freezer for kid's ice-creams, well liked bar food from sandwiches to good steaks and fresh fish (own fishing business), Brains, Felinfoel and Greene King, separate games room with juke box; seats on heated terrace overlooking harbour, self-catering cottage in village, open all day from 9.30am for breakfast, till 1am Fri, Sat. *(Pete Flower, Geoff and Linda Payne)*

PUMSAINT   SN6540
Dolaucothi Arms   (01558) 650237
A482 Lampeter-Llandovery; SA19 8UW National Trust-owned pub (part of the Dolaucothi Estate) recently reopened after long closure, local beers and straightforward home-made food (not Sun evening), flagstoned bar with two woodburners, muddy walkers and dogs welcome (pub cat Lily), garden overlooking Cothi River (pub has 4 miles of fishing rights), two bedrooms, closed Mon, lunchtime Tues, otherwise open all day. *(Anon)*

RHANDIRMWYN   SN7843
Royal Oak   (01550) 760201
7 miles N of Llandovery; SA20 0NY Friendly 17th-c stone-built inn in remote and peaceful walking country, comfortable traditional bar with log fire, four well kept local ales, ciders and perries, good variety of popular sensibly priced food sourced locally,

big dining area, pool room; children and dogs welcome, hill views from garden and bedrooms, handy for Brecon Beacons. *(Andy Beveridge)*

GLAMORGAN

BISHOPSTON   SS5789
Joiners Arms   (01792) 232658
Bishopston Road, just off B4436 SW of Swansea; SA3 3EJ Thriving local brewing its own good value Swansea ales along with well kept guests, reasonably priced straightforward food (not Sun evening, Mon), friendly staff, unpretentious quarry-tiled bar with massive solid-fuel stove, comfortable lounge; TV for rugby; children welcome, open all day (from 3pm Mon, Tues). *(Anon)*

BRIDGEND   SS9379
White Horse   (01656) 652583
Heol-Y-Capel; CF35 5HD Popular Brains pub in attractive village setting, their beers and guests, wide range of good value food including Sun carvery, prompt service even when busy; open all day. *(R C Vincent)*

CAERPHILLY   ST1484
✶ Black Cock   (02920) 880534
Watford; Tongwynlais exit from M4 junction 32, then right just after church; CF83 1NF Welcoming beamed country pub with series of interconnecting rooms, large back dining extension, good choice of enjoyable pub food all day (not Sun evening) including children's, well kept welsh ales, cheerful staff, woodburners; background music; dogs welcome in bar, disabled access, sizeable terraced garden among trees with good play area, up in the hills just below Caerphilly Common, popular with walkers and riders (there's a hitching rail), open all day. *(R T and J C Moggridge)*

CARDIFF   ST1876
Cottage   (029) 2033 7195
St Mary Street, near Howells; CF10 1AA 18th-c Brains pub with their full range kept well, long neat bar with narrow frontage and back eating area, lots of polished wood, glass and mirrors, pictures on papered walls, straightforward home-made food (Sun till 6pm) including all-day breakfast and other bargains, good cheerful service and relaxed friendly atmosphere even Fri and Sat when crowded (gets packed on rugby international days); open all day. *(David and Sue Atkinson, Roger and Donna Huggins)*

CARDIFF   ST1876
Goat Major   (029) 2033 7161
High Street, opposite castle; CF10 1PU Named for Royal Welsh Regiment mascot (plenty of pictures), Victorian-style décor with dark panelling and green leatherette wall seats, shiny floor tiles around bar, carpets beyond, Brains beers kept well,

pie-based menu, friendly young staff; background music, silent TVs showing subtitled news; open all day. *(Roger and Donna Huggins, Jeremy King)*

COWBRIDGE   SS9974
* **Bear** (01446) 774814
High Street, with car park behind off North Street; signed off A48; CF71 7AF Busy Georgian coaching inn in smart village, well kept Brains, Hancocks and guests, decent house wines, enjoyable usual food from good sandwiches and wraps up, young uniformed staff, three attractively furnished bars with flagstones, bare boards or carpet, some stripped stone and panelling, big hot open fires, barrel-vaulted cellar restaurant; children and dogs (in one bar) welcome, courtyard tables, comfortable quiet bedrooms, open all day. *(Dennis Jenkin)*

COWBRIDGE   SS9974
Duke of Wellington (01446) 773592
High Street; CF71 7AG Popular 16th-c half-timbered building with wide oak-panelled rooms and airy back conservatory, good food cooked to order (so may be a wait) from extensive and imaginative menu, efficient waitress service, Brains beers; nice one-street Vale of Glamorgan town. *(Peter Hacker)*

GWAELOD-Y-GARTH   ST1183
Gwaelod y Garth Inn
(029) 2081 0408 *Main Road; CF15 9HH* Meaning 'foot of the mountain', this stone-built village pub has wonderful valley views and is popular with walkers on on Taff Ely Ridgeway Path; popular well presented home-made food (not Sun evening), friendly efficient service, own-brew beer along with Wye Valley and guests from pine-clad bar, log fires, upstairs restaurant (disabled access from back car park); table skittles, pool, digital juke box; children and dogs welcome, three bedrooms, open all day. *(Roy Payne)*

KENFIG   SS8081
* **Prince of Wales** (01656) 740356
2.2 miles from M4 junction 37; A4229 towards Porthcawl, then right when dual carriageway narrows on bend, signed Maudlam and Kenfig; CF33 4PR Ancient local with plenty of individuality by historic sand dunes, cheerful welcoming landlord, well kept ales tapped from the cask, decent wines and good choice of malts, enjoyable straightforward generous food at low prices, chatty panelled room off main bar (dogs allowed here), log fires, stripped stone, lots of wreck pictures, restaurant with upstairs overspill room, several ghosts; TV for special rugby events; children till 9pm, handy for nature reserve (June orchids), open all day. *(Anon)*

LISVANE   ST1883
Ty Mawr Arms (01222) 754456
From B4562 on E edge turn N into

Church Road, bear left into Llwyn y Pia Road, keep on along Graig Road; *CF14 0UF* Large welcoming country pub with good choice of popular food, well kept Brains and guest ales, decent wines by the glass, teas and coffees, friendly service, great views over Cardiff from spacious bay-windowed dining area off traditional log-fire bar; children welcome, disabled access with help to main bar area, big attractive garden with pond, open all day. *(Colin McKerrow)*

LLANBLETHIAN   SS9873
Cross (01446) 772995
Church Road; CF71 7JF Former staging inn cheerfully refurbished by present friendly owners, well kept Wye Valley and guests (beer festivals), enjoyable freshly made food from pubby choices up in comfortable bar or light airy restaurant, reasonable prices, open fire and woodburner; children and dogs welcome, terrace seats, open all day. *(Clive Roberts)*

LLANCARFAN   ST0570
Fox & Hounds (01446) 781287
Signed off A4226; can also be reached from A48 from Bonvilston or B4265 via Llancadle; CF62 3AD Good carefully cooked food using local ingredients in neat comfortably modernised village pub, Brains beers kept well and nice choice of wines, friendly staff; unobtrusive background music; tables on covered terrace, pretty streamside setting by interesting church, eight comfortable bedrooms, good breakfast, closed Sun evening. *(Jillian and Martin Rolls, J D and A P)*

LLANGYNWYD   SS8588
Old House (01656) 733310
Off A4063 S of Maesteg; pub behind church, nearly a mile W of modern village; CF34 9SB Thatched and beamed dining pub, well kept Flowers and decent wines by the glass, good choice of malt whiskies, reasonably priced food from pubby choices to specials, nice staff, sporting pictures, lots of jugs and brassware, huge fireplace, attractive conservatory extension; children welcome, garden tables, nearby huge churchyard and valley views worth a look. *(Ian Phillips)*

LLANMADOC   SS4493
Britannia (01792) 386624
The Gower, near Whiteford Burrows (NT); SA3 1DB Busy summer pub right out on the peninsula, enjoyable locally sourced food and well kept beers, nice coffee, gleaming copper stove in beamed and tiled bar, steps up to stripped-stone dining area; children and dogs welcome, tables out in front and in big garden behind, great estuary views, lovely walks. *(Ann and Adrian Bulley, Tom and Ruth Rees)*

LLANSAMLET SS6897
Plough & Harrow (01792) 772263
Church Road; SA7 9RL Friendly open-plan pub with well kept Marstons-related ales such as Banks's Sunbeam and Jennings Cocker Hoop, good value generous pub food including deals, carvery (Weds, Sun), quiz Weds. *(R T and J C Moggridge)*

MUMBLES SS6188
Park Inn (01792) 366738
Park Street; SA3 4DA Cosy two-bar Victorian backstreet local with good mix of customers, five interesting well kept beers, lots of photographs of old Mumbles Railway, piano and open fire, back games room; open all day Fri-Sun, from 4pm other days. *(Darren)*

OGMORE SS8876
Pelican (01656) 880049
Ogmore Road (B4524); CF32 0QP Nice spot above ruined castle, beamery, bare boards and welcoming fire, popular all-day food, Sharps Doom Bar and Wye Valley, cheerful service; may try to keep your credit card while you eat; dogs allowed in lounge (flagstone floor), tables on small front terrace, rather grand smokers' hut, views and quite handy for beaches. *(Anon)*

OLDWALLS SS4891
Greyhound (01792) 391027
W of Llanrhidian; SA3 1HA 19th-c pub with spacious beamed and dark-panelled carpeted lounge bar, well kept ales including own Gower brews, decent wine and coffee, popular reasonably priced pub food including good Sun roasts, friendly staff, hot coal fires, back dining room and upstairs overspill/ function room; children and dogs welcome, picnic-sets in big garden with terrace, play area and good views, open all day. *(M G Hart)*

PONTNEDDFECHAN SN8907
Angel (01639) 722013
Just off A465; Pontneathvaughan Road; SA11 5NR Comfortably opened up 16th-c pub with friendly staff and atmosphere, well kept ales such as Neath Witch Hunter, enjoyable reasonably priced pub food (good lamb cawl), masses of jugs on beams, ancient houseware and old kitchen range, separate flagstoned bar; terrace tables, good walks including the waterfalls. *(R T and J C Moggridge)*

REYNOLDSTON SS4889
⋆ King Arthur (01792) 390775
Higher Green, off A4118; SA3 1AD Cheerful pub-hotel with timbered main bar and hall, back family summer dining area (games room with pool in winter), good fairly priced food with some emphasis on fish, friendly helpful staff coping well when busy, Felinfoel and guests, country house bric-a-brac, log fire, lively local atmosphere

evenings; background music; tables out on green, play area, 19 bedrooms and self-catering cottage, open all day. *(Anon)*

SWANSEA SS6492
Brunswick (01792) 465676
Duke Street; SA1 4HS Large rambling local with lots of artwork and prints for sale, bargain popular weekday food till 7.30pm, Courage, Greene King and a guest (usually local), friendly helpful service, regular live music; open all day. *(Jan Masson)*

SWANSEA SS6592
Queens (01792) 521531
Gloucester Place; SA1 1TY Well kept Brains, Theakstons and a guest, basic but very cheap pub food, plenty of local atmosphere and friendly service, live music Sat; handy for museums and Dylan Thomas Centre. *(R T and J C Moggridge, Darren)*

GWENT

ABERGAVENNY SO2914
Angel (01873) 857121
Cross Street, by town hall; NP7 5EN Comfortable late Georgian coaching inn with good friendly staff and thriving local atmosphere, lovely bevelled glass behind servery, some big settees, enjoyable varied food in bar and restaurant; pretty courtyard, 35 bedrooms (some in other buildings). *(Eryl and Keith Dykes)*

ABERGAVENNY SO3111
⋆ Hardwick (01873) 854220
Hardwick; B4598 SE, off A40 at A465/ A4042 exit – coming from E on A40, go right round the exit system, as B4598 is final road out; NP7 9AA Restaurant-with-rooms, and you'll need to book for owner-chef's highly regarded imaginative food; drinkers welcome in simple bar with spindleback chairs around pub tables, stripped brickwork by fireplace and small corner counter serving Rhymney and Wye Valley, local perry and a dozen wines by the glass, two dining rooms, one with beams, bare boards and huge fireplace, the other in lighter carpeted extension, friendly service; background music; no under-8s in restaurant after 8pm, teak tables and chairs under umbrellas by car park, neat garden, bedrooms, open all day (till 10pm Sun), closed Mon in winter and second week in Jan. *(M E and F J Thomasson, Lucien Perring, Lori Kelley, Duncan Cloud)*

CAERLEON ST3490
⋆ Bell (01633) 420613
Bulmore Road; off M4 junction 24 via B4237 and B4236; NP18 1QQ Nicely furnished linked beamed areas in old stone coaching inn, good popular food using local ingredients (best to book weekends), well kept Timothy Taylors Landlord, Wye Valley

HPA and a guest, excellent choice of welsh ciders and perries, big open fireplace; unobtrusive background music (live Sun afternoon); children welcome, pretty back terrace with koi tank, open all day. *(M G Hart)*

CHEPSTOW ST5394
Three Tuns (01291) 645797
Bridge Street; NP16 5EY Dating from early 17th c and a pub for much of that time; refurbished bare-boards interior with painted farmhouse pine furniture, a couple of mismatched sofas by woodburner, dresser with china plates, local ales and ciders from nice wooden counter at unusual angle, very reasonably priced home-made bar food, friendly staff; background music (live Sat); dogs welcome, three bedrooms, open all day (till 10pm Mon-Thurs). *(Anon)*

GROSMONT SO4024
Angel (01981) 240646
Corner of B4347 and Poorscript Lane; NP7 8EP Friendly little 17th-c local owned by village co-operative, rustic interior with simple wooden furniture, Fullers, Tomos Watkins and Wye Valley, real ciders, decent good value straightforward bar food (not Sun or Mon), evening food more ambitious, pool room with darts, live music (instruments provided); no lavatories – public ones close by; a couple of garden tables and boules behind, seats out by ancient market cross on attractive steep single street in sight of castle, good local walks, open all day Sat, closed Mon lunchtime. *(Guy Vowles)*

LLANDENNY SO4103
✶ Raglan Arms (01291) 690800
Centre of village; NP15 1DL Well run dining pub with good interesting fresh food (not Sun evening), Wye Valley Butty Bach and good selection of wines, friendly welcoming young staff, big pine tables and a couple of leather sofas in linked dining rooms leading through to conservatory, log fire in flagstoned bar's handsome stone fireplace, relaxed informal atmosphere; children welcome, garden tables, closed Mon. *(Anon)*

LLANGATTOCK LINGOED SO3620
Hunters Moon (01873) 821499
Off B4521 just E of Llanvetherine; NP7 8RR Attractive tucked-away pub dating from 13th c, beams, dark stripped stone and flagstones, woodburner, friendly licensees and locals, welsh ales tapped from the cask, separate dining room, enjoyable straightforward food (Thurs and Fri evenings, Sat, lunchtime Sun); children welcome, tables out on deck and in charming dell with ducks, waterfall, four comfortable bedrooms, glorious country on Offa's Dyke Path, closed Mon and weekday lunchtimes. *(David Harris, Neil and Anita Christopher)*

LLANGYBI ST3797
White Hart (01633) 450258
On main road; NP15 1NP Friendly village dining pub in delightful 12th-c monastery building, part of Jane Seymour's dowry, pubby bar with roaring log fire, steps up to pleasant light restaurant, good if not particularly cheap food (not Sun evening), afternoon tea, several well kept mainly welsh ales, good choice of wines by the glass; children welcome, two bedrooms, open all day, closed Mon. *(Anon)*

LLANOVER SO2907
✶ Goose & Cuckoo (01873) 880277
Upper Llanover signed up track off A4042 S of Abergavenny; after 0.5 miles take first left; NP7 9ER Unchanging simple pub much loved by walkers (Monmouthshire & Brecon Canal towpath nearby, or over hilltops towards Blorenge and Blaenavon); essentially one small room with rustic furniture and woodburner, Rhymney and guests, 75 malt whiskies, wholesome Aga-cooked bar food, friendly landlady, small picture-window extension making most of valley view, daily papers, darts and board games; no credit cards; children and dogs welcome, they keep sheep, goats, geese and chickens, may have honey for sale, one bedroom, self-catering cottage and camping, open all day Fri-Sun, closed Mon. *(Guy Vowles)*

LLANTHONY SO2827
✶ Priory Hotel (01873) 890487
Aka Abbey Hotel, Llanthony Priory; off A465, back road Llanvihangel Crucorney–Hay; NP7 7NN Magical setting for plain bar in dimly lit vaulted flagstoned crypt of graceful ruined Norman abbey, lovely in summer, with lawns around and the peaceful border hills beyond; well kept ales such as Brains, Felinfoel and Newmans, summer farm cider, good coffee, simple lunchtime bar food (can be long queue on fine summer days, but number system works well), evening restaurant, occasional live music; no dogs; children welcome but not in hotel area with four bedrooms in restored parts of abbey walls, open all day Sat and summer Sun, closed winter Mon-Thurs, Sun evening. *(David and Sue Atkinson, MLR)*

LLANTRISANT FAWR ST3997
Greyhound (01291) 672505
Off A449 near Usk; NP15 1LE Prettily set 17th-c country inn with relaxed homely feel in three linked beamed rooms, steps between two, nice mix of furnishings and rustic decorations, enjoyable home cooking at sensible prices, efficient service, two or more well kept ales, decent wines by the glass, log fires, pleasant panelled dining room; muddy boots/dogs welcome in stable bar, attractive garden with big fountain,

hill views, comfortable bedrooms in small attached motel, closed Sun evening. *(Dr Peter Clinch)*

MAMHILAD   SO3004
Horseshoe (01873) 880542
Old Abergavenny Road; NP4 8QZ Old beamed country pub improved under new owners; slate-floor bar with traditional pubby furniture, a couple of unusual posts acting as elbow-tables, original Hancocks pub sign, ornate woodburner in stone fireplace, good fairly priced food (not Sun evening) from lunchtime baguettes up, Sharps Doom Bar and a local guest, Blaengawney cider; children welcome, dogs away from dining area, lovely views particularly from tables by car park over road, open all day Fri-Sun, closed Mon. *(Mr N and Mr G Webb)*

MONMOUTH   SO5012
Robin Hood (01600) 715423
Monnow Street; NP25 3EQ Ancient pub with low-beamed panelled bar, popular food from sandwiches to specials, well kept ales including Bass and Greene King, friendly service, restaurant; children welcome, tables and play area outside, open all day. *(Anon)*

PENALLT   SO5209
Inn at Penallt (01600) 772765
Village signed off B4293; at crossroads in village turn left; NP25 4SE Refurbished 17th-c stone pub, good home-made bar and restaurant food with emphasis on local produce, also local ales and cider, well priced wine list, courteous efficient service, airy slate-floored bar with woodburner, restaurant and small back conservatory; children and dogs welcome, big garden with terrace and play area, Wye Valley views, four bedrooms, closed Mon, lunchtime Tues (and lunchtimes Weds, Thurs in winter). *(Anon)*

RAGLAN   SO4107
Beaufort Arms (01291) 690412
High Street; NP15 2DY Pub-hotel (former 16th-c coaching inn) with two character beamed bars, one with big stone fireplace and comfortable seats on slate floor, well kept Fullers London Pride and Wye Valley Butty Bach, good varied range of locally sourced food including set lunch/early evening menu, light airy brasserie, friendly attentive service; background music; children welcome, terrace tables, 17 good bedrooms. *(Chris Flynn, Wendy Jones, LM, Duncan Cloud, Eryl and Keith Dykes)*

REDBROOK   SO5309
★ Boat (01600) 712615
Car park signed on A466 Chepstow–Monmouth, then 30-metre footbridge over Wye; or very narrow steep car access from Penallt in Wales; NP25 4AJ Beautifully set riverside pub with well kept Wye Valley and guests tapped from the cask, lots of ciders, perries and country wines, enjoyable good value simple food from baguettes and baked potatoes up (nothing fried), helpful staff, unchanging interior with stripped-stone walls, flagstones and roaring woodburner; children and dogs welcome, rough home-built seats in informal tiered suntrap garden with stream spilling down waterfall cliffs into duck pond, open all day. *(Steve and Liz Tilley)*

TINTERN   SO5200
Moon & Sixpence (01291) 689284
A466 Chepstow–Monmouth; NP16 6SG Stripped stone, beams, open fires and woodburners, lots of bric-a-brac and antiques for sale, two dining areas, another room with sofas, natural spring feeding indoor goldfish pool, well kept Wye Valley ales and two ciders from back bar, enjoyable pubby food including good value Sun roasts, friendly staff; background music, sports TV; children welcome, terrace with views along River Wye to abbey, good walks, open all day; long-serving owners approaching retirement, so things may change. *(Neil and Anita Christopher)*

TRELLECK   SO5005
Lion (01600) 860322
B4293 6 miles S of Monmouth; NP25 4PA Open-plan bar with one or two low black beams, nice mix of old furniture, two log fires, ales such as Butcombe, Felinfoel and Wye Valley, wide range of good inexpensive food including hungarian and thai specialities, Fri evening fish and chips, traditional games such as shove-ha'penny, ring the bull and table skittles, background music; children and dogs welcome, picnic-sets on grass, side courtyard overlooking church, self-catering cottage, open all day Fri, Sat, closed Sun evening. *(Anon)*

TRELLECK GRANGE   SO5001
Fountain (01291) 689303
Minor road Tintern–Llanishen, SE of village; NP16 6QW Traditional 17th-c country pub under friendly licensees, some sympathetic refurbishment, enjoyable local food from pub favourites to game specials, three well kept welsh ales, farm cider and perry, roomy low-beamed flagstoned bar with log fire; dogs welcome, small walled garden, peaceful spot on small windy road, comfortable bedrooms, open all day, closed Mon. *(Peter Martin)*

USK   SO3700
Cross Keys (01291) 672535
Bridge Street; NP15 1BG Small two-bar stone pub dating from the 14th c, wide choice of popular good value food including OAP deal, well kept Brains and Hancocks, good service and friendly atmosphere, log fire in handsome fireplace, oak beams, wall plaques marking past flood levels, daily newspapers; sports TV; children and dogs (not during

food times) welcome, back terrace, disabled access, five comfortable bedrooms, good breakfast, open all day. *(Anon)*

USK
SO3700
Kings Head (01291) 672963
Old Market Street; NP15 1AL Chatty relaxed atmosphere, good generously served food and well kept beers, friendly efficient staff, huge log fire in superb fireplace; sports TV; bedrooms, open all day. *(Anon)*

GWYNEDD

ABERDOVEY
SN6196
Britannia (01654) 767426
Sea View Terrace; LL35 0EF
Friendly busting harbourside inn; great estuary and distant mountain views from upstairs restaurant with balcony, good range of enjoyable well priced food including fresh crab, downstairs locals' bar with real ales, darts and TV, woodburner in cosy back snug; children welcome (not in bar), three bedrooms, open all day. *(Michael Butler, Jean and Douglas Troup)*

ABERDOVEY
SN6196
✶ Penhelig Arms (01654) 767215
Opposite Penhelig Station; LL35 0LT
Fine harbourside location for this 18th-c hotel, traditional bar with warm fire in central stone fireplace, some panelling, Brains ales and a guest, good choice of wines and malt whiskies, enjoyable food including good fish and chips, attentive staff; children welcome, dogs allowed in bar and comfortable bedrooms (some have balconies overlooking estuary, ones nearest road can be noisy), open all day. *(Henry Pursehouse-Tranter, Bob and Tanya Ekers, Michael Butler, Mr and Mrs P R Thomas, David Glynne-Jones, Richard Osborne-Fardon and others)*

BETWS-Y-COED
SH7955
✶ Ty Gwyn (01690) 710383
A5 just S of bridge to village; LL24 0SG
Restaurant-with-rooms rather than pub (you must eat or stay overnight to be served alcohol), but pubby feel in beamed lounge bar with ancient cooking range, easy chairs, antiques, silver, cut-glass, old prints and interesting bric-a-brac, really good interesting food using local produce including own fruit and vegetables, beers such as Adnams, Brains and Great Orme, friendly professional service; background music; children welcome, 12 comfortable bedrooms and holiday cottage, closed Mon-Weds in Jan. *(Ann and Adrian Bulley)*

BLAENAU FFESTINIOG
SH7041
Pengwern Arms (01766) 762200
Church Square, Ffestiniog; LL41 4PB
Co-operative-owned village pub being restored in stages; panelled bar with well kept/priced Llyn or Purple Moose and a

guest, dining area serving weekend food including bargain Sun lunch, friendly local atmosphere, Mon quiz; fine views from back garden. *(Mike and Eleanor Anderson)*

CAERNARFON
SH4762
✶ Black Buoy (01286) 673604
Northgate Street; LL55 1RW Busy traditional pub by castle walls, renamed losing its historical connection (properly Black Boy, from King Charles II's nickname in its Kings Head days); cheery fire, beams from ships wrecked here in the 16th c, bare floors and thick walls, lots of welsh chat, enjoyable generous food all day from baguettes and doorstep sandwiches to interesting fish and vegetarian dishes, well kept ales such as Brains, Conwy and Purple Moose, good friendly service, character lounge bar, restaurant, public bar with TV; a few pavement picnic-sets, nice bedrooms. *(Jamie Price, John and Gloria Isaacs, Dave Webster, Sue Holland)*

CAPEL CURIG
SH7257
✶ Bryn Tyrch (01690) 720223
A5 E; LL24 0EL Family-owned inn perfectly placed for the mountains of Snowdonia; bare-stone walkers' bar with big communal tables and amazing picture-windows views, two Great Orme ales and a guest beer, quite a few malt whiskies, comprehensive choice of good well presented food including packed lunches and hampers; second bar with big menu boards, leather sofas and mix of tables on floorboards, coal fire; children and dogs welcome, steep little side garden, more seats on terrace and across road by stream, country-style bedrooms, open all day weekends, from 4.30pm weekdays (midday during holidays). *(Anon)*

CAPEL CURIG
SH7357
Tyn y Coed (01690) 720331
A5 SE of village; LL24 0EE Friendly inn across road from River Llugwy; enjoyable good value home-made food using local produce, well kept Purple Moose and three guests, pleasant quick service, log fires, pool room with juke box; nice side terrace, good surrounding walks, comfortable bedrooms, closed weekday lunchtimes out of season, otherwise open all day. *(Chris and Val Ramstedt)*

CONWY
SH7777
Albion (01492) 582484
Uppergate Street; LL32 8RF Sensitively restored 1920s pub thriving under the collective ownership of four welsh brewers – Bragd'yr, Conwy, Great Orme and Purple Moose, their beers and guests kept well, interesting building with plenty of well preserved features including stained glass and huge baronial fireplace, quieter back room with serving hatch. *(Chris and Angela Buckell)*

LLANDUDNO
SH7882
Cottage Loaf (01492) 870762
Market Street; LL30 2SR Friendly former bakery with big log fire, flagstones, bare boards and salvaged ship's timbers, mix of individual tables and chairs, enjoyable good value food, five well kept local ales such as Great Orme. *(Rod and Sue Forrester, Roy Bowman, Derek Wason)*

LLANUWCHLLYN
SH8730
Eagles (01678) 540278
Aka Eryrod; A494/B4403; LL23 7UB Family-run and welcoming with good reasonably priced food (bilingual menu) using produce from own farm, opened-up slate-floor bar with log fire, beams and some stripped stone, back picture-window view of mountains with Lake Bala in distance, ales such as Purple Moose, limited wine choice in small bottles; sports TV; children welcome, picnic-sets under parasols on flower-filled back terrace, open all day summer (afternoon break Mon). *(Anon)*

MAENTWROG
SH6640
Grapes (01766) 590208
A496; village signed from A470; LL41 4HN Sadly closed as we went to press – news please.

PENMAENPOOL
SH6918
George III (01341) 422525
Just off A493, near Dolgellau; LL40 1YD Attractive inn dating from 1650, lovely views over Mawddach estuary from civilised partly panelled upstairs bar opening into cosy inglenook lounge, more basic beamed and flagstoned downstairs bar for peak times, well kept ale such as Black Sheep, Fullers and Purple Moose, enjoyable good value food including specials, restaurant; they ask to keep a credit card if you run a tab; dogs and children welcome, sheltered terrace, 11 good bedrooms including some in converted train station (line now a walkway), open all day. *(Michael Butler, Phil and Helen Holt)*

PORTH DINLLAEN
SH2741
✳ Ty Coch (01758) 720498
Beach car park signed from Morfa Nefyn, then 15-minute walk; LL53 6DB Idyllic location right on beach with great view along coast to mountains, far from roads and only reached on foot; bar crammed with nautical paraphernalia, pewter, old miners' and railway lamps, RNLI memorabilia and so forth, simple furnishings and coal fire, a couple of real ales (served in plastic as worried about glass on beach), short lunchtime bar menu; children and dogs welcome, open all day in season (till 4pm Sun), 12-4pm Oct-Easter. *(Theocsbrian, Matt Williams)*

PORTHMADOG
SH5738
Spooners (01766) 516032
Harbour Station; LL49 9NF Platform café-bar at steam line terminus, lots of railway memorabilia including a former working engine (Princess) in one corner, Marstons-related ales and welsh guests like Purple Moose, good value pub food including popular Sun lunch, evening meals Tues-Sat (all week in high season); children welcome, platform tables, open all day. *(Tony Hobden, Mike and Eleanor Anderson, Phil Bryant)*

TREFRIW
SH7863
Old Ship (01492) 640013
B5106; LL27 0JH Well run old pub with nice staff and cheerful local atmosphere, good home-made food from changing blackboard menu, particularly well kept Marstons-related beers and local guests, good selection of wines/malt whiskies, log fire and inglenook woodburner; garden with picnic-sets by stream, children welcome, open all day weekends, closed Mon. *(Martin Cawley, Claes Mauroy, Mike Proctor, Mike and Wena Stevenson)*

TUDWEILIOG
SH2336
Lion (01758) 659724
Nefyn Road (B4417), Lleyn Peninsula; LL53 8ND Cheerful village inn with enjoyable sensibly priced food from baguettes to blackboard specials, lounge bar and two dining rooms (one for families), quick friendly service, real ales such as Purple Moose (up to three in summer), dozens of malt whiskies, decent wines, games in public bar; pleasant front garden, four bedrooms, open all day in season. *(John and Louise Gittins)*

POWYS

BERRIEW
SJ1800
Lion (01686) 640452
B4390; village signed off A483 Welshpool–Newtown; SY21 8PQ Black and white beamed 17th-c coaching inn in attractive riverside village (with lively sculpture gallery), friendly welcome from mother-and-daughter team, old-fashioned inglenook public bar and partly stripped-stone lounge, enjoyable food here or in restaurant from sandwiches up, helpful cheerful service, well kept Banks's and Jennings, decent house wines, dominoes; quiet background music; children and dogs (in bar) welcome, seven bedrooms, open all day Fri, Sat. *(David Glynne-Jones, Clare Tagg)*

We can always use photos of pubs on our website – why not e-mail us one – feedback@thegoodpubguide.co.uk

BLEDDFA   SO2068

Hundred House (01547) 550441

A488 Knighton–Penybont; LD7 1PA
Refurbished 16th-c pub (former courthouse)
opposite village green, friendly newish
licensees, carpeted lounge bar with
woodburner in big inglenook, L-shaped
room with lower flagstoned bar, another
big fireplace in cosy dining room, enjoyable
locally sourced food, Radnorshire ales;
background music; children welcome,
tables in side garden with play area,
lovely countryside, closed Mon, otherwise
open all day. *(Anon)*

CAERSWS   SO0391

Buck (01686) 688267

Main Street; SY17 5EL Friendly
refurbished and extended old inn, good
sensibly priced home-made food (evenings
Thurs-Sat, lunchtime Sun) in bar and
restaurant, local ales; bedrooms, open
all day weekends, from 5pm weekdays.
(Jean and Douglas Troup)

CARNO   SN9696

Aleppo Merchant (01686) 420210

A470 Newtown–Machynlleth; SY17 5LL
Good choice of reasonably priced pub food
from sandwiches up (open for breakfast
too), helpful friendly staff, Boddingtons and
a guest, plushly modernised stripped-stone
bar, peaceful lounge on right with open fire,
restaurant (well behaved children allowed
here), back extension with big-screen TV in
games room; background music; disabled
access, steps up to tables in back garden,
bedrooms, nice countryside, open all day.
(Mike and Mary Carter)

CRICKHOWELL   SO2118

Dragon (01873) 810362

High Street; NP8 1BE Welcoming old inn
(more hotel-restaurant than pub but with
small bar), enjoyable food from new chef,
prompt friendly service, Rhymney, log fire;
15 comfortable bedrooms. *(Tony and Gill
Powell, Eryl and Keith Dykes)*

DERWENLAS   SN7299

★ Black Lion (01654) 703913

A487 just S of Machynlleth; SY20 8TN
Cosy 16th-c country pub with good range
of enjoyable well priced food including
children's menu, friendly staff coping well
at busy times, Wye Valley Butty Bach and
a guest, decent wines, heavy black beams,
thick walls and black timbering, attractive
pictures, brasses and lion models, tartan
carpet over big slate flagstones, good log
fire; background music; garden behind with
play area and steps up into woods, limited
parking, bedrooms, closed Mon. *(Anon)*

DINAS MAWDDWY   SH8514

Red Lion (01650) 531247

Dyfi Road; off A470 (N of A458

junction); SY20 9JA Two small traditional
front bars and more modern back extension,
changing ales including some from small
local brewers, good generous home-made
food including specials, reasonable prices
and friendly efficient service, open fire,
beams and lots of brass; children welcome,
simple bedrooms, pub named in welsh
(Llew Coch). *(Peter and Anne Hollindale)*

GLADESTRY   SO2355

Royal Oak (01544) 370669

B4594; HR5 3NR Old-fashioned village pub
on Offa's Dyke Path with friendly licensees,
simple stripped-stone slate-floored walkers'
bar, beams hung with tankards and lanterns,
piano, darts, carpeted lounge, open fires,
ales from Golden Valley and Wye Valley,
uncomplicated home-made food; no credit
cards; children welcome, dogs in bar (and
bedrooms by arrangement), sheltered back
garden, camping, closed Mon and evenings
Tues, Thurs, Sun (may also shut if quiet but
will open if you ring the bell). *(Ann and
Colin Hunt)*

GLASBURY   SO1839

Harp (01497) 847373

*B4350 towards Hay, just N of A438;
HR3 5NR* Welcoming, relaxed and homely
old place with good value pubby food (not
Mon) cooked by landlady including proper
pies, log-fire lounge with eating areas, airy
bar, well kept local ales, picture windows
over wooded garden sloping to River Wye,
some acoustic music, darts; river views
from terrace and back bedrooms, good
breakfast. *(Mike Ashley)*

HAY-ON-WYE   SO2242

Blue Boar (01497) 820884

Castle Street/Oxford Road; HR3 5DF
Medieval bar in character pub, cosy corners,
dark panelling, pews and country chairs,
open fire in Edwardian fireplace, four ales
including a house beer from Hydes, organic
bottled cider and several wines by the glass,
enjoyable food (from breakfast on) in quite
different long open café dining room, bright
light décor, local artwork for sale and another
open fire; background music; children and
dogs welcome, tables in tree-shaded garden,
open all day from 9am. *(Mark Sykes, David and
Sue Atkinson)*

HAY-ON-WYE   SO2342

★ Old Black Lion (01497) 820841

Lion Street; HR3 5AD Comfortable low-
beamed bar with old pine tables and original
fireplace, mostly laid for dining, good bar
and restaurant food available throughout,
Wye Valley Butty Bach (labelled as Old Black
Lion) and a guest, friendly helpful service;
no dogs; children over 5 allowed if eating,
sheltered back terrace, ten bedrooms
(some above bar), good breakfast, open
all day. *(Anon)*

HAY-ON-WYE   SO2242
⋆ **Three Tuns** (01497) 821855
Broad Street; HR3 5DB Popular freshly
prepared food (not Sun evening) in big pub
with low beams and inglenook woodburners,
lighter sofa area, ancient stairs to raftered
restaurant, well kept ales and good wine
choice, prompt helpful service; may ask for a
credit card if you run a tab, no dogs; children
welcome till 7pm, disabled facilities, seats
under big parasols in sheltered courtyard,
open all day weekends, closed Mon and Tues
out of season. *(Martin and Sue Day)*

POWYS
HUNDRED HOUSE   SO1154
Hundred House Inn (01982) 570231
A481 NE of Builth Wells; LD1 5RY
Old-fashioned two-room roadside country pub
with welcoming landlord, one or more well
kept ales, good choice of straightforward food
(deals most nights), woodburner in public
bar; no dogs; garden picnic-sets. *(Ann and
Colin Hunt)*

KNIGHTON   SO2872
Horse & Jockey (01547) 520062
Wylcwm Place; LD7 1AE Popular old
family-run pub with several cosy areas, one
with log fire, enjoyable good value food from
traditional choices and pizzas up in bar
and adjoining restaurant, cheerful service,
well kept beers; tables in pleasant medieval
courtyard, six bedrooms, handy for Offa's
Dyke Path. *(Ann and Colin Hunt)*

LLANBEDR   SO2320
Red Lion (01873) 810754
Off A40 at Crickhowell; NP8 1SR Quaint,
welcoming old local in pretty little village
set in dell, heavy beams, antique settles in
lounge and snug, log fires, Rhymney, Wye
Valley and a guest ale, front dining area with
good value home-made food; good walking
country (porch for muddy boots), closed
weekday lunchtime (except 2-5pm Weds),
open all day weekends. *(Anon)*

LLANFIHANGEL-NANT-
MELAN   SO1958
Red Lion (01544) 350220
A44 10 miles W of Kington; LD8 2TN
Stripped-stone and beamed 16th-c roadside
dining pub, roomy main bar with flagstones
and woodburner, carpeted restaurant,
front sun porch, reasonably priced home-
made food from sandwiches to Sun roasts,
vegetarian options, Brains and changing
guests, back bar with woodburner, pool

and darts; children and dogs welcome,
pleasant garden with nice country views,
seven bedrooms (three in annexe), handy
for Radnor Forest walks, near impressive
waterfall, open all day Sun till 9pm, closed
Tues. *(Ann and Colin Hunt)*

LLANFRYNACH   SO0725
White Swan (01874) 665276
*Village signposted from B4558, off A40
E of Brecon – take second turn to village,
which is also signed to pub; LD3 7BZ*
Comfortably upmarket country dining pub
in heart of Brecon Beacons; original part
with stripped stone and flagstones, sturdy
oak tables, leather sofas and armchairs
at low tables, woodburner, Brains, Sharps
and a guest, Addlestone's cider, decent
wines and coffees, good food with plenty of
variety (simpler at lunchtime), overflow into
more modern high-ceilinged bare-boards
extension; background music; children
and dogs welcome, charming back terrace
attractively divided by low privet hedges,
towpath walks along canal, closed Mon
winter. *(Anon)*

LLANGEDWYN   SJ1924
⋆ **Green Inn** (01691) 828234
B4396 E of village; SY10 9JW Ancient
country dining pub with various snug alcoves,
nooks and crannies, good mix of furnishings
including oak settles and leather sofas,
blazing log fire, helpful friendly staff, up to
four changing ales and good wines by the
glass, enjoyable well prepared food, plenty of
events from music to comedy; children and
dogs welcome, attractive garden over road
running down towards River Tanat (fishing
permits available), camping, open all day
weekends, closed Tues. *(Mike Walker, Jill
Sparrow)*

LLANGURIG   SN9079
Blue Bell (01686) 440254
A44 opposite church; SY18 6SG Friendly
old-fashioned country inn with well kept
Brains Rev James and Wye Valley Butty
Bach, Thatcher's cider, ample helpings
of enjoyable good value pubby food,
comfortable flagstoned bar, games room
with darts, dominoes and pool, small dining
room; background music, no dogs; children
welcome, nine inexpensive simple bedrooms,
open all day. *(Anon)*

LLANIDLOES   SN9584
Crown & Anchor (01686) 412398
Long Bridge Street; SY18 6EF Friendly
unspoilt town-centre pub known locally
as Rubys after landlady who has run it for
48 years, well kept Brains Rev James and

Post Office address codings confusingly give the impression that some pubs
are in Gwent or Powys, Wales, when they're really in Gloucestershire or Shropshire
(which is where we list them).

Worthington Bitter, chatty locals' bar, lounge, snug, and two other rooms, one with pool and games machine separated by central hallway; open all day; up for sale so things may change. *(Anon)*

LLANWRTYD WELLS　　　SN8746
Neuadd Arms　(01591) 610236
The Square; LD5 4RB Sizeable 19th-c hotel (friendly and by no means upmarket) brewing its own good value Heart of Wales beers in back stable block, enjoyable straightforward home-made food, log fires in lounge and small tiled public bar still with its old service bells, restaurant, games room; lots of outdoor events (some rather outré such as bogsnorkelling and man v horse); well behaved dogs welcome in bars, a few tables out in front, 21 bedrooms (front ones can be noisy), engaging very small town in good walking area, open all day. *(Taff Thomas)*

LLOWES　　　SO1941
Radnor Arms　(01497) 847460
A438 Brecon–Hereford; HR3 5JA Attractive little stone-built country pub, well kept Wye Valley Butty Bach and a guest, extensive choice of bottled beers, good blackboard food including fresh fish, children's menu, traditional beamed bar with stripped stone and log fire, two small dining rooms; dogs welcome, tables in garden looking over fields to the Black Mountains, small campsite, closed Sun evening, Mon, Tues, lunchtimes Weds and Thurs. *(Clare Williams, Reg Fowle, Helen Rickwood)*

PAINSCASTLE　　　SO1646
★ Roast Ox　(01497) 851398
Off A470 Brecon–Builth Wells, or from A438 at Clyro; LD2 3JL Well restored pub with beams, flagstones, stripped stone, appropriate simple furnishings and some rustic bric-a-brac, well kept ales tapped from the cask and good range of farm ciders, popular freshly made food, friendly quick service; children and dogs welcome, picnic-sets outside, attractive hill country, ten comfortable bedrooms. *(T and F Melhuish)*

PENCELLI　　　SO0925
Royal Oak　(01874) 665396
B4558 SE of Brecon; LD3 7LX Unpretentious and friendly with two small bars, low beams, assorted pine furniture on polished flagstones, autographed sporting memorabilia, log fires, well kept Brains Rev James and a guest, small blackboard choice of enjoyable home-made food (standard times in summer, Thurs-Sat evenings and weekend lunchtimes in winter), simple modern candlelit dining room; children welcome, terraces backing on to Monmouth & Brecon Canal, nearby moorings, lovely canalside walks and handy for Taff Trail, closed Mon-Weds out of season. *(Brian and Anna Marsden)*

PEN-Y-CAE　　　SN8313
Ancient Briton　(01639) 730273
Brecon Road (A4067); SA9 1YY Friendly opened-up roadside pub, six or more well kept ales from far and wide, local cider, enjoyable reasonably priced home-made food; outside seats and play area, campsite, handy for Dan-yr-Ogof caves, Henrhyd Waterfall and Carig-y-Nos Country Park, open all day. *(Quentin and Carol Williamson, MLR)*

PRESTEIGNE　　　SO3164
Radnorshire Arms　(01544) 267406
High Street (B4355 N of centre); LD8 2BE Fine Elizabethan timbered hotel full of rambling individuality and historical charm; relaxed bar, venerable dark oak panelling, latticed windows, elegantly moulded black oak beams, polished copper pans and measures, a handful of armchairs, lovely dining room, enjoyable well priced pubby food, decent choice of real ales and ciders, friendly efficient staff; background music, pool room; children welcome, outside play area, 16 bedrooms (eight in garden lodge), open all day. *(Anon)*

RHAYADER　　　SN9668
★ Triangle　(01597) 810537
Cwmdauddwr, B4518 by bridge over River Wye, SW of centre; LD6 5AR Interesting mainly 16th-c pub, small and spotless with nice chatty atmosphere and welcoming helpful service, shortish choice of good value home-made pubby food (best to book evenings), well kept Brains Rev James and Hancocks HB, small selection of reasonably priced wines, dining area with nice view over park to Wye, darts and quiz nights; three tables on small front terrace. *(Di and Mike Gillam, Taff Thomas)*

TALYBONT-ON-USK　　　SO1122
★ Star　(01874) 676635
B4558; LD3 7YX Old-fashioned canalside inn unashamedly stronger on character than creature comforts, five changing ales served by enthusiastic landlord, real cider, fair-priced standard bar food, good mix of customers including walkers with dogs, several plainly furnished pubby rooms, open fires (one in splendid stone fireplace); sports TV, juke box, live music last Fri of month, quiz Weds in winter; children and dogs welcome, picnic sets in sizeable tree-ringed garden with path leading to river, lovely village surrounded by Brecon Beacons National Park, two bedrooms, open all day summer. *(Brian and Anna Marsden, Taff Thomas)*

A little further afield

CHANNEL ISLANDS

GUERNSEY
KING'S MILLS
⋆**Fleur du Jardin** (01481) 257996
King's Mills Road; GY5 7JT Lovely
country hotel in attractive walled garden
with solar-heated swimming pool, relaxing
low-beamed flagstoned bar with good log
fire, old prints and subdued lighting, good
food strong on local produce and seafood,
friendly helpful service, several real ales
such as Adnams Broadside and Liberation,
good choice of wines by the glass, local cider,
restaurant; background music; children and
small dogs welcome, plenty of tables on back
terrace, 15 clean comfortable bedrooms,
open all day. *(Anon)*

ST PETER PORT
Ship & Crown (01481) 728994
Opposite Crown Pier, Esplanade;
GY1 2NB Bustling town pub with bay
windows overlooking harbour, very popular
with yachting people and smarter locals;
interesting photographs (especially of World
War II occupation, also boats and local
shipwrecks), good value all-day bar food from
sandwiches up, three changing ales and a
proper cider, welcoming prompt service even
when busy, more modern-feel Crow's Nest
brasserie upstairs with fine views; sports TVs
in bar; open all day from 10am till late.
(MLR)

VALE
Houmet (01481) 242214
Grande Havre; GY6 8JR Modern
building overlooking Grande Havre Bay,
front restaurant-bar with conservatory, good
choice of reasonably priced popular food
(best to book) including fresh local fish and
seafood, friendly service, a couple of real
ales and several wines by the glass, back
public bar with pool and big screen sports
TV (dogs allowed here); children welcome,
tables out on decking, open all day (till 8pm
Sun). *(MLR)*

JERSEY
GRÈVE DE LECQ
⋆**Moulin de Lecq** (01534) 482818
Mont de la Grève de Lecq; JE3 2DT
Cheerful family-friendly converted mill
dating from 12th c with massive waterwheel
dominating the softly lit beamed bar, good
pubby food, four changing ales and a couple
of real ciders, prompt friendly service, lots of
board games, pool in upstairs games room,
restaurant extension; dogs welcome in bar,
terrace picnic-sets and good adventure
playground, quiet streamside spot with nice
walks, open all day in summer. *(Anon)*

ST AUBIN
Boat House (01534) 747141
North Quay; JE3 8BS Modern steel
and timber clad harbourside building,
refurbished with new larger bar area, good
local ales, modern food cooked using Josper
oven ranging from tapas to flame-grilled
steaks in light and airy upstairs restaurant,
great views (window tables for diners);
balcony and decked terrace, open all day.
(Anon)

ST AUBIN
⋆**Old Court House Inn**
(01534) 746433 *Harbour Boulevard;*
JE3 8AB Pubby low-beamed downstairs
bar with open fire, other rambling areas
including smarter bar partly built from
schooner's gig, food from pubby snacks to
lots of good fresh fish, well kept real ales
and nice wines by the glass, handsome
upstairs restaurant, glorious views across
harbour to St Helier; children welcome,
front deck overloooking harbour, more seats
in floral courtyard behind, ten comfortable
bedrooms, open all day (food all day in
summer). *(Anon)*

ST BRELADE
Old Smugglers (01534) 741510
Ouaisne Bay; OS map reference
595476; JE3 8AW Happily unpretentious
black-beamed pub, well kept Bass and two
guests, farm cider, enjoyable reasonably
priced pubby food (good steaks), friendly

service, log fires, traditional built-in settles, darts, cribbage and dominoes, restaurant; occasional live music, sports TV; children and dogs welcome, sun porch with interesting coast views, just above Ouaisne beach, open all day. *(John Evans)*

ST HELIER
★ **Lamplighter** (01534) 723119
Mulcaster Street; JE2 3NJ Small pub with up to eight well kept ales including Liberation, local cider, around 160 whiskies, bargain simple food such as crab sandwiches, heavy timbers, rough panelling and scrubbed pine tables; sports TV, can get very busy; interesting façade (with only Union Flag visible during Nazi occupation), open all day. *(Steve and Claire Harvey, MLR)*

ISLE OF MAN

LAXEY   SC4382
Shore (01624) 861509
Old Laxey Hill; IM4 7DA Friendly nautically themed village pub brewing its own Old Laxey Bosuns Bitter, good value wines by the glass, enjoyable pubby lunchtime food (also Tues curry and Thurs steak nights); children welcome till 9pm, picnic-sets out by lovely stream, nice walk to Laxey Waterwheel, open all day. *(Dr J Barrie Jones)*

PEEL   SC2484
Creek (01624) 842216
Station Place/North Quay; IM5 1AT In lovely setting on the ancient quayside opposite the House of Manannan heritage centre, welcoming relaxed atmosphere, wide choice of sensibly priced food all day including fish, crab and lobsters fresh from the boats, good local kippers too, well kept Okells and nine guest ales, nautical-themed lounge bar with etched mirrors and mainly old woodwork, public bar with TVs and weekend live music; children welcome, tables outside overlooking harbour, open all day. *(Steve Homer)*

PORT ERIN
Falcon's Nest (01624) 834077
Station Road; IM9 6AF Friendly family-run hotel overlooking the bay, good sensibly priced food including local fish/seafood, five well kept ales (May beer festival) and some 70 malt whiskies, two bars, one with open fire and conservatory, restaurant; children welcome, 39 bedrooms many with sea view, also eight self-catering apartments, handy for steam rail terminus, open all day. *(Dr J Barrie Jones)*

Pubs that serve food all day

We list here all the pubs that have told us they plan to serve food all day, even if it's only one day of the week. The individual entries for the pubs themselves show the actual details.

Bedfordshire
Clophill, Flying Horse
Ireland, Black Horse
Oakley, Bedford Arms

Berkshire
Cookham Dean, Chequers
Kintbury, Dundas Arms
Peasemore, Fox
Sonning, Bull
White Waltham, Beehive

Buckinghamshire
Coleshill, Harte & Magpies
Forty Green, Royal Standard of England
Wooburn Common, Chequers

Cambridgeshire
Bourn, Willow Tree
Cambridge, Punter
Peterborough, Brewery Tap
Stilton, Bell

Cheshire
Aldford, Grosvenor Arms
Allostock, Three Greyhounds
Astbury, Egerton Arms
Aston, Bhurtpore
Bickley Moss, Cholmondeley Arms
Bunbury, Dysart Arms
Burleydam, Combermere Arms
Burwardsley, Pheasant
Chester, Architect, Mill, Old Harkers Arms
Cotebrook, Fox & Barrel
Delamere, Fishpool
Eaton, Plough
Macclesfield, Sutton Hall
Marton, Davenport Arms
Mobberley, Bulls Head
Mottram St Andrew, Bulls Head
Nether Alderley, Wizard
Peover Heath, Dog
Spurstow, Yew Tree
Tarporley, Rising Sun
Thelwall, Little Manor
Warmingham, Bears Paw

Cornwall
Crafthole, Finnygook
Mylor Bridge, Pandora
Porthtowan, Blue

Cumbria
Cartmel Fell, Masons Arms
Crosthwaite, Punch Bowl
Elterwater, Britannia

Ings, Watermill
Levens, Strickland Arms
Lupton, Plough
Ravenstonedale, Black Swan

Derbyshire

Alderwasley, Bear
Beeley, Devonshire Arms
Chelmorton, Church Inn
Fenny Bentley, Coach & Horses
Hathersage, Plough, Scotsmans Pack
Hayfield, Lantern Pike, Royal
Ladybower Reservoir, Ladybower Inn, Yorkshire Bridge
Litton, Red Lion

Devon

Avonwick, Turtley Corn Mill
Cockwood, Anchor
Iddesleigh, Duke of York
Postbridge, Warren House
Sidbury, Hare & Hounds

Dorset

Tarrant Monkton, Langton Arms
Weymouth, Red Lion
Worth Matravers, Square & Compass

Essex

Aythorpe Roding, Axe & Compasses
Feering, Sun
Little Walden, Crown
Peldon, Rose
South Hanningfield, Old Windmill

Gloucestershire

Broad Campden, Bakers Arms
Coates, Tunnel House
Ford, Plough

Guiting Power, Hollow Bottom
Nailsworth, Egypt Mill, Weighbridge
Sheepscombe, Butchers Arms

Hampshire

Bransgore, Three Tuns
Portsmouth, Old Customs House

Hertfordshire

Aldbury, Valiant Trooper
Barnet, Duke of York

Isle of Wight

Arreton, White Lion
Fishbourne, Fishbourne Inn
Ningwood, Horse & Groom
Niton, Buddle
Seaview, Boathouse
Shorwell, Crown

Kent

Brookland, Woolpack
Hollingbourne, Windmill
Langton Green, Hare
Penshurst, Bottle House
Sevenoaks, White Hart
Stalisfield Green, Plough
Stowting, Tiger

Lancashire

Bashall Eaves, Red Pump
Bispham Green, Eagle & Child
Great Mitton, Three Fishes
Liverpool, Philharmonic Dining Rooms
Manchester, Dukes 92, Wharf
Nether Burrow, Highwayman
Pleasington, Clog & Billycock
Stalybridge, Station Buffet
Uppermill, Church Inn
Waddington, Lower Buck
Whalley, Swan

Leicestershire

Coleorton, George
Lyddington, Marquess of Exeter
Swithland, Griffin
Woodhouse Eaves, Wheatsheaf
Lincolnshire
Kirkby la Thorpe, Queens Head

Norfolk

Brancaster Staithe, Jolly Sailors
King's Lynn, Bank House
Larling, Angel
Morston, Anchor
Salthouse, Dun Cow
Stiffkey, Red Lion
Swanton Morley, Darbys
Thorpe Market, Gunton Arms
Woodbastwick, Fur & Feather
Northamptonshire
Ashby St Ledgers, Olde Coach House
Oundle, Ship

Northumbria

Aycliffe, County
Carterway Heads, Manor House Inn
Cotherstone, Fox & Hounds
New York, Shiremoor Farm
Weldon Bridge, Anglers Arms

Nottinghamshire

Nottingham, Olde Trip to Jerusalem

Oxfordshire

Kingham, Plough
Oxford, Bear, Punter

Shropshire

Chetwynd Aston, Fox
Shrewsbury, Armoury

Somerset

Dunster, Luttrell Arms
Hinton St George, Lord Poulett Arms
Stanton Wick, Carpenters Arms
Staffordshire
Salt, Holly Bush
Wrinehill, Hand & Trumpet

Suffolk

Chelmondiston, Butt & Oyster
Southwold, Harbour Inn
Stoke-by-Nayland, Crown
Waldringfield, Maybush

Surrey

Buckland, Jolly Farmers
Elstead, Mill at Elstead
Milford, Refectory
Outwood, Bell

Sussex

Alfriston, George
Ashurst, Fountain
Blackboys, Blackboys Inn
Charlton, Fox Goes Free
Chiddingly, Six Bells
East Chiltington, Jolly Sportsman
Eridge Green, Nevill Crest & Gun
Horsham, Black Jug
Lodsworth, Halfway Bridge Inn
Mayfield, Rose & Crown
Ringmer, Cock

Warwickshire

Birmingham, Old Joint Stock
Farnborough, Inn at Farnborough
Long Compton, Red Lion
Stratford-upon-Avon, Encore
Welford-on-Avon, Bell

Yorkshire

Blakey Ridge, Lion
Bradfield, Strines Inn
Broughton, Bull
Elslack, Tempest Arms
Grinton, Bridge Inn
Halifax, Shibden Mill
Hartshead, Gray Ox
Ledsham, Chequers
Linton in Craven, Fountaine
Widdop, Pack Horse

London

Central London, Bountiful Cow,
Dog & Duck, Old Bank of England,
Olde Mitre, Seven Stars

North London, Holly Bush

South London, Greenwich Union

West London, Churchill Arms,
Dove, Duke of Sussex, Old
Orchard, Portobello Gold, White
Horse, Windsor Castle

Scotland

Applecross, Applecross Inn
Edinburgh, Abbotsford
Gairloch, Old Inn
Glasgow, Babbity Bowster,
Bon Accord
Glencoe, Clachaig
Houston, Fox & Hounds
Kippen, Cross Keys
Pitlochry, Moulin
Shieldaig, Tigh an Eilean Hotel
Thornhill, Lion & Unicorn
Scottish Islands
Carbost, Old Inn
Sligachan, Sligachan Hotel

Wales

Colwyn Bay, Pen-y-Bryn
Gresford, Pant-yr-Ochain
Jameston, Tudor Lodge
Llandudno Junction, Queens Head
Llangollen, Corn Mill
Mold, Glasfryn
Overton Bridge, Cross Foxes
Pontypridd, Bunch of Grapes
Tresaith, Ship

Pubs near motorway junctions

The number at the start of each line is the number of the junction.

Detailed directions are given in the entry for each pub. In this section, to help you find the pubs quickly before you're past the junction, we give the name of the chapter where you'll find the text.

M1

9: Redbourn, Cricketers (Hertfordshire) 3.2 miles

13: Woburn, Birch (Bedfordshire) 3.5 miles

16: Weedon, Narrow Boat (Northamptonshire) 3.9 miles; Nether Heyford, Olde Sun (Northamptonshire) 1.8 miles

18: Ashby St Ledgers, Olde Coach House (Northamptonshire) 4 miles

M3

1: Sunbury, Flower Pot (Surrey) 1.6 miles

3: West End, Inn at West End (Surrey) 2.4 miles

5: North Warnborough, Mill House (Hampshire) 1 mile; Hook, Hogget (Hampshire) 1.1 miles

7: North Waltham, Fox (Hampshire) 3 miles

9: Easton, Chestnut Horse (Hampshire) 3.6 miles

M4

9: Bray, Crown (Berkshire) 1.75 miles; Bray, Hinds Head (Berkshire) 1.75 miles

13: Winterbourne, Winterbourne Arms (Berkshire) 3.7 miles; Peasemore, Fox (Berkshire) 4 miles

14: Shefford Woodlands, Pheasant (Berkshire) 0.3 miles; East Garston, Queens Arms (Berkshire) 3.5 miles

17: Norton, Vine Tree (Wiltshire) 4 miles

M5

4: Holy Cross, Bell & Cross (Worcestershire) 4 miles; Coombe Hill, Gloucester Old Spot (Gloucestershire) 1 mile

19: Clapton-in-Gordano, Black Horse (Somerset) 4 miles

26: Clayhidon, Merry Harriers (Devon) 3.1 miles

30: Woodbury Salterton, Diggers Rest (Devon) 3.5 miles

M6

17: Sandbach, Old Hall (Cheshire) 1.2 miles

18: Allostock, Three Greyhounds (Cheshire) 4.7 miles

19: Mobberley, Bulls Head (Cheshire) 4 miles

36: Lupton, Plough (Cumbria) 2 miles; Levens, Strickland Arms (Cumbria) 4 miles

40: Yanwath, Gate Inn (Cumbria) 2.25 miles; Tirril, Queens Head (Cumbria) 3.5 miles

M11

7: Hastingwood, Rainbow & Dove (Essex) 0.25 miles

9: Hinxton, Red Lion (Cambridgeshire) 2 miles; Great Chesterford, Crown & Thistle (Essex) 1.5 miles

10: Whittlesford, Tickell Arms (Cambridgeshire) 2.4 miles

M20

8: Hollingbourne, Windmill (Kent) 1 mile

11: Stowting, Tiger (Kent) 3.7 miles

M25

5: Chipstead, George & Dragon (Kent) 1.25 miles

16: Denham, Swan (Buckinghamshire) 0.75 miles

18: Chenies, Red Lion (Buckinghamshire) 2 miles; Flaunden, Bricklayers Arms (Hertfordshire) 4 miles

21A: Potters Crouch, Holly Bush (Hertfordshire) 2.3 miles

M27

1: Fritham, Royal Oak (Hampshire) 4 miles

M40

2: Hedgerley, White Horse (Buckinghamshire) 2.4 miles; Forty Green, Royal Standard of England (Buckinghamshire) 3.5 miles

12: Gaydon, Malt Shovel (Warwickshire) 0.9 miles

M42

5: Barston, Malt Shovel (Warwickshire) 3 miles

6: Hampton in Arden, White Lion (Warwickshire) 1.25 miles

M50

3: Kilcot, Kilcot Inn (Gloucestershire) 2.3 miles

M62

25: Hartshead, Gray Ox (Yorkshire) 3.5 miles

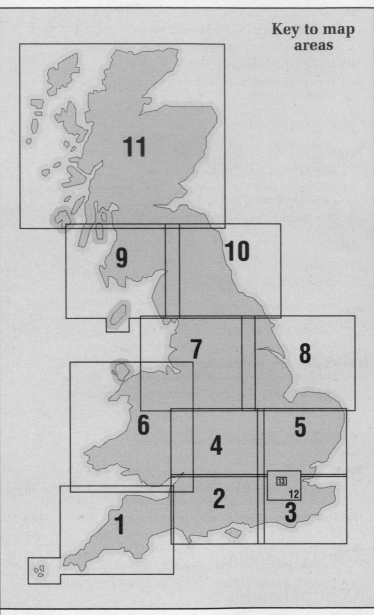

Key to map areas

Reference to sectional maps

	Motorway	●	Main Entry
	Major road	◉	Main Entry with accommodation
	County boundary	■	Place name to assist navigation

MAPS

1

- Main Entry
- Main Entry with accommodation
- Place name to assist navigation

Channel Islands

ALDERNEY

F R A N C E

ST PETER PORT

SARK

GUERNSEY

JERSEY

ST HELIER

0   10
Miles

BUDE

The Scilly Isles

ST MARTIN'S

TRESCO   **SV**

ST MARY'S

ST AGNES

0   3
MILES

Wainhouse Corner

Boscastle

LAUNCESTON

Port Isaac

Blisland

St Merryn

WADEBRIDGE

CORNWALL

BODMIN

LISKEARD

NEWQUAY

Lostwithiel

SW

Trevaunance Cove

ST AUSTELL

POWEY

Crafthol

Porthtowan

TRURO

Polkerris

Polperro

REDRUTH

Devoran

Gurnards Head

Perranwell

Mylor Bridge

Penzance

FALMOUTH

Perranuthnoe

Helston

Constantine

Mousehole

Cadgwith

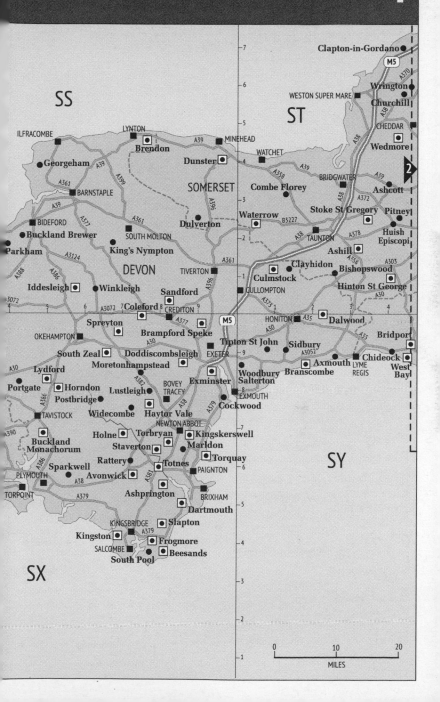

2

- Main Entry
- Main Entry with accommodation
- Place name to assist navigation

Tetbury
Oldbury-on-Severn
Crudwell
4 Cricklade
GLOUCESTERSHIRE
Leighterton
Sherston
MALMESBURY
Norton
Swindon
Grittleton
Broad Hinton
Ford
CHIPPENHAM
Compton Bassett
Bristol
Corsham
Lacock
CALNE
Marlborough
Sandy Lane
Manton
Stanton Wick
Bath
South Wraxall
MELKSHAM
Wrington
Winsley
Broughton Gifford
Midford
BRADFORD-ON-AVON
DEVIZES
Combe Hay
TROWBRIDGE
WILTSHIRE
Hinton Charterhouse
Poulshot
MIDSOMER NORTON
West Lavington
CHEDDAR
Holcombe
Priddy
FROME
East Chisenbury
Wells
Mells
Croscombe
WARMINSTER
SHEPTON MALLET
SOMERSET
Upton Lovell
Newton Tony
GLASTONBURY
Batcombe
AMESBURY
WYLYE
ST
Fonthill Gifford
Babcary
WINCANTON
East Knoyle
Chicksgrove
Salisbury
Pitton
Corton Denham
West Stour
Charlton Horethorne
SHAFTESBURY
Berwick St John
Trent
YEOVIL
Tollard Royal
Rockbourne
Odcombe
Sherborne
FORDINGBRIDGE
Fritham
Farnham
Middlemarsh
BLANDFORD FORUM
DORSET
Tarrant Monkton
Evershot
Cerne Abbas
Plush
RINGWOOD
Powerstock
Wimborne Minster
Bransgore
Nettlecombe
Sydling St Nicholas
CHRISTCHURCH
Askerswell
Bridport
DORCHESTER
POOLE
BOURNEMOUTH
Mudeford
Burton Bradstock
WAREHAM
Weymouth
Church Knowle
SWANAGE
SY
Worth Matravers

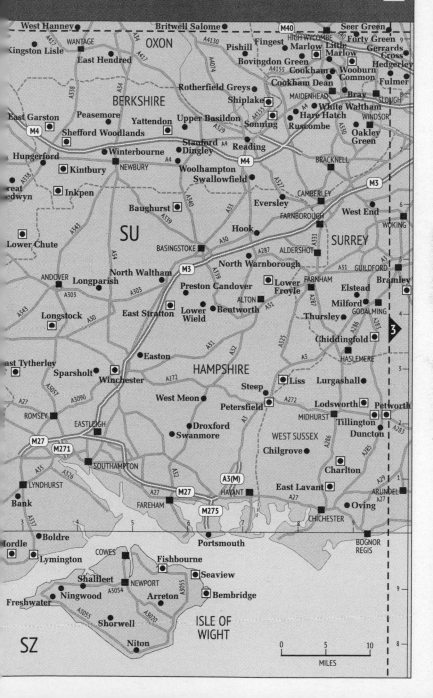

3
- ● Main Entry
- ◉ Main Entry with accommodation
- ■ Place name to assist navigation

BUCKS
● Chenies
Gerrards
Cross ◉
Hedgerley ●
■ UXBRIDGE
● Denham
Harefield (see West London)
GREATER LONDON
M40
Fulmer ●
M1
M11
5
M25
● Horndon-on-
-the-Hill
A127
A13
A128
BERKS
M4
M25
■ STAINES
■ TILBURY
■ GRAVESEND
DARTFORD
■
ROCHESTER
A2
M2
M3
◉ Sunbury
Esher ● ● Thames Ditton
Claygate
M25
M20
M20
M27
A228
WOKING ■
A3
M25
● Chipstead
Chipstead ●
M26
M20
A227
MAIDSTONE
SURREY
◉ Mickleham
WESTERHAM
A25
Sevenoaks ●
● Ivy Hatch
A25
DORKING
● Buckland
A24
Bramley ◉
REIGATE
A25
A31
■ TONBRIDGE
TO
Leigh ● ● Outwood
A22
Penshurst ● ● Speldhurst
● Goudhurst
A262
● Shamley Green
A281
◉ Cranleigh
CRAWLEY
A264
M23
A264
EAST GRINSTEAD
Langton Green ●
Eridge Green ●
Tunbridge
Wells ◉
A267
A21
2
● Horsham
West Hoathly ◉
CROWBOROUGH
A26
A27
A21
◉ Ticehurst
● Warninglid
HAYWARDS
HEATH
● Danehill
Fletching ◉
● Mayfield
Salehur
A265
Petworth ◉
A283
● Dial Post
● Ashurst
A24
A272
A23
A273
● East Chiltington
BURGESS HILL
UCKFIELD ■
Blackboys ●
● Chiddingly
Heathfield ●
● Robertsbridge
EAST
SUSSEX
A271
A21
WEST SUSSEX
A29
A283
A27
A275
LEWES
● Ringmer
HAILSHAM
● Wartling ◉
A259
BEXHILL
ARUNDEL ■
A259
WORTHING
BRIGHTON
A259
NEWHAVEN
Alciston ◉
A27
EASTBOURNE
◉ Alfriston
◉ East Dean

TV

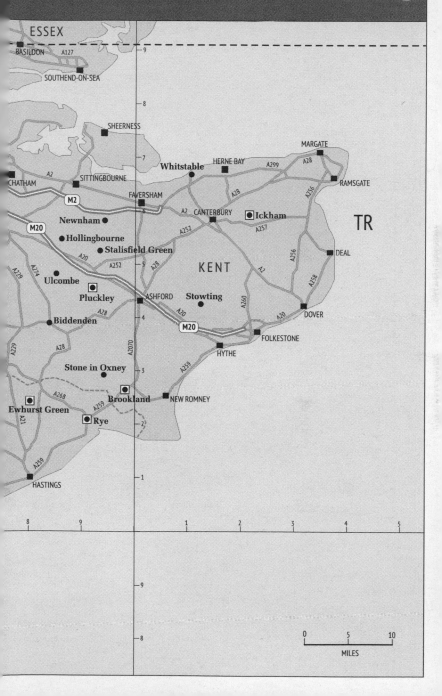

7

4
- Main Entry
- Main Entry with accommodation
- Place name to assist navigation

Shrewsbury
TELFORD
STAFFS
M54
M6
LICHFIELD
TAMWORTH
A5
SJ
M6 Toll
A5
MILES
0 5 10
A458
A5
A38
Ironbridge
A442
Coalport
M6
A41
A454
WOLVERHAMPTON
M42
Much Wenlock
Norton
Cardington
SHROPSHIRE
Bridgnorth
A4123
M6
A458
Birmingham
A441
A38
M5
A449
Hampton in Arden
M42
A34
Ludlow
A4117
Bewdley
A456
Clent
Barston
A49
KIDDERMINSTER
Holy Cross
M42
A456
A449
A448
M42
M40
A443
A4189
Tenbury Wells
A449
M5
REDDITCH
Preston Bagot
A3400
A46
WORCESTERSHIRE
A455
LEOMINSTER
Alcester
Knightwick
WORCESTER
A46
Stratford-upon-Avon
A44
A412
Ardens Grafton
A422
Little Cowarne
Bransford
A38
Welford-on-Avon
B439
6
Newland
A4103
A449
A44
Alderminster
HEREFORDSHIRE
Malvern
Ilmington
A46
A3400
HEREFORD
SO
Upper Colwall
A4104
Bretforton
A438
EVESHAM
Ebrington
Ledbury
A46
Chipping Campden
Woolhope
A438
Broadway
B4632
Broad Campden
A49
Carey
Stanton
M50
Bourton-on-the-Hill
A417
A449
TEWKESBURY
Gretton
MORETON-IN-MARSH
A455
Ford
Upper Oddington
Ross-on-Wye
Ashleworth
A38
Coombe Hill
Lower Slaughter
A44
Kilcot
Guiting Power
STOW-ON-THE-WOLD
Walford
Clifford's Mesne
Cheltenham
A456
Bledington
A40
Brockhampton
A429
Nether Westcote
A466
Symonds Yat
A4136
Blaisdon
Gloucester
Great Rissington
A474
MONMOUTH
Cowley
Northleach
Burford
GLOUCESTERSHIRE
Sheepscombe
Fossebridge
Shilton
Newland
Duntisbourne Abbots
North Cerney
Filkins
Tintern
STROUD
A419
Sapperton
B4425
Barnsley
Langford
A48
CIRENCESTER
A417
Southrop
Dursley
A4135
Nailsworth
Coates
A419
Fairford
Marston Meysey
A466
Oldbury-on-Severn
M5
A46
Tetbury
A429
Crudwell
Cricklade
CHEPSTOW

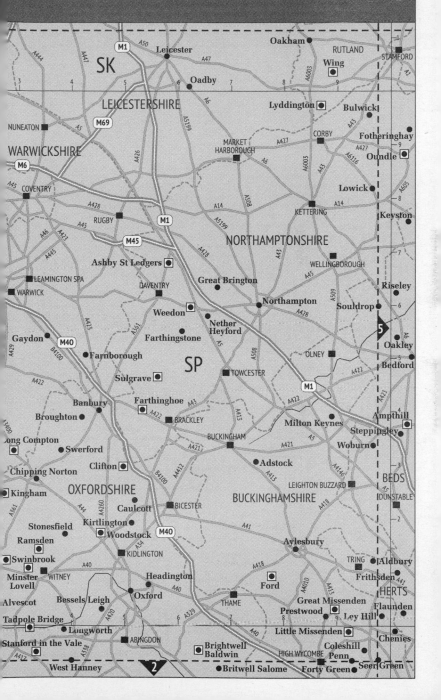

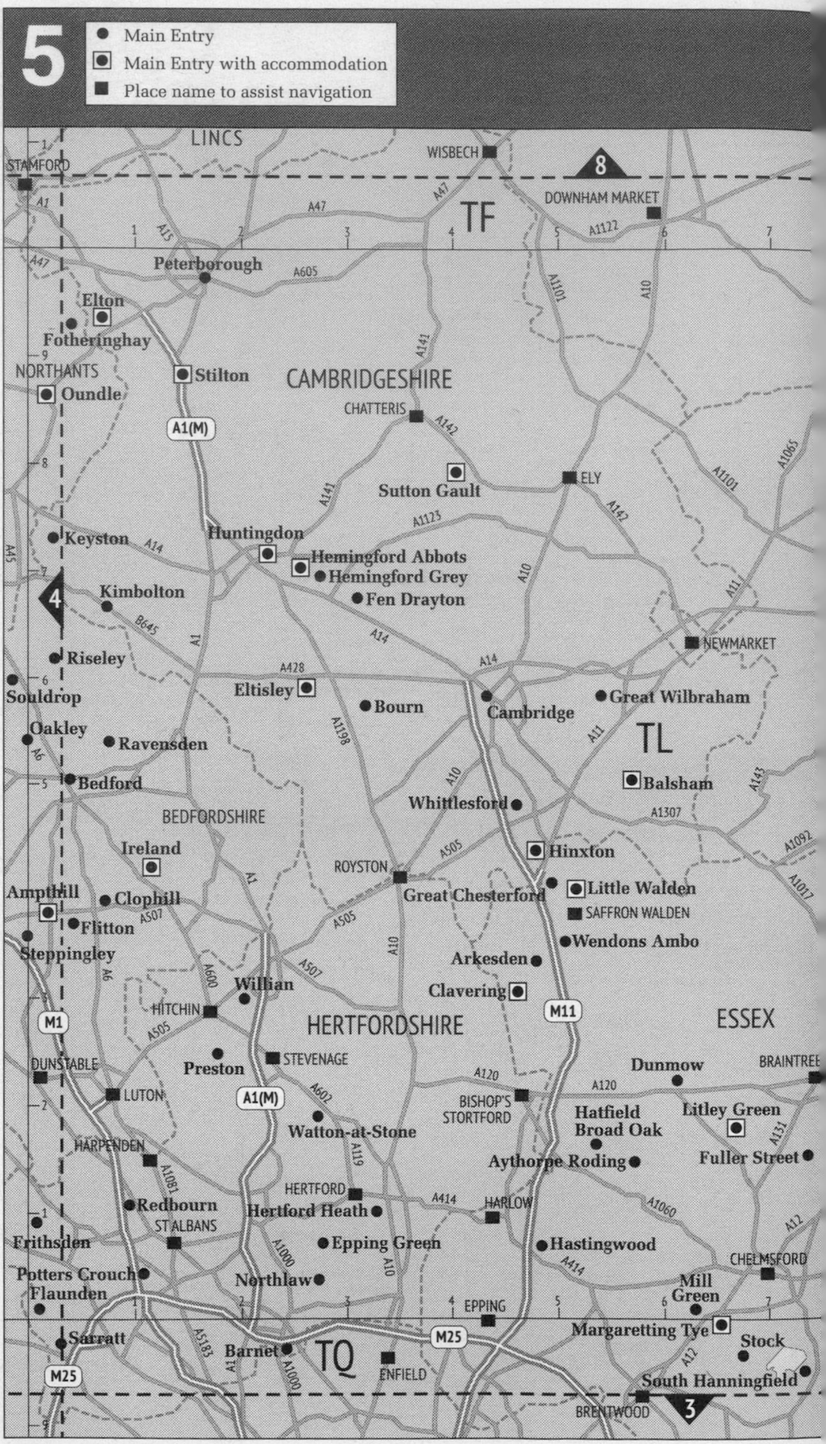
5
Main Entry
Main Entry with accommodation
Place name to assist navigation
LINCS
STAMFORD
WISBECH
8
DOWNHAM MARKET
TF
Peterborough
Elton
Fotheringhay
NORTHANTS
Stilton
Oundle
CAMBRIDGESHIRE
CHATTERIS
A1(M)
Sutton Gault
ELY
Keyston
Huntingdon
Hemingford Abbots
Hemingford Grey
Fen Drayton
4
Kimbolton
Riseley
NEWMARKET
Souldrop
Eltisley
Bourn
Cambridge
Great Wilbraham
Oakley
Ravensden
TL
Balsham
Bedford
Whittlesford
BEDFORDSHIRE
Ireland
Hinxton
ROYSTON
Ampthill
Clophill
Great Chesterford
Little Walden
SAFFRON WALDEN
Flitton
Steppingley
Wendons Ambo
Arkesden
Willian
Clavering
M11
HITCHIN
HERTFORDSHIRE
ESSEX
M1
Preston
STEVENAGE
DUNSTABLE
Dunmow
BRAINTREE
LUTON
A1(M)
BISHOP'S STORTFORD
Hatfield Broad Oak
Litley Green
Watton-at-Stone
HARPENDEN
Aythorpe Roding
Fuller Street
HERTFORD
Redbourn
Hertford Heath
HARLOW
ST ALBANS
Frithsden
Epping Green
Hastingwood
CHELMSFORD
Potters Crouch
Northlaw
Mill Green
Flaunden
EPPING
Margaretting Tye
Sarratt
Barnet
M25
TQ
Stock
ENFIELD
M25
South Hanningfield
BRENTWOOD
3

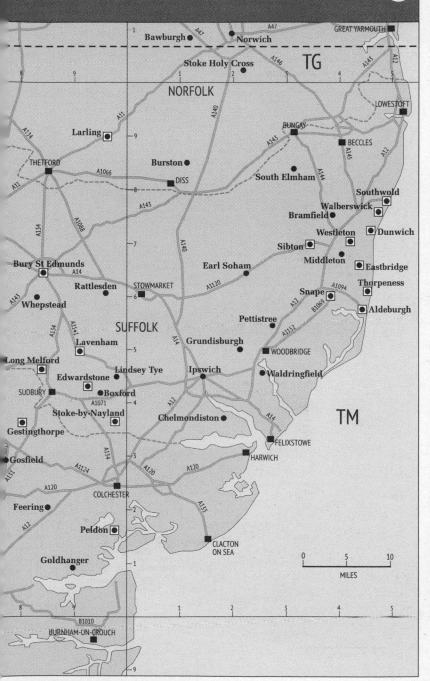

Bawburgh ● ● Norwich · · · · · · GREAT YARMOUTH ■

Stoke Holy Cross ● · · · · · · · TG

NORFOLK · · · · · · · · · · · · LOWESTOFT ■

Larling ▣ · · · · · · · · · · · · · BUNGAY ■ · · · · BECCLES ■

THETFORD ■ · · · · · · · · Burston ● · · · · · · South Elmham ●

· · · · · · · · · · · · · DISS ■ · · · · · · · · Southwold ▣

· Walberswick ▣

· · · · · · · · · · · · · · Bramfield ● · · · · Westleton ▣ · Dunwich ▣

· · · · · · · · · · · · · · · · · Sibton ▣ · Middleton ● Eastbridge ▣

Bury St Edmunds ▣ · · · · Earl Soham ● · · · · · · Thorpeness ▣

· · · Rattlesden ● · · STOWMARKET ■ · · · · Snape ● · Aldeburgh ▣

Whepstead ● · · · · · · SUFFOLK · · · · Pettistree ●

· · · · · · · · · · · · · · · · Grundisburgh ● · · WOODBRIDGE ■

Lavenham ▣ · · · Lindsey Tye · · Ipswich ● · · Waldringfield ●

Long Melford ▣ · · · · · · · · · · · · · · · · · TM

Edwardstone ▣ · Boxford ● · · · · · · · · · · · ·

SUDBURY ■ · · · · · · · · · · · Chelmondiston ●

Gestingthorpe ▣ · Stoke-by-Nayland ▣ · · · · · · · · FELIXSTOWE ■

Gosfield ● · · · · · · · · · · · · HARWICH ■

Feering ● · · · COLCHESTER ■

· · · · · Peldon ▣ · · · · · · · · CLACTON ON SEA ■

Goldhanger ● · · · · · · · · · · · · 0 · · · 5 · · · 10

· MILES

BURNHAM-ON-CROUCH ■

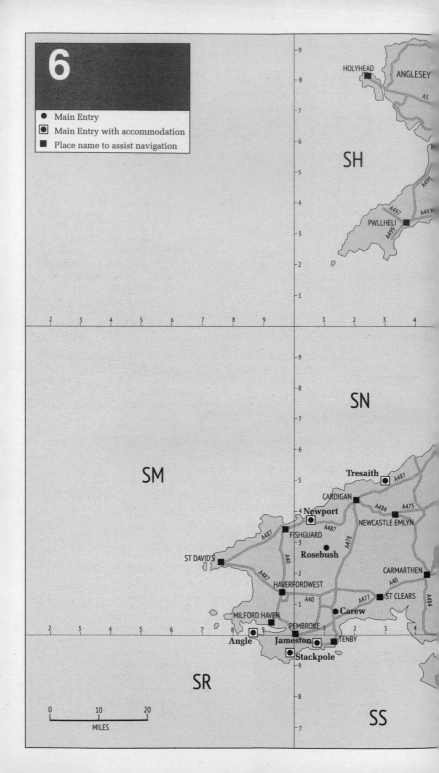

6

- Main Entry
- Main Entry with accommodation
- Place name to assist navigation

SH

HOLYHEAD ANGLESEY
A5

A499

A497 A497

PWLLHELI
A499

SN

SM

Tresaith A487

CARDIGAN
A484 A475

Newport
A487 NEWCASTLE EMLYN

FISHGUARD

A487

A40 **Rosebush**

ST DAVID'S

A478

CARMARTHEN

A487
HAVERFORDWEST
A40 A40

A477 ST CLEARS A484

A40

MILFORD HAVEN

Carew

PEMBROKE

Angle **Jameston** TENBY

Stackpole

SR

SS

0   10   20
MILES

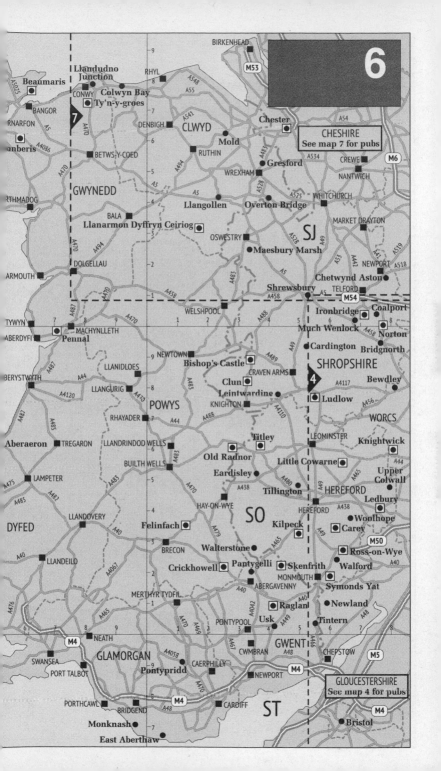

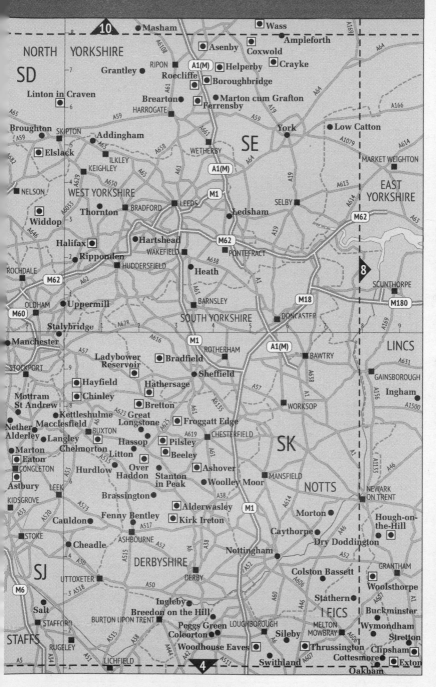

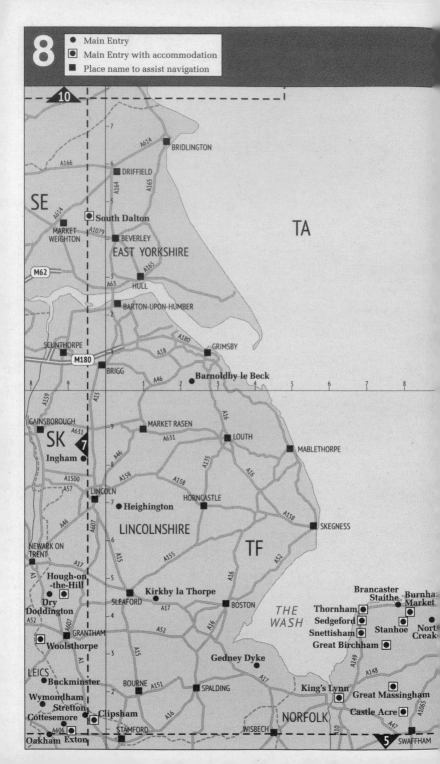

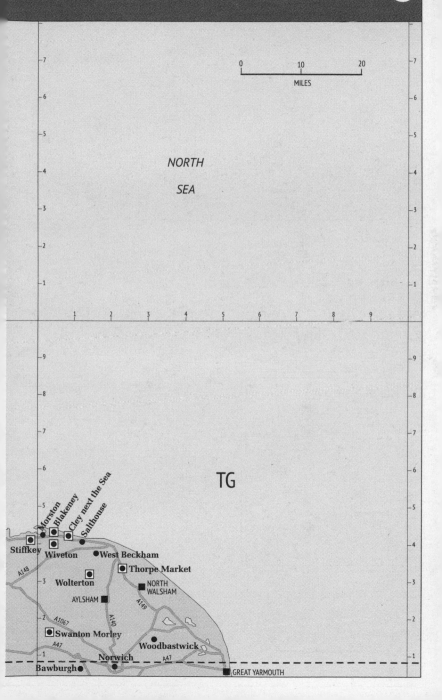

0   10   20
MILES

NORTH

SEA

TG

Morston
Blakeney
Cley next the Sea
Salthouse
Stiffkey
Wiveton
West Beckham
Thorpe Market
Wolterton
NORTH WALSHAM
AYLSHAM
A1067
A140
A148
A149
Swanton Morley
A47
Woodbastwick
Norwich
Bawburgh
GREAT YARMOUTH

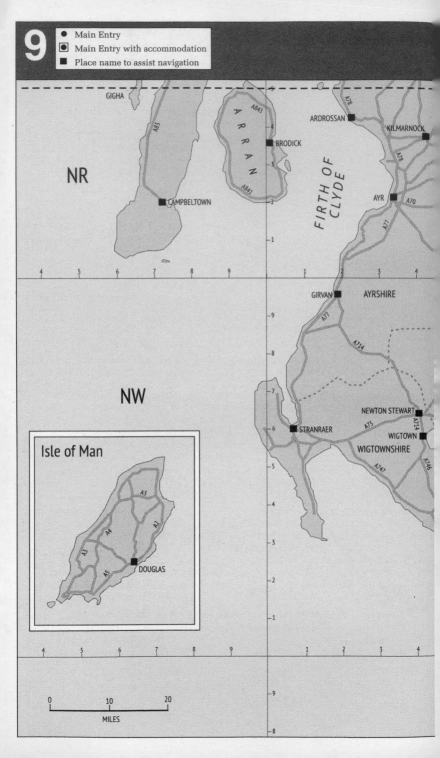

9

- ● Main Entry
- ◉ Main Entry with accommodation
- ■ Place name to assist navigation

GIGHA

A841

A R R A N

BRODICK

ARDROSSAN

KILMARNOCK

A78

A78

NR

FIRTH OF CLYDE

CAMPBELTOWN

AYR

A70

A77

4 5 6 7 8 9   1 2 3 4

GIRVAN   AYRSHIRE

A77

A714

NW

NEWTON STEWART

Isle of Man

A714

STRANRAER

WIGTOWN

A75

A3

WIGTOWNSHIRE

A146

A747

A2

A4

A8

A5

DOUGLAS

4 5 6 7 8 9   1 2 3 4

0   10   20

MILES

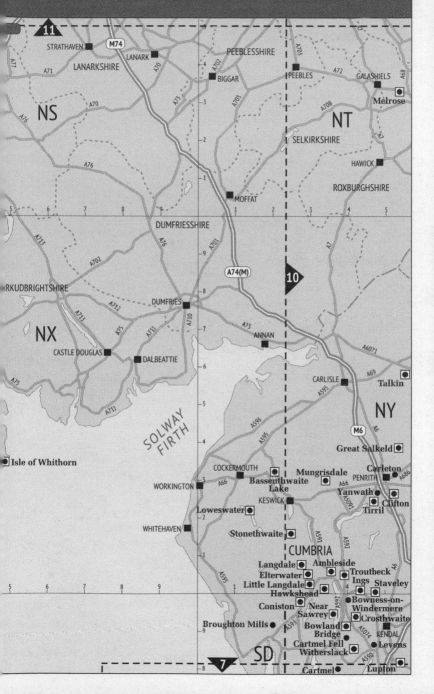

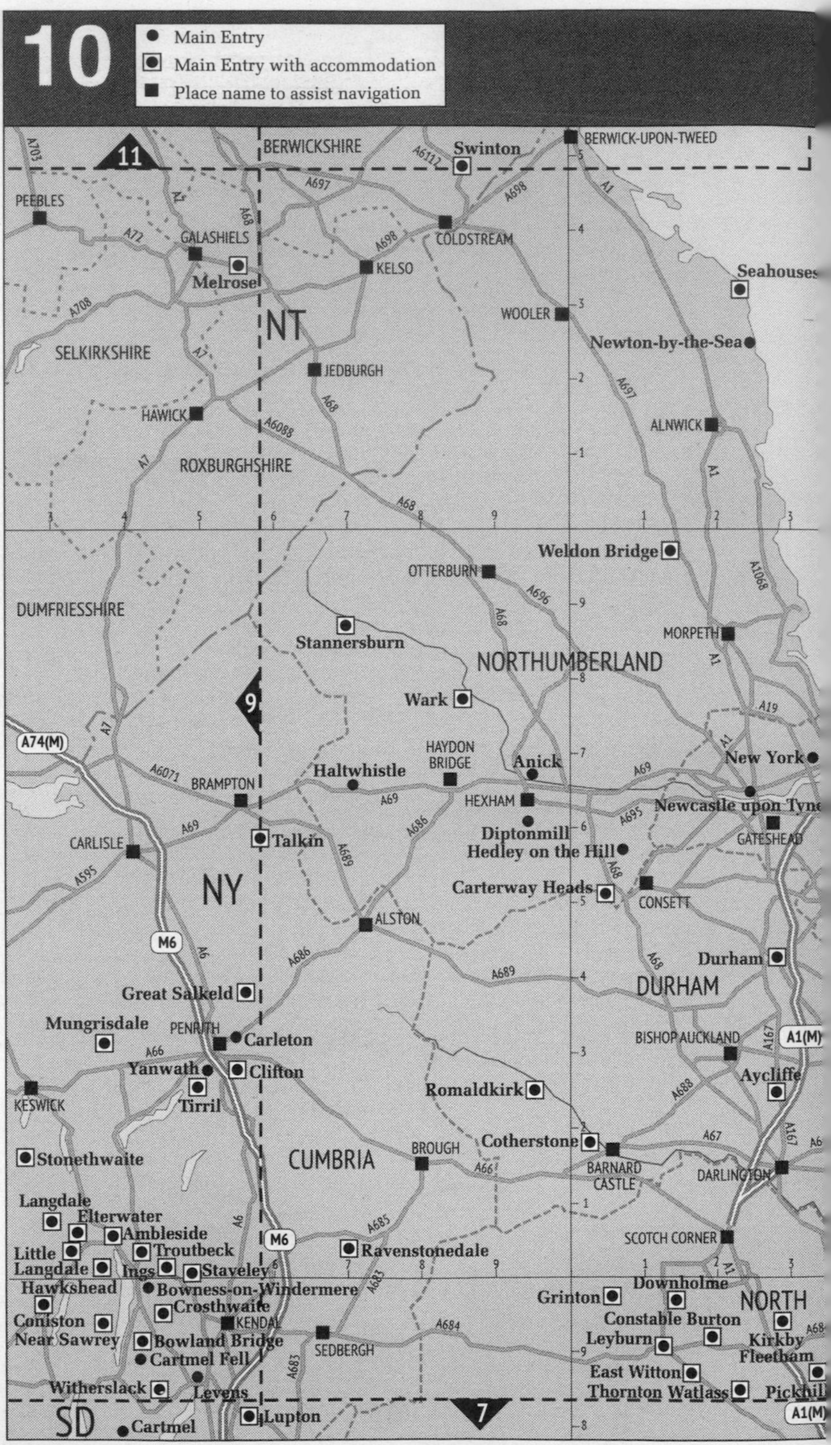
10
Main Entry
Main Entry with accommodation
Place name to assist navigation
11
BERWICKSHIRE
Swinton
BERWICK-UPON-TWEED
PEEBLES
GALASHIELS
Melrose
KELSO
COLDSTREAM
Seahouses
NT
WOOLER
Newton-by-the-Sea
SELKIRKSHIRE
JEDBURGH
HAWICK
ALNWICK
ROXBURGHSHIRE
Weldon Bridge
OTTERBURN
DUMFRIESSHIRE
Stannersburn
MORPETH
NORTHUMBERLAND
Wark
9
A74(M)
HAYDON BRIDGE
Anick
New York
Haltwhistle
BRAMPTON
HEXHAM
Newcastle upon Tyne
Diptonmill
GATESHEAD
Talkin
Hedley on the Hill
CARLISLE
NY
Carterway Heads
CONSETT
ALSTON
M6
Durham
DURHAM
Great Salkeld
Mungrisdale
PENRITH
Carleton
BISHOP AUCKLAND
A1(M)
Yanwath
Clifton
Aycliffe
KESWICK
Tirril
Romaldkirk
Stonethwaite
CUMBRIA
BROUGH
Cotherstone
BARNARD CASTLE
DARLINGTON
Langdale
Elterwater
Ambleside
Little Langdale
Troutbeck
Ings
Staveley
Ravenstonedale
SCOTCH CORNER
Hawkshead
Bowness-on-Windermere
Grinton
Downholme
NORTH
Crosthwaite
Coniston
KENDAL
Constable Burton
Near Sawrey
Bowland Bridge
SEDBERGH
Leyburn
Kirkby Fleetham
Cartmel Fell
East Witton
Witherslack
Levens
Thornton Watlass
Pickhill
SD
Cartmel
Lupton
7

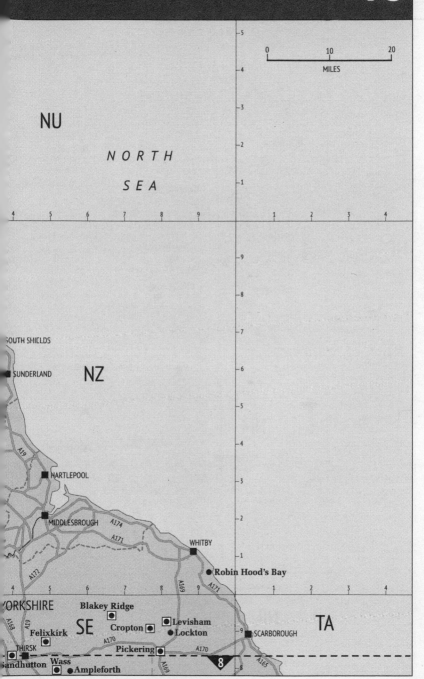

NU

N O R T H

S E A

0   10   20
MILES

4   5   6   7   8   9 | 1   2   3   4

9

8

7

SOUTH SHIELDS

SUNDERLAND   NZ   6

5

4

A19   3

HARTLEPOOL   3

2

MIDDLESBROUGH   A174   2

A171

WHITBY   1

● Robin Hood's Bay

4   5   6   7   8   9 | 1   2   3   4

ORKSHIRE   Blakey Ridge

SE   ● Levisham   TA

Felixkirk   Cropton ●   ● Lockton   SCARBOROUGH   9

THIRSK   A170

andhutton   Wass   Pickering ●   A170   A165   8

● Ampleforth   ▼8

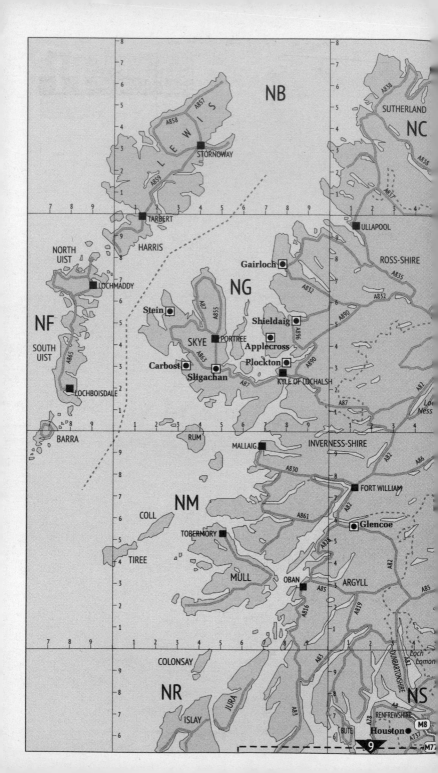

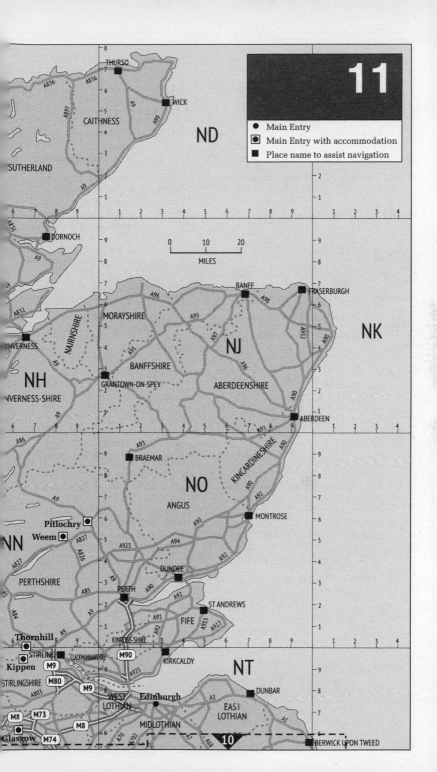

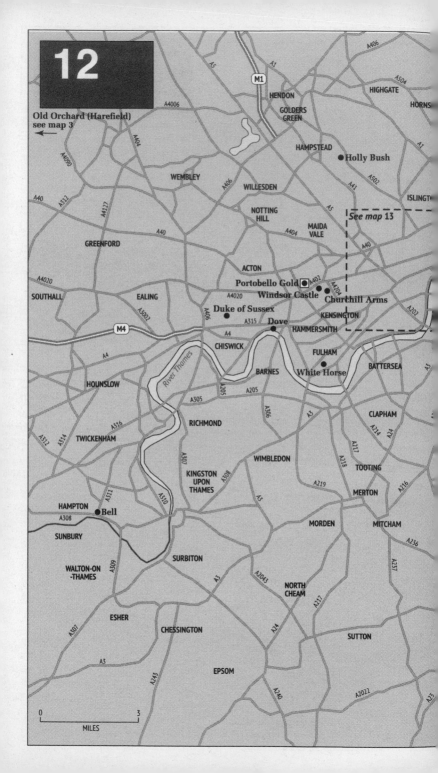

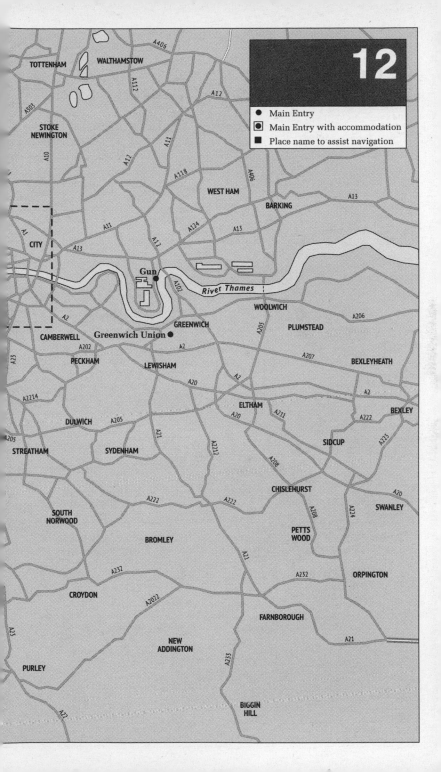

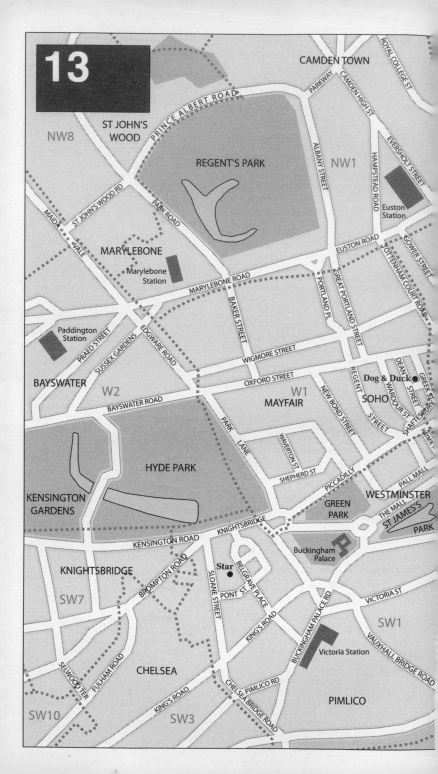

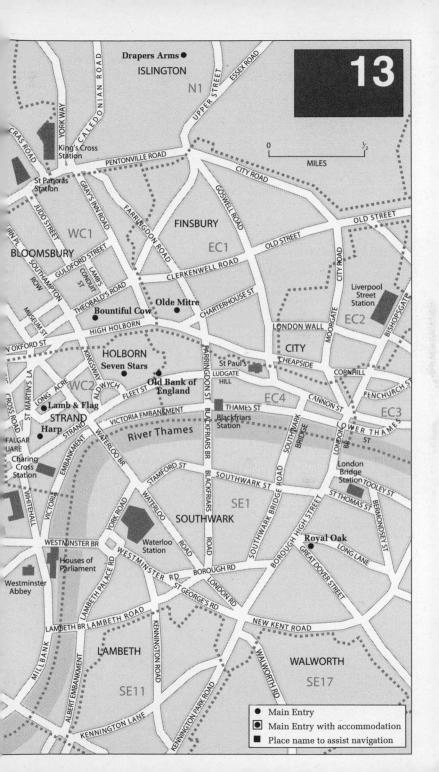

REPORT FORMS

We would very much appreciate hearing about your visits to pubs in this *Guide*, whether you have found them as described and recommend them for continued inclusion or noticed a fall in standards.

We'd also be glad to hear of any new pubs that you think we should know about. Readers' reports are very valuable to us, and sometimes pubs are dropped simply because we have had no up-to-date news on them.

You can use the tear-out forms on the following pages, email us at feedback@goodguides.co.uk or send us comments via our website (www.thegoodpubguide.co.uk) or app. We include two types of forms: one for you to simply list pubs you have visited and confirm that our review is accurate, and the other for you to give us more detailed information on individual pubs. If you would like more forms, please write to us at:

The Good Pub Guide

FREEPOST TN1569

WADHURST

East Sussex TN5 7BR

Though we try to answer all letters, please understand if there's a delay (particularly in summer, our busiest period).

We'll assume we can print your name or initials as a recommender unless you tell us otherwise.

MAIN ENTRY OR 'ALSO WORTH A VISIT'?

Please try to gauge whether a pub should be a Main Entry or go in the Also Worth a Visit section (and tick the relevant box). Main Entries need to have qualities that would make it worth other readers' while to travel some distance to them. If a pub is an entirely new recommendation, the Also Worth a Visit section may be the best place for it to start its career in the *Guide* – to encourage other readers to report on it.

The more detail you can put into your description of a pub, the better. Any information on how good the landlord or landlady is, what it looks like inside, what you like about the atmosphere and character, the quality and type of food, which real ales are available and whether they're well kept, whether bedrooms are available, and how big/attractive the garden is. Other helpful information includes prices for food and bedrooms, food service and opening hours, and if children or dogs are welcome.

If the food or accommodation is outstanding, tick the FOOD AWARD or the STAY AWARD box.

If you're in a position to gauge a pub's suitability or otherwise for disabled people, do please tell us about that.

If you can, give the full address or directions for any pub not currently in the *Guide* – most of all, please give us its postcode. If we can't find a pub's postcode, we don't include it in the *Guide*.

I have been to the following pubs in *The Good Pub Guide 2014* in the last few months, found them as described, and confirm that they deserve continued inclusion:

continued overleaf

PLEASE GIVE YOUR NAME AND ADDRESS ON THE BACK OF THIS FORM

Pubs visited continued..........

_____

By returning this form, you consent to the collection, recording and use of the information you submit, by The Random House Group Ltd. Any personal details which you provide from which we can identify you are held and processed in accordance with the Data Protection Act 1998 and will not be passed on to any third parties. The Random House Group Ltd may wish to send you further information on their associated products.

Please tick box if you do not wish to receive any such information. ☐

Your own name and address (block capitals please)

....

....

....

Postcode..

In returning this form I confirm my agreement that the information I provide may be used by The Random House Group Ltd, its assignees and/or licensees in any media or medium whatsoever.

Please return to

The Good Pub Guide
FREEPOST TN1569
WADHURST
East Sussex
TN5 7BR

IF YOU PREFER, YOU CAN SEND
US REPORTS BY EMAIL:

feedback@goodguides.com

I have been to the following pubs in *The Good Pub Guide 2014* in the last few months, found them as described, and confirm that they deserve continued inclusion:

continued overleaf

PLEASE GIVE YOUR NAME AND ADDRESS ON THE BACK OF THIS FORM

Pubs visited continued..........

Your own name and address (block capitals please)

....

....

....

Postcode...

Please return to

The Good Pub Guide
FREEPOST TN1569
WADHURST
East Sussex
TN5 7BR

IF YOU PREFER, YOU CAN SEND
US REPORTS BY EMAIL:

feedback@goodguides.com

I have been to the following pubs in *The Good Pub Guide 2014* in the last few months, found them as described, and confirm that they deserve continued inclusion:

continued overleaf

PLEASE GIVE YOUR NAME AND ADDRESS ON THE BACK OF THIS FORM

Pubs visited continued..........

By returning this form, you consent to the collection, recording and use of the information you submit, by The Random House Group Ltd. Any personal details which you provide from which we can identify you are held and processed in accordance with the Data Protection Act 1998 and will not be passed on to any third parties. The Random House Group Ltd may wish to send you further information on their associated products.

Please tick box if you do not wish to receive any such information. ☐

Your own name and address (block capitals please)

....

....

....

Postcode..

In returning this form I confirm my agreement that the information I provide may be used by The Random House Group Ltd, its assignees and/or licensees in any media or medium whatsoever.

Please return to

The Good Pub Guide
FREEPOST TN1569
WADHURST
East Sussex
TN5 7BR

IF YOU PREFER, YOU CAN SEND
US REPORTS BY EMAIL:

feedback@goodguides.com

I have been to the following pubs in *The Good Pub Guide 2014* in the last few months, found them as described, and confirm that they deserve continued inclusion:

continued overleaf

PLEASE GIVE YOUR NAME AND ADDRESS ON THE BACK OF THIS FORM

Pubs visited continued..........

Your own name and address (block capitals please)

....

....

....

Postcode...

Please return to

The Good Pub Guide
FREEPOST TN1569
WADHURST
East Sussex
TN5 7BR

IF YOU PREFER, YOU CAN SEND
US REPORTS BY EMAIL:

feedback@goodguides.com

I have been to the following pubs in *The Good Pub Guide 2014* in the last few months, found them as described, and confirm that they deserve continued inclusion:

continued overleaf

PLEASE GIVE YOUR NAME AND ADDRESS ON THE BACK OF THIS FORM

Pubs visited continued..........

Your own name and address (block capitals please)

....

....

....

Postcode..

Please return to

The Good Pub Guide
FREEPOST TN1569
WADHURST
East Sussex
TN5 7BR

IF YOU PREFER, YOU CAN SEND
US REPORTS BY EMAIL:

feedback@goodguides.com

I have been to the following pubs in *The Good Pub Guide 2014* in the last few months, found them as described, and confirm that they deserve continued inclusion:

continued overleaf

PLEASE GIVE YOUR NAME AND ADDRESS ON THE BACK OF THIS FORM

Pubs visited continued..........

Your own name and address (block capitals please)

....

....

....

Postcode...

Please return to

The Good Pub Guide
FREEPOST TN1569
WADHURST
East Sussex
TN5 7BR

IF YOU PREFER, YOU CAN SEND
US REPORTS BY EMAIL:

feedback@goodguides.com

I have been to the following pubs in *The Good Pub Guide 2014* in the last few months, found them as described, and confirm that they deserve continued inclusion:

continued overleaf

PLEASE GIVE YOUR NAME AND ADDRESS ON THE BACK OF THIS FORM

Pubs visited continued..........

Your own name and address (block capitals please)

....

....

....

Postcode...

Please return to

The Good Pub Guide
FREEPOST TN1569
WADHURST
East Sussex
TN5 7BR

IF YOU PREFER, YOU CAN SEND
US REPORTS BY EMAIL:

feedback@goodguides.com

Report On (pub's name)

....

Pub's address

....

☐ YES MAIN ENTRY ☐ YES WORTH A VISIT ☐ NO don't include

Please tick one of these boxes to show your verdict, and give reasons, descriptive comments, prices and the date of your visit

☐ Deserves **FOOD Award** ☐ Deserves **STAY Award** 2014:1

PLEASE GIVE YOUR NAME AND ADDRESS ON THE BACK OF THIS FORM

✂ ....

Report On (pub's name)

....

Pub's address

....

☐ YES MAIN ENTRY ☐ YES WORTH A VISIT ☐ NO don't include

Please tick one of these boxes to show your verdict, and give reasons, descriptive comments, prices and the date of your visit

☐ Deserves **FOOD Award** ☐ Deserves **STAY Award** 2014:2

PLEASE GIVE YOUR NAME AND ADDRESS ON THE BACK OF THIS FORM

Your own name and address *(block capitals please)*

In returning this form I confirm my agreement that the information I provide may be used by The Random House Group Ltd, its assignees and/or licensees in any media or medium whatsoever.

DO NOT USE THIS SIDE OF THE PAGE FOR WRITING ABOUT PUBS

✂ ....

Your own name and address *(block capitals please)*

In returning this form I confirm my agreement that the information I provide may be used by The Random House Group Ltd, its assignees and/or licensees in any media or medium whatsoever.

DO NOT USE THIS SIDE OF THE PAGE FOR WRITING ABOUT PUBS

Report On (pub's name)

....

Pub's address

....

☐ YES MAIN ENTRY   ☐ YES WORTH A VISIT   ☐ NO don't include

Please tick one of these boxes to show your verdict, and give reasons,
descriptive comments, prices and the date of your visit

☐ Deserves **FOOD Award**   ☐ Deserves **STAY Award**   2014:3

PLEASE GIVE YOUR NAME AND ADDRESS ON THE BACK OF THIS FORM

✂ ....

Report On (pub's name)

....

Pub's address

....

☐ YES MAIN ENTRY   ☐ YES WORTH A VISIT   ☐ NO don't include

Please tick one of these boxes to show your verdict, and give reasons,
descriptive comments, prices and the date of your visit

☐ Deserves **FOOD Award**   ☐ Deserves **STAY Award**   2014:4

PLEASE GIVE YOUR NAME AND ADDRESS ON THE BACK OF THIS FORM

Your own name and address *(block capitals please)*

In returning this form I confirm my agreement that the information I provide may be used by The Random House Group Ltd, its assignees and/or licensees in any media or medium whatsoever.

DO NOT USE THIS SIDE OF THE PAGE FOR WRITING ABOUT PUBS

✂ ....

Your own name and address *(block capitals please)*

In returning this form I confirm my agreement that the information I provide may be used by The Random House Group Ltd, its assignees and/or licensees in any media or medium whatsoever.

DO NOT USE THIS SIDE OF THE PAGE FOR WRITING ABOUT PUBS

Report On (pub's name)

....

Pub's address

....

☐ YES MAIN ENTRY ☐ YES WORTH A VISIT ☐ NO don't include

Please tick one of these boxes to show your verdict, and give reasons, descriptive comments, prices and the date of your visit

☐ Deserves **FOOD Award** ☐ Deserves **STAY Award** 2014:5

PLEASE GIVE YOUR NAME AND ADDRESS ON THE BACK OF THIS FORM

✂ ....

Report On (pub's name)

....

Pub's address

....

☐ YES MAIN ENTRY ☐ YES WORTH A VISIT ☐ NO don't include

Please tick one of these boxes to show your verdict, and give reasons, descriptive comments, prices and the date of your visit

☐ Deserves **FOOD Award** ☐ Deserves **STAY Award** 2014:6

PLEASE GIVE YOUR NAME AND ADDRESS ON THE BACK OF THIS FORM

Your own name and address *(block capitals please)*

In returning this form I confirm my agreement that the information I provide may be used by The Random House Group Ltd, its assignees and/or licensees in any media or medium whatsoever.

DO NOT USE THIS SIDE OF THE PAGE FOR WRITING ABOUT PUBS

✂ ....

Your own name and address *(block capitals please)*

In returning this form I confirm my agreement that the information I provide may be used by The Random House Group Ltd, its assignees and/or licensees in any media or medium whatsoever.

DO NOT USE THIS SIDE OF THE PAGE FOR WRITING ABOUT PUBS

Report On (pub's name)

....

Pub's address

....

☐ YES MAIN ENTRY ☐ YES WORTH A VISIT ☐ NO don't include

Please tick one of these boxes to show your verdict, and give reasons, descriptive comments, prices and the date of your visit

☐ Deserves **FOOD Award** ☐ Deserves **STAY Award** 2014:7

PLEASE GIVE YOUR NAME AND ADDRESS ON THE BACK OF THIS FORM

✂ ....

Report On (pub's name)

....

Pub's address

....

☐ YES MAIN ENTRY ☐ YES WORTH A VISIT ☐ NO don't include

Please tick one of these boxes to show your verdict, and give reasons, descriptive comments, prices and the date of your visit

☐ Deserves **FOOD Award** ☐ Deserves **STAY Award** 2014:8

PLEASE GIVE YOUR NAME AND ADDRESS ON THE BACK OF THIS FORM

Your own name and address *(block capitals please)*

In returning this form I confirm my agreement that the information I provide may be used by The Random House Group Ltd, its assignees and/or licensees in any media or medium whatsoever.

DO NOT USE THIS SIDE OF THE PAGE FOR WRITING ABOUT PUBS

By returning this form, you consent to the collection, recording and use of the information you submit, by The Random House Group Ltd. Any personal details which you provide from which we can identify you are held and processed in accordance with the Data Protection Act 1998 and will not be passed on to any third parties. The Random House Group Ltd may wish to send you further information on their associated products. Please tick box if you do not wish to receive any such information.

✂ ....

Your own name and address *(block capitals please)*

In returning this form I confirm my agreement that the information I provide may be used by The Random House Group Ltd, its assignees and/or licensees in any media or medium whatsoever.

DO NOT USE THIS SIDE OF THE PAGE FOR WRITING ABOUT PUBS

By returning this form, you consent to the collection, recording and use of the information you submit, by The Random House Group Ltd. Any personal details which you provide from which we can identify you are held and processed in accordance with the Data Protection Act 1998 and will not be passed on to any third parties. The Random House Group Ltd may wish to send you further information on their associated products. Please tick box if you do not wish to receive any such information.

Report On (pub's name)

....

Pub's address

....

☐ YES MAIN ENTRY   ☐ YES WORTH A VISIT   ☐ NO don't include

Please tick one of these boxes to show your verdict, and give reasons,
descriptive comments, prices and the date of your visit

☐ Deserves **FOOD Award**   ☐ Deserves **STAY Award**   2014:9

PLEASE GIVE YOUR NAME AND ADDRESS ON THE BACK OF THIS FORM

✂ ....

Report On (pub's name)

....

Pub's address

....

☐ YES MAIN ENTRY   ☐ YES WORTH A VISIT   ☐ NO don't include

Please tick one of these boxes to show your verdict, and give reasons,
descriptive comments, prices and the date of your visit

☐ Deserves **FOOD Award**   ☐ Deserves **STAY Award**   2014:10

PLEASE GIVE YOUR NAME AND ADDRESS ON THE BACK OF THIS FORM

Your own name and address *(block capitals please)*

In returning this form I confirm my agreement that the information I provide may be used by The Random House Group Ltd, its assignees and/or licensees in any media or medium whatsoever.

DO NOT USE THIS SIDE OF THE PAGE FOR WRITING ABOUT PUBS

✂ ....

Your own name and address *(block capitals please)*

In returning this form I confirm my agreement that the information I provide may be used by The Random House Group Ltd, its assignees and/or licensees in any media or medium whatsoever.

DO NOT USE THIS SIDE OF THE PAGE FOR WRITING ABOUT PUBS

Report On (pub's name)

....

Pub's address

....

☐ YES MAIN ENTRY   ☐ YES WORTH A VISIT   ☐ NO don't include

Please tick one of these boxes to show your verdict, and give reasons,
descriptive comments, prices and the date of your visit

☐ Deserves **FOOD Award**   ☐ Deserves **STAY Award**   2014:11

PLEASE GIVE YOUR NAME AND ADDRESS ON THE BACK OF THIS FORM

✂ ....

Report On (pub's name)

....

Pub's address

....

☐ YES MAIN ENTRY   ☐ YES WORTH A VISIT   ☐ NO don't include

Please tick one of these boxes to show your verdict, and give reasons,
descriptive comments, prices and the date of your visit

☐ Deserves **FOOD Award**   ☐ Deserves **STAY Award**   2014:12

PLEASE GIVE YOUR NAME AND ADDRESS ON THE BACK OF THIS FORM

Your own name and address *(block capitals please)*

In returning this form I confirm my agreement that the information I provide may be used by The Random House Group Ltd, its assignees and/or licensees in any media or medium whatsoever.

DO NOT USE THIS SIDE OF THE PAGE FOR WRITING ABOUT PUBS

By returning this form, you consent to the collection, recording and use of the information you submit, by The Random House Group Ltd. Any personal details which you provide from which we can identify you are held and processed in accordance with the Data Protection Act 1998 and will not be passed on to any third parties. The Random House Group Ltd may wish to send you further information on their associated products. Please tick box if you do not wish to receive any such information.

✂ ....

Your own name and address *(block capitals please)*

In returning this form I confirm my agreement that the information I provide may be used by The Random House Group Ltd, its assignees and/or licensees in any media or medium whatsoever.

DO NOT USE THIS SIDE OF THE PAGE FOR WRITING ABOUT PUBS

By returning this form, you consent to the collection, recording and use of the information you submit, by The Random House Group Ltd. Any personal details which you provide from which we can identify you are held and processed in accordance with the Data Protection Act 1998 and will not be passed on to any third parties. The Random House Group Ltd may wish to send you further information on their associated products. Please tick box if you do not wish to receive any such information.

Report On (pub's name)

....

Pub's address

....

☐ YES MAIN ENTRY   ☐ YES WORTH A VISIT   ☐ NO don't include

Please tick one of these boxes to show your verdict, and give reasons,
descriptive comments, prices and the date of your visit

☐ Deserves **FOOD Award**   ☐ Deserves **STAY Award**   2014:13

PLEASE GIVE YOUR NAME AND ADDRESS ON THE BACK OF THIS FORM

✂ ....

Report On (pub's name)

....

Pub's address

....

☐ YES MAIN ENTRY   ☐ YES WORTH A VISIT   ☐ NO don't include

Please tick one of these boxes to show your verdict, and give reasons,
descriptive comments, prices and the date of your visit

☐ Deserves **FOOD Award**   ☐ Deserves **STAY Award**   2014:14

PLEASE GIVE YOUR NAME AND ADDRESS ON THE BACK OF THIS FORM

Your own name and address *(block capitals please)*

In returning this form I confirm my agreement that the information I provide may be used by The Random House Group Ltd, its assignees and/or licensees in any media or medium whatsoever.

DO NOT USE THIS SIDE OF THE PAGE FOR WRITING ABOUT PUBS

By returning this form, you consent to the collection, recording and use of the information you submit, by The Random House Group Ltd. Any personal details which you provide from which we can identify you are held and processed in accordance with the Data Protection Act 1998 and will not be passed on to any third parties. The Random House Group Ltd may wish to send you further information on their associated products. Please tick box if you do not wish to receive any such information.

✂ ....

Your own name and address *(block capitals please)*

In returning this form I confirm my agreement that the information I provide may be used by The Random House Group Ltd, its assignees and/or licensees in any media or medium whatsoever.

DO NOT USE THIS SIDE OF THE PAGE FOR WRITING ABOUT PUBS

By returning this form, you consent to the collection, recording and use of the information you submit, by The Random House Group Ltd. Any personal details which you provide from which we can identify you are held and processed in accordance with the Data Protection Act 1998 and will not be passed on to any third parties. The Random House Group Ltd may wish to send you further information on their associated products. Please tick box if you do not wish to receive any such information.

Report On (pub's name)

....

Pub's address

....

☐ YES MAIN ENTRY ☐ YES WORTH A VISIT ☐ NO don't include

Please tick one of these boxes to show your verdict, and give reasons, descriptive comments, prices and the date of your visit

☐ Deserves **FOOD Award** ☐ Deserves **STAY Award** 2014:15

PLEASE GIVE YOUR NAME AND ADDRESS ON THE BACK OF THIS FORM

✂ ....

Report On (pub's name)

....

Pub's address

....

☐ YES MAIN ENTRY ☐ YES WORTH A VISIT ☐ NO don't include

Please tick one of these boxes to show your verdict, and give reasons, descriptive comments, prices and the date of your visit

☐ Deserves **FOOD Award** ☐ Deserves **STAY Award** 201416

PLEASE GIVE YOUR NAME AND ADDRESS ON THE BACK OF THIS FORM

Your own name and address *(block capitals please)*

In returning this form I confirm my agreement that the information I provide may be used by The Random House Group Ltd, its assignees and/or licensees in any media or medium whatsoever.

DO NOT USE THIS SIDE OF THE PAGE FOR WRITING ABOUT PUBS

✂ ....

Your own name and address *(block capitals please)*

In returning this form I confirm my agreement that the information I provide may be used by The Random House Group Ltd, its assignees and/or licensees in any media or medium whatsoever.

DO NOT USE THIS SIDE OF THE PAGE FOR WRITING ABOUT PUBS

Report On _____ (pub's name)

....

Pub's address

....

☐ YES MAIN ENTRY   ☐ YES WORTH A VISIT   ☐ NO don't include

Please tick one of these boxes to show your verdict, and give reasons,
descriptive comments, prices and the date of your visit

☐ Deserves **FOOD Award**   ☐ Deserves **STAY Award**   2014:17

PLEASE GIVE YOUR NAME AND ADDRESS ON THE BACK OF THIS FORM

✂ ....

Report On _____ (pub's name)

....

Pub's address

....

☐ YES MAIN ENTRY   ☐ YES WORTH A VISIT   ☐ NO don't include

Please tick one of these boxes to show your verdict, and give reasons,
descriptive comments, prices and the date of your visit

☐ Deserves **FOOD Award**   ☐ Deserves **STAY Award**   2014:18

PLEASE GIVE YOUR NAME AND ADDRESS ON THE BACK OF THIS FORM

Your own name and address *(block capitals please)*

In returning this form I confirm my agreement that the information I provide may be used by The Random House Group Ltd, its assignees and/or licensees in any media or medium whatsoever.

DO NOT USE THIS SIDE OF THE PAGE FOR WRITING ABOUT PUBS

By returning this form, you consent to the collection, recording and use of the information you submit, by The Random House Group Ltd. Any personal details which you provide from which we can identify you are held and processed in accordance with the Data Protection Act 1998 and will not be passed on to any third parties. The Random House Group Ltd may wish to send you further information on their associated products. Please tick box if you do not wish to receive any such information.

✂ ....

Your own name and address *(block capitals please)*

In returning this form I confirm my agreement that the information I provide may be used by The Random House Group Ltd, its assignees and/or licensees in any media or medium whatsoever.

DO NOT USE THIS SIDE OF THE PAGE FOR WRITING ABOUT PUBS

By returning this form, you consent to the collection, recording and use of the information you submit, by The Random House Group Ltd. Any personal details which you provide from which we can identify you are held and processed in accordance with the Data Protection Act 1998 and will not be passed on to any third parties. The Random House Group Ltd may wish to send you further information on their associated products. Please tick box if you do not wish to receive any such information.

Report On   (pub's name)

....

Pub's address

....

☐ YES MAIN ENTRY   ☐ YES WORTH A VISIT   ☐ NO don't include

Please tick one of these boxes to show your verdict, and give reasons,
descriptive comments, prices and the date of your visit

☐ Deserves **FOOD Award**   ☐ Deserves **STAY Award**   2014:19

PLEASE GIVE YOUR NAME AND ADDRESS ON THE BACK OF THIS FORM

✂ ....

Report On   (pub's name)

....

Pub's address

....

☐ YES MAIN ENTRY   ☐ YES WORTH A VISIT   ☐ NO don't include

Please tick one of these boxes to show your verdict, and give reasons,
descriptive comments, prices and the date of your visit

☐ Deserves **FOOD Award**   ☐ Deserves **STAY Award**   2014:20

PLEASE GIVE YOUR NAME AND ADDRESS ON THE BACK OF THIS FORM

Your own name and address *(block capitals please)*

In returning this form I confirm my agreement that the information I provide may be used by The Random House Group Ltd, its assignees and/or licensees in any media or medium whatsoever.

DO NOT USE THIS SIDE OF THE PAGE FOR WRITING ABOUT PUBS

✄ ....

Your own name and address *(block capitals please)*

In returning this form I confirm my agreement that the information I provide may be used by The Random House Group Ltd, its assignees and/or licensees in any media or medium whatsoever.

DO NOT USE THIS SIDE OF THE PAGE FOR WRITING ABOUT PUBS

By returning this form, you consent to the collection, recording and use of the information you submit, by The Random House Group Ltd. Any personal details which you provide from which we can identify you are held and processed in accordance with the Data Protection Act 1998 and will not be passed on to any third parties. The Random House Group Ltd may wish to send you further information on their associated products. Please tick box if you do not wish to receive any such information.

Report On (pub's name)

....

Pub's address

....

☐ YES MAIN ENTRY ☐ YES WORTH A VISIT ☐ NO don't include

Please tick one of these boxes to show your verdict, and give reasons, descriptive comments, prices and the date of your visit

☐ Deserves **FOOD Award** ☐ Deserves **STAY Award** 2014:21

PLEASE GIVE YOUR NAME AND ADDRESS ON THE BACK OF THIS FORM

✂ ....

Report On (pub's name)

....

Pub's address

....

☐ YES MAIN ENTRY ☐ YES WORTH A VISIT ☐ NO don't include

Please tick one of these boxes to show your verdict, and give reasons, descriptive comments, prices and the date of your visit

☐ Deserves **FOOD Award** ☐ Deserves **STAY Award** 2014:22

PLEASE GIVE YOUR NAME AND ADDRESS ON THE BACK OF THIS FORM

Your own name and address *(block capitals please)*

In returning this form I confirm my agreement that the information I provide may be used by The Random House Group Ltd, its assignees and/or licensees in any media or medium whatsoever.

DO NOT USE THIS SIDE OF THE PAGE FOR WRITING ABOUT PUBS

✂ ....

Your own name and address *(block capitals please)*

In returning this form I confirm my agreement that the information I provide may be used by The Random House Group Ltd, its assignees and/or licensees in any media or medium whatsoever.

DO NOT USE THIS SIDE OF THE PAGE FOR WRITING ABOUT PUBS

Index of advertisers